THE EUROPEAN FOOTBALL YEARBOOK 2017/18

THE EUROPEAN FOOTBALL YEARBOOK 2017/18

General Editor
Mike Hammond

The only authoritative annual on the European game

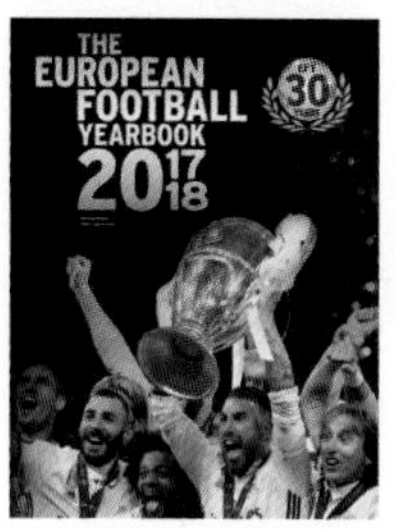

Further copies of The European Football Yearbook 2017/18
are available from:
www.carltonbooks.co.uk
hotline number +44 (0) 141 306 3100

The European Football Yearbook 2017/18

First published by Carlton Books Ltd, England in 2017

Printed by mpress ltd, England

ISBN 978-1-78097-973-1

UEFA – the Union of European Football Associations – is the governing body of football on the continent of Europe. UEFA's core mission is to promote, protect and develop European football at every level of the game, to promote the principles of unity and solidarity, and to deal with all questions relating to European football.

UEFA is an association of associations based on representative democracy, and is the governing body of European football.

UEFA
Route de Genève 46
Case postale
CH-1260 Nyon 2
Switzerland

Tel: +41 (0) 848 00 2727
Web: UEFA.com

Media Desk
Tel: +41 (0) 848 04 2727

All views expressed in the European Football Yearbook do not necessarily reflect those of UEFA. Every effort has been made to ensure the accuracy of the data in the European Football Yearbook, official and unofficial.

Front cover image: Real Madrid captain Sergio Ramos lifts the UEFA Champions League trophy after his team's 4-1 victory against Juventus in Cardiff

The European Football Yearbook 2012/13, 2013/14, 2014/15, 2015/16, 2016/17
are available from:
www.calmproductions.com
orders@calmproductions.com
UK hotline 0845 408 2606

THE EUROPEAN FOOTBALL YEARBOOK 2017/18

General Editor
Mike Hammond

Assistant Editor
Jesper Krogshede Sørensen

Nation-by-nation

Correspondents and Researchers

Nikolai Belov (Russia), Xavi Bonet (Andorra), Daniel Briskman (Israel), José Del Olmo (Spain), Sean DeLoughry (Republic of Ireland), Tamás Dénes (Hungary), Mike Farrugia (Malta), Arno Funck (Luxembourg), Stoyan Georgiev (Bulgaria), GFT (Julian Fortuna, Aaron Payas, Sean Mascarenhas, Ryan Gonzalez) (Gibraltar), Marshall Gillespie (Northern Ireland), Clas Glenning (France, Sweden), Miron Goihman (Moldova), Elia Gorini (San Marino), Marcel Haisma (Netherlands), Michael Hansen (Denmark), Diturie Hoxha (Kosovo), Romeo Ionescu (Romania), Mikael Kirakosyan (Armenia), Igor Kramarsić (Croatia), Jesper Krogshede Sørensen (Faroe Islands, Italy), Fedja Krvavac (Bosnia & Herzegovina), Zdeněk Kučera (Czech Republic), Ambrosius Kutschera (Austria), Almantas Laužadis (Lithuania), Tarmo Lehiste (Estonia), Dag Lindholm (Norway), Ewan Macdonald (Scotland), Ivica Madžarović (Montenegro), Erlan Manashev (Kazakhstan), Goran Mancevski (FYR Macedonia), Rasim Mövsümov (Azerbaijan), Giovanni Nappi (Albania), Kazimierz Oleszek (Poland), Olexandr Pauk (Belarus, Ukraine), Luca Pelliccioni (San Marino), Humberto Pereira Silva (Portugal), Mike Ritter & Silvia Schäfer (Germany), Grega Sever (Slovenia), Revaz Shengelia (Georgia), Vídir Sigurdsson (Iceland), Erdinç Sivritepe (Turkey), Vlastimir Stevanović (Serbia), Edouard Stutz (Switzerland), Matej Széher (Slovakia), Mel Thomas (Wales), Vesa Tikander (Finland), Serge Van Hoof (Belgium), Victor Vassallo (Malta), Georgios J Vassalos (Cyprus, Greece), Sergey Vorobyov (Latvia); additional assistance Emil Gasevski, Charlie Hammond, Gabriel Mantz, Sveinur Tróndarson

Photography

Getty Images, Getty Images/AFP, Getty Images/Bongarts, Sportsfile; additional assistance Domenic Aquilina, Mateo Beusan, Brit Maria Tael Photography, Vadim Caftanat, Jens Dresling/Polfoto, Álvur Haraldsen/Sosialurin, Símun á Høvdanum/Klips.fo, Stephen Ignacio, Yevhen Kraws, Pavlo Kubanov, Arban Osmani, Filippo Pruccoli/FSGC, worldsport.ge

UEFA

Editorial

Wayne Harrison, Michael Harrold, Patrick Hart, Simon Hart, Andrew Haslam, Conrad Leach, Anthony Naughton, Paul Saffer, Jim Wirth

Data

Andy Lockwood, Rob Esteva, Craig Steeples, Jim Agnew

Production

Print

m press ltd, England; Cliff Moulder

Distribution

Carlton Books Ltd; Martin Corteel, Jim Greenhough, Owen Hazell

Design

Keith Jackson

Graphics

Mikhail Sipovich

Data extraction

Delta3 (Emiliano Borello, Paolo Calva, Edoardo Masci)

Foreword

Zinédine Zidane

National three-letter codes

There are many instances throughout the European Football Yearbook where country names are abbreviated using three-letter codes. These codes are shown below, listed alphabetically by nation and divided into Europe and the Rest of the World.

Europe

ALB	Alb	Albania
AND	And	Andorra
ARM	Arm	Armenia
AUT	Aut	Austria
AZE	Aze	Azerbaijan
BLR	Blr	Belarus
BEL	Bel	Belgium
BIH	Bih	Bosnia & Herzegovina
BUL	Bul	Bulgaria
CRO	Cro	Croatia
CYP	Cyp	Cyprus
CZE	Cze	Czech Republic
DEN	Den	Denmark
ENG	Eng	England
EST	Est	Estonia
FRO	Fro	Faroe Islands
FIN	Fin	Finland
FRA	Fra	France
GEO	Geo	Georgia
GER	Ger	Germany
GIB	Gib	Gibraltar
GRE	Gre	Greece
HUN	Hun	Hungary
ISL	Isl	Iceland
ISR	Isr	Israel
ITA	Ita	Italy
KAZ	Kaz	Kazakhstan
KOS	Kos	Kosovo
LVA	Lva	Latvia
LIE	Lie	Liechtenstein
LTU	Ltu	Lithuania
LUX	Lux	Luxembourg
MKD	Mkd	Former Yugoslav Republic of Macedonia
MLT	Mlt	Malta
MDA	Mda	Moldova
MNE	Mne	Montenegro
NED	Ned	Netherlands
NIR	Nir	Northern Ireland
NOR	Nor	Norway
POL	Pol	Poland
POR	Por	Portugal
IRL	Irl	Republic of Ireland
ROU	Rou	Romania
RUS	Rus	Russia
SMR	Smr	San Marino
SCO	Sco	Scotland
SRB	Srb	Serbia
SVK	Svk	Slovakia
SVN	Svn	Slovenia
ESP	Esp	Spain
SWE	Swe	Sweden
SUI	Sui	Switzerland
TUR	Tur	Turkey
UKR	Ukr	Ukraine
WAL	Wal	Wales

Rest of the World

AFG	Afg	Afghanistan
ALG	Alg	Algeria
ANG	Ang	Angola
ATG	Atg	Antigua & Barbuda
ARG	Arg	Argentina
ARU	Aru	Aruba
AUS	Aus	Australia
BAH	Bah	Bahamas
BHR	Bhr	Bahrain
BAN	Ban	Bangladesh
BRB	Brb	Barbados
BEN	Ben	Benin
BER	Ber	Bermuda
BOL	Bol	Bolivia
BOT	Bot	Botswana
BRA	Bra	Brazil
BFA	Bfa	Burkina Faso
BDI	Bdi	Burundi
CMR	Cmr	Cameroon
CAN	Can	Canada
CPV	Cpv	Cape Verde Islands
CAY	Cay	Cayman Islands
CTA	Cta	Central African Republic
CHA	Cha	Chad
CHI	Chi	Chile
CHN	Chn	China
TPE	Tpe	Chinese Taipei
COL	Col	Colombia
COM	Com	Comoros
CGO	Cgo	Congo
COD	Cod	Congo DR
CRC	Crc	Costa Rica
CUB	Cub	Cuba
CUW	Cuw	Curacao
DJI	Dji	Djibouti
DOM	Dom	Dominican Republic
ECU	Ecu	Ecuador
EGY	Egy	Egypt
SLV	Slv	El Salvador
EQG	Eqg	Equatorial Guinea
ERI	Eri	Eritrea
ETH	Eth	Ethiopia
FIJ	Fij	Fiji
GAB	Gab	Gabon
GAM	Gam	Gambia
GHA	Gha	Ghana
GRN	Grn	Grenada
GUM	Gum	Guam
GUA	Gua	Guatemala
GUI	Gui	Guinea
GNB	Gnb	Guinea-Bissau
GUY	Guy	Guyana
HAI	Hai	Haiti
HON	Hon	Honduras
HKG	Hkg	Hong Kong
IND	Ind	India
IDN	Idn	Indonesia
IRN	Irn	Iran
IRQ	Irq	Iraq
CIV	Civ	Ivory Coast
JAM	Jam	Jamaica
JPN	Jpn	Japan
JOR	Jor	Jordan
KEN	Ken	Kenya
KUW	Kuw	Kuwait
KGZ	Kgz	Kyrgyzstan
LIB	Lib	Lebanon
LBR	Lbr	Liberia
LBY	Lby	Libya
MAD	Mad	Madagascar
MWI	Mwi	Malawi
MAS	Mas	Malaysia
MLI	Mli	Mali
MTQ	Mtq	Martinique
MTN	Mtn	Mauritania
MRI	Mri	Mauritius
MEX	Mex	Mexico
MSR	Msr	Montserrat
MAR	Mar	Morocco
MOZ	Moz	Mozambique
NAM	Nam	Namibia
ANT	Ant	Netherlands Antilles
NCL	Ncl	New Caledonia
NZL	Nzl	New Zealand
NCA	Nca	Nicaragua
NIG	Nig	Niger
NGA	Nga	Nigeria
PRK	Prk	North Korea
OMA	Oma	Oman
PAK	Pak	Pakistan
PLE	Ple	Palestine
PAN	Pan	Panama
PAR	Par	Paraguay
PER	Per	Peru
PHI	Phi	Philippines
PUR	Pur	Puerto Rico
QAT	Qat	Qatar
RWA	Rwa	Rwanda
STP	Stp	Sao Tome & Principe
KSA	Ksa	Saudi Arabia
SEN	Sen	Senegal
SLE	Sle	Sierra Leone
SIN	Sin	Singapore
SOL	Sol	Solomon Islands
SOM	Som	Somalia
RSA	Rsa	South Africa
KOR	Kor	South Korea
SKN	Skn	St Kitts & Nevis
VIN	Vin	St Vincent & Grenadines
SDN	Sdn	Sudan
SUR	Sur	Surinam
SYR	Syr	Syria
TAH	Tah	Tahiti
TJK	Tjk	Tajikistan
TAN	Tan	Tanzania
THA	Tha	Thailand
TOG	Tog	Togo
TRI	Tri	Trinidad & Tobago
TUN	Tun	Tunisia
TKM	Tkm	Turkmenistan
UGA	Uga	Uganda
UAE	Uae	United Arab Emirates
USA	Usa	United States
URU	Uru	Uruguay
UZB	Uzb	Uzbekistan
VEN	Ven	Venezuela
VIE	Vie	Vietnam
YEM	Yem	Yemen
ZAM	Zam	Zambia
ZIM	Zim	Zimbabwe

THE EUROPEAN FOOTBALL YEARBOOK 2017 18

Contents

Foreword

I am honoured to have been asked to write the foreword to the European Football Yearbook, which, with this edition, reaches its landmark 30th year.

My playing career was only just starting when the first such Yearbook came out in 1988, and a great deal has happened both to me and to European football in the three decades that have passed since then.

I stopped playing this beautiful game back in 2006, but for the best part of the last two years it has been my great privilege to serve as head coach to the club I consider to be the biggest and best in the world.

I am so grateful to be able to work on a daily basis with some of the greatest footballers on the planet, indeed some of the greatest to have ever played the game, and for us to have been crowned kings of Europe two years in a row – an unprecedented feat in the UEFA Champions League era – as well as reclaiming the Spanish Liga title, ensures that this Real Madrid team will occupy a place in the annals of European and world football for ever more.

Football is a team game, and winning football matches is never down to one individual, it is all about everyone involved pulling together in the same direction and doing everything to achieve a collective goal.

In 2016/17, as in 2015/16, my players, my coaching staff, my president, all the club´s employees and all the many fans who follow and support this great club made life easy for me by matching my desire for victory – both on the domestic front and, especially, in the most important club competition in the world.

Our run to the Cardiff final was not without its ups and downs. Unusually, we did not win our group, but we stayed strong to eliminate very difficult opponents in Napoli, Bayern München and our city rivals Atlético. Then, with the world watching us on the biggest stage of all, we rose to the occasion against Juventus to win 4-1 and lift the treasured trophy for the second time in just over a year.

Now, of course, our next target is to claim a UEFA Champions League hat-trick...

Looking back, though, is as much a part of the joy of football as looking forward. Future achievement can only truly be measured by what has happened in the past.

And that is why the service provided by the European Football Yearbook, which has stood alone in archiving the stories and statistics of a whole continent over the past 30 years, is so essential to this great and glorious game of ours.

I will obviously read through this edition with particular pleasure and enthusiasm – as, I hope, will coaches, players, administrators and fans of other clubs who fulfilled their football dreams, however big or small, in 2016/17.

Zinédine Zidane
Head coach
Real Madrid CF
UEFA Champions League winners 2016/17

Introduction

From the General Editor

Welcome to the 2017/18 edition of the European Football Yearbook.

As you will ascertain from the logo that adorns this page, the front cover and elsewhere, the Yearbook celebrates its 30th birthday with this edition.

That is a landmark I have long been working towards, and I am delighted that it has been reached with what I hope, and believe, is another edition worthy of both the cover price and the publication's heritage.

Thirty years. That's a long time. More than half of my life - and, dare I surmise, of most readers' too.

When I started working on the very first European Football Yearbook, way back in 1987, I could never have imagined that it would still be a going concern three decades later – or indeed that I would still be its General Editor.

Overseeing the Yearbook's growth and development during the past 30 years has helped me to make a living in a fascinating and rewarding profession, but it has also been a labour of love with immense job satisfaction.

The journey to this point has not always been straightforward. The second, third and 17th editions, although written, edited and ready for print, never saw the light of day, and there was even a change of name – to the European Book of Football – for a couple of years before UEFA took the publication under their wing in 2007. But it has certainly been worth it.

Those of you who have purchased every edition – or even most of them – since that ambitious inaugural effort with Ruud Gullit and Marco van Basten on the cover have my profound thanks. Your support is beyond admirable and very much appreciated, and while your bookshelves might be creaking a bit from the collective weight, especially since we changed format and went heavy-duty a few years ago, I hope your collection is well-thumbed and continues to serve its purpose.

I would like to think that despite the internet and its myriad wonders the European Football Yearbook retains its appeal, charm and value. It has no competition as such in printed form – and never really has had despite some very short-lived rival efforts in its early days – and therefore still lives up to the 'Unique' part of the slogan that has promoted it since day one.

The 'Comprehensive' bit of that 30-year-old strapline also still stands. Indeed, in this edition the Yearbook features more countries than ever before, with Kosovo, the 55th member association of UEFA, receiving the same in-depth coverage as every other nation. It is no easy task to obtain reliable and accurate data from some of Europe's 'smaller' leagues, especially in regard to player appearances and goals, but we are a tenacious bunch here at the EFY and seldom take no for an answer.

Back in 1987 there were just 33 countries playing in UEFA competitions, so we have had a 40 per cent increase since then, and that has required a similar expansion of European Football Yearbook personnel.

All of the contributors to this 2017/18 edition are listed on page five. As you can see, it is quite a team. It goes without saying that I am grateful to each and every one of them for their help, but, as ever, my special thanks go to Jesper Krogshede Sørensen, whose enthusiasm, tireless effort and eagle eye make him the perfect – and I mean perfect – assistant, and designer Keith Jackson, whose discipline and dedication are second to none. Without this dream 'team within a team' there would be no European Football Yearbook.

Jesper and Keith both belong at the top of the list of people who have been of most help to me in making the Yearbook what it is over the past 30 years. Others that deserve a particular mention – in roughly chronological order – are Nick Facer (RIP), Rob Kendrew, Jan Buitenga, Bernard Gallagher, Jon Hare, Chris Nawrat (RIP), Cliff Moulder, John Robinson and David Farrelly.

Additionally, I cannot overstate the importance of my family – Sue, Rebecca and Charlie – whose unflinching love and support has kept me going all these years.

I am unsure what the future holds for the European Football Yearbook, but I sincerely hope you enjoy looking through this special anniversary edition as much as I enjoyed putting it together.

Mike Hammond
efyhammond@gmail.com
August 2017

RESPECT
7
2

2016/17 season summary

Real Madrid began the 2016/17 season as they finished it – by lifting a European trophy. Indeed, their thrilling 3-2 UEFA Super Cup triumph against Sevilla in Trondheim, Norway, in August was a portent of things to come as Zinédine Zidane's exciting side stayed true to their attacking instincts to become the first team to make a successful defence of the European title in the UEFA Champions League era. Their 4-1 win against Juventus in the Cardiff final was their record 12th European Cup success and included two more goals from Cristiano Ronaldo, who earlier in the season had become the first player to score 100 in the competition.

If the name added to the UEFA Champions League roll of honour was familiar, there was a new team inscribed on the UEFA Europa League trophy, albeit one accustomed to European success. Manchester United's 2-0 win against Ajax in Stockholm was their first European title since winning the UEFA Champions League in 2008, and it enabled them to become the fifth club, after Ajax, Bayern München, Chelsea and Juventus, to have won the three major continental prizes.

On the international stage, the two main events of the summer were the 2017 UEFA Women's EURO and the 2017 UEFA European Under-21 Championship. If Germany were finally dethroned in the former, they proudly prevailed in the latter for the first time since 2009. A Spain side boasting several high-profile players, including five-goal top scorer Saúl Ñiguez, were most people's favourites to lift the trophy in Poland, but Stefan Kuntz's team upset the odds and defeated them 1-0 in the Krakow final.

Spain had been given reason to celebrate earlier in the summer when they beat England on penalties to win the 2017 UEFA European Under-17 Championship in Varazdin, Croatia – their record third title at that level. England did not, however, have long to wait for success of their own, the Under-19s following on from the Under-20s' victory at the FIFA U-20 World Cup by winning the 2017 UEFA European Under-19 Championship for the first time, courtesy of a 2-1 final win against Portugal in Georgia.

There were upsets galore at the 2017 UEFA Women's EURO as host nation the Netherlands lifted the trophy for the first time after a thrilling 4-2 victory over Denmark in front of a full house in Enschede. While Denmark's quarter-final victory against Germany, winners of the six previous tournaments, was the biggest shock, France's elimination at the same stage by England was also a surprise given their domination of the women's club scene in 2016/17.

For the first time in a decade there were no German representatives in the UEFA Women's Champions League final as Lyon and Paris Saint-Germain imposed themselves

with victories against Wolfsburg and Bayern München respectively in the quarter-finals. Those two would meet in the final, where holders Lyon triumphed for the fourth time, winning on penalties for the second year in a row.

Germany, though, did not go through the season empty-handed as they claimed a record sixth title at the UEFA Women's European Under-17 Championship with victory against Spain on penalties in the final in the Czech Republic.

Also on the honours board in 2016/17 were Salzburg, who greatly impressed in the UEFA Youth League finals week by seeing off Barcelona in the last four then Benfica in the final to win the trophy for the first time. In futsal, meanwhile, Spanish powerhouse Inter FS won the UEFA Futsal Cup for a record fourth time, while at amateur level Croatian side Zagreb captured the UEFA Regions' Cup.

CLUBS CHAMP
ROPÉENS
Emirates
CHAMPIONS LEAGUE
FINAL CARDIFF
adidas

Zinédine Zidane's team secure historic trophy defence

Juventus overpowered in second half of Cardiff final

Competition debutants Leicester reach quarter-finals

Real Madrid reign supreme

History was made in the 25th year of the UEFA Champions League as for the very first time since the European Cup was revamped and rebranded in 1992 the holders made a successful defence of the trophy. Four defending champions had previously returned to the final a year later but all had suffered defeat. Now, in 2017, Real Madrid, the most successful club in the history of Europe's flagship club competition, lifted the curse, overcoming previously undefeated Juventus 4-1 with a masterful second-half display in the Cardiff final.

Zinédine Zidane's second season as Madrid coach thus ended with a repeat triumph – both for him and a team that had barely changed from the one that ascended to European club football's summit the year before with their penalty shoot-out victory over Atlético Madrid in Milan. The spirit, togetherness and collective ruthlessness of the team was once again on repeated show throughout a run to Cardiff in which they were beaten only once – 2-1 at Atlético in the second leg of the semi-final – and scored in every game.

At the forefront of Madrid's success, not for the first time, was the great Cristiano Ronaldo, who topped the competition's goal charts for the fifth season in a row – with one more goal than eternal rival Lionel Messi – thanks to his double in the final against Juventus. The 32-year-old's contribution was fairly low-key in the early stages, scoring only twice as Madrid were demoted to second place in their group by Borussia Dortmund, but he came spectacularly alive at the business end of the competition, scoring five goals against Bayern München in an extended quarter-final and a hat-trick in the first leg of the semi against Atlético before hogging the limelight once again in the final.

While Madrid were indebted above all to their prolific attack – the team's final tally of 36 goals was the second highest registered by a UEFA Champions League-winning team, behind only their own record figure of 41 in 2013/14 – Juventus progressed all the way to Cardiff thanks predominantly to a rock-solid defence. Up until the final they conceded just three goals, keeping nine clean sheets, including six in succession. Massimiliano Allegri's side looked every bit Madrid's equal – until the second half in Cardiff when they simply had no answer to the strength of the attacking armoury aligned against them.

Monaco were consistent crowd-pleasers in reaching the semi-finals, Leonardo Jardim's side knocking out two English clubs – Tottenham Hotspur and Manchester City – before seeing off Borussia Dortmund in a quarter-final scarred by a terrorist attack on the German club's team bus prior to the first leg in Germany. Highly-fancied Bayern and Barcelona also fell at that stage, to the eventual finalists, the Catalans having defied improbable odds with a record-breaking comeback win over Paris Saint-Germain in the last 16. Another noteworthy reversal of fortune in that round was provided by Leicester City, the Premier League champions and competition newcomers, who, after topping their group in style, overturned a first-leg defeat at Sevilla to knock out the perennial UEFA Europa League winners with a momentous 2-0 home win and reach the quarter-finals as England's last surviving representatives.

All in all, the 2016/17 UEFA Champions League season was one of the best yet. On top of all the entertainment and excitement, a total of 380 goals were scored from the group stage to the final, which was the most in a 125-match campaign, yielding an average of over three goals per game for the first time – a fitting way in which to mark the first quarter of a century of a competition whose appeal and prestige has never been greater.

Opposite: Sergio Ramos raises the famous trophy as Real Madrid make history with their second successive UEFA Champions League triumph

Qualifying rounds

The qualifying phase of the 2016/17 competition, staged over four rounds from late June to the third week of August, involved 56 clubs competing at various points of entry for ten places in the group stage, where the successful teams would join the 22 clubs exempt from qualification.

There was an early bombshell when Lincoln, the champions of Gibraltar, not only eliminated Estonia's Flora Tallinn in the first qualifying round but then sensationally beat Celtic – in new manager Brendan Rodgers' first competitive fixture – 1-0 at home in the first leg of their next tie. Unsurprisingly, the Scottish champions recovered from that embarrassment to make further progress with a 3-0 win in Glasgow, and they would even go on to reach the group stage, their home form again proving decisive in closely contested match-ups with FC Astana and, in the play-offs, Hapoel Beer Sheva.

Celtic were one of five participants in the second qualifying round who made it through to the competition proper, Ludogorets Razgrad, FC København, Legia Warszawa and Dinamo Zagreb following suit. The latter were within three minutes of losing their play-off against Salzburg, but a late equaliser followed by an extra-time winner broke the hearts of the Austrian champions, whose bid to compete in the group stage for the first time once again fell agonisingly short.

One newcomer did make it through from the qualifying phase, and in some style too, as Russian Premier-Liga runners-up Rostov eliminated their more experienced counterparts from Belgium and the Netherlands, overcoming first Anderlecht – with a 2-0 win in Brussels – then Ajax – with a swaggering 4-1 victory on home soil. Other group stage regulars unable to return were BATE Borisov, Shakhtar Donetsk, Fenerbahçe and Olympiacos, who all dropped out in the third qualifying round before Roma joined them in the play-offs.

The Serie A side looked well set to qualify when they drew the first leg of their tie away to FC Porto, but a second-leg collapse at the Stadio Olimpico allowed their Portuguese visitors to romp to a 3-0 win. Italy were not the only major country to surrender one of their number, Villarreal losing home and away to Monaco and therefore failing to join the other four Spanish teams automatically qualified for the group stage. There was never a question of England or Germany not having a full complement among the elite 32 as Manchester City and Borussia Mönchengladbach both cruised through their play-off engagements, posting aggregate winning scores of 6-0 and 9-2 against Steaua Bucureşti and Young Boys, respectively.

Steaua goalkeeper Valentin Cojocaru is beaten by Manchester City's Fabian Delph (No18) in the second leg of the play-offs

Group stage

There was something of an unbalanced look to **Group A**, with Bulgarian qualifiers Ludogorets and Swiss champions Basel being drawn alongside two European heavyweights in Arsenal and Paris Saint-Germain. Sure enough, the section would be dominated by the teams from the English and French capitals.

Matchday one brought the two favourites face to face at the Parc des Princes, and it took Paris striker Edinson Cavani a mere 42 seconds to open the scoring – and register the first goal of the group stage – as he headed in Serge Aurier's measured right-wing cross. The Uruguayan had many more chances to double his tally over the course of the evening but he missed them all, and his team paid the price when Alexis Sánchez fired Arsenal level 12 minutes from time to snatch an unlikely point.

The 1-1 draw was no bad result for either team, however, as they would both take nine points from their next three fixtures, leaving Basel and Ludogorets on just the one apiece they had claimed from their opening 1-1 draw in Switzerland. Arsenal and Paris were comfortable winners on matchdays two and three but both required late goals away from home to maintain their victory run on matchday four, the Gunners overturning a two-goal deficit in Bulgaria to beat Ludogorets with a brilliant 88th-minute individual strike from Mesut Özil, who had already scored a hat-trick against the same opponents in a 6-0 rout two weeks earlier. PSG left it even later in Basel, Thomas Meunier's sliced volley on the stroke of full time giving the visitors a 2-1 win that ensured both they and Arsenal would qualify with two games to spare.

A 2-2 draw in north London took Paris to the top of the table but they could not stay there, a repeat scoreline at home to Ludogorets enabling Arsenal, with a closing 4-1 win at Basel featuring a Lucas Pérez hat-trick, to win the group – the first time they had done so for five years. Ludogorets finished third to qualify for the UEFA Europa League with just three points – a tally that would have been considerably greater had they possessed the wherewithal to hang on to leads.

Unlike Group A, **Group B** possessed no clear favourites. All four teams – Benfica, Beşiktaş, Napoli and Dynamo Kyiv – had

KEY FACT

7

Carlo Ancelotti became the first coach to lead seven different clubs in the UEFA Champions League, his first outing with Bayern München coming after stints with Parma, Juventus, Milan, Chelsea, Paris Saint-Germain and Real Madrid. His fellow-Italian Claudio Ranieri, meanwhile, joined Rafel Benítez in Ancelotti's slipstream by coaching a sixth different club in the competition, Leicester City following on from Chelsea, Valencia, Juventus, Roma and Inter.

received direct entry to the group stage, with the Italian side the only non-national champions among them.

It was Maurizio Sarri's side, however, that made the best start, a double for new Polish striker Arkadiusz Milik swinging victory Napoli's way on opening night at Dynamo Kyiv before Benfica were comprehensively beaten at the Stadio San Paolo, Milik again among the scorers in a 4-2 win. Beşiktaş kicked off with two 1-1 draws, the first of them snatched in extremis away to Benfica thanks to a brilliant free-kick from Talisca, who was on loan to them from the Lisbon club, before setting the cat among the pigeons when they overcame Napoli in southern Italy, Vincent Aboubakar's second goal of the game bringing the Turkish champions an unexpected 3-2 victory after Lorenzo Insigne had missed a penalty for the home side.

Benfica used their double header with Dynamo Kyiv to get back into contention, Eduardo Salvio scoring twice from the spot to help his team to six precious points and Ederson saving a penalty in the 1-0 home win – a result that effectively removed the winless Ukrainians from contention. With Napoli drawing 1-1 at Beşiktaş in the return fixture – courtesy of skipper Marek Hamšík's terrific equaliser – only one point separated the top three teams with two games to go, and it remained that way when Napoli were held 0-0 at home by Dynamo and Beşiktaş staged a stunning comeback from three goals down to share the spoils with Benfica in Istanbul.

Napoli, Benfica and Beşiktaş all knew that victory on matchday six would guarantee their progress while a draw could be enough depending on the other result. As it transpired, even a home defeat did not eliminate Benfica, Napoli's 2-1 win in the Portuguese capital combining with Beşiktaş's ten-man submission in Kyiv, where they were routed 6-0, to give the Italian side first place in the group and their hosts the runners-up spot – albeit with just eight points, the lowest final tally of any of the 16 qualifiers.

There were no pre-matchday six permutations needed in **Group C,** where all four final placings were decided a round in advance of its conclusion. Barcelona, as expected, finished first, topping their group for the tenth season in a row and 18th in all – both competition records – while Manchester City, led by ex-Barça boss Pep Guardiola, seized the runners-up spot, Borussia Mönchengladbach took third place and winless Celtic ended up bottom.

The star of the show, not for the first time, was Lionel Messi, who scored ten of Barcelona's 20 goals (a personal-best group stage haul), including two hat-tricks – his sixth and seventh in the UEFA Champions League. The first of those came on the opening night when Barcelona thrashed Celtic 7-0 at the Camp Nou, giving the home side their highest-scoring win in the competition while subjecting the visitors to the heaviest European defeat in their history. The Argentinian maestro missed Barça's 2-1 victory at Mönchengladbach on matchday two but returned to grab three more goals in a 4-0 demolition of Manchester City – thus scoring back-to-back UEFA Champions League hat-tricks for the first time – and went on to find the net in every subsequent fixture too.

Arguably the best of Messi's ten goals came in the one game Barça lost – a brilliant counter-attacking effort to open the scoring in Manchester – where City staged a rousing comeback – aided by two İlkay Gündoğan goals and the odd touch of good fortune – to win 3-1, giving Guardiola a first victory against the club that groomed him. Barcelona recovered quickly from the wounds of defeat, returning to British shores to defeat Celtic 2-0 in Glasgow – with a Messi double – and clinch top spot, while City made sure of second place with a 1-1 draw at Gladbach, the team they had defeated 4-0 on matchday one – with a Sergio Agüero hat-trick - in a game postponed for 24 hours because of a waterlogged pitch.

Lionel Messi waltzes past Claudio Bravo to score the first goal of his Camp Nou hat-trick for Barcelona against Manchester City

Bayern München began their bid for European glory in **Group D** with a home fixture against group stage debutants Rostov. The outcome was wholly predictable, with the German champions cruising to victory – a competition-record 13th in succession at home – as two Joshua Kimmich headers helped them defeat the Russian side 5-0.

Next time out, however, Bayern were beaten. Atlético Madrid, the club that had eliminated them the previous season in the semi-finals, again got the better of them at the Estadio Vicente Calderón, repeating the 1-0 scoreline of a few months earlier thanks to Yannick Carrasco's 35th-minute strike, with Antoine Griezmann even missing a late penalty that he smashed against the crossbar. Having also won their opening fixture 1-0, at PSV Eindhoven, Atlético were now in the driving seat and that was where they remained after doing the double over Rostov, firstly with another 1-0 win – and another fine Carrasco goal – in Russia, then with a last-ditch 2-1 home success in which Griezmann scored twice, his second goal not arriving until the third minute of stoppage time.

With Bayern also taking maximum points at the expense of PSV thanks to another easy home win (4-1) and a Robert Lewandowski double that brought a comeback victory in the Netherlands (2-1), the two qualifying places were settled with two fixtures remaining. Bayern got their revenge on Atlético with a 1-0 win of their own in the final round, Lewandowski again doing the honours with his fifth goal of the campaign, but the result had no bearing on the final placings, with Atlético having already sealed top spot a fortnight earlier when they made it five wins out of five in beating PSV 2-0 at home while Bayern stumbled to a shock 3-2 defeat in Rostov. The Russian side took confidence from that landmark victory into their final fixture, in Eindhoven, where they got the draw they needed (0-0) to protect third place and qualify for the UEFA Europa League.

CSKA Moskva were the only reigning domestic champions in **Group E**, which also included Bayer Leverkusen, Monaco and Tottenham Hotspur, who, with building work for a new stadium taking place next to White Hart Lane, switched their home games in the competition to Wembley Stadium.

Spurs' record at the reconstructed Wembley was unimpressive, and talk of the national stadium having a jinx on the club intensified when Mauricio Pochettino's side lost there to Monaco on opening night, goals from Bernardo Silva and Thomas Lemar earning a deserved 2-1 victory for a team that arrived high on confidence after a perfect start to the new Ligue 1 campaign. With Leverkusen simultaneously squandering a two-goal lead to draw 2-2 at home to CSKA, Monaco were the early leaders. It was a position they would never relinquish.

Late goals from Kamil Glik – with the last kick of the game – at home to Leverkusen and Bernardo Silva at CSKA preserved Monaco's unbeaten record before they clinched top spot with back-to-back home wins, defeating CSKA 3-0 thanks to a couple of goals from a revitalised Radamel Falcao and Spurs 2-1 with another winning goal from Lemar – just a minute after Harry Kane had drawn the visitors level from the penalty spot.

That defeat on the French Riviera ended Tottenham's qualifying hopes, the Wembley wobbles having afflicted them again earlier that month when they lost 1-0 to Leverkusen – the German club's first victory after three successive draws, which included a goalless stalemate at home to the north Londoners notable for an astonishing goal-line save from visiting keeper Hugo Lloris. Slovenian international Kevin Kampl scored the only goal at Wembley to give Leverkusen a two-point advantage over Spurs, and they increased that to an unassailable three with yet another draw, 1-1 at winless CSKA, guaranteeing their qualification as group runners-up. The Rhinelanders defeated a second-string Monaco 3-0 on matchday six, while Tottenham finally won at Wembley, coming from behind to defeat CSKA 3-1 and pip the Russian side to a UEFA Europa League spot while also condemning ooposition keeper Igor Akinfeev to his 43rd consecutive UEFA Champions League appearance without a clean sheet.

Radamel Falcao celebrates scoring for Monaco against CSKA Moskva

KEY FACT

12

Borussia Dortmund's 8-4 win at home to Legia Warszawa was the highest-scoring UEFA Champions League match of all time, the 12 goals beating the 11 registered in Monaco's 8-3 victory over Deportivo La Coruña in November 2003. Furthermore, Dortmund became only the fourth team to score eight goals in a match. Apart from Monaco, the other two occasions were 8-0 wins for Liverpool (v Beşiktaş in November 2007) and Real Madrid (v Malmö FF in December 2015).

Group F was headed by holders Real Madrid, who were making their record 20th successive appearance in the group stage of the competition. For company they had Borussia Dortmund, Sporting Clube de Portugal and the only domestic champions in the section, Legia Warszawa of Poland.

Madrid would come through the group unbeaten but not without several scares and indeed not in first place, ceding that honour to Dortmund, with whom they shared two highly entertaining 2-2 draws. The second of those, at the Estadio Santiago Bernabéu on matchday six, came after the German club had recovered a two-goal deficit and, with Marco Reus's late equaliser, set a new record for the number of goals scored by a team in a UEFA Champions League group, that being their 21st – one more than the final tally of four other teams, including Barcelona, who had equalled the record 24 hours earlier.

Two thirds of Dortmund's goals were scored against Legia, an opening 6-0 win in Poland supplemented in the return fixture by eight more, with Thomas Tuchel's side eventually prevailing 8-4 on an extraordinary, record-breaking night in the Ruhr. The 51 goals scored in Group F's 12 fixtures also constituted a competition high, no previous group having ever reached the half-century.

Given the proliferation of goals, it was perhaps surprising that Cristiano Ronaldo only contributed two of them. His first rescued Madrid from a possible opening-day defeat at home to Sporting – before Álvaro Morata pounced with a 94th-minute winner – and his second opened the scoring in Dortmund. He failed to cash in against Legia, who, after losing 5-1 in the Bernabéu, almost pulled off a shock win behind closed doors in Warsaw before settling for a 3-3 draw. The Polish side equalled the record for the number of goals conceded in a group but managed to avoid having it all to themselves when they defeated Sporting 1-0 at home in their final fixture – a result that enabled them to leapfrog their opponents into third place and the UEFA Europa League.

Leicester City, the reigning champions of England, made their UEFA Champions League debut in **Group G**. It was the club's first European campaign in 16 years and only their fourth ever. But if they were an unknown quantity at the highest level, that description certainly didn't apply to their manager, Claudio Ranieri, who had already taken five previous clubs into the group stage of Europe's elite club competition.

Seeded in the draw, Leicester were not unhappy to be grouped with FC København, Club Brugge and FC Porto, but few could have predicted that they would make such a whirlwind start, winger Marc Albrighton putting them ahead five minutes into their opening game in Bruges before Riyad Mahrez exploited two fouls on Jamie Vardy to score a free-kick and a penalty and bring the Foxes their first European victory for 55 years.

That was just the start for the shock Premier League winners. Despite a troublesome run on the domestic front, they came alive on European nights, beating both Porto and København 1-0 in front of raucous home support to take a commanding lead at the top of the table before consolidating their position with a fourth successive clean sheet – a record for a UEFA Champions League debutant – in a 0-0 draw at Parken, where the home side had not lost in 30 matches. Brilliant late saves by goalkeeper Kasper Schmeichel from his fellow Danish international Andreas Cornelius in both games against FCK were crucial in Leicester's march to the knockout phase, and they secured their place in the last 16, as group winners, with a game to spare by beating Club Brugge 2-1 – their third home win out of three.

Shinji Kagawa heads in the first of Dortmund's eight goals in their record-breaking 8-4 win against Legia Warszawa

With Leicester commanding the group and Club Brugge propping it up, an interesting battle for second place developed between Porto and København. The Portuguese side held the advantage going into the final fixture following a goalless draw between the two teams in the Danish capital, and with Ranieri sending out a second XI in the Estádio do Dragão, Porto duly sealed the win they needed in some comfort, routing the group winners 5-0 with an irresistible attacking display and rendering their rivals' 2-0 win in Bruges academic.

Juventus, the Italian champions, and Sevilla, the three-in-a-row UEFA Europa League winners, were the fancied teams to reach the round of 16 from **Group H**. However, they both found themselves two points adrift of Lyon after matchday one, the French side's easy 3-0 win at home to Dinamo Zagreb coinciding with a goalless draw between the two favourites in Turin – a match in which overworked Sevilla goalkeeper Sergio Rico was the standout performer.

By the halfway point of the group, though, that stalemate felt like one point gained rather than two lost, with Juve and Sevilla prevailing in each of their next two games, including a 1-0 win apiece over Lyon. The French side could count themselves extremely unfortunate to be beaten at home by the Bianconeri on a night when Gianluigi Buffon was at his brilliant best, pulling off three world-class saves, including one from an Alexandre Lacazette penalty, before Juan Cuadrado scored the visitors' winning goal. Lyon fought back well to draw 1-1 in the return, with Corentin Tolisso striking a late equaliser, but an even later miss by Lacazette left Bruno Génésio's men again reflecting on what might have been.

Juventus clinched qualification on matchday five by winning 3-1 at Sevilla. The Spanish side had not conceded in their first four matches, but although they took an early lead, the 36th-minute dismissal of Franco Vázquez completely turned the game and Juve, having equalised with a penalty on the stroke of half-time, added two more goals late on, through Leonardo Bonucci and Mario Mandžukić, to claim their third successive away win.

With Lyon simultaneously beating hapless Dinamo, 1-0 in Zagreb, Sevilla were not yet through, but if they avoided defeat by two goals in France on the final day, they would not be returning to the UEFA Europa League to defend their trophy. Another clean sheet, in an oddly uneventful 0-0 draw, did the job, while Juve also kept their goal intact by winning 2-0 against Dinamo, who thus became only the second team in UEFA Champions League history to lose all six group matches without scoring a goal.

Round of 16

The first round of the knockout phase, spread over a month and a day in early spring, could hardly have been more exciting. It was thrill-a-minute stuff all the way, with the 16 matches delivering no fewer than 62 goals – a record for that stage of the competition – and a multitude of incidents and talking points. The round also produced the greatest second-leg comeback the UEFA Champions League had ever witnessed.

Barcelona looked almost certain to depart the competition before the quarter-finals for the first time in a decade. They were blitzed in their first leg at the Parc des Princes by a Paris Saint-Germain side at the absolute pinnacle of their form, the home side harrying their illustrious visitors out of their stride and scoring four goals without reply, including two from Ángel Di María and one from Cavani, both of whom were celebrating their birthday. Paris's midfield trio of Adrien Rabiot, Marco Verratti and Blaise Matuidi all had the game of their lives in a wondrous all-round team performance that had the fans in the French capital in raptures.

Three weeks later, however, that ecstasy turned to agony as PSG inconceivably allowed their huge advantage to be overturned at the Camp Nou. No team had ever retrieved a four-goal first-leg deficit in UEFA Champions League history, but Barcelona, backed by a fervent and noisy crowd that never doubted the possibility of history being made despite coach Luis Enrique's mid-tie announcement that he would be leaving at the end of the season, pulled it off. When Cavani made it 3-1 on the night just after the hour and the scoreline remained that way with two minutes of normal time remaining, the outcome looked settled. But a brilliant Neymar free-kick gave the home side renewed hope and in added time the Brazilian took over, scoring a penalty before, in the final play of the game, he lifted an exquisite ball over the panicky Paris defence for Sergi Roberto to bring the house down with an immaculate volleyed finish. It was Barça's sixth goal of the evening and one that will undoubtedly go down in club legend for ever more.

Bayern München made it through to a record 16th quarter-final with rather less bother, subjecting Arsène Wenger's Arsenal to their most humiliating UEFA Champions League experience as the Londoners exited at the round of 16 stage for the seventh year running with a 10-2 aggregate defeat. Two second-half capitulations without their key defender Laurent Koscielny – injured in Munich, sent off in London – allowed Bayern to score for fun, and they did just that, reaching double figures for the tie with Arturo Vidal's late double in the second leg that brought a repeat of the 5-1 scoreline from the first.

Borussia Dortmund ensured a double German presence in the last eight by overpowering Benfica 4-0 at home after losing the first leg 1-0 in Lisbon. Pierre-Emerick Aubameyang endured a miserable night in the Portuguese capital, missing several gilt-edged chances, including a penalty, but he atoned on home soil, firing his team into the next round with a timely hat-trick. One Bundesliga side did drop out, however, Bayer Leverkusen losing 4-2 at home to Atlético Madrid in the first leg before finding goalkeeper Jan Oblak in unbeatable form in the goalless return.

Arturo Vidal chips past David Ospina as Bayern finish off Arsenal in London

KEY FACT

6

Manchester City went out of the competition despite scoring six goals against Monaco – the most ever registered by an eliminated side in a UEFA Champions League knockout phase tie. Three clubs had previously scored five.

Real Madrid, embarking on a record 20th successive knockout phase campaign, beat Napoli 3-1 in both legs, but they fell a goal behind in each, Lorenzo Insigne's brilliantly opportunistic 40-yard strike opening the scoring in the Bernabéu before Karim Benzema, Toni Kroos and – with a wonder goal of his own – Casemiro put the defending champions back in charge. Skipper Sergio Ramos was Madrid's goalscoring hero in Naples, heading in an equaliser and then forcing an own-goal from Napoli's earlier scorer Dries Mertens to ensure his club's further progress. Juventus kept Italian interest alive, although they were helped on their way into the quarter-finals by a Porto side who had players red-carded in the first half of each game, Alex Telles departing early in Porto and Maxi Pereira doing likewise in Turin. Juve took full advantage, substitutes Marko Pjaca and Dani Alves scoring in the 2-0 first-leg win and Paulo Dybala's penalty proving sufficient for victory in the return.

Leicester, the only one of the 16 teams that had never previously participated in the UEFA Champions League knockout phase, were going through a dreadful run of form in the Premier League when they took on Sevilla, and for much of the first leg in Andalusia they were under the cosh, relying on the goalkeeping expertise of Schmeichel, whose many fine saves included one from a Joaquín Correa penalty, to keep them afloat. The Dane was eventually beaten twice, by Pablo Sarabia and Correa, but out of the blue Leicester got back into the tie with a tremendous goal of geometrical precision finished off by Jamie Vardy.

Leicester captain Wes Morgan turns to celebrate after putting his team 1-0 up at home to Sevilla in the round of 16 second leg

By the time the second leg came around, Leicester had dismissed their title-winning manager Ranieri. They were a revived force under the Italian's replacement and erstwhile assistant Craig Shakespeare, and they produced one of the greatest performances in the club's history to overturn their 2-1 first-leg defeat, captain Wes Morgan making it 1-0 from close range, winger Marc Albrighton doubling the lead with a well-taken second and – after Samir Nasri had been sent off – Schmeichel pulling off another penalty save, this time from Steven N'Zonzi, before the final whistle brought unfettered jubilation in the stands.

Leicester's remarkable achievement in reaching the quarter-finals at the expense of the team that had won the UEFA Europa League three years running was magnified the following day when they became the last English team standing, Manchester City losing out on the away-goals rule to Monaco at the end of a magnificent tie that yielded a dozen goals, repeatedly swung one way then the other and revealed to the world a potential global superstar in Monaco's 18-year-old striker Kylian Mbappé.

The multi-talented youngster scored in both legs, putting Monaco 2-1 ahead in a frenzied first encounter in Manchester, which featured two special goals from Radamel Falcao – who also missed a penalty – and a brilliant comeback from Guardiola's team, who scored three times in the last 20 minutes to win the game 5-3. Monaco utterly dominated the first half of the second leg at the Stade Louis II, scoring twice through Mbappé and Fabinho, but City again fought back after the interval and appeared to have made the decisive breakthrough when Leroy Sané restored their aggregate lead. The last word, though, went to Monaco, midfielder Tiémoué Bakayoko heading home a free-kick 13 minutes from time that earned his club a record-equalling fifth away-goals success in the UEFA Champions League.

Quarter-finals

The last-eight line-up comprised three Spanish clubs – for the fifth successive year – plus two from Germany and one apiece from England, France and Italy, leaving no room for teams outside Europe's big five leagues. Leicester's presence had landmark significance, not only for them but for the competition as a whole as they were the 50th different club to reach the UEFA Champions League quarter-finals and the eighth from England – the most from any single nation.

Atlético Madrid were not the opposition Leicester were hoping for as they had been responsible for ending two of the English club's three previous European adventures. The Spaniards, making their fourth successive quarter-final appearance, would prove to be their bogey side once again, although not without a gallant effort from the English underdogs. A Griezmann penalty – awarded for a foul that video footage showed to be outside, rather than inside, the area – was the only goal of the first leg in Madrid, but Leicester were left needing to score three times in front of their own fans when a superb Saúl Ñíguez header doubled Atlético's advantage 26 minutes into the return. A gutsy second-half onslaught brought an equaliser from Vardy and a couple of further chances, but Atlético's celebrated defence, led by the irrepressible Diego Godín, weathered the storm, enabling Diego Simeone's side to take their place in the semi-finals and bring the curtain down on Leicester's memorable UEFA Champions League debut.

Real Madrid joined Atlético in the last four but only after an epic battle with Bayern. Cristiano Ronaldo, without a goal in the competition since matchday two, burst back into life with a match-winning double in Munich, turning the tie in the holders' favour after Vidal, who had put the home side ahead with a thumping header, sent a penalty over the bar and Javi Martínez was sent off. The 2-1 defeat ended Bayern's record run of 16 successive home wins, but they were not dead yet, and coach Carlo Ancelotti's return to the Bernabéu so very nearly became a triumphant one. Indeed, had luck gone for Bayern rather than against them on a number of key occasions, they might indeed have savoured a famous comeback victory. As it was, Bayern

KEY FACT

2

Quarter-final wins for Real Madrid and Atlético Madrid meant that Spain took two teams into the UEFA Champions League semi-finals for the seventh season in a row. The only other country to have had double representation in the last four during that time was Germany in 2012/13, when that nation also provided both finalists. 2016/17 was the first season without a German semi-finalist since 2008/09.

took the game to extra time, but they did so with ten men after losing Vidal to an unfortunate red card and eventually paid the price as Ronaldo scored twice to become the first player to reach 100 UEFA Champions League goals and take his team through on what would eventually be a comfortable 6-3 aggregate.

That was also the final two-legged scoreline in the other tie involving a German club, with Dortmund following Bayern out of the competition after losing both legs to Monaco. The tie was utterly overshadowed, however, by a terrorist attack on the Dortmund team bus prior to the first leg in Germany. The match was postponed for a day, with one Dortmund player, defender Marc Bartra, being hospitalised with a broken wrist. The casualty list could have been far, far worse, but the trauma of the experience evidently took its toll on the Dortmund players, who underperformed in a 3-2 defeat in which Mbappé was once again the Monaco star, scoring twice, his second goal a sublime finish on the run. The teenager was on target once again a week later just three minutes in, and when Falcao made it 2-0 on the night with a magnificent flying header, there was no way back for Dortmund, Leonardo Jardim's exciting young team eventually going through in style, having scored six goals for the second round in succession.

Juventus against Barcelona was a repeat of the 2015 final, which the Catalans had won 3-1 in Berlin. This time, though, it was the perennial Serie A champions who prevailed. As in the round of 16, Barcelona proved terrible travellers, Dybala twice piercing their defence with his rapier-like left foot before Giorgio Chiellini headed in a third goal that, with Buffon performing brilliantly in goal to keep another clean sheet, would normally have given the Bianconeri an unassailable advantage going into the second leg. But against Barcelona, it seemed, no lead was big enough. Juventus, though, were the masters of protecting what they had, and there would be no second miraculous comeback at the Camp Nou. Indeed, Barça would fail even to win the match – for the first time in 16 UEFA Champions League fixtures at the venue – as Buffon and co magisterially denied Messi and co to get what they came for – a goalless draw that put them through to the semi-finals and inflicted on their opponents a second successive quarter-final elimination.

Gonzalo Higuaín puts Juventus 1-0 up against Monaco in the Stade Louis II

Semi-finals

The draw for the semi-finals ensured that there would be no possibility of a third all-Madrid final in four years as Real and Atlético were paired together, with Juventus taking on Monaco in the other tie.

It was nevertheless the fourth time in as many seasons that the two rivals from the Spanish capital had been placed in UEFA Champions League opposition, with Real winning all three of the previous ties. A fourth looked to be something of a foregone conclusion after a one-sided first leg in the Bernabéu, during which Ronaldo helped himself to a second successive hat-trick to give the defending champions a 3-0 lead.

The Portuguese superstar headed in his first goal after just ten minutes as Real got off to a flier, pinning Atlético in their own half with a series of fast, fluent attacks. Whether or not it was the unfamiliar black and yellow kit they were wearing, Atlético took a long time to get going, but after creating, and wasting, a couple of chances before the interval, they eventually managed to get a foothold, only for Ronaldo to take centre stage in the final 20 minutes and score twice more as Real went in for the kill. The goal that completed his 42nd hat-trick for the Merengues was also his 399th for the club and took his total for the European season to ten – one shy of Messi's leading tally.

The second leg was Atlético's farewell European match at the Vicente Calderón before their move to a new stadium. It was always going to be an emotional occasion, but the prospects of it being a celebratory one were unexpectedly raised as Simeone's men scored twice in the opening 16 minutes, Saúl powering in a header before Griezmann fortuitously found the net from a mis-struck penalty awarded after Raphaël Varane had tangled with Fernando Torres. It was game on now for sure, but Real Madrid had scored in every match they had played in 2016/17 and three minutes before the end of an increasingly aggressive first half, they duly kept that run going, Isco turning the ball home from close range after Oblak had saved a low shot from Kroos following brilliant approach work on the left by Benzema. With that goal the tie effectively ended as a contest. Atlético, like opponents Leicester the round before, had to score three goals without reply in the second half. They could not manage one, the match eventually concluding in a violent thunderstorm that somehow seemed appropriate for the occasion.

Jardim's free-scoring, spectator-friendly Monaco side had been the revelation of both the French and the European season, but they met their match when Juventus visited the Principality for the first leg of the club's first UEFA Champions League semi-final for 13 years. Massimiliano Allegri's wily Italian side closed down their vibrant hosts at every opportunity, cramping their style sufficiently to keep a sixth successive European clean sheet and also scoring two marvellous goals themselves. Gonzalo Higuaín was responsible for both of them, Dani Alves on each occasion supplying him with the assist. The first, on 29 minutes, was a counter-attacking goal of lethal precision, the second, just before the hour, a smart left-footed finish to a brilliant right-wing cross.

KEY FACT

690

Juventus went 690 minutes without conceding a goal in the competition until Kylian Mbappé's consolation effort for Monaco in Turin in the second leg of the semi-final. It was the second-longest sequence in the competition's history, albeit some way behind Arsenal's 2005/06 record of 995 minutes.

With a 2-0 advantage in a stadium where they had not lost in 50 matches, and with a perfect record in 11 two-legged ties against French opposition, Juventus were presumably undaunted by the fact that Monaco had scored three times away from home in each of the previous two rounds. It certainly appeared that way as they treated their fans to another first-half masterclass, several chances going begging before Mario Mandžukić broke the deadlock from yet another Dani Alves assist and then the Brazilian full-back scored himself with a majestically struck volley to increase Juve's aggregate lead to 4-0. The second half was nowhere near as enthralling, but Monaco did manage to score a goal, through Mbappé's close-range strike, which ended Juve's long run without conceding on 690 minutes.

Final

The 25th UEFA Champions League final, staged under a closed roof at the National Stadium of Wales in Cardiff, brought together the record champions of Italy and Spain. On paper there was little to choose between Real Madrid and Juventus. Both were in ebullient form, having just won another domestic title, both were at full strength – with the possible exception of Madrid's Gareth Bale, the local Welsh hero, who, after a six-week injury lay-off, was deemed fit enough only to start on the bench – and both were appearing in their sixth UEFA Champions League final, matching AC Milan's record. The only significant difference was that Madrid had been triumphant on each of their five previous visits, whereas Juventus had won only one – and that on penalties back in 1996.

Juve were seeking the first treble in their history, whereas Madrid were bidding for a first European Cup and domestic league double since 1958. They were also eager to become European club champions for a record-extending 12th time and in so doing lay claim to being the first team ever to make a successful defence of club football's most treasured trophy since the competition was renamed as the UEFA Champions League in 1992.

Juve made the brighter start, testing Madrid keeper Keylor Navas three times in the opening minutes, but it was the holders, with their first meaningful attack, and their first shot, who opened the scoring, the inevitable Ronaldo sweeping home a first-time right-footer from Daniel Carvajal's pull-back that took the slightest of deflections before beating Buffon. It was a historic strike for both Madrid – their 500th UEFA Champions League goal – and their talismanic striker as he became the first player to score in three UEFA Champions League finals. Seven minutes later the Bianconeri responded to that setback with a quite majestic goal, as brilliant in its creation as it was in its execution, with Alex Santos volleying Bonucci's 50-yard diagonal pass back across the area for Higuaín, who then, also on the volley, fed Mandžukić. The Croatian international was tightly marked but he controlled the ball superbly before beating Navas with an audacious and spectacular overhead kick.

KEY FACT

4

Cristiano Ronaldo joined Clarence Seedorf as a record four-time winner of the UEFA Champions League. His double for Real Madrid against Juventus in Cardiff also enabled him to become the first player to score in three UEFA Champions League finals and the sixth to score a double. With four goals in total he also became the fixture's record marksman.

Level at half-time, the contest was intriguingly poised, but the second half would be completely dominated by Madrid. It needed a slice of good fortune for Zinédine Zidane's side to retake the lead, Casemiro's speculative shot taking a huge deflection off Sami Khedira before squeezing into the corner past Buffon's outstretched right hand, but three minutes later Ronaldo was at it again, tucking home Luka Modrić's pull-back with a deft near-post half-volley to make it 3-1 and in the process lift his total for the season to 12 goals, one more than Messi at the head of the scorers' chart. Juve were out for the count, and Zidane was able to bring on Bale for a late cameo. The Cardiff-born winger did not score, but his team did, another substitute, Marco Asensio, making it 4-1 late in the game after a clever run on the left by Marcelo, the Italians having at that stage been reduced to ten men following Juan Cuadrado's 84th-minute red card.

Madrid's majestic second-half display simply blew Juventus away. While Ronaldo, with his two goals, was evidently the star of the show, the victory was a magnificent team effort from front to back. It was also a personal triumph for Zidane, the first coach – just as Real Madrid were the first club – to win the UEFA Champions League two years in succession.

Cristiano Ronaldo leaves the Juventus defence in shreds with his second goal in Real Madrid's 4-1 victory

UEFA Champions League

First qualifying round

28/06/16, A. Le Coq Arena, Tallinn
FC Flora Tallinn 2-1 Lincoln FC
06/07/16, Victoria Stadium, Gibraltar
Lincoln FC 2-0 FC Flora Tallinn
Aggregate: 3-2; Lincoln FC qualify.

28/06/16, Park Hall, Oswestry
The New Saints FC 2-1 SP Tre Penne
05/07/16, San Marino Stadium, Serravalle
SP Tre Penne 0-3 The New Saints FC
Aggregate: 1-5; The New Saints FC qualify.

28/06/16, Hibernians Stadium, Paola
Valletta FC 1-0 B36 Tórshavn
05/07/16, Gundadalur, Torshavn
B36 Tórshavn 2-1 Valletta FC
Aggregate: 2-2; Valletta FC qualify on away goal.

28/06/16, Estadi Comunal, Andorra la Vella
FC Santa Coloma 0-0 Alashkert FC
05/07/16, Vazgen Sargsyan anvan Hanrapetakan Marzadasht, Yerevan
Alashkert FC 3-0 FC Santa Coloma
Aggregate: 3-0; Alashkert FC qualify.

Second qualifying round

12/07/16, NK Zrinjski, Mostar
HŠK Zrinjski 1-1 Legia Warszawa
19/07/16, Stadion Wojska Polskiego, Warsaw
Legia Warszawa 2-0 HŠK Zrinjski
Aggregate: 3-1; Legia Warszawa qualify.

12/07/16, Park Hall, Oswestry
The New Saints FC 0-0 APOEL FC
19/07/16, GSP, Nicosia
APOEL FC 3-0 The New Saints FC
Aggregate: 3-0; APOEL FC qualify.

12/07/16, Hibernians Stadium, Paola
Valletta FC 1-2 FK Crvena zvezda
19/07/16, Stadion Rajko Mitić, Belgrade
FK Crvena zvezda 2-1 Valletta FC
Aggregate: 4-2; FK Crvena zvezda qualify.

12/07/16, Victoria Stadium, Gibraltar
Lincoln FC 1-0 Celtic FC
20/07/16, Celtic Park, Glasgow
Celtic FC 3-0 Lincoln FC
Aggregate: 3-1; Celtic FC qualify.

12/07/16, Stadion Salzburg, Salzburg
FC Salzburg 1-0 FK Liepāja
19/07/16, Daugava, Liepaja
FK Liepāja 0-2 FC Salzburg
Aggregate: 0-3; FC Salzburg qualify.

12/07/16, Nacionalna Arena Filip II Makedonski, Skopje
FK Vardar 1-2 GNK Dinamo Zagreb
20/07/16, Stadion Maksimir, Zagreb
GNK Dinamo Zagreb 3-2 FK Vardar
Aggregate: 5-3; GNK Dinamo Zagreb qualify.

12/07/16, Turner Stadium, Beer Sheva
Hapoel Beer-Sheva FC 3-2 FC Sheriff
19/07/16, Stadionul Sheriff, Tiraspol
FC Sheriff 0-0 Hapoel Beer-Sheva FC
Aggregate: 2-3; Hapoel Beer-Sheva FC qualify.

12/07/16, Tofiq Bähramov Republican stadium, Baku
Qarabağ FK 2-0 F91 Dudelange
20/07/16, Jos Nosbaum, Dudelange
F91 Dudelange 1-1 Qarabağ FK
Aggregate: 1-3; Qarabağ FK qualify.

12/07/16, Boris Paichadze Dinamo Arena, Tbilisi
FC Dinamo Tbilisi 2-0 Alashkert FC
19/07/16, Vazgen Sargsyan anvan Hanrapetakan Marzadasht, Yerevan
Alashkert FC 1-1 FC Dinamo Tbilisi
Aggregate: 1-3; FC Dinamo Tbilisi qualify.

12/07/16, Borisov-Arena, Borisov
FC BATE Borisov 2-0 SJK Seinäjoki
19/07/16, OmaSP Stadion, Seinajoki
SJK Seinäjoki 2-2 FC BATE Borisov
Aggregate: 2-4; FC BATE Borisov qualify.

13/07/16, Seaview, Belfast
Crusaders FC 0-3 FC København
19/07/16, Parken, Copenhagen
FC København 6-0 Crusaders FC
Aggregate: 9-0; FC København qualify.

13/07/16, Lerkendal Stadion, Trondheim
Rosenborg BK 3-1 IFK Norrköping
20/07/16, Norrköpings Idrottsparken, Norrkoping
IFK Norrköping 3-2 Rosenborg BK
Aggregate: 4-5; Rosenborg BK qualify.

13/07/16, Oriel Park, Dundalk
Dundalk FC 1-1 FH Hafnarfjördur
20/07/16, Kaplakrikavöllur, Hafnarfjördur
FH Hafnarfjördur 2-2 Dundalk FC
Aggregate: 3-3; Dundalk FC qualify on away goals.

13/07/16, Elbasan Arena, Elbasan
FK Partizani 1-1 Ferencvárosi TC
20/07/16, Groupama Aréna, Budapest
Ferencvárosi TC 1-1 FK Partizani (aet)
Aggregate: 2-2; FK Partizani qualify 3-1 on penalties.

13/07/16, LFF stadionas, Vilnius
FK Žalgiris Vilnius 0-0 FC Astana
20/07/16, Astana Arena, Astana
FC Astana 2-1 FK Žalgiris Vilnius
Aggregate: 2-1; FC Astana qualify.

13/07/16, Stadion Stožice, Ljubljana
NK Olimpija Ljubljana 3-4 FK AS Trenčín
20/07/16, Štadión MŠK Žilina, Zilina
FK AS Trenčín 2-3 NK Olimpija Ljubljana
Aggregate: 6-6; FK AS Trenčín qualify on away goals.

13/07/16, Ludogorets Arena, Razgrad
PFC Ludogorets Razgrad 2-0 FK Mladost Podgorica
19/07/16, Gradski Stadion Podgorica, Podgorica
FK Mladost Podgorica 0-3 PFC Ludogorets Razgrad
Aggregate: 0-5; PFC Ludogorets Razgrad qualify.

Patrick Roberts makes it 3-0 for Celtic at home to Lincoln

Third qualifying round

26/07/16, Generali Arena, Prague
AC Sparta Praha 1-1 FC Steaua Bucureşti
03/08/16, Arena Națională, Bucharest
FC Steaua Bucureşti 2-0 AC Sparta Praha
Aggregate: 3-1; FC Steaua Bucureşti qualify.

26/07/16, Doosan Arena, Plzen
FC Viktoria Plzeň 0-0 Qarabağ FK
02/08/16, Tofig Bahramov Republican stadium, Baku
Qarabağ FK 1-1 FC Viktoria Plzeň
Aggregate: 1-1; FC Viktoria Plzeň qualify on away goal.

26/07/16, Elbasan Arena, Elbasan
FK Partizani 0-1 FC Salzburg
03/08/16, Stadion Salzburg, Salzburg
FC Salzburg 2-0 FK Partizani
Aggregate: 3-0; FC Salzburg qualify.

26/07/16, Stadion Maksimir, Zagreb
GNK Dinamo Zagreb 2-0 FC Dinamo Tbilisi
02/08/16, Boris Paichadze Dinamo Arena, Tbilisi
FC Dinamo Tbilisi 0-1 GNK Dinamo Zagreb
Aggregate: 0-3; GNK Dinamo Zagreb qualify.

26/07/16, Amsterdam ArenA, Amsterdam
AFC Ajax 1-1 PAOK FC
03/08/16, Stadio Toumba, Salonika
PAOK FC 1-2 AFC Ajax
Aggregate: 2-3; AFC Ajax qualify.

26/07/16, Borisov-Arena, Borisov
FC BATE Borisov 1-0 Dundalk FC
02/08/16, Tallaght Stadium, Dublin
Dundalk FC 3-0 FC BATE Borisov
Aggregate: 3-1; Dundalk FC qualify.

26/07/16, Ludogorets Arena, Razgrad
PFC Ludogorets Razgrad 2-2 FK Crvena zvezda
02/08/16, Stadion Rajko Mitić, Belgrade
FK Crvena zvezda 2-4 PFC Ludogorets Razgrad (aet)
Aggregate: 4-6; PFC Ludogorets Razgrad qualify.

26/07/16, Olimp 2, Rostov-on-Don
FC Rostov 2-2 RSC Anderlecht
03/08/16, Constant Vanden Stock Stadium, Brussels
RSC Anderlecht 0-2 FC Rostov
Aggregate: 2-4; FC Rostov qualify.

26/07/16, Arena Lviv, Lviv
FC Shakhtar Donetsk 2-0 BSC Young Boys
03/08/16, Stade de Suisse, Berne
BSC Young Boys 2-0 FC Shakhtar Donetsk (aet)
Aggregate: 2-2; BSC Young Boys qualify 4-2 on penalties.

27/07/16, Lerkendal Stadion, Trondheim
Rosenborg BK 2-1 APOEL FC
02/08/16, GSP, Nicosia
APOEL FC 3-0 Rosenborg BK
Aggregate: 4-2; APOEL FC qualify.

27/07/16, Astana Arena, Astana
FC Astana 1-1 Celtic FC
03/08/16, Celtic Park, Glasgow
Celtic FC 2-1 FC Astana
Aggregate: 3-2; Celtic FC qualify.

27/07/16, Štadión MŠK Žilina, Zilina
FK AS Trenčín 0-1 Legia Warszawa
03/08/16, Stadion Wojska Polskiego, Warsaw
Legia Warszawa 0-0 FK AS Trenčín
Aggregate: 1-0; Legia Warszawa qualify.

27/07/16, Marin Anastasovici, Giurgiu
FC Astra Giurgiu 1-1 FC København
03/08/16, Parken, Copenhagen
FC København 3-0 FC Astra Giurgiu
Aggregate: 4-1; FC København qualify.

27/07/16, Şükrü Saracoğlu, Istanbul
Fenerbahçe SK 2-1 AS Monaco FC
03/08/16, Stade Louis II, Monaco
AS Monaco FC 3-1 Fenerbahçe SK
Aggregate: 4-3; AS Monaco FC qualify.

27/07/16, Stadio Georgios Karaiskakis, Piraeus
Olympiacos FC 0-0 Hapoel Beer-Sheva FC
03/08/16, Turner Stadium, Beer Sheva
Hapoel Beer-Sheva FC 1-0 Olympiacos FC
Aggregate: 1-0; Hapoel Beer-Sheva FC qualify.

Play-offs

16/08/16, Parken, Copenhagen
FC København 1-0 APOEL FC
Goal: 1-0 Pavlović 43
24/08/16, GSP, Nicosia
APOEL FC 1-1 FC København
Goals: 1-0 Sotiriou 69, 1-1 Santander 86
Aggregate: 1-2; FC København qualify.

16/08/16, Stadion Maksimir, Zagreb
GNK Dinamo Zagreb 1-1 FC Salzburg
Goals: 0-1 Lazaro 59, 1-1 Rog 76(p)
24/08/16, Stadion Salzburg, Salzburg
FC Salzburg 1-2 GNK Dinamo Zagreb (aet)
Goals: 1-0 Lazaro 22, 1-1 Fernandes 87, 1-2 Soudani 95
Aggregate: 2-3; GNK Dinamo Zagreb qualify.

16/08/16, Amsterdam ArenA, Amsterdam
AFC Ajax 1-1 FC Rostov
Goals: 0-1 Noboa 13, 1-1 Klaassen 38(p)
24/08/16, Olimp 2, Rostov-on-Don
FC Rostov 4-1 AFC Ajax
Goals: 1-0 Azmoun 34, 2-0 Yerokhin 52, 3-0 Noboa 60, 4-0 Poloz 66, 4-1 Klaassen 84(p)
Aggregate: 5-2; FC Rostov qualify.

16/08/16, Stade de Suisse, Berne
BSC Young Boys 1-3 VfL Borussia Mönchengladbach
Goals: 0-1 Raffael 11, 1-1 Sulejmani 56, 1-2 Hahn 67, 1-3 Rochat 69(og)
24/08/16, Borussia-Park, Monchengladbach
VfL Borussia Mönchengladbach 6-1 BSC Young Boys
Goals: 1-0 Hazard 9, 2-0 Raffael 33, 3-0 Raffael 40, 4-0 Hazard 64, 5-0 Raffael 77, 5-1 Ravet 79, 6-1 Hazard 84
Aggregate: 9-2; VfL Borussia Mönchengladbach qualify.

16/08/16, Arena Națională, Bucharest
FC Steaua București 0-5 Manchester City FC
Goals: 0-1 Silva 13, 0-2 Agüero 41, 0-3 Nolito 49, 0-4 Agüero 78, 0-5 Agüero 89
24/08/16, City of Manchester Stadium, Manchester
Manchester City FC 1-0 FC Steaua București
Goal: 1-0 Delph 56
Aggregate: 6-0; Manchester City FC qualify.

17/08/16, Celtic Park, Glasgow
Celtic FC 5-2 Hapoel Beer-Sheva FC
Goals: 1-0 Rogic 9, 2-0 Griffiths 39, 3-0 Griffiths 45+1, 3-1 Lúcio Maranhão 55, 3-2 Melikson 57, 4-2 Dembélé 73, 5-2 Brown 85
23/08/16, Turner Stadium, Beer Sheva
Hapoel Beer-Sheva FC 2-0 Celtic FC
Goals: 1-0 Sahar 21, 2-0 Hoban 48
Aggregate: 4-5; Celtic FC qualify.

17/08/16, Aviva Stadium, Dublin
Dundalk FC 0-2 Legia Warszawa
Goals: 0-1 Nikolić 56(p), 0-2 Prijović 90+4
23/08/16, Stadion Wojska Polskiego, Warsaw
Legia Warszawa 1-1 Dundalk FC
Goals: 0-1 Benson 19, 1-1 Kucharczyk 90+2
Aggregate: 3-1; Legia Warszawa qualify.

Mönchengladbach's Thorgan Hazard on the ball against Young Boys in the play-offs

17/08/16, Estádio do Dragão, Porto
FC Porto 1-1 AS Roma
Goals: 0-1 Felipe 21(og), 1-1 André Silva 61(p)
23/08/16, Stadio Olimpico, Rome
AS Roma 0-3 FC Porto
Goals: 0-1 Felipe 8, 0-2 Layún 73, 0-3 Corona 75
Aggregate: 1-4; FC Porto qualify.

17/08/16, Estadio de la Cerámica, Villarreal
Villarreal CF 1-2 AS Monaco FC
Goals: 0-1 Fabinho 3(p), 1-1 Pato 36, 1-2 Bernardo Silva 72
23/08/16, Stade Louis II, Monaco
AS Monaco FC 1-0 Villarreal CF
Goal: 1-0 Fabinho 90+1(p)
Aggregate: 3-1; AS Monaco FC qualify.

17/08/16, Natsionalen Stadion Vasil Levski, Sofia
PFC Ludogorets Razgrad 2-0 FC Viktoria Plzeň
Goals: 1-0 Moți 51(p), 2-0 Misidjan 64
23/08/16, Doosan Arena, Plzen
FC Viktoria Plzeň 2-2 PFC Ludogorets Razgrad
Goals: 1-0 Ďuriš 7, 1-1 Misidjan 17, 2-1 Matějů 64, 2-2 Keşerü 90+5
Aggregate: 2-4; PFC Ludogorets Razgrad qualify.

Group stage

Group A

13/09/16, Parc des Princes, Paris (att: 46,440)
Paris Saint-Germain 1-1 Arsenal FC
Goals: 1-0 Cavani 1, 1-1 Alexis Sánchez 78
Referee: Kassai (HUN)

13/09/16, St Jakob-Park, Basel (att: 30,852)
FC Basel 1893 1-1 PFC Ludogorets Razgrad
Goals: 0-1 Jonathan Cafú 45, 1-1 Steffen 79
Referee: Kulbakov (BLR)

28/09/16, Arsenal Stadium, London (att: 59,993)
Arsenal FC 2-0 FC Basel 1893
Goals: 1-0 Walcott 7, 2-0 Walcott 26
Referee: Makkelie (NED)

28/09/16, Natsionalen Stadion Vasil Levski, Sofia (att: 17,155)
PFC Ludogorets Razgrad 1-3 Paris Saint-Germain
Goals: 1-0 Natanael 16, 1-1 Matuidi 41, 1-2 Cavani 56, 1-3 Cavani 60
Referee: Královec (CZE)

19/10/16, Arsenal Stadium, London (att: 59,944)
Arsenal FC 6-0 PFC Ludogorets Razgrad
Goals: 1-0 Alexis Sánchez 13, 2-0 Walcott 42, 3-0 Oxlade-Chamberlain 47, 4-0 Özil 56, 5-0 Özil 83, 6-0 Özil 87
Referee: Artur Dias (POR)

19/10/16, Parc des Princes, Paris (att: 46,488)
Paris Saint-Germain 3-0 FC Basel 1893
Goals: 1-0 Di María 40, 2-0 Lucas 62, 3-0 Cavani 90+3(p)
Referee: Aytekin (GER)

01/11/16, St Jakob-Park, Basel (att: 34,639)
FC Basel 1893 1-2 Paris Saint-Germain
Goals: 0-1 Matuidi 43, 1-1 Zuffi 76, 1-2 Meunier 90
Referee: Hațegan (ROU)

01/11/16, Natsionalen Stadion Vasil Levski, Sofia (att: 30,862)
PFC Ludogorets Razgrad 2-3 Arsenal FC
Goals: 1-0 Jonathan Cafú 12, 2-0 Keşerü 15, 2-1 Xhaka 20, 2-2 Giroud 42, 2-3 Özil 88
Referee: Nijhuis (NED)

23/11/16, Arsenal Stadium, London (att: 59,628)
Arsenal FC 2-2 Paris Saint-Germain
Goals: 0-1 Cavani 18, 1-1 Giroud 45+1(p), 2-1 Verratti 60(og), 2-2 Iwobi 77(og)
Referee: Brych (GER)

23/11/16, Natsionalen Stadion Vasil Levski, Sofia (att: 20,821)
PFC Ludogorets Razgrad 0-0 FC Basel 1893
Referee: Atkinson (ENG)

06/12/16, Parc des Princes, Paris (att: 42,650)
Paris Saint-Germain 2-2 PFC Ludogorets Razgrad
Goals: 0-1 Misidjan 15, 1-1 Cavani 61, 1-2 Wanderson 69, 2-2 Di María 90+2
Referee: Sidiropoulos (GRE)

06/12/16, St Jakob-Park, Basel (att: 36,000)
FC Basel 1893 1-4 Arsenal FC
Goals: 0-1 Lucas Pérez 8, 0-2 Lucas Pérez 16, 0-3 Lucas Pérez 47, 0-4 Iwobi 53, 1-4 Doumbia 78
Referee: Manuel De Sousa (POR)

Group B

13/09/16, Estádio do Sport Lisboa e Benfica, Lisbon (att: 42,126)
SL Benfica 1-1 Beşiktaş JK
Goals: 1-0 Cervi 12, 1-1 Talisca 90+3
Referee: Mažić (SRB)

13/09/16, NSK Olimpiyskyi, Kyiv (att: 35,137)
FC Dynamo Kyiv 1-2 SSC Napoli
Goals: 1-0 Garmash 26, 1-1 Milik 36, 1-2 Milik 45+2
Referee: Collum (SCO)

28/09/16, Stadio San Paolo, Naples (att: 41,281)
SSC Napoli 4-2 SL Benfica
Goals: 1-0 Hamšík 20, 2-0 Mertens 51, 3-0 Milik 54(p), 4-0 Mertens 58, 4-1 Gonçalo Guedes 70, 4-2 Salvio 86
Referee: Brych (GER)

28/09/16, Beşiktaş Arena, Istanbul (att: 33,938)
Beşiktaş JK 1-1 FC Dynamo Kyiv
Goals: 1-0 Ricardo Quaresma 29, 1-1 Tsygankov 65
Referee: Zwayer (GER)

19/10/16, Stadio San Paolo, Naples (att: 28,502)
SSC Napoli 2-3 Beşiktaş JK
Goals: 0-1 Adriano 12, 1-1 Mertens 30, 1-2 Aboubakar 38, 2-2 Gabbiadini 69(p), 2-3 Aboubakar 86
Referee: Karasev (RUS)

19/10/16, NSK Olimpiyskyi, Kyiv (att: 25,911)
FC Dynamo Kyiv 0-2 SL Benfica
Goals: 0-1 Salvio 9(p), 0-2 Cervi 55
Referee: Fernández Borbalán (ESP)

01/11/16, Estádio do Sport Lisboa e Benfica, Lisbon (att: 51,641)
SL Benfica 1-0 FC Dynamo Kyiv
Goal: 1-0 Salvio 45+2(p)
Referee: Turpin (FRA)

01/11/16, Beşiktaş Arena, Istanbul (att: 35,552)
Beşiktaş JK 1-1 SSC Napoli
Goals: 1-0 Ricardo Quaresma 79(p), 1-1 Hamšík 82
Referee: Clattenburg (ENG)

23/11/16, Stadio San Paolo, Naples (att: 33,736)
SSC Napoli 0-0 FC Dynamo Kyiv
Referee: Haţegan (ROU)

23/11/16, Beşiktaş Arena, Istanbul (att: 36,063)
Beşiktaş JK 3-3 SL Benfica
Goals: 0-1 Gonçalo Guedes 10, 0-2 Nélson Semedo 25, 0-3 Fejsa 31, 1-3 Cenk Tosun 58, 2-3 Ricardo Quaresma 83(p), 3-3 Aboubakar 89
Referee: Skomina (SVN)

06/12/16, Estádio do Sport Lisboa e Benfica, Lisbon (att: 55,364)
SL Benfica 1-2 SSC Napoli
Goals: 0-1 Callejón 60, 0-2 Mertens 79, 1-2 Jiménez 87
Referee: Mateu Lahoz (ESP)

06/12/16, NSK Olimpiyskyi, Kyiv (att: 14,036)
FC Dynamo Kyiv 6-0 Beşiktaş JK
Goals: 1-0 Besedin 9, 2-0 Yarmolenko 30(p), 3-0 Buyalskiy 32, 4-0 González 45+3, 5-0 Sydorchuk 60, 6-0 Júnior Moraes 77
Referee: Thomson (SCO)

Group C

13/09/16, Camp Nou, Barcelona (att: 73,290)
FC Barcelona 7-0 Celtic FC
Goals: 1-0 Messi 3, 2-0 Messi 27, 3-0 Neymar 50, 4-0 Iniesta 59, 5-0 Messi 60, 6-0 Suárez 75, 7-0 Suárez 88
Referee: Haţegan (ROU)

14/09/16, City of Manchester Stadium, Manchester (att: 30,270)
Manchester City FC 4-0 VfL Borussia Mönchengladbach
Goals: 1-0 Agüero 9, 2-0 Agüero 28(p), 3-0 Agüero 77, 4-0 Iheanacho 90+1
Referee: Kuipers (NED)

28/09/16, Celtic Park, Glasgow (att: 57,952)
Celtic FC 3-3 Manchester City FC
Goals: 1-0 Dembélé 3, 1-1 Fernandinho 12, 2-1 Sterling 20(og), 2-2 Sterling 28, 3-2 Dembélé 47, 3-3 Nolito 55
Referee: Rizzoli (ITA)

28/09/16, Borussia-Park, Monchengladbach (att: 46,283)
VfL Borussia Mönchengladbach 1-2 FC Barcelona
Goals: 1-0 Hazard 34, 1-1 Arda Turan 65, 1-2 Piqué 74
Referee: Skomina (SVN)

Joshua Kimmich (in red) finds the net from close range as Bayern take a 3-0 lead at home to Rostov

19/10/16, Celtic Park, Glasgow (att: 57,814)
Celtic FC 0-2 VfL Borussia Mönchengladbach
Goals: 0-1 Stindl 57, 0-2 Hahn 77
Referee: Sidiropoulos (GRE)

19/10/16, Camp Nou, Barcelona (att: 96,920)
FC Barcelona 4-0 Manchester City FC
Goals: 1-0 Messi 17, 2-0 Messi 61, 3-0 Messi 69, 4-0 Neymar 89
Referee: Mažić (SRB)

01/11/16, City of Manchester Stadium, Manchester (att: 53,340)
Manchester City FC 3-1 FC Barcelona
Goals: 0-1 Messi 21, 1-1 Gündoğan 39, 2-1 De Bruyne 51, 3-1 Gündoğan 74
Referee: Kassai (HUN)

01/11/16, Borussia-Park, Monchengladbach (att: 46,283)
VfL Borussia Mönchengladbach 1-1 Celtic FC
Goals: 1-0 Stindl 32, 1-1 Dembélé 76(p)
Referee: Manuel De Sousa (POR)

23/11/16, Celtic Park, Glasgow (att: 57,937)
Celtic FC 0-2 FC Barcelona
Goals: 0-1 Messi 24, 0-2 Messi 56(p)
Referee: Orsato (ITA)

23/11/16, Borussia-Park, Monchengladbach (att: 45,921)
VfL Borussia Mönchengladbach 1-1 Manchester City FC
Goals: 1-0 Raffael 23, 1-1 Silva 45+1
Referee: Çakır (TUR)

06/12/16, City of Manchester Stadium, Manchester (att: 51,297)
Manchester City FC 1-1 Celtic FC
Goals: 0-1 Roberts 4, 1-1 Iheanacho 8
Referee: Vinčić (SVN)

06/12/16, Camp Nou, Barcelona (att: 67,157)
FC Barcelona 4-0 VfL Borussia Mönchengladbach
Goals: 1-0 Messi 16, 2-0 Arda Turan 50, 3-0 Arda Turan 53, 4-0 Arda Turan 67
Referee: Karasev (RUS)

Group D

13/09/16, Fußball Arena München, Munich (att: 70,000)
FC Bayern München 5-0 FC Rostov
Goals: 1-0 Lewandowski 28(p), 2-0 Müller 45+2, 3-0 Kimmich 53, 4-0 Kimmich 60, 5-0 Bernat 90
Referee: Taylor (ENG)

13/09/16, PSV Stadion, Eindhoven (att: 33,989)
PSV Eindhoven 0-1 Club Atlético de Madrid
Goal: 0-1 Saúl Ñíguez 43
Referee: Atkinson (ENG)

28/09/16, Estadio Vicente Calderón, Madrid (att: 48,242)
Club Atlético de Madrid 1-0 FC Bayern München
Goal: 1-0 Carrasco 35
Referee: Marciniak (POL)

28/09/16, Olimp 2, Rostov-on-Don (att: 12,646)
FC Rostov 2-2 PSV Eindhoven
Goals: 1-0 Poloz 8, 1-1 Pröpper 14, 2-1 Poloz 37, 2-2 L de Jong 45+1
Referee: Turpin (FRA)

19/10/16, Fußball Arena München, Munich (att: 70,000)
FC Bayern München 4-1 PSV Eindhoven
Goals: 1-0 Müller 13, 2-0 Kimmich 21, 2-1 Narsingh 41, 3-1 Lewandowski 59, 4-1 Robben 84
Referee: Collum (SCO)

19/10/16, Olimp 2, Rostov-on-Don (att: 15,300)
FC Rostov 0-1 Club Atlético de Madrid
Goal: 0-1 Carrasco 62
Referee: Orsato (ITA)

01/11/16, Estadio Vicente Calderón, Madrid (att: 40,392)
Club Atlético de Madrid 2-1 FC Rostov
Goals: 1-0 Griezmann 28, 1-1 Azmoun 30, 2-1 Griezmann 90+3
Referee: Thomson (SCO)

01/11/16, PSV Stadion, Eindhoven (att: 35,000)
PSV Eindhoven 1-2 FC Bayern München
Goals: 1-0 Arias 14, 1-1 Lewandowski 34(p), 1-2 Lewandowski 74
Referee: Rocchi (ITA)

23/11/16, Olimp 2, Rostov-on-Don (att: 15,211)
FC Rostov 3-2 FC Bayern München
Goals: 0-1 Douglas Costa 35, 1-1 Azmoun 44, 2-1 Poloz 50(p), 2-2 Bernat 52, 3-2 Noboa 67
Referee: Artur Dias (POR)

23/11/16, Estadio Vicente Calderón, Madrid (att: 37,891)
Club Atlético de Madrid 2-0 PSV Eindhoven
Goals: 1-0 Gameiro 55, 2-0 Griezmann 66
Referee: Kulbakov (BLR)

06/12/16, Fußball Arena München, Munich (att: 70,000)
FC Bayern München 1-0 Club Atlético de Madrid
Goal: 1-0 Lewandowski 28
Referee: Turpin (FRA)

06/12/16, PSV Stadion, Eindhoven (att: 33,400)
PSV Eindhoven 0-0 FC Rostov
Referee: Aytekin (GER)

Group E

14/09/16, Wembley Stadium, London (att: 81,011)
Tottenham Hotspur FC 1-2 AS Monaco FC
Goals: 0-1 Bernardo Silva 15, 0-2 Lemar 31, 1-2 Alderweireld 45
Referee: Rocchi (ITA)

14/09/16, BayArena, Leverkusen (att: 23,459)
Bayer 04 Leverkusen 2-2 PFC CSKA Moskva
Goals: 1-0 Mehmedi 9, 2-0 Hakan Çalhanoğlu 15, 2-1 Dzagoev 36, 2-2 Eremenko 38
Referee: Orsato (ITA)

27/09/16, Stade Louis II, Monaco (att: 8,100)
AS Monaco FC 1-1 Bayer 04 Leverkusen
Goals: 0-1 Hernández 74, 1-1 Glik 90+4
Referee: Fernández Borbalán (ESP)

27/09/16, Stadion CSKA Moskva, Moscow (att: 26,153)
PFC CSKA Moskva 0-1 Tottenham Hotspur FC
Goal: 0-1 Son 71
Referee: Mateu Lahoz (ESP)

18/10/16, BayArena, Leverkusen (att: 28,887)
Bayer 04 Leverkusen 0-0 Tottenham Hotspur FC
Referee: Çakır (TUR)

18/10/16, Stadion CSKA Moskva, Moscow (att: 24,100)
PFC CSKA Moskva 1-1 AS Monaco FC
Goals: 1-0 Traoré 34, 1-1 Bernardo Silva 87
Referee: Strömbergsson (SWE)

02/11/16, Wembley Stadium, London (att: 85,512)
Tottenham Hotspur FC 0-1 Bayer 04 Leverkusen
Goal: 0-1 Kampl 65
Referee: Eriksson (SWE)

02/11/16, Stade Louis II, Monaco (att: 10,029)
AS Monaco FC 3-0 PFC CSKA Moskva
Goals: 1-0 Germain 13, 2-0 Falcao 29, 3-0 Falcao 41
Referee: Jug (SVN)

Kevin Kampl scores Leverkusen's winner against Tottenham at Wembley

22/11/16, Stadion CSKA Moskva, Moscow (att: 19,164)
PFC CSKA Moskva 1-1 Bayer 04 Leverkusen
Goals: 0-1 Volland 16, 1-1 Natcho 76(p)
Referee: Undiano Mallenco (ESP)

22/11/16, Stade Louis II, Monaco (att: 13,100)
AS Monaco FC 2-1 Tottenham Hotspur FC
Goals: 1-0 Sidibé 48, 1-1 Kane 52(p), 2-1 Lemar 53
Referee: Kuipers (NED)

07/12/16, Wembley Stadium, London (att: 62,034)
Tottenham Hotspur FC 3-1 PFC CSKA Moskva
Goals: 0-1 Dzagoev 33, 1-1 Alli 38, 2-1 Kane 45+1, 3-1 Akinfeev 77(og)
Referee: Rizzoli (ITA)

07/12/16, BayArena, Leverkusen (att: 21,928)
Bayer 04 Leverkusen 3-0 AS Monaco FC
Goals: 1-0 Yurchenko 30, 2-0 Brandt 48, 3-0 De Sanctis 82(og)
Referee: Mažeika (LTU)

Group F

14/09/16, Estadio Santiago Bernabéu, Madrid (att: 72,179)
Real Madrid CF 2-1 Sporting Clube de Portugal
Goals: 0-1 Bruno César 48, 1-1 Cristiano Ronaldo 89, 2-1 Morata 90+4
Referee: Tagliavento (ITA)

14/09/16, Stadion Wojska Polskiego, Warsaw (att: 27,304)
Legia Warszawa 0-6 Borussia Dortmund
Goals: 0-1 Götze 7, 0-2 Papastathopoulos 15, 0-3 Bartra 17, 0-4 Raphaël Guerreiro 51, 0-5 Castro 76, 0-6 Aubameyang 87
Referee: Karasev (RUS)

27/09/16, José Alvalade, Lisbon (att: 40,094)
Sporting Clube de Portugal 2-0 Legia Warszawa
Goals: 1-0 B Ruiz 28, 2-0 Dost 37
Referee: Oliver (ENG)

27/09/16, BVB Stadion Dortmund, Dortmund (att: 65,849)
Borussia Dortmund 2-2 Real Madrid CF
Goals: 0-1 Cristiano Ronaldo 17, 1-1 Aubameyang 43, 1-2 Varane 68, 2-2 Schürrle 87
Referee: Clattenburg (ENG)

18/10/16, José Alvalade, Lisbon (att: 46,609)
Sporting Clube de Portugal 1-2 Borussia Dortmund
Goals: 0-1 Aubameyang 9, 0-2 Weigl 43, 1-2 Bruno César 67
Referee: Skomina (SVN)

18/10/16, Estadio Santiago Bernabéu, Madrid (att: 70,251)
Real Madrid CF 5-1 Legia Warszawa
Goals: 1-0 Bale 16, 2-0 Jodłowiec 20(og), 2-1 Radović 22(p), 3-1 Marco Asensio 37, 4-1 Lucas Vázquez 68, 5-1 Morata 84
Referee: Buquet (FRA)

02/11/16, BVB Stadion Dortmund, Dortmund (att: 65,849)
Borussia Dortmund 1-0 Sporting Clube de Portugal
Goal: 1-0 Ramos 12
Referee: Makkelie (NED)

02/11/16, Stadion Wojska Polskiego, Warsaw
Legia Warszawa 3-3 Real Madrid CF
Goals: 0-1 Bale 1, 0-2 Benzema 35, 1-2 Odjidja-Ofoe 40, 2-2 Radović 58, 3-2 Moulin 83, 3-3 Kovačić 85
Referee: Královec (CZE)

22/11/16, José Alvalade, Lisbon (att: 50,046)
Sporting Clube de Portugal 1-2 Real Madrid CF
Goals: 0-1 Varane 29, 1-1 Adrien Silva 80(p), 1-2 Benzema 87
Referee: Collum (SCO)

22/11/16, BVB Stadion Dortmund, Dortmund (att: 55,094)
Borussia Dortmund 8-4 Legia Warszawa
Goals: 0-1 Prijović 10, 1-1 Kagawa 17, 2-1 Kagawa 18, 3-1 Nuri Şahin 20, 3-2 Prijović 24, 4-2 Dembélé 29, 5-2 Reus 32, 6-2 Reus 52, 6-3 Kucharczyk 57, 7-3 Passlack 81, 7-4 Nikolić 83, 8-4 Rzeźniczak 90+2(og)
Referee: Strömbergsson (SWE)

07/12/16, Estadio Santiago Bernabéu, Madrid (att: 76,894)
Real Madrid CF 2-2 Borussia Dortmund
Goals: 1-0 Benzema 28, 2-0 Benzema 53, 2-1 Aubameyang 60, 2-2 Reus 88
Referee: Marciniak (POL)

07/12/16, Stadion Wojska Polskiego, Warsaw (att: 28,232)
Legia Warszawa 1-0 Sporting Clube de Portugal
Goal: 1-0 Guilherme 30
Referee: Rocchi (ITA)

Group G

14/09/16, Estádio do Dragão, Porto (att: 34,325)
FC Porto 1-1 FC København
Goals: 1-0 Otávio 13, 1-1 Cornelius 52
Referee: Jug (SVN)

14/09/16, Jan Breydelstadion, Bruges (att: 20,917)
Club Brugge KV 0-3 Leicester City FC
Goals: 0-1 Albrighton 5, 0-2 Mahrez 29, 0-3 Mahrez 61(p)
Referee: Sidiropoulos (GRE)

27/09/16, Leicester City Stadium, Leicester (att: 31,805)
Leicester City FC 1-0 FC Porto
Goal: 1-0 Slimani 25
Referee: Çakır (TUR)

27/09/16, Parken, Copenhagen (att: 25,605)
FC København 4-0 Club Brugge KV
Goals: 1-0 Denswil 53(og), 2-0 Delaney 64, 3-0 Santander 69, 4-0 Jørgensen 90+2
Referee: Thomson (SCO)

18/10/16, Leicester City Stadium, Leicester (att: 31,037)
Leicester City FC 1-0 FC København
Goal: 1-0 Mahrez 40
Referee: Rizzoli (ITA)

18/10/16, Jan Breydelstadion, Bruges (att: 23,325)
Club Brugge KV 1-2 FC Porto
Goals: 1-0 Vossen 12, 1-1 Layún 68, 1-2 André Silva 90+3(p)
Referee: Tagliavento (ITA)

02/11/16, Estádio do Dragão, Porto (att: 32,310)
FC Porto 1-0 Club Brugge KV
Goal: 1-0 André Silva 37
Referee: Undiano Mallenco (ESP)

02/11/16, Parken, Copenhagen (att: 34,146)
FC København 0-0 Leicester City FC
Referee: Brych (GER)

22/11/16, Leicester City Stadium, Leicester (att: 31,443)
Leicester City FC 2-1 Club Brugge KV
Goals: 1-0 Okazaki 5, 2-0 Mahrez 30(p), 2-1 Izquierdo 52
Referee: Buquet (FRA)

22/11/16, Parken, Copenhagen (att: 32,036)
FC København 0-0 FC Porto
Referee: Mažić (SRB)

07/12/16, Estádio do Dragão, Porto (att: 39,310)
FC Porto 5-0 Leicester City FC
Goals: 1-0 André Silva 6, 2-0 Corona 26, 3-0 Brahimi 44, 4-0 André Silva 64(p), 5-0 Diogo Jota 77
Referee: Zwayer (GER)

07/12/16, Jan Breydelstadion, Bruges (att: 18,981)
Club Brugge KV 0-2 FC København
Goals: 0-1 Mechele 8(og), 0-2 Jørgensen 15
Referee: Oliver (ENG)

Group H

14/09/16, Stade de Lyon, Decines (att: 43,754)
Olympique Lyonnais 3-0 GNK Dinamo Zagreb
Goals: 1-0 Tolisso 13, 2-0 Ferri 49, 3-0 Cornet 57
Referee: Strömbergsson (SWE)

14/09/16, Juventus Stadium, Turin (att: 33,261)
Juventus 0-0 Sevilla FC
Referee: Aytekin (GER)

27/09/16, Estadio Ramón Sánchez Pizjuán, Seville (att: 36,741)
Sevilla FC 1-0 Olympique Lyonnais
Goal: 1-0 Ben Yedder 53
Referee: Nijhuis (NED)

27/09/16, Stadion Maksimir, Zagreb (att: 25,320)
GNK Dinamo Zagreb 0-4 Juventus
Goals: 0-1 Pjanić 24, 0-2 Higuaín 31, 0-3 Dybala 57, 0-4 Dani Alves 85
Referee: Manuel De Sousa (POR)

18/10/16, Stadion Maksimir, Zagreb (att: 6,021)
GNK Dinamo Zagreb 0-1 Sevilla FC
Goal: 0-1 Nasri 37
Referee: Oliver (ENG)

18/10/16, Stade de Lyon, Decines (att: 53,907)
Olympique Lyonnais 0-1 Juventus
Goal: 0-1 Cuadrado 76
Referee: Marciniak (POL)

02/11/16, Estadio Ramón Sánchez Pizjuán, Seville (att: 35,215)
Sevilla FC 4-0 GNK Dinamo Zagreb
Goals: 1-0 Vietto 31, 2-0 Sergio Escudero 66, 3-0 N'Zonzi 80, 4-0 Ben Yedder 87
Referee: Zwayer (GER)

02/11/16, Juventus Stadium, Turin (att: 40,356)
Juventus 1-1 Olympique Lyonnais
Goals: 1-0 Higuaín 13(p), 1-1 Tolisso 85
Referee: Kuipers (NED)

22/11/16, Stadion Maksimir, Zagreb (att: 7,834)
GNK Dinamo Zagreb 0-1 Olympique Lyonnais
Goal: 0-1 Lacazette 72
Referee: Královec (CZE)

22/11/16, Estadio Ramón Sánchez Pizjuán, Seville (att: 38,942)
Sevilla FC 1-3 Juventus
Goals: 1-0 Pareja 9, 1-1 Marchisio 45+2(p), 1-2 Bonucci 84, 1-3 Mandžukić 90+4
Referee: Clattenburg (ENG)

07/12/16, Stade de Lyon, Decines (att: 52,423)
Olympique Lyonnais 0-0 Sevilla FC
Referee: Eriksson (SWE)

07/12/16, Juventus Stadium, Turin (att: 39,380)
Juventus 2-0 GNK Dinamo Zagreb
Goals: 1-0 Higuaín 52, 2-0 Rugani 73
Referee: Taylor (ENG)

Final group tables

Group A

			Home					Away					Total					
		Pld	W	D	L	F	A	W	D	L	F	A	W	D	L	F	A	Pts
1	Arsenal FC	6	2	1	0	10	2	2	1	0	8	4	4	2	0	18	6	14
2	Paris Saint-Germain	6	1	2	0	6	3	2	1	0	7	4	3	3	0	13	7	12
3	PFC Ludogorets Razgrad	6	0	1	2	3	6	0	2	1	3	9	0	3	3	6	15	3
4	FC Basel 1893	6	0	1	2	3	7	0	1	2	0	5	0	2	4	3	12	2

Group B

			Home					Away					Total					
		Pld	W	D	L	F	A	W	D	L	F	A	W	D	L	F	A	Pts
1	SSC Napoli	6	1	1	1	6	5	2	1	0	5	3	3	2	1	11	8	11
2	SL Benfica	6	1	1	1	3	3	1	1	1	7	7	2	2	2	10	10	8
3	Beşiktaş JK	6	0	3	0	5	5	1	1	1	4	9	1	4	1	9	14	7
4	FC Dynamo Kyiv	6	1	0	2	7	4	0	2	1	1	2	1	2	3	8	6	5

Group C

			Home					Away					Total					
		Pld	W	D	L	F	A	W	D	L	F	A	W	D	L	F	A	Pts
1	FC Barcelona	6	3	0	0	15	0	2	0	1	5	4	5	0	1	20	4	15
2	Manchester City FC	6	2	1	0	8	2	0	2	1	4	8	2	3	1	12	10	9
3	VfL Borussia Mönchengladbach	6	0	2	1	3	4	1	0	2	2	8	1	2	3	5	12	5
4	Celtic FC	6	0	1	2	3	7	0	2	1	2	9	0	3	3	5	16	3

Group D

			Home					Away					Total					
		Pld	W	D	L	F	A	W	D	L	F	A	W	D	L	F	A	Pts
1	Club Atlético de Madrid	6	3	0	0	5	1	2	0	1	2	1	5	0	1	7	2	15
2	FC Bayern München	6	3	0	0	10	1	1	0	2	4	5	4	0	2	14	6	12
3	FC Rostov	6	1	1	1	5	5	0	1	2	1	7	1	2	3	6	12	5
4	PSV Eindhoven	6	0	1	2	1	3	0	1	2	3	8	0	2	4	4	11	2

Group E

			Home					Away					Total					
		Pld	W	D	L	F	A	W	D	L	F	A	W	D	L	F	A	Pts
1	AS Monaco FC	6	2	1	0	6	2	1	1	1	3	5	3	2	1	9	7	11
2	Bayer 04 Leverkusen	6	1	2	0	5	2	1	2	0	3	2	2	4	0	8	4	10
3	Tottenham Hotspur FC	6	1	0	2	4	4	1	1	1	2	2	2	1	3	6	6	7
4	PFC CSKA Moskva	6	0	2	1	2	3	0	1	2	3	8	0	3	3	5	11	3

Group F

			Home					Away					Total					
		Pld	W	D	L	F	A	W	D	L	F	A	W	D	L	F	A	Pts
1	Borussia Dortmund	6	2	1	0	11	6	2	1	0	10	3	4	2	0	21	9	14
2	Real Madrid CF	6	2	1	0	9	4	1	2	0	7	6	3	3	0	16	10	12
3	Legia Warszawa	6	1	1	1	4	9	0	0	3	5	15	1	1	4	9	24	4
4	Sporting Clube de Portugal	6	1	0	2	4	4	0	0	3	1	4	1	0	5	5	8	3

Group G

			Home					Away					Total					
		Pld	W	D	L	F	A	W	D	L	F	A	W	D	L	F	A	Pts
1	Leicester City FC	6	3	0	0	4	1	1	1	1	3	5	4	1	1	7	6	13
2	FC Porto	6	2	1	0	7	1	1	1	1	2	2	3	2	1	9	3	11
3	FC København	6	1	2	0	4	0	1	1	1	3	2	2	3	1	7	2	9
4	Club Brugge KV	6	0	0	3	1	7	0	0	3	1	7	0	0	6	2	14	0

Group H

			Home					Away					Total					
		Pld	W	D	L	F	A	W	D	L	F	A	W	D	L	F	A	Pts
1	Juventus	6	1	2	0	3	1	3	0	0	8	1	4	2	0	11	2	14
2	Sevilla FC	6	2	0	1	6	3	1	2	0	1	0	3	2	1	7	3	11
3	Olympique Lyonnais	6	1	1	1	3	1	1	1	1	2	2	2	2	2	5	3	8
4	GNK Dinamo Zagreb	6	0	0	3	0	6	0	0	3	0	9	0	0	6	0	15	0

Top goalscorers (after group stage)

10	Lionel Messi (Barcelona)
6	Edinson Cavani (Paris)
5	Robert Lewandowski (Bayern)
4	Mesut Özil (Arsenal) Arda Turan (Barcelona) Pierre-Emerick Aubameyang (Dortmund) Riyad Mahrez (Leicester) Dries Mertens (Napoli) André Silva (Porto) Karim Benzema (Real Madrid)

Round of 16

14/02/17, Estádio do Sport Lisboa e Benfica, Lisbon (att: 55,124)
SL Benfica 1-0 Borussia Dortmund
Goal: 1-0 Mitroglou 48
Referee: Rizzoli (ITA)
08/03/17, BVB Stadion Dortmund, Dortmund (att: 65,849)
Borussia Dortmund 4-0 SL Benfica
Goals: 1-0 Aubameyang 4, 2-0 Pulisic 59, 3-0 Aubameyang 61, 4-0 Aubameyang 85
Referee: Atkinson (ENG)
Aggregate: 4-1; Borussia Dortmund qualify.

14/02/17, Parc des Princes, Paris (att: 46,565)
Paris Saint-Germain 4-0 FC Barcelona
Goals: 1-0 Di María 18, 2-0 Draxler 40, 3-0 Di María 55, 4-0 Cavani 72
Referee: Marciniak (POL)
08/03/17, Camp Nou, Barcelona (att: 96,290)
FC Barcelona 6-1 Paris Saint-Germain
Goals: 1-0 Suárez 3, 2-0 Kurzawa 40(og), 3-0 Messi 50(p), 3-1 Cavani 62, 4-1 Neymar 88, 5-1 Neymar 90+1(p), 6-1 Sergi Roberto 90+5
Referee: Aytekin (GER)
Aggregate: 6-5; FC Barcelona qualify.

15/02/17, Estadio Santiago Bernabéu, Madrid (att: 78,000)
Real Madrid CF 3-1 SSC Napoli
Goals: 0-1 Insigne 8, 1-1 Benzema 18, 2-1 Kroos 49, 3-1 Casemiro 54
Referee: Skomina (SVN)
07/03/17, Stadio San Paolo, Naples (att: 56,695)
SSC Napoli 1-3 Real Madrid CF
Goals: 1-0 Mertens 24, 1-1 Sergio Ramos 52, 1-2 Mertens 57(og), 1-3 Morata 90+1
Referee: Çakır (TUR)
Aggregate: 2-6; Real Madrid CF qualify.

15/02/17, Fußball Arena München, Munich (att: 70,000)
FC Bayern München 5-1 Arsenal FC
Goals: 1-0 Robben 11, 1-1 Alexis Sánchez 30, 2-1 Lewandowski 53, 3-1 Thiago 56, 4-1 Thiago 63, 5-1 Müller 88
Referee: Mažić (SRB)
07/03/17, Arsenal Stadium, London (att: 59,911)
Arsenal FC 1-5 FC Bayern München
Goals: 1-0 Walcott 20, 1-1 Lewandowski 55(p), 1-2 Robben 68, 1-3 Douglas Costa 78, 1-4 Vidal 80, 1-5 Vidal 85
Referee: Sidiropoulos (GRE)
Aggregate: 2-10; FC Bayern München qualify.

21/02/17, City of Manchester Stadium, Manchester (att: 53,351)
Manchester City FC 5-3 AS Monaco FC
Goals: 1-0 Sterling 26, 1-1 Falcao 32, 1-2 Mbappé 40, 2-2 Agüero 58, 2-3 Falcao 61, 3-3 Agüero 71, 4-3 Stones 77, 5-3 Sané 82
Referee: Mateu Lahoz (ESP)
15/03/17, Stade Louis II, Monaco (att: 15,700)
AS Monaco FC 3-1 Manchester City FC
Goals: 1-0 Mbappé 8, 2-0 Fabinho 29, 2-1 Sané 71, 3-1 Bakayoko 77
Referee: Rocchi (ITA)
Aggregate: 6-6; AS Monaco FC qualify on away goals.

21/02/17, BayArena, Leverkusen (att: 29,300)
Bayer 04 Leverkusen 2-4 Club Atlético de Madrid
Goals: 0-1 Saúl Ñíguez 17, 0-2 Griezmann 25, 1-2 Bellarabi 48, 1-3 Gameiro 59(p), 2-3 Savić 68(og), 2-4 Fernando Torres 86
Referee: Collum (SCO)

Valère Germain completes the scoring as Monaco defeat Dortmund to reach the semi-finals

15/03/17, Estadio Vicente Calderón, Madrid (att: 49,133)
Club Atlético de Madrid 0-0 Bayer 04 Leverkusen
Referee: Karasev (RUS)
Aggregate: 4-2; Club Atlético de Madrid qualify.

22/02/17, Estádio do Dragão, Porto (att: 49,229)
FC Porto 0-2 Juventus
Goals: 0-1 Pjaca 72, 0-2 Dani Alves 74
Referee: Brych (GER)
14/03/17, Juventus Stadium, Turin (att: 41,161)
Juventus 1-0 FC Porto
Goal: 1-0 Dybala 42(p)
Referee: Hațegan (ROU)
Aggregate: 3-0; Juventus qualify.

22/02/17, Estadio Ramón Sánchez Pizjuán, Seville (att: 38,834)
Sevilla FC 2-1 Leicester City FC
Goals: 1-0 Sarabia 25, 2-0 Correa 62, 2-1 Vardy 73
Referee: Turpin (FRA)
14/03/17, Leicester City Stadium, Leicester (att: 31,520)
Leicester City FC 2-0 Sevilla FC
Goals: 1-0 Morgan 27, 2-0 Albrighton 54
Referee: Orsato (ITA)
Aggregate: 3-2; Leicester City FC qualify.

Quarter-finals

11/04/17, Juventus Stadium, Turin (att: 41,092)
Juventus 3-0 FC Barcelona
Goals: 1-0 Dybala 7, 2-0 Dybala 22, 3-0 Chiellini 55
Referee: Marciniak (POL)
19/04/17, Camp Nou, Barcelona (att: 96,290)
FC Barcelona 0-0 Juventus
Referee: Kuipers (NED)
Aggregate: 0-3; Juventus qualify.

12/04/17, BVB Stadion Dortmund, Dortmund (att: 65,849)
Borussia Dortmund 2-3 AS Monaco FC
Goals: 0-1 Mbappé 19, 0-2 Bender 35(og), 1-2 Dembélé 57, 1-3 Mbappé 79, 2-3 Kagawa 84
Referee: Orsato (ITA)
19/04/17, Stade Louis II, Monaco (att: 17,135)
AS Monaco FC 3-1 Borussia Dortmund
Goals: 1-0 Mbappé 3, 2-0 Falcao 17, 2-1 Reus 48, 3-1 Germain 81
Referee: Skomina (SVN)
Aggregate: 6-3; AS Monaco FC qualify.

12/04/17, Estadio Vicente Calderón, Madrid (att: 51,423)
Club Atlético de Madrid 1-0 Leicester City FC
Goal: 1-0 Griezmann 28(p)
Referee: Eriksson (SWE)
18/04/17, Leicester City Stadium, Leicester (att: 31,548)
Leicester City FC 1-1 Club Atlético de Madrid
Goals: 0-1 Saúl Ñíguez 26, 1-1 Vardy 61
Referee: Rocchi (ITA)
Aggregate: 1-2; Club Atlético de Madrid qualify.

12/04/17, Fußball Arena München, Munich (att: 70,000)
FC Bayern München 1-2 Real Madrid CF
Goals: 1-0 Vidal 25, 1-1 Cristiano Ronaldo 47, 1-2 Cristiano Ronaldo 77
Referee: Rizzoli (ITA)
18/04/17, Estadio Santiago Bernabéu, Madrid (att: 78,346)
Real Madrid CF 4-2 FC Bayern München (aet)
Goals: 0-1 Lewandowski 53(p), 1-1 Cristiano Ronaldo 76, 1-2 Sergio Ramos 78(og), 2-2 Cristiano Ronaldo 105, 3-2 Cristiano Ronaldo 110, 4-2 Marco Asensio 112
Referee: Kassai (HUN)
Aggregate: 6-3; Real Madrid CF qualify.

Semi-finals

02/05/17, Estadio Santiago Bernabéu, Madrid (att: 77,609)
Real Madrid CF 3-0 Club Atlético de Madrid
Goals: 1-0 Cristiano Ronaldo 10, 2-0 Cristiano Ronaldo 73, 3-0 Cristiano Ronaldo 86
Referee: Atkinson (ENG)
10/05/17, Estadio Vicente Calderón, Madrid (att: 53,422)
Club Atlético de Madrid 2-1 Real Madrid CF
Goals: 1-0 Saúl Ñíguez 12, 2-0 Griezmann 16(p), 2-1 Isco 42
Referee: Çakır (TUR)
Aggregate: 2-4; Real Madrid CF qualify.

03/05/17, Stade Louis II, Monaco (att: 16,762)
AS Monaco FC 0-2 Juventus
Goals: 0-1 Higuaín 29, 0-2 Higuaín 59
Referee: Mateu Lahoz (ESP)
09/05/17, Juventus Stadium, Turin (att: 40,244)
Juventus 2-1 AS Monaco FC
Goals: 1-0 Mandžukić 33, 2-0 Dani Alves 44, 2-1 Mbappé 69
Referee: Kuipers (NED)
Aggregate: 4-1; Juventus qualify.

Final

03/06/17, The National Stadium of Wales, Cardiff (att: 65,842)
Juventus 1-4 Real Madrid CF
Goals: 0-1 Cristiano Ronaldo 20, 1-1 Mandžukić 27, 1-2 Casemiro 61, 1-3 Cristiano Ronaldo 64, 1-4 Marco Asensio 90
Referee: Brych (GER)
Juventus: Buffon, Chiellini, Pjanić (Marchisio 71), Khedira, Higuaín, Alex Sandro, Barzagli (Cuadrado 66), Mandžukić, Bonucci, Dybala (Lemina 78), Dani Alves. Coach: Massimiliano Allegri (ITA)
Real Madrid: Navas, Carvajal, Sergio Ramos, Varane, Cristiano Ronaldo, Kroos (Morata 89), Benzema (Bale 77), Marcelo, Casemiro, Modrić, Isco (Marco Asensio 82). Coach: Zinédine Zidane (FRA)
Red card: Cuadrado 84 (Juventus)
Yellow cards: Dybala 12 (Juventus), Sergio Ramos 31 (Real Madrid), Carvajal 42 (Real Madrid), Kroos 53 (Real Madrid), Pjanić 66 (Juventus), Alex Sandro 70 (Juventus), Cuadrado 72 (Juventus), Cuadrado 84 (Juventus), Marco Asensio 90+1 (Real Madrid)

Top goalscorers

12	Cristiano Ronaldo (Real Madrid)
11	Lionel Messi (Barcelona)
8	Robert Lewandowski (Bayern) Edinson Cavani (Paris)
7	Pierre-Emerick Aubameyang (Dortmund)
6	Antoine Griezmann (Atlético) Kylian Mbappé (Monaco)
5	Gonzalo Higuaín (Juventus) Sergio Agüero (Man. City) Radamel Falcao (Monaco) Dries Mertens (Napoli) Karim Benzema (Real Madrid)

Marco Asensio steers the ball home to stretch Real Madrid's lead over Juventus to 4-1 in the last minute of the UEFA Champions League final

Squads/Appearances/Goals

Arsenal FC

No	Name	Nat	DoB	Aps	(s)	Gls
Goalkeepers						
13	David Ospina	COL	31/08/88	8		
Defenders						
24	Héctor Bellerín	ESP	19/03/95	5		
5	Gabriel	BRA	26/11/90	1	(1)	
3	Kieran Gibbs		26/09/89	5	(1)	
16	Rob Holding		20/09/95	1		
25	Carl Jenkinson		08/02/92	2		
6	Laurent Koscielny	FRA	10/09/85	8		
18	Nacho Monreal	ESP	26/02/86	3		
20	Shkodran Mustafi	GER	17/04/92	7		
Midfielders						
34	Francis Coquelin	FRA	13/05/91	5	(1)	
35	Mohamed Elneny	EGY	11/07/92		(5)	
17	Alex Iwobi	NGA	03/05/96	5	(2)	1
15	Alex Oxlade-Chamberlain		15/08/93	4	(3)	1
11	Mesut Özil	GER	15/10/88	7	(1)	4
8	Aaron Ramsey	WAL	26/12/90	4		
19	Santi Cazorla	ESP	13/12/84	3		
29	Granit Xhaka	SUI	27/09/92	5	(2)	1
Forwards						
7	Alexis Sánchez	CHI	19/12/88	8		3
12	Olivier Giroud	FRA	30/09/86	3	(3)	2
9	Lucas Pérez	ESP	10/09/88	1	(2)	3
14	Theo Walcott		16/03/89	3	(3)	4

Club Atlético de Madrid

No	Name	Nat	DoB	Aps	(s)	Gls
Goalkeepers						
1	Miguel Ángel Moyá		02/04/84	1		
13	Jan Oblak	SVN	07/01/93	11		
Defenders						
3	Filipe Luís	BRA	09/08/85	10		
24	José María Giménez	URU	20/01/95	6		
2	Diego Godín	URU	16/02/86	11		
20	Juanfran		09/01/85	5	(1)	
19	Lucas Hernández	FRA	14/02/96	3	(1)	
15	Stefan Savić	MNE	08/01/91	9	(1)	
16	Šime Vrsaljko	CRO	10/01/92	5		
Midfielders						
10	Yannick Carrasco	BEL	04/09/93	11	(1)	2
14	Gabi		10/07/83	11		
23	Nicolás Gaitán	ARG	23/02/88	2	(3)	
6	Koke		08/01/92	12		
8	Saúl Ñíguez		21/11/94	10	(2)	4
22	Thomas	GHA	13/06/93	1	(5)	
5	Tiago	POR	02/05/81	1	(2)	
Forwards						
11	Ángel Correa	ARG	09/03/95	2	(7)	
9	Fernando Torres		20/03/84	5	(4)	1
21	Kevin Gameiro	FRA	09/05/87	4	(5)	2
7	Antoine Griezmann	FRA	21/03/91	12		6

FC Barcelona

No	Name	Nat	DoB	Aps	(s)	Gls
Goalkeepers						
13	Jasper Cillessen	NED	22/04/89	1		
1	Marc-André ter Stegen	GER	30/04/92	9		
Defenders						
22	Aleix Vidal		21/08/89	1		
19	Lucas Digne	FRA	20/07/93	2	(2)	
18	Jordi Alba		21/03/89	6		
33	Marlon	BRA	07/09/95		(1)	
14	Javier Mascherano	ARG	08/06/84	7	(1)	
24	Jérémy Mathieu	FRA	29/10/83	1	(1)	
3	Gerard Piqué		02/02/87	8		1
20	Sergi Roberto		07/02/92	7	(1)	1
23	Samuel Umtiti	FRA	14/11/93	8		
Midfielders						
21	André Gomes	POR	30/07/93	5	(3)	
7	Arda Turan	TUR	30/01/87	1	(4)	4
5	Sergio Busquets		16/07/88	8		
6	Denis Suárez		06/01/94	1		
8	Andrés Iniesta		11/05/84	7	(1)	1
12	Rafinha	BRA	12/02/93	1	(5)	
4	Ivan Rakitić	CRO	10/03/88	8	(1)	
Forwards						
29	Marc Cardona		08/07/95		(1)	
10	Lionel Messi	ARG	24/06/87	9		11
11	Neymar	BRA	05/02/92	9		4
17	Paco Alcácer		30/08/93	2	(1)	
9	Luis Suárez	URU	24/01/87	9		3

FC Basel 1893

No	Name	Nat	DoB	Aps	(s)	Gls
Goalkeepers						
1	Tomáš Vaclík	CZE	29/03/89	6		
Defenders						
23	Éder Balanta	COL	28/02/93	6		
4	Omar Gaber	EGY	30/01/92	1		
5	Michael Lang		08/02/91	5		
17	Marek Suchý	CZE	29/03/88	6		
3	Adama Traoré	CIV	03/02/90	6		
Midfielders						
8	Birkir Bjarnason	ISL	27/05/88	5		
39	Davide Callà		06/10/84		(3)	
10	Matías Delgado	ARG	15/12/82	5	(1)	
24	Mohamed Elyounoussi	NOR	04/08/94	2	(1)	
15	Alexander Fransson	SWE	02/04/94	1	(1)	
6	Serey Dié	CIV	07/11/84	3		
11	Renato Steffen		03/11/91	5		1
34	Taulant Xhaka	ALB	28/03/91	6		
7	Luca Zuffi		27/03/90	3	(3)	1
Forwards						
88	Seydou Doumbia	CIV	31/12/87	4	(2)	1
21	Marc Janko	AUT	25/06/83	2	(3)	
9	Andraž Šporar	SVN	27/02/94		(4)	

Bayer 04 Leverkusen

No	Name	Nat	DoB	Aps	(s)	Gls
Goalkeepers						
1	Bernd Leno		04/03/92	7		
28	Ramazan Özcan	AUT	28/06/84	1		
Defenders						
23	Danny Da Costa		13/07/93	1		
6	Aleksandar Dragovic	AUT	06/03/91	3		
39	Benjamin Henrichs		23/02/97	6	(1)	
13	Roberto Hilbert		16/10/84	1		
16	Tin Jedvaj	CRO	28/11/95	3	(1)	
21	Ömer Toprak	TUR	21/07/89	6		
4	Jonathan Tah		11/02/96	5		
18	Wendell	BRA	20/07/93	5		
Midfielders						
20	Charles Aránguiz	CHI	17/04/89	5	(3)	
15	Julian Baumgartlinger	AUT	02/01/88	3	(3)	
38	Karim Bellarabi		08/04/90	2		1
8	Lars Bender		27/04/89	3		
19	Julian Brandt		02/05/96	7	(1)	1
10	Hakan Çalhanoğlu	TUR	08/02/94	5	(1)	1
29	Kai Havertz		11/06/99	1	(2)	
44	Kevin Kampl	SVN	09/10/90	7		1
35	Vladlen Yurchenko	UKR	22/01/94	1		1
Forwards						
9	Leon Bailey	JAM	09/08/97		(2)	
7	Javier Hernández	MEX	01/06/88	8		1
11	Stefan Kiessling		25/01/84	2	(1)	
27	Robbie Kruse	AUS	05/10/88		(1)	
14	Admir Mehmedi	SUI	16/03/91	3	(3)	1
17	Joel Pohjanpalo	FIN	13/09/94		(2)	
31	Kevin Volland		30/07/92	3	(3)	1

FC Bayern München

No	Name	Nat	DoB	Aps	(s)	Gls
Goalkeepers						
1	Manuel Neuer		27/03/86	9		
26	Sven Ulreich		03/08/88	1		
Defenders						
27	David Alaba	AUT	24/06/92	9		
28	Holger Badstuber		13/03/89	1		
18	Juan Bernat	ESP	01/03/93	2	(2)	2
17	Jérôme Boateng		03/09/88	6		
5	Mats Hummels		16/12/88	7	(2)	
8	Javi Martínez	ESP	02/09/88	5	(2)	
21	Philipp Lahm		11/11/83	7		
13	Rafinha	BRA	07/09/85	4	(1)	
Midfielders						
29	Kingsley Coman	FRA	13/06/96		(2)	
11	Douglas Costa	BRA	14/09/90	4	(5)	2
32	Joshua Kimmich		08/02/95	3	(5)	3
35	Renato Sanches	POR	18/08/97	2	(4)	
7	Franck Ribéry	FRA	07/04/83	5	(1)	
10	Arjen Robben	NED	23/01/84	7	(1)	3
6	Thiago Alcántara	ESP	11/04/91	9		2
23	Arturo Vidal	CHI	22/05/87	8		3
14	Xabi Alonso	ESP	25/11/81	7		
Forwards						
9	Robert Lewandowski	POL	21/08/88	9		8
25	Thomas Müller		13/09/89	5	(4)	3

SL Benfica

No	Name	Nat	DoB	Aps	(s)	Gls
Goalkeepers						
1	Ederson	BRA	17/08/93	7		
12	Júlio César	BRA	03/09/79	1		
Defenders						
3	Álex Grimaldo	ESP	20/09/95	4		
19	Eliseu		01/10/83	3	(1)	
14	Victor Lindelöf	SWE	17/07/94	8		
2	Lisandro López	ARG	01/09/89	2		
4	Luisão	BRA	13/02/81	6		
50	Nélson Semedo		16/11/93	8		1
Midfielders						
34	André Almeida		10/09/90	3	(1)	
8	André Horta		07/11/96	2		
28	Guillermo Celis	COL	08/05/93		(2)	
22	Franco Cervi	ARG	26/05/94	6	(1)	2
5	Ljubomir Fejsa	SRB	14/08/88	7		1
6	Filipe Augusto	BRA	12/08/93		(1)	
21	Pizzi		06/10/89	8		
27	Rafa Silva		17/05/93	1	(2)	
18	Eduardo Salvio	ARG	13/07/90	7	(1)	3
7	Andreas Samaris	GRE	13/06/89	1	(3)	
17	Andrija Živković	SRB	11/07/96		(1)	
Forwards						
15	André Carrillo	PER	14/06/91	2	(1)	
20	Gonçalo Guedes		29/11/96	5	(1)	2
9	Raúl Jiménez	MEX	05/05/91	1	(5)	1
10	Jonas	BRA	01/04/84		(1)	
70	José Gomes		08/04/99		(1)	
11	Kostas Mitroglou	GRE	12/03/88	6	(1)	1

Beşiktaş JK

No	Name	Nat	DoB	Aps	(s)	Gls
Goalkeepers						
1	Fabricio	ESP	31/12/87	5		
29	Tolga Zengin		10/10/83	1		
Defenders						
3	Adriano	BRA	26/10/84	6		1
33	Atınç Nukan		20/07/93		(1)	
32	Andreas Beck	GER	13/03/87	6		
88	Caner Erkin		04/10/88	3		
77	Gökhan Gönül		04/01/85	1	(1)	
30	Marcelo	BRA	20/05/87	6		
44	Rhodolfo	BRA	11/08/86	1		
6	Duško Tošić	SRB	19/01/85	6		
Midfielders						
18	Tolgay Arslan	GER	16/08/90	5		
13	Atiba Hutchinson	CAN	08/02/83	6		
80	Gökhan Inler	SUI	27/06/84	2	(3)	
21	Kerim Koyunlu		19/11/93		(2)	
20	Necip Uysal		24/01/91	1		
15	Oğuzhan Özyakup		23/09/92	3	(1)	
10	Olcay Şahan		26/05/87	1	(1)	
7	Ricardo Quaresma	POR	26/09/83	6		3
94	Talisca	BRA	01/02/94	1	(2)	1
Forwards						
9	Vincent Aboubakar	CMR	22/01/92	6		3
23	Cenk Tosun		07/06/91		(6)	1

Borussia Dortmund

No	Name	Nat	DoB	Aps	(s)	Gls
Goalkeepers						
38	Roman Bürki	SUI	14/11/90	8		
1	Roman Weidenfeller		06/08/80	2		
Defenders						
5	Marc Bartra	ESP	15/01/91	7		1
37	Erik Durm		12/05/92	3	(1)	
28	Matthias Ginter		19/01/94	6	(2)	
25	Sokratis Papastathopoulos	GRE	09/06/88	9		1
30	Felix Passlack		29/05/98	2		1
26	Łukasz Piszczek	POL	03/06/85	7	(2)	
29	Marcel Schmelzer		22/01/88	6	(1)	
Midfielders						
6	Sven Bender		27/04/89	1		
32	Dzenis Burnic		22/05/98		(1)	
27	Gonzalo Castro		11/06/87	5	(2)	1
7	Ousmane Dembélé	FRA	15/05/97	9	(1)	2
9	Emre Mor	TUR	24/07/97		(3)	
10	Mario Götze		03/06/92	4		1
23	Shinji Kagawa	JPN	17/03/89	4	(1)	3
8	Nuri Şahin	TUR	05/09/88	2	(1)	1
22	Christian Pulisic	USA	18/09/98	6	(4)	1
13	Raphaël Guerreiro	POR	22/12/93	6		1
11	Marco Reus		31/05/89	3	(1)	4
18	Sebastian Rode		11/10/90	1	(3)	
21	André Schürrle		06/11/90	1	(5)	1
33	Julian Weigl		08/09/95	9		1
Forwards						
17	Pierre-Emerick Aubameyang	GAB	18/06/89	8	(1)	7
20	Adrián Ramos	COL	22/01/86	1		1

Celtic FC

No	Name	Nat	DoB	Aps	(s)	Gls
Goalkeepers						
24	Dorus de Vries	NED	29/12/80	1		
1	Craig Gordon		31/12/82	5		
Defenders						
12	Cristian Gamboa	CRC	24/10/89	2		
3	Emilio Izaguirre	HON	10/05/86	3		
23	Mikael Lustig	SWE	13/12/86	6		
34	Eoghan O'Connell	IRL	13/08/95		(1)	
5	Jozo Šimunović	CRO	04/08/94	2		
28	Erik Sviatchenko	DEN	04/10/91	6		
63	Kieran Tierney		05/06/97	3		
2	Kolo Touré	CIV	19/03/81	3		
Midfielders						
14	Stuart Armstrong		30/03/92	3	(2)	
6	Nir Biton	ISR	30/10/91	3	(1)	
8	Scott Brown		25/06/85	6		
49	James Forrest		07/07/91	4	(1)	
53	Liam Henderson		25/04/96		(1)	
16	Gary Mackay-Steven		31/08/90		(1)	
42	Callum McGregor		14/06/93	1	(3)	
27	Patrick Roberts	ENG	05/02/97	2	(4)	1
18	Tom Rogic	AUS	16/12/92	5		
11	Scott Sinclair	ENG	25/03/89	5		
Forwards						
10	Moussa Dembélé	FRA	12/07/96	6		3
9	Leigh Griffiths		20/08/90		(3)	

PFC CSKA Moskva

No	Name	Nat	DoB	Aps	(s)	Gls
Goalkeepers						
35	Igor Akinfeev		08/04/86	6		
Defenders						
6	Aleksei Berezutski		20/06/82	3	(2)	
24	Vasili Berezutski		20/06/82	5		
4	Sergei Ignashevich		14/07/79	4		
2	Mário Fernandes		19/09/90	5		
14	Kirill Nababkin		08/09/86	1	(1)	
42	Georgi Schennikov		27/04/91	6		
Midfielders						
10	Alan Dzagoev		17/06/90	3		2
25	Roman Eremenko	FIN	19/03/87	2		1
17	Aleksandr Golovin		30/05/96	6		
72	Astemir Gordyushenko		30/03/97		(2)	
8	Georgi Milanov	BUL	19/02/92	3	(3)	
66	Bebras Natcho	ISR	18/02/88	4	(1)	1
7	Zoran Tošić	SRB	28/04/87	4		
3	Pontus Wernbloom	SWE	25/06/86	5		
Forwards						
63	Fedor Chalov		10/04/98	1	(1)	
11	Aleksei Ionov		18/02/89	3		
23	Carlos Strandberg	SWE	14/04/96	1	(4)	
9	Lacina Traoré	CIV	20/08/90	4	(2)	1

VfL Borussia Mönchengladbach

No	Name	Nat	DoB	Aps	(s)	Gls
Goalkeepers						
1	Yann Sommer	SUI	17/12/88	6		
Defenders						
3	Andreas Christensen	DEN	10/04/96	4		
30	Nico Elvedi	SUI	30/09/96	6		
24	Tony Jantschke		07/04/90	2	(1)	
27	Julian Korb		21/03/92	4	(1)	
4	Jannik Vestergaard	DEN	03/08/92	3	(1)	
17	Oscar Wendt	SWE	24/10/85	5		
Midfielders						
8	Mahmoud Dahoud		01/01/96	4		
28	André Hahn		13/08/90	4	(2)	1
10	Thorgan Hazard	BEL	29/03/93	3	(1)	1
7	Patrick Herrmann		12/02/91		(3)	
23	Jonas Hofmann		14/07/92	1	(1)	
19	Fabian Johnson	USA	11/12/87	3	(2)	
6	Christoph Kramer		19/02/91	4	(1)	
14	Nico Schulz		01/04/93	1	(1)	
5	Tobias Strobl		12/05/90	5		
16	Ibrahima Traoré	GUI	21/04/88	3	(1)	
Forwards						
11	Raffael	BRA	28/03/85	3	(2)	1
13	Lars Stindl		26/08/88	5		2

Club Brugge KV

No	Name	Nat	DoB	Aps	(s)	Gls
Goalkeepers						
1	Ludovic Butelle	FRA	03/04/83	6		
Defenders						
21	Dion Cools		04/06/96	3		
28	Laurens De Bock		07/11/92	3		
24	Stefano Denswil	NED	07/05/93	5		
4	Björn Engels		15/09/94	1		
44	Brandon Mechele		28/01/93	2		
5	Benoît Poulain	FRA	24/07/87	4	(1)	
2	Ricardo van Rhijn	NED	13/06/91	5	(1)	
Midfielders						
63	Boli Bolingoli-Mbombo		01/07/95	2	(1)	
6	Claudemir	BRA	27/03/88	5		
19	Felipe Gedoz	BRA	12/07/93	1	(3)	
11	José Izquierdo	COL	07/07/92	3	(1)	1
17	Anthony Limbombe		15/07/94	1	(3)	
15	Tomás Pina	ESP	14/10/87	5		
8	Lior Refaelov	ISR	26/04/86	1		
3	Timmy Simons		11/12/76	4		
20	Hans Vanaken		24/08/92	4	(2)	
25	Ruud Vormer	NED	11/05/88	4	(1)	
Forwards						
10	Abdoulay Diaby	MLI	21/05/91	2		
9	Jelle Vossen		22/03/89	3	(1)	1
7	Wesley	BRA	26/11/96	2	(3)	

GNK Dinamo Zagreb

No	Name	Nat	DoB	Aps	(s)	Gls
Goalkeepers						
40	Dominik Livaković		09/01/95	4		
98	Adrian Šemper		12/01/98	2		
Defenders						
26	Filip Benković		13/07/97	5		
77	Alexandru Mățel	ROU	17/10/89	1	(2)	
55	Dino Perić		12/07/94		(1)	
19	Josip Pivarić		30/01/89	5		
23	Gordon Schildenfeld		18/03/85	5		
22	Leonardo Sigali	ARG	29/05/87	5		
35	Borna Sosa		21/01/98	1		
37	Petar Stojanovič	SVN	07/10/95	3	(1)	
Midfielders						
8	Domagoj Antolić		30/06/90	2		
24	Ante Ćorić		14/04/97	4		
29	Ivan Fiolić		29/04/96		(4)	
14	Amer Gojak	BIH	13/02/97	2	(1)	
5	Jonas	BRA	08/10/91	2	(2)	
25	Bojan Knežević		28/01/97	3		
27	Nikola Moro		12/03/98	1		
10	Paulo Machado	POR	31/03/86	2	(2)	
18	Domagoj Pavičić		09/03/94	5		
7	Mario Šitum		04/04/92	3	(2)	
Forwards						
15	Armin Hodžić	BIH	17/11/94		(1)	
11	Júnior Fernandes	CHI	10/04/88	6		
9	Ángelo Henríquez	CHI	13/04/94		(2)	
2	El Arabi Hillel Soudani	ALG	25/11/87	5		

FC Dynamo Kyiv

No	Name	Nat	DoB	Aps	(s)	Gls
Goalkeepers						
72	Artur Rudko		07/05/92	5		
1	Olexandr Shovkovskiy		02/01/75	1		
Defenders						
5	Antunes	POR	01/04/87	4		
26	Mykyta Burda		24/03/95	1		
2	Danilo Silva	BRA	24/11/86	1		
34	Yevhen Khacheridi		28/07/87	6		
27	Yevhen Makarenko		21/05/91	3		
9	Mykola Morozyuk		17/01/88	3		
24	Domagoj Vida	CRO	29/04/89	6		
Midfielders						
29	Vitaliy Buyalskiy		06/01/93	3	(1)	1
32	Valeriy Fedorchuk		05/10/88	1		
19	Denys Garmash		19/04/90	3		1
25	Derlis González	PAR	20/03/94	4	(1)	1
77	Artem Gromov		14/01/90		(1)	
20	Oleh Gusev		25/04/83		(1)	
18	Nikita Korzun	BLR	06/03/95	1	(3)	
48	Pavlo Orikhovskiy		13/05/96		(2)	
17	Serhiy Rybalka		01/04/90	5		
16	Serhiy Sydorchuk		02/05/91	5		1
15	Viktor Tsygankov		15/11/97	3	(3)	1
10	Andriy Yarmolenko		23/10/89	5		1
Forwards						
41	Artem Besedin		31/03/96	2	(1)	1
7	Olexandr Gladkiy		24/08/87		(3)	
11	Júnior Moraes	BRA	04/04/87	4	(2)	1

FC København

No	Name	Nat	DoB	Aps	(s)	Gls
Goalkeepers						
31	Robin Olsen	SWE	08/01/90	6		
Defenders						
22	Peter Ankersen		22/09/90	6		
15	Mikael Antonsson	SWE	31/05/81		(1)	
3	Ludwig Augustinsson	SWE	21/04/94	6		
2	Tom Høgli	NOR	24/02/84		(1)	
5	Erik Johansson	SWE	30/12/88	6		
25	Mathias "Zanka" Jørgensen		23/04/90	6		2
Midfielders						
32	Danny Amankwaa		30/01/94		(1)	
8	Thomas Delaney		03/09/91	6		1
33	Rasmus Falk		15/01/92	4	(2)	
16	Ján Greguš	SVK	29/01/91	1	(3)	
35	Aboubakar Keita	CIV	05/11/97		(1)	
17	Kasper Kusk		10/11/91		(2)	
6	William Kvist		24/02/85	6		
24	Youssef Toutouh		06/10/92	4	(2)	
7	Benjamin Verbič	SVN	27/11/93	4	(1)	
Forwards						
11	Andreas Cornelius		16/03/93	5		1
23	Andrija Pavlović	SRB	16/11/93	2	(2)	
19	Federico Santander	PAR	04/06/91	4		1

Leicester City FC

No	Name	Nat	DoB	Aps	(s)	Gls
Goalkeepers						
12	Ben Hamer		20/11/87	1		
1	Kasper Schmeichel	DEN	05/11/86	8		
21	Ron-Robert Zieler	GER	12/02/89	1		
Defenders						
29	Yohan Benalouane	TUN	28/03/87	2		
3	Ben Chilwell		21/12/96	1	(1)	
28	Christian Fuchs	AUT	07/04/86	9		
6	Robert Huth	GER	18/08/84	8		
2	Luis Hernández	ESP	14/04/89	4		
5	Wes Morgan	JAM	21/01/84	9		1
17	Danny Simpson		04/01/87	6		
27	Marcin Wasilewski	POL	09/06/80	1		
Midfielders						
11	Marc Albrighton		18/11/89	8	(1)	2
13	Daniel Amartey	GHA	21/12/94	3	(5)	
39	Harvey Barnes		09/12/97		(1)	
4	Danny Drinkwater		05/03/90	10		
22	Demarai Gray		28/06/96	1	(4)	
10	Andy King	WAL	29/10/88	2	(2)	
26	Riyad Mahrez	ALG	21/02/91	9		4
24	Nampalys Mendy	FRA	23/06/92	1		
25	Wilfred Ndidi	NGA	16/12/96	4		
15	Jeff Schlupp	GHA	23/12/92	2	(1)	
Forwards						
7	Ahmed Musa	NGA	14/10/92	3	(2)	
20	Shinji Okazaki	JPN	16/04/86	5	(2)	1
19	Islam Slimani	ALG	18/06/88	3	(2)	1
23	Leonardo Ulloa	ARG	27/07/86		(4)	
9	Jamie Vardy		11/01/87	9		2

Juventus FC

No	Name	Nat	DoB	Aps	(s)	Gls
Goalkeepers						
1	Gianluigi Buffon		28/01/78	12		
25	Neto	BRA	19/07/89	1		
Defenders						
12	Alex Sandro	BRA	26/01/91	9	(2)	
15	Andrea Barzagli		08/05/81	8	(3)	
4	Medhi Benatia	MAR	17/04/87	2	(3)	
19	Leonardo Bonucci		01/05/87	11		1
3	Giorgio Chiellini		14/08/84	8	(1)	1
23	Dani Alves	BRA	06/05/83	11	(1)	3
33	Patrice Evra	FRA	15/05/81	6		
26	Stephan Lichtsteiner	SUI	16/01/84	1		
24	Daniele Rugani		29/07/94	2		1
Midfielders						
22	Kwadwo Asamoah	GHA	09/12/88	2	(1)	
7	Juan Cuadrado	COL	26/05/88	6	(6)	1
11	Hernanes	BRA	29/05/85	1	(1)	
6	Sami Khedira	GER	04/04/87	11		
18	Mario Lemina	GAB	01/09/93	3	(4)	
8	Claudio Marchisio		19/01/86	5	(3)	1
20	Marko Pjaca	CRO	06/05/95		(4)	1
5	Miralem Pjanić	BIH	02/04/90	11	(1)	1
28	Tomás Rincón	VEN	13/01/88		(3)	
27	Stefano Sturaro		09/03/93	1	(3)	
Forwards						
21	Paulo Dybala	ARG	15/11/93	10	(1)	4
9	Gonzalo Higuaín	ARG	10/12/87	12		5
34	Moise Kean		28/02/00		(1)	
17	Mario Mandžukić	CRO	21/05/86	10	(1)	3

Legia Warszawa

No	Name	Nat	DoB	Aps	(s)	Gls
Goalkeepers						
33	Radosław Cierzniak		24/04/83	1		
1	Arkadiusz Malarz		19/06/80	5		
Defenders						
19	Bartosz Bereszyński		12/07/92	6		
4	Jakub Czerwiński		06/08/91	4		
5	Maciej Dąbrowski		20/04/87	1	(1)	
14	Adam Hloušek	CZE	20/12/88	4		
2	Michał Pazdan		21/09/87	3		
25	Jakub Rzeźniczak		26/10/86	5		
52	Mateusz Wieteska		11/02/97		(1)	
Midfielders						
77	Mihail Alexandrov	BUL	11/06/89		(2)	
6	Guilherme	BRA	21/05/91	6		1
22	Kasper Hämäläinen	FIN	08/08/86		(1)	
3	Tomasz Jodłowiec		08/09/85	3	(2)	
9	Valeri Kazaishvili	GEO	29/01/93	1	(1)	
15	Michał Kopczyński		15/06/92	3	(2)	
18	Michał Kucharczyk		20/03/91	2	(2)	1
7	Steeven Langil	FRA	04/03/88	2		
75	Thibault Moulin	FRA	13/01/90	5		1
8	Vadis Odjidja-Ofoe	BEL	21/02/89	5	(1)	1
32	Miroslav Radović		16/01/84	5	(1)	2
Forwards						
11	Nemanja Nikolić	HUN	31/12/87	2	(3)	1
99	Aleksandar Prijović	SRB	21/04/90	3	(1)	2

PFC Ludogorets Razgrad

No	Name	Nat	DoB	Aps	(s)	Gls
Goalkeepers						
1	Milan Borjan	CAN	23/10/87	1		
21	Vladislav Stoyanov		08/06/87	5		
Defenders						
4	Cicinho	BRA	26/12/88	2		
25	Yordan Minev		14/10/80	4		
27	Cosmin Moţi	ROU	03/12/84	6		
6	Natanael	BRA	25/12/90	6		1
5	José Luis Palomino	ARG	05/01/90	5		
32	Ihor Plastun	UKR	20/08/90	1	(2)	
77	Vitinha	POR	11/02/86		(1)	
Midfielders						
12	Anicet Abel	MAD	16/03/90	6		
18	Svetoslav Dyakov		31/05/84	6		
10	Gustavo Campanharo	BRA	04/04/92		(2)	
8	Lucas Sasha	BRA	01/03/90		(1)	
92	Jody Lukoki	COD	15/11/92		(4)	
84	Marcelinho		24/08/84	5		
93	Virgil Misidjan	NED	24/07/93	5	(1)	1
88	Wanderson	BRA	02/01/88	6		1
Forwards						
22	Jonathan Cafú	BRA	10/07/91	6		2
28	Claudiu Keşerü	ROU	02/12/86	2	(3)	1

Olympique Lyonnais

No	Name	Nat	DoB	Aps	(s)	Gls
Goalkeepers						
1	Anthony Lopes	POR	01/10/90	6		
Defenders						
5	Mouctar Diakhaby		19/12/96	3		
23	Jordy Gaspar		23/04/97	1		
4	Emanuel Mammana	ARG	10/02/96	1		
15	Jérémy Morel		02/04/84	6		
3	Nicolas N'Koulou	CMR	27/03/90	4		
20	Rafael	BRA	09/07/90	5		
31	Maciej Rybus	POL	19/08/89	3	(1)	
2	Mapou Yanga-Mbiwa		15/05/89	5		
Midfielders						
14	Sergi Darder	ESP	22/12/93	5	(1)	
18	Nabil Fekir		18/07/93	3	(2)	
12	Jordan Ferri		12/03/92	2	(1)	1
11	Rachid Ghezzal	ALG	09/05/92	2	(3)	
21	Maxime Gonalons		10/03/89	6		
7	Clément Grenier		07/01/91		(1)	
8	Corentin Tolisso		03/08/94	5	(1)	2
29	Lucas Tousart		29/04/97		(1)	
28	Mathieu Valbuena		28/09/84	2	(1)	
Forwards						
27	Maxwel Cornet	CIV	27/09/96	3	(3)	1
26	Aldo Kalulu		21/01/96		(2)	
10	Alexandre Lacazette		28/05/91	4		1

AS Monaco FC

No	Name	Nat	DoB	Aps	(s)	Gls
Goalkeepers						
16	Morgan De Sanctis	ITA	26/03/77	1		
1	Danijel Subašić	CRO	27/10/84	11		
Defenders						
34	Abdou Diallo		04/05/96	1		
25	Kamil Glik	POL	03/02/88	10		1
5	Jemerson	BRA	24/08/92	11		
23	Benjamin Mendy		17/07/94	6	(1)	
24	Andrea Raggi	ITA	24/06/84	8	(3)	
19	Djibril Sidibé		29/07/92	9		1
38	Almamy Touré	MLI	28/04/96	3	(2)	
Midfielders						
14	Tiémoué Bakayoko		17/08/94	10		1
10	Bernardo Silva	POR	10/08/94	11		2
26	Boschilia	BRA	05/03/96	1	(1)	
7	Nabil Dirar	MAR	25/02/86	3	(4)	
2	Fabinho	BRA	23/10/93	9	(1)	1
8	João Moutinho	POR	08/09/86	7	(4)	
27	Thomas Lemar		12/11/95	9	(3)	2
35	Kévin N'Doram		22/01/96	1		
20	Adama Traoré	MLI	28/06/95		(1)	
Forwards						
11	Guido Carrillo	ARG	25/05/91	1	(4)	
9	Radamel Falcao	COL	10/02/86	8		5
18	Valère Germain		17/04/90	5	(7)	2
28	Corentin Jean		15/07/95	1		
29	Kylian Mbappé		20/12/98	6	(3)	6

Paris Saint-Germain

No	Name	Nat	DoB	Aps	(s)	Gls
Goalkeepers						
16	Alphonse Areola		27/02/93	6		
1	Kevin Trapp	GER	08/07/90	2		
Defenders						
19	Serge Aurier	CIV	24/12/92	3	(2)	
3	Presnel Kimpembe		13/08/95	1		
20	Layvin Kurzawa		04/09/92	4	(1)	
5	Marquinhos	BRA	14/05/94	8		
17	Maxwell	BRA	27/08/81	4		
12	Thomas Meunier	BEL	12/09/91	5	(1)	1
2	Thiago Silva	BRA	22/09/84	7		
Midfielders						
21	Hatem Ben Arfa		07/03/87	1	(2)	
11	Ángel Di María	ARG	14/02/88	6	(1)	4
23	Julian Draxler	GER	20/09/93	2		1
36	Jonathan Ikoné		02/05/98		(1)	
4	Grzegorz Krychowiak	POL	29/01/90	2	(4)	
7	Lucas	BRA	13/08/92	6	(1)	1
14	Blaise Matuidi		09/04/87	8		2
24	Christopher Nkunku		14/11/97		(1)	
10	Javier Pastore	ARG	20/06/89		(2)	
25	Adrien Rabiot		03/04/95	4	(1)	
8	Thiago Motta	ITA	28/08/82	4	(1)	
6	Marco Verratti	ITA	05/11/92	7		
Forwards						
29	Jean-Kévin Augustin		16/06/97		(1)	
9	Edinson Cavani	URU	14/02/87	8		8
22	Jesé	ESP	26/02/93		(4)	

Manchester City FC

No	Name	Nat	DoB	Aps	(s)	Gls
Goalkeepers						
1	Claudio Bravo	CHI	13/04/83	4		
13	Willy Caballero	ARG	28/09/81	4	(1)	
Defenders						
53	Tosin Adarabioyo		24/09/97	1		
22	Gaël Clichy	FRA	26/07/85	3	(2)	
11	Aleksandar Kolarov	SRB	10/11/85	6		
50	Pablo Maffeo	ESP	12/07/97	1		
30	Nicolás Otamendi	ARG	12/02/88	6		
3	Bacary Sagna	FRA	14/02/83	3	(1)	
24	John Stones		28/05/94	6	(1)	1
5	Pablo Zabaleta	ARG	16/01/85	5	(1)	
Midfielders						
17	Kevin De Bruyne	BEL	28/06/91	6		1
25	Fernandinho	BRA	04/05/85	7		1
6	Fernando	BRA	25/07/87	1	(3)	
8	İlkay Gündoğan	GER	24/10/90	6		2
15	Jesús Navas	ESP	21/11/85	2	(3)	
19	Leroy Sané	GER	11/01/96	3	(1)	2
21	David Silva	ESP	08/01/86	6		1
7	Raheem Sterling		08/12/94	7		2
42	Yaya Touré	CIV	13/05/83	1		
Forwards						
10	Sergio Agüero	ARG	02/06/88	6	(1)	5
72	Kelechi Iheanacho	NGA	03/10/96	1	(2)	2
9	Nolito	ESP	15/10/86	3	(1)	1

SSC Napoli

No	Name	Nat	DoB	Aps	(s)	Gls
Goalkeepers						
25	Pepe Reina	ESP	31/08/82	8		
Defenders						
33	Raúl Albiol	ESP	04/09/85	6		
21	Vlad Chiricheş	ROU	14/11/89	1		
31	Faouzi Ghoulam	ALG	01/02/91	8		
2	Elseid Hysaj	ALB	20/02/94	7		
26	Kalidou Koulibaly	SEN	20/06/91	8		
11	Christian Maggio		11/02/82	1		
19	Nikola Maksimović	SRB	25/11/91	1	(1)	
Midfielders						
5	Allan	BRA	08/01/91	5	(3)	
7	José Callejón	ESP	11/02/87	8		1
42	Amadou Diawara	GUI	17/07/97	4	(2)	
4	Emanuele Giaccherini		05/05/85		(2)	
17	Marek Hamšík	SVK	27/07/87	8		2
8	Jorginho		20/12/91	4		
30	Marko Rog	CRO	19/07/95		(2)	
20	Piotr Zieliński	POL	20/05/94	3	(4)	
Forwards						
23	Manolo Gabbiadini		26/11/91	2	(3)	1
24	Lorenzo Insigne		04/06/91	6	(2)	1
14	Dries Mertens	BEL	06/05/87	6	(2)	5
99	Arkadiusz Milik	POL	28/02/94	2	(2)	3

FC Porto

No	Name	Nat	DoB	Aps	(s)	Gls
Goalkeepers						
1	Iker Casillas	ESP	20/05/81	8		
Defenders						
13	Alex Telles	BRA	15/12/92	7		
4	Willy Boly	FRA	03/02/91		(1)	
28	Felipe	BRA	16/05/89	8		
21	Miguel Layún	MEX	25/06/88	4	(2)	1
5	Iván Marcano	ESP	23/06/87	8		
2	Maxi Pereira	URU	08/06/84	5		
Midfielders						
20	André André		26/08/89	2	(1)	
8	Yacine Brahimi	ALG	08/02/90	3	(2)	1
22	Danilo Pereira		09/09/91	8		
15	Evandro	BRA	23/08/86		(1)	
16	Héctor Herrera	MEX	19/04/90	4	(2)	
30	Óliver Torres	ESP	10/11/94	7		
25	Otávio	BRA	09/02/95	5	(1)	1
6	Rúben Neves		13/03/97	1	(2)	
Forwards						
11	Adrián López	ESP	08/01/88	1		
10	André Silva		06/11/95	8		4
17	Jesús Corona	MEX	06/01/93	3	(4)	1
9	Laurent Depoitre	BEL	07/12/88		(1)	
19	Diogo Jota		04/12/96	4	(4)	1
29	Francisco Soares	BRA	17/01/91	2		
59	Rui Pedro		20/03/98		(1)	
7	Silvestre Varela		02/02/85		(1)	

PSV Eindhoven

No	Name	Nat	DoB	Aps	(s)	Gls
	Goalkeepers					
22	Remko Pasveer		08/11/83	1		
1	Jeroen Zoet		06/01/91	5		
	Defenders					
4	Santiago Arias	COL	13/01/92	4		1
20	Joshua Brenet		20/03/94	3	(1)	
30	Jordy de Wijs		08/01/95		(1)	
2	Nicolas Isimat-Mirin	FRA	15/11/91	5	(1)	
3	Héctor Moreno	MEX	17/01/88	6		
5	Daniel Schwaab	GER	23/08/88	6		
15	Jetro Willems		30/03/94	5		
	Midfielders					
10	Siem de Jong		28/01/89	1	(2)	
18	Andrés Guardado	MEX	28/09/86	4		
8	Jorrit Hendrix		06/02/95	2		
38	Ramon Lundqvist	SWE	10/05/97		(1)	
7	Gastón Pereiro	URU	11/06/95	3	(2)	
6	Davy Pröpper		02/09/91	6		1
23	Bart Ramselaar		29/06/96	3	(1)	
25	Olexandr Zinchenko	UKR	15/12/96	2	(2)	
	Forwards					
27	Steven Bergwijn		08/10/97	2	(4)	
9	Luuk de Jong		27/08/90	5		1
11	Luciano Narsingh		13/09/90	3	(2)	1

FC Rostov

No	Name	Nat	DoB	Aps	(s)	Gls
	Goalkeepers					
35	Soslan Dzhanaev		13/03/87	6		
	Defenders					
44	César Navas	ESP	14/02/80	6		
4	Vladimir Granat		22/05/87	6		
30	Fedor Kudryashov		05/04/87	4		
23	Miha Mevlja	SVN	12/06/90	6		
5	Denis Terentyev		13/08/92	2	(3)	
	Midfielders					
10	Moussa Doumbia	MLI	15/08/94		(4)	
6	Saeid Ezatolahi	IRN	01/10/96		(2)	
84	Alexandru Gatcan	MDA	27/03/84	6		
9	Maksim Grigoryev		06/07/90		(1)	
2	Timofei Kalachev	BLR	01/05/81	5		
8	Igor Kireev		17/02/92	1		
16	Christian Noboa	ECU	08/04/85	6		1
28	Andrei Prepeliţă	ROU	08/12/85		(4)	
89	Aleksandr Yerokhin		13/10/89	6		
	Forwards					
20	Sardar Azmoun	IRN	01/01/95	6		2
11	Aleksandr Bukharov		12/03/85		(1)	
7	Dmitri Poloz		12/07/91	6		3

Sporting Clube de Portugal

No	Name	Nat	DoB	Aps	(s)	Gls
	Goalkeepers					
1	Rui Patrício		15/02/88	6		
	Defenders					
13	Sebastián Coates	URU	07/10/90	6		
4	Jefferson	BRA	05/07/88	1		
21	João Pereira		25/02/84	3		
15	Paulo Oliveira		08/01/92	2		
47	Ricardo Esgaio		16/05/93		(1)	
35	Rúben Semedo		04/04/94	6		
2	Ezequiel Schelotto	ITA	23/05/89	2	(1)	
31	Marvin Zeegelaar	NED	12/08/90	5		
	Midfielders					
23	Adrien Silva		15/03/89	4	(1)	1
11	Bruno César	BRA	03/11/88	5	(1)	2
22	Elías	BRA	16/05/85	1	(1)	
77	Gelson Martins		11/05/95	6		
3	Lazar Marković	SRB	02/03/94	2	(3)	
8	Radosav Petrović	SRB	08/03/89		(1)	
10	Bryan Ruiz	CRC	18/08/85	5	(1)	1
14	William Carvalho		07/04/92	6		
	Forwards					
16	André	BRA	27/09/90		(3)	
7	Joel Campbell	CRC	26/06/92		(4)	
20	Luc Castaignos	NED	27/09/92	1		
28	Bas Dost	NED	31/05/89	5	(1)	1

Real Madrid CF

No	Name	Nat	DoB	Aps	(s)	Gls
	Goalkeepers					
13	Kiko Casilla		02/10/86	1		
1	Keylor Navas	CRC	15/12/86	12		
	Defenders					
2	Daniel Carvajal		11/01/92	11		
23	Danilo	BRA	15/07/91	3		
15	Fábio Coentrão	POR	11/03/88	1	(1)	
12	Marcelo	BRA	12/05/88	11		
6	Nacho		18/01/90	3	(1)	
3	Pepe	POR	26/02/83	2	(1)	
4	Sergio Ramos		30/03/86	11		1
5	Raphaël Varane	FRA	25/04/93	10		2
	Midfielders					
14	Casemiro	BRA	23/02/92	9		2
22	Isco		21/04/92	5	(1)	1
10	James Rodríguez	COL	12/07/91	4	(2)	
16	Mateo Kovačić	CRO	06/05/94	2	(4)	1
8	Toni Kroos	GER	04/01/90	11	(1)	1
17	Lucas Vázquez		01/07/91	2	(8)	1
20	Marco Asensio		21/01/96	1	(7)	3
19	Luka Modrić	CRO	09/09/85	11		
	Forwards					
11	Gareth Bale	WAL	16/07/89	7	(1)	2
9	Karim Benzema	FRA	19/12/87	12	(1)	5
7	Cristiano Ronaldo	POR	05/02/85	13		12
18	Mariano Díaz	DOM	01/08/93		(1)	
21	Álvaro Morata		23/10/92	1	(8)	3

Sevilla FC

No	Name	Nat	DoB	Aps	(s)	Gls
	Goalkeepers					
1	Sergio Rico		01/09/93	8		
	Defenders					
6	Daniel Carriço	POR	04/08/88		(2)	
5	Timothée Kolodziejczak	FRA	01/10/91		(1)	
45	Clément Lenglet	FRA	17/06/95	1		
3	Mariano	BRA	23/06/86	6	(2)	
24	Gabriel Mercado	ARG	18/03/87	7		
21	Nicolás Pareja	ARG	19/01/84	6		1
23	Adil Rami	FRA	27/12/85	7		
18	Sergio Escudero		02/09/89	8		1
	Midfielders					
11	Joaquín Correa	ARG	13/08/94	1	(2)	1
19	Ganso	BRA	12/10/89	1		
8	Vicente Iborra		16/01/88	4	(3)	
14	Hiroshi Kiyotake	JPN	12/11/89		(1)	
4	Matías Kranevitter	ARG	21/05/93	2	(2)	
15	Steven N'Zonzi	FRA	15/12/88	8		1
10	Samir Nasri	FRA	26/06/87	5		1
17	Pablo Sarabia		11/05/92	4	(3)	1
22	Franco Vázquez	ITA	22/02/89	5		
20	Vitolo		02/11/89	8		
	Forwards					
12	Wissam Ben Yedder	FRA	12/08/90	2	(3)	2
16	Stevan Jovetić	MNE	02/11/89	1	(1)	
9	Luciano Vietto	ARG	05/12/93	4		1

Tottenham Hotspur FC

No	Name	Nat	DoB	Aps	(s)	Gls
	Goalkeepers					
1	Hugo Lloris	FRA	26/12/86	6		
	Defenders					
4	Toby Alderweireld	BEL	02/03/89	2	(1)	1
33	Ben Davies	WAL	24/04/93	3		
15	Eric Dier		15/01/94	5		
3	Danny Rose		02/07/90	3		
16	Kieran Trippier		19/09/90	3		
5	Jan Vertonghen	BEL	24/04/87	5		
2	Kyle Walker		28/05/90	3		
27	Kevin Wimmer	AUT	15/11/92	1		
	Midfielders					
20	Dele Alli		11/04/96	6		1
19	Mousa Dembélé	BEL	16/07/87	2	(2)	
23	Christian Eriksen	DEN	14/02/92	5	(1)	
11	Erik Lamela	ARG	04/03/92	3		
14	Georges-Kévin N'Koudou	FRA	13/02/95		(3)	
25	Josh Onomah		27/04/97		(2)	
17	Moussa Sissoko	FRA	16/08/89	1	(3)	
12	Victor Wanyama	KEN	25/06/91	5		
29	Harry Winks		02/02/96	2	(2)	
	Forwards					
9	Vincent Janssen	NED	15/06/94	2	(3)	
10	Harry Kane		28/07/93	3		2
7	Son Heung-min	KOR	08/07/92	6		1

STOCKHOLM FINAL 2017

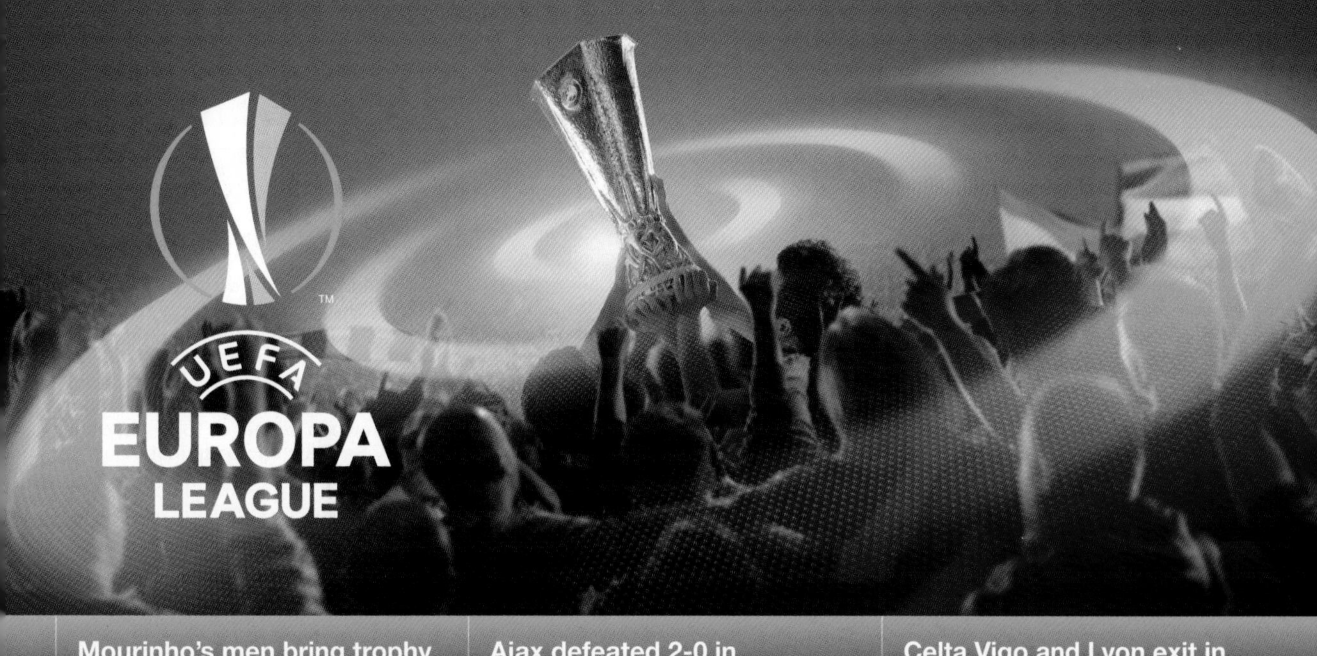

United complete the set

A new name was carved on to the UEFA Europa League trophy – formerly known as the UEFA Cup – as Manchester United captured the one major piece of silverware missing from their well-stocked cabinet with a 2-0 victory over Ajax in the Stockholm final.

A tactical masterclass from José Mourinho and his players in the Swedish capital, supplemented by a goal in each half, brought the trophy back to Manchester – a city in mourning following a terrorist atrocity earlier in the week that had left many, including children, dead and severely injured.

United's triumph came with the added bonus of a place in the 2017/18 UEFA Champions League group stage – a prize the club had missed out on via the domestic path after finishing outside the top four in the Premier League. It was the second UEFA Europa League success for England, with Chelsea having won it four years earlier – the last time any club other than Sevilla had laid hands on the trophy.

Spanish hopes of claiming a sixth victory in the revamped competition's eight-year history ended with the semi-final elimination of competition debutants Celta Vigo, who gave United an almighty late scare at Old Trafford before going down 2-1 on aggregate. Ajax were also relieved to hear the final whistle at the end of another epic semi-final against Olympique Lyonnais, having seemingly taken control of the tie with a brilliant first-leg 4-1 victory in Amsterdam.

All four quarter-finals also went thrillingly to the wire, with three requiring extra time and one of those resulting in the UEFA Europa League's longest ever penalty shoot-out as Lyon overcame Beşiktaş 7-6 in Istanbul. Belgium lost two teams at that stage of the competition, with Genk, who had started their campaign in the second qualifying round, falling to Celta and Anderlecht going out after a stirring second leg at Old Trafford. Ajax ended German hopes with a ten-man great escape at Schalke, who had eliminated fellow Bundesliga side Borussia Mönchengladbach in equally dramatic fashion the round before.

Shakhtar Donetsk were the standout team of the group stage, winning all six matches and scoring 21 goals in the process. Schalke and Zenit also won their first five fixtures before succumbing to defeat in the sixth. United, meanwhile, lost twice in their group, including their opening game at Feyenoord, and could only finish second to Fenerbahçe, but they went unbeaten during the knockout phase, conceding just four times in nine games and scoring themselves in all of them.

Mourinho became, at the age of 54 years and 118 days, the oldest UEFA Europa League-winning coach – one year and 97 days older than 2013 winner Rafa Benítez (Chelsea) – while Marcus Rashford, who scored crucial goals in the quarter-final against Anderlecht and semi-final against Celta, became the youngest winning player, aged 19 years and 205 days, eclipsing the previous record of Eduardo Salvio, who was 98 days older when he helped Atlético Madrid win the inaugural final of 2010 against Fulham.

The 2016/17 UEFA Europa League season was packed not just with great sporting drama but also a healthy number of goals, the final tally of 565, at an average of 2.76 per match, surpassing every previous season bar one (2011/12). The two most important came in Stockholm and, fittingly, were scored by arguably Manchester United's two most prominent contributors over the entire campaign, ever-present French midfielder Paul Pogba and their top-scoring Armenian, six-goal Henrikh Mkhitaryan.

Opposite: Captain Wayne Rooney holds aloft the trophy as Manchester United celebrate their UEFA Europa League triumph in Stockholm

Group stage

The qualifying process for the 2016/17 group stage was unchanged from the previous season, with 16 teams – from 12 different countries – gaining automatic entry, 22 qualifying via the play-offs and another ten crossing over from the UEFA Champions League.

Sevilla, the winners in each of the previous three seasons, were not among the 48-team field, having used their 2016 victory to secure group stage involvement in the UEFA Champions League; nor were the team they defeated in the final, Liverpool being absent from Europe altogether. The two beaten semi-finalists from the previous season were present, however, with Villarreal, who lost their UEFA Champions League play-off to Monaco, going on to set a new record for the number of matches played in the UEFA Europa League, and Shakhtar Donetsk proceeding to become the eighth team – and seventh club – to go through their group with a 100% record.

Group H turned out to be a breeze for Shakhtar, who not only amassed 18 points but also won it by a margin of ten. In so doing they also scored 21 times – just one short of the group stage record number set a year earlier by Napoli. The Ukrainian club scored five goals in both fixtures against Gent, yet it was the Belgian side that accompanied them through to the round of 32 thanks to a brilliantly improvised 94th-minute winner from striker Kalifa Coulibaly in their final fixture away to Konyaspor. That goal sent Gent through at the expense of former finalists Braga, whose game at home to Shakhtar (2-4) had already concluded. Barring Coulibaly's late intervention, Braga would have qualified – with just a third of Shakhtar's points tally – thanks to an away-goals head-to-head advantage over Gent.

Villarreal had a much tougher time of it in **Group L**, where, remarkably, the four teams were separated by a single point prior to matchday six. Turkish newcomers Osmanlıspor had upset the apple cart by claiming a famous 2-1 win in Spain to end Villarreal's eight-game winning home streak in the competition, and they held a one-point lead over the other three going into the final fixtures. It was an advantage they duly protected, defeating Swiss second-tier outfit FC Zürich 2-0 in Ankara to top the section, while Villarreal needed an 88th-minute strike from midfielder Manu Trigueros to get the win they sought at home to Steaua Bucureşti – although the other result meant that the 1-1 draw they were heading towards at that point would have sufficed.

The other two Spanish participants, 2012 runners-up Athletic Club and competition newcomers Celta Vigo, also advanced as group runners-up. Athletic had to accept second billing in **Group F** to Genk despite beating them 5-3 in Bilbao – a match in which Aritz Aduriz set a new UEFA Europa League record by scoring five goals. Genk had won the previous meeting 2-0 in Belgium, but another victory by the same scoreline on the final day at Sassuolo, Italy's European debutants, ensured that they finished top by two points – rather than head-to-head records – as Athletic could only draw 1-1 at Rapid Wien.

Celta were tested fully in **Group G**, but they avoided a complicated mathematical shake-up with Standard Liège – with whom they had drawn both games 1-1 – thanks to a last-day 2-0 win in Athens against bottom-placed Panathinaikos, whose defeat set a new competition record of 13 matches without a win. Ajax, the only team to have competed in all eight UEFA Europa League campaigns, were comfortable group winners, their closing 1-1 draw in Liege ensuring that they would be one of just four teams to progress to the next round undefeated and one of ten with a flawless record at home.

Osmanlıspor's Raul Rusescu (centre) is congratulated after scoring his team's winning goal at Villarreal

KEY FACT

10.69

The first goal scored in the 2016/17 UEFA Europa League group stage was also the fastest in the competition's history, Jan Sýkora's strike for Slovan Liberec at Qarabağ coming after just 10.69 seconds – and therefore beating the previous fastest of 13.21 seconds set by Sevilla's Vitolo against Villarreal in March 2015.

Fenerbahçe and Manchester United both progressed from **Group A** with three home wins out of three. The Turkish club were the only one of the four sides in the section required to pre-qualify, but they ended up looking down on United as well as Feyenoord and Zorya Luhansk, wrapping up qualification as well as top spot with a 1-0 win in Rotterdam. United had opened their campaign with a 1-0 defeat in the same city, but they gained ample revenge on Feyenoord in the return fixture, romping to a 4-0 win. Fenerbahçe had also conceded four goals at Old Trafford, but their 2-1 success in the return left United vulnerable to an early exit when they travelled to Odessa to take on already-eliminated Zorya. Happily for José Mourinho and his side, they returned to winning ways on the road – though Feyenoord's simultaneous home defeat ultimately made their 2-0 victory academic.

With West Ham having surprisingly been eliminated in qualifying by Romanian club Astra Giurgiu for the second successive summer, only one other English club joined United in the group stage – Southampton. They began their **Group K** campaign with a bang, beating Sparta Praha 3-0 at home, but their campaign would end prematurely amidst late drama at the same venue three months later as Israeli champions Hapoel Beer Sheva earned the 1-1 draw they needed to go through at the Premier League side's expense. A repeat of the goalless stalemate the two sides had produced in Israel would have favoured Southampton, but Maor Buzaglo's fine 79th-minute goal ultimately proved decisive. Sparta, meanwhile, ended their campaign as they started it, in defeat, but still topped the group, four wins in the interim, including all three in Prague, having pre-booked their place in the round of

32. The section's major surprise was the poor showing of Internazionale, beaten home and away by Beer Sheva and never properly in contention to prolong their campaign beyond Christmas.

As Inter and Sassuolo exited, two other Serie A sides – Roma and Fiorentina – advanced, in each case as convincing section winners. **Group E** provided the Giallorossi with few moments of concern as they saw off Astra, Viktoria Plzeň and Austria Wien to finish first with an unbeaten record. Astra accompanied them through after Austria fell to their third successive defeat, 3-2 at already-eliminated Plzeň. **Group J** belonged to the Viola, who scored more than twice as many goals as any of their three opponents. The other teams – PAOK, Qarabağ and Slovan Liberec – were all still striving to finish second with a game to go, but it was the Greek side who prevailed, their 2-0 home win over Liberec coinciding with the Tuscans' 2-1 win in Baku, where a home win would have taken the champions of Azerbaijan through instead of PAOK.

Qarabağ outperformed domestic rivals Qäbälä, who, having travelled all the way from the first qualifying round, lost all six matches in **Group C**, thus becoming only the fourth side to suffer a UEFA Europa League group stage whitewash. The two qualifying places went to Saint-Étienne, who avoided defeat, and Anderlecht, who scored 16 goals, twice as many as the team that pipped them to first place, including half a dozen in Brussels against Mainz.

A year after bossing their UEFA Champions League section, Zenit staged an encore in the UEFA Europa League, winning their first five fixtures in **Group D** before closing with a defeat. Inspired by six-goal Brazilian Giuliano, the Russian club now coached by ex-Shakhtar boss Mircea Lucescu took confidence from an extraordinary comeback in their opening fixture, away to Maccabi Tel-Aviv, which they won 4-3 having been three goals down entering the final 15 minutes. Surprise qualifiers Dundalk compounded the Israeli side's misery on matchday two by defeating them 1-0 in Dublin – the first victory by an Irish club in a European group stage – to add to an encouraging opening 1-1 draw at AZ Alkmaar, but defeats in all of their remaining games left Stephen Kenny's side propping up the section, with the Dutch side advancing ahead of Tel-Aviv thanks to a crucial 3-2 home win over Zenit on matchday six.

PAOK's José Cañas protects the ball from fellow Spaniard Borja Valero of Fiorentina

Like Zenit, Schalke qualified early from **Group I** by winning their first five matches before closing with a defeat. The loss came in Salzburg, where the home side had left themselves with too much to do after losing their opening three matches, finishing third behind FC Krasnodar on head-to-head results, a late equaliser from Russian international Fedor Smolov having fatally damaged the Austrian champions' chances of progress on matchday five.

Arguably the most surprising of the 12 group winners were Cypriot champions APOEL, who registered four wins in **Group B** to finish ahead of Olympiacos, Young Boys and FC Astana. A perfect record in Nicosia was supplemented by a famous 1-0 victory over Olympiacos in Piraeus. Fortunately for the Greek giants, they procured enough points from their other four games to take second spot, French striker Guillaume Hoarau's five goals for Young Boys thus ultimately proving in vain.

Round of 32

The first round of the knockout phase was to provide shocks and surprises galore as seven of the 12 group winners crashed out of the competition along with three of the eight teams that had parachuted in from the UEFA Champions League. There was plenty of excitement and late drama, too, plus large crowds, hat-tricks and a new record for the number of goals scored by a team in both a UEFA Europa League match and a knockout phase tie.

Those latter landmarks went to Lyon, who annihilated AZ 4-1 away and then 7-1 at home. No side had ever scored more than six goals in a UEFA Europa League game or more than ten over two legs, but the French side showed no mercy against their outclassed Eredivisie opponents to keep the French flag flying after local rivals Saint-Étienne had exited without scoring against Manchester United. Mourinho's side were indebted to a rather fortuitous hat-trick from Zlatan Ibrahimović at Old Trafford and a single Henrikh Mkhitaryan strike in a raucous Stade Geoffroy Guichard.

As one English side stayed in, another went out, Tottenham drawing over 80,000 fans to Wembley Stadium for their second leg against Gent but, as in the UEFA Champions League, failing to perform in their temporary European home, the Belgian side's French striker Jérémy Perbet proving the tie-winning hero with crucial goals in both legs. Another unexpected Belgian success was provided by Anderlecht as they knocked out Zenit on the away-goals rule thanks to a 90th-minute goal in St Petersburg from new signing Isaac Kiese Thelin. The Russian side appeared to have turned the tie around when a Giuliano double put them 3-2 up on aggregate, but the young Swede's perfectly placed header proved decisive. Genk, meanwhile, made it three out of three Belgian qualifiers, at the expense of Astra.

Spain, the competition's dominant nation, came within a whisker of losing all three participants. Villarreal's proud home record in Europe took a battering as Roma's Edin Džeko moved level with Giuliano at the top of the scoring charts with a superb hat-trick in a remarkable 4-0 win at the Estadio de la Cerámica (formerly El Madrigal), while Athletic became the latest victims of Cypriot giantkillers APOEL, who prevailed 4-3 on aggregate. Celta were on the brink of

KEY FACT

7

Lyon became the first team to score seven goals in a UEFA Europa League game, group stage to final, as they trounced AZ Alkmaar 7-1. The eight goals scored in that game also equalled a competition high, as did the six-goal margin of victory, while Lyon's aggregate of 11 goals in their two matches against AZ was also a record for a knockout phase tie.

going out, too, before a generous penalty awarded to them in added time of their second leg against Shakhtar. The Ukrainian side had made it seven wins out of seven with a 1-0 victory in Vigo, but Iago Aspas's successful spot kick in Kharkiv took the tie into extra time, where defender Gustavo Cabral settled the outcome in the visitors' favour.

Another home side stunned into submission were Fiorentina, who, after winning 1-0 at Borussia Mönchengladbach with a magnificent long-range free-kick from Federico Bernardeschi, added two further goals in Florence before visiting skipper Lars Stindl transformed the tie with an 11-minute hat-trick – the second fastest in UEFA Europa League history – to catapult the German side into the round of 16, where they were joined by Schalke, comfortable conquerors of PAOK.

Russia, like Germany, carried two teams forward, Krasnodar and Rostov both advancing further than ever before in Europe as they took care, respectively, of Fenerbahçe and Sparta Praha. Osmanlıspor were another group winner to bite the dust, against Olympiacos, but Beşiktaş ensured a continued Turkish presence by routinely dismissing Hapoel Beer Sheva, while in the only tie between two UEFA Champions League outcasts, FC København narrowly got the better of Ludogorets – as did Ajax against another competition latecomer, Legia Warszawa.

Round of 16

There were 12 nations represented in the round of 16 – a UEFA Europa League record – with Cyprus and Denmark featuring for the first time in the respective shape of APOEL and FC København, earlier opponents in the UEFA Champions League play-offs. Furthermore, not one of the remaining teams had ever gone as far as the semi-finals in the rebranded competition, with Lyon and Schalke the only two to have previously reached the last eight.

Belgium had more surviving clubs than any other country, but two of those, Gent and Genk, were paired together. A closely-matched contest was anticipated but it proved anything but as Genk ran out 5-2 winners away from home in the first leg, Gent thus conceding five goals in a game for the third time in the campaign.

The two remaining German clubs, Mönchengladbach and Schalke, were also drawn together, and between them they produced an enthralling tie packed with incident and controversy. Gladbach keeper Yann Sommer kept his team afloat in the first leg with a series of saves as they drew 1-1 in Gelsenkirchen, and they appeared to be quarter-final-bound when a stunning long-range strike from Mahmoud Dahoud put them 3-1 up on aggregate in the second leg. However, the luck was with Schalke in the second half and two fortunate goals, the second from the penalty spot, took them through despite the fact they had never led in the tie.

Lyon striker Alexandre Lacazette leaves Roma defender Federico Fazio floored in the teams' round of 16 clash

Russia, the only other country with two teams still standing, lost both as Krasnodar were beaten in both legs by Celta Vigo and Rostov bowed out to Manchester United, their cause not helped by a barely playable surface for the first leg and a depleted squad for the second. United were not at their best at Old Trafford but came through 2-1 on aggregate thanks to a Juan Mata goal and a brilliant Sergio Romero save from the last kick of the game.

The tie of the round resulted in victory for Lyon against Roma thanks chiefly to a formidable first-leg comeback on home turf that brought three wonderful second-half goals from Corentin Tolisso, Nabil Fekir and, in added time, Alexandre Lacazette. The French side increased the aggregate score to 5-2 in Rome before the Giallorossi produced a fightback of their own, only to fall one goal short and therefore end Italian interest in the competition for another year.

The last 16 was the end of the road too for APOEL and København, the former losing both legs 1-0 to Anderlecht, while the Danish champions conceded at home for the first time in seven European ties, with one of their own, Ajax's young Danish striker Kasper Dolberg, scoring the all-important away goal in the Amsterdammers' 3-2 aggregate success. Beşiktaş completed the quarter-final line-up in a rare match-up between the champions of Turkey and Greece, drawing 1-1 at Olympiacos before seeing them off 4-1 in Istanbul despite playing much of the game with ten men following Vincent Aboubakar's red card.

Quarter-finals

The eight remaining teams were all bidding to become first-time UEFA Europa League semi-finalists, and the collective determination to break new ground produced four captivating ties, three of which went to extra time and one to a penalty shoot-out.

Lyon and Beşiktaş were the only two surviving clubs from the eight that had contested the UEFA Champions League group stage, and they were drawn together for what would be an unyieldingly dramatic tie. Alas, major crowd disorder resulted in a lengthy delay to kick-off in the first leg in France, which brought an early goal for Beşiktaş, from an excellent Ryan Babel finish – the Dutchman's third goal in two games – and a second-half onslaught from the home side that bore fruit late on with two goals in as many minutes courtesy of uncharacteristically bad Beşiktaş defending.

No Lyon supporters were present in Istanbul for the return leg, but Bruno

KEY FACT

7

Seven nations were represented in the quarter-finals – a UEFA Europa League high – with only Belgium having more than one surviving club. The previous largest number had been six – the case in each of the previous four seasons.

Génésio's team performed admirably without them, Lacazette scoring another excellent goal to equalise Talisca's opener before the Brazilian levelled the tie up at 3-3 just before the hour. Lacazette was twice denied by the woodwork, which meant extra time and, subsequently, penalties. The first 12 kicks were all successfully converted, but the next three were missed, with Lyon keeper Anthony Lopes saving from defenders Duško Tošić and Matej Mitrović before skipper Maxime Gonalons saved team-mate Christophe Jallet's blushes by finding the target and giving the French side a 7-6 victory.

Mkhitaryan opened the scoring for Manchester United for the third successive away fixture in the knockout phase to give his team control of their quarter-final against Anderlecht, but despite a dominant display Mourinho's team could not hold on for the victory, Leander Dendoncker's flying header giving the Brussels side an unexpected lifeline four minutes from time. The same sequence of events transpired a week later at Old Trafford as Mkhitaryan gave United the lead before Anderlecht equalised, this time through Sofiane Hanni. The English side suffered a double blow with serious injuries to Marcos Rojo and the talismanic Ibrahimović, but they eventually edged home thanks to a Marcus Rashford strike in extra time – though not before Romero had pulled off another couple of vital late saves.

Ajax should have had far more than two unanswered Davy Klaassen goals to show for a brilliant, one-sided display against Schalke at the Amsterdam ArenA, but a succession of fine saves from visiting keeper Ralf Fährmann kept the German team in the tie, and the following week they not only recovered the two-goal deficit but, with Ajax reduced to ten men, moved purposefully towards the last four when Daniel Caligiuri headed them into a 3-2 aggregate lead 11 minutes into extra time. Peter Bosz's men would not be denied, though, scoring not once but twice in the second additional period to silence the crowd and turn a potentially galling defeat into a magnificent aggregate victory.

Celta maintained Spanish hopes of a sixth UEFA Europa League triumph with a 4-3 victory over the two legs against Genk. A late Thomas Buffel goal in Galicia had given the Belgian side hope for the return leg, and although Celta's young Danish star Pione Sisto restored his team's two-goal advantage in Belgium, Genk struck back almost immediately and were just one more goal away from qualification when the final whistle sounded.

Semi-finals

Clubs from four different countries filled the UEFA Europa League semi-final slots for only the second time (after 2012/13), with only one of the four participants – Ajax – having previously contested a final in the competition's former guise of the UEFA Cup, winning it in 1992. Lyon were bidding to reach a first European final, as were Celta, who had never previously reached the last four.

A public holiday in the Netherlands brought the first leg of the Ajax-Lyon tie forward a day. With Europe's full focus on the Amsterdam ArenA, the home side rose magnificently to the occasion, Bosz's young charges treating the capacity crowd and television viewers to a sumptuous attacking display that brought four goals and umpteen near misses. Loan striker Bertrand Traoré scored the first and last of those goals, crowning an inspired individual display, with the equally impressive Dolberg and another youngster, Amin Younes, grabbing the others.

A joyous Bertrand Traoré is hugged by team-mate Hakim Ziyech after scoring Ajax's fourth goal at home to Lyon

Lyon also played their part in a remarkably open game and had a goal to take back to France thanks to Mathieu Valbuena's exquisite finish, but when Dolberg struck after 27 minutes in the return, boosting Ajax's aggregate lead to 5-1, that appeared to be that. Lyon, though, had fought back valiantly in front of their fans against Roma and Beşiktaş, and they did so again, Lacazette scoring twice in a minute just before the interval and substitute Rachid Ghezzal leaving the home side just one goal short when he made it 3-1 on the night nine minutes from time. Ajax's discomfort was further intensified when they lost Nick Viergever to a red card, but somehow they held on to squeeze through to their first European final for 22 years.

Manchester United also looked to be in total command of their semi-final halfway through, an excellent performance in Vigo earning them a 1-0 win that would have been more comprehensive but for the excellence of Celta goalkeeper Sergio Álvarez. The only time he was beaten was from Marcus Rashford's stunning 67th-minute free-kick, but with United having never lost a European tie after they had won the first leg away from home, that solitary strike looked like it was enough to place at least one of their feet in the final.

United strengthened their position when Marouane Fellaini headed home a Rashford cross 17 minutes into the second leg at Old Trafford, but Celta refused to crack. Playing far better than on home soil, they came back at United and eventually found the goal their efforts deserved five minutes from time when defender Facundo Roncaglia glanced in a Claudio Beauvue cross. The Argentine defender was sent off soon afterwards, along with United counterpart Eric Bailly, following an unseemly mass brawl in the centre circle. United appeared to have scored again, through Ander Herrera, four minutes into added time, but the goal was ruled out for a foul and moments later, in the last play of the match, Beauvue penetrated the United defence, but rather than shoot he laid the ball square for John Guidetti, who miscued with the goal at his mercy. For the third round in a row, United had survived a late second-leg scare at Old Trafford and were now through to their seventh major European final.

Final

The eighth UEFA Europa League final, staged at the Friends Arena in the Stockholm suburb of Solna, was overshadowed by the tragic terrorist attack in Manchester two days earlier. There was an understandably subdued mood to proceedings, but it was mixed with defiance, and with a major European trophy and a guaranteed place in the group stage of the 2017/18 UEFA Champions League at stake, Manchester United and Ajax both had much still to play for.

There was a predictably cautious, nervous start from both sides, but on 18 minutes United went ahead. It was a fortuitous goal, Paul Pogba's speculative strike taking a huge deflection off Ajax defender Davinson Sánchez before sending goalkeeper André Onana the wrong way. Once in front, Mourinho's team made defending that lead their absolute priority. Ajax could not find any rhythm, misplacing passes here, there and everywhere as United repeatedly hounded and pressed them into errors.

One-nil up at the interval, United doubled their advantage three minutes after the restart, Mkhitaryan hooking the ball home from close range after Chris Smalling had headed a Mata corner goalwards. That second goal effectively sealed Ajax's fate, United becoming even more eager to deny them a way back into the game with a brilliantly disciplined defensive performance epitomised in the centre of midfield by the indefatigable Ander Herrera.

The Dutch side barely created a chance of note in response, and United comfortably saw the game out, prompting uncharacteristically wild celebrations from Mourinho, who knew how much victory meant towards defining his first season as Manchester United manager. With two major trophies – he had also won the English League Cup – and qualification for the UEFA Champions League, he was more than entitled to claim it as a success – despite the club's modest sixth-place finish in the Premier League. As for Ajax and coach Bosz, they ended the season empty-handed. They had not turned up on their big night, but, more to the point, United had not allowed them to, suffocating them with a superb, tactically perfect performance and deservedly taking back to a troubled city the one major international trophy missing from their copious collection.

KEY FACT

8

Manchester United kept eight clean sheets in their 15 matches, a record number for a UEFA Europa League-winning side that began their campaign in the group stage – as was their concession of just eight goals. They also scored in 14 of those 15 games, equalling the feats of FC Porto (2010/11) and Atlético Madrid (2011/12).

Henrikh Mkhitaryan (No22) puts Manchester United 2-0 up against Ajax in the UEFA Europa League final

First qualifying round

28/06/16, Nacionalna Arena Filip II Makedonski, Skopje
FK Rabotnicki 1-1 FK Budućnost Podgorica
07/07/16, Gradski Stadion Podgorica, Podgorica
FK Budućnost Podgorica 1-0 FK Rabotnicki
Aggregate: 2-1; FK Budućnost Podgorica qualify.

28/06/16, Elbasan Arena, Elbasan
FK Partizani 0-0 ŠK Slovan Bratislava
Second leg not played; ŠK Slovan Bratislava qualify as FK Partizani transferred to UEFA Champions League.

28/06/16, Richmond Park, Dublin
Saint Patrick's Athletic FC 1-0 AS Jeunesse Esch
05/07/16, La Frontière, Esch-sur-Alzette
AS Jeunesse Esch 2-1 Saint Patrick's Athletic FC
Aggregate: 2-2; Saint Patrick's Athletic FC qualify on away goal.

28/06/16, Dalga Stadium, Baku
Käpäz PFK 0-0 FC Dacia Chisinau
07/07/16, Speia, Speia
FC Dacia Chisinau 0-1 Käpäz PFK
Aggregate: 0-1; Käpäz PFK qualify.

30/06/16, Estadi Comunal, Andorra la Vella
UE Santa Coloma 1-3 NK Lokomotiva Zagreb
07/07/16, Zagreb, Zagreb
NK Lokomotiva Zagreb 4-1 UE Santa Coloma
Aggregate: 7-2; NK Lokomotiva Zagreb qualify.

30/06/16, NV Arena, St Polten
FC Admira Wacker Mödling 1-1 TJ Spartak Myjava
07/07/16, Spartak Myjava, Myjava
TJ Spartak Myjava 2-3 FC Admira Wacker Mödling
Aggregate: 3-4; FC Admira Wacker Mödling qualify.

30/06/16, Pod Malim Brdom, Budva
FK Bokelj 1-1 FK Vojvodina
07/07/16, Karadjordje, Novi Sad
FK Vojvodina 5-0 FK Bokelj
Aggregate: 6-1; FK Vojvodina qualify.

30/06/16, Ventspils Olimpiskais Centrs, Ventspils
FK Ventspils 2-0 Víkingur
07/07/16, Toftir, Toftir
Víkingur 0-2 FK Ventspils
Aggregate: 0-4; FK Ventspils qualify.

30/06/16, Tengiz Burjanadze Stadioni, Gori
FC Dila Gori 1-0 FC Shirak
07/07/16, Gyumri City, Gyumri
FC Shirak 1-0 FC Dila Gori (aet)
Aggregate: 1-1; FC Shirak qualify 4-1 on penalties.

30/06/16, Pancho stadium, Felcsut
Videoton FC 3-0 FC Zaria Balti
07/07/16, Stadionul Zimbru, Chisinau
FC Zaria Balti 2-0 Videoton FC
Aggregate: 2-3; Videoton FC qualify.

30/06/16, Stadion Bilino polje, Zenica
FK Sloboda Tuzla 0-0 Beitar Jerusalem FC
07/07/16, Itztadion Teddy, Jerusalem
Beitar Jerusalem FC 1-0 FK Sloboda Tuzla
Aggregate: 1-0; Beitar Jerusalem FC qualify.

30/06/16, Hibernians Stadium, Paola
Balzan FC 0-2 Neftçi PFK
07/07/16, 8KM Stadium, Baku
Neftçi PFK 1-2 Balzan FC
Aggregate: 3-2; Neftçi PFK qualify.

30/06/16, Gamla Ullevi, Gothenburg
IFK Göteborg 5-0 Llandudno FC
07/07/16, Nantporth, Bangor
Llandudno FC 1-2 IFK Göteborg
Aggregate: 1-7; IFK Göteborg qualify.

30/06/16, Stockholms, Stockholm
AIK 2-0 Bala Town FC
07/07/16, Belle Vue, Rhyl
Bala Town FC 0-2 AIK
Aggregate: 0-4; AIK qualify.

30/06/16, Victoria Stadium, Gibraltar
Europa FC 2-0 FC Pyunik
07/07/16, Vazgen Sargsyan anvan Hanrapetakan Marzadasht, Yerevan
FC Pyunik 2-1 Europa FC
Aggregate: 2-3; Europa FC qualify.

30/06/16, Arena Herning, Herning
FC Midtjylland 1-0 FK Sūduva
07/07/16, Stadium of Marijampole football club, Marijampole
FK Sūduva 0-1 FC Midtjylland
Aggregate: 0-2; FC Midtjylland qualify.

30/06/16, Kadriorg, Tallinn
FC Levadia Tallinn 1-1 HB Tórshavn
07/07/16, Gundadalur, Torshavn
HB Tórshavn 0-2 FC Levadia Tallinn
Aggregate: 1-3; FC Levadia Tallinn qualify.

30/06/16, Klaipėdosmiesto Centrinis, Klaipeda
FK Atlantas 0-2 HJK Helsinki
07/07/16, Helsinki Football Stadium, Helsinki
HJK Helsinki 1-1 FK Atlantas
Aggregate: 3-1; HJK Helsinki qualify.

30/06/16, LFF stadionas, Vilnius
FK Trakai 2-1 Nõmme Kalju FC
07/07/16, Kadriorg, Tallinn
Nõmme Kalju FC 4-1 FK Trakai
Aggregate: 5-3; Nõmme Kalju FC qualify.

30/06/16, Traktor, Minsk
FC Dinamo Minsk 2-1 FK Spartaks Jūrmala
07/07/16, Sloka, Jurmala
FK Spartaks Jūrmala 0-2 FC Dinamo Minsk
Aggregate: 1-4; FC Dinamo Minsk qualify.

30/06/16, Toftir, Toftir
NSÍ Runavík 0-2 FC Shakhtyor Soligorsk
07/07/16, Stroitel, Soligorsk
FC Shakhtyor Soligorsk 5-0 NSÍ Runavík
Aggregate: 7-0; FC Shakhtyor Soligorsk qualify.

30/06/16, Stade Municipal de Differdange, Differdange
FC Differdange 03 1-1 Cliftonville FC
07/07/16, Solitude, Belfast
Cliftonville FC 2-0 FC Differdange 03
Aggregate: 3-1; Cliftonville FC qualify.

30/06/16, Odd, Skien
Odds BK 2-0 IFK Mariehamn
07/07/16, Wiklöf Holding Arena, Mariehamn
IFK Mariehamn 1-1 Odds BK
Aggregate: 1-3; Odds BK qualify.

30/06/16, Pecara, Siroki Brijeg
NK Široki Brijeg 1-1 Birkirkara FC
05/07/16, Hibernians Stadium, Paola
Birkirkara FC 2-0 NK Široki Brijeg
Aggregate: 3-1; Birkirkara FC qualify.

30/06/16, Elbasan Arena, Elbasan
FK Kukësi 1-1 FK Rudar Pljevlja
07/07/16, Gradski, Niksic
FK Rudar Pljevlja 0-1 FK Kukësi
Aggregate: 1-2; FK Kukësi qualify.

Tom Laterza of Fola Esch turns away from Aberdeen's Jonny Hayes in the first qualifying round

30/06/16, Rheinpark Stadion, Vaduz
FC Vaduz 3-1 FK Sileks
07/07/16, Nacionalna Arena Filip II Makedonski, Skopje
FK Sileks 1-2 FC Vaduz
Aggregate: 2-5; FC Vaduz qualify.

30/06/16, Tsentralniy, Aktobe
FC Aktobe 1-1 MTK Budapest
07/07/16, Gyirmóti Stadion, Gyor
MTK Budapest 2-0 FC Aktobe
Aggregate: 3-1; MTK Budapest qualify.

30/06/16, Belle Vue, Rhyl
Connah's Quay FC 0-0 Stabæk Fotball
07/07/16, Fredrikstad, Fredrikstad
Stabæk Fotball 0-1 Connah's Quay FC
Aggregate: 0-1; Connah's Quay FC qualify.

30/06/16, KR-völlur, Reykjavik
KR Reykjavík 2-1 Glenavon FC
07/07/16, Mourneview Park, Lurgan
Glenavon FC 0-6 KR Reykjavík
Aggregate: 1-8; KR Reykjavík qualify.

30/06/16, Kópavogsvöllur, Kopavogur
Breidablik 2-3 FK Jelgava
07/07/16, Zemgales Olympic Centre, Jelgava
FK Jelgava 2-2 Breidablik
Aggregate: 5-4; FK Jelgava qualify.

30/06/16, Natsionalen Stadion Vasil Levski, Sofia
PFC Slavia Sofia 1-0 Zagłębie Lubin
07/07/16, Zaglebia, Lubin
Zagłębie Lubin 3-0 PFC Slavia Sofia
Aggregate: 3-1; Zagłębie Lubin qualify.

30/06/16, Windsor Park, Belfast
Linfield FC 0-1 Cork City FC
07/07/16, Turner's Cross, Cork
Cork City FC 1-1 Linfield FC
Aggregate: 2-1; Cork City FC qualify.

30/06/16, Pittodrie, Aberdeen
Aberdeen FC 3-1 CS Fola Esch
07/07/16, Stade Josy Barthel, Luxembourg
CS Fola Esch 1-0 Aberdeen FC
Aggregate: 2-3; Aberdeen FC qualify.

30/06/16, Tynecastle, Edinburgh
Heart of Midlothian FC 2-1 FCI Tallinn
06/07/16, A. Le Coq Arena, Tallinn
FCI Tallinn 2-4 Heart of Midlothian FC
Aggregate: 3-6; Heart of Midlothian FC qualify.

30/06/16, Tallaght Stadium, Dublin
Shamrock Rovers FC 0-2 RoPS Rovaniemi
07/07/16, Keskuskenttä, Rovaniemi
RoPS Rovaniemi 1-1 Shamrock Rovers FC
Aggregate: 3-1; RoPS Rovaniemi qualify.

30/06/16, Športni park, Domzale
NK Domžale 3-1 FC Lusitans
07/07/16, Estadi Comunal, Andorra la Vella
FC Lusitans 1-2 NK Domžale
Aggregate: 2-5; NK Domžale qualify.

30/06/16, Antonis Papadopoulos, Larnaca
AEK Larnaca FC 3-0 SS Folgore
07/07/16, San Marino Stadium, Serravalle
SS Folgore 1-3 AEK Larnaca FC
Aggregate: 1-6; AEK Larnaca FC qualify.

30/06/16, Stadionul Zimbru, Chisinau
FC Zimbru Chisinau 0-1 FC Chikhura Sachkhere
05/07/16, David Abashidze, Zestaponi
FC Chikhura Sachkhere 2-3 FC Zimbru Chisinau
Aggregate: 3-3; FC Zimbru Chisinau qualify on away goals.

30/06/16, Niko Dovana, Durres
KF Teuta 0-1 FC Kairat Almaty
07/07/16, Almaty Ortalyk Stadion, Almaty
FC Kairat Almaty 5-0 KF Teuta
Aggregate: 6-0; FC Kairat Almaty qualify.

30/06/16, Vazgen Sargsyan anvan Hanrapetakan Marzadasht, Yerevan
FC Banants 0-1 AC Omonia
07/07/16, GSP, Nicosia
AC Omonia 4-1 FC Banants (aet)
Aggregate: 5-1; AC Omonia qualify.

30/06/16, Netanya Municipal Stadium, Netanya
Maccabi Tel-Aviv FC 3-0 ND Gorica
07/07/16, Športni Park, Nova Gorica
ND Gorica 0-1 Maccabi Tel-Aviv FC
Aggregate: 0-4; Maccabi Tel-Aviv FC qualify.

30/06/16, Štadión Antona Malatinského, Trnava
FC Spartak Trnava 3-0 Hibernians FC
07/07/16, Hibernians Stadium, Paola
Hibernians FC 0-3 FC Spartak Trnava
Aggregate: 0-6; FC Spartak Trnava qualify.

30/06/16, FK Čukarički, Belgrade
FK Čukarički 3-0 FC Ordabasy Shymkent
07/07/16, Kazhimukan Munaytpasov, Shymkent
FC Ordabasy Shymkent 3-3 FK Čukarički
Aggregate: 3-6; FK Čukarički qualify.

30/06/16, Beroe, Stara Zagora
PFC Beroe Stara Zagora 0-0 FK Radnik Bijeljina
07/07/16, Gradski Stadium Banja Luka, Banja Luka
FK Radnik Bijeljina 0-2 PFC Beroe Stara Zagora
Aggregate: 0-2; PFC Beroe Stara Zagora qualify.

30/06/16, San Marino Stadium, Serravalle
SP La Fiorita 0-5 Debreceni VSC
07/07/16, Debrecen Stadion, Debrecen
Debreceni VSC 2-0 SP La Fiorita
Aggregate: 7-0; Debreceni VSC qualify.

30/06/16, Hlídarendi, Reykjavik
Valur Reykjavík 1-4 Brøndby IF
07/07/16, Brøndby, Brondby
Brøndby IF 6-0 Valur Reykjavík
Aggregate: 10-1; Brøndby IF qualify.

30/06/16, 8KM Stadium, Baku
Qäbälä FK 5-1 FC Samtredia
07/07/16, David Abashidze, Zestaponi
FC Samtredia 2-1 Qäbälä FK
Aggregate: 3-6; Qäbälä FK qualify.

30/06/16, Nacionalna Arena Filip II Makedonski, Skopje
KF Shkëndija 2-0 MKS Cracovia Kraków
07/07/16, Marszałek Piłsudski, Krakow
MKS Cracovia Kraków 1-2 KF Shkëndija
Aggregate: 1-4; KF Shkëndija qualify.

UEFA Europa League

Second qualifying round

14/07/16, Gyumri City, Gyumri
FC Shirak 1-1 FC Spartak Trnava
21/07/16, Štadión Antona Malatinského, Trnava
FC Spartak Trnava 2-0 FC Shirak
Aggregate: 3-1; FC Spartak Trnava qualify.

14/07/16, Traktor, Minsk
FC Dinamo Minsk 1-1 Saint Patrick's Athletic FC
21/07/16, Richmond Park, Dublin
Saint Patrick's Athletic FC 0-1 FC Dinamo Minsk
Aggregate: 1-2; FC Dinamo Minsk qualify.

14/07/16, Arena Herning, Herning
FC Midtjylland 3-0 FC Vaduz
21/07/16, Rheinpark Stadion, Vaduz
FC Vaduz 2-2 FC Midtjylland
Aggregate: 2-5; FC Midtjylland qualify.

14/07/16, Debrecen Stadion, Debrecen
Debreceni VSC 1-2 FC Torpedo Zhodino
21/07/16, Torpedo, Zhodino
FC Torpedo Zhodino 1-0 Debreceni VSC
Aggregate: 3-1; FC Torpedo Zhodino qualify.

14/07/16, Keskuskenttä, Rovaniemi
RoPS Rovaniemi 1-1 NK Lokomotiva Zagreb
21/07/16, Zagreb, Zagreb
NK Lokomotiva Zagreb 3-0 RoPS Rovaniemi
Aggregate: 4-1; NK Lokomotiva Zagreb qualify.

14/07/16, NV Arena, St Polten
FC Admira Wacker Mödling 1-0 Käpäz PFK
20/07/16, Dalga Stadium, Baku
Käpäz PFK 0-2 FC Admira Wacker Mödling
Aggregate: 0-3; FC Admira Wacker Mödling qualify.

14/07/16, Bravida Stadium, Gothenburg
BK Häcken 1-1 Cork City FC
21/07/16, Turner's Cross, Cork
Cork City FC 1-0 BK Häcken
Aggregate: 2-1; Cork City FC qualify.

14/07/16, Friends Arena, Solna
AIK 1-0 Europa FC
21/07/16, Victoria Stadium, Gibraltar
Europa FC 0-1 AIK
Aggregate: 0-2; AIK qualify.

14/07/16, Kadriorg, Tallinn
FC Levadia Tallinn 3-1 SK Slavia Praha
21/07/16, Eden Arena, Prague
SK Slavia Praha 2-0 FC Levadia Tallinn
Aggregate: 3-3; SK Slavia Praha qualify on away goal.

14/07/16, Haderslev, Haderslev
SønderjyskE 2-1 Strømsgodset IF
21/07/16, Marienlyst, Drammen
Strømsgodset IF 2-2 SønderjyskE (aet)
Aggregate: 3-4; SønderjyskE qualify.

14/07/16, KR-völlur, Reykjavik
KR Reykjavík 3-3 Grasshopper Club Zürich
21/07/16, Stadion Letzigrund, Zurich
Grasshopper Club Zürich 2-1 KR Reykjavík
Aggregate: 5-4; Grasshopper Club Zürich qualify.

14/07/16, Easter Road Stadium, Edinburgh
Hibernian FC 0-1 Brøndby IF
21/07/16, Brøndby, Brondby
Brøndby IF 0-1 Hibernian FC (aet)
Aggregate: 1-1; Brøndby IF qualify 5-3 on penalties.

14/07/16, Pittodrie, Aberdeen
Aberdeen FC 3-0 FK Ventspils
21/07/16, Ventspils Olimpiskais Centrs, Ventspils
FK Ventspils 0-1 Aberdeen FC
Aggregate: 0-4; Aberdeen FC qualify.

14/07/16, Solitude, Belfast
Cliftonville FC 2-3 AEK Larnaca FC
21/07/16, Antonis Papadopoulos, Larnaca
AEK Larnaca FC 2-0 Cliftonville FC
Aggregate: 5-2; AEK Larnaca FC qualify.

14/07/16, Karadjordje, Novi Sad
FK Vojvodina 1-0 Connah's Quay FC
21/07/16, Belle Vue, Rhyl
Connah's Quay FC 1-2 FK Vojvodina
Aggregate: 1-3; FK Vojvodina qualify.

14/07/16, Netanya Municipal Stadium, Netanya
Maccabi Haifa FC 1-1 Nõmme Kalju FC
21/07/16, Kadriorg, Tallinn
Nõmme Kalju FC 1-1 Maccabi Haifa FC (aet)
Aggregate: 2-2; Nõmme Kalju FC qualify 5-3 on penalties.

14/07/16, 8KM Stadium, Baku
Neftçi PFK 0-0 KF Shkëndija
21/07/16, Nacionalna Arena Filip II Makedonski, Skopje
KF Shkëndija 1-0 Neftçi PFK
Aggregate: 1-0; KF Shkëndija qualify.

14/07/16, Stadionul Zimbru, Chisinau
FC Zimbru Chisinau 2-2 Osmanlıspor
21/07/16, Osmanlı Stadı, Ankara
Osmanlıspor 5-0 FC Zimbru Chisinau
Aggregate: 7-2; Osmanlıspor qualify.

14/07/16, Stadion Ljudski vrt, Maribor
NK Maribor 0-0 PFC Levski Sofia
21/07/16, Georgi Asparuhov Stadion, Sofia
PFC Levski Sofia 1-1 NK Maribor
Aggregate: 1-1; NK Maribor qualify on away goal.

14/07/16, Itztadion Teddy, Jerusalem
Beitar Jerusalem FC 1-0 AC Omonia
21/07/16, GSP, Nicosia
AC Omonia 3-2 Beitar Jerusalem FC
Aggregate: 3-3; Beitar Jerusalem FC qualify on away goals.

14/07/16, KRC Genk Arena, Genk
KRC Genk 2-0 FK Budućnost Podgorica
21/07/16, Gradski Stadion Podgorica, Podgorica
FK Budućnost Podgorica 2-0 KRC Genk (aet)
Aggregate: 2-2; KRC Genk qualify 4-2 on penalties.

14/07/16, Stadion FK Partizan, Belgrade
FK Partizan 0-0 Zagłębie Lubin
21/07/16, Zaglebia, Lubin
Zagłębie Lubin 0-0 FK Partizan (aet)
Aggregate: 0-0; Zagłębie Lubin qualify 4-3 on penalties.

14/07/16, Štadión Pasienky, Bratislava
ŠK Slovan Bratislava 0-0 FK Jelgava
21/07/16, Zemgales Olympic Centre, Jelgava
FK Jelgava 3-0 ŠK Slovan Bratislava
Aggregate: 3-0; FK Jelgava qualify.

14/07/16, Stroitel, Soligorsk
FC Shakhtyor Soligorsk 1-1 NK Domžale
21/07/16, Sportni park, Domzale
NK Domžale 2-1 FC Shakhtyor Soligorsk
Aggregate: 3-2; NK Domžale qualify.

14/07/16, Gyirmóti Stadion, Gyor
MTK Budapest 1-2 Qäbälä FK
21/07/16, 8KM Stadium, Baku
Qäbälä FK 2-0 MTK Budapest
Aggregate: 4-1; Qäbälä FK qualify.

14/07/16, Beroe, Stara Zagora
PFC Beroe Stara Zagora 1-1 HJK Helsinki
21/07/16, Helsinki Football Stadium, Helsinki
HJK Helsinki 1-0 PFC Beroe Stara Zagora
Aggregate: 2-1; HJK Helsinki qualify.

14/07/16, Hibernians Stadium, Paola
Birkirkara FC 0-0 Heart of Midlothian FC
21/07/16, Tynecastle, Edinburgh
Heart of Midlothian FC 1-2 Birkirkara FC
Aggregate: 1-2; Birkirkara FC qualify.

14/07/16, Pancho stadium, Felcsut
Videoton FC 2-0 FK Čukarički
21/07/16, FK Čukarički, Belgrade
FK Čukarički 1-1 Videoton FC
Aggregate: 1-3; Videoton FC qualify.

14/07/16, Piast, Gliwice
GKS Piast Gliwice 0-3 IFK Göteborg
21/07/16, Gamla Ullevi, Gothenburg
IFK Göteborg 0-0 GKS Piast Gliwice
Aggregate: 3-0; IFK Göteborg qualify.

14/07/16, Almaty Ortalyk Stadion, Almaty
FC Kairat Almaty 1-1 Maccabi Tel-Aviv FC
21/07/16, Netanya Municipal Stadium, Netanya
Maccabi Tel-Aviv FC 2-1 FC Kairat Almaty
Aggregate: 3-2; Maccabi Tel-Aviv FC qualify.

14/07/16, Zossimades, Ioannina
PAS Giannina FC 3-0 Odds BK
21/07/16, Odd, Skien
Odds BK 3-1 PAS Giannina FC (aet)
Aggregate: 3-4; PAS Giannina FC qualify.

14/07/16, Emil Alexandrescu, Iasi
CSMS Iaşi 2-2 HNK Hajduk Split
21/07/16, Stadion Poljud, Split
HNK Hajduk Split 2-1 CSMS Iaşi
Aggregate: 4-3; HNK Hajduk Split qualify.

14/07/16, Ernst-Happel-Stadion, Vienna
FK Austria Wien 1-0 FK Kukësi
21/07/16, Elbasan Arena, Elbasan
FK Kukësi 1-4 FK Austria Wien
Aggregate: 1-5; FK Austria Wien qualify.

Christian Bubalović of Birkirkara (No3) rifles a shot through the Hearts defence to help his team to a shock 2-1 win in Edinburgh

Third qualifying round

28/07/16, Antonis Papadopoulos, Larnaca
AEK Larnaca FC 1-1 FC Spartak Moskva
04/08/16, Otkrytie Arena, Moscow
FC Spartak Moskva 0-1 AEK Larnaca FC
Aggregate: 1-2; AEK Larnaca FC qualify.

28/07/16, Polman-Stadion, Almelo
Heracles Almelo 1-1 FC Arouca
04/08/16, Arouca Municipal Stadium, Arouca
FC Arouca 0-0 Heracles Almelo
Aggregate: 1-1; FC Arouca qualify on away goal.

28/07/16, Stadion Maksimir, Zagreb
NK Lokomotiva Zagreb 0-0 FC Vorskla Poltava
04/08/16, Stadion Vorskla im. Olexiy Butovskiy, Poltava
FC Vorskla Poltava 2-3 NK Lokomotiva Zagreb
Aggregate: 2-3; NK Lokomotiva Zagreb qualify.

28/07/16, Zaglebia, Lubin
Zagłębie Lubin 1-2 SønderjyskE
04/08/16, Haderslev, Haderslev
SønderjyskE 1-1 Zagłębie Lubin
Aggregate: 3-2; SønderjyskE qualify.

28/07/16, Eden Arena, Prague
SK Slavia Praha 0-0 Rio Ave FC
04/08/16, Rio Ave, Vila do Conde
Rio Ave FC 1-1 SK Slavia Praha
Aggregate: 1-1; SK Slavia Praha qualify on away goal.

28/07/16, Ernst-Happel-Stadion, Vienna
FK Austria Wien 0-1 FC Spartak Trnava
04/08/16, Štadión Antona Malatinského, Trnava
FC Spartak Trnava 0-1 FK Austria Wien (aet)
Aggregate: 1-1; FK Austria Wien qualify 5-4 on penalties.

28/07/16, Lille Métropole, Lille
LOSC Lille 1-1 Qäbälä FK
04/08/16, 8KM Stadium, Baku
Qäbälä FK 1-0 LOSC Lille
Aggregate: 2-1; Qäbälä FK qualify.

28/07/16, Gamla Ullevi, Gothenburg
IFK Göteborg 1-2 HJK Helsinki
04/08/16, Helsinki Football Stadium, Helsinki
HJK Helsinki 0-2 IFK Göteborg
Aggregate: 2-3; IFK Göteborg qualify.

28/07/16, Hibernians Stadium, Paola
Birkirkara FC 0-3 FC Krasnodar
04/08/16, Kuban, Krasnodar
FC Krasnodar 3-1 Birkirkara FC
Aggregate: 6-1; FC Krasnodar qualify.

28/07/16, Nika, Oleksandria
FC Olexandriya 0-3 HNK Hajduk Split
04/08/16, Stadion Poljud, Split
HNK Hajduk Split 3-1 FC Olexandriya
Aggregate: 6-1; HNK Hajduk Split qualify.

28/07/16, Swissporarena, Lucerne
FC Luzern 1-1 US Sassuolo Calcio
04/08/16, Stadio Città del Tricolore, Reggio Emilia
US Sassuolo Calcio 3-0 FC Luzern
Aggregate: 4-1; US Sassuolo Calcio qualify.

28/07/16, Pittodrie, Aberdeen
Aberdeen FC 1-1 NK Maribor
04/08/16, Stadion Ljudski vrt, Maribor
NK Maribor 1-0 Aberdeen FC
Aggregate: 2-1; NK Maribor qualify.

28/07/16, AFG Arena, St Gallen
Grasshopper Club Zürich 2-1 Apollon Limassol FC
04/08/16, GSP, Nicosia
Apollon Limassol FC 3-3 Grasshopper Club Zürich (aet)
Aggregate: 4-5; Grasshopper Club Zürich qualify.

Sofiane Feghouli of West Ham gets in front of Domžale's Kenan Horić

28/07/16, Karadjordje, Novi Sad
FK Vojvodina 1-1 FC Dinamo Minsk
04/08/16, Brestsky, Brest
FC Dinamo Minsk 0-2 FK Vojvodina
Aggregate: 1-3; FK Vojvodina qualify.

28/07/16, Skonto Stadions, Riga
FK Jelgava 1-1 Beitar Jerusalem FC
04/08/16, Itztadion Teddy, Jerusalem
Beitar Jerusalem FC 3-0 FK Jelgava
Aggregate: 4-1; Beitar Jerusalem FC qualify.

28/07/16, Torpedo, Zhodino
FC Torpedo Zhodino 0-0 SK Rapid Wien
04/08/16, Weststadion, Vienna
SK Rapid Wien 3-0 FC Torpedo Zhodino
Aggregate: 3-0; SK Rapid Wien qualify.

28/07/16, KRC Genk Arena, Genk
KRC Genk 1-0 Cork City FC
04/08/16, Turner's Cross, Cork
Cork City FC 1-2 KRC Genk
Aggregate: 1-3; KRC Genk qualify.

28/07/16, Nacionalna Arena Filip II Makedonski, Skopje
KF Shkëndija 2-0 FK Mladá Boleslav
04/08/16, Mestský, Mlada Boleslav
FK Mladá Boleslav 1-0 KF Shkëndija
Aggregate: 1-2; KF Shkëndija qualify.

28/07/16, Friedrich-Ludwig-Jahn-Sportpark, Berlin
Hertha BSC Berlin 1-0 Brøndby IF
04/08/16, Brøndby, Brondby
Brøndby IF 3-1 Hertha BSC Berlin
Aggregate: 3-2; Brøndby IF qualify.

28/07/16, Başakşehir Fatih Terim Stadyumu, Istanbul
İstanbul Başakşehir 0-0 HNK Rijeka
04/08/16, Stadion HNK Rijeka, Rijeka
HNK Rijeka 2-2 İstanbul Başakşehir
Aggregate: 2-2; İstanbul Başakşehir qualify on away goals.

28/07/16, Pancho stadium, Felcsut
Videoton FC 0-1 FC Midtjylland
04/08/16, Arena Herning, Herning
FC Midtjylland 1-1 Videoton FC (aet)
Aggregate: 2-1; FC Midtjylland qualify.

28/07/16, KAA Gent Stadium, Ghent
KAA Gent 5-0 FC Viitorul Constanţa
04/08/16, Central Stadium Hagi Academy, Ovidiu
FC Viitorul Constanţa 0-0 KAA Gent
Aggregate: 0-5; KAA Gent qualify.

28/07/16, AZ Stadion, Alkmaar
AZ Alkmaar 1-0 PAS Giannina FC
04/08/16, Peristeri, Athens
PAS Giannina FC 1-2 AZ Alkmaar
Aggregate: 1-3; AZ Alkmaar qualify.

28/07/16, Stadion Stožice, Ljubljana
NK Domžale 2-1 West Ham United FC
04/08/16, London Stadium, London
West Ham United FC 3-0 NK Domžale
Aggregate: 4-2; West Ham United FC qualify.

28/07/16, Stade Geoffroy Guichard, Saint-Etienne
AS Saint-Étienne 0-0 AEK Athens FC
04/08/16, OAKA Spiros Louis, Athens
AEK Athens FC 0-1 AS Saint-Étienne
Aggregate: 0-1; AS Saint-Étienne qualify.

28/07/16, Stadionul Municipal, Drobeta-Turnu Severin
CS Pandurii Târgu Jiu 1-3 Maccabi Tel-Aviv FC
04/08/16, Netanya Municipal Stadium, Netanya
Maccabi Tel-Aviv FC 2-1 CS Pandurii Târgu Jiu
Aggregate: 5-2; Maccabi Tel-Aviv FC qualify.

28/07/16, Apostolos Nikolaidis, Athens
Panathinaikos FC 1-0 AIK
04/08/16, Stockholms, Stockholm
AIK 0-2 Panathinaikos FC
Aggregate: 0-3; Panathinaikos FC qualify.

28/07/16, Osmanlı Stadı, Ankara
Osmanlıspor 1-0 Nõmme Kalju FC
04/08/16, Kadriorg, Tallinn
Nõmme Kalju FC 0-2 Osmanlıspor
Aggregate: 0-3; Osmanlıspor qualify.

28/07/16, Bundesstadion Südstadt, Maria Enzersdorf
FC Admira Wacker Mödling 1-2 FC Slovan Liberec
03/08/16, U Nisy, Liberec
FC Slovan Liberec 2-0 FC Admira Wacker Mödling
Aggregate: 4-1; FC Slovan Liberec qualify.

Play-offs

17/08/16, Itztadion Teddy, Jerusalem
Beitar Jerusalem FC 1-2 AS Saint-Étienne
25/08/16, Stade Geoffroy Guichard, Saint-Etienne
AS Saint-Étienne 0-0 Beitar Jerusalem FC
Aggregate: 2-1; AS Saint-Étienne qualify.

18/08/16, Haderslev, Haderslev
SønderjyskE 0-0 AC Sparta Praha
25/08/16, Generali Arena, Prague
AC Sparta Praha 3-2 SønderjyskE
Aggregate: 3-2; AC Sparta Praha qualify.

18/08/16, Arena Herning, Herning
FC Midtjylland 0-1 Osmanlıspor
25/08/16, Osmanlı Stadı, Ankara
Osmanlıspor 2-0 FC Midtjylland
Aggregate: 3-0; Osmanlıspor qualify.

UEFA Europa League

18/08/16, Ernst-Happel-Stadion, Vienna
FK Austria Wien 2-1 Rosenborg BK
25/08/16, Lerkendal Stadion, Trondheim
Rosenborg BK 1-2 FK Austria Wien
Aggregate: 2-4; FK Austria Wien qualify.

18/08/16, Eden Arena, Prague
SK Slavia Praha 0-3 RSC Anderlecht
25/08/16, Constant Vanden Stock Stadium, Brussels
RSC Anderlecht 3-0 SK Slavia Praha
Aggregate: 6-0; RSC Anderlecht qualify.

18/08/16, Gamla Ullevi, Gothenburg
IFK Göteborg 1-0 Qarabağ FK
25/08/16, Tofiq Bähramov Republican stadium, Baku
Qarabağ FK 3-0 IFK Göteborg
Aggregate: 3-1; Qarabağ FK qualify.

18/08/16, Kuban, Krasnodar
FC Krasnodar 4-0 FK Partizani
25/08/16, Elbasan Arena, Elbasan
FK Partizani 0-0 FC Krasnodar
Aggregate: 0-4; FC Krasnodar qualify.

18/08/16, Astana Arena, Astana
FC Astana 2-0 FC BATE Borisov
25/08/16, Borisov-Arena, Borisov
FC BATE Borisov 2-2 FC Astana
Aggregate: 2-4; FC Astana qualify.

18/08/16, Arouca Municipal Stadium, Arouca
FC Arouca 0-1 Olympiacos FC
25/08/16, Stadio Georgios Karaiskakis, Piraeus
Olympiacos FC 2-1 FC Arouca (aet)
Aggregate: 3-1; Olympiacos FC qualify.

18/08/16, Stadion Maksimir, Zagreb
NK Lokomotiva Zagreb 2-2 KRC Genk
25/08/16, KRC Genk Arena, Genk
KRC Genk 2-0 NK Lokomotiva Zagreb
Aggregate: 4-2; KRC Genk qualify.

18/08/16, Antonis Papadopoulos, Larnaca
AEK Larnaca FC 0-1 FC Slovan Liberec
25/08/16, U Nisy, Liberec
FC Slovan Liberec 3-0 AEK Larnaca FC
Aggregate: 4-0; FC Slovan Liberec qualify.

18/08/16, Boris Paichadze Dinamo Arena, Tbilisi
FC Dinamo Tbilisi 0-3 PAOK FC
25/08/16, Stadio Toumba, Salonika
PAOK FC 2-0 FC Dinamo Tbilisi
Aggregate: 5-0; PAOK FC qualify.

18/08/16, Karadjordje, Novi Sad
FK Vojvodina 0-3 AZ Alkmaar
25/08/16, AZ Stadion, Alkmaar
AZ Alkmaar 0-0 FK Vojvodina
Aggregate: 3-0; AZ Alkmaar qualify.

18/08/16, Netanya Municipal Stadium, Netanya
Maccabi Tel-Aviv FC 2-1 HNK Hajduk Split
25/08/16, Stadion Poljud, Split
HNK Hajduk Split 2-1 Maccabi Tel-Aviv FC (aet)
Aggregate: 3-3; Maccabi Tel-Aviv FC qualify 4-3 on penalties.

18/08/16, KAA Gent Stadium, Ghent
KAA Gent 2-1 KF Shkëndija
25/08/16, Nacionalna Arena Filip II Makedonski, Skopje
KF Shkëndija 0-4 KAA Gent
Aggregate: 1-6; KAA Gent qualify.

18/08/16, Başakşehir Fatih Terim Stadyumu, Istanbul
İstanbul Başakşehir 1-2 FC Shakhtar Donetsk
25/08/16, Arena Lviv, Lviv
FC Shakhtar Donetsk 2-0 İstanbul Başakşehir
Aggregate: 4-1; FC Shakhtar Donetsk qualify.

18/08/16, Stadio Città del Tricolore, Reggio Emilia
US Sassuolo Calcio 3-0 FK Crvena zvezda
25/08/16, Stadion Rajko Mitić, Belgrade
FK Crvena zvezda 1-1 US Sassuolo Calcio
Aggregate: 1-4; US Sassuolo Calcio qualify.

18/08/16, Dalga Stadium, Baku
Qäbälä FK 3-1 NK Maribor
25/08/16, Stadion Ljudski vrt, Maribor
NK Maribor 1-0 Qäbälä FK
Aggregate: 2-3; Qäbälä FK qualify.

18/08/16, Şükrü Saracoğlu, Istanbul
Fenerbahçe SK 3-0 Grasshopper Club Zürich
25/08/16, Stadion Letzigrund, Zurich
Grasshopper Club Zürich 0-2 Fenerbahçe SK
Aggregate: 0-5; Fenerbahçe SK qualify.

18/08/16, Apostolos Nikolaidis, Athens
Panathinaikos FC 3-0 Brøndby IF
25/08/16, Brøndby, Brondby
Brøndby IF 1-1 Panathinaikos FC
Aggregate: 1-4; Panathinaikos FC qualify.

18/08/16, Štadión MŠK Žilina, Zilina
FK AS Trenčín 0-4 SK Rapid Wien
25/08/16, Weststadion, Vienna
SK Rapid Wien 0-2 FK AS Trenčín
Aggregate: 4-2; SK Rapid Wien qualify.

18/08/16, Marin Anastasovici, Giurgiu
FC Astra Giurgiu 1-1 West Ham United FC
25/08/16, London Stadium, London
West Ham United FC 0-1 FC Astra Giurgiu
Aggregate: 1-2; FC Astra Giurgiu qualify.

Group stage

Group A

15/09/16, Stadion Feijenoord, Rotterdam
Feyenoord 1-0 Manchester United FC
Goal: 1-0 Trindade de Vilhena 79

15/09/16, Stadion Chornomorets, Odessa
FC Zorya Luhansk 1-1 Fenerbahçe SK
Goals: 1-0 Grechishkin 52, 1-1 Kjær 90+5

29/09/16, Old Trafford, Manchester
Manchester United FC 1-0 FC Zorya Luhansk
Goal: 1-0 Ibrahimović 69

29/09/16, Şükrü Saracoğlu, Istanbul
Fenerbahçe SK 1-0 Feyenoord
Goal: 1-0 Emenike 18

20/10/16, Old Trafford, Manchester
Manchester United FC 4-1 Fenerbahçe SK
Goals: 1-0 Pogba 31(p), 2-0 Martial 34(p), 3-0 Pogba 45+1, 4-0 Lingard 48, 4-1 Van Persie 83

20/10/16, Stadion Feijenoord, Rotterdam
Feyenoord 1-0 FC Zorya Luhansk
Goal: 1-0 Jørgensen 55

03/11/16, Stadion Chornomorets, Odessa
FC Zorya Luhansk 1-1 Feyenoord
Goals: 0-1 Jørgensen 15, 1-1 Rafael Forster 44

03/11/16, Şükrü Saracoğlu, Istanbul
Fenerbahçe SK 2-1 Manchester United FC
Goals: 1-0 Sow 2, 2-0 Lens 59, 2-1 Rooney 89

24/11/16, Şükrü Saracoğlu, Istanbul
Fenerbahçe SK 2-0 FC Zorya Luhansk
Goals: 1-0 Stoch 59, 2-0 Kjær 67

Miroslav Stoch celebrates opening the scoring for Fenerbahçe against Zorya in Istanbul

24/11/16, Old Trafford, Manchester
Manchester United FC 4-0 Feyenoord
Goals: 1-0 Rooney 35, 2-0 Mata 69, 3-0 Jones 75(og), 4-0 Lingard 90+2

08/12/16, Stadion Feijenoord, Rotterdam
Feyenoord 0-1 Fenerbahçe SK
Goal: 0-1 Sow 22

08/12/16, Stadion Chornomorets, Odessa
FC Zorya Luhansk 0-2 Manchester United FC
Goals: 0-1 Mkhitaryan 48, 0-2 Ibrahimović 88

Group B

15/09/16, Stade de Suisse, Berne
BSC Young Boys 0-1 Olympiacos FC
Goal: 0-1 Cambiasso 42

15/09/16, GSP, Nicosia
APOEL FC 2-1 FC Astana
Goals: 0-1 Maksimović 45+1, 1-1 Vinícius 75, 2-1 De Camargo 87

29/09/16, Astana Arena, Astana
FC Astana 0-0 BSC Young Boys

29/09/16, Stadio Georgios Karaiskakis, Piraeus
Olympiacos FC 0-1 APOEL FC
Goal: 0-1 Sotiriou 10

20/10/16, Stade de Suisse, Berne
BSC Young Boys 3-1 APOEL FC
Goals: 0-1 Efrem 14, 1-1 Hoarau 18, 2-1 Hoarau 52, 3-1 Hoarau 82(p)

20/10/16, Stadio Georgios Karaiskakis, Piraeus
Olympiacos FC 4-1 FC Astana
Goals: 1-0 Diogo Figueiras 25, 2-0 Elyounoussi 33, 3-0 Sebá 34, 3-1 Kabananga 54, 4-1 Sebá 65

03/11/16, GSP, Nicosia
APOEL FC 1-0 BSC Young Boys
Goal: 1-0 Sotiriou 69

03/11/16, Astana Arena, Astana
FC Astana 1-1 Olympiacos FC
Goals: 1-0 Despotović 8, 1-1 Sebá 30

24/11/16, Astana Arena, Astana
FC Astana 2-1 APOEL FC
Goals: 0-1 Efrem 31, 1-1 Aničić 59, 2-1 Despotović 84

24/11/16, Stadio Georgios Karaiskakis, Piraeus
Olympiacos FC 1-1 BSC Young Boys
Goals: 1-0 Fortounis 48, 1-1 Hoarau 58

08/12/16, Stade de Suisse, Berne
BSC Young Boys 3-0 FC Astana
Goals: 1-0 Frey 63, 2-0 Hoarau 66, 3-0 Schick 71

08/12/16, GSP, Nicosia
APOEL FC 2-0 Olympiacos FC
Goals: 1-0 Manuel Da Costa 19(og), 2-0 De Camargo 83

Group C

15/09/16, Mainz Arena, Mainz
1. FSV Mainz 05 1-1 AS Saint-Étienne
Goals: 1-0 Bungert 57, 1-1 Berič 88

15/09/16, Constant Vanden Stock Stadium, Brussels
RSC Anderlecht 3-1 Qäbälä FK
Goals: 1-0 Teodorczyk 14, 1-1 Dabo 20, 2-1 Rafael 41(og), 3-1 Diego Capel 77

29/09/16, 8KM Stadium, Baku
Qäbälä FK 2-3 1. FSV Mainz 05
Goals: 0-1 Muto 41, 1-1 R Qurbanov 57(p), 2-1 Zenjov 62, 2-2 Córdoba 68, 2-3 Öztunali 78

29/09/16, Stade Geoffroy Guichard, Saint-Etienne
AS Saint-Étienne 1-1 RSC Anderlecht
Goals: 0-1 Tielemans 62(p), 1-1 Roux 90+4

20/10/16, Stade Geoffroy Guichard, Saint-Etienne
AS Saint-Étienne 1-0 Qäbälä FK
Goal: 1-0 Ricardinho 70(og)

20/10/16, Mainz Arena, Mainz
1. FSV Mainz 05 1-1 RSC Anderlecht
Goals: 1-0 Yunus Mallı 10(p), 1-1 Teodorczyk 65

03/11/16, Constant Vanden Stock Stadium, Brussels
RSC Anderlecht 6-1 1. FSV Mainz 05
Goals: 1-0 Stanciu 9, 1-1 De Blasis 15, 2-1 Stanciu 41, 3-1 Tielemans 62, 4-1 Teodorczyk 89, 5-1 Bruno 90+2, 6-1 Teodorczyk 90+4(p)

03/11/16, 8KM Stadium, Baku
Qäbälä FK 1-2 AS Saint-Étienne
Goals: 1-0 R Qurbanov 39, 1-1 Tannane 45+1, 1-2 Berič 53

24/11/16, 8KM Stadium, Baku
Qäbälä FK 1-3 RSC Anderlecht
Goals: 0-1 Tielemans 11, 1-1 Ricardinho 15(p), 1-2 Bruno 90, 1-3 Teodorczyk 90+4

24/11/16, Stade Geoffroy Guichard, Saint-Etienne
AS Saint-Étienne 0-0 1. FSV Mainz 05

08/12/16, Mainz Arena, Mainz
1. FSV Mainz 05 2-0 Qäbälä FK
Goals: 1-0 Hack 30, 2-0 De Blasis 40

08/12/16, Constant Vanden Stock Stadium, Brussels
RSC Anderlecht 2-3 AS Saint-Étienne
Goals: 1-0 Chipciu 21, 2-0 Stanciu 31, 2-1 Søderlund 62, 2-2 Søderlund 67, 2-3 Monnet-Paquet 74

Group D

15/09/16, AZ Stadion, Alkmaar
AZ Alkmaar 1-1 Dundalk FC
Goals: 1-0 Wuytens 61, 1-1 Kilduff 89

15/09/16, Netanya Municipal Stadium, Netanya
Maccabi Tel-Aviv FC 3-4 FC Zenit
Goals: 1-0 Medunjanin 26, 2-0 Kjartansson 50, 3-0 Medunjanin 70, 3-1 Kokorin 77, 3-2 Maurício 84, 3-3 Giuliano 86, 3-4 Djordjević 90+2

29/09/16, Tallaght Stadium, Dublin
Dundalk FC 1-0 Maccabi Tel-Aviv FC
Goal: 1-0 Kilduff 72

29/09/16, Stadion Petrovski, St Petersburg
FC Zenit 5-0 AZ Alkmaar
Goals: 1-0 Kokorin 26, 2-0 Giuliano 48, 3-0 Kokorin 59, 4-0 Criscito 66(p), 5-0 Shatov 80

20/10/16, Tallaght Stadium, Dublin
Dundalk FC 1-2 FC Zenit
Goals: 1-0 Benson 52, 1-1 Mak 71, 1-2 Giuliano 77

20/10/16, AZ Stadion, Alkmaar
AZ Alkmaar 1-2 Maccabi Tel-Aviv FC
Goals: 0-1 Scarione 24, 1-1 Mühren 72, 1-2 Golasa 82

03/11/16, Netanya Municipal Stadium, Netanya
Maccabi Tel-Aviv FC 0-0 AZ Alkmaar

03/11/16, Stadion Petrovski, St Petersburg
FC Zenit 2-1 Dundalk FC
Goals: 1-0 Giuliano 42, 1-1 Horgan 52, 2-1 Giuliano 78

24/11/16, Stadion Petrovski, St Petersburg
FC Zenit 2-0 Maccabi Tel-Aviv FC
Goals: 1-0 Kokorin 44, 2-0 A Kerzhakov 90+1

24/11/16, Tallaght Stadium, Dublin
Dundalk FC 0-1 AZ Alkmaar
Goal: 0-1 Weghorst 9

08/12/16, AZ Stadion, Alkmaar
AZ Alkmaar 3-2 FC Zenit
Goals: 1-0 Rienstra 7, 2-0 Haps 43, 2-1 Giuliano 58, 3-1 Tankovic 68, 3-2 Wuytens 80(og)

08/12/16, Netanya Municipal Stadium, Netanya
Maccabi Tel-Aviv FC 2-1 Dundalk FC
Goals: 1-0 Ben Haim (II) 21(p), 1-1 Dasa 27(og), 2-1 Micha 38

Anderlecht's Youri Tielemans shields the ball from Daniel Brosinski of Mainz

Group E

15/09/16, Doosan Arena, Plzen
FC Viktoria Plzeň 1-1 AS Roma
Goals: 0-1 Perotti 4(p), 1-1 Bakoš 11

15/09/16, Arena Națională, Bucharest
FC Astra Giurgiu 2-3 FK Austria Wien
Goals: 0-1 Holzhauser 16(p), 1-1 Alibec 18, 1-2 Friesenbichler 33, 1-3 Grünwald 58, 2-3 Săpunaru 74

29/09/16, Ernst-Happel-Stadion, Vienna
FK Austria Wien 0-0 FC Viktoria Plzeň

29/09/16, Stadio Olimpico, Rome
AS Roma 4-0 FC Astra Giurgiu
Goals: 1-0 Strootman 15, 2-0 Fazio 45+2, 3-0 Fabrício 47(og), 4-0 Salah 55

20/10/16, Stadio Olimpico, Rome
AS Roma 3-3 FK Austria Wien
Goals: 0-1 Holzhauser 16, 1-1 El Shaarawy 19, 2-1 El Shaarawy 34, 3-1 Florenzi 69, 3-2 Prokop 82, 3-3 Kayode 84

20/10/16, Doosan Arena, Plzen
FC Viktoria Plzeň 1-2 FC Astra Giurgiu
Goals: 0-1 Alibec 41, 0-2 Hořava 64(og), 1-2 Hořava 86

03/11/16, Ernst-Happel-Stadion, Vienna
FK Austria Wien 2-4 AS Roma
Goals: 1-0 Kayode 2, 1-1 Džeko 5, 1-2 De Rossi 18, 1-3 Džeko 65, 1-4 Nainggolan 78, 2-4 Grünwald 89

03/11/16, Arena Națională, Bucharest
FC Astra Giurgiu 1-1 FC Viktoria Plzeň
Goals: 1-0 Stan 19, 1-1 Krmenčík 25

24/11/16, Stadio Olimpico, Rome
AS Roma 4-1 FC Viktoria Plzeň
Goals: 1-0 Džeko 11, 1-1 Zeman 18, 2-1 Džeko 61, 3-1 Matějů 82(og), 4-1 Džeko 88

24/11/16, Ernst-Happel-Stadion, Vienna
FK Austria Wien 1-2 FC Astra Giurgiu
Goals: 1-0 Rotpuller 57, 1-1 Florea 79, 1-2 Budescu 88(p)

08/12/16, Doosan Arena, Plzen
FC Viktoria Plzeň 3-2 FK Austria Wien
Goals: 0-1 Holzhauser 19(p), 0-2 Rotpuller 40, 1-2 Hořava 44, 2-2 Ďuriš 72, 3-2 Ďuriš 84

08/12/16, Arena Națională, Bucharest
FC Astra Giurgiu 0-0 AS Roma

Group F

15/09/16, Weststadion, Vienna
SK Rapid Wien 3-2 KRC Genk
Goals: 0-1 Bailey 29, 1-1 Schwab 51, 2-1 Joelinton 59, 3-1 Colley 60(og), 3-2 Bailey 90(p)

15/09/16, Stadio Città del Tricolore, Reggio Emilia
US Sassuolo Calcio 3-0 Athletic Club
Goals: 1-0 Pol Lirola 60, 2-0 Defrel 75, 3-0 Politano 82

29/09/16, Estadio de San Mamés, Bilbao
Athletic Club 1-0 SK Rapid Wien
Goal: 1-0 Beñat Etxebarria 59

29/09/16, KRC Genk Arena, Genk
KRC Genk 3-1 US Sassuolo Calcio
Goals: 1-0 Karelis 8, 2-0 Bailey 25, 3-0 Buffel 61, 3-1 Politano 65

UEFA Europa League

20/10/16, KRC Genk Arena, Genk
KRC Genk 2-0 Athletic Club
Goals: 1-0 Brabec 40, 2-0 Ndidi 83

20/10/16, Weststadion, Vienna
SK Rapid Wien 1-1 US Sassuolo Calcio
Goals: 1-0 Schaub 7, 1-1 Schrammel 66(og)

03/11/16, Estadio de San Mamés, Bilbao
Athletic Club 5-3 KRC Genk
Goals: 1-0 Aduriz 8, 2-0 Aduriz 24(p), 2-1 Bailey 28, 3-1 Aduriz 44(p), 3-2 Ndidi 51, 4-2 Aduriz 74, 4-3 Sušić 80, 5-3 Aduriz 90+4(p)

03/11/16, Stadio Città del Tricolore, Reggio Emilia
US Sassuolo Calcio 2-2 SK Rapid Wien
Goals: 1-0 Defrel 34, 2-0 Pellegrini 45+2, 2-1 Jelić 86, 2-2 Kvilitaia 90

24/11/16, KRC Genk Arena, Genk
KRC Genk 1-0 SK Rapid Wien
Goal: 1-0 Karelis 11

24/11/16, Estadio de San Mamés, Bilbao
Athletic Club 3-2 US Sassuolo Calcio
Goals: 0-1 Balenziaga 2(og), 1-1 Raúl García 10, 2-1 Aduriz 58, 3-1 Lekue 79, 3-2 Ragusa 83

08/12/16, Weststadion, Vienna
SK Rapid Wien 1-1 Athletic Club
Goals: 1-0 Joelinton 72, 1-1 Saborit 84

09/12/16, Stadio Città del Tricolore, Reggio Emilia
US Sassuolo Calcio 0-2 KRC Genk
Goals: 0-1 Heynen 58, 0-2 Trossard 80

Group G

15/09/16, Stade Maurice Dufrasne, Liege
R. Standard de Liège 1-1 RC Celta de Vigo
Goals: 1-0 Dossevi 3, 1-1 Rossi 13

15/09/16, Apostolos Nikolaidis, Athens
Panathinaikos FC 1-2 AFC Ajax
Goals: 1-0 Berg 5, 1-1 Traoré 33, 1-2 Riedewald 67

29/09/16, Amsterdam ArenA, Amsterdam
AFC Ajax 1-0 R. Standard de Liège
Goal: 1-0 Dolberg 28

29/09/16, Balaídos, Vigo
RC Celta de Vigo 2-0 Panathinaikos FC
Goals: 1-0 Guidetti 84, 2-0 Wass 89

20/10/16, Balaídos, Vigo
RC Celta de Vigo 2-2 AFC Ajax
Goals: 0-1 Ziyech 22, 1-1 Fontàs 29, 1-2 Younes 71, 2-2 Orellana 82

20/10/16, Stade Maurice Dufrasne, Liege
R. Standard de Liège 2-2 Panathinaikos FC
Goals: 0-1 Ibarbo 12, 0-2 Ibarbo 36, 1-2 Edmilson Junior 45+1(p), 2-2 Belfodil 82

03/11/16, Amsterdam ArenA, Amsterdam
AFC Ajax 3-2 RC Celta de Vigo
Goals: 1-0 Dolberg 41, 2-0 Ziyech 68, 3-0 Younes 71, 3-1 Guidetti 79, 3-2 Iago Aspas 86

03/11/16, Apostolos Nikolaidis, Athens
Panathinaikos FC 0-3 R. Standard de Liège
Goals: 0-1 Cisse 61, 0-2 Belfodil 76, 0-3 Belfodil 90+3

24/11/16, Balaídos, Vigo
RC Celta de Vigo 1-1 R. Standard de Liège
Goals: 1-0 Iago Aspas 8, 1-1 Laifis 81

Ajax's Kasper Dolberg hurdles Standard Liège goalkeeper Jean-François Gillet

24/11/16, Amsterdam ArenA, Amsterdam
AFC Ajax 2-0 Panathinaikos FC
Goals: 1-0 Schöne 40, 2-0 Tete 50

08/12/16, Stade Maurice Dufrasne, Liege
R. Standard de Liège 1-1 AFC Ajax
Goals: 0-1 El Ghazi 27, 1-1 Raman 85

08/12/16, Apostolos Nikolaidis, Athens
Panathinaikos FC 0-2 RC Celta de Vigo
Goals: 0-1 Guidetti 4, 0-2 Orellana 76(p)

Group H

15/09/16, Estádio Municipal de Braga, Braga
SC Braga 1-1 KAA Gent
Goals: 0-1 Miličević 6, 1-1 André Pinto 24

15/09/16, Konya Büyükşehir Belediyesi Stadyumu, Konya
Konyaspor 0-1 FC Shakhtar Donetsk
Goal: 0-1 Ferreyra 75

29/09/16, KAA Gent Stadium, Ghent
KAA Gent 2-0 Konyaspor
Goals: 1-0 Saief 17, 2-0 Renato Neto 33

29/09/16, Arena Lviv, Lviv
FC Shakhtar Donetsk 2-0 SC Braga
Goals: 1-0 Stepanenko 5, 2-0 Kovalenko 56

20/10/16, Arena Lviv, Lviv
FC Shakhtar Donetsk 5-0 KAA Gent
Goals: 1-0 Kovalenko 12, 2-0 Ferreyra 30, 3-0 Bernard 46, 4-0 Taison 75, 5-0 Malyshev 85

20/10/16, Konya Büyükşehir Belediyesi Stadyumu, Konya
Konyaspor 1-1 SC Braga
Goals: 1-0 Milošević 9, 1-1 Hassan 55

03/11/16, Estádio Municipal de Braga, Braga
SC Braga 3-1 Konyaspor
Goals: 0-1 Rangelov 30, 1-1 Velázquez 34, 2-1 Wilson Eduardo 45+1, 3-1 Ricardo Horta 90+7

03/11/16, KAA Gent Stadium, Ghent
KAA Gent 3-5 FC Shakhtar Donetsk
Goals: 1-0 Coulibaly 1, 1-1 Marlos 36(p), 1-2 Taison 41, 1-3 Stepanenko 45+3, 1-4 Fred 68, 2-4 Perbet 83, 2-5 Ferreyra 87, 3-5 Miličević 89

24/11/16, KAA Gent Stadium, Ghent
KAA Gent 2-2 SC Braga
Goals: 0-1 Stojiljković 14, 1-1 Coulibaly 32, 1-2 Hassan 36, 2-2 Miličević 40

24/11/16, Arena Lviv, Lviv
FC Shakhtar Donetsk 4-0 Konyaspor
Goals: 1-0 Abdülkerim Bardakcı 11(og), 2-0 Dentinho 36, 3-0 Eduardo 66, 4-0 Bernard 74

08/12/16, Estádio Municipal de Braga, Braga
SC Braga 2-4 FC Shakhtar Donetsk
Goals: 0-1 Krivtsov 22, 0-2 Taison 39, 1-2 Stojiljković 43, 1-3 Krivtsov 62, 1-4 Taison 66, 2-4 Vukčević 89

08/12/16, Konya Büyükşehir Belediyesi Stadyumu, Konya
Konyaspor 0-1 KAA Gent
Goal: 0-1 Coulibaly 90+4

Group I

15/09/16, Stadion Salzburg, Salzburg
FC Salzburg 0-1 FC Krasnodar
Goal: 0-1 Joãozinho 37

15/09/16, Stade de Nice, Nice
OGC Nice 0-1 FC Schalke 04
Goal: 0-1 Rahman 75

29/09/16, Arena AufSchalke, Gelsenkirchen
FC Schalke 04 3-1 FC Salzburg
Goals: 1-0 Goretzka 15, 2-0 Ćaleta-Car 47(og), 3-0 Höwedes 58, 3-1 Jonatan Soriano 72

29/09/16, Kuban, Krasnodar
FC Krasnodar 5-2 OGC Nice
Goals: 1-0 Smolov 22, 2-0 Joãozinho 33, 2-1 Balotelli 43, 3-1 Joãozinho 65(p), 3-2 Cyprien 71, 4-2 Ari 86, 5-2 Ari 90+3

20/10/16, Stadion Salzburg, Salzburg
FC Salzburg 0-1 OGC Nice
Goal: 0-1 Pléa 13

20/10/16, Krasnodar Stadium, Krasnodar
FC Krasnodar 0-1 FC Schalke 04
Goal: 0-1 Konoplyanka 11

03/11/16, Arena AufSchalke, Gelsenkirchen
FC Schalke 04 2-0 FC Krasnodar
Goals: 1-0 Júnior Caiçara 25, 2-0 Bentaleb 28

03/11/16, Stade de Nice, Nice
OGC Nice 0-2 FC Salzburg
Goals: 0-1 Hwang 72, 0-2 Hwang 73

24/11/16, Arena AufSchalke, Gelsenkirchen
FC Schalke 04 2-0 OGC Nice
Goals: 1-0 Konoplyanka 14, 2-0 Aogo 80(p)

24/11/16, Krasnodar Stadium, Krasnodar
FC Krasnodar 1-1 FC Salzburg
Goals: 0-1 Dabbur 37, 1-1 Smolov 85

08/12/16, Stadion Salzburg, Salzburg
FC Salzburg 2-0 FC Schalke 04
Goals: 1-0 Schlager 22, 2-0 Radošević 90+4

08/12/16, Stade de Nice, Nice
OGC Nice 2-1 FC Krasnodar
Goals: 0-1 Smolov 52, 1-1 Bosetti 64(p), 2-1 Le Marchand 77

Group J

15/09/16, Dalga Stadium, Baku
Qarabağ FK 2-2 FC Slovan Liberec
Goals: 0-1 Sýkora 1, 1-1 Míchel 7, 1-2 Baroš 68, 2-2 Sadıqov 90+4

15/09/16, Stadio Toumba, Salonika
PAOK FC 0-0 ACF Fiorentina

29/09/16, Stadio Artemio Franchi, Florence
ACF Fiorentina 5-1 Qarabağ FK
Goals: 1-0 Babacar 39, 2-0 Kalinić 43, 3-0 Babacar 45+2, 4-0 Zárate 63, 5-0 Zárate 78, 5-1 Ndlovu 90+2

29/09/16, U Nisy, Liberec
FC Slovan Liberec 1-2 PAOK FC
Goals: 1-0 Komlichenko 1, 1-1 Athanasiadis 10(p), 1-2 Athanasiadis 82

20/10/16, U Nisy, Liberec
FC Slovan Liberec 1-3 ACF Fiorentina
Goals: 0-1 Kalinić 8, 0-2 Kalinić 23, 1-2 Ševčík 58, 1-3 Babacar 70

20/10/16, Tofiq Bähramov Republican stadium, Baku
Qarabağ FK 2-0 PAOK FC
Goals: 1-0 Dani Quintana 56, 2-0 Ämirquliyev 87

03/11/16, Stadio Artemio Franchi, Florence
ACF Fiorentina 3-0 FC Slovan Liberec
Goals: 1-0 Iličič 30(p), 2-0 Kalinić 43, 3-0 Cristóforo 73

03/11/16, Stadio Toumba, Salonika
PAOK FC 0-1 Qarabağ FK
Goal: 0-1 Míchel 69

24/11/16, U Nisy, Liberec
FC Slovan Liberec 3-0 Qarabağ FK
Goals: 1-0 Vůch 11, 2-0 Komlichenko 57(p), 3-0 Komlichenko 63

24/11/16, Stadio Artemio Franchi, Florence
ACF Fiorentina 2-3 PAOK FC
Goals: 0-1 Shakhov 5, 0-2 Djalma 26, 1-2 Bernardeschi 33, 2-2 Babacar 50, 2-3 Mendes Rodrigues 90+3

08/12/16, Stadio Toumba, Salonika
PAOK FC 2-0 FC Slovan Liberec
Goals: 1-0 Mendes Rodrigues 29, 2-0 Pelkas 67

08/12/16, Tofiq Bähramov Republican stadium, Baku
Qarabağ FK 1-2 ACF Fiorentina
Goals: 0-1 Vecino 60, 1-1 Reynaldo 73, 1-2 Chiesa 76

Group K

15/09/16, St Mary's Stadium, Southampton
Southampton FC 3-0 AC Sparta Praha
Goals: 1-0 Austin 5(p), 2-0 Austin 27, 3-0 Rodriguez 90+2

15/09/16, Stadio San Siro, Milan
FC Internazionale Milano 0-2 Hapoel Beer Sheva FC
Goals: 0-1 Miguel Vítor 54, 0-2 Buzaglo 69

29/09/16, Generali Arena, Prague
AC Sparta Praha 3-1 FC Internazionale Milano
Goals: 1-0 V Kadlec 7, 2-0 V Kadlec 25, 2-1 Palacio 71, 3-1 Holek 76

29/09/16, Turner Stadium, Beer Sheva
Hapoel Beer Sheva FC 0-0 Southampton FC

20/10/16, Stadio San Siro, Milan
FC Internazionale Milano 1-0 Southampton FC
Goal: 1-0 Candreva 67

20/10/16, Turner Stadium, Beer Sheva
Hapoel Beer Sheva FC 0-1 AC Sparta Praha
Goal: 0-1 Pulkrab 71

03/11/16, St Mary's Stadium, Southampton
Southampton FC 2-1 FC Internazionale Milano
Goals: 0-1 Icardi 33, 1-1 Van Dijk 64, 2-1 Nagatomo 70(og)

03/11/16, Generali Arena, Prague
AC Sparta Praha 2-0 Hapoel Beer Sheva FC
Goals: 1-0 Biton 23(og), 2-0 Lafata 38

24/11/16, Generali Arena, Prague
AC Sparta Praha 1-0 Southampton FC
Goal: 1-0 Nhamoinesu 11

24/11/16, Turner Stadium, Beer Sheva
Hapoel Beer Sheva FC 3-2 FC Internazionale Milano
Goals: 0-1 Icardi 13, 0-2 Brozović 25, 1-2 Lúcio Maranhão 58, 2-2 Nwakaeme 71(p), 3-2 Sahar 90+3

08/12/16, St Mary's Stadium, Southampton
Southampton FC 1-1 Hapoel Beer Sheva FC
Goals: 0-1 Buzaglo 79, 1-1 Van Dijk 90+1

08/12/16, Stadio San Siro, Milan
FC Internazionale Milano 2-1 AC Sparta Praha
Goals: 1-0 Éder 23, 1-1 Mareček 54, 2-1 Éder 90

Group L

15/09/16, Estadio de la Cerámica, Villarreal
Villarreal CF 2-1 FC Zürich
Goals: 0-1 Sadiku 2, 1-1 Pato 28, 2-1 Jonathan dos Santos 45+1

15/09/16, Osmanlı Stadı, Ankara
Osmanlıspor 2-0 FC Steaua Bucureşti
Goals: 1-0 Diabaté 64(p), 2-0 Umar 74

29/09/16, Stadion Letzigrund, Zurich
FC Zürich 2-1 Osmanlıspor
Goals: 1-0 Schönbächler 45+1, 1-1 Maher 73, 2-1 Čavuševič 79

29/09/16, Arena Naţională, Bucharest
FC Steaua Bucureşti 1-1 Villarreal CF
Goals: 0-1 Borré 9, 1-1 Muniru 19

20/10/16, Arena Naţională, Bucharest
FC Steaua Bucureşti 1-1 FC Zürich
Goals: 1-0 Golubović 63, 1-1 Koné 86

20/10/16, Osmanlı Stadı, Ankara
Osmanlıspor 2-2 Villarreal CF
Goals: 1-0 Rusescu 23, 2-0 Rusescu 24, 2-1 N'Diaye 56, 2-2 Pato 74

03/11/16, Stadion Letzigrund, Zurich
FC Zürich 0-0 FC Steaua Bucureşti

03/11/16, Estadio de la Cerámica, Villarreal
Villarreal CF 1-2 Osmanlıspor
Goals: 0-1 Webó 8, 1-1 Rodri Hernández 48, 1-2 Rusescu 75

24/11/16, Stadion Letzigrund, Zurich
FC Zürich 1-1 Villarreal CF
Goals: 0-1 Bruno Soriano 14, 1-1 Rodriguez 87(p)

24/11/16, Arena Naţională, Bucharest
FC Steaua Bucureşti 2-1 Osmanlıspor
Goals: 0-1 Ndiaye 30, 1-1 Momčilović 68, 2-1 Tamaş 86

08/12/16, Estadio de la Cerámica, Villarreal
Villarreal CF 2-1 FC Steaua Bucureşti
Goals: 1-0 Sansone 16, 1-1 Achim 55, 2-1 Trigueros 88

08/12/16, Osmanlı Stadı, Ankara
Osmanlıspor 2-0 FC Zürich
Goals: 1-0 Delarge 73, 2-0 Erdal Kılıçaslan 89

Southampton's Nathan Redmond holds off Hapoel Beer Sheva's Ben Biton in a decisive Group K fixture

UEFA Europa League

Final group tables

Group A

			Home					Away					Total					
		Pld	W	D	L	F	A	W	D	L	F	A	W	D	L	F	A	Pts
1	Fenerbahçe SK	6	3	0	0	5	1	1	1	1	3	5	4	1	1	8	6	13
2	Manchester United FC	6	3	0	0	9	1	1	0	2	3	3	4	0	2	12	4	12
3	Feyenoord	6	2	0	1	2	1	0	1	2	1	6	2	1	3	3	7	7
4	FC Zorya Luhansk	6	0	2	1	2	4	0	0	3	0	4	0	2	4	2	8	2

Group B

			Home					Away					Total					
		Pld	W	D	L	F	A	W	D	L	F	A	W	D	L	F	A	Pts
1	APOEL FC	6	3	0	0	5	1	1	0	2	3	5	4	0	2	8	6	12
2	Olympiacos FC	6	1	1	1	5	3	1	1	1	2	3	2	2	2	7	6	8
3	BSC Young Boys	6	2	0	1	6	2	0	2	1	1	2	2	2	2	7	4	8
4	FC Astana	6	1	2	0	3	2	0	0	3	2	9	1	2	3	5	11	5

Group C

			Home					Away					Total					
		Pld	W	D	L	F	A	W	D	L	F	A	W	D	L	F	A	Pts
1	AS Saint-Étienne	6	1	2	0	2	1	2	1	0	6	4	3	3	0	8	5	12
2	RSC Anderlecht	6	2	0	1	11	5	1	2	0	5	3	3	2	1	16	8	11
3	1. FSV Mainz 05	6	1	2	0	4	2	1	1	1	4	8	2	3	1	8	10	9
4	Qäbälä FK	6	0	0	3	4	8	0	0	3	1	6	0	0	6	5	14	0

Group D

			Home					Away					Total					
		Pld	W	D	L	F	A	W	D	L	F	A	W	D	L	F	A	Pts
1	FC Zenit	6	3	0	0	9	1	2	0	1	8	7	5	0	1	17	8	15
2	AZ Alkmaar	6	1	1	1	5	5	1	1	1	1	5	2	2	2	6	10	8
3	Maccabi Tel-Aviv FC	6	1	1	1	5	5	1	0	2	2	4	2	1	3	7	9	7
4	Dundalk FC	6	1	0	2	2	3	0	1	2	3	5	1	1	4	5	8	4

Group E

			Home					Away					Total					
		Pld	W	D	L	F	A	W	D	L	F	A	W	D	L	F	A	Pts
1	AS Roma	6	2	1	0	11	4	1	2	0	5	3	3	3	0	16	7	12
2	FC Astra Giurgiu	6	0	2	1	3	4	2	0	1	4	6	2	2	2	7	10	8
3	FC Viktoria Plzeň	6	1	1	1	5	5	0	2	1	2	5	1	3	2	7	10	6
4	FK Austria Wien	6	0	1	2	3	6	1	1	1	8	8	1	2	3	11	14	5

Group F

			Home					Away					Total					
		Pld	W	D	L	F	A	W	D	L	F	A	W	D	L	F	A	Pts
1	KRC Genk	6	3	0	0	6	1	1	0	2	7	8	4	0	2	13	9	12
2	Athletic Club	6	3	0	0	9	5	0	1	2	1	6	3	1	2	10	11	10
3	SK Rapid Wien	6	1	2	0	5	4	0	1	2	2	4	1	3	2	7	8	6
4	US Sassuolo Calcio	6	1	1	1	5	4	0	1	2	4	7	1	2	3	9	11	5

Group G

			Home					Away					Total					
		Pld	W	D	L	F	A	W	D	L	F	A	W	D	L	F	A	Pts
1	AFC Ajax	6	3	0	0	6	2	1	2	0	5	4	4	2	0	11	6	14
2	RC Celta de Vigo	6	1	2	0	5	3	1	1	1	5	4	2	3	1	10	7	9
3	R. Standard de Liège	6	0	3	0	4	4	1	1	1	4	2	1	4	1	8	6	7
4	Panathinaikos FC	6	0	0	3	1	7	0	1	2	2	6	0	1	5	3	13	1

Group H

			Home					Away					Total					
		Pld	W	D	L	F	A	W	D	L	F	A	W	D	L	F	A	Pts
1	FC Shakhtar Donetsk	6	3	0	0	11	0	3	0	0	10	5	6	0	0	21	5	18
2	KAA Gent	6	1	1	1	7	7	1	1	1	2	6	2	2	2	9	13	8
3	SC Braga	6	1	1	1	6	6	0	2	1	3	5	1	3	2	9	11	6
4	Konyaspor	6	0	1	2	1	3	0	0	3	1	9	0	1	5	2	12	1

Group I

			Home					Away					Total					
		Pld	W	D	L	F	A	W	D	L	F	A	W	D	L	F	A	Pts
1	FC Schalke 04	6	3	0	0	7	1	2	0	1	2	2	5	0	1	9	3	15
2	FC Krasnodar	6	1	1	1	6	4	1	0	2	2	4	2	1	3	8	8	7
3	FC Salzburg	6	1	0	2	2	2	1	1	1	4	4	2	1	3	6	6	7
4	OGC Nice	6	1	0	2	2	4	1	0	2	3	7	2	0	4	5	11	6

Group J

			Home					Away					Total					
		Pld	W	D	L	F	A	W	D	L	F	A	W	D	L	F	A	Pts
1	ACF Fiorentina	6	2	0	1	10	4	2	1	0	5	2	4	1	1	15	6	13
2	PAOK FC	6	1	1	1	2	1	2	0	1	5	5	3	1	2	7	6	10
3	Qarabağ FK	6	1	1	1	5	4	1	0	2	2	8	2	1	3	7	12	7
4	FC Slovan Liberec	6	1	0	2	5	5	0	1	2	2	7	1	1	4	7	12	4

Group K

			Home					Away					Total					
		Pld	W	D	L	F	A	W	D	L	F	A	W	D	L	F	A	Pts
1	AC Sparta Praha	6	3	0	0	6	1	1	0	2	2	5	4	0	2	8	6	12
2	Hapoel Beer Sheva FC	6	1	1	1	3	3	1	1	1	3	3	2	2	2	6	6	8
3	Southampton FC	6	2	1	0	6	2	0	1	2	0	2	2	2	2	6	4	8
4	FC Internazionale Milano	6	2	0	1	3	3	0	0	3	4	8	2	0	4	7	11	6

Group L

			Home					Away					Total					
		Pld	W	D	L	F	A	W	D	L	F	A	W	D	L	F	A	Pts
1	Osmanlıspor	6	2	1	0	6	2	1	0	2	4	5	3	1	2	10	7	10
2	Villarreal CF	6	2	0	1	5	4	0	3	0	4	4	2	3	1	9	8	9
3	FC Zürich	6	1	2	0	3	2	0	1	2	2	5	1	3	2	5	7	6
4	FC Steaua Bucureşti	6	1	2	0	4	3	0	1	2	1	4	1	3	2	5	7	6

Top goalscorers (after group stage)

6 Aritz Aduriz (Athletic)
Giuliano (Zenit)

5 Łukasz Teodorczyk (Anderlecht)
Edin Džeko (Roma)
Guillaume Hoarau (Young Boys)

4 Khouma Babacar (Fiorentina)
Nikola Kalinić (Fiorentina)
Leon Bailey (Genk)
Taison (Shakhtar Donetsk)
Aleksandr Kokorin (Zenit)

Round of 32

16/02/17, Balaídos, Vigo (att: 18,318)
RC Celta de Vigo 0-1 FC Shakhtar Donetsk
Goal: 0-1 Blanco 27
Referee: Mažeika (LTU)
23/02/17, Metalist Stadium, Kharkiv (att: 33,117)
FC Shakhtar Donetsk 0-2 RC Celta de Vigo (aet)
Goals: 0-1 Iago Aspas 90+1(p), 0-2 Cabral 108
Referee: Vinčić (SVN)
Aggregate: 1-2; RC Celta de Vigo qualify.

16/02/17, KAA Gent Stadium, Ghent (att: 19,267)
KAA Gent 1-0 Tottenham Hotspur FC
Goal: 1-0 Perbet 59
Referee: Bastien (FRA)
23/02/17, Wembley Stadium, London (att: 80,465)
Tottenham Hotspur FC 2-2 KAA Gent
Goals: 1-0 Eriksen 10, 1-1 Kane 20(og), 2-1 Wanyama 61, 2-2 Perbet 82
Referee: Manuel de Sousa (POR)
Aggregate: 2-3; KAA Gent qualify.

16/02/17, Krasnodar Stadium, Krasnodar (att: 32,460)
FC Krasnodar 1-0 Fenerbahçe SK
Goal: 1-0 Claesson 4
Referee: Kružliak (SVK)
22/02/17, Şükrü Saracoğlu, Istanbul (att: 21,788)
Fenerbahçe SK 1-1 FC Krasnodar
Goals: 0-1 Smolov 7, 1-1 Souza 41
Referee: Raczkowski (POL)
Aggregate: 1-2; FC Krasnodar qualify.

16/02/17, Borussia-Park, Monchengladbach (att: 41,863)
VfL Borussia Mönchengladbach 0-1 ACF Fiorentina
Goal: 0-1 Bernardeschi 44
Referee: Gil Manzano (ESP)
23/02/17, Stadio Artemio Franchi, Florence (att: 24,712)
ACF Fiorentina 2-4 VfL Borussia Mönchengladbach
Goals: 1-0 Kalinić 16, 2-0 Borja Valero 29, 2-1 Stindl 44(p), 2-2 Stindl 47, 2-3 Stindl 55, 2-4 Christensen 60
Referee: Artur Dias (POR)
Aggregate: 3-4; VfL Borussia Mönchengladbach qualify.

16/02/17, AZ Stadion, Alkmaar (att: 16,098)
AZ Alkmaar 1-4 Olympique Lyonnais
Goals: 0-1 Tousart 26, 0-2 Lacazette 45+2, 0-3 Lacazette 57, 1-3 Jahanbakhsh 68(p), 1-4 Ferri 90+5
Referee: Madden (SCO)
23/02/17, Stade de Lyon, Decines (att: 25,743)
Olympique Lyonnais 7-1 AZ Alkmaar
Goals: 1-0 Fekir 5, 2-0 Cornet 17, 2-1 Garcia 26, 3-1 Fekir 27, 4-1 Darder 34, 5-1 Fekir 78, 6-1 Aouar 87, 7-1 Diakhaby 89
Referee: Kulbakov (BLR)
Aggregate: 11-2; Olympique Lyonnais qualify.

16/02/17, Marin Anastasovici, Giurgiu (att: 3,775)
FC Astra Giurgiu 2-2 KRC Genk
Goals: 0-1 Castagne 25, 1-1 Budescu 43, 1-2 Trossard 83, 2-2 Seto 90
Referee: Moen (NOR)
23/02/17, KRC Genk Arena, Genk (att: 8,804)
KRC Genk 1-0 FC Astra Giurgiu
Goal: 1-0 Pozuelo 67
Referee: Gözübüyük (NED)
Aggregate: 3-2; KRC Genk qualify.

16/02/17, Natsionalen Stadion Vasil Levski, Sofia (att: 14,500)
PFC Ludogorets Razgrad 1-2 FC København
Goals: 0-1 Anicet Abel 2(og), 0-2 Toutouh 53, 1-2 Keşerü 81
Referee: Bebek (CRO)
23/02/17, Parken, Copenhagen (att: 17,064)
FC København 0-0 PFC Ludogorets Razgrad
Referee: Zelinka (CZE)
Aggregate: 2-1; FC København qualify.

16/02/17, Stadio Georgios Karaiskakis, Piraeus (att: 24,478)
Olympiacos FC 0-0 Osmanlıspor
Referee: Buquet (FRA)
23/02/17, Osmanlı Stadı, Ankara (att: 17,500)
Osmanlıspor 0-3 Olympiacos FC
Goals: 0-1 Ansarifard 47, 0-2 Elyounoussi 70, 0-3 Ansarifard 86
Referee: Vad (HUN)
Aggregate: 0-3; Olympiacos FC qualify.

16/02/17, Old Trafford, Manchester (att: 67,192)
Manchester United FC 3-0 AS Saint-Étienne
Goals: 1-0 Ibrahimović 15, 2-0 Ibrahimović 75, 3-0 Ibrahimović 88(p)
Referee: Královec (CZE)
22/02/17, Stade Geoffroy Guichard, Saint-Etienne (att: 41,492)
AS Saint-Étienne 0-1 Manchester United FC
Goal: 0-1 Mkhitaryan 17
Referee: Aytekin (GER)
Aggregate: 0-4; Manchester United FC qualify.

16/02/17, Olimp 2, Rostov-on-Don (att: 6,160)
FC Rostov 4-0 AC Sparta Praha
Goals: 1-0 Mevlja 15, 2-0 Poloz 38, 3-0 Noboa 40, 4-0 Azmoun 68
Referee: Nijhuis (NED)
23/02/17, Generali Arena, Prague (att: 13,413)
AC Sparta Praha 1-1 FC Rostov
Goals: 0-1 Poloz 13, 1-1 Karavaev 84
Referee: Göçek (TUR)
Aggregate: 1-5; FC Rostov qualify.

16/02/17, Estadio de San Mamés, Bilbao (att: 32,675)
Athletic Club 3-2 APOEL FC
Goals: 0-1 Efrem 36, 1-1 Merkis 38(og), 2-1 Aduriz 61, 3-1 Iñaki Williams 72, 3-2 Gianniotas 89
Referee: Eriksson (SWE)
23/02/17, GSP, Nicosia (att: 15,275)
APOEL FC 2-0 Athletic Club
Goals: 1-0 Sotiriou 46, 2-0 Gianniotas 54(p)
Referee: Bezborodov (RUS)
Aggregate: 4-3; APOEL FC qualify.

Timoty Castagne puts Genk 1-0 up away to Astra Giurgiu

16/02/17, Stadion Wojska Polskiego, Warsaw (att: 28,742)
Legia Warszawa 0-0 AFC Ajax
Referee: Fernández Borbalán (ESP)
23/02/17, Amsterdam ArenA, Amsterdam (att: 52,285)
AFC Ajax 1-0 Legia Warszawa
Goal: 1-0 Viergever 49
Referee: Taylor (ENG)
Aggregate: 1-0; AFC Ajax qualify.

16/02/17, Constant Vanden Stock Stadium, Brussels (att: 13,415)
RSC Anderlecht 2-0 FC Zenit
Goals: 1-0 Acheampong 5, 2-0 Acheampong 31
Referee: Oliver (ENG)
23/02/17, Stadion Petrovski, St Petersburg (att: 17,992)
FC Zenit 3-1 RSC Anderlecht
Goals: 1-0 Giuliano 24, 2-0 Dzyuba 72, 3-0 Giuliano 78, 3-1 Kiese Thelin 90
Referee: Sidiropoulos (GRE)
Aggregate: 3-3; RSC Anderlecht qualify on away goal.

16/02/17, Estadio de la Cerámica, Villarreal (att: 17,960)
Villarreal CF 0-4 AS Roma
Goals: 0-1 Emerson 32, 0-2 Džeko 65, 0-3 Džeko 79, 0-4 Džeko 86
Referee: Makkelie (NED)
23/02/17, Stadio Olimpico, Rome (att: 19,495)
AS Roma 0-1 Villarreal CF
Goal: 0-1 Borré 15
Referee: Zwayer (GER)
Aggregate: 4-1; AS Roma qualify.

16/02/17, Turner Stadium, Beer Sheva (att: 15,347)
Hapoel Beer Sheva FC 1-3 Beşiktaş JK
Goals: 0-1 William 42(og), 1-1 Barda 44, 1-2 Cenk Tosun 60, 1-3 Hutchinson 90+3
Referee: Atkinson (ENG)
23/02/17, Beşiktaş Arena, Istanbul (att: 27,892)
Beşiktaş JK 2-1 Hapoel Beer Sheva FC
Goals: 1-0 Aboubakar 17, 1-1 Nwakaeme 64, 2-1 Cenk Tosun 87
Referee: Jug (SVN)
Aggregate: 5-2; Beşiktaş JK qualify.

16/02/17, Stadio Toumba, Salonika (att: 25,593)
PAOK FC 0-3 FC Schalke 04
Goals: 0-1 Burgstaller 27, 0-2 Meyer 81, 0-3 Huntelaar 89
Referee: Estrada (ESP)
22/02/17, Arena AufSchalke, Gelsenkirchen (att: 50,619)
FC Schalke 04 1-1 PAOK FC
Goals: 1-0 Schöpf 23, 1-1 Nastasić 25(og)
Referee: Banti (ITA)
Aggregate: 4-1; FC Schalke 04 qualify.

Round of 16

09/03/17, Parken, Copenhagen (att: 31,189)
FC København 2-1 AFC Ajax
Goals: 1-0 Falk 1, 1-1 Dolberg 32, 2-1 Cornelius 60
Referee: Artur Dias (POR)
16/03/17, Amsterdam ArenA, Amsterdam (att: 52,270)
AFC Ajax 2-0 FC København
Goals: 1-0 Traoré 23, 2-0 Dolberg 45+2(p)
Referee: Kružliak (SVK)
Aggregate: 3-2; AFC Ajax qualify.

09/03/17, GSP, Nicosia (att: 19,327)
APOEL FC 0-1 RSC Anderlecht
Goal: 0-1 Stanciu 29
Referee: Manuel de Sousa (POR)
16/03/17, Constant Vanden Stock Stadium, Brussels (att: 15,662)
RSC Anderlecht 1-0 APOEL FC
Goal: 1-0 Acheampong 65
Referee: Kulbakov (BLR)
Aggregate: 2-0; RSC Anderlecht qualify.

09/03/17, Olimp 2, Rostov-on-Don (att: 14,223)
FC Rostov 1-1 Manchester United FC
Goals: 0-1 Mkhitaryan 35, 1-1 Bukharov 53
Referee: Zwayer (GER)
16/03/17, Old Trafford, Manchester (att: 64,361)
Manchester United FC 1-0 FC Rostov
Goal: 1-0 Mata 70
Referee: Mažeika (LTU)
Aggregate: 2-1; Manchester United FC qualify.

09/03/17, Balaídos, Vigo (att: 18,414)
RC Celta de Vigo 2-1 FC Krasnodar
Goals: 1-0 Wass 50, 1-1 Claesson 56, 2-1 Beauvue 90
Referee: Thomson (SCO)
16/03/17, Krasnodar Stadium, Krasnodar (att: 33,318)
FC Krasnodar 0-2 RC Celta de Vigo
Goals: 0-1 Hugo Mallo 52, 0-2 Iago Aspas 80
Referee: Buquet (FRA)
Aggregate: 1-4; RC Celta de Vigo qualify.

09/03/17, Arena AufSchalke, Gelsenkirchen (att: 52,412)
FC Schalke 04 1-1 VfL Borussia Mönchengladbach
Goals: 0-1 Hofmann 15, 1-1 Burgstaller 25
Referee: Kuipers (NED)
16/03/17, Borussia-Park, Monchengladbach (att: 46,283)
VfL Borussia Mönchengladbach 2-2 FC Schalke 04
Goals: 1-0 Christensen 26, 2-0 Dahoud 45+2, 2-1 Goretzka 54, 2-2 Bentaleb 68(p)
Referee: Clattenburg (ENG)
Aggregate: 3-3; FC Schalke 04 qualify on away goals.

09/03/17, Stade de Lyon, Decines (att: 50,588)
Olympique Lyonnais 4-2 AS Roma
Goals: 1-0 Diakhaby 8, 1-1 Salah 20, 1-2 Fazio 33, 2-2 Tolisso 47, 3-2 Fekir 74, 4-2 Lacazette 90+2
Referee: Taylor (ENG)
16/03/17, Stadio Olimpico, Rome (att: 46,453)
AS Roma 2-1 Olympique Lyonnais
Goals: 0-1 Diakhaby 16, 1-1 Strootman 17, 2-1 Tousart 60(og)
Referee: Kassai (HUN)
Aggregate: 4-5; Olympique Lyonnais qualify.

09/03/17, KAA Gent Stadium, Ghent (att: 17,112)
KAA Gent 2-5 KRC Genk
Goals: 0-1 Malinovskiy 21, 1-1 Kalu 27, 1-2 Colley 33, 1-3 Samatta 41, 1-4 Uronen 45+2, 2-4 Coulibaly 61, 2-5 Samatta 72
Referee: Tagliavento (ITA)
16/03/17, KRC Genk Arena, Genk (att: 16,028)
KRC Genk 1-1 KAA Gent
Goals: 1-0 Castagne 20, 1-1 Verstraete 84
Referee: Undiano Mallenco (ESP)
Aggregate: 6-3; KRC Genk qualify.

09/03/17, Stadio Georgios Karaiskakis, Piraeus (att: 25,515)
Olympiacos FC 1-1 Beşiktaş JK
Goals: 1-0 Cambiasso 36, 1-1 Aboubakar 53
Referee: Makkelie (NED)
16/03/17, Beşiktaş Arena, Istanbul (att: 37,966)
Beşiktaş JK 4-1 Olympiacos FC
Goals: 1-0 Aboubakar 10, 2-0 Babel 22, 2-1 Elyounoussi 31, 3-1 Babel 75, 4-1 Cenk Tosun 84
Referee: Oliver (ENG)
Aggregate: 5-2; Beşiktaş JK qualify.

Quarter-finals

13/04/17, Constant Vanden Stock Stadium, Brussels (att: 20,060)
RSC Anderlecht 1-1 Manchester United FC
Goals: 0-1 Mkhitaryan 37, 1-1 Dendoncker 86
Referee: Brych (GER)
20/04/17, Old Trafford, Manchester (att: 71,496)
Manchester United FC 2-1 RSC Anderlecht (aet)
Goals: 1-0 Mkhitaryan 10, 1-1 Hanni 32, 2-1 Rashford 107
Referee: Undiano Mallenco (ESP)
Aggregate: 3-2; Manchester United FC qualify.

13/04/17, Balaídos, Vigo (att: 21,608)
RC Celta de Vigo 3-2 KRC Genk
Goals: 0-1 Boëtius 10, 1-1 Sisto 15, 2-1 Iago Aspas 18, 3-1 Guidetti 38, 3-2 Buffel 67
Referee: Turpin (FRA)
20/04/17, KRC Genk Arena, Genk (att: 18,833)
KRC Genk 1-1 RC Celta de Vigo
Goals: 0-1 Sisto 63, 1-1 Trossard 67
Referee: Collum (SCO)
Aggregate: 3-4; RC Celta de Vigo qualify.

13/04/17, Amsterdam ArenA, Amsterdam (att: 52,384)
AFC Ajax 2-0 FC Schalke 04
Goals: 1-0 Klaassen 23(p), 2-0 Klaassen 52
Referee: Karasev (RUS)
20/04/17, Arena AufSchalke, Gelsenkirchen (att: 53,701)
FC Schalke 04 3-2 AFC Ajax (aet)
Goals: 1-0 Goretzka 53, 2-0 Burgstaller 56, 3-0 Caligiuri 101, 3-1 Viergever 111, 3-2 Younes 120
Referee: Haţegan (ROU)
Aggregate: 3-4; AFC Ajax qualify.

13/04/17, Stade de Lyon, Decines (att: 55,452)
Olympique Lyonnais 2-1 Beşiktaş JK
Goals: 0-1 Babel 15, 1-1 Tolisso 83, 2-1 Morel 85
Referee: Mateu Lahoz (ESP)
20/04/17, Beşiktaş Arena, Istanbul (att: 39,623)
Beşiktaş JK 2-1 Olympique Lyonnais (aet)
Goals: 1-0 Talisca 27, 1-1 Lacazette 34, 2-1 Talisca 58
Referee: Mažić (SRB)
Aggregate: 3-3; Olympique Lyonnais qualify 7-6 on penalties.

Semi-finals

03/05/17, Amsterdam ArenA, Amsterdam (att: 52,141)
AFC Ajax 4-1 Olympique Lyonnais
Goals: 1-0 Traoré 25, 2-0 Dolberg 34, 3-0 Younes 49, 3-1 Valbuena 66, 4-1 Traoré 71
Referee: Rocchi (ITA)
11/05/17, Stade de Lyon, Decines (att: 53,810)
Olympique Lyonnais 3-1 AFC Ajax
Goals: 0-1 Dolberg 27, 1-1 Lacazette 45(p), 2-1 Lacazette 45+1, 3-1 Ghezzal 81
Referee: Marciniak (POL)
Aggregate: 4-5; AFC Ajax qualify.

04/05/17, Balaídos, Vigo (att: 26,202)
RC Celta de Vigo 0-1 Manchester United FC
Goal: 0-1 Rashford 67
Referee: Karasev (RUS)
11/05/17, Old Trafford, Manchester (att: 75,138)
Manchester United FC 1-1 RC Celta de Vigo
Goals: 1-0 Fellaini 17, 1-1 Roncaglia 85
Referee: Haţegan (ROU)
Aggregate: 2-1; Manchester United FC qualify.

Final

24/05/17, Friends Arena, Stockholm (att: 46,961)
AFC Ajax 0-2 Manchester United FC
Goals: 0-1 Pogba 18, 0-2 Mkhitaryan 48
Referee: Skomina (SVN)
Ajax: Onana, Veltman, Riedewald (De Jong 82), Sánchez, Traoré, Klaassen, Younes, Schöne (Van de Beek 70), Ziyech, Dolberg (David Neres 62), De Ligt. Coach: Peter Bosz (NED)
Man. United: Romero, Pogba, Mata (Rooney 90), Smalling, Blind, Rashford (Martial 84), Ander Herrera, Mkhitaryan (Lingard 74), Valencia, Fellaini, Darmian. Coach: José Mourinho (POR)
Yellow cards: Mkhitaryan 31 (Man. United), Fellaini 52 (Man. United), Veltman 58 (Ajax), Younes 64 (Ajax), Riedewald 78 (Ajax), Juan Mata 78 (Man. United)

Top goalscorers

Edin Džeko

Giuliano

8	Edin Džeko (Roma)
	Giuliano (Zenit)
7	Aritz Aduriz (Athletic)
6	Kasper Dolberg (Ajax)
	Alexandre Lacazette (Lyon)
	Henrikh Mkhitaryan (Man. United)
5	Łukasz Teodorczyk (Anderlecht)
	Iago Aspas (Celta)
	Nikola Kalinić (Fiorentina)
	Zlatan Ibrahimović (Man. United)
	Guillaume Hoarau (Young Boys)

Squads/Appearances/Goals

AFC Ajax

No	Name	Nat	DoB	Aps	(s)	Gls
Goalkeepers						
33	Diederik Boer		24/09/80	1		
24	André Onana	CMR	02/04/96	14		
Defenders						
36	Matthijs de Ligt		12/08/99	8	(1)	
35	Mitchell Dijks		09/02/93	3		
4	Jaïro Riedewald		09/09/96	6	(1)	1
5	Davinson Sánchez	COL	12/06/96	12		
2	Kenny Tete		09/10/95	5	(3)	1
3	Joël Veltman		15/01/92	10		
26	Nick Viergever		03/08/89	10		2
16	Heiko Westermann	GER	14/08/83	1	(1)	
Midfielders						
6	Riechedly Bazoer		12/10/96		(1)	
21	Frenkie de Jong		12/05/97		(4)	
27	Nemanja Gudelj	SRB	16/11/91	3	(1)	
10	Davy Klaassen		21/02/93	13		2
34	Abdelhak Nouri		02/04/97	2	(1)	
20	Lasse Schöne	DEN	27/05/86	11	(1)	1
8	Daley Sinkgraven		04/07/95	6	(1)	
30	Donny van de Beek		18/04/97	5	(5)	
11	Amin Younes	GER	06/08/93	15		4
22	Hakim Ziyech	MAR	19/03/93	11	(2)	2
Forwards						
19	Mateo Çassierra	COL	13/04/97	2	(3)	
17	Václav Černý	CZE	17/10/97	1		
44	Pelle Clement		19/05/96		(1)	
77	David Neres	BRA	03/03/97		(4)	
25	Kasper Dolberg	DEN	06/10/97	10	(3)	6
7	Anwar El Ghazi		03/05/95	1	(1)	1
45	Justin Kluivert		05/05/99	2	(4)	
9	Bertrand Traoré	BFA	06/09/95	13		4

RSC Anderlecht

No	Name	Nat	DoB	Aps	(s)	Gls
Goalkeepers						
23	Frank Boeckx		27/09/86	1		
1	Davy Roef		06/02/94	5		
30	Rubén	ESP	22/06/84	6		
Defenders						
12	Dennis Appiah	FRA	09/06/92	4		
3	Olivier Deschacht		16/02/81	4		
4	Serigne Mbodji	SEN	11/11/89	7		
7	Andy Najar	HON	16/03/93	4	(1)	
14	Bram Nuytinck	NED	04/05/90	7	(1)	
37	Ivan Obradović	SRB	25/07/88	6		
41	Emmanuel Sowah	GHA	16/01/98	4		
5	Uroš Spajić	SRB	13/02/98	9		
Midfielders						
18	Frank Acheampong	GHA	16/10/93	10	(2)	3
8	Stéphane Badji	SEN	18/01/90	1	(4)	
10	Massimo Bruno		17/09/93	2	(7)	2
11	Alexandru Chipciu	ROU	18/05/89	8	(2)	1
32	Leander Dendoncker		15/04/95	12		1
17	Diego Capel	ESP	16/02/88	1	(5)	1
22	Idrissa Doumbia	CIV	14/04/98		(1)	
94	Sofiane Hanni	ALG	29/12/90	7	(4)	1
73	Nicolae Stanciu	ROU	07/05/93	11	(1)	4
31	Youri Tielemans		07/05/97	11		3
Forwards						
9	Hamdi Harbaoui	TUN	05/01/85		(2)	
24	Isaac Kiese Thelin	SWE	24/06/92	3	(3)	1
91	Łukasz Teodorczyk	POL	03/06/91	8	(3)	5
49	Jorn Vancamp		28/10/98	1		

APOEL FC

No	Name	Nat	DoB	Aps	(s)	Gls
Goalkeepers						
99	Boy Waterman	NED	24/01/84	10		
Defenders						
11	Nektarios Alexandrou		19/12/83	1		
5	Carlão	BRA	19/01/86	6		
44	Nicholas Ioannou		10/11/95	4		
23	Iñaki Astiz	ESP	05/11/83	6	(2)	
30	Georgios Merkis		30/07/84	6	(1)	
21	Zhivko Milanov	BUL	15/07/84	10		
3	Roberto Lago	ESP	30/08/85	6	(1)	
90	Cédric Yambéré	FRA	06/11/90	1	(1)	
Midfielders						
46	Efstathios Aloneftis		29/03/83	3	(1)	
4	Kostakis Artymatas		15/04/93	1	(3)	
10	Facundo Bertoglio	ARG	30/06/90	4	(3)	
6	Lorenzo Ebecilio	NED	24/09/91	2	(1)	
7	Georgios Efrem		05/07/89	8	(1)	3
70	Ioannis Gianniotas	GRE	29/04/93	6	(4)	2
26	Nuno Morais	POR	29/01/84	9		
8	Andrea Orlandi	ESP	03/08/84	1	(1)	
88	Renan Bressan	BLR	03/11/88	1	(1)	
77	Vander	BRA	03/10/88	2	(5)	
16	Vinícius	BRA	16/05/86	8		1
Forwards						
17	David Barral	ESP	10/05/83	3		
9	Igor De Camargo	BEL	12/05/83	3	(5)	2
20	Pieros Sotiriou		13/01/93	9		3

FC Astra Giurgiu

No	Name	Nat	DoB	Aps	(s)	Gls
Goalkeepers						
1	Silviu Lung		04/06/89	8		
Defenders						
4	Fabrício	BRA	20/02/90	5		
2	Geraldo Alves	POR	08/11/80	7		
13	Júnior Morais	BRA	22/07/86	7		
5	Vlatko Lazic	NED	01/05/89	2		
15	Cristian Oroş		15/10/84	3	(1)	
22	Cristian Săpunaru		05/04/84	8		1
77	Alexandru Stan		07/02/89	5		1
Midfielders						
24	Damien Boudjemaa	FRA	07/06/85	1		
10	Constantin Budescu		19/02/89	7	(1)	2
80	Filipe Teixeira	POR	02/10/80	7		
31	Alexandru Ioniţă		14/12/94	1	(3)	
20	Florin Lovin		11/02/82	5	(2)	
19	Boubacar Mansaly	SEN	04/02/88	5	(1)	
17	Viorel Nicoară		27/09/87	2	(4)	
8	Takayuki Seto	JPN	05/02/86	7	(1)	1
Forwards						
7	Denis Alibec		05/01/91	5		2
9	Sergiu Buş		20/11/92		(2)	
11	Daniel Florea		17/04/88		(6)	1
21	Daniel Niculae		06/10/82	3	(3)	

FK Austria Wien

No	Name	Nat	DoB	Aps	(s)	Gls
Goalkeepers						
1	Robert Almer		20/03/84	2		
31	Osman Hadzikic		12/03/96	4	(1)	
Defenders						
23	David De Paula	ESP	03/05/84	1		
4	Petar Filipovic	GER	14/09/90	6		
28	Christoph Martschinko		13/02/94	5		
33	Lukas Rotpuller		31/03/91	4		2
25	Thomas Salamon		18/01/89	1		
18	Patrizio Stronati	CZE	17/11/94	2		
17	Jens Stryger	DEN	21/02/91	5	(1)	
Midfielders						
95	Felipe Pires	BRA	18/04/95	6		
10	Alexander Grünwald		01/05/89	5		2
26	Raphael Holzhauser		16/02/93	6		3
16	Dominik Prokop		02/06/97	1	(2)	1
15	Tarkan Serbest		02/05/94	6		
7	Ismael Tajouri	LBY	28/03/94	1	(5)	
Forwards						
9	Kevin Friesenbichler		06/05/94	1	(4)	1
8	Olarenwaju Kayode	NGA	08/05/93	5	(1)	2
27	Marko Kvasina		20/12/96		(1)	
11	Lucas Venuto	BRA	14/01/95	5	(1)	

FC Astana

No	Name	Nat	DoB	Aps	(s)	Gls
Goalkeepers						
1	Nenad Erić		26/05/82	6		
Defenders						
5	Marin Aničić	BIH	17/08/89	4		1
15	Abzal Beysebekov		30/11/92	6		
28	Birzhan Kulbekov		22/04/94		(1)	
27	Yuri Logvinenko		22/07/88	4		
25	Sergei Maliy		05/06/90	4	(2)	
14	Igor Shitov	BLR	24/10/86	5	(1)	
77	Dmitri Shomko		19/03/90	6		
Midfielders						
88	Roger Cañas	COL	27/03/90	5		
6	Nemanja Maksimović	SRB	26/01/95	5		1
7	Serikzhan Muzhikov		17/06/89	5	(1)	
12	Gevorg Najaryan		06/01/98		(2)	
13	Azat Nurgaliyev		30/06/86		(2)	
8	Askhat Tagybergen		09/08/90	1	(2)	
31	Abay Zhunusov		15/03/95		(1)	
Forwards						
10	Djordje Despotović	SRB	04/03/92	5	(1)	2
30	Junior Kabananga	COD	04/04/89	6		1
17	Tanat Nuserbayev		01/01/87	1	(3)	
23	Patrick Twumasi	GHA	09/05/94	3	(1)	

Athletic Club

No	Name	Nat	DoB	Aps	(s)	Gls
Goalkeepers						
1	Gorka Iraizoz		06/03/81	3		
13	Iago Herrerín		25/01/88	5		
Defenders						
24	Mikel Balenziaga		29/02/88	7		
2	Eneko Bóveda		14/12/88		(1)	
18	Óscar De Marcos		14/04/89	5		
16	Xabier Etxeita		31/10/87	2		
4	Aymeric Laporte	FRA	27/05/94	6		
15	Iñigo Lekue		04/05/93	3	(2)	1
25	Enric Saborit		27/04/92	1	(1)	1
27	Yeray Álvarez		24/01/95	8		
Midfielders						
7	Beñat Etxebarria		19/02/87	5	(1)	1
3	Gorka Elustondo		18/03/87		(1)	
5	Javier Eraso		22/03/90	1	(1)	
8	Ander Iturraspe		08/03/89	4	(1)	
17	Mikel Rico		04/11/84	2	(2)	
10	Iker Muniain		19/12/92	7	(1)	
22	Raúl García		11/07/86	7		1
6	Mikel San José		30/05/89	4	(2)	
14	Markel Susaeta		14/12/87	3	(4)	
12	Mikel Vesga		08/04/93	1		
Forwards						
20	Aritz Aduriz		11/02/81	5	(1)	7
11	Iñaki Williams		15/06/94	7	(1)	1
19	Sabin Merino		04/01/92	2	(3)	
28	Asier Villalibre		30/09/97		(2)	

AZ Alkmaar

No	Name	Nat	DoB	Aps	(s)	Gls
Goalkeepers						
1	Tim Krul		03/04/88	2		
1	Sergio Rochet	URU	23/03/93	6		
Defenders						
5	Ridgeciano Haps		12/06/93	8		1
2	Mattias Johansson	SWE	16/02/92	6		
29	Fernando Lewis		31/01/93	1		
22	Thomas Ouwejan		30/09/96		(1)	
3	Rens van Eijden		03/03/88	5	(1)	
4	Ron Vlaar		16/02/85	5		
Midfielders						
18	Iliass Bel Hassani		16/09/92	5	(2)	
19	Dabney dos Santos		31/07/96	2	(3)	
28	Levi Garcia	TRI	20/11/97	2	(2)	1
23	Derrick Luckassen		03/07/95	8		
6	Ben Rienstra		05/06/90	6	(2)	1
20	Mats Seuntjens		17/04/92	3	(2)	
15	Guus Til		22/12/97		(1)	
8	Joris van Overeem		01/06/94	3	(2)	
30	Stijn Wuytens	BEL	08/10/89	8		1
Forwards						
27	Fred Friday	NGA	22/05/95	4	(3)	
7	Alireza Jahanbakhsh	IRN	11/08/93	4	(1)	1
21	Robert Mühren		18/05/89	2	(1)	1
11	Muamer Tankovic	SWE	22/02/95	3		1
9	Wout Weghorst		07/08/92	5	(3)	1

Beşiktaş JK

No	Name	Nat	DoB	Aps	(s)	Gls
Goalkeepers						
1	Fabricio	ESP	31/12/87	6		
Defenders						
3	Adriano	BRA	26/10/84	4		
33	Atınç Nukan		20/07/93	1		
32	Andreas Beck	GER	13/03/87	1	(1)	
77	Gökhan Gönül		04/01/85	5		
30	Marcelo	BRA	20/05/87	4		
2	Matej Mitrović	CRO	10/11/93	4		
6	Duško Tošić	SRB	19/01/85	6		
Midfielders						
18	Tolgay Arslan	GER	16/08/90	2	(3)	
49	Ryan Babel	NED	19/12/86	6		3
13	Atiba Hutchinson	CAN	08/02/83	5		1
80	Gökhan Inler	SUI	27/06/84	1	(4)	
20	Necip Uysal		24/01/91	2	(3)	
15	Oğuzhan Özyakup		23/09/92	3	(2)	
7	Ricardo Quaresma	POR	26/09/83	5		
94	Talisca	BRA	01/02/94	5	(1)	2
Forwards						
9	Vincent Aboubakar	CMR	22/01/92	3		3
23	Cenk Tosun		07/06/91	3	(3)	3
17	Ömer Şişmanoğlu		01/08/89		(1)	

SC Braga

No	Name	Nat	DoB	Aps	(s)	Gls
Goalkeepers						
28	Marafona		08/05/87	2		
92	Matheus	BRA	29/03/92	4		
Defenders						
6	André Pinto		05/10/89	3		1
44	Artur Jorge		14/08/94	1	(1)	
15	Baiano	BRA	23/02/87	6		
87	Marcelo Goiano	BRA	13/10/87	6		
3	Lazar Rosić	SRB	29/06/93	6		
2	Emiliano Velázquez	URU	30/04/94	2		1
Midfielders						
30	Alan	BRA	19/09/79	1	(3)	
8	Marko Bakić	MNE	01/11/93	1	(1)	
10	Tomas Martínez	ARG	07/03/95		(1)	
63	Mauro	BRA	31/10/90	4		
23	Pedro Santos		22/04/88	3	(2)	
25	Pedro Tiba		31/08/88	3	(1)	
21	Ricardo Horta		15/09/94	4	(1)	1
35	Nikola Vukčević	MNE	13/12/91	5	(1)	1
7	Wilson Eduardo		08/07/90	6		1
Forwards						
26	Óscar Benítez	ARG	14/01/93		(1)	
9	Ahmed Hassan	EGY	05/03/93	5	(1)	2
17	Rui Fonte		23/04/90	2	(2)	
19	Nikola Stojiljković	SRB	17/08/92	2	(3)	2

Dundalk FC

No	Name	Nat	DoB	Aps	(s)	Gls
Goalkeepers						
1	Gary Rogers		25/09/81	5		
22	Gabriel Sava	ITA	15/10/86	1		
Defenders						
15	Paddy Barrett		22/07/93		(1)	
4	Andy Boyle		07/03/91	6		
2	Sean Gannon		11/07/91	6		
3	Brian Gartland		04/11/86	6		
14	Dane Massey		17/04/88	6		
Midfielders						
18	Robbie Benson		07/05/92	4	(1)	1
10	Ronan Finn		21/12/87	6		
7	Daryl Horgan		10/08/92	6		1
11	Patrick McEleney		26/09/92	6		
8	John Mountney		22/02/93	2	(3)	
6	Stephen O'Donnell		15/01/86	2	(2)	
5	Chris Shields		27/12/90	4	(1)	
19	Dean Shiels	NIR	01/02/85		(4)	
Forwards						
16	Ciaran Kilduff		29/09/88	1	(5)	2
9	David McMillan		14/12/88	5	(1)	

VfL Borussia Mönchengladbach

No	Name	Nat	DoB	Aps	(s)	Gls
Goalkeepers						
1	Yann Sommer	SUI	17/12/88	4		
Defenders						
3	Andreas Christensen	DEN	10/04/96	3		2
24	Tony Jantschke		07/04/90	4		
2	Timothée Kolodziejczak	FRA	01/10/91	1		
27	Julian Korb		21/03/92		(1)	
4	Jannik Vestergaard	DEN	03/08/92	4		
17	Oscar Wendt	SWE	24/10/85	4		
Midfielders						
8	Mahmoud Dahoud		01/01/96	4		1
28	André Hahn		13/08/90		(3)	
10	Thorgan Hazard	BEL	29/03/93	2		
7	Patrick Herrmann		12/02/91	3	(1)	
23	Jonas Hofmann		14/07/92	2	(1)	1
19	Fabian Johnson	USA	11/12/87	3	(1)	
6	Christoph Kramer		19/02/91	3		
14	Nico Schulz		01/04/93		(1)	
5	Tobias Strobl		12/05/90	1	(2)	
Forwards						
9	Josip Drmic	SUI	08/08/92	1	(2)	
11	Raffael	BRA	28/03/85	2		
13	Lars Stindl		26/08/88	3		3

RC Celta de Vigo

No	Name	Nat	DoB	Aps	(s)	Gls
Goalkeepers						
13	Rubén Blanco		25/07/95	4		
1	Sergio Álvarez		03/08/86	10		
Defenders						
22	Gustavo Cabral	ARG	14/10/85	12		1
4	David Costas		26/03/95	1		
3	Andreu Fontàs		14/11/89	8		1
2	Hugo Mallo		22/06/91	12		1
19	Jonny		03/03/94	12		
21	Carles Planas		04/03/91	2		
24	Facundo Roncaglia	ARG	10/02/87	7	(2)	1
20	Sergi Gómez		28/03/92	3	(2)	
Midfielders						
12	Claudio Beauvue	FRA	16/04/88		(6)	1
7	Théo Bongonda	BEL	20/11/95	3	(3)	
5	Marcelo Díaz	CHI	30/12/86	4	(1)	
8	Pablo Hernández	CHI	24/10/86	12		
16	Jozabed		08/03/91		(8)	
15	Álvaro Lemos		30/03/93	3		
17	José Naranjo		28/07/94	2		
14	Fabián Orellana	CHI	27/01/86	1	(1)	2
6	Nemanja Radoja	SRB	06/02/93	11	(1)	
23	Josep Señé		10/12/91	3		
11	Pione Sisto	DEN	04/02/95	10	(3)	2
18	Daniel Wass	DEN	31/05/89	10	(4)	2
Forwards						
9	John Guidetti	SWE	15/04/92	12	(1)	4
10	Iago Aspas		01/08/87	9	(3)	5
25	Giuseppe Rossi	ITA	01/02/87	3	(4)	1

Fenerbahçe SK

No	Name	Nat	DoB	Aps	(s)	Gls
Goalkeepers						
40	Fabiano	BRA	29/02/88		(1)	
1	Volkan Demirel		27/10/81	8		
Defenders						
3	Hasan Ali Kaldırım		09/12/89	7		
22	İsmail Köybaşı		10/07/89	1	(3)	
4	Simon Kjær	DEN	26/03/89	8		2
19	Şener Özbayraklı		23/01/90	7		
37	Martin Škrtel	SVK	15/12/84	7		
23	Gregory van der Wiel	NED	03/02/88	1		
Midfielders						
7	Alper Potuk		08/04/91	7	(1)	
77	Jeremain Lens	NED	24/11/87	5		1
5	Mehmet Topal		03/03/86	8		
33	Roman Neustädter	RUS	18/02/88	2	(3)	
8	Ozan Tufan		23/03/95	1	(2)	
48	Salih Uçan		06/01/94	1	(1)	
6	Souza	BRA	11/02/89	8		1
99	Miroslav Stoch	SVK	19/10/89	1	(1)	1
20	Volkan Şen		07/07/87	3	(2)	
Forwards						
29	Emmanuel Emenike	NGA	10/05/87	3	(4)	1
9	Fernandão	BRA	27/03/87		(2)	
17	Moussa Sow	SEN	19/01/86	7		2
10	Robin van Persie	NED	06/08/83	3	(2)	1

Feyenoord

No	Name	Nat	DoB	Aps	(s)	Gls
Goalkeepers						
25	Brad Jones	AUS	19/03/82	6		
Defenders						
33	Eric Botteghin	BRA	31/08/87	5		
31	Wessel Dammers		01/03/95	1		
2	Rick Karsdorp		11/02/95	6		
4	Terence Kongolo		14/02/94	4		
18	Miguel Nelom		22/09/90	2	(1)	
26	Bart Nieuwkoop		07/03/96		(2)	
6	Jan-Arie van der Heijden		03/03/88	6		
Midfielders						
8	Karim El Ahmadi	MAR	27/01/85	4		
7	Dirk Kuyt		22/07/80	5		
20	Renato Tapia	PER	28/07/95	3		
10	Tonny Trindade de Vilhena		03/01/95	5		1
5	Marko Vejinovic		03/02/90	1		
Forwards						
19	Steven Berghuis		19/12/91	2	(1)	
14	Bilal Başacıkoğlu	TUR	26/03/95	1	(5)	
11	Eljero Elia		13/02/87	3		
9	Nicolai Jørgensen	DEN	15/01/91	6		2
29	Michiel Kramer		03/12/88		(4)	
28	Jens Toornstra		04/04/89	6		

KRC Genk

No	Name	Nat	DoB	Aps	(s)	Gls
Goalkeepers						
1	Marco Bizot	NED	10/03/91	5		
30	Nordin Jackers		05/09/97	1		
70	Mathew Ryan	AUS	08/04/92	6		
Defenders						
2	Jakub Brabec	CZE	06/08/92	11		1
41	Timoty Castagne		05/12/95	10		2
4	Omar Colley	GAM	24/10/92	11		1
6	Sebastien Dewaest		27/05/91	2	(1)	
32	Christophe Janssens		09/03/98		(1)	
3	Bojan Nastić	SRB	06/07/94	4		
21	Jere Uronen	FIN	13/07/94	7		1
5	Sandy Walsh	NED	14/03/95	3	(1)	
Midfielders						
27	Sander Berge	NOR	14/02/98	5	(1)	
9	Jean-Paul Boëtius	NED	22/03/94	3	(3)	1
19	Thomas Buffel		19/02/81	7	(5)	2
28	Bryan Heynen		06/02/97	3	(4)	1
18	Ruslan Malinovskiy	UKR	04/05/93	5		1
25	Wilfred Ndidi	NGA	16/12/96	6		2
24	Alejandro Pozuelo	ESP	20/09/91	11		1
20	Paolo Sabak		10/02/99		(1)	
10	Tino-Sven Sušić	BIH	13/02/92	4	(1)	1
14	Leandro Trossard		04/12/94	5	(7)	3
8	Bennard Yao Kumordzi	GHA	21/03/85	1	(3)	
Forwards						
31	Leon Bailey	JAM	09/08/97	6		4
7	Nikolaos Karelis	GRE	24/02/92	4	(2)	2
77	Mbwana Samatta	TAN	13/12/92	9	(3)	2
22	Siebe Schrijvers		18/07/96	3	(3)	

Hapoel Beer Sheva FC

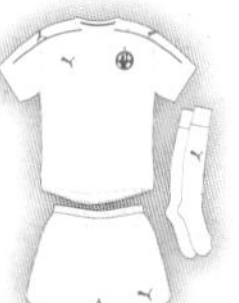

No	Name	Nat	DoB	Aps	(s)	Gls
Goalkeepers						
1	Dudu Goresh		01/02/80	8		
Defenders						
2	Ben Biton		03/01/91	7		
69	Mihály Korhut	HUN	01/12/88	6		
4	Miguel Vítor	POR	30/06/89	6		1
17	Matan Ohayon		25/02/86	1		
20	Loai Taha		26/11/89	4		
3	Ben Turgeman		09/01/89	2	(1)	
5	Shir Tzedek		22/08/89	8		
25	William	BRA	07/02/85	2		
Midfielders						
15	Vladimir Broun		06/05/89	1		
11	Maor Buzaglo		14/01/88	4	(3)	2
12	Ovidiu Hoban	ROU	27/12/82	7	(1)	
24	Maor Melikson		30/10/84	4	(2)	
30	John Ogu	NGA	20/04/88	7		
18	Michael Ohana		04/10/95		(1)	
7	Mahran Radi		01/07/82	5	(1)	
21	Yuval Shabtai		18/12/86		(2)	
Forwards						
10	Elyaniv Barda		15/12/81	1	(1)	1
8	Mohammad Ghadir		21/01/91	1	(5)	
22	Lúcio Maranhão	BRA	28/09/88	5	(1)	1
9	Anthony Nwakaeme	NGA	21/03/89	7		2
14	Ben Sahar		10/08/89	2	(6)	1

ACF Fiorentina

No	Name	Nat	DoB	Aps	(s)	Gls
Goalkeepers						
1	Luca Lezzerini		24/03/95	1		
12	Ciprian Tătăruşanu	ROU	09/02/86	7		
Defenders						
13	Davide Astori		07/01/87	6		
4	Sebastian De Maio	FRA	05/03/87	2		
2	Gonzalo Rodríguez	ARG	10/04/84	7		
31	Hrvoje Milić	CRO	10/05/89	2		
15	Maximiliano Olivera		05/03/92	6		
18	Carlos Salcedo	MEX	29/09/93	2		
40	Nenad Tomović	SRB	30/08/87	6	(1)	
Midfielders						
5	Milan Badelj	CRO	25/02/89	6		
10	Federico Bernardeschi		16/02/94	5	(3)	2
20	Borja Valero	ESP	12/01/85	5	(1)	1
25	Federico Chiesa		25/10/97	3	(2)	1
19	Sebastián Cristóforo	URU	23/08/93	5	(1)	1
72	Josip Iličič	SVN	29/01/88	2	(2)	1
6	Carlos Sánchez	COL	06/02/86	4	(4)	
16	Cristian Tello	ESP	11/08/91	3	(2)	
8	Matías Vecino	URU	24/08/91	5	(2)	1
Forwards						
30	Khouma Babacar	SEN	17/03/93	5	(3)	4
9	Nikola Kalinić	CRO	05/01/88	6	(1)	5
7	Mauro Zárate	ARG	18/03/87		(1)	2

KAA Gent

No	Name	Nat	DoB	Aps	(s)	Gls
Goalkeepers						
91	Lovre Kalinić	CRO	03/04/90	4		
1	Jacob Rinne	SWE	20/06/93	5		
20	Yannick Thoelen		18/07/90	1		
Defenders						
21	Nana Asare	GHA	11/07/86	6		
5	Ofir Davidzada	ISR	05/05/91		(2)	
29	Thibault De Smet		05/06/98	1		
55	Rami Gershon	ISR	12/08/88	7	(1)	
4	Samuel Gigot	FRA	12/10/93	4		
13	Stefan Mitrović	SRB	22/05/90	9		
23	Lasse Nielsen	DEN	08/01/88	4		
Midfielders						
19	Brecht Dejaegere		29/05/91	4	(3)	
44	Anderson Esiti	NGA	24/05/94	6	(2)	
32	Thomas Foket		25/09/94	8	(1)	
40	Rabiu Ibrahim	NGA	15/03/91	1	(2)	
18	Samuel Kalu	NGA	26/08/97	2	(1)	1
8	Thomas Matton		24/10/85	2	(2)	
77	Danijel Milićević	BIH	05/01/86	8		3
10	Renato Neto	BRA	27/09/91	6		1
15	Kenny Saief	USA	17/12/93	8	(1)	1
17	Hannes Van der Bruggen		01/04/93	3		
33	Louis Verstraete		04/05/99	1	(2)	1
Forwards						
7	Kalifa Coulibaly	MLI	21/08/91	6	(4)	4
88	Dieumerci Ndongala	COD	14/06/91	1	(1)	
24	Jérémy Perbet	FRA	12/12/84	6	(4)	3
27	Moses Simon	NGA	12/07/95	7	(1)	

FC Internazionale Milano

No	Name	Nat	DoB	Aps	(s)	Gls
Goalkeepers						
30	Juan Pablo Carrizo	ARG	06/05/84	1	(1)	
1	Samir Handanovič	SVN	14/07/84	5		
Defenders						
2	Marco Andreolli		10/06/86	1		
15	Cristian Ansaldi	ARG	20/09/86	1	(2)	
33	Danilo D'Ambrosio		09/09/88	4	(1)	
95	Senna Miangue	BEL	05/02/97	2		
25	Miranda	BRA	07/09/84	3		
24	Jeison Murillo	COL	27/05/92	5		
55	Yuto Nagatomo	JPN	12/09/86	4		
13	Andrea Ranocchia		16/02/88	4		
21	Davide Santon		02/01/91	1		
Midfielders						
77	Marcelo Brozović	CRO	16/11/92	3		1
87	Antonio Candreva		28/02/87	4	(1)	1
19	Éver Banega	ARG	29/06/88	3	(1)	
5	Felipe Melo	BRA	26/06/83	4	(1)	
27	Assane Gnoukouri	CIV	28/09/96	3	(1)	
17	Gary Medel	CHI	03/08/87	3		
44	Ivan Perišić	CRO	02/02/89	1	(4)	
Forwards						
93	Axel Bakayoko	FRA	06/01/98		(1)	
11	Jonathan Biabiany	FRA	28/04/88	2	(1)	
23	Éder		15/11/86	5	(1)	2
9	Mauro Icardi	ARG	19/02/93	3	(2)	2
8	Rodrigo Palacio	ARG	05/02/82	3		1
99	Andrea Pinamonti		19/05/99	1		

UEFA Europa League

FC København

No	Name	Nat	DoB	Aps	(s)	Gls
	Goalkeepers					
31	Robin Olsen	SWE	08/01/90	4		
	Defenders					
22	Peter Ankersen		22/09/90	4		
3	Ludwig Augustinsson	SWE	21/04/94	4		
20	Nicolai Boilesen		16/02/92		(2)	
2	Tom Høgli	NOR	24/02/84		(1)	
5	Erik Johansson	SWE	30/12/88	4		
25	Mathias "Zanka" Jørgensen		23/04/90	3		
26	Jores Okore		11/08/92	1		
	Midfielders					
33	Rasmus Falk		15/01/92	3		1
16	Ján Greguš	SVK	29/01/91	1	(1)	
35	Aboubakar Keita	CIV	05/11/97	1		
17	Kasper Kusk		10/11/91		(2)	
6	William Kvist		24/02/85	3		
88	Uroš Matić	SRB	23/05/90	4		
24	Youssef Toutouh		06/10/92	4		1
7	Benjamin Verbič	SVN	27/11/93		(1)	
	Forwards					
11	Andreas Cornelius		16/03/93	4		1
23	Andrija Pavlović	SRB	16/11/93		(3)	
19	Federico Santander	PAR	04/06/91	4		

FC Krasnodar

No	Name	Nat	DoB	Aps	(s)	Gls
	Goalkeepers					
1	Stanislav Kritsyuk		01/12/90	8		
88	Andrei Sinitsin		23/06/88	2		
	Defenders					
6	Andreas Granqvist	SWE	16/04/85	9		
55	Artur Jędrzejczyk	POL	04/11/87	5		
17	Vitali Kaleshin		03/10/80	3	(3)	
4	Aleksandr Martynovich	BLR	26/08/87	5		
3	Naldo	BRA	25/08/88	9		
98	Sergei Petrov		02/01/91	4		
12	Cristian Ramírez	ECU	12/08/94	3		
	Midfielders					
10	Odil Akhmedov	UZB	25/11/87	6		
16	Viktor Claesson	SWE	02/01/92	4		2
8	Yuri Gazinski		20/07/89	5	(4)	
2	Marat Izmailov		21/09/82		(2)	
22	Joãozinho	BRA	25/12/88	6	(1)	3
77	Charles Kaboré	FRA	09/02/88	8		
38	Eboué Kouassi	CIV	13/12/97	6		
21	Ricardo Laborde	COL	16/02/88		(9)	
7	Pavel Mamaev		17/09/88		(3)	
33	Mauricio Pereyra	URU	15/03/90	4	(2)	
11	Vyacheslav Podberyozkin		21/06/92	8		
5	Dmitri Torbinski		28/04/84	3	(1)	
15	Ilya Zhigulev		01/02/96	1		
	Forwards					
9	Ari	BRA	11/12/85	1	(1)	2
90	Fedor Smolov		09/02/90	6		4
14	Wanderson	BRA	18/02/86	4		

PFC Ludogorets Razgrad

No	Name	Nat	DoB	Aps	(s)	Gls
	Goalkeepers					
21	Vladislav Stoyanov		08/06/87	2		
	Defenders					
25	Yordan Minev		14/10/80	2		
27	Cosmin Moţi	ROU	03/12/84	2		
6	Natanael	BRA	25/12/90	2		
5	José Luis Palomino	ARG	05/01/90	2		
	Midfielders					
12	Anicet Abel	MAD	16/03/90	2		
18	Svetoslav Dyakov		31/05/84	2		
11	Juninho Quixadá	BRA	12/12/85		(1)	
84	Marcelinho		24/08/84	2		
93	Virgil Misidjan	NED	24/07/93	1	(1)	
88	Wanderson	BRA	02/01/88	2		
	Forwards					
37	João Paulo	BRA	02/06/88		(2)	
22	Jonathan Cafú	BRA	10/07/91	2		
28	Claudiu Keşerü	ROU	02/12/86	1	(1)	1

Konyaspor

No	Name	Nat	DoB	Aps	(s)	Gls
	Goalkeepers					
30	Serkan Kırıntılı		15/02/85	6		
	Defenders					
42	Abdülkerim Bardakcı		07/09/94	2		
4	Ali Turan		06/09/83	4		
3	Barry Douglas	SCO	04/09/89	4		
54	Mehmet Uslu		25/02/88	2		
5	Selim Ay		31/07/91	2		
89	Nejc Skubic	SVN	13/06/89	5		
26	Jagoš Vuković	SRB	10/06/88	4		
	Midfielders					
8	Ali Çamdalı		22/02/84	4	(1)	
18	Amir Hadžiahmetović	BIH	08/03/97	5	(1)	
6	Jens Jønsson	DEN	10/01/93	4		
14	Marc Mbamba	CMR	15/10/88	2		
27	Alban Meha	KOS	26/04/86	2	(4)	
11	Deni Milošević	BIH	09/03/95	5	(1)	1
7	Ömer Ali Şahiner		02/01/92	5	(1)	
2	Volkan Fındıklı		13/10/90	4	(1)	
	Forwards					
10	Riad Bajić	BIH	06/05/94	3	(3)	
61	Halil İbrahim Sönmez		01/10/90		(4)	
88	Ioan Hora	ROU	21/08/88	2	(1)	
9	Dimitar Rangelov	BUL	09/02/83	1		1

Legia Warszawa

No	Name	Nat	DoB	Aps	(s)	Gls
	Goalkeepers					
1	Arkadiusz Malarz		19/06/80	2		
	Defenders					
28	Łukasz Broź		17/12/85	2		
5	Maciej Dąbrowski		20/04/87	2		
14	Adam Hloušek	CZE	20/12/88	2		
2	Michał Pazdan		21/09/87	2		
	Midfielders					
6	Guilherme	BRA	21/05/91	1	(1)	
22	Kasper Hämäläinen	FIN	08/08/86		(1)	
3	Tomasz Jodłowiec		08/09/85	2		
9	Valeri Kazaishvili	GEO	29/01/93	2		
15	Michał Kopczyński		15/06/92	2		
18	Michał Kucharczyk		20/03/91	1	(1)	
75	Thibault Moulin	FRA	13/01/90		(1)	
8	Vadis Odjidja-Ofoe	BEL	21/02/89	2		
32	Miroslav Radović		16/01/84	1		
	Forwards					
27	Daniel Chima	NGA	04/04/91		(1)	
24	Tomáš Necid	CZE	13/08/89	1	(1)	

Olympique Lyonnais

No	Name	Nat	DoB	Aps	(s)	Gls
	Goalkeepers					
1	Anthony Lopes	POR	01/10/90	8		
	Defenders					
5	Mouctar Diakhaby		19/12/96	8		3
13	Christophe Jallet		31/10/83	5	(2)	
4	Emanuel Mammana	ARG	10/02/96	4		
15	Jérémy Morel		02/04/84	6		1
3	Nicolas N'Koulou	CMR	27/03/90	3		
20	Rafael	BRA	09/07/90	4	(2)	
31	Maciej Rybus	POL	19/08/89	1	(2)	
2	Mapou Yanga-Mbiwa		15/05/89	1	(1)	
	Midfielders					
25	Houssem Aouar		30/06/98		(2)	1
14	Sergi Darder	ESP	22/12/93	2		1
18	Nabil Fekir		18/07/93	5	(3)	4
12	Jordan Ferri		12/03/92	1	(1)	1
11	Rachid Ghezzal	ALG	09/05/92	3	(3)	1
21	Maxime Gonalons		10/03/89	6		
8	Corentin Tolisso		03/08/94	7	(1)	2
29	Lucas Tousart		29/04/97	7		1
28	Mathieu Valbuena		28/09/84	6		1
	Forwards					
27	Maxwel Cornet	CIV	27/09/96	5	(3)	1
10	Alexandre Lacazette		28/05/91	6	(2)	6

Maccabi Tel-Aviv FC

No	Name	Nat	DoB	Aps	(s)	Gls
	Goalkeepers					
95	Predrag Rajković	SRB	31/10/95	6		
	Defenders					
26	Tal Ben Haim (I)		31/03/82	5		
20	Omri Ben Harush		07/03/90	6		
2	Eli Dasa		03/12/92	5		
21	Yegor Filipenko	BLR	10/04/88	2	(1)	
22	Avi Rikan		10/09/88		(1)	
18	Eitan Tibi		16/11/87	5		
	Midfielders					
6	Gal Alberman		17/04/83	4	(1)	
51	Yossi Benayoun		05/05/80	1	(4)	
23	Eyal Golasa		07/10/91	3		1
40	Emmanuel Nosa Igiebor	NGA	09/11/90	4	(2)	
4	Haris Medunjanin	BIH	08/03/85	6		2
15	Dor Micha		02/03/92	2	(3)	1
42	Dor Peretz		17/05/95	1	(1)	
45	Eliel Peretz		18/11/96		(1)	
5	Ezequiel Scarione	ARG	14/07/85	4		1
	Forwards					
9	Eden Ben Basat		08/09/86	1	(2)	
11	Tal Ben Haim (II)		05/08/89	6		1
10	Barak Itzhaki		25/09/84		(1)	
24	Vidar Örn Kjartansson	ISL	11/03/90	5		1
17	Sagiv Yehezkel		21/03/95		(1)	

1. FSV Mainz 05

No	Name	Nat	DoB	Aps	(s)	Gls
	Goalkeepers					
33	Jannik Huth		15/04/94	1		
1	Jonas Lössl	DEN	01/02/89	5		
	Defenders					
22	André Ramalho	BRA	16/02/92	2		
3	Leon Balogun	NGA	28/06/88	2		
16	Stefan Bell		24/08/91	6		
18	Daniel Brosinski		17/07/88	3	(1)	
26	Niko Bungert		24/10/86	2		1
24	Gaëtan Bussmann	FRA	02/02/91	5		
2	Giulio Donati	ITA	05/02/90	4		
42	Alexander Hack		08/09/93	2		1
	Midfielders					
27	Christian Clemens		04/08/91	2		
32	Pablo De Blasis	ARG	04/02/88	5		2
20	Fabian Frei	SUI	08/01/89	2	(2)	
25	Jean-Philippe Gbamin	CIV	25/09/95	5		
38	Gerrit Holtmann		25/03/95		(1)	
17	Jairo Samperio	ESP	11/07/93	1	(3)	
5	José Rodríguez	ESP	16/12/94	1		
21	Karim Onisiwo	AUT	17/03/92	3		
8	Levin Öztunali		15/03/96	1	(4)	1
45	Suat Serdar		11/04/97	3	(1)	
10	Yunus Mallı	TUR	24/02/92	5	(1)	1
	Forwards					
15	Jhon Córdoba	COL	11/05/93	4	(2)	1
9	Yoshinori Muto	JPN	15/07/92	2		1
36	Aaron Seydel		07/02/96		(2)	

Manchester United FC

No	Name	Nat	DoB	Aps	(s)	Gls
	Goalkeepers					
1	David de Gea	ESP	07/11/90	3		
20	Sergio Romero	ARG	22/02/87	12		
	Defenders					
3	Eric Bailly	CIV	12/04/94	11		
17	Daley Blind	NED	09/03/90	10	(1)	
36	Matteo Darmian	ITA	02/12/89	7		
24	Timothy Fosu-Mensah	NED	02/01/98	1	(3)	
4	Phil Jones		21/02/92	2	(1)	
5	Marcos Rojo	ARG	20/03/90	8	(2)	
23	Luke Shaw		12/07/95	4		
12	Chris Smalling		22/11/89	8	(2)	
25	Antonio Valencia	ECU	04/08/85	8	(1)	
	Midfielders					
21	Ander Herrera	ESP	14/08/89	9		
16	Michael Carrick		28/07/81	5	(2)	
27	Marouane Fellaini	BEL	22/11/87	7	(4)	1
14	Jesse Lingard		15/12/92	6	(4)	2
8	Juan Mata	ESP	28/04/88	9	(1)	2
22	Henrikh Mkhitaryan	ARM	21/01/89	10	(1)	6
6	Paul Pogba	FRA	15/03/93	15		3
28	Morgan Schneiderlin	FRA	08/11/89	2		
31	Bastian Schweinsteiger	GER	01/08/84		(1)	
18	Ashley Young		09/07/85	3	(4)	
	Forwards					
7	Memphis Depay	NED	13/02/94		(3)	
9	Zlatan Ibrahimović	SWE	03/10/81	9	(2)	5
11	Anthony Martial	FRA	05/12/95	4	(6)	1
19	Marcus Rashford		31/10/97	8	(3)	2
10	Wayne Rooney		24/10/85	4	(3)	2

OGC Nice

No	Name	Nat	DoB	Aps	(s)	Gls
	Goalkeepers					
40	Walter Benítez	ARG	19/01/93	1		
30	Yoan Cardinale		27/03/94	5		
	Defenders					
4	Paul Baysse		18/05/88	3		
28	Olivier Boscagli		18/11/97	2		
29	Dalbert	BRA	08/09/93	4		
31	Dante	BRA	18/10/83	5		
20	Maxime Le Marchand		10/10/89	1		1
36	Romain Perraud		22/09/97	1		
21	Ricardo	POR	06/10/93	5		
34	Malang Sarr		23/01/99	4		
2	Arnaud Souquet		12/02/92	3		
	Midfielders					
5	Younès Belhanda		25/02/90	3	(2)	
24	Mathieu Bodmer		22/11/82	3	(1)	
35	Patrick Burner		11/04/96	1		
25	Wylan Cyprien		28/01/95	2	(2)	1
13	Valentin Eysseric		25/03/92	2	(2)	
26	Vincent Koziello		28/10/95	5		
8	Arnaud Lusamba		04/01/97	1		
39	Hicham Mahou		02/07/99		(1)	
33	Vincent Marcel		09/04/97	1	(1)	
12	Albert Rafetraniaina		09/09/96		(1)	
6	Jean Michaël Seri	CIV	19/07/91	3	(1)	
18	Rémi Walter		26/04/95	2	(2)	
	Forwards					
9	Mario Balotelli	ITA	12/08/90	4		1
23	Alexy Bosetti		23/04/93		(1)	1
22	Anastasios Donis	GRE	29/08/96	2	(1)	
14	Alassane Pléa		10/03/93	3	(2)	1

Olympiacos FC

No	Name	Nat	DoB	Aps	(s)	Gls
	Goalkeepers					
31	Nicola Leali	ITA	17/02/93	10		
	Defenders					
3	Alberto Botía	ESP	27/01/89	8		
36	Bruno Viana	BRA	05/02/95	3		
22	Aly Cissokho	FRA	15/09/87	4		
24	Alberto de la Bella	ESP	02/12/85	3		
77	Diogo Figueiras	POR	07/01/91	9		1
14	Omar Elabdellaoui	NOR	05/12/91	1		
6	Manuel da Costa	MAR	06/05/86	7	(1)	
45	Panagiotis Retsos		09/08/98	7		
	Midfielders					
28	André Martins	POR	21/01/90	6	(4)	
32	Athanasios Androutsos		06/05/97	1	(3)	
8	Andreas Bouhalakis		05/04/93	1	(1)	
19	Esteban Cambiasso	ARG	18/08/80	5	(1)	2
10	Alejandro Domínguez	ARG	10/06/81		(1)	
18	Tarik Elyounoussi	NOR	23/02/88	7	(2)	3
7	Kostas Fortounis		16/10/92	8		1
52	Georgios Manthatis		11/05/97	3	(5)	
11	Marko Marin	GER	13/03/89	2	(2)	
5	Luka Milivojević	SRB	07/04/91	4		
4	Alaixys Romao	TOG	18/01/84	3	(4)	
92	Sebá	BRA	08/06/92	8	(1)	3
	Forwards					
17	Karim Ansarifard	IRN	02/04/90	3	(1)	2
9	Óscar Cardozo	PAR	20/05/83	3	(2)	
99	Brown Ideye	NGA	10/10/88	4		

Osmanlıspor

No	Name	Nat	DoB	Aps	(s)	Gls
	Goalkeepers					
1	Hakan Arıkan		17/08/82	2		
99	Žydrūnas Karčemarskas	LTU	24/05/83	6		
	Defenders					
5	Aykut Demir		22/10/88	3	(1)	
4	Koray Altınay		11/10/91	1		
33	Muhammed Bayır		05/02/89	1	(2)	
61	Numan Çürüksu		02/12/84	8		
21	Václav Procházka	CZE	08/05/84	5	(1)	
15	Tiago Pinto	POR	01/02/88	8		
2	Avdija Vršajević	BIH	06/03/86	6		
	Midfielders					
28	Dzon Delarge	CGO	24/06/90	6	(2)	1
11	Erdal Kılıçaslan		23/08/84		(2)	1
8	Raheem Lawal	NGA	04/05/89	3	(1)	
20	Luíz Carlos	BRA	05/07/85	1		
93	Adam Maher	NED	20/07/93	5	(3)	1
6	Mehmet Güven		30/07/87	1	(3)	
35	Musa Çağıran		17/11/92	6		
10	Pape Alioune Ndiaye	SEN	27/10/90	8		1
17	Adrien Regattin	MAR	22/08/91	6	(2)	
27	Aminu Umar	NGA	06/03/95	3	(2)	1
	Forwards					
39	Thievy Bifouma	CGO	13/05/92	2		
14	Cheick Diabaté	MLI	25/04/88	1	(1)	1
24	Raul Rusescu	ROU	09/07/88	3	(4)	3
9	Pierre Webó	CMR	20/01/82	3		1

UEFA Europa League

Panathinaikos FC

No	Name	Nat	DoB	Aps	(s)	Gls
Goalkeepers						
15	Luke Steele	ENG	24/09/84	6		
Defenders						
3	Diamantis Chouchoumis		17/07/94	2		
78	Ousmane Coulibaly	MLI	09/07/89	4		
51	Ivan Ivanov	BUL	25/02/88	3	(2)	
4	Georgios Koutroumbis		10/02/91	5	(1)	
27	Giandomenico Mesto	ITA	25/05/82	3		
31	Rodrigo Moledo	BRA	27/10/87	6		
6	Christopher Samba	CGO	28/03/84	3	(1)	
Midfielders						
39	Anastasios Hatzigiovannis		31/05/97		(1)	
23	Niklas Hult	SWE	13/02/90	3		
24	Cristian Ledesma	ITA	24/09/82	3	(1)	
11	Sebastián Leto	ARG	30/08/86	1	(3)	
17	Robin Lod	FIN	17/04/93	5	(1)	
40	Paul-José M'Poku	COD	19/04/92	2	(2)	
19	Lucas Villafáñez	ARG	04/10/91	4	(1)	
22	Wakaso Mubarak	GHA	25/07/90	3		
10	Zeca		31/08/88	5		
Forwards						
9	Marcus Berg	SWE	17/08/86	3		1
8	Víctor Ibarbo	COL	19/05/90	4	(1)	2
20	Lautaro Rinaldi	ARG	30/12/93	1	(2)	

Qarabağ FK

No	Name	Nat	DoB	Aps	(s)	Gls
Goalkeepers						
13	Ibrahim Šehić	BIH	02/09/88	6		
Defenders						
25	Ansi Agolli	ALB	11/10/82	6		
21	Arif Daşdämirov		10/02/87	1		
55	Bädavi Hüseynov		11/07/91	4	(1)	
5	Maksim Medvedev		29/09/89	5		
18	İlqar Qurbanov		25/04/86	1		
14	Räşad F Sadıqov		16/06/82	5		1
32	Elvin Yunuszadä		22/08/92	2		
Midfielders						
20	Richard Almeida		20/03/89	6		
15	Rahid Ämirquliyev		01/09/89	4		1
99	Dani Quintana	ESP	08/03/87	6		1
22	Afran İsmayılov		08/10/88	1	(4)	
8	Míchel	ESP	08/11/85	3	(1)	2
10	Muarem Muarem	MKD	22/10/88	4	(2)	
2	Qara Qarayev		12/10/92	5		
Forwards						
17	Namiq Äläsgärov		03/02/95		(1)	
11	Mahir Mädätov		01/07/97		(3)	
71	Vüqar Nadirov		15/06/87		(1)	
6	Dino Ndlovu	RSA	15/02/90	5	(1)	1
9	Reynaldo	BRA	24/08/89	2	(3)	1

SK Rapid Wien

No	Name	Nat	DoB	Aps	(s)	Gls
Goalkeepers						
21	Tobias Knoflach		30/12/93	1		
1	Ján Novota	SVK	29/11/83	1		
30	Richard Strebinger		14/02/93	4		
Defenders						
24	Stephan Auer		11/01/91	1		
17	Christopher Dibon		02/11/90	5		
20	Maximilian Hofmann		07/08/93	2	(1)	
22	Mario Pavelic		19/09/93	3		
3	Christoph Schösswendter		16/07/88	4		
4	Thomas Schrammel		05/09/87	6		
6	Mario Sonnleitner		08/10/86	3		
38	Manuel Thurnwald		16/07/98	2		
39	Maximilian Wöber		04/02/98	2		
Midfielders						
15	Srdjan Grahovac	BIH	19/09/92	4	(1)	
11	Steffen Hofmann	GER	09/09/80		(2)	
16	Philipp Malicsek		03/06/97	1		
26	Ivan Močinić	CRO	30/04/93	4		
29	Thomas Murg		14/11/94	2	(1)	
10	Louis Schaub		29/12/94	5	(1)	1
7	Philipp Schobesberger		10/12/93		(1)	
8	Stefan Schwab		27/09/90	3		1
18	Tamás Szántó	HUN	18/02/96	1	(2)	
23	Arnór Ingvi Traustason	ISL	30/04/93	5		
Forwards						
9	Matej Jelić	CRO	05/11/90	1	(3)	1
34	Joelinton	BRA	14/08/96	5	(1)	2
13	Giorgi Kvilitaia	GEO	01/10/93		(5)	1
28	Tomi Correa	ESP	05/12/84	1		

PAOK FC

No	Name	Nat	DoB	Aps	(s)	Gls
Goalkeepers						
23	Željko Brkić	SRB	09/07/86	1		
71	Panagiotis Glykos		10/10/86	7		
Defenders						
15	José Ángel Crespo	ESP	09/02/87	5	(2)	
70	Stilianos Kitsiou		28/09/93	1		
3	Léo Matos	BRA	02/04/86	7		
4	Marin Leovac	CRO	07/08/88	7		
13	Stilianos Malezas		11/03/85	2	(1)	
44	Achilleas Pougouras		13/12/95	1		
31	Georgios Tzavellas		26/11/87	3		
43	Fernando Varela	CPV	26/11/87	7		
Midfielders						
21	Diego Biseswar	NED	08/03/88	2	(2)	
87	José Cañas	ESP	27/05/87	6		
16	Gojko Cimirot	BIH	19/12/92	8		
24	Garry Mendes Rodrigues	CPV	27/11/90	6		2
11	Pedro Henrique	BRA	16/06/90		(2)	
77	Dimitrios Pelkas		26/10/93	2	(2)	1
14	Facundo Pereyra	ARG	03/09/87		(2)	
28	Yevhen Shakhov	UKR	30/11/90	5	(3)	1
74	Amr Warda	EGY	17/09/93	1	(1)	
Forwards						
33	Stefanos Athanasiadis		24/12/88	5		2
10	Djalma	ANG	30/05/87	6	(1)	1
20	Efthimios Koulouris		06/03/96	2	(2)	
27	Ioannis Mystakidis		07/12/94	3	(2)	
7	Mame Baba Thiam	SEN	09/10/92	1	(4)	

Qäbälä FK

No	Name	Nat	DoB	Aps	(s)	Gls
Goalkeepers						
22	Dmytro Bezotosniy	UKR	15/11/83	6		
Defenders						
34	Ürfan Abbasov		14/10/92	3		
17	Mähämmäd Mirzäbäyov		16/11/90	4		
44	Rafael Santos	BRA	10/11/84	3		
20	Ricardinho	BRA	09/09/84	6		1
3	Vojislav Stanković	SRB	22/09/87	5		
15	Vitaliy Vernydub	UKR	17/10/87	6		
Midfielders						
4	Elvin Camalov		04/02/95		(2)	
32	Räşad Eyubov		03/12/92	2	(2)	
30	Petar Franjić	CRO	21/08/91		(4)	
21	Roman Hüseynov		26/12/97		(1)	
7	Nika Kvekveskiri	GEO	29/05/92	2	(1)	
11	Asif Mämmädov		05/08/86	3	(3)	
19	Filip Ozobić	CRO	08/04/91	6		
6	Räşad Ä Sadiqov		08/10/83	4		
27	Theo Weeks	LBR	19/01/90	4		
Forwards						
18	Bagaliy Dabo	FRA	27/07/88	3		1
10	Ruslan Qurbanov		12/09/91	4	(2)	2
9	Sergei Zenjov	EST	20/04/89	5		1

AS Roma

No	Name	Nat	DoB	Aps	(s)	Gls
Goalkeepers						
19	Alisson	BRA	02/10/92	10		
Defenders						
13	Bruno Peres	BRA	01/03/90	9		
33	Emerson	BRA	03/08/94	4	(1)	1
20	Federico Fazio		17/03/87	7	(1)	2
24	Alessandro Florenzi		11/03/91	1	(2)	1
3	Juan	BRA	10/06/91	7	(1)	
44	Kostas Manolas	GRE	14/06/91	7		
91	Riccardo Marchizza		26/03/98		(1)	
21	Mário Rui	POR	27/05/91	2		
2	Antonio Rüdiger	GER	03/03/93	4	(1)	
17	Moustapha Seck	SEN	23/02/96	1		
15	Thomas Vermaelen	BEL	14/11/85	2		
Midfielders						
16	Daniele De Rossi		24/07/83	5	(1)	1
30	Gerson	BRA	20/05/97	3	(3)	
4	Radja Nainggolan	BEL	04/05/88	7	(3)	1
5	Leandro Paredes	ARG	29/06/94	6	(2)	
8	Diego Perotti	ESP	26/07/88	4	(3)	1
6	Kevin Strootman	NED	13/02/90	7		2
Forwards						
9	Edin Džeko	BIH	17/03/86	5	(3)	8
92	Stephan El Shaarawy		27/10/92	6	(2)	2
7	Juan Manuel Iturbe	PAR	04/06/93	5	(1)	
11	Mohamed Salah	EGY	15/06/92	4	(2)	2
10	Francesco Totti		27/09/76	4	(2)	

FC Rostov

No	Name	Nat	DoB	Aps	(s)	Gls
Goalkeepers						
77	Nikita Medvedev		17/12/94	4		
Defenders						
44	César Navas	ESP	14/02/80	4		
4	Vladimir Granat		22/05/87	3		
30	Fedor Kudryashov		05/04/87	4		
23	Miha Mevlja	SVN	12/06/90	4		1
5	Denis Terentyev		13/08/92	1	(2)	
Midfielders						
19	Khoren Bayramyan		07/01/92	1		
84	Alexandru Gatcan	MDA	27/03/84	3		
2	Timofei Kalachev	BLR	01/05/81	3		
8	Igor Kireev		17/02/92		(1)	
16	Christian Noboa	ECU	08/04/85	4		1
28	Andrei Prepeliță	ROU	08/12/85	1	(2)	
89	Aleksandr Yerokhin		13/10/89	4		
Forwards						
20	Sardar Azmoun	IRN	01/01/95	1	(3)	1
11	Aleksandr Bukharov		12/03/85	3	(1)	1
33	Marko Dević	UKR	28/10/83		(2)	
7	Dmitri Poloz		12/07/91	4		2

FC Salzburg

No	Name	Nat	DoB	Aps	(s)	Gls
Goalkeepers						
1	Cican Stankovic		04/11/92	1		
33	Alexander Walke	GER	06/06/83	5		
Defenders						
5	Duje Ćaleta-Car	CRO	17/09/96	3		
22	Stefan Lainer		27/08/92	3	(2)	
3	Paulo Miranda	BRA	16/08/88	5		
6	Christian Schwegler	SUI	06/06/84	1		
17	Andreas Ulmer		30/10/85	5		
4	Dayot Upamecano	FRA	27/10/98	4		
47	Andre Wisdom	ENG	09/05/93	5		
Midfielders						
14	Valon Berisha	KOS	07/02/93	3		
27	Konrad Laimer		27/05/97	4		
10	Valentino Lazaro		24/03/96	6		
25	Josip Radošević	CRO	03/04/94	4	(1)	1
11	Marc Rzatkowski	GER	02/03/90	3	(1)	
8	Diadie Samassékou	MLI	11/01/96	2	(1)	
42	Xaver Schlager		28/09/97	1	(1)	1
94	Wanderson	BEL	07/10/94	1	(1)	
7	Reinhold Yabo	GER	10/02/92		(1)	
Forwards						
9	Munas Dabbur	ISR	14/05/92	2	(2)	1
21	Fredrik Gulbrandsen	NOR	10/09/92	3		
19	Hwang Hee-chan	KOR	26/01/96		(3)	2
26	Jonatan Soriano	ESP	24/09/85	3	(1)	1
18	Takumi Minamino	JPN	16/01/95	2	(2)	
13	Hannes Wolf		16/04/99		(1)	

FC Schalke 04

No	Name	Nat	DoB	Aps	(s)	Gls
Goalkeepers						
1	Ralf Fährmann		27/09/88	11		
34	Fabian Giefer		17/05/90	1		
Defenders						
15	Dennis Aogo		14/01/87	5		1
24	Holger Badstuber		13/03/89		(1)	
4	Benedikt Höwedes		29/02/88	11		1
3	Júnior Caiçara	BUL	27/04/89	4		1
20	Thilo Kehrer		21/09/96	5	(3)	
6	Sead Kolašinac	BIH	20/06/93	6	(2)	
29	Naldo	BRA	10/09/82	7		
31	Matija Nastasić	SRB	28/03/93	10		
14	Abdul Baba Rahman	GHA	02/07/94	5	(1)	1
27	Sascha Riether		23/03/83	3		
22	Atsuto Uchida	JPN	27/03/88		(1)	
Midfielders						
10	Nabil Bentaleb	ALG	24/11/94	7	(2)	2
2	Daniel Caligiuri	ITA	15/01/88	5		1
5	Johannes Geis		17/08/93	4	(1)	
8	Leon Goretzka		06/02/95	7	(2)	3
11	Yevhen Konoplyanka	UKR	29/09/89	4	(4)	2
7	Max Meyer		18/09/95	7	(2)	1
18	Sidney Sam		31/01/88		(1)	
21	Alessandro Schöpf	AUT	07/02/94	6	(4)	1
17	Benjamin Stambouli	FRA	13/08/90	8	(3)	
Forwards						
33	Donis Avdijaj	KOS	25/08/96	1	(2)	
19	Guido Burgstaller	AUT	29/04/89	5		3
13	Eric Maxim Choupo-Moting	CMR	23/03/89	4	(1)	
9	Franco Di Santo	ARG	07/04/89	1	(1)	
36	Breel Embolo	SUI	14/02/97	2		
25	Klaas-Jan Huntelaar	NED	12/08/83	1	(4)	1
16	Fabian Reese		29/11/97	1	(1)	
32	Bernard Tekpetey	GHA	03/09/97	1		

AS Saint-Étienne

No	Name	Nat	DoB	Aps	(s)	Gls
Goalkeepers						
30	Jessy Moulin		13/01/86	3		
16	Stéphane Ruffier		27/09/86	5		
Defenders						
32	Benjamin Karamoko	CIV	17/05/95	1		
4	Léo Lacroix	SUI	27/02/92	2	(1)	
12	Cheikh M'Bengue	SEN	23/07/88	2		
25	Kévin Malcuit		31/07/91	6		
24	Loïc Perrin		07/08/85	6		
19	Florentin Pogba	GUI	19/08/90	7		
3	Pierre-Yves Polomat		27/12/93	2		
2	Kévin Théophile-Catherine		28/10/89	6		
Midfielders						
6	Jérémy Clément		26/08/84	1		
8	Benjamin Corgnet		06/04/87		(1)	
7	Bryan Dabo		18/02/92	3		
21	Romain Hamouma		29/03/87	4	(1)	
18	Fabien Lemoine		16/03/87	1	(1)	
35	Arnaud Nordin		17/06/98	1	(1)	
5	Vincent Pajot		19/08/90	3	(4)	
11	Henri Saivet	SEN	26/10/90	7		
17	Ole Kristian Selnæs	NOR	07/07/94	4	(1)	
10	Oussama Tannane	MAR	23/03/94	3	(3)	1
14	Jordan Veretout		01/03/93	6	(1)	
Forwards						
27	Robert Berič	SVN	17/06/91	3	(2)	2
26	Jorginho	POR	21/09/95	1	(1)	
22	Kévin Monnet-Paquet		19/08/88	7		1
9	Nolan Roux		01/03/88	3	(3)	1
23	Alexander Søderlund	NOR	03/08/87	1	(3)	2

US Sassuolo Calcio

No	Name	Nat	DoB	Aps	(s)	Gls
Goalkeepers						
47	Andrea Consigli		27/01/87	5		
79	Gianluca Pegolo		25/03/81	1		
Defenders						
15	Francesco Acerbi		10/02/88	6		
5	Luca Antei		19/04/92	2		
28	Paolo Cannavaro		26/06/81	3		
23	Marcello Gazzola		03/04/85	2		
55	Timo Letschert	NED	25/05/93	2		
13	Federico Peluso		20/01/84	3		
20	Pol Lirola	ESP	13/08/97	6		1
Midfielders						
98	Claud Adjapong		06/05/98	2	(1)	
8	Davide Biondini		24/01/83	4		
32	Alfred Duncan	GHA	10/03/93		(1)	
4	Francesco Magnanelli		12/11/84	4	(1)	
22	Luca Mazzitelli		15/11/95	3	(1)	
7	Simone Missiroli		23/05/86	1	(1)	
6	Lorenzo Pellegrini		19/06/96	4	(1)	1
Forwards						
31	Simone Caputo		25/07/98	1	(1)	
11	Grégoire Defrel	FRA	17/06/91	4	(1)	2
33	Simone Franchini		30/03/98		(1)	
10	Alessandro Matri		19/08/84	3	(2)	
16	Matteo Politano		03/08/93	3	(2)	2
90	Antonino Ragusa		27/03/90	4	(2)	1
27	Federico Ricci		27/05/94	3	(3)	

FC Shakhtar Donetsk

No	Name	Nat	DoB	Aps	(s)	Gls
Goalkeepers						
30	Andriy Pyatov		28/06/84	6		
26	Mykyta Shevchenko		26/01/93	2		
Defenders						
2	Bohdan Butko		13/01/91	3		
31	Ismaily	BRA	11/01/90	6		
38	Serhiy Krivtsov		15/03/91	2		2
5	Olexandr Kucher		22/10/82	4		
25	Mykola Matviyenko		02/05/96	2		
18	Ivan Ordets		08/07/92	5	(1)	
44	Yaroslav Rakitskiy		03/08/89	5		
33	Darijo Srna	CRO	01/05/82	5		
Midfielders						
10	Bernard	BRA	08/09/92	5	(3)	2
9	Dentinho	BRA	19/01/89	3	(3)	1
8	Fred	BRA	05/03/93	5	(1)	1
74	Viktor Kovalenko		14/02/96	5	(1)	2
17	Maxym Malyshev		24/12/92	5	(3)	1
66	Márcio Azevedo	BRA	05/02/86		(1)	
11	Marlos	BRA	07/06/88	7		1
6	Taras Stepanenko		08/08/89	4	(2)	2
28	Taison	BRA	13/01/88	5	(3)	4
24	Vyacheslav Tankovskiy		16/08/95	1	(1)	
Forwards						
99	Gustavo Blanco	ARG	05/11/91	2		1
41	Andriy Boryachuk		23/04/96	2	(1)	
22	Eduardo	CRO	25/02/83		(3)	1
19	Facundo Ferreyra	ARG	14/03/91	4	(1)	3

UEFA Europa League

FC Slovan Liberec

No	Name	Nat	DoB	Aps	(s)	Gls
Goalkeepers						
19	Martin Dúbravka	SVK	15/01/89	5		
17	Václav Hladký		14/11/90	1		
Defenders						
26	Lukáš Bartošák		03/07/90	5	(1)	
5	Vladimír Coufal		22/08/92	6		
11	David Hovorka		07/08/93	4		
4	Ondřej Karafiát		01/12/94	3	(2)	
31	Martin Latka		28/09/84	2		
7	Milan Nitrianský		13/12/90		(2)	
29	Lukáš Pokorný		05/07/93	2		
Midfielders						
24	Daniel Bartl		05/07/89	3	(3)	
14	Ondřej Bláha		22/08/96		(1)	
2	Radim Breite		10/08/89	5		
28	Ubong Ekpai	NGA	17/10/95	2	(1)	
10	Zdeněk Folprecht		07/01/91	6		
18	Ilya Kubyshkin	RUS	12/01/96		(1)	
9	Jan Navrátil		13/04/90	1	(2)	
22	Petr Ševčík		04/05/94	4		1
16	Igor Súkenník	SVK	25/10/89	1	(1)	
6	Jan Sýkora		29/12/93	4	(1)	1
23	Egon Vůch		01/02/91	6		1
Forwards						
27	Milan Baroš		28/10/81	1	(1)	1
21	Nikolai Komlichenko	RUS	29/06/95	4	(1)	3
13	Miroslav Marković	SRB	04/11/89	1	(1)	

AC Sparta Praha

No	Name	Nat	DoB	Aps	(s)	Gls
Goalkeepers						
33	Tomáš Koubek		26/08/92	8		
Defenders						
25	Mario Holek		28/10/86	7	(1)	1
78	Matěj Hybš		03/01/93		(2)	
3	Michal Kadlec		13/12/84	8		
46	Milan Kadlec		27/02/95		(1)	
4	Vyacheslav Karavaev	RUS	20/05/95	8		1
47	Daniel Köstl		23/05/98		(1)	
2	Ondřej Mazuch		15/03/89	7		
26	Costa Nhamoinesu	ZIM	06/01/86	6		1
Midfielders						
17	Aleš Čermák		01/10/94	3		
9	Bořek Dočkal		30/09/88	6		
43	Václav Dudl		22/09/99		(4)	
14	Martin Frýdek		24/03/92	2		
45	Filip Havelka		21/01/98		(2)	
22	Daniel Holzer		18/08/95	4		
18	Tiémoko Konaté	CIV	19/04/90	1		
11	Lukáš Mareček		17/04/90	4	(1)	1
16	Michal Sáček		19/09/96	4	(1)	
23	Josef Šural		30/05/90	1	(1)	
6	Lukáš Vácha		13/05/89	2		
28	Ondřej Zahustel		18/06/91	1		
Forwards						
30	Lukáš Juliš		02/12/94	7	(1)	
77	Václav Kadlec		20/05/92	3		2
21	David Lafata		18/09/81	3	(4)	1
15	Néstor Albiach	ESP	18/08/92	2		
24	Matěj Pulkrab		23/05/97	1	(5)	1

FC Steaua Bucureşti

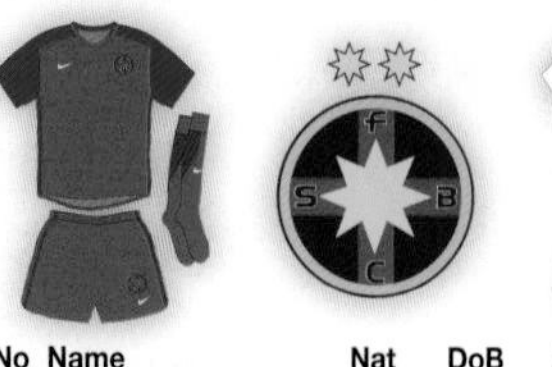

No	Name	Nat	DoB	Aps	(s)	Gls
Goalkeepers						
1	Florin Niță		03/07/87	6		
Defenders						
44	Gabriel Enache		18/08/90	3		
3	Bogdan Mitrea		29/09/87		(1)	
21	Wilfried Moke	COD	12/02/88	5		
15	Marko Momčilović	SRB	11/06/87	5		1
23	Ovidiu Popescu		27/02/94	1	(2)	
4	Gabriel Tamaş		09/11/83	6		1
13	Alin Toşca		14/03/92	6		
Midfielders						
20	Vlad Achim		07/04/89		(3)	1
19	Adnan Aganović	CRO	03/10/87	1	(1)	
55	Alexandru Bourceanu		24/04/85	5	(1)	
27	Fernando Boldrin	BRA	23/02/89	6		
17	Antonio Jakoliš	CRO	28/02/92		(3)	
11	Sulley Muniru	GHA	25/10/92	4		1
6	Mihai Pintilii		09/11/84	2		
77	Adrian Popa		24/07/88	6		
10	Florin Tănase		30/12/94		(2)	
29	William	BRA	15/12/91	6		
Forwards						
14	Bojan Golubović	SRB	22/08/83	4	(2)	1
9	Alexandru Tudorie		19/03/96		(2)	

Southampton FC

No	Name	Nat	DoB	Aps	(s)	Gls
Goalkeepers						
1	Fraser Forster		17/03/88	6		
Defenders						
21	Ryan Bertrand		05/08/89	1		
2	Cédric	POR	31/08/91	1		
15	Cuco Martina	CUW	25/09/89	5		
38	Sam McQueen		06/02/95	3		
33	Matt Targett		18/09/95	2		
17	Virgil van Dijk	NED	08/07/91	6		2
3	Maya Yoshida	JPN	24/08/88	6		
Midfielders						
19	Sofiane Boufal	MAR	17/09/93		(2)	
4	Jordy Clasie	NED	27/06/91	2		
8	Steven Davis	NIR	01/01/85	1	(3)	
42	Jake Hesketh		27/03/96	1		
23	Pierre Højbjerg	DEN	05/08/95	5	(1)	
22	Nathan Redmond		06/03/94	4	(1)	
14	Oriol Romeu	ESP	24/09/91	5	(1)	
39	Josh Sims		28/03/97	1		
11	Dušan Tadić	SRB	20/11/88	3	(2)	
16	James Ward-Prowse		01/11/94	5	(1)	
Forwards						
10	Charlie Austin		05/07/89	2	(3)	2
7	Shane Long	IRL	22/01/87	4	(1)	
9	Jay Rodriguez		29/07/89	3	(1)	1

R. Standard de Liège

No	Name	Nat	DoB	Aps	(s)	Gls
Goalkeepers						
1	Jean-François Gillet		31/05/79	3		
28	Guillaume Hubert		11/01/94	3		
Defenders						
27	Darwin Andrade	COL	11/02/91	2		
5	Elderson Echiéjilé	NGA	20/01/88	2	(1)	
32	Collins Fai	CMR	13/08/92	5		
24	Corentin Fiore		24/03/95	2	(2)	
2	Réginal Goreux	HAI	31/12/87	1		
34	Konstantinos Laifis	CYP	19/05/93	6		1
13	Alexander Scholz	DEN	24/10/92	6		
Midfielders						
44	Ibrahima Cissé		28/02/94	3		1
10	Jean-Luc Dompé	FRA	12/08/95	1	(1)	
7	Mathieu Dossevi	TOG	12/02/88	3		1
22	Edmilson Junior		19/08/94	6		1
21	Eyong Enoh	CMR	23/03/86	3	(1)	
30	Jonathan Legear		13/04/87		(1)	
8	Benito Raman		07/11/94	4	(1)	1
23	Adrien Trebel	FRA	03/03/91	6		
Forwards						
12	Beni Badibanga		19/02/96		(3)	
99	Ishak Belfodil	ALG	12/01/92	5		3
14	Isaac Mbenza		08/03/96	1	(5)	
70	Orlando Sá	POR	26/05/88	4	(1)	

Tottenham Hotspur FC

No	Name	Nat	DoB	Aps	(s)	Gls
Goalkeepers						
1	Hugo Lloris	FRA	26/12/86	2		
Defenders						
4	Toby Alderweireld	BEL	02/03/89	2		
33	Ben Davies	WAL	24/04/93	2		
15	Eric Dier		15/01/94	2		
5	Jan Vertonghen	BEL	24/04/87	1		
2	Kyle Walker		28/05/90	2		
Midfielders						
20	Dele Alli		11/04/96	2		
19	Mousa Dembélé	BEL	16/07/87	2		
23	Christian Eriksen	DEN	14/02/92	1	(1)	1
14	Georges-Kévin N'Koudou	FRA	13/02/95		(1)	
17	Moussa Sissoko	FRA	16/08/89	1		
12	Victor Wanyama	KEN	25/06/91	2		1
29	Harry Winks		02/02/96	1	(1)	
Forwards						
9	Vincent Janssen	NED	15/06/94		(1)	
10	Harry Kane		28/07/93	2		
7	Son Heung-min	KOR	08/07/92		(2)	

FC Viktoria Plzeň

No	Name	Nat	DoB	Aps	(s)	Gls
	Goalkeepers					
13	Petr Bolek		13/06/84	1		
1	Matúš Kozáčik	SVK	27/12/83	5		
	Defenders					
22	Jan Baránek		26/06/93	1		
2	Lukáš Hejda		09/03/90	6		
4	Roman Hubník		06/06/84	3		
8	David Limberský		06/10/83	4		
3	Aleš Matějů		03/06/96	4		
14	Radim Řezník		20/01/89	3		
	Midfielders					
7	Tomáš Hořava		29/05/88	4	(1)	2
25	Jakub Hromada	SVK	25/05/96	3	(1)	
17	Patrik Hrošovský	SVK	22/04/92	3		
20	Ergys Kaçe	ALB	08/07/93	4		
10	Jan Kopic		04/06/90	3	(2)	
19	Jan Kovařík		19/06/88	3	(1)	
11	Milan Petržela		19/06/83	5	(1)	
9	Martin Zeman		28/03/89	5		1
	Forwards					
23	Marek Bakoš	SVK	15/04/83	3	(3)	1
12	Michal Ďuriš	SVK	01/06/88	2	(2)	2
15	Michael Krmenčík		15/03/93	3	(3)	1
18	Tomáš Poznar		27/09/88	1	(3)	

BSC Young Boys

No	Name	Nat	DoB	Aps	(s)	Gls
	Goalkeepers					
18	Yvon Mvogo		06/06/94	6		
	Defenders					
80	Loris Benito		07/01/92	1	(1)	
8	Jan Lecjaks	CZE	09/08/90	5		
43	Kevin Mbabu		19/04/95		(1)	
24	Kasim Nuhu	GHA	22/06/95	4		
32	Linus Obexer		05/06/97	1		
21	Alain Rochat		01/02/83	1		
23	Scott Sutter		13/05/86	6		
5	Steve von Bergen		10/06/83	6		
	Midfielders					
51	Michel Aebischer		06/01/97	1	(1)	
6	Leonardo Bertone		14/03/94	4	(2)	
34	Kwadwo Duah		24/02/97		(5)	
10	Yoric Ravet	FRA	12/09/89	4		
35	Sékou Sanogo	CIV	05/05/89	4		
19	Thorsten Schick	AUT	19/05/90	4	(2)	1
7	Miralem Sulejmani	SRB	05/12/88	3		
28	Denis Zakaria		20/11/96	5		
	Forwards					
11	Michael Frey		19/07/94	2	(4)	1
9	Alexander Gerndt	SWE	14/07/86	1	(1)	
99	Guillaume Hoarau	FRA	05/03/84	4		5
31	Yuya Kubo	JPN	24/12/93	4		

FC Zorya Luhansk

No	Name	Nat	DoB	Aps	(s)	Gls
	Goalkeepers					
91	Ihor Levchenko		23/02/91	1		
1	Olexiy Shevchenko		24/02/92	5		
	Defenders					
6	Mykyta Kamenyuka		03/06/85	4	(1)	
39	Yevhen Opanasenko		25/08/90	2	(2)	
12	Rafael Forster	BRA	23/07/90	6		1
3	Mikhail Sivakov	BLR	16/01/88	5		
95	Eduard Sobol		20/04/95	5		
2	Artem Sukhovskiy		06/12/92	1		
	Midfielders					
4	Ihor Chaikovskiy		07/10/91	5		
24	Dmytro Grechishkin		22/09/91	5	(1)	1
5	Artem Hordiyenko		04/03/91	1	(2)	
20	Olexandr Karavayev		02/06/92	6		
8	Ihor Kharatin		02/02/95	3	(1)	
10	Jaba Lipartia	GEO	16/11/87	1	(2)	
22	Željko Ljubenović	SRB	09/07/81	4	(1)	
7	Ivan Petryak		13/03/94	6		
	Forwards					
21	Denys Bezborodko		31/05/94	1		
42	Emmanuel Bonaventure	NGA	15/11/97	1	(2)	
9	Vladyslav Kulach		07/05/93	4	(1)	
11	Paulinho	BRA	29/05/93		(5)	

Villarreal CF

No	Name	Nat	DoB	Aps	(s)	Gls
	Goalkeepers					
13	Andrés Fernández		17/12/86	5		
1	Sergio Asenjo		28/06/89	3		
	Defenders					
12	Álvaro González		08/01/90	4	(1)	
23	Daniele Bonera	ITA	31/05/81	3		
11	Jaume Costa		18/03/88	2		
3	José Ángel		05/09/89	6		
2	Mario Gaspar		24/11/90	2		
5	Mateo Musacchio	ARG	26/08/90	4		
22	Antonio Rukavina	SRB	26/01/84	6		
6	Víctor Ruiz		25/01/89	5		
	Midfielders					
21	Bruno Soriano		12/06/84	8		1
7	Denis Cheryshev	RUS	26/12/90	5	(1)	
8	Jonathan dos Santos	MEX	26/04/90	7	(1)	1
4	Alfred N'Diaye	SEN	06/03/90	3		1
16	Rodri Hernández		22/06/96	2	(2)	1
19	Samu Castillejo		18/01/95	2	(4)	
20	Roberto Soriano	ITA	08/02/91	2	(3)	
14	Manu Trigueros		17/10/91	3		1
	Forwards					
15	Adrián López		08/01/88		(2)	
17	Cédric Bakambu	COD	11/04/91	4	(3)	
24	Rafael Borré	COL	15/09/95	5	(2)	2
10	Pato	BRA	02/09/89	4	(1)	2
18	Nicola Sansone	ITA	10/09/91	2	(4)	1
9	Roberto Soldado		27/05/85	1		

FC Zenit

No	Name	Nat	DoB	Aps	(s)	Gls
	Goalkeepers					
41	Mikhail Kerzhakov		28/01/87	1		
1	Yuri Lodygin		26/05/90	7		
	Defenders					
2	Aleksandr Anyukov		28/09/82	4		
4	Domenico Criscito	ITA	30/12/86	7		1
60	Branislav Ivanović	SRB	22/02/84	1		
6	Nicolas Lombaerts	BEL	20/03/85	4	(1)	
13	Luís Neto	POR	26/05/88	7		
3	Ivan Novoseltsev		25/08/91	2	(1)	
19	Igor Smolnikov		08/08/88	2		
81	Yuri Zhirkov		20/08/83	5	(1)	
	Midfielders					
7	Giuliano	BRA	31/05/90	8		8
33	Hernâni	BRA	27/03/94	1		
21	Javi García	ESP	08/02/87	7		
29	Róbert Mak	SVK	08/03/91	5	(3)	1
8	Maurício	BRA	21/10/88	2	(3)	1
17	Oleg Shatov		29/07/90	3	(1)	1
28	Axel Witsel	BEL	12/01/89	6		
14	Artur Yusupov		01/09/89		(2)	
	Forwards					
10	Danny	POR	07/08/83	1	(1)	
77	Luka Djordjević	MNE	09/07/94	2	(4)	1
22	Artem Dzyuba		22/08/88	5	(1)	1
11	Aleksandr Kerzhakov		27/11/82	2	(1)	1
9	Aleksandr Kokorin		19/03/91	6	(2)	4

FC Zürich

No	Name	Nat	DoB	Aps	(s)	Gls
	Goalkeepers					
1	Andris Vaņins	LVA	30/04/80	6		
	Defenders					
22	Umaru Bangura	SLE	07/10/87	3		
26	Cédric Brunner		17/02/94	6		
25	Ivan Kecojević	MNE	10/04/88	6		
13	Alain Nef		06/02/82	6		
28	Nicolas Stettler		28/04/96		(1)	
41	Kay Voser		04/01/87	6		
	Midfielders					
15	Oliver Buff		03/08/92	3		
20	Burim Kukeli	ALB	16/01/84	5		
8	Antonio Marchesano		18/01/91	1	(1)	
34	Roberto Rodriguez		28/07/90	4	(2)	1
29	Sangoné Sarr	SEN	07/07/92	6		
27	Marco Schönbächler		11/01/90	2	(4)	1
7	Adrian Winter		08/07/86	4	(2)	
37	Gilles Yapi Yapo	CIV	30/01/82	1	(2)	
	Forwards					
21	Džengis Čavuševič	SVN	26/11/87	3	(2)	1
4	Moussa Koné	SEN	30/12/96	3	(2)	1
11	Armando Sadiku	ALB	27/05/91	1	(2)	1

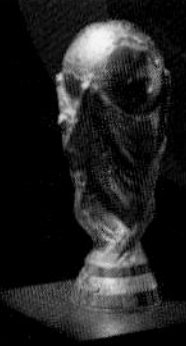

2018 FIFA WORLD CUP

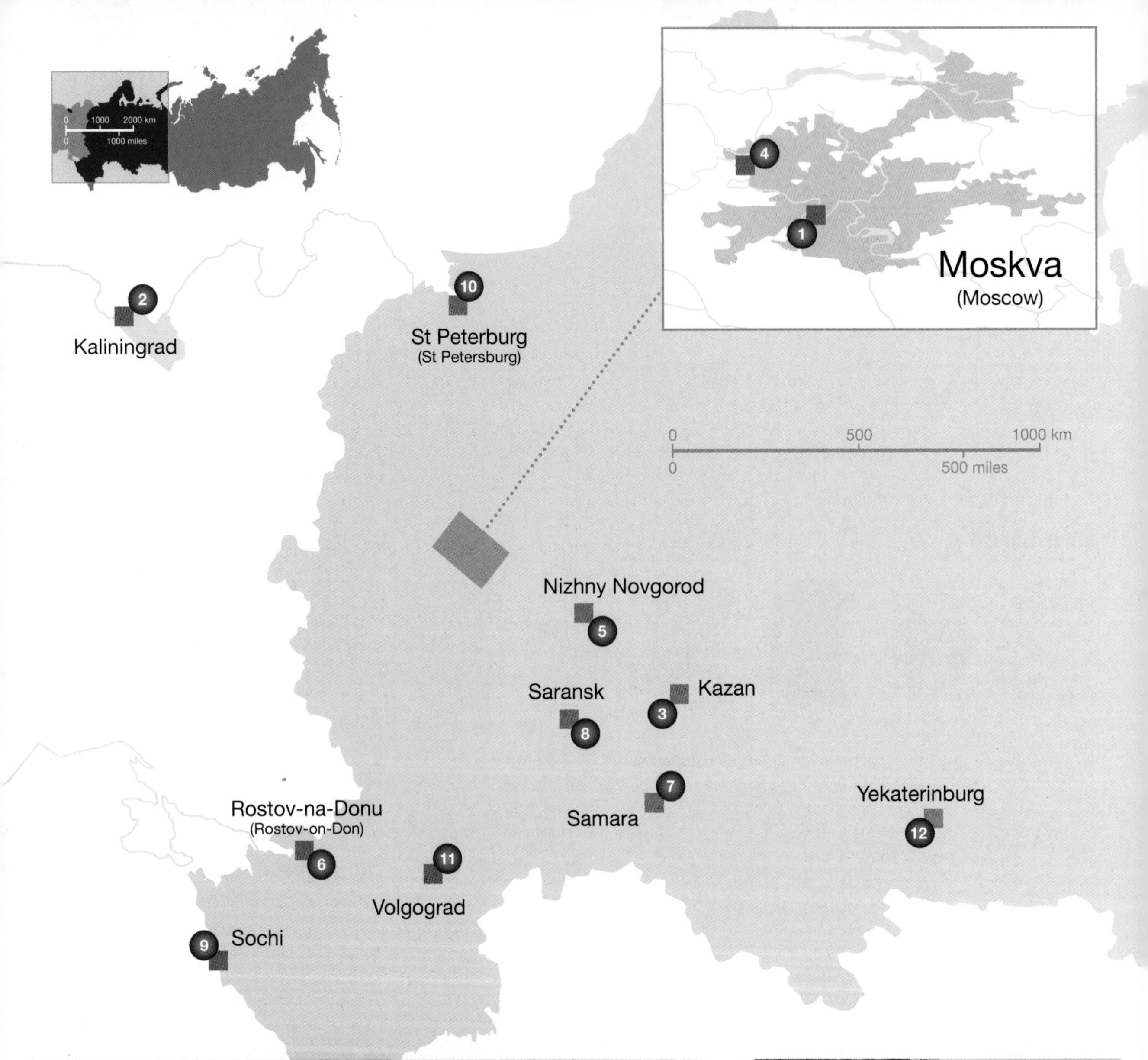

0 1000 2000 km
0 1000 miles
Moskva
(Moscow)
1
4
2
Kaliningrad
10
St Peterburg
(St Petersburg)
0 500 1000 km
0 500 miles
Nizhny Novgorod
5
Saransk
8
Kazan
3
7
Samara
Yekaterinburg
12
Rostov-na-Donu
(Rostov-on-Don)
6
11
Volgograd
9
Sochi

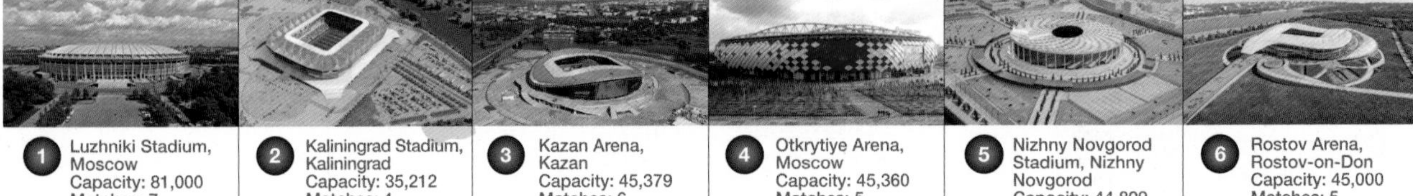

1 Luzhniki Stadium, Moscow
Capacity: 81,000
Matches: 7

2 Kaliningrad Stadium, Kaliningrad
Capacity: 35,212
Matches: 4

3 Kazan Arena, Kazan
Capacity: 45,379
Matches: 6

4 Otkrytiye Arena, Moscow
Capacity: 45,360
Matches: 5

5 Nizhny Novgorod Stadium, Nizhny Novgorod
Capacity: 44,899
Matches: 6

6 Rostov Arena, Rostov-on-Don
Capacity: 45,000
Matches: 5

RUSSIA

Match schedule

Group A

Date	Venue	Teams	Time	Match no.
14/06/18	Moscow / Luzhniki	Russia - A2	16:00	1
15/06/18	Yekaterinburg	A3 - A4	13:00	2
19/06/18	St Petersburg	Russia - A3	19:00	17
20/06/18	Rostov-on-Don	A4 - A2	16:00	18
25/06/18	Samara	A4 - Russia	15:00	33
25/06/18	Volgograd	A2 - A3	15:00	34

Group B

Date	Venue	Teams	Time	Match no.
15/06/18	St Petersburg	B3 - B4	16:00	4
15/06/18	Sochi	B1 - B2	19:00	3
20/06/18	Moscow / Luzhniki	B1 - B3	13:00	19
20/06/18	Kazan	B4 - B2	19:00	20
25/06/18	Saransk	B4 - B1	19:00	35
25/06/18	Kaliningrad	B2 - B3	19:00	36

Group C

Date	Venue	Teams	Time	Match no.
16/06/18	Kazan	C1 - C2	11:00	5
16/06/18	Saransk	C3 - C4	17:00	6
21/06/18	Yekaterinburg	C1 - C3	13:00	21
21/06/18	Samara	C4 - C2	16:00	22
26/06/18	Moscow / Luzhniki	C4 - C1	15:00	37
26/06/18	Sochi	C2 - C3	15:00	38

Group D

Date	Venue	Teams	Time	Match no.
16/06/18	Moscow / Otkrytiye	D1 - D2	14:00	7
16/06/18	Kaliningrad	D3 - D4	20:00	8
21/06/18	Nizhny Novgorod	D1 - D3	19:00	23
22/06/18	Volgograd	D4 - D2	16:00	24
26/06/18	St Petersburg	D4 - D1	19:00	39
26/06/18	Rostov-on-Don	D2 - D3	19:00	40

Group E

Date	Venue	Teams	Time	Match no.
17/06/18	Samara	E3 - E4	13:00	10
17/06/18	Rostov-on-Don	E1 - E2	19:00	9
22/06/18	St Petersburg	E1 - E3	13:00	25
22/06/18	Kaliningrad	E4 - E2	19:00	26
27/06/18	Moscow / Otkrytiye	E4 - E1	19:00	41
27/06/18	Nizhny Novgorod	E2 - E3	19:00	42

Group F

Date	Venue	Teams	Time	Match no.
17/06/18	Moscow / Luzhniki	F1 - F2	16:00	11
18/06/18	Nizhny Novgorod	F3 - F4	13:00	12
23/06/18	Sochi	F1 - F3	16:00	27
23/06/18	Rostov-on-Don	F4 - F2	19:00	28
27/06/18	Kazan	F4 - F1	15:00	43
27/06/18	Yekaterinburg	F2 - F3	15:00	44

Group G

Date	Venue	Teams	Time	Match no.
18/06/18	Sochi	G1 - G2	16:00	13
18/06/18	Volgograd	G3 - G4	19:00	14
23/06/18	Moscow / Otkrytiye	G1 - G3	13:00	29
24/06/18	Nizhny Novgorod	G4 - G2	13:00	30
28/06/18	Kaliningrad	G4 - G1	19:00	45
28/06/18	Saransk	G2 - G3	19:00	46

Group H

Date	Venue	Teams	Time	Match no.
19/06/18	Moscow / Otkrytiye	H1 - H2	13:00	15
19/06/18	Saransk	H3 - H4	16:00	16
24/06/18	Yekaterinburg	H4 - H2	16:00	32
24/06/18	Kazan	H1 - H3	19:00	31
28/06/18	Volgograd	H4 - H1	15:00	47
28/06/18	Samara	H2 - H3	15:00	48

Round of 16

Date	Venue	Teams	Time	Match no.
30/06/18	Kazan	Winner Group C - Runner-up Group D	15:00	50
30/06/18	Sochi	Winner Group A - Runner-up Group B	19:00	49
01/07/18	Moscow / Luzhniki	Winner Group B - Runner-up Group A	15:00	51
01/07/18	Nizhny Novgorod	Winner Group D - Runner-up Group C	19:00	52
02/07/18	Samara	Winner Group E - Runner-up Group F	15:00	53
02/07/18	Rostov-on-Don	Winner Group G - Runner-up Group H	19:00	54
03/07/18	St Petersburg	Winner Group F - Runner-up Group E	15:00	55
03/07/18	Moscow / Otkrytiye	Winner Group H - Runner-up Group G	19:00	56

Quarter-finals

Date	Venue	Teams	Time	Match no.
06/07/18	Nizhny Novgorod	Winner 49 - Winner 50	15:00	57
06/07/18	Kazan	Winner 53 - Winner 54	19:00	58
07/07/18	Samara	Winner 55 - Winner 56	15:00	60
07/07/18	Sochi	Winner 51 - Winner 52	19:00	59

Semi-finals

Date	Venue	Teams	Time	Match no.
10/07/18	St Petersburg	Winner 57 - Winner 58	19:00	61
11/07/18	Moscow / Luzhniki	Winner 59 - Winner 60	19:00	62

Third place play-off

Date	Venue	Teams	Time	Match no.
14/07/18	St Petersburg	Loser 61 - Loser 62	15:00	63

Final

Date	Venue	Teams	Time	Match no.
15/07/18	Moscow / Luzhniki	Winner 61 - Winner 62	16:00	64

NB All kick-off times are CET (subtract one hour for BST).

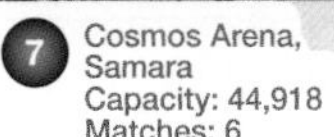

7 Cosmos Arena, Samara
Capacity: 44,918
Matches: 6

8 Mordovia Arena, Saransk
Capacity: 45,015
Matches: 4

9 Fisht Olympic Stadium, Sochi
Capacity: 47,659
Matches: 6

10 Krestovsky Stadium, St Petersburg
68,134
Matches: 7

11 Volgograd Arena, Volgograd
Capacity: 45,568
Matches: 4

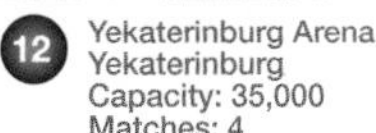

12 Yekaterinburg Arena, Yekaterinburg
Capacity: 35,000
Matches: 4

Fifty-four European teams battle for 13 qualifying places

Eleven nations unbeaten after six matchdays

Maximum points for Germany and Switzerland

Plots thicken on road to Russia

With just 13 places at the 2018 FIFA World Cup finals available to the 54 teams participating in the European qualifying zone – as opposed to the 23 on offer to 53 in UEFA EURO 2016 qualification – the battle to line up alongside hosts Russia and 18 other countries from around the world was always going to be keenly fought with little margin for error.

After six of the ten matchdays – with two double-header Weeks of Football to come in the early autumn – no European teams had guaranteed their place at the final tournament. It was all but certain, however, that Germany would be there in Russia to defend the trophy they had lifted in Brazil, Joachim Löw's side having won all of their matches in Group C with 27 goals scored – the largest number in any of the nine groups – and just one conceded.

Switzerland, in Group B, were the only other team to have maximum points on the board as the qualifying competition paused for its summer break, but Vladimir Petković's side had European champions Portugal, spearheaded by the remarkable Cristiano Ronaldo, breathing down their neck, so their invitation to the global party in June and July 2018 was anything but assured.

Germany and Switzerland were two of 11 teams yet to be beaten with 60 per cent of their qualifying programme completed. Those included the two qualifying specialists in Group G, Spain and Italy, whose only dropped points came against each other, in Turin (1-1), and Group E front-runners Poland, who, driven by the prolific goalscoring of Robert Lewandowski, boasted the biggest lead of any section – six points – as they sought to reach the World Cup finals for the first time since 2006.

Robert Lewandowski (No9) towers above the Romania defence to score one of his 11 qualifying goals for Group E leaders Poland

There were three undefeated teams in a tightly-contested Group D, with Serbia and the Republic of Ireland both four points clear of UEFA EURO 2016 semi-finalists Wales, while England, who alone kept clean sheets in their first five fixtures, headed Group F by two points and Belgium, with just two points dropped, ran in 24 goals to open up a four-point lead over another unbeaten team, Greece, in Group H.

Of the countries yet to appear at the World Cup, Iceland, the surprise package of the European finals in France, were the most favourably placed, level on points with Group I leaders Croatia, while Montenegro stood second in Group E. On the other hand, the Netherlands, World Cup runners-up in 2010 and bronze medalists in 2014 but absent altogether from UEFA EURO 2016, risked a second successive qualifying failure as they sat third three points in arrears of both Sweden and France in Group A, which, like every other section, was fascinatingly poised with four matchdays to go.

Group A

France, the UEFA EURO 2016 runners-up, appeared to be making serene progress towards their sixth successive World Cup until the 93rd minute of their sixth match, away to Sweden, when goalkeeper Hugo Lloris miscued a clearance that was returned into his net from the centre circle, with a magnificently precise first-time strike, by Swedish striker Ola Toivonen. That spectacular goal, the third of an absorbing encounter at the Friends Arena following first-half stunners from Olivier Giroud and Jimmy Durmaz, gave the hosts a 2-1 victory that not only put them level with Didier Deschamps' star-studded side – instead of keeping them three points in arrears – but also placed them on top of the table on goal difference.

It was the second meeting of the two teams and a mirror image of the first, at the Stade de France in November, when Les Bleus had come from behind – after a superb Emil Forsberg free-kick – thanks to Dimitri Payet, who provided the assist for Paul Pogba's equalising header before coolly scoring the winner himself following a handling error from Robin Olsen. Sweden's new No1 had actually been the team's star performer in their opening fixture, a 1-1 draw against the Netherlands, and he also kept clean sheets in their other three games as they defeated Luxembourg 1-0 away before comprehensively dismantling Bulgaria (3-0) and Belarus (4-0) at home, enabling new coach Jan Andersson to feel confident about steering Sweden to their first World Cup appearance in 12 years.

After starting with a goalless draw in Belarus, where they missed countless chances, France reeled off four successive wins, the highlight an impressive 1-0 victory over the Netherlands in Amsterdam secured by a long-range Pogba drive. That result induced a degree of disquiet in the Dutch camp, and when the Oranje lost again, 2-0 in Bulgaria, coach Danny Blind was given the sack, paving the way for Dick Advocaat to return for a third spell. His first game was a routine 5-0 home win over Luxembourg, which, allied with Sweden's last-gasp win against France, put the Netherlands back in the qualifying mix ahead of a huge encounter at the Stade de France on 31 August.

Group B

Portugal went into their first competitive game as European champions without Cristiano Ronaldo, their captain still nursing the injury he sustained against France in the UEFA EURO 2016 final, and

Ola Toivonen celebrates his spectacular last-gasp winner for Sweden at home to France

it did not go well for Fernando Santos's side as they lost 2-0 to Switzerland in Basel. It was the first defeat in 15 competitive games for the Portugal coach but a magnificent start to Switzerland's bid to reach a fourth successive World Cup, first-half goals from Breel Embolo – a follow-up header after a Ricardo Rodriguez free-kick had struck the bar – and Admir Mehemdi – a brilliant curling shot into the top corner – putting Vladimir Petković's side firmly in the Group B driving seat.

Over the next five matchdays Switzerland and Portugal – with Ronaldo back on board – would win all of their fixtures, effectively eliminating the other four teams. Hungary, who had topped Portugal's group at UEFA EURO 2016, seemed discharged of confidence after drawing 0-0 in the Faroe Islands, and a late goal conceded to Switzerland in Budapest on matchday two – with Valentin Stocker scrambling home the winner a minute after coming off the bench – left Bernd Storck's side with an uphill struggle that they all but abandoned when Andorra, astonishingly, beat them 1-0 in June.

It was the second positive result in succession for the Pyrenean minnows, their 0-0 draw at home to the Faroe Islands having ended a run of 58 consecutive qualifying defeats. It even lifted them off the bottom of the table, where they were replaced by a Latvia side on a run of five successive losses, including two against Portugal, the second of which, in Riga, featured Ronaldo's 10th and 11th goals of the campaign. Those were two simple close-range efforts, but the four finishes with which the Real Madrid maestro found the net in a 6-0 win at home to Andorra in September were all out of the top drawer. He also weighed in with a couple of beauties in the 3-0 home win over Hungary, although it was his new strike partner André Silva who stole the show in the Faroe Islands, scoring a first-half hat-trick on only his second international start.

While Portugal went gung-ho, Switzerland collected their points more pragmatically, with just seven goals – from seven different scorers – sufficing to see off Andorra, Latvia and the Faroe Islands (twice). With a three-point advantage over Portugal but a vastly inferior goal difference, Switzerland's hopes of remaining in top spot looked likely to depend on avoiding defeat in their final fixture, a 10 October showdown in Lisbon's Estádio da Luz.

Group C

With only two World Cup qualifying defeats in their history, reigning champions Germany never looked likely to be over-troubled in a group containing the Czech Republic, Northern Ireland, Norway, Azerbaijan and San Marino as they sought to defend their trophy in Russia. And so it proved with six straightforward wins out of six for Joachim Löw's side and a barrage of goals for good measure, albeit the majority of them against minnows San Marino. The only player to score against them was a player based in Germany, Erzgebirge Aue midfielder Dimitrij Nazarov, and that was just a consolation in Azerbaijan's 4-1 home defeat.

Thomas Müller took his tally of World Cup goals to 19 (out of 37 in total for Germany) by scoring in that game to add to doubles in each of his team's opening 3-0 victories against Norway in Oslo and the Czech Republic in Hamburg. Northern Ireland looked set for a pounding when they conceded two early goals to the world champions in Hanover on matchday three, but to their credit Michael O'Neill's side kept the final scoreline at 2-0 and, suitably buoyed, went on to win their next three matches without conceding as they overcame previously unbeaten Azerbaijan 4-0 at Windsor Park, defeated Norway 2-0 at the same venue and then, in June, snatched a crucial added-time winner in Baku that kept them in second place with a four-point cushion over the third-placed Czechs.

After six matches the only goals conceded by Northern Ireland had been the two scored by Germany's Julian Draxler and Sami Khedira. They kicked off their campaign with a goalless draw in Prague against Karel Jarolím's new-look Czech side, who took until matchday four to record their first goal, scored 11 minutes into his debut by Viktoria Plzeň striker Michael Krmenčík. With Slavia Praha's Jaromír Zmrhal also scoring his first international goal – from a peach of a pass by Bořek Dočkal – Jarolím's men had their first win, 2-1 at home to Norway. The return fixture in Oslo ended 1-1, with Norway, now coached by ex-Sweden and Iceland boss Lars Lagerbäck, missing a golden opportunity to reverse the Prague scoreline when Tarik Elyounoussi squandered a late two-on-one breakaway chance. It was in the same Ullevaal Stadion eight months earlier that Norway had conceded an equalising goal to San Marino – the minnows' first in an away qualifier for 15 years.

Group D

There was no clear favourite at the outset of Group D, with Wales, the seeded side, one of three UEFA EURO 2016 participants alongside Austria and the Republic of Ireland, and Serbia, a team of talented individuals now under the experienced guidance of Slavoljub Muslin, the darkest of dark horses.

The tightness of the section was evident from the proliferation of drawn matches. When all three June fixtures finished level, it meant that half of the 18 games had ended with the points shared. Wales, who opened their campaign by beating Moldova 4-0 at home, were involved in five of those draws and led in four of them, including both games against Serbia, before Aleksandar Mitrović equalised. Although holding Ireland 0-0 in Dublin and Serbia 1-1 in Belgrade were not bad results in themselves, Chris Coleman's European semi-finalists found themselves four points behind both those opponents with just four games remaining.

Austria, too, had the same amount of ground to make up, their campaign having hit the rocks with successive autumn defeats against Serbia in Belgrade and Ireland in Vienna. The first of those two encounters was one of the most exciting of the whole European qualifying campaign, with Muslin's men twice going in front through Mitrović but twice having that lead cancelled out before man of the match Dušan Tadić, who had set up the first two Serbia goals, crowned a majestic display by scoring their decisive third in a crucial 3-2 win.

A breakaway goal from James McClean, who had already scored twice in a 3-1 win in Moldova, gave Ireland a 1-0 victory in Vienna, but having already drawn in Belgrade on matchday one – with first international goals for Jeff Hendrick and Daryl Murphy – then claimed a fortuitous 1-0 home win against Georgia – with skipper Séamus Coleman's first goal for his country – Martin O'Neill's team could manage only home draws against Wales (0-0) – in which Coleman suffered a horrendous leg break – and Austria (1-1), which, while maintaining their unbeaten record, left them second on goal difference behind Serbia, the next visitors to Dublin in early September.

Group E

Poland scored the first goal of the European qualifying campaign, through Bartosz Kapustka, but although they surrendered a two-goal lead in that opening fixture against Kazakhstan to draw 2-2, those would be the only points surrendered by Adam Nawałka's lively side in their first six qualifiers, and with all of their group rivals dropping important points in unlikely places, Poland's five successive wins lifted them into an almost unassailable six-point lead at the Group E summit.

Aleksandar Mitrović slots home to bring Serbia level against Wales in Belgrade

The goals of Robert Lewandowski, bidding to participate at his first World Cup, were the key to their success, the Bayern München striker carrying on where he had left off in the qualifying competition for UEFA EURO 2016 to find the net in every one of Poland's opening six matches, scoring 11 goals in total including hat-tricks at home to Romania and Denmark. That made it a staggering 11 successive European Qualifiers in which Lewandowski had been on target, accumulating 20 goals during that run. The two hat-tricks were huge, as indeed was his double against Romania in Bucharest which came after he had been struck by a flare thrown from the crowd. But his most important goal was arguably the 95th-minute header that he powered home on matchday three in Warsaw against Armenia, giving Poland a 2-1 win barely a minute after they had survived a massive scare at the other end when Aras Özbiliz broke through one-on-one but swept his shot wastefully wide.

With just six points from six games, both Armenia and goal-shy Romania, under new German coach Christoph Daum, appeared to have too much to do even to make the play-offs. As they both lost in June, Denmark and Montenegro both won to move on to ten points and seemingly into a duel for second place. Montenegro, having lost 3-2 to Armenia in Yerevan with the last kick of the game, avenged that defeat with a fine 4-1 win in Podgorica thanks to a brilliant treble from Stevan Jovetić – the first hat-trick in the team's history – while Denmark won 3-1 in Kazakhstan to add to their earlier 4-1 victory over the same opponents in Copenhagen. Åge Hareide's team had lost at home to Montenegro in the autumn, however, going down to a single Fatos Bećiraj goal beautifully crafted by Jovetić – a result they would possibly need to reverse on their visit to Podgorica in October in order to reach the play-offs.

Group F

Undefeated in each of their previous three qualifying campaigns, England managed to prolong that run after six matches on the road to the 2018 World Cup despite the turbulence caused by the departure of their new coach, Sam Allardyce, after just one game and his replacement – after an initial caretaker period – by Under-21s boss Gareth Southgate. With four games to go, England led second-placed Slovakia by two points and third-placed Slovenia by three, while Scotland, still kicking themselves for allowing the Auld Enemy

New England coach Gareth Southgate congratulates his match-saving skipper Harry Kane after the final whistle of a 2-2 draw with Scotland in Glasgow

to snatch a late equaliser in a 2-2 draw at Hampden, were a worrying six points off the pace in fourth.

The one game under Allardyce – before he was forced to stand down over some ill-advised comments caught on camera by a national newspaper – had the potential to be England's most important of all as a 95th-minute winner from Adam Lallana, who had never previously scored in 26 internationals, earned a 1-0 win over Slovakia in Trnava. Southgate's first and last qualifiers in temporary charge brought comfortable, if not entirely convincing, home wins over Malta (2-0) and Scotland (3-0), but he had goalkeeper Joe Hart to thank for a goalless draw against Slovenia in Ljubljana.

Recalled veteran striker Jermain Defoe scored on his return to international action as England posted their fifth straight clean sheet with a 2-0 home win over Lithuania in Southgate's first qualifier as permanent coach, and it looked as if the gates to Russia had opened wide for the Three Lions when Alex Oxlade-Chamberlain came off the bench to put them 1-0 up in Glasgow, but that was before an extraordinary sequence of events late in the game. Leigh Griffiths, the Celtic striker who had never scored for his country, beat Hart with a couple of superb free-kicks to seemingly snatch victory from the jaws of defeat for a Scotland side that had also won their previous home game, against Slovenia, with a late goal from Chris Martin. However, panic in the Scotland defence allowed Harry Kane to steal in and volley home Raheem Sterling's cross with virtually the last kick of the game and deny Gordon Strachan's team a famous victory.

Slovakia responded superbly to defeats in their opening two fixtures – they lost 1-0 in Slovenia after conceding that late heartbreaker against England – by chalking up four successive victories, the first of them 3-0 in Trnava against Scotland. Slovenia, meanwhile, kept a third home clean sheet with a 2-0 win in Ljubljana against point-less Malta to stay in touch with the top two, both of whom they were due to visit in the early autumn.

Group G

Spain, who had not lost a World Cup qualifier since 1993, and Italy, undefeated in any qualifying fixture since September 2006, went into battle eager to prolong those impressive sequences but also, more importantly, to secure Group G's one automatic qualifying spot for the 2018 finals. The last major tournament either of the two countries had failed to qualify for was EURO '92 in Sweden, from which they were both absent, so although both nations embarked on the road to Russia with new coaches, Julen Lopetegui for Spain and Giampiero Ventura for Italy, the chances of the other four teams in the section – Albania, Israel, FYR Macedonia and Liechtenstein – getting a look-in seemed pretty remote from the outset.

Sure enough, after six matchdays the top two had created a seven-point gap between themselves and the rest. Furthermore, the two southern European superpowers were locked together on 16 points, with Spain topping the table on goal difference. The first of the two head-to-head encounters, in Turin, on matchday two, ended 1-1 – a good result on paper for Spain although they left the field frustrated after having the better of the contest against the side that had ended their eight-year reign as European champions at UEFA EURO 2016. Vitolo put the visitors ahead after an uncharacteristic faux pas from Italy captain Gianluigi Buffon, who raced out of his goal to intercept a through-ball and failed to make contact, but a foul by Spain skipper Sergio Ramos gave the Azzurri a late penalty, which Daniele De Rossi expertly converted.

The two front-runners did not err elsewhere, although both teams made hard work of beating FYR Macedonia in Skopje, Italy prevailing 3-2 only after a 92nd-minute winner from Ciro Immobile while Spain appeared to be coasting after going 2-0 up until a brilliant solo goal from Stefan Ristovski reduced the deficit and induced some late anxiety for Lopetegui's team. Immobile, with five goals, and Andrea Belotti, with four, appeared to have formed an excellent new forward partnership for Italy, while Diego Costa, also on five goals, finally established himself as Spain's main man in attack.

In the scrap for the minor placings Albania and Israel traded 3-0 away wins, with both of them beating FYR Macedonia and Liechtenstein. The last 14 minutes of Albania's opening game against FYR Macedonia in Shkoder had to be postponed until the next day, at 1-1, because of a torrential downpour, and the home side took advantage when Bekim Balaj, who had scored Albania's winner away to Portugal in their opening UEFA EURO 2016 qualifier, struck an 89th-minute winner.

Group H

The appointment of ex-Everton manager Roberto Martínez as Belgium's new head coach took many by surprise, but with six 2018 World Cup qualifiers played his team were sitting pretty at the top of Group H having scored 24 goals and surrendered just two points – in a 1-1 draw at home to Greece, who, also undefeated and also under a new foreign coach in German Michael Skibbe, went into the summer as their closest challengers four points in arrears.

Only an 89th-minute equaliser from Romelu Lukaku – his sixth goal of the competition – enabled Martínez's men to salvage a draw at home to a Greek side down to ten men for much of the second half after they had snatched the lead just 19 seconds into it from Kostas Mitroglou. Lukaku had begun the campaign by netting twice in an opening 3-0 win in Cyprus before completing the scoring the following month in a superb 4-0 win at home to Bosnia & Herzegovina.

Belgium's next two fixtures yielded 14 further goals, a 6-0 win away to Gibraltar – in which Christian Benteke scored the fastest-ever goal in a World Cup qualifier, after 8.1 seconds, en route to a first international hat-trick – followed by an 8-1 demolition of Estonia in Brussels. Dries Mertens scored two goals against the Estonians at home and another to help his team to a 2-0 win in Tallinn in June, which gave Belgium their third win on the road without conceding and put them in control of the section – albeit with trips to Greece and Bosnia & Herzegovina still to come.

Those two teams helped Belgium's cause by drawing twice against each other, 1-1 in Piraeus and 0-0 in Zenica. The first game featured a red card for each side and a stunning stoppage-time strike from Greece left-back Georgios Tzavellas that cancelled out an earlier free-kick from Miralem Pjanić that struck the post and the body of Greece goalkeeper Orestis Karnezis before entering the net.

Group I

A gripping finale beckoned in Group I as just two points separated the top four teams. Croatia and Iceland, with 13 points, headed Turkey and Ukraine, both on 11, with all permutations possible. The only certainly was that Finland and competition debutants Kosovo, with just one point apiece, would not be going to Russia.

Ante Čačić's Croatia, impressive performers at UEFA EURO 2016, were obliged to play their first two home games behind closed doors as punishment for fan misbehaviour. They dropped two points in the first of them, against Turkey, as Hakan Çalhanoğlu's deflected free-kick cancelled out an Ivan Rakitić penalty, but against Iceland a first international double from midfielder Marcelo Brozović – with two fine strikes from the edge of the area – brought a 2-0 win that, combined with victories in Kosovo (6-0) and Finland (1-0), put Croatia on top of the group.

The supporters were back in the Maksimir stadium to see Čačić's side strengthen their position with a 1-0 win over Ukraine – thanks to Nikola Kalinić's excellent finish – but with 90 minutes on the clock in the season's final fixture, in Reykjavik, Iceland bundled in a winning goal off the shoulder of defender Hördur Magnússon and suddenly Croatia, defeated for the first time, had company at the top of the standings.

It was not the first time that Iceland, the shock UEFA EURO 2016 quarter-finalists, had scored late to claim three points at the Laugardalsvöllur. Indeed their brinksmanship on matchday two had been even more dramatic as they entered added time 2-1 down against Finland only to pull the rabbit out of the hat thanks to timely strikes from Alfred Finnbogason and – with another scrappy close-range effort – Ragnar Sigurdsson. Less problematic for Heimir Hallgrímsson's side was a 2-0 home win against Turkey, who appeared to be out for the count with just two points from their opening three games but rallied to win their next three, albeit two of them against Kosovo, whose only point came in their opening fixture against Finland in Turku.

Unlike the fourth-placed teams in the other eight groups, Ukraine, now coached by legendary striker Andriy Shevchenko, were still very much in the qualifying frame. Although they were held 1-1 at home by Iceland – in a deserted stadium – and lost in Croatia, they drew 2-2 in Turkey and beat Kosovo 3-0 in neighbouring Poland – with skipper Andriy Yarmolenko's third goal in as many games – before winning home and away against Finland to set themselves up for a couple of enthralling Weeks of Football in September and October.

Iceland's Gylfi Sigurdsson (left) and Croatia's Mateo Kovačić vie for possession in the top-of-the-table Group I clash in Reykjavik

Qualifying round

Group A

06/09/16, Borisov-Arena, Borisov (att: 12,920)
Belarus 0-0 France
Referee: Haţegan (ROU)
Belarus: Gorbunov, Polyakov, Politevich, Korzun, Stasevich (Krivets 69), Gordeichuk (M Volodko 85), Sivakov, Mayevski, Bordachev, Signevich (Kornilenko 81), Kalachev. Coach: Aleksandr Khatskevich (BLR)
France: Mandanda, Kurzawa, Varane, Pogba, Griezmann, Giroud (Gameiro 83), Martial (Payet 57), Kanté, Sissoko (Dembélé 69), Sidibé, Koscielny. Coach: Didier Deschamps (FRA)

06/09/16, Natsionalen Stadion Vasil Levski, Sofia (att: 4,202)
Bulgaria 4-3 Luxembourg
Goals: 1-0 Rangelov 16, 1-1 Joachim 60, 1-2 Joachim 62, 2-2 Marcelinho 65, 3-2 I Popov 79, 3-3 Bohnert 90+1, 4-3 Tonev 90+2
Referee: Mažeika (LTU)
Bulgaria: Stoyanov, S Popov, Nedyalkov, Chorbadzhiyski, M Alexandrov (Chochev 56), Rangelov, I Popov (Bozhilov 85), Marcelinho, Ivanov, G Milanov (Tonev 64), Dyakov. Coach: Ivaylo Petev (BUL)
Luxembourg: Joubert, Chanot, Malget, Philipps (Deville 84), Gerson, Martins, Da Mota (Bohnert 68), V Thill (Turpel 59), Mutsch, Jans, Joachim. Coach: Luc Holtz (LUX)

06/09/16, Friends Arena, Solna (att: 36,128)
Sweden 1-1 Netherlands
Goals: 1-0 Berg 42, 1-1 Sneijder 67
Referee: Orsato (ITA)
Sweden: Olsen, Lustig, Lindelöf, Granqvist, Rohdén (Kujovic 76), Berg (Durmaz 87), Forsberg, Guidetti (Nyman 64), Hiljemark, Wendt, Fransson. Coach: Jan Andersson (SWE)
Netherlands: Zoet, Janmaat, Bruma, Van Dijk, Blind, Strootman, Klaassen, Wijnaldum (Dost 66), Janssen, Sneijder, Promes (Berghuis 78). Coach: Danny Blind (NED)

07/10/16, Stade de France, Saint-Denis (att: 65,475)
France 4-1 Bulgaria
Goals: 0-1 M Alexandrov 6(p), 1-1 Gameiro 23, 2-1 Payet 26, 3-1 Griezmann 38, 4-1 Gameiro 59
Referee: Banti (ITA)
France: Lloris, Kurzawa, Varane, Pogba, Griezmann (Fekir 83), Payet, Gameiro (Gignac 72), Matuidi, Sissoko, Sagna (Sidibé 27), Koscielny. Coach: Didier Deschamps (FRA)
Bulgaria: Stoyanov, S Popov, A Aleksandrov, M Alexandrov (Nedelev 76), Kostadinov, I Popov (Tonev 68), Marcelinho (Rangelov 62), Pirgov, Z Milanov, G Milanov, Dyakov. Coach: Petar Hubchev (BUL)

07/10/16, De Kuip, Rotterdam (att: 41,200)
Netherlands 4-1 Belarus
Goals: 1-0 Promes 15, 2-0 Promes 31, 2-1 Rios 47, 3-1 Klaassen 56, 4-1 Janssen 64
Referee: Thomson (SCO)
Netherlands: Stekelenburg, Karsdorp, Bruma, Van Dijk, Blind, Strootman (Clasie 79), Klaassen, Wijnaldum, Janssen (Dost 83), Sneijder (Pröpper 46), Promes. Coach: Danny Blind (NED)
Belarus: Gorbunov, Polyakov, Politevich, Korzun, Kornilenko, Gordeichuk (M Volodko 74), Krivets (Kislyak 67), Rios, Sivakov, Mayevski (Hleb 46), Bordachev. Coach: Aleksandr Khatskevich (BLR)

Memphis Depay scores for the Netherlands away to Luxembourg

07/10/16, Stade Josy Barthel, Luxembourg (att: 5,057)
Luxembourg 0-1 Sweden
Goal: 0-1 Lustig 58
Referee: Bebek (CRO)
Luxembourg: Moris, Malget, Bohnert, Philipps, Martins, V Thill (Turpel 66), Carlson, Mutsch, Jans, Deville (Da Mota 66), Joachim. Coach: Luc Holtz (LUX)
Sweden: Olsen, Lustig, Lindelöf, Granqvist, M Olsson, Ekdal (Fransson 79), Berg, Forsberg, Guidetti (Toivonen 70), Hiljemark, Durmaz (Nyman 88). Coach: Jan Andersson (SWE)
Red card: Malget 82 (Luxembourg)

10/10/16, Borisov-Arena, Borisov (att: 9,011)
Belarus 1-1 Luxembourg
Goals: 1-0 Savitski 80, 1-1 Joachim 85
Referee: Welz (GER)
Belarus: Gorbunov, Martynovich, Polyakov, Korzun, Hleb, Gordeichuk, Mayevski (Savitski 71), Bordachev (M Volodko 78), Signevich (Kornilenko 60), Filipenko, Kalachev. Coach: Aleksandr Khatskevich (BLR)
Luxembourg: Moris, Bohnert (Turpel 72), Philipps, Martins (Veiga 35), Da Mota, V Thill (Jänisch 46), Carlson, Delgado, Mutsch, Jans, Joachim. Coach: Luc Holtz (LUX)
Red card: Carlson 44 (Luxembourg)

10/10/16, Amsterdam ArenA, Amsterdam (att: 50,220)
Netherlands 0-1 France
Goal: 0-1 Pogba 30
Referee: Skomina (SVN)
Netherlands: Stekelenburg, Karsdorp, Bruma, Van Dijk, Blind, Strootman, Klaassen, Wijnaldum (Dost 62), Janssen, Pröpper (Willems 84), Promes (Depay 16). Coach: Danny Blind (NED)
France: Lloris, Sidibé, Kurzawa, Varane, Pogba, Griezmann (Kanté 90+3), Payet (Martial 67), Gameiro (Gignac 79), Matuidi, Sissoko, Koscielny. Coach: Didier Deschamps (FRA)

10/10/16, Friends Arena, Solna (att: 21,777)
Sweden 3-0 Bulgaria
Goals: 1-0 Toivonen 39, 2-0 Hiljemark 45, 3-0 Lindelöf 58
Referee: Oliver (ENG)
Sweden: Olsen, Lindelöf, Granqvist, M Olsson (Augustinsson 63), Ekdal, Berg (Guidetti 85), Forsberg (Wendt 74), Hiljemark, Krafth, Toivonen, Durmaz. Coach: Jan Andersson (SWE)
Bulgaria: Stoyanov, S Popov, A Aleksandrov, Bozhikov, Slavchev (Raynov 89), Kostadinov (M Alexandrov 53), I Popov, Nedyalkov, G Milanov, Chochev (Marcelinho 72), Dyakov. Coach: Petar Hubchev (BUL)

13/11/16, Natsionalen Stadion Vasil Levski, Sofia (att: 1,994)
Bulgaria 1-0 Belarus
Goal: 1-0 I Popov 10
Referee: Klossner (SUI)
Bulgaria: Stoyanov, S Popov, A Aleksandrov, Zanev, Slavchev, Delev, I Popov (Yordanov 75), Bozhikov, G Milanov (Chochev 53), Tonev (Kirilov 66), Dyakov. Coach: Petar Hubchev (BUL)
Belarus: Gorbunov, Martynovich (Shitov 36), Polyakov, Politevich, Hleb, Gordeichuk, Nekhaichik (Savitski 61), Kendysh, Mayevski (Kornilenko 74), Filipenko, Laptev. Coach: Aleksandr Khatskevich (BLR)
Red card: Hleb 90+1 (Belarus)

11/11/16, Stade de France, Saint-Denis (att: 80,000)
France 2-1 Sweden
Goals: 0-1 Forsberg 55, 1-1 Pogba 58, 2-1 Payet 65
Referee: Mažić (SRB)
France: Lloris, Evra, Varane, Pogba, Griezmann (Kanté 88), Payet, Giroud, Matuidi, Sissoko, Sidibé, Koscielny. Coach: Didier Deschamps (FRA)
Sweden: Olsen, Lindelöf, Granqvist, Augustinsson, Ekdal (Hiljemark 66), Forsberg, Guidetti (Kiese Thelin 73), Johansson, Krafth, Toivonen, Durmaz (Jansson 87). Coach: Jan Andersson (SWE)

13/11/16, Stade Josy Barthel, Luxembourg (att: 8,000)
Luxembourg 1-3 Netherlands
Goals: 0-1 Robben 36, 1-1 Chanot 44(p), 1-2 Depay 58, 1-3 Depay 84
Referee: Taylor (ENG)
Luxembourg: Schon, Chanot, Mahmutovic, Malget, Bohnert, Philipps, Da Mota (Kerger 75), Bensi (V Thill 82), Mutsch, Jans (Jänisch 26), Turpel. Coach: Luc Holtz (LUX)
Netherlands: Stekelenburg, Brenet, Bruma, Van Dijk, Blind, Ramselaar (De Roon 88), Klaassen, Wijnaldum, Dost, Sneijder (Depay 46), Robben (Berghuis 46). Coach: Danny Blind (NED)

25/03/17, Natsionalen Stadion Vasil Levski, Sofia (att: 10,900)
Bulgaria 2-0 Netherlands
Goals: 1-0 Delev 5, 2-0 Delev 20
Referee: Collum (SCO)
Bulgaria: Mihaylov,S Popov, Zanev (Nedyalkov 86), Chorbadzhiyski, Slavchev, Kostadinov, Delev (Bodurov 88), I Popov (Kraev 67), Manolev, Bozhikov, Tonev. Coach: Petar Hubchev (BUL)
Netherlands: Zoet, Karsdorp, De Ligt (Hoedt 46), Martins Indi, Blind, Strootman, Promes (L de Jong 68), Wijnaldum (Sneijder 46), Dost, Klaassen, Robben. Coach: Danny Blind (NED)

25/03/17, Stade Josy Barthel, Luxembourg (att: 8,000)
Luxembourg 1-3 France
Goals: 0-1 Giroud 28, 1-1 Joachim 34(p), 1-2 Griezmann 37(p), 1-3 Giroud 77
Referee: Treimanis (LVA)
Luxembourg: Moris (Schon 21), Chanot, Malget, Philipps, Gerson, Martins, Da Mota (Rodrigues 81), Bensi, Mutsch (Bohnert 62), Jans, Joachim. Coach: Luc Holtz (LUX)
France: Lloris, Griezmann, Payet (Mbappé 78), Giroud, Dembélé, Kanté, Matuidi (Rabiot 83), Mendy, Sidibé (Jallet 62), Koscielny, Umtiti. Coach: Didier Deschamps (FRA)

25/03/17, Friends Arena, Solna (att: 31,243)
Sweden 4-0 Belarus
Goals: 1-0 Forsberg 19(p), 2-0 Forsberg 49, 3-0 Berg 57, 4-0 Kiese Thelin 78
Referee: Lechner (AUT)
Sweden: Olsen, Lustig, Granqvist, Augustinsson, Ekdal (Johansson 69), Berg, Forsberg, Hiljemark, Jansson, Toivonen (Kiese Thelin 74), Durmaz (Claesson 85). Coach: Jan Andersson (SWE)
Belarus: Gorbunov, Martynovich, Shitov, Politevich, Renan Bressan, Gordeichuk, Signevich (Rodionov 71), Rios, Mayevski (Dragun 65), Bordachev (M Volodko 69), Filipenko. Coach: Igor Kriushenko (BLR)

09/06/17, Borisov-Arena, Borisov (att: 6,150)
Belarus 2-1 Bulgaria
Goals: 1-0 Sivakov 33(p), 2-0 Savitski 80, 2-1 Kostadinov 90+1
Referee: Jug (SVN)
Belarus: Chernik, Dragun, Matveichik, Aliseiko, Politevich, Savitski (Skavysh 82), Sivakov, Mayevski (Gordeichuk 89), Laptev (Bykov 74), Filipenko, Balanovich. Coach: Igor Kriushenko (BLR)
Bulgaria: Mihaylov, S Popov, Zanev, Chorbadzhiyski, Kostadinov, Delev (Galabinov 54), I Popov (Chochev 64), Manolev (G Milanov 81), Bozhikov, Tonev, Dyakov. Coach: Petar Hubchev (BUL)

09/06/17, De Kuip, Rotterdam (att: 41,300)
Netherlands 5-0 Luxembourg
Goals: 1-0 Robben 21, 2-0 Sneijder 34, 3-0 Wijnaldum 62, 4-0 Promes 70, 5-0 Janssen 84(p)
Referee: Frankowski (POL)
Netherlands: Cillessen, Veltman, De Vrij, Hoedt, Blind, Strootman, Depay (Promes 66), Wijnaldum, Janssen, Sneijder (Aké 82), Robben (Lens 73). Coach: Dick Advocaat (NED)
Luxembourg: Schon, Chanot (Delgado 25), Mahmutovic, Malget, Martins, V Thill (Gerson 54), Bensi, Rodrigues (Bohnert 85), S Thill, Jans, Turpel. Coach: Luc Holtz (LUX)

09/06/17, Friends Arena, Stockholm (att: 48,783)
Sweden 2-1 France
Goals: 0-1 Giroud 37, 1-1 Durmaz 43, 2-1 Toivonen 90+3
Referee: Atkinson (ENG)
Sweden: Olsen, Lustig, Lindelöf, Granqvist, Augustinsson, Ekdal (Sebastian Larsson 77), Berg (Guidetti 88), Forsberg, Johansson, Toivonen, Durmaz (Claesson 76). Coach: Jan Andersson (SWE)
France: Lloris, Mendy, Varane, Pogba, Griezmann (Mbappé 75), Giroud, Payet (Lemar 76), Matuidi, Sissoko, Sidibé, Koscielny. Coach: Didier Deschamps (FRA)

Remaining fixtures

31/08/17
Bulgaria - Sweden
France - Netherlands
Luxembourg - Belarus

03/09/17
Belarus - Sweden
France - Luxembourg
Netherlands - Bulgaria

07/10/17
Belarus - Netherlands
Bulgaria - France
Sweden - Luxembourg

10/10/17
France - Belarus
Luxembourg - Bulgaria
Netherlands - Sweden

Group B

06/09/16, Estadi Nacional, Andorra la Vella (att: 1,115)
Andorra 0-1 Latvia
Goal: 0-1 Šabala 48
Referee: Pisani (MLT)
Andorra: Pol, C Martínez, Vales, Lima, Vieira, Riera (Rebés 30), Clemente (Pujol 78), Aláez (Moreira 83), Llovera, M García, Jordi Rubio. Coach: Koldo Alvarez (AND)
Latvia: Vaņins, Maksimenko, Gabovs, A Višņakovs, Lazdiņš (Laizāns 45+1), Šabala, Gorkšs, J Ikaunieks, D Ikaunieks (Torres 63), Zjuzins (Karašausks 74), Jagodinskis. Coach: Marians Pahars (LVA)

06/09/16, Tórsvøllur, Torshavn (att: 4,066)
Faroe Islands 0-0 Hungary
Referee: Vinčić (SVN)
Faroe Islands: Nielsen, V Davidsen, Gregersen, Nattestad, Hansson (Vatnsdal 90+1), Benjaminsen, B Olsen, Vatnhamar, Edmundsson, Joensen, Hansen. Coach: Lars Olsen (DEN)
Hungary: Gulácsi, Lang, Kádár, Fiola, Elek, Dzsudzsák, Á Nagy, Németh (Nikolić 70), Kleinheisler (Stieber 80), Priskin (Szalai 27), Guzmics. Coach: Bernd Storck (GER)

06/09/16, St. Jakob-Park, Basel (att: 36,000)
Switzerland 2-0 Portugal
Goals: 1-0 Embolo 24, 2-0 Mehmedi 30
Referee: Mateu Lahoz (ESP)
Switzerland: Sommer, Lichtsteiner (Widmer 70), Embolo, Seferovic (Derdiyok 78), Xhaka, Behrami, Rodriguez, Dzemaili (G Fernandes 89), Mehmedi, Djourou, Schär. Coach: Vladimir Petković (SUI)
Portugal: Rui Patrício, Pepe, Raphaël Guerreiro, José Fonte, João Moutinho (Ricardo Quaresma 68), Éder (André Silva 46), Bernardo Silva, William Carvalho (João Mário 46), Nani, Cédric, Adrien Silva. Coach: Fernando Santos (POR)
Red card: Xhaka 90+3 (Switzerland)

07/10/16, Skonto Stadions, Riga (att: 4,823)
Latvia 0-2 Faroe Islands
Goals: 0-1 Nattestad 19, 0-2 Edmundsson 70
Referee: Boiko (UKR)
Latvia: Vaņins, Maksimenko, Laizāns, Gabovs, A Višņakovs, Šabala, Gorkšs, Lukjanovs (D Ikaunieks 76), Jagodinskis, Kļuškins (Zjuzins 72), Gutkovskis (Karlsons 64). Coach: Marians Pahars (LVA)
Faroe Islands: Nielsen, Næs, V Davidsen, Gregersen, Nattestad, Hansson, Benjaminsen, B Olsen (P Justinussen 88), Vatnhamar, Edmundsson (Klettskard 90+2), Joensen (Sørensen 73). Coach: Lars Olsen (DEN)

07/10/16, Groupama Aréna, Budapest (att: 21,668)
Hungary 2-3 Switzerland
Goals: 0-1 Seferovic 51, 1-1 Szalai 53, 1-2 Rodriguez 67, 2-2 Szalai 71, 2-3 Stocker 89
Referee: Kuipers (NED)
Hungary: Gulácsi, Lang, Kádár, Fiola, Dzsudzsák, Á Nagy, Szalai (Nikolić 87), Gera, Kleinheisler (Németh 76), Stieber, Guzmics. Coach: Bernd Storck (GER)
Switzerland: Sommer, Lichtsteiner, Elvedi, Embolo, Seferovic (Derdiyok 72), Behrami, Rodriguez, Dzemaili, Mehmedi (Stocker 88), Schär, Shaqiri (G Fernandes 81). Coach: Vladimir Petković (SUI)

07/10/16, Estádio Municipal de Aveiro, Aveiro (att: 25,120)
Portugal 6-0 Andorra
Goals: 1-0 Cristiano Ronaldo 2, 2-0 Cristiano Ronaldo 4, 3-0 João Cancelo 44, 4-0 Cristiano Ronaldo 47, 5-0 Cristiano Ronaldo 68, 6-0 André Silva 86
Referee: Drachta (AUT)
Portugal: Rui Patrício, Pepe (Gelson Martins 72), Raphaël Guerreiro (Antunes 52), José Fonte, Cristiano Ronaldo, João Moutinho, Bernardo Silva, André Gomes (João Mário 66), André Silva, Ricardo Quaresma, João Cancelo. Coach: Fernando Santos (POR)

Cristiano Ronaldo scores one of his four goals for Portugal against Andorra in Aveiro

Andorra: Gomes, C Martínez (Moreira 76), Vales, Rebés, Lima, Vieira, Aláez (Pujol 73), Llovera, M García (San Nicolás 49), Rodríguez, Jordi Rubio. Coach: Koldo Alvarez (AND)
Red cards: Jordi Rubio 62 (Andorra), Rebés 71 (Andorra)

10/10/16, Estadi Nacional, Andorra la Vella (att: 2,014)
Andorra 1-2 Switzerland
Goals: 0-1 Schär 19(p), 0-2 Mehmedi 77, 1-2 A Martínez 90+1
Referee: Beaton (SCO)
Andorra: Gomes, Vales, E García, Lima, Pujol (Riera 84), Vieira (C Martínez 80), Clemente (A Martínez 73), San Nicolás, Llovera, Rodríguez, Jesús Rubio. Coach: Koldo Alvarez (AND)
Switzerland: Bürki, Klose (Elvedi 46), Lang, Embolo, Seferovic, Xhaka, Rodriguez, G Fernandes (Zakaria 66), Mehmedi, Schär, Shaqiri (Stocker 80). Coach: Vladimir Petković (SUI)

10/10/16, Tórsvøllur, Torshavn (att: 4,780)
Faroe Islands 0-6 Portugal
Goals: 0-1 André Silva 12, 0-2 André Silva 22, 0-3 André Silva 37, 0-4 Cristiano Ronaldo 65, 0-5 João Moutinho 90+1, 0-6 João Cancelo 90+3
Referee: Mažeika (LTU)
Faroe Islands: Nielsen, V Davidsen, Gregersen (J Davidsen 72), Nattestad, Hansson, Benjaminsen, B Olsen (Bartalsstovu 79), Sørensen (Joensen 66), Vatnhamar, Edmundsson, Hansen. Coach: Lars Olsen (DEN)
Portugal: Rui Patrício, Pepe, Antunes, José Fonte, Cristiano Ronaldo, João Mário (João Moutinho 81), William Carvalho, André Gomes, André Silva (Éder 79), Ricardo Quaresma (Gelson Martins 67), João Cancelo. Coach: Fernando Santos (POR)

10/10/16, Skonto Stadions, Riga (att: 4,715)
Latvia 0-2 Hungary
Goals: 0-1 Gyurcsó 10, 0-2 Szalai 77
Referee: Gil (POL)
Latvia: Vaņins, Maksimenko, Laizāns (Karašausks 77), Gabovs, A Višņakovs (Zjuzins 57), D Ikaunieks, Šabala, Gorkšs, Tarasovs, Jagodinskis, Kļuškins (J Ikaunieks 68). Coach: Marians Pahars (LVA)
Hungary: Gulácsi, Korhut, Kádár, Dzsudzsák, Á Nagy, Szalai, Gera (Vida 83), Gyurcsó, Bese, Nikolić (Kleinheisler 46), Guzmics. Coach: Bernd Storck (GER)

13/11/16, Groupama Aréna, Budapest (att: 20,479)
Hungary 4-0 Andorra
Goals: 1-0 Gera 34, 2-0 Lang 43, 3-0 Gyurcsó 73, 4-0 Szalai 88
Referee: Nicolaides (CYP)
Hungary: Gulácsi, Lang, Korhut, Dzsudzsák, Á Nagy, Szalai, Gera (Böde 84), Kleinheisler (Stieber 74), Gyurcsó (Németh 81), Guzmics, Bese. Coach: Bernd Storck (GER)
Andorra: Gomes, C Martínez (A Martínez 67), Vales, E García, Pujol (Sánchez 87), Vieira, Aláez, San Nicolás, Jesús Rubio, Llovera, Rodríguez (Moreira 83). Coach: Koldo Alvarez (AND)

13/11/16, Estádio Algarve, Faro (att: 20,744)
Portugal 4-1 Latvia
Goals: 1-0 Cristiano Ronaldo 28(p), 1-1 Zjuzins 67, 2-1 William Carvalho 70, 3-1 Cristiano Ronaldo 85, 4-1 Bruno Alves 90+2
Referee: Madden (SCO)
Portugal: Rui Patrício, Bruno Alves, Raphaël Guerreiro, José Fonte, Cristiano Ronaldo, João Mário (Gelson Martins 71), William Carvalho, João Cancelo, Nani (Ricardo Quaresma 65), André Silva, André Gomes (Renato Sanches 87). Coach: Fernando Santos (POR)
Latvia: Vaņins, Maksimenko, Freimanis, Laizāns, Gabovs, D Ikaunieks (Zjuzins 59), Gorkšs, Rudņevs (Gutkovskis 87), Tarasovs, Jagodinskis, Kļuškins (A Višņakovs 79). Coach: Marians Pahars (LVA)

Breel Embolo celebrates opening the scoring for Switzerland against Portugal

13/11/16, Swissporarena, Lucerne (att: 14,800)
Switzerland 2-0 Faroe Islands
Goals: 1-0 Derdiyok 27, 2-0 Lichtsteiner 83
Referee: Delferiere (BEL)
Switzerland: Sommer, Lichtsteiner, Xhaka, Behrami, Rodriguez, Stocker (E Fernandes 69), Dzemaili (Steffen 80), Mehmedi, Derdiyok (Seferovic 87), Djourou, Schär. Coach: Vladimir Petković (SUI)
Faroe Islands: Nielsen, Næs, Gregersen, Nattestad, Hansson, Benjaminsen (Færø 89), B Olsen, Sørensen (Joensen 78), Vatnhamar (A Olsen 81), Edmundsson, Hansen. Coach: Lars Olsen (DEN)

25/03/17, Estadi Nacional, Andorra la Vella (att: 1,755)
Andorra 0-0 Faroe Islands
Referee: Valjić (BIH)
Andorra: Gomes, C Martínez, Vales, Lima, Pujol (A Martínez 54), Vieira, Aláez, San Nicolás, Jesús Rubio (M García 46), Llovera, Jordi Rubio (Clemente 77). Coach: Koldo Alvarez (AND)
Faroe Islands: Nielsen, Næs, V Davidsen, Gregersen, Hansson, Bartalsstovu (Hansen 70), Sørensen (P Justinussen 82), Vatnhamar, Edmundsson, J Davidsen, Klettskard. Coach: Lars Olsen (DEN)
Red card: Edmundsson 74 (Faroe Islands)

25/03/17, Estádio do Sport Lisboa e Benfica, Lisbon (att: 57,816)
Portugal 3-0 Hungary
Goals: 1-0 André Silva 32, 2-0 Cristiano Ronaldo 36, 3-0 Cristiano Ronaldo 65
Referee: Marciniak (POL)
Portugal: Rui Patrício, Pepe, Raphaël Guerreiro, José Fonte, Cristiano Ronaldo, João Mário (João Moutinho 83), William Carvalho, André Gomes (Pizzi 86), André Silva (Bernardo Silva 67), Ricardo Quaresma, Cédric. Coach: Fernando Santos (POR)
Hungary: Gulácsi, Lang (Lovrencsics 46), Korhut, Kádár, Dzsudzsák, Á Nagy, Szalai, Gera (Pintér 85), Gyurcsó (Kalmár 69), Paulo Vinícius, Bese. Coach: Bernd Storck (GER)

25/03/17, Stade de Genève, Geneva (att: 25,000)
Switzerland 1-0 Latvia
Goal: 1-0 Drmic 66
Referee: Bezborodov (RUS)
Switzerland: Sommer, Lichtsteiner, Moubandje, Seferovic (Freuler 83), Xhaka, Dzemaili, G Fernandes (Drmic 64), Mehmedi, Djourou, Schär, Shaqiri (Zuber 77). Coach: Vladimir Petković (SUI)
Latvia: Vaņins, Freimanis, Laizāns, A Višņakovs (Gabovs 56), Lazdiņš (Gutkovskis 77), D Ikaunieks (Rakels 69), Šabala, Solovjovs, Gorkšs, Jagodinskis, Kļuškins. Coach: Marians Pahars (LVA)

09/06/17, Estadi Nacional, Andorra la Vella (att: 2,376)
Andorra 1-0 Hungary
Goal: 1-0 Rebés 26
Referee: Kalogeropoulos (GRE)
Andorra: Gomes, Vales, Rebés, Lima, Pujol (Ayala 88), Clemente (Riera 83), Aláez (Maneiro 68), San Nicolás, A Martínez, Llovera, Jesús Rubio. Coach: Koldo Alvarez (AND)
Hungary: Gulácsi, Lang (Balogh 56), Paulo Vinícius, Dzsudzsák, A Nagy, Eppel, Kleinheisler, Gyurcsó (Sallai 71), Stieber (D Nagy 21), Bese, Tóth. Coach: Bernd Storck (GER)

09/06/17, Tórsvøllur, Torshavn (att: 4,594)
Faroe Islands 0-2 Switzerland
Goals: 0-1 Xhaka 36, 0-2 Shaqiri 59
Referee: Mazzoleni (ITA)
Faroe Islands: Nielsen, Næs, V Davidsen, Gregersen, J Davidsen (Færø 70), Hansson (Løkin 66), Benjaminsen, K Olsen (Joensen 61), Sørensen, Vatnhamar, F Justinussen. Coach: Lars Olsen (DEN)
Switzerland: Sommer, Lichtsteiner, Moubandje, Seferovic (Derdiyok 78), Xhaka, Behrami, Akanji, Dzemaili (Freuler 86), Mehmedi (Zuber 62), Djourou, Shaqiri. Coach: Vladimir Petković (SUI)

09/06/17, Skonto Stadions, Riga (att: 8,179)
Latvia 0-3 Portugal
Goals: 0-1 Cristiano Ronaldo 41, 0-2 Cristiano Ronaldo 63, 0-3 André Silva 67
Referee: Kovács (ROU)
Latvia: Vaņins, Maksimenko, Laizāns, D Ikaunieks (Rakels 68), Šabala, Solovjovs, Gorkšs, Kazačoks (Vardanjans 72), Koļesovs, Jagodinskis, Kļuškins (Indrāns 62). Coach: Aleksandrs Starkovs (LVA)
Portugal: Rui Patrício, Bruno Alves, Raphaël Guerreiro, José Fonte, Cristiano Ronaldo, João Moutinho, André Silva (Nani 80), William Carvalho, André Gomes, Gelson Martins (Ricardo Quaresma 57), Cédric (Nélson Semedo 71). Coach: Fernando Santos (POR)

Remaining fixtures

31/08/17
Hungary - Latvia
Portugal - Faroe Islands
Switzerland - Andorra

03/09/17
Faroe Islands - Andorra
Hungary - Portugal
Latvia - Switzerland

07/10/17
Andorra - Portugal
Faroe Islands - Latvia
Switzerland - Hungary

10/10/17
Hungary - Faroe Islands
Latvia - Andorra
Portugal - Switzerland

Thomas Müller grabs his second goal of the game as Germany defeat Czech Republic 3-0 in Hamburg

Group C

04/09/16, GENERALI Arena, Prague (att: 10,731)
Czech Republic 0-0 Northern Ireland
Referee: Sidiropoulos (GRE)
Czech Republic: Vaclík, Kadeřábek, M Kadlec, Darida, Skalák (Kopic 77), Pavelka, V Kadlec (Vydra 83), Suchý, Krejčí, Škoda (Necid 68), Novák. Coach: Karel Jarolím (CZE)
Northern Ireland: McGovern, C McLaughlin, Ferguson (Hodson 66), McAuley, J Evans, Davis, K Lafferty (Magennis 59), Dallas, Norwood, McNair, Ward (McGinn 74). Coach: Michael O'Neill (NIR)

04/09/16, Ullevaal Stadion, Oslo (att: 26,793)
Norway 0-3 Germany
Goals: 0-1 Müller 15, 0-2 Kimmich 45, 0-3 Müller 60
Referee: Collum (SCO)
Norway: Jarstein, Aleesami, Hovland, Tettey, Nordtveit, King (Sørloth 72), Johansen (Yttergård Jenssen 67), Henriksen (Selnæs 61), Svensson, Berisha, Diomandé. Coach: Per-Mathias Høgmo (NOR)
Germany: Neuer, Hector, Höwedes, Hummels, Khedira (Weigl 84), Kroos, Özil, Draxler (Meyer 84), Müller, Götze (Brandt 72), Kimmich. Coach: Joachim Löw (GER)

04/09/16, San Marino Stadium, Serravalle (att: 886)
San Marino 0-1 Azerbaijan
Goal: 0-1 Qurbanov 45
Referee: Delferiere (BEL)
San Marino: A Simoncini, Cesarini, Brolli, D Simoncini, M Vitaioli (Valentini 86), Hirsch, Palazzi, Tosi, M Berardi, F Berardi (Rinaldi 73), Chiaruzzi (L Gasperoni 54). Coach: Pierangelo Manzaroli (SMR)
Azerbaijan: K Ağayev, Qarayev, Mirzäbäyov, Medvedev, Qurbanov (Äläsgärov 69), Nazarov (Mahmudov 78), R F Sadıqov, Ramazanov (Şeydayev 89), Ämirquliyev, Daşdämirov, İsmayılov. Coach: Robert Prosinečki (CRO)
Red card: Brolli 52 (San Marino)

08/10/16, Bakı Olimpiya Stadionu, Baku (att: 35,000)
Azerbaijan 1-0 Norway
Goal: 1-0 Medvedev 11
Referee: Liany (ISR)
Azerbaijan: K Ağayev, Qarayev, Mirzäbäyov, Medvedev, İsrafilov (Äläsgärov 65), Qurbanov (Şeydayev 80), Nazarov, R F Sadıqov, Ramazanov (B Hüseynov 90), Ämirquliyev, Daşdämirov. Coach: Robert Prosinečki (CRO)
Norway: Jarstein, Aleesami, Hovland, Strandberg, King (Sørloth 61), Henriksen, Skjelbred (Johansen 84), Svensson, Selnæs, Diomandé, Helland (Berget 71). Coach: Per-Mathias Høgmo (NOR)

08/10/16, Volksparkstadion, Hamburg (att: 51,299)
Germany 3-0 Czech Republic
Goals: 1-0 Müller 13, 2-0 Kroos 49, 3-0 Müller 65
Referee: Hațegan (ROU)
Germany: Neuer, Hector (Höwedes 68), Hummels, Khedira, Draxler (Brandt 80), Kroos (Gündoğan 76), Özil, Müller, Boateng, Kimmich, Götze. Coach: Joachim Löw (GER)
Czech Republic: Vaclík, Kadeřábek, Sivok, Novák, Dočkal, Petržela (Skalák 69), Pavelka (Droppa 63), Suchý, Hořava, Krejčí, Vydra (V Kadlec 76). Coach: Karel Jarolím (CZE)

08/10/16, Windsor Park, Belfast (att: 18,234)
Northern Ireland 4-0 San Marino
Goals: 1-0 Davis 26(p), 2-0 K Lafferty 79, 3-0 Ward 85, 4-0 K Lafferty 90+4
Referee: Kovács (ROU)
Northern Ireland: McGovern, C McLaughlin (McNair 77), Ferguson, McAuley, J Evans, McGinn, Davis, Dallas (Washington 65), Norwood, Ward, Magennis (K Lafferty 72). Coach: Michael O'Neill (NIR)
San Marino: A Simoncini, M Berardi, Coppini (E Golinucci 71), F Vitaioli, D Simoncini, M Vitaioli, Hirsch (Cesarini 56), Stefanelli (Zafferani 88), Della Valle, Tosi, Palazzi. Coach: Pierangelo Manzaroli (SMR)
Red card: Palazzi 49 (San Marino)

11/10/16, Městský Stadion, Ostrava (att: 12,148)
Czech Republic 0-0 Azerbaijan
Referee: Jug (SVN)
Czech Republic: Vaclík, Droppa, Gebre Selassie, Brabec, Sivok, Dočkal, Skalák (Zmrhal 74), V Kadlec, Sýkora, Krejčí (Petržela 64), Schick (Škoda 66). Coach: Karel Jarolím (CZE)
Azerbaijan: K Ağayev, Qarayev, Mirzäbäyov, Medvedev, B Hüseynov, Äläsgärov (Ramazanov 71), Qurbanov (Abdullayev 87), Nazarov, Ämirquliyev, Şeydayev (İsrafilov 90+1), Daşdämirov. Coach: Robert Prosinečki (CRO)

11/10/16, HDI Arena, Hanover (att: 42,132)
Germany 2-0 Northern Ireland
Goals: 1-0 Draxler 13, 2-0 Khedira 17
Referee: Tagliavento (ITA)
Germany: Neuer, Hector (Volland 81), Hummels, Khedira, Draxler, Kroos, Özil (Gündoğan 46), Müller, Boateng (Mustafi 69), Kimmich, Götze. Coach: Joachim Löw (GER)
Northern Ireland: McGovern, Ferguson, McAuley, J Evans, Hodson, Davis, C Evans, Norwood (McNair 73), Hughes, Ward (McGinn 61), Magennis (K Lafferty 76). Coach: Michael O'Neill (NIR)

11/10/16, Ullevaal Stadion, Oslo (att: 8,214)
Norway 4-1 San Marino
Goals: 1-0 D Simoncini 12(og), 1-1 Stefanelli 54, 2-1 Diomandé 77, 3-1 Samuelsen 82, 4-1 King 83
Referee: Bastien (FRA)
Norway: Jarstein, Aleesami, Hovland, Strandberg, Tettey (Samuelsen 67), King, Henriksen (Diomandé 46), Skjelbred, Svensson, Selnæs, Berget (Sørloth 73). Coach: Per-Mathias Høgmo (NOR)
San Marino: A Simoncini, Valentini (Hirsch 68), F Vitaioli, D Simoncini, Brolli, Stefanelli (Selva 82), Della Valle, Zafferani, Rinaldi (M Berardi 46), Tosi, Mazza. Coach: Pierangelo Manzaroli (SMR)

11/11/16, Eden Arena, Prague (att: 16,411)
Czech Republic 2-1 Norway
Goals: 1-0 Krmenčík 11, 2-0 Zmrhal 47, 2-1 King 87
Referee: Nijhuis (NED)
Czech Republic: Vaclík, Kadeřábek, Droppa (Pavelka 81), Sivok, Zmrhal, Dočkal, Krmenčík (Schick 81), Brabec, Hořava, Krejčí (Skalák 86), Novák. Coach: Karel Jarolím (CZE)
Norway: Jarstein, Aleesami, Hovland, Tettey, King, Johansen, Henriksen (Diomandé 61), Elabdellaoui, Skjelbred (Dæhli 51), Forren, Berget (T Elyounoussi 71). Coach: Per-Mathias Høgmo (NOR)

11/11/16, Windsor Park, Belfast (att: 18,404)
Northern Ireland 4-0 Azerbaijan
Goals: 1-0 K Lafferty 27, 2-0 McAuley 40, 3-0 C McLaughlin 66, 4-0 Brunt 83
Referee: Turpin (FRA)
Northern Ireland: McGovern, C McLaughlin, Ferguson (McGinn 73), McAuley, J Evans, Davis, K Lafferty (Grigg 61), Brunt, C Evans (McNair 81), Norwood, Magennis. Coach: Michael O'Neill (NIR)
Azerbaijan: K Ağayev, Qarayev, Mirzäbäyov, Medvedev, B Hüseynov, Qurbanov (Ramazanov 75), Mahmudov (Nazarov 70), Ämirquliyev, Şeydayev (Yılmaz 46), Daşdämirov, İsmayılov. Coach: Robert Prosinečki (CRO)

11/11/16, San Marino Stadium, Serravalle (att: 3,851)
San Marino 0-8 Germany
Goals: 0-1 Khedira 7, 0-2 Gnabry 9, 0-3 Hector 32, 0-4 Gnabry 58, 0-5 Hector 65, 0-6 Gnabry 76, 0-7 Stefanelli 82(og), 0-8 Volland 85
Referee: Kuchin (KAZ)
San Marino: A Simoncini, F Vitaioli, D Simoncini, M Vitaioli (Hirsch 90+1), A Gasperoni, Stefanelli, Zafferani (Brolli 83), M Berardi, Cesarini, Tosi (Domeniconi 58), Palazzi. Coach: Pierangelo Manzaroli (SMR)

Germany: Ter Stegen, Hector, Hummels, Khedira (Goretzka 77), Gnabry, Müller, Henrichs, Kimmich, Götze (Meyer 71), Gündoğan, Gomez (Volland 71). Coach: Joachim Löw (GER)

26/03/17, Tofiq Bähramov adına Respublika stadionu, Baku (att: 30,000)
Azerbaijan 1-4 Germany
Goals: 0-1 Schürrle 19, 1-1 Nazarov 31, 1-2 Müller 36, 1-3 Gomez 45, 1-4 Schürrle 81
Referee: Orsato (ITA)
Azerbaijan: K Ağayev, Qarayev, Mirzäbäyov, Paşayev, B Hüseynov, Nazarov, R F Sadıqov, C Hüseynov, Ämirquliyev (İsrafilov 87), Şeydayev (Yılmaz 67), İsmayılov (Qurbanov 81). Coach: Robert Prosinečki (CRO)
Germany: Leno, Hector, Höwedes, Hummels, Khedira, Draxler (Sané 84), Kroos (Rudy 89), Schürrle, Müller, Kimmich, Gomez (Özil 61). Coach: Joachim Löw (GER)

26/03/17, Windsor Park, Belfast (att: 18,161)
Northern Ireland 2-0 Norway
Goals: 1-0 Ward 2, 2-0 Washington 33
Referee: Göçek (TUR)
Northern Ireland: McGovern, C McLaughlin, McAuley, J Evans, Davis, Washington (K Lafferty 85), Brunt, Dallas (Lund 88), Norwood, Ward (McGinn 80), Cathcart. Coach: Michael O'Neill (NIR)
Norway: Jarstein, Skjelvik, Hovland, Valsvik, Nordtveit, King, Johansen (Berge 75), Søderlund (Diomandé 63), T Elyounoussi (Dæhli 53), Elabdellaoui, M Elyounoussi. Coach: Lars Lagerbäck (SWE)

26/03/17, San Marino Stadium, Serravalle (att: 1,023)
San Marino 0-6 Czech Republic
Goals: 0-1 Barák 17, 0-2 Darida 19, 0-3 Barák 24, 0-4 Gebre Selassie 26, 0-5 Krmenčík 43, 0-6 Darida 77(p)
Referee: Tohver (EST)
San Marino: A Simoncini, Cesarini, F Vitaioli, D Simoncini, M Vitaioli, Domeniconi, Stefanelli (Mazza 84), Zafferani, Cervellini (Battistini 90+1), Rinaldi (Tomassini 62), Palazzi. Coach: Pierangelo Manzaroli (SMR)
Czech Republic: Vaclík, Gebre Selassie, Brabec, Sivok, Darida, Dočkal, Krmenčík (Škoda 68), Jankto (Zmrhal 68), Krejčí, Barák (Hořava 76), Novák. Coach: Karel Jarolím (CZE)

10/06/17, Tofig Bahramov Republican stadium, Baku (att: 27,978)
Azerbaijan 0-1 Northern Ireland
Goal: 0-1 Dallas 90+2
Referee: Estrada (ESP)
Azerbaijan: K Ağayev, Qarayev, Paşayev, Medvedev, B Hüseynov, Şeydayev (Abdullayev 90), Nazarov (Äläsgärov 77), R F Sadıqov, C Hüseynov, Almeida, İsmayılov (Ämirquliyev 84). Coach: Robert Prosinečki (CRO)
Northern Ireland: McGovern, C McLaughlin, McAuley (McGinn 25; Hodson 86), J Evans, Davis, Boyce (K Lafferty 77), Brunt, Dallas, Norwood, Hughes, Magennis. Coach: Michael O'Neill (NIR)

10/06/17, Stadion Nürnberg, Nuremberg (att: 32,467)
Germany 7-0 San Marino
Goals: 1-0 Draxler 11, 2-0 Wagner 16, 3-0 Wagner 29, 4-0 Younes 38, 5-0 Mustafi 47, 6-0 Brandt 72, 7-0 Wagner 85
Referee: Petrescu (ROU)
Germany: Ter Stegen, Mustafi, Hector (Plattenhardt 55), Draxler (Demme 76), Goretzka, Wagner, Stindl (Werner 55), Can, Younes, Kimmich, Brandt. Coach: Joachim Löw (GER)
San Marino: Benedettini, Cesarini (Brolli 87), Palazzi, A Golinucci, Bonini, Mazza (Bernardi 69), Zafferani, Della Valle, Cervellini, Rinaldi (Hirsch 78), Biordi. Coach: Pierangelo Manzaroli (SMR)

10/06/17, Ullevaal Stadion, Oslo (att: 12,179)
Norway 1-1 Czech Republic
Goals: 0-1 Gebre Selassie 36, 1-1 Søderlund 55(p)
Referee: Marriner (ENG)
Norway: Jarstein, Aleesami, Reginiussen (Valsvik 33), Nordtveit, Johansen, Søderlund (Johnsen 71), T Elyounoussi, M Elyounoussi, Berge, Svensson, Berget (Dæhli 61). Coach: Lars Lagerbäck (SWE)
Czech Republic: Vaclík, Kadeřábek, Gebre Selassie, Brabec, Sivok, Zmrhal (Jankto 43), Darida (Hořava 79), Dočkal, Krmenčík (Schick 63), Souček, Krejčí. Coach: Karel Jarolím (CZE)

Remaining fixtures

01/09/17
Czech Republic - Germany
Norway - Azerbaijan
San Marino - Northern Ireland

04/09/17
Azerbaijan - San Marino
Germany - Norway
Northern Ireland - Czech Republic

05/10/17
Azerbaijan - Czech Republic
Northern Ireland - Germany
San Marino - Norway

08/10/17
Czech Republic - San Marino
Germany - Azerbaijan
Norway - Northern Ireland

Group D

05/09/16, Boris Paichadze Dinamo Arena, Tbilisi (att: 28,500)
Georgia 1-2 Austria
Goals: 0-1 Hinteregger 16, 0-2 Janko 42, 1-2 Ananidze 78
Referee: Kulbakov (BLR)
Georgia: Loria, U Lobjanidze (Chanturia 84), Kverkvelia, Kashia, Amisulashvili (Okriashvili 76), Daushvili, Ananidze, Kazaishvili, Dvalishvili (Skhirtladze 63), Jigauri, Navalovski. Coach: Vladimír Weiss (SVK)
Austria: Almer, Dragovic, Hinteregger, Arnautovic, Alaba, Junuzovic (Schöpf 67), Harnik (Sabitzer 72), Suttner, Baumgartlinger, Klein, Janko (Gregoritsch 76). Coach: Marcel Koller (SUI)

05/09/16, Stadion Rajko Mitić, Belgrade (att: 7,896)
Serbia 2-2 Republic of Ireland
Goals: 0-1 Hendrick 3, 1-1 Kostić 62, 2-1 Tadić 69(p), 2-2 Murphy 81
Referee: Kassai (HUN)
Serbia: Rajković, Rukavina, Gudelj, Nastasić, Ivanović, A Mitrović (Pavlović 59), Tadić, Mladenović (D Tošić 76), Milivojević, Kostić (Katai 82), Vuković. Coach: Slavoljub Muslin (SRB)
Republic of Ireland: Randolph, Coleman, O'Shea, Keogh, Whelan, S Long (Clark 90+1), Brady, McClean, Hendrick (Murphy 75), Ward (Quinn 70), Walters. Coach: Martin O'Neill (NIR)

05/09/16, Cardiff City Stadium, Cardiff (att: 31,731)
Wales 4-0 Moldova
Goals: 1-0 Vokes 38, 2-0 Allen 44, 3-0 Bale 51, 4-0 Bale 90+5(p)
Referee: Liany (ISR)
Wales: Hennessey, Gunter, Taylor, Davies, Chester, A Williams (Collins 82), Allen, King, Bale, Ledley (Huws 67), Vokes (Robson-Kanu 75). Coach: Chris Coleman (WAL)
Moldova: Cebanu, Armas, Epureanu, Ionita, Gatcan, Cebotari (Sidorenco 75), Dedov (Mihaliov 85), Ginsari (Bugaiov 75), Cascaval, Cojocari, Jardan. Coach: Igor Dobrovolski (RUS)

06/10/16, Ernst-Happel-Stadion, Vienna (att: 44,200)
Austria 2-2 Wales
Goals: 0-1 Allen 22, 1-1 Arnautovic 28, 1-2 Wimmer 45+1(og), 2-2 Arnautovic 48
Referee: Çakır (TUR)
Austria: Almer (Özcan 58), Dragovic, Hinteregger, Wimmer, Arnautovic (Schaub 87), Alaba, Sabitzer, Junuzovic (Schöpf 79), Baumgartlinger, Klein, Janko. Coach: Marcel Koller (SUI)
Wales: Hennessey, Gunter, Taylor (Huws 90+1), Davies, Chester, A Williams, Allen (Edwards 56), King, Bale, Ledley, Vokes (Robson-Kanu 77). Coach: Chris Coleman (WAL)

06/10/16, Stadionul Zimbru, Chisinau (att: 6,192)
Moldova 0-3 Serbia
Goals: 0-1 Kostić 19, 0-2 Ivanović 37, 0-3 Tadić 59
Referee: Kulbakov (BLR)
Moldova: Cebanu, Carp, Racu, Epureanu, Cojocari, Gatcan, Cebotari (Ginsari 77), Dedov (Sidorenco 63), Bolohan, G Andronic (Mihaliov 69), Bugaiov. Coach: Igor Dobrovolski (RUS)
Serbia: Stojković, Rukavina, Gudelj, Nastasić, Ivanović, Tadić, Kolarov, Milivojević, Kostić (Z Tošić 69), Pavlović (Katai 46), Vuković (S Mitrović 69). Coach: Slavoljub Muslin (SRB)

Gareth Bale puts Wales 3-0 up in their opening qualifier at home to Moldova

06/10/16, Aviva Stadium, Dublin (att: 39,793)
Republic of Ireland 1-0 Georgia
Goal: 1-0 Coleman 56
Referee: Chapron (FRA)
Republic of Ireland: Randolph, Coleman, Clark, Duffy, McCarthy, S Long (O'Shea 90+4), Brady (Whelan 79), McClean, Hendrick, Ward, Walters. Coach: Martin O'Neill (NIR)
Georgia: Loria, Kakabadze, Kashia, Kverkvelia, Daushvili (Kacharava 90+3), Ananidze (Skhirtladze 73), Kazaishvili, Okriashvili, Gvilia, Navalovski (Kobakhidze 89), Mchedlidze. Coach: Vladimír Weiss (SVK)

09/10/16, Stadionul Zimbru, Chisinau (att: 6,089)
Moldova 1-3 Republic of Ireland
Goals: 0-1 S Long 2, 1-1 Bugaiov 45+1, 1-2 McClean 69, 1-3 McClean 76
Referee: Kehlet (DEN)
Moldova: Calancea, Armas (Golovatenco 36), Cojocari, Gatcan, Dedov, Bordian, Posmac, Bolohan, G Andronic (Sidorenco 83), Bugaiov, Zasavitschi (Cebotari 61). Coach: Igor Dobrovolski (RUS)
Republic of Ireland: Randolph, Coleman, Clark, Whelan, Duffy, McCarthy (Meyler 80), S Long (O'Dowda 63), McClean, Hoolahan (O'Kane 86), Ward, Walters. Coach: Martin O'Neill (NIR)

09/10/16, Stadion Rajko Mitić, Belgrade (att: 14,200)
Serbia 3-2 Austria
Goals: 1-0 A Mitrović 6, 1-1 Sabitzer 16, 2-1 A Mitrović 23, 2-2 Janko 62, 3-2 Tadić 74
Referee: Eriksson (SWE)
Serbia: Stojković, Rukavina (Maksimović 89), Nastasić, Ivanović, A Mitrović (Gudelj 77), Tadić, Kolarov, S Mitrović, Fejsa, Milivojević, Kostić (Katai 65). Coach: Slavoljub Muslin (SRB)
Austria: Özcan, Dragovic (Prödl 71), Hinteregger, Wimmer, Arnautovic, Alaba, Sabitzer, Junuzovic (Schöpf 63), Baumgartlinger (Ilsanker 58), Klein, Janko. Coach: Marcel Koller (SUI)

09/10/16, Cardiff City Stadium, Cardiff (att: 32,652)
Wales 1-1 Georgia
Goals: 1-0 Bale 10, 1-1 Okriashvili 57
Referee: Mazzoleni (ITA)
Wales: Hennessey, Gunter, Taylor (Cotterill 70), Davies, Chester, A Williams, King (Robson-Kanu 61), Bale, Edwards, Ledley (Huws 73), Vokes. Coach: Chris Coleman (WAL)
Georgia: Loria, Kakabadze, Kashia, Kverkvelia, Daushvili, Ananidze (Kacharava 90+3), Kazaishvili, Okriashvili (Jigauri 90+1), Gvilia, Navalovski, Mchedlidze (Dvalishvili 75). Coach: Vladimír Weiss (SVK)

12/11/16, Ernst-Happel-Stadion, Vienna (att: 48,500)
Austria 0-1 Republic of Ireland
Goal: 0-1 McClean 48
Referee: Karasev (RUS)
Austria: Özcan, Dragovic, Hinteregger, Wimmer (Ilsanker 78), Arnautovic, Alaba, Sabitzer (Harnik 73), Baumgartlinger, Klein, Schöpf (Schaub 57), Janko. Coach: Marcel Koller (SUI)
Republic of Ireland: Randolph, Coleman, Clark, Whelan (Meyler 24), Arter, Brady, McClean (McGeady 85), Hendrick, Hoolahan (McGoldrick 78), Duffy, Walters. Coach: Martin O'Neill (NIR)

12/11/16, Boris Paichadze Dinamo Arena, Tbilisi (att: 40,642)
Georgia 1-1 Moldova
Goals: 1-0 Kazaishvili 16, 1-1 Gatcan 78
Referee: Kabakov (BUL)
Georgia: Loria, Kashia, Kverkvelia, Daushvili, Kazaishvili (Skhirtladze 80), Okriashvili, Chanturia, Kvilitaia (Kankava 64), Gvilia (Dvalishvili 71), Kakabadze, Navalovski. Coach: Vladimír Weiss (SVK)

Joy for Aleksandar Mitrović after he gives Serbia the lead against Austria in Belgrade

Moldova: Cebanu, Posmac, Jardan, Epureanu, Racu (Golovatenco 41), Gatcan, Bordian, Bolohan, Mihaliov (G Andronic 77), Sidorenco (A Antoniuc 70), Bugaiov. Coach: Igor Dobrovolski (RUS)

12/11/16, Cardiff City Stadium, Cardiff (att: 32,879)
Wales 1-1 Serbia
Goals: 1-0 Bale 30, 1-1 A Mitrović 86
Referee: Undiano Mallenco (ESP)
Wales: Hennessey, Gunter, Taylor, Chester, A Williams, Allen, Robson-Kanu (Lawrence 68), Ramsey, Bale, Ledley (Edwards 84), Vokes. Coach: Chris Coleman (WAL)
Serbia: Stojković, Rukavina, Nastasić, Ivanović, A Mitrović (Gudelj 88), Tadić, Milivojević, Kostić (Katai 70), Maksimović, Matić, Obradović. Coach: Slavoljub Muslin (SRB)

24/03/17, Ernst-Happel-Stadion, Vienna (att: 21,000)
Austria 2-0 Moldova
Goals: 1-0 Arnautovic 75, 2-0 Harnik 90
Referee: Vad (HUN)
Austria: Lindner, Dragovic, Hinteregger, Ilsanker, Arnautovic (Suttner 90+3), Alaba, Sabitzer, Junuzovic, Prödl, Burgstaller (Harnik 82), Lazaro (Janko 69). Coach: Marcel Koller (SUI)
Moldova: Namasco, Golovatenco (Racu 80), Epureanu, Gatcan, Cebotari, Dedov, Ginsari, Posmac, A Antoniuc (Ionita 62), Bolohan (Mihaliov 90), Bugaiov. Coach: Igor Dobrovolski (RUS)

24/03/17, Boris Paichadze Dinamo Arena, Tbilisi (att: 31,328)
Georgia 1-3 Serbia
Goals: 1-0 Kacharava 6, 1-1 Tadić 45(p), 1-2 A Mitrović 64, 1-3 Gaćinović 86
Referee: Zwayer (GER)
Georgia: Loria, Kashia, Kverkvelia, Kvekveskiri, Kankava, Kazaishvili (Kvilitaia 83), Ananidze, Kacharava, Gvilia (Jigauri 90), Kakabadze (Arabidze 70), Navalovski. Coach: Vladimír Weiss (SVK)
Serbia: Stojković, Rukavina, Ivanović, A Mitrović (Gudelj 71), Tadić, Kolarov, Milivojević, Kostić (Gaćinović 81), Maksimović, Matić, Obradović (Vuković 47). Coach: Slavoljub Muslin (SRB)

24/03/17, Aviva Stadium, Dublin (att: 49,989)
Republic of Ireland 0-0 Wales
Referee: Rizzoli (ITA)
Republic of Ireland: Randolph, Coleman (Christie 72), Keogh, O'Shea, McClean, Whelan, S Long, Hendrick, Ward, Meyler (McGeady 79), Walters. Coach: Martin O'Neill (NIR)
Wales: Hennessey, Taylor, Allen, Ledley (Richards 72), Chester, Robson-Kanu (Vokes 46), Bale, Gunter, Davies, A Williams, Ramsey. Coach: Chris Coleman (WAL)
Red card: Taylor 69 (Wales)

11/06/17, Stadionul Zimbru, Chisinau (att: 4,803)
Moldova 2-2 Georgia
Goals: 1-0 Ginsari 15, 2-0 Dedov 36, 2-1 Merebashvili 65, 2-2 Kazaishvili 70
Referee: Ekberg (SWE)
Moldova: Namasco, Posmac, Carp (Cojocari 73), Epureanu, Tigirlas (Racu 78), Cebotari, Dedov, Ginsari, Bordian, A Antoniuc, Cociuc (Bugaiov 73). Coach: Igor Dobrovolski (RUS)
Georgia: Makaridze, U Lobjanidze (Kvekveskiri 35), Tabidze, Kashia, Kverkvelia, Daushvili (Kazaishvili 46), Kankava, Dvalishvili (Merebashvili 65), Kacharava, Arabidze, Navalovski. Coach: Vladimír Weiss (SVK)

11/06/17, Aviva Stadium, Dublin (att: 50,000)
Republic of Ireland 1-1 Austria
Goals: 0-1 Hinteregger 31, 1-1 Walters 85
Referee: Fernández Borbalán (ESP)
Republic of Ireland: Randolph, Christie, Whelan (McGeady 77), Brady, McClean, Hendrick, Ward (Murphy 56), K Long, Walters, Duffy, Arter (Hoolahan 71). Coach: Martin O'Neill (NIR)
Austria: Lindner, Lainer, Dragovic, Hinteregger, Alaba, Kainz (Gregoritsch 90), Junuzovic (Grillitsch 79), Baumgartlinger, Prödl, Burgstaller (Harnik 75), Lazaro. Coach: Marcel Koller (SUI)

11/06/17, Stadion Rajko Mitić, Belgrade (att: 42,100)
Serbia 1-1 Wales
Goals: 0-1 Ramsey 35(p), 1-1 A Mitrović 74
Referee: Manuel De Sousa (POR)
Serbia: Stojković, Rukavina, Nastasić, Ivanović, A Mitrović, Tadić, Kolarov, Vuković, Milivojević (Gudelj 63), Kostić (Prijović 67), Matić. Coach: Slavoljub Muslin (SRB)
Wales: Hennessey, Gunter, Davies, Chester, A Williams, Allen, Ramsey, Edwards (Huws 73), Ledley, Richards, Vokes (Lawrence 86). Coach: Chris Coleman (WAL)

Remaining fixtures

02/09/17
Georgia - Republic of Ireland
Serbia - Moldova
Wales - Austria

05/09/17
Austria - Georgia
Moldova - Wales
Republic of Ireland - Serbia

06/10/17
Austria - Serbia
Georgia - Wales
Republic of Ireland - Moldova

09/10/17
Moldova - Austria
Serbia - Georgia
Wales - Republic of Ireland

Group E

04/09/16, Parken, Copenhagen (att: 21,745)
Denmark 1-0 Armenia
Goal: 1-0 Eriksen 17
Referee: Lechner (AUT)
Denmark: Rønnow, Ankersen, Vestergaard, Kjær, Durmisi, Christensen, Kvist, N Jørgensen (Poulsen 66), Eriksen, Fischer, Højbjerg (Delaney 81). Coach: Åge Hareide (NOR)
Armenia: Beglaryan, G Hovhannisyan, Haroyan, Andonyan, Kadimyan, Mkoyan, Artak Yedigaryan, Hambardzumyan, Arshakyan (Pizzelli 70), Malakyan (Manoyan 77), Özbiliz (Ghazaryan 41). Coach: Varuzhan Sukiasyan (ARM)

04/09/16, Astana Arena, Astana (att: 19,905)
Kazakhstan 2-2 Poland
Goals: 0-1 Kapustka 9, 0-2 Lewandowski 35(p), 1-2 Khizhnichenko 51, 2-2 Khizhnichenko 58
Referee: Gözübüyük (NED)
Kazakhstan: Pokatilov, Maliy, Kislitsyn, Kuat, Akhmetov (Abdulin 61), Islamkhan (Tagybergen 79), Muzhikov, Bayzhanov (Nurgaliyev 69), Shomko, Khizhnichenko, Beysebekov. Coach: Talgat Baysufinov (KAZ)
Poland: Fabiański, Milik, Lewandowski, Krychowiak, Rybus, Glik, Błaszczykowski, Salamon, Zieliński, Piszczek, Kapustka (Linetty 83). Coach: Adam Nawałka (POL)

04/09/16, Cluj Arena, Cluj-Napoca (att: 25,468)
Romania 1-1 Montenegro
Goals: 1-0 Popa 85, 1-1 Jovetić 87
Referee: Taylor (ENG)
Romania: Pantilimon, Filip, Moţi, Hoban, Benzar, Andone (Torje 70), Bicfalvi (Popa 76), Stancu (Keşerü 90), Grigore, Săpunaru, Stanciu. Coach: Christoph Daum (GER)
Montenegro: Božović, Vukčević, Tomašević, Vešović (Kojašević 80), Bakić (Mugoša 68), Jovetić, Bećiraj (Nikolić 90+2), Savić, Šćekić, Simić, Marušić. Coach: Ljubiša Tumbaković (SRB)

08/10/16, Vazgen Sargsyan anvan Hanrapetakan Marzadasht, Yerevan (att: 5,500)
Armenia 0-5 Romania
Goals: 0-1 Stancu 4(p), 0-2 Popa 10, 0-3 Marin 12, 0-4 Stanciu 29, 0-5 Chipciu 60
Referee: Bezborodov (RUS)
Armenia: Beglaryan, Haroyan, Andonyan (Voskanyan 39), Pizzelli, Malakyan, Poghosyan (Muradyan 33), Grigoryan, Mkoyan, Hayrapetyan, Manoyan, Özbiliz (K Hovhannisyan 64). Coach: Varuzhan Sukiasyan (ARM)
Romania: Tătăruşanu, Benzar, Latovlevici, Hoban, Chipciu (Rotariu 67), Popa, Marin, Stancu (Keşerü 57), Grigore, Săpunaru, Stanciu (Bicfalvi 82). Coach: Christoph Daum (GER)
Red card: Malakyan 3 (Armenia)

08/10/16, Gradski Stadion Podgorica, Podgorica (att: 8,517)
Montenegro 5-0 Kazakhstan
Goals: 1-0 Tomašević 24, 2-0 Vukčević 59, 3-0 Jovetić 64, 4-0 Bećiraj 73, 5-0 Savić 78
Referee: Schörgenhofer (AUT)
Montenegro: Božović, Vukčević (Nikolić 68), Tomašević, Vešović, Jovetić, Bećiraj (Raičević 76), Savić, Kojašević, Šćekić (Bakić 83), Simić, Marušić. Coach: Ljubiša Tumbaković (SRB)
Kazakhstan: Pokatilov, Maliy, Kislitsyn, Kuat (Tagybergen 76), Mukhutdinov, Islamkhan (Muzhikov 64), Nurgaliyev, Shomko, Khizhnichenko (Murtazayev 85), Beysebekov, Logvinenko. Coach: Talgat Baysufinov (KAZ)

08/10/16, PGE Narodowy, Warsaw (att: 56,811)
Poland 3-2 Denmark
Goals: 1-0 Lewandowski 20, 2-0 Lewandowski 36(p), 3-0 Lewandowski 48, 3-1 Glik 49(og), 3-2 Y Poulsen 69
Referee: Rocchi (ITA)
Poland: Fabiański, Jędrzejczyk, Cionek, Milik (Linetty 46), Lewandowski, Krychowiak, Grosicki (Rybus 74), Glik, Błaszczykowski (Peszko 89), Zieliński, Piszczek. Coach: Adam Nawałka (POL)
Denmark: Schmeichel, Ankersen, Vestergaard (Delaney 82), Kjær, Durmisi, Christensen, Kvist, N Jørgensen (Poulsen 46), Eriksen, Fischer (Sisto 75), Højbjerg. Coach: Åge Hareide (NOR)

11/10/16, Parken, Copenhagen (att: 20,582)
Denmark 0-1 Montenegro
Goal: 0-1 Bećiraj 32
Referee: Undiano Mallenco (ESP)
Denmark: Schmeichel, Ankersen, Kjær, Durmisi, Christensen, Delaney, Eriksen, Fischer (Cornelius 70), M Jørgensen (N Jørgensen 83), Poulsen, Højbjerg (Sisto 63). Coach: Åge Hareide (DEN)
Montenegro: Božović, Vukčević, Tomašević, Vešović (Mijušković 90), Jovetić, Bećiraj, Savić, Kojašević (Jovović 63), Šćekić, Simić (Šofranac 70), Marušić. Coach: Ljubiša Tumbaković (SRB)

11/10/16, Astana Arena, Astana (att: 12,346)
Kazakhstan 0-0 Romania
Referee: Manuel De Sousa (POR)
Kazakhstan: Pokatilov, Maliy, Kuat (Tagybergen 86), Akhmetov, Smakov, Muzhikov, Bayzhanov (Nurgaliyev 66), Shomko, Khizhnichenko (Murtazayev 82), Beysebekov, Logvinenko. Coach: Talgat Baysufinov (KAZ)
Romania: Tătăruşanu, Benzar, Hoban, Toşca, Chipciu (Enache 46), Popa (Andone 84), Marin, Stancu, Grigore (Moţi 26), Săpunaru, Stanciu. Coach: Christoph Daum (GER)

11/10/16, PGE Narodowy, Warsaw (att: 44,786)
Poland 2-1 Armenia
Goals: 1-0 Mkoyan 48(og), 1-1 Pizzelli 50, 2-1 Lewandowski 90+5
Referee: Kružliak (SVK)
Poland: Fabiański, Jędrzejczyk (Wszołek 34), Cionek, Lewandowski, Krychowiak, Grosicki (Kapustka 70), Rybus, Teodorczyk (Wilczek 85), Glik, Błaszczykowski, Zieliński. Coach: Adam Nawałka (POL)
Armenia: Beglaryan, Haroyan, Andonyan, Pizzelli (Hakobyan 85), Grigoryan, K Hovhannisyan (Özbiliz 61), Mkoyan, Minasyan, Muradyan (Voskanyan 34), Hayrapetyan, Manoyan. Coach: Varuzhan Sukiasyan (ARM)
Red card: Andonyan 30 (Armenia)

11/11/16, Vazgen Sargsyan anvan Hanrapetakan Marzadasht, Yerevan (att: 3,500)
Armenia 3-2 Montenegro
Goals: 0-1 Kojašević 36, 0-2 Jovetić 38, 1-2 Grigoryan 50, 2-2 Haroyan 74, 3-2 Ghazaryan 90+3
Referee: Královec (CZE)
Armenia: Beglaryan, Haroyan, Voskanyan, Malakyan, Pizzelli (K Hovhannisyan 81), Koryan (Sarkisov 59), Ghazaryan, Grigoryan, Mkoyan, Mkhitaryan, Hayrapetyan. Coach: Artur Petrosyan (ARM)
Montenegro: Božović, Vukčević (Zverotić 63), Baša, Vešović (Mugoša 86), Jovetić, Bećiraj, Savić, Kojašević (Jovović 74), Šćekić, Stojković, Marušić. Coach: Ljubiša Tumbaković (SRB)

11/11/16, Parken, Copenhagen (att: 18,901)
Denmark 4-1 Kazakhstan
Goals: 1-0 Cornelius 15, 1-1 Suyumbayev 17, 2-1 Eriksen 36(p), 3-1 Ankersen 78, 4-1 Eriksen 90+2
Referee: Yefet (ISR)
Denmark: Rønnow, Ankersen, Kjær, Durmisi, Kvist, Delaney, N Jørgensen, Eriksen, Bjelland, Poulsen, Cornelius (Dolberg 82). Coach: Åge Hareide (NOR)
Kazakhstan: Pokatilov, Maliy, Akhmetov, Mukhutdinov, Islamkhan (Murtazayev 70), Muzhikov (Tunggyshbayev 81), Bayzhanov, Suyumbayev, Shomko, Khizhnichenko (Moldakaraev 60), Logvinenko. Coach: Talgat Baysufinov (KAZ)

11/11/16, Arena Naţională, Bucharest (att: 48,531)
Romania 0-3 Poland
Goals: 0-1 Grosicki 11, 0-2 Lewandowski 83, 0-3 Lewandowski 90+1(p)
Referee: Skomina (SVN)
Romania: Tătăruşanu, Benzar, Toşca, Hoban (Prepeliţă 46), Chiricheş, Chipciu, Popa (Andone 46), Marin, Stancu, Grigore, Stanciu (Keşerü 82). Coach: Christoph Daum (GER)
Poland: Fabiański, Pazdan, Jędrzejczyk, Linetty (Mączyński 70), Lewandowski, Krychowiak, Grosicki (Peszko 89), Glik, Błaszczykowski, Zieliński (Teodorczyk 80), Piszczek. Coach: Adam Nawałka (POL)

Scorer Fatos Bećiraj (right) leads the celebrations as Montenegro go 4-0 up at home to Kazakhstan

26/03/17, Vazgen Sargsyan anvan Hanrapetakan Marzadasht, Yerevan (att: 11,500)
Armenia 2-0 Kazakhstan
Goals: 1-0 Mkhitaryan 73, 2-0 Özbiliz 75
Referee: Stavrev (MKD)
Armenia: Beglaryan, Haroyan, Voskanyan, Andonyan, Malakyan, Pizzelli (E Manucharyan 65), Ghazaryan (Barseghyan 5), Sarkisov (Özbiliz 70), K Hovhannisyan, Mkhitaryan, Hayrapetyan. Coach: Artur Petrosyan (ARM)
Kazakhstan: Loria, Maliy, Kuat (Dmitrenko 82), Tunggyshbayev (Muzhikov 79), Tagybergen, Islamkhan (Bayzhanov 87), Nurgaliyev, Suyumbayev, Nuserbayev, Shomko, Beysebekov. Coach: Aleksandr Borodyuk (RUS)
Red card: Maliy 64 (Kazakhstan)

26/03/17, Gradski Stadion Podgorica, Podgorica (att: 10,439)
Montenegro 1-2 Poland
Goals: 0-1 Lewandowski 40, 1-1 Mugoša 63, 1-2 Piszczek 82
Referee: Kassai (HUN)
Montenegro: Božović, Šofranac, Vukčević, Vešović, Mugoša, Bećiraj, Savić, Kojašević (Ivanić 81), Šćekić (Djordjević 86), Stojković, Marušić (Vučinić 90+2). Coach: Ljubiša Tumbaković (SRB)
Poland: Fabiański, Pazdan, Jędrzejczyk, Mączyński (Cionek 90+2), Linetty (Teodorczyk 78), Lewandowski, Grosicki (Peszko 90+5), Glik, Błaszczykowski, Zieliński, Piszczek. Coach: Adam Nawałka (POL)

26/03/17, Cluj Arena, Cluj-Napoca (att: 26,895)
Romania 0-0 Denmark
Referee: Atkinson (ENG)
Romania: Tătăruşanu, Benzar, Toşca, Chiricheş, Chipciu (Ivan 85), Pintilii, Keşerü (Alibec 63), Latovlevici (Rotariu 76), Marin, Săpunaru, Stanciu. Coach: Christoph Daum (GER)
Denmark: Schmeichel, Ankersen, Vestergaard, Kjær (M Jørgensen 46), Durmisi, Christensen, Kvist, Delaney, Eriksen, Schöne (Braithwaite 69), Cornelius. Coach: Åge Hareide (NOR)

10/06/17, Almaty Ortalyk Stadion, Almaty (att: 19,065)
Kazakhstan 1-3 Denmark
Goals: 0-1 N Jørgensen 27, 0-2 Eriksen 51(p), 1-2 Kuat 76, 1-3 Dolberg 81
Referee: Bezborodov (RUS)
Kazakhstan: Loria, Kuat, Akhmetov, Islamkhan, Zhukov, Muzhikov, Nurgaliyev (Beysebekov 56), Suyumbayev, Nuserbayev (Tunggyshbayev 74), Shomko (Vorogovskiy 67), Logvinenko. Coach: Aleksandr Borodyuk (RUS)
Denmark: Rønnow, Vestergaard, Kjær, Durmisi, Kvist (Schöne 46), Delaney, N Jørgensen, Eriksen, Braithwaite, Stryger (Dalsgaard 82), Poulsen (Dolberg 68). Coach: Åge Hareide (NOR)
Red card: Islamkhan 43 (Kazakhstan)

10/06/17, Gradski Stadion Podgorica, Podgorica (att: 6,861)
Montenegro 4-1 Armenia
Goals: 1-0 Bećiraj 2, 2-0 Jovetić 28, 3-0 Jovetić 54, 4-0 Jovetić 82, 4-1 Koryan 89
Referee: Blom (NED)
Montenegro: Petković, Jovović (Hakšabanović 84), Vukčević (Šćekić 71), Tomašević (Klimenta 75), Kosović, Janković, Jovetić, Bećiraj, Savić, Simić, Marušić. Coach: Ljubiša Tumbakovic (SRB)
Armenia: Beglaryan, Daghbashyan, Voskanyan, Andonyan, Pizzelli (Barseghyan 73), Koryan, K Hovhannisyan, Grigoryan, Mkoyan (Artak Yedigaryan 46), Mkhitaryan, Özbiliz (E Manucharyan 59). Coach: Artur Petrosyan (ARM)

10/06/17, Stadion Narodowy, Warsaw (att: 57,128)
Poland 3-1 Romania
Goals: 1-0 Lewandowski 29(p), 2-0 Lewandowski 57, 3-0 Lewandowski 62(p), 3-1 Stancu 77
Referee: Buquet (FRA)
Poland: Szczęsny, Pazdan, Jędrzejczyk, Cionek, Mączyński (Krychowiak 44), Linetty (Milik 72), Lewandowski, Grosicki, Błaszczykowski, Zieliński (Teodorczyk 81), Piszczek. Coach: Adam Nawałka (POL)
Romania: Tătăruşanu, Benzar, Toşca, Chiricheş, Chipciu (Stanciu 60), Pintilii, Andone, Latovlevici (Grozav 60), Marin (Hanca 79), Stancu, Săpunaru. Coach: Christoph Daum (GER)

Denmark's Christian Eriksen (No10) is mobbed by team-mates after scoring his team's winning goal against Armenia in Copenhagen

Remaining fixtures

01/09/17
Denmark - Poland
Kazakhstan - Montenegro
Romania - Armenia

04/09/17
Armenia - Denmark
Montenegro - Romania
Poland - Kazakhstan

05/10/17
Armenia - Poland
Montenegro - Denmark
Romania - Kazakhstan

08/10/17
Denmark - Romania
Kazakhstan - Armenia
Poland - Montenegro

Group F

04/09/16, LFF stadionas, Vilnius (att: 4,114)
Lithuania 2-2 Slovenia
Goals: 1-0 Černych 32, 2-0 Slivka 34, 2-1 Krhin 77, 2-2 Cesar 90+3
Referee: Artur Dias (POR)
Lithuania: Šetkus, Freidgeimas, Girdvainis, Slavickas, Vaitkūnas, Novikovas, Slivka (Chvedukas 79), Kuklys, Žulpa, Valskis (Matulevičius 85), Černych (Grigaravičius 70). Coach: Edgaras Jankauskas (LTU)
Slovenia: Oblak, Skubic, Samardžič, Cesar, Krhin, Berič (Iličič 46), Birsa, Jokič, Bezjak, Kampl, Verbič (Novakovič 56). Coach: Srečko Katanec (SVN)

04/09/16, National Stadium, Ta' Qali (att: 15,069)
Malta 1-5 Scotland
Goals: 0-1 Snodgrass 10, 1-1 Effiong 14, 1-2 C Martin 53, 1-3 Snodgrass 61(p), 1-4 S Fletcher 78, 1-5 Snodgrass 85
Referee: Aranovskiy (UKR)
Malta: Hogg, Caruana, Zerafa, Sciberras, Agius, P Fenech, Gambin, Schembri (Briffa 66), Borg, Scicluna (R Camilleri 79), Effiong (Mifsud 89). Coach: Pietro Ghedin (ITA)
Scotland: Marshall, Paterson, Robertson, R Martin, Hanley, Bannan, D Fletcher, Burke (Forrest 66), C Martin (S Fletcher 69), Snodgrass, Ritchie (Anya 86). Coach: Gordon Strachan (SCO)
Red cards: Caruana 59 (Malta), Gambin 90+1 (Malta)

04/09/16, Štadión Antona Malatinského, Trnava (att: 18,111)
Slovakia 0-1 England
Goal: 0-1 Lallana 90+5
Referee: Mažić (SRB)
Slovakia: Kozáčik, Pekarík, Škrtel, Ďurica, Greguš, Hubočan, Hamšík, Švento (Kiss 78), Mak (Kubík 71), Ďuriš, Pečovský (Gyömbér 55). Coach: Ján Kozák (SVK)
England: Hart, Walker, Rose, Dier, Cahill, Stones, Sterling (Walcott 71), Henderson (Alli 64), Kane (Sturridge 82), Rooney, Lallana. Coach: Sam Allardyce (ENG)
Red card: Škrtel 57 (Slovakia)

08/10/16, Wembley Stadium, London (att: 81,781)
England 2-0 Malta
Goals: 1-0 Sturridge 29, 2-0 Alli 38
Referee: Johannesson (SWE)
England: Hart, Walker, Bertrand (Rose 19), Henderson, Cahill, Stones, Walcott (Rashford 68), Alli, Sturridge (Vardy 73), Rooney, Lingard. Coach: Gareth Southgate (ENG)
Malta: Hogg, Sciberras, Agius, Borg, P Fenech, Schembri (R Muscat 86), R Camilleri, Kristensen, Effiong (Mifsud 76), Z Muscat, A Muscat. Coach: Pietro Ghedin (ITA)

08/10/16, Hampden Park, Glasgow (att: 35,966)
Scotland 1-1 Lithuania
Goals: 0-1 Černych 59, 1-1 McArthur 89
Referee: Stieler (GER)
Scotland: Marshall, Paterson, Robertson, R Martin, Hanley, Bannan, D Fletcher (McArthur 46), Burke (Forrest 57), C Martin, Snodgrass, Ritchie (Griffiths 71). Coach: Gordon Strachan (SCO)
Lithuania: Šetkus, Freidgeimas, Girdvainis, Vaitkūnas, Novikovas, Slivka, Slavickas (Andriuškevičius 64), Kuklys, Žulpa (Chvedukas 65), Valskis (Grigaravičius 85), Černych. Coach: Edgaras Jankauskas (LTU)

08/10/16, Stadion Stožice, Ljubljana (att: 10,492)
Slovenia 1-0 Slovakia
Goal: 1-0 Kronaveter 74
Referee: Rizzoli (ITA)
Slovenia: Oblak, Samardžič, Cesar, Krhin, Iličič, Kurtič (Kronaveter 72), Birsa (Novakovič 68), Jokič, Bezjak (Mevlja 90+1), Verbič, Aljaž Struna. Coach: Srečko Katanec (SVN)
Slovakia: Kozáčik, Ďurica, Greguš, Hrošovský (Ďuriš 79), Pauschek (Sabo 79), Hubočan, Saláta, Hamšík, Švento (Holúbek 79), Kucka, Mak. Coach: Ján Kozák (SVK)

11/10/16, LFF stadionas, Vilnius (att: 5,067)
Lithuania 2-0 Malta
Goals: 1-0 Černych 76, 2-0 Novikovas 84(p)
Referee: Gil Manzano (ESP)
Lithuania: Šetkus, Freidgeimas, Mikuckis, Vaitkūnas, Novikovas (Grigaravičius 87), Slivka, Kuklys (Chvedukas 79), Žulpa, Valskis (Matulevičius 62), Černych, Andriuškevičius. Coach: Edgaras Jankauskas (LTU)
Malta: Hogg, Caruana, Zerafa, Sciberras, Agius, Borg, P Fenech (Pisani 85), Mifsud, Schembri (R Muscat 83), Kristensen (Effiong 80), Z Muscat. Coach: Pietro Ghedin (ITA)
Red card: Caruana 82 (Malta)

11/10/16, Štadión Antona Malatinského, Trnava (att: 11,098)
Slovakia 3-0 Scotland
Goals: 1-0 Mak 18, 2-0 Mak 56, 3-0 Nemec 68
Referee: Strömbergsson (SWE)
Slovakia: Kozáčik, Škrtel, Ďurica, Sabo, Nemec (Bakoš 69), Škriniar, Hamšík (Kiss 87), Kucka, Mak (Švento 80), Ďuriš, Holúbek. Coach: Ján Kozák (SVK)
Scotland: Marshall, Paterson, Tierney, R Martin, Hanley, Bannan, D Fletcher (Griffiths 64), McArthur, S Fletcher (McGinn 76), Snodgrass, Ritchie (Anya 64). Coach: Gordon Strachan (SCO)

11/10/16, Stadion Stožice, Ljubljana (att: 13,274)
Slovenia 0-0 England
Referee: Aytekin (GER)
Slovenia: Oblak, Samardžič, Cesar (Mevlja 68), Krhin (Omladič 84), Iličič, Kurtič, Birsa (Kronaveter 59), Jokič, Bezjak, Verbič, Aljaž Struna. Coach: Srečko Katanec (SVN)
England: Hart, Walker, Rose, Henderson, Cahill, Stones, Walcott (Townsend 62), Dier, Sturridge (Rashford 82), Alli (Rooney 73), Lingard. Coach: Gareth Southgate (ENG)

11/11/16, Wembley Stadium, London (att: 87,258)
England 3-0 Scotland
Goals: 1-0 Sturridge 23, 2-0 Lallana 50, 3-0 Cahill 61
Referee: Çakır (TUR)
England: Hart, Walker, Rose, Dier, Cahill, Stones, Sterling, Henderson, Sturridge (Vardy 74), Rooney, Lallana. Coach: Gareth Southgate (ENG)
Scotland: Gordon, Anya (Paterson 79), Wallace, Berra, Hanley, Forrest, D Fletcher, Brown, Griffiths, Snodgrass (Ritchie 82), Morrison (McArthur 66). Coach: Gordon Strachan (SCO)

Milivoje Novakovič is overjoyed after scoring against Malta in his farewell international for Slovenia

11/11/16, National Stadium, Ta' Qali (att: 4,207)
Malta 0-1 Slovenia
Goal: 0-1 Verbič 47
Referee: Raczkowski (POL)
Malta: Hogg, Magri, Zerafa, Sciberras, Agius, Mifsud (Farrugia 77), Gambin, R Muscat, Schembri, R Camilleri (Borg 68), Z Muscat. Coach: Pietro Ghedin (ITA)
Slovenia: Oblak, Skubic, Samardžič, Cesar, Krhin, Iličič, Kurtič, Birsa (Omladič 71), Novakovič (Šporar 83), Trajkovski (Jovič 63), Verbič. Coach: Srečko Katanec (SVN)

11/11/16, Štadión Antona Malatinského, Trnava (att: 9,653)
Slovakia 4-0 Lithuania
Goals: 1-0 Nemec 12, 2-0 Kucka 15, 3-0 Škrtel 36, 4-0 Hamšík 86
Referee: Sidiropoulos (GRE)
Slovakia: Kozáčik, Pekarík, Škrtel, Ďurica, Weiss (Bero 89), Nemec (Ďuriš 77), Škriniar, Hubočan, Hamšík, Kucka, Mak (Švento 83). Coach: Ján Kozák (SVK)
Lithuania: Šetkus, Freidgeimas, Girdvainis, Vaitkūnas, Žulpa (Chvedukas 33), Novikovas, Slivka, Kuklys, Valskis (Ruzgis 87), Černych, Andriuškevičius. Coach: Edgaras Jankauskas (LTU)

26/03/17, Wembley Stadium, London (att: 77,690)
England 2-0 Lithuania
Goals: 1-0 Defoe 22, 2-0 Vardy 66
Referee: Buquet (FRA)
England: Hart, Walker, Bertrand, Dier, Keane, Stones, Sterling (Rashford 60), Oxlade-Chamberlain, Defoe (Vardy 60), Alli, Lallana. Coach: Gareth Southgate (ENG)
Lithuania: Šetkus, L Klimavičius, Slavickas, Kijanskas, Vaitkūnas, Žulpa, Novikovas (Grigaravičius 54), Slivka (Paulius 87), Kuklys, Valskis (Matulevičius 74), Černych. Coach: Edgaras Jankauskas (LTU)

26/03/17, National Stadium, Ta' Qali (att: 4,980)
Malta 1-3 Slovakia
Goals: 0-1 Weiss 2, 1-1 Farrugia 14, 1-2 Greguš 41, 1-3 Nemec 84
Referee: Palabıyık (TUR)
Malta: Hogg, Magri, Sciberras, P Fenech, Schembri (Montebello 90+1), Gambin (Kristensen 73), Farrugia, R Camilleri (Gatt Baldacchino 81), Zerafa, Z Muscat, Attard. Coach: Pietro Ghedin (ITA)
Slovakia: Kozáčik, Pekarík, Škrtel, Greguš, Weiss (Rusnák 86), Nemec, Hrošovský, Škriniar, Hubočan, Kucka (Ďuriš 74), Mak (Hamšík 50). Coach: Ján Kozák (SVK)
Red cards: Farrugia 79 (Malta), Nemec 90+1 (Slovakia)

26/03/17, Hampden Park, Glasgow (att: 20,435)
Scotland 1-0 Slovenia
Goal: 1-0 C Martin 88
Referee: Kuipers (NED)
Scotland: Gordon, Tierney, Robertson, R Martin, Mulgrew, Armstrong, Morrison (C Martin 82), Brown, Griffiths (Naismith 50), Snodgrass (Anya 75), Forrest. Coach: Gordon Strachan (SCO)
Slovenia: Oblak, Samardžič, Cesar, Krhin, Iličič, Kurtič, Birsa (Berič 69), Jokič, Bezjak (Verbič 58), Kampl (Omladič 87), Aljaž Struna. Coach: Srečko Katanec (SVN)

10/06/17, LFF stadionas, Vilnius (att: 4,083)
Lithuania 1-2 Slovakia
Goals: 0-1 Weiss 32, 0-2 Hamšík 58, 1-0 Novikovas 90+3
Referee: Gräfe (GER)
Lithuania: Zubas, L Klimavičius, Kijanskas, Slavickas, Šernas, Novikovas, Slivka (Dapkus 75), Kuklys, Valskis (Matulevičius 72), Borovskij, Černych. Coach: Edgaras Jankauskas (LTU)
Slovakia: Dúbravka, Pekarík, Škrtel, Ďurica, Greguš, Weiss, Duda (Bénes 89), Škriniar, Hubočan (Gyömbér 58), Hamšík, Mak (Rusnák 77). Coach: Ján Kozák (SVK)

10/06/17, Hampden Park, Glasgow (att: 48,520)
Scotland 2-2 England
Goals: 0-1 Oxlade-Chamberlain 70, 1-1 Griffiths 87, 2-1 Griffiths 90, 2-2 Kane 90+3
Referee: Tagliavento (ITA)
Scotland: Gordon, Tierney, Robertson, Berra, Mulgrew, Morrison (McArthur 46), Armstrong, Brown, Griffiths, Snodgrass (Fraser 67), Anya (C Martin 81). Coach: Gordon Strachan (SCO)
England: Hart, Walker, Bertrand, Dier, Cahill, Smalling, Rashford (Oxlade-Chamberlain 65), Livermore (Defoe 90+2), Kane, Alli (Sterling 84), Lallana. Coach: Gareth Southgate (ENG)

10/06/17, Stadion Stožice, Ljubljana (att: 7,839)
Slovenia 2-0 Malta
Goals: 1-0 Iličič 45+2, 2-0 Novakovič 84
Referee: Evans (WAL)
Slovenia: Oblak, Skubic (Palčič 89), Delamea Mlinar, Krhin, Iličič, Kurtič, Berič (Novakovič 64), Jokič, Bezjak (Omladič 59), Mevlja, Verbič. Coach: Srečko Katanec (SVN)
Malta: Hogg, Borg (Magri 89), Agius, R Fenech, Failla, Schembri (Mifsud 62), Kristensen (Gambin 46), Effiong, Z Muscat, Pisani, A Muscat. Coach: Pietro Ghedin (ITA)

Remaining fixtures

01/09/17
Malta - England
Lithuania - Scotland
Slovakia - Slovenia

04/09/17
England - Slovakia
Scotland - Malta
Slovenia - Lithuania

05/10/17
England - Slovenia
Malta - Lithuania
Scotland - Slovakia

08/10/17
Lithuania - England
Slovakia - Malta
Slovenia - Scotland

European Qualifiers

Group G

05 & 06/09/16, Loro Boriçi Stadium, Shkoder (att: 14,667)
Albania 2-1 FYR Macedonia
Goals: 1-0 Sadiku 9, 1-1 Alioski 51, 2-1 Balaj 89
Referee: Göçek (TUR)
Albania: Berisha, Hysaj, Djimsiti, Agolli, Sadiku, Gashi (Memushaj 60), Kukeli, Xhaka, Mavraj, Hyka (Roshi 67), Abrashi (Balaj 60). Coach: Gianni De Biasi (ITA)
FYR Macedonia: Zahov, Zhuta, Ristevski, Mojsov (Ibraimi 89), Sikov, Alioski, Pandev, Hasani (Gjorgjev 74), Ristovski, Stjepanovic (Petrovic 61), Spirovski. Coach: Igor Angelovski (MKD)

05/09/16, Sammy Ofer Stadium, Haifa (att: 29,300)
Israel 1-3 Italy
Goals: 0-1 Pellè 14, 0-2 Candreva 31(p), 1-2 Ben Haim II 35, 1-3 Immobile 83
Referee: Karasev (RUS)
Israel: Goresh, Davidzada, N Biton (Atzili 57), Zahavi, Kayal, Hemed, Ben Haim II (Kehat 62), Yeini, Tzedek, Tibi (Gershon 50), B Biton. Coach: Elisha Levi (ISR)
Italy: Buffon, Chiellini, Candreva (Florenzi 67), Bonaventura (Ogbonna 63), Pellè, Verratti, Antonelli, Barzagli, Parolo, Éder (Immobile 70), Bonucci. Coach: Giampiero Ventura (ITA)
Red card: Chiellini 55 (Italy)

05/09/16, Estadio Municipal Reino de León, Leon (att: 12,139)
Spain 8-0 Liechtenstein
Goals: 1-0 Diego Costa 10, 2-0 Sergi Roberto 55, 3-0 Silva 59, 4-0 Vitolo 60, 5-0 Diego Costa 66, 6-0 Morata 82, 7-0 Morata 83, 8-0 Silva 90+1
Referee: Evans (WAL)
Spain: De Gea, Piqué, Busquets, Sergi Roberto, Koke, Thiago (Nolito 46), Vitolo (Marco Asensio 79), Sergio Ramos, Jordi Alba, Diego Costa (Morata 68), Silva. Coach: Julen Lopetegui (ESP)
Liechtenstein: Jehle, Göppel, Kaufmann, Rechsteiner (Yildiz 71), Marcel Büchel, Wieser, Burgmeier, Martin Büchel (Gubser 83), Hasler, Salanovic (Wolfinger 77), Polverino. Coach: René Pauritsch (AUT)

06/10/16, Juventus Stadium, Turin (att: 38,470)
Italy 1-1 Spain
Goals: 0-1 Vitolo 55, 1-1 De Rossi 82(p)
Referee: Brych (GER)
Italy: Buffon, De Sciglio, Romagnoli, Florenzi, Pellè (Immobile 59), Barzagli, De Rossi, Éder, Montolivo (Bonaventura 30), Bonucci, Parolo (Belotti 76). Coach: Giampiero Ventura (ITA)
Spain: De Gea, Carvajal, Piqué, Busquets, Iniesta, Koke, Vitolo (Thiago 84), Sergio Ramos, Jordi Alba (Nacho 22), Diego Costa (Morata 67), Silva. Coach: Julen Lopetegui (ESP)

06/10/16, Rheinpark Stadion, Vaduz (att: 5,864)
Liechtenstein 0-2 Albania
Goals: 0-1 Jehle 12(og), 0-2 Balaj 71
Referee: Bognar (HUN)
Liechtenstein: Jehle, Göppel, Kaufmann, Marcel Büchel, Wieser, Burgmeier, Oehri, Gubser (Frick 59), Hasler, Salanovic (Kühne 73), Polverino (Rechsteiner 46). Coach: René Pauritsch (AUT)
Albania: Berisha, Hysaj, Djimsiti, Llullaku (Çikalleshi 69), Kukeli (Basha 44), Mavraj, Aliji, Hyka, Balaj, Roshi, Abrashi (Lila 46). Coach: Gianni De Biasi (ITA)

06/10/16, Filip II Arena, Skopje (att: 6,500)
FYR Macedonia 1-2 Israel
Goals: 0-1 Hemed 25, 0-2 Ben Haim II 43, 1-2 Nestorovski 63
Referee: Marriner (ENG)
FYR Macedonia: Bogatinov, Zhuta, Ristevski, Mojsov, Sikov (Ibraimi 51), Alioski, Nestorovski, Pandev (Jahovic 76), Hasani, Ristovski, Petrovic (Spirovski 46). Coach: Igor Angelovski (MKD)
Israel: Goresh, Dasa, Davidzada, N Biton, Zahavi, Cohen, Hemed (Abed 75), Ben Haim II (Buzaglo 68), Golasa (Einbinder 72), Tzedek, Tibi. Coach: Elisha Levi (ISR)
Red card: Tibi 90+4 (Israel)

09/10/16, Loro Boriçi Stadium, Shkoder (att: 15,425)
Albania 0-2 Spain
Goals: 0-1 Diego Costa 55, 0-2 Nolito 63
Referee: Nijhuis (NED)
Albania: Berisha, Lila, Lenjani (Aliji 46), Hysaj, Djimsiti, Agolli, Memushaj (Basha 68), Xhaka (Hyka 75), Mavraj, Balaj, Roshi. Coach: Gianni De Biasi (ITA)
Spain: De Gea, Piqué, Busquets, Iniesta (Isco 78), Koke, Thiago, Vitolo (Nolito 60), Sergio Ramos (Iñigo Martínez 80), Monreal, Diego Costa, Silva. Coach: Julen Lopetegui (ESP)

09/10/16, Itztadion Teddy, Jerusalem (att: 9,000)
Israel 2-1 Liechtenstein
Goals: 1-0 Hemed 4, 2-0 Hemed 16, 2-1 Göppel 49
Referee: Pisani (MLT)
Israel: Goresh, Dasa, Gershon, Zahavi, Cohen, Hemed (Kehat 75), Buzaglo (Atzili 63), Ben Haim II (Dabbur 81), Golasa, Tzedek, Ben Harush. Coach: Elisha Levi (ISR)
Liechtenstein: Jehle, Göppel, Kaufmann, Rechsteiner, Marcel Büchel (Salanovic 88), Christen, Wieser, Burgmeier (Kühne 81), Martin Büchel, Gubser (Frick 75), Hasler. Coach: René Pauritsch (AUT)

09/10/16, Filip II Arena, Skopje (att: 19,195)
FYR Macedonia 2-3 Italy
Goals: 0-1 Belotti 24, 1-1 Nestorovski 57, 2-1 Hasani 59, 2-2 Immobile 75, 2-3 Immobile 90+2
Referee: Makkelie (NED)
FYR Macedonia: Bogatinov, Zhuta (Ibraimi 46), Ristevski, Mojsov, Sikov, Alioski, Nestorovski (Petrovic 68), Pandev, Hasani (Trajcevski 84), Ristovski, Spirovski. Coach: Igor Angelovski (MKD)
Italy: Buffon, De Sciglio, Romagnoli, Candreva, Bonaventura (Parolo 64), Verratti, Immobile, Barzagli, Bonucci, Bernardeschi (Sansone 64), Belotti (Éder 84). Coach: Giampiero Ventura (ITA)

Sergio Ramos (left) congratulates goalscorer Diego Costa as Spain go 3-0 up at home to Israel

12/11/16, Elbasan Arena, Elbasan (att: 7,600)
Albania 0-3 Israel
Goals: 0-1 Zahavi 18(p), 0-2 Einbinder 66, 0-3 Atar 83
Referee: Aytekin (GER)
Albania: Berisha, Hysaj (Çani 79), Djimsiti, Agolli, Memushaj, Llullaku (Hoxha 57), Kukeli, Xhaka (Manaj 82), Mavraj, Balaj, Roshi. Coach: Gianni De Biasi (ITA)
Israel: Goresh, Dasa, Gershon, Natcho, Zahavi, Cohen, Einbinder (Hemed 70), Ben Haim II (Atar 75), Sahar (Buzaglo 64), Tzedek, Tibi. Coach: Elisha Levi (ISR)
Red cards: Djimsiti 17 (Albania), Berisha 55 (Albania)

12/11/16, Rheinpark Stadion, Vaduz (att: 5,864)
Liechtenstein 0-4 Italy
Goals: 0-1 Belotti 11, 0-2 Immobile 12, 0-3 Candreva 32, 0-4 Belotti 44
Referee: Bebek (CRO)
Liechtenstein: Jehle, Kaufmann, Rechsteiner, Marcel Büchel, Christen, Wieser, Burgmeier, Martin Büchel, Oehri, Salanovic, Polverino. Coach: René Pauritsch (AUT)
Italy: Buffon, De Sciglio, Romagnoli, Candreva (Éder 74), Bonaventura (Insigne 67), Belotti, Verratti, Immobile (Zaza 81), De Rossi, Bonucci, Zappacosta. Coach: Giampiero Ventura (ITA)

12/11/16, Estadio Nuevo Los Cármenes, Granada (att: 16,622)
Spain 4-0 FYR Macedonia
Goals: 1-0 Velkovski 34(og), 2-0 Vitolo 63, 3-0 Monreal 84, 4-0 Aduriz 85
Referee: Schörgenhofer (AUT)
Spain: De Gea, Bartra, Busquets, Nacho, Morata (Aduriz 60), Koke (Isco 71), Thiago, Vitolo (Callejón 87), Carvajal, Monreal, Silva. Coach: Julen Lopetegui (ESP)
FYR Macedonia: Dimitrievski, Ristevski, Mojsov, Bardi, Alioski, Nestorovski (Ibraimi 82), Pandev, Hasani (Gjorgjev 87), Ristovski, Velkovski, Spirovski (Zhuta 60). Coach: Igor Angelovski (MKD)

24/03/17, Renzo Barbera, Palermo (att: 33,136)
Italy 2-0 Albania
Goals: 1-0 De Rossi 12(p), 2-0 Immobile 80
Referee: Vinčič (SVN)
Italy: Buffon, De Sciglio, Candreva, Insigne, Belotti, Verratti, Immobile, Barzagli, De Rossi, Bonucci, Zappacosta. Coach: Giampiero Ventura (ITA)
Albania: Strakosha, Lila (Sadiku 77), Hysaj, Veseli, Agolli, Basha (Latifi 90+6), Memushaj, Kukeli, Çikalleshi, Ajeti, Roshi (Grezda 87). Coach: Gianni De Biasi (ITA)

24/03/17, Rheinpark Stadion, Vaduz (att: 4,517)
Liechtenstein 0-3 FYR Macedonia
Goals: 0-1 Nikolov 43, 0-2 Nestorovski 68, 0-3 Nestorovski 73
Referee: Lardot (BEL)
Liechtenstein: Jehle, Göppel, Malin, Rechsteiner (Wolfinger 78), Marcel Büchel, Burgmeier, Martin Büchel (A Sele 83), Gubser, Hasler, Salanovic (Brändle 87), Frick. Coach: René Pauritsch (AUT)
FYR Macedonia: Dimitrievski, Ristevski, Sikov, Trickovski (Babunski 78), Pandev, Ibraimi (Trajkovski 64), Ristovski, Velkoski, Nikolov, Spirovski (Gjorgjev 85), Nestorovski. Coach: Igor Angelovski (MKD)

24/03/17, El Molinón, Gijon (att: 20,321)
Spain 4-1 Israel
Goals: 1-0 Silva 13, 2-0 Vitolo 45+1, 3-0 Diego Costa 51, 3-1 Refaelov 76, 4-1 Isco 88
Referee: Oliver (ENG)
Spain: De Gea, Piqué, Busquets, Iniesta (Isco 70), Thiago (Koke 63), Vitolo (Iago Aspas 83), Sergio Ramos, Jordi Alba, Diego Costa, Carvajal, Silva. Coach: Julen Lopetegui (ESP)

Israel: Marciano, Dasa, Gershon, Natcho, Zahavi, Cohen, Refaelov, Ben Haim II (Hemed 64), Einbinder (Keltjens 60), Tzedek, Tibi (Tawatha 19). Coach: Elisha Levi (ISR)

11/06/17, Stadio Friuli, Udine (att: 20,514)
Italy 5-0 Liechtenstein
Goals: 1-0 Insigne 35, 2-0 Belotti 52, 3-0 Éder 74, 4-0 Bernardeschi 83, 5-0 Gabbiadini 90+1
Referee: Clancy (SCO)
Italy: Buffon, Chiellini, Darmian, Pellegrini, Candreva (Bernardeschi 60), Spinazzola, Belotti (Gabbiadini 75), Insigne, Immobile (Éder 67), Barzagli, De Rossi. Coach: Giampiero Ventura (ITA)
Liechtenstein: Jehle, Göppel, Rechsteiner, Burgmeier (Wolfinger 68), Martin Büchel, Malin, Gubser, Hasler, Salanovic (Brändle 59), Frick, Polverino (Quintans 87). Coach: René Pauritsch (AUT)

11/06/17, Sammy Ofer Stadium, Haifa (att: 15,150)
Israel 0-3 Albania
Goals: 0-1 Sadiku 22, 0-2 Sadiku 44, 0-3 Memushaj 71
Referee: Kulbakov (BLR)
Israel: Goresh, Dasa, Tzedek , Natcho, Zahavi, Cohen, Refaelov (Vered 57), Tawatha, Sahar (Benayoun 67), Tibi, Golasa (Shechter 53). Coach: Elisha Levi (ISR)
Albania: Strakosha, Hysaj, Djimsiti, Memushaj , Sadiku (Çikalleshi 70), Kukeli (Veseli 82), Hyka, Mavraj, Aliji, Roshi (Lila 53), Abrashi. Coach: Gianni De Biasi (ITA)

11/06/17, Filip II Arena, Skopje (att: 20,675)
FYR Macedonia 1-2 Spain
Goals: 0-1 Silva 15, 0-2 Diego Costa 27, 1-2 Ristovski 66
Referee: Gil (POL)
FYR Macedonia: Dimitrievski, Tosevski (Trajkovski 74), Ristevski, Mojsov (Trickovski 85), Sikov, Alioski, Pandev, Ristovski, Stjepanovic (Elmas 46), Spirovski, Nestorovski. Coach: Igor Angelovski (MKD)
Spain: De Gea, Piqué, Busquets, Iniesta (Saúl Ñíguez 90+2), Thiago (Koke 74), Sergio Ramos, Jordi Alba, Diego Costa, Carvajal, Silva (Pedro 69), Isco. Coach: Julen Lopetegui (ESP)

Remaining fixtures

02/09/17
Albania - Liechtenstein
Israel - FYR Macedonia
Spain - Italy

05/09/17
Italy - Israel
Liechtenstein - Spain
FYR Macedonia - Albania

06/10/17
Italy - FYR Macedonia
Liechtenstein - Israel
Spain - Albania

09/10/17
Albania - Italy
Israel - Spain
FYR Macedonia - Liechtenstein

Group H

06/09/16, Stadion Bilino polje, Zenica (att: 8,820)
Bosnia & Herzegovina 5-0 Estonia
Goals: 1-0 Spahić 7, 2-0 Džeko 23(p), 3-0 Medunjanin 71, 4-0 Ibišević 83, 5-0 Spahić 90+2
Referee: Zelinka (CZE)
Bosnia & Herzegovina: Begović, Spahić, Kolašinac, Vranješ (Bičakčić 62), Medunjanin, Ibišević, Pjanić, Džeko (Djurić 81), Lulić, Zukanović, Višća (Miličević 75). Coach: Mehmed Baždarević (BIH)
Estonia: Aksalu, Pikk, Zenjov (Anier 71), Vassiljev, Klavan, Antonov (Sappinen 86), Mets, Kallaste, Kams (Kruglov 46), Baranov, Teniste. Coach: Magnus Pehrsson (SWE)

Belgium captain Eden Hazard scores the third of his country's goals in an 8-1 victory against Estonia in Brussels

06/09/16, GSP, Nicosia (att: 12,029)
Cyprus 0-3 Belgium
Goals: 0-1 R Lukaku 13, 0-2 R Lukaku 61, 0-3 Carrasco 81
Referee: Zwayer (GER)
Cyprus: Panagi, Dossa Júnior, Demetriou, Sotiriou (Mytidis 69), Charalambides, Alexandrou, Laban (Artymatas 69), Kyriakou, Efrem, Laifis, Kastanos (Makris 78). Coach: Christakis Christoforou (CYP)
Belgium: Courtois, Alderweireld, Vermaelen, Vertonghen, Witsel, De Bruyne, Fellaini (Nainggolan 84), R Lukaku (Batshuayi 73), Hazard, Meunier, Carrasco. Coach: Roberto Martínez (ESP)

06/09/16, Estádio Algarve, Faro (att: 460)
Gibraltar 1-4 Greece
Goals: 0-1 Mitroglou 10, 1-1 Walker 26, 1-2 Wiseman 44(og), 1-3 Fortounis 45, 1-4 Torosidis 45+2
Referee: Kehlet (DEN)
Gibraltar: J Perez, Wiseman, J Chipolina, R Casciaro, R Chipolina, Walker, Bosio (K Casciaro 71), L Casciaro, Hernandez, Coombes (Yome 85), Garcia. Coach: Jeff Wood (ENG)
Greece: Karnezis, Maniatis (Tziolis 71), Tzavellas, Manolas, Fortounis, Mitroglou (Vellios 73), Bakasetas, Torosidis, Mantalos (Gianniotas 62), Papastathopoulos, Samaris. Coach: Michael Skibbe (GER)

07/10/16, King Baudouin Stadium, Brussels (att: 42,653)
Belgium 4-0 Bosnia & Herzegovina
Goals: 1-0 Spahić 26(og), 2-0 Hazard 29, 3-0 Alderweireld 60, 4-0 R Lukaku 79
Referee: Atkinson (ENG)
Belgium: Courtois, Alderweireld, Vertonghen, Witsel, Carrasco, Fellaini, R Lukaku (Benteke 82), Hazard (Mirallas 87), Mertens, Meunier, J Lukaku (Ciman 21). Coach: Roberto Martínez (ESP)
Bosnia & Herzegovina: Begović, Bičakčić, Spahić, Kolašinac, Medunjanin, Ibišević (Djurić 64), Pjanić (Cimirot 81), Džeko, Lulić, Zukanović, Jajalo (Višća 73). Coach: Mehmed Baždarević (BIH)

07/10/16, A. Le Coq Arena, Tallinn (att: 4,678)
Estonia 4-0 Gibraltar
Goals: 1-0 Käit 47, 2-0 Vassiljev 52, 3-0 Käit 70, 4-0 Mošnikov 88
Referee: Eskov (RUS)
Estonia: Aksalu, Käit (Lepistu 80), Kruglov, Anier, Zenjov (Henrik Ojamaa 65), Vassiljev (Mošnikov 61), Klavan, Luts, Mets, Baranov, Teniste. Coach: Martin Reim (EST)

Gibraltar: J Perez, J Chipolina (K Casciaro 89), R Casciaro, R Chipolina, L Casciaro, Walker, Mascarenhas-Olivero, Bosio (Payas 58), Bardon, Priestley (Coombes 65), Garcia. Coach: Jeff Wood (ENG)

07/10/16, Stadio Georgios Karaiskakis, Piraeus (att: 16,512)
Greece 2-0 Cyprus
Goals: 1-0 Mitroglou 12, 2-0 Mantalos 42
Referee: Královec (CZE)
Greece: Karnezis, Maniatis, Tzavellas (Karelis 88), Manolas, Fortounis, Mitroglou, Bakasetas (Holebas 77), Torosidis, Mantalos, Papastathopoulos, Stafylidis (Papadopoulos 70). Coach: Michael Skibbe (GER)
Cyprus: Panagi, Dossa Júnior, Charalambous, Demetriou, Charalambides (Christofi 66), Mytidis (Makris 83), Laban, Efrem, Artymatas (Kyriakou 78), Laifis, Kastanos. Coach: Christakis Christoforou (CYP)

10/10/16, Stadion Bilino polje, Zenica (att: 8,900)
Bosnia & Herzegovina 2-0 Cyprus
Goals: 1-0 Džeko 70, 2-0 Džeko 81
Referee: Estrada (ESP)
Bosnia & Herzegovina: Begović, Spahić, Kolašinac (Hajrović 64), Vranješ, Medunjanin, Pjanić, Džeko, Šunjić, Lulić, Djurić (Ibišević 81), Višća (Sušić 78). Coach: Mehmed Baždarević (BIH)
Cyprus: Panagi, Dossa Júnior, Demetriou, Sotiriou, Christofi (Charalambides 77), Alexandrou, Laban, Artymatas (Mytidis 85), Laifis, Kastanos, Makris (Efrem 72). Coach: Christakis Christoforou (CYP)

10/10/16, A. Le Coq Arena, Tallinn (att: 4,467)
Estonia 0-2 Greece
Goals: 0-1 Torosidis 2, 0-2 Stafylidis 60
Referee: Vad (HUN)
Estonia: Aksalu, Aleksandr Dmitrijev (Mošnikov 79), Marin, Zenjov, Vassiljev, Klavan, Luts (Purje 69), Mets, Kallaste, Baranov, Teniste (Kams 31). Coach: Martin Reim (EST)
Greece: Karnezis, Maniatis (Tziolis 86), Manolas, Papadopoulos, Karelis, Mitroglou, Bakasetas, Torosidis (Oikonomou 18), Mantalos, Papastathopoulos (Tachtsidis 6), Stafylidis. Coach: Michael Skibbe (GER)

European Qualifiers

Remaining fixtures

02/09/17
Croatia - Kosovo
Finland - Iceland
Ukraine - Turkey

05/09/17
Iceland - Ukraine
Kosovo - Finland
Turkey - Croatia

06/10/17
Croatia - Finland
Kosovo - Ukraine
Turkey - Iceland

09/10/17
Iceland - Kosovo
Finland - Turkey
Ukraine – Croatia

Top goalscorers (after matchday six)

Robert Lewandowski

Cristiano Ronaldo

11	Robert Lewandowski (Poland)
	Cristiano Ronaldo (Portugal)
6	Romelu Lukaku (Belgium)
	Stevan Jovetić (Montenegro)
	André Silva (Portugal)
5	Thomas Müller (Germany)
	Ciro Immobile (Italy)
	Aleksandar Mitrović (Serbia)
	Diego Costa (Spain)

Tables (after matchday six)

Group A

		Home					Away					Total					
	Pld	W	D	L	F	A	W	D	L	F	A	W	D	L	F	A	Pts
1 Sweden	6	3	1	0	10	2	1	0	1	2	2	4	1	1	12	4	13
2 France	6	2	0	0	6	2	2	1	1	5	3	4	1	1	11	5	13
3 Netherlands	6	2	0	1	9	2	1	1	1	4	4	3	1	2	13	6	10
4 Bulgaria	6	3	0	0	7	3	0	0	3	2	9	3	0	3	9	12	9
5 Belarus	6	1	2	0	3	2	0	0	3	1	9	1	2	3	4	11	5
6 Luxembourg	6	0	0	3	2	7	0	1	2	4	10	0	1	5	6	17	1

Group B

		Home					Away					Total					
	Pld	W	D	L	F	A	W	D	L	F	A	W	D	L	F	A	Pts
1 Switzerland	6	3	0	0	5	0	3	0	0	7	3	6	0	0	12	3	18
2 Portugal	6	3	0	0	13	1	2	0	1	9	2	5	0	1	22	3	15
3 Hungary	6	1	0	1	6	3	1	1	2	2	4	2	1	3	8	7	7
4 Faroe Islands	6	0	1	2	0	8	1	1	1	2	2	1	2	3	2	10	5
5 Andorra	6	1	1	2	2	3	0	0	2	0	10	1	1	4	2	13	4
6 Latvia	6	0	0	3	0	7	1	0	2	2	5	1	0	5	2	12	3

Group C

		Home					Away					Total					
	Pld	W	D	L	F	A	W	D	L	F	A	W	D	L	F	A	Pts
1 Germany	6	3	0	0	12	0	3	0	0	15	1	6	0	0	27	1	18
2 Northern Ireland	6	3	0	0	10	0	1	1	1	1	2	4	1	1	11	2	13
3 Czech Republic	6	1	2	0	2	1	1	1	1	7	4	2	3	1	9	5	9
4 Azerbaijan	6	1	0	2	2	5	1	1	1	1	4	2	1	3	3	9	7
5 Norway	6	1	1	1	5	5	0	0	3	1	5	1	1	4	6	10	4
6 San Marino	6	0	0	3	0	15	0	0	3	1	15	0	0	6	1	30	0

Group D

		Home					Away					Total					
	Pld	W	D	L	F	A	W	D	L	F	A	W	D	L	F	A	Pts
1 Serbia	6	1	2	0	6	5	2	1	0	7	2	3	3	0	13	7	12
2 Republic of Ireland	6	1	2	0	2	1	2	1	0	6	3	3	3	0	8	4	12
3 Wales	6	1	2	0	6	2	0	3	0	3	3	1	5	0	9	5	8
4 Austria	6	1	1	1	4	3	1	1	1	5	5	2	2	2	9	8	8
5 Georgia	6	0	1	2	3	6	0	2	1	3	4	0	3	3	6	10	3
6 Moldova	6	0	1	2	3	8	0	1	2	1	7	0	2	4	4	15	2

Group E

		Home					Away					Total					
	Pld	W	D	L	F	A	W	D	L	F	A	W	D	L	F	A	Pts
1 Poland	6	3	0	0	8	4	2	1	0	7	3	5	1	0	15	7	16
2 Montenegro	6	2	0	1	10	3	1	1	1	4	4	3	1	2	14	7	10
3 Denmark	6	2	0	1	5	2	1	1	1	5	4	3	1	2	10	6	10
4 Romania	6	0	2	1	1	4	1	1	1	6	3	1	3	2	7	7	6
5 Armenia	6	2	0	1	5	7	0	0	3	2	7	2	0	4	7	14	6
6 Kazakhstan	6	0	2	1	3	5	0	0	3	1	11	0	2	4	4	16	2

Group F

		Home					Away					Total					
	Pld	W	D	L	F	A	W	D	L	F	A	W	D	L	F	A	Pts
1 England	6	3	0	0	7	0	1	2	0	3	2	4	2	0	10	2	14
2 Slovakia	6	2	0	1	7	1	2	0	1	5	3	4	0	2	12	4	12
3 Slovenia	6	2	1	0	3	0	1	1	1	3	3	3	2	1	6	3	11
4 Scotland	6	1	2	0	4	3	1	0	2	5	7	2	2	2	9	10	8
5 Lithuania	6	1	1	1	5	4	0	1	2	1	7	1	2	3	6	11	5
6 Malta	6	0	0	3	2	9	0	0	3	0	6	0	0	6	2	15	0

Group G

		Home					Away					Total					
	Pld	W	D	L	F	A	W	D	L	F	A	W	D	L	F	A	Pts
1 Spain	6	3	0	0	16	1	2	1	0	5	2	5	1	0	21	3	16
2 Italy	6	2	1	0	8	1	3	0	0	10	3	5	1	0	18	4	16
3 Albania	6	1	0	2	2	6	2	0	1	5	2	3	0	3	7	8	9
4 Israel	6	1	0	2	3	7	2	0	1	6	5	3	0	3	9	12	9
5 FYR Macedonia	6	0	0	3	4	7	1	0	2	4	6	1	0	5	8	13	3
6 Liechtenstein	6	0	0	3	0	9	0	0	3	1	15	0	0	6	1	24	0

Group H

		Home					Away					Total					
	Pld	W	D	L	F	A	W	D	L	F	A	W	D	L	F	A	Pts
1 Belgium	6	2	1	0	13	2	3	0	0	11	0	5	1	0	24	2	16
2 Greece	6	1	1	0	3	1	2	2	0	7	2	3	3	0	10	3	12
3 Bosnia & Herzegovina	6	3	1	0	12	0	0	1	1	1	5	3	2	1	13	5	11
4 Cyprus	6	1	1	1	3	4	1	0	2	2	5	2	1	3	5	9	7
5 Estonia	6	1	0	2	4	4	0	1	2	1	13	1	1	4	5	17	4
6 Gibraltar	6	0	0	3	2	12	0	0	3	1	12	0	0	6	3	24	0

Group I

		Home					Away					Total					
	Pld	W	D	L	F	A	W	D	L	F	A	W	D	L	F	A	Pts
1 Croatia	6	2	1	0	4	1	2	0	1	7	1	4	1	1	11	2	13
2 Iceland	6	3	0	0	6	2	1	1	1	3	4	4	1	1	9	6	13
3 Turkey	6	2	1	0	6	2	1	1	1	5	4	3	2	1	11	6	11
4 Ukraine	6	2	1	0	5	1	1	1	1	4	4	3	2	1	9	5	11
5 Finland	6	0	1	2	2	4	0	0	3	2	6	0	1	5	4	10	1
6 Kosovo	6	0	0	3	2	12	0	1	2	1	6	0	1	5	3	18	1

NB The nine group winners advance directly to the final tournament. The eight best runners-up, calculated from results against the teams finishing first, third, fourth and fifth in their group, proceed to the play-offs in November 2017 to decide the remaining four berths. Russia, as tournament hosts, are exempt from qualification.

SUPER CUP

Sevilla beaten after extra time in Trondheim

Defenders do damage with last-gasp strikes

Second win in three years for Los Blancos

Real Madrid leave it late

If events in Basel and Milan the previous May had not been conclusive enough, the 2016 UEFA Super Cup served to reinforce Spain's dominance of the European club scene.

Real Madrid and Sevilla staged a repeat of their 2014 encounter in Cardiff, and the outcome was the same as a defiant Madrid came from behind to win a five-goal extra-time thriller in Trondheim, becoming the 13th Spanish winner of the competition and taking the trophy for the third time themselves. Alas for their opponents, it was a third defeat in as many years and their fourth in a row after winning it on their first visit, in 2006.

The Andalusians were entering the new campaign with a new coach, Jorge Sampaoli, the successor to triple UEFA Europa League-winning boss Unai Emery. Real Madrid, meanwhile, were fresh from securing their 11th European Cup, and despite the absence of the injured Cristiano Ronaldo they surged in front through the Portuguese superstar's replacement, Marco Asensio, on 21 minutes, the youngster finding the top corner with a confident strike. When Franco Vázquez squeezed in the equaliser just before half-time, however, it was the prelude to roller-coaster excitement at the Lerkendal Stadion – the setting for Norway's first UEFA club final.

Yevhen Konoplyanka's 72nd-minute penalty turned the game in Sevilla's favour, but just as it seemed that they would gain revenge for their 2-0 defeat by Madrid two years earlier, Merengues centre-back and skipper Sergio Ramos headed home in the same third minute of stoppage time in which he had denied Atlético Madrid UEFA Champions League glory in the 2014 final in Lisbon.

Real Madrid skipper Sergio Ramos lifts the UEFA Super Cup in Trondheim

Timothée Kolodziejczak's second booking three minutes into extra time dealt Sevilla a further heavy blow, and they were clinging on in increasing desperation when, 60 seconds from a penalty shoot-out, right-back Dani Carvajal waltzed through the overworked Sevilla rearguard to score superbly and clinch a dramatic victory for Zinédine Zidane's side.

Final

09/08/16, Lerkendal Stadion, Trondheim (att: 17,939)

Real Madrid CF 3-2 Sevilla FC (aet)

Goals: 1-0 Marco Asensio 21, 1-1 Vázquez 41, 1-2 Konoplyanka 72(p), 2-2 Sergio Ramos 90+3, 3-2 Carvajal 119

Referee: Mažić (SRB)

Real Madrid: Casilla, Carvajal, Sergio Ramos, Varane, Marcelo, Casemiro, Kovačić (James Rodríguez 73), Lucas Vázquez, Morata (Benzema 62), Isco (Modrić 66), Marco Asensio. Coach: Zinédine Zidane (FRA)

Sevilla: Sergio Rico, Kolodziejczak, Daniel Carriço (Rami 51), Iborra (Kranevitter 74), Vietto (Konoplyanka 67), Kiyotake, N'Zonzi, Vitolo, Pareja, Vázquez, Mariano. Coach: Jorge Sampaoli (ARG)

Red card: Kolodziejczak 93 (Sevilla)

Yellow cards: Vitolo 39 (Sevilla), Carvajal 84 (Real Madrid), Marco Asensio 86 (Real Madrid), Kolodziejczak 90 (Sevilla), Kolodziejczak 93 (Sevilla), James Rodríguez 93 (Real Madrid)

Austrian club overcome Benfica in final

Substitutes strike in 2-1 comeback win

Barcelona and Real Madrid go out in semi-finals

Salzburg storm to victory

A new name was added to the UEFA Youth League's embryonic roll of honour as Salzburg emerged triumphant in the now traditional setting of the Stade Colovray at UEFA HQ by the banks of Lake Geneva in Switzerland.

The Austrian club joined inaugural victors Barcelona and two-time champions Chelsea as winners of the Lennart Johansson Trophy. They did it the hard way too, eliminating several high-profile teams en route to Nyon – namely Manchester City, Paris Saint-Germain and Atlético Madrid – having eased past Vardar and Kairat Almaty in the Domestic Champions path.

The calibre of opposition Salzburg overcame in Switzerland was equally impressive. Trailing 1-0 to Barcelona until just after the hour, Marco Rose's side responded with two unanswered goals, substitute Daka Patson scoring the second of them on his competition debut. That was the cue for a flurry of celebratory back-flips from a player who had fired Zambia to victory at the Africa U-20 Cup of Nations the previous month.

The narrative for the final was strikingly similar, only this time Salzburg were a goal down against Benfica until the 72nd minute, when Patson headed in the equaliser. His fellow substitute Alexander Schmidt, making his first appearance since November because of injury, completed the turnaround as Benfica endured their second defeat in the final, having also succumbed to Barcelona three years earlier.

Success amounted to a belated birthday present for Salzburg captain Sandro Ingolitsch, who turned 20 six days before the final. It also meant Rose's charges finished the campaign nine matches unbeaten, having amassed a competition-high tally of 29 goals.

Hannes Wolf, who provided three assists and a goal in Nyon, and his fellow forward Mergim Berisha scored seven apiece over the campaign. They were two of three players in Rose's finals squad with first-team experience. The other, Amadou Haidara, had struck on his senior debut in an Austrian Cup tie less than three weeks before travelling to Nyon.

Salzburg celebrate their UEFA Youth League triumph

Benfica defeated Real Madrid 4-2 in the other semi-final with doubles from João Félix and João Filipe, condemning Los Blancos to their third last-four loss following reverses in 2014 and 2016. The Spanish teams headed home disappointed, although Barcelona's Jordi Mboula, on target against Salzburg, at least had the personal consolation of finishing as the campaign's joint eight-goal leading scorer alongside Ajax's Kaj Sierhuis.

Overall, 40 countries, up three from the previous season, were represented in the 2016/17 edition. For the first time there were entrants from FYR Macedonia, the Republic of Ireland and Montenegro.

The competition was partly designed to bridge the gap between youth and senior teams, and for 16 players that step was taken in 2016/17 as they also featured in the UEFA Champions League. Among that number were Fedor Chalov from quarter-finalists CSKA Moskva, Benfica's José Gomes (their goalscorer in the final), and Borussia Dortmund defender Felix Passlack.

Group stage

Group A

13/09/16, Leichtathletik Stadion St. Jakob, Basel
FC Basel 1893 1-0 PFC Ludogorets Razgrad

13/09/16, Stade Georges-Lefèvre, Saint-Germain-en-Laye
Paris Saint-Germain 0-0 Arsenal FC

28/09/16, Meadow Park, Borehamwood
Arsenal FC 1-2 FC Basel 1893

28/09/16, Georgi Asparuhov Stadion, Sofia
PFC Ludogorets Razgrad 1-8 Paris Saint-Germain

19/10/16, Meadow Park, Borehamwood
Arsenal FC 3-0 PFC Ludogorets Razgrad

19/10/16, Stade Georges-Lefèvre, Saint-Germain-en-Laye
Paris Saint-Germain 4-1 FC Basel 1893

01/11/16, Georgi Asparuhov Stadion, Sofia
PFC Ludogorets Razgrad 1-1 Arsenal FC

01/11/16, Leichtathletik Stadion St. Jakob, Basel
FC Basel 1893 2-3 Paris Saint-Germain

23/11/16, Meadow Park, Borehamwood
Arsenal FC 2-2 Paris Saint-Germain

23/11/16, Georgi Asparuhov Stadion, Sofia
PFC Ludogorets Razgrad 0-4 FC Basel 1893

06/12/16, Stade Georges-Lefèvre, Saint-Germain-en-Laye
Paris Saint-Germain 4-1 PFC Ludogorets Razgrad

06/12/16, Leichtathletik Stadion St. Jakob, Basel
FC Basel 1893 1-1 Arsenal FC

	Pld	W	D	L	F	A	Pts
1 Paris Saint-Germain	6	4	2	0	21	7	14
2 FC Basel 1893	6	3	1	2	11	9	10
3 Arsenal FC	6	1	4	1	8	6	7
4 PFC Ludogorets Razgrad	6	0	1	5	3	21	1

Group B

13/09/16, Stadion Dynamo im. Valeriy Lobanovskiy, Kyiv
FC Dynamo Kyiv 4-1 SSC Napoli

13/09/16, Caixa Futebol Campus, Seixal
SL Benfica 0-0 Beşiktaş JK

28/09/16, Yusuf Ziya Öniş, Istanbul
Beşiktaş JK 3-3 FC Dynamo Kyiv

28/09/16, Pasquale Ianniello, Frattamaggiore
SSC Napoli 2-3 SL Benfica

19/10/16, Stadion Dynamo im. Valeriy Lobanovskiy, Kyiv
FC Dynamo Kyiv 2-1 SL Benfica

19/10/16, Pasquale Ianniello, Frattamaggiore
SSC Napoli 2-2 Beşiktaş JK

01/11/16, Yusuf Ziya Öniş, Istanbul
Beşiktaş JK 0-1 SSC Napoli

01/11/16, Caixa Futebol Campus, Seixal
SL Benfica 1-2 FC Dynamo Kyiv

23/11/16, Yusuf Ziya Öniş, Istanbul
Beşiktaş JK 0-3 SL Benfica

23/11/16, Pasquale Ianniello, Frattamaggiore
SSC Napoli 0-2 FC Dynamo Kyiv

06/12/16, Stadion Dynamo im. Valeriy Lobanovskiy, Kyiv
FC Dynamo Kyiv 3-1 Beşiktaş JK

06/12/16, Caixa Futebol Campus, Seixal
SL Benfica 2-0 SSC Napoli

CSKA Moskva's Khetag Khosonov holds off Tottenham's Keanen Bennetts

	Pld	W	D	L	F	A	Pts
1 FC Dynamo Kyiv	6	5	1	0	16	7	16
2 SL Benfica	6	3	1	2	10	6	10
3 SSC Napoli	6	1	1	4	6	13	4
4 Beşiktaş JK	6	0	3	3	6	12	3

Group C

13/09/16, Mini-Stadium, Manchester
Manchester City FC 4-1 VfL Borussia Mönchengladbach

13/09/16, Mini Estadi, Barcelona
FC Barcelona 2-1 Celtic FC

28/09/16, Fohlenplatz, Monchengladbach
VfL Borussia Mönchengladbach 1-3 FC Barcelona

28/09/16, Cappielow Park, Greenock
Celtic FC 0-4 Manchester City FC

19/10/16, Cappielow Park, Greenock
Celtic FC 1-1 VfL Borussia Mönchengladbach

19/10/16, Mini Estadi, Barcelona
FC Barcelona 1-0 Manchester City FC

01/11/16, Fohlenplatz, Monchengladbach
VfL Borussia Mönchengladbach 4-1 Celtic FC

01/11/16, Mini-Stadium, Manchester
Manchester City FC 0-2 FC Barcelona

23/11/16, Cappielow Park, Greenock
Celtic FC 1-4 FC Barcelona

23/11/16, Fohlenplatz, Monchengladbach
VfL Borussia Mönchengladbach 1-2 Manchester City FC

06/12/16, Mini-Stadium, Manchester
Manchester City FC 3-2 Celtic FC

06/12/16, Mini Estadi, Barcelona
FC Barcelona 1-2 VfL Borussia Mönchengladbach

	Pld	W	D	L	F	A	Pts
1 FC Barcelona	6	5	0	1	13	5	15
2 Manchester City FC	6	4	0	2	13	7	12
3 VfL Borussia Mönchengladbach	6	2	1	3	10	12	7
4 Celtic FC	6	0	1	5	6	18	1

Group D

13/09/16, an der Grünwalderstrasse, Munich
FC Bayern München 4-2 FC Rostov

13/09/16, Sportcomplex de Herdgang, Eindhoven
PSV Eindhoven 0-0 Club Atlético de Madrid

28/09/16, Lokomotiv Stadion, Bataysk
FC Rostov 0-6 PSV Eindhoven

28/09/16, Ciudad Deportiva Cerro Del Espino, Majadahonda
Club Atlético de Madrid 1-3 FC Bayern München

19/10/16, Lokomotiv Stadion, Bataysk
FC Rostov 1-3 Club Atlético de Madrid

19/10/16, an der Grünwalderstrasse, Munich
FC Bayern München 0-2 PSV Eindhoven

01/11/16, Ciudad Deportiva Cerro Del Espino, Majadahonda
Club Atlético de Madrid 1-0 FC Rostov

01/11/16, Sportcomplex de Herdgang, Eindhoven
PSV Eindhoven 2-0 FC Bayern München

23/11/16, Lokomotiv Stadion, Bataysk
FC Rostov 0-1 FC Bayern München

23/11/16, Ciudad Deportiva Cerro Del Espino, Majadahonda
Club Atlético de Madrid 2-0 PSV Eindhoven

06/12/16, an der Grünwalderstrasse, Munich
FC Bayern München 1-1 Club Atlético de Madrid

06/12/16, Sportcomplex de Herdgang, Eindhoven
PSV Eindhoven 6-0 FC Rostov

	Pld	W	D	L	F	A	Pts
1 PSV Eindhoven	6	4	1	1	16	2	13
2 Club Atlético de Madrid	6	3	2	1	8	5	11
3 FC Bayern München	6	3	1	2	9	8	10
4 FC Rostov	6	0	0	6	3	21	0

Group E

14/09/16, Ulrich Haberland Stadion, Leverkusen
Bayer 04 Leverkusen 2-1 PFC CSKA Moskva

14/09/16, Tottenham Training Centre, Enfield
Tottenham Hotspur FC 2-3 AS Monaco FC

27/09/16, Stadium «Oktyabr», Moscow
PFC CSKA Moskva 3-2 Tottenham Hotspur FC

27/09/16, Stade de formation AS Monaco 1, La Turbie
AS Monaco FC 2-1 Bayer 04 Leverkusen

18/10/16, Stadium Oktyabr Artificial Turf, Moscow
PFC CSKA Moskva 4-1 AS Monaco FC

18/10/16, Ulrich Haberland Stadion, Leverkusen
Bayer 04 Leverkusen 3-1 Tottenham Hotspur FC

02/11/16, Stade de formation AS Monaco 1, La Turbie
AS Monaco FC 0-5 PFC CSKA Moskva

02/11/16, Tottenham Training Centre, Enfield
Tottenham Hotspur FC 2-1 Bayer 04 Leverkusen

22/11/16, Stadium Oktyabr Artificial Turf, Moscow
PFC CSKA Moskva 2-1 Bayer 04 Leverkusen

22/11/16, Stade de formation AS Monaco 1, La Turbie
AS Monaco FC 2-1 Tottenham Hotspur FC

07/12/16, Ulrich Haberland Stadion, Leverkusen
Bayer 04 Leverkusen 1-2 AS Monaco FC

07/12/16, Tottenham Training Centre, Enfield
Tottenham Hotspur FC 0-0 PFC CSKA Moskva

	Pld	W	D	L	F	A	Pts
1 PFC CSKA Moskva	6	4	1	1	15	6	13
2 AS Monaco FC	6	4	0	2	10	14	12
3 Bayer 04 Leverkusen	6	2	0	4	9	10	6
4 Tottenham Hotspur FC	6	1	1	4	8	12	4

UEFA Youth League

Group F

14/09/16, Miejski Osrodek Sportu, Zabki
Legia Warszawa 0-2 Borussia Dortmund

14/09/16, Estadio Alfredo Di Stefano, Madrid
Real Madrid CF 1-1 Sporting Clube de Portugal

27/09/16, CGD Stadium Aurelio Pereira, Alcochete
Sporting Clube de Portugal 2-2 Legia Warszawa

27/09/16, Montanhydraulik-Stadion, Holzwickede
Borussia Dortmund 2-5 Real Madrid CF

18/10/16, CGD Stadium Aurelio Pereira, Alcochete
Sporting Clube de Portugal 1-1 Borussia Dortmund

18/10/16, Estadio Alfredo Di Stefano, Madrid
Real Madrid CF 3-2 Legia Warszawa

02/11/16, Montanhydraulik-Stadion, Holzwickede
Borussia Dortmund 0-1 Sporting Clube de Portugal

02/11/16, Miejski Osrodek Sportu, Zabki
Legia Warszawa 1-2 Real Madrid CF

22/11/16, CGD Stadium Aurelio Pereira, Alcochete
Sporting Clube de Portugal 1-3 Real Madrid CF

22/11/16, Dortmund Brackel Training Ground, Dortmund
Borussia Dortmund 3-3 Legia Warszawa

07/12/16, MZOS Znicz, Pruszkow
Legia Warszawa 2-0 Sporting Clube de Portugal

07/12/16, Estadio Alfredo Di Stefano, Madrid
Real Madrid CF 1-3 Borussia Dortmund

	Pld	W	D	L	F	A	Pts
1 Real Madrid CF	6	4	1	1	15	10	13
2 Borussia Dortmund	6	2	2	2	11	11	8
3 Sporting Clube de Portugal	6	1	3	2	6	9	6
4 Legia Warszawa	6	1	2	3	10	12	5

Group G

13/09/16, Schiervelde, Roeselare
Club Brugge KV 2-1 Leicester City FC

14/09/16, Centro de Treinos e Formação Desportiva, Vila Nova de Gaia (Porto)
FC Porto 4-1 FC København

27/09/16, University Stadium, Loughborough
Leicester City FC 0-2 FC Porto

27/09/16, Østerbro, Copenhagen
FC København 0-0 Club Brugge KV

18/10/16, University Stadium, Loughborough
Leicester City FC 3-2 FC København

18/10/16, Schiervelde, Roeselare
Club Brugge KV 0-2 FC Porto

02/11/16, Centro de Treinos e Formação Desportiva, Vila Nova de Gaia (Porto)
FC Porto 1-3 Club Brugge KV

02/11/16, Østerbro, Copenhagen
FC København 3-2 Leicester City FC

22/11/16, Leicester City Training Ground, Leicester
Leicester City FC 2-3 Club Brugge KV

22/11/16, Østerbro, Copenhagen
FC København 3-1 FC Porto

07/12/16, Centro de Treinos e Formação Desportiva, Vila Nova de Gaia (Porto)
FC Porto 2-1 Leicester City FC

07/12/16, Schiervelde, Roeselare
Club Brugge KV 0-3 FC København

	Pld	W	D	L	F	A	Pts
1 FC Porto	6	4	0	2	12	8	12
2 FC København	6	3	1	2	12	10	10
3 Club Brugge KV	6	3	1	2	8	9	10
4 Leicester City FC	6	1	0	5	9	14	3

Group H

14/09/16, Groupama Academy Stadium, Decines
Olympique Lyonnais 2-0 GNK Dinamo Zagreb

14/09/16, Juventus Training Ground, Turin
Juventus 2-1 Sevilla FC

27/09/16, Felipe del Valle, San Jose de la Rinconada
Sevilla FC 2-1 Olympique Lyonnais

27/09/16, Hitrec-Kacijan, Zagreb
GNK Dinamo Zagreb 2-1 Juventus

18/10/16, Groupama Academy Stadium, Decines
Olympique Lyonnais 0-3 Juventus

18/10/16, Hitrec-Kacijan, Zagreb
GNK Dinamo Zagreb 2-4 Sevilla FC

02/11/16, Felipe del Valle, San Jose de la Rinconada
Sevilla FC 1-1 GNK Dinamo Zagreb

02/11/16, Juventus Training Ground, Turin
Juventus 0-1 Olympique Lyonnais

22/11/16, Hitrec-Kacijan, Zagreb
GNK Dinamo Zagreb 1-2 Olympique Lyonnais

22/11/16, Felipe del Valle, San Jose de la Rinconada
Sevilla FC 0-2 Juventus

07/12/16, Groupama Academy Stadium, Decines
Olympique Lyonnais 0-1 Sevilla FC

07/12/16, Juventus Stadium, Turin
Juventus 0-1 GNK Dinamo Zagreb

	Pld	W	D	L	F	A	Pts
1 Sevilla FC	6	3	1	2	9	8	10
2 Juventus	6	3	0	3	8	5	9
3 Olympique Lyonnais	6	3	0	3	6	7	9
4 GNK Dinamo Zagreb	6	2	1	3	7	10	7

First round

21/09/16, Qäbälä Şähär Stadionu, Qäbälä
Gabala SC 0-2 FC Dinamo Moskva
19/10/16, Rodina, Khimki
FC Dinamo Moskva 5-0 Gabala SC
Aggregate: 7-0; FC Dinamo Moskva qualify.

27/09/16, Untersberg Arena, Grödig
FC Salzburg 5-0 FK Vardar
19/10/16, Nacionalna Arena Filip II Makedonski, Skopje
FK Vardar 0-3 FC Salzburg
Aggregate: 0-8; FC Salzburg qualify.

27/09/16, Constant Vanden Stock Stadium, Brussels
RSC Anderlecht 0-0 FC Midtjylland
19/10/16, Arena Herning, Herning
FC Midtjylland 3-1 RSC Anderlecht
Aggregate: 3-1; FC Midtjylland qualify.

28/09/16, FK Viktoria Žižkov, Prague
AC Sparta Praha 4-0 FK Mladost Podgorica
19/10/16, Gradski Stadion Podgorica, Podgorica
FK Mladost Podgorica 0-5 AC Sparta Praha
Aggregate: 0-9; AC Sparta Praha qualify.

28/09/16, Makarion, Nicosia
APOEL FC 0-3 AS Roma
19/10/16, Campo Agostino Di Bartolomei, Rome
AS Roma 6-1 APOEL FC
Aggregate: 9-1; AS Roma qualify.

28/09/16, Kópavogsvöllur, Kopavogur
Breidablik 0-3 AFC Ajax
19/10/16, De Toekomst, Duivendrecht
AFC Ajax 4-0 Breidablik
Aggregate: 7-0; AFC Ajax qualify.

28/09/16, Štadión FC Nitra, Nitra
FC Nitra 2-3 Málaga CF
19/10/16, La Rosaleda, Malaga
Málaga CF 5-0 FC Nitra
Aggregate: 8-2; Málaga CF qualify.

28/09/16, Pancho stadium, Felcsut
Puskás Akadémia Felcsút 1-1 PAOK FC
19/10/16, Kaftanzoglio, Salonika
PAOK FC 0-0 Puskás Akadémia Felcsút
Aggregate: 1-1; PAOK FC qualify on away goal.

28/09/16, Športni park, Domzale
NK Domžale 1-1 FK Čukarički
19/10/16, FK Čukarički, Belgrade
FK Čukarički 4-1 NK Domžale
Aggregate: 5-2; FK Čukarički qualify.

28/09/16, Lerkendal Stadion, Trondheim
Rosenborg BK 0-0 AIK
19/10/16, Skytteholm IP, Skytteholm - Stockholm
AIK 1-3 Rosenborg BK
Aggregate: 1-3; Rosenborg BK qualify.

28/09/16, NK Zrinjski, Mostar
HŠK Zrinjski Mostar 0-3 FC Zürich
19/10/16, Utogrund, Zurich
FC Zürich 6-0 HŠK Zrinjski Mostar
Aggregate: 9-0; FC Zürich qualify.

28/09/16, Atatürk, Izmir
Altınordu 5-0 PFC Levski Sofia
19/10/16, Georgi Asparuhov Stadion, Sofia
PFC Levski Sofia 1-1 Altınordu
Aggregate: 1-6; Altınordu qualify.

28/09/16, Helsinki Football Stadium, Helsinki
HJK Helsinki 0-0 Cork City FC
19/10/16, Turner's Cross, Cork
Cork City FC 1-0 HJK Helsinki
Aggregate: 1-0; Cork City FC qualify.

28/09/16, Central Stadium Hagi Academy, Ovidiu
FC Viitorul 4-1 FC Sheriff
19/10/16, Sheriff small Arena, Tiraspol
FC Sheriff 0-1 FC Viitorul
Aggregate: 1-5; FC Viitorul qualify.

29/09/16, Boris Paichadze Dinamo Arena, Tbilisi
FC Dinamo Tbilisi 0-3 FC Kairat Almaty
19/10/16, Almaty Ortalyk Stadion, Almaty
FC Kairat Almaty 5-1 FC Dinamo Tbilisi
Aggregate: 8-1; FC Kairat Almaty qualify.

05/10/16, Sammy Ofer Stadium, Haifa
Maccabi Haifa FC 5-0 FC Shakhtyor Soligorsk
19/10/16, Stroitel, Soligorsk
FC Shakhtyor Soligorsk 2-3 Maccabi Haifa FC
Aggregate: 2-8; Maccabi Haifa FC qualify.

Second round

02/11/16, Kaftanzoglio, Salonika
PAOK FC 0-2 AFC Ajax
22/11/16, De Toekomst, Duivendrecht
AFC Ajax 2-1 PAOK FC
Aggregate: 4-1; AFC Ajax qualify.

02/11/16, Estadio Ciudad de Málaga, Malaga
Málaga CF 2-0 FC Midtjylland
23/11/16, Arena Herning, Herning
FC Midtjylland 4-0 Málaga CF
Aggregate: 4-2; FC Midtjylland qualify.

02/11/16, Lerkendal Stadion, Trondheim
Rosenborg BK 0-1 FK Čukarički
23/11/16, FK Čukarički, Belgrade
FK Čukarički 0-2 Rosenborg BK
Aggregate: 1-2; Rosenborg BK qualify.

02/11/16, Central Stadium Hagi Academy, Ovidiu
FC Viitorul 5-0 FC Zürich
23/11/16, Utogrund, Zurich
FC Zürich 2-0 FC Viitorul
Aggregate: 2-5; FC Viitorul qualify.

02/11/16, Stadion Salzburg, Salzburg
FC Salzburg 8-1 FC Kairat Almaty
23/11/16, Almaty Ortalyk Stadion, Almaty
FC Kairat Almaty 0-1 FC Salzburg
Aggregate: 1-9; FC Salzburg qualify.

02/11/16, Turner's Cross, Cork
Cork City FC 1-3 AS Roma
23/11/16, Tre Fontane, Rome
AS Roma 1-0 Cork City FC
Aggregate: 4-1; AS Roma qualify.

09/11/16, Bornova Stadyumu, Izmir
Altınordu 6-2 AC Sparta Praha
30/11/16, FK Viktoria Žižkov, Prague
AC Sparta Praha 3-2 Altınordu
Aggregate: 5-8; Altınordu qualify.

16/11/16, Sammy Ofer Stadium, Haifa
Maccabi Haifa FC 0-0 FC Dinamo Moskva
23/11/16, Rodina, Khimki
FC Dinamo Moskva 1-1 Maccabi Haifa FC
Aggregate: 1-1; Maccabi Haifa FC qualify on away goal.

Play-offs

07/02/17, Arena Herning, Herning
FC Midtjylland 1-1 SL Benfica (aet; 5-6 on pens)
Goals: 0-1 Diogo Gonçalves 42, 1-1 Torp 84

07/02/17, Sammy Ofer Stadium, Haifa
Maccabi Haifa FC 0-1 Borussia Dortmund
Goal: 0-1 Schwermann 60

07/02/17, De Toekomst, Duivendrecht
AFC Ajax 2-0 Juventus
Goals: 1-0 Eiting 44, 2-0 Sierhuis 48

08/02/17, Tre Fontane, Rome
AS Roma 1-2 AS Monaco FC
Goals: 1-0 Grossi 12, 1-1 Bongiovanni 56(p), 1-2 Sylla 58

08/02/17, Central Stadium Hagi Academy, Ovidiu
FC Viitorul 4-2 FC København
Goals: 1-0 Casap 32, 1-1 Holse 35, 2-1 C Ene 67, 3-1 Coman 79, 4-1 Casap 83, 4-2 Wind 90+2

08/02/17, Stadion Salzburg, Salzburg
FC Salzburg 1-1 Manchester City FC (aet; 4-3 on pens)
Goals: 1-0 Wolf 12, 1-1 Nmecha 30

08/02/17, Lerkendal Stadion Training Ground, Trondheim
Rosenborg BK 1-0 FC Basel 1893
Goal: 1-0 Solli 76

08/02/17, Bornova Stadyumu, Izmir
Altınordu 0-2 Club Atlético de Madrid
Goals: 0-1 Toni Moya 12(p), 0-2 De Castro 90

Round of 16

21/02/17, Centro de Treinos e Formação Desportiva, Vila Nova de Gaia (Porto)
FC Porto 3-0 FC Viitorul
Goals: 1-0 Abou 54, 2-0 Rui Pedro 69, 3-0 Madi Queta 90+1

Alexander Schmidt of Salzburg celebrates scoring the winner during the final against Benfica

21/02/17, Ciudad Deportiva Cerro Del Espino, Majadahonda
Club Atlético de Madrid 3-2 Sevilla FC
Goals: 1-0 Acosta 13, 1-1 Amo 57(p), 2-1 Salomón 63, 2-2 Amo 83(p), 3-2 Clemente Mues 86

21/02/17, De Toekomst, Duivendrecht
AFC Ajax 3-0 FC Dynamo Kyiv
Goals: 1-0 Sierhuis 11, 2-0 D de Wit 62, 3-0 Sierhuis 87

21/02/17, Stadion Salzburg, Salzburg
FC Salzburg 5-0 Paris Saint-Germain
Goals: 1-0 Wolf 15, 2-0 Filip 31, 3-0 Filip 34, 4-0 Filip 61, 5-0 Mensah 73

21/02/17, PSV Stadion, Eindhoven
PSV Eindhoven 1-1 SL Benfica (aet; 4-5 on pens)
Goals: 1-0 Piroe 44, 1-1 João Félix 47

22/02/17, Stadium Oktyabr Artificial Turf, Moscow
PFC CSKA Moskva 2-1 Rosenborg BK
Goals: 1-0 Zhamaletdinov 26, 1-1 Vinje 36(p), 2-1 Pukhov 89(p)

22/02/17, Stade Louis II, Monaco
AS Monaco FC 3-4 Real Madrid CF
Goals: 1-0 Cardona 24(p), 2-0 Mbae 33, 2-1 Peeters 57, 2-2 Sergio Díaz 67(p), 2-3 Dani Gómez 71, 2-4 Peeters 90, 3-4 Bongiovanni 90+4

22/02/17, Mini Estadi, Barcelona
FC Barcelona 4-1 Borussia Dortmund
Goals: 0-1 Wanner 6, 1-1 Carles Pérez 41, 2-1 Ruiz 51, 3-1 Lee 62, 4-1 Mboula 68

Quarter-finals

07/03/17, Stadium Oktyabr Artificial Turf, Moscow (att: 400)
PFC CSKA Moskva 0-2 SL Benfica
Goals: 0-1 Diogo Gonçalves 16, 0-2 Leonov 47(og)

07/03/17, Stadion Salzburg, Salzburg (att: 5,380)
FC Salzburg 2-1 Club Atlético de Madrid
Goals: 1-0 Igor 48, 2-0 Wolf 61, 2-1 Navarro 79

07/03/17, Mini Estadi, Barcelona (att: 2,133)
FC Barcelona 2-1 FC Porto
Goals: 0-1 Bruno Costa 62, 1-1 Ruiz 75, 2-1 Mboula 87(p)

08/03/17, Estadio Alfredo Di Stefano, Madrid (att: 830)
Real Madrid CF 2-1 AFC Ajax
Goals: 1-0 Dani Gómez 5, 1-1 Lang 66, 2-1 Álex Martín 78(p)

Semi-finals

21/04/17, Colovray Sports Centre, Nyon
FC Barcelona 1-2 FC Salzburg
Goals: 1-0 Mboula 19, 1-1 Wolf 63, 1-2 Patson 84

21/04/17, Colovray Sports Centre, Nyon
Real Madrid CF 2-4 SL Benfica
Goals: 0-1 João Félix 5, 0-2 João Filipe 17, 0-3 João Félix 19, 1-3 Dani Gómez 28, 2-3 Seoane 55, 2-4 João Filipe 90+6

Final

24/04/17, Colovray Sports Centre, Nyon (att: 4,000)
SL Benfica 1-2 FC Salzburg
Goals: 1-0 José Gomes 29, 1-1 Patson 72, 1-2 Schmidt 76
Referee: Palabıyık (TUR)
Benfica: Fábio Duarte, Buta, Rúben Dias, Kalaica, Ricardo Araujo (Mesaque Dju 87), Florentino, João Filipe (Vinícius Jaú 83), Gedson Fernandes, José Gomes, Diogo Gonçalves, João Félix (David Tavares 73). Coach: João Tralhão (POR)
Salzburg: Żynel, Meisl, Gorzel, Berisha, Wolf (Lugonja 90+6), Sturm (Schmidt 68), Mensah, Haidara, Meister (Patson 55), Ingolitsch, Igor. Coach: Marco Rose (GER)
Red card: Ingolitsch 90+4 (Salzburg)
Yellow cards: Haidara 62 (Salzburg), Buta 67 (Benfica), Ingolitsch 89 (Salzburg), Florentino 89 (Benfica), José Gomes 90+1 (Benfica), Ingolitsch 90+4 (Salzburg)

Top goalscorers

Kaj Sierhuis

Jordi Mboula

8	Kaj Sierhuis (Ajax) Jordi Mboula (Barcelona)
7	Rui Pedro (Porto) Hannes Wolf (Salzburg) Mergim Berisha (Salzburg)

POLAND 2017
RESPECT
adidas

Stefan Kuntz's side triumph in Krakow

Favourites Spain defeated 1-0 in final

Group winners England and Italy exit in semi-finals

Germany find a way to win

The 2017 UEFA European Under-21 Championship kicked off on 26 March 2015 when the Republic of Ireland defeated Andorra 1-0 in the first of 254 qualifying matches. Two years and three months later, the competition ended with another 1-0 win as Germany defeated Spain in Krakow to win the trophy for the second time.

Germany's success, courtesy of Mitchell Weiser's superbly-placed glancing header, came at the conclusion of an enlarged, 12-team final round. Stefan Kuntz's side, who had qualified in style as the only team with a 100% winning record, saved their best performance in Poland for last, stifling Spanish flair and scoring at a vital time – five minutes before the interval – before diligent and determined defending saw them home.

German efficiency was very much to the fore in the final, yet they had got there only after finishing as the best of the three group runners-up – thanks partly to the advantage of being drawn in Group C, whose matches were played after those in Groups A and B. A 1-0 defeat by Italy in their final group fixture was an acceptable result as it enabled both teams to progress – at the expense of unfortunate Group A runners-up Slovakia. Kuntz's team then overcame Group A winners England in a semi-final penalty shoot-out after a 2-2 draw in Tychy before raising their game to another level to outplay Spain in the final and add a second U21 crown to their 2009 triumph in Sweden.

Spain had qualified less impressively for Poland, squeezing past Austria on away goals in a play-off after finishing second in their group behind Sweden, yet they lit up the tournament with their attacking football. Albert Celades's side won all four games prior to the final, with Real Madrid's Marco Asensio and Atlético Madrid's Saúl Ñíguez each scoring a hat-trick along the way, the latter in a 3-1 semi-final triumph over Italy that helped him win the Golden Boot.

Arguably the most impressive feat in the qualifying phase was achieved by Bladoja Milevski's FYR Macedonia as they secured their nation's first appearance in any UEFA final tournament by winning Group C ahead of France and Iceland. Denmark and Italy qualified with the best defensive records, while the Czech Republic's campaign was illuminated by an unsurpassed ten goals from striker Patrik Schick.

When the final tournament began on 16 June, it featured four teams more than in previous editions. With only a third of them advancing to the semi-finals, points and goals were at a premium.

In Group A, England emerged as the strongest side, securing their progress with a 3-0 win over disappointing hosts Poland. Slovakia, with two victories, ended as runners-up, but six points would not be enough – a fate that also befell Portugal in Group B as they paid the price for a 3-1 defeat in their middle fixture against Spain.

In Group C, Italy and Germany both took six points, with Luigi Di Biagio's side claiming first place on head-to-head thanks to Federico Bernardeschi's winner. With six points already in the bag, Germany's chief concern against the Azzurrini was to preserve their goal difference advantage over Slovakia.

Having duly overcome that obstacle with characteristic pragmatism, Kuntz's men were on their way. Although penalties were needed to see off England – a repeat of the EURO 96 semi-final scenario at senior level when Kuntz was involved as a player – Germany were the better team during the preceding two hours, and it was the same story again over the 90 minutes of the final against Spain.

Opposite: Germany are European champions at Under-21 level for the second time after defeating Spain 1-0 in Krakow

Final tournament

The attention on the opening day of the 2017 UEFA European Under-21 Championship was focused on the hosts and the holders, and neither had it their own way in Group A. Well-supported defending champions Sweden squandered an opportunity to open with a victory when England goalkeeper Jordan Pickford saved Linus Wahlqvist's late penalty in a goalless draw, while Poland suffered even greater frustration as Slovakia substitute Pavol Šafranko's late goal inflicted a 2-1 defeat on the tournament hosts, who had opened the scoring to fervent acclaim through striker Patryk Lypski in the very first minute.

In Group B, FYR Macedonia made their final tournament debut against Spain and received a salutary lesson in efficiency. Although Blagoja Milevski's side racked up 24 goal attempts, they lost 5-0 to the four-time winners, with Marco Asensio hitting a hat-trick. Portugal suggested they would be Spain's most serious challengers by defeating Serbia 2-0 in Bydgoszcz, and there were identical victories in Group C for Germany and Italy, who overcame Czech Republic and Denmark respectively, the Azzurrini with the help of Lorenzo Pellegrini's brilliant overhead kick.

Matchday two in Group A produced plenty of twists and turns as England came from behind to beat Slovakia 2-1 in Kielce thanks to goals from Alfie Mawson and Nathan Redmond, while Poland surrendered an early lead once more before snatching a point against Sweden through Dawid Kownacki's last-ditch penalty. There was a similarly dramatic 2-2 draw in Group B the following day as Serbia forward Uroš Djurdjević's 90th-minute header denied FYR Macedonia a historic victory.

One of the tournament's finest spectacles then unfolded in Gdynia, where Spain and Portugal crossed swords. A high-quality encounter ended Spain's way, with substitute Iñaki Williams' excellent added-time strike sealing a 3-1 victory that enabled the 2011 and 2013 champions to become the first team guaranteed a semi-final place and leave Portugal, despite a brilliant volleyed goal from Bruma, with only the best runners-up spot to play for.

By contrast, the plot thickened in Group C after Czech Republic hit two late goals – the second a Michael Lüftner thunderbolt – to beat Italy 3-1 and climb level on points with their vanquished opponents as Germany went top by defeating Denmark 3-0, all three of their goals coming in a dominant second-half display.

Group A concluded with two equally comprehensive results. England followed Spain into the semi-finals by beating Poland 3-0, recalled Leicester City winger Demarai Gray sending Aidy Boothroyd's ever-improving side on their way with a fine sixth-minute strike, while Slovakia's identical victory over Sweden eliminated the holders and left Pavel Hapal's enterprising second-placed side having to hang around for a couple of days and anxiously wait to see whether their six points and +3 goal difference would suffice to keep them in Poland as the best runners-up.

To oust Slovakia, Portugal needed to beat FYR Macedonia by a three-goal margin and score at least four goals. Ultimately, they fell just short, a 4-2 success against commendably committed opponents leaving Rui Jorge's attractive side three points behind Spain, who maintained their perfect record by defeating Serbia 1-0.

There were still two semi-final places up for grabs in advance of the final two fixtures in Group C. A fascinating number of permutations remained open to determine which combination of Germany, Italy, the Czech Republic and Slovakia would join England and Spain in the last four. For both Italy and Czech Republic, it was a case of win or bust, with Italy needing victory over Germany by a margin of 3-1 or better to guarantee their safe passage. Otherwise only Germany were fully in charge of their own destiny, a win, a draw or defeat by a one-goal margin ensuring their

Mitchell Weiser heads in Germany's winning goal against Spain in the Krakow final

progress. There was even the intriguing possibility of both the Czech Republic and Slovakia going through if the Czechs beat Denmark and Italy defeated Germany 2-0, whereas an Italy victory over Germany by 4-2 or 5-3 etc would guarantee both teams' progress

In the event, with Czech Republic going down 4-2 to Denmark in Tychy, and Italy taking a 31st-minute lead in Krakow, neither Italy nor Germany had any urgent need to alter the scoreline. The final few minutes of the contest were played out – much to Slovakia's chagrin – at a stroll, enabling Italy, as group winners, to face Spain in Krakow, and Germany, the best runners-up (with six points and a +4 goal difference), to take on England in Tychy.

Italy gave a good account of themselves against Spain in an even and goalless first half but fell behind to a spectacular Saúl Ñíguez strike and, after losing Roberto Gagliardini to a red card, were eventually swept away by their numerically superior opponents, with Saúl completing a superb hat-trick in a 3-1 win. The other semi-final between England and Germany was rich in drama too, the former coming from behind to lead 2-1, with goals from Gray and Tammy Abraham, before a dominant German side grabbed a deserved equaliser and repeatedly threatened a late winner against their heavy-legged opponents. England's penalty shoot-out curse, which was born in two semi-finals against Germany at senior level in the 1990s, now struck again, with misses from Abraham and Redmond enabling Germany to prevail 4-3 and move into their third U21 final.

Three days later, Stefan Kuntz's side faced Spain as underdogs, but in front of over 14,000 spectators at Krakow Stadium an assertive, aggressive display from the men in white upset the form book. Albert Celades's side were hustled out of their stride, and when Mitchell Weiser's looping header found the net just before the interval, this time, unlike against England, Germany successfully battened down the hatches, circulated the ball with economy and skill and, in the end, comfortably protected their lead.

Spain would boast the Player of the Tournament in midfielder Dani Ceballos and the five-goal Golden Boot winner in Saúl, but the main prize, that of European Under-21 champions, belonged to Germany.

Qualifying round

Group 1

Belgium 2-1 Moldova
Moldova 0-0 Malta
Montenegro 1-0 Moldova
Latvia 1-2 Malta
Moldova 1-0 Montenegro
Czech Republic 4-1 Malta
Latvia 0-2 Belgium
Latvia 1-1 Czech Republic
Montenegro 0-0 Malta
Belgium 2-0 Malta
Moldova 0-3 Latvia
Czech Republic 3-3 Montenegro
Czech Republic 1-0 Belgium
Montenegro 3-3 Latvia
Moldova 1-3 Czech Republic
Moldova 0-2 Belgium
Malta 0-1 Montenegro
Czech Republic 2-1 Latvia
Belgium 1-2 Montenegro
Malta 0-7 Czech Republic

01/09/16, Gradski Stadion Podgorica, Podgorica
Montenegro 0-3 Czech Republic
Goals: 0-1 Schick 6(p), 0-2 Schick 9, 0-3 Čermák 16

02/09/16, Zemgales Olympic Centre, Jelgava
Latvia 0-2 Moldova
Goals: 0-1 Zommers 65(og), 0-2 Graur 90+1

02/09/16, Hibernians Stadium, Paola
Malta 2-3 Belgium
Goals: 0-1 Tielemans 3(p), 0-2 Bongonda 24, 1-2 Degabriele 74, 2-2 Heylen 84(og), 2-3 Engels 90

06/09/16, Zemgales Olympic Centre, Jelgava
Latvia 0-0 Montenegro

06/09/16, Den Dreef, Louvain
Belgium 2-1 Czech Republic
Goals: 1-0 Praet 12, 1-1 Čermák 21, 2-1 Tielemans 88

07/10/16, Znojmo Stadium, Znojmo
Czech Republic 4-1 Moldova
Goals: 1-0 Jankto 45+1, 2-0 Juliš 67, 3-0 Jankto 74, 4-0 Černý 77, 4-1 Rebenja 90+2

07/10/16, Hibernians Stadium, Paola
Malta 1-0 Latvia
Goal: 1-0 J Grech 46

07/10/16, Gradski, Niksic
Montenegro 3-0 Belgium
Goals: 1-0 Jovović 17, 2-0 Boljević 26, 3-0 Boljević 37

11/10/16, Hibernians Stadium, Paola
Malta 3-2 Moldova
Goals: 1-0 Borg 40, 2-0 Camenzuli 45, 2-1 Taras 53, 2-2 Svinarenco 65(p), 3-2 Mbong 67

11/10/16, Den Dreef, Louvain
Belgium 0-1 Latvia
Goal: 0-1 Černomordijs 88

Group 2

Republic of Ireland 1-0 Andorra
Slovenia 4-0 Andorra
Andorra 1-0 Lithuania
Slovenia 3-0 Lithuania
Andorra 0-2 Republic of Ireland
Italy 1-0 Slovenia
Serbia 5-0 Lithuania

Patrik Schick of Czech Republic – the top scorer in qualifying with ten goals

Serbia 5-0 Andorra
Slovenia 0-3 Italy
Republic of Ireland 3-0 Lithuania
Italy 1-0 Republic of Ireland
Andorra 0-5 Slovenia
Lithuania 0-2 Serbia
Serbia 1-1 Italy
Lithuania 3-1 Republic of Ireland
Slovenia 2-0 Serbia
Italy 2-0 Lithuania
Republic of Ireland 1-4 Italy
Andorra 0-4 Serbia
Slovenia 3-1 Republic of Ireland
Andorra 0-1 Italy

01/09/16, LFF stadionas, Vilnius
Lithuania 1-0 Andorra
Goal: 1-0 Sirgėdas 34

02/09/16, Romeo Menti, Vicenza
Italy 1-1 Serbia
Goals: 0-1 Gajić 33, 1-1 Cerri 54(p)

02/09/16, Regional Sports Centre, Waterford
Republic of Ireland 2-0 Slovenia
Goals: 1-0 Charsley 87, 2-0 Maguire 90+1(p)

06/09/16, Karadjordje, Novi Sad
Serbia 3-2 Republic of Ireland
Goals: 1-0 Djurdjević 12, 2-0 Lazić 65, 2-1 O'Dowda 69, 3-1 Djurdjević 72(p), 3-2 Maguire 81

06/09/16, Stadium Alberto Picco, La Spezia
Italy 3-0 Andorra
Goals: 1-0 Di Francesco 48, 2-0 Di Francesco 73, 3-0 Pellegrini 88

07/10/16, Regional Sports Centre, Waterford
Republic of Ireland 1-3 Serbia
Goals: 1-0 Duffus 49, 1-1 Mihajlović 64, 1-2 Gaćinović 67, 1-3 Lukić 88

07/10/16, Dariaus ir Girėno stadionas, Kaunas
Lithuania 1-0 Slovenia
Goal: 1-0 Ruzgis 72

11/10/16, FK Metalac, Gornji Milanovac
Serbia 3-1 Slovenia
Goals: 1-0 Djurdjević 8, 1-1 Lotrič 19, 2-1 Djurdjević 25(p), 3-1 Djurdjević 86

11/10/16, Dariaus ir Girėno stadionas, Kaunas
Lithuania 0-0 Italy

UEFA European Under-21 Championship

Group 3

Iceland 3-0 FYR Macedonia
Iceland 3-2 France
Northern Ireland 1-2 Scotland
FYR Macedonia 1-0 Ukraine
Iceland 1-1 Northern Ireland
Ukraine 0-1 Iceland
Scotland 1-2 France
Northern Ireland 1-2 FYR Macedonia
Scotland 0-0 Iceland
France 2-0 Ukraine
France 1-0 Northern Ireland
Scotland 2-2 Ukraine
FYR Macedonia 2-2 France
Northern Ireland 1-2 Ukraine
FYR Macedonia 0-0 Iceland
France 2-0 Scotland
France 1-1 FYR Macedonia
Scotland 3-1 Northern Ireland
Ukraine 0-2 FYR Macedonia

02/09/16, Mourneview Park, Lurgan
Northern Ireland 0-1 Iceland
Goal: 0-1 Ægisson 87

02/09/16, Tynecastle, Edinburgh
Scotland 0-1 FYR Macedonia
Goal: 0-1 Markoski 18

02/09/16, Obolon, Kyiv
Ukraine 1-0 France
Goal: 1-0 Vakulko 90+2

06/09/16, Obolon, Kyiv
Ukraine 4-0 Scotland
Goals: 1-0 Blyznychenko 26, 2-0 Besedin 69, 3-0 Besedin 77, 4-0 Boryachuk 90+2(p)

06/09/16, Michel-d'Ornano, Caen
France 2-0 Iceland
Goals: 1-0 Tolisso 11, 2-0 Tolisso 62

06/09/16, Nacionalna Arena Filip II Makedonski, Skopje
FYR Macedonia 2-0 Northern Ireland
Goals: 1-0 Doherty 37(og), 2-0 Markoski 85

05/10/16, Víkingsvöllur, Reykjavik
Iceland 2-0 Scotland
Goals: 1-0 Thrándarson 47, 2-0 E Ómarsson 66

06/10/16, Obolon, Kyiv
Ukraine 1-1 Northern Ireland
Goals: 0-1 Smyth 12, 1-1 Besedin 15

11/10/16, Laugardalsvöllur, Reykjavik
Iceland 2-4 Ukraine
Goals: 1-0 Grétarsson 22, 1-1 Boryachuk 56, 1-2 Besedin 75, 2-2 E Ómarsson 88, 2-3 Boryachuk 90, 2-4 Zubkov 90+4

11/10/16, Windsor Park, Belfast
Northern Ireland 0-3 France
Goals: 0-1 Augustin 16, 0-2 Augustin 42, 0-3 Dembélé 89

11/10/16, Nacionalna Arena Filip II Makedonski, Skopje
FYR Macedonia 2-0 Scotland
Goals: 1-0 Markoski 18, 2-0 Bardi 22

Group 4

Liechtenstein 0-2 Albania
Liechtenstein 0-4 Israel
Albania 1-1 Israel
Liechtenstein 0-6 Hungary
Liechtenstein 0-2 Greece
Albania 1-6 Portugal
Portugal 2-0 Hungary
Greece 0-4 Portugal
Hungary 2-2 Albania
Greece 5-0 Liechtenstein
Portugal 4-0 Albania
Israel 3-0 Hungary
Hungary 2-1 Greece
Albania 2-0 Liechtenstein
Israel 0-3 Portugal
Portugal 4-0 Liechtenstein
Albania 0-0 Greece
Hungary 0-0 Israel
Greece 0-1 Israel
Albania 2-1 Hungary

01/09/16, Gyirmóti Stadion, Gyor
Hungary 4-0 Liechtenstein
Goals: 1-0 Mervó 18, 2-0 Berecz 60, 3-0 Mervó 68, 4-0 Frick 79(og)

02/09/16, A Mata Real, Pacos de Ferreira
Portugal 0-0 Israel

02/09/16, Peristeri, Athens
Greece 2-1 Albania
Goals: 0-1 Latifi 22, 1-1 Ioannidis 44(p), 2-1 Tsilianidis 90

06/09/16, Cidade de Barcelos, Barcelos
Portugal 1-0 Greece
Goal: 1-0 Gelson Martins 54

06/09/16, Ha Moshava, Petah Tikva
Israel 4-0 Liechtenstein
Goals: 1-0 E Peretz 35, 2-0 Ohana 43, 3-0 Barshatzki 61, 4-0 Ohana 63

06/10/16, Gyirmóti Stadion, Gyor
Hungary 3-3 Portugal
Goals: 0-1 Diogo Jota 10, 0-2 João Carvalho 13, 1-2 D Nagy 28(p), 1-3 Daniel Podence 48, 2-3 Prosser 62, 3-3 Balogh 78

06/10/16, Turner Stadium, Beer Sheva
Israel 4-0 Greece
Goals: 1-0 Altman 27, 2-0 Gozlan 42, 3-0 D Peretz 55, 4-0 Altman 60(p)

10/10/16, Peristeri, Athens
Greece 3-1 Hungary
Goals: 1-0 Donis 28, 1-1 Mervó 56, 2-1 Koulouris 69, 3-1 Charisis 83

10/10/16, Ha Moshava, Petah Tikva
Israel 4-0 Albania
Goals: 1-0 Gozlan 18, 2-0 Altman 43, 3-0 Biton 55, 4-0 Hugy 70

11/10/16, Rheinpark Stadion, Vaduz
Liechtenstein 1-7 Portugal
Goals: 1-0 Salanovic 3, 1-1 Bruno Fernandes 20, 1-2 Daniel Podence 24, 1-3 Gonçalo Guedes 26, 1-4 João Carvalho 28, 1-5 Gonçalo Guedes 53, 1-6 Rúben Neves 75, 1-7 Ruben Semedo 84

Group 5

Wales 3-1 Bulgaria
Romania 3-0 Armenia
Luxembourg 1-3 Wales
Romania 0-2 Bulgaria
Armenia 2-3 Romania
Bulgaria 3-0 Luxembourg
Luxembourg 0-1 Romania
Denmark 0-0 Wales
Bulgaria 2-0 Armenia
Armenia 1-1 Luxembourg
Denmark 1-0 Bulgaria
Wales 2-1 Armenia
Romania 0-3 Denmark
Wales 1-1 Romania
Denmark 2-0 Armenia
Luxembourg 0-1 Denmark
Bulgaria 0-0 Wales
Luxembourg 0-0 Bulgaria
Romania 2-1 Wales
Armenia 1-3 Denmark

02/09/16, The Racecourse Ground, Wrexham
Wales 0-4 Denmark
Goals: 0-1 Ingvartsen 21, 0-2 Sisto 40, 0-3 Sisto 49, 0-4 Dolberg 83

02/09/16, Gaz Metan, Medias
Romania 4-0 Luxembourg
Goals: 1-0 Ţîru 13, 2-0 Bumba 29, 3-0 Ioniţă 45, 4-0 Popescu 75

06/09/16, Nantporth, Bangor
Wales 1-1 Luxembourg
Goals: 0-1 Kerger 15, 1-1 Charles 90+1

06/09/16, FFA Academy Stadium, Yerevan
Armenia 0-1 Bulgaria
Goal: 0-1 Nenov 79

06/09/16, Aalborg Stadion, Aalborg
Denmark 3-1 Romania
Goals: 1-0 Sisto 10, 2-0 Ingvartsen 35(p), 3-0 Ingvartsen 39, 3-1 Miron 68

07/10/16, La Frontière, Esch-sur-Alzette
Luxembourg 1-0 Armenia
Goal: 1-0 Todorovic 83

07/10/16, Beroe, Stara Zagora
Bulgaria 0-3 Denmark
Goals: 0-1 Ingvartsen 13(p), 0-2 Ingvartsen 28, 0-3 Ingvartsen 62

11/10/16, Beroe, Stara Zagora
Bulgaria 2-0 Romania
Goals: 1-0 Tasev 16, 2-0 A Georgiev 35

Marcus Ingvartsen scored eight goals for Group 5 winners Denmark

11/10/16, Aalborg Stadion, Aalborg
Denmark 4-1 Luxembourg
Goals: 1-0 Ingvartsen 71, 2-0 Hjulsager 73, 3-0 Marcondes 76, 4-0 Mahmutovic 79(og), 4-1 Gomes Borges 90+3

11/10/16, FFA Academy Stadium, Yerevan
Armenia 1-3 Wales
Goals: 0-1 Harrison 19, 0-2 Shakhnazaryan 67(og), 1-2 Simonyan 69, 1-3 O'Sullivan 90

Group 6

San Marino 0-3 Georgia
Estonia 0-0 San Marino
Estonia 0-2 Spain
Croatia 1-0 Georgia
Sweden 3-0 San Marino
Estonia 0-4 Croatia
San Marino 0-3 Croatia
Georgia 2-5 Spain
Sweden 5-0 Estonia
Spain 1-1 Sweden
Georgia 3-0 Estonia
Croatia 4-0 San Marino
Spain 5-0 Georgia
San Marino 1-2 Estonia
Georgia 0-1 Sweden
Croatia 2-3 Spain
Georgia 4-0 San Marino
Spain 0-3 Croatia
San Marino 0-2 Sweden
Croatia 2-1 Estonia
Sweden 3-2 Georgia

01/09/16, Gradski stadion Koprivnica, Koprivnica
Croatia 1-1 Sweden
Goals: 0-1 Cibicki 57, 1-1 Perica 78

01/09/16, Castalia, Castellon
Spain 6-0 San Marino
Goals: 1-0 Diego González 14, 2-0 Munir 17, 3-0 Munir 36, 4-0 Santi Mina 45, 5-0 Santi Mina 84, 6-0 Iñaki Williams 88

01/09/16, A. Le Coq Arena, Tallinn
Estonia 0-1 Georgia
Goal: 0-1 Kacharava 39

05/09/16, Malmö New Stadium, Malmo
Sweden 1-1 Spain
Goals: 0-1 Deulofeu 50, 1-1 Mikel Merino 86(og)

06/09/16, David Abashidze, Zestaponi
Georgia 2-2 Croatia
Goals: 1-0 Papunashvili 1, 1-1 Perica 43, 2-1 Livaković 50(og), 2-2 Perica 61

05/10/16, San Marino Stadium, Serravalle
San Marino 0-3 Spain
Goals: 0-1 Munir 16, 0-2 Denis Suárez 68, 0-3 Jorge Meré 79

06/10/16, Pärnu Rannastaadion, Parnu
Estonia 0-3 Sweden
Goals: 0-1 Dagerstål 9, 0-2 Tankovic 44, 0-3 Asoro 53

10/10/16, Pasarón, Pontevedra
Spain 5-0 Estonia
Goals: 1-0 Denis Suárez 36, 2-0 Marco Asensio 38, 3-0 Munir 86, 4-0 Marco Asensio 90, 5-0 Munir 90+3

10/10/16, Vångavallen, Trelleborg
Sweden 4-2 Croatia
Goals: 0-1 Perica 23, 1-1 Wahlqvist 26(p), 2-1 Olsson 53, 3-1 Hallberg 58, 4-1 Strandberg 64, 4-2 Benković 67

Group 7

Faroe Islands 0-1 Azerbaijan
Finland 2-0 Russia
Azerbaijan 0-2 Austria
Austria 4-3 Russia
Finland 3-0 Faroe Islands
Azerbaijan 0-3 Germany
Austria 7-0 Azerbaijan
Germany 4-0 Finland
Faroe Islands 0-6 Germany
Azerbaijan 0-1 Finland
Russia 2-0 Faroe Islands
Germany 3-1 Azerbaijan
Austria 2-0 Finland
Azerbaijan 3-0 Russia
Germany 4-2 Austria
Russia 2-2 Azerbaijan
Germany 4-1 Faroe Islands
Austria 1-0 Faroe Islands
Russia 0-2 Germany
Faroe Islands 1-6 Finland

01/09/16, Toftir, Toftir
Faroe Islands 0-3 Russia
Goals: 0-1 Komlichenko 8, 0-2 Karpov 30, 0-3 Evseev 43

02/09/16, Hietalahti, Vaasa
Finland 0-1 Austria
Goal: 0-1 Dovedan 90+1

06/09/16, Arena Khimki, Khimki
Russia 1-1 Austria
Goals: 1-0 Zuev 33, 1-1 Jakupovic 55

06/09/16, Dalga Stadium, Baku
Azerbaijan 1-1 Faroe Islands
Goals: 0-1 Jonsson 40, 1-1 Mädätov 88

06/09/16, OmaSP Stadion, Seinajoki
Finland 0-1 Germany
Goal: 0-1 Väisänen 41(og)

07/10/16, Toftir, Toftir
Faroe Islands 0-1 Austria
Goal: 0-1 Schoissengeyer 44

07/10/16, Sportpark, Ingolstadt
Germany 4-3 Russia
Goals: 1-0 Arnold 12, 2-0 Gnabry 34, 2-1 Lystsov 35, 3-1 Selke 36, 3-2 Evseev 45, 4-2 Arnold 57(p), 4-3 Bezdenezhnykh 60

07/10/16, Töölön jalkapallostadion, Helsinki
Finland 0-0 Azerbaijan

11/10/16, NV Arena, St Polten
Austria 1-4 Germany
Goals: 0-1 Arnold 12, 0-2 Öztunali 52, 0-3 Selke 58, 0-4 Haberer 78(p), 1-4 Lienhart 86

11/10/16, Arena Khimki, Khimki
Russia 1-1 Finland
Goals: 1-0 Palienko 3, 1-1 Viitikko 64

Group 8

Netherlands 4-0 Cyprus
Belarus 1-0 Slovakia
Turkey 0-1 Netherlands
Slovakia 2-0 Cyprus
Belarus 0-2 Turkey
Netherlands 1-3 Slovakia
Cyprus 0-1 Belarus
Cyprus 0-3 Turkey
Netherlands 1-0 Belarus
Slovakia 4-2 Netherlands
Belarus 2-2 Cyprus
Slovakia 5-0 Turkey

Davie Selke found the net seven times for Germany as they won all ten of their qualifying matches

01/09/16, Osmanlı Stadı, Ankara
Turkey 0-1 Cyprus
Goal: 0-1 Katelaris 22

02/09/16, FC Minsk, Minsk
Belarus 2-2 Netherlands
Goals: 1-0 Savitski 18(p), 1-1 El Ghazi 68, 2-1 Savitski 76, 2-2 Luckassen 78

05/09/16, Ammochostos, Larnaca
Cyprus 0-3 Slovakia
Goals: 0-1 Chrien 1, 0-2 Bero 58, 0-3 Rusnák 72

06/09/16, Osmanlı Stadı, Ankara
Turkey 1-0 Belarus
Goal: 1-0 Oğulcan Çağlayan 30

06/10/16, AZ Stadion, Alkmaar
Netherlands 0-0 Turkey

07/10/16, Spartak Myjava, Myjava
Slovakia 3-1 Belarus
Goals: 1-0 Šafranko 36, 2-0 Šafranko 61, 2-1 Yablonski 72, 3-1 Chrien 90+1

11/10/16, Ammochostos, Larnaca
Cyprus 1-4 Netherlands
Goals: 0-1 Van de Beek 17, 1-1 N Ioannou 20, 1-2 Bergwijn 41, 1-3 Bazoer 57, 1-4 Bergwijn 66

11/10/16, Oba Stadyumu, Alanya
Turkey 1-1 Slovakia
Goals: 1-0 Hruška 44(og), 1-1 Lobotka 70(p)

Group 9

Norway 2-0 Bosnia & Herzegovina
Bosnia & Herzegovina 1-2 Kazakhstan
Norway 0-1 England
Kazakhstan 0-1 Switzerland
Switzerland 3-1 Bosnia & Herzegovina
Norway 2-1 Kazakhstan

UEFA European Under-21 Championship

Switzerland 1-1 Norway
England 3-0 Kazakhstan
Bosnia & Herzegovina 0-0 England
England 3-1 Switzerland
Kazakhstan 0-0 Bosnia & Herzegovina
Switzerland 1-1 England

02/09/16, Grbavica, Sarajevo
Bosnia & Herzegovina 0-1 Norway
Goal: 0-1 M Elyounoussi 57

02/09/16, Biel/Bienne, Biel
Switzerland 3-0 Kazakhstan
Goals: 1-0 Khelifi 28, 2-0 Angha 41, 3-0 Fernandes 63

06/09/16, Grbavica, Sarajevo
Bosnia & Herzegovina 0-0 Switzerland

06/09/16, Community, Colchester
England 6-1 Norway
Goals: 1-0 Rashford 29, 2-0 Chalobah 38, 3-0 Loftus-Cheek 64, 4-0 Rashford 66, 4-1 Zahid 68, 5-1 Rashford 72(p), 6-1 Baker 86

06/10/16, Tsentralniy, Aktobe
Kazakhstan 0-1 England
Goal: 0-1 Gray 6

07/10/16, Marienlyst, Drammen
Norway 2-1 Switzerland
Goals: 1-0 Zahid 44, 1-1 Fernandes 66, 2-1 Elyounoussi 79

11/10/16, Bescot Stadium, Walsall
England 5-0 Bosnia & Herzegovina
Goals: 1-0 Swift 14, 2-0 Abraham 18, 3-0 Onomah 49, 4-0 Watmore 62, 5-0 Abraham 68

11/10/16, Tsentralniy, Aktobe
Kazakhstan 0-3 Norway
Goals: 0-1 Ødegaard 53, 0-2 Zahid 68, 0-3 Ødegaard 85

Play-offs

11/11/16, Stadion FK Partizan, Belgrade (att: 8,450)
Serbia 2-0 Norway
Goals: 1-0 Djurdjević 6, 2-0 Haraldseid 69(og)
15/11/16, Marienlyst, Drammen (att: 4,838)
Norway 1-0 Serbia
Goal: 1-0 M Elyounoussi 70
Aggregate: 1-2; Serbia qualify.

11/11/16, NV Arena, St Polten (att: 1,503)
Austria 1-1 Spain
Goals: 0-1 Deulofeu 45+2(p), 1-1 Jonny 61(og)
15/11/16, Carlos Belmonte, Albacete (att: 12,500)
Spain 0-0 Austria
Aggregate: 1-1; Spain qualify on away goal.

Top goalscorers

(Qualifying round/Play-offs)

10	Patrik Schick (Czech Republic)
9	Michael Gregoritsch (Austria)
	Uroš Djurdjević (Serbia)
8	Marcus Ingvartsen (Denmark)
	Gerard Deulofeu (Spain)
7	Stipe Perica (Croatia)
	Davie Selke (Germany)
	Munir El Haddadi (Spain)

Final tables

Group 1

		Home					Away					Total					
	Pld	W	D	L	F	A	W	D	L	F	A	W	D	L	F	A	Pts
1 Czech Republic	10	4	1	0	14	6	3	1	1	15	4	7	2	1	29	10	23
2 Belgium	10	3	0	2	7	5	3	0	2	7	6	6	0	4	14	11	18
3 Montenegro	10	2	2	1	7	6	2	2	1	6	5	4	4	2	13	11	16
4 Malta	10	2	0	3	6	13	1	2	2	3	7	3	2	5	9	20	11
5 Latvia	10	0	2	3	2	7	2	1	2	8	6	2	3	5	10	13	9
6 Moldova	10	1	1	3	2	8	1	0	4	6	10	2	1	7	8	18	7

Group 2

		Home					Away					Total					
	Pld	W	D	L	F	A	W	D	L	F	A	W	D	L	F	A	Pts
1 Italy	10	4	1	0	8	1	3	2	0	9	2	7	3	0	17	3	24
2 Serbia	10	4	1	0	17	4	3	1	1	10	4	7	2	1	27	8	23
3 Slovenia	10	4	0	1	12	4	1	0	4	6	7	5	0	5	18	11	15
4 Republic of Ireland	10	3	0	2	8	7	1	0	4	6	10	4	0	6	14	17	12
5 Lithuania	10	3	1	1	5	3	0	0	5	0	14	3	1	6	5	17	10
6 Andorra	10	1	0	4	1	12	0	0	5	0	14	1	0	9	1	26	3

Group 3

		Home					Away					Total					
	Pld	W	D	L	F	A	W	D	L	F	A	W	D	L	F	A	Pts
1 FYR Macedonia	10	3	2	0	7	2	3	1	1	6	5	6	3	1	13	7	21
2 France	10	4	1	0	8	1	2	1	2	9	7	6	2	2	17	8	20
3 Iceland	10	3	1	1	11	7	2	2	1	2	2	5	3	2	13	9	18
4 Ukraine	10	2	1	2	6	4	2	1	2	8	8	4	2	4	14	12	14
5 Scotland	10	1	2	2	6	6	1	0	4	2	11	2	2	6	8	17	8
6 Northern Ireland	10	0	0	5	3	10	0	2	3	3	8	0	2	8	6	18	2

Group 4

		Home					Away					Total					
	Pld	W	D	L	F	A	W	D	L	F	A	W	D	L	F	A	Pts
1 Portugal	10	4	1	0	11	0	4	1	0	23	5	8	2	0	34	5	26
2 Israel	10	4	0	1	15	3	2	3	0	6	1	6	3	1	21	4	21
3 Greece	10	3	0	2	10	7	1	1	3	3	7	4	1	5	13	14	13
4 Albania	10	2	2	1	6	8	1	1	3	5	12	3	3	4	11	20	12
5 Hungary	10	2	3	0	11	6	1	0	4	8	10	3	3	4	19	16	12
6 Liechtenstein	10	0	0	5	1	21	0	0	5	0	19	0	0	10	1	40	0

Group 5

		Home					Away					Total					
	Pld	W	D	L	F	A	W	D	L	F	A	W	D	L	F	A	Pts
1 Denmark	10	4	1	0	10	2	5	0	0	14	1	9	1	0	24	3	28
2 Bulgaria	10	3	1	1	7	3	2	1	2	4	4	5	2	3	11	7	17
3 Romania	10	3	0	2	9	6	2	1	2	6	8	5	1	4	15	14	16
4 Wales	10	2	2	1	7	8	2	2	1	7	4	4	4	2	14	12	16
5 Luxembourg	10	1	1	3	2	5	0	2	3	3	13	1	3	6	5	18	6
6 Armenia	10	0	1	4	5	11	0	0	5	1	10	0	1	9	6	21	1

Group 6

		Home					Away					Total					
	Pld	W	D	L	F	A	W	D	L	F	A	W	D	L	F	A	Pts
1 Sweden	10	4	1	0	16	5	3	2	0	8	2	7	3	0	24	7	24
2 Spain	10	3	1	1	17	4	4	1	0	14	5	7	2	1	31	9	23
3 Croatia	10	3	1	1	10	5	3	1	1	14	6	6	2	2	24	11	20
4 Georgia	10	2	1	2	11	8	2	0	3	6	9	4	1	5	17	17	13
5 Estonia	10	0	1	4	0	10	1	0	4	3	16	1	1	8	3	26	4
6 San Marino	10	0	0	5	1	13	0	1	4	0	17	0	1	9	1	30	1

Group 7

		Home					Away					Total					
	Pld	W	D	L	F	A	W	D	L	F	A	W	D	L	F	A	Pts
1 Germany	10	5	0	0	19	7	5	0	0	16	1	10	0	0	35	8	30
2 Austria	10	4	0	1	15	7	3	1	1	7	5	7	1	2	22	12	22
3 Finland	10	2	1	2	5	2	2	1	2	8	8	4	2	4	13	10	14
4 Azerbaijan	10	1	1	3	4	7	1	2	2	4	12	2	3	5	8	19	9
5 Russia	10	1	3	1	6	6	1	0	4	9	13	2	3	5	15	19	9
6 Faroe Islands	10	0	0	5	1	17	0	1	4	2	11	0	1	9	3	28	1

Group 8

		Home					Away					Total					
	Pld	W	D	L	F	A	W	D	L	F	A	W	D	L	F	A	Pts
1 Slovakia	8	4	0	0	14	3	2	1	1	7	3	6	1	1	21	6	19
2 Netherlands	8	2	1	1	6	3	2	1	1	9	7	4	2	2	15	10	14
3 Turkey	8	1	1	2	2	3	2	1	1	5	5	3	2	3	7	8	11
4 Belarus	8	1	2	1	5	6	1	0	3	2	5	2	2	4	7	11	8
5 Cyprus	8	0	0	4	1	11	1	1	2	3	8	1	1	6	4	19	4

Group 9

		Home					Away					Total					
	Pld	W	D	L	F	A	W	D	L	F	A	W	D	L	F	A	Pts
1 England	8	4	0	0	17	2	2	2	0	3	1	6	2	0	20	3	20
2 Norway	8	3	0	1	6	3	2	1	1	6	7	5	1	2	12	10	16
3 Switzerland	8	2	2	0	8	3	1	1	2	3	5	3	3	2	11	8	12
4 Kazakhstan	8	0	1	3	0	5	1	0	3	3	9	1	1	6	3	14	4
5 Bosnia & Herzegovina	8	0	2	2	1	3	0	1	3	1	10	0	3	5	2	13	3

England's Tammy Abraham (right) takes on Slovakia's Milan Škriniar in the Group A encounter

Final tournament

Group A

16/06/17, Kielce Stadium, Kielce (att: 11,672)
Sweden 0-0 England
Referee: Stieler (GER)
Sweden: Cajtoft, Wahlqvist, Une Larsson, Lundqvist, Tibbling (Tankovic 85), Fransson (Mrabti 73), Olsson, Engvall (Strandberg 59), Dagerstål, Hallberg, Cibicki. Coach: Håkan Ericson (SWE)
England: Pickford, Holgate, Chilwell, Chalobah, Chambers, Ward-Prowse, Abraham, Baker, Redmond, Murphy (Gray 70), Mawson. Coach: Aidy Boothroyd (ENG)

16/06/17, Lublin Stadium, Lublin (att: 14,911)
Poland 1-2 Slovakia
Goals: 1-0 Lipski 1, 1-1 Valjent 20, 1-2 Šafranko 78
Referee: Gözübüyük (NED)
Poland: Wrąbel, Jaroszyński, Kędziora, Bednarek, Linetty, Stępiński (Piątek 84), Lipski (Niezgoda 82), Frankowski, Jach, Dawidowicz, Kapustka (Moneta 59). Coach: Marcin Dorna (POL)
Slovakia: Chovan, Niňaj, Škriniar, Valjent, Lobotka, Mihalík (Haraslín 82), Chrien, Rusnák, Mazáň, Zreľák (Šafranko 73), Bero (Bénes 90+2). Coach: Pavel Hapal (CZE)
Yellow cards: Škriniar 71 (Slovakia), Šafranko 81 (Slovakia)

19/06/17, Kielce Stadium, Kielce (att: 12,087)
Slovakia 1-2 England
Goals: 1-0 Chrien 23, 1-1 Mawson 50, 1-2 Redmond 61
Referee: Mažeika (LTU)
Slovakia: Chovan, Niňaj, Škriniar, Valjent, Lobotka, Mihalík (Haraslín 73), Chrien (Bénes 66), Rusnák, Mazáň, Zreľák (Šafranko 65), Bero. Coach: Pavel Hapal (CZE)
England: Pickford, Holgate (Murphy 46), Chilwell, Chalobah, Chambers, Ward-Prowse, Abraham (Woodrow 88), Baker, Redmond, Swift (Gray 79), Mawson. Coach: Aidy Boothroyd (ENG)
Yellow cards: Bero 13 (Slovakia), Ward-Prowse 27 (England), Mazáň 65 (Slovakia), Murphy 86 (England), Baker 90+4 (England)

19/06/17, Lublin Stadium, Lublin (att: 14,561)
Poland 2-2 Sweden
Goals: 1-0 Moneta 6, 1-1 Strandberg 36, 1-2 Une Larsson 41, 2-2 Kownacki 90+1(p)
Referee: Vinčić (SVN)
Poland: Wrąbel, Jaroszyński, Kędziora, Bednarek, Linetty, Stępiński (Niezgoda 58), Frankowski, Moneta (Lipski 74), Kownacki, Jach, Dawidowicz (Piątek 88). Coach: Marcin Dorna (POL)
Sweden: Cajtoft, Wahlqvist, Une Larsson, Lundqvist, Tibbling (Tankovic 61), Fransson (Mrabti 87), Olsson, Strandberg (Engvall 69), Dagerstål, Hallberg, Cibicki. Coach: Håkan Ericson (SWE)
Yellow cards: Olsson 19 (Sweden), Strandberg 24 (Sweden), Cibicki 29 (Sweden), Kownacki 46 (Poland), Niezgoda 65 (Poland), Bednarek 71 (Poland), Linetty 86 (Poland), Hallberg 89 (Sweden), Dagerstål 90 (Sweden), Wahlqvist 90+5 (Sweden)

22/06/17, Kielce Stadium, Kielce (att: 13,176)
England 3-0 Poland
Goals: 1-0 Gray 6, 2-0 Murphy 69, 3-0 Baker 82(p)
Referee: Lechner (AUT)
England: Pickford, Holgate, Chilwell, Chalobah (Hughes 39), Chambers, Gray, Ward-Prowse (Abraham 72), Baker, Redmond (Murphy 46), Swift, Mawson. Coach: Aidy Boothroyd (ENG)
Poland: Wrąbel, Jaroszyński, Kędziora, Bednarek, Linetty, Murawski, Frankowski, Moneta (Lipski 46), Kownacki (Stępiński 73), Jach, Piątek (Niezgoda 64). Coach: Marcin Dorna (POL)
Red card: Bednarek 82 (Poland)
Yellow cards: Mawson 65 (England), Bednarek 79 (Poland), Bednarek 82 (Poland)

22/06/17, Lublin Stadium, Lublin (att: 11,203)
Slovakia 3-0 Sweden
Goals: 1-0 Chrien 5, 2-0 Mihalík 22, 3-0 Šatka 73
Referee: Gil Manzano (ESP)
Slovakia: Chovan, Niňaj, Škriniar, Lobotka, Mihalík (Haraslín 90), Chrien, Rusnák, Šatka, Mazáň, Zreľák (Šafranko 69), Bero (Bénes 85). Coach: Pavel Hapal (CZE)
Sweden: Cajtoft, Wahlqvist, Une Larsson, Fransson, Olsson (Asoro 72), Strandberg, Brorsson, Hallberg (Tankovic 46), Mrabti, Cibicki (Eliasson 46), Binaku. Coach: Håkan Ericson (SWE)
Yellow cards: Mrabti 56 (Sweden), Wahlqvist 86 (Sweden)

	Pld	W	D	L	F	A	Pts
1 England	3	2	1	0	5	1	7
2 Slovakia	3	2	0	1	6	3	6
3 Sweden	3	0	2	1	2	5	2
4 Poland	3	0	1	2	3	7	1

Group B

17/06/17, Bydgoszcz Stadium, Bydgoszcz (att: 10,724)
Portugal 2-0 Serbia
Goals: 1-0 Gonçalo Guedes 37, 2-0 Bruno Fernandes 88
Referee: Bastien (FRA)
Portugal: Bruno Varela, João Cancelo, Edgar Ié, Rúben Semedo, Rúben Neves, Daniel Podence (Iuri Medeiros 68), Bruno Fernandes, Rodrigues, Gonçalo Guedes, Diogo Jota (Bruma 46), João Carvalho (Renato Sanches 59). Coach: Rui Jorge (POR)
Serbia: Milinković-Savić, Gajić, Antonov, Veljković, Maksimović, Djurdjević (Ožegović 74), Gaćinović, Čavrić (Plavšić 46), Jovanović, Grujić (Radonjić 68), Živković. Coach: Nenad Lalatović (SRB)
Yellow cards: Grujić 4 (Serbia), Rúben Semedo 19 (Portugal), Gaćinović 51 (Serbia), Antonov 55 (Serbia), Gajić 70 (Serbia), Bruma 78 (Portugal), Bruno Fernandes 81 (Portugal)

17/06/17, Gdynia Stadium, Gdynia (att: 8,269)
Spain 5-0 FYR Macedonia
Goals: 1-0 Saúl Ñíguez 10, 2-0 Marco Asensio 16, 3-0 Deulofeu 35(p), 4-0 Marco Asensio 54, 5-0 Marco Asensio 72
Referee: Lechner (AUT)
Spain: Arrizabalaga, Bellerín, José Gayà, Jorge Meré, Jesús Vallejo, Deulofeu (Dani Ceballos 63), Saúl Ñíguez, Denis Suárez, Marco Asensio (Oyarzábal 81), Sandro Ramírez (Iñaki Williams 74), Llorente. Coach: Albert Celades (ESP)
FYR Macedonia: Aleksovski, Zajkov, Bardi, Nikolov, Radeski, Babunski (Kostadinov 76), Velkovski, Bejtulai, Markoski (Gjorgjev 46), Angelov (Elmas 46), Demiri. Coach: Blagoja Milevski (MKD)
Yellow card: Jorge Meré 2 (Spain)

20/06/17, Bydgoszcz Stadium, Bydgoszcz (att: 5,121)
Serbia 2-2 FYR Macedonia
Goals: 1-0 Gaćinović 24, 1-1 Bardi 64(p), 1-2 Gjorgjev 83, 2-2 Djurdjević 90
Referee: Madden (SCO)
Serbia: Milinković-Savić, Gajić (Filipović 46), Antonov (Ožegović 77), Veljković, Maksimović, Djurdjević, Gaćinović, Jovanović, Grujić (Ristić 52), Živković, Plavšić. Coach: Nenad Lalatović (SRB)
FYR Macedonia: Aleksovski, Zajkov, Bardi, Nikolov, Radeski (Pivkovski 86), Babunski (Elmas 58), Avramovski (Gjorgjev 46), Velkovski, Markoski, Demiri, Murati. Coach: Blagoja Milevski (MKD)
Red card: Pankov 90+5 (Serbia)
Yellow cards: Markoski 14 (FYR Macedonia), Grujić 23 (Serbia), Elmas 60 (FYR Macedonia), Plavšić 85 (Serbia), Jovanović 85 (Serbia), Veljković 90+4 (Serbia), Milinković-Savić 90+5 (Serbia), Pankov 90+5 (Serbia)

20/06/17, Gdynia Stadium, Gdynia (att: 13,862)
Portugal 1-3 Spain
Goals: 0-1 Saúl Ñíguez 21, 0-2 Sandro Ramírez 65, 1-2 Bruma 77, 1-3 Iñaki Williams 90+3
Referee: Stieler (GER)
Portugal: Bruno Varela, João Cancelo, Edgar Ié, Rúben Semedo, Rúben Neves, Daniel Podence (Bruma 57), Bruno Fernandes, Rodrigues, Renato Sanches (Ricardo Horta 73), Gonçalo Guedes, João Carvalho (Gonçalo Paciência 66). Coach: Rui Jorge (POR)
Spain: Arrizabalaga, Bellerín, Jorge Meré, Jesús Vallejo, Dani Ceballos, Deulofeu (Denis Suárez 82), Saúl Ñíguez, Marco Asensio (Mikel Merino 90), Sandro Ramírez (Iñaki Williams 75), Jonny, Llorente. Coach: Albert Celades (ESP)
Yellow cards: Rúben Neves 4 (Portugal), Dani Ceballos 57 (Spain), Bruno Fernandes 70 (Portugal), Gonçalo Paciência 75 (Portugal), Rúben Semedo 79 (Portugal)

23/06/17, Gdynia Stadium, Gdynia (att: 7,533)
FYR Macedonia 2-4 Portugal
Goals: 0-1 Edgar Ié 2, 0-2 Bruma 22, 1-2 Bardi 40, 1-3 Daniel Podence 57, 2-3 Markoski 80, 2-4 Bruma 90+1
Referee: Kružliak (SVK)
FYR Macedonia: Siskovski, Popzlatanov, Zajkov, Bardi, Nikolov, Radeski (Musliu 28), Babunski (Markoski 74), Bejtulai, Angelov (Elmas 57), Murati, Gjorgjev. Coach: Blagoja Milevski (MKD)
Portugal: Bruno Varela, João Cancelo, Edgar Ié, Tobias Figueiredo, Rúben Neves, Daniel Podence (Diogo Jota 69), Gonçalo Paciência, Iuri Medeiros, Pedro Rebocho (Rodrigues 18), Renato Sanches (Ricardo Horta 55), Bruma. Coach: Rui Jorge (POR)
Red card: Diogo Jota 90+2 (Portugal)
Yellow cards: Babunski 49 (FYR Macedonia), Musliu 63 (FYR Macedonia), Gonçalo Paciência 86 (Portugal), Siskovski 88 (FYR Macedonia), Bardi 90+5 (FYR Macedonia), Tobias Figueiredo 90+7 (Portugal)

23/06/17, Bydgoszcz Stadium, Bydgoszcz (att: 12,058)
Serbia 0-1 Spain
Goal: 0-1 Denis Suárez 38
Referee: Mažeika (LTU)
Serbia: Manojlović, Antonov, Veljković, Maksimović, Djurdjević, Gaćinović, Jovanović, Filipović, Živković, Lukić (Plavšić 87), Radonjić (Ristić 71). Coach: Nenad Lalatović (SRB)
Spain: Pau López, José Gayà, Borja Mayoral, Denis Suárez, Mikel Merino, Iñaki Williams, Odriozola, Oyarzábal, Carlos Soler, Rodri Hernández, Diego González. Coach: Albert Celades (ESP)
Red card: Djurdjević 41 (Serbia)
Yellow cards: Djurdjević 21 (Serbia), Jovanović 40 (Serbia), Djurdjević 41 (Serbia), Mikel Merino 90 (Spain)

Portugal's Bruma (right) fends off a challenge from FYR Macedonia's Jovan Popzlatanov in his country's 4-2 win

	Pld	W	D	L	F	A	Pts
1 Spain	3	3	0	0	9	1	9
2 Portugal	3	2	0	1	7	5	6
3 Serbia	3	0	1	2	2	5	1
4 FYR Macedonia	3	0	1	2	4	11	1

Group C

18/06/17, Tychy Stadium, Tychy (att: 14,051)
Germany 2-0 Czech Republic
Goals: 1-0 Meyer 44, 2-0 Gnabry 50
Referee: Gil Manzano (ESP)
Germany: Pollersbeck, Toljan, Gerhardt, Stark, Meyer, Dahoud (Jung 66), Selke, Arnold (Haberer 86), Gnabry, Kempf, Weiser (Philipp 76). Coach: Stefan Kuntz (GER)
Czech Republic: Zima, Simič, Sáček (Chorý 81), Souček, Lüftner, Trávník, Jankto, Schick, Černý (Hašek 72), Ševčík (Barák 56), Havel. Coach: Vítězslav Lavička (CZE)
Yellow cards: Trávník 83 (Czech Republic), Jankto 89 (Czech Republic)

18/06/17, Krakow Stadium, Krakow (att: 8,754)
Denmark 0-2 Italy
Goals: 0-1 Pellegrini 54, 0-2 Petagna 86
Referee: Kružliak (SVK)
Denmark: Højbjerg, Holst, Maxsø, Banggaard, Nørgaard, Hjulsager, Vigen Christensen, Ingvartsen (Zohore 72), Andersen (Marcondes 80), Børsting (Duelund 79), Rasmussen. Coach: Niels Frederiksen (DEN)
Italy: Donnarumma, Barreca, Rugani, Pellegrini, Berardi (Chiesa 67), Bernardeschi, Petagna (Cerri 88), Conti, Caldara, Benassi (Grassi 73), Gagliardini. Coach: Luigi Di Biagio (ITA)
Yellow cards: Nørgaard 26 (Denmark), Holst 83 (Denmark)

21/06/17, Tychy Stadium, Tychy (att: 13,251)
Czech Republic 3-1 Italy
Goals: 1-0 Trávník 24, 1-1 Berardi 70, 2-1 Havlík 79, 3-1 Lüftner 85
Referee: Bastien (FRA)
Czech Republic: Zima, Simič, Souček, Lüftner, Trávník, Jankto, Hubínek (Chorý 77), Schick (Sáček 83), Havel, Hašek (Havlík 66), Holzer. Coach: Vítězslav Lavička (CZE)
Italy: Donnarumma, Calabria, Rugani, Cataldi (Cerri 83), Pellegrini, Berardi, Grassi (Chiesa 54), Bernardeschi (Gagliardini 75), Petagna, Conti, Ferrari. Coach: Luigi Di Biagio (ITA)
Yellow cards: Hubínek 18 (Czech Republic), Berardi 29 (Italy), Cataldi 34 (Italy), Conti 73 (Italy), Havlík 76 (Czech Republic), Cerri 87 (Italy)

21/06/17, Krakow Stadium, Krakow (att: 9,298)
Germany 3-0 Denmark
Goals: 1-0 Selke 53, 2-0 Kempf 73, 3-0 Amiri 79
Referee: Gözübüyük (NED)
Germany: Pollersbeck, Toljan, Gerhardt, Stark, Meyer, Dahoud, Selke, Arnold (Amiri 65), Gnabry (Öztunali 80), Kempf, Weiser (Jung 66). Coach: Stefan Kuntz (GER)
Denmark: Højbjerg, Holst, Maxsø, Banggaard, Blåbjerg (Pedersen 62), Nørgaard, Hjulsager (Jensen 80), Vigen Christensen, Ingvartsen, Nielsen (Zohore 56), Duelund. Coach: Niels Frederiksen (DEN)
Yellow cards: Vigen Christensen 13 (Denmark), Duelund 46 (Denmark), Banggaard 63 (Denmark), Jung 76 (Germany), Toljan 84 (Germany), Stark 90+2 (Germany)

Julian Pollersbeck seals Germany's penalty shoot-out victory against England with the decisive save from Nathan Redmond's spot kick

24/06/17, Krakow Stadium, Krakow (att: 14,039)
Italy 1-0 Germany
Goal: 1-0 Bernardeschi 31
Referee: Vinčić (SVN)
Italy: Donnarumma, Barreca, Rugani, Pellegrini, Berardi (Locatelli 86), Bernardeschi, Conti, Caldara, Benassi, Gagliardini, Chiesa (Petagna 78). Coach: Luigi Di Biagio (ITA)
Germany: Pollersbeck, Toljan, Gerhardt, Stark, Meyer (Philipp 67), Dahoud (Jung 72), Selke, Arnold, Gnabry, Kempf, Weiser (Amiri 76). Coach: Stefan Kuntz (GER)
Yellow cards: Kempf 25 (Germany), Berardi 32 (Italy), Arnold 32 (Germany), Chiesa 34 (Italy), Bernardeschi 38 (Italy), Conti 45+1 (Italy), Gerhardt 84 (Germany)

24/06/17, Tychy Stadium, Tychy (att: 9,047)
Czech Republic 2-4 Denmark
Goals: 0-1 Andersen 23, 1-1 Schick 27, 1-2 Zohore 35, 2-2 Chorý 54, 2-3 Zohore 73, 2-4 Ingvartsen 90+1
Referee: Madden (SCO)
Czech Republic: Zima, Simič, Souček, Lüftner, Trávník, Jankto (Juliš 64), Schick, Černý, Havel, Hašek (Chorý 46), Holzer (Havlík 78). Coach: Vítězslav Lavička (CZE)
Denmark: Højbjerg, Maxsø, Banggaard, Nørgaard, Hjulsager (Ingvartsen 65), Vigen Christensen (Nielsen 57), Andersen, Zohore, Nissen, Pedersen (Blåbjerg 74), Jensen. Coach: Niels Frederiksen (DEN)
Yellow cards: Ingvartsen 69 (Denmark), Černý 79 (Czech Republic), Simič 82 (Czech Republic), Souček 88 (Czech Republic)

	Pld	W	D	L	F	A	Pts
1 Italy	3	2	0	1	4	3	6
2 Germany	3	2	0	1	5	1	6
3 Denmark	3	1	0	2	4	7	3
4 Czech Republic	3	1	0	2	5	7	3

Semi-finals

27/06/17, Tychy Stadium, Tychy (att: 13,214)
England 2-2 Germany (aet; 3-4 on pens)
Goals: 0-1 Selke 35, 1-1 Gray 41, 2-1 Abraham 50, 2-2 Platte 70
Referee: Mažeika (LTU)
England: Pickford, Holgate (Iorfa 106), Chilwell, Chalobah (Murphy 66), Chambers, Gray (Redmond 73), Ward-Prowse, Abraham, Baker, Hughes (Swift 86), Mawson. Coach: Aidy Boothroyd (ENG)
Germany: Pollersbeck, Toljan, Gerhardt, Jung (Kehrer 80), Meyer, Selke (Platte 63), Arnold, Gnabry (Amiri 87), Kempf, Haberer (Kohr 102), Philipp. Coach: Stefan Kuntz (GER)
Yellow cards: Hughes 11 (England), Selke 19 (Germany), Chilwell 59 (England), Gnabry 81 (Germany), Holgate 84 (England), Kempf 108 (Germany), Arnold 113 (Germany)

27/06/17, Krakow Stadium, Krakow (att: 13,105)
Spain 3-1 Italy
Goals: 1-0 Saúl Ñíguez 53, 1-1 Bernardeschi 62, 2-1 Saúl Ñíguez 65, 3-1 Saúl Ñíguez 74
Referee: Vinčić (SVN)
Spain: Arrizabalaga, Bellerín, Jorge Meré, Jesús Vallejo, Dani Ceballos (Oyarzábal 88), Deulofeu (Denis Suárez 82), Saúl Ñíguez, Marco Asensio, Sandro Ramírez (Iñaki Williams 78), Jonny, Llorente. Coach: Albert Celades (ESP)
Italy: Donnarumma, Calabria, Barreca, Rugani, Pellegrini, Bernardeschi, Petagna (Cerri 72), Caldara, Benassi (Garritano 87), Gagliardini, Chiesa (Locatelli 61). Coach: Luigi Di Biagio (ITA)
Red card: Gagliardini 58 (Italy)
Yellow cards: Benassi 45+1 (Italy), Gagliardini 50 (Italy), Calabria 56 (Italy), Gagliardini 58 (Italy), Cerri 77 (Italy)

Final

30/06/17, Krakow Stadium, Krakow (att: 14,059)
Germany 1-0 Spain
Goal: 1-0 Weiser 40
Referee: Bastien (FRA)
Germany: Pollersbeck, Toljan, Gerhardt, Stark, Meyer, Arnold, Gnabry (Amiri 81), Kempf, Weiser, Haberer (Kohr 82), Philipp (Öztunali 87). Coach: Stefan Kuntz (GER)
Spain: Arrizabalaga, Bellerín, Jorge Meré, Jesús Vallejo, Dani Ceballos, Deulofeu, Saúl Ñíguez, Marco Asensio, Sandro Ramírez (Iñaki Williams 71), Jonny (José Gayà 51), Llorente (Borja Mayoral 83). Coach: Albert Celades (ESP)
Yellow cards: Saúl Ñíguez 43 (Spain), Arnold 47 (Germany), Haberer 50 (Germany), Stark 52 (Germany), Llorente 54 (Spain), Meyer 78 (Germany), Jesús Vallejo 89 (Spain)

Top goalscorers (Final tournament)

5	Saúl Ñíguez (Spain)
3	Bruma (Portugal)
	Marco Asensio (Spain)
2	Kenneth Zohore (Denmark)
	Demarai Gray (England)
	Davie Selke (Germany)
	Federico Bernardeschi (Italy)
	Enis Bardi (FYR Macedonia)
	Martin Chrien (Slovakia)

UEFA European Under-21 Championship

Squads/Appearances/Goals

Czech Republic

No	Name	DoB	Aps	(s)	Gls	Club
Goalkeepers						
23	Patrik Macej	11/06/94				Michalovce (SVK)
1	Luděk Vejmola	03/11/94				Mladá Boleslav
16	Lukáš Zima	09/01/94	3			Genoa (ITA)
Defenders						
19	Milan Havel	07/08/94	3			Bohemians 1905
21	Daniel Holzer	18/08/95	2			Sparta Praha
22	Filip Kaša	01/01/94				Žilina (SVK)
6	Michael Lüftner	14/03/94	3		1	Slavia Praha
4	Michal Sáček	19/09/96	1	(1)		Sparta Praha
2	Stefan Simič	20/01/95	3			Mouscron (BEL)
15	Patrizio Stronati	17/11/94				Mladá Boleslav
Midfielders						
8	Antonín Barák	03/12/94		(1)		Slavia Praha
17	Václav Černý	17/10/97	2			Ajax (NED)
20	Martin Hašek	03/10/95	2	(1)		Bohemians 1905
3	Marek Havlík	08/07/95		(2)	1	Slovácko
12	Michal Hubínek	10/11/94	1			Bohemians 1905
11	Jakub Jankto	19/01/96	3			Udinese (ITA)
13	Jakub Nečas	26/01/95				Mladá Boleslav
18	Petr Ševčík	04/05/94	1			Liberec
5	Tomáš Souček	27/02/95	3			Slavia Praha
10	Michal Trávník	17/05/94	3		1	Jablonec
Forwards						
9	Tomáš Chorý	26/01/95		(3)	1	Sigma
7	Lukáš Juliš	02/12/94		(1)		Sparta Praha
14	Patrik Schick	24/01/96	3		1	Sampdoria (ITA)

Denmark

No	Name	DoB	Aps	(s)	Gls	Club
Goalkeepers						
16	Thomas Hagelskjær	04/02/95				AGF
1	Jeppe Højbjerg	30/04/95	3			Esbjerg
22	Daniel Iversen	19/07/97				Esbjerg
Defenders						
13	Joachim Andersen	31/05/96				Twente (NED)
4	Patrick Banggaard	04/04/94	3			Darmstadt (GER)
5	Jakob Blåbjerg	11/01/95	1	(1)		AaB
2	Frederik Holst	24/09/94	2			Brøndby
3	Andreas Maxsø	18/03/94	3			Nordsjælland
12	Rasmus Nissen	11/07/97	1			Midtjylland
15	Mads Pedersen	01/09/96	1	(1)		Nordsjælland
20	Jacob Rasmussen	28/05/97	1			Rosenborg (NOR)
Midfielders						
19	Frederik Børsting	13/02/95	1			AaB
7	Andrew Hjulsager	15/01/95	3			Celta (ESP)
17	Mathias Jensen	01/01/96	1	(1)		Nordsjælland
18	Emiliano Marcondes	09/03/95		(1)		Nordsjælland
14	Casper Nielsen	29/04/94	1	(1)		OB
6	Christian Nørgaard	10/03/94	3			Brøndby
8	Lasse Vigen Christensen	15/08/94	3			Burton (ENG)
Forwards						
10	Lucas Andersen	13/09/94	2		1	Grasshoppers (SUI)
23	Mikkel Duelund	29/06/97	1	(1)		Midtjylland
9	Marcus Ingvartsen	04/01/96	2	(1)	1	Nordsjælland
21	Kasper Junker	05/03/94				AGF
11	Kenneth Zohore	31/01/94	1	(2)	2	Cardiff (ENG)

England

No	Name	DoB	Aps	(s)	Gls	Club
Goalkeepers						
13	Angus Gunn	22/01/96				Man. City
21	Jonathan Mitchell	24/11/94				Derby
1	Jordan Pickford	07/03/94	4			Sunderland
Defenders						
5	Calum Chambers	20/01/95	4			Middlesbrough
3	Ben Chilwell	21/12/96	4			Leicester
17	Kortney Hause	16/07/95				Wolves
16	Rob Holding	20/09/95				Arsenal
2	Mason Holgate	22/10/96	4			Everton
18	Dominic Iorfa	24/06/95		(1)		Wolves
23	Alfie Mawson	19/01/94	4		1	Swansea
6	Jack Stephens	27/01/94				Southampton
12	Matt Targett	18/09/95				Southampton
Midfielders						
10	Lewis Baker	25/04/95	4		1	Vitesse (NED)
4	Nathaniel Chalobah	12/12/94	4			Chelsea
20	Jack Grealish	10/09/95				Aston Villa
19	Will Hughes	17/04/95	1	(1)		Derby
11	Nathan Redmond	06/03/94	3	(1)	1	Southampton
15	John Swift	23/06/95	2	(1)		Reading
8	James Ward-Prowse	01/11/94	4			Southampton
Forwards						
9	Tammy Abraham	02/10/97	3	(1)	1	Bristol City
7	Demarai Gray	28/06/96	2	(2)	2	Leicester
14	Jacob Murphy	24/02/95	1	(3)	1	Norwich
22	Cauley Woodrow	02/12/94		(1)		Burton

Germany

No	Name	DoB	Aps	(s)	Gls	Club
Goalkeepers						
12	Julian Pollersbeck	16/08/94	5			Kaiserslautern
1	Marvin Schwäbe	25/04/95				Dynamo Dresden
23	Odysseas Vlachodimos	26/04/94				Panathinaikos (GRE)
Defenders						
4	Waldemar Anton	20/07/96				Hannover
3	Yannick Gerhardt	13/03/94	5			Wolfsburg
6	Gideon Jung	12/09/94	1	(3)		Hamburg
16	Thilo Kehrer	21/09/96		(1)		Schalke
15	Marc-Oliver Kempf	28/01/95	5		1	Freiburg
14	Lukas Klünter	26/05/96				Köln
5	Niklas Stark	14/04/95	4			Hertha
2	Jeremy Toljan	08/08/94	5			Hoffenheim
Midfielders						
18	Nadiem Amiri	27/10/96		(4)	1	Hoffenheim
10	Maximilian Arnold	27/05/94	5			Wolfsburg
8	Mahmoud Dahoud	01/01/96	3			Mönchengladbach
11	Serge Gnabry	14/07/95	5		1	Bremen
19	Janik Haberer	02/04/94	2	(1)		Freiburg
21	Dominik Kohr	31/01/94		(2)		Augsburg
7	Max Meyer	18/09/95	5		1	Schalke
20	Levin Öztunali	15/03/96		(2)		Mainz
17	Mitchell Weiser	21/04/94	4		1	Hertha
Forwards						
22	Maximilian Philipp	01/03/94	2	(2)		Freiburg
13	Felix Platte	11/02/96		(1)	1	Darmstadt
9	Davie Selke	20/01/95	4		2	RB Leipzig

Italy

No	Name	DoB	Aps	(s)	Gls	Club
Goalkeepers						
17	Alessio Cragno	28/06/94				Benevento
1	Gianluigi Donnarumma	25/02/99	4			Milan
19	Simone Scuffet	31/05/96				Udinese
Defenders						
3	Antonio Barreca	18/03/95	3			Torino
14	Davide Biraschi	02/07/94				Genoa
2	Davide Calabria	06/12/96	2			Milan
13	Mattia Caldara	05/05/94	3			Atalanta
12	Andrea Conti	02/03/94	3			Atalanta
22	Alex Ferrari	01/07/94	1			Verona
23	Giuseppe Pezzella	29/11/97				Palermo
4	Daniele Rugani	29/07/94	4			Juventus
Midfielders						
15	Marco Benassi	08/09/94	3			Torino
5	Danilo Cataldi	06/08/94	1			Genoa
18	Roberto Gagliardini	07/04/94	3	(1)		Internazionale
8	Alberto Grassi	07/03/95	1	(1)		Atalanta
21	Manuel Locatelli	08/01/98		(2)		Milan
6	Lorenzo Pellegrini	19/06/96	4		1	Sassuolo
Forwards						
7	Domenico Berardi	01/08/94	3		1	Sassuolo
10	Federico Bernardeschi	16/02/94	4		2	Fiorentina
9	Alberto Cerri	16/04/96		(3)		Pescara
20	Federico Chiesa	25/10/97	2	(2)		Fiorentina
16	Luca Garritano	11/02/94		(1)		Cesena
11	Andrea Petagna	30/06/95	3	(1)	1	Atalanta

FYR Macedonia

No	Name	DoB	Aps	(s)	Gls	Club
Goalkeepers						
1	Igor Aleksovski	24/02/95	2			Vardar
13	Filip Ilic	26/01/97				Gandzasar (ARM)
12	Damjan Siskovski	18/03/95	1			Rabotnicki
Defenders						
6	Aleksa Amanovic	24/10/96				Javor (SRB)
15	Egzon Bejtulai	07/01/94	2			Shkëndija
19	Besir Demiri	01/08/94	2			Shkëndija
21	Mevlan Murati	05/03/94	2			Shkëndija
4	Visar Musliu	13/11/94		(1)		Renova
3	Jovan Popzlatanov	06/07/96	1			Pelister
14	Darko Velkovski	21/06/95	2			Vardar
5	Gjoko Zajkov	10/02/95	3			Charleroi (BEL)
Midfielders						
7	Enis Bardi	02/07/95	3		2	Újpest (HUN)
10	David Babunski	01/03/94	3			Yokohama F Marinos (JPN)
2	Eljif Elmas	24/09/99		(3)		Rabotnicki
22	Nikola Gjorgjev	22/08/97	1	(2)	1	Grasshoppers (SUI)
20	Tihomir Kostadinov	04/03/96		(1)		Zlaté Moravce (SVK)
17	Kire Markoski	20/02/95	2	(1)	1	Rabotnicki
8	Boban Nikolov	28/07/94	3			Vardar
16	Petar Petkovski	03/01/97				Vardar
9	Marjan Radeski	10/02/95	3			Shkëndija
Forwards						
18	Viktor Angelov	27/03/94	2			Újpest (HUN)
11	Daniel Avramovski	20/02/95	1			Olimpija Ljubljana (SVN)
23	Filip Pivkovski	31/01/94		(1)		Landskrona (SWE)

Poland

No	Name	DoB	Aps	(s)	Gls	Club
Goalkeepers						
1	Bartłomiej Drągowski	19/08/97				Fiorentina (ITA)
22	Maksymilian Stryjek	18/07/96				Sunderland (ENG)
12	Jakub Wrąbel	08/06/96	3			Olimpia Grudziądz
Defenders						
6	Jan Bednarek	12/04/96	3			Lech
15	Jarosław Jach	17/02/94	3			Zagłębie
2	Paweł Jaroszyński	02/10/94	3			Cracovia
4	Tomasz Kędziora	11/06/94	3			Lech
5	Igor Łasicki	26/06/95				Carpi (ITA)
23	Przemysław Szymiński	24/06/94				Wisła Płock
Midfielders						
3	Krystian Bielik	04/01/98				Birmingham (ENG)
17	Paweł Dawidowicz	20/05/95	2			Bochum (GER)
11	Przemysław Frankowski	12/04/95	3			Jagiellonia
19	Bartosz Kapustka	23/12/96	1			Leicester (ENG)
14	Dawid Kownacki	14/03/97	2		1	Lech
20	Jarosław Kubicki	07/08/95				Zagłębie
7	Karol Linetty	02/02/95	3			Sampdoria (ITA)
10	Patryk Lipski	12/06/94	1	(2)	1	Ruch
13	Łukasz Moneta	13/05/94	2	(1)	1	Ruch
8	Radosław Murawski	22/04/94	1			Piast
18	Jarosław Niezgoda	15/03/95		(3)		Ruch
Forwards						
21	Adam Buksa	12/07/96				Zagłębie
16	Krzysztof Piątek	01/07/95	1	(2)		Cracovia
9	Mariusz Stępiński	12/05/95	2	(1)		Nantes (FRA)

Serbia

No	Name	DoB	Aps	(s)	Gls	Club
Goalkeepers						
1	Filip Manojlović	25/04/96	1			Crvena zvezda
12	Djordje Nikolić	13/04/97				Basel (SUI)
23	Vanja Milinković-Savić	20/02/97	2			Lechia (POL)
Defenders						
3	Nemanja Antonov	06/05/95	3			Grasshoppers (SUI)
13	Miroslav Bogosavac	14/10/96				Partizan
15	Aleksandar Filipović	20/12/94	1	(1)		Voždovac
2	Milan Gajić	28/01/96	2			Bordeaux (FRA)
4	Nikola Milenković	12/10/97				Partizan
6	Radovan Pankov	05/08/95				Ural (RUS)
14	Vukašin Jovanović	17/05/96	3			Bordeaux (FRA)
5	Miloš Veljković	26/09/95	3			Bremen (GER)
Midfielders						
10	Mijat Gaćinović	08/02/95	3		1	Eintracht Frankfurt (GER)
16	Marko Grujić	13/04/96	2			Liverpool (ENG)
19	Saša Lukić	13/08/96	1			Torino (ITA)
8	Nemanja Maksimović	26/01/95	3			Astana (KAZ)
18	Dejan Meleg	01/10/94				Vojvodina
21	Nemanja Radonjić	15/02/96	1	(1)		Čukarički
20	Mihailo Ristić	31/10/95		(2)		Crvena zvezda
17	Andrija Živković	11/07/96	3			Benfica (POR)
Forwards						
11	Aleksandar Čavrić	18/05/94	1			Slovan Bratislava (SVK)
9	Uroš Djurdjević	02/03/94	3		1	Partizan
7	Ognjen Ožegović	09/06/94		(2)		Čukarički
22	Srdjan Plavšić	03/12/95	1	(2)		Crvena zvezda

Spain

No	Name	DoB	Aps	(s)	Gls	Club
Goalkeepers						
1	Kepa Arrizabalaga	03/10/94	4			Athletic
16	Pau López	13/12/94	1			Tottenham (ENG)
13	Rubén Blanco	25/07/95				Celta
Defenders						
2	Héctor Bellerín	19/03/95	4			Arsenal (ENG)
23	Diego González	28/01/95	1			Sevilla
5	Jesús Vallejo	05/01/97	4			Eintracht Frankfurt (GER)
3	José Gayà	25/05/95	2	(1)		Valencia
19	Jonny	03/03/94	3			Celta
4	Jorge Meré	17/04/97	4			Sporting Gijón
14	Mikel Merino	22/06/96	1	(1)		Dortmund (GER)
17	Álvaro Odriozola	14/12/95	1			Real Sociedad
Midfielders						
20	Carlos Soler	02/01/97	1			Valencia
6	Dani Ceballos	07/08/96	3	(1)		Betis
10	Denis Suárez	06/01/94	2	(2)	1	Barcelona
7	Gerard Deulofeu	13/03/94	4		1	Milan (ITA)
22	Marcos Llorente	30/01/95	4			Alavés
11	Marco Asensio	21/01/96	4		3	Real Madrid
18	Mikel Oyarzábal	21/04/97	1	(2)		Real Sociedad
21	Rodri Hernández	22/06/96	1			Villarreal
8	Saúl Ñíguez	21/11/94	4		5	Atlético
Forwards						
9	Borja Mayoral	05/04/97	1	(1)		Wolfsburg (GER)
15	Iñaki Williams	15/06/94	1	(4)	1	Athletic
12	Sandro Ramírez	09/07/95	4		1	Málaga

Portugal

No	Name	DoB	Aps	(s)	Gls	Club
Goalkeepers						
1	Bruno Varela	04/11/94	3			Setúbal
22	Joel Pereira	28/06/96				Man. United (ENG)
12	Miguel Silva	07/04/95				Guimarães
Defenders						
3	Edgar Ié	01/05/94	3		1	Belenenses
15	Fernando Fonseca	14/03/97				Porto
2	João Cancelo	27/05/94	3			Valencia (ESP)
14	Pedro Rebocho	23/01/95	1			Moreirense
13	Kévin Rodrigues	05/03/94	2	(1)		Real Sociedad (ESP)
5	Rúben Semedo	04/04/94	2			Sporting CP
4	Tobias Figueiredo	02/02/94	1			Nacional
Midfielders						
10	Bruno Fernandes	08/09/94	2		1	Sampdoria (ITA)
8	Francisco Geraldes	18/04/95				Sporting CP
17	Francisco Ramos	10/04/95				Porto
11	Iuri Medeiros	10/07/94	1	(1)		Boavista
23	João Carvalho	09/03/97	2			Setúbal
16	Renato Sanches	18/08/97	2	(1)		Bayern (GER)
6	Rúben Neves	13/03/97	3			Porto
Forwards						
20	Bruma	24/10/94	1	(2)	3	Galatasaray (TUR)
7	Daniel Podence	21/10/95	3		1	Sporting CP
19	Diogo Jota	04/12/96	1	(1)		Porto
18	Gonçalo Guedes	29/11/96	2		1	Paris (FRA)
9	Gonçalo Paciência	01/08/94	1	(1)		Rio Ave
21	Ricardo Horta	15/09/94		(2)		Braga

Slovakia

No	Name	DoB	Aps	(s)	Gls	Club
Goalkeepers						
1	Adrián Chovan	08/10/95	3			Trenčín
23	Adam Jakubech	02/01/97				Spartak Trnava
12	Marek Rodák	13/12/96				Fulham (ENG)
Defenders						
5	Tomáš Huk	22/12/94				Dunajská Streda
14	Róbert Mazáň	09/02/94	3			Žilina
2	Branislav Niňaj	17/05/94	3			Lokeren (BEL)
13	Ľubomír Šatka	02/12/95	1		1	Newcastle (ENG)
16	Lukáš Skovajsa	27/03/94				Trenčín
3	Milan Škriniar	11/02/95	3			Sampdoria (ITA)
4	Martin Valjent	11/12/95	2		1	Ternana (ITA)
19	Denis Vavro	10/04/96				Žilina
Midfielders						
22	László Bénes	09/09/97		(3)		Mönchengladbach (GER)
21	Matúš Bero	06/09/95	3			Trabzonspor (TUR)
8	Martin Chrien	08/09/95	3		2	Ružomberok
17	Lukáš Haraslín	26/05/96		(3)		Lechia (POL)
20	Miroslav Káčer	02/02/96				Žilina
6	Stanislav Lobotka	25/11/94	3			Nordsjælland (DEN)
7	Jaroslav Mihalík	27/07/94	3		1	Cracovia (POL)
10	Albert Rusnák	07/07/94	3			Real Salt Lake (USA)
11	Nikolas Špalek	12/02/97				Žilina
Forwards						
18	Pavol Šafranko	16/11/94		(3)	1	Dunajská Streda
9	Tomáš Vestenický	06/04/96				Cracovia (POL)
15	Adam Zreľák	05/05/94	3			Jablonec (CZE)

Sweden

No	Name	DoB	Aps	(s)	Gls	Club
Goalkeepers						
12	Anton Cajtoft	13/02/94	3			Jönköping
23	Pontus Dahlberg	21/01/99				Göteborg
1	Tim Erlandsson	25/12/96				Eskilstuna
Defenders						
20	Egzon Binaku	27/08/95	1			Häcken
15	Franz Brorsson	30/01/96	1			Malmö
14	Filip Dagerstål	01/02/97	2			Norrköping
5	Adam Lundqvist	20/03/94	2			Elfsborg
4	Joakim Nilsson	06/02/94				Elfsborg
13	Isak Ssewankambo	27/02/96				Molde (NOR)
3	Jacob Une Larsson	08/04/94	3		1	Djurgården
2	Linus Wahlqvist	11/11/96	3			Norrköping
Midfielders						
22	Amin Affane	21/01/94				AIK
19	Niclas Eliasson	07/12/95		(1)		Norrköping
7	Alexander Fransson	02/04/94	3			Basel (SUI)
16	Melker Hallberg	20/10/95	3			Kalmar
17	Kerim Mrabti	20/05/94	1	(2)		Djurgården
8	Kristoffer Olsson	30/06/95	3			AIK
9	Muamer Tankovic	22/02/95		(3)		AZ (NED)
6	Simon Tibbling	07/09/94	2			Groningen (NED)
Forwards						
21	Joel Asoro	27/04/99		(1)		Sunderland (ENG)
18	Pawel Cibicki	09/01/94	3			Malmö
11	Gustav Engvall	29/04/96	1	(1)		Djurgården
10	Carlos Strandberg	14/04/96	2	(1)	1	Westerlo (BEL)

Flawless form in Georgia brings first U19 title

Keith Downing's team defeat Portugal 2-1 in final

Surprises galore in qualifying competition

England on the march

For the first time since 2013 there was a new name on the UEFA European Under-19 Championship trophy as England defeated Portugal 2-1 in the Georgian city of Gori to add the title to that of the FIFA U-20 World Cup claimed a month earlier in South Korea.

Neither of the two finalists had been crowned U19 European champions before, but they had twice been runners-up, so there was an eagerness in both camps to avoid becoming the first country to lose a third final. After a goalless first half it was England who struck first when centre-back Easah Suliman headed in after Mason Mount's free-kick had come back off the post. Although Dujon Sterling's own goal quickly brought Portugal level, Keith Downing's team restored their lead via a lightning counterattack, the impressive Mount drawing two defenders and the goalkeeper before setting up Lukas Nmecha to score the goal that would prove decisive despite England having midfielder Tayo Edun sent off four minutes from time.

England's long-awaited first U19 title was a fitting climax to a competition that provided an abundance of unlikely results – especially in the qualifying competition. Holders France and 2016 runners-up Italy were among the big-name elite round casualties, both finishing bottom of their group, while England, for the second season running, knocked out seven-time champions Spain.

Germany, therefore, were the only former winners to qualify, but it would not be a good tournament for the two-time champions. They were up against it from the outset in Group B, Joël Piroe's hat-trick giving the Netherlands an opening 4-1 win. England, meanwhile, made serene progress, opening with a 2-0 victory against Bulgaria before substitute Ben Brereton struck late against the Dutch. The same player and Ryan Sessegnon then each scored twice as Germany were dismantled 4-1. That result, coupled with the Netherlands' 1-1 draw against Bulgaria, enabled the Dutch to progress to the semi-finals in England's wake.

England lift the European U19 trophy for the first time

Portugal took control of Group A, Rui Pedro scoring winning goals against hosts Georgia and the Czech Republic to take his country through as group winners with a match to spare. The Czechs held firm in the face of a 24,000-strong crowd in Tbilisi to beat Georgia 2-0 and go through at the hosts' expense, while debutants Sweden finished bottom despite Viktor Gyökeres's feat of scoring in every game.

Both semi-finals proved tight affairs. Portugal struck the decisive blow against the Netherlands thanks to Gedson Fernandes' 24th-minute strike, and there was a dramatic conclusion to the second semi-final as England's Marcus Edwards set up fellow substitute Nmecha for a back-heeled finish with seconds left in stoppage time for the only goal against the Czechs. It was England's fourth win out of four in Georgia. They would make it five out of five against Portugal three days later.

Qualifying round

Group 1
06-11/10/16 Tessenderlo, Maasmechelen, Beringen
Russia 1-1 Finland, Kazakhstan 0-5 Belgium, Belgium 2-2 Finland, Russia 5-0 Kazakhstan, Belgium 2-2 Russia, Finland 6-0 Kazakhstan

	Pld	W	D	L	F	A	Pts
1 Belgium	3	1	2	0	9	4	5
2 Finland	3	1	2	0	9	3	5
3 Russia	3	1	2	0	8	3	5
4 Kazakhstan	3	0	0	3	0	16	0

Group 2
06-11/10/16 Vriezenveen, Hardenberg
San Marino 0-9 Norway, Netherlands 2-1 Romania, Norway 3-1 Romania, Netherlands 4-0 San Marino, Norway 0-1 Netherlands, Romania 6-0 San Marino

	Pld	W	D	L	F	A	Pts
1 Netherlands	3	3	0	0	7	1	9
2 Norway	3	2	0	1	12	2	6
3 Romania	3	1	0	2	8	5	3
4 San Marino	3	0	0	3	0	19	0

Group 3
25-30/10/16 Andorra la Vella
Liechtenstein 0-1 Scotland, Israel 3-2 Andorra, Israel 5-0 Liechtenstein, Scotland 1-0 Andorra, Scotland 0-1 Israel, Andorra 4-2 Liechtenstein

	Pld	W	D	L	F	A	Pts
1 Israel	3	3	0	0	9	2	9
2 Scotland	3	2	0	1	2	1	6
3 Andorra	3	1	0	2	6	6	3
4 Liechtenstein	3	0	0	3	2	10	0

Group 4
06-11/10/16 Tirana, Durres
Albania 0-1 Republic of Ireland, Germany 5-0 Gibraltar, Republic of Ireland 5-0 Gibraltar, Germany 3-2 Albania, Republic of Ireland 0-4 Germany, Gibraltar 0-1 Albania

	Pld	W	D	L	F	A	Pts
1 Germany	3	3	0	0	12	2	9
2 Republic of Ireland	3	2	0	1	6	4	6
3 Albania	3	1	0	2	3	4	3
4 Gibraltar	3	0	0	3	0	11	0

Group 5
04-09/10/16 Marijampole, Alytus
Austria 4-1 Azerbaijan, Lithuania 0-3 Bosnia & Herzegovina, Bosnia & Herzegovina 2-1 Azerbaijan, Austria 3-2 Lithuania, Bosnia & Herzegovina 1-3 Austria, Azerbaijan 2-0 Lithuania

	Pld	W	D	L	F	A	Pts
1 Austria	3	3	0	0	10	4	9
2 Bosnia & Herzegovina	3	2	0	1	6	4	6
3 Azerbaijan	3	1	0	2	4	6	3
4 Lithuania	3	0	0	3	2	8	0

Group 6
10-15/11/16 Wrexham, Rhyl, Bangor
Wales 0-2 Greece, England 2-0 Luxembourg, Greece 5-0 Luxembourg, England 2-3 Wales, Greece 0-2 England, Luxembourg 2-6 Wales

	Pld	W	D	L	F	A	Pts
1 England	3	2	0	1	6	3	6
2 Greece	3	2	0	1	7	2	6
3 Wales	3	2	0	1	9	6	6
4 Luxembourg	3	0	0	3	2	13	0

Group 7
10-15/11/16 Yerevan
Switzerland 4-0 Armenia, Hungary 0-1 Italy, Italy 2-1 Armenia, Switzerland 1-2 Hungary, Italy 1-1 Switzerland, Armenia 0-4 Hungary

	Pld	W	D	L	F	A	Pts
1 Italy	3	2	1	0	4	2	7
2 Hungary	3	2	0	1	6	2	6
3 Switzerland	3	1	1	1	6	3	4
4 Armenia	3	0	0	3	1	10	0

Group 8
10-15/11/16 Sliven, Stara Zagora
Bulgaria 1-0 Portugal, Denmark 5-0 Belarus, Portugal 1-1 Belarus, Denmark 1-3 Bulgaria, Portugal 2-1 Denmark, Belarus 1-0 Bulgaria

	Pld	W	D	L	F	A	Pts
1 Bulgaria	3	2	0	1	4	2	6
2 Portugal	3	1	1	1	3	3	4
3 Belarus	3	1	1	1	2	6	4
4 Denmark	3	1	0	2	7	5	3

Group 9
06-11/10/16 Chomutov, Teplice, Usti nad Labem
France 1-1 Slovenia, Estonia 0-5 Czech Republic, France 4-0 Estonia, Czech Republic 2-1 Slovenia, Czech Republic 0-2 France, Slovenia 5-0 Estonia

	Pld	W	D	L	F	A	Pts
1 France	3	2	1	0	7	1	7
2 Czech Republic	3	2	0	1	7	3	6
3 Slovenia	3	1	1	1	7	3	4
4 Estonia	3	0	0	3	0	14	0

Group 10
09-14/11/16 Belgrade, Stara Pazova
Sweden 4-0 Malta, Moldova 0-2 Serbia, Sweden 1-0 Moldova, Serbia 1-0 Malta, Serbia 2-3 Sweden, Malta 1-0 Moldova

	Pld	W	D	L	F	A	Pts
1 Sweden	3	3	0	0	8	2	9
2 Serbia	3	2	0	1	5	3	6
3 Malta	3	1	0	2	1	5	3
4 Moldova	3	0	0	3	0	4	0

Group 11
06-11/10/16 Torun, Szubin, Inowrocław
Northern Ireland 0-1 Slovakia, FYR Macedonia 0-4 Poland, FYR Macedonia 1-2 Northern Ireland, Slovakia 1-0 Poland, Slovakia 2-0 FYR Macedonia, Poland 3-0 Northern Ireland

	Pld	W	D	L	F	A	Pts
1 Slovakia	3	3	0	0	4	0	9
2 Poland	3	2	0	1	7	1	6
3 Northern Ireland	3	1	0	2	2	5	3
4 FYR Macedonia	3	0	0	3	1	8	0

Group 12
09-14/11/16 Podgorica, Budva
Croatia 4-0 Cyprus, Faroe Islands 2-1 Montenegro, Croatia 5-0 Faroe Islands, Montenegro 0-1 Cyprus, Montenegro 1-2 Croatia, Cyprus 1-0 Faroe Islands

	Pld	W	D	L	F	A	Pts
1 Croatia	3	3	0	0	11	1	9
2 Cyprus	3	2	0	1	2	4	6
3 Faroe Islands	3	1	0	2	2	7	3
4 Montenegro	3	0	0	3	2	5	0

Group 13
06-11/10/16 Borispol, Bucha
Ukraine 2-0 Iceland, Latvia 2-2 Turkey, Ukraine 3-0 Latvia, Turkey 2-1 Iceland, Turkey 3-1 Ukraine, Iceland 2-0 Latvia

	Pld	W	D	L	F	A	Pts
1 Turkey	3	2	1	0	7	4	7
2 Ukraine	3	2	0	1	6	3	6
3 Iceland	3	1	0	2	3	4	3
4 Latvia	3	0	1	2	2	7	1

Elite round

Group 1
23-28/03/17 Assen, Harkema
Netherlands 1-0 Finland, Ukraine 2-0 Greece, Greece 4-1 Finland, Netherlands 2-0 Ukraine, Greece 0-0 Netherlands, Finland 2-1 Ukraine

	Pld	W	D	L	F	A	Pts
1 Netherlands	3	2	1	0	3	0	7
2 Greece	3	1	1	1	4	3	4
3 Finland	3	1	0	2	3	6	3
4 Ukraine	3	1	0	2	3	4	3

Group 2
23-28/03/17 Rüsselsheim am Main, Kelsterbach, Frankfurt am Main
Germany 2-1 Cyprus, Serbia 1-0 Slovakia, Germany 2-0 Serbia, Slovakia 5-0 Cyprus, Slovakia 0-4 Germany, Cyprus 0-0 Serbia

	Pld	W	D	L	F	A	Pts
1 Germany	3	3	0	0	8	1	9
2 Serbia	3	1	1	1	1	2	4
3 Slovakia	3	1	0	2	5	5	3
4 Cyprus	3	0	1	2	1	7	1

Group 3
22-27/03/17 Burton-on-Trent, Leek
Spain 5-0 Belarus, England 3-0 Norway, Spain 0-3 England, Norway 2-1 Belarus, Norway 0-2 Spain, Belarus 1-5 England

	Pld	W	D	L	F	A	Pts
1 England	3	3	0	0	11	1	9
2 Spain	3	2	0	1	7	3	6
3 Norway	3	1	0	2	2	6	3
4 Belarus	3	0	0	3	2	12	0

Group 4
23-28/03/17 Fão, Pacos de Ferreira, Vila do Conde, Felgueiras, Barcelos
Poland 1-0 Turkey, Croatia 1-2 Portugal, Croatia 2-0 Poland, Turkey 2-1 Portugal, Turkey 0-0 Croatia, Portugal 3-1 Poland

	Pld	W	D	L	F	A	Pts
1 Portugal	3	2	0	1	6	4	6
2 Croatia	3	1	1	1	3	2	4
3 Turkey	3	1	1	1	2	2	4
4 Poland	3	1	0	2	2	5	3

Group 5
22-27/03/17 Romorantin, Blois, Vineuil
Bosnia & Herzegovina 2-0 France, Israel 1-1 Bulgaria, Israel 1-1 Bosnia & Herzegovina, France 1-2 Bulgaria, France 0-0 Israel, Bulgaria 3-1 Bosnia & Herzegovina

	Pld	W	D	L	F	A	Pts
1 Bulgaria	3	2	1	0	6	3	7
2 Bosnia & Herzegovina	3	1	1	1	4	4	4
3 Israel	3	0	3	0	2	2	3
4 France	3	0	1	2	1	4	1

Group 6

22-27/03/17 Zlin, Uherske Hradiste
Austria 3-0 Scotland, Hungary 1-2 Czech Republic, Austria 1-3 Hungary, Czech Republic 1-0 Scotland, Czech Republic 3-0 Austria, Scotland 1-2 Hungary

	Pld	W	D	L	F	A	Pts
1 Czech Republic	3	3	0	0	6	1	9
2 Hungary	3	2	0	1	6	4	6
3 Austria	3	1	0	2	4	6	3
4 Scotland	3	0	0	3	1	6	0

Group 7

23-28/03/17 Beveren, Hamme
Sweden 1-2 Belgium, Republic of Ireland 2-0 Italy, Sweden 3-0 Republic of Ireland, Italy 1-1 Belgium, Italy 0-1 Sweden, Belgium 0-1 Republic of Ireland

	Pld	W	D	L	F	A	Pts
1 Sweden	3	2	0	1	5	2	6
2 Republic of Ireland	3	2	0	1	3	3	6
3 Belgium	3	1	1	1	3	3	4
4 Italy	3	0	1	2	1	4	1

Top goalscorers (Qualifying/Elite rounds)

5	Lassi Lappalainen (Finland)
	Birk Risa (Norway)
	Nathan Broadhead (Wales)
4	Arnel Jakupovic (Austria)
	Matthias Verreth (Belgium)
	Trent Arnold (England)
	Etienne Amenyido (Germany)

Final tournament

Group A

02/07/17, Mikheil Meskhi Stadioni, Tbilisi
Sweden 1-2 Czech Republic
Goals: 0-1 Turyna 42, 0-2 Turyna 55, 1-2 Gyökeres 77
Referee: Lapochkin (RUS)

02/07/17, Tengiz Burjanadze Stadioni, Gori
Georgia 0-1 Portugal
Goal: 0-1 Rui Pedro 66
Referee: Massa (ITA)

05/07/17, Mikheil Meskhi Stadioni, Tbilisi
Georgia 2-1 Sweden
Goals: 1-0 Kokhreidze 3, 2-0 Chakvetadze 31, 2-1 Gyökeres 47
Referee: Jovanović (SRB)

05/07/17, David Petriashvili Stadium, Tbilisi
Czech Republic 1-2 Portugal
Goals: 0-1 Mesaque Dju 35, 1-1 Graiciar 40, 1-2 Rui Pedro 74
Referee: Palabıyık (TUR)

08/07/17, Mikheil Meskhi Stadioni, Tbilisi
Czech Republic 2-0 Georgia
Goals: 1-0 Šašinka 45+1, 2-0 Holík 70
Referee: Kristoffersen (DEN)

08/07/17, Tengiz Burjanadze Stadioni, Gori
Portugal 2-2 Sweden
Goals: 0-1 Gyökeres 43, 0-2 Karlsson 61, 1-2 Rafael Leão 70, 2-2 João Filipe 87(p)
Referee: Nilsen (NOR)

	Pld	W	D	L	F	A	Pts
1 Portugal	3	2	1	0	5	3	7
2 Czech Republic	3	2	0	1	5	3	6
3 Georgia	3	1	0	2	2	4	3
4 Sweden	3	0	1	2	4	6	1

Group B

03/07/17, Mikheil Meskhi-2, Tbilisi
Bulgaria 0-2 England
Goals: 0-1 Mount 1, 0-2 Sessegnon 48
Referee: Nilsen (NOR)

03/07/17, David Petriashvili Stadium, Tbilisi
Germany 1-4 Netherlands
Goals: 1-0 Barkok 46, 1-1 Piroe 49, 1-2 Piroe 65, 1-3 Piroe 79, 1-4 Grot 90+1
Referee: Kristoffersen (DEN)

06/07/17, Mikheil Meskhi Stadioni, Tbilisi
England 1-0 Netherlands
Goal: 1-0 Brereton 84
Referee: Massa (ITA)

06/07/17, Tengiz Burjanadze Stadioni, Gori
Germany 3-0 Bulgaria
Goals: 1-0 Amenyido 10, 2-0 Gül 19(p), 3-0 Friede 54(p)
Referee: Lapochkin (RUS)

09/07/17, David Petriashvili Stadium, Tbilisi
England 4-1 Germany
Goals: 1-0 Brereton 52(p), 2-0 Brereton 64, 2-1 Warschewski 76, 3-1 Sessegnon 80, 4-1 Sessegnon 84
Referee: Palabıyık (TUR)

09/07/17, Tengiz Burjanadze Stadioni, Gori
Netherlands 1-1 Bulgaria
Goals: 1-0 Kongolo 50, 1-1 Rusev 55
Referee: Jovanović (SRB)

	Pld	W	D	L	F	A	Pts
1 England	3	3	0	0	7	1	9
2 Netherlands	3	1	1	1	5	3	4
3 Germany	3	1	0	2	5	8	3
4 Bulgaria	3	0	1	2	1	6	1

Semi-finals

12/07/17, David Petriashvili Stadium, Tbilisi
Portugal 1-0 Netherlands
Goals: 1-0 Gedson Fernandes 24
Referee: Kristoffersen (DEN)

12/07/17, Mikheil Meskhi Stadioni, Tbilisi
England 1-0 Czech Republic
Goals: 1-0 Nmecha 90+3
Referee: Massa (ITA)

Final

15/07/17, Tengiz Burjanadze Stadioni, Gori
(att: 4,100)
Portugal 1-2 England
Goals: 0-1 Suliman 50, 1-1 Sterling 56(og), 1-2 Nmecha 68
Referee: Jovanović (SRB)
Portugal: Diogo Costa, Diogo Dalot, Diogo Queirós, Abdu Conté (Madi Queta 78), Rui Pires, João Filipe (Rafael Leão 56), Gedson Fernandes, Mesaque Dju (Miguel Luis 75), Rui Pedro, João Queirós, Quina. Coach: Hélio Sousa (POR)
England: Ramsdale, Sterling, Jay DaSilva, Edun, Suliman, Buckley-Ricketts (Edwards 84), Dozzell (Josh Da Silva 77), Mount, Sessegnon, Nmecha (Brereton 73), Johnson. Coach: Keith Downing (ENG)
Red card: Edun 86 (England)
Yellow cards: Edun 54 (England), Rui Pires 67 (Portugal), Edun 86 (England), Ramsdale 90+1 (England)

Top goalscorers (Final tournament)

3	Ben Brereton (England)
	Ryan Sessegnon (England)
	Joël Piroe (Netherlands)
	Viktor Gyökeres (Sweden)
2	Daniel Turyna (Czech Republic)
	Lukas Nmecha (England)
	Rui Pedro (Portugal)

Squads/Appearances/Goals

Bulgaria

No	Name	DoB	Aps	(s)	Gls	Club
Goalkeepers						
1	Daniel Naumov	29/03/98	2			Ludogorets
12	Dimitar Sheytanov	15/03/99	1			Levski
Defenders						
2	Andrea Hristov	01/03/99	2			Slavia Sofia
18	Mariyan Dimitrov	28/09/98		(1)		Septemvri
3	Vasil Dobrev	05/01/98	2	(1)		Septemvri
5	Petar Genchev	29/03/98	3			Septemvri
4	Angel Lyaskov	16/03/98	3			CSKA Sofia
15	Petko Hristov	01/03/99	3			Slavia Sofia
20	Mateo Stamatov	22/03/99		(1)		Espanyol (ESP)
Midfielders						
6	Ivaylo Klimentov	03/02/98		(2)		Ludogorets
11	Svetoslav Kovachev	14/03/98	1			Ludogorets
7	Ivaylo Naydenov	22/03/98	3			Levski
22	Ivan Tilev	05/01/99	3			Septemvri
8	Georgi Yanev	04/01/98	2	(1)		Levski
Forwards						
16	Kaloyan Krastev	24/01/99	3			Slavia Sofia
10	Georgi Rusev	02/07/98	2		1	Elche (ESP)
19	Stanislav Ivanov	16/04/99	1	(2)		Levski
9	Tonislav Yordanov	27/11/98	2	(1)		CSKA Sofia

Czech Republic

No	Name	DoB	Aps	(s)	Gls	Club
Goalkeepers						
16	Martin Jedlička	24/01/98	4			Mladá Boleslav
1	Jan Plachý	07/05/98				Teplice
Defenders						
3	Matěj Chaluš	02/02/98	4			Příbram
18	Denis Granečný	07/09/98	2	(1)		Baník Ostrava
4	Libor Holík	12/05/98	4		1	Slavia Praha
13	Alex Král	19/05/98	4			Teplice
Midfielders						
15	Ondřej Chvěja	17/07/98	3	(1)		Baník Ostrava
14	Filip Havelka	21/01/98	4			Sparta Praha
20	Michal Hlavatý	17/06/98	1	(1)		Baník Sokolov
5	Daniel Mareček	30/05/98	3			Sparta Praha
8	Michal Sadílek	31/05/99	4			PSV (NED)
6	Emil Tischler	13/03/98	3			Slovácko
Forwards						
19	Martin Graiciar	11/04/99	1	(2)	1	Liberec
9	Ondřej Lingr	07/10/98	1	(1)		Karviná
12	Ondřej Novotný	05/02/98		(1)		Sparta Praha
10	Ondřej Šašinka	21/03/98	3	(1)	1	Baník Ostrava
7	Daniel Turyna	26/02/98	3	(1)	2	Sparta Praha

England

No	Name	DoB	Aps	(s)	Gls	Club
Goalkeepers						
1	Aaron Ramsdale	14/05/98	5			Bournemouth
13	Nathan Trott	21/11/98				West Ham
Defenders						
5	Trevoh Chalobah	05/07/99	3			Chelsea
18	Reece James	08/12/99	1	(1)		Chelsea
3	Jay DaSilva	22/04/98	5			Chelsea
16	Darnell Johnson	03/09/98	2	(1)		Leicester
2	Dujon Sterling	24/10/99	5			Chelsea
6	Easah Suliman	26/01/98	5		1	Aston Villa
Midfielders						
15	Josh Da Silva	23/10/98		(3)		Arsenal
8	Andre Dozzell	02/05/99	4			Ipswich
4	Tayo Edun	14/05/98	5			Fulham
14	Marcus Edwards	03/12/98	1	(3)		Tottenham
17	Jacob Maddox	03/11/98	1	(1)		Chelsea
10	Mason Mount	10/01/99	5		1	Chelsea
Forwards						
9	Ben Brereton	18/04/99	3	(2)	3	Nottingham Forest
7	Isaac Buckley-Ricketts	14/03/98	3	(2)		Man. City
12	Lukas Nmecha	14/12/98	2	(2)	2	Man. City
11	Ryan Sessegnon	18/05/00	5		3	Fulham

Germany

No	Name	DoB	Aps	(s)	Gls	Club
Goalkeepers						
12	Eike Bansen	21/02/98	3			Dortmund
1	Markus Schubert	12/06/98				Dynamo Dresden
Defenders						
19	Maxime Awoudja	02/02/98	1	(1)		Bayern
2	Jonas Busam	03/05/98	3			Freiburg
5	Julian Chabot	12/02/98	2			Sparta Rotterdam (NED)
3	Dominik Franke	05/10/98	2			RB Leipzig
4	Gökhan Gül	17/07/98	3		1	Düsseldorf
17	Mats Köhlert	02/05/98	1			Hamburg
Midfielders						
16	Bote Baku	08/04/98		(2)		Mainz
8	Sidney Friede	12/04/98	3		1	Hertha
6	Dennis Geiger	10/06/98	3			Hoffenheim
14	Felix Götze	11/02/98		(1)		Bayern
13	David Raum	21/04/98		(3)		Greuther Fürth
15	Görkem Saglam	11/04/98	3			Bochum
Forwards						
9	Etienne Amenyido	01/03/98	3		1	Dortmund
7	Aymen Barkok	21/05/98	3		1	Eintracht Frankfurt
11	Robin Hack	27/08/98	3			Hoffenheim
18	Tobias Warschewski	06/02/98		(2)	1	Preussen Münster

Portugal

No	Name	DoB	Aps	(s)	Gls	Club
Goalkeepers						
1	Diogo Costa	19/09/99	4			Porto
12	Daniel Figueira	20/07/98	1			Guimarães
Defenders						
5	Abdu Conté	24/03/98	5			Sporting
10	Bruno Paz	23/04/98	1	(2)		Sporting
2	Diogo Dalot	18/03/99	4	(1)		Porto
4	Diogo Leite	23/01/99	1			Porto
3	Diogo Queirós	05/01/99	4			Porto
15	João Queirós	22/04/98	5			Porto
Midfielders						
14	Florentino	19/08/99	1	(2)		Benfica
8	Gedson Fernandes	09/01/99	4		1	Benfica
16	Miguel Luis	27/02/99	2	(3)		Sporting
18	Quina	18/11/99	4	(1)		West Ham (ENG)
6	Rui Pires	22/03/98	4			Porto
Forwards						
7	João Filipe	30/03/99	4	(1)	1	Benfica
9	Madi Queta	21/10/98	1	(1)		Porto
11	Mesaque Dju	18/03/99	4	(1)	1	Benfica
17	Rafael Leão	10/06/99	2	(3)	1	Sporting
13	Rui Pedro	20/03/98	4		2	Porto

Georgia

No	Name	DoB	Aps	(s)	Gls	Club
Goalkeepers						
1	Giorgi Chochishvili	07/05/98	3			Shevardeni
12	Luka Gugeshashvili	29/04/99				Jagiellonia (POL)
Defenders						
3	Shalva Burjanadze	29/10/98	3			Torpedo Kutaisi
4	Aleksandr Kakhidze	24/04/99				Spartak Moskva (RUS)
13	Toma Khubashvili	29/07/98		(1)		Saburtalo
5	David Kobouri	24/01/98	3			Dinamo Tbilisi
21	Luka Lakvekheliani	20/10/98	3			Saburtalo
2	Nikoloz Mali	27/01/99	3			Saburtalo
Midfielders						
9	Vato Arveladze	04/03/98		(2)		Locomotive Tbilisi
14	Giorgi Kochorashvili	29/06/99	2	(1)		Saburtalo
6	Giorgi Kutsia	27/10/99	3			Dinamo Tbilisi
8	David Samurkasovi	05/02/98	3			Locomotive Tbilisi
Forwards						
20	Giorgi Arabidze	04/03/98	3			Shakhtar Donetsk (UKR)
10	Giorgi Chakvetadze	29/08/99	3		1	Dinamo Tbilisi
18	Temur Chogadze	05/05/98		(2)		Saburtalo
17	Nika Kvantaliani	06/02/98		(1)		Dinamo Batumi
7	Giorgi Kokhreidze	18/11/98	3		1	Saburtalo
11	Gabriel Sagrishvili	17/06/98	1	(2)		Torpedo Kutaisi

Netherlands

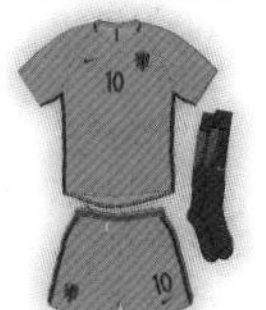

No	Name	DoB	Aps	(s)	Gls	Club
Goalkeepers						
1	Justin Bijlow	22/01/98	4			Feyenoord
16	Maarten Paes	14/05/98				NEC
Defenders						
13	Navajo Bakboord	29/01/99	4			Ajax
5	Jurich Carolina	15/07/98	4			PSV
2	Tristan Dekker	27/03/98	3			VVV
15	Boy Kemper	21/06/99	1			Ajax
4	Armando Obispo	05/03/99	3			PSV
3	Robin Zwartjens	17/03/98	1	(1)		Utrecht
Midfielders						
6	Dani de Wit	28/01/98	4			Ajax
10	Ferdi Kadioglu	07/10/99	4			NEC
12	Rodney Kongolo	09/01/98	2	(2)	1	Man. City (ENG)
8	Teun Koopmeiners	28/02/98	4			AZ
18	Noa Lang	17/06/99		(3)		Ajax
14	Justin Lonwijk	21/12/99		(2)		PSV
Forwards						
11	Javairo Dilrosun	22/06/98	4			Man. City (ENG)
7	Jay-Roy Grot	13/03/98	1	(3)	1	NEC
17	Che Nunnely	04/02/99	3	(1)		Ajax
9	Joël Piroe	02/08/99	2		3	PSV

Sweden

No	Name	DoB	Aps	(s)	Gls	Club
Goalkeepers						
12	Viktor Johansson	14/09/98	1			Aston Villa (ENG)
1	Marko Johansson	25/08/98	2			Trelleborg
Defenders						
5	Anel Ahmedhodzic	26/03/99	1	(2)		Nottingham Forest (ENG)
4	Joseph Colley	13/04/99	2	(1)		Chelsea (ENG)
7	Thomas Isherwood	28/01/98	3			Bayern (GER)
6	Anton Kralj	03/12/98	3			Malmö
2	Mattias Andersson	13/03/98	3			Juventus (ITA)
3	Charlie Weberg	22/05/98				Helsingborg
Midfielders						
16	Samuel Adrian	02/03/98	2	(1)		Malmö
13	Joseph Ceesay	03/06/98	1			Vasalund
14	Dusan Jajic	04/07/98	3			Hammarby
10	Carl Johansson	17/06/98	2			Kalmar
15	Besard Sabovic	05/01/98	2			Brommapojkarna
9	Max Svensson	19/06/98	2			Helsingborg
Forwards						
8	Teddy Bergqvist	16/03/99		(2)		Malmö
17	Viktor Gyökeres	04/06/98	3		3	Brommapojkarna
11	Jesper Karlsson	25/07/98	2	(1)	1	Elfsborg
18	Isac Lidberg	08/09/98	1	(2)		Åtvidaberg

Penalty triumphs lead to record third title

England denied at the death in dramatic final

Record goal haul for France's Amine Gouiri

Spain prevail on penalties

Spain won the UEFA European Under-17 Championship for a record third time when they defeated England 4-1 on penalties in the northern Croatian town of Varazdin. For the fifth time in six years, spot kicks were required to settle the outcome of the final, the match having finished 2-2 moments earlier following Spain substitute Nacho Díaz's equalising header in the sixth additional minute.

The title hat-trick was completed ten years after a team featuring Bojan Krkić and David de Gea landed Spain's first U17 silverware, also at England's expense in the final. Spain, triumphant again in 2008, thus moved ahead of England and four other countries with two victories to their name – France, the Netherlands, Portugal and Russia – on the competition's roll of honour.

At the other end of the scale, the Faroe Islands were in a UEFA final tournament for the first time. Unsurprisingly, Áki Johansen's North Atlantic minnows finished bottom of Group B after losing all three games without scoring. Fellow U17 finals newcomers Norway and hosts Croatia fared only slightly better, managing a solitary point apiece in Groups D and A respectively.

The Faroe islands were on the receiving end of a 7-0 rout by France, the biggest win in a U17 EURO finals – matched four days later by Germany against the Republic of Ireland. Jann-Fiete Arp registered his second hat-trick of the tournament in the latter game, having struck three times in 13 minutes during a 5-0 victory over Bosnia & Herzegovina in Germany's Group C opener. Ireland nevertheless qualified for the knockout stage on goals scored in a three-way head-to-head with Bosnia & Herzegovina and Serbia. Germany, like England in Group D, collected maximum points.

Spain rejoice after winning a third European U17 title

France's Amine Gouiri won the golden boot, seven of his record tally of nine goals in Croatia coming in the group stage. France succumbed 3-1 to Spain in the quarter-finals, but Gouiri was on target once more in his side's 1-0 play-off win over Hungary for a place in the 2017 FIFA U-17 World Cup.

England (1-0 v Republic of Ireland), Germany (2-1 v Netherlands) and Turkey (1-0 v Hungary) edged through in the other quarter-finals, also securing a 2017 World Cup spot, and the semi-finals were equally tight. Jadon Sancho's fifth goal at the tournament helped England beat Turkey 2-1, while Spain eliminated Germany on penalties after a goalless draw.

The third U17 EURO final between Spain and England, after 2007 and 2010, did not disappoint. When Phil Foden put England 2-1 up just before the hour, the Young Lions were not only on course for a 12th successive win in the competition but a third title of their own. Díaz, though, changed all that, and – just as they had done at the same venue three nights before – Spain, unlike England, held their nerve from the spot.

Qualifying round

Group 1

23-28/09/16 Orhei, Chisinau

Bosnia & Herzegovina 3-0 Latvia, Moldova 0-5 Russia, Bosnia & Herzegovina 1-0 Moldova, Russia 1-0 Latvia, Russia 2-1 Bosnia & Herzegovina, Latvia 2-0 Moldova

	Pld	W	D	L	F	A	Pts
1 Russia	3	3	0	0	8	1	9
2 Bosnia & Herzegovina	3	2	0	1	5	2	6
3 Latvia	3	1	0	2	2	4	3
4 Moldova	3	0	0	3	0	8	0

Group 2

15-20/10/16 Andorra la Vella

Kazakhstan 0-1 Greece, Republic of Ireland 5-1 Andorra, Republic of Ireland 3-1 Kazakhstan, Greece 3-0 Andorra, Greece 0-1 Republic of Ireland, Andorra 0-2 Kazakhstan

	Pld	W	D	L	F	A	Pts
1 Republic of Ireland	3	3	0	0	9	2	9
2 Greece	3	2	0	1	4	1	6
3 Kazakhstan	3	1	0	2	3	4	3
4 Andorra	3	0	0	3	1	10	0

Group 3

21-26/10/16 Esch-sur-Alzette, Wiltz, Niedercorn

Switzerland 2-1 Luxembourg, Faroe Islands 2-0 Czech Republic, Switzerland 3-0 Faroe Islands, Czech Republic 2-0 Luxembourg, Czech Republic 3-3 Switzerland, Luxembourg 2-2 Faroe Islands

	Pld	W	D	L	F	A	Pts
1 Switzerland	3	2	1	0	8	4	7
2 Faroe Islands	3	1	1	1	4	5	4
3 Czech Republic	3	1	1	1	5	5	4
4 Luxembourg	3	0	1	2	3	6	1

Group 4

26-31/10/16 Russi, Ravenna, Forlì

Serbia 3-1 FYR Macedonia, Albania 0-1 Italy, Serbia 2-0 Albania, Italy 0-0 FYR Macedonia, Italy 2-0 Serbia, FYR Macedonia 2-1 Albania

	Pld	W	D	L	F	A	Pts
1 Italy	3	2	1	0	3	0	7
2 Serbia	3	2	0	1	5	3	6
3 FYR Macedonia	3	1	1	1	3	4	4
4 Albania	3	0	0	3	1	5	0

Group 5

20-25/10/16 Kranj, Domzale

Slovenia 4-1 Estonia, Montenegro 1-2 France, France 7-0 Estonia, Slovenia 2-2 Montenegro, France 1-1 Slovenia, Estonia 1-2 Montenegro

	Pld	W	D	L	F	A	Pts
1 France	3	2	1	0	10	2	7
2 Slovenia	3	1	2	0	7	4	5
3 Montenegro	3	1	1	1	5	5	4
4 Estonia	3	0	0	3	2	13	0

Group 6

25-30/10/16 Buftea, Voluntari

Romania 1-2 Austria, England 2-0 Azerbaijan, England 3-0 Romania, Austria 3-1 Azerbaijan, Austria 2-3 England, Azerbaijan 1-0 Romania

	Pld	W	D	L	F	A	Pts
1 England	3	3	0	0	8	2	9
2 Austria	3	2	0	1	7	5	6
3 Azerbaijan	3	1	0	2	2	5	3
4 Romania	3	0	0	3	1	6	0

England's Rhian Brewster (right) takes on Austria's Lion Schuster in the qualifying round

Group 7

28/09-03/10/16 Telki, Dabas, Csákvár

Hungary 3-0 Liechtenstein, Denmark 0-2 Netherlands, Hungary 3-1 Denmark, Netherlands 9-0 Liechtenstein, Netherlands 4-0 Hungary, Liechtenstein 0-11 Denmark

	Pld	W	D	L	F	A	Pts
1 Netherlands	3	3	0	0	15	0	9
2 Hungary	3	2	0	1	6	5	6
3 Denmark	3	1	0	2	12	5	3
4 Liechtenstein	3	0	0	3	0	23	0

Group 8

28/09-03/10/16 Kempele, Oulu, Raahe

Georgia 0-1 Bulgaria, Finland 0-5 Sweden, Sweden 3-1 Bulgaria, Georgia 0-2 Finland, Sweden 4-0 Georgia, Bulgaria 0-1 Finland

	Pld	W	D	L	F	A	Pts
1 Sweden	3	3	0	0	12	1	9
2 Finland	3	2	0	1	3	5	6
3 Bulgaria	3	1	0	2	2	4	3
4 Georgia	3	0	0	3	0	7	0

Group 9

19-24/09/16 Dungannon, Lurgan, Belfast

San Marino 0-4 Slovakia, Spain 4-0 Northern Ireland, Spain 3-0 San Marino, Slovakia 4-3 Northern Ireland, Slovakia 0-6 Spain, Northern Ireland 2-1 San Marino

	Pld	W	D	L	F	A	Pts
1 Spain	3	3	0	0	13	0	9
2 Slovakia	3	2	0	1	8	9	6
3 Northern Ireland	3	1	0	2	5	9	3
4 San Marino	3	0	0	3	1	9	0

Group 10

16-21/09/16 Febres, Pampilhosa, Coimbra

Scotland 6-0 Malta, Wales 0-2 Portugal, Scotland 1-0 Wales, Portugal 5-0 Malta, Portugal 0-1 Scotland, Malta 0-3 Wales

	Pld	W	D	L	F	A	Pts
1 Scotland	3	3	0	0	8	0	9
2 Portugal	3	2	0	1	7	1	6
3 Wales	3	1	0	2	3	3	3
4 Malta	3	0	0	3	0	14	0

Group 11

26-31/10/16 Paphos

Belarus 0-1 Cyprus, Gibraltar 0-2 Belgium, Belarus 3-1 Gibraltar, Belgium 0-1 Cyprus, Belgium 0-0 Belarus, Cyprus 2-0 Gibraltar

	Pld	W	D	L	F	A	Pts
1 Cyprus	3	3	0	0	4	0	9
2 Belarus	3	1	1	1	3	2	4
3 Belgium	3	1	1	1	2	1	4
4 Gibraltar	3	0	0	3	1	7	0

Group 12

01-06/11/16 Shefayim, Herzliya

Poland 1-1 Armenia, Iceland 0-2 Israel, Poland 2-0 Iceland, Israel 2-0 Armenia, Israel 3-1 Poland, Armenia 3-2 Iceland

	Pld	W	D	L	F	A	Pts
1 Israel	3	3	0	0	7	1	9
2 Poland	3	1	1	1	4	4	4
3 Armenia	3	1	1	1	4	5	4
4 Iceland	3	0	0	3	2	7	0

Group 13

23-28/09/16 Kaunas, Alytus

Turkey 2-0 Norway, Ukraine 1-1 Lithuania, Ukraine 0-1 Turkey, Norway 2-1 Lithuania, Norway 2-2 Ukraine, Lithuania 0-1 Turkey

	Pld	W	D	L	F	A	Pts
1 Turkey	3	3	0	0	4	0	9
2 Norway	3	1	1	1	4	5	4
3 Ukraine	3	0	2	1	3	4	2
4 Lithuania	3	0	1	2	2	4	1

Elite round

Group 1

23-28/03/17 Manavgat

Germany 10-1 Armenia, Finland 1-4 Turkey, Germany 6-2 Finland, Turkey 6-0 Armenia, Turkey 1-3 Germany, Armenia 0-5 Finland

	Pld	W	D	L	F	A	Pts
1 Germany	3	3	0	0	19	4	9
2 Turkey	3	2	0	1	11	4	6
3 Finland	3	1	0	2	8	10	3
4 Armenia	3	0	0	3	1	21	0

Group 2

21-26/03/17 Dabas, Telki, Budapest

Russia 2-2 Norway, Hungary 0-1 Israel, Israel 0-3 Norway, Russia 1-2 Hungary, Israel 0-0 Russia, Norway 0-1 Hungary

	Pld	W	D	L	F	A	Pts
1 Hungary	3	2	0	1	3	2	6
2 Norway	3	1	1	1	5	3	4
3 Israel	3	1	1	1	1	3	4
4 Russia	3	0	2	1	3	4	2

Group 3

10-15/03/17 Nazare, Marinha Grande, Rio Maior

Greece 0-4 Portugal, Spain 3-1 Poland, Spain 0-1 Greece, Portugal 3-3 Poland, Portugal 0-2 Spain, Poland 3-0 Greece

	Pld	W	D	L	F	A	Pts
1 Spain	3	2	0	1	5	2	6
2 Portugal	3	1	1	1	7	5	4
3 Poland	3	1	1	1	7	6	4
4 Greece	3	1	0	2	1	7	3

UEFA European Under-17 Championship

Group 4

17-22/03/17 Greenock, Paisley

Serbia 2-1 Switzerland, Scotland 6-1 Montenegro, Switzerland 3-1 Montenegro, Scotland 1-0 Serbia, Switzerland 0-1 Scotland, Montenegro 0-1 Serbia

	Pld	W	D	L	F	A	Pts
1 Scotland	3	3	0	0	8	1	9
2 Serbia	3	2	0	1	3	2	6
3 Switzerland	3	1	0	2	4	4	3
4 Montenegro	3	0	0	3	2	10	0

Group 5

14-19/03/17 Uden, Groesbeek

Netherlands 2-0 Belgium, Belarus 0-3 Italy, Netherlands 3-2 Belarus, Italy 1-0 Belgium, Italy 1-2 Netherlands, Belgium 1-2 Belarus

	Pld	W	D	L	F	A	Pts
1 Netherlands	3	3	0	0	7	3	9
2 Italy	3	2	0	1	5	2	6
3 Belarus	3	1	0	2	4	7	3
4 Belgium	3	0	0	3	1	5	0

Group 6

23-28/03/17 Gleisdorf, Rohrbach an der Lafnitz, Bad Waltersdorf

Sweden 1-2 Ukraine, Austria 1-1 France, France 3-1 Ukraine, Sweden 1-3 Austria, France 2-0 Sweden, Ukraine 2-1 Austria

	Pld	W	D	L	F	A	Pts
1 France	3	2	1	0	6	2	7
2 Ukraine	3	2	0	1	5	5	6
3 Austria	3	1	1	1	5	4	4
4 Sweden	3	0	0	3	2	7	0

Group 7

23-28/03/17 Bijeljina

England 5-3 Czech Republic, Slovenia 0-0 Bosnia & Herzegovina, England 4-0 Slovenia, Bosnia & Herzegovina 2-1 Czech Republic, Bosnia & Herzegovina 0-1 England, Czech Republic 2-2 Slovenia

	Pld	W	D	L	F	A	Pts
1 England	3	3	0	0	10	3	9
2 Bosnia & Herzegovina	3	1	1	1	2	2	4
3 Slovenia	3	0	2	1	2	6	2
4 Czech Republic	3	0	1	2	6	9	1

Group 8

15-20/03/17 Paphos

Republic of Ireland 4-0 Faroe Islands, Slovakia 2-1 Cyprus, Republic of Ireland 1-0 Slovakia, Cyprus 0-0 Faroe Islands, Cyprus 0-2 Republic of Ireland, Faroe Islands 2-1 Slovakia

	Pld	W	D	L	F	A	Pts
1 Republic of Ireland	3	3	0	0	7	0	9
2 Faroe Islands	3	1	1	1	2	5	4
3 Slovakia	3	1	0	2	3	4	3
4 Cyprus	3	0	1	2	1	4	1

Top goalscorers (Qualifying/Elite rounds)

7 Aaron Connolly (Republic of Ireland)

6 Maximo Tolonen (Finland)
Abel Ruiz (Spain)

5 Elias Abouchabaka (Germany)
Glenn Middleton (Scotland)
Filston Mawana (Sweden)
Atalay Babacan (Turkey)

Final tournament

Group A

03/05/17, Stadion HNK Rijeka, Rijeka
Turkey 2-3 Spain
Goals: 1-0 Umut Güneş 5, 2-0 Malik Karaahmet 11, 2-1 Sergio Gómez 24, 2-2 Ruiz 33(p), 2-3 Morey 72
Referee: Ouschan (AUT)

03/05/17, Stadion HNK Rijeka, Rijeka
Croatia 0-1 Italy
Goal: 0-1 Kean 78
Referee: Verissimo (POR)

06/05/17, Stadion HNK Rijeka, Rijeka
Croatia 1-4 Turkey
Goals: 0-1 Malik Karaahmet 18, 0-2 Recep Gül 49, 1-2 Marin 67, 1-3 Ozan Kabak 69, 1-4 Yunus Akgün 80
Referee: Laforge (BEL)

06/05/17, Stadion HNK Rijeka, Rijeka
Spain 3-1 Italy
Goals: 1-0 Sergio Gómez 36, 2-0 Ruiz 68(p), 3-0 Ruiz 80, 3-1 Nicolussi Caviglia 80+2
Referee: Papapetrou (GRE)

09/05/17, Pomorac Kostrena, Kostrena
Spain 1-1 Croatia
Goals: 0-1 Čolina 56, 1-1 Blanco 80+1
Referee: Al-Hakim (SWE)

09/05/17, Stadion HNK Rijeka, Rijeka
Italy 1-2 Turkey
Goals: 0-1 Malik Karaahmet 5, 1-1 Pellegri 15, 1-2 Atalay Babacan 74
Referee: Maae (DEN)

	Pld	W	D	L	F	A	Pts
1 Spain	3	2	1	0	7	4	7
2 Turkey	3	2	0	1	8	5	6
3 Italy	3	1	0	2	3	5	3
4 Croatia	3	0	1	2	2	6	1

Group B

03/05/17, Lučko, Lučko
Scotland 2-0 Faroe Islands
Goals: 1-0 Cameron 59, 2-0 Aitchison 68
Referee: Rumšas (LTU)

03/05/17, SRC Velika Gorika, Velika Gorica
Hungary 3-2 France
Goals: 0-1 Gouiri 36, 1-1 Csoboth 38, 2-1 Csoboth 41, 3-1 Bencze 52, 3-2 Gouiri 80+4(p)
Referee: Massias (CYP)

06/05/17, NK Inter Zaprešić, Zapresic
France 7-0 Faroe Islands
Goals: 1-0 Gouiri 1, 2-0 Caqueret 4, 3-0 Gouiri 10, 4-0 Picouleau 15, 5-0 Gouiri 33, 6-0 Caqueret 46, 7-0 Adli 54
Referee: Maae (DEN)

06/05/17, Lučko, Lučko
Scotland 1-1 Hungary
Goals: 1-0 Rudden 30, 1-1 Szerető 52
Referee: Al-Hakim (SWE)

09/05/17, SRC Velika Gorika, Velika Gorica
France 2-1 Scotland
Goals: 1-0 Gouiri 35, 1-1 Rudden 42, 2-1 Gouiri 80
Referee: Laforge (BEL)

09/05/17, Lučko, Lučko
Faroe Islands 0-4 Hungary
Goals: 0-1 Torvund 24, 0-2 Szoboszlai 26, 0-3 Edmundsson 29(og), 0-4 Szoboszlai 48
Referee: Jović (CRO)

	Pld	W	D	L	F	A	Pts
1 Hungary	3	2	1	0	8	3	7
2 France	3	2	0	1	11	4	6
3 Scotland	3	1	1	1	4	3	4
4 Faroe Islands	3	0	0	3	0	13	0

Group C

04/05/17, Pomorac Kostrena, Kostrena
Germany 5-0 Bosnia & Herzegovina
Goals: 1-0 Mai 2, 2-0 Keitel 16, 3-0 Arp 50, 4-0 Arp 51, 5-0 Arp 62
Referee: Laforge (BEL)

04/05/17, Pomorac Kostrena, Kostrena
Serbia 1-0 Republic of Ireland
Goal: 1-0 Gavrić 72
Referee: Papapetrou (GRE)

07/05/17, Pomorac Kostrena, Kostrena
Germany 3-1 Serbia
Goals: 1-0 Abouchabaka 7(p), 2-0 Yeboah 39, 3-0 Majetschak 61, 3-1 Stuparević 75(p)
Referee: Ouschan (AUT)

07/05/17, Pomorac Kostrena, Kostrena
Republic of Ireland 2-1 Bosnia & Herzegovina
Goals: 1-0 Roache 7, 1-1 Vještica 13, 2-1 Idah 29(p)
Referee: Verissimo (POR)

10/05/17, Stadion HNK Rijeka, Rijeka
Republic of Ireland 0-7 Germany
Goals: 0-1 Abouchabaka 8, 0-2 Arp 15, 0-3 L O'Connor 21(og), 0-4 Arp 45, 0-5 Arp 49, 0-6 Awuku 73, 0-7 Hottmann 76
Referee: Verissimo (POR)

10/05/17, Pomorac Kostrena, Kostrena
Bosnia & Herzegovina 1-0 Serbia
Goal: 1-0 Imamović 80
Referee: Rumšas (LTU)

	Pld	W	D	L	F	A	Pts
1 Germany	3	3	0	0	15	1	9
2 Republic of Ireland	3	1	0	2	2	9	3
3 Bosnia & Herzegovina	3	1	0	2	2	7	3
4 Serbia	3	1	0	2	2	4	3

Group D

04/05/17, Sv. Josip Radnik, Sesvete
Netherlands 1-0 Ukraine
Goal: 1-0 El Bouchataoui 61
Referee: Maae (DEN)

04/05/17, SRC Velika Gorika, Velika Gorica
Norway 1-3 England
Goals: 1-0 Guehi 8(og), 1-1 Brewster 10, 1-2 Brewster 35, 1-3 Foden 78
Referee: Al-Hakim (SWE)

07/05/17, Sv. Josip Radnik, Sesvete
England 4-0 Ukraine
Goals: 1-0 McEachran 20, 2-0 Brewster 32, 3-0 Sancho 36, 4-0 Barlow 69
Referee: Rumšas (LTU)

07/05/17, SRC Velika Gorika, Velika Gorica
Netherlands 2-2 Norway
Goals: 1-0 Aboukhlal 11, 1-1 Larsen 50, 1-2 Stenevik 55, 2-2 El Bouchataoui 80+2(p)
Referee: Massias (CYP)

10/05/17, NK Inter Zaprešić, Zapresic
England 3-0 Netherlands
Goals: 1-0 Sancho 23, 2-0 Sancho 48(p), 3-0 Hudson-Odoi 80
Referee: Papapetrou (GRE)

10/05/17, Sv. Josip Radnik, Sesvete
Ukraine 2-0 Norway
Goals: 1-0 Kashchuk 78, 2-0 Kholod 80+1
Referee: Ouschan (AUT)

	Pld	W	D	L	F	A	Pts
1 England	3	3	0	0	10	1	9
2 Netherlands	3	1	1	1	3	5	4
3 Ukraine	3	1	0	2	2	5	3
4 Norway	3	0	1	2	3	7	1

Quarter-finals

12/05/17, SRC Velika Gorika, Velika Gorica
Hungary 0-1 Turkey
Goal: 0-1 Csonka 20(og)
Referee: Rumšas (LTU)

12/05/17, NK Varaždin, Varazdin
Spain 3-1 France
Goals: 0-1 Gouiri 9, 1-1 Morey 17, 2-1 Ruiz 35(p), 3-1 Sergio Gómez 56
Referee: Jović (CRO)

13/05/17, SRC Velika Gorika, Velika Gorica
England 1-0 Republic of Ireland
Goal: 1-0 Sancho 13
Referee: Laforge (BEL)

13/05/17, NK Inter Zaprešić, Zapresic
Germany 2-1 Netherlands
Goals: 0-1 Aboukhlal 40+1, 1-1 Abouchabaka 66, 2-1 Arp 79
Referee: Al-Hakim (SWE)

FIFA U-17 World Cup play-off

16/05/17, Sv. Josip Radnik, Sesvete
Hungary 0-1 France
Goal: 0-1 Gouiri 26
Referee: Papapetrou (GRE)

Semi-finals

16/05/17, NK Inter Zaprešić, Zapresic
Turkey 1-2 England
Goals: 0-1 Hudson-Odoi 11, 0-2 Sancho 37, 1-2 Kerem Kesgin 40+13
Referee: Verissimo (POR)

16/05/17, NK Varaždin, Varazdin
Spain 0-0 Germany (4-2 on pens)
Referee: Ouschan (AUT)

Final

19/05/17, NK Varaždin, Varazdin (att: 8,187)
Spain 2-2 England (4-1 on pens)
Goals: 0-1 Hudson-Odoi 18, 1-1 Morey 38, 1-2 Foden 58, 2-2 Díaz 80+6
Referee: Maae (DEN)
Spain: Fernández, Morey, Miranda, Guillamón, Chust, Blanco (José Alonso 60), Torres, Moha (Díaz 78), Ruiz, Sergio Gómez, Orellana (Beitia 56). Coach: Santi Denia (ESP)
England: Bursik, Gibson, McEachran, Guehi, Panzo, Foden (Loader 80), Brewster, Hudson-Odoi (Barlow 76), Sancho (Vokins 80+3), Denny, Latibeaudiere. Coach: Steven Cooper (ENG)
Yellow cards: Blanco 37 (Spain), Latibeaudiere 67 (England), Miranda 70 (Spain), Morey 80+3 (Spain), Panzo 80+4 (England), Fernández 80+4 (Spain)

Top goalscorers (Final tournament)

9	Amine Gouiri (France)
7	Jann-Fiete Arp (Germany)
5	Jadon Sancho (England)
4	Abel Ruiz (Spain)

Squads/Appearances/Goals

Bosnia & Herzegovina

No	Name	DoB	Aps	(s)	Gls	Club
	Goalkeepers					
1	Jasmin Kršić	02/03/00	3			Željezničar
12	Matej Perković	06/05/00				Široki Brijeg
	Defenders					
6	Jusuf Gazibegović	11/03/00	3			Salzburg (AUT)
4	Dino-Samuel Kurbegović	21/12/00				Mainz (GER)
16	Domagoj Marušić	19/03/00	1	(2)		Široki Brijeg
5	Rijad Sadiku	18/01/00	3			Sarajevo
3	Dobrica Tegeltija	06/10/00	2	(1)		Vojvodina (SRB)
15	Nemanja Vještica	01/02/00	3		1	Partizan (SRB)
2	Enio Zilić	12/07/00	1	(1)		Željezničar
	Midfielders					
7	Marko Brkić	11/04/00		(3)		Crvena zvezda (SRB)
14	Armin Imamović	17/02/00	3		1	Sarajevo
11	Eldin Omerović	26/05/00	2			Sloboda Tuzla
9	Džani Salčin	19/03/00	2			Sarajevo
8	Stefan Santrač	24/01/00	3			Crvena zvezda (SRB)
18	Milan Savić	19/05/00	2			Crvena zvezda (SRB)
13	Emir Sejdović	25/04/00	2			FSV Frankfurt (GER)
	Forwards					
17	Elvis Mehanović	10/04/00	1	(1)		Genk (BEL)
10	Milan Šikanjić	03/01/00	2	(1)		Crvena zvezda (SRB)

Croatia

No	Name	DoB	Aps	(s)	Gls	Club
	Goalkeepers					
12	Vice Baždarić	14/02/00				Hajduk Split
1	Dominik Kotarski	10/02/00	3			Dinamo Zagreb
	Defenders					
3	David Čolina	19/07/00	3		1	Dinamo Zagreb
2	Filip Hlevnjak	05/08/00	2			Slaven Koprivnica
14	Tin Hrvoj	06/06/01	1			Dinamo Zagreb
4	Ivan Nekić	24/12/00	2			Rijeka
5	Stipe Radić	10/06/00	3			Hajduk Split
13	Mario Vušković	16/11/01	1			Hajduk Split
	Midfielders					
6	Bartol Franjić	14/01/00	3			Dinamo Zagreb
8	Marko Hanuljak	31/01/00	3			Osijek
18	Tomislav Krizmanić	21/04/01	1	(2)		Dinamo Zagreb
15	Juraj Ljubić	26/05/00				Dinamo Zagreb
10	Jurica Pršir	29/05/00	2	(1)		Dinamo Zagreb
	Forwards					
17	Roko Baturina	20/06/00	1	(2)		Split
7	Leon Kreković	07/05/00	2	(1)		Hajduk Split
9	Antonio Marin	09/01/01	2	(1)	1	Dinamo Zagreb
16	Josip Mitrović	11/06/00	1	(2)		Rijeka
11	Michele Šego	05/08/00	3			Hajduk Split

England

No	Name	DoB	Aps	(s)	Gls	Club
	Goalkeepers					
13	Curtis Anderson	27/09/00				Man. City
1	Josef Bursik	12/07/00	6			Wimbledon
	Defenders					
2	Timothy Eyoma	29/01/00	5			Tottenham
3	Lewis Gibson	19/07/00	6			Newcastle
5	Marc Guehi	13/07/00	6			Chelsea
19	Joel Latibeaudiere	06/01/00	1			Man. City
6	Jonathan Panzo	25/10/00	6			Chelsea
14	Jake Vokins	17/03/00		(1)		Southampton
	Midfielders					
17	Aidan Barlow	10/01/00		(3)	1	Man. United
15	Alexander Denny	12/04/00	1	(1)		Everton
7	Phil Foden	28/05/00	6		2	Man. City
10	Callum Hudson-Odoi	07/11/00	6		3	Chelsea
4	George McEachran	30/08/00	6		1	Chelsea
8	Tashan Oakley-Boothe	14/02/00	5			Tottenham
11	Jadon Sancho	25/03/00	6		5	Man. City
18	Emile Smith-Rowe	28/07/00		(3)		Arsenal
	Forwards					
9	Rhian Brewster	01/04/00	6		3	Liverpool
12	Reo Griffiths	27/06/00		(1)		Tottenham
16	Daniel Loader	28/08/00		(5)		Reading

Faroe Islands

No	Name	DoB	Aps	(s)	Gls	Club
	Goalkeepers					
1	Bárdur Á Reynatrød	08/01/00	2			Víkingur
12	Bjarti Vitalis Mørk	07/06/01	1			HB
	Defenders					
14	Bjarni Brimnes	21/05/00		(3)		HB
3	Andrias Edmundsson	18/12/00	3			B68
4	Dann Fródason	27/04/00	3			07 Vestur
8	Asbjørn Hedinsson	19/12/00	2			07 Vestur
17	Sveinur Lava Olsen	14/01/01		(2)		HB
2	Sjúrdur Pauli Chin Nielsen	18/04/00	3			NSÍ
	Midfielders					
11	Elias El Moustage	30/05/01	3			AaB (DEN)
6	Magnus Holm Jacobsen	23/05/00	2			B36
20	Jákup Joensen	27/02/00		(2)		Skála
19	Filip í Lida	06/11/00		(2)		AB
18	Sølvi Sigvardsen	18/10/00	3			NSÍ
16	Símun Sólheim	25/02/01	2			HB
7	Hanus Sørensen	19/02/01	3			Midtjylland (DEN)
	Forwards					
15	Tórur Jacobsen	24/04/00	2			KÍ
13	Steffan Abrahamsson Løkin	13/11/00	1			NSÍ
9	Stefan Radosavljevic	08/09/00	3			TB / FCS / Royn

France

No	Name	DoB	Aps	(s)	Gls	Club
	Goalkeepers					
1	Nathan Cremillieux	09/01/00	4			St-Étienne
16	Yahia Fofana	21/08/00	1			Le Havre
	Defenders					
4	William Bianda	30/04/00	4			Lens
2	Vincent Collet	23/03/00	5			Metz
15	John Da	03/03/00	1	(1)		Nancy
3	Hakim Guenouche	30/05/00	3			Nancy
17	Maxence Lacroix	06/04/00	3	(1)		Sochaux
5	Andy Pelmard	12/03/00	4			Nice
	Midfielders					
7	Yacine Adli	29/07/00	5		1	Paris
10	Maxence Caqueret	15/02/00	5		2	Lyon
11	Willem Geubbels	16/08/01	2	(1)		Lyon
6	Claudio Gomes	23/07/00	5			Paris
14	Mathis Picouleau	08/05/00	3		1	Rennes
8	Aurélien Tchouaemi	27/01/00	2	(1)		Bordeaux
	Forwards					
13	Alexis Flips	18/01/00	1	(4)		LOSC
9	Amine Gouiri	16/02/00	5		9	Lyon
18	Wilson Isidor	27/08/00		(5)		Rennes
12	Alan Kereoudan	12/01/00	2	(2)		Rennes

Hungary

No	Name	DoB	Aps	(s)	Gls	Club
	Goalkeepers					
1	Balázs Ásványi	13/05/01	4			Puskás Akadémia
22	István Oroszi	14/09/00	1			Ferencváros
	Defenders					
23	Dominik Alex Arday	08/12/00	1	(1)		Vasas
15	Gergő Bolla	22/02/00	3	(1)		Illés Akadémia
2	Krisztián Kovács	29/05/00	5			Győr
3	Martin Majnovics	26/10/00	4			Mattersburg (AUT)
14	Attila Mocsi	29/05/00	4			Győr
4	Balázs Opavszky	18/02/00	4			Vasas
	Midfielders					
11	Márk Bencze	30/01/00	4	(1)	1	Vitesse (NED)
8	András Csonka	01/05/00	4			Ferencváros
20	Tamás Kiss	24/11/00	1	(3)		Illés Akadémia
10	Szabolcs Schön	27/09/00	4			Ajax (NED)
6	Dominik Szoboszlai	25/10/00	2		2	Salzburg (AUT)
	Forwards					
17	Kevin Csoboth	20/06/00	4	(1)	2	Benfica (POR)
9	Norbert Szendrei	27/03/00	1	(2)		Honvéd
7	Krisztofer Szerető	10/01/00	5		1	Stoke (ENG)
21	Norman Timári	18/02/00		(5)		Puskás Akadémia
19	Alexander Torvund	01/08/00	4	(1)	1	Vasas

Netherlands

No	Name	DoB	Aps	(s)	Gls	Club
	Goalkeepers					
16	Fabian de Keijzer	10/05/00				Utrecht
1	Jasper Schendelaar	02/09/00	4			AZ
	Defenders					
4	Micthel Bakker	20/06/00	4			Ajax
3	Tijn Daverveld	29/04/00	2			PSV
13	Justin de Haas	01/02/00		(2)		AZ
2	Lutsharel Geertruida	18/07/00	4			Feyenoord
5	Kik Pierie	20/07/00	4			Heerenveen
12	Tommy St Jago	03/01/00	2	(1)		Utrecht
	Midfielders					
6	Achraf El Bouchataoui	12/01/00	4		2	Feyenoord
10	Juan Familio-Castillo	13/01/00	3	(1)		Chelsea (ENG)
8	Dogucan Haspolat	11/02/00	2	(1)		Excelsior
18	Delano Ladan	09/02/00	1	(2)		Den Haag
15	Andrew Mendonça	09/07/00		(1)		PSV
14	Thijs Oosting	02/05/00	4			AZ
	Forwards					
11	Zakaria Aboukhlal	18/02/00	4		2	Willem II
17	Myron Boadu	14/01/01		(1)		AZ
9	Thomas Buitink	14/06/00	2	(2)		Vitesse
7	Mohamed Mallahi	13/02/00	3			Utrecht
19	Bradly van Hoeven	17/04/00	1			Sparta

Germany

No	Name	DoB	Aps	(s)	Gls	Club
	Goalkeepers					
12	Luis Klatte	01/03/00				Hertha
1	Luca Plogmann	10/03/00	5			Bremen
	Defenders					
4	Dominik Becker	09/01/00	2	(1)		Köln
5	Jan Boller	14/03/00	4			Leverkusen
3	Pascal Hackethal	27/01/00	4			Bremen
15	Kilian Ludewig	05/03/00	4	(1)		RB Leipzig
16	Lars Lukas Mai	31/03/00	5		1	Bayern
2	Alexander Nitzl	11/07/00	2	(3)		Bayern
	Midfielders					
10	Elias Abouchabaka	31/03/00	4	(1)	3	RB Leipzig
7	Sahverdi Cetin	28/09/00	3			Eintracht Frankfurt
13	Dennis Jastrzembski	20/02/00	4			Hertha
14	Yannik Keitel	15/02/00	4		1	Freiburg
8	Erik Majetschak	01/03/00	3	(2)	1	RB Leipzig
18	John Yeboah	23/06/00	4		1	Wolfsburg
	Forwards					
9	Jann-Fiete Arp	06/01/00	5		7	Hamburg
6	Noah Awuku	09/01/00	1	(2)	1	Kiel
11	Eric Hottmann	08/02/00		(3)	1	Stuttgart
17	Maurice Malone	17/08/00	1	(2)		Augsburg

Italy

No	Name	DoB	Aps	(s)	Gls	Club
	Goalkeepers					
12	Marco Carnesecchi	01/07/00				Cesena
22	Luca Gemello	03/07/00				Torino
1	Simone Ghidotti	19/03/00	3			Fiorentina
	Defenders					
5	Matteo Anzolin	11/11/00	3			Vicenza
2	Raoul Bellanova	17/05/00	1			Milan
13	Gabriele Bellodi	02/09/00		(1)		Milan
6	Davide Bettella	07/04/00	3			Internazionale
3	Axel Campeol	05/03/00	2	(1)		Milan
15	Antonio Candela	27/04/00	3			Spezia
	Midfielders					
10	Roberto Biancu	19/01/00	2	(1)		Cagliari
8	Fabrizio Caligara	12/04/00	2			Juventus
17	Manolo Portanova	02/06/00	3			Lazio
4	Andrea Rizzo Pinna	13/01/00	3			Atalanta
7	Elia Visconti	30/06/00	2	(1)		Internazionale
	Forwards					
20	Flavio Junior Bianchi	24/01/00		(1)		Genoa
9	Moise Kean	28/02/00	1		1	Juventus
11	Davide Merola	27/03/00	2	(1)		Internazionale
14	Hans Nicolussi Caviglia	18/06/00		(1)	1	Juventus
18	Pietro Pellegri	17/03/01	2		1	Genoa
16	Emanuel Vignato	24/08/00	1	(2)		Chievo

Norway

No	Name	DoB	Aps	(s)	Gls	Club
	Goalkeepers					
1	Mads Christiansen	21/10/00	3			Lillestrøm
12	Lars Kvarekvål	05/02/00				Stabæk
	Defenders					
15	Jesper Daland	06/01/00		(1)		Stabæk
3	Emil Kalsaas	07/07/00	3			Fyllingsdalen
2	Fabian Rimestad	13/01/00	3			Fana
4	Colin Rösler	22/04/00	3			Man. City (ENG)
5	Erik Tobias Sandberg	27/02/00	3			Lillestrøm
17	Andreas Uran	01/02/00		(1)		Molde
8	Anders Waagan	18/02/00	1	(2)		Aalesund
	Midfielders					
11	Håkon Evjen	14/02/00	1	(1)		Bodø/Glimt
18	Elias Flø	16/01/00	1			Hødd
6	Johan Hove	07/09/00	3			Sogndal
16	Halldor Stenevik	02/02/00	2		1	Brann
13	Edvard Sandvik Tagseth	23/01/01	2	(1)		Liverpool (ENG)
7	Mikael Ugland	24/01/00	2			Start
	Forwards					
9	Erik Botheim	10/01/00	2	(1)		Rosenborg
14	Erling Håland	21/07/00	2	(1)		Molde
10	Jørgen Larsen	06/02/00	2	(1)	1	Sarpsborg

Republic of Ireland

No	Name	DoB	Aps	(s)	Gls	Club
Goalkeepers						
16	Kian Clarke	09/05/01				Bohemians
1	Brian Maher	01/11/00	4			St Patrick's
Defenders						
5	Nathan Collins	30/04/01	4			Cherry Orchard
4	Jordan Doherty	29/08/00	4			Sheffield United (ENG)
3	Kameron Ledwidge	07/04/01	4			St Kevins Boys
2	Lee O'Connor	28/07/00	2			Man. United (ENG)
13	Darryl Walsh	14/06/00				Waterford
Midfielders						
6	Aaron Bolger	02/02/00	4			Shamrock Rovers
12	Brandon Kavanagh	21/09/00		(2)		Bohemians
17	Gavin Kilkenny	01/02/00	1	(1)		Bournemouth (ENG)
7	Luke Nolan	21/08/00	4			St Patrick's
14	Richard O'Farrell	18/09/00	4			St Patrick's
15	Joseph Redmond	23/01/00	1			Birmingham (ENG)
9	Rowan Roache	09/02/00	3	(1)	1	Blackpool (ENG)
18	Tyreik Samuel Wright	22/09/01		(1)		Lakewood
Forwards						
11	Aaron Connolly	28/01/00	3	(1)		Brighton (ENG)
10	Adam Idah	11/02/01	4		1	College Corinthians
8	Callum Thompson	20/04/01	2	(2)		Wolves (ENG)

Serbia

No	Name	DoB	Aps	(s)	Gls	Club
Goalkeepers						
1	Miloš Gordić	05/03/00	3			Crvena zvezda
12	Aleksa Milojević	08/01/00				Jagodina
Defenders						
7	Marko Janković	29/08/00	3			Crvena zvezda
16	Dimitrije Kamenović	16/07/00	3			Čukarički
2	Aleksandar Kostić	24/01/00	3			Crvena zvezda
5	Svetozar Marković	23/03/00	2			Partizan
6	Jovan Vladimir Pavlović	11/02/00	3			Sport Team Banja Luka (BIH)
3	Zlatan Šehović	08/08/00				Partizan
Midfielders						
10	Armin Djerlek	15/07/00	3			Partizan
8	Željko Gavrić	05/12/00	3		1	Crvena zvezda
4	Ivan Ilić	17/03/01	2			Crvena zvezda
11	Mihajlo Nešković	09/02/00	1	(2)		Vojvodina
17	Milutin Vidosavljević	21/02/01	1			Čukarički
20	Mateja Zuvić	13/02/00	1	(2)		Partizan
14	Vanja Zvekanov	25/05/00		(2)		Spartak Subotica
Forwards						
15	Jovan Kokir	25/04/00		(2)		Partizan
9	Filip Stuparević	30/08/00	3		1	Voždovac
18	Slobodan Tedić	13/04/00	2	(1)		Vojvodina

Turkey

No	Name	DoB	Aps	(s)	Gls	Club
Goalkeepers						
1	Berke Özer	25/05/00	5			Altınordu
12	Ozan Can Oruç	26/05/00				Altınordu
Defenders						
4	Abdussamed Karnuçu	04/02/00	3			Galatasaray
13	Berk Cetin	02/02/00	4	(1)		Mönchengladbach (GER)
15	Berkehan Biçer	01/01/00	1			Altınordu
5	Ozan Kabak	25/03/00	5		1	Galatasaray
2	Ramazan Civelek	05/01/00	5			Galatasaray
Midfielders						
10	Atalay Babacan	28/06/00	5		1	Galatasaray
17	Enes Ilkin	11/01/00		(2)		Samsunspor
16	Egehan Gök	27/02/00		(3)		Altınordu
18	Hasan Adıgüzel	03/04/00	3	(2)		Akhisar
8	Kerem Kesgin	05/11/00	4		1	Bucaspor
6	Sefa Akgün	30/06/00	4			Trabzonspor
14	Umut Güneş	16/03/00	1	(4)	1	Stuttgart (GER)
Forwards						
3	Ali Göçmen	15/03/00		(2)		Kasımpaşa
9	Malik Karaahmet	18/01/00	5		3	Eintracht Frankfurt (GER)
7	Recep Gül	05/11/00	5		1	Galatasaray
11	Yunus Akgün	07/07/00	5		1	Galatasaray

Scotland

No	Name	DoB	Aps	(s)	Gls	Club
Goalkeepers						
1	Jon Mccracken	24/05/00	3			Norwich (ENG)
12	Ryan Mullen	18/05/01				Celtic
Defenders						
3	Daniel Church	21/07/00	3			Celtic
5	Robbie Deas	27/02/00		(2)		Celtic
17	Jordan Houston	28/01/00	3			Rangers
2	Lewis Mayo	19/03/00	3			Rangers
18	Aaron Reid	05/01/00		(1)		Hearts
4	Stephen Welsh	19/01/00	3			Celtic
Midfielders						
16	Kerr McInroy	31/08/00	2			Celtic
6	Jonathan Mitchell	16/03/00	3			Falkirk
13	Sebastian Ross	20/01/00	2	(1)		Aberdeen
15	Lewis Smith	16/03/00	1			Hamilton
8	Elliot Watt	11/03/00	2	(1)		Wolves (ENG)
Forwards						
7	Jack Aitchison	05/03/00	3		1	Celtic
14	Innes Cameron	22/08/00		(3)	1	Kilmarnock
10	Lewis Hutchison	19/02/00		(1)		Aberdeen
11	Glenn Middleton	01/01/00	3			Norwich (ENG)
9	Zak Rudden	06/02/00	2		2	Rangers

Spain

No	Name	DoB	Aps	(s)	Gls	Club
Goalkeepers						
1	Álvaro Fernández	10/04/00	5			CD San Félix
13	Mohamet Ramos	13/04/00	1			Real Madrid
Defenders						
5	Víctor Chust	05/03/00	5			Real Madrid
15	Eric García Martret	09/01/01	1	(1)		Barcelona
12	Victor Gomez Perea	01/04/00	2	(1)		Espanyol
4	Hugo Guillamón	31/01/00	6			Valencia
3	Juan Miranda	19/01/00	5			Barcelona
2	Mateu Morey	02/03/00	5		3	Barcelona
Midfielders						
19	Carlos Beitia	15/02/00		(1)		CD Roda
6	Antonio Blanco	23/07/00	5	(1)	1	Real Madrid
18	César Gelabert	31/10/00	1	(1)		Real Madrid
14	Alvaro Garcia Segovia	01/06/00	1	(3)		Albacete
17	José Alonso	07/03/00	2	(4)		Sevilla
8	Moha Aiman	06/02/00	5			Real Madrid
10	Sergio Gómez	04/09/00	6		3	Barcelona
Forwards						
11	Nacho Díaz	27/06/00	1	(2)	1	CD Roda
16	Jandro Orellana	07/08/00	5	(1)		Barcelona
9	Abel Ruiz	28/01/00	5	(1)	4	Barcelona
7	Ferrán Torres	29/02/00	5	(1)		Valencia

Ukraine

No	Name	DoB	Aps	(s)	Gls	Club
Goalkeepers						
1	Viktor Babichyn	22/08/00				Dnipro
12	Dany Ltaif	01/05/00	3			Olimpik Donetsk
Defenders						
15	Petro Kharzhevskiy	03/01/00	3			Karpaty
19	Bohdan Kurtiak	11/03/00		(1)		Karpaty
13	Illia Malyshkin	10/03/00	3			Dynamo Kyiv
3	Roman Slyva	23/09/00	3			Karpaty
4	Ihor Snurnitsyn	07/03/00	3			Olimpik Donetsk
5	Oleksandr Syrota	11/06/00				Dynamo Kyiv
Midfielders						
18	Bohdan Biloshevskiy	12/01/00	3			Dynamo Kyiv
11	Ievgenii Isaienko	07/08/00	3			Dynamo Kyiv
17	Artem Kholod	22/01/00		(2)	1	Shakhtar Donetsk
14	Mykyta Titaievskiy	13/01/00		(2)		Chornomorets Odesa
10	Heorhii Tsitaishvili	18/11/00	2	(1)		Dynamo Kyiv
9	Artur Vashchyshyn	11/06/00	3			Dynamo Kyiv
16	Vikentii Voloshyn	17/04/01		(1)		Dynamo Kyiv
Forwards						
8	Olexiy Kashchuk	29/06/00	3		1	Shakhtar Donetsk
22	Vadym Mashchenko	26/07/00	1	(2)		Dynamo Kyiv
7	Vladyslav Supriaha	15/02/00	3			Dnipro

2015 runners-up become first Croatian winners

Irish side Region 2 defeated 1-0 in final

Hosts Istanbul eliminated in group stage

Zagreb claim amateur crown

"I don't like to use the word 'revenge'," said Zagreb Region coach Tomislav Gričar ahead of the 2017 UEFA Regions' Cup final. However, if his team's 1-0 victory against the Republic of Ireland's Region 2 – a team featuring several players from the Eastern Region side that had defeated Zagreb in the 2015 final in Dublin – did not quite belong in that category, it certainly tasted very sweet.

Zagreb's Toni Adžić scored the only goal on 26 minutes at the Turkish Football Association's Riva complex on the outskirts of Istanbul, with Gerry Davis's side going agonisingly close to a last-gasp equaliser when Shane Daly-Butz struck the crossbar deep into added time. The first side to reach two successive finals of the prestigious biennial amateur tournament, Zagreb thus become the first Croatian winners of a trophy previously lifted by teams from Italy (three times), Spain (twice), Czech Republic, Poland, Portugal and Ireland.

In total, 38 teams competed in the landmark tenth edition of the competition. Zagreb marked themselves out as ones to watch in qualifying, scoring 12 goals without reply in Hungary to join Region 2, 2009 winners Castilla y León (Spain), Ingulec (Ukraine), Lisboa (Portugal), Olomouc (Czech Republic), South Region (Russia), and hosts Istanbul (Turkey) in the final tournament.

Zagreb had a tough start in Group A, drawing 2-2 after twice being pegged back by Lisboa, but their path to the final opened up when they triumphed 2-0 against Istanbul – 3-0 winners against Ingulec in their opening game – on matchday two. Needing a win against Ingulec on the final day to be sure of their progress to the final, they sailed through, with captain and fearsome front man Željko Štulec among the scorers in a 4-1 success. Istanbul, meanwhile, snatched a late equaliser against Lisboa in the other game to finish second.

Zagreb of Croatia lift the 2017 UEFA Regions' Cup

Group B was tighter. While Region 2 won 1-0 against South Region on the opening day, Castilla y León were quickly installed as favourites after they comfortably defeated Olomouc 4-1. However, the Spanish side's fortunes waned following an exhausting goalless draw against Region 2, the Irish side showing immense resilience to hold off their advances, while in the other encounter South Region rallied to beat Olomouc 2-1.

Those results left three sides still in the running for a final place on the closing day. At the interval, with Castilla y León 2-0 up against South Region – thanks to a double from tournament top scorer Roberto García Puente – and Region 2 leading 2-1 against eliminated Olomouc, the Spanish side had the edge thanks to a superior scoring record. By full time, however, the final group table painted a very different picture, the Irish side having extended their advantage to win 4-1 while South Region staged an extraordinary comeback, with ten men, to beat Castilla y León 3-2 and leapfrog them into second place.

Preliminary round

Group A

21-25/05/16 Kaunas

FC Tartu 1-4 Region of Gothenburg, East West Central Scotland 1-1 FK Nevėžis, East West Central Scotland 9-0 FC Tartu, Region of Gothenburg 0-2 FK Nevėžis, Region of Gothenburg 0-1 East West Central Scotland, FK Nevėžis 5-2 FC Tartu

	Pld	W	D	L	F	A	Pts
1 East West Central Scotland	3	2	1	0	11	1	7
2 FK Nevėžis	3	2	1	0	8	3	7
3 Region of Gothenburg	3	1	0	2	4	4	3
4 FC Tartu	3	0	0	3	3	18	0

Group B

03-07/06/16 San Marino, Serravalle

San Marino 4-0 South Wales Football Association, ZSMK 0-4 Xanthi Region, South Wales Football Association 3-2 Xanthi Region, ZSMK 0-3 San Marino, South Wales Football Association 2-3 ZSMK, Xanthi Region 1-1 San Marino

	Pld	W	D	L	F	A	Pts
1 San Marino	3	2	1	0	8	1	7
2 Xanthi Region	3	1	1	1	7	4	4
3 ZSMK	3	1	0	2	3	9	3
4 South Wales Football Association	3	1	0	2	5	9	3

Intermediate round

Group 1

05-09/10/16 Gozo

Ligue Paris Ile de France 1-2 Ingulee, Kirovograd Region, Gozo Region 0-5 East West Central Scotland, Ligue Paris Ile de France 0-0 Gozo Region, East West Central Scotland 0-3 Ingulee, Kirovograd Region, East West Central Scotland 0-4 Ligue Paris Ile de France, Ingulee, Kirovograd Region 3-1 Gozo Region

	Pld	W	D	L	F	A	Pts
1 Ingulee, Kirovograd Region	3	3	0	0	8	2	9
2 Ligue Paris Ile de France	3	1	1	1	5	2	4
3 East West Central Scotland	3	1	0	2	5	7	3
4 Gozo Region	3	0	1	2	1	8	1

Group 2

27-31/10/16 Simitli, Razlog

Castilla y León 4-0 South-West Region, NZ Tuzlanskog Kantona 0-1 San Marino, Castilla y León 3-0 NZ Tuzlanskog Kantona , San Marino 1-5 South-West Region, San Marino 1-0 Castilla y León, South-West Region 2-0 NZ Tuzlanskog Kantona

	Pld	W	D	L	F	A	Pts
1 Castilla y León	3	2	0	1	7	1	6
2 South-West Region	3	2	0	1	7	5	6
3 San Marino	3	2	0	1	3	5	6
4 NZ Tuzlanskog Kantona	3	0	0	3	0	6	0

Group 3

20-24/09/16 Buftea, Voluntari

Prahova Muntenia 1-2 West Yorkshire League, South Region Russia 4-3 FA of Vojvodina, West Yorkshire League 1-1 FA of Vojvodina, South Region Russia 2-1 Prahova Muntenia, West Yorkshire League 2-2 South Region Russia, FA of Vojvodina 3-1 Prahova Muntenia

	Pld	W	D	L	F	A	Pts
1 South Region Russia	3	2	1	0	8	6	7
2 West Yorkshire League	3	1	2	0	5	4	5
3 FA of Vojvodina	3	1	1	1	7	6	4
4 Prahova Muntenia	3	0	0	3	3	7	0

Group 4

24-28/09/16 Legnica, Polkowice

Lisboa 2-0 Dolnośląski Region, FC Caramba Riga 1-1 FC Zvezda - FOTS Victoria, Lisboa 2-0 FC Caramba Riga, FC Zvezda - FOTS Victoria 1-3 Dolnośląski Region, FC Zvezda - FOTS Victoria 0-1 Lisboa, Dolnośląski Region 7-0 FC Caramba Riga

	Pld	W	D	L	F	A	Pts
1 Lisboa	3	3	0	0	5	0	9
2 Dolnośląski Region	3	2	0	1	10	3	6
3 FC Zvezda - FOTS Victoria	3	0	1	2	2	5	1
4 FC Caramba Riga	3	0	1	2	1	10	1

Group 5

14-18/11/16 Orhei, Chisinau

Istanbul 2-0 Western Region, ARF Soroca 0-1 Genève Amateur, Istanbul 0-0 ARF Soroca, Genève Amateur 2-1 Western Region, Genève Amateur 0-1 Istanbul, Western Region 1-2 ARF Soroca

	Pld	W	D	L	F	A	Pts
1 Istanbul	3	2	1	0	3	0	7
2 Genève Amateur	3	2	0	1	3	2	6
3 ARF Soroca	3	1	1	1	2	2	4
4 Western Region	3	0	0	3	2	6	0

Group 6

21-25/09/16 Repcin, Olomouc

Hapoel Jordan Valley 1-1 West Slovak Football Associations, Olomouc Region Selection 2-2 Bremer Fußball-Verband, West Slovak Football Associations 0-0 Bremer Fußball-Verband, Olomouc Region Selection 3-0 Hapoel Jordan Valley, West Slovak Football Associations 0-0 Olomouc Region Selection, Bremer Fußball-Verband 3-1 Hapoel Jordan Valley

	Pld	W	D	L	F	A	Pts
1 Olomouc Region Selection	3	1	2	0	5	2	5
2 Bremer Fußball-Verband	3	1	2	0	5	3	5
3 West Slovak Football Associations	3	0	3	0	1	1	3
4 Hapoel Jordan Valley	3	0	1	2	2	7	1

Group 7

28/09-02/10/16 Gorgonzola, Seregno, San Giovanni, Inveruno, Solbiate Arno, Carvaggio

Lombardia Regional FA 0-1 Region 2, MNZ Maribor 0-0 RAT North-East Macedonia, Lombardia Regional FA 4-1 MNZ Maribor, RAT North-East Macedonia 0-2 Region 2, RAT North-East Macedonia 0-1 Lombardia Regional FA, Region 2 0-0 MNZ Maribor

	Pld	W	D	L	F	A	Pts
1 Region 2	3	2	1	0	3	0	7
2 Lombardia Regional FA	3	2	0	1	5	2	6
3 MNZ Maribor	3	0	2	1	1	4	2
4 RAT North-East Macedonia	3	0	1	2	0	3	1

Group 8

24-28/10/16 Kisvarda, Nyiregyhaza

East Region Selection 0-4 Zagreb Region, Sharur 0-3 East District Team, East Region Selection 6-0 Sharur, East District Team 0-5 Zagreb Region, East District Team 0-2 East Region Selection, Zagreb Region 3-0 Sharur

	Pld	W	D	L	F	A	Pts
1 Zagreb Region	3	3	0	0	12	0	9
2 East Region Selection	3	2	0	1	8	4	6
3 East District Team	3	1	0	2	3	7	3
4 Sharur	3	0	0	3	0	12	0

Top goalscorers (Preliminary/Intermediate rounds)

6 Enea Jaupi (San Marino)
Željko Štulec (Zagreb)

4 Damian Niedojad (Dolnośląski)
David Kneale (East West Central Scotland)
Kristijan Lovrić (Zagreb)

Final tournament

Group A

01/07/17, TFF Riva, Istanbul
Zagreb Region 2-2 Lisboa
Goals: 1-0 Štulec 24, 1-1 David Cardoso 36, 2-1 Adžić 41, 2-2 Tiago Honrado 57

01/07/17, TFF Riva, Istanbul
Istanbul 3-0 Ingulec, Kirovograd Region
Goals: 1-0 Serkan Uysal 34, 2-0 Ufuk Özcan 52, 3-0 Semih Akgöz 90+2(p)

03/07/17, TFF Riva, Istanbul
Ingulec, Kirovograd Region 3-3 Lisboa
Goals: 1-0 Horshchynskyi 8, 1-1 Flecha 23, 2-1 Sorokyn 33(p), 2-2 Flecha 38, 3-2 Bozhenko 78, 3-3 Flecha 88

03/07/17, TFF Riva, Istanbul
Istanbul 0-2 Zagreb Region
Goals: 0-1 Adžić 16, 0-2 Šimunić 67

06/07/17, TFF Riva, Istanbul
Lisboa 1-1 Istanbul
Goals: 1-0 David Cardoso 41, 1-1 Ramazan Kallıoğlu 90+5

06/07/17, Sarıyer Yusuf Ziya Öniş Stadyumu, Istanbul
Ingulec, Kirovograd Region 1-4 Zagreb Region
Goals: 0-1 Filipović 43, 0-2 Mohač 45, 0-3 Štulec 83, 1-3 Bozhenko 90, 1-4 Krajačić 90+1

	Pld	W	D	L	F	A	Pts
1 Zagreb Region	3	2	1	0	8	3	7
2 Istanbul	3	1	1	1	4	3	4
3 Lisboa	3	0	3	0	6	6	3
4 Ingulec, Kirovograd Region	3	0	1	2	4	10	1

Group B

01/07/17, Maltepe, Istanbul
Castilla y León 4-1 Olomouc Region Selection
Goals: 1-0 García Puente 3, 2-0 García Puente 45, 2-1 P Navrátil 58, 3-1 Rodriguez Ramos 64, 4-1 Jorge Vegas 90+1

01/07/17, Sarıyer Yusuf Ziya Öniş Stadyumu, Istanbul
Region 2 1-0 South Region Russia
Goal: 1-0 Hayes 26

03/07/17, Maltepe, Istanbul
Castilla y León 0-0 Region 2

03/07/17, Sarıyer Yusuf Ziya Öniş Stadyumu, Istanbul
Olomouc Region Selection 1-2 South Region Russia
Goals: 0-1 Donskov 14, 1-1 Woitek 45, 1-2 Lomovtsev 54

06/07/17, TFF Riva, Istanbul
South Region Russia 3-2 Castilla y León
Goals: 0-1 García Puente 16, 0-2 García Puente 19, 1-2 Nastavshev 64, 2-2 Khodzhumyan 76(p), 3-2 Sokolov 90+2

06/07/17, Maltepe, Istanbul
Olomouc Region Selection 1-4 Region 2
Goals: 0-1 Kelly 22, 1-1 P Navrátil 35, 1-2 Hayes 39, 1-3 Hayes 51, 1-4 Carr 83

	Pld	W	D	L	F	A	Pts
1 Region 2	3	2	1	0	5	1	7
2 South Region Russia	3	2	0	1	5	4	6
3 Castilla y León	3	1	1	1	6	4	4
4 Olomouc Region Selection	3	0	0	3	3	10	0

Final

09/07/17, TFF Riva, Istanbul
Zagreb Region 1-0 Region 2
Goal: 1-0 Adžić 26
Referee: Kuchin (KAZ)
Zagreb: Durdek, Vrbat, Ivkovčić, Adžić (Švigir 74), Štulec, Čibarić, Soldo (Filipović 61), Lihić, Brujić (Krznar 87), Mislimi, Mohač. Coach: Tomislav Gričar (CRO)
Region 2: O'Connell, Higgins, Hoey, Kelly, Horgan, Carr, Stack (Chris 77), O' Donovan, Hayes, O' Connell (Hoban 71), Daly-Butz. Coach: Gerry Davis (IRL)
Yellow cards: Horgan 67 (Region 2), Štulec 89 (Zagreb)

Top goalscorers (Final tournament)

4 Roberto García Puente (Castilla y León)

3 Flecha (Lisboa)
Eoin Hayes (Region 2)
Toni Adžić (Zagreb Region)

WOMEN'S EURO 2017
THE NETHERLANDS

Netherlands take trophy for first time

Denmark defeated 4-2 in Enschede final

Germany's 22-year reign comes to an end

Dutch delight on home soil

The new expanded UEFA Women's EURO, containing 16 teams, was a historic and triumphant occasion for tournament hosts the Netherlands, who won all of their games and became only the fourth different nation to win the trophy, their crowning glory coming in the final with a thrilling 4-2 victory over Denmark, the quarter-final conquerors of long-time champions Germany.

Concerns prior to the tournament that the increased number of participants might affect the balance of the competition proved unfounded as the lower-ranked teams did not just compete with the traditional powers but largely dominated the finals.

The biggest upset was the quarter-final elimination of Germany, winners of each of the previous six UEFA Women's EUROs, by Denmark, who went on to meet their all-conquering hosts in the Enschede final.

A record 46 teams competed for the 15 qualifying spots in the Netherlands. Debutants Andorra were one of six to fall in the preliminary stages as Moldova and Georgia progressed to the main qualifying round.

That the 2017 tournament would come to be characterised by upsets was not so evident en route to the finals as Germany and France qualified without dropping a point or conceding a goal, and 11 of the 12 finalists from 2013 made it through, invariably with ease. The odd ones out were Finland, victims of a major shock when they surrendered a 2-0 lead to lose 3-2 against Portugal, a fourth-seeded side who then defeated Romania with an extra-time away goal in the play-off.

Like Portugal, four other nations – Belgium, Switzerland, Austria and Scotland – made their finals debut in the Netherlands, and all would gain at least one victory. In fact, only two teams failed to get a point – injury-hit Iceland and, to widespread amazement, 2013 runners-up Norway.

Boasting star striker Ada Hegerberg, Norway were widely tipped to go all the way, but they never recovered from an opening 1-0 defeat by the hosts and exited without scoring a goal after further losses to Belgium and Denmark, the latter, like Group A winners the Netherlands, entering the last eight as underdogs.

Theresa Nielsen (No8) jumps for joy after scoring Denmark's winning goal against Germany

Germany and Sweden, on the other hand, both emerged as expected from Group B, but they would be surprised in the quarter-finals.

The Netherlands comprehensively beat Sweden 2-0, and in a game postponed until the following day because of torrential rain Denmark came from behind to beat Germany 2-1 and end their bid for a seventh straight title.

In the other half of the draw, Austria were the shock winners of Group C ahead of France, who only just beat Switzerland to second place. England and Spain, as predicted, qualified from Group D, but while the Lionesses won all three games, Spain only just edged out Scotland in a three-way tie on three points with Portugal. Spain then went out to Austria on penalties while England won 1-0 against France with a fifth goal of the tournament from Jodie Taylor.

In the first of the semi-finals, Austria lost on penalties after a 0-0 draw against Denmark before the meeting of the two teams with 100% records resulted in an impressive 3-0 win for the Netherlands against England.

Back in Enschede for the final three days later, Sarina Wiegman's team fell behind early but rallied to beat Denmark 4-2 in a pulsating match that showcased women's international football at its finest, two Vivianne Miedema goals ensuring joyous celebrations amidst the swathes of orange-bedecked supporters in the sold-out crowd.

Opposite: Mandy van den Berg (left) and Sherida Spitse lift the UEFA Women's EURO trophy in front of their Netherlands team-mates

Final tournament

If the theme of the tournament was the Netherlands entertaining and enthralling packed stadiums, the overture was Group A's opening game in Utrecht as the hosts' adventurous wing play tore Norway apart, and the Dutch women's record 21,731 crowd rejoiced in Shanice van de Sanden's winner. Denmark made the most of an early goal to beat Belgium 1-0, but the debutants recovered to stun Norway 2-0. Denmark then lost 1-0 to the hosts, a Sherida Spitse penalty deciding the outcome, but their 1-0 victory against Norway took them through as the Netherlands overcame Belgium 2-1.

In Group B, Russia were the early leaders after beating Italy 2-1 as Germany and Sweden drew 0-0, but both favourites would leapfrog them four days later, Germany eliminating Italy with a 2-1 win and Sweden beating Russia 2-0. That proved a vital victory for Sweden as they then lost 3-2 to Italy and had Germany to thank for ending Russia's hopes with two penalties in a 2-0 victory.

On a tight opening day in Group C, Austria surprised Switzerland 1-0 with a Nina Burger goal while France needed an 86th-minute Eugénie Le Sommer penalty to pip Iceland. Switzerland then ended Iceland's hopes with a 2-1 comeback win as Austria again exceeded expectations with a 1-1 draw against France. The increasing confidence of Dominik Thalhammer's side helped them to blow away Iceland 3-0, which earned them first place ahead of Olivier Echouafni's France, who only just scraped through thanks to Camille Abily's late equaliser against Switzerland.

Records tumbled in Utrecht as Mark Sampson's England beat Scotland by a UEFA Women's EURO record 6-0 margin in Group D, Jodie Taylor scoring the first hat-trick recorded at the finals since 1997. Spain beat Portugal 2-0 but then lost by the same score to England, with Taylor again finding the net. Tenacious Portugal found a way to beat Scotland 1-0 but then lost 2-1 to a much-changed England side. Scotland simultaneously beat Spain, but the 1-0 victory margin was not enough for Anna Signeul's team and their defeated opponents progressed as runners-up with just three points.

Only one of the two scheduled Saturday quarter-finals took place, with the Netherlands seeing off Sweden 2-0 thanks to a goal in each half from Lieke Martens and Vivianne Miedema. Torrential Rotterdam rain forced Germany's game with Denmark to be postponed until the following afternoon, but it was worth the wait as an inspired Denmark came from behind through the superb Nadia Nadim and Theresa Nielsen to end Germany's long reign. Austria, boasting several Germany-based players, did make it through to the last four, after a 0-0 draw against Spain, prevailing 5-3 on penalties with five perfect spot-kicks before another Taylor goal proved sufficient for England to beat France, the new favourites, for the first time since 1974.

At the 2013 finals Denmark had won their quarter-final on penalties but then been felled in the semis by the same method. This time they inflicted the same fate on Austria, whose spot-kick luck deserted them not only in normal time, through Sarah Puntigam, but then also in the shoot-out as, in complete contrast to the quarter-final, they failed to convert a single kick, enabling Nils Nielsen's side to win 3-0. In the second semi-final the Dutch attendance record from the opening game was eclipsed by the 27,093 that watched the Netherlands defeat a distraught England thanks to a header from Miedema and a well-struck second from Danielle van de Donk, with an added-time own goal from Millie Bright completing a raucously celebrated 3-0 win.

The best match of the tournament was duly saved until last. Nadim's early penalty was quickly cancelled out by Miedema, and after Martens, later named Player of the Tournament, had put the Netherlands ahead, Pernille Harder equalised for Denmark – all before half-time. Shortly after the interval a Spitse free-kick restored the hosts' lead, and Denmark's hopes were finally crushed in the 89th minute as local golden girl Miedema rifled in her second goal of the game, and fourth of the tournament, to complete a magnificent 4-2 win and confirm the Netherlands as the women's champions of Europe for the first time.

Sherida Spitse converts a free-kick to put the Netherlands 3-2 up against Denmark in the final

Qualifying group stage

Group 1

Slovenia 0-3 Scotland
Iceland 2-0 Belarus
Slovenia 3-0 Belarus
FYR Macedonia 0-4 Iceland
Scotland 7-0 Belarus
Slovenia 0-6 Iceland
FYR Macedonia 1-4 Scotland
FYR Macedonia 0-2 Belarus
Scotland 10-0 FYR Macedonia
Scotland 3-1 Slovenia
Belarus 0-5 Iceland
Slovenia 8-1 FYR Macedonia
FYR Macedonia 0-9 Slovenia
Scotland 0-4 Iceland
Belarus 0-1 Scotland
Iceland 8-0 FYR Macedonia

15/09/16, FC Minsk, Minsk
Belarus 6-2 FYR Macedonia
Goals: 1-0 Slesarchik 14, 2-0 Shcherbachenia 15, 3-0 Avkhimovich 17, 3-1 Jakovska 23, 4-1 Linnik 28, 5-1 Urazaeva 52, 5-2 Krstanovska 55, 6-2 Shuppo 70

16/09/16, Laugardalsvöllur, Reykjavik
Iceland 4-0 Slovenia
Goals: 1-0 Gísladóttir 11, 2-0 Brynjarsdóttir 21, 3-0 Brynjarsdóttir 46, 4-0 Jónsdóttir 68

20/09/16, Laugardalsvöllur, Reykjavik
Iceland 1-2 Scotland
Goals: 0-1 J Ross 25, 1-1 Fridriksdóttir 40, 1-2 J Ross 56(p)

20/09/16, FC Minsk, Minsk
Belarus 2-0 Slovenia
Goals: 1-0 Slesarchik 38, 2-0 Slesarchik 84

	Pld	W	D	L	F	A	Pts
1 Iceland	8	7	0	1	34	2	21
2 Scotland	8	7	0	1	30	7	21
3 Slovenia	8	3	0	5	21	19	9
4 Belarus	8	3	0	5	10	20	9
5 FYR Macedonia	8	0	0	8	4	51	0

Group 2

Finland 1-0 Montenegro
Republic of Ireland 0-2 Finland
Portugal 1-2 Republic of Ireland
Finland 1-2 Spain
Republic of Ireland 0-3 Spain
Portugal 6-1 Montenegro
Spain 2-0 Portugal
Montenegro 0-7 Spain
Montenegro 0-5 Republic of Ireland
Portugal 1-4 Spain
Montenegro 1-7 Finland
Spain 3-0 Republic of Ireland
Finland 4-1 Republic of Ireland
Montenegro 0-3 Portugal
Finland 0-0 Portugal
Republic of Ireland 9-0 Montenegro

15/09/16, Pabellón de la Ciudad del Fútbol 1, Madrid
Spain 13-0 Montenegro
Goals: 1-0 Verónica Boquete 2, 2-0 Verónica Boquete 7, 3-0 Sonia 10, 4-0 Sampedro 16, 5-0 Sonia 20, 6-0 Sonia 23, 7-0 Corredera 25,

Marie-Laure Delie completes the scoring for France in a 6-0 victory against Albania that took the winners through to the Netherlands with a perfect record

8-0 Verónica Boquete 45, 9-0 Verónica Boquete 46, 10-0 Sonia 52, 11-0 Losada 74, 12-0 Alexia 80, 13-0 Sonia 90+3

16/09/16, CD Trofense, Trofa
Portugal 3-2 Finland
Goals: 0-1 Alanen 21(p), 0-2 Franssi 27, 1-2 Cláudia Neto 29, 2-2 Cláudia Neto 45(p), 3-2 Cláudia Neto 84(p)

20/09/16, Tallaght Stadium, Dublin
Republic of Ireland 0-1 Portugal
Goal: 0-1 Cláudia Neto 78

20/09/16, Estadio Butarque, Madrid
Spain 5-0 Finland
Goals: 1-0 Torrejón 28, 2-0 Paredes 66(p), 3-0 Paredes 82, 4-0 Sampedro 88(p), 5-0 Hermoso 90+1

	Pld	W	D	L	F	A	Pts
1 Spain	8	8	0	0	39	2	24
2 Portugal	8	4	1	3	15	11	13
3 Finland	8	4	1	3	17	12	13
4 Republic of Ireland	8	3	0	5	17	14	9
5 Montenegro	8	0	0	8	2	51	0

Group 3

France 3-0 Romania
Albania 1-4 Greece
Ukraine 2-2 Romania
Romania 3-0 Albania
Ukraine 0-3 France
Greece 1-3 Romania
Albania 0-6 France
Greece 0-3 France
Greece 3-2 Albania
Albania 0-4 Ukraine
Greece 1-3 Ukraine
Ukraine 2-0 Albania
Romania 0-1 France
France 4-0 Ukraine
Albania 0-3 Romania
France 1-0 Greece
Ukraine 2-0 Greece

15/09/16, Stadionul Dr. Constantin Rădulescu, Cluj-Napoca
Romania 2-1 Ukraine
Goals: 1-0 Havristiuc 4, 1-1 Ovdiychuk 8, 2-1 Duşa 11

20/09/16, Stadionul Dr. Constantin Rădulescu, Cluj-Napoca
Romania 4-0 Greece
Goals: 1-0 Lunca 5, 2-0 Ficzay 15, 3-0 Vătafu 76, 4-0 Bătea 79

20/09/16, Stade Jean Bouin, Paris
France 6-0 Albania
Goals: 1-0 Le Bihan 18, 2-0 Hamraoui 21, 3-0 Le Sommer 45+1, 4-0 Hamraoui 60, 5-0 Le Sommer 64(p), 6-0 Delie 77

	Pld	W	D	L	F	A	Pts
1 France	8	8	0	0	27	0	24
2 Romania	8	5	1	2	17	8	16
3 Ukraine	8	4	1	3	14	12	13
4 Greece	8	2	0	6	9	19	6
5 Albania	8	0	0	8	3	31	0

Group 4

Moldova 0-3 Sweden
Sweden 3-0 Poland
Poland 2-0 Slovakia
Denmark 4-0 Moldova
Slovakia 4-0 Moldova
Sweden 1-0 Denmark
Slovakia 0-1 Denmark
Moldova 1-3 Poland
Moldova 0-4 Slovakia
Poland 0-0 Denmark
Slovakia 0-3 Sweden
Slovakia 2-1 Poland
Poland 0-4 Sweden
Denmark 4-0 Slovakia
Sweden 6-0 Moldova
Denmark 6-0 Poland

15/09/16, Gamla Ullevi, Gothenburg
Sweden 2-1 Slovakia
Goals: 1-0 Appelquist 23, 1-1 Fischerová 59, 2-1 Hammarlund 65

15/09/16, Stadionul Zimbru, Chisinau
Moldova 0-5 Denmark
Goals: 0-1 Nadim 3, 0-2 Harder 18, 0-3 Harder 33, 0-4 Nadim 68, 0-5 Harder 74

20/09/16, Osrodek Sportu i Rekreacji, Wloclawek
Poland 4-0 Moldova
Goals: 1-0 Pajor 43, 2-0 Daleszczyk 64, 3-0 Arnautu 68(og), 4-0 Winczo 90+1

20/09/16, Viborg Stadion, Viborg
Denmark 2-0 Sweden
Goals: 1-0 Rasmussen 12, 2-0 Nadim 47

	Pld	W	D	L	F	A	Pts
1 Sweden	8	7	0	1	22	3	21
2 Denmark	8	6	1	1	22	1	19
3 Poland	8	3	1	4	10	16	10
4 Slovakia	8	3	0	5	11	13	9
5 Moldova	8	0	0	8	1	33	0

Group 5

Turkey 1-4 Croatia
Germany 12-0 Hungary
Croatia 0-1 Germany
Hungary 1-0 Turkey
Germany 2-0 Russia
Germany 7-0 Turkey
Croatia 1-1 Hungary
Turkey 0-0 Russia
Hungary 0-1 Russia
Croatia 3-0 Turkey
Turkey 0-6 Germany
Hungary 2-0 Croatia
Germany 2-0 Croatia
Russia 3-3 Hungary
Russia 2-0 Turkey
Turkey 2-1 Hungary
Croatia 0-3 Russia

16/09/16, Arena Khimki, Khimki
Russia 0-4 Germany
Goals: 0-1 Tsybutovich 7(og), 0-2 Maier 14, 0-3 Hendrich 26, 0-4 Petermann 78

20/09/16, Gyirmóti Stadion, Gyor
Hungary 0-1 Germany
Goal: 0-1 V Szabó 29(og)

20/09/16, Arena Khimki, Khimki
Russia 5-0 Croatia
Goals: 1-0 Pantyukhina 6, 2-0 Chernomyrdina 12, 3-0 Danilova 25, 4-0 Danilova 44, 5-0 Sochneva 75

	Pld	W	D	L	F	A	Pts
1 Germany	8	8	0	0	35	0	24
2 Russia	8	4	2	2	14	9	14
3 Hungary	8	2	2	4	8	20	8
4 Croatia	8	2	1	5	8	15	7
5 Turkey	8	1	1	6	3	24	4

Leonie Maier (left) congratulates goalscorer Lena Petermann as Germany go 4-0 up in their penultimate qualifier away to Russia

Group 6

Italy 6-1 Georgia
Georgia 0-3 Czech Republic
Italy 0-3 Switzerland
Georgia 0-3 Northern Ireland
Czech Republic 0-3 Italy
Switzerland 4-0 Georgia
Northern Ireland 1-8 Switzerland
Switzerland 5-1 Czech Republic
Switzerland 2-1 Italy
Czech Republic 4-1 Georgia
Italy 3-1 Northern Ireland
Northern Ireland 4-0 Georgia
Czech Republic 0-5 Switzerland
Georgia 0-7 Italy
Czech Republic 3-0 Northern Ireland

03/08/16, Mourneview Park, Lurgan
Northern Ireland 1-1 Czech Republic
Goals: 0-1 Chlastáková 35, 1-1 Furness 55(p)

15/09/16, Tengiz Burjanadze Stadioni, Gori
Georgia 0-3 Switzerland
Goals: 0-1 Crnogorčević 18(p), 0-2 Humm 34, 0-3 Dickenmann 90+4

16/09/16, Mourneview Park, Lurgan
Northern Ireland 0-3 Italy
Goals: 0-1 Girelli 45+1, 0-2 Gabbiadini 76, 0-3 Girelli 90+4

20/09/16, Stadio Silvio Piola, Vercelli
Italy 3-1 Czech Republic
Goals: 1-0 Mauro 6, 1-1 Voňková 13, 2-1 Mauro 14, 3-1 Guagni 62

20/09/16, Biel/Bienne, Biel
Switzerland 4-0 Northern Ireland
Goals: 1-0 Bernauer 17, 2-0 Kiwic 42, 3-0 Bernauer 46, 4-0 Rinast 54

	Pld	W	D	L	F	A	Pts
1 Switzerland	8	8	0	0	34	3	24
2 Italy	8	6	0	2	26	8	18
3 Czech Republic	8	3	1	4	13	18	10
4 Northern Ireland	8	2	1	5	10	22	7
5 Georgia	8	0	0	8	2	34	0

Group 7

Estonia 0-1 Serbia
Estonia 0-8 England
Belgium 6-0 Bosnia & Herzegovina
Bosnia & Herzegovina 4-0 Estonia
Serbia 3-0 Estonia
Bosnia & Herzegovina 0-5 Belgium
Serbia 0-1 Bosnia & Herzegovina
England 1-0 Bosnia & Herzegovina
Belgium 1-1 Serbia

England 1-1 Belgium
Bosnia & Herzegovina 0-1 England
Belgium 6-0 Estonia
Estonia 0-5 Belgium
England 7-0 Serbia
Estonia 0-1 Bosnia & Herzegovina
Serbia 0-7 England

15/09/16, Sports Center of FA of Serbia, Stara Pazova
Serbia 1-3 Belgium
Goals: 0-1 De Caigny 13, 1-1 Tenkov 31, 1-2 Deloose 52, 1-3 Van Gorp 74

15/09/16, Meadow Lane, Nottingham
England 5-0 Estonia
Goals: 1-0 Carter 9, 2-0 J Scott 13, 3-0 Carter 17, 4-0 Carter 56, 5-0 Carney 90+4(p)

20/09/16, FF BH Football Training Centre, Zenica
Bosnia & Herzegovina 2-4 Serbia
Goals: 0-1 Slović 9, 1-1 Medić 40, 1-2 Tenkov 48, 1-3 Čubrilo 54, 1-4 Tenkov 69, 2-4 Nikolić 84(p)

20/09/16, Den Dreef, Louvain
Belgium 0-2 England
Goals: 0-1 Parris 65, 0-2 Carney 85

	Pld	W	D	L	F	A	Pts
1 England	8	7	1	0	32	1	22
2 Belgium	8	5	2	1	27	5	17
3 Serbia	8	3	1	4	10	21	10
4 Bosnia & Herzegovina	8	3	0	5	8	17	9
5 Estonia	8	0	0	8	0	33	0

Group 8

Kazakhstan 0-2 Austria
Kazakhstan 0-4 Norway
Austria 3-0 Wales
Israel 0-0 Kazakhstan
Norway 4-0 Wales
Israel 0-1 Austria
Wales 4-0 Kazakhstan
Israel 2-2 Wales
Israel 0-1 Norway
Austria 6-1 Kazakhstan
Austria 0-1 Norway
Kazakhstan 0-4 Wales
Kazakhstan 1-0 Israel
Norway 2-2 Austria
Austria 4-0 Israel
Wales 0-2 Norway

Isabella Herlovsen (No9) is poised to score one of her three goals in Norway's 10-0 victory at home to Kazakhstan

15/09/16, Molde Stadion, Molde
Norway 10-0 Kazakhstan
Goals: 1-0 Ada Hegerberg 8, 2-0 Herlovsen 10, 3-0 Herlovsen 12, 4-0 Reinås 21, 5-0 Mjelde 23, 6-0 Graham Hansen 29, 7-0 Mjelde 45+1, 8-0 Isaksen 77, 9-0 Herlovsen 79, 10-0 An Hegerberg 81

15/09/16, Newport County AFC, Newport
Wales 3-0 Israel
Goals: 1-0 Ward 16, 2-0 Ward 32, 3-0 Estcourt 59

19/09/16, Hoddvoll Stadion, Ulsteinvik
Norway 5-0 Israel
Goals: 1-0 Ada Hegerberg 43, 2-0 Ada Hegerberg 48, 3-0 Ada Hegerberg 52, 4-0 Bøe Risa 71, 5-0 Herlovsen 80

20/09/16, Newport County AFC, Newport
Wales 0-0 Austria

	Pld	W	D	L	F	A	Pts
1 Norway	8	7	1	0	29	2	22
2 Austria	8	5	2	1	18	4	17
3 Wales	8	3	2	3	13	11	11
4 Kazakhstan	8	1	1	6	2	30	4
5 Israel	8	0	2	6	2	17	2

Play-off

21/10/16, Restelo, Lisbon
Portugal 0-0 Romania
25/10/16, Stadionul Dr Constantin Rădulescu, Cluj-Napoca
Romania 1-1 Portugal (aet)
Goals: 0-1 Andreia Norton 105+1, 1-1 Rus 111
Aggregate: 1-1; Portugal qualify on away goal.

Top goalscorers (Qualifying round/Play-offs)

10 Harpa Thorsteinsdóttir (Iceland)
Ada Hegerberg (Norway)
Jane Ross (Scotland)

8 Eugénie Le Sommer (France)
Verónica Boquete (Spain)

7 Nadia Nadim (Denmark)
Pernille Harder (Denmark)
Dagný Brynjarsdóttir (Iceland)
Isabell Herlovsen (Norway)
Ana-Maria Crnogorčević (Switzerland)
Helen Ward (Wales)

Harpa Thorsteinsdóttir

Ada Hegerberg

Jane Ross

Final tournament

Group A

16/07/17, Stadion Galgenwaard, Utrecht (att: 21,731)
Netherlands 1-0 Norway
Goal: 1-0 Van de Sanden 66
Referee: Frappart (FRA)
Netherlands: Van Veenendaal, Van Lunteren, Van den Berg (Van der Gragt 80), Van Es, Dekker, Van de Sanden (Beerensteyn 77), Spitse, Miedema, Van de Donk (Roord 90+1), Martens, Groenen. Coach: Sarina Wiegman (NED)
Norway: Hjelmseth, Wold, Thorisdottir, Mjelde, Schjelderup (Reiten 75), Thorsnes, Graham Hansen, Holstad Berge, Ada Hegerberg, Minde (Haavi 66), Maanum (Isaksen 58). Coach: Martin Sjögren (SWE)
Yellow cards: Ada Hegerberg 9 (Norway), Groenen 90+1 (Netherlands)

16/07/17, Stadion De Vijverberg, Doetinchem (att: 4,565)
Denmark 1-0 Belgium
Goal: 1-0 Troelsgaard 6
Referee: Monzul (UKR)
Denmark: Petersen, Røddik, Arnth, Boye Sørensen, Troelsgaard, Nielsen, Nadim (Thøgersen 71), Harder, Veje, Larsen (Kildemoes 60), Jensen. Coach: Nils Nielsen (DEN)
Belgium: Odeurs, Philtjens (Daniels 86), Jaques, Coutereels, De Caigny, Van Gorp (Vanmechelen 62), Onzia, Wullaert, Zeler, Cayman, Biesmans (Coryn 82). Coach: Ives Serneels (BEL)
Yellow cards: Nadim 51 (Denmark), Røddik 65 (Denmark), Philtjens 83 (Belgium), Nielsen 86 (Denmark), Kildemoes 89 (Denmark)

20/07/17, Rat Verlegh Stadion, Breda (att: 8,477)
Norway 0-2 Belgium
Goals: 0-1 Van Gorp 59, 0-2 Cayman 67
Referee: Mularczyk (POL)
Norway: Hjelmseth, Wold (Sønstevold 46), Mjelde, Schjelderup (Utland 78), Andrine Hegerberg, Thorsnes (Haavi 75), Graham Hansen, Holstad Berge, Ada Hegerberg, Minde, Spord. Coach: Martin Sjögren (SWE)
Belgium: Odeurs, Philtjens (Coryn 76), Jaques, Coutereels, De Caigny, Van Gorp (Daniels 88), Onzia, Wullaert, Zeler, Cayman (Biesmans 90+5), Deloose. Coach: Ives Serneels (BEL)
Yellow cards: Zeler 23 (Belgium), Jaques 48 (Belgium), Sønstevold 90 (Norway)

20/07/17, Sparta Stadion, Rotterdam (att: 10,078)
Netherlands 1-0 Denmark
Goal: 1-0 Spitse 20(p)
Referee: Hussein (GER)
Netherlands: Van Veenendaal, Van Lunteren, Van den Berg (Van der Gragt 54), Van Es, Dekker, Van de Sanden (Beerensteyn 88), Spitse, Miedema, Van de Donk, Martens (R Jansen 78), Groenen. Coach: Sarina Wiegman (NED)
Denmark: Petersen, Boye Sørensen, Christiansen (Kildemoes 64), Troelsgaard, Nielsen, Nadim, Harder, Veje (Larsen 69), Jensen, Jans, Sandvej. Coach: Nils Nielsen (DEN)
Yellow cards: Troelsgaard 49 (Denmark), Kildemoes 77 (Denmark), Boye Sørensen 82 (Denmark)

24/07/17, Willem II Stadion, Tilburg (att: 12,697)
Belgium 1-2 Netherlands
Goals: 0-1 Spitse 27(p), 1-1 Wullaert 59, 1-2 Martens 74
Referee: Steinhaus (GER)
Belgium: Odeurs, Philtjens, Jaques, Coutereels (Vanmechelen 46), De Caigny, Van Gorp (Coryn 57), Onzia (Daniels 76), Wullaert, Zeler, Cayman, Deloose. Coach: Ives Serneels (BEL)
Netherlands: Van Veenendaal, Van der Gragt, Van Es, Dekker, Van de Sanden, Spitse, Miedema (Lewerissa 86), Van de Donk (Zeeman 75), Martens, Groenen (Roord 80), Van der Most. Coach: Sarina Wiegman (NED)
Yellow cards: Dekker 32 (Netherlands), Deloose 54 (Belgium), Van de Donk 61 (Netherlands), Miedema 72 (Netherlands), Van der Gragt 88 (Netherlands)

24/07/17, Stadion De Adelaarshorst, Deventer (att: 5,885)
Norway 0-1 Denmark
Goal: 0-1 Veje 5
Referee: Frappart (FRA)
Norway: Hjelmseth, Wold, Thorisdottir, Reiten, Mjelde, Schjelderup (Maanum 56), Graham Hansen, Holstad Berge, Ada Hegerberg, Minde, Spord (Utland 79). Coach: Martin Sjögren (SWE)
Denmark: Petersen, Røddik, Boye Sørensen, Troelsgaard, Nielsen, Nadim (Sandvej 81), Harder, Veje (Christiansen 90+2), Larsen, Thøgersen (Sørensen 78), Jensen. Coach: Nils Nielsen (DEN)
Yellow card: Mjelde 90+5 (Norway)

	Pld	W	D	L	F	A	Pts
1 Netherlands	3	3	0	0	4	1	9
2 Denmark	3	2	0	1	2	1	6
3 Belgium	3	1	0	2	3	3	3
4 Norway	3	0	0	3	0	4	0

Group B

17/07/17, Sparta Stadion, Rotterdam (att: 637)
Italy 1-2 Russia
Goals: 0-1 Danilova 9, 0-2 Morozova 26, 1-2 Mauro 88
Referee: Adámková (CZE)
Italy: Marchitelli, Salvai, Gama (Tucceri Cimini 27), Stracchi, Linari, Guagni (Bonansea 71), Gabbiadini, Mauro, Bartoli, Giugliano, Carissimi (Girelli 61). Coach: Antonio Cabrini (ITA)
Russia: Shcherbak, Solodkaya, Kozhnikova, Makarenko, Cholovyaga (Pantyukhina 59), Smirnova, Sochneva (Kiskonen 90), Danilova (Karpova 74), Ziyastinova, Chernomyrdina, Morozova. Coach: Elena Fomina (RUS)
Yellow cards: Shcherbak 61 (Russia), Linari 69 (Italy), Bartoli 90 (Italy)

17/07/17, Rat Verlegh Stadion, Breda (att: 9,267)
Germany 0-0 Sweden
Referee: Kulcsár (HUN)
Germany: Schult, Henning, Peter, Demann, Simon, Marozsán, Mittag (Kayikci 65), Däbritz, Blässe (Maier 73), Huth (Islacker 39), Magull. Coach: Steffi Jones (GER)
Sweden: Lindahl, Andersson (Ericsson 87), Sembrant, Fischer, Dahlkvist, Schelin, Asllani, Samuelsson, Seger, Rolfö (Blackstenius 56), Schough (Rubensson 56). Coach: Pia Sundhage (SWE)
Yellow card: Magull 75 (Germany)

21/07/17, Stadion De Adelaarshorst, Deventer (att: 5,764)
Sweden 2-0 Russia
Goals: 1-0 Schelin 22, 2-0 Blackstenius 51
Referee: Frappart (FRA)
Sweden: Lindahl, Sembrant, Fischer, Ericsson, Dahlkvist (Folkesson 63), Schelin, Asllani, Blackstenius (Hammarlund 73), Samuelsson, Seger, Schough (Rolfö 46). Coach: Pia Sundhage (SWE)
Russia: Shcherbak, Solodkaya, Kozhnikova, Makarenko, Cholovyaga, Smirnova, Sochneva (Kiskonen 81), Danilova (Karpova 72), Ziyastinova, Chernomyrdina (Fedorova 66), Morozova. Coach: Elena Fomina (RUS)
Yellow cards: Ericsson 17 (Sweden), Sochneva 21 (Russia), Morozova 55 (Russia)

Sweden's Elin Rubensson pulls clear of Germany's Hasret Kayikci (left) and Mandy Islacker during the Group B goalless draw in Breda

21/07/17, Willem II Stadion, Tilburg (att: 7,108)
Germany 2-1 Italy
Goals: 1-0 Henning 19, 1-1 Mauro 29, 2-1 Peter 67(p)
Referee: Monzul (UKR)
Germany: Schult, Henning (Hendrich 46), Maier, Peter, Demann, Islacker (Petermann 79), Marozsán, Mittag, Däbritz, Dallmann (Magull 88), Ierschowski. Coach: Steffi Jones (GER)
Italy: Giuliani, Salvai, Stracchi, Linari, Guagni, Gabbiadini (Sabatino 84), Mauro (Girelli 45+2), Bonansea, Bartoli, Cernoia (Tucceri Cimini 73), Carissimi. Coach: Antonio Cabrini (ITA)
Red card: Bartoli 69 (Italy)
Yellow cards: Henning 39 (Germany), Carissimi 53 (Italy), Bartoli 64 (Italy), Stracchi 66 (Italy), Bartoli 69 (Italy), Maier 81 (Germany), Mittag 85 (Germany)

25/07/17, Stadion Galgenwaard, Utrecht (att: 6,458)
Russia 0-2 Germany
Goals: 0-1 Peter 10(p), 0-2 Marozsán 56(p)
Referee: Mularczyk (POL)
Russia: Shcherbak, Solodkaya, Kozhnikova, Makarenko (Morozova 28), Cholovyaga, Smirnova (Fedorova 46), Sochneva, Danilova, Ziyastinova, Chernomyrdina (Karpova 63), Morozova. Coach: Elena Fomina (RUS)
Germany: Schult, Peter, Demann, Simon, Gössling, Islacker (Kayikci 46), Marozsán, Mittag (Kemme 75), Däbritz (Magull 68), Blässe, Doorsoun-Khajeh. Coach: Steffi Jones (GER)
Yellow card: Kozhnikova 43 (Russia)

25/07/17, Stadion De Vijverberg, Doetinchem (att: 3,776)
Sweden 2-3 Italy
Goals: 0-1 Sabatino 4, 1-1 Schelin 14(p), 1-2 Sabatino 37, 2-2 Blackstenius 47, 2-3 Girelli 85
Referee: Staubli (SUI)
Sweden: Lindahl, Andersson, Sembrant, Ericsson, Schelin, Asllani (Rolfö 46), Blackstenius, Folkesson, Seger (Dahlkvist 46), Schough (Spetsmark 79), Rubensson. Coach: Pia Sundhage (SWE)
Italy: Giuliani, Stracchi, Linari, Guagni, Gabbiadini, Rosucci (Carissimi 84), Bonansea, Tucceri Cimini (Giugliano 60), Di Criscio, Sabatino (Girelli 77), Galli. Coach: Antonio Cabrini (ITA)
Yellow cards: Di Criscio 13 (Italy), Tucceri Cimini 26 (Italy)

	Pld	W	D	L	F	A	Pts
1 Germany	3	2	1	0	4	1	7
2 Sweden	3	1	1	1	4	3	4
3 Russia	3	1	0	2	2	5	3
4 Italy	3	1	0	2	5	6	3

Group C

18/07/17, Stadion De Adelaarshorst, Deventer (att: 4,781)
Austria 1-0 Switzerland
Goal: 1-0 Burger 15
Referee: Steinhaus (GER)
Austria: Zinsberger, Schiechtl (Schnaderbeck 77), Wenninger, Zadrazil, Burger, Kirchberger, Billa (Pinther 83), Puntigam, Feiersinger, Aschauer, Makas (Prohaska 39). Coach: Dominik Thalhammer (AUT)
Switzerland: Thalmann, Maritz, Reuteler (Brunner 62), Moser, Crnogorčević, Bachmann, Dickenmann, Wälti, Kiwic, Abbé (Bernauer 57), Humm (Aigbogun 57). Coach: Martina Voss-Tecklenburg (SUI)
Red card: Kiwic 60 (Switzerland)
Yellow cards: Abbé 19 (Switzerland), Kirchberger 55 (Austria), Burger 71 (Austria)

Lisa Makas (No20) fires Austria into the lead in their 1-1 draw against France in Utrecht

18/07/17, Willem II Stadion, Tilburg (att: 4,894)
France 1-0 Iceland
Goal: 1-0 Le Sommer 86(p)
Referee: Vitulano (ITA)
France: Bouhaddi, Renard, Georges, Henry, Le Bihan (Diani 43), Houara-D'Hommeaux, Le Sommer, Abily, Thomis (Delie 77), Bussaglia (Thiney 64), Karchaoui. Coach: Olivier Echouafni (FRA)
Iceland: G Gunnarsdóttir, Atladóttir, I Sigurdardóttir, Viggósdóttir, Jónsdóttir, Gunnarsdóttir, Gardarsdóttir (Thorsteinsdóttir 75), Brynjarsdóttir, Gísladóttir, Albertsdóttir (Ásbjörnsdóttir 61), Fridriksdóttir (Jensen 82). Coach: Freyr Alexandersson (ISL)
Yellow cards: Renard 17 (France), I Sigurdardóttir 34 (Iceland), Albertsdóttir 54 (Iceland)

22/07/17, Stadion De Vijverberg, Doetinchem (att: 5,647)
Iceland 1-2 Switzerland
Goals: 1-0 Fridriksdóttir 33, 1-1 Dickenmann 43, 1-2 Bachmann 52
Referee: Pustovoitova (RUS)
Iceland: G Gunnarsdóttir, Atladóttir, I Sigurdardóttir, Viggósdóttir, Jónsdóttir (Magnúsdóttir 83), Gunnarsdóttir, Gardarsdóttir (Thorsteinsdóttir 88), Ásbjörnsdóttir (Albertsdóttir 66), Brynjarsdóttir, Gísladóttir, Fridriksdóttir. Coach: Freyr Alexandersson (ISL)
Switzerland: Thalmann, Brunner, Maritz, Moser (Aigbogun 57), Zehnder, Crnogorčević, Bachmann (Rinast 90+10), Dickenmann, Wälti, Bernauer, Bürki (Humm 76). Coach: Martina Voss-Tecklenburg (SUI)
Yellow cards: Dickenmann 7 (Switzerland), Jónsdóttir 44 (Iceland)

22/07/17, Stadion Galgenwaard, Utrecht (att: 4,387)
France 1-1 Austria
Goals: 0-1 Makas 27, 1-1 Henry 51
Referee: Adámková (CZE)
France: Bouhaddi, Perisset, Renard, Henry, Houara-D'Hommeaux (Karchaoui 63), Le Sommer, Bussaglia (Abily 78), Thiney (Diani 70), Delie, M'Bock Bathy, Geyoro. Coach: Olivier Echouafni (FRA)
Austria: Zinsberger, Schiechtl, Wenninger, Burger (Pinther 75), Schnaderbeck, Kirchberger, Billa (Eder 85), Puntigam, Feiersinger, Aschauer, Makas (Prohaska 69). Coach: Dominik Thalhammer (AUT)
Yellow cards: Feiersinger 20 (Austria), Houara-D'Hommeaux 44 (France)

26/07/17, Rat Verlegh Stadion, Breda (att: 3,545)
Switzerland 1-1 France
Goals: 1-0 Crnogorčević 19, 1-1 Abily 76
Referee: Kulcsár (HUN)
Switzerland: Thalmann, Maritz, Moser (Calligaris 65), Zehnder (Reuteler 79), Crnogorčević, Bachmann, Dickenmann, Wälti, Kiwic, Aigbogun (Terchoun 79), Bernauer. Coach: Martina Voss-Tecklenburg (SUI)
France: Bouhaddi, Perisset, Renard, Henry, Le Sommer, Abily (Thiney 87), Lavogez (Delie 71), M'Bock Bathy, Diani (Houara-D'Hommeaux 83), Karchaoui, Geyoro. Coach: Olivier Echouafni (FRA)
Red card: Perisset 17 (France)
Yellow cards: Renard 14 (France), Henry 43 (France), Bernauer 66 (Switzerland), Calligaris 68 (Switzerland), Dickenmann 72 (Switzerland)

26/07/17, Sparta Stadion, Rotterdam (att: 4,120)
Iceland 0-3 Austria
Goals: 0-1 Zadrazil 36, 0-2 Burger 44, 0-3 Enzinger 89
Referee: Hussein (GER)
Iceland: G Gunnarsdóttir, Atladóttir, Viggósdóttir, Magnúsdóttir (Jónsdóttir 51), Gunnarsdóttir, Brynjarsdóttir, Gísladóttir, Thorsteinsdóttir (Thorvaldsdóttir 71), Albertsdóttir (Jessen 83), Kristjansdóttir, Fridriksdóttir. Coach: Freyr Alexandersson (ISL)
Austria: Zinsberger, Schiechtl, Wenninger, Zadrazil (Schnaderbeck 72), Burger, Kirchberger, Billa (Enzinger 86), Puntigam, Feiersinger, Aschauer, Makas (Prohaska 56). Coach: Dominik Thalhammer (AUT)
Yellow cards: Kristjansdóttir 48 (Iceland), Zadrazil 54 (Austria)

	Pld	W	D	L	F	A	Pts
1 Austria	3	2	1	0	5	1	7
2 France	3	1	2	0	3	2	5
3 Switzerland	3	1	1	1	3	3	4
4 Iceland	3	0	0	3	1	6	0

Group D

19/07/17, Stadion De Vijverberg, Doetinchem (att: 2,424)
Spain 2-0 Portugal
Goals: 1-0 Losada 23, 2-0 Sampedro 42
Referee: Larsson (SWE)
Spain: Paños, Torrejón, Paredes, Pereira, Sampedro, Hermoso (María Paz 65), Alexia (Latorre 81), Losada, Silvia Meseguer, Ouahabi (María León 89), Mariona. Coach: Jorge Vilda (ESP)
Portugal: Patricia Morais, Sílvia Rebelo, Cláudia Neto, Ana Borges, Ana Leite (Carolina Mendes 59), Tatiana Pinto, Dolores Silva, Carole Costa, Diana Silva (Laura Luís 85), Vanessa Marques, Suzane Pires (Antunes 71). Coach: Francisco Neto (POR)

19/07/17, Stadion Galgenwaard, Utrecht (att: 5,587)
England 6-0 Scotland
Goals: 1-0 Taylor 11, 2-0 Taylor 26, 3-0 White 32, 4-0 Taylor 53, 5-0 Nobbs 87, 6-0 Duggan 90+3
Referee: Staubli (SUI)
England: Bardsley, Bronze, Stokes, J Scott, Houghton, Nobbs, Taylor (Duggan 59), Moore, Bright, White (Carney 74), Kirby (Parris 65). Coach: Mark Sampson (WAL)
Scotland: Fay, Barsley, Dieke, Weir, Crichton, Evans, J Ross (Cuthbert 63), Corsie (Love 76), Brown, Brown (Clelland 46), Arthur. Coach: Anna Signeul (SWE)
Yellow cards: Houghton 55 (England), J Scott 62 (England), Weir 84 (Scotland)

23/07/17, Sparta Stadion, Rotterdam (att: 3,123)
Scotland 1-2 Portugal
Goals: 0-1 Carolina Mendes 27, 1-1 Cuthbert 68, 1-2 Ana Leite 72
Referee: Kulcsár (HUN)
Scotland: Fay, Barsley, Dieke, Weir, Crichton, Evans, Corsie, McLauchlan (Love 82), Clelland (Cuthbert 54), Smith, Brown (Lauder 67). Coach: Anna Signeul (SWE)
Portugal: Patricia Morais, Sílvia Rebelo, Cláudia Neto, Ana Borges, Tatiana Pinto, Dolores Silva, Carole Costa, Diana Silva (Laura Luís 90+2), Vanessa Marques, Carolina Mendes (Ana Leite 70), Amanda da Costa (Suzane Pires 76). Coach: Francisco Neto (POR)
Yellow cards: Carole Costa 2 (Portugal), Diana Silva 47 (Portugal), Corsie 74 (Scotland), Sílvia Rebelo 76 (Portugal), Patricia Morais 86 (Portugal), Cláudia Neto 89 (Portugal)

23/07/17, Rat Verlegh Stadion, Breda (att: 4,879)
England 2-0 Spain
Goals: 1-0 Kirby 2, 2-0 Taylor 85
Referee: Vitulano (ITA)
England: Bardsley, Bronze, Stokes, J Scott, Houghton, Nobbs, Taylor (Potter 89), Moore, Bright, White (Duggan 79), Kirby (Christiansen 69). Coach: Mark Sampson (WAL)
Spain: Paños, Torrejón, Paredes, Pereira, Corredera, Sampedro (Virginia 89), Hermoso, Alexia, Losada (García 73), Silvia Meseguer, Ouahabi (Latorre 89). Coach: Jorge Vilda (ESP)
Yellow cards: Paredes 31 (Spain), Pereira 69 (Spain)

27/07/17, Willem II Stadion, Tilburg (att: 3,335)
Portugal 1-2 England
Goals: 0-1 Duggan 7, 1-1 Carolina Mendes 17, 1-2 Parris 48
Referee: Monzul (UKR)
Portugal: Patricia Morais, Sílvia Rebelo, Cláudia Neto, Ana Borges, Tatiana Pinto, Dolores Silva, Carole Costa, Diana Silva (Laura Luís 87), Carolina Mendes (Ana Leite 64), Suzane Pires (Amanda da Costa 79), Antunes. Coach: Francisco Neto (POR)
England: Chamberlain, Potter, Christiansen, Williams, Carney, Bassett, Bright (Nobbs 60), Parris, Duggan (Stokes 81), Greenwood, A Scott. Coach: Mark Sampson (WAL)
Yellow cards: Williams 5 (England), Christiansen 27 (England)

27/07/17, Stadion De Adelaarshorst, Deventer (att: 4,840)
Scotland 1-0 Spain
Goal: 1-0 Weir 42
Referee: Adámková (CZE)
Scotland: Fay, Dieke, L Ross (Clelland 46), Love (Brown 73), Cuthbert, Weir, Crichton, Evans, Corsie, Brown, Arthur. Coach: Anna Signeul (SWE)
Spain: Paños, Torrejón, Paredes, Pereira, Sampedro, Hermoso (María Paz 46), Alexia, Losada, Silvia Meseguer, Ouahabi (Corredera 56), Mariona (Latorre 79). Coach: Jorge Vilda (ESP)
Yellow cards: Fay 40 (Scotland), Brown 44 (Scotland), Ouahabi 54 (Spain)

	Pld	W	D	L	F	A	Pts
1 England	3	3	0	0	10	1	9
2 Spain	3	1	0	2	2	3	3
3 Scotland	3	1	0	2	2	8	3
4 Portugal	3	1	0	2	3	5	3

England captain Steph Houghton heads goalwards in the Lionesses' opening 6-0 victory over Scotland

Quarter-finals

29/07/17, Stadion De Vijverberg, Doetinchem (att: 11,106)
Netherlands 2-0 Sweden
Goals: 1-0 Martens 33, 2-0 Miedema 64
Referee: Steinhaus (GER)
Netherlands: Van Veenendaal, Van Lunteren, Van der Gragt (Van den Berg 46), Van Es, Dekker, Van de Sanden (R Jansen 76), Spitse, Miedema, Van de Donk, Martens (Beerensteyn 87), Groenen. Coach: Sarina Wiegman (NED)
Sweden: Lindahl, Andersson (Larsson 81), Sembrant, Fischer, Dahlkvist, Schelin, Asllani, Blackstenius, Samuelsson, Seger, Rolfö (Folkesson 73). Coach: Pia Sundhage (SWE)
Yellow cards: Samuelsson 43 (Sweden), Asllani 90+1 (Sweden)

30/07/17, Sparta Stadion, Rotterdam (att: 5,251)
Germany 1-2 Denmark
Goals: 1-0 I Kerschowski 3, 1-1 Nadim 49, 1-2 Nielsen 83
Referee: Kulcsár (HUN)
Germany: Schult, Peter, Demann (Islacker 62), Gössling, Marozsán, Mittag, Däbritz, Blässe, Doorsoun-Khajeh (Magull 46), Dallmann (Petermann 88), Kerschowski. Coach: Steffi Jones (GER)
Denmark: Petersen, Røddik (Sandvej 69), Kildemoes (Thøgersen 66), Boye Sørensen, Troelsgaard, Nielsen, Nadim, Harder, Veje, Larsen, Jensen. Coach: Nils Nielsen (DEN)

30/07/17, Willem II Stadion, Tilburg (att: 3,488)
Austria 0-0 Spain (aet; 5-3 on pens)
Referee: Frappart (FRA)
Austria: Zinsberger, Schiechtl, Wenninger, Zadrazil (Pinther 110), Burger, Schnaderbeck, Billa (Kirchberger 81), Puntigam, Feiersinger, Aschauer, Makas (Prohaska 42). Coach: Dominik Thalhammer (AUT)
Spain: Paños, Torrejón, Paredes, Corredera, Sampedro, María Paz (Virginia 112), Losada (Alexia 68), Silvia Meseguer, Latorre (Hermoso 76), María León, Mariona (García 56). Coach: Jorge Vilda (ESP)
Yellow cards: María León 30 (Spain), Wenninger 75 (Austria), Torrejón 88 (Spain), Aschauer 119 (Austria)

30/07/17, Stadion De Adelaarshorst, Deventer (att: 6,283)
England 1-0 France
Goal: 1-0 Taylor 60
Referee: Staubli (SUI)
England: Bardsley (Chamberlain 75), Bronze, Stokes, J Scott, Houghton, Nobbs, Taylor, Moore, Bright, White, Kirby. Coach: Mark Sampson (WAL)
France: Bouhaddi, Georges, Henry, Houara-D'Hommeaux, Le Sommer, Abily (Lavogez 78), Delie (Le Bihan 90), M'Bock Bathy, Diani (Thomis 65), Karchaoui, Geyoro. Coach: Olivier Echouafni (FRA)
Yellow cards: J Scott 33 (England), Taylor 62 (England), M'Bock Bathy 81 (France)

Semi-finals

03/08/17, Rat Verlegh Stadion, Breda (att: 10,184)
Denmark 0-0 Austria (aet; 3-0 on pens)
Referee: Monzul (UKR)
Denmark: Petersen, Røddik (Sandvej 46), Kildemoes (Thøgersen 52), Boye Sørensen, Troelsgaard, Nielsen, Nadim, Harder, Veje (Sørensen 120+1), Larsen, Jensen (Pedersen 69) Coach: Nils Nielsen (DEN)

Austria: Zinsberger, Schiechtl, Wenninger, Zadrazil, Burger, Schnaderbeck, Kirchberger, Billa (Prohaska 39), Puntigam (Pinther 91), Feiersinger, Aschauer. Coach: Dominik Thalhammer (AUT)
Yellow cards: Kildemoes 36 (Denmark), Schiechtl 56 (Austria), Harder 80 (Denmark), Zadrazil 97 (Austria)

03/08/17, FC Twente Stadion, Enschede (att: 27,093)
Netherlands 3-0 England
Goals: 1-0 Miedema 22, 2-0 Van de Donk 62, 3-0 Bright 90+3(og)
Referee: Frappart (FRA)
Netherlands: Van Veenendaal, Van Lunteren, Van der Gragt (Zeeman 70), Van Es, Dekker, Van de Sanden (Jansen 89), Spitse, Miedema, Van de Donk (Roord 90+1), Martens, Groenen. Coach: Sarina Wiegman (NED)
England: Chamberlain, Bronze, Stokes, Houghton, Nobbs, Taylor, Williams (Duggan 67), Moore (Carney 76), Bright, White, Kirby. Coach: Mark Sampson (WAL)
Yellow cards: Van Lunteren 13 (Netherlands), Bright 15 (England), Moore 47 (England), Van de Donk 59 (Netherlands)

Final

06/08/17, FC Twente Stadion, Enschede (att: 28,182)
Netherlands 4-2 Denmark
Goals: 0-1 Nadim 6(p), 1-1 Miedema 10, 2-1 Martens 28, 2-2 Harder 33, 3-2 Spitse 51, 4-2 Miedema 89
Referee: Staubli (SUI)
Netherlands: Van Veenendaal, Van Lunteren (Janssen 57), Van der Gragt, Van Es (Van den Berg 90+4), Dekker, Van de Sanden (Jansen 90), Spitse, Miedema, Van de Donk, Martens, Groenen. Coach: Sarina Wiegman (NED)
Denmark: Petersen, Kildemoes (Thøgersen 61), Boye Sørensen (Røddik 77), Troelsgaard, Nielsen, Nadim, Harder, Veje, Larsen, Pedersen (Christiansen 82), Sandvej. Coach: Nils Nielsen (DEN)
Yellow cards: Groenen 21 (Netherlands), Dekker 43 (Netherlands), Nadim 45 (Denmark), Van der Gragt 72 (Netherlands)

Top goalscorers (Final tournament)

5	Jodie Taylor (England)
4	Vivianne Miedema (Netherlands)
3	Lieke Martens (Netherlands) Sherida Spitse (Netherlands)

Squads/Appearances/Goals

Austria

No	Name	DoB	Aps	(s)	Gls	Club
Goalkeepers						
23	Carolin Grössinger	10/05/97				Bergheim
21	Jasmin Pfeiler	28/07/84				Altenmarkt
1	Manuela Zinsberger	19/10/95	5			Bayern (GER)
Defenders						
19	Verena Aschauer	20/01/94	5			Sand (GER)
2	Marina Georgieva	13/04/97				Potsdam (GER)
13	Virginia Kirchberger	25/05/93	4	(1)		Duisburg (GER)
5	Sophie Maierhofer	09/08/96				Kansas University (USA)
3	Katharina Naschenweng	16/12/97				Sturm
11	Viktoria Schnaderbeck	04/01/91	3	(2)		Bayern (GER)
6	Katharina Schiechtl	27/02/93	5			Bremen (GER)
7	Carina Wenninger	06/02/91	5			Bayern (GER)
Midfielders						
14	Barbara Dunst	25/09/97				Leverkusen (GER)
16	Jasmin Eder	08/10/92		(1)		St Pölten
18	Laura Feiersinger	05/04/93	5			Sand (GER)
22	Jennifer Klein	11/01/99				Neulengbach
20	Lisa Makas	11/05/92	4		1	Duisburg (GER)
8	Nadine Prohaska	15/08/90		(5)		St Pölten
17	Sarah Puntigam	13/10/92	5			Freiburg (GER)
9	Sarah Zadrazil	19/02/93	4		1	Potsdam (GER)
Forwards						
15	Nicole Billa	05/03/96	5			Hoffenheim (GER)
10	Nina Burger	27/12/87	5		2	Sand (GER)
12	Stefanie Enzinger	25/11/90		(1)	1	Sturm
4	Viktoria Pinther	16/10/98		(4)		St Pölten

Belgium

No	Name	DoB	Aps	(s)	Gls	Club
Goalkeepers						
21	Nicky Evrard	26/05/95				Twente (NED)
12	Diede Lemey	07/10/96				Anderlecht
1	Justien Odeurs	30/05/97	3			Jena (GER)
Defenders						
19	Imke Courtois	14/03/88				Standard
4	Maud Coutereels	21/05/86	3			LOSC (FRA)
22	Laura Deloose	18/06/93	2			Anderlecht
3	Heleen Jaques	20/04/88	3			Anderlecht
2	Davina Philtjens	26/02/89	3			Ajax (NED)
5	Lorca Van de Putte	03/04/88				Kristianstads (SWE)
23	Elien Van Wynendaele	19/02/95				Gent
10	Aline Zeler	02/06/83	3			Anderlecht
Midfielders						
20	Julie Biesmans	04/05/94	1	(1)		Standard
6	Tine De Caigny	09/06/97	3			Anderlecht
18	Laura Deneve	09/10/94				Anderlecht
8	Lenie Onzia	30/05/89	3			Anderlecht
16	Nicky Van den Abbeele	21/02/94				Anderlecht
7	Elke Van Gorp	12/05/95	3		1	Anderlecht
13	Sara Yuceil	22/06/88				PSV (NED)
Forwards						
11	Janice Cayman	12/10/88	3		1	Montpellier (FRA)
17	Jana Coryn	26/06/92		(3)		LOSC (FRA)
15	Yana Daniels	08/05/92		(3)		Bristol City (ENG)
14	Davinia Vanmechelen	30/08/99		(2)		Genk
9	Tessa Wullaert	19/03/93	3		1	Wolfsburg (GER)

Denmark

No	Name	DoB	Aps	(s)	Gls	Club
Goalkeepers						
16	Maria Christensen	03/07/95				Fortuna
22	Line Johansen	26/07/89				Velje
1	Stina Lykke Petersen	03/02/86	6			KoldingQ
Defenders						
3	Janni Arnth	15/10/86	1			Linköping (SWE)
5	Simone Boye Sørensen	03/03/92	6			Rosengård (SWE)
23	Luna Gewitz	03/03/94				Fortuna
18	Mie Jans	06/02/94	1			Man. City (ENG)
12	Stine Larsen	24/01/96	5	(1)		Brøndby
8	Theresa Nielsen	20/07/86	6		1	Vålerenga (NOR)
20	Stine Pedersen	03/01/94				Skovbakken
2	Line Røddik	31/01/88	4	(1)		Barcelona (ESP)
19	Cecilie Sandvej	13/06/90	2	(3)		Frankfurt (GER)
Midfielders						
6	Nanna Christiansen	17/06/89	1	(2)		Brøndby
21	Sarah Hansen	14/09/96				Fortuna
17	Line Jensen	23/08/91	5			Washington Spirit (USA)
4	Maja Kildemoes	15/08/96	3	(2)		Linköping (SWE)
13	Sofie Pedersen	24/04/92	1	(1)		Rosengård (SWE)
15	Frederikke Thøgersen	24/07/95	1	(4)		Fortuna
7	Sanne Troelsgaard	15/08/88	6		1	Rosengård (SWE)
11	Katrine Veje	19/06/91	6		1	Montpellier (FRA)
Forwards						
10	Pernille Harder	15/11/92	6		1	Wolfsburg (GER)
9	Nadia Nadim	02/01/88	6		2	Portland Thorns (USA)
14	Nicoline Sørensen	15/08/97		(2)		Brøndby

England

No	Name	DoB	Aps	(s)	Gls	Club
Goalkeepers						
1	Karen Bardsley	14/10/84	3			Man. City
13	Siobhan Chamberlain	15/08/83	2	(1)		Liverpool
21	Carly Telford	07/07/87				Chelsea
Defenders						
15	Laura Bassett	02/08/83	1			Unattached
16	Millie Bright	21/08/93	5			Chelsea
2	Lucy Bronze	28/10/91	4			Man. City
20	Alex Greenwood	07/09/93	1			Liverpool
5	Steph Houghton	23/04/88	4			Man. City
22	Alex Scott	14/10/84	1			Arsenal
3	Demi Stokes	12/12/91	4	(1)		Man. City
12	Casey Stoney	13/05/82				Liverpool
Midfielders						
14	Karen Carney	01/08/87	1	(2)		Chelsea
8	Isobel Christiansen	20/09/91	1	(1)		Man. City
23	Fran Kirby	29/06/93	4		1	Chelsea
11	Jade Moore	22/10/90	4			Reading
7	Jordan Nobbs	08/12/92	4	(1)	1	Arsenal
6	Jo Potter	13/11/84	1	(1)		Reading
4	Jill Scott	02/02/87	3			Man. City
18	Ellen White	09/05/89	4		1	Birmingham
10	Fara Williams	25/01/84	2			Arsenal
Forwards						
19	Toni Duggan	25/07/91	1	(3)	2	Barcelona (ESP)
17	Nikita Parris	10/03/94	1	(1)	1	Man. City
9	Jodie Taylor	17/05/86	4		5	Arsenal

France

No	Name	DoB	Aps	(s)	Gls	Club
Goalkeepers						
16	Sarah Bouhaddi	17/10/86	4			Lyon
21	Méline Gérard	30/05/90				Montpellier
1	Laetitia Philippe	30/04/91				Montpellier
Defenders						
4	Laura Georges	20/08/84	2			Paris
22	Sakina Karchaoui	26/01/96	3	(1)		Montpellier
8	Jessica Houara-D'Hommeaux	29/09/87	3	(1)		Lyon
19	Griedge M'Bock Bathy	26/02/95	3			Lyon
2	Eve Perisset	24/12/94	2			Paris
3	Wendie Renard	20/07/90	3			Lyon
14	Aissatou Tounkara	16/03/95				Paris FC
Midfielders						
10	Camille Abily	05/12/84	3	(1)	1	Lyon
15	Élise Bussaglia	24/09/85	2			Barcelona (ESP)
23	Grace Geyoro	02/07/97	3			Paris
6	Amandine Henry	28/09/89	4		1	Portland Thorns (USA)
11	Claire Lavogez	18/06/94	1	(1)		Lyon
7	Clarisse Le Bihan	14/12/94	1	(1)		Montpellier
12	Élodie Thomis	13/08/86	1	(1)		Lyon
5	Sandie Toletti	13/07/95				Montpellier
Forwards						
13	Camille Catala	06/05/91				Paris FC
18	Marie-Laure Delie	29/01/88	2	(2)		Paris
20	Kadidiatou Diani	01/04/95	2	(2)		Paris FC
9	Eugénie Le Sommer	18/05/89	4		1	Lyon
17	Gaëtane Thiney	28/10/85	1	(2)		Paris FC

Germany

No	Name	DoB	Aps	(s)	Gls	Club
Goalkeepers						
12	Laura Benkarth	14/10/92				Wolfsburg
1	Almuth Schult	09/02/91	4			Wolfsburg
21	Lisa Weiss	29/10/87				Essen
Defenders						
14	Anna Blässe	27/02/87	3			Wolfsburg
8	Lena Gössling	08/03/86	2			Wolfsburg
3	Kathrin-Julia Hendrich	06/04/92		(1)		Frankfurt
2	Josephine Henning	08/09/89	2		1	Lyon (FRA)
22	Tabea Kemme	14/12/91		(1)		Potsdam
17	Isabel Kerschowski	22/01/88	2		1	Wolfsburg
4	Leonie Maier	29/09/92	1	(1)		Bayern
5	Babett Peter	12/05/88	4		2	Wolfsburg
7	Carolin Simon	24/11/92	2			Freiburg
Midfielders						
13	Sara Däbritz	15/02/95	4			Bayern
6	Kristin Demann	07/04/93	4			Bayern
15	Sara Doorsoun-Khajeh	17/11/91	2			Essen
20	Lina Magull	15/08/94	1	(3)		Freiburg
10	Dzsenifer Marozsán	18/04/92	4		1	Lyon (FRA)
Forwards						
16	Linda Dallmann	02/09/94	2			Essen
19	Svenja Huth	25/01/91	1			Potsdam
9	Mandy Islacker	08/08/88	2	(2)		Frankfurt
23	Hasret Kayikci	06/11/91		(2)		Freiburg
11	Anja Mittag	16/05/85	4			Rosengård (SWE)
18	Lena Petermann	05/02/94		(2)		Freiburg

Iceland

No	Name	DoB	Aps	(s)	Gls	Club
Goalkeepers						
1	Gudbjörg Gunnarsdóttir	18/05/85	3			Djurgården (SWE)
12	Sandra Sigurdardóttir	02/10/86				Valur
13	Sonny Thrainsdóttir	09/12/86				Breidablik
Defenders						
21	Arna Ásgrímsdóttir	12/08/92				Valur
2	Sif Atladóttir	15/07/85	3			Kristianstads (SWE)
19	Anna Bjork Kristjansdóttir	14/10/89	1			IF Limhamn Bunkeflo 2007 (SWE)
3	Ingibjörg Sigurdardóttir	07/10/97	2			Breidablik
14	Málfrídur Erna Sigurdardóttir	30/05/84				Valur
4	Glódís Viggósdóttir	27/06/95	3			Eskilstuna (SWE)
Midfielders						
17	Agla Maria Albertsdóttir	05/08/99	2	(1)		Stjarnan
9	Katrin Ásbjörnsdóttir	11/12/92	1	(1)		Stjarnan
10	Dagný Brynjarsdóttir	10/08/91	3			Portland Thorns (USA)
8	Sigrídur Gardarsdóttir	11/03/94	2			IBV
11	Hallbera Gísladóttir	14/09/86	3			Djurgården (SWE)
7	Sara Bjork Gunnarsdóttir	29/09/90	3			Wolfsburg (GER)
18	Sandra Jessen	18/01/95		(1)		Thór/KA
5	Gunnhildur Jónsdóttir	28/09/88	2	(1)		Vålerenga (NOR)
6	Hólmfrídur Magnúsdóttir	20/09/84	1	(1)		KR
Forwards						
23	Fanndís Fridriksdóttir	09/05/90	3		1	Breidablik
22	Rakel Hönnudóttir	30/12/88				Breidablik
15	Elín Jensen	01/03/95		(1)		Valur
16	Harpa Thorsteinsdóttir	27/06/86	1	(2)		Stjarnan
20	Berglind Thorvaldsdóttir	18/01/92		(1)		Breidablik

Italy

No	Name	DoB	Aps	(s)	Gls	Club
Goalkeepers						
1	Laura Giuliani	05/06/93	2			Freiburg (GER)
12	Chiara Marchitelli	04/05/85	1			Brescia
22	Katja Schroffenegger	28/04/91				Unterland
Defenders						
13	Elisa Bartoli	07/05/91	2			Fiorentina
17	Federica Di Criscio	12/05/93	1			Verona
3	Sara Gama	27/03/89	1			Brescia
7	Alia Guagni	01/10/87	3			Fiorentina
5	Elena Linari	15/04/94	3			Fiorentina
2	Cecilia Salvai	02/12/93	2			Brescia
14	Linda Tucceri Cimini	04/04/91	1	(2)		San Zaccaria
Midfielders						
11	Barbara Bonansea	13/06/91	2	(1)		Brescia
21	Marta Carissimi	03/05/87	2	(1)		Fiorentina
20	Valentina Cernoia	22/06/91	1			Brescia
15	Laura Fusetti	08/10/90				Como
19	Aurora Galli	13/12/96	1			Verona
16	Manuela Giugliano	18/08/97	1	(1)		Verona
10	Martina Rosucci	09/05/92	1			Brescia
4	Daniela Stracchi	02/09/83	3			Mozzanica
Forwards						
8	Melania Gabbiadini	28/08/83	3			Verona
23	Cristiana Girelli	23/04/90		(3)	1	Brescia
6	Sandy Iannella	06/04/87				Cuneo
9	Ilaria Mauro	22/05/88	2		2	Fiorentina
18	Daniela Sabatino	26/06/85	1	(1)	2	Brescia

Netherlands

No	Name	DoB	Aps	(s)	Gls	Club
Goalkeepers						
16	Angela Christ	06/03/89				PSV
23	Loes Geurts	12/01/86				Paris (FRA)
1	Sari van Veenendaal	03/04/90	6			Arsenal (ENG)
Defenders						
6	Anouk Dekker	15/11/86	6			Montpellier (FRA)
20	Dominique Janssen	17/01/95		(1)		Arsenal (ENG)
4	Mandy van den Berg	26/08/90	2	(2)		Reading (ENG)
3	Stephanie van der Gragt	16/08/92	4	(2)		Ajax
22	Liza van der Most	08/10/93	1			Ajax
5	Kika van Es	11/10/91	6			Twente
2	Desiree van Lunteren	30/12/92	5			Ajax
17	Kelly Zeeman	19/11/93		(2)		Ajax
Midfielders						
15	Sisca Folkertsma	21/05/97				Ajax
14	Jackie Groenen	17/12/94	6			Frankfurt (GER)
12	Jill Roord	22/04/97		(3)		Bayern (GER)
8	Sherida Spitse	29/05/90	6		3	Twente
10	Danielle van de Donk	05/08/91	6		1	Arsenal (ENG)
19	Sheila van den Bulk	06/04/89				Djurgården (SWE)
Forwards						
21	Lineth Beerensteyn	11/10/96		(3)		Bayern (GER)
13	Renate Jansen	07/12/90		(4)		Twente
18	Vanity Lewerissa	01/04/91		(1)		PSV
11	Lieke Martens	16/12/92	6		3	Barcelona (ESP)
9	Vivianne Miedema	15/07/96	6		4	Arsenal (ENG)
7	Shanice van de Sanden	02/10/92	6		1	Liverpool (ENG)

Norway

No	Name	DoB	Aps	(s)	Gls	Club
Goalkeepers						
23	Oda Bogstad	24/04/96				Klepp
12	Cecilie Fiskerstrand	20/03/96				LSK
1	Ingrid Hjelmseth	10/04/80	3			Stabæk
Defenders						
11	Nora Holstad Berge	26/03/87	3			Bayern (GER)
21	Kristine Leine	06/08/96				Røa
18	Frida Maanum	16/07/99	1	(1)		Stabæk
6	Maren Mjelde	06/11/89	3			Chelsea (ENG)
13	Stine Pettersen Reinås	15/07/94				Stabæk
16	Anja Sønstevold	21/06/92		(1)		LSK
3	Maria Thorisdottir	05/06/93	2			Klepp
9	Elise Thorsnes	14/08/88	2			Avaldsnes
2	Ingrid Wold	29/01/90	3			LSK
Midfielders						
5	Tuva Hansen	04/08/97				Klepp
8	Andrine Hegerberg	06/06/93	1			Birmingham (ENG)
19	Ingvild Isaksen	10/02/89		(1)		Stabæk
17	Kristine Minde	08/08/92	3			Linköping (SWE)
4	Guro Reiten	26/07/94	1	(1)		LSK
7	Ingrid Schjelderup	21/12/87	3			Eskilstuna (SWE)
22	Ingrid Marie Spord	12/07/94	2			LSK
Forwards						
10	Caroline Graham Hansen	18/02/95	3			Wolfsburg (GER)
20	Emilie Haavi	16/06/92		(2)		Boston Breakers (USA)
14	Ada Hegerberg	10/07/95	3			Lyon (FRA)
15	Lisa-Marie Utland	19/09/92		(2)		Røa

Portugal

No	Name	DoB	Aps	(s)	Gls	Club
	Goalkeepers					
1	Jamila Marreiros	30/05/88				Futebol Benfica
12	Patricia Morais	17/06/92	3			Sporting
22	Rute Costa	01/06/94				Braga
	Defenders					
9	Ana Borges	15/06/90	3			Sporting
15	Carole Costa	03/05/90	3			Cloppenburg (GER)
21	Diana Gomes	26/07/98				Valadares Gaia
14	Dolores Silva	07/08/91	3			Jena (GER)
5	Matilde Fidalgo	15/05/94				Futebol Benfica
2	Mónica Mendes	16/06/93				Neunkirch (SUI)
3	Raquel Infante	19/09/90				Levante (ESP)
4	Sílvia Rebelo	20/05/89	3			Braga
	Midfielders					
19	Amanda da Costa	07/10/89	1	(1)		Boston Breakers (USA)
10	Ana Leite	23/10/91	1	(2)	1	Leverkusen (GER)
23	Melissa Antunes	08/01/90	1	(1)		Braga
7	Cláudia Neto	18/04/88	3			Linköping (SWE)
13	Fátima Pinto	16/01/96				Sporting
8	Laura Luís	15/08/92		(3)		Jena (GER)
11	Tatiana Pinto	28/03/94	3			Sporting
	Forwards					
6	Andreia Norton	15/08/96				Braga
18	Carolina Mendes	27/11/87	2	(1)	1	Grindavík (ISL)
16	Diana Silva	04/06/95	3			Sporting
20	Suzane Pires	17/08/92	2	(1)		Santos (BRA)
17	Vanessa Marques	12/04/96	2			Braga

Scotland

No	Name	DoB	Aps	(s)	Gls	Club
	Goalkeepers					
21	Lee Alexander	23/09/91				Glasgow City
1	Gemma Fay	09/12/81	3			Stjarnan (ISL)
12	Shannon Lynn	22/10/85				Vittsjö (SWE)
	Defenders					
23	Chloe Arthur	21/01/95	2			Bristol City (ENG)
2	Vaila Barsley	15/09/87	2			Eskilstuna (SWE)
17	Frankie Brown	08/10/87	2			Bristol City (ENG)
4	Ifeoma Dieke	25/02/81	3			Vittsjö (SWE)
15	Sophie Howard	17/09/93				Hoffenheim (GER)
18	Rachel McLauchlan	07/07/97	1			Hibernian
3	Joelle Murray	07/11/86				Hibernian
20	Kirsty Smith	06/01/94	1			Hibernian
	Midfielders					
19	Lana Clelland	26/01/93	1	(2)		Tavagnacco (ITA)
14	Rachel Corsie	17/08/89	3			Seattle Reign (USA)
10	Leanne Crichton	06/08/87	3			Glasgow City
8	Erin Cuthbert	19/07/98	1	(2)	1	Chelsea (ENG)
7	Hayley Lauder	04/06/90		(1)		Glasgow City
6	Joanne Love	06/12/85	1	(2)		Glasgow City
5	Leanne Ross	08/07/81	1			Glasgow City
9	Caroline Weir	20/06/95	3		1	Liverpool (ENG)
	Forwards					
22	Fiona Brown	31/03/95	2	(1)		Eskilstuna (SWE)
16	Christie Murray	03/05/90				Doncaster (ENG)
11	Lisa Evans	21/05/92	3			Arsenal (ENG)
13	Jane Ross	18/09/89	1			Man. City (ENG)

Sweden

No	Name	DoB	Aps	(s)	Gls	Club
	Goalkeepers					
12	Hilda Carlén	13/08/91				Piteå
1	Hedvig Lindahl	29/04/83	4			Chelsea (ENG)
21	Emelie Lundberg	10/03/93				Eskilstuna
	Defenders					
2	Jonna Andersson	02/01/93	3			Linköping
4	Emma Berglund	19/12/88				Paris FC (FRA)
6	Magdalena Ericsson	08/09/93	2	(1)		Linköping
5	Nilla Fischer	02/08/84	3			Wolfsburg (GER)
16	Hanna Glas	16/04/93				Eskilstuna
15	Jessica Samuelsson	30/01/92	3			Linköping
3	Linda Sembrant	15/05/87	4			Montpellier (FRA)
	Midfielders					
9	Kosovare Asllani	29/07/89	4			Man. City (ENG)
7	Lisa Dahlkvist	06/02/87	3	(1)		Örebro
14	Hanna Folkesson	15/06/88	1	(2)		Rosengård
13	Josefin Johansson	17/03/88				Piteå
23	Elin Rubensson	11/05/93	1	(1)		Kopparbergs/ Göteborg FC
22	Olivia Schough	11/03/91	3			Eskilstuna
17	Caroline Seger	19/03/85	4			Lyon (FRA)
10	Julia Spetsmark	30/06/89		(1)		Örebro
	Forwards					
11	Stina Blackstenius	05/02/96	3	(1)	2	Montpellier (FRA)
19	Pauline Hammarlund	07/05/94		(1)		Kopparbergs/ Göteborg FC
20	Mimmi Larsson	09/04/94		(1)		Eskilstuna
18	Fridolina Rolfö	24/11/93	2	(2)		Bayern (GER)
8	Lotta Schelin	27/02/84	4		2	Rosengård

Russia

No	Name	DoB	Aps	(s)	Gls	Club
	Goalkeepers					
12	Alena Belyaeva	13/02/92				Chertanovo
21	Yulia Grichenko	10/03/90				CSKA Moskva
1	Tatyana Shcherbak	22/10/97	3			Kubanochka
	Defenders					
13	Anna Belomyttseva	24/11/96				Ryazan-VDV
14	Nasiba Gasanova	15/12/94				Kubanochka
3	Anna Kozhnikova	10/07/87	3			CSKA Moskva
8	Daria Makarenko	07/03/92	3			Ryazan-VDV
19	Ekaterina Morozova	26/03/91		(1)		Chertanovo
5	Viktoriya Shkoda	21/12/99				Kubanochka
2	Natalya Solodkaya	04/04/95	3			Kubanochka
18	Elvira Ziyastinova	13/02/91	3			CSKA Moskva
	Midfielders					
20	Margarita Chernomyrdina	06/03/96	3			Chertanovo
9	Anna Cholovyaga	08/05/92	3			CSKA Moskva
23	Elena Morozova	15/03/87	3		1	Kubanochka
7	Anastasia Pozdeeva	12/06/93				Zvezda 2005
4	Tatiana Sheykina	14/11/91				Ryazan-VDV
11	Ekaterina Sochneva	12/08/85	3			CSKA Moskva
10	Nadezhda Smirnova	22/02/96	3			CSKA Moskva
	Forwards					
15	Elena Danilova	17/06/87	3		1	Ryazan-VDV
16	Marina Fedorova	10/05/97		(2)		Ryazan-VDV
6	Nadezhda Karpova	09/03/95		(3)		Chertanovo
22	Marina Kiskonen	19/03/94		(2)		Chertanovo
17	Ekaterina Pantyukhina	09/04/93		(1)		Zvezda 2005

Spain

No	Name	DoB	Aps	(s)	Gls	Club
	Goalkeepers					
1	Dolores Gallardo	10/06/93				Atlético
12	Mariasun	29/10/96				Real Sociedad
13	Sandra Paños	04/11/92	4			Barcelona
	Defenders					
16	Alexandra	28/02/89				Atlético
2	Celia Jiménez	20/06/95				Alabama (USA)
20	María León	13/06/95	1	(1)		Atlético
21	Leila Ouahabi	22/03/93	3			Barcelona
4	Irene Paredes	04/07/91	4			Paris (FRA)
5	Andrea Pereira	19/09/93	3			Atlético
3	Marta Torrejón	27/02/90	4			Barcelona
	Midfielders					
11	Alexia Putellas	04/02/94	3	(1)		Barcelona
14	Vicky Losada	05/03/91	4		1	Barcelona
22	Mariona Caldentey	19/03/96	3			Barcelona
23	Paula Nicart	08/09/94				Valencia
8	Amanda Sampedro	26/06/93	4		1	Atlético
15	Silvia Meseguer	12/03/89	4			Atlético
6	Virginia Torrecilla	04/09/94		(2)		Montpellier (FRA)
	Forwards					
7	Marta Corredera	08/08/91	2	(1)		Atlético
18	Esther González	08/12/92				Atlético
17	Olga García	01/06/92		(2)		Barcelona
10	Jennifer Hermoso	09/05/90	3	(1)		Barcelona
19	Bárbara Latorre	14/03/93	1	(3)		Barcelona
9	María Paz	01/02/88	1	(2)		Valencia

Switzerland

No	Name	DoB	Aps	(s)	Gls	Club
	Goalkeepers					
21	Seraina Friedli	20/03/93				Zürich
12	Stenia Michel	23/10/87				Basel
1	Gaëlle Thalmann	18/01/86	3			Verona (ITA)
	Defenders					
15	Caroline Abbé	13/01/88	1			Zürich
17	Sandra Betschart	30/03/89				Duisburg (GER)
2	Jana Brunner	20/01/97	1	(1)		Basel
9	Ana-Maria Crnogorčević	03/10/90	3		1	Frankfurt (GER)
14	Rahel Kiwic	05/01/91	2			Potsdam (GER)
5	Noelle Maritz	23/12/95	3			Wolfsburg (GER)
4	Rachel Rinast	02/06/91		(1)		Basel
13	Lia Wälti	19/04/93	3			Potsdam (GER)
	Midfielders					
22	Vanessa Bernauer	23/03/88	2	(1)		Wolfsburg (GER)
18	Viola Calligaris	17/03/96		(1)		Young Boys
11	Lara Dickenmann	27/11/85	3		1	Wolfsburg (GER)
20	Sandrine Mauron	19/12/96				Zürich
7	Martina Moser	09/04/86	3			Zürich
8	Cinzia Zehnder	04/08/97	2			Zürich
	Forwards					
19	Eseosa Aigbogun	23/05/93	1	(2)		Potsdam (GER)
10	Ramona Bachmann	25/12/90	3		1	Chelsea (ENG)
23	Vanessa Bürki	01/04/86	1			Bayern (GER)
16	Fabienne Humm	20/12/86	1	(1)		Zürich
6	Géraldine Reuteler	21/04/99	1	(1)		Luzern
3	Meriame Terchoun	27/10/95		(1)		Zürich

OLYMPIQUE LYONNAIS
FINAL·CARDIFF·2017

Paris Saint-Germain defeated in all-French final

Goalless draw precedes marathon shoot-out in Cardiff

German interest ends prematurely in quarter-finals

Lyon enter the record books

The 2016/17 UEFA Women's Champions League season brought record-equalling success for Lyon as the French club matched FFC Frankfurt's landmark achievements of six final appearances and four titles – although for the second year running they needed a penalty shoot-out to emerge victorious in the final.

For only the third time in the competition's 16-year history, no German teams were present at its conclusion. However, for the seventh time in the eight finals since the UEFA Women's Cup was rebranded, there was French representation. Furthermore, France supplied both finalists as Lyon took on Paris Saint-Germain, led by former OL boss Patrice Lair, in front of 22,433 spectators at Cardiff City Stadium.

Only a few days earlier, the sides had met in the French Cup final, with Lyon winning a penalty shoot-out that went to the 16th kick, only a fine performance from Paris goalkeeper Katarzyna Kiedrzynek having kept the illustrious Lyon attack at bay and taken the contest to penalties.

As in their domestic encounter, the teams could not score a goal between them in a disappointingly low-quality encounter in the Welsh capital. Neither could they be separated after seven penalties apiece. Then Kiedrzynek, who had been very active on the goal-line attempting to put off the Lyon kickers, stepped up and scuffed her shot wide. She had an immediate chance at redemption, but opposite number Sarah Bouhaddi kept her nerve to convert her effort and give Lyon a 7-6 victory.

Bouhaddi, Wendie Renard, Camille Abily and Le Sommer all secured their fourth European title with Lyon, the first team to claim a second successful title defence, having previously won back-to-back crowns in 2011 and 2012 to match Umeå's feat in 2003 and 2004. Lyon coach Gérard Prêcheur stepped down after the final, having led the club to the unprecedented achievement of two straight trebles.

The competition's record entry of 55 clubs included first Kosovan entrants Hajvalia, who drew two of their three qualifying round games, while Norway's Avaldsnes were the only one of the six debutants to survive that stage. Some big names were pitted together in the early stages of the knockout phase, with Wolfsburg beating Chelsea in the round of 32 thanks to a first-leg hat-trick at Stamford Bridge by Zsanett Jakabfi, who was to finish up as the competition's eight-goal joint top scorer alongside Bayern München's Vivianne Miedema on eight goals.

Meanwhile, Brescia ousted Medyk Konin on away goals after a 6-6 aggregate draw in which both teams had two-goal advantages wiped out. However, in the round of 16, Brescia were eliminated by 2003 runners-up Fortuna Hjørring, who therefore ended a run of seven straight exits at that stage.

Fortuna fell in the quarter-finals to newcomers Manchester City, who had taken out Zvezda-2005 and the other Danish entrants Brøndby in an impressive debut campaign. It was France 2 Germany 0 in the last eight as Lyon saw off Wolfsburg in a rematch of the 2016 final and Paris defeated Bayern München, while Barcelona reached their first semi-final with a convincing 3-0 aggregate win over Sweden's Rosengård.

Paris, though, proved too much for Barcelona in the semis, avenging their male team's harrowing UEFA Champions League last 16 defeat by winning 3-1 in Spain and 2-0 at Parc des Princes. City lost 3-1 at home to Lyon but gave notice of their promise with a 1-0 victory in the return against the holders and ultimately successful defending champions.

Opposite: Jubilation for four-time UEFA Women's Champions League winners Lyon

Qualifying round

Group 1

23-28/08/16 Paphos, Limassol
Apollon Ladies FC 5-0 Klaksvíkar Ítrottarfelag, FC PAOK Thessaloniki 1-1 WFC Hajvalia, Klaksvíkar Ítrottarfelag 1-1 FC PAOK Thessaloniki, Apollon Ladies FC 1-0 WFC Hajvalia, FC PAOK Thessaloniki 3-3 Apollon Ladies FC, WFC Hajvalia 1-1 Klaksvíkar Ítrottarfelag

	Pld	W	D	L	F	A	Pts
1 Apollon Ladies FC	3	2	1	0	9	3	7
2 FC PAOK Thessaloniki	3	0	3	0	5	5	3
3 WFC Hajvalia	3	0	2	1	2	3	2
4 Klaksvíkar Ítrottarfelag	3	0	2	1	2	7	2

Group 2

23-28/08/16 Osijek, Vinkovci
R. Standard de Liège 1-3 ZFK Minsk, ŽNK Osijek 14-1 ŽFK Dragon 2014, R. Standard de Liège 11-0 ŽFK Dragon 2014, ZFK Minsk 5-0 ŽNK Osijek, ŽNK Osijek 1-1 R. Standard de Liège, ŽFK Dragon 2014 0-9 ZFK Minsk

	Pld	W	D	L	F	A	Pts
1 ZFK Minsk	3	3	0	0	17	1	9
2 R. Standard de Liège	3	1	1	1	13	4	4
3 ŽNK Osijek	3	1	1	1	15	7	4
4 ŽFK Dragon 2014	3	0	0	3	1	34	0

Group 3

23-28/08/16 Cardiff, Barry
FC NSA 0-4 Cardiff Met Ladies FC, ZFK Spartak Subotica 1-1 Breidablik, Breidablik 5-0 FC NSA, ZFK Spartak Subotica 3-2 Cardiff Met Ladies FC, FC NSA 0-2 ZFK Spartak Subotica, Cardiff Met Ladies FC 0-8 Breidablik

	Pld	W	D	L	F	A	Pts
1 Breidablik	3	2	1	0	14	1	7
2 ZFK Spartak Subotica	3	2	1	0	6	3	7
3 Cardiff Met Ladies FC	3	1	0	2	6	11	3
4 FC NSA	3	0	0	3	0	11	0

Group 4

23-28/08/16 Konin, Wrzesnia
CFF Olimpia Cluj 7-1 Pärnu Jalgpalliklubi, KKPK Medyk Konin 9-0 FK Breznica Pljevlja, CFF Olimpia Cluj 10-0 FK Breznica Pljevlja, Pärnu Jalgpalliklubi 0-1 KKPK Medyk Konin, KKPK Medyk Konin 3-1 CFF Olimpia Cluj, FK Breznica Pljevlja 2-2 Pärnu Jalgpalliklubi

	Pld	W	D	L	F	A	Pts
1 KKPK Medyk Konin	3	3	0	0	13	1	9
2 CFF Olimpia Cluj	3	2	0	1	18	4	6
3 Pärnu Jalgpalliklubi	3	0	1	2	3	10	1
4 FK Breznica Pljevlja	3	0	1	2	2	21	1

BIIK-Kazygurt celebrate their 3-1 win at Wexford in the qualifying round

Group 5

23-28/08/16 Beltinci, Lendava
FC Zürich Frauen 3-1 ŠK Slovan Bratislava, ŽNK Pomurje 6-1 KS Vllaznia, FC Zürich Frauen 3-0 KS Vllaznia, ŠK Slovan Bratislava 2-4 ŽNK Pomurje, ŽNK Pomurje 0-5 FC Zürich Frauen, KS Vllaznia 1-2 ŠK Slovan Bratislava

	Pld	W	D	L	F	A	Pts
1 FC Zürich Frauen	3	3	0	0	11	1	9
2 ŽNK Pomurje	3	2	0	1	10	8	6
3 ŠK Slovan Bratislava	3	1	0	2	5	8	3
4 KS Vllaznia	3	0	0	3	2	11	0

Group 6

23-28/08/16 Sarajevo
SFK 2000 Sarajevo 1-0 WFC Ramat Hasharon, WFC Kharkiv 2-0 Rīgas FS, WFC Ramat Hasharon 1-0 WFC Kharkiv, SFK 2000 Sarajevo 3-0 Rīgas FS, WFC Kharkiv 2-2 SFK 2000 Sarajevo, Rīgas FS 0-4 WFC Ramat Hasharon

	Pld	W	D	L	F	A	Pts
1 SFK 2000 Sarajevo	3	2	1	0	6	2	7
2 WFC Ramat Hasharon	3	2	0	1	5	1	6
3 WFC Kharkiv	3	1	1	1	4	3	4
4 Rīgas FS	3	0	0	3	0	9	0

Group 7

23-28/08/16 Waterford, Wexford
Gintra Universitetas 13-0 ARF Criuleni, WFC BIIK-Kazygurt 3-1 Wexford Youths Women's FC, WFC BIIK-Kazygurt 3-0 ARF Criuleni, Wexford Youths Women's FC 1-2 Gintra Universitetas, Gintra Universitetas 0-3 WFC BIIK-Kazygurt, ARF Criuleni 0-0 Wexford Youths Women's FC

	Pld	W	D	L	F	A	Pts
1 WFC BIIK-Kazygurt	3	3	0	0	9	1	9
2 Gintra Universitetas	3	2	0	1	15	4	6
3 Wexford Youths Women's FC	3	0	1	2	2	5	1
4 ARF Criuleni	3	0	1	2	0	16	1

Group 8

23-28/08/16 Vantaa, Helsinki
Avaldsnes Idrettslag 11-0 Newry City Ladies, PK-35 Vantaa 1-2 Clube Futebol Benfica, Clube Futebol Benfica 1-6 Avaldsnes Idrettslag, PK-35 Vantaa 2-0 Newry City Ladies, Avaldsnes Idrettslag 2-0 PK-35 Vantaa, Newry City Ladies 0-5 Clube Futebol Benfica

	Pld	W	D	L	F	A	Pts
1 Avaldsnes Idrettslag	3	3	0	0	19	1	9
2 Clube Futebol Benfica	3	2	0	1	8	7	6
3 PK-35 Vantaa	3	1	0	2	3	4	3
4 Newry City Ladies	3	0	0	3	0	18	0

Group 9

23-28/08/16 Geesteren, Oldenzaal
FC Twente '65 2-1 Ferencvárosi TC, Konak Belediyespor 5-0 Hibernians FC, FC Twente '65 9-0 Hibernians FC, Ferencvárosi TC 2-0 Konak Belediyespor, Konak Belediyespor 2-6 FC Twente '65, Hibernians FC 0-4 Ferencvárosi TC

	Pld	W	D	L	F	A	Pts
1 FC Twente '65	3	3	0	0	17	3	9
2 Ferencvárosi TC	3	2	0	1	7	2	6
3 Konak Belediyespor	3	1	0	2	7	8	3
4 Hibernians FC	3	0	0	3	0	18	0

Round of 32

05/10/16, BIIK Stadium, Shymkent
WFC BIIK-Kazygurt 3-1 ASD Verona
Goals: 1-0 Adule 3, 2-0 Gabelia 12, 2-1 Gabbiadini 53, 3-1 Gabelia 80
Referee: Urban (HUN)
12/10/16, Marc'Antonio Bentegodi, Verona
ASD Verona 1-1 WFC BIIK-Kazygurt
Goals: 0-1 Gabelia 40, 1-1 Gabbiadini 58(p)
Referee: Valentová (SVK)
Aggregate: 2-4; WFC BIIK-Kazygurt qualify.

05/10/16, Kópavogsvöllur, Kopavogur
Breidablik 0-1 FC Rosengård
Goal: 0-1 Schelin 8
Referee: Karagiorgi (CYP)
12/10/16, Malmö Idrottsplats, Malmo
FC Rosengård 0-0 Breidablik
Referee: Clark (SCO)
Aggregate: 1-0; FC Rosengård qualify.

05/10/16, Miejski im. Złotej Jedenastki, Konin
KKPK Medyk Konin 4-3 Brescia Femminile
Goals: 0-1 Bonansea 18, 1-1 Kostova 29, 1-2 Cernoia 36, 1-3 Sabatino 70, 2-3 Sikora 76, 3-3 Gawrońska 79, 4-3 Kostova 84
Referee: Chudá (SVK)
13/10/16, Mario Rigamonti, Brescia
Brescia Femminile 3-2 KKPK Medyk Konin
Goals: 0-1 Kostova 5, 1-1 Slavcheva 15(og), 1-2 Sikora 53, 2-2 Girelli 69, 3-2 Sabatino 83
Referee: Raudziņa (LVA)
Aggregate: 6-6; Brescia Femminile qualify on away goals.

05/10/16, Asim Ferhatović Hase Stadion, Sarajevo
SFK 2000 Sarajevo 0-0 FC Rossiyanka
Referee: Otte (BEL)
13/10/16, Rodina, Khimki
FC Rossiyanka 2-1 SFK 2000 Sarajevo
Goals: 1-0 N'Rehy 50, 1-1 Djoković 70(p), 2-1 Nahi 90+4
Referee: Grundbacher (SUI)
Aggregate: 2-1; FC Rossiyanka qualify.

05/10/16, Stadion Graz Liebenau, Graz
SK Sturm Graz Damen 0-6 FC Zürich Frauen
Goals: 0-1 Leon 2, 0-2 Leon 32, 0-3 Franssi 63, 0-4 Leon 67, 0-5 Kuster 72(p), 0-6 Humm 90+1
Referee: Adámková (CZE)
12/10/16, Stadion Letzigrund, Zurich
FC Zürich Frauen 3-0 SK Sturm Graz Damen
Goals: 1-0 Humm 21, 2-0 Humm 28, 3-0 Deplazes 74
Referee: Lehtovaara (FIN)
Aggregate: 9-0; FC Zürich Frauen qualify.

05/10/16, Haugesund, Haugesund
Avaldsnes Idrettslag 2-5 Olympique Lyonnais
Goals: 0-1 Kumagai 7(p), 0-2 Le Sommer 20, 1-2 Thorsnes 23, 1-3 Abily 48, 2-3 Hansen 52, 2-4 Abily 62, 2-5 Ada Hegerberg 86
Referee: Albon (ROU)
12/10/16, Stade de Lyon, Decines
Olympique Lyonnais 5-0 Avaldsnes Idrettslag
Goals: 1-0 Renard 3, 2-0 Marozsán 41, 3-0 D Cascarino 59, 4-0 Le Sommer 64, 5-0 Le Sommer 74
Referee: Kováčová (SVK)
Aggregate: 10-2; Olympique Lyonnais qualify.

05/10/16, Stamford Bridge, London
Chelsea LFC 0-3 VfL Wolfsburg
Goals: 0-1 Jakabfi 12, 0-2 Jakabfi 39, 0-3 Jakabfi 54
Referee: Mitsi (GRE)
12/10/16, AOK stadium, Wolfsburg
VfL Wolfsburg 1-1 Chelsea LFC
Goals: 0-1 Aluko 43, 1-1 Gunnarsdóttir 80
Referee: Vitulano (ITA)
Aggregate: 4-1; VfL Wolfsburg qualify.

05/10/16, FC Twente Stadion, Enschede
FC Twente '65 2-0 AC Sparta Praha
Goals: 1-0 Waldus 79, 2-0 Roord 90+1
Referee: Huerta De Aza (ESP)
12/10/16, Generali Arena, Prague
AC Sparta Praha 1-3 FC Twente '65
Goals: 0-1 Odehnalová 28(og), 1-1 Stašková 34, 1-2 R Jansen 82, 1-3 Roord 89
Referee: Andersson (SWE)
Aggregate: 1-5; FC Twente '65 qualify.

05/10/16, Paphiakos Stadium, Paphos
Apollon Ladies FC 1-1 SK Slavia Praha
Goals: 1-0 Alborghetti 53(p), 1-1 Pincová 90+5
Referee: Nurmustafina (KAZ)
12/10/16, Eden Arena, Prague
SK Slavia Praha 3-2 Apollon Ladies FC
Goals: 0-1 Witteman 10, 0-2 Witteman 14, 1-2 Divišová 19, 2-2 Svitková 41, 3-2 Svitková 82
Referee: Peeters (NED)
Aggregate: 4-3; SK Slavia Praha qualify.

05/10/16, Estadio de San Mamés, Bilbao
Athletic Club 2-1 Fortuna Hjørring
Goals: 1-0 Corres 34, 1-1 Smidt 71, 2-1 Oroz 83
Referee: Dorcioman (ROU)
12/10/16, Hjørring Stadion, Hjorring
Fortuna Hjørring 3-1 Athletic Club (aet)
Goals: 1-0 Damjanović 49, 1-1 Erika Vázquez 69, 2-1 Larsen 84, 3-1 Tamires 119
Referee: Kulcsár (HUN)
Aggregate: 4-3; Fortuna Hjørring qualify.

05/10/16, Easter Road Stadium, Edinburgh
Hibernian Ladies FC 0-6 FC Bayern München
Goals: 0-1 Van der Gragt 6, 0-2 Miedema 26, 0-3 Leupolz 38, 0-4 Miedema 57, 0-5 Leupolz 63, 0-6 Behringer 67(p)
Referee: Staubli (SUI)
12/10/16, an der Grünwalderstrasse, Munich
FC Bayern München 4-1 Hibernian Ladies FC
Goals: 1-0 Gerhardt 6, 2-0 Evans 33, 3-0 Gerhardt 38, 3-1 Harrison 39, 4-1 Miedema 72
Referee: Sørø (NOR)
Aggregate: 10-1; FC Bayern München qualify.

05/10/16, NV Arena, St Polten
SKN St Pölten Frauen 0-2 Brøndby IF
Goals: 0-1 N Sørensen 21, 0-2 N Sørensen 63
Referee: Larsson (SWE)
12/10/16, Brøndby, Brondby
Brøndby IF 2-2 SKN St Pölten Frauen
Goals: 0-1 Vágó 55, 1-1 Boye Sørensen 61, 1-2 Pinther 82, 2-2 N Sørensen 88
Referee: Gaál (HUN)
Aggregate: 4-2; Brøndby IF qualify.

Action from the round of 32 as Wolfsburg's Nilla Fischer challenges for an aerial ball with Chelsea's Millie Bright and Niamh Fahey

06/10/16, FC Minsk, Minsk
ZFK Minsk 0-3 FC Barcelona
Goals: 0-1 Hermoso 5, 0-2 Torrejón 32, 0-3 Hermoso 90+1
Referee: Guillemin (FRA)
12/10/16, Mini Estadi, Barcelona
FC Barcelona 2-1 ZFK Minsk
Goals: 0-1 Ogbiagbevha 51, 1-1 Hermoso 61(p), 2-1 Andressa Alves 75
Referee: Milkova (BUL)
Aggregate: 5-1; FC Barcelona qualify.

06/10/16, Åråsen, Lillestrom
LSK Kvinner FK 3-1 Paris Saint-Germain
Goals: 0-1 Paredes 35, 1-1 Haavi 67, 2-1 Mykjåland 82, 3-1 Spord 88
Referee: Monzul (UKR)
13/10/16, Charlety, Paris
Paris Saint-Germain 4-1 LSK Kvinner FK
Goals: 1-0 Verónica Boquete 4(p), 2-0 Cristiane 20, 3-0 Cristiane 49, 4-0 Cristiane 74, 4-1 Berget 90+2
Referee: Persson (SWE)
Aggregate: 5-4; Paris Saint-Germain qualify.

06/10/16, Tunavallen, Eskilstuna
Eskilstuna United DFF 1-0 Glasgow City FC
Goal: 1-0 Larsson 52
Referee: Fernandes Morais (LUX)
13/10/16, Excelsior Stadium, Airdrie
Glasgow City FC 1-2 Eskilstuna United DFF
Goals: 0-1 Schough 7, 1-1 Crilly 46, 1-2 Schough 58
Referee: Frappart (FRA)
Aggregate: 1-3; Eskilstuna United DFF qualify.

06/10/16, Mini-Stadium, Manchester
Manchester City Women's FC 2-0 WFC Zvezda-2005
Goals: 1-0 J Scott 34, 2-0 Bronze 90+3
Referee: Mularczyk (POL)
12/10/16, Zvezda, Perm
WFC Zvezda-2005 0-4 Manchester City Women's FC
Goals: 0-1 Beattie 23, 0-2 Bronze 32, 0-3 Beattie 52, 0-4 Christiansen 74
Referee: Hussein (GER)
Aggregate: 0-6; Manchester City Women's FC qualify.

Round of 16

09/11/16, an der Grünwalderstrasse, Munich
FC Bayern München 4-0 FC Rossiyanka
Goals: 1-0 Evans 41, 2-0 Rolser 45+2, 3-0 Miedema 52, 4-0 Miedema 75
Referee: Bastos (POR)
17/11/16, Rodina, Khimki
FC Rossiyanka 0-4 FC Bayern München
Goals: 0-1 Miedema 42, 0-2 Miedema 52, 0-3 Däbritz 72, 0-4 Holstad Berge 90+2
Referee: Frappart (FRA)
Aggregate: 0-8; FC Bayern München qualify.

09/11/16, Stade de Lyon, Decines
Olympique Lyonnais 8-0 FC Zürich Frauen
Goals: 1-0 Le Sommer 22, 2-0 M'Bock Bathy 26, 3-0 Ada Hegerberg 29, 4-0 Ada Hegerberg 30, 5-0 Le Sommer 35, 6-0 Ada Hegerberg 41, 7-0 Tarrieu 90, 8-0 Lavogez 90+3
Referee: Azzopardi (MLT)
16/11/16, Stadion Letzigrund, Zurich
FC Zürich Frauen 0-9 Olympique Lyonnais
Goals: 0-1 Abily 18, 0-2 Seger 20, 0-3 Abily 39, 0-4 Kumagai 42, 0-5 Lavogez 62, 0-6 Lavogez 63, 0-7 Tarrieu 64, 0-8 Renard 80, 0-9 Petit 88
Referee: Sørø (NOR)
Aggregate: 0-17; Olympique Lyonnais qualify.

Jill Scott of Manchester City (left) takes on Zvezda 2005's Anastasia Akimova

09/11/16, Mini Estadi, Barcelona
FC Barcelona 1-0 FC Twente '65
Goal: 1-0 Hermoso 10
Referee: Steinhaus (GER)
16/11/16, FC Twente Stadion, Enschede
FC Twente '65 0-4 FC Barcelona
Goals: 0-1 Torrejón 18, 0-2 Andressa Alves 37, 0-3 Latorre 79, 0-4 Nguessan 86
Referee: Mitsi (GRE)
Aggregate: 0-5; FC Barcelona qualify.

09/11/16, Mini-Stadium, Manchester
Manchester City Women's FC 1-0 Brøndby IF
Goal: 1-0 Walsh 74
Referee: Albon (ROU)
16/11/16, Brøndby, Brondby
Brøndby IF 1-1 Manchester City Women's FC
Goals: 0-1 Duggan 65, 1-1 N Christiansen 67
Referee: Vitulano (ITA)
Aggregate: 1-2; Manchester City Women's FC qualify.

09/11/16, Mario Rigamonti, Brescia
Brescia Femminile 0-1 Fortuna Hjørring
Goal: 0-1 Tamires 42
Referee: Larsson (SWE)
16/11/16, Hjørring Stadion, Hjorring
Fortuna Hjørring 3-1 Brescia Femminile
Goals: 1-0 Olar 36, 2-0 Larsen 49, 3-0 Larsen 67, 3-1 Manieri 81
Referee: Monzul (UKR)
Aggregate: 4-1; Fortuna Hjørring qualify.

10/11/16, BIIK Stadium, Shymkent
WFC BIIK-Kazygurt 0-3 Paris Saint-Germain
Goals: 0-1 Verónica Boquete 17, 0-2 Paredes 45+1, 0-3 Paredes 59
Referee: Zadinová (CZE)
17/11/16, Charlety, Paris
Paris Saint-Germain 4-1 WFC BIIK-Kazygurt
Goals: 1-0 Cruz Traña 43, 2-0 Sarr 45+1, 2-1 Adule 67, 3-1 Delie 70, 4-1 Sarr 79
Referee: Clark (SCO)
Aggregate: 7-1; Paris Saint-Germain qualify.

10/11/16, FK Viktoria Žižkov, Prague
SK Slavia Praha 1-3 FC Rosengård
Goals: 0-1 Masar 33, 0-2 Nilsson 36, 0-3 Enganamouit 44(p), 1-3 Svitková 90+2
Referee: Lehtovaara (FIN)
16/11/16, Malmö Idrottsplats, Malmo
FC Rosengård 3-0 SK Slavia Praha
Goals: 1-0 Masar 3, 2-0 Enganamouit 18, 3-0 Enganamouit 19
Referee: Pustovoitova (RUS)
Aggregate: 6-1; FC Rosengård qualify.

Leila Ouahabi is lifted in celebration by Marta Unzué after scoring for Barcelona against Rosengård

10/11/16, Tunavallen, Eskilstuna
Eskilstuna United DFF 1-5 VfL Wolfsburg
Goals: 0-1 Jakabfi 5, 0-2 Jakabfi 17, 1-2 Banušić 31, 1-3 Jakabfi 52, 1-4 Jakabfi 63, 1-5 Popp 76
Referee: Dorcioman (ROU)
17/11/16, AOK stadium, Wolfsburg
VfL Wolfsburg 3-0 Eskilstuna United DFF
Goals: 1-0 Dickenmann 38, 2-0 Jakabfi 62, 3-0 Bernauer 85
Referee: Staubli (SUI)
Aggregate: 8-1; VfL Wolfsburg qualify.

Quarter-finals

22/03/17, Malmö Idrottsplats, Malmo
FC Rosengård 0-1 FC Barcelona
Goal: 0-1 Ouahabi 45+2
Referee: Frappart (FRA)
29/03/17, Mini Estadi, Barcelona
FC Barcelona 2-0 FC Rosengård
Goals: 1-0 Hermoso 52, 2-0 Mariona 90+4
Referee: Monzul (UKR)
Aggregate: 3-0; FC Barcelona qualify.

23/03/17, Hjørring Stadion, Hjorring
Fortuna Hjørring 0-1 Manchester City Women's FC
Goal: 0-1 Lloyd 36
Referee: Hussein (GER)
30/03/17, Mini-Stadium, Manchester
Manchester City Women's FC 1-0 Fortuna Hjørring
Goal: 1-0 Bronze 41
Referee: Pustovoitova (RUS)
Aggregate: 2-0; Manchester City Women's FC qualify.

23/03/17, an der Grünwalderstrasse, Munich
FC Bayern München 1-0 Paris Saint-Germain
Goal: 1-0 Miedema 72
Referee: Larsson (SWE)
29/03/17, Parc des Princes, Paris
Paris Saint-Germain 4-0 FC Bayern München
Goals: 1-0 Delie 4, 2-0 Cristiane 12, 3-0 Cruz Traña 42, 4-0 Cristiane 52
Referee: Vitulano (ITA)
Aggregate: 4-1; Paris Saint-Germain qualify.

23/03/17, AOK stadium, Wolfsburg
VfL Wolfsburg 0-2 Olympique Lyonnais
Goals: 0-1 Abily 62, 0-2 Marozsán 74
Referee: Adámková (CZE)
29/03/17, Stade de Lyon, Décines
Olympique Lyonnais 0-1 VfL Wolfsburg
Goal: 0-1 Graham Hansen 82(p)
Referee: Mularczyk (POL)
Aggregate: 2-1; Olympique Lyonnais qualify.

Semi-finals

22/04/17, Mini-Stadium, Manchester
Manchester City Women's FC 1-3 Olympique Lyonnais
Goals: 0-1 Kumagai 2(p), 1-1 Asllani 10, 1-2 Marozsán 16, 1-3 Le Sommer 68
Referee: Kulcsár (HUN)
29/04/17, Stade de Lyon, Decines
Olympique Lyonnais 0-1 Manchester City Women's FC
Goal: 0-1 Lloyd 57
Referee: Staubli (SUI)
Aggregate: 3-2; Olympique Lyonnais qualify.

Paris Saint-Germain goalkeeper Katarzyna Kiedrzynek is beaten by her opposite number Sarah Bouhaddi's decisive spot kick for Lyon in the Cardiff final

22/04/17, Mini Estadi, Barcelona
FC Barcelona 1-3 Paris Saint-Germain
Goals: 0-1 Delie 26, 0-2 Cristiane 36, 0-3 Cruz Traña 53, 1-3 Latorre 89
Referee: Albon (ROU)
29/04/17, Parc des Princes, Paris
Paris Saint-Germain 2-0 FC Barcelona
Goals: 1-0 Delannoy 55(p), 2-0 Diéguez 61(og)
Referee: Adámková (CZE)
Aggregate: 5-1; Paris Saint-Germain qualify.

Final

01/06/17, Cardiff City Stadium, Cardiff (att: 22,433)
Olympique Lyonnais 0-0 Paris Saint-Germain (aet; 7-6 on pens)
Referee: Steinhaus (GER)
Lyon: Bouhaddi, Renard, Kumagai, Majri, Le Sommer, Marozsán, Ada Hegerberg (Bremer 60), Buchanan, Abily, M'Bock Bathy, Morgan (Thomis 23; Lavogez 17). Coach: Gérard Prêcheur (FRA)
Paris: Kiedrzynek, Delannoy, Diallo (Verónica Boquete 57), Cristiane, Lawrence, Paredes, Perisset (Morroni 90+4), Delie, Formiga, Geyoro, Cruz Traña (Georges 80). Coach: Patrice Lair (FRA)
Yellow cards: Diallo 55 (Paris), Kumagai 66 (Lyon), Georges 81 (Paris), Morroni 115 (Paris)

Top goalscorers

Vivianne Miedema

Zsanett Jakabfi

8	Vivianne Miedema (Bayern) Zsanett Jakabfi (Wolfsburg)
6	Cristiane (Paris) Eugénie Le Sommer (Lyon)
5	Jennifer Hermoso (Barcelona) Camille Abily (Lyon)
4	Ada Hegerberg (Lyon)

Penalty shoot-outs decide semi-final and final

Record sixth title from ten tournaments

Spain finish runners-up for fourth time

Familiar routine for Germany

A new system for penalty shoot-outs was trialled for the first time at the 2017 UEFA European Women's Under-17 Championship in the Czech Republic - the tenth staging of the event – but there was nothing remotely unfamiliar about the outcome.

As in 2015/16, and indeed 2013/14, Germany overcame Spain in the final on spot kicks – having also prevailed by the same method against Norway in the semi-finals – to lift the trophy and thus maintain their perfect record of six wins in six Women's U17 final appearances, with four of those victories having come against three-time winners Spain.

There was a debut for Malta in the qualifying competition, but no major surprises as such on the road to the Czech Republic, with all of the eight teams that proceeded to the finals – Germany, Spain, France, the Netherlands, Norway, England, the Republic of Ireland and the hosts – having already competed in previous Women's U17 tournaments.

A competition-record attendance of 10,219 watched on as France pipped the Czech Republic 2-1 on the opening day in Plzen, with Germany later seeing off Spain with improbable ease, 4-1 in Prestice. The holders then beat France 2-1 and the hosts 5-1 to top the section, with Spain overcoming the Czechs 5-1 and then getting the draw they needed against Les Bleues (1-1) to qualify as runners-up on goal difference.

The Netherlands progressed from Group B with a game to spare after defeating Norway 3-1 and England 2-1. England had cruised past Ireland, wining 5-1, but Norway also beat the Irish, 1-0 with a late winner, to set up a final-day showdown, in which they downed England 2-0 to reach the last four.

Germany are Women's Under-17 champions of Europe for the sixth time

Norway then looked on course for a first ever appearance in the final as they led Germany at half-time in their semi-final in Pribram through Olaug Tvedten's early strike, but Sydney Lohmann's leveller forced penalties. Under a new shoot-out system, teams took turns to go first in each 'round' of kicks. That appeared to unsettle Germany, who missed their first three efforts to trail 2-0. But the tide soon turned, with Norway then failing to find the net three times in succession while Germany, in contrast, became flawless, defender Andrea Brunner converting the decisive kick in sudden death.

It was a more straightforward passage to the final for Spain as two first-half goals from Carla Piqueras Bautista (a penalty) and Claudia Pina took them past the Netherlands and into a fourth straight final. Yet, as in the previous season's showpiece between Germany and Spain in Borisov, the 80 minutes ended goalless, leading straight to penalties. Now it was Spain's turn to miss their first three kicks, and Germany did not let them off the hook, tournament top scorer (with three goals) Melissa Kössler slotting home her effort to secure a 3-1 shoot-out triumph for the holders.

Qualifying round

Group 1

20-25/09/16 Shefayim, Ramat Gan

Slovakia 1-6 Denmark, Switzerland 1-0 Israel, Switzerland 3-0 Slovakia, Denmark 2-0 Israel, Denmark 4-1 Switzerland, Israel 0-1 Slovakia

	Pld	W	D	L	F	A	Pts
1 Denmark	3	3	0	0	12	2	9
2 Switzerland	3	2	0	1	5	4	6
3 Slovakia	3	1	0	2	2	9	3
4 Israel	3	0	0	3	0	4	0

Group 2

06-11/10/16 Patras, Nafpaktos

Sweden 3-0 Malta, Montenegro 0-4 Greece, Sweden 2-1 Montenegro, Greece 2-0 Malta, Greece 1-1 Sweden, Malta 2-1 Montenegro

	Pld	W	D	L	F	A	Pts
1 Greece	3	2	1	0	7	1	7
2 Sweden	3	2	1	0	6	2	7
3 Malta	3	1	0	2	2	6	3
4 Montenegro	3	0	0	3	2	8	0

Group 3

08-13/10/16 Szombathely, Buk

Poland 7-0 Estonia, Azerbaijan 0-3 Hungary, Poland 4-0 Azerbaijan, Hungary 3-1 Estonia, Hungary 2-2 Poland, Estonia 0-1 Azerbaijan

	Pld	W	D	L	F	A	Pts
1 Poland	3	2	1	0	13	2	7
2 Hungary	3	2	1	0	8	3	7
3 Azerbaijan	3	1	0	2	1	7	3
4 Estonia	3	0	0	3	1	11	0

Group 4

21-26/10/16 Chisinau, Orhei

Norway 6-0 Moldova, Bulgaria 0-11 Netherlands, Norway 4-0 Bulgaria, Netherlands 13-0 Moldova, Moldova 0-1 Bulgaria, Netherlands 0-2 Norway

	Pld	W	D	L	F	A	Pts
1 Norway	3	3	0	0	12	0	9
2 Netherlands	3	2	0	1	24	2	6
3 Bulgaria	3	1	0	2	1	15	3
4 Moldova	3	0	0	3	0	20	0

Group 5

26-31/10/16 Cruz Quebrada, Mafra

Italy 8-0 Georgia, Portugal 1-1 Finland, Finland 8-0 Georgia, Italy 1-1 Portugal, Finland 0-0 Italy, Georgia 0-7 Portugal

	Pld	W	D	L	F	A	Pts
1 Portugal	3	1	2	0	9	2	5
2 Italy	3	1	2	0	9	1	5
3 Finland	3	1	2	0	9	1	5
4 Georgia	3	0	0	3	0	23	0

Group 6

10-15/10/16 Edinburgh

France 17-0 Kazakhstan, Croatia 0-4 Scotland, France 4-0 Croatia, Scotland 8-0 Kazakhstan, Kazakhstan 0-3 Croatia, Scotland 0-4 France

Joëlle Smits of the Netherlands takes aim against Moldova

	Pld	W	D	L	F	A	Pts
1 France	3	3	0	0	25	0	9
2 Scotland	3	2	0	1	12	4	6
3 Croatia	3	1	0	2	3	8	3
4 Kazakhstan	3	0	0	3	0	28	0

Group 7

02-07/10/16 Riga, Ogre

Wales 2-1 Turkey, Germany 6-0 Latvia, Germany 6-0 Wales, Turkey 2-1 Latvia, Turkey 0-4 Germany, Latvia 1-1 Wales

	Pld	W	D	L	F	A	Pts
1 Germany	3	3	0	0	16	0	9
2 Wales	3	1	1	1	3	8	4
3 Turkey	3	1	0	2	3	7	3
4 Latvia	3	0	1	2	2	9	1

Group 8

24-29/10/16 Marijampole, Kaunas

Slovenia 0-1 Russia, England 14-0 Lithuania, England 0-1 Slovenia, Russia 2-0 Lithuania, Russia 0-1 England, Lithuania 0-3 Slovenia

	Pld	W	D	L	F	A	Pts
1 England	3	2	0	1	15	1	6
2 Slovenia	3	2	0	1	4	1	6
3 Russia	3	2	0	1	3	1	6
4 Lithuania	3	0	0	3	0	19	0

Group 9

26/09-01/10/16 Pecinci, Stara Pazova

Belgium 4-0 Ukraine, Romania 0-1 Serbia, Belgium 0-1 Romania, Serbia 1-1 Ukraine, Serbia 0-1 Belgium, Ukraine 2-1 Romania

	Pld	W	D	L	F	A	Pts
1 Belgium	3	2	0	1	5	1	6
2 Serbia	3	1	1	1	2	2	4
3 Ukraine	3	1	1	1	3	6	4
4 Romania	3	1	0	2	2	3	3

Group 10

26-31/10/16 Cork, Cobh

Belarus 0-4 Iceland, Republic of Ireland 6-0 Faroe Islands, Iceland 4-0 Faroe Islands, Republic of Ireland 2-0 Belarus, Iceland 1-4 Republic of Ireland, Faroe Islands 2-1 Belarus

	Pld	W	D	L	F	A	Pts
1 Republic of Ireland	3	3	0	0	12	1	9
2 Iceland	3	2	0	1	9	4	6
3 Faroe Islands	3	1	0	2	2	11	3
4 Belarus	3	0	0	3	1	8	0

Group 11

30/09-05/10/16 Skopje

Austria 7-0 FYR Macedonia, Bosnia & Herzegovina 4-0 Northern Ireland, Austria 4-1 Bosnia & Herzegovina, Northern Ireland 4-0 FYR Macedonia, Northern Ireland 0-4 Austria, FYR Macedonia 0-4 Bosnia & Herzegovina

	Pld	W	D	L	F	A	Pts
1 Austria	3	3	0	0	15	1	9
2 Bosnia & Herzegovina	3	2	0	1	9	4	6
3 Northern Ireland	3	1	0	2	4	8	3
4 FYR Macedonia	3	0	0	3	0	15	0

Elite round

Group 1

27/03-01/04/17 Veen, Zaltbommel

Austria 0-2 Switzerland, Slovenia 0-3 Netherlands, Austria 0-1 Slovenia, Netherlands 1-1 Switzerland, Netherlands 2-1 Austria, Switzerland 1-2 Slovenia

	Pld	W	D	L	F	A	Pts
1 Netherlands	3	2	1	0	6	2	7
2 Slovenia	3	2	0	1	3	4	6
3 Switzerland	3	1	1	1	4	3	4
4 Austria	3	0	0	3	1	5	0

Group 2

20-25/03/17 Sarajevo, Kakanj

Norway 8-1 Wales, Bosnia & Herzegovina 1-2 Denmark, Norway 2-1 Bosnia & Herzegovina, Denmark 2-0 Wales, Denmark 1-6 Norway, Wales 1-0 Bosnia & Herzegovina

	Pld	W	D	L	F	A	Pts
1 Norway	3	3	0	0	16	3	9
2 Denmark	3	2	0	1	5	7	6
3 Wales	3	1	0	2	2	10	3
4 Bosnia & Herzegovina	3	0	0	3	2	5	0

Group 3

25-30/03/17 Cannock, Telford, Burton-on-Trent

Germany 3-1 Italy, England 2-0 Poland, Germany 1-2 England, Poland 0-2 Italy, Poland 0-4 Germany, Italy 0-0 England

	Pld	W	D	L	F	A	Pts
1 England	3	2	1	0	4	1	7
2 Germany	3	2	0	1	8	3	6
3 Italy	3	1	1	1	3	3	4
4 Poland	3	0	0	3	0	8	0

Group 4

13-18/03/17 Stara Pazova, Belgrade

Republic of Ireland 1-0 Serbia, Scotland 1-1 Hungary, Republic of Ireland 0-0 Scotland, Hungary 1-0 Serbia, Hungary 0-1 Republic of Ireland, Serbia 1-2 Scotland

	Pld	W	D	L	F	A	Pts
1 Republic of Ireland	3	2	1	0	2	0	7
2 Scotland	3	1	2	0	3	2	5
3 Hungary	3	1	1	1	2	2	4
4 Serbia	3	0	0	3	1	4	0

Holders Spain lead way to Ljubljana

Spotless records for Kazakhstan and Russia

France and Georgia reach play-offs

Seven secure passage to Slovenia

UEFA Futsal EURO 2018 in Slovenia will mark the end of an era as the tournament will in future be played every four years, rather than two, expanding from 12 to 16 teams as part of a package of reforms introducing youth and women's European competitions to the five-a-side sport.

For now, though, the European futsal focus is on Ljubljana, where the 2018 finals will be staged from 30 January to 10 February. Eight of the 12 contenders were decided in April 2017, with hosts Slovenia being joined by main round group winners Italy, Azerbaijan, Ukraine, Portugal, Spain (the holders), Kazakhstan and Russia, all of whom were also present at the 2016 finals in Belgrade.

The path remained open, however, for a couple of tournament debutants as France and Georgia reached the play-offs for the first time. They joined Hungary, Croatia, Romania, Serbia, Poland and the Czech Republic, with the two-legged ties in September determining the last four finalists.

France and Georgia both began the competition in the preliminary round, coming through those ties in January and February 2017 alongside Moldova, Latvia, Albania, Denmark and Montenegro.

The heavyweight contenders entered in the main round, from which only the seven group winners qualified automatically. Italy, the 2014 champions, and Russia, the 2016 runners-up, both advanced with a game to spare, and it was in Russia's group that France beat Turkey and Slovakia to make the play-offs, with Georgia holding the Azzurri 2-2 in their final fixture to finish ahead of Belarus and the Netherlands.

Russia went on to record three wins and ten unanswered goals, a feat bettered by Kazakhstan, who, having reached the 2016 semis on their finals debut, now made it to Slovenia by scoring 11 and conceding none. That included a 3-0 last-day defeat of the Czech Republic, whose crucial result had been the opening 5-4 win against Denmark, secured with a goal three seconds from time.

Emulating Russia and Kazakhstan with maximum points were Azerbaijan, Ukraine and Portugal but not Spain, who surprisingly drew their last game 1-1 with Poland. As Serbia overcame Moldova 7-3 to come second in that group, Poland's point was precious as it enabled them to book into the play-offs as the best third-placed team by a single goal ahead of Finland.

Luck was not on Finland's side as they conceded with four seconds left to draw 5-5 with Romania. They then lost 5-1 to Portugal, and their 4-3 win against Latvia left them not only a goal behind Poland but also in arrears of group runners-up Romania by the same narrow margin. Croatia also just missed out on automatic qualification as they conceded a late winning goal to Ukraine when a draw would have ensured a direct passage across the border to Slovenia.

Holders Spain topped their main round group to qualify for UEFA Futsal EURO 2018

Preliminary round

Group A

24-27/01/17 Tbilisi
Switzerland 6-2 Scotland, Georgia 3-0 Israel, Israel 0-3 Switzerland, Georgia 11-0 Scotland, Scotland 2-6 Israel, Switzerland 3-6 Georgia

	Pld	W	D	L	F	A	Pts
1 Georgia	3	3	0	0	20	3	9
2 Switzerland	3	2	0	1	12	8	6
3 Israel	3	1	0	2	6	8	3
4 Scotland	3	0	0	3	4	23	0

Group B

26-29/01/17 Hereford
Greece 3-2 San Marino, Wales 1-6 Moldova, Moldova 4-0 Greece, Wales 8-1 San Marino, San Marino 0-6 Moldova, Greece 2-2 Wales

	Pld	W	D	L	F	A	Pts
1 Moldova	3	3	0	0	16	1	9
2 Wales	3	1	1	1	11	9	4
3 Greece	3	1	1	1	5	8	4
4 San Marino	3	0	0	3	3	17	0

Group C

26-29/01/17 Jelgava
Armenia 5-3 Germany, Latvia 4-2 Estonia, Estonia 1-5 Armenia, Latvia 3-3 Germany, Germany 5-4 Estonia, Armenia 1-4 Latvia

	Pld	W	D	L	F	A	Pts
1 Latvia	3	2	1	0	11	6	7
2 Armenia	3	2	0	1	11	8	6
3 Germany	3	1	1	1	11	12	4
4 Estonia	3	0	0	3	7	14	0

Group D

24-27/01/17 Varna
England 6-1 Malta, Bulgaria 1-7 Albania, Albania 5-1 England, Bulgaria 6-1 Malta, Malta 2-3 Albania, England 4-1 Bulgaria

	Pld	W	D	L	F	A	Pts
1 Albania	3	3	0	0	15	4	9
2 England	3	2	0	1	11	7	6
3 Bulgaria	3	1	0	2	8	12	3
4 Malta	3	0	0	3	4	15	0

Group E

30/01-02/02/17 Nicosia
Norway 1-5 Kosovo, Cyprus 3-2 Denmark, Denmark 2-1 Norway, Cyprus 1-3 Kosovo, Kosovo 1-2 Denmark, Norway 4-4 Cyprus

	Pld	W	D	L	F	A	Pts
1 Denmark	3	2	0	1	6	5	6
2 Kosovo	3	2	0	1	9	4	6
3 Cyprus	3	1	1	1	8	9	4
4 Norway	3	0	1	2	6	11	1

Group F

27-29/01/17 Vilnius
Lithuania 5-1 Andorra, Andorra 0-5 France, France 3-1 Lithuania

	Pld	W	D	L	F	A	Pts
1 France	2	2	0	0	8	1	6
2 Lithuania	2	1	0	1	6	4	3
3 Andorra	2	0	0	2	1	10	0

Action from the preliminary round fixture between Gibraltar (in red) and Montenegro

Group G

28-30/01/17 Gibraltar
Gibraltar 1-8 Montenegro, Montenegro 11-4 Sweden, Sweden 5-1 Gibraltar

	Pld	W	D	L	F	A	Pts
1 Montenegro	2	2	0	0	19	5	6
2 Sweden	2	1	0	1	9	12	3
3 Gibraltar	2	0	0	2	2	13	0

Main round

Group A

08-11/04/17 Tbilisi
Italy 2-1 Belarus, Georgia 1-1 Netherlands, Netherlands 2-4 Italy, Georgia 1-1 Belarus, Belarus 3-3 Netherlands, Italy 2-2 Georgia

	Pld	W	D	L	F	A	Pts
1 Italy	3	2	1	0	8	5	7
2 Georgia	3	0	3	0	4	4	3
3 Belarus	3	0	2	1	5	6	2
4 Netherlands	3	0	2	1	6	8	2

Group B

08-11/04/17 Baku
Hungary 4-3 Albania, Azerbaijan 5-4 Bosnia & Herzegovina, Bosnia & Herzegovina 2-2 Hungary, Azerbaijan 5-0 Albania, Albania 6-6 Bosnia & Herzegovina, Hungary 1-6 Azerbaijan

	Pld	W	D	L	F	A	Pts
1 Azerbaijan	3	3	0	0	16	5	9
2 Hungary	3	1	1	1	7	11	4
3 Bosnia & Herzegovina	3	0	2	1	12	13	2
4 Albania	3	0	1	2	9	15	1

Ukraine pipped Croatia to top spot in Group C

Group C

08-11/04/17 Kyiv
Croatia 4-0 Montenegro, Ukraine 1-0 Belgium, Belgium 1-6 Croatia, Ukraine 4-2 Montenegro, Montenegro 1-2 Belgium, Croatia 1-2 Ukraine

	Pld	W	D	L	F	A	Pts
1 Ukraine	3	3	0	0	7	3	9
2 Croatia	3	2	0	1	11	3	6
3 Belgium	3	1	0	2	3	8	3
4 Montenegro	3	0	0	3	3	10	0

Group D

08-11/04/17 Calarasi
Portugal 2-1 Latvia, Romania 5-5 Finland, Finland 1-5 Portugal, Romania 3-1 Latvia, Latvia 3-4 Finland, Portugal 4-0 Romania

	Pld	W	D	L	F	A	Pts
1 Portugal	3	3	0	0	11	2	9
2 Romania	3	1	1	1	8	10	4
3 Finland	3	1	1	1	10	13	4
4 Latvia	3	0	0	3	5	9	0

Group E

08-11/04/17 Elblag
Spain 7-0 Moldova, Poland 0-4 Serbia, Serbia 0-6 Spain, Poland 4-2 Moldova, Moldova 3-7 Serbia, Spain 1-1 Poland

	Pld	W	D	L	F	A	Pts
1 Spain	3	2	1	0	14	1	7
2 Serbia	3	2	0	1	11	9	6
3 Poland	3	1	1	1	5	7	4
4 Moldova	3	0	0	3	5	18	0

Group F

08-11/04/17 Almaty
Czech Republic 5-4 Denmark, Kazakhstan 3-0 FYR Macedonia, FYR Macedonia 3-7 Czech Republic, Kazakhstan 5-0 Denmark, Denmark 3-4 FYR Macedonia, Czech Republic 0-3 Kazakhstan

	Pld	W	D	L	F	A	Pts
1 Kazakhstan	3	3	0	0	11	0	9
2 Czech Republic	3	2	0	1	12	10	6
3 FYR Macedonia	3	1	0	2	7	13	3
4 Denmark	3	0	0	3	7	14	0

Group G

08-11/04/17 Kocaeli
Turkey 1-8 Slovakia, Russia 5-0 France, Turkey 1-5 France, Slovakia 0-1 Russia, France 4-1 Slovakia, Russia 4-0 Turkey

	Pld	W	D	L	F	A	Pts
1 Russia	3	3	0	0	10	0	9
2 France	3	2	0	1	9	7	6
3 Slovakia	3	1	0	2	9	6	3
4 Turkey	3	0	0	3	2	17	0

Play-offs

10-13 & 24-27 September, 2017
Czech Republic v Serbia
France v Croatia
Romania v Georgia
Hungary v Poland

Spanish club rout Sporting in one-sided final

Eight-year wait for trophy ends in Almaty

Hosts Kairat take bronze medal on penalties

Record fourth title for Inter

Inter FS, the illustrious futsal club from the Madrid satellite town of Torrejon de Ardoz, returned to the pinnacle of the European game by winning their fourth UEFA Futsal Cup, thus ending eight years of frustration that included a shock final defeat to Russian debutants Ugra Yugorsk 12 months earlier.

Victory in Kazakhstan took the Spanish side two wins clear of any other club in the competition's roll of honour, and they returned to the top place on the podium in commanding fashion, destroying Sporting Clube de Portugal by a record 7-0 margin in the final.

In addition to Inter and Sporting, holders Ugra qualified for the final four along with Kairat Almaty, the 2013 and 2015 champions, who were chosen to host the event, having also done so previously in 2011.

Sporting, the sole survivors from the main round – the second of the four tournament stages – went into their semi-final against Ugra as outsiders but never looked it once play got under way. The Portuguese team tore into their opponents and, despite a nervous finish, were full value for their 2-1 victory – Ugra's first European defeat in their 12th fixture.

Immediately afterwards came the much-anticipated showdown between Inter and Kairat, backed by a crowd of 10,238, the second highest in UEFA Futsal Cup history. A magical Ricardinho goal, one of two strikes in the game for the celebrated Portuguese winger, aided Inter to a comeback 3-2 success, with Ortiz turning in a deflected late winner to put Inter into their seventh final – another record.

Despite their disappointment, around 8,000 spectators were back at the Almaty Arena two days later to see Kairat tackle Ugra for bronze. The two teams played out a riveting spectacle, drawing 5-5 before the hosts delighted the majority of the audience by prevailing 3-2 on penalties.

While the first three games were closely contested, the final was anything but. Gadeia and Lolo put Inter 2-0 up at half-time and Rafael and Mario Rivillos extended the lead following clever free-kick moves. With Sporting throwing caution to the wind, Inter scored three times from their own half to seal the win. The final two goals came from Ricardinho, who thus became one of only a handful of players to have won the trophy twice, having previously helped Benfica beat Inter in Lisbon in 2010.

The competition is set to undergo a revamp in 2017/18 ahead of being renamed the UEFA Futsal Champions League in 2018/19. The three highest-ranked nations (Spain, Russia and Portugal) will receive two automatic entries for the first time, with Italy also entitled to two berths thanks to Inter's win – the eighth Spanish triumph in the event's 16 seasons.

Inter FS pose for the camera after their record-breaking fourth UEFA Futsal Cup triumph

Preliminary round

Group A

17-20/08/16 Yerevan

FC APOEL Nicosia 9-7 AFM Futsal Maniacs, ASUE 4-6 JB Futsal Gentofte, JB Futsal Gentofte 3-4 FC APOEL Nicosia, ASUE 3-2 AFM Futsal Maniacs, AFM Futsal Maniacs 2-8 JB Futsal Gentofte, FC APOEL Nicosia 7-7 ASUE

	Pld	W	D	L	F	A	Pts
1 FC APOEL Nicosia	3	2	1	0	20	17	7
2 JB Futsal Gentofte	3	2	0	1	17	10	6
3 ASUE	3	1	1	1	14	15	4
4 AFM Futsal Maniacs	3	0	0	3	11	20	0

Group B

16-19/08/16 Podgorica

Athina '90 3-2 SS Tre Fiori FC, Military Futsal Team 3-1 Blue Magic, Blue Magic 2-4 Athina '90, Military Futsal Team 5-0 SS Tre Fiori FC, SS Tre Fiori FC 3-3 Blue Magic, Athina '90 7-6 Military Futsal Team

	Pld	W	D	L	F	A	Pts
1 Athina '90	3	3	0	0	14	10	9
2 Military Futsal Team	3	2	0	1	14	8	6
3 Blue Magic	3	0	1	2	6	10	1
4 SS Tre Fiori FC	3	0	1	2	5	11	1

Group C

18-21/08/16 Ciorescu

Hamburg Panthers 6-2 Cardiff University, FCA Classic Chisinau 2-2 Sandefjord Fotball, Sandefjord Fotball 2-2 Hamburg Panthers, FCA Classic Chisinau 1-0 Cardiff University, Cardiff University 4-4 Sandefjord Fotball, Hamburg Panthers 4-2 FCA Classic Chisinau

	Pld	W	D	L	F	A	Pts
1 Hamburg Panthers	3	2	1	0	12	6	7
2 FCA Classic Chisinau	3	1	1	1	5	6	4
3 Sandefjord Fotball	3	0	3	0	8	8	3
4 Cardiff University	3	0	1	2	6	11	1

Group D

17-20/08/16 Panevezys

MNK Centar Sarajevo 9-3 Lynx FC, FC Baltija 6-3 Istanbul Üniversitesi SK, Istanbul Üniversitesi SK 3-9 MNK Centar Sarajevo, FC Baltija 4-2 Lynx FC, Lynx FC 4-8 Istanbul Üniversitesi SK, MNK Centar Sarajevo 4-1 FC Baltija

	Pld	W	D	L	F	A	Pts
1 MNK Centar Sarajevo	3	3	0	0	22	7	9
2 FC Baltija	3	2	0	1	11	9	6
3 Istanbul Üniversitesi SK	3	1	0	2	14	19	3
4 Lynx FC	3	0	0	3	9	21	0

Group E

17-20/08/16 Vienna

Amsterdam SV 11-2 FC Cosmos, Futsal Club Liberta Wien 1-2 IFK Göteborg Futsal, IFK Göteborg Futsal 3-2 Amsterdam SV, Futsal Club Liberta Wien 3-2 FC Cosmos, FC Cosmos 1-2 IFK Göteborg Futsal, Amsterdam SV 5-4 Futsal Club Liberta Wien

Győr players rejoice after scoring a decisive goal against Energy Lviv

	Pld	W	D	L	F	A	Pts
1 IFK Göteborg Futsal	3	3	0	0	7	4	9
2 Amsterdam SV	3	2	0	1	18	9	6
3 Futsal Club Liberta Wien	3	1	0	2	8	9	3
4 FC Cosmos	3	0	0	3	5	16	0

Group F

17-20/08/16 Ylivieska

Tbilisi State University 12-4 Wattcell Futsal Club, Sievi Futsal 7-3 Valletta FC, Valletta FC 0-6 Tbilisi State University, Sievi Futsal 13-3 Wattcell Futsal Club, Wattcell Futsal Club 3-9 Valletta FC, Tbilisi State University 5-4 Sievi Futsal

	Pld	W	D	L	F	A	Pts
1 Tbilisi State University	3	3	0	0	23	8	9
2 Sievi Futsal	3	2	0	1	24	11	6
3 Valletta FC	3	1	0	2	12	16	3
4 Wattcell Futsal Club	3	0	0	3	10	34	0

Group G

17-20/08/16 Maribor

Zdunska Wola 10-4 ALSS Munsbach, SD Brezje Maribor 4-2 KF Tirana, KF Tirana 3-8 Zdunska Wola, SD Brezje Maribor 14-2 ALSS Munsbach, ALSS Munsbach 5-1 KF Tirana, Zdunska Wola 4-6 SD Brezje Maribor

	Pld	W	D	L	F	A	Pts
1 SD Brezje Maribor	3	3	0	0	24	8	9
2 Zdunska Wola	3	2	0	1	22	13	6
3 ALSS Munsbach	3	1	0	2	11	25	3
4 KF Tirana	3	0	0	3	6	17	0

Group H

17-20/08/16 Andorra la Vella

Oxford City Lions Futsal Club 2-3 FC Feniks, FC Encamp 1-2 Tel Aviv Owl, Tel Aviv Owl 0-5 Oxford City Lions Futsal Club, FC Encamp 0-12 FC Feniks, FC Feniks 6-0 Tel Aviv Owl, Oxford City Lions Futsal Club 6-2 FC Encamp

	Pld	W	D	L	F	A	Pts
1 FC Feniks	3	3	0	0	21	2	9
2 Oxford City Lions Futsal Club	3	2	0	1	13	5	6
3 Tel Aviv Owl	3	1	0	2	2	12	3
4 FC Encamp	3	0	0	3	3	20	0

Main round

Group 1

12-15/10/16 Lviv

Győri ETO FC 4-0 SD Brezje Maribor, Energy Lviv 4-1 Kremlin Bicêtre United, Kremlin Bicêtre United 3-10 Győri ETO FC, Energy Lviv 2-6 SD Brezje Maribor, SD Brezje Maribor 1-2 Kremlin Bicêtre United, Győri ETO FC 3-2 Energy Lviv

	Pld	W	D	L	F	A	Pts
1 Győri ETO FC	3	3	0	0	17	5	9
2 SD Brezje Maribor	3	1	0	2	7	8	3
3 Energy Lviv	3	1	0	2	8	10	3
4 Kremlin Bicêtre United	3	1	0	2	6	15	3

Group 2

11-14/10/16 Skopje

Araz Naxçivan 7-1 Tbilisi State University , KMF Zelezarec Skopje 0-5 FC Feniks, FC Feniks 0-1 Araz Naxçivan, KMF Zelezarec Skopje 0-10 Tbilisi State University , Tbilisi State University 3-7 FC Feniks, Araz Naxçivan 15-4 KMF Zelezarec Skopje

	Pld	W	D	L	F	A	Pts
1 Araz Naxçivan	3	3	0	0	23	5	9
2 FC Feniks	3	2	0	1	12	4	6
3 Tbilisi State University	3	1	0	2	14	14	3
4 KMF Zelezarec Skopje	3	0	0	3	4	30	0

Group 3

12-15/10/16 Varna

FK Nikars Riga 5-2 IFK Göteborg Futsal, FC Grand Pro Varna 4-5 Hamburg Panthers, Hamburg Panthers 1-5 FK Nikars Riga, FC Grand Pro Varna 5-6 IFK Göteborg Futsal, IFK Göteborg Futsal 3-4 Hamburg Panthers, FK Nikars Riga 2-1 FC Grand Pro Varna

	Pld	W	D	L	F	A	Pts
1 FK Nikars Riga	3	3	0	0	12	4	9
2 Hamburg Panthers	3	2	0	1	10	12	6
3 IFK Göteborg Futsal	3	1	0	2	11	14	3
4 FC Grand Pro Varna	3	0	0	3	10	13	0

Group 4

12-15/10/16 Kragujevac

Lidselmash Lida 3-1 Athina '90, KMF Ekonomac Kragujevac 5-1 Nacional Zagreb FC, Nacional Zagreb FC 1-0 Lidselmash Lida, KMF Ekonomac Kragujevac 5-2 Athina '90, Athina '90 0-6 Nacional Zagreb FC, Lidselmash Lida 0-1 KMF Ekonomac Kragujevac

	Pld	W	D	L	F	A	Pts
1 KMF Ekonomac Kragujevac	3	3	0	0	11	3	9
2 Nacional Zagreb FC	3	2	0	1	8	5	6
3 Lidselmash Lida	3	1	0	2	3	3	3
4 Athina '90	3	0	0	3	3	14	0

Group 5

12-15/10/16 Foligno

Sporting Clube de Portugal 7-1 MNK Centar Sarajevo, Real Rieti 2-2 FP Halle-Gooik, FP Halle-Gooik 1-5 Sporting Clube de Portugal, Real Rieti 7-3 MNK Centar Sarajevo, MNK Centar Sarajevo 3-4 FP Halle-Gooik, Sporting Clube de Portugal 4-0 Real Rieti

	Pld	W	D	L	F	A	Pts
1 Sporting Clube de Portugal	3	3	0	0	16	2	9
2 Real Rieti	3	1	1	1	9	9	4
3 FP Halle-Gooik	3	1	1	1	7	10	4
4 MNK Centar Sarajevo	3	0	0	3	7	18	0

Group 6

11-14/10/16 Chrudim

City'US Târgu Mureş 3-3 FC APOEL Nicosia, FK EP Chrudim 4-1 Pinerola Bratislava, Pinerola Bratislava 3-8 City'US Târgu Mureş, FK EP Chrudim 7-0 FC APOEL Nicosia, FC APOEL Nicosia 6-5 Pinerola Bratislava, City'US Târgu Mureş 0-3 FK EP Chrudim

	Pld	W	D	L	F	A	Pts
1 FK EP Chrudim	3	3	0	0	14	1	9
2 City'US Târgu Mureş	3	1	1	1	11	9	4
3 FC APOEL Nicosia	3	1	1	1	9	15	4
4 Pinerola Bratislava	3	0	0	3	9	18	0

Elite round

Group A

24-27/11/16 Almaty

FK Nikars Riga 4-3 FC Feniks, Kairat Almaty 3-2 Real Rieti, Real Rieti 7-0 FK Nikars Riga, Kairat Almaty 6-0 FC Feniks, FC Feniks 3-6 Real Rieti, FK Nikars Riga 1-4 Kairat Almaty

	Pld	W	D	L	F	A	Pts
1 Kairat Almaty	3	3	0	0	13	3	9
2 Real Rieti	3	2	0	1	15	6	6
3 FK Nikars Riga	3	1	0	2	5	14	3
4 FC Feniks	3	0	0	3	6	16	0

Group B

23-26/11/16 Zagreb

Ugra Yugorsk 4-0 Hamburg Panthers, Nacional Zagreb FC 2-1 Araz Naxçivan, Araz Naxçivan 0-4 Ugra Yugorsk, Nacional Zagreb FC 11-1 Hamburg Panthers, Hamburg Panthers 1-5 Araz Naxçivan, Ugra Yugorsk 5-1 Nacional Zagreb FC

	Pld	W	D	L	F	A	Pts
1 Ugra Yugorsk	3	3	0	0	13	1	9
2 Nacional Zagreb FC	3	2	0	1	14	7	6
3 Araz Naxçivan	3	1	0	2	6	7	3
4 Hamburg Panthers	3	0	0	3	2	20	0

Pola of Inter (left) takes on Sporting's Caio during the final at the Almaty Arena

Group C

23-26/11/16 Maribor

Inter FS 2-0 FK EP Chrudim, SD Brezje Maribor 6-2 KMF Ekonomac Kragujevac, KMF Ekonomac Kragujevac 1-8 Inter FS, SD Brezje Maribor 1-4 FK EP Chrudim, FK EP Chrudim 0-1 KMF Ekonomac Kragujevac, Inter FS 3-1 SD Brezje Maribor

	Pld	W	D	L	F	A	Pts
1 Inter FS	3	3	0	0	13	2	9
2 FK EP Chrudim	3	1	0	2	4	4	3
3 SD Brezje Maribor	3	1	0	2	8	9	3
4 KMF Ekonomac Kragujevac	3	1	0	2	4	14	3

Group D

24-27/11/16 Odivelas

FC Dynamo 11-1 City'US Târgu Mureş, Sporting Clube de Portugal 4-1 Győri ETO FC, Győri ETO FC 1-5 FC Dynamo, Sporting Clube de Portugal 16-1 City'US Târgu Mureş, City'US Târgu Mureş 0-5 Győri ETO FC, FC Dynamo 3-3 Sporting Clube de Portugal

	Pld	W	D	L	F	A	Pts
1 Sporting Clube de Portugal	3	2	1	0	23	5	7
2 FC Dynamo	3	2	1	0	19	5	7
3 Győri ETO FC	3	1	0	2	7	9	3
4 City'US Târgu Mureş	3	0	0	3	2	32	0

Semi-finals

28/04/17, Almaty Arena, Almaty

Ugra Yugorsk 1-2 Sporting Clube de Portugal

Goals: 0-1 Alex Merlim 24, 0-2 Dieguinho 33, 1-2 Shayakhmetov 38

28/04/17, Almaty Arena, Almaty

Inter FS 3-2 Kairat Almaty

Goals: 0-1 Cabreúva 4, 1-1 Ricardinho 12, 1-2 Igor 15, 2-2 Ricardinho 22(p), 3-2 Ortiz 38

Third place play-off

30/04/17, Almaty Arena, Almaty

Ugra Yugorsk 5-5 Kairat Almaty (aet; 2-3 on pens)

Goals: 1-0 Shayakhmetov 1, 1-1 Dróth 8, 2-1 Caio 13, 2-2 Davydov 15(og), 3-2 Lyskov 22, 3-3 Tayebi 24, 3-4 Cabreúva 32, 4-4 Divanei 36(og), 4-5 Divanei 38, 5-5 Marcênio 39

Final

30/04/17, Almaty Arena, Almaty (att: 6,353)

Sporting Clube de Portugal 0-7 Inter FS

Goals: 0-1 Bastezini 6, 0-2 Lolo 15, 0-3 Rafael 22, 0-4 Mario Rivillos 23, 0-5 Mario Rivillos 31, 0-6 Ricardinho 33, 0-7 Ricardinho 36

Referee: Bogdan Sorescu (ROU)/ Saša Tomić (CRO)

Sporting CP: André Sousa, Marcão, Paulinho, João Matos, Leo, Cavinato, Edgar Varela, Diogo, Déo, Caio, Alex Merlim, Anilton Varela. Coach: Nuno Dias (POR)

Inter: Jesús Herrero, Gonzalez, Ortiz, Humberto, Ricardinho, Rafael, Lolo, Bastezini, Shiraishi, Pola, Mario Rivillos, Borja. Coach: Jesús Velasco (ESP)

Yellow cards: Alex Merlim 2 (Sporting CP), Leo 16 (Sporting CP)

Top goalscorers (Final tournament)

4	Ricardinho (Inter)
2	Mario Rivillos (Inter)
	Cabreúva (Kairat)
	Vladislav Shayakhmetov (Ugra)

THE EUROPEAN FOOTBALL YEARBOOK 2017/18

TOP 100 PLAYERS

Welcome to the Top 100 Players of the Season chapter.

Turn the page and you will find an alphabetical list of the players who have been voted into the 2017/18 European Football Yearbook's Top 100.

On the pages that follow, each of the players selected is given a short narrative profile that summarises his notable achievements during the 2016/17 season. That is followed by an assortment of vital statistics covering his international and club career plus key appearances/goals figures for the season in question.

While the European Football Yearbook is 30 years old, the Top 100 Players section is now in its 13th year. The list bears no official stamp or sponsor, and there is no order of merit within it, although I am aware of some readers who enjoy creating their own personal classification and indeed logging how many times the players have been included in previous editions and overall.

As always, the selection process was lengthy, considered and democratic. While the majority of the players on the list staked an obvious claim for inclusion, others just edged in – or were edged out – on a borderline decision.

Should you wish to send in your feedback on the choices we have made, please make contact on the email address below.

Please note that the deadline for club and honours data is 4 August 2017.

Enjoy the read.

Mike Hammond
General Editor
efyhammond@gmail.com

Top 100 players

Sergio Agüero (Manchester City FC/Argentina)
Alex Sandro (Juventus FC/Brazil)
Alexis Sánchez (Arsenal FC/Chile)
Dele Alli (Tottenham Hotspur FC/England)
Marcos Alonso (Chelsea FC/Spain)
André Silva (FC Porto/Portugal)
Pierre-Emerick Aubameyang (Borussia Dortmund/Gabon)
César Azpilicueta (Chelsea FC/Spain)
Andrea Belotti (Torino FC/Italy)
Karim Benzema (Real Madrid CF/France)
Marcus Berg (Panathinaikos FC/Sweden)
Federico Bernardeschi (ACF Fiorentina/Italy)
Bernardo Silva (AS Monaco FC/Portugal)
Leonardo Bonucci (Juventus FC/Italy)
Gianluigi Buffon (Juventus FC/Italy)
Gary Cahill (Chelsea FC/England)
Daniel Carvajal (Real Madrid CF/Spain)
Edinson Cavani (Paris Saint-Germain/Uruguay)
Giorgio Chiellini (Juventus FC/Italy)
Cristiano Ronaldo (Real Madrid CF/Portugal)
Dani Alves (Juventus FC/Brazil)
David Luiz (Chelsea FC/Brazil)
Kevin De Bruyne (Manchester City FC/Belgium)
David de Gea (Manchester United FC/Spain)
Ousmane Dembélé (Borussia Dortmund/France)
Leander Dendoncker (RSC Anderlecht/Belgium)
Diego Costa (Chelsea FC/Spain)
Kasper Dolberg (AFC Ajax/Denmark)
Gianluigi Donnarumma (AC Milan/Italy)
Bas Dost (Sporting Clube de Portugal/Netherlands)
Paulo Dybala (Juventus FC/Argentina)
Edin Džeko (AS Roma/Bosnia & Herzegovina)
Ederson (SL Benfica/Brazil)
Christian Eriksen (Tottenham Hotspur FC/Denmark)
Radamel Falcao (AS Monaco FC/Colombia)
Emil Forsberg (RB Leipzig/Sweden)
Kamil Glik (AS Monaco FC/Poland)
Denis Glushakov (FC Spartak Moskva/Russia)
Diego Godín (Club Atlético de Madrid/Uruguay)
Alejandro Gómez (Atalanta BC/Argentina)
Antoine Griezmann (Club Atlético de Madrid/France)
Marek Hamšík (SSC Napoli/Slovakia)
Eden Hazard (Chelsea FC/Belgium)
Gonzalo Higuaín (Juventus FC/Argentina)
Mats Hummels (FC Bayern München/Germany)
Iago Aspas (RC Celta de Vigo/Spain)
Zlatan Ibrahimović (Manchester United FC/Sweden)
Mauro Icardi (FC Internazionale Milano/Argentina)
Ciro Immobile (SS Lazio/Italy)
Isco (Real Madrid CF/Spain)
Nicolai Jørgensen (Feyenoord/Denmark)
Harry Kane (Tottenham Hotspur FC/England)
N'Golo Kanté (Chelsea FC/France)
Naby Keïta (RB Leipzig/Guinea)
Joshua Kimmich (FC Bayern München/Germany)
Davy Klaassen (AFC Ajax/Netherlands)
Toni Kroos (Real Madrid CF/Germany)
Alexandre Lacazette (Olympique Lyonnais/France)
Philipp Lahm (FC Bayern München/Germany)
Thomas Lemar (AS Monaco FC/France)
Robert Lewandowski (FC Bayern München/Poland)
Victor Lindelöf (SL Benfica/Sweden)
Romelu Lukaku (Everton FC/Belgium)
Mario Mandžukić (Juventus FC/Croatia)
Sadio Mané (Liverpool FC/Senegal)
Marcelo (Real Madrid CF/Brazil)
Kylian Mbappé (AS Monaco FC/France)
Benjamin Mendy (AS Monaco FC/France)
Dries Mertens (SSC Napoli/Belgium)
Lionel Messi (FC Barcelona/Argentina)
Henrikh Mkhitaryan (Manchester United FC/Armenia)
Anthony Modeste (1. FC Köln/France)
Luka Modrić (Real Madrid CF/Croatia)
Radja Nainggolan (AS Roma/Belgium)
Neymar (FC Barcelona/Brazil)
Jan Oblak (Club Atlético de Madrid/Slovenia)
Miralem Pjanić (Juventus FC/Bosnia & Herzegovina)
Paul Pogba (Manchester United FC/France)
Quincy Promes (FC Spartak Moskva/Netherlands)
Raphaël Guerreiro (Borussia Dortmund/Portugal)
Arjen Robben (FC Bayern München/Netherlands)
Saúl Ñíguez (Club Atlético de Madrid/Spain)
Patrik Schick (UC Sampdoria/Czech Republic)
Kasper Schmeichel (Leicester City FC/Denmark)
Sergio Ramos (Real Madrid CF/Spain)
Djibril Sidibé (AS Monaco FC/France)
Gylfi Thór Sigurdsson (Swansea City AFC/Iceland)
David Silva (Manchester City FC/Spain)
Fedor Smolov (FC Krasnodar/Russia)
Lars Stindl (VfL Borussia Mönchengladbach/Germany)
Luis Suárez (FC Barcelona/Uruguay)
Niklas Süle (TSG 1899 Hoffenheim/Germany)
Talisca (Beşiktaş JK/Brazil)
Łukasz Teodorczyk (RSC Anderlecht/Poland)
Thiago Alcántara (FC Bayern München/Spain)
Youri Tielemans (RSC Anderlecht/Belgium)
Corentin Tolisso (Olympique Lyonnais/France)
Marco Verratti (Paris Saint-Germain/Italy)
Arturo Vidal (FC Bayern München/Chile)
Timo Werner (RB Leipzig/Germany)

NB Clubs indicated are those the players belonged to in the 2016/17 season.

Key to competitions:

WCF = FIFA World Cup final tournament
WCQ = FIFA World Cup qualifying round
ECF = UEFA EURO final tournament
ECQ = UEFA EURO qualifying round
CC = FIFA Confederations Cup
CA = Copa América
ANF = Africa Cup of Nations final tournament
ANQ = Africa Cup of Nations qualifying round
CGC = CONCACAF Gold Cup

Sergio Agüero

Striker, Height 172cm
Born 02/06/88, Quilmes, Argentina

Agüero's sixth season at Manchester City did not always go to plan, but despite a couple of Premier League suspensions and a spell during which the club's new coach, Pep Guardiola, decided to demote him to the bench, the 2016/17 campaign provided further confirmation of the 28-year-old Argentinian's standing as one of the most lethal strikers in the game. His aggregate tally of 35 goals across all competitions for City was higher than in any of his previous seasons and incorporated 20 Premier League strikes plus goal-a-game records in both the UEFA Champions League and the FA Cup.

International career

ARGENTINA
Debut 03/09/06 v Brazil (n, London, friendly), lost 0-3
First goal 17/11/07 v Bolivia (h, Buenos Aires, WCQ), won 3-0
Caps 82 **Goals** 33
Major tournaments FIFA World Cup 2010; Copa América 2011; FIFA World Cup 2014; Copa América 2015; Copa América 2016

Club career

Major honours *UEFA Europa League (2010); UEFA Super Cup (2010); English League (2012, 2014); English League Cup (2014, 2016)*
Clubs 02-06 CA Independiente; 06-11 Club Atlético de Madrid (ESP); 11- Manchester City FC (ENG)

2016/17 appearances/goals

Domestic league English Premier League 25(6)/20
Europe UEFA Champions League 6(1)/5; UEFA Champions League play-offs 1/3
National team FIFA World Cup qualifying 4(1)/-

Alex Sandro

Left-back, Height 181cm
Born 26/01/91, Catanduva, Brazil

A relatively discreet first season at Juventus was followed by a fabulous second as Alex Sandro evoked comparisons with Brazilian compatriot Roberto Carlos, his enterprise and expertise at left-back helping the Turin club to retain both of Italy's major domestic trophies and reach the final of the UEFA Champions League. The 26-year-old former Porto player showed his versatility, performing superbly both as a wing-back and, when required, on the left flank in a conventional back four. He particularly stood out in Europe, where his galloping runs and pin-point diagonals were a regular feature of Juve's play.

International career

BRAZIL
Debut 10/11/11 v Gabon (a, Libreville, friendly), won 2-0
Caps 7 **Goals** 0

Club career

Major honours *Libertadores Cup (2011); Portuguese League (2012, 2013); Italian League (2016, 2017); Brazilian Cup (2010); Italian Cup (2016, 2017)*
Clubs 08-10 Atlético Paranaense; 10-11 Deportivo Maldonado (URU); 10-11 Santos FC (loan); 11-15 FC Porto (POR); 15- Juventus FC (ITA)

2016/17 appearances/goals

Domestic league Italian Serie A 25(2)/3
Europe UEFA Champions League 9(2)/-
National team Friendlies 1/-

Alexis Sánchez

Striker/Attacking midfielder, Height 169cm
Born 19/12/88, Tocopilla, Chile

Reunited with his favoured No7 shirt after two seasons wearing No17, Alexis enjoyed his most productive campaign yet for Arsenal. While it was a bad season for the club in the Premier League as they finished fifth – their lowest placing for 21 years – it was a good one for their clever, cunning Chilean forward, who struck 24 goals to finish third in the golden boot standings. The Gunners' match-winner in the FA Cup semi-final against Manchester City, he also opened the scoring in the final against Chelsea with his 30th goal of the season, winning the trophy for the second time after Arsenal's 2-1 victory at Wembley.

International career

CHILE
Major honours *Copa América (2015, 2016)*
Debut 27/04/06 v New Zealand (h, La Calera, friendly), won 1-0
First goal 07/09/07 v Switzerland (n, Vienna, friendly), lost 1-2
Caps 115 **Goals** 38
Major tournaments FIFA World Cup 2010; Copa América 2011; FIFA World Cup 2014; Copa América 2015; Copa América 2016; FIFA Confederations Cup 2017

Club career

Major honours *UEFA Super Cup (2011); FIFA Club World Cup (2011); Chilean League (clausura 2006, apertura 2007); Argentinian League (clausura 2008); Spanish League (2013); Spanish Cup (2012); English FA Cup (2015, 2017)*
Clubs 05-06 CD Cobreloa; 06-11 Udinese Calcio (ITA); 06-07 Colo-Colo (loan); 07-08 CA River Plate (ARG, loan); 11-14 FC Barcelona (ESP); 14- Arsenal FC (ENG)

2016/17 appearances/goals

Domestic league English Premier League 36(2)/24
Europe UEFA Champions League 8/3
National team FIFA World Cup qualifying 7/3; FIFA Confederations Cup 4(1)/1; Friendlies 1(1)/-

Dele Alli

Midfielder, Height 188cm
Born 11/04/96, Milton Keynes, England

The title of PFA Young Player of the Year went to Alli for the second successive season in 2016/17, enabling the Tottenham midfielder to become the first player since Wayne Rooney, 11 years earlier, to retain the prestigious prize. The 21-year-old cemented his growing reputation as one of English football's brightest young talents by helping Spurs finish runners-up in the Premier League. His 18 goals included eight in six games around the turn of the year, highlighted by a match-winning double against Chelsea that ended their London rivals' record-equalling run of 13 successive victories.

International career

ENGLAND
Debut 09/10/15 v Estonia (h, London, ECQ), won 2-0
First goal 17/11/15 v France (h, London, friendly), won 2-0
Caps 19 **Goals** 2
Major tournaments UEFA EURO 2016

Club career

Clubs 11-15 Milton Keynes Dons FC; 15- Tottenham Hotspur FC

2016/17 appearances/goals

Domestic league English Premier League 35(2)/18
Europe UEFA Champions League 6/1; UEFA Europa League 2/-
National team FIFA World Cup qualifying 4(1)/1; Friendlies 2/-

Marcos Alonso

Left-back/Midfielder, Height 188cm
Born 28/12/90, Madrid, Spain

There was widespread surprise among English football followers when Chelsea announced at the end of the 2016 summer transfer window that they had spent £26m to buy Alonso from Fiorentina. Though excellent for the Viola, the elegant left-footer had done little during previous spells in England with Bolton and Sunderland to suggest that he warranted such a fee. It proved, however, to be an extremely smart piece of business by new Blues boss Antonio Conte, the 26-year-old Spaniard developing into a key component of his Premier League title-winning side as an assiduous and adventurous left wing-back.

International career

SPAIN
Uncapped

Club career

Major honours *English League (2017)*
Clubs 08-10 Real Madrid CF B; 10 Real Madrid CF; 10-13 Bolton Wanderers FC (ENG); 13-16 ACF Fiorentina (ITA); 14 Sunderland AFC (ENG, loan); 16- Chelsea FC (ENG)

2016/17 appearances/goals

Domestic league English Premier League 30(1)/6

André Silva

Striker, Height 185cm
Born 06/11/95, Baguim do Monte, Portugal

Portuguese football hailed a new star in 2016/17 as André Silva rose rapidly from the rank and file at FC Porto to become not only the club's top goalscorer, but also Cristiano Ronaldo's chief attacking accomplice in the national team. Already capped multiple times for various youth selections, he was still only 20 when he won his first senior international cap, scored his first goal and then, on only his fourth appearance, against the Faroe Islands, bagged his first hat-trick. His remarkable breakthrough season ended at the FIFA Confederations Cup in Russia after he had signed a five-year contract for AC Milan.

International career

PORTUGAL
Debut 01/09/16 v Gibraltar (h, Porto, friendly), won 5-0
First goal 07/10/16 v Andorra (h, Aveiro, WCQ), won 6-0
Caps 13 **Goals** 8
Major tournaments FIFA Confederations Cup 2017

Club career

Clubs 13-16 FC Porto B; 15-17 FC Porto; 17- AC Milan (ITA)

2016/17 appearances/goals

Domestic league Portuguese Liga 28(4)/16
Europe UEFA Champions League 8/4; UEFA Champions League play-offs 2/1
National team FIFA World Cup qualifying 5(1)/6; FIFA Confederations Cup 4(1)/2; Friendlies 1(1)/1

Pierre-Emerick Aubameyang

Striker, Height 187cm
Born 18/06/89, Laval, France

A second successive season of ceaseless goalscoring for Borussia Dortmund elevated Aubameyang's standing to that of a truly world-class striker. Even with the interruption of a mid-season trip back home to participate in the 2017 Africa Cup of Nations, the pacy Gabonese striker amassed 40 goals for his club, including a Bundesliga-best tally of 31 – the highest total since Dieter Müller's 34 for Köln in 1976/77 – and the winner in the German Cup final against Eintracht Frankfurt. His seven European goals included one in each group game against Real Madrid and a round of 16 hat-trick against Benfica.

International career

GABON
Debut 28/03/09 v Morocco (a, Casablanca, WCQ), won 2-1
First goal 28/03/09 v Morocco (a, Casablanca, WCQ), won 2-1
Caps 53 **Goals** 23
Major tournaments Africa Cup of Nations 2010; Africa Cup of Nations 2012; Africa Cup of Nations 2015; Africa Cup of Nations 2017

Club career

Major honours *French League Cup (2013); German Cup (2017)*
Clubs 08-11 AC Milan (ITA); 08-09 Dijon FCO (FRA, loan); 09-10 LOSC Lille (FRA, loan); 10-11 AS Monaco FC (FRA, loan); 11-13 AS Saint-Étienne (FRA); 13- Borussia Dortmund (GER)

2016/17 appearances/goals

Domestic league German Bundesliga 31(1)/31
Europe UEFA Champions League 8(1)/7
National team FIFA World Cup qualifying 2/-; Africa Cup of Nations 3/2; Friendlies 1/1

César Azpilicueta

Full-back/Centre-back, Height 178cm
Born 28/08/89, Pamplona, Spain

Antonio Conte fielded virtually the same XI from one game to the next as Chelsea cruised to the Premier League title, but only one player started all 38 matches, and that was Azpilicueta. The versatile, unassuming Spanish defender started his fifth season at Stamford Bridge in the familiar position of left-back, but once Conte changed his system, the former Marseille man regularly operated as the right-sided defender in a back three. The transition was seamless, with the 27-year-old going about his work in consistent, dependable fashion and even scoring a goal in the title-celebrating 4-3 win at home to Watford.

International career

SPAIN
Debut 06/02/13 v Uruguay (n, Doha, friendly), won 3-1
Caps 19 **Goals** 0
Major tournaments FIFA Confederations Cup 2013; FIFA World Cup 2014; UEFA EURO 2016

Club career

Major honours *UEFA Europa League (2013); English League (2015, 2017); French League Cup (2011, 2012); English League Cup (2015)*
Clubs 07-10 CA Osasuna; 10-12 Olympique de Marseille (FRA); 12- Chelsea FC (ENG)

2016/17 appearances/goals

Domestic league English Premier League 38/1
National team Friendlies 2(1)/-

Andrea Belotti

Striker, Height 181cm
Born 20/12/93, Calcinate, Italy

Italy managed only six goals in five matches at UEFA EURO 2016, so there was clearly a need to improve the Azzurri's scoring potential. New boss Giampiero Ventura gambled on Belotti, with whom he had worked at Torino in 2015/16, and the dynamic young striker, who had been a prolific marksman for the national Under-21 team, repaid his faith by scoring four FIFA World Cup qualifying goals. At club level, too, the 23-year-old striker was in explosive form, scoring 26 Serie A goals for Torino – the third-highest total in the division – and consequently courting interest from the big clubs of Italy and beyond.

International career

ITALY
Debut 01/09/16 v France (h, Bari, friendly), lost 1-3
First goal 09/10/16 v FYR Macedonia (a, Skopje, WCQ), won 3-2
Caps 9 **Goals** 4

Club career

Clubs 12-13 UC AlbinoLeffe; 13-15 US Città di Palermo; 15- Torino FC

2016/17 appearances/goals

Domestic league Italian Serie A 34(1)/26
National team FIFA World Cup qualifying 4(1)/4; Friendlies 2(2)/-

Karim Benzema

Striker, Height 183cm
Born 17/12/87, Lyon, France

Benzema's eighth season at Real Madrid was far from his most prolific, but it was his most successful as he helped the club to their first UEFA Champions League/Liga double since 1958. The Frenchman continued to wear the club's prestigious No9 shirt with distinction and his goals, though less frequent than in 2015/16, were often vital, such as the two he scored away to Celta Vigo and Málaga in Madrid's last two league games and the five he delivered in a run of four UEFA Champions League games to bypass 50 in total and therefore become the competition's highest-scoring Frenchman, eclipsing Thierry Henry.

International career

FRANCE
Debut 28/03/07 v Austria (h, Paris, friendly), won 1-0
First goal 28/03/07 v Austria (h, Paris, friendly), won 1-0
Caps 81 **Goals** 27
Major tournaments UEFA EURO 2008; UEFA EURO 2012; FIFA World Cup 2014

Club career

Major honours *UEFA Champions League (2014, 2016, 2017); UEFA Super Cup (2014, 2016); FIFA Club World Cup (2014,2016); French League (2005, 2006, 2007, 2008); Spanish League (2012, 2017); French Cup (2008); Spanish Cup (2011, 2014)*
Clubs 04-09 Olympique Lyonnais; 09- Real Madrid CF (ESP)

2016/17 appearances/goals

Domestic league Spanish Liga 23(6)/11
Europe UEFA Champions League 12(1)/5

Marcus Berg

Striker, Height 183cm
Born 17/08/86, Torsby, Sweden

With a final haul of 22 goals for Panathinaikos, almost half of the club's total, Berg was a convincing winner of the 2016/17 Greek Superleague golden boot. As in each of his previous three seasons, the Swedish striker was the Greens' most fertile source of goals, his prodigious tally including the winner against champions Olympiacos. Unfortunately, he was banned for the final four games of the UEFA Champions League qualifying play-offs and left Athens in June for United Arab Emirates club Al-Ain. He also performed well for Sweden, scoring with a delightful chip in their opening FIFA World Cup qualifier against the Netherlands.

International career

SWEDEN
Debut 06/02/08 v Turkey (a, Istanbul, friendly), drew 0-0
First goal 10/06/09 v Malta (h, Gothenburg, WCQ), won 4-0
Caps 47 **Goals** 12

Club career

Major honours *Swedish League (2007); Greek Cup (2014)*
Clubs 05-07 IFK Göteborg; 07-09 FC Groningen (NED); 09-13 Hamburger SV (GER); 10-11 PSV Eindhoven (NED, loan); 13-17 Panathinaikos FC (GRE); 17- Al-Ain FC (UAE)

2016/17 appearances/goals

Domestic league Greek Superleague 28/22
Europe UEFA Europa League 3/1; UEFA Europa League qualifying/play-offs 4/3
National team FIFA World Cup qualifying 5/2; Friendlies (1)/-

Federico Bernardeschi

Attacking midfielder/Winger, Height 183cm
Born 16/02/94, Carrara, Italy

A stunning match-winning free-kick for Fiorentina against Borussia Mönchengladbach in the UEFA Europa League was one of many standout moments from Bernardeschi during a season in which the gifted young Tuscan emerged as one of Serie A's most exciting performers, eventually earning himself a lucrative summer transfer to Juventus. A member of Italy's UEFA EURO 2016 squad, the left-footed schemer/winger registered his first senior Azzurri goal against Liechtenstein shortly before representing his country at the UEFA European Under-21 Championship, where he scored against both finalists, Germany and Spain.

International career

ITALY
Debut 24/03/16 v Spain (h, Udine, friendly), drew 1-1
First goal 11/06/17 v Liechtenstein (h, Udine, WCQ), won 5-0
Caps 9 **Goals** 1
Major tournaments UEFA EURO 2016

Club career

Clubs 13-17 ACF Fiorentina; 13-14 FC Crotone (loan); 17- Juventus FC

2016/17 appearances/goals

Domestic league Italian Serie A 27(5)/11
Europe UEFA Europa League 5(3)/2
National team FIFA World Cup qualifying 1(1)/1; Friendlies (2)/-

Bernardo Silva

Attacking midfielder, Height 173cm
Born 10/08/94, Lisbon, Portugal

Bernardo Silva's frustration at missing out on Portugal's UEFA EURO 2016 triumph through injury was considerably eased by his achievements over the 12 months that followed. The skilful left-footer was one of the star turns in the Monaco side, coached by his compatriot Leonardo Jardim, that won the French title and reached the semi-finals of the UEFA Champions League. Indeed, his superb last-minute equaliser away to defending champions Paris Saint-Germain was probably the defining moment of the entire Ligue 1 campaign. The season had barely finished when he signed a five-year deal to move to Manchester City.

International career

PORTUGAL
Debut 31/03/15 v Cape Verde (h, Estoril, friendly), lost 0-2
First goal 01/09/16 v Gibraltar (h, Porto, friendly), won 5-0
Caps 15 **Goals** 2
Major tournaments FIFA Confederations Cup 2017

Club career

Major honours *Portuguese League (2014); French League (2017); Portuguese Cup (2014)*
Clubs 13-14 SL Benfica; 14 AS Monaco FC (FRA, loan); 15-17 AS Monaco FC (FRA); 17- Manchester City FC (ENG)

2016/17 appearances/goals

Domestic league French Ligue 1 33(4)/8
Europe UEFA Champions League 11/2; UEFA Champions League qualifying/play-offs 2(2)/1
National team FIFA World Cup qualifying 2(1)/-; FIFA Confederations Cup 3/1; Friendlies 2(1)/1

Leonardo Bonucci

Centre-back, Height 190cm
Born 01/05/87, Viterbo, Italy

The complete defender, Bonucci had another fabulous season in 2016/17. For the sixth successive year the Italian international helped Juventus to the Serie A title, and there was a hat-trick of domestic doubles to celebrate also as he scored Juve's second goal in the Coppa Italia final against Lazio (2-0). His best efforts could not alas bring to Turin the trophy his club desired most as they lost the UEFA Champions League final to Real Madrid, but his form was formidable on the road to Cardiff. It was with a mixture of shock and sadness that Juve fans learnt in July that he had signed a five-year deal with AC Milan.

International career

ITALY
Debut 03/03/10 v Cameroon (n, Monaco, friendly), drew 0-0
First goal 03/06/10 v Mexico (n, Brussels, friendly), lost 1-2
Caps 70 **Goals** 5
Major tournaments FIFA World Cup 2010; UEFA EURO 2012; FIFA Confederations Cup 2013; FIFA World Cup 2014; UEFA EURO 2016

Club career

Major honours *Italian League (2006, 2012, 2013, 2014, 2015, 2016, 2017); Italian Cup (2015, 2016, 2017)*
Clubs 05-07 FC Internazionale Milano; 07-09 FC Treviso; 09 AC Pisa (loan); 09-10 AS Bari; 10-17 Juventus FC; 17- AC Milan

2016/17 appearances/goals

Domestic league Italian Serie A 26(3)/3
Europe UEFA Champions League 11/1
National team FIFA World Cup qualifying 5/-; Friendlies 3/1

Gianluigi Buffon

Goalkeeper, Height 191cm
Born 28/01/78, Carrara, Italy

There was a double celebration for Buffon when he led Italy out in Palermo for a FIFA World Cup qualifier against Albania on 24 March 2017. It was the 39-year-old goalkeeper's 1,000th match as a senior professional and also his 168th international cap, the largest number ever attributed to a European player. Typically, he kept a clean sheet as Italy won 2-0. At the time he was in the midst of a brilliant run of shutouts for Juventus in Europe, eventually going 600 minutes without conceding. A UEFA Champions League winner's medal would sadly elude him once again, but his eighth Serie A title equalled the all-time record.

International career

ITALY
Major honours *FIFA World Cup (2006)*
Debut 29/10/97 v Russia (a, Moscow, WCQ), drew 1-1
Caps 169 **Goals** 0
Major tournaments FIFA World Cup 1998; FIFA World Cup 2002; UEFA EURO 2004; FIFA World Cup 2006; UEFA EURO 2008; FIFA Confederations Cup 2009; FIFA World Cup 2010; UEFA EURO 2012; FIFA Confederations Cup 2013; FIFA World Cup 2014; UEFA EURO 2016

Club career

Major honours *UEFA Cup (1999); Italian League (2002, 2003, 2012, 2013, 2014, 2015, 2016, 2017); Italian Cup (1999, 2015, 2016, 2017)*
Clubs 95-01 Parma FC; 01- Juventus FC

2016/17 appearances/goals

Domestic league Italian Serie A 30/-
Europe UEFA Champions League 12/-
National team FIFA World Cup qualifying 6/-; Friendlies 2/-

Gary Cahill

Centre-back, Height 193cm
Born 19/12/85, Dronfield, England

With club captain John Terry unable to find a place in new Chelsea boss Antonio Conte's three-man defence, Cahill was Chelsea's regular on-field skipper during the 2016/17 Premier League title-winning campaign. The England international started 36 of the 38 games and chipped in with a personal-best tally of six goals, the first of them in a 4-0 win over Manchester United on old boss José Mourinho's return to Stamford Bridge. Capped for the 50th time by England in a FIFA World Cup qualifier in Slovenia, he scored the third of three headed goals for his country in a 3-0 win against Scotland a month later at Wembley.

International career

ENGLAND
Debut 03/09/10 v Bulgaria (h, London, ECQ), won 4-0
First goal 02/09/11 v Bulgaria (a, Sofia, ECQ), won 3-0
Caps 55 **Goals** 4
Major tournaments FIFA World Cup 2014; UEFA EURO 2016

Club career

Major honours *UEFA Champions League (2012); UEFA Europa League (2013); English League (2015, 2017); English FA Cup (2012); English League Cup (2015)*
Clubs 04-08 Aston Villa FC; 04-05 Burnley FC (loan); 07-08 Sheffield United FC (loan); 08-12 Bolton Wanderers FC; 12- Chelsea FC

2016/17 appearances/goals

Domestic league English Premier League 36(1)/6
National team FIFA World Cup qualifying 5/1; Friendlies 3/-

Daniel Carvajal

Right-back, Height 173cm
Born 11/01/92, Leganes, Spain

The 2016/17 season began with a bang for 'Dani' Carvajal as he scored a superb 119th-minute solo goal in the UEFA Super Cup to give Real Madrid a dramatic 3-2 win over Sevilla in Trondheim. It also ended sweetly for the 25-year-old as he returned from a thigh strain just in time to play the full 90 minutes of Madrid's UEFA Champions League final triumph against Juventus. In between he established himself as the first-choice right-back in Zinédine Zidane's star-spangled side with a series of enterprising and efficient performances that also earned him a Liga winner's medal and a regular berth in the Spanish national side.

International career

SPAIN
Debut 04/09/14 v France (a, Saint-Denis, friendly), lost 0-1
Caps 12 **Goals** 0

Club career

Major honours *UEFA Champions League (2014, 2016, 2017); UEFA Super Cup (2014, 2016); FIFA Club World Cup (2014, 2016); Spanish League (2017); Spanish Cup (2014)*
Clubs 10-12 Real Madrid CF B; 12-13 Bayer 04 Leverkusen (GER); 13- Real Madrid CF

2016/17 appearances/goals

Domestic league Spanish Liga 21(2)/-
Europe UEFA Champions League 11/-
National team FIFA World Cup qualifying 5/-; Friendlies 2/-

Edinson Cavani

Striker, Height 188cm
Born 14/02/87, Salto, Uruguay

Monaco succeeded Paris Saint-Germain as the champions of France, but the official Ligue 1 player of the year was its top marksman. Cavani scored 35 league goals for the Parisian club and 49 in total, including eight in eight UEFA Champions League games. He scored in the first minute of PSG's opening European clash against Arsenal but missed so many chances thereafter that concerns were raised that he would not fill the huge gap left by the departed Zlatan Ibrahimović. Not a bit of it. His goalscoring was prolific all season, with Barcelona and Monaco among those who felt the force of the Uruguayan's finishing power.

International career

URUGUAY
Major honours *Copa América (2011)*
Debut 06/02/08 v Colombia (h, Montevideo, friendly), drew 2-2
First goal 06/02/08 v Colombia (h, Montevideo, friendly), drew 2-2
Caps 92 **Goals** 38
Major tournaments FIFA World Cup 2010; Copa América 2011; FIFA Confederations Cup 2013; FIFA World Cup 2014; Copa América 2015; Copa América 2016

Club career

Major honours *Uruguayan League (apertura 2006); French League (2014, 2015, 2016); Italian Cup (2012); French Cup (2015, 2016, 2017); French League Cup (2014, 2015, 2016, 2017)*
Clubs 06-07 Danubio FC; 07-10 US Città di Palermo (ITA); 10-13 SSC Napoli (ITA); 13- Paris Saint-Germain (FRA)

2016/17 appearances/goals

Domestic league French Ligue 1 35(1)/35
Europe UEFA Champions League 8/8
National team FIFA World Cup qualifying 7/6; Friendlies 1/-

Giorgio Chiellini

Centre-back, Height 186cm
Born 14/08/84, Pisa, Italy

The archetypal Italian 'hard man' defender had something of a stop-start season in 2016/17 – his 12th consecutive campaign with Juventus – but when he was there alongside Andrea Barzagli and Leonardo Bonucci in the Bianconeri's famous 'BBC' back three, Juve invariably proved tougher to score against. He made his 300th Serie A appearance for the club in April – shortly before collecting his sixth successive league winner's medal – and also scored a memorable header against Barcelona in the quarter-finals of the UEFA Champions League. Like all of his team-mates, however, the final in Cardiff was a night he would rather forget.

International career

ITALY
Debut 17/11/04 v Finland (h, Messina, friendly), won 1-0
First goal 21/11/07 v Faroe Islands (h, Modena, ECQ), won 3-1
Caps 92 **Goals** 7
Major tournaments UEFA EURO 2008; FIFA Confederations Cup 2009; FIFA World Cup 2010; UEFA EURO 2012; FIFA Confederations Cup 2013; FIFA World Cup 2014; UEFA EURO 2016

Club career

Major honours *Italian League (2012, 2013, 2014, 2015, 2016, 2017); Italian Cup (2015, 2016, 2017)*
Clubs 00-04 AS Livorno Calcio; 04-05 AFC Fiorentina; 05- Juventus FC

2016/17 appearances/goals

Domestic league Italian Serie A 20(1)/2
Europe UEFA Champions League 8(1)/1
National team FIFA World Cup qualifying 2/-; Friendlies 1(1)/-

Cristiano Ronaldo

Striker, Height 184cm
Born 05/02/85, Funchal, Madeira, Portugal

Most footballers begin to decline when they enter their thirties, but at 32 Cristiano Ronaldo remains a phenomenon. His scoring feats continue to astonish, and in 2016/17 he added another 42 goals for Real Madrid – including top-scoring tallies in triumphant UEFA Champions League and FIFA Club World Cup campaigns – to lift his eight-year tally in all competitions to a staggering 406 in 394 matches. For Portugal he was in hotter form than ever, finding the net 14 times to become, with 75 goals, the joint-second highest European international scorer of all time – behind only the late great Ferenc Puskás of Hungary.

International career

PORTUGAL
Major honours *UEFA European Championship (2016)*
Debut 20/08/03 v Kazakhstan (h, Chaves, friendly), won 1-0
First goal 12/06/04 v Greece (h, Porto, ECF), lost 1-2
Caps 143 **Goals** 75
Major tournaments UEFA EURO 2004; FIFA World Cup 2006; UEFA EURO 2008; FIFA World Cup 2010; UEFA EURO 2012; FIFA World Cup 2014; UEFA EURO 2016; FIFA Confederations Cup 2017

Club career

Major honours *UEFA Champions League (2008, 2014, 2016, 2017); UEFA Super Cup (2014); FIFA Club World Cup (2008, 2014, 2016); English League (2007, 2008, 2009); Spanish League (2012, 2017); English FA Cup (2004); Spanish Cup (2011, 2014); English League Cup (2006, 2009)*
Clubs 02-03 Sporting Clube de Portugal; 03-09 Manchester United FC (ENG); 09- Real Madrid CF (ESP)

2016/17 appearances/goals

Domestic league Spanish Liga 29/25
Europe UEFA Champions League 13/12
National team FIFA World Cup qualifying 5/1; FIFA Confederations Cup 4/2; Friendlies 1/1

Dani Alves

Right-back, Height 171cm
Born 06/05/83, Juazeiro, Brazil

After eight seasons of serial trophy-collecting with Barcelona, Dani Alves left Catalonia for north-west Italy and continued the trend with Juventus, adding Serie A and Coppa Italia triumphs to his honours list. Although his domestic season was interrupted in mid-campaign when he fractured a fibula, he missed only one game in Europe, where he played a prominent role in helping Juve to the UEFA Champions League final, notably in the semi-final against Monaco, when he supplied three assists before scoring a spectacular fourth goal. His first season in Turin would be his last, however, as he signed a two-year deal with Paris Saint-Germain in July.

International career

BRAZIL
Major honours *Copa América (2007); FIFA Confederations Cup (2009, 2013)*
Debut 10/10/06 v Ecuador (n, Solna, friendly), won 2-1
First goal 15/7/07 v Argentina (n, Maracaibo, CA), won 3-0
Caps 100 **Goals** 7
Major tournaments Copa América 2007; FIFA Confederations Cup 2009; FIFA World Cup 2010; Copa América 2011; FIFA Confederations Cup 2013; FIFA World Cup 2014; Copa América 2015; Copa América 2016

Club career

Major honours *UEFA Champions League (2009, 2011, 2015); UEFA Cup (2006, 2007); UEFA Super Cup (2006, 2009, 2011, 2015); FIFA Club World Cup (2009, 2011, 2015); Spanish League (2009, 2010, 2011, 2013, 2015, 2016); Italian League (2017); Spanish Cup (2007, 2009, 2012, 2015, 2016); Italian Cup (2017)*
Clubs: 01-02 EC Bahia; 02-08 Sevilla FC (ESP); 08-16 FC Barcelona (ESP); 16-17 Juventus FC (ITA); 17- Paris Saint-Germain (FRA)

2016/17 appearances/goals

Domestic league Italian Serie A 15(4)/2
Europe UEFA Champions League 11(1)/3
National team FIFA World Cup qualifying 7/-

David Luiz

Centre-back, Height 188cm
Born 22/04/87, Diadema, Brazil

When Chelsea repurchased David Luiz from Paris Saint-Germain in August 2016, many questioned the wisdom of bringing back a player whose defensive ability had been widely criticised during his first spell in west London. But as the season progressed it was plain to see that the bushy-haired Brazilian had come on in leaps and bounds during his two years in the French capital and was the perfect fit at the heart of Antonio Conte's three-man defence. He commanded the Blues' back line with calmness, skill and authority and was one of four Chelsea players named in the PFA Premier League team of the year.

International career

BRAZIL
Major honours *FIFA Confederations Cup (2013)*
Debut 10/08/10 v United States (a, East Rutherford, friendly), won 2-0
First goal 28/06/14 v Chile (h, Belo Horizonte, WCF), drew 1-1
Caps 57 **Goals** 3
Major tournaments Copa América 2011; FIFA Confederations Cup 2013; FIFA World Cup 2014; Copa América 2015

Club career

Major honours *UEFA Champions League (2012); UEFA Europa League (2013); Portuguese League (2010); French League (2015, 2016); English League (2017); English FA Cup (2012); French Cup (2015, 2016); French League Cup (2015, 2016)*
Clubs 06-07 EC Vitória; 07-11 SL Benfica (POR); 11-14 Chelsea FC (ENG); 14-16 Paris Saint-Germain (FRA); 16- Chelsea FC (ENG)

2016/17 appearances/goals

Domestic league English Premier League 33/1
National team Friendlies 1/-

Kevin De Bruyne

Attacking midfielder, Height 181cm
Born 28/06/91, Drongen, Belgium

The 2016/17 Premier League's king of assists with 18, De Bruyne was a class act throughout his second season at Manchester City, maintaining the same high measure of consistency under Pep Guardiola that he had displayed on debut under Manuel Pellegrini. A willing ball-carrier with the ability to penetrate any defence with a single pass or cross, the Belgian international was right on top of his game in the early weeks, notably with a man-of-the-match performance away to Manchester United. His one goal in the UEFA Champions League was a stunning free-kick that helped City to a crucial 3-1 victory over Barcelona.

International career

BELGIUM
Debut 11/08/10 v Finland (a, Turku, friendly), lost 0-1
First goal 12/10/12 v Serbia (a, Belgrade, WCQ), won 3-0
Caps 52 **Goals** 13
Major tournaments FIFA World Cup 2014; UEFA EURO 2016

Club career

Major honours *Belgian League (2011); German Cup (2015); English League Cup (2016)*
Clubs 08-12 KRC Genk; 12-14 Chelsea FC (ENG); 12 KRC Genk (loan); 12-13 SV Werder Bremen (GER, loan); 14-15 VfL Wolfsburg (GER); 15- Manchester City FC (ENG)

2016/17 appearances/goals

Domestic league English Premier League 33(3)/6
Europe UEFA Champions League 6/1; UEFA Champions League play-offs 1/-
National team FIFA World Cup qualifying 3/-; Friendlies 3/-

David de Gea

Goalkeeper, Height 190cm
Born 07/11/90, Madrid, Spain

Voted by the PFA as the Premier League's goalkeeper of the year for the third time in a row – and fourth in all – De Gea earned the recognition with another commanding season for Manchester United. While his understudy Sergio Romero was one of United's top performers in their UEFA Europa League triumph, going unbeaten in a dozen games, the Spain No1 was the man José Mourinho counted on in the Premier League, helping the team post a 25-match unbeaten run from late October to early May. During that time he also won the EFL Cup to complete a clean sweep of domestic trophies during his six years in England.

International career

SPAIN
Debut 07/06/14 v El Salvador (n, Landover, USA, friendly), won 2-0
Caps 21 **Goals** 0
Major tournaments FIFA World Cup 2014; UEFA EURO 2016

Club career

Major honours *UEFA Europa League (2010, 2017); UEFA Super Cup (2010); English League (2013); English FA Cup (2016); English League Cup (2017)*
Clubs 09-11 Club Atlético de Madrid; 11- Manchester United FC (ENG)

2016/17 appearances/goals

Domestic league English Premier League 35/-
Europe UEFA Europa League 3/-
National team FIFA World Cup qualifying 6/-; Friendlies 2/-

Ousmane Dembélé

Attacking midfielder, Height 177cm
Born 15/05/97, Vernon, France

After just one, albeit brilliant, debut season in Ligue 1 with Rennes, concerns were voiced in France that Dembélé was taking a risk in leaving his homeland at just 19 to join Borussia Dortmund. But the gifted teenager was unperturbed, settling quickly at his new club and going on to enchant and entertain Bundesliga crowds with his pace and two-footed trickery. The pick of Dortmund's sizeable new intake, he crowned an outstanding debut campaign in Germany with crucial DFB-Pokal goals against Bayern München and Eintracht Frankfurt before adding a first international strike for France to win an end-of-season friendly against England.

International career

FRANCE
Debut 01/09/16 v Italy (a, Bari, friendly), won 3-1
First goal 13/06/17 v England (h, Saint-Denis, friendly), won 3-2
Caps 7 **Goals** 1

Club career

Clubs 15-16 Stade Rennais FC; 16- Borussia Dortmund (GER)

2016/17 appearances/goals

Domestic league German Bundesliga 22(10)/6
Europe UEFA Champions League 9(1)/2
National team FIFA World Cup qualifying 1(1)/-; Friendlies 3(2)/1

Leander Dendoncker

Midfielder, Height 188cm
Born 15/04/95, Passendale, Belgium

Dendoncker's third season as a regular first-teamer with Anderlecht was considerably busier than the first two as the 22-year-old holding midfielder chalked up 58 appearances in all competitions, including the maximum 40 in Belgium's top division. The only ever-present in René Weiler's title-winning side, his influence was profound, mixing strength and industry with tremendous tactical awareness and also providing a goal threat from set pieces. His most prominent goal of the campaign was a brilliant bullet header on the run at home to Manchester United in the UEFA Europa League, which he followed up with an excellent performance at Old Trafford.

International career

BELGIUM
Debut 07/06/15 v France (a, Saint-Denis, friendly), won 4-3
Caps 2 **Goals** 0

Club career

Major honours *Belgian League (2017)*
Clubs 13- RSC Anderlecht

2016/17 appearances/goals

Domestic league Belgian Pro League 40/5
Europe UEFA Champions League qualifying 2/-; UEFA Europa League 12/1; UEFA Europa League play-offs 2/-
National team FIFA World Cup qualifying 1/-

Diego Costa

Striker, Height 188cm
Born 07/10/88, Lagarto, Brazil

As in Chelsea's 2014/15 Premier League title triumph, Diego Costa was the team's top scorer with 20 goals as they regained the trophy in 2016/17. The Brazilian-born Spanish international was back to his belligerent best, getting under the skin of opposition defenders – not to mention supporters – with his muscular aggression and power and scoring some exquisite goals. It appeared as if he might leave in January for China but instead he stayed on at Stamford Bridge to collect his second Premier League winner's medal. It was a good season also for the striker at international level as he scored five FIFA World Cup qualifying goals for Spain.

International career

BRAZIL
Debut 21/03/13 v Italy (n, Geneva, friendly), drew 2-2
Caps 2 **Goals** 0
SPAIN
Debut 05/03/14 v Italy (h, Madrid, friendly), won 1-0
First goal 12/10/14 v Luxembourg (a, Luxembourg, ECQ), won 4-0
Caps 16 **Goals** 6
Major tournaments FIFA World Cup 2014

Club career

Major honours *UEFA Super Cup (2010, 2012); Spanish League (2014); English League (2015, 2017); Spanish Cup (2013); English League Cup (2015)*
Clubs 06-07 SC Braga (POR); 06 FC Penafiel (POR, loan); 07-09 Club Atlético de Madrid; 07 SC Braga (POR, loan); 07-08 RC Celta de Vigo (loan); 08-09 Albacete Balompié (loan); 09-10 Real Valladolid CF; 10-14 Club Atlético de Madrid; 12 Rayo Vallecano de Madrid (loan); 14- Chelsea FC (ENG)

2016/17 appearances/goals

Domestic league English Premier League 35/20
National team FIFA World Cup qualifying 5/5; Friendlies (1)/-

Kasper Dolberg

Striker, Height 187cm
Born 06/10/97, Silkeborg, Denmark

Ajax won no trophies in 2016/17, finishing runners-up in both the Eredivisie and UEFA Europa League, but regular visitors to the Amsterdam ArenA found some solace in the meteoric rise of 19-year-old academy graduate Dolberg. The elegant young Danish striker had yet to make a first-team appearance when the season began, but by the end of it he was the club's top marksman, scoring 16 goals in the domestic league and seven in Europe, including one in each leg of the UEFA Europa League semi-final against Lyon. Fast-tracked into the Denmark side, he scored his first international goal, away to Kazakhstan, in June.

International career

DENMARK
Debut 11/11/16 v Kazakhstan (h, Copenhagen, WCQ), won 4-1
First goal 10/06/17 v Kazakhstan (a, Almaty, WCQ), won 3-1
Caps 3 **Goals** 1

Club career

Clubs 14-15 Silkeborg IF; 16- AFC Ajax (NED)

2016/17 appearances/goals

Domestic league Dutch Eredivisie 26(3)/16
Europe UEFA Champions League qualifying/play-offs 2(2)/1; UEFA Europa League 10(3)/6
National team FIFA World Cup qualifying (2)/1; Friendlies (1)/-

Gianluigi Donnarumma

Goalkeeper, Height 196cm
Born 25/02/99, Castellammare di Stabia, Italy

In the same season that 39-year-old Gianluigi Buffon won his landmark 168th Italian cap, his successor-in-waiting picked up his first, Donnarumma's debut against France – after substituting Buffon – making him, at 17 years and 189 days, the youngest goalkeeper ever to play for the Azzurri. Replacing a legend over twice as old as him is earmarked for after the 2018 FIFA World Cup, but equally important in the career progress of the young giant who played for his country at the 2017 UEFA European Under-21 finals is to consolidate his spectacular beginnings at AC Milan, for whom he started all 38 Serie A games in 2016/17.

International career

ITALY
Debut 01/09/16 v France (h, Bari, friendly), lost 1-3
Caps 4 **Goals** 0

Club career

Clubs 15- AC Milan

2016/17 appearances/goals

Domestic league Italian Serie A 38/-
National team Friendlies 2(2)/-

Bas Dost

Striker, Height 196cm
Born 31/05/89, Deventer, Netherlands

Once the scorer of 32 goals in a single Eredivisie campaign for FC Groningen, which prompted a move to German club Wolfsburg, Dost returned to those giddy heights in his first season with Sporting CP, finding the net with increased regularity as the months passed, four hat-tricks in his last ten games boosting his final Primeira Liga goal tally to 34, which was 15 more than anyone else in the division and also precisely 50 per cent of his team's entire output. The Dutchman's scoring exploits could take Sporting no higher than third place, however, after they prematurely dropped out of a title race won by Lisbon rivals Benfica.

International career

NETHERLANDS
Debut 28/03/15 v Turkey (h, Amsterdam, ECQ), drew 1-1
First goal 13/11/15 v Wales (a, Cardiff, friendly), won 3-2
Caps 15 **Goals** 1

Club career

Major honours *German Cup (2015)*
Clubs 07-08 Emmen; 08-10 Heracles Almelo; 10-12 sc Heerenveen; 12-16 VfL Wolfsburg (GER); 16- Sporting Clube de Portugal (POR)

2016/17 appearances/goals

Domestic league Portuguese Liga 30(1)/34
Europe UEFA Champions League 5(1)/1
National team FIFA World Cup qualifying 2(3)/-; Friendlies (4)/-

Paulo Dybala

Striker, Height 179cm
Born 15/11/93, Cordoba, Argentina

Juventus's leading Serie A scorer in 2015/16, with 19 goals, Dybala was somewhat outshone in that department by his newly arrived compatriot Gonzalo Higuaín in 2016/17, but the skilful young Argentine found a deeper role in Massimiliano Allegri's team that still allowed his marvellous talent to flourish. That was never more apparent than in the first leg of Juve's UEFA Champions League quarter-final at home to Barcelona, when he stole the show with two brilliant left-footed strikes in a momentous 3-0 victory. It was no great surprise when just two days later Juventus renewed the 23-year-old's contract.

International career

ARGENTINA
Debut 13/10/15 v Paraguay (a, Asunción, WCQ), drew 0-0
Caps 8 **Goals** 0

Club career

Major honours *Italian League (2016, 2017); Italian Cup (2016, 2017)*
Clubs 11-12 Instituto de Córdoba; 12-15 US Città di Palermo (ITA); 15- Juventus FC (ITA)

2016/17 appearances/goals

Domestic league Italian Serie A 26(5)/11
Europe UEFA Champions League 10(1)/4
National team FIFA World Cup qualifying 3/-; Friendlies 2/-

Edin Džeko

Striker, Height 193cm
Born 17/03/86, Doboj, Bosnia & Herzegovina

An erratic debut season with Roma was quickly forgotten as Džeko went goal-crazy in his second, topping the Serie A charts with 29 strikes and sharing top spot in the UEFA Europa League listings on eight with Zenit midfielder Giuliano. His aggregate tally of 39 goals across all competitions was a club record, cementing the 31-year-old striker's place in the Roma history books. Only two Serie A teams, Juventus and Lazio, did not concede to him in an astonishingly prolific season that also brought him four goals for Bosnia & Herzegovina, enabling him to reach the landmark figure of 50 for his country.

International career

BOSNIA & HERZEGOVINA
Debut 02/06/07 v Turkey (h, Sarajevo, ECQ), won 3-2
First goal 02/06/07 v Turkey (h, Sarajevo, ECQ), won 3-2
Caps 85 **Goals** 50
Major tournaments FIFA World Cup 2014

Club career

Major honours *German League (2009); English League (2012, 2014); English FA Cup (2011); English League Cup (2014)*
Clubs 03-05 FK Željezničar; 05 FK Ústí nad Labem (CZE); 06-07 FK Teplice (CZE); 07-11 VfL Wolfsburg (GER); 11-16 Manchester City FC (ENG); 15-16 AS Roma (ITA, loan); 16- AS Roma (ITA)

2016/17 appearances/goals

Domestic league Italian Serie A 33(4)/29
Europe UEFA Champions League play-offs 2/-; UEFA Europa League 5(3)/8
National team FIFA World Cup qualifying 5/3; Friendlies 1/1

Ederson

Goalkeeper, Height 188cm
Born 17/08/93, Osasco, Brazil

The understudy to compatriot Júlio César for most of Benfica's 2015/16 Primeira Liga title-wining campaign, Ederson emerged as the Eagles' No1 goalkeeper in 2016/17, making a major contribution towards the retention of the Portuguese title and also distinguishing himself repeatedly in Europe. Young, brave and agile, his finest performance was probably the first leg of Benfica's UEFA Champions League round of 16 encounter with Borussia Dortmund, in which he made a string of saves, including one from a Pierre-Emerick Aubameyang penalty. He left Benfica for Manchester City in the summer for a £35m fee.

International career

BRAZIL
Uncapped

Club career

Major honours *Portuguese League (2016, 2017); Portuguese Cup (2017)*
Clubs 11-12 GD Riberão (POR); 12-15 Rio Ave FC (POR); 15-17 SL Benfica (POR); 17- Manchester City FC (ENG)

2016/17 appearances/goals

Domestic league Portuguese Liga 27/-
Europe UEFA Champions League 7/-

Christian Eriksen

Midfielder, Height 180cm
Born 14/02/92, Middelfart, Denmark

After four seasons in London with Tottenham Hotspur, Eriksen was still waiting to add to an honours list containing three Eredivisie titles and one Dutch Cup with Ajax, but his Premier League career continued to blossom in 2016/17 as he helped Spurs finish runners-up – their highest position in England's top division for 54 years. Clever and creative, the 25-year-old schemer set up 15 league goals and scored eight himself. The most talented Danish player of his generation, he was also on form for his country in the FIFA World Cup qualifiers, scoring four goals, all of them in victories, to bolster Denmark's bid for a place in Russia.

International career

DENMARK
Debut 03/03/10 v Austria (a, Vienna, friendly), lost 1-2
First goal 04/06/11 v Iceland (a, Reykjavik, ECQ), won 2-0
Caps 69 **Goals** 14
Major tournaments FIFA World Cup 2010; UEFA EURO 2012

Club career

Major honours *Dutch League (2011, 2012, 2013); Dutch Cup (2010)*
Clubs 10-13 AFC Ajax (NED); 13- Tottenham Hotspur FC (ENG)

2016/17 appearances/goals

Domestic league English Premier League 36/8
Europe UEFA Champions League 5(1)/-; UEFA Europa League 1(1)/1
National team FIFA World Cup qualifying 6/4; Friendlies 2/1

Radamel Falcao

Striker, Height 175cm
Born 10/02/86, Magdalena, Colombia

Two fallow seasons on loan in England at Manchester United and Chelsea appeared to have signalled the beginning of the end of Falcao's career, but the Colombian striker was back to his fearsome best in 2016/17 as the inspirational captain of an exciting young Monaco side that won the French title and reached the semi-finals of the UEFA Champions League. With 30 goals in all competitions, the 31-year-old returned to the form of his prime at FC Porto and Atlético Madrid. There were some delightful strikes among that number, including a magnificent chip against Manchester City and a spectacular flying header against Borussia Dortmund.

International career

COLOMBIA
Debut 07/02/07 v Uruguay (h, Cucuta, friendly), lost 1-3
First goal 03/06/07 v Montenegro (n, Matsumoto, Kirin Cup), won 1-0
Caps 66 **Goals** 26
Major tournaments Copa América 2011; Copa América 2015

Club career

Major honours *UEFA Europa League (2011, 2012); UEFA Super Cup (2012); Argentinian League (clausura 2008); Portuguese League (2011); French League (2017); Portuguese Cup (2010, 2011); Spanish Cup (2013)*
Clubs 05-09 CA River Plate (ARG); 09-11 FC Porto (POR); 11-13 Club Atlético de Madrid (ESP); 13- AS Monaco FC (FRA); 14-15 Manchester United FC (ENG, loan); 15-16 Chelsea FC (ENG, loan)

2016/17 appearances/goals

Domestic league French Ligue 1 22(7)/21
Europe UEFA Champions League 8/5
National team FIFA World Cup qualifying 1(1)/-; Friendlies 1(1)/1

Emil Forsberg

Attacking midfielder/Winger, Height 179cm
Born 23/10/91, Sundsvall, Sweden

Voted the best player in the 2015/16 Zweite Bundesliga, from which RB Leipzig won promotion, Forsberg was also a big hit on his debut season in Germany's top flight, registering a Bundesliga-best tally of 19 assists, to which he added eight goals, as Leipzig shook up the established order and finished runners-up to perennial champions Bayern München. Whether stationed in the 'hole' behind the strikers or in his favoured left-sided role, the 25-year-old was a constant threat with his purposeful probing and precise passing. He also enjoyed an excellent season with Sweden, having confidently taken possession of Zlatan Ibrahimović's No10 shirt.

International career

SWEDEN
Debut 17/01/14 v Moldova (n, Abu Dhabi, friendly), won 2-1
First goal 14/11/15 v Denmark (h, Solna, ECQ), won 2-1
Caps 27 **Goals** 5
Major tournaments UEFA EURO 2016

Club career

Major honours *Swedish League (2013, 2014)*
Clubs 09-13 GIF Sundsvall; 09 Medskogsbron BK (loan); 13-15 Malmö FF; 15- RB Leipzig (GER)

2016/17 appearances/goals

Domestic league German Bundesliga 27(3)/8
National team FIFA World Cup qualifying 6/3; Friendlies (1)/-

Kamil Glik

Centre-back, Height 190cm
Born 03/02/88, Jastrzebie Zdroj, Poland

After six years in Italy, five of them with Torino, Glik sought pastures new and found fertile ground in the south of France with Monaco. The big, powerful Polish centre-back enjoyed a wonderful season, claiming the first major trophy of his career as the Monégasques shocked Paris Saint-Germain by unseating them as Ligue 1 champions and also making an impressive debut in the UEFA Champions League as Leonardo Jardim's young team swaggered their way into the semi-finals. There were happy days too for the 29-year-old at national team level as he helped Poland build a big lead in their FIFA World Cup qualifying group.

International career

POLAND
Debut 20/01/10 v Thailand (a, Nakhon Ratchasima, friendly), won 3-1
First goal 20/01/10 v Thailand (a, Nakhon Ratchasima, friendly), won 3-1
Caps 51 **Goals** 3
Major tournaments UEFA EURO 2016

Club career

Major honours *French League (2017)*
Clubs 06 UD Horadada (ESP); 07-08 Real Madrid CF C (ESP); 08-10 GKS Piast Gliwice; 10-11 US Città di Palermo (ITA); 11 AS Bari (ITA, loan); 11-16 Torino FC (ITA); 16- AS Monaco FC (FRA)

2016/17 appearances/goals

Domestic league French Ligue 1 35/6
Europe UEFA Champions League 10/1
National team FIFA World Cup qualifying 5/-

Denis Glushakov

Midfielder, Height 182cm
Born 27/01/87, Millerovo, Russia

Russia will be desperately seeking heroes at the 2018 FIFA World Cup, and while Glushakov, an unfussy thirtysomething defensive midfielder, may not be the most glamorous footballer to tie up his bootlaces and enter the arena for the host nation next summer, he could turn out to be one of their most important. He was certainly among Russia's better performers at the 2017 FIFA Confederations Cup, where he played every minute, and also one of the stars of the show for Spartak Moskva in 2016/17 – both in defence and attack – as the Red-and-Whites renewed acquaintance with the Premier-Liga trophy after a 16-year wait.

International career

RUSSIA
Debut 29/03/11 v Qatar (a, Doha, friendly), drew 1-1
First goal 11/10/11 v Andorra (h, Moscow, ECQ), won 6-0
Caps 54 **Goals** 5
Major tournaments UEFA EURO 2012; FIFA World Cup 2014; UEFA EURO 2016; FIFA Confederations Cup 2017

Club career

Major honours *Russian League (2017)*
Clubs 05 FC Nika Moskva; 05-13 FC Lokomotiv Moskva; 06 SKA Rostov-na-Donu (loan); 07 FC Zvezda Irkutsk (loan); 13- FC Spartak Moskva

2016/17 appearances/goals

Domestic league Russian Premier-Liga 24(1)/8
Europe UEFA Europa League qualifying 1(1)/-
National team FIFA Confederations Cup 3/-; Friendlies 4(1)/-

Diego Godín

Centre-back, Height 186cm
Born 16/02/86, Rosario, Uruguay

A Uruguayan international with over 100 caps and experience at seven major tournaments, Godín has made his name in Europe with Atlético Madrid, and his iconic status with the locals was reinforced still further with another outstanding season of rugged resilience on both the domestic and European front in 2016/17. The 31-year-old centre-back was once again the linchpin of the Spanish Liga's number one defence, and with him at the back Atlético conceded just three goals in nine UEFA Champions League games until Real Madrid's Cristiano Ronaldo doubled that number in the first leg of the semi-final.

International career

URUGUAY
Major honours *Copa América (2011)*
Debut 26/10/05 v Mexico (a, Guadalajara, friendly), lost 1-3
First goal 27/05/06 v Serbia & Montenegro (a, Belgrade, friendly), drew 1-1
Caps 108 **Goals** 8
Major tournaments Copa América 2007; FIFA World Cup 2010; Copa América 2011; FIFA Confederations Cup 2013; FIFA World Cup 2014; Copa América 2015; Copa América 2016

Club career

Major honours *UEFA Europa League (2012); UEFA Super Cup (2010, 2012); Spanish League (2014); Spanish Cup (2013)*
Clubs 03-06 CA Cerro; 06-07 Club Nacional; 07-10 Villarreal CF (ESP); 10- Club Atlético de Madrid (ESP)

2016/17 appearances/goals

Domestic league Spanish Liga 30(1)/3
Europe UEFA Champions League 11/-
National team FIFA World Cup qualifying 8/-

Alejandro Gómez

Attacking midfielder, Height 165cm
Born 15/02/88, Buenos Aires, Argentina

In the northern Italian region of Lombardy football conversation is normally dominated by Internazionale and AC Milan, but in 2016/17 much of the talk was about the remarkable exploits of Bergamo side Atalanta, who defied logic and reason to finish fourth in Serie A – above both Milanese giants. Central to their success was 'Papu' Gómez, a diminutive Argentinian playmaker and dribbler who in his third season at the club took his game to impressive new heights both as a maker and scorer of goals, assisting ten and putting his name on another 16 to become the top marksman for Gian Piero Gasperini's overachieving provincials.

International career

ARGENTINA
Debut 13/06/17 v Singapore (a, Singapore, friendly), won 6-0
First goal 13/06/17 v Singapore (a, Singapore, friendly), won 6-0
Caps 1 **Goals** 1

Club career

Major honours *Copa Sudamericana (2007)*
Clubs 05-09 Arsenal de Sarandí; 09-10 CA San Lorenzo; 10-13 Calcio Catania (ITA); 13-14 FC Metalist Kharkiv (UKR); 14- Atalanta BC (ITA)

2016/17 appearances/goals

Domestic league Italian Serie A 37/16
National team Friendlies 1/1

Antoine Griezmann

Striker/Attacking midfielder, Height 176cm
Born 21/03/91, Macon, France

The best player and top scorer at UEFA EURO 2016 was rewarded during the tournament with a substantially improved new contract at Atlético Madrid. A year later, after another fine season for Diego Simeone's side, Griezmann had that contract revised and extended once again, silencing widespread rumours that the skilful left-footer might be on the move to Manchester United. As the French international's hair grew, so the goals continued to flow, with a purple patch in the spring helping Atlético put together a good run in the Liga, where they overhauled Sevilla to finish third, and also reach the last four of the UEFA Champions League.

International career

FRANCE
Debut 05/03/14 v Netherlands (h, Paris, friendly), won 2-0
First goal 01/06/14 v Paraguay (h, Nice, friendly), drew 1-1
Caps 43 **Goals** 16
Major tournaments FIFA World Cup 2014; UEFA EURO 2016

Club career

Clubs 09-14 Real Sociedad de Fútbol (ESP); 14- Club Atlético de Madrid (ESP)

2016/17 appearances/goals

Domestic league Spanish Liga 36/16
Europe UEFA Champions League 12/6
National team FIFA World Cup qualifying 6/2; Friendlies 3/1

Marek Hamšík

Attacking midfielder, Height 180cm
Born 27/07/87, Banska Bystrica, Slovakia

Hamšík completed a tenth successive Serie A season with Napoli in May 2017. The captain of Slovakia, who joined the club just before his 20th birthday, has long been considered a Neapolitan legend, but there was no resting on his laurels in his landmark season. On the contrary, he enjoyed one of his finest campaigns, playing in all 38 Serie A games and scoring 12 goals, which, supplemented by three in other competitions, not only added up to the most prolific season of his career but also lifted him into second place in Napoli's all-time scorer charts with 113 goals – just two behind the great Diego Maradona.

International career

SLOVAKIA
Debut 07/02/07 v Poland (n, Jerez, friendly), drew 2-2
First goal 13/10/07 v San Marino (h, Dubnica, ECQ), won 7-0
Caps 97 **Goals** 21
Major tournaments FIFA World Cup 2010; UEFA EURO 2016

Club career

Major honours *Italian Cup (2012, 2014)*
Clubs 04 ŠK Slovan Bratislava; 04-07 Brescia Calcio (ITA); 07- SSC Napoli (ITA)

2016/17 appearances/goals

Domestic league Italian Serie A 37(1)/12
Europe UEFA Champions League 8/2
National team FIFA World Cup qualifying 5(1)/2

Eden Hazard

Winger/Attacking midfielder, Height 170cm
Born 07/01/91, La Louviere, Belgium

The zip and zest of old returned to Hazard's play in 2016/17 as the dazzling Belgian dribbler left the disturbing form slump of the previous season far behind him en route to a second Premier League title triumph in three years with Chelsea. New manager Antonio Conte gave the 26-year-old licence to roam and the result was a collection of vintage performances and a personal-best top-flight tally of 16 goals. Two of those came in a fantastic 5-0 win at home to Everton, and he also treated the Stamford Bridge faithful to a sumptuous solo strike against Arsenal plus a match-winning double against Manchester City.

International career

BELGIUM
Debut 19/11/08 v Luxembourg (a, Luxembourg, friendly), drew 1-1
First goal 07/10/11 v Kazakhstan (h, Brussels, ECQ), won 4-1
Caps 77 **Goals** 17
Major tournaments FIFA World Cup 2014, UEFA EURO 2016

Club career

Major honours *UEFA Europa League (2013); French League (2011); English League (2015, 2017); French Cup (2011); English League Cup (2015)*
Clubs 07-12 LOSC Lille (FRA); 12- Chelsea FC (ENG)

2016/17 appearances/goals

Domestic league English Premier League 36/16
National team FIFA World Cup qualifying 4/3; Friendlies 2/-

Gonzalo Higuaín

Striker, Height 184cm
Born 10/12/87, Brest, France

Juventus paid a reported €90m to Napoli to lure the 2015/16 Serie A top scorer to Turin, but if the size of the fee brought added pressure on Higuaín to succeed at his new club, it was barely evident. The 29-year-old Argentinian did exactly what he was bought for, scoring important goals in big games. Unfortunately for Napoli and their irate fans, four of his 32 goals were scored against them – a crucial late winning strike in Serie A and three in the semi-final of the Coppa Italia. His five UEFA Champions League goals included two characteristically clinical finishes in Juve's 2-0 win at Monaco in the first leg of the semi-final.

International career

ARGENTINA
Debut 10/10/09 v Peru (h, Buenos Aires, WCQ), won 2-1
First goal 10/10/09 v Peru (h, Buenos Aires, WCQ), won 2-1
Caps 69 **Goals** 31
Major tournaments FIFA World Cup 2010; Copa América 2011; FIFA World Cup 2014; Copa América 2015; Copa América 2016

Club career

Major honours *Spanish League (2007, 2008, 2012); Italian League (2017); Spanish Cup (2011); Italian Cup (2014, 2017)*
Clubs 04-06 CA River Plate; 07-13 Real Madrid CF (ESP); 13-16 SSC Napoli (ITA); 16- Juventus FC (ITA)

2016/17 appearances/goals

Domestic league Italian Serie A 32(6)/24
Europe UEFA Champions League 12/5
National team FIFA World Cup qualifying 4(1)/1; Friendlies 1/-

Mats Hummels

Centre-back, Height 192cm
Born 16/12/88, Bergisch Gladbach, Germany

The return of Hummels to his first club Bayern München after eight and a half seasons at Borussia Dortmund did not sit easily with many German fans, dismayed as they were to see the country's strongest club becoming even stronger. Their fears of further Bayern domination were duly realised as they powered to a fifth successive Bundesliga title, with their new German international centre-back a key and decisive figure. The 28-year-old was his usual elegant, unflustered, authoritative self, winning the third league title of his career and also helping his country to almost certain qualification for the 2018 FIFA World Cup.

International career

GERMANY
Major honours *FIFA World Cup (2014)*
Debut 13/05/10 v Malta (h, Aachen, friendly), won 3-0
First goal 26/05/12 v Switzerland (a, Basel, friendly), lost 3-5
Caps 57 **Goals** 4
Major tournaments UEFA EURO 2012; FIFA World Cup 2014; UEFA EURO 2016

Club career

Major honours *German League (2011, 2012, 2017); German Cup (2012)*
Clubs 07-09 FC Bayern München; 08-09 Borussia Dortmund (loan); 09-16 Borussia Dortmund; 16- FC Bayern München

2016/17 appearances/goals

Domestic league German Bundesliga 24(3)/1
Europe UEFA Champions League 7(2)/-
National team FIFA World Cup qualifying 5/-; Friendlies 2/-

Iago Aspas

Striker, Height 176cm
Born 01/08/87, Moana, Spain

With 19 Liga goals for Celta Vigo in 2016/17, Iago Aspas was the highest-scoring Spaniard in the division, with only the cream of the foreign crop, Lionel Messi, Luis Suárez and Cristiano Ronaldo, finishing above him, but it was not only in domestic competition that the ex-Liverpool striker excelled. He scored five goals in the UEFA Europa League to help Celta reach the semi-finals, including a nerveless last-minute penalty away to Shakhtar Donetsk, and also found the net on his international debut with a classy left-foot curler that helped Spain come from behind to salvage a late 2-2 draw with England at Wembley.

International career

SPAIN
Debut 15/11/16 v England (a, London, friendly), drew 2-2
First goal 15/11/16 v England (a, London, friendly), drew 2-2
Caps 4 **Goals** 1

Club career

Major honours *UEFA Europa League (2015)*
Clubs 06-09 RC Celta de Vigo B; 08-13 RC Celta de Vigo; 13-15 Liverpool FC (ENG); 14-15 Sevilla FC (loan); 15- RC Celta de Vigo

2016/17 appearances/goals

Domestic league Spanish Liga 25(7)/19
Europe UEFA Europa League 9(3)/5
National team FIFA World Cup qualifying (1)/-; Friendlies 1(2)/1

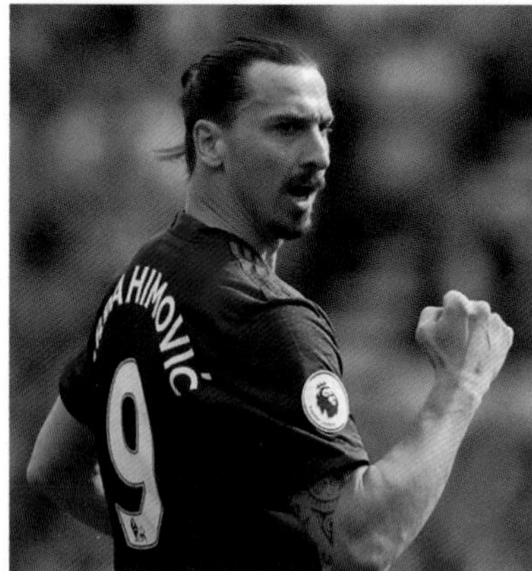

Zlatan Ibrahimović

Striker, Height 192cm
Born 03/10/81, Malmo, Sweden

After four glorious years at Paris Saint-Germain, Ibrahimović joined Manchester United on a one-year contract. At the age of 35, retired from international football, he arrived at Old Trafford unburdened by great expectations, but right from day one the big striker's world-class talent endeared him not only to United fans but also to a sceptical English public. He was the stand-out player in José Mourinho's side, scoring 17 Premier League goals and two in the EFL Cup final win against Southampton. A serious injury to his right knee cruelly cut short his season, denying him UEFA Europa League final participation in his native Sweden.

International career

SWEDEN
Debut 31/01/01 v Faroe Islands (h, Vaxjo, friendly), drew 0-0
First goal 07/10/01 v Azerbaijan (h, Solna, WCQ), won 3-0
Caps 116 **Goals** 62
Major tournaments FIFA World Cup 2002; UEFA EURO 2004; FIFA World Cup 2006; UEFA EURO 2008; UEFA EURO 2012; UEFA EURO 2016

Club career

Major honours *UEFA Europa League (2017); UEFA Super Cup (2009); FIFA Club World Cup (2009); Dutch League (2002, 2004); Italian League (2007, 2008, 2009, 2011); Spanish League (2010); French League (2013, 2014, 2015, 2016); Dutch Cup (2002); French Cup (2015, 2016); French League Cup (2014, 2015, 2016); English League Cup (2017)*
Clubs 99-01 Malmö FF; 01-04 AFC Ajax (NED); 04-06 Juventus FC (ITA); 06-09 FC Internazionale Milano (ITA); 09-11 FC Barcelona (ESP); 10-11 AC Milan (ITA, loan); 11-12 AC Milan (ITA); 12-16 Paris Saint-Germain (FRA); 16-17 Manchester United FC (ENG)

2016/17 appearances/goals

Domestic league English Premier League 27(1)/17
Europe UEFA Europa League 9(2)/5

Mauro Icardi

Striker, Height 181cm
Born 19/02/93, Rosario, Argentina

The captain of Internazionale, Icardi got into some hot water with the Nerazzurri fans after the publication of his autobiography in October 2016, but the matter was eventually resolved and the young Argentinian striker showed no ill effects as he powered his way to a personal-best tally of 24 Serie A goals. That was an impressive figure given the instability of Inter's season in which they sacked two coaches, Frank de Boer and Stefano Pioli, and finished out of Europe in seventh place. Among the striker's highlights were a seventh goal in eight games against Juventus (in a 2-1 victory) and a hat-trick in a 7-1 win against Atalanta.

International career

ARGENTINA
Debut 15/10/13 v Uruguay (a, Montevideo, WCQ), lost 2-3
Caps 1 **Goals** 0

Club career

Clubs 11-13 UC Sampdoria (ITA); 13- FC Internazionale Milano (ITA)

2016/17 appearances/goals

Domestic league Italian Serie A 34/24
Europe UEFA Europa League 3(2)/2

Ciro Immobile

Striker, Height 185cm
Born 20/02/90, Torre Annunziata, Italy

Changing clubs from one year to the next after a brilliant 2013/14 campaign with Torino had stagnated Immobile's career progress, but after unsatisfactory spells in Germany and Spain a return home to Lazio in July 2016 finally gave the striker the lift he needed. A goal on his debut against Atalanta was the first of 23 he would score in Serie A – one more than he had managed in becoming capocannoniere three years earlier. He was also Lazio's two-goal hero against Roma in the Coppa Italia semi-final and, after reuniting with ex-Torino boss Giampiero Ventura, scored five goals in six FIFA World Cup qualifiers for Italy.

International career

ITALY
Debut 05/03/14 v Spain (a, Madrid, friendly), lost 0-1
First goal 04/09/14 v Netherlands (h, Bari, friendly), won 2-0
Caps 24 **Goals** 6
Major tournaments FIFA World Cup 2014; UEFA EURO 2016

Club career

Clubs 09-12 Juventus FC; 10-11 AC Siena (loan); 11 US Grosseto (loan); 11-12 Pescara Calcio (loan); 12-13 Genoa CFC; 13-14 Torino FC; 14-15 Borussia Dortmund (GER); 15-16 Sevilla FC (ESP); 16 Torino FC (loan); 16- SS Lazio

2016/17 appearances/goals

Domestic league Italian Serie A 35(1)/23
National team FIFA World Cup qualifying 4(2)/5; Friendlies 3/-

Isco

Attacking midfielder, Height 176cm
Born 21/04/92, Benalmadena, Spain

Isco's creative talent was one of the key factors in taking Real Madrid over the line in their triumphant 2016/17 Liga campaign. The 25-year-old playmaker was especially influential in the second half of the season, popping up at vital moments to score a decisive goal or supply the killer pass. It was his crucial away goal also that enabled Madrid to halt neighbours Atlético's comeback in the second leg of the UEFA Champions League semi-final, and he ensured an undefeated debut season for Spain coach Julen Lopetegui with a last-gasp equaliser in a November friendly against England at Wembley.

International career

SPAIN
Debut 06/02/13 v Uruguay (n, Doha, friendly), won 3-1
First goal 15/11/14 v Belarus (h, Huelva, ECQ), won 3-0
Caps 20 **Goals** 3

Club career

Major honours *UEFA Champions League (2014, 2016, 2017); UEFA Super Cup (2014, 2016); FIFA Club World Cup (2014, 2016); Spanish League (2017); Spanish Cup (2014)*
Clubs 10-11 Valencia CF; 11-13 Málaga CF; 13- Real Madrid CF

2016/17 appearances/goals

Domestic league Spanish Liga 18(12)/10
Europe UEFA Champions League 5(1)/1
National team FIFA World Cup qualifying 1(3)/1; Friendlies 1(1)/1

Nicolai Jørgensen

Striker, Height 190cm
Born 15/01/91, Ballerup, Denmark

The €3.5m that Feyenoord paid FC København for Jørgensen turned out to be a bargain as the Danish striker spearheaded the Rotterdam club to their first Eredivisie title for 18 years. Tall and powerful, the 26-year-old had been FCK's leading marksman in their 2015/16 Superliga-winning campaign and he repeated the trick in his new colours, scoring 21 goals, which was also enough to pip Vitesse's Ricky van Wolfswinkel to the Eredivisie's golden boot. The last Feyenoord player to have claimed the prize was none other than last-day hat-trick hero Dirk Kuyt, who had scored 29 goals in 2004/05 during his first spell at the club.

International career

DENMARK
Debut 11/11/11 v Sweden (h, Copenhagen, friendly), won 2-0
First goal 14/11/15 v Sweden (a, Solna, ECQ), lost 1-2
Caps 24 **Goals** 7

Club career

Major honours *Danish League (2013, 2016); Dutch League (2017); Danish Cup (2015, 2016)*
Clubs 09-10 AB Gladsaxe; 10-12 Bayer 04 Leverkusen (GER); 12 1. FC Kaiserslautern (GER, loan); 12 FC København (loan); 12-16 FC København; 16- Feyenoord (NED)

2016/17 appearances/goals

Domestic league Dutch Eredivisie 32/21
Europe UEFA Europa League 6/2
National team FIFA World Cup qualifying 4(1)/1; Friendlies 3/3

Harry Kane

Striker, Height 188cm
Born 28/07/93, London, England

With eight goals in his last three games, Kane overtook Romelu Lukaku to become the Premier League's top scorer for the second season in a row. The Tottenham striker might have saved his best until the title race had already been run, but without his prolific goalscoring Spurs' challenge to Chelsea would never have got off the ground. He was badly missed through injury in the autumn – both domestically and in Europe – but after returning to fitness he was irrepressible, ending up with 29 goals in as many starts. His late-season purple patch also extended to England duty. Handed the captaincy, he scored three goals in two games, including a vital late equaliser against Scotland.

International career

ENGLAND
Debut 27/03/15 v Lithuania (h, London, ECQ), won 4-0
First goal 27/03/15 v Lithuania (h, London, ECQ), won 4-0
Caps 19 **Goals** 8
Major tournaments UEFA EURO 2016

Club career

Clubs 09- Tottenham Hotspur FC; 11 Leyton Orient FC (loan); 12 Millwall FC (loan); 12-13 Norwich City FC (loan); 13 Leicester City FC (loan)

2016/17 appearances/goals

Domestic league English Premier League 29(1)/29
Europe UEFA Champions League 3/2; UEFA Europa League 2/-
National team FIFA World Cup qualifying 2/1; Friendlies 1/2

N'Golo Kanté

Midfielder, Height 169cm
Born 29/03/91, Paris, France

A Premier League champion two years in succession, in debut seasons with two different clubs, Kanté was duly showered with all of English football's main individual accolades – PFA Player of the Year, FWA Footballer of the Year and Premier League Player of the Season. Leicester City's loss was very much Chelsea's gain as the west Londoners' new signing took no time to settle at Stamford Bridge and establish himself as the team's ubiquitous and energetic midfield fulcrum, the 26-year-old Frenchman's renowned attributes of tackling and intercepting matched by exceptional mobility, intelligent ball distribution and even the occasional assist and goal.

International career

FRANCE
Debut 25/03/16 v Netherlands (a, Amsterdam, friendly), won 3-2
First goal 29/03/16 v Russia (h, Saint-Denis, friendly), won 4-2
Caps 17 **Goals** 1
Major tournaments UEFA EURO 2016

Club career

Major honours *English League (2016, 2017)*
Clubs 11-13 US Boulogne; 13-15 SM Caen; 15-16 Leicester City FC (ENG); 16- Chelsea FC (ENG)

2016/17 appearances/goals

Domestic league English Premier League 35/1
National team FIFA World Cup qualifying 2(2)/-; Friendlies 4(1)/-

Naby Keïta

Midfielder, Height 172cm
Born 10/02/95, Conakry, Guinea

Transferred from FC Salzburg to German 'sister' club RB Leipzig after winning successive Austrian doubles, Keïta had the local fans in raptures when he scored the winning goal against Borussia Dortmund on his home debut. There would be plenty more adulation to follow over the course of a brilliant Bundesliga campaign, in which he inspired his new club to an unexpected second-place finish. A do-it-all midfielder of silk and steel, the diminutive Guinean international registered eight goals and seven assists, with the consistent quality and diversity of the 22-year-old's play raising his market value on an almost weekly basis.

International career

GUINEA
Debut 25/05/14 v Mali (n, Paris, friendly), won 2-1
First goal 12/11/15 v Namibia (a, Windhoek, WCQ), won 1-0
Caps 24 **Goals** 3
Major tournaments Africa Cup of Nations 2015

Club career

Major honours *Austrian League (2015, 2016); Austrian Cup (2015, 2016)*
Clubs 12-13 Horoya AC; 13-14 FC Istres (FRA); 14-16 FC Salzburg (AUT); 16- RB Leipzig (GER)

2016/17 appearances/goals

Domestic league German Bundesliga 29(2)/8
National team FIFA World Cup qualifying 2/-; Africa Cup of Nations qualifying 1/1; Friendlies 1/-

Joshua Kimmich

Right-back/Midfielder, Height 176cm
Born 08/02/95, Rottweil, Germany

Germany played 15 international matches in 2016/17, and Kimmich was on the field from start to finish of every one. The team's first competitive fixture of the season, a FIFA World Cup qualifier in Norway, brought him a first international goal, and the last of them earned him a first international honour as Joachim Löw's side defeated Chile 1-0 in the FIFA Confederations Cup final. The versatile 22-year-old made the same number of Bundesliga starts for Bayern München as he did for his country, scoring six goals to add to the three he plundered on his first two starts in the UEFA Champions League group stage.

International career

GERMANY
Major honours *FIFA Confederations Cup (2017)*
Debut 29/05/16 v Slovakia (h, Augsburg, friendly), lost 1-3
First goal 04/09/16 v Norway (a, Oslo, WCQ), won 3-0
Caps 20 **Goals** 2
Major tournaments UEFA EURO 2016; FIFA Confederations Cup 2017

Club career

Major honours *German League (2016, 2017); German Cup (2016)*
Clubs 13-15 RB Leipzig; 15- FC Bayern München

2016/17 appearances/goals

Domestic league German Bundesliga 15(12)/6
Europe UEFA Champions League 3(5)/3
National team FIFA World Cup qualifying 6/1; FIFA Confederations Cup 5/-; Friendlies 4/1

Davy Klaassen

Attacking midfielder, Height 185cm
Born 22/02/93, Hilversum, Netherlands

Klaassen's Ajax career came to an end on 15 June 2017 when he signed a five-year contract to play in the English Premier League under fellow Dutchman Ronald Koeman at Everton. Unfortunately, his final season in Amsterdam did not end with a trophy-lift, but the Ajax captain certainly left the club with a soaring reputation after an excellent season from an individual perspective in which he scored more goals than ever before (20), led an extremely young team to the final of the UEFA Europa League and a runners-up spot in the Eredivisie, and also became a fixture in the Netherlands national team.

International career

NETHERLANDS
Debut 05/03/14 v France (a, Saint-Denis, friendly), lost 0-2
First goal 31/03/15 v Spain (h, Amsterdam, friendly), won 2-0
Caps 14 **Goals** 4

Club career

Major honours *Dutch League (2012, 2013, 2014)*
Clubs 11-17 AFC Ajax; 17- Everton FC (ENG)

2016/17 appearances/goals

Domestic league Dutch Eredivisie 33/14
Europe UEFA Champions League qualifying/play-offs 4/4; UEFA Europa League 13/2
National team FIFA World Cup qualifying 5/1; Friendlies 3(1)/2

Toni Kroos

Midfielder, Height 182cm
Born 04/01/90, Greifswald, Germany

Real Madrid's master strategist reaffirmed his stature as one of the game's great midfield generals with another magnificent season that brought him a third victory in both the UEFA Champions League and FIFA World Club Cup and a first Spanish domestic league title to go with the three Bundesliga crowns he had claimed with Bayern München. Kroos offered one perfectly polished performance after another in Madrid's all-conquering campaign. The 27-year-old already has one FIFA World Cup winner's medal, but with him on board Germany have every chance of retaining football's most treasured trophy in Russia.

International career

GERMANY
Major honours *FIFA World Cup (2014)*
Debut 03/03/10 v Argentina (h, Munich, friendly), lost 0-1
First goal 06/09/11 v Poland (a, Gdansk, friendly), drew 2-2
Caps 76 **Goals** 12
Major tournaments FIFA World Cup 2010; UEFA EURO 2012; FIFA World Cup 2014; UEFA EURO 2016

Club career

Major honours *UEFA Champions League (2013, 2016, 2017); UEFA Super Cup (2013, 2016); FIFA Club World Cup (2013, 2014, 2016); German League (2008, 2013, 2014); Spanish League (2017); German Cup (2008, 2013, 2014)*
Clubs 07-14 FC Bayern München; 09-10 Bayer 04 Leverkusen (loan); 14- Real Madrid CF (ESP)

2016/17 appearances/goals

Domestic league Spanish Liga 28(1)/3
Europe UEFA Champions League 11(1)/1
National team FIFA World Cup qualifying 4/1; Friendlies 1/-

Alexandre Lacazette

Striker, Height 175cm
Born 28/05/91, Lyon, France

It says a lot about the depth of talent available to France coach Didier Deschamps that Lacazette, a scorer of 37 goals for Olympique Lyonnais in 2016/17, was restricted to just 17 minutes of a friendly during Les Bleus' first post-UEFA EURO 2016 season. The 26-year-old striker left Lyon in the summer for Arsenal having scored precisely 100 Ligue 1 goals for the club. Twenty-eight of those came in his swansong campaign, which also featured half a dozen strikes in the UEFA Europa League, a competition in which his sharp-shooting prowess was frequently in the spotlight as Bruno Genésio's team reached the semi-finals.

International career

FRANCE
Debut 05/06/13 v Uruguay (a, Montevideo, friendly), lost 0-1
First goal 29/03/15 v Denmark (h, Saint-Etienne, friendly), won 2-0
Caps 11 **Goals** 1

Club career

Major honours *French Cup (2012)*
Clubs 10-17 Olympique Lyonnais; 17- Arsenal FC (ENG)

2016/17 appearances/goals

Domestic league French Ligue 1 28(2)/28
Europe UEFA Champions League 4/1; UEFA Europa League 6(2)/6
National team Friendlies (1)/-

Philipp Lahm

Full-back, Height 170cm
Born 11/11/83, Munich, Germany

One of the finest players of his generation, and the man who lifted the FIFA World Cup for Germany in 2014, Lahm announced his imminent retirement from the game in February 2017 – three days after making his 500th appearance for Bayern München. Although still with much to offer at only 33, the Bayern skipper duly played his last match as a professional at home to Freiburg on 20 May, departing the field to an emotional ovation on a day when team-mate Xabi Alonso also made his farewell appearance. The Bundesliga title he won in 2016/17 was his eighth, equalling the all-time record held by three other Bayern players.

International career

GERMANY
Major honours *FIFA World Cup (2014)*
Debut 18/02/04 v Croatia (a, Split, friendly), won 2-1
First goal 28/04/04 v Romania (a, Bucharest, friendly), lost 1-5
Caps 113 **Goals** 5
Major tournaments UEFA EURO 2004; FIFA World Cup 2006; UEFA EURO 2008; FIFA World Cup 2010; UEFA EURO 2012; FIFA World Cup 2014

Club career

Major honours *UEFA Champions League (2013); UEFA Super Cup (2013); FIFA Club World Cup (2013); German League (2006, 2008, 2010, 2013, 2014, 2015, 2016, 2017); German Cup (2006, 2008, 2010, 2013, 2014, 2016)*
Clubs; 02-17 FC Bayern München; 03-05 VfB Stuttgart (loan)

2016/17 appearances/goals

Domestic league German Bundesliga 24(2)/1
Europe UEFA Champions League 7/-

Thomas Lemar

Attacking midfielder, Height 170cm
Born 12/11/95, Baie-Mahault, Guadeloupe

One of several Monaco players to come thrillingly to the fore in the club's magnificent 2016/17 season, Lemar projected his talent on to the European stage with a couple of fine goals against Tottenham Hotspur in the UEFA Champions League group stage, and the 21-year-old from Guadeloupe featured prominently too in the knockout phase wins over Manchester City and Borussia Dortmund that carried Monaco into the last four. Domestically, the gifted left-footer was equally eye-catching, contributing nine goals, ten assists and countless moments of crowd-pleasing skill to the club's first Ligue 1 title triumph for 17 years.

International career

FRANCE
Debut 15/11/16 v Ivory Coast (h, Lens, friendly), drew 0-0
Caps 5 **Goals** 0

Club career

Major honours *French League (2017)*
Clubs 13-15 SM Caen; 15- AS Monaco FC

2016/17 appearances/goals

Domestic league French Ligue 1 28(6)/9
Europe UEFA Champions League 9(3)/2; UEFA Champions League qualifying/play-offs 4/-
National team FIFA World Cup qualifying (1)/-; Friendlies 1(3)/-

Robert Lewandowski

Striker, Height 184cm
Born 21/08/88, Warsaw, Poland

Football in the 21st century has been blessed with two all-time greats in Lionel Messi and Cristiano Ronaldo, but as far as traditional centre-forwards go, there have not been many better over the past decade than Lewandowski. The Polish international became his country's second-highest scorer, on 46 goals, by adding 11 to his total during the first six games of the 2018 FIFA World Cup qualifying campaign, a figure that included hat-tricks against Denmark and Romania. Furthermore, for his club, Bayern München, he scored 30 Bundesliga goals for a second successive season – a feat managed by only one other player, Bayern legend Gerd Müller.

International career

POLAND
Debut 10/09/08 v San Marino (a, Serravalle, WCQ), won 2-0
First goal 10/09/08 v San Marino (a, Serravalle, WCQ), won 2-0
Caps 87 **Goals** 46
Major tournaments UEFA EURO 2012; UEFA EURO 2016

Club career

Major honours *Polish League (2010); German League (2011, 2012, 2015, 2016, 2017); Polish Cup (2009); German Cup (2012, 2016)*
Clubs 06-08 Znicz Pruszków; 08-10 KKS Lech Poznań; 10-14 Borussia Dortmund (GER); 14- FC Bayern München (GER)

2016/17 appearances/goals

Domestic league German Bundesliga 31(2)/30
Europe UEFA Champions League 9/8
National team FIFA World Cup qualifying 6/11

Victor Lindelöf

Centre-back, Height 187cm
Born 17/07/94, Vasteras, Sweden

A Benfica player since the age of 17, Lindelöf did not make his first-team breakthrough until the second half of the 2015/16 season, but in the follow-up campaign he was a fixture in Rui Vitória's side, the dominant figure in a defence that shipped only 18 goals in 34 matches en route to defending the Primeira Liga title. The Swedish international, a European champion at Under-21 level in 2015, also helped the Eagles complete the double with victory in the Taça de Portugal while making a name for himself with some uncompromising displays in the UEFA Champions League. In June he signed a four-year contract with Manchester United.

International career

SWEDEN
Debut 24/03/16 v Turkey (a, Antalya, friendly), lost 1-2
First goal 10/10/16 v Bulgaria (h, Solna, WCQ), won 3-0
Caps 12 **Goals** 1
Major tournaments UEFA EURO 2016

Club career

Major honours *Portuguese League (2014, 2016, 2017); Portuguese Cup (2014, 2017)*
Clubs 09-12 Västerås SK; 12-15 SL Benfica B (POR); 13-17 SL Benfica (POR); 17- Manchester United FC (ENG)

2016/17 appearances/goals

Domestic league Portuguese Liga 32(1)/1
Europe UEFA Champions League 8/-
National team FIFA World Cup qualifying 5/1; Friendlies (1)/-

Romelu Lukaku

Striker, Height 190cm
Born 13/05/93, Antwerp, Belgium

Lukaku spent the 2016/17 season breaking a whole list of scoring records for Everton, becoming among other things the club's all-time top Premier League marksman. The powerful 24-year-old left-footer ended the season with 25 league goals, the highest figure in his career and second only to Tottenham's Harry Kane in the final golden boot standings. An uneasy truce, however, existed between the Belgian international striker and the Merseyside club in the final months of the season after he shunned a new contract offer and expressed his intention to leave. In July he got his wish, signing a lucrative five-year deal with Manchester United.

International career

BELGIUM
Debut 03/03/10 v Croatia (h, Brussels, friendly), lost 0-1
First goal 17/11/10 v Russia (a, Voronezh, friendly), won 2-0
Caps 60 **Goals** 23
Major tournaments FIFA World Cup 2014; UEFA EURO 2016

Club career

Major honours *Belgian League (2010); English FA Cup (2012)*
Clubs 09-11 RSC Anderlecht; 11-14 Chelsea FC (ENG); 12-13 West Bromwich Albion (ENG, loan); 13-14 Everton FC (ENG, loan); 14-17 Everton FC (ENG); 17- Manchester United FC (ENG)

2016/17 appearances/goals

Domestic league English Premier League 36(1)/25
National team FIFA World Cup qualifying 5/6; Friendlies 1(3)/-

Mario Mandžukić

Striker/Attacking midfielder, Height 186cm
Born 21/05/86, Slavonski Brod, Croatia

Shunted out of his place at the point of the Juventus attack by the arrival of Gonzalo Higuaín, Mandžukić eventually reclaimed his berth in Massimiliano Allegri's side as a wide-left attacking midfielder – a role he had filled early in his career with Dinamo Zagreb and one he would return to with efficiency and panache, helping the Bianconeri to another Serie A/Coppa Italia double. The Croatian international remained in that position for the UEFA Champions League final against Real Madrid in Cardiff, where he scored a majestic overhead volley to level the scores at 1-1 before the holders swept Juve aside in the second half.

International career

CROATIA
Debut 17/11/07 v FYR Macedonia (a, Skopje, ECQ), lost 0-2
First goal 10/09/08 v England (h, Zagreb, WCQ), lost 1-4
Caps 76 **Goals** 29
Major tournaments UEFA EURO 2012; FIFA World Cup 2014; UEFA EURO 2016

Club career

Major honours *UEFA Champions League (2013); UEFA Super Cup (2013); FIFA Club World Cup (2013); Croatian League (2008, 2009, 2010); German League (2013, 2014); Italian League (2016, 2017); Croatian Cup (2008, 2009); German Cup (2013, 2014); Italian Cup (2016, 2017)*
Clubs 04-05 NK Marsonia; 05-07 NK Zagreb; 07-10 GNK Dinamo Zagreb; 10-12 VfL Wolfsburg (GER); 12-14 FC Bayern München (GER); 14-15 Club Atlético de Madrid (ESP); 15- Juventus FC (ITA)

2016/17 appearances/goals

Domestic league Italian Serie A 28(6)/7
Europe UEFA Champions League 10(1)/3
National team FIFA World Cup qualifying 6/4; Friendlies 1/1

Sadio Mané

Attacking midfielder/Winger, Height 175cm
Born 10/04/92, Sedhiou, Senegal

Mané became the subject of the most expensive transfer involving an African footballer when he joined Liverpool from Southampton in June 2016 for £34m. The Senegal international thus became the latest in a long line of players to make that particular move, including new team-mates Nathaniel Clyne, Adam Lallana and Dejan Lovren, and he proved to be arguably the best of the bunch, scoring 13 Premier League goals from his advanced midfield position, including one in each Merseyside derby against Everton, despite a mid-season trip to the Africa Cup of Nations and an injury that ruled him out of the last eight matches.

International career

SENEGAL
Debut 25/05/12 v Morocco (a, Marrakech, friendly), won 1-0
First goal 02/06/12 v Liberia (h, Dakar, WCQ), won 3-1
Caps 45 **Goals** 13
Major tournaments Africa Cup of Nations 2015; Africa Cup of Nations 2017

Club career

Major honours *Austrian League (2014); Austrian Cup (2014)*
Clubs 11-12 FC Metz (FRA); 12-14 FC Salzburg (AUT); 14-16 Southampton FC (ENG); 16- Liverpool FC (ENG)

2016/17 appearances/goals

Domestic league English Premier League 26(1)/13
National team FIFA World Cup qualifying 2/-; Africa Cup of Nations 3/2; Africa Cup of Nations qualifying 1/-; Friendlies 2(1)/1

Marcelo

Left-back, Height 174cm
Born 12/05/88, Rio de Janeiro, Brazil

Marcelo completed a decade as a Real Madrid player midway through a 2016/17 season that possibly brought him more satisfaction than any of his previous ten campaigns. Not only did the Brazilian left-back pick up more major trophies than ever before (four), but few Madrid fans could recall a season in which he had been so brilliant from start to finish. It was his dazzling forward raids down the left flank that particularly caught the eye, one of which led to Madrid's fourth goal in the UEFA Champions League final. Back in the Brazil squad, the effervescent 29-year-old could be a major star at the 2018 FIFA World Cup.

International career

BRAZIL
Major honours *FIFA Confederations Cup (2013)*
Debut 05/09/06 v Wales (n, London, friendly), won 2-0
First goal 05/09/06 v Wales (n, London, friendly), won 2-0
Caps 47 **Goals** 5
Major tournaments FIFA Confederations Cup 2013; FIFA World Cup 2014

Club career

Major honours *UEFA Champions League (2014, 2016, 2017); UEFA Super Cup (2014, 2016); FIFA Club World Cup (2014, 2016); Spanish League (2007, 2008, 2012, 2017); Spanish Cup (2011, 2014)*
Clubs 05-06 Fluminense FC; 07- Real Madrid CF (ESP)

2016/17 appearances/goals

Domestic league Spanish Liga 26(4)/2
Europe UEFA Champions League 11/-
National team FIFA World Cup qualifying 5/1

Kylian Mbappé

Striker, Height 178cm
Born 20/12/98, Bondy, France

It was difficult to play down the hype surrounding 18-year-old Mbappé during a season in which the extravagantly gifted, lightning-fast Monaco striker emerged as the hottest young prospect in the game. Although initially handled with care by Leonardo Jardim, the Monaco boss was so seduced by the youngster's talent that he selected him regularly in the first XI after Christmas. The reward for his faith was 15 goals in the team's triumphant Ligue 1 campaign and six in as many games during the knockout phase of the UEFA Champions League. A glittering career of many titles and trophies, a Ballon d'Or or two perhaps among them, lie in wait for this teenage sensation.

International career

FRANCE
Debut 25/03/17 v Luxembourg (a, Luxembourg, WCQ), won 3-1
Caps 4 **Goals** 0

Club career

Major honours *French League (2017)*
Clubs 15- AS Monaco FC

2016/17 appearances/goals

Domestic league French Ligue 1 17(12)/15
Europe UEFA Champions League 6(3)/6
National team FIFA World Cup qualifying (2)/-; Friendlies 2/-

Benjamin Mendy

Left-back, Height 185cm
Born 17/07/94, Longjumeau, France

After three seasons at Marseille, where he made over 100 appearances, Mendy left for Monaco in a transfer that made few waves outside the south of France. The left-back was known for the speed of his forward runs and the accuracy of his crosses, but at the time no foreign club showed an interest. A year later, however, after a stunning season at the Stade Louis II, during which he took his career to a whole new level, winning the Ligue 1 title, reaching the UEFA Champions League semi-finals and becoming a senior French international, the 23-year-old was being feted as the most expensive defender of all time following a £52m transfer to Manchester City.

International career

FRANCE
Debut 25/03/17 v Luxembourg (a, Luxembourg, WCQ), won 3-1
Caps 4 **Goals** 0

Club career

Major honours *French League (2017)*
Clubs 10-13 Le Havre AC; 13-16 Olympique de Marseille; 16-17 AS Monaco FC; 17- Manchester City FC (ENG)

2016/17 appearances/goals

Domestic league French Ligue 1 24(1)/-
Europe UEFA Champions League 6(1)/-; UEFA Champions League qualifying/play-offs 3/-
National team FIFA World Cup qualifying 2/-; Friendlies 2/-

Dries Mertens

Attacking midfielder/Striker, Height 169cm
Born 06/05/87, Leuven, Belgium

The 2016/17 season was one that Mertens will never forget. Aside from being named by fans of the Belgian national side as their 2016 player of the year, he won no silverware. Indeed, there was disappointment that his Napoli side finished third, rather than second, in Serie A. But with a remarkable tally of 28 goals in Italy's top division, the 30-year-old had the time of his life. Pressed into service up front following an injury to new signing Arkadiusz Milik, he could not stop scoring. There were five goals from him in the UEFA Champions League too, including one against Real Madrid, plus another four in FIFA World Cup qualifiers for Belgium.

International career

BELGIUM
Debut 09/02/11 v Finland (h, Ghent, friendly), drew 1-1
First goal 15/08/12 v Netherlands (h, Brussels, friendly), won 4-2
Caps 59 **Goals** 12
Major tournaments FIFA World Cup 2014; UEFA EURO 2016

Club career

Major honours *Dutch Cup (2012); Italian Cup (2014)*
Clubs 04-07 KAA Gent; 05-06 KSC Eendracht Aalst (loan); 06-07 AGOVV Apeldoorn (NED, loan); 07-09 AGOVV Apeldoorn (NED); 09-11 FC Utrecht (NED); 11-13 PSV Eindhoven (NED); 13- SSC Napoli (ITA)

2016/17 appearances/goals

Domestic league Italian Serie A 28(7)/28
Europe UEFA Champions League 6(2)/5
National team FIFA World Cup qualifying 5/4; Friendlies 1(2)/-

Lionel Messi

Striker, Height 170cm
Born 24/06/87, Rosario, Argentina

For the fourth time in his incomparable career with Barcelona, Messi completed the season with more goals than appearances. There were 54 altogether in 52 matches, with 37 of them scored in the Spanish Liga – which earned him a fourth Pichichi and ESM Golden Shoe – and 11 of them in the UEFA Champions League, including an unprecedented ten in the group stage. Despite all the goals and a great deal of other glorious moments besides, the only major trophy that came his way in 2016/17 was the Copa del Rey. Inevitably he played a key role in Barça's triumph, turning in a brilliant man-of-the-match performance against Alavés in the final.

International career

ARGENTINA
Debut 17/08/05 v Hungary (a, Budapest, friendly), won 2-1
First goal 01/03/06 v Croatia (n, Basel, friendly), lost 2-3
Caps 118 **Goals** 58
Major tournaments FIFA World Cup 2006; Copa América 2007; FIFA World Cup 2010; Copa América 2011; FIFA World Cup 2014; Copa América 2015; Copa América 2016

Club career

Major honours *UEFA Champions League (2006, 2009, 2011, 2015); UEFA Super Cup (2009, 2011, 2015); FIFA Club World Cup (2009, 2011, 2015); Spanish League (2005, 2006, 2009, 2010, 2011, 2013, 2015, 2016); Spanish Cup (2009, 2012, 2015, 2016, 2017)*
Clubs 04- FC Barcelona (ESP)

2016/17 appearances/goals

Domestic league Spanish Liga 32(2)/37
Europe UEFA Champions League 9/11
National team FIFA World Cup qualifying 4/3; Friendlies 1/-

Henrikh Mkhitaryan

Attacking midfielder, Height 178cm
Born 21/01/89, Yerevan, Armenia

Armenia's greatest ever footballer became the first from his country to play in the English Premier League when he joined Manchester United from Borussia Dortmund on a four-year contract in July 2016. He did not have it easy at first under United's new manager José Mourinho, but as the season progressed the 28-year-old's form and discipline improved to such a degree that he became the team's chief creative force. He was especially productive in the UEFA Europa League, scoring six goals, five of them away from Old Trafford including the one that doubled United's lead in the Stockholm final against Ajax.

International career

ARMENIA
Debut 14/01/07 v Panama (n, Los Angeles, friendly), drew 1-1
First goal 28/03/09 v Estonia (h, Yerevan, WCQ), drew 2-2
Caps 64 **Goals** 22

Club career

Major honours *UEFA Europa League (2017); Armenian League (2006, 2007, 2008, 2009); Ukrainian League (2011, 2012, 2013); Armenian Cup (2009); Ukrainian Cup (2011, 2012, 2013); English League Cup (2017)*
Clubs 06-09 FC Pyunik; 09-10 FC Metalurh Donetsk (UKR); 10-13 FC Shakhtar Donetsk (UKR); 13-16 Borussia Dortmund (GER); 16- Manchester United (ENG)

2016/17 appearances/goals

Domestic league English Premier League 15(9)/4
Europe UEFA Europa League 10(1)/6
National team FIFA World Cup qualifying 3/1; Friendlies 2/2

Anthony Modeste

Striker, Height 187cm
Born 14/04/88, Cannes, France

The goals flowed from Modeste like never before in 2016/17 as the 29-year-old striker powered Köln back into Europe for the first time in a quarter of a century, their fifth-place finish in the Bundesliga securing a group stage berth in the UEFA Europa League. He had struck 15 goals in his first season for the Rhinelanders, and that was raised to 25 in his second, his copious haul including an equaliser away to Bayern and hat-tricks against Hamburg and Hertha Berlin. There would be no first taste of European football for the Frenchman, however, as he opted to continue his career in China, agreeing a two-year loan to Tianjin Quanjian.

International career

FRANCE
Uncapped

Club career

Clubs 07-10 OGC Nice; 09-10 Angers SCO (loan); 10-13 FC Girondins de Bordeaux; 12 Blackburn Rovers FC (ENG, loan); 12-13 SC Bastia (loan); 13-15 TSG 1899 Hoffenheim (GER); 15- 1. FC Köln (GER); 17- Tianjin Quanjian FC (CHN, loan)

2016/17 appearances/goals

Domestic league German Bundesliga 34/25

Luka Modrić

Midfielder, Height 174cm
Born 09/09/85, Zadar, Croatia

The 2016/17 season brought Modrić a whole cluster of winner's medals to add to his already sizeable collection. The UEFA Super Cup, FIFA Club World Cup and UEFA Champions League had all been won before, but victory in the Spanish Liga was a novel experience for the 31-year-old schemer, giving him a first national title since the third of his Croatian league crowns with Dinamo Zagreb in 2008. Pivotal to all of Madrid's successes, he was particularly prominent in the latter stages of the UEFA Champions League, putting in colossal shifts against Bayern München, Atlético Madrid and, in the Cardiff final, Juventus.

International career

CROATIA
Debut 01/03/06 v Argentina (n, Basel, friendly), won 3-2
First goal 16/08/06 v Italy (a, Livorno, friendly), won 2-0
Caps 97 **Goals** 11
Major tournaments FIFA World Cup 2006; UEFA EURO 2008; UEFA EURO 2012; FIFA World Cup 2014; UEFA EURO 2016

Club career

Major honours *UEFA Champions League (2014, 2016, 2017); UEFA Super Cup (2014, 2016); FIFA Club World Cup (2014, 2016); Croatian League (2006, 2007, 2008); Spanish League (2017); Croatian Cup (2007, 2008); Spanish Cup (2014)*
Clubs 02-08 GNK Dinamo Zagreb; 03-04 HŠK Zrinjski (BIH, loan); 04-05 NK Inter Zaprešić (loan); 08-12 Tottenham Hotspur FC (ENG); 12- Real Madrid CF (ESP)

2016/17 appearances/goals

Domestic league Spanish Liga 22(3)/1
Europe UEFA Champions League 11/-
National team FIFA World Cup qualifying 3(1)/-

Radja Nainggolan

Midfielder, Height 175cm
Born 04/05/88, Antwerp, Belgium

Roma's tigerish, tattoo-heavy Belgian midfielder enjoyed another splendid season in the Eternal City to help the Giallorossi finish runners-up to Juventus in Serie A and secure guaranteed group stage UEFA Champions League football at the Stadio Olimpico in 2017/18. To his natural aggression and energy the 28-year-old added an increased attacking threat, scoring 11 league goals – the same number as in the previous two seasons combined – plus the first of his career in Europe. Given his great form in Italy, it was a surprise that new Belgium boss Roberto Martínez used him so sparingly during the FIFA World Cup qualifying campaign.

International career

BELGIUM
Debut 29/05/09 v Chile (n, Chiba, Kirin Cup), drew 1-1
First goal 05/03/14 v Ivory Coast (h, Brussels, friendly), drew 2-2
Caps 29 **Goals** 6
Major tournaments UEFA EURO 2016

Club career

Clubs 06-10 Piacenza Calcio (ITA); 10 Cagliari Calcio (ITA, loan); 10-14 Cagliari Calcio (ITA); 14 AS Roma (ITA, loan); 14- AS Roma (ITA)

2016/17 appearances/goals

Domestic league Italian Serie A 35(2)/11
Europe UEFA Champions League play-offs 2/-; UEFA Europa League 7(3)/1
National team FIFA World Cup qualifying 1(1)/-; Friendlies 3/-

Neymar

Striker, Height 174cm
Born 05/02/92, Mogi das Cruzes, Brazil

The football world shook on its axis when it was announced in early August 2017 that Neymar wanted to leave Barcelona. Four years at the Camp Nou, during which he scored 105 goals but was never fully able to step out of the shadow of the great Lionel Messi, was apparently long enough. The last of the Brazilian international's seasons in Catalonia was not his best, but it certainly provided his greatest performance – the UEFA Champions League round of 16 second leg against Paris Saint-Germain, which he turned around almost single-handedly to give Barça a historic, record-breaking victory. No wonder PSG were prepared to move heaven and earth to sign him.

International career

BRAZIL
Major honours *FIFA Confederations Cup (2013)*
Debut 10/08/10 v United States (a, East Rutherford, friendly), won 2-0
First goal 10/08/10 v United States (a, East Rutherford, friendly), won 2-0
Caps 77 **Goals** 52
Major tournaments Copa América 2011; FIFA Confederations Cup 2013; FIFA World Cup 2014; Copa América 2015

Club career

Major honours *UEFA Champions League (2015); Libertadores Cup (2011); Recopa Sudamericana (2012); UEFA Super Cup (2015); FIFA Club World Cup (2015); Spanish League (2015, 2016); Brazilian Cup (2010); Spanish Cup (2015, 2016, 2017)*
Clubs 09-13 Santos FC; 13-17 FC Barcelona (ESP); 17- Paris Saint-Germain (FRA)

2016/17 appearances/goals

Domestic league Spanish Liga 30/13
Europe UEFA Champions League 9/4
National team FIFA World Cup qualifying 7/6

Jan Oblak

Goalkeeper, Height 186cm
Born 07/01/93, Skofla Loka, Slovenia

Having convinced national team boss Srečko Katanec to make him Slovenia's first-choice goalkeeper – ahead of Samir Handanovič – for the 2018 FIFA World Cup qualifying campaign, and then repaid that faith by conceding just three goals in six games, Oblak furthered his growing reputation as one of Europe's top shot-stoppers with another excellent season between the posts for Atlético Madrid. He retained the Zamora trophy after conceding just 21 goals in the Spanish Liga and also kept six clean sheets in the UEFA Champions League, including four out of five matches at home, to help his team through to the semi-finals.

International career

SLOVENIA
Debut 11/09/12 v Norway (a, Oslo, WCQ), lost 1-2
Caps 14 **Goals** 0

Club career

Major honours *Portuguese League (2014); Portuguese Cup (2014)*
Clubs 09-10 NK Olimpija Ljubljana; 10-14 SL Benfica (POR); 10 SC Beira Mar (POR, loan); 11 SC Olhanense (POR, loan); 11-12 UD Leiria (POR, loan); 12-13 Rio Ave FC (POR, loan); 14- Club Atlético de Madrid (ESP)

2016/17 appearances/goals

Domestic league Spanish Liga 30/-
Europe UEFA Champions League 11/-
National team FIFA World Cup qualifying 6/-

Miralem Pjanić

Midfielder, Height 180cm
Born 02/04/90, Tuzla, Bosnia & Herzegovina

After three years with Lyon and five with Roma, Pjanić was still seeking the first major honour of his career. A summer 2016 transfer to Juventus changed all that. The Bosnia & Herzegovina international cost €32m, but on the evidence of his first season in Turin the money was well spent. Buoyed by the early settler of a goal on his debut, against Sassuolo, he proceeded to pull the strings in midfield for Juve just as he had done for Roma. In the second half of the season he operated in a deeper role, which reduced his goal threat, but his contribution towards the team's Serie A and Coppa Italia triumphs was no less influential.

International career

BOSNIA & HERZEGOVINA
Debut 20/08/08 v Bulgaria (h, Zenica, friendly), lost 1-2
First goal 03/03/10 v Ghana (h, Sarajevo, friendly), won 2-1
Caps 74 **Goals** 11
Major tournaments FIFA World Cup 2014

Club career

Major honours *Italian League (2017); Italian Cup (2017)*
Clubs 07-08 FC Metz (FRA); 08-11 Olympique Lyonnais (FRA); 11-16 AS Roma (ITA); 16- Juventus FC (ITA)

2016/17 appearances/goals

Domestic league Italian Serie A 25(5)/5
Europe UEFA Champions League 11(1)/1
National team FIFA World Cup qualifying 6/-

Paul Pogba

Midfielder, Height 186cm
Born 15/03/93, Lagny-sur-Marne, France

Back at his first club Manchester United after four years at Juventus, Pogba initially found it difficult to cope with the world-record price tag of €105m that was hanging around his neck. The expectation, both at Old Trafford and among English football followers at large, was understandably huge. The Frenchman improved as the season progressed, but as the Premier League largely passed United by, the UEFA Europa League became his stage. He started all 15 matches, scoring three goals, the last of them to give United the lead against Ajax in the final and propel them to victory in the one major competition they had never won.

International career

FRANCE
Debut 22/03/13 v Georgia (h, Paris, WCQ), won 3-1
First goal 10/09/13 v Belarus (a, Gomel, WCQ), won 4-2
Caps 47 **Goals** 8
Major tournaments FIFA World Cup 2014; UEFA EURO 2016

Club career

Major honours *UEFA Europa League (2017); Italian League (2013, 2014, 2015, 2016); Italian Cup (2015, 2016); English League Cup (2017)*
Clubs 11-12 Manchester United FC (ENG); 12-16 Juventus FC (ITA); 16- Manchester United FC (ENG)

2016/17 appearances/goals

Domestic league English Premier League 29(1)/5
Europe UEFA Europa League 15/3
National team FIFA World Cup qualifying 5/2; Friendlies 4/-

Quincy Promes

Winger/Striker, Height 174cm
Born 04/01/92, Amsterdam, Netherlands

Bought by Spartak Moskva from FC Twente in 2014, Dutch winger Promes impressed in Russia almost from day one and in 2016/17, with his standing firmly established as one of the Premier-Liga's leading attractions, he added substance to the style by helping Spartak win the title. With 12 goals he was the team's top scorer for the third season in a row, setting up another nine for his team-mates. His speed, skill and shooting power were also frequently on show for the Netherlands during a season in which he scored his first four international goals, breaking his duck with a double in a FIFA World Cup qualifier at home to Belarus.

International career

NETHERLANDS
Debut 05/03/14 v France (a, Saint-Denis, friendly), lost 0-2
First goal 07/10/16 v Belarus (h, Rotterdam, WCQ), won 4-1
Caps 21 **Goals** 4

Club career

Major honours *Russian League (2017)*
Clubs 12-14 FC Twente; 12-13 Go Ahead Eagles (loan); 14- FC Spartak Moskva (RUS)

2016/17 appearances/goals

Domestic league Russian Premier-Liga 25(1)/12
Europe UEFA Europa League qualifying 2/-
National team FIFA World Cup qualifying 4(1)/3; Friendlies 3(1)/1

Raphaël Guerreiro

Left-back/Midfielder, Height 170cm
Born 22/12/93, Le Blanc-Mesnil, France

His star in the ascendancy after a tremendous UEFA EURO 2016, Raphaël Guerreiro began a new chapter to his career in Germany with Borussia Dortmund. His transfer from Lorient had already been completed before Portugal's triumph in France – the country in which he was born and had spent his entire career. The new twin challenge of the Bundesliga and the UEFA Champions League was one he rose to with impressive speed and confidence. Dortmund boss Thomas Tuchel got the best of the 23-year-old by switching him from left-back to a central midfield role, and it was in that position that he helped the Schwarzgelben to victory in the German Cup.

International career

PORTUGAL
Major honours *UEFA European Championship (2016)*
Debut 14/11/14 v Armenia (h, Faro, ECQ), won 1-0
First goal 18/11/14 v Argentina (n, Manchester, friendly), won 1-0
Caps 20 **Goals** 2
Major tournaments UEFA EURO 2016; FIFA Confederations Cup 2017

Club career

Major honours *German Cup (2017)*
Clubs 10-13 SM Caen (FRA); 13-16 FC Lorient (FRA); 16- Borussia Dortmund (GER)

2016/17 appearances/goals

Domestic league German Bundesliga 17(7)/6
Europe UEFA Champions League 6/1
National team FIFA World Cup qualifying 5/-; FIFA Confederations Cup 2/-; Friendlies 1/-

Arjen Robben

Winger, Height 180cm
Born 23/01/84, Bedum, Netherlands

Robben won the tenth national title of his illustrious career as he helped Bayern München to their fifth successive Bundesliga triumph. The 2016/17 season was one of the very best of his eight in Munich. At 33 and with a body battered over the years by an assortment of injuries, the Dutchman proved that he is still one of the most gifted wingers in the game. He was second only to Robert Lewandowski in Bayern's scoring charts, registering 13 Bundesliga goals and three more in the UEFA Champions League. All were scored in singles, including home and away strikes against Arsenal and a dramatic stoppage-time winner at RB Leipzig.

International career

NETHERLANDS
Debut 30/04/03 v Portugal (h, Eindhoven, friendly), drew 1-1
First goal 11/10/03 v Moldova (h, Eindhoven, ECQ), won 5-0
Caps 92 **Goals** 33
Major tournaments UEFA EURO 2004; FIFA World Cup 2006; UEFA EURO 2008; FIFA World Cup 2010; UEFA EURO 2012; FIFA World Cup 2014

Club career

Major honours *UEFA Champions League (2013); UEFA Super Cup (2013); FIFA Club World Cup (2013); Dutch League (2003); English League (2005, 2006); Spanish League (2008); German League (2010, 2013, 2014, 2015, 2016, 2017); English FA Cup (2007); German Cup (2010, 2013, 2014, 2016); English League Cup (2005, 2007)*
Clubs 00-02 FC Groningen; 02-04 PSV Eindhoven; 04-07 Chelsea FC (ENG); 07-09 Real Madrid CF (ESP); 09- FC Bayern München (GER)

2016/17 appearances/goals

Domestic league German Bundesliga 21(5)/13
Europe UEFA Champions League 7(1)/3
National team FIFA World Cup qualifying 3/2; Friendlies 1/1

Saúl Ñíguez

Attacking midfielder, Height 182cm
Born 21/11/94, Elche, Spain

Granted a long-awaited first senior cap for Spain at the start of the 2016/17 season, Saúl ended it by starring for his country at the UEFA European Under-21 Championship. The Atlético Madrid midfielder was on fire in Poland, scoring a tournament-high tally of five goals, most of them spectacular, including a semi-final hat-trick against Italy. He returned home to find Atlético eager to tie him to a new long-term contract, which, to the consternation of several of Europe's top clubs, he duly signed. Another excellent season for Diego Simeone's side featured four crucial UEFA Champions League goals, including a rare header away to Leicester in the quarter-final.

International career

SPAIN
Debut 01/09/16 v Belgium (a, Brussels, friendly), won 2-0
Caps 3 **Goals** 0

Club career

Major honours *Spanish Cup (2013)*
Clubs 10-13 Club Atlético de Madrid B; 12- Club Atlético de Madrid; 13-14 Rayo Vallecano de Madrid (loan)

2016/17 appearances/goals

Domestic league Spanish Liga 29(4)/4
Europe UEFA Champions League 10(2)/4
National team FIFA World Cup qualifying (1)/-; Friendlies (2)/-

Patrik Schick

Striker, Height 187cm
Born 24/01/96, Prague, Czech Republic

Serie A followers, especially those of Sampdoria, were seduced by Schick's graceful skill and scoring touch as the young Czech striker made a dramatic impact on his first season in Italy. Just 20 when he arrived in Genoa from Sparta Praha, the tall, elegant striker scored 11 league goals for Samp, most of them displaying a touch of class including one exquisite effort against Crotone. He was also the top scorer in the UEFA European Under-21 Championship qualifying campaign, netting ten goals for the Czech Republic. He added another at the finals, against Denmark, but in a 4-2 defeat that eliminated his team at the group stage.

International career

CZECH REPUBLIC
Debut 27/05/16 v Malta (n, Kufstein, friendly), won 6-0
First goal 27/05/16 v Malta (n, Kufstein, friendly), won 6-0
Caps 5 **Goals** 1

Club career

Major honours *Czech League (2014); Czech Cup (2014)*
Clubs 14-16 AC Sparta Praha; 15-16 Bohemians Praha 1905 (loan); 16- UC Sampdoria (ITA)

2016/17 appearances/goals

Domestic league Italian Serie A 14(18)/11
National team FIFA World Cup qualifying 1(2)/-; Friendlies 1/-

Kasper Schmeichel

Goalkeeper, Height 189cm
Born 05/11/86, Copenhagen, Denmark

While most Leicester City players struggled to replicate their remarkable 2015/16 form in the season after their Premier League triumph, Schmeichel's standards never dropped. The Danish goalkeeper proved to be a particularly formidable last line of defence in the UEFA Champions League, drawing favourable comparison with his famous father Peter by keeping clean sheets in his first four games – despite playing with a broken hand against FC København on his return to the city of his birth, an injury that sidelined him for several weeks. He was back to his heroic best in the round of 16, saving penalties in both legs of Leicester's momentous victory over Sevilla.

International career

DENMARK
Debut 06/02/13 v FYR Macedonia (a, Skopje, friendly), lost 0-3
Caps 25 **Goals** 0

Club career

Major honours *English League (2016)*
Clubs 05-09 Manchester City FC (ENG); 06 Darlington FC (ENG, loan); 06 Bury FC (ENG, loan); 07 Falkirk FC (SCO, loan); 07-08 Cardiff City FC (ENG, loan); 08 Coventry City FC (ENG, loan); 09-10 Notts County FC (ENG); 10-11 Leeds United AFC (ENG); 11- Leicester City FC (ENG)

2016/17 appearances/goals

Domestic league English Premier League 30/-
Europe UEFA Champions League 8/-
National team FIFA World Cup qualifying 3/-

Sergio Ramos

Centre-back, Height 183cm
Born 30/03/86, Seville, Spain

The first captain to lift the European Cup two years running in the UEFA Champions League era, Sergio Ramos concluded arguably the finest season of his career in Cardiff. It was the fourth major trophy he had raised in 2016/17, the trend starting in August in Norway when he scored a late equaliser against former club Sevilla en route to a dramatic UEFA Super Cup triumph. The Madrid skipper scored ten goals over the campaign – a personal-best haul – and many of them were all-important late strikes, such as his 90th-minute equalising header away to Barcelona in December and the stoppage-time winner at Deportivo seven days later.

International career

SPAIN
Major honours *FIFA World Cup (2010); UEFA European Championship (2008, 2012)*
Debut 26/03/05 v China (h, Salamanca, friendly), won 3-0
First goal 13/10/05 v San Marino (a, Serravalle, WCQ), won 6-0
Caps 143 **Goals** 10
Major tournaments FIFA World Cup 2006; UEFA EURO 2008; FIFA Confederations Cup 2009; FIFA World Cup 2010; UEFA EURO 2012; FIFA Confederations Cup 2013; FIFA World Cup 2014; UEFA EURO 2016

Club career

Major honours *UEFA Champions League (2014, 2016, 2017); UEFA Super Cup (2014, 2016); FIFA Club World Cup (2014, 2016); Spanish League (2007, 2008, 2012, 2017); Spanish Cup (2011, 2014)*
Clubs 02-05 Sevilla FC; 05- Real Madrid CF

2016/17 appearances/goals

Domestic league Spanish Liga 28/7
Europe UEFA Champions League 11/1
National team FIFA World Cup qualifying 5/-; Friendlies 2/-

Djibril Sidibé

Right-back, Height 182cm
Born 29/07/92, Troyes, France

France found a new right-back and Monaco a Ligue 1-winning warrior as Sidibé's career soared to spectacular new heights in 2016/17. Newly recruited from Lille on a five-year contract, he was the perfect fit for Leonardo Jardim's audacious high-rollers, his swashbuckling right-touchline raids and vicious outswinging crosses sourcing several of the many goals Monaco scored en route to capturing the French title, reaching the final of the League Cup and the last four of both the UEFA Champions League and Coupe de France. His season ended on an appropriate high with his first international goal – in a 3-2 friendly win against England.

International career

FRANCE
Debut 01/09/16 v Italy (a, Bari, friendly), won 3-1
First goal 13/06/17 v England (h, Saint-Denis, friendly), won 3-2
Caps 10 **Goals** 1

Club career

Major honours *French League (2017)*
Clubs 10-12 ES Troyes AC; 12-16 LOSC Lille; 16- AS Monaco FC

2016/17 appearances/goals

Domestic league French Ligue 1 25(3)/2
Europe UEFA Champions League 9/1; UEFA Champions League qualifying/play-offs 3/-
National team FIFA World Cup qualifying 5(1)/-; Friendlies 4/1

Gylfi Thór Sigurdsson

Midfielder, Height 186cm
Born 08/09/89, Reykjavik, Iceland

A key member of the Iceland side that stunned Europe by reaching the last eight of UEFA EURO 2016, Sigurdsson continued his good work by helping his country take 13 points from their opening six FIFA World Cup qualifiers, a crucial 1-0 win at home to Croatia coming on his 50th appearance. At club level the 27-year-old was arguably the difference between Swansea City staying in the Premier League and submitting to relegation. Ever-present and routinely excellent, he scored nine goals, away strikes at Arsenal, Liverpool, Manchester City and Manchester United among them, to become a wanted man in the summer transfer market.

International career

ICELAND
Debut 29/05/10 v Andorra (h, Reykjavik, friendly), won 4-0
First goal 07/10/11 v Portugal (a, Porto, ECQ), lost 3-5
Caps 50 **Goals** 15
Major tournaments UEFA EURO 2016

Club career

Clubs 08-10 Reading FC (ENG); 08 Shrewsbury Town FC (ENG, loan); 09 Crewe Alexandra FC (ENG, loan); 10-12 TSG 1899 Hoffenheim (GER); 12 Swansea City AFC (ENG, loan); 12-14 Tottenham Hotspur FC (ENG); 14- Swansea City AFC (ENG)

2016/17 appearances/goals

Domestic league English Premier League 37(1)/9
National team FIFA World Cup qualifying 6/1

David Silva

Attacking midfielder, Height 170cm
Born 08/01/86, Arguinegin, Gran Canaria, Spain

Sergio Agüero scored more goals and Kevin De Bruyne provided more assists, but the best Manchester City player in 2016/17, according to an official club fan vote, was Silva. His first season under compatriot Pep Guardiola brought no trophies, yet the view of the locals was that the slippery, skilful 31-year-old left-footer had never played better. That was true also of his performances for Spain, for whom he scored eight goals in coach Julen Lopetegui's first season, four of them in FIFA World Cup qualifiers and the deadlock-breaking strike in each of his country's first four internationals of 2017, which made him Spain's fourth-highest scorer of all time.

International career

SPAIN
Major honours *FIFA World Cup (2010); UEFA European Championship (2008, 2012)*
Debut 15/11/06 v Romania (h, Cadiz, friendly), lost 0-1
First goal 22/08/07 v Greece (a, Thessaloniki, friendly), won 3-2
Caps 113 **Goals** 32
Major tournaments UEFA EURO 2008; FIFA Confederations Cup 2009; FIFA World Cup 2010; UEFA EURO 2012; FIFA Confederations Cup 2013; FIFA World Cup 2014; UEFA EURO 2016

Club career

Major honours *English League (2012, 2014); Spanish Cup (2008); English FA Cup (2011); English League Cup (2014, 2016)*
Clubs 03-04 Valencia CF B; 04-10 Valencia CF; 04-05 SD Éibar (loan); 05-06 RC Celta de Vigo (loan); 10- Manchester City FC (ENG)

2016/17 appearances/goals

Domestic league English Premier League 31(3)/4
Europe UEFA Champions League 6/1
National team FIFA World Cup qualifying 6/4; Friendlies 3(1)/4

Fedor Smolov

Striker, Height 187cm
Born 09/02/90, Saratov, Russia

Russia have struggled for goals in their recent tournament appearances, scoring just eight in their last 11 matches, the 2017 FIFA Confederations Cup included. That does not bode well for the 2018 FIFA World Cup, but the man Russian fans will be counting on to reverse that trend when the country hosts football's biggest event is Smolov. The FC Krasnodar striker topped the Premier-Liga scoring charts for the second successive season in 2016/17, with 18 goals, and also added six in Europe. The 27-year-old also found the net three times for his country, in wins against Ghana, Hungary and New Zealand. No player will be under greater pressure next summer.

International career

RUSSIA
Debut 14/11/12 v United States (h, Krasnodar, friendly), drew 2-2
First goal 14/11/12 v United States (h, Krasnodar, friendly), drew 2-2
Caps 24 **Goals** 8
Major tournaments UEFA EURO 2016; FIFA Confederations Cup 2017

Club career

Clubs 07-15 FC Dinamo Moskva; 10 Feyenoord (NED, loan); 12-13 & 14 FC Anji (loan); 14-15 FC Ural Yekaterinburg (loan); 15- FC Krasnodar

2016/17 appearances/goals

Domestic league Russian Premier-Liga 21(1)/18
Europe UEFA Europa League 6/4; UEFA Europa League qualifying/play-offs 2/2
National team FIFA Confederations Cup 3/1; Friendlies 4/2

Lars Stindl

Attacking midfielder/Striker, Height 180cm
Born 26/08/88, Speyer, Germany

It was not quite the same as scoring the winning goal in a FIFA World Cup final, but Lars Stindl's tap-in against Chile in St Petersburg enabled Germany to beat the South American champions 1-0 and win the FIFA Confederations Cup for the first time. It was the Borussia Mönchengladbach captain's third goal at a tournament in which he, like several other fringe players, boosted his chances of breaking into the Germany squad that will return to Russia to defend the World Cup in 2018. A first international call-up at 28 was earned by an excellent season at Gladbach, with an 11-minute UEFA Europa League hat-trick against Fiorentina among its highlights.

International career

GERMANY
Major honours *FIFA Confederations Cup (2017)*
Debut 06/06/17 v Denmark (a, Brondby, friendly), drew 1-1
First goal 19/06/17 v Australia (n, Sochi, CC), won 3-2
Caps 6 **Goals** 3
Major tournaments FIFA Confederations Cup 2017

Club career

Clubs 07-10 Karlsruher SC; 10-15 Hannover 96; 15- VfL Borussia Mönchengladbach

2016/17 appearances/goals

Domestic league German Bundesliga 29(1)/11
Europe UEFA Champions League 5/2; UEFA Champions League play-offs 2/-; UEFA Europa League 3/3
National team FIFA World Cup qualifying 1/-; FIFA Confederations Cup 4/3; Friendlies 1/-

Luis Suárez

Striker, Height 181cm
Born 24/01/87, Salto, Uruguay

With 59 goals for Barcelona in 2015/16, Suárez gave himself a hard act to follow. The Uruguayan started the season in determined mood by scoring a hat-trick in his first Liga game, against Real Betis, and two goals on his first UEFA Champions League outing, against Celtic, but matching that tally was never a realistic possibility. In the end he had to be content with 29 in the league – second to team-mate Lionel Messi on the Pichichi list – and three in Europe. He also struck six goals in the Copa del Rey, including one against Athletic Club that brought up his century for Barça, but missed the final, a 3-1 win against Alavés, through suspension.

International career

URUGUAY
Major honours *Copa América (2011)*
Debut 07/02/07 v Colombia (a, Cucuta, friendly), won 3-1
First goal 13/10/07 v Bolivia (h, Montevideo, WCQ), won 5-0
Caps 91 **Goals** 46
Major tournaments FIFA World Cup 2010; Copa América 2011; FIFA Confederations Cup 2013; FIFA World Cup 2014; Copa América 2016

Club career

Major honours *UEFA Champions League (2015); UEFA Super Cup (2015); FIFA Club World Cup (2015); Uruguayan League (2006); Dutch League (2011); Spanish League (2015, 2016); Dutch Cup (2010); Spanish Cup (2015, 2016, 2017); English League Cup (2012)*
Clubs 05-06 Club Nacional; 06-07 FC Groningen (NED); 07-11 AFC Ajax (NED); 11-14 Liverpool FC (ENG); 14- FC Barcelona (ESP)

2016/17 appearances/goals

Domestic league Spanish Liga 34(1)/29
Europe UEFA Champions League 9/3
National team FIFA World Cup qualifying 7/2

Niklas Süle

Centre-back, Height 195cm
Born 03/09/95, Frankfurt am Main, Germany

An Olympic silver medallist with Germany in Rio de Janeiro, Süle built on his reputation as one of Germany's finest young defensive talents by helping Hoffenheim to defy the odds and finish fourth in the Bundesliga – the highest position in the club's history. Midway through the campaign he agreed a deal to join Bayern München in the summer. It had no ill effect on his performances. On the contrary, any swelling to his pride was channelled positively, and he even helped Hoffenheim to a memorable 1-0 win over his future employers before going to Russia at the end of term and helping Germany win the FIFA Confederations Cup.

International career

GERMANY
Major honours *FIFA Confederations Cup (2017)*
Debut 31/08/16 v Finland (h, Monchengladbach, friendly), won 2-0
Caps 6 **Goals** 0
Major tournaments FIFA Confederations Cup 2017

Club career

Clubs 12-17 TSG 1899 Hoffenheim; 17- FC Bayern München

2016/17 appearances/goals

Domestic league German Bundesliga 33/2
National team FIFA Confederations Cup 2(2)/-; Friendlies 2/-

Talisca

Attacking midfielder, Height 191cm
Born 01/02/94, Feira de Santana, Brazil

While his parent club Benfica retained the Portuguese Primeira Liga title without him, Talisca helped Beşiktaş achieve the equivalent feat in Turkey – although not before he had returned to Lisbon to score a brilliant late equaliser against Benfica in the UEFA Champions League. The tall, languid left-footer was a welcome addition not only to Beşiktaş but also to the Süper Lig as a whole, his natural Brazilian flair bewitching Turkish fans of all parishes and persuasions. He scored 13 league goals, including the winner away to Galatasaray, and also showed his class in helping the Black Eagles to the quarter-finals of the UEFA Europa League.

International career

BRAZIL
Uncapped

Club career

Major honours *Portuguese League (2015, 2016); Turkish League (2017)*
Clubs 13-14 EC Bahia; 14- SL Benfica (POR); 16-17 Beşiktaş JK (loan)

2016/17 appearances/goals

Domestic league Turkish Süper Lig 21(1)/13
Europe UEFA Champions League 1(2)/1; UEFA Europa League 5(1)/2

Łukasz Teodorczyk

Striker, Height 185cm
Born 03/06/91, Zuromin, Poland

On loan to Anderlecht from Dynamo Kyiv for the duration of the 2016/17 season, Teodorczyk took so well to life at the Brussels club that he was able to engineer a permanent move from the Ukrainian capital several weeks before the campaign had concluded. Curiously the goals that had flowed from August to March dried up once the Polish striker had settled his future, but he did return to form with a double in the 3-1 win at Charleroi that wrapped up Anderlecht's 34th Belgian title, giving him a total of 22 for the season, enough for a share of the golden boot with Eupen's Henry Onyekuru.

International career

POLAND
Debut 02/02/13 v Romania B (n, Malaga, friendly), won 4-1
First goal 02/02/13 v Romania B (n, Malaga, friendly), won 4-1
Caps 13 **Goals** 4

Club career

Major honours *Ukrainian League (2015, 2016); Belgian League (2017); Ukrainian Cup (2015)*
Clubs 10-12 Polonia Warszawa; 13-14 KKS Lech Poznań; 14-17 FC Dynamo Kyiv (UKR); 16-17 RSC Anderlecht (BEL, loan); 17- RSC Anderlecht (BEL)

2016/17 appearances/goals

Domestic league Belgian Pro League 36(2)/22
Europe UEFA Europa League 8(3)/5; UEFA Europa League play-offs 2/2
National team FIFA World Cup qualifying 1(3)/-; Friendlies 1/1

Thiago Alcántara

Midfielder, Height 172cm
Born 11/04/91, San Pietro Vernotico, Italy

Fears that the departure of his mentor Pep Guardiola to Manchester City might have an adverse effect on Thiago's performances for Bayern München could hardly have been wider of the mark. The challenge of working for a different coach, with different ideas, instead brought out the best in the 26-year-old as Carlo Ancelotti prepared for the imminent retirement of Xabi Alonso by making the ex-Barcelona man his main distribution hub in midfield – with hugely positive results. A masterclass in the crucial 3-0 win over RB Leipzig just before Christmas was just one of many sparkling displays by the stylish Spanish international.

International career

SPAIN
Debut 10/08/11 v Italy (a, Bari, friendly), lost 1-2
Caps 21 **Goals** 0
Major tournaments UEFA EURO 2016

Club career

Major honours *UEFA Champions League (2011); UEFA Super Cup (2009, 2011, 2013); FIFA Club World Cup (2009, 2011, 2013); Spanish League (2009, 2010, 2011, 2013); German League (2014, 2015, 2016, 2017); Spanish Cup (2009, 2012); German Cup (2014, 2016)*
Clubs 08-11 FC Barcelona B; 09-13 FC Barcelona; 13- FC Bayern München (GER)

2016/17 appearances/goals

Domestic league German Bundesliga 26(1)/6
Europe UEFA Champions League 9/2
National team FIFA World Cup qualifying 5(1)/-; Friendlies 2(1)/-

Youri Tielemans

Midfielder, Height 176cm
Born 07/05/97, Sint-Pieters-Leeuw, Belgium

Hailed as the brightest new star in the Belgian firmament ever since he made his Anderlecht debut at 16, Tielemans was still not out of his teens for the majority of the 2016/17 season, yet he was the best player in the country by a distance as he inspired the Brussels club to their first national title in three years as well as a place in the quarter-finals of the UEFA Europa League. His youthful energy and enthusiasm served him well in a punishing season that required him to play 53 matches – in which he scored 18 goals – plus another four for Belgium. The season had only just finished when he signed a five-year contract with Monaco.

International career

BELGIUM
Debut 09/11/16 v Netherlands (a, Amsterdam, friendly), drew 1-1
Caps 4 **Goals** 0

Club career

Major honours *Belgian League (2014, 2017)*
Clubs 13-17 RSC Anderlecht; 17- AS Monaco FC (FRA)

2016/17 appearances/goals

Domestic league Belgian Pro League 35(2)/13
Europe UEFA Champions League qualifying 2/1; UEFA Europa League 11/3; UEFA Europa League play-offs 2/1
National team FIFA World Cup qualifying (1)/-; Friendlies 2(1)/-

Corentin Tolisso

Attacking midfielder, Height 181cm
Born 03/08/94, Tarare, France

A first senior cap for a France side already bursting at the seams with midfield talent was one of two rewards for Tolisso's excellent 2016/17 campaign with Lyon. The second came three months later when Bayern München forked out a Bundesliga-record fee of €41.5m to bring the talented youngster to Germany. Versatile and unpredictable, the former France Under-21 captain had been tried out in a number of positions during his first two seasons as a Lyon regular, but it was in an advanced midfield role that he excelled in his third, scoring 14 goals in all competitions, which doubled his tally from the previous two campaigns put together.

International career

FRANCE
Debut 28/03/17 v Spain (h, Saint-Denis, friendly), lost 0-2
Caps 1 **Goals** 0

Club career

Clubs 13-17 Olympique Lyonnais; 17- FC Bayern München (GER)

2016/17 appearances/goals

Domestic league French Ligue 1 29(2)/8
Europe UEFA Champions League 5(1)/2; UEFA Europa League 7(1)/2
National team Friendlies 1/-

Marco Verratti

Midfielder, Height 165cm
Born 05/11/92, Pescara, Italy

For the first time in his Paris Saint-Germain career there was no Ligue 1 winner's medal for Verratti, yet the indefatigable Italian midfielder still earned a fifth successive selection in the official Ligue 1 team of the year. He also won a fourth Coupe de la Ligue and third Coupe de France, starting and starring for Unai Emery's side in both finals. Like many of his PSG team-mates, his best performance of the season came in the 4-0 home win over Barcelona and his worst in the 6-1 away defeat that followed. After missing UEFA EURO 2016 with injury, the 24-year-old re-established himself as an Azzurri regular in the 2018 FIFA World Cup qualifiers.

International career

ITALY
Debut 15/08/12 v England (n, Berne, friendly), lost 1-2
First goal 06/02/13 v Netherlands (a, Amsterdam, friendly), drew 1-1
Caps 21 **Goals** 1
Major tournaments FIFA World Cup 2014

Club career

Major honours *French League (2013, 2014, 2015, 2016); French Cup (2015, 2016, 2017); French League Cup (2014, 2015, 2016, 2017)*
Clubs 08-12 Pescara Calcio; 12- Paris Saint-Germain (FRA)

2016/17 appearances/goals

Domestic league French Ligue 1 25(3)/3
Europe UEFA Champions League 7/-
National team FIFA World Cup qualifying 4/-; Friendlies 1(1)/-

Arturo Vidal

Midfielder, Height 181cm
Born 22/05/87, Santiago, Chile

Vidal made it six national titles in as many seasons as he strung a second Bundesliga crown with Bayern München on to a run of four straight Serie A successes with Juventus. Not at his best in 2015/16, under Pep Guardiola, the combative Chilean midfielder came alive with Carlo Ancelotti at the controls. His energy and passion proved infectious, especially in the UEFA Champions League – which he has never won – and he carried those fighting qualities through to the FIFA Confederations Cup, where he was one of the tournament's outstanding performers, albeit a figure of frustration at the end after Chile's unlucky defeat in the final against Germany.

International career

CHILE
Major honours *Copa América (2015, 2016)*
Debut 07/02/07 v Venezuela (a, Maracaibo, friendly), won 1-0
First goal 05/09/09 v Venezuela (h, Santiago, WCQ), drew 2-2
Caps 95 **Goals** 23
Major tournaments FIFA World Cup 2010; Copa América 2011; FIFA World Cup 2014; Copa América 2015; Copa América 2016; FIFA Confederations Cup 2017

Club career

Major honours *Chilean League (apertura 2006; clausura 2006; apertura 2007); Italian League (2012, 2013, 2014, 2015); German League (2016, 2017); Italian Cup (2015); German Cup (2016)*
Clubs 05-07 CSD Colo-Colo; 07-11 Bayer 04 Leverkusen (GER); 11-15 Juventus FC (ITA); 15- FC Bayern München (GER)

2016/17 appearances/goals

Domestic league German Bundesliga 21(6)/4
Europe UEFA Champions League 8/3
National team FIFA World Cup qualifying 7/3; FIFA Confederations Cup 5/1; Friendlies 2(1)/2

Timo Werner

Striker, Height 181cm
Born 06/03/96, Stuttgart, Germany

Relegated from the Bundesliga with VfB Stuttgart in 2015/16, Werner was a runner-up 12 months later with newly-promoted RB Leipzig, his €10m move having paid dividends far richer than either he or his new club could have imagined. The dynamic 21-year-old striker was a pest to Bundesliga back lines all season long with his terrific pace and tenacious pressing. His finishing skills were also of the highest order as he struck 21 goals – the fourth-highest figure in the division. A first cap for Germany was inevitable, and he starred in the team's FIFA Confederations Cup triumph, scoring three goals and setting up the winner against Chile in the final.

International career

GERMANY
Major honours *FIFA Confederations Cup (2017)*
Debut 22/03/17 v England (h, Dortmund, friendly), won 1-0
First goal 25/06/17 v Cameroon (n, Sochi, CC), won 3-1
Caps 6 **Goals** 3
Major tournaments FIFA Confederations Cup 2017

Club career

Clubs 13-16 VfB Stuttgart; 16- RB Leipzig

2016/17 appearances/goals

Domestic league German Bundesliga 28(3)/21
National team FIFA World Cup qualifying (1)/-; FIFA Confederations Cup 3(1)/3; Friendlies 1/-

Nation-by-nation

Welcome to the Nation-by-nation section of the European Football Yearbook.

Here you will find separate chapters, alphabetically arranged, on each UEFA member association containing the following information.

Association directory

The member association's official logo, name, address, contact details, senior officials, year of formation and, where applicable, national stadium as of July 2017.

Map/Club index

A map of the country illustrating the locations of its top-division clubs, which are listed in alphabetical order, plus any clubs promoted to the top division at the end of the 2016/17 (2016) season. Teams qualified for the 2017/18 UEFA Champions League and UEFA Europa League are indicated as such with colour coding, as are relegated teams. Official logos are set beside all clubs.

NB Locations are those where the club played all or the majority of their home matches during the 2016/17 (2016) season.

Review

A narrative review of the season, headed by an appropriate photo, is divided into four sections – Domestic league, Domestic cup, Europe and National team.

DOMESTIC SEASON AT A GLANCE

Domestic league final table

The final standings of the member association's top division including home, away and total records. The champions are indicated in bold type.

Key: Pld = matches played, W = matches won, D = matches drawn, L = matches lost, F = goals for (scored), A = goals against (conceded), Pts = points

··············· = play-off line

- - - - - - - - - = relegation line

Any peculiarities, such as the deduction of points, clubs withdrawn or relegation issues, are indicated as *NB* at the foot of the table.

European qualification

The clubs qualified for the 2017/18 UEFA Champions League and UEFA Europa League are indicated, together with (in brackets) the round for which they have qualified. Champions and Cup winners are highlighted.

The league's top scorer(s), promoted club(s), relegated club(s) and the result of the domestic cup final(s) are listed in summary.

Player of the season
Newcomer of the season
Team of the season

These are either official selections or personal choices of the correspondents.

NATIONAL TEAM

Home (left) and away (right) playing kits, international honours and major international tournament appearances head this section. Also included are the member association's top five all-time international cap-holders and goalscorers. Players active in 2016/17 are highlighted in bold.

Results 2016/17

Details on all senior international matches played between August 2016 and June 2017 with date, opponent, venue, result, scorer(s) and goal time(s).

Key: H = home, A = away, N = neutral,
W = won, D = drawn, L = lost,
og = own goal, *p* = penalty,
(aet) = after extra time,
(WCQ) = 2018 FIFA World Cup qualification,
(CC) = FIFA Confederations Cup

Appearances 2016/17

Details on all participants in the aforementioned matches (coaches and players), including name, date of birth and, for each player, club(s), match-by-match appearances and all-time international caps and goals scored.

Opponents are ranged across the top and abbreviated with the appropriate three-letter country code – capital letters identify a competitive match (i.e. FIFA World Cup qualifier or FIFA Confederations Cup).

Changes of national team coach are indicated with the appropriate appointment dates; temporary coaches are indicated in brackets.

Non-native coaches and clubs are indicated with the appropriate three-letter country code.

Key: G = goalkeeper, D = defender,
M = midfielder, A = attacker,
s = substitute, * = red card.

The number appearing after the letter indicates the minute in which a substitution took place. The number preceding an asterisk indicates the minute in which a red card occurred.

EUROPE

Details including opponent, result, scorers, goaltimes, lineups and red cards of all matches played by the member association's clubs in the 2016/17 UEFA Champions League and UEFA Europa League, including qualifying rounds and play-offs. Each team's entry is headed by home and away playing kits (those used in 2016/17) and the club logo. The home kit is on the left.

Key: *(aet)* = after extra time

DOMESTIC LEAGUE CLUB-BY-CLUB

Information on each top-division club, displayed in alphabetical order, is provided in six parts:

1) Club name and a circular swatch indicating shirt and short colours.

2) The year in which the club was founded, the home stadium(s) used during the season (with capacity) and, where applicable, the official club website.

3) Major honours, including European, international and domestic competitions. National 'super cups', secondary leagues and minor or age-restricted knockout competitions are not included.

4) The coach(es)/manager(s) used during the season and, in the case of new appointments, the dates on which they took place. Non-native coaches/ managers are indicated with the appropriate three-letter country code.

5) League fixtures chronologically listed, including dates, opponents, results and goalscorers.

   Key: h = home, a = away, W = won, D = drawn, L = lost, *og* = own goal, *(p)* = penalty, *(w/o)* = walkover/forfeit

6) A list of all players used in the league campaign, including name, nationality (where non-native), date of birth, principal playing position, appearances and goals. Where applicable, squad numbers are also included.

   Key: No = squad (shirt) number, Name = first name and family name, or, in some instances, 'football name', Nat = nationality (native unless listed with three-letter country code), DoB = date of birth, Pos = playing position, Aps = number of appearances in the starting lineup, (s) = number of appearances as a substitute, Gls = number of goals scored, G = goalkeeper, D = defender, M = midfielder, A = attacker.

Top goalscorers

A list of the top ten (and equal) goalscorers in the member association's top division. The figures refer to league goals only.

Promoted club(s)

Information on each promoted club is provided in four parts:

1) Club name and a circular swatch indicating shirt and short colours.

2) The year in which the club was founded, the home stadium(s) used during the season (with capacity) and, where applicable, the official club website.

3) Major honours, including European, international and domestic competitions. National 'super cups', secondary leagues and minor or age-restricted knockout competitions are not included.

4) The coach(es)/manager(s) used during the season and, in the case of new appointments, the dates on which they took place. Non-native coaches/ managers are indicated with the appropriate three-letter country code.

Second level final table

The final classification of the member association's second level (i.e. feeder league to the top division) table(s). Play-off details, where applicable, are also indicated.

Key: Pld = matches played, W = matches won, D = matches drawn, L = matches lost, F = goals for (scored), A = goals against (conceded), Pts = points.

- - - - - - - - - = promotion line (at the top)

··············· = play-off line

- - - - - - - - - = relegation line (at the bottom)

Any peculiarities, such as the deduction of points, clubs withdrawn or promotion issues, are indicated as *NB* at the foot of the final league table.

DOMESTIC CUP(S)

Results from the member association's principal domestic knockout competition, beginning at the round in which the top-division clubs (or some of them) enter.

Goalscorers and goaltimes are indicated from the quarter-final stage, with complete lineups, referees and red cards added for the final.

Details of the latter stages of significant secondary knockout competitions are also included for some member associations.

Key: *(aet)* = after extra time, *(w/o)* = walkover/forfeit

NB A complete key to all three-letter country codes can be found on page 6.

Page index

ALBANIA

Federata Shqiptarë e Futbollit (FShF)

Address	Rruga e Elbasanit AL-1000 Tiranë
Tel	+355 42 346 605
Fax	+355 42 346 609
E-mail	fshf@fshf.org.al
Website	fshf.org

President	Armand Duka
General secretary	Ilir Shulku
Media officer	Tritan Kokona
Year of formation	1930
National stadium	Elbasan Arena, Elbasan (15,000)

KATEGORIA SUPERIORE CLUBS

  1 **KS Flamurtari**

 2 **KS Korabi**

 3 **FK Kukësi**

 4 **KF Laçi**

 5 **KS Luftëtari**

 6 **FK Partizani**

 7 **KF Skënderbeu**

 8 **KF Teuta**

 9 **KF Tirana**

 10 **KF Vllaznia**

PROMOTED CLUBS

 11 **FC Kamza**

 12 **KS Lushnja**

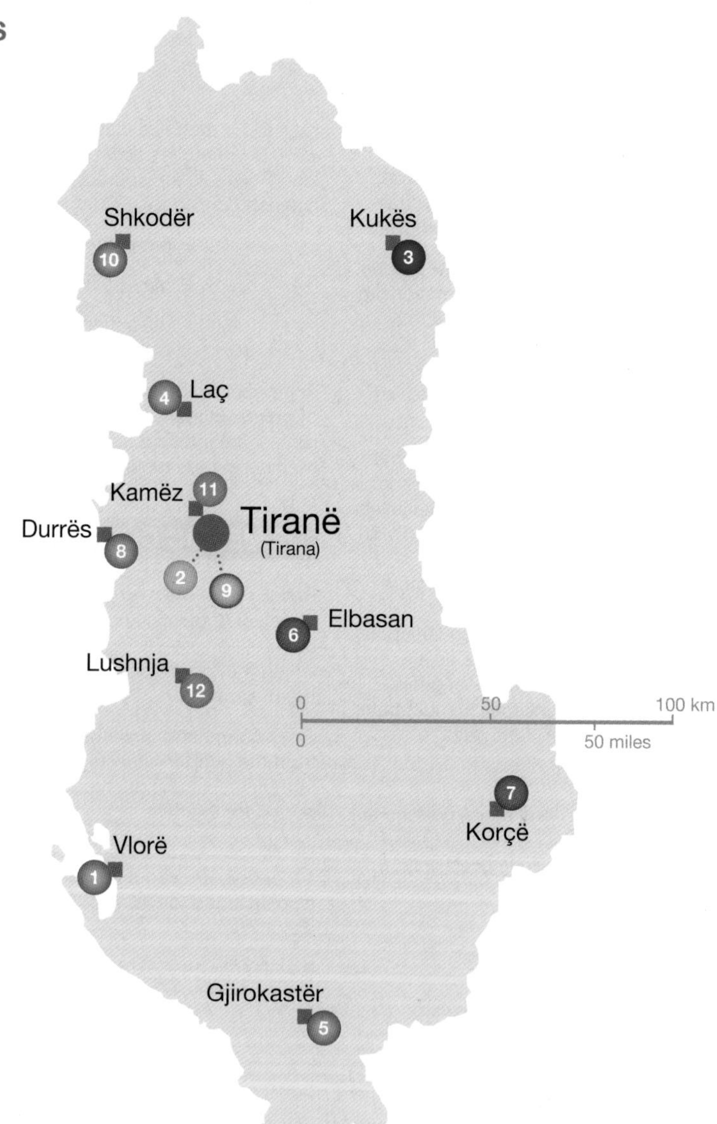

KEY

- UEFA Champions League
- UEFA Europa League
- Promoted
- Relegated
- Relegated club in UEFA Europa League

Kukës come to the party

After three runners-up placings in their first four seasons of Kategoria Superiore football, perennial bridesmaids FK Kukësi became the bride in 2016/17, withstanding the twin challenge of FK Partizani and the team that had lifted the title in each of the previous six campaigns, KF Skënderbeu.

Kukës were undefeated until the final day, by which stage they were already champions after beating Skënderbeu 2-0 in an incident-packed penultimate fixture. KF Tirana, Albania's most decorated club, suffered a shock relegation but picked themselves up to win the Albanian Cup.

First national league title for north-eastern club

Skënderbeu's six-year reign comes to an end

Tirana suffer first relegation but win the cup

Domestic league

Kukës had been passive onlookers in the 2015/16 title race, and a similar story looked set to develop when they trailed Skënderbeu by eight points after just six matches. Kukës, under unheralded new coach Ernest Gjoka, did not lose any of those games but drew four of them whereas Skënderbeu, now under the coach who had challenged the Korce club for the previous season's title with Partizani, Andrea Agostinelli, won all six.

The holders' early fire fizzled out, however, and Kukës, who had brought prolific Croatian striker Pero Pejić back from Iran, gradually clawed back the deficit so that by the winter break they actually led the table by a point. Furthermore, it was not Skënderbeu in second place but Partizani, revitalised after a shabby start following the reappointment of Sulejman Starova, the man replaced halfway through the previous season by Agostinelli.

The spring campaign was fiercely contested, with all three contenders increasingly fancying their chances as the weeks passed. Crucially, though, Kukës were dogged front-runners, refusing both to be beaten and to surrender their position. It all came down to their final home game, against Skënderbeu, a victory in which would give them an unassailable four-point lead over their in-form rivals with one fixture remaining. Not unexpectedly, with so much at stake, the match became overheated, a penalty from Pejić stoking the ire of the visitors, who ended the game with nine men and another goal in their net as the big Croatian struck a late second to seal the title.

Kukës' unbeaten run ended a week later at Luftëtari, the newly-promoted side that finished a creditable fourth – albeit 28 points distant of third-placed Skënderbeu, who could only draw 2-2 at home to Partizani and therefore ceded the runners-up spot on head-to-head, the holders' eight games against the top two having failed to produce a single victory. A much costlier last-day draw was Tirana's 0-0 stalemate at Vllaznia, which, with Laç and Flamurtari both winning, relegated the 24-time champions for the first time in their history. The man who took them down was Mirel Josa, Skënderbeu's coach in each of their past four title-winning campaigns.

Domestic cup

The trauma of relegation did not, however, prevent Josa and his players from defeating Skënderbeu in the Albanian Cup final four days later, Tirana lifting the trophy for a record 16th time (one more than city rivals Partizani) thanks to a trio of African goalscorers. Nigerian Ifeanyi Ede opened the scoring before Congo pair Justalain Nkounkou and Merveille Ndockyt both struck in extra time after Marko Radaš's late equaliser for Skënderbeu, who thus made it five defeats in as many cup final appearances.

Europe

Skënderbeu were belatedly banned from participating in the 2016/17 UEFA Champions League, which enabled Partizani to take their place midway through a UEFA Europa League first qualifying round tie with Slovan Bratislava. A penalty shoot-out win over Ferencváros enabled them to return, ultimately, to the competition in which they began, with FC Krasnodar blocking their route to the group stage.

National team

Albania's hopes of following up their surprise qualification for UEFA EURO 2016 with a repeat run to the FIFA World Cup in Russia were always fated to be forlorn once they found Italy and Spain in their qualifying group, but by the summer their record of three wins and three defeats was a respectable return, especially as their opening game against FYR Macedonia was abandoned and completed a day later due to heavy rain in Shkoder and their final outing of the season brought a 3-0 win in Israel against the team that had embarrassed them by the same score in Elbasan.

DOMESTIC SEASON AT A GLANCE

Kategoria Superiore 2016/17 final table

			Home					Away					Total					
		Pld	W	D	L	F	A	W	D	L	F	A	W	D	L	F	A	Pts
1	**FK Kukësi**	**36**	**15**	**3**	**0**	**32**	**5**	**5**	**12**	**1**	**19**	**13**	**20**	**15**	**1**	**51**	**18**	**75**
2	FK Partizani	36	12	6	0	27	5	7	9	2	19	12	19	15	2	46	17	72
3	KF Skënderbeu	36	13	4	1	29	10	8	5	5	16	12	21	9	6	45	22	72
4	KS Luftëtari	36	8	8	2	20	12	3	3	12	17	33	11	11	14	37	45	44
5	KF Teuta	36	6	5	7	14	14	4	5	9	13	20	10	10	16	27	34	40
6	KF Laçi	36	8	5	5	17	16	2	5	11	6	19	10	10	16	23	35	40
7	KF Vllaznia	36	5	9	4	18	14	3	7	8	11	21	8	16	12	29	35	40
8	KS Flamurtari	36	9	6	3	29	9	3	4	11	13	25	12	10	14	42	34	40
9	KF Tirana	36	7	8	3	23	13	1	7	10	6	19	8	15	13	29	32	39
10	KS Korabi	36	1	5	12	5	28	1	2	15	6	40	2	7	27	11	68	13

NB KS Flamurtari – 6 pts deducted.

European qualification 2017/18

FK Kukësi (second qualifying round)

Cup winner: KF Tirana (first qualifying round)
FK Partizani (first qualifying round)
KF Skënderbeu (first qualifying round)

Top scorer Pero Pejić (Kukës), 28 goals
Relegated clubs KS Korabi, KF Tirana
Promoted clubs FC Kamza, KS Lushnja
Cup final KF Tirana 3-1 KF Skënderbeu *(aet)*

Player of the season

Pero Pejić
(FK Kukësi)

Back at the club for whom he had scored a league-high tally of 31 goals in the 2014/15 season before trying his luck – not particularly successfully – in Iran with Esteghlal, Pejić was once again an unrivalled winner of the Kategoria Superiore's golden boot. This time the tall Croatian striker found the net 28 times, a dozen of those goals coming during the final quarter of the campaign, including both in the 2-0 win over his former club Skënderbeu that clinched the Albanian title – the first for Kukës and the fourth for him personally.

Newcomer of the season

Albi Alla
(FK Kukësi)

An Albanian centre-back who began his career in Greece, Alla returned to his homeland in 2015 to join Skënderbeu but failed to get a game and was sent on loan to Bylis, who were relegated. Kukës subsequently took a chance on him and it was a gamble that would pay handsome dividends as the 24-year-old proved to be a revelation in defence, his strength and aerial presence helping the club to the promised land of a first Albanian league title. Kukës were unable to keep him, however, as he moved back to Greece, joining Superleague side Larissa.

Team of the season
(4-4-2)

Coach: Gjoka *(Kukës)*

NATIONAL TEAM

International tournament appearances
UEFA European Championship (1) 2016

Top five all-time caps
Lorik Cana (92); Altin Lala (78); Klodian Duro (76); Erjon Bogdani & Ervin Skela (75)

Top five all-time goals
Erjon Bogdani (18); Alban Bushi (14); Ervin Skela (13); Altin Rraklli & Hamdi Salihi (11)

Results 2016/17

31/08/16	Morocco	H	Shkoder	D	0-0	
05&06/09/16	FYR Macedonia (WCQ)	H	Shkoder	W	2-1	*Sadiku (9), Balaj (89)*
06/10/16	Liechtenstein (WCQ)	A	Vaduz	W	2-0	*Jehle (11og), Balaj (71)*
09/10/16	Spain (WCQ)	H	Shkoder	L	0-2	
12/11/16	Israel (WCQ)	H	Elbasan	L	0-3	
24/03/17	Italy (WCQ)	A	Palermo	L	0-2	
28/03/17	Bosnia & Herzegovina	H	Elbasan	L	1-2	*Balaj (68)*
04/06/17	Luxembourg	A	Luxembourg	L	1-2	*Roshi (52)*
11/06/17	Israel (WCQ)	A	Haifa	W	3-0	*Sadiku (22, 44), Memushaj (71)*

Appearances 2016/17

Coach: Gianni De Biasi (ITA)	16/06/56		Mar	MKD	LIE	ESP	ISR	ITA	Bih	Lux	ISR	Caps	Goals
Etrit Berisha	10/03/89	Atalanta (ITA)	G	G	G	G	G 55*					42	-
Elseid Hysaj	20/02/94	Napoli (ITA)	D	D	D	D	D79	D	D	M	D	31	-
Berat Djimsiti	19/02/93	Avellino (ITA)	D	D	D	D	D 17*			D	D	13	1
Mërgim Mavraj	09/06/86	Köln (GER) /Hamburg (GER)	D	D	D	D	D			D	D	36	3
Ermir Lenjani	05/08/89	Rennes (FRA)	D59			M46				M62		24	3
Taulant Xhaka	28/03/91	Basel (SUI)	M60	M		M75	M82					17	-
Shkëlzen Gashi	15/07/88	Colorado Rapids (USA)	M60	M60								16	1
Migjen Basha	05/01/87	Bari (ITA)	M72		s44	s68		M96	M	s46		25	3
Amir Abrashi	27/03/90	Freiburg (GER)	M60	M60	M46					M77	M	26	1
Jahmir Hyka	08/03/88	Luzern (SUI) /San Jose Earthquakes (USA)	M59	M67	M	s75			M71		M	44	2
Sokol Çikalleshi	27/07/90	İstanbul Başakşehir (TUR) /Akhisar (TUR)	A		s69			A	s79	A46	s70	25	2
Ansi Agolli	11/10/82	Qarabağ (AZE)	s59	D		D	D	D				69	2
Frederic Veseli	20/11/92	Empoli (ITA)	s59					D	D		s82	7	-
Burim Kukeli	16/01/84	Zürich (SUI)	s60	M	M44		M	M	M	D	M82	25	-
Ledian Memushaj	07/12/86	Pescara (ITA)	s60	s60		M68	M	M	M59	M	M	23	1
Armando Sadiku	27/05/91	Zürich (SUI) /Lugano (SUI)	s60	A				s77		s46	A70	27	9
Ergys Kaçe	08/07/93	Plzeň (CZE) /PAOK (GRE)	s72							M46		19	2
Bekim Balaj	11/01/91	Terek (RUS)		s60	A	A	A		A			21	4
Odhise Roshi	22/05/91	Terek (RUS)		s67	M	M	M	M87	s59	A62	M53	42	2
Naser Aliji	27/12/93	Kaiserslautern (GER)			D	s46			D	s62	D	9	-
Azdren Llullaku	15/02/88	Gaz Metan (ROU) /Astana (KAZ)			M69		M57		M79			3	-
Andi Lila	12/02/86	Giannina (GRE)			s46	M		M77			s53	63	-
Alban Hoxha	23/11/87	Partizani					s57		s46			3	-
Edgar Çani	22/07/89	Pisa (ITA)					s79					16	4
Rey Manaj	24/02/97	Pescara (ITA)					s82					2	-
Thomas Strakosha	19/03/95	Lazio (ITA)						G	G46	G	G	4	-
Arlind Ajeti	25/09/93	Torino (ITA)						D	s46			13	1
Eros Grezda	15/04/95	Lokomotiva Zagreb (CRO)						s87		s62		2	-
Liridon Latifi	06/02/94	Skënderbeu						s96	s71	s77		3	-
Albi Alla	01/02/93	Kukës							D46			1	-

EUROPE

FK Partizani

First qualifying round - ŠK Slovan Bratislava (SVK)
H 0-0
Hoxha, Arapi, Krasniqi, Fili (Jaupaj 87), Batha, Ramadani, Trashi, Ibrahimi, Torassa (Bardhi 83), Vila, Kalari (Atanda 87). Coach: Klevis Dalipi (ALB)

NB Partizani transferred to the UEFA Champions League midway through the tie following the expulsion of KF Skënderbeu.

CHAMPIONS LEAGUE

Second qualifying round - Ferencvárosi TC (HUN)
H 1-1 *Fili (47)*
Hoxha, Arapi, Krasniqi, Fili (Volaš 85), Batha, Ramadani, Trashi, Ibrahimi, Torassa (Ekuban 67), Vila (Atanda 82), Kalari. Coach: Adolfo Sormani (ITA)
A 1-1 (aet; 3-1 on pens) *Hüsing (40og)*
Hoxha, Arapi, Krasniqi, Fili (Bardhi 82), Batha (Ekuban 26), Ramadani, Trashi, Ibrahimi, Torassa (Atanda 71), Vila, Kalari. Coach: Adolfo Sormani (ITA)

Third qualifying round - FC Salzburg (AUT)
H 0-1
Hoxha, Arapi, Krasniqi, Fili (Batha 57), Ramadani, Trashi, Ibrahimi, Torassa (Bardhi 82), Ekuban, Vila, Kalari. Coach: Adolfo Sormani (ITA)
Red card: Kalari 73
A 0-2
Hoxha, Arapi, Krasniqi, Fili (Volaš 78), Ramadani, Trashi, Ibrahimi, Torassa (Batha 63), Atanda (Bertoni 88), Ekuban, Vila. Coach: Adolfo Sormani (ITA)

Play-offs - FC Krasnodar (RUS)
A 0-4
Hoxha, Arapi, Krasniqi, Batha, Bardhi (Fili 64), Ramadani, Trashi, Ibrahimi (Fejzullahu 64), Torassa, Ekuban, Vila. Coach: Adolfo Sormani (ITA)
H 0-0
Hoxha, Krasniqi, Batha, Ramadani (Bertoni 22), Trashi (Vatnikaj 74), Ibrahimi, Torassa, Fejzullahu (Bardhi 64), Atanda, Ekuban, Vila. Coach: Adolfo Sormani (ITA)

FK Kukësi

EUROPA LEAGUE

First qualifying round - FK Rudar Pljevlja (MNE)
H 1-1 *Rangel (32)*
Koliqi, Shameti, Muca (Greca 82), Mici, Emini, Jean Carioca (Philippe Guimarães 75), Hallaçi, Rangel, Dvorneković (Dema 65), Musolli, Malota. Coach: Hasan Lika (ALB)
A 1-0 *Guri (79)*
Koliqi, Shameti, Mici, Emini, Jean Carioca, Dema (Greca 54), Hallaçi, Rangel, Dvorneković (Guri 63), Musolli (Muca 77), Malota. Coach: Hasan Lika (ALB)
Red card: Greca 65

Second qualifying round - FK Austria Wien (AUT)
A 0-1
Koliqi, Shameti, Lilaj, Mici, Jean Carioca (Emini 73), Hallaçi, Latifi, Rangel (Guri 70), Musolli, Malota, Fukui (Dvorneković 81). Coach: Hasan Lika (ALB)
H 1-4 *Hallaçi (78)*
Koliqi, Shameti, Lilaj, Mici, Jean Carioca (Dvorneković 46), Hallaçi, Latifi, Rangel (Emini 33), Musolli, Malota, Fukui (Guri 61). Coach: Hasan Lika (ALB)

KF Teuta

EUROPA LEAGUE

First qualifying round - FC Kairat Almaty (KAZ)
H 0-1
Moçka, Shkalla, R Hoxha, Çyrbja, Lena (Lamçja 65), E Hoxha, Kotobelli, Magani (Rraboshta 76), Hila, Musta, Hodo (Gripshi 82). Coach: Hito Hitaj (ALB)
A 0-5
Moçka, Shkalla (Gripshi 66), R Hoxha, Çyrbja (Rraboshta 52), Lena, E Hoxha (Shehi 54), Kotobelli, Magani, Hila, Musta, Hodo. Coach: Hito Hitaj (ALB)

DOMESTIC LEAGUE CLUB-BY-CLUB

KS Flamurtari

1923 • Flamurtari (9,000) • skflamurtari.com
Major honours
Albanian League (1) 1991; Albanian Cup (4) 1985, 1988, 2009, 2014
Coach: Gugash Magani; (18/10/16) (Gentian Mezani); (16/02/17) Shpëtim Duro

Date		Opponent	Res	Score	Scorers
2016					
07/09	a	Skënderbeu	L	1-2	*Shkodra*
11/09	h	Luftëtari	W	5-0	*Shkodra 2, Bušić, Galić, Shehaj*
18/09	a	Vllaznia	L	0-2	
24/09	h	Teuta	D	0-0	
02/10	a	Tirana	L	0-3	
12/10	h	Kukës	D	1-1	*Berisha*
17/10	a	Partizani	L	0-4	
22/10	a	Laç	D	1-1	*Radović*
30/10	h	Korabi	W	4-1	*Shkodra, Telushi (p), Bušić, Fazliu*
05/11	h	Skënderbeu	W	2-0	*Shkodra, Bušić*
20/11	a	Luftëtari	D	1-1	*Galić*
25/11	h	Vllaznia	L	0-1	
30/11	a	Teuta	W	2-1	*Galić, og (Moçka)*
06/12	h	Tirana	W	1-0	*Shkodra*
10/12	a	Kukës	L	0-1	
14/12	h	Partizani	D	1-1	*Danilo Alves*
18/12	h	Laç	W	1-0	*Shehaj*
22/12	a	Korabi	L	0-1	
2017					
28/01	a	Skënderbeu	L	0-1	
06/02	h	Luftëtari	W	2-1	*Veliu, Bušić*
11/02	a	Vllaznia	L	2-3	*Bušić 2*
19/02	h	Teuta	L	0-1	
26/02	a	Tirana	D	0-0	
05/03	h	Kukës	D	1-1	*Danilo Alves*
11/03	a	Partizani	L	1-2	*Danilo Alves*
18/03	a	Laç	L	0-1	
01/04	h	Korabi	W	6-0	*Shkodra, Telushi (p), Bušić 2, Neziraj, og (A Peposhi)*
10/04	h	Skënderbeu	L	0-1	
15/04	a	Luftëtari	W	2-1	*Shkodra, Telushi (p)*
22/04	h	Vllaznia	W	2-0	*Bušić, Danilo Alves*
30/04	a	Teuta	D	0-0	
06/05	h	Tirana	W	2-0	*Shkodra, Bušić*
10/05	a	Kukës	L	0-1	
14/05	h	Partizani	D	1-1	*Telushi (p)*
20/05	h	Laç	D	0-0	
27/05	a	Korabi	W	3-0	*Danilo Alves (p), Veliu, Lynneeker*

No	Name	Nat	DoB	Pos	Aps	(s)	Gls
16	Arbri Beqaj		29/09/89	D	13	(3)	
5	Ilir Berisha	KOS	25/06/91	D	17		1
14	Tomislav Bušić	CRO	02/02/86	A	27	(1)	10
99	Danilo Alves	BRA	11/04/91	A	29		5
44	Nikola Djurić	SRB	06/11/89	D		(1)	
7	Rigers Dushku		08/09/91	M	3	(14)	
7	Astrit Fazliu	KOS	08/10/87	M	18	(8)	1
80	Stivi Frashëri		29/08/90	G	10	(1)	
97	Ivan Galić	CRO	09/01/95	M	15	(12)	3
24	Julian Gjinaj		24/10/96	D		(2)	
1	Argjend Halilaj		16/11/82	G	26		
26	Nertil Hoxhaj		21/05/97	D		(3)	
26	Alessio Hyseni		04/11/97	M	10	(5)	
23	Onlis Idrizaj		23/02/91	D		(3)	
18	Masaki Iinuma	JPN	27/11/92	M		(1)	
13	Ivan Jakovljević	SRB	28/05/89	D	16		
20	Taulant Kuqi		11/11/85	D	19	(8)	
16	Aldo Llambi		06/06/96	M		(3)	
44	Slavko Lukić	SRB	14/03/89	D	5		
77	Lynneeker	BRA	11/01/93	D	1	(6)	1
3	Kristi Marku		13/04/95	D	2	(2)	
4	Mauricio Leal	BRA	11/06/87	D	10	(1)	
3	Ergys Mersini		30/09/88	M	17		
21	Haxhi Neziraj		16/03/93	M	12	(5)	1
6	Jurgen Qarri		02/07/98	A		(1)	
22	Balša Radović	MNE	04/01/91	M	8	(5)	1
25	Miloš Rnić	SRB	24/01/89	D	15	(3)	
9	Ardit Shehaj		23/09/90	A	20	(13)	2
10	Donjet Shkodra	KOS	30/04/89	M	25	(1)	9
17	Bruno Telushi		14/11/90	M	31		4
11	Franc Veliu		11/11/88	D	31		2
19	Hajr Zeqiri		11/10/88	M	16		

KS Korabi

1930 • Selman Stërmasi, Tirana (9,200); Zeqir Ymeri, Kukes (4,500); Elbasan Arena, Elbasan (15,000); Niko Dovana, Durres (8,000); Loro Boriçi, Shkoder (16,500) • no website

Coach: Artan Mërgjyshi; (31/10/16) (Artion Poçi); (08/11/16) Gerd Haxhiu (13/04/17) Artion Poçi

Date		Opponent		Score	Scorers
2016					
07/09	h	Laç	D	0-0	
11/09	h	Skënderbeu	L	0-2	
17/09	a	Luftëtari	L	0-1	
24/09	h	Vllaznia	D	0-0	
02/10	a	Teuta	W	3-2	*Plaku, Nedzipi, Kaja*
12/10	h	Tirana	L	0-1	
16/10	a	Kukës	L	0-2	
22/10	h	Partizani	L	0-1	
30/10	a	Flamurtari	L	1-4	*Nedzipi*
05/11	a	Laç	L	0-1	
20/11	a	Skënderbeu	L	0-1	
26/11	h	Luftëtari	D	1-1	*Mziu*
30/11	a	Vllaznia	L	0-3	
04/12	h	Teuta	L	0-1	
10/12	a	Tirana	D	1-1	*Plaku*
14/12	h	Kukës	D	1-1	*Gavazaj*
18/12	a	Partizani	L	0-1	
22/12	h	Flamurtari	W	1-0	*Plaku*
2017					
28/01	h	Laç	L	0-1	
06/02	h	Skënderbeu	L	0-1	
12/02	a	Luftëtari	L	0-2	
19/02	h	Vllaznia	L	0-2	
25/02	a	Teuta	L	0-1	
04/03	h	Tirana	D	1-1	*Kaja*
11/03	a	Kukës	L	0-4	
18/03	h	Partizani	L	0-2	
01/04	a	Flamurtari	L	0-6	
09/04	a	Laç	L	0-2	
15/04	a	Skënderbeu	L	0-3	
22/04	h	Luftëtari	L	0-4	
29/04	a	Vllaznia	D	1-1	*Premçi*
06/05	h	Teuta	L	0-4	
10/05	a	Tirana	L	0-2	
14/05	h	Kukës	L	1-3	*E Kaloshi*
21/05	a	Partizani	L	0-3	
27/05	h	Flamurtari	L	0-3	

No	Name	Nat	DoB	Pos	Aps	(s)	Gls
88	Abraham Adelaya	NGA	31/01/88	A	2	(3)	
14	Besmir Arifaj		06/05/86	M	17		
3	Aurel Bitri		08/01/90	D		(2)	
17	Dejvis Çangu		11/08/94	M	3	(2)	
3	Emiljano Çela		21/07/85	D	21		
77	Duško Dukić	SRB	21/06/85	D	10	(1)	
10	Alush Gavazaj		24/03/95	M	21	(3)	1
2	Klajdi Hoxha		26/07/95	D		(1)	
11	Ardit Hoxhaj		20/07/94	A	15		
28	Paolo Ivani		12/01/97	M	4	(7)	
20	Daniel Jubani		07/12/93	M	10	(11)	
29	Ervis Kaja		29/07/87	D	28	(2)	2
32	Dejvis Kalemi		24/05/97	M		(4)	
16	Emrush Kaloshi		12/12/95	A	11	(10)	1
23	Geraldo Kaloshi		13/11/95	M	4	(4)	
6	Ergys Kraja		13/07/96	M	4	(5)	
95	Ted Laço		01/02/95	G	6		
97	Xhon Marinaj		12/10/97	M		(8)	
13	Gebriel Mezini		05/02/94	M		(1)	
99	Armend Murrja		06/01/99	M		(6)	
7	Sokol Mziu		21/07/87	M	20	(6)	1
6	Rudin Nako		20/05/87	D	10	(1)	
11	Nderim Nedzipi	MKD	22/05/84	M	13	(3)	2
25	Ardit Peposhi		14/03/93	D	29	(0)	
9	Denis Peposhi		01/02/95	A	10	(10)	
99	Sebino Plaku		20/05/85	A	15	(1)	3
5	Elvis Premçi		26/06/93	D	24	(2)	1
13	Endrit Prençi		30/06/96	G	9		
24	Andi Prifti		01/08/88	D	8	(1)	
8	Veton Shabani	KOS	05/05/90	D	17		
4	Arjan Sheta		13/02/81	D	17		
1	Erkan Spahija		03/04/94	G	2		
28	Emiljano Veliaj		09/02/85	M	11	(1)	
21	Miroslav Vujadinović	MNE	22/04/83	G	19	(1)	
22	Alfred Zefi		20/08/91	M	27	(2)	
8	Vangjel Zguro		04/03/93	D	9	(1)	

FK Kukësi

1930 • Zeqir Ymeri (4,500) • fk-kukesi.al

Major honours
Albanian League (1) 2017; Albanian Cup (1) 2016

Coach: Hasan Lika; (24/07/16) Ernest Gjoka

Date		Opponent		Score	Scorers
2016					
08/09	a	Vllaznia	D	0-0	
12/09	h	Teuta	W	3-0	*Pejić 2 (1p), Greca*
17/09	a	Tirana	D	2-2	*Pejić (p), Emini*
24/09	a	Laç	D	0-0	
01/10	h	Partizani	W	1-0	*Pejić*
12/10	a	Flamurtari	D	1-1	*Pejić*
16/10	h	Korabi	W	2-0	*Dvorneković, Pejić*
22/10	a	Skënderbeu	D	0-0	
29/10	h	Luftëtari	W	1-0	*Emini*
06/11	h	Vllaznia	W	3-1	*Pejić 2 (1p), Guri*
21/11	a	Teuta	W	2-1	*Rangel, Lushtaku*
26/11	h	Tirana	D	0-0	
30/11	h	Laç	W	2-0	*Dvorneković, Emini*
06/12	a	Partizani	D	0-0	
10/12	h	Flamurtari	W	1-0	*Emini*
14/12	a	Korabi	D	1-1	*Lushtaku*
18/12	h	Skënderbeu	W	2-0	*Pejić 2 (1p)*
22/12	a	Luftëtari	D	2-2	*Pejić (p), Emini*
2017					
27/01	a	Vllaznia	W	1-0	*Pejić*
05/02	h	Teuta	W	1-0	*Emini*
11/02	a	Tirana	W	2-1	*Pejić, Emini*
20/02	a	Laç	D	0-0	
26/02	h	Partizani	D	0-0	
05/03	a	Flamurtari	D	1-1	*Guri*
11/03	h	Korabi	W	4-0	*Pejić 2 (1p), Elton Calé, Dvorneković*
17/03	a	Skënderbeu	D	1-1	*Elton Calé*
02/04	h	Luftëtari	W	3-2	*Shameti, og (Boyom), Pejić*
09/04	h	Vllaznia	D	0-0	
15/04	a	Teuta	W	2-0	*Pejić 2 (1p)*
23/04	h	Tirana	W	4-1	*Emini, Pejić 2 (1p), Jean Carioca*
29/04	h	Laç	W	2-1	*Pejić 2*
05/05	a	Partizani	D	1-1	*Dvorneković*
10/05	h	Flamurtari	W	1-0	*Pejić*
14/05	a	Korabi	W	3-1	*Pejić 3 (1p)*
20/05	h	Skënderbeu	W	2-0	*Pejić 2 (1p)*
27/05	a	Luftëtari	L	0-1	

No	Name	Nat	DoB	Pos	Aps	(s)	Gls
6	Albi Alla		01/02/93	D	30		
31	Polizoi Arbëri		09/09/88	D	1		
18	Klaudio Cema		22/04/95	M		(1)	
11	Bekim Dema		30/03/93	D	1	(4)	
21	Matija Dvorneković	CRO	01/01/89	A	26	(7)	4
11	Elton Calé	BRA	12/07/88	A	8	(7)	2
8	Izair Emini	MKD	04/10/85	M	28	(2)	8
15	Felipe Moreira	BRA	28/11/88	M		(2)	
7	Bedri Greca		23/10/90	M	7	(10)	1
9	Sindrit Guri		23/10/93	A	5	(20)	2
13	Rrahman Hallaçi		12/11/83	D	32	(1)	
16	Edon Hasani		09/01/92	M	17	(2)	
19	Eni Imami		19/12/92	M	20	(2)	
10	Jean Carioca	BRA	01/06/88	M	30	(3)	1
12	Ervis Koçi		13/11/84	G	1		
97	Albi Koldashi		06/07/97	M		(1)	
1	Enea Koliqi		13/03/86	G	35		
17	Nijaz Lena	MKD	25/06/86	M	28	(2)	
99	Kushtrim Lushtaku		08/10/89	M	2	(17)	2
3	Rexhep Memini		10/04/94	D	8	(5)	
23	Besar Musolli	KOS	28/02/89	M	32	(1)	
5	Entonio Pashaj		10/11/84	D	14	(3)	
22	Pero Pejić	CRO	28/11/82	A	35		28
24	Rangel	BRA	29/12/94	M		(17)	1
20	Simon Rrumbullaku		30/12/91	D	10		
4	Ylli Shameti		07/06/84	D	26		1

KF Laçi

1960 • Laçi (5,000) • no website

Major honours
Albanian Cup (2) 2013, 2015

Coach: Marcelo Troisi (BRA); (03/10/16) Ramazan Ndreu; (08/01/17) Bledar Sinella; (24/04/17) Stavri Nica

Date		Opponent		Score	Scorers
2016					
07/09	a	Korabi	D	0-0	
11/09	h	Tirana	D	0-0	
17/09	a	Skënderbeu	L	0-1	
24/09	h	Kukës	D	0-0	
01/10	a	Luftëtari	L	0-1	
13/10	h	Partizani	L	0-2	
17/10	a	Vllaznia	W	2-1	*Toski, Lulaj*
22/10	h	Flamurtari	D	1-1	*Lulaj*
30/10	a	Teuta	L	1-3	*Pericles*
05/11	h	Korabi	W	1-0	*Çelhaka*
20/11	a	Tirana	L	0-1	
26/11	h	Skënderbeu	L	0-1	
30/11	a	Kukës	L	0-2	
04/12	h	Luftëtari	D	2-2	*Bruno Aquino 2*
10/12	a	Partizani	L	0-2	
14/12	h	Vllaznia	W	1-0	*Bruno Aquino*
18/12	a	Flamurtari	L	0-1	
22/12	h	Teuta	L	0-2	
2017					
28/01	a	Korabi	W	1-0	*Lushkja*
05/02	h	Tirana	W	1-0	*Mensah*
11/02	a	Skënderbeu	L	0-1	
20/02	h	Kukës	D	0-0	
25/02	a	Luftëtari	D	1-1	*Jonuzi*
05/03	h	Partizani	L	0-1	
12/03	a	Vllaznia	L	0-1	
18/03	h	Flamurtari	W	1-0	*Nika*
01/04	a	Teuta	L	0-2	
09/04	h	Korabi	W	2-0	*Lushkja, Gjoni*
15/04	a	Tirana	D	0-0	
23/04	h	Skënderbeu	L	1-5	*Mensah*
29/04	a	Kukës	L	1-2	*Jonuzi*
06/05	h	Luftëtari	W	2-1	*Qaqi, Serginho*
11/05	a	Partizani	D	0-0	
14/05	h	Vllaznia	W	3-0	*Vucaj (p), Qaqi, Mensah*
20/05	a	Flamurtari	D	0-0	
27/05	h	Teuta	W	2-1	*Jonuzi, Mensah*

No	Name	Nat	DoB	Pos	Aps	(s)	Gls
33	Abraham Alechenwu	NGA	26/03/86	D	10	(12)	
6	Kejvi Bardhi		07/08/96	A		(2)	
22	Denis Biba		17/06/95	D	2	(6)	
17	Bruno Agnello	BRA	07/12/85	M	3	(3)	
28	Bruno Aquino	BRA	21/06/91	A	15		3
22	Ded Bushi		02/10/98	M		(2)	
7	Alked Çelhaka		07/08/94	M	13	(11)	1
33	Bekim Dema		30/03/93	D	1	(2)	
9	Abdurrahman Fangaj		12/10/97	D	3	(9)	
16	Eglantin Gjoni		02/12/92	D	26	(2)	1
14	Kristi Hyseni		21/02/98	M		(3)	
7	Emiljano Hysi		16/06/96	M		(1)	
9	Fjoart Jonuzi		09/07/96	D	17	(1)	3
11	Alush Kanapari		17/10/94	A	2	(4)	
6	Ilir Kastrati		20/07/94	M	8	(6)	
21	Bruno Lipi		07/04/94	M	7	(3)	
4	Bruno Lulaj		02/04/95	D	28	(1)	2
19	Regi Lushkja		17/05/96	M	30	(1)	2
6	Enco Malindi		15/01/88	A	4	(2)	
20	Emmanuel Mensah	GHA	30/06/94	A	17		4
18	Drilon Musaj	KOS	11/09/94	M	33	(1)	
14	Ansi Nika		22/08/90	M	15		1
11	Thomas Nyameke	GHA	04/09/98	A	1		
8	Pericles	BRA	04/11/89	M	10		1
4	Klevis Përkeqi		06/03/98	M		(1)	
9	Rudolf Popaj		03/09/99	A		(1)	
5	Harallamb Qaqi		17/09/93	D	34	(1)	2
28	Blažo Rajović	MNE	26/03/86	D	1		
6	Taulant Sefgjini		21/07/86	D	10	(3)	
1	Gentian Selmani		09/03/98	G	33		
17	Serginho	BRA	06/04/95	A	14	(3)	1
3	Arbër Shala	KOS	23/12/91	D	22	(7)	
9	Taubaté	BRA	15/09/91	A	6	(1)	
2	Klajdi Toska		31/10/96	D	4	(7)	
20	Faton Toski	GER	17/02/87	M	9		1
1	Elton Vata		13/04/98	G	3		
10	Erjon Vucaj		25/12/90	M	15		1

ALBANIA

KS Luftëtari

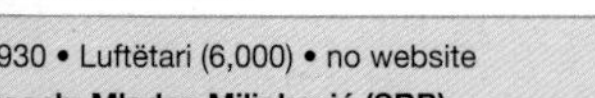

1930 • Luftëtari (6,000) • no website

Coach: Mladen Milinković (SRB)

Date		Opponent			Scorers
2016					
07/09	a	Partizani	L	0-1	
11/09	a	Flamurtari	L	0-5	
17/09	h	Korabi	W	1-0	*Montero*
24/09	a	Skënderbeu	L	0-1	
01/10	h	Laç	W	1-0	*Ramadani (p)*
12/10	h	Vllaznia	D	1-1	*Abazaj*
17/10	a	Teuta	L	0-2	
23/10	h	Tirana	W	2-1	*Reginaldo, Bregu*
29/10	a	Kukës	L	0-1	
05/11	h	Partizani	D	1-1	*Bregu*
20/11	h	Flamurtari	D	1-1	*Reginaldo*
26/11	a	Korabi	D	1-1	*Reginaldo*
30/11	h	Skënderbeu	D	0-0	
04/12	a	Laç	D	2-2	*Boyom, Bregu*
10/12	a	Vllaznia	W	3-2	*og (Cicmil), Reginaldo 2*
14/12	h	Teuta	W	1-0	*Bregu*
18/12	a	Tirana	L	0-2	
22/12	h	Kukës	D	2-2	*Reginaldo, Rrapo*
2017					
29/01	h	Partizani	W	2-0	*Ramadani (p), Abazaj*
06/02	a	Flamurtari	L	1-2	*Rroca*
12/02	h	Korabi	W	2-0	*Bregu, Abazaj*
19/02	a	Skënderbeu	L	0-3	
25/02	h	Laç	D	1-1	*Ramadani (p)*
04/03	h	Vllaznia	D	0-0	
12/03	a	Teuta	W	1-0	*Rroca*
19/03	h	Tirana	W	2-1	*Lamçja, Bregu*
02/04	a	Kukës	L	2-3	*Lamçja, Beqiri*
08/04	a	Partizani	L	0-2	
15/04	h	Flamurtari	L	1-2	*Bregu*
22/04	a	Korabi	W	4-0	*Brahimaj, Bregu, Bengui, Reginaldo*
30/04	h	Skënderbeu	L	0-1	
06/05	a	Laç	L	1-2	*Aleksi (p)*
10/05	a	Vllaznia	D	2-2	*Boyom, Reginaldo*
14/05	h	Teuta	D	1-1	*Ramadani (p)*
20/05	a	Tirana	L	0-2	
27/05	h	Kukës	W	1-0	*Bregu (p)*

No	Name	Nat	DoB	Pos	Aps	(s)	Gls
25	Kristal Abazaj		06/07/96	A	30	(3)	3
5	Albano Aleksi		10/10/92	M	21	(3)	1
9	Pedro Bengui	ANG	02/03/93	A	2	(6)	1
20	Oriad Beqiri		21/02/85	D	30	(1)	1
44	Edy-Nicolas Boyom	CMR	12/12/88	D	30		2
30	Brixhild Brahimaj		05/12/95	M	6	(8)	1
21	Dejvi Bregu		24/10/95	M	30	(2)	9
7	Dany	ANG	14/01/90	M	12	(3)	
9	Baptiste Faye	SEN	18/08/87	A	1	(9)	
27	Eri Lamçja		10/03/94	A	9	(6)	2
19	Silvio Liçaj		19/01/87	M	29	(2)	
14	Julian Lluka		14/02/91	M		(3)	
8	Ergys Mersini		30/09/88	M	16	(1)	
1	Festim Miraka		31/12/87	G	18		
11	Andrés Montero	VEN	05/03/94	M	4	(4)	1
6	Ussama Mutumane	MOZ	01/03/91	A	7	(4)	
16	Behar Ramadani		06/04/90	M	22	(2)	4
77	Reginaldo	MOZ	04/06/90	A	29	(3)	8
4	Oltion Rrapa		30/09/89	D	33		
23	Donald Rrapo		04/10/90	D	12	(14)	1
10	Eduard Rroca		28/07/93	M	19	(3)	2
12	Shkëlzen Ruçi		01/07/92	G	18		
15	Emiljano Shehu		10/06/98	M	1	(1)	
3	Marjus Topi		19/10/95	D	2	(4)	
8	Vangjel Zguro		04/03/93	D	13	(2)	
22	Silvio Zogaj		25/07/97	M	2	(11)	

FK Partizani

1946 • Elbasan Arena, Elbasan (15,000); Selman Stërmasi (9,200) • partizani.al

Major honours

Albanian League (15) 1947, 1948, 1949, 1954, 1957, 1958, 1959, 1961, 1963, 1964, 1971, 1979, 1981, 1987, 1993; Albanian Cup (15) 1948, 1949, 1957, 1958, 1961, 1964, 1966, 1968, 1970, 1973, 1980, 1991, 1993, 1997, 2004

Coach: (Gentian Stojku); (01/07/16) Adolfo Sormani (ITA); (09/10/16) Sulejman Starova

Date		Opponent			Scorers
2016					
07/09	h	Luftëtari	W	1-0	*Batha (p)*
12/09	h	Vllaznia	D	0-0	
18/09	a	Teuta	W	2-0	*Atanda, Ekuban*
25/09	h	Tirana	D	0-0	
01/10	a	Kukës	L	0-1	
13/10	a	Laç	W	2-0	*Ekuban 2*
17/10	h	Flamurtari	W	4-0	*Ekuban, Trashi, Vila, Bardhi*
22/10	a	Korabi	W	1-0	*Ekuban*
30/10	h	Skënderbeu	D	0-0	
05/11	a	Luftëtari	D	1-1	*Ibrahimi*
20/11	a	Vllaznia	D	1-1	*Batha*
26/11	h	Teuta	W	1-0	*Ekuban*
01/12	a	Tirana	D	0-0	
06/12	h	Kukës	D	0-0	
10/12	h	Laç	W	2-0	*Ekuban, Torassa (p)*
14/12	a	Flamurtari	D	1-1	*Batha*
18/12	h	Korabi	W	1-0	*Azubel*
22/12	a	Skënderbeu	W	2-1	*Ekuban 2*
2017					
29/01	a	Luftëtari	L	0-2	
05/02	h	Vllaznia	W	2-1	*Bardhi, Batha (p)*
10/02	a	Teuta	D	0-0	
20/02	h	Tirana	W	2-1	*Malota, Ekuban*
26/02	a	Kukës	D	0-0	
05/03	a	Laç	W	1-0	*Krasniqi*
11/03	h	Flamurtari	W	2-1	*Mazrekaj, Trashi (p)*
18/03	a	Korabi	W	2-0	*og (Premçi), Ekuban*
02/04	h	Skënderbeu	W	1-0	*Batha*
08/04	h	Luftëtari	W	2-0	*Batha (p), Ekuban*
15/04	a	Vllaznia	D	1-1	*Ekuban*
23/04	h	Teuta	W	5-1	*Torassa 2, Ekuban 2, Sukaj (p)*
28/04	a	Tirana	W	2-1	*Batha (p), Sukaj*
05/05	h	Kukës	D	1-1	*og (Shameti)*
11/05	h	Laç	D	0-0	
14/05	a	Flamurtari	D	1-1	*Ekuban*
21/05	h	Korabi	W	3-0	*Četković, Ekuban, Krasniqi*
27/05	a	Skënderbeu	D	2-2	*Batha, Kalari*

No	Name	Nat	DoB	Pos	Aps	(s)	Gls
36	Sodiq Atanda	NGA	26/08/93	D	26	(2)	1
9	Ben Azubel	ISR	19/09/93	A	2	(5)	1
11	Jurgen Bardhi		06/11/97	M	7	(17)	2
10	Idriz Batha		28/03/92	M	31		8
70	Luca Bertoni	ITA	19/06/92	M	4		
9	Mathew Boniface	NGA	05/10/94	A		(7)	
21	Marko Četković	MNE	10/07/86	M	11	(5)	1
45	Caleb Ekuban	GHA	23/03/93	A	34		17
31	Arbnor Fejzullahu		08/04/93	D	24	(2)	
7	Realdo Fili		04/05/96	A	7	(11)	
4	Esin Hakaj		06/12/96	D		(1)	
12	Alban Hoxha		23/11/87	G	34		
22	Labinot Ibrahimi	KOS	25/06/86	D	19	(6)	1
91	Ardit Jaupaj		06/06/96	A	1	(3)	
99	Renaldo Kalari		25/06/84	D	23	(3)	1
5	Gëzim Krasniqi		05/01/90	D	27		2
13	Renato Malota		24/06/86	D	18	(2)	1
3	Kristi Marku		13/04/95	D		(1)	
14	Mentor Mazrekaj	KOS	08/02/89	M	6	(9)	1
16	Ylber Ramadani	KOS	12/04/96	M	22	(10)	
20	Xhevahir Sukaj		05/10/87	A		(8)	2
27	Agustín Torassa	ARG	20/10/88	A	31	(2)	3
19	Lorenc Trashi		19/05/92	M	34		2
8	Jurgen Vatnikaj		08/08/95	M		(1)	
88	Emiljano Vila		12/03/87	M	33	(2)	1
1	Dashamir Xhika		23/05/89	G	2		

KF Skënderbeu

1909 • Skënderbeu (7,000) • kfskenderbeu.al

Major honours

Albanian League (7) 1933, 2011, 2012, 2013, 2014, 2015, 2016

Coach: Andrea Agostinelli (ITA); (03/01/17) Ilir Daja

Date		Opponent			Scorers
2016					
07/09	h	Flamurtari	W	2-1	*Salihi 2 (1p)*
11/09	a	Korabi	W	2-0	*Jashanica, Salihi*
17/09	h	Laç	W	1-0	*Serginho*
24/09	h	Luftëtari	W	1-0	*Adeniyi*
01/10	h	Vllaznia	W	3-0	*Adeniyi, Salihi 2*
12/10	h	Teuta	W	1-0	*Nimaga*
16/10	a	Tirana	L	1-2	*Latifi*
22/10	h	Kukës	D	0-0	
30/10	a	Partizani	D	0-0	
05/11	a	Flamurtari	L	0-2	
20/11	h	Korabi	W	1-0	*Adeniyi*
26/11	a	Laç	W	1-0	*Latifi*
30/11	a	Luftëtari	D	0-0	
04/12	a	Vllaznia	D	0-0	
09/12	a	Teuta	D	0-0	
14/12	h	Tirana	W	2-0	*Salihi, Latifi*
18/12	a	Kukës	L	0-2	
22/12	h	Partizani	L	1-2	*Adeniyi*
2017					
28/01	h	Flamurtari	W	1-0	*Jashanica*
06/02	a	Korabi	W	1-0	*Salihi (p)*
11/02	h	Laç	W	1-0	*Salihi*
19/02	h	Luftëtari	W	3-0	*Muzaka, Latifi, Radaš*
25/02	a	Vllaznia	W	1-0	*Latifi*
04/03	h	Teuta	D	1-1	*Adeniyi*
10/03	a	Tirana	D	2-2	*Salihi 2 (1p)*
17/03	h	Kukës	D	1-1	*Latifi*
02/04	a	Partizani	L	0-1	
10/04	a	Flamurtari	W	1-0	*Latifi*
15/04	h	Korabi	W	3-0	*Jashanica, Salihi, Nimaga*
23/04	a	Laç	W	5-1	*Latifi 3, Adeniyi, Salihi*
30/04	a	Luftëtari	W	1-0	*Adeniyi*
06/05	h	Vllaznia	W	4-3	*Salihi 2 (1p), Muzaka, Latifi (p)*
10/05	a	Teuta	W	1-0	*Adeniyi*
14/05	h	Tirana	W	1-0	*Salihi (p)*
20/05	a	Kukës	L	0-2	
27/05	h	Partizani	D	2-2	*Plaku, Gripshi*

No	Name	Nat	DoB	Pos	Aps	(s)	Gls
11	Leonit Abazi	KOS	05/07/93	D		(2)	
78	James Adeniyi	NGA	20/12/92	A	27	(5)	8
99	Masato Fukui	JPN	14/11/88	M	10	(4)	
7	Enis Gavazaj		21/03/95	A	14	(10)	
18	Nazmi Gripshi		05/07/97	M		(10)	1
70	Ardit Hoxhaj		20/07/94	A		(2)	
20	Hektor Idrizaj		15/04/89	D	3	(3)	
5	Bajram Jashanica	KOS	25/09/90	D	30	(1)	3
77	Reza Karimi	IRN	23/08/98	A		(6)	
27	Liridon Latifi		06/02/94	M	33	(1)	11
88	Sabien Lilaj		18/02/89	M	25		
23	Argjend Malaj	KOS	16/10/93	M	3	(6)	
3	Gledi Mici		06/02/91	D	32		
21	Argjend Mustafa	KOS	30/08/92	M	5	(4)	
17	Gjergji Muzaka		26/09/84	M	7	(6)	2
8	Bakary Nimaga	MLI	06/12/94	M	11	(8)	2
38	Marvin Ogunjimi	BEL	12/10/87	A	1	(5)	
80	Nuredeen Orelesi	NGA	10/04/89	M	31	(2)	
19	Tefik Osmani		08/06/85	D	22	(4)	
23	Anteo Osmanllari		11/11/98	A		(1)	
9	Sebino Plaku		20/05/85	A	4	(3)	1
22	Cornel Predescu	ROU	21/12/87	M	2	(5)	
33	Marko Radaš	CRO	26/10/83	D	27		1
14	Hamdi Salihi		19/01/84	A	32	(1)	15
49	Serginho	BRA	06/04/95	A	7	(6)	1
1	Orges Shehi		25/09/77	G	36		
32	Kristi Vangjeli		05/09/85	D	33		
78	Agim Zeka		06/09/98	M	1	(2)	

KF Teuta

1925 • Niko Dovana (8,000) • kfteuta.com

Major honours
Albanian League (1) 1994; Albanian Cup (3) 1995, 2000, 2005

Coach: (Julian Ahmataj); (18/07/16) (Gentian Begeja); (01/09/16) Cesare Beggi (ITA); (26/09/16) (Gentian Begeja); (09/10/16) Roberto Cevoli (ITA); (25/10/16) Gugash Magani

2016

07/09 h Tirana D 0-0
12/09 a Kukës L 0-3
18/09 h Partizani L 0-2
24/09 a Flamurtari D 0-0
02/10 h Korabi L 2-3 *Čmajčanin, Kotobelli*
12/10 a Skënderbeu L 0-1
17/10 h Luftëtari W 2-0 *Faisal Bangal, Çyrbja*
23/10 a Vllaznia L 0-1
30/10 h Laç W 3-1 *Magani, Faisal Bangal, Çyrbja*
06/11 a Tirana L 1-3 *Gripshi*
21/11 h Kukës L 1-2 *Faisal Bangal*
26/11 a Partizani L 0-1
30/11 h Flamurtari L 1-2 *Ribaj*
04/12 a Korabi W 1-0 *Magani*
09/12 h Skënderbeu D 0-0
14/12 a Luftëtari L 0-1
18/12 h Vllaznia D 0-0
22/12 a Laç W 2-0 *Ribaj 2 (1p)*

2017

28/01 h Tirana W 1-0 *Hila*
05/02 a Kukës L 0-1
10/02 h Partizani D 0-0
19/02 a Flamurtari W 1-0 *Čmajčanin*
25/02 h Korabi W 1-0 *Ribaj (p)*
04/03 a Skënderbeu D 1-1 *Musta*
12/03 h Luftëtari L 0-1
19/03 a Vllaznia D 0-0
01/04 h Laç W 2-0 *Dita, Marković*
10/04 a Tirana D 0-0
15/04 h Kukës L 0-2
23/04 a Partizani L 1-5 *Çyrbja*
30/04 h Flamurtari D 0-0
06/05 a Korabi W 4-0 *Papa, Magani, Progni, Çyrbja*
10/05 h Skënderbeu L 0-1
14/05 a Luftëtari D 1-1 *Faisal Bangal*
20/05 h Vllaznia W 1-0 *Progni*
27/05 a Laç L 1-2 *Çyrbja*

No	Name	Nat	DoB	Pos	Aps	(s)	Gls
11	Eko Barine	NGA	12/05/97	A		(1)	
19	Fabio Beqja		15/02/94	M	17	(6)	
6	Ergi Borshi		09/08/97	M	6	(2)	
10	Tarik Čmajčanin	SRB	18/06/94	M	23	(2)	2
7	Arbër Çyrbja		18/09/93	M	14	(15)	5
22	Bruno Dita		18/02/93	D	21	(3)	1
54	Faisal Bangal	MOZ	05/01/95	A	18	(10)	4
8	Nazmi Gripshi		05/07/97	M	16	(3)	1
17	Fabio Hasa		12/08/96	A	1	(4)	
27	Arjan Hila		06/01/93	M	26	(2)	1
30	Bledar Hodo		21/09/85	M	15	(1)	
14	Erand Hoxha		25/04/85	D	8	(1)	
5	Rustem Hoxha		04/07/91	D	27		
12	Elhan Kastrati		02/02/97	G	13		
15	Blerim Kotobelli		10/08/92	D	33	(1)	1
18	Xhonatan Lajthia		01/02/99	M	1		
17	Eri Lamçja		10/03/94	A	3	(4)	
23	Granuel Lika		22/10/98	M	1		
16	Artur Magani		08/07/94	A	21	(10)	3
11	Elidon Mara		27/06/97	A		(1)	
4	Bojan Marković	BIH	12/11/85	D	16		1
12	Shpëtim Moçka		20/10/89	G	23		
29	Emiljano Musta		31/01/92	M	24	(7)	1
20	Enriko Papa		12/03/93	M	4	(4)	1
77	Gerhard Progni		06/11/86	M	13	(2)	2
4	Valdrin Rashica	KOS	14/12/92	M	4	(6)	
9	Andi Ribaj		21/11/89	A	16	(10)	4
9	Jasmin Rraboshta		30/04/90	A		(1)	
2	Dajan Shehi		19/09/97	D	4	(1)	
3	Silvester Shkalla		10/08/95	D	18	(7)	
5	Mateus Shkreta		16/04/94	D	1		
24	Arsen Sykaj		16/04/90	D	8	(3)	
8	Lorenco Vila		14/12/98	D	1		

KF Tirana

1920 • Selman Stërmasi (9,200) • kftirana.al

Major honours
Albanian League (24) 1930, 1931, 1932, 1934, 1936, 1937, 1965, 1966, 1968, 1970, 1982, 1985, 1988, 1989, 1995, 1996, 1997, 1999, 2000, 2003, 2004, 2005, 2007, 2009; Albanian Cup (16) 1939, 1963, 1976, 1977, 1983, 1984, 1986, 1994, 1996, 1999, 2001, 2002, 2006, 2011, 2012, 2017

Coach: Ilir Daja; (01/11/16) Mirel Josa

2016

07/09 a Teuta D 0-0
11/09 a Laç D 0-0
17/09 h Kukës D 2-2 *Taku, Ndockyt*
25/09 a Partizani D 0-0
02/10 h Flamurtari W 3-0 *Ede, Taku 2*
12/10 a Korabi W 1-0 *Muzaka*
16/10 h Skënderbeu W 2-1 *Ndockyt, Nkounkou*
23/10 a Luftëtari L 1-2 *Taku*
30/10 h Vllaznia D 0-0
06/11 h Teuta W 3-1 *Hoxhallari, Muça, Taku*
20/11 h Laç W 1-0 *Ndockyt*
26/11 a Kukës D 0-0
01/12 h Partizani D 0-0
06/12 a Flamurtari L 0-1
10/12 h Korabi D 1-1 *Taku*
14/12 a Skënderbeu L 0-2
18/12 h Luftëtari W 2-0 *Taku, Ndockyt*
22/12 a Vllaznia D 0-0

2017

28/01 a Teuta L 0-1
05/02 a Laç L 0-1
11/02 h Kukës L 1-2 *Taku*
20/02 a Partizani L 1-2 *Teqja*
26/02 h Flamurtari D 0-0
04/03 a Korabi D 1-1 *Ede*
10/03 h Skënderbeu D 2-2 *Ede, Hoxhallari*
19/03 a Luftëtari L 1-2 *Cissé*
31/03 h Vllaznia L 1-2 *Cissé*
10/04 h Teuta D 0-0
15/04 h Laç D 0-0
23/04 a Kukës L 1-4 *Turtulli*
28/04 h Partizani L 1-2 *Ede*
06/05 a Flamurtari L 0-2
10/05 h Korabi W 2-0 *Ede, Taku*
14/05 a Skënderbeu L 0-1
20/05 h Luftëtari W 2-0 *Ede, Ndockyt*
27/05 a Vllaznia D 0-0

No	Name	Nat	DoB	Pos	Aps	(s)	Gls
45	Reuben Acquah	GHA	03/11/96	M	16	(8)	
23	Flamur Bajrami	KOS	10/02/97	M		(3)	
25	Klisman Cake		02/05/99	D	7	(2)	
3	Moctar Cissé	MLI	10/03/93	A	15	(8)	2
14	Asjon Daja		14/03/90	M	30	(1)	
15	Fjoralb Deliaj		04/04/97	M	2	(5)	
17	Albi Doka		26/06/97	D	16	(1)	
6	David Domgjoni	KOS	21/05/97	D	8	(4)	
11	Ifeanyi Ede	NGA	24/12/96	A	18	(3)	6
9	Grent Halili		24/05/98	A	5	(10)	
28	Erjon Hoxhallari		15/10/95	D	34		2
13	Erando Karabeci		06/09/88	M	21	(2)	
18	Dorian Kërçiku		30/08/93	M	16	(4)	
7	Gilman Lika		13/01/87	M	9	(11)	
1	Ilion Lika		17/05/80	G	36		
4	Gentian Muça		13/05/97	D	18		1
17	Gjergji Muzaka		26/09/84	M	5	(7)	1
19	Merveille Ndockyt	CGO	20/07/98	M	28	(2)	5
77	Ansi Nika		22/08/90	A	4	(4)	
22	Justalain Nkounkou	CGO	02/08/96	A	27	(5)	1
8	Romuald Ntsitsigui	GAB	08/04/91	M	2	(4)	
2	Marlind Nuriu		05/07/97	D		(2)	
25	Majkëll Peçi		29/08/96	A	1	(1)	
26	Afrim Taku		04/08/89	M	34		9
21	Olsi Teqja		27/07/88	D	29		1
5	Marvin Turtulli		17/10/94	D	10	(2)	1
10	Erjon Vucaj		25/12/90	M	5	(5)	

KF Vllaznia

1919 • Loro Boriçi (16,500); Reshit Rusi (3,500) • vllaznia.al

Major honours
Albanian League (9) 1945, 1946, 1972, 1974, 1978, 1983, 1992, 1998, 2001; Albanian Cup (6) 1965, 1972, 1979, 1981, 1987, 2008

Coach: Armando Cungu

2016

08/09 h Kukës D 0-0
12/09 a Partizani D 0-0
18/09 h Flamurtari W 2-0 *Tafili (p), Hebaj*
24/09 a Korabi D 0-0
01/10 a Skënderbeu L 0-3
12/10 a Luftëtari D 1-1 *Shtupina*
17/10 h Laç L 1-2 *Shtupina*
23/10 h Teuta W 1-0 *Vrapi*
30/10 a Tirana D 0-0
06/11 a Kukës L 1-3 *Shtupina*
20/11 h Partizani D 1-1 *Çinari*
25/11 a Flamurtari W 1-0 *Cicmil*
30/11 h Korabi W 3-0 *Shtupina, Bardhulla, Tafili*
04/12 h Skënderbeu D 0-0
10/12 h Luftëtari L 2-3 *Shtupina, Marku*
14/12 a Laç L 0-1
18/12 a Teuta D 0-0
22/12 h Tirana D 0-0

2017

27/01 h Kukës L 0-1
05/02 a Partizani L 1-2 *Bakaj*
11/02 h Flamurtari W 3-2 *Hebaj, Bakaj, Pjeshka*
19/02 a Korabi W 2-0 *Bakaj, Hebaj*
25/02 h Skënderbeu L 0-1
04/03 a Luftëtari D 0-0
12/03 h Laç W 1-0 *Bakaj (p)*
19/03 h Teuta D 0-0
31/03 a Tirana W 2-1 *Gocaj (p), Gurishta*
09/04 a Kukës D 0-0
15/04 h Partizani D 1-1 *Hebaj*
22/04 a Flamurtari L 0-2
29/04 h Korabi D 1-1 *Gurishta*
06/05 a Skënderbeu L 3-4 *Çinari, Tafili (p), Bakaj*
10/05 h Luftëtari D 2-2 *Bakaj (p), Shtupina*
14/05 a Laç L 0-3
20/05 a Teuta L 0-1
27/05 h Tirana D 0-0

No	Name	Nat	DoB	Pos	Aps	(s)	Gls
12	Jasmin Agović	MNE	13/03/91	G	22		
20	Elis Bakaj		25/06/87	A	13	(1)	6
7	Florind Bardhulla		19/11/92	M	25	(3)	1
15	Ditmar Bicaj		26/02/89	D	29		
59	Stefan Cicmil	MNE	16/08/90	D	17	(2)	1
11	Erald Çinari		11/10/92	A	24	(3)	2
9	Arenc Dibra		11/05/90	A		(3)	
17	Denis Dyca		11/01/96	M	1	(5)	
21	Olsi Gocaj		30/09/88	M	31	(2)	1
2	Erdenis Gurishta		24/04/95	D	15	(5)	2
18	Arsen Hajdari		25/02/89	A	1	(3)	
7	Rudin Hebaj		30/07/98	M	8	(15)	4
20	Yll Hoxha	KOS	26/12/87	M	2	(5)	
19	Arlind Kalaja		27/12/95	A	20	(3)	
4	Ambroz Kapaklija		30/11/96	M		(1)	
14	Arsid Kruja		08/06/93	A	7	(8)	
6	Ardit Krymi		02/05/96	M	29		
3	Antonio Marku		24/03/92	D	11	(3)	1
4	Landry Mulemo	COD	17/09/86	D	2	(6)	
18	Brunild Pepa		22/11/90	A	9	(7)	
5	Denis Pjeshka		28/05/95	D	20	(5)	1
1	Erind Selimaj		22/05/89	G	14		
10	Ndriçim Shtupina		18/03/87	M	33	(1)	6
40	Alsid Tafili		20/08/87	M	31	(1)	3
17	Uendi Vecaj		18/02/97	M	5	(9)	
44	Endrit Vrapi		23/05/82	D	22	(6)	1
8	Ivor Weitzer	CRO	24/05/88	M	5	(6)	

ALBANIA

Top goalscorers

28	Pero Pejić (Kukës)
17	Caleb Ekuban (Partizani)
15	Hamdi Salihi (Skënderbeu)
11	Liridon Latifi (Skënderbeu)
10	Tomislav Bušić (Flamurtari)
9	Donjet Shkodra (Flamurtari) Dejvi Bregu (Luftëtari) Afrim Taku (Tirana)
8	Izair Emini (Kukës) Reginaldo (Luftëtari) Idriz Batha (Partizani) James Adeniyi (Skënderbeu)

Promoted clubs

FC Kamza

1936 • Fuat Toptani (4,500) • no website
Coach: Bledar Devolli; (25/03/17) Ramadan Ndreu

KS Lushnja

1927 • Abdurrahman "Roza" Haxhiu (7,000) • no website
Coach: Artan Bano

Second level final tables 2016/17

Group A Regular season

		Pld	W	D	L	F	A	Pts
1	FC Kamza	18	15	2	1	25	7	47
2	KS Besëlidhja	18	11	6	1	26	11	39
3	KF Erzeni	18	12	1	5	32	14	37
4	KS Burreli	18	7	5	6	18	16	26
5	KF Shenkolli	18	7	2	9	16	23	23
6	KS Kastrioti	18	5	7	6	18	14	22
7	KS Besa	18	5	3	10	10	18	18
8	KF Adriatiku	18	3	5	10	12	25	14
9	KF Iliria	18	3	5	10	12	26	14
10	KF Tërbuni	18	2	4	12	6	21	10

Group A Promotion play-offs

		Pld	W	D	L	F	A	Pts
1	FC Kamza	8	4	4	0	12	6	40
2	KS Besëlidhja	8	6	2	0	14	3	40
3	KF Erzeni	8	1	2	5	13	21	24
4	KS Burreli	8	2	2	4	11	12	21
5	FK Shënkolli	8	0	4	4	11	19	16

Group B Regular season

		Pld	W	D	L	F	A	Pts
1	KS Lushnja	18	12	5	1	31	12	41
2	FK Bylis	18	11	5	2	23	10	38
3	KF Pogradeci	18	8	5	5	21	16	29
4	FK Tomori	18	6	5	7	11	12	23
5	KS Shkumbini	18	7	1	10	10	18	22
6	KF Apolonia	18	6	4	8	19	20	22
7	KS Turbina	18	6	3	9	16	20	21
8	FK Dinamo Tirana	18	4	6	8	12	13	18
9	KF Sopoti	18	2	10	6	17	26	16
10	KF Elbasani	18	4	4	10	15	28	16

Group B Promotion play-offs

		Pld	W	D	L	F	A	Pts
1	KS Lushnja	8	6	2	0	13	6	41
2	FK Bylis	8	6	1	1	17	5	38
3	KF Pogradeci	8	2	3	3	10	12	24
4	KS Shkumbini	8	1	2	5	8	18	16
5	FK Tomori	8	1	0	7	10	17	15

NB After 18 rounds the top five clubs enter promotion play-offs, carrying forward half of their points total (half points rounded upwards).

DOMESTIC CUP

Kupa e Shqipërisë 2016/17

FIRST ROUND

(28/09/16 & 05/10/16)
Besa 1-1, 1-4 Tërbuni *(aet; 2-5)*
Burreli 3-1, 1-4 Kastrioti *(4-5)*
Butrinti 1-1, 0-8 Skënderbeu *(1-9)*
Dinamo 2-1, 1-1 Pogradec *(3-2)*
Elbasan 0-1, 2-2 Luftëtari *(2-3)*
Erzeni 1-3, 2-2 Besëlidhja *(3-5)*
Iliria 1-0, 0-6 Flamurtari *(1-6)*
Kamza 1-1, 2-0 Korabi *(3-1)*
Lushnja 1-3, 0-1 Apolonia *(1-4)*
Mamurrasi 0-3, 0-4 Vllaznia *(0-7)*
Shënkolli 0-0, 0-2 Teuta *(0-2)*
Shkumbini 1-3, 0-4 Bylis *(1-7)*
Sopoti 1-1, 0-7 Tirana *(1-8)*
Tomori 0-3, 0-1 Kukës *(0-4)*
Turbina 0-2, 0-3 Laç *(0-5)*

(28/09/16 & 06/10/16)
Kevitan 1-5, 0-4 Partizani *(1-9)*

SECOND ROUND

(26/10/16 & 16/11/16)
Apolonia 2-1, 0-3 Skënderbeu *(2-4)*
Besëlidhja 1-0, 1-1 Partizani *(2-1)*
Bylis 1-1, 0-3 Laç *(1-4)*
Dinamo 0-2, 0-0 Kukës *(0-2)*
Kamza 0-2, 0-6 Vllaznia *(0-8)*
Kastrioti 2-1, 1-3 Teuta *(3-4)*
Luftëtari 1-4, 0-1 Tirana *(1-5)*
Tërbuni 3-3, 0-2 Flamurtari *(3-5)*

QUARTER-FINALS

(01/02/17 & 15/02/17)
Flamurtari 1-2 Besëlidhja *(Smajlaj 74og; Camara 19, Marashi 47)*
Besëlidhja 0-0 Flamurtari
(Besëlidhja 2-1)

Laç 1-1Skënderbeu *(Kanapari 69; Osmani 90)*
Skënderbeu 1-0 Laç *(Gavazaj 57)*
(Skënderbeu 2-1)

Tirana 2-1 Kukës *(Halili 30, Taku 45; Imami 47)*
Kukës 0-0 Tirana
(Tirana 2-1)

Vllaznia 1-0 Teuta *(Tafili 23)*
Teuta 2-0 Vllaznia *(Hila 81p, Progni 83)*
(Teuta 2-1)

SEMI-FINALS

(05/04/17 & 19/04/17)
Besëlidhja 1-1 Tirana *(Marashi 67; Ndockyt 59)*
Tirana 2-0 Besëlidhja *(Taku 24p, Hoxhallari 40)*
(Tirana 3-1)

(06/04/17 & 19/04/17)
Skënderbeu 1-0 Teuta *(Vangjeli 86)*
Teuta 0-1 Skënderbeu *(Latifi 51)*
(Skënderbeu 2-0)

FINAL

(31/05/17)
Elbasan Arena, Elbasan
KF TIRANA 3 *(Ede 20, Nkounkou 102, Ndockyt 112p)*
KF SKËNDERBEU 1 *(Radaš 86)*
(aet)
Referee: *Meta*
TIRANA: *I Lika, Doka (Halili 83), Teqja, Turtulli, Hoxhallari, Acquah, Karabeci, Kërçiku, G Lika (Daja 63), Ndockyt, Ede (Nkounkou 79)*
SKËNDERBEU: *Shehi, Vangjeli, Jashanica, Radaš, Mici (Idrizaj 63), Nimaga, Muzaka, Latifi (Gripshi 77), Gavazaj (Karimi 77), Plaku, Adeniyi*

Tirana partly made up for their relegation with victory in the Albanian Cup

ANDORRA

Federació Andorrana de Fútbol (FAF)

Address	c/ Batlle Tomàs, 4 Baixos AD-700 Escaldes-Engordany	**President**	Victor Manuel Domingos dos Santos
Tel	+376 805 830	**General secretary**	Tomás Gea
Fax	+376 862 006	**Media officer**	Xavi Bonet
E-mail	info@faf.ad	**Year of formation**	1994
Website	faf.ad	**National stadium**	Estadi Nacional, Andorra la Vella (3,306)

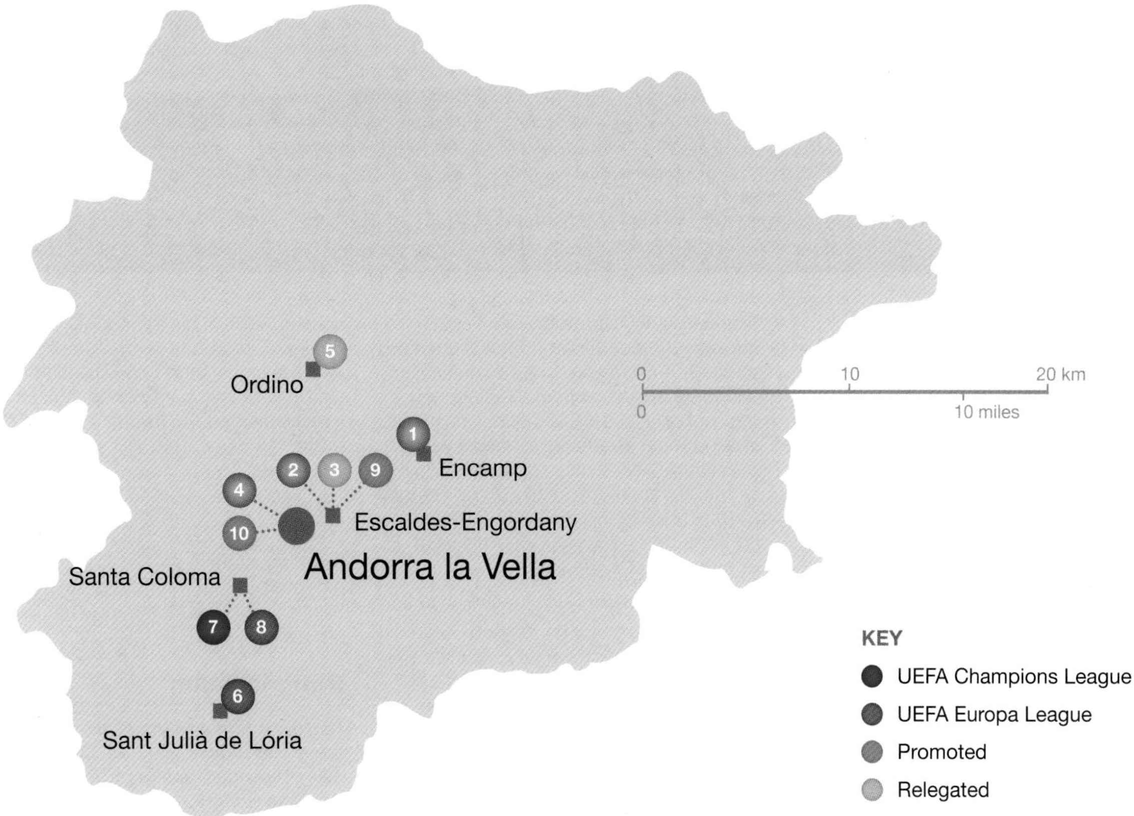

Ordino
Encamp
Escaldes-Engordany
Andorra la Vella
Santa Coloma
Sant Julià de Lória

0 10 20 km
0 10 miles

KEY
UEFA Champions League
UEFA Europa League
Promoted
Relegated

PRIMERA DIVISIÓ CLUBS

1 **FC Encamp**

2 **UE Engordany**

3 **CE Jenlai**

4 **FC Lusitans**

5 **FC Ordino**

6 **UE Sant Julià**

7 **FC Santa Coloma**

8 **UE Santa Coloma**

PROMOTED CLUBS

9 **Inter Club d'Escaldes**

10 **Penya Encarnada d'Andorra**

Four in a row for FC Santa Coloma

The 2016/17 season in Andorra was practically a repeat of the previous campaign as FC Santa Coloma retained their Primera Divisió title, winning it for an unprecedented fourth successive year, while local rivals UE Santa Coloma kept hold of the Copa Constitució.

There was unexpected news elsewhere, however, as the Andorran national team not only brought a long run of defeats in European Qualifiers to an end but followed up a goalless draw against the Faroe Islands with an incredible 1-0 win against UEFA EURO 2016 participants Hungary.

LLIGA NACIONAL DE [illegible]OL CA[illegible]NS

FAF

www.faf.ad

Strong finish secures record 11th league crown

UE Santa Coloma double up in Andorran Cup

Losing streak finally ends for national side

Domestic league

There was a change to the Primera Divisió fixture schedule in 2016/17, with the eight teams playing each other three times rather than two during the first phase of the competition. For the first half of it, FC Santa Coloma looked far from certain to make a successful defence of their title.

The club's previous three campaigns under coach Richard Imbernón had all resulted in glory, but a sloppy start, in which they won just two of their opening six matches and only received three points from their next fixture because newly-promoted Jenlai failed to turn up, left them playing catch-up on regular rivals UE Santa Coloma, Sant Julià and Lusitans. By the turn of the year just one point separated the top three, Lusitans having slipped off the pace, but the defending champions had registered six successive wins in the run-up to Christmas and they carried that form into the new year. By the time of the split they had constructed a four-point lead.

The same four teams as in the previous seven seasons entered the Championship pool, but there was no contest at the top. Imbernón's side not only protected their position during the final six games but extended their advantage to a whopping ten points at the finish. A mixture of Andorrans and Spaniards, FC Santa Coloma's squad even contained a FIFA World Cup and UEFA European Championship winner in 39-year-old ex-Spain international Joan Capdevila. For all his international honours, he had never previously won a national championship winner's medal. It was the third, though, for his defensive partner, 37-year-old Ildefons Lima – one of four Andorran internationals in the side.

At the bottom Jenlai were so cast adrift and disgruntled that by the end of the season they were taking the field without a full starting XI, departing with a 15-1 defeat by Encamp, who avoided the relegation play-off place on head-to-head results with Ordino. Penya Ercanada d'Andorra had endured a similarly forgettable top-flight experience the previous season, but they were happy to come back for more, finishing a close second to automatically-promoted Inter d'Escaldes before turning their play-off around with a remarkable 5-1 second-leg win at Ordino.

Domestic cup

UE Santa Coloma retained the Copa Constitució thanks to a 1-0 win in the final over the recrowned champions. Their match-winner was Spanish striker Víctor Bernat, who had just topped the Primera Divisió scoring charts for the second season running and had also scored twice in his team's 3-0 win against Engordany in the 2016 final. It was the club's third cup win, all of those victories having come since their local rivals last lifted the trophy.

Europe

A familiar collective misadventure in Europe befell Andorra's clubs, with all three again falling at the first hurdle, the only non-defeat a goalless draw for FC Santa Coloma at home to Armenian champions Alashkert.

National team

Two wins and one draw in their first three matches of 2017 constituted a mind-blowing transformation in the fortunes of the Andorran national team. A 2-0 friendly win away to San Marino in February – which ended an 86-game wait for a win of any kind – was followed by a 0-0 draw at home to Faroe Islands – which ended a run of 58 successive European Qualifier defeats. With confidence now at an all-time high, and skipper Lima set to equal Óscar Sonejee's record figure of 106 caps, Koldo Alvarez's side recorded arguably the greatest result in Andorra's history, a momentous looping header from FC Santa Coloma midfielder Marc Rebés not only beating Hungary 1-0 but also lifting the team off the bottom of their FIFA World Cup qualifying group.

DOMESTIC SEASON AT A GLANCE

Primera Divisió 2016/17 final tables

FIRST PHASE

		Pld	W	D	L	F	A	Pts
1	FC Santa Coloma	21	15	3	3	44	14	48
2	UE Sant Julià	21	13	5	3	49	16	44
3	UE Santa Coloma	21	13	5	3	54	22	44
4	FC Lusitans	21	11	6	4	40	20	39
5	UE Engordany	21	8	6	7	35	27	30
6	FC Encamp	21	4	3	14	18	31	15
7	FC Ordino	21	3	3	15	24	49	12
8	CE Jenlai	21	1	1	19	10	95	1

SECOND PHASE

Championship pool

		Pld	W	D	L	F	A	Pts
1	**FC Santa Coloma**	**27**	**18**	**6**	**3**	**57**	**21**	**60**
2	UE Sant Julià	27	14	8	5	55	23	50
3	UE Santa Coloma	27	14	6	7	62	34	48
4	FC Lusitans	27	13	9	5	49	30	48

Relegation pool

		Pld	W	D	L	F	A	Pts
5	UE Engordany	27	10	6	11	46	39	36
6	FC Encamp	27	8	3	16	45	37	27
7	FC Ordino	27	8	3	16	45	56	27
8	CE Jenlai	27	2	1	24	18	137	4

NB CE Jenlai – 3 pts deducted.

European qualification 2017/18

Champion: FC Santa Coloma (first qualifying round)

Cup winner: UE Santa Coloma (first qualifying round)
UE Sant Julià (first qualifying round)

Top scorer Víctor Bernat (UE Santa Coloma), 18 goals
Relegated clubs CE Jenlai, FC Ordino
Promoted clubs Inter Club d'Escaldes, Penya Encarnada d'Andorra
Cup final UE Santa Coloma 1-0 FC Santa Coloma

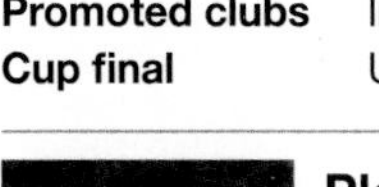

Player of the season

Juanfer
(FC Santa Coloma)

Barcelona-born Juan Fernando Láin González made it four Andorran championship titles in four seasons at FC Santa Coloma, and the 34-year-old attacking midfielder made the 2016/17 season a particularly special one with an avalanche of goals. He had scored 13 in total over the three previous seasons put together, but he matched that figure in one campaign to become his club's leading marksman – with three more than Andorran international Gabriel Riera – and the second highest scorer in the Primera Divisió – behind UE Santa Coloma's Víctor Bernat.

Newcomer of the season

Isaac Padilla
(UE Sant Julià)

Sant Julià were unable to maintain the lead at the top of the Primera Divisió table that they held at the winter break, but they received a considerable boost to their attacking armoury for the second half of the campaign when they brought in Padilla, an FC Barcelona academy trainee, on loan from Spanish club Sabadell. The 21-year-old scored nine goals, including a hat-trick in the opening game of the championship play-off series that earned his team a 3-3 draw against FC Santa Coloma, plus a double that brought a 2-1 win against UE Santa Coloma.

Team of the season

(4-3-3)

Coach: Imbernón *(FC Santa Coloma)*

ANDORRA

NATIONAL TEAM

Top five all-time caps

Ildefons Lima & Óscar Sonejee (106); **Josep Manel Ayala** (85); Manolo Jiménez (80) Koldo Álvarez (79)

Top five all-time goals

Ildefons Lima (11); Óscar Sonejee (4); Jesús Julián Lucendo (3); Emiliano González, **Cristian Martínez**, **Marc Pujol**, Justo Ruiz & Fernando Silva (2)

Results 2016/17

06/09/16	Latvia (WCQ)	H	Andorra la Vella	L	0-1	
07/10/16	Portugal (WCQ)	A	Aveiro	L	0-6	
10/10/16	Switzerland (WCQ)	H	Andorra la Vella	L	1-2	*A Martínez (90+1)*
13/11/16	Hungary (WCQ)	A	Budapest	L	0-4	
22/02/17	San Marino	A	Serravalle	W	2-0	*Lima (28), C Martínez (66)*
25/03/17	Faroe Islands (WCQ)	H	Andorra la Vella	D	0-0	
09/06/17	Hungary (WCQ)	H	Andorra la Vella	W	1-0	*Rebés (26)*

Appearances 2016/17

Coach: Koldo Alvarez	**04/09/70**		**LVA**	**POR**	**SUI**	**HUN**	**Smr**	**FRO**	**HUN**	**Caps**	**Goals**
Ferran Pol	28/02/83	FC Andorra (ESP)	G				G			25	-
Jordi Rubio	01/11/87	UE Santa Coloma	D	D 62*				M77		34	-
Ildefons Lima	10/12/79	FC Santa Coloma	D	D	D		D	D	D	106	11
Max Llovera	08/01/97	Lleida Esportiu (ESP)	D	D	D	D	D88	D	D	12	-
Marc García	21/03/88	Manlleu (ESP)	D	D49			D67	s46		35	-
Marc Vales	04/04/90	SJK (FIN)	M	M	M	D	M	M	M	49	-
Ludovic Clemente	09/05/86	FC Andorra (ESP)	M78		M73		s78	s77	M83	19	-
Jordi Aláez	23/01/98	FC Andorra (ESP)	M83	A73		A	s57	A	A68	8	-
Márcio Vieira	10/10/84	Atlético Monzón (ESP)	M	M	M80	M	M	M		73	-
Cristian Martínez	16/10/89	FC Andorra (ESP)	M	M76	s80	M67	M78	M		44	2
Gabriel Riera	05/06/85	FC Santa Coloma	A30		s84				s83	37	1
Marc Rebés	03/07/94	FC Santa Coloma	s30	M 71*					M	9	1
Marc Pujol	21/08/82	FC Andorra (ESP)	s78	s73	A84	A87	M82	M54	M88	75	2
Victor Hugo Moreira	05/10/82	FC Andorra (ESP)	s83	s76		s83				19	-
José Antonio Gomes	03/12/85	Illescas (ESP)		G	G	G		G	G	40	-
Victor Rodríguez	07/09/87	FC Santa Coloma		M	M	M83	M75			16	-
Moisés San Nicolás	17/09/93	Lusitans		s49	D	D	s67	D	D	26	-
Emili García	11/01/89	FC Andorra (ESP)			D	D	s82			35	1
Jesús Rubio	09/09/94	UE Santa Coloma			D	D	D	D46	D	6	-
Alexandre Martínez	10/10/98	FC Andorra (ESP)			s73	s67	A57	s54	A	7	1
Juli Sánchez	20/06/78	UE Santa Coloma				s87				66	1
Sergio Moreno	25/11/87	FC Andorra (ESP)					s75			55	-
Adrián Rodrigues	14/08/88	Villarrobledo (ESP)					s88			16	-
David Maneiro	16/02/89	UE Santa Coloma							s68	12	-
Josep Manel Ayala	08/04/80	UE Santa Coloma							s88	85	-

EUROPE

FC Santa Coloma

First qualifying round - Alashkert FC (ARM)
H 0-0
Casals, Wagner, A Ramos, Rebés (Noguerol 61), Lima, Pujol, C Martínez, Armero (Juanfer 66), Capdevila, González, Rodríguez (J Toscano 80). Coach: Richard Imbernón (AND)
A 0-3
Casals, C Martínez, Lima, R Ramos (Juanfer 72), A Ramos (Mercadé 83), González, Parra, Capdevila, Rebés (Noguerol 64), Rodríguez, Armero. Coach: Richard Imbernón (AND)
Red cards: González 60, C Martínez 90, Parra 90+4

UE Santa Coloma

First qualifying round - NK Lokomotiva Zagreb (CRO)
H 1-3 *Pedro Reis (90+3)*
Periánez, Jesús Rubio, Martínez, Ayala, Antón (Bousenine 74), Pedro Reis, Salomó (Jordi Rubio 62), Bernat, Aloy (Orosa 81), Ruiz, Crespo. Coach: Emilio Gómez (ESP)
A 1-4 *Salomó (89)*
Fernández, Jesús Rubio, Maneiro (Salomó 69), Martínez, Jordi Rubio, Antón, Bernat (Pereira 59), Ruiz, Crespo (Nazzaro 62), Bousenine, Orosa. Coach: Emilio Gómez (ESP)

FC Lusitans

First qualifying round - NK Domžale (SVN)
A 1-3 *Luizão (5)*
Coca, Acosta (Pousa 66), M San Nicolás, Muñoz, Pinto, Luizão (L San Nicolás 84), Dos Reis (Lucas Maciel 56), Aguilar, Molina, Bruninho, Léo Maciel. Coach: Raúl Cañete (ESP)
H 1-2 *Luizão (18)*
Coca, M San Nicolás, Lucas Maciel, Muñoz, Pinto, Luizão (Dos Reis 69), Aguilar, Molina, Bruninho (L San Nicolás 82), Pousa (Acosta 68), Léo Maciel. Coach: Raúl Cañete (ESP)

DOMESTIC LEAGUE CLUB-BY-CLUB

Stadium

Centre d'Entrenament FAF - Borda Mateu, Andorra la Vella (500)

FC Encamp

1950 • fcencamp.org
Major honours
Andorran League (2) 1996, 2002
Coach: Vicenç Marquès (ESP)

Date	Opponent	Res	Score	Scorers
2016				
18/09	FC Santa Coloma	W	1-0	*Vieira*
25/09	Engordany	D	1-1	*Prat*
02/10	Lusitans	L	0-1	
16/10	Jenlai	L	1-2	*Varela*
23/10	Sant Julià	L	0-1	
30/10	Ordino	L	1-2	*Najera*
06/11	UE Santa Coloma	L	0-2	
20/11	FC Santa Coloma	L	0-1	
27/11	Engordany	L	1-3	*Najera*
04/12	Lusitans	L	1-2	*Najera*
11/12	Jenlai	W	5-0	*Vieira 3, Bueno, G Garcia*
18/12	Sant Julià	D	1-1	*Paredes*
2017				
22/01	Ordino	W	1-0	*Najera*
05/02	UE Santa Coloma	L	1-2	*Paredes*
12/02	FC Santa Coloma	L	0-1	
18/02	Engordany	L	0-3	
26/02	Lusitans	L	1-3	*Najera*
05/03	Jenlai	W	1-0	*De la Torre*
11/03	Sant Julià	L	0-1	
14/03	Ordino	D	2-2	*Reyes, G Garcia*
19/03	UE Santa Coloma	L	0-3	
09/04	Engordany	W	2-0	*Vieira 2*
23/04	Ordino	W	3-1	*C Bové, De la Torre, Najera*
30/04	Jenlai	W	5-0	*Reyes, Varela 2, Peppe, Prat*
07/05	Engordany	L	1-2	*Varela*
14/05	Ordino	L	1-2	*Fontan*
21/05	Jenlai	W	15-1	*Najera 3, Villanueva, De la Torre, G Garcia, Varela 3, Fontan, Bueno 2, Barra, Reyes, Peppe*

No	Name	Nat	DoB	Pos	Aps	(s)	Gls
2	André Marinho	POR	26/03/93	D	17	(2)	
17	Jordi Barra		10/07/78	M	6	(6)	1
11	Aleix Bové		08/03/96	D	7	(7)	
20	Claudi Bové		08/03/96	D	5	(1)	1
15	Víctor Bueno		23/07/94	M	8	(9)	3
9	Ángel De la Torre	MEX	04/01/91	A	8	(5)	3
13	Hugo Do Paço		10/06/84	G	8		
7	Roberto Dos Santos		20/04/94	M	12	(5)	
4	Yael Fontan	ESP	24/02/80	D	23		2
8	Genís Garcia		18/05/78	M	11	(6)	3
22	Txema Garcia		04/12/74	D	5	(7)	
1	Elias Lomeli	MEX	15/01/88	G	11		
18	Diego Najera	MEX	11/12/94	A	25	(1)	9
3	Christian Paredes	PER	16/04/87	D	15	(2)	2
12	Edu Peppe		28/01/83	M	25	(1)	2
21	Xavier Prat		28/04/92	A	17	(7)	2
20	Albert Ramírez		05/02/87	M	4	(4)	
14	Albert Reyes		24/03/96	M	16	(2)	3
13	Alberto Usubiaga		06/11/94	G	8	(1)	
16	Oriol Vales		23/12/97	M	3	(2)	
5	Sebas Varela	URU	23/09/80	D	23		7
10	Xavier Vieira		14/01/92	M	16	(1)	6
6	David Villanueva	ESP	12/02/96	D	24		1

UE Engordany

2001 • ueengordauny.jimdo.com
Coach: Otger Canals (ESP)

Date	Opponent	Res	Score	Scorers
2016				
18/09	UE Santa Coloma	L	1-2	*Lampereur*
25/09	Encamp	D	1-1	*Ruiz*
02/10	FC Santa Coloma	L	0-1	
16/10	Lusitans	D	1-1	*Sanguina (p)*
23/10	Jenlai	W	3-0	*Martins 2, J Pinto*
30/10	Sant Julià	L	1-3	*Mbang*
06/11	Ordino	W	6-1	*Martins, Mbang 2, Lampereur, Sanguina 2 (1p)*
20/11	UE Santa Coloma	L	1-2	*Liébana*
27/11	Encamp	W	3-1	*Mbang 2, Lampereur*
04/12	FC Santa Coloma	L	1-4	*Bousenine*
11/12	Lusitans	D	1-1	*og (Muñoz)*
18/12	Jenlai	W	2-1	*Bousenine, Lampereur*
2017				
22/01	Sant Julià	W	2-1	*Ryahi, Amarilla*
05/02	Ordino	W	4-2	*Begeorgi, Amarilla 2, Spano*
12/02	UE Santa Coloma	D	1-1	*Benhaim*
18/02	Encamp	W	3-0	*Benhaim, Amarilla 2*
26/02	FC Santa Coloma	L	1-2	*Amarilla*
05/03	Lusitans	D	1-1	*Benhaim*
11/03	Jenlai	W	1-0	*Sala*
14/03	Sant Julià	L	0-1	
19/03	Ordino	D	1-1	*Amarilla*
09/04	Encamp	L	0-2	
23/04	Jenlai	W	8-2	*Benhaim 2, Peña 2, Guida 3, Spano*
29/04	Ordino	L	0-2	
07/05	Encamp	W	2-1	*Benhaim, Peña*
14/05	Jenlai	L	1-2	*Guida*
21/05	Ordino	L	0-3	

No	Name	Nat	DoB	Pos	Aps	(s)	Gls
9	Éver Amarilla	PAR	03/10/84	A	10		7
14	Fabrice Begeorgi	FRA	20/04/87	D	15	(1)	1
3	Julien Benhaim	FRA	25/10/96	A	13		6
13	Andrés Benítez	PAR	01/01/83	G	15		
17	Samïr Bousenine		07/02/91	M	14	(5)	2
5	Barthelémy Casanova	FRA	02/03/92	M	8		
13	Roberto García	ESP	09/01/87	G	2		
11	Rodrigo Guida		24/08/82	A	3	(7)	4
7	Jérémy Lampereur	FRA	29/11/87	M	23		4
3	Óscar Liébana	ESP	29/10/90	D	12		1
24	Rafa Martins		07/11/91	M	12	(7)	3
19	Gilles Mbang	GAB	19/10/85	A	4	(2)	5
16	Críspulo Peña	PAR	21/04/91	M	10	(3)	3
4	Jorge Pinto		15/05/94	D	8	(5)	1
20	Luis Pinto		05/03/87	M	16	(5)	
16	Bryan Pubill		26/07/00	M		(3)	
13	Jordi Rodríguez		01/12/93	G	3		
9	Adrián Ruiz	ESP	18/03/94	A	2	(1)	1
8	Hamza Ryahi	ESP	11/03/94	M	25		1
5	Marc Sala	ESP	09/03/95	D	13	(1)	1
22	Carlos Javier Sanguina	PAR	22/05/95	A	10	(2)	3
1	Pol Serrat	ESP	20/05/96	G	7		
25	Mario Valentín Spano	ITA	07/02/86	D	23		2
10	Brian Felipe Teixeira		26/06/95	A	13	(6)	
6	Quentin Van Damme	FRA	20/11/95	M	17	(4)	
2	Walter Wagner	ARG	12/01/81	D	19		

ANDORRA

CE Jenlai

2008 • no website

Coach: Llorenç Codoñes (ESP); (07/11/16) Jordi Pascual (ESP)

Date	Opponent	Result	Scorers
2016			
18/09	Sant Julià	L 1-3	*Nuno Machado*
25/09	Ordino	D 0-0	
02/10	UE Santa Coloma	L 0-5	
16/10	Encamp	W 2-1	*Pisculichi 2 (1p)*
23/10	Engordany	L 0-3	
30/10	Lusitans	L 0-2	
06/11	FC Santa Coloma	L 0-3	*(w/o)*
20/11	Sant Julià	L 0-9	
27/11	Ordino	L 1-4	*Ribeiro*
04/12	UE Santa Coloma	L 2-7	*Pisculichi, Albino*
11/12	Encamp	L 0-5	
18/12	Engordany	L 1-2	*Antonio Lopes*
2017			
22/01	Lusitans	L 1-6	*Ribeiro*
05/02	FC Santa Coloma	L 0-9	
12/02	Sant Julià	L 0-5	
19/02	Ordino	L 1-6	*Pisculichi*
25/02	UE Santa Coloma	L 1-10	*Pisculichi*
05/03	Encamp	L 0-1	
11/03	Engordany	L 0-1	
14/03	Lusitans	L 0-7	
19/03	FC Santa Coloma	L 0-6	
09/04	Ordino	L 0-3	
23/04	Engordany	L 2-8	*Bríñez (p), M Garcia*
30/04	Encamp	L 0-5	
07/05	Ordino	L 3-10	*Ruiz (p), Albino (p), Léo Correia*
14/05	Engordany	W 2-1	*Bríñez, M Garcia*
21/05	Encamp	L 1-15	*M Garcia*

No	Name	Nat	DoB	Pos	Aps	(s)	Gls
20	Cristovao Albino		27/01/95	M	23	(1)	2
2	Antonio Lopes	POR	29/04/85	D	8	(2)	1
10	Andrés Bríñez	COL	14/07/96	A	13	(2)	2
15	Jordi Català	ESP	15/11/90	D	5		
16	José María Da Costa		31/07/88	M	23	(1)	
13	Hugo Do Paço		10/06/84	G	6		
5	Duarte Pires	POR	07/05/89	D	3		
20	Maurizio Falzone	ITA	27/01/76	M	4	(3)	
25	Arnau Fernández	ESP	14/09/89	G	2		
14	Ivan García	ESP	01/04/91	D	8	(4)	
8	Miguel Ángel Garcia		17/08/90	M	17	(6)	3
13	Dídac Giribet		07/07/94	G	2		
15	Jefferson	BRA	06/02/95	M	13	(1)	
4	João Veloso	POR	04/07/75	D	15	(2)	
5	Favio Lucas Laurino	ITA	14/01/89	D	9		
21	Léo Correia	POR	10/07/83	A	22	(1)	1
1	Eric Saúl León	MEX	10/11/94	G	7	(1)	
7	Vicente López		26/11/91	D	6	(1)	
22	Nuno Machado	POR	18/08/87	D	23	(1)	1
10	Dominic Pereira		04/05/94	M	4		
9	Federico Pisculichi	ARG	27/06/89	A	24		5
11	Albert Pous	ESP	05/02/90	A	4	(3)	
15	Daniel Ribeiro		09/01/92	M	18	(2)	2
17	Jaime Andrés Ruiz	COL	20/11/94	A	8		1
12	Francesc Vicente	ESP	25/01/94	M	4		
12	Roger Zambrano	ECU	21/03/88	G	9	(1)	
12	Roger Zambrano	ECU	21/03/88	M		(1)	

FC Lusitans

1999 • fclusitans.com

Major honours

Andorran League (2) 2012, 2013; Andorran Cup (1) 2002

Coach: Raúl Cañete (ESP); (10/03/17) Miguel Ángel Lozano (ESP)

Date	Opponent	Result	Scorers
2016			
18/09	Ordino	W 1-0	*Riera*
25/09	UE Santa Coloma	D 1-1	*Dos Reis*
02/10	Encamp	W 1-0	*Aguilar*
16/10	Engordany	D 1-1	*Luizão*
23/10	FC Santa Coloma	W 3-2	*Muñoz, Riera 2*
30/10	Jenlai	W 2-0	*Aguilar 2*
06/11	Sant Julià	L 1-2	*L San Nicolás*
20/11	Ordino	W 2-1	*L San Nicolás, Aguilar*
27/11	UE Santa Coloma	L 1-2	*Dos Reis*
04/12	Encamp	W 2-1	*Peralta 2*
11/12	Engordany	D 1-1	*Bruninho*
18/12	FC Santa Coloma	L 1-2	*Peralta*
2017			
22/01	Jenlai	W 6-1	*og (João Veloso), Luizão, Bruninho 2, Riera, Peralta (p)*
05/02	Sant Julià	D 1-1	*Njoya*
12/02	Ordino	W 2-1	*og (Gómez), Rúben Silvestre*
18/02	UE Santa Coloma	L 1-2	*Marquinhos*
26/02	Encamp	W 3-1	*Luizão 2, Bruninho*
05/03	Engordany	D 1-1	*Luizão*
11/03	FC Santa Coloma	D 0-0	
14/03	Jenlai	W 7-0	*Riera, Peralta, Léo Maciel, L San Nicolás 2, Gastão, Pousa*
19/03	Sant Julià	W 2-0	*Riera, L San Nicolás*
09/04	UE Santa Coloma	D 3-3	*Molina (p), Riera, Pousa*
23/04	Sant Julià	D 0-0	
03/04	FC Santa Coloma	L 1-4	*Pousa (p)*
07/05	UE Santa Coloma	W 3-2	*Peralta 2 (1p), Luizão*
14/05	Sant Julià	W 1-0	*Gastão*
21/05	FC Santa Coloma	D 1-1	*L San Nicolás*

No	Name	Nat	DoB	Pos	Aps	(s)	Gls
8	Carlos Acosta	ESP	15/08/89	M	5	(2)	
11	José Antonio Aguilar	ESP	11/10/89	A	8	(1)	4
19	Bruninho	POR	11/01/86	A	21	(5)	4
1	Jesús Coca	ESP	22/05/89	G	27		
10	Luís dos Reis	POR	22/03/81	A	12	(7)	2
27	Gastão	MOZ	01/05/95	M	4	(3)	2
9	Luizão	BRA	25/02/90	A	14	(9)	6
24	Léo Maciel	POR	02/07/82	D	17	(1)	1
4	Lucas Maciel	POR	06/03/91	D	17	(1)	
13	Marquinhos	POR	26/01/86	M	13		1
14	Alberto Molina	ESP	21/04/88	M	20		1
5	Pedro Muñoz	ESP	09/01/88	D	20		1
18	Aboubakar Njoya	CMR	26/03/95	M	21		1
16	Eugenio Peralta	PAR	16/12/77	A	8	(10)	7
23	Cristopher Pousa		29/06/92	M	10	(6)	3
15	Óscar Reyes	ESP	12/03/88	D	14	(1)	
11	Riera	POR	15/09/86	A	20	(2)	7
17	Rúben Silvestre	POR	21/01/94	M	8	(2)	1
7	Luigi San Nicolás		28/06/92	M	9	(12)	6
3	Moisés San Nicolás		17/09/93	D	24		
22	Tiago	POR	13/10/93	D	5	(1)	

FC Ordino

2010 • futbolclubordino.com

Coach: Dani Luque (ESP)

Date	Opponent	Result	Scorers
2016			
18/09	Lusitans	L 0-1	
25/09	Jenlai	D 0-0	
02/10	Sant Julià	L 1-7	*Parra*
16/10	FC Santa Coloma	L 1-2	*J Toscano*
23/10	UE Santa Coloma	L 0-1	
30/10	Encamp	W 2-1	*Aranyó, Idris*
06/11	Engordany	L 1-6	*J Toscano (p)*
20/11	Lusitans	L 1-2	*Bertrán*
27/11	Jenlai	W 4-1	*Edgar, Andrés, Idris, Parra (p)*
04/12	Sant Julià	L 0-3	
11/12	FC Santa Coloma	L 0-1	
18/12	UE Santa Coloma	L 2-5	*Bertrán 2*
2017			
22/01	Encamp	L 0-1	
05/02	Engordany	L 2-4	*Bahamonde, Parra*
12/02	Lusitans	L 1-2	*Parra*
19/02	Jenlai	W 6-1	*Luís Martins 3, Bahamonde, Parra, Forzinetti*
26/02	Sant Julià	L 0-3	
05/03	FC Santa Coloma	L 0-2	
11/03	UE Santa Coloma	L 0-3	
14/03	Encamp	D 2-2	*Gómez, J Toscano*
19/03	Engordany	D 1-1	*Bahamonde*
09/04	Jenlai	W 3-0	*Parra, Luís Martins, J Toscano*
23/04	Encamp	L 1-3	*J Toscano*
29/04	Engordany	W 2-0	*Alborch, Gonçalves*
07/05	Jenlai	W 10-3	*Edgar, Parra, Bahamonde 5, og (João Veloso), Gómez 2 (1p)*
14/05	Encamp	W 2-1	*Bahamonde 2*
21/05	Engordany	W 3-0	*Edgar, Gómez, J Toscano*

No	Name	Nat	DoB	Pos	Aps	(s)	Gls
22	Diego Abdián	ESP	22/11/82	D	7		
23	Dimitrios Achladis	GRE	08/10/91	D	1	(2)	
14	Daniel Alborch	ESP	15/07/90	D	8	(2)	1
16	Daniel Alves		13/05/97	D	7		
21	Marc Andrés		13/03/89	D	17	(1)	1
9	Marc Aranyó	ESP	13/01/93	A	8		1
9	Álex Bahamonde	ESP	20/01/90	A	9	(2)	10
10	Sebastià Bertrán		10/12/92	M	19	(1)	3
18	Jules Bidau	FRA	03/07/96	M	7		
7	Èric Buixó		07/02/89	M	10	(7)	
12	Dario Córdoba	ARG	03/01/95	D	9		
1	José Francisco Domingo		12/02/99	G	10		
6	Edgar Fernández	ESP	24/08/96	M	23	(1)	3
5	Robert Flotats		11/11/97	M	10	(2)	
22	Remo Forzinetti	ESP	03/03/84	M	6	(2)	1
4	Walter Eduardo Gómez	ARG	26/08/91	D	10		4
3	Jonathan Gonçalves		21/02/96	D	20	(2)	1
8	Jacobo Gracia	ECU	25/03/88	M	9	(4)	
4	Rashid Idris	GHA	30/09/89	A	6	(3)	2
18	Manu Jiménez	ESP	16/12/96	M	10	(2)	
11	Luís Martins	BRA	11/06/98	M	3	(2)	4
11	Roger Marsal		26/05/99	M	4	(3)	
11	Aaron Parra	ESP	09/11/95	A	22	(1)	7
14	Gilbert Sánchez		06/07/91	D	4	(1)	
21	Manu Sepulveda	CHI	20/08/84	D	20		
13	Francisco Toscano		05/02/83	G	4		
23	Juan Carlos Toscano		14/08/84	A	20	(3)	6
13	Houssain Zain	MAR	20/01/96	G	13	(1)	
13	Houssain Zain	MAR	20/01/96	M	1		

UE Sant Julià

1982 • no website

Major honours

Andorran League (2) 2005, 2009; Andorran Cup (5) 2008, 2010, 2011, 2014, 2015

Coach: Luis Blanco (ESP)

Date	Opponent		Score	Scorers
2016				
18/09	Jenlai	W	3-1	*Villanueva (p), Rafa Santos, Baffoe*
25/09	FC Santa Coloma	D	1-1	*Baffoe*
02/10	Ordino	W	7-1	*Baffoe 3, Villanueva (p), Serra, Marinho 2*
16/10	UE Santa Coloma	D	1-1	*Villanueva*
23/10	Encamp	W	1-0	*Serra*
30/10	Engordany	W	3-1	*Villanueva (p), Baffoe, E Rodríguez*
06/11	Lusitans	W	2-1	*Baffoe, Gomes*
20/11	Jenlai	W	9-0	*Serra, Villanueva 3, M Rodríguez, Baffoe 2, Marinho (p), E Rodríguez*
27/11	FC Santa Coloma	L	1-2	*Girau*
04/12	Ordino	W	3-0	*E Rodríguez, Serra, Blanco*
11/12	UE Santa Coloma	W	3-1	*Villanueva (p), Rafa Santos, Blanco*
18/12	Encamp	D	1-1	*Blanco*
2017				
22/01	Engordany	L	1-2	*Villanueva*
05/02	Lusitans	D	1-1	*Padilla*
12/02	Jenlai	W	5-0	*Vigo, Blanco 2, M Rodríguez 2*
18/02	FC Santa Coloma	W	1-0	*Zarioh*
26/02	Ordino	W	3-0	*Padilla 2, Alves*
05/03	UE Santa Coloma	D	1-1	*M Rodríguez*
11/03	Encamp	W	1-0	*Padilla*
14/03	Engordany	W	1-0	*Girau*
19/03	Lusitans	L	0-2	
08/04	FC Santa Coloma	D	3-3	*Padilla 3 (2p)*
23/04	Lusitans	D	0-0	
30/04	UE Santa Coloma	W	2-1	*Padilla 2*
07/05	FC Santa Coloma	D	1-1	*Baffoe*
14/05	Lusitans	L	0-1	
21/05	UE Santa Coloma	L	0-1	

No	Name	Nat	DoB	Pos	Aps	(s)	Gls
5	Leo Alves		28/09/93	M	6	(4)	1
21	Noah Baffoe	GHA	21/05/93	A	24	(2)	10
10	Luis Blanco		15/01/90	M	22	(4)	5
25	Germán Canal		21/10/83	G	1	(1)	
18	Christian Ariel Cellay	ARG	05/09/81	D	6		
7	Kiko Girau	ESP	03/06/85	M	26		2
11	Carlos Gomes		18/10/93	M	1	(5)	1
20	Joao Lopes		09/10/91	M	5	(6)	
23	Diego Rafael Marinho		16/06/92	M		(12)	3
19	Julco Ngoma	GAB	19/09/97	M	20	(1)	
3	Isaac Padilla	ESP	23/03/96	A	13	(2)	9
6	Rafa Santos	POR	21/10/83	D	22		2
14	Eric Rodríguez		27/04/93	D	20	(4)	3
13	Mateo Rodríguez	URU	25/05/93	D	24		4
8	Rayco Rodríguez		12/07/89	M	2	(8)	
17	Fábio Serra	POR	24/08/84	A	22	(1)	4
1	Manu Vidal	ESP	07/09/90	G	26		
22	Ivan Vigo	ESP	07/09/86	D	14	(1)	1
9	José Antonio Villanueva	ESP	16/08/85	A	19	(1)	9
4	Jamal Zarioh		30/01/89	D	19	(5)	1
16	Nikola Zugic	POR	30/01/90	M	5		

FC Santa Coloma

1986 • fclubsantacoloma.net

Major honours

Andorran League (11) 1995, 2001, 2003, 2004, 2008, 2010, 2011, 2014, 2015, 2016, 2017; Andorran Cup (8) 2001, 2003, 2004, 2005, 2006, 2007, 2009, 2012

Coach: Richard Imbernón

Date	Opponent		Score	Scorers
2016				
18/09	Encamp	L	0-1	
25/09	Sant Julià	D	1-1	*Riera*
02/10	Engordany	W	1-0	*Noguerol*
16/10	Ordino	W	2-1	*Juanfer, Riera*
23/10	Lusitans	L	2-3	*Parra 2 (1p)*
30/10	UE Santa Coloma	D	1-1	*Parra (p)*
06/11	Jenlai	W	3-0	*(w/o)*
20/11	Encamp	W	1-0	*Parra*
27/11	Sant Julià	W	2-1	*Juanfer 2*
04/12	Engordany	W	4-1	*Juanfer, Riera, Parra, Rodríguez*
11/12	Ordino	W	1-0	*Santos*
18/12	Lusitans	W	2-1	*og (Muñoz), Riera*
2017				
22/01	UE Santa Coloma	W	2-1	*Riera 2*
05/02	Jenlai	W	9-0	*Juanfer 3, Villagrasa, Mercadé, og (Da Costa), Sosa, Capdevila (p), A Ramos*
12/02	Encamp	W	1-0	*Juanfer*
18/02	Sant Julià	L	0-1	
26/02	Engordany	W	2-1	*Capdevila (p), Juanfer*
05/03	Ordino	W	2-0	*Rodríguez, Noguerol*
11/03	Lusitans	D	0-0	
14/03	UE Santa Coloma	W	2-1	*Parra, Juanfer*
19/03	Jenlai	W	6-0	*A Ramos, Rebés, Riera 3, Juanfer*
08/04	Sant Julià	D	3-3	*Sosa, Parra, Santos*
23/04	UE Santa Coloma	W	1-0	*Parra*
30/04	Lusitans	W	4-1	*Juanfer, Sosa, Riera, A Ramos (p)*
07/05	Sant Julià	D	1-1	*A Ramos*
14/05	UE Santa Coloma	W	3-1	*Sosa, Juanfer, Noguerol*
21/05	Lusitans	D	1-1	*A Ramos*

No	Name	Nat	DoB	Pos	Aps	(s)	Gls
19	Joan Capdevila	ESP	03/02/78	D	25		2
1	Eloy Casals	ESP	22/10/82	G	21		
3	Oriol Fité		02/02/89	D	8	(6)	
23	Juanfer	ESP	05/05/83	M	22	(4)	13
6	Ildefons Lima		10/12/79	D	19		
8	Joel Martínez		31/12/88	M	8	(8)	
14	Andreu Matos		01/12/95	M	4	(5)	
11	Albert Mercadé	ESP	23/01/85	A	8	(5)	1
20	Jaime Noguerol	ESP	24/02/84	M	19	(5)	3
9	Iban Parra	ESP	18/10/77	A	17	(4)	8
4	Andreu Ramos	ESP	19/01/89	D	26		5
24	Robert Ramos	ESP	11/12/92	D	16	(2)	
5	Marc Rebés		03/07/94	M	20	(3)	1
21	Gabriel Riera		05/06/85	A	16	(7)	10
25	Víctor Rodríguez		07/09/87	M	12	(10)	2
10	Pedro Santos	ESP	01/06/93	M	6	(2)	2
13	Víctor Silverio		15/04/97	G	5	(4)	
7	Jesús David Sosa	ESP	05/01/94	M	13	(2)	4
22	Enric Triquell		20/03/93	D	2	(3)	
7	Carles Valls	ESP	24/12/87	M	1	(2)	
16	Álex Villagrasa		26/03/97	M	18	(4)	1

UE Santa Coloma

1986 • uesantacoloma.com

Major honours

Andorran Cup (3) 2013, 2016, 2017

Coach: Emiliano González (ESP)

Date	Opponent		Score	Scorers
2016				
18/09	Engordany	W	2-1	*Bernat, Sánchez*
25/09	Lusitans	D	1-1	*Salomó*
02/10	Jenlai	W	5-0	*Jordi Rubio 2, Bernat 2, Roca*
16/10	Sant Julià	D	1-1	*Bernat*
23/10	Ordino	W	1-0	*Jordi Rubio*
30/10	FC Santa Coloma	D	1-1	*Bernat*
06/11	Encamp	W	2-0	*Ayala, Salomó*
20/11	Engordany	W	2-1	*Jordi Rubio 2*
27/11	Lusitans	W	2-1	*Antón, Jesús Rubio*
04/12	Jenlai	W	7-2	*Jordi Rubio 2, Bernat 2, Antón, Sánchez, Maneiro*
11/12	Sant Julià	L	1-3	*Bernat*
18/12	Ordino	W	5-2	*Antón, Jordi Rubio, Bernat 2, Alves*
2017				
22/01	FC Santa Coloma	L	1-2	*Martínez*
05/02	Encamp	W	2-1	*Bernat 2*
12/02	Engordany	D	1-1	*Ayala*
18/02	Lusitans	W	2-1	*Bernat, Ruiz*
25/02	Jenlai	W	10-1	*Jordi Rubio, Nazzaro, Bernat 3, Jesús Rubio, Antón, Maneiro, Crespo 2*
05/03	Sant Julià	D	1-1	*Jordi Rubio*
11/03	Ordino	W	3-0	*Salomó 2, Bernat*
14/03	FC Santa Coloma	L	1-2	*Ayala*
19/03	Encamp	W	3-0	*Salomó 2, Antón*
09/04	Lusitans	D	3-3	*Salomó 2, Jordi Rubio*
23/04	FC Santa Coloma	L	0-1	
30/04	Sant Julià	L	1-2	*Martínez*
07/05	Lusitans	L	2-3	*Salomó, Bernat*
14/05	FC Santa Coloma	L	1-3	*Sánchez*
21/05	Sant Julià	W	1-0	*Salomó*

No	Name	Nat	DoB	Pos	Aps	(s)	Gls
17	Gerard Aloy		17/04/89	D	9		
4	Marc Amat		26/06/93	D		(3)	
9	Boris Antón		27/02/87	A	24	(3)	5
16	Leonel Alves		28/09/93	A		(7)	1
8	Josep Manel Ayala		08/04/80	M	21	(1)	3
14	Víctor Bernat	ESP	17/05/87	A	24	(2)	18
24	Walid Bousenine		07/04/93	M		(1)	
22	Sergio Crespo		29/09/92	M	16	(10)	2
13	Ricard Fernández	ESP	26/05/75	G	14		
21	Sandro Gutiérrez		02/01/96	M	5	(8)	
3	David Maneiro		16/02/89	D	18	(2)	2
5	Alex Martínez		04/03/87	D	19	(1)	2
19	Roger Nazzaro		07/04/97	M	9	(11)	1
25	Cristian Orosa		12/12/90	D	13	(2)	
10	Pedro Reis	POR	08/02/85	A	10	(11)	
1	Ivan Periánez		25/01/82	G	13		
6	Álex Roca		04/07/91	D	11	(5)	1
2	Jesús Rubio		09/09/94	D	16		2
7	Jordi Rubio		01/11/87	M	23	(3)	11
18	Miguel Ruiz	ESP	16/07/82	D	25		1
11	Joan Salomó	ESP	20/12/93	A	20	(5)	10
23	Juli Sánchez		20/06/78	A	7	(4)	3

ANDORRA

Top goalscorers

18	Víctor Bernat (UE Santa Coloma)
13	Juanfer (FC Santa Coloma)
11	Jordi Rubio (UE Santa Coloma)
10	Álex Bahamonde (Ordino) Noah Baffoe (Sant Julià) Gabriel Riera (FC Santa Coloma) Joan Salomó (UE Santa Coloma)
9	Diego Najera (Encamp) Isaac Padilla (Sant Julià) José Antonio Villanueva (Sant Julià)

Promoted clubs

Inter Club d'Escaldes

1991 • no website
Coach: Álex Somoza

Penya Encarnada d'Andorra

2009 • penyaencarnada.com
Coach: Yulian Vladimirov (BUL)

Second level final tables 2016/17

First stage

		Pld	W	D	L	F	A	Pts
1	Inter Club d'Escaldes	18	14	1	3	54	12	43
2	Penya Encarnada d'Andorra	18	13	3	2	66	24	42
3	CF Atlètic Amèrica	18	11	4	3	43	22	37
4	FC Encamp B	18	10	2	6	43	35	32
5	Atlètic Club d'Escaldes	18	8	3	7	55	31	27
6	FC Santa Coloma B	18	7	2	9	28	39	23
7	FS La Massana	18	6	3	9	41	43	21
8	UE Santa Coloma B	18	6	1	11	28	47	19
9	Ranger's FC	18	3	1	14	17	57	10
10	FC Lusitans B	18	2	0	16	21	86	6

NB After 18 rounds the six clubs eligible for promotion (i.e. no 'B' teams) enter the promotion play-offs.

Promotion play-offs

		Pld	W	D	L	F	A	Pts
1	Inter Club d'Escaldes	23	18	2	3	82	16	56
2	Penya Encarnada d'Andorra	23	17	4	2	89	27	55
3	CF Atlètic Amèrica	23	13	4	6	57	42	43
4	Atlètic Club d'Escaldes	23	11	3	9	81	41	36
5	FS La Massana	23	7	3	13	49	69	24
6	Ranger's FC	23	3	1	19	22	100	10

Promotion/Relegation play-offs

(28/05/17 & 31/05/17)
Penya Encarnada d'Andorra 0-2 Ordino
Ordino 1-5 Penya Encarnada d'Andorra
(Penya Encarnada d'Andorra 5-3)

DOMESTIC CUP

Copa Constitució 2017

FIRST ROUND

(07/02/17)
Ordino 6-0 Atlètic Club d'Escaldes

(08/02/17)
Engordany 5-0 Inter Club d'Escaldes

(09/02/17)
Jenlai 1-1 Atlètic Amèrica *(aet; 3-4 on pens)*

(15/02/17)
Encamp 1-0 Penya Encarnada d'Andorra

QUARTER-FINALS

(22/03/17)
Atlètic Amèrcia 0-6 Lusitans *(Rúben Silvestre 13, Peralta 33, Luizão 58, 80, 87, Lucas Maciel 53)*

(02/04/17)
Encamp 0-1 FC Santa Coloma *(Parra 71)*

Engordany 0-1 UE Santa Coloma *(Ayala 47)*

Ordino 3-2 Sant Julià *(Parra 26, 47, Gómez 100p; Padilla 73p, Ngoma 83) (aet)*

SEMI-FINALS

(12/04/17)
Ordino 0-6 FC Santa Coloma *(Parra 3, 81, Rodríguez 48, Juanfer 50, Riera 65, Capdevila 70)*

(13/04/17)
UE Santa Coloma 2-1 Lusitans *(Bernat 22, Jordi Rubio 47; Pousa 72)*

FINAL

(28/05/17)
Estadi Nacional, Andorra la Vella
UE SANTA COLOMA 1 *(Bernat 25)*
FC SANTA COLOMA 0
Referee: *Do Nascimento*
UE SANTA COLOMA: *Periánez, Martínez, Aloy, Ruiz, Maneiro, Jordi Rubio, Ayala, Antón (Orosa 85), Salomó, Bernat (Pedro Reis 75), Sánchez (Crespo 73)*
FC SANTA COLOMA: *Casals, Fité (Villagrasa 64), Lima, Capdevila, A Ramos, Rebés (Rodríguez 81), Sosa, Santos, Noguerol, Mercadé (Juanfer 55), Riera*

UE Santa Coloma make their Andorran Cup celebrations a family affair

ARMENIA

Hayastani Futboli Federacia (HFF)

Address	Khanjyan Street 27 AM-0010 Yerevan	**President**	Ruben Hayrapetyan
Tel	+374 10 568883	**Vice-president**	Armen Minasyan
Fax	+374 10 547173	**Media officer**	Hayk Karapetyan
E-mail	ffa@ffa.am	**Year of formation**	1992
Website	ffa.am	**National stadium**	Hanrapetakan, Yerevan (14,400)

Gyumri
6

KEY
UEFA Champions League
UEFA Europa League

1 2 3 5
Yerevan

PREMIER LEAGUE CLUBS

  1 **Alashkert FC**

  2 **FC Ararat**

  3 **FC Banants**

  4 **FC Gandzasar**

  5 **FC Pyunik**

 6 **FC Shirak**

All's well that ends well for Alashkert

The Armenian Premier League was reduced to just six participating clubs in 2016/17, making it the smallest top division in Europe. Each team played the others six times, which brought a degree of over-familiarity but also a worthy champion in Alashkert FC, who retained the title they had won for the first time 12 months earlier.

Gandzasar finished second in the league – their highest-ever final placing – while autumn pacesetters Shirak, the only other non-Yerevan club among the elite, fell away in the spring only to recover in time to win the Armenian Cup with a 3-0 victory over Pyunik.

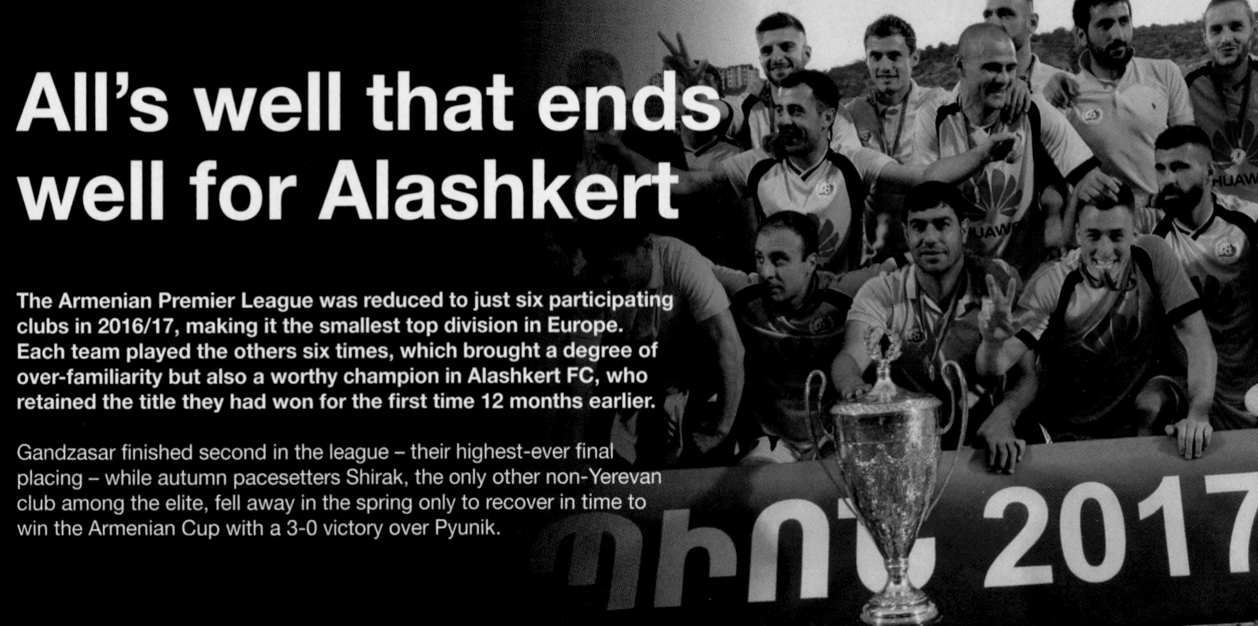

Yerevan outfit come from behind to retain crown

Shirak surrender lead in league but win the cup

Only six teams take part in top division

Domestic league

Led into battle once again by their 2015/16 title-winning coach Abraham Khashmanyan, Alashkert's path to a successful championship defence was not without its pitfalls. A shock early defeat to Ararat, who would win only two other games all season, upset the team's rhythm, and two further losses in quick succession at the end of October, the first of them a 4-0 thumping at home to Gandzasar, suggested that Alashkert's bid to become the first back-to-back Armenian champions since Pyunik won their tenth title in a row in 2010 was unlikely to come to fruition.

The spring, however, would see a very different Alashkert side – one that racked up the points with ruthless efficiency, losing again at home to Gandzasar but winning eight of their other nine games following the resumption. However, their rivals from the south-east were on a similar roll, and when the two teams met for the sixth and last time, at the Hanrapetakan stadium in Yerevan, Alashkert were just two points ahead of Gandzasar.

By the final whistle, the champions' lead was up to five, a 69th-minute own goal from Gandzasar's Colombian midfielder Wbeymar Angulo giving Alashkert victory and a relatively free run to the title, which they secured with a 3-1 win at home to Shirak in the penultimate round thanks to goals from their leading scorers Artak Yedigaryan and Mihran Manasyan (two).

With a final tally of 59 goals scored, Alashkert boasted far and away the division's most productive attack, and it was that consistent ability to find the net, allied to a phenomenal away record (12 wins and just one defeat in 15 matches), which ultimately made the difference.

Domestic cup

Shirak's title challenge hit the rocks when they lost five games out of seven in March and April, but the team from the north-western town of Gyumri, led for the sixth successive season by coach Vardan Bichakhchyan, maintained their momentum in the Armenian Independence Cup, eliminating Gandzasar 2-1 on aggregate in the semi-finals before making mincemeat of Pyunik in the final, three first-half goals securing a revenge win over the team that had defeated them on their most recent appearance in the fixture, in 2013, when Shirak had gone into the final as holders.

Europe

Several months earlier Pyunik had suffered embarrassment in Europe when they were knocked out of the UEFA Europa League by Europa FC of Gibraltar. Shirak made it through that round on penalties against Dila Gori but it was another Georgian club, Dinamo Tbilisi, that ended Alashkert's UEFA Champions League adventure in the second qualifying round.

National team

Varuzhan Sukiasyan's tenure as head coach of the Armenian national team lasted less than a year, defeats in each of the team's first three FIFA World Cup qualifiers, including a heaviest ever at home (0-5 against Romania), triggering his dismissal. Artur Petrosyan, an illustrious ex-player with 69 caps and 11 goals, took over and promptly led the side to a memorable 3-2 comeback win against Montenegro. The team's points tally was doubled with another home success in the spring, 2-0 against Kazakhstan, in which superstar skipper Henrikh Mkhitaryan scored his 20th international goal, but a 4-1 revenge defeat by Montenegro in June served to nip any remote qualifying hopes abruptly in the bud.

Mkhitaryan's UEFA Europa League triumph with Manchester United – in which he played a predominant role, top-scoring with six goals – was once again the most widely celebrated success for an Armenian player in 2016/17. A couple of months earlier the 28-year-old schemer had been voted Armenian Footballer of the Year for the sixth season in a row and seventh time in all.

DOMESTIC SEASON AT A GLANCE

Premier League 2016/17 final table

			Home					Away					Total					
		Pld	W	D	L	F	A	W	D	L	F	A	W	D	L	F	A	Pts
1	**Alashkert FC**	**30**	**7**	**5**	**3**	**28**	**17**	**12**	**2**	**1**	**31**	**9**	**19**	**7**	**4**	**59**	**26**	**64**
2	FC Gandzasar	30	10	1	4	21	11	7	5	3	17	13	17	6	7	38	24	57
3	FC Shirak	30	7	3	5	13	10	9	2	4	18	14	16	5	9	31	24	53
4	FC Pyunik	30	6	4	5	19	15	6	5	4	16	12	12	9	9	35	27	45
5	FC Banants	30	3	3	9	10	21	2	3	10	8	23	5	6	19	18	44	21
6	FC Ararat	30	2	2	11	9	24	1	1	13	8	29	3	3	24	17	53	12

European qualification 2017/18

Champion: Alashkert FC (first qualifying round)

Cup winner: FC Shirak (first qualifying round)

FC Gandzasar (first qualifying round)
FC Pyunik (first qualifying round)

Top scorer Mihran Minasyan (Alashkert) & Artak Yedigaryan (Alashkert), 13 goals
Relegated clubs none
Promoted clubs none
Cup final FC Shirak 3-0 FC Pyunik

Player of the season

Artak Yedigaryan
(Alashkert FC)

A switch from left-back into midfield worked wonders for Yedigaryan in 2016/17 as the 27-year-old suddenly displayed a previously undiscovered knack of scoring goals. He had managed only two in his first season for Alashkert, but his second yielded no fewer than 13, which, had his team-mate Mihran Manasyan not found the net twice in the final game of the season, would have made him the Premier League's top scorer alone. A four-time national champion with Pyunik, he added to his new-found reputation in June by scoring his first international goal for Armenia.

Newcomer of the season

Vahan Bichakhchyan
(FC Shirak)

Talk spread through Armenia and beyond during the 2016/17 season that a 'new Mkhitaryan' might have been found. The son of long-serving Shirak coach Vardan Bichakhchyan was still only 16 when he came off the bench to score a decisive goal for his club in a UEFA Europa League victory over Dila Gori. Talented beyond his years, he would add four further goals in the Armenian Premier League – all in 1-0 wins – before rounding off a hugely promising debut season by scoring Shirak's second goal in the cup final victory against Pyunik.

Team of the season
(4-3-3)

Coach: Khashmanyan *(Alashkert)*

ARMENIA

NATIONAL TEAM

Top five all-time caps

Sargis Hovsepyan (131); Roman Berezovski (94); Robert Arzumanyan (74); Artur Petrosyan (69); **Henrikh Mkhitaryan** (64)

Top five all-time goals

Henrikh Mkhitaryan (22); Artur Petrosyan (11); **Gevorg Ghazaryan** (10), **Edgar Manucharyan**, Yura Movsisyan & **Marcos Pizzelli** (9)

Results 2016/17

31/08/16	Czech Republic	A	Mlada Boleslav	L	0-3	
04/09/16	Denmark (WCQ)	A	Copenhagen	L	0-1	
08/10/16	Romania (WCQ)	H	Yerevan	L	0-5	
11/10/16	Poland (WCQ)	A	Warsaw	L	1-2	*Pizzelli (50)*
11/11/16	Montenegro (WCQ)	H	Yerevan	W	3-2	*Grigoryan (50), Haroyan (74), Ghazaryan (90+3)*
26/03/17	Kazakhstan (WCQ)	H	Yerevan	W	2-0	*Mkhitaryan (73), Özbiliz (75)*
04/06/17	St Kitts & Nevis	H	Yerevan	W	5-0	*Koryan (20), Mkhitaryan (30, 40), Sarkisov (68), Yedigaryan (89)*
10/06/17	Montenegro (WCQ)	A	Podgorica	L	1-4	*Koryan (89)*

Appearances 2016/17

Coach: Varuzhan Sukiasyan /(01/11/16) Artur Petrosyan	**05/08/56 17/12/71**		**Cze**	**DEN**	**ROU**	**POL**	**MNE**	**KAZ**	**Skn**	**MNE**	**Caps**	**Goals**
Arsen Beglaryan	18/02/93	Alashkert	G	G	G	G	G	G	G	G	11	-
Hovhannes Hambardzumyan	04/10/90	Vardar (MKD)	D	D							16	1
Gael Andonyan	07/02/95	Marseille (FRA)	D46	D	D39	D 30*						
		/Veria (GRE)						D	D	D	16	-
Varazdat Haroyan	24/08/92	Padideh (IRN)	D	D	D	D	D	D			27	1
Hrayr Mkoyan	02/09/86	Esteghlal (IRN)	D	D	D	D	D		s59	D46	43	1
Gegam Kadimyan	19/10/92	Karpaty (UKR)	M50	M							5	2
Gor Malakyan	12/06/94	Stal (UKR)	M76	M77	M 3*		M	M			8	-
Karlen Mkrtchyan	25/11/88	Anji (RUS)	M70								46	2
Gevorg Ghazaryan	05/04/88	Marítimo (POR)	M46	s41			M	M5			53	10
Henrikh Mkhitaryan	21/01/89	Man. United (ENG)	M38				M	M	M46	M	64	22
Marcos Pizzelli	03/10/84	Al-Fujairah (UAE)	A61	s70	M	A85	M81					
		/Xanthi (GRE)						M65	M	M73	57	9
Artak Yedigaryan	18/03/90	Alashkert	s38	M					D	s46	23	1
Davit Manoyan	05/07/90	Karmiotissa (CYP)	s46	s77	M	M					24	-
Aras Özbiliz	09/03/90	Beşiktaş (TUR)	s46	M41	M64	s61		s70	M70	M59	31	5
Artur Sarkisov	19/01/87	Mordovia (RUS)	s50				s59					
		/Enisey (RUS)						A70	s46		38	6
Ruslan Koryan	15/06/88	SKA-Khabarovsk (RUS)	s61				A59		A46	A	8	2
Taron Voskanyan	22/02/93	Karmiotissa (CYP)	s70		s39	s34	D	D	D70	D	22	-
Davit Hakobyan	21/03/93	Shirak	s76			s85					3	-
Gevorg Hovhannisyan	16/06/83	Shirak		D							1	-
David Arshakyan	16/08/94	Chicago Fire (USA)		A70							1	-
Levon Hayrapetyan	17/04/89	Paykan (IRN)			D	D	D	D	s72		39	1
Artak Grigoryan	19/10/87	Alashkert			M	M	M		M	M	7	1
Vardan Poghosyan	08/03/92	Pyunik			A33						3	-
Karen Muradyan	01/11/92	Alashkert			s33	M34					4	-
Kamo Hovhannisyan	05/10/92	Pyunik			s64	M61	s81					
		/Torpedo Zhodino (BLR)						M		M	32	-
Vahagn Minasyan	25/04/85	Alashkert				D					13	1
Tigran Barseghyan	22/09/93	Vardar (MKD)						s5	s46	s73	6	1
Edgar Manucharyan	19/01/87	Ural (RUS)						s65	A59	s59	53	9
Gagik Daghbashyan	19/10/90	Alashkert							D72	D	3	-
Narek Aslanyan	04/01/96	Pyunik							s70		1	-
Armen Manucharyan	03/02/95	Pyunik							s70		1	-

EUROPE

Alashkert FC

First qualifying round - FC Santa Coloma (AND)

A 0-0

Kasparov, Khovbosha, Tasić, Muradyan, Manasyan, Veranyan, Gevorg Poghosyan, Artak Yedigaryan (Avagyan 76), Savin (Dashyan 69), Minasyan, Grigoryan (Gyozalyan 80). Coach: Abraham Khashmanyan (ARM)

H 3-0 *Minasyan (12), Gyozalyan (84), Artur Yedigaryan (88)*

Kasparov, Tasić, Muradyan, Manasyan, Dashyan (Gyozalyan 72), Veranyan (Ghazaryan 78), Gevorg Poghosyan, Artak Yedigaryan, Savin (Artur Yedigaryan 87), Minasyan, Grigoryan. Coach: Abraham Khashmanyan (ARM)

Red card: Manasyan 26

Second qualifying round - FC Dinamo Tbilisi (GEO)

A 0-2

Kasparov, Voskanyan, Tasić (Bareghamyan 46), Muradyan, Dashyan, Gevorg Poghosyan, Artak Yedigaryan, Savin (Artur Yedigaryan 64), Minasyan, Grigoryan, Gyozalyan (Melkonyan 83). Coach: Abraham Khashmanyan (ARM)

H 1-1 *Gyozalyan (51)*

Kasparov, Voskanyan, Tasić, Muradyan, Dashyan (Ghazaryan 76), Kvekveskiri, Artak Yedigaryan, Minasyan, Artur Yedigaryan (Melkonyan 65), Grigoryan (Veranyan 84), Gyozalyan. Coach: Abraham Khashmanyan (ARM)

FC Banants

First qualifying round - AC Omonia (CYP)

H 0-1

Ghazaryan, Kalmanov, Hakobyan, Kachmazov, Poghosyan (Oganesyan 78), Torrejón, Badoyan (Movsisyan 85), Ayvazyan (Avetisyan 81), Drobarov, Adams, Buraev. Coach: Tito Ramallo (ESP)

A 1-4 (aet) *Buraev (71)*

Ghazaryan, Kalmanov, Hakobyan, Kachmazov (Avetisyan 100), Poghosyan (Ayvazyan 56), Torrejón, Mecinovic, Badoyan (Movsisyan 89), Drobarov, Adams, Buraev. Coach: Tito Ramallo (ESP)

FC Shirak

First qualifying round - FC Dila Gori (GEO)

A 0-1

Ayvazov, A Hovhannisyan, Mikaelyan, Hovsepyan (Diarrassouba 58), Kouakou (Muradyan 87), Hakobyan (Brou 78), Udo, G Hovhannisyan, Darbinyan, Kaba, Stošković. Coach: Vardan Bichakhchyan (ARM)

H 1-0 (aet; 4-1 on pens) *Bichakhchyan (84)*

Ayvazov, Mikaelyan, Hovsepyan, Kouakou (Ayvazyan 69), Hakobyan, Udo, G Hovhannisyan, Darbinyan, Davoyan (A Hovhannisyan 71), Diarrassouba, Stošković (Bichakhchyan 65). Coach: Vardan Bichakhchyan (ARM)

Second qualifying round - FC Spartak Trnava (SVK)

H 1-1 *Hakobyan (16)*

Ayvazov, Mikaelyan, Kouakou, Hakobyan, Udo, G Hovhannisyan, Darbinyan, Davoyan (A Hovhannisyan 83), Kaba, Diarrassouba (Poghosyan 75), Stošković (Bichakhchyan 63). Coach: Vardan Bichakhchyan (ARM)

A 0-2

Ayvazov, A Hovhannisyan (Davoyan 76), Mikaelyan, Hovsepyan (Poghosyan 65), Kouakou, Udo, G Hovhannisyan, Darbinyan, Kaba, Diarrassouba, Stošković (Ayvazyan 65). Coach: Vardan Bichakhchyan (ARM)

FC Pyunik

First qualifying round - Europa FC (GIB)

A 0-2

Manukyan, Grigoryan, Kartashyan, Manucharyan, Hovhannisyan, Razmik Hakobyan (Petrosyan 46), Manoyan, Yusbashyan (Minasyan 71), Arakelyan, Satumyan (H Harutyunyan 46), T Voskanyan. Coach: Sargis Hovsepyan (ARM)

Red card: Grigoryan 79

H 2-1 *Arakelyan (25), Razmik Hakobyan (56)*

Manukyan, Kartashyan, Manucharyan, Hovhannisyan, Panosyan, Manoyan, Yusbashyan (Razmik Hakobyan 54), Robert Hakobyan, Arakelyan, Minasyan (Satumyan 64), H Harutyunyan (Aslanyan 90+3). Coach: Sargis Hovsepyan (ARM)

DOMESTIC LEAGUE CLUB-BY-CLUB

Alashkert FC

2011 • Nairi (2,500) • fcalashkert.am

Major honours

Armenian League (2) 2016, 2017

Coach: Abraham Khashmanyan

Date		Opponent	Res	Score	Scorers
2016					
07/08	h	Gandzasar	D	0-0	
13/08	a	Pyunik	W	2-1	*Artak Yedigaryan, Manasyan*
21/08	h	Banants	W	3-0	*Dashyan, Artur Yedigaryan, Fomenko*
27/08	a	Shirak	D	2-2	*Kvekveskiri, Tasić*
10/09	h	Ararat	L	1-3	*Artur Yedigaryan*
18/09	a	Gandzasar	W	2-0	*og (Meliksetyan), Fomenko*
27/09	h	Pyunik	D	0-0	
02/10	a	Banants	W	3-0	*Artur Yedigaryan 2, Manasyan*
16/10	h	Shirak	D	1-1	*Gyozalyan (p)*
22/10	a	Ararat	W	2-1	*Manasyan, Minasyan*
27/10	h	Gandzasar	L	0-4	
30/10	a	Pyunik	L	1-2	*Artak Yedigaryan*
05/11	h	Banants	W	4-1	*Artak Yedigaryan 2, Veranyan, Grigoryan*
20/11	a	Shirak	D	0-0	
23/11	h	Ararat	W	4-1	*Manasyan 4 (1p)*
27/11	a	Gandzasar	W	2-1	*Dashyan, Artak Yedigaryan (p)*
04/12	h	Pyunik	D	0-0	
2017					
04/03	a	Banants	W	2-1	*Minasyan, Nenadović*
12/03	h	Shirak	W	3-0	*Artak Yedigaryan, Dashyan, Nenadović*
17/03	a	Ararat	W	3-0	*Manasyan 2, Badoyan*
30/03	h	Gandzasar	L	1-2	*og (Khachatryan)*
07/04	a	Pyunik	W	3-0	*Nenadović, Minasyan, Artak Yedigaryan (p)*
14/04	h	Banants	W	2-0	*Artak Yedigaryan 2*
23/04	a	Shirak	W	1-0	*Arakelyan*
29/04	h	Ararat	W	3-1	*Artak Yedigaryan 2 (1p), Badoyan*
06/05	a	Gandzasar	W	1-0	*og (Angulo)*
13/05	h	Pyunik	D	3-3	*Badoyan, Dashyan 2 (1p)*
19/05	a	Banants	W	3-0	*Manasyan, Artak Yedigaryan, Dashyan*
28/05	h	Shirak	W	3-1	*Artak Yedigaryan, Manasyan, Nenadović*
31/05	a	Ararat	W	4-1	*Manasyan 2, N Beglaryan, Nranyan*

No	Name	Nat	DoB	Pos	Aps	(s)	Gls
6	Ararat Arakelyan		01/02/84	D	16		1
17	Zaven Badoyan		22/12/89	M	3	(4)	3
21	Arsen Balabekyan		24/11/86	M	1	(1)	
1	Arsen Beglaryan		18/02/93	G	20		
14	Narek Beglaryan		01/09/85	A		(1)	1
12	Atsamaz Buraev	RUS	05/02/90	A		(4)	
16	Marat Butuev	RUS	08/05/92	D	2		
8	Gagik Daghbashyan		19/10/90	D	22	(1)	
20	Artak Dashyan		20/11/89	M	19	(8)	6
4	Saša Filipović	SRB	30/04/93	M	2	(2)	
13	Yuriy Fomenko	UKR	31/12/86	A	4	(11)	2
21	Artak G Grigoryan		19/10/87	M	24	(2)	1
22	Norayr Gyozalyan		15/03/90	A	4	(2)	1
23	Alen Hambartsumyan		02/03/92	D	1		
12	Benik Hovhannisyan		01/05/93	M	1	(2)	
15	Aram Hovsepyan		06/06/91	M	1		
1	Gevorg Kasparov		25/07/80	G	10		
17	Mikayel Khashmanyan		05/08/96	D	1		
2	Dmytro Khovbosha	UKR	05/02/89	D	19		
13	Irakli Kvekveskiri	GEO	12/03/90	M	18	(7)	1
7	Mihran Manasyan		13/06/89	A	24	(3)	13
14	Samvel Melkonyan		15/03/94	A	1	(3)	
19	Vahagn Minasyan		25/04/85	D	22	(1)	3
5	Karen Muradyan		01/11/92	M	6	(2)	
15	Uroš Nenadović	SRB	28/01/94	A	10	(1)	4
9	Gevorg Nranyan		08/03/86	A		(1)	1
14	Lester Peltier	TRI	13/09/88	A	6	(4)	
18	Anton Savin	UKR	07/02/90	M	2	(1)	
5	Danijel Stojković	SRB	14/08/90	D	10		
4	Aleksandar Tasić	SRB	06/04/88	D	7	(2)	1
10	Khoren Veranyan		04/09/86	M	12	(11)	1
3	Andranik Voskanyan		11/04/90	D	23		
17	Artak Yedigaryan		18/03/90	M	27	(1)	13
20	Artur Yedigaryan		26/07/87	M	12	(15)	4

ARMENIA

FC Ararat

1935 • Hanrapetakan (14,400); Banants-3 (1,500); MF (7,140) • fcararat.am

Major honours
USSR League (1) 1973; Armenian League (1) 1993; USSR Cup (2) 1973, 1975; Armenian Cup (5) 1993, 1994, 1995, 1997, 2008

Coach: Arkadi Andreasyan

2016

Date		Opponent		Score	Scorers
06/08	a	Banants	L	0-1	
13/08	a	Gandzasar	L	0-2	
20/08	a	Shirak	L	0-1	
27/08	h	Pyunik	D	0-0	
10/09	a	Alashkert	W	3-1	*Nwabueze 2, Kpenia*
17/09	h	Banants	L	0-2	
25/09	h	Gandzasar	L	0-2	
01/10	h	Shirak	L	0-1	
15/10	a	Pyunik	L	0-4	
22/10	h	Alashkert	L	1-2	*A Loretsyan*
26/10	a	Banants	D	0-0	
30/10	a	Gandzasar	L	0-1	
04/11	a	Shirak	L	0-2	
19/11	h	Pyunik	L	1-2	*S Mkrtchyan*
23/11	a	Alashkert	L	1-4	*Safaryan*
27/11	h	Banants	D	1-1	*Sahakyan*
03/12	h	Gandzasar	L	0-1	

2017

Date		Opponent		Score	Scorers
05/03	h	Shirak	L	0-1	
10/03	a	Pyunik	L	0-3	
17/03	h	Alashkert	L	0-3	
31/03	a	Banants	L	1-2	*Tumbaryan*
08/04	a	Gandzasar	L	1-2	*Kocharyan*
15/04	a	Shirak	L	0-1	
21/04	h	Pyunik	W	1-0	*Tumbaryan*
29/04	a	Alashkert	L	1-3	*E Mkrtchyan*
06/05	h	Banants	W	1-0	*Minasyan*
13/05	h	Gandzasar	L	1-2	*Yeghiazaryan*
20/05	h	Shirak	L	2-3	*Safaryan, Arzoyan*
27/05	a	Pyunik	L	1-2	*Tumbaryan*
31/05	h	Alashkert	L	1-4	*Arustamyan*

No	Name	Nat	DoB	Pos	Aps	(s)	Gls
7	Mikael Arustamyan		14/10/91	M		(2)	1
8	Vardan Arzoyan		30/04/95	D	15	(4)	1
3	Sergey Avagimyan		05/07/89	D	2		
2	Ruslan Avagyan		24/06/95	D	2	(6)	
15	Norik Avdalyan	RUS	01/01/96	A		(1)	
4	Karen Avoyan		22/08/86	M	10		
1	Poghos Ayvazyan		09/06/95	G	9		
10	Areg Azatyan		29/06/90	A	3	(2)	
15	Kouadio Brou	CIV	25/12/95	M	5	(1)	
14	Marat Daudov	UKR	03/08/89	M	7	(3)	
3	Armen Derdzyan		17/11/93	M	7	(2)	
12	Gor Elazyan		01/06/91	G	4		
11	Yuri Gareginyan		03/02/94	M	20	(4)	
21	David Ghandilyan		04/07/93	A	1	(1)	
11	Rafael Ghazaryan		17/05/90	M	7	(3)	
11	Davit G Grigoryan		17/07/89	M	2	(4)	
5	Norayr Grigoryan		07/06/83	D	7		
77	Aram Hayrapetyan		22/11/86	G	14		
41	Andranik Hovhannisyan	BEL	17/05/88	M		(1)	
8	Aram Hovsepyan		06/06/91	M	1		
10	Oumarou Kaina	CMR	16/10/96	M	7		
18	Gorik Khachatryan		16/06/88	M	3	(3)	
7	Garegin Kirakosyan		22/11/95	M	3	(5)	
9	Andranik Kocharyan		29/01/94	A	7	(1)	1
4	Souleymane Koné	CIV	05/01/92	D	4		
19	Aaron Kpenia	CIV	20/12/96	M	7	(2)	1
7	Aram Loretsyan		07/03/93	M	9	(2)	1
7	Hakob Loretsyan		16/03/94	D	2	(2)	
2	Davit Markosyan		07/10/95	M	4		
2	Vahe Martirosyan		19/01/88	D	3		
16	Arman Meliksetyan		21/07/95	G	3		
19	Sargis Metoyan		01/01/97	A	8	(6)	
14	David Minasyan		09/03/93	M	6	(5)	1
10	Edgar Mkrtchyan		14/07/94	A	8	(1)	1
15	Sergei Mkrtchyan		09/02/83	M	10	(3)	1
16	Edmond Muradyan		29/03/96	A		(2)	
18	Erik Nazaryan		14/03/96	M		(1)	
9	Gevorg Nranyan		09/03/86	A	2	(3)	
23	Kieran Nwabueze	USA	12/11/92	A	4	(2)	2
20	Paul Oshie	NGA	27/09/96	A	1		
9	Hovhannes Papazyan		14/07/96	A	4	(4)	
25	Narek Papoyan		09/04/96	M	1		
6	Argishti Petrosyan		16/10/92	D	23	(1)	
21	Gevorg Poghosyan		20/08/86	D	22	(3)	
23	Gor Poghosyan		11/06/88	D	12	(1)	
20	Rafael Safaryan		30/01/86	D	18		2
8	Mher Sahakyan		15/07/95	M	8	(1)	1
14	Happy Simelela	RSA	17/10/94	M	4	(1)	
8	Artur Stepanyan		06/10/89	D		(10)	
13	Gegham Tumbaryan		13/05/96	M	19	(9)	3
2	Revik Yeghiazaryan		01/01/91	M	12		1

FC Banants

1992 • Banants-1 (4,860); Banants-3 (1,500) • fcbanants.am

Major honours
Armenian League (1) 2014; Armenian Cup (3) 1992, 2007, 2016

Coach: Tito Ramallo (ESP); (03/10/16) Aram Voskanyan

2016

Date		Opponent		Score	Scorers
06/08	h	Ararat	W	1-0	*Laércio*
14/08	h	Shirak	L	0-1	
21/08	a	Alashkert	L	0-3	
28/08	h	Gandzasar	W	4-1	*Badoyan, Satumyan, Laércio (p), Buraev*
11/09	a	Pyunik	L	1-2	*Drobarov*
17/09	a	Ararat	W	2-0	*Badoyan, Oganesyan*
27/09	a	Shirak	W	1-0	*Minasyan*
02/10	h	Alashkert	L	0-3	
15/10	a	Gandzasar	L	0-4	
23/10	h	Pyunik	L	0-1	
26/10	h	Ararat	D	0-0	
29/10	h	Shirak	L	1-2	*Aghekyan*
05/11	a	Alashkert	L	1-4	*Ayvazyan*
19/11	h	Gandzasar	D	1-1	*Kocharyan*
22/11	a	Pyunik	D	1-1	*Ilangyozyan*
27/11	a	Ararat	D	1-1	*Laércio (p)*
03/12	h	Shirak	L	0-1	

2017

Date		Opponent		Score	Scorers
04/03	h	Alashkert	L	1-2	*Melkonyan*
11/03	a	Gandzasar	L	0-1	
19/03	h	Pyunik	L	0-3	
31/03	h	Ararat	W	2-1	*Injac 2*
07/04	a	Shirak	L	0-1	
14/04	a	Alashkert	L	0-2	
22/04	h	Gandzasar	D	0-0	
30/04	a	Pyunik	D	0-0	
06/05	a	Ararat	L	0-1	
14/05	a	Shirak	L	0-1	
19/05	h	Alashkert	L	0-3	
27/05	a	Gandzasar	L	1-2	*Yeghiazaryan*
31/05	h	Pyunik	L	0-2	

No	Name	Nat	DoB	Pos	Aps	(s)	Gls
55	Lionel Adams	RUS	09/08/94	D	15	(1)	
31	Ashot Adamyan		15/06/97	M		(2)	
13	Grigor Aghekyan		06/04/96	A	7	(5)	1
15	Artur A Avagyan		04/07/87	D	13	(3)	
16	Henry Avagyan		16/01/96	G	4		
18	Vahagn Ayvazyan		16/04/92	M	17	(6)	1
17	Zaven Badoyan		22/12/89	M	11	(1)	2
17	Aram Bareghamyan		06/01/88	M	21	(2)	
90	Atsamaz Buraev	RUS	05/02/90	A	8	(4)	1
3	Vlatko Drobarov	MKD	02/11/92	D	27	(2)	1
88	Stepan Ghazaryan		11/01/85	G	16		
42	Martin Grigoryan		25/09/00	M		(3)	
23	Norayr Gyozalyan		15/03/90	A	10	(1)	
24	Hakob Hakobyan		29/03/97	D	12	(4)	
18	Hakob Hambardzumyan		26/05/97	D	15	(1)	
25	Orbeli Hambardzumyan		26/03/96	A	2	(3)	
20	Karen Harutyunyan		05/08/86	M	8	(5)	
22	Aram Hayrapetyan		22/11/86	G	8	(1)	
19	Hovhannes Ilangyozyan		14/01/97	M	7	(6)	1
26	Nenad Injac	SRB	04/09/85	A	10		2
5	Soslan Kachmazov	RUS	14/07/91	D	6	(1)	
2	Aslan Kalmanov	RUS	05/06/94	D	3	(1)	
25	Aram Khamoyan		10/01/00	M		(5)	
3	Gevorg Khuloyan		18/08/96	D	15	(1)	
28	Aram Kocharyan		05/03/96	M	4	(2)	1
14	Laércio	BRA	03/03/90	M	16		3
29	Aram Loretsyan		07/03/93	M	3	(1)	
22	Gagik Maghakyan		07/02/96	D	2		
1	Grigor Makaryan		19/04/95	G	2	(1)	
18	Zhirayr Margaryan		13/09/97	D	5		
32	Karen Melkonyan		25/03/99	M	1	(5)	1
11	Nairi Minasyan		26/08/95	M	11	(4)	1
28	Edgar Movsisyan		09/09/98	A	1	(3)	
4	Aleksandr Oganesyan		20/07/96	M	8	(2)	1
31	Aghavard Petrosyan		16/04/97	D	2		
18	Narek Petrosyan		25/01/96	D	6	(7)	
8	Valter Poghosyan		16/05/92	M	3	(2)	
23	Vardan Safaryan		22/04/97	M		(1)	
29	Hayk Sargsyan		12/03/98	D	1		
9	Vardges Satumyan		07/02/90	M	8	(4)	1
14	Claudio Torrejón	PER	14/05/93	M	13		
30	Erik Vardanyan		08/03/99	M		(3)	
35	Hayk Voskanyan		23/06/96	M	4	(3)	
23	Emil Yeghiazaryan		03/11/97	M	5	(7)	1

FC Gandzasar

2002 • Gandzasar (3,500); Armenian Football Academy (1,428); Hanrapetakan (14,400) • no website

Coach: Ashot Barseghyan

2016

Date		Opponent		Score	Scorers
07/08	a	Alashkert	D	0-0	
13/08	h	Ararat	W	2-0	*Claudir, Harutyunyan*
21/08	a	Pyunik	L	0-3	
28/08	a	Banants	L	1-4	*Musonda*
11/09	h	Shirak	L	0-1	
18/09	h	Alashkert	L	0-2	
25/09	a	Ararat	W	2-0	*Musonda, Khachatryan (p)*
01/10	h	Pyunik	W	1-0	*Ishkhanyan*
15/10	h	Banants	W	4-0	*Claudir, Memović, Gogatishvili, Walmerson*
22/10	a	Shirak	L	0-1	
27/10	a	Alashkert	W	4-0	*Claudir, Harutyunyan 2, og (Grigoryan)*
30/10	h	Ararat	W	1-0	*Harutyunyan*
05/11	a	Pyunik	D	0-0	
19/11	a	Banants	D	1-1	*Harutyunyan*
23/11	h	Shirak	W	1-0	*Harutyunyan*
27/11	h	Alashkert	L	1-2	*Harutyunyan*
03/12	a	Ararat	W	1-0	*Claudir*

2017

Date		Opponent		Score	Scorers
05/03	h	Pyunik	W	2-0	*Claudir. Harutyunyan*
11/03	h	Banants	W	1-0	*Walmerson*
18/03	a	Shirak	W	2-1	*Bakalyan, Ishkhanyan*
30/03	a	Alashkert	W	2-1	*Harutyunyan, Walmerson*
08/04	h	Ararat	W	2-1	*Harutyunyan, Claudir*
16/04	a	Pyunik	W	2-1	*Musonda, Khachatryan (p)*
22/04	a	Banants	D	0-0	
29/04	h	Shirak	W	3-2	*Musonda, Claudir, Walmerson*
06/05	h	Alashkert	L	0-1	
13/05	a	Ararat	W	2-1	*Musonda, Claudir*
20/05	h	Pyunik	D	1-1	*Harutyunyan*
27/05	h	Banants	W	2-1	*Harutyunyan (p), Walmerson*
31/05	a	Shirak	D	0-0	

No	Name	Nat	DoB	Pos	Aps	(s)	Gls
2	Artur Adamyan	RUS	22/04/92	M	1	(2)	
4	Artak Aleksanyan		10/03/91	M	6	(1)	
6	Wbeymar Angulo	COL	06/03/92	M	28	(1)	
3	Hamlet Asoyan		13/06/95	M	6	(6)	
24	Vardan Bakalyan		04/04/95	A	1	(10)	1
14	Claudir	BRA	06/08/92	A	27		8
15	Rafael Ghazaryan		17/05/90	M	3	(8)	
9	Gogita Gogatishvili	GEO	02/02/90	M	11	(3)	1
22	Gegham Harutyunyan		23/08/90	A	20	(9)	12
1	Filip Ilic	MKD	26/01/97	G	1		
21	Hayk Ishkhanyan		24/07/89	D	17	(4)	2
25	Ashot Karapetyan		12/05/93	D	2	(13)	
16	Ara Khachatryan		21/10/81	D	30		2
5	Edward Kpodo	GHA	14/07/90	D	4	(6)	
1	Grigor Meliksetyan		18/08/86	G	29		
13	Damir Memović	SRB	19/01/89	D	28	(1)	1
18	Vaspurak Minasyan		29/06/94	D	18	(3)	
89	Lubambo Musonda	ZAM	01/01/95	M	29		5
22	Gevorg Ohanyan		31/03/92	M		(7)	
15	Alexander Petrosyan		28/05/86	D	22		
2	Armen S Petrosyan		26/09/85	M	9	(3)	
30	Sargis Shahinyan		10/09/95	M	5	(6)	
4	Gegham Simonyan		09/09/00	M		(1)	
17	Walmerson	BRA	13/01/94	A	20	(4)	5
16	Artur Yusbashyan		07/09/89	M	13		

FC Pyunik

1992 • Armenian Football Academy (1,428); Pyunik s/s (2,000) • fcpyunik.am

Major honours
Armenian League (14) 1992 (shared), 1996, 1997, 2001, 2002, 2003, 2004, 2005, 2006, 2007, 2008, 2009, 2010, 2015; Armenian Cup (8) 1996, 2002, 2004, 2009, 2010, 2013, 2014, 2015

Coach: Sargis Hovsepyan; (01/08/16) Artak Oseyan

2016

06/08	a	Shirak	L	1-3	*Manoyan (p)*
13/08	h	Alashkert	L	1-2	*Arakelyan*
21/08	h	Gandzasar	W	3-0	*Arakelyan 2 (1p), Petrosyan*
27/08	a	Ararat	D	0-0	
11/09	h	Banants	W	2-1	*V Poghosyan, Petrosyan*
18/09	h	Shirak	D	0-0	
27/09	a	Alashkert	D	0-0	
01/10	a	Gandzasar	L	0-1	
15/10	h	Ararat	W	4-0	*V Poghosyan 2, Avetisyan, Hovhannisyan*
23/10	a	Banants	W	1-0	*Shahnazaryan*
26/10	a	Shirak	W	1-0	*Kartashyan*
30/10	h	Alashkert	W	2-1	*Manucharyan, V Poghosyan (p)*
05/11	h	Gandzasar	D	0-0	
19/11	a	Ararat	W	2-1	*Arakelyan, Manucharyan*
22/11	h	Banants	D	1-1	*Hovhannisyan*
26/11	h	Shirak	L	0-2	
04/12	a	Alashkert	D	0-0	

2017

05/03	a	Gandzasar	L	0-2	
10/03	h	Ararat	W	3-0	*G Harutyunyan, Razmik Hakobyan, Nadiryan*
19/03	a	Banants	W	3-0	*Hayrapetyan, V Poghosyan (p), Nahapetyan*
01/04	a	Shirak	W	2-0	*Kartashyan, Avetisyan (p)*
07/04	h	Alashkert	L	0-3	
16/04	h	Gandzasar	L	1-2	*Kartashyan*
21/04	a	Ararat	L	0-1	
30/04	h	Banants	D	0-0	
06/05	h	Shirak	L	0-2	
13/05	a	Alashkert	D	3-3	*Kartashyan, V Poghosyan, Aslanyan*
20/05	a	Gandzasar	D	1-1	*Arakelyan*
27/05	h	Ararat	W	2-1	*H Harutyunyan 2*
31/05	a	Banants	W	2-0	*Spertsyan, Begoyan*

No	Name	Nat	DoB	Pos	Aps	(s)	Gls
18	Alik Arakelyan		21/05/96	M	24	(2)	5
5	Narek Aslanyan		04/01/96	M	23	(3)	1
4	Petros Avetisyan		07/01/96	M	20	(4)	2
3	Vigen Begoyan		08/09/97	M		(3)	1
2	Serob Grigoryan		04/02/95	D	28		
26	Razmik Hakobyan		09/02/96	A	16	(3)	1
16	Robert Hakobyan		22/10/96	D	9	(6)	
8	Gevorg Harutyunyan	RUS	21/02/97	M	10	(3)	1
6	Hovhannes Harutyunyan		25/05/99	M	3	(17)	2
30	Vahagn Hayrapetyan		14/06/97	M	20	(5)	1
7	Kamo Hovhannisyan		05/10/92	D	10	(4)	2
18	Artur Kartashyan		08/01/97	D	28		4
11	Davit Manoyan		05/07/90	M	1		1
4	Armen Manucharyan		03/02/95	D	27	(3)	2
12	Gor Manukyan		27/09/93	G	13		
7	Robert Minasyan		08/04/97	A		(5)	
21	Artur Nadiryan		27/03/98	M	5	(6)	1
14	Armen Nahapetyan		24/07/99	M		(10)	1
19	Hovhannes Nazaryan		11/03/98	D	1	(1)	
15	Hovhannes Panosyan		25/03/89	M		(2)	
17	Erik Petrosyan		19/02/98	A	3	(21)	2
16	Hovhannes Poghosyan		17/12/97	A	15	(1)	
17	Vardan Poghosyan		08/03/92	A	26	(1)	6
29	Aram Shahnazaryan		21/04/94	D	24	(3)	1
19	Samvel Spertsyan		24/05/98	M	3	(3)	1
23	Erik Vardanyan		07/06/98	M	4	(5)	
25	Valeriy Voskonyan	UKR	06/04/94	G	17		

FC Shirak

1958 • Gyumri City (3,500) • fcshirak.am

Major honours
Armenian League (4) 1992 (shared), 1994, 1999, 2013; Armenian Cup (2) 2012, 2017

Coach: Vardan Bichakhchyan

2016

06/08	h	Pyunik	W	3-1	*Ayvazyan 2, Muradyan*
14/08	a	Banants	W	1-0	*Hakobyan*
20/08	h	Ararat	W	1-0	*Bichakhchyan*
27/08	a	Alashkert	D	2-2	*og (Daghbashyan), Ayvazyan*
11/09	h	Gandzasar	W	1-0	*Muradyan*
18/09	a	Pyunik	D	0-0	
27/09	h	Banants	L	0-1	
01/10	a	Ararat	W	1-0	*Hovsepyan*
16/10	a	Alashkert	D	1-1	*Gogichaev*
22/10	a	Gandzasar	W	1-0	*De la Fuente*
26/10	h	Pyunik	L	0-1	
29/10	a	Banants	W	2-1	*Ayvazyan (p), Kaba*
04/11	h	Ararat	W	2-0	*Ayvazyan, Poghosyan*
20/11	h	Alashkert	D	0-0	
23/11	a	Gandzasar	L	0-1	
26/11	a	Pyunik	W	2-0	*Ayvazyan 2*
03/12	a	Banants	W	1-0	*Bichakhchyan*

2017

05/03	a	Ararat	W	1-0	*Bichakhchyan*
12/03	a	Alashkert	L	0-3	
18/03	h	Gandzasar	L	1-2	*Bakayoko*
01/04	h	Pyunik	L	0-2	
07/04	h	Banants	W	1-0	*Nwabueze*
15/04	h	Ararat	W	1-0	*Bichakhchyan*
23/04	h	Alashkert	L	0-1	
29/04	a	Gandzasar	L	2-3	*Hovsepyan (p), Bakayoko*
06/05	a	Pyunik	W	2-0	*Ayvazyan, Poghosyan*
14/05	h	Banants	W	1-0	*Udo*
20/05	a	Ararat	W	3-2	*Hovsepyan, Prljević, Poghosyan*
28/05	a	Alashkert	L	1-3	*Muradyan*
31/05	h	Gandzasar	D	0-0	

No	Name	Nat	DoB	Pos	Aps	(s)	Gls
1	Norayr Abrahamyan		30/10/85	G	1		
15	Karen Aleksanyan		17/06/80	M	3	(2)	
31	Arman Aslanyan		30/01/94	M		(1)	
3	Anatoliy Ayvazov		08/06/96	G	27		
7	Viulen Ayvazyan		01/01/95	A	23	(5)	8
4	Moussa Bakayoko	CIV	27/12/96	M	6	(5)	2
17	Vahan Bichakhchyan		09/07/99	M	4	(18)	4
2	Robert Darbinyan		04/10/95	D	12		
12	Semen Datsenko	UKR	10/05/94	D	3	(3)	
25	Aghvan Davoyan		21/03/90	D	23		
1	Vsevolod Ermakov	RUS	06/01/96	G	2		
16	Bryan de la Fuente	MEX	01/07/92	M	6	(6)	1
19	Georgi Gogichaev	RUS	16/01/91	M	5	(6)	1
10	Davit Hakobyan		21/03/93	M	14	(2)	1
29	Arman Hovhannisyan		07/07/93	D	19	(2)	
21	Gevorg Hovhannisyan		16/06/83	D	15		
7	Rumyan Hovsepyan		13/11/91	M	24	(4)	3
23	Milutin Ivanović	SRB	30/10/90	A	4		
28	Mohamed Kaba	CIV	05/04/89	M	20	(2)	1
22	Oumarou Kaina	CMR	16/10/96	M	7	(3)	
3	Artyom Mikaelyan		12/07/91	D	26	(1)	
23	Artush Mirzakhanyan		30/09/98	M		(1)	
29	Rudik Mkrtchyan		26/10/98	M	1	(1)	
18	Aram Muradyan		01/01/96	A	5	(20)	3
24	Kieran Nwabueze	USA	12/11/92	A	9	(1)	1
29	Ghukas Poghosyan		06/02/94	A	5	(13)	3
34	Marko Prljević	SRB	02/08/88	D	19		1
18	Fatawu Safiu	GHA	16/07/94	A	6	(1)	
4	Kostyantyn Shults	UKR	24/06/93	D	3	(1)	
4	Nemanja Stošković	SRB	21/02/90	M	8	(6)	
22	Arman Tadevosyan		26/09/94	D	1	(2)	
31	Arlen Tsaturyan		05/01/99	M	1	(1)	
25	Solomon Udo	NGA	15/07/95	M	28		1

Top goalscorers

Mihran Manasyan

Artak Yedigaryan

13	Mihran Manasyan (Alashkert) Artak Yedigaryan (Alashkert)
12	Gegham Harutyunyan (Gandzasar)
8	Claudir (Gandzasar) Viulen Ayvazyan (Shirak)
6	Artak Dashyan (Alashkert) Vardan Poghosyan (Pyunik)
5	Lubambo Musonda (Gandzasar) Walmerson (Gandzasar) Alik Arakelyan (Pyunik) Zaven Badoyan (Banants/Alashkert)

Second level

Second level final table 2016/17

		Pld	W	D	L	F	A	Pts
1	FC Banants-2	24	17	4	3	63	23	55
2	FC Pyunik-2	24	14	5	5	65	28	47
3	FC Ararat-2	24	11	9	4	36	20	42
4	FC Gandzasar-2	24	11	5	8	33	37	38
5	Alashkert FC-2	24	5	7	12	25	40	22
6	FC Shirak-2	24	6	3	15	23	46	21
7	Erebuni SC	24	2	3	19	20	71	9
8	FC Kotayk	0	0	0	0	0	0	0

NB FC Kotayk withdrew after round 7 - all their matches were annulled; no promotion.

DOMESTIC CUP

Armenian Independence Cup 2016/17

QUARTER-FINALS

(21/09/16 & 18/10/16)
Ararat 1-2 Banants *(Kpenia 73; O Hambardzumyan 6, Movsisyan 46)*
Banants 0-1 Ararat *(Tumbaryan 63)*
(2-2; Banants on away goals)

(21/09/16 & 19/10/16)
Alashkert 1-2 Pyunik *(Fomenko 47; Arakelyan 5, Hovhannisyan 13)*
Pyunik 1-0 Alashkert *(Hovhannisyan 87)*
(Pyunik 3-1)

(22/09/16 & 19/10/16)
Kotayk 0-0 Shirak
Shirak 3-0 Kotayk *(w/o)*
(Shirak 3-0)

(09/10/16 & 18/10/16)
Gandzasar w/o Erebuni

SEMI-FINALS

(11/04/17 & 25/04/17)
Pyunik 2-1 Banants *(Avetisyan 36, Bareghamyan 52og; Injac 28)*
Banants 0-1 Pyunik *(Shahnazaryan 50)*
(Pyunik 3-1)

(12/04/17 & 26/04/17)
Gandzasar 0-1 Shirak *(Kaina 45)*
Shirak 1-1 Gandzasar *(Minasyan 66og; Musonda 40p)*
(Shirak 2-1)

FINAL

(24/05/17)
Hanrapetakan, Yerevan
FC SHIRAK 3 *(Nwabueze 6, 38, Bichakhchyan 28)*
FC PYUNIK 0
Referee: *Hovhannisyan*
SHIRAK: *Ermakov, Darbinyan, Prljević, G Hovhannisyan, Davoyan (Mikaelyan 74), Udo, Hovsepyan (Kaba 87), Bakayoko, Bichakhchyan, Poghosyan (Ayvazyan 64), Nwabueze*
PYUNIK: *Voskonyan, Manucharyan, Shahnazaryan, Kartashyan, Grigoryan, Aslanyan (H Harutyunyan 55), Hayrapetyan, Arakelyan (Nahapetyan 71), Avetisyan (Petrosyan 71), G Harutyunyan (Vardanyan 55), V Poghosyan*

Shirak players celebrate their 3-0 victory against Pyunik in the Armenian Independence Cup final

AUSTRIA

Österreichischer Fussball-Bund (ÖFB)

Address	Ernst-Happel-Stadion Sektor A/F, Meiereistrasse 7 AT-1020 Wien	**President**	Leo Windtner
		General secretary	Thomas Hollerer
		Media officer	Iris Stöckelmayr
Tel	+43 1 727 180	**Year of formation**	1904
Fax	+43 1 728 1632	**National stadium**	Ernst-Happel-Stadion, Vienna (50,865)
E-mail	office@oefb.at		
Website	oefb.at		

KEY
- UEFA Champions League
- UEFA Europa League
- Promoted
- Relegated

Ried im Innkreis 6
Pasching 11
St Pölten 8
Wien (Vienna) 3 5
Mödling 1
Salzburg 7
Mattersburg 4

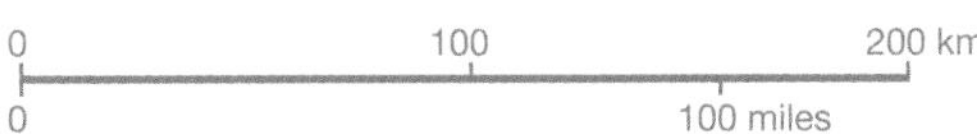

BUNDESLIGA CLUBS

1 **FC Admira Wacker Mödling**

2 **SCR Altach**

3 **FK Austria Wien**

 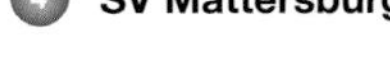
4 **SV Mattersburg**

5 **SK Rapid Wien**

6 **SV Ried**

7 **FC Salzburg**

8 **SKN St Pölten**

9 **SK Sturm Graz**

10 **Wolfsberger AC**

PROMOTED CLUB

11 **LASK Linz**

Salzburg remain out of reach

There was no change to an increasingly familiar script in 2016/17 as FC Salzburg agonisingly failed to qualify for the UEFA Champions League group stage but again proved all-conquering on the domestic scene, winning the Austrian league and cup double for the fourth year in a row.

Europe was not entirely a dead loss for Salzburg, however, as they unexpectedly won the UEFA Youth League, and there was another surprise as unheralded SCR Altach led the Bundesliga at the winter break – only to fall away dramatically during the spring.

Fourth successive double for serial trophy-winners

Youth League win atones for European failure

Altach top Bundesliga standings at winter break

Domestic league

Salzburg's domination of the Bundesliga received an unexpected challenge during the autumn, with both Altach and Sturm Graz keeping them off the top of the table in an intriguing title race. However, in the second half of the season there was only one team in it, Óscar García's side racking up one victory after another as the form of their erstwhile rivals took a nosedive.

At the winter break Altach, astonishingly, led Salzburg by two points, but by the end of the season the minnows from the western state of Vorarlberg had dropped so far out of contention that there was a 28-point gap separating them from the summit. Salzburg were simply on a different plane from the other nine teams in the division – and this despite the sale of their prolific Spanish striker/skipper Jonatan Soriano, who departed in late February for Chinese club Beijing Guoan.

Salzburg's 11th title – and eighth in 11 years – was duly sealed with three rounds to spare thanks to a 1-0 home win over Rapid Wien. The champions won their last three games as well to make it 25 victories out of 36, with South Korean striker Hwang Hee-chan finishing up as the club's leading marksman on 12 goals, one more than Takumi Minamino of Japan. Salzburg were a multi-national entity, but there was still room for homegrown talent to shine, teenage midfielder Konrad Laimer particularly excelling alongside Austrian internationals Valentino Lazaro and Stefan Lainer.

Austria Wien finished 18 points in arrears of Salzburg but did enough to take the runners-up spot, German coach Thorsten Fink just eclipsing his long-serving compatriot at Sturm, Franco Foda, thanks to a 6-1 win at Admira on the final day. Another little victory for the Violetten was the golden boot claimed by their 17-goal striker Olarenwaju Kayode. The Nigerian edged out Sturm's Deni Alar, who had led the listings virtually all season until the goals dried up late on.

Domestic cup

Runners-up to Salzburg in the previous three Bundesliga campaigns, Rapid lost more games than they won in 2016/17 and could finish only fifth. To requalify for Europe, at Altach's expense, the country's best-supported club had to win the Austrian Cup for the first time in 22 years. They reached the final with an added-time winner against runaway second division champions LASK Linz but could not repeat the trick in the Klagenfurt final against Salzburg, Hwang and Lazaro scoring the goals that gave the champions a 2-1 win and completed yet another domestic double, giving coach Óscar his second in as many seasons.

Europe

The bad news for Salzburg fans came in August when the team put them through the annual ordeal of narrowly missing out on a first-ever qualification for the UEFA Champions League group stage. Poised to achieve their long-targeted objective at the end of a play-off tie against Dinamo Zagreb that they dominated, Salzburg conceded once in normal time then again in extra time to drop into the UEFA Europa League, where, like fellow Austrian combatants Rapid and Austria Wien, they were unable to progress beyond the group stage.

National team

The fall-out from Austria's UEFA EURO 2016 disappointment was felt in the qualifying campaign for the 2018 FIFA World Cup, with Marcel Koller's side dropping five points in their first two home fixtures – 2-2 against Wales and 0-1 versus the Republic of Ireland – and, in between, suffering their first defeat in 13 European Qualifiers (11 of them won) as they lost 3-2 in a Belgrade thriller against Serbia. By the summer, after conceding a late equaliser in Dublin and thus remaining four points off second place, Austria's chances of participating in Russia looked slim.

DOMESTIC SEASON AT A GLANCE

Bundesliga 2016/17 final table

		Pld	Home W	D	L	F	A	Away W	D	L	F	A	Total W	D	L	F	A	Pts
1	**FC Salzburg**	**36**	**14**	**2**	**2**	**34**	**8**	**11**	**4**	**3**	**40**	**16**	**25**	**6**	**5**	**74**	**24**	**81**
2	FK Austria Wien	36	10	1	7	36	25	10	2	6	36	25	20	3	13	72	50	63
3	SK Sturm Graz	36	11	2	5	32	21	8	1	9	23	18	19	3	14	55	39	60
4	SCR Altach	36	10	4	4	27	18	5	4	9	19	31	15	8	13	46	49	53
5	SK Rapid Wien	36	9	4	5	29	12	3	6	9	23	30	12	10	14	52	42	46
6	FC Admira Wacker Mödling	36	8	3	7	22	29	5	4	9	14	26	13	7	16	36	55	46
7	SV Mattersburg	36	9	3	6	21	21	3	4	11	18	33	12	7	17	39	54	43
8	Wolfsberger AC	36	8	6	4	24	20	3	3	12	16	39	11	9	16	40	59	42
9	SKN St Pölten	36	5	6	7	24	33	4	4	10	17	27	9	10	17	41	60	37
10	SV Ried	36	8	3	7	24	28	2	2	14	9	28	10	5	21	33	56	35

European qualification 2017/18

Champion/Cup winner: FC Salzburg (second qualifying round)

FK Austria Wien (third qualifying round)
SK Sturm Graz (second qualifying round)
SCR Altach (first qualifying round)

Top scorer Olarenwaju Kayode (Austria Wien), 17 goals
Relegated club SV Ried
Promoted club LASK Linz
Cup final FC Salzburg 2-1 SK Rapid Wien

Player of the season

Konrad Laimer
(FC Salzburg)

Introduced gently to the Salzburg first team in 2015/16, Laimer became not only a fully-fledged starting XI regular in 2016/17 but also one of the key figures in the club's Bundesliga/ÖFB Pokal double-winning campaign. In fact, so profound was the 19-year-old defensive midfielder's impact that he was officially voted Bundesliga player of the season at the end of term. Additional post-season rewards included a first call-up for Austrian senior national duty – though no first cap – plus a four-year contract with Salzburg's German partner club, RB Leipzig.

Newcomer of the season

Christoph Monschein
(FC Admira Wacker Mödling)

Admira finished sixth in the 2016/17 Bundesliga – two places lower than the previous season – but the campaign proved extremely rewarding for the development of their pacy 24-year-old striker, who top-scored with ten goals, including four in successive games during a prolific November that featured a winner against Salzburg. Most of his goals were highly significant, including his first of the campaign that brought Admira a 2-1 win over Austria Wien – the club that decided to add Monschein to their ranks in the summer, luring him to the capital on a four-year deal.

Team of the season
(4-4-2)

Coach: Baumgartner *(Mattersburg)*

AUSTRIA

NATIONAL TEAM

International tournament appearances

FIFA World Cup (7) 1934 (4th), 1954 (3rd), 1958, 1978 (2nd phase), 1982 (2nd phase), 1990, 1998
UEFA European Championship (2) 2008, 2016

Top five all-time caps

Andreas Herzog (103); Anton Polster (95); Gerhard Hanappi (93); Karl Koller (86); Friedl Koncilia & Bruno Pezzey (84)

Top five all-time goals

Anton Polster (44); Hans Krankl (34); Erich Hof, Johann Horvath & **Marc Janko** (28)

Results 2016/17

05/09/16	Georgia (WCQ)	A	Tbilisi	W	2-1	*Hinteregger (16), Janko (42)*
06/10/16	Wales (WCQ)	H	Vienna	D	2-2	*Arnautovic (28, 48)*
09/10/16	Serbia (WCQ)	A	Belgrade	L	2-3	*Sabitzer (16), Janko (62)*
12/11/16	Republic of Ireland (WCQ)	H	Vienna	L	0-1	
15/11/16	Slovakia	H	Vienna	D	0-0	
24/03/17	Moldova (WCQ)	H	Vienna	W	2-0	*Arnautovic (75), Harnik (90)*
28/03/17	Finland	H	Innsbruck	D	1-1	*Arnautovic (62)*
11/06/17	Republic of Ireland (WCQ)	A	Dublin	D	1-1	*Hinteregger (31)*

Appearances 2016/17

Coach: Marcel Koller (SUI)	**11/11/60**		**GEO**	**WAL**	**SRB**	**IRL**	**Svk**	**MDA**	**Fin**	**IRL**	**Caps**	**Goals**
Robert Almer	20/03/84	Austria Wien	G	G58							33	-
Florian Klein	17/11/86	Stuttgart (GER)	D	D	D	D	s46				45	-
Aleksandar Dragovic	06/03/91	Leverkusen (GER)	D	D	D71	D	D	D	D	D	57	1
Martin Hinteregger	07/09/92	Augsburg GER)	D	D	D	D	s46	D	D	D	25	2
Markus Suttner	16/04/87	Ingolstadt GER)	D				D69	s93	M46		20	-
Martin Harnik	10/06/87	Hannover (GER)	M72			s73	A46	s82	A46	s75	66	15
Julian Baumgartlinger	02/01/88	Leverkusen (GER)	M	M	M58	M	M46			M	54	1
David Alaba	24/06/92	Bayern (GER)	M	M	M	M	s46	M	M46	M	57	11
Marko Arnautovic	19/04/89	Stoke (ENG)	M	M87	M	M	M	A93	s46		62	15
Zlatko Junuzovic	26/09/87	Bremen (GER)	M67	M79	M63			M	M81	M79	55	7
Marc Janko	25/06/83	Basel (SUI)	A76	A	A	A	s69	s69	s46		63	28
Alessandro Schöpf	07/02/94	Schalke (GER)	s67	s79	s63	M57			M72		12	2
Marcel Sabitzer	17/03/94	RB Leipzig (GER)	s72	M	M	M73		A	A46		27	4
Michael Gregoritsch	18/04/94	Hamburg (GER)	s76						s72	s90	3	-
Kevin Wimmer	15/11/92	Tottenham (ENG)		D	D	D78	s84				8	-
Ramazan Özcan	28/06/84	Leverkusen (GER)		s58	G	G					10	-
Louis Schaub	29/12/94	Rapid Wien		s87		s57					2	-
Stefan Ilsanker	18/05/89	RB Leipzig (GER)			s58	s78	M46	M	s81		23	-
Sebastian Prödl	21/06/87	Watford (ENG)			s71			D	D	D	63	4
Andreas Lukse	08/11/87	Altach					G				1	-
Valentino Lazaro	24/03/96	Salzburg					D	M69	M	M	8	-
Michael Madl	21/03/88	Fulham (ENG)					D				1	-
Lukas Hinterseer	28/03/91	Ingolstadt (GER)					M69				12	-
Karim Onisiwo	17/03/92	Mainz (GER)					M84				2	-
Stefan Stangl	20/10/91	Salzburg					s69				1	-
Heinz Lindner	17/07/90	Eintracht Frankfurt (GER)						G	G	G	11	-
Guido Burgstaller	29/04/89	Schalke (GER)						A82		A75	11	-
Florian Grillitsch	07/08/95	Bremen (GER)							s46	s79	2	-
Stefan Lainer	27/08/92	Salzburg							s46	D	2	-
Florian Kainz	24/10/92	Bremen (GER)								M90	2	-

EUROPE

FC Salzburg

CHAMPIONS LEAGUE

Second qualifying round - FK Liepāja (LVA)
H 1-0 *Jonatan Soriano (83)*
Walke, Paulo Miranda, Schwegler, Dabbur, Lazaro (Reyna 70), V Berisha, Ulmer, Jonatan Soriano, Laimer (Samassékou 64), Hinteregger, Bernardo. Coach: Óscar García (ESP)
A 2-0 *V Berisha (35), Bernardo (65)*
Walke, Paulo Miranda (Ćaleta-Car 83), Schwegler, Dabbur, Lazaro, V Berisha, Ulmer, Jonatan Soriano, Laimer (Samassékou 59), Hinteregger, Bernardo (Upamecano 87). Coach: Óscar García (ESP)

Third qualifying round - FK Partizani (ALB)
A 1-0 *Jonatan Soriano (70p)*
Walke, Ćaleta-Car, Schwegler, Samassékou, Dabbur (Laimer 55), Lazaro (Lainer 89), V Berisha, Ulmer, Jonatan Soriano (Gulbrandsen 74), Hinteregger, Bernardo. Coach: Óscar García (ESP)
Red card: Samassékou 54
H 2-0 *Jonatan Soriano (76), Wanderson (81)*
Walke, Ćaleta-Car, Schwegler, Dabbur (Wanderson 46), Lazaro (Lainer 74), V Berisha, Ulmer, Jonatan Soriano (Gulbrandsen 84), Laimer, Hinteregger, Bernardo. Coach: Óscar García (ESP)

Play-offs - GNK Dinamo Zagreb (CRO)
A 1-1 *Lazaro (59)*
Walke, Ćaleta-Car, Schwegler, Lazaro, V Berisha, Ulmer, Jonatan Soriano (Gulbrandsen 63), Laimer, Hinteregger, Wanderson (Lainer 78), Bernardo. Coach: Óscar García (ESP)
H 1-2 (aet) *Lazaro (22)*
Walke, Ćaleta-Car, Schwegler (Lainer 46), Lazaro (Samassékou 61), V Berisha, Ulmer, Jonatan Soriano, Laimer, Hinteregger, Wanderson (Minamino 66), Bernardo. Coach: Óscar García (ESP)
Red card: Schwegler 106

EUROPA LEAGUE

Group I
Match 1 - FC Krasnodar (RUS)
H 0-1
Walke, Paulo Miranda, Upamecano, Ćaleta-Car, Samassékou (Dabbur 73), Lazaro, V Berisha, Ulmer, Minamino, Jonatan Soriano, Wisdom (Lainer 30; Wanderson 80). Coach: Óscar García (ESP)
Match 2 - FC Schalke 04 (GER)
A 1-3 *Jonatan Soriano (72)*
Walke, Paulo Miranda, Upamecano, Ćaleta-Car, Lazaro (Minamino 65), V Berisha, Ulmer, Lainer, Jonatan Soriano, Laimer (Radošević 65), Wanderson (Rzatkowski 89). Coach: Óscar García (ESP)
Match 3 - OGC Nice (FRA)
H 0-1
Walke, Paulo Miranda, Lazaro (Minamino 80), Rzatkowski, Ulmer, Gulbrandsen (Hwang 83), Lainer, Radošević, Jonatan Soriano (Dabbur 83), Laimer, Wisdom. Coach: Óscar García (ESP)
Match 4 - OGC Nice (FRA)
A 2-0 *Hwang (72, 73)*
Walke, Paulo Miranda, Upamecano, Dabbur (Jonatan Soriano 83), Lazaro, Rzatkowski (Lainer 76), Ulmer, Gulbrandsen (Hwang 62), Radošević, Laimer, Wisdom. Coach: Óscar García (ESP)
Match 5 - FC Krasnodar (RUS)
A 1-1 *Dabbur (37)*
Walke, Paulo Miranda, Upamecano, Samassékou, Dabbur, Lazaro, V Berisha (Schlager 88), Ulmer, Gulbrandsen (Hwang 73), Radošević, Wisdom. Coach: Óscar García (ESP)
Match 6 - FC Schalke 04 (GER)
H 2-0 *Schlager (22), Radošević (90+4)*
Stankovic, Ćaleta-Car, Schwegler, Lazaro (Wolf 75), Rzatkowski, Minamino, Lainer, Radošević, Laimer (Samassékou 60), Schlager (Yabo 86), Wisdom. Coach: Óscar García (ESP)

SK Rapid Wien

EUROPA LEAGUE

Third qualifying round - FC Torpedo Zhodino (BLR)
A 0-0
Novota, Schösswendter, Schrammel, Schobesberger (Traustason 70), Schwab, Schaub, Grahovac, Dibon, Pavelic, Murg (Močinić 85), Joelinton. Coach: Mike Büskens (GER)
H 3-0 *Pavelic (26), Schrammel (36), Schaub (90+2)*
Novota, Schösswendter, Schrammel, Schwab, Schaub, Dibon, Pavelic, Traustason (Grahovac 68), Močinić (Szántó 80), Murg, Joelinton (Schobesberger 71). Coach: Mike Büskens (GER)

Play-offs - FK AS Trenčín (SVK)
A 4-0 *Schaub (32, 54, 83), Schwab (73)*
Novota, Schösswendter, Schrammel, Schobesberger (Murg 50), Schwab, Schaub (Auer 85), Grahovac, Dibon, Pavelic, Močinić, Joelinton (Entrup 84). Coach: Mike Büskens (GER)
H 0-2
Novota, Schaub (S Hofmann 90+2), Grahovac, Dibon, M Hofmann, Pavelic, Traustason (Schrammel 83), Auer, Močinić, Murg (Schwab 46), Joelinton. Coach: Mike Büskens (GER)

Group F
Match 1 - KRC Genk (BEL)
H 3-2 *Schwab (51), Joelinton (59), Colley (60og)*
Strebinger, Schösswendter, Schrammel, Schwab, Schaub, Dibon, Szántó (S Hofmann 63), Pavelic, Traustason (Murg 79), Močinić, Joelinton (Kvilitaia 86). Coach: Mike Büskens (GER)
Match 2 - Athletic Club (ESP)
A 0-1
Strebinger, Schösswendter, Schrammel, Schwab, Schaub, Grahovac, Dibon, Pavelic, Traustason (Szántó 72), Močinić (S Hofmann 67), Joelinton (Kvilitaia 84). Coach: Mike Büskens (GER)
Match 3 - US Sassuolo Calcio (ITA)
H 1-1 *Schaub (7)*
Strebinger, Schösswendter, Schrammel, Schwab, Schaub, Dibon (M Hofmann 46), Pavelic, Traustason (Jelić 73), Močinić, Murg (Grahovac 64), Joelinton. Coach: Mike Büskens (GER)
Match 4 - US Sassuolo Calcio (ITA)
A 2-2 *Jelić (86), Kvilitaia (90)*
Strebinger, Schrammel, Sonnleitner, Schaub, Grahovac, M Hofmann, Traustason, Močinić (Szántó 85), Murg (Jelić 61), Joelinton (Kvilitaia 61), Thurnwald. Coach: Mike Büskens (GER)
Match 5 - KRC Genk (BEL)
A 0-1
Novota, Schösswendter, Schrammel, Sonnleitner, Schaub (Jelić 84), Grahovac, Dibon, Traustason, Joelinton (Schobesberger 63), Thurnwald (Kvilitaia 72), Wöber. Coach: Damir Canadi (AUT)
Match 6 - Athletic Club (ESP)
H 1-1 *Joelinton (72)*
Knoflach, Schrammel, Sonnleitner, Jelić (Joelinton 57), Grahovac, Malicsek, Dibon (Schaub 69), M Hofmann, Auer, Tomi Correa (Kvilitaia 57), Wöber. Coach: Damir Canadi (AUT)

FK Austria Wien

EUROPA LEAGUE

Second qualifying round - FK Kukësi (ALB)
H 1-0 *Felipe Pires (24)*
Hadzikic, Filipovic, Kayode (Vukojević 90+2), Lucas Venuto, Serbest, Prokop (Kvasina 69), Stryger, Holzhauser, Martschinko, Rotpuller, Felipe Pires (De Paula 85). Coach: Thorsten Fink (GER)
A 4-1 *Kayode (16, 58), Holzhauser (67), Martschinko (90+4)*
Almer, Filipovic, Kayode (Kvasina 70), Lucas Venuto, Serbest, Stryger, Kehat, Holzhauser (Vukojević 79), Martschinko, Rotpuller, Felipe Pires (Tajouri 79). Coach: Thorsten Fink (GER)

Third qualifying round - FC Spartak Trnava (SVK)
H 0-1
Almer, Filipovic, Kayode (Friesenbichler 85), Lucas Venuto, Serbest, Stryger, Kehat (Grünwald 61), Holzhauser, Martschinko, Rotpuller, Felipe Pires (Tajouri 72). Coach: Thorsten Fink (GER)
A 1-0 (aet; 5-4 on pens) *Friesenbichler (88)*
Almer, Filipovic, Kayode, Grünwald, Lucas Venuto (Kvasina 86), Serbest, Stryger, Holzhauser (Friesenbichler 71), Martschinko, Rotpuller, Felipe Pires (Tajouri 71). Coach: Thorsten Fink (GER)

Play-offs - Rosenborg BK (NOR)
H 2-1 *Grünwald (51), Felipe Pires (53)*
Almer, Filipovic, Kayode (Friesenbichler 90), Grünwald (Windbichler 81), Lucas Venuto (De Paula 84), Serbest, Stryger, Holzhauser, Martschinko, Rotpuller, Felipe Pires. Coach: Thorsten Fink (GER)
A 2-1 *Grünwald (58), Kayode (69)*
Almer, Filipovic, Kayode (Friesenbichler 78), Grünwald, Lucas Venuto (De Paula 76), Serbest, Stryger (Tajouri 89), Holzhauser, Martschinko, Rotpuller, Felipe Pires. Coach: Thorsten Fink (GER)

Group E
Match 1 - FC Astra Giurgiu (ROU)
A 3-2 *Holzhauser (16p), Friesenbichler (33), Grünwald (58)*
Hadzikic, Filipovic, Tajouri, Friesenbichler (Kayode 82), Grünwald, Serbest, De Paula (Stryger 37), Salamon, Holzhauser, Rotpuller, Felipe Pires (Lucas Venuto 62). Coach: Thorsten Fink (GER)
Red card: Rotpuller 79

Match 2 - FC Viktoria Plzeň (CZE)
H 0-0
Almer, Filipovic, Kayode (Friesenbichler 85), Grünwald, Lucas Venuto (Tajouri 79), Serbest, Stryger, Stronati, Holzhauser, Martschinko, Felipe Pires. Coach: Thorsten Fink (GER)
Match 3 - AS Roma (ITA)
A 3-3 *Holzhauser (16), Prokop (82), Kayode (84)*
Almer (Hadzikic 25), Filipovic, Kayode, Grünwald (Prokop 78), Lucas Venuto (Tajouri 76), Serbest, Stryger, Stronati, Holzhauser, Martschinko, Felipe Pires. Coach: Thorsten Fink (GER)
Match 4 - AS Roma (ITA)
H 2-4 *Kayode (2), Grünwald (89)*
Hadzikic, Filipovic, Kayode (Friesenbichler 71), Grünwald, Lucas Venuto (Tajouri 86), Serbest (Prokop 84), Stryger, Holzhauser, Martschinko, Rotpuller, Felipe Pires. Coach: Thorsten Fink (GER)
Match 5 - FC Astra Giurgiu (ROU)
H 1-2 *Rotpuller (57)*
Hadzikic, Filipovic, Kayode (Friesenbichler 90), Grünwald, Lucas Venuto (Tajouri 90), Serbest, Stryger, Holzhauser, Martschinko, Rotpuller, Felipe Pires. Coach: Thorsten Fink (GER)
Red card: Grünwald 65
Match 6 - FC Viktoria Plzeň (CZE)
A 2-3 *Holzhauser (19p), Rotpuller (40)*
Hadzikic, Filipovic, Kayode, Lucas Venuto (Kvasina 85), Serbest, Prokop (Friesenbichler 70), Stryger, Holzhauser, Martschinko, Rotpuller, Felipe Pires (Tajouri 77). Coach: Thorsten Fink (GER)

FC Admira Wacker Mödling

UEFA EUROPA LEAGUE

First qualifying round - TJ Spartak Myjava (SVK)
H 1-1 *Bajrami (34)*
Siebenhandl, Zwierschitz, Ebner, Lackner, Knasmüllner, Toth, Monschein (Vastic 59), Starkl (Pavic 74), Wostry, Bajrami, Spiridonovic. Coach: Oliver Lederer (AUT)
A 3-2 *Wostry (2), Starkl (27), Zwierschitz (57)*
Siebenhandl, Strauss, Zwierschitz, Ebner, Lackner, Knasmüllner (Toth 66), Grozurek (Sax 46), Starkl (Monschein 80), Pavic, Wostry, Bajrami. Coach: Oliver Lederer (AUT)

Second qualifying round - Käpäz PFK (AZE)
H 1-0 *Starkl (41)*
Siebenhandl, Strauss, Zwierschitz, Ebner, Lackner, Sax (Spiridonovic 58), Knasmüllner, Starkl (Monschein 75), Pavic, Wostry, Bajrami. Coach: Oliver Lederer (AUT)
A 2-0 *Knasmüllner (17), Schmidt (76)*
Siebenhandl, Zwierschitz, Ebner, Lackner, Sax (Ayyildiz 54), Knasmüllner (Fischerauer 75), Toth, Starkl (Schmidt 38), Pavic, Wostry, Bajrami. Coach: Oliver Lederer (AUT)

Third qualifying round - FC Slovan Liberec (CZE)
H 1-2 *Knasmüllner (7)*
Kuttin, Strauss, Zwierschitz, Ebner, Lackner, Sax, Knasmüllner, Toth (Vastic 56), Starkl, Wostry, Bajrami (Spiridonovic 56). Coach: Oliver Lederer (AUT)
Red card: Vastic 90
A 0-2
Kuttin, Strauss, Zwierschitz, Ebner, Lackner (Roguljić 88), Knasmüllner, Starkl (Grozurek 62), Wostry, Bajrami, Posch, Spiridonovic. Coach: Oliver Lederer (AUT)

DOMESTIC LEAGUE CLUB-BY-CLUB

FC Admira Wacker Mödling

1905 • BSFZ-Arena (12,000) • admirawacker.at

Major honours
Austrian League (9) 1927, 1928, 1932, 1934, 1936, 1937, 1939, 1947, 1966; Austrian Cup (6) 1928, 1932, 1934, 1947, 1964, 1966

Coach: Oliver Lederer;
(03/01/17) Damir Burić (CRO)

Date		Opponent		Score	Scorers
2016					
24/07	a	Mattersburg	W	1-0	*Knasmüllner*
31/07	a	St Pölten	L	1-2	*Spiridonovic (p)*
06/08	h	Altach	L	1-2	*Grozurek*
13/08	a	Rapid	L	0-4	
20/08	h	Ried	W	1-0	*Grozurek*
27/08	a	Wolfsberg	L	0-5	
11/09	h	Salzburg	L	0-4	
17/09	h	Sturm	L	0-3	
24/09	a	Austria Wien	W	2-1	*Sax, Monschein*
01/10	h	Mattersburg	W	1-0	*og (Mahrer)*
15/10	h	St Pölten	D	1-1	*Lackner*
22/10	a	Altach	L	0-2	
29/10	h	Rapid	L	1-2	*Knasmüllner*
05/11	a	Ried	L	1-2	*Monschein*
19/11	h	Wolfsberg	W	4-1	*Knasmüllner, Ebner 2, Monschein*
27/11	a	Salzburg	W	1-0	*Monschein*
30/11	a	Sturm	W	2-0	*Monschein, Sax*
03/12	h	Austria Wien	L	0-2	
10/12	a	Mattersburg	L	0-2	
17/12	a	St Pölten	D	2-2	*Monschein 2*
2017					
11/02	h	Altach	D	1-1	*Monschein*
18/02	a	Rapid	D	0-0	
25/02	h	Ried	W	1-0	*Starkl*
04/03	a	Wolfsberg	D	1-1	*Knasmüllner (p)*
11/03	h	Salzburg	D	1-1	*Sax*
18/03	h	Sturm	W	1-0	*Monschein*
01/04	a	Austria Wien	W	2-0	*Zwierschitz, Starkl*
08/04	h	Mattersburg	L	0-2	
15/04	h	St Pölten	W	2-0	*Knasmüllner 2*
22/04	a	Altach	D	0-0	
30/04	h	Rapid	W	3-2	*Sax, Knasmüllner (p), Monschein*
06/05	a	Ried	L	0-1	
13/05	h	Wolfsberg	W	3-2	*Sax, Zwierschitz, Schmidt*
20/05	a	Salzburg	L	0-2	
25/05	a	Sturm	L	1-2	*Sax*
28/05	h	Austria Wien	L	1-6	*Knasmüllner (p)*

No	Name	Nat	DoB	Pos	Aps	(s)	Gls
55	Ilter Ayyildiz		31/07/92	M	1	(2)	
27	Eldis Bajrami	MKD	12/12/92	M	18	(11)	
13	Markus Blutsch		01/06/95	M		(5)	
5	Thomas Ebner		22/02/92	D	33		2
11	Lukas Grozurek		22/12/91	M	8	(11)	2
31	Ione Cabrera	ESP	13/10/85	D	2		
8	Christoph Knasmüllner		30/04/92	M	31	(4)	8
29	Manuel Kuttin		17/12/93	G	8		
6	Markus Lackner		05/04/91	M	33		1
1	Andreas Leitner		25/03/94	G	27		
19	Nico Löffler		05/07/97	M		(1)	
22	Marcus Maier		18/12/95	M	2	(2)	
12	Lukas Malicsek		06/06/99	D		(1)	
15	Manuel Maranda		09/07/97	D	10	(3)	
14	Christoph Monschein		22/10/92	A	26	(2)	10
20	Markus Pavic		26/03/95	D	8		
32	Philipp Posch		09/01/94	D	7	(5)	
44	Ante Roguljić	CRO	11/03/96	M	2	(1)	
7	Maximilian Sax		22/11/92	M	25	(4)	6
16	Patrick Schmidt		22/07/98	A	4	(11)	1
28	Jörg Siebenhandl		18/01/90	G	1		
93	Srdjan Spiridonovic		13/10/93	M	10	(8)	1
17	Dominik Starkl		06/11/93	A	13	(13)	2
2	Fabio Strauss		06/08/94	D	22	(1)	
10	Daniel Toth		10/06/87	M	29	(3)	
9	Toni Vastic		17/01/93	A	3	(11)	
25	Patrick Wessely		27/03/94	D	5	(3)	
21	Markus Wostry		19/07/92	D	33		
4	Stephan Zwierschitz		17/09/90	D	35		2

SCR Altach

1929 • Cashpoint-Arena (8,500) • scra.at

Coach: Damir Canadi;
(11/11/16) (Werner Grabherr);
(23/12/16) Martin Scherb

Date		Opponent		Score	Scorers
2016					
23/07	h	Wolfsberg	W	1-0	*Oberlin*
31/07	h	Rapid	W	1-0	*Salomon*
06/08	a	Admira	W	2-1	*Oberlin 2*
13/08	h	St Pölten	W	3-1	*Oberlin 2, Dovedan*
21/08	a	Austria Wien	L	1-3	*Oberlin*
27/08	a	Sturm	L	1-3	*Dovedan*
10/09	h	Mattersburg	W	2-1	*Zivotic 2*
17/09	a	Ried	L	1-2	*Ngwat-Mahop*
25/09	h	Salzburg	D	0-0	
01/10	a	Wolfsberg	W	2-1	*Ngamaleu, Oberlin (p)*
15/10	a	Rapid	D	1-1	*Ngamaleu*
22/10	h	Admira	W	2-0	*Netzer, Dovedan*
29/10	a	St Pölten	W	1-0	*Salomon*
06/11	h	Austria Wien	W	5-1	*Ngamaleu, Dovedan 2, Lienhart, Oberlin*
19/11	h	Sturm	D	1-1	*Oberlin*
26/11	a	Mattersburg	W	2-1	*Dovedan, Ngwat-Mahop*
29/11	h	Ried	W	1-0	*Prokopic*
03/12	a	Salzburg	L	1-4	*og (Paulo Miranda)*
10/12	h	Wolfsberg	W	2-1	*Prokopic, Ngwat-Mahop*
18/12	h	Rapid	W	3-1	*Netzer 2, Dovedan*
2017					
11/02	a	Admira	D	1-1	*Ngamaleu (p)*
18/02	h	St Pölten	L	1-2	*Ngamaleu*
25/02	a	Austria Wien	W	3-1	*Ngamaleu, Dovedan 2 (1p)*
04/03	a	Sturm	L	0-3	
11/03	h	Mattersburg	W	3-0	*Aigner, Sakic, Ngamaleu*
18/03	a	Ried	L	0-2	
02/04	h	Salzburg	L	0-5	
08/04	a	Wolfsberg	D	0-0	
15/04	a	Rapid	L	0-3	
22/04	h	Admira	D	0-0	
29/04	a	St Pölten	D	3-3	*Ngwat-Mahop, Zwischenbrugger, Aigner (p)*
07/05	h	Austria Wien	D	1-1	*Dovedan*
14/05	h	Sturm	L	1-2	*Netzer*
20/05	a	Mattersburg	L	0-1	
25/05	h	Ried	L	0-2	
28/05	a	Salzburg	L	0-1	

No	Name	Nat	DoB	Pos	Aps	(s)	Gls
25	Hannes Aigner		16/03/81	A	7	(6)	2
4	César Ortiz	ESP	30/01/89	D	4	(2)	
11	Nikola Dovedan		06/07/94	M	25	(7)	10
9	Martin Harrer		19/05/92	A	3	(12)	
22	Lukas Jäger		12/02/94	D	33	(1)	
32	Bernhard Janeczek		10/03/92	D	8	(1)	
1	Martin Kobras		19/06/86	G	9	(1)	
7	Andreas Lienhart		28/01/86	M	29	(2)	1
3	Lucas Galvão	BRA	22/06/91	D	27		
15	Gabriel Lüchinger		18/12/92	M		(2)	
12	Andreas Lukse		08/11/87	G	27		
21	Daniel Luxbacher		13/03/92	M	17	(9)	
17	Valentino Müller		19/01/99	M	3	(5)	
5	Philipp Netzer		02/10/85	D	33		4
13	Nicolas Ngamaleu	CMR	09/07/94	M	24	(4)	7
29	Louis Ngwat-Mahop	CMR	16/09/87	A	25	(3)	4
20	Daniel Nussbaumer		29/11/99	M		(1)	
37	Dimitri Oberlin	SUI	27/09/97	A	14	(6)	9
28	Boris Prokopic		29/03/88	M	17	(1)	2
6	Emanuel Sakic		25/01/91	M	8	(8)	1
10	Patrick Salomon		10/06/88	M	21	(9)	2
27	Christian Schilling		06/01/92	D	1	(2)	
16	Emanuel Schreiner		02/02/89	M	26		
23	Benedikt Zech		03/11/90	D	27		
14	Nikola Zivotic		26/01/96	A	1	(19)	2
18	Jan Zwischenbrugger		16/06/90	D	7	(7)	1

FK Austria Wien

1911 • Ernst-Happel-Stadion (50,865) • fk-austria.at

Major honours
Austrian League (24) 1924, 1926, 1949, 1950, 1953, 1961, 1962, 1963, 1969, 1970, 1976, 1978, 1979, 1980, 1981, 1984, 1985, 1986, 1991, 1992, 1993, 2003, 2006, 2013; Austrian Cup (27) 1921, 1924, 1925, 1926, 1933, 1935, 1936, 1948, 1949, 1960, 1962, 1963, 1967, 1971, 1974, 1977, 1980, 1982, 1986, 1990, 1992, 1994, 2003, 2005, 2006, 2007, 2009

Coach: Thorsten Fink (GER)

Date		Opponent		Score	Scorers
2016					
24/07	a	St Pölten	W	2-1	*Kayode, Tajouri*
31/07	h	Mattersburg	W	3-1	*Lucas Venuto 2 (1p), Tajouri*
07/08	h	Rapid	L	1-4	*Kayode*
14/08	a	Sturm	L	1-3	*Filipovic*
21/08	h	Altach	W	3-1	*Tajouri, Friesenbichler 2*
28/08	a	Ried	D	1-1	*Tajouri*
10/09	h	Wolfsberg	W	4-1	*Lucas Venuto, Holzhauser, Grünwald 2*
18/09	a	Salzburg	L	1-4	*Grünwald*
24/09	h	Admira	L	1-2	*Tajouri*
02/10	h	St Pölten	W	2-1	*Serbest, Kayode*
16/10	a	Mattersburg	W	2-0	*Grünwald, Martschinko*
23/10	a	Rapid	W	2-0	*Holzhauser (p), Grünwald*
30/10	h	Sturm	W	2-0	*Holzhauser (p), Kayode*
06/11	a	Altach	L	1-5	*Filipovic*
19/11	h	Ried	W	2-0	*Grünwald, Kayode*
27/11	a	Wolfsberg	W	3-0	*Tajouri, Lucas Venuto, Friesenbichler*
30/11	h	Salzburg	L	1-3	*Kayode*
03/12	a	Admira	W	2-0	*Kayode, Holzhauser (p)*
11/12	a	St Pölten	L	1-2	*Holzhauser*
17/12	h	Mattersburg	W	2-0	*Lucas Venuto, Filipovic*
2017					
12/02	h	Rapid	D	1-1	*Rotpuller*
18/02	a	Sturm	W	4-0	*Grünwald, Rotpuller, Friesenbichler, Felipe Pires*
25/02	h	Altach	L	1-3	*Holzhauser (p)*
04/03	a	Ried	W	3-0	*Holzhauser, Kayode, Lucas Venuto*
11/03	h	Wolfsberg	W	3-0	*og (Sollbauer), Grünwald, Kayode*
19/03	a	Salzburg	L	0-5	
01/04	h	Admira	L	0-2	
08/04	h	St Pölten	L	1-2	*Kayode*
16/04	a	Mattersburg	W	3-0	*Kayode, Grünwald, Felipe Pires*
23/04	a	Rapid	W	2-0	*Lucas Venuto, Felipe Pires*
29/04	h	Sturm	W	4-1	*Tajouri, Filipovic, Kayode 2*
07/05	a	Altach	D	1-1	*Kayode*
13/05	h	Ried	W	3-0	*Kayode 2, Serbest*
20/05	a	Wolfsberg	L	1-2	*Felipe Pires*
25/05	h	Salzburg	L	2-3	*og (Ulmer), Kayode*
28/05	a	Admira	W	6-1	*Grünwald 2, Holzhauser (p), Prokop, Tajouri, Friesenbichler*

No	Name	Nat	DoB	Pos	Aps	(s)	Gls
1	Robert Almer		20/03/84	G	9		
19	Michael Blauensteiner		11/02/95	M		(1)	
24	Alexandar Borkovic		11/06/99	D	1	(1)	
23	David De Paula	ESP	03/05/84	D	6	(6)	
95	Felipe Pires	BRA	18/04/95	M	30	(4)	4
4	Petar Filipovic	GER	14/09/90	D	31		4
9	Kevin Friesenbichler		06/05/94	A	11	(21)	5
2	Petar Gluhakovic		25/03/96	D		(1)	
10	Alexander Grünwald		01/05/89	M	33	(3)	11
31	Osman Hadzikic		12/03/96	G	27		
26	Raphael Holzhauser		16/02/93	M	35		8
8	Olarenwaju Kayode	NGA	08/05/93	A	27	(6)	17
19	Roi Kehat	ISR	12/05/92	M	1		
27	Marko Kvasina		20/12/96	A	1	(15)	
11	Lucas Venuto	BRA	14/01/95	M	26	(3)	7
28	Christoph Martschinko		13/02/94	D	22	(1)	1
6	Abdul Mohammed	GHA	07/03/96	M	6	(4)	
16	Dominik Prokop		02/06/97	M	2	(11)	1
33	Lukas Rotpuller		31/03/91	D	29		2
25	Thomas Salamon		18/01/89	D	14	(2)	
15	Tarkan Serbest		02/05/94	M	31	(2)	2
18	Patrizio Stronati	CZE	17/11/94	D		(2)	
17	Jens Stryger	DEN	21/02/91	D	29		
7	Ismael Tajouri	LBY	28/03/94	M	15	(17)	8
5	Ognjen Vukojević	CRO	20/12/83	M	3		
3	Richard Windbichler		02/04/91	D	7	(4)	

SV Mattersburg

1922 • Pappelstadion (15,700) • svm.at

Coach: Ivica Vastic; (02/01/17) Gerald Baumgartner

Date		Opponent		Score	Scorers
2016					
24/07	h	Admira	L	0-1	
31/07	a	Austria Wien	L	1-3	*Bürger*
06/08	h	Sturm	L	0-2	
13/08	h	Wolfsberg	W	3-1	*Perlak 2 (2p), Pink*
20/08	a	Salzburg	L	1-3	*Röcher*
27/08	h	St Pölten	D	1-1	*Mahrer*
10/09	a	Altach	L	1-2	*Perlak (p)*
18/09	a	Rapid	L	0-3	
24/09	h	Ried	D	1-1	*Grgic*
01/10	a	Admira	L	0-1	
16/10	h	Austria Wien	L	0-2	
22/10	a	Sturm	D	2-2	*Bürger, Fran*
29/10	a	Wolfsberg	L	0-3	
06/11	h	Salzburg	W	2-1	*Erhardt, Jano*
19/11	a	St Pölten	D	2-2	*Varga, Röcher*
26/11	h	Altach	L	1-2	*Templ*
30/11	h	Rapid	D	1-1	*Jano*
03/12	a	Ried	L	1-2	*Bürger*
10/12	h	Admira	W	2-0	*Fran, Templ*
17/12	a	Austria Wien	L	0-2	
2017					
11/02	h	Sturm	W	1-0	*Röcher*
18/02	h	Wolfsberg	W	2-1	*Röcher, Maierhofer*
25/02	a	Salzburg	L	0-1	
04/03	h	St Pölten	W	1-0	*Fran*
11/03	a	Altach	L	0-3	
18/03	a	Rapid	D	1-1	*Atanga*
01/04	h	Ried	W	2-1	*Bürger 2*
08/04	a	Admira	W	2-0	*Röcher, Bürger*
16/04	h	Austria Wien	L	0-3	
22/04	a	Sturm	W	2-0	*Atanga, Bürger*
29/04	a	Wolfsberg	D	2-2	*Röcher, Höller*
06/05	h	Salzburg	W	2-1	*Maierhofer, Atanga*
13/05	a	St Pölten	L	0-1	
20/05	h	Altach	W	1-0	*Höller*
25/05	h	Rapid	L	1-3	*Höller*
28/05	a	Ried	W	3-2	*Perlak, Bürger, Seidl*

No	Name	Nat	DoB	Pos	Aps	(s)	Gls
29	David Atanga	GHA	25/12/96	M	15		3
22	Markus Böcskör		01/10/82	G	6		
33	Patrick Bürger		27/06/87	A	17	(14)	8
5	César Ortiz	ESP	30/01/89	D	12		
6	Philipp Erhardt		10/09/93	D	24	(1)	1
23	Julius Ertlthaler		25/04/97	M	2	(7)	
17	Patrick Farkas		09/09/92	M	22	(5)	
26	Fran	ESP	08/02/90	D	6	(7)	3
16	Mario Grgic		10/09/91	M	6	(9)	1
8	Alois Höller		15/03/89	D	32	(1)	3
11	Alexander Ibser		19/02/91	M	5	(9)	
10	Jano	ESP	23/12/86	M	34	(1)	2
21	Markus Kuster		22/02/94	G	30		
28	Francesco Lovric		05/10/95	M	1		
31	Thorsten Mahrer		22/01/90	D	12	(7)	1
19	Stefan Maierhofer		16/08/82	A	11	(3)	2
2	Vitālijs Maksimenko	LVA	08/12/90	D	17	(1)	
4	Nedeljko Malić	BIH	15/05/88	D	25		
25	Michael Novak		30/12/90	D	14	(2)	
20	Michael Perlak		26/12/85	M	18	(5)	4
32	Markus Pink		24/02/91	A	3	(11)	1
18	Lukas Rath		18/01/92	D	25	(1)	
27	Thorsten Röcher		11/06/91	M	31	(3)	6
7	Manuel Seidl		26/10/88	M	2	(3)	1
15	Sven Sprangler		27/03/95	M	12	(2)	
13	Florian Templ		01/10/88	A	9	(9)	2
9	Barnabás Varga	HUN	25/01/94	A	5	(6)	1

SK Rapid Wien

1899 • Allianz Stadion (28,000) • skrapid.at

Major honours
Austrian League (32) 1912, 1913, 1916, 1917, 1919, 1920, 1921, 1923, 1929, 1930, 1935, 1938, 1940, 1941, 1946, 1948, 1951, 1952, 1954, 1956, 1957, 1960, 1964, 1967, 1968, 1982, 1983, 1987, 1988, 1996, 2005, 2008; German League (1) 1941; Austrian Cup (14) 1919, 1920, 1927, 1946, 1961, 1968, 1969, 1972, 1976, 1983, 1984, 1985, 1987, 1995; German Cup (1) 1938

Coach: Mike Büskens (GER); (11/11/16) Damir Canadi (10/04/17) (Goran Djuricin)

Date		Opponent		Score	Scorers
2016					
23/07	h	Ried	W	5-0	*Schösswendter, Schaub, Murg 2, Joelinton*
31/07	a	Altach	L	0-1	
07/08	a	Austria Wien	W	4-1	*Traustason, Schaub, Grahovac, Joelinton*
13/08	h	Admira	W	4-0	*Schaub 2, Schwab 2*
21/08	a	Wolfsberg	D	1-1	*Schösswendter*
28/08	h	Salzburg	D	0-0	
10/09	a	Sturm	D	1-1	*Szántó*
18/09	h	Mattersburg	W	3-0	*Schaub, Szántó, Pavelic*
24/09	a	St Pölten	D	1-1	*Joelinton (p)*
02/10	a	Ried	L	2-4	*Schwab 2*
15/10	h	Altach	D	1-1	*Schösswendter*
23/10	h	Austria Wien	L	0-2	
29/10	a	Admira	W	2-1	*Szántó, Murg*
06/11	h	Wolfsberg	L	0-1	
20/11	a	Salzburg	L	1-2	*Tomi Correa (p)*
27/11	h	Sturm	L	1-2	*Kvilitaia*
30/11	a	Mattersburg	D	1-1	*Malicsek*
03/12	h	St Pölten	W	1-0	*Traustason*
11/12	h	Ried	W	3-1	*Sonnleitner, Kvilitaia 2 (1p)*
18/12	a	Altach	L	1-3	*Grahovac*
2017					
12/02	a	Austria Wien	D	1-1	*Kvilitaia*
18/02	h	Admira	D	0-0	
25/02	a	Wolfsberg	L	1-2	*Sonnleitner*
05/03	h	Salzburg	L	0-1	
12/03	a	Sturm	L	1-2	*Joelinton*
18/03	h	Mattersburg	D	1-1	*Kvilitaia*
01/04	a	St Pölten	D	1-1	*Joelinton*
08/04	a	Ried	L	0-3	
15/04	h	Altach	W	3-0	*S Hofmann 2 (1p), Malicsek*
23/04	h	Austria Wien	L	0-2	
30/04	a	Admira	L	2-3	*Szántó, Joelinton*
06/05	h	Wolfsberg	W	4-0	*Kvilitaia 2, Joelinton, Schwab*
13/05	a	Salzburg	L	0-1	
21/05	h	Sturm	W	1-0	*Szántó*
25/05	a	Mattersburg	W	3-1	*Joelinton, Traustason, og (Malić)*
28/05	h	St Pölten	W	2-1	*Dibon, Schösswendter*

No	Name	Nat	DoB	Pos	Aps	(s)	Gls
36	Kelvin Arase		15/01/99	M		(2)	
24	Stephan Auer		11/01/91	D	15	(3)	
17	Christopher Dibon		02/11/90	D	26		1
25	Andreas Dober		31/03/86	D	1		
99	Maximilian Entrup		25/07/97	A		(2)	
15	Srdjan Grahovac	BIH	19/09/92	M	12	(8)	2
20	Maximilian Hofmann		07/08/93	D	16	(3)	
11	Steffen Hofmann	GER	09/09/80	M	7	(8)	2
9	Matej Jelić	CRO	05/11/90	A	5	(5)	
34	Joelinton	BRA	14/08/96	A	26	(7)	8
21	Tobias Knoflach		30/12/93	G	15		
27	Andreas Kuen		24/03/95	M	8		
13	Giorgi Kvilitaia	GEO	01/10/93	A	17	(9)	7
16	Philipp Malicsek		03/06/97	M	2	(7)	2
26	Ivan Močinić	CRO	30/04/93	M	11	(3)	
29	Thomas Murg		14/11/94	M	19	(7)	3
1	Ján Novota	SVK	29/11/83	G	4		
41	Osarenren Okungbowa		13/05/94	M	1	(1)	
22	Mario Pavelic		19/09/93	D	28		1
10	Louis Schaub		29/12/94	M	26	(2)	5
7	Philipp Schobesberger		10/12/93	M	4	(1)	
3	Christoph Schösswendter		16/07/88	D	20	(2)	4
4	Thomas Schrammel		05/09/87	D	22	(4)	
8	Stefan Schwab		27/09/90	M	27		5
43	Alex Sobczyk		20/05/97	A		(1)	
6	Mario Sonnleitner		08/10/86	D	17	(3)	2
30	Richard Strebinger		14/02/93	G	17		
18	Tamás Szántó	HUN	18/02/96	M	18	(11)	5
38	Manuel Thurnwald		16/07/98	D	9	(2)	
28	Tomi Correa	ESP	05/12/84	A		(2)	1
23	Arnór Ingvi Traustason	ISL	30/04/93	M	14	(8)	3
39	Maximilian Wöber		04/02/98	D	9	(2)	

AUSTRIA

SV Ried

1912 • Keine Sorgen Arena (7,680) • svried.at

Major honours
Austrian Cup (2) 1998, 2011

Coach: Christian Benbennek (GER); (01/03/17) Lassaad Chabbi

Date		Opponent		Score	Scorers
2016					
23/07	a	Rapid	L	0-5	
30/07	h	Sturm	W	1-0	*Zulj*
06/08	a	Wolfsberg	L	0-1	
13/08	h	Salzburg	L	0-2	
20/08	a	Admira	L	0-1	
28/08	h	Austria Wien	D	1-1	*Honsak*
10/09	a	St Pölten	W	3-2	*Walch 2, Ademi*
17/09	h	Altach	W	2-1	*Walch, Ronny Marcos*
24/09	a	Mattersburg	D	1-1	*Zulj (p)*
02/10	h	Rapid	W	4-2	*Honsak, Zulj, Reifeltshammer, Nutz*
15/10	a	Sturm	L	0-1	
22/10	h	Wolfsberg	L	0-1	
29/10	a	Salzburg	L	0-1	
05/11	h	Admira	W	2-1	*og (Wostry), Möschl*
19/11	a	Austria Wien	L	0-2	
26/11	h	St Pölten	L	1-2	*Reifeltshammer*
29/11	a	Altach	L	0-1	
03/12	h	Mattersburg	W	2-1	*Möschl, Reifeltshammer*
11/12	a	Rapid	L	1-3	*Elsneg*
17/12	h	Sturm	L	0-3	
2017					
11/02	a	Wolfsberg	L	0-1	
19/02	h	Salzburg	L	1-6	*Egho*
25/02	a	Admira	L	0-1	
04/03	h	Austria Wien	L	0-3	
11/03	a	St Pölten	L	0-1	
18/03	h	Altach	W	2-0	*Möschl, Honsak*
01/04	a	Mattersburg	L	1-2	*Ademi*
08/04	h	Rapid	W	3-0	*Elsneg, Zulj, Hart*
15/04	a	Sturm	L	0-1	
22/04	h	Wolfsberg	D	1-1	*Ademi*
29/04	a	Salzburg	D	1-1	*Zulj (p)*
06/05	h	Admira	W	1-0	*Fröschl*
13/05	a	Austria Wien	L	0-3	
20/05	h	St Pölten	D	1-1	*Reifeltshammer*
25/05	a	Altach	W	2-0	*Möschl, Zulj*
28/05	h	Mattersburg	L	2-3	*Nutz, Möschl*

No	Name	Nat	DoB	Pos	Aps	(s)	Gls
9	Orhan Ademi	SUI	28/10/91	A	23	(5)	3
24	Alberto Prada	ESP	19/01/89	D	12	(8)	
5	Nico Antonitsch		30/09/91	D	3	(3)	
14	Thomas Bergmann		20/09/89	D	10	(6)	
13	Michael Brandner		13/02/95	M	7	(9)	
15	Dennis Chessa	GER	19/10/92	D	19	(2)	
34	Reuf Duraković	BIH	21/03/94	G	5		
17	Marvin Egho		09/05/94	A	4	(6)	1
20	Dieter Elsneg		04/02/90	M	25	(8)	2
19	Thomas Fröschl		20/09/88	A	6	(18)	1
1	Thomas Gebauer	GER	30/06/82	G	31		
12	Florian Hart		11/05/90	D	28		1
11	Mathias Honsak		20/12/96	M	19	(5)	3
25	Patrick Möschl		06/03/93	M	22	(9)	5
7	Stefan Nutz		15/02/92	M	15	(5)	2
6	Özgür Özdemir	TUR	10/01/95	D	31	(1)	
28	Thomas Reifeltshammer		03/07/88	D	35		4
3	Ronny Marcos	MOZ	01/10/93	D	16	(3)	1
22	Fabian Schubert		29/08/94	A		(2)	
8	Gernot Trauner		25/03/92	M	8	(2)	
33	Clemens Walch		10/07/87	M	17	(8)	3
4	Marcel Ziegl		20/12/92	M	30	(1)	
10	Peter Zulj		09/06/93	M	30	(3)	6

FC Salzburg

1933 • Bullen Arena Wals-Siezenheim (30,900) • redbullsalzburg.at

Major honours
Austrian League (11) 1994, 1995, 1997, 2007, 2009, 2010, 2012, 2014, 2015, 2016, 2017; Austrian Cup (5) 2012, 2014, 2015, 2016, 2017

Coach: Óscar García (ESP)

Date		Opponent		Score	Scorers
2016					
23/07	a	Sturm	L	1-3	*Gulbrandsen*
30/07	h	Wolfsberg	D	1-1	*Jonatan Soriano (p)*
06/08	h	St Pölten	W	2-0	*Dabbur, Lainer*
13/08	a	Ried	W	2-0	*Bernardo, V Berisha*
20/08	h	Mattersburg	W	3-1	*Minamino, Lainer, Laimer*
28/08	a	Rapid	D	0-0	
11/09	a	Admira	W	4-0	*Jonatan Soriano, Paulo Miranda, Minamino 2*
18/09	h	Austria Wien	W	4-1	*Jonatan Soriano 3, Wanderson*
25/09	a	Altach	D	0-0	
02/10	h	Sturm	L	0-1	
15/10	a	Wolfsberg	D	2-2	*Lazaro, Jonatan Soriano*
23/10	a	St Pölten	W	5-1	*Hwang 2, Rzatkowski, Lainer, Gulbrandsen*
29/10	h	Ried	W	1-0	*Hwang*
06/11	a	Mattersburg	L	1-2	*V Berisha*
20/11	h	Rapid	W	2-1	*Dabbur, Lainer*
27/11	h	Admira	L	0-1	
30/11	a	Austria Wien	W	3-1	*og (Martschinko), Laimer, Minamino*
03/12	h	Altach	W	4-1	*Lainer, V Berisha, Paulo Miranda, Hwang*
11/12	a	Sturm	W	1-0	*V Berisha*
17/12	h	Wolfsberg	W	3-0	*Minamino 2, Ulmer*
2017					
11/02	h	St Pölten	W	2-0	*Jonatan Soriano, Laimer*
19/02	a	Ried	W	6-1	*Jonatan Soriano, Minamino 3, Radošević, Hwang (p)*
25/02	h	Mattersburg	W	1-0	*Oberlin*
05/03	a	Rapid	W	1-0	*V Berisha*
11/03	a	Admira	D	1-1	*Schlager*
19/03	h	Austria Wien	W	5-0	*V Berisha, Ulmer, Hwang 2, Radošević*
02/04	a	Altach	W	5-0	*Ulmer 2, og (Netzer), Minamino 2*
09/04	h	Sturm	W	1-0	*Radošević*
15/04	a	Wolfsberg	W	2-0	*V Berisha (p), Lainer*
22/04	a	St Pölten	W	2-1	*Hwang, Wanderson*
29/04	h	Ried	D	1-1	*Hwang*
06/05	a	Mattersburg	L	1-2	*Wanderson*
13/05	h	Rapid	W	1-0	*Lazaro*
20/05	h	Admira	W	2-0	*Hwang 2*
25/05	a	Austria Wien	W	3-2	*Haidara, Hwang, Lazaro*
28/05	h	Altach	W	1-0	*og (Zivotic)*

No	Name	Nat	DoB	Pos	Aps	(s)	Gls
37	Mergim Berisha	KOS	11/05/98	A		(1)	
14	Valon Berisha	KOS	07/02/93	M	33	(1)	7
95	Bernardo	BRA	14/05/95	D	3		1
5	Duje Ćaleta-Car	CRO	17/09/96	D	17	(1)	
9	Munas Dabbur	ISR	14/05/92	A	12	(3)	2
21	Fredrik Gulbrandsen	NOR	10/09/92	A	4	(5)	2
4	Amadou Haidara	MLI	31/01/98	M	1	(4)	1
36	Martin Hinteregger		07/09/92	D	5		
19	Hwang Hee-chan	KOR	26/01/96	A	20	(6)	12
44	Igor	BRA	02/07/98	D	1		
26	Jonatan Soriano	ESP	24/09/85	A	12	(1)	8
27	Konrad Laimer		27/05/97	M	27	(4)	3
22	Stefan Lainer		27/08/92	D	30	(1)	6
10	Valentino Lazaro		24/03/96	M	26	(3)	3
24	Christoph Leitgeb		14/04/85	M	1	(7)	
18	Takumi Minamino	JPN	16/01/95	A	11	(10)	11
77	Dimitri Oberlin	SUI	27/09/97	A	1	(4)	1
3	Paulo Miranda	BRA	16/08/88	D	27		2
25	Josip Radošević	CRO	03/04/94	M	8	(12)	3
15	Yordy Reyna	PER	17/09/93	A	2		
11	Marc Rzatkowski	GER	02/03/90	M	6	(1)	1
8	Diadie Samassékou	MLI	11/01/96	M	24	(3)	
42	Xaver Schlager		28/09/97	M	7	(6)	1
6	Christian Schwegler	SUI	06/06/84	D	10	(3)	
23	Stefan Stangl		20/10/91	D	5	(1)	
1	Cican Stankovic		04/11/92	G	2		
17	Andreas Ulmer		30/10/85	D	29	(1)	4
4	Dayot Upamecano	FRA	27/10/98	D	15		
33	Alexander Walke	GER	06/06/83	G	34		
94	Wanderson	BEL	07/10/94	M	9	(11)	3
47	Andre Wisdom	ENG	09/05/93	D	13	(3)	
13	Hannes Wolf		16/04/99	A	1	(2)	
7	Reinhold Yabo	GER	10/02/92	M		(2)	

SKN St Pölten

2000 • NV-Arena (8,000) • skn-stpoelten.at

Coach: Karl Daxbacher; (25/10/16) Jochen Fallmann

Date		Opponent		Score	Scorers
2016					
24/07	h	Austria Wien	L	1-2	*Hartl*
31/07	h	Admira	W	2-1	*Hartl, Schütz*
06/08	a	Salzburg	L	0-2	
13/08	a	Altach	L	1-3	*Schütz*
20/08	h	Sturm	L	1-3	*Daniel Lucas*
27/08	a	Mattersburg	D	1-1	*Daniel Lucas*
10/09	h	Ried	L	2-3	*Dober, Daniel Lucas*
17/09	a	Wolfsberg	D	1-1	*Perchtold*
24/09	h	Rapid	D	1-1	*Petrovic*
02/10	a	Austria Wien	L	1-2	*Lumu*
15/10	a	Admira	D	1-1	*Luckassen*
23/10	h	Salzburg	L	1-5	*Luckassen*
29/10	h	Altach	L	0-1	
05/11	a	Sturm	W	2-1	*Holzmann, Ambichl*
19/11	h	Mattersburg	D	2-2	*Holzmann, Keita (p)*
26/11	a	Ried	W	2-1	*Petrovic, Lumu*
30/11	h	Wolfsberg	L	0-4	
03/12	a	Rapid	L	0-1	
11/12	h	Austria Wien	W	2-1	*Schütz, Keita*
17/12	h	Admira	D	2-2	*Thürauer, Daniel Lucas (p)*
2017					
11/02	a	Salzburg	L	0-2	
18/02	a	Altach	W	2-1	*Dieng, Thürauer*
26/02	h	Sturm	W	2-1	*Doumbouya (p), Hartl*
04/03	a	Mattersburg	L	0-1	
11/03	h	Ried	W	1-0	*Perchtold*
18/03	a	Wolfsberg	L	0-1	
01/04	h	Rapid	D	1-1	*Huber*
08/04	a	Austria Wien	W	2-1	*og (Stryger), Doumbouya (p)*
15/04	a	Admira	L	0-2	
22/04	h	Salzburg	L	1-2	*Thürauer*
29/04	h	Altach	D	3-3	*Luckassen 2, Martic*
06/05	a	Sturm	L	2-3	*Schütz, Petrovic*
13/05	h	Mattersburg	W	1-0	*Martic*
20/05	a	Ried	D	1-1	*Perchtold*
25/05	h	Wolfsberg	D	1-1	*Ambichl*
28/05	a	Rapid	L	1-2	*Doumbouya (p)*

No	Name	Nat	DoB	Pos	Aps	(s)	Gls
8	Michael Ambichl		26/04/91	M	23	(5)	2
7	Peter Brandl		17/07/88	M	4	(5)	
12	Daniel Lucas	ESP	23/05/85	A	11	(6)	4
21	Babacar Diallo	SEN	25/03/89	D	12		
10	Cheikhou Dieng	SEN	23/11/93	M	12	(1)	1
25	Andreas Dober		31/03/86	D	11	(3)	1
87	Lonsana Doumbouya	GUI	26/09/90	A	11	(2)	3
11	Christopher Drazan		02/10/90	A	4	(5)	
15	Martin Grasegger		10/01/89	D	12	(2)	
19	Manuel Hartl		31/12/85	M	14	(7)	3
5	Kai Heerings	NED	12/01/90	D	2	(3)	
23	Marcel Holzmann		03/09/90	D	6		2
3	Michael Huber		14/01/90	D	30	(1)	1
99	Alhassane Keita	GUI	26/06/83	A	8	(3)	2
55	Ümit Korkmaz		17/09/85	M	4	(7)	
9	Kevin Luckassen	NED	26/07/93	A	12	(11)	4
27	Jeroen Lumu	NED	27/05/95	M	5	(7)	2
10	Florian Mader		14/09/82	M	11	(2)	
17	Manuel Martic		15/08/95	M	19	(4)	2
4	Adi Mehremić	BIH	26/04/92	D	11	(2)	
77	Mario Mosböck		07/05/96	A		(1)	
2	Ahmet Muhamedbegovic		30/10/98	D	1		
18	Paul Pârvulescu	ROU	11/08/88	D	17	(3)	
26	Marco Perchtold		21/09/88	M	18	(5)	3
6	Danijel Petrovic		27/11/92	D	24	(2)	3
1	Christoph Riegler		30/03/92	G	27		
20	Daniel Schütz		19/06/91	M	25	(3)	4
29	David Stec		10/05/94	D	34		
13	Lukas Thürauer		21/12/87	M	19	(8)	3
32	Thomas Vollnhofer		02/09/84	G	9	(1)	
28	Aleksandar Vucenovic		10/10/97	A		(1)	

SK Sturm Graz

1909 • Merkur-Arena (16,600) • sksturm.at

Major honours
Austrian League (3) 1998, 1999, 2011; Austrian Cup (4) 1996, 1997, 1999, 2010

Coach: Franco Foda (GER)

Date		Opponent		Score	Scorers
2016					
23/07	h	Salzburg	W	3-1	*Matić, Schmerböck, Alar*
30/07	a	Ried	L	0-1	
06/08	a	Mattersburg	W	2-0	*Alar, Edomwonyi*
14/08	h	Austria Wien	W	3-1	*Alar 2, Huspek*
20/08	a	St Pölten	W	3-1	*Edomwonyi, Spendlhofer, Matić*
27/08	h	Altach	W	3-1	*Schulz, Alar, Hierländer*
10/09	h	Rapid	D	1-1	*Schulz*
17/09	a	Admira	W	3-0	*Alar 2, Spendlhofer*
24/09	h	Wolfsberg	W	3-0	*Alar 2, Edomwonyi*
02/10	a	Salzburg	W	1-0	*Alar*
15/10	h	Ried	W	1-0	*Edomwonyi*
22/10	h	Mattersburg	D	2-2	*Alar, Hierländer*
30/10	a	Austria Wien	L	0-2	
05/11	h	St Pölten	L	1-2	*Koch*
19/11	a	Altach	D	1-1	*Koch*
27/11	a	Rapid	W	2-1	*Lykogiannis, Schmerböck*
30/11	h	Admira	L	0-2	
04/12	a	Wolfsberg	W	4-0	*Schmerböck, Lykogiannis, Koch, Hierländer*
11/12	h	Salzburg	L	0-1	
17/12	a	Ried	W	3-0	*Alar 2, Matić*
2017					
11/02	a	Mattersburg	L	0-1	
18/02	h	Austria Wien	L	0-4	
26/02	a	St Pölten	L	1-2	*Schoissengeyr*
04/03	h	Altach	W	3-0	*Hierländer, Barış, Schmerböck*
12/03	h	Rapid	W	2-1	*Alar (p), Lykogiannis*
18/03	a	Admira	L	0-1	
01/04	h	Wolfsberg	W	4-0	*Barış, Piesinger, Alar, Schmerböck*
09/04	a	Salzburg	L	0-1	
15/04	h	Ried	W	1-0	*Zulechner*
22/04	h	Mattersburg	L	0-2	
29/04	a	Austria Wien	L	1-4	*Barış*
06/05	h	St Pölten	W	3-2	*Hierländer, Alar, Schmerböck*
14/05	a	Altach	W	2-1	*Schulz, Barış*
21/05	a	Rapid	L	0-1	
25/05	h	Admira	W	2-1	*Barış, Zulechner*
28/05	a	Wolfsberg	L	0-1	

No	Name	Nat	DoB	Pos	Aps	(s)	Gls
9	Deni Alar		18/01/90	A	32	(2)	16
28	Barış Atik	TUR	09/01/95	M	13	(3)	5
36	Seifedin Chabbi		04/07/93	A		(7)	
37	Kristijan Dobras		09/10/92	M	2	(11)	
34	Bright Edomwonyi	NGA	24/07/94	A	14	(4)	4
1	Christian Gratzei		19/09/81	G	35		
22	Andreas Gruber		29/06/95	M	1	(4)	
25	Stefan Hierländer		03/02/91	M	27	(3)	5
29	Sascha Horvath		22/08/96	M	10	(13)	
18	Philipp Huspek		05/02/91	M	17	(9)	1
6	James Jeggo	AUS	12/02/92	M	32		
42	Roman Kienast		29/03/84	A	1	(9)	
26	Fabian Koch		24/06/89	D	36		3
30	Sandi Lovric		28/03/98	M	2	(1)	
33	Daniel Lück	GER	18/05/91	G	1	(1)	
14	Charalampos Lykogiannis	GRE	22/10/93	D	34		3
35	Dario Maresic		29/09/99	D	5		
8	Uroš Matić	SRB	23/05/90	M	20		3
16	Martin Ovenstad	NOR	18/04/94	M	2	(2)	
13	Simon Piesinger		13/05/92	M	13	(1)	1
19	Marvin Potzmann		07/12/93	D	4	(8)	
24	Marc-Andre Schmerböck		01/04/94	M	24	(6)	6
39	Romano Schmid		27/01/00	M		(1)	
5	Christian Schoissengeyr		18/10/94	D	6	(5)	1
20	Christian Schulz	GER	01/04/83	D	30		3
23	Lukas Spendlhofer		02/06/93	D	32		2
10	Marko Stankovic		17/02/86	M		(4)	
11	Philipp Zulechner		12/04/90	A	3	(12)	2

Wolfsberger AC

1931 • Lavanttal Arena (7,300) • rzpelletswac.at

Coach: Heimo Pfeifenberger

Date		Opponent		Score	Scorers
2016					
23/07	a	Altach	L	0-1	
30/07	a	Salzburg	D	1-1	*Hellquist*
06/08	h	Ried	W	1-0	*Hüttenbrenner*
13/08	a	Mattersburg	L	1-3	*Nutz*
21/08	h	Rapid	D	1-1	*Prosenik*
27/08	h	Admira	W	5-0	*Prosenik 3, Hellquist, Topčagić (p)*
10/09	a	Austria Wien	L	1-4	*Prosenik*
17/09	h	St Pölten	D	1-1	*Sanogo*
24/09	a	Sturm	L	0-3	
01/10	h	Altach	L	1-2	*Wernitznig*
15/10	h	Salzburg	D	2-2	*Hüttenbrenner, Jacobo (p)*
22/10	a	Ried	W	1-0	*Nutz*
29/10	h	Mattersburg	W	3-0	*Hüttenbrenner, Prosenik, Wernitznig*
06/11	a	Rapid	W	1-0	*Prosenik*
19/11	a	Admira	L	1-4	*Wernitznig*
27/11	h	Austria Wien	L	0-3	
30/11	a	St Pölten	W	4-0	*Topčagić, Drescher, Hellquist 2*
04/12	h	Sturm	L	0-4	
10/12	a	Altach	L	1-2	*Nutz*
17/12	a	Salzburg	L	0-3	
2017					
11/02	h	Ried	W	1-0	*Klem*
18/02	a	Mattersburg	L	1-2	*Orgill*
25/02	h	Rapid	W	2-1	*Tschernegg, Leitgeb*
04/03	h	Admira	D	1-1	*Sollbauer*
11/03	a	Austria Wien	L	0-3	
18/03	h	St Pölten	W	1-0	*Klem*
01/04	a	Sturm	L	0-4	
08/04	h	Altach	D	0-0	
15/04	h	Salzburg	L	0-2	
22/04	a	Ried	D	1-1	*og (Özgür)*
29/04	h	Mattersburg	D	2-2	*Offenbacher 2*
06/05	a	Rapid	L	0-4	
13/05	a	Admira	L	2-3	*Tschernegg 2*
20/05	h	Austria Wien	W	2-1	*Offenbacher (p), Tschernegg*
25/05	a	St Pölten	D	1-1	*Klem*
28/05	h	Sturm	W	1-0	*Orgill*

No	Name	Nat	DoB	Pos	Aps	(s)	Gls
2	Michael Augustin		29/07/98	D		(1)	
7	Dario Baldauf		27/03/85	D	15	(2)	
1	Christian Dobnik		10/07/86	G	10		
27	Daniel Drescher		07/10/89	D	10		1
9	Philip Hellquist	SWE	12/05/91	A	8	(11)	4
5	Marcek Holzer		06/10/98	A	1	(2)	
16	Boris Hüttenbrenner		23/09/85	M	21		3
11	Jacobo	ESP	04/02/84	M	7	(13)	1
21	Christian Klem		21/04/91	D	32		3
31	Alexander Kofler		06/11/86	G	25		
18	Mario Leitgeb		30/06/88	M	9	(3)	1
29	Gerald Nutz		25/01/94	M	23	(5)	3
10	Daniel Offenbacher		18/02/92	M	19	(11)	3
12	Dever Orgill	JAM	08/03/90	A	11	(3)	2
33	Issiaka Ouédraogo	BFA	19/08/88	A	7	(3)	
4	Stephan Palla	PHI	15/05/89	D	12	(3)	
19	Florian Prohart		12/01/99	A		(1)	
14	Philipp Prosenik		01/03/93	A	22	(11)	7
20	Christoph Rabitsch		10/04/96	M	5	(7)	
15	Nemanja Rnić	SRB	30/09/84	D	27		
22	Benjamin Rosenberger		15/06/96	M		(1)	
35	Raphael Sallinger		08/12/95	G	1		
6	Zakaria Sanogo	BFA	11/12/96	M	10	(7)	1
26	Michael Sollbauer		15/05/90	D	23		1
25	Joachim Standfest		30/05/80	D	28	(3)	
8	Mihret Topčagić	BIH	21/06/88	A	7	(10)	2
23	Peter Tschernegg		23/07/92	M	29		4
24	Christopher Wernitznig		24/02/90	M	15	(5)	3
28	Thomas Zündel		24/12/87	M	19	(1)	

Top goalscorers

17 Olarenwaju Kayode (Austria Wien)

16 Deni Alar (Sturm)

12 Hwang Hee-chan (Salzburg)

11 Alexander Grünwald (Austria Wien)
Takumi Minamino (Salzburg)

10 Christoph Monschein (Admira)
Nikola Dovedan (Altach)
Dimitri Oberlin (Altach/Salzburg)

8 Christoph Knasmüllner (Admira)
Raphael Holzhauser (Austria Wien)
Ismael Tajouri (Austria Wien)
Patrick Bürger (Mattersburg)
Joelinton (Rapid)
Jonatan Soriano (Salzburg)

Promoted club

LASK Linz

1908 • Waldstadion, Pasching (7,152) • lask.at

Major honours
Austrian League (1) 1965; Austrian Cup (1) 1965

Coach: Oliver Glasner

Second level final table 2016/17

		Pld	W	D	L	F	A	Pts
1	LASK Linz	36	23	8	5	77	42	77
2	FC Liefering	36	17	9	10	58	49	60
3	SC Austria Lustenau	36	15	12	9	58	49	57
4	FC Wacker Innsbruck	36	15	9	12	58	53	54
5	WSG Wattens	36	13	12	11	56	54	51
6	Kapfenberger SV	36	12	9	15	47	57	41
7	FC Blau-Weiss Linz	36	8	15	13	41	45	39
8	SC Wiener Neustadt	36	11	6	19	40	62	39
9	Floridsdorfer AC	36	10	8	18	39	48	38
10	SV Horn	36	9	6	21	42	57	33

NB Kapfenberger SV – 4 pts deducted.

DOMESTIC CUP

ÖFB-Cup 2016/17

FIRST ROUND

(08/07/16)
Karabakh Wien 1-3 Rapid

(15/07/16)
Amstetten 3-0 Wienerberg *(aet)*
ATSV Wolfsberg 0-3 Floridsdorfer AC
Bad Wimsbach 3-1 Austria Salzburg
Deutschlandsberg 1-3 Lafnitz
Ebreichsdorf 1-0 Wolfsberg
Gleisdorf 2-2 Hartberg *(aet; 3-5 on pens)*
Grieskirchen 0-2 Wiener Neustadt
Kalsdorf 4-0 Austria Klagenfurt
Krems 0-2 St Pölten
Neusiedl 3-5 Wattens *(aet)*
Parndorf 2-3 LASK *(aet)*
Purgstall 0-6 Kapfenberg
Stadlau 0-2 Sturm Graz
Vienna 6-0 Treibach
Vorwärts Steyr 1-3 Salzburg
Wiener Sportklub 0-3 Ritzing

(16/07/16)
Anif 0-1 Altach
Ferlach 1-6 Austria Lustenau
Hard 0-1 St Florian
Hohenems 0-4 Grödig
Kufstein 1-4 Ried
Leobendorf 0-0 Allerheiligen *(aet; 3-1 on pens)*
Schwaz 4-3 Bergheim
St Johann 0-3 Gurten
Stadl-Paura 0-1 Blau-Weiss Linz
Traiskirchen 1-3 Horn

(17/07/16)
Dornbirner SV 1-4 Admira
FC Dornbirn 0-6 Austria Wien
Mannsdorf 3-3 Wacker Innsbruck *(aet; 4-3 on pens)*
Rudersdorf 0-7 Mattersburg
Wörgl 2-4 Kitzbühel *(aet)*

SECOND ROUND

(20/09/16)
Amstetten 2-2 Austria Lustenau *(aet; 3-2 on pens)*
Grödig 2-2 Horn *(aet; 4-2 on pens)*
Gurten 2-4 Kapfenberg
Hartberg 1-1 Wattens *(aet; 4-5 on pens)*
Kalsdorf 1-2 LASK
Kitzbühel 1-2 Blau-Weiss Linz
Schwaz 0-1 Floridsdorfer AC
St Florian 0-3 Wiener Neustadt *(aet)*
St Pölten 2-1 Ried

(21/09/16)
Bad Wimsbach 0-5 Sturm Graz
Ebreichsdorf 3-0 Altach
Lafnitz 0-0 Mattersburg *(aet; 4-3 on pens)*
Leobendorf 0-1 Rapid
Mannsdorf 1-7 Salzburg
Ritzing 1-3 Admira
Vienna 1-3 Austria Wien *(aet)*

THIRD ROUND

(25/10/16)
Amstetten 3-4 LASK *(aet)*
Grödig 1-0 Wattens
Lafnitz 1-5 Kapfenberg
Wiener Neustadt 1-3 Admira

(26/10/16)
Blau-Weiss Linz 0-4 Rapid
Ebreichsdorf 4-5 Austria Wien *(aet)*
Salzburg 2-0 Floridsdorfer AC
St Pölten 1-1 Sturm Graz *(aet; 4-3 on pens)*

QUARTER-FINALS

(04/04/17)
Grödig 0-3 LASK *(Rep 64, Imbongo 88, Fabiano 90+1)*

(05/04/17)
Austria Wien 1-2 Admira *(Friesenbichler 33; Knasmüllner 6, Monschein 14)*

Salzburg 2-1 Kapfenberg *(Radošević 20, Haidara 110; João Victor 8) (aet)*

St Pölten 1-3 Rapid *(Wöber 90+6og; Wöber 18, Pavelic 74, Schwab 84)*

SEMI-FINALS

(26/04/17)
Admira 0-5 Salzburg *(Minamino 7, 86, Wanderson 29, Laimer 48, Lazaro 60)*

Rapid 2-1 LASK *(Murg 76, Joelinton 90+3; Gartler 90)*

FINAL

(01/06/17)
Wörthersee-Stadion, Klagenfurt
FC SALZBURG 2 *(Hwang 51, Lazaro 85)*
SK RAPID WIEN 1 *(Joelinton 56)*
Referee: *Hameter*
SALZBURG: Stankovic, Lainer, Wisdom, Paulo Miranda, Ulmer (Schwegler 70), Lazaro (Ćaleta-Car 90+1), Laimer, Samassékou, V Berisha, Wanderson (Haidara 84), Hwang
RAPID: Knoflach, Pavelic, Dibon, Wöber, Schrammel, Schwab, Auer, Schaub (Kuen 71), Szántó (Traustason 73), Murg (Schösswendter 86), Joelinton

More joy for serial Austrian Cup winners Salzburg as they celebrate a fourth successive domestic double

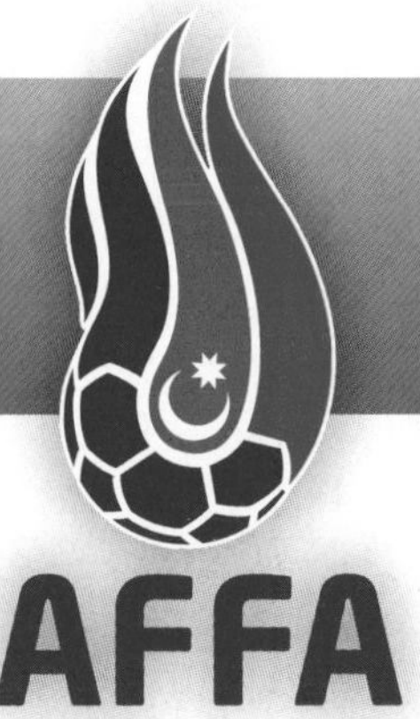

AZERBAIJAN

Azärbaycan Futbol Federasiyaları Assosiasiyası (AFFA)

Address	Nobel Prospekti 2208 AZ-1025 Bakı
Tel	+994 12 404 27 77
Fax	+994 12 404 27 72
E-mail	info@affa.az
Website	affa.az

President	Rövnaq Abdullayev
General secretary	Elkhan Mämmädov
Media officer	Mikayıl Narimanoğlu
Year of formation	1992
National stadium	Bakı Olimpiya Stadionu, Baku (68,700)

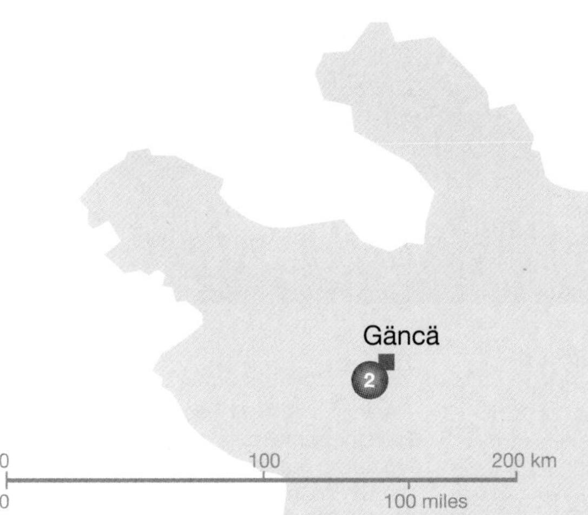

PREMYER LİQA CLUBS

1 İnter Bakı PİK

2 Käpäz PFK

3 Neftçi PFK

4 Olimpik-Şüvälan PFK

5 Qarabağ FK

6 Qäbälä FK

7 Sumqayıt FK

8 Zirä FK

PROMOTED CLUB

9 Säbail FK

Qarabağ continue to call the shots

Qarabağ FK's monopoly of the Premyer Liqa title stretched to a fourth successive season as they saw off a concerted challenge from Qäbälä with a powerful surge in the final quarter of a season that comprised only 28 matches following the reduction in the number of participating teams from ten to eight.

Qurban Qurbanov's side also denied Qäbälä a first major trophy by defeating them 2-0 in the final of the cup. The country's top two clubs did Azerbaijan proud by reaching the group stage of the UEFA Europa League in tandem for the second season in a row.

Third straight double for Qurban Qurbanov's team

Qäbälä challenge seen off in finishing straight

Top two clubs fly flag again in Europe

Domestic league

There was little to choose between the two contenders during the first half of the campaign, with each team defeating the other at home. Qäbälä drew first blood with a 2-0 victory in early October before Qarabağ bit back in late November, a 2-1 win thus halting their rivals' 12-match undefeated run. At the winter break the defending champions led by a point, with İnter Bakı six further points back in third.

Led again by Ukrainian coach Roman Hryhorchuk, Qäbälä seemed certain to finish higher in the Premyer Liqa than ever before – their loftiest placing had been third in each of the previous three seasons – but in the early spring, with their Croatian star Filip Ozobić scoring freely, including his third goal in as many games against Qarabağ, a first title was very much in the provincial club's sights. Indeed, with a quarter of the season remaining, Hryhorchuk's team were on top of the table with a one-point lead.

Alas for Qäbälä, that was as good as it got. A 1-0 defeat at Neftçi sent them into a tailspin from which there was no escape, Qarabağ eventually racing clear to complete a hat-trick of successful title defences with two games to spare. A 3-0 home win against İnter featuring two goals from top-scoring South African striker Dino Ndlovu sealed the deal, and two further wins left them with a ten-point victory margin – some way short of the 22-point advantage from the previous (36-match) season but a comprehensive triumph all the same.

Qäbälä in turn finished with a nine-point cushion over İnter, who, like fourth-placed Zirä, qualified for the UEFA Europa League having been refused entry a year earlier. Record champions Neftçi endured a miserable campaign, with just one team finishing below them – Olimpik-Şüvälan, who totalled just ten points and were relegated, to be replaced not by second-tier champions Turan Tovuz, who were declined a top-flight licence, but by runners-up Säbail.

Domestic cup

Defeated on penalties by Neftçi in their only previous Azerbaijan Cup final, in 2014, Qäbälä were hoping for better fortune when they took on Qarabağ in Naxcivan. That first major trophy would remain elusive, however, as the cup winners of the previous two years completed the hat-trick, two goals early in the second half bringing Qarabağ the trophy for the sixth time – just one short of Neftçi's record.

Europe

Qarabağ's 2016/17 European campaign took the same route as the previous two, starting in the second qualifying round of the UEFA Champions League and ending five months later on matchday six of the UEFA Europa League group stage. It would have extended into the spring for the first time had they won, not lost, their final fixture, at home to Fiorentina, but the seven points they accumulated was their best tally yet. It was also seven more than Qäbälä managed as they suffered a group stage whitewash – a complete contrast to their qualifying form, which brought them victories over Samtredia, MTK, Lille and Maribor and an unprecedented second successive run from the first qualifying round to the group stage.

National team

Azerbaijan made a blockbusting start to their 2018 FIFA World Cup qualifying campaign, taking seven points from their first three matches while keeping three clean sheets. A best-ever campaign looked to be on the cards, but a heavy defeat in Northern Ireland was followed by further losses in Baku against Germany and – to a last-minute winner – Northern Ireland again, leaving coach Robert Prosinečki with the difficult challenge of lifting the squad – most of them home-based, many with Qarabağ – for the final four fixtures.

DOMESTIC SEASON AT A GLANCE

Premyer Liqa 2016/17 final table

			Home					Away					Total					
		Pld	W	D	L	F	A	W	D	L	F	A	W	D	L	F	A	Pts
1	**Qarabağ FK**	**28**	**10**	**3**	**1**	**25**	**5**	**9**	**2**	**3**	**21**	**9**	**19**	**5**	**4**	**46**	**14**	**62**
2	Qäbälä FK	28	11	3	0	27	7	3	7	4	21	14	14	10	4	48	21	52
3	İnter Bakı PİK	28	7	4	3	23	18	4	6	4	16	15	11	10	7	39	33	43
4	Zirä FK	28	7	4	3	18	11	3	5	6	11	15	10	9	9	29	26	39
5	Käpäz PFK	28	7	6	1	14	4	2	3	9	10	23	9	9	10	24	27	36
6	Sumqayıt FK	28	6	5	3	19	17	3	3	8	9	18	9	8	11	28	35	35
7	Neftçi PFK	28	6	1	7	15	20	3	1	10	9	25	9	2	17	24	45	29
8	Olimpik-Şüvälan PFK	28	0	4	10	7	21	1	3	10	6	29	1	7	20	13	50	10

European qualification 2017/18

Champion/Cup winner: Qarabağ FK (second qualifying round)

Qäbälä FK (second qualifying round)
İnter Bakı PİK (first qualifying round)
Zirä FK (first qualifying round)

Top scorer	Rauf Äliyev (İnter) & Filip Ozobić (Qäbälä), 11 goals
Relegated club	Olimpik-Şüvälan PFK
Promoted club	Säbail FK
Cup final	Qarabağ FK 2-0 Qäbälä FK

Player of the season

Filip Ozobić
(Qäbälä FK)

Treading water in the Croatian top flight with Slaven Koprivnica, Ozobić decided to move to Azerbaijan in the summer of 2016 and try his luck with Qäbälä. It proved to be a smart move for both player and club, the lively attacking midfielder endearing himself to his new fans early on with a couple of important European goals against MTK and Lille before taking the Premyer Liqası by storm and ending up as the division's joint-leading scorer – alongside İnter Bakı's Azerbaijan international Rauf Äliyev – on 11 goals, three of them against champions Qarabağ.

Newcomer of the season

Mirabdulla Abbasov
(Sumqayıt FK)

There was not a great deal to shout about in 2016/17 for the supporters of Sumqayıt. They were thrashed 11-2 by Qarabağ in the quarter-finals of the cup and won only nine of their 28 Premyer Ligası matches, finishing sixth. That, however, was one place higher than Neftçi, the club that had provided them with Abbasov on a season-long loan and would live to regret it as the 21-year-old schemer-cum-striker scored eight league goals, including one in a 2-0 win against his parent club. Unsurprisingly, he was recalled by Neftçi in the summer.

Team of the season

(3-5-2)

Coach: Qurbanov *(Qarabağ)*

AZERBAIJAN

NATIONAL TEAM

Top five all-time caps
Räşad F Sadıqov (106); Aslan Kärimov (79); Mahir Şükürov (76); Tärlan Ähmädov (73); Mahmud Qurbanov (72)

Top five all-time goals
Qurban Qurbanov (12); Vaqif Cavadov (9); **Rauf Äliyev**, **Elvin Mämmädov** & Branimir Subašić (7)

Results 2016/17

04/09/16	San Marino (WCQ)	A	Serravalle	W	1-0	*Qurbanov (45)*
08/10/16	Norway (WCQ)	H	Baku	W	1-0	*Medvedev (11)*
11/10/16	Czech Republic (WCQ)	A	Ostrava	D	0-0	
11/11/16	Northern Ireland (WCQ)	A	Belfast	L	0-4	
09/03/17	Qatar	A	Doha	W	2-1	*Quliyev (52), Abdullayev (62)*
26/03/17	Germany (WCQ)	H	Baku	L	1-4	*Nazarov (31)*
10/06/17	Northern Ireland (WCQ)	H	Baku	L	0-1	

Appearances 2016/17

Coach: Robert Prosinečki (CRO)	12/01/69		SMR	NOR	CZE	NIR	Qat	GER	NIR	Caps	Goals
Kamran Ağayev	09/02/86	Sumqayıt	G								
		/Boavista (POR)		G	G	G		G			
		/unattached							G	65	-
Mähämmäd Mirzäbäyov	16/11/90	Qäbälä	D	D	D	D	D	D		15	-
Maksim Medvedev	29/09/89	Qarabağ	D	D	D	D			D	40	1
Räşad F Sadıqov	16/06/82	Qarabağ	D	D			D46	D	D	106	4
Arif Daşdämirov	10/02/87	Qarabağ	D	D	D	D				14	-
Qara Qarayev	12/10/92	Qarabağ	M	M	M	M	M	M	M	31	-
Äfran İsmayılov	08/10/88	Qarabağ	M			M		M81	M84	33	2
Rahid Ämirquliyev	01/09/89	Qarabağ	M	M	M	M	M	M87	s84	55	3
Dimitrij Nazarov	04/04/90	Erzgebirge Aue (GER)	M78	M	M	s70		M	M77	24	6
Ruslan Qurbanov	12/09/91	Qäbälä	M69	M80	M87	M75	A46	s81		17	1
Ağabala Ramazanov	20/01/93	İnter Bakı	A89	A90	s71	s75					
		/Qarabağ					M68			11	1
Namiq Äläsgärov	03/02/95	Qarabağ	s69	s65	M71						
		/Neftçi					M46		s77	8	-
Emin Mahmudov	27/04/92	Boavista (POR)	s78			M70				2	-
Ramil Şeydayev	15/03/96	Trabzonspor (TUR)	s89	s80	A91	A46					
		/Žilina (SVK)						A67	A90	6	-
Eddy İsrafilov	02/08/92	Cádiz (ESP)		M65	s91			s87		8	-
Bädavi Hüseynov	11/07/91	Qarabağ		s90	D	D	D	D	D	29	-
Araz Abdullayev	18/04/92	Neftçi			s87						
		/Qäbälä					s46		s90	22	1
Deniz Yılmaz	26/02/88	Bursaspor (TUR)				s46		s67		2	-
Sälahät Ağayev	04/01/91	İnter Bakı					G			9	-
Tellur Mütällimov	08/04/95	Qäbälä					D68			1	-
Cavid Hüseynov	09/03/88	Qäbälä					M81	M	M	47	2
Tärlan Quliyev	19/04/92	İnter Bakı					s46			7	1
Rauf Äliyev	12/02/89	İnter Bakı					s46			43	7
Ürfan Abbasov	14/10/92	Qäbälä					s68			2	-
Mahir Mädätov	01/07/97	Qarabağ					s68			1	-
Elvin Mämmädov	18/07/88	Zirä					s81			36	7
Pavlo Paşayev	04/01/88	Stal (UKR)						D	D	5	-
Richard Almeida	20/03/89	Qarabağ							M	1	-

EUROPE

Qarabağ FK

Second qualifying round - F91 Dudelange (LUX)
H 2-0 *Almeida (10p, 27)*
Šehić, Qarayev, Medvedev, Míchel, Muarem (İsmayılov 74), Mädätov (Reynaldo 63), Sadıqov, Almeida, Agolli, Hüseynov, Dani Quintana (Ämirquliyev 83). Coach: Qurban Qurbanov (AZE)
A 1-1 *Reynaldo (90+4)*
Šehić, Qarayev (Diniyev 82), Medvedev, Míchel, Reynaldo, Muarem (Mädätov 70), Sadıqov, Almeida, Agolli, Hüseynov, Dani Quintana (İsmayılov 90+5). Coach: Qurban Qurbanov (AZE)

Third qualifying round - FC Viktoria Plzeň (CZE)
A 0-0
Šehić, Qarayev, Medvedev, Míchel, Reynaldo, Mädätov (Muarem 46), Sadıqov, Almeida, Agolli (Qurbanov 79), Hüseynov, Dani Quintana (İsmayılov 67). Coach: Qurban Qurbanov (AZE)
H 1-1 *Muarem (28)*
Šehić, Qarayev, Medvedev, Míchel, Reynaldo, Muarem (İsmayılov 70), Sadıqov, Almeida (Yunuszadä 84), Agolli, Hüseynov, Dani Quintana (El Jadeyaoui 82). Coach: Qurban Qurbanov (AZE)

Play-offs - IFK Göteborg (SWE)
A 0-1
Šehić, Qarayev, Medvedev, Míchel, Reynaldo, Muarem (Äläsgärov 72), Sadıqov, Almeida, Agolli, Hüseynov, Dani Quintana. Coach: Qurban Qurbanov (AZE)
H 3-0 *Sadıqov (19), Muarem (26), Dani Quintana (51)*
Šehić, Qarayev, Medvedev, Míchel, Reynaldo (Äläsgärov 90), Muarem (Ndlovu 83), Sadıqov, Almeida (Ämirquliyev 88), Agolli, Yunuszadä, Dani Quintana. Coach: Qurban Qurbanov (AZE)

Group J
Match 1 - FC Slovan Liberec (CZE)
H 2-2 *Míchel (7), Sadıqov (90+4)*
Šehić, Qarayev (İsmayılov 76), Medvedev, Ndlovu (Muarem 66), Míchel, Reynaldo, Sadıqov, Almeida, Agolli (Mädätov 86), Yunuszadä, Dani Quintana. Coach: Qurban Qurbanov (AZE)
Match 2 - ACF Fiorentina (ITA)
A 1-5 *Ndlovu (90+2)*
Šehić, Medvedev, Míchel, Reynaldo (Ndlovu 84), Sadıqov, Ämirquliyev, Almeida, İsmayılov (Muarem 60), Agolli, Yunuszadä, Dani Quintana (Hüseynov 46). Coach: Qurban Qurbanov (AZE)
Red card: Yunuszadä 30
Match 3 - PAOK FC (GRE)
H 2-0 *Dani Quintana (56), Ämirquliyev (87)*
Šehić, Qarayev, Medvedev, Ndlovu (Mädätov 76), Muarem (Nadirov 90+2), Sadıqov, Ämirquliyev, Almeida, Agolli, Hüseynov, Dani Quintana (Äläsgärov 90). Coach: Qurban Qurbanov (AZE)
Match 4 - PAOK FC (GRE)
A 1-0 *Míchel (69)*
Šehić, Qarayev, Medvedev, Ndlovu (Reynaldo 76), Muarem (İsmayılov 88), Sadıqov, Ämirquliyev (Míchel 64), Almeida, Agolli, Hüseynov, Dani Quintana. Coach: Qurban Qurbanov (AZE)
Match 5 - FC Slovan Liberec (CZE)
A 0-3
Šehić, Qarayev, Medvedev, Ndlovu, Míchel (İsmayılov 52), Muarem (Reynaldo 60), Almeida, Daşdämirov, Agolli, Hüseynov, Dani Quintana. Coach: Qurban Qurbanov (AZE)
Match 6 - ACF Fiorentina (ITA)
H 1-2 *Reynaldo (73)*
Šehić, Qarayev, Ndlovu (Mädätov 71), Muarem (İsmayılov 46), Sadıqov, Ämirquliyev (Reynaldo 62), Qurbanov, Almeida, Agolli, Hüseynov, Dani Quintana. Coach: Qurban Qurbanov (AZE)

Qäbälä FK

First qualifying round - FC Samtredia (GEO)
H 5-1 *Stanković (16), Zenjov (19), Weeks (30, 69, 72)*
Bezotosniy, Stanković, Sadiqov, Kvekveskiri, Zenjov (Mütällimov 83), Vernydub, Dabo (Eyubov 77), Ozobić, Ricardinho, Weeks (Alıyev 86), Abbasov. Coach: Roman Hryhorchuk (UKR)
A 1-2 *Weeks (42)*
Bezotosniy, Stanković, Sadiqov (Camalov 69), Kvekveskiri, Zenjov, Vernydub (Rafael Santos 46), Dabo, Ozobić (Mütällimov 52), Ricardinho, Weeks, Abbasov. Coach: Roman Hryhorchuk (UKR)

Second qualifying round - MTK Budapest (HUN)
A 2-1 *Kvekveskiri (25), Ozobić (63)*
Bezotosniy, Stanković, Sadiqov, Kvekveskiri, Zenjov, Vernydub, Mirzäbäyov, Dabo (Mämmädov 86), Ozobić, Ricardinho, Weeks. Coach: Roman Hryhorchuk (UKR)
H 2-0 *Zenjov (7), Weeks (37)*
Bezotosniy, Stanković (Rafael Santos 88), Sadiqov, Kvekveskiri (Camalov 79), Zenjov (Mämmädov 77), Vernydub, Mirzäbäyov, Dabo, Ozobić, Ricardinho, Weeks. Coach: Roman Hryhorchuk (UKR)

Third qualifying round - LOSC Lille (FRA)
A 1-1 *Vernydub (13)*
Bezotosniy, Stanković (Rafael Santos 76), Sadiqov, Kvekveskiri, Zenjov (Mämmädov 81), Vernydub, Mirzäbäyov, Dabo (Eyubov 90+3), Ozobić, Ricardinho, Weeks. Coach: Roman Hryhorchuk (UKR)
H 1-0 *Ozobić (34)*
Bezotosniy, Stanković, Sadiqov, Kvekveskiri, Zenjov, Vernydub, Mirzäbäyov, Dabo, Ozobić (Mämmädov 77), Ricardinho, Weeks. Coach: Roman Hryhorchuk (UKR)

Play-offs - NK Maribor (SVN)
H 3-1 *Zenjov (37), Dabo (50, 52)*
Bezotosniy, Stanković, Kvekveskiri, Zenjov, Vernydub (Camalov 90), Mirzäbäyov, Dabo, Ozobić (Mämmädov 80), Ricardinho, Weeks (Eyubov 90+2), Rafael Santos. Coach: Roman Hryhorchuk (UKR)
A 0-1
Bezotosniy, Stanković, Kvekveskiri, Zenjov (Mämmädov 86), Vernydub, Mirzäbäyov, Dabo (Eyubov 90+6), Ozobić, Ricardinho, Weeks, Rafael Santos. Coach: Roman Hryhorchuk (UKR)
Red card: Weeks 69

Group C
Match 1 - RSC Anderlecht (BEL)
A 1-3 *Dabo (20)*
Bezotosniy, Stanković, Sadiqov, Zenjov (Eyubov 90+2), R Qurbanov (Mämmädov 46), Vernydub (Franjić 59), Mirzäbäyov, Dabo, Ozobić, Ricardinho, Rafael Santos. Coach: Roman Hryhorchuk (UKR)
Match 2 - 1. FSV Mainz 05 (GER)
H 2-3 *R Qurbanov (57p), Zenjov (62)*
Bezotosniy, Stanković, Sadiqov (Mämmädov 81), Zenjov, R Qurbanov (Franjić 81), Vernydub (Camalov 86), Mirzäbäyov, Dabo, Ozobić, Ricardinho, Rafael Santos. Coach: Roman Hryhorchuk (UKR)
Match 3 - AS Saint-Étienne (FRA)
A 0-1
Bezotosniy, Stanković, Zenjov (Franjić 80), R Qurbanov, Mämmädov (Eyubov 80), Vernydub, Mirzäbäyov, Ozobić, Ricardinho, Weeks, Abbasov. Coach: Roman Hryhorchuk (UKR)
Match 4 - AS Saint-Étienne (FRA)
H 1-2 *R Qurbanov (39)*
Bezotosniy, Stanković, Sadiqov (Kvekveskiri 84), Zenjov (Mämmädov 61), R Qurbanov, Vernydub, Mirzäbäyov, Ozobić, Ricardinho, Weeks, Eyubov (Franjić 65). Coach: Roman Hryhorchuk (UKR)
Match 5 - RSC Anderlecht (BEL)
H 1-3 *Ricardinho (15p)*
Bezotosniy, Kvekveskiri, Mämmädov, Vernydub, Dabo (R Qurbanov 52), Ozobić, Ricardinho, Weeks, Eyubov, Abbasov, Rafael Santos. Coach:
Red card: Eyubov 89
Match 6 - 1. FSV Mainz 05 (GER)
A 0-2
Bezotosniy, Stanković, Sadiqov (R Qurbanov 46), Kvekveskiri, Zenjov (Hüseynov 77), Mämmädov, Vernydub, Ozobić, Ricardinho, Weeks (Camalov 86), Abbasov. Coach: Roman Hryhorchuk (UKR)

Käpäz PFK

First qualifying round - FC Dacia Chisinau (MDA)

H 0-0

Simaitis, Diniyev, Bäybalayev (Cavadov 73), Dário Júnior, Ş Rähimov, Qurbanov (O Äliyev 70), Axundov, Ş Äliyev, Renan, Serginho (Qürbätov 79), Ebah. Coach: Şahin Diniyev (AZE)

A 1-0 *Dário Júnior (57)*

Simaitis, Diniyev, Bäybalayev (Cavadov 67), Dário Júnior, Ş Rähimov, Qurbanov (Kärimov 82), Axundov, Ş Äliyev, Renan, Serginho (Qürbätov 73), Ebah. Coach: Şahin Diniyev (AZE)

Second qualifying round - FC Admira Wacker Mödling (AUT)

A 0-1

Simaitis, Diniyev, Bäybalayev (O Äliyev 73), Dário Júnior, Ş Rähimov, Qurbanov (Cavadov 73), Axundov, Ş Äliyev, Renan, Serginho (Qürbätov 88), Ebah. Coach: Şahin Diniyev (AZE)

H 0-2

Simaitis, Diniyev, Bäybalayev (Cavadov 46), Dário Júnior, Ş Rähimov, Qurbanov (O Äliyev 69), Axundov, Ş Äliyev, Renan, Serginho (Qürbätov 82), Ebah. Coach: Şahin Diniyev (AZE)

Neftçi PFK

First qualifying round - Balzan FC (MLT)

A 2-0 *Hacıyev (14), R Qurbanov (84p)*

Santini, Jairo, A Abdullayev (Muradbäyli 81), E Abdullayev, R Qurbanov, Ağayev, Hacıyev (İmamverdiyev 75), Sikov, İsayev, Melnjak, Castillo (Mämmädov 90+4). Coach: Väli Qasımov (AZE)

H 1-2 *Jairo (20)*

Santini, Jairo, A Abdullayev (Muradbäyli 77), E Abdullayev (Mämmädov 90), R Qurbanov (İmamverdiyev 69), Ağayev, Hacıyev, Sikov, İsayev, Melnjak, Castillo. Coach: Väli Qasımov (AZE)

Second qualifying round - KF Shkëndija (MKD)

H 0-0

Santini, Jairo, A Abdullayev, R Qurbanov (E Abdullayev 86), Ağayev (İmamverdiyev 78), Hacıyev, Muradbäyli, Sikov, İsayev, Melnjak, Castillo. Coach: Väli Qasımov (AZE)

A 0-1

Santini, Jairo, A Abdullayev, R Qurbanov (Mämmädov 87), Ağayev, Hacıyev (İmamverdiyev 80), Muradbäyli (A Qurbanlı 85), Sikov, İsayev, Melnjak, Castillo. Coach: Väli Qasımov (AZE)

Red card: Sikov 70

DOMESTIC LEAGUE CLUB-BY-CLUB

İnter Bakı PİK

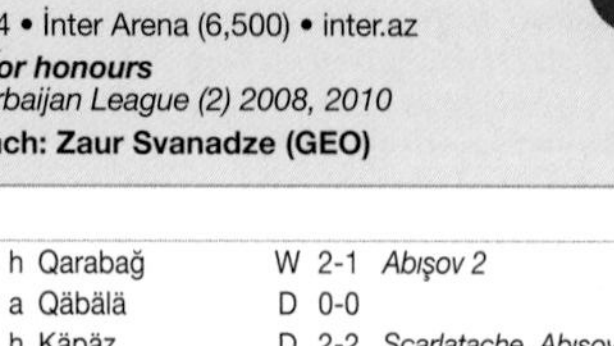

2004 • İnter Arena (6,500) • inter.az

Major honours
Azerbaijan League (2) 2008, 2010

Coach: Zaur Svanadze (GEO)

2016					
07/08	h	Qarabağ	W	2-1	*Abışov 2*
12/08	a	Qäbälä	D	0-0	
19/08	h	Käpäz	D	2-2	*Scarlatache, Abışov*
11/09	a	Sumqayıt	W	2-1	*Dênis Silva, Ramazanov*
18/09	h	Neftçi	W	2-1	*Äliyev 2*
24/09	a	Olimpik-Şüvälan	W	3-1	*Hacıyev (p), Äliyev, Ramazanov*
30/09	h	Zirä	D	1-1	*Ramazanov*
15/10	h	Qäbälä	D	1-1	*Ramazanov*
23/10	a	Käpäz	D	0-0	
30/10	h	Sumqayıt	W	3-1	*Khizanishvili, Hacıyev 2*
05/11	a	Neftçi	L	1-2	*Khizanishvili*
20/11	h	Olimpik-Şüvälan	W	3-0	*Abışov (p), Qırtımov, Alxasov*
28/11	a	Zirä	D	1-1	*Abışov*
17/12	a	Qarabağ	D	0-0	
2017					
28/01	h	Käpäz	W	4-1	*Hacıyev, Bayramov, Hüseynov, Äliyev*
04/02	a	Sumqayıt	D	2-2	*Qırtımov, Äliyev*
09/02	h	Neftçi	L	1-3	*Äliyev*
13/02	a	Olimpik-Şüvälan	W	1-0	*Hacıyev*
18/02	h	Zirä	D	1-1	*Äliyev*
28/02	a	Qarabağ	W	1-0	*Khizanishvili*
04/03	h	Qäbälä	L	0-2	
13/03	h	Sumqayıt	W	1-0	*Hacıyev*
18/03	a	Neftçi	L	1-2	*Hacıyev*
02/04	h	Olimpik-Şüvälan	W	2-1	*Dênis Silva, Äliyev*
10/04	a	Zirä	D	1-1	*Äliyev*
16/04	h	Qarabağ	L	0-3	
24/04	a	Qäbälä	L	3-4	*Äliyev 2, Abdullayev*
29/04	a	Käpäz	L	0-1	

No	Name	Nat	DoB	Pos	Aps	(s)	Gls
7	Mirsahib Abbasov		19/01/93	M	9	(4)	
10	Elnur Abdullayev		16/02/86	M	20	(3)	1
15	Ruslan Abışov		10/10/87	M	11	(2)	5
1	Sälahät Ağayev		04/01/91	G	22		
4	Slavik Alxasov		06/02/93	D	16	(2)	1
11	Rauf Äliyev		12/02/89	A	25	(1)	11
65	Cabir Ämirli		06/01/97	M	1	(1)	
24	Fuad H Bayramov		30/11/94	M	24		1
3	Dênis Silva	BRA	28/12/85	D	21	(4)	2
9	Pardis Fardjad-Azad		12/04/88	A	8	(15)	
8	Nizami Hacıyev		08/02/88	M	21	(3)	7
17	Abbas Hüseynov		13/06/95	D	9	(6)	1
14	Zurab Khizanishvili	GEO	06/10/81	D	26		3
98	Qara İ Qarayev		05/03/98	A		(1)	
66	Murad Qayalı		09/03/99	D		(1)	
22	İlkin Qırtımov		04/11/90	D	24		2
88	Mämmäd Quliyev		25/08/95	M	2	(5)	
33	Tärlan Quliyev		19/04/92	D	23		
55	Ağabala Ramazanov		20/01/93	M	13		4
13	Orxan Sadıqlı		19/03/93	G	6		
27	Adrian Scarlatache	ROU	05/12/86	D	16	(3)	1
19	Mirhüseyn Seyidov		10/08/92	M	3	(3)	
2	Sertan Taşkın		08/10/97	D	3	(8)	
6	Samir Zärgärov		29/08/86	M	5	(14)	

Käpäz PFK

1959 • Gäncä şähär stadionu (27,830) • kapazpfc.az

Major honours
Azerbaijan League (3) 1995, 1998, 1999; Azerbaijan Cup (4) 1994, 1997, 1998, 2000

Coach: Şahin Diniyev

2016					
08/08	a	Qäbälä	L	0-2	
13/08	h	Olimpik-Şüvälan	D	0-0	
19/08	a	İnter	D	2-2	*Axundov (p), Ebah*
11/09	h	Zirä	W	2-0	*Ebah, Ş Rähimov*
18/09	a	Sumqayıt	D	1-1	*Diniyev*
25/09	h	Qarabağ	D	1-1	*Dário Júnior*
01/10	a	Neftçi	L	0-2	
16/10	a	Olimpik-Şüvälan	W	1-0	*Ebah*
23/10	h	İnter	D	0-0	
30/10	a	Zirä	L	0-2	
05/11	h	Sumqayıt	D	0-0	
19/11	a	Qarabağ	L	0-1	
27/11	h	Neftçi	W	2-0	*O Äliyev, Ebah*
17/12	a	Qäbälä	L	1-2	*Axundov (p)*
2017					
28/01	a	İnter	L	1-4	*Axundov*
04/02	a	Zirä	L	0-1	
09/02	a	Sumqayıt	L	1-3	*Diniyev*
12/02	h	Qarabağ	L	0-1	
18/02	a	Neftçi	D	0-0	
28/02	h	Qäbälä	D	1-1	*Ş Rähimov*
05/03	h	Olimpik-Şüvälan	D	1-1	*Ş Äliyev*
13/03	h	Zirä	W	1-0	*Ebah*
18/03	h	Sumqayıt	W	1-0	*Dário Júnior*
02/04	a	Qarabağ	L	1-2	*Diniyev*
09/04	h	Neftçi	W	2-0	*Axundov 2 (2p)*
16/04	h	Qäbälä	W	2-0	*Ebah, Dário Júnior*
23/04	a	Olimpik-Şüvälan	W	2-1	*Serginho 2*
29/04	h	İnter	W	1-0	*Dário Júnior*

No	Name	Nat	DoB	Pos	Aps	(s)	Gls
18	Tural Axundov		01/08/88	D	25		5
19	Orxan Äliyev		21/12/95	M	27		1
25	Şähriyar Äliyev		25/12/92	D	17		1
7	Vüqar Bäybalayev		05/08/93	M	9	(10)	
6	Ceyhun Cavadov		05/10/92	M	7	(11)	
10	Dário Júnior	BRA	11/09/91	M	20	(2)	4
5	Kärim Diniyev		05/09/93	M	26		3
90	Julien Ebah	CMR	03/09/88	A	25	(3)	6
30	Davud Kärimi		08/10/84	G	11		
15	Azad Kärimov		31/10/94	D	12	(9)	
21	Novruz Mämmädov		20/03/90	D	16	(4)	
23	Tural Närimanov		27/10/89	D	3	(1)	
68	Äli Nuri		02/01/96	M	1	(1)	
17	Nicat Qurbanov		17/02/92	M	12	(10)	
9	Tural Qürbätov		01/03/93	A	4	(10)	
8	Elcan Rähimov		06/08/98	D		(1)	
13	Şähriyar Rähimov		06/04/89	M	27		2
36	Renan	BRA	17/12/92	D	24		
80	Tural Rzayev		26/08/93	A		(16)	
99	Äli Sämädov		06/09/97	M		(1)	
77	Serginho	POR	21/02/91	A	25	(2)	2
88	Tadas Simaitis	LTU	29/12/90	G	17		
16	Emin Zamanov		26/12/97	M		(1)	

Neftçi PFK

1937 • Älincä Arena (13,000); Bakcell Arena (11,000); Dalğa Arena (6,700) • neftchipfk.com

Major honours

Azerbaijan League (8) 1992, 1996, 1997, 2004, 2005, 2011, 2012, 2013; Azerbaijan Cup (7) 1995, 1996, 1999, 2002, 2004, 2013, 2014

Coach: Väli Qasımov; (14/09/16) Elxan Abdullayev

Date		Opponent		Score	Scorers
2016					
06/08	a	Olimpik-Şüvälan	W	2-0	*Bädälov, Hacıyev*
14/08	h	Zirä	L	0-1	
21/08	a	Qarabağ	L	0-3	
10/09	h	Qäbälä	L	0-8	
18/09	a	İnter	L	1-2	*Abdullayev (p)*
27/09	h	Sumqayıt	L	1-2	*İmamverdiyev*
01/10	h	Käpäz	W	2-0	*Denílson, Ţîră*
16/10	a	Zirä	L	0-2	
25/10	h	Qarabağ	L	0-2	
29/10	a	Qäbälä	L	1-4	*Abdullayev*
05/11	h	İnter	W	2-1	*Jonas Pessalli, Abdullayev (p)*
20/11	a	Sumqayıt	L	0-2	
27/11	a	Käpäz	L	0-2	
17/12	h	Olimpik-Şüvälan	L	0-1	
2017					
29/01	a	Qarabağ	D	1-1	*İmamverdiyev*
03/02	a	Qäbälä	L	0-1	
09/02	a	İnter	W	3-1	*Daniel Lucas, Äläsgärov, Herrera*
13/02	h	Sumqayıt	W	1-0	*Bargas*
18/02	h	Käpäz	D	0-0	
27/02	a	Olimpik-Şüvälan	W	1-0	*Daniel Lucas*
05/03	h	Zirä	L	1-2	*Daniel Lucas (p)*
14/03	h	Qäbälä	W	1-0	*Äläsgärov*
18/03	h	İnter	W	2-1	*Bargas, Hacıyev*
02/04	a	Sumqayıt	L	0-2	
09/04	a	Käpäz	L	0-2	
14/04	h	Olimpik-Şüvälan	W	4-0	*Folprecht, Daniel Lucas, Herrera, Hacıyev*
23/04	a	Zirä	L	0-3	*(w/o; original result 2-2 Herrera, Daniel Lucas)*
29/04	h	Qarabağ	L	1-2	*Herrera*

No	Name	Nat	DoB	Pos	Aps	(s)	Gls
7	Araz Abdullayev		18/04/92	M	9	(2)	3
15	Ruslan Abışov		10/10/87	M	9		
13	Murad Ağayev		09/02/93	M	6	(2)	
7	Namiq Äläsgärov		03/02/95	A	12		2
66	İbrahim Äliyev		07/06/99	A		(2)	
33	Boban Bajković	MNE	15/03/85	G	14		
9	Hugo Bargas	FRA	22/10/86	A	3	(10)	2
95	Elvin Bädälov		14/06/95	D	13	(3)	1
23	Tärzin Cahangirov		17/01/92	M	13	(4)	
80	Edson Castillo	VEN	18/05/94	M	16	(4)	
12	Daniel Lucas	ESP	23/05/85	A	11	(2)	5
99	Denílson	BRA	18/07/95	A	7	(2)	1
6	Pavel Dreksa	CZE	17/09/89	D	11		
8	Zdeněk Folprecht	CZE	01/07/91	M	13	(1)	1
17	Rähman Hacıyev		25/07/93	M	22	(5)	3
11	Ignacio Herrera	CHI	14/10/87	A	12	(1)	4
10	Cavid İmamverdiyev		08/01/90	M	13	(7)	2
27	Mäqsäd İsayev		07/06/94	D	21	(1)	
3	Jairo	BRA	31/12/92	D	12	(1)	
90	Jonas Pessalli	BRA	24/09/90	M	3	(4)	1
4	Rahil Mämmädov		24/11/95	D	7	(1)	
30	Dario Melnjak	CRO	31/10/92	D	10		
19	Fähmin Muradbäyli		16/03/96	M	11	(8)	
29	Giorgi Navalovski	GEO	28/06/86	D	13	(1)	
25	Kyrylo Petrov	UKR	22/06/90	M	10		
88	Orxan Qurbanlı		12/07/95	M		(1)	
26	Kamal Qurbanov		06/05/94	D	5	(5)	
11	Ruslan Qurbanov		12/09/91	A	2	(1)	
1	Krševan Santini	CRO	11/04/87	G	8		
6	Vance Sikov	MKD	19/07/85	D	5		
22	Mahir Şükürov		12/12/82	D	4	(3)	
9	Cătălin Ţîră	ROU	18/06/94	A	4	(4)	1
53	Maksim Vaylo		13/05/95	G	6	(1)	
20	Eltun Yaqublu		19/08/91	D	3	(1)	

Olimpik-Şüvälan PFK

2004 • AZAL Arena (3,000) • azalpfc.az

Coach: Tärlan Ähmädov

Date		Opponent		Score	Scorers
2016					
06/08	h	Neftçi	L	0-2	
13/08	a	Käpäz	D	0-0	
19/08	a	Zirä	L	1-3	*Janelidze*
09/09	a	Qarabağ	L	0-6	
19/09	a	Qäbälä	L	0-3	
24/09	h	İnter	L	1-3	*Kvirtia*
01/10	a	Sumqayıt	D	1-1	*Äläkbärov*
16/10	h	Käpäz	L	0-1	
24/10	h	Zirä	D	1-1	*Janelidze*
29/10	h	Qarabağ	L	0-1	
06/11	h	Qäbälä	D	0-0	
20/11	a	İnter	L	0-3	
27/11	h	Sumqayıt	D	1-1	*Kvirtia*
17/12	a	Neftçi	W	1-0	*Janelidze*
2017					
29/01	a	Zirä	L	1-2	*Abdullayev*
03/02	h	Qarabağ	L	1-2	*Abdullayev*
08/02	a	Qäbälä	L	0-2	
13/02	h	İnter	L	0-1	
19/02	a	Sumqayıt	L	0-1	
27/02	h	Neftçi	L	0-1	
05/03	a	Käpäz	D	1-1	*Cavadov*
14/03	a	Qarabağ	L	0-1	
19/03	h	Qäbälä	D	1-1	*Kvirtia*
02/04	a	İnter	L	1-2	*Ämircanov*
10/04	h	Sumqayıt	L	1-2	*Ämircanov*
15/04	a	Neftçi	L	0-4	
23/04	h	Käpäz	L	1-2	*Madou*
29/04	h	Zirä	L	0-3	

No	Name	Nat	DoB	Pos	Aps	(s)	Gls
17	Räşad Abdullayev		01/10/81	M	14	(3)	2
33	Seyidräzi Ağayev		18/01/96	M	1		
36	Renat Aşurov		18/07/96	A	1		
14	İlqar Äläkbärov		06/10/93	M	16		1
55	Qeyrät Äliyev		08/11/88	D	3	(1)	
18	Ruslan Ämircanov		01/02/85	D	23	(3)	2
1	Räşad Äzizli		01/01/94	G	2		
51	Fuad Bayramov		20/05/98	D	1		
70	Vaqif Cavadov		25/05/89	M	6	(3)	1
24	Emin Cäfärquliyev		17/06/90	D	25		
77	Adan Coronado	USA	20/04/90	D	11	(1)	
15	Brian Fok	HKG	08/03/94	D	2	(1)	
77	Arkadi Galperin	RUS	21/05/92	M	10	(3)	
22	Tural Hümbätov		24/01/94	D	16	(1)	
27	Eltun Hüseynov		27/02/93	D	4	(4)	
5	Kamil Hüseynov		04/02/92	M	22		
88	Mirzağa Hüseynpur		11/03/90	A	1	(7)	
21	David Janelidze	GEO	12/09/89	A	6	(6)	3
10	Nugzar Kvirtia	GEO	16/09/84	M	16	(10)	3
11	Franck Madou	CIV	15/09/87	A	2	(6)	1
2	Elşad Manafov		08/03/92	D	10		
4	Qvanzav Maqomedov		08/06/94	D	8		
23	Aqil Mämmädov		01/05/89	G	25		
95	Şirmämmäd Mämmädov		03/03/95	M	1	(1)	
21	Samir Mäsimov		25/08/95	M	3	(5)	
7	Kamal Mirzäyev		14/09/94	M	21		
9	Röyal Näcäfov		09/07/90	A	16	(7)	
11	Ruslan Näsirli		12/01/95	M	7	(3)	
6	Taqim Novruzov		21/11/86	M	1	(1)	
1	Tärlan Qasımzadä		01/01/95	G	1		
44	Omega Roberts	LBR	12/12/89	D	5		
6	Bäxtiyar Soltanov		21/06/89	M	4	(1)	
19	Elnur Süleymanov		17/09/96	M	7	(9)	
91	Mehdi Taouil	MAR	20/05/83	M	5		
8	Sadio Tounkara	MLI	27/04/92	A	12	(1)	

Qarabağ FK

1987 • Älincä Arena (13,000); Azärsun Arena (5,900); Tofiq Bähramov adına Respublika stadionu (32,000) • qarabagh.com

Major honours

Azerbaijan League (5) 1993, 2014, 2015, 2016, 2017; Azerbaijan Cup (6) 1993, 2006, 2009, 2015, 2016, 2017

Coach: Qurban Qurbanov

Date		Opponent		Score	Scorers
2016					
07/08	a	İnter	L	1-2	*Reynaldo*
11/08	a	Sumqayıt	W	2-0	*Muarem, Dani Quintana*
21/08	h	Neftçi	W	3-0	*og (Jairo), Mädätov, El Jadeyaoui*
09/09	h	Olimpik-Şüvälan	W	6-0	*Reynaldo 2, Medvedev 2, Míchel, Dani Quintana*
19/09	h	Zirä	W	2-0	*Ämirquliyev 2*
25/09	a	Käpäz	D	1-1	*Reynaldo*
02/10	a	Qäbälä	L	0-2	
15/10	h	Sumqayıt	W	3-0	*Míchel, Qurbanov, Ndlovu*
25/10	a	Neftçi	W	2-0	*Ämirquliyev, og (Jairo)*
29/10	a	Olimpik-Şüvälan	W	1-0	*Muarem*
06/11	a	Zirä	W	2-0	*Dani Quintana, Yunuszadä*
19/11	h	Käpäz	W	1-0	*Ndlovu*
29/11	h	Qäbälä	W	2-1	*Almeida (p), Ndlovu*
17/12	h	İnter	D	0-0	
2017					
29/01	h	Neftçi	D	1-1	*Ndlovu (p)*
03/02	a	Olimpik-Şüvälan	W	2-1	*Medvedev, Diniyev*
08/02	h	Zirä	W	2-0	*İsmayılov, Ndlovu*
12/02	a	Käpäz	W	1-0	*Mädätov*
19/02	a	Qäbälä	L	0-2	
28/02	h	İnter	L	0-1	
04/03	a	Sumqayıt	W	4-0	*Míchel, Almeida (p), Muarem, Hüseynov*
14/03	h	Olimpik-Şüvälan	W	1-0	*Ndlovu*
19/03	a	Zirä	D	0-0	
02/04	h	Käpäz	W	2-1	*Ndlovu, Míchel*
09/04	h	Qäbälä	D	0-0	
16/04	a	İnter	W	3-0	*Mädätov, Ndlovu 2*
23/04	h	Sumqayıt	W	2-1	*Muarem, Abdullayev*
29/04	a	Neftçi	W	2-1	*Ndlovu, og (Abışov)*

No	Name	Nat	DoB	Pos	Aps	(s)	Gls
77	Elşän Abdullayev		05/02/94	M	1	(1)	1
25	Ansi Agolli	ALB	11/10/82	D	20	(1)	
17	Namiq Äläsgärov		03/02/95	A	2	(6)	
20	Richard Almeida		20/03/89	M	20		2
15	Rahid Ämirquliyev		01/09/89	M	12	(8)	3
99	Dani Quintana	ESP	08/03/87	M	13	(2)	3
21	Arif Daşdämirov		10/02/87	D	11		
91	Coşqun Diniyev		13/09/95	M	16	(5)	1
67	Alharbi El Jadeyaoui	MAR	08/08/86	M	1		1
55	Bädavi Hüseynov		11/07/91	D	20		1
22	Äfran İsmayılov		08/10/88	M	10	(11)	1
11	Mahir Mädätov		01/07/97	A	8	(13)	3
12	Şahrudin Mähämmädäliyev		12/06/94	G	7		
5	Maksim Medvedev		29/09/89	D	19	(1)	3
8	Míchel	ESP	08/11/85	M	21	(4)	4
10	Muarem Muarem	MKD	22/10/88	M	15	(8)	4
71	Vüqar Nadirov		15/06/87	M	1	(1)	
6	Dino Ndlovu	RSA	15/02/90	A	20	(3)	10
2	Qara E Qarayev		12/10/92	M	14	(6)	
18	İlqar Qurbanov		25/04/86	D	15	(1)	1
44	Ağabala Ramazanov		20/01/93	M	8	(4)	
9	Reynaldo	BRA	24/08/89	A	7	(3)	4
14	Räşad F Sadıqov		16/06/82	D	14		
1	Bojan Šaranov	SRB	22/09/87	G	2		
13	Ibrahim Šehić	BIH	02/09/88	G	19		
32	Elvin Yunuszadä		22/08/92	D	12	(1)	1

Qäbälä FK

2005 • Dalğa Arena (6,700); Qäbälä şähär stadionu (4,500) • gabalafc.az

Coach: Roman Hryhorchuk (UKR)

Date		Opponent	Res	Score	Scorers
2016					
08/08	h	Käpäz	W	2-0	*Mütällimov, Dabo*
12/08	h	İnter	D	0-0	
10/09	a	Neftçi	W	8-0	*Dabo 3, Vernydub, Ozobić, Qurbanov 2, og (Jairo)*
19/09	h	Olimpik-Şüvälan	W	3-0	*Ozobić, Qurbanov, R Hüseynov*
22/09	h	Sumqayıt	W	2-0	*Dabo 2*
25/09	a	Zirä	W	2-0	*Weeks 2*
02/10	h	Qarabağ	W	2-0	*Ozobić, Dabo*
15/10	a	İnter	D	1-1	*Zenjov*
25/10	a	Sumqayıt	D	2-2	*Eyubov, Ozobić*
29/10	h	Neftçi	W	4-1	*Zenjov 2, Mämmädov, Eyubov*
06/11	a	Olimpik-Şüvälan	D	0-0	
19/11	h	Zirä	W	1-0	*Ozobić*
29/11	a	Qarabağ	L	1-2	*Ozobić*
17/12	h	Käpäz	W	2-1	*Ozobić (p), Qurbanov (p)*
2017					
28/01	h	Sumqayıt	D	1-1	*Vernydub*
03/02	h	Neftçi	W	1-0	*Subotic*
08/02	h	Olimpik-Şüvälan	W	2-0	*Ozobić 2 (1p)*
12/02	a	Zirä	D	2-2	*Subotic, Ozobić*
19/02	h	Qarabağ	W	2-0	*Zenjov, Ozobić*
28/02	a	Käpäz	D	1-1	*og (Renan)*
04/03	a	İnter	W	2-0	*Mütällimov, Subotic*
14/03	a	Neftçi	L	0-1	
19/03	a	Olimpik-Şüvälan	D	1-1	*Mütällimov*
02/04	h	Zirä	D	1-1	*Zenjov*
09/04	a	Qarabağ	D	0-0	
16/04	a	Käpäz	L	0-2	
24/04	h	İnter	W	4-3	*Ricardinho, Zenjov, og (Scarlatache), Mütällimov*
29/04	a	Sumqayıt	L	1-2	*Mämmädov*

No	Name	Nat	DoB	Pos	Aps	(s)	Gls
34	Ürfan Abbasov		14/10/92	D	18	(2)	
77	Araz Abdullayev		18/04/92	M	7	(2)	
8	Qismät Alıyev		24/10/96	M	2	(1)	
22	Dmytro Bezotosniy	UKR	15/11/83	G	27		
4	Elvin Camalov		04/02/95	M	11	(2)	
18	Bagaliy Dabo	FRA	27/07/88	A	10	(6)	7
32	Räşad Eyubov		03/12/92	M	6	(2)	2
30	Petar Franjić	CRO	21/08/91	M	2	(2)	
90	Ramil Hasanov	UKR	15/02/96	A		(1)	
14	Cavid Hüseynov		09/03/88	M	10	(6)	
21	Roman Hüseynov		26/12/97	M	2	(4)	1
26	Ülvi İbazadä		26/08/96	M	1		
7	Nika Kvekveskiri	GEO	29/05/92	M	13	(1)	
11	Asif Mämmädov		05/08/86	M	17	(3)	2
17	Mähämmäd Mirzäbäyov		16/11/90	D	14	(7)	
13	Murad Musayev		13/06/94	D	2	(2)	
88	Tellur Mütällimov		08/04/95	D	15	(2)	4
70	Färid Näbiyev		22/07/99	A		(1)	
19	Filip Ozobić	CRO	08/04/91	M	26	(1)	11
33	Dawid Pietrzkiewicz	POL	09/02/88	G	1		
39	Sadiq Quliyev		09/03/95	D		(1)	
10	Ruslan Qurbanov		12/09/91	A	14	(7)	4
44	Rafael Santos	BRA	10/11/84	D	8	(1)	
5	Rasim Ramaldanov		24/01/86	D	6		
20	Ricardinho	BRA	09/09/84	D	10		1
6	Räşad Ä Sadiqov		08/10/83	M	17	(4)	
3	Vojislav Stanković	SRB	22/09/87	D	23		
31	Danijel Subotic	SUI	31/01/89	A	7	(4)	3
15	Vitaliy Vernydub	UKR	17/10/87	D	14		2
27	Theo Weeks	LBR	19/01/90	M	11	(5)	2
9	Sergei Zenjov	EST	20/04/89	A	14	(7)	6

Sumqayıt FK

2010 • Kapital Bank Arena (1,326) • sumqayitpfc.az

Coach: Samir Abasov

Date		Opponent	Res	Score	Scorers
2016					
06/08	a	Zirä	W	1-0	*Cavadov*
11/08	h	Qarabağ	L	0-2	
11/09	h	İnter	L	1-2	*Cavadov*
18/09	h	Käpäz	D	1-1	*Cavadov*
22/09	a	Qäbälä	L	0-2	
27/09	a	Neftçi	W	2-1	*Näbiyev, Äsädov*
01/10	h	Olimpik-Şüvälan	D	1-1	*Abbasov*
15/10	a	Qarabağ	L	0-3	
25/10	h	Qäbälä	D	2-2	*Näbiyev, Yunanov (p)*
30/10	a	İnter	L	1-3	*Abbasov*
05/11	a	Käpäz	D	0-0	
20/11	h	Neftçi	W	2-0	*Quluzadä, Abbasov*
27/11	a	Olimpik-Şüvälan	D	1-1	*Yunanov (p)*
17/12	h	Zirä	W	1-0	*Abbasov*
2017					
28/01	a	Qäbälä	D	1-1	*Qurbanov*
04/02	h	İnter	D	2-2	*Abbasov (p), Muxtarov*
09/02	h	Käpäz	W	3-1	*Chernyshev, Salahlı, Qurbanov*
13/02	a	Neftçi	L	0-1	
19/02	h	Olimpik-Şüvälan	W	1-0	*Näbiyev*
27/02	a	Zirä	L	0-1	
04/03	h	Qarabağ	L	0-4	
13/03	a	İnter	L	0-1	
18/03	a	Käpäz	L	0-1	
02/04	h	Neftçi	W	2-0	*Häsänalızadä, Yunanov*
10/04	a	Olimpik-Şüvälan	W	2-1	*Yunanov, Abbasov*
15/04	h	Zirä	D	1-1	*Abbasov*
23/04	a	Qarabağ	L	1-2	*Yunanov*
29/04	h	Qäbälä	W	2-1	*Yunanov, Abbasov*

No	Name	Nat	DoB	Pos	Aps	(s)	Gls
22	Mirabdulla Abbasov		27/04/95	M	19	(8)	8
42	Kamran Abdullazadä		20/03/95	M	8	(2)	
11	Ebrahim Abednezhad	IRN	22/08/92	M	4	(1)	
21	Nasir Abilayev	RUS	19/11/95	M	1	(5)	
18	Süleyman Ähmädov		25/11/99	M	1	(2)	
5	Seymur Äsädov		05/05/94	M	6	(8)	1
39	Tural Bayramlı		07/01/98	M		(2)	
7	Vaqif Cavadov		25/05/89	M	10	(3)	3
7	Sergei Chernyshev	RUS	27/04/90	M	6	(3)	1
66	Afshin Esmaeilzadeh	IRN	21/04/92	M	5	(5)	
17	Vaquf Güläliyev		11/05/93	D		(1)	
20	Farkhad Gystarov	RUS	21/11/94	M	8		
14	Bäxtiyar Häsänalızadä		29/12/92	D	24		1
3	Vurğun Hüseynov		25/04/88	D	27		
2	Rail Mälikov		18/12/85	D	24		
25	Ayaz Mehdiyev		22/02/93	M	11	(5)	
13	Bählul Mustafazadä		27/02/97	D	2	(2)	
8	Nicat Muxtarov		01/06/95	M	15	(6)	1
74	Yusif Näbiyev		03/09/97	D	15	(3)	3
97	Xäyal Näcäfov		19/12/97	M	14	(5)	
24	Amit Quluzadä		20/11/92	M	13		1
10	Mähämmäd Qurbanov		11/04/92	A	21	(1)	2
19	Azär Salahlı		11/04/94	D	26	(2)	1
77	Ehtiram Şahverdiyev		01/10/96	M	7	(5)	
1	Färhad Väliyev		01/11/80	G	28		
29	Amil Yunanov		06/01/93	A	13	(10)	6

Zirä FK

2014 • Zirä qäsäbä Olimpiya Kompleksinin stadionu (1,512) • fczire.az

Coach: Adil Şükürov; (27/12/16) Ayxan Abbasov

Date		Opponent	Res	Score	Scorers
2016					
06/08	h	Sumqayıt	L	0-1	
14/08	a	Neftçi	W	1-0	*Mustafayev*
19/08	h	Olimpik-Şüvälan	W	3-1	*Progni 2, Mämmädov (p)*
11/09	a	Käpäz	L	0-2	
19/09	a	Qarabağ	L	0-2	
25/09	h	Qäbälä	L	0-2	
30/09	a	İnter	D	1-1	*Igbekoyi*
16/10	h	Neftçi	W	2-0	*Krneta (p), Nağıyev*
24/10	a	Olimpik-Şüvälan	D	1-1	*Meza (p)*
30/10	h	Käpäz	W	2-0	*Tağıyev, Mämmädov (p)*
06/11	h	Qarabağ	L	0-2	
19/11	a	Qäbälä	L	0-1	
28/11	h	İnter	D	1-1	*Krneta*
17/12	a	Sumqayıt	L	0-1	
2017					
29/01	h	Olimpik-Şüvälan	W	2-1	*Meza 2*
04/02	h	Käpäz	W	1-0	*Novruzov*
08/02	a	Qarabağ	L	0-2	
12/02	h	Qäbälä	D	2-2	*Igbekoyi, Gadze*
18/02	a	İnter	D	1-1	*og (Dênis Silva)*
27/02	h	Sumqayıt	W	1-0	*Gadze*
05/03	a	Neftçi	W	2-1	*og (Navalovski), Djurić*
13/03	a	Käpäz	L	0-1	
19/03	h	Qarabağ	D	0-0	
02/04	a	Qäbälä	D	1-1	*Meza*
10/04	h	İnter	D	1-1	*Gadze*
15/04	a	Sumqayıt	D	1-1	*Djurić (p)*
23/04	h	Neftçi	W	3-0	*(w/o; original result 2-2 Xälilzadä, Latifu)*
29/04	a	Olimpik-Şüvälan	W	3-0	*Mämmädov, Djurić, Xälilzadä (p)*

No	Name	Nat	DoB	Pos	Aps	(s)	Gls
85	Kamal Bayramov		15/08/85	G	5	(1)	
18	Tural Cälilov		28/11/86	D	5	(4)	
8	Milan Djurić	SRB	03/10/87	M	24	(2)	3
43	Richard Gadze	GHA	23/08/94	A	11	(1)	3
26	Giorgi Gorozia	GEO	26/03/95	M		(5)	
11	Victor Igbekoyi	NGA	01/09/86	M	17	(6)	2
90	Vüsal İsgändärli		03/11/95	M		(15)	
99	Yasyn Khamid	UKR	10/01/93	A		(3)	
23	Jovan Krneta	SRB	04/05/92	D	24		2
16	Akeem Latifu	NGA	16/11/89	D	11		1
10	Elvin Mämmädov		18/07/88	M	20	(5)	3
20	César Meza	PAR	05/10/91	M	18	(2)	4
44	Miguel Lourenço	POR	27/05/92	D	21		
38	İlkin Muradov		05/03/96	M		(1)	
6	Vüqar Mustafayev		05/08/94	M	21	(4)	1
5	Adil Nağıyev		11/09/95	D	21	(1)	1
96	Elgün Näbiyev		04/01/96	A		(2)	
1	Anar Näzirov		08/09/85	G	23		
19	Nurlan Novruzov		03/03/93	A	15	(8)	1
7	Gerhard Progni	ALB	06/11/86	M	12	(2)	2
39	Sadiq Quliyev		09/03/95	D	12		
7	Ben Sangaré	FRA	12/11/90	M	5	(4)	
21	Murad Sättarlı		09/05/92	A	4	(5)	
13	Aleksandr Şemonayev		01/04/85	D	6	(4)	
92	Cavid Tağıyev		22/07/92	M	6	(6)	1
28	Tämkin Xälilzadä		06/08/93	M	27		2

Top goalscorers

Rauf Äliyev

Filip Ozobić

11	Rauf Äliyev (İnter) Filip Ozobić (Qäbälä)
10	Dino Ndlovu (Qarabağ)
8	Mirabdulla Abbasov (Sumqayıt)
7	Nizami Hacıyev (İnter) Bagaliy Dabo (Qäbälä)
6	Julien Ebah (Käpäz) Amil Yunanov (Sumqayıt) Sergei Zenjov (Qäbälä)
5	Ruslan Abışov (İnter) Tural Axundov (Käpäz) Daniel Lucas (Neftçi)

Promoted club

Säbail FK

2016 • Bayıl Arena (3,000) • no website
Coach: Elman Sultanov

Second level final table 2016/17

		Pld	W	D	L	F	A	Pts
1	Turan Tovuz İK	26	18	7	1	62	11	61
2	Säbail FK	26	18	3	5	80	25	57
3	Ağsu FK	26	16	5	5	63	21	53
4	Qaradağ Lökbatan FK	26	17	1	8	64	31	52
5	Zaqatala PFK	26	15	4	7	69	31	49
6	Şämkir FK	26	15	3	8	41	20	48
7	Mil-Muğan İmişli FK	26	13	5	8	53	33	44
8	MOİK Bakı PFK	26	10	6	10	47	31	36
9	Şahdağ Qusar FK	26	8	6	12	36	45	30
10	Şärurspor PFK	26	7	4	15	36	54	25
11	Energetik Mingäçevir FK	26	5	5	16	25	86	20
12	Bakılı Bakı PFK	26	3	2	21	30	99	11
13	Rävan Bakı FK	26	6	1	19	24	70	10
14	Göyäzän Qazax FK	26	2	4	20	20	99	10

NB Rävan Bakı FK – 9 pts deducted; Rävan Bakı FK and Şärurspor PFK withdrew after round 19 – their remaining matches were awarded as 0-3 defeats; Turan Tovuz İK did not obtain licence for Premyer Liqası 2017/18; Säbail FK promoted instead.

DOMESTIC CUP

Azärbaycan kuboku 2016/17

1/8 FINALS

(02/12/16)
İnter 5-1 Qaradağ Lökbatan
MOİK 0-2 Sumqayıt
Neftçi 2-0 Şärurspor
Olimpik-Şüvälan 4-0 Rävan

(03/12/16)
Qarabağ 5-0 Säbail
Qäbälä 2-2 Zaqatala *(aet; 4-1 on pens)*
Şahdağ 1-5 Käpäz
Turan Tovuz 0-1 Zirä

QUARTER-FINALS

(13/12/16 & 21/12/16)
İnter 2-0 Käpäz *(Äliyev 58, Hacıyev 61)*
Käpäz 0-0 İnter
(İnter 2-0)

Qarabağ 6-0 Sumqayıt *(Almeida 25p, Ndlovu 34p, Diniyev 42, Mädätov 64, 79, Äläsgärov 67)*
Sumqayıt 2-5 Qarabağ *(Yunanov 14, 80; Äläsgärov 8, 16, 82, Nadirov 70, Ämirquliyev 90)*
(Qarabağ 11-2)

Qäbälä 2-1 Olimpik-Şüvälan *(Ozobić 61, Qurbanov 74; Hüseynpur 37)*
Olimpik-Şüvälan 0-1 Qäbälä *(Mämmädov 53)*
(Qäbälä 3-1)

Zirä 0-3 Neftçi *(Jonas Pessalli 44, 58p, 63p)*
Neftçi 1-2 Zirä *(Mämmädov 40; Djurić 34, Novruzov 85)*
(Neftçi 4-2)

SEMI-FINALS

(30/03/17 & 05/04/17)
İnter 1-3 Qäbälä *(Scarlatache 18; Subotic 14p, 47, Ozobić 88p)*
Qäbälä 2-0 İnter *(Subotic 12, Dabo 33)*
(Qäbälä 5-1)

Neftçi 0-2 Qarabağ *(Muarem 13, Ndlovu 28)*
Qarabağ 0-0 Neftçi
(Qarabağ 2-0)

FINAL

(05/05/17)
Naxçıvan Muxtar Respublika stadionu, Naxcivan
QARABAĞ FK 2 *(Mädätov 52, Abbasov 68og)*
QÄBÄLÄ FK 0
Referee: *Yusifov*
QARABAĞ: *Šehić, Medvedev, Sadıqov (Diniyev 54), Hüseynov, Agolli, Qarayev, Almeida (Ämirquliyev 85), Míchel, İsmayılov, Muarem, Mädätov (Ramazanov 74)*
QÄBÄLÄ: *Bezotosniy, Mütällimov (R Hüseynov 26), Stanković, Sadiqov, Abbasov, Weeks (Mirzäbäyov 27), Kvekveskiri, Ozobić, C Hüseynov, Abdullayev (Dabo 73), Zenjov*

Qarabağ completed a hat-trick of domestic cup triumphs with a 2-0 win against Qäbälä

BELARUS

Belorusskaja Federacija Futbola (BFF)

Address	Prospekt Pobeditelei 20/3 BY-220020 Minsk	**President**	Sergei Roumas
Tel	+375 17 2545 600	**General secretary**	Sergei Safaryan
Fax	+375 17 2509 636	**Media officer**	Aleksandr Aleinik
E-mail	info@bff.by	**Year of formation**	1989
Website	bff.by	**National stadium**	Borisov Arena, Borisov (13,126)

PREMIER LEAGUE CLUBS

 1 **FC BATE Borisov**

 2 **FC Belshina Bobruisk**

 3 **FC Dinamo Brest**

 4 **FC Dinamo Minsk**

 5 **FC Gorodeya**

 6 **FC Granit Mikashevichi**

 7 **FC Isloch**

 8 **FC Krumkachy**

 9 **FC Minsk**

 10 **FC Naftan Novopolotsk**

 11 **FC Neman Grodno**

 12 **FC Shakhtyor Soligorsk**

 13 **FC Slavia-Mozyr**

 14 **SFC Slutsk**

 15 **FC Torpedo Zhodino**

 16 **FC Vitebsk**

PROMOTED CLUBS

 17 **FC Gomel**

 18 **FC Dnepr Mogilev**

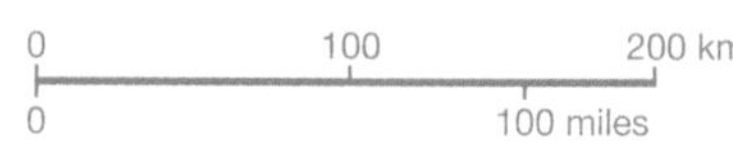

KEY

- UEFA Champions League
- UEFA Europa League
- Promoted
- Relegated

Record 13th crown for relentless BATE

FC BATE Borisov had a rare year off from group stage European football in 2016, but despite an increase from 14 to 16 teams there was no change to the script in the Belarusian Premier League as their sequence of successive victories in the competition stretched to an 11th year, giving them a record-extending 13th title in all.

There was little competition for BATE in the league, but in the cup they were eliminated in the semi-finals by Dinamo Brest, who went on to lift the trophy for the first time in a decade after a penalty shoot-out win over Shakhtyor Soligorsk.

Borisov club claim 11th successive league title

Domestic triumph atones for European disappointment

Cup glory goes to Dinamo Brest

Domestic league

The outcome of Aleksandr Yermakovich's third full season as BATE head coach never looked likely to differ from those of the previous two once the serial champions had kicked off with six wins and a draw from their first seven fixtures. Although the only points they dropped during that opening sequence came in a thrilling 3-3 draw at home to Dinamo Minsk, the previous season's runners-up would share the points in five successive fixtures during the first two months and effectively relinquish all hope of mounting a challenge to BATE.

Dinamo switched coach in mid-campaign, with Sergei Borovski, a two-time national team boss of Belarus, replacing Serbian Vuk Rašović, but they were unable to finish higher than third – four points behind Shakhtyor (Borovski's ex-club), who, thanks to the league's best defence and a closing 13-match unbeaten run, reclaimed the runners-up spot they had last filled in 2013.

BATE were never properly challenged. Not for the first time they made mathematically certain of the title long before the league's conclusion, a 1-0 win at lowly Granit Mikashevichi – courtesy of substitute Nikolai Signevich's late strike – settling matters with five of their 30 fixtures still to complete. That was BATE's sixth three-pointer in a row – their longest winning sequence of the campaign – and although they eased off thereafter, they still ended up with an 11-point winning margin over Shakhtyor. Furthermore they scored 73 goals, with strikers Vitali Rodionov and Mikhail Gordeichuk both supplying 15 apiece to share the Premier League's golden boot. At the other end, BATE used four goalkeepers in conceding 25 goals – five more than Shakhtyor.

Gomel, the only team relegated in 2015, won immediate promotion, finishing above second-tier runners-up Dnepr Mogilev on the head-to-head rule after their rivals had a point removed for financial irregularities. At the foot of the Premier League, Belshina Bobruisk and Granit also finished level on points, but 25 apiece meant relegation for both, while the three top-flight newcomers – Isloch, Gorodeya and Krumkachy – all surprisingly stayed up.

Domestic cup

It was a mid-table Premier League side, Dinamo Brest, that lifted the 2016/17 Belarusian Cup, the team from the south-west border overcoming Shakhtyor just up the road in Grodno at the end of a marathon penalty shoot-out. The two hours of regulation play in the final ended goalless, but there was no lack of precision from the spot as only one of the 20 outfield players active at the end of extra time missed his kick – the 20th and last taker, Shakhtyor's Aleksei Yanushkevich. Having ousted Dinamo Minsk and BATE in the previous two rounds, it was a worthy second cup triumph for Brest, led to victory by their new (ex-Shakhtyor) coach, Vladimir Zhuravel.

Europe

After becoming accustomed to regular group stage involvement, BATE's 2016/17 European campaign was one of grave disappointment. Yermakovich's troops fell to Dundalk in the UEFA Champions League third qualifying round before losing to FC Astana in the UEFA Europa League play-offs. That defeat ended Belarusian interest, with the nation's other three clubs having all bowed out during the UEFA Europa League qualifying phase.

National team

Belarus's hopes of participating in the 2018 FIFA World Cup in neighbouring Russia always looked slim given the strength of their qualifying group, and despite an opening 0-0 draw against France, coach Aleksandr Khatskevich was removed from his post when the next three fixtures yielded just one further point – from a 1-1 home draw with Luxembourg. New boss Igor Kriushenko (ex-BATE, 2005-07) eventually led the team to their first win, 2-1 against Bulgaria in Borisov, thanks to a splendid winning strike from Pavel Savitski.

DOMESTIC SEASON AT A GLANCE

Premier League 2016 final table

		Pld	Home W	Home D	Home L	Home F	Home A	Away W	Away D	Away L	Away F	Away A	Total W	Total D	Total L	Total F	Total A	Pts
1	**FC BATE Borisov**	**30**	**12**	**2**	**1**	**43**	**9**	**10**	**2**	**3**	**30**	**16**	**22**	**4**	**4**	**73**	**25**	**70**
2	FC Shakhtyor Soligorsk	30	9	4	2	27	8	8	4	3	19	12	17	8	5	46	20	59
3	FC Dinamo Minsk	30	10	3	2	25	10	5	7	3	21	18	15	10	5	46	28	55
4	FC Minsk	30	7	4	4	24	12	8	4	3	25	12	15	8	7	49	24	53
5	FC Torpedo Zhodino	30	6	4	5	22	15	7	5	3	25	18	13	9	8	47	33	48
6	FC Vitebsk	30	6	4	5	15	14	6	2	7	15	12	12	6	12	30	26	42
7	FC Isloch	30	6	3	6	19	22	5	5	5	14	17	11	8	11	33	39	41
8	FC Dinamo Brest	30	5	5	5	18	21	6	2	7	20	17	11	7	12	38	38	40
9	FC Gorodeya	30	5	7	3	21	15	3	7	5	15	24	8	14	8	36	39	38
10	FC Slavia-Mozyr	30	7	3	5	22	23	2	5	8	11	26	9	8	13	33	49	35
11	FC Krumkachy	30	7	1	7	14	16	2	5	8	10	23	9	6	15	24	39	33
12	SFC Slutsk	30	5	6	4	14	13	1	6	8	8	21	6	12	12	22	34	30
13	FC Naftan Novopolotsk	30	5	6	4	16	16	2	2	11	9	30	7	8	15	25	46	29
14	FC Neman Grodno	30	4	4	7	14	19	3	4	8	7	17	7	8	15	21	36	29
15	FC Belshina Bobruisk	30	2	6	7	14	21	3	4	8	20	24	5	10	15	34	45	25
16	FC Granit Mikashevichi	30	2	6	7	9	26	3	4	8	11	30	5	10	15	20	56	25

European qualification 2017/18

Champion: FC BATE Borisov (second qualifying round)

Cup winner: FC Dinamo Brest (second qualifying round)

FC Shakhtyor Soligorsk (first qualifying round)
FC Dinamo Minsk (first qualifying round)

Top scorer	Mikhail Gordeichuk (BATE) & Vitali Rodionov (BATE), 15 goals
Relegated clubs	FC Granit Mikashevichi, FC Belshina Bobruisk
Promoted clubs	FC Gomel, FC Dnepr Mogilev
Cup final	FC Dinamo Brest 0-0 FC Shakhtyor Soligorsk *(aet; 10-9 on pens)*

Player of the season

Vitali Rodionov
(FC BATE Borisov)

Involved in every one of BATE's 11 successive Belarusian title triumphs, Rodionov, who joined the club from Torpedo Zhodino in 2005, claimed a third Premier League golden boot, sharing the prize – on 15 goals apiece – with club colleague Mikhail Gordeichuk. The 32-year-old Belarus international striker had previously won the award in 2008 (shared) and 2013, and his durable talent, which has also brought him 20 European goals, was much in evidence in the 2016 season, during which he also provided eight assists (two more than Gordeichuk).

Newcomer of the season

Joel Fameyeh
(FC Belshina Bobruisk/ FC Dinamo Brest)

The top-scoring foreigner in the 2016 Belarusian Premier League, Fameyeh split his ten goals evenly between two clubs, Belshina and Dinamo Brest, as he made the most of his loan spell from Ghanaian club Asokwa Deportivo. The 19-year-old striker scored his first goal for Belshina against BATE, but he left in mid-campaign for Brest, helping his new team to mid-table safety while his former charges slipped out of the division. He then helped Dinamo to victory in the 2016/17 Belarusian Cup, scoring the decisive goal against BATE in the semi-finals.

Team of the season

(4-3-3)

Coach: Yermakovich *(BATE)*

NATIONAL TEAM

Top five all-time caps

Aleksandr Kulchy (102); Sergei Gurenko (80); **Sergei Kornilenko** (78); **Aleksandr Hleb** (77); **Timofei Kalachev** (76)

Top five all-time goals

Maksim Romashchenko (20); **Sergei Kornilenko** (17); Vitali Kutuzov (13); Vyacheslav Hleb (12); Valentin Belkevich, **Timofei Kalachev**, **Vitali Rodionov** & Roman Vasilyuk (10)

Results 2016/17

31/08/16	Norway	A	Oslo	W	1-0	*Krivets (56)*
06/09/16	France (WCQ)	H	Borisov	D	0-0	
07/10/16	Netherlands (WCQ)	A	Rotterdam	L	1-4	*Rios (47)*
10/10/16	Luxembourg (WCQ)	H	Borisov	D	1-1	*Savitski (80)*
09/11/16	Greece	A	Piraeus	W	1-0	*Politevich (14)*
13/11/16	Bulgaria (WCQ)	A	Sofia	L	0-1	
25/03/17	Sweden (WCQ)	A	Solna	L	0-4	
28/03/17	FYR Macedonia	A	Skopje	L	0-3	
01/06/17	Switzerland	A	Neuchatel	L	0-1	
09/06/17	Bulgaria (WCQ)	H	Borisov	W	2-1	*Sivakov (33p), Savitski (80)*
12/06/17	New Zealand	H	Minsk	W	1-0	*Polyakov (47)*

Appearances 2016/17

Coach: Aleksandr Khatskevich /(01/03/17) Igor Kriushenko	**19/10/73 10/02/64**		**Nor**	**FRA**	**NED**	**LUX**	**Gre**	**BUL**	**SWE**	**Mkd**	**Sui**	**BUL**	**Nzl**	**Caps**	**Goals**
Andrei Gorbunov	25/05/83	Atromitos (GRE)	G	G	G	G		G	G					13	-
Igor Shitov	24/10/86	Astana (KAZ)	D				D	s36	D					54	1
Aleksandr Martynovich	26/08/87	Krasnodar (RUS)	D46			D	s46	D36	D	s84				56	2
Mikhail Sivakov	16/01/88	Zorya (UKR) /Orenburg (RUS)	D	D	D					D84	D	D		16	1
Denis Polyakov	17/04/91	BATE	D	D	D	D	D46	D		D			D86	26	1
Ivan Mayevski	05/05/88	Anji (RUS) /Astana (KAZ)	M	M	M46	M71	M	M74	M65			M89	M79	14	-
Sergei Kislyak	06/08/87	Gaziantepspor (TUR)	M87		s67					D75				63	9
Timofei Kalachev	01/05/81	Rostov (RUS)	M46	M		M								76	10
Mikhail Gordeichuk	23/10/89	BATE	A	A85	A74	A	s57	A	A	s58	A46	s89	A62	24	4
Maksim Volodko	10/11/92	BATE	M46	s85	s74	s78	s46		s69	D				18	1
Nikolai Signevich	20/02/92	BATE /Platanias (GRE)	A70	A81		A60			A71	s59				11	1
Yegor Filipenko	10/04/88	M. Tel-Aviv (ISR)	s46 /74			D	D	D	D		D	D		50	1
Sergei Krivets	08/06/86	Wisla Plock (POL)	s46	s69	M67									38	5
Aleksei Rios	14/05/87	BATE	s46		M		s72		M	s75			M71	6	1
Sergei Kornilenko	14/06/83	Krylya Sovetov (RUS)	s70	s81	A	s60	s62	s74						78	17
Sergei Politevich	09/04/90	Gençlerbirliği (TUR)	s74	D	D		D46	D	D	D46		D	D	19	1
Stanislav Dragun	04/06/88	Dinamo Moskva (RUS) /Orenburg (RUS)	s87						s65	M	M	M		42	5
Maksim Bordachev	18/06/86	Tom (RUS) /Orenburg (RUS)		D	D	D78			D69					44	2
Igor Stasevich	21/10/85	BATE		M69						M				31	2
Nikita Korzun	06/03/95	Dynamo Kyiv (UKR)		M	M	M	s62						M	7	-
Aleksandr Hleb	01/05/81	BATE			s46	M	M57	M 91*						77	6
Pavel Savitski	12/07/94	Neman				s71	M72	s61		M58	s46	A82	s62	10	4
Sergei Chernik	20/07/88	Nancy (FRA)					G				G	G		11	-
Yuri Kendysh	10/06/90	BATE					M62	M		M71				3	-
Pavel Nekhaichik	15/07/88	Orenburg (RUS)					M	M61						21	1
Denis Laptev	01/08/91	Shakhtyor Soligorsk					A62	A			s46	A74	s62	6	-
Renan Bressan	03/11/88	Chaves (POR)							M	s71				26	3
Vitali Rodionov	11/12/83	BATE							s71	A59				48	10
Aleksandr Gutor	18/04/89	Orenburg (RUS)								G				8	-
Maksim Skavysh	13/11/89	Torpedo Zhodino								s46	A46	s82	A62	7	-
Aleksandr Sachivko	05/01/86	Dinamo Minsk									D61		D	2	-
Igor Burko	08/09/88	Shakhtyor Soligorsk									M46		M71	2	-
Oleg Yevdokimov	25/02/94	Minsk									M46			1	-
Aleksei Legchilin	11/04/92	Dinamo Brest									M46			1	-
Sergei Balanovich	29/08/87	Amkar (RUS)									A	A		27	2
Dmitri Aliseiko	28/08/92	Dinamo Brest									s46	M	s71	3	-
Artem Bykov	19/10/92	Dinamo Minsk									s46	s74	M	5	-
Sergei Matveichik	05/06/88	Shakhtyor Soligorsk									s46	M	s71	5	-
Aleksandr Pavlovets	13/08/96	Torpedo Zhodino									s61		s86	2	-
Andrei Klimovich	27/08/88	Dinamo Minsk											G	1	-
Evgeni Berezkin	05/07/96	BATE											s79	1	-

EUROPE

FC BATE Borisov

Second qualifying round - SJK Seinäjoki (FIN)
H 2-0 *Kendysh (32), Rodionov (68)*
Veremko, Gaiduchik, Karnitski (Gvilia 84), A Volodko (Ivanić 74), Pikk, Zhavnerchik, Rodionov, Stasevich, Polyakov, Gordeichuk (Rios 69), Kendysh. Coach: Aleksandr Yermakovich (BLR)
A 2-2 *Karnitski (15), Rios (29)*
Veremko, Gaiduchik, Karnitski, A Volodko (Ivanić 54), Pikk, Zhavnerchik, Rios (Gordeichuk 69), Rodionov (M Volodko 85), Stasevich, Polyakov, Kendysh. Coach: Aleksandr Yermakovich (BLR)

Third qualifying round - Dundalk FC (IRL)
H 1-0 *Gordeichuk (70)*
Veremko, Dubra, Karnitski (A Volodko 88), Ivanić (Gordeichuk 68), Pikk, Zhavnerchik (Hleb 60), Rios, Rodionov, Stasevich, Polyakov, Kendysh. Coach: Aleksandr Yermakovich (BLR)
A 0-3
Veremko, Dubra, Karnitski (Hleb 46), Ivanić, Pikk (Gordeichuk 65), Zhavnerchik (Signevich 81), Rios, Rodionov, Stasevich, Polyakov, Kendysh. Coach: Aleksandr Yermakovich (BLR)

Play-offs - FC Astana (KAZ)
A 0-2
Veremko, Gaiduchik, Karnitski (Signevich 80), Zhavnerchik, Rios, Rodionov, Polyakov, Gordeichuk, Kendysh, Gvilia (Yablonski 46), Hleb (Ivanić 39). Coach: Aleksandr Yermakovich (BLR)
H 2-2 *Gordeichuk (27), Stasevich (89p)*
Soroko, Gaiduchik, Ivanić, Zhavnerchik, Rios, Rodionov (Pikk 86), Stasevich, Polyakov, M Volodko (Signevich 55), Gordeichuk (Mozolevski 73), Kendysh. Coach: Aleksandr Yermakovich (BLR)
Red card: Rios 82

FC Torpedo Zhodino

Second qualifying round - Debreceni VSC (HUN)
A 2-1 *Zaginaylov (23), Klopotski (88)*
Fomichev, Chelyadinski, Klopotski, Pankovets, Shapoval, Khachaturyan (Pavlyukovets 80), Lutsevich, Shcherbo (Chelyadko 85), Zaginaylov (Trapashko 69), Afanasiyev, Demidovich. Coach: Igor Kriushenko (BLR)
H 1-0 *Demidovich (25)*
Fomichev, Chelyadinski, Klopotski, Pankovets, Shapoval, Khachaturyan, Lutsevich, Golenkov (Chelyadko 66), Zaginaylov (Trapashko 78), Afanasiyev (Belevich 87), Demidovich. Coach: Igor Kriushenko (BLR)

Third qualifying round - SK Rapid Wien (AUT)
H 0-0
Fomichev, Chelyadinski, Klopotski, Pankovets, Shapoval, Khachaturyan, Lutsevich, Zaginaylov (Golenkov 71), Imerekov, Afanasiyev (Shcherbo 87), Demidovich (Belevich 90+1). Coach: Igor Kriushenko (BLR)
A 0-3
Fomichev, Chelyadinski, Klopotski, Pankovets (Shcherbo 46), Shapoval, Khachaturyan, Lutsevich, Zaginaylov (Trapashko 57), Imerekov, Afanasiyev (Chelyadko 66), Demidovich. Coach: Igor Kriushenko (BLR)

FC Dinamo Minsk

First qualifying round - FK Spartaks Jūrmala (LVA)
H 2-1 *Bykov (18, 82)*
Ignatovich, Ostroukh, Premudrov, Bykov, Rassadkin, Korytko (Rotković 66), Zhukovski (Shramchenko 86), Noyok, Habovda, Khvashchinski, Kaplenko. Coach: Vuk Rašović (SRB)
A 2-0 *Khvashchinski (11), El Monir (90+1)*
Ignatovich, Ostroukh, Premudrov, Bykov, Rassadkin (Rotković 90+3), Korytko, Zhukovski (El Monir 82), Noyok, Habovda, Khvashchinski (Shramchenko 68), Kaplenko. Coach: Vuk Rašović (SRB)

Second qualifying round - Saint Patrick's Athletic FC (IRL)
H 1-1 *Korytko (25)*
Ignatovich, Ostroukh, Premudrov, Bykov, Rassadkin, Korytko (Shramchenko 79), Zhukovski (Rotković 70), Noyok, Habovda, Khvashchinski (El Monir 57), Kaplenko. Coach: Vuk Rašović (SRB)
A 1-0 *Rassadkin (18)*
Ignatovich, Ostroukh, Bykov, Rassadkin (Rotković 58), Korytko, Zhukovski (Shramchenko 79), El Monir (Premudrov 90+2), Noyok, Habovda, Kaplenko, Sverchinski. Coach: Sergei Borovski (BLR)
Red card: Khvashchinski 84

Third qualifying round - FK Vojvodina (SRB)
A 1-1 *Budnyk (83)*
Ignatovich, Ostroukh, Bykov, Korytko, Zhukovski (Karpovich 64), El Monir (Shramchenko 84), Noyok, Habovda, Kontsevoi, Sverchinski, Rotković (Budnyk 64). Coach: Sergei Borovski (BLR)
H 0-2
Ignatovich, Ostroukh, Bykov, Budnyk (Rotković 84), Korytko (Zhukovski 70), El Monir, Karpovich, Noyok, Habovda, Kontsevoi, Sverchinski. Coach: Sergei Borovski (BLR)
Red card: El Monir 55

FC Shakhtyor Soligorsk

First qualifying round - NSÍ Runavík (FRO)
A 2-0 *Starhorodskiy (45+1p, 84p)*
Bushma, Matveichik, Yurevich, Burko (Shibun 65), Osipenko (Yelezarenko 79), Rudyka (Pavlov 58), Starhorodskiy, Ignjatijević, Rybak, Kuzmenok, Kovalev. Coach: Mikhail Markhel (BLR)
H 5-0 *Burko (20), Rudyka (42), Shibun (81p), Yelezarenko (86), Yanushkevich (90)*
Bushma, Yanushkevich, Yurevich (Yelezarenko 67), Burko (Shibun 69), Osipenko (Pavlov 79), Rudyka, Starhorodskiy, Ignjatijević, Rybak, Kuzmenok, Kovalev. Coach: Mikhail Markhel (BLR)

Second qualifying round - NK Domžale (SVN)
H 1-1 *Ignjatijević (35)*
Bushma, Yanushkevich, Yurevich, Burko, Osipenko (Yanush 55), Rudyka (Laptev 75), Starhorodskiy, Ignjatijević, Rybak, Kuzmenok, Kovalev (Yelezarenko 66). Coach: Mikhail Markhel (BLR)
A 1-2 *Laptev (61)*
Bushma, Yurevich, Burko, Yanush, Starhorodskiy, Ignjatijević, Rybak (Osipenko 72), Kuzmenok, Yelezarenko (Rudyka 77), Kovalev, Shibun (Laptev 46). Coach: Mikhail Markhel (BLR)

DOMESTIC LEAGUE CLUB-BY-CLUB

FC BATE Borisov

1996 • Borisov Arena (13,126) • fcbate.by

Major honours

Belarusian League (13) 1999, 2002, 2006, 2007, 2008, 2009, 2010, 2011, 2012, 2013, 2014, 2015, 2016; Belarusian Cup (3) 2006, 2010, 2015

Coach: Aleksandr Yermakovich

2016

Date		Opponent		Score	Scorers
02/04	a	Dinamo Brest	W	4-1	*Gordeichuk, Stasevich 2, Rios*
11/04	h	Shakhtyor	W	2-0	*Rodionov, Yablonski*
16/04	a	Minsk	W	3-2	*Gordeichuk, Ivanić, Milunović*
24/04	h	Dinamo Minsk	D	3-3	*Stasevich, Milunović, Gordeichuk (p)*
29/04	a	Belshina	W	3-2	*A Volodko, Rodionov, Dubra*
08/05	h	Slutsk	W	3-0	*M Volodko, Gordeichuk, Ivanić*
12/05	a	Neman	W	1-0	*Gordeichuk*
16/05	a	Naftan	L	2-3	*A Volodko, Dubra*
05/06	h	Granit	W	4-0	*Karnitski, Ivanić 2, Gordeichuk*
10/06	a	Slavia-Mozyr	L	1-2	*Stasevich*
15/06	h	Krumkachy	W	5-0	*Kendysh, Gordeichuk 2 (1p), Stasevich, Rodionov*
19/06	a	Torpedo	W	2-1	*Rodionov, Rios*
25/06	h	Vitebsk	W	1-0	*A Volodko*
02/07	a	Gorodeya	D	1-1	*Dubra*
07/07	a	Isloch	W	3-1	*A Volodko, Rodionov 2*
29/07	h	Dinamo Brest	W	2-0	*Gordeichuk (p), Dubra*
08/08	a	Shakhtyor	W	2-0	*Rodionov 2*
13/08	h	Minsk	W	3-1	*Gvilia, Rodionov, Dubra*
21/08	a	Dinamo Minsk	D	1-1	*Gordeichuk*
28/08	h	Belshina	W	2-1	*Gvilia, Rodionov*
10/09	a	Slutsk	W	2-0	*Kendysh, A Volodko*
17/09	h	Neman	W	4-0	*Gaiduchik, Gordeichuk, Rodionov, Ivanić*
25/09	h	Naftan	W	4-1	*Rodionov 2, Gvilia, Gordeichuk*
02/10	h	Isloch	W	4-1	*Gordeichuk, Gvilia, Stasevich, Rodionov*
14/10	a	Granit	W	1-0	*Signevich*
23/10	h	Slavia-Mozyr	D	0-0	
28/10	a	Krumkachy	W	3-0	*Signevich 2, M Volodko*
05/11	h	Torpedo	L	1-2	*Gordeichuk*
19/11	a	Vitebsk	L	1-2	*Signevich*
27/11	h	Gorodeya	W	5-0	*Rodionov, Gordeichuk, Ivanić, A Volodko, Kendysh*

No	Name	Nat	DoB	Pos	Aps	(s)	Gls
11	Dmitri Antilevski		12/06/97	A		(4)	
16	Sergei Chernik		20/07/88	G	12		
4	Kaspars Dubra	LVA	20/12/90	D	15	(1)	5
49	Aleksandr Dzhygero		15/04/96	M	1	(6)	
3	Vitali Gaiduchik		12/07/89	D	10	(1)	1
62	Mikhail Gordeichuk		23/10/89	A	25	(3)	15
80	Valerian Gvilia	GEO	24/05/94	M	9	(5)	4
81	Aleksandr Hleb		01/05/81	M	3	(3)	
10	Mirko Ivanić	MNE	13/09/93	M	22	(4)	6
7	Aleksandr Karnitski		14/02/89	M	7	(8)	1
77	Yuri Kendysh		10/06/90	M	23		3
44	Vladislav Malkevich		04/12/99	D		(1)	
19	Nemanja Milunović	SRB	31/05/89	D	10	(1)	2
18	Dmitri Mozolevski		30/04/85	A	5	(10)	
23	Edgar Olekhnovich		17/05/87	M	4	(1)	
14	Artur Pikk	EST	05/03/93	D	15	(2)	
33	Denis Polyakov		17/04/91	D	21		
17	Aleksei Rios		14/05/87	D	17	(7)	2
20	Vitali Rodionov		11/12/83	A	22	(3)	15
48	Denis Shcherbitski		14/04/96	G	5		
13	Nikolai Signevich		20/02/92	A	6	(9)	4
34	Artem Soroko		01/04/92	G	7		
22	Igor Stasevich		21/10/85	M	24	(2)	6
16	Sergei Veremko		16/10/82	G	6		
8	Aleksandr Volodko		18/06/86	M	14	(2)	6
42	Maksim Volodko		10/11/92	M	14	(10)	2
5	Evgeni Yablonski		10/05/95	M	14	(6)	1
15	Maksim Zhavnerchik		09/02/85	D	19		

FC Belshina Bobruisk

1976 • im. Aleksandr Prokopenko (1,500); Spartak (3,700) • fcbelshina.by

Major honours

Belarusian League (1) 2001; Belarusian Cup (3) 1997, 1999, 2001

Coach: Vladimir Yezhurov (RUS); (11/04/16) Vyacheslav Gerashchenko; (20/07/16) Vitali Pavlov

2016

Date		Opponent		Score	Scorers
02/04	h	Krumkachy	D	1-1	*Yushin*
11/04	h	Vitebsk	L	0-1	
16/04	h	Dinamo Brest	W	4-2	*Afanasiyev 2, Bulyga 2*
24/04	a	Minsk	D	1-1	*Bulyga*
29/04	h	BATE	L	2-3	*Matveyenko, Fameyeh*
07/05	h	Neman	D	1-1	*Bulyga*
12/05	a	Isloch	W	3-2	*Kontsevoi, Komarovski, Fameyeh*
17/05	h	Slavia-Mozyr	D	2-2	*Fameyeh, Bulyga (p)*
25/05	a	Torpedo	D	2-2	*Bulyga, Matveyenko*
03/06	h	Gorodeya	L	0-2	
10/06	a	Shakhtyor	L	0-3	
15/06	h	Dinamo Minsk	L	1-2	*Matveyenko*
19/06	a	Slutsk	L	1-2	*Gavrilovich*
25/06	h	Naftan	W	1-0	*Zaragoza*
03/07	a	Granit	W	4-0	*Fameyeh 2, Zamarián, Shakurov*
31/07	a	Krumkachy	L	1-2	*Gerasimov*
08/08	a	Vitebsk	L	0-1	
13/08	a	Dinamo Brest	L	1-2	*Shreitor*
21/08	h	Minsk	L	0-2	
28/08	a	BATE	L	1-2	*Yasinski*
10/09	a	Neman	L	0-1	
17/09	h	Isloch	D	0-0	
26/09	a	Slavia-Mozyr	W	2-0	*Zinovich, Shreitor*
01/10	h	Torpedo	L	1-3	*Shreitor*
16/10	a	Gorodeya	D	1-1	*Kadiyev*
23/10	h	Shakhtyor	L	0-1	
29/10	a	Dinamo Minsk	L	1-3	*Murikhin*
06/11	h	Slutsk	D	0-0	
19/11	a	Naftan	D	2-2	*Yasinski, Gerasimov*
27/11	h	Granit	D	1-1	*og (Zabelin)*

No	Name	Nat	DoB	Pos	Aps	(s)	Gls
7	Mikhail Afanasiyev		04/11/86	M	8	(1)	2
1	Anton Amelchenko		27/03/85	G	8	(1)	
5	Henri Belle	CMR	25/01/89	A	3	(8)	
88	Nikita Bukatkin		07/03/88	M	12		
10	Vitali Bulyga		12/01/80	A	12	(2)	6
8	Danila Buranov	RUS	11/02/96	M	1	(3)	
17	Joel Fameyeh	GHA	14/05/97	A	5	(7)	5
4	Aleksei Gavrilovich		05/01/90	D	13	(1)	1
5	Aleksei Gerasimov	RUS	15/04/93	D	14		2
57	Pavel Grechishko		23/03/89	D	12	(2)	
10	Dzhabrail Kadiyev	RUS	21/01/94	D	7	(4)	1
22	Oleh Karamushka	UKR	03/04/84	D	14		
11	Valeri Karnitski		20/08/91	M	5	(3)	
35	Andrei Khachaturyan		02/09/87	M	5		
15	Dmitri Komarovski		10/10/86	A	8	(2)	1
26	Sergei Kontsevoi		21/06/86	D	14		1
11	Anton Matveyenko		03/09/86	M	11	(4)	3
8	Stanislav Murikhin	RUS	21/01/92	A	5	(4)	1
30	Boris Pankratov		30/12/82	G	20		
88	Aleksandr Puzevich		02/08/95	D		(5)	
18	Kirill Shakurov		07/04/94	A	1	(16)	1
14	Vadym Shevchuk	UKR	21/10/95	D	13		
22	Kirill Shreitor		06/08/86	A	12	(2)	3
23	Aleksei Skvernyuk		13/10/85	M	26		
16	Maksim Tanko		18/02/94	G	2		
20	Leandro Torres	ARG	04/11/88	M	11	(2)	
20	Dmitri Turlin		08/09/85	M	11	(3)	
7	Sergei Vodyanovich		02/05/95	M	12	(2)	
9	Igor Yasinski		04/07/90	M	13		2
55	Aleksandr Yushin	RUS	04/04/95	M	12	(9)	1
14	Facundo Zamarián	ARG	25/12/95	M	6	(3)	1
9	Matías Zaragoza	ARG	20/09/95	D	4	(1)	1
35	Hleb Zheleznikov		31/07/97	D		(1)	
4	Ivan Zhestkin		08/05/91	M	12	(1)	
17	Eduard Zhevnerov		01/11/87	D	7	(2)	
26	Dmitri Zinovich		29/03/95	D	11		1

FC Dinamo Brest

1960 • GOSK Brestski (10,080) • dynamo-brest.by

Major honours

Belarusian Cup (2) 2007, 2017

Coach: Sergei Kovalchuk

2016

Date		Opponent		Score	Scorers
02/04	h	BATE	L	1-4	*Isayev*
10/04	h	Minsk	L	0-3	
16/04	a	Belshina	L	2-4	*Demeshko (p), Nazarenko*
23/04	h	Neman	W	2-0	*Demeshko 2*
30/04	a	Isloch	W	3-0	*(w/o; original result 4-2 Demeshko 2 (1p), Ergashev, Pobudei)*
07/05	h	Slavia-Mozyr	D	0-0	
30/05	h	Torpedo	W	3-2	*Chizh, Demeshko, German*
16/05	h	Gorodeya	D	1-1	*Novik*
22/05	a	Shakhtyor	L	1-3	*Chizh*
04/06	h	Dinamo Minsk	L	1-4	*German*
09/06	a	Slutsk	W	1-0	*Chizh*
15/06	h	Naftan	D	1-1	*Isayev*
19/06	a	Granit	L	1-2	*Karnitski*
24/06	h	Krumkachy	L	1-2	*Tymonyuk*
02/07	a	Vitebsk	L	0-1	
29/07	a	BATE	L	0-2	
07/08	a	Minsk	W	1-0	*Fameyeh*
13/08	h	Belshina	W	2-1	*Kouyaté 2*
19/08	a	Neman	W	4-0	*og (Leshko), Fameyeh 2, Amadu*
26/08	h	Isloch	D	1-1	*Kouyaté*
10/09	a	Slavia-Mozyr	W	4-1	*German, Kouyaté, Torres, Afoakwa*
17/09	a	Torpedo	W	1-0	*Fameyeh*
26/09	a	Gorodeya	D	1-1	*Torres*
02/10	h	Shakhtyor	L	1-2	*Torres*
15/10	a	Dinamo Minsk	L	1-2	*Fameyeh*
23/10	h	Slutsk	D	0-0	
29/10	a	Naftan	L	0-1	
05/11	h	Granit	W	1-0	*Kouyaté*
19/11	a	Krumkachy	D	0-0	
27/11	h	Vitebsk	W	3-0	*German, Sedko, Pobudei*

No	Name	Nat	DoB	Pos	Aps	(s)	Gls
45	Dickson Afoakwa	GHA	24/04/98	A	3	(7)	1
11	Latif Amadu	GHA	20/08/93	A	2	(6)	1
64	Dmitri Asnin		06/07/84	G	25	(1)	
65	Adrian Avramia	MDA	31/01/92	D	9		
8	Nikita Bukatkin		07/03/88	M	13		
31	Maksim Chizh		08/10/93	M	20	(4)	3
1	Denis Dechko		26/04/90	G	4		
9	Aleksandr Demeshko		07/11/86	A	14	(9)	6
62	Jahongir Ergashev	TJK	06/03/94	M	6	(6)	1
20	Joel Fameyeh	GHA	14/05/97	A	14	(1)	5
4	Aleksei Gavrilovich		05/01/90	D	14		
88	Dmitri German		12/06/88	M	26	(1)	4
19	Ramazan Isayev	RUS	17/01/98	A	3	(9)	2
97	Aleksei Ivanov		19/02/97	D	15		
7	Valeri Karnitski		20/08/91	M	7	(1)	1
10	Aleksandr Komlev		26/06/94	A	3	(9)	
6	Boris Konevega		06/08/95	M	11	(1)	
77	Idrissa Kouyaté	CIV	27/04/91	A	12	(1)	5
12	Vladislav Kuzhal		12/02/98	G	1		
13	Pavel Nazarenko		20/01/95	D	26		1
2	Aleksandr Novik		15/10/94	D	13		1
5	Simon Ogar	NGA	24/04/87	M	8	(4)	
34	Pavel Pampukha		23/05/95	A		(1)	
21	Vadim Pobudei		17/12/94	M	15	(6)	2
17	Pavel Sedko		03/04/98	M	4	(8)	1
3	Anton Shepelev		08/11/89	D	15		
80	Vasili Sumnakayev	RUS	17/11/95	M		(1)	
23	Leandro Torres	ARG	04/11/88	M	15		3
4	Andrei Tsevan		15/03/86	M	1		
22	Igor Tymonyuk		31/03/94	D	19	(1)	1
10	Roman Vasilyuk		23/11/78	A	2	(7)	
4	Sergei Vodyanovich		02/05/95	M	1	(4)	
18	Giorgi Zabedashvili	GEO	01/01/96	D	1		
33	Dmitri Zinovich		29/03/95	D	8	(1)	

BELARUS

FC Dinamo Minsk

1927 • Traktor (17,600) • dinamo-minsk.by

Major honours
USSR League (1) 1982; Belarusian League (7) 1992, 1993, 1994, 1995 (spring), 1995 (autumn), 1997, 2004; Belarusian Cup (3) 1992, 1994, 2003

Coach: Vuk Rašović (SRB); (16/07/16) Sergei Borovski

2016

Date		Opponent		Score	Scorers
02/04	a	Torpedo	W	2-0	*Adamović, Zubovich*
10/04	h	Gorodeya	W	2-0	*Begunov, Zhukovski*
16/04	a	Shakhtyor	D	0-0	
24/04	a	BATE	D	3-3	*Zhukovski 2 (1p), Rassadkin*
29/04	h	Slutsk	D	1-1	*Yarotski*
08/05	a	Naftan	D	1-1	*Zubovich*
13/05	a	Granit	D	1-1	*Rotković*
17/05	a	Krumkachy	L	1-4	*og (Shchegrikovich)*
22/05	h	Vitebsk	W	1-0	*Premudrov*
04/06	a	Dinamo Brest	W	4-1	*Rotković 2, Khvashchinski, Adamović*
10/06	h	Minsk	W	1-0	*Rotković (p)*
15/06	a	Belshina	W	2-1	*Rassadkin, Bykov*
20/06	h	Neman	L	0-1	
25/06	a	Isloch	L	1-3	*Rotković*
03/07	h	Slavia-Mozyr	W	1-0	*Rassadkin*
08/08	a	Gorodeya	D	0-0	
13/08	h	Shakhtyor	L	1-3	*Habovda*
21/08	h	BATE	D	1-1	*Shramchenko*
28/08	a	Slutsk	D	1-1	*og (Golyatkin)*
10/09	h	Naftan	W	3-1	*Habovda, Zubovich, Bykov*
17/09	h	Granit	W	5-0	*Premudrov, Budnyk, Zubovich 2, Korytko*
25/09	h	Krumkachy	W	2-0	*Bykov, Khvashchinski*
02/10	a	Vitebsk	W	2-0	*Khvashchinski, Premudrov*
08/10	h	Torpedo	D	1-1	*Budnyk*
15/10	h	Dinamo Brest	W	2-1	*Khvashchinski 2*
23/10	a	Minsk	D	0-0	
29/10	h	Belshina	W	3-1	*Khvashchinski 2, Habovda*
06/11	a	Neman	W	3-2	*Korytko, Khvashchinski, Chelyadinski*
19/11	h	Isloch	W	1-0	*Budnyk*
27/11	a	Slavia-Mozyr	L	0-1	

No	Name	Nat	DoB	Pos	Aps	(s)	Gls
88	Nenad Adamović	SRB	12/01/89	M	9	(3)	2
17	Umaru Bangura	SLE	07/10/87	D	13		
22	Roman Begunov		22/03/93	D	14	(3)	1
9	Yevhen Budnyk	UKR	04/09/90	A	9	(2)	3
7	Artem Bykov		19/10/92	M	19	(1)	3
3	Artem Chelyadinski		29/12/77	D	9		1
13	Mohamed El Monir	LBY	08/04/92	D	13	(6)	
52	Viktor Genev	BUL	27/10/88	D	1	(1)	
30	Aleksandr Gutor		18/04/89	G	14		
19	Yuriy Habovda	UKR	06/05/89	M	22	(3)	3
35	Sergei Ignatovich		29/06/92	G	16		
24	Nikita Kaplenko		18/09/95	M	16		
16	Sergei Karpovich		29/03/94	D	4		
23	Vladimir Khvashchinski		10/05/90	A	14	(7)	8
25	Artem Kiyko		13/01/96	A		(1)	
26	Sergei Kontsevoi		21/06/86	D	11	(2)	
10	Vladimir Korytko		06/07/79	M	11	(4)	2
14	Aleksei Kozlov		11/07/89	D	1	(3)	
30	Uroš Nikolić	SRB	14/12/92	M	9		
18	Olexandr Noyok	UKR	15/05/92	D	29		
5	Yuri Ostroukh		21/01/88	D	14	(2)	
6	Kirill Premudrov		11/06/92	M	25	(3)	3
8	Hleb Rassadkin		05/04/95	A	12	(7)	3
15	Luka Rotković	MNE	05/07/88	A	10	(6)	5
28	Anton Shramchenko		12/03/93	A	3	(3)	1
2	Maksim Shvetsov		02/04/98	D	2	(1)	
44	Aleksandr Sverchinski		16/09/91	D	5		
26	Yan Tigorev		10/03/84	M	1		
9	Yaroslav Yarotski		28/03/96	M	4	(8)	1
11	Valeri Zhukovski		21/05/84	M	13	(6)	3
27	Yegor Zubovich		01/06/89	A	7	(14)	5

FC Gorodeya

2004 • RCOP-BGU, Minsk (1,500); Urozhai, Nesvizh (2,224); Gorodeya (1,625) • fcgorodeya.by

Coach: Sergei Yaromko

2016

Date		Opponent		Score	Scorers
02/04	h	Shakhtyor	L	0-1	
10/04	a	Dinamo Minsk	L	0-2	
17/04	h	Slutsk	W	2-0	*Pavlyuchek, Saroka*
24/04	a	Naftan	D	0-0	
30/04	a	Granit	D	0-0	
07/05	a	Krumkachy	W	1-0	*Saroka*
12/05	h	Vitebsk	L	0-2	
16/05	a	Dinamo Brest	D	1-1	*Martynets*
23/05	h	Minsk	L	1-2	*Petrov*
03/06	a	Belshina	W	2-0	*Milovanović, Saroka*
09/06	h	Neman	W	2-1	*Saroka, Lebedev*
16/06	a	Isloch	L	0-2	
20/06	h	Slavia-Mozyr	W	4-2	*Tupchiy, Saroka, Lebedev 2*
26/06	a	Torpedo	W	3-1	*Lebedev, Saroka, Parkhachev*
02/07	h	BATE	D	1-1	*Pavlyuchek*
31/07	a	Shakhtyor	D	2-2	*Lebedev, Tupchiy*
08/08	h	Dinamo Minsk	D	0-0	
14/08	a	Slutsk	D	1-1	*Parkhachev*
20/08	h	Naftan	W	3-0	*Ignatenko, Lebedev 2*
27/08	h	Granit	W	2-0	*Parkhachev, Ignatenko*
10/09	h	Krumkachy	D	1-1	*Saroka*
17/09	a	Vitebsk	D	1-1	*Kolyadko*
26/09	h	Dinamo Brest	D	1-1	*Ignatenko*
02/10	a	Minsk	L	1-3	*Parkhachev*
16/10	h	Belshina	D	1-1	*Pavlyuchek*
22/10	a	Neman	L	0-3	
30/10	h	Isloch	D	0-0	
07/11	a	Slavia-Mozyr	D	3-3	*Saroka, Ignatenko, Pavlyuchek*
19/11	h	Torpedo	D	3-3	*Lebedev, Plaskonny, Parkhachev*
27/11	a	BATE	L	0-5	

No	Name	Nat	DoB	Pos	Aps	(s)	Gls
30	Pavel Chesnovski		04/03/86	G	30		
2	Dmitri Ignatenko		24/10/88	M	14		4
19	Aleksei Khaletski		19/06/84	D		(6)	
33	Ilya Kolpachuk		09/10/90	D	2	(4)	
11	Mikhail Kolyadko		21/11/88	M	17	(5)	1
99	Dmitri Kovb		20/01/87	A	6	(3)	
10	Dmitri Lebedev		13/05/86	M	27	(1)	8
20	Aleksei Martynets		13/06/85	M	6	(8)	1
9	Nemanja Milovanović	SRB	12/06/91	M	21		1
85	Dmitri Parkhachev		30/12/84	M	24	(3)	5
16	Kirill Pavlyuchek		27/06/84	D	27		4
35	Aleksei Petrov		30/04/91	A	3	(22)	1
3	Pavel Plaskonny		29/01/85	D	27		1
7	Anton Saroka		05/03/92	A	23	(2)	8
4	Semen Shestilovski		20/05/94	D	15	(1)	
14	Evgeni Shidlovski		13/01/91	D	3	(2)	
5	Olexiy Tupchiy	UKR	22/08/86	M	24	(3)	2
8	Sergei Usenya		04/03/88	D	28		
21	Yuri Volovik		19/06/93	M	4	(11)	
31	Denis Yakubovich		31/03/88	M	11	(7)	
18	Vyacheslav Yaroslavski		14/05/85	D	18	(7)	

FC Granit Mikashevichi

1978 • Polesiye, Luninets (3,090) • fcgranit.by

Coach: Valeri Bokhno

2016

Date		Opponent		Score	Scorers
03/04	a	Neman	D	1-1	*Ignatenko*
09/04	h	Isloch	L	0-1	
15/04	a	Slavia-Mozyr	W	3-1	*Ignatenko (p), Sheryakov, Babyr*
25/04	h	Torpedo	D	1-1	*Klimovich*
30/04	h	Gorodeya	D	0-0	
07/05	h	Shakhtyor	D	1-1	*Klimovich*
13/05	h	Dinamo Minsk	D	1-1	*Sheryakov (p)*
17/05	h	Slutsk	W	2-1	*Yusov, Lutsevich*
23/05	a	Naftan	D	1-1	*Babyr*
05/06	a	BATE	L	0-4	
09/06	h	Krumkachy	D	1-1	*Sheryakov (p)*
15/06	a	Vitebsk	W	1-0	*Lutsevich*
19/06	h	Dinamo Brest	W	2-1	*Kosmynin, Babyr*
24/06	a	Minsk	D	0-0	
03/07	h	Belshina	L	0-4	
29/07	h	Neman	L	0-1	
06/08	a	Isloch	L	2-3	*Krivitski, Kovalyuk*
14/08	h	Slavia-Mozyr	D	0-0	
20/08	a	Torpedo	L	0-5	
27/08	a	Gorodeya	L	0-2	
10/09	a	Shakhtyor	L	0-4	
17/09	a	Dinamo Minsk	L	0-5	
25/09	a	Slutsk	W	1-0	*Kovalyuk*
01/10	h	Naftan	L	1-3	*Kovalyuk*
14/10	h	BATE	L	0-1	
21/10	a	Krumkachy	L	1-2	*Zagvozdin*
29/10	h	Vitebsk	L	0-3	
05/11	a	Dinamo Brest	L	0-1	
19/11	h	Minsk	L	0-7	
27/11	a	Belshina	D	1-1	*Zabelin*

No	Name	Nat	DoB	Pos	Aps	(s)	Gls
19	Olexiy Babyr	UKR	15/03/90	A	13		3
9	Viktor Bruyevich	RUS	08/03/97	M	8	(1)	
1	Dmitri Dudar		08/11/91	G	14		
3	Oleg Garapuchik		29/05/97	D	2	(2)	
3	Sergei Golyatkin	RUS	04/05/88	D	10		
7	Dmitri Ignatenko		24/10/88	M	10	(1)	2
28	Igor Khomlyak		20/05/88	G	1		
18	Vitali Kibuk		07/01/89	A	5	(9)	
6	Pavel Kirilchik		04/01/81	M	12	(2)	
26	Dmitri Klimovich		09/02/84	D	15		2
5	Vladislav Kosmynin		17/01/90	D	14		1
6	Sergei Kovalyuk		07/01/80	M	13		3
5	Aleksandr Krasiy		17/03/90	D	13		
19	Vladislav Krivitski		03/07/95	D	10		1
26	Vadim Kurlovich		30/10/92	M	15		
11	Ilya Leskin	RUS	04/05/94	A	7	(5)	
21	Igor Lisitsa		10/04/88	D	5	(7)	
14	Terenti Lutsevich		19/04/91	D	15		2
15	Nikita Metlitski		06/02/95	M	1	(9)	
10	Nicolae Milinceanu	MDA	01/08/92	A	7		
23	Olexandr Nasonov	UKR	28/04/91	D		(2)	
22	Dmytro Osadchiy	UKR	05/08/92	M		(3)	
21	Aleksei Plyasunov		03/01/91	M	11	(4)	
11	Aleksei Pyshinski		28/04/93	M		(1)	
2	Pavel Secrier	MDA	11/01/91	A	15		
7	Boris Shavlokhov	RUS	12/06/96	D	14		
10	Andrei Sheryakov		10/11/82	A	14		3
22	Antonio Siyaka		27/01/96	M	1	(5)	
28	Rodion Syamuk	UKR	11/03/89	G	6		
19	Aleksandr Tarasenia		25/09/96	A		(1)	
15	Igor Trukhov		19/08/76	M	15		
1	Vladislav Vasilyuchek		28/03/94	G	9		
9	Pavel Yevseyenko		30/10/80	M	10	(3)	
11	Dmytro Yusov	UKR	11/05/93	M	10		1
30	Pavel Zabelin		30/06/95	M	14		1
17	Nikolai Zagvozdin		31/08/91	M	14		1
18	Evgeni Zemko		16/02/96	A	5	(4)	
17	Nikolai Zenko		11/03/89	A	2	(9)	

FC Isloch

2007 • City, Molodechno (4,800); FC Minsk (3,000); FC Minsk artificial (600) • fcisloch.by

Coach: Vitali Zhukovski

2016					
01/04	h	Naftan	W	2-0	*Lebedev, Belov*
09/04	a	Granit	W	1-0	*Misyuk*
17/04	h	Krumkachy	D	0-0	
23/04	a	Vitebsk	W	2-1	*Denisevich, Lebedev*
30/04	h	Dinamo Brest	L	0-3	*(w/o; original result 2-4 Alumona (p), Lebedev)*
08/05	a	Minsk	W	1-0	*Shagoiko*
12/05	h	Belshina	L	2-3	*Papush, Shagoiko (p)*
17/05	a	Neman	L	1-2	*Yasyukevich*
05/06	h	Slavia-Mozyr	L	0-1	
10/06	a	Torpedo	D	1-1	*Alumona*
16/06	h	Gorodeya	W	2-0	*Alumona 2*
20/06	a	Shakhtyor	L	0-3	
25/06	h	Dinamo Minsk	W	3-1	*Ryzhko, Alumona, Bubnov*
02/07	a	Slutsk	D	2-2	*Shagoiko (p), Lebedev*
07/07	h	BATE	L	1-3	*Makar*
30/07	a	Naftan	W	2-0	*Papush, Tishkevich*
06/08	h	Granit	W	3-2	*Tishkevich, Shagoiko 2 (1p)*
12/08	a	Krumkachy	W	1-0	*Shagoiko*
21/08	h	Vitebsk	D	0-0	
26/08	a	Dinamo Brest	D	1-1	*Papush*
10/09	h	Minsk	L	0-4	
17/09	a	Belshina	D	0-0	
25/09	h	Neman	D	0-0	
02/10	a	BATE	L	1-4	*Komarovski*
15/10	a	Slavia-Mozyr	L	1-2	*Komarovski*
22/10	h	Torpedo	W	3-2	*Bubnov, Bliznyuk 2*
30/10	a	Gorodeya	D	0-0	
06/11	h	Shakhtyor	L	1-3	*Krotov*
19/11	a	Dinamo Minsk	L	0-1	
27/11	h	Slutsk	W	2-0	*Ryzhko, Komarovski*

No	Name	Nat	DoB	Pos	Aps	(s)	Gls
17	Aleksandr Alumona	RUS	18/12/83	A	9	(3)	5
23	Konstantin Belov	RUS	04/01/90	A	3	(2)	1
1	Artem Belyi		28/04/97	G		(1)	
10	Gennadi Bliznyuk		30/07/80	A	10	(1)	2
21	Igor Borozdin	RUS	15/10/88	M	4	(5)	
32	Anton Bubnov		23/11/88	M	18	(6)	2
98	Aleksandr Budakov	RUS	10/02/85	G	14		
9	Ivan Denisevich		09/11/84	M	20	(5)	1
44	Aleksei Dovgel		28/07/94	M		(1)	
16	Vladislav Fedotov		08/02/97	M		(6)	
11	Aleksandr Kholodinski		16/10/91	M	23	(4)	
33	Pavel Kirilchik		04/01/81	M	6		
15	Dmitri Komarovski		10/10/86	A	9	(2)	3
17	Aleksandr Krotov		19/04/95	M	3	(7)	1
14	Aleksandr Lebedev		14/04/85	A	8	(4)	4
7	Dmitri Makar		01/10/81	D	6	(5)	1
6	Sergei Marinich		03/06/98	M		(1)	
26	Bojan Mihajlović	BIH	15/09/88	D	15		
9	Andrei Misyuk		20/03/81	M	12	(6)	1
5	Olexandr Papush	UKR	14/01/85	D	25		3
6	Oleg Patotski		24/06/91	M	11	(1)	
15	Andrei Poryvaev		03/01/82	D	5	(2)	
69	Nikita Rochev		06/11/92	D	17	(2)	
31	Konstantin Rudenok		15/12/90	G	12		
50	Yuri Ryzhko		10/10/89	D	22	(1)	2
2	Aleksandr Shagoiko		27/07/80	M	25		6
13	Artur Slabashevich		09/02/89	M	12	(2)	
10	Aleksandr Tishkevich		16/02/86	M	9	(4)	2
19	Valeri Tsyganenko		21/07/81	A	6	(11)	
24	Sergei Turanok		29/03/86	G	4		
20	Vladislav Yasyukevich		30/05/94	D	22	(3)	1

FC Krumkachy

2011 • FC Minsk (3,000) • krumka.by

Coach: Oleg Dulub;
(05/10/16) Yakov Zalevski & Vasili Khomutovski

2016					
02/04	a	Belshina	D	1-1	*Shikavka*
09/04	h	Neman	W	2-1	*Hleb, Shchegrikovich*
17/04	a	Isloch	D	0-0	
23/04	h	Slavia-Mozyr	W	1-0	*Ivanov (p)*
30/04	a	Torpedo	L	0-3	
07/05	h	Gorodeya	L	0-1	
11/05	a	Shakhtyor	W	2-0	*Hleb, Shikavka*
17/05	h	Dinamo Minsk	W	4-1	*Korsak, Shchegrikovich, Hleb, Shikavka*
23/05	a	Slutsk	L	0-2	
04/06	h	Naftan	W	2-0	*Vasilevski, Batyshchev*
09/06	a	Granit	D	1-1	*Vasilevski*
15/06	a	BATE	L	0-5	
19/06	h	Vitebsk	W	1-0	*Korsak*
24/06	a	Dinamo Brest	W	2-1	*Vasilevski, Shikavka*
01/07	h	Minsk	L	0-1	
31/07	h	Belshina	W	2-1	*Hleb 2*
07/08	a	Neman	D	2-2	*Hleb 2 (1p)*
12/08	h	Isloch	L	0-1	
19/08	a	Slavia-Mozyr	L	0-1	
26/08	h	Torpedo	L	0-2	
10/09	a	Gorodeya	D	1-1	*Korsak*
18/09	h	Shakhtyor	L	0-1	
25/09	a	Dinamo Minsk	L	0-2	
30/09	h	Slutsk	L	0-3	
14/10	a	Naftan	L	0-1	
21/10	h	Granit	W	2-1	*Semenov, Klimovich*
28/10	h	BATE	L	0-3	
05/11	a	Vitebsk	L	1-2	*Ivanov (p)*
19/11	h	Dinamo Brest	D	0-0	
27/11	a	Minsk	L	0-1	

No	Name	Nat	DoB	Pos	Aps	(s)	Gls
9	Olexandr Batyshchev	UKR	14/09/91	M	29		1
1	Andriy Fedorenko	UKR	09/01/84	G	27		
20	Aleksandr Filanovich		01/12/92	A		(1)	
3	Roman Gayev		20/01/89	D	6	(2)	
99	Vyacheslav Hleb		12/02/83	M	23	(5)	7
10	Filipp Ivanov		21/07/90	A	23	(4)	2
73	Mykhailo Kalugin	UKR	20/11/94	D	24	(1)	
11	Vladimir Karp		09/10/94	A	5	(5)	
13	Dmitri Klimovich		09/02/84	D	13		1
7	Sergei Korsak		24/02/89	M	10	(12)	3
66	Sergei Koshel		14/03/86	A	1	(7)	
69	Evgeni Kostyukevich		19/12/89	G	3	(1)	
27	Aleksei Rudenok		25/02/93	M		(1)	
29	Maksim Sanets		04/04/97	A	2	(13)	
8	Yegor Semenov		06/01/88	M	9	(16)	1
22	Sergei Shchegrikovich		19/12/90	D	29		2
23	Evgeni Shikavka		15/10/92	M	24	(5)	4
18	David Simbo	SLE	28/09/89	D	3		
17	Aleksandr Skshinetski		28/02/90	M	24	(1)	
19	Maksim Taleiko		20/02/93	M	22	(6)	
5	Aleksei Vasilevski		02/06/93	D	20	(2)	3
21	Ihor Voronkov	UKR	24/04/81	M	8		
88	Dmitri Yashin	RUS	25/04/93	D	24	(1)	
12	Pavel Zuyevich		12/07/97	A	1	(3)	

FC Minsk

2006 • FC Minsk (3,000) • fcminsk.by

Major honours
Belarusian Cup (1) 2013

Coach: Georgi Kondratiev

2016					
02/04	h	Vitebsk	W	1-0	*Legchilin*
10/04	a	Dinamo Brest	W	3-0	*Gvilia, Vasiliyev, Bessmertnyi*
16/04	h	BATE	L	2-3	*Čović, Trubilo*
24/04	h	Belshina	D	1-1	*Gvilia*
29/04	a	Neman	W	1-0	*Kovel*
08/05	h	Isloch	L	0-1	
12/05	a	Slavia-Mozyr	L	2-6	*Sachivko (p), Gvilia*
16/05	h	Torpedo	D	0-0	
23/05	a	Gorodeya	W	2-1	*Shevchenko, Kovel*
05/06	h	Shakhtyor	W	1-0	*Čović*
10/06	a	Dinamo Minsk	L	0-1	
15/06	h	Slutsk	W	5-2	*Čović 2, Legchilin, og (Bamba), Gvilia (p)*
19/06	a	Naftan	D	1-1	*Legchilin*
24/06	h	Granit	D	0-0	
01/07	a	Krumkachy	W	1-0	*Shevchenko*
31/07	a	Vitebsk	D	0-0	
07/08	h	Dinamo Brest	L	0-1	
13/08	a	BATE	L	1-3	*Sachivko*
21/08	a	Belshina	W	2-0	*Makarov, og (Gerasimov)*
27/08	h	Neman	L	0-1	
10/09	a	Isloch	W	4-0	*Legchilin, og (Rochev), Vasiliyev, Veretilo*
16/09	h	Slavia-Mozyr	W	6-2	*Yevdokimov, Kovel, Sachivko 3 (2p), Omelyanchuk*
25/09	a	Torpedo	D	0-0	
02/10	h	Gorodeya	W	3-1	*Čović 2, Kovel*
15/10	a	Shakhtyor	D	0-0	
23/10	h	Dinamo Minsk	D	0-0	
30/10	a	Slutsk	W	1-0	*Kovel*
05/11	h	Naftan	W	4-0	*Čović, Yevdokimov, Matveyenko, Kovel*
19/11	a	Granit	W	7-0	*Makarov, Yevdokimov, Kovel, Čović, Legchilin, Sachivko, Shevchenko*
27/11	h	Krumkachy	W	1-0	*Matveyenko*

No	Name	Nat	DoB	Pos	Aps	(s)	Gls
17	Ivan Bakhar		10/07/98	M		(1)	
15	Dmitri Bessmertnyi		03/01/97	M	7	(11)	1
91	Nemanja Čović	SRB	18/06/91	A	23	(1)	8
23	Valeri Gromyko		23/01/97	M	3	(20)	
10	Valerian Gvilia	GEO	24/05/94	M	14	(1)	4
19	Pavel Holovenko		12/01/97	G		(1)	
16	Sergei Karpovich		29/03/94	D	13	(1)	
1	Andrei Klimovich		27/08/88	G	30		
18	Yehor Klymenchuk	UKR	11/11/97	M	3	(1)	
11	Leonid Kovel		29/07/86	A	23	(6)	7
95	Serhiy Kulinich	UKR	09/01/95	D	10	(9)	
46	Aleksei Legchilin		11/04/92	M	26		5
9	Sergei Makarov	RUS	03/10/96	M	30		2
10	Anton Matveyenko		03/09/86	M	15		2
8	Sergei Omelyanchuk		08/08/80	D	25		1
7	Sergei Rusak		03/09/93	M	3	(7)	
20	Aleksandr Sachivko		05/01/86	D	28		6
96	Evgeni Shevchenko		06/06/96	A	8	(9)	3
5	Igor Shumilov		20/10/93	D	4	(6)	
24	Vitali Trubilo		07/01/85	D	28		1
32	Aleksei Vakulich		24/06/98	M		(1)	
97	Artem Vasiliyev		23/01/97	A		(9)	2
21	Oleg Veretilo		10/07/88	D	12	(1)	1
14	Oleg Yevdokimov		25/02/94	M	25	(1)	3

BELARUS

FC Naftan Novopolotsk

1963 • Atlant (5,300); Atlant artificial (500) • fcnaftan.com

Major honours
Belarusian Cup (2) 2009, 2012

Coach: Valeri Stripeikis; (23/08/16) Oleg Sidorenkov

2016

01/04	a	Isloch	L	0-2	
10/04	h	Slavia-Mozyr	L	0-1	
16/04	a	Torpedo	L	1-2	*Zyulev*
24/04	h	Gorodeya	D	0-0	
29/04	a	Shakhtyor	L	0-2	
08/05	h	Dinamo Minsk	D	1-1	*Teverov*
12/05	h	Slutsk	W	1-0	*Yakimov*
16/05	h	BATE	W	3-2	*Zyulev, Berezkin, Yakimov*
23/05	h	Granit	D	1-1	*Lebedev*
04/06	a	Krumkachy	L	0-2	
09/06	h	Vitebsk	L	1-2	*Zyulev*
15/06	a	Dinamo Brest	D	1-1	*Gorbachev*
19/06	h	Minsk	D	1-1	*Borisov*
25/06	a	Belshina	L	0-1	
02/07	h	Neman	W	2-0	*Lebedev, Borisov*
30/07	h	Isloch	L	0-2	
06/08	a	Slavia-Mozyr	L	0-2	
14/08	h	Torpedo	L	1-3	*Borisov*
20/08	a	Gorodeya	L	0-3	
28/08	h	Shakhtyor	D	1-1	*Yakimov*
10/09	a	Dinamo Minsk	L	1-3	*Suchkov*
16/09	a	Slutsk	D	1-1	*Kolyaev*
25/09	a	BATE	L	1-4	*Teplov*
01/10	a	Granit	W	3-1	*Lebedev 2, Trukhov*
14/10	h	Krumkachy	W	1-0	*Berezkin*
22/10	a	Vitebsk	L	0-2	
29/10	h	Dinamo Brest	W	1-0	*Trukhov*
05/11	a	Minsk	L	0-4	
19/11	h	Belshina	D	2-2	*Trukhov, Zyulev*
27/11	a	Neman	W	1-0	*Borisov*

No	Name	Nat	DoB	Pos	Aps	(s)	Gls
8	Evgeni Berezkin		05/07/96	M	21	(7)	2
2	Dmitri Borisov		08/01/95	D	15	(5)	4
1	Igor Dovgyallo		17/07/85	G	28		
4	Mikhail Gorbachev		29/07/83	D	27		1
35	Ruslan Hunchak	UKR	09/08/79	D	29	(1)	
25	Mikhail Khodunov		08/12/94	M		(2)	
3	Yehor Klymenchuk	UKR	11/11/97	M		(3)	
5	Nikita Kolyaev	RUS	23/07/89	A	8	(3)	1
13	Sergei Kondratiev		02/02/90	D	25	(2)	
77	Anton Kotlyar	UKR	07/03/93	M	7	(5)	
12	Aleksandr Krovetski		02/10/96	A		(2)	
20	Abdulaziz Lawal	NGA	20/12/92	M	9	(7)	
14	Evgeni Lebedev		29/12/94	A	13	(9)	4
16	Artur Semenov		21/10/94	G		(1)	
10	Oleg Shkabara		15/02/83	M	14	(3)	
81	Nikita Shugunkov		17/04/92	A	5	(19)	
34	Roman Stepanov		06/08/91	G	2		
17	Aleksei Suchkov		10/06/81	M	26		1
37	Artem Teplov		14/01/92	D	22	(3)	1
9	Ruslan Teverov		01/05/94	A	13	(2)	1
9	Igor Trukhov		19/08/76	M	14	(1)	3
3	Dmitri Turlin		08/09/85	M	1	(2)	
7	Andrei Yakimov		17/11/89	M	21	(6)	3
25	Igor Yasinski		04/07/90	M	2	(1)	
33	Igor Zyulev		05/01/84	D	28		4

FC Neman Grodno

1964 • Central Sportkomplex Neman (8,404) • fcneman.by

Major honours
Belarusian Cup (1) 1993

Coach: Sergei Solodovnikov; (26/04/16) Oleg Kirenya; (17/06/16) Igor Kovalevich

2016

03/04	h	Granit	D	1-1	*Vasilyuk*
09/04	a	Krumkachy	L	1-2	*Vasilyuk*
15/04	h	Vitebsk	D	0-0	
23/04	a	Dinamo Brest	L	0-2	
29/04	h	Minsk	L	0-1	
07/05	a	Belshina	D	1-1	*Bombel*
12/05	h	BATE	L	0-1	
17/05	h	Isloch	W	2-1	*Kontsevoi, Vasilyuk (p)*
22/05	a	Slavia-Mozyr	L	0-1	
04/06	h	Torpedo	L	0-3	
09/06	a	Gorodeya	L	1-2	*Savitski*
16/06	h	Shakhtyor	L	0-1	
20/06	a	Dinamo Minsk	W	1-0	*Gorbach*
26/06	h	Slutsk	D	0-0	
02/07	a	Naftan	L	0-2	
29/07	a	Granit	W	1-0	*Savitski*
07/08	h	Krumkachy	D	2-2	*Kontsevoi, Yarotski*
12/08	a	Vitebsk	D	1-1	*Bombel*
19/08	h	Dinamo Brest	L	0-4	
27/08	a	Minsk	W	1-0	*Savitski*
10/09	h	Belshina	W	1-0	*Vaskov*
17/09	a	BATE	L	0-4	
25/09	a	Isloch	D	0-0	
30/09	h	Slavia-Mozyr	W	3-1	*Rudik, Savitski, Anyukevich*
15/10	a	Torpedo	L	0-1	
22/10	h	Gorodeya	W	3-0	*Kosmynin, Savitski 2*
29/10	a	Shakhtyor	L	0-1	
06/11	h	Dinamo Minsk	L	2-3	*Rudik, Bombel*
19/11	a	Slutsk	D	0-0	
27/11	h	Naftan	L	0-1	

No	Name	Nat	DoB	Pos	Aps	(s)	Gls
14	Aleksandr Anyukevich		10/04/92	D	19	(3)	1
8	Paul Bebey	CMR	09/11/86	D	22	(1)	
29	Artur Bombel		14/12/92	A	14	(10)	3
20	Andrei Chukhlei		02/10/87	M	4	(1)	
31	Taras Durai	UKR	31/07/84	M	11		
32	Andrei Gorbach		20/05/85	D	12	(10)	1
24	Vladislav Klimovich		12/06/96	A	3	(2)	
77	Artem Kontsevoi		20/05/83	A	23		2
18	Vladislav Kosmynin		17/01/90	D	10	(1)	1
10	Dmitri Kovalenok		03/11/77	A	1	(10)	
7	Sergei Kovalyuk		07/01/80	M	13	(1)	
19	Sergei Kurganski		15/05/86	G	29		
25	Evgeni Leshko		24/06/96	D	10	(5)	
23	Aleksei Nosko		15/08/96	M		(1)	
13	Aleksandr Pavlovets		13/08/96	D	15		
6	Aleksandr Poznyak		23/07/94	D	27		
4	Serhiy Rozhok	UKR	25/04/85	M	10		
7	Filipp Rudik		22/03/87	M	14		2
20	Ivan Rudnytskiy	UKR	05/07/91	M	1	(2)	
88	Pavel Savitski		12/07/94	M	21	(4)	6
33	Evgeni Savostyanov		30/01/88	M	15	(4)	
17	Yan Senkevich		18/02/95	M		(4)	
31	Semen Smunev		14/09/95	M		(1)	
21	Anton Sorokin		21/02/96	M		(1)	
3	Sergei Sosnovski		14/08/81	D	16	(3)	
78	Roman Vasilyuk		23/11/78	A	10	(3)	3
16	Artem Vaskov		21/10/88	M	19	(4)	1
9	Kirill Vergeichik		23/08/91	A	2	(9)	
28	Yaroslav Yarotski		28/03/96	M	8	(3)	1
11	Vasili Zhurnevich		21/02/95	A		(2)	
1	Vladimir Zhurov		09/03/91	G	1	(1)	

FC Shakhtyor Soligorsk

1961 • Stroitel (4,200) • fcshakhter.by

Major honours
Belarusian League (1) 2005; Belarusian Cup (2) 2004, 2014

Coach: Sergei Nikiforenko

2016

02/04	a	Gorodeya	W	1-0	*Yanush*
11/04	a	BATE	L	0-2	
16/04	h	Dinamo Minsk	D	0-0	
24/04	a	Slutsk	L	0-1	
29/04	h	Naftan	W	2-0	*Lisakovich, Yanush*
07/05	a	Granit	D	1-1	*Pavlov*
11/05	h	Krumkachy	L	0-2	
16/05	a	Vitebsk	W	3-1	*Yanush 2, Burko*
22/05	h	Dinamo Brest	W	3-1	*Yanush (p), Kuzmenok, Starhorodskiy*
05/06	a	Minsk	L	0-1	
10/06	h	Belshina	W	3-0	*Yanush, Yelezarenko, Pavlov*
16/06	a	Neman	W	1-0	*Yanush*
20/06	h	Isloch	W	3-0	*Starhorodskiy, Yanush, Rybak*
25/06	a	Slavia-Mozyr	D	1-1	*Osipenko*
04/07	h	Torpedo	W	3-0	*Rudyka, Kovalev, Yelezarenko*
31/07	h	Gorodeya	D	2-2	*Starhorodskiy, Yanush*
08/08	h	BATE	L	0-2	
13/08	a	Dinamo Minsk	W	3-1	*Starhorodskiy, Laptev, Burko*
21/08	h	Slutsk	D	0-0	
28/08	a	Naftan	D	1-1	*Laptev*
10/09	h	Granit	W	4-0	*og (Zemko), Starhorodskiy (p), Pavlov, Kovalev*
18/09	a	Krumkachy	W	1-0	*Rybak*
25/09	h	Vitebsk	W	1-0	*Laptev*
02/10	a	Dinamo Brest	W	2-1	*Laptev 2*
15/10	h	Minsk	D	0-0	
23/10	a	Belshina	W	1-0	*Teverov*
29/10	h	Neman	W	1-0	*Burko*
06/11	a	Isloch	W	3-1	*Yanush, Burko, Yurevich*
19/11	h	Slavia-Mozyr	W	5-1	*Yanush, Kovalev 2, Laptev, Burko*
27/11	a	Torpedo	D	1-1	*Yanush*

No	Name	Nat	DoB	Pos	Aps	(s)	Gls
6	Igor Burko		08/09/88	D	28	(2)	5
16	Vladimir Bushma		24/11/83	G	29		
12	Nikola Ignjatijević	SRB	12/12/83	D	22		
1	Artur Kotenko	EST	20/08/81	G	1		
23	Yuri Kovalev		27/01/93	M	17	(12)	4
19	Igor Kuzmenok		06/07/90	D	28		1
15	Denis Laptev		01/08/91	A	7	(7)	6
99	Vitali Lisakovich		08/02/98	A	3	(8)	1
3	Sergei Matveichik		05/06/88	D	25		
7	Dmitri Osipenko		12/12/82	A	9	(12)	1
17	Aleksandr Pavlov		18/08/84	M	13	(8)	3
9	Serhiy Rudyka	UKR	14/06/88	M	8	(5)	1
18	Pavel Rybak		11/09/83	D	24		2
8	Aleksandr Selyava		17/05/92	M	11	(3)	
31	Mikhail Shibun		01/01/96	M	4	(1)	
11	Artem Starhorodskiy	UKR	17/01/82	M	25	(1)	5
23	Ruslan Teverov		01/05/94	A	3	(10)	1
81	Aleksei Timoshenko		09/12/86	M	4	(6)	
10	Nikolai Yanush		09/09/84	A	22	(2)	12
4	Aleksei Yanushkevich		15/01/86	D	7	(4)	
21	Evgeni Yelezarenko		04/07/93	M	12	(8)	2
5	Aleksandr Yurevich		08/08/79	M	28	(1)	1

FC Slavia-Mozyr

1987 • Yunost (5,253) • fcslavia.by

Major honours
Belarusian League (2) 1996, 2000; Belarusian Cup (2) 1996, 2000

Coach: Yuri Puntus

2016

02/04	h	Slutsk	D	1-1	*Laptev*
10/04	a	Naftan	W	1-0	*Laptev (p)*
15/04	h	Granit	L	1-3	*Lemiechevski*
23/04	a	Krumkachy	L	0-1	
30/04	h	Vitebsk	L	0-4	
07/05	a	Dinamo Brest	D	0-0	
12/05	h	Minsk	W	6-2	*Mosemgvdlishvili 2, Kovalevski, Lemiechevski, Costrov, Shkurko*
17/05	a	Belshina	D	2-2	*Costrov, Laptev*
22/05	h	Neman	W	1-0	*Kovalevski*
05/06	a	Isloch	W	1-0	*Zhuk*
10/06	h	BATE	W	2-1	*Strakhanovich, Mosemgvdlishvili*
15/06	h	Torpedo	L	0-1	
20/06	a	Gorodeya	L	2-4	*Shkurko, Strakhanovich*
25/06	h	Shakhtyor	D	1-1	*Voronkov*
03/07	a	Dinamo Minsk	L	0-1	
29/07	a	Slutsk	L	0-1	
06/08	h	Naftan	W	2-0	*Strakhanovich, Shkurko*
14/08	a	Granit	D	0-0	
19/08	h	Krumkachy	W	1-0	*Kovalevski*
27/08	a	Vitebsk	D	1-1	*Kovalevski*
10/09	h	Dinamo Brest	L	1-4	*Hodovaniy*
16/09	a	Minsk	L	2-6	*og (Omelyanchuk), Voronkov (p)*
26/09	h	Belshina	L	0-2	
30/09	a	Neman	L	1-3	*Shkurko*
15/10	h	Isloch	W	2-1	*Voronkov, Strakhanovich*
23/10	a	BATE	D	0-0	
30/10	a	Torpedo	L	0-2	
07/11	h	Gorodeya	D	3-3	*Kotlyarov, Voronkov (p), Zhuk*
19/11	a	Shakhtyor	L	1-5	*Rayevski*
27/11	h	Dinamo Minsk	W	1-0	*Kotlyarov*

No	Name	Nat	DoB	Pos	Aps	(s)	Gls
77	Iakob Apkhazava	GEO	30/04/91	A	3	(2)	
14	Vladislav Borisenko		05/03/97	D	8		
13	Igor Costrov	MDA	03/08/87	M	22	(5)	2
3	Roman Hodovaniy	UKR	04/10/90	D	8		1
11	Aleksandr Kobets		11/06/81	M	14	(2)	
67	Sergei Koshel		14/03/86	A		(2)	
7	Aleksandr Kotlyarov		30/01/93	M	10	(6)	2
45	Denis Kovalevski		02/05/92	D	25		4
23	Evgeni Kuntsevich		16/08/88	D	19		
15	Denis Laptev		01/08/91	A	10	(5)	3
24	Bruno Lemiechevski	ESP	03/04/94	A	5	(16)	2
4	Igor Maltsev		11/03/86	D	25		
5	Papuna Mosemgvdlishvili	GEO	27/04/94	D	15	(2)	3
17	Maksim Pavlovets		08/08/96	M	3	(9)	
27	Aleksandr Rayevski		19/06/88	D	18	(5)	1
84	Nikolai Romanyuk		02/06/84	G	30		
9	Hleb Shevchenko		17/02/99	M		(2)	
16	Yaroslav Shkurko		08/02/91	M	24	(5)	4
8	Oleg Strakhanovich		13/10/79	M	20	(5)	4
26	Ivan Sulim		04/05/89	D	22		
77	Pavel Sultanov	RUS	07/07/93	M	4	(5)	
20	Dmytro Vorobei	UKR	10/05/85	M	6		
88	Andrei Voronkov		08/02/89	A	20	(6)	4
18	Vladislav Zhuk		11/06/94	M	19	(9)	2

SFC Slutsk

1998 • City (1,896) • sfc-slutsk.by

Coach: Vyacheslav Grigorov

2016

02/04	a	Slavia-Mozyr	D	1-1	*Aliseiko*
10/04	h	Torpedo	D	1-1	*Tsvetinski*
17/04	a	Gorodeya	L	0-2	
24/04	h	Shakhtyor	W	1-0	*Bobko*
29/04	a	Dinamo Minsk	D	1-1	*Hlebko*
08/05	a	BATE	L	0-3	
12/05	a	Naftan	L	0-1	
17/05	a	Granit	L	1-2	*Bamba*
23/05	h	Krumkachy	W	2-0	*Shchegrikovich, Bylina*
03/06	a	Vitebsk	L	0-2	
09/06	h	Dinamo Brest	L	0-1	
15/06	a	Minsk	L	2-5	*Perepechko, Demidchik*
19/06	h	Belshina	W	2-1	*Kugan, Bobko*
26/06	a	Neman	D	0-0	
02/07	h	Isloch	D	2-2	*Bobko, Yatskevich*
29/07	h	Slavia-Mozyr	W	1-0	*Kibuk*
08/08	a	Torpedo	L	0-2	
14/08	h	Gorodeya	D	1-1	*Kibuk*
21/08	a	Shakhtyor	D	0-0	
28/08	h	Dinamo Minsk	D	1-1	*Hlebko*
10/09	h	BATE	L	0-2	
16/09	h	Naftan	D	1-1	*Aliseiko (p)*
25/09	h	Granit	L	0-1	
30/09	a	Krumkachy	W	3-0	*Aleksei Zaleski, Sebai, Kibuk*
16/10	h	Vitebsk	W	2-1	*Sebai, Golyatkin*
23/10	a	Dinamo Brest	D	0-0	
30/10	h	Minsk	L	0-1	
06/11	a	Belshina	D	0-0	
19/11	h	Neman	D	0-0	
27/11	a	Isloch	L	0-2	

No	Name	Nat	DoB	Pos	Aps	(s)	Gls
16	Dmitri Aliseiko		28/08/92	D	23		2
11	Konan Auye	CIV	12/06/94	D	9	(1)	
14	Fousseni Bamba	CIV	19/04/90	D	9		1
23	Igor Bobko		09/09/85	M	25	(1)	3
30	Ilya Branovets		16/04/90	G	5		
3	Aleksandr Bylina		26/03/81	D	15	(3)	1
29	Pavel Demidchik		30/01/96	A		(3)	1
10	Sekou Doumbia	CIV	16/11/88	M	2	(2)	
1	Dmitri Dudar		08/11/91	G	13	(1)	
27	Sergei Golyatkin	RUS	04/05/88	D	13		1
17	Sergei Hlebko		23/08/92	A	17	(5)	2
7	Vitali Kibuk		07/01/89	A	11	(3)	3
55	Gnohoré Kriso	CIV	20/06/97	A	5	(4)	
20	Aleksandr Kugan		26/05/91	M	7	(8)	1
7	Vadim Kurlovich		30/10/92	M	2	(7)	
27	Artur Lesko		25/05/84	G	8		
6	Sergei Levitski		17/03/90	M	10	(1)	
10	Evgeni Loshankov		02/01/79	M	1	(4)	
4	Vadym Milko	UKR	22/08/86	M	25	(2)	
8	Aleksandr Perepechko		07/04/89	M	10	(9)	1
1	Konstantin Rudenok		15/12/90	G	4	(1)	
15	Bohdan Rudyuk	UKR	19/04/94	D	10		
14	Vitali Rushnitski		17/01/90	M	2	(4)	
19	Senin Sebai	CIV	18/12/93	A	8	(5)	2
5	Dmitri Shchegrikovich		07/12/83	M	22	(4)	1
18	Sergei Tsvetinski		22/02/84	D	10		1
9	Pavel Vakulich		14/09/96	M		(2)	
2	Ihor Voronkov	UKR	24/04/81	M	4	(1)	
12	Aleksandr Yatskevich		04/01/85	A	11	(9)	1
22	Aleksei Zaleski		07/10/94	D	21	(3)	1
13	Andrei Zaleski		20/01/91	D	28		

FC Torpedo Zhodino

1961 • Torpedo (6,542) • torpedo-belaz.by

Major honours
Belarusian Cup (1) 2016

Coach: Igor Kriushenko

2016

02/04	h	Dinamo Minsk	L	0-2	
10/04	a	Slutsk	D	1-1	*Skavysh*
16/04	h	Naftan	W	2-1	*Chumak (p), Demidovich*
25/04	a	Granit	D	1-1	*Skavysh*
30/04	h	Krumkachy	W	3-0	*Skavysh, Kvashuk, Golenkov*
08/05	a	Vitebsk	W	1-0	*Skavysh*
16/05	a	Minsk	D	0-0	
25/05	h	Belshina	D	2-2	*Skavysh, Demidovich*
30/05	a	Dinamo Brest	L	2-3	*Chelyadinski, Shcherbo*
04/06	a	Neman	W	3-0	*Skavysh, Demidovich 2 (1p)*
10/06	h	Isloch	D	1-1	*Skavysh*
15/06	a	Slavia-Mozyr	W	1-0	*Chelyadinski*
19/06	h	BATE	L	1-2	*Chelyadinski*
26/06	h	Gorodeya	L	1-3	*Trapashko*
04/07	a	Shakhtyor	L	0-3	
08/08	h	Slutsk	W	2-0	*Afanasiyev, Demidovich*
14/08	a	Naftan	W	3-1	*Khachaturyan, Karshakevich, Imerekov*
20/08	h	Granit	W	5-0	*Demidovich 2, Afanasiyev, Imerekov, Lutsevich*
26/08	a	Krumkachy	W	2-0	*Afanasiyev, Demidovich*
09/09	h	Vitebsk	L	1-2	*Klopotski*
17/09	h	Dinamo Brest	L	0-1	
25/09	h	Minsk	D	0-0	
01/10	a	Belshina	W	3-1	*Afanasiyev 2, Demidovich*
08/10	a	Dinamo Minsk	D	1-1	*Rekish*
15/10	h	Neman	W	1-0	*Lutsevich*
22/10	a	Isloch	L	2-3	*Lutsevich 2*
30/10	h	Slavia-Mozyr	W	2-0	*Demidovich 2 (1p)*
05/11	a	BATE	W	2-1	*Demidovich, Rekish*
19/11	a	Gorodeya	D	3-3	*Lutsevich, Golenkov, Shcherbo*
27/11	h	Shakhtyor	D	1-1	*Lutsevich*

No	Name	Nat	DoB	Pos	Aps	(s)	Gls
77	Mikhail Afanasiyev		04/11/86	M	15		5
99	Aleksei Belevich		26/01/95	M	1	(4)	
10	Gennadi Bliznyuk		30/07/80	A	11	(2)	
2	Artem Chelyadinski		29/12/77	D	12		3
30	Pavel Chelyadko		03/03/93	D	7	(7)	
28	Yevhen Chumak	UKR	25/08/95	M	11		1
87	Vadim Demidovich		20/09/85	A	23	(7)	12
23	Valeri Fomichev		23/03/88	G	24		
9	Soslan Gatagov	RUS	29/09/92	D	7		
17	Anton Golenkov		17/12/89	M	16	(10)	2
44	Maxym Imerekov	UKR	23/01/91	D	15		2
21	Valeri Karshakevich		15/02/88	D	20		1
10	Andrei Khachaturyan		02/09/87	M	15		1
35	Yegor Khatkevich		09/07/88	G	6		
4	Evgeni Klopotski		12/08/93	D	22		1
77	Vitaliy Kvashuk	UKR	01/04/93	M	5	(7)	1
14	Terenti Lutsevich		19/04/91	D	7	(7)	6
6	Aleksei Pankovets		18/04/81	D	29	(1)	
22	Aleksandr Pavlovets		13/08/96	D	7	(2)	
31	Yuri Pavlyukovets		24/06/94	M	2	(4)	
15	Dmitri Rekish		14/09/88	M	8	(7)	2
7	Serhiy Shapoval	UKR	07/02/90	M	23	(2)	
18	Vladimir Shcherbo		01/04/86	D	21	(5)	2
13	Maksim Skavysh		13/11/89	A	12	(2)	7
8	Andrei Solovei		13/12/94	M	1	(6)	
50	Denis Trapashko		17/05/90	A	1	(12)	1
28	Serhiy Zaginaylov	UKR	03/01/91	M	9	(3)	

BELARUS

FC Vitebsk

1960 • Central (8,100) • fc.vitebsk.by

Major honours

Belarusian Cup (1) 1998

Coach: Sergei Yasinski

2016

02/04	a	Minsk	L	0-1	
11/04	a	Belshina	W	1-0	*Solovei*
15/04	a	Neman	D	0-0	
23/04	h	Isloch	L	1-2	*og (Shagoiko)*
30/04	a	Slavia-Mozyr	W	4-0	*Solovei 2, og (Sulim), Babychev*
08/05	h	Torpedo	L	0-1	
12/05	a	Gorodeya	W	2-0	*Naumov, Volkov*
16/05	h	Shakhtyor	L	1-3	*Marakhovski*
22/05	a	Dinamo Minsk	L	0-1	
03/06	h	Slutsk	W	2-0	*Kalinin, Solovei*
09/06	a	Naftan	W	2-1	*Volkov 2*
15/06	h	Granit	L	0-1	
19/06	a	Krumkachy	L	0-1	
25/06	a	BATE	L	0-1	
02/07	h	Dinamo Brest	W	1-0	*Solovei*
31/07	h	Minsk	D	0-0	
08/08	h	Belshina	D	1-1	*Karamushka*
12/08	h	Neman	D	1-1	*Lebedev*
21/08	a	Isloch	D	0-0	
27/08	h	Slavia-Mozyr	D	1-1	*Volkov*
09/09	a	Torpedo	W	2-1	*Solovei, Tikhonovski*
17/09	h	Gorodeya	W	1-0	*Vergeichik*
25/09	a	Shakhtyor	L	0-1	
02/10	h	Dinamo Minsk	L	0-2	
16/10	a	Slutsk	L	1-2	*Volkov*
22/10	h	Naftan	W	2-0	*Volkov, Vinogradov*
29/10	a	Granit	W	3-0	*Volkov, Vergeichik, Solovei*
05/11	h	Krumkachy	W	2-1	*Volkov 2*
19/11	h	BATE	W	2-1	*Solovei, Karamushka*
27/11	a	Dinamo Brest	L	0-3	

No	Name	Nat	DoB	Pos	Aps	(s)	Gls
30	Aleksandr Aleksandrovich		06/07/97	M		(2)	
6	Mikhail Babychev		02/02/95	M	20	(8)	1
22	Andrei Baranok		20/07/79	M	11	(8)	
1	Dmitri Gushchenko		12/05/88	G	29		
11	Evgeni Kalinin		15/08/93	M	10	(3)	1
25	Oleh Karamushka	UKR	03/04/84	D	14		2
17	Mikhail Kozlov		12/02/90	M	16	(2)	
26	Aleksandr Kucherov		22/01/95	A		(1)	
2	Andrei Lebedev		01/02/91	D	12	(13)	1
10	Igor Lisitsa		10/04/88	M	15		
5	Vitali Marakhovski	RUS	14/01/88	D	17	(2)	1
23	Nikita Naumov		15/11/89	D	19	(1)	1
16	Andrei Shcherbakov		31/01/91	G	1		
7	Serhiy Shevchuk	UKR	21/09/90	M	9	(7)	
25	Kirill Sidorenko		25/08/95	A		(12)	
4	Artem Skitov		21/01/91	D	27		
13	Artur Slabashevich		09/02/89	D	10	(3)	
15	Artem Solovei		01/11/90	M	29		8
10	Vyacheslav Sushkin	RUS	11/03/91	M	7	(4)	
8	Sergei Tikhonovski		26/06/90	M	23	(5)	1
77	Kirill Vergeichik		23/08/91	A	8	(6)	2
23	Sergei Vinogradov	RUS	17/11/81	M	15		1
19	Roman Volkov		08/01/87	A	26	(1)	9
35	Nikolai Zolotov		11/11/94	D	12	(11)	

Top goalscorers

15	Mikhail Gordeichuk (BATE) Vitali Rodionov (BATE)
12	Nikolai Yanush (Shakhtyor) Vadim Demidovich (Torpedo)
10	Joel Fameyeh (Belshina/Dinamo Brest)
9	Denis Laptev (Slavia-Mozyr/Shakhtyor) Roman Volkov (Vitebsk)
8	Vladimir Khvashchinski (Dinamo Minsk) Dmitri Lebedev (Gorodeya) Anton Saroka (Gorodeya) Terenti Lutsevich (Granit/Torpedo) Nemanja Čović (Minsk) Valerian Gvilia (Minsk/BATE) Artem Solovei (Vitebsk)

Promoted clubs

FC Gomel

1959 • Central Sportkomplex (CSK) (14,307) • fcgomel.by

Major honours

Belarusian League (1) 2003; Belarusian Cup (2) 2002, 2011

Coach: Vladimir Zhuravel

FC Dnepr Mogilev

1960 • Spartak (7,350) • fcdnepr.by

Major honours

Belarusian League (1) 1998

Coach: Aleksandr Sednev

Second level final table 2016

		Pld	W	D	L	F	A	Pts
1	FC Gomel	26	19	6	1	48	11	63
2	FC Dnepr Mogilev	26	20	4	2	61	19	63
3	FC Gomelzheldortrans Gomel	26	12	8	6	33	24	44
4	FC Luch Minsk	26	12	5	9	38	28	41
5	FC Smorgon	26	10	8	8	40	39	38
6	FC Lida	26	11	5	10	26	33	38
7	FC Orsha	26	9	10	7	43	34	37
8	FC Smolevichi-STI	26	9	7	10	38	29	34
9	FC Torpedo Minsk	26	9	6	11	35	36	33
10	FC Zvezda-BGU Minsk	26	9	6	11	33	41	33
11	FC Slonim	26	6	6	14	36	49	24
12	FC Khimik Svetlogorsk	26	6	5	15	26	49	23
13	FC Baranovichi	26	5	7	14	35	51	22
14	FC Oshmyany	26	2	1	23	15	64	7

NB FC Dnepr Mogilev – 1 pt deducted.

DOMESTIC CUP

Kubok Belarusii 2016/17

SECOND ROUND

(06/07/16)
Orsha 0-4 Minsk
Slonim 0-2 Dinamo Brest

(07/07/16)
Neman-Agro Stolbtsy 0-5 Neman

(08/07/16)
Smolevichi-STI 0-1 Vitebsk
Zvezda-BGU 0-0 Gorodeya *(aet; 2-3 on pens)*

(09/07/16)
Baranovichi 3-2 Belshina *(aet)*
Gomelzheldortrans 2-1 Krumkachy
Khimik Svetlogorsk 0-4 Slutsk
Senno 0-1 Naftan
Smorgon 3-0 Granit
Volna 0-4 Torpedo Zhodino

(10/07/16)
Torpedo Minsk 0-2 Slavia-Mozyr

(26/07/16)
Vertikal Kalinkovichi 1-6 Isloch

(01/09/16)
Gomel 0-1 Dinamo Minsk

(06/09/16)
Lida 0-2 Shakhtyor

(14/09/16)
Torpedo Mogilev 0-4 BATE

THIRD ROUND

(21/09/16)
Baranovichi 2-3 Minsk *(aet)*
BATE 4-2 Isloch
Dinamo Brest 2-1 Naftan
Gomelzheldortrans 0-0 Slavia-Mozyr *(aet; 3-0 on pens)*
Gorodeya 0-0 Dinamo Minsk *(aet; 1-4 on pens)*
Neman 1-2 Shakhtyor *(aet)*
Slutsk 3-0 Smorgon
Torpedo Zhodino 2-1 Vitebsk

QUARTER-FINALS

(12/03/17 & 18/03/17)
Lokomotiv Gomel 0-3 Shakhtyor *(Laptev 62, 86, Aleksiyevich 82)*
Shakhtyor 2-1 Lokomotiv Gomel *(Khizhnichenko 57p, Yanush 59; Kleshchenok 55)*
(Shakhtyor 5-1)

Dinamo Minsk 2-2 Dinamo Brest *(Premudrov 12, Galović 40; Fameyeh 49, Osuchukwu 56)*
Dinamo Brest 0-0 Dinamo Minsk
(2-2; Dinamo Brest on away goals)

(15/03/17 & 19/03/17)
Minsk 0-1 BATE *(Gordeichuk 4)*
BATE 2-1 Minsk *(Rios 40, Rodionov 67; Ostojić 61og)*
(BATE 3-1)

Torpedo Zhodino 1-0 Slutsk *(Makas 47)*
Slutsk 2-0 Torpedo Zhodino *(Yusov 60, Shcherbo 81og)*
(Slutsk 2-1)

NB Gomelzheldortrans renamed Lokomotiv Gomel for 2017 season.

SEMI-FINALS

(05/04/17 & 26/04/17)
Dinamo Brest 2-0 BATE *(Torres 2, Fameyeh 58)*
BATE 1-0 Dinamo Brest *(Ivanić 64)*
(Dinamo Brest 2-1)

Slutsk 1-2 Shakhtyor *(Yusov 20; Yanush 12, Bagarić 25)*
Shakhtyor 1-1 Slutsk *(Soiri 31; Sebai 85)*
(Shakhtyor 3-2)

FINAL

(28/05/17)
CSK Neman, Grodno
FC DINAMO BREST 1*(Legchilin 82)*
FC SHAKHTYOR SOLIGORSK 1 *(Lisakovich 69)*
(aet; 10-9 on pens)
Referee: *Kulbakov*
DINAMO BREST: *Malherbe, Aliseiko, Avramia, Lebedev, Vitus, Legchilin, Bukatkin (Sedko 77), Chizh (Mozolevski 74), Osuchukwu (Afoakwa 106), Torres, Fameyeh*
SHAKHTYOR: *Bushma, Burko, Yanushkevich, Rybak, Matveichik, Olekhnovich, Crepulja, Bagarić (Kovalev 76), Aleksiyevich, Soiri (Lisakovich 52), Laptev (Yanush 81)*

BELGIUM

Union Royale Belge des Sociétés de Football Association (URBSFA) / Koninklijke Belgische Voetbalbond (KBVB)

Address 145 Avenue Houba de Strooper
BE-1020 Bruxelles
Tel +32 2 477 1211
Fax +32 2 478 2391
E-mail urbsfa.kbvb@footbel.com
Website belgiumfootball.be

President	Gérard Linard
General secretary	Koen De Brabander
Media officer	Pierre Cornez
Year of formation	1895
National stadium	King Baudouin, Brussels (50,122)

KEY

- UEFA Champions League
- UEFA Europa League
- Promoted
- Relegated

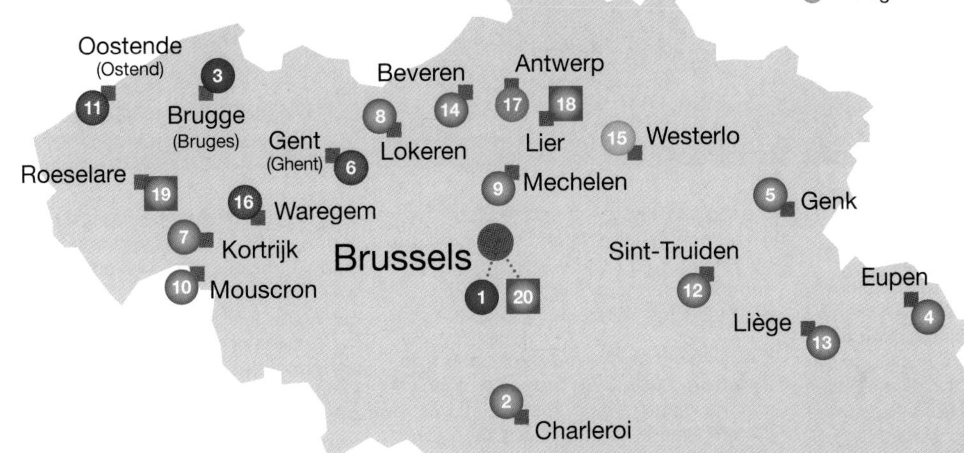

PRO LEAGUE CLUBS

1 **RSC Anderlecht**

2 **R. Charleroi SC**

3 **Club Brugge KV**

4 **KAS Eupen**

5 **KRC Genk**

6 **KAA Gent**

7 **KV Kortrijk**

8 **KSC Lokeren OV**

9 **KV Mechelen**

10 **R. Excel Mouscron**

11 **KV Oostende**

12 **K. Sint-Truidense VV**

13 **R. Standard de Liège**

14 **Waasland-Beveren**

15 **KVC Westerlo**

16 **SV Zulte Waregem**

PROMOTED CLUB

17 **R. Antwerp FC**

ADDITIONAL CLUBS

18 **K. Lierse SK**

19 **KSV Roeselare**

20 **R. Union Saint-Gilloise**

Anderlecht back where they belong

Belgium's most decorated club were back in possession of the country's most prestigious football trophy in 2016/17 as Anderlecht, led by new Swiss coach René Weiler, came storming through the play-off section of the two-tiered Pro League to win their 34th top-flight title.

Defending champions Club Brugge finished second, with 2014/15 winners Gent, the best of the rest in the play-offs, taking third spot to qualify for the UEFA Europa League, where they were joined by Belgian Cup winners Zulte Waregem and the team defeated on penalties in the final, Oostende.

New coach Weiler leads Brussels giants to 34th title

Zulte Waregem beat Oostende on penalties in cup final

2018 World Cup beckons free-scoring national side

Domestic league

Quizzical looks greeted the relatively unknown Weiler as he arrived in Brussels having narrowly failed to take Nürnberg into the German Bundesliga following a play-off defeat by Eintracht Frankfurt. Anderlecht were keen to avoid going three consecutive seasons without a title for the first time in the 21st century, but their ambitions appeared to be veering off course when, after a fair-to-middling start – in which only on-loan Polish striker Łukasz Teodorczyk of a handful of interesting new signings settled fast – their form sagged in mid-autumn with three successive away defeats, at Club Brugge, Waasland-Beveren and Zulte Waregem.

There was widespread media talk of Weiler being shown the door, but the club kept faith and were handsomely rewarded as the 43-year-old former defender rallied his troops and guided them on an impressive 13-match unbeaten run over the winter that took them to the summit of the newly-named First Division A table before that particular stage of the Pro League came to a conclusion in mid-March. Club Brugge, still led by 2015/16 title-winning boss Michel Preud'homme, had put together a 13-match winning streak of their own, from mid-October to late January, and as the league entered its second phase, with points halved and the top six playing-off for the title, Anderlecht led the defending champions by a point, with Zulte Waregem, the early front-runners, a further three points back in third.

It was now that Weiler's team came into their own. While Club Brugge suddenly lost the winning habit, Anderlecht got the results they wanted – not always in the style that the club's illustrious tradition demanded but with discipline, strength of character and efficiency – qualities epitomised by the team's two young midfield stars Leander Dendoncker and Youri Tielemans. Club Brugge were defeated 2-0 in Brussels, in-form Gent were held 0-0 away and Zulte Waregem beaten twice. Only Charleroi, the one newcomer to the top half-dozen from the previous season (in place of Genk), gave Anderlecht a scare, beating them 1-0 at the Constant Vanden Stock stadium, but in the rematch two goals from Teodorczyk – his 21st and 22nd of the campaign – inspired the Mauves to a 3-1 win that clinched the title with a game to spare.

With just four goals conceded in those first nine play-off matches, Anderlecht's defenders deserved a particular pat on the back, notably central pillars Uroš Spajić – a Serbian loanee from Toulouse – and Serigne 'Kara' Mbodji – a Senegal international formerly with Genk. Defensive midfielder Dendoncker, who started all 40 matches and was never substituted, also had a heroic season, while Tielemans, who only turned 20 in early May, fulfilled his potential with a succession of commanding performances that displayed maturity beyond his years. Skipper Sofiane Hanni, a high-profile new recruit from Mechelen, also had his moments, the Algerian international mixing flair with pace and scoring ten goals.

While Anderlecht's title earned direct access to the UEFA Champions League group stage, Club Brugge's final-day 2-1 win against Gent at the Jan Breydelstadion earned them a place in the third qualifying round of Europe's blue riband club competition. That was a decent consolation prize for Preud'homme's team, who never managed to hit the heights of the previous campaign despite their admirable refusal to be beaten in front of their own fans.

Gent's defeat in Bruges was one of only two that Hein Vanhaezebrouck's side suffered in the play-offs, enabling them to move up a place and secure a UEFA Europa League berth without recourse to a play-off. That was the fate of fourth-placed Oostende, but they came through it successfully, home advantage helping Yves Vanderhaeghe's enterprising side to a 3-1 win over Genk, who had finished top of their play-off table – by an 11-point margin – and then beaten the other group winners Sint-Truiden 3-0 to earn the right to that final showdown by the North Sea.

An idiosyncratic new format was devised for the Belgian second tier, with the newly-named First Division B containing just eight clubs, who played each other home and away in two separate phases of the competition, with the winners of each phase – 'Opening' and 'Closing' – facing-off in a two-legged play-off for one automatic promotion place to First Division A. Roeselare and Antwerp duly met in early March, with the latter winning both legs to return to the elite for the first time in 13 years. Lierse had good reason to feel hard done by as they had outpointed both Antwerp and Roeselare over the two phases combined, but their only reward was a two-month extension to their season in the labyrinthine UEFA Europa League qualification process. Like Antwerp, however, Westerlo's campaign was over in March as they finished bottom of First Division A – one point below Excel Mouscron – and were automatically relegated.

Domestic cup

Staged in mid-March before the league play-offs got under way, the Belgian Cup final brought together Zulte Waregem and Oostende, the latter making their first appearance in the fixture. A crowd of 35,000 in the King Baudouin stadium were treated to a cracking contest that swung one way then the other, with Oostende twice taking the lead in normal time through their charismatic teenager Landry Dimata only to be pegged back by their opponents, who then went 3-2 ahead nine minutes from the end of extra time before a Knowledge Musona penalty levelled it up at 3-3. Musona, however, would miss a second spot kick, Zulte Waregem goalkeeper Sammy Bossut saving from the Zimbabwean in the shoot-out before team-mate Brian Hamalainen converted the winning kick.

Oostende's defeat completed a chain of misfortune following Anderlecht's last-16 elimination on penalties by Charleroi, who were then defeated in the quarter-finals by Genk, who in turn lost in the semis to Oostende. Zulte Waregem, meanwhile, had their hands on the trophy for the second time, their previous win in 2005/06 having also been masterminded by coach Francky Dury during the first of his two spells in charge.

Europe

There were some long European campaigns for Belgian clubs to contend with alongside their marathon domestic season in 2016/17, although not for Club Brugge, whose first UEFA Champions League group stage campaign for 11 years ended in a whitewash, their six defeats yielding just two goals.

In contrast, the UEFA Europa League provided 50 matches with Pro League interest, including two in which Belgian clubs came into direct opposition – for only the second time in European club competition history – as Gent met Genk in the round of 16. The latter prevailed comfortably, 6-3 on aggregate, but their 18-match odyssey from the second qualifying round reached its end in the quarter-finals with defeat by Celta Vigo.

Anderlecht, beaten by Rostov in the UEFA Champions League third qualifying round, found solace in an extensive UEFA Europa League journey that took in a 6-1 home win against Mainz, a last-gasp away-goal success against Zenit and a double over Cypriot champions APOEL before coming to a halt in extra time at Old Trafford against eventual winners Manchester United. Weiler's men came agonisingly close to claiming a second Belgian success against English opposition following Gent's memorable 2-2 draw at Wembley Stadium that knocked out Tottenham Hotspur in the round of 32.

National team

A new era for the Belgian national side began with the arrival of Roberto Martínez as the replacement coach for Marc Wilmots. Things did not start too well for the ex-Everton manager when his team were booed off at the end of his first game, a friendly at home to his native Spain that ended in a 2-0 defeat. However, that was to be the only loss endured by Martínez in a season that brought 16 points from a possible 18 – plus an average return of four goals per game – in the qualifying competition for the 2018 FIFA World Cup

Although the head coach was new – as was his assistant, legendary French striker Thierry Henry – the squad of players at Martínez's disposal was practically the same as before, and several of its many top-class individuals, among them English Premier League luminaries like Eden Hazard, Jan Vertonghen and six-goal Romelu Lukaku and Serie A stars such as Dries Mertens and Radja Nainggolan, evidently enjoyed themselves under the new regime. A third major tournament qualification in a row – after five successive failures – was clearly Belgium's for the taking as they led Group H by four points with four games to play.

Romelu Lukaku heads home his second goal in Belgium's 3-0 win against Cyprus in Nicosia

DOMESTIC SEASON AT A GLANCE

Pro League 2016/17 final tables

Championship play-offs

			Home					Away					Total					
		Pld	W	D	L	F	A	W	D	L	F	A	W	D	L	F	A	Pts
1	**RSC Anderlecht**	**10**	**3**	**1**	**1**	**7**	**3**	**3**	**2**	**0**	**7**	**3**	**6**	**3**	**1**	**14**	**6**	**52**
2	Club Brugge KV	10	3	2	0	9	5	1	1	3	7	9	4	3	3	16	14	45
3	KAA Gent	10	2	3	0	9	5	2	1	2	7	6	4	4	2	16	11	41
4	KV Oostende	10	3	1	1	8	6	0	2	3	6	11	3	3	4	14	17	37
5	R. Charleroi SC	10	1	1	3	5	8	1	3	1	5	5	2	4	4	10	13	35
6	SV Zulte Waregem	10	1	2	2	8	9	0	1	4	4	12	1	3	6	12	21	33

First phase

			Home					Away					Total					
		Pld	W	D	L	F	A	W	D	L	F	A	W	D	L	F	A	Pts
1	RSC Anderlecht	30	10	4	1	38	11	8	3	4	29	19	18	7	5	67	30	61
2	Club Brugge KV	30	12	3	0	39	12	6	2	7	17	12	18	5	7	56	24	59
3	SV Zulte Waregem	30	8	7	0	23	10	7	2	6	26	28	15	9	6	49	38	54
4	KAA Gent	30	12	1	2	31	9	2	7	6	14	20	14	8	8	45	29	50
5	KV Oostende	30	8	4	3	30	17	6	4	5	22	20	14	8	8	52	37	50
6	R. Charleroi SC	30	10	3	2	21	14	3	7	5	13	15	13	10	7	34	29	49
7	KV Mechelen	30	10	1	4	24	13	4	5	6	17	23	14	6	10	41	36	48
8	KRC Genk	30	10	3	2	24	13	4	3	8	16	22	14	6	10	40	35	48
9	R. Standard de Liège	30	7	5	3	27	16	3	7	5	20	22	10	12	8	47	38	39
10	KV Kortrijk	30	5	3	7	23	25	3	4	8	15	30	8	7	15	38	55	31
11	KSC Lokeren OV	30	5	6	4	12	11	2	4	9	12	23	7	10	13	24	34	31
12	K. Sint-Truidense VV	30	7	4	4	23	18	1	2	12	12	30	8	6	16	35	48	30
13	KAS Eupen	30	4	5	6	24	32	4	1	10	16	32	8	6	16	40	64	30
14	Waasland-Beveren	30	4	6	5	16	16	3	3	9	12	27	7	9	14	28	43	30
15	R. Excel Mouscron	30	4	2	9	15	26	3	1	11	14	27	7	3	20	29	53	24
16	KVC Westerlo	30	3	3	9	16	29	2	5	8	17	36	5	8	17	33	65	23

NB After 30 rounds the top six clubs enter a championship play-off, carrying forward half of their points total (half points rounded upwards); clubs placed 7-15 enter two play-off groups with three second level clubs; R. Standard de Liège – 3 pts deducted.

European qualification 2017/18

Champion: RSC Anderlecht (group stage)

Club Brugge KV (third qualifying round)

Cup winner: SV Zulte Waregem (group stage)

KAA Gent (third qualifying round)

KV Oostende (third qualifying round)

Top scorer	Łukasz Teodorczyk (Anderlecht) & Henry Onyekuru (Eupen), 22 goals
Relegated club	KVC Westerlo
Promoted club	R. Antwerp FC
Cup final	SV Zulte Waregem 3-3 KV Oostende *(aet; 4-2 on pens)*

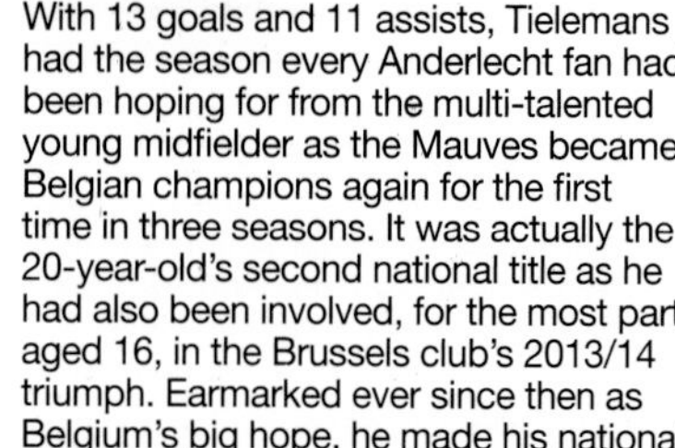

Player of the season

Youri Tielemans
(RSC Anderlecht)

With 13 goals and 11 assists, Tielemans had the season every Anderlecht fan had been hoping for from the multi-talented young midfielder as the Mauves became Belgian champions again for the first time in three seasons. It was actually the 20-year-old's second national title as he had also been involved, for the most part aged 16, in the Brussels club's 2013/14 triumph. Earmarked ever since then as Belgium's big hope, he made his national team debut in November 2016 and six months later was transferred for a reported €25m to French champions Monaco.

Newcomer of the season

Henry Onyekuru
(KAS Eupen)

Having helped Eupen win promotion in 2015/16, Onyekuru shone brightly for the club in Belgium's top flight, starting all but two of the club's 40 matches over the two phases of the league campaign and helping himself to 22 goals – the same number as Anderlecht's Łukasz Teodorczyk at the top of the Pro League scorers' chart. The month of June started with the young striker winning his first senior cap for Nigeria, against Togo, and ended with an out-of-the-blue transfer to Everton, albeit with the 2017/18 season being spent on loan at Anderlecht.

Team of the season
(4-2-3-1)

Coach: Weiler *(Anderlecht)*

NATIONAL TEAM

International tournament appearances

FIFA World Cup (12) 1930, 1934, 1938, 1954, 1970, 1982 (2nd phase), 1986 (4th), 1990 (2nd round), 1994 (2nd round), 1998, 2002 (2nd round), 2014 (qtr-finals)
UEFA European Championship (5) 1972 (3rd), 1980 (runners-up), 1984, 2000, 2016 (qtr-finals)

Top five all-time caps

Jan Ceulemans (96); **Timmy Simons** (94); **Jan Vertonghen** (93); Eric Gerets & Franky Van Der Elst (86)

Top five all-time goals

Paul Van Himst & Bernard Voorhoof (30); Marc Wilmots (28); Jef Mermans (27); Raymond Braine & Robert De Veen (26))

Results 2016/17

01/09/16	Spain	H	Brussels	L	0-2	
06/09/16	Cyprus (WCQ)	A	Nicosia	W	3-0	*R Lukaku (13, 61), Carrasco (81)*
07/10/16	Bosnia & Herzegovina (WCQ)	H	Brussels	W	4-0	*Spahić (26og), E Hazard (29), Alderweireld (60), R Lukaku (79)*
10/10/16	Gibraltar (WCQ)	A	Faro (POR)	W	6-0	*Benteke (1, 43, 56), Witsel (19), Mertens (51), E Hazard (79)*
09/11/16	Netherlands	A	Amsterdam	D	1-1	*Carrasco (82)*
13/11/16	Estonia (WCQ)	H	Brussels	W	8-1	*Meunier (8), Mertens (16, 68), E Hazard (25), Carrasco (62), Klavan (64og), R Lukaku (83, 88)*
25/03/17	Greece (WCQ)	H	Brussels	D	1-1	*R Lukaku (89)*
28/03/17	Russia	A	Sochi	D	3-3	*Mirallas (17p), Benteke (42, 45)*
05/06/17	Czech Republic	H	Brussels	W	2-1	*Batshuayi (25), Fellaini (52)*
09/06/17	Estonia (WCQ)	A	Tallinn	W	2-0	*Mertens (31), Chadli (86)*

Appearances 2016/17

Coach: Roberto Martínez (ESP)	**13/07/73**		**Esp**	**CYP**	**BIH**	**GIB**	**Ned**	**EST**	**GRE**	**Rus**	**Cze**	**EST**	**Caps**	**Goals**
Thibaut Courtois	11/05/92	Chelsea (ENG)	G	G	G	G		G	G		G	G	50	-
Thomas Meunier	12/09/91	Paris (FRA)	D	D	D	M	M46	M					15	1
Toby Alderweireld	02/03/89	Tottenham (ENG)	D	D	D	D			D	D	D	D	69	3
Jan Vertonghen	24/04/87	Tottenham (ENG)	D	D	D	D	D	D	D	D	D	D	93	6
Jordan Lukaku	25/07/94	Lazio (ITA)	D		D21								7	-
Radja Nainggolan	04/05/88	Roma (ITA)	M46	s84					M	M	M46		29	6
Axel Witsel	12/01/89	Zenit (RUS) /Tianjin Quanjian (CHN)	M	M	M	M	M	M88	M	s66		M	83	8
Yannick Carrasco	04/09/93	Atlético (ESP)	M77	M	M	M53	M	M	M	s77	M87	M	19	4
Kevin De Bruyne	28/06/91	Man. City (ENG)	M87	M			A64	M			M	A	52	13
Eden Hazard	07/01/91	Chelsea (ENG)	M	M	M87	A	A	A73					77	17
Divock Origi	18/04/95	Liverpool (ENG)	A67										23	3
Mousa Dembélé	16/07/87	Tottenham (ENG)	s46						s66	M85			69	5
Romelu Lukaku	13/05/93	Everton (ENG)	s67	A73	A82		s64	A	A	s77	A46	A	60	23
Kevin Mirallas	05/10/87	Everton (ENG)	s77		s87	s64		s73	s84	A66	s46		58	10
Steven Defour	15/04/88	Burnley (ENG)	s87			M	M84						51	2
Thomas Vermaelen	14/11/85	Roma (ITA)		D						D90	s46		61	1
Marouane Fellaini	22/11/87	Man. United (ENG)		M84	M				M66		s46	M	78	16
Michy Batshuayi	02/10/93	Chelsea (ENG)		s73		s80					A46	s81	11	4
Dries Mertens	06/05/87	Napoli (ITA)			M	A64	A64	A79	A	s66	s46	A81	59	12
Laurent Ciman	05/08/85	Montreal Impact (USA)			s21	D	D	D	D84				17	1
Christian Benteke	03/12/90	Crystal Palace (ENG)			s82	A80				A77	s46		33	12
Nacer Chadli	02/08/89	West Brom (ENG)				s53			M	M77	M	M	37	5
Simon Mignolet	06/03/88	Liverpool (ENG)					G			G			19	-
Christian Kabasele	24/02/91	Watford (ENG)					D						1	-
Thomas Foket	25/09/94	Gent					s46			M			2	-
Thorgan Hazard	29/03/93	Mönchengladbach (GER)					s64			s85	s87		4	-
Youri Tielemans	07/05/97	Anderlecht					s84	s79		M66	M46		4	-
Leander Dendoncker	15/04/95	Anderlecht						D					2	-
Timmy Simons	11/12/76	Club Brugge						s88					94	6
Dedryck Boyata	28/11/90	Celtic (SCO)								s90			3	-
Vincent Kompany	10/04/86	Man. City (ENG)									D46	D	74	4

EUROPE

Club Brugge KV

Group G

Match 1 - Leicester City FC (ENG)

H 0-3

Butelle, Van Rhijn, Simons, Engels (Poulain 53), Diaby (Vossen 62), Izquierdo (Felipe Gedoz 77), Pina, Vanaken, Denswil, Vormer, De Bock. Coach: Michel Preud'homme (BEL)

Match 2 - FC København (DEN)

A 0-4

Butelle, Van Rhijn, Simons, Poulain, Claudemir, Vossen (Wesley 63), Izquierdo (Felipe Gedoz 79), Vanaken (Limbombe 46), Denswil, Vormer, De Bock. Coach: Michel Preud'homme (BEL)

Match 3 - FC Porto (POR)

H 1-2 *Vossen (12)*

Butelle, Van Rhijn, Simons, Poulain, Claudemir, Vossen (Wesley 84), Pina (Felipe Gedoz 78), Limbombe (Bolingoli-Mbombo 82), Vanaken, Denswil, Vormer. Coach: Michel Preud'homme (BEL)

Match 4 - FC Porto (POR)

A 0-1

Butelle, Van Rhijn, Poulain, Claudemir, Wesley (Izquierdo 77), Diaby (Limbombe 46), Pina, Cools, Denswil, Vormer, Bolingoli-Mbombo (Vanaken 65). Coach: Michel Preud'homme (BEL)

Match 5 - Leicester City FC (ENG)

A 1-2 *Izquierdo (52)*

Butelle, Simons, Poulain, Claudemir (Wesley 85), Vossen, Izquierdo, Pina (Limbombe 61), Vanaken, Cools, De Bock (Van Rhijn 70), Mechele. Coach: Michel Preud'homme (BEL)

Match 6 - FC København (DEN)

H 0-2

Butelle, Van Rhijn (Vormer 77), Claudemir, Wesley, Refaelov (Vanaken 66), Pina, Felipe Gedoz, Cools, Denswil, Mechele, Bolingoli-Mbombo. Coach: Michel Preud'homme (BEL)

RSC Anderlecht

Third qualifying round - FC Rostov (RUS)

A 2-2 *Hanni (3), Tielemans (52)*

Roef, De Maio, Chipciu (Acheampong 69), Appiah, Nuytinck, Defour (Heylen 90+4), N'Sakala, Sylla, Tielemans, Dendoncker, Hanni (Hassan 80). Coach: René Weiler (SUI)

H 0-2

Roef, De Maio, Chipciu, Appiah, Nuytinck (Kabasele 60), Defour, N'Sakala (Acheampong 54), Sylla, Tielemans, Dendoncker, Hanni (Hassan 77). Coach: René Weiler (SUI)

Play-offs - SK Slavia Praha (CZE)

A 3-0 *Sylla (49), Teodorczyk (60), Hanni (71)*

Roef, Praet (Badji 68), Chipciu, Appiah (Heylen 73), Nuytinck, Acheampong, Sylla (Diego Capel 78), Tielemans, Dendoncker, Teodorczyk, Hanni. Coach: René Weiler (SUI)

H 3-0 *Tielemans (22p), Teodorczyk (40p), Heylen (61)*

Roef, Badji, Chipciu, Nuytinck, Diego Capel, Acheampong, Heylen, Tielemans (Doumbia 62), Dendoncker, Teodorczyk (Sylla 56), Hanni (Sowah 70). Coach: René Weiler (SUI)

Group C

Match 1 - Qäbälä FK (AZE)

H 3-1 *Teodorczyk (14), Rafael (41og), Diego Capel (77)*

Roef, Mbodji, Spajić, Chipciu (Diego Capel 73), Nuytinck, Acheampong, Tielemans (Badji 18), Dendoncker, Stanciu, Teodorczyk (Harbaoui 80), Hanni. Coach: René Weiler (SUI)

Match 2 - AS Saint-Étienne (FRA)

A 1-1 *Tielemans (62p)*

Roef, Mbodji, Spajić, Chipciu, Nuytinck, Acheampong, Tielemans, Dendoncker, Stanciu (Diego Capel 82), Teodorczyk (Harbaoui 69), Hanni (Badji 75). Coach: René Weiler (SUI)

Match 3 - 1. FSV Mainz 05 (GER)

A 1-1 *Teodorczyk (65)*

Roef, Deschacht, Mbodji, Nuytinck, Acheampong, Tielemans, Dendoncker, Sowah (Bruno 82), Stanciu (Diego Capel 60), Teodorczyk (Badji 76), Hanni. Coach: René Weiler (SUI)

Match 4 - 1. FSV Mainz 05 (GER)

H 6-1 *Stanciu (9, 41), Tielemans (62), Teodorczyk (89, 90+4p), Bruno (90+2)*

Roef, Deschacht, Mbodji, Chipciu (Diego Capel 56), Acheampong, Tielemans (Bruno 89), Dendoncker, Sowah, Stanciu (Badji 67), Teodorczyk, Hanni. Coach: René Weiler (SUI)

Match 5 - Qäbälä FK (AZE)

A 3-1 *Tielemans (11), Bruno (90), Teodorczyk (90+4)*

Boeckx, Spajić, Nuytinck, Diego Capel (Bruno 60), Acheampong (Doumbia 90+4), Tielemans, Dendoncker, Obradović, Sowah, Stanciu (Hanni 70), Teodorczyk. Coach: René Weiler (SUI)

Match 6 - AS Saint-Étienne (FRA)

H 2-3 *Chipciu (21), Stanciu (31)*

Roef, Spajić, Badji, Chipciu (Najar 60), Nuytinck, Acheampong (Hanni 66), Dendoncker, Obradović, Sowah, Vancamp (Teodorczyk 60), Stanciu. Coach: René Weiler (SUI)

Round of 32 - FC Zenit (RUS)

H 2-0 *Acheampong (5, 31)*

Rubén, Deschacht, Spajić, Najar, Bruno, Acheampong (Chipciu 60), Kiese Thelin (Teodorczyk 80), Tielemans, Dendoncker, Obradović, Stanciu (Hanni 74). Coach: René Weiler (SUI)

A 1-3 *Kiese Thelin (90)*

Rubén, Deschacht, Spajić, Najar, Chipciu (Nuytinck 84), Acheampong (Diego Capel 89), Kiese Thelin, Tielemans, Dendoncker, Obradović, Stanciu (Bruno 73). Coach: René Weiler (SUI)

Round of 16 - APOEL FC (CYP)

A 1-0 *Stanciu (29)*

Rubén, Spajić, Najar, Chipciu (Bruno 88), Appiah, Nuytinck, Tielemans, Dendoncker, Stanciu (Acheampong 80), Teodorczyk (Kiese Thelin 59), Hanni. Coach: René Weiler (SUI)

H 1-0 *Acheampong (65)*

Rubén, Mbodji, Spajić, Najar, Chipciu (Bruno 89), Appiah, Tielemans, Dendoncker, Stanciu (Acheampong 64), Teodorczyk (Kiese Thelin 75), Hanni. Coach: René Weiler (SUI)

Quarter-finals - Manchester United FC (ENG)

H 1-1 *Dendoncker (86)*

Rubén, Mbodji, Bruno (Chipciu 58), Appiah, Nuytinck, Acheampong, Kiese Thelin (Teodorczyk 75), Tielemans, Dendoncker, Obradović, Stanciu (Hanni 65). Coach: René Weiler (SUI)

A 1-2 (aet) *Hanni (32)*

Rubén, Mbodji, Spajić, Chipciu (Bruno 64), Appiah, Acheampong, Tielemans, Dendoncker, Obradović, Teodorczyk (Kiese Thelin 79), Hanni (Stanciu 64). Coach: René Weiler (SUI)

R. Standard de Liège

Group G

Match 1 - RC Celta de Vigo (ESP)

H 1-1 *Dossevi (3)*

Gillet, Echiéjilé (Fiore 86), Dossevi, Raman (Mbenza 68), Scholz, Enoh, Edmilson Junior, Trebel, Fai, Laifis, Belfodil (Orlando Sá 82). Coach: Aleksandar Janković (SRB)

Match 2 - AFC Ajax (NED)

A 0-1

Gillet, Dossevi (Legear 80), Raman (Dompé 69), Scholz, Enoh, Edmilson Junior (Mbenza 69), Trebel, Andrade, Fai, Laifis, Belfodil. Coach: Aleksandar Janković (SRB)

Match 3 - Panathinaikos FC (GRE)

H 2-2 *Edmilson Junior (45+1p), Belfodil (82)*

Gillet, Dossevi (Mbenza 63), Scholz, Edmilson Junior, Trebel, Andrade, Fai, Laifis, Cissé (Enoh 72), Orlando Sá, Belfodil. Coach: Aleksandar Janković (SRB)

Match 4 - Panathinaikos FC (GRE)

A 3-0 Cissé (61), Belfodil (76, 90+3)

Hubert, Echiéjilé (Fiore 46), Raman (Badibanga 62), Scholz, Edmilson Junior (Mbenza 88), Trebel, Fai, Laifis, Cissé, Orlando Sá, Belfodil. Coach: Aleksandar Janković (SRB)

Match 5 - RC Celta de Vigo (ESP)
A 1-1 *Laifis (81)*
Hubert, Raman (Badibanga 89), Scholz, Edmilson Junior (Mbenza 62), Trebel, Fiore, Fai, Laifis, Cissé, Orlando Sá, Belfodil. Coach: Aleksandar Janković (SRB)
Match 6 - AFC Ajax (NED)
H 1-1 *Raman (85)*
Hubert, Goreux, Dompé (Raman 57), Scholz, Mbenza, Enoh, Edmilson Junior (Badibanga 66), Trebel, Fiore (Echiéjilé 57), Laifis, Orlando Sá. Coach: Aleksandar Janković (SRB)

KAA Gent

Third qualifying round - FC Viitorul (ROU)
H 5-0 *Mitrović (16), Coulibaly (37, 50), Depoitre (56), Renato Neto (66)*
Rinne, Coulibaly, Matton (Miličević 65), Depoitre (Perbet 69), Renato Neto, Mitrović, Kums (Schoofs 76), Saief, Nielsen, Foket, Gershon. Coach: Hein Vanhaezebrouck (BEL)
A 0-0
Thoelen, Renato Neto (Schoofs 64), Kujovic, Mitrović (Nielsen 46), Saief, Schoofs, Perbet, Horemans, Foket (Ndongala 72), Gershon, Miličević. Coach: Hein Vanhaezebrouck (BEL)

Play-offs - KF Shkëndija (MKD)
H 2-1 *Matton (45+2), Coulibaly (90+2)*
Rinne, Coulibaly, Matton (Simon 73), Renato Neto, Kujovic (Miličević 64), Mitrović, Kums, Saief, Nielsen, Foket, Gershon (Perbet 85). Coach: Hein Vanhaezebrouck (BEL)
A 4-0 *Coulibaly (60, 69), Perbet (81), Renato Neto (86)*
Rinne, Coulibaly (Perbet 75), Renato Neto, Mitrović, Kums, Saief, Nielsen (Asare 46), Simon, Foket, Gershon, Miličević (Matton 71). Coach: Hein Vanhaezebrouck (BEL)

Group H
Match 1 - SC Braga (POR)
A 1-1 *Miličević (6)*
Rinne, Renato Neto, Mitrović, Saief, Asare, Perbet (Davidzada 70), Simon (Coulibaly 40), Foket, Esiti, Gershon, Miličević. Coach: Hein Vanhaezebrouck (BEL)
Match 2 - Konyaspor (TUR)
H 2-0 *Saief (17), Renato Neto (33)*
Rinne, Coulibaly, Renato Neto, Mitrović, Saief (Davidzada 88), Van der Bruggen, Asare, Nielsen, Gershon, Miličević (Perbet 46), Ndongala (Esiti 72). Coach: Hein Vanhaezebrouck (BEL)
Match 3 - FC Shakhtar Donetsk (UKR)
A 0-5
Rinne, Renato Neto, Mitrović, Saief, Van der Bruggen (Ibrahim 64), Asare, Perbet (Coulibaly 46), Simon, Foket, Gershon, Miličević (Dejaegere 72). Coach: Hein Vanhaezebrouck (BEL)
Match 4 - FC Shakhtar Donetsk (UKR)
H 3-5 *Coulibaly (1), Perbet (83), Miličević (89)*
Rinne, Coulibaly (Perbet 74), Renato Neto, Dejaegere (Saief 70), Asare, Nielsen, Simon (Ndongala 77), Foket, Esiti, Gershon, Miličević. Coach: Hein Vanhaezebrouck (BEL)
Match 5 - SC Braga (POR)
H 2-2 *Coulibaly (32), Miličević (40)*
Thoelen, Coulibaly, Renato Neto, Mitrović, Saief (Matton 90), Asare, Nielsen, Simon (Dejaegere 70), Foket, Esiti (Perbet 85), Miličević. Coach: Hein Vanhaezebrouck (BEL)
Match 6 - Konyaspor (TUR)
A 1-0 *Coulibaly (90+4)*
Rinne, Matton (Dejaegere 66), Renato Neto (Esiti 69), Mitrović, Saief, Van der Bruggen, Nielsen, Perbet (Coulibaly 66), Foket, Gershon, Miličević. Coach: Hein Vanhaezebrouck (BEL)

Round of 32 - Tottenham Hotspur FC (ENG)
H 1-0 *Perbet (59)*
Kalinić, Gigot, Mitrović, Saief, Dejaegere, Asare (Gershon 80), Perbet (Coulibaly 75), Simon (Kalu 74), Foket, Esiti, Miličević. Coach: Hein Vanhaezebrouck (BEL)
A 2-2 *Kane (20og), Perbet (82)*
Kalinić, Gigot, Coulibaly, Mitrović, Saief, Dejaegere (L Verstraete 56), Simon (Perbet 75), Foket, Esiti, Gershon, Miličević (Matton 46). Coach: Hein Vanhaezebrouck (BEL)

Round of 16 - KRC Genk (BEL)
H 2-5 *Kalu (27), Coulibaly (61)*
Kalinić, Gigot, Coulibaly, Matton, Mitrović, Saief (Simon 76), Kalu, Perbet (Foket 76), L Verstraete (Ibrahim 46), Esiti, Gershon. Coach: Hein Vanhaezebrouck (BEL)
Red card: Esiti 84
A 1-1 *Verstraete (84)*
Kalinić, Gigot, Coulibaly, Mitrović, Kalu, Dejaegere, Perbet (L Verstraete 62), Simon, De Smet, Foket, Ibrahim. Coach: Hein Vanhaezebrouck (BEL)

KRC Genk

Second qualifying round - FK Budućnost Podgorica (MNE)
H 2-0 *Kebano (17p), Samatta (79)*
Bizot, Dewaest, Yao Kumordzi, Buffel, Uronen, Ndidi, Bailey, Castagne, Buyens (Heynen 74), Samatta (Trossard 88), Kebano (Karelis 76). Coach: Peter Maes (BEL)
A 0-2 (aet; 4-2 on pens)
Bizot, Dewaest, Karelis (Wouters 75), Yao Kumordzi, Buffel, Uronen, Ndidi, Bailey, Castagne (Walsh 67), Buyens (Heynen 46), Samatta. Coach: Peter Maes (BEL)
Red card: Yao Kumordzi 74

Third qualifying round - Cork City FC (IRL)
H 1-0 *Bailey (31)*
Bizot, Walsh, Dewaest, Karelis (Kebano 73), Wouters, Buffel, Uronen, Pozuelo (Heynen 82), Ndidi, Bailey, Samatta. Coach: Peter Maes (BEL)
A 2-1 *Buffel (13), Dewaest (41)*
Bizot, Walsh, Dewaest, Wouters, Buffel (Tshimanga 83), Uronen, Pozuelo, Ndidi, Bailey (Trossard 65), Samatta (Heynen 77), Kebano. Coach: Peter Maes (BEL)

Play-offs - NK Lokomotiva Zagreb (CRO)
A 2-2 *Bailey (35p), Samatta (47)*
Bizot, Colley, Walsh, Dewaest, Buffel (Trossard 42), Uronen, Pozuelo, Ndidi, Heynen, Bailey, Samatta (Karelis 83). Coach: Peter Maes (BEL)
H 2-0 *Samatta (2), Bailey (50)*
Bizot, Colley, Walsh, Dewaest, Trossard, Uronen, Pozuelo (Yao Kumordzi 82), Ndidi, Heynen, Bailey (Kebano 74), Samatta (Karelis 80). Coach: Peter Maes (BEL)

Group F
Match 1 - SK Rapid Wien (AUT)
A 2-3 *Bailey (29, 90p)*
Bizot, Colley, Walsh, Dewaest, Buffel (Trossard 66), Uronen, Pozuelo, Ndidi, Heynen (Sušić 78), Bailey, Samatta (Karelis 78). Coach: Peter Maes (BEL)
Match 2 - US Sassuolo Calcio (ITA)
H 3-1 *Karelis (8), Bailey (25), Buffel (61)*
Bizot, Brabec, Nastić, Colley, Walsh, Karelis (Samatta 75), Sušić (Yao Kumordzi 82), Buffel (Trossard 87), Pozuelo, Ndidi, Bailey. Coach: Peter Maes (BEL)
Match 3 - Athletic Club (ESP)
H 2-0 *Brabec (40), Ndidi (83)*
Bizot, Brabec, Nastić, Colley, Karelis (Trossard 84), Sušić (Heynen 78), Buffel (Samatta 56), Pozuelo, Ndidi, Bailey, Castagne. Coach: Peter Maes (BEL)
Match 4 - Athletic Club (ESP)
A 3-5 *Bailey (28), Ndidi (51), Sušić (80)*
Bizot, Brabec, Nastić (Walsh 75), Colley, Sušić, Buffel (Trossard 75), Pozuelo, Ndidi, Bailey, Castagne, Samatta (Karelis 83). Coach: Peter Maes (BEL)
Match 5 - SK Rapid Wien (AUT)
H 1-0 *Karelis (11)*
Bizot, Brabec, Nastić, Colley, Karelis (Samatta 84), Sušić (Heynen 79), Buffel (Trossard 90), Pozuelo, Ndidi, Bailey, Castagne. Coach: Peter Maes (BEL)
Match 6 - US Sassuolo Calcio (ITA)
A 2-0 *Heynen (58), Trossard (80)*
Jackers, Brabec, Walsh, Dewaest, Karelis (Sabak 90+3), Trossard, Ndidi, Heynen (Yao Kumordzi 89), Bailey (Buffel 81), Castagne, Samatta. Coach: Peter Maes (BEL)

Round of 32 - FC Astra Giurgiu (ROU)
A 2-2 *Castagne (25), Trossard (83)*
Ryan, Brabec, Colley, Yao Kumordzi (Berge 64), Trossard (Buffel 88), Uronen, Schrijvers, Pozuelo (Boëtius 74), Heynen, Castagne, Samatta. Coach: Albert Stuivenberg (NED)
H 1-0 *Pozuelo (67)*
Ryan, Brabec, Colley, Trossard, Malinovskiy (Boëtius 90), Uronen, Schrijvers (Buffel 77), Pozuelo (Yao Kumordzi 89), Berge, Castagne, Samatta. Coach: Albert Stuivenberg (NED)

Round of 16 - KAA Gent (BEL)
A 5-2 *Malinovskiy (21), Colley (33), Samatta (41, 72), Uronen (45+2)*
Ryan, Brabec, Colley, Boëtius (Buffel 46), Malinovskiy (Heynen 81), Uronen, Schrijvers (Trossard 90), Pozuelo, Berge, Castagne, Samatta. Coach: Albert Stuivenberg (NED)
H 1-1 *Castagne (20)*
Ryan, Brabec, Colley, Boëtius, Malinovskiy, Buffel (Trossard 74), Uronen (Janssens 81), Pozuelo (Schrijvers 46), Berge, Castagne, Samatta. Coach: Albert Stuivenberg (NED)

Quarter-finals - RC Celta de Vigo (ESP)
A 2-3 *Boëtius (10), Buffel (67)*
Ryan, Brabec, Colley, Boëtius (Buffel 62), Trossard (Schrijvers 82), Malinovskiy (Heynen 90+2), Uronen, Pozuelo, Berge, Castagne, Samatta. Coach: Albert Stuivenberg (NED)
H 1-1 *Trossard (67)*
Ryan, Brabec (Dewaest 81), Colley, Trossard, Malinovskiy (Schrijvers 72), Buffel (Boëtius 72), Uronen, Pozuelo, Berge, Castagne, Samatta. Coach: Albert Stuivenberg (NED)

DOMESTIC LEAGUE CLUB-BY-CLUB

RSC Anderlecht

1908 • Constant Vanden Stock (28,063) • rsca.be

Major honours
UEFA Cup Winners' Cup (2) 1976, 1978;
UEFA Cup (1) 1983;
UEFA Super Cup (2) 1976, 1978;
Belgian League (34) 1947, 1949, 1950, 1951, 1954, 1955, 1956, 1959, 1962, 1964, 1965, 1966, 1967, 1968, 1972, 1974, 1981, 1985, 1986, 1987, 1991, 1993, 1994, 1995, 2000, 2001, 2004, 2006, 2007, 2010, 2012, 2013, 2014, 2017;
Belgian Cup (9) 1965, 1972, 1973, 1975, 1976, 1988, 1989, 1994, 2008

Coach: René Weiler (SUI)

2016					
30/07	a	Mouscron	W	2-1	*Acheampong, Sylla*
07/08	h	Kortrijk	W	5-1	*Hanni, Teodorczyck, Chipciu, Defour, Sylla*
12/08	a	Sint-Truiden	D	0-0	
21/08	a	Eupen	D	2-2	*Diego Capel, Teodorczyk*
28/08	h	Gent	D	2-2	*Tielemans (p), Teodorczyk*
11/09	h	Charleroi	W	3-2	*Teodorczyk, Hanni, Tielemans*
18/09	a	Genk	W	2-0	*Mbodji, Harbaoui*
25/09	h	Westerlo	L	1-2	*Hanni*
02/10	a	Standard	W	1-0	*Teodorczyk*
16/10	h	Lokeren	W	1-0	*Teodorczyk*
23/10	a	Club Brugge	L	1-2	*Teodorczyk*
26/10	h	Mechelen	W	2-0	*Teodorczyk, Tielemans (p)*
30/10	a	Waasland-Beveren	L	1-2	*Teodorczyk*
06/11	h	Oostende	D	1-1	*Tielemans (p)*
20/11	a	Zulte Waregem	L	2-3	*Teodorczyk 2*
27/11	h	Mouscron	W	7-0	*Teodorczyk, Hanni, og (Hubert), Stanciu, Tielemans (p), Spajić, Bruno*
04/12	a	Kortrijk	W	3-1	*Stanciu, Teodorczyk, Obradović*
11/12	h	Club Brugge	D	0-0	
18/12	h	Eupen	W	4-0	*Hanni 2, Dendoncker 2*
22/12	a	Gent	W	3-2	*Teodorczyk 2, Chipciu*
26/12	a	Charleroi	W	2-0	*Teodorczyk, Acheampong*
2017					
22/01	h	Sint-Truiden	W	3-1	*Tielemans 2 (1p), Stanciu*
25/01	a	Westerlo	W	4-2	*Teodorczyk, Stanciu, Dendoncker, Tielemans*
29/01	h	Standard	D	0-0	
03/02	a	Lokeren	D	0-0	
12/02	h	Zulte Waregem	W	4-2	*Hanni, Bruno, Tielemans, Chipciu*
19/02	a	Oostende	W	4-1	*Hanni, Tielemans 2, Teodorczyk*
26/02	h	Genk	W	2-0	*Mbodji, Tielemans*
04/03	a	Mechelen	L	2-3	*Teodorczyk, Nuytinck*
12/03	h	Waasland-Beveren	W	3-0	*Bruno, Teodorczyk, Mbodji*
31/03	a	Zulte Waregem	W	2-1	*Chipciu, Tielemans*
09/04	h	Gent	D	0-0	
16/04	a	Oostende	W	1-0	*Hanni*
23/04	h	Club Brugge	W	2-0	*Dendoncker, Mbodji*
27/04	h	Charleroi	L	0-1	
30/04	a	Gent	D	0-0	
07/05	h	Zulte Waregem	W	2-0	*Chipciu, Kiese Thelin*
14/05	a	Club Brugge	D	1-1	*Hanni*
18/05	a	Charleroi	W	3-1	*Teodorczyk 2, Bruno*
21/05	h	Oostende	W	3-2	*og (Rozehnal), Dendoncker, Acheampong*

No	Name	Nat	DoB	Pos	Aps	(s)	Gls
18	Frank Acheampong	GHA	16/10/93	M	16	(13)	3
12	Dennis Appiah	FRA	09/06/92	D	17		
8	Stéphane Badji	SEN	18/01/90	M	6	(4)	
23	Frank Boeckx		27/09/86	G	24		
10	Massimo Bruno		17/09/93	M	13	(15)	4
11	Alexandru Chipciu	ROU	18/05/89	M	31	(1)	5
5	Sebastien De Maio	FRA	05/03/87	D	2		
16	Steven Defour		15/04/88	M	1	(1)	1
32	Leander Dendoncker		15/04/95	M	40		5
3	Olivier Deschacht		16/02/81	D	5	(11)	
17	Diego Capel	ESP	16/02/88	M	5	(10)	1
22	Idrissa Doumbia	CIV	14/04/98	M	1	(1)	
94	Sofiane Hanni	ALG	29/12/90	M	35	(3)	10
9	Hamdi Harbaoui	TUN	05/01/85	A	1	(7)	1
27	Mahmoud Hassan	EGY	01/10/94	M		(1)	
24	Michaël Heylen		03/01/94	D		(2)	
77	Nathan Kabasele		14/01/94	A		(1)	
24	Isaac Kiese Thelin	SWE	24/06/92	A	2	(14)	1
4	Serigne Mbodji	SEN	11/11/89	D	29		4
21	Fabrice N'Sakala	COD	21/07/90	D	2		
7	Andy Najar	HON	16/03/93	D	7	(2)	
14	Bram Nuytinck	NED	04/05/90	D	28	(2)	1
37	Ivan Obradović	SRB	25/07/88	D	26		1
10	Dennis Praet		14/05/94	M		(1)	
1	Davy Roef		06/02/94	G	15		
1	Rubén	ESP	22/06/84	G	1		
41	Emmanuel Sowah	GHA	16/01/98	D	5	(4)	
5	Uroš Spajić	SRB	13/02/93	D	24	(4)	1
73	Nicolae Stanciu	ROU	07/05/93	M	20	(4)	4
26	Idrissa Sylla	GUI	03/12/90	A	1	(3)	2
91	Łukasz Teodorczyk	POL	03/06/91	A	36	(2)	22
31	Youri Tielemans		07/05/97	M	35	(2)	13
25	Adrien Trebel	FRA	03/03/91	M	12	(5)	
49	Jorn Vancamp		28/10/98	A		(1)	

R. Charleroi SC

1904 • Pays de Charleroi (15,000) • sporting-charleroi.be

Coach: Felice Mazzu

2016					
30/07	h	Waasland-Beveren	W	1-0	*Willems*
06/08	a	Mouscron	W	1-0	*Tainmont*
13/08	h	Gent	D	1-1	*Pollet*
19/08	a	Standard	D	0-0	
26/08	h	Eupen	W	3-2	*Willems, Pollet 2*
11/09	a	Anderlecht	L	2-3	*Bakar, Baby*
16/09	h	Mechelen	D	0-0	
24/09	h	Oostende	W	2-1	*Fall, Bedia*
01/10	a	Zulte Waregem	D	1-1	*Bedia (p)*
14/10	h	Club Brugge	W	1-0	*Bedia*
22/10	a	Westerlo	D	0-0	
26/10	h	Genk	W	2-1	*Ninis, Diandy*
29/10	a	Sint-Truiden	D	2-2	*Ninis, Pollet*
04/11	a	Kortrijk	L	1-2	*Pollet*
20/11	h	Lokeren	W	2-1	*Fall, Pollet*
26/11	a	Waasland-Beveren	W	1-0	*Baby*
04/12	h	Standard	L	1-3	*Bakar (match abandoned after 68 mins; result stood)*
10/12	a	Eupen	D	2-2	*og (Niasse), Fall*
17/12	h	Mouscron	W	2-0	*Baby, N'Ganga*
20/12	a	Mechelen	L	0-1	
26/12	h	Anderlecht	L	0-2	
2017					
20/01	a	Gent	L	0-1	
24/01	a	Oostende	W	2-1	*Harbaoui, Benavente*
27/01	h	Zulte Waregem	W	2-1	*Harbaoui, Remacle*
05/02	a	Club Brugge	L	0-1	
11/02	h	Westerlo	W	2-1	*Marcq, Benavente*
19/02	a	Genk	D	1-1	*Marinos*
25/02	h	Sint-Truiden	W	1-0	*Harbaoui*
04/03	h	Kortrijk	D	1-1	*Dessoleil*
12/03	a	Lokeren	D	0-0	
01/04	h	Oostende	D	1-1	*Clinton Mata*
08/04	a	Club Brugge	D	1-1	*Bedia (p)*
17/04	h	Gent	L	0-1	
22/04	h	Zulte Waregem	W	2-0	*Baby, Pollet*
27/04	a	Anderlecht	W	1-0	*Harbaoui*
30/04	a	Oostende	L	0-1	
05/05	h	Club Brugge	L	1-3	*Pollet*
14/05	a	Gent	D	1-1	*Saglik*
18/05	h	Anderlecht	L	1-3	*Bedia*
21/05	a	Zulte Waregem	D	2-2	*Benavente 2*

No	Name	Nat	DoB	Pos	Aps	(s)	Gls
18	Amara Baby	SEN	23/02/89	M	22	(10)	4
21	Djamel Bakar	FRA	06/04/89	A	8	(7)	2
99	Chris Bedia	CIV	05/03/96	A	19	(16)	5
14	Cristian Benavente	PER	19/05/94	M	9	(16)	4
5	Benjamin Boulenger	FRA	01/03/90	D	4	(2)	
19	Clinton Mata	ANG	07/11/92	D	34	(2)	1
24	Dorian Dessoleil		07/08/92	D	17	(2)	1
13	Christophe Diandy	SEN	25/11/90	M	37	(1)	1
77	Mamadou Fall	SEN	31/12/91	M	23	(8)	3
45	Roman Ferber		29/05/93	A		(2)	
20	Hamdi Harbaoui	TUN	05/01/85	A	13	(1)	4
22	Gaëtan Hendrickx		30/03/95	M	9	(5)	
35	Parfait Mandanda	COD	10/10/89	G	2		
25	Damien Marcq	FRA	08/12/88	M	34		1
17	Stergos Marinos	GRE	17/09/87	D	5	(6)	1
8	Martos	ESP	04/01/84	D	40		
41	Francis N'Ganga	CGO	16/06/85	D	32	(2)	1
29	Sotiris Ninis	GRE	03/04/90	M	9	(4)	2
1	Nicolas Penneteau	FRA	20/02/81	G	38		
10	David Pollet		12/08/88	A	24	(8)	8
29	Jordan Remacle		14/02/87	M	3	(6)	1
28	Enes Saglik		08/07/91	M	5	(5)	1
7	Clément Tainmont	FRA	12/02/86	M	21	(11)	1
23	Steeven Willems	FRA	31/08/90	D	31	(1)	2
6	Gjoko Zajkov	MKD	10/02/95	D	1		

Club Brugge KV

1891 • Jan Breydelstadion (29,042) • clubbrugge.be

Major honours
Belgian League (14) 1920, 1973, 1976, 1977, 1978, 1980, 1988, 1990, 1992, 1996, 1998, 2003, 2005, 2016; Belgian Cup (11) 1968, 1970, 1977, 1986, 1991, 1995, 1996, 2002, 2004, 2007, 2015

Coach: Michel Preud'homme

2016
29/07 a Mechelen W 2-0 *Izquierdo, Cools*
05/08 a Oostende L 0-1
14/08 h Lokeren W 1-0 *Refaelov (p)*
20/08 a Kortrijk L 1-2 *Vanaken*
28/08 h Standard D 2-2 *Felipe Gedoz, Engels*
09/09 a Waasland-Beveren L 0-1
17/09 h Eupen W 3-2 *Vossen 2 (2p), Denswil*
23/09 a Mouscron W 3-0 *Izquierdo 2, Vossen*
02/10 h Gent W 1-0 *Van Rhijn*
14/10 a Charleroi L 0-1
23/10 h Anderlecht W 2-1 *Vanaken, Vormer*
26/10 h Westerlo W 4-0 *Cools 2, Vormer, Pina*
29/10 a Zulte Waregem D 0-0
06/11 h Genk D 1-1 *Vossen*
18/11 a Sint-Truiden W 1-0 *Vossen (p)*
25/11 h Mechelen W 6-1 *Vossen 4 (1p), Izquierdo, Vanaken*
03/12 h Oostende W 2-0 *Izquierdo, Vossen (p)*
11/12 a Anderlecht D 0-0
18/12 h Kortrijk W 5-1 *Van Rhijn, Refaelov, Vanaken, Vossen, Vormer*
21/12 a Eupen W 4-1 *Vormer 2, og (Blondelle), Izquierdo*
26/12 h Mouscron W 2-1 *Van Rhijn, Vossen*

2017
22/01 a Standard W 3-0 *Vossen, Vormer, Wesley*
25/01 h Waasland-Beveren W 2-1 *Immers, Izquierdo*
29/01 a Gent L 0-2
05/02 h Charleroi W 1-0 *Vossen*
12/02 a Lokeren L 0-1
17/02 a Westerlo W 2-1 *og (Miletić), Vanaken*
24/02 h Zulte Waregem W 5-0 *Vormer 2, Engels, Izquierdo, Vossen (p)*
04/03 a Genk L 1-2 *Izquierdo*
12/03 h Sint-Truiden D 2-2 *Vanaken, Claudemir*
02/04 a Gent L 1-2 *Wesley*
08/04 h Charleroi D 1-1 *Wesley*
17/04 a Zulte Waregem D 2-2 *Vanaken, Wesley*
23/04 a Anderlecht L 0-2
26/04 h Oostende W 3-1 *Vossen, Izquierdo 2*
01/05 h Zulte Waregem W 2-1 *Vanaken, Rotariu*
05/05 a Charleroi W 3-1 *Izquierdo 3*
14/05 h Anderlecht D 1-1 *Vormer*
18/05 a Oostende L 1-2 *Wesley*
21/05 h Gent W 2-1 *Wesley, Vanaken*

No	Name	Nat	DoB	Pos	Aps	(s)	Gls
63	Boli Bolingoli-Mbombo		01/07/95	M	4	(4)	
1	Ludovic Butelle	FRA	03/04/83	G	36		
6	Claudemir	BRA	27/03/88	M	25	(8)	1
21	Dion Cools		04/06/96	D	22	(2)	3
28	Laurens De Bock		07/11/92	D	18		
24	Stefano Denswil	NED	07/05/93	D	39		1
10	Abdoulay Diaby	MLI	21/05/91	A	6	(10)	
4	Björn Engels		15/09/94	D	18	(4)	2
19	Felipe Gedoz	BRA	12/07/93	M	2	(3)	1
22	Ethan Horvath	USA	09/06/95	G	4		
27	Lex Immers	NED	08/06/86	M	3	(7)	1
22	José Izquierdo	COL	07/07/92	M	26	(2)	14
17	Anthony Limbombe		15/07/94	M	12	(10)	
18	Helibelton Palacios	COL	11/06/93	D	9	(2)	
15	Tomás Pina	ESP	14/10/87	M	4	(2)	1
5	Benoît Poulain	FRA	24/07/87	D	19	(1)	
8	Lior Refaelov	ISR	26/04/86	M	14	(7)	2
29	Dorin Rotariu	ROU	29/07/95	M	7	(5)	1
3	Timmy Simons		11/12/76	M	33	(2)	
42	Nikola Storm		30/09/94	A		(5)	
96	Ahmed Touba		13/03/98	D	3	(2)	
2	Ricardo van Rhijn	NED	13/06/91	D	21		3
20	Hans Vanaken		24/08/92	M	37	(2)	9
93	Thibault Vlietinck		19/08/97	M		(2)	
25	Ruud Vormer	NED	11/05/88	M	38		9
9	Jelle Vossen		22/03/89	A	30	(9)	16
7	Wesley	BRA	26/11/96	A	10	(15)	6

KAS Eupen

1945• Kehrwegstadion (8,363) • as-eupen.be

Coach: Jordi Condom Aulí (ESP)

2016
30/07 a Zulte Waregem L 0-3
06/08 h Mechelen L 0-2
13/08 a Westerlo W 2-1 *Taulemesse, Onyekuru*
21/08 h Anderlecht D 2-2 *Sylla, og (Roef)*
26/08 a Charleroi L 2-3 *og (Marcq), Onyekuru*
10/09 h Oostende W 2-1 *Sylla, Ocansey*
17/09 a Club Brugge L 2-3 *Onyekuru, Luis García (p)*
25/09 a Standard L 0-3
01/10 h Mouscron L 1-4 *Onyekuru*
15/10 a Waasland-Beveren L 2-4 *Ocansey 2*
23/10 h Gent W 3-2 *Sylla, Cases, Taulemesse*
26/10 a Kortrijk D 1-1 *Luis García*
29/10 h Lokeren D 2-2 *Onyekuru, Sylla*
05/11 h Sint-Truiden W 4-2 *Sylla 2, Amani, Onyekuru*
19/11 a Genk L 0-2
26/11 h Westerlo D 3-3 *Amani, Bassey, Onyekuru*
02/12 a Mechelen L 0-1
10/12 h Charleroi D 2-2 *Sylla (p), Onyekuru*
18/12 a Anderlecht L 0-4
21/12 h Club Brugge L 1-4 *Sylla*
26/12 a Oostende W 3-1 *Onyekuru 2, Sylla*

2017
21/01 h Genk L 0-1
26/01 h Standard D 2-2 *og (Laifis), Sylla*
29/01 a Mouscron L 0-3
04/02 h Waasland-Beveren L 0-2
11/02 a Gent W 1-0 *Onyekuru*
18/02 h Kortrijk W 1-0 *Wagué*
25/02 a Lokeren W 2-1 *Ocansey, Onyekuru*
04/03 a Sint-Truiden L 1-2 *Sylla*
12/03 h Zulte Waregem L 1-3 *Luis García (p)*
01/04 h Roeselare D 2-2 *Onyekuru 2*
08/04 a Mouscron W 2-0 *Onyekuru, Sylla*
15/04 h Lokeren D 3-3 *Luis García (p), Brüls, og (Maric)*
22/04 a Kortrijk D 3-3 *Ocansey, Onyekuru, Luis García*
26/04 h Genk D 1-1 *Luis García (p)*
29/04 a Lokeren L 1-4 *Luis García (p)*
07/05 a Genk L 1-2 *Onyekuru*
13/05 h Kortrijk W 3-2 *Suárez, Onyekuru 2*
17/05 h Mouscron W 2-0 *Suárez, Onyekuru*
20/05 a Roeselare L 2-3 *Onyekuru 2*

No	Name	Nat	DoB	Pos	Aps	(s)	Gls
3	Fahad Al-Abdulrahman	QAT	06/04/95	D	29		
8	Jean Amani	CIV	07/03/98	M	22	(4)	2
11	Anthony Bassey	NGA	20/07/94	M	16	(11)	1
22	Siebe Blondelle		20/04/86	D	36		
19	Christian Brüls		30/09/88	M	14	(2)	1
91	José Maria Cases	ESP	23/11/86	M	6	(17)	1
5	Diawandou Diagne	SEN	28/07/94	M	38		
2	Ibrahim Diallo	MLI	12/08/96	D	31		
4	Ibrahima Diedhiou	SEN	13/10/94	D	1		
7	Jean-Luc Dompé	FRA	12/08/95	M		(2)	
18	Guy Dufour		14/03/87	M	5	(7)	
42	Peter Hackenberg	GER	06/02/89	D	17	(6)	
6	Raoul Kenne	CMR	25/03/94	D	1		
10	Luis García	ESP	06/02/81	M	37		7
24	Silas Gnaka	CIV	18/12/98	D	1	(1)	
13	Damien Mouchamps		10/01/96	A		(5)	
31	Samba Ndiaye	SEN	12/01/94	M		(1)	
30	Babacar Niasse	SEN	20/12/96	G	5	(1)	
28	Eric Ocansey	GHA	22/08/97	M	22	(2)	5
25	George Odeni	NGA	18/05/95	D	14	(8)	
21	Henry Onyekuru	NGA	05/06/97	M	38		22
27	Ntuthuko Radebe	RSA	29/09/94	D	1		
25	Abdoulaye Sanogo	MLI	14/10/96	M		(3)	
9	Jeffren Suárez	VEN	20/01/88	M	15	(11)	2
20	Mamadou Sylla	SEN	20/03/94	A	33	(2)	12
19	Florian Taulemesse	FRA	31/01/86	A	10	(8)	2
92	Nicolas Timmermans		04/11/82	D	1	(4)	
1	Hendrik Van Crombrugge		30/04/93	G	35		
15	Moussa Wagué	SEN	04/10/98	D	12	(2)	1

KRC Genk

1988 • Luminus Arena (23,718) • krcgenk.be

Major honours
Belgian League (3) 1999, 2002, 2011; Belgian Cup (4) 1998, 2000, 2009, 2013

Coach: Peter Maes; (26/12/16) Albert Stuivenberg (NED)

2016
31/07 h Oostende W 2-1 *Karelis, Samatta*
07/08 a Gent L 0-1
13/08 h Waasland-Beveren D 2-2 *Karelis, og (Jans)*
21/08 a Lokeren W 3-0 *Samatta 2, Bailey*
28/08 h Zulte Waregem W 1-0 *Pozuelo*
11/09 a Standard L 0-2
18/09 h Anderlecht L 0-2
25/09 a Kortrijk L 1-4 *Trossard*
02/10 h Mechelen W 2-1 *Karelis (p), Bailey*
15/10 a Mouscron D 2-2 *Karelis 2*
23/10 h Sint-Truiden W 1-0 *Karelis*
26/10 a Charleroi L 1-2 *Karelis*
29/10 h Westerlo W 2-1 *Pozuelo, Karelis (p)*
06/11 a Club Brugge D 1-1 *Buffel*
19/11 h Eupen W 2-0 *og (Diallo), Pozuelo*
27/11 a Oostende L 0-6
04/12 h Lokeren L 1-2 *Trossard*
18/12 h Standard D 2-2 *Colley, Samatta*
21/12 a Zulte Waregem L 0-1
27/12 h Gent W 2-0 *Pozuelo, Karelis*

2017
21/01 a Eupen W 1-0 *Samatta*
24/01 h Kortrijk W 3-0 *Schrijvers, Samatta, Pozuelo*
28/01 a Mechelen L 0-1
04/02 h Mouscron W 1-0 *Naranjo*
07/02 a Waasland-Beveren D 0-0
10/02 a Sint-Truiden W 3-0 *Pozuelo, Samatta, Malinovskiy*
19/02 h Charleroi D 1-1 *Trossard (p)*
26/02 a Anderlecht L 0-2
04/03 h Club Brugge W 2-1 *Samatta 2*
12/03 a Westerlo W 4-0 *Samatta, Buffel, Colley, Malinovskiy*
01/04 h Lokeren W 4-0 *Pozuelo, Samatta, Boëtius, Naranjo*
08/04 a Roeselare W 1-0 *Naranjo*
15/04 a Kortrijk W 3-0 *Malinovskiy, Colley, Yao Kumordzi*
23/04 h Mouscron W 6-0 *Walsh, Trossard 2, Naranjo 3*
26/04 a Eupen D 1-1 *Malinovskiy*
29/04 h Kortrijk W 3-0 *Trossard (p), Schrijvers 2*
07/05 h Eupen W 2-1 *Uronen, Samatta*
14/05 a Mouscron W 2-0 *Malinovskiy, Boëtius*
17/05 h Roeselare W 3-1 *Brabec, Buffel, Boëtius*
20/05 a Lokeren D 1-1 *og (Persoons)*
27/05 h Sint-Truiden W 3-0 *Buffel, Boëtius, Samatta*
31/05 a Oostende L 1-3 *Schrijvers (p)*

No	Name	Nat	DoB	Pos	Aps	(s)	Gls
31	Leon Bailey	JAM	09/08/97	A	17	(2)	2
25	Sander Berge	NOR	14/02/98	M	15	(4)	
1	Marco Bizot	NED	10/03/91	G	22		
9	Jean-Paul Boëtius	NED	22/03/94	M	12	(5)	4
2	Jakub Brabec	CZE	06/08/92	D	24	(1)	1
19	Thomas Buffel		19/02/81	M	25	(6)	4
41	Timothy Castagne		05/12/95	D	31	(1)	
15	Omar Colley	GAM	24/10/92	D	35		3
6	Sebastien Dewaest		27/05/91	D	20	(1)	
28	Bryan Heynen		06/02/97	M	20	(13)	
30	Nordin Jackers		05/09/97	G	3	(1)	
32	Christophe Janssens		09/03/98	D		(2)	
7	Nikolaos Karelis	GRE	24/02/92	A	14	(4)	9
92	Neeskens Kebano	COD	10/03/92	M	3		
18	Ruslan Malinovskiy	UKR	04/05/93	M	19	(1)	5
11	José Naranjo	ESP	28/07/94	A	6	(14)	6
3	Bojan Nastić	SRB	06/07/94	D	10	(4)	
25	Wilfred Ndidi	NGA	16/12/96	M	19		
24	Alejandro Pozuelo	ESP	20/09/91	M	33		7
26	Mathew Ryan	AUS	08/04/92	G	17		
20	Paolo Sabak		10/02/99	M	1	(2)	
77	Mbwana Samatta	TAN	13/12/92	A	24	(13)	13
22	Siebe Schrijvers		18/07/96	A	15	(3)	4
23	Rubin Seigers		11/01/98	D	1	(1)	
10	Tino-Sven Sušić	BIH	13/02/92	M	10	(5)	
14	Leandro Trossard		04/12/94	M	19	(12)	6
17	Holly Tshimanga		25/04/97	A		(1)	
21	Jere Uronen	FIN	13/07/94	D	27	(1)	1
16	Dante Vanzeir		16/04/98	A		(1)	
27	Laurens Vermijl		01/01/97	M		(1)	
5	Sandy Walsh	NED	14/03/95	D	13	(4)	1
4	Dries Wouters		28/01/97	D	5	(3)	
8	Bennard Yao Kumordzi	GHA	21/03/85	M	2	(10)	1

BELGIUM

KAA Gent

1900 • Ghelamco Arena (20,000) • kaagent.be

Major honours
Belgian League (1) 2015; Belgian Cup (3) 1964, 1984, 2010

Coach: Hein Vanhaezebrouck

2016

Date		Opponent		Score	Scorers
31/07	a	Kortrijk	D	1-1	*Renato Neto*
07/08	h	Genk	W	1-0	*Perbet*
13/08	a	Charleroi	D	1-1	*Renato Neto*
21/08	h	Westerlo	W	4-2	*Perbet 2, Miličević, Saief (p)*
28/08	a	Anderlecht	D	2-2	*Simon, Asare*
11/09	h	Lokeren	W	3-0	*og (Ňinaj), Coulibaly, Simon*
18/09	a	Oostende	L	0-1	
24/09	h	Sint-Truiden	W	2-1	*Perbet, Schoofs*
02/10	a	Club Brugge	L	0-1	
16/10	h	Zulte Waregem	W	3-0	*Coulibaly, Simon, Van der Bruggen*
23/10	a	Eupen	L	2-3	*Miličević (p), Renato Neto*
27/10	h	Standard	W	1-0	*Coulibaly*
30/10	a	Mechelen	L	0-2	
06/11	h	Waasland-Beveren	W	2-0	*Dejaegere, Saief*
19/11	a	Mouscron	W	2-0	*Perbet, Saief (p)*
27/11	h	Kortrijk	W	3-0	*Perbet, Renato Neto, Saief*
03/12	a	Westerlo	D	0-0	
11/12	h	Oostende	D	1-1	*Coulibaly*
17/12	a	Sint-Truiden	L	1-3	*Mitrović*
22/12	h	Anderlecht	L	2-3	*Miličević 2 (1p)*
27/12	a	Genk	L	0-2	

2017

Date		Opponent		Score	Scorers
20/01	h	Charleroi	W	1-0	*Miličević*
25/01	a	Lokeren	D	0-0	
29/01	h	Club Brugge	W	2-0	*Kubo, Coulibaly*
05/02	a	Zulte Waregem	D	1-1	*Kubo (p)*
11/02	h	Eupen	L	0-1	
19/02	a	Standard	D	1-1	*Mitrović*
26/02	h	Mouscron	W	3-1	*Kalu, Kubo, Perbet (p)*
04/03	a	Waasland-Beveren	W	3-2	*Perbet 2, Kubo*
12/03	h	Mechelen	W	3-0	*Perbet, Kubo, Kalu*
02/04	h	Club Brugge	W	2-1	*Simon 2 (1p)*
09/04	a	Anderlecht	D	0-0	
17/04	a	Charleroi	W	1-0	*Kubo*
21/04	h	Oostende	D	1-1	*Kubo*
25/04	a	Zulte Waregem	W	2-0	*Kubo, Coulibaly*
30/04	h	Anderlecht	D	0-0	
07/05	a	Oostende	L	3-4	*Saief, Miličević, Kubo*
14/05	h	Charleroi	D	1-1	*Kubo (p)*
18/05	h	Zulte Waregem	W	5-2	*Coulibaly 2, Saief, Kalu, Kubo*
21/05	a	Club Brugge	L	1-2	*Saief*

No	Name	Nat	DoB	Pos	Aps	(s)	Gls
21	Nana Asare	GHA	11/07/86	D	24	(1)	1
30	Darko Bjedov	SRB	28/03/98	A	2	(1)	
7	Kalifa Coulibaly	MLI	21/08/91	A	25	(8)	8
5	Ofir Davidzada	ISR	05/05/91	D	1	(2)	
29	Thibault De Smet		05/06/98	D	1	(3)	
19	Brecht Dejaegere		29/05/91	M	18	(7)	1
9	Laurent Depoitre		07/12/88	A	2		
44	Anderson Esiti	NGA	24/05/94	M	19	(6)	
32	Thomas Foket		25/09/94	M	25	(10)	
55	Rami Gershon	ISR	12/08/88	D	26	(3)	
23	Samuel Gigot	FRA	12/10/93	D	16		
28	Siebe Horemans		02/06/98	D	1		
40	Rabiu Ibrahim	NGA	15/03/91	M	1	(3)	
91	Lovre Kalinić	CRO	03/04/90	G	19		
18	Samuel Kalu	NGA	26/08/97	M	11	(5)	3
31	Yuya Kubo	JPN	24/12/93	A	17		11
11	Emir Kujovic	SWE	22/06/88	A		(1)	
14	Sven Kums		26/02/88	M	5		
8	Thomas Matton		24/10/85	M	10	(7)	
77	Danijel Miličević	BIH	05/01/86	M	28	(5)	6
13	Stefan Mitrović	SRB	22/05/90	D	36	(1)	2
88	Dieumerci Ndongala	COD	14/06/91	A	3	(6)	
23	Lasse Nielsen	DEN	08/01/88	D	16	(2)	
24	Jérémy Perbet	FRA	12/12/84	A	16	(11)	10
10	Renato Neto	BRA	27/09/91	M	24		4
1	Jacob Rinne	SWE	20/06/93	G	12		
15	Kenny Saief	USA	17/12/93	M	23	(8)	7
16	Rob Schoofs		23/03/94	M	9	(5)	1
27	Moses Simon	NGA	12/07/95	A	24	(6)	5
2	Jérémy Taravel	FRA	17/04/87	D	2	(1)	
20	Yannick Thoelen		18/07/90	G	9		
4	William Troost-Ekong	NGA	01/09/93	D	7	(1)	
17	Hannes Van der Bruggen		01/04/93	M	6	(1)	1
6	Birger Verstraete		16/04/94	M	2	(6)	
33	Louis Verstraete		04/05/99	M		(7)	

KV Kortrijk

1971 • Guldensporenstadion (9,399) • kvk.be

Coach: Karim Belhocine (FRA); (29/08/16) Bart Van Lancker; (08/03/17) Karim Belhocine (FRA)

2016

Date		Opponent		Score	Scorers
31/07	h	Gent	D	1-1	*Ouali*
07/08	a	Anderlecht	L	1-5	*Kagé*
13/08	a	Mechelen	D	0-0	
20/08	h	Club Brugge	W	2-1	*Saadi 2*
27/08	a	Sint-Truiden	W	2-1	*Mercier, Kagé*
10/09	h	Westerlo	W	4-1	*Saadi 2, Kagé 2*
17/09	a	Zulte Waregem	L	1-2	*Saadi*
25/09	h	Genk	W	4-1	*Totovytskiy, Mercier, Saadi 2*
01/10	a	Lokeren	L	1-2	*Gigot*
15/10	h	Standard	D	3-3	*Saadi, Kagé, Totovytskiy*
21/10	a	Oostende	D	2-2	*Ouali, Gigot*
26/10	h	Eupen	D	1-1	*Rolland*
29/10	a	Mouscron	W	1-0	*Kagé*
04/11	h	Charleroi	W	2-1	*Saadi, Ouali*
19/11	a	Waasland-Beveren	D	1-1	*Kagé*
27/11	a	Gent	L	0-3	
04/12	h	Anderlecht	L	1-3	*Saadi*
10/12	h	Sint-Truiden	L	0-1	
18/12	a	Club Brugge	L	1-5	*Veldwijk*
21/12	h	Oostende	L	0-2	
26/12	a	Westerlo	L	1-4	*De Smet (p)*

2017

Date		Opponent		Score	Scorers
21/01	h	Zulte Waregem	L	2-3	*Chevalier, Pavlović*
24/01	a	Genk	L	0-3	
28/01	h	Lokeren	W	2-1	*Chevalier 2*
04/02	a	Standard	W	3-0	*Chevalier, Saadi 2*
11/02	h	Mechelen	L	0-2	
18/02	a	Eupen	L	0-1	
25/02	h	Waasland-Beveren	L	1-2	*Saadi*
04/03	a	Charleroi	D	1-1	*Saadi*
12/03	h	Mouscron	L	0-2	
01/04	h	Mouscron	W	2-1	*Mercier, Barbarić*
08/04	a	Lokeren	D	0-0	
15/04	h	Genk	L	0-3	
22/04	h	Eupen	D	3-3	*De Smet (p), Totovytskiy, Sarr*
25/04	a	Roeselare	W	3-2	*De Smet 2, Totovytskiy*
30/04	a	Genk	L	0-3	
06/05	h	Roeselare	L	0-3	
13/05	a	Eupen	L	2-3	*Rolland, Totovytskiy*
17/05	h	Lokeren	D	4-4	*Stojanović, Mercier, Saadi, Kovačević*
20/05	a	Mouscron	W	1-0	*Saadi (p)*

No	Name	Nat	DoB	Pos	Aps	(s)	Gls
16	Tomislav Barbarić	CRO	29/03/89	D	10		1
3	Fabien Boyer	FRA	12/04/91	D		(1)	
9	Teddy Chevalier	FRA	28/06/87	A	15	(4)	4
30	Kristof D'Haene		06/06/90	M	20	(10)	
17	Gertjan De Mets		02/04/87	M	6	(2)	
7	Stijn De Smet		27/03/85	M	17	(8)	4
20	Samuel Gigot	FRA	12/10/93	D	20		2
6	Dimitrios Goutas	GRE	04/04/94	D	25	(1)	
12	Medjon Hoxha		27/07/99	M		(2)	
2	Marvin Ivanof		18/02/96	D	3	(1)	
23	Joãozinho	POR	02/07/89	D	26		
10	Hervé Kagé	COD	10/04/89	M	21	(6)	7
28	Thomas Kaminski		23/10/92	G	32		
5	Vladimir Kovačević	SRB	11/11/92	D	6	(4)	1
25	Xavier Mercier	FRA	25/07/89	M	20	(10)	4
15	Romain Métanire	FRA	28/03/90	D	18		
27	Idir Ouali	FRA	21/05/88	M	26	(7)	3
9	Sakis Papazoglou	GRE	30/03/88	A	3	(7)	
8	Nebojša Pavlović	SRB	09/04/81	M	17	(1)	1
26	Elohim Rolland	FRA	03/03/89	M	33	(1)	2
24	Lucas Rougeaux	FRA	10/03/94	D	11	(2)	
11	Idriss Saadi	ALG	08/02/92	A	30	(7)	16
88	Sidy Sarr	SEN	05/06/96	M	8	(22)	1
13	Mihail Sifakis	GRE	09/09/84	G	8		
20	Jovan Stojanović	SRB	21/04/94	M	2	(7)	1
29	Andriy Totovytskiy	UKR	20/01/93	M	12	(9)	5
14	Hannes Van der Bruggen		01/04/93	M	17		
31	Anthony Van Loo		05/10/88	D	12		
39	Lars Veldwijk	RSA	21/08/91	A	2	(7)	1
5	Birger Verstraete		16/04/94	M	20		

KSC Lokeren OV

1970 • Daknamstadion (12,136) • sporting.be

Major honours
Belgian Cup (2) 2012, 2014

Coach: Georges Leekens; (27/10/16) Rúnar Kristinsson (ISL)

2016

Date		Opponent		Score	Scorers
30/07	a	Sint-Truiden	L	0-1	
07/08	h	Westerlo	W	3-0	*De Sutter, Maric (p), Bolbat*
14/08	a	Club Brugge	L	0-1	
21/08	h	Genk	L	0-3	
27/08	h	Mouscron	W	2-1	*og (Essikal), Jajá*
11/09	a	Gent	L	0-3	
18/09	h	Standard	L	0-1	
24/09	a	Waasland-Beveren	D	1-1	*Skúlason (p)*
01/10	h	Kortrijk	W	2-1	*Jajá, Mirić*
16/10	a	Anderlecht	L	0-1	
22/10	a	Zulte Waregem	L	0-2	
25/10	h	Oostende	L	1-2	*Bolbat*
29/10	a	Eupen	D	2-2	*Terki, Straetman*
05/11	h	Mechelen	D	0-0	
20/11	a	Charleroi	L	1-2	*Mirić*
26/11	h	Sint-Truiden	W	1-0	*Maric (p)*
04/12	a	Genk	W	2-1	*Terki, Bolbat*
09/12	h	Zulte Waregem	D	1-1	*Skúlason*
17/12	a	Westerlo	W	3-1	*De Sutter, Terki, De Ridder*
21/12	a	Standard	D	1-1	*Maric*
26/12	h	Waasland-Beveren	D	0-0	

2017

Date		Opponent		Score	Scorers
21/01	a	Mouscron	L	1-2	*og (Vojvoda)*
25/01	h	Gent	D	0-0	
28/01	a	Kortrijk	L	1-2	*De Sutter*
03/02	h	Anderlecht	D	0-0	
12/02	h	Club Brugge	W	1-0	*De Sutter*
18/02	a	Mechelen	L	0-3	
25/02	h	Eupen	L	1-2	*Maric (p)*
04/03	a	Oostende	D	0-0	
12/03	h	Charleroi	D	0-0	
01/04	a	Genk	L	0-4	
08/04	h	Kortrijk	D	0-0	
15/04	a	Eupen	D	3-3	*De Sutter, Straetman, Mirić*
22/04	h	Roeselare	W	2-1	*Maric, De Sutter*
26/04	a	Mouscron	D	2-2	*Persoons, De Sutter*
29/04	h	Eupen	W	4-1	*De Sutter 2, Maric (p), Hupperts*
06/05	h	Mouscron	D	2-2	*Persoons, Mirić*
13/05	a	Roeselare	W	3-2	*Hupperts, Mirić, De Ridder*
17/05	a	Kortrijk	D	4-4	*Hupperts, De Sutter, Persoons, Enoh*
20/05	h	Genk	D	1-1	*De Sutter*

No	Name	Nat	DoB	Pos	Aps	(s)	Gls
3	Eugene Ansah	GHA	16/12/94	A		(4)	
1	Boubacar Barry	CIV	30/12/79	G	26		
50	Serhiy Bolbat	UKR	13/06/93	M	11	(10)	3
12	Ortwin De Wolf		23/04/96	G	1		
34	Sander De Pryker		28/02/98	D		(1)	
22	Steve De Ridder		25/02/87	A	25	(7)	2
9	Tom De Sutter		03/07/85	A	28	(5)	11
29	Lewis Enoh	CMR	23/10/92	A	4	(7)	1
11	Georgios Galitsios	GRE	06/07/86	D	34		
17	Guus Hupperts	NED	25/04/92	M	25	(2)	3
15	Sverrir Ingi Ingason	ISL	05/08/93	D	19	(2)	
70	Jajá	BRA	28/02/86	A	12		2
23	Nikola Jambor	CRO	25/09/95	M	6	(3)	
30	João Carlos	BRA	01/01/82	D	5		
5	Mijat Maric	SUI	30/04/84	D	30		6
18	Gary Martin	ENG	10/10/98	A	5	(9)	
21	Marko Mirić	SRB	26/03/87	A	16	(13)	5
27	Arno Monsecour		19/01/96	D	4	(2)	
25	Branislav Ňinaj	SVK	17/05/94	D	18	(3)	
15	Mohamed Ofkir	NOR	04/08/96	M	5	(4)	
7	Killian Overmeire		06/12/85	M	21		
10	Ayanda Patosi	RSA	31/10/92	M	7	(1)	
8	Koen Persoons		12/07/83	M	23	(3)	3
20	Joher Rassoul	SEN	31/12/95	M	14	(7)	
6	Ari Freyr Skúlason	ISL	14/05/87	D	26	(2)	2
34	Bob Straetman		19/12/97	M	12	(13)	2
14	Mehdi Terki	ALG	27/09/91	M	30	(6)	3
19	Mario Tičinović	CRO	20/08/91	D	20	(11)	
33	Joran Triest		08/04/97	A		(1)	
13	Davino Verhulst		25/11/87	G	13		

KV Mechelen

1904 • AFAS Stadion (16,672) • kvmechelen.be

Major honours
UEFA Cup Winners' Cup (1) 1988; UEFA Super Cup (1) 1989; Belgian League (4) 1943, 1946, 1948, 1989; Belgian Cup (1) 1987

Coach: Aleksandar Janković (SRB); (12/09/16) Yannick Ferrera

2016					
29/07	h	Club Brugge	L	0-2	
06/08	a	Eupen	W	2-0	*Verdier, Matthys*
13/08	h	Kortrijk	D	0-0	
20/08	a	Waasland-Beveren	D	2-2	*Bjelica, Verdier*
27/08	a	Westerlo	W	2-1	*Croizet, Rits*
10/09	h	Sint-Truiden	W	2-0	*Verdier, Kolovos*
16/09	a	Charleroi	D	0-0	
24/09	h	Zulte Waregem	L	2-3	*Verdier, Croizet*
01/10	a	Genk	L	1-2	*Verdier*
16/10	h	Oostende	L	2-3	*Verdier, De Witte (p)*
22/10	h	Mouscron	W	2-0	*Croizet, Kolovos*
26/10	a	Anderlecht	L	0-2	
30/10	h	Gent	W	2-0	*Filipovič, Vitas (p)*
05/11	a	Lokeren	D	0-0	
20/11	h	Standard	W	2-1	*Rits, Verdier*
25/11	a	Club Brugge	L	1-6	*Bjelica*
02/12	h	Eupen	W	1-0	*Jaadi*
10/12	a	Mouscron	W	4-1	*Kolovos, Matthys, Bjelica, Vitas (p)*
17/12	h	Waasland-Beveren	W	2-0	*Schouterden, Claes*
20/12	h	Charleroi	W	1-0	*Rits*
26/12	a	Zulte Waregem	D	0-0	
2017					
22/01	h	Westerlo	L	1-2	*Kolovos*
25/01	a	Sint-Truiden	L	1-2	*Verdier*
28/01	h	Genk	W	1-0	*De Witte*
04/02	a	Oostende	L	0-2	
11/02	a	Kortrijk	W	2-0	*Vitas 2*
18/02	h	Lokeren	W	3-0	*Verdier, Kolovos, Osaguona*
26/02	a	Standard	D	2-2	*Rits 2*
04/03	h	Anderlecht	W	3-2	*De Witte (p), Vanlerberghe, Matthys*
12/03	a	Gent	L	0-3	
01/04	a	Saint-Gilloise	L	0-3	
09/04	h	Lierse	W	1-0	*Vitas*
16/04	a	Waasland-Beveren	W	2-1	*Vitas (p), Jaadi*
22/04	h	Standard	W	1-0	*Vanlerberghe*
26/04	h	Sint-Truiden	W	1-0	*Schouterden*
29/04	a	Lierse	D	0-0	
06/05	h	Waasland-Beveren	L	1-3	*og (Moren)*
12/05	a	Standard	L	0-2	
16/05	h	Saint-Gilloise	W	1-0	*Peffer*
19/05	a	Sint-Truiden	L	0-7	

No	Name	Nat	DoB	Pos	Aps	(s)	Gls
16	Aleksandar Bjelica	SRB	07/01/94	D	25	(1)	3
33	Jeff Callebaut		23/01/97	M		(4)	
14	Xavier Chen	TPE	05/10/83	D	13	(2)	
77	Glen Claes		08/03/94	M	13	(13)	1
22	Elias Cobbaut		21/11/97	D	12	(5)	
15	Edin Cocalić	BIH	05/12/87	D	36		
26	Colin Coosemans		03/08/92	G	28		
10	Yohan Croizet	FRA	15/02/92	M	31	(6)	3
4	Seth De Witte		18/10/87	D	13	(2)	3
3	Ahmed El Messaoudi	MAR	03/08/95	D	21	(6)	
55	Željko Filipovič	SVN	03/10/88	M	18	(6)	1
39	Reda Jaadi		14/02/95	M		(11)	2
17	Dimitrios Kolovos	GRE	27/04/93	M	22	(5)	5
8	Randall Leal	CRC	14/01/97	M	3	(3)	
7	Tim Matthys		23/12/83	M	25	(12)	3
49	Anthony Moris	LUX	29/04/90	G	12		
21	Sotiris Ninis	GRE	03/04/90	M		(1)	
12	Christian Osaguona	NGA	10/10/90	A	4	(11)	1
2	Laurens Paulussen		19/07/90	D	17	(3)	
27	Jordy Peffer		04/11/96	A	2	(5)	1
11	Mats Rits		18/07/93	M	37		5
18	Nils Schouterden		14/12/88	M	26	(3)	2
29	Jules Van Cleemput		11/04/97	D	8	(2)	
30	Jordi Vanlerberghe		27/03/96	D	17	(5)	2
99	Nicolas Verdier	FRA	17/01/87	A	29	(6)	9
9	Dalibor Veselinović	SRB	21/09/87	A	1	(7)	
23	Uroš Vitas	SRB	28/09/92	D	27	(1)	6

R. Excel Mouscron

1922 • Le Canonnier (10,800) • excel.foot.be

Coach: Glen De Boeck; (07/12/16) Mircea Rednic (ROU)

2016					
30/07	h	Anderlecht	L	1-2	*Marković*
06/08	h	Charleroi	L	0-1	
14/08	a	Oostende	L	1-2	*Marković*
20/08	h	Sint-Truiden	W	2-1	*Stojanović, Marković*
27/08	a	Lokeren	L	1-2	*Marković*
10/09	h	Zulte Waregem	L	1-5	*Ferber*
17/09	a	Westerlo	W	3-1	*Stojanović, Hassan, Simič*
23/09	h	Club Brugge	L	0-3	
01/10	a	Eupen	W	4-1	*Diédhiou 3, Stojanović*
15/10	h	Genk	D	2-2	*Hassan, Viola*
22/10	a	Mechelen	L	0-2	
27/10	a	Waasland-Beveren	D	0-0	
29/10	h	Kortrijk	L	0-1	
06/11	a	Standard	L	1-2	*Hassan*
19/11	h	Gent	L	0-2	
27/11	a	Anderlecht	L	0-7	
03/12	a	Sint-Truiden	L	0-1	
10/12	h	Mechelen	L	1-4	*Marković*
17/12	a	Charleroi	L	0-2	
20/12	h	Westerlo	D	0-0	
26/12	a	Club Brugge	L	1-2	*Nkaka*
2017					
21/01	h	Lokeren	W	2-1	*Hubert (p), Arslanagic*
24/01	a	Zulte Waregem	L	0-1	
29/01	h	Eupen	W	3-0	*Matulevičius, Marković, Diédhiou*
04/02	a	Genk	L	0-1	
11/02	h	Oostende	L	1-2	*Matulevičius*
18/02	h	Waasland-Beveren	L	1-2	*Kabasele*
26/02	a	Gent	L	1-3	*Stojanović*
04/03	h	Standard	W	1-0	*Diédhiou*
12/03	a	Kortrijk	W	2-0	*Hassan, og (Kovačević)*
01/04	a	Kortrijk	L	1-2	*Vojvoda*
08/04	h	Eupen	L	0-2	
15/04	a	Roeselare	W	5-3	*Diédhiou, Hassan 2, Matulevičius, og (Zolotić)*
23/04	a	Genk	L	0-6	
26/04	h	Lokeren	D	2-2	*Kabasele, Peyre*
29/04	h	Roeselare	W	1-0	*Matulevičius*
06/05	a	Lokeren	D	2-2	*Nkaka, Kabasele*
14/05	h	Genk	L	0-2	
17/05	a	Eupen	L	0-2	
20/05	h	Kortrijk	L	0-1	

No	Name	Nat	DoB	Pos	Aps	(s)	Gls
36	Dino Arslanagic		24/04/93	D	17	(1)	1
9	Anice Badri	FRA	18/09/90	M	1		
25	Agustín Cedrés	URU	28/05/98	M		(2)	
16	Noam Debaisseux		15/12/99	D		(2)	
33	Théo Defourny		25/04/92	G	5		
21	Matej Delač	CRO	20/08/92	G	28		
3	Thomas Demol		11/05/98	D		(1)	
20	Simon Diédhiou	SEN	10/07/91	A	32	(3)	6
17	Babacar Dione		22/03/97	A	1		
6	Noë Dussenne		07/04/92	D	4		
4	Karim Essikal	MAR	08/02/96	M	5	(2)	
9	Roman Ferber		29/11/93	A	4	(3)	1
99	Islam Feruz	SCO	10/09/95	A	1	(6)	
15	Daniel Graovac	BIH	08/08/93	D	1	(1)	
24	Nikola Gulan	SRB	23/03/89	D	17	(8)	
10	Mahmoud Hassan	EGY	01/10/94	M	25	(1)	6
5	David Hubert		12/08/88	M	29	(1)	1
28	Jérémy Huyghebaert		07/01/89	D	26	(3)	
94	Nathan Kabasele		14/01/94	A	8	(7)	3
6	Cristian Manea	ROU	09/08/97	D	7	(1)	
7	Filip Marković	SRB	03/03/92	M	25	(3)	6
99	Deivydas Matulevičius	LTU	08/04/89	A	8	(7)	4
10	Julian Michel	FRA	19/02/92	M	1		
18	Farouk Miya	UGA	26/11/97	M	1	(2)	
11	Dimitri Mohamed	FRA	11/06/89	M	25	(7)	
45	Fejsal Mulić	SRB	03/10/94	A	3	(9)	
26	Aristote Nkaka		01/07/96	M	18	(6)	2
8	Fabrice Olinga	CMR	12/05/96	M	7	(10)	
29	Thibault Peyre	FRA	03/10/92	D	27	(2)	1
19	Martin Selak		22/06/95	D	1	(1)	
34	Stefan Simič	CZE	20/01/95	D	29	(1)	1
14	Sebastjan Spahiu		30/10/99	A	1		
22	Luka Stojanović	SRB	04/01/94	M	18	(11)	4
23	Mickaël Tirpan		23/10/93	D	25	(1)	
1	Vagner	BRA	06/06/86	G	7		
30	Benjamin Van Durmen		20/03/97	D	2	(2)	
16	Valentín Viola	ARG	28/08/91	A	8	(6)	1
27	Mërgim Vojvoda	KOS	01/02/95	D	23	(7)	1

KV Oostende

1981 • Versluys Arena (8,400) • kvo.be

Coach: Yves Vanderhaeghe

2016					
31/07	a	Genk	L	1-2	*Musona*
05/08	h	Club Brugge	W	1-0	*El Ghanassy*
14/08	h	Mouscron	W	2-1	*Musona (p), Marušić*
20/08	a	Zulte Waregem	D	1-1	*Marušić*
27/08	h	Waasland-Beveren	W	2-1	*og (Camacho), Musona*
10/09	a	Eupen	L	1-2	*El Ghanassy*
18/09	h	Gent	W	1-0	*Cyriac*
24/09	a	Charleroi	L	1-2	*Musona (p)*
30/09	h	Sint-Truiden	D	2-2	*Cyriac (p), Musona*
16/10	a	Mechelen	W	3-2	*Musona, Godeau, Conté*
21/10	h	Kortrijk	D	2-2	*Dimata, og (Gigot)*
25/10	a	Lokeren	W	2-1	*Dimata, Milić*
30/10	h	Standard	W	3-1	*Dimata, Berrier 2*
06/11	a	Anderlecht	D	1-1	*Berrier (p)*
19/11	h	Westerlo	W	5-0	*Milić 2, Musona, Dimata, Fernando Canesin*
27/11	h	Genk	W	6-0	*Berrier, Milić, Musona, Dimata 2, Cyriac*
03/12	a	Club Brugge	L	0-2	
11/12	a	Gent	D	1-1	*El Ghanassy*
17/12	h	Zulte Waregem	D	1-1	*Berrier (p)*
21/12	a	Kortrijk	W	2-0	*Cyriac (p), El Ghanassy*
26/12	h	Eupen	L	1-3	*Dimata*
2017					
21/01	a	Waasland-Beveren	W	1-0	*Dimata*
24/01	h	Charleroi	L	1-2	*Jonckheere*
28/01	a	Sint-Truiden	L	0-3	
04/02	h	Mechelen	W	2-0	*og (Vanlerberghe), og (De Witte)*
11/02	a	Mouscron	W	2-1	*Dimata, Rozehnal*
19/02	h	Anderlecht	L	1-4	*Dimata (p)*
25/02	a	Westerlo	W	4-0	*Dimata (p), Musona, Jonckheere, Marušić*
04/03	h	Lokeren	D	0-0	
12/03	a	Standard	D	2-2	*Bossaerts, Akpala*
01/04	a	Charleroi	D	1-1	*Musona*
07/04	h	Zulte Waregem	D	1-1	*Berrier*
16/04	h	Anderlecht	L	0-1	
21/04	a	Gent	D	1-1	*Berrier*
26/04	a	Club Brugge	L	1-3	*Dimata*
30/04	h	Charleroi	W	1-0	*Siani (p)*
07/05	h	Gent	W	4-3	*Siani, Marušić, Berrier, Rozehnal*
12/05	a	Zulte Waregem	L	1-3	*Marušić*
18/05	h	Club Brugge	W	2-1	*Rozehnal, Akpala*
21/05	a	Anderlecht	L	2-3	*Milić, Akpala*
31/05	h	Genk	W	3-1	*Akpala, Rozehnal, Jali*

No	Name	Nat	DoB	Pos	Aps	(s)	Gls
17	Joseph Akpala	NGA	24/08/86	A	4	(14)	4
4	Fabien Antunes	FRA	19/11/91	D	12	(5)	
10	Franck Berrier	FRA	02/02/84	M	30	(7)	8
6	Matthias Bossaerts		10/07/96	D	9	(1)	1
27	Brecht Capon		24/04/88	D	22	(1)	
22	Ibrahima Conté	GUI	03/04/91	A	3	(5)	1
9	Cyriac	CIV	15/08/90	A	10	(11)	4
19	Landry Dimata		01/09/97	A	26	(3)	12
28	William Dutoît	FRA	18/09/88	G	13	(1)	
8	Yassine El Ghanassy		12/07/90	M	26	(10)	4
55	Fernando Canesin	BRA	27/02/92	M	23	(11)	1
31	Bruno Godeau		10/05/92	D	15	(5)	1
36	Hasan Özkan	TUR	14/11/97	M	1	(7)	
15	Andile Jali	RSA	10/04/90	M	12	(3)	1
20	Michiel Jonckheere		03/01/90	M	24	(4)	2
77	Adam Marušić	MNE	17/10/92	D	34	(2)	5
44	Antonio Milić	CRO	10/03/94	D	27	(2)	5
11	Knowledge Musona	ZIM	21/06/90	M	27	(3)	10
1	Didier Ovono	GAB	23/01/83	G	7		
14	Nicklas Pedersen	DEN	10/10/87	A		(12)	
1	Silvio Proto		23/05/83	G	21		
18	David Rozehnal	CZE	05/07/80	D	28		4
7	Sébastien Siani	CMR	21/12/86	M	28	(3)	2
33	Žarko Tomašević	MNE	22/02/90	D	19	(3)	
24	Siebe Van der Heyden		30/05/98	M		(1)	
26	Kevin Vandendriessche	FRA	07/08/89	M	30	(6)	

BELGIUM

K. Sint-Truidense VV

1924 • Stayen (17,850) • stvv.com

Coach: Ivan Leko (CRO)

Date		Opponent		Score	Scorers
2016					
30/07	h	Lokeren	W	1-0	*Proschwitz*
06/08	a	Standard	L	0-2	
12/08	h	Anderlecht	D	0-0	
20/08	a	Mouscron	L	1-2	*Pulido*
27/08	h	Kortrijk	L	1-2	*De Petter*
10/09	a	Mechelen	L	0-2	
17/09	h	Waasland-Beveren	W	4-1	*Boli 2, Bamba 2*
24/09	a	Gent	L	1-2	*Peeters*
30/09	a	Oostende	D	2-2	*Peeters, Gerkens*
15/10	h	Westerlo	D	2-2	*Rúben Fernandes, Boli*
23/10	a	Genk	L	0-1	
26/10	h	Zulte Waregem	L	0-2	
29/10	h	Charleroi	D	2-2	*Peeters, Pulido*
05/11	a	Eupen	L	2-4	*Koubemba, Boli*
18/11	h	Club Brugge	L	0-1	
26/11	a	Lokeren	L	0-1	
03/12	h	Mouscron	W	1-0	*Rúben Fernandes*
10/12	a	Kortrijk	W	1-0	*Janssens*
17/12	h	Gent	W	3-1	*Gerkens 2, Janssens*
20/12	a	Waasland-Beveren	L	1-3	*Boli (p)*
27/12	h	Standard	D	2-2	*Ceballos, Boli*
2017					
22/01	a	Anderlecht	L	1-3	*Gerkens*
25/01	h	Mechelen	W	2-1	*Vetokele, Peeters*
28/01	h	Oostende	W	3-0	*Mechele, Vetokele 2*
05/02	a	Westerlo	L	0-1	
10/02	h	Genk	L	0-3	
18/02	a	Zulte Waregem	L	1-4	*De Petter*
25/02	a	Charleroi	L	0-1	
04/03	h	Eupen	W	2-1	*Vetokele, Gerkens*
12/03	a	Club Brugge	D	2-2	*De Petter, Gerkens*
01/04	h	Waasland-Beveren	W	3-0	*Peeters, Bezus, Gerkens (p)*
08/04	a	Standard	D	2-2	*Mechele, Gerkens*
15/04	h	Lierse	W	2-1	*Gerkens 2*
22/04	h	Saint-Gilloise	L	0-1	
26/04	a	Mechelen	L	0-1	
29/04	a	Waasland-Beveren	W	1-0	*Gerkens*
06/05	h	Standard	W	1-0	*Gerkens*
13/05	a	Saint-Gilloise	W	4-1	*Vetokele 2 (1p), Ceballos 2*
16/05	a	Lierse	W	3-1	*Gerkens, Vetokele (p), Ceballos*
19/05	h	Mechelen	W	7-0	*Vetokele, Rúben Fernandes, Gerkens, Ceballos, Abrahams 3*
27/05	a	Genk	L	0-3	

No	Name	Nat	DoB	Pos	Aps	(s)	Gls
25	Kurt Abrahams	RSA	30/12/96	A	1	(6)	3
18	Mamadou Bagayoko	CIV	31/12/89	D	21	(4)	
17	Jonathan Bamba	FRA	26/03/96	A	7	(1)	2
10	Roman Bezus	UKR	26/09/90	M	14	(6)	1
11	Yohan Boli	FRA	17/11/93	A	16	(8)	6
31	Boli Bolingoli-Mbombo		01/07/95	M	16	(2)	
13	Sébastien Bruzzese		01/03/89	G	5		
19	Cristian Ceballos	ESP	03/12/92	M	22	(7)	5
16	Cristian Cuevas	CHI	02/04/95	D	17	(3)	
3	Djené Dakonam	TOG	31/12/91	D	24	(2)	
6	Steven De Petter		22/11/85	M	33	(2)	3
5	Alexis De Sart		12/11/96	M	5	(6)	
20	Damien Dussaut	FRA	08/11/94	D	12	(4)	
28	William Dutoît	FRA	18/09/88	G	14		
14	Pieter Gerkens		17/02/95	M	28	(10)	14
22	Wolke Janssens		11/01/95	A	8	(15)	2
23	Sascha Kotysch	GER	02/10/88	M	26	(1)	
77	Kevin Koubemba	CGO	23/03/93	D	4	(4)	1
2	Brandon Mechele		28/01/93	D	18		2
25	Yuji Ono	JPN	22/12/92	M	4	(2)	
8	Stef Peeters		09/02/92	M	32	(5)	5
21	Lucas Pirard		10/03/95	G	22		
9	Nick Proschwitz	GER	28/11/86	A	10	(8)	1
4	Jorge Pulido	ESP	08/04/91	D	12	(1)	2
26	Rúben Fernandes	POR	06/05/86	D	37	(1)	3
27	Iebe Swers		27/12/96	M	8	(5)	
29	Salimo Sylla	FRA	25/01/94	D	7		
7	Fabien Tchenkoua	CMR	01/10/92	M	3	(11)	
24	Pierrick Valdivia	FRA	18/04/88	M	10	(3)	
28	Igor Vetokele	ANG	23/03/92	A	15	(2)	8

R. Standard de Liège

1898 • Maurice Dufrasne (27,670) • standard.be

Major honours

Belgian League (10) 1958, 1961, 1963, 1969, 1970, 1971, 1982, 1983, 2008, 2009;
Belgian Cup (7) 1954, 1966, 1967, 1981, 1993, 2011, 2016

Coach: Yannick Ferrera;
(06/09/16) Aleksandar Janković (SRB);
(17/04/17) (José Jeunechamps)

Date		Opponent		Score	Scorers
2016					
31/07	a	Westerlo	D	2-2	*Santini, Legear*
06/08	h	Sint-Truiden	W	2-0	*og (Pulido), Edmilson Junior (p)*
14/08	a	Zulte Waregem	L	0-1	
19/08	h	Charleroi	D	0-0	
28/08	a	Club Brugge	D	2-2	*Touré, Edmilson Junior*
11/09	h	Genk	W	2-0	*Belfodil, Orlando Sá*
18/09	a	Lokeren	W	1-0	*Raman*
25/09	h	Eupen	W	3-0	*Raman, Edmilson Junior, Belfodil*
02/10	h	Anderlecht	L	0-1	
15/10	a	Kortrijk	D	3-3	*Orlando Sá 2, Trebel*
23/10	h	Waasland-Beveren	W	5-0	*Raman 2, Orlando Sá 2, Emond (p)*
27/10	a	Gent	L	0-1	
30/10	a	Oostende	L	1-3	*Orlando Sá*
06/11	h	Mouscron	W	2-1	*Belfodil, Edmilson Junior*
20/11	a	Mechelen	L	1-2	*Orlando Sá*
27/11	h	Zulte Waregem	W	4-1	*Scholz, Belfodil, Emond, Edmilson Junior*
04/12	a	Charleroi	W	3-1	*Orlando Sá 2, Belfodil (match abandoned after 68 mins; result stood)*
11/12	h	Westerlo	W	3-1	*Orlando Sá (p), Laifis, Mbenza*
18/12	a	Genk	D	2-2	*Orlando Sá, Belfodil*
21/12	h	Lokeren	D	1-1	*Goreux*
27/12	a	Sint-Truiden	D	2-2	*Trebel, Belfodil (p)*
2017					
22/01	h	Club Brugge	L	0-3	
26/01	a	Eupen	D	2-2	*Belfodil 2*
29/01	a	Anderlecht	D	0-0	
04/02	h	Kortrijk	L	0-3	
12/02	a	Waasland-Beveren	W	1-0	*Orlando Sá*
19/02	h	Gent	D	1-1	*Orlando Sá*
26/02	h	Mechelen	D	2-2	*Kosanović, Orlando Sá*
04/03	a	Mouscron	L	0-1	
12/03	h	Oostende	D	2-2	*Belfodil 2 (1p)*
02/04	a	Lierse	L	0-1	
08/04	h	Sint-Truiden	D	2-2	*Belfodil, Marin*
14/04	a	Saint-Gilloise	D	2-2	*Orlando Sá, Belfodil*
22/04	a	Mechelen	L	0-1	
25/04	h	Waasland-Beveren	L	0-2	
28/04	h	Saint-Gilloise	W	3-1	*Orlando Sá, Luyindama, Belfodil*
06/05	a	Sint-Truiden	L	0-1	
12/05	h	Mechelen	W	2-0	*Luchkevych, Andrade*
16/05	a	Waasland-Beveren	W	3-1	*Emond, R Mmaee A Nwambeben, Edmilson Junior*
19/05	h	Lierse	W	2-0	*Orlando Sá, Marin*

No	Name	Nat	DoB	Pos	Aps	(s)	Gls
27	Darwin Andrade	COL	11/02/91	D	16		1
36	Dino Arslanagic		24/04/93	D	1		
12	Beni Badibanga		19/02/96	A		(2)	
52	Ibrahima Bah		01/01/99	A		(1)	
99	Ishak Belfodil	ALG	12/01/92	A	32		14
16	Arnaud Bodart		11/03/98	G	2		
15	Merveille Bokadi	COD	21/05/92	M	2		
11	Jonathan Bolingi	COD	30/06/94	A	2	(4)	
38	Alexandro Cavagnera		01/12/98	M		(1)	
44	Ibrahima Cissé		28/02/94	M	16	(6)	
5	Danilo	BRA	28/02/96	M	2	(4)	
40	Jérôme Deom		19/04/99	M	5	(4)	
10	Jean-Luc Dompé	FRA	12/08/95	M	4	(3)	
7	Mathieu Dossevi	TOG	12/02/88	M	20	(3)	
5	Elderson Echiéjilé	NGA	20/01/88	D	6		
22	Edmilson Junior		19/08/94	M	26	(5)	6
9	Renaud Emond		05/12/91	A	5	(9)	3
21	Eyong Enoh	CMR	23/03/86	M	20		
32	Collins Fai	CMR	13/08/92	D	18		
24	Corentin Fiore		24/03/95	D	15	(2)	
1	Jean-François Gillet		31/05/79	G	28		
2	Réginal Goreux	HAI	31/12/87	D	20	(3)	1
28	Guillaume Hubert		11/01/94	G	10		
33	Miloš Kosanović	SRB	28/05/90	D	15	(2)	1
34	Konstantinos Laifis	CYP	19/05/93	D	28	(2)	1
30	Jonathan Legear		13/04/87	M	4	(10)	1
77	Valeriy Luchkevych	UKR	11/01/96	M	6	(4)	1
26	Christian Luyindama	COD	08/01/94	M	6		1
18	Răzvan Marin	ROU	23/05/96	M	10	(8)	2
14	Isaac Mbenza		08/03/96	A	2	(19)	1
15	Farouk Miya	UGA	26/11/97	M		(1)	
25	Filip Mladenović	SRB	15/08/91	D	5		
17	Ryan Mmaee A Nwambeben	MAR	01/04/97	A	6	(1)	1
20	Samy Mmaee A Nwambeben		08/09/96	D		(1)	
10	Dieumerci Ndongala		14/06/91	A	3	(2)	
70	Orlando Sá	POR	26/05/88	A	24	(4)	17
8	Benito Raman		07/11/94	M	20	(5)	4
18	Ivan Santini	CRO	21/05/89	A	1		1
13	Alexander Scholz	DEN	24/10/92	D	33		1
11	Benjamin Tetteh	GHA	10/07/97	A	1		
60	Birama Touré	MLI	06/06/92	M	1	(2)	1
23	Adrien Trebel	FRA	03/03/91	M	20		2
42	Wallyson Mallmann	BRA	16/02/94	M		(2)	
31	William	BRA	07/02/85	D	5	(1)	

Waasland-Beveren

2010 • Freethiel (8,190) • waasland-beveren.be

Coach: Stijn Vreven; (28/10/16) (Bart Wilmssen); (07/11/16) Cedomir Janevski (MKD)

Date		Opponent		Score	Scorers
2016					
30/07	a	Charleroi	L	0-1	
06/08	h	Zulte Waregem	L	0-2	
13/08	a	Genk	D	2-2	*Seck, Buatu*
20/08	h	Mechelen	D	2-2	*Schrijvers, Seck*
27/08	a	Oostende	L	1-2	*Jans*
09/09	h	Club Brugge	W	1-0	*Schrijvers*
17/09	a	Sint-Truiden	L	1-4	*Gano*
24/09	h	Lokeren	D	1-1	*Schrijvers (p)*
01/10	a	Westerlo	L	0-1	
15/10	h	Eupen	W	4-2	*Marquet, Schrijvers, Demir, Schwartz*
23/10	a	Standard	L	0-5	
27/10	h	Mouscron	D	0-0	
30/10	h	Anderlecht	W	2-1	*Gano, Cools*
06/11	a	Gent	L	0-2	
19/11	h	Kortrijk	D	1-1	*Schrijvers (p)*
26/11	h	Charleroi	L	0-1	
03/12	a	Zulte Waregem	D	1-1	*Gano*
17/12	a	Mechelen	L	0-2	
20/12	h	Sint-Truiden	W	3-1	*Gano, Buatu, Cerigioni*
26/12	a	Lokeren	D	0-0	
2017					
21/01	h	Oostende	L	0-1	
25/01	a	Club Brugge	L	1-2	*Gano*
28/01	h	Westerlo	D	0-0	
04/02	a	Eupen	W	2-0	*Myny 2*
07/02	h	Genk	D	0-0	
12/02	h	Standard	L	0-1	
18/02	a	Mouscron	W	2-1	*Camacho (p), Langil*
25/02	a	Kortrijk	W	2-1	*Cerigioni 2*
04/03	h	Gent	L	2-3	*Myny 2*
12/03	a	Anderlecht	L	0-3	
01/04	a	Sint-Truiden	L	0-3	
08/04	h	Saint-Gilloise	L	1-4	*Gano*
15/04	h	Mechelen	L	1-2	*Cools*
22/04	a	Lierse	W	3-2	*Seck, Boljević, Gano*
25/04	a	Standard	W	2-0	*Moren, Gano*
29/04	h	Sint-Truiden	L	0-1	
06/05	a	Mechelen	W	3-1	*Gano 2, Cools*
13/05	h	Lierse	W	3-2	*Camacho (p), Cools, Langil*
16/05	h	Standard	L	1-3	*Gano*
19/05	a	Saint-Gilloise	W	3-1	*Ampomah 2, Borry*

No	Name	Nat	DoB	Pos	Aps	(s)	Gls
22	Opoku Ampomah	GHA	02/01/96	M	2	(16)	2
7	Aleksandar Boljević	MNE	12/12/95	M	19	(11)	1
25	Kjetil Borry		16/08/94	D	1		1
5	Jonathan Buatu	ANG	27/09/93	D	25	(3)	2
69	Rudy Camacho	FRA	05/03/91	D	35		2
23	Maximiliano Caufriez		16/02/97	D	5		
11	Alessandro Cerigioni		30/09/92	A	16	(11)	3
17	Ibrahima Conté	GUI	03/04/91	M	5		
24	Jens Cools		16/10/90	M	27	(9)	4
3	Niels De Schutter		08/08/88	D	12	(5)	
2	Erdin Demir	SWE	27/03/90	D	31	(1)	1
20	Aaron Dhondt		19/12/95	A	4	(7)	
9	Zino Gano		13/10/93	A	35	(1)	11
18	Merveille Goblet		20/11/94	G	18		
21	Laurent Jans	LUX	05/08/92	D	37		1
26	László Köteles	HUN	01/09/84	G	22		
10	Steven Langil	FRA	04/03/88	M	9	(5)	2
8	François Marquet		17/04/95	M	17	(6)	1
12	Julian Michel	FRA	19/02/92	M	20	(4)	
4	Valtteri Moren	FIN	15/06/91	D	13	(7)	1
32	Olivier Myny		10/11/94	M	20	(6)	4
16	Cherif Ndiaye	SEN	23/01/96	A		(4)	
27	Maxim Nys		28/10/96	D	3	(2)	
10	Siebe Schrijvers		18/07/96	A	19		5
19	Ronnie Schwartz	DEN	29/08/89	A	2	(10)	1
15	Ibrahima Seck	SEN	10/08/89	M	34		3
30	Gilles Van Remoortere		08/11/96	M		(1)	
28	Floriano Vanzo		22/04/94	M	9	(4)	

KVC Westerlo

1933 • Het Kuipje (8,035) • kvcwesterlo.be

Major honours

Belgian Cup (1) 2001

Coach: Bob Peeters; (13/09/16) Jacky Mathijssen

Date		Opponent		Score	Scorers
2016					
31/07	h	Standard	D	2-2	*Acolatse, Ganvoula*
07/08	a	Lokeren	L	0-3	
13/08	h	Eupen	L	1-2	*Manias*
21/08	a	Gent	L	2-4	*Daems, Acolatse*
27/08	h	Mechelen	L	1-2	*Ganvoula*
10/09	a	Kortrijk	L	1-4	*Schuermans*
17/09	h	Mouscron	L	1-3	*Manias*
25/09	a	Anderlecht	W	2-1	*Heylen, Rommens*
01/10	h	Waasland-Beveren	W	1-0	*Annys*
15/10	a	Sint-Truiden	D	2-2	*Acolatse, Ganvoula*
22/10	h	Charleroi	D	0-0	
26/10	a	Club Brugge	L	0-4	
29/10	a	Genk	L	1-2	*Molenberghs*
05/11	h	Zulte Waregem	L	1-2	*Annys*
19/11	a	Oostende	L	0-5	
26/11	a	Eupen	D	3-3	*Ganvoula, Buyens, De Ceulaer*
03/12	h	Gent	D	0-0	
11/12	a	Standard	L	1-3	*Hyland*
17/12	h	Lokeren	L	1-3	*Acolatse*
20/12	a	Mouscron	D	0-0	
26/12	h	Kortrijk	W	4-1	*Ganvoula 2, Rommens, Daems*
2017					
22/01	a	Mechelen	W	2-1	*Rommens, Hyland*
25/01	h	Anderlecht	L	2-4	*Strandberg, Ganvoula*
28/01	a	Waasland-Beveren	D	0-0	
05/02	h	Sint-Truiden	W	1-0	*Acolatse*
11/02	a	Charleroi	L	1-2	*Acolatse*
17/02	h	Club Brugge	L	1-2	*Ganvoula*
25/02	h	Oostende	L	0-4	
04/03	a	Zulte Waregem	D	2-2	*De Ceulaer, Ganvoula*
12/03	h	Genk	L	0-4	

No	Name	Nat	DoB	Pos	Aps	(s)	Gls
9	Elton Acolatse	NED	25/07/95	M	23	(5)	6
8	Maxime Annys		24/07/86	M	13	(3)	2
2	Mitch Apau	NED	27/04/90	D	19	(4)	
29	Yoni Buyens		10/03/88	M	13	(8)	1
19	Daniel Christensen	DEN	19/09/88	D	15	(3)	
3	Filip Daems		31/10/78	D	28	(1)	2
10	Benjamin De Ceulaer		19/12/83	A	11	(1)	2
35	Silvère Ganvoula	CGO	22/06/96	A	25	(1)	9
6	Robin Henkens		12/09/88	M	13	(9)	
24	Michaël Heylen		03/01/94	D	24		1
18	Daan Heymans		15/06/99	M		(1)	
11	Khaleem Hyland	TRI	05/06/89	M	27	(1)	2
7	Eric Lanini	ITA	25/02/94	A		(4)	
33	Michalis Manias	GRE	20/02/90	A	5	(9)	2
44	Hervé Matthys		19/01/96	D	4	(2)	
73	Nemanja Miletić	SRB	16/01/91	D	20		
23	Jarno Molenberghs		11/12/89	M	9	(6)	1
16	Jordan Mustoe	ENG	28/01/91	D	14		
7	Marko Nikolic	SWE	17/09/97	M		(1)	
28	Nicolas Rommens		17/12/94	M	21	(5)	3
22	Gilles Ruyssen		18/06/94	D	4	(6)	
17	Kenneth Schuermans		25/05/91	D	10	(5)	1
97	Carlos Strandberg	SWE	14/04/96	A	2	(6)	1
1	Kristof Van Hout		09/02/87	G	2		
30	Koen Van Langendonck		09/06/89	G	28		

SV Zulte Waregem

2001 • Regenboogstadion (12,250) • essevee.be

Major honours

Belgian Cup (2) 2006, 2017

Coach: Francky Dury

Date		Opponent		Score	Scorers
2016					
30/07	h	Eupen	W	3-0	*Leye (p), Derijck, Lepoint*
06/08	a	Waasland-Beveren	W	2-0	*Lepoint, Kaya*
14/08	h	Standard	W	1-0	*Derijck*
20/08	h	Oostende	D	1-1	*Leye*
28/08	a	Genk	L	0-1	
10/09	a	Mouscron	W	5-1	*Leye 2, og (Vagner), Cordaro, Naessens*
17/09	h	Kortrijk	W	2-1	*Kaya, og (Kaminski)*
24/09	a	Mechelen	W	3-2	*Lerager 2, Coopman*
01/10	h	Charleroi	D	1-1	*Derijck*
16/10	a	Gent	L	0-3	
22/10	h	Lokeren	W	2-0	*Cordaro, Lerager*
26/10	a	Sint-Truiden	W	2-0	*Lerager, De Fauw*
29/10	h	Club Brugge	D	0-0	
05/11	a	Westerlo	W	2-1	*Derijck (p), De Fauw*
20/11	h	Anderlecht	W	3-2	*Cordaro, Derijck (p), Leye*
27/11	a	Standard	L	1-4	*Oularé*
03/12	h	Waasland-Beveren	D	1-1	*Leye*
09/12	a	Lokeren	D	1-1	*Hamalainen*
17/12	a	Oostende	D	1-1	*Lerager*
21/12	h	Genk	W	1-0	*Meïté*
26/12	h	Mechelen	D	0-0	
2017					
21/01	a	Kortrijk	W	3-2	*Leye, De Fauw, Derijck (p)*
24/01	h	Mouscron	W	1-0	*Leye*
27/01	a	Charleroi	L	1-2	*Gueye*
05/02	h	Gent	D	1-1	*Dalsgaard*
12/02	a	Anderlecht	L	2-4	*Leye 2 (1p)*
18/02	h	Sint-Truiden	W	4-1	*Lerager, Gueye, Leye, Kaya*
24/02	a	Club Brugge	L	0-5	
04/03	h	Westerlo	D	2-2	*Cordaro, Coopman*
12/03	a	Eupen	W	3-1	*Leye 2, Mühren*
31/03	h	Anderlecht	L	1-2	*Dalsgaard*
07/04	a	Oostende	D	1-1	*Dalsgaard*
17/04	h	Club Brugge	D	2-2	*Leye (p), Dalsgaard*
22/04	a	Charleroi	L	0-2	
25/04	h	Gent	L	0-2	
01/05	a	Club Brugge	L	1-2	*Derijck*
07/05	a	Anderlecht	L	0-2	
13/05	h	Oostende	W	3-1	*Kaya, Hamalainen, Leye*
18/05	a	Gent	L	2-5	*Leye, Dalsgaard*
21/05	h	Charleroi	D	2-2	*Dalsgaard, Mühren*

No	Name	Nat	DoB	Pos	Aps	(s)	Gls
30	Jakob Ankersen	DEN	22/09/90	M		(1)	
7	Aliko Bala	NGA	27/02/97	M		(6)	
3	Marvin Baudry	CGO	26/01/90	D	35	(2)	
1	Sammy Bossut		11/08/85	G	18		
25	Louis Bostyn		04/10/93	G	3		
33	Sébastien Brebels		05/05/95	M	1		
43	Sander Coopman		12/03/95	M	16	(15)	2
29	Alessandro Cordaro		02/05/86	M	25	(1)	4
14	Henrik Dalsgaard	DEN	27/07/89	D	14	(2)	6
2	Davy De Fauw		08/07/81	D	27		3
6	Timothy Derijck		25/05/87	D	30		7
19	Babacar Gueye	SEN	31/12/94	A	3	(9)	2
31	Brian Hamalainen	DEN	29/05/89	D	35		2
10	Onur Kaya		20/04/86	M	33	(7)	4
23	Christophe Lepoint		24/10/84	M	27	(9)	2
8	Lukas Lerager	DEN	12/07/93	M	38	(1)	6
9	Mbaye Leye	SEN	01/12/82	A	40		16
15	Kingsley Madu	NGA	12/12/95	D	3	(9)	
4	Luca Marrone	ITA	28/03/90	M	18	(7)	
17	Soualiho Meïté	FRA	17/03/94	M	39	(1)	1
21	Robert Mühren	NED	18/05/89	A	4	(8)	2
11	Jens Naessens		01/04/91	A	1	(10)	1
16	Obbi Oularé		08/01/96	A		(10)	1
5	Yoan Severin	FRA	24/01/97	D	4		
22	Kenny Steppe		14/11/88	G	19		
5	Bryan Verboom		30/01/92	D	2	(3)	
7	Igor Vetokele	ANG	23/03/92	A	5	(9)	

BELGIUM

Mid-table play-offs 2016/17

Play-off 2A final table

		Home						Away					Total					
	Pld	W	D	L	F	A	W	D	L	F	A	W	D	L	F	A	Pts
1	K. Sint-Truidense VV	10	4	0	1	13	2	3	1	1	10	5	7	1	2	23	7	22
2	KV Mechelen	10	4	0	1	5	3	1	1	3	2	13	5	1	4	7	16	16
3	Waasland-Beveren	10	1	0	4	6	12	4	0	1	11	7	5	0	5	17	19	15
4	R. Standard de Liège	10	3	1	1	9	5	1	1	3	5	6	4	2	4	14	11	14
5	R. Union Saint-Gilloise	10	1	1	3	8	12	2	0	3	7	7	3	1	6	15	19	10
6	K. Lierse SK	10	2	1	2	6	7	1	0	4	6	9	3	1	6	12	16	10

Play-off 2B final table

		Home						Away					Total					
	Pld	W	D	L	F	A	W	D	L	F	A	W	D	L	F	A	Pts
1	KRC Genk	10	5	0	0	18	2	3	2	0	8	2	8	2	0	26	4	26
2	KSC Lokeren OV	10	2	3	0	9	5	1	3	1	12	15	3	6	1	21	20	15
3	KAS Eupen	10	2	3	0	11	8	1	1	3	9	12	3	4	3	20	20	13
4	KV Kortrijk	10	1	2	2	9	14	2	1	2	6	8	3	3	4	15	22	12
5	R. Excel Mouscron	10	1	1	3	3	7	1	1	3	8	15	2	2	6	11	22	8
6	KSV Roeselare	10	1	0	4	10	14	1	1	3	7	8	2	1	7	17	22	7

UEFA Europa League qualification play-offs

FIRST ROUND

(27/05/17)
Genk 3-0 Sint-Truiden

SECOND ROUND

(31/05/17)
Oostende 3-1 Genk

Top goalscorers

Łukasz Teodorczyk — Henry Onyekuru

22	Łukasz Teodorczyk (Anderlecht) Henry Onyekuru (Eupen)
17	Orlando Sá (Standard)
16	Jelle Vossen (Club Brugge) Idriss Saadi (Kortrijk) Mbaye Leye (Zulte Waregem)
14	José Izquierdo (Club Brugge) Pieter Gerkens (Sint-Truiden) Ishak Belfodil (Standard)
13	Youri Tielemans (Anderlecht) Mbwana Samatta (Genk)

Additional clubs

K. Lierse SK

1906 • Herman Vanderpoortenstadion (14,538) • lierse.com

Major honours
Belgian League (4) 1932, 1942, 1960, 1997; Belgian Cup (2) 1969, 1999

Coach: Eric Van Meir

2017

02/04	h Standard	W	1-0	*Benson*
09/04	a Mechelen	L	0-1	
15/04	a Sint-Truiden	L	1-2	*Tahiri*
22/04	h Waasland-Beveren	L	2-3	*Benson, Tahiri (p)*
25/04	a Saint-Gilloise	W	3-1	*Frans, Benson, El-Gabbas*
29/04	h Mechelen	D	0-0	
06/05	h Saint-Gilloise	W	2-1	*Vinck, og (Mpati)*
13/05	a Waasland-Beveren	L	2-3	*og (Gano), De Belder*
16/05	h Sint-Truiden	L	1-3	*Benson*
19/05	a Standard	L	0-2	

No	Name	Nat	DoB	Pos	Aps	(s)	Gls
20	Charles Ankomah	GHA	10/04/96	M	2	(2)	
11	Manuel Benson		28/03/97	M	9		4
21	Sabir Bougrine	FRA	10/07/96	M	9	(1)	
47	Othman Boussaid		07/03/00	A	1	(2)	
3	Ibrahim Brik		11/01/97	D	1	(2)	
13	Ludovic Buyssens		13/03/86	D	4	(1)	
9	Dylan De Belder		03/04/92	A	7		1
24	Boubacar Diarra	MLI	18/04/94	M	8		
77	Mohamed El-Gabbas	EGY	01/01/88	A	5	(4)	1
4	Frédéric Frans		03/01/89	D	9		1
30	Nathan Goris		30/03/90	G	1		
22	Aurélien Joachim	LUX	10/08/86	A	5		
12	Faysel Kasmi		31/10/95	M	8	(1)	
27	Charles Kwateng		27/05/97	A		(4)	
41	Mehdi Lehaire		22/01/00	A		(1)	
19	Kyriakos Mazoulouxis	GRE	01/05/97	D	4		
16	Joeri Poelmans		08/09/95	D	3	(3)	
10	Anas Tahiri		05/05/95	M	4	(2)	2
31	Mike Vanhamel		16/11/89	G	9		
2	Jonas Vinck		25/06/95	D	8		1
17	Koen Weuts		18/09/90	D	6	(3)	
14	Issahaku Yakubu	GHA	17/06/94	D	7	(1)	

KSV Roeselare

1999 • Schiervelde (9,461) • ksvroeselare.be

Coach: Arnauld Mercier (FRA)

2017

01/04	a Eupen	D	2-2	*Kehli, Lecomte*
08/04	h Genk	L	0-1	
15/04	h Mouscron	L	3-5	*og (Gulan), Cornet, Lépicier*
22/04	a Lokeren	L	1-2	*Brouwers*
25/04	h Kortrijk	L	2-3	*Van Eenoo 2*
29/04	a Mouscron	L	0-1	
06/05	a Kortrijk	W	3-0	*Kehli, Godwin, Brouwers*
13/05	h Lokeren	L	2-3	*Van Acker, Cornet (p)*
17/05	a Genk	L	1-3	*Cornet*
20/05	h Eupen	W	3-2	*Godwin, Brouwers, Zolotić*

No	Name	Nat	DoB	Pos	Aps	(s)	Gls
1	Wouter Biebauw		21/05/84	G	5		
26	Lilian Bochet	FRA	03/04/91	M	2	(3)	
7	Davy Brouwers		03/02/98	A	6	(1)	3
39	Jo Coppens		21/12/90	G	5		
24	Mathieu Cornet		08/08/90	A	4	(4)	3
13	Carlo Damman		18/03/93	D	5	(1)	
30	Saviour Godwin	NGA	22/08/96	M	7	(1)	2
17	Grégory Grisez		17/08/89	D	8		
4	Marin Jakoliš	CRO	26/12/96	A	1	(1)	
10	Sami Kehli	FRA	27/01/91	M	7		2
3	Kevin Kis		26/09/90	D	3	(1)	
27	François Kompany		28/09/89	D	1		
3	Dylan Lambrecht		13/11/92	M		(1)	
9	Raphaël Lecomte		22/05/88	M	7		1
18	Maël Lépicier	CGO	14/01/86	M	10		1
2	Martijn Monteyne		12/11/84	D	4		
19	EmileSamijn		28/04/97	A	3	(2)	
12	Ebrahima Ibou Sawaneh	GAM	07/09/86	A	2	(4)	
6	Baptiste Schmisser	FRA	26/02/86	D	7		
8	Mickaël Seoudi	FRA	28/01/86	M	3		
8	Florent Stevance	FRA	08/10/88	A		(3)	
25	Sun Weizhe	CHN	01/01/97	M		(5)	
6	Thibaut Van Acker		21/11/91	M	6	(2)	1
30	Lukas Van Eenoo		06/02/91	M	5	(1)	2
14	Nermin Zolotić	BIH	07/07/93	D	9		1

R. Union Saint-Gilloise

1897 • King Baudouin (50,122) • rusg.be

Major honours
Belgian League (11) 1904, 1905, 1906, 1907, 1909, 1910, 1913, 1923, 1933, 1934, 1935; Belgian Cup (2) 1913, 1914

Coach: Marc Grosjean

2017

01/04	h Mechelen	W	3-0	*Mombongo-Dues, Vendiepenbeeck,Rajsel (p)*
08/04	a Waasland-Beveren	W	4-1	*Martens, Morren, Aoulad, Rajsel*
14/04	h Standard	D	2-2	*Aguemon, Perdichizzi*
22/04	a Sint-Truiden	W	1-0	*Aoulad*
25/04	h Lierse	L	1-3	*Martens*
28/04	a Standard	L	1-3	*Rajsel*
06/05	a Lierse	L	1-2	*Aoulad*
13/05	h Sint-Truiden	L	1-4	*Perdichizzi*
16/05	a Mechelen	L	0-1	
19/05	h Waasland-Beveren	L	1-3	*Augusto da Silva*

No	Name	Nat	DoB	Pos	Aps	(s)	Gls
20	Yannick Aguemon	FRA	11/02/92	M	10		1
91	Mohammmed Aoulad		29/08/91	A	4	(6)	3
10	Augusto da Silva	BRA	17/11/83	M	9		1
6	Pierre-Baptiste Baherlé	FRA	07/07/91	M	4	(3)	
11	Geoffrey Cabeke		05/11/88	D	8		
9	Cédric Fauré	FRA	14/02/79	A		(1)	
96	Matthias Fixelles		11/08/96	M	3	(2)	
21	Gertjan Martens		20/09/88	D	8		2
23	Jordan Massengo	CGO	31/01/90	M	10		
24	Freddy Mombongo-Dues	COD	30/08/85	A	5	(1)	1
16	Charles Morren		28/02/92	M	4	(1)	1
12	Tracy Mpati		21/03/92	D	10		
5	Grégoire Neels		02/08/82	D	1	(4)	
6	Quentin Ngakoutou	CTA	10/05/94	A		(1)	
31	Georgios Kaminiaris		20/10/88	D	2	(2)	
93	Jonathan Okita		05/10/95	M	2	(4)	
2	Pietro Perdichizzi		16/12/92	D	6	(2)	2
32	Nicolas Rajsel	SVN	31/05/93	M	8		3
19	Anthony Sadin		24/01/89	G	3	(1)	
8	Yassine Salah	MAR	27/03/88	M		(2)	
26	Adrien Saussez		25/08/91	G	7		
13	Vincent Vandiepenbeeck	FRA	14/12/84	D	6		1

Promoted club

R. Antwerp FC

1880 • Bosuilstadion (12,975) • royalantwerpfc.be

Major honours
Belgian League (4) 1929, 1931, 1944, 1957; Belgian Cup (2) 1955, 1992

Coach: Frederik Vanderbiest; (15/10/16) David Gevaert; (17/11/16) Wim De Decker

Second level final tables 2016/17

Opening phase

		Pld	W	D	L	F	A	Pts
1	KSV Roeselare	14	9	3	2	24	15	30
2	K. Lierse SK	14	8	4	2	26	14	28
3	R. Antwerp FC	14	5	5	4	19	15	20
4	R. Union Saint-Gilloise	14	5	3	6	22	22	18
5	AFC Tubize	14	5	2	7	23	29	17
6	Oud-Heverlee Leuven	14	3	6	5	18	21	15
7	Lommel United	14	3	4	7	20	27	13
8	Cercle Brugge KSV	14	3	3	8	18	27	12

Closing phase

		Pld	W	D	L	F	A	Pts
1	R. Antwerp FC	14	8	5	1	21	11	29
2	K. Lierse SK	14	7	6	1	25	11	27
3	Cercle Brugge KSV	14	6	3	5	14	13	21
4	KSV Roeselare	14	5	5	4	18	17	20
5	AFC Tubize	14	5	2	7	19	24	17
6	R. Union Saint-Gilloise	14	4	5	5	11	12	17
7	Oud-Heverlee Leuven	14	4	3	7	15	21	15
8	Lommel United	14	0	5	9	11	25	5

NB The winners of the Opening and Closing phases play off for promotion.

Promotion play-offs

(05/03/17 & 11/03/17)
Antwerp 3-1 Roeselare
Roeselare 1-2 Antwerp
(Antwerp 5-2)

Final aggregate table

		Pld	W	D	L	F	A	Pts
1	K. Lierse SK	28	15	10	3	51	25	55
2	KSV Roeselare	28	14	8	6	42	32	50
3	R. Antwerp FC	28	13	10	5	40	26	49
4	R. Union Saint-Gilloise	28	9	8	11	33	34	35
5	AFC Tubize	28	10	4	14	42	53	34
6	Cercle Brugge KSV	28	9	6	13	32	40	33
7	Oud-Heverlee Leuven	28	7	9	12	33	42	30
8	Lommel United	28	3	9	16	31	52	18

NB The three best-placed teams on aggregate (over the Opening and Closing phases combined), excluding the promotion play-off winner, enter play-offs for UEFA Europa League qualification with nine top-division clubs.

DOMESTIC CUP

Coupe de Belgique/Beker van België 2016/17

SIXTH ROUND

(20/09/16)
Club Brugge 3-1 Lommel
Dessel Sport 3-3 Mouscron *(aet; 7-8 on pens)*

(21/09/16)
Aalst 0-4 Genk
Anderlecht 1-0 Leuven
Antwerp 0-2 Oostende
Cappellen 1-2 Zulte Waregem
Charleroi 5-0 Bocholt
Geel 2-1 Standard
Harelbeke 1-6 Sint-Truiden
Hasselt 2-3 KV Mechelen
Kortrijk 2-0 Sprimont Comblain
Lierse 1-2 Gent
Lokeren 3-2 Cercle Brugge
Roeselare 2-3 Eupen
Waasland-Beveren 2-0 Oosterzonen
Westerlo 0-1 Tubize

SEVENTH ROUND

(29/11/16)
Eupen 3-2 Club Brugge
Sint-Truiden 2-2 KV Mechelen *(aet; 4-3 on pens)*

(30/11/16)
Geel 1-2 Zulte Waregem *(aet)*
Gent 1-0 Lokeren
Kortrijk 1-0 Mouscron
Tubize 3-4 Oostende *(aet)*
Waasland-Beveren 1-3 Genk

(01/12/16)
Charleroi 2-2 Anderlecht *(aet; 5-3 on pens)*

QUARTER-FINALS

(13/12/16)
Eupen 4-0 Kortrijk *(Diallo 9, Luis García 57p, Sylla 70p, Onyekuru 90)*

(14/12/16)
Charleroi 1-3 Genk *(Willems 83; Karelis 69, 94, 116) (aet)*

Oostende 1-0 Gent *(Cyriac 65)*

Zulte Waregem 2-0 Sint-Truiden *(Leye 22, Madu 89)*

SEMI-FINALS

(17/01/17 & 31/01/17)
Oostende 1-1 Genk *(Vandendriessche 21; Malinovskiy 55)*
Genk 0-1 Oostende *(Musona 8)*
(Oostende 2-1)

(18/01/17 & 01/02/17)
Zulte Waregem 1-0 Eupen *(Coopman 86)*
Eupen 0-2 Zulte Waregem *(Hamalainen 77, Marrone 89)*
(Zulte Waregem 3-0)

FINAL

(18/03/17)
King Baudouin, Brussels
SV ZULTE WAREGEM 3 *(Derijck 25, Coopman 64, Gueye 111)*
KV OOSTENDE 3 *(Dimata 19, 54, Musona 116p)*
(aet; 4-2 on pens)
Referee: *Delferière*
ZULTE WAREGEM: *Bossut, Dalsgaard, Derijck, Baudry, Hamalainen, Lerager, Meïté, Cordaro (Coopman 57), Lepoint (Gueye 57), Kaya (Mühren 83), Leye*
OOSTENDE: *Dutoît, Capon, Rozehnal, Godeau, Marušić, Jonckheere (Fernando Canesin 71), Siani, Vandendriessche, Berrier (El Ghanassy 87), Musona, Dimata (Akpala 97)*

Zulte Waregem overcame Oostende on penalties after a thrilling 3-3 draw in the Belgian Cup final

BOSNIA & HERZEGOVINA

Nogometni / Fudbalski savez Bosne i Hercegovine (NFSBiH)

Address	Ulica Ferhadija 30 BA-71000 Saarajevo
Tel	+387 33 276 660
Fax	+387 33 444 332
E-mail	info@nsbih.ba
Website	nfsbih.ba

President	Elvedin Begić
General secretary	Jasmin Baković
Media officer	Slavica Pecikoza
Year of formation	1992
National stadium	Bilino Polje, Zenica (13,000)

PREMIJER LIGA CLUBS

 1 **NK Čelik Zenica**

 2 **FK Krupa**

 3 **NK Metalleghe-BSI**

 4 **FK Mladost Doboj Kakanj**

 5 **FK Olimpic Sarajevo**

 6 **FK Radnik Bijeljina**

 7 **FK Sarajevo**

 8 **FK Sloboda Tuzla**

 9 **NK Široki Brijeg**

 10 **NK Vitez**

 11 **HŠK Zrinjski**

 12 **FK Željezničar**

PROMOTED CLUBS

 13 **NK GOŠK Gabela**

 14 **FK Borac Banja Luka**

KEY

- UEFA Champions League
- UEFA Europa League
- Promoted
- Relegated

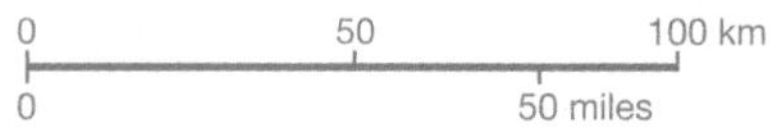

Zrinjski go back-to-back

A pulsating finish to the 2016/17 Premijer Liga title race resulted in victory for defending champions HŠK Zrinjski, the team from Mostar needing – and getting – wins in each of their last three fixtures to finish a point ahead of FK Željezničar, the club they consequently joined at the head of the competition's roll of honour with five titles.

Široki Brijeg failed to reach the championship pool in the new two-stage, 12-team top flight but they made amends by winning the cup, albeit only on penalties after an attritional two-legged final with FK Sarajevo, who finished third in the league.

Mostar club claim record-equalling fifth title

Željezničar and Sarajevo pipped at the post

Edin Džeko scores 50th international goal

Domestic league

Zrinjski's quest for a third Premijer Liga title in four years looked destined to reach a satisfactory conclusion when they built up a formidable lead during the autumn. Under the command once more of Vinko Marinović, their 2015/16 title-winning coach, they recovered from an early loss at Sarajevo to go undefeated through their next 14 matches, winning nine of them. Everything was going pretty much to plan until round 17 and a home fixture with Željezničar.

Zrinjski had not lost at home in the league since April 2013 – a run of 55 matches – but that sequence screeched to a halt as they were thrashed 4-0 by the visitors from the capital, who took the lead just before half-time and added three further goals in the second half with Zrinjski down to ten men. It was a huge turning point in the season because it not only allowed Željezničar and an improving Sarajevo to relaunch their title ambitions but also, a few weeks later, led to the dismissal of Marinović.

Ivica Barbarić, his replacement, did not last long, resigning after the shame of another home defeat – this one to lowly Premijer Liga first-timers Metalleghe-BSI, who would be relegated alongside Olimpic Sarajevo – and handing over the reigns to Mostar native and former Marseille midfielder Blaž Slišković, who thus returned for his third spell in charge. Things did not greatly improve, and after another defeat against Slavko Petrović's Željezničar, 2-1 away, the champions found themselves four points in arrears of their conquerors – and one behind Sarajevo – with just three games to go.

A miraculous turnaround was needed, and that is what transpired, Zrinjski beating Sarejevo 3-2 and then, a week later, scoring a disputed last-minute penalty at Radnik while Sarajevo were beating Željezničar 1-0 – also with a contentious spot kick – to suddenly find themselves back on top of the table with one fixture remaining. It was a second chance they gleefully seized, beating Sloboda 3-0 with two goals from Nemanja Bilbija and one from his strike partner Jasmin Mešanović. Both Zrinjski scorers ended the season in double figures, albeit some way behind Željezničar's Croatian hitman Ivan Lendrić, who topped the golden boot charts with 19 goals.

Domestic cup

The only two-legged domestic cup final in Europe was unable to produce a winner over its 180 minutes, with Široki Brijeg winning the first leg 1-0 in Sarajevo but then losing by the same scoreline at home. FK Sarajevo were bidding, like Zrinjski in the league, to match Željezničar's record tally of five wins in the competition, but two missed spot kicks in the ensuing penalty shoot-out, as opposed to just one by their hosts, resulted in Široki Brijeg's third cup triumph.

Europe

European competition for Premijer Liga clubs in 2016/17 was a washout, with all four teams failing to negotiate their opening ties, each one of them drawing the first leg before losing the second.

National team

Bosnia & Herzegovina were the second seeds in their 2018 FIFA World Cup qualifying group, behind Belgium, but the team's chances of taking the runners-up spot were severely compromised by a late equaliser conceded in a 1-1 draw away to Greece and a goalless stalemate at home to the same opposition that ended their 100% record in Zenica following earlier wins against Estonia, Cyprus and Gibraltar. The Albanian city of Elbasan was the stage for Edin Džeko's 50th international goal, a penalty in a 2-1 friendly win, and the Bosnia & Herzegovina captain, who received a bizarre red card in Piraeus, would prove that at 31 his predatory powers remained intact by topping the 2016/17 Serie A capocannonieri listings with 29 goals for Roma.

DOMESTIC SEASON AT A GLANCE

Premijer Liga 2016/17 final table

			Home					Away					Total					
		Pld	W	D	L	F	A	W	D	L	F	A	W	D	L	F	A	Pts
1	**HŠK Zrinjski**	**32**	**12**	**2**	**2**	**32**	**13**	**6**	**8**	**2**	**22**	**12**	**18**	**10**	**4**	**54**	**25**	**64**
2	FK Željezničar	32	11	3	2	24	13	7	6	3	17	9	18	9	5	41	22	63
3	FK Sarajevo	32	10	5	1	25	10	6	6	4	16	12	16	11	5	41	22	59
4	FK Krupa	32	7	7	2	19	8	5	3	8	21	26	12	10	10	40	34	46
5	FK Sloboda Tuzla	32	9	4	3	25	14	2	6	8	14	28	11	10	11	39	42	43
6	FK Radnik Bijeljina	32	5	5	6	18	19	5	5	6	19	20	10	10	12	37	39	40
7	NK Široki Brijeg	32	7	7	2	28	15	2	3	11	6	20	9	10	13	34	35	37
8	FK Mladost Doboj Kakanj	32	7	6	3	26	16	1	7	8	16	29	8	13	11	42	45	37
9	NK Vitez	32	2	7	7	8	16	6	4	6	12	14	8	11	13	20	30	35
10	NK Čelik Zenica	32	5	5	6	17	16	3	6	7	11	23	8	11	13	28	39	35
11	NK Metalleghe-BSI	32	2	8	6	7	15	5	3	8	18	19	7	11	14	25	34	32
12	FK Olimpic Sarajevo	32	4	3	9	17	28	1	5	10	11	34	5	8	19	28	62	23

NB League splits into top and bottom halves after 22 games, after which the clubs play exclusively against teams in their group.

European qualification 2017/18

Champion: HŠK Zrinjski (second qualifying round)

Cup winner: NK Široki Brijeg (first qualifying round)

FK Željezničar (first qualifying round)
FK Sarajevo (first qualifying round)

Top scorer Ivan Lendrić (Željezničar), 19 goals
Relegated clubs FK Olimpic Sarajevo, NK Metalleghe-BSI
Promoted clubs NK GOŠK Gabela, FK Borac Banja Luka
Cup final FK Sarajevo 0-1; 1-0 NK Široki Brijeg *(agg 1-1; 2-4 on pens)*

Player of the season

Miroslav Stevanović
(FK Željezničar)

While midfielder Tomislav Tomić was arguably the leading light in Zrinjski's title-winning team, the most consistently impressive performer in the Premijer Liga as a whole was Stevanović, his efforts for Željezničar earning him the official player of the year award as well as a recall to the Bosnia & Herzegovina national team. Having returned to his homeland in January 2016 after unsuccessful spells in Spain, Hungary and Greece, the 26-year-old right-sided midfielder became a favourite of the Željo fans and started all but one league match in 2016/17.

Newcomer of the season

Marko Mihojević
(FK Sarajevo)

An international for Bosnia & Herzegovina at every youth level from Under-17 to U21, Mihojević found the Premijer Liga stage to his liking as he became a first-team regular at the age of 20 in Mehmed Janjoš's FK Sarajevo side, helping the club to a third-place finish in the league as well as a runners-up spot in the domestic cup, where only a penalty shoot-out defeat denied him a first major honour. Strong and tenacious, the young centre-back appears to have a bright future, with a move abroad to one of Europe's major leagues far from out of the question.

Team of the season
(4-4-2)

Coach: Starčević *(Krupa)*

NATIONAL TEAM

International tournament appearances
FIFA World Cup (1) 2014

Top five all-time caps
Emir Spahić (93); **Edin Džeko** (85); Zvjezdan Misimović (83); **Vedad Ibišević** (79); **Miralem Pjanić** (74)

Top five all-time goals
Edin Džeko (50); **Vedad Ibišević** (28); Zvjezdan Misimović (25); Elvir Bolić (22); Sergej Barbarez (17)

Results 2016/17

06/09/16	Estonia (WCQ)	H	Zenica	W	5-0	*Spahić (7, 90+2), Džeko (23p), Medunjanin (71), Ibišević (83)*
07/10/16	Belgium (WCQ)	A	Brussels	L	0-4	
10/10/16	Cyprus (WCQ)	H	Zenica	W	2-0	*Džeko (70, 81)*
13/11/16	Greece (WCQ)	A	Piraeus	D	1-1	*Karnezis (32og)*
25/03/17	Gibraltar (WCQ)	H	Zenica	W	5-0	*Ibišević (4, 43), Vršajević (52), Višća (56), Bičakčić (90+4)*
28/03/17	Albania	A	Elbasan	W	2-1	*Džeko (7p), Lulić (42)*
09/06/17	Greece (WCQ)	H	Zenica	D	0-0	

Appearances 2016/17

Coach: Mehmed Baždarević	28/09/60		EST	BEL	CYP	GRE	GIB	Alb	GRE	Caps	Goals
Asmir Begović	20/06/87	Chelsea (ENG)	G	G	G	G	G	G	G	57	-
Ognjen Vranješ	24/10/89	Tom (RUS) /AEK Athens (GRE)	D62		D	D		D40	D	30	-
Emir Spahić	18/08/80	Hamburg (GER)	D	D	D	D70				93	6
Ervin Zukanović	11/02/87	Atalanta (ITA)	D	D		D	D	D	D	21	-
Sead Kolašinac	20/06/93	Schalke (GER)	D	D	D64	D	D46			18	-
Edin Višća	17/02/90	İstanbul Başakşehir (TUR)	M75	s73	M78		M		M	30	3
Miralem Pjanić	02/04/90	Juventus (ITA)	M	M81	M	M	M57		M	74	11
Haris Medunjanin	08/03/85	M. Tel-Aviv (ISR)	M	M	M					54	8
Senad Lulić	18/01/86	Lazio (ITA)	M	M	M	M		M72	M21	54	3
Vedad Ibišević	06/08/84	Hertha (GER)	A	A64	s81	A84	A		A	79	28
Edin Džeko	17/03/86	Roma (ITA)	A81	A	A	A 78*		A59	A	85	50
Ermin Bičakčić	24/01/90	Hoffenheim (GER)	s62	D		s87	D		D	19	3
Danijel Milićević	05/01/86	Gent (BEL)	s75							1	-
Milan Djurić	22/05/90	Cesena (ITA)	s81	s64	A81	s84				14	7
Mato Jajalo	25/05/88	Palermo (ITA)		M73		M		M72	M	4	-
Gojko Cimirot	19/12/92	PAOK (GRE)		s81			M	s46		5	-
Toni Šunjić	15/12/88	Stuttgart (GER) /Palermo (ITA)			D	s70		D	D69	27	-
Izet Hajrović	04/08/91	Bremen (GER)			s64	M87				22	3
Tino-Sven Sušić	13/02/92	Genk (BEL)			s78					9	-
Edin Cocalić	05/12/87	Mechelen (BEL)					D			8	-
Avdija Vršajević	06/03/86	Osmanlıspor (TUR)					M75			17	2
Armin Hodžić	17/11/94	Dinamo Zagreb (CRO)					M			4	-
Daniel Pavlović	22/04/88	Sampdoria (ITA)					s46	s78		2	-
Mario Vrančić	23/05/89	Darmstadt (GER)					s57	s72		6	-
Riad Bajić	06/05/94	Konyaspor (TUR)					s75	s59		2	-
Dario Dumić	30/01/92	NEC (NED)						D	s69	2	-
Sanjin Prcić	20/11/93	Rennes (FRA)						M46		6	-
Rade Krunić	07/10/93	Empoli (ITA)						M		2	-
Kenan Kodro	19/08/93	Osasuna (ESP)						A78	s21 /77	2	-
Miroslav Stevanović	29/07/90	Željezničar						s40		13	1
Haris Duljević	16/11/93	Sarajevo						s72		6	-
Muhamed Bešić	10/09/92	Everton (ENG)							s77	27	-

EUROPE

HŠK Zrinjski

UEFA CHAMPIONS LEAGUE

Second qualifying round - Legia Warszawa (POL)

H 1-1 *Katanec (57)*

Kozić, Peko (Žeravica 81), Tomić, Barić, Stojkić, Todorović (Filipović 69), Mešanović, Petrak, Jakovljević, Katanec, Bilbija (Arežina 87). Coach: Vinko Marinović (BIH)

A 0-2

Kozić, Peko, Tomić, Barić, Stojkić, Todorović (Filipović 78), Mešanović, Petrak, Jakovljević, Katanec (Radeljić 45+4), Bilbija (Žeravica 75). Coach: Vinko Marinović (BIH)

FK Sloboda Tuzla

UEFA EUROPA LEAGUE

First qualifying round - Beitar Jerusalem FC (ISR)

H 0-0

Pirić, Kostić, Džidić, Karić, Efendić, Zeba, Ordagić, Stjepanović, Govedarica (Veselinović 80), Mehidić (Grahovac 85), Merzić. Coach: Husref Musemić (BIH)

A 0-1

Pirić, Kostić, Džidić, Karić, Efendić, Zeba, Ordagić, Stjepanović (Krpić 81), Mehidić (Govedarica 73), Veselinović, Merzić. Coach: Husref Musemić (BIH)

Red card: Džidić 87

FK Radnik Bijeljina

UEFA EUROPA LEAGUE

First qualifying round - PFC Beroe Stara Zagora (BUL)

A 0-0

Lučić, Čelebić (Ostojić 59), Memišević, Martinović, D Beširović, Vasić, Stokić (Peco 79), Zeljković, Kojić, Obradović, Djurić (Janković 65). Coach: Slavko Petrović (SRB)

H 0-2

Lučić, Čelebić, Memišević, Martinović, D Beširović (Janković 76), Vasić, Stokić (Peco 76), Zeljković, Kojić, Obradović, Djurić. Coach: Slavko Petrović (SRB)

NK Široki Brijeg

UEFA EUROPA LEAGUE

First qualifying round - Birkirkara FC (MLT)

H 1-1 *Baraban (45)*

Soldo, Pandža, Ćorić, Krstanović, Ivanković (Plazonić 70), Baraban (Menalo 85), Čorluka (Wagner 46), Sesar, Brekalo, Crnov, Marković. Coach: Slaven Musa (BIH)

A 0-2

Soldo, Pandža (Barišić 46), Ćorić, Plazonić (Ivanković 46), Krstanović, Baraban (Menalo 78), Wagner, Sesar, Brekalo, Crnov, Marković. Coach: Slaven Musa (BIH)

DOMESTIC LEAGUE CLUB-BY-CLUB

NK Čelik Zenica

1945 • Bilino Polje (13,000) • nkcelik.ba

Coach: Kemal Alispahić;
(19/09/16) Ivo Ištuk;
(02/11/16) Nedim Jusufbegović;
(19/03/17) Boris Pavić (CRO)

2016					
23/07	h	Metalleghe-BSI	L	1-3	*Brković*
31/07	a	Radnik	W	3-2	*Pezer, M Popović, Brković*
06/08	h	Sarajevo	D	1-1	*Smriko*
10/08	a	Olimpic	L	0-3	
13/08	h	Široki Brijeg	L	0-1	
20/08	a	Sloboda	L	0-2	
27/08	h	Željezničar	D	1-1	*M Popović*
10/09	a	Zrinjski	L	0-4	
17/09	h	Vitez	L	0-1	
24/09	h	Krupa	L	1-2	*Marković*
30/09	a	Mladost	L	0-1	
15/10	a	Metalleghe-BSI	D	1-1	*Smriko*
23/10	h	Radnik	L	0-1	
30/10	a	Sarajevo	L	0-4	
06/11	h	Olimpic	W	3-0	*Brković, Smriko, Pliska*
20/11	a	Široki Brijeg	L	0-1	
26/11	h	Sloboda	L	0-2	
03/12	a	Željezničar	L	0-1	
2017					
25/02	h	Zrinjski	D	1-1	*Dilaver (p)*
04/03	a	Vitez	D	0-0	
11/03	h	Krupa	D	0-0	
18/03	a	Mladost	D	2-2	*Pezer, Stokić*
01/04	a	Mladost	D	3-3	*Karić (p), Dilaver, Brković*
05/04	h	Vitez	W	1-0	*Dilaver*
09/04	a	Metalleghe-BSI	D	0-0	
14/04	a	Olimpic	W	1-0	*Brković*
22/04	h	Široki Brijeg	W	1-0	*Regoje*
29/04	h	Mladost	W	1-0	*Smriko*
06/05	a	Vitez	W	2-0	*Jusić, Haurdić*
13/05	h	Metalleghe-BSI	D	0-0	
15/05	h	Olimpic	W	4-1	*Regoje, Dilaver 3*
27/05	a	Široki Brijeg	D	1-1	*Karić*

No	Name	Nat	DoB	Pos	Aps	(s)	Gls
9	Hanan Adilović		08/08/96	A		(1)	
27	Tarik Adilović		31/07/97	M		(4)	
11	Danijal Brković	CRO	03/06/91	A	24	(3)	5
1	Semir Bukvić		21/05/91	G	6		
16	Dženan Bureković		29/05/95	D	9		
9	Haris Dilaver		06/02/90	M	14		6
1	Ratko Dujković		16/03/83	G	3		
26	Anes Duraković		22/12/96	D	5	(4)	
5	Armin Duvnjak		15/02/90	M	1	(3)	
18	Ahmed Džafić		28/02/93	A		(1)	
8	Dino Hasanović		21/01/96	M	11	(2)	
24	Anes Haurdić		01/03/90	M	11	(7)	1
20	Haris Hećo		20/05/87	M	26	(2)	
28	Ante Hrkać	CRO	11/03/92	M	14	(4)	
15	Dženis Huseinspahić		30/09/91	A	3	(3)	
15	Senad Husić		12/04/90	D	2	(3)	
6	Vernes Islamagić		27/07/94	D	2	(2)	
24	Dino Jurković		02/07/95	D	2	(2)	
5	Emir Jusić		13/06/86	D	24		1
7	Mahir Karić		14/12/86	M	12	(2)	2
21	Bojan Marković		12/11/85	D	15		1
25	Eldin Mašić		02/01/87	D		(4)	
17	Ammar Nadžak		28/07/93	M		(1)	
19	Semir Pezer		18/08/92	A	26	(1)	2
16	Almir Pliska		12/08/87	A	8	(4)	1
14	Goran Popović		11/01/88	D	14	(2)	
7	Marin Popović		18/08/94	M	16	(1)	2
4	Bojan Regoje		02/12/81	D	13		2
89	Branislav Ružić	SRB	02/04/89	G	23		
17	Enis Sadiković		21/03/90	A	12		
18	Duško Sakan		03/03/89	M	3	(4)	
10	Fenan Salčinović		26/06/87	M	18	(2)	
18	Jasmin Smriko		20/01/91	A	8	(15)	4
14	Joco Stokić		07/04/87	A	1	(4)	1
24	Aldin Šišić		29/09/90	M	11	(1)	
3	Safet Šivšić		16/02/93	D	14	(1)	
15	Faris Zeljković		09/08/93	D	1	(3)	

FK Krupa

1983 • Gradski (2,000) • no website

Coach: Slobodan Starčević

Date		Opponent		Score	Scorers
2016					
24/07	h	Mladost	D	1-1	*Koljić*
30/07	a	Metalleghe-BSI	W	2-0	*Koljić, Perić*
06/08	h	Radnik	D	2-2	*Koljić 2*
10/08	a	Sarajevo	L	2-3	*Koljić, Marušić*
13/08	h	Olimpic	W	2-0	*Koljić 2*
21/08	a	Široki Brijeg	L	1-3	*Jašarević*
27/08	h	Sloboda	W	3-0	*Mirković (p), Redžić, Perić*
10/09	a	Željezničar	L	1-2	*Milutinović (p)*
17/09	h	Zrinjski	D	0-0	
24/09	a	Čelik	W	2-1	*Kajkut, Ljubenović*
01/10	h	Vitez	W	2-0	*Kajkut 2 (2p)*
15/10	a	Mladost	W	1-0	*Kajkut*
22/10	h	Metalleghe-BSI	W	1-0	*Milutinović*
29/10	a	Radnik	L	1-3	*Kajkut*
05/11	h	Sarajevo	L	0-1	
20/11	a	Olimpic	W	3-0	*Milutinović (p), Koljić (p), Ljubenović*
26/11	h	Široki Brijeg	W	1-0	*Dujaković*
03/12	a	Sloboda	L	1-2	*Mirković*
2017					
26/02	h	Željezničar	L	0-1	
04/03	a	Zrinjski	L	1-3	*Koljić*
11/03	h	Čelik	D	0-0	
18/03	a	Vitez	D	0-0	
01/04	a	Zrinjski	L	0-4	
05/04	h	Radnik	D	1-1	*Ljubenović*
08/04	a	Željezničar	L	0-1	
15/04	h	Sloboda	W	3-0	*Vukotić, Dujaković, Šamara*
23/04	a	Sarajevo	D	1-1	*Koljić*
29/04	h	Zrinjski	D	1-1	*Koljić*
07/05	a	Radnik	D	2-2	*Barić, Milutinović (p)*
14/05	h	Željezničar	D	1-1	*Barić*
20/05	a	Sloboda	W	3-1	*Koljić 2, Redžić*
28/05	h	Sarajevo	W	1-0	*Dujaković*

No	Name	Nat	DoB	Pos	Aps	(s)	Gls
26	Radoslav Aleksić	SRB	06/03/86	D	29		
77	Stefan Barić	SRB	17/02/91	M	5	(8)	2
18	Obren Cvijanović		30/08/94	M	2	(4)	
17	Denis Čomor		03/01/90	D	21	(1)	
5	Nemanja Damjanović		27/09/86	D	2		
10	Nikola Dujaković		27/06/96	M	25	(3)	3
20	Dejan Gavrić		10/06/97	M		(3)	
22	Adel Halilović		17/03/96	D	1		
1	Mladen Ilić		07/11/96	G	10		
6	Irfan Jašarević		24/08/95	D	27		1
12	Saša Kajkut		07/07/84	A	4	(4)	5
24	Nemanja Kartal		17/07/94	D	2		
7	Elvir Koljić		08/07/95	A	24	(2)	13
16	Jovan Kutić		19/05/94	G	20		
8	Miljan Ljubenović		18/09/95	M	26	(2)	3
3	Stojan Maksimović		06/01/96	D	3		
21	Srdjan Malinović		14/03/91	M		(1)	
52	Zoran Marušić	SRB	29/11/93	D	1	(9)	1
22	Dušan Mijić	SRB	22/06/93	D	16	(1)	
27	Slobodan Milanović	SRB	27/07/92	A	15	(2)	
13	Zoran Milutinović		01/03/88	M	30		4
88	Uroš Mirković	SRB	08/08/90	M	19	(12)	2
35	Milorad Nikolić	SRB	06/02/84	G	2		
9	Ozren Perić		04/04/87	A	3	(17)	2
4	Ajdin Redžić		25/01/97	M	26	(3)	2
14	Enis Sadiković		21/03/93	M		(10)	
20	Stefan Savić	SRB	19/11/92	M		(6)	
97	Zoran Šamara		25/04/97	M		(2)	1
2	Nemanja Vidović		25/09/93	D		(2)	
15	Aleksandar Vukotić	SRB	22/07/95	D	29		1
11	Dragan Vuković		22/06/88	D	10	(1)	

NK Metalleghe-BSI

2009 • Pirota, Travnik (4,000); Gradski, Banja Luka (9,730) • nkmetalleghe-bsi.com

Coach: Nermin Bašić; (14/11/16) Mato Neretljak (CRO)

Date		Opponent		Score	Scorers
2016					
23/07	a	Čelik	W	3-1	*Dujaković 2 (1p), Popović*
30/07	h	Krupa	L	0-2	
07/08	a	Mladost	L	2-3	*Radulović 2*
10/08	a	Vitez	L	0-1	
14/08	h	Radnik	L	1-2	*Smajić (p)*
22/08	a	Sarajevo	W	2-1	*og (Ahmetović), Kovač*
27/08	h	Olimpic	D	1-1	*Popović*
11/09	a	Široki Brijeg	L	1-3	*Rašić*
18/09	h	Sloboda	D	0-0	
25/09	a	Željezničar	L	1-2	*Smiljanič*
01/10	h	Zrinjski	L	0-4	
15/10	h	Čelik	D	1-1	*Kovač*
22/10	a	Krupa	L	0-1	
29/10	h	Mladost	W	2-0	*Pezo, Smajić (p)*
05/11	h	Vitez	L	0-1	
19/11	a	Radnik	L	0-1	
27/11	h	Sarajevo	L	0-2	
03/12	a	Olimpic	W	2-0	*Dujaković, Smajić*
2017					
25/02	h	Široki Brijeg	W	1-0	*Vidović*
04/03	a	Sloboda	L	1-2	*Vidović*
11/03	h	Željezničar	L	0-1	
18/03	a	Zrinjski	W	2-0	*Zeba, Jovanović*
01/04	a	Vitez	D	1-1	*Vidović*
05/04	a	Olimpic	L	0-1	
09/04	h	Čelik	D	0-0	
15/04	a	Široki Brijeg	W	1-0	*Aletić*
22/04	h	Mladost	D	0-0	
30/04	h	Vitez	D	0-0	
06/05	h	Olimpic	D	1-1	*Vidović (p)*
13/05	a	Čelik	D	0-0	
21/05	h	Široki Brijeg	D	0-0	
27/05	a	Mladost	D	2-2	*Rašić, Vidović*

No	Name	Nat	DoB	Pos	Aps	(s)	Gls
8	Elvedin Aletić		01/03/95	M	9	(1)	1
15	Nemanja Asanović	MNE	23/09/90	A	2	(4)	
21	Dženis Beganović		23/03/96	A	12	(1)	
3	Vukašin Benović		31/07/87	D	23		
8	Elvis Bibić		04/03/92	M	9	(4)	
18	Dino Deak		12/08/91	D	13		
18	Siniša Dujaković		22/11/91	M	13	(1)	3
7	Dženan Durak		04/02/91	M	11	(12)	
1	Nevres Fejzić		04/11/90	G	31		
15	Armin Helvida		20/02/86	D	15		
25	Demir Jakupović		16/02/96	A	6	(13)	
6	Stanoje Jovanović	SRB	21/08/93	M	11	(2)	1
31	Josip Jozić	CRO	10/01/95	M	4	(3)	
13	Kenan Karadjuz		01/11/90	D	7	(3)	
9	Mirza Kovač		23/05/92	M	18	(8)	2
41	Željko Kuzmić	SRB	02/11/84	G	1		
31	Toni Pezo	CRO	14/02/87	M	9	(1)	1
10	Rijad Pljevljak		31/05/91	M	1	(4)	
77	Nebojša Popović	CRO	04/04/92	A	12	(2)	2
24	Aleksandar Radulović		09/02/87	M	14	(3)	2
22	Danijel Rašić	CRO	05/10/88	D	27	(3)	2
21	Duško Sakan		03/03/89	D	9	(3)	
24	Ante Sarić	CRO	17/06/92	D	12		
23	Marko Savinović	SRB	13/01/91	D	2		
16	Vernes Selimović		08/05/83	A	10	(5)	
11	Sulejman Smajić		13/08/84	M	21	(1)	3
23	Stefan Smiljanič	SVN	10/07/91	M	1	(6)	1
29	Dragoslav Stakić		20/09/85	D	17	(4)	
5	Ivan Tankuljić		04/02/99	M		(5)	
86	Srdjan Vidaković	CRO	13/10/86	M	4	(1)	
16	Antonio Vidović		25/07/89	A	10	(2)	5
14	Emir Zeba		10/06/89	M	18	(1)	1

FK Mladost Doboj Kakanj

1959 • Gradski (3,000) • no website

Coach: Ibro Rahimić; (27/09/16) Husref Musemić

Date		Opponent		Score	Scorers
2016					
24/07	a	Krupa	D	1-1	*Ramović*
30/07	a	Vitez	D	1-1	*Rizvanović*
07/08	h	Metalleghe-BSI	W	3-2	*Asanović, Brkić 2*
10/08	a	Radnik	D	0-0	
13/08	h	Sarajevo	D	0-0	
20/08	a	Olimpic	W	3-2	*Husić, Brkić, Isaković*
28/08	h	Široki Brijeg	W	3-1	*Husić 2, Brkić*
11/09	a	Sloboda	D	1-1	*Aladin Šišić*
17/09	h	Željezničar	D	0-0	
24/09	a	Zrinjski	L	1-2	*Kuzmanović*
30/09	h	Čelik	W	1-0	*Brkić*
15/10	h	Krupa	L	0-1	
22/10	h	Vitez	L	1-2	*Asanović*
29/10	a	Metalleghe-BSI	L	0-2	
06/11	h	Radnik	D	0-0	
20/11	a	Sarajevo	L	3-4	*Aladin Šišić, Maksimović 2*
26/11	h	Olimpic	W	3-0	*Maksimović, Husić, Laštro*
04/12	a	Široki Brijeg	L	1-2	*Ramović*
2017					
25/02	h	Sloboda	W	3-1	*Kuzmanović, Ramović, Maksimović*
04/03	a	Željezničar	L	0-1	
15/03	h	Zrinjski	L	0-1	
18/03	a	Čelik	D	2-2	*Aladin Šišić, Maksimović*
01/04	h	Čelik	D	3-3	*Kuzmanović, Brkić 2 (1p)*
05/04	a	Široki Brijeg	L	0-4	
08/04	h	Olimpic	D	2-2	*Ramović, Brkić (p)*
15/04	h	Vitez	W	4-1	*Ramović, Husić, Aladin Šišić, Brkić*
22/04	a	Metalleghe-BSI	D	0-0	
29/04	a	Čelik	L	0-1	
06/05	h	Široki Brijeg	W	1-0	*Aganspahić*
13/05	a	Olimpic	D	3-3	*Husić 2, Brkić*
21/05	a	Vitez	L	0-3	
27/05	h	Metalleghe-BSI	D	2-2	*Maksimović, Isaković*

No	Name	Nat	DoB	Pos	Aps	(s)	Gls
9	Almir Aganspahić		12/09/96	A	10	(2)	1
9	Nemanja Asanović	MNE	23/09/90	A	2	(6)	2
6	Darko Bošković	SRB	16/09/87	M	4	(6)	
29	Goran Brkić	SRB	28/04/91	M	29		10
4	Faruk Gačan		08/01/94	D	15	(7)	
2	Marin Galić		21/09/95	D	26	(1)	
88	Adnan Hadžić		15/01/88	G	16		
22	Adnan Hodžić		01/06/90	M	2	(5)	
37	Adnan Hrelja		10/10/93	M	1		
7	Anel Husić		12/12/94	A	16	(10)	7
99	Aladin Isaković		28/07/85	D	27		2
42	Ervin Jusufović		07/05/95	M	5	(1)	
95	Lazar Kalajanović	SRB	25/08/94	M		(1)	
80	Senad Karahmet		23/02/92	D	14		
11	Mićo Kuzmanović		18/03/96	A	22	(6)	3
1	Franko Lalić	CRO	05/02/91	G	5		
5	Neven Laštro		01/10/88	D	19	(2)	1
10	Milivoje Lazić		19/09/92	A	4	(5)	
21	Dejan Maksimović		11/10/95	M	14	(5)	6
16	Omer Musić		11/04/93	D	16	(6)	
77	Sinan Ramović		13/10/92	M	24	(1)	5
20	Mirza Rizvanović		27/09/86	D	14	(5)	1
6	Imad Rondić		16/02/99	M	1	(2)	
8	Pavle Sušić	SRB	15/04/88	M	11	(9)	
22	Adnan Šećerović		01/12/91	M	11		
17	Aladin Šišić		28/09/91	A	17	(5)	4
10	Aldin Šišić		29/09/90	M	15	(2)	
19	Anes Vazda		24/07/97	M	1	(2)	
28	Emil Velić		06/02/95	G	11		

FK Olimpic Sarajevo

1993 • Otoka (3,500) • no website

Major honours
Bosnian-Herzegovinian Cup (1) 2015

Coach: Faik Kolar;
(06/09/16) Dragan Radović;
(02/11/16) Asim Saračević;
(09/11/16) Darko Dražić (CRO);
(27/12/16) Faruk Kulović
(12/03/17) Dragan Radović

Date		Opponent		Score	Scorers
2016					
23/07	a	Sloboda	L	0-3	
30/07	h	Željezničar	L	0-2	
06/08	a	Zrinjski	L	1-4	*Hadžić*
10/08	h	Čelik	W	3-0	*Lelić, Mahović, Kobiljar*
13/08	a	Krupa	L	0-2	
20/08	h	Mladost	L	2-3	*Lelić, Regoje (p)*
27/08	a	Metalleghe-BSI	D	1-1	*Regoje (p)*
11/09	h	Radnik	L	0-3	
18/09	a	Sarajevo	L	0-1	
24/09	a	Vitez	D	0-0	
01/10	h	Široki Brijeg	W	3-1	*Mahović, Osmanović, Plakalo*
15/10	h	Sloboda	D	3-3	*Mašić, Isić, Regoje*
22/10	a	Željezničar	L	2-3	*Lelić, Plakalo*
29/10	h	Zrinjski	L	0-5	
06/11	a	Čelik	L	0-3	
20/11	h	Krupa	L	0-3	
26/11	a	Mladost	L	0-3	
03/12	h	Metalleghe-BSI	L	0-2	
2017					
25/02	a	Radnik	L	0-2	
04/03	h	Sarajevo	L	0-1	
11/03	h	Vitez	D	0-0	
18/03	a	Široki Brijeg	D	0-0	
02/04	a	Široki Brijeg	L	1-5	*Osmanović*
05/04	h	Metalleghe-BSI	W	1-0	*Svraka*
08/04	a	Mladost	D	2-2	*Svraka, Govedarica*
14/04	h	Čelik	L	0-1	
22/04	a	Vitez	W	2-0	*Osmanović 2*
30/04	h	Široki Brijeg	W	2-0	*Čolić, Kojić*
06/05	a	Metalleghe-BSI	D	1-1	*Uzelac*
13/05	h	Mladost	D	3-3	*Svraka 2, Govedarica*
21/05	a	Čelik	L	1-4	*Džugurdić*
27/05	h	Vitez	L	0-1	

No	Name	Nat	DoB	Pos	Aps	(s)	Gls
21	Irfan Ajdinović		01/03/97	M		(2)	
7	Vahidin Alešević		02/07/97	M		(2)	
1	Dejan Bandović		11/06/83	G	26		
20	Alden Bešić		19/12/94	M		(2)	
3	Dino Bevab		13/01/93	D	11		
5	Advan Bjelak		25/02/99	M	2	(1)	
25	Jasmin Bogdanović		10/05/90	D	6	(3)	
17	Benjamin Čolić		23/07/91	D	13		1
15	Amer Drljević		18/05/94	M	8	(2)	
30	Ratko Dujković		16/03/93	G	4		
14	Miloš Džugurdić	SRB	02/12/92	M	2	(3)	1
22	Miljan Govedarica		26/05/94	A	7	(3)	2
11	Emir Hadžić		19/07/84	A	14	(4)	1
8	Tarik Handžić		28/07/96	A	1		
5	Filip Holi	CRO	07/02/93	D	5	(1)	
2	Ermin Imamović		30/04/95	D	7		
23	Tarik Isić		08/10/94	D	9	(2)	1
69	Aleksandar Jovanović	SRB	25/02/92	G	2		
10	Mahir Karić		05/03/92	M	25	(1)	
88	Nenad Kiso		30/04/89	D	3	(2)	
8	Rijad Kobiljar		08/04/96	M	15		1
13	Jovo Kojić		08/04/88	D	12		1
24	Sanjin Lelić		11/01/97	A	15		3
9	Armin Mahović		28/11/91	A	9	(11)	2
23	Eldin Mašić		02/01/87	M	13	(1)	1
5	Alen Mikuličić	CRO	18/01/91	D	6	(1)	
20	Djoko Milović		16/09/92	D	15	(2)	
20	Damir Osmanković	CRO	12/09/93	D	1	(1)	
11	Adnan Osmanović		20/03/97	M	14	(6)	4
11	Mile Pehar		24/01/91	M	19	(3)	
15	Alem Plakalo		01/05/94	A	2	(12)	2
55	Omer Pršeš		07/05/95	M	3	(7)	
21	Marinko Rastoka		10/06/91	D	3	(2)	
6	Bojan Regoje		26/07/81	D	13		3
45	Anel Rikalo		18/04/95	D		(1)	
27	Muamer Svraka		14/02/88	A	12		4
5	Tarik Šahović		29/03/97	D	3		
7	Nedo Turković		23/10/89	A	3	(2)	
33	Stefan Udovičić		20/09/91	D	3	(2)	
5	Dejan Uzelac	SRB	29/11/93	D	3	(1)	1
8	Mario Vrdoljak		21/07/93	D	21	(3)	
4	Dejan Vukomanović		31/10/90	M	7	(4)	
28	Faris Zeljković		09/08/93	D	1	(1)	
33	Amir Zolj		24/11/89	M	10	(1)	
14	Sandi Zulčić		05/11/95	D	4	(4)	

FK Radnik Bijeljina

1945 • Gradski (4,000) • fkradnik.ba

Major honours
Bosnian-Herzegovinian Cup (1) 2016

Coach: Slavko Petrović (SRB)
(25/08/16) Nebojša Milošević (SRB);
(10/05/17) Mladen Žižović

Date		Opponent		Score	Scorers
2016					
24/07	a	Zrinjski	L	1-2	*Obradović*
31/07	h	Čelik	L	2-3	*Obradović, og (Hrkać)*
06/08	a	Krupa	D	2-2	*Kojić, Obradović*
10/08	h	Mladost	D	0-0	
14/08	a	Metalleghe-BSI	W	2-1	*Peco, og (Pezo)*
21/08	a	Vitez	W	4-1	*Obradović, Jakovljević, Peco, Djurić*
27/08	h	Sarajevo	D	0-0	
11/09	a	Olimpic	W	3-0	*Obradović, Janković, Simeunović*
17/09	h	Široki Brijeg	W	2-1	*Janković, Kojić*
24/09	a	Sloboda	W	1-0	*Martinović*
01/10	h	Željezničar	L	1-2	*Obradović*
15/10	h	Zrinjski	D	1-1	*Martinović*
23/10	a	Čelik	W	1-0	*Obradović*
29/10	h	Krupa	W	3-1	*Martinović, Simeunović, Djurić*
06/11	a	Mladost	D	0-0	
19/11	h	Metalleghe-BSI	W	1-0	*Obradović*
26/11	h	Vitez	D	1-1	*Bajić*
04/12	a	Sarajevo	L	0-2	
2017					
25/02	h	Olimpic	W	2-0	*Obradović, Janković*
04/03	a	Široki Brijeg	D	2-2	*Stojanović, Djurić*
11/03	h	Sloboda	W	2-1	*Stojanović, Obradović*
18/03	a	Željezničar	L	0-2	
02/04	a	Sarajevo	D	1-1	*Okić*
05/04	a	Krupa	D	1-1	*Djurić*
08/04	h	Sloboda	L	0-1	
15/04	a	Zrinjski	L	0-2	
23/04	h	Željezničar	L	0-1	
29/04	h	Sarajevo	L	0-3	
07/05	h	Krupa	D	2-2	*Stojanović 2 (1p)*
13/05	a	Sloboda	L	0-2	
20/05	h	Zrinjski	L	1-2	*D Beširović*
28/05	a	Željezničar	L	1-2	*Peco*

No	Name	Nat	DoB	Pos	Aps	(s)	Gls
28	Edin Ademović	SRB	02/10/87	A	1	(8)	
4	Davor Arnautović		03/09/91	M	6	(2)	
21	Delimir Bajić		27/03/84	D	8	(3)	1
11	Abdurahman Beširović		05/06/97	M		(1)	
8	Dino Beširović		31/01/94	M	29		1
3	Nikola Čelebić	MNE	04/07/89	D	2	(1)	
22	Velibor Djurić		05/05/82	M	26	(4)	4
2	Eldin Faćić		03/09/94	M		(5)	
4	Domagoj Franić	CRO	12/04/89	M	7	(1)	
20	Aleksandar Glišić		03/09/92	M		(15)	
27	Samed Hodžić		02/10/99	G	1		
21	Ivan Jakovljević	SRB	26/05/89	D	15		1
6	Dejan Janković	SRB	06/01/86	M	13	(5)	3
10	Aleksandar Kitanović		20/01/95	M		(3)	
13	Jovica Kojić		08/06/88	D	10		2
21	Aleksandar Kosorić		30/01/87	D	14		
11	Željko Krsmanović		11/12/90	D	7	(6)	
1	Mladen Lučić		06/07/85	G	31		
6	Dušan Martinović	SRB	22/12/87	M	16		3
5	Samir Memišević		13/08/93	M	1		
19	Jovan Motika		11/09/98	A	1	(4)	
16	Marko Obradović	MNE	30/06/91	A	31		10
25	Šefko Okić		27/07/88	A	16	(2)	1
18	Stanko Ostojić	SRB	15/01/85	D	25	(1)	
14	Damir Peco		31/07/98	M	12	(2)	3
7	Deni Simeunović	CRO	12/02/92	M	2	(8)	2
19	Nenad Srećković	SRB	11/04/88	M	14	(5)	
7	Filip Stojanović	SRB	19/05/88	M	12		4
26	Besim Šerbečić		01/05/98	D	10	(3)	
9	Aleksandar Vasić		04/01/85	M	14	(8)	
12	Mladen Zeljković	SRB	18/11/87	D	26		
3	Nemanja Zlatković	SRB	21/08/88	D	2	(4)	

FK Sarajevo

1946 • Olimpijski Asim Ferhatović Hase (34,600) • fksarajevo.ba

Major honours
Yugoslav League (2) 1967, 1985; Bosnian-Herzegovinian League (2) 2007, 2015; Bosnian-Herzegovinian Cup (3) 2002, 2005, 2014

Coach: Almir Hurtić;
(29/08/16) Mehmed Janjoš

Date		Opponent		Score	Scorers
2016					
23/07	a	Željezničar	D	1-1	*Ahmetović*
31/07	h	Zrinjski	W	2-0	*Duljević, Ahmetović*
06/08	a	Čelik	D	1-1	*Ćetković*
10/08	h	Krupa	W	3-2	*Radovac, Sarić (p), Kadušić*
13/08	a	Mladost	D	0-0	
22/08	h	Metalleghe-BSI	L	1-2	*Ahmetović*
27/08	a	Radnik	D	0-0	
11/09	a	Vitez	W	1-0	*Ahmetović*
18/09	h	Olimpic	W	1-0	*Balić*
25/09	a	Široki Brijeg	D	2-2	*Novaković, Crnkić*
01/10	h	Sloboda	D	1-1	*Ahmetović*
16/10	h	Željezničar	D	0-0	
22/10	a	Zrinjski	L	0-1	
30/10	h	Čelik	W	4-0	*Hebibović, Crnkić 2, Ahmetović*
05/11	a	Krupa	W	1-0	*Ahmetović*
20/11	h	Mladost	W	4-3	*Crnkić 2, Amer Bekić, Hebibović*
27/11	a	Metalleghe-BSI	W	2-0	*Sarić, Ahmetović*
04/12	h	Radnik	W	2-0	*Ahmetović, Hebibović*
2017					
26/02	h	Vitez	W	1-0	*Hebibović*
04/03	a	Olimpic	W	1-0	*Husejinović*
11/03	h	Široki Brijeg	W	2-0	*Hebibović, Novaković*
18/03	a	Sloboda	L	0-3	
02/04	h	Radnik	D	1-1	*Amer Bekić*
05/04	a	Sloboda	W	2-0	*Hebibović, Sarić*
09/04	h	Zrinjski	D	0-0	
15/04	a	Željezničar	D	0-0	
23/04	h	Krupa	D	1-1	*Ahmetović (p)*
29/04	a	Radnik	W	3-0	*Hodžić, Crnkić 2*
05/05	h	Sloboda	W	1-0	*Crnkić*
13/05	a	Zrinjski	L	2-3	*Crnkić, Sarić*
20/05	h	Željezničar	W	1-0	*Amer Bekić (p)*
28/05	a	Krupa	L	0-1	

No	Name	Nat	DoB	Pos	Aps	(s)	Gls
34	Adi Adilović		20/02/83	G	2		
24	Mersudin Ahmetović		19/03/85	A	29	(1)	10
22	Nemanja Andjušić		17/10/96	M	2	(15)	
14	Saša Balić	MNE	20/01/90	D	14	(1)	1
19	Almir Bekić		01/06/89	D	24	(2)	
8	Amer Bekić		05/08/92	A	7	(15)	3
9	Nermin Crnkić		31/08/92	M	25	(2)	9
20	Marko Ćetković	MNE	10/07/86	M	7	(3)	1
17	Haris Duljević		16/11/93	M	24	(2)	1
9	Nedim Hadžić		19/03/99	A		(1)	
13	Anel Hebibović		07/07/90	M	23	(4)	6
97	Elvedin Herić		02/09/97	M		(3)	
2	Dušan Hodžić		31/10/93	D	24	(3)	1
10	Said Husejinović		13/05/88	M	3	(6)	1
29	Perica Ivetić		28/11/86	D	20	(3)	
3	Advan Kadušić		14/10/97	D	12	(6)	1
5	Adnan Kovačević		09/09/93	D	8	(1)	
21	Sanjin Lelić		11/01/97	M		(5)	
23	Frank Liivak	EST	07/07/96	M		(2)	
16	Marko Mihojević		21/04/96	D	21	(1)	
18	Nihad Mujakić		15/04/98	D		(1)	
6	Saša Novaković	CRO	27/05/91	D	28		2
30	Bojan Pavlović	SRB	08/11/86	G	30		
88	Samir Radovac		25/01/96	M	7	(7)	1
4	Edin Rustemović		06/01/93	M	19	(3)	
8	Elvis Sarić	CRO	21/06/90	M	23	(4)	4

FK Sloboda Tuzla

1919 • Tušanj (8,000) • fksloboda.ba

Coach: Husref Musemić;
(11/09/16) (Amir Spahic);
(11/10/16) Vlado Jagodić

2016

23/07	h	Olimpic	W	3-0	*Krpić 2, Kostić*
31/07	a	Široki Brijeg	D	2-2	*Karić, Krpić*
05/08	h	Vitez	W	1-0	*Veselinović*
10/08	h	Željezničar	W	2-0	*Veselinović, Stjepanović*
13/08	a	Zrinjski	L	0-2	
20/08	h	Čelik	W	2-0	*Subić, Zec*
27/08	a	Krupa	L	0-3	
11/09	h	Mladost	D	1-1	*Krpić*
18/09	a	Metalleghe-BSI	D	0-0	
24/09	h	Radnik	L	0-1	
01/10	a	Sarajevo	D	1-1	*Krpić*
15/10	a	Olimpic	D	3-3	*Krpić 2, Mehmedagić*
22/10	h	Široki Brijeg	W	1-0	*Krpić*
29/10	a	Vitez	D	0-0	
05/11	a	Željezničar	D	1-1	*Krpić*
19/11	h	Zrinjski	D	3-3	*Subić, Mehmedagić, Krpić*
26/11	a	Čelik	W	2-0	*Krpić, Zec*
03/12	h	Krupa	W	2-1	*Subić, Mehmedagić*

2017

25/02	a	Mladost	L	1-3	*Zec*
04/03	h	Metalleghe-BSI	W	2-1	*Zec, Tandir*
11/03	a	Radnik	L	1-2	*Zec*
18/03	h	Sarajevo	w	3-0	*Zec, Tandir, Ziljkić*
01/04	a	Željezničar	L	2-4	*Zec, Subić*
05/04	h	Sarajevo	L	0-2	
08/04	a	Radnik	W	1-0	*Tandir*
15/04	a	Krupa	L	0-3	
22/04	h	Zrinjski	D	0-0	
30/04	h	Željezničar	D	2-2	*Zec 2*
05/05	a	Sarajevo	L	0-1	
13/05	h	Radnik	W	2-0	*Kalezić, Salihović*
20/05	h	Krupa	L	1-3	*Todorović*
28/05	a	Zrinjski	L	0-3	

No	Name	Nat	DoB	Pos	Aps	(s)	Gls
16	Amar Beganović		25/11/99	D		(2)	
12	Adnan Bobić		04/02/87	G	3		
5	Aldin Džidić		30/08/83	M	6	(1)	
8	Samir Efendić		10/05/91	D	24	(1)	
12	Filip Erić		10/10/94	G	4		
6	Ivan Fatić	MNE	21/08/88	D	4	(5)	
22	Miljan Govedarica		26/05/94	M	1	(6)	
14	Vladimir Grahovac		12/01/95	M	14	(13)	
1	Adnan Hadžić		15/01/88	G	6		
25	Ismar Hairlahović		04/03/96	M	8	(2)	
18	Eldar Hasanović		12/01/90	M	4	(2)	
23	Dino Hodžić		06/07/99	M		(1)	
19	Adnan Jahić		28/02/85	M	3		
30	Miloš Kalezić	SRB	09/08/93	M	9	(1)	1
7	Mahir Karić		14/11/86	A	9		1
3	Ivan Kostić	SRB	24/06/89	D	10	(1)	1
9	Sulejman Krpić		01/01/91	A	14	(5)	11
15	Aleksandar Lazevski	MKD	21/01/88	D	18		
23	Damir Mehidić		07/01/92	M	1	(2)	
17	Haris Mehmedagić		29/03/88	D	23		3
28	Samir Merzić		29/06/84	D	8	(5)	
13	Azir Muminović		18/04/97	G	4		
19	Amer Ordagić		05/05/93	M	24	(1)	
12	Kenan Pirić		07/07/94	G	15		
5	Adnan Salihović		18/10/92	D	8	(1)	1
24	Edis Smajić		10/09/99	M	3	(13)	
20	Nemanja Stjepanović	SRB	07/02/84	M	21	(5)	1
11	Aleksandar Subić		27/09/93	D	20	(2)	4
4	Ibrahim Škahić		25/10/93	D	19	(1)	
18	Ismar Tandir		19/08/95	A	9	(2)	3
25	Darko Todorović		05/05/97	D	14	(2)	1
27	Mladen Veselinović		04/01/93	M	14	(7)	2
10	Zajko Zeba		22/05/83	M	8		
26	Asim Zec		23/01/94	A	18	(9)	9
9	Almedin Ziljkić		25/02/96	M	6	(5)	1

NK Široki Brijeg

1948 • Pecara (7,000) • nk-sirokibrijeg.com

Major honours
Bosnian-Herzegovinian League (2) 2004, 2006;
Bosnian-Herzegovinian Cup (3) 2007, 2013, 2017

Coach: Slaven Musa;
(08/07/16) Branko Karačić (CRO);
(13/10/16) (Denis Corić);
(17/01/17) Goran Sablić (CRO)

2016

24/07	h	Vitez	D	1-1	*Krstanović*
31/07	h	Sloboda	D	2-2	*Baraban, Wagner*
06/08	a	Željezničar	L	0-2	
10/08	h	Zrinjski	D	1-1	*Baraban*
13/08	a	Čelik	W	1-0	*Menalo*
21/08	h	Krupa	W	3-1	*Bralić, Baraban, Barić*
28/08	a	Mladost	L	1-3	*Wagner*
11/09	h	Metalleghe-BSI	W	3-1	*Wagner 2, Menalo*
17/09	a	Radnik	L	1-2	*Krstanović*
25/09	h	Sarajevo	D	2-2	*Pandža, Menalo*
01/10	a	Olimpic	L	1-3	*Menalo*
15/10	a	Vitez	W	1-0	*Wagner*
22/10	a	Sloboda	L	0-1	
30/10	h	Željezničar	W	1-0	*Wagner*
05/11	a	Zrinjski	D	0-0	
20/11	h	Čelik	W	1-0	*Wagner*
26/11	a	Krupa	L	0-1	
04/12	h	Mladost	W	2-1	*Menalo, Wagner*

2017

25/02	a	Metalleghe-BSI	L	0-1	
04/03	h	Radnik	D	2-2	*Zlomislić, Čabraja*
11/03	a	Sarajevo	L	0-2	
18/03	h	Olimpic	L	0-0	
02/04	h	Olimpic	W	5-1	*Menalo 2, Zlomislić, Sivrić, og (Kojić)*
05/04	h	Mladost	W	4-0	*Menalo 2, Wagner, Čabraja*
08/04	a	Vitez	D	1-1	*Čabraja*
15/04	h	Metalleghe-BSI	L	0-1	
22/04	a	Čelik	L	0-1	
30/04	a	Olimpic	L	0-2	
06/05	a	Mladost	L	0-1	
12/05	h	Vitez	L	0-1	
21/05	a	Metalleghe-BSI	D	0-0	
27/05	h	Čelik	D	1-1	*og (Sadiković)*

No	Name	Nat	DoB	Pos	Aps	(s)	Gls
11	Ivan Baraban	CRO	22/01/88	M	16	(3)	3
22	Stefan Barić	SRB	17/02/91	D	3	(5)	1
6	Josip Barišić		12/08/83	D	12	(4)	
12	Luka Bilobrk		08/12/85	G	8		
28	Slavko Bralić	CRO	15/12/92	D	22	(1)	1
21	Slavko Brekalo		25/02/90	D	14		
30	Ivan Crnov	CRO	14/08/88	M	8	(3)	
9	Dejan Čabraja		22/08/93	M	7	(3)	3
16	Josip Čorluka		03/03/95	M	16	(3)	
7	Dino Ćorić		30/06/90	D	19	(1)	
10	Jure Ivanković	CRO	15/11/85	M	17	(6)	
27	Luka Juričić		25/11/96	A	1	(4)	
4	Danijel Kožul		01/08/88	M	6	(5)	
9	Ivan Krstanović	CRO	05/01/83	A	24	(1)	2
24	Stipe Lončar		10/11/96	M	13	(10)	
14	Mateo Marić		18/03/98	D	1	(2)	
30	Mario Marina		03/08/89	M	7	(3)	
33	Stipo Marković		03/12/93	D	25	(2)	
17	Luka Menalo		22/07/96	M	19	(9)	9
18	Ivan Milićević		16/07/98	M	5		
32	Toni Nikić		27/03/98	M	4		
5	Boris Pandža		15/12/86	D	17		1
8	Zoran Plazonić	CRO	01/02/89	M	7	(3)	
20	Antonio Repić	CRO	30/03/91	M	4	(8)	
19	Ivan Sesar		23/01/89	M	16	(6)	
22	Matej Sivrić	CRO	31/01/90	M	9	(2)	1
23	Antonio Soldo		12/01/88	G	24		
15	Wagner	BRA	01/01/78	M	18	(6)	9
8	Damir Zlomislić		20/07/91	M	10		2

NK Vitez

1947 • Gradski (2,000) • nkvitez.com

Coach: Boris Pavić (CRO);
(04/10/16) Slaven Musa

2016

24/07	a	Široki Brijeg	D	1-1	*Kapetan*
30/07	h	Mladost	D	1-1	*Varupa*
05/08	a	Sloboda	L	0-1	
10/08	h	Metalleghe-BSI	W	1-0	*Dedić*
14/08	a	Željezničar	W	2-0	*Kapetan, Kokot*
21/08	h	Radnik	L	1-4	*og (Jakovljević)*
27/08	a	Zrinjski	L	1-2	*Barišić*
11/09	h	Sarajevo	L	0-1	
17/09	a	Čelik	W	1-0	*Kokot*
24/09	h	Olimpic	D	0-0	
01/10	a	Krupa	L	0-2	
15/10	h	Široki Brijeg	L	0-1	
22/10	a	Mladost	W	2-1	*Dedić, Mamić*
29/10	h	Sloboda	D	0-0	
05/11	a	Metalleghe-BSI	W	1-0	*Kapetan*
19/11	h	Željezničar	L	0-2	
26/11	a	Radnik	D	1-1	*Dedić*
02/12	h	Zrinjski	L	0-1	

2017

26/02	a	Sarajevo	L	0-1	
04/03	h	Čelik	D	0-0	
11/03	a	Olimpic	D	0-0	
18/03	h	Krupa	D	0-0	
01/04	h	Metalleghe-BSI	D	1-1	*Kapetan*
05/04	a	Čelik	L	0-1	
08/04	h	Široki Brijeg	D	1-1	*Kokot*
15/04	a	Mladost	L	1-4	*Kapetan*
22/04	h	Olimpic	L	0-2	
30/04	a	Metalleghe-BSI	D	0-0	
06/05	h	Čelik	L	0-2	
12/05	a	Široki Brijeg	W	1-0	*Barišić*
21/05	h	Mladost	W	3-0	*og (Rizvanović), Kokot, Livančić*
27/05	a	Olimpic	W	1-0	*Dedić*

No	Name	Nat	DoB	Pos	Aps	(s)	Gls
14	Namir Alispahić		16/04/95	A	4	(8)	
19	Hrvoje Barišić	CRO	03/02/91	D	23	(2)	2
11	Elvis Bibić		04/03/92	M	1	(1)	
10	Anel Dedić		02/05/91	M	22	(3)	4
17	Boban Djerić		20/08/93	A	15	(11)	
6	Marko Franjić		30/05/97	M		(1)	
32	Emir Hodžurda		12/11/90	D	20	(1)	
5	Marko Jevtić	SRB	21/05/82	D	19		
21	Armin Kapetan		11/03/86	M	27	(3)	5
9	Zoran Kokot		09/12/85	A	23	(5)	4
7	Ivan Livaja		01/10/87	D	13	(13)	
15	Toni Livančić		11/12/94	M	18	(3)	1
16	Ivan Mamić		15/09/90	M	15	(10)	1
18	Jakov Milas	CRO	19/01/97	D	1	(2)	
8	Milan Muminović		02/10/83	M	28		
18	Leopold Novak	CRO	03/12/90	A	2	(3)	
12	David Nwolokor	NGA	10/01/96	G	26		
11	Juraj Petrović		02/07/97	M		(2)	
6	Kristijan Ramljak		26/11/97	M		(2)	
4	Damir Rašić	CRO	05/10/88	M	22	(3)	
20	Elvis Sadiković		29/10/83	D	31	(1)	
25	Vernes Selimović		08/05/83	A	10	(4)	
2	Ivan Stanić		30/06/96	D	12	(9)	
1	Ivan Tirić		15/04/93	G	6		
14	Nermin Varupa		18/04/91	M	1	(5)	1
3	Vedran Vrhovac		20/11/98	D	13	(3)	

BOSNIA & HERZEGOVINA

HŠK Zrinjski

1905 • Bijeli Brijeg (15,000) • hskzrinjski.ba

Major honours
Bosnian-Herzegovinian League (5) 2005, 2009, 2014, 2016, 2017; Bosnian-Herzegovinian Cup (1) 2008

Coach: Vinko Marinović; (03/01/17) Ivica Barbarić; (23/03/17) Blaž Slišković

2016

Date		Opponent		Score	Scorers
24/07	h	Radnik	W	2-1	*Jakovljević, Bilbija*
31/07	a	Sarajevo	L	0-2	
06/08	h	Olimpic	W	4-1	*Mešanović 3 (1p), Katanec*
10/08	a	Široki Brijeg	D	1-1	*Peko*
13/08	h	Sloboda	W	2-0	*Tomić, Stojanović*
20/08	a	Željezničar	W	1-0	*Bilbija*
27/08	h	Vitez	W	2-1	*Bilbija, Mešanović*
10/09	h	Čelik	W	4-0	*Todorović 2, Petrak, Tomić*
17/09	a	Krupa	D	0-0	
24/09	h	Mladost	W	2-1	*Mešanović, Filipović*
01/10	a	Metalleghe-BSI	W	4-0	*Jakovljević, Mešanović, Tomić, Todorović*
15/10	a	Radnik	D	1-1	*Bilbija*
22/10	h	Sarajevo	W	1-0	*Jakovljević*
29/10	a	Olimpic	W	5-0	*Mešanović, Stojanović, Bilbija, Todorović 2*
05/11	h	Široki Brijeg	D	0-0	
19/11	a	Sloboda	D	3-3	*Mešanović, Petrak, Bilbija*
26/11	h	Željezničar	L	0-4	
02/12	a	Vitez	W	1-0	*Jović*

2017

Date		Opponent		Score	Scorers
25/02	a	Čelik	D	1-1	*Tomić*
04/03	h	Krupa	W	3-1	*Stojkić, Todorović, Bilbija*
11/03	a	Mladost	W	1-0	*Petrak*
18/03	h	Metalleghe-BSI	L	0-2	
01/04	h	Krupa	W	4-0	*Mešanović, Bilbija, Todorović, Petrak*
05/04	h	Željezničar	D	0-0	
09/04	a	Sarajevo	D	0-0	
15/04	h	Radnik	W	2-0	*Filipović, Petrak*
22/04	a	Sloboda	D	0-0	
29/04	a	Krupa	D	1-1	*Kukoč*
06/05	a	Željezničar	L	1-2	*Filipović*
13/05	h	Sarajevo	W	3-2	*Mešanović, Stojkić, Tomić*
20/05	a	Radnik	W	2-1	*Kajkut 2 (1p)*
28/05	h	Sloboda	W	3-0	*Bilbija 2, Mešanović*

No	Name	Nat	DoB	Pos	Aps	(s)	Gls
19	Miloš Aćimović		06/07/97	A		(1)	
12	Krešimir Bandić		16/09/95	G		(1)	
9	Mario Barić	CRO	15/04/85	D	19	(1)	
99	Nemanja Bilbija		02/11/90	A	31		10
2	Zvonimir Blaić	CRO	02/01/91	D	3		
7	Jasmin Bogdanović		10/05/90	D	1		
15	Benjamin Čolić		23/07/91	D	7		
10	Marijan Ćavar		02/02/98	M		(1)	
55	Miloš Filipović	SRB	06/05/90	M	5	(8)	3
5	Daniel Graovac		08/08/93	D	11		
27	Slobodan Jakovljević	SRB	26/05/89	D	22		3
24	Nermin Jamak		25/08/86	M	7	(4)	
11	Toni Jović	CRO	02/09/92	M	7	(9)	1
10	Saša Kajkut		07/07/84	A	2	(8)	2
32	Matija Katanec	CRO	04/05/90	D	26		1
96	Rijad Kobiljar		08/04/96	M		(4)	
22	Germain Kouadio	CIV	27/12/92	M		(1)	
30	Dalibor Kozić		10/02/88	G	17		
33	Tonći Kukoč	CRO	25/09/90	D	3	(2)	1
14	Luka Lučić	CRO	02/01/95	D	6	(2)	
21	Jasmin Mešanović		21/06/92	A	27	(2)	11
18	Josip Miketek		22/08/97	M		(3)	
77	Momčilo Mrkajić		21/09/90	A	1	(8)	
8	Mate Pehar	CRO	25/02/88	M	2	(13)	
4	Ivan Peko		05/01/90	M	22	(2)	1
25	Oliver Petrak	CRO	06/02/91	M	31		5
22	Kenan Pirić		07/07/94	G	14		
6	Anto Radeljić		31/12/90	D	3	(2)	
24	Matej Sivrić	CRO	31/01/90	M	4	(3)	
20	Danijel Stojanović	CRO	18/08/84	D	3	(4)	2
16	Pero Stojkić		09/12/86	D	25		2
17	Ognjen Todorović		24/03/89	M	21	(3)	7
7	Tomislav Tomić		16/11/90	M	30		5
1	Nikola Vasilj		02/12/95	G	1		
10	Miloš Žeravica	SRB	22/07/88	M	1	(11)	

FK Željezničar

1921 • Grbavica (14,000) • fkzeljeznicar.ba

Major honours
Yugoslav League (1) 1972; Bosnian-Herzegovinian League (5) 2001, 2002, 2010, 2012, 2013; Bosnian-Herzegovinian Cup (5) 2000, 2001, 2003, 2011, 2012

Coach: Miloš Kostič (SVN); (24/08/16) Slavko Petrović (SRB)

2016

Date		Opponent		Score	Scorers
23/07	h	Sarajevo	D	1-1	*Lendrić*
30/07	a	Olimpic	W	2-0	*Lendrić, Boccaccini*
06/08	h	Široki Brijeg	W	2-0	*Lendrić, Nikolić*
10/08	a	Sloboda	L	0-2	
14/08	h	Vitez	L	0-2	
20/08	h	Zrinjski	L	0-1	
27/08	a	Čelik	D	1-1	*Bekrić*
10/09	h	Krupa	W	2-1	*Križman, Marković*
17/09	a	Mladost	D	0-0	
25/09	h	Metalleghe-BSI	W	2-1	*Lendrić, Križman*
01/10	a	Radnik	W	2-1	*Križman, Nikolić*
16/10	a	Sarajevo	D	0-0	
22/10	h	Olimpic	W	3-2	*Lendrić 2, M Stevanović*
30/10	a	Široki Brijeg	L	0-1	
05/11	h	Sloboda	D	1-1	*Lendrić*
19/11	a	Vitez	W	2-0	*Lendrić 2*
26/11	a	Zrinjski	W	4-0	*Lendrić, Bekrić, Križman (p), M Stevanović*
03/12	h	Čelik	W	1-0	*Marković*

2017

Date		Opponent		Score	Scorers
26/02	a	Krupa	W	1-0	*Lendrić*
04/03	h	Mladost	W	1-0	*Lendrić*
11/03	a	Metalleghe-BSI	W	1-0	*Zeba*
18/03	h	Radnik	W	2-0	*Zakarić, Lendrić*
01/04	h	Sloboda	W	4-2	*Lendrić 3, Stanić*
05/04	a	Zrinjski	D	0-0	
08/04	h	Krupa	W	1-0	*Lendrić*
15/04	h	Sarajevo	D	0-0	
23/04	a	Radnik	W	1-0	*Zeba*
30/04	a	Sloboda	D	2-2	*Crnov, Nikolić*
06/05	h	Zrinjski	W	2-1	*Lendrić, Marković*
14/05	a	Krupa	D	1-1	*Bekrić*
20/05	a	Sarajevo	L	0-1	
28/05	h	Radnik	W	2-1	*Lendrić, Zakarić*

No	Name	Nat	DoB	Pos	Aps	(s)	Gls
21	Dženis Beganović		23/05/96	A	4	(5)	
10	Samir Bekrić		20/10/84	M	12	(8)	3
14	Dino Bevab		13/01/93	D	4	(2)	
11	Jovan Blagojević	SRB	15/03/88	M	25	(2)	
4	Matteo Boccaccini	ITA	08/02/93	D	16	(3)	1
15	Jadranko Bogičević		11/03/83	D	18		
7	Ivan Crnov	CRO	01/02/90	M	5	(4)	1
1	Irfan Fejzić		01/07/86	G	3		
17	Mirza Halvadzic	SWE	15/02/96	A		(1)	
32	Dino Hasanović		21/01/96	M	1	(5)	
70	Senad Husić		12/04/90	D	4		
7	Sanel Jahić		10/12/81	D	4	(1)	
19	Semir Kerla		26/09/87	D	10		
13	Vedran Kjosevski		22/05/95	G	29		
5	Aleksandar Kosorić		30/01/87	D	15	(1)	
80	Sandi Križman	CRO	17/08/89	M	10	(1)	4
92	Milivoje Lazić		19/09/92	M	1	(8)	
24	Ivan Lendrić	CRO	08/08/91	A	32		19
8	Darko Marković	MNE	15/05/87	M	22	(1)	3
6	Kerim Memija		06/01/96	D	12		
22	Musa Muhammed	NGA	31/10/96	D	1	(5)	
29	Ajdin Mujagić		03/01/98	A		(2)	
23	Stevo Nikolić		04/12/84	A	6	(14)	3
27	Kemal Osmanković		04/03/97	D	1	(1)	
31	Denis Pozder	GER	11/12/89	A	2	(3)	
25	Uglješa Radinović	SRB	25/08/93	M	13	(9)	
16	Srdjan Stanić		06/07/89	D	13	(3)	1
88	Miroslav Stevanović		29/07/90	M	31		2
2	Siniša Stevanović	SRB	12/01/89	D	25	(1)	
18	Danijel Stojanović		18/08/84	D	7	(1)	
22	Adnan Šećerović		01/12/91	A	4	(4)	
33	Dimitrios Toskas	GRE	13/03/91	M		(1)	
17	Goran Zakarić		07/11/92	M	9	(5)	2
20	Zajko Zeba		22/05/83	M	13		2
39	Denis Žerić		21/03/98	M		(3)	

Top goalscorers

Goals	Player
19	Ivan Lendrić (Željezničar)
13	Elvir Koljić (Krupa)
11	Sulejman Krpić (Sloboda)
	Jasmin Mešanović (Zrinjski)
10	Goran Brkić (Mladost)
	Marko Obradović (Radnik)
	Mersudin Ahmetović (Sarajevo)
	Nemanja Bilbija (Zrinjski)
9	Nermin Crnkić (Sarajevo)
	Asim Zec (Sloboda)
	Luka Menalo (Široki Brijeg)
	Wagner (Široki Brijeg)

Promoted clubs

NK GOŠK Gabela

1919 • Perica Pero Pavlović (3,500) • nkgoskgabela.weebly.com

Coach: Nedim Jusufbegović; (19/09/16) Zlatko Križanović (07/01/17) Darko Vojvodić

FK Borac Banja Luka

1926 • Gradski (9,730) • fkborac.net

Major honours
Bosnian-Herzegovinian League (1) 2011; Yugoslav Cup (1) 1988; Bosnian-Herzegovinian Cup (1) 2010

Coach: Zoran Dragišić; (23/08/16) Vlado Jagodić; (11/10/16) Vule Trivunović; (01/06/17) ŽeljkoVranješ

Second level final tables 2016/17

Prva liga FBIH	Pld	W	D	L	F	A	Pts
1 NK GOŠK Gabela	30	16	8	6	50	26	56
2 NK Bosna Visoko	30	15	5	10	39	29	50
3 FK Sloga Simin Han	30	15	3	12	43	36	48
4 FK Rudar Kakanj	30	13	7	10	40	28	46
5 HNK Čapljina	30	13	7	10	34	25	46
6 NK Travnik	30	12	10	8	44	36	46
7 NK Bratstvo Gračanica	30	13	6	11	43	34	45
8 NK Zvijezda Gradačac	30	13	6	11	40	32	45
9 HNK Orašje	30	12	8	10	40	42	44
10 NK Jedinstvo Bihać	30	12	8	10	34	37	44
11 FK Velež	30	11	10	9	39	33	43
12 FK Goražde	30	12	7	11	35	32	43
13 FK Radnički Lukavac	30	11	3	16	37	51	36
14 FK Budućnost Banovići	30	10	5	15	36	40	35
15 FK Bosna Sema Sarajevo	30	9	5	16	38	46	32
16 NK Novi Travnik	30	2	4	24	14	79	10

Prva liga RS	Pld	W	D	L	F	A	Pts
1 FK Borac Banja Luka	32	25	6	1	61	12	81
2 FK Podrinje Janja	32	18	5	9	47	29	59
3 FK Rudar Prijedor	32	15	7	10	59	40	52
4 FK Drina Zvornik	32	15	7	10	39	29	52
5 FK Kozara Gradiška	32	10	6	16	39	44	36
6 FK Tekstilac Derventa	32	8	12	12	18	26	36
7 FK Sloga Doboj	32	13	8	11	61	52	47
8 FK Sloboda Mrkonjić Grad	32	13	7	12	43	51	46
9 FK Slavija Sarajevo	32	12	6	14	51	41	42
10 FK Zvijezda 09 Stanišići	32	13	3	16	36	51	42
11 FK Sutjeska Foča	32	9	6	17	30	52	33
12 FK Borac Šamac	32	2	5	25	24	81	11

NB League splits into top and bottom halves after 22 games, after which the clubs play exclusively against teams in their group.

DOMESTIC CUP

Kup Bosne i Hercegovine 2016/17

1/16 FINALS

(21/09/16)
Brotnjo 0-7 Željezničar
Čelik 1-1 Bosna Sema *(4-5 on pens)*
Goražde 1-1 Zvijezda Gradačac *(4-3 on pens)*
GOŠK Gabela 0-1 Radnik Bijeljina
Kozara Gradiška 0-0 Olimpic Sarajevo *(3-2 on pens)*
Krupa 1-3 Travnik
Metalleghe-BSI 1-2 Velež
Mladost Doboj Kakanj 1-0 Rudar Prijedor
Orašje 3-2 Karanovac
Podrinje Janja 0-1 Sloboda Tuzla
Radnički Lukavac 3-1 Drina Zvornik
Rudar Kakanj 5-1 Sloboda Novi Grad
Sarajevo 2-0 Bratstvo
Slavija Sarajevo 0-0 Vitez *(5-4 on pens)*
Široki Brijeg 5-0 Čapljina
Zrinjski 5-0 Borac Banja Luka

1/8 FINALS

(18/10/16 & 25/10/16)
Orašje 1-1, 1-3 Travnik *(2-4)*

(19/10/16 & 26/10/16)
Mladost Doboj Kakanj 6-1, 2-0 Slavija Sarajevo *(8-1)*
Sarajevo 3-1, 5-0 Kozara Gradiska *(8-1)*
Sloboda Tuzla 1-0, 0-2 Široki Brijeg *(1-2)*
Rudar Kakanj 0-1, 1-5 Radnik Bijeljina *(1-6)*
Zrinjski 3-0, 2-1 Velež *(5-1)*
Željezničar 5-1, 3-0 Goražde *(8-1)*

(20/10/16 & 26/10/16)
Bosna Sema 6-0, 2-3 Radnički Lukavac *(8-3)*

QUARTER-FINALS

(08/03/17 & 15/03/17)
Mladost Doboj Kakanj 6-3 Bosna Sema *(Sinanović 10og, Husić 44, Aganspahić 64, Aladin Šišić 68, 84, Ramović 70; Oglečevac 73, Murga 76p, Ćatić 88)*
Bosna Sema 2-3 Mladost Doboj Kakanj *(Oglečevac 15, Mujić 79p; Maksimović 4p, 68, Husić 47)*
(Mladost Doboj Kakanj 9-5)

Radnik Bijeljina 2-2 Željezničar *(Franić 37, Obradović 59; Lendrić 48, Marković 68)*
Željezničar 2-0 Radnik Bijeljina *(Nikolić 71, Bekrić 82)*
(Željezničar 4-2)

Sarajevo 2-0 Travnik *(Amer Bekić 4, 33)*
Travnik 2-2 Sarajevo *(Jusufbašić 16, Kadrić 58; Husejinović 5, Ahmetović 55)*
(Sarajevo 4-2)

Zrinjski 0-2 Široki Brijeg *(Wagner 19, 38)*
Široki Brijeg 1-0 Zrinjski *(Krstanović 34p)*
(Široki Brijeg 3-0)

SEMI-FINALS

(12/04/17 & 19/04/17)
Sarajevo 1-1 Mladost Doboj Kakanj *(Ahmetović 42; Kuzmanović 12)*
Mladost Doboj Kakanj 2-3 Sarajevo *(Brkić 88, 90; Duljević 46, Crnkić 61, Kovačević 83)*
(Sarajevo 4-3)

(12/04/17 & 26/04/17)
Široki Brijeg 1-0 Željezničar *(Krstanović 55)*
Željezničar 0-3 Široki Brijeg *(Krstanović 5, Pandža 11, Čabraja 55)*
(Široki Brijeg 4-0)

FINAL

(10/05/17)
Olimpijski Asim Ferhatović Hase, Sarajevo
FK SARAJEVO 0
NK ŠIROKI BRIJEG 1 *(Barišić 45)*
Referee: *Valjić*
SARAJEVO: *Pavlović, Hodžić, Novaković, Kovačević, Almir Bekić, Sarić, Mihojević (Radovac 66), Hebibović (Amer Bekić 59), Duljević (Ivetić 69), Crnkić, Ahmetović*
ŠIROKI BRIJEG: *Bilobrk, Ćorluka, Pandža, Barišić, Bralić, Marković, Zlomislić, Čabraja (Brekalo 89), Lončar (Kožul 82), Menalo (Ivanković 84), Krstanović*

(17/05/17)
Pecara, Siroki Brijeg
NK ŠIROKI BRIJEG 0
FK SARAJEVO 1 *(Amer Bekić 65p)*
Referee: *Jakupović*
ŠIROKI BRIJEG: *Bilobrk, Ćorluka (Ivanković 90), Pandža, Barišić, Bralić, Marković, Zlomislić (Kožul 80), Čabraja, Lončar, Wagner (Ćorić 66), Krstanović*
SARAJEVO: *Pavlović, Hodžić, Mihojević, Novaković, Almir Bekić, Sarić, Ivetić (Rustemović 89), Hebibović (Ahmetović 87), Duljević, Crnkić (Husejinović 89), Amer Bekić*

(1-1; Široki Brijeg 4-2 on pens)

Široki Brijeg's third domestic cup triumph came after a penalty shoot-win in the final against Sarajevo

BULGARIA

Bulgarski Futbolen Soyuz (BFS)

Address	26 Tzar Ivan Assen II Street BG-1124 Sofia
Tel	+359 2 942 6202
Fax	+359 2 942 6200
E-mail	bfu@bfunion.bg
Website	bfunion.bg

President	Borislav Mihaylov
General secretary	Borislav Popov
Media officer	Yordan Grozdanov
Year of formation	1923
National stadium	Vasil Levski, Sofia (43,230)

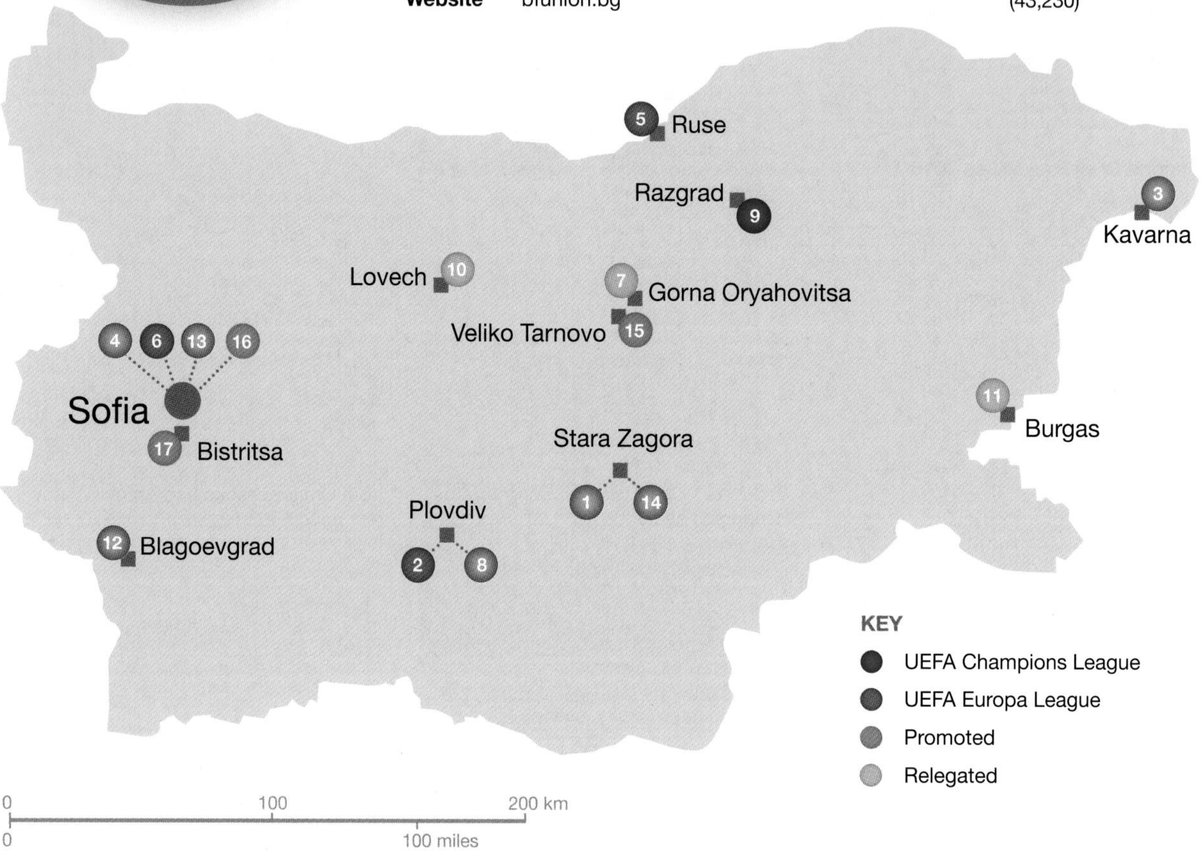

PARVA LIGA CLUBS

  1 **PFC Beroe Stara Zagora**

2 **PFC Botev Plovdiv**

 3 **PFC Cherno More Varna**

 4 **PFC CSKA Sofia**

 5 **PFC Dunav Ruse**

 6 **PFC Levski Sofia**

 7 **FC Lokomotiv Gorna Oryahovitsa**

 8 **PFC Lokomotiv Plovdiv**

 9 **PFC Ludogorets Razgrad**

 10 **PFC Montana 1921**

 11 **PFC Neftochimic Burgas**

 12 **OFC Pirin Blagoevgrad**

 13 **PFC Slavia Sofia**

 14 **FC Vereya Stara Zagora**

PROMOTED CLUBS

  15 **FC Etar Veliko Tarnovo**

  16 **PFC Septemvri Sofia**

 17 **FC Vitosha Bistritsa**

Ludogorets on a different level

Ludogorets Razgrad romped to another one-sided Bulgarian league title in 2016/17, claiming their sixth championship crown in as many years. Levski Sofia offered up a challenge early on, but Georgi Dermendhiev's free-scoring side set a standard that no other team could match.

The title was wrapped up halfway through the second phase of a new league structure in which the top six teams played 36 matches. Ludogorets' busy schedule included 14 European games plus six more in the Bulgarian Cup, but it was Botev Plovdiv who won the trophy, denying them the double with a surprise 2-1 victory.

Sixth title in succession for Razgrad club

Extended European stay for Dermendzhiev's side

Botev Plovdiv deny champions in cup final

Domestic league

With the same coach and a largely unchanged playing staff from the previous season, Ludogorets were the new-look Parva Liga's overwhelming title favourites. Five dropped points in their opening two away fixtures, the first of them a 1-0 defeat at Levski, raised eyebrows, but 13 successive victories thereafter soon restored normality. Levski actually topped the table for several weeks, but when their first defeat, at home to Lokomotiv Plovdiv, was immediately followed by a second, at Ludogorets, their title bid effectively ended.

Ludogorets increased their points tally in every match until they lost 1-0 at home to the season's surprise package, newly-promoted Dunav Ruse, in the first game of the championship play-offs. Dermendzhiev's side entered that phase with a 16-point lead, their sixth straight title already a foregone conclusion. Draws against Levski and CSKA Sofia merely delayed the inevitable, which came on 5 May when they won 3-0 at Lokomotiv Plovdiv.

Ludogorets retained their 16-point winning margin at the finish, with CSKA leapfrogging arch-rivals Levski to claim second place. The champions' 36 matches yielded a staggering 87 goals – an average of one a game more than CSKA – with four of their players contributing double-figure tallies. Romanian striker Claudiu Keşerü topped the league's scoring charts with 22 goals – thus denying a sixth golden boot to Lokomotiv Plovdiv veteran Martin Kamburov – while Brazilian wing wizards Wanderson and Jonathan Cafú chipped in with 14 and ten, respectively. Playmaker Marcelinho also struck 14 times in a vintage campaign, while long-serving skipper Svetoslav Dyakov was another key contributor whose form seldom wavered.

CSKA, back in the top flight and back, after some extensive administrative manoeuvres, with their former identity, did not, however, receive international clearance to return to European competition. Their ineligibility complicated the qualification procedure for the UEFA Europa League, but ultimately the three spots went to cup winners Botev, play-off winners Levski – who overcame a resurgent Vereya 9-8 on penalties in a dramatic final – and, retrospectively, thanks to their fourth-place finish, Veselin Velkov's overachieving Dunav.

Domestic cup

Botev went into the Bulgarian Cup final as rank outsiders. Their record in the fixture was woeful, with nine defeats and just two wins. More pertinently, opponents Ludogorets came to the Vasil Levski stadium not only as recrowned champions but with an astonishing record in their run to the final of 23 goals for and none against. Botev had lost their prolific Brazilian striker João Paulo to Ludogorets in the winter, and perhaps it was the lingering resentment over that move that powered the underdogs to victory, goals from Omar Kossoko and Antonio Vutov rendering a late reply from Keşerü redundant and bringing about the biggest upset of the Bulgarian season.

Europe

Ludogorets reached the UEFA Champions League group stage for the second time in three years, going unbeaten through three qualifying ties. They won no further matches, but opened the scoring in four of their group games, including twice against Paris Saint-Germain, and their final tally of three points was enough to take them forward into the UEFA Europa League round of 32, where they were eliminated by FC København.

National team

Bulgaria's first six 2018 FIFA World Cup qualifying games produced three home wins and three away defeats. The highlight was a 2-0 victory over the Netherlands in which striker Spas Delev scored his first two international goals. That provided coach Petar Hubchev with a much-needed boost after his first two games had brought heavy defeats in France and Sweden. The ex-Beroe Stara Zagora coach – and ever-present member of Bulgaria's legendary 1994 World Cup team – took charge when Ivaylo Petev suddenly upped and left to join Dinamo Zagreb.

DOMESTIC SEASON AT A GLANCE

Parva Liga 2016/17 final tables

Championship play-offs

		Pld	Home W	Home D	Home L	Home F	Home A	Away W	Away D	Away L	Away F	Away A	Total W	Total D	Total L	Total F	Total A	Pts
1	**PFC Ludogorets Razgard**	**36**	**12**	**4**	**2**	**38**	**12**	**13**	**4**	**1**	**49**	**16**	**25**	**8**	**3**	**87**	**28**	**83**
2	PFC CSKA Sofia	36	11	5	2	32	9	8	5	5	19	12	19	10	7	51	21	67
3	PFC Levski Sofia	36	11	4	3	29	13	7	5	6	21	18	18	9	9	50	31	63
4	PFC Dunav Ruse	36	7	6	5	25	22	8	4	6	21	22	15	10	11	46	44	55
5	PFC Lokomotiv Plovdiv	36	7	7	4	27	23	7	3	8	23	29	14	10	12	50	52	52
6	PFC Cherno More Varna	36	8	4	6	19	18	5	4	9	20	27	13	8	15	39	45	47

First phase final table

		Pld	Home W	Home D	Home L	Home F	Home A	Away W	Away D	Away L	Away F	Away A	Total W	Total D	Total L	Total F	Total A	Pts
1	PFC Ludogorets Razgard	26	11	2	0	32	8	10	2	1	37	11	21	4	1	69	19	67
2	PFC Levski Sofia	26	10	2	1	20	4	5	4	4	18	13	15	6	5	38	17	51
3	PFC CSKA Sofia	26	8	3	2	23	7	5	4	4	12	9	13	7	6	35	16	46
4	PFC Cherno More Varna	26	7	4	2	14	9	5	3	5	16	15	12	7	7	30	24	43
5	PFC Lokomotiv Plovdiv	26	5	7	1	19	12	5	2	6	16	18	10	9	7	35	30	39
6	PFC Dunav Ruse	26	5	5	3	19	16	5	3	5	13	15	10	8	8	32	31	38
7	PFC Botev Plovdiv	26	7	3	3	23	16	3	2	8	13	26	10	5	11	36	42	35
8	PFC Beroe Stara Zagora	26	6	3	4	15	13	4	2	7	12	15	10	5	11	27	28	35
9	OFC Pirin Blagoevgrad	26	8	3	2	21	12	2	1	10	9	24	10	4	12	30	36	34
10	FC Vereya Stara Zagora	26	8	2	3	15	8	0	4	9	7	28	8	6	12	22	36	30
11	PFC Slavia Sofia	26	7	0	6	22	22	1	4	8	8	23	8	4	14	30	45	28
12	PFC Neftochimic Burgas	26	6	2	5	19	14	1	3	9	8	23	7	5	14	27	37	26
13	FC Lokomotiv Gorna Oryahovitsa	26	4	3	6	11	14	1	4	8	11	25	5	7	14	22	39	22
14	PFC Montana 1921	26	2	1	10	12	29	1	2	10	4	20	3	3	20	16	49	12

NB After 26 rounds the top six clubs enter a championship play-off, with clubs placed 7-14 entering two play-off groups. Full points and goals totals are carried forward.

European qualification 2017/18

Champion: PFC Ludogorets Razgrad (second qualifying round)

Cup winner: PFC Botev Plovdiv (first qualifying round)

PFC Levski Sofia (first qualifying round)
PFC Dunav Ruse (first qualifying round)

Top scorer Claudiu Keşerü (Ludogorets), 22 goals
Relegated clubs FC Lokomotiv Gorna Oryahovitsa, PFC Neftochimic Burgas, PFC Montana 1921
Promoted clubs FC Etar Veliko Tarnovo, PFC Septemvri Sofia, FC Vitosha Bistritsa
Cup final PFC Botev Plovdiv 2-1 PFC Ludogorets Razgrad

Player of the season

Marcelinho
(PFC Ludogorets Razgrad)

A stalwart figure in all six of Ludogorets' Bulgarian championship triumphs, Marcelinho was better than ever in 2016/17, supplementing his crafty, inspirational midfield play with a personal-best haul of 14 goals. He did not add to that tally in Europe but started all bar one of the team's 14 matches, proving his worth against continental heavyweights Arsenal and Paris Saint-Germain. Born in the Amazonas region of Brazil but qualified to play for Bulgaria, the 32-year-old scored on his FIFA World Cup debut – in a dramatic 4-3 victory over Luxembourg.

Newcomer of the season

Bozhidar Chorbadzhiyski
(PFC CSKA Sofia)

A domestic cup winner with CSKA in 2016, Chorbadzhiyski was new to the Bulgarian top flight when the club were reinvited back after an enforced year's absence. The 21-year-old central defender rose to the challenge so rapidly that he was handed his senior international debut for Bulgaria in their opening FIFA World Cup qualifier against Luxembourg. As the season progressed, he became an ever more dependable and influential figure in a CSKA defence that conceded just 21 goals and kept 19 clean sheets in their 36 Parva Liga fixtures.

Team of the season
(4-2-3-1)

Coach: Dermendzhiev *(Ludogorets)*

NATIONAL TEAM

International tournament appearances
FIFA World Cup (7) 1962, 1966, 1970, 1974, 1986 (2nd round), 1994 (4th), 1998
UEFA European Championship (2) 1996, 2004

Top five all-time caps
Stiliyan Petrov (106); Borislav Mihaylov (102); Hristo Bonev (96); Krasimir Balakov (92); Martin Petrov (91)

Top five all-time goals
Dimitar Berbatov (48); Hristo Bonev (47); Hristo Stoichkov (37); Emil Kostadinov (26); Lyubomir Angelov, Ivan Kolev & Petar Zhekov (25)

Results 2016/7

06/09/16	Luxembourg (WCQ)	H	Sofia	W	4-3	*Rangelov (16), Marcelinho (65), I Popov (79), Tonev (90+2)*
07/10/16	France (WQC)	A	Saint-Denis	L	1-4	*M Alexandrov (6p)*
10/10/16	Sweden (WCQ)	A	Solna	L	0-3	
13/11/16	Belarus (WCQ)	H	Sofia	W	1-0	*I Popov (10)*
25/03/17	Netherlands (WCQ)	H	Sofia	W	2-0	*Delev (5, 20)*
09/06/17	Belarus (WCQ)	A	Borisov	L	1-2	*Kostadinov (90+1)*

Appearances 2016/17

Coach: Ivaylo Petev /(28/09/16) Petar Hubchev	**09/07/75 26/02/64**		**LUX**	**FRA**	**SWE**	**BLR**	**NED**	**BLR**	**Caps**	**Goals**
Vladislav Stoyanov	08/06/87	Ludogorets	G	G	G	G			19	-
Strahil Popov	31/08/90	Kasımpaşa (TUR)	D	D	D	D	D	D	12	-
Bozhidar Chorbadzhiyski	08/08/95	CSKA Sofia	D				D	D	3	-
Ivan Ivanov	25/02/88	Panathinaikos (GRE)	D						41	3
Anton Nedyalkov	30/04/93	CSKA Sofia	D		D		s86		3	-
Georgi Milanov	19/02/92	CSKA Moskva (RUS)	M64	M	M	M53		s81	35	2
Svetoslav Dyakov	31/05/84	Ludogorets	M	M	M	M		M	36	-
Marcelinho	24/08/84	Ludogorets	M	M62	s72				7	2
Mihail Alexandrov	11/06/89	Legia (POL)	M56	M76	s53				18	3
Dimitar Rangelov	09/02/83	Konyaspor (TUR)	A	s62					41	6
Ivelin Popov	26/10/87	Spartak Moskva (RUS)	A85	A68	A	A75	A67	A64	69	14
Ivaylo Chochev	18/02/93	Palermo (ITA)	s56		M72	s53		s64	12	1
Alexander Tonev	03/02/90	Crotone (ITA)	s64	s68		M66	M	M	27	5
Georgi Bozhilov	12/02/87	Beroe	s85						2	-
Alexander D Alexandrov	13/04/86	Levski		D	D	D			15	-
Dimitar Pirgov	26/10/89	Levski		D					1	-
Zhivko Milanov	15/07/84	APOEL (CYP)		D					28	-
Georgi Kostadinov	07/09/90	Levski		M	M53		M	M	4	1
Todor Nedelev	07/02/93	Botev Plovdiv		s76					11	-
Vasil Bozhikov	02/06/88	Kasımpaşa (TUR)			D	D	D	D	7	-
Simeon Slavchev	25/09/93	Lechia (POL)			M89	M	M		10	-
Martin Raynov	25/04/92	Lokomotiv Plovdiv			s89				1	-
Petar Zanev	18/10/85	Amkar (RUS)				D	D86	D	30	-
Spas Delev	22/09/89	Pogoń (POL)				A	A88	A54	15	2
Radoslav Kirilov	29/06/92	Beroe				s66			1	-
Preslav Yordanov	21/07/89	CSKA Sofia				s75			1	-
Nikolay Mihaylov	28/06/88	Mersin (TUR)					G	G	34	-
Stanislav Manolev	16/12/85	CSKA Sofia					M	M81	48	4
Bozhidar Kraev	23/06/97	Levski					s67		1	-
Nikolay Bodurov	30/05/86	CSKA Sofia					s88		37	1
Andrey Galabinov	27/11/88	Novara (ITA)						s54	7	2

EUROPE

PFC Ludogorets Razgrad

Second qualifying round - FK Mladost Podgorica (MNE)
H 2-0 *Moţi (13p), Lukoki (26)*
Stoyanov, Cicinho, Natanael, Juninho Quixadá (Lucas Sasha 81), Dyakov (Anicet Abel 90+3), Jonathan Cafú, Moţi, Plastun, Marcelinho, Wanderson (Keşerü 80), Lukoki. Coach: Georgi Dermendzhiev (BUL)
A 3-0 *Lukoki (39, 64), Wanderson (48)*
Stoyanov, Natanael, Lucas Sasha (Anicet Abel 84), Dyakov, Jonathan Cafú, Minev, Moţi, Plastun, Marcelinho (Prepeliţă 76), Wanderson (Keşerü 65), Lukoki. Coach: Georgi Dermendzhiev (BUL)

Third qualifying round - FK Crvena zvezda (SRB)
H 2-2 *Jonathan Cafú (43), Keşerü (76)*
Stoyanov, Natanael, Lucas Sasha (Juninho Quixadá 75), Dyakov, Jonathan Cafú, Minev, Moţi, Plastun, Marcelinho, Wanderson, Lukoki (Keşerü 67). Coach: Georgi Dermendzhiev (BUL)
A 4-2 (aet) *Jonathan Cafú (24), Wanderson (40, 92, 97)*
Stoyanov, Natanael, Anicet Abel, Dyakov, Jonathan Cafú (Misidjan 70), Minev, Moţi, Keşerü (Palomino 46), Plastun, Marcelinho (Lucas Sasha 101), Wanderson. Coach: Georgi Dermendzhiev (BUL)
Red card: Plastun 44

Play-offs - FC Viktoria Plzeň (CZE)
H 2-0 *Moţi (51p), Misidjan (64)*
Stoyanov, Palomino, Natanael, Lucas Sasha, Dyakov, Jonathan Cafú (Juninho Quixadá 90+3), Minev, Moţi, Marcelinho, Wanderson (Gustavo Campanharo 90), Misidjan (Keşerü 81). Coach: Georgi Dermendzhiev (BUL)
A 2-2 *Misidjan (17), Keşerü (90+5)*
Stoyanov, Palomino, Natanael, Lucas Sasha, Dyakov (Gustavo Campanharo 80), Jonathan Cafú, Minev, Moţi, Marcelinho, Wanderson (Plastun 85), Misidjan (Keşerü 76). Coach: Georgi Dermendzhiev (BUL)

Group A
Match 1 - FC Basel 1893 (SUI)
A 1-1 *Jonathan Cafú (45)*
Stoyanov, Palomino, Natanael (Vitinha 80), Anicet Abel, Dyakov (Lucas Sasha 90+1), Jonathan Cafú, Minev, Moţi, Marcelinho, Wanderson (Plastun 85), Misidjan. Coach: Georgi Dermendzhiev (BUL)
Match 2 - Paris Saint-Germain (FRA)
H 1-3 *Natanael (16)*
Stoyanov, Palomino, Natanael, Anicet Abel, Dyakov, Jonathan Cafú, Minev, Moţi, Marcelinho, Wanderson (Keşerü 88), Misidjan (Lukoki 74). Coach: Georgi Dermendzhiev (BUL)
Match 3 - Arsenal FC (ENG)
A 0-6
Stoyanov, Palomino, Natanael, Anicet Abel, Dyakov, Jonathan Cafú, Minev, Moţi, Marcelinho, Wanderson (Lukoki 80), Misidjan (Keşerü 69). Coach: Georgi Dermendzhiev (BUL)
Match 4 - Arsenal FC (ENG)
H 2-3 *Jonathan Cafú (12), Keşerü (15)*
Borjan, Palomino, Natanael, Anicet Abel, Dyakov, Jonathan Cafú, Minev, Moţi, Keşerü (Misidjan 80), Marcelinho, Wanderson. Coach: Georgi Dermendzhiev (BUL)
Match 5 - FC Basel 1893 (SUI)
H 0-0
Stoyanov, Cicinho, Palomino, Natanael, Anicet Abel, Dyakov, Jonathan Cafú, Moţi, Keşerü (Plastun 90+2), Wanderson (Gustavo Campanharo 90+3), Misidjan (Lukoki 84). Coach: Georgi Dermendzhiev (BUL)
Match 6 - Paris Saint-Germain (FRA)
A 2-2 *Misidjan (15), Wanderson (69)*
Stoyanov, Cicinho, Palomino, Natanael, Anicet Abel, Dyakov, Jonathan Cafú, Moţi, Plastun, Marcelinho (Gustavo Campanharo 86), Wanderson (Keşerü 90+5), Misidjan (Lukoki 72). Coach: Georgi Dermendzhiev (BUL)

Round of 32 - FC København (DEN)
H 1-2 *Keşerü (81)*
Stoyanov, Palomino, Natanael, Anicet Abel, Dyakov, Jonathan Cafú, Minev, Moţi, Marcelinho, Wanderson (João Paulo 80), Misidjan (Keşerü 62). Coach: Georgi Dermendzhiev (BUL)
A 0-0
Stoyanov, Palomino, Natanael, Anicet Abel (Juninho Quixadá 65), Dyakov, Jonathan Cafú (Misidjan 75), Minev, Moţi, Keşerü, Marcelinho, Wanderson (João Paulo 83). Coach: Georgi Dermendzhiev (BUL)

PFC Levski Sofia

Second qualifying round - NK Maribor (SVN)
A 0-0
Jorgačević, Pirgov, A D Alexandrov, Narh, De Nooijer, Hristov (Adeniji 71), Minev, Procházka, Añete (Orachev 85), A E Alexandrov, Kostadinov. Coach: Ljupko Petrović (SRB)
H 1-1 *Narh (22)*
Jorgačević, Pirgov, A D Alexandrov, Narh, De Nooijer, Hristov, Minev, Procházka, Añete (Deza 86), A E Alexandrov, Kostadinov (Adeniji 79). Coach: Ljupko Petrović (SRB)

PFC Beroe Stara Zagora

First qualifying round - FK Radnik Bijeljina (BIH)
H 0-0
Makendzhiev, Kolev, Panayotov (Tom 54), Milisavljević (Dryanov 71), Bozhilov, A Vasilev (Pedro Marques 83), V Vasilev, Hubchev, Penev, Milanov, Pochanski. Coach: Ivaylo Yordanov (BUL)
A 2-0 *Pochanski (79, 80)*
Makendzhiev, Ivanov, Panayotov, Milisavljević, Bozhilov, Pedro Marques (A Vasilev 89), V Vasilev, Penev, Tom (Dinkov 85), Milanov, Pochanski (Kolev 90+2). Coach: Ivaylo Yordanov (BUL)

Second qualifying round - HJK Helsinki (FIN)
H 1-1 *Penev (49)*
Makendzhiev, Kato, Ivanov, Kirilov, Milisavljević (Kolev 89), Bozhilov, V Vasilev (A Vasilev 76), Penev, Tom (Panayotov 89), Milanov, Pochanski. Coach: Ivaylo Yordanov (BUL)
A 0-1
Makendzhiev, Kato, Ivanov, Kirilov (Kolev 84), Milisavljević (Pedro Marques 65), Bozhilov, V Vasilev, Penev, Tom (Dryanov 84), Milanov, Pochanski. Coach: Ivaylo Yordanov (BUL)

PFC Slavia Sofia

First qualifying round - Zagłębie Lubin (POL)
H 1-0 *Serderov (85)*
Kirev, Baldzhiyski (Karabelyov 55), Vasev, Serderov, Pashov, Velkov, Krastev (I Dimitrov 56), Martinov, Yomov (P Hristov 90), Sergeev, Khamis. Coach: Aleksandr Tarkhanov (RUS)
A 0-3
Kirev, Baldzhiyski, Vasev, Serderov, Karabelyov (Yomov 46), Pashov, Velkov, I Dimitrov (Stankev 67), Martinov (Krastev 82), Sergeev, Khamis. Coach: Aleksandr Tarkhanov (RUS)

DOMESTIC LEAGUE CLUB-BY-CLUB

PFC Beroe Stara Zagora

1916 • Beroe (12,128) • beroe.bg

Major honours

Bulgarian League (1) 1986; Bulgarian Cup (2) 2010, 2013

Coach: Alexander Dimitrov; (18/10/16) (Plamen Lipenski); (26/10/16) Ferario Spasov

2016

Date		Opponent		Score	Scorers
07/08	a	Slavia	W	2-1	*A Vasilev, Bozhilov*
13/08	h	Vereya	W	1-0	*Bozhilov*
21/08	a	Neftochimic	L	0-1	
26/08	h	Pirin	W	1-0	*Kato*
12/09	a	Lokomotiv GO	W	1-0	*Manga*
18/09	h	Dunav	D	0-0	
25/09	a	CSKA	L	0-4	
30/09	h	Cherno More	L	0-1	
16/10	h	Botev	L	3-4	*Mapuku 3 (1p)*
22/10	a	Levski	L	0-2	
29/10	h	Montana	W	2-1	*Zehirov, Mapuku*
02/11	a	Lok Plovdiv	D	1-1	*Ohene*
16/11	h	Ludogorets	L	0-2	
19/11	a	Ludogorets	L	0-1	
27/11	h	Slavia	D	1-1	*V Vasilev*
01/12	a	Vereya	L	0-1	
04/12	h	Neftochimic	W	2-0	*Ivanov, Pochanski*
12/12	a	Pirin	D	1-1	*Mapuku*
15/12	h	Lokomotiv GO	D	1-1	*Manga*

2017

Date		Opponent		Score	Scorers
17/02	a	Dunav	W	4-0	*Karachanakov 2, Mapuku, Salmikivi*
25/02	h	CSKA	L	0-1	
02/03	h	Cherno More	L	0-1	
06/03	a	Botev	L	0-2	
12/03	h	Levski	W	1-0	*Raynov*
17/03	a	Montana	W	3-0	*Tsonev 2, Mapuku*
01/04	h	Lok Plovdiv	W	3-2	*og (Petrov), Karachanakov, Delić*
08/04	h	Lokomotiv GO	L	2-3	*Mapuku 2*
14/04	h	Pirin	D	1-1	*Mapuku*
21/04	a	Neftochimic	D	0-0	
29/04	a	Lokomotiv GO	W	1-0	*og (Zhelev)*
06/05	a	Pirin	D	1-1	*Mapuku*
11/05	h	Neftochimic	W	3-0	*V Vasilev, Karachanakov, Georgiev*

No	Name	Nat	DoB	Pos	Aps	(s)	Gls
13	Emin Ahmed		10/03/96	D	1	(3)	
14	Georgi Bozhilov		12/02/87	A	12	(9)	2
24	Mateas Delić	CRO	17/06/88	M	7	(3)	1
15	Georgi Dinkov		20/05/91	D	13	(4)	
10	Stanislav Dryanov		04/02/92	M		(2)	
23	Emil Gargorov		15/02/81	M	2		
13	Nikola Gavov		19/03/99	M		(1)	
5	Asen Georgiev		13/02/89	D	10	(1)	1
6	Ivo Ivanov		11/03/85	D	24		1
17	Anton Karachanakov		17/01/92	M	10		4
4	Kohei Kato	JPN	14/06/89	M	25	(1)	1
9	Radoslav Kirilov		26/09/92	M	11	(6)	
7	Alexander Kolev		08/12/92	A	2	(9)	
22	Blagoy Makendzhiev		11/07/88	G	19		
77	David Manga	CTA	03/02/89	M	3	(6)	2
30	Junior Mapuku	COD	07/01/90	A	23		11
27	Marquitos	ESP	21/03/87	M	1	(2)	
1	Mihail Mihaylov		16/06/97	G	1		
71	Iliya Milanov		19/02/92	D	11	(2)	
11	Nemanja Milisavljević	SRB	01/11/84	M	10	(1)	
3	Carlos Ohene	GHA	21/07/93	M	19	(3)	1
8	Vasil Panayotov		16/07/90	M	3		
17	Pedro Marques	POR	31/03/88	M	1	(2)	
28	Veselin Penev		11/08/82	D	28		
12	Dušan Perniš	SVK	28/11/84	G	12		
91	Erik Pochanski		05/04/92	M	10	(6)	1
7	Martin Raynov		25/04/92	M	11		1
11	Ville Salmikivi	FIN	20/05/92	A	2	(10)	1
27	Denislav Stanchev		28/03/00	M		(2)	
19	Plamen Tenev		13/06/95	D	7		
70	Tom	BRA	18/03/86	M	3	(4)	
23	Borislav Tsonev		29/04/95	M	10	(9)	2
19	Alexander Vasilev		27/04/95	M	11	(4)	1
21	Ventsislav Vasilev		08/07/88	D	30		2
18	Atanas Zehirov		13/02/89	M	20	(5)	1

PFC Botev Plovdiv

1912 • Komatevo (3,300) • botevplovdiv.bg

Major honours

Bulgarian League (2) 1929, 1967; Bulgarian Cup (3) 1962, 1981, 2017

Coach: Nikolay Kostov; (25/08/16) Nikolay Kirov

2016

Date		Opponent		Score	Scorers
30/07	h	Lok Plovdiv	D	1-1	*I Stoyanov*
06/08	a	Ludogorets	L	1-4	*Sténio*
15/08	h	Slavia	W	3-2	*Nedelev 2 (1p), João Paulo*
22/08	a	Vereya	L	0-1	
27/08	h	Neftochimic	W	2-1	*João Paulo, Yusein*
11/09	a	Pirin	L	1-2	*Nedelev (p)*
17/09	h	Lokomotiv GO	W	4-0	*João Paulo 3, Yusein*
24/09	a	Dunav	W	2-1	*Felipe Brisola, João Paulo*
01/10	h	CSKA	D	0-0	
16/10	a	Beroe	W	4-3	*Kossoko, Nedelev 2, João Paulo*
22/10	h	Cherno More	L	2-3	*Yusein, Terziev*
30/10	h	Levski	D	1-1	*João Paulo*
03/11	a	Montana	L	1-3	*João Paulo*
20/11	a	Lok Plovdiv	L	0-2	
26/11	h	Ludogorets	L	1-3	*João Paulo*
30/11	a	Slavia	L	2-3	*I Stoyanov (p), Nedelev*
05/12	h	Vereya	W	2-1	*Nedelev (p), João Paulo*
09/12	a	Neftochimic	L	0-4	
15/12	h	Pirin	W	3-2	*Nedelev (p), Kossoko, João Paulo*

2017

Date		Opponent		Score	Scorers
18/02	a	Lokomotiv GO	W	1-0	*Fernando Viana*
24/02	h	Dunav	L	0-2	
28/02	a	CSKA	D	0-0	
06/03	h	Beroe	W	2-0	*Fernando Viana 2*
11/03	a	Cherno More	D	1-1	*Baltanov*
19/03	a	Levski	L	0-2	
31/03	h	Montana	W	2-0	*Nedelev (p), Fernando Viana*
07/04	h	Montana	W	7-1	*Krum Stoyanov, Baltanov, Vutov 2, Nedelev 2, Dobrev*
14/04	h	Vereya	L	0-1	
22/04	a	Slavia	W	3-0	*Kossoko 2, Vutov*
30/04	a	Montana	L	1-2	*Kossoko*
05/05	a	Vereya	L	1-3	*Yusein*
10/05	h	Slavia	W	3-1	*Felipe Brisola, Fernando Viana, Kossoko*

No	Name	Nat	DoB	Pos	Aps	(s)	Gls
26	Radoslav Apostolov		15/06/98	M	2	(3)	
17	Lachezar Baltanov		11/07/88	M	12	(1)	2
23	Petar Chalakov		15/06/98	M		(1)	
9	Asen Chandarov		13/11/98	M	2	(3)	
99	Ivan Čvorović		21/09/85	G	10		
19	Zdravko Dermenov		05/09/98	D		(1)	
5	Kristian Dimitrov		27/02/97	D	7	(4)	
11	Kristian Dobrev		27/04/01	A		(4)	1
7	Felipe Brisola	BRA	06/06/90	M	18	(4)	2
9	Fernando Viana	BRA	20/02/92	A	10	(1)	5
44	Viktor Genev		27/10/88	D	12		
22	Georgi Georgiev		12/10/88	G	22	(1)	
22	Milko Georgiev		03/08/98	M	1	(9)	
37	João Paulo	BRA	02/06/88	A	19		12
71	Milen Kikarin		18/08/92	D	4	(2)	
15	Ivan Kirev		12/12/98	A		(2)	
20	Omar Kossoko	BEN	10/03/88	M	14	(7)	6
88	Daniel Kutev		06/03/91	A	1	(14)	
24	Lazar Marin		09/02/94	D	10	(3)	
45	Nasko Milev		18/07/96	A	1	(12)	
8	Todor Nedelev		07/02/93	M	30	(1)	11
14	Meledje Omnibes	CIV	25/09/97	M	18	(8)	
2	Tsvetomir Panov		17/04/97	D	27		
16	Sténio	CPV	06/05/88	M	15	(1)	1
73	Ivan Stoyanov		24/07/83	M	16	(1)	2
15	Kostadin Stoyanov		02/05/86	D	2	(1)	
25	Krum Stoyanov		01/08/91	D	24	(2)	1
3	Atanas Tasholov		09/09/98	D		(1)	
18	Radoslav Terziev		06/08/94	D	28		1
19	Boris Tyutyukov		28/10/97	M		(4)	
39	Antonio Vutov		06/06/96	M	10	(1)	3
20	Serkan Yusein		31/03/96	M	25	(5)	4
6	Daniel Zlatkov		06/03/89	D	12		

PFC Cherno More Varna

1913 • Kavarna (8,000) • chernomorepfc.bg

Major honours

Bulgarian Cup (1) 2015

Coach: Georgi Ivanov

2016

Date		Opponent		Score	Scorers
31/07	a	Pirin	W	3-1	*G Iliev 2 (1p), Kuzma*
08/08	h	Montana	W	1-0	*Nikolov*
14/08	a	Lokomotiv GO	D	2-2	*Bacari 2*
19/08	h	Lok Plovdiv	W	2-0	*Kuzma 2*
27/08	a	Dunav	L	0-3	
09/09	h	Ludogorets	L	1-3	*og (Palomino)*
18/09	a	CSKA	L	0-1	
25/09	h	Slavia	D	0-0	
30/09	a	Beroe	W	1-0	*Kokonov*
14/10	h	Vereya	W	2-1	*og (Zafirov), Kuzma*
22/10	a	Botev	W	3-2	*Kokonov, Georgiev, Hugo Seco*
30/10	h	Neftochimic	W	3-1	*G Iliev, Hugo Seco, Nikolov*
04/11	a	Levski	L	0-1	
18/11	h	Pirin	D	0-0	
26/11	a	Montana	W	2-0	*Bacari, Palankov*
29/11	h	Lokomotiv GO	D	1-1	*Trayanov*
02/12	a	Lok Plovdiv	L	0-1	
11/12	h	Dunav	W	1-0	*Tsvetkov*
14/12	a	Ludogorets	D	1-1	*Kuzma*

2017

Date		Opponent		Score	Scorers
19/02	h	CSKA	L	0-2	
26/02	a	Slavia	L	1-2	*Bacari*
02/03	h	Beroe	W	1-0	*Baldzhiyski*
05/03	a	Vereya	D	0-0	
11/03	h	Botev	D	1-1	*Kuzma*
19/03	a	Neftochimic	W	3-1	*Kuzma 2, Pirulo*
01/04	h	Levski	W	1-0	*Tsvetkov*
08/04	a	CSKA	L	1-3	*Kokonov*
15/04	a	Dunav	L	0-1	
23/04	h	Lok Plovdiv	W	2-3	*Stanchev, og (Vezalov), Kuzma*
01/05	a	Ludogorets	L	0-4	
07/05	h	Levski	L	0-1	
13/05	h	CSKA	L	0-1	
17/05	h	Dunav	L	1-2	*Venkov*
21/05	a	Lok Plovdiv	L	1-2	*Minkov*
28/05	h	Ludogorets	L	1-3	*Kuzma*
31/05	a	Levski	D	2-2	*Kostadinov, Kasabov*

No	Name	Nat	DoB	Pos	Aps	(s)	Gls
71	Georgi Andonov		28/06/83	A		(4)	
9	Bubacar Bacari	ESP	14/03/88	A	14	(4)	4
7	Borislav Baldzhiyski		12/10/90	M	11	(5)	1
40	Aleksandar Čanović	SRB	18/02/83	G	5		
25	Ivan Dyulgerov		15/07/99	G	1		
3	Daniel Georgiev		06/11/82	M	15	(6)	1
66	Filip Hlúpik	CZE	30/04/91	M	2	(2)	
7	Hugo Seco	POR	17/06/88	M	18		2
21	Georgi Iliev		05/09/81	M	27	(3)	3
10	Ilian Iliev		20/08/99	M		(3)	
36	Rumen Kasabov		15/11/99	M		(1)	1
13	Ivan Kokonov		17/08/91	M	25	(7)	3
17	Martin Kostadinov		13/05/96	D	11	(3)	1
31	Přemysl Kovář	CZE	14/10/85	G	12		
29	Marek Kuzma	SVK	22/06/88	A	26	(10)	10
8	Jan Malík	CZE	11/02/92	M	2	(8)	
38	Alexander Mihaylov		13/08/98	M		(1)	
33	Emil Mihaylov		01/05/88	G	13		
35	Martin Minchev		22/04/01	A	2	(2)	
97	Nikolay Minkov		13/08/97	M	4	(6)	1
22	Plamen Nikolov		12/06/85	D	25	(2)	2
84	Todor Palankov		13/01/84	M	28	(1)	1
77	Pirulo	ESP	17/04/92	M	8	(7)	1
11	Vladislav Romanov		07/02/88	M	3	(3)	
30	Vojtěch Šrom	CZE	03/05/88	G	5		
5	Stefan Stanchev		26/04/89	D	24	(1)	1
73	Ondřej Sukup	CZE	08/12/88	D	34		
37	Ertan Tombak		01/01/98	M	1		
15	Trayan Trayanov		03/08/87	D	12	(8)	1
6	Alexander Tsvetkov		31/08/90	M	31		2
4	Mihail Venkov		28/07/83	D	28		1
34	Emil Yanchev		08/02/99	M	2	(1)	
98	Valentin Yoskov		05/06/98	A	4	(12)	
66	Daniel Zlatkov		06/03/89	D	3	(1)	

BULGARIA

PFC CSKA Sofia

1948 • Bulgarska Armia (22,000) • cska.bg

Major honours

Bulgarian League (31) 1948, 1951, 1952, 1954, 1955, 1956, 1957, 1958, 1959, 1960, 1961, 1962, 1966, 1969, 1971, 1972, 1973, 1975, 1976, 1980, 1981, 1982, 1983, 1987, 1989, 1990, 1992, 1997, 2003, 2005, 2008; Bulgarian Cup (20) 1951, 1954, 1955, 1961, 1965, 1969, 1972, 1973, 1974, 1983, 1985, 1987, 1988, 1989, 1993, 1997, 1999, 2006, 2011, 2016

Coach: Hristo Yanev; (22/08/16) Edward Iordănescu (ROU); (30/11/16) Stamen Belchev

2016

Date		Opponent		Score	Scorers
29/07	h	Slavia	W	2-0	*Diogo Viana 2*
06/08	a	Vereya	L	0-1	
14/08	h	Neftochimic	W	5-1	*P Yordanov, Arsénio, Diogo Viana 2, Chorbadzhiyski*
20/08	a	Pirin	D	1-1	*Arsénio*
27/08	h	Lokomotiv GO	W	2-0	*Culma, Chorbadzhiyski*
11/09	a	Dunav	L	0-2	
18/09	h	Cherno More	W	1-0	*Culma*
25/09	h	Beroe	W	4-0	*David Simão (p), Culma, Diogo Viana, Rui Pedro*
01/10	a	Botev	D	0-0	
15/10	h	Levski	D	1-1	*P Yordanov (p)*
21/10	a	Montana	W	2-0	*Angelov 2*
29/10	h	Lok Plovdiv	L	0-1	
05/11	a	Ludogorets	L	1-2	*Culma*
19/11	a	Slavia	W	1-0	*Angelov*
27/11	h	Vereya	D	1-1	*Boumal*
01/12	a	Neftochimic	W	2-0	*Pérez, Culma*
04/12	h	Pirin	W	2-0	*P Yordanov, Angelov*
11/12	a	Lokomotiv GO	D	0-0	
16/12	h	Dunav	W	3-0	*Rúben Pinto, Chorbadzhiyski, Dyulgerov*

2017

Date		Opponent		Score	Scorers
19/02	a	Cherno More	W	2-0	*Rui Pedro 2*
25/02	a	Beroe	W	1-0	*Rui Pedro*
28/02	h	Botev	D	0-0	
04/03	a	Levski	L	1-2	*Arsénio*
11/03	h	Montana	W	2-1	*Mercado, Despodov*
18/03	a	Lok Plovdiv	D	1-1	*Despodov*
01/04	h	Ludogorets	L	0-2	
08/04	h	Cherno More	W	3-1	*Fernando Karanga 2, Despodov*
13/04	a	Lok Plovdiv	W	2-1	*Bodurov, Culma*
23/04	h	Ludogorets	D	1-1	*Boumal (p)*
29/04	a	Levski	W	3-0	*Arsénio, Despodov, Fernando Karanga*
07/05	h	Dunav	W	2-0	*Fernando Karanga, Rúben Pinto*
13/05	a	Cherno More	W	1-0	*Fernando Karanga*
17/05	h	Lok Plovdiv	D	0-0	
20/05	a	Ludogorets	D	1-1	*Fernando Karanga*
28/05	h	Levski	W	3-0	*David Simão 2, Culma*
31/05	a	Dunav	L	0-1	

No	Name	Nat	DoB	Pos	Aps	(s)	Gls
73	Milcho Angelov		02/01/95	A	1	(9)	4
10	Arsénio	POR	30/08/89	M	25	(3)	4
2	Stoycho Atanasov		14/05/97	D	7		
14	Samis Ayass		24/12/90	M		(4)	
14	Nikolay Bodurov		30/05/86	D	16		1
20	Petrus Boumal	CMR	20/04/93	M	17	(5)	2
4	Bozhidar Chorbadzhiyski		08/08/95	D	31		3
28	Gustavo Culma	COL	20/04/93	A	26	(4)	7
17	David Simão	POR	15/05/90	M	17	(5)	3
19	Kiril Despodov		11/11/96	A	15	(10)	4
7	Diogo Viana	POR	22/02/90	M	15	(3)	5
23	Alexander Dyulgerov		19/04/90	D	14	(5)	1
8	Fernando Karanga	BRA	14/01/91	A	12		6
28	Plamen Galabov		02/11/95	D	1	(1)	
8	Boris Galchev		31/10/83	M	6	(2)	
19	Alexander Georgiev		10/10/97	M	2	(4)	
21	Radoslav Iliev		30/07/00	M		(1)	
25	Wilmar Jordán	COL	17/10/90	A	1	(2)	
12	Georgi Kitanov		06/03/95	G	33		
22	Nikola Kolev		06/06/95	M	5	(4)	
30	Alexander Konov		03/09/93	G	3		
8	Kevin Koubemba	CGO	23/03/93	A	6	(6)	
20	Stanislav Malamov		21/09/89	D	2	(2)	
15	Kristiyan Malinov		30/03/94	M	8	(9)	
29	Milen Manchev		01/04/00	D		(1)	
11	Stanislav Manolev		16/12/85	D	23	(1)	
7	Kevin Mercado	ECU	28/01/95	M	4	(10)	1
21	Ivan Minchev		28/05/91	M		(1)	
19	Mitko Mitkov		28/08/00	M		(1)	
3	Anton Nedyalkov		30/04/93	D	34		
5	Rafael Pérez	COL	09/01/90	D	16		1
6	Rúben Pinto	POR	24/4/92	M	25	(2)	2
21	Rui Pedro	POR	02/07/88	M	16	(9)	4
10	Rumen Rumenov		07/06/93	M	1		
5	Martin Simeonov		20/08/98	D	1		
6	Krasimir Stanoev		14/09/94	M	1	(1)	
26	Georgi Tartov		03/12/98	M	1		
16	Petar Vitanov		10/03/95	M	1		
9	Preslav Yordanov		21/07/89	A	9	(2)	3
25	Tonislav Yordanov		27/11/98	A	1		

PFC Dunav Ruse

2010 • Ludogorets Arena, Razgrad (6,500); Gradski (13,000) • fcdunav.eu

Coach: Veselin Velikov

2016

Date		Opponent		Score	Scorers
30/07	h	Vereya	D	0-0	
05/08	a	Neftochimic	W	2-1	*Nenov, Milchev*
12/08	h	Pirin	W	1-0	*Nenov*
19/08	a	Lokomotiv GO	W	2-0	*Ognyanov, Budinov*
27/08	h	Cherno More	W	3-0	*Ognyanov, Dimov, Budinov*
11/09	h	CSKA	W	2-0	*Shopov, Ognyanov*
18/09	a	Beroe	D	0-0	
24/09	h	Botev	L	1-2	*Ognyanov*
02/10	a	Levski	L	0-2	
16/10	h	Montana	D	1-1	*Shopov*
21/10	a	Lok Plovdiv	D	0-0	
28/10	h	Ludogorets	L	3-5	*Budinov, Shopov, Patev*
02/11	a	Slavia	W	2-0	*Kostadinov, Shopov*
19/11	a	Vereya	L	0-1	
27/11	h	Neftochimic	W	3-0	*Dimov, Budinov 2*
30/11	a	Pirin	L	1-4	*Dimov*
03/12	h	Lokomotiv GO	W	1-0	*Kostadinov*
11/12	a	Cherno More	L	0-1	
16/12	a	CSKA	L	0-3	

2017

Date		Opponent		Score	Scorers
17/02	h	Beroe	L	0-4	
24/02	a	Botev	W	2-0	*Karageren 2*
28/02	h	Levski	D	2-2	*Karageren, Budinov*
04/03	a	Montana	W	2-1	*Budinov (p), Mujeci*
10/03	h	Lok Plovdiv	D	1-1	*Shopov*
18/03	a	Ludogorets	D	2-2	*Kostadinov, Karageren*
02/04	h	Slavia	D	1-1	*Larin*
09/04	a	Ludogorets	W	1-0	*Ayass*
15/04	h	Cherno More	W	1-0	*Budinov*
21/04	a	Levski	D	1-1	*Ayass*
28/04	h	Lok Plovdiv	L	2-3	*Kostadinov 2*
07/05	a	CSKA	L	0-2	
12/05	h	Ludogorets	D	2-2	*Shopov, Karagaren*
17/05	a	Cherno More	W	2-1	*Budinov, Kostadinov*
21/05	h	Levski	L	0-1	
28/05	a	Lok Plovdiv	W	4-3	*Nenov, Ayass, Budinov (p), Kostadinov*
31/05	h	CSKA	W	1-0	*Ayass*

No	Name	Nat	DoB	Pos	Aps	(s)	Gls
86	Stanislav Antonov		21/03/86	G	16		
28	Atanas Atanasov		14/07/85	D	16	(1)	
14	Samir Ayass		24/12/90	M	27		4
9	Miroslav Budinov		23/01/86	A	31	(3)	10
12	Svetoslav Chitakov		10/01/92	M		(4)	
91	Nuriddin Davronov	TJK	16/01/91	M		(8)	
15	Diyan Dimov		27/09/85	M	34	(1)	3
66	Iskandar Dzhalilov	TJK	01/06/92	D	23	(2)	
17	Spas Georgiev		21/06/92	M	1	(6)	
23	Hristofor Hubchev		24/11/95	D	13	(2)	
7	Birsent Karageren		06/12/92	M	17		5
7	Nikolay Kolev		29/03/90	M		(14)	
21	Branimir Kostadinov		04/03/91	M	19	(13)	7
21	Olexiy Larin	UKR	04/06/94	D	9	(1)	1
1	Martin Lukov		05/07/93	G	20		
5	Teynur Marem		24/09/94	D	15	(4)	
22	Mihail Milchev		18/06/88	D	33		1
10	Ndue Mujeci	ALB	24/02/93	A	2	(13)	1
94	Yulian Nenov		17/11/94	M	24	(11)	3
18	Anton Ognyanov		30/06/88	M	18		4
4	Petar Patev		21/05/93	D	26	(5)	1
3	Mario Petkov		04/12/96	D	9	(6)	
8	Ivaylo Radentsov		29/05/83	M	10	(10)	
10	Vasil Shopov		09/11/91	M	32	(1)	6
15	Darko Stojanov	MKD	11/12/90	D	1		

PFC Levski Sofia

1914 • Vivacom Arena - Georgi Asparuhov (28,000) • levski.bg

Major honours

Bulgarian League (26) 1933, 1937, 1942, 1946, 1947, 1949, 1950, 1953, 1965, 1968, 1970, 1974, 1977, 1979, 1984, 1985, 1988, 1993, 1994, 1995, 2000, 2001, 2002, 2006, 2007, 2009; Bulgarian Cup (25) 1942, 1946, 1947, 1949, 1950, 1956, 1957, 1959, 1967, 1970, 1971, 1976, 1977, 1979, 1984, 1986, 1991, 1992, 1994, 1998, 2000, 2002, 2003, 2005, 2007

Coach: Ljupko Petrović (SRB); (24/10/16) (Elin Topuzakov); (02/03/17) Nikolay Mitov

2016

Date		Opponent		Score	Scorers
31/07	h	Montana	D	0-0	
07/08	a	Lok Plovdiv	D	2-2	*Narh, Adeniji*
13/08	h	Ludogorets	W	1-0	*Kraev*
21/08	a	Slavia	W	4-0	*Añete, Adeniji, Kostadinov, Kraev*
28/08	h	Vereya	W	4-0	*Narh, Kraev, og (Hassani), Añete*
10/09	a	Neftochimic	W	2-1	*Procházka 2 (2p)*
17/09	h	Pirin	W	2-0	*Pirgov, Adeniji*
26/09	a	Lokomotiv GO	W	1-0	*og (Kavdanski)*
02/10	h	Dunav	W	2-0	*Kostadinov 2*
15/10	a	CSKA	D	1-1	*Narh*
22/10	h	Beroe	W	2-0	*Añete, Kostadinov*
30/10	a	Botev	D	1-1	*Procházka*
04/11	h	Cherno More	W	1-0	*Procházka*
20/11	a	Montana	W	3-1	*Kraev, Pirgov, Mitsanski*
26/11	h	Lok Plovdiv	L	1-2	*og (El Kharroubi)*
30/11	a	Ludogorets	L	1-2	*Adeniji*
03/12	h	Slavia	W	1-0	*Bourabia*
10/12	a	Vereya	W	1-0	*Añete*
14/12	h	Neftochimic	W	1-0	*Adeniji*

2017

Date		Opponent		Score	Scorers
18/02	a	Pirin	L	0-1	
25/02	h	Lokomotiv GO	D	1-1	*Adeniji*
28/02	a	Dunav	D	2-2	*Ognyanov, Procházka (p)*
04/03	h	CSKA	W	2-1	*Procházka (p), Jablonský*
12/03	a	Beroe	L	0-1	
19/03	h	Botev	W	2-0	*Procházka, Adeniji*
01/04	a	Cherno More	L	0-1	
09/04	h	Lok Plovdiv	W	5-0	*Añete, Kraev 4*
14/04	a	Ludogorets	D	0-0	
21/04	h	Dunav	D	1-1	*og (Budinov)*
29/04	h	CSKA	L	0-3	
07/05	a	Cherno More	W	1-0	*Soukouna*
12/05	a	Lok Plovdiv	L	1-2	*Bourabia*
16/05	h	Ludogorets	L	1-3	*Jablonský*
21/05	a	Dunav	W	1-0	*Kraev*
28/05	a	CSKA	L	0-3	
31/05	h	Cherno More	D	2-2	*Kraev, Procházka*

No	Name	Nat	DoB	Pos	Aps	(s)	Gls
17	Tunde Adeniji	NGA	17/09/95	A	33	(3)	7
5	Alexander Dragimirov Alexandrov		13/04/86	D	24	(1)	
25	Alexander Emilov Alexandrov		30/07/86	D	32	(1)	
20	Añete	ESP	01/10/85	M	25	(5)	5
75	Aleks Borimirov		13/05/98	M	1	(3)	
27	Mehdi Bourabia	FRA	07/08/91	M	20	(9)	2
8	Jeremy de Nooijer	CUW	15/03/92	M	21		
11	Jean Deza	PER	09/06/93	M	2	(8)	
44	Viktor Genev		27/10/88	D	2	(2)	
91	Ventsislav Hristov		09/11/88	A	1	(3)	
10	Galin Ivanov		15/04/88	M	1	(2)	
99	Stanislav Ivanov		16/04/99	M	4	(8)	
28	David Jablonský	CZE	08/10/91	D	11	(1)	2
29	Bojan Jorgačević	SRB	12/02/82	G	21		
16	Atanas Kabov		11/04/99	M	1	(2)	
70	Georgi Kostadinov		07/09/90	M	19	(1)	4
12	Bozhidar Kraev		23/06/97	M	24	(10)	10
89	Nikolay Krastev		06/12/96	G	14		
2	Srdjan Luchin	ROU	04/03/86	D	11	(1)	
14	Veselin Minev		14/10/80	D	24		
21	Bozhidar Mitrev		31/03/87	G	1		
9	Iliyan Mitsanski		20/12/85	A		(9)	1
47	Francis Narh	GHA	18/04/94	M	31	(5)	3
6	Ivaylo Naydenov		22/03/98	M	5	(3)	
18	Anton Ognyanov		30/06/88	M	7	(7)	1
4	Miki Orachev		19/03/96	D	1	(2)	
3	Dimitar Pirgov		26/10/89	D	25	(2)	2
15	Roman Procházka	SVK	14/03/89	D	29		8
23	Simon Sandberg	SWE	25/03/94	D	2	(3)	
26	Amadou Soukouna	FRA	24/06/92	A	4	(6)	1
24	Iliya Yurukov		22/09/99	A		(2)	

FC Lokomotiv Gorna Oryahovitsa

1932 • Gradski (7,000) • no website

Coach: Angel Chervenkov; (28/09/16) Ivan Kolev; (02/03/17) (Milcho Sirmov); (14/03/17) Alexander Dimitrov

Date		Opponent		Score	Scorers
2016					
29/07	h	Neftochimic	D	0-0	
05/08	a	Pirin	L	1-2	*Fidanin*
14/08	h	Cherno More	D	2-2	*Trifonov, Smirnov*
19/08	h	Dunav	L	0-2	
27/08	a	CSKA	L	0-2	
12/09	h	Beroe	L	0-1	
17/09	a	Botev	L	0-4	
26/09	h	Levski	L	0-1	
01/10	a	Montana	W	4-2	*Coureur 2, Kifoueti, Atanasov*
17/10	h	Lok Plovdiv	W	2-1	*Coureur, Kifoueti*
22/10	a	Ludogorets	L	0-4	
28/10	h	Slavia	W	1-0	*Apostolov*
04/11	a	Vereya	L	0-1	
21/11	a	Neftochimic	D	1-1	*Fidanin*
25/11	h	Pirin	W	1-0	*Atanasov*
29/11	a	Cherno More	D	1-1	*Djoman*
03/12	a	Dunav	L	0-1	
11/12	h	CSKA	D	0-0	
15/12	a	Beroe	D	1-1	*Uzunov*
2017					
18/02	h	Botev	L	0-1	
25/02	a	Levski	D	1-1	*Kifoueti*
01/03	h	Montana	L	0-1	
04/03	a	Lok Plovdiv	L	1-2	*Moussa*
12/03	h	Ludogorets	L	0-5	
16/03	a	Slavia	L	1-3	*N'Dongala*
02/04	h	Vereya	W	5-0	*Kifoueti 2, Djoman, N'Dongala 2 (1p)*
08/04	a	Beroe	W	3-2	*Kifoueti, N'Dongala, Uzunov*
13/04	h	Neftochimic	D	1-1	*N'Dongala*
24/04	a	Pirin	D	1-1	*Kifoueti*
29/04	h	Beroe	L	0-1	
06/05	a	Neftochimic	L	1-4	*Fidanin (p)*
11/05	h	Pirin	W	4-3	*Tsonkov 2, N'Dongala, Moussa*

No	Name	Nat	DoB	Pos	Aps	(s)	Gls
15	Jean Ambrose	FRA	01/06/91	D	10		
88	Yordan Apostolov		30/11/89	M	9	(4)	1
30	Dimo Atanasov		24/10/85	M	10	(5)	2
66	Antoniy Balakov		14/12/88	M		(2)	
91	Nikolay Bankov		19/11/90	G	26		
28	Mohammed Ben Othman	TUN	18/11/89	M	15	(5)	
19	Mathias Coureur	MTQ	22/03/88	A	10	(1)	3
16	Petar Denchev		16/03/89	G	1	(1)	
27	Igor Djoman	FRA	01/05/86	M	20	(1)	2
75	Mehdi Fennouche	ALG	20/02/93	M	4	(1)	
6	Atanas Fidanin		09/08/86	D	24	(1)	3
77	Lyubomor Genchev		13/04/96	M	4	(13)	
18	Tsvetan Genkov		08/02/84	A	9	(1)	
4	Nikolay Hristov		01/08/89	M	14	(4)	
9	Tihomir Kanev		03/01/86	A	6	(3)	
15	Georgi Karaneychev		09/06/88	M	1	(3)	
5	Martin Kavdanski		13/02/87	D	29		
37	Ventsislav Kerchev		02/06/97	D	21	(3)	
14	Rahavi Kifoueti	CGO	12/03/89	A	23	(1)	7
1	Stefano Kunchev		20/04/91	G	5		
22	Karl Madianga	FRA	30/01/94	M	3	(2)	
7	Simeon Mechev		16/03/90	M	15	(3)	
9	Sofien Moussa	TUN	06/02/88	A	6	(6)	2
38	Aristote N'Dongala	COD	19/01/94	M	10	(1)	6
24	Ulysse Ndong	GAB	24/11/92	M	20		
10	Bedri Ryustemov		17/11/95	M		(1)	
99	Viktor Shishkov		07/09/86	A		(1)	
71	Yanaki Smirnov		20/12/92	A	5	(3)	1
11	Krasen Trifonov		05/12/83	M	7	(3)	1
33	Stefan Tsonkov		24/01/95	D	7	(4)	2
23	Vladislav Uzunov		25/05/91	M	9	(13)	2
8	Milen Zhelev		17/07/93	D	29	(2)	

PFC Lokomotiv Plovdiv

1926 • Lokomotiv (10,000) • lokomotivpd.com

Major honours
Bulgarian League (1) 2004

Coach: Ilian Iliev; (18/10/16) (Hristo Kolev); (31/10/16) Eduard Eranosyan; (10/04/17) (Stoyan Kolev); (19/04/17) Voin Voinov

Date		Opponent		Score	Scorers
2016					
30/07	a	Botev	D	1-1	*Kiki*
07/08	h	Levski	D	2-2	*Marchev, Kamburov (p)*
12/08	a	Montana	W	3-0	*Kiki, Karageren, Kamburov (p)*
19/08	a	Cherno More	L	0-2	
28/08	h	Ludogorets	D	2-2	*Kamburov, Raykov*
10/09	a	Slavia	L	2-5	*Kiki, Kamburov (p)*
16/09	h	Vereya	W	3-1	*Kamburov, Umarbaev, Kotev*
24/09	a	Neftochimic	W	2-1	*Raynov, Bakalov*
30/09	h	Pirin	L	2-3	*Bakalov, Raynov*
17/10	a	Lokomotiv GO	L	1-2	*Kamburov*
21/10	h	Dunav	D	0-0	
29/10	a	CSKA	W	1-0	*Kiki*
02/11	h	Beroe	D	1-1	*Kamburov*
20/11	h	Botev	W	2-0	*Kamburov, Umarbaev*
26/11	a	Levski	W	2-1	*Marchev, Kamburov (p)*
29/11	h	Montana	W	2-0	*Marchev, Kamburov*
02/12	h	Cherno More	W	1-0	*Kiki*
10/12	a	Ludogorets	L	0-1	
14/12	h	Slavia	D	1-1	*Kotev*
2017					
20/02	a	Vereya	W	1-0	*Umarbaev*
25/02	h	Neftochimic	D	0-0	
01/03	a	Pirin	L	0-1	
04/03	h	Lokomotiv GO	W	2-1	*Martinovič 2*
10/03	a	Dunav	D	1-1	*Martinovič*
18/03	h	CSKA	D	1-1	*Kiki*
01/04	a	Beroe	L	2-3	*Vidanov, Bakalov*
09/04	a	Levski	L	0-5	
13/04	h	CSKA	L	1-2	*Bakalov*
23/04	a	Cherno More	L	2-3	*Kamburov, Bakalov*
28/04	a	Dunav	W	3-2	*Marchev 2, Kamburov*
05/05	h	Ludogorets	L	0-3	
12/05	h	Levski	W	2-1	*Kamburov, Jevtoski*
17/05	a	CSKA	D	0-0	
21/05	h	Cherno More	W	2-1	*Kamburov, Martinovič*
28/05	h	Dunav	L	3-4	*Martinovič 2, Kamburov (p)*
31/05	a	Ludogorets	W	2-1	*Kamburov (p), Martinovič*

No	Name	Nat	DoB	Pos	Aps	(s)	Gls
29	Yassine Amrioui	FRA	21/02/95	D	3	(1)	
27	Dimo Bakalov		19/12/88	M	20	(13)	5
23	Choco	BRA	18/01/90	D	3	(4)	
16	Yassine El Kharroubi	MAR	29/03/90	G	20		
14	Ivan Goranov		10/06/92	D	28	(1)	
9	Petar Glavchev		19/08/99	M		(1)	
77	Iyad Hamud		24/07/01	M	2	(1)	
4	Stefan Jevtoski	MKD	02/09/97	M	10	(7)	1
11	Martin Kamburov		13/10/80	A	32	(1)	16
21	Birsent Karageren		06/12/92	M	3	(3)	1
9	Dani Kiki		08/01/88	M	26	(7)	6
6	Kiril Kotev		18/04/82	D	29	(1)	2
71	Plamen Krumov		04/11/85	D	29		
10	Veselin Marchev		07/02/90	M	28	(4)	5
77	Dino Martinovič	SVN	20/07/90	M	7	(8)	7
23	Miguel Luque	ESP	23/07/90	M	6	(2)	
24	Robert Petrov	MKD	02/06/78	D	2		
20	Paulo Teles	POR	30/09/93	M	4	(5)	
28	Ilko Pirgov		10/06/92	G	16		
22	Osama Rachid	IRQ	17/01/92	M	2	(3)	
13	Simeon Raykov		11/11/89	M	6	(3)	1
18	Martin Raynov		25/04/92	M	12	(4)	2
93	Aymen Souda	FRA	28/02/93	A		(2)	
23	Vanco Trajanov	MKD	09/08/78	M	28	(1)	
3	Alexander Tunchev		10/07/81	D	2	(1)	
39	Perviz Umarbaev	TJK	01/11/94	M	15	(18)	3
5	Georgi Valchev		07/03/91	D	8	(1)	
19	Dimitar Velkovski		22/01/95	M	11	(9)	
15	Dimitar Vezalov		13/04/87	D	20	(2)	
5	Pavel Vidanov		01/08/88	D	24	(1)	1
37	Dimitar Zakonov		20/06/99	M		(1)	

PFC Ludogorets Razgrad

1945 • Ludogorets Arena (6,500) • ludogorets.com

Major honours
Bulgarian League (6) 2012, 2013, 2014, 2015, 2016, 2017; Bulgarian Cup (2) 2012, 2014

Coach: Georgi Dermendzhiev

Date		Opponent		Score	Scorers
2016					
06/08	h	Botev	W	4-1	*Cicinho, Marcelinho, Keşerü (p), Juninho Quixadá*
13/08	a	Levski	L	0-1	
20/08	h	Montana	W	2-0	*Shokolarov, Keşerü*
28/08	a	Lok Plovdiv	D	2-2	*Plastun, Keşerü*
09/09	a	Cherno More	W	3-1	*Wanderson, Marcelinho 2*
17/09	h	Slavia	W	3-1	*Moţi (p), Wanderson, Jonathan Cafú*
23/09	a	Vereya	W	5-1	*Misidjan, Jonathan Cafú 2, Wanderson, Marcelinho*
02/10	h	Neftochimic	W	3-1	*Wanderson, Lucas Sasha, Keşerü*
14/10	a	Pirin	W	3-1	*Moţi (p), Jonathan Cafú, og (Bashliev)*
22/10	h	Lokomotiv GO	W	4-0	*Keşerü 2, Marcelinho, Juninho Quixadá*
28/10	a	Dunav	W	5-3	*Keşerü 3, Wanderson, Jonathan Cafú*
05/11	h	CSKA	W	2-1	*Wanderson, Moţi*
16/11	a	Beroe	W	2-0	*Keşerü, Marcelinho*
19/11	h	Beroe	W	1-0	*Jonathan Cafú*
26/11	a	Botev	W	3-1	*Lukoki, Gustavo Campanharo, Keşerü*
30/11	h	Levski	W	2-1	*Wanderson, Marcelinho*
10/12	h	Lok Plovdiv	W	1-0	*Jonathan Cafú*
14/12	h	Cherno More	D	1-1	*Keşerü*
2017					
12/02	a	Montana	W	4-0	*Marcelinho 2, Wanderson, Jonathan Cafú*
20/02	a	Slavia	W	2-0	*Keşerü, Juninho Quixadá*
26/02	h	Vereya	W	4-0	*Gustavo Campanharo, Wanderson, João Paulo, Marcelinho*
01/03	a	Neftochimic	D	1-1	*Marcelinho*
05/03	h	Pirin	W	3-0	*Jonathan Cafú, Keşerü 2*
12/03	a	Lokomotiv GO	W	5-0	*Marcelinho, Keşerü 3, Wanderson*
18/03	h	Dunav	D	2-2	*Palomino, Keşerü*
01/04	a	CSKA	W	2-0	*Moţi, Jonathan Cafú*
09/04	h	Dunav	L	0-1	
14/04	h	Levski	D	0-0	
23/04	a	CSKA	D	1-1	*Marcelinho*
01/05	h	Cherno More	W	4-0	*Keşerü 2 (1p), Palomino, Wanderson*
05/05	a	Lok Plovdiv	W	3-0	*Anicet Abel, Wanderson, Natanael*
12/05	a	Dunav	D	2-2	*Keşerü, og (Milchev)*
16/05	a	Levski	W	3-1	*Marcelinho, Wanderson 2*
20/05	h	CSKA	D	1-1	*Dyakov*
28/05	a	Cherno More	W	3-1	*Plastun, Grigorov, K Dimitrov*
31/05	h	Lok Plovdiv	L	1-2	*Tsvyatkov*

No	Name	Nat	DoB	Pos	Aps	(s)	Gls
80	Denislav Alexandrov		19/07/97	A	1	(2)	
12	Anicet Abel	MAD	16/03/90	M	16	(9)	1
1	Milan Borjan	CAN	23/10/87	G	7		
23	Tsvetelin Chunchukov		26/12/94	A	2	(1)	
4	Cicinho	BRA	26/12/88	D	18	(1)	1
73	Kristiyan Dimitrov		16/04/93	D	2		1
34	Oleg Dimitrov		06/03/96	M	2	(1)	
18	Svetoslav Dyakov		31/05/84	M	22		1
99	Kristiyan Grigorov		27/10/90	D	2		1
10	Gustavo Campanharo	BRA	04/04/92	M	15	(10)	2
37	João Paulo	BRA	02/06/88	A	1	(5)	1
22	Jonathan Cafú	BRA	10/07/91	A	28	(2)	10
11	Juninho Quixadá	BRA	12/12/85	M	7	(17)	3
85	Atanas Karacharov		18/06/98	M		(1)	
28	Claudiu Keşerü	ROU	02/12/86	A	25	(5)	22
36	Kristiyan Kitov		14/10/96	M	2		
45	Ivaylo Klimentov		03/02/98	M		(1)	
98	Svetoslav Kovachev		14/03/98	M	3		
8	Lucas Sasha	BRA	01/03/90	M	19	(6)	1
92	Jody Lukoki	COD	15/11/92	M	3	(11)	1
84	Marcelinho		24/08/84	M	30	(2)	14
25	Yordan Minev		14/10/80	D	12	(1)	
93	Virgil Misidjan	NED	24/07/93	M	12	(15)	1
27	Cosmin Moţi	ROU	03/12/84	D	22		4
6	Natanael	BRA	25/12/90	D	26		1
29	Daniel Naumov		29/03/98	G	2		
5	José Luis Palomino	ARG	05/01/90	D	27		2
24	Preslav Petrov		01/05/95	D	2		
32	Ihor Plastun	UKR	20/08/90	D	18	(3)	2
33	Renan	BRA	18/05/89	G	9		
14	Slavcho Shokolarov		20/08/89	M	3		1
21	Vladislav Stoyanov		08/06/87	G	18		
55	Georgi Terziev		18/04/92	D	3		
97	Tomas Tsvyatkov		01/06/97	A		(2)	1
19	Alexander Vasilev		27/04/95	M	4	(1)	
77	Vitinha	POR	11/02/86	D	2	(2)	
88	Wanderson	BRA	02/01/88	M	31		14
76	Serdar Yusufov		02/10/98	M		(1)	

BULGARIA

PFC Montana 1921

1921 • Gradski, Lovech (7,000) • pfcmontana.bg

Coach: Stevica Kuzmanovski (MKD); (03/10/16) Atanas Dzhambazki; (17/04/17) (Dilyan Ivanov); (20/04/17) Atanas Atanasov

Date		Opponent		Score	Scorers
2016					
31/07	a	Levski	D	0-0	
08/08	a	Cherno More	L	0-1	
12/08	h	Lok Plovdiv	L	0-3	
20/08	a	Ludogorets	L	0-2	
26/08	h	Slavia	L	1-2	*Marquinhos*
09/09	a	Vereya	L	0-3	
16/09	h	Neftochimic	W	2-0	*Petkov, Vasev*
23/09	a	Pirin	L	0-1	
01/10	h	Lokomotiv GO	L	2-4	*Petkov, Danillo Bala*
16/10	a	Dunav	D	1-1	*Mihov*
21/10	h	CSKA	L	0-2	
29/10	a	Beroe	L	1-2	*Petkov*
03/11	h	Botev	W	3-1	*Petkov 2, Georgiev*
20/11	h	Levski	L	1-3	*Dyakov*
26/11	h	Cherno More	L	0-2	
29/11	a	Lok Plovdiv	L	0-2	
10/12	a	Slavia	L	0-2	
13/12	h	Vereya	D	1-1	*Iliev*
2017					
12/02	h	Ludogorets	L	0-4	
18/02	a	Neftochimic	L	0-2	
26/02	h	Pirin	L	1-2	*Genov*
01/03	a	Lokomotiv GO	W	1-0	*Vasev*
04/03	h	Dunav	L	1-2	*Petkov*
11/03	a	CSKA	L	1-2	*Atanasov*
17/03	h	Beroe	L	0-3	
31/03	a	Botev	L	0-2	
07/04	a	Botev	L	1-7	*Sène*
15/04	h	Slavia	L	3-4	*Iliev, og (A Hristov), Sène*
22/04	a	Vereya	L	0-1	
30/04	h	Botev	W	2-1	*Petkov, Atanasov*
05/05	a	Slavia	L	0-1	
10/05	h	Vereya	L	2-3	*Georgiev, Sène*

No	Name	Nat	DoB	Pos	Aps	(s)	Gls
1	Evgeni Alexandrov		14/06/88	G	4		
10	Petar Atanasov		13/10/90	M	22	(7)	2
12	Corrin Brooks-Meade	MSR	19/03/88	G	7	(1)	
19	Yuliyan Chapaev		03/07/96	D	2	(2)	
20	Nikolay Chipev		20/02/89	M	9		
23	Choco	BRA	18/01/90	D	18		
8	Borislav Damyanov		11/04/98	A		(1)	
4	Danillo Bala	BRA	05/05/93	A		(2)	1
29	Bamba Diarrassouba	FRA	29/03/89	D	20		
25	Kostadin Dyakov		22/08/85	M	19	(4)	1
24	Fernando Silva	BRA	18/05/91	A	4	(8)	
6	Daniel Gadzhev		21/06/85	M	8		
7	Daniel Genov		19/05/89	A	17	(9)	1
22	Sergey Georgiev		05/05/92	M	26	(5)	2
17	Blažo Igumanović	MNE	19/01/86	D	10		
9	Atanas Iliev		09/10/94	A	6	(12)	2
77	Nebojša Ivančević	SRB	01/09/94	A		(3)	
4	Antoni Ivanov		11/09/95	M	5	(6)	
1	Hristo Ivanov		06/04/82	G	14		
21	Ivan Ivanov		13/08/92	M	3		
26	Djordje Ivelja	SRB	30/06/84	M	2	(5)	
2	Marko Jakolič	SVN	16/04/91	M	6	(3)	
14	Christos Kontochristos	GRE	03/01/91	D	11		
8	Georgi Korudzhiev		02/03/88	M	13	(3)	
28	Marquinhos		30/04/82	M	9	(6)	1
3	Ivan Mihov		08/06/91	D	29		1
13	Raif Muradov		10/12/93	D	5		
16	Stivan Petkov		07/05/95	A	14	(9)	7
5	Anton Polyutkin	RUS	02/02/93	M	7		
5	Birahim Sarr	FRA	27/07/91	D	10		
33	Nemanja Šćekić	MNE	17/12/91	G	3		
28	Saër Sène	FRA	04/11/86	A	5	(2)	3
6	Tihomir Trifonov		25/11/86	D	11		
11	Andreas Vasev		01/03/91	M	22	(5)	2
33	Ivaylo Vasilev		15/01/91	G	4		
17	Alexander Veselinov		01/01/97	A		(2)	
24	Santiago Villafañe	ARG	19/05/88	D	7		

PFC Neftochimic Burgas

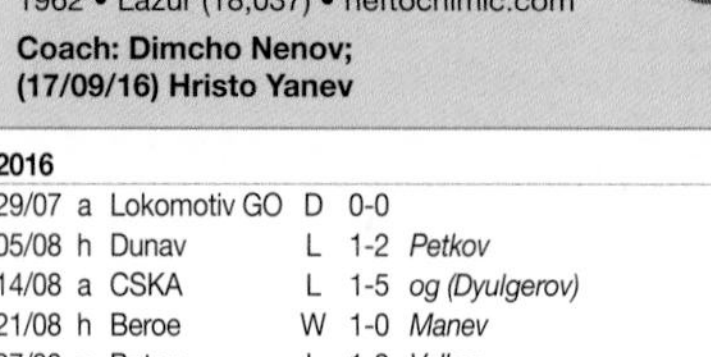

1962 • Lazur (18,037) • neftochimic.com

Coach: Dimcho Nenov; (17/09/16) Hristo Yanev

Date		Opponent		Score	Scorers
2016					
29/07	a	Lokomotiv GO	D	0-0	
05/08	h	Dunav	L	1-2	*Petkov*
14/08	a	CSKA	L	1-5	*og (Dyulgerov)*
21/08	h	Beroe	W	1-0	*Manev*
27/08	a	Botev	L	1-2	*Velkov*
10/09	h	Levski	L	1-2	*Valchanov*
16/09	a	Montana	L	0-2	
24/09	h	Lok Plovdiv	L	1-2	*Hristov*
02/10	a	Ludogorets	L	1-3	*Dyulgerov*
15/10	h	Slavia	W	2-0	*Hristov, Manev*
23/10	a	Vereya	D	1-1	*Manev*
30/10	a	Cherno More	L	1-3	*Valchanov*
04/11	h	Pirin	W	3-1	*Valchanov, Randjelović, Hazurov (p)*
21/11	h	Lokomotiv GO	D	1-1	*Malamov*
27/11	a	Dunav	L	0-3	
01/12	h	CSKA	L	0-2	
04/12	a	Beroe	L	0-2	
09/12	h	Botev	W	4-0	*Bozhinov, Dyulgerov, Ognyanov, Hristov*
14/12	a	Levski	L	0-1	
2017					
18/02	h	Montana	W	2-0	*Ivanov 2*
25/02	a	Lok Plovdiv	D	0-0	
01/03	h	Ludogorets	D	1-1	*Milanov*
05/03	a	Slavia	W	3-0	*Valchanov, Dyulgerov, Ivanov*
13/03	h	Vereya	W	1-0	*Valchev*
19/03	h	Cherno More	L	1-3	*Valchev*
31/03	a	Pirin	L	0-1	
07/04	a	Pirin	L	1-2	*Valchanov*
13/04	a	Lokomotiv GO	D	1-1	*Hristov*
21/04	h	beroe	D	0-0	
28/04	h	Pirin	L	0-3	
06/05	h	Lokomotiv GO	W	4-1	*Valchanov, Ivanov, Romanov 2*
11/05	a	Beroe	L	0-3	

No	Name	Nat	DoB	Pos	Aps	(s)	Gls
10	Alexander Alexandrov		28/03/94	M	4	(1)	
32	Lyubomir Bozhinov		16/05/86	M	11	(9)	1
61	Georgi Chakarov		13/01/89	A	2	(2)	
11	Atanas Chepilov		06/02/87	A		(6)	
8	Nikolay Dyulgerov		10/03/88	M	28		3
1	Yanko Georgiev		22/10/88	G	27		
16	Bojan Gjorgievski	MKD	25/01/92	D	3	(1)	
25	Angel Granchov		16/10/92	D	21	(3)	
5	Zhivko Hadzhiev		09/11/94	D	1		
3	Georgi Hashev		26/03/90	D	5	(2)	
24	Kostadin Hazurov		05/08/85	A	7	(11)	1
26	Sergiu Homei	ROU	06/07/87	D	25		
91	Ventsislav Hristov		09/11/88	A	11	(4)	4
10	Galin Ivanov		15/04/88	M	9	(1)	4
12	Stoyan Kolev		03/02/89	G	4		
89	Stanislav Malamov		21/09/89	M	5	(3)	1
3	Ivo Malinov		29/01/93	D	6	(1)	
22	Emanuil Manev		19/04/92	M	13	(9)	3
71	Iliya Milanov		19/02/92	D	6	(3)	1
7	Mariyan Ognyanov		30/07/88	M	18	(1)	1
17	Randy Onuoha	NED	01/04/94	D	9	(1)	
19	Mihael Orachev		03/10/95	M	16	(4)	
19	Kristian Parashkevov		07/02/99	M		(3)	
20	Yani Pehlivanov		14/07/88	D	20	(1)	
15	Zhivko Petkov		15/02/93	A	6	(14)	1
6	Marko Randjelović	SRB	16/08/84	D	11	(3)	1
23	Mario Rašić	CRO	20/05/89	M		(2)	
73	Vladislav Romanov		07/02/88	M	12	(1)	2
17	Rumen Rumenov		07/06/93	M	6	(5)	
5	Simeon Rusev		26/08/98	M	1		
7	Ivan Valchanov		28/09/91	M	25	(4)	6
5	Georgi Valchev		07/03/91	D	7		2
33	Ivaylo Vasilev		15/01/91	G	1		
2	Kostadin Velkov		26/03/89	D	14		1
12	Yordan Yordanov		14/04/92	M	18	(1)	

OFC Pirin Blagoevgrad

1922 • Hristo Botev (7,500) • pirinfc.com

Coach: Stefan Genov; (13/01/17) Milen Radukanov

Date		Opponent		Score	Scorers
2016					
31/07	h	Cherno More	L	1-3	*Zlatinov*
05/08	h	Lokomotiv GO	W	2-1	*Zlatinov (p), S Kostov*
12/08	a	Dunav	L	0-1	
20/08	h	CSKA	D	1-1	*Blagov*
26/08	a	Beroe	L	0-1	
11/09	h	Botev	W	2-1	*D Mladenov, Bashliev*
17/09	a	Levski	L	0-2	
23/09	h	Montana	W	1-0	*Nikolov*
30/09	a	Lok Plovdiv	W	3-2	*D Mladenov 2, S Kostov*
14/10	h	Ludogorets	L	1-3	*D Mladenov*
23/10	a	Slavia	L	1-3	*D Mladenov*
31/10	h	Vereya	D	1-1	*Bashliev*
04/11	a	Neftochimic	L	1-3	*Zlatinov*
18/11	a	Cherno More	D	0-0	
25/11	a	Lokomotiv GO	L	0-1	
30/11	h	Dunav	W	4-1	*D Mladenov 2, S Kostov 2*
04/12	a	CSKA	L	0-2	
12/12	h	Beroe	D	1-1	*Starokin*
15/12	a	Botev	L	2-3	*S Kostov 2*
2017					
18/02	h	Levski	W	1-0	*Souda*
26/02	a	Montana	W	2-1	*D Mladenov, Tsvetkov*
01/03	h	Lok Plovdiv	W	1-0	*Starokin*
05/03	a	Ludogorets	L	0-3	
12/03	h	Slavia	W	4-0	*Tsvetkov (p), Starokin, Sandev, S Kostov*
18/03	a	Vereya	L	0-2	
31/03	h	Neftochimic	W	1-0	*S Kostov*
07/04	h	Neftochimic	W	2-1	*Popev, Tsvetkov (p)*
14/04	a	Beroe	D	1-1	*Blagov*
24/04	h	Lokomotiv GO	D	1-1	*D Mladenov (p)*
28/04	a	Neftochimic	W	3-0	*D Mladenov 2, Tsvetkov*
06/05	h	Beroe	D	1-1	*S Kostov*
11/05	a	Lokomotiv GO	L	3-4	*Blagov, S Kostov, Tsvetkov*

No	Name	Nat	DoB	Pos	Aps	(s)	Gls
29	Alexandre	BRA	18/06/94	D	6		
31	Georgi Argilashki		13/06/91	G	5		
21	Alexander Bashliev		16/11/89	D	27	(1)	2
16	Ventsislav Bengyuzov		22/01/91	M	1	(5)	
15	Dimitar Blagov		30/03/92	M	22	(3)	3
8	Iliya Dimitrov		10/07/96	A		(3)	
29	Kiril Grozdanov		27/09/97	A	2	(9)	
24	Antonio Hadzhiivanov		16/01/90	A			
9	Ross Jenkins	ENG	09/11/90	M	9		
24	Anton Kostadinov		24/06/82	M	16	(7)	
76	Krasimir Kostov		01/09/85	G	16		
19	Stanislav Kostov		02/10/91	A	26	(4)	10
4	Kristián Koštrna	SVK	15/12/93	D	29	(1)	
22	Blagoy Makendzhiev		11/07/88	G	11		
9	Daniel Mladenov		25/05/87	M	20	(4)	11
5	Hristo Mladenov		22/03/98	M		(1)	
10	Ndue Mujeci	ALB	24/02/93	A	6	(5)	
27	Kostadin Nichev		22/07/88	D	10	(9)	
14	Stiliyan Nikolov		16/07/91	D	28		1
18	Yulian Popev		06/07/86	D	19	(3)	1
3	Rumen Sandev		19/11/88	D	28		1
93	Aymen Souda	FRA	28/02/93	A	3	(1)	1
6	Orlin Starokin		08/01/87	M	22	(2)	3
7	Toni Tasev		25/03/94	M	25	(4)	
17	Mario Topuzov		25/07/99	M		(2)	
23	Todor Trayanov		30/05/95	M	13	(11)	
8	Ivan Tsvetkov		31/08/79	A	3	(9)	5
9	Vladislav Zlatinov		23/03/83	A	5	(6)	3

PFC Slavia Sofia

1913 • Vasil Levski (43,230) • pfcslavia.com

Major honours
Bulgarian League (7) 1928, 1930, 1936, 1939, 1941, 1943, 1996; Bulgarian Cup (7) 1952, 1963, 1964, 1966, 1975, 1980, 1996

Coach: Aleksandr Tarkhanov (RUS); (03/11/16) Vladimir Ivanov; (12/05/17) Zlatomir Zagorčić

2016

29/07	a	CSKA	L	0-2	
07/08	h	Beroe	L	1-2	*Serderov*
15/08	a	Botev	L	2-3	*Serderov, I Dimitrov (p)*
21/08	h	Levski	L	0-4	
26/08	a	Montana	W	2-1	*Yomov, Baldzhiyski*
10/09	h	Lok Plovdiv	W	5-2	*P Hristov, Serderov, I Dimitrov 2 (1p), Yomov*
17/09	a	Ludogorets	L	1-3	*Velkov*
25/09	a	Cherno More	D	0-0	
01/10	h	Vereya	W	3-1	*Minchev, Vasev 2*
15/10	a	Neftochimic	L	0-2	
23/10	h	Pirin	W	3-1	*Domovchiyski 2, Serderov*
28/10	a	Lokomotiv GO	L	0-1	
02/11	h	Dunav	L	0-2	
19/11	h	CSKA	L	0-1	
27/11	a	Beroe	D	1-1	*Minchev*
30/11	h	Botev	W	3-2	*Serderov, Domovchiyski, Baldzhiyski*
03/12	a	Levski	L	0-1	
10/12	h	Montana	W	2-0	*N Dimitrov, Domovchiyski*
14/12	a	Lok Plovdiv	D	1-1	*Vasev*

2017

20/02	h	Ludogorets	L	0-2	
26/02	h	Cherno More	W	2-1	*Serderov, Minchev*
02/03	a	Vereya	L	0-3	
05/03	h	Neftochimic	L	0-3	
12/03	a	Pirin	L	0-4	
16/03	h	Lokomotiv GO	W	3-1	*I Dimitrov (p), Serderov, Vasev*
02/04	a	Dunav	D	1-1	*Serderov*
10/04	a	Vereya	W	1-0	*I Dimitrov*
15/04	a	Montana	W	4-3	*Milev, Minchev 2, Krastev*
22/04	h	Botev	L	0-3	
01/05	h	Vereya	L	0-1	
05/05	h	Montana	W	1-0	*Velev*
10/05	a	Botev	L	1-3	*og (Apostolov)*

No	Name	Nat	DoB	Pos	Aps	(s)	Gls
11	Borislav Baldzhiyski		12/10/90	M	8	(4)	2
6	Alexander Branekov		31/05/87	D	9		
5	Dimitar Burov		31/08/97	D	2		
14	Ivaylo Dimitrov		26/03/89	M	13	(7)	5
77	Nikolay Dimitrov		15/10/96	M	10	(1)	1
24	Valeri Domovchiyski		05/10/86	A	11	(1)	4
5	Alexandru Giurgiu	ROU	25/09/92	D	1	(3)	
4	Andrea Hristov		01/03/99	D	14	(2)	
15	Petko Hristov		01/03/99	D	24	(1)	1
15	Georg Iliev		23/10/94	M		(1)	
10	Yanis Karabelyov		08/03/96	M	15	(6)	
66	Aboud Omar Khamis	KEN	09/09/92	D	27		
13	Mario Kirev		15/08/89	G	11	(1)	
19	Kaloyan Krastev		24/01/99	A	9	(14)	1
27	Emil Martinov		18/03/92	M	29		
18	Daniil Maykov	RUS	14/04/97	D	3		
45	Nasko Milev		18/07/96	A	3	(5)	1
73	Ivan Minchev		28/05/91	M	19	(4)	5
11	Georgi Pashov		04/03/90	D	27		
1	Georgi Petkov		14/03/76	G	16	(1)	
22	Vladimir Semerdzhiev		27/05/95	M	11	(4)	
9	Serder Serderov	RUS	10/03/94	M	24	(3)	8
21	Martin Stankev		29/07/89	M	1	(2)	
32	Antonis Stergiakis	GRE	16/03/99	G	5	(3)	
71	Emil Stoev		17/01/96	M	1	(1)	
18	Evgeni Tyukalov	RUS	07/08/92	A	1	(2)	
8	Bozhidar Vasev		14/03/93	M	23	(5)	4
33	Kitan Vasilev		19/02/97	A		(3)	
17	Stefan Velev		02/05/89	M	8		1
13	Stefan Velkov		12/12/96	D	18	(1)	1
35	Georgi Yomov		06/07/97	M	9	(16)	2

FC Vereya Stara Zagora

2001 • Trace Arena (2,214) • fcvereya.bg

Coach: Alexander Tomash

2016

30/07	a	Dunav	L	0-0	
06/08	h	CSKA	W	1-0	*Soukouna*
13/08	a	Beroe	L	0-1	
22/08	h	Botev	W	1-0	*Kostov*
28/08	a	Levski	L	0-4	
09/09	h	Montana	W	3-0	*Yordanov, Andonov 2 (1p)*
16/09	a	Lok Plovdiv	L	1-3	*Tsvetanov*
23/09	h	Ludogorets	L	1-5	*Elias (p)*
01/10	a	Slavia	L	1-3	*Soukouna*
14/10	a	Cherno More	L	1-2	*Munin*
23/10	h	Neftochimic	D	1-1	*Angelov*
31/10	a	Pirin	D	1-1	*Tsvetanov*
04/11	h	Lokomotiv GO	W	1-0	*Tsvetanov*
19/11	h	Dunav	W	1-0	*Soukouna*
27/11	a	CSKA	D	1-1	*Tsvetanov*
01/12	h	Beroe	W	1-0	*Soukouna*
05/12	a	Botev	L	1-2	*Tsvetanov*
10/12	h	Levski	L	0-1	
13/12	a	Montana	D	1-1	*Angelov*

2017

20/02	h	Lok Plovdiv	L	0-1	
26/02	a	Ludogorets	L	0-4	
02/03	h	Slavia	W	3-0	*Andonov (p), Ivanov 2*
05/03	h	Cherno More	D	0-0	
13/03	a	Neftochimic	L	0-1	
18/03	h	Pirin	W	2-0	*Domovchiyski, Pedro Eugénio*
02/04	a	Lokomotiv GO	L	0-5	
10/04	h	Slavia	L	0-1	
14/04	a	Botev	W	1-0	*Pedro Eugénio*
22/04	h	Montana	W	1-0	*Bengyuzov*
01/05	a	Slavia	W	1-0	*Pedro Eugénio*
05/05	h	Botev	W	3-1	*Andonov, Kaloyanov, Yordanov*
10/05	a	Montana	W	3-2	*Baldé, Kerkar, Ben Djemia*

No	Name	Nat	DoB	Pos	Aps	(s)	Gls
71	Georgi Andonov		28/06/83	A	19	(3)	4
25	Georgi Angelov		12/11/90	M	27	(1)	2
33	Georgi Argilashki		13/06/91	G	2		
8	Ousmane Baldé	GUI	30/12/89	M	10	(6)	1
71	Ivan Bandalovski		23/11/86	D	7		
4	Selim Ben Djemia	TUN	29/01/89	D	7		1
16	Ventsislav Bengyuzov		22/01/91	M	10		1
27	Svetoslav Dikov		18/04/92	M		(6)	
24	Valeri Domovchiyski		05/10/86	A	6	(2)	1
10	Elias	BRA	04/09/81	M	19	(6)	1
71	Emre Emin		19/06/98	M		(2)	
33	Miroslav Enchev		08/08/91	D	4	(8)	
6	Ilias Hassani	FRA	08/11/95	D	19	(4)	
21	Zdravko Iliev		19/10/84	D	26	(3)	
89	Samuel Inkoom	GHA	01/06/89	D	6	(3)	
18	Yanislav Ivanov		06/03/92	M	3	(6)	2
32	Vasil Kaloyanov		13/07/88	A	6	(6)	1
12	Ivan Karadzhov		12/07/89	G	16		
26	Salim Kerkar	FRA	04/08/87	M	7	(8)	1
1	Plamen Kolev		09/02/88	G	14		
39	Metodi Kostov		04/04/90	A	4	(7)	1
5	Iliya Munin		16/01/93	D	15	(1)	1
8	Alexandru Pascenco	MDA	28/05/89	M	1	(4)	
77	Pedro Eugénio	POR	26/06/90	M	26	(3)	3
15	Kostadin Slaev		02/10/89	D	24	(1)	
9	Amadou Soukouna	FRA	21/06/92	A	18		4
7	Momchil Tsvetanov		03/12/90	M	16	(2)	5
71	Ivan Vinkov		08/01/92	M		(1)	
26	Alexander Yakimov		27/04/89	M		(4)	
11	Iliyan Yordanov		03/04/89	M	17	(7)	2
3	Vladimir Zafirov		21/03/83	D	23		

Top goalscorers

22	Claudiu Keşerü (Ludogorets)
16	Martin Kamburov (Lokomotiv Plovdiv)
14	Marcelinho (Ludogorets) Wanderson (Ludogorets)
13	João Paulo (Botev/Ludogorets)
11	Junior Mapuku (Beroe) Todor Nedelev (Botev) Daniel Mladenov (Pirin)
10	Marek Kuzma (Cherno More) Miroslav Budinov (Dunav) Bozhidar Kraev (Levski) Jonathan Cafú (Ludogorets) Stanislav Kostov (Pirin)

Promoted clubs

FC Etar Veliko Tarnovo

2013 • Ivaylo (18,000) • etarvt.bg

Coach: Sasho Angelov; (10/08/17) (Iliyan Kiryakov); (21/08/17) Georgi Vasilev; (12/01/17) Stanislav Genchev

PFC Septemvri Sofia

1944 • Dragalevtsi (2,000) • fcseptemvri.com

Coach: Nikolay Mitov; (02/03/17) Hristo Arangelov

FC Vitosha Bistritsa

1958 • Bistritsa (1,700) • fcvitosha.bg

Coach: Kostadin Angelov

Second level final table 2016/17

		Pld	W	D	L	F	A	Pts
1	FC Etar Veliko Tarnovo	30	17	10	3	52	27	61
2	PFC Septemvri Sofia	30	17	8	5	52	26	59
3	FC Vitosha Bistritsa	30	15	8	7	37	23	53
4	FC Sozopol	30	14	8	8	38	25	50
5	FC Tsarsko Selo Sofia	30	14	6	10	54	39	48
6	FC Lokomotiv Sofia	30	13	8	9	47	34	47
7	OFC Pomorie	30	14	5	11	36	32	47
8	PFC Ludogorets Razgrad II	30	13	5	12	39	33	44
9	OFC Nesebar	30	11	7	12	39	47	40
10	OFC Botev Vratsa	30	9	11	10	42	41	38
11	FC Oborishte Panagyurishte	30	10	7	13	30	39	37
12	FC Botev Galabovo	30	9	7	14	28	39	34
13	PFC CSKA Sofia II	30	9	6	15	44	49	33
14	PFC Spartak Pleven	30	9	6	15	44	52	33
15	PFC Bansko 1951	30	6	7	17	26	55	25
16	FC Levski Karlovo	30	5	1	24	24	71	16

Continued over the page

BULGARIA

Promotion/Relegation play-offs

FIRST ROUND

(18/05/17 & 22/05/17)
Lokomotiv GO 0-3 Slavia
Slavia 1-1 Lokomotiv GO
(Slavia 4-1)

Montana 1-3 Neftochimic
Neftochimic 2-1 Montana
(Neftochimic 5-2)

SECOND ROUND

(26/05/17 & 29/05/17)
Montana 1-1 Lokomotiv GO
Lokomotiv GO 0-3 Montana
(Montana 4-1)

Neftochimic 0-1 Slavia
Slavia 5-2 Neftochimic
(Slavia 6-2)

THIRD ROUND

(02/06/17)
Neftochimic 0-1 Vitosha Bistritsa

(03/06/17)
Montana 1-2 Septemvri

Mid-table play-offs 2016/17

Play-off Group 1 final table

			Home					Away					Total					
		Pld	W	D	L	F	A	W	D	L	F	A	W	D	L	F	A	Pts
1	FC Vereya Stara Zagora	32	10	2	4	19	10	3	4	9	12	30	13	6	13	31	40	45
2	PFC Botev Plovdiv	32	9	3	4	33	19	4	2	10	18	31	13	5	14	51	50	44
3	PFC Slavia Sofia	32	8	0	8	23	26	3	4	9	14	29	11	4	17	37	55	37
4	PFC Montana 1921	32	3	1	12	19	37	1	2	13	5	29	4	3	25	24	66	15

Play-off Group 2 final table

			Home					Away					Total					
		Pld	W	D	L	F	A	W	D	L	F	A	W	D	L	F	A	Pts
1	PFC Beroe Stara Zagora	32	7	4	5	21	17	5	4	7	14	16	12	8	12	35	33	44
2	OFC Pirin Blagoevgrad	32	9	5	2	25	15	3	2	11	16	29	12	7	13	41	44	43
3	PFC Neftochimic Burgas	32	7	3	6	23	18	1	4	11	10	29	8	7	17	33	47	31
4	FC Lokomotiv Gorna Oryahovitsa	32	5	4	7	16	19	2	5	9	16	32	7	9	16	32	51	30

UEFA Europa League qualification play-offs

FIRST ROUND

(15/05/17 & 19/05/17)
Botev 3-0 Beroe *(Kossoko 14, Fernando Viana 45, Vutov 81)*
Beroe 2-1 Botev *(Dimitrov 15og, Mapuku 75; Vutov 64)*
(Botev 4-2)

(16/05/17 & 20/05/17)
Pirin 1-1 Vereya *(Tsvetkov 81; Bandalovski 90)*
Vereya 1-0 Pirin *(Kaloyanov 44)*
(Vereya 2-1)

SECOND ROUND

(27/05/17 & 30/05/17)
Vereya w/o Botev

NB Vereya received a bye as Botev won the Bulgarian Cup.

THIRD ROUND

(04/06/17)
Levski 1-1 Vereya *(Kraev 44; Bandalovski 90+2)* *(aet; 9-8 on pens)*

DOMESTIC CUP

Kupa na Bulgariya 2016/17

FIRST ROUND

(20/09/16)
Botev Galabovo 2-3 Montana
Botev Vratsa 0-4 Ludogorets Razgrad
Chernomorets Balchik 2-5 Lokomotiv Plovdiv
Etar Veliko Tarnovo 1-1 Neftochimic Burgas *(aet; 3-4 on pens)*
Levski Karlovo 0-2 Vereya Stara Zagora
Spartak Pleven 2-3 Pirin Blagoevgrad

(21/09/16)
Bansko 0-1 Sozopol
Litex Lovech 2-0 Slavia Sofia
Lokomotiv Sofia 2-1 CSKA Sofia
Nesebar 1-2 Pomorie
Pirin Gotse Delchev 3-6 Botev Plovdiv
Rozova Dolina Kazanlak 1-2 Cherno More Varna
Septemvri Sofia 2-0 Beroe Stara Zagora
Vitosha Bistritsa 1-1 Dunav Ruse *(aet; 7-8 on pens)*

(22/09/16)
Oborishte Panagyurishte 2-0 Lokomotiv Gorna Oryahovitsa
Tsarsko Selo Sofia 0-2 Levski Sofia

SECOND ROUND

(25/10/16)
Lokomotiv Plovdiv 6-0 Oborishte Panagyurishte
Montana 0-4 Ludogorets Razgrad
Septemvri Sofia 0-2 Dunav Ruse

(26/10/16)
Levski Sofia 2-3 Cherno More Varna *(aet)*
Litex Lovech 1-1 Lokomotiv Sofia *(aet; 4-2 on pens)*

(26/10/16)
Botev Plovdiv 3-0 Neftochimic Burgas
Sozopol 0-1 Pirin Blagoevgrad
Vereya Stara Zagora 1-0 Pomorie

QUARTER-FINALS

(04/04/17)
Pirin Blagoevgrad 0-1 Botev Plovdiv *(Baltanov 27)*

(05/04/17)
Litex Lovech 1-1 Cherno More Varna *(Kostov, 22p; Venkov 34) (aet; 5-3 on pens)*

Lokomotiv Plovdiv 0-4 Ludogorets Razgrad *(Marcelinho 32, Wanderson 59, Vidanov 62og, Misidjan 78)*

(06/04/17)
Vereya Stara Zagora 2-0 Dunav Ruse *(Pedro Eugénio 22, 73)*

SEMI-FINALS

(18/04/17 & 27/04/17)
Ludogorets Razgrad 4-0 Litex Lovech *(Misidjan 2, Gustavo Campanharo 26, Vasilev 29, Juninho Quixadá 34)*
Litex Lovech 0-7 Ludogorets Razgrad *(João Paulo 12, 52, 82, Keșerü 24, 68, 90p, Misidjan 38)*
(Ludogorets 11-0)

(19/04/17 & 26/04/17)
Vereya Stara Zagora 0-1 Botev Plovdiv *(Nedelev 90p)*
Botev Plovdiv 1-1 Vereya Stara Zagora *(Vutov 34; Kaloyanov 61)*
(Botev 2-1)

FINAL

(24/05/17)
Vasil Levski, Sofia
PFC BOTEV PLOVDIV 2 *(Kossoko 44, Vutov 52)*
PFC LUDOGORETS RAZGRAD 1 *(Keșerü 80)*
Referee: *Popov*
BOTEV: *Čvorović, Panov, Terziev, Genev, Marin, Omnibes, Nedelev, Baltanov, Kossoko (Felipe Brisola 70), Krum Stoyanov (Yusein 84), Vutov (Fernando Viana 64)*
Red card: *Fernando Viana (90+2)*
LUDOGORETS: *Renan, Cicinho, Moți, Palomino, Natanael, Dyakov, Gustavo Campanharo (Juninho Quixadá 55), Misidjan (Keșerü 55), Marcelinho (Anicet Abel 67), Wanderson, Jonathan Cafú*

CROATIA

Hrvatski Nogometni Savez (HNS)

Address	Vukovarska 269A HR-10000 Zagreb
Tel	+385 1 2361 555
Fax	+385 1 2441 501
E-mail	info@hns-cff.hr
Website	hns-cff.hr

President	Davor Šuker
General secretary	Damir Vrbanović
Media officer	Tomislav Pacak
Year of formation	1912
National stadium	Maksimir, Zagreb (35,123)

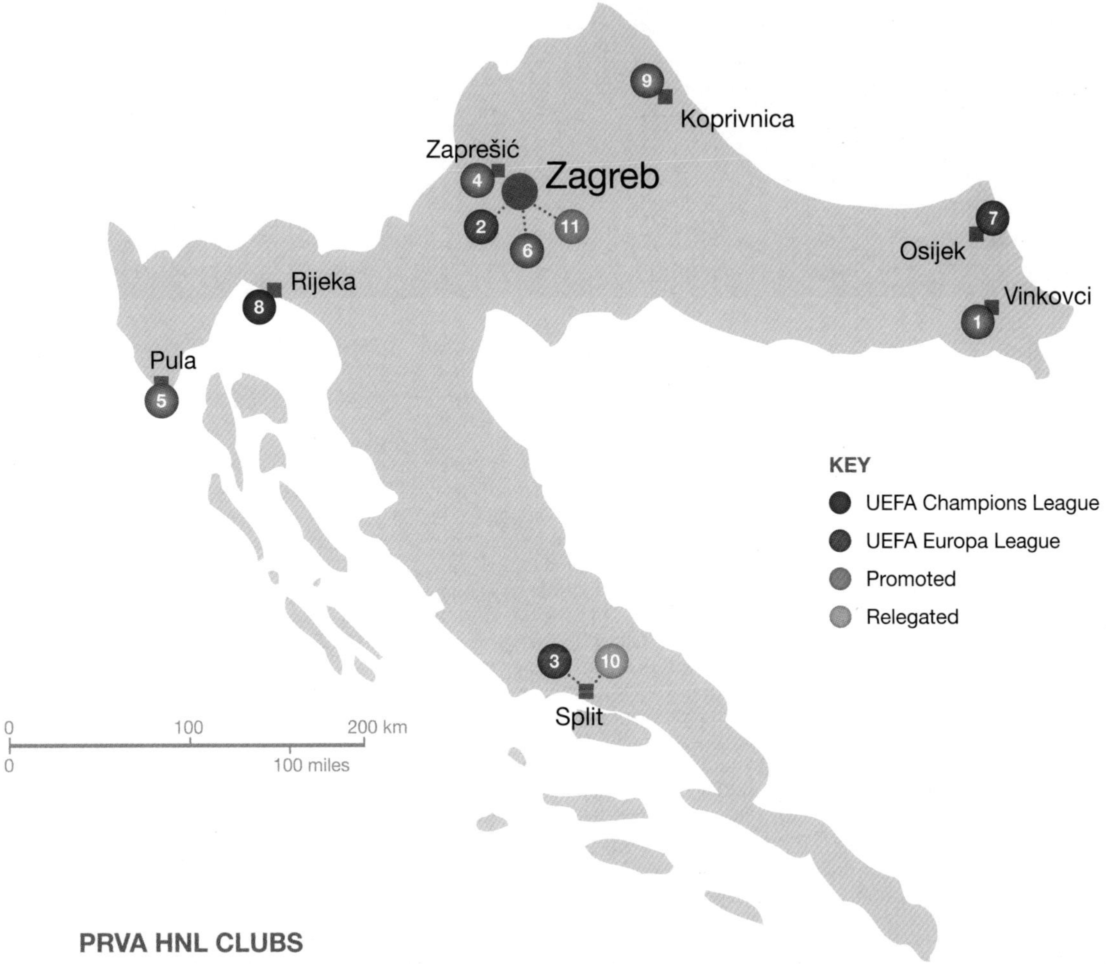

Koprivnica
Zaprešić
Zagreb
Osijek
Vinkovci
Rijeka
Pula
Split

KEY
- UEFA Champions League
- UEFA Europa League
- Promoted
- Relegated

0 100 200 km
0 100 miles

PRVA HNL CLUBS

1 **HNK Cibalia**

2 **GNK Dinamo Zagreb**

3 **HNK Hajduk Split**

4 **NK Inter Zaprešić**

5 **NK Istra 1961**

6 **NK Lokomotiva Zagreb**

7 **NK Osijek**

8 **HNK Rijeka**

9 **NK Slaven Koprivnica**

10 **RNK Split**

PROMOTED CLUB

11 **NK Rudeš**

Rijeka write a new script

A refreshing wind of change blew through Croatian football in 2016/17 as HNK Rijeka brought to an end one of Europe's longest-running title-winning sequences, dethroning Dinamo Zagreb, who had won the league in each of the previous 11 seasons, before completing the double by beating them 3-1 in the final of the Croatian Cup.

The first league title in Rijeka's history was masterminded by Slovenian coach Matjaž Kek in his fourth season at the club. Dinamo, meanwhile, used three new coaches, none of whom could get them either a point or a goal in the UEFA Champions League group stage.

First-time champions end Dinamo's 11-year reign

Cup final win earns Matjaž Kek's team the double

Dinamo fail to score in Champions League group

Domestic league

Rijeka had given Dinamo a good run for their money in 2015/16, losing just once all season, and Kek's team were back to their tough-to-beat best right from the outset, rattling off a succession of impressive results that included a momentous 5-2 victory at home to Dinamo. That was the second shattering defeat in just over a week for the perennial champions. Eight days earlier they had lost a league game at home for the first time since July 2010 – a run of 103 fixtures – when Osijek beat them 1-0. A 0-0 draw against eternal rivals Hajduk Split in their next home game enabled Rijeka to open up a six-point lead at the top of the Prva HNL table, and with the two clubs matching each other result for result over the next two months, that remained the status quo at the winter break.

Points were accumulated with similar regularity on the resumption in the spring, but the pressure of the chase eventually got to Dinamo and they lost back-to-back fixtures again when Hajduk beat them 2-0 in Zagreb and three days later a last-minute winner enabled Slaven Koprivnica to snatch a famous 2-1 victory. By then Rijeka were still undefeated, but with the winning post in sight Kek's men finally succumbed, losing 1-0 at Lokomotiva Zagreb.

Fortunately for them, though, it was only a temporary hitch. Rijeka won their next three matches, securing the title in the last of them with a nerveless 4-0 win at home to lowly Cibalia.

It was a tremendous achievement. They would be defeated 5-2 by Dinamo on the final day, but it was the deadest of dead rubbers. Rijeka's final tally of 88 points was the same number as Dinamo had managed in their invincible 2014/15 campaign. Fifty-two of those were claimed at home, where Rijeka were in temporary accommodation because of reconstruction work on their Kantrida stadium. They boasted the league's best attack and defence and most of its outstanding individual performers, not least top-scoring midfielder Franko Andrijašević, ever-present goalkeeper Andrej Prskalo and Croatian international centre-back Matej Mitrović, who only saw half the season before leaving for Beşiktaş, where he also won the Turkish title.

Domestic cup

Far more significant than the meeting of the top two on the last day of the league was their rematch four days later in Varazdin for the Croatian Cup final. Dinamo had lifted the trophy in each of the previous two years, but Rijeka were to deny them a hat-trick, two goals from Swiss striker Mario Gavranovic powering the league champions to a 3-1 win and a dream-fulfilling double.

Europe

Rijeka's historic season was perhaps aided by an early European exit. Hajduk and Lokomotiva both outlasted them to reach the UEFA Europa League play-offs, whereas Dinamo, thanks to an extra-time win in Salzburg, earned a sixth shot at the UEFA Champions League group stage. It was not a rewarding experience, their six matches against Lyon, Juventus and Sevilla all ending in defeat and without even a consolation goal to show for their efforts.

National team

After a positive if prematurely terminated UEFA EURO 2016, Ante Čačić's Croatia were making excellent headway towards the 2018 FIFA World Cup in Russia until the last minute of their sixth qualifying match when Iceland bundled in a last-minute winner in Reykjavik to join them on 13 points at the summit of Group I. It was a flat end to a fine season in which several Croatian players performed extremely well for club and country, with two of the most prominent, Real Madrid's Luka Modrić and Juventus's Mario Mandžukić, meeting, and starring, in the UEFA Champions League final.

DOMESTIC SEASON AT A GLANCE

Prva HNL 2016/17 final table

			Home					Away					Total					
		Pld	W	D	L	F	A	W	D	L	F	A	W	D	L	F	A	Pts
1	**HNK Rijeka**	**36**	**17**	**1**	**0**	**41**	**8**	**10**	**6**	**2**	**30**	**15**	**27**	**7**	**2**	**71**	**23**	**88**
2	GNK Dinamo Zagreb	36	12	4	2	37	13	15	1	2	31	11	27	5	4	68	24	86
3	HNK Hajduk Split	36	12	3	3	48	17	8	6	4	22	14	20	9	7	70	31	69
4	NK Osijek	36	11	3	4	28	12	9	3	6	24	25	20	6	10	52	37	66
5	NK Lokomotiva Zagreb	36	9	2	7	24	16	3	6	9	17	22	12	8	16	41	38	44
6	NK Istra 1961	36	6	5	7	16	20	4	4	10	17	29	10	9	17	33	49	39
7	NK Slaven Koprivnica	36	8	3	7	26	19	1	8	9	10	26	9	11	16	36	45	38
8	NK Inter Zaprešić	36	4	8	6	17	24	1	5	12	9	33	5	13	18	26	57	28
9	HNK Cibalia	36	3	7	8	15	27	1	2	15	11	52	4	9	23	26	79	21
10	RNK Split	36	2	7	9	8	19	1	2	15	4	33	3	9	24	12	52	18

European qualification 2017/18

Champion/Cup winner: HNK Rijeka (second qualifying round)

GNK Dinamo Zagreb (third qualifying round)
HNK Hajduk Split (second qualifying round)
NK Osijek (first qualifying round)

Top scorer Márkó Futács (Hajduk), 18 goals
Relegated club RNK Split
Promoted club NK Rudeš
Cup final HNK Rijeka 3-1 GNK Dinamo Zagreb

Player of the season

Franko Andrijašević
(HNK Rijeka)

Once the subject of a heated transfer from Hajduk Split to Dinamo Zagreb, Andrijašević had a fine season on loan at Lokomotiva in 2015/16, but it was only after moving on to Rijeka that the football public in Croatia got to see the very best of him. The 25-year-old midfielder turned out to be the driving force in his new club's historic double-winning campaign, scoring 16 goals in the league and another couple in the cup. He also netted a first international goal for Croatia – against Chile – and was transferred to Belgian club Gent in the summer.

Newcomer of the season

Márkó Futács
(HNK Hajduk Split)

A giant Hungarian striker whose career had incorporated brief sojourns in Germany, England and Turkey, Futács finally found a club, and a league, where his traditional centre-forward-style talent was able to flourish. Hajduk Split took a chance on him and were amply rewarded as the 27-year-old scored 18 goals in the Croatian top flight, including one in a long-awaited victory at arch-rivals Dinamo Zagreb, to scoop the golden boot, thus becoming the first Hajduk player to win the prize since Ardian Kozniku in the inaugural Prva HNL of 1992.

Team of the season

(4-3-3)

Coach: Kek *(Rijeka)*

CROATIA

NATIONAL TEAM

International tournament appearances

FIFA World Cup (4) 1998 (3rd), 2002, 2006, 2014
UEFA European Championship (5) 1996 (qtr-finals), 2004, 2008 (qtr-finals), 2012, 2016 (round of 16)

Top five all-time caps

Darijo Srna (134); Stipe Pletikosa (114); Josip Šimunić (105); Ivica Olić (104); Dario Šimić (100)

Top five all-time goals

Davor Šuker (45); Eduardo & **Mario Mandžukić** (29); Darijo Srna (22); Ivica Olić (20)

Results 2016/17

05/09/16	Turkey (WCQ)	H	Zagreb	D	1-1	*Rakitić (44p)*
06/10/16	Kosovo (WCQ)	A	Shkoder (ALB)	W	6-0	*Mandžukić (6, 24, 35), Mitrović (68), Perišić (83), N Kalinić (90+2)*
09/10/16	Finland (WCQ)	A	Tampere	W	1-0	*Mandžukić (18)*
12/11/16	Iceland (WCQ)	H	Zagreb	W	2-0	*Brozović (15, 90+1)*
15/11/16	Northern Ireland	A	Belfast	W	3-0	*Mandžukić (9), Čop (35), Kramarić (68)*
11/01/17	Chile	N	Nanning (CHN)	D	1-1	*Andrijašević (76) (1-4 on pens)*
14/01/17	China	A	Nanning	D	1-1	*Ivanušec (36) (3-4 on pens)*
24/03/17	Ukraine (WCQ)	H	Zagreb	W	1-0	*N Kalinić (38)*
28/03/17	Estonia	A	Tallinn	L	0-3	
27/05/17	Mexico	N	Los Angeles (USA)	W	2-1	*Čop (36), Tudor (37)*
11/06/17	Iceland (WCQ)	A	Reykjavik	L	0-1	

Appearances 2016/17

Coach: Ante Čačić	29/09/53		TUR	KOS	FIN	ISL	Nir	Chi	Chn	UKR	Est	Mex	ISL	Caps	Goals
Lovre Kalinić	03/04/90	Hajduk Split /Gent (BEL)	G				G82				G	G	G	9	-
Šime Vrsaljko	10/01/92	Atlético (ESP)	D	D	D	D	s59							26	-
Vedran Ćorluka	05/02/86	Lokomotiv Moskva (RUS)	D	D46		D								95	4
Domagoj Vida	29/04/89	Dynamo Kyiv (UKR)	D	D	D	D	D59			D	D84		D	49	1
Ivan Strinić	17/07/87	Napoli (ITA)	D											39	-
Milan Badelj	25/02/89	Fiorentina (ITA)	M	M	M	M	M52			M	s58		M	32	1
Luka Modrić	09/09/85	Real Madrid (ESP)	M			s46				M			M	97	11
Marko Pjaca	06/05/95	Juventus (ITA)	M80								M66			13	1
Ivan Rakitić	10/03/88	Barcelona (ESP)	M64			M85				M79				83	13
Ivan Perišić	02/02/89	Internazionale (ITA)	M	M	M	M 94*					M		M	57	16
Mario Mandžukić	21/05/86	Juventus (ITA)	A85	A59	A87	A92	A72			M			M88	76	29
Marcelo Brozović	16/11/92	Internazionale (ITA)	s64	M	M71	M	s52			M91			s63	27	6
Nikola Kalinić	05/01/88	Fiorentina (ITA)	s80	s59	s87					A87			A63	36	14
Andrej Kramarić	19/06/91	Hoffenheim (GER)	s85	A71	A81	s85	A			s87	A			21	5
Danijel Subašić	27/10/84	Monaco (FRA)		G	G	G				G				29	-
Josip Pivarić	30/01/89	Dinamo Zagreb		D	D	D	s87	D	D	D	s58		D	14	-
Mateo Kovačić	06/05/94	Real Madrid (ESP)		M	M	M46				s79	M		M	35	1
Matej Mitrović	10/11/93	Rijeka /Beşiktaş (TUR)		s46	D		D			D	D			6	1
Marko Rog	19/07/95	Napoli (ITA)		s71	s81		M87			s91	M58			9	-
Duje Čop	01/02/90	Sporting Gijón (ESP)			s71	s92	A				A	A93		10	2
Tin Jedvaj	28/11/95	Leverkusen (GER)					D			D	s84	D	D	9	-
Marin Leovac	07/08/88	PAOK (GRE)					D							4	-
Filip Bradarić	11/01/92	Rijeka					M				M58			2	-
Ante Ćorić	14/04/97	Dinamo Zagreb					s72				s66			4	-
Ivan Vargić	15/03/87	Lazio (ITA)					s82							3	-
Dominik Livaković	09/01/95	Dinamo Zagreb						G						1	-
Nikola Matas	22/06/87	Osijek						D	s80					2	-
Jakov Filipović	17/10/92	Inter Zaprešić						D	D			D		3	-
Mateo Barać	20/07/94	Osijek						D						1	-
Josip Mišić	28/06/94	Rijeka						M	M					2	-
Domagoj Antolić	30/06/90	Dinamo Zagreb						M	M64					6	-
Antonio Perošević	06/03/92	Osijek						M57	s64					2	-
Filip Ozobić	08/04/91	Qäbälä (AZE)						M57	s90					2	-
Franko Andrijašević	22/06/91	Rijeka						M90	s46					3	1
Mario Šitum	04/04/92	Dinamo Zagreb						A64	s68					2	-
Mirko Marić	16/05/95	Lokomotiva Zagreb						s57	A46					2	-
Fran Tudor	27/09/95	Hajduk Split						s57	M68			M71		3	1
Borna Barišić	10/11/92	Osijek						s64	M90			D		3	-
Luka Ivanušec	26/11/98	Lokomotiva Zagreb						s90	M80					2	1
Andrej Prskalo	01/05/87	Rijeka							G					1	-
Josip Juranović	16/08/95	Hajduk Split							D					1	-
Toni Datković	06/11/93	Koper (SVN)							D					1	-
Marko Lešković	27/04/91	Dinamo Zagreb									D			4	-
Zoran Nižić	11/10/89	Hajduk Split										D		1	-
Nikola Vlašić	04/10/97	Hajduk Split										M90		1	-
Ivan Šunjić	09/10/96	Lokomotiva Zagreb										M		1	-
Mile Škorić	19/06/91	Osijek										M 77*		1	-
Ivan Santini	21/05/89	Caen (FRA)										A82	s88	2	-
Denis Kolinger	14/01/94	Lokomotiva Zagreb										s71		1	-
Nikola Katić	10/10/96	Slaven Koprivnica										s82		1	-
Mato Miloš	30/06/93	Istra 1961										s90		1	-
Lovro Majer	17/01/98	Lokomotiva Zagreb										s93		1	-
Dejan Lovren	05/07/89	Liverpool (ENG)											D	32	2

EUROPE

GNK Dinamo Zagreb

Second qualifying round - FK Vardar (MKD)
A 2-1 *Mijušković (21og), Rog (30)*
Ježina, Soudani, Antolić, Henríquez (Ćorić 65), Paulo Machado, Fernandes, Sigali, Schildenfeld, Rog (Šovšić 80), Stojanovič, Măţel (Sosa 66). Coach: Zlatko Kranjčar (CRO)
H 3-2 *Pjaca (55p, 70p), Paulo Machado (78)*
Ježina, Soudani, Antolić, Paulo Machado, Hodžić (Benković 68), Pjaca (Pivarić 85), Sigali, Schildenfeld, Rog (Fernandes 81), Stojanovič, Măţel. Coach: Zlatko Kranjčar (CRO)

Third qualifying round - FC Dinamo Tbilisi (GEO)
H 2-0 *Soudani (39), Ćorić (42)*
Eduardo, Soudani, Antolić, Paulo Machado (Fernandes 9), Hodžić (Jonas 62), Pivarić, Sigali, Ćorić (Henríquez 74), Benković, Rog, Stojanovič. Coach: Zlatko Kranjčar (CRO)
A 1-0 *Rog (8)*
Eduardo, Soudani, Jonas (Ćorić 77), Antolić, Fernandes (Pavičić 72), Sigali, Schildenfeld, Benković, Rog, Sosa (Măţel 53), Stojanovič. Coach: Zlatko Kranjčar (CRO)

Play-offs - FC Salzburg (AUT)
H 1-1 *Rog (76p)*
Eduardo, Soudani, Jonas, Antolić (Ćorić 65), Fernandes (Henríquez 78), Sigali, Kneževič (Pavičić 57), Benković, Rog, Stojanovič, Măţel. Coach: Zlatko Kranjčar (CRO)
A 2-1 (aet) *Fernandes (87), Soudani (95)*
Eduardo, Soudani, Jonas (Pavičić 73), Antolić (Schildenfeld 83), Henríquez (Ćorić 62), Fernandes, Pivarić, Sigali, Benković, Rog, Stojanovič. Coach: Zlatko Kranjčar (CRO)

Group H
Match 1 - Olympique Lyonnais (FRA)
A 0-3
Šemper, Soudani, Jonas (Gojak 85), Paulo Machado (Šitum 67), Fernandes, Pavičić, Pivarić, Schildenfeld, Ćorić (Fiolić 53), Benković, Stojanovič. Coach: Zlatko Kranjčar (CRO)
Match 2 - Juventus (ITA)
H 0-4
Šemper, Soudani, Jonas (Fiolić 48), Šitum, Antolić (Paulo Machado 72), Fernandes (Hodžić 58), Pavičić, Pivarić, Sigali, Schildenfeld, Benković. Coach: Željko Sopić (CRO)
Match 3 - Sevilla FC (ESP)
H 0-1
Livaković, Soudani, Antolić (Fiolić 15), Fernandes, Pavičić (Jonas 51), Sigali, Schildenfeld, Kneževič (Henríquez 87), Benković, Sosa, Stojanovič. Coach: Ivaylo Petev (BUL)
Match 4 - Sevilla FC (ESP)
A 0-4
Livaković, Soudani (Măţel 46), Paulo Machado (Perić 60), Fernandes, Pavičić, Pivarić, Sigali, Schildenfeld, Ćorić (Šitum 53), Benković, Stojanovič. Coach: Ivaylo Petev (BUL)
Red card: Stojanovič 45+1
Match 5 - Olympique Lyonnais (FRA)
H 0-1
Livaković, Šitum, Fernandes, Gojak, Pavičić (Paulo Machado 73), Pivarić, Sigali, Ćorić (Jonas 52), Kneževič, Benković, Măţel (Henríquez 14). Coach: Ivaylo Petev (BUL)
Match 6 - Juventus (ITA)
A 0-2
Livaković, Soudani (Stojanovič 74), Šitum, Fernandes, Gojak (Fiolić 57), Pivarić, Sigali, Schildenfeld, Ćorić, Kneževič, Moro (Măţel 85). Coach: Ivaylo Petev (BUL)

HNK Rijeka

Third qualifying round - İstanbul Başakşehir (TUR)
A 0-0
Prskalo, Ristovski, Tomasov (Mišić 80), Zhuta, Bezjak, Mitrović, Gavranovic (Matei 61), Elez, Maleš, Bradarić, Vešović (Handžić 86). Coach: Matjaž Kek (SVN)
H 2-2 *Bezjak (24, 50p)*
Prskalo, Ristovski (Čanadjija 90+2), Tomasov , Zhuta, Bezjak, Mitrović, Gavranovic, Elez, Maleš, J Mišić (Handžić 83), Vešović (Matei 67). Coach: Matjaž Kek (SVN)

HNK Hajduk Split

Second qualifying round – CSM Politehnica Iaşi (ROU)
A 2-2 *Ohandza (48), Said (90+4)*
Stipica, Jefferson, Vlašić, Mastelić (Ohandza 46), Juranović, Kožulj, Milić, Nižić, Bašić (Mujan 57), Tudor (Said 68), Ćosić. Coach: Marijan Pušnik (SVN)
H 2-1 *Tudor (22), Ohandza (90)*
Stipica, Jefferson (Biliy 68), Vlašić, Juranović, Kožulj, Milić, Said (Ohandza 46), Nižić, Sušić (Bašić 60), Tudor, Ćosić. Coach: Marijan Pušnik (SVN)

Third qualifying round - FC Olexandriya (UKR)
A 3-0 *Ćosić (52), Erceg (82), Ohandza (90)*
Kalinić, Biliy (Bašić 64), Jefferson, Vlašić (Erceg 71), Juranović, Kožulj, Milić, Said (Ohandza 68), Nižić, Sušić, Ćosić. Coach: Marijan Pušnik (SVN)
H 3-1 *Nižić (21), Sušić (52p, 56)*
Kalinić, Biliy (Bašić 61), Jefferson, Vlašić, Juranović, Kožulj, Milić, Said (Ohandza 66), Nižić, Sušić (Tudor 77), Ćosić. Coach: Marijan Pušnik (SVN)

Play-offs - Maccabi Tel-Aviv FC (ISR)
A 1-2 *Said (56)*
Kalinić, Jefferson, Vlašić, Kožulj (Biliy 73), Said (Ohandza 62), Nižić, Memolla, Sušić, Ismajli, Ćosić, Gentsoglou (Bašić 87). Coach: Marijan Pušnik (SVN)
H 2-1 (aet; 3-4 on pens) *Ćosić (40, 59)*
Kalinić, Šimić, Jefferson, Vlašić, Kožulj (Tudor 69), Said (Ohandza 63), Memolla, Sušić, Ismajli, Ćosić, Gentsoglou. Coach: Marijan Pušnik (SVN)

NK Lokomotiva Zagreb

First qualifying round - UE Santa Coloma (AND)
A 3-1 *Marić (20, 73), Prenga (65)*
Filipović, Bartolec, Marić (Puljić 79), Fiolić, Bručić, Ivanušec (Ćorić 60), Perić, Çekiçi, Grezda (Majer 76), Prenga, Capan. Coach: Mario Tokić (CRO)
H 4-1 *Ćorić (8), Prenga (18p), Marić (48), Perić (57)*
Filipović, Bartolec, Karačić, Marić, Fiolić, Perić, Ćorić, Çekiçi (Doležal 72), Grezda, Prenga (Oluić 81), Capan (Majer 60). Coach: Mario Tokić (CRO)

Second qualifying round - RoPS Rovaniemi (FIN)
A 1-1 *Jammeh (73og)*
Filipović, Bartolec, Rožman, Marić, Fiolić (Puljić 90+3), Perić, Ćorić (Šunjić 82), Çekiçi, Grezda (Bočkaj 66), Prenga, Capan. Coach: Mario Tokić (CRO)
H 3-0 *Fiolić (44), Marić (49, 83)*
Filipović, Bartolec, Rožman, Marić, Fiolić, Perić, Ćorić (Antunović 85), Çekiçi (Bočkaj 65), Grezda, Prenga, Capan (Šunjić 71). Coach: Mario Tokić (CRO)

Third qualifying round - FC Vorskla Poltava (UKR)
H 0-0
Zagorac, Bartolec, Rožman, Marić (Radonjić 67), Fiolić, Ivanušec, Perić, Ćorić, Grezda (Çekiçi 89), Capan (Šunjić 80), Majstorović. Coach: Tomislav Ivković (CRO)
A 3-2 *Bočkaj (1), Fiolić (53), Perić (64)*
Zagorac, Bartolec, Rožman, Marić (Radonjić 65), Fiolić (Šunjić 81), Perić, Ćorić, Grezda, Capan, Bočkaj (Çekiçi 68), Majstorović. Coach: Tomislav Ivković (CRO)

Play-offs - KRC Genk (BEL)
H 2-2 *Marić (52p), Fiolić (59)*
Zagorac, Bartolec, Rožman, Marić, Fiolić, Perić, Ćorić (Ivanušec 46), Grezda, Šunjić, Bočkaj (Çekiçi 87), Majstorović. Coach: Tomislav Ivković (CRO)
A 0-2
Zagorac, Bartolec, Rožman, Marić, Fiolić, Perić, Grezda (Ćorić 46), Šunjić, Capan (Ivanušec 66), Bočkaj (Çekiçi 72), Majstorović. Coach: Tomislav Ivković (CRO)

DOMESTIC LEAGUE CLUB-BY-CLUB

HNK Cibalia

1919 • Cibalia (12,000) • hnk-cibalia.hr

Coach: Stanko Mršić;
(13/11/16) (Siniša Sesar);
(07/01/17) Peter Pacult (AUT)
(27/03/17) Mladen Bartolović

Date		Opponent	Res	Score	Scorers
2016					
17/07	h	Hajduk	L	0-2	
23/07	a	Slaven	L	2-3	*Vitaić, Tiago*
30/07	h	Inter	D	3-3	*Ugrina, Baša, Vitaić*
06/08	h	Dinamo	L	0-2	
12/08	a	Split	D	2-2	*Vitaić, og (Fuštar)*
20/08	h	Istra 1961	D	1-1	*Vitaić*
27/08	a	Osijek	L	0-2	
11/09	h	Rijeka	D	0-0	
16/09	a	Lokomotiva	L	0-4	
24/09	a	Hajduk	L	1-6	*Dabro*
02/10	h	Slaven	D	0-0	
15/10	a	Inter	L	0-1	
22/10	a	Dinamo	L	0-3	
31/10	h	Split	W	1-0	*Tomašević*
06/11	a	Istra 1961	L	2-3	*Pervan, M Mišić*
20/11	h	Osijek	L	0-2	
26/11	a	Rijeka	L	0-2	
03/12	h	Lokomotiva	L	1-4	*Tiago*
10/12	h	Hajduk	L	1-2	*Baša*
18/12	a	Slaven	L	0-4	
2017					
18/02	h	Inter	D	1-1	*Glavica*
26/02	h	Dinamo	L	1-2	*Zgrablić*
05/03	a	Split	L	0-1	
12/03	h	Istra 1961	L	0-2	
18/03	a	Osijek	L	0-2	
02/04	h	Rijeka	L	0-3	
07/04	a	Lokomotiva	L	1-4	*Glavica*
14/04	a	Hajduk	L	0-3	
21/04	h	Slaven	W	3-1	*Glavica, Vitaić 2 (2p)*
26/04	a	Inter	D	1-1	*Brekalo*
29/04	a	Dinamo	L	0-6	
07/05	h	Split	W	1-0	*Baša*
12/05	a	Istra 1961	W	2-1	*Pervan, Baša*
16/05	h	Osijek	D	1-1	*Vitaić (p)*
21/05	a	Rijeka	L	0-4	
26/05	h	Lokomotiva	D	1-1	*Baša*

No	Name	Nat	DoB	Pos	Aps	(s)	Gls
13	Edi Baša		29/06/93	A	31	(3)	5
3	Marko Brekalo		24/11/92	A	4	(6)	1
15	Mate Crnčević		20/03/95	M	14	(5)	
19	Tomislav Čuljak		25/05/87	D	19	(2)	
9	Marko Dabro		28/03/97	A	7	(6)	1
26	Zvonimir Filipović		10/04/97	M	4	(7)	
11	Dejan Glavica		20/08/91	M	13		3
24	Matej Grafina		11/03/94	A		(4)	
5	Jure Jerbić		28/06/90	D	17		
2	Matej Karačić	BIH	04/08/93	M	6	(10)	
3	Krešimir Kelez		14/03/95	D		(1)	
14	Jamal Khatib	ISR	20/09/95	M		(1)	
20	Marko Kraljević		04/11/95	A		(1)	
5	Toni Markić	BIH	25/10/90	D	5		
25	Ivan Mastelić		02/01/96	A	7	(2)	
89	Mladen Matković		12/05/89	G	35		
17	Luka Mijoković		30/08/94	M	22	(6)	
28	Matija Mišić		30/01/92	M	24	(6)	1
20	Petar Mišić		24/07/94	M	14	(1)	
27	Marko Mlakić		29/03/98	M	1	(6)	
7	Luka Muženjak		04/07/93	D	19	(2)	
7	Marko Pervan		04/04/96	M	11	(5)	2
8	Ivan Prskalo		29/03/95	A		(4)	
26	Danijel Romić		19/03/93	D	7		
9	Petar Rubić		03/07/98	D	4	(2)	
3	Perica Šare		06/02/91	D	10	(4)	
21	Vlatko Šimunac		01/02/90	A	7	(7)	
1	Zvonimir Šubarić		25/05/97	G	1	(1)	
11	Fran Šutalo		22/03/97	D	1		
7	Tiago	BRA	30/05/89	A	4	(8)	2
14	Toni Tipuric	AUT	10/09/90	D	7		
6	Josip Tomašević		26/09/93	M	25	(3)	1
11	Sandro Ugrina		10/08/91	A	8	(1)	1
25	Filip Uremović		11/02/97	D	2	(1)	
22	Frane Vitaić		07/06/82	M	19	(1)	7
4	Ivan Zgrablić		15/03/91	D	27	(2)	1
18	Filip Žderić		11/12/91	D	21		

GNK Dinamo Zagreb

1945 • Maksimir (35,123) • gnkdinamo.hr

Major honours
Inter Cities Fairs Cup (1) 1967;
Yugoslav League (4) 1948, 1954, 1958, 1982;
Croatian League (18) 1993, 1996, 1997, 1998, 1999, 2000, 2003, 2006, 2007, 2008, 2009, 2010, 2011, 2012, 2013, 2014, 2015, 2016;
Yugoslav Cup (7) 1951, 1960, 1963, 1965, 1969, 1980, 1983;
Croatian Cup (14) 1994, 1996, 1997, 1998, 2001, 2002, 2004, 2007, 2008, 2009, 2011, 2012, 2015, 2016

Coach: Zlatko Kranjčar;
(19/09/16) Željko Sopić;
(29/09/16) Ivaylo Petev (BUL)

Date		Opponent	Res	Score	Scorers
2016					
17/07	h	Lokomotiva	W	3-1	*Soudani, Hodžić 2*
29/07	h	Slaven	D	1-1	*Benković*
06/08	a	Cibalia	W	2-0	*Soudani, og (Vitaić)*
10/08	a	Hajduk	W	4-0	*Rog 2, Fernandes 2*
13/08	h	Inter	W	2-1	*Soudani, Fernandes*
19/08	h	Split	W	1-0	*Antolić*
28/08	a	Istra 1961	W	2-1	*Ćorić, Soudani*
10/09	h	Osijek	L	0-1	
18/09	a	Rijeka	L	2-5	*Soudani, Pavičić*
23/09	a	Lokomotiva	W	1-0	*Benković*
02/10	h	Hajduk	D	0-0	
14/10	a	Slaven	W	1-0	*Fernandes*
22/10	h	Cibalia	W	3-0	*Soudani, Henríquez, Šitum*
29/10	a	Inter	W	1-0	*Ćorić*
06/11	a	Split	W	1-0	*Stojanovič*
18/11	h	Istra 1961	D	1-1	*Fernandes (p)*
27/11	a	Osijek	W	2-0	*Ćorić, Soudani*
03/12	h	Rijeka	D	1-1	*Sigali*
11/12	h	Lokomotiva	W	3-1	*Soudani 2, Fiolić*
17/12	a	Hajduk	W	1-0	*Soudani*
2017					
18/02	h	Slaven	W	1-0	*Hodžić*
26/02	a	Cibalia	W	2-1	*Hodžić 2*
04/03	h	Inter	W	2-0	*Pivarić, Hodžić*
11/03	h	Split	W	4-0	*Hodžić 2, Sammir, Ćorić*
19/03	a	Istra 1961	W	3-0	*Soudani, Hodžić 2*
01/04	h	Osijek	W	2-1	*Pavičić, Lešković*
08/04	a	Rijeka	D	1-1	*Soudani*
14/04	a	Lokomotiva	W	2-1	*Hodžić 2*
22/04	h	Hajduk	L	0-2	
25/04	a	Slaven	L	1-2	*Moro*
29/04	h	Cibalia	W	6-0	*Gojak 4, Soudani, Antolić*
04/05	a	Inter	W	3-0	*Hodžić, Soudani, Antolić*
12/05	a	Split	W	1-0	*Hodžić*
17/05	h	Istra 1961	W	2-1	*Antolić, Hodžić*
20/05	a	Osijek	W	1-0	*Sigali*
27/05	h	Rijeka	W	5-2	*Soudani 3, Dani Olmo, Hodžić*

No	Name	Nat	DoB	Pos	Aps	(s)	Gls
8	Domagoj Antolić		30/06/90	M	22	(1)	4
26	Filip Benković		13/07/97	D	18		2
24	Ante Ćorić		14/04/97	M	19	(4)	4
21	Dani Olmo	ESP	07/05/98	A	8	(6)	1
34	Eduardo	POR	19/09/82	G	4		
11	Júnior Fernandes	CHI	10/04/88	A	15	(3)	5
29	Ivan Fiolić		29/04/96	M	4	(4)	1
14	Amer Gojak	BIH	13/02/97	M	10	(12)	4
9	Ángelo Henríquez	CHI	13/04/94	A	11	(9)	1
15	Armin Hodžić	BIH	17/11/94	A	22	(3)	16
1	Antonijo Ježina		05/06/89	G	1		
5	Jonas	BRA	08/10/91	M	13		
66	Ali Karimi	IRN	11/02/94	M		(1)	
25	Bojan Knežević		28/01/97	M	5	(6)	
31	Marko Lešković		27/04/91	D	15		1
40	Dominik Livaković		09/01/95	G	22		
11	Marcos Guilherme	BRA	05/08/95	M	5	(6)	
77	Alexandru Mățel	ROU	17/10/89	D	17	(1)	
27	Nikola Moro		12/03/98	M	12	(3)	1
4	Darick Kobie Morris		15/07/95	D	1		
10	Paulo Machado	POR	31/03/86	M	8	(9)	
18	Domagoj Pavičić		09/03/94	M	15	(9)	2
55	Dino Perić		12/07/94	D	6	(4)	
19	Josip Pivarić		30/01/89	D	22	(2)	1
20	Marko Pjaca		06/05/95	A	1		
30	Marko Rog		19/07/95	M	4	(2)	2
20	Sammir		23/04/87	M	8	(4)	1
23	Gordon Schildenfeld		18/03/85	D	15	(1)	
22	Leonardo Sigali	ARG	29/05/87	D	19		2
6	Vinko Soldo		15/02/98	D	2	(2)	
35	Borna Sosa		21/01/98	D	7	(1)	
2	El Arabi Hillel Soudani	ALG	25/11/87	A	28	(1)	17
37	Petar Stojanovič	SVN	07/10/95	D	18	(5)	1
98	Adrian Šemper		12/01/98	G	6		
7	Mario Šitum		04/04/92	M	10	(9)	1
1	Danijel Zagorac		07/02/87	G	3		

HNK Hajduk Split

1911 • Poljud (34,200) • hajduk.hr

Major honours

Yugoslav League (9) 1927, 1929, 1950, 1952, 1955, 1971, 1974, 1975, 1979; Croatian League (6) 1992, 1994, 1995, 2001, 2004, 2005; Yugoslav Cup (9) 1967, 1972, 1973, 1974, 1976, 1977, 1984, 1987, 1991; Croatian Cup (6) 1993, 1995, 2000, 2003, 2010, 2013

Coach: Marijan Pušnik (SVN); (02/12/16) (Marko Lozo); (05/12/16) Joan Carrillo (ESP)

2016

17/07	a	Cibalia	W 2-0	*Bašić, Kožulj*
31/07	a	Split	W 1-0	*Ohandza*
07/08	h	Istra 1961	W 4-0	*Ohandza (p), Erceg, Tudor, og (Žižić)*
10/08	h	Dinamo	L 0-4	
14/08	a	Osijek	D 1-1	*Erceg*
21/08	h	Rijeka	L 2-4	*Ohandza (p), Ismajli*
28/08	a	Lokomotiva	W 2-0	*Erceg, og (Karačić)*
09/09	a	Inter	D 1-1	*Tudor*
17/09	h	Slaven	W 4-0	*Said 2, Erceg, Futács*
24/09	h	Cibalia	W 6-1	*Said, Ohandza 2, Kožulj, Futács, Jefferson*
02/10	a	Dinamo	D 0-0	
16/10	h	Split	W 2-1	*Futács (p), Bašić*
22/10	a	Istra 1961	D 0-0	
30/10	h	Osijek	W 1-0	*Futács*
05/11	a	Rijeka	L 1-2	*Futács*
19/11	h	Lokomotiva	W 1-0	*Barry*
27/11	h	Inter	W 2-0	*Erceg, Kožulj*
04/12	a	Slaven	L 1-2	*Said*
10/12	a	Cibalia	W 2-1	*Futács 2*
17/12	h	Dinamo	L 0-1	

2017

19/02	a	Split	D 1-1	*Erceg*
24/02	h	Istra 1961	W 4-0	*Erceg, Vlašić, Said, Futács*
05/03	a	Osijek	L 1-2	*Futács*
11/03	h	Rijeka	D 1-1	*Barry*
17/03	a	Lokomotiva	D 0-0	
31/03	a	Inter	W 3-1	*Bašić, Nižić, Ohandza*
08/04	h	Slaven	D 1-1	*Ohandza*
14/04	h	Cibalia	W 3-0	*og (Zgrablić), Kožulj, Vlašić*
22/04	a	Dinamo	W 2-0	*Erceg, Futács*
26/04	h	Split	W 5-2	*Vlašić (p), Nižić, Erceg, Said, Ohandza*
30/04	a	Istra 1961	W 2-0	*Erceg, Futács*
06/05	h	Osijek	W 5-1	*Bašić 2, Futács, Erceg, Said*
13/05	a	Rijeka	L 0-2	
17/05	h	Lokomotiva	D 1-1	*Barry*
20/05	h	Inter	W 6-0	*Futács 4, Tudor, Vlašić*
26/05	a	Slaven	W 2-1	*Futács 2*

No	Name	Nat	DoB	Pos	Aps	(s)	Gls
19	Hamza Barry	GAM	15/10/94	M	21	(6)	3
26	Toma Bašić		25/11/96	M	17	(11)	5
4	Maxym Biliy	UKR	21/06/90	D	3	(1)	
4	Petar Bosančić		19/04/96	D	1	(1)	
44	Marko Ćosić		02/03/94	D	16		
50	Ante Erceg		12/12/89	M	27	(2)	11
9	Márkó Futács	HUN	22/02/90	A	20	(6)	18
90	Savvas Gentsoglou	GRE	19/09/90	M	23	(1)	
34	Ardian Ismajli	KOS	30/09/96	D	11	(7)	1
21	Robert Jandrek		30/08/95	M		(5)	
6	Jefferson	BRA	14/04/93	M	22	(5)	1
17	Josip Juranović		16/08/95	D	17	(1)	
91	Lovre Kalinić		03/04/90	G	13		
18	Zvonimir Kožulj	BIH	15/11/93	M	18	(8)	4
3	Josip Kvesić	BIH	21/09/90	D	9		
15	Ignacio Maganto	ESP	02/01/92	M	2	(7)	
27	Hysen Memolla	ALB	03/07/92	D	24		
14	Tonći Mujan		19/07/95	A		(3)	
23	Zoran Nižić		11/10/89	D	28		2
11	Franck Ohandza	CMR	28/09/91	A	8	(16)	8
24	Marko Pejić		24/02/95	D	4		
7	Ivan Prtajin		14/05/96	A		(1)	
22	Ahmed Said	ITA	20/04/93	A	16	(12)	7
1	Dante Stipica		30/05/91	G	23		
31	Tino-Sven Sušić	BIH	13/02/92	A	2		
5	Lorenco Šimić		15/07/96	D	13		
55	Georgi Terziev	BUL	18/04/92	D	8		
32	Fran Tudor		27/09/95	D	20	(7)	3
8	Nikola Vlašić		04/10/97	M	27	(3)	4
88	Frane Vojković		20/12/96	A	3	(3)	

NK Inter Zaprešić

1929 • ŠRC Zaprešić (5,000) • inter.hr

Major honours

Croatian Cup (1) 1992

Coach: Samir Toplak

2016

15/07	a	Slaven	L 0-2	
23/07	h	Osijek	L 0-2	
30/07	a	Cibalia	D 3-3	*Filipović, Brlečić, Puljić*
07/08	h	Rijeka	D 1-1	*Puljić (p)*
13/08	a	Dinamo	L 1-2	*Blažević*
21/08	h	Lokomotiva	W 2-1	*Puljić 2*
26/08	a	Split	D 0-0	
09/09	h	Hajduk	D 1-1	*Puljić*
17/09	a	Istra 1961	L 1-4	*og (Georgiev)*
24/09	h	Slaven	D 1-1	*Blažević*
01/10	a	Osijek	D 1-1	*Šarić*
15/10	h	Cibalia	W 1-0	*Puljić*
23/10	a	Rijeka	L 0-1	
29/10	h	Dinamo	L 0-1	
04/11	a	Lokomotiva	W 1-0	*Kolar*
19/11	h	Split	W 2-0	*Kolar 2*
27/11	a	Hajduk	L 0-2	
05/12	h	Istra 1961	D 2-2	*Puljić 2*
09/12	a	Slaven	L 0-2	
16/12	h	Osijek	D 2-2	*Filipović, Puljić (p)*

2017

18/02	a	Cibalia	D 1-1	*Blažević*
26/02	h	Rijeka	L 1-2	*Filipović*
04/03	a	Dinamo	L 0-2	
10/03	h	Lokomotiva	D 0-0	
18/03	a	Split	D 0-0	
31/03	h	Hajduk	L 1-3	*Kolar*
09/04	a	Istra 1961	L 0-1	
15/04	h	Slaven	D 1-1	*Puljić*
21/04	a	Osijek	L 1-2	*Mamut*
26/04	h	Cibalia	D 1-1	*Puljić*
29/04	a	Rijeka	L 0-2	
04/05	h	Dinamo	L 0-3	
13/05	a	Lokomotiva	L 0-2	
17/05	h	Split	W 1-0	*Kolar*
20/05	a	Hajduk	L 0-6	
27/05	h	Istra 1961	L 0-3	

No	Name	Nat	DoB	Pos	Aps	(s)	Gls
99	Marjan Altiparmakovski	MKD	18/07/91	A	5	(5)	
4	Silvije Begić		03/06/93	D	17	(4)	
10	Ivan Blažević		25/07/92	M	22	(2)	3
26	Antonio Bosec		28/08/97	D	24	(2)	
23	Mario Brlečić		10/01/89	M	16	(8)	1
5	Hrvoje Čale		04/03/85	D	6	(1)	
13	Ivan Čeliković		10/04/89	D	14	(4)	
1	Ivan Čović		17/09/90	G	31		
27	Zoran Danoski	MKD	20/10/90	A	1	(4)	
22	Jakov Filipović		17/10/92	D	33		3
29	Tomislav Hanžek		31/05/96	D		(5)	
13	Franko Knez		26/03/98	D		(2)	
9	Marko Kolar		31/05/95	A	27	(2)	5
15	Mislav Komorski		17/04/92	D	25		
36	Ivan Madžar		17/03/98	G		(1)	
11	Ivan Mamut		30/04/97	A	5	(10)	1
28	Tomislav Mazalović		10/06/90	M	27	(1)	
27	Joseph Essien Mbong	MLT	15/07/97	A		(1)	
20	Khaled Mesfin	GER	02/06/92	D	20	(7)	
34	Petar Mikulić		14/07/00	D	1	(3)	
1	Ante Mrmić		06/08/92	G	5	(1)	
18	Abid Mujagič	BIH	05/08/93	A	6	(3)	
8	Andrea Ottochian		28/06/88	M	13	(2)	
32	Luca Polizzi	BEL	28/05/96	M	8	(11)	
7	Igor Postonjski		04/02/95	D	13	(2)	
21	Jakov Puljić		04/08/93	A	30	(1)	11
25	Tomislav Šarić		24/06/90	M	25		1
29	Frane Šiljić		08/03/99	M	3	(4)	
7	Josip Šoljić		18/06/87	M	11	(3)	
14	Jerko Zadro		24/05/98	D	1		
19	Marin Zulim		26/10/91	A	7	(16)	

NK Istra 1961

1961 • Aldo Drosina (8,923) • nkistra1961.hr

Coach: Andrej Panadić; (22/07/16) Goran Tomić; (30/11/16) (Darko Raić-Sudar); (30/12/16) Marijo Tot; (19/05/17) (Darko Raić-Sudar)

2016

16/07	h	Osijek	L 0-1	
22/07	a	Rijeka	L 1-4	*Roce*
31/07	h	Lokomotiva	D 1-1	*Solomon*
07/08	a	Hajduk	L 0-4	
14/08	h	Slaven	D 0-0	
20/08	a	Cibalia	D 1-1	*Solomon*
28/08	h	Dinamo	L 1-2	*Ljubanović*
10/09	a	Split	W 3-0	*Gržan, Stepčić (p), Solomon*
17/09	h	Inter	W 4-1	*Bertoša, Gržan, Stepčić (p), Solomon*
25/09	a	Osijek	D 1-1	*Stepčić*
30/09	h	Rijeka	L 0-2	
15/10	a	Lokomotiva	L 1-2	*Roce*
22/10	h	Hajduk	D 0-0	
29/10	a	Slaven	L 0-2	
06/11	h	Cibalia	W 3-2	*Parački, Solomon, Gržan*
18/11	a	Dinamo	D 1-1	*Roce (p)*
26/11	h	Split	W 1-0	*og (Jurendić)*
05/12	a	Inter	D 2-2	*Roce, Mário Lúcio*
10/12	h	Osijek	L 1-3	*og (Škorić)*
17/12	a	Rijeka	L 0-1	

2017

17/02	h	Lokomotiva	W 1-0	*Roce*
24/02	a	Hajduk	L 0-4	
03/03	h	Slaven	D 0-0	
12/03	a	Cibalia	W 2-0	*Solomon, Pavić*
19/03	h	Dinamo	L 0-3	
02/04	a	Split	W 1-0	*Gržan*
09/04	h	Inter	W 1-0	*Roce (p)*
15/04	a	Osijek	L 0-2	
22/04	h	Rijeka	D 1-1	*Gržan (p)*
26/04	a	Lokomotiva	L 0-1	
30/04	h	Hajduk	L 0-2	
07/05	a	Slaven	L 0-2	
12/05	h	Cibalia	L 1-2	*Mitrevski*
17/05	a	Dinamo	L 1-2	*Prelčec*
22/05	h	Split	W 1-0	*Puclin*
27/05	a	Inter	W 3-0	*Roce 2, Solomon*

No	Name	Nat	DoB	Pos	Aps	(s)	Gls
13	Mateo Bertoša		10/08/88	D	9	(1)	1
10	Abdelhakim Bouhna	BEL	24/05/91	A	7	(10)	
1	Ivan Brkić		29/06/95	G	1		
98	Vladimir Burić		13/01/98	M	3	(10)	
99	Jamilu Collins	NGA	05/08/94	D	10	(1)	
1	Marijan Ćorić		06/02/95	G	1		
18	Asen Georgiev	BUL	09/07/93	D	18		
2	Renato Gojković	BIH	10/09/95	D	14	(5)	
77	Šime Gržan		06/04/94	A	27	(5)	5
25	Kenan Hadžić		07/05/94	D	5		
17	Hong Sung-min	KOR	14/10/92	M	2		
12	Vanja Iveša		21/07/77	G	12		
33	Ivica Ivušić		01/02/95	G	22	(1)	
5	Ivica Jurkić		22/02/94	D	6		
22	Lirim Kelmendi	GER	28/01/96	D		(1)	
17	Tome Kitanovski	MKD	21/05/92	D	4	(2)	
24	Ivor Ljubanović		29/12/98	A	2	(10)	1
30	Viktor Marić		18/03/98	M		(1)	
7	Mário Lúcio	BRA	11/12/89	M	21	(3)	1
4	Paolo Matteoni		04/06/98	M		(1)	
6	Jakov Medić		07/09/98	D		(2)	
23	Mato Miloš		30/06/93	D	25		
20	Darko Mišić		27/06/91	D	3		
15	Risto Mitrevski	MKD	05/10/91	D	26	(3)	1
35	Goran Parački		21/01/87	M	34		1
3	Antonio Pavić		18/11/94	D	14		1
4	Dejan Polić		21/04/93	M	4	(2)	
8	Nikola Prelčec		12/11/89	M	5	(21)	1
92	David Puclin		17/06/92	M	17	(5)	1
11	Goran Roce		12/04/86	A	27	(4)	8
9	Theophilus Solomon	NGA	18/01/96	A	30	(1)	7
21	Valentino Stepčić		16/01/90	M	16	(5)	3
27	Marko Trojak		28/03/88	M	1	(6)	
28	Saša Urošević		26/01/99	M	1	(4)	
16	Nikola Žižić		23/01/88	D	29		

CROATIA

NK Lokomotiva Zagreb

1914 • Kranjčevićeva (8,850) • nklokomotiva.hr

Coach: (Mario Tokić); (25/07/16) Tomislav Ivković; (14/11/16) Mario Tokić

Date		Opponent		Score	Scorers
2016					
17/07	a	Dinamo	L	1-3	*Fiolić*
24/07	h	Split	D	0-0	
31/07	a	Istra 1961	D	1-1	*Radonjić*
08/08	h	Osijek	L	2-3	*Karačić, Ćorić (p)*
13/08	a	Rijeka	L	0-1	
21/08	a	Inter	L	1-2	*Çekiçi*
28/08	h	Hajduk	L	0-2	
11/09	a	Slaven	W	3-2	*Majer, Antunović, Karačić*
16/09	h	Cibalia	W	4-0	*Doležal, Marić, Bočkaj, Grezda*
23/09	h	Dinamo	L	0-1	
01/10	a	Split	W	2-0	*Grezda 2*
15/10	h	Istra 1961	W	2-1	*Rožman, Marić*
23/10	a	Osijek	L	0-1	
30/10	h	Rijeka	L	0-2	
04/11	h	Inter	L	0-1	
19/11	a	Hajduk	L	0-1	
25/11	h	Slaven	L	0-2	
03/12	a	Cibalia	W	4-1	*Çekiçi, Ćorić (p), Ivanušec, Marić*
11/12	a	Dinamo	L	1-3	*Antunović*
18/12	h	Split	W	3-0	*Doležal, Ćorić (p), Rrahmani*
2017					
17/02	a	Istra 1961	L	0-1	
25/02	h	Osijek	W	2-0	*Çekiçi, Ćorić*
04/03	a	Rijeka	L	1-2	*Ćorić*
10/03	a	Inter	D	0-0	
17/03	h	Hajduk	D	0-0	
01/04	a	Slaven	D	1-1	*Antunović*
07/04	h	Cibalia	W	4-1	*Ćorić (p), Doležal, Grezda, Bočkaj*
14/04	h	Dinamo	L	1-2	*Grezda*
23/04	a	Split	D	0-0	
26/04	h	Istra 1961	W	1-0	*Karimi*
01/05	a	Osijek	L	0-1	
06/05	h	Rijeka	W	1-0	*Majer*
13/05	h	Inter	W	2-0	*Karačić, Šunjić*
16/05	a	Hajduk	D	1-1	*Doležal*
20/05	h	Slaven	W	2-1	*Majer (p), Capan*
26/05	a	Cibalia	D	1-1	*Doležal*

No	Name	Nat	DoB	Pos	Aps	(s)	Gls
11	Ivan Antunović		16/10/95	A	6	(13)	3
2	Karlo Bartolec		20/04/95	D	5		
8	Luka Begonja		23/05/92	M		(1)	
40	Petar Bočkaj		23/07/96	D	16	(11)	2
34	Toni Brezina		18/01/99	M		(1)	
31	Luka Capan		06/04/95	D	22	(3)	1
17	Endri Çekiçi	ALB	23/11/96	M	17	(6)	3
22	Chiquinho	POR	19/07/95	M	1	(5)	
16	Josip Ćorić	BIH	09/11/88	M	16	(4)	6
25	Jan Doležal		12/02/93	A	21	(5)	5
23	Ivan Filipović		13/11/94	G	2		
10	Ivan Fiolić		29/04/96	M	5	(2)	1
18	Eros Grezda	ALB	15/04/95	M	27	(3)	5
21	Tibor Halilović		18/03/95	M	7	(11)	
35	Luka Hujber		16/06/99	D	1		
14	Luka Ivanušec		26/11/98	M	17	(5)	1
3	Fran Karačić		12/05/96	D	17	(2)	3
6	Ali Karimi	IRN	11/02/94	M	7	(1)	1
2	Dino Kluk		13/05/91	D	1	(1)	
20	Denis Kolinger		14/01/94	D	19	(2)	
31	Nikola Krajinović		09/11/99	M		(1)	
15	Kristijan Lovrić		01/12/95	M		(1)	
7	Lovro Majer		17/01/98	M	18	(5)	3
44	Ante Majstorović		06/11/93	D	29		
9	Mirko Marić		16/05/95	A	15	(3)	3
92	Filip Mihaljević		09/03/92	A	3	(1)	
28	Maksim Oluić		20/05/98	D	1	(1)	
15	Dino Perić		12/07/94	D	5		
19	Herdi Prenga	ALB	31/08/94	D	2		
36	Dejan Radonjić		23/07/90	A	2	(4)	1
32	Bruno Rihtar		26/03/98	A		(1)	
5	Siniša Rožman		16/10/90	D	23	(3)	1
13	Amir Rrahmani	KOS	24/02/94	D	28		1
15	Ivan Skansi		29/01/99	A		(1)	
24	Marko Stolnik		08/07/96	D	2	(1)	
98	Adrian Šemper		12/01/98	G	16		
30	Ivan Šunjić		09/10/96	M	22	(1)	1
4	Tomislav Valentić		04/06/94	D	5	(2)	
12	Danijel Zagorac		07/02/87	G	18		

NK Osijek

1947 • Gradski vrt (19,500) • nk-osijek.hr

Major honours
Croatian Cup (1) 1999

Coach: Zoran Zekić

Date		Opponent		Score	Scorers
2016					
16/07	a	Istra 1961	W	1-0	*Perošević*
23/07	a	Inter	W	2-0	*Vojnović, Boban*
31/07	h	Rijeka	L	0-1	
08/08	a	Lokomotiva	W	3-2	*Matas, Lulić, Džolan*
14/08	h	Hajduk	D	1-1	*Ejupi*
20/08	a	Slaven	W	3-2	*Ejupi 2, og (Štiglec)*
27/08	h	Cibalia	W	2-0	*Mioč, Knežević*
10/09	a	Dinamo	W	1-0	*Knežević*
18/09	h	Split	W	3-0	*Perošević, Vojnović 2*
25/09	h	Istra 1961	D	1-1	*Ejupi*
01/10	h	Inter	D	1-1	*Ejupi (p)*
16/10	a	Rijeka	L	0-3	
23/10	h	Lokomotiva	W	1-0	*Perošević*
30/10	a	Hajduk	L	0-1	
05/11	h	Slaven	W	1-0	*Perošević*
20/11	a	Cibalia	W	2-0	*Ejupi, Boban*
27/11	h	Dinamo	L	0-2	
04/12	a	Split	D	1-1	*Lesjak*
10/12	a	Istra 1961	W	3-1	*Perošević, Barišić, Ejupi*
16/12	a	Inter	D	2-2	*Ejupi, Boban*
2017					
19/02	h	Rijeka	L	2-3	*Lyopa, Ejupi*
25/02	a	Lokomotiva	L	0-2	
05/03	h	Hajduk	W	2-1	*Ejupi 2*
12/03	a	Slaven	W	2-1	*Lesjak, Ejupi*
18/03	h	Cibalia	W	2-0	*Lyopa 2*
01/04	a	Dinamo	L	1-2	*Barać*
09/04	h	Split	W	4-0	*Lyopa, Lukić, Perošević, Grgić*
15/04	h	Istra 1961	W	2-0	*Lyopa 2*
21/04	h	Inter	W	2-1	*Lyopa, Lukić*
25/04	a	Rijeka	L	0-2	
01/05	h	Lokomotiva	W	1-0	*Perošević (p)*
06/05	a	Hajduk	L	1-5	*Boban*
13/05	h	Slaven	W	3-0	*Ejupi 2 (1p), Lyopa*
16/05	a	Cibalia	D	1-1	*Knežević*
21/05	h	Dinamo	L	0-1	
26/05	a	Split	W	1-0	*Knežević*

No	Name	Nat	DoB	Pos	Aps	(s)	Gls
15	Zoran Arsenić		02/06/94	D	13	(4)	
4	Mateo Barać		20/07/94	D	23	(1)	1
3	Borna Barišić		10/11/92	D	32		1
7	Gabrijel Boban		23/07/89	A	23	(8)	4
16	Josip Čikvar		15/04/98	A		(1)	
6	Ivica Džolan		11/10/88	D	1	(1)	1
9	Muzafer Ejupi	MKD	16/09/88	A	29		14
23	Alen Grgić		10/08/94	A	9	(14)	1
29	Ivan Ikić		13/09/99	M		(1)	
11	Mihael Klepač		19/09/97	M		(1)	
30	Josip Knežević		03/10/88	M	27	(4)	4
17	Mislav Leko		19/12/87	D	2	(2)	
19	Zoran Lesjak		01/02/88	D	13	(5)	2
6	Filip Lišnić		17/02/99	D	1		
2	Danijel Lončar		26/06/97	D	1		
28	Andrej Lukić		02/04/94	D	23	(6)	2
24	Karlo Lulić		10/05/96	M	2	(9)	1
27	Dmytro Lyopa	UKR	23/11/88	M	19	(2)	8
13	Marko Malenica		08/02/94	G	10		
9	Nikola Mandić		19/03/95	A		(1)	
14	Luka Marin		16/03/98	M	1	(1)	
26	Nikola Matas		22/06/87	D	28	(2)	1
1	Zvonimir Mikulić		05/02/90	G	26		
5	Benedik Mioč		06/10/94	M	27	(5)	1
10	Antonio Perošević		06/03/92	A	20	(6)	7
25	Milovan Petrovic	MKD	23/01/90	M	17	(2)	
22	Domagoj Pušić		24/10/91	M	8	(14)	
18	Andrej Šimunec		02/03/95	D	1	(3)	
21	Mile Škorić		19/06/91	D	21	(1)	
11	Josip Špoljarić		05/01/97	M		(1)	
18	Tomislav Štrkalj		02/08/96	A		(1)	
8	Aljoša Vojnović		24/10/85	M	19	(11)	3

HNK Rijeka

1946 • HNK Rijeka (8,500) • nk-rijeka.hr

Major honours
Yugoslav Cup (2) 1978, 1979; Croatian League (1) 2017; Croatian Cup (4) 2005, 2006, 2014, 2017

Coach: Matjaž Kek (SVN)

Date		Opponent		Score	Scorers
2016					
16/07	a	Split	W	3-0	*Bezjak 2, Tomasov*
22/07	h	Istra 1961	W	4-1	*Gavranovic 2, Bezjak 2*
31/07	a	Osijek	W	1-0	*Mišić*
07/08	a	Inter	D	1-1	*Gavranovic*
13/08	h	Lokomotiva	W	1-0	*Mitrović*
21/08	a	Hajduk	W	4-2	*Gavranovic, Bezjak 2 (1p), Andrijašević*
27/08	h	Slaven	W	2-0	*Matei, Bezjak (p)*
11/09	a	Cibalia	D	0-0	
18/09	h	Dinamo	W	5-2	*Gavranovic, Gorgon 2, Vešović 2*
25/09	h	Split	W	2-0	*Gorgon, Andrijašević*
30/09	a	Istra 1961	W	2-0	*Črnic, Gorgon*
16/10	h	Osijek	W	3-0	*Andrijašević, Gavranovic, Gorgon*
23/10	h	Inter	W	1-0	*Andrijašević*
30/10	a	Lokomotiva	W	2-0	*Andrijašević, Gorgon*
05/11	h	Hajduk	W	2-1	*Elez 2*
20/11	a	Slaven	D	0-0	
26/11	h	Cibalia	W	2-0	*Gorgon (p), Matei (p)*
03/12	a	Dinamo	D	1-1	*Gorgon*
11/12	a	Split	W	2-0	*Andrijašević 2 (1p)*
17/12	h	Istra 1961	W	1-0	*Andrijašević*
2017					
19/02	a	Osijek	W	3-2	*Gavranovic, Andrijašević 2*
26/02	a	Inter	W	2-1	*Mišić, og (Filipović)*
04/03	h	Lokomotiva	W	2-1	*Bradarić, Gorgon*
11/03	a	Hajduk	D	1-1	*Bezjak (p)*
19/03	h	Slaven	W	3-2	*Andrijašević, og (Jovičić), Vešović*
02/04	a	Cibalia	W	3-0	*Bradarić, Andrijašević, Gorgon*
08/04	h	Dinamo	D	1-1	*Andrijašević*
15/04	h	Split	W	2-0	*Gorgon, Vešović*
22/04	a	Istra 1961	D	1-1	*Gorgon*
25/04	h	Osijek	W	2-0	*Bezjak (p), Andrijašević (p)*
29/04	h	Inter	W	2-0	*Gavranovic, Bezjak (p)*
06/05	a	Lokomotiva	L	0-1	
13/05	h	Hajduk	W	2-0	*Maleš, Gavranovic*
17/05	a	Slaven	W	2-0	*Andrijašević, Vešović*
21/05	h	Cibalia	W	4-0	*Gavranovic 2, Bezjak, Župarić*
27/05	a	Dinamo	L	2-5	*Vešović, Andrijašević*

No	Name	Nat	DoB	Pos	Aps	(s)	Gls
21	Goodness Ajayi	NGA	06/10/94	A		(7)	
23	Franko Andrijašević		22/06/91	M	28		16
11	Roman Bezjak	SVN	21/02/89	A	17	(6)	11
28	Filip Bradarić		11/01/92	M	33		2
5	Dario Čanadjija		17/04/94	M		(24)	
3	Jasmin Čeliković	BIH	07/01/99	M		(1)	
11	Matic Črnic	SVN	12/06/92	M	1	(10)	1
18	Josip Elez		25/04/94	D	34		2
17	Mario Gavranovic	SUI	24/11/89	A	27	(2)	11
20	Alexander Gorgon	AUT	28/10/88	A	21	(4)	12
99	Haris Handžić		20/06/90	A	1	(3)	
4	Ante Kulušić		06/06/86	D	3	(2)	
26	Mate Maleš		11/03/89	M	16	(9)	1
77	Ivan Martic		02/10/90	D	6	(11)	
10	Florentin Matei	ROU	15/04/93	M	9	(9)	2
27	Josip Mišić		28/06/94	M	28	(6)	2
15	Matej Mitrović		10/11/93	D	20		1
16	Ivan Močinić		30/04/93	M		(1)	
32	Andrej Prskalo		01/05/87	G	36		
6	Stefan Ristovski	MKD	12/02/92	D	33		
23	Odhise Roshi	ALB	22/05/91	M		(1)	
22	Aleksandar Šofranac	MNE	21/10/90	D	4	(3)	
7	Marin Tomasov		31/08/87	A	2		1
29	Marko Vešović	MNE	28/08/91	D	32	(1)	6
8	Leonard Zhuta	MKD	09/08/92	D	34	(1)	
13	Dario Župarić		03/05/92	D	11		1

NK Slaven Koprivnica

1907 • Gradski (3,800) • nk-slaven-belupo.hr

Coach: Željko Kopić

Date		Opponent		Score	Scorers
2016					
15/07	h	Inter	W	2-0	*Štiglec, Arap*
23/07	h	Cibalia	W	3-2	*Ivanovski 2, Barić*
29/07	a	Dinamo	D	1-1	*Jovičić*
05/08	h	Split	D	0-0	
14/08	a	Istra 1961	D	0-0	
20/08	h	Osijek	L	2-3	*Ivanovski, Savic*
27/08	a	Rijeka	L	0-2	
11/09	h	Lokomotiva	L	2-3	*Ivanovski 2*
17/09	a	Hajduk	L	0-4	
24/09	a	Inter	D	1-1	*Bouadla*
02/10	a	Cibalia	D	0-0	
14/10	h	Dinamo	L	0-1	
21/10	a	Split	L	0-3	
29/10	h	Istra 1961	W	2-0	*Barić, Héber*
05/11	a	Osijek	L	0-1	
20/11	h	Rijeka	D	0-0	
25/11	a	Lokomotiva	W	2-0	*Héber 2*
04/12	h	Hajduk	W	2-1	*Burić, Ivanovski (p)*
09/12	h	Inter	W	2-0	*Arap, Héber*
18/12	h	Cibalia	W	4-0	*Héber 3, Savic*
2017					
18/02	a	Dinamo	L	0-1	
25/02	h	Split	L	0-1	
03/03	a	Istra 1961	D	0-0	
12/03	h	Osijek	L	1-2	*Melnjak*
19/03	a	Rijeka	L	2-3	*Tadić, Héber*
01/04	h	Lokomotiva	D	1-1	*Héber*
08/04	a	Hajduk	D	1-1	*Ivanovski (p)*
15/04	a	Inter	D	1-1	*Burić*
21/04	a	Cibalia	L	1-3	*Ivanovski (p)*
25/04	h	Dinamo	W	2-1	*Héber, Bogojević*
30/04	a	Split	D	0-0	
07/05	h	Istra 1961	W	2-0	*Katić, Ivanovski*
13/05	a	Osijek	L	0-3	
17/05	h	Rijeka	L	0-2	
20/05	a	Lokomotiva	L	1-2	*Ivanovski*
26/05	h	Hajduk	L	1-2	*Medjimorec*

No	Name	Nat	DoB	Pos	Aps	(s)	Gls
15	Fidan Aliti	KOS	03/10/93	D	16	(6)	
13	David Arap		09/03/95	M	8	(13)	2
18	Gordan Barić		11/08/94	D	14	(11)	2
21	Kristijan Bistrović		09/04/98	M		(2)	
1	Goran Blažević		07/06/86	G	24		
30	Bruno Bogojević		29/06/98	A		(9)	1
11	Selim Bouadla	FRA	26/08/88	M	20	(2)	1
17	Mario Burić		25/10/91	M	24	(6)	2
8	Søren Christensen	DEN	29/06/86	M	28	(2)	
9	Muzafer Ejupi	MKD	16/09/88	A	4		
20	Mario Gregurina		23/03/88	M	9	(5)	
9	Héber	BRA	10/08/91	A	28	(2)	10
23	Helder	BRA	01/08/91	M		(2)	
22	Mirko Ivanovski	MKD	31/10/89	A	30	(3)	10
5	Aleksandar Jovičić	BIH	18/07/95	D	19	(3)	1
19	Nikola Katić		10/10/96	D	27	(2)	1
12	Antun Marković		04/07/92	G	12		
3	Marko Martinaga		27/05/98	D		(2)	
4	Vinko Medjimorec		01/06/96	D	4	(4)	1
23	Dario Melnjak		31/10/92	D	10	(3)	1
7	Mihael Mladen		28/09/99	A		(1)	
26	Božo Musa		15/09/88	D	31		
10	Nikola Pokrivač		26/11/85	M	4		
16	Vedran Purić		16/03/86	D	30	(1)	
27	Dominik Radić		26/07/96	A		(5)	
7	Stefan Savic	AUT	09/01/94	M	11	(8)	2
6	Dalibor Stevanovič	SVN	27/09/84	M	11	(1)	
24	Dino Štiglec		03/10/90	D	20		1
21	Josip Tadić		22/08/87	A	10	(2)	1
21	Goran Zakarić	BIH	07/11/92	M	2	(5)	

RNK Split

1912 • Park mladeži (8,000) • rnksplit.hr

Coach: Goran Sablić; (18/07/16) Vjekoslav Lokica; (13/02/17) Bruno Akrapović (BiH)

Date		Opponent		Score	Scorers
2016					
16/07	h	Rijeka	L	0-3	
24/07	a	Lokomotiva	D	0-0	
31/07	h	Hajduk	L	0-1	
05/08	a	Slaven	D	0-0	
12/08	h	Cibalia	D	2-2	*Bakaj, Jurendić*
19/08	a	Dinamo	L	0-1	
26/08	h	Inter	D	0-0	
10/09	h	Istra 1961	L	0-3	
18/09	a	Osijek	L	0-3	
25/09	a	Rijeka	L	0-2	
01/10	h	Lokomotiva	L	0-2	
16/10	a	Hajduk	L	1-2	*Pešić*
21/10	h	Slaven	W	3-0	*Boljat, Ugrina, Pavlovski*
31/10	a	Cibalia	L	0-1	
06/11	h	Dinamo	L	0-1	
19/11	a	Inter	L	0-2	
26/11	a	Istra 1961	L	0-1	
04/12	h	Osijek	D	1-1	*Jurendić*
11/12	h	Rijeka	L	0-2	
18/12	a	Lokomotiva	L	0-3	
2017					
19/02	h	Hajduk	D	1-1	*Pešić*
25/02	a	Slaven	W	1-0	*Tomičić*
05/03	h	Cibalia	W	1-0	*og (Žderić)*
11/03	a	Dinamo	L	0-4	
18/03	h	Inter	D	0-0	
02/04	h	Istra 1961	L	0-1	
09/04	a	Osijek	L	0-4	
15/04	a	Rijeka	L	0-2	
23/04	h	Lokomotiva	D	0-0	
26/04	a	Hajduk	L	2-5	*Tomičić, Ugrina*
30/04	h	Slaven	D	0-0	
07/05	a	Cibalia	L	0-1	
12/05	h	Dinamo	L	0-1	
17/05	a	Inter	L	0-1	
22/05	a	Istra 1961	L	0-1	
26/05	h	Osijek	L	0-1	

No	Name	Nat	DoB	Pos	Aps	(s)	Gls
15	Mohammed Aliyu	NGA	05/09/95	A	3	(4)	
11	Dražen Bagarić		12/11/92	A	2	(1)	
9	Elis Bakaj	ALB	25/06/87	A	9	(1)	1
30	Mateo Baturina		18/06/96	M		(2)	
15	Roko Baturina		20/06/00	A		(1)	
9	Filip Bojić		05/10/92	A	2	(5)	
22	Domagoj Boljat		25/01/91	M	23	(3)	1
15	Karolis Chvedukas	LTU	21/04/91	M	9	(4)	
15	Ardit Deliu	ALB	26/10/97	M		(1)	
1	Tomislav Duka		07/09/92	G	29		
6	Amer Dupovac	BIH	29/05/91	D	23		
55	Ivan Fuštar		18/08/89	D	8	(2)	
11	Mihovil Geljić		25/02/92	A	1	(1)	
3	Toni Grković		29/12/90	M	1		
20	Luka Grubišić		09/11/97	M	6	(3)	
4	Kristijan Jakić		14/05/97	M	19	(5)	
9	Ivan Jovanović		22/05/91	A	8	(8)	
7	Ivan Jukić		21/06/96	M	3	(3)	
22	Matej Jukić		07/04/97	M		(3)	
13	Josip Jurendić		26/04/87	D	24		2
8	Luka Kapetanović		12/09/90	M		(4)	
12	Luka Kukić		16/05/96	G	7	(1)	
6	Frane Maglica		02/07/97	D	19	(4)	
4	Ante Majstorović		06/11/93	D	1		
15	Alem Merajić	BIH	04/02/94	D	8	(5)	
5	Božo Mikulić		29/01/97	D	25	(2)	
10	Petar Mišić		24/07/94	A	2	(3)	
44	Jure Obšivač		28/05/90	D	7		
16	Marko Pavlovski	SRB	07/02/94	M	21	(3)	1
8	Marko Perković		30/08/91	D	9		
21	Ivan Pešić		06/04/92	A	30	(1)	2
14	Marin Roglić		16/06/97	A	3	(7)	
18	Amir Rrahmani	KOS	24/02/94	D	7		
7	Antonio Samac		30/07/97	M		(5)	
21	Tomislav Šarić		24/06/90	M	1		
3	Dino Škvorc		02/02/90	D	4	(1)	
17	Dino Špehar		08/02/94	A	8	(3)	
30	Ivan Tomičić		01/03/93	M	11	(1)	2
11	Sandro Ugrina		10/08/91	A	18	(5)	2
14	Ivan Anton Vasilj		05/04/91	D	12	(3)	
24	Miloš Vidović	SRB	03/10/89	M	16	(1)	
13	Santiago Villafañe	ARG	19/05/88	D	1		
3	Maksim Vitus	BLR	11/02/89	D	11		
14	Josip Vuković		02/05/92	M	3	(7)	
22	Adnan Zahirović	BIH	23/03/90	M	2		

Top goalscorers

18	Márkó Futács (Hajduk)
17	El Arabi Hillel Soudani (Dinamo)
16	Armin Hodžić (Dinamo)
	Franko Andrijašević (Rijeka)
14	Muzafer Ejupi (Osijek)
12	Alexander Gorgon (Rijeka)
11	Ante Erceg (Hajduk)
	Jakov Puljić (Inter)
	Roman Bezjak (Rijeka)
	Mario Gavranovic (Rijeka)

Promoted club

NK Rudeš

1957 • ŠC Rudeš (2,500) • nk-rudes.hr
Coach: Igor Bišćan

Second level final table 2016/17

		Pld	W	D	L	F	A	Pts
1	NK Rudeš	33	17	9	7	43	28	60
2	HNK Gorica	33	15	12	6	53	31	57
3	NK Solin	33	16	7	10	40	36	55
4	NK Sesvete	33	15	7	11	53	36	52
5	GNK Dinamo Zagreb II	33	12	11	10	39	32	47
6	NK Dugopolje	33	12	10	11	36	32	46
7	HNK Šibenik	33	12	9	12	32	33	45
8	NK Novigrad	33	11	9	13	28	35	42
9	NK Lučko	33	9	11	13	34	48	38
10	NK Hrvatski dragovoljac	33	9	9	15	30	39	36
11	NK Imotski	33	8	7	18	36	58	31
12	NK Zagreb	33	6	11	16	34	50	29

Promotion/Relegation play-off

(04/06/17 & 07/06/17)
Gorica 0-2 Cibalia
Cibalia 3-1 Gorica
(Cibalia 5-1)

DOMESTIC CUP

Hrvatski Nogometni Kup 2016/17

SECOND ROUND

(20/09/16)
Bijelo Brdo 2-3 Inter
Krk 0-2 Lokomotiva
Medimurje 1-2 Šibenik *(aet)*
Samobor 1-6 Cibalia *(aet)*
Veli Vrh 0-5 Dinamo

(21/09/16)
Bjelovar 4-0 Zagreb
Djakovo-Croatia 0-3 Rijeka
Jalžabet 0-6 Hajduk
Libertas 2-5 Vinogradar
Neretvanac Opuzen 1-3 Istra 1961
Novigrad 4-0 Zelina
Rudeš 3-0 GOŠK Dubrovnik
Slavija Pleternica 1-2 Split
Solin 1-0 Zadar
Varaždin 2-2 Slaven *(aet; 2-4 on pens)*
Vukovar 1-4 Osijek

THIRD ROUND

(25/10/16)
Bjelovar 1-2 Dinamo
Istra 1961 1-3 Split *(aet)*
Novigrad 0-1 Slaven

(26/10/16)
Inter 1-0 Cibalia
Rudeš 3-5 Rijeka *(aet)*
Solin 1-2 Hajduk
Šibenik 1-2 Osijek
Vinogradar 1-2 Lokomotiva

QUARTER-FINALS

(29/11/16)
Lokomotiva 1-3 Rijeka *(Çekiçi 79; Maleš 21, Ristovski 38, Gorgon 41p)*

(30/11/16)
Inter 0-1 Dinamo *(Perić 68)*

Osijek 1-0 Slaven *(Perošević 81)*

Split 2-1 Hajduk *(Ugrina 91, 106; Barry 25) (aet)*

SEMI-FINALS

(01/03/17 & 14/03/17)
Dinamo 6-0 Split *(Ćorić 25, 78, Hodžić 37, 51, 66, 81p)*
Split 0-0 Dinamo
(Dinamo 6-0)

(01/03/17 & 15/03/17)
Rijeka 3-1 Osijek *(Gavranovic 9, 23, 71; Perošević 75p)*
Osijek 0-2 Rijeka *(Škorić 52og, Andrijašević 57)*
(Rijeka 5-1)

FINAL

(31/05/17)
Gradski stadion Andjelko Herjavec, Varazdin
HNK RIJEKA 3 *(Gavranovic 24, 46, Župarić 73)*
GNK DINAMO ZAGREB 1 *(Dani Olmo 37)*
Referee: *Vučemilović-Šimunović*
RIJEKA: *Prskalo, Ristovski (Zhuta 85), Župarić, Vešović, Elez, Andrijašević (Maleš 60), Bradarić, Mišić, Gorgon (Čanadjija 73), Gavranovic, Bezjak*
DINAMO: *Zagorac, Måţel, Lešković (Soldo 53), Schildenfeld, Pivarić, Gojak (Sammir 59), Paulo Machado, Pavičić, Hodžić (Henríquez 75), Dani Olmo, Soudani*

Champions Rijeka clinched a league and cup double with a 3-1 win over Dinamo Zagreb in Varazdin

CYPRUS

Kypriaki Omospondia Podosfairon (KOP)/ Cyprus Football Association (CFA)

Address	10 Achaion Street 2413 Engomi, PO Box 25071 CY-1306 Nicosia	**President**	Costakis Koutsokoumnis
		General secretary	Phivos Vakis
Tel	+357 22 352 341	**Media officer**	Kyriacos Giorgallis
Fax	+357 22 590 544	**Year of formation**	1934
E-mail	info@cfa.com.cy	**National stadium**	GSP, Nicosia (23,700)
Website	cfa.com.cy		

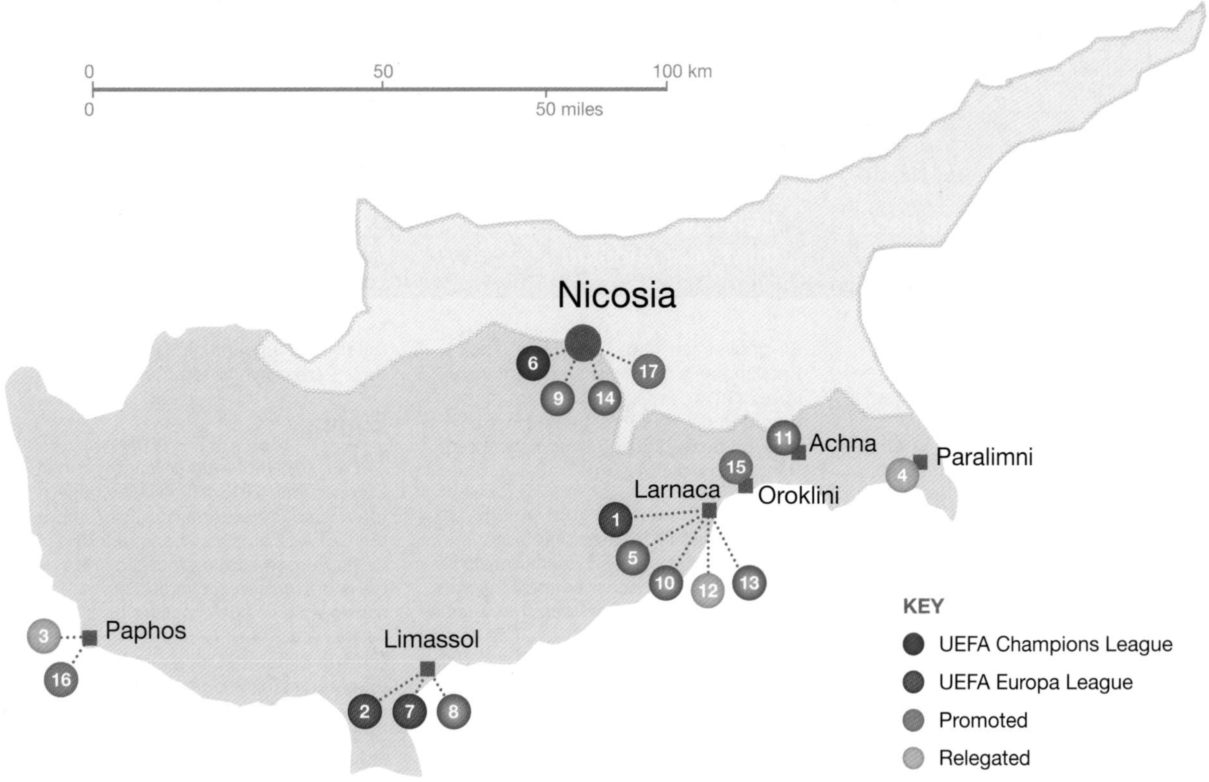

0 50 100 km
0 50 miles

Nicosia
Achna
Paralimni
Larnaca
Oroklini
Paphos
Limassol

KEY
- UEFA Champions League
- UEFA Europa League
- Promoted
- Relegated

A KATIGORIA CLUBS

1 **AEK Larnaca FC**

2 **AEL Limassol FC**

3 **AEZ Zakakiou FC**

4 **Anagennisis Derynia FC**

5 **Anorthosis Famagusta FC**

6 **APOEL FC**

7 **Apollon Limassol FC**

8 **Aris Limassol FC**

9 **Doxa Katokopia FC**

10 **Ermis Aradippou FC**

11 **Ethnikos Achnas FC**

12 **Karmiotissa Pano Polemidia FC**

13 **Nea Salamis Famagusta FC**

14 **AC Omonia**

PROMOTED CLUBS

15 **Alki Oroklini FC**

16 **Pafos FC**

17 **Olympiakos Nicosia FC**

Five in a row for APOEL

APOEL FC made it five Cypriot league titles on the trot, equalling a club record set back in 1940. Despite a heavy European schedule the Nicosia team proved irrepressible front-runners under their new coach Thomas Christiansen, lured to the capital from AEK Larnaca, who finished runners-up for the third successive season.

Apollon Limassol retained the Cypriot Cup for the first time in half a century, denying APOEL the double with a 1-0 win in the final under their impressive novice coach Sofronis Avgousti, who had replaced Pedro Emanuel in mid-season

Nicosia heavyweights secure record 26th title

AEK finish runners-up for third year running

Apollon upset champions to retain Cypriot Cup

Domestic league

AEK replaced Christiansen with another Spaniard, Imanol Idiakez, and the ex-Lleida coach could hardly have made a better start to his first assignment abroad, steering the team to eight successive wins. The run was halted by a 1-1 draw against APOEL, who at the time were also undefeated and just two points in arrears. By Christmas, AEK still held that advantage, but a 3-1 defeat at home to Apollon in the first match of the new year allowed the defending champions to supplant them at the summit. It was a position they would never surrender.

While AEK got bogged down by a succession of draws in January and February, which allowed AEL Limassol and a resurgent Apollon to challenge their position, APOEL charged clear with a series of high-scoring victories. By the 26-game cut-off point APOEL held a four-point lead. They would win only half of their remaining ten fixtures but it would be enough to get them over the line, their fifth and final win of the play-off series, 3-1 against local rivals Omonia, seeing them home with a game to spare.

The winning goal against Omonia was scored by APOEL's leading scorer Pieros Sotiriou. It was the 24-year-old's 21st of a sparkling campaign, although that tally was insufficient to win him the golden boot, which went instead to Omonia's 24-goal striker Matt Derbyshire. The Englishman's consistent marksmanship could not, however, lift his team higher than fifth place, a total freefall in the play-off phase leaving Omonia without European football in 2017/18.

There was never any doubt which teams would fill the two automatic relegation places. AEZ Zakakiou and Anagennisis Derynia managed the sum total of one victory between them – and that in AEZ's opening fixture. The other newly-promoted club, Karmiotissa Pano Polemidia, did significantly better but ended up sharing the same fate after losing out at the end of the play-off series to Doxa Katokopia, who finished above them only on head-to-head goal difference.

Domestic cup

Appointed only on a caretaker basis in mid-December, ex-Apollon player Avgousti made a storming start to his coaching career with wins in his opening eight league games and further success in the Cypriot Cup, a 6-0 victory against Anorthosis in the first leg of the semi-final pre-booking a final date with APOEL. Despite playing in their home GSP Stadium, where they had not lost in the league all season, the champions were to endure an off-day, with holders Apollon claiming a 1-0 victory thanks to a 78th-minute goal from Brazilian defender Paulo Vinícius at a time when they were down to ten men.

Europe

APOEL enjoyed another lengthy run in Europe, their 2016/17 odyssey taking them from the second qualifying round of the UEFA Champions League to the UEFA Europa League round of 16. Christiansen's men claimed some memorable scalps en route, beating Olympiacos twice and knocking out Athletic Bilbao before a rare home defeat triggered elimination by Anderlecht. AEK also upset the odds by overcoming Spartak Moskva, only to temper that achievement by succumbing meekly in the next round to Slovan Liberec.

National team

Christakis Christoforou's spell in charge of Cyprus lasted just 18 months, the 53-year-old ex-AEL and Apollon coach standing down after a FIFA World Cup qualifier against Gibraltar in which victory was only salvaged with a late Sotiriou strike. That took Cyprus's points total to seven. It had been zero after three games, although not much more was expected from encounters at home to Belgium and away to Greece and Bosnia & Herzegovina. The return fixtures against those three nations would see a new man on the Cyprus bench – experienced Israeli coach Ran Ben Shimon.

DOMESTIC SEASON AT A GLANCE

A Katigoria 2016/17 final table

		Pld	Home W	Home D	Home L	Home F	Home A	Away W	Away D	Away L	Away F	Away A	Total W	Total D	Total L	Total F	Total A	Pts
1	**APOEL FC**	**36**	**13**	**5**	**0**	**41**	**8**	**11**	**3**	**4**	**36**	**16**	**24**	**8**	**4**	**77**	**24**	**80**
2	AEK Larnaca FC	36	13	4	1	38	12	9	6	3	28	16	22	10	4	66	28	76
3	Apollon Limassol FC	36	12	5	1	35	12	9	5	4	36	18	21	10	5	71	30	73
4	AEL Limassol FC	36	11	5	2	28	14	8	4	6	25	22	19	9	8	53	36	66
5	AC Omonia	36	12	1	5	40	24	5	5	8	28	33	17	6	13	68	57	57
6	Anorthosis Famagusta FC	36	6	7	5	25	17	6	4	8	23	24	12	11	13	48	41	47
7	Nea Salamis Famagusta FC	36	6	4	8	16	24	6	5	7	17	20	12	9	15	33	44	45
8	Ethnikos Achnas FC	36	7	6	5	31	29	4	4	10	26	37	11	10	15	57	66	43
9	Ermis Aradippou FC	36	9	2	7	31	30	5	4	9	20	31	14	6	16	51	61	42
10	Aris Limassol FC	36	6	4	8	28	28	5	4	9	19	37	11	8	17	47	65	41
11	Doxa Katokopia FC	36	4	5	9	18	25	6	2	10	22	27	10	7	19	40	52	37
12	Karmiotissa Pano Polemidia FC	36	6	4	8	26	30	4	3	11	21	41	10	7	19	47	71	37
13	AEZ Zakakiou FC	26	1	2	10	13	40	0	6	7	7	23	1	8	17	20	63	11
14	Anagennisis Derynia FC	26	0	4	9	11	22	0	3	10	7	36	0	7	19	18	58	7

NB After 26 matches the top 12 clubs split into two groups of six, after which they play exclusively against teams in their group; Ermis Aradippou FC – 6 pts deducted.

European qualification 2017/18

Champion: APOEL FC (second qualifying round)

Cup winner: Apollon Limassol FC (second qualifying round)
AEK Larnaca FC (first qualifying round)
AEL Limassol FC (first qualifying round)

Top scorer Matt Derbyshire (Omonia), 24 goals
Relegated clubs Anagennisis Derynia FC, AEZ Zakakiou FC, Karmiotissa Pano Polemidia FC
Promoted clubs Alki Oroklini FC, Pafos FC, Olympiakos Nicosia FC
Cup final Apollon Limassol FC 1-0 APOEL FC

Player of the season

Pieros Sotiriou
(APOEL FC)

There was only one contender for the Cyprus FA player of the season award. Sotiriou fired APOEL to the league title with 21 goals – seven more than he had managed in his three previous seasons combined – and also excelled in the club's 16-match European run, scoring vital goals against Olympiacos, Young Boys and Athletic. Additionally, he opened his international account for Cyprus with a goal in each game against Gibraltar. A player in form and in demand, he was recruited in the summer by Danish champions FC København on a five-year contract.

Newcomer of the season

Fanos Katelaris
(AC Omonia)

Promoted to the Omonia first-team squad in 2016/17 after being farmed out on loan to Alki Larnaca and second division Olympiakos Nicosia, Katelaris caught the eye on a number of occasions with his diligent defensive midfield play. Energetic, effervescent and economical in possession, the Cypriot Under-21 international was promoted to senior duty by coach Christakis Christoforou and he made the most of the unexpected opportunity, scoring on his debut, still aged 20, in a 3-1 friendly win against Kazakhstan in Larnaca.

Team of the season
(4-4-2)

Coach: Avgousti *(Apollon)*

NATIONAL TEAM

Top five all-time caps
Ioannis Okkas (104); **Kostas Charalambides** (90); Michalis Konstantinou (87); Pambos Pittas (82); Konstantinos Makrides (77)

Top five all-time goals
Michalis Konstantinou (32); Ioannis Okkas (26); **Kostas Charalambides** (12); Marios Agathokleous & Efstathios Aloneftis (10)

Results 2016/17

06/09/16	Belgium (WCQ)	H	Nicosia	L	0-3	
07/10/16	Greece (WCQ)	A	Piraeus	L	0-2	
10/10/16	Bosnia & Herzegovina (WCQ)	A	Zenica	L	0-2	
13/11/16	Gibraltar (WCQ)	H	Nicosia	W	3-1	*Laifis (29), Sotiriou (65), Sielis (87)*
22/03/17	Kazakhstan	H	Larnaca	W	3-1	*Mytidis (55), Katelaris (62), Christofi (67)*
25/03/17	Estonia (WCQ)	H	Nicosia	D	0-0	
03/06/17	Portugal	A	Estoril	L	0-4	
09/06/17	Gibraltar (WCQ)	A	Faro (POR)	W	2-1	*R Chipolina (10og), Sotiriou (87)*

Appearances 2016/17

Coach: Christakis Christoforou	26/01/64		BEL	GRE	BIH	GIB	Kaz	EST	Por	GIB	Caps	Goals
Konstantinos Panagi	08/10/94	Omonia	G	G	G	G	G	G		G	8	-
Jason Demetriou	18/11/87	Southend (ENG)	D	D	D	D			D82	D	37	1
Dossa Júnior	28/07/86	AEL	D	D	D						23	1
Konstantinos Laifis	19/05/93	Standard Liège (BEL)	D	D	D	D		D	D	D	15	1
Nektarios Alexandrou	19/12/83	APOEL	D		D		D		D68	s61	37	-
Vincent Laban	09/09/84	AEK Larnaca	M69	M	M		M58	M82			29	2
Charalambos Kyriakou	09/02/95	Apollon	M	s78		M91	s68	M	M60	M	10	-
Kostas Charalambides	25/07/81	AEK Larnaca	M	M66	s77	s73	M58		M60	M	90	12
Grigoris Kastanos	30/01/98	Juventus (ITA) /Pescara (ITA)	M78	M	M	M	M68	M			8	-
Georgios Efrem	05/07/89	APOEL	M	M	s72	M73					36	3
Pieros Sotiriou	13/01/93	APOEL	A69		A	A86			A75	A	21	2
Kostakis Artymatas	15/04/93	APOEL	s69	M78	M85	M	M	M	M	M82	16	-
Nestoras Mytidis	01/06/91	Roda (NED) /AEK Larnaca	s69	A83	s85	s86	A68	A88	s60	s82	29	5
Andreas Makris	27/11/95	Walsall (ENG)	s78	s83	M72		M81	s88	M70	s73	17	-
Ilias Charalambous	25/09/80	AEK Larnaca		D		D		D			69	-
Dimitris Christofi	28/09/88	Omonia		s66	M77	M	s58	M		M73	44	7
Valentinos Sielis	01/03/90	AEL /Gangwon (KOR)				D	D				14	1
Marios Nicolaou	04/10/83	AEL				s91					54	1
Marios Stylianou	23/09/93	Apollon					D77	D72	s82		6	-
Fanos Katelaris	26/08/96	Omonia					D		D		2	1
Renato Margaça	17/07/85	Omonia					s58		M	M61	3	-
Andreas Avraam	06/06/87	Larissa (GRE)					s68	s72	s60		32	5
Andreas Panagiotou	31/05/95	Omonia					s77				1	-
Onisiforos Roushias	15/07/92	Omonia					s81	s82			3	-
Georgios Merkis	30/07/84	APOEL						D		D	35	1
Antonis Georgallides	30/01/82	AEK Larnaca							G		65	-
Nicholas Ioannou	10/11/95	APOEL							s68	D	2	-
Nikos Englezou	11/07/93	Nea Salamis							s70		4	-
Georgios Oikonomidis	10/04/90	Anorthosis							s75		7	-

EUROPE

APOEL FC

Second qualifying round - The New Saints FC (WAL)
A 0-0
Waterman, Carlão, Efrem (Aloneftis 83), De Vincenti, Alexandrou, Vinícius (Orlandi 71), Sotiriou, Milanov, Iñaki Astiz, Nuno Morais, Vander. Coach: Thomas Christiansen (ESP)
H 3-0 *Alexandrou (54), Sotiriou (73), De Vincenti (90+5p)*
Waterman, Carlão, Efrem (Orlandi 78), De Vincenti, Alexandrou, Vinícius (Renan Bressan 58), Sotiriou, Iñaki Astiz, Nuno Morais, Mário Sérgio (Milanov 85), Vander. Coach: Thomas Christiansen (ESP)

Third qualifying round - Rosenborg BK (NOR)
A 1-2 *Efrem (67)*
Waterman, Artymatas (Orlandi 59), Carlão, Alexandrou, Vinícius, Sotiriou (De Camargo 77), Milanov, Iñaki Astiz, Nuno Morais, Gianniotas, Vander (Efrem 65). Coach: Thomas Christiansen (ESP)
H 3-0 *Gianniotas (90+1), Vander (90+6), De Vincenti (90+9)*
Waterman, Carlão, Efrem (Vander 71), De Vincenti, Alexandrou, Vinícius (Orlandi 71), Sotiriou (De Camargo 77), Milanov, Iñaki Astiz, Nuno Morais, Gianniotas. Coach: Thomas Christiansen (ESP)

Play-offs - FC København (DEN)
A 0-1
Waterman, Carlão (Merkis 46), Efrem (Vander 56), Orlandi, Alexandrou, Vinícius, Sotiriou (De Camargo 75), Milanov, Iñaki Astiz, Nuno Morais, Gianniotas. Coach: Thomas Christiansen (ESP)
H 1-1 *Sotiriou (69)*
Waterman, Carlão, Efrem (Vander 59), Orlandi (Renan Bressan 75), Alexandrou (De Camargo 89), Vinícius, Sotiriou, Milanov, Iñaki Astiz, Nuno Morais, Gianniotas. Coach: Thomas Christiansen (ESP)

EUROPA LEAGUE

Group B
Match 1 - FC Astana (KAZ)
H 2-1 *Vinícius (75), De Camargo (87)*
Waterman, Roberto Lago, Carlão, Efrem (De Camargo 70), Orlandi (Bertoglio 56), Vinícius, Sotiriou, Milanov, Iñaki Astiz, Nuno Morais, Gianniotas (Vander 78). Coach: Thomas Christiansen (ESP)
Match 2 - Olympiacos FC (GRE)
A 1-0 *Sotiriou (10)*
Waterman, Roberto Lago, Carlão, Bertoglio (Artymatas 65), Vinícius, Sotiriou, Milanov, Nuno Morais, Merkis, Gianniotas (Iñaki Astiz 82), Vander (Efrem 68). Coach: Thomas Christiansen (ESP)
Match 3 - BSC Young Boys (SUI)
A 1-3 *Efrem (14)*
Waterman, Roberto Lago, Carlão (Merkis 50), Efrem, Bertoglio (Renan Bressan 78), Vinícius, Sotiriou, Milanov, Iñaki Astiz, Nuno Morais, Vander (Gianniotas 68). Coach: Thomas Christiansen (ESP)
Match 4 - BSC Young Boys (SUI)
H 1-0 *Sotiriou (69)*
Waterman, Roberto Lago, Carlão, Efrem, Vinícius, Sotiriou (De Camargo 83), Milanov, Iñaki Astiz, Nuno Morais, Aloneftis (Gianniotas 66), Renan Bressan (Bertoglio 59). Coach: Thomas Christiansen (ESP)
Match 5 - FC Astana (KAZ)
A 1-2 *Efrem (31)*
Waterman, Roberto Lago, Carlão, Efrem (Gianniotas 81), De Camargo (Vander 63), Vinícius, Sotiriou, Milanov, Iñaki Astiz, Nuno Morais, Aloneftis (Artymatas 35). Coach: Thomas Christiansen (ESP)
Red card: Iñaki Astiz 33
Match 6 - Olympiacos FC (GRE)
H 2-0 *Manuel Da Costa (19og), De Camargo (83)*
Waterman, Carlão, Efrem (Gianniotas 59), Bertoglio (Orlandi 67), Alexandrou, Vinícius, Sotiriou (De Camargo 80), Milanov, Nuno Morais, Merkis, Aloneftis. Coach: Thomas Christiansen (ESP)

Round of 32 - Athletic Club (ESP)
A 2-3 *Efrem (36), Gianniotas (89)*
Waterman, Efrem (Aloneftis 73), Bertoglio (De Camargo 60), Vinícius, Sotiriou (Iñaki Astiz 77), Milanov, Nuno Morais, Merkis, Ioannou, Gianniotas, Yambéré. Coach: Thomas Christiansen (ESP)
H 2-0 *Sotiriou (46), Gianniotas (54p)*
Waterman, Efrem (Vander 71), Vinícius (Ebecilio 76), Barral (De Camargo 61), Sotiriou, Milanov, Iñaki Astiz, Nuno Morais, Merkis, Ioannou, Gianniotas. Coach: Thomas Christiansen (ESP)
Red card: Sotiriou 65

Round of 16 - RSC Anderlecht (BEL)
H 0-1
Waterman, Ebecilio (Artymatas 72), Efrem (Vander 55), De Camargo, Barral, Milanov, Iñaki Astiz (Roberto Lago 40), Nuno Morais, Merkis, Ioannou, Gianniotas. Coach: Thomas Christiansen (ESP)
A 0-1
Waterman, Roberto Lago, Artymatas, Ebecilio (Yambéré 57), De Camargo (Bertoglio 72), Barral (Vander 77), Sotiriou, Milanov, Merkis, Ioannou, Gianniotas. Coach: Thomas Christiansen (ESP)

Apollon Limassol FC

Third qualifying round - Grasshopper Club Zürich (SUI)
A 1-2 *Gneki Guié (76)*
Bruno Vale, Alex, Bedoya (Barbaro 90+1), João Pedro, Gneki Guié (Maglica 83), Kyriakou, Angeli, Stylianou, Pittas (Sachetti 63), Paulo Vinícius, Vasiliou. Coach: Pedro Emanuel (POR)
Red card: Sachetti 87
H 3-3 (aet) *Paulo Vinícius (73), Papoulis (87), Gneki Guié (101)*
Bruno Vale, Alex, Bedoya, João Pedro, Gneki Guié, Kyriakou (Papoulis 68), Angeli, Stylianou, Paulo Vinícius, Vasiliou (Dudu Paraíba 84), Maglica (Piech 39). Coach: Pedro Emanuel (POR)

AEK Larnaca FC

First qualifying round - SS Folgore (SMR)
H 3-0 *Trickovski (22, 34), André Alves (31)*
Taudul, Mojsov (Murillo 74), David Català, Jorge Larena, André Alves, Joan Tomàs, Tete (Charalambides 63), Trickovski, Laban, Charalambous (Englezou 84), Mintikkis. Coach: Imanol Idiakez (ESP)
A 3-1 *Trickovski (51, 55), André Alves (65p)*
Taudul, David Català, Jorge Larena, André Alves, Joan Tomàs, Trickovski (Konstantinou 86), Murillo, Laban (Boljević 73), Charalambous, Charalambides (Tete 67), Mintikkis. Coach: Imanol Idiakez (ESP)

Second qualifying round - Cliftonville FC (NIR)
A 3-2 *Trickovski (59), Charalambous (64), Joan Tomàs (77)*
Rubén Miño, Mojsov, David Català, Jorge Larena, André Alves (Charalambides 72), Joan Tomàs, Tete (Englezou 84), Trickovski, Juanma Ortiz, Laban (Boljević 81), Charalambous. Coach: Imanol Idiakez (ESP)
H 2-0 *Boljević (45), Joan Tomàs (48)*
Rubén Miño, Mojsov (André Alves 46), David Català, Jorge Larena, Joan Tomàs, Tete (Ioannou 77), Trickovski (Englezou 69), Boljević, Juanma Ortiz, Murillo, Charalambides. Coach: Imanol Idiakez (ESP)

Third qualifying round - FC Spartak Moskva (RUS)
H 1-1 *André Alves (65)*
Rubén Miño, Mojsov, David Català, Jorge Larena, André Alves, Joan Tomàs, Tete (Charalambides 76), Trickovski, Boljević, Juanma Ortiz, Charalambous (Ioannou 84). Coach: Imanol Idiakez (ESP)
A 1-0 *Trickovski (89)*
Rubén Miño, Mojsov, David Català, Jorge Larena, André Alves, Joan Tomàs, Tete (Englezou 89), Trickovski, Boljević (Acorán 84), Juanma Ortiz, Murillo (Charalambides 81). Coach: Imanol Idiakez (ESP)

Play-offs - FC Slovan Liberec (CZE)
H 0-1
Rubén Miño, Truyols (Charalambous 34), Mojsov, Jorge Larena, André Alves (Charalambides 75), Joan Tomàs, Tete (Acorán 82), Trickovski, Boljević, Juanma Ortiz, Murillo. Coach: Imanol Idiakez (ESP)
Red card: Juanma Ortiz 65
A 0-3
Rubén Miño, Mojsov, Jorge Larena, André Alves, Joan Tomàs, Tete (Englezou 59), Trickovski, Boljević, Murillo, Charalambous (Acorán 46), Mintikkis (Charalambides 46). Coach: Imanol Idiakez (ESP)
Red card: Murillo 90

DOMESTIC LEAGUE CLUB-BY-CLUB

AC Omonia

EUROPA LEAGUE

First qualifying round - FC Banants (ARM)

A 1-0 *Derbyshire (26)*

Panagi, Carlitos, Panteliadis, Sheridan (Cleyton 70), Fylaktou, Derbyshire, Renato Margaça, Badibanga (Panagiotou 90+1), Florescu, Oršulić, Christofi (Agaiev 17). Coach: John Carver (ENG)

H 4-1 (aet) *Roushias (93, 108), Derbyshire (114), Cleyton (120+1)*

Panagi, Carlitos, Panteliadis, Sheridan, Agaiev (Roushias 85), Fylaktou, Derbyshire, Renato Margaça, Badibanga (Cleyton 73), Florescu (Katelaris 73), Oršulić. Coach: John Carver (ENG)

Second qualifying round - Beitar Jerusalem FC (ISR)

A 0-1

Panagi, Carlitos, Panteliadis, Sheridan, Cleyton, Agaiev (Touré 68), Fylaktou, Derbyshire, Renato Margaça, Florescu, Oršulić. Coach: John Carver (ENG)

H 3-2 *Agaiev (26), Sheridan (45+3p), Roushias (81)*

Panagi, Bruno Nascimento, Carlitos, Sheridan (Roushias 65), Cleyton, Agaiev (Touré 55), Fylaktou (Soiledis 55), Derbyshire, Renato Margaça, Florescu, Oršulić. Coach: John Carver (ENG)

AEK Larnaca FC

1994 • Neo GSZ (13,032); AEK Arena (7,400) • aek.com.cy

Major honours
Cypriot Cup (1) 2004

Coach: Imanol Idiakez (ESP)

2016

10/09	h	Karmiotissa	W	3-0	*Jorge Larena, Trickovski, Joan Tomàs*
14/09	h	Doxa	W	2-0	*Juanma Ortiz, og (Serrán)*
18/09	a	Apollon	W	1-0	*Tete*
21/09	a	Ethnikos	W	3-0	*Boljević, Mojsov, Charalambides*
25/09	h	Anorthosis	W	4-1	*Trickovski, Murillo, Boljević, Jorge Larena*
02/10	a	Nea Salamis	W	1-0	*Acorán*
17/10	h	Aris	W	4-0	*Jorge Larena, André Alves 2, Joan Tomàs*
23/10	a	AEZ	W	5-2	*André Alves 2, Trickovski 2, Acorán*
29/10	h	APOEL	D	1-1	*André Alves*
05/11	h	AEL	W	2-1	*Acorán, Tete*
20/11	a	Omonia	L	1-2	*Acorán*
26/11	h	Ermis	W	1-0	*og (Da Sylva)*
03/12	a	Anagennisis	D	0-0	
11/12	a	Doxa	D	1-1	*Charalambides*
17/12	h	Ethnikos	W	1-0	*Trickovski (p)*
21/12	a	Karmiotissa	W	3-0	*Trickovski, André Alves, Acorán*

2017

03/01	h	Apollon	L	1-3	*Trickovski*
07/01	a	Anorthosis	W	1-0	*Trickovski (p)*
14/01	h	Nea Salamis	W	2-0	*Truyols, Trickovski*
21/01	a	Aris	D	1-1	*Trickovski*
29/01	h	AEZ	D	1-1	*Acorán*
05/02	a	APOEL	D	1-1	*Taulemesse*
12/02	a	AEL	D	1-1	*Trickovski*
19/02	h	Omonia	W	4-2	*Murillo, Acorán, Trickovski, Taulemesse*
26/02	a	Ermis	W	3-2	*Trickovski 2 (1p), Hevel*
05/03	h	Anagennisis	W	6-0	*David Català 2, Mytides 2, Hevel, Charalambous*
13/03	h	Omonia	D	1-1	*David Català*
18/03	a	Apollon	L	2-3	*Taulemesse, Garrido*
01/04	h	APOEL	W	2-1	*Mytides, Jorge Larena*
09/04	a	AEL	L	1-2	*Taulemesse*
12/04	h	Anorthosis	W	1-0	*Charalambides*
22/04	a	Omonia	W	2-1	*Truyols, og (Katelaris)*
30/04	h	Apollon	W	1-0	*Acorán*
07/05	a	APOEL	D	0-0	
13/05	h	AEL	D	1-1	*Jorge Larena (p)*
20/05	a	Anorthosis	W	1-0	*Acorán*

No	Name	Nat	DoB	Pos	Aps	(s)	Gls
8	Acorán	ESP	31/01/83	M	29	(6)	9
9	André Alves	BRA	15/10/83	A	13	(5)	6
14	Vladimir Boljević	MNE	17/01/88	M	22	(11)	2
10	Kostas Charalambides		25/07/81	M	5	(17)	3
33	Ilias Charalambous		25/09/80	D	11	(1)	1
6	David Català	ESP	03/05/80	D	26	(3)	3
21	Nikos Englezou		11/07/93	M	4	(11)	
19	Javier Garrido	ESP	15/03/85	D	20	(2)	1
1	Antonis Georgallides		30/01/82	G	10	(2)	
13	Hector Hevel	NED	15/05/96	M	9		2
21	Thomas Ioannou		19/07/95	D	1	(1)	
10	Joan Tomàs	ESP	17/05/85	M	10	(8)	2
7	Jorge Larena	ESP	29/09/81	M	30	(2)	5
30	Juan Pablo	ESP	02/09/78	G	5		
17	Juanma Ortiz	ESP	01/03/82	D	30	(1)	1
20	Vincent Laban		09/09/84	M	26	(1)	
22	Elvir Maloku	ALB	14/05/96	A	2	(12)	
77	Konstantinos Mintikkis		08/06/89	D	2	(1)	
50	Daniel Mojsov	MKD	25/12/87	D	28	(3)	1
18	Ander Murillo	ESP	26/07/83	D	20		2
25	Nestoras Mytides		01/06/91	A	2	(12)	3
15	Rubén Miño	ESP	18/01/89	G	21		
23	Florian Taulemesse	FRA	31/01/86	A	13		4
11	Tete	ESP	26/05/85	M	20	(3)	2
12	Ivan Trickovski	MKD	18/04/87	A	24	(2)	14
4	Guillem Truyols	ESP	11/11/89	D	13	(2)	2

AEL Limassol FC

1930 • Tsirion (13,331) • ael-fc.com

Major honours
Cypriot League (6) 1941, 1953, 1955, 1956, 1968, 2012; Cypriot Cup (6) 1939, 1940, 1948, 1985, 1987, 1989

Coach: Charalambos Christodoulou; (08/03/17) (Dionysis Dionysiou); (22/03/17) Bruno Baltazar (BRA)

2016

21/08	h	Anagennisis	W	1-0	*Danilo Bueno (p)*
27/08	a	Doxa	W	3-1	*Savane, Mesca, Lucas Souza*
12/09	h	Ethnikos	D	0-0	
19/09	a	Karmiotissa	W	1-0	*Dossa Júnior*
24/09	h	Apollon	W	2-1	*Marco Soares, Arruabarrena*
01/10	a	Anorthosis	D	0-0	
15/10	h	Nea Salamis	W	3-0	*Arruabarrena 2 (1p), Sielis*
23/10	a	Aris	W	3-0	*Lafrance, Marco Soares, Savane*
30/10	h	AEZ	D	1-1	*Lucas Souza*
05/11	a	AEK	L	1-2	*Dossa Júnior*
19/11	h	APOEL	W	1-0	*Arruabarrena (p)*
26/11	h	Omonia	W	1-0	*Lafrance*
04/12	a	Ermis	W	1-0	*Lafrance*
10/12	a	Anagennisis	W	3-1	*Mesca, Danilo Bueno, Lucas Souza*
17/12	h	Doxa	W	1-0	*Arruabarrena (p)*
22/12	a	Ethnikos	D	2-2	*Danilo Bueno (p), Lucas Souza*

2017

04/01	h	Karmiotissa	W	4-1	*Arruabarrena 2, Lucas Souza, Wellington*
07/01	a	Apollon	L	0-2	
15/01	h	Anorthosis	D	0-0	
22/01	a	Nea Salamis	W	3-1	*Piti 2, Mesca*
30/01	h	Aris	W	3-0	*Sassi, Lafrance, Dossa Júnior*
04/02	a	AEZ	W	3-0	*Nicolaou, Mesca, Arruabarrena (p)*
12/02	h	AEK	D	1-1	*Arruabarrena*
20/02	a	APOEL	L	0-3	
25/02	a	Omonia	L	1-4	*Sassi*
05/03	h	Ermis	L	1-2	*Mavrou*
11/03	h	Apollon	D	1-1	*og (Paulo Vinícius)*
20/03	a	APOEL	L	0-2	
02/04	a	Anorthosis	W	1-0	*A Kyriakou*
09/04	h	AEK	W	2-1	*Arruabarrena 2*
12/04	a	Omonia	L	1-2	*Piti*
23/04	a	Apollon	D	1-1	*Piti*
30/04	h	APOEL	L	1-4	*Mitrea (p)*
08/05	h	Anorthosis	W	2-0	*Sassi 2*
13/05	a	AEK	D	1-1	*Piti (p)*
21/05	h	Omonia	W	3-2	*Sassi, Gerolemou, Marco Soares*

No	Name	Nat	DoB	Pos	Aps	(s)	Gls
9	Aguinaldo	ANG	25/03/89	A		(2)	
11	Mikel Arruabarrena	ESP	09/02/83	A	23	(4)	11
5	Babanco	CPV	27/07/85	M	5	(2)	
83	Danilo Bueno	BRA	07/12/83	M	13	(4)	3
2	Dossa Júnior		28/07/86	D	19		3
90	Alain Eizmendi	ESP	10/06/90	M	7	(4)	
35	Marios Elia		19/05/96	A	2	(8)	
87	Georgios K Georgiadis	GRE	14/11/87	A	15	(13)	
40	Evangelos Georgiou		01/01/95	G	1		
24	Giannis Gerolemou		27/01/00	M		(1)	1
31	Andreas Kittos		09/09/90	G	1		
45	Andreas Kyriakou		05/02/94	D	5		1
40	Charalambos Kyriakou		15/10/89	D	10	(4)	
13	Kevin Lafrance	HAI	13/01/90	D	20	(2)	4
8	Lucas Souza	BRA	04/07/90	M	18		5
21	Marco Airosa	ANG	06/08/84	D	27		
60	Marco Soares	CPV	16/06/84	M	33	(2)	3
19	Ioannis Mavrou		19/07/94	A	3	(7)	1
17	Mesca	POR	06/05/93	M	27	(2)	4
29	Bogdan Mitrea	ROU	29/09/87	D	12	(2)	1
98	Andreas Neophytou		07/07/98	M	1	(1)	
83	Marios Nicolaou		04/10/83	M	21	(11)	1
25	Núrio Fortuna	POR	24/03/95	D	33		
70	Stylianos Panteli		07/08/99	M	1	(1)	
77	Piti	ESP	26/05/81	M	12	(5)	5
1	Rafael Romo	VEN	25/02/90	G	34		
7	Emmanuel Sarki	HAI	26/12/87	M		(5)	
22	Ismail Sassi	TUN	24/12/91	A	12	(4)	5
10	Aly Savane	CIV	11/01/90	M	16	(12)	2
4	Valentinos Sielis		01/03/90	D	18		1
33	Sotiris Vasiliou		29/12/95	M		(1)	
99	Wellington	BRA	05/10/87	A	7	(11)	1

AEZ Zakakiou FC

1956 • Pafiako, Paphos (7,650) • no website

Coach: Nikolas Martides;
(16/11/16) (Alexandros Garpozis);
(12/12/16) Demetris Demetriou

2016

21/08	h	Ethnikos	W	3-1	*Pangalos 3*
28/08	a	Karmiotissa	D	0-0	
11/09	h	Apollon	L	0-4	
17/09	a	Anorthosis	D	2-2	*Pangalos, Gbedinyessi*
24/09	h	Nea Salamis	L	1-5	*Pangalos*
01/10	a	Aris	D	0-0	
15/10	h	APOEL	L	1-4	*Pangalos*
23/10	h	AEK	L	2-5	*Pangalos, Sassi*
30/10	a	AEL	D	1-1	*Sassi*
05/11	h	Omonia	L	0-1	
19/11	a	Ermis	L	1-2	*Sakellariou*
27/11	h	Anagennisis	D	1-1	*Di Franco*
05/12	a	Doxa	L	0-1	
11/12	a	Ethnikos	L	1-3	*Villafañe*
16/12	h	Karmiotissa	D	3-3	*Sassi, Marco Aurélio (p), Pangalos (p)*
21/12	a	Apollon	L	1-2	*Sassi*

2017

03/01	h	Anorthosis	L	0-2	
09/01	a	Nea Salamis	L	0-2	
16/01	h	Aris	L	2-3	*Andreou, Sassi*
22/01	a	APOEL	L	0-7	
29/01	a	AEK	D	1-1	*Lisandro Semedo*
04/02	h	AEL	L	0-3	
11/02	a	Omonia	L	0-2	
18/02	h	Ermis	L	0-4	
25/02	a	Anagennisis	D	0-0	
04/03	h	Doxa	L	0-4	

No	Name	Nat	DoB	Pos	Aps	(s)	Gls
99	Kristis Andreou		12/08/94	A	19	(2)	1
22	Christos Antoniou		11/07/97	D	3		
4	Tawonga Chimodzi	MWI	26/06/88	M	15	(1)	
2	Andreas Christou		12/03/94	A	6		
31	Athos Chrysostomou		08/07/81	G	8		
28	Francisco Di Franco	ARG	28/01/95	A	4	(4)	1
25	Douglas	BRA	07/05/91	D	16		
24	Antonis Eleftheriou		01/02/93	D	2		
95	Endrick	BRA	07/03/95	M	12	(2)	
88	Félicien Gbedinyessi	CIV	02/05/88	M	19	(3)	1
18	Andreas Iakovou		15/12/95	A		(2)	
32	Antonis Katsis		06/09/89	M	12	(4)	
30	Simos Krassas		10/07/82	M		(3)	
20	Pantelis Kyriakou		20/04/91	D	17	(1)	
14	Lisandro Semedo	POR	12/03/96	A	11	(4)	1
29	Andreas Mammidis		10/06/88	D	19	(3)	
8	Marco Aurélio	BRA	27/03/83	M	13	(2)	1
11	Giannis Pachipis		11/04/94	A	3	(1)	
70	Emilios Panagiotou		22/09/92	M	2	(5)	
6	Sergios Panagiotou		18/03/94	M	2	(1)	
23	Konstantinos Pangalos	GRE	03/07/87	A	14	(1)	8
60	Marios Papachristoforou		15/01/96	A		(4)	
13	Stavros Paraskeva		21/11/96	D	3	(2)	
9	Andreas Pittaras		25/09/90	A	3	(7)	
91	Vilim Posinković	CRO	10/01/91	A	6	(2)	
89	Romão	BRA	31/07/89	A		(1)	
3	Eleftherios Sakellariou	GRE	17/02/87	D	12	(1)	1
7	Ismail Sassi	TUN	24/12/91	A	14	(2)	5
4	Nebojša Skopljak	SRB	12/05/87	D	11	(4)	
90	Ellinas Sofroniou		29/01/96	G	11		
77	Anthos Solomou		30/11/85	M	2	(2)	
33	Archontis Stoyanov	BUL	29/03/96	M	3		
17	Dmytro Strelkovskiy	UKR	03/03/95	D	3	(2)	
12	Stylianos Stylianou		06/07/95	A	9	(2)	
1	Mateusz Taudul	POL	12/01/94	G	7	(1)	
34	Kyriakos Theodosiou		11/04/97	D		(1)	
10	Nicolás Villafañe	ARG	19/05/88	M	5	(4)	1

Anagennisis Derynia FC

1920 • Tasos Markou, Paralimni (8,000) • no website

Coach: Adamos Adamou;
(18/10/16) (Christos Siailis);
(24/10/16) Savvas Poursaitidis (GRE);
(25/01/17) Zouvanis Zouvani

2016

21/08	a	AEL	L	0-1	
27/08	h	Omonia	D	2-2	*Kyprianou, Rúben Brígido*
11/09	a	Ermis	L	0-1	
18/09	a	APOEL	L	0-2	
25/09	h	Doxa	L	0-1	
01/10	a	Ethnikos	L	3-5	*Wesllem, og (Bogatinov), José Furtado*
16/10	h	Karmiotissa	L	0-1	
22/10	a	Apollon	L	0-4	
31/10	h	Anorthosis	L	1-2	*Wesllem*
06/11	a	Nea Salamis	L	0-2	
20/11	h	Aris	L	1-2	*Giannakou*
27/11	a	AEZ	D	1-1	*José Furtado*
03/12	h	AEK	D	0-0	
10/12	h	AEL	L	1-3	*Wesllem*
17/12	a	Omonia	L	1-5	*José Furtado*
21/12	h	Ermis	D	2-2	*José Furtado (p), Rúben Brígido*

2017

03/01	h	APOEL	L	2-4	*Wesllem, Rúben Brígido*
07/01	a	Doxa	D	0-0	
15/01	h	Ethnikos	L	2-3	*G Christodoulou, José Furtado (p)*
22/01	a	Karmiotissa	D	2-2	*José Furtado, Rivas González*
28/01	h	Apollon	L	0-1	
05/02	a	Anorthosis	L	0-3	
12/02	h	Nea Salamis	L	0-1	
18/02	a	Aris	L	0-4	
25/02	h	AEZ	D	0-0	
05/03	a	AEK	L	0-6	

No	Name	Nat	DoB	Pos	Aps	(s)	Gls
25	Rafael Anastasiou		09/06/97	D	18		
19	Nikolaos Barboudis	GRE	06/03/89	D	12	(1)	
97	Andreas Christodoulou		05/02/96	A		(1)	
45	Georgios Christodoulou		17/08/97	M	18	(2)	1
99	Lysandros Christodoulou		24/01/99	D		(3)	
8	Issaga Diallo	FRA	26/01/87	D	21		
3	Nikos Efthymiou		04/02/93	D	18	(1)	
2	Nikolas Fotiou		11/11/89	D	14	(5)	
5	Georgios Giannakou		02/09/83	D	4		1
70	Vasilios Hadjiyiannakou		10/04/91	A	1	(2)	
98	Sion Ioannou		18/01/98	D	4	(4)	
54	Jorge Vieira	POR	08/01/91	G	2		
20	José Furtado	POR	14/03/83	A	11	(9)	6
11	Vasko Kalezić	MNE	14/03/94	M	7	(7)	
34	Georgios Kolanis		04/11/80	M	1	(12)	
23	Sergei Kundik	RUS	10/07/95	A	4		
9	Andreas Kyprianou		05/12/88	A	2	(2)	1
4	Tomas Maricić	CRO	16/04/95	D	1		
1	Christakis Mastrou		30/01/88	G	24		
10	Alexandros Natsiopoulos	GRE	05/01/91	M	12	(6)	
90	Konstantinos Pafitis		03/10/00	M	1	(1)	
18	Luka Ratković	SRB	09/04/97	A	6	(4)	
50	Rodrigo Rivas González	COL	11/04/97	A	5	(3)	1
7	Rúben Brígido	POR	23/06/91	M	20	(1)	3
29	Georgios Siathas		07/03/96	A		(1)	
56	Alistair Slowe	ENG	16/10/88	M		(4)	
16	Modestos Sotiriou		26/03/93	D	14	(4)	
7	Prodromos Therapontos		25/03/89	M	13	(3)	
14	Nikos Vlassopoulos	GRE	30/05/88	M	23	(1)	
21	Wesllem	BRA	21/04/85	M	21		4
22	Artur Yusbashyan	ARM	07/09/89	M	9	(1)	

Anorthosis Famagusta FC

1911 • Antonis Papadopoulos (10,230) • anorthosisfc.com.cy

Major honours
Cypriot League (13) 1950, 1957, 1958, 1960, 1962, 1963, 1995, 1997, 1998, 1999, 2000, 2005, 2008; Cypriot Cup (10) 1949, 1959, 1962, 1964, 1971, 1975, 1998, 2002, 2003, 2007

Coach: Antonio Puche (ESP);
(18/10/16) (Antonio Saravia) (ESP);
(27/10/16) Ronny Levi (ISR)

2016

27/08	h	Nea Salamis	D	0-0	
11/09	a	Aris	W	2-1	*Colunga (p), Cabrera*
17/09	h	AEZ	D	2-2	*Rayo, Íñigo Calderón*
21/09	h	APOEL	D	0-0	
25/09	a	AEK	L	1-4	*Cabrera*
01/10	h	AEL	D	0-0	
15/10	a	Omonia	L	0-2	
23/10	h	Ermis	D	2-2	*Esmaël Gonçalves (p), Cabrera*
31/10	a	Anagennisis	W	2-1	*Pelé, Esmaël Gonçalves*
06/11	h	Doxa	W	3-0	*Esmaël Gonçalves, Cabrera, Shehu*
21/11	a	Ethnikos	L	1-2	*Rayo (p)*
27/11	h	Karmiotissa	L	0-1	
04/12	a	Apollon	D	1-1	*Cabrera*
12/12	a	APOEL	L	1-2	*Esmaël Gonçalves*
16/12	a	Nea Salamis	L	1-2	*Rayo*
22/12	h	Aris	W	2-0	*Esmaël Gonçalves 2 (1p)*

2017

03/01	a	AEZ	W	2-0	*Pelé, Carlitos*
07/01	h	AEK	L	0-1	
15/01	a	AEL	D	0-0	
21/01	h	Omonia	D	2-2	*João Victor, Íñigo Calderón*
28/01	a	Ermis	W	4-1	*João Victor, Esmaël Gonçalves 2, Shehu*
05/02	h	Anagennisis	W	3-0	*Gabriel, André Alves, Rayo*
13/02	a	Doxa	W	2-0	*Filipe Oliveira, Cabrera*
19/02	h	Ethnikos	W	4-2	*André Alves 3, João Victor*
26/02	a	Karmiotissa	W	4-1	*André Alves, Rayo 2 (1p), Filipe Oliveira*
05/03	h	Apollon	D	0-0	
12/03	h	APOEL	L	0-1	
18/03	a	Omonia	L	0-2	
02/04	h	AEL	L	0-1	
08/04	h	Apollon	W	3-1	*Chus Herrero, Rayo, og (Pelagias)*
12/04	a	AEK	L	0-1	
23/04	a	APOEL	D	1-1	*Íñigo Calderón*
29/04	h	Omonia	W	4-3	*Mitrović, João Victor, Filipe Oliveira, André Alves*
08/05	a	AEL	L	0-2	
14/05	a	Apollon	D	1-1	*Rayo*
20/05	h	AEK	L	0-1	

No	Name	Nat	DoB	Pos	Aps	(s)	Gls
22	Alberto Aguilar	ESP	12/07/84	D	12	(2)	
29	André Alves	BRA	15/10/83	A	10	(4)	6
16	Charalambos Aristotelous		26/01/95	D	1	(7)	
9	Airam Cabrera	ESP	21/10/87	A	18	(14)	6
7	Carlitos	POR	09/03/93	M	24	(4)	1
5	Chus Herrero	ESP	10/02/84	D	29		1
27	Adrián Colunga	ESP	17/11/84	A	8	(10)	1
43	Lazaros Efthimiou		19/04/99	D	1		
77	Esmaël Gonçalves	POR	25/06/91	A	19		8
6	Filipe Oliveira	POR	27/05/84	A	11	(3)	3
2	Gabriel	BRA	18/06/88	D	32	(2)	1
31	Dimitrios Giannoulis	GRE	17/10/95	D	3	(5)	
33	Guilherme Santos	BRA	05/02/88	D	29		
39	Christos Hadjipaschalis		01/08/99	M		(1)	
17	Íñigo Calderón	ESP	04/01/82	D	21	(7)	3
48	Michalis Ioannou		30/06/00	M		(1)	
19	João Victor	BRA	17/11/88	M	33		4
88	Jan Koprivec	SVN	15/07/88	G	33		
44	Pavlos Korrea		14/07/98	D	1		
38	Fytos Kyriakou		29/10/97	A	2	(8)	
26	Nikola Mitrović	SRB	02/01/87	M	14	(1)	1
20	Marios Nicolaou		26/07/96	D	3	(2)	
23	Georgios Oikonomidis		10/04/90	M	22	(6)	
91	Georgios Papadopoulos		24/04/91	G	3	(1)	
4	Pelé	POR	14/09/87	M	9	(5)	2
10	Rayo	ESP	21/06/86	M	27	(3)	8
11	José Antonio Ríos	ESP	10/05/90	D	4	(7)	
15	Abdullahi Shehu	NGA	12/03/93	M	27	(2)	2

CYPRUS

APOEL FC

1926 • GSP (23,700) • apoelfc.com.cy

Major honours
Cypriot League (26) 1936, 1937, 1938, 1939, 1940, 1947, 1948, 1949, 1952, 1965, 1973, 1980, 1986, 1990, 1992, 1996, 2002, 2004, 2007, 2009, 2011, 2013, 2014, 2015, 2016, 2017; Cypriot Cup (21) 1937, 1941, 1947, 1951, 1963, 1968, 1969, 1973, 1976, 1978, 1979, 1984, 1993, 1995, 1996, 1997, 1999, 2006, 2008, 2014, 2015

Coach: Thomas Christiansen (ESP)

Date		Opponent			Scorers
2016					
28/08	h	Ermis	W	3-0	*Nuno Morais, Gianniotas, Efrem*
10/09	a	Nea Salamis	W	4-0	*Sotiriou 2, De Camargo, Efrem*
18/09	h	Anagennisis	W	2-0	*De Camargo, Vander*
21/09	a	Anorthosis	D	0-0	
25/09	a	Aris	W	3-0	*Gianniotas, Vinícius, Merkis*
02/10	h	Doxa	W	2-0	*Efrem, Gianniotas*
15/10	a	AEZ	W	4-1	*Bertoglio, Sotiriou, Efrem 2*
24/10	h	Ethnikos	W	2-0	*Sotiriou 2*
29/10	a	AEK	D	1-1	*Vinícius*
06/11	h	Karmiotissa	W	4-1	*Sotiriou 2, Aloneftis, Renan Bressan*
19/11	a	AEL	L	0-1	
28/11	h	Apollon	D	1-1	*Bertoglio*
03/12	a	Omonia	W	4-1	*Efrem (p), Sotiriou 2, Vinícius*
12/12	h	Anorthosis	W	2-1	*De Camargo, Iñaki Astiz*
17/12	a	Ermis	D	1-1	*Bertoglio*
21/12	h	Nea Salamis	W	1-0	*De Camargo*
2017					
03/01	a	Anagennisis	W	4-2	*Aloneftis, Vinícius 2, Gianniotas*
08/01	h	Aris	W	5-0	*Sotiriou 3 (1p), Efrem 2*
14/01	a	Doxa	W	2-0	*De Camargo, Sotiriou*
22/01	h	AEZ	W	7-0	*Aloneftis, Barral 2, Sotiriou, Merkis, De Camargo 2*
29/01	a	Ethnikos	W	3-2	*De Camargo, Iñaki Astiz, Gianniotas*
05/02	h	AEK	D	1-1	*Sotiriou*
11/02	a	Karmiotissa	W	1-0	*Bertoglio*
20/02	h	AEL	W	3-0	*Vinícius, Nuno Morais, De Camargo (p)*
27/02	a	Apollon	L	0-2	
04/03	h	Omonia	W	2-1	*Sotiriou (p), Barral (p)*
12/03	a	Anorthosis	W	1-0	*Sotiriou*
20/03	h	AEL	W	2-0	*Sotiriou (p), Cañas*
01/04	a	AEK	L	1-2	*Nuno Morais*
09/04	h	Omonia	W	1-0	*Ebecilio*
13/04	a	Apollon	L	0-1	
23/04	h	Anorthosis	D	1-1	*Yambéré*
30/04	a	AEL	W	4-1	*Vander, Ebecilio, Sotiriou 2*
07/05	h	AEK	D	0-0	
13/05	a	Omonia	W	3-1	*Aloneftis, Sotiriou, Vander*
20/05	h	Apollon	D	2-2	*Bertoglio, De Camargo*

No	Name	Nat	DoB	Pos	Aps	(s)	Gls
11	Nektarios Alexandrou		19/12/83	D	11	(1)	
46	Efstathios Aloneftis		29/03/83	M	14	(14)	4
4	Kostakis Artymatas		15/04/93	M	9	(6)	
17	David Barral	ESP	10/05/83	A	5	(7)	3
23	Facundo Bertoglio	ARG	30/06/90	M	15	(11)	5
80	Roger Cañas	COL	27/03/90	M	12	(1)	1
5	Carlão	BRA	19/01/86	D	15		
4	Kypros Christoforou		24/04/93	D	2		
9	Igor De Camargo	BEL	12/05/83	A	12	(15)	10
6	Lorenzo Ebecilio	NED	24/09/91	M	3	(5)	2
7	Georgios Efrem		05/07/89	M	17	(8)	8
70	Ioannis Gianniotas	GRE	29/04/93	M	19	(10)	5
23	Iñaki Astiz	ESP	05/11/83	D	26	(1)	2
44	Nicholas Ioannou		10/11/95	D	17		
28	Mário Sérgio	POR	28/07/81	D	1	(2)	
30	Georgios Merkis		30/07/84	D	18	(2)	2
21	Zhivko Milanov	BUL	15/07/84	D	27		
26	Nuno Morais	POR	29/01/84	M	33		3
8	Andrea Orlandi	ESP	03/08/84	M	3	(6)	
31	Vasilios Papafotis		10/08/95	A	1	(2)	
88	Renan Bressan	BLR	03/11/88	M	3	(3)	1
3	Roberto Lago	ESP	30/08/85	D	16	(1)	
20	Pieros Sotiriou		13/01/93	A	31	(1)	21
78	Urko Pardo	ESP	28/01/83	G	2		
77	Vander	BRA	03/10/88	M	20	(8)	3
16	Vinícius	BRA	16/05/86	M	25	(2)	6
99	Boy Waterman	NED	24/01/84	G	34		
90	Cédric Yambéré	FRA	06/11/90	D	5	(2)	1

Apollon Limassol FC

1954 • Tsirion (13,331) • apollon.com.cy

Major honours
Cypriot League (3) 1991, 1994, 2006; Cypriot Cup (9) 1966, 1967, 1986, 1992, 2001, 2010, 2013, 2016, 2017

Coach: Pedro Emanuel (POR); (12/12/16) (Sofronis Avgousti)

Date		Opponent			Scorers
2016					
20/08	a	Nea Salamis	W	3-0	*Gneki Guié, João Pedro, Alex*
27/08	h	Aris	D	0-0	
11/09	a	AEZ	W	4-0	*Papoulis 2, Gneki Guié, Alex*
18/09	h	AEK	L	0-1	
24/09	a	AEL	L	1-2	*Papoulis*
02/10	h	Omonia	W	2-1	*Gneki Guié, Alex (p)*
16/10	a	Ermis	L	2-3	*Papoulis, Gneki Guié*
22/10	h	Anagennisis	W	4-0	*Gneki Guié, Maglica, Papoulis, Paulo Vinícius*
30/10	a	Doxa	W	1-0	*Paulo Vinícius*
06/11	h	Ethnikos	W	3-2	*Angeli, Bedoya, Alex*
20/11	a	Karmiotissa	W	6-0	*Papoulis 2, Alex (p), Maglica, Piech, C Kyriakou*
28/11	a	APOEL	D	1-1	*Alex (p)*
04/12	h	Anorthosis	D	1-1	*Papoulis*
10/12	h	Nea Salamis	D	1-1	*Piech*
16/12	a	Aris	W	4-1	*Papoulis, Alex, Angeli, Piech*
21/12	h	AEZ	W	2-1	*Maglica, Papoulis*
2017					
03/01	a	AEK	W	3-1	*Papoulis, Maglica, Alex (p)*
07/01	h	AEL	W	2-0	*Piech, Papoulis (p)*
15/01	a	Omonia	W	2-1	*Adrián Sardinero 2*
22/01	h	Ermis	W	3-0	*Alex (p), João Pedro, Maglica*
28/01	a	Anagennisis	W	1-0	*Maglica*
04/02	h	Doxa	W	3-1	*Paulo Vinícius, Adrián Sardinero, Piech*
12/02	a	Ethnikos	D	2-2	*Alex (p), Maglica*
19/02	h	Karmiotissa	W	3-0	*Piech 2, Alex*
27/02	h	APOEL	W	2-0	*Maglica, João Pedro*
05/03	a	Anorthosis	D	0-0	
11/03	a	AEL	D	1-1	*Paulo Vinícius*
18/03	h	AEK	W	3-2	*Vasiliou, Paulo Vinícius, Gneki Guié*
02/04	a	Omonia	W	2-0	*Adrián Sardinero, Piech*
08/04	a	Anorthosis	L	1-3	*Papoulis*
13/04	h	APOEL	W	1-0	*Papoulis*
23/04	h	AEL	D	1-1	*Pittas*
30/04	a	AEK	L	0-1	
07/05	h	Omonia	W	3-0	*Maglica, Alex (p), Paulo Vinícius*
14/05	h	Anorthosis	D	1-1	*Semedo*
20/05	a	APOEL	D	2-2	*Piech, Pittas*

No	Name	Nat	DoB	Pos	Aps	(s)	Gls
77	Adrián Sardinero	ESP	13/10/90	M	21	(10)	4
10	Alex	BRA	15/08/83	M	34	(1)	12
58	Marios Andreou		26/08/98	D	1	(1)	
27	Angelis Angeli		31/05/89	D	5		2
65	Olymbios Antoniadis		29/09/98	A		(1)	
51	Konstantinos Aristotelous		08/11/97	D		(1)	
11	Alejandro Barbaro	ARG	20/01/92	M		(9)	
16	Miguel Bedoya	ESP	15/04/86	M	21	(3)	1
83	Bruno Vale	POR	08/04/83	G	33		
12	Dudu Paraíba	BRA	11/03/85	D		(2)	
19	Abraham Gneki Guié	CIV	25/07/86	A	13	(3)	6
17	João Pedro	POR	04/05/86	D	24	(6)	3
6	Andreas Karo		09/09/96	D	1		
46	Tasos Kissas		18/01/88	G	3		
25	Charalambos Kyriakou		09/02/95	M	19	(5)	1
56	Leonidas Kyriakou		24/02/98	D	1		
99	Anton Maglica	CRO	11/11/91	A	19	(6)	9
28	Mário Sérgio	POR	28/07/81	D	11	(5)	
3	Nuno Lopes	POR	19/12/86	D	7	(1)	
62	Konstantinos Papamichail		17/05/99	D	1		
26	Fotios Papoulis	GRE	22/01/85	M	31	(2)	14
55	Paulo Vinícius	BRA	12/08/84	D	33		6
33	Georgios Pelagias		10/05/85	D	3	(2)	
18	Arkadiusz Piech	POL	07/06/85	A	12	(14)	9
52	Ioannis Pittas		10/07/96	M	2	(5)	2
57	Petros Psychas		28/08/98	A	1	(1)	
20	Alastair Reynolds	SCO	02/09/96	M	2	(8)	
22	Valentin Roberge	FRA	09/06/87	D	25		
5	Esteban Sachetti	ARG	21/11/85	M	29		
66	Semedo	CPV	23/02/88	M	4	(8)	1
59	Evdoras Silvestros		19/06/98	M		(1)	
28	Marios Stylianou		23/09/93	D	7	(5)	
30	Tiago Gomes	POR	29/07/86	D	16	(2)	
88	Georgios Vasiliou		12/06/84	D	17	(4)	1

Aris Limassol FC

1930 • Tsirion (13,331) • no website

Coach: Thalis Theodoridis (GRE); (24/10/16) (Nikos Andreou); (31/10/16) Frederik Vanderbiest (BEL); (04/01/17) Nikolas Martides

Date		Opponent			Scorers
2016					
22/08	h	Karmiotissa	D	1-1	*Maragoudakis*
27/08	a	Apollon	D	0-0	
11/09	h	Anorthosis	L	1-2	*Antoniou*
18/09	a	Nea Salamis	D	0-0	
25/09	h	APOEL	L	0-3	
01/10	h	AEZ	D	0-0	
17/10	a	AEK	L	0-4	
23/10	h	AEL	L	0-3	
29/10	a	Omonia	L	1-3	*Shkurtaj*
05/11	h	Ermis	L	0-2	
20/11	a	Anagennisis	W	2-1	*González, Rogério Martins*
27/11	h	Doxa	W	4-0	*og (Serrán), Antoniou, Fragkou, Onyilo*
04/12	a	Ethnikos	L	0-2	
11/12	a	Karmiotissa	D	3-3	*González, Maragoudakis, Ikande (p)*
16/12	h	Apollon	L	1-4	*Antoniou*
22/12	a	Anorthosis	L	0-2	

Date		Opponent			Scorers
2017					
03/01	h	Nea Salamis	L	1-2	*Antoniou*
08/01	a	APOEL	L	0-5	
16/01	a	AEZ	W	3-2	*Shkurtaj, Marco Aurélio (p), Rogério Martins*
21/01	h	AEK	D	1-1	*Rogério Martins*
30/01	a	AEL	L	0-3	
05/02	h	Omonia	L	2-4	*Marco Aurélio, Shkurtaj*
11/02	a	Ermis	W	2-1	*Maragoudakis, Youssef*
18/02	h	Anagennisis	W	4-0	*Shkurtaj, Rogério Martins, González 2*
25/02	a	Doxa	L	1-3	*Rogério Martins (p)*
04/03	h	Ethnikos	W	3-1	*Rogério Martins 3 (3p)*
11/03	a	Nea Salamis	W	3-0	*Maragoudakis, Rogério Martins, González*
19/03	h	Doxa	W	4-1	*Maragoudakis, Youssef 2, Fragkou*
01/04	h	Ethnikos	L	0-1	
09/04	a	Ermis	L	1-2	*Rogério Martins (p)*
12/04	h	Karmiotissa	W	3-2	*Wełna, Rogério Martins (p), Maragoudakis*
22/04	h	Nea Salamis	D	1-1	*González*
29/04	a	Doxa	W	1-0	*Antoniou*
06/05	a	Ethnikos	D	1-1	*Antoniou*
08/05	h	Ermis	W	2-0	*Rogério Martins (p), Antoniou*
21/05	a	Karmiotissa	L	1-5	*Rogério Martins (p)*

No	Name	Nat	DoB	Pos	Aps	(s)	Gls
15	Alain Álvarez	ESP	13/11/89	D	29		
22	Minas Antoniou		22/02/94	M	21	(12)	7
7	Mariano Berriex	ARG	29/04/89	A	5		
19	Sadat Bukari	GHA	12/04/89	A		(1)	
25	Sofoklis Christodoulou		30/06/97	D		(1)	
4	Kypros Christoforou		24/04/93	D	1		
3	Ioannis Efstathiou		14/02/93	D	25	(2)	
8	Andreas Fragkou		19/01/97	M	13	(15)	2
31	Nikolaos Giannakopoulos	GRE	19/02/93	G	23		
99	Silvio González	ARG	08/06/80	A	8	(14)	6
1	Gott	BRA	16/01/91	G	13		
71	Óscar Guerrero	COL	01/03/85	A	3	(6)	
70	Harmony Ikande	NGA	17/09/90	M	11	(1)	1
17	Theodosis Kyprou		24/02/92	A	2		
32	Evangelos Kyriakou		03/02/94	D	14	(5)	
11	Markos Maragoudakis	GRE	28/01/82	A	27	(2)	6
8	Marco Aurélio	BRA	27/03/83	M	14	(1)	2
77	Stefanos Martsakis	GRE	24/05/90	A		(3)	
80	Andreas Masonos		21/11/98	M	1		
93	Donneil Moukanza	FRA	27/02/91	M		(3)	
23	Ifeanyi Onyilo	NGA	31/10/90	A	2	(7)	1
6	Andreas Pachipis		16/12/94	M	27	(2)	
30	Kyriakos Panagi		22/04/96	M	8	(9)	
5	Nikolaos Pantidos	GRE	19/04/91	D	10		
28	Kyriakos Pavlou		04/09/86	M	4	(5)	
16	Andrei Radu	ROU	21/06/96	D	21	(3)	
10	Rogério Martins	BRA	19/11/84	M	31	(2)	13
12	Vasil Shkurtaj	ALB	27/02/92	A	15	(3)	4
92	Rasmus Sjöstedt	SWE	28/02/92	D	13		
21	Christos Theophilou		30/04/81	D	24	(1)	
27	Tomasz Wełna	POL	27/01/91	D	9	(5)	1
87	Christer Youssef	SWE	01/12/87	M	22	(4)	3

Doxa Katokopia FC

1954 • Makario, Nicosia (16,000) • doxafc.com.cy

Coach: Loukas Hadjiloukas; (01/12/16) Carlos Corberán (ESP); (25/01/17) Savvas Poursaitidis (GRE); (01/05/17) Loukas Hadjiloukas

Date		Opponent		Score	Scorers
2016					
27/08	h	AEL	L	1-3	*Peralta*
10/09	a	Omonia	D	1-1	*Rudy*
14/09	a	AEK	L	0-2	
18/09	h	Ermis	L	1-2	*Bebeto*
25/09	a	Anagennisis	W	1-0	*Carles Coto*
02/10	a	APOEL	L	0-2	
16/10	h	Ethnikos	D	0-0	
22/10	a	Karmiotissa	L	0-1	
30/10	h	Apollon	L	0-1	
06/11	a	Anorthosis	L	0-3	
20/11	h	Nea Salamis	D	0-0	
27/11	a	Aris	L	0-4	
05/12	h	AEZ	W	1-0	*Rudy*
11/12	h	AEK	D	1-1	*Wilson Kenidy*
17/12	a	AEL	L	0-1	
21/12	h	Omonia	L	2-3	*Fofana, Rudy*
2017					
04/01	a	Ermis	L	0-1	
07/01	h	Anagennisis	D	0-0	
14/01	h	APOEL	L	0-2	
23/01	a	Ethnikos	L	0-2	
29/01	h	Karmiotissa	L	1-2	*Braulio (p)*
04/02	a	Apollon	L	1-3	*Coro*
13/02	h	Anorthosis	L	0-2	
18/02	a	Nea Salamis	W	3-1	*Braulio 2, Serrán*
25/02	h	Aris	W	3-1	*og (Álvarez), Braulio (p), Coro*
04/03	a	AEZ	W	4-0	*Fofana, Tiago Gomes, Braulio, Coro*
12/03	h	Ermis	W	2-1	*Serrán, Braulio*
19/03	a	Aris	L	1-4	*Braulio*
01/04	h	Karmiotissa	W	3-0	*Fofana, Coro, Tiago Gomes*
08/04	h	Ethnikos	D	3-3	*Braulio 2, Eninful*
13/04	a	Nea Salamis	D	0-0	
22/04	a	Ermis	W	5-1	*Braulio, Redondo, Coro, Castro, Tiago Gomes (p)*
29/04	h	Aris	L	0-1	
07/05	a	Karmiotissa	W	2-1	*Goulon, Eninful*
14/05	a	Ethnikos	W	4-0	*Tiago Gomes, Castro 2, João Leonardo*
21/05	h	Nea Salamis	L	0-3	

No	Name	Nat	DoB	Pos	Aps	(s)	Gls
37	Andreas Andreou		05/02/97	A	1		
20	Kyriakos Aretas	GRE	31/03/97	M	1	(2)	
91	Bebeto	SEN	31/12/91	A	9	(7)	1
85	Braulio	ESP	18/09/85	A	14	(1)	10
7	Carles Coto	ESP	11/02/88	M	6	(2)	1
13	Carlos Marques	POR	06/02/83	D		(1)	
7	Yair Castro	COL	10/04/97	M	9	(16)	3
21	Konstantinos Christodoulou		22/03/96	M	1		
23	Coro	ESP	05/01/83	A	18		5
3	Stelios Demetriou		04/10/90	D	16	(1)	
19	Edmar	BRA	09/04/82	D	19	(6)	
30	Henri Eninful	TOG	21/07/92	M	23	(4)	2
26	Gaoussou Fofana	CIV	14/04/84	M	26	(8)	3
93	Hérold Goulon	FRA	12/06/88	D	14	(1)	1
99	Evagoras Hadjifrangiskou		29/10/86	G	3	(1)	
25	João Leonardo	BRA	25/06/85	D	26	(5)	1
1	Alexandre Negri		27/03/81	G	33		
2	Paulinho	BRA	24/08/83	D	23	(4)	
9	Luis Peralta	COL	30/07/92	A	7	(5)	1
38	Marios Poutziouris		08/12/93	M	29	(1)	
6	Manuel Redondo	ESP	11/01/85	D	29	(1)	1
11	Rodrigo Rivas González	COL	11/04/97	A		(2)	
5	Rudy	POR	05/01/89	M	27	(8)	3
4	Emilio Sánchez	ESP	30/04/85	M	3	(2)	
33	Alberto Serrán	ESP	17/07/84	D	24	(1)	2
15	Paolo Stylianou		11/06/97	D		(1)	
22	Tiago Gomes	POR	18/08/85	M	25	(3)	4
14	Wilson Kenidy	ANG	02/02/93	M	10	(15)	1

Ermis Aradippou FC

1958 • Antonis Papadopoulos, Larnaca (10,230) • ermisfc.com.cy

Coach: Nicos Panayiotou; (09/01/17) Georgios Kosma; (29/01/17) Carlos Corberán (ESP)

Date		Opponent		Score	Scorers
2016					
20/08	a	Omonia	L	1-3	*Ibson*
28/08	a	APOEL	L	0-3	
11/09	h	Anagennisis	W	1-0	*Da Sylva*
18/09	a	Doxa	W	2-1	*Martynyuk, Ibson*
26/09	h	Ethnikos	W	2-1	*Martynyuk 2*
02/10	a	Karmiotissa	L	0-3	
16/10	h	Apollon	W	3-2	*Alexiou, og (Paulo Vinícius), Martynyuk*
23/10	a	Anorthosis	D	2-2	*Alba (p), Da Sylva*
30/10	h	Nea Salamis	L	1-2	*Mashinya*
05/11	a	Aris	W	2-0	*Da Sylva, Alba*
19/11	h	AEZ	W	2-1	*Ibson, Alba (p)*
26/11	a	AEK	L	0-1	
04/12	h	AEL	L	0-1	
10/12	h	Omonia	D	2-2	*Lillis, Mashinya*
17/12	h	APOEL	D	1-1	*Mashinya*
21/12	a	Anagennisis	D	2-2	*Mashinya 2*
2017					
04/01	h	Doxa	W	1-0	*Artabe*
08/01	a	Ethnikos	L	1-3	*Sîrghi*
15/01	h	Karmiotissa	W	2-0	*og (Taralidis), Froxylias*
22/01	a	Apollon	L	0-3	
28/01	h	Anorthosis	L	1-4	*Benga*
04/02	a	Nea Salamis	D	0-0	
11/02	h	Aris	L	1-2	*Da Sylva*
18/02	a	AEZ	W	4-0	*Mashinya 3, Grandin*
26/02	h	AEK	L	2-3	*Ibson (p), Bouwman*
05/03	a	AEL	W	2-1	*Ibson, Mashinya*
12/03	a	Doxa	L	1-2	*Mashinya*
19/03	h	Karmiotissa	W	3-1	*Mashinya, Bouwman, Psaltis*
03/04	a	Nea Salamis	L	1-4	*Martynyuk (p)*
09/04	h	Aris	W	2-1	*Ibson, Martynyuk*
12/04	a	Ethnikos	D	1-1	*Martynyuk*
22/04	h	Doxa	L	1-5	*Grandin*
29/04	a	Karmiotissa	W	1-0	*Martynyuk (p)*
06/05	h	Nea Salamis	W	3-0	*Artabe, Ibson, Martynyuk*
14/05	a	Aris	L	0-2	
21/05	h	Ethnikos	L	3-4	*Grandin, Mashinya 2*

No	Name	Nat	DoB	Pos	Aps	(s)	Gls
10	Miguel Alba	ARG	11/08/88	M	9	(3)	3
88	Nicolas Alexiou		06/12/94	A	8	(8)	1
92	Anastasios Andreou		26/05/98	A		(2)	
26	Giannis Antoniou		21/01/90	D	4	(7)	
6	Alfonso Artabe	ESP	18/08/88	M	23	(10)	2
4	Alexandru Benga	ROU	15/06/89	D	26	(1)	1
24	Pim Bouwman	NED	30/01/91	M	23	(2)	2
23	Carles Coto	ESP	11/02/88	M	13	(3)	
89	Vytautas Černiauskas	LTU	12/03/89	G	2		
27	Sergis Chatzidemetriou		08/12/98	D	2	(3)	
28	Nicolas Christaki		12/11/01	M		(1)	
17	Martinos Christofi		26/07/93	D	26	(1)	
29	Dominique Da Sylva	MTN	16/08/89	A	16	(5)	4
14	Emmerik De Vriese	BEL	14/02/85	D	23	(1)	
1	Jordy Deckers	NED	20/06/89	G	1		
12	Elliot Grandin	FRA	17/10/87	M	7	(6)	3
9	Elson Hooi	CUW	01/10/91	A	5	(2)	
11	Yordan Hristov	BUL	12/02/84	D	25	(2)	
80	Dimitris Froxylias		28/06/93	M	3	(2)	1
7	Ibson	BRA	08/11/89	M	35	(1)	7
5	Fotis Kezos		25/07/95	M	6	(5)	
20	Georgios Kyprianou		22/09/94	M	2		
77	Leandros Lillis		13/09/96	M	7	(13)	1
41	Savvas Lytra		16/01/00	A		(2)	
18	Irakli Maisuradze	GEO	22/08/88	M	20	(3)	
8	Yaroslav Martynyuk	UKR	20/02/89	M	32	(1)	9
37	Edward Mashinya	ZIM	22/02/84	A	16	(10)	13
19	Muller Fernandes	BRA	14/03/89	A	2	(3)	
15	Edin Nuredinoski	MKD	21/04/82	G	9		
33	Georgios Panagi		16/07/95	G	3		
13	Paulo Pina	CPV	04/01/81	D	6		
22	Paris Psaltis		12/11/96	D	10	(3)	1
16	Cristian Sîrghi	ROU	23/11/86	D	8	(1)	1
50	Dimitris Stylianou		05/07/84	G	21		
21	Rafael Yiangoudakis		03/08/90	M	3	(3)	

Ethnikos Achnas FC

1968 • Dasaki (5,000) • ethnikosachnafc.com

Coach: Danilo Dončić (SRB); (28/09/16) (Panayiotis Engomitis); (04/10/16) Valdas Ivanauskas (LTU)

Date		Opponent		Score	Scorers
2016					
21/08	a	AEZ	L	1-3	*Filipov*
12/09	a	AEL	D	0-0	
17/09	h	Omonia	L	1-2	*Chatzivasilis*
21/09	h	AEK	L	0-3	
26/09	a	Ermis	L	1-2	*Chatzivasilis*
01/10	h	Anagennisis	W	5-3	*Kipiani, Eduardo Pincelli 2 (2p), Kyprianou, Zelaya*
16/10	a	Doxa	D	0-0	
24/10	a	APOEL	L	0-2	
29/10	h	Karmiotissa	W	4-2	*Kacharava 4*
06/11	a	Apollon	L	2-3	*Zelaya 2*
21/11	h	Anorthosis	W	2-1	*Zelaya, Eduardo Pincelli (p)*
26/11	a	Nea Salamis	L	0-1	
04/12	h	Aris	W	2-0	*Kacharava 2*
11/12	h	AEZ	W	3-1	*Kacharava 2, Chatzivasilis*
17/12	a	AEK	L	0-1	
22/12	h	AEL	D	2-2	*Zelaya, Kacharava*
2017					
04/01	a	Omonia	L	2-3	*Zelaya, Kacharava*
08/01	h	Ermis	W	3-1	*Filipov, Zelaya, Kacharava*
15/01	a	Anagennisis	W	3-2	*Zelaya, Chatzivasilis, Kipiani*
23/01	h	Doxa	W	2-0	*Stoychev, Zelaya*
29/01	h	APOEL	L	2-3	*Chatzivasilis, Eduardo Pincelli (p)*
06/02	a	Karmiotissa	D	2-2	*Zelaya 2*
12/02	h	Apollon	D	2-2	*Zelaya, Kacharava*
19/02	a	Anorthosis	L	2-4	*Zelaya, og (Guilherme Santos)*
26/02	h	Nea Salamis	D	0-0	
04/03	a	Aris	L	1-3	*Eduardo Pincelli (p)*
12/03	a	Karmiotissa	L	3-5	*Kipiani 2, Kacharava*
19/03	h	Nea Salamis	L	0-2	
01/04	a	Aris	W	1-0	*Zelaya*
08/04	a	Doxa	D	3-3	*Kipiani, Zelaya, Kyprianou*
12/04	h	Ermis	D	1-1	*Kyprianou*
22/04	h	Karmiotissa	D	1-1	*Krachunov*
30/04	a	Nea Salamis	W	1-0	*Kacharava*
06/05	h	Aris	D	1-1	*Kacharava*
14/05	h	Doxa	L	0-4	
21/05	a	Ermis	W	4-3	*Kacharava, Kipiani, Filipov, Elia*

No	Name	Nat	DoB	Pos	Aps	(s)	Gls
88	Georgios Aresti		02/09/94	M	11	(9)	
22	Martin Bogatinov	MKD	26/04/86	G	20		
6	Bruno Arrabal	BRA	23/02/92	M	20	(5)	
13	Petros Chatziaros		10/08/82	D	3		
19	Giannis Chatzivasilis		26/04/90	A	26	(3)	5
26	Mite Cikarski	MKD	06/01/93	D	18	(5)	
90	Aleksandr Dovbnya	RUS	14/02/96	D	19	(2)	
5	Eduardo Pincelli	BRA	23/04/83	M	26		5
35	Andreas Elia		09/08/97	A		(1)	1
22	Andrei Enescu	ROU	12/10/87	M	21	(7)	
28	Filip Filipov	BUL	02/08/88	D	32		3
77	Bogdan Gavrilă	ROU	06/02/92	A	3	(9)	
5	Gia Grigalava	GEO	05/08/89	D	8	(1)	
21	Giorgi Iluridze	GEO	20/02/92	A	6	(14)	
11	Jefinho	BRA	23/02/89	A	1		
9	Nika Kacharava	GEO	13/01/94	A	26	(1)	16
7	Nikolai Kipiani	RUS	25/01/97	M	28	(4)	6
66	Plamen Krachunov	BUL	11/01/89	D	25	(3)	1
23	Dimitris Kyprianou		02/02/93	M	26	(6)	3
55	Dimitris Moulazimis		15/01/92	A	5	(4)	
43	Georgios Papageorgiou		07/06/97	D	2	(13)	
10	Christos Poyiatzis		12/04/78	M		(5)	
95	Patryk Procek	POL	01/03/95	G	16	(1)	
2	Borislav Stoychev	BUL	26/11/86	D	26	(1)	1
99	Emilio Zelaya	ARG	30/07/87	A	28	(2)	15

CYPRUS

Karmiotissa Pano Polemidia FC

1979 • Neo GSZ, Larnaca (13,032) • karmiotissafc.com

Coach: Liasos Louka

Date		Opponent		Score	Scorers
2016					
22/08	a	Aris	D	1-1	*Vattis*
28/08	h	AEZ	D	0-0	
10/09	a	AEK	L	0-3	
19/09	h	AEL	L	0-1	
24/09	a	Omonia	L	2-4	*Ordoš, Taralidis*
02/10	h	Ermis	W	3-0	*Vattis, Adamović, Taralidis (p)*
16/10	a	Anagennisis	W	1-0	*Vattis*
22/10	h	Doxa	W	1-0	*Ordoš*
29/10	a	Ethnikos	L	2-4	*Poljanec, Vattis (p)*
06/11	a	APOEL	L	1-4	*Poljanec*
20/11	h	Apollon	L	0-6	
27/11	a	Anorthosis	W	1-0	*Stavrou*
03/12	h	Nea Salamis	W	1-0	*Poljanec*
11/12	h	Aris	D	3-3	*Poljanec, Vattis, Taralidis (p)*
16/12	a	AEZ	D	3-3	*Stavrou, Logombe, Arocha*
21/12	h	AEK	L	0-3	
2017					
04/01	a	AEL	L	1-4	*Wheeler*
08/01	h	Omonia	L	0-1	
15/01	a	Ermis	L	0-2	
22/01	h	Anagennisis	D	2-2	*Poljanec, Pašek*
29/01	a	Doxa	W	2-1	*Adamović, Pašek*
06/02	h	Ethnikos	D	2-2	*Vattis, Barbaro*
11/02	h	APOEL	L	0-1	
19/02	a	Apollon	L	0-3	
26/02	h	Anorthosis	L	1-4	*Adamović*
04/03	a	Nea Salamis	W	3-1	*Barbaro, Demetriou, Pašek*
12/03	h	Ethnikos	W	5-3	*Ordoš 2, Poljanec, Adamović 2*
19/03	a	Ermis	L	1-3	*Pantos*
01/04	a	Doxa	L	0-3	
08/04	h	Nea Salamis	W	2-0	*Adamović, Poljanec*
12/04	a	Aris	L	2-3	*og (Rogério Martins), Vattis*
22/04	a	Ethnikos	D	1-1	*Manoyan*
29/04	h	Ermis	L	0-1	
07/05	h	Doxa	L	1-2	*Poljanec*
14/05	a	Nea Salamis	L	0-1	
21/05	h	Aris	W	5-1	*Barbaro 3, Pantos 2 (1p)*

No	Name	Nat	DoB	Pos	Aps	(s)	Gls
16	Marko Adamović	SRB	11/03/91	M	31		6
18	Rubén Arocha	VEN	21/04/87	M	21	(4)	1
15	Alejandro Barbaro	ARG	20/01/92	M	15	(2)	5
14	Alkiviadis Christofi		20/01/92	A	13	(11)	
17	Konstantinos Demetriou		29/03/93	D	5	(3)	1
1	Andrija Dragojević	MNE	25/12/91	G	21		
19	Charalambos Kairinos		06/06/82	G	15		
42	Mohamed Kone	CIV	12/12/93	D	9	(1)	
11	Savvas Kyprou		02/05/82	D		(4)	
10	Andreas Kyriakou		21/04/90	M	1	(7)	
8	Evgenios Kyriakou		14/05/92	M	1	(5)	
21	Alain Logombe	COD	21/03/90	D	23		1
91	Davit Manoyan	ARM	05/07/90	M	17	(5)	1
77	Michal Ordoš	CZE	27/01/83	A	26	(6)	4
6	Ivan Ostojić	SRB	26/06/89	D	7		
9	Stamatios Pantos		22/03/90	A	4	(18)	3
18	Vasilios Papadopoulos	GRE	28/01/95	A		(3)	
28	David Pašek	CZE	27/10/89	M	7	(9)	3
24	Kleanthis Pieri		05/10/99	D		(1)	
27	David Poljanec	SVN	27/11/86	A	32		8
96	Stilianos Pozoglou	GRE	22/01/96	M		(1)	
34	Emmanouil Saliakas	GRE	12/09/96	D	27	(3)	
20	Andreas Stavrou		27/10/88	M	17	(11)	2
5	Ioannis Taralidis	GRE	17/05/81	M	23	(2)	3
97	Ioannis Tsolakidis	GRE	26/01/96	M		(2)	
7	Ilias Vattis		28/02/86	M	25	(8)	7
3	Taron Voskanyan	ARM	22/02/93	D	28		
12	Christos Wheeler		29/06/97	D	28	(1)	1

Nea Salamis Famagusta FC

1948 • Ammochostos (4,000) • neasalamina.com

Major honours

Cypriot Cup (1) 1990

Coach: Eugen Neagoe (ROU); (21/09/16) Staikos Vergetis (GRE); (08/03/17) (Kostas Mina); (16/03/17) Toni Conceição (POR)

Date		Opponent		Score	Scorers
2016					
20/08	h	Apollon	L	0-3	
27/08	a	Anorthosis	D	0-0	
10/09	h	APOEL	L	0-4	
18/09	h	Aris	D	0-0	
24/09	a	AEZ	W	5-1	*Skopelitis, Maachi 4*
02/10	h	AEK	L	0-1	
15/10	a	AEL	L	0-3	
22/10	h	Omonia	D	1-1	*Tsabouris*
30/10	a	Ermis	W	2-1	*og (Artabe), Kolokoudias*
06/11	h	Anagennisis	W	2-0	*Kolokoudias, Maachi*
20/11	a	Doxa	D	0-0	
26/11	h	Ethnikos	W	1-0	*Makriev (p)*
03/12	a	Karmiotissa	L	0-1	
10/12	a	Apollon	D	1-1	*Makriev*
16/12	h	Anorthosis	W	2-1	*Makriev, Maachi*
21/12	a	APOEL	L	0-1	
2017					
03/01	a	Aris	W	2-1	*Tsabouris, Makriev*
09/01	h	AEZ	W	2-0	*Makriev, Maachi*
14/01	a	AEK	L	0-2	
22/01	h	AEL	L	1-3	*Kolokoudias*
28/01	a	Omonia	L	0-3	
04/02	h	Ermis	D	0-0	
12/02	a	Anagennisis	W	1-0	*Maachi*
18/02	h	Doxa	L	1-3	*Grassi*
26/02	a	Ethnikos	D	0-0	
04/03	h	Karmiotissa	L	1-3	*Makriev (p)*
11/03	h	Aris	L	0-3	
19/03	a	Ethnikos	W	2-0	*Makriev, Englezou*
03/04	h	Ermis	W	4-1	*Makriev 2, Dudú, Kousoulos*
08/04	a	Karmiotissa	L	0-2	
13/04	h	Doxa	D	0-0	
22/04	a	Aris	D	1-1	*Grassi*
30/04	h	Ethnikos	L	0-1	
06/05	a	Ermis	L	0-3	
14/05	h	Karmiotissa	W	1-0	*Makriev*
21/05	a	Doxa	W	3-0	*Maachi 3*

No	Name	Nat	DoB	Pos	Aps	(s)	Gls
38	Matías Abelairas	ARG	18/06/85	M	19	(6)	
17	Goran Antonić	SRB	03/11/90	D	26	(2)	
82	China	POR	15/04/82	D	28	(1)	
90	Mattia Cinquini	ITA	11/05/90	D	1		
8	Ivan Ćurjurić	CRO	29/09/89	M	18	(7)	
2	Dudú	BRA	14/03/89	M	9	(4)	1
27	Georgios Eleftheriou		30/09/84	M	7	(2)	
30	Nikos Englezou		11/07/93	M	10	(1)	1
10	Dimitris Froxylias		28/06/93	M		(1)	
15	Emiliano Fusco	ARG	02/03/86	D	10	(5)	
21	Davide Grassi	ITA	13/01/86	D	28	(1)	2
29	Georgios Kolokoudias		03/05/89	A	15	(11)	3
70	Alex Konstantinou		11/04/92	M	7	(13)	
30	Ioannis Kostis		17/03/00	A		(1)	
13	Giannis Kousoulos		14/06/96	D	26	(2)	1
3	Luciano Bebê	BRA	11/03/81	M	15	(11)	
16	Nassir Maachi	NED	09/09/85	M	24	(11)	11
9	Dimitar Makriev	BUL	07/01/84	A	30	(5)	10
93	Neofytos Michael		16/12/93	G	5		
6	Ionuț Neagu	ROU	26/10/89	M	6	(9)	
11	Koullis Pavlou		04/09/86	M	2	(3)	
7	Pedrito	ESP	28/04/89	M	6	(5)	
19	Iasonas Piki		11/11/00	A		(1)	
7	Rúben Brígido	POR	23/06/91	M	10	(4)	
2	Konstantinos Sergiou		02/10/00	D	1		
22	Theodosis Siathas		16/12/98	A		(1)	
20	Giannis Skopelitis	GRE	02/05/78	M	32	(1)	1
31	Savvas Tsabouris	GRE	16/07/86	D	30		2
33	Róbert Veselovský	SVK	02/09/85	G	31		

AC Omonia

1948 • GSP (23,700) • omonoia.com.cy

Major honours

Cypriot League (20) 1961, 1966, 1972, 1974, 1975, 1976, 1977, 1978, 1979, 1981, 1982, 1983, 1984, 1985, 1987, 1989, 1993, 2001, 2003, 2010; Cypriot Cup (14) 1965, 1972, 1974, 1980, 1981, 1982, 1983, 1988, 1991, 1994, 2000, 2005, 2011, 2012

Coach: John Carver (ENG); (23/02/17) Akis Ioakim

Date		Opponent		Score	Scorers
2016					
22/08	h	Ermis	W	3-1	*Derbyshire (p), Agaiev 2*
27/08	a	Anagennisis	D	2-2	*Derbyshire 2*
10/09	h	Doxa	D	1-1	*Sheridan (p)*
17/09	a	Ethnikos	W	2-1	*Sheridan 2*
24/09	h	Karmiotissa	W	4-2	*Sheridan (p), Derbyshire 2, Renato Margaça*
02/10	a	Apollon	L	1-2	*Katelaris*
15/10	h	Anorthosis	W	2-0	*Sheridan (p), Cleyton*
22/10	a	Nea Salamis	D	1-1	*Derbyshire*
29/10	h	Aris	W	3-1	*Sheridan, Derbyshire 2*
05/11	a	AEZ	W	1-0	*Christofi*
20/11	h	AEK	W	2-1	*Katelaris, Derbyshire*
26/11	a	AEL	L	0-1	
03/12	h	APOEL	L	1-4	*Renato Margaça*
10/12	a	Ermis	D	2-2	*Renato Margaça, Cleyton*
17/12	h	Anagennisis	W	5-1	*og (Efthymiou), og (Diallo), Derbyshire 2, Cleyton*
21/12	a	Doxa	W	3-2	*Sheridan, Derbyshire, Katelaris*
2017					
04/01	h	Ethnikos	W	3-2	*Derbyshire 3*
08/01	a	Karmiotissa	W	1-0	*Derbyshire*
15/01	h	Apollon	L	1-2	*Carlitos*
21/01	a	Anorthosis	D	2-2	*Renato Margaça, Christofi*
28/01	h	Nea Salamis	W	3-0	*Sheridan, og (Fusco), Derbyshire*
05/02	a	Aris	W	4-2	*Árnason, Christofi, Vyntra, Derbyshire*
11/02	h	AEZ	W	2-0	*Christofi, Cleyton*
19/02	a	AEK	L	2-4	*Christofi, Breeveld*
25/02	h	AEL	W	4-1	*Cleyton 2, Christofi, Derbyshire*
04/03	a	APOEL	L	1-2	*Derbyshire*
13/03	a	AEK	D	1-1	*Vyntra*
18/03	h	Anorthosis	W	2-0	*Derbyshire, Christofi*
02/04	h	Apollon	L	0-2	
09/04	a	APOEL	L	0-1	
12/04	h	AEL	W	2-1	*Christofi, Derbyshire*
22/04	h	AEK	L	1-2	*Cleyton*
29/04	a	Anorthosis	L	3-4	*Cleyton, Touré, Derbyshire*
07/05	a	Apollon	L	0-3	
13/05	h	APOEL	L	1-3	*Derbyshire*
21/05	a	AEL	L	2-3	*Árnason, Katsantonis*

No	Name	Nat	DoB	Pos	Aps	(s)	Gls
11	Amir Agaiev	ISR	10/02/92	M	5	(1)	2
21	Kári Árnason	ISL	13/10/82	D	8		2
29	Stephane Aziz Ki	BFA	03/03/96	M	7	(6)	
71	Nicandro Breeveld	SUR	07/10/86	M	8	(6)	1
2	Bruno Nascimento	BRA	30/05/91	D	6	(3)	
23	Carlitos	CPV	23/04/85	D	18	(7)	1
16	Dimosthenis Chantzaras	GRE	08/01/97	M		(1)	
60	Christos Charalambous		20/06/98	M		(1)	
25	Andreas Christodoulou		26/03/97	G	4	(1)	
77	Dimitris Christofi		28/09/88	A	20	(8)	8
10	Cleyton	BRA	08/03/83	M	30	(3)	8
7	Marios Demetriou		25/12/92	D	9	(1)	
27	Matt Derbyshire	ENG	14/04/86	A	32	(1)	24
67	Sotiris Fiakas		08/09/98	M		(1)	
40	George Florescu	ROU	21/05/84	M	20	(6)	
68	Andreas Frangeskou		26/02/96	D	1		
20	Gerasimos Fylaktou		24/07/91	M	4	(9)	
49	Fanos Katelaris		26/08/96	M	17	(9)	3
65	Andreas Katsantonis		16/02/00	M	1	(1)	1
22	Dimitrios Konstantinidis	GRE	02/06/94	D	17	(1)	
18	Dario Krešić	CRO	11/01/84	G	3		
99	Theodosis Kyprou		24/02/92	A	7	(9)	
48	Marin Oršulić	CRO	25/08/87	D	13	(2)	
1	Konstantinos Panagi		08/10/94	G	29		
19	Andreas Panagiotou		31/05/95	D	9	(5)	
5	Athanasios Panteliadis	GRE	06/09/87	D	6	(1)	
28	Renato Margaça		17/07/85	M	33		4
8	Onisiforos Roushias		15/07/92	A	2	(11)	
9	Cillian Sheridan	IRL	23/02/89	A	17	(6)	8
3	Aristidis Soiledis	GRE	08/02/91	D	18	(2)	
17	Blati Touré	BFA	04/08/94	M	25	(2)	1
64	Apollonas Vasiliou		29/03/97	A	1		
24	Loukas Vyntra	GRE	05/02/81	D	26	(2)	2

Top goalscorers

24	Matt Derbyshire (Omonia)
21	Pieros Sotiriou (APOEL)
16	Nika Kacharava (Ethnikos)
15	Emilio Zelaya (Ethnikos)
14	Ivan Trickovski (AEK) Fotios Papoulis (Apollon)
13	Rogério Martins (Aris) Edward Mashinya (Ermis)
12	André Alves (AEK/Anorthosis) Alex (Apollon)

Promoted clubs

Alki Oroklini FC

2014 • Oroklini Municipal (1,500) • no website
Coach: Savvas Damianou

Pafos FC

2014 • Pafiako (7,650) • no website
Coach: Dimitris Ioannou

Olympiakos Nicosia FC

1931 • Makario (16,000) • olympiakos.com.cy
Major honours
Cypriot League (3) 1967, 1969, 1971; Cypriot Cup (1) 1977
Coach: Savvas Paraskeva; (04/11/16) Chrysis Michail

Second level final table 2016/17

		Pld	W	D	L	F	A	Pts
1	Alki Oroklini FC	26	21	3	2	60	15	66
2	Pafos FC	26	17	6	3	51	24	57
3	Olympiakos Nicosia FC	26	16	6	4	44	23	54
4	Othellos Athienou FC	26	15	4	7	53	33	49
5	Ayia Napa FC	26	13	7	6	51	28	46
6	Enosis Neon Paralimni FC	26	12	8	6	41	32	44
7	ENTHOI Lakatamia FC	26	9	6	11	32	33	33
8	ASIL Lysi FC	26	8	6	12	27	33	30
9	PAEEK FC	26	6	8	12	26	37	26
10	Omonia Aradippou FC	26	5	7	14	16	30	22
11	Ethnikos Assias FC	26	6	4	16	23	52	22
12	Akritas Chlorakas FC	26	5	4	17	24	45	19
13	ENAD Polis-Chrysochous FC	26	4	7	15	26	52	19
14	Enosis Neon Parekklisias FC	26	4	6	16	27	64	15

NB Enosis Neon Parekklisias FC – 3 pts deducted.

DOMESTIC CUP

Cyprus Cup 2016/17

FIRST ROUND

(26/10/16)
Anorthosis 2-1 Othellos *(aet)*
Aris 6-0 Akritas Chlorakas
Doxa 3-2 Ermis
Karmiotissa 3-1 Ayia Napa
Omonia Aradippou 0-3 AEK
Paralimni 2-4 AEZ

(02/11/16)
Alki Oroklini 1-2 AEL

(23/11/16)
Pafos 2-3 Anagennisis Derynia *(aet)*

(30/11/16)
Nea Salamis 2-0 PAEEK

Byes – APOEL, Apollon, ASIL Lysi, Ethnikos Achnas, Ethnikos Assias, Olympiakos, Omonia

SECOND ROUND

(11/01/17 & 18/01/17)
AEK 2-1, 6-1 Karmiotissa *(8-2)*
Olympiakos 2-0, 3-0 Ethnikos Assias *(5-0)*
Omonia 0-0, 1-1 Ethnikos Achnas *(1-1; Omonia on away goal)*

(11/01/17 & 25/01/17)
Anorthosis 2-0, 5-0 ASIL Lysi *(7-0)*
Aris 0-2, 0-1 AEL *(0-3)*

(18/01/17 & 25/01/17)
APOEL 2-1, 2-1 Nea Salamis *(4-2)*

(01/02/17 & 08/02/17)
Apollon 2-0, 2-0 AEZ *(4-0)*
Doxa 2-1, 3-0 Anagennisis Derynia *(5-1)*

QUARTER-FINALS

(15/02/17 & 22/02/17)
Omonia 2-2 Apollon *(Cleyton 58, Christofi 63; Maglica 10, Alex 21)*
Apollon 3-0 Omonia *(w/o; original match abandoned after 82 mins at 3-1; Maglica 7, Alex 26, João Pedro 68; Sheridan 45+2p)*
(Apollon 5-2)

(22/02/17 & 08/03/17)
AEK 1-3 Anorthosis *(Trickovski 48; Rayo 5, 12, Filipe Oliveira 59)*
Anorthosis 2-2 AEK *(Shehu 64, André Alves 72; Mytides 69, Taulemesse 88)*
(Anorthosis 5-3)

Olympiakos 1-1 Doxa *(Pachipis 56; Wilson Kenidy 45)*
Doxa 2-1 Olympiakos *(Coro 14, Braulio 105; Christodoulou 28) (aet)*
(Doxa 3-2)

(05/04/17 & 19/04/17)
APOEL 0-0 AEL
AEL 1-1 APOEL *(Arruabarrena 81; Barral 53)*
(1-1; APOEL on away goal)

SEMI-FINALS

(26/04/17 & 03/05/17)
Apollon 6-0 Anorthosis *(Maglica 13, Adrián Sardinero 34, Paulo Vinícius 37, Papoulis 54p, Makrides 88, Piech 90)*
Anorthosis 1-0 Apollon *(Filipe Oliveira 34)*
(Apollon 6-1)

Doxa 0-2 APOEL *(Barral 45, Iñaki Astiz 62)*
APOEL 5-0 Doxa *(Aloneftis 13, Artymatas 22, Bertoglio 42, De Camargo 71, Vinícius 80)*
(APOEL 7-0)

FINAL

(24/05/17)
GSP, Nicosia
APOLLON LIMASSOL FC 1 *(Paulo Vinícius 78)*
APOEL FC 0
Referee: *Sotiriou*
APOLLON: *Bruno Vale, João Pedro (Mário Sérgio 90+5), Paulo Vinícius, Roberge, Vasiliou, Sachetti, C Kyriakou, Adrián Sardinero, Alex, Papoulis (Gneki Guié 63), Maglica*
Red card: *Alex (61)*
APOEL: *Urko Pardo, Milanov, Merkis, Ioannou (De Camargo 78), Roberto Lago, Gianniotas (Vander 63), Nuno Morais, Vinícius, Aloneftis, Efrem (Bertoglio 72), Sotiriou*

Apollon retained the Cyprus Cup for the first time in 50 years

CZECH REPUBLIC

Fotbalová asociace České republiky (FAČR)

Address	Diskařská 2431/4 CZ-160 17 Praha
Tel	+420 2 3302 9111
Fax	+420 2 3335 3107
E-mail	facr@fotbal.cz
Website	fotbal.cz

President	vacant
General secretary	Rudolf Řepka
Media officer	Michal Jurman
Year of formation	1901

0 100 200 km
0 100 miles

Liberec 10
4
Teplice 12
Jablonec nad Nisou
6
Mladá Boleslav
3
Hradec Králové
8
2
11
1
Praha
(Prague)
Plzeň 13
7
Příbram
Ostrava 18
Karviná 5
Olomouc 17
Jihlava 14
Zlín 16
Brno 15
9
Uherské Hradiště

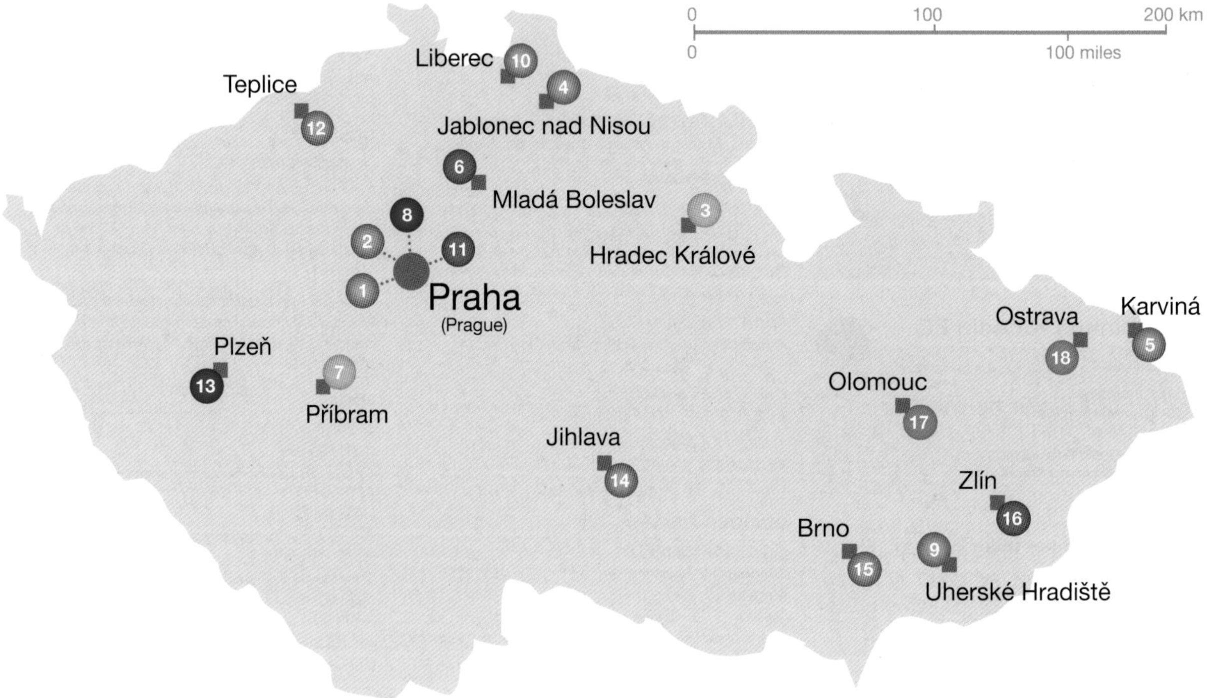

1. LIGA CLUBS

1 **Bohemians Praha 1905**

2 **FK Dukla Praha**

3 **FC Hradec Králové**

4 **FK Jablonec**

5 **MFK Karviná**

6 **FK Mladá Boleslav**

7 **1. FK Příbram**

8 **SK Slavia Praha**

9 **1. FC Slovácko**

10 **FC Slovan Liberec**

11 **AC Sparta Praha**

12 **FK Teplice**

13 **FC Viktoria Plzeň**

14 **FC Vysočina Jihlava**

15 **FC Zbrojovka Brno**

16 **FC Zlín**

PROMOTED CLUBS

17 **SK Sigma Olomouc**

18 **FC Baník Ostrava**

KEY

- UEFA Champions League
- UEFA Europa League
- Promoted
- Relegated

Slavia see it through

An absorbing two-pronged tussle for the Czech 1. Liga title concluded with victory for Slavia Praha over defending champions Viktoria Plzeň, the club from the capital holding their nerve to take the title on the final day with a 4-0 home win against Zbrojovka Brno.

A remarkable run of 26 games undefeated under new coach Jaroslav Šilhavý secured Slavia's first league triumph for eight years, but they lost their Czech Cup semi-final to FC Zlín, who went on to win the trophy, defeating another surprise finalist, second-tier SFC Opava, 1-0 in Olomouc.

Šilhavý steers champions to 26-game unbeaten run

Viktoria Plzeň edged out in thrilling title race

Zlín beat fellow giant-killers Opava in cup final

Domestic league

Slavia had endured some bleak times since last winning the title in 2008/09, but even though new Chinese ownership had stabilised the club financially, which had funded a draft of new signings, there was little evidence to suggest that the team that finished fifth in 2015/16 would be strong enough to compete with Plzeň or city rivals Sparta for the league title.

A poor start under Dušan Uhrin Jr, highlighted by a 3-1 defeat in Plzen, reinforced that viewpoint. It led to a change of coach, with Šilhavý, an ex-Slavia player who had led Slovan Liberec to the 2011/12 title, whisked in from Dukla Praha. Slavia's fortunes were suddenly transformed as the new man oversaw a run of six successive victories, among them a 2-0 win away to Sparta – a result that sparked a coaching change there too, with Zdeněk Šćasný losing his job.

Plzeň, under new management themselves, with Roman Pivarník having replaced 2015/16 title-winning boss Karel Krejčí, were beaten early on by Bohumil Páník's Zlín, the surprise early leaders, but they recovered well and at the winter break topped the table by a point from Slavia with a game in hand.

The two title contenders jostled for pole position throughout the spring. Crucially Slavia won the head-to-head at the Eden Arena, defender Michal Frydrych scoring an 88th-minute winner to delight the majority of the 19,084 spectators (the 1. Liga's largest attendance of the season). Slavia would test their fans' nerves again on several further occasions, notably when Milan Škoda scored a last-minute penalty to earn a 1-1 draw against Sparta, but they kept their unbeaten run going and remained neck-and-neck with Plzeň, who surprisingly axed Pivarník after a 2-2 home draw with Teplice. Šilhavý's side eventually sneaked into a two-point lead and protected it with a comprehensive last-day victory against Brno to claim their 17th national title.

With 65 goals, Slavia possessed by far the most prolific attack, the three teams immediately below them all scoring a modest 47 in comparison. Škoda, with 15 goals, shared the golden boot with Sparta's evergreen David Lafata, top of the charts for the fifth time in six seasons. Another familiar tale was yo-yo club Hradec Králové switching divisions again, while Sigma Olomouc and Baník Ostrava both made an immediate top-flight return a year after relegation.

Domestic cup

Shocks abounded in the Czech Cup, with Zlín taking on Opava, who would narrowly miss out on promotion, in the final. Zlín knocked out Sparta, Liberec and Slavia, while Opava's giant-killing spree claimed four top-division victims, including Plzeň and holders Mladá Boleslav. The final was settled by a single goal from Zlín midfielder Robert Bartolomeu, giving the club their first domestic cup triumph since 1970.

Europe

For the second straight season Plzeň, Sparta and Liberec all reached the UEFA Europa League group stage. Only Sparta, however, made it into the knockout phase, impressively topping a group that included Internazionale and Southampton thanks to perfect results in Prague, but they could not repeat their run to the quarter-final of the season before, a 4-0 defeat in Rostov cutting their campaign short in the round of 32.

National team

A new era for the Czech national team under Karel Jarolím – Slavia's 2007/08 and 2008/09 title-winning coach – began badly as two 0-0 draws at home to Northern Ireland and Azerbaijan plus a 3-0 defeat in Germany scarred the start of their 2018 FIFA World Cup qualifying campaign. A win and draw against Norway offered hope of better things to come, but with a four-point deficit to make up on second place and just four games remaining, another World Cup qualifying failure appeared to be staring the Czech Republic in the face.

DOMESTIC SEASON AT A GLANCE

1. Liga 2016/17 final table

			Home					Away					Total					
		Pld	W	D	L	F	A	W	D	L	F	A	W	D	L	F	A	Pts
1	**SK Slavia Praha**	**30**	**10**	**5**	**0**	**28**	**9**	**10**	**4**	**1**	**37**	**13**	**20**	**9**	**1**	**65**	**22**	**69**
2	FC Viktoria Plzeň	30	11	3	1	29	11	9	4	2	18	10	20	7	3	47	21	67
3	AC Sparta Praha	30	12	2	1	31	11	4	7	4	16	15	16	9	5	47	26	57
4	FK Mladá Boleslav	30	6	6	3	23	14	7	4	4	24	23	13	10	7	47	37	49
5	FK Teplice	30	7	4	4	18	11	6	5	4	20	14	13	9	8	38	25	48
6	FC Zlín	30	4	5	6	16	22	7	3	5	18	13	11	8	11	34	35	41
7	FK Dukla Praha	30	7	2	6	24	16	4	5	6	15	19	11	7	12	39	35	40
8	FK Jablonec	30	6	6	3	29	18	3	6	6	14	20	9	12	9	43	38	39
9	FC Slovan Liberec	30	7	7	1	25	10	3	2	10	6	18	10	9	11	31	28	39
10	MFK Karviná	30	6	4	5	22	18	3	3	9	17	31	9	7	14	39	49	34
11	1. FC Slovácko	30	3	8	4	14	17	3	6	6	15	21	6	14	10	29	38	32
12	FC Zbrojovka Brno	30	4	8	3	17	16	2	6	7	15	29	6	14	10	32	45	32
13	Bohemians Praha 1905	30	6	1	8	14	18	1	6	8	8	21	7	7	16	22	39	28
14	FC Vysočina Jihlava	30	5	5	5	18	19	1	4	10	8	28	6	9	15	26	47	27
15	FC Hradec Králové	30	4	2	9	11	20	4	1	10	18	31	8	3	19	29	51	27
16	1. FK Příbram	30	5	1	9	18	30	1	3	11	11	31	6	4	20	29	61	22

European qualification 2017/18

Champion: SK Slavia Praha (third qualifying round)

FC Viktoria Plzeň (third qualifying round)

Cup winner: FC Zlín (group stage)

AC Sparta Praha (third qualifying round)
FK Mladá Boleslav (second qualifying round)

Top scorer Milan Škoda (Slavia) & David Lafata (Sparta), 15 goals
Relegated clubs 1. FK Příbram, FC Hradec Králové
Promoted clubs SK Sigma Olomouc, FC Baník Ostrava
Cup final FC Zlín 1-0 SFC Opava

Team of the season

(4-4-2)

Coach: Šilhavý *(Slavia)*

Player of the season

Milan Škoda
(SK Slavia Praha)

A loyal servant to Slavia through good times and bad, Czech Republic international Škoda was rewarded at the end of his fifth season at the club with the first major honour of his career. The powerful 31-year-old Prague-born striker proved to be a talismanic figure for a new-look Slavia team. He was also a consistent provider of goals throughout the title-winning campaign, scoring 15 in total, most of them decisive, to win a share of the golden boot with Sparta's David Lafata. The prize of 1. Liga player of the season, however, was his alone.

Newcomer of the season

Michal Sáček
(AC Sparta Praha)

The 2016/17 season was not a memorable one for Sparta Praha as they watched Slavia and Viktoria Plzeň slug it out for the title. However, there was some comfort to be found in the emergence of 20-year-old Sáček, who, having begun the season as a fringe squad member, seized the opportunity when it came his way and by the spring, under Petr Rada, the club's fifth coach of the campaign, had become a regular starter in midfield. He also received a first call-up for the Czech Republic in June before representing his country at the UEFA European Under-21 Championship in Poland.

NATIONAL TEAM

International honours*
UEFA European Championship (1) 1976.

International tournament appearances*
FIFA World Cup (9) 1934 (runners-up), 1938 (qtr-finals), 1954, 1958, 1962 (runners-up), 1970, 1982, 1990 (qtr-finals), 2006
UEFA European Championship (9) 1960 (3rd), 1976 (Winners), 1980 (3rd), 1996 (runners-up), 2000, 2004 (semi-finals), 2008, 2012 (qtr-finals), 2016.

Top five all-time caps
Petr Čech (124); Karel Poborský (118); Tomáš Rosický (105); Jaroslav Plašil (103); Milan Baroš (93)

Top five all-time goals
Jan Koller (55); Milan Baroš (41); Antonín Puč (35); Zdeněk Nehoda (31); Pavel Kuka & Oldřich Nejedlý (29)

(before 1996 as Czechoslovakia)*

Results 2016/17

31/08/16	Armenia	H	Mlada Boleslav	W	3-0	*Krejčí (4), V Kadlec (34), Kopic (86)*
04/09/16	Northern Ireland (WCQ)	H	Prague	D	0-0	
08/10/16	Germany (WCQ)	A	Hamburg	L	0-3	
11/10/16	Azerbaijan (WCQ)	H	Ostrava	D	0-0	
11/11/16	Norway (WCQ)	H	Prague	W	2-1	*Krmenčík (11), Zmrhal (47)*
15/11/16	Denmark	H	Mlada Boleslav	D	1-1	*Barák (8)*
22/03/17	Lithuania	H	Usti nad Labem	W	3-0	*Hořava (48p), Jankto (65), Krmenčík (79)*
26/03/17	San Marino (WCQ)	A	Serravalle	W	6-0	*Barák (17, 24), Darida (19, 77p), Gebre Selassie (26), Krmenčík (43)*
05/06/17	Belgium	A	Brussels	L	1-2	*Krmenčík (29)*
10/06/17	Norway (WCQ)	A	Oslo	D	1-1	*Gebre Selassie (36)*

Appearances 2016/17

Coach: Karel Jarolím	23/08/56		Arm	NIR	GER	AZE	NOR	Den	Ltu	SMR	Bel	NOR	Caps	Goals
Tomáš Vaclík	29/03/89	Basel (SUI)	G46	G	G	G	G		G46	G	G33	G	15	-
Pavel Kadeřábek	25/04/92	Hoffenheim (GER)	D46	D	D		D	s66			D46	D	28	2
Marek Suchý	29/03/88	Basel (SUI)	D46	D	D			D	s46				32	1
Lukáš Pokorný	05/07/93	Liberec	D46										1	-
Daniel Pudil	27/09/85	Sheffield Wednesday (ENG)	D46					D					35	2
Jiří Skalák	12/03/92	Brighton (ENG)	M46	M77	s69	M74	s86						16	-
Vladimír Darida	08/08/90	Hertha (GER)	M46	M					M46	M	M	M79	45	3
David Pavelka	18/05/91	Kasımpaşa (TUR)	M46	M	M63		s81						14	-
Ladislav Krejčí	05/07/92	Bologna (ITA)	M46	M	M	M64	M86		M46	M	M46	M	35	5
Václav Kadlec	20/05/92	Midtjylland (DEN)	A46											
		/Sparta Praha		A83	s76	A							15	3
Milan Škoda	16/01/86	Slavia Praha	A46	A68		s66		A46	A46	s68	s64		18	4
Martin Frýdek	24/03/92	Sparta Praha	s46										3	-
Michal Kadlec	13/12/84	Sparta Praha	s46	D									67	8
Tomáš Kalas	15/05/93	Fulham (ENG)	s46					D	s46		D		7	-
Jan Kopic	04/06/90	Plzeň	s46	s77				M					5	1
Tomáš Koubek	26/08/92	Sparta Praha	s46					G46	s46				5	-
Tomáš Necid	13/08/89	Bursaspor (TUR)	s46	s68									44	12
Filip Novák	26/06/90	Midtjylland (DEN)	s46	D	D		D		D46	D			8	-
Josef Šural	30/05/90	Sparta Praha	s46										15	1
Jan Sýkora	29/12/93	Liberec	s46			D		M46						
		/Slavia Praha							s46				4	-
Matěj Vydra	01/05/92	Derby (ENG)	s46	s83	A76								20	5
Ondřej Zahustel	18/06/91	Sparta Praha	s46										3	1
Tomáš Sivok	15/09/83	Bursaspor (TUR)			D	D	D		D46	D		D	64	5
Bořek Dočkal	30/09/88	Sparta Praha			M	M	M	M						
		/Henan Jianye (CHN)							M46	M	s46	M	33	6
Tomáš Hořava	29/05/88	Plzeň			M		M		s46	s76		s79	10	3
Milan Petržela	19/06/83	Plzeň			M69	s64							19	-
Lukáš Droppa	22/04/89	Tom (RUS)			s63	M	M81	s81					4	-
Theodor Gebre Selassie	24/12/86	Bremen (GER)				D		D66	D46	D	D	D	43	3
Jakub Brabec	06/08/92	Genk (BEL)				D	D		D46	D	D	D	7	-
Patrik Schick	24/01/96	Sampdoria (ITA)				A66	s81				A64	s63	5	1
Jaromír Zmrhal	02/08/93	Slavia Praha				s74	M	M66	M46	s68	M77	M43	7	1
Michael Krmenčík	15/03/93	Plzeň					A81	s46	s46	A68	A46	A63	6	4
Antonín Barák	03/12/94	Slavia Praha						M81	M46	M76			3	3
Petr Mareš	17/01/91	Mladá Boleslav						s46	s46		s77		3	-
Jiří Pavlenka	14/04/92	Slavia Praha						s46			s33		2	-
Tomáš Souček	27/02/95	Slavia Praha						s66						
		/Liberec									M	M	3	-
Ondřej Čelůstka	18/06/89	Antalyaspor (TUR)							s46		s46		3	1
Adam Hloušek	20/12/88	Legia (POL)							s46				8	-
Josef Hušbauer	16/03/90	Slavia Praha							s46				10	1
Jakub Jankto	19/01/96	Udinese (ITA)							s46	M68	s46	s43	4	1

EUROPE

FC Viktoria Plzeň

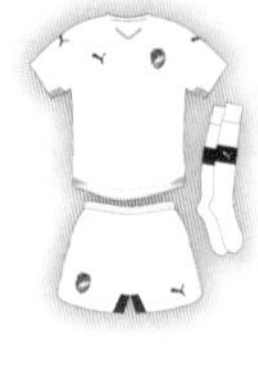

Third qualifying round - Qarabağ FK (AZE)
H 0-0
Kozáčik, Matějů, Hubník, Hořava, Limberský, Petržela, Ďuriš (Krmenčík 62), Hrošovský, Kovařík (Kopic 72), Baránek, Kolář (Hejda 79). Coach: Roman Pivarník (CZE)
Red card: Baránek 75
A 1-1 *Krmenčík (85)*
Kozáčik, Hejda, Matějů, Hubník, Hořava, Limberský, Petržela, Ďuriš (Bakoš 79), Hrošovský, Kovařík (Kopic 57), Kolář (Krmenčík 63). Coach: Roman Pivarník (CZE)

Play-offs - PFC Ludogorets Razgrad (BUL)
A 0-2
Kozáčik, Hejda, Matějů, Hubník, Limberský, Kopic, Ďuriš (Hořava 68), Hrošovský, Kovařík, Bakoš (Krmenčík 77), Hromada (Kolář 82). Coach: Roman Pivarník (CZE)
H 2-2 *Ďuriš (7), Matějů (64)*
Kozáčik, Hejda, Matějů, Hubník, Hořava (Baránek 88), Limberský, Kopic, Petržela (Kovařík 83), Ďuriš (Krmenčík 84), Bakoš, Hromada. Coach: Roman Pivarník (CZE)

Group E
Match 1 - AS Roma (ITA)
H 1-1 *Bakoš (11)*
Bolek, Hejda, Matějů, Hubník, Hořava, Limberský, Zeman (Petržela 72), Kopic, Ďuriš (Krmenčík 78), Kaçe, Bakoš (Poznar 84). Coach: Roman Pivarník (CZE)
Match 2 - FK Austria Wien (AUT)
A 0-0
Kozáčik, Hejda, Matějů, Hubník, Hořava, Limberský, Zeman, Petržela (Kopic 57), Poznar, Kaçe (Hromada 90+1), Bakoš (Krmenčík 66). Coach: Roman Pivarník (CZE)
Match 3 - FC Astra Giurgiu (ROU)
H 1-2 *Hořava (86)*
Kozáčik, Hejda, Hořava, Limberský, Zeman (Kovařík 76), Petržela, Ďuriš (Poznar 53), Řezník, Kaçe, Baránek, Bakoš (Krmenčík 65). Coach: Roman Pivarník (CZE)
Match 4 - FC Astra Giurgiu (ROU)
A 1-1 *Krmenčík (25)*
Kozáčik, Hejda, Matějů, Hubník, Petržela, Řezník, Krmenčík, Hrošovský, Kovařík (Kopic 67), Kaçe (Hořava 62), Hromada (Bakoš 87). Coach: Roman Pivarník (CZE)
Match 5 - AS Roma (ITA)
A 1-4 *Zeman (18)*
Kozáčik, Hejda, Matějů, Limberský, Zeman, Kopic (Ďuriš 63), Petržela, Krmenčík (Bakoš 75), Hrošovský, Kovařík, Hromada. Coach: Roman Pivarník (CZE)
Match 6 - FK Austria Wien (AUT)
H 3-2 *Hořava (44), Ďuriš (72, 84)*
Kozáčik, Hejda, Hořava (Poznar 90+1), Zeman, Kopic (Bakoš 83), Petržela, Řezník, Krmenčík (Ďuriš 58), Hrošovský, Kovařík, Hromada. Coach: Roman Pivarník (CZE)
Red card: Hejda 19

AC Sparta Praha

Third qualifying round - FC Steaua Bucureşti (ROU)
H 1-1 *Šural (35)*
Bičík, Michal Kadlec, Brabec, Dočkal, M Frýdek, Čermák (Matějovský 63), Konaté, Lafata, Šural (Fatai 59), Holek, Zahustel (Nhamoinesu 80). Coach: Zdeněk Ščasný (CZE)
A 0-2
Bičík, Michal Kadlec, Brabec, Vácha, Dočkal, M Frýdek, Konaté, Lafata (Mareček 83), Šural (Juliš 63), Nhamoinesu, Zahustel. Coach: Zdeněk Ščasný (CZE)
Red card: Brabec 51

Play-offs - SønderjyskE (DEN)
A 0-0
Koubek, Mazuch, Michal Kadlec, Vácha, Dočkal, Mareček, Holzer (M Frýdek 46), Šural (Pulkrab 80), Nhamoinesu, Zahustel, Juliš. Coach: Zdeněk Ščasný (CZE)
H 3-2 Lafata (44), Šural (69), Brabec (85)
Koubek, Michal Kadlec, Karavaev (Brabec 85), Vácha, Mareček (Juliš 46), M Frýdek, Lafata, Šural, Pulkrab (Zahustel 82), Holek, Nhamoinesu. Coach: Zdeněk Ščasný (CZE)

Group K
Match 1 - Southampton FC (ENG)
A 0-3
Koubek, Michal Kadlec, Karavaev, Vácha (Mareček 64), M Frýdek, Sáček, Šural (Pulkrab 74), Holek, Nhamoinesu, Juliš (Lafata 46), V Kadlec. Coach: Zdeněk Ščasný (CZE)
Match 2 - FC Internazionale Milano (ITA)
H 3-1 *V Kadlec (7, 25), Holek (76)*
Koubek, Mazuch, Michal Kadlec (Pulkrab 73), Karavaev, Dočkal, M Frýdek (Juliš 66), Sáček, Čermák (Lafata 88), Holzer, Holek, V Kadlec. Coach: David Holoubek (CZE)
Match 3 - Hapoel Beer-Sheva FC (ISR)
A 1-0 *Pulkrab (71)*
Koubek, Mazuch, Michal Kadlec, Karavaev, Dočkal, Mareček, Holzer (Pulkrab 46), Holek, Zahustel, Juliš (Lafata 77), V Kadlec (Dudl 90+2). Coach: David Holoubek (CZE)
Match 4 - Hapoel Beer-Sheva FC (ISR)
H 2-0 *Bitton (23og), Lafata (38)*
Koubek, Mazuch, Michal Kadlec, Karavaev, Dočkal, Mareček, Lafata (Pulkrab 80), Holzer (Milan Kadlec 90+1), Holek, Nhamoinesu, Juliš (Dudl 72). Coach: David Holoubek (CZE)
Match 5 - Southampton FC (ENG)
H 1-0 *Nhamoinesu (11)*
Koubek, Mazuch, Michal Kadlec, Karavaev, Dočkal, Mareček, Lafata (Havelka 88), Holzer (Dudl 90+1), Holek, Nhamoinesu, Juliš (Köstl 90+3). Coach: David Holoubek (CZE)
Match 6 - FC Internazionale Milano (ITA)
A 1-2 *Mareček (54)*
Koubek, Mazuch, Michal Kadlec, Karavaev, Dočkal, Mareček, Čermák (Sáček 78), Lafata (Pulkrab 74), Holek, Nhamoinesu, Juliš (Dudl 89). Coach: Zdeněk Svoboda (CZE)

Round of 32 - FC Rostov (RUS)
A 0-4
Koubek, Mazuch, Michal Kadlec, Karavaev, Vácha (Holek 80), Dočkal (Lafata 87), Néstor Albiach (Hybš 76), Sáček, Konaté, Nhamoinesu, Juliš. Coach: Tomáš Požár (CZE)
Red card: Konaté 32
H 1-1 *Karavaev (84)*
Koubek, Mazuch (Havelka 46), Michal Kadlec, Karavaev, Néstor Albiach (Hybš 70), Sáček, Čermák, Pulkrab (Šural 40), Holek, Nhamoinesu, Juliš. Coach: Tomáš Požár (CZE)
Red card: Nhamoinesu 67

FK Mladá Boleslav

Third qualifying round - KF Shkëndija (MKD)
A 0-2
Diviš, Fleišman, Jánoš, Kalabiška, Kúdela, Magera (Takács 82), Pauschek, Rada, Mebrahtu (Chramosta 46; Kerestеš 59), Hůlka, Vukadinović. Coach: Karel Jarolím (CZE)
Red card: Hůlka 52
H 1-0 *Magera (82)*
Diviš, Fleišman, Douglas, Jánoš, Kalabiška (Kerestеš 61), Kúdela, Magera, Chramosta, Pauschek (Mebrahtu 46), Rada, Vukadinović (Takács 69). Coach: Karel Jarolím (CZE)

FC Slovan Liberec

Third qualifying round - FC Admira Wacker Mödling (AUT)
A 2-1 *Vůch (11, 69)*
Dúbravka, Breite, Coufal, Sýkora, Folprecht, Hovorka, Komlichenko (Baroš 60), Ševčík, Vůch (Navrátil 88), Bartl (Nitrianský 78), Pokorný. Coach: Jindřich Trpišovský (CZE)
H 2-0 *Coufal (20), Komlichenko (34p)*
Dúbravka, Breite, Coufal, Sýkora, Folprecht, Hovorka, Komlichenko (Baroš 62), Ševčík (Lesniak 83), Vůch, Bartl (Navrátil 76), Pokorný. Coach: Jindřich Trpišovský (CZE)

Play-offs - AEK Larnaca FC (CYP)
A 1-0 *Coufal (29)*
Dúbravka, Breite (Kubyshkin 85), Coufal, Sýkora, Folprecht, Hovorka, Komlichenko, Vůch (Navrátil 60), Bartl, Bartošák (Súkenník 70), Pokorný. Coach: Jindřich Trpišovský (CZE)
H 3-0 *Sýkora (8, 15, 41)*
Dúbravka, Breite, Coufal, Sýkora, Folprecht, Hovorka, Vůch (Súkenník 89), Bartl (Navrátil 79), Bartošák, Baroš (Komlichenko 83), Pokorný. Coach: Jaroslav Köstl (CZE)

Group J
Match 1 - Qarabağ FK (AZE)
A 2-2 *Sýkora (1), Baroš (68)*
Dúbravka, Breite, Coufal, Sýkora (Nitrianský 85), Folprecht, Hovorka, Vůch, Bartl (Karafiát 65), Bartošák, Baroš (Súkenník 75), Latka. Coach: Jindřich Trpišovský (CZE)

FK Mladá Boleslav

1902 • Adidas Arena (5,000) • fkmb.cz

Major honours
Czech Cup (2) 2011, 2016

Coach: Karel Jarolím;
(10/08/16) Leoš Kalvoda;
(16/12/16) Martin Svědík

Date		Opponent			Scorers
2016					
31/07	h	Liberec	W	3-0	*Chramosta 3*
07/08	a	Příbram	W	1-0	*Rada*
13/08	h	Karviná	L	1-2	*Rada*
19/08	a	Teplice	W	2-1	*Magera, Mebrahtu*
26/08	h	Hradec Králové	W	2-0	*Hůlka, Magera*
10/09	a	Sparta	D	2-2	*Mebrahtu, Chramosta*
17/09	h	Slovácko	W	3-0	*Chramosta 2, Mebrahtu*
23/09	a	Jablonec	W	2-1	*Mebrahtu, Přikryl*
01/10	h	Dukla	W	1-0	*Klobása*
14/10	a	Bohemians 1905	W	3-1	*Matějovský, Chramosta, Přikryl*
22/10	h	Brno	D	3-3	*Přikryl, Douglas, Mareš*
29/10	h	Zlín	L	1-2	*Mebrahtu*
04/11	a	Jihlava	L	1-2	*Klobása*
19/11	h	Plzeň	D	0-0	
26/11	a	Slavia	L	1-2	*Magera (p)*
04/12	h	Příbram	D	2-2	*Fabián, Chramosta*
2017					
19/02	a	Karviná	D	1-1	*Takács*
27/02	h	Teplice	D	1-1	*Nečas*
04/03	a	Hradec Králové	D	0-0	
12/03	h	Sparta	W	1-0	*Douglas*
18/03	a	Slovácko	L	1-2	*Přikryl*
31/03	h	Jablonec	D	0-0	
07/04	a	Dukla	W	2-1	*Železník, og (Podaný)*
15/04	h	Bohemians 1905	D	1-1	*Železník*
22/04	a	Brno	W	3-2	*Mebrahtu 3 (1p)*
29/04	a	Zlín	W	2-1	*Magera, Douglas*
07/05	h	Jihlava	W	3-1	*Železník, Mareš, Přikryl*
12/05	a	Plzeň	D	3-3	*Levin, Kysela, Jánoš*
20/05	h	Slavia	L	1-2	*Chramosta*
27/05	a	Liberec	L	0-4	

No	Name	Nat	DoB	Pos	Aps	(s)	Gls
19	Jan Chramosta		12/10/90	A	18	(5)	9
24	Pavel Čmovš		29/06/90	D	3	(5)	
23	Jakub Diviš		27/07/86	G	16		
4	Douglas	BRA	07/03/84	D	24	(1)	3
5	Tomáš Fabián		10/09/89	M	7		1
3	Jiří Fleišman		02/10/84	D	30		
28	Lukáš Hůlka		31/03/95	D	9		1
6	Adam Jánoš		20/07/92	D	17	(5)	1
9	Jan Kalabiška		22/12/86	M	3	(6)	
29	Miroslav Keresteš	SVK	30/07/89	D	1	(2)	
31	Stanislav Klobása		07/03/94	A	3	(7)	2
11	Ondřej Kúdela		26/03/87	M	16		
20	Jan Kysela		17/12/85	D	3	(1)	1
16	Vladislav Levin	RUS	28/03/95	M	7	(1)	1
18	Lukáš Magera		17/01/83	A	9	(12)	4
30	Kevin Malpon	FRA	01/03/96	M	1		
17	Petr Mareš		17/01/91	M	22	(1)	2
8	Marek Matějovský		20/12/81	M	9	(4)	1
26	Golgol Mebrahtu	AUS	28/08/90	A	11	(10)	8
33	Jakub Nečas		26/01/95	A	3	(5)	1
21	Lukáš Pauschek	SVK	09/12/92	D	21	(1)	
14	Tomáš Přikryl		04/07/92	M	23	(3)	5
25	Jakub Rada		05/05/87	M	5		2
12	Jan Šeda		17/12/85	G	5		
15	Patrizio Stronati		17/11/94	D	14		
22	Laco Takács		15/07/96	D	16	(7)	1
11,7	Jiří Valenta		14/02/88	M	4	(4)	
1	Luděk Vejmola		03/11/94	G	9		
30	Miljan Vukadinović	SRB	27/12/92	M	11	(5)	
7	Lukáš Železník		18/06/90	A	10	(2)	3

1. FK Příbram

1928 • Energon Arena (9,100) • fkpribram.cz

Coach: Martin Pulpit;
(22/08/16) Petr Rada;
(07/01/17) Kamil Tobiáš

Date		Opponent			Scorers
2016					
30/07	a	Zlín	L	0-2	
07/08	h	Mladá Boleslav	L	0-1	
12/08	h	Plzeň	L	0-3	
21/08	a	Slavia	L	0-3	
28/08	h	Liberec	L	0-1	
10/09	a	Hradec Králové	L	0-2	
17/09	h	Teplice	W	3-2	*Majtán, Brandner, Mahmutović*
24/09	a	Bohemians 1905	L	0-1	
01/10	h	Slovácko	L	0-1	
15/10	a	Karviná	L	0-2	
22/10	h	Jablonec	L	2-4	*T Pilík, Kacafírek*
29/10	a	Sparta	L	0-4	
05/11	h	Dukla	W	3-1	*Brandner, T Pilík 2*
19/11	a	Brno	D	2-2	*T Pilík (p), Brandner*
26/11	h	Jihlava	D	0-0	
04/12	a	Mladá Boleslav	D	2-2	*Rezek, Tregler*
2017					
18/02	a	Plzeň	L	0-1	
25/02	h	Slavia	L	1-8	*Divíšek*
05/03	a	Liberec	L	1-2	*Tregler*
11/03	h	Hradec Králové	W	1-0	*T Pilík (p)*
18/03	a	Teplice	L	0-3	
01/04	h	Bohemians 1905	W	1-0	*T Pilík*
08/04	a	Slovácko	L	0-1	
15/04	h	Karviná	W	4-2	*Jiránek, Suchan, Rezek, Linhart*
23/04	a	Jablonec	W	4-2	*T Pilík, Rezek 2, Suchan*
28/04	h	Sparta	L	1-2	*Rezek*
05/05	a	Dukla	L	1-3	*Suchan*
13/05	h	Brno	L	2-3	*T Pilík, P Pilík*
20/05	a	Jihlava	D	1-1	*og (Štěpánek)*
27/05	h	Zlín	L	0-2	

No	Name	Nat	DoB	Pos	Aps	(s)	Gls
15	Karsten Ayong		20/01/98	A	3	(8)	
8	Josef Bazal		06/11/93	M	9	(2)	
32	Tomáš Borek		04/04/86	M	3	(2)	
15	Faouzi Bourenane	ALG	24/08/94	M		(2)	
7	Patrik Brandner		04/01/94	A	7	(6)	3
28	José Casado	ESP	14/01/88	M		(2)	
27	Matěj Chaluš		02/02/98	D	26	(1)	
24	Josef Divíšek		24/09/90	D	27		1
12	Marco Ferrara	ITA	05/05/94	D	7	(1)	
14	Štěpán Holý		18/08/96	D		(1)	
13	Aleš Hruška		23/11/85	G	29		
16	Jiří Januška		11/10/97	M		(5)	
25	Martin Jiránek		25/05/79	D	21		1
23	Štěpán Kacafírek		29/09/89	A	4	(13)	1
26	Ondřej Kočí		07/04/95	G	1		
19	Martin Krameš		17/08/93	M	15	(7)	
12	Davor Kukec	CRO	16/03/86	M	5	(1)	
3	Roman Květ		17/12/97	M	7	(1)	
9	Jan Kvída		17/01/91	D	8		
11	Denis Laňka		13/05/97	A	2	(5)	
14	Zdeněk Linhart		05/03/94	A	9	(1)	1
5	Lukáš Lupták	SVK	28/07/90	M	3	(1)	
9	Aidin Mahmutović	BIH	06/04/86	A	6	(7)	1
18	Tomáš Majtán	SVK	30/03/87	A	10	(6)	1
21	Jiří Mareš		16/02/92	M	2		
5	Miloš Nikolić	SRB	22/02/89	D	2		
17	Michal Pecháček		14/04/96	M	9	(1)	
14	Lester Peltier	TRI	13/09/88	A	5		
21	Pavel Pilík		13/02/92	M	3	(5)	1
6	Tomáš Pilík		20/12/88	M	26	(3)	8
10	Jan Rezek		05/05/82	M	29		5
14	Lukáš Ric		18/07/98	M		(1)	
7	Jan Suchan		18/01/96	M	10		3
22	Petr Trapp		06/12/85	D	15	(2)	
20	Jaroslav Tregler		01/12/95	D	27		2

SK Slavia Praha

1892 • Eden Arena (20,232) • slavia.cz

Major honours
Czechoslovakian/Czech League (17) 1925, 1929, 1930, 1931, 1933, 1934, 1935, 1937, 1940, 1941, 1942, 1943, 1947, 1996, 2008, 2009, 2017; Czech Cup (3) 1997, 1999, 2002

Coach: Dušan Uhrin Jr;
(05/09/16) Jaroslav Šilhavý

Date		Opponent			Scorers
2016					
08/08	h	Zlín	D	2-2	*Van Kessel, Mešanović*
14/08	a	Jihlava	D	1-1	*Van Kessel*
21/08	h	Příbram	W	3-0	*Mešanović, Škoda, Hušbauer*
28/08	a	Plzeň	L	1-3	*Bílek*
11/09	a	Teplice	D	2-2	*Mešanović, Mihalík*
19/09	h	Liberec	W	1-0	*Škoda*
25/09	a	Sparta	W	2-0	*Mešanović, Zmrhal*
01/10	h	Karviná	W	1-0	*Mešanović*
15/10	a	Hradec Králové	W	3-0	*Škoda, Zmrhal, Barák*
19/10	a	Brno	W	4-1	*Barák 2, Frydrych, Škoda*
22/10	h	Slovácko	W	1-0	*Zmrhal*
30/10	a	Jablonec	D	0-0	
05/11	h	Bohemians 1905	D	1-1	*Škoda*
18/11	a	Dukla	W	2-1	*Mešanović, Škoda*
26/11	h	Mladá Boleslav	W	2-1	*Ngadeu, Zmrhal*
02/12	a	Zlín	W	4-0	*Škoda 2 (1p), Mešanović, Zmrhal*
2017					
18/02	h	Jihlava	W	2-0	*Škoda 2 (1p)*
25/02	a	Příbram	W	8-1	*Škoda, Sýkora, Hušbauer, Ngadeu 3 (1p), Mešanović, Bořil*
05/03	h	Plzeň	W	1-0	*Frydrych*
12/03	h	Teplice	W	2-1	*Škoda, og (Vaněček)*
18/03	a	Liberec	D	1-1	*Zmrhal*
02/04	h	Sparta	D	1-1	*Škoda (p)*
08/04	a	Karviná	W	2-1	*Mešanović 2*
17/04	h	Hradec Králové	W	4-0	*Frydrych, Škoda (p), Mingazov, Hušbauer*
21/04	a	Slovácko	W	2-0	*Škoda, Deli*
30/04	h	Jablonec	D	1-1	*Mešanović*
06/05	a	Bohemians 1905	W	3-1	*Mingazov, Zmrhal, Sýkora*
13/05	h	Dukla	D	2-2	*Mešanović, Barák (p)*
20/05	a	Mladá Boleslav	W	2-1	*Ngadeu, Mingazov*
27/05	h	Brno	W	4-0	*Frydrych, Tecl 2, Ngadeu*

No	Name	Nat	DoB	Pos	Aps	(s)	Gls
27	Antonín Barák		03/12/94	M	18	(7)	4
12	Martin Berkovec		12/02/89	G	2		
20	Jan Bílek		04/11/83	D	16	(1)	1
18	Jan Bořil		11/01/91	D	22	(2)	1
19	Simon Deli	CIV	27/10/91	D	25		1
15	Per-Egil Flo	NOR	18/01/89	D	10	(1)	
25	Michal Frydrych		27/02/90	D	24	(1)	4
10	Josef Hušbauer		16/03/90	M	29		3
11	Levan Kenia	GEO	18/10/90	M	1		
26	Michael Lüftner		14/03/94	D	14		
24	Muris Mešanović	BIH	04/07/90	A	11	(15)	12
17	Jaroslav Mihalík	SVK	27/07/94	M	4	(5)	1
3	Jan Mikula		05/01/92	D	4		
9	Ruslan Mingazov	TKM	23/11/91	M	8	(8)	3
13	Michael Ngadeu	CMR	23/11/90	M	26	(1)	6
1	Jiří Pavlenka		14/04/92	G	28		
23	Jasmin Ščuk	BIH	14/07/90	M	4	(13)	
21	Milan Škoda		16/01/86	A	27	(2)	15
22	Tomáš Souček		27/02/95	M	5	(2)	
81	Dušan Švento	SVK	01/08/85	M	7	(5)	
6	Jan Sýkora		29/12/93	M	10	(1)	2
17	Stanislav Tecl		01/09/90	A	3	(8)	2
14	Mick van Buren	NED	14/08/92	A		(10)	
99	Gino van Kessel	CUW	09/03/93	A	5	(2)	2
2	Lukáš Železník		18/06/90	A		(2)	
8	Jaromír Zmrhal		02/08/93	M	27	(3)	7

CZECH REPUBLIC

1. FC Slovácko

1927 • Městský fotbalový stadion Miroslava Valenty (8,000) • fcslovacko.cz

Coach: Stanislav Levý

2016

30/07	a Sparta	L	2-3	*Diviš 2*
06/08	h Dukla	D	2-2	*Košút, Zajíc*
13/08	a Jablonec	D	2-2	*Rada, Havlík*
20/08	h Bohemians 1905	W	2-0	*Kerbr, Diviš*
27/08	a Brno	L	0-1	
09/09	h Zlín	L	1-3	*Čivić*
17/09	a Mladá Boleslav	L	0-3	
24/09	h Jihlava	D	1-1	*Havlík*
01/10	a Příbram	W	1-0	*Ťok*
15/10	h Plzeň	D	1-1	*Havlík*
22/10	a Slavia	L	0-1	
29/10	h Teplice	D	1-1	*Daníček*
06/11	a Karviná	W	1-0	*Koné*
19/11	h Hradec Králové	L	1-3	*Zajíc (p)*
27/11	a Liberec	D	2-2	*Koné, Hlúpik*
04/12	a Dukla	W	3-2	*Tetteh, Koné, Zajíc*

2017

18/02	h Jablonec	D	0-0	
25/02	a Bohemians 1905	D	0-0	
04/03	h Brno	D	0-0	
11/03	a Zlín	D	1-1	*Navrátil*
18/03	h Mladá Boleslav	W	2-1	*Zajíc, Havlík*
01/04	a Jihlava	D	0-0	
08/04	h Příbram	W	1-0	*Sumulikoski*
16/04	a Plzeň	L	0-2	
21/04	h Slavia	L	0-2	
30/04	a Teplice	D	2-2	*Zajíc, Navrátil*
06/05	h Karviná	D	1-1	*Havlík*
13/05	a Hradec Králové	L	1-2	*Navrátil*
20/05	h Liberec	L	0-1	
27/05	h Sparta	D	1-1	*Sumulikoski*

No	Name	Nat	DoB	Pos	Aps	(s)	Gls
14	Matěj Biolek		09/02/91	M	2	(5)	
19	Tomáš Břečka		12/05/94	D	15		
8	Juraj Chvátal	SVK	13/07/96	D	5	(2)	
24	Petr Chýla		05/05/94	D	1		
3	Eldar Čivić	BIH	28/05/96	M	19	(1)	1
25	Michal Daněk		06/07/83	G	9		
28	Vlastimil Daníček		15/07/91	M	26		1
9	Jaroslav Diviš		09/07/86	M	14	(2)	3
20	Marek Havlík		08/07/95	M	26	(3)	5
29	Milan Heča		23/03/91	G	21		
8	Filip Hlúpik		30/04/91	M	2	(1)	1
6	Stanislav Hofmann		17/06/90	D	15	(1)	
10	Luboš Kalouda		20/05/87	M	1	(1)	
21	Milan Kerbr		10/09/89	A	10	(1)	1
26	Francis Koné	TOG	22/11/90	A	14	(7)	3
22	Tomáš Košút	SVK	13/01/90	D	15		1
21	Filip Kubala		02/09/99	M		(1)	
8, 18	David Machalík		21/06/96	M	13		
9	Jan Navrátil		13/04/90	M	14		3
4	Tomáš Rada		15/02/83	D	14	(2)	1
23	Petr Reinberk		23/05/89	D	25	(1)	
18	Jan Rezek		29/05/98	M	2	(7)	
16	Patrik Šimko	SVK	08/07/91	D	17	(3)	
14	Michal Suchý		29/07/96	D	1		
5	Velice Sumulikoski	MKD	24/04/81	M	29		2
19	Benjamin Tetteh	GHA	10/07/97	A	4	(9)	1
11	Tomáš Ťok		02/02/95	M	4	(10)	1
14	Yu Kang-hyun	KOR	27/04/96	A		(1)	
17	Tomáš Zajíc		12/08/96	A	12	(13)	5

FC Slovan Liberec

1958 • U Nisy (9,900) • fcslovanliberec.cz

Major honours

Czech League (3) 2002, 2006, 2012; Czech Cup (2) 2000, 2015

Coach: Jindřich Trpišovský

2016

31/07	a Mladá Boleslav	L	0-3	
07/08	h Jihlava	D	1-1	*Baroš*
13/08	a Zlín	L	1-2	*Bartl*
21/08	h Brno	D	0-0	
28/08	a Příbram	W	1-0	*Hovorka*
10/09	h Plzeň	L	1-2	*Komlichenko*
19/09	a Slavia	L	0-1	
02/10	h Teplice	W	2-0	*Folprecht, Breite*
15/10	a Dukla	D	0-0	
23/10	h Hradec Králové	W	2-0	*Bartl 2*
26/10	a Karviná	D	0-0	
30/10	a Bohemians 1905	L	1-2	*Breite*
06/11	h Sparta	D	0-0	
19/11	a Jablonec	L	0-3	
27/11	h Slovácko	D	2-2	*Komlichenko 2 (2p)*
03/12	a Jihlava	L	0-1	

2017

20/02	h Zlín	D	0-0	
25/02	a Brno	L	0-1	
05/03	h Příbram	W	2-1	*Baroš, Vůch*
11/03	a Plzeň	L	0-1	
18/03	h Slavia	D	1-1	*Ekpai*
01/04	h Karviná	W	2-0	*Bartl, Potočný*
08/04	a Teplice	L	1-3	*Mikula*
16/04	h Dukla	W	3-1	*Mikula, Kerbr, Kouřil*
22/04	a Hradec Králové	W	1-0	*Kerbr (p)*
01/05	h Bohemians 1905	W	4-1	*Ekpai 2, Baroš, Voltr*
07/05	a Sparta	L	0-1	
13/05	h Jablonec	D	1-1	*Breite*
20/05	a Slovácko	W	1-0	*Ekpai*
27/05	h Mladá Boleslav	W	4-0	*Baroš 2, Kerbr (p), Potočný*

No	Name	Nat	DoB	Pos	Aps	(s)	Gls
27	Milan Baroš		28/10/81	A	21	(5)	5
24	Daniel Bartl		05/07/89	M	16	(2)	4
26	Lukáš Bartošák		03/07/90	D	10	(2)	
14	Ondřej Bláha		22/08/96	M		(1)	
10	Miloš Bosančić	SRB	22/05/88	M	5	(3)	
2	Radim Breite		10/08/89	M	22	(4)	3
5	Vladimír Coufal		22/08/92	D	15	(2)	
19	Martin Dúbravka	SVK	15/01/89	G	28		
28	Ubong Ekpai	NGA	17/10/95	M	11	(4)	4
10	Zdeněk Folprecht		07/01/91	M	11	(3)	1
8	Martin Graiciar		11/04/99	A	2	(4)	
15	Vojtěch Hadaščok		08/01/92	A	2	(1)	
16	Václav Hladký		14/11/90	G	2		
11	David Hovorka		07/08/93	D	11		1
4	Ondřej Karafiát		01/12/94	D	20	(2)	
37	Milan Kerbr		10/09/89	A	13		3
21	Nikolai Komlichenko	RUS	29/06/95	A	6	(6)	3
21	Martin Kouřil		24/02/91	D		(3)	1
18	Ilya Kubyshkin	RUS	12/01/96	M	1		
15	Ondřej Kúdela		26/03/87	M	14		
31	Martin Latka		28/09/84	D	9	(1)	
8	Filip Lesniak	SVK	14/05/96	M		(1)	
25	Ondřej Machuča		13/04/96	M	1	(2)	
13	Miroslav Marković	SRB	04/11/89	A	4	(3)	
3	Jan Mikula		05/01/92	D	13		2
9	Jan Navrátil		13/04/90	M	8	(2)	
7	Milan Nitrianský		13/12/90	D	4	(3)	
20	Michal Obročník	SVK	04/06/91	M	2	(2)	
29	Lukáš Pokorný		05/07/93	D	8		
13	Roman Potočný		25/04/91	A	8	(2)	2
22	Petr Ševčík		04/05/94	M	16	(6)	
29	Tomáš Souček		27/02/95	M	12		
16	Igor Súkenník	SVK	25/10/89	M	3	(2)	
6	Jan Šulc		02/06/98	M		(2)	
6	Jan Sýkora		29/12/93	M	10	(3)	
9	Radek Voltr		28/11/91	A	4	(9)	1
23	Egon Vůch		01/02/91	M	15	(2)	1
3	Wesley	BRA	03/06/96	M	3	(3)	

AC Sparta Praha

1893 • GENERALI Arena (18,887) • sparta.cz

Major honours

Czechoslovakian/Czech League (33) 1926, 1927, 1932, 1936, 1938, 1939, 1944, 1946, 1948, 1952, 1954, 1965, 1967, 1984, 1985, 1987, 1988, 1989, 1990, 1991, 1993, 1994, 1995, 1997, 1998, 1999, 2000, 2001, 2003, 2005, 2007, 2010, 2014; Czechoslovakian/Czech Cup (14) 1964, 1972, 1976, 1980, 1984, 1988, 1989, 1992, 1996, 2004, 2006, 2007, 2008, 2014

Coach: Zdeněk Ščasný;
(26/09/16) (David Holoubek);
(27/11/16) (Zdeněk Svoboda);
(21/12/16) (Tomáš Požár);
(14/03/17) Petr Rada

2016

30/07	h Slovácko	W	3-2	*Dočkal 2 (1p), Konaté*
07/08	a Teplice	D	0-0	
13/08	a Bohemians 1905	W	2-0	*Juliš, Dočkal*
21/08	h Jablonec	W	3-0	*Lafata 2, Pulkrab*
28/08	a Dukla	W	2-0	*M Frýdek 2*
10/09	h Mladá Boleslav	D	2-2	*Lafata, Šural*
19/09	a Zlín	D	1-1	*V Kadlec*
25/09	h Slavia	L	0-2	
02/10	a Brno	D	3-3	*Mazuch, Dočkal, Pulkrab*
16/10	h Jihlava	W	3-0	*Lafata 2, Karavaev*
23/10	a Plzeň	L	0-1	
29/10	h Příbram	W	4-0	*Karavaev, Lafata 3*
06/11	a Liberec	D	0-0	
20/11	h Karviná	W	3-0	*Holzer, Pulkrab, Lafata*
27/11	a Hradec Králové	W	2-1	*Juliš, Pulkrab*
03/12	h Teplice	W	2-1	*M Kadlec, Lafata*

2017

19/02	h Bohemians 1905	W	1-0	*Čermák*
26/02	a Jablonec	L	1-3	*Lafata (p)*
04/03	h Dukla	W	1-0	*Šural*
12/03	a Mladá Boleslav	L	0-1	
17/03	h Zlín	D	0-0	
02/04	a Slavia	D	1-1	*V Kadlec*
09/04	h Brno	W	3-2	*M Kadlec, Lafata 2 (1p)*
15/04	a Jihlava	L	0-1	
23/04	h Plzeň	W	2-0	*Šural, Karavaev*
28/04	a Příbram	W	2-1	*Šural 2*
07/05	h Liberec	W	1-0	*Lafata*
12/05	a Karviná	D	1-1	*M Kadlec*
20/05	h Hradec Králové	W	3-2	*V Kadlec, Šural, Lafata*
27/05	a Slovácko	D	1-1	*Juliš*

No	Name	Nat	DoB	Pos	Aps	(s)	Gls
35	David Bičík		06/04/81	G	7		
5	Jakub Brabec		06/08/92	D	1	(1)	
17	Aleš Čermák		01/10/94	M	12	(5)	1
9	Bořek Dočkal		30/09/88	M	12		4
43	Václav Dudl		22/09/99	M		(5)	
20	Christián Frýdek		01/02/99	M		(1)	
14	Martin Frýdek		24/03/92	M	5	(4)	2
45	Filip Havelka		21/01/98	M	1	(3)	
25	Mario Holek		28/10/86	D	23	(3)	
22	Daniel Holzer		18/08/95	M	8	(5)	1
29	Matěj Hybš		03/01/93	D	9	(1)	
30	Lukáš Juliš		02/12/94	A	12	(10)	3
3	Michal Kadlec		13/12/84	D	27	(1)	3
77	Václav Kadlec		20/05/92	A	12	(2)	3
4	Vyacheslav Karavaev	RUS	20/05/95	D	27		3
18	Tiémoko Konaté	CIV	19/04/90	M	12	(1)	1
33	Tomáš Koubek		26/08/92	G	23		
21	David Lafata		18/09/81	A	25	(3)	15
11	Lukáš Mareček		17/04/90	M	18	(4)	
47	Martin Matoušek		02/05/95	M		(1)	
27	Ondřej Mazuch		15/03/89	D	14		1
32	Zinedin Mustedanagić	BIH	01/08/98	M		(5)	
15	Néstor Albiach	ESP	18/08/92	A	4	(2)	
26	Costa Nhamoinesu	ZIM	06/01/86	D	14	(2)	
19	Martin Nový		23/06/93	D		(1)	
24	Matěj Pulkrab		23/05/97	A	6	(9)	4
10	Tomáš Rosický		04/10/80	M		(1)	
16	Michal Sáček		19/09/96	M	14	(1)	
23	Josef Šural		30/05/90	M	18	(3)	6
6	Lukáš Vácha		13/05/89	M	14	(2)	
88	Bogdan Vătăjelu	ROU	24/04/92	D	6		
28	Ondřej Zahustel		18/06/91	M	6	(7)	

FK Teplice

1945 • AGC Arena Na Stínadlech (18,221) • fkteplice.cz

Major honours
Czech Cup (2) 2003, 2009

Coach: Daniel Šmejkal

2016				
29/07	a Dukla	W	1-0	*Potočný*
07/08	h Sparta	D	0-0	
13/08	a Brno	D	0-0	
19/08	h Mladá Boleslav	L	1-2	*Fillo*
26/08	a Jihlava	W	2-0	*Ljevaković, Hora*
11/09	h Slavia	D	2-2	*Vondrášek, Vaněček*
17/09	a Příbram	L	2-3	*Vaněček 2*
24/09	h Plzeň	L	0-1	
02/10	a Liberec	L	0-2	
15/10	h Zlín	W	2-0	*Potočný, Vaněček*
22/10	a Karviná	W	4-1	*og (Dreksa), Vaněček, Fillo, Lüftner*
29/10	a Slovácko	D	1-1	*Jeřábek*
05/11	h Hradec Králové	L	0-1	
19/11	a Bohemians 1905	W	1-0	*Hora*
26/11	h Jablonec	W	1-0	*Kučera*
03/12	a Sparta	L	1-2	*Vaněček*
2017				
18/02	h Brno	D	1-1	*Fillo*
27/02	a Mladá Boleslav	D	1-1	*Červenka*
04/03	h Jihlava	W	1-0	*Fillo (p)*
12/03	a Slavia	L	1-2	*Fillo*
18/03	h Příbram	W	3-0	*Nivaldo, Hora, Červenka*
01/04	a Plzeň	D	2-2	*Červenka, Vošahlík*
08/04	h Liberec	W	3-1	*Červenka, Hora, Vošahlík*
15/04	a Zlín	W	2-0	*Fillo, Jeřábek*
22/04	h Karviná	W	1-0	*Hora*
30/04	h Slovácko	D	2-2	*Fillo 2 (1p)*
07/05	a Hradec Králové	W	2-0	*Vošahlík, Vaněček*
14/05	h Bohemians 1905	W	1-0	*Jeřábek*
20/05	a Jablonec	D	0-0	
27/05	h Dukla	L	0-1	

No	Name	Nat	DoB	Pos	Aps	(s)	Gls
11	Marek Červenka		17/12/92	A	11	(4)	4
23	Martin Chudý	SVK	23/04/89	G	4		
15	Patrik Dressler		30/10/90	D		(4)	
7	Martin Fillo		07/02/86	M	28		8
30	Tomáš Grigar		01/02/83	G	26		
13	Jakub Hora		23/02/91	M	26		5
20	Robert Hrubý		27/04/94	D	8		
16	Alois Hyčka		22/07/90	D	6	(4)	
18	Michal Jeřábek		10/09/93	D	29		3
22	Petr Kodeš		31/01/96	M	4	(5)	
20	Alex Král		19/05/98	M	1	(2)	
24	Jan Krob		27/04/87	D	23	(1)	
27	Tomáš Kučera		20/07/91	M	22		1
14	Davor Kukec	CRO	16/03/86	M		(3)	
5	Admir Ljevaković	BIH	07/08/84	M	26		1
6	Michael Lüftner		14/03/94	D	14		1
10	Nivaldo	CPV	10/07/88	M	6	(4)	1
31	Jan Plachý		07/05/98	G		(1)	
26	Roman Potočný		25/04/91	A	5	(9)	2
19	Soune Soungole	CIV	26/02/95	M	10	(2)	
15	Aleksandar Šušnjar	SRB	19/08/95	D	13		
23	Zurab Tsiskaridze	GEO	08/09/86	D	1	(1)	
2	Otto Urma		17/08/94	D	11		
8	Štěpán Vachoušek		26/07/79	M	5	(17)	
28	David Vaněček		09/03/91	A	14	(14)	7
17	Tomáš Vondrášek		26/10/87	D	29		1
26	Jan Vošahlík		08/03/89	A	8	(6)	3

FC Viktoria Plzeň

1911 • Doosan Arena (11,700) • fcviktoria.cz

Major honours
Czech League (4) 2011, 2013, 2015, 2016; Czech Cup (1) 2010

Coach: Roman Pivarník; (02/04/17) (Zdeněk Bečka)

2016				
30/07	a Jihlava	W	2-1	*Kučera, Kopic*
07/08	h Bohemians 1905	D	1-1	*Kopic*
12/08	a Příbram	W	3-0	*Bakoš (p), Ďuriš, Kovařík*
20/08	h Zlín	L	0-2	
28/08	h Slavia	W	3-1	*Petržela, Hejda, Krmenčík*
10/09	a Liberec	W	2-1	*Hromada, Ďuriš*
18/09	h Karviná	W	2-0	*Hořava 2 (1p)*
24/09	a Teplice	W	1-0	*Bakoš*
02/10	h Hradec Králové	W	4-1	*Hejda, Krmenčík 2, og (Chleboun)*
15/10	a Slovácko	D	1-1	*Hejda*
23/10	h Sparta	W	1-0	*Krmenčík*
30/10	a Dukla	W	1-0	*Hořava*
06/11	h Jablonec	W	3-1	*Hořava, Hrošovský, Hejda*
19/11	a Mladá Boleslav	D	0-0	
27/11	h Brno	W	2-0	*Krmenčík, Ďuriš*
2017				
18/02	h Příbram	W	1-0	*Krmenčík*
25/02	a Zlín	D	0-0	
05/03	a Slavia	L	0-1	
11/03	h Liberec	W	1-0	*og (Kúdela)*
15/03	a Bohemians 1905	W	1-0	*Bakoš*
19/03	a Karviná	W	3-2	*Bakoš, Ivanschitz, Hořava*
01/04	h Teplice	D	2-2	*Hořava, Bakoš*
07/04	a Hradec Králové	W	1-0	*Hejda*
16/04	h Slovácko	W	2-0	*Krmenčík, Bakoš (p)*
23/04	a Sparta	L	0-2	
29/04	h Dukla	W	2-0	*Petržela, Bakoš (p)*
06/05	a Jablonec	D	2-2	*Ivanschitz 2*
12/05	h Mladá Boleslav	D	3-3	*Krmenčík 2, Hejda*
20/05	a Brno	W	1-0	*Krmenčík*
27/05	h Jihlava	W	2-0	*Bakoš, og (Štěpánek)*

No	Name	Nat	DoB	Pos	Aps	(s)	Gls
23	Marek Bakoš	SVK	15/04/83	A	16	(6)	8
22	Jan Baránek		26/06/93	D	3	(4)	
13	Petr Bolek		13/06/84	G	4		
20	Martin Chrien	SVK	08/09/95	M	1	(2)	
12	Michal Ďuriš	SVK	01/06/88	A	5	(6)	3
21	Tomáš Hájek		01/12/91	D	3	(2)	
2	Lukáš Hejda		09/03/90	D	27		6
7	Tomáš Hořava		29/05/88	M	28		6
25	Jakub Hromada	SVK	25/05/96	M	14	(4)	1
17	Patrik Hrošovský	SVK	22/04/92	M	22	(3)	1
4	Roman Hubník		06/06/84	D	28	(1)	
33	Andreas Ivanschitz	AUT	15/10/83	M	5	(3)	3
5	Erik Janža	SVK	21/06/93	D	3		
20	Ergys Kaçe	ALB	08/07/93	M	2	(2)	
26	Daniel Kolář		27/10/85	M	3		
10	Jan Kopic		04/06/90	M	17	(5)	2
19	Jan Kovařík		19/06/88	M	6	(12)	1
1	Matúš Kozáčik	SVK	27/12/83	G	26		
15	Michael Krmenčík		15/03/93	A	16	(9)	10
29	Tomáš Kučera		20/07/91	M	2	(1)	1
8	David Limberský		06/10/83	D	24		
3	Aleš Matějů		03/06/96	D	14	(2)	
11	Milan Petržela		19/06/83	M	21	(2)	2
6	Václav Pilař		13/12/88	M	2	(4)	
18	Tomáš Poznar		27/09/88	A	6	(10)	
27	František Rajtoral		12/03/86	D	2	(1)	
14	Radim Řezník		20/01/89	D	16	(2)	
30	Dominik Sváček		24/02/97	G		(1)	
9	Martin Zeman		28/03/89	M	14	(2)	

FC Vysočina Jihlava

1948 • Stadion v Jiráskově ulici (4,500) • fcvysocina.cz

Coach: Michal Hipp (SVK); (14/09/16) Michal Bílek; (11/04/17) Josef Jinoch

2016				
30/07	h Plzeň	L	1-2	*Ikaunieks*
07/08	a Liberec	D	1-1	*Urdinov (p)*
14/08	h Slavia	D	1-1	*Ikaunieks*
20/08	a Hradec Králové	L	0-1	
26/08	h Teplice	L	0-2	
10/09	a Karviná	L	0-3	
17/09	h Jablonec	D	1-1	*Rabušic*
24/09	a Slovácko	D	1-1	*Ikaunieks*
30/09	h Bohemians 1905	L	0-2	
16/10	a Sparta	L	0-3	
21/10	h Dukla	D	1-1	*Zoubele*
29/10	a Brno	D	1-1	*Dvořák*
04/11	h Mladá Boleslav	W	2-1	*Rabušic, Urblík*
18/11	h Zlín	L	1-3	*Dvořák*
26/11	a Příbram	D	0-0	
03/12	h Liberec	W	1-0	*Hronek*
2017				
18/02	a Slavia	L	0-2	
24/02	h Hradec Králové	W	3-1	*Ikaunieks 2, Dvořák*
04/03	a Teplice	L	0-1	
11/03	h Karviná	L	2-4	*Hronek, Dvořák*
19/03	a Jablonec	L	0-5	
01/04	h Slovácko	D	0-0	
08/04	a Bohemians 1905	L	0-1	
15/04	h Sparta	W	1-0	*Ikaunieks*
21/04	a Dukla	L	1-4	*Hronek*
28/04	h Brno	W	3-0	*Zoubele, Fulnek, Ikaunieks*
07/05	a Mladá Boleslav	L	1-3	*Popović*
13/05	a Zlín	W	3-0	*og (Hubáček), Ikaunieks 2*
20/05	h Příbram	D	1-1	*Hronek*
27/05	a Plzeň	L	0-2	

No	Name	Nat	DoB	Pos	Aps	(s)	Gls
27	Augusto Batioja	ECU	04/05/90	M	16	(8)	
2	Zvonimir Blaić	CRO	02/01/91	D	8	(1)	
21	Tomáš Duba		21/01/96	A		(3)	
28	Pavel Dvořák		19/02/89	A	20	(10)	4
22	Jakub Fulnek		26/04/94	M	9	(3)	1
1	Jan Hanuš		24/04/88	G	26		
21	Haris Harba	BIH	14/07/88	A		(1)	
2	Vojtěch Hron		15/04/95	D		(1)	
7	Petr Hronek		04/07/93	M	20	(3)	4
24	Dāvis Ikaunieks	LVA	07/01/94	M	22	(7)	9
5	Jiří Krejčí		22/03/86	D	28		
15	Lukáš Kryštůfek		11/08/92	D	2	(1)	
23	Milan Mišůn		21/02/90	D	12	(2)	
8	Filip Novotný		17/08/95	M	3	(1)	
9	Martin Popović	BIH	18/08/94	M	5	(5)	1
14	Michael Rabušic		17/09/89	A	20	(7)	2
34	Matej Rakovan	SVK	14/03/90	G	4	(1)	
25	Antonín Rosa		12/11/86	D	23	(1)	
9	Rostislav Šamánek		09/08/89	A		(6)	
12	David Štěpánek		30/03/97	M	20	(4)	
20	Peter Šulek	SVK	21/09/88	D	6		
17	Petr Tlustý		17/01/86	D	17	(2)	
30	Jozef Urblík	SVK	22/08/96	M	15		1
18	Yani Urdinov	MKD	28/03/91	D	18	(1)	1
11	Lukáš Vaculík		06/06/83	M	23	(3)	
16	Čestmír Vitásek		17/02/97	M		(2)	
10	Jan Záviška		21/08/95	M		(6)	
19	Lukáš Zoubele		20/12/85	M	13	(7)	2

CZECH REPUBLIC

FC Zbrojovka Brno

1913 • Městský fotbalový stadion Srbská (10,200) • fczbrno.cz

Major honours
Czechoslovakian League (1) 1978

Coach: Svatopluk Habanec

Date		Opponent	Res	Score	Scorers
2016					
06/08	a	Karviná	D	1-1	*Řezníček*
13/08	h	Teplice	D	0-0	
21/08	a	Liberec	D	0-0	
27/08	h	Slovácko	W	1-0	*Polák*
11/09	a	Bohemians 1905	L	0-3	
17/09	h	Hradec Králové	D	1-1	*Škoda*
24/09	a	Dukla	L	2-4	*Škoda 2*
02/10	h	Sparta	D	3-3	*Škoda, Přichystal, Hyčka*
15/10	a	Jablonec	W	2-1	*Škoda, Řezníček*
19/10	h	Slavia	L	1-4	*Přichystal*
22/10	a	Mladá Boleslav	D	3-3	*Řezníček, og (Fleišman), Škoda*
29/10	h	Jihlava	D	1-1	*Škoda*
05/11	a	Zlín	L	1-2	*Škoda*
19/11	h	Příbram	D	2-2	*Škoda 2*
27/11	a	Plzeň	L	0-2	
03/12	h	Karviná	D	1-1	*Vraštil*
2017					
18/02	a	Teplice	D	1-1	*og (Vondrášek)*
25/02	h	Liberec	W	1-0	*Řezníček*
04/03	a	Slovácko	D	0-0	
11/03	h	Bohemians 1905	D	0-0	
19/03	a	Hradec Králové	D	0-0	
01/04	h	Dukla	D	0-0	
09/04	a	Sparta	L	2-3	*Polák, Tashchy*
15/04	h	Jablonec	W	2-0	*Tashchy, Řezníček*
22/04	h	Mladá Boleslav	L	2-3	*Přichystal, Zavadil*
28/04	a	Jihlava	L	0-3	
07/05	h	Zlín	W	2-0	*Řezníček, Pavlík*
13/05	a	Příbram	W	3-2	*Zavadil, Lutonský, Řezníček*
20/05	h	Plzeň	L	0-1	
27/05	a	Slavia	L	0-4	

No	Name	Nat	DoB	Pos	Aps	(s)	Gls
10	Musefiu Ashiru	NGA	26/06/94	M	10	(1)	
26	Radek Buchta		22/04/89	M	4	(5)	
24	Alois Hyčka		22/07/90	D	16		1
18	Tomáš Jablonský		21/06/87	D	11	(2)	
6	Mihailo Jovanović	SRB	14/02/89	D	2		
2	Tadas Kijanskas	LTU	06/09/85	D	25	(2)	
11	Ladislav Krejčí		20/04/99	M	7	(6)	
28	Matúš Lacko	SVK	14/04/87	M	8	(4)	
29	Francis Litsingi	CGO	09/10/86	M	3	(8)	
19	Milan Lutonský		10/08/93	M	24	(4)	1
1	Dušan Melichárek		29/11/83	G	30		
25	David Pašek		27/10/89	M	1	(9)	
4	Petr Pavlík		22/07/87	D	14		1
8	Jan Polák		14/03/81	M	24		2
21	Jakub Přichystal		25/10/95	A	12	(9)	3
37	Jakub Řezníček		26/05/88	A	29		7
32	Antonín Růsek		22/03/99	M		(3)	
14	Petr Rybička		14/01/96	A		(2)	
16	Jan Sedlák		25/10/94	D	12	(8)	
23	Michal Škoda		01/03/88	A	19	(1)	10
17	Jan Štohanzl		20/03/85	M	9	(2)	
15	Jakub Šural		01/07/96	D	23	(2)	
93	Borys Tashchy	UKR	26/07/93	A	9	(3)	2
9	Stanislav Vávra		20/07/93	A	4	(3)	
20	Vlastimil Veselý		06/05/93	G		(1)	
13	Lukáš Vraštil		07/03/94	D	20	(1)	1
10	Tomáš Weber		26/05/96	M		(1)	
7	Pavel Zavadil		30/04/78	M	14	(2)	2

FC Zlín

1919 • Letná (5,783) • fcfastavzlin.cz

Major honours
Czechoslovakian/Czech Cup (2) 1970, 2017

Coach: Bohumil Páník

Date		Opponent	Res	Score	Scorers
2016					
30/07	h	Příbram	W	2-0	*Hájek, Jugas*
08/08	a	Slavia	D	2-2	*Poznar, Holík*
13/08	h	Liberec	W	2-1	*Jugas, Hájek*
20/08	a	Plzeň	W	2-0	*Poznar, Diop*
29/08	h	Karviná	W	3-0	*Diop 2, Holík*
09/09	a	Slovácko	W	3-1	*Harba 2, Jordan*
19/09	h	Sparta	D	1-1	*Jugas*
24/09	a	Hradec Králové	W	2-0	*Diop, Vukadinović*
01/10	h	Jablonec	D	2-2	*Harba 2*
15/10	a	Teplice	L	0-2	
21/10	h	Bohemians 1905	D	1-1	*Kopečný*
29/10	a	Mladá Boleslav	W	2-1	*Vukadinović, Harba*
05/11	h	Brno	W	2-1	*Harba, Štípek*
18/11	a	Jihlava	W	3-1	*Diop, Hnaníček, Jordan*
26/11	h	Dukla	L	0-1	
02/12	h	Slavia	L	0-4	
2017					
20/02	a	Liberec	D	0-0	
25/02	h	Plzeň	D	0-0	
05/03	a	Karviná	L	0-1	
11/03	h	Slovácko	D	1-1	*Beauguel*
17/03	a	Sparta	D	0-0	
01/04	h	Hradec Králové	L	1-3	*Beauguel*
09/04	a	Jablonec	L	0-2	
15/04	h	Teplice	L	0-2	
22/04	a	Bohemians 1905	W	2-0	*Kopečný, Bartolomeu*
29/04	h	Mladá Boleslav	L	1-2	*Hnaníček*
07/05	a	Brno	L	0-2	
13/05	h	Jihlava	L	0-3	
20/05	a	Dukla	L	0-1	
27/05	a	Příbram	W	2-0	*Bartolomeu, Vukadinović*

No	Name	Nat	DoB	Pos	Aps	(s)	Gls
27	Ondřej Bačo		25/03/96	D	4	(1)	
25	Robert Bartolomeu		03/12/93	M	4	(5)	2
10	Jean-David Beauguel	FRA	21/03/92	A	3	(4)	2
29	Martin Blanař		22/09/95	D	1		
38	Šimon Chwaszcz		28/05/96	A		(3)	
7	Dame Diop	SEN	15/03/93	A	15	(3)	5
30	Stanislav Dostál		30/06/91	G	24		
15	Antonín Fantiš		15/04/92	M	8	(9)	
18	Zoran Gajić	SRB	15/05/90	D	13		
18	Tomáš Hájek		01/12/91	D	15		2
28	Haris Harba	BIH	14/07/88	A	10	(1)	6
8	Patrik Helebrand		16/05/99	M	1		
21	Josef Hnaníček		28/12/86	M	22	(2)	2
9	Lukáš Holík		23/08/92	M	22	(6)	2
4	David Hubáček		23/07/77	D	6	(5)	
13	Tomáš Janíček		07/09/82	D	8	(9)	
29	Marko Jordan	CRO	27/10/90	A	3	(9)	2
24	Jakub Jugas		05/05/92	D	27		3
23	Miloš Kopečný		26/12/93	D	18	(7)	2
36	Tomáš Masař		22/10/96	M		(2)	
16	Róbert Matejov	SVK	05/07/88	D	25		
26	Vít Mlýnek		20/02/97	M		(2)	
20	Lukáš Pazdera		06/03/87	D	19	(2)	
10	Tomáš Poznar		27/09/88	A	5		2
6	David Štípek		31/05/92	M	16	(3)	1
44	Milan Švenger		06/07/86	G	6		
12	Ibrahim Traoré	CIV	16/09/88	M	18	(5)	
11	Vukadin Vukadinović	SRB	14/12/90	M	24	(5)	3
22	Diego Živulić	CRO	23/03/92	M	13	(1)	

Top goalscorers

Goals	Player
15	Milan Škoda (Slavia)
	David Lafata (Sparta)
12	Muris Mešanović (Slavia)
10	Michael Krmenčík (Plzeň)
	Michal Škoda (Brno)
9	Jan Chramosta (Mladá Boleslav)
	Dāvis Ikaunieks (Jihlava)
8	Martin Doležal (Jablonec)
	Golgol Mebrahtu (Mladá Boleslav)
	Tomáš Pilík (Příbram)
	Martin Fillo (Teplice)
	Marek Bakoš (Plzeň)

Promoted clubs

SK Sigma Olomouc

1919 • Andrův stadion (12,541) • sigmafotbal.cz

Major honours
Czech Cup (1) 2012

Coach: Václav Jílek

FC Baník Ostrava

1922 • Městský stadion (15,123) • fcb.cz

Major honours
Czechoslovakian/Czech League (4) 1976, 1980, 1981, 2004; Czechoslovakian/Czech Cup (4) 1973, 1978, 1991, 2005

Coach: Vlastimil Petržela

Second level final table 2016/17

		Pld	W	D	L	F	A	Pts
1	SK Sigma Olomouc	30	21	6	3	59	22	69
2	FC Baník Ostrava	30	18	10	2	48	20	64
3	SFC Opava	30	19	6	5	61	33	63
4	FC Vlašim	30	16	6	8	61	34	54
5	SK Dynamo České Budějovice	30	12	10	8	39	31	46
6	1. SC Znojmo	30	11	8	11	49	47	41
7	FK Pardubice	30	10	9	11	31	33	39
8	FK Ústí nad Labem	30	10	7	13	34	41	37
9	FK Viktoria Žižkov	30	10	9	11	49	41	36
10	FC MAS Táborsko	30	9	9	12	38	48	36
11	FK Varnsdorf	30	10	5	15	44	46	35
12	FK Fotbal Třinec	30	9	7	14	40	52	34
13	FK Baník Sokolov	30	7	11	12	28	44	32
14	FC Vítkovice	30	9	4	17	35	47	31
15	MFK Frýdek-Místek	30	7	8	15	40	57	29
16	1. SK Prostějov	30	3	3	24	20	80	12

NB FK Viktoria Žižkov – 3 pts deducted.

DOMESTIC CUP

Pohár FAČR 2016/17

SECOND ROUND

(09/08/16)
Nový Jičín 1-2 Karviná

(10/08/16)
Admira Praha 1-4 Hradec Králové
Benátky nad Jizerou 2-5 Vlašim *(aet)*
Český Brod 3-4 České Budějovice
Chrudim 1-0 Vítkovice *(aet)*
Hlučín 2-1 Frýdek-Místek *(aet)*
Jiskra Domažlice 1-4 Jablonec
Klatovy 1-9 Vysočina Jihlava
Králův Dvůr 1-0 Teplice
Líšeň 1-3 Prostějov
Loko Vltavín 1-2 Táborsko
Písek 3-0 Varnsdorf
Převýšov 0-3 Dukla Praha
Slavičín 1-3 Zbrojovka Brno
Slavoj Polná 1-10 Sigma Olomouc
Sokol Živanice 0-1 Pardubice
Spartak Hulín 2-1 Znojmo
Štěchovice 2-3 Bohemians 1905
Šumperk 1-4 Opava
Tachov 1-1 Viktoria Žižkov *(aet; 5-4 on pens)*
Uničov 1-3 Slovácko

(16/08/16)
Litoměřicko 3-1 Příbram

(17/08/16)
Velké Meziříčí 2-1 Fotbal Třinec

(23/08/16)
Benešov 2-4 Ústí nad Labem
Břeclav 0-6 Baník Ostrava
Třebíč 0-4 Zlín

(24/08/16)
Sokol Zápy 2-1 Baník Sokolov

Byes – Mladá Boleslav, Slavia Praha, Slovan Liberec, Sparta Praha, Viktoria Plzeň

THIRD ROUND

(14/09/16)
Sokol Zápy 1-2 Mladá Boleslav

(20/09/16)
Pardubice 1-3 Vysočina Jihlava
Sigma Olomouc 1-2 Táborsko
Spartak Hulín 0-2 Bohemians 1905
Vlašim 0-1 Hradec Králové

(21/09/16)
Hlučín 0-7 Viktoria Plzeň
Litoměřicko 2-1 Baník Ostrava
Ústí nad Labem 1-4 Zbrojovka Brno
Velké Meziříčí 1-2 Dukla Praha

(27/09/16)
Karviná 2-0 Prostějov *(aet)*

(28/09/16)
Chrudim 1-3 Slavia Praha

(05/10/16)
Tachov 0-4 Zlín

(11/10/16)
Králův Dvůr 1-1 Jablonec *(aet; 5-3 on pens)*
Slovácko 3-4 Opava *(aet)*

(12/10/16)
České Budějovice 1-2 Sparta Praha
Písek 1-5 Slovan Liberec

FOURTH ROUND

(26/10/16)
Bohemians 1905 3-1 Králův Dvůr
Mladá Boleslav 4-2 Hradec Králové
Opava 4-2 Viktoria Plzeň
Slavia Praha 7-0 Litoměřicko
Zbrojovka Brno 2-1 Vysočina Jihlava
Zlín 3-1 Sparta Praha *(aet)*

(30/11/16)
Karviná 2-2 Dukla Praha *(aet; 3-2 on pens)*

(01/03/17)
Táborsko 1-3 Slovan Liberec

QUARTER-FINALS

(26/03/17)
Opava 2-1 Zbrojovka Brno *(Janietzký 65, Schaffartzik 76; Řezníček 45)*

(04/04/17)
Bohemians 1905 1-1 Mladá Boleslav *(Mašek 75; Magera 59) (aet; 3-4 on pens)*

(05/04/17)
Slovan Liberec 2-4 Zlín *(Gajić 11og, Voltr 60; Vukadinović 52p, Matejov 57, Holík 95, Kopečný 119) (aet)*

(12/04/17)
Slavia Praha 5-2 Karviná *(Frydrych 24, Ščuk 38, Mingazov 49, Tecl 63, Bořil 68; Wágner 34, Lüftner 53og)*

SEMI-FINALS

(25/04/17)
Slavia Praha 0-1 Zlín *(Holík 31)*

(26/04/17)
Mladá Boleslav 0-2 Opava *(Helebrand 22, Jurečka 42)*

FINAL

(17/05/17)
Andrův stadion, Olomouc
FC ZLÍN 1 *(Bartolomeu 20)*
SFC OPAVA 0
Referee: *Příhoda*
ZLÍN: *Dostál, Kopečný, Jugas, Gajić, Matejov, Traoré, Hnaníček (Janíček 77), Vukadinović (Fantiš 86), Holík, Bartolomeu, Beauguel (Bačo 90+4)*
Red card: *Jugas (90+4)*
OPAVA: *Fendrich, Hrabina, Simerský, Žídek, Čelůstka (Pospěch 72), Janetzký, Radić (Jursa 55), Schaffartzik, Zapalač, Smola, Kuzmanović (Jurečka 60)*

Celebration time for the players of surprise Czech Cup winners FC Zlín

DENMARK

Dansk Boldspil-Union (DBU)

Address	House of Football DBU Allé 1 DK-2605 Brøndby
Tel	+45 43 262 222
Fax	+45 43 262 245
E-mail	dbu@dbu.dk
Website	dbu.dk

President	Jesper Møller Christensen
Chief executive	Claus Bretton-Meyer
Media officer	Jacob Høyer
Year of formation	1889
National stadium	Telia Parken (38,065)

SUPERLIGA CLUBS

 1 **Aalborg BK**

 2 **AGF Aarhus**

 3 **Brøndby IF**

 4 **Esbjerg fB**

 5 **AC Horsens**

 6 **FC København**

 7 **Lyngby BK**

 8 **FC Midtjylland**

 9 **FC Nordsjælland**

 10 **Odense BK**

 11 **Randers FC**

 12 **Silkeborg IF**

 13 **SønderjyskE**

 14 **Viborg FF**

PROMOTED CLUBS

 15 **Hobro IK**

 16 **FC Helsingør**

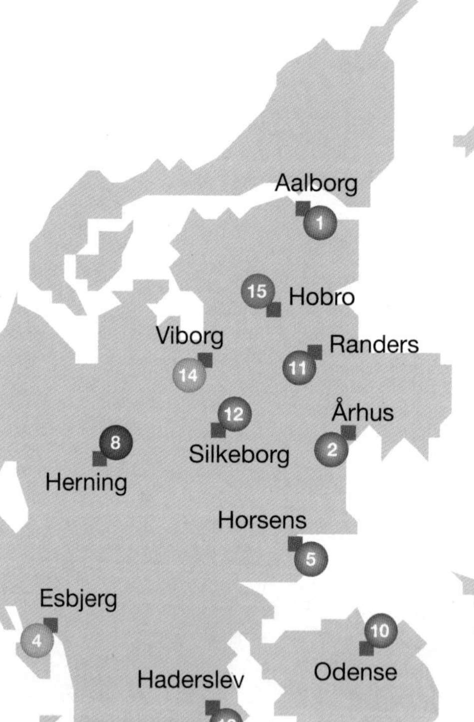

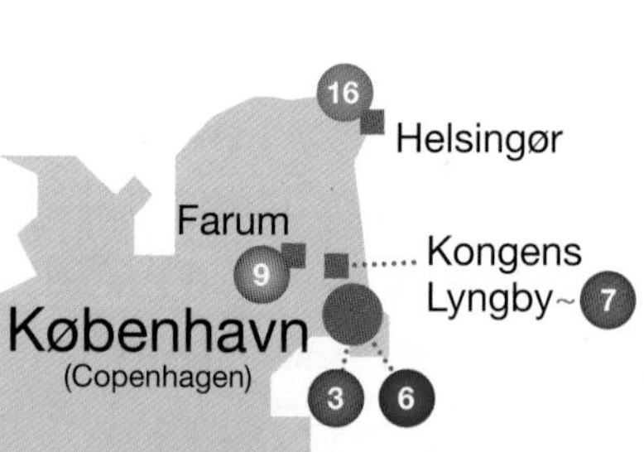

KEY

- UEFA Champions League
- UEFA Europa League
- Promoted
- Relegated

0 100 200 km
0 100 miles

Double double for FC København

A class apart from the competition, FC København defended their Superliga title with the utmost ease, Ståle Solbakken's side remaining undefeated until victory was complete despite a lengthy spell of overtime in Europe.

A reconfigured Superliga, based on the Belgian model with its multi-phase play-off structure and enlarged to include 14 clubs rather than the traditional 12, suffered from FCK's dominance, but there was excitement in the cup final, with the champions scoring twice late on to beat Brøndby, the distant league runners-up, and complete a second successive domestic double.

Capital club cruise unopposed to 12th league title

Cup final win against Brøndby seals repeat double

Play-offs all the rage in new-look Superliga

Domestic league

Having won their first league title for three years, and sixth in total under Solbakken's command, in 2015/16, there was never any chance of FCK resting on their laurels. Suitably reinforced in the summer transfer market, they started confidently and before long had opened up a big gap at the Superliga summit. Even with a busy schedule in the UEFA Champions League to negotiate, they reeled off nine straight wins in late autumn, which put them 11 points clear of Brøndby at the winter break.

By the end of the first phase, with 26 matches played and not one defeat staining their record, the defending champions' advantage was up to 12 points and a record 12th title was all but in the bag. Although Solbakken's team were the most prolific in the division with 74 goals, twin strikers Andreas Cornelius and Federico Santander scoring a dozen apiece, the crux of their success was a magnificent defence. It barely altered from game to game, with goalkeeper Robin Olsen, the new Sweden No1, protected by a rock-solid back four of Peter Ankersen, Mathias "Zanka" Jørgensen, Erik Johansson and Ludwig Augustinsson, and, in the midfield holding role, captain William Kvist.

The figures said it all. FCK conceded just 20 goals in their 36 matches and a mere four in their Telia Parken fortress, where they went unbreached for over six months in mid-campaign. It was only after the title was wrapped up that the champions lost a game, Midtjylland and Lyngby both doing the honours in FCK's last two away fixtures when their minds might have been focused on the upcoming Danish Cup final. Likewise Brøndby, who, having repeatedly impressed under their new German coach Alexander Zorniger, securing second place, lost their last five games.

In contrast, newly-promoted Lyngby won their last five to finish third and qualify for Europe. Midtjylland joined them and Brøndby in the UEFA Europa League but only after winning a play-off against Randers, who worked their way diligently through ten post-Superleague fixtures, only to end up short of their ultimate objective after a 3-0 defeat in Herning. Viborg and Esbjerg also fell foul of the new league system, surrendering their top-flight status in the promotion/relegation play-offs.

Domestic cup

FCK were seeking a Danish Cup hat-trick when they took on Brøndby at Telia Parken. It was only the second time the two Copenhagen clubs had met in the fixture, Brøndby having previously prevailed 4-1 in 1998. A Cornelius strike looked to have won the day for the champions until Brøndby's 20-goal scorer in the league, Finnish international Teemu Pukki, equalised nine minutes from time. But the underdogs were not level for long and further goals from Santander and Cornelius ensured an eighth cup win for their club – one behind AGF's all-time record.

Europe

FC København's formidable defence was a factor also in Europe, where the club played 16 games and lost only two – to Leicester City in the UEFA Champions League and Ajax in the last 16 of the UEFA Europa League. Astonishingly, the Dutch club were the only one of eight visitors to Telia Parken to score there, and somewhat ironically it was a Dane, Kasper Dolberg, who got the goal.

National team

Dolberg, who enjoyed a tremendous debut season in Amsterdam, was belatedly introduced to the Danish national side by Åge Hareide after a disappointing start to the 2018 FIFA World Cup qualifying campaign that brought back-to-back defeats against Poland away and, more damagingly, Montenegro at home. Ten points out of 18 left Denmark well adrift of leaders Poland but level on points with Montenegro and firmly in contention for a play-off berth.

DOMESTIC SEASON AT A GLANCE

Superliga 2016/17 final tables

Championship play-offs	Pld	Home W	D	L	F	A	Away W	D	L	F	A	Total W	D	L	F	A	Pts
1 FC København	**36**	**15**	**3**	**0**	**43**	**4**	**10**	**6**	**2**	**31**	**16**	**25**	**9**	**2**	**74**	**20**	**84**
2 Brøndby IF	36	9	4	5	35	22	9	4	5	27	18	18	8	10	62	40	62
3 Lyngby BK	36	8	5	5	19	14	9	2	7	23	21	17	7	12	42	35	58
4 FC Midtjylland	36	9	5	4	37	25	6	4	8	30	28	15	9	12	67	53	54
5 FC Nordsjælland	36	7	4	7	32	27	6	6	6	27	28	13	10	13	59	55	49
6 SønderjyskE	36	7	5	6	24	20	5	5	8	20	34	12	10	14	44	54	46

First phase	Pld	Home W	D	L	F	A	Away W	D	L	F	A	Total W	D	L	F	A	Pts
1 FC København	26	11	2	0	33	2	8	5	0	24	8	19	7	0	57	10	64
2 Brøndby IF	26	8	3	2	30	14	7	4	2	22	9	15	7	4	52	23	52
3 Lyngby BK	26	5	4	4	9	8	6	2	5	16	15	11	6	9	25	23	39
4 SønderjyskE	26	5	5	3	13	10	5	4	4	17	22	10	9	7	30	32	39
5 FC Midtjylland	26	5	5	3	24	16	5	3	5	20	13	10	8	8	44	29	38
6 FC Nordsjælland	26	5	3	5	23	21	4	5	4	18	20	9	8	9	41	41	35
7 Randers FC	26	6	2	5	14	15	3	4	6	12	17	9	6	11	26	32	33
8 Aalborg BK	26	6	4	3	17	12	3	2	8	11	26	9	6	11	28	38	33
9 Silkeborg IF	26	6	3	4	20	22	1	6	6	11	24	7	9	10	31	46	30
10 AC Horsens	26	4	4	5	15	22	3	4	6	14	23	7	8	11	29	45	29
11 Odense BK	26	5	2	6	14	11	2	5	6	12	21	7	7	12	26	32	28
12 AGF Aarhus	26	3	3	7	17	23	3	4	6	16	17	6	7	13	33	40	25
13 Viborg FF	26	2	5	6	12	21	4	2	7	17	19	6	7	13	29	40	25
14 Esbjerg fB	26	3	7	3	20	21	2	2	9	8	27	5	9	12	28	48	24

NB After 26 rounds the top six clubs enter a championship play-off, with clubs placed 7-14 entering two play-off groups. Full points and goals totals are carried forward.

European qualification 2017/18

Champion/Cup winner: FC København (second qualifying round)

Brøndby IF (second qualifying round)
Lyngby BK (first qualifying round)
FC Midtjylland (first qualifying round)

Top scorer Marcus Ingvartsen (Nordsjælland), 23 goals
Relegated clubs Esbjerg fB, Viborg FF
Promoted clubs Hobro IK, FC Helsingør
Cup final FC København 3-1 Brøndby IF

Player of the season

Hany Mukhtar
(Brøndby IF)

A German youth international at every age group, Mukhtar did not find his way into his country's triumphant Under-21 squad in Poland, but many followers of Danish football would have been wondering why after the young attacking midfielder's scintillating debut season in the Superliga with Brøndby. While FC København were unquestionably the best team in the land, their arch-rivals boasted arguably the most entertaining individual in the 22-year-old schemer who was on loan to the club from Benfica. In April that move was made permanent.

Newcomer of the season

Marcus Ingvartsen
(FC Nordsjælland)

Nordsjælland only won as many games as they lost in 2016/17, finishing fifth, but the 2011/12 Danish champions would have been in a much more difficult situation had it not been for the sudden emergence in their ranks of a serial goalscorer. Tall, raw and largely unknown, Ingvartsen rattled in 23 Superliga goals to claim the golden boot. He also found the net with impressive regularity for the Danish Under-21 side, helping them qualify in style for the finals in Poland, where he scored again in the team's closing 4-2 win against the Czech Republic.

Team of the season
(4-4-2)

Coach: Nielsen *(Lyngby)*

NATIONAL TEAM

International honours
UEFA European Championship (1) 1992

International tournament appearances
FIFA World Cup (4) 1986 (2nd round), 1998 (qtr-finals), 2002 (2nd round), 2010
UEFA European Championship (8) 1964 (4th), 1984 (semi-finals), 1988, 1992 (Winners), 1996, 2000, 2004 (qtr-finals), 2012

Top five all-time caps
Peter Schmeichel (129); Dennis Rommedahl (126); Jon Dahl Tomasson (112); Thomas Helveg (109); Michael Laudrup (104)

Top five all-time goals
Poul "Tist" Nielsen & Jon Dahl Tomasson (52); Pauli Jørgensen (44); Ole Madsen (42); Preben Elkjær (38)

Results 2016/17

Date	Opponent		Venue		Score	Scorers
31/08/16	Liechtenstein	H	Horsens	W	5-0	*N Jørgensen (30, 33), Cornelius (49), Fischer (62), Stryger (84)*
04/09/16	Armenia (WCQ)	H	Copenhagen	W	1-0	*Eriksen (17)*
08/10/16	Poland (WCQ)	A	Warsaw	L	2-3	*Glik (49og), Poulsen (69)*
11/10/16	Montenegro (WCQ)	H	Copenhagen	L	0-1	
11/11/16	Kazakhstan (WCQ)	H	Copenhagen	W	4-1	*Cornelius (15), Eriksen (36p, 90+2), Ankersen (78)*
15/11/16	Czech Republic	A	Mlada Boleslav	D	1-1	*N Jørgensen (38)*
26/03/17	Romania (WCQ)	A	Cluj-Napoca	D	0-0	
06/06/17	Germany	H	Brondby	D	1-1	*Eriksen (18)*
10/06/17	Kazakhstan (WCQ)	A	Almaty	W	3-1	*N Jørgensen (27), Eriksen (51p), Dolberg (81)*

Appearances 2016/17

Coach: Åge Hareide (NOR)	23/09/53		Lie	ARM	POL	MNE	KAZ	Cze	ROU	Ger	KAZ	Caps	Goals
Frederik Rønnow	04/08/92	Brøndby	G	G			G	G		G	G	6	-
Simon Kjær	26/03/89	Fenerbahçe (TUR)	D46	D	D	D	D	D78	D46		D	68	3
Andreas Christensen	10/04/96	Mönchengladbach (GER)	D	D	D	D			D	D46		12	-
Jannik Vestergaard	03/08/92	Mönchengladbach (GER)	D	D	D82			s46	D	D	D	15	1
Peter Ankersen	22/09/90	København	M	M	M	M	D	s78	M			19	1
William Kvist	24/02/85	København	M65	M	M		M		M	M46	M46	71	2
Pierre Højbjerg	05/08/95	Southampton (ENG)	M46	M81	M	M63						21	1
Christian Eriksen	14/02/92	Tottenham (ENG)	M	M	M	M	M		A	M65	M	69	14
Riza Durmisi	08/01/94	Betis (ESP)	M65	M	M	M	D	M	M	D65	D	20	-
Nicolai Jørgensen	15/01/91	Feyenoord (NED)	A76	A66	A46	s83	A	A46		A76	A	24	7
Viktor Fischer	09/06/94	Middlesbrough (ENG)	A65	A	A75	A70		A				15	3
Andreas Cornelius	16/03/93	København	s46			s70	A82		A			12	3
Thomas Delaney	03/09/91	København /Bremen (GER)	s46	s81	s82	M	M		M	M	M	17	-
Mathias "Zanka" Jørgensen	23/04/90	København	s65			D83		D	s46	s46		11	-
Jens Stryger	21/02/91	Austria Wien (AUT)	s65					M		D	D82	4	1
Daniel Wass	31/05/89	Celta (ESP)	s65					M66				16	-
Yussuf Poulsen	15/06/94	RB Leipzig (GER)	s76	s66	s46	A	A			A76	A68	20	3
Kasper Schmeichel	05/11/86	Leicester (ENG)			G	G			G			25	-
Pione Sisto	04/02/95	Celta (ESP)			s75	s63						4	-
Andreas Bjelland	11/07/88	Brentford (ENG)					D	D46				23	2
Kasper Dolberg	06/10/97	Ajax (NED)					s82			s76	s68	3	1
Mike Jensen	19/02/88	Rosenborg (NOR)						M				4	-
Lasse Schöne	27/05/86	Ajax (NED)						M	M69	s46	s46	30	3
Christian Gytkjær	06/05/90	Rosenborg (NOR)						s46				1	-
Lucas Andersen	13/09/94	Grasshoppers (SUI)						s66				3	-
Martin Braithwaite	05/06/91	Toulouse (FRA)							s69	A	A	17	1
Lukas Lerager	12/07/93	Zulte Waregem (BEL)								s65		1	-
Frederik Sørensen	14/04/92	Köln (GER)								s65		1	-
Lasse Vibe	22/02/87	Brentford (ENG)								s76		11	1
Henrik Dalsgaard	27/07/89	Zulte Waregem (BEL)									s82	4	-

EUROPE

FC København

Second qualifying round - Crusaders FC (NIR)
A 3-0 *Santander (6), Cornelius (40), Falk (53)*
Olsen, Augustinsson, Johansson, Kvist (Greguš 59), Delaney, Cornelius, Kusk (Toutouh 76), Santander (Kadrii 73), Ankersen, Jørgensen, Falk. Coach: Ståle Solbakken (NOR)
H 6-0 *Pavlović (15), Mitchell (45+1og), Cornelius (48, 76), Falk (58), Greguš (68)*
Andersen, Augustinsson, Cornelius, Antonsson, Greguš, Kusk, Remmer, Pavlović (Kadrii 63), Toutouh, Jørgensen (Keita 63), Falk (Amankwaa 63). Coach: Ståle Solbakken (NOR)

Third qualifying round - FC Astra Giurgiu (ROU)
A 1-1 *Delaney (64)*
Olsen, Augustinsson, Johansson, Kvist, Verbič (Amankwaa 80), Delaney, Cornelius, Santander, Ankersen, Toutouh (Falk 61), Jørgensen. Coach: Ståle Solbakken (NOR)
H 3-0 *Cornelius (14, 45+1), Santander (34)*
Olsen, Augustinsson, Johansson, Kvist, Verbič, Delaney, Cornelius (Pavlović 61), Santander (Kusk 83), Ankersen, Jørgensen, Falk (Toutouh 70). Coach: Ståle Solbakken (NOR)

Play-offs - APOEL FC (CYP)
H 1-0 *Pavlović (43)*
Olsen, Augustinsson, Johansson, Kvist, Verbič (Greguš 88), Delaney, Santander, Ankersen, Pavlović (Cornelius 67), Jørgensen, Falk (Toutouh 79). Coach: Ståle Solbakken (NOR)
A 1-1 *Santander (86)*
Olsen, Augustinsson, Johansson, Kvist, Verbič (Greguš 88), Delaney, Cornelius (Pavlović 80), Santander, Ankersen, Jørgensen, Falk (Toutouh 46). Coach: Ståle Solbakken (NOR)

Group G
Match 1 - FC Porto (POR)
A 1-1 *Cornelius (52)*
Olsen, Augustinsson, Johansson, Kvist (Antonsson 90+3), Delaney, Cornelius, Greguš, Santander (Verbič 69), Ankersen, Toutouh (Falk 77), Jørgensen. Coach: Ståle Solbakken (NOR)
Red card: Greguš 66
Match 2 - Club Brugge KV (BEL)
H 4-0 *Denswil (53og), Delaney (64), Santander (69), Jørgensen (90+2)*
Olsen, Augustinsson, Johansson, Kvist, Verbič (Toutouh 67), Delaney, Cornelius, Santander (Pavlović 79), Ankersen, Jørgensen, Falk (Amankwaa 84). Coach: Ståle Solbakken (NOR)
Match 3 - Leicester City FC (ENG)
A 0-1
Olsen, Augustinsson, Johansson, Kvist, Verbič (Falk 66), Delaney, Cornelius, Santander, Ankersen (Greguš 87), Toutouh (Pavlović 85), Jørgensen. Coach: Ståle Solbakken (NOR)
Match 4 - Leicester City FC (ENG)
H 0-0
Olsen, Augustinsson, Johansson, Kvist, Verbič (Kusk 83), Delaney, Cornelius, Santander, Ankersen, Jørgensen, Falk (Toutouh 65). Coach: Ståle Solbakken (NOR)
Match 5 - FC Porto (POR)
H 0-0
Olsen, Augustinsson, Johansson, Kvist, Verbič, Delaney, Ankersen, Pavlović, Toutouh (Greguš 75), Jørgensen, Falk (Kusk 75). Coach: Ståle Solbakken (NOR)
Match 6 - Club Brugge KV (BEL)
A 2-0 *Mechele (8og), Jørgensen (15)*
Olsen, Augustinsson, Johansson, Kvist, Delaney, Cornelius, Ankersen (Høgli 89), Pavlović (Keita 88), Toutouh, Jørgensen, Falk (Greguš 58). Coach: Ståle Solbakken (NOR)

Round of 32 - PFC Ludogorets Razgrad (BUL)
A 2-1 *Anicet Abel (2og), Toutouh (53)*
Olsen, Augustinsson, Johansson, Kvist, Cornelius, Santander (Pavlović 71), Ankersen, Toutouh (Høgli 90), Jørgensen, Falk (Greguš 71), Matic. Coach: Ståle Solbakken (NOR)
Red card: Greguš 90+6
H 0-0
Olsen, Augustinsson, Johansson, Cornelius, Santander (Pavlović 80), Ankersen, Toutouh, Jørgensen, Falk (Boilesen 89), Keita (Kusk 66), Matic. Coach: Ståle Solbakken (NOR)

Round of 16 - AFC Ajax (NED)
H 2-1 *Falk (1), Cornelius (60)*
Olsen, Augustinsson, Johansson, Kvist, Cornelius, Santander (Pavlović 63), Ankersen, Toutouh, Jørgensen, Falk, Matic. Coach: Ståle Solbakken (NOR)
A 0-2
Olsen, Augustinsson, Johansson, Kvist, Cornelius, Greguš (Verbič 57), Santander, Ankersen, Toutouh (Kusk 77), Okore (Boilesen 46), Matic. Coach: Ståle Solbakken (NOR)

SønderjyskE

Second qualifying round - Strømsgodset IF (NOR)
H 2-1 *Kløve (9), Uhre (82)*
Skender, Pedersen, Kroon, Dal Hende, Drachmann, Bechmann (Ritter 76), Kløve (Olesen 56), Guira, Kanstrup, Rømer (Uhre 63), Maak. Coach: Jakob Michelsen (DEN)
A 2-2 (aet) *Uhre (69), Kløve (120)*
Skender, Pedersen (Hedegaard 118), Kroon, Dal Hende, Drachmann, Absalonsen (Kløve 71), Uhre (Bechmann 80), Guira, Kanstrup, Rømer, Maak. Coach: Jakob Michelsen (DEN)

Third qualifying round - Zagłębie Lubin (POL)
A 2-1 *Kroon (19), Dal Hende (36)*
Skender, Pedersen, Kroon (Kløve 68), Dal Hende, Drachmann, Bechmann (Uhre 64), Absalonsen, Guira, Kanstrup, Rømer (Madsen 74), Maak. Coach: Jakob Michelsen (DEN)
H 1-1 *Pedersen (65)*
Skender, Pedersen, Kroon (Kløve 76), Dal Hende, Bechmann (Uhre 81), Madsen, Absalonsen, Guira, Kanstrup, Rømer, Maak. Coach: Jakob Michelsen (DEN)

Play-offs - AC Sparta Praha (CZE)
H 0-0
Skender, Pedersen, Dal Hende, Drachmann, Madsen, Absalonsen, Uhre (Kløve 74), Guira, Kanstrup, Rømer (Kroon 73), Maak. Coach: Jakob Michelsen (DEN)
A 2-3 *Uhre (35), Kløve (40)*
Skender, Pedersen, Dal Hende, Drachmann, Madsen, Absalonsen (Luijckx 87), Kløve (Kroon 76), Uhre, Kanstrup, Rømer (Mattila 83), Maak. Coach: Jakob Michelsen (DEN)

FC Midtjylland

First qualifying round - FK Sūduva (LTU)
H 1-0 *Onuachu (56)*
Dahlin, Hansen, Sparv (Halsti 90+1), J Poulsen, Pusic, Olsson (Duelund 55), Banggaard, Sisto (Kadlec 77), Onuachu, Nissen, Novák. Coach: Jess Thorup (DEN)
A 1-0 *Novák (16)*
Dahlin, Hansen (Riis 64), Halsti (Rømer 76), J Poulsen, Pusic, Olsson, Banggaard, Sisto, Hassan (Kadlec 55), Nissen, Novák. Coach: Jess Thorup (DEN)

Second qualifying round - FC Vaduz (LIE)
H 3-0 *Sisto (20, 82), Onuachu (73)*
Dahlin, Hansen, Halsti, J Poulsen, Pusic (Onuachu 68), Olsson, Banggaard, Sisto (Duelund 87), Hassan (Kadlec 72), Nissen, Novák. Coach: Jess Thorup (DEN)
A 2-2 *Sisto (41, 68)*
Dahlin, Hansen (Riis 57), Halsti (Olsson 69), J Poulsen, Kadlec, Banggaard, Sisto, Rømer, Onuachu (Duelund 57), Hassan, Nissen. Coach: Jess Thorup (DEN)
Red card: J Poulsen 45+2

Third qualifying round - Videoton FC (HUN)
A 1-0 *Novák (55)*
Dahlin, Hansen, Halsti, Kadlec (Rømer 71), Olsson, Banggaard, Sisto (Duelund 88), Onuachu, Hassan, Nissen, Novák. Coach: Jess Thorup (DEN)
H 1-1 (aet) *Novák (104)*
Dahlin, Hansen, Halsti, Kadlec (Duelund 69), Olsson (Larsen 109), Banggaard, Rømer (Pusic 80), Onuachu, Hassan, Nissen, Novák. Coach: Jess Thorup (DEN)

Play-offs - Osmanlıspor (TUR)
H 0-1
Dahlin, Hansen, Halsti (Rømer 61), J Poulsen, Kadlec, Olsson (Pusic 53), Banggaard, Onuachu (Duelund 78), Hassan, Nissen, Novák. Coach: Jess Thorup (DEN)
A 0-2
Dahlin, Hansen, Halsti, J Poulsen (Pusic 55), Kadlec (Van der Vaart 72), Olsson, Banggaard, Rømer, Hassan, Nissen, Novák (Duelund 62). Coach: Jess Thorup (DEN)

DOMESTIC LEAGUE CLUB-BY-CLUB

Brøndby IF

First qualifying round - Valur Reykjavík (ISL)

A 4-1 *Wilczek (47, 54), Pukki (61), Jakobsen (79)*

Rønnow, Juelsgård, Röcker, Pukki (Borring 69), Larsson, Boysen (Phiri 46), Nørgaard, Wilczek, Hjulsager (Holst 83), Jakobsen, Crone. Coach: Alexander Zorniger (GER)

H 6-0 *Wilczek (5), Hjulsager (15), Pukki (26, 57), Stückler (71, 90+3)*

Rønnow, Juelsgård, Röcker, Pukki, Larsson, Phiri (Holst 61), Nørgaard, Wilczek (Stückler 46), Hjulsager, Jakobsen (Da Silva 73), Crone. Coach: Alexander Zorniger (GER)

Second qualifying round - Hibernian FC (SCO)

A 1-0 *Wilczek (1)*

Rønnow, Röcker, Albrechtsen, Austin (Hjulsager 43), Holst, Larsson, Nørgaard, Wilczek, Da Silva, Stückler (Pukki 52), Jakobsen (Juelsgård 84). Coach: Alexander Zorniger (GER)

H 0-1 (aet; 5-3 on pens)

Rønnow, Röcker, Albrechtsen, Pukki (Stückler 114), Larsson, Phiri (Corlu 102), Nørgaard, Wilczek, Hjulsager, Jakobsen (Holst 64), Crone. Coach: Alexander Zorniger (GER)

Third qualifying round - Hertha BSC Berlin (GER)

A 0-1

Rønnow, Röcker, Albrechtsen, Pukki, Holst (Mukhtar 58), Larsson, Phiri, Nørgaard (Austin 78), Wilczek (Jakobsen 84), Hjulsager, Crone. Coach: Alexander Zorniger (GER)

H 3-1 *Pukki (3, 34, 52)*

Rønnow, Röcker, Albrechtsen, Pukki (Ureña 76), Mukhtar (Jakobsen 67), Larsson, Phiri, Nørgaard (Austin 76), Wilczek, Hjulsager, Crone. Coach: Alexander Zorniger (GER)

Play-offs - Panathinaikos FC (GRE)

A 0-3

Rønnow, Röcker, Albrechtsen, Pukki (Toppel 53), Mukhtar (Juelsgård 46), Larsson, Phiri, Nørgaard, Wilczek (Hermannsson 72), Hjulsager, Crone. Coach: Alexander Zorniger (GER)

Red cards: Crone 33, Rønnow 50

H 1-1 *Mukhtar (35)*

Toppel, Röcker, Hermannsson, Pukki (Jakobsen 83), Mukhtar, Holst (Ureña 67), Larsson, Phiri (Corlu 75), Nørgaard, Wilczek, Hjulsager. Coach: Alexander Zorniger (GER)

Aalborg BK

1885 • Aalborg Portland Park (13,800) • fodbold.aabsport.dk

Major honours
Danish League (4) 1995, 1999, 2008, 2014; Danish Cup (3) 1966, 1970, 2014

Coach: Lars Søndergaard; (02/01/17) Morten Wieghorst

2016

17/07	h	Horsens	D	1-1	*Holgersson*
24/07	a	Randers	W	1-0	*Meilinger*
01/08	h	OB	D	2-2	*Bassogog, Würtz*
07/08	a	Nordsjælland	W	2-1	*Meilinger, Holgersson*
15/08	h	Esbjerg	W	2-1	*Risgård, Enevoldsen*
20/08	a	København	D	1-1	*Bassogog*
28/08	h	AGF	W	2-1	*Flores, Bassogog*
11/09	h	Brøndby	L	0-1	
19/09	a	Lyngby	L	0-1	
22/09	h	Viborg	W	1-0	*Pedersen*
26/09	a	Silkeborg	L	3-5	*Meilinger, Pedersen, Blåbjerg*
02/10	h	SønderjyskE	L	0-1	
16/10	a	Midtjylland	L	0-2	
21/10	h	Nordsjælland	D	1-1	*Mæhle*
30/10	a	Brøndby	L	0-2	
04/11	a	Esbjerg	L	0-3	
18/11	h	København	L	1-2	*Børsting*
25/11	h	Randers	W	2-1	*og (Fenger), Børsting*
29/11	a	SønderjyskE	D	1-1	*Risgård (p)*
05/12	h	Lyngby	W	1-0	*Bassogog*
09/12	a	Horsens	L	0-3	

2017

19/02	a	AGF	W	2-1	*Sylvestr, Pohl*
26/02	h	Silkeborg	W	3-0	*Sylvestr 3*
06/03	a	OB	L	0-4	
13/03	h	Midtjylland	D	1-1	*Børsting*
19/03	a	Viborg	L	1-2	*Sylvestr (p)*
01/04	a	Silkeborg	D	0-0	
08/04	h	Viborg	L	0-1	
17/04	h	AGF	W	1-0	*Thellufsen*
24/04	a	AGF	L	0-4	
30/04	a	Viborg	D	1-1	*Børsting*
07/05	h	Silkeborg	L	0-1	

No	Name	Nat	DoB	Pos	Aps	(s)	Gls
27	Oliver Abildgaard		10/06/96	M	4	(7)	
3	Jakob Ahlmann		18/01/91	D	19	(3)	
17	Christian Bassogog	CMR	18/10/95	A	20	(1)	4
4	Jakob Blåbjerg		11/01/95	D	21		1
25	Frederik Børsting		13/02/95	M	20	(7)	4
16	Magnus Christensen		20/08/97	A	17	(7)	
7	Thomas Enevoldsen		27/07/87	M	10	(5)	1
10	Edison Flores	PER	14/05/94	M	8	(8)	1
29	Sebastian Grønning		03/02/97	A		(12)	
11	Nicklas Helenius		08/05/91	A	1	(2)	
5	Markus Holgersson	SWE	16/04/85	D	26		2
2	Patrick Kristensen		28/04/87	D	23	(4)	
1	Nicolai Larsen		09/03/91	G	32		
20	Marco Meilinger	AUT	08/08/91	M	26	(2)	3
31	Joakim Mæhle		20/05/97	D	19	(3)	1
32	Kasper Pedersen		13/01/93	D	21	(2)	2
9	Jannik Pohl		06/04/96	A	7	(10)	1
19	Marco Ramkilde		09/05/98	A		(2)	
21	Kasper Risgård		04/01/83	M	22	(4)	2
14	Casper Sloth		26/03/92	M	10	(10)	
11	Jakub Sylvestr	SVK	02/02/89	A	9	(2)	5
15	Gilli Sørensen	FRO	11/08/92	A	3		
18	Rasmus Thellufsen		09/01/97	D	8	(4)	1
8	Rasmus Würtz		18/09/83	M	26		1

AGF Aarhus

1880 • Ceres Park (20,032) • agf.dk

Major honours
Danish League (5) 1955, 1956, 1957, 1960, 1986; Danish Cup (9) 1955, 1957, 1960, 1961, 1965, 1987, 1988, 1992, 1996

Coach: Glen Riddersholm

2016

17/07	a	SønderjyskE	W	2-1	*Petersen, Amini*
22/07	h	Viborg	W	2-1	*Junker, Backman*
31/07	h	Randers	L	1-2	*Khodzhaniyazov*
08/08	a	Esbjerg	D	2-2	*Amini, Soares*
12/08	a	Lyngby	D	0-0	
21/08	h	Brøndby	L	0-7	
28/08	a	AaB	L	1-2	*Andersen*
12/09	h	Nordsjælland	W	3-1	*M Rasmussen 2, Juelsgård*
17/09	a	Silkeborg	L	0-1	
21/09	h	Midtjylland	D	1-1	*M Rasmussen*
24/09	a	København	L	0-2	
30/09	a	OB	L	1-2	*Amini*
14/10	h	Horsens	D	1-1	*Olsen*
23/10	a	Brøndby	L	0-1	
31/10	h	Esbjerg	W	6-2	*Juelsgård, Junker, Spelmann 2, Sverrisson, Andersen*
04/11	h	Silkeborg	D	0-0	
19/11	a	Nordsjælland	L	2-3	*Stage, Junker*
25/11	a	Horsens	W	5-1	*Sverrisson, M Rasmussen 3, Amini*
29/11	h	Lyngby	L	0-1	
04/12	a	Midtjylland	W	1-0	*Andersen*
11/12	h	København	L	0-1	

2017

19/02	h	AaB	L	1-2	*Ikonomidis*
27/02	a	Viborg	D	1-1	*Amini*
04/03	h	SønderjyskE	L	1-2	*M Rasmussen*
10/03	a	Randers	D	1-1	*M Rasmussen (p)*
19/03	h	OB	L	1-2	*M Rasmussen (p)*
02/04	a	Viborg	W	4-2	*Bundu, Olsen, Bjarnason, Petersen*
10/04	h	Silkeborg	L	1-3	*Olsen*
17/04	a	AaB	L	0-1	
24/04	h	AaB	W	4-0	*M Rasmussen 2 (1p), Juel-Nielsen 2*
01/05	a	Silkeborg	W	2-0	*M Rasmussen 2 (2p)*
07/05	h	Viborg	W	1-0	*Sverrisson*

No	Name	Nat	DoB	Pos	Aps	(s)	Gls
8	Mustafa Amini	AUS	20/04/93	M	29	(3)	5
5	Alexander Juel Andersen		29/01/91	D	21	(2)	3
3	Niklas Backman	SWE	13/11/88	D	21	(1)	1
20	Theódór Elmar Bjarnason	ISL	04/03/87	M	20	(6)	1
19	Mustapha Bundu	SLE	28/02/97	M	3	(6)	1
17	Oskar Buur		31/03/98	D		(1)	
6	Daniel Christensen		19/09/88	D	3	(1)	
34	Nimo Gribenco		23/01/97	M		(1)	
22	Benjamin Hvidt		12/03/00	M		(1)	
16	Christopher Ikonomidis	AUS	04/05/95	M	11	(7)	1
26	Aleksandar Jovanović	SRB	06/12/92	G	30		
21	Thomas Juel-Nielsen		18/06/90	D	4	(2)	2
18	Jesper Juelsgård		26/01/89	D	23		2
9	Kasper Junker		05/03/94	A	17	(9)	3
16	Jens Jønsson		10/01/93	M	4		
28	Dzhamaldin Khodzhaniyazov	RUS	18/07/96	D	19	(1)	1
2	Dino Mikanović	CRO	07/05/94	D	24	(1)	
11	Danny Olsen		11/06/85	M	12	(11)	3
4	Daniel Pedersen		27/07/92	M	14	(8)	
7	Stephan Petersen		15/11/85	M	10	(9)	2
15	Mikkel Rask		22/06/83	D	3	(1)	
13	Morten "Duncan" Rasmussen		31/01/85	A	22	(2)	13
1	Steffen Rasmussen		30/09/82	G	2	(1)	
15	Anthony Soares	USA	28/11/88	D	5	(1)	1
10	Martin Spelmann		21/03/87	M	25	(1)	2
14	Jens Stage		08/11/96	M	9	(7)	1
6	Björn Daníel Sverrisson	ISL	29/05/90	M	20	(4)	3
27	Michael Zacho		11/11/96	M	1	(8)	

DENMARK

Brøndby IF

1964 • Brøndby Stadion (28,000) • brondby.com

Major honours
Danish League (10) 1985, 1987, 1988, 1990, 1991, 1996, 1997, 1998, 2002, 2005; Danish Cup (6) 1989, 1994, 1998, 2003, 2005, 2008

Coach: Alexander Zorniger (GER)

Date		Opponent		Score	Scorers
2016					
17/07	h	Esbjerg	W	4-0	*Pukki, Wilczek, Hjulsager, Holst*
24/07	a	Silkeborg	W	2-0	*Hjulsager, Holst*
31/07	h	Horsens	D	2-2	*Hjulsager, Wilczek*
07/08	a	Midtjylland	D	3-3	*Pukki 3*
14/08	h	SønderjyskE	W	4-0	*Pukki 2, Hermannsson, Wilczek*
21/08	a	AGF	W	7-0	*Wilczek, og (Backman), Hjulsager 2, Mukhtar, Pukki 2 (1p)*
28/08	h	København	D	1-1	*Hjulsager*
11/09	a	AaB	W	1-0	*Wilczek*
18/09	h	Viborg	L	1-2	*Wilczek*
22/09	a	Lyngby	L	0-1	
25/09	h	OB	W	3-0	*Nørgaard, Mukhtar, Pukki*
02/10	h	Randers	D	2-2	*Wilczek, Mukhtar*
16/10	a	Nordsjælland	D	1-1	*Kliment*
23/10	h	AGF	W	1-0	*Mukhtar*
30/10	h	AaB	W	2-0	*Pukki (p), Wilczek*
06/11	a	Viborg	W	2-1	*Wilczek, Hjulsager*
20/11	a	OB	L	0-1	
27/11	h	Silkeborg	W	3-1	*Mukhtar, Pukki, Wilczek*
30/11	a	Randers	W	1-0	*Jakobsen*
04/12	a	Esbjerg	D	1-1	*Pukki*
11/12	h	Midtjylland	W	2-1	*Pukki 2*
2017					
19/02	a	København	D	0-0	
26/02	a	SønderjyskE	W	2-1	*Pukki (p), Nørgaard*
05/03	h	Nordsjælland	L	2-3	*Mukhtar, Pukki*
12/03	a	Horsens	W	2-0	*Austin, Nørgaard*
19/03	h	Lyngby	W	3-2	*Wilczek 3*
02/04	h	Midtjylland	W	3-2	*Phiri, Larsson, Nørgaard*
09/04	a	Lyngby	W	2-1	*Pukki 2*
17/04	h	København	L	0-1	
23/04	a	Nordsjælland	W	1-0	*Larsson*
30/04	h	SønderjyskE	D	1-1	*Nilsson*
07/05	a	Midtjylland	L	2-4	*Mensah, Pukki*
14/05	a	København	L	0-1	
18/05	h	Lyngby	L	0-2	
21/05	a	SønderjyskE	L	0-3	
28/05	h	Nordsjælland	L	1-2	*Pukki*

No	Name	Nat	DoB	Pos	Aps	(s)	Gls
5	Martin Albrechtsen		31/03/80	D		(2)	
23	Paulus Arajuuri	FIN	15/06/88	D	6	(2)	
8	Rodolph Austin	JAM	01/06/85	M	11	(12)	1
11	Jonas Borring		04/01/85	M		(1)	
17	Rezan Corlu		07/08/97	M	1	(3)	
27	Svenn Crone		20/05/95	D	22	(7)	
23	Patrick da Silva		23/10/94	D	1		
34	Christian Enemark		20/01/99	D	1	(1)	
6	Hjörtur Hermannsson	ISL	08/02/95	D	32		1
21	Andrew Hjulsager		15/01/95	M	18	(1)	7
12	Frederik Holst		24/09/94	M	17	(7)	2
25	Christian Jakobsen		27/03/93	M	3	(13)	1
2	Jesper Juelsgård		26/01/89	D	4		
7	Thomas Kahlenberg		20/03/83	M	1	(1)	
11	Zsolt Kalmár	HUN	09/06/95	M	8	(4)	
29	Jan Kliment	CZE	01/09/93	A	4	(14)	1
16	Adam Larsen Kwarasey	GHA	12/12/87	G	2		
13	Johan Larsson	SWE	05/05/90	D	33	(2)	2
14	Kevin Mensah		15/05/91	M	1	(7)	1
10	Hany Mukhtar	GER	21/03/95	M	28	(1)	6
22	Gustaf Nilsson	SWE	23/05/97	A	4	(7)	1
19	Christian Nørgaard		10/03/94	M	30	(1)	4
18	Lebogang Phiri	RSA	09/11/94	M	30	(4)	1
9	Teemu Pukki	FIN	29/03/90	A	31	(3)	20
4	Benedikt Röcker	GER	19/11/89	D	33	(1)	
1	Frederik Rønnow		04/08/92	G	34		
5	Gregor Sikošek	SVN	13/02/94	D	9	(1)	
24	Daniel Stückler		13/04/97	A	1		
15	Marcos Ureña	CRC	05/03/90	A	2	(11)	
36	Magnus Warming		08/06/00	A		(1)	
20	Kamil Wilczek	POL	14/01/88	A	29	(1)	13

Esbjerg fB

1924 • Blue Water Arena (16,942) • efb.dk

Major honours
Danish League (5) 1961, 1962, 1963, 1965, 1979; Danish Cup (3) 1964, 1976, 2013

Coach: Colin Todd (ENG); (05/12/16) Lars Lungi Sørensen

Date		Opponent		Score	Scorers
2016					
17/07	a	Brøndby	L	0-4	
23/07	h	København	L	0-4	
29/07	a	Viborg	L	1-2	*Pálsson*
08/08	h	AGF	D	2-2	*Mensah, Andersen*
15/08	a	AaB	L	1-2	*Nordvik*
22/08	h	OB	W	3-2	*Andersen, Hvilsom, Paulsen*
28/08	a	SønderjyskE	D	1-1	*Paulsen*
09/09	a	Midtjylland	L	0-3	
16/09	h	Randers	D	1-1	*Nordvik*
20/09	h	Silkeborg	D	0-0	
25/09	a	Nordsjælland	L	0-3	
01/10	a	Horsens	L	0-1	
17/10	h	Lyngby	D	2-2	*Lund, og (Christjansen)*
24/10	h	Midtjylland	L	1-3	*Mabil*
31/10	a	AGF	L	2-6	*Söder, Hvilsom*
04/11	h	AaB	W	3-0	*Pálsson, Söder 2*
21/11	a	Silkeborg	L	0-3	
27/11	h	Nordsjælland	D	2-2	*Söder, McGrath*
01/12	a	OB	W	1-0	*Jørgensen (p)*
04/12	h	Brøndby	D	1-1	*Söder*
11/12	a	Randers	W	2-0	*Mabil, Söder*
2017					
17/02	h	SønderjyskE	W	3-0	*Söder, Mabil, Tsimikas*
27/02	a	Lyngby	D	0-0	
03/03	h	Viborg	L	1-3	*Söder*
12/03	a	København	L	0-2	
19/03	h	Horsens	D	1-1	*Söder*
02/04	h	Randers	D	0-0	
07/04	a	OB	L	0-3	
15/04	h	Horsens	L	0-1	
22/04	a	Horsens	W	3-1	*Dreyer, Tsimikas, Söder*
28/04	a	Randers	D	0-0	
08/05	h	OB	D	1-1	*Mabil*

No	Name	Nat	DoB	Pos	Aps	(s)	Gls
8	Jeppe Andersen		06/12/92	M	12		2
40	Daniel Anyembe		22/07/98	D		(1)	
25	Jeppe Brinch		30/04/95	D	8		
21	Mark Brink		15/03/98	M	3	(9)	
39	Anders Dreyer		02/05/98	A	4	(2)	1
17	Emmanuel Oti Essigba	GHA	24/09/96	M	3	(1)	
32	Nikolaj Hagelskjær		06/05/90	D	12	(2)	
9	Mads Hvilsom		23/08/92	A	13	(11)	2
16	Jeppe Højbjerg		30/04/95	G	24		
1	Jonas Jensen		25/10/85	G	8		
18	Leon Jessen		11/06/86	D	12	(2)	
7	Jesper Jørgensen		09/05/84	M	14	(3)	1
2	Otar Kakabadze	GEO	27/06/95	D	9		
5	Georgios Katsikas	GRE	14/06/90	D	10		
26	Mathias Kristensen		21/03/97	M	6	(4)	
14	Jesper Lauridsen		27/03/91	D	8	(6)	
15	Ryan Laursen		14/04/92	D	11	(1)	
6	Magnus Lekven	NOR	13/01/88	M	1	(1)	
24	Marco Lund		30/06/96	D	19	(4)	1
10	Awer Mabil	AUS	15/09/95	M	18	(7)	4
22	Brent McGrath	AUS	18/06/91	A	11	(6)	1
33	Kevin Mensah		15/05/91	M	12	(1)	1
17	Casper Nielsen		29/04/94	M	16	(1)	
23	Andreas Nordvik	NOR	18/03/87	D	24		2
4	Gudlaugur Victor Pálsson	ISL	30/04/91	M	29	(1)	2
6	Lasha Parunashvili	GEO	14/02/93	M		(2)	
5	Bjørn Paulsen		02/07/91	M	16	(4)	2
3	Daniel Stenderup		31/05/89	D	7	(1)	
27	Robin Söder	SWE	01/04/91	A	24	(4)	10
38	Jacob Lungi Sørensen		03/03/98	D	7	(1)	
3	Konstantinos Tsimikas	GRE	12/05/96	D	8	(1)	2
11	Budu Zivzivadze	GEO	10/03/94	A	3	(4)	

AC Horsens

1994 • Casa Arena (10,495) • achorsens.dk

Coach: Bo Henriksen

Date		Opponent		Score	Scorers
2016					
17/07	a	AaB	D	1-1	*Sanneh*
24/07	h	SønderjyskE	D	1-1	*Sanneh*
31/07	a	Brøndby	D	2-2	*Finnbogason, Aabech*
05/08	a	Randers	L	0-1	
13/08	h	Silkeborg	D	3-3	*Aabech, Bjerregaard, Sanneh*
19/08	h	Lyngby	W	2-1	*Aabech, Finnbogason*
28/08	a	OB	W	1-0	*Hansson*
10/09	a	Viborg	W	4-2	*Kryger 2, Finnbogason (p), Bjerregaard*
18/09	h	København	L	0-2	
21/09	h	Nordsjælland	D	0-0	
25/09	a	Midtjylland	L	2-5	*Aabech (p), Hansson*
01/10	h	Esbjerg	W	1-0	*Finnbogason*
14/10	a	AGF	D	1-1	*Sanneh*
23/10	h	Randers	W	1-0	*Bjerregaard*
30/10	a	SønderjyskE	L	0-2	
06/11	h	Midtjylland	L	1-5	*Jespersen*
18/11	a	Lyngby	W	1-0	*Aabech (p)*
25/11	h	AGF	L	1-5	*Finnbogason*
30/11	a	Nordsjælland	L	1-2	*Aabech*
03/12	h	Viborg	L	1-2	*Hansson*
09/12	h	AaB	W	3-0	*Finnbogason, Aabech, O'Brien*
2017					
18/02	a	Silkeborg	L	0-1	
25/02	h	OB	D	1-1	*Hansson*
05/03	a	København	L	0-5	
12/03	h	Brøndby	L	0-2	
19/03	a	Esbjerg	D	1-1	*Finnbogason*
31/03	h	OB	D	0-0	
07/04	a	Randers	L	0-2	
15/04	a	Esbjerg	W	1-0	*Møller*
22/04	h	Esbjerg	L	1-3	*Kortegaard*
28/04	a	OB	L	1-2	*Helgason*
08/05	h	Randers	W	2-1	*Finnbogason, og (Bager)*

No	Name	Nat	DoB	Pos	Aps	(s)	Gls
19	Kim Aabech		31/05/83	A	23	(7)	7
3	Martin Albrechtsen		31/03/80	D	1	(1)	
29	André Bjerregaard		03/09/91	A	26	(5)	3
21	Steve Clark	USA	14/04/86	G	11		
1	Nicklas Dannevang		11/09/90	G	21		
24	Nicolai Dohn		18/08/98	M		(1)	
9	Kjartan Henry Finnbogason	ISL	09/07/86	A	14	(16)	8
14	Jonas Gemmer		31/01/96	M	5	(14)	
17	Hallur Hansson	FRO	08/07/92	M	29		4
2	Elfar Freyr Helgason	ISL	27/07/89	D	4	(1)	1
2	Doneil Henry	CAN	20/04/93	D	2	(2)	
8	Mikkel Jespersen		11/06/91	M	8	(15)	1
13	Thomas Kortegaard		02/07/84	M	10	(4)	1
10	Lasse Kryger		03/11/82	M	24	(2)	2
18	Jeppe Mehl		21/09/86	M	6	(9)	
12	Joseph Mensah	GHA	29/09/94	M		(7)	
5	Frederik Møller		08/07/93	D	30		1
7	Mathias Nielsen		02/03/91	D	22		
11	Peter Nymann		22/08/82	D	31		
4	Conor O'Brien	USA	20/10/88	M	30	(1)	1
20	Mikkel Qvist		22/04/93	D		(2)	
15	Bubacarr Sanneh	GAM	14/11/94	D	31		4
22	Mads Bech Sørensen		07/01/99	D	2	(4)	
16	Delphin Tshiembe	COD	07/12/91	M	22	(2)	
21	Patryk Wolański	POL	15/08/91	G		(1)	

FC København

1992 • Telia Parken (38,065) • fck.dk

Major honours
Danish League (12) 1993, 2001, 2003, 2004, 2006, 2007, 2009, 2010, 2011, 2013, 2016, 2017; Danish Cup (8) 1995, 1997, 2004, 2009, 2012, 2015, 2016, 2017

Coach: Ståle Solbakken (NOR)

Date		Opponent		Score	Scorers
2016					
16/07	h	Lyngby	W	3-0	*Toutouh, Verbič, Delaney*
23/07	a	Esbjerg	W	4-0	*Verbič, Falk, Delaney, Kusk*
30/07	h	Nordsjælland	W	4-0	*Pavlović, Falk, Kusk 2*
07/08	a	SønderjyskE	D	1-1	*Verbič*
13/08	h	Midtjylland	W	3-1	*Johansson, og (Dahlin), Toutouh*
20/08	h	AaB	D	1-1	*Cornelius*
28/08	a	Brøndby	D	1-1	*Pavlović*
10/09	h	OB	W	2-0	*Augustinsson (p), Cornelius*
18/09	a	Horsens	W	2-0	*Cornelius, Delaney*
21/09	a	Randers	D	2-2	*Santander 2*
24/09	h	AGF	W	2-0	*Santander, Kusk*
02/10	a	Viborg	D	0-0	
15/10	h	Silkeborg	W	2-0	*Falk, Cornelius*
23/10	a	OB	W	3-0	*Verbič, og (Tingager), Delaney*
30/10	a	Midtjylland	W	3-1	*Santander 2, Cornelius*
06/11	h	SønderjyskE	W	4-0	*Cornelius, Toutouh 2, Delaney*
18/11	a	AaB	W	2-1	*Delaney, Falk*
26/11	a	Lyngby	W	1-0	*Toutouh*
29/11	h	Viborg	W	4-0	*Greguš 2, Kusk, Ankersen*
03/12	h	Randers	W	1-0	*Falk*
11/12	a	AGF	W	1-0	*og (Andersen)*
2017					
19/02	h	Brøndby	D	0-0	
26/02	a	Nordsjælland	D	1-1	*Santander*
05/03	h	Horsens	W	5-0	*Santander 2, Ankersen, Cornelius, Toutouh, Pavlović*
12/03	h	Esbjerg	W	2-0	*Santander, Cornelius*
19/03	a	Silkeborg	W	3-1	*Santander, Cornelius, Matić*
03/04	a	SønderjyskE	W	2-1	*Pavlović, Santander*
09/04	h	Nordsjælland	D	1-1	*Verbič (p)*
17/04	a	Brøndby	W	1-0	*Verbič*
23/04	h	Midtjylland	W	3-1	*Cornelius 2, Ankersen*
30/04	h	Lyngby	W	3-0	*Pavlović 3*
05/05	a	Nordsjælland	D	1-1	*Cornelius*
14/05	h	Brøndby	W	1-0	*Kusk*
17/05	a	Midtjylland	L	2-3	*Ankersen 2*
21/05	a	Lyngby	L	1-3	*Pavlović*
28/05	h	SønderjyskE	W	2-0	*Santander, Matić*

No	Name	Nat	DoB	Pos	Aps	(s)	Gls
32	Danny Amankwaa		30/01/94	M		(8)	
1	Stephan Andersen		26/11/81	G	3		
22	Peter Ankersen		22/09/90	D	32		5
15	Mikael Antonsson	SWE	31/05/81	D	6	(2)	
3	Ludwig Augustinsson	SWE	21/04/94	D	31	(1)	1
20	Nicolai Boilesen		16/02/92	D	5	(3)	
11	Andreas Cornelius		16/03/93	A	21	(9)	12
8	Thomas Delaney		03/09/91	M	18	(1)	6
33	Rasmus Falk		15/01/92	M	16	(6)	5
16	Ján Greguš	SVK	29/01/91	M	12	(16)	2
2	Tom Høgli	NOR	24/02/84	D	4	(5)	
5	Erik Johansson	SWE	30/12/88	D	28		1
25	Mathias "Zanka" Jørgensen		23/04/90	D	33		
9	Bashkim Kadrii		09/07/91	M		(1)	
35	Aboubakar Keita	CIV	05/11/97	M		(2)	
17	Kasper Kusk		10/11/91	M	14	(16)	6
6	William Kvist		24/02/85	M	29	(1)	
8	Uroš Matić	SRB	23/05/90	M	13	(2)	2
26	Jores Okore		11/08/92	D	3	(2)	
31	Robin Olsen	SWE	08/01/90	G	33		
23	Andrija Pavlović	SRB	16/11/93	A	25	(10)	8
27	Mads Roerslev		24/06/99	D	2	(1)	
19	Federico Santander	PAR	04/06/91	A	24	(4)	12
24	Youssef Toutouh		06/10/92	M	23	(10)	5
7	Benjamin Verbič	SVN	27/11/93	M	21	(6)	6

Lyngby BK

1921 • Lyngby Stadion (10,000) • lyngby-boldklub.dk

Major honours
Danish League (2) 1983, 1992; Danish Cup (3) 1984, 1985, 1990

Coach: David Nielsen

Date		Opponent		Score	Scorers
2016					
16/07	a	København	L	0-3	
24/07	h	OB	D	2-2	*Kjær 2*
31/07	a	SønderjyskE	W	1-0	*Rygaard*
05/08	a	Silkeborg	W	4-0	*Christjansen, K Larsen, Kjær, Fosgaard*
12/08	h	AGF	D	0-0	
19/08	a	Horsens	L	1-2	*Rygaard*
26/08	h	Nordsjælland	L	0-1	
09/09	a	Randers	L	0-2	
19/09	h	AaB	W	1-0	*K Larsen*
22/09	h	Brøndby	W	1-0	*Kjær*
25/09	a	Viborg	W	1-0	*Kjær*
02/10	h	Midtjylland	W	1-0	*K Larsen*
17/10	a	Esbjerg	D	2-2	*Rygaard, Christjansen*
22/10	h	SønderjyskE	W	2-0	*Ojo, Christjansen*
29/10	h	Randers	L	0-2	
06/11	a	OB	W	2-1	*Kjær 2*
18/11	h	Horsens	L	0-1	
26/11	h	København	L	0-1	
29/11	a	AGF	W	1-0	*Kjær*
05/12	a	AaB	L	0-1	
10/12	h	Silkeborg	D	1-1	*Blume*
2017					
17/02	a	Nordsjælland	W	1-0	*Boysen*
27/02	h	Esbjerg	D	0-0	
03/03	a	Midtjylland	D	1-1	*Kjær*
11/03	h	Viborg	W	1-0	*Brandrup*
19/03	a	Brøndby	L	2-3	*Kjær, Odgaard*
31/03	a	Nordsjælland	L	0-2	
09/04	h	Brøndby	L	1-2	*Christjansen*
16/04	h	Midtjylland	D	2-2	*og (Hansen), Odgaard*
21/04	a	SønderjyskE	W	2-1	*Lumb, Tauber*
30/04	a	København	L	0-3	
07/05	h	SønderjyskE	W	2-0	*Brandrup, Ojo*
12/05	h	Nordsjælland	W	2-1	*Ojo, Boysen (p)*
18/05	a	Brøndby	W	2-0	*Ørnskov, K Larsen*
21/05	h	København	W	3-1	*Rygaard, Jónasson, Odgaard*
28/05	a	Midtjylland	W	3-0	*Blume, Rygaard, Kjær*

No	Name	Nat	DoB	Pos	Aps	(s)	Gls
11	Danilo Arrieta		10/02/87	M		(2)	
22	Bror Blume		22/01/92	A	20	(8)	2
21	David Boysen		30/04/91	M	13	(1)	2
20	Jeppe Brandrup		03/06/85	D	28		2
2	Thomas Guldborg Christensen		20/01/84	D	1	(1)	
7	Jesper Christjansen		29/12/87	M	33	(1)	4
9	Lasse Fosgaard		06/09/86	M	21	(8)	1
26	Frederik Gytkjær		16/03/93	M	3	(8)	
1	Jesper Hansen		31/03/85	G	35		
30	Hallgrímur Jónasson	ISL	04/05/86	D	17	(4)	1
15	Jeppe Kjær		06/11/85	A	23	(6)	11
28	Oliver Kjærgaard		11/07/98	M		(3)	
16	Andreas Larsen		22/05/90	G	1	(1)	
25	Emil Larsen		22/06/91	M	3	(1)	
19	Kristoffer Larsen	NOR	19/01/92	M	19	(8)	4
3	Michael Lumb		09/01/88	D	32		1
33	Gustav Marcussen		12/06/98	M		(2)	
13	Alexander Munksgaard		13/12/97	D	8	(2)	
17	Casper Højer Nielsen		20/11/94	D	5	(4)	
12	Mads Nordam		14/05/95	D	1	(1)	
23	Jens Odgaard		31/03/99	A	4	(12)	3
27	Kim Ojo	NGA	09/12/88	A	8	(8)	3
14	Philip Rasmussen		12/01/89	M	4	(9)	
8	Lasse Rise		09/06/86	M	1	(8)	
21,10	Mikkel Rygaard		25/12/90	M	31	(3)	5
24	Thomas Sørensen		01/08/84	D	29	(1)	
4	Mathias Tauber		24/08/84	D	25		1
5	Martin Ørnskov		10/10/85	M	31		1

FC Midtjylland

1999 • MCH Arena (11,809) • fcm.dk

Major honours
Danish League (1) 2015

Coach: Jess Thorup

Date		Opponent		Score	Scorers
2016					
18/07	h	Randers	D	2-2	*Kadlec, Onuachu*
24/07	a	Nordsjælland	W	4-0	*J Poulsen (p), Sisto 2 (1p), Novák*
31/07	h	Silkeborg	W	3-0	*Duelund, Kadlec 2*
07/08	h	Brøndby	D	3-3	*Onuachu, J Poulsen 2 (2p)*
13/08	a	København	L	1-3	*J Poulsen*
21/08	h	SønderjyskE	D	2-2	*og (Kanstrup), Novák*
28/08	a	Viborg	D	0-0	
09/09	h	Esbjerg	W	3-0	*Pusic (p), Rømer, Borring*
18/09	a	OB	W	1-0	*Olsson*
21/09	a	AGF	D	1-1	*Novák*
25/09	h	Horsens	W	5-2	*Wikheim, Van der Vaart, Duelund 2, Onuachu*
02/10	a	Lyngby	L	0-1	
16/10	h	AaB	W	2-0	*Banggaard, Wikheim*
24/10	a	Esbjerg	W	3-1	*Borring, J Poulsen, Duelund*
30/10	h	København	L	1-3	*Pusic*
06/11	a	Horsens	W	5-1	*Onuachu 2, Borring, Hassan, Novák*
20/11	a	SønderjyskE	L	0-1	
28/11	h	OB	W	1-0	*Nissen*
01/12	a	Silkeborg	L	1-2	*Onuachu*
04/12	h	AGF	L	0-1	
11/12	a	Brøndby	L	1-2	*Van der Vaart*
2017					
19/02	h	Viborg	D	0-0	
24/02	a	Randers	W	2-0	*Duelund, Onuachu*
03/03	h	Lyngby	D	1-1	*J Poulsen*
13/03	a	AaB	D	1-1	*Onuachu*
19/03	h	Nordsjælland	L	1-2	*Onuachu*
02/04	a	Brøndby	L	2-3	*Onuachu 2*
09/04	h	SønderjyskE	W	3-1	*Onuachu, Hassan, Nissen*
16/04	a	Lyngby	D	2-2	*Hansen, Duelund*
23/04	a	København	L	1-3	*Wikheim*
29/04	h	Nordsjælland	W	3-1	*Hansen, Novák, Onuachu*
07/05	h	Brøndby	W	4-2	*Onuachu, Hassan, Duelund 2*
12/05	a	SønderjyskE	L	2-5	*Hassan, Wikheim*
17/05	h	København	W	3-2	*og (Johansson), Rømer, Onuachu*
20/05	a	Nordsjælland	W	3-2	*Onuachu 2, Rømer*
28/05	h	Lyngby	L	0-3	

No	Name	Nat	DoB	Pos	Aps	(s)	Gls
31	Mikkel Andersen		17/12/88	G	12	(1)	
34	Mikael Anderson		01/07/98	M		(2)	
26	Patrick Banggaard		04/04/94	D	20		1
11	Jonas Borring		04/01/85	M	22	(11)	3
77	Bruninho	BRA	29/09/89	A	1	(10)	
16	Johan Dahlin	SWE	08/09/86	G	24		
5	Marc Dal Hende		06/11/90	D	1	(3)	
9	Janus Drachmann		11/05/88	M	9		
22	Mikkel Duelund		29/06/97	M	24	(8)	8
6	Markus Halsti	FIN	19/03/84	D	14	(1)	
2	Kian Hansen		03/03/89	D	30		2
36	Rilwan Hassan	NGA	09/02/91	M	30	(4)	4
14	Václav Kadlec	CZE	20/05/92	A	5	(2)	3
21	Kaan Kairinen	FIN	22/12/98	M		(2)	
14	Simon Kroon	SWE	16/06/93	M		(5)	
19	Marco Larsen		15/05/93	M		(1)	
13	Alexander Munksgaard		13/12/97	D		(1)	
20	Rasmus Nicolaisen		16/03/97	D	5	(2)	
43	Rasmus Nissen		11/07/97	M	32	(1)	2
70	Filip Novák	CZE	26/06/90	D	33		5
17	Kristoffer Olsson	SWE	30/06/95	M	5	(8)	1
33	Paul Onuachu	NGA	28/05/94	A	28	(7)	17
40	Andreas Poulsen		13/10/99	D	1		
7	Jakob Poulsen		07/07/83	M	35		6
10	Martin Pusic	AUT	24/10/87	A	5	(7)	2
18	Kristian Riis		17/02/97	D	9	(5)	
28	André Rømer		18/07/93	D	26	(5)	3
27	Pione Sisto		04/02/95	M	1	(1)	2
3	Tim Sparv	FIN	20/02/87	M	3	(1)	
24	Mads Døhr Thychosen		27/06/97	A		(4)	
8	Rafael van der Vaart	NED	11/02/83	M	10	(5)	2
88	Gustav Wikheim	NOR	18/03/93	M	11	(10)	4

DENMARK

FC Nordsjælland

2003 • Right to Dream Park (10,300) • fcn.dk

Major honours
Danish League (1) 2012; Danish Cup (2) 2010, 2011

Coach: Kasper Hjulmand

2016

Date		Opponent		Score	Scorers
15/07	a	Viborg	W	4-0	*Mikkelsen, Ingvartsen, Ramón, John*
24/07	h	Midtjylland	L	0-4	
30/07	a	København	L	0-4	
07/08	h	AaB	L	1-2	*Jensen*
14/08	a	OB	L	1-3	*Ingvartsen*
19/08	h	Randers	D	1-1	*Donyoh*
26/08	a	Lyngby	W	1-0	*Ingvartsen*
12/09	a	AGF	L	1-3	*Ingvartsen*
18/09	h	SønderjyskE	L	2-3	*Asante, og (Fernandes)*
21/09	a	Horsens	D	0-0	
25/09	h	Esbjerg	W	3-0	*Ingvartsen 2 (1p), Donyoh*
30/09	a	Silkeborg	D	2-2	*Donyoh, Ingvartsen*
16/10	h	Brøndby	D	1-1	*Donyoh*
21/10	a	AaB	D	1-1	*Ingvartsen*
28/10	h	Viborg	W	4-3	*Asante, Donyoh, Marcondes 2*
05/11	a	Randers	L	1-2	*Ingvartsen*
19/11	h	AGF	W	3-2	*Marcondes 2, Ingvartsen*
27/11	a	Esbjerg	D	2-2	*Ingvartsen, Asante*
30/11	h	Horsens	W	2-1	*Marcondes, Ingvartsen (p)*
04/12	h	OB	L	0-1	
09/12	a	SønderjyskE	D	0-0	

2017

Date		Opponent		Score	Scorers
17/02	h	Lyngby	L	0-1	
26/02	h	København	D	1-1	*Marcondes*
05/03	a	Brøndby	W	3-2	*Donyoh, Marcondes, Asante*
10/03	h	Silkeborg	W	5-1	*Donyoh 2, Marcondes, og (Flinta), Ingvartsen*
19/03	a	Midtjylland	W	2-1	*Ingvartsen, Marcondes*
31/03	h	Lyngby	W	2-0	*Ingvartsen, Donyoh*
09/04	a	København	D	1-1	*Ingvartsen*
14/04	a	SønderjyskE	W	4-1	*Marcondes 2, Ingvartsen 2*
23/04	h	Brøndby	L	0-1	
29/04	a	Midtjylland	L	1-3	*Ingvartsen*
05/05	h	København	D	1-1	*Ingvartsen*
12/05	a	Lyngby	L	1-2	*Ingvartsen*
16/05	h	SønderjyskE	W	4-1	*Asante, Marcondes, Ingvartsen (p), Jensen*
20/05	h	Midtjylland	L	2-3	*Bartolec, Maxsø*
28/05	a	Brøndby	W	2-1	*Ingvartsen, Rasmussen*

No	Name	Nat	DoB	Pos	Aps	(s)	Gls
12	Ernest Asante	GHA	06/11/88	A	19	(11)	5
2	Karlo Bartolec	CRO	20/04/95	D	21		1
1	Patrik Carlgren	SWE	08/01/92	G	5		
20	Patrick da Silva		23/10/94	D	1	(1)	
31	Godsway Donyoh	GHA	14/10/94	A	23	(3)	9
11	Mohammed Fellah	NOR	24/05/89	M	6	(6)	
34	Martin Frese		04/01/98	M	1		
3	Pascal Gregor		18/02/94	D	17	(1)	
21	Indy Groothuizen	NED	22/07/96	G	11	(1)	
19	Marcus Ingvartsen		04/01/96	A	34	(1)	23
23	Mathias Jensen		01/01/96	M	17	(5)	2
35	Jakob Johansson		06/08/98	A	1	(2)	
12	Joshua John	NED	01/10/88	A	3		1
24	Christian Køhler		10/04/96	M	11	(8)	
7	Stanislav Lobotka	SVK	25/11/94	M	35		
29	Benjamin Lund		12/03/97	D	5	(2)	
18,10	Emiliano Marcondes		09/03/95	M	19	(6)	12
4	Andreas Maxsø		18/03/94	D	33		1
9	Tobias Mikkelsen		18/09/86	M	7	(12)	1
25	Adnan Mohammad		02/07/96	A	4	(6)	
20	Nicklas Mouritsen		15/03/95	D	2	(1)	
8	Patrick Mtiliga		28/01/81	D	13	(2)	
30	Abdul Mumin	GHA	06/06/98	D	1	(2)	
15	Divine Naah	GHA	20/04/96	M	4	(1)	
36	Victor Nelsson		14/10/98	M	12	(11)	
34	Dominic Oduro	GHA	23/01/95	D	1		
22,5	Mads Pedersen		01/09/96	D	25		
6	Lasse Petry		19/09/92	M	4		
5	Ramón	BRA	22/08/90	D	6		1
14	Mathias Rasmussen	NOR	25/11/97	M	3	(11)	1
16	Rúnar Alex Rúnarsson	ISL	18/02/95	G	20		
17	Andreas Skovgaard		27/03/97	D	18	(6)	
33	Collins Tanor	GHA	04/01/98	M		(3)	
32	Viktor Tranberg		26/02/97	D	14	(2)	

Odense BK

1887 • EWII Park (15,790) • ob.dk

Major honours
Danish League (3) 1977, 1982, 1989; Danish Cup (5) 1983, 1991, 1993, 2002, 2007

Coach: Kent Nielsen

2016

Date		Opponent		Score	Scorers
15/07	h	Silkeborg	D	0-0	
24/07	a	Lyngby	D	2-2	*Petersen (p), Festersen*
01/08	a	AaB	D	2-2	*Edmundsson 2*
06/08	h	Viborg	D	0-0	
14/08	h	Nordsjælland	W	3-1	*Mikkelsen 2, Petersen*
22/08	a	Esbjerg	L	2-3	*Festersen, Edmundsson*
28/08	h	Horsens	L	0-1	
10/09	a	København	L	0-2	
18/09	h	Midtjylland	L	0-1	
22/09	a	SønderjyskE	L	0-1	
25/09	a	Brøndby	L	0-3	
30/09	h	AGF	W	2-1	*Tingager, Jönsson*
16/10	a	Randers	L	0-3	
23/10	h	København	L	0-3	
28/10	a	Silkeborg	D	1-1	*Thrane*
06/11	h	Lyngby	L	1-2	*Edmundsson*
20/11	h	Brøndby	W	1-0	*Jacobsen*
28/11	a	Midtjylland	L	0-1	
01/12	h	Esbjerg	L	0-1	
04/12	a	Nordsjælland	W	1-0	*Festersen*
11/12	a	Viborg	D	1-1	*Thomasen*

2017

Date		Opponent		Score	Scorers
20/02	h	Randers	W	3-0	*Edmundsson, Jönsson 2*
25/02	a	Horsens	D	1-1	*Jönsson*
06/03	h	AaB	W	4-0	*Nielsen, Edmundsson 2, Jönsson*
12/03	h	SønderjyskE	L	0-1	
19/03	a	AGF	W	2-1	*Edmundsson, Tingager*
31/03	a	Horsens	D	0-0	
07/04	h	Esbjerg	W	3-0	*Festersen 2 (1p), Jacobsen*
18/04	h	Randers	W	1-0	*Jönsson*
23/04	a	Randers	L	0-4	
28/04	h	Horsens	W	2-1	*Greve, Thomasen*
08/05	a	Esbjerg	D	1-1	*Edmundsson*

No	Name	Nat	DoB	Pos	Aps	(s)	Gls
19	Mikkel Desler		19/02/95	D	29	(1)	
26	Yao Dieudonne	CIV	14/02/97	M	1	(12)	
7	Jóan Símun Edmundsson	FRO	26/07/91	A	24	(3)	9
8	Mohamed El Makrini	NED	06/07/87	M	16		
1	Michael Falkesgaard		09/04/91	G	2	(1)	
10	Rasmus Festersen		26/08/86	A	24	(2)	5
21	Mathias Greve		11/02/95	M	9	(16)	1
13	Sten Grytebust	NOR	25/10/89	G	30		
28	Anders Jacobsen		27/10/89	A	21	(6)	2
5	João Pereira	POR	10/05/90	D	10		
9	Rasmus Jönsson	SWE	27/01/90	M	30	(2)	6
20	Jacob Barrett Laursen		17/11/94	D	18	(3)	
4	Ryan Laursen		14/04/92	D	1	(2)	
24	Oliver Lund		21/08/90	D	11	(7)	
23	Thomas Mikkelsen		19/01/90	A	3	(9)	2
11	Casper Nielsen		29/04/94	M	9		1
2	Kenneth Emil Petersen		15/01/85	D	21		2
14	Jens Jakob Thomasen		25/06/96	M	19	(2)	2
18	Mathias Thrane		04/09/93	M	4	(14)	1
3	Frederik Tingager		22/02/93	D	20	(3)	2
6	Jeppe Tverskov		12/03/93	D	29	(1)	
15	Izunna Uzochukwu	NGA	11/04/90	M	17	(5)	
22	Nana Welbeck	GHA	24/11/94	M	4	(7)	

Randers FC

2003 • BioNutria Park (10,300) • randersfc.dk

Major honours
Danish Cup (1) 2006

Coach: Ólafur Kristjánsson (ISL)

2016

Date		Opponent		Score	Scorers
18/07	a	Midtjylland	D	2-2	*Fisker, Masango*
24/07	h	AaB	L	0-1	
31/07	a	AGF	W	2-1	*Kauko, Ishak*
05/08	h	Horsens	W	1-0	*Lundberg*
12/08	a	Viborg	W	1-0	*Lundberg*
19/08	a	Nordsjælland	D	1-1	*Kallesøe*
26/08	h	Silkeborg	W	1-0	*Kallesøe*
09/09	h	Lyngby	W	2-0	*Marxen, Ishak*
16/09	a	Esbjerg	D	1-1	*Lundberg*
21/09	h	København	D	2-2	*Pourie, Marxen*
25/09	h	SønderjyskE	L	0-4	
02/10	a	Brøndby	D	2-2	*Kallesøe, Ishak*
16/10	h	OB	W	3-0	*George, Ishak 2*
23/10	a	Horsens	L	0-1	
29/10	a	Lyngby	W	2-0	*Ishak, Pourie*
05/11	h	Nordsjælland	W	2-1	*Ishak, Olsen*
20/11	h	Viborg	W	2-1	*Ishak, Pourie*
25/11	a	AaB	L	1-2	*Enghardt*
30/11	h	Brøndby	L	0-1	
03/12	a	København	L	0-1	
11/12	h	Esbjerg	L	0-2	

2017

Date		Opponent		Score	Scorers
20/02	a	OB	L	0-3	
24/02	h	Midtjylland	L	0-2	
05/03	a	Silkeborg	L	0-2	
10/03	h	AGF	D	1-1	*George*
19/03	a	SønderjyskE	L	0-1	
02/04	a	Esbjerg	D	0-0	
07/04	h	Horsens	W	2-0	*Pourie 2*
18/04	a	OB	L	0-1	
23/04	h	OB	W	4-0	*og (Tverskov), Fisker, Fischer, Pourie*
28/04	h	Esbjerg	D	0-0	
08/05	a	Horsens	L	1-2	*Pourie*

No	Name	Nat	DoB	Pos	Aps	(s)	Gls
5	Mads Agesen		17/03/83	D	26	(1)	
20	Joel Allansson	SWE	03/11/92	M	21	(3)	
7	Edgar Babayan		28/10/95	M	3	(5)	
24	Jonas Bager		18/07/96	D	15	(6)	
7	Andreas Bruhn		17/02/94	M	1	(8)	
28	Nikola Djurdjić	SRB	01/04/86	A	2	(2)	
22	Frederik Due		18/07/92	G	2		
2	Kasper Enghardt		27/05/92	D	19	(8)	1
13	Mads Fenger		10/09/90	D	23	(1)	
21	Alexander Fischer		16/09/86	D	11	(1)	1
16	Kasper Fisker		22/05/88	M	31		2
9	Mayron George	CRC	23/10/93	A	4	(11)	2
1	Hannes Thór Halldórsson	ISL	27/04/84	G	30		
18	Lucas Haren		13/10/97	M	1	(1)	
10	Mikael Ishak	SWE	31/03/93	A	17		8
19	Mikkel Kallesøe		20/04/97	M	13	(4)	3
6	Joni Kauko	FIN	12/07/90	M	12	(8)	1
23	Viktor Lundberg	SWE	04/03/91	A	20	(6)	3
15	Sam Lundholm	SWE	01/07/94	M	1		
11	Erik Marxen		02/12/90	D	24	(1)	2
17	Mandla Masango	RSA	18/07/89	M	2		1
92	Marko Mitrovic	SWE	27/06/92	A	3	(7)	
70	Marcus Mølvadgaard		03/08/99	A	1	(5)	
8	Brandur H Olsen	FRO	19/12/95	M	1	(4)	1
38	Nicolai Poulsen		15/08/93	M	21	(4)	
14,10	Marvin Pourie	GER	08/01/91	A	19	(7)	7
4	Johnny Thomsen		26/02/82	D	29		

Silkeborg IF

1917 • Mascot Park (10,000) • silkeborgif.com

Major honours

Danish League (1) 1994; Danish Cup (1) 2001

Coach: Peter Sørensen

2016

15/07 a OB D 0-0
24/07 h Brøndby L 0-2
31/07 a Midtjylland L 0-3
05/08 h Lyngby L 0-4
13/08 a Horsens D 3-3 *Skhirtladze 2, Gammelby*
21/08 h Viborg L 1-5 *Albers (p)*
26/08 a Randers L 0-1
11/09 a SønderjyskE D 2-2 *Albers, Helenius*
17/09 h AGF W 1-0 *Albers*
20/09 a Esbjerg D 0-0
26/09 h AaB W 5-3 *Skhirtladze 2, Skov, Helenius, Albers*
30/09 h Nordsjælland D 2-2 *Scheel, Helenius*
15/10 a København L 0-2
21/10 a Viborg W 3-1 *Skhirtladze 3*
28/10 h OB D 1-1 *Gammelby*
04/11 a AGF D 0-0
21/11 h Esbjerg W 3-0 *Skov 2, Scheel*
27/11 a Brøndby L 1-3 *Helenius*
01/12 h Midtjylland W 2-1 *Helenius 2 (1p)*
05/12 h SønderjyskE D 1-1 *Skov*
10/12 a Lyngby D 1-1 *Skov*

2017

18/02 h Horsens W 1-0 *Helenius (p)*
26/02 a AaB L 0-3
05/03 h Randers W 2-0 *Skov, Albers*
10/03 a Nordsjælland L 1-5 *Rubin*
19/03 h København L 1-3 *Moro*
01/04 h AaB D 0-0
10/04 a AGF W 3-1 *Helenius 2, Skytte*
17/04 a Viborg D 0-0
21/04 h Viborg L 1-2 *Skov*
01/05 h AGF L 0-2
07/05 a AaB W 1-0 *Skov*

No	Name	Nat	DoB	Pos	Aps	(s)	Gls
7	Nicolaj Agger		23/10/88	A	8	(12)	
9	Andreas Albers		23/03/90	A	7	(24)	5
5	Mikkel Cramer		25/01/92	D	21	(3)	
15	Gustav Dahl		21/01/96	D	11	(1)	
14	Dennis Flinta		14/11/83	D	31		
11	Ulrik Flo	NOR	06/10/88	A		(3)	
6	Jens Martin Gammelby		05/02/95	D	31		2
20	Frank Hansen		23/02/83	D		(3)	
11	Nicklas Helenius		08/05/91	A	27		9
4	Simon Jakobsen		17/11/90	D	31		
17	Emil Lyng		03/08/89	M	2	(16)	
21	Mads Emil Madsen		14/01/98	M		(2)	
18	Ibrahim Moro	GHA	10/11/93	M	24		1
1	Thomas Nørgaard		07/01/87	G	29		
23	Jeppe Okkels		27/07/99	A		(5)	
31	Jens Rinke		16/04/90	G	3		
20	Rubio Rubin	USA	01/03/96	A		(3)	1
28	Tobias Salquist		18/05/95	D	3	(3)	
10	Emil Scheel		18/03/90	M	28	(4)	2
22,8	Davit Skhirtladze	GEO	16/03/93	M	28	(2)	7
29	Robert Skov		20/05/96	M	26	(1)	8
19,2	Sammy Skytte		20/02/97	M	14	(3)	1
8	Martin Thomsen		06/08/82	A	7		
13	Mikkel Vendelbo		15/08/87	M	21	(5)	

SønderjyskE

2004 • Sydbank Park (10,000) • soenderjyske.dk

Coach: Jakob Michelsen; (05/01/17) Claus Nørgaard

2016

17/07 h AGF L 1-2 *Kroon*
24/07 a Horsens D 1-1 *Dal Hende*
31/07 h Lyngby L 0-1
07/08 h København D 1-1 *Kroon*
14/08 a Brøndby L 0-4
21/08 a Midtjylland D 2-2 *Madsen, og (Hansen)*
28/08 h Esbjerg D 1-1 *Uhre*
11/09 h Silkeborg D 2-2 *Madsen, Absalonsen*
18/09 a Nordsjælland W 3-2 *Uhre, Drachmann, Luijckx*
22/09 h OB W 1-0 *Kroon*
25/09 a Randers W 4-0 *Dal Hende, Madsen, Pedersen, Luijckx*
02/10 a AaB W 1-0 *Kroon (p)*
14/10 h Viborg W 1-0 *Kanstrup (p)*
22/10 a Lyngby L 0-2
30/10 h Horsens W 2-0 *Uhre, Rømer*
06/11 a København L 0-4
20/11 h Midtjylland W 1-0 *Zinckernagel*
26/11 a Viborg D 2-2 *Kløve, Mattila*
29/11 h AaB D 1-1 *Dal Hende*
05/12 a Silkeborg D 1-1 *Absalonsen*
09/12 h Nordsjælland D 0-0

2017

17/02 a Esbjerg L 0-3
26/02 h Brøndby L 1-2 *Uhre*
04/03 a AGF W 2-1 *Rømer, Hedegaard*
12/03 a OB W 1-0 *Pedersen*
19/03 h Randers W 1-0 *Hedegaard*
03/04 h København L 1-2 *Kløve*
09/04 a Midtjylland L 1-3 *Mitrovic*
14/04 h Nordsjælland L 1-4 *Absalonsen*
21/04 h Lyngby L 1-2 *Simonsen*
30/04 a Brøndby D 1-1 *Absalonsen (p)*
07/05 a Lyngby L 0-2
12/05 h Midtjylland W 5-2 *og (Halsti), Absalonsen 2, Uhre, Songani*
16/05 a Nordsjælland L 1-4 *Absalonsen*
21/05 h Brøndby W 3-0 *Jakobsen 3*
28/05 a København L 0-2

No	Name	Nat	DoB	Pos	Aps	(s)	Gls
11	Johan Absalonsen		16/09/85	M	24	(3)	7
9	Tommy Bechmann		22/12/81	A	3	(7)	
7	Marc Dal Hende		06/11/90	D	18		3
8	Janus Drachmann		11/05/88	M	16		1
28	Lukas Fernandes		01/03/93	G	27		
18	Adama Guira	BFA	24/04/88	M	7		
14	Mikkel Hedegaard		03/07/96	D	8	(10)	2
8	Christian Jakobsen		27/03/93	M	13	(1)	3
26	Pierre Kanstrup		21/02/89	D	36		1
15	Troels Kløve		23/10/90	M	28	(4)	2
6	Simon Kroon	SWE	16/06/93	M	10	(4)	4
5	Kees Luijckx	NED	11/02/86	D	24		2
31	Matthias Maak	AUT	12/05/92	D	8	(4)	
10	Nicolaj Madsen		16/07/88	M	27	(3)	3
18	Nicholas Marfelt		15/09/94	D	5	(5)	
16	Sakari Mattila	FIN	14/07/89	M	9	(9)	1
9	Marko Mitrovic	SWE	27/06/92	A	3	(6)	1
25	Emmanuel Okwi	UGA	25/12/92	A	2		
13	Casper Olesen		10/05/96	A		(2)	
3	Marc Pedersen		31/07/89	D	26		2
7	Simon Busk Poulsen		07/10/84	D	10		
4	Ramón	BRA	22/08/90	D	8	(4)	
2	Nicolaj Ritter		08/05/92	D	3	(7)	
30	Marcel Rømer		08/08/91	M	31	(2)	2
21	Jeppe Simonsen		21/11/95	A	1	(3)	1
1	Marin Skender	CRO	12/08/79	G	9		
23	Silas Songani	ZIM	28/06/89	A	1	(2)	1
17	Mikael Uhre		30/09/94	A	29	(5)	5
29	Rasmus Vinderslev		12/08/97	M		(2)	
19	Philip Zinckernagel		16/12/94	A	10	(14)	1

Viborg FF

1896 • Energi Viborg Arena (10,000) • vff.dk

Major honours

Danish Cup (1) 2000

Coach: Johnny Mølby

2016

15/07 h Nordsjælland L 0-4
22/07 a AGF L 1-2 *Park*
29/07 h Esbjerg W 2-1 *Kamper, Thychosen*
06/08 a OB D 0-0
12/08 h Randers L 0-1
21/08 a Silkeborg W 5-1 *Rask 2, Thychosen, Kamper 2*
28/08 h Midtjylland D 0-0
10/09 h Horsens L 2-4 *Deblé 2*
18/09 a Brøndby W 2-1 *Rask, og (Larsson)*
22/09 a AaB L 0-1
25/09 h Lyngby L 0-1
02/10 h København D 0-0
14/10 a SønderjyskE L 0-1
21/10 h Silkeborg L 1-3 *Rask*
28/10 a Nordsjælland L 3-4 *Keller, Frederiksen (p), Stankov*
06/11 h Brøndby L 1-2 *Sivebæk*
20/11 a Randers L 1-2 *Reese*
26/11 h SønderjyskE D 2-2 *Deblé, Frederiksen (p)*
29/11 a København L 0-4
03/12 a Horsens W 2-1 *Deblé, Sivebæk*
12/12 h OB D 1-1 *Frederiksen*

2017

19/02 a Midtjylland D 0-0
27/02 h AGF D 1-1 *Frederiksen (p)*
05/03 a Esbjerg W 3-1 *Jakobsen, Vestergaard, Kamper*
11/03 a Lyngby L 0-1
19/03 h AaB W 2-1 *Reese, Deblé*
02/04 h AGF L 2-4 *Frederiksen, Curth*
08/04 a AaB W 1-0 *Curth*
17/04 h Silkeborg D 0-0
21/04 a Silkeborg W 2-1 *Frederiksen, Vestergaard*
30/04 h AaB D 1-1 *Akharraz*
07/05 a AGF L 0-1

No	Name	Nat	DoB	Pos	Aps	(s)	Gls
21	Osama Akharraz		26/11/90	M		(3)	1
4	Jacob Dehn Andersen		04/08/95	D	1	(2)	
17	Andreas Bruhn		17/02/94	M	4	(9)	
10	Jeppe Curth		21/03/84	A	12	(6)	2
28	Serge Deblé	CIV	01/10/89	A	24	(2)	5
8	George Fochive	USA	24/03/92	M	9	(3)	
25	Søren Frederiksen		08/07/89	M	23	(5)	6
18	Donny Gorter	NED	15/06/88	D		(1)	
13	Jeppe Grønning		24/05/91	M	30	(1)	
70	Alexander Jakobsen	EGY	18/03/94	M	9	(1)	1
1	Peter Friis Jensen		02/05/88	G	27		
11	Jonas Kamper		03/05/83	M	28	(2)	4
3	Christian Keller		17/08/80	M	18	(4)	1
5	Erik Moberg	SWE	05/07/86	D	11		
6	Kristoffer Pallesen		30/04/90	D	29		
14	Park Jung-Bin	KOR	22/02/94	A	17	(8)	1
5	Mikkel Rask		22/06/83	D	21		4
20	Søren Reese		29/07/93	D	28		2
23	Christian Sivebæk		19/02/88	M	7	(11)	2
16	Aleksandar Stankov	MKD	19/02/91	A	1	(8)	1
2	Jonas Thorsen		19/04/90	D	30	(1)	
9	Oliver Thychosen		17/01/93	M	6	(1)	2
18	Mate Vatsadze	GEO	17/12/88	A	5	(2)	
26	Jeroen Veldmate	NED	08/11/88	D	4		
29	Mikkel Vestergaard		22/11/92	A		(10)	2
12	Walter Viitala	FIN	09/01/92	G	5		
7	Mathias Wichmann		06/08/91	M	3	(10)	

DENMARK

Top goalscorers

23	Marcus Ingvartsen (Nordsjælland)
20	Teemu Pukki (Brøndby)
17	Paul Onuachu (Midtjylland)
13	Morten "Duncan" Rasmussen (AGF) Kamil Wilczek (Brøndby)
12	Andreas Cornelius (København) Federico Santander (København) Emiliano Marcondes (Nordsjælland)
11	Jeppe Kjær (Lyngby)
10	Robin Söder (Esbjerg)

Promoted clubs

Hobro IK

1913 • DS Arena (10,700) • hikfodbold.dk
Coach: Ove Pedersen;
(04/01/17) Thomas Thomasberg

FC Helsingør

2005 • Helsingør Stadion (4,500) • fchelsingor.dk
Coach: Christian Lønstrup

Second level final table 2016/17

		Pld	W	D	L	F	A	Pts
1	Hobro IK	33	17	7	9	54	34	58
2	Vendsyssel FF	33	16	7	10	51	39	55
3	FC Helsingør	33	14	11	8	43	31	53
4	FC Roskilde	33	14	8	11	44	43	50
5	Skive IK	33	15	4	14	41	51	49
6	HB Køge	33	11	14	8	33	27	47
7	Nykøbing FC	33	13	7	13	50	51	46
8	FC Fredericia	33	11	10	12	36	43	43
9	Vejle BK	33	10	11	12	49	46	41
10	BK Fremad Amager	33	10	11	12	42	45	41
11	Næstved BK	33	9	8	16	45	51	35
12	Akademisk BK	33	6	6	21	34	61	24

Promotion/Relegation play-offs

FIRST ROUND

(12/05/17 & 16/05/17)
Viborg 3-0 Horsens
Horsens 1-0 Viborg
(Viborg 3-1)

(14/05/17 & 17/05/17)
Esbjerg 0-0 AGF
AGF 3-1 Esbjerg
(AGF 3-1)

SECOND ROUND

(20/05/17 & 28/05/17)
Esbjerg 1-1 Horsens
Horsens 3-2 Esbjerg
(Horsens 4-3)

(22/05/17 & 28/05/17)
Viborg 2-2 AGF
AGF 1-0 Viborg
(AGF 3-2)

THIRD ROUND

(31/05/17 & 04/06/17)
Helsingør 1-1 Viborg
Viborg 2-2 Helsingør *(aet)*
(3-3; Helsingør on away goals)

Horsens 0-0 Vendsyssel
Vendsyssel 1-3 Horsens
(Horsens 3-1)

Mid-table play-offs 2016/17

Play-off Group 1 final table			Home					Away					Total					
		Pld	W	D	L	F	A	W	D	L	F	A	W	D	L	F	A	Pts
1	Randers FC	32	8	3	5	20	15	3	5	8	13	20	11	8	13	33	35	41
2	Odense BK	32	8	2	6	20	12	2	7	7	13	26	10	9	13	33	38	39
3	AC Horsens	32	5	5	6	18	26	4	4	8	16	27	9	9	14	34	53	36
4	Esbjerg fB	32	3	9	4	21	23	3	3	10	11	31	6	12	14	32	54	30

Play-off Group 2 final table			Home					Away					Total					
		Pld	W	D	L	F	A	W	D	L	F	A	W	D	L	F	A	Pts
1	Silkeborg IF	32	6	4	6	21	26	3	7	6	15	25	9	11	12	36	51	38
2	Aalborg BK	32	7	4	5	18	14	3	4	9	12	31	10	8	14	30	45	38
3	AGF Aarhus	32	5	3	8	23	26	5	4	7	22	20	10	7	15	45	46	37
4	Viborg FF	32	2	7	7	15	26	6	2	8	20	21	8	9	15	35	47	33

UEFA Europa League qualification play-offs

FIRST ROUND

(12/05/17 & 17/05/17)
AaB 0-2 Randers *(Pourie 26, 32)*
Randers 2-1 AaB *(Djurdjić 34, Lundberg 66; Thellufsen 55)*
(Randers 4-1)

(13/05/17 & 16/05/17)
OB 3-1 Silkeborg *(Jönsson 18, Greve 68, Festersen 75; Helenius 34)*
Silkeborg 2-1 OB *(Skov 51, 72; Desler 70)*
(OB 4-3)

SECOND ROUND

(20/05/17 & 29/05/17)
OB 1-1 Randers *(Jönsson 83; Allansson 54)*
Randers 2-0 OB *(Pourie 90+1, Lundberg 90+5)*
(Randers 3-1)

THIRD ROUND

(01/06/17)
Midtjylland 3-0 Randers *(Onuachu 37, Nicolaisen 67, Borring 69)*

DOMESTIC CUP

Landspokalturneringen 2016/17

SECOND ROUND

(30/08/16)
Aabyhøj 0-9 Silkeborg
Birkerød 0-3 HIK
Dalum 0-1 Holbæk
KFUM Roskilde 1-4 B93
Kjellerup 2-0 Odder
Ledøje-Smørum 2-7 AB
NB Bornholm 0-4 Frem
Otterup 0-4 Hvidovre
Tårnby 1-4 Nordsjælland
Varde 1-2 Jammerbugt
VSK Århus 4-3 Kolding IF *(aet)*

(31/08/16)
Aalborg Freja 0-5 AGF
B1908 1-5 Marienlyst
B1909 0-6 Skive
Fredensborg 0-4 Helsingør
Frederiksværk 1-3 Lyngby
Haarby/Flemløse 0-5 Esbjerg fB
Lyseng 1-4 Horsens *(aet)*
Lystrup 2-6 Randers
OKS 0-2 Viborg
VB 1968 0-2 Fremad Amager

(05/09/16)
Nykøbing 2-2 Næstved *(aet; 3-4 on pens)*

(07/09/16)
Brabrand 2-4 Fredericia
Døllefjelde Musse 0-3 HB Køge
Nørresundby 1-5 AaB
Skovshoved 1-3 FC Roskilde
Vejle 0-4 OB
Vendsyssel 2-0 Hobro

Byes – Brøndby, København, Midtjylland, SønderjyskE

THIRD ROUND

(11/10/16)
HIK 1-3 Randers *(aet)*

(12/10/16)
Skive 1-3 Silkeborg *(aet)*

(13/10/16)
B93 1-0 Esbjerg fB

(19/10/16)
Vendsyssel 2-1 OB

(25/10/16)
Hvidovre 0-2 SønderjyskE
Kjellerup 4-3 Lyngby *(aet)*

(26/10/16)
Frem 1-2 Brøndby
Helsingør 0-1 Horsens
Holbæk 1-3 AGF
Jammerbugt 1-6 København
Marienlyst 2-2 AB *(aet; 4-2 on pens)*
FC Roskilde 2-1 Fredericia
VSK Århus 0-1 AaB

(27/10/16)
Fremad Amager 1-3 Midtjylland

(02/11/16)
HB Køge 2-1 Viborg
Næstved 1-0 Nordsjælland

FOURTH ROUND

(28/02/17)
Vendsyssel 4-0 HB Køge

(01/03/17)
B93 0-3 København

(02/03/17)
AaB 5-0 Silkeborg

(07/03/17)
Kjellerup 0-3 Midtjylland

(08/03/17)
Marienlyst 1-4 Brøndby
Næstved 3-2 FC Roskilde

(15/03/17)
Horsens 1-3 AGF
Randers 1-0 SønderjyskE

QUARTER-FINALS

(05/04/17)
AaB 2-3 Midtjylland *(Würtz 33p, Risgård 77; Onuachu 22, 29, Novák 52)*
Næstved 1-2 Vendsyssel *(Timm 19; Tiago 15p, Moses 76)*

(06/04/17)
København 2-1 AGF *(Pavlović 45, Augustinsson 82; Spelmann 48)*

(13/04/17)
Randers 2-4 Brøndby *(Bruhn 15, Pourie 39; Wilczek 5, Mukhtar 89, 93, Kalmár 97) (aet)*

SEMI-FINALS

(27/04/17)
Vendsyssel 0-2 København *(Greguš 20, Kusk 74)*

(04/05/17)
Midtjylland 1-2 Brøndby *(J Poulsen 29p; Pukki 34, Nørgaard 90)*

FINAL

(25/05/17)
Telia Parken, Copenhagen
FC KØBENHAVN 3 *(Cornelius 51, 85, Santander 83)*
BRØNDBY IF 1 *(Pukki 61)*
Referee: *Maae*
KØBENHAVN: *Andersen, Boilesen, Jørgensen, Johansson, Augustinsson, Verbič, Kvist, Greguš (Matić 77), Toutouh, Santander, Cornelius (Pavlović 90+1)*
BRØNDBY: *Rønnow, Larsson, Röcker, Hermannsson, Crone, Austin (Mensah 86), Nørgaard, Holst (Kalmár 72), Mukhtar, Pukki, Wilczek (Nilsson 86)*

FC København defender "Zanka" Jørgensen lifts the Danish Cup after his team's 3-1 victory in the final against arch-rivals Brøndby

ENGLAND

The Football Association (FA)

Address	Wembley Stadium PO Box 1966 GB-London SW1P 9EQ
Tel	+44 844 980 8200
Fax	+44 844 980 8201
E-mail	info@thefa.com
Website	thefa.com

Chairman	Greg Clarke
Chief executive	Martin Glenn
Media officer	Andy Walker
Year of formation	1863
National stadium	Wembley Stadium, London (90,000)

PREMIER LEAGUE CLUBS

 1 **Arsenal FC**

 2 **AFC Bournemouth**

 3 **Burnley FC**

 4 **Chelsea FC**

 5 **Crystal Palace FC**

 6 **Everton FC**

 7 **Hull City AFC**

 8 **Leicester City FC**

 9 **Liverpool FC**

 10 **Manchester City FC**

 11 **Manchester United FC**

 12 **Middlesbrough FC**

 13 **Southampton FC**

 14 **Stoke City FC**

 15 **Sunderland AFC**

 16 **Swansea City AFC**

 17 **Tottenham Hotspur FC**

 18 **Watford FC**

 19 **West Bromwich Albion FC**

 20 **West Ham United FC**

PROMOTED CLUBS

 21 **Newcastle United FC**

 22 **Brighton & Hove Albion FC**

23 **Huddersfield Town AFC**

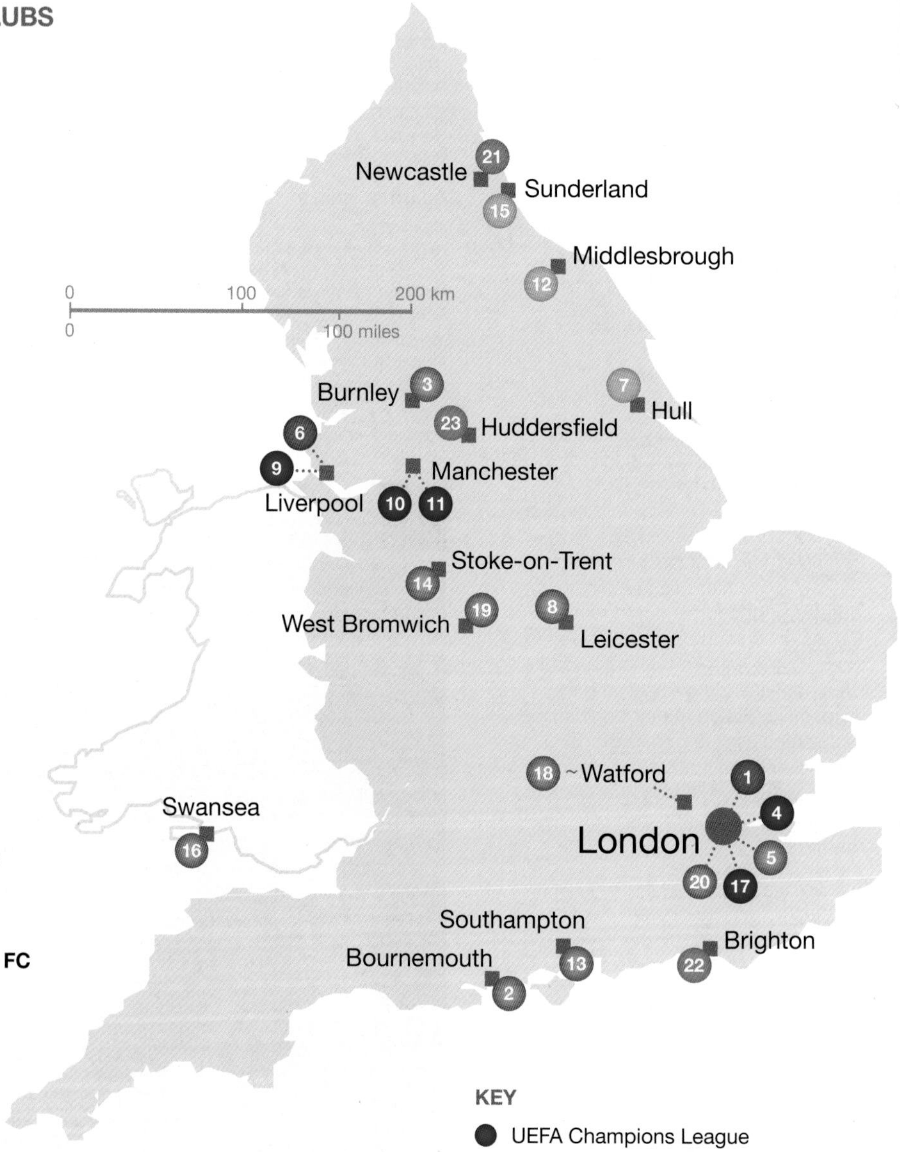

Newcastle 21
Sunderland 15
Middlesbrough 12
Burnley 3
Hull 7
Huddersfield 23
Liverpool 6 9
Manchester 10 11
Stoke-on-Trent 14
West Bromwich 19
Leicester 8
Watford 18
London 1 4 5 17 20
Swansea 16
Southampton 13
Bournemouth 2
Brighton 22

0 100 200 km
0 100 miles

KEY

- UEFA Champions League
- UEFA Europa League
- Promoted
- Relegated

Recharged Chelsea back with a bang

After Leicester City's out-of-nowhere title triumph in 2015/16, it was back to business as usual for the Premier League as the country's six biggest clubs broke clear of the pack and Chelsea, the 2014/15 champions, regained the trophy under their new Italian coach Antonio Conte.

Tottenham Hotspur finished runners-up for the second season in a row, but neither they nor fellow top-four finishers Manchester City and Liverpool picked up a trophy. Manchester United, on the other hand, made up for a poor league campaign by winning the EFL Cup and UEFA Europa League while Arsenal, out of the UEFA Champions League qualifying places for the first time in two decades, won the FA Cup for a record 13th time.

New boss Conte masterminds Premier League triumph

Two major trophies for Mourinho's Manchester United

Fifth-placed Arsenal find solace in record FA Cup win

Domestic league

The arrival of Conte at Chelsea, José Mourinho at Manchester United and Pep Guardiola at Manchester City, supplemented by a large influx of new players, showed that English football's heavyweight clubs were in no mood for any more Premier League fairytales. Only one team, of course, could follow Leicester on to the competition's roll of honour, and with Tottenham and Liverpool already well set with their respective foreign managers, Mauricio Pochettino and Jürgen Klopp, and Arsenal celebrating Arsène Wenger's 20 years at the club, a fascinating six-pronged battle for Premier League supremacy beckoned.

Initially at least, it was anyone's guess as to which of the half-dozen contenders would take the title. Manchester City made the best start, the Guardiola-effect inspiring the team to six successive victories, including a majestic 2-1 win across town at Old Trafford, but a 2-0 defeat at Tottenham brought their progress to an abrupt halt. Liverpool, who kicked off their first full season under Klopp with a pulsating 4-3 win at Arsenal, also won 2-1 at Chelsea thanks to a brilliant strike from new skipper Jordan Henderson before moving to the top of the table in early November.

However, it was Conte's Chelsea who made the decisive move. Beaten 3-0 at Arsenal a week after the home defeat by Liverpool, the manager decided it was necessary to alter the team's formation, reverting to the three-man defence that had served him so well with Juventus and the Italian national side. The impact was immediate and remarkable. Free from European distractions after finishing tenth in 2015/16, the new-look Chelsea at once appeared liberated and irresistible. A rousing 4-0 win over Manchester United – and returning former boss Mourinho – at Stamford Bridge was followed by an even better home display as the Blues celebrated Bonfire Night with one of the most spectacular Premier League performances of all time, overwhelming Ronald Koeman's Everton 5-0. That was not the end of the fireworks, either, as Conte's men won 2-1 at home to Tottenham, beat Manchester City 3-1 away and prolonged their victory charge all the way to the turn of the year. From 1 October to 31 December they won 13 league games in a row, equalling an English top-flight record, and as 2016 became 2017 they held a six-point lead at the top of the table.

Liverpool were Chelsea's closest pursuers at the time, but after beating a stuttering Manchester City 1-0 at Anfield on New Year's Eve, Klopp's team suffered a hangover that would last for several weeks, eliminating them from title contention for good. Tottenham did their best to keep the title race alive by ending Chelsea's winning run with a couple of Dele Alli goals in a stirring 2-0 victory at White Hart Lane, but four successive draws in the autumn had stalled Spurs' challenge and they were still seven points in arrears of their London rivals. They needed Chelsea to start slipping up more often, but Conte's men would not lose again for another three months, by which stage their lead over Spurs had stretched into double figures and every other club was effectively out of the running.

As in the previous season, when another team in all-blue led by an Italian manager had thwarted their bid for a first English league title since 1961, Tottenham could not apply sufficient pressure to take the contest through to the finish, a Friday-night defeat at neighbours West Ham ending their nine-match winning run and all but handing the trophy to Chelsea, who, despite losing at home to Crystal Palace and away to Manchester United, maintained a healthy advantage thanks to a crucial 3-0 win at Everton in arguably their toughest fixture during the run-in. Precisely seven days after Spurs' defeat at the London (née Olympic) Stadium the show was over, substitute Michy

ENGLAND

Batshuayi's late goal at West Bromwich Albion giving Chelsea a 1-0 win that made their sixth English title a mathematical certainty with two games to spare.

Again like Leicester the season before, Chelsea benefited from a settled side seldom troubled by injuries or suspensions. There was no room for long-serving club captain John Terry in Conte's three-man defence, with re-signed David Luiz operating in the middle alongside stand-in skipper Gary Cahill and the versatile César Azpilicueta in front of goalkeeper Thibaut Courtois. The two wing-back positions were filled by Marcos Alonso – newly recruited from Fiorentina – on the left and Victor Moses – back at the club after three loan spells – on the right. N'Golo Kanté, the midfield inspiration behind Leicester's title triumph, served up an encore for Chelsea, forming a perfectly balanced little-and-large central pairing with Nemanja Matić that gave wide midfielders Pedro and a revitalised Eden Hazard free rein to support abrasive spearhead Diego Costa in attack. Cesc Fàbregas and Willian also made useful contributions, but Batshuayi, another newcomer, was mostly confined to the bench alongside Terry, while two former regulars, Branislav Ivanović and Oscar, were both sold in January.

Unlike the previous season, Tottenham did not fall apart at the finish. On the contrary, they treated their fans to a fitting farewell at White Hart Lane – set for demolition to make way for an adjacent new superstadium – with a 2-1 win over Manchester United, their 14th successive league victory there, before running riot at Leicester and Hull, with 6-1 and 7-1 wins respectively. Seven of those 13 goals were scored by Harry Kane, increasing his total to 29, which won him the golden boot for the second successive year. Alli also enjoyed another fine campaign, finding the net 18 times, while Christian Eriksen and Son Heung-min offered excellent support. Tottenham's late goal blitz enabled them to end up with the Premier League's best attack as well as the best defence. They also succumbed to the fewest defeats, although critically they lacked Chelsea's knack of turning draws into wins.

Manchester City finished almost as well as they started to take third place, but overall it was an underwhelming first season in England for the much-lauded Guardiola – the first of his coaching career to end without silverware. While Sergio Agüero, David Silva and Kevin De Bruyne were as productive and entertaining as ever, the club's heavy pre-season outlay on new signings paid small dividends, with only young German winger Leroy Sané making a positive impression. Liverpool, on the other hand, found a new Anfield hero in Sadio Mané, the club's latest buy from Southampton, while Philippe Coutinho and Adam Lallana also excelled as Klopp's team achieved their season's objective of finishing in the top four.

Arsenal's campaign was one of general dissatisfaction and supporter unrest. Not only did they finish below arch-rivals Spurs for the first time in 22 Premier League campaigns, their final position of fifth ended a run of 19 successive participations in the UEFA Champions League – a sequence bettered only by Real Madrid. Alexis Sánchez had another splendid season, scoring 24 goals, but just five points from a possible 24 against the four teams that finished above them was not what the ever-demanding Gunners fans were hoping for. The supporters of Manchester United, who finished sixth, 24 points behind Chelsea, also expected much more from Mourinho's first season, especially after the club had paid a world-record fee to Juventus for Paul Pogba, but despite the evergreen artistry and goalscoring talent of another newcomer, Zlatan Ibrahimović, United were never in the title hunt. They actually went 25 games undefeated after that 4-0 mauling at Chelsea but 12 of those were drawn, nine of them at Old Trafford.

Everton, in Koeman's first season, did well to finish seventh, the 25 goals of Romelu Lukaku transporting them back into Europe. Koeman's former club, Southampton, were one place behind Everton but 15 points in arrears and closer to the relegation zone, which was filled by three teams from the north-east – bottom club Sunderland and two newly-promoted sides, Middlesbrough and Hull. As many as a dozen clubs were threatened by relegation at some point, and those included defending champions Leicester, whose decision to sack title-winning boss Claudio Ranieri in February following a dreadful run of five successive defeats without a goal proved fully vindicated as his assistant Craig Shakespeare led a resurgent team to five straight wins and ultimately to mid-table safety. Swansea and Crystal Palace also benefited from managerial changes, with Paul Clement and Sam Allardyce respectively keeping their teams among the elite for the 2017/18 season, where they would be doing battle with Championship winners Newcastle United – back after one season away – and two newcomers to the Premier League in Brighton & Hove Albion and Huddersfield Town.

Chelsea midfield duo Nemanja Matić (No21) and N'Golo Kanté (7) in action during their team's 4-0 home win against Manchester United in the Premier League

Domestic cups

Winners of the pre-season FA Community Shield, 2-1 against Leicester thanks to a late Ibrahimović winner, Manchester United repeated the trick in the final of the newly-named EFL (formerly League) Cup, with the Swedish striker scoring the second of his two goals against Southampton at Wembley in the 87th minute to earn his side a 3-2 win and give Mourinho the trophy for a record-equalling fourth time (alongside Brian Clough and Alex Ferguson). The Saints had earlier eliminated Arsenal and Liverpool but two goals from new Italian striker Manolo Gabbiadini were insufficient to bring the club a first major trophy in 41 years.

The FA Cup was won for the third time in four years by Arsenal, and a record 13th in all, seven of those during Wenger's long reign. The Gunners avenged Southampton with a 5-0 away win in the fourth round but thereafter got the luck of the draw as they were paired with two fifth-tier sides in Sutton United and Lincoln City, the latter becoming the first non-league club to reach the quarter-finals for over a century. After all the giant-killing the semi-finals brought together four Premier League powerhouses, with Chelsea beating Spurs 4-2 and Arsenal coming from behind to beat Manchester City 2-1 after extra time. Another 2-1 win at Wembley five weeks later enabled Arsenal to deny champions Chelsea the double, with midfielder Aaron Ramsey scoring the winning goal – just as he had done in the 2014 final against Hull.

Europe

Manchester United became the first English club to win a European trophy for four years as they followed Chelsea on to the UEFA Europa League roll of honour with a comfortable 2-0 victory over Ajax in the final. Undefeated in the knockout phase after finishing second in their group, United nevertheless lived dangerously at Old Trafford against Rostov, Anderlecht and Celta Vigo, but goalkeeper Sergio Romero, David de Gea's understudy, repeatedly saved the day, while the ever-present Pogba and top scorer Henrikh Mkhitaryan both enjoyed outstanding campaigns, scoring the goals in Stockholm that would earn United the one major trophy they had never won while also qualifying them for the UEFA Champions League.

Dele Alli (left) looks on as Jermain Defoe opens the scoring for England against Lithuania on his return to international action after a lengthy absence

Once again English teams were found wanting in the biggest club competition of all. Tottenham, playing home games at Wembley, crashed out in the group stage, Arsenal were battered by Bayern München as they exited in the round of 16 for the seventh season in a row, while Manchester City went out at the same stage on the away goals rule despite scoring six times in a rollercoaster tie against Monaco. That left just one English team in the quarter-finals – competition debutants Leicester. Although their Premier League defence left a lot to be desired, the Foxes found their form of old on the European stage, winning their first three matches and keeping clean sheets in their first four before progressing as group winners and knocking out European specialists Sevilla 3-2 on aggregate with a wonderful 2-0 second-leg home win in Shakespeare's first European game as manager. A valiant effort against Atlético Madrid in the quarter-finals ensured that Leicester departed the competition, unlike the other three English teams, with their heads held high.

National team

England kicked off their 2018 FIFA World Cup qualifying campaign under new management, Allardyce having replaced Roy Hodgson after the embarrassment of UEFA EURO 2016. However, the new manager became an old one after just one match – a 1-0 win in Slovakia secured in added time by Lallana's first international goal – when he was caught in a newspaper sting and forced to resign. Under-21 boss Gareth Southgate was summoned to take over as caretaker, and he added seven further points to England's total in the three autumn qualifiers, which duly earned him permanent elevation to the job.

A 2-0 win against Lithuania, in which Jermain Defoe returned from a lengthy international exile to score his 20th England goal, secured a fifth successive clean sheet, but two late free-kicks from Scotland's Leigh Griffiths at Hampden in June ended that streak and appeared to have turned the game only for Kane, captain for the day, to save England's blushes with a stoppage-time equaliser that stretched his country's unbeaten run in qualifying matches to 35 and kept them two points clear at the top of Group F.

A day after that 2-2 draw in Glasgow, England were crowned champions of the world at Under-20 level as Paul Simpson's team defeated Venezuela 1-0 in South Korea. Later that month Aidy Boothroyd's Under-21 side reached the European semi-finals in Poland, and in July another England selection, led by Keith Downing, won the UEFA European Under-19 Championship in Georgia. It remains to be seen whether the youngsters who shone in those tournaments will develop into stars for the senior team, but for the Football Association and all those working to bring success to the English game at every level, the summer of 2017 is unlikely to be forgotten in a hurry.

DOMESTIC SEASON AT A GLANCE

Premier League 2016/17 final table

			Home					Away					Total					
		Pld	W	D	L	F	A	W	D	L	F	A	W	D	L	F	A	Pts
1	**Chelsea FC**	**38**	**17**	**0**	**2**	**55**	**17**	**13**	**3**	**3**	**30**	**16**	**30**	**3**	**5**	**85**	**33**	**93**
2	Tottenham Hotspur FC	38	17	2	0	47	9	9	6	4	39	17	26	8	4	86	26	86
3	Manchester City FC	38	11	7	1	37	17	12	2	5	43	22	23	9	6	80	39	78
4	Liverpool FC	38	12	5	2	45	18	10	5	4	33	24	22	10	6	78	42	76
5	Arsenal FC	38	14	3	2	39	16	9	3	7	38	28	23	6	9	77	44	75
6	Manchester United FC	38	8	10	1	26	12	10	5	4	28	17	18	15	5	54	29	69
7	Everton FC	38	13	4	2	42	16	4	6	9	20	28	17	10	11	62	44	61
8	Southampton FC	38	6	6	7	17	21	6	4	9	24	27	12	10	16	41	48	46
9	AFC Bournemouth	38	9	4	6	35	29	3	6	10	20	38	12	10	16	55	67	46
10	West Bromwich Albion FC	38	9	2	8	27	22	3	7	9	16	29	12	9	17	43	51	45
11	West Ham United FC	38	7	4	8	19	31	5	5	9	28	33	12	9	17	47	64	45
12	Leicester City FC	38	10	4	5	31	25	2	4	13	17	38	12	8	18	48	63	44
13	Stoke City FC	38	7	6	6	24	24	4	5	10	17	32	11	11	16	41	56	44
14	Crystal Palace FC	38	6	2	11	24	25	6	3	10	26	38	12	5	21	50	63	41
15	Swansea City AFC	38	8	3	8	27	34	4	2	13	18	36	12	5	21	45	70	41
16	Burnley FC	38	10	3	6	26	20	1	4	14	13	35	11	7	20	39	55	40
17	Watford FC	38	8	4	7	25	29	3	3	13	15	39	11	7	20	40	68	40
18	Hull City AFC	38	8	4	7	28	35	1	3	15	9	45	9	7	22	37	80	34
19	Middlesbrough FC	38	4	6	9	17	23	1	7	11	10	30	5	13	20	27	53	28
20	Sunderland AFC	38	3	5	11	16	34	3	1	15	13	35	6	6	26	29	69	24

European qualification 2017/18

Champion: Chelsea FC (group stage)
Tottenham Hotspur FC (group stage)
Manchester City FC (group stage)
Manchester United FC (group stage)
Liverpool FC (play-offs)

Cup winner: Arsenal FC (group stage)
Everton FC (third qualifying round)

Top scorer Harry Kane (Tottenham), 29 goals
Relegated clubs Sunderland AFC, Middlesbrough FC, Hull City AFC
Promoted clubs Newcastle United FC, Brighton & Hove Albion FC, Huddersfield Town AFC
FA Cup final Arsenal FC 2-1 Chelsea FC
EFL Cup final Manchester United FC 3-2 Southampton FC

Player of the season

N'Golo Kanté
(Chelsea FC)

The driving force behind Leicester City's 2015/16 Premier League triumph, Kanté left after just one season, but while the East Midlands failed adequately to replace him, the diminutive, all-action French midfielder went on to star again for Chelsea, the £32m they paid for him proving a snip as he inspired the west Londoners to the title, becoming the first player to be crowned champion of England in successive years with different clubs since his compatriot Éric Cantona in 1993. The 26-year-old was also the recipient of all three of England's prestigious player of the year awards.

Newcomer of the season

Jordan Pickford
(Sunderland AFC)

A look at the final 2016/17 Premier League table would suggest that Sunderland could hardly have endured a worse season had they tried, but without the goals of Jermain Defoe and the athletic brilliance between the posts of Pickford, they certainly would have done. The Academy graduate replaced Vito Mannone and went on to become not only Sunderland's first-choice keeper but also the No1 for the England Under-21 side. By the time he starred for his country at the European finals in Poland he had already left the relegated Wearsiders for Everton in a £30m move.

Team of the season
(4-1-3-2)

Manager: Conte *(Chelsea)*

NATIONAL TEAM

International honours
FIFA World Cup (1) 1966.

International tournament appearances
FIFA World Cup (14) 1950, 1954 (qtr-finals), 1958, 1962 (qtr-finals), 1966 (Winners), 1970 (qtr-finals), 1982 (2nd phase), 1986 (qtr-finals), 1990 (4th), 1998 (2nd round), 2002 (qtr-finals), 2006 (qtr-finals), 2010 (2nd round), 2014

UEFA European Championship (9) 1968 (3rd), 1980, 1988, 1992, 1996 (semi-finals), 2000, 2004 (qtr-finals), 2012 (qtr-finals), 2016 (round of 16)

Top five all-time caps
Peter Shilton (125); **Wayne Rooney** (119); David Beckham (115); Steven Gerrard (114); Bobby Moore (108)

Top five all-time goals
Wayne Rooney (53); Bobby Charlton (49); Gary Lineker (48); Jimmy Greaves (44); Michael Owen (40)

Results 2016/17

04/09/16	Slovakia (WCQ)	A	Trnava	W	1-0	*Lallana (90+5)*
08/10/16	Malta (WCQ)	H	London	W	2-0	*Sturridge (29), Alli (38)*
11/10/16	Slovenia (WCQ)	A	Ljubljana	D	0-0	
11/11/16	Scotland (WCQ)	H	London	W	3-0	*Sturridge (23), Lallana (50), Cahill (61)*
15/11/16	Spain	H	London	D	2-2	*Lallana (9p), Vardy (48)*
22/03/17	Germany	A	Dortmund	L	0-1	
26/03/17	Lithuania (WCQ)	H	London	W	2-0	*Defoe (22), Vardy (66)*
10/06/17	Scotland (WCQ)	A	Glasgow	D	2-2	*Oxlade-Chamberlain (70), Kane (90+3)*
13/06/17	France	A	Saint-Denis	L	2-3	*Kane (9, 48p)*

Appearances 2016/17

Coach: Sam Allardyce /(27/09/16) Gareth Southgate	**19/10/54 03/09/70**		**SVK**	**MLT**	**SVN**	**SCO**	**Esp**	**Ger**	**LTU**	**SCO**	**Fra**	**Caps**	**Goals**
Joe Hart	19/04/87	Torino (ITA)	G	G	G	G	G46	G	G	G		71	-
Kyle Walker	28/05/90	Tottenham	D	D	D	D		M	D	D	s46	27	-
Gary Cahill	19/12/85	Chelsea	D	D	D	D	D46	D		D	D	55	4
John Stones	28/05/94	Man. City	D	D	D	D	D	s84	D		D	18	-
Danny Rose	02/07/90	Tottenham	D	s19	D	D	D79					12	-
Jordan Henderson	17/06/90	Liverpool	M64	M	M	M	M					32	-
Eric Dier	15/01/94	Tottenham	M		M	M	M	M	M	M	M	19	2
Wayne Rooney	24/10/85	Man. United	M	M	s73	M						119	53
Raheem Sterling	08/12/94	Man. City	A71			M	M65		M60	s84	M	32	2
Harry Kane	28/07/93	Tottenham	A82							A	A	19	8
Adam Lallana	10/05/88	Liverpool	A			M	M27	A66	M	M	s76	33	3
Dele Alli	11/04/96	Tottenham	s64	M	M73			A71	M	M84	M	19	2
Theo Walcott	16/03/89	Arsenal	s71	A68	M62		s27					47	8
Daniel Sturridge	01/09/89	Liverpool	s82	A73	A82	A74						25	8
Ryan Bertrand	05/08/89	Southampton		D19				M83	D	D	M46	14	-
Jesse Lingard	15/12/92	Man. United		A	M		M	s71				4	-
Marcus Rashford	31/10/97	Man. United		s68	s82		s67	s70	s60	M65		9	1
Jamie Vardy	11/01/87	Leicester		s73		s74	A67	A70	s60			16	6
Andros Townsend	16/07/91	Crystal Palace			s62		s65					13	3
Nathaniel Clyne	05/04/91	Liverpool					D					14	-
Tom Heaton	15/04/86	Burnley					s46				G46	3	-
Phil Jagielka	17/08/82	Everton					s46					40	3
Aaron Cresswell	15/12/89	West Ham					s79				s82	2	-
Chris Smalling	22/11/89	Man. United						D84		D		31	1
Michael Keane	11/01/93	Burnley						D	D			2	-
Jake Livermore	14/11/89	West Brom						M83		M92		3	-
Nathan Redmond	06/03/94	Southampton						s66				1	-
Luke Shaw	12/07/95	Man. United						s83				7	-
James Ward-Prowse	01/11/94	Southampton						s83				1	-
Alex Oxlade-Chamberlain	15/08/93	Arsenal							M	s65	M	27	6
Jermain Defoe	07/10/82	Sunderland							A60	s92		57	20
Phil Jones	21/02/92	Man. United									D82	21	-
Kieran Trippier	19/09/90	Tottenham									M76	1	-
Jack Butland	10/03/93	Stoke									s46	5	-

EUROPE

Leicester City FC

CHAMPIONS LEAGUE

Group G
Match 1 - Club Brugge KV (BEL)
A 3-0 *Albrighton (5), Mahrez (29, 61p)*
Schmeichel, Luis Hernández, Drinkwater, Morgan, Huth, Vardy (Musa 70), Albrighton, Amartey, Slimani (Ulloa 62), Mahrez (Gray 81), Fuchs. Coach: Claudio Ranieri (ITA)
Match 2 - FC Porto (POR)
H 1-0 *Slimani (25)*
Schmeichel, Luis Hernández, Drinkwater, Morgan, Huth, Vardy (Musa 90+4), Albrighton, Amartey, Slimani (King 82), Mahrez (Gray 88), Fuchs. Coach: Claudio Ranieri (ITA)
Match 3 - FC København (DEN)
H 1-0 *Mahrez (40)*
Schmeichel, Drinkwater, Morgan, Huth, Vardy (Okazaki 85), King, Albrighton, Simpson, Slimani (Ulloa 88), Mahrez (Amartey 90+2), Fuchs. Coach: Claudio Ranieri (ITA)
Match 4 - FC København (DEN)
A 0-0
Schmeichel, Luis Hernández, Drinkwater, Morgan, Huth, Musa, Vardy, Amartey, Schlupp (Okazaki 71), Mahrez, Fuchs. Coach: Claudio Ranieri (ITA)
Match 5 - Club Brugge KV (BEL)
H 2-1 *Okazaki (5), Mahrez (30p)*
Zieler, Drinkwater, Morgan, Huth, Vardy, King, Albrighton (Amartey 78), Simpson, Okazaki (Gray 68), Mahrez (Schlupp 68), Fuchs. Coach: Claudio Ranieri (ITA)
Match 6 - FC Porto (POR)
A 0-5
Hamer, Luis Hernández, Chilwell, Drinkwater (Barnes 76), Morgan, Musa (Ulloa 46), Schlupp (Albrighton 46), Okazaki, Gray, Mendy, Wasilewski. Coach: Claudio Ranieri (ITA)

Round of 16 - Sevilla FC (ESP)
A 1-2 *Vardy (73)*
Schmeichel, Drinkwater, Morgan, Huth, Musa (Gray 58), Vardy, Albrighton (Amartey 88), Simpson, Ndidi, Mahrez, Fuchs. Coach: Claudio Ranieri (ITA)
H 2-0 *Morgan (27), Albrighton (54)*
Schmeichel, Drinkwater, Morgan, Huth, Vardy, Albrighton, Simpson, Okazaki (Slimani 64), Ndidi, Mahrez (Amartey 90), Fuchs. Coach: Craig Shakespeare (ENG)

Quarter-finals - Club Atlético de Madrid (ESP)
A 0-1
Schmeichel, Drinkwater, Huth, Vardy (Slimani 77), Albrighton, Simpson, Okazaki (King 46), Ndidi, Mahrez, Fuchs, Benalouane. Coach: Craig Shakespeare (ENG)
H 1-1 *Vardy (61)*
Schmeichel, Drinkwater, Morgan (Amartey 84), Vardy, Albrighton, Simpson, Okazaki (Ulloa 46), Ndidi, Mahrez, Fuchs, Benalouane (Chilwell 46). Coach: Craig Shakespeare (ENG)

Arsenal FC

CHAMPIONS LEAGUE

Group A
Match 1 - Paris Saint-Germain (FRA)
A 1-1 *Alexis Sánchez (78)*
Ospina, Koscielny, Alexis Sánchez, Özil (Elneny 85), Oxlade-Chamberlain (Giroud 63), Iwobi, Monreal, Santi Cazorla, Mustafi, Bellerín, Coquelin (Xhaka 71). Coach: Arsène Wenger (FRA)
Red card: Giroud 90+3
Match 2 - FC Basel 1893 (SUI)
H 2-0 *Walcott (7, 26)*
Ospina, Koscielny, Alexis Sánchez, Özil, Walcott (Oxlade-Chamberlain 70), Iwobi (Elneny 70), Monreal (Gibbs 75), Santi Cazorla, Mustafi, Bellerín, Xhaka. Coach: Arsène Wenger (FRA)
Match 3 - PFC Ludogorets Razgrad (BUL)
H 6-0 *Alexis Sánchez (13), Walcott (42), Oxlade-Chamberlain (47), Özil (56, 83, 87)*
Ospina, Gibbs, Koscielny, Alexis Sánchez (Iwobi 73), Özil, Walcott (Lucas Pérez 62), Oxlade-Chamberlain, Santi Cazorla (Elneny 57), Mustafi, Bellerín, Coquelin. Coach: Arsène Wenger (FRA)
Match 4 - PFC Ludogorets Razgrad (BUL)
A 3-2 *Xhaka (20), Giroud (42), Özil (88)*
Ospina, Gibbs, Koscielny, Alexis Sánchez (Iwobi 90), Ramsey (Oxlade-Chamberlain 75), Özil, Giroud, Mustafi, Jenkinson, Xhaka (Elneny 87), Coquelin. Coach: Arsène Wenger (FRA)
Match 5 - Paris Saint-Germain (FRA)
H 2-2 *Giroud (45+1p), Verratti (60og)*
Ospina, Gibbs, Koscielny, Alexis Sánchez, Ramsey, Özil, Giroud, Iwobi (Xhaka 77), Mustafi, Jenkinson (Oxlade-Chamberlain 81), Coquelin (Walcott 80). Coach: Arsène Wenger (FRA)
Match 6 - FC Basel 1893 (SUI)
A 4-1 *Lucas Pérez (8, 16, 47), Iwobi (53)*
Ospina, Gibbs, Gabriel, Koscielny, Alexis Sánchez (Elneny 70), Ramsey (Giroud 70), Lucas Pérez, Özil (Walcott 74), Holding, Iwobi, Xhaka. Coach: Arsène Wenger (FRA)

Round of 16 - FC Bayern München (GER)
A 1-5 *Alexis Sánchez (30)*
Ospina, Gibbs, Koscielny (Gabriel 49), Alexis Sánchez, Özil, Oxlade-Chamberlain, Iwobi (Walcott 66), Mustafi, Bellerín, Xhaka, Coquelin (Giroud 77). Coach: Arsène Wenger (FRA)
H 1-5 *Walcott (20)*
Ospina, Koscielny, Alexis Sánchez (Lucas Pérez 72), Ramsey (Coquelin 72), Giroud (Özil 72), Walcott, Oxlade-Chamberlain, Monreal, Mustafi, Bellerín, Xhaka. Coach: Arsène Wenger (FRA)
Red card: Koscielny 53

Tottenham Hotspur FC

CHAMPIONS LEAGUE

Group E
Match 1 - AS Monaco FC (FRA)
H 1-2 *Alderweireld (45)*
Lloris, Walker, Alderweireld, Vertonghen, Son (Dembélé 46), Kane, Lamela (Janssen 71), Dier (Sissoko 81), Alli, Eriksen, Davies. Coach: Mauricio Pochettino (ARG)
Match 2 - PFC CSKA Moskva (RUS)
A 1-0 *Son (71)*
Lloris, Alderweireld, Vertonghen, Son, Janssen (N'Koudou 67), Lamela, Wanyama, Trippier, Alli (Winks 82), Eriksen, Davies. Coach: Mauricio Pochettino (ARG)
Match 3 - Bayer 04 Leverkusen (GER)
A 0-0
Lloris, Rose, Vertonghen, Son (Onomah 90), Janssen (Dembélé 65), Lamela (Sissoko 71), Wanyama, Dier, Trippier, Alli, Eriksen. Coach: Mauricio Pochettino (ARG)
Match 4 - Bayer 04 Leverkusen (GER)
H 0-1
Lloris, Walker, Vertonghen, Son (N'Koudou 73), Wanyama, Dier, Sissoko, Dembélé (Janssen 30), Alli, Eriksen (Winks 65), Davies. Coach: Mauricio Pochettino (ARG)
Match 5 - AS Monaco FC (FRA)
A 1-2 *Kane (52p)*
Lloris, Rose, Son (Janssen 65), Kane, Wanyama, Dier, Trippier, Dembélé (Eriksen 65), Alli, Wimmer, Winks (Sissoko 74). Coach: Mauricio Pochettino (ARG)
Match 6 - PFC CSKA Moskva (RUS)
H 3-1 *Alli (38), Kane (45+1), Akinfeev (77og)*
Lloris, Walker, Rose, Vertonghen, Son (N'Koudou 61), Kane (Onomah 83), Wanyama (Alderweireld 68), Dier, Alli, Eriksen, Winks. Coach: Mauricio Pochettino (ARG)

EUROPA LEAGUE

Round of 32 - KAA Gent (BEL)
A 0-1
Lloris, Walker, Alderweireld, Kane, Wanyama, Dier, Sissoko (N'Koudou 71), Dembélé (Son 68), Alli, Winks (Eriksen 80), Davies. Coach: Mauricio Pochettino (ARG)
H 2-2 *Eriksen (10), Wanyama (61)*
Lloris, Walker, Alderweireld, Vertonghen, Kane, Wanyama, Dier (Janssen 89), Dembélé (Winks 75), Alli, Eriksen, Davies (Son 58). Coach: Mauricio Pochettino (ARG)
Red card: Alli 40

Manchester City FC

Play-offs - FC Steaua Bucureşti (ROU)
A 5-0 *Silva (13), Agüero (41, 78, 89), Nolito (49)*
Caballero, Zabaleta (Sagna 70), Sterling, Nolito, Agüero, Kolarov (Clichy 75), De Bruyne (Fernando 80), Silva, Stones, Fernandinho, Otamendi. Coach: Pep Guardiola (ESP)
H 1-0 *Delph (56)*
Hart, Fernando, Nolito (Angeliño 60), Kolarov, Jesús Navas, Delph, Clichy, Stones (Adarabioyo 60), Touré, Maffeo, Iheanacho (Fernandinho 76). Coach: Pep Guardiola (ESP)

Group C
Match 1 - VfL Borussia Mönchengladbach (GER)
H 4-0 *Agüero (9, 28p, 77), Iheanacho (90+1)*
Bravo, Zabaleta, Sterling (Sané 79), Gündoğan (Clichy 81), Agüero (Iheanacho 83), Kolarov, Jesús Navas, De Bruyne, Stones, Fernandinho, Otamendi. Coach: Pep Guardiola (ESP)
Match 2 - Celtic FC (SCO)
A 3-3 *Fernandinho (12), Sterling (28), Nolito (55)*
Bravo, Zabaleta, Sterling, Gündoğan, Nolito (Fernando 76), Agüero, Kolarov, Silva, Clichy (Stones 73), Fernandinho, Otamendi. Coach: Pep Guardiola (ESP)
Match 3 - FC Barcelona (ESP)
A 0-4
Bravo, Zabaleta (Caballero 57), Sterling, Gündoğan (Agüero 79), Nolito (Clichy 57), Kolarov, De Bruyne, Silva, Stones, Fernandinho, Otamendi. Coach: Pep Guardiola (ESP)
Red card: Bravo 53
Match 4 - FC Barcelona (ESP)
H 3-1 *Gündoğan (39, 74), De Bruyne (51)*
Caballero, Zabaleta, Sterling (Jesús Navas 71), Gündoğan, Agüero, Kolarov, De Bruyne (Nolito 89), Silva, Stones, Fernandinho (Fernando 60), Otamendi. Coach: Pep Guardiola (ESP)
Match 5 - VfL Borussia Mönchengladbach (GER)
A 1-1 *Silva (45+1)*
Bravo, Sterling (Sagna 68), Gündoğan, Agüero, Kolarov, Jesús Navas, De Bruyne, Silva, Stones, Fernandinho, Otamendi. Coach: Pep Guardiola (ESP)
Red card: Fernandinho 63
Match 6 - Celtic FC (SCO)
H 1-1 *Iheanacho (8)*
Caballero, Sagna, Zabaleta, Fernando, Gündoğan, Nolito, Sané, Clichy, Maffeo (Jesús Navas 62), Adarabioyo, Iheanacho. Coach: Pep Guardiola (ESP)

Round of 16 - AS Monaco FC (FRA)
H 5-3 *Sterling (26), Agüero (58, 71), Stones (77), Sané (82)*
Caballero, Sagna, Sterling (Jesús Navas 89), Agüero (Fernando 87), De Bruyne, Sané, Silva, Stones, Fernandinho (Zabaleta 62), Otamendi, Touré. Coach: Pep Guardiola (ESP)
A 1-3 *Sané (71)*
Caballero, Sagna, Sterling, Agüero, Kolarov, De Bruyne, Sané, Silva, Clichy (Iheanacho 84), Stones, Fernandinho. Coach: Pep Guardiola (ESP)

Manchester United FC

Group A
Match 1 - Feyenoord (NED)
A 0-1
De Gea, Bailly, Rojo, Pogba, Mata (Young 63), Martial (Depay 63), Smalling, Rashford (Ibrahimović 63), Ander Herrera, Schneiderlin, Darmian. Coach: José Mourinho (POR)
Match 2 - FC Zorya Luhansk (UKR)
H 1-0 *Ibrahimović (69)*
Romero, Bailly, Rojo, Pogba, Mata (Young 74), Ibrahimović, Smalling, Lingard (Rooney 68), Rashford, Fosu-Mensah (Martial 74), Fellaini. Coach: José Mourinho (POR)
Match 3 - Fenerbahçe SK (TUR)
H 4-1 *Pogba (31p, 45+1), Martial (34p), Lingard (48)*
De Gea, Bailly, Pogba (Fosu-Mensah 75), Mata, Rooney, Martial, Smalling (Rojo 46), Lingard (Depay 66), Carrick, Shaw, Darmian. Coach: José Mourinho (POR)
Match 4 - Fenerbahçe SK (TUR)
A 1-2 *Rooney (89)*
De Gea, Rojo, Pogba (Ibrahimović 30), Rooney, Martial, Blind, Rashford (Mkhitaryan 61), Ander Herrera, Shaw, Schneiderlin (Mata 46), Darmian. Coach: José Mourinho (POR)
Match 5 - Feyenoord (NED)
H 4-0 *Rooney (35), Mata (69), Jones (75og), Lingard (90+2)*
Romero, Jones, Pogba, Mata (Rashford 70), Ibrahimović, Rooney (Depay 82), Carrick, Blind, Mkhitaryan (Lingard 82), Shaw, Valencia. Coach: José Mourinho (POR)
Match 6 - FC Zorya Luhansk (UKR)
A 2-0 *Mkhitaryan (48), Ibrahimović (88)*
Romero, Bailly, Rojo, Pogba, Mata (Lingard 65), Ibrahimović, Rooney (Fellaini 70), Blind, Young, Ander Herrera, Mkhitaryan (Fosu-Mensah 85). Coach: José Mourinho (POR)

Round of 32 - AS Saint-Étienne (FRA)
H 3-0 *Ibrahimović (15, 75, 88p)*
Romero, Bailly, Pogba, Mata (Rashford 70), Ibrahimović, Martial (Young 84), Smalling, Blind, Ander Herrera, Valencia, Fellaini (Lingard 45+1). Coach: José Mourinho (POR)
A 1-0 *Mkhitaryan (17)*
Romero, Bailly, Pogba, Mata (Rojo 64), Ibrahimović, Smalling, Carrick (Schweinsteiger 62), Blind, Young, Mkhitaryan (Rashford 25), Fellaini. Coach: José Mourinho (POR)
Red card: Bailly 63

Round of 16 - FC Rostov (RUS)
A 1-1 *Mkhitaryan (35)*
Romero, Jones, Rojo, Pogba, Ibrahimović, Smalling, Blind (Valencia 90+2), Young, Ander Herrera (Carrick 90+2), Mkhitaryan (Martial 67), Fellaini. Coach: José Mourinho (POR)
H 1-0 *Mata (70)*
Romero, Bailly, Rojo, Pogba (Fellaini 48), Mata, Ibrahimović, Smalling, Blind (Jones 64), Ander Herrera, Mkhitaryan, Valencia. Coach: José Mourinho (POR)

Quarter-finals - RSC Anderlecht (BEL)
A 1-1 *Mkhitaryan (37)*
Romero, Bailly, Rojo, Pogba, Ibrahimović, Lingard (Martial 63), Carrick, Rashford (Fellaini 75), Mkhitaryan (Fosu-Mensah 90+1), Valencia, Darmian. Coach: José Mourinho (POR)
H 2-1 (aet) *Mkhitaryan (10), Rashford (107)*
Romero, Bailly, Rojo (Blind 23), Pogba, Ibrahimović (Martial 90+3), Lingard (Fellaini 60), Carrick, Rashford, Mkhitaryan, Shaw, Valencia. Coach: José Mourinho (POR)

Semi-finals - RC Celta de Vigo (ESP)
A 1-0 *Rashford (67)*
Romero, Bailly, Pogba, Lingard, Blind, Rashford (Martial 80), Ander Herrera, Mkhitaryan (Young 78; Smalling 90), Valencia, Fellaini, Darmian. Coach: José Mourinho (POR)
H 1-1 *Fellaini (17)*
Romero, Bailly, Pogba, Lingard (Rooney 86), Blind, Rashford (Smalling 89), Ander Herrera, Mkhitaryan (Carrick 77), Valencia, Fellaini, Darmian. Coach: José Mourinho (POR)
Red card: Bailly 88

Final - AFC Ajax (NED)
N 2-0 *Pogba (18), Mkhitaryan (48)*
Romero, Pogba, Mata (Rooney 90), Smalling, Blind, Rashford (Martial 84), Ander Herrera, Mkhitaryan (Lingard 74), Valencia, Fellaini, Darmian. Coach: José Mourinho (POR)

Southampton FC

Group K
Match 1 - AC Sparta Praha (CZE)
H 3-0 *Austin (5p, 27), Rodriguez (90+2)*
Forster, Yoshida, Long, Austin (Rodriguez 77), Tadić (Redmond 70), Romeu (Davis 83), Martina, Ward-Prowse, Van Dijk, Højbjerg, Targett. Coach: Claude Puel (FRA)
Match 2 - Hapoel Beer-Sheva FC (ISR)
A 0-0
Forster, Yoshida, Clasie, Long, Romeu, Martina, Ward-Prowse, Van Dijk, Redmond (Højbjerg 85), Targett, Hesketh (Tadić 35). Coach: Claude Puel (FRA)
Match 3 - FC Internazionale Milano (ITA)
A 0-1
Forster, Yoshida, Long (Austin 48), Rodriguez (Davis 78), Tadić (Boufal 73), Romeu, Martina, Ward-Prowse, Van Dijk, Højbjerg, McQueen. Coach: Claude Puel (FRA)
Match 4 - FC Internazionale Milano (ITA)
H 2-1 *Van Dijk (64), Nagatomo (70og)*
Forster, Yoshida, Rodriguez (Austin 59), Tadić (Davis 77), Romeu, Martina, Ward-Prowse, Van Dijk, Redmond, Højbjerg, McQueen. Coach: Claude Puel (FRA)
Match 5 - AC Sparta Praha (CZE)
A 0-1
Forster, Yoshida, Clasie (Austin 72), Long, Rodriguez (Boufal 55), Martina, Ward-Prowse, Van Dijk, Redmond, Højbjerg (Romeu 55), McQueen. Coach: Claude Puel (FRA)
Match 6 - Hapoel Beer-Sheva FC (ISR)
H 1-1 *Van Dijk (90+1)*
Forster, Cédric, Yoshida, Davis, Austin (Long 39), Romeu, Van Dijk, Bertrand, Redmond, Højbjerg (Ward-Prowse 82), Sims (Tadić 59). Coach: Claude Puel (FRA)

DOMESTIC LEAGUE CLUB-BY-CLUB

West Ham United FC

Third qualifying round - NK Domžale (SVN)

A 1-2 *Noble (18p)*

Adrián, Reid, Nordtveit, Feghouli, Kouyaté, Carroll, Valencia, Pedro Obiang, Noble, Byram, Antonio (Quina 80). Coach: Nikola Jurčević (CRO)

H 3-0 *Kouyaté (8, 25), Feghouli (81)*

Randolph, Reid, Nordtveit, Feghouli (Quina 87), Kouyaté (Pedro Obiang 79), Carroll (Fletcher 90), Valencia, Noble, Byram, Antonio, Oxford. Coach: Slaven Bilić (CRO)

Play-offs - FC Astra Giurgiu (ROU)

A 1-1 *Noble (45p)*

Randolph, Valencia (Carroll 62), Pedro Obiang, Noble, Gökhan Töre (Browne 75), Ogbonna, Byram, Calleri (Collins 63), Antonio, Burke, Oxford. Coach: Slaven Bilić (CRO)

H 0-1

Randolph, Reid, Nordtveit (Valencia 46), Kouyaté, Pedro Obiang, Gökhan Töre, Ogbonna, Byram, Calleri (Fletcher 61), Antonio, Burke (Collins 88). Coach: Slaven Bilić (CRO)

Arsenal FC

1886 • Emirates Stadium (60,432) • arsenal.com

Major honours

UEFA Cup Winners' Cup (1) 1994; Inter Cities Fairs Cup (1) 1970; English League (13) 1931, 1933, 1934, 1935, 1938, 1948, 1953, 1971, 1989, 1991, 1998, 2002, 2004; FA Cup (13) 1930, 1936, 1950, 1971, 1979, 1993, 1998, 2002, 2003, 2005, 2014, 2015, 2017; League Cup (2) 1987, 1993

Manager: Arsène Wenger (FRA)

Date		Opponent		Score	Scorers
2016					
14/08	h	Liverpool	L	3-4	*Walcott, Oxlade-Chamberlain, Chambers*
20/08	a	Leicester	D	0-0	
27/08	a	Watford	W	3-1	*Santi Cazorla (p), Alexis Sánchez, Özil*
10/09	h	Southampton	W	2-1	*Koscielny, Santi Cazorla (p)*
17/09	a	Hull	W	4-1	*Alexis Sánchez 2, Walcott, Xhaka*
24/09	h	Chelsea	W	3-0	*Alexis Sánchez, Walcott, Özil*
02/10	a	Burnley	W	1-0	*Koscielny*
15/10	h	Swansea	W	3-2	*Walcott 2, Özil*
22/10	h	Middlesbrough	D	0-0	
29/10	a	Sunderland	W	4-1	*Alexis Sánchez 2, Giroud 2*
06/11	h	Tottenham	D	1-1	*og (Wimmer)*
19/11	a	Man. United	D	1-1	*Giroud*
27/11	h	Bournemouth	W	3-1	*Alexis Sánchez 2, Walcott*
03/12	a	West Ham	W	5-1	*Özil, Alexis Sánchez 3, Oxlade-Chamberlain*
10/12	h	Stoke	W	3-1	*Walcott, Özil, Iwobi*
13/12	a	Everton	L	1-2	*Alexis Sánchez*
18/12	a	Man. City	L	1-2	*Walcott*
26/12	h	West Brom	W	1-0	*Giroud*
2017					
01/01	h	Crystal Palace	W	2-0	*Giroud, Iwobi*
03/01	a	Bournemouth	D	3-3	*Alexis Sánchez, Lucas Pérez, Giroud*
14/01	a	Swansea	W	4-0	*Giroud, og (Cork), og (Naughton), Alexis Sánchez*
22/01	h	Burnley	W	2-1	*Mustafi, Alexis Sánchez (p)*
31/01	h	Watford	L	1-2	*Iwobi*
04/02	a	Chelsea	L	1-3	*Giroud*
11/02	h	Hull	W	2-0	*Alexis Sánchez 2 (1p)*
04/03	a	Liverpool	L	1-3	*Welbeck*
18/03	a	West Brom	L	1-3	*Alexis Sánchez*
02/04	h	Man. City	D	2-2	*Walcott, Mustafi*
05/04	h	West Ham	W	3-0	*Özil, Walcott, Giroud*
10/04	a	Crystal Palace	L	0-3	
17/04	a	Middlesbrough	W	2-1	*Alexis Sánchez, Özil*
26/04	h	Leicester	W	1-0	*og (Huth)*
30/04	a	Tottenham	L	0-2	
07/05	h	Man. United	W	2-0	*Xhaka, Welbeck*
10/05	a	Southampton	W	2-0	*Alexis Sánchez, Giroud*
13/05	a	Stoke	W	4-1	*Giroud 2, Özil, Alexis Sánchez*
16/05	h	Sunderland	W	2-0	*Alexis Sánchez 2*
21/05	h	Everton	W	3-1	*Bellerín, Alexis Sánchez, Ramsey*

No	Name	Nat	DoB	Pos	Aps	(s)	Gls
7	Alexis Sánchez	CHI	19/12/88	A	36	(2)	24
24	Héctor Bellerín	ESP	19/03/95	D	27	(6)	1
33	Petr Čech	CZE	20/05/82	G	35		
21	Calum Chambers		20/01/95	D	1		1
34	Francis Coquelin	FRA	13/05/91	M	22	(7)	
2	Mathieu Debuchy	FRA	28/07/85	D	1		
35	Mohamed Elneny	EGY	11/07/92	M	8	(6)	
5	Gabriel	BRA	26/11/90	D	15	(4)	
3	Kieran Gibbs		26/09/89	D	8	(3)	
12	Olivier Giroud	FRA	30/09/86	A	11	(18)	12
16	Rob Holding		20/09/95	D	9		
17	Alex Iwobi	NGA	03/05/96	M	18	(8)	3
25	Carl Jenkinson		08/02/92	D	1		
6	Laurent Koscielny	FRA	10/09/85	D	33		2
9	Lucas Pérez	ESP	10/09/88	A	2	(9)	1
55	Ainsley Maitland-Niles		29/08/97	M		(1)	
26	Emiliano Martínez	ARG	02/09/92	G	2		
4	Per Mertesacker	GER	29/09/84	D		(1)	
18	Nacho Monreal	ESP	26/02/86	D	35	(1)	
20	Shkodran Mustafi	GER	17/04/92	D	26		2
13	David Ospina	COL	31/08/88	G	1	(1)	
15	Alex Oxlade-Chamberlain		15/08/93	M	16	(13)	2
11	Mesut Özil	GER	15/10/88	M	32	(1)	8
8	Aaron Ramsey	WAL	26/12/90	M	13	(10)	1
19	Santi Cazorla	ESP	13/12/84	M	7	(1)	2
14	Theo Walcott		16/03/89	A	23	(5)	10
23	Danny Welbeck		26/11/90	A	8	(8)	2
10	Jack Wilshere		01/01/92	M		(2)	
29	Granit Xhaka	SUI	27/09/92	M	28	(4)	2

AFC Bournemouth

1890 • Vitality Stadium (11,464) • afcb.co.uk

Manager: Eddie Howe

Date		Opponent		Score	Scorers
2016					
14/08	h	Man. United	L	1-3	*A Smith*
21/08	a	West Ham	L	0-1	
27/08	a	Crystal Palace	D	1-1	*King*
10/09	h	West Brom	W	1-0	*Wilson*
17/09	a	Man. City	L	0-4	
24/09	h	Everton	W	1-0	*Stanislas*
01/10	a	Watford	D	2-2	*Wilson, King*
15/10	h	Hull	W	6-1	*Daniels, S Cook, Stanislas 2 (1p), Wilson, Gosling*
22/10	h	Tottenham	D	0-0	
29/10	a	Middlesbrough	L	0-2	
05/11	h	Sunderland	L	1-2	*Gosling*
19/11	a	Stoke	W	1-0	*Aké*
27/11	a	Arsenal	L	1-3	*Wilson (p)*
04/12	h	Liverpool	W	4-3	*Wilson (p), Fraser, S Cook, Aké*
10/12	a	Burnley	L	2-3	*Afobe, Daniels*
13/12	h	Leicester	W	1-0	*Pugh*
18/12	h	Southampton	L	1-3	*Aké*
26/12	a	Chelsea	L	0-3	
31/12	a	Swansea	W	3-0	*Afobe, Fraser, King*
2017					
03/01	h	Arsenal	D	3-3	*Daniels, Wilson (p), Fraser*
14/01	a	Hull	L	1-3	*Stanislas (p)*
21/01	h	Watford	D	2-2	*King, Afobe*
31/01	h	Crystal Palace	L	0-2	
04/02	a	Everton	L	3-6	*King 2, Arter*
13/02	h	Man. City	L	0-2	
25/02	a	West Brom	L	1-2	*King (p)*
04/03	a	Man. United	D	1-1	*King (p)*
11/03	h	West Ham	W	3-2	*King 3*
18/03	h	Swansea	W	2-0	*og (Mawson), Afobe*
01/04	a	Southampton	D	0-0	
05/04	a	Liverpool	D	2-2	*Afobe, King*
08/04	h	Chelsea	L	1-3	*King*
15/04	a	Tottenham	L	0-4	
22/04	h	Middlesbrough	W	4-0	*King, Afobe, Pugh, Daniels*
29/04	a	Sunderland	W	1-0	*King*
06/05	h	Stoke	D	2-2	*Stanislas, og (Shawcross)*
13/05	h	Burnley	W	2-1	*Stanislas, King*
21/05	a	Leicester	D	1-1	*Stanislas*

No	Name	Nat	DoB	Pos	Aps	(s)	Gls
9	Benik Afobe	COD	12/02/93	A	14	(17)	6
5	Nathan Aké	NED	18/02/95	D	8	(2)	3
21	Ryan Allsop		17/06/92	G	1		
8	Harry Arter	IRL	28/12/89	M	33	(2)	1
1	Artur Boruc	POL	20/02/80	G	35		
38	Baily Cargill		05/07/95	D		(1)	
18	Lewis Cook		03/02/97	M	4	(2)	
3	Steve Cook		19/04/91	D	38		2
11	Charlie Daniels		07/09/86	D	34		4
23	Adam Federici	AUS	31/01/85	G	2		
2	Simon Francis		16/02/85	D	34		
24	Ryan Fraser	SCO	24/02/94	M	19	(9)	3
4	Dan Gosling		02/02/90	M	14	(13)	2
28	Lewis Grabban		12/01/88	A		(3)	
10	Max Gradel	CIV	30/11/87	A		(11)	
33	Jordon Ibe		08/12/95	M	13	(12)	
17	Joshua King	NOR	15/01/92	A	31	(5)	16
26	Tyrone Mings		13/03/93	D	5	(2)	
31	Lys Mousset	FRA	08/02/96	A	3	(8)	
7	Marc Pugh		02/04/87	M	16	(5)	2
15	Adam Smith		29/04/91	D	34	(2)	1
14	Brad Smith	AUS	09/04/94	D	3	(2)	
19	Junior Stanislas		26/11/89	M	18	(3)	7
6	Andrew Surman		20/08/86	M	21	(1)	
32	Jack Wilshere		01/01/92	M	22	(5)	
13	Callum Wilson		27/02/92	A	16	(4)	6
58	Matt Worthington		18/12/97	M		(1)	

Burnley FC

1882 • Turf Moor (22,546) • burnleyfootballclub.com

Major honours
English League (2) 1921, 1960; FA Cup (1) 1914

Manager: Sean Dyche

Date		Opponent		Score	Scorers
2016					
13/08	h	Swansea	L	0-1	
20/08	h	Liverpool	W	2-0	*Vokes, Gray*
27/08	a	Chelsea	L	0-3	
10/09	h	Hull	D	1-1	*Defour*
17/09	a	Leicester	L	0-3	
26/09	h	Watford	W	2-0	*Hendrick, Keane*
02/10	h	Arsenal	L	0-1	
16/10	a	Southampton	L	1-3	*Vokes (p)*
22/10	h	Everton	W	2-1	*Vokes, Arfield*
29/10	a	Man. United	D	0-0	
05/11	h	Crystal Palace	W	3-2	*Vokes, Gudmundsson, Barnes*
21/11	a	West Brom	L	0-4	
26/11	h	Man. City	L	1-2	*Marney*
03/12	a	Stoke	L	0-2	
10/12	h	Bournemouth	W	3-2	*Hendrick, Ward, Boyd*
14/12	a	West Ham	L	0-1	
18/12	a	Tottenham	L	1-2	*Barnes*
26/12	h	Middlesbrough	W	1-0	*Gray*
31/12	h	Sunderland	W	4-1	*Gray 3, Barnes (p)*
2017					
02/01	a	Man. City	L	1-2	*Mee*
14/01	h	Southampton	W	1-0	*Barton*
22/01	a	Arsenal	L	1-2	*Gray (p)*
31/01	h	Leicester	W	1-0	*Vokes*
04/02	a	Watford	L	1-2	*Barnes (p)*
12/02	h	Chelsea	D	1-1	*Brady*
25/02	a	Hull	D	1-1	*Keane*
04/03	a	Swansea	L	2-3	*Gray 2 (1p)*
12/03	a	Liverpool	L	1-2	*Barnes*
18/03	a	Sunderland	D	0-0	
01/04	h	Tottenham	L	0-2	
04/04	h	Stoke	W	1-0	*Boyd*
08/04	a	Middlesbrough	D	0-0	
15/04	a	Everton	L	1-3	*Vokes (p)*
23/04	h	Man. United	L	0-2	
29/04	a	Crystal Palace	W	2-0	*Barnes, Gray*
06/05	h	West Brom	D	2-2	*Vokes 2*
13/05	a	Bournemouth	L	1-2	*Vokes*
21/05	h	West Ham	L	1-2	*Vokes*

No	Name	Nat	DoB	Pos	Aps	(s)	Gls
32	Dan Agyei		01/06/97	A		(3)	
37	Scott Arfield	CAN	01/11/88	M	23	(8)	1
15	Patrick Bamford		05/09/93	A		(6)	
10	Ashley Barnes	AUT	30/10/89	A	20	(8)	6
19	Joey Barton		02/09/82	M	12	(2)	1
21	George Boyd	SCO	02/10/85	M	33	(3)	2
12	Robbie Brady	IRL	14/01/92	M	7	(7)	1
16	Steven Defour	BEL	15/04/88	M	16	(5)	1
4	Jon Flanagan		01/01/93	D	3	(3)	
7	Andre Gray		26/06/91	A	26	(6)	9
25	Jóhann Berg Gudmundsson	ISL	27/10/90	M	10	(10)	1
1	Tom Heaton		15/04/86	G	35		
13	Jeff Hendrick	IRL	31/01/92	M	31	(1)	2
14	David Jones		04/11/84	M	1		
28	Lukas Jutkiewicz		28/03/89	A		(2)	
5	Michael Keane		11/01/93	D	35		2
11	Michael Kightly		24/01/86	M	1	(4)	
28	Kevin Long	IRL	18/08/90	D	3		
2	Matthew Lowton		09/06/89	D	36		
8	Dean Marney		31/01/84	M	21		1
6	Ben Mee		21/09/89	D	34		1
41	Aiden O'Neill	AUS	04/07/98	M		(3)	
17	Paul Robinson		15/10/79	G	3		
26	James Tarkowski		19/11/92	D	4	(15)	
9	Sam Vokes	WAL	21/10/89	A	21	(16)	10
23	Stephen Ward	IRL	20/08/85	D	37		1
18	Ashley Westwood		01/04/90	M	6	(3)	

Chelsea FC

1905 • Stamford Bridge (41,623) • chelseafc.com

Major honours
UEFA Champions League (1) 2012; UEFA Cup Winners' Cup (2) 1971, 1998; UEFA Europa League (1) 2013; UEFA Super Cup (1) 1998; English League (6) 1955, 2005, 2006, 2010, 2015, 2017; FA Cup (7) 1970, 1997, 2000, 2007, 2009, 2010, 2012; League Cup (5) 1965, 1998, 2005, 2007, 2015

Manager: Antonio Conte (ITA)

Date		Opponent		Score	Scorers
2016					
15/08	h	West Ham	W	2-1	*Hazard (p), Diego Costa*
20/08	a	Watford	W	2-1	*Batshuayi, Diego Costa*
27/08	h	Burnley	W	3-0	*Hazard, Willian, Moses*
11/09	a	Swansea	D	2-2	*Diego Costa 2*
16/09	h	Liverpool	L	1-2	*Diego Costa*
24/09	a	Arsenal	L	0-3	
01/10	a	Hull	W	2-0	*Willian, Diego Costa*
15/10	h	Leicester	W	3-0	*Diego Costa, Hazard, Moses*
23/10	h	Man. United	W	4-0	*Pedro, Cahill, Hazard, Kanté*
30/10	a	Southampton	W	2-0	*Hazard, Diego Costa*
05/11	h	Everton	W	5-0	*Hazard 2, Alonso, Diego Costa, Pedro*
20/11	a	Middlesbrough	W	1-0	*Diego Costa*
26/11	h	Tottenham	W	2-1	*Pedro, Moses*
03/12	a	Man. City	W	3-1	*Diego Costa, Willian, Hazard*
11/12	h	West Brom	W	1-0	*Diego Costa*
14/12	a	Sunderland	W	1-0	*Fàbregas*
17/12	a	Crystal Palace	W	1-0	*Diego Costa*
26/12	h	Bournemouth	W	3-0	*Pedro, Hazard (p), og (S Cook)*
31/12	h	Stoke	W	4-2	*Cahill, Willian 2, Diego Costa*
2017					
04/01	a	Tottenham	L	0-2	
14/01	a	Leicester	W	3-0	*Alonso 2, Pedro*
22/01	h	Hull	W	2-0	*Diego Costa, Cahill*
31/01	a	Liverpool	D	1-1	*David Luiz*
04/02	h	Arsenal	W	3-1	*Alonso, Hazard, Fàbregas*
12/02	a	Burnley	D	1-1	*Pedro*
25/02	h	Swansea	W	3-1	*Fàbregas, Pedro, Diego Costa*
06/03	a	West Ham	W	2-1	*Hazard, Diego Costa*
18/03	a	Stoke	W	2-1	*Willian, Cahill*
01/04	h	Crystal Palace	L	1-2	*Fàbregas*
05/04	h	Man. City	W	2-1	*Hazard 2*
08/04	a	Bournemouth	W	3-1	*og (A Smith), Hazard, Alonso*
16/04	a	Man. United	L	0-2	
25/04	h	Southampton	W	4-2	*Hazard, Cahill, Diego Costa 2*
30/04	a	Everton	W	3-0	*Pedro, Cahill, Willian*
08/05	h	Middlesbrough	W	3-0	*Diego Costa, Alonso, Matić*
12/05	a	West Brom	W	1-0	*Batshuayi*
15/05	h	Watford	W	4-3	*Terry, Azpilicueta, Batshuayi, Fàbregas*
21/05	h	Sunderland	W	5-1	*Willian, Hazard, Pedro, Batshuayi 2*

No	Name	Nat	DoB	Pos	Aps	(s)	Gls
34	Ola Aina		08/10/96	D		(3)	
6	Nathan Aké	NED	18/02/95	D	1	(1)	
3	Marcos Alonso	ESP	28/12/90	M	30	(1)	6
28	César Azpilicueta	ESP	28/08/89	D	38		1
23	Michy Batshuayi	BEL	02/10/93	A	1	(19)	5
1	Asmir Begović	BIH	20/06/87	G	2		
24	Gary Cahill		19/12/85	D	36	(1)	6
29	Nathaniel Chalobah		12/12/94	M	1	(9)	
13	Thibaut Courtois	BEL	11/05/92	G	36		
30	David Luiz	BRA	22/04/87	D	33		1
19	Diego Costa	ESP	07/10/88	A	35		20
4	Cesc Fàbregas	ESP	04/05/87	M	13	(16)	5
10	Eden Hazard	BEL	07/01/91	M	36		16
2	Branislav Ivanović	SRB	22/02/84	D	6	(7)	
7	N'Golo Kanté	FRA	29/03/91	M	35		1
16	Kenedy	BRA	08/02/96	M	1		
14	Ruben Loftus-Cheek		23/01/96	M		(6)	
21	Nemanja Matić	SRB	01/08/88	M	30	(5)	1
15	Victor Moses	NGA	12/12/90	M	29	(5)	3
8	Oscar	BRA	09/09/91	M	5	(4)	
11	Pedro Rodríguez	ESP	28/07/87	A	26	(9)	9
26	John Terry		07/12/80	D	6	(3)	1
22	Willian	BRA	09/08/88	M	15	(19)	8
5	Kurt Zouma	FRA	27/10/94	D	3	(6)	

Crystal Palace FC

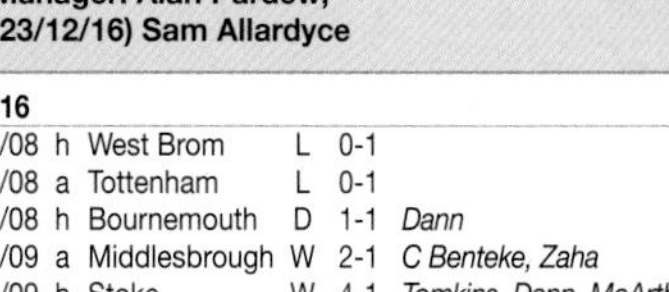

1905 • Selhurst Park (26,309) • cpfc.co.uk

Manager: Alan Pardew; (23/12/16) Sam Allardyce

Date		Opponent		Score	Scorers
2016					
13/08	h	West Brom	L	0-1	
20/08	a	Tottenham	L	0-1	
27/08	h	Bournemouth	D	1-1	*Dann*
10/09	a	Middlesbrough	W	2-1	*C Benteke, Zaha*
18/09	h	Stoke	W	4-1	*Tomkins, Dann, McArthur, Townsend*
24/09	a	Sunderland	W	3-2	*Ledley, McArthur, C Benteke*
30/09	a	Everton	D	1-1	*C Benteke*
15/10	h	West Ham	L	0-1	
22/10	a	Leicester	L	1-3	*Cabaye*
29/10	h	Liverpool	L	2-4	*McArthur 2*
05/11	a	Burnley	L	2-3	*Wickham, C Benteke (p)*
19/11	h	Man. City	L	1-2	*Wickham*
26/11	a	Swansea	L	4-5	*Zaha, Tomkins, og (Cork), C Benteke*
03/12	h	Southampton	W	3-0	*C Benteke 2, Tomkins*
10/12	a	Hull	D	3-3	*C Benteke (p), Zaha, Campbell*
14/12	h	Man. United	L	1-2	*McArthur*
17/12	h	Chelsea	L	0-1	
26/12	a	Watford	D	1-1	*Cabaye*
2017					
01/01	a	Arsenal	L	0-2	
03/01	h	Swansea	L	1-2	*Zaha*
14/01	a	West Ham	L	0-3	
21/01	h	Everton	L	0-1	
31/01	a	Bournemouth	W	2-0	*Dann, C Benteke*
04/02	h	Sunderland	L	0-4	
11/02	a	Stoke	L	0-1	
25/02	h	Middlesbrough	W	1-0	*Van Aanholt*
04/03	a	West Brom	W	2-0	*Zaha, Townsend*
18/03	h	Watford	W	1-0	*og (Deeney)*
01/04	a	Chelsea	W	2-1	*Zaha, C Benteke*
05/04	a	Southampton	L	1-3	*C Benteke*
10/04	h	Arsenal	W	3-0	*Townsend, Cabaye, Milivojević (p)*
15/04	h	Leicester	D	2-2	*Cabaye, C Benteke*
23/04	a	Liverpool	W	2-1	*C Benteke 2*
26/04	h	Tottenham	L	0-1	
29/04	h	Burnley	L	0-2	
06/05	a	Man. City	L	0-5	
14/05	h	Hull	W	4-0	*Zaha, C Benteke, Milivojević (p), Van Aanholt*
21/05	a	Man. United	L	0-2	

No	Name	Nat	DoB	Pos	Aps	(s)	Gls
17	Christian Benteke	BEL	03/12/90	A	36		15
15	Jonathan Benteke	BEL	28/04/95	A		(1)	
10	Yannick Bolasie	COD	24/05/89	M		(1)	
7	Yohan Cabaye	FRA	14/01/86	M	25	(7)	4
9	Fraizer Campbell		13/09/87	A		(12)	1
6	Scott Dann		14/02/87	D	19	(4)	3
27	Damien Delaney	IRL	29/07/81	D	21	(9)	
20	Mathieu Flamini	FRA	07/03/84	M	3	(7)	
19	Zeki Fryers		09/09/92	D		(8)	
13	Wayne Hennessey	WAL	24/01/87	G	29		
15	Mile Jedinak	AUS	03/08/84	M	1		
25	Sullay Kaikai		26/08/95	M		(1)	
34	Martin Kelly		27/04/90	D	25	(4)	
16	Joe Ledley	WAL	23/01/87	M	13	(5)	1
14	Lee Chung-yong	KOR	02/07/88	M	4	(11)	
30	Steve Mandanda	FRA	28/03/85	G	9		
18	James McArthur	SCO	07/10/87	M	24	(5)	5
28	Luka Milivojević	SRB	07/04/91	M	14		2
22	Jordon Mutch		02/12/91	M		(4)	
42	Jason Puncheon		26/06/86	M	35	(1)	
8	Loïc Rémy	FRA	02/01/87	A	1	(4)	
12	Mamadou Sakho	FRA	13/02/90	D	8		
26	Bakary Sako	MLI	24/04/88	M		(7)	
31	Jeff Schlupp	GHA	23/12/92	M	11	(4)	
23	Pape Souaré	SEN	06/06/90	D	3		
5	James Tomkins		29/03/89	D	23	(1)	3
10	Andros Townsend		16/07/91	M	30	(6)	3
3	Patrick van Aanholt	NED	29/08/90	D	8	(3)	2
2	Joel Ward		29/10/89	D	38		
21	Connor Wickham		31/03/93	A	4	(4)	2
11	Wilfried Zaha	CIV	10/11/92	M	34	(1)	7

ENGLAND

Everton FC

1878 • Goodison Park (40,569) • evertonfc.com

Major honours
UEFA Cup Winners' Cup (1) 1985; English League (9) 1891, 1915, 1928, 1932, 1939, 1963, 1970, 1985, 1987; FA Cup (5) 1906, 1933, 1966, 1984, 1995

Manager: Ronald Koeman (NED)

Date		Opponent		Score	Scorers
2016					
13/08	h	Tottenham	D	1-1	*Barkley*
20/08	a	West Brom	W	2-1	*Mirallas, Barry*
27/08	h	Stoke	W	1-0	*og (Given)*
12/09	a	Sunderland	W	3-0	*Lukaku 3*
17/09	h	Middlesbrough	W	3-1	*Barry, Coleman, Lukaku*
24/09	a	Bournemouth	L	0-1	
30/09	h	Crystal Palace	D	1-1	*Lukaku*
15/10	a	Man. City	D	1-1	*Lukaku*
22/10	a	Burnley	L	1-2	*Bolasie*
30/10	h	West Ham	W	2-0	*Lukaku, Barkley*
05/11	a	Chelsea	L	0-5	
19/11	h	Swansea	D	1-1	*Coleman*
27/11	a	Southampton	L	0-1	
04/12	h	Man. United	D	1-1	*Baines (p)*
10/12	a	Watford	L	2-3	*Lukaku 2*
13/12	h	Arsenal	W	2-1	*Coleman, Williams*
19/12	h	Liverpool	L	0-1	
26/12	a	Leicester	W	2-0	*Mirallas, Lukaku*
30/12	a	Hull	D	2-2	*og (Marshall), Barkley*
2017					
02/01	h	Southampton	W	3-0	*Valencia, Baines (p), Lukaku*
15/01	h	Man. City	W	4-0	*Lukaku, Mirallas, Davies, Lookman*
21/01	a	Crystal Palace	W	1-0	*Coleman*
01/02	a	Stoke	D	1-1	*og (Shawcross)*
04/02	h	Bournemouth	W	6-3	*Lukaku 4, McCarthy, Barkley*
11/02	a	Middlesbrough	D	0-0	
25/02	h	Sunderland	W	2-0	*Gueye, Lukaku*
05/03	a	Tottenham	L	2-3	*Lukaku, Valencia*
11/03	h	West Brom	W	3-0	*Mirallas, Schneiderlin, Lukaku*
18/03	h	Hull	W	4-0	*Calvert-Lewin, Valencia, Lukaku 2*
01/04	a	Liverpool	L	1-3	*Pennington*
04/04	a	Man. United	D	1-1	*Jagielka*
09/04	h	Leicester	W	4-2	*Davies, Lukaku 2, Jagielka*
15/04	h	Burnley	W	3-1	*Jagielka, og (Mee), Lukaku*
22/04	a	West Ham	D	0-0	
30/04	h	Chelsea	L	0-3	
06/05	a	Swansea	L	0-1	
12/05	h	Watford	W	1-0	*Barkley*
21/05	a	Arsenal	L	1-3	*Lukaku (p)*

No	Name	Nat	DoB	Pos	Aps	(s)	Gls
3	Leighton Baines		11/12/84	D	32		2
8	Ross Barkley		05/12/93	M	32	(4)	5
18	Gareth Barry		23/02/81	M	23	(10)	2
14	Yannick Bolasie	COD	24/05/89	M	12	(1)	1
29	Dominic Calvert-Lewin		16/03/97	A	5	(6)	1
15	Tom Cleverley		12/08/89	M	4	(6)	
23	Séamus Coleman	IRL	11/10/88	D	26		4
26	Tom Davies		30/06/98	M	18	(6)	2
7	Gerard Deulofeu	ESP	13/03/94	A	4	(7)	
25	Ramiro Funes Mori	ARG	05/03/91	D	16	(7)	
17	Idrissa Gueye	SEN	26/09/89	M	32	(1)	1
30	Mason Holgate		22/10/96	D	16	(2)	
6	Phil Jagielka		17/08/82	D	25	(2)	3
1	Joel Robles	ESP	17/06/90	G	19	(1)	
43	Jonjoe Kenny		15/03/97	D		(1)	
9	Arouna Koné	CIV	11/11/83	A		(6)	
12	Aaron Lennon		16/04/87	M	6	(5)	
31	Ademola Lookman		20/10/97	A	3	(5)	1
10	Romelu Lukaku	BEL	13/05/93	A	36	(1)	25
16	James McCarthy	IRL	12/11/90	M	7	(5)	1
11	Kevin Mirallas	BEL	05/10/87	M	23	(12)	4
20	Bryan Oviedo	CRC	18/02/90	D	6		
38	Matthew Pennington		06/10/94	D	2	(1)	1
2	Morgan Schneiderlin	FRA	08/11/89	M	12	(2)	1
22	Maarten Stekelenburg	NED	22/09/82	G	19		
19	Enner Valencia	ECU	04/11/89	A	5	(16)	3
5	Ashley Williams	WAL	23/08/84	D	35	(1)	1

Hull City AFC

1904 • KCOM Stadium (25,404) • hullcitytigers.com

Manager: Mike Phelan; (04/01/17) Marco Silva (POR)

Date		Opponent		Score	Scorers
2016					
13/08	h	Leicester	W	2-1	*Diomandé, Snodgrass*
20/08	a	Swansea	W	2-0	*Maloney, Hernández*
27/08	h	Man. United	L	0-1	
10/09	a	Burnley	D	1-1	*Snodgrass*
17/09	h	Arsenal	L	1-4	*Snodgrass (p)*
24/09	a	Liverpool	L	1-5	*Meyler*
01/10	h	Chelsea	L	0-2	
15/10	a	Bournemouth	L	1-6	*Mason*
22/10	h	Stoke	L	0-2	
29/10	a	Watford	L	0-1	
06/11	h	Southampton	W	2-1	*Snodgrass, Dawson*
19/11	a	Sunderland	L	0-3	
26/11	h	West Brom	D	1-1	*Dawson*
05/12	a	Middlesbrough	L	0-1	
10/12	h	Crystal Palace	D	3-3	*Snodgrass (p), Diomandé, Livermore*
14/12	a	Tottenham	L	0-3	
17/12	a	West Ham	L	0-1	
26/12	h	Man. City	L	0-3	
30/12	h	Everton	D	2-2	*Dawson, Snodgrass*
2017					
02/01	a	West Brom	L	1-3	*Snodgrass*
14/01	h	Bournemouth	W	3-1	*Hernández 2, og (Mings)*
22/01	a	Chelsea	L	0-2	
01/02	a	Man. United	D	0-0	
04/02	h	Liverpool	W	2-0	*N'Diaye, Niasse*
11/02	a	Arsenal	L	0-2	
25/02	h	Burnley	D	1-1	*Huddlestone (p)*
04/03	a	Leicester	L	1-3	*Clucas*
11/03	h	Swansea	W	2-1	*Niasse 2*
18/03	a	Everton	L	0-4	
01/04	h	West Ham	W	2-1	*Robertson, Ranocchia*
05/04	h	Middlesbrough	W	4-2	*Marković, Niasse, Hernández, Maguire*
08/04	a	Man. City	L	1-3	*Ranocchia*
15/04	a	Stoke	L	1-3	*Maguire*
22/04	h	Watford	W	2-0	*Marković, Clucas*
29/04	a	Southampton	D	0-0	
06/05	h	Sunderland	L	0-2	
14/05	a	Crystal Palace	L	0-4	
21/05	h	Tottenham	L	1-7	*Clucas*

No	Name	Nat	DoB	Pos	Aps	(s)	Gls
29	Jarrod Bowen		20/12/96	A	1	(6)	
11	Sam Clucas		25/09/90	M	36	(1)	3
6	Curtis Davies		15/03/85	D	25	(1)	
21	Michael Dawson		18/11/83	D	19	(3)	3
20	Adama Diomandé	NOR	14/02/90	A	13	(9)	2
14	Omar Elabdellaoui	NOR	05/12/91	D	7	(1)	
27	Ahmed Elmohamady	EGY	09/09/87	M	28	(5)	
40	Evandro	BRA	23/08/86	M	7	(4)	
17	Kamil Grosicki	POL	08/06/88	M	12	(3)	
22	Markus Henriksen	NOR	25/07/92	M	6	(9)	
9	Abel Hernández	URU	08/08/90	A	16	(8)	4
8	Tom Huddlestone		28/12/86	M	23	(8)	1
16	Eldin Jakupovic	SUI	02/10/84	G	22		
19	Will Keane		11/01/93	A	4	(1)	
14	Jake Livermore		14/11/89	M	20	(1)	1
5	Harry Maguire		05/03/93	D	25	(4)	2
15	Shaun Maloney	SCO	24/01/83	M	2	(7)	1
50	Lazar Marković	SRB	02/03/94	M	12		2
23	David Marshall	SCO	05/03/85	G	16		
25	Ryan Mason		13/06/91	M	11	(5)	1
18	Dieumerci Mbokani	COD	22/11/85	A	8	(4)	
7	David Meyler	IRL	29/05/89	M	9	(11)	1
10	Alfred N'Diaye	SEN	06/03/90	M	15		1
24	Oumar Niasse	SEN	18/04/90	A	12	(5)	4
13	Andrea Ranocchia	ITA	16/02/88	D	15	(1)	2
3	Andrew Robertson	SCO	11/03/94	D	31	(2)	1
10	Robert Snodgrass	SCO	07/09/87	M	19	(1)	7
28	Josh Tymon		22/05/99	D	4	(1)	

Leicester City FC

1884 • King Power Stadium (32,500) • lcfc.com

Major honours
English League (1) 2016; League Cup (3) 1964, 1997, 2000

Manager: Claudio Ranieri (ITA); (23/02/17) Craig Shakespeare

Date		Opponent		Score	Scorers
2016					
13/08	a	Hull	L	1-2	*Mahrez (p)*
20/08	h	Arsenal	D	0-0	
27/08	h	Swansea	W	2-1	*Vardy, Morgan*
10/09	a	Liverpool	L	1-4	*Vardy*
17/09	h	Burnley	W	3-0	*Slimani 2, og (Mee)*
24/09	a	Man. United	L	1-4	*Gray*
02/10	h	Southampton	D	0-0	
15/10	a	Chelsea	L	0-3	
22/10	h	Crystal Palace	W	3-1	*Musa, Okazaki, Fuchs*
29/10	a	Tottenham	D	1-1	*Musa*
06/11	h	West Brom	L	1-2	*Slimani*
19/11	a	Watford	L	1-2	*Mahrez (p)*
26/11	h	Middlesbrough	D	2-2	*Mahrez (p), Slimani (p)*
03/12	a	Sunderland	L	1-2	*Okazaki*
10/12	h	Man. City	W	4-2	*Vardy 3, King*
13/12	a	Bournemouth	L	0-1	
17/12	a	Stoke	D	2-2	*Ulloa, Amartey*
26/12	h	Everton	L	0-2	
31/12	h	West Ham	W	1-0	*Slimani*
2017					
02/01	a	Middlesbrough	D	0-0	
14/01	h	Chelsea	L	0-3	
22/01	a	Southampton	L	0-3	
31/01	a	Burnley	L	0-1	
05/02	h	Man. United	L	0-3	
12/02	a	Swansea	L	0-2	
27/02	h	Liverpool	W	3-1	*Vardy 2, Drinkwater*
04/03	h	Hull	W	3-1	*Fuchs, Mahrez, og (Huddlestone)*
18/03	a	West Ham	W	3-2	*Mahrez, Huth, Vardy*
01/04	h	Stoke	W	2-0	*Ndidi, Vardy*
04/04	h	Sunderland	W	2-0	*Slimani, Vardy*
09/04	a	Everton	L	2-4	*Slimani, Albrighton*
15/04	a	Crystal Palace	D	2-2	*Huth, Vardy*
26/04	a	Arsenal	L	0-1	
29/04	a	West Brom	W	1-0	*Vardy*
06/05	h	Watford	W	3-0	*Ndidi, Mahrez, Albrighton*
13/05	a	Man. City	L	1-2	*Okazaki*
18/05	h	Tottenham	L	1-6	*Chilwell*
21/05	h	Bournemouth	D	1-1	*Vardy*

No	Name	Nat	DoB	Pos	Aps	(s)	Gls
11	Marc Albrighton		18/11/89	M	29	(4)	2
13	Daniel Amartey	GHA	21/12/94	M	17	(7)	1
29	Yohan Benalouane	TUN	28/03/87	D	11		
3	Ben Chilwell		21/12/96	D	7	(5)	1
4	Danny Drinkwater		05/03/90	M	27	(2)	1
28	Christian Fuchs	AUT	07/04/86	D	35	(1)	2
22	Demarai Gray		28/06/96	M	9	(21)	1
6	Robert Huth	GER	18/08/84	D	33		2
8	Matty James		22/07/91	M		(1)	
10	Andy King	WAL	29/10/88	M	15	(8)	1
2	Luis Hernández	ESP	14/04/89	D	3	(1)	
26	Riyad Mahrez	ALG	21/02/91	M	33	(3)	6
24	Nampalys Mendy	FRA	23/06/92	M	4		
5	Wes Morgan	JAM	21/01/84	D	27		1
7	Ahmed Musa	NGA	14/10/92	A	7	(14)	2
25	Wilfred Ndidi	NGA	16/12/96	M	17		2
20	Shinji Okazaki	JPN	16/04/86	A	21	(9)	3
15	Jeff Schlupp	GHA	23/12/92	M	1	(3)	
1	Kasper Schmeichel	DEN	05/11/86	G	30		
17	Danny Simpson		04/01/87	D	34	(1)	
19	Islam Slimani	ALG	18/06/88	A	13	(10)	7
23	Leonardo Ulloa	ARG	26/07/86	A	3	(13)	1
9	Jamie Vardy		11/01/87	A	33	(2)	13
27	Marcin Wasilewski	POL	09/06/80	D	1		
21	Ron-Robert Zieler	GER	12/02/89	G	8	(1)	

Liverpool FC

1892 • Anfield (54,074) • liverpoolfc.com

Major honours
European Champion Clubs' Cup/UEFA Champions League (5) 1977, 1978, 1981, 1984, 2005; UEFA Cup (3) 1973, 1976, 2001; UEFA Super Cup (3) 1977, 2001, 2005; English League (18) 1901, 1906, 1922, 1923, 1947, 1964, 1966, 1973, 1976, 1977, 1979, 1980, 1982, 1983, 1984, 1986, 1988, 1990; FA Cup (7) 1965, 1974, 1986, 1989, 1992, 2001, 2006; League Cup (8) 1981, 1982, 1983, 1984, 1995, 2001, 2003, 2012

Manager: Jürgen Klopp (GER)

2016					
14/08	a	Arsenal	W	4-3	*Coutinho 2, Lallana, Mané*
20/08	a	Burnley	L	0-2	
27/08	a	Tottenham	D	1-1	*Milner (p)*
10/09	h	Leicester	W	4-1	*Roberto Firmino 2, Mané, Lallana*
16/09	a	Chelsea	W	2-1	*Lovren, Henderson*
24/09	h	Hull	W	5-1	*Lallana, Milner 2 (2p), Mané, Coutinho*
01/10	a	Swansea	W	2-1	*Roberto Firmino, Milner (p)*
17/10	h	Man. United	D	0-0	
22/10	h	West Brom	W	2-1	*Mané, Coutinho*
29/10	a	Crystal Palace	W	4-2	*Can, Lovren, Matip, Roberto Firmino*
06/11	h	Watford	W	6-1	*Mané 2, Coutinho, Can, Roberto Firmino, Wijnaldum*
19/11	a	Southampton	D	0-0	
26/11	h	Sunderland	W	2-0	*Origi, Milner (p)*
04/12	a	Bournemouth	L	3-4	*Mané, Origi, Can*
11/12	h	West Ham	D	2-2	*Lallana, Origi*
14/12	a	Middlesbrough	W	3-0	*Lallana 2, Origi*
19/12	a	Everton	W	1-0	*Mané*
27/12	h	Stoke	W	4-1	*Lallana, Roberto Firmino, og (Imbula), Sturridge*
31/12	h	Man. City	W	1-0	*Wijnaldum*
2017					
02/01	a	Sunderland	D	2-2	*Sturridge, Mané*
15/01	a	Man. United	D	1-1	*Milner (p)*
21/01	h	Swansea	L	2-3	*Roberto Firmino 2*
31/01	h	Chelsea	D	1-1	*Wijnaldum*
04/02	a	Hull	L	0-2	
11/02	h	Tottenham	W	2-0	*Mané 2*
27/02	a	Leicester	L	1-3	*Coutinho*
04/03	h	Arsenal	W	3-1	*Roberto Firmino, Mané, Wijnaldum*
12/03	h	Burnley	W	2-1	*Wijnaldum, Can*
19/03	a	Man. City	D	1-1	*Milner (p)*
01/04	h	Everton	W	3-1	*Mané, Coutinho, Origi*
05/04	h	Bournemouth	D	2-2	*Coutinho, Origi*
08/04	a	Stoke	W	2-1	*Coutinho, Roberto Firmino*
16/04	a	West Brom	W	1-0	*Roberto Firmino*
23/04	h	Crystal Palace	L	1-2	*Coutinho*
01/05	a	Watford	W	1-0	*Can*
07/05	h	Southampton	D	0-0	
14/05	a	West Ham	W	4-0	*Sturridge, Coutinho 2, Origi*
21/05	h	Middlesbrough	W	3-0	*Wijnaldum, Coutinho, Lallana*

No	Name	Nat	DoB	Pos	Aps	(s)	Gls
66	Trent Alexander-Arnold		17/10/98	D	2	(5)	
23	Emre Can	GER	12/01/94	M	26	(6)	5
2	Nathaniel Clyne		05/04/91	D	37		
10	Philippe Coutinho	BRA	12/06/92	M	28	(3)	13
53	Ovie Ejaria		18/11/97	M		(2)	
16	Marko Grujić	SRB	13/04/96	M		(5)	
14	Jordan Henderson		17/06/90	M	24		1
1	Loris Karius	GER	22/06/93	G	10		
17	Ragnar Klavan	EST	30/10/85	D	15	(5)	
20	Adam Lallana		10/05/88	M	27	(4)	8
6	Dejan Lovren	CRO	05/07/89	D	29		2
21	Lucas Leiva	BRA	09/01/87	M	12	(12)	
19	Sadio Mané	SEN	10/04/92	M	26	(1)	13
32	Joël Matip	CMR	08/08/91	D	27	(2)	1
22	Simon Mignolet	BEL	06/03/88	G	28		
7	James Milner		04/01/86	D	36		7
18	Alberto Moreno	ESP	05/07/92	D	2	(10)	
27	Divock Origi	BEL	18/04/95	A	14	(20)	7
11	Roberto Firmino	BRA	02/10/91	A	34	(1)	11
35	Kevin Stewart		07/09/93	M		(4)	
15	Daniel Sturridge		01/09/89	A	7	(13)	3
5	Georginio Wijnaldum	NED	11/11/90	M	33	(3)	6
58	Ben Woodburn	WAL	15/10/99	A	1	(4)	

Manchester City FC

1894 • Etihad Stadium (55,097) • mancity.com

Major honours
UEFA Cup Winners' Cup (1) 1970; English League (4) 1937, 1968, 2012, 2014; FA Cup (5) 1904, 1934, 1956, 1969, 2011; League Cup (4) 1970, 1976, 2014, 2016

Manager: Pep Guardiola (ESP)

2016					
13/08	h	Sunderland	W	2-1	*Agüero (p), og (McNair)*
20/08	a	Stoke	W	4-1	*Agüero 2 (1p), Nolito 2*
28/08	h	West Ham	W	3-1	*Sterling 2, Fernandinho*
10/09	a	Man. United	W	2-1	*De Bruyne, Iheanacho*
17/09	h	Bournemouth	W	4-0	*De Bruyne, Iheanacho, Sterling, Gündoğan*
24/09	a	Swansea	W	3-1	*Agüero 2 (1p), Sterling*
02/10	a	Tottenham	L	0-2	
15/10	h	Everton	D	1-1	*Nolito*
23/10	h	Southampton	D	1-1	*Iheanacho*
29/10	a	West Brom	W	4-0	*Agüero 2, Gündoğan 2*
05/11	h	Middlesbrough	D	1-1	*Agüero*
19/11	a	Crystal Palace	W	2-1	*Touré 2*
26/11	a	Burnley	W	2-1	*Agüero 2*
03/12	h	Chelsea	L	1-3	*og (Cahill)*
10/12	a	Leicester	L	2-4	*Kolarov, Nolito*
14/12	h	Watford	W	2-0	*Zabaleta, Silva*
18/12	h	Arsenal	W	2-1	*Sané, Sterling*
26/12	a	Hull	W	3-0	*Touré (p), Iheanacho, og (Davies)*
31/12	a	Liverpool	L	0-1	
2017					
02/01	h	Burnley	W	2-1	*Clichy, Agüero*
15/01	a	Everton	L	0-4	
21/01	h	Tottenham	D	2-2	*Sané, De Bruyne*
01/02	a	West Ham	W	4-0	*De Bruyne, Silva, Gabriel Jesus, Touré (p)*
05/02	h	Swansea	W	2-1	*Gabriel Jesus 2*
13/02	a	Bournemouth	W	2-0	*Sterling, og (Mings)*
05/03	a	Sunderland	W	2-0	*Agüero, Sané*
08/03	h	Stoke	D	0-0	
19/03	h	Liverpool	D	1-1	*Agüero*
02/04	a	Arsenal	D	2-2	*Sané, Agüero*
05/04	a	Chelsea	L	1-2	*Agüero*
08/04	h	Hull	W	3-1	*og (Elmohamady), Agüero, Delph*
15/04	a	Southampton	W	3-0	*Kompany, Sané, Agüero*
27/04	h	Man. United	D	0-0	
30/04	a	Middlesbrough	D	2-2	*Agüero (p), Gabriel Jesus*
06/05	h	Crystal Palace	W	5-0	*Silva, Kompany, De Bruyne, Sterling, Otamendi*
13/05	h	Leicester	W	2-1	*Silva, Gabriel Jesus (p)*
16/05	h	West Brom	W	3-1	*Gabriel Jesus, De Bruyne, Touré*
21/05	a	Watford	W	5-0	*Kompany, Agüero 2, Fernandinho, Gabriel Jesus*

No	Name	Nat	DoB	Pos	Aps	(s)	Gls
10	Sergio Agüero	ARG	02/06/88	A	25	(6)	20
1	Claudio Bravo	CHI	13/04/83	G	22		
13	Willy Caballero	ARG	28/09/81	G	16	(1)	
22	Gaël Clichy	FRA	26/07/85	D	24	(1)	1
17	Kevin De Bruyne	BEL	28/06/91	M	33	(3)	6
18	Fabian Delph		21/11/89	M	2	(5)	1
25	Fernandinho	BRA	04/05/85	M	31	(1)	2
6	Fernando	BRA	25/07/87	M	5	(10)	
33	Gabriel Jesus	BRA	03/04/97	A	8	(2)	7
75	Aleix García	ESP	28/06/97	M	1	(3)	
8	İlkay Gündoğan	GER	24/10/90	M	9	(1)	3
72	Kelechi Iheanacho	NGA	03/10/96	A	5	(15)	4
15	Jesús Navas	ESP	21/11/85	M	12	(12)	
11	Aleksandar Kolarov	SRB	10/11/85	D	27	(2)	1
4	Vincent Kompany	BEL	10/04/86	D	10	(1)	3
8	Samir Nasri	FRA	26/06/87	M		(1)	
9	Nolito	ESP	15/10/86	A	9	(10)	4
30	Nicolás Otamendi	ARG	12/02/88	D	29	(1)	1
3	Bacary Sagna	FRA	14/02/83	D	14	(3)	
19	Leroy Sané	GER	11/01/96	M	20	(6)	5
21	David Silva	ESP	08/01/86	M	31	(3)	4
7	Raheem Sterling		08/12/94	M	29	(4)	7
24	John Stones		28/05/94	D	23	(4)	
42	Yaya Touré	CIV	13/05/83	M	22	(3)	5
5	Pablo Zabaleta	ARG	16/01/85	D	11	(9)	1

Manchester United FC

1878 • Old Trafford (76,100) • manutd.com

Major honours
European Champion Clubs' Cup/UEFA Champions League (3) 1968, 1999, 2008; UEFA Cup Winners' Cup (1) 1991; UEFA Europa League (1) 2017; UEFA Super Cup (1) 1991; European/South American Cup (1) 1999; FIFA Club World Cup (1) 2008; English League (20) 1908, 1911, 1952, 1956, 1957, 1965, 1967, 1993, 1994, 1996, 1997, 1999, 2000, 2001, 2003, 2007, 2008, 2009, 2011, 2013; FA Cup (12) 1909, 1948, 1963, 1977, 1983, 1985, 1990, 1994, 1996, 1999, 2004, 2016; League Cup (5) 1992, 2006, 2009, 2010, 2017

Manager: José Mourinho (POR)

2016					
14/08	a	Bournemouth	W	3-1	*Mata, Rooney, Ibrahimović*
19/08	h	Southampton	W	2-0	*Ibrahimović 2 (1p)*
27/08	a	Hull	W	1-0	*Rashford*
10/09	h	Man. City	L	1-2	*Ibrahimović*
18/09	a	Watford	L	1-3	*Rashford*
24/09	h	Leicester	W	4-1	*Smalling, Mata, Rashford, Pogba*
02/10	h	Stoke	D	1-1	*Martial*
17/10	a	Liverpool	D	0-0	
23/10	a	Chelsea	L	0-4	
29/10	h	Burnley	D	0-0	
06/11	a	Swansea	W	3-1	*Pogba, Ibrahimović 2*
19/11	h	Arsenal	D	1-1	*Mata*
27/11	h	West Ham	D	1-1	*Ibrahimović*
04/12	a	Everton	D	1-1	*Ibrahimović*
11/12	h	Tottenham	W	1-0	*Mkhitaryan*
14/12	a	Crystal Palace	W	2-1	*Pogba, Ibrahimović*
17/12	a	West Brom	W	2-0	*Ibrahimović 2*
26/12	h	Sunderland	W	3-1	*Blind, Ibrahimović, Mkhitaryan*
31/12	h	Middlesbrough	W	2-1	*Martial, Pogba*
2017					
02/01	a	West Ham	W	2-0	*Mata, Ibrahimović*
15/01	h	Liverpool	D	1-1	*Ibrahimović*
21/01	a	Stoke	D	1-1	*Rooney*
01/02	h	Hull	D	0-0	
05/02	a	Leicester	W	3-0	*Mkhitaryan, Ibrahimović, Mata*
11/02	h	Watford	W	2-0	*Mata, Martial*
04/03	h	Bournemouth	D	1-1	*Rojo*
19/03	a	Middlesbrough	W	3-1	*Fellaini, Lingard, Valencia*
01/04	h	West Brom	D	0-0	
04/04	h	Everton	D	1-1	*Ibrahimović (p)*
09/04	a	Sunderland	W	3-0	*Ibrahimović, Mkhitaryan, Rashford*
16/04	h	Chelsea	W	2-0	*Rashford, Ander Herrera*
23/04	a	Burnley	W	2-0	*Martial, Rooney*
27/04	a	Man. City	D	0-0	
30/04	h	Swansea	D	1-1	*Rooney (p)*
07/05	a	Arsenal	L	0-2	
14/05	a	Tottenham	L	1-2	*Rooney*
17/05	a	Southampton	D	0-0	
21/05	h	Crystal Palace	W	2-0	*Harrop, Pogba*

No	Name	Nat	DoB	Pos	Aps	(s)	Gls
21	Ander Herrera	ESP	14/08/89	M	27	(4)	1
3	Eric Bailly	CIV	12/04/94	D	24	(1)	
17	Daley Blind	NED	09/03/90	D	20	(3)	1
16	Michael Carrick		28/07/81	M	18	(5)	
36	Matteo Darmian	ITA	02/12/89	D	15	(3)	
1	David de Gea	ESP	07/11/90	G	35		
7	Memphis Depay	NED	13/02/94	A		(4)	
27	Marouane Fellaini	BEL	22/11/87	M	18	(10)	1
24	Timothy Fosu-Mensah	NED	02/01/98	D	1	(3)	
47	Angel Gomes		31/08/00	M		(1)	
46	Josh Harrop		15/12/95	A	1		1
9	Zlatan Ibrahimović	SWE	03/10/81	A	27	(1)	17
40	Joel Pereira	POR	28/08/96	G	1		
4	Phil Jones		21/02/92	D	18		
14	Jesse Lingard		15/12/92	M	18	(7)	1
11	Anthony Martial	FRA	05/12/95	A	18	(7)	4
8	Juan Mata	ESP	28/04/88	M	19	(6)	6
39	Scott McTominay	SCO	08/12/96	M	1	(1)	
35	Demetri Mitchell		11/01/97	D	1		
22	Henrikh Mkhitaryan	ARM	21/01/89	M	15	(9)	4
6	Paul Pogba	FRA	15/03/93	M	29	(1)	5
19	Marcus Rashford		31/10/97	A	16	(16)	5
5	Marcos Rojo	ARG	20/03/90	D	18	(3)	1
20	Sergio Romero	ARG	22/02/87	G	2		
10	Wayne Rooney		24/10/85	A	15	(10)	5
28	Morgan Schneiderlin	FRA	08/11/89	M		(3)	
23	Luke Shaw		12/07/95	D	9	(2)	
12	Chris Smalling		22/11/89	D	13	(5)	1
38	Axel Tuanzebe		14/11/97	D	4		
25	Antonio Valencia	ECU	04/08/85	D	27	(1)	1
18	Ashley Young		09/07/85	M	8	(4)	

ENGLAND

Middlesbrough FC

1876 • Riverside Stadium (35,100) • mfc.co.uk

Major honours
League Cup (1) 2004

Manager: Aitor Karanka (ESP); (16/03/17) (Steve Agnew)

2016

Date		Opponent		Score	Scorers
13/08	h	Stoke	D	1-1	*Negredo*
21/08	a	Sunderland	W	2-1	*Stuani 2*
28/08	a	West Brom	D	0-0	
10/09	h	Crystal Palace	L	1-2	*Ayala*
17/09	a	Everton	L	1-3	*og (Stekelenburg)*
24/09	h	Tottenham	L	1-2	*Gibson*
01/10	a	West Ham	D	1-1	*Stuani*
16/10	h	Watford	L	0-1	
22/10	a	Arsenal	D	0-0	
29/10	h	Bournemouth	W	2-0	*Ramírez, Downing*
05/11	a	Man. City	D	1-1	*De Roon*
20/11	h	Chelsea	L	0-1	
26/11	a	Leicester	D	2-2	*Negredo 2*
05/12	h	Hull	W	1-0	*Ramírez*
11/12	a	Southampton	L	0-1	
14/12	h	Liverpool	L	0-3	
17/12	h	Swansea	W	3-0	*Negredo 2 (1p), De Roon*
26/12	a	Burnley	L	0-1	
31/12	a	Man. United	L	1-2	*Leadbitter*

2017

Date		Opponent		Score	Scorers
02/01	h	Leicester	D	0-0	
14/01	a	Watford	D	0-0	
21/01	h	West Ham	L	1-3	*Stuani*
31/01	h	West Brom	D	1-1	*Negredo (p)*
04/02	a	Tottenham	L	0-1	
11/02	h	Everton	D	0-0	
25/02	a	Crystal Palace	L	0-1	
04/03	a	Stoke	L	0-2	
19/03	h	Man. United	L	1-3	*Gestede*
02/04	a	Swansea	D	0-0	
05/04	a	Hull	L	2-4	*Negredo, De Roon*
08/04	h	Burnley	D	0-0	
17/04	h	Arsenal	L	1-2	*Negredo*
22/04	a	Bournemouth	L	0-4	
26/04	h	Sunderland	W	1-0	*De Roon*
30/04	h	Man. City	D	2-2	*Negredo, Chambers*
08/05	a	Chelsea	L	0-3	
13/05	h	Southampton	L	1-2	*Bamford*
21/05	a	Liverpool	L	0-3	

No	Name	Nat	DoB	Pos	Aps	(s)	Gls
27	Albert Adomah	GHA	13/12/87	M	1	(1)	
14	Daniel Ayala	ESP	07/11/90	D	11	(3)	1
20	Patrick Bamford		05/09/93	A	2	(6)	1
17	Antonio Barragán	ESP	12/06/87	D	26		
25	Calum Chambers		20/01/95	D	24		1
8	Adam Clayton		14/01/89	M	32	(2)	
14	Marten de Roon	NED	29/03/91	M	32	(1)	4
19	Stewart Downing		22/07/84	M	24	(6)	1
5	Bernardo Espinosa	COL	11/07/89	D	10	(1)	
2	Fábio	BRA	09/07/90	D	21	(3)	
11	Viktor Fischer	DEN	09/06/94	A	6	(7)	
34	Adam Forshaw		08/10/91	M	30	(4)	
3	George Friend		17/10/87	D	20	(4)	
29	Rudy Gestede	BEN	10/10/88	A	4	(12)	1
6	Ben Gibson		15/01/93	D	38		1
27	Adlène Guedioura	ALG	12/11/85	M		(5)	
12	Brad Guzan	USA	09/09/84	G	10		
40	James Husband		03/01/94	D	1		
7	Grant Leadbitter		07/01/86	M	7	(6)	1
10	Álvaro Negredo	ESP	20/08/85	A	33	(3)	9
24	Emilio Nsue	EQG	30/09/89	M	4		
35	David Nugent		02/05/85	A		(4)	
21	Gastón Ramírez	URU	02/12/90	M	20	(4)	2
9	Jordan Rhodes	SCO	05/02/90	A	2	(4)	
18	Cristhian Stuani	URU	12/10/86	A	16	(7)	4
37	Adama Traoré	ESP	25/01/96	M	16	(11)	
26	Víctor Valdés	ESP	14/01/82	G	28		

Southampton FC

1885 • St Mary's Stadium (32,689) • southamptonfc.com

Major honours
FA Cup (1) 1976

Manager: Claude Puel (FRA)

2016

Date		Opponent		Score	Scorers
13/08	h	Watford	D	1-1	*Redmond*
19/08	a	Man. United	L	0-2	
27/08	h	Sunderland	D	1-1	*Rodriguez*
10/09	a	Arsenal	L	1-2	*og (Čech)*
18/09	h	Swansea	W	1-0	*Austin*
25/09	a	West Ham	W	3-0	*Austin, Tadić, Ward-Prowse*
02/10	a	Leicester	D	0-0	
16/10	h	Burnley	W	3-1	*Austin 2 (1p), Redmond*
23/10	a	Man. City	D	1-1	*Redmond*
30/10	h	Chelsea	L	0-2	
06/11	a	Hull	L	1-2	*Austin (p)*
19/11	h	Liverpool	D	0-0	
27/11	h	Everton	W	1-0	*Austin*
03/12	a	Crystal Palace	L	0-3	
11/12	h	Middlesbrough	W	1-0	*Boufal*
14/12	a	Stoke	D	0-0	
18/12	a	Bournemouth	W	3-1	*Bertrand, Rodriguez 2*
28/12	h	Tottenham	L	1-4	*Van Dijk*
31/12	h	West Brom	L	1-2	*Long*

2017

Date		Opponent		Score	Scorers
02/01	a	Everton	L	0-3	
14/01	a	Burnley	L	0-1	
22/01	h	Leicester	W	3-0	*Ward-Prowse, Rodriguez, Tadić (p)*
31/01	a	Swansea	L	1-2	*Long*
04/02	h	West Ham	L	1-3	*Gabbiadini*
11/02	a	Sunderland	W	4-0	*Gabbiadini 2, og (Denayer), Long*
04/03	a	Watford	W	4-3	*Tadić, Redmond 2, Gabbiadini*
19/03	a	Tottenham	L	1-2	*Ward-Prowse*
01/04	h	Bournemouth	D	0-0	
05/04	h	Crystal Palace	W	3-1	*Redmond, Yoshida, Ward-Prowse*
08/04	a	West Brom	W	1-0	*Clasie*
15/04	h	Man. City	L	0-3	
25/04	a	Chelsea	L	2-4	*Romeu, Bertrand*
29/04	h	Hull	D	0-0	
07/05	a	Liverpool	D	0-0	
10/05	h	Arsenal	L	0-2	
13/05	a	Middlesbrough	W	2-1	*Rodriguez, Redmond*
17/05	h	Man. United	D	0-0	
21/05	h	Stoke	L	0-1	

No	Name	Nat	DoB	Pos	Aps	(s)	Gls
10	Charlie Austin		05/07/89	A	11	(4)	6
21	Ryan Bertrand		05/08/89	D	28		2
19	Sofiane Boufal	MAR	17/09/93	M	12	(12)	1
12	Martín Cáceres	URU	07/04/87	D	1		
2	Cédric	POR	31/08/91	D	30		
4	Jordy Clasie	NED	27/06/91	M	12	(4)	1
8	Steven Davis	NIR	01/01/85	M	29	(3)	
1	Fraser Forster		17/03/88	G	38		
20	Manolo Gabbiadini	ITA	26/11/91	A	10	(1)	4
23	Pierre Højbjerg	DEN	05/08/95	M	14	(8)	
6	José Fonte	POR	22/12/83	D	17		
7	Shane Long	IRL	22/01/87	A	10	(22)	3
15	Cuco Martina	CUW	25/09/89	D	6	(3)	
38	Sam McQueen		06/02/95	D	5	(8)	
26	Jérémy Pied	FRA	23/02/89	D	1	(3)	
22	Nathan Redmond		06/03/94	M	32	(5)	7
18	Harrison Reed		27/01/95	M	1	(2)	
9	Jay Rodriguez		29/07/89	A	9	(15)	5
14	Oriol Romeu	ESP	24/09/91	M	35		1
39	Josh Sims		28/03/97	M	1	(6)	
24	Jack Stephens		27/01/94	D	15	(2)	
11	Dušan Tadić	SRB	20/11/88	M	30	(3)	3
33	Matt Targett		18/09/95	D	5		
17	Virgil van Dijk	NED	08/07/91	D	21		1
16	James Ward-Prowse		01/11/94	M	22	(8)	4
3	Maya Yoshida	JPN	24/08/88	D	23		1

Stoke City FC

1863 • bet365 Stadium (28,383) • stokecityfc.com

Major honours
League Cup (1) 1972

Manager: Mark Hughes (WAL)

2016

Date		Opponent		Score	Scorers
13/08	a	Middlesbrough	D	1-1	*Shaqiri*
20/08	h	Man. City	L	1-4	*Bojan (p)*
27/08	a	Everton	L	0-1	
10/09	h	Tottenham	L	0-4	
18/09	a	Crystal Palace	L	1-4	*Arnautovic*
24/09	h	West Brom	D	1-1	*Allen*
02/10	a	Man. United	D	1-1	*Allen*
15/10	h	Sunderland	W	2-0	*Allen 2*
22/10	a	Hull	W	2-0	*Shaqiri 2*
31/10	h	Swansea	W	3-1	*Bony 2, og (Mawson)*
05/11	a	West Ham	D	1-1	*Bojan*
19/11	h	Bournemouth	L	0-1	
27/11	a	Watford	W	1-0	*og (Gomes)*
03/12	h	Burnley	W	2-0	*Walters, Muniesa*
10/12	a	Arsenal	L	1-3	*Adam (p)*
14/12	h	Southampton	D	0-0	
17/12	h	Leicester	D	2-2	*Bojan (p), Allen*
27/12	a	Liverpool	L	1-4	*Walters*
31/12	a	Chelsea	L	2-4	*Martins Indi, Crouch*

2017

Date		Opponent		Score	Scorers
03/01	h	Watford	W	2-0	*Shawcross, Crouch*
14/01	a	Sunderland	W	3-1	*Arnautovic 2, Crouch*
21/01	h	Man. United	D	1-1	*og (Mata)*
01/02	h	Everton	D	1-1	*Crouch*
04/02	a	West Brom	L	0-1	
11/02	h	Crystal Palace	W	1-0	*Allen*
26/02	a	Tottenham	L	0-4	
04/03	h	Middlesbrough	W	2-0	*Arnautovic 2*
08/03	a	Man. City	D	0-0	
18/03	h	Chelsea	L	1-2	*Walters (p)*
01/04	a	Leicester	L	0-2	
04/04	a	Burnley	L	0-1	
08/04	h	Liverpool	L	1-2	*Walters*
15/04	h	Hull	W	3-1	*Arnautovic, Crouch, Shaqiri*
22/04	a	Swansea	L	0-2	
29/04	h	West Ham	D	0-0	
06/05	a	Bournemouth	D	2-2	*og (Mousset), Diouf*
13/05	h	Arsenal	L	1-4	*Crouch*
21/05	a	Southampton	W	1-0	*Crouch*

No	Name	Nat	DoB	Pos	Aps	(s)	Gls
16	Charlie Adam	SCO	10/12/85	M	17	(7)	1
14	Ibrahim Afellay	NED	02/04/86	M	3	(9)	
4	Joe Allen	WAL	14/03/90	M	34	(2)	6
10	Marko Arnautovic	AUT	19/04/89	A	32		6
2	Phil Bardsley	SCO	28/06/85	D	14	(1)	
9	Saido Berahino		04/08/93	A	8	(5)	
27	Bojan Krkić	ESP	28/08/90	A	5	(4)	3
12	Wilfried Bony	CIV	10/12/88	A	9	(1)	2
1	Jack Butland		10/03/93	G	5		
20	Geoff Cameron	USA	11/07/85	D	18	(1)	
25	Peter Crouch		30/01/81	A	13	(14)	7
18	Mame Biram Diouf	SEN	16/12/87	A	15	(12)	1
24	Shay Given	IRL	20/04/76	G	5		
33	Lee Grant		27/01/83	G	28		
21	Giannelli Imbula	FRA	12/09/92	M	9	(3)	
8	Glen Johnson		23/08/84	D	21	(2)	
15	Bruno Martins Indi	NED	08/02/92	D	35		1
5	Marc Muniesa	ESP	27/03/92	D	7	(3)	1
45	Julien Ngoy	BEL	02/11/97	A		(5)	
3	Erik Pieters	NED	07/08/88	D	35	(1)	
22	Xherdan Shaqiri	SUI	10/10/91	A	21		4
17	Ryan Shawcross		04/10/87	D	35		1
32	Ramadan Sobhi	EGY	27/06/97	M	8	(9)	
19	Jonathan Walters	IRL	20/09/83	A	13	(10)	4
6	Glenn Whelan	IRL	13/01/84	M	26	(4)	
26	Philipp Wollscheid	GER	06/03/89	D	2		

Sunderland AFC

1879 • Stadium of Light (49,000) • safc.com

Major honours
English League (6) 1892, 1893, 1895, 1902, 1913, 1936; FA Cup (2) 1937, 1973

Manager: David Moyes (SCO)

Date		Opponent			Scorers
2016					
13/08	a	Man. City	L	1-2	*Defoe*
21/08	h	Middlesbrough	L	1-2	*Van Aanholt*
27/08	a	Southampton	D	1-1	*Defoe (p)*
12/09	h	Everton	L	0-3	
18/09	a	Tottenham	L	0-1	
24/09	h	Crystal Palace	L	2-3	*Defoe 2*
01/10	h	West Brom	D	1-1	*Van Aanholt*
15/10	a	Stoke	L	0-2	
22/10	a	West Ham	L	0-1	
29/10	h	Arsenal	L	1-4	*Defoe (p)*
05/11	a	Bournemouth	W	2-1	*Anichebe, Defoe (p)*
19/11	h	Hull	W	3-0	*Defoe, Anichebe 2*
26/11	a	Liverpool	L	0-2	
03/12	h	Leicester	W	2-1	*og (Huth), Defoe*
10/12	a	Swansea	L	0-3	
14/12	h	Chelsea	L	0-1	
17/12	h	Watford	W	1-0	*Van Aanholt*
26/12	a	Man. United	L	1-3	*Borini*
31/12	a	Burnley	L	1-4	*Defoe*
2017					
02/01	h	Liverpool	D	2-2	*Defoe 2 (2p)*
14/01	h	Stoke	L	1-3	*Defoe*
21/01	a	West Brom	L	0-2	
31/01	h	Tottenham	D	0-0	
04/02	a	Crystal Palace	W	4-0	*Koné, N'Dong, Defoe 2*
11/02	h	Southampton	L	0-4	
25/02	a	Everton	L	0-2	
05/03	h	Man. City	L	0-2	
18/03	h	Burnley	D	0-0	
01/04	a	Watford	L	0-1	
04/04	a	Leicester	L	0-2	
09/04	h	Man. United	L	0-3	
15/04	h	West Ham	D	2-2	*Khazri, Borini*
26/04	a	Middlesbrough	L	0-1	
29/04	h	Bournemouth	L	0-1	
06/05	a	Hull	W	2-0	*Jones, Defoe*
13/05	h	Swansea	L	0-2	
16/05	a	Arsenal	L	0-2	
21/05	a	Chelsea	L	1-5	*Javi Manquillo*

No	Name	Nat	DoB	Pos	Aps	(s)	Gls
28	Victor Anichebe	NGA	23/04/88	A	14	(4)	3
29	Joel Asoro	SWE	27/04/99	M		(1)	
9	Fabio Borini	ITA	29/03/91	A	19	(5)	2
6	Lee Cattermole		21/03/88	M	8		
18	Jermain Defoe		07/10/82	A	37		15
4	Jason Denayer	BEL	28/06/95	D	22	(2)	
5	Papy Djilobodji	SEN	01/12/88	D	17	(1)	
24	Darron Gibson	IRL	25/10/87	M	7	(5)	
46	Lynden Gooch	USA	24/12/95	M	4	(7)	
39	George Honeyman		08/09/94	M	2	(3)	
44	Adnan Januzaj	BEL	05/02/95	M	18	(7)	
21	Javi Manquillo	ESP	05/05/94	D	15	(5)	1
2	Billy Jones		24/03/87	D	25	(2)	1
15	Younès Kaboul	FRA	04/01/86	D	1		
10	Wahbi Khazri	TUN	08/02/91	M	7	(14)	1
27	Jan Kirchhoff	GER	01/10/90	M	5	(2)	
23	Lamine Koné	CIV	01/02/89	D	29	(1)	1
7	Sebastian Larsson	SWE	06/06/85	M	17	(4)	
17	Jeremain Lens	NED	24/11/87	M		(2)	
15	Joleon Lescott		16/08/82	D	1	(1)	
22	Donald Love	SCO	02/12/94	D	6	(6)	
1	Vito Mannone	ITA	02/03/88	G	9		
19	Paddy McNair	NIR	27/04/95	D	5	(4)	
17	Didier N'Dong	GAB	17/06/94	M	27	(4)	1
16	John O'Shea	IRL	30/04/81	D	26	(2)	
3	Bryan Oviedo	CRC	18/02/90	D	10		
13	Jordan Pickford		07/03/94	G	29		
20	Steven Pienaar	RSA	17/03/82	M	10	(5)	
8	Jack Rodwell		11/03/91	M	17	(3)	
3	Patrick van Aanholt	NED	29/08/90	D	20	(1)	3
14	Duncan Watmore		08/03/94	M	11	(3)	

Swansea City AFC

1912 • Liberty Stadium (20,972) • swanseacity.net

Major honours
League Cup (1) 2013; Welsh Cup (10) 1913, 1932, 1950, 1961, 1966, 1981, 1982, 1983, 1989, 1991

Manager: Francesco Guidolin (ITA); (03/10/16) Bob Bradley (USA); (27/12/16) (Alan Curtis (WAL)); (03/01/17) Paul Clement

Date		Opponent			Scorers
2016					
13/08	a	Burnley	W	1-0	*Fer*
20/08	h	Hull	L	0-2	
27/08	a	Leicester	L	1-2	*Fer*
11/09	h	Chelsea	D	2-2	*Sigurdsson (p), Fer*
18/09	a	Southampton	L	0-1	
24/09	h	Man. City	L	1-3	*Llorente*
01/10	h	Liverpool	L	1-2	*Fer*
15/10	a	Arsenal	L	2-3	*Sigurdsson, Borja Bastón*
22/10	h	Watford	D	0-0	
31/10	a	Stoke	L	1-3	*Routledge*
06/11	h	Man. United	L	1-3	*Van der Hoorn*
19/11	a	Everton	D	1-1	*Sigurdsson (p)*
26/11	h	Crystal Palace	W	5-4	*Sigurdsson, Fer 2, Llorente 2*
03/12	a	Tottenham	L	0-5	
10/12	h	Sunderland	W	3-0	*Sigurdsson (p), Llorente 2*
14/12	a	West Brom	L	1-3	*Routledge*
17/12	a	Middlesbrough	L	0-3	
26/12	h	West Ham	L	1-4	*Llorente*
31/12	h	Bournemouth	L	0-3	
2017					
03/01	a	Crystal Palace	W	2-1	*Mawson, Rangel*
14/01	h	Arsenal	L	0-4	
21/01	a	Liverpool	W	3-2	*Llorente 2, Sigurdsson*
31/01	h	Southampton	W	2-1	*Mawson, Sigurdsson*
05/02	a	Man. City	L	1-2	*Sigurdsson*
12/02	h	Leicester	W	2-0	*Mawson, Olsson*
25/02	a	Chelsea	L	1-3	*Llorente*
04/03	h	Burnley	W	3-2	*Llorente 2, Olsson*
11/03	a	Hull	L	1-2	*Mawson*
18/03	a	Bournemouth	L	0-2	
02/04	h	Middlesbrough	D	0-0	
05/04	h	Tottenham	L	1-3	*Routledge*
08/04	a	West Ham	L	0-1	
15/04	a	Watford	L	0-1	
22/04	h	Stoke	W	2-0	*Llorente, Carroll*
30/04	a	Man. United	D	1-1	*Sigurdsson*
06/05	h	Everton	W	1-0	*Llorente*
13/05	a	Sunderland	W	2-0	*Llorente, Naughton*
21/05	h	West Brom	W	2-1	*Ayew, Llorente*

No	Name	Nat	DoB	Pos	Aps	(s)	Gls
3	Jordan Ayew	GHA	11/09/91	A	9	(5)	1
17	Modou Barrow	GAM	13/10/92	A	12	(6)	
10	Borja Bastón	ESP	25/08/92	A	4	(14)	1
7	Leon Britton		16/09/82	M	16		
42	Tom Carroll		28/05/92	M	16	(1)	1
24	Jack Cork		25/06/89	M	25	(5)	
12	Nathan Dyer		29/11/87	M	3	(5)	
1	Łukasz Fabiański	POL	18/04/85	G	37		
8	Leroy Fer	NED	05/01/90	M	27	(7)	6
33	Federico Fernández	ARG	21/02/89	D	27		
56	Jay Fulton	SCO	01/04/94	M	9	(2)	
2	Jordi Amat	ESP	21/03/92	D	15	(2)	
4	Ki Sung-yueng	KOR	24/01/89	M	13	(10)	
35	Stephen Kingsley	SCO	23/07/94	D	12	(1)	
9	Fernando Llorente	ESP	26/02/85	A	28	(5)	15
6	Alfie Mawson		19/01/94	D	27		4
62	Oliver McBurnie	SCO	04/06/96	A		(5)	
20	Jefferson Montero	ECU	01/09/89	M	2	(11)	
28	Luciano Narsingh	NED	13/09/90	M	3	(10)	
26	Kyle Naughton		11/11/88	D	31		1
13	Kristoffer Nordfeldt	SWE	23/06/89	G	1		
16	Martin Olsson	SWE	17/05/88	D	14	(1)	2
22	Ángel Rangel	ESP	28/10/82	D	8	(10)	1
15	Wayne Routledge		07/01/85	M	24	(3)	3
23	Gylfi Thór Sigurdsson	ISL	08/09/89	M	37	(1)	9
3	Neil Taylor	WAL	07/02/89	D	11		
5	Mike van der Hoorn	NED	15/10/92	D	7	(1)	1

Tottenham Hotspur FC

1882 • White Hart Lane (32,000) • tottenhamhotspur.com

Major honours
UEFA Cup Winners' Cup (1) 1963; UEFA Cup (2) 1972, 1984; English League (2) 1951, 1961; FA Cup (8) 1901, 1921, 1961, 1962, 1967, 1981, 1982, 1991; League Cup (4) 1971, 1973, 1999, 2008

Manager: Mauricio Pochettino (ARG)

Date		Opponent			Scorers
2016					
13/08	a	Everton	D	1-1	*Lamela*
20/08	h	Crystal Palace	W	1-0	*Wanyama*
27/08	h	Liverpool	D	1-1	*Rose*
10/09	a	Stoke	W	4-0	*Son 2, Alli, Kane*
18/09	h	Sunderland	W	1-0	*Kane*
24/09	a	Middlesbrough	W	2-1	*Son 2*
02/10	h	Man. City	W	2-0	*og (Kolarov), Alli*
15/10	a	West Brom	D	1-1	*Alli*
22/10	a	Bournemouth	D	0-0	
29/10	h	Leicester	D	1-1	*Janssen (p)*
06/11	a	Arsenal	D	1-1	*Kane (p)*
19/11	h	West Ham	W	3-2	*Winks, Kane 2 (1p)*
26/11	a	Chelsea	L	1-2	*Eriksen*
03/12	h	Swansea	W	5-0	*Kane 2 (1p), Son, Eriksen 2*
11/12	a	Man. United	L	0-1	
14/12	h	Hull	W	3-0	*Eriksen 2, Wanyama*
18/12	h	Burnley	W	2-1	*Alli, Rose*
28/12	a	Southampton	W	4-1	*Alli 2, Kane, Son*
2017					
01/01	a	Watford	W	4-1	*Kane 2, Alli 2*
04/01	h	Chelsea	W	2-0	*Alli 2*
14/01	h	West Brom	W	4-0	*Kane 3, og (McAuley)*
23/01	a	Man. City	D	2-2	*Alli, Son*
31/01	a	Sunderland	D	0-0	
04/02	h	Middlesbrough	W	1-0	*Kane (p)*
11/02	a	Liverpool	L	0-2	
26/02	h	Stoke	W	4-0	*Kane 3, Alli*
05/03	h	Everton	W	3-2	*Kane 2, Alli*
19/03	h	Southampton	W	2-1	*Eriksen, Alli (p)*
01/04	a	Burnley	W	2-0	*Dier, Son*
05/04	a	Swansea	W	3-1	*Alli, Son, Eriksen*
08/04	h	Watford	W	4-0	*Alli, Dier, Son 2*
15/04	h	Bournemouth	W	4-0	*Dembélé, Son, Kane, Janssen*
26/04	a	Crystal Palace	W	1-0	*Eriksen*
30/04	h	Arsenal	W	2-0	*Alli, Kane (p)*
05/05	a	West Ham	L	0-1	
14/05	h	Man. United	W	2-1	*Wanyama, Kane*
18/05	a	Leicester	W	6-1	*Kane 4, Son 2*
21/05	a	Hull	W	7-1	*Kane 3, Alli, Wanyama, Davies, Alderweireld*

No	Name	Nat	DoB	Pos	Aps	(s)	Gls
4	Toby Alderweireld	BEL	02/03/89	D	30		1
20	Dele Alli		11/04/96	M	35	(2)	18
28	Tom Carroll		28/05/92	M		(1)	
33	Ben Davies	WAL	24/04/93	D	18	(5)	1
19	Mousa Dembélé	BEL	16/07/87	M	24	(6)	1
15	Eric Dier		15/01/94	D	34	(2)	2
23	Christian Eriksen	DEN	14/02/92	M	36		8
9	Vincent Janssen	NED	15/06/94	A	7	(20)	2
10	Harry Kane		28/07/93	A	29	(1)	29
11	Erik Lamela	ARG	04/03/92	M	6	(3)	1
44	Filip Lesniak	SVK	14/05/96	M		(1)	
1	Hugo Lloris	FRA	26/12/86	G	34		
14	Georges-Kévin N'Koudou	FRA	13/02/95	M		(8)	
25	Josh Onomah		27/04/97	M		(5)	
3	Danny Rose		02/07/90	D	18		2
17	Moussa Sissoko	FRA	16/08/89	M	8	(17)	
7	Son Heung-min	KOR	08/07/92	A	23	(11)	14
16	Kieran Trippier		19/09/90	D	6	(6)	
5	Jan Vertonghen	BEL	24/04/87	D	33		
13	Michel Vorm	NED	20/10/83	G	4	(1)	
2	Kyle Walker		28/05/90	D	31	(2)	
12	Victor Wanyama	KEN	25/06/91	M	35	(1)	4
27	Kevin Wimmer	AUT	15/11/92	D	4	(1)	
29	Harry Winks		02/02/96	M	3	(18)	1

Watford FC

1881 • Vicarage Road (21,977) • watfordfc.com

Manager: Walter Mazzarri (ITA)

Date		Opponent		Score	Scorers
2016					
13/08	a	Southampton	D	1-1	*Capoue*
20/08	h	Chelsea	L	1-2	*Capoue*
27/08	h	Arsenal	L	1-3	*Pereyra*
10/09	a	West Ham	W	4-2	*Ighalo, Deeney, Capoue, Holebas*
18/09	h	Man. United	W	3-1	*Capoue, Zúñiga, Deeney (p)*
26/09	a	Burnley	L	0-2	
01/10	h	Bournemouth	D	2-2	*Deeney, Success*
16/10	a	Middlesbrough	W	1-0	*Holebas*
22/10	a	Swansea	D	0-0	
29/10	h	Hull	W	1-0	*og (Dawson)*
06/11	a	Liverpool	L	1-6	*Janmaat*
19/11	h	Leicester	W	2-1	*Capoue, Pereyra*
27/11	h	Stoke	L	0-1	
03/12	a	West Brom	L	1-3	*Kabasele*
10/12	h	Everton	W	3-2	*Okaka 2, Prödl*
14/12	a	Man. City	L	0-2	
17/12	a	Sunderland	L	0-1	
26/12	h	Crystal Palace	D	1-1	*Deeney (p)*
2017					
01/01	h	Tottenham	L	1-4	*Kaboul*
03/01	a	Stoke	L	0-2	
14/01	h	Middlesbrough	D	0-0	
21/01	a	Bournemouth	D	2-2	*Kabasele, Deeney*
31/01	a	Arsenal	W	2-1	*Kaboul, Deeney*
04/02	h	Burnley	W	2-1	*Deeney, Niang*
11/02	a	Man. United	L	0-2	
25/02	h	West Ham	D	1-1	*Deeney (p)*
04/03	h	Southampton	L	3-4	*Deeney, Okaka, Doucouré*
18/03	a	Crystal Palace	L	0-1	
01/04	h	Sunderland	W	1-0	*Britos*
04/04	h	West Brom	W	2-0	*Niang, Deeney*
08/04	a	Tottenham	L	0-4	
15/04	h	Swansea	W	1-0	*Capoue*
22/04	a	Hull	L	0-2	
01/05	h	Liverpool	L	0-1	
06/05	a	Leicester	L	0-3	
12/05	a	Everton	L	0-1	
15/05	a	Chelsea	L	3-4	*Capoue, Janmaat, Okaka*
21/05	h	Man. City	L	0-5	

No	Name	Nat	DoB	Pos	Aps	(s)	Gls
7	Nordin Amrabat	MAR	31/03/87	M	25	(4)	
21	Ikechi Anya	SCO	03/01/88	M		(1)	
11	Valon Behrami	SUI	19/04/85	M	26	(1)	
3	Miguel Britos	URU	17/07/85	D	27		1
29	Étienne Capoue	FRA	11/07/88	M	37		7
15	Craig Cathcart	NIR	06/02/89	D	13	(2)	
8	Tom Cleverley		12/08/89	M	16	(1)	
9	Troy Deeney		29/06/88	A	31	(6)	10
16	Abdoulaye Doucouré	FRA	01/01/93	M	14	(6)	1
42	Andrew Eleftheriou		08/11/97	D		(1)	
39	Michael Folivi		25/02/98	A		(1)	
1	Heurelho Gomes	BRA	15/02/81	G	38		
17	Adlène Guedioura	ALG	12/11/85	M	9	(3)	
25	José Holebas	GRE	27/06/84	D	33		2
24	Odion Ighalo	NGA	16/06/89	A	14	(4)	1
22	Daryl Janmaat	NED	22/07/89	D	18	(9)	2
27	Christian Kabasele	BEL	24/02/91	D	7	(9)	2
4	Younès Kaboul	FRA	04/01/86	D	22		2
12	Kenedy	BRA	08/02/96	M		(1)	
6	Adrian Mariappa	JAM	03/10/86	D	6	(1)	
32	Brandon Mason		30/09/97	D	1	(1)	
21	M'Baye Niang	FRA	19/12/94	A	15	(1)	2
33	Stefano Okaka	ITA	09/08/89	A	10	(9)	4
30	Costel Pantilimon	ROU	01/02/87	G		(2)	
47	Dion Pereira		25/03/99	M		(2)	
37	Roberto Pereyra	ARG	07/01/91	M	12	(1)	2
5	Sebastian Prödl	AUT	21/06/87	D	32	(1)	1
19	Jerome Sinclair		20/09/96	A	1	(4)	
10	Isaac Success	NGA	07/01/96	A	2	(17)	1
20	Matěj Vydra	CZE	01/05/92	A		(1)	
23	Ben Watson		09/07/85	M		(4)	
20	Mauro Zárate	ARG	18/03/87	A	3		
18	Juan Zúñiga	COL	14/12/85	D	6	(15)	1

West Bromwich Albion FC

1878 • The Hawthorns (26,500) • wba.co.uk

Major honours
English League (1) 1920; FA Cup (5) 1888, 1892, 1931, 1954, 1968; League Cup (1) 1966

Manager: Tony Pulis (WAL)

Date		Opponent		Score	Scorers
2016					
13/08	a	Crystal Palace	W	1-0	*Rondón*
20/08	h	Everton	L	1-2	*McAuley*
28/08	h	Middlesbrough	D	0-0	
10/09	a	Bournemouth	L	0-1	
17/09	h	West Ham	W	4-2	*Chadli 2, Rondón, McClean*
24/09	a	Stoke	D	1-1	*Rondón*
01/10	a	Sunderland	D	1-1	*Chadli*
15/10	h	Tottenham	D	1-1	*Chadli*
22/10	a	Liverpool	L	1-2	*McAuley*
29/10	h	Man. City	L	0-4	
06/11	a	Leicester	W	2-1	*Morrison, Phillips*
21/11	h	Burnley	W	4-0	*Phillips, Morrison, Fletcher, Rondón*
26/11	a	Hull	D	1-1	*McAuley*
03/12	h	Watford	W	3-1	*Evans, Brunt, Phillips*
11/12	a	Chelsea	L	0-1	
14/12	h	Swansea	W	3-1	*Rondón 3*
17/12	h	Man. United	L	0-2	
26/12	a	Arsenal	L	0-1	
31/12	a	Southampton	W	2-1	*Phillips, Robson-Kanu*
2017					
02/01	h	Hull	W	3-1	*Brunt, McAuley, Morrison*
14/01	a	Tottenham	L	0-4	
21/01	h	Sunderland	W	2-0	*Fletcher, Brunt*
31/01	a	Middlesbrough	D	1-1	*Morrison*
04/02	h	Stoke	W	1-0	*Morrison*
11/02	a	West Ham	D	2-2	*Chadli, McAuley*
25/02	h	Bournemouth	W	2-1	*Dawson, McAuley*
04/03	h	Crystal Palace	L	0-2	
11/03	a	Everton	L	0-3	
18/03	h	Arsenal	W	3-1	*Dawson 2, Robson-Kanu*
01/04	a	Man. United	D	0-0	
04/04	a	Watford	L	0-2	
08/04	h	Southampton	L	0-1	
16/04	h	Liverpool	L	0-1	
29/04	a	Leicester	L	0-1	
06/05	a	Burnley	D	2-2	*Rondón, Dawson*
12/05	h	Chelsea	L	0-1	
16/05	a	Man. City	L	1-3	*Robson-Kanu*
21/05	a	Swansea	L	1-2	*Evans*

No	Name	Nat	DoB	Pos	Aps	(s)	Gls
18	Saido Berahino		04/08/93	A	3	(1)	
11	Chris Brunt	NIR	14/12/84	D	27	(4)	3
22	Nacer Chadli	BEL	02/08/89	M	27	(4)	5
25	Craig Dawson		06/05/90	D	37		4
6	Jonny Evans	NIR	03/01/88	D	30	(1)	2
47	Sam Field		08/05/98	M	4	(4)	
24	Darren Fletcher	SCO	01/02/84	M	37	(1)	2
1	Ben Foster		03/04/83	G	38		
20	Brendan Galloway		17/03/96	D	3		
8	Craig Gardner		25/11/86	M	2	(7)	
17	Rickie Lambert		16/02/82	A		(1)	
45	Jonathan Leko		24/04/99	A		(9)	
8	Jake Livermore		14/11/89	M	15	(1)	
23	Gareth McAuley	NIR	05/12/79	D	36		6
14	James McClean	IRL	22/04/89	M	13	(21)	1
7	James Morrison	SCO	25/05/86	M	17	(14)	5
2	Allan Nyom	CMR	10/05/88	D	29	(3)	
3	Jonas Olsson	SWE	10/03/83	D	7		
10	Matt Phillips	SCO	13/03/91	M	26	(1)	4
4	Hal Robson-Kanu	WAL	21/05/89	A	5	(24)	3
9	José Salomón Rondón	VEN	16/09/89	A	32	(6)	8
12	Marc Wilson	IRL	17/08/87	D	3	(1)	
5	Claudio Yacob	ARG	18/07/87	M	27	(6)	

West Ham United FC

1895 • London Stadium (57,000) • whufc.com

Major honours
UEFA Cup Winners' Cup (1) 1965; FA Cup (3) 1964, 1975, 1980

Manager: Slaven Bilić (CRO)

Date		Opponent		Score	Scorers
2016					
15/08	a	Chelsea	L	1-2	*Collins*
21/08	h	Bournemouth	W	1-0	*Antonio*
28/08	a	Man. City	L	1-3	*Antonio*
10/09	h	Watford	L	2-4	*Antonio 2*
17/09	a	West Brom	L	2-4	*Antonio, Lanzini (p)*
25/09	h	Southampton	L	0-3	
01/10	h	Middlesbrough	D	1-1	*Payet*
15/10	a	Crystal Palace	W	1-0	*Lanzini*
22/10	h	Sunderland	W	1-0	*Reid*
30/10	a	Everton	L	0-2	
05/11	h	Stoke	D	1-1	*og (Whelan)*
19/11	a	Tottenham	L	2-3	*Antonio, Lanzini (p)*
27/11	a	Man. United	D	1-1	*Sakho*
03/12	h	Arsenal	L	1-5	*Carroll*
11/12	a	Liverpool	D	2-2	*Payet, Antonio*
14/12	h	Burnley	W	1-0	*Noble*
17/12	h	Hull	W	1-0	*Noble (p)*
26/12	a	Swansea	W	4-1	*Ayew, Reid, Antonio, Carroll*
31/12	a	Leicester	L	0-1	
2017					
02/01	h	Man. United	L	0-2	
14/01	h	Crystal Palace	W	3-0	*Feghouli, Carroll, Lanzini*
21/01	a	Middlesbrough	W	3-1	*Carroll 2, Calleri*
01/02	h	Man. City	L	0-4	
04/02	a	Southampton	W	3-1	*Carroll, Pedro Obiang, Noble*
11/02	h	West Brom	D	2-2	*Feghouli, Lanzini*
25/02	a	Watford	D	1-1	*Ayew*
06/03	h	Chelsea	L	1-2	*Lanzini*
11/03	a	Bournemouth	L	2-3	*Antonio, Ayew*
18/03	h	Leicester	L	2-3	*Lanzini, Ayew*
01/04	a	Hull	L	1-2	*Carroll*
05/04	a	Arsenal	L	0-3	
08/04	h	Swansea	W	1-0	*Kouyaté*
15/04	a	Sunderland	D	2-2	*Ayew, Collins*
22/04	h	Everton	D	0-0	
29/04	a	Stoke	D	0-0	
05/05	h	Tottenham	W	1-0	*Lanzini*
14/05	h	Liverpool	L	0-4	
21/05	a	Burnley	W	2-1	*Feghouli, Ayew*

No	Name	Nat	DoB	Pos	Aps	(s)	Gls
13	Adrián	ESP	03/01/87	G	16		
30	Michail Antonio		28/03/90	M	29		9
5	Álvaro Arbeloa	ESP	17/01/83	D	1	(2)	
20	André Ayew	GHA	17/12/89	A	16	(9)	6
22	Sam Byram		16/09/93	D	13	(5)	
28	Jonathan Calleri	ARG	23/09/93	A	4	(12)	1
9	Andy Carroll		06/01/89	A	15	(3)	7
19	James Collins	WAL	23/08/83	D	19	(3)	2
3	Aaron Cresswell		15/12/89	D	24	(2)	
7	Sofiane Feghouli	ALG	26/12/89	M	11	(10)	3
31	Edimilson Fernandes	SUI	15/04/96	M	8	(20)	
24	Ashley Fletcher		02/10/95	A	2	(14)	
17	Gökhan Töre	TUR	20/01/92	M	3	(2)	
23	José Fonte	POR	22/12/83	D	16		
8	Cheikhou Kouyaté	SEN	21/12/89	M	31		1
10	Manuel Lanzini	ARG	15/02/93	M	31	(4)	8
26	Arthur Masuaku	FRA	07/11/93	D	11	(2)	
16	Mark Noble		08/05/87	M	29	(1)	3
4	Håvard Nordtveit	NOR	21/06/90	D	11	(5)	
21	Angelo Ogbonna	ITA	23/05/88	D	20		
27	Dimitri Payet	FRA	29/03/87	M	17	(1)	2
14	Pedro Obiang	ESP	27/03/92	M	21	(1)	1
1	Darren Randolph	IRL	12/05/87	G	22		
2	Winston Reid	NZL	03/07/88	D	30		2
41	Declan Rice	IRL	14/01/99	D		(1)	
15	Diafra Sakho	SEN	24/12/89	A	2	(2)	1
11	Robert Snodgrass	SCO	07/09/87	M	8	(7)	
11	Enner Valencia	ECU	04/11/89	A	3		
11	Simone Zaza	ITA	25/06/91	A	5	(3)	

Top goalscorers

29	Harry Kane (Tottenham)
25	Romelu Lukaku (Everton)
24	Alexis Sánchez (Arsenal)
20	Diego Costa (Chelsea) Sergio Agüero (Man. City)
18	Dele Alli (Tottenham)
17	Zlatan Ibrahimović (Man. United)
16	Joshua King (Bournemouth) Eden Hazard (Chelsea)
15	Christian Benteke (Crystal Palace) Jermain Defoe (Sunderland) Fernando Llorente (Swansea)

Promoted clubs

Newcastle United FC

1881 • St James' Park (52,354) • nufc.co.uk

Major honours
Inter Cities Fairs Cup (1) 1969; English League (4) 1905, 1907, 1909, 1927; FA Cup (6) 1910, 1924, 1932, 1951, 1952, 1955

Manager: Rafael Benítez (ESP)

Brighton & Hove Albion FC

1901 • AMEX Stadium (30,278) • seagulls.co.uk

Manager: Chris Hughton

Huddersfield Town AFC

1908 • John Smith's Stadium (24,500) • htafc.com

Major honours
English League (3) 1924, 1925, 1926; FA Cup (1) 1922

Manager: David Wagner (USA)

Second level final table 2016/17

		Pld	W	D	L	F	A	Pts
1	Newcastle United FC	46	29	7	10	85	40	94
2	Brighton & Hove Albion FC	46	28	9	9	74	40	93
3	Reading FC	46	26	7	13	68	64	85
4	Sheffield Wednesday FC	46	24	9	13	60	45	81
5	Huddersfield Town AFC	46	25	6	15	56	58	81
6	Fulham FC	46	22	14	10	85	57	80
7	Leeds United AFC	46	22	9	15	61	47	75
8	Norwich City FC	46	20	10	16	85	69	70
9	Derby County FC	46	18	13	15	54	50	67
10	Brentford FC	46	18	10	18	75	65	64
11	Preston North End FC	46	16	14	16	64	63	62
12	Cardiff City FC	46	17	11	18	60	61	62
13	Aston Villa FC	46	16	14	16	47	48	62
14	Barnsley FC	46	15	13	18	64	67	58
15	Wolverhampton Wanderers FC	46	16	10	20	54	58	58
16	Ipswich Town FC	46	13	16	17	48	58	55
17	Bristol City FC	46	15	9	22	60	66	54
18	Queens Park Rangers FC	46	15	8	23	52	66	53
19	Birmingham City FC	46	13	14	19	45	64	53
20	Burton Albion FC	46	13	13	20	49	63	52
21	Nottingham Forest FC	46	14	9	23	62	72	51
22	Blackburn Rovers FC	46	12	15	19	53	65	51
23	Wigan Athletic FC	46	10	12	24	40	57	42
24	Rotherham United FC	46	5	8	33	40	98	23

Promotion play-offs

(13/05/17 & 16/05/17)
Fulham 1-1 Reading
Reading 1-0 Fulham
(Reading 2-1)

(14/05/17 & 17/05/17)
Huddersfield 0-0 Sheffield Wednesday
Sheffield Wednesday 1-1 Huddersfield *(aet)*
(1-1; Huddersfield 4-3 on pens)

(29/05/17)
Huddersfield 0-0 Reading *(aet; 4-3 on pens)*

DOMESTIC CUPS

FA Cup 2016/17

THIRD ROUND

(06/01/17)
West Ham 0-5 Man. City

(07/01/17)
Accrington 2-1 Luton
Barrow 0-2 Rochdale
Birmingham 1-1 Newcastle
Blackpool 0-0 Barnsley
Bolton 0-0 Crystal Palace
Brentford 5-1 Eastleigh
Brighton 2-0 MK Dons
Bristol City 0-0 Fleetwood
Everton 1-2 Leicester
Huddersfield 4-0 Port Vale
Hull 2-0 Swansea
Ipswich 2-2 Lincoln
Man. United 4-0 Reading
Millwall 3-0 Bournemouth
Norwich 2-2 Southampton
Preston 1-2 Arsenal
QPR 1-2 Blackburn
Rotherham 2-3 Oxford
Stoke 0-2 Wolverhampton
Sunderland 0-0 Burnley
Sutton 0-0 Wimbledon
Watford 2-0 Burton
West Brom 1-2 Derby
Wigan 2-0 Nottingham Forest
Wycombe 2-1 Stourbridge

(08/01/17)
Cardiff 1-2 Fulham
Chelsea 4-1 Peterborough
Liverpool 0-0 Plymouth
Middlesbrough 3-0 Sheffield Wednesday
Tottenham 2-0 Aston Villa

(09/01/17)
Cambridge United 1-2 Leeds

Replays

(17/01/17)
Barnsley 1-2 Blackpool *(aet)*
Burnley 2-0 Sunderland
Crystal Palace 2-1 Bolton
Fleetwood 0-1 Bristol City
Lincoln 1-0 Ipswich
Wimbledon 1-3 Sutton

(18/01/17)
Newcastle 3-1 Birmingham
Plymouth 0-1 Liverpool
Southampton 1-0 Norwich

FOURTH ROUND

(27/01/17)
Derby 2-2 Leicester

(28/01/17)
Blackburn 2-0 Blackpool
Burnley 2-0 Bristol City
Chelsea 4-0 Brentford
Crystal Palace 0-3 Man. City
Lincoln 3-1 Brighton
Liverpool 1-2 Wolverhampton
Middlesbrough 1-0 Accrington
Oxford 3-0 Newcastle
Rochdale 0-4 Huddersfield

Continued over the page

Per Mertesacker (centre) returned from a season-long injury to skipper Arsenal to a 2-1 victory over champions Chelsea and a record-breaking 13th FA Cup triumph

Southampton 0-5 Arsenal
Tottenham 4-3 Wycombe

(29/01/17)
Fulham 4-1 Hull
Man. United 4-0 Wigan
Millwall 1-0 Watford
Sutton 1-0 Leeds

Replay

(08/02/17)
Leicester 3-1 Derby *(aet)*

FIFTH ROUND

((18/02/17)
Burnley 0-1 Lincoln
Huddersfield 0-0 Man. City
Middlesbrough 3-2 Oxford
Millwall 1-0 Leicester
Wolverhampton 0-2 Chelsea

(19/02/17)
Blackburn 1-2 Man. United
Fulham 0-3 Tottenham

(20/02/17)
Sutton 0-2 Arsenal

Replay

(01/03/17)
Man. City 5-1 Huddersfield

QUARTER-FINALS

(11/03/17)
Arsenal 5-0 Lincoln *(Walcott 45, Giroud 53, Waterfall 58og, Alexis Sánchez 72, Ramsey 75)*

Middlesbrough 0-2 Man. City *(Silva 3, Agüero 67)*

(12/03/17)
Tottenham 6-0 Millwall *(Eriksen 31, Son 41, 54, 90+2, Alli 72, Janssen 79)*

(13/03/17)
Chelsea 1-0 Man. United *(Kanté 51)*

SEMI-FINALS

(22/04/17)
Chelsea 4-2 Tottenham *(Willian 5, 43p, Hazard 75, Matić 80; Kane 18, Alli 52)*

(23/04/17)
Arsenal 2-1 Man. City *(Monreal 71, Alexis Sánchez 101; Agüero 62) (aet)*

FINAL

(27/05/17)
Wembley Stadium, London
ARSENAL FC 2 (*Alexis Sánchez 4, Ramsey 79)*
CHELSEA FC 1 (*Diego Costa 76)*
Referee: *Taylor*
ARSENAL: *Ospina, Holding, Mertesacker, Monreal, Bellerín, Ramsey, Xhaka, Oxlade-Chamberlain (Coquelin 82), Özil, Alexis Sánchez (Elneny 90+3), Welbeck (Giroud 78)*
CHELSEA: *Courtois, Azpilicueta, David Luiz, Cahill, Moses, Kanté, Matić (Fàbregas 61), Alonso, Pedro (Willian 72), Hazard, Diego Costa (Batshuayi 88)*
Red card: *Moses (68)*

EFL Cup 2016/17

QUARTER-FINALS

(29/11/16)
Hull 1-1 Newcastle 1 *(Snodgrass 99; Diamé 98) (aet; 3-1 on pens)*

Liverpool 2-0 Leeds *(Origi 76, Woodburn 81)*

(30/11/16)
Arsenal 0-2 Southampton *(Clasie 13, Bertrand 38)*

Man. United 4-1 West Ham *(Ibrahimović 2, 90, Martial 48, 62; Fletcher 35)*

SEMI-FINALS

((10/01/17 & 26/01/17)
Man. United 2-0 Hull *(Mata 56, Fellaini 87)*
Hull 2-1 Man. United *(Huudlestone 35p, Niasse 85; Pogba 66)*
(Man. United 3-2)

(11/01/17 & 25/01/17)
Southampton 1-0 Liverpool *(Redmond 20)*
Liverpool 0-1 Southampton *(Long 90+1)*
(Southampton 2-0)

FINAL

(26/02/17)
Wembley Stadium, London
MANCHESTER UNITED FC 3 *(Ibrahimović 19, 87, Lingard 38)*
SOUTHAMPTON FC 2 *(Gabbiadini 45+1, 48)*
Referee: *Marriner*
MAN. UNITED: *De Gea, Valencia, Bailly, Smalling, Rojo, Ander Herrera, Pogba, Mata (Carrick 46), Lingard (Rashford 77), Martial (Fellaini 90), Ibrahimović*
SOUTHAMPTON: *Forster, Cédric, Stephens, Yoshida, Bertrand, Ward-Prowse, Romeu, Davis (Rodriguez 90), Redmond, Tadić (Boufal 77), Gabbiadini (Long 83)*

Wayne Rooney lifts the EFL Cup for Manchester United

ESTONIA

Eesti Jalgpalli Liit (EJL)

Address	A. Le Coq Arena, Asula 4c EE-11312 Tallinn
Tel	+372 627 9960
Fax	+372 627 9969
E-mail	efa@jalgpall.ee
Website	jalgpall.ee

President	Aivar Pohlak
General secretary	Anne Rei
Media officer	Mihkel Uiboleht
Year of formation	1921
National stadium	A. Le Coq Arena, Tallinn (9,692)

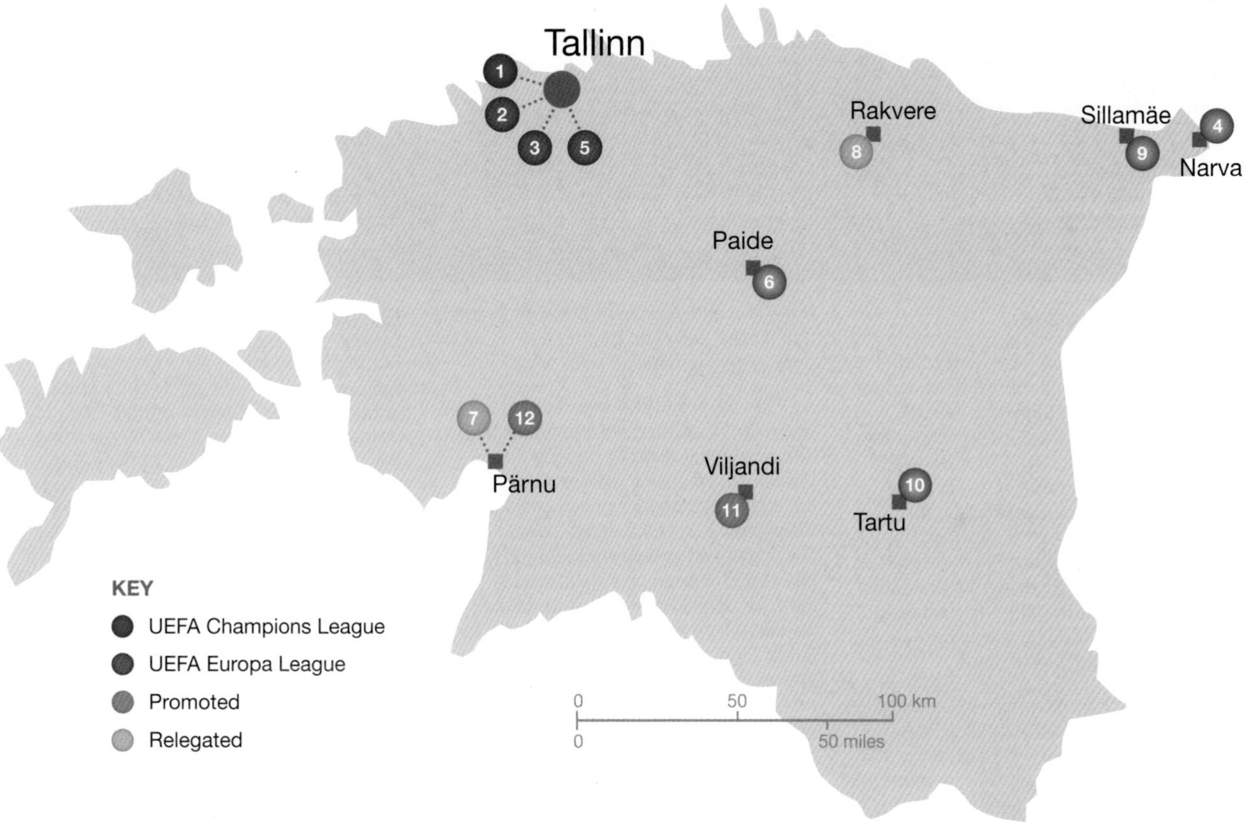

Tallinn
Rakvere
Sillamäe
Narva
Paide
Pärnu
Viljandi
Tartu

KEY
- UEFA Champions League
- UEFA Europa League
- Promoted
- Relegated

0 50 100 km
0 50 miles

MEISTRILIIGA CLUBS

1 **FCI Tallinn**

2 **FC Flora Tallinn**

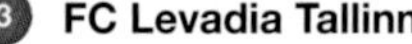
3 **FC Levadia Tallinn**

4 **JK Narva Trans**

5 **Nõmme Kalju FC**

6 **Paide Linnameeskond**

7 **Pärnu Linnameeskond**

8 **Rakvere JK Tarvas**

9 **JK Sillamäe Kalev**

10 **JK Tammeka Tartu**

PROMOTED CLUBS

11 **JK Tulevik Viljandi**

12 **Pärnu JK Vaprus**

FCI Tallinn on the rise

After Flora Tallinn's record-breaking tenth title in 2015, a new name was carved on to the Meistriliiga trophy 12 months later as FCI, in only their fourth top-flight campaign, held their nerve to take the spoils on the final day, edging another club from the capital, Levadia, into the runners-up spot after a 2-1 win against third-placed Nõmme Kalju.

There was further joy a little over six months later for the club formerly known by their sponsors' name of FC Infonet as they added the Estonian Cup with a 2-0 victory in the final over Tammeka Tartu.

Maiden Meistriliiga crown for Puštov's men

Four-strong title tussle goes to the wire

New champions also triumph in Estonian Cup

Domestic league

Formed in 2002 and promoted to the Meistriliiga for the first time, under coach Aleksandr Puštov, ten years later, FCI made steady progress in their first three top-level seasons, finishing sixth in 2013, fifth in 2014 and fourth in 2015, which earned them a first qualification for Europe. But despite their upward mobility, plus a significantly reinforced playing staff, few gave them a chance of infiltrating the established title-chasing triumvirate of Flora, Levadia and Kalju, let alone finishing above all three.

However, with Puštov still in command, that is precisely what they did. They powered to the top of the standings at the start with four straight wins, then shrugged off away defeats at both Levadia and Kalju to surge clear with a 14-match unbeaten streak that contained 12 victories, ten of them in succession, including thrilling home successes against Levadia (3-2) and Flora (4-3).

With the pressure mounting, FCI stood resolute, and on a tense final day they came from behind to win 2-1 away at Kalju (who were still in the title mix) with second-half goals from Ghanaian defender Mike Ofosu-Appiah and midfielder Sergei Mošnikov and finish two points clear of Levadia, who had also overturned a deficit to beat Flora at home by the same score. Had any two of the three title challengers at the start of the day finished level on points, a championship play-off beckoned.

As FCI's 39-year-old skipper Andrei Kalimullin celebrated his 500th Meistriliiga appearance by lifting the league trophy, Levadia, the club with whom he had won the same prize on six previous occasions, were left to lick their wounds after just missing out on a record-equalling tenth title. A mid-season change of coach – Igor Prins for Sergei Ratnikov – had not had the desired effect, and it was a not dissimilar tale at Flora, whose replacement of 2015 title-winning boss Norbert Hurt with Argo Arbeiter considerably boosted the team's goal output but could not ultimately lift them higher than the fourth place they occupied when he took over.

Domestic cup

A succession of unlikely results in the 2016/17 Estonian Cup paved the way for FCI's delayed domestic double, although it was the champions themselves who ousted Levadia and Kajlu, the latter on penalties in the quarter-finals, before seeing off giant-killing Narva United in the semis and fellow first-time finalists Tammeka in the main event. Veteran Estonia midfielder Dmitri Kruglov opened the scoring in the A. Le Coq Arena before Tartu-born new signing (and ex-Tammeka player) Albert Prosa doubled FCI's advantage just after the interval.

Europe

For the fourth successive year Nõmme Kalju were Estonia's last team standing in Europe. They outlasted their domestic rivals once again by reaching the third qualifying round of the UEFA Europa League, with new Russian coach Sergei Frantsev overseeing a dramatic penalty shoot-out victory over Maccabi Haifa. Levadia almost caused another upset in the same round against Slavia Praha, but there was no proud exit from the UEFA Champions League for Flora, humbled on entry by Lincoln of Gibraltar.

National team

There was a change of coach after just one fixture of Estonia's 2018 FIFA World Cup qualifying campaign as record cap-holder Martin Reim was promoted from the Under-21s to replace Magnus Pehrsson following an opening 5-0 defeat in Bosnia & Herzegovina. Reim kicked off his reign with an easy 4-0 win against Gibraltar but just one further point was eked from the next four qualifiers, which included a crushing 8-1 loss in Belgium. A 3-0 friendly victory against Croatia was the season's highlight, featuring a 23rd international goal for Konstantin Vassiljev, who also enjoyed a splendid club campaign in Poland with Jagiellonia Białystok.

DOMESTIC SEASON AT A GLANCE

Meistriliiga 2016 final table

			Home					Away					Total					
		Pld	W	D	L	F	A	W	D	L	F	A	W	D	L	F	A	Pts
1	**FCI Tallinn**	**36**	**14**	**4**	**0**	**45**	**18**	**10**	**4**	**4**	**29**	**15**	**24**	**8**	**4**	**74**	**33**	**80**
2	FC Levadia Tallinn	36	13	4	1	42	10	11	2	5	35	20	24	6	6	77	30	78
3	Nõmme Kalju FC	36	12	3	3	36	13	10	6	2	34	15	22	9	5	70	28	75
4	FC Flora Tallinn	36	11	6	1	48	9	10	4	4	48	22	21	10	5	96	31	73
5	JK Sillamäe Kalev	36	8	4	6	34	26	6	5	7	31	29	14	9	13	65	55	51
6	Paide Linnameeskond	36	9	3	6	36	26	5	3	10	22	35	14	6	16	58	61	48
7	JK Tammeka Tartu	36	7	2	9	27	29	5	3	10	16	36	12	5	19	43	65	41
8	JK Narva Trans	36	6	6	6	33	30	5	2	11	27	38	11	8	17	60	68	41
9	Pärnu Linnameeskond	36	4	0	14	14	50	1	2	15	10	48	5	2	29	24	98	17
10	Rakvere JK Tarvas	36	0	1	17	6	50	0	2	16	9	63	0	3	33	15	113	3

European qualification 2017/18

Champion/Cup winner: FCI Tallinn (first qualifying round)

FC Levadia Tallinn (first qualifying round)
Nõmme Kalju FC (first qualifying round)
FC Flora Tallinn (first qualifying round)

Top scorer Evgeni Kabaev (Sillamäe), 25 goals
Relegated clubs Rakvere JK Tarvas, Pärnu Linnameeskond (withdrawn)
Promoted clubs JK Tulevik Viljandi, Pärnu JK Vaprus
Cup final FCI Tallinn 2-0 JK Tammeka Tartu

Player of the season

Evgeni Kabaev
(JK Sillamäe Kalev)

With 12 goals in the last nine games of the season, Kabaev guaranteed himself a comfortable victory in the race for the Meistriliiga golden boot, ending up with a final tally of 25 – six more than Flora's 20-year-old rising star Rauno Sappinen and Paide Linnameeskond's retiring 35-year-old Vjatšeslav Zahovaiko. The Russian striker thus regained the prize he had won in scoring 36 times for Sillamäe in 2014. Officially voted 2016 Meistriliiga player of the year, he left Estonia soon afterwards to join Czech top-flight club Bohemians 1905.

Newcomer of the season

Mike Ofosu-Appiah
(FCI Tallinn)

The Ghanaian centre-back was one of several new signings made by FCI in the build-up to the 2016 Meistriliiga campaign – others included Estonian international stalwarts Dmitri Kruglov and Vladmir Voskoboinikov – and he turned out to be arguably the best of the bunch. Not only did the ex-Skonto FC defender play a decisive role at the back, he also struck eight goals in FCI's surprise title triumph, including the winner on his home debut against Nõmme Kalju and the equaliser in the final-day showdown against the same opposition.

Team of the season

(4-5-1)

Coach: Puštov *(FCI)*

ESTONIA

NATIONAL TEAM

Top five all-time caps
Martin Reim (157); Marko Kristal (143); Andres Oper (134); Enar Jääger (121); Mart Poom (120)

Top five all-time goals
Andres Oper (38); Indrek Zelinski (27); **Konstantin Vassiljev** (23); Eduard Ellmann-Eelma (21); Richard Kuremaa (19)

Results 2016/17

Date	Opponent		Venue		Score	Goals
31/08/16	Malta	H	Parnu	D	1-1	*Zenjov (57)*
06/09/16	Bosnia & Herzegovina (WCQ)	A	Zenica	L	0-5	
07/10/16	Gibraltar (WCQ)	H	Tallinn	W	4-0	*Käit (47, 70), Vassiljev (52), Mošnikov (88)*
10/10/16	Greece (WCQ)	H	Tallinn	L	0-2	
13/11/16	Belgium (WCQ)	A	Brussels	L	1-8	*Anier (29)*
19/11/16	St Kitts & Nevis	A	Basseterre	D	1-1	*Sappinen (41)*
22/11/16	Antigua & Barbuda	A	St John's	W	1-0	*Marin (7)*
25/03/17	Cyprus (WCQ)	A	Nicosia	D	0-0	
28/03/17	Croatia	H	Tallinn	W	3-0	*Luts (1), Vassiljev (81), Zenjov (84)*
09/06/17	Belgium (WCQ)	H	Tallinn	L	0-2	
12/06/17	Latvia	A	Riga	W	2-1	*Zenjov (51), Purje (77)*

Appearances 2016/17

Coach: Magnus Pehrsson (SWE) /(14/09/17) Martin Reim	**25/05/76 14/05/71**		**Mlt**	**BIH**	**GIB**	**GRE**	**BEL**	**Skn**	**Atg**	**CYP**	**Cro**	**BEL**	**Lva**	**Caps**	**Goals**
Mihkel Aksalu	07/11/84	SJK (FIN)	G	G	G	G	G			G	G46	G		32	-
Taijo Teniste	31/01/88	Sogndal (NOR)	D	D	D	D31	D			D	D86	D	D	56	-
Nikita Baranov	19/08/92	Flora /Kristiansund (NOR)	D	D	D	D	D	D	D	D	D	D	D	20	-
Ken Kallaste	31/08/88	Korona (POL)	D	M		D	D				D	s75	D69	35	-
Artur Pikk	05/03/93	BATE (BLR)	D77	D								D		18	1
Gert Kams	25/05/85	Flora	M62	M46		s31	s63	D84	s65					48	2
Karol Mets	16/05/93	Viking (NOR)	M	M	M	M	M	D	M	D	M	D	D	40	-
Aleksandr Dmitrijev	18/02/82	FCI	M69			M79	M			M			M84	104	-
Konstantin Vassiljev	16/08/84	Jagiellonia (POL)	M	M	M61	M	M			M91	s76	A	s57	97	23
Sergei Zenjov	20/04/89	Qäbälä (AZE)	M	A71	M65	A				M79	s70	M79	s46	58	12
Ats Purje	03/08/85	Kalju /KuPS (FIN)	A68			s69		s61	A74				s69	61	9
Maksim Gussev	20/07/94	Flora	s62											9	1
Rauno Sappinen	23/01/96	Flora	s68	s86				M61						11	1
Ilja Antonov	05/12/92	Levadia /Horn (AUT)	s69	M86							s86			31	1
Dmitri Kruglov	24/05/84	FCI	s77	s46	D					D			s69	108	4
Ragnar Klavan	30/10/85	Liverpool (ENG)		D	D	D	D			D	D	D		119	3
Henri Anier	17/12/90	Kalmar (SWE) /Inverness (SCO)		s71	A		A85	A	s74	s91	A70	s85	A46	38	7
Mattias Käit	29/06/98	Fulham (ENG)			M80					A	M	M85	M57	6	2
Siim Luts	12/03/89	Bohemians 1905 (CZE)			M	M69	M84			s65	M	M75	M81	31	2
Sergei Mošnikov	07/01/88	FCI /Minsk (BLR)			s61	s79	M63	M61	s74				s84	29	1
Henrik Ojamaa	20/05/91	Go Ahead Eagles (NED) /Dundee (SCO)			s65		s85			M65		s79		27	-
Brent Lepistu	26/03/93	Flora			s80			M					s81	4	-
Pavel Marin	14/06/95	Levadia				M	s84	M77	M65					8	1
Andreas Vaikla	19/02/97	unattached						G						2	-
Markus Jürgenson	09/09/87	Flora						D						9	-
Artjom Dmitrijev	14/11/88	Kalju						M	s46		M86	M 44*		5	-
Pavel Dõmov	31/12/93	FCI						s61	M46					2	-
Janar Toomet	10/08/89	Kalju						s77	M80	s79	M76		M69	5	-
Karl Mööl	04/03/92	Kalju						s84	D		s86			4	-
Marko Meerits	26/04/92	Tarvas /VPS (FIN)							G		s46		G	7	-
Joonas Tamm	02/02/92	Flora							D					7	-
Trevor Elhi	11/04/93	Kalju							D					1	-
Martin Miller	25/09/97	Tammeka							M74					1	-
Hindrek Ojamaa	12/06/95	Levadia							s80					2	-
Madis Vihmann	05/10/95	Flora											D	1	-

EUROPE

FC Flora Tallinn

First qualifying round - Lincoln FC (GIB)

H 2-1 *Alliku (35), Sappinen (49)*

Toom, Kokla, Alliku, Sappinen, Jürgenson, Kams, Gussev (Saliste 85), Vihmann, Baranov, Ainsalu (Lepistu 68), Beglarishvili (Prosa 71). Coach: Norbert Hurt (EST)

A 0-2

Toom, Kokla (Šlein 82), Alliku, Lepistu, Sappinen, Jürgenson, Kams, Gussev, Vihmann (Tamm 60), Baranov, Beglarishvili (Prosa 53). Coach: Norbert Hurt (EST)

FC Levadia Tallinn

First qualifying round - HB Tórshavn (FRO)

H 1-1 *Marin (65)*

Lepmets, Tabi Manga, Antonov, Marin, Gando, Miranchuk (Gatagov 70), Ratnikov, Podholjuzin, Morozov, Hunt, Kobzar (Luts 46). Coach: Sergei Ratnikov (EST)

A 2-0 *Kobzar (71), Miranchuk (90+2)*

Lepmets, Tabi Manga, Antonov, Gando, Miranchuk, Luts, Kaljumäe, Podholjuzin, Morozov, Hunt, Kobzar (Raudsepp 75). Coach: Sergei Ratnikov (EST)

Second qualifying round - SK Slavia Praha (CZE)

H 3-1 *Hunt (35), Gando (67), Antonov (90)*

Lepmets, Tabi Manga, Antonov, Gando, Miranchuk, Luts, Kaljumäe, Podholjuzin, Morozov, Hunt, Kobzar (Raudsepp 68). Coach: Igor Prins (EST)

A 0-2

Lepmets, Tabi Manga, Antonov, Gando, Miranchuk, Luts, Kaljumäe (Raudsepp 80), Podholjuzin, Morozov, Hunt, Kobzar (Gatagov 80). Coach: Igor Prins (EST)

Nõmme Kalju FC

First qualifying round - FK Trakai (LTU)

A 1-2 *Wakui (6p)*

Teleš, Uggè, Jorge Rodrigues, Mbu Alidor, Dmitrijev, Toomet (Järva 77), Klein (Neemelo 80), Sidorenkov, Mööl, Wakui, Quintieri (Sinyavskiy 45). Coach: Sergei Frantsev (RUS)

H 4-1 *Jorge Rodrigues (66), Sidorenkov (69), Neemelo (87, 90+2)*

Teleš, Uggè, Jorge Rodrigues, Mbu Alidor, Dmitrijev, Toomet, Klein (Neemelo 46), Sidorenkov, Mööl, Wakui (E Puri 66), Quintieri (Purje 59). Coach: Sergei Frantsev (RUS)

Second qualifying round - Maccabi Haifa FC (ISR)

A 1-1 *Toomet (47)*

Teleš, Uggè, Jorge Rodrigues, Mbu Alidor, Dmitrijev, Purje (Neemelo 79), Toomet (Subbotin 68), Valikaev, Sidorenkov, Mööl, Quintieri (E Puri 59). Coach: Sergei Frantsev (RUS)

H 1-1 (aet; 5-3 on pens) *Neemelo (90)*

Teleš, Uggè, Jorge Rodrigues, Mbu Alidor, Dmitrijev, Purje, Toomet (Subbotin 71), Valikaev (Wakui 84), Sidorenkov, Mööl, Quintieri (Neemelo 63). Coach: Sergei Frantsev (RUS)

Third qualifying round - Osmanlıspor (TUR)

A 0-1

Teleš, Uggè, Jorge Rodrigues, Mbu Alidor, Dmitrijev, Purje (Neemelo 67), Toomet (E Puri 75), Valikaev, Sidorenkov, Mööl, Quintieri (Subbotin 64). Coach: Sergei Frantsev (RUS)

H 0-2

Teleš, Uggè, Jorge Rodrigues, Mbu Alidor, Dmitrijev, Purje, Toomet (Subbotin 46), Valikaev (Wakui 79), Sidorenkov, Mööl, Quintieri (Neemelo 63). Coach: Sergei Frantsev (RUS)

FCI Tallinn

First qualifying round - Heart of Midlothian FC (SCO)

A 1-2 *Harin (21)*

Igonen, Kalimullin, Avilov, Ofosu-Appiah, Volodin, Voskoboinikov, Harin (Kulinitš 83), Mošnikov, Kruglov, Dmitrijev, Mashichev (Draman 61). Coach: Aleksandr Puštov (EST)

H 2-4 *Harin (51), Voskoboinikov (63)*

Igonen, Kalimullin, Avilov (Dõmov 46), Ofosu-Appiah, Volodin (Kulinitš 75), Voskoboinikov, Harin, Mošnikov (Draman 46), Kruglov, Dmitrijev, Mashichev. Coach: Aleksandr Puštov (EST)

DOMESTIC LEAGUE CLUB-BY-CLUB

FCI Tallinn

2002 • Infonet Lasnamäe (500); Sportland Arena (540) • fcinfonet.com

Major honours

Estonian League (1) 2016; Estonian Cup (1) 2017

Coach: Aleksandr Puštov

2016

05/03	a	Paide	W	2-0	*og (Rähn), Voskoboinikov*
09/03	h	Kalju	W	2-1	*og (Jorge Rodrigues), Ofosu-Appiah*
12/03	h	Tammeka	W	4-0	*Ofosu-Appiah, Mashichev, Draman, Voskoboinikov*
19/03	a	Pärnu	W	2-0	*Rättel, Ofosu-Appiah*
01/04	h	Flora	D	1-1	*Kruglov (p)*
04/04	a	Sillamäe	D	2-2	*Golovljov, Harin*
09/04	a	Levadia	L	0-1	
16/04	h	Rakvere Tarvas	W	4-1	*Mashichev, Ofosu-Appiah, Voskoboinikov 2*
23/04	a	Trans	W	3-0	*Rättel 2, Ofosu-Appiah*
26/04	a	Kalju	L	1-2	*Volodin*
30/04	h	Sillamäe	D	0-0	
07/05	a	Rakvere Tarvas	W	1-0	*Mashichev (p)*
10/05	a	Paide	W	4-1	*Volodin, Mashichev, Kulinitš, Rättel*
14/05	h	Levadia	W	3-2	*Harin, Ofosu-Appiah, Avilov*
17/05	h	Trans	W	2-1	*Harin, Avilov*
23/05	a	Tammeka	W	2-1	*Harin, Voskoboinikov*
19/06	h	Pärnu	W	3-1	*Kulinitš 2, Voskoboinikov*
10/07	h	Flora	W	4-3	*Kruglov, Voskoboinikov, Mashichev (p), Harin*
23/07	h	Rakvere Tarvas	W	6-0	*Draman, Harin, Kalimullin, Voskoboinikov 2 (1p), Volodin*
30/07	h	Trans	W	4-3	*Voskoboinikov, Mošnikov, Harin, Mashichev (p)*
05/08	a	Tammeka	W	1-0	*Voskoboinikov*
13/08	h	Levadia	D	0-0	
16/08	a	Pärnu	W	5-0	*Draman, Kruglov, Harin, Mošnikov, Voskoboinikov*
19/08	h	Paide	W	1-0	*og (Rähn)*
23/08	a	Flora	L	0-3	
27/08	a	Sillamäe	D	0-0	
10/09	h	Sillamäe	W	4-2	*Mošnikov 2, Dõmov, Avilov*
13/09	a	Flora	L	1-2	*Kulinitš*
17/09	a	Rakvere Tarvas	W	1-0	*Kulinitš*
23/09	h	Pärnu	W	1-0	*Mashichev*
27/09	h	Kalju	D	2-2	*Ofosu-Appiah, og (Sidorenkov)*
01/10	a	Levadia	D	2-2	*Kruglov, Kulinitš*
14/10	h	Tammeka	W	1-0	*Kulinitš*
21/10	a	Trans	D	0-0	
28/10	h	Paide	W	3-1	*Mošnikov, Harin, Tumasyan*
05/11	a	Kalju	W	2-1	*Ofosu-Appiah, Mošnikov*

Name	Nat	DoB	Pos	Aps	(s)	Gls
Vladimir Avilov		10/03/95	D	29	(3)	3
Aleksandr Dmitrijev		18/02/82	M	32		
Pavel Dõmov		31/12/93	M	17	(2)	1
Haminu Draman	GHA	01/04/86	M	13	(10)	3
Eduard Golovljov		25/01/97	A	1	(10)	1
Jevgeni Harin	RUS	11/06/95	M	26	(4)	9
Matvei Igonen		02/10/96	G	34		
Juri Jevdokimov		03/06/88	A		(6)	
Andrei Kalimullin		06/10/77	D	21	(8)	1
Dmitri Kruglov		24/05/84	D	33	(1)	4
Aleksandr Kulinitš		24/05/92	D	23	(10)	7
Mihhail Lavrentjev		22/02/90	G	2		
Nikolai Mashichev		05/12/88	M	29	(1)	7
Sergei Mošnikov		07/01/88	M	27	(1)	6
Mike Ofosu-Appiah	GHA	29/12/89	D	24	(1)	8
Artur Rättel		08/02/93	A	17	(11)	4
Roman Sobtšenko		25/01/94	M	4	(11)	
Sergei Tumasyan	RUS	31/01/90	M	8	(2)	1
Evgeny Tyukalov	RUS	07/08/92	A	8	(5)	
Denis Vnukov		01/11/91	M	4	(5)	
Aleksandr Volodin		29/03/88	D	24	(2)	3
Vladimir Voskoboinikov		02/02/83	A	20	(10)	12

ESTONIA

FC Flora Tallinn

1990 • A. Le Coq Arena (9,600); Sportland Arena (540) • fcflora.ee

Major honours
Estonian League (10) 1994, 1995, 1998, 1998 (autumn), 2001, 2002, 2003, 2010, 2011, 2015; Estonian Cup (7) 1995, 1998, 2008, 2009, 2011, 2013, 2016

Coach: Norbert Hurt; (08/07/16) (Jürgen Henn); (13/07/16) Argo Arbeiter

2016					
05/03	a	Levadia	D	0-0	
08/03	h	Rakvere Tarvas	W	6-0	*Tukiainen 5, Jürgenson (p)*
12/03	h	Trans	W	3-0	*Jürgenson, Prosa, Sappinen*
19/03	a	Kalju	L	0-2	
01/04	a	FCI	D	1-1	*Prosa*
04/04	h	Tammeka	D	0-0	
08/04	h	Sillamäe	D	0-0	
16/04	a	Paide	D	1-1	*Gussev*
22/04	a	Pärnu	W	3-0	*Frolov (p), Sappinen 2*
26/04	h	Levadia	L	1-2	*Tamm*
29/04	h	Pärnu	W	6-0	*Tamm, Prosa, Beglarishvili, Saliste, Baranov, Tukiainen*
06/05	h	Paide	W	2-0	*og (Lomp), Prosa*
10/05	h	Kalju	D	0-0	
13/05	a	Sillamäe	W	4-2	*Prosa 3, Sappinen*
16/05	h	Tammeka	D	0-0	
24/05	a	Trans	W	2-1	*og (Proshin), Lepistu*
19/06	a	Rakvere Tarvas	W	5-0	*Alliku 4, Prosa (p)*
10/07	a	FCI	L	3-4	*Prosa 2, Saliste*
22/07	a	Tammeka	W	4-0	*Sappinen 2, Alliku 2*
29/07	a	Paide	W	3-0	*Tukiainen 3*
01/08	h	Levadia	W	6-1	*Tukiainen, Alliku 2, Sappinen 2, Gussev*
06/08	h	Trans	W	4-1	*Sappinen, Tukiainen, Gussev, Riiberg*
12/08	h	Pärnu	W	3-0	*Alliku 2, Gussev*
16/08	a	Rakvere Tarvas	W	4-1	*Tukiainen 2, Sappinen, Jürgenson*
19/08	a	Sillamäe	W	4-1	*Sappinen, Alliku, Kams, og (Dudarev)*
23/08	h	FCI	W	3-0	*Jürgenson, Sappinen, Riiberg*
27/08	a	Kalju	D	3-3	*Gussev, Kams 2*
10/09	h	Kalju	D	1-1	*Gussev*
13/09	h	FCI	W	2-1	*Sappinen 2*
16/09	a	Tammeka	L	2-3	*Ainsalu, Riiberg*
23/09	h	Rakvere Tarvas	W	4-0	*Beglarishvili 2, Vihmann, Riiberg*
01/10	a	Pärnu	W	6-1	*Alliku 3, Sappinen 2, Riiberg*
15/10	a	Trans	W	2-0	*(w/o; original result 2-0 Sappinen, Alliku)*
22/10	h	Paide	W	4-0	*Gussev, Ainsalu, Beglarishvili, Sappinen*
29/10	h	Sillamäe	D	3-3	*Gussev, Jürgenson, Tukiainen*
05/11	a	Levadia	L	1-2	*Sappinen*

Name	Nat	DoB	Pos	Aps	(s)	Gls
Mihkel Ainsalu		08/03/96	M	21	(5)	2
Richard Aland		15/03/94	G	16		
Rauno Alliku		02/03/90	M	25	(6)	15
Kevin Aloe		07/05/95	D	6	(1)	
Hannes Anier		16/01/93	M	1	(3)	
Nikita Baranov		19/08/92	D	31	(1)	1
Zakaria Beglarishvili	GEO	30/04/90	M	29	(2)	4
Andre Frolov		18/04/88	M	13	(7)	1
Maksim Gussev		20/07/94	M	20	(9)	8
Henri Järvelaid		11/12/98	A		(1)	
Markus Jürgenson		09/09/87	D	31	(1)	5
Gert Kams		25/05/85	D	31		3
Jan Kokla		29/05/97	M	10	(2)	
Brent Lepistu		26/03/93	M	21	(9)	1
Markus Poom		27/02/99	M	1	(5)	
Albert Prosa		01/10/90	A	13	(4)	10
Herol Riiberg		14/04/97	M	4	(8)	5
Joseph Saliste		10/04/95	M	9	(13)	2
Rauno Sappinen		23/01/96	A	31	(1)	19
German Šlein		28/03/96	M	10	(5)	
Erik Sorga		09/07/99	A		(2)	
Joonas Tamm		02/02/92	D	30	(1)	2
Mait Toom		07/05/90	G	20		
Sakari Tukiainen	FIN	02/10/91	A	12	(14)	14
Madis Vihmann		05/10/95	D	11	(3)	1

FC Levadia Tallinn

1998 • Kadriorg (5,000); Sportland Arena (540) • fclevadia.ee

Major honours
Estonian League (9) 1999, 2000, 2004, 2006, 2007, 2008, 2009, 2013, 2014; Estonian Cup (8) 1999, 2000, 2004, 2005, 2007, 2010, 2012, 2014

Coach: Sergei Ratnikov; (11/07/16) Igor Prins

2016					
05/03	h	Flora	D	0-0	
08/03	h	Pärnu	W	1-0	*Marin*
12/03	a	Paide	W	1-0	*Luts*
18/03	a	Trans	D	1-1	*Gando*
02/04	h	Kalju	D	1-1	*Luts*
05/04	h	Rakvere Tarvas	W	2-0	*Miranchuk, Kobzar*
09/04	h	FCI	W	1-0	*Morozov*
16/04	a	Sillamäe	W	2-0	*Luts, Morozov*
22/04	h	Tammeka	D	1-1	*Morozov*
26/04	a	Flora	W	2-1	*Kobzar, og (Baranov)*
29/04	a	Tammeka	W	4-1	*Morozov, Miranchuk, Marin 2*
07/05	h	Sillamäe	W	2-1	*Antonov, Hunt*
10/05	h	Trans	W	1-0	*og (Nesterovski)*
14/05	a	FCI	L	2-3	*Miranchuk 2 (1p)*
17/05	a	Rakvere Tarvas	W	4-0	*Tabi Manga 2, Miranchuk (p), Kaljumäe*
24/05	a	Kalju	W	1-0	*Miranchuk*
19/06	h	Paide	W	4-0	*Hunt 2, Kobzar, Morozov*
10/07	a	Pärnu	L	0-1	
24/07	h	Paide	W	7-1	*Miranchuk 3 (1p), Gando, Kauber 2, Tabi Manga*
29/07	a	Pärnu	W	4-0	*Miranchuk, Gando, Tabi Manga, Kobzar*
01/08	a	Flora	L	1-6	*Kobzar*
06/08	h	Sillamäe	W	2-1	*Kobzar, Gando*
13/08	a	FCI	D	0-0	
16/08	a	Tammeka	W	2-1	*Miranchuk (p), Gando*
20/08	h	Rakvere Tarvas	W	4-0	*Gatagov, Kaljumäe 2, Kauber*
23/08	h	Kalju	L	1-2	*Kauber*
26/08	a	Trans	L	1-3	*Gando*
10/09	h	Trans	W	5-0	*Kobzar 2, Gando, Gatagov, Kauber*
13/09	a	Kalju	W	3-0	*Kobzar, Morozov, Hunt*
17/09	a	Paide	W	4-0	*Hunt 2, Marin, Kauber*
24/09	h	Tammeka	W	4-0	*Podholjuzin, Marin, Miranchuk, Hunt*
01/10	h	FCI	D	2-2	*Miranchuk, Marin*
15/10	a	Sillamäe	L	2-3	*Kauber, Gando*
22/10	h	Pärnu	W	2-0	*Miranchuk (p), Kaljumäe*
29/10	a	Rakvere Tarvas	W	1-0	*Gando*
05/11	h	Flora	W	2-1	*Kobzar, Kauber*

Name	Nat	DoB	Pos	Aps	(s)	Gls
Ilja Antonov		05/12/92	M	27	(2)	1
Aimé Gando	CMR	27/02/97	D	29	(6)	9
Alan Gatagov	RUS	23/01/91	M	19	(2)	2
Rimo Hunt		05/11/85	A	32		7
Marek Kaljumäe		18/02/91	M	24	(12)	4
Kevin Kauber		23/03/95	A	7	(9)	8
Evgeni Kobzar	RUS	09/08/92	A	30	(3)	10
Nikita Koger		06/05/94	A	1	(1)	
Cristofer Kuusma		16/06/98	M		(1)	
Sergei Lepmets		05/04/87	G	35		
Siim Luts		12/03/89	M	12	(1)	3
Pavel Marin		14/06/95	M	16	(13)	6
Anton Miranchuk	RUS	17/10/95	M	28	(2)	14
Igor Morozov		27/05/89	D	32		6
Kaspar Mutso		01/08/98	M	1	(1)	
Hindrek Ojamaa		12/06/95	D	16	(6)	
Rasmus Peetson		03/05/95	M		(2)	
Priit Pikker		15/03/86	G	1		
Maksim Podholjuzin		13/11/92	D	32	(1)	1
Daniil Ratnikov		10/02/88	M	14		
Andreas Raudsepp		13/12/93	M	15	(10)	
Luc Tabi Manga	CMR	17/11/94	D	25	(5)	4
Markus Vaherna		27/01/99	M		(1)	
Magnar Vainumäe		19/04/98	M		(2)	

JK Narva Trans

1979 • Kreenholm (1,080); Fama Kalev (1,200) • fctrans.ee

Major honours
Estonian Cup (1) 2001

Adyam Kuzyaev (RUS)

2016					
04/03	a	Tammeka	D	2-2	*Proshin, Nesterov*
08/03	h	Sillamäe	D	3-3	*Nesterov 2, Nesterovski (p)*
12/03	a	Flora	L	0-3	
18/03	h	Levadia	D	1-1	*Umarov*
02/04	h	Rakvere Tarvas	D	2-2	*Nesterovski (p), Jakovlev*
05/04	h	Paide	L	2-3	*Umarov, Nesterovski*
09/04	a	Kalju	L	0-6	
16/04	h	Pärnu	W	4-0	*Jakovlev, Proshin, Umarov, Nesterovski (p)*
23/04	h	FCI	L	0-3	
29/04	a	Rakvere Tarvas	W	1-0	*Proshin*
06/05	a	Pärnu	W	1-0	*Plotnikov*
10/05	a	Levadia	L	0-1	
14/05	h	Kalju	D	1-1	*Umarov*
17/05	a	FCI	L	1-2	*og (Vnukov)*
24/05	h	Flora	L	1-2	*Škinjov*
19/06	h	Tammeka	W	4-1	*Umarov 3, Proshin*
02/07	a	Paide	L	2-3	*Proshin 2*
08/07	a	Sillamäe	L	0-3	
16/07	h	Paide	W	3-1	*Umarov, Škinjov, Proshin*
23/07	h	Sillamäe	L	1-3	*og (Sukharov)*
30/07	a	FCI	L	3-4	*Chernukhin, Barkov, Nesterovski (p)*
06/08	a	Flora	L	1-4	*Nesterovski*
12/08	h	Rakvere Tarvas	D	1-1	*Barkov*
15/08	a	Kalju	L	0-2	
19/08	h	Pärnu	W	3-1	*Proshin 2, Barkov*
23/08	a	Tammeka	W	2-0	*Škinjov, Barkov*
26/08	h	Levadia	W	3-1	*Nesterov, Umarov, Nesterovski*
10/09	a	Levadia	L	0-5	
13/09	h	Tammeka	W	4-2	*Barkov 2, Jakovlev, Proshin*
17/09	a	Sillamäe	L	1-2	*Proshin*
24/09	h	Kalju	L	0-3	
01/10	a	Rakvere Tarvas	W	6-0	*Irié, Barkov 2, Proshin 2, og (Meerits)*
15/10	h	Flora	L	0-2	*(w/o; original result 0-2)*
21/10	h	FCI	D	0-0	
29/10	a	Pärnu	W	7-1	*Barkov 3, Umarov 2, Nesterov, Proshin*
05/11	a	Paide	D	0-0	

Name	Nat	DoB	Pos	Aps	(s)	Gls
Vitali Andreev	RUS	22/02/86	D	11	(1)	
Dmitri Barkov	RUS	19/06/92	A	16	(2)	11
Dmitri Chernukhin	RUS	17/11/88	D	20		1
Khurshed-Timur Dzhuraev	RUS	21/09/97	M	10	(13)	
Bi Sehi Elysée Irié	CIV	13/09/89	M	9		1
Vladislav Ivanov	RUS	24/01/86	M	14	(2)	
Svjatoslav Jakovlev		24/04/96	M	28	(6)	3
Dmytro Kalininskiy	UKR	13/04/95	D		(1)	
Sergei Kapustin	RUS	06/03/98	M		(1)	
Arnold Kreger	RUS	22/12/90	G	13		
Ruslan Kuzyaev	RUS	07/08/87	M	13	(1)	
German-Guri Lvov		16/01/96	A	8	(16)	
Aleksei Matrossov		06/04/91	G	23		
Vadim Mihhailov		06/06/98	M	3	(13)	
Kirill Nesterov	RUS	21/07/89	D	32		5
Roman Nesterovski		09/06/89	D	36		7
Igor Ovsjannikov		23/02/92	D	22	(3)	
Viktor Plotnikov		14/07/89	M	25		1
Dmitri Proshin	RUS	06/01/84	M	34		14
Nikita Savenkov		28/07/98	D	18	(8)	
Artjom Škinjov		30/01/96	M	20	(11)	3
Tanel Tamberg		06/06/92	D	10	(3)	
Nikita Tokaitšuk		12/03/96	M		(1)	
Georgi Tunjov		17/04/01	A	1	(5)	
Rizvan Umarov	AZE	05/04/93	A	30		11

Nõmme Kalju FC

1923 • Hiiu (700) • jkkalju.ee

Major honours

Estonian League (1) 2012; Estonian Cup (1) 2015

Coach: Sergei Frantsev (RUS)

2016

Date		Opponent		Score	Scorers
05/03	h	Sillamäe	W	2-0	*Elhi, Sidorenkov*
09/03	a	FCI	L	1-2	*Dmitrijev*
12/03	h	Rakvere Tarvas	W	3-1	*Mööl 2, Jorge Rodrigues*
19/03	h	Flora	W	2-0	*Uggè, Neemelo*
02/04	a	Levadia	D	1-1	*Quintieri*
05/04	a	Pärnu	W	1-0	*Sidorenkov (p)*
09/04	h	Trans	W	6-0	*Quintieri, Dmitrijev 2, Listmann 2, Purje*
15/04	a	Tammeka	W	3-0	*Uggè, Mööl, Purje*
23/04	h	Paide	W	1-0	*Jorge Rodrigues*
26/04	h	FCI	W	2-1	*Neemelo, Sidorenkov*
30/04	a	Paide	D	1-1	*Kirss*
07/05	h	Tammeka	W	2-0	*Kirss, Wakui*
10/05	a	Flora	D	0-0	
14/05	a	Trans	D	1-1	*Mööl*
17/05	h	Pärnu	W	3-0	*Purje, Dmitrijev 2*
24/05	h	Levadia	L	0-1	
19/06	a	Sillamäe	W	3-1	*Klein, Neemelo, Alex*
10/07	a	Rakvere Tarvas	W	6-1	*Mööl, Wakui (p), Purje 3, Dmitrijev*
24/07	h	Pärnu	D	0-0	
07/08	h	Paide	D	1-1	*Pürg*
12/08	a	Sillamäe	W	1-0	*Uggè*
15/08	h	Trans	W	2-0	*Purje, Toomet*
20/08	h	Tammeka	W	3-0	*Purje, Quintieri, Valikaev*
23/08	a	Levadia	W	2-1	*Purje, Dmitrijev*
27/08	h	Flora	D	3-3	*Valikaev, Mööl, Neemelo*
10/09	a	Flora	D	1-1	*Purje*
13/09	h	Levadia	L	0-3	
17/09	a	Pärnu	W	5-1	*Purje, Sidorenkov 3, Neemelo*
24/09	a	Trans	W	3-0	*Toomet, Subbotin, Klein*
27/09	a	FCI	D	2-2	*Toomet, Purje*
01/10	h	Sillamäe	W	3-1	*Kirss, S Puri, Neemelo*
15/10	a	Paide	L	0-2	
22/10	h	Rakvere Tarvas	W	2-0	*Wakui (p), Dmitrijev (p)*
25/10	a	Rakvere Tarvas	W	2-1	*Purje, Uggè*
29/10	a	Tammeka	W	1-0	*S Puri*
05/11	h	FCI	L	1-2	*Purje*

Name	Nat	DoB	Pos	Aps	(s)	Gls
Alex	BRA	16/01/87	D	3		1
Artjom Dmitrijev		14/11/88	M	33		8
Trevor Elhi		11/04/93	D	9	(5)	1
Andre Järva		21/11/96	A	3	(13)	
Jorge Rodrigues	POR	19/03/82	D	21	(1)	2
Sören Kaldma		03/07/96	M		(4)	
Robert Kirss		03/09/94	A	12		3
Peeter Klein		28/01/97	A	3	(1)	2
Märten Kuusk		05/04/96	D	1		
Erik Listmann		09/02/95	M	11	(2)	2
Reginald Mbu Alidor	FRA	15/05/93	M	28	(1)	
Karl Mööl		04/03/92	D	35		6
Tarmo Neemelo		10/02/82	A		(33)	6
Henrik Pürg		03/06/96	D	16		1
Eino Puri		07/05/88	M	19	(6)	
Sander Puri		07/05/88	M	8	(5)	2
Ats Purje		03/08/85	A	24	(4)	14
Damiano Quintieri	ITA	04/05/90	M	19	(5)	3
Andrei Sidorenkov		12/02/84	D	29		6
Vlasiy Sinyavskiy		27/11/96	M	6	(4)	
Igor Subbotin		26/06/90	M	12	(4)	1
Vitali Teleš		17/10/83	G	36		
Janar Toomet		10/08/89	M	11	(6)	3
Maximiliano Uggè	ITA	24/09/91	D	33		4
Artur Valikaev	RUS	08/01/88	M	14	(3)	2
Hidetoshi Wakui	JPN	12/02/83	M	10	(5)	3

Paide Linnameeskond

2004 • Paide (450); Paide kunstmurustaadion (200) • paidelinnameeskond.ee

Coach: Meelis Rooba

2016

Date		Opponent		Score	Scorers
05/03	h	FCI	L	0-2	
08/03	a	Tammeka	L	0-2	
12/03	h	Levadia	L	0-1	
19/03	a	Sillamäe	D	1-1	*Roosnupp*
02/04	h	Pärnu	W	4-0	*Uwaegbulam (p), Zahovaiko (p), Lomp, Kase*
05/04	a	Trans	W	3-2	*Zahovaiko, Uwaegbulam, Lomp*
09/04	a	Rakvere Tarvas	W	5-0	*og (Kaasik), Uwaegbulam, Kase 2, Lomp*
16/04	h	Flora	D	1-1	*Zahovaiko (p)*
23/04	a	Kalju	L	0-1	
30/04	h	Kalju	D	1-1	*Uwaegbulam (p)*
06/05	a	Flora	L	0-2	
10/05	h	FCI	L	1-4	*Roosnupp*
13/05	h	Rakvere Tarvas	W	4-2	*Zahovaiko 3 (1p), Roosnupp*
17/05	a	Sillamäe	D	0-0	
24/05	a	Pärnu	W	3-0	*Varendi, Juha, Uwaegbulam*
19/06	a	Levadia	L	0-4	
02/07	h	Trans	W	3-2	*Rähn, Zahovaiko, Uwaegbulam (p)*
09/07	h	Tammeka	W	3-0	*Zahovaiko 3 (1p)*
16/07	a	Trans	L	1-3	*Roosnupp*
24/07	a	Levadia	L	1-7	*Sinilaid*
29/07	h	Flora	L	0-3	
07/08	a	Kalju	D	1-1	*Rähn*
13/08	h	Tammeka	W	3-1	*Zahovaiko 2, Saarlas*
16/08	h	Sillamäe	L	1-3	*El Hussieny*
19/08	a	FCI	L	0-1	
23/08	h	Rakvere Tarvas	W	7-0	*Sinilaid 2, Zahovaiko (p), Rähn, El Hussieny 2, Uwaegbulam*
27/08	a	Pärnu	L	1-3	*Jevdokimov*
09/09	h	Pärnu	W	4-1	*Zahovaiko 3, Sinilaid*
12/09	a	Rakvere Tarvas	W	1-0	*Zahovaiko*
17/09	h	Levadia	L	0-4	
24/09	h	Sillamäe	W	2-1	*Uwaegbulam, El Hussieny (p)*
30/09	a	Tammeka	W	4-1	*Zahovaiko 2, Valge, El Hussieny*
15/10	h	Kalju	W	2-0	*Valge, Roosnupp*
22/10	a	Flora	L	0-4	
28/10	a	FCI	L	1-3	*Juha*
05/11	h	Trans	D	0-0	

Name	Nat	DoB	Pos	Aps	(s)	Gls
Omar El Hussieny	EGY	03/11/85	M	17		5
Juri Jevdokimov		03/06/88	A	12	(3)	1
Joosep Juha		05/09/96	D	25	(4)	2
Gerdo Juhkam		19/06/94	D	2	(2)	
Martin Kase		02/09/93	A	25	(4)	3
Ervin Köll		18/03/89	M		(1)	
Johannes Kukebal		19/07/93	D		(7)	
Kert Kütt		09/10/80	G	34		
Michael Lilander		10/06/97	D	33	(1)	
Timo Lomp		26/07/88	D	30		3
Andre Mägi		14/01/88	D	1		
Martin Naggel		22/05/90	D		(4)	
Mart-Mattis Niinepuu		23/07/92	G	1		
Nikita Novopashin	RUS	16/06/97	D	31	(3)	
Meelis Peitre		27/03/90	D	6	(2)	
Taavi Rähn		16/05/81	D	28	(1)	3
Mark Oliver Roosnupp		12/05/97	M	26	(5)	5
Marten Saarlas		29/03/95	M	1	(9)	1
Sander Sinilaid		07/10/90	M	25	(7)	4
Roman Starikov	RUS	15/02/97	M	1	(2)	
Rasmus Tomson		13/08/85	M	2	(11)	
Janar Toomet		10/08/89	M	3	(9)	
Martin Ustaal		06/02/93	M	11	(2)	
Jasper Uwaegbulam	NGA	12/12/94	M	26	(5)	8
Sten-Marten Vahi		28/03/97	G	1		
Ander Ott Valge		20/10/98	A	7	(9)	2
Lauri Varendi		29/12/88	M	26	(6)	1
Vjatšeslav Zahovaiko		29/12/81	A	22	(9)	19

Pärnu Linnameeskond

2010 • Raeküla (450); Pärnu kunstmurustaadion (200); Pärnu Rannastaadion (1,501) • parnulm.ee

Coach: Marko Lelov

2016

Date		Opponent		Score	Scorers
05/03	h	Rakvere Tarvas	W	3-0	*Laurits (p), Tutk, Melts*
08/03	a	Levadia	L	0-1	
12/03	a	Sillamäe	L	1-4	*Laurits*
19/03	h	FCI	L	0-2	
02/04	a	Paide	L	0-4	
05/04	h	Kalju	L	0-1	
09/04	h	Tammeka	L	0-1	
16/04	a	Trans	L	0-4	
22/04	h	Flora	L	0-3	
29/04	a	Flora	L	0-6	
06/05	h	Trans	L	0-1	
13/05	a	Tammeka	L	1-2	*Hanson*
17/05	a	Kalju	L	0-3	
24/05	h	Paide	L	0-3	
09/06	h	Sillamäe	L	0-2	
19/06	a	FCI	L	1-3	*Mägi*
02/07	a	Rakvere Tarvas	W	2-1	*Vunk (p), Tutk*
10/07	h	Levadia	W	1-0	*Pent*
16/07	a	Tammeka	L	0-2	
24/07	a	Kalju	D	0-0	
29/07	h	Levadia	L	0-4	
05/08	h	Rakvere Tarvas	W	2-1	*Saarts, Rando Leokin*
12/08	a	Flora	L	0-3	
16/08	h	FCI	L	0-5	
19/08	a	Trans	L	1-3	*Raido Leokin*
22/08	h	Sillamäe	L	2-5	*Pent, Hanson*
27/08	h	Paide	W	3-1	*Hanson 2, Pent*
09/09	a	Paide	L	1-4	*Saarts*
13/09	a	Sillamäe	L	2-4	*Hanson, Lenk*
17/09	h	Kalju	L	1-5	*Vunk*
23/09	a	FCI	L	0-1	
01/10	h	Flora	L	1-6	*Hanson*
15/10	a	Rakvere Tarvas	D	1-1	*Tutk*
22/10	a	Levadia	L	0-2	
29/10	h	Trans	L	1-7	*Tutk (p)*
05/11	h	Tammeka	L	0-3	

Name	Nat	DoB	Pos	Aps	(s)	Gls
Hevar Aas		27/10/92	D	1	(1)	
Henri Hanson		18/04/95	A	22	(7)	6
Henri Hansson		18/08/97	A		(2)	
Jako Kanter		09/01/98	D	18	(3)	
Greger Könninge		23/01/91	M	10	(8)	
Taavi Laurits		23/01/90	A	9	(9)	2
Kristian Lenk		20/05/97	A	13	(13)	1
Raido Leokin		05/03/92	D	14	(6)	1
Rando Leokin		05/03/92	M	12	(12)	1
Marco Lukka		04/12/96	D	33		
Martin Mägi		18/06/96	D	30	(1)	1
Martin Mardiste		13/02/97	M		(2)	
Tanel Melts		20/11/88	M	12		1
Karl Palatu		05/12/82	D	24	(1)	
Risto Pärnat		11/10/92	M	4	(5)	
Toomas Pent		28/09/90	M	24		3
Kristen Saarts		28/10/94	A	27	(3)	2
Joosep Sarapuu		30/07/94	D	15	(4)	
Kristjan Tamme		21/09/95	G	18		
Rauno Tutk		10/04/88	M	30	(2)	4
Joel Vabrit		09/09/87	G	2	(1)	
Hendrik Vainu		03/04/96	G	16	(1)	
Karmo Valk		16/06/97	M		(4)	
Tõnis Vihmoja		15/01/93	M	13	(13)	
Magnus Villota		11/02/98	D	28		
Martin Vunk		21/08/84	M	21	(6)	2

ESTONIA

Rakvere JK Tarvas

2004 • Rakvere linnastaadion (1,785) • jktarvas.ee

Coach: Valeri Bondarenko; (04/06/16) Urmas Kirs

2016					
05/03	a	Pärnu	L	0-3	
08/03	a	Flora	L	0-6	
12/03	a	Kalju	L	1-3	*Goldberg*
19/03	a	Tammeka	L	1-3	*Rannamäe*
02/04	a	Trans	D	2-2	*Kuusk 2*
05/04	a	Levadia	L	0-2	
09/04	h	Paide	L	0-5	
16/04	a	FCI	L	1-4	*Gull*
23/04	a	Sillamäe	L	0-1	
29/04	h	Trans	L	0-1	
07/05	h	FCI	L	0-1	
13/05	a	Paide	L	2-4	*Siim, Rannamäe*
17/05	h	Levadia	L	0-4	
24/05	h	Sillamäe	L	0-3	
09/06	h	Tammeka	L	0-1	
19/06	h	Flora	L	0-5	
02/07	h	Pärnu	L	1-2	*Kaasik*
10/07	h	Kalju	L	1-6	*og (Elhi)*
15/07	a	Sillamäe	L	0-4	
23/07	a	FCI	L	0-6	
05/08	a	Pärnu	L	1-2	*Aunapuu*
12/08	a	Trans	D	1-1	*Sepp*
16/08	h	Flora	L	1-4	*Larin*
20/08	a	Levadia	L	0-4	
23/08	a	Paide	L	0-7	
26/08	h	Tammeka	L	1-3	*Siim*
09/09	a	Tammeka	L	0-5	
12/09	h	Paide	L	0-1	
17/09	h	FCI	L	0-1	
23/09	a	Flora	L	0-4	
01/10	h	Trans	L	0-6	
15/10	h	Pärnu	D	1-1	*Kuokkanen*
22/10	a	Kalju	L	0-2	
25/10	h	Kalju	L	1-2	*Madis Reimal*
29/10	h	Levadia	L	0-1	
05/11	h	Sillamäe	L	0-3	

Name	Nat	DoB	Pos	Aps	(s)	Gls
Alari Aunapuu		23/12/89	M	10	(3)	1
Stanislav Goldberg		30/10/92	M	10		1
Mihkel Gull		16/03/88	D	26	(6)	1
Henri Hang		28/08/91	A	1	(4)	
Jaanus Kaasik		22/06/90	D	30	(1)	1
Rauno Kald		11/03/91	M	13		
Toomas Kiis		11/08/92	M		(12)	
Mihhail Kolesnikov		06/02/95	G		(1)	
Yao Sylvain Kouassi	CIV	08/06/88	M	3	(6)	
Erkki Kubber		30/04/94	M	6	(2)	
Mario Kuokkanen		17/06/99	M	24	(8)	1
Märten Kuusk		05/04/96	D	14		2
Aleksei Larin		29/03/92	D	28	(2)	1
Joonas Ljaš		03/09/90	M	17	(8)	
Marko Meerits		26/04/92	G	10		
Taavi Münter		22/12/92	D	21	(6)	
Siim Rannamäe		16/03/90	A	16		2
Madis Reimal		23/02/93	M	14	(11)	1
Martti Reimal		30/04/97	A		(1)	
Kaarel Saar		19/03/90	D	14	(2)	
Mihkel Saar		30/09/82	D	12	(9)	
Kert Saarmets		13/03/00	M		(1)	
Alex Sander Sepp		08/04/95	M	18	(1)	1
Juhan Jograf Siim		22/04/96	A	17	(3)	2
Sander Susi		24/04/92	G	26		
Hans Joosep Tammerik		30/09/95	D	2		
Sten Tammik		15/03/95	A	1	(1)	
Alari Tovstik		31/07/84	M	4		
Elar Tovstik		31/10/81	D	21	(4)	
Taavi Trasberg		17/07/93	M	26	(1)	
Samuel Vard		30/12/96	M	12	(5)	
Rainer Võsaste		12/06/90	A		(1)	

JK Sillamäe Kalev

1951 • Kalev (1,000); Sillamäe kunstmurustaadion (490) • fcsillamae.ee

Coach: Denis Ugarov (RUS); (22/05/16) Algimantas Briaunys (LTU)

2016					
05/03	a	Kalju	L	0-2	
08/03	a	Trans	D	3-3	*Semakhin, Malov (p), Dudarev*
12/03	h	Pärnu	W	4-1	*Ziļs, Lipin, og (Lenk), Volkov*
19/03	h	Paide	D	1-1	*Ziļs*
01/04	a	Tammeka	L	0-4	
04/04	h	FCI	D	2-2	*Savin, Malov*
08/04	a	Flora	D	0-0	
16/04	h	Levadia	L	0-2	
23/04	h	Rakvere Tarvas	W	1-0	*Paponov*
30/04	a	FCI	D	0-0	
07/05	a	Levadia	L	1-2	*Volkov*
13/05	h	Flora	L	2-4	*Kabaev 2 (1p)*
17/05	h	Paide	D	0-0	
24/05	a	Rakvere Tarvas	W	3-0	*Kabaev 2, Volkov*
09/06	a	Pärnu	W	2-0	*Ziļs 2*
19/06	h	Kalju	L	1-3	*Savin*
01/07	a	Tammeka	D	0-0	
08/07	h	Trans	W	3-0	*Kabaev, Aidara, Paponov*
15/07	h	Rakvere Tarvas	W	4-0	*Aidara 2, Volkov, Kabaev*
23/07	a	Trans	W	3-1	*Paponov, Kabaev, Panov*
30/07	h	Tammeka	W	5-1	*Kabaev 4, Paponov*
06/08	a	Levadia	L	1-2	*Savin*
12/08	h	Kalju	L	0-1	
16/08	a	Paide	W	3-1	*Aidara 2, La Vecchia*
19/08	h	Flora	L	1-4	*Kabaev*
22/08	a	Pärnu	W	5-2	*Savin, Kabaev, Sukharov, Paponov, Abu Bakr*
27/08	h	FCI	D	0-0	
10/09	a	FCI	L	2-4	*Savin, Kabaev*
13/09	h	Pärnu	W	4-2	*Kabaev 2, Lipin, Savin*
17/09	h	Trans	W	2-1	*Volkov, Kabaev (p)*
24/09	a	Paide	L	1-2	*Tjapkin*
01/10	a	Kalju	L	1-3	*Kabaev*
15/10	h	Levadia	W	3-2	*Kabaev 2 (1p), Savin*
22/10	h	Tammeka	L	1-2	*Kabaev*
29/10	a	Flora	D	3-3	*Kabaev 2, Solovjovs*
05/11	a	Rakvere Tarvas	W	3-0	*La Vecchia, Kabaev 2*

Name	Nat	DoB	Pos	Aps	(s)	Gls
Radanfah Abu Bakr	TRI	12/02/87	D	15		1
Kassim Aidara	FRA	12/05/87	M	27	(1)	5
Pavel Aleksejev		24/02/91	D		(1)	
Aleksei Cherkasov	RUS	01/09/94	D	18	(9)	
Artjom Davõdov		04/03/99	D	1	(8)	
Igor Dudarev	RUS	12/08/93	D	25	(1)	1
Roman Grigorevski	RUS	11/06/97	M		(6)	
Aleksandr Ivanjušin		07/09/95	D	19	(4)	
Evgeni Kabaev	RUS	28/02/88	A	26	(2)	25
Dmitri Kolipov		16/05/96	M		(1)	
Alessandro La Vecchia	ITA	10/01/85	M	4	(2)	2
Maksim Lipin		17/03/92	M	31	(3)	2
Deniss Malov		08/06/80	M	28	(3)	2
Daniil Mironov		27/12/96	M		(10)	
Anton Panov		22/08/96	D	7	(15)	1
Maksim Paponov		11/06/90	M	22	(2)	5
Aleksandr Savin	RUS	20/10/84	A	23	(2)	7
Aleksandr Semakhin	RUS	10/01/95	M	6	(1)	1
Aleksandrs Solovjovs	LVA	25/02/88	D	19		1
Mihhail Starodubtsev		14/08/82	G	32	(1)	
Olexandr Sukharov	UKR	08/02/94	D	15		1
Deniss Tjapkin		30/01/91	D	31		1
Irakli Torinava	RUS	12/04/94	A		(3)	
Eduard Usikov-Orehov		06/12/89	G	4	(1)	
Eduard Usikov-Orehov		06/12/89	M		(1)	
Aleksandr Volkov		11/10/94	A	28	(5)	5
Vitālijs Ziļs	LVA	19/08/87	A	15	(2)	4

JK Tammeka Tartu

1989 • Tamme (1,645); Annelinna kunstmuruväljak (500) • jktammeka.ee

Coach: Indrek Koser

2016					
04/03	h	Trans	D	2-2	*Tauts, Tekko*
08/03	h	Paide	W	2-0	*Tiirik, Jõgi*
12/03	a	FCI	L	0-4	
19/03	h	Rakvere Tarvas	W	3-1	*Koskor 2, Rääbis*
01/04	h	Sillamäe	W	4-0	*Kiidron, Tiirik 2, Rääbis*
04/04	a	Flora	D	0-0	
09/04	a	Pärnu	W	1-0	*Rääbis*
15/04	h	Kalju	L	0-3	
22/04	a	Levadia	D	1-1	*Jõgi*
29/04	h	Levadia	L	1-4	*Tiirik*
07/05	a	Kalju	L	0-2	
13/05	h	Pärnu	W	2-1	*Tiirik (p), Koskor*
16/05	a	Flora	D	0-0	
23/05	h	FCI	L	1-2	*Tauts*
09/06	a	Rakvere Tarvas	W	1-0	*Tiirik*
19/06	a	Trans	L	1-4	*Tiirik (p)*
01/07	h	Sillamäe	D	0-0	
09/07	a	Paide	L	0-3	
16/07	h	Pärnu	W	2-0	*Tiirik, Tauts*
22/07	h	Flora	L	0-4	
30/07	a	Sillamäe	L	1-5	*Tšernjavski*
05/08	h	FCI	L	0-1	
13/08	a	Paide	L	1-3	*Miller*
16/08	h	Levadia	L	1-2	*Lorenz*
20/08	a	Kalju	L	0-3	
23/08	h	Trans	L	0-2	
26/08	a	Rakvere Tarvas	W	3-1	*Paur, Tiirik (p), Kapper*
09/09	h	Rakvere Tarvas	W	5-0	*Paur 3, Grauberg, Tiirik*
13/09	a	Trans	L	2-4	*Tiirik, Tšernjavski*
16/09	h	Flora	W	3-2	*Tšernjavski, Rande, Kiidron*
24/09	a	Levadia	L	0-4	
30/09	h	Paide	L	1-4	*Miller*
14/10	a	FCI	L	0-1	
22/10	a	Sillamäe	W	2-1	*Tiirik, Miller*
29/10	h	Kalju	L	0-1	
05/11	a	Pärnu	W	3-0	*Läll, Tšernjavski, Tekko*

Name	Nat	DoB	Pos	Aps	(s)	Gls
Martin Aasmäe		10/05/96	M	1	(4)	
Kevin Anderson		10/11/93	D	21	(2)	
Silver Grauberg		26/11/96	D	14	(1)	1
Georgi Ivanov		19/06/92	A		(1)	
Martin Jõgi		05/01/95	D	13	(5)	2
Sander Kapper		08/12/94	M	9	(7)	1
Kaarel Kiidron		30/04/90	D	34		2
Karlo Korss		19/03/98	D		(1)	
Tristan Koskor		28/11/95	A	25	(2)	3
Reio Laabus		14/03/90	M	30	(2)	
Rait Läll		31/12/99	A	7	(8)	1
Erko Litvjakov		22/07/99	M		(3)	
Jürgen Lorenz		11/05/93	D	36		1
Martin Miller		25/09/97	M	35	(1)	3
Erki Mõttus		15/01/97	M	1	(9)	
Andre Paju		05/01/95	D	32		
Kaspar Paur		16/02/95	M	9	(2)	4
Karl Johan Pechter		02/03/96	G	35		
Kevin Rääbis		02/01/94	M	6	(2)	3
Randin Rande		28/07/97	M	1	(5)	1
Andrei Sadovoi		21/02/97	M	1	(2)	
Geir-Kristjan Suurpere		26/02/95	M	2	(4)	
Sander Taan		16/03/98	D		(1)	
Rasmus Tauts		07/01/97	M	17	(1)	3
Tauno Tekko		14/12/94	M	24	(6)	2
Kristjan Tiirik		25/08/82	M	35		12
Marek Tšernjavski		15/05/92	A	7	(12)	4
Karl Vaabel		25/08/97	G	1		

Top goalscorers

25 Evgeni Kabaev (Sillamäe)

19 Rauno Sappinen (Flora)
Vjatšeslav Zahovaiko (Paide)

15 Rauno Alliku (Flora)

14 Sakari Tukiainen (Flora)
Anton Miranchuk (Levadia)
Dmitri Proshin (Trans)
Ats Purje (Kalju)

12 Vladimir Voskoboinikov (FCI)
Kristjan Tiirik (Tammeka)

Promoted clubs

JK Tulevik Viljandi

1912 • Viljandi linnastaadion (1,084) • jktulevik.ee
Coach: Aivar Lillevere

Pärnu JK Vaprus

1922 • Pärnu Rannastaadion (1,501) • vaprus.ee
Coach: Marko Lelov

Second level final table 2016

		Pld	W	D	L	F	A	Pts
1	JK Tulevik Viljandi	36	28	5	3	106	38	89
2	FC Flora Tallinn U21	36	20	8	8	78	47	68
3	FCI Tallinn II	36	18	2	16	98	81	56
4	Maardu Linnameeskond	36	16	6	14	83	75	54
5	FC Levadia Tallinn U21	36	15	5	16	81	69	50
6	FC Santos Tartu	36	16	1	19	63	70	49
7	JK Tallinna Kalev	36	13	6	17	56	58	45
8	Nõmme Kalju FC U21	36	12	5	19	62	86	41
9	JK Vaprus Vändra	36	8	8	20	48	96	32
10	JK Järve Kohtla-Järve	36	8	6	22	42	97	30

Promotion/Relegation play-offs

(12/11/16 & 19/11/16)
Maardu 1-5 Pärnu
Pärnu 4-3 Maardu
(Pärnu 9-4)

NB Pärnu JK Vaprus replaced Pärnu Linnameeskond in 2017 Meistriliiga.

DOMESTIC CUP

Eesti Karikas 2016/17

FIRST ROUND

(31/05/16)
Depoo 0-6 FCI-2
Järva-Jaani w/o Ararat TTÜ
Järve 3-0 Kohtla-Nõmme
Poseidon 7-0 Enamasti Pealekata
Rakvere Tarvas 13-0 FC Sssolutions

(02/06/16)
Raplamaa Märjamaa 4-0 Navi
Sillamäe w/o Roosu

(04/06/16)
Puhkus Mehhikos 0-2 Flora U19 *(aet)*

(05/06/16)
Elva 13-0 IceBears
Piraaja 11-1 Wolves Tallinn
Soccernet 8-1 Wolves Jõgeva-2

(06/06/16)
Olympic Olybet 2-3 TransferWise *(aet)*

(07/06/16)
Castovanni Eagles-2 0-4 Ambla
Fellin 0-1 Keila
Flora 11-0 Peedu
Levadia-3 8-0 Raudteetöölised
Tääksi 3-2 Helios Tartu
Twister 7-0 Warrior
Wolves Jõgeva 7-0 Reaal

(08/06/16)
Kadakas 2-1 Rasmus Värk
Otepää 1-2 Narva United

(09/06/16)
Koeru 0-2 Tannem
Lelle 1-6 Molycorp Silmet
Nõmme United 24-0 Õismäe Torm

(12/06/16)
Forza 0-8 Kalju
(15/06/16)
Rada 0-4 Raplamaa

(16/06/16)
Igiliikur 0-6 Welco
Tallinna Kalev 14-0 Illi
Tammeka 2-0 Santos

(18/06/16)
Castovanni Eagles w/o Pedajamäe
Tallinna Kalev-3 0-4 Tulevik

(19/06/16)
Eston Villa w/o Kaitseliit Kalev

(22/06/16)
Merkuur 6-4 Zenit

(26/06/16)
Kuressaare w/o Väätsa
Tammeka U21 1-4 Pärnu

(28/06/16)
Reliikvia 1-2 Terav Sats

(03/07/16)
Charma 1-2 Maardu

SECOND ROUND

(09/07/16)
Tääksi 5-0 Jalgpallihaigla

(17/07/16)
Welco 0-8 Flora

(20/07/16)
Soccernet 1-5 Kuressaare

(24/07/16)
Ambla 2-5 Tõrva
EMÜ w/o Castovanni Eagles
Jalgpalliselts 0-3 TÜ Fauna
Lokomotiv 1-1 Flora U19 *(aet; 3-5 on pens)*
Molycorp Silmet w/o Forss

(26/07/16)
FCI 9-0 Piraaja
Järva-Jaani 1-4 Narva United
Maardu United 2-10 Sillamäe
Rakvere Tarvas 5-1 Maardu

(02/08/16)
Kose 0-2 Poseidon
Laagri 6-1 Wolves Jõgeva
Paide 1-0 Nõmme United
Tammeka 3-0 Läänemaa

(03/08/16)
Elva 2-3 Tallinna Kalev
Järve w/o Twister
Joker 4-3 Raplamaa *(aet)*
Legion 1-0 Ganvix
Raplamaa Märjamaa 2-1 Irbis
Terav Sats w/o Noorus-96
Viimsi-2 0-5 FCI-2

(04/08/16)
Kadakas 5-3 Tannem *(aet)*

(07/08/16)
Tulevik 13-0 Loo

(08/08/16)
TransferWise 1-6 Viimsi

(09/08/16)
Pärnu 2-4 Levadia

(10/08/16)
Kalju-3 0-5 Flora U21
Merkuur 3-4 Rumori Calcio *(aet)*

(17/08/16)
Eston Villa 4-4 Tartu *(aet; 5-6 on pens)*
Levadia-3 4-1 Keila

(20/09/16)
Trans 0-2 Kalju

THIRD ROUND

(24/08/16)
TÜ Fauna 4-6 EMÜ

(01/09/16)
Laagri 0-3 FCI-2
Tulevik 1-0 Sillamäe

(04/09/16)
Kuressaare 3-2 Legion
Rumori Calcio 4-3 Kadakas
Terav Sats 0-2 Raplamaa Märjamaa

(06/09/16)
Tartu 0-11 FCI

(07/09/16)
Tallinna Kalev 5-0 Tääksi

(20/09/16)
Levadia-3 1-8 Tammeka
Rakvere Tarvas 2-3 Paide

(21/09/16)
Järve 0-2 Flora U21
Molycorp Silmet 6-5 Flora U19 *(aet)*
Narva United 0-0 Viimsi JK *(aet; 3-2 on pens)*

(27/09/16)
Levadia 7-0 Joker

(28/09/16)
Flora 5-0 Tõrva

(05/10/16)
Kalju 10-0 Poseidon

FOURTH ROUND

(05/10/16)
Tammeka 5-1 Rumori Calcio

(12/10/16)
Kuressaare 5-0 Raplamaa Märjamaa

(16/10/16)
EMÜ 0-5 Tulevik

(18/10/16)
FCI 2-1 Levadia

(19/10/16)
Flora U21 1-3 Narva United
FCI-2 1-4 Paide
Kalju 1-0 Flora

(15/11/16)
Molycorp Silmet 0-11 Tallinna Kalev

QUARTER-FINALS

(11/04/17)
Tallinna Kalev 0-3 Paide *(Sinilaid 30, Kriisa 32og, Hanson 37)*

Tulevik 0-1 Tammeka *(Aasmäe 120) (aet)*

(12/04/17)
Kalju 1-1 FCI *(Tjapkin 71; Nesterov 87) (aet; 3-5 on pens)*

Narva United 3-1 Kuressaare *(Seleznjov 24, Andreev 71, Novikov 87; Suursaar 45)*

SEMI-FINALS

(09/05/17)
Tammeka 0-0 Paide *(aet; 4-2 on pens)*

(10/05/17)
FCI 2-0 Narva United *(Nesterov 3, Voskoboinikov 87)*

FINAL

(27/05/17)
A. Le Coq Arena, Tallinn
FCI TALLINN 2 *(Kruglov 9, Prosa 47)*
JK TAMMEKA TARTU 0
Referee: *Martin*
FCI: *Igonen, Avilov, Ofosu-Appiah, Kulinitš, Kruglov, Nesterov, Harin, Dõmov (Volodin 79), Dmitrijev, Voskoboinikov, Prosa (Kalimullin 90+4)*
TAMMEKA: *Pechter, Paju, Kiidron, Lorenz, Anderson, Laabus, Tekko (Puri 64), Kapper (Grauberg 75), Aasmäe, Rande (Tšernjavski 61), Jõgi*

FAROE ISLANDS

Fótbóltssamband Føroya (FSF)

Address	Gundadalur, PO Box 3028 FO-110 Tórshavn
Tel	+298 351979
Fax	+298 319079
E-mail	fsf@football.fo
Website	football.fo

President	Christian Andreasen
General secretary	Virgar Hvidbro
Media officer	Kristin Dam Ziska
Year of formation	1979
National stadium	Tórsvøllur, Torshavn (6,040)

MEISTARADEILDIN CLUBS

1 **AB Argir**

2 **B36 Tórshavn**

3 **B68 Toftir**

4 **HB Tórshavn**

5 **ÍF Fuglafjørdur**

6 **KÍ Klaksvík**

7 **NSÍ Runavík**

8 **Skála ÍF**

9 **TB Tvøroyri**
NB Merged with FC Suduroy & Royn to become TB/FCS/Royn for 2017 season

10 **Víkingur**

PROMOTED CLUBS

11 **EB/Streymur**

12 **07 Vestur**

Eidi
Fuglafjørdur
Klaksvík
Gøta
Skáli
Toftir
Runavík
Sandavágur
Tórshavn
Argir
Tvøroyri

0 20 40 km
0 20 miles

KEY

- UEFA Champions League
- UEFA Europa League
- Promoted
- Relegated

Víkingur surge to historic victory

Having won six national titles under their previous guise as GÍ Gøta, Víkingur added a seventh in 2016 to conclude a 20-year wait. It was not until their final fixture, a 3-1 win at relegated AB Argir, that their triumph was confirmed, KÍ Klaksvík having ceded the initiative during the run-in after topping the table for the majority of the campaign.

KÍ did, however, end Víkingur's four-year monopoly of the domestic cup, defeating their rivals on penalties in the final to claim their first trophy of the 21st century. It was a season to forget, however, for Torshavn clubs B36 and HB.

New name on the Meistaradeildin trophy

Long-time leaders KÍ miss out by a point

Klaksvik club end Víkingur's cup-winning run

Domestic league

A domestic title-winning coach with both HB (in 2009) and B36 (in 2014), Sámal Erik Hentze was appointed by Víkingur with the fixed goal of transforming the club from cup specialists into champions. He got off to a modest start, though, and when his side lost 2-0 both home and away to KÍ, it looked as if the title was heading to Klaksvik for the first time since 1999.

The month-long summer break, however, re-energised Víkingur and before long they were back in business. By the time they met KÍ again, at home, seven successive victories had propelled them to within a point of Mikkjal Thomassen's front-runners, who, powered by the goals of Páll Ándrasson Klettskard and Jóannes Bjartalíd, had won 13 of their previous 15 matches. A Klettskard double would give KÍ a 2-1 win, complete a clean sweep over Víkingur and increase their lead to four points with just four games to go.

A fortnight later, however, it was Víkingur, not KÍ, who topped the table, the leaders having dropped five points in two matches, the second of them a 3-1 defeat at lowly AB. As chance would have it, Víkingur's final fixture was also at AB – their first away fixture after four in a row at home – but they did not make the same mistake as KÍ, reversing that 3-1 scoreline in their favour with timely goals from Sølvi Vatnhamar and Andreas Lava Olsen (two) to retain the one-point advantage they had held at kick-off.

It was Víkingur's 11th win in 12 matches, and they had needed every one of them to take the title. KÍ, with their perfect record against the champions, had every reason to feel aggrieved, but they did lose two out of three against third-placed NSÍ, who yet again, for the fourth straight year, provided the league's leading marksman in Klæmint Andrasson Olsen, his final goal tally amounting to a personal-best 23. B36, the champions of the previous two seasons, finished fourth, one place ahead of local rivals HB, who actually led early on before going seven games without a victory. B68, who went down with AB, failed to win all season, swapping divisions for the second successive winter with EB/Streymur, promoted alongside 07 Vestur.

Domestic cup

Víkingur's determined late run in the league was perhaps triggered by the concession to KÍ in late August of the Faroe Islands Cup – a trophy they had come to consider almost as their own. Having flirted with elimination in the quarter-finals, when they only overcame HB on penalties, they were unable to repeat their shoot-out escapology in the Tórsvøllur final, with KÍ prevailing 5-3 after a 1-1 draw to win the competition for the first time in 17 years.

Europe

The Meistaradeildin experienced a European whitewash for the second straight year as B36, Víkingur, NSÍ and HB all repeated their experience of the previous summer by departing on entry from their respective competitions. There was just one win between them, but B36's 2-1 success at home to Valletta in the first qualifying round of the UEFA Champions League amounted to failure (on the away goals rule) after they had lost 1-0 in Malta.

National team

Five points from six matches and fourth place in their FIFA World Cup qualifying group was a generally acceptable state of affairs for the Faroe Islands, although there was disappointment that Lars Olsen's side failed to score in their three home games and were unable to build on an excellent early 2-0 win in Latvia, a 6-0 defeat in Torshavn by European champions Portugal following just three days later.

DOMESTIC SEASON AT A GLANCE

Meistaradeildin 2016 final table

		Pld	Home					Away					Total					Pts
			W	D	L	F	A	W	D	L	F	A	W	D	L	F	A	
1	**Víkingur**	**27**	**12**	**0**	**2**	**33**	**8**	**7**	**4**	**2**	**26**	**17**	**19**	**4**	**4**	**59**	**25**	**61**
2	KÍ Klaksvík	27	11	2	2	41	12	8	1	3	23	14	19	3	5	64	26	60
3	NSÍ Runavík	27	11	1	2	36	14	7	0	6	24	22	18	1	8	60	36	55
4	B36 Tórshavn	27	9	3	2	31	16	5	4	4	15	12	14	7	6	46	28	49
5	HB Tórshavn	27	7	3	4	28	16	5	4	4	16	14	12	7	8	44	30	43
6	ÍF Fuglafjørdur	27	4	5	4	20	21	5	0	9	22	38	9	5	13	42	59	32
7	TB Tvøroyri	27	6	2	4	16	14	1	4	10	15	34	7	6	14	31	48	27
8	Skála ÍF	27	5	2	6	16	16	1	6	7	9	25	6	8	13	25	41	26
9	AB Argir	27	3	4	6	21	21	1	2	11	10	28	4	6	17	31	49	18
10	B68 Toftir	27	0	5	8	12	30	0	2	12	8	50	0	7	20	20	80	7

European qualification 2017/18

Champion: Víkingur (first qualifying round)

Cup winner: KÍ Klaksvík (first qualifying round)
NSÍ Runavík (first qualifying round)
B36 Tórshavn (first qualifying round)

Top scorer Klæmint Andrasson Olsen (NSÍ), 23 goals
Relegated clubs B68 Toftir, AB Argir
Promoted clubs EB/Streymur, 07 Vestur
Cup final KÍ Klaksvík 1-1 Víkingur *(aet; 5-3 on pens)*

Player of the season

Sølvi Vatnhamar
(Víkingur)

At the age of 30, Vatnhamar reached a career peak by helping Víkingur to victory in the Meistaradeildin. The long-serving midfielder had already won five domestic cups with the club, but he took his game to a new level in 2016, scoring 14 league goals, including two hat-tricks, to end up as the champions' leading marksman – four ahead of his Serbian partner Filip Djordjević. His outstanding club form earned him a regular spot in the Faroe Islands national team for the 2018 FIFA World Cup qualifying campaign.

Newcomer of the season

Teit Jacobsen
(HB Tórshavn)

A fringe player for HB in the 2015 Meistaradeildin, Jacobsen claimed a fixed berth in the Torshavn club's midfield during the 2016 campaign at the age of 18 and he further endeared himself to the club's fans by scoring in two of the three derbies against B36. Already a Faroe Islands international at youth level, his impressive club performances earned him regular selection for the Under-21 team. Senior recognition also appeared to be on the horizon when he made a move to Danish Superliga side SønderjyskE in January 2017.

Team of the season
(4-4-2)

Coach: Hentze *(Víkingur)*

NATIONAL TEAM

Top five all-time caps

Fródi Benjaminsen (92); Óli Johannesen (83); Jákup Mikkelsen (73); Jens Martin Knudsen (65); Julian Johnsson (62)

Top five all-time goals

Rógvi Jacobsen (10); Todi Jónsson (9); Uni Arge (8); **Fródi Benjaminsen, Jóan Símun Edmundsson**, Christian Lamhauge Holst & John Petersen (6)

Results 2016/17

06/09/16	Hungary (WCQ)	H	Torshavn	D	0-0	
07/10/16	Latvia (WCQ)	A	Riga	W	2-0	*Nattestad (19), Edmundsson (70)*
10/10/16	Portugal (WCQ)	H	Torshavn	L	0-6	
13/11/16	Switzerland (WCQ)	A	Lucerne	L	0-2	
25/03/17	Andorra (WCQ)	A	Andorra la Vella	D	0-0	
09/06/17	Switzerland (WCQ)	H	Torshavn	L	0-2	

Appearances 2016/17

Coach: Lars Olsen (DEN)	**02/02/61**		**HUN**	**LVA**	**POR**	**SUI**	**AND**	**SUI**	**Caps**	**Goals**
Gunnar Nielsen	07/10/86	FH (ISL)	G	G	G	G	G	G	39	-
Bárdur J Hansen	13/03/92	Fremad Amager (DEN) /NSÍ	D		D	D	s70		6	-
Atli Gregersen	15/06/82	Víkingur	D	D	D72	D	D	D	37	-
Sonni Nattestad	05/08/94	Fylkir (ISL)	D	D	D	D			17	1
Viljormur Davidsen	19/07/91	Vejle (DEN)	D	D	D		D	D	20	-
Sølvi Vatnhamar	05/05/86	Víkingur	M	M	M	M81	M	M	17	1
Fródi Benjaminsen	14/12/77	HB /Víkingur	M	M	M	M89		M	92	6
Hallur Hansson	08/07/92	Horsens (DEN)	M91	M	M	M	M	M66	29	4
René S Joensen	08/02/93	Vendsyssel (DEN)	M	M73	s66	s78		s61	11	-
Brandur H Olsen	19/12/95	Randers (DEN)	M	M88	M79	M			14	2
Jóan Símun Edmundsson	26/07/91	OB (DEN)	A	A92	A	A	M 74*		42	6
Heini Vatnsdal	18/10/91	Fremad Amager (DEN)	s91						7	-
Jónas Tór Næs	27/12/86	B36 /ÍBV (ISL)		D		D	D	D	51	-
Gilli Sørensen	11/08/92	Brann (NOR)		s73	M66	M78	M82	M	17	-
Pól Jóhannus Justinussen	13/01/89	NSÍ		s88			s82		26	-
Páll A Klettskard	17/05/90	KÍ		s92			A		14	-
Jóhan Troest Davidsen	31/01/88	HB			s72		D	D70	35	-
Kaj Leo í Bartalsstovu	23/06/91	FH (ISL) /ÍBV (ISL)			s79		M70		11	-
Andreas Lava Olsen	09/10/87	Víkingur				s81			10	1
Odmar Færø	01/11/89	B36				s89		s70	16	-
Finnur Justinussen	30/03/89	Fremad Amager (DEN)						A	4	-
Klæmint A Olsen	17/07/90	NSÍ						A61	10	-
Karl Løkin	19/04/91	NSÍ						s66	5	-

EUROPE

B36 Tórshavn

First qualifying round - Valletta FC (MLT)

A 0-1

T Askham, Eriksen, Næs, Færø, Mellemgaard (Cieślewicz 74), H Askham, Borg (Pingel 82), Jakobsen, Dam, Eysturoy, Thorleifsson (Agnarsson 71). Coach: Eydun Klakstein (FRO)

H 2-1 *Thorleifsson (10), Agnarsson (66)*

T Askham, Eriksen, Næs, Færø, Mellemgaard (P Petersen 89), H Askham, Borg (Agnarsson 62), Jakobsen, Cieślewicz, Eysturoy, Thorleifsson (Pingel 81). Coach: Eydun Klakstein (FRO)

NSÍ Runavík

First qualifying round - FC Shakhtyor Soligorsk (BLR)

H 0-2

S Hansen, Langgaard, M Jacobsen, Joensen, J Mortensen (J Olsen 71), K Olsen (M Olsen 52), Justinussen, Køhlert, J Jacobsen, P Knudsen (J Benjaminsen 88), Madsen. Coach: Anders Gerber (DEN)

Red card: Joensen 47

A 0-5

S Hansen, Langgaard, M Jacobsen, J Mortensen (J Benjaminsen 75), K Olsen, Justinussen, Køhlert, J Jacobsen, P Knudsen (M Mortensen 87), M Olsen, Madsen (Gaardbo 84). Coach: Anders Gerber (DEN)

Víkingur

First qualifying round - FK Ventspils (LVA)

A 0-2

Túri, A Olsen (Poulsen 75), Gregersen, Djordjević (J Olsen 86), S Vatnhamar, Samuelsen (Anghel 62), B Hansen, E Jacobsen, Djurhuus, Justinussen, G Hansen. Coach: Sámal Erik Hentze (FRO)

H 0-2

Túri, A Olsen, Gregersen, Djordjević (J Olsen 68), S Vatnhamar, B Hansen, E Jacobsen, Djurhuus, Justinussen, Anghel (G Vatnhamar 71), G Hansen. Coach: Sámal Erik Hentze (FRO)

Red cards: A Olsen 52, Djurhuus 58

HB Tórshavn

First qualifying round - FC Levadia Tallinn (EST)

A 1-1 *Tabi Manga (21og)*

Gestsson, Jógvan Davidsen, Jóhan Davidsen, Egilsson (Wardum 66), Benjaminsen, Jensen, Mouritsen, Jacobsen, Jespersen (Justinussen 90+3), Jónsson, Olsen (Joensen 84). Coach: Jan Christian Dam (FRO)

H 0-2

Gestsson, Jógvan Davidsen, Jóhan Davidsen, Egilsson, Benjaminsen, Jensen, Mouritsen (Wardum 37), Jacobsen, Justinussen (Dalbúd 79), Jónsson, Olsen (Joensen 79). Coach: Jan Christian Dam (FRO)

DOMESTIC LEAGUE CLUB-BY-CLUB

AB Argir

1973 • Blue Water Arena (2,000) • argjaboltfelag.com

Coach: Trygvi Mortensen

2016					
06/03	h	B68	D	1-1	*Johannesen (p)*
13/03	a	ÍF	L	0-1	
20/03	a	TB	L	0-1	
03/04	a	B36	L	1-2	*Danielsen*
10/04	h	Víkingur	D	2-2	*Højgaard, Á Nielsen*
17/04	a	HB	D	0-0	
21/04	h	KÍ	D	1-1	*Símun Samuelsen*
28/04	h	Skála	D	0-0	
01/05	a	NSÍ	L	1-2	*Sørensen*
12/05	h	B36	L	2-3	*Janković, Johannesen (p)*
16/05	h	TB	W	3-2	*Soylu, Sørensen, Johannesen*
22/05	a	B68	D	2-2	*B Nielsen, Johannesen*
29/05	h	ÍF	L	2-3	*Á Nielsen, Johannesen*
12/06	a	Skála	L	0-1	
19/06	h	HB	L	0-1	
24/06	a	KÍ	L	1-5	*Á Nielsen*
24/07	a	Víkingur	L	0-3	
27/07	h	NSÍ	L	1-2	*Johannesen*
07/08	a	B36	L	1-2	*Johannesen*
14/08	a	TB	L	1-2	*Símun Samuelsen*
21/08	h	B68	W	5-0	*Johannesen, Soylu, Hansen 2, Símun Samuelsen*
11/09	a	ÍF	L	0-2	
18/09	h	Skála	L	0-2	
25/09	a	HB	W	2-1	*Johannesen, Splidt*
02/10	h	KÍ	W	3-1	*Johannesen (p), Splidt 2*
16/10	a	NSÍ	L	1-4	*Hansen (p)*
22/10	h	Víkingur	L	1-3	*Johannesen*

No	Name	Nat	DoB	Pos	Aps	(s)	Gls
2	Andri Freyr Björnsson	ISL	12/08/86	D	2		
14	Aron Clementsen		17/11/96	M	12	(1)	
3	Rói Danielsen		18/02/89	D	18		1
14	Jobin Drangastein		01/11/90	M	3	(6)	
9	Nicolaj Lindholm Eriksen	DEN	01/08/86	A		(2)	
12	Sandri Færø		04/03/92	M	18	(3)	
9	Símin Hansen		11/12/82	A	10		3
4	Gunnar Højgaard Haraldsen		21/11/87	D		(2)	
22	Beinir Henriksen		16/02/97	D		(1)	
20	Karstin Højgaard		23/02/94	M	8		1
6	Dmitrije Janković	SRB	05/11/75	D	22	(3)	1
11	Patrik Johannesen		07/09/95	A	26		11
15	Høgni Midjord		04/02/91	M		(2)	
18	Martin Midjord		25/12/89	D		(3)	
20	Hørdur Mouritzarson Mohr		06/03/93	M		(1)	
17	Árni Guldborg Nielsen		22/06/93	M	4	(12)	3
22	Bjarki Christiansson Nielsen		02/11/98	M	4	(5)	1
5	Kári Nielsen		03/03/81	D	16	(3)	
8	Bárdur Olsen		05/12/85	M	18	(3)	
20	Teitur Olsen		27/01/98	M		(3)	
5	Rógvi Poulsen		31/10/89	M	1	(1)	
10	Símun Samuelsen		21/05/85	M	17	(2)	3
19	Sørin Nygaard Samuelsen		29/04/92	D	20	(1)	
21	Bjarni Skála		14/11/97	M		(5)	
7	Dan í Soylu		09/07/96	M	25	(1)	2
18	Dion Brynjolf Splidt		05/06/89	M	9	(3)	3
16	Hedin Stenberg		14/01/89	G	27		
13	Jónas Stenberg		07/04/87	D	22	(3)	
23	Rasmus Dan Sørensen		27/05/95	A	13	(8)	2
2	Andras Brixen Vágsheyg		01/01/92	D	2		

B36 Tórshavn

1936 • Gundadalur (5,000) • b36.fo

Major honours
Faroe Islands League (11) 1946, 1948, 1950, 1959, 1962, 1997, 2001, 2005, 2011, 2014, 2015; Faroe Islands Cup (5) 1965, 1991, 2001, 2003, 2006

Coach: Eydun Klakstein

2016

Date		Opponent		Score	Scorers
05/03	h	ÍF	W	4-1	*Dam, Nolsøe 2, Pingel*
12/03	a	Skála	L	0-1	
20/03	a	B68	W	4-1	*Jakobsen 2 (1p), Cieślewicz, Pingel*
03/04	h	AB	W	2-1	*Cieślewicz, Pingel*
10/04	h	TB	D	0-0	
17/04	a	KÍ	D	1-1	*Jakobsen*
21/04	h	NSÍ	W	3-1	*Pingel, Jakobsen (p), Cieślewicz*
28/04	h	HB	W	3-2	*H Askham, Eysturoy 2*
01/05	a	Víkingur	L	0-1	
12/05	a	AB	W	3-2	*Nolsøe 2, Jakobsen (p)*
16/05	h	B68	W	3-1	*Nolsøe, Agnarsson, Jakobsen*
22/05	a	ÍF	D	0-0	
29/05	h	Skála	D	1-1	*Pingel*
12/06	a	HB	D	0-0	
19/06	h	KÍ	L	0-1	
23/06	a	NSÍ	L	1-2	*Eysturoy*
24/07	a	TB	W	1-0	*Færø*
29/07	h	Víkingur	L	0-2	
07/08	h	AB	W	2-1	*Jakobsen, Thorleifsson*
14/08	a	B68	W	1-0	*Cieślewicz*
21/08	h	ÍF	W	4-1	*Pingel, Dam, H Askham, Cieślewicz*
11/09	a	Skála	W	2-0	*Jakobsen 2*
18/09	h	HB	D	2-2	*Thorleifsson, Pingel*
25/09	a	KÍ	D	2-2	*Pingel, Færø*
02/10	h	NSÍ	W	2-0	*Jakobsen (p), Agnarsson*
16/10	a	Víkingur	L	0-2	
22/10	h	TB	W	5-2	*Borg, B Petersen, Pingel 2, Færø*

No	Name	Nat	DoB	Pos	Aps	(s)	Gls
15	Hannes Agnarsson		26/02/99	M	13	(3)	2
8	Hørdur Askham		22/09/94	D	22	(3)	2
25	Trygvi Askham		28/03/88	G	5	(2)	
9	Jákup á Borg		26/10/79	A	7	(1)	1
4	Robert Hedin Brockie		21/12/92	D	2		
11	Łukasz Cieślewicz	POL	15/11/87	M	22		5
13	Gestur Bogason Dam		17/09/94	D	24	(1)	2
2	Andrias Høgnason Eriksen		22/02/94	D	24		
20	Høgni Eysturoy		14/07/90	D	12	(5)	3
5	Odmar Færø		01/11/89	D	11		3
18	Benjamin Heinesen		26/03/96	M	10	(8)	
10	Róaldur Jakobsen		23/01/91	M	26		10
6	Høgni Madsen		04/02/85	M	9	(1)	
19	Erlendur Magnussen		02/07/98	D	1	(2)	
7	Alex Mellemgaard		27/11/91	D	8	(5)	
6	Eli Falkvard Nielsen		23/09/92	M	7	(3)	
23	Jógvan Andrias Nolsøe		20/05/92	A	12	(8)	5
3	Jónas Tór Næs		27/02/86	D	26		
16	Bjarni Petersen		12/08/98	M	6	(2)	1
14	Pætur Joensson Petersen		29/03/98	M	3	(16)	
22	Sebastian Pingel	DEN	11/05/93	A	17	(3)	10
22	Fródi Rasmussen		10/02/00	D		(1)	
4	Gilli Samuelsen		12/02/99	M		(1)	
24	Hugin Samuelsen		12/02/99	M		(1)	
4	Jóhan Eiler Simonsen		10/09/98	D		(1)	
1	Tórdur Thomsen		11/06/86	G	22		
24	Hanus Thorleifsson		19/12/85	M	8	(5)	2

B68 Toftir

1962 • Svangarskard (5,000) • b68.fo

Major honours
Faroe Islands League (3) 1984, 1985, 1992

Coach: Páll Gudlaugsson (ISL);
(04/07/16) Oddur Olsen;
(30/07/16) Eliesar Jónsson Olsen & Oddur Olsen

2016

Date		Opponent		Score	Scorers
06/03	a	AB	D	1-1	*Edmundsson*
13/03	h	TB	D	1-1	*Edmundsson*
20/03	h	B36	L	1-4	*O Petersen*
03/04	a	Víkingur	L	0-4	
10/04	h	NSÍ	L	0-5	
17/04	a	Skála	D	0-0	
20/04	a	HB	L	0-1	
28/04	h	ÍF	L	1-2	*Przybylski*
01/05	a	KÍ	L	1-4	*Andreassen*
12/05	h	Víkingur	D	2-2	*Herrero, O Petersen*
16/05	a	B36	L	1-3	*og (Magnussen)*
22/05	h	AB	D	2-2	*Edmundsson, Przybylski*
29/05	h	TB	D	3-3	*J Petersen, Przybylski, Ó Olsen (p)*
12/06	a	ÍF	L	0-4	
19/06	h	Skála	D	1-1	*Albert Johannesen*
24/06	a	HB	L	1-6	*Ó Olsen (p)*
24/07	a	NSÍ	L	1-2	*Ó Olsen*
31/07	h	KÍ	L	0-3	
07/08	a	Víkingur	L	1-5	*Yüksel*
14/08	h	B36	L	0-1	
21/08	a	AB	L	0-5	
11/09	a	TB	L	1-4	*Blé*
18/09	h	ÍF	L	0-2	
25/09	a	Skála	L	1-5	*Yüksel*
02/10	h	HB	L	0-1	
16/10	a	KÍ	L	0-6	
22/10	h	NSÍ	L	1-3	*Yüksel*

No	Name	Nat	DoB	Pos	Aps	(s)	Gls
8	Kristian Anton Andreassen		30/08/85	M	20	(5)	1
2	Pedro Tarancon Anton	ESP	18/12/85	D	20		
14	Líggjas Bjartalíd		22/12/88	A	2	(1)	
77	Evrard Blé	CIV	02/01/82	M	17	(5)	1
15	Esmar Petur Clementsen		29/09/96	M	1	(8)	
14	Hákun Edmundsson		21/03/96	M	14		3
19	Jógvan Ingvard Hansen		12/01/93	D	6	(1)	
18	Jóhannus Hansen		25/04/96	M	6	(11)	
16	Carlos Quintana Herrero	ESP	07/02/87	A	12	(3)	1
9	Búi í Hjøllum		30/03/90	A		(3)	
4	Jóhan Dávur Højgaard		11/06/82	D	22	(2)	
20	Leivur Højgaard		03/01/96	M	6	(8)	
22	Oddur Árnason Højgaard		12/09/89	D	6		
22	Ivan Joensen		20/02/92	M	4		
13	Albert Róin Johannesen		29/03/95	D	15	(5)	1
5	Ari Johannesen		07/06/96	D	24		
17	Bergur Johannesen		03/05/99	D		(1)	
22	Helgi Johannesen		28/06/97	D	2	(2)	
1	Ragnar Lindholm		17/08/93	G	22		
11	André Olsen		23/10/90	M	5	(1)	
10	Óli Højgaard Olsen		24/11/85	A	24	(1)	3
6	Jann Ingi Petersen		07/01/84	M	11		1
23	Otto Reinert Petersen		21/12/95	M	13	(7)	2
3	Niklas Poulsen		30/03/89	D	13		
7	Michał Przybylski	POL	29/12/97	M	22	(2)	3
12	Frídi Sigurdsson		09/09/95	G	5		
14	Damir Ibrić Yüksel	BIH	30/03/84	A	5	(2)	3

HB Tórshavn

1904 • Gundadalur (5,000) • hb.fo

Major honours
Faroe Islands League (22) 1955, 1960, 1963, 1964, 1965, 1971, 1973, 1974, 1975, 1978, 1981, 1982, 1988, 1990, 1998, 2002, 2003, 2004, 2006, 2009, 2010, 2013; Faroe Islands Cup (26) 1955, 1957, 1959, 1962, 1963, 1964, 1968, 1969, 1971, 1972, 1973, 1975, 1976, 1978, 1979, 1980, 1981, 1982, 1984, 1987, 1988, 1989, 1992, 1995, 1998, 2004

Coach: Jan Christian Dam

2016

Date		Opponent		Score	Scorers
05/03	a	NSÍ	W	2-1	*Olsen, Egilsson*
13/03	h	Víkingur	D	1-1	*Jespersen*
20/03	h	KÍ	W	4-2	*Mouritsen 2 (2p), Ingason 2*
03/04	a	TB	W	1-0	*Jespersen*
09/04	a	Skála	W	3-0	*Dalbúd 3*
17/04	h	AB	D	0-0	
20/04	h	B68	W	1-0	*Jóhan Davidsen*
28/04	a	B36	L	2-3	*Dalbúd, Jacobsen*
01/05	a	ÍF	L	2-4	*Mouritsen (p), J Hansen*
12/05	a	TB	D	0-0	
16/05	a	KÍ	L	0-1	
22/05	h	NSÍ	L	3-4	*Ingason 2, Dalbúd (p)*
29/05	a	Víkingur	L	0-1	
12/06	h	B36	D	0-0	
19/06	a	AB	W	1-0	*Jespersen*
24/06	h	B68	W	6-1	*Olsen 3, Mouritsen 2, Justinussen*
24/07	h	Skála	W	1-0	*Jóhan Davidsen*
28/07	h	ÍF	W	1-0	*Olsen*
07/08	h	TB	W	4-1	*Dalbúd 2, Olsen, Joensen*
14/08	h	KÍ	L	2-3	*Jespersen, Olsen*
21/08	a	NSÍ	D	0-0	
11/09	h	Víkingur	L	0-1	
18/09	a	B36	D	2-2	*Jacobsen, Jóhan Davidsen*
25/09	h	AB	L	1-2	*Dalbúd*
02/10	a	B68	W	1-0	*Dalbúd*
16/10	h	ÍF	W	4-1	*Benjaminsen, Wardum, Dalbúd 2*
22/10	a	Skála	D	2-2	*Dalbúd 2*

No	Name	Nat	DoB	Pos	Aps	(s)	Gls
7	Fródi Benjaminsen		14/12/77	M	17	(5)	1
12	Øssur Meinhardtsson Dalbúd		28/03/89	A	13	(8)	13
3	Jógvan Rói Davidsen		09/10/91	D	27		
5	Jóhan Troest Davidsen		31/01/88	D	25		3
4	Hjalti Kárason Djurhuus		14/07/98	M	3		
6	Magnus Egilsson		19/03/94	M	13	(6)	1
22	Rói av Fløtum		30/12/94	M		(1)	
1	Teitur Matras Gestsson		19/08/92	G	27		
8	Arnbjørn Theodor Hansen		27/02/86	A	2	(2)	
2	Jákup Finnsson Hansen		24/06/96	D	6	(5)	1
27	Símin Hansen		11/12/82	A		(3)	
20	Poul Ingason		28/09/95	A	3	(6)	4
14	Teit Jacobsen		16/03/98	M	24	(1)	2
9	Tróndur Jensen		06/02/93	M	20	(5)	
19	Rókur av Fløtum Jespersen		16/03/85	M	20		4
18	Pál Mohr Joensen		20/08/92	D	10	(7)	1
26	Daniel Johansen		09/07/98	M		(2)	
22	Ári Mohr Jónsson		22/07/94	D	19		
21	Adrian Justinussen		21/07/98	M	5	(12)	1
15	Andrias Mikkelsen		02/04/00	D		(1)	
11	Christian Restorff Mouritsen		03/12/88	M	21	(1)	5
23	Ari Mohr Olsen		16/12/97	A	22	(3)	7
24	Tóri Rasmussen		21/06/95	M		(2)	
17	Bartal Wardum		03/05/97	D	20	(5)	1

FAROE ISLANDS

ÍF Fuglafjørdur

1946 • Fløtugerdi (2,000) • if.fo

Major honours
Faroe Islands League (1) 1979

Coach: Jógvan Martin Olsen;
(26/04/16) Jákup Mikkelsen;
(08/05/16) Símun Eliasen & Jákup Mikkelsen

2016					
05/03	a	B36	L	1-4	*B Petersen*
13/03	h	AB	W	1-0	*Olsen*
19/03	h	Víkingur	D	2-2	*Clayton, Olsen*
02/04	a	NSÍ	L	1-6	*Clayton*
10/04	h	KÍ	L	0-4	
17/04	a	TB	W	3-0	*P Mikkelsen, Lawal, Lakjuni*
21/04	h	Skála	D	2-2	*og (Jakobsen), Clayton*
28/04	a	B68	W	2-1	*Lawal, B Petersen*
01/05	h	HB	W	4-2	*Lawal 3, B Petersen*
12/05	h	NSÍ	L	0-2	
16/05	a	Víkingur	L	1-3	*og (S Vatnhamar)*
22/05	h	B36	D	0-0	
29/05	a	AB	W	3-2	*Lakjuni, Clayton, B Petersen (p)*
12/06	h	B68	W	4-0	*A Ellingsgaard, Lakjuni, Lawal, og (Edmundsson)*
19/06	h	TB	D	2-2	*J Ellingsgaard, Lawal*
24/06	a	Skála	L	0-1	
24/07	a	KÍ	W	4-2	*Lawal 3, Jakobsen*
28/07	a	HB	L	0-1	
07/08	a	NSÍ	L	1-7	*Lawal*
12/08	h	Víkingur	L	1-3	*Lakjuni*
21/08	a	B36	L	1-4	*Joensen*
11/09	h	AB	W	2-0	*Lawal, Løkin*
18/09	a	B68	W	2-0	*Alex, A Ellingsgaard*
25/09	a	TB	L	2-3	*Løkin, J Ellingsgaard*
02/10	h	Skála	D	1-1	*Olsen*
16/10	a	HB	L	1-4	*Clayton*
22/10	h	KÍ	L	1-3	*Lawal*

No	Name	Nat	DoB	Pos	Aps	(s)	Gls
4	Alex	BRA	28/03/81	D	25	(1)	1
2	Gunnar Christiansen		08/08/92	D	7	(5)	
18	Clayton	BRA	24/11/78	A	24	(2)	5
28	Hanus Eliasen		09/05/84	M		(9)	
10	Ari Ólavsson Ellingsgaard		03/02/93	M	19	(5)	2
37	Jan Ólavsson Ellingsgaard		26/06/90	D	23		2
5	John Daniel Gudjónsson		17/09/96	D	17	(4)	
13	Hallgrím Gregersen Hansen		24/12/94	G	2	(1)	
14	Dánjal Pauli Højgaard		27/12/83	M	6	(7)	
9	Kristoffur Jakobsen		07/11/88	M	24	(2)	1
17	Leivur Joensen		07/02/94	D	15	(7)	1
15	Oliver Korch	DEN	18/06/94	G	12		
7	Dánjal á Lakjuni		22/09/90	M	12	(11)	4
30	Adeshina Lawal	NGA	17/10/84	A	21	(3)	13
6	Karl Abrahamson Løkin		19/04/91	M	25		2
13	Jákup Mikkelsen		14/08/70	G	1		
3	Poul Nolsøe Mikkelsen		19/04/95	D	8	(1)	1
23	Andy Ólavur Olsen		03/12/84	M	26	(1)	3
8	Bogi Reinert Petersen		20/02/93	M	13	(1)	4
17	Jóhan Petersen		13/08/98	M		(4)	
1	Andrias Poulsen		03/08/97	M		(4)	
12	Elias Rasmussen		13/05/96	G	9		
22	Ingi Sørensen		24/11/90	M	4	(1)	
27	Margeir Toftegaard		29/06/94	M	1	(2)	
80	Tóri Tórmódsson Tradará		16/07/96	G	3		

KÍ Klaksvík

1904 • Djúpumýra (3,000) • ki.fo

Major honours
Faroe Islands League (17) 1942, 1945, 1952, 1953, 1954, 1956, 1957, 1958, 1961, 1966, 1967, 1968, 1969, 1970, 1972, 1991, 1999; Faroe Islands Cup (6) 1966, 1967, 1990, 1994, 1999, 2016

Coach: Mikkjal Thomassen

2016					
05/03	h	TB	W	1-0	*Klakstein*
13/03	h	NSÍ	L	1-3	*Klettskard*
20/03	a	HB	L	2-4	*Bjartalíd, Rasmussen*
03/04	h	Skála	W	2-0	*Klettskard, Hadžibulić*
10/04	a	ÍF	W	4-0	*Mujdragić, Klettskard 2, Bjartalíd*
17/04	h	B36	D	1-1	*Klettskard*
21/04	a	AB	D	1-1	*Klettskard*
28/04	a	Víkingur	W	2-0	*Bjartalíd 2*
01/05	h	B68	W	4-1	*Bjartalíd 3, Elttør*
12/05	a	Skála	W	1-0	*Klettskard*
16/05	h	HB	W	1-0	*Klettskard*
22/05	h	TB	W	1-0	*Bjartalíd*
05/06	h	NSÍ	W	4-0	*Bjartalíd 3 (1p), Klettskard*
12/06	h	Víkingur	W	2-0	*Bjartalíd, Klettskard*
19/06	a	B36	W	1-0	*Hadžibulić*
24/06	h	AB	W	5-1	*Elttør, Mujdragić, Bjartalíd 2, Rasmussen*
24/07	h	ÍF	L	2-4	*Klettskard, J Andreasen*
31/07	a	B68	W	3-0	*J Andreasen, Elttør, Bjartalíd*
05/08	h	Skála	W	5-0	*Olsen, Klettskard 3, Hadžibulić*
14/08	a	HB	W	3-2	*Bjartalíd (p), og (Jóhan Davidsen), Olsen*
21/08	h	TB	W	4-0	*Olsen 2, Klettskard, N Danielsen*
11/09	a	NSÍ	L	0-2	
18/09	a	Víkingur	W	2-1	*Klettskard 2*
25/09	h	B36	D	2-2	*Bjartalíd, og (Thomsen)*
02/10	a	AB	L	1-3	*Kalsø*
16/10	h	B68	W	6-0	*Olsen 2, Klettskard 3 (1p), Justesen*
22/10	a	ÍF	W	3-1	*Klettskard (p), N Danielsen 2*

No	Name	Nat	DoB	Pos	Aps	(s)	Gls
20	Mayowa Oladele Alli	USA	21/03/92	D	14	(2)	
19	Jákup Biskopstø Andreasen		31/05/98	M	23	(2)	2
13	Petur Andreasen		19/02/94	A	1	(1)	
8	Jóannes Bjartalíd		10/07/96	M	25	(1)	17
23	Aksel Danielsen		03/04/99	M		(1)	
11	Atli Danielsen		15/08/83	D	1	(8)	
17	Niels Pauli Bjartalíd Danielsen		18/01/89	A	8	(17)	3
10	Hjalgrím Elttør		03/03/83	M	21	(6)	3
22	Semir Hadžibulić	SRB	16/08/86	M	21		3
1	Kristian Joensen		21/12/92	G	26		
16	Meinhardt Joensen		27/11/79	G	1		
14	Tórur Justesen		04/01/95	M	1	(10)	1
6	Sørmundur Árni Kalsø		20/01/92	D	26		1
21	Hedin Klakstein		30/04/92	M	12	(14)	1
9	Páll Andrasson Klettskard		17/05/90	A	27		21
2	Dávid Langgaard		30/03/95	D	9	(10)	
5	Ahmed Mujdragić	SRB	13/03/86	D	20	(1)	2
18	Ólavur Niclasen		07/07/98	D	1	(2)	
7	Súni Olsen		07/03/81	M	16	(3)	6
4	Jonas Flindt Rasmussen	DEN	07/11/88	D	25		2
3	Ísak Simonsen		12/10/93	D	19	(1)	

NSÍ Runavík

1957 • Vid Løkin (2,000) • nsi.fo

Major honours
Faroe Islands League (1) 2007; Faroe Islands Cup (2) 1986, 2002

Coach: Anders Gerber (DEN)

2016					
05/03	h	HB	L	1-2	*K Olsen*
13/03	a	KÍ	W	3-1	*og (Rasmussen), Frederiksberg, K Olsen*
19/03	h	Skála	W	2-0	*Langgaard, P Knudsen*
02/04	h	ÍF	W	6-1	*K Olsen 2, E Hansen, Frederiksberg, P Knudsen, Joensen*
10/04	a	B68	W	5-0	*K Olsen 3, P Knudsen, Justinussen*
17/04	h	Víkingur	L	1-3	*Frederiksberg*
21/04	a	B36	L	1-3	*K Olsen*
27/04	a	TB	L	1-2	*Frederiksberg (p)*
01/05	h	AB	W	2-1	*M Olsen, K Olsen (p)*
12/05	a	ÍF	W	2-0	*K Olsen 2*
16/05	h	Skála	W	1-0	*K Olsen*
22/05	a	HB	W	4-3	*Justinussen 2, K Olsen (p), P Knudsen*
05/06	a	KÍ	L	0-4	
12/06	a	TB	L	1-3	*Justinussen*
18/06	h	Víkingur	W	4-2	*Frederiksberg 2, K Olsen 2*
23/06	h	B36	W	2-1	*K Olsen 2 (1p)*
24/07	h	B68	W	2-1	*og (O Højgaard), Køhlert*
27/07	a	AB	W	2-1	*Højgaard, K Olsen*
07/08	h	ÍF	W	7-1	*K Olsen, M Olsen, og (P Mikkelsen), Frederiksberg 2, Justinussen, P Knudsen*
14/08	a	Skála	W	2-0	*B Hansen, K Olsen (p)*
21/08	h	HB	D	0-0	
11/09	h	KÍ	W	2-0	*Langgaard, Frederiksberg*
18/09	h	TB	W	2-1	*Frederiksberg, K Olsen*
25/09	a	Víkingur	L	0-2	
02/10	a	B36	L	0-2	
16/10	h	AB	W	4-1	*A Benjaminsen, Frederiksberg, J Mortensen, K Olsen*
22/10	a	B68	W	3-1	*Justinussen 2, K Olsen*

No	Name	Nat	DoB	Pos	Aps	(s)	Gls
21	Andri Benjaminsen		12/01/99	M	1	(3)	1
17	Jann Julian Benjaminsen		02/03/97	M	4	(5)	
19	Hans Marius Davidsen		12/05/98	A		(8)	
11	Árni Frederiksberg		13/06/92	M	27		11
5	Jákup Andrias Gaardbo		22/09/95	D	6	(2)	
24	Betuel Hansen		14/03/97	M	9		1
12	Einar Tróndargjógv Hansen		02/04/88	D	14	(1)	1
29	Karstin Hansen		05/10/97	G	2		
1	Símun Rógvi Hansen		10/04/87	G	25		
9	Jonleif Højgaard		26/10/88	M	6	(11)	1
15	Johan Jacobsen		02/07/92	D	16		
3	Monrad Holm Jacobsen		23/04/91	D	23	(1)	
4	Jens Joensen		17/05/89	D	22	(1)	1
13	Pól Jóhannus Justinussen		13/01/89	M	25		7
12	Aron Knudsen		05/11/99	M	1		
16	Petur Knudsen		24/04/98	M	15	(10)	5
14	Nikolaj Køhlert	DEN	21/01/93	M	20	(2)	1
2	Per Langgaard		30/05/91	D	23		2
22	Høgni Madsen		04/02/85	M	2	(1)	
7	Jann Martin Mortensen		18/07/89	M	5	(5)	1
20	Mórits Heini Mortensen		25/03/99	M	2	(1)	
25	Tobias Olesen	DEN	19/04/96	D	7	(1)	
23	Jannik Olsen		28/12/98	M	8	(2)	
10	Klæmint Andrasson Olsen		17/07/90	A	27		23
18	Magnus Hendriksson Olsen		26/10/86	M	7	(7)	2

Skála ÍF

1965 • Undir Mýruhjalla (2,000) • skalaif.fo

Coach: Pauli Poulsen

2016					
06/03	a	Víkingur	L	1-4	*E Jacobsen*
12/03	h	B36	W	1-0	*Christiansen*
19/03	a	NSÍ	L	0-2	
03/04	a	KÍ	L	0-2	
09/04	h	HB	L	0-3	
17/04	h	B68	D	0-0	
21/04	a	ÍF	D	2-2	*B Jacobsen, Lambanum*
28/04	a	AB	D	0-0	
01/05	h	TB	W	5-1	*Frederiksberg 3, Christiansen, Jákup Johansen*
12/05	h	KÍ	L	0-1	
16/05	a	NSÍ	L	0-1	
21/05	h	Víkingur	L	1-3	*Christiansen (p)*
29/05	a	B36	D	1-1	*B Jacobsen*
12/06	h	AB	W	1-0	*Olsen*
19/06	a	B68	D	1-1	*P Jacobsen*
24/06	h	ÍF	W	1-0	*Jákup Johansen*
24/07	a	HB	L	0-1	
31/07	h	TB	L	0-1	
05/08	a	KÍ	L	0-5	
14/08	h	NSÍ	L	0-2	
21/08	a	Víkingur	L	0-4	
11/09	h	B36	L	0-2	
18/09	a	AB	W	2-0	*B Jacobsen, E Jacobsen*
25/09	h	B68	W	5-1	*Mikkelsen, E Jacobsen 2, Andersson 2*
02/10	a	ÍF	D	1-1	*Poulsen*
16/10	a	TB	D	1-1	*P Jacobsen (p)*
22/10	h	HB	D	2-2	*B Jacobsen, Olsen*

No	Name	Nat	DoB	Pos	Aps	(s)	Gls
9	Rasmus Andersson	SWE	17/04/93	D	3	(6)	2
22	Arnhold Berg		07/09/83	D		(6)	
11	Álvur Fuglø Christiansen		29/05/89	M	18	(1)	3
17	Jónhard Frederiksberg		27/08/80	M	27		3
14	Hendrik á Frídriksmørk		29/10/94	M		(6)	
1	András Gángó	HUN	02/03/84	G	27		
18	Jan Ingason Hansen		08/10/97	M	3	(15)	
16	Pauli Gregersen Hansen		09/04/80	M	10	(2)	
9	Andreas Jacobsen		25/11/99	A		(1)	
9	Brian Jacobsen		04/11/91	A	18	(4)	4
20	Edvin Jacobsen		12/04/91	M	26		4
6	Pætur Dam Jacobsen		05/12/82	D	27		2
4	Jákup Jakobsen		22/11/92	D	23		
15	Jákup Joensen		27/02/00	M		(5)	
19	Teitur Reinert Joensen		10/11/86	M	15	(3)	
4	Jákup Johansen		27/04/93	M	16	(2)	2
19	Jóhan Bergsson Johansen		11/06/93	A		(1)	
5	Fritleif í Lambanum		13/04/86	D	19	(4)	1
7	Ólavur Mikkelsen		11/01/92	M	23	(2)	1
3	Rógvi Egilstoft Nielsen		07/12/92	D	10		
2	Ari Olsen		09/09/98	D	16	(9)	2
8	Símun Petur Poulsen		16/11/94	M	16	(7)	1

TB Tvøroyri

1892 • Vid Stórá (3,000) • tb.fo

Major honours

Faroe Islands League (7) 1943, 1949, 1951, 1976, 1977, 1980, 1987; Faroe Islands Cup (5) 1956, 1958, 1960, 1961, 1977

Coach: Robert Roelofsen (NED); (06/06/16) Sigfrídur Clementsen

2016					
05/03	a	KÍ	L	0-1	
13/03	a	B68	D	1-1	*Rógvi Joensen*
20/03	h	AB	W	1-0	*Rógvi Joensen*
03/04	h	HB	L	0-1	
10/04	a	B36	D	0-0	
17/04	h	ÍF	L	0-3	
20/04	a	Víkingur	L	1-2	*Adu*
27/04	h	NSÍ	W	2-1	*S Bech, Adu*
01/05	a	Skála	L	1-5	*Justinussen*
12/05	h	HB	D	0-0	
16/05	a	AB	L	2-3	*Heini Mortensen, Adu*
22/05	a	KÍ	L	0-1	
29/05	a	B68	D	3-3	*Adu, S Bech 2*
12/06	h	NSÍ	W	3-1	*S Bech, Adu 2*
19/06	a	ÍF	D	2-2	*Adu, S Bech*
24/06	h	Víkingur	L	0-2	
24/07	h	B36	L	0-1	
31/07	a	Skála	W	1-0	*Adu*
07/08	a	HB	L	1-4	*Adu (p)*
14/08	h	AB	W	2-1	*S Bech, Adu*
21/08	a	KÍ	L	0-4	
11/09	h	B68	W	4-1	*Adu 2, Justinussen, Appiah*
18/09	a	NSÍ	L	1-2	*S Bech*
25/09	h	ÍF	W	3-2	*S Bech, Adu, Ingason*
02/10	a	Víkingur	L	0-1	
16/10	h	Skála	D	1-1	*Ingason (p)*
22/10	a	B36	L	2-5	*Heini Mortensen 2*

No	Name	Nat	DoB	Pos	Aps	(s)	Gls
10	Albert Adu	NED	08/08/88	A	26		13
8	Hávar Albinus		19/02/98	M		(2)	
19	Kofi Appiah	GHA	24/12/88	M	19	(5)	1
24	Carl Mikkjal Bech		15/01/89	D	7	(2)	
9	Salmundur Bech		16/01/96	M	25		8
27	Jákup Pauli Breckmann		16/04/98	M	9	(2)	
20	Bárdur Annfinnur Dimon		09/07/83	M	3	(3)	
23	Hervé Din Din	CMR	17/04/91	A	9	(4)	
2	Absalon Eliasen		30/05/97	D	4	(5)	
11	Eirikur Magnusarson Ellendersen		05/03/94	D	19	(3)	
21	Ndende Adama Gueye	SEN	05/01/83	M	26		
17	Poul Ingason		28/09/95	A	7	(2)	2
14	Andreas Jacobsen		27/05/97	M	1	(1)	
1	Meinhard Joensen		27/11/79	G	3		
5	Ragnar Joensen		14/07/93	D	17	(5)	
6	Rógvi Joensen		14/07/93	M	12	(2)	2
7	Teitur Wiberg Justinussen		08/04/93	M	17	(3)	2
1	Predrag Marković	SRB	01/02/77	G	2		
30	Joslain Mayebi	CMR	14/10/86	G	11		
27	Martin Midjord		16/08/93	A		(1)	
14	Heri Hjalt Mohr		13/05/97	D	9		
9	Dan Mortensen		31/10/78	A		(1)	
2	Hanus Mortensen		26/02/91	A	1	(2)	
24	Heine Mortensen		26/02/91	D	7		
18	Heini Mikal Mortensen		20/09/94	D	12	(9)	3
17	Petur Mortensen		20/04/90	M		(3)	
3	Signar Hermansson Olsen		25/11/93	M	3	(6)	
15	Teitur Jespersen Olsen		10/05/95	D	24		
1	Casper Radza	DEN	26/02/94	G	11		
14	Andrias Sørensen		17/02/00	M		(1)	
4	Aron Sørensen		22/12/88	A	1	(3)	
4	Árni Rúnar Örvarsson	ISL	21/03/94	D	12	(2)	

Víkingur

2008 • Sarpugerdi (2,000) • vikingur.fo

Major honours

Faroe Islands League (7) 1983, 1986, 1993, 1994, 1995, 1996 (as GÍ Gøta), 2016; Faroe Islands Cup (11) 1983, 1985, 1996, 1997, 2000, 2005 (as GÍ Gøta), 2009, 2012, 2013, 2014, 2015

Coach: Sámal Erik Hentze

2016					
06/03	h	Skála	W	4-1	*A Olsen, Djordjević 2, J Olsen*
13/03	a	HB	D	1-1	*G Hansen*
19/03	a	ÍF	D	2-2	*G Hansen, S Vatnhamar*
03/04	h	B68	W	4-0	*Djordjević 2, Jarnskor, E Jacobsen*
10/04	a	AB	D	2-2	*Djordjević, Poulsen*
17/04	a	NSÍ	W	3-1	*G Hansen, Samuelsen, S Vatnhamar*
20/04	h	TB	W	2-1	*A Olsen, Samuelsen (p)*
28/04	h	KÍ	L	0-2	
01/05	h	B36	W	1-0	*Djordjević*
12/05	a	B68	D	2-2	*Lervig, Jarnskor*
16/05	h	ÍF	W	3-1	*S Vatnhamar 3*
21/05	a	Skála	W	3-1	*A Olsen, Samuelsen 2 (1p)*
29/05	h	HB	W	1-0	*S Vatnhamar*
12/06	a	KÍ	L	0-2	
18/06	a	NSÍ	L	2-4	*Samuelsen 2*
24/06	a	TB	W	2-0	*Djordjević, S Vatnhamar*
24/07	h	AB	W	3-0	*Justinussen, H Jacobsen, S Vatnhamar*
29/07	a	B36	W	2-0	*Djordjević, og (H Askham)*
07/08	h	B68	W	5-1	*S Vatnhamar 2, H Jacobsen, Samuelsen (p), Poulsen*
12/08	a	ÍF	W	3-1	*Anghel, E Jacobsen (p), Djordjević*
21/08	h	Skála	W	4-0	*A Olsen, S Vatnhamar 3*
11/09	a	HB	W	1-0	*Djordjević*
18/09	h	KÍ	L	1-2	*G Hansen*
25/09	h	NSÍ	W	2-0	*A Olsen, Samuelsen*
02/10	h	TB	W	1-0	*H Jacobsen*
16/10	h	B36	W	2-0	*A Olsen 2*
22/10	a	AB	W	3-1	*S Vatnhamar, A Olsen 2*

No	Name	Nat	DoB	Pos	Aps	(s)	Gls
21	Sorin Vasile Anghel		16/07/79	M	12		1
9	Filip Djordjević	SRB	07/03/94	M	24	(2)	10
16	Hans Jørgin Djurhuus		29/11/78	M	14	(1)	
19	Jobin Drangastein		01/11/90	M	1	(6)	
4	Atli Gregersen		15/06/82	D	24		
12	Bárdur Jógvansson Hansen		13/03/92	D	15		
21	Gert Åge Hansen		25/07/84	D	24	(1)	4
8	Hedin Hansen		30/07/93	M	16	(6)	
13	Erling Dávidsson Jacobsen		13/02/90	D	27		2
3	Hanus Jacobsen		25/05/85	D	17		3
14	Magnus Jarnskor		14/12/95	M	5	(7)	2
6	Sámal Jákup Joensen		07/04/93	M	1	(3)	
17	Finnur Justinussen		30/03/89	A	4	(1)	1
5	Dánjal Pauli Lervig		26/04/91	D	1		1
2	Andreas Lava Olsen		09/10/87	A	20	(5)	9
15	Jákup Vatnhamar Olsen		30/05/96	M	9	(9)	1
7	Jón Krosslá Poulsen		17/02/88	A	1	(18)	2
27	Elias Rasmussen		13/05/96	G	1	(1)	
11	Hans Pauli Samuelsen		18/10/84	M	25	(1)	8
1	Géza Túri	HUN	11/03/74	G	26		
24	Gunnar Vatnhamar		29/03/95	D	4	(12)	
10	Sølvi Vatnhamar		05/05/86	M	26		14

FAROE ISLANDS

Top goalscorers

23	Klæmint Andrasson Olsen (NSÍ)
21	Páll Andrasson Klettskard (KÍ)
17	Jóannes Bjartalíd (KÍ)
14	Sølvi Vatnhamar (Víkingur)
13	Øssur Meinhardtsson Dalbúd (HB) Adeshina Lawal (ÍF) Albert Adu (TB)
11	Patrik Johannesen (AB) Árni Frederiksberg (NSÍ)
10	Róaldur Jakobsen (B36) Sebastian Pingel (B36) Filip Djordjević (Víkingur)

Promoted clubs

EB/Streymur

1993 • Vid Margáir (3,000) • eb-streymur.fo

Major honours
Faroe Islands League (2) 2008, 2012; Faroe Islands Cup (4) 2007, 2008, 2010, 2011

Coach: Olgar Danielsen

07 Vestur

2007 • Á Dungasandi (1,000) • 07vestur.fo

Coach: Hegga Samuelsen

Second level final table 2016

		Pld	W	D	L	F	A	Pts
1	EB/Streymur	27	21	4	2	105	28	67
2	07 Vestur	27	21	2	4	98	34	65
3	FC Suduroy	27	17	3	7	67	40	54
4	Giza/Hoyvík	27	15	3	9	60	40	48
5	NSÍ Runavík II	27	11	1	15	59	83	34
6	KÍ Klaksvík II	27	10	3	14	53	67	33
7	Víkingur II	27	9	4	14	42	60	31
8	HB Tórshavn II	27	9	3	15	50	69	30
9	AB Argir II	27	3	5	19	22	73	14
10	B71 Sandoy	27	3	4	20	36	98	13

DOMESTIC CUP

Løgmanssteypid 2016

SECOND ROUND

(23/04/16)
Giza/Hoyvík 2-0 B68

(24/04/16)
AB 1-2 B36
EB/Streymur 2-1 07 Vestur
HB 9-1 B71
ÍF 0-4 KÍ
Suduroy 2-3 Víkingur
TB 1-2 NSÍ
Undrid 0-6 Skála

QUARTER-FINALS

(07/05/16)
Giza/Hoyvík 1-2 Skála *(Joensen 90; P Jacobsen 10, Jákup Johansen 85)*

(08/05/16)
Víkingur 3-3 HB *(S Vatnhamar 2, 20, A Olsen 71; Ingason 44, 45, Dalbúd 88p) (aet; 4-3 on pens)*

KÍ 2-1 B36 *(Olsen 4, Bjartalíd 23; Mellemgaard 86)*

NSÍ 2-0 EB/Streymur *(Frederiksberg 44, P Knudsen 85)*

SEMI-FINALS

(25/05/16 & 15/06/16)
Skála 0-1 Víkingur *(E Jacobsen 88)*
Víkingur 1-1 Skála *(S Vatnhamar 27; Mikkelsen 22)*
(Víkingur 2-1)

(26/05/16 & 15/06/16)
KÍ 4-1 NSÍ *(Hadžibulić 16, Bjartalíd 26, 35p, Klettskard 52; Justinussen 8)*
NSÍ 0-0 KÍ
(KÍ 4-1)

FINAL

(27/08/16)
Tórsvøllur, Torshavn
KÍ KLAKSVÍK 1 *(Gregersen 14og)*
VÍKINGUR 1 *(A Olsen 31)*
(aet; 5-3 on pens)
Referee: *Troleis*
KÍ: *K Joensen, Mujdragić, Kalsø, Rasmussen, Simonsen (Klakstein 91), Alli, Hadžibulić (N Danielsen 116), J Andreasen, Bjartalíd, Elttør (Olsen 64), Klettskard*
VÍKINGUR: *Túri, G Hansen, Gregersen, H Jacobsen, E Jacobsen, Samuelsen (Jarnskor 116), S Vatnhamar, H Hansen (J Olsen 102), Djordjević, Anghel (G Vatnhamar 87), A Olsen*

KÍ denied Víkingur a fifth successive cup triumph with a penalty shoot-out victory in Torshavn

FINLAND

Suomen Palloliitto – Finlands Bollförbund (SPL-FBF)

Address	Urheilukatu 5, PO Box 191 FI-00251 Helsinki
Tel	+358 9 742 151
Fax	+358 9 454 3352
E-mail	sami.terava@palloliitto.fi
Website	palloliitto.fi

President	Pertti Alaja
General secretary	Marco Casagrande
Media officer	Sami Terävä
Year of formation	1907

VEIKKAUSLIIGA CLUBS

  1 **HIFK Helsinki**

 2 **HJK Helsinki**

 3 **Ilves Tampere**

 4 **FC Inter Turku**

 5 **PS Kemi**

 6 **KuPS Kuopio**

 7 **FC Lahti**

 8 **IFK Mariehamn**

 9 **PK-35 Vantaa**

 10 **RoPS Rovaniemi**

 11 **SJK Seinäjoki**

 12 **VPS Vaasa**

PROMOTED CLUB

 13 **JJK Jyväskylä**

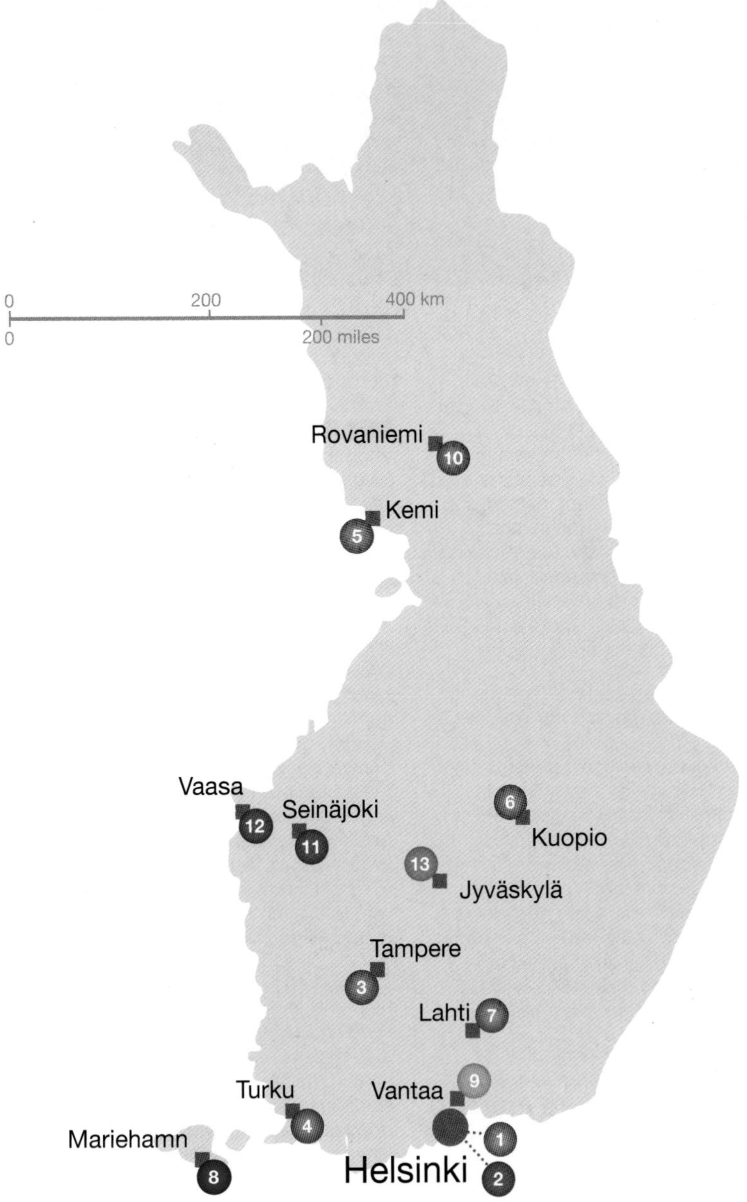

0 200 400 km
0 200 miles

Rovaniemi 10
Kemi 5
Vaasa 12
Seinäjoki 11
Kuopio 6
Jyväskylä 13
Tampere 3
Lahti 7
Turku 4
Vantaa 9
Mariehamn 8
Helsinki 1 2

KEY

- UEFA Champions League
- UEFA Europa League
- Promoted
- Relegated

Mariehamn conquer the mainland

The Aland Islanders of IFK Mariehamn followed up their maiden Finnish Cup win in 2015 by capturing the even more coveted prize of the Veikkausliiga title for the first time in the club's 97-year history.

Under the command of new coaching duo Peter Lundberg and Kari Virtanen, Mariehamn valiantly withstood the twin assault of record champions HJK and title holders SJK, who met in the Finnish Cup final, the latter claiming the trophy for the first time after a lengthy penalty shoot-out in Tampere.

First national league title for Aland Islands club

Three-way Veikkausliiga battle goes to the wire

SJK defeat HJK in extended cup final shoot-out

Domestic league

Mariehamn embarked on a new era in 2016. It was their first season in 14 years without resident coach Pekka Lyyski, who retired after leading the club to their historic cup triumph. He was succeeded by Lundberg, his assistant, and ex-Finland international Virtanen, and although his son Jani, the team's captain, maintained a family presence, few envisaged that Lyyski's departure would herald a season of even more astounding achievement than the previous one.

HJK defeated Mariehamn 2-0 on the opening day and the club from the capital, led again by 2014 double-winning boss Mika Lehkosuo, seemed hell-bent on regaining their title as they stormed to the summit in the early weeks. Mariehamn, however, recovered from that early defeat and never allowed HJK to steal a march on them. A captivating two-way contest eventually attracted a third contender as the leading pair both faltered while SJK, handicapped by a disastrous start to their title defence, finally flowered in the closing weeks.

With a game to go just two points separated the three challengers, with Mariehamn in the driving seat a point ahead of HJK, who in turn held the same advantage over SJK – the side they hosted in their final fixture. Mariehamn signed off at home to the season's surprise package, Ilves, and knew that victory would secure their first title. If they dropped points, the winner of the game in Helsinki would leapfrog them into top spot. In the event, that Sonera Stadium showdown finished goalless, but the league leaders did not leave their fate to chance, beating Ilves 2-1 thanks to a 75th-minute winner from Brazilian midfielder Diego Assis – their two-goal match-winner in the 2015 cup final.

The champions scored just 40 goals but conceded a mere 25 – the fewest in the division – and it was in defence where their most consistent performers operated, with captain Lyyski and Kristian Kojola a doughty combination in front of ever-present goalkeeper Walter Viitala. The team's top scorer was Jamaican striker Dever Orgill, who supplemented his dozen goals with seven assists. SJK provided the Veikkausliiga's leading marksman in 17-goal Finnish international Roope Riski, with HJK's impressive new Colombian import Alfredo Morelos just one adrift.

Domestic cup

Riski and Morelos also proved prolific in the Finnish Cup, the two of them both finding the net in the quarter-finals and semi-finals before scoring again in opposition at Tampere's Ratinan stadion, where the final was staged for the first time. Two hours of football could not separate the two teams. Neither could the five regulation penalties, with HJK defender Ivan Tatomirović failing to convert the kick that would have given his team the trophy before his team-mate Ville Jalasto followed suit in sudden-death to give SJK a 7-6 win and a first cup triumph.

Europe

There was little joy for the Finnish contingent in European competition, with HJK as ever providing the most resistance but ultimately missing out on extended UEFA Europa League participation after losing at home to fellow Scandinavians IFK Göteborg. That 0-2 defeat followed an excellent 2-1 victory in Sweden, the winning goal scored by the ever-reliable Morelos, who had also netted important away goals in the two previous rounds.

National team

The 2016/17 season was a thoroughly depressing one for the Finnish national side as they plundered one measly point from six European Qualifiers – and that from an opening 1-1 draw in Turku against FIFA World Cup debutants Kosovo. Iceland, Croatia, Turkey and Ukraine (twice) were all too good for them, and even the removal of Hans Backe after less than a year in charge and the reinstatement of his caretaker predecessor Markku Kanerva did little to change the team's fortunes.

DOMESTIC SEASON AT A GLANCE

Veikkausliiga 2016 final table

			Home					Away					Total					
		Pld	W	D	L	F	A	W	D	L	F	A	W	D	L	F	A	Pts
1	**IFK Mariehamn**	**33**	**9**	**6**	**2**	**23**	**15**	**8**	**4**	**4**	**17**	**10**	**17**	**10**	**6**	**40**	**25**	**61**
2	HJK Helsinki	33	11	4	2	35	19	5	6	5	17	17	16	10	7	52	36	58
3	SJK Seinäjoki	33	13	1	3	32	13	4	5	7	17	23	17	6	10	49	36	57
4	VPS Vaasa	33	9	3	4	20	10	6	5	6	16	17	15	8	10	36	27	53
5	Ilves Tampere	33	9	5	2	20	10	6	2	9	16	25	15	7	11	36	35	52
6	RoPS Rovaniemi	33	9	6	2	24	10	4	5	7	19	23	13	11	9	43	33	50
7	KuPS Kuopio	33	9	3	4	19	11	5	4	8	18	20	14	7	12	37	31	49
8	FC Lahti	33	7	6	4	23	15	3	6	7	19	28	10	12	11	42	43	42
9	PS Kemi	33	7	1	8	21	25	3	4	10	8	23	10	5	18	29	48	35
10	HIFK Helsinki	33	4	5	7	17	19	4	5	8	18	20	8	10	15	35	39	34
11	FC Inter Turku	33	4	7	6	15	20	3	4	9	13	21	7	11	15	28	41	32
12	PK-35 Vantaa	33	2	5	9	16	27	2	2	13	16	38	4	7	22	32	65	13

NB PK-35 Vantaa – 6 pts deducted.

European qualification 2017/18

Champion: IFK Mariehamn (second qualifying round)

Cup winner: SJK Seinäjoki (first qualifying round)
HJK Helsinki (first qualifying round)
VPS Vaasa (first qualifying round)

Top scorers	Roope Riski (SJK), 17 goals
Relegated club	PK-35 Vantaa
Promoted club	JJK Jyväskylä
Cup final	SJK Seinäjoki 1-1 HJK Helsinki *(aet; 7-6 on pens)*

Player of the season

Emile Paul Tendeng
(Ilves Tampere)

With seven goals and a league-best tally of eight assists, Tendeng played a crucial role in the uplifting 2016 season of Tampere club Ilves, a team widely tipped for relegation on the eve of the campaign. The 24-year-old Senegalese midfielder joined the club in February, his only previous spell in Europe having been a brief stay on loan at Romanian club FC Vaslui in 2013. He operated mostly in the No10 role but proved equally at ease in all attacking positions and was duly voted players' player of the year.

Newcomer of the season

Mikael Soisalo
(Ilves Tampere)

Unhappy with his prospects at HJK, 18-year-old Soisalo was lured to Ilves in early 2016 by Jarkko Wiss, who had previously coached him at Finnish national youth team level. The pacy winger made an immediate impact in the Veikkausliiga and went on to supply seven goals and five assists. Such was the speed of his progress that a move to greener pastures was inevitable, and in January 2017 the blond-haired youngster joined the academy side of English Premier League club Middlesbrough on a three-year contract.

Team of the season

(4-4-2)

Coach: Wiss *(Ilves)*

FINLAND

NATIONAL TEAM

Top five all-time caps
Jari Litmanen (137); Sami Hyypiä & Jonatan Johansson (105); Ari Hjelm (100); Joonas Kolkka (98)

Top five all-time goals
Jari Litmanen (32); Mikael Forssell (29); Jonatan Johansson (22); Ari Hjelm (20); Mixu Paatelainen (18)

Results 2016/17

31/08/16	Germany	A	Monchengladbach	L	0-2	
05/09/16	Kosovo (WCQ)	H	Turku	D	1-1	*Arajuuri (18)*
06/10/16	Iceland (WCQ)	A	Reykjavik	L	2-3	*Pukki (21), Lod (39)*
09/10/16	Croatia (WCQ)	H	Tampere	L	0-1	
12/11/16	Ukraine (WCQ)	A	Odessa	L	0-1	
09/01/17	Morocco	N	Al Ain (UAE)	W	1-0	*Ojala (45+1)*
13/01/17	Slovenia B	N	Abu Dhabi (UAE)	L	0-2	
24/03/17	Turkey (WCQ)	A	Antalya	L	0-2	
28/03/17	Austria	A	Innsbruck	D	1-1	*Jensen (76)*
07/06/17	Liechtenstein	H	Turku	D	1-1	*M Hetemaj (17)*
11/06/17	Ukraine (WCQ)	H	Tampere	L	1-2	*Pohjanpalo (72)*

Appearances 2016/17

Coach: Hans Backe (SWE) /(12/12/16) Markku Kanerva	**14/02/52 24/05/64**		Ger	KOS	ISL	CRO	UKR	Mar	Svn	TUR	Aut	Lie	UKR	Caps	Goals
Lukas Hradecky	24/11/89	Eintracht Frankfurt (GER)	G	G	G	G	G			G	G		G	37	-
Jukka Raitala	15/09/88	Sogndal (NOR) /Columbus Crew (USA)	D	D	s85	D	D				D	D	D	39	-
Thomas Lam	18/12/93	Nottingham Forest (ENG)	D	D65		s67	s63				M	M70	M	12	-
Paulus Arajuuri	15/06/88	Lech (POL) /Brøndby (DEN)	D81	D	D	D	D			D	D46			22	2
Niklas Moisander	29/09/85	Bremen (GER)	D	D	D	M				D	D	D	D	59	2
Jere Uronen	13/07/94	Genk (BEL)	D60	D						D	M46	D46	M84	25	-
Alexander Ring	09/04/91	Kaiserslautern (GER) /New York City (USA)	M	s65	M94	M67	M46			M84				43	1
Markus Halsti	19/03/84	Midtjylland (DEN)	M72	M	D		M63	D				s55		34	-
Robin Lod	17/04/93	Panathinaikos (GRE)	M60	M88	M	M	M			M		M51	M68	15	1
Kasper Hämäläinen	08/08/86	Legia (POL)	A46	s73	A56							s51	M	57	8
Joel Pohjanpalo	13/09/94	Leverkusen (GER)	A72	A						A72	s58	A	s68	26	5
Teemu Pukki	29/03/90	Brøndby (DEN)	s46	A73	A	A	A			A	A58	A54	A68	58	9
Janne Saksela	14/03/93	RoPS /Sparta (NED)	s60			M	s83				M58			8	-
Rasmus Schüller	18/06/91	Häcken (SWE)	s60	s88	s94	s46		M65	M					23	-
Sakari Mattila	14/07/89	SønderjyskE (DEN)	s72				M	M73	s72	M67	s65			15	-
Eero Markkanen	03/07/91	AIK (SWE)	s72		s56 /85		s46		A67	s72		s70	s84	12	-
Juhani Ojala	19/06/89	unattached /SJK /Häcken (SWE)	s81			D		D				D46	D	20	1
Roman Eremenko	19/03/87	CSKA Moskva (RUS)		M										73	5
Kari Arkivuo	23/06/83	Häcken (SWE)			D	D46	D	D82	D80	D	s46	s46	D	55	1
Sauli Väisänen	05/06/94	AIK (SWE)			D	D87	D83		D		s46	s46		6	-
Perparim Hetemaj	12/12/86	Chievo (ITA)			M					M	M			46	4
Roope Riski	16/08/91	SJK				s87								5	1
Joona Toivio	10/03/88	Molde (NOR)					D				D			40	2
Walter Viitala	09/01/92	Viborg (DEN)						G	G52					2	-
Juha Pirinen	22/10/91	HJK						D79	s80					4	-
Matej Hradecky	17/04/95	SJK						M						2	-
Petteri Forsell	16/10/90	Miedź (POL)						M56	s60	s84				9	1
Tim Väyrynen	30/03/93	Dynamo Dresden (GER)						A85	s67					8	-
Simon Skrabb	19/01/95	Norrköping (SWE)						A	s60					3	-
Robert Taylor	21/10/94	RoPS						s56	M60					2	-
Joni Kauko	12/07/90	Randers (DEN)						s65	M72					9	-
Jasse Tuominen	12/11/95	Lahti						s73	M60					2	-
Albin Granlund	01/09/89	Mariehamn						s79						1	-
Mikko Sumusalo	12/03/90	RW Erfurt (GER)						s82	D					6	1
Akseli Pelvas	08/02/89	HJK						s85	A					5	-
Kristian Kojola	12/09/86	Mariehamn							D					1	-
Mika Hilander	17/08/83	Ilves							s52					2	-
Moshtagh Yaghoubi	08/11/94	HJK								s67	M65		M	3	-
Fredrik Jensen	09/09/97	Twente (NED)									s58	s54	s68	3	1
Anssi Jaakkola	13/03/87	Reading (ENG)										G		2	-
Mehmet Hetemaj	08/12/87	SJK										M55		6	1
Riku Riski	16/08/89	Odd (NOR)										M		27	4

EUROPE

SJK Seinäjoki

Second qualifying round - FC BATE Borisov (BLR)
A 0-2
Aksalu, Aalto, Hradecky, Laaksonen, Vasara (Klinga 76), Ngueukam (Tahvanainen 76), Riski, Penninkangas (Rahimi 90+2), Hurme, Méïté, Hetemaj. Coach: Simo Valakari (FIN)
H 2-2 *Ngueukam (44), Riski (61)*
Aksalu, Aalto, Hradecky (Ahde 75), Tahvanainen (Kane 46), Laaksonen, Vasara (Rahimi 59), Ngueukam, Riski, Hurme, Méïté, Hetemaj. Coach: Simo Valakari (FIN)

IFK Mariehamn

First qualifying round - Odds BK (NOR)
A 0-2
Viitala, Granlund, Kojola, Orgill, Lyyski, Span, Petrovic, Ekhalie (Wirtanen 90), Dafaa (Sparrdal Mantilla 59), Diego Assis (Kangaskolkka 69), Friberg da Cruz. Coach: Peter Lundberg (FIN) & Kari Virtanen (FIN)
H 1-1 *Sparrdal Mantilla (4)*
Viitala, Granlund, Kojola, Sparrdal Mantilla (Mäkinen 88), Orgill, Lyyski, Span (Sid 70), Petrovic (Diego Assis 80), Ekhalie, Kangaskolkka, Friberg da Cruz. Coach: Peter Lundberg (FIN) & Kari Virtanen (FIN)

RoPS Rovaniemi

First qualifying round - Shamrock Rovers FC (IRL)
A 2-0 *Lahdenmäki (27), Saksela (74)*
Reguero, Lahdenmäki, Saksela, Pirinen, Taylor, Nganbe Nganbe (Muinonen 70), Saine (Mäkitalo 82), Mravec, Hämäläinen, John (Kokko 68), Jammeh. Coach: Juha Malinen (FIN)
H 1-1 *Muinonen (27)*
Reguero, Lahdenmäki, Saksela, Pirinen, Taylor, Muinonen, Saine (Mäkitalo 46; Nganbe Nganbe 53), Mravec, Hämäläinen, John (Kokko 46), Jammeh. Coach: Juha Malinen (FIN)

Second qualifying round - NK Lokomotiva Zagreb (CRO)
H 1-1 *Prenga (87og)*
Reguero, Saksela, Pirinen, Taylor, Nganbe Nganbe (Okkonen 73), Kokko (Heikkilä 60), Muinonen, Mravec, Hämäläinen, John (Osei 81), Jammeh. Coach: Juha Malinen (FIN)
A 0-3
Reguero, Saksela, Pirinen, Mäkitalo (Nganbe Nganbe 62), Taylor, Kokko (Okkonen 45+2), Muinonen, Mravec (Lahdenmäki 75), Hämäläinen, John, Jammeh. Coach: Juha Malinen (FIN)
Red cards: Pirinen 33, Jammeh 89

HJK Helsinki

First qualifying round - FK Atlantas (LTU)
A 2-0 *Morelos (53, 85)*
Dähne, Taiwo, Medo, Rexhepi, Malolo, Alho (Gadze 24; Sorsa 82), Tanaka, Morelos, Tatomirović, Jalasto, Oduamadi (Kolehmainen 88). Coach: Mika Lehkosuo (FIN)
H 1-1 *Taiwo (30p)*
Dähne, Taiwo, Medo, Rexhepi, Malolo, Alho (Sorsa 82), Morelos (Forssell 67), Kolehmainen, Tatomirović, Jalasto, Gadze (Oduamadi 75). Coach: Mika Lehkosuo (FIN)

Second qualifying round - PFC Beroe Stara Zagora (BUL)
A 1-1 *Morelos (38)*
Dähne, Taiwo, Medo (Annan 80), Rexhepi, Alho (Malolo 73), Tanaka, Morelos, Tatomirović, Jalasto, Sorsa, Dahlström. Coach: Mika Lehkosuo (FIN)
H 1-0 *Tanaka (25)*
Dähne, Taiwo (Sorsa 79), Medo (Dahlström 90+2), Rexhepi, Alho, Tanaka, Morelos, Tatomirović, Jalasto, Annan, Oduamadi. Coach: Mika Lehkosuo (FIN)

Third qualifying round - IFK Göteborg (SWE)
A 2-1 *Tanaka (47), Morelos (75)*
Dähne, Medo, Rexhepi, Alho, Tanaka (Kolehmainen 77), Morelos, Tatomirović, Jalasto, Annan, Sorsa, Gadze (Malolo 87). Coach: Mika Lehkosuo (FIN)
H 0-2
Dähne, Medo, Alho, Morelos, Tatomirović, Jalasto, Halme, Annan, Sorsa, Gadze (Kolehmainen 67), Oduamadi. Coach: Mika Lehkosuo (FIN)

DOMESTIC LEAGUE CLUB-BY-CLUB

HIFK Helsinki

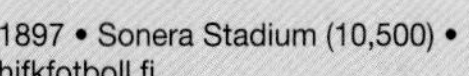

1897 • Sonera Stadium (10,500) • hifkfotboll.fi

Major honours
Finnish League (7) 1930, 1931, 1933, 1937, 1947, 1959, 1961

Coach: Jani Honkavaara; (28/07/16) Antti Muurinen

2016					
09/04	a	PK-35	W	2-0	*Mäkelä, Bäckman*
14/04	h	Inter	L	1-2	*Salmikivi*
18/04	a	Lahti	D	2-2	*Mäkelä, Pirttijoki*
25/04	h	Kemi	D	0-0	
28/04	h	KuPS	W	3-2	*Aho, Mäkelä 2*
04/05	a	VPS	L	1-3	*Sihvola*
09/05	h	RoPS	D	1-1	*Korhonen*
14/05	a	SJK	L	1-2	*Mäkelä (p)*
20/05	h	Mariehamn	L	0-1	
26/05	a	HJK	L	1-2	*Terävä*
29/05	h	Ilves	L	0-1	
09/06	h	PK-35	L	1-2	*Salmikivi*
12/06	a	Inter	L	0-1	
18/06	h	Lahti	D	2-2	*Terävä, Hänninen*
03/07	a	Kemi	W	2-1	*Vesala 2*
10/07	a	KuPS	L	0-1	
18/07	h	VPS	L	0-1	
24/07	a	RoPS	L	0-1	
30/07	h	SJK	D	1-1	*Salmikivi*
07/08	a	Mariehamn	W	5-2	*Sihvola 3, Salmikivi 2*
10/08	h	HJK	D	0-0	
13/08	a	Ilves	L	1-3	*Sihvola*
21/08	a	Mariehamn	L	0-1	
27/08	h	SJK	W	3-1	*Sihvola, Bäckman, Salmikivi*
09/09	h	VPS	L	0-1	
12/09	a	Inter	D	0-0	
16/09	h	Kemi	W	3-1	*Ristola, Kuusijärvi, Mäkelä*
20/09	a	PK-35	W	2-0	*Mäkelä, Sihvola*
26/09	a	Lahti	D	0-0	
30/09	h	HJK	W	2-1	*Mäkelä, Sihvola*
14/10	a	Ilves	D	1-1	*Anyamele*
17/10	h	KuPS	L	0-2	
23/10	a	RoPS	D	0-0	

No	Name	Nat	DoB	Pos	Aps	(s)	Gls
2	Tuomas Aho		27/05/81	D	20		1
27	Nnaemeka Anyamele		16/05/94	M	17	(5)	1
17	Jani Bäckman		20/03/88	A	5	(13)	2
71	Carljohan Eriksson		25/04/95	G	20		
6	Xhevdet Gela		14/11/89	M	26	(1)	
8	Jukka Halme		29/05/85	M	6	(2)	
18	Matias Hänninen		15/03/91	D	21	(3)	1
12	Otto-Pekka Jurvainen		01/02/85	D	7	(6)	
31	Joni Korhonen		08/02/87	A	22	(7)	1
3	Pauli Kuusijärvi		21/03/86	D	26	(1)	1
22	Fredrik Lassas		01/10/96	M	17	(4)	
1	Tomi Maanoja		12/09/86	G	13		
20	Rickson Mansiamina	SWE	09/07/97	A	6	(3)	
16	Tuomas Mustonen		04/06/85	A		(5)	
10	Juho Mäkelä		23/06/83	A	21	(7)	8
11	Eero Peltonen		22/12/86	M	8	(3)	
15	Juho Pirttijoki		30/07/96	D	25		1
7	Daniel Rantanen		11/05/98	M	2	(2)	
19	Aleksi Ristola		06/11/89	M	8	(1)	1
26	Ville Salmikivi		20/05/92	A	14	(10)	6
9	Pekka Sihvola		22/04/84	A	22	(9)	8
5	Jukka Sinisalo		21/05/82	D	10	(1)	
21	Ville Taulo		14/08/85	M	5	(2)	
13	Esa Terävä		08/11/87	A	12	(10)	2
4	Tommi Vesala		12/01/86	D	17	(2)	2
23	Mika Väyrynen		28/12/81	M	13	(1)	

FINLAND

HJK Helsinki

1907 • Sonera Stadium (10,800) • hjk.fi

Major honours
Finnish League (27) 1911, 1912, 1917, 1918, 1919, 1923, 1925, 1936, 1938, 1964, 1973, 1978, 1981, 1985, 1987, 1988, 1990, 1992, 1997, 2002, 2003, 2009, 2010, 2011, 2012, 2013, 2014; Finnish Cup (12) 1966, 1981, 1984, 1993, 1996, 1998, 2000, 2003, 2006, 2008, 2011, 2014

Coach: Mika Lehkosuo

2016

Date		Opponent		Score	Scorers
02/04	h	Mariehamn	W	2-0	*Tanaka 2*
08/04	h	VPS	W	3-1	*Morelos, Medo, Tanaka*
14/04	a	RoPS	D	2-2	*Morelos 2*
18/04	h	SJK	W	2-1	*Morelos, Tanaka*
24/04	a	Mariehamn	D	0-0	
29/04	a	Kemi	L	0-1	
04/05	h	Ilves	W	5-1	*Forssell 2 (1p), Oduamadi, Dahlström, Jalasto*
07/05	a	PK-35	W	2-1	*Oduamadi, Taiwo*
16/05	h	Inter	W	3-1	*Alho, Taiwo 2*
20/05	a	Lahti	W	2-1	*Oduamadi, Taiwo (p)*
26/05	h	HIFK	W	2-1	*Morelos, Oduamadi*
29/05	a	KuPS	D	0-0	
09/06	a	VPS	L	0-3	
12/06	h	RoPS	D	1-1	*Taiwo (p)*
18/06	a	SJK	W	3-2	*Morelos, Taiwo, Tanaka*
10/07	h	Kemi	W	2-0	*Oduamadi, Alho*
17/07	a	Ilves	L	0-1	
24/07	h	PK-35	W	4-2	*Morelos, Alho, Dahlström, Oduamadi*
31/07	a	Inter	D	0-0	
07/08	h	Lahti	D	2-2	*Forssell, Morelos*
10/08	a	HIFK	D	0-0	
15/08	h	KuPS	L	2-3	*Morelos 2*
21/08	a	VPS	D	0-0	
24/08	h	PK-35	W	2-0	*Jallow 2 (1p)*
28/08	h	KuPS	W	1-0	*Morelos*
09/09	a	Kemi	W	2-0	*Morelos, og (Räihä)*
12/09	h	Lahti	L	1-4	*Morelos*
16/09	a	Inter	L	2-3	*Pelvas 2 (1p)*
21/09	h	RoPS	W	2-1	*Morelos, Pelvas (p)*
30/09	a	HIFK	L	1-2	*Morelos*
14/10	h	Mariehamn	D	1-1	*Morelos*
17/10	a	Ilves	W	3-1	*Rafinha, Oduamadi, Dahlström*
23/10	h	SJK	D	0-0	

No	Name	Nat	DoB	Pos	Aps	(s)	Gls
7	Nikolai Alho		12/03/93	A	21	(3)	3
22	Anthony Annan	GHA	21/07/86	M	13	(2)	
38	Sebastian Dahlström		05/11/96	M	16	(5)	3
21	Thomas Dähne	GER	04/01/94	G	28		
9	Mikael Forssell		15/03/81	A	4	(15)	3
43	Richard Gadze	GHA	23/08/93	A	4	(10)	
16	Aapo Halme		22/05/98	D	10	(4)	
15	Ville Jalasto		19/04/86	D	24		1
17	Ousman Jallow	GAM	21/10/88	A	3		2
13	Toni Kolehmainen		20/07/88	D	13	(2)	
25	Jiri Koski		20/04/95	G		(1)	
34	Lassi Lappalainen		24/08/98	A	5	(9)	
19	Lucas Lingman		25/01/98	M		(6)	
6	Obed Malolo		18/04/97	M	13	(2)	
4	Medo	SLE	16/11/87	M	19	(2)	1
77	Evans Mensah	GHA	09/02/98	A		(3)	
11	Alfredo Morelos	COL	21/06/96	A	27	(3)	16
90	Nnamdi Oduamadi	NGA	17/10/90	M	26	(2)	7
20	Vincent Onovo	NGA	10/12/95	M	7	(2)	
18	Roni Peiponen		09/04/97	D	6	(5)	
31	Akseli Pelvas		08/02/89	A	8		3
8	Rafinha	BRA	29/06/82	M	12	(1)	1
5	Lum Rexhepi	KOS	03/08/92	D	21	(1)	
27	Sebastian Sorsa		25/01/84	D	17	(3)	
3	Taye Taiwo	NGA	16/04/85	D	21		6
10	Atomu Tanaka	JPN	04/10/87	M	16	(1)	5
14	Ivan Tatomirović	SRB	11/01/89	D	22	(1)	
29	Markus Uusitalo		15/05/97	G	5	(1)	
31	Leo Väisänen		23/07/97	D	2	(1)	

Ilves Tampere

1931 • Tammelan stadion (5,000) • ilvesedustus.fi

Major honours
Finnish League (1) 1983; Finnish Cup (2) 1979, 1990

Coach: Jarkko Wiss

2016

Date		Opponent		Score	Scorers
09/04	a	KuPS	W	1-0	*Tendeng*
24/04	a	SJK	W	2-0	*Lahtinen (p), Tendeng*
29/04	h	Mariehamn	L	0-1	
04/05	a	HJK	L	1-5	*Siira*
07/05	a	Kemi	L	0-1	
13/05	h	PK-35	W	2-0	*Siira, Soisalo*
21/05	a	Inter	L	0-1	
25/05	h	Lahti	W	2-0	*Hynynen, Soisalo*
29/05	a	HIFK	W	1-0	*Miettunen*
09/06	h	KuPS	W	1-0	*Tendeng (p)*
12/06	h	VPS	W	1-0	*Tendeng*
18/06	a	RoPS	L	0-1	
28/06	a	VPS	L	0-2	
02/07	h	SJK	W	2-1	*Ala-Myllymäki, Siira*
10/07	a	Mariehamn	L	1-3	*Hilska*
17/07	h	HJK	W	1-0	*Tendeng (p)*
24/07	h	Kemi	D	1-1	*Ala-Myllymäki*
02/08	a	PK-35	D	1-1	*Milosavljević*
06/08	h	Inter	D	0-0	
10/08	a	Lahti	L	2-3	*Soisalo, Ala-Myllymäki*
13/08	h	HIFK	W	3-1	*Soisalo, Ly, Sentamu*
20/08	a	SJK	L	0-4	
24/08	h	RoPS	D	1-1	*Soisalo*
27/08	a	Inter	W	1-0	*Ala-Myllymäki*
09/09	h	RoPS	W	2-1	*Ala-Myllymäki, Tendeng*
12/09	a	PK-35	W	3-1	*Tendeng, Ala-Myllymäki, Aspegren*
16/09	h	VPS	D	0-0	
21/09	a	KuPS	W	2-1	*Soisalo (p), Ala-Myllymäki*
25/09	h	Kemi	W	2-0	*Soisalo (p), Juuti*
02/10	a	Lahti	D	0-0	
14/10	h	HIFK	D	1-1	*Ala-Myllymäki (p)*
17/10	h	HJK	L	1-3	*Ala-Myllymäki*
23/10	a	Mariehamn	L	1-2	*Siira*

No	Name	Nat	DoB	Pos	Aps	(s)	Gls
3	Heikki Aho		16/03/83	D	10	(3)	
15	Lauri Ala-Myllymäki		04/06/97	M	22	(9)	9
4	Felipe Aspegren		12/02/94	D	25	(2)	1
20	Reuben Ayarna	GHA	22/10/85	M	29	(1)	
17	Yero Bello	NGA	11/12/87	A	2		
27	Martti Haukioja		06/10/99	D	2	(1)	
1	Mika Hilander		17/08/83	G	32		
26	Antto Hilska		22/09/93	A	10	(9)	1
9	Jonne Hjelm		14/01/88	A	13	(13)	
2	Antti Hynynen		30/05/84	D	23		1
19	Jaakko Juuti		13/08/87	M	9	(12)	1
8	Eero Korte		20/09/87	M	1	(2)	
25	Antti Koskinen		19/07/88	D	9	(3)	
32	Antti Kuusinen		30/11/96	G	1		
23	Mika Lahtinen		30/04/85	A	6	(8)	1
30	Yoro Lamine Ly	SEN	27/08/88	A	7	(3)	1
7	Marco Matrone		02/07/87	M	19	(5)	
16	Tatu Miettunen		24/04/95	M	32		1
5	Pavle Milosavljević	SRB	21/06/87	D	30		1
6	Samu Nieminen		14/01/92	D	1	(1)	
10	Tomi Petrescu		24/07/86	M		(1)	
13	Yunus Sentamu	UGA	13/08/94	A	5	(9)	1
14	Tuure Siira		25/10/94	M	21	(9)	4
11	Mikael Soisalo		24/04/98	M	26	(5)	7
22	Emile Paul Tendeng	SEN	09/03/92	M	28		7
18	Diogo Tomas		31/07/97	D		(3)	

FC Inter Turku

1990 • Veritas Stadion (8,072) • fcinter.fi

Major honours
Finnish League (1) 2008; Finnish Cup (1) 2009

Coach: Job Dragtsma (NED); (26/05/16) (Jami Wallenius); (03/08/16) Shefki Kuqi

2016

Date		Opponent		Score	Scorers
09/04	h	Lahti	D	1-1	*Belica*
14/04	a	HIFK	W	2-1	*Njoku, Belica*
18/04	h	KuPS	W	3-1	*Belica, Källman, Mannström*
24/04	a	VPS	D	0-0	
28/04	h	RoPS	L	1-2	*Nwanganga*
05/05	a	SJK	L	0-1	
09/05	h	Mariehamn	L	0-2	
16/05	a	HJK	L	1-3	*Duah*
21/05	h	Ilves	W	1-0	*Gnabouyou*
25/05	a	PK-35	L	1-3	*Gnabouyou*
28/05	h	Kemi	L	0-2	
09/06	a	Lahti	L	0-1	
12/06	h	HIFK	W	1-0	*Nwanganga*
19/06	a	KuPS	L	1-2	*Källman*
28/06	h	SJK	L	1-3	*Gnabouyou*
04/07	h	VPS	L	0-2	
10/07	a	RoPS	L	1-2	*Duah*
25/07	a	Mariehamn	D	0-0	
31/07	h	HJK	D	0-0	
06/08	a	Ilves	D	0-0	
10/08	h	PK-35	D	2-2	*Kuqi 2*
13/08	a	Kemi	L	1-3	*Kuqi*
21/08	a	Lahti	W	2-1	*Nwanganga, Duah*
27/08	h	Ilves	L	0-1	
09/09	a	SJK	L	0-1	
12/09	h	HIFK	D	0-0	
16/09	h	HJK	W	3-2	*Nwanganga, Kuqi 2*
21/09	a	Mariehamn	D	1-1	*Kuqi (p)*
26/09	h	VPS	D	1-1	*Kuqi*
02/10	a	KuPS	W	2-0	*Duah, Manev*
14/10	h	Kemi	D	0-0	
17/10	h	RoPS	D	1-1	*Kuqi*
23/10	a	PK-35	L	1-2	*Nebihi*

No	Name	Nat	DoB	Pos	Aps	(s)	Gls
18	Albion Ademi		19/02/99	M		(2)	
14	Joni Aho		12/04/86	D	22	(4)	
2	Egzon Belica	MKD	03/09/90	D	29		3
20	Markus Blomqvist		03/01/97	A		(2)	
21	Solomon Duah		07/01/93	M	24	(7)	4
11	Alban Ferati		01/11/91	M		(2)	
23	Lucas García	ARG	13/01/88	M	5	(4)	
10	Guy Gnabouyou	FRA	01/12/89	A	19	(9)	3
15	Tuomas Happonen		28/01/96	M		(1)	
22	Arttu Hoskonen		16/04/97	M	13	(5)	
6	Petros Kanakoudis	GRE	16/04/84	D	16	(2)	
16	Kalle Kauppi		06/05/92	M	11	(9)	
99	Njazi Kuqi		25/03/83	A	13		8
9	Benjamin Källman		17/06/98	A	13	(9)	2
29	Henri Lehtonen		28/07/80	M	19	(3)	
12	Jukka Lehtovaara		15/03/88	G	22		
26	Kosta Manev		07/04/93	D	9	(1)	1
8	Sebastian Mannström		29/10/88	M	19	(1)	1
13	Aati Marttinen		26/12/97	G	2	(2)	
1	Henrik Moisander		29/09/85	G	8		
33	David Monsalve	CAN	21/12/88	G	1		
8	Bajram Nebihi	GER	05/08/88	M	5	(3)	1
23	Marios Nicolaou	CYP	04/10/83	M	4	(3)	
25	Philip Njoku	NGA	03/06/96	A	9	(3)	1
27	Kennedy Nwanganga	NGA	15/08/90	A	20	(8)	4
7	Ari Nyman		07/02/84	M	23	(4)	
30	Faith Obilor	NGA	05/03/91	D	31		
24	Juho Salminen		08/08/95	D	3	(7)	
5	Pape Sow	SEN	02/12/85	D	5		
3	Adama Tamboura	MLI	18/05/85	D	6		
17	Erfan Zeneli		28/12/86	M	12	(2)	

PS Kemi

1999 • Sauvosaaren urheilupuisto (4,500) • pskemi.fi

Coach: Jari Åhman

2016

Date		Opponent		Score	Scorers
09/04	h	SJK	W	3-0	*(w/o; original result 0-2)*
17/04	h	Mariehamn	L	1-2	*Kaby Djaló*
25/04	a	HIFK	D	0-0	
29/04	h	HJK	W	1-0	*Gilligan*
04/05	a	KuPS	L	0-2	
07/05	h	Ilves	W	1-0	*Ions*
13/05	a	VPS	W	1-0	*Ions*
21/05	a	PK-35	D	2-2	*Ions 2*
28/05	a	Inter	W	2-0	*Könönen, Ions*
09/06	a	SJK	L	0-1	
12/06	h	Lahti	W	2-1	*Stewart, Gullsten*
19/06	a	Mariehamn	L	0-2	
23/06	h	RoPS	L	0-2	
29/06	a	Lahti	L	0-1	
03/07	h	HIFK	L	1-2	*Ions*
10/07	a	HJK	L	0-2	
16/07	h	KuPS	L	0-2	
24/07	a	Ilves	D	1-1	*Bitsindou*
30/07	h	VPS	D	0-0	
06/08	h	PK-35	W	2-1	*Ions, Taimi*
10/08	a	RoPS	L	0-5	
13/08	h	Inter	W	3-1	*Ions, Törnros, Eissele (p)*
20/08	h	RoPS	W	3-1	*Törnros 2, Savić*
26/08	a	PK-35	W	1-0	*Törnros*
09/09	h	HJK	L	0-2	
12/09	a	Mariehamn	L	0-1	
16/09	a	HIFK	L	1-3	*Törnros*
21/09	h	Lahti	L	2-4	*Törnros, Valenčič*
25/09	a	Ilves	L	0-2	
01/10	h	SJK	L	1-3	*Törnros*
14/10	a	Inter	D	0-0	
17/10	h	VPS	L	1-4	*Törnros*
23/10	a	KuPS	L	0-1	

No	Name	Nat	DoB	Pos	Aps	(s)	Gls
21	Juho-Teppo Berg		25/11/92	A		(1)	
2	David Bitsindou	FRA	26/03/89	D	28	(1)	1
5	Christian Eissele	USA	23/06/92	M	11	(15)	1
87	Ryan Gilligan	ENG	18/01/87	M	28		1
17	Aleksi Gullsten		22/03/93	M	22	(9)	1
12	Jusa Impiö		16/11/91	G	2		
9	Billy Ions	ENG	11/03/94	M	21		8
19	Paavo Jokinen		30/08/96	M		(1)	
22	Saša Jovović	MNE	06/09/86	A	1		
10	Kaby Djaló	GNB	05/02/92	M	16	(1)	1
6	Saku Kvist		18/04/95	M	14	(10)	
88	Tuomo Könönen		29/12/77	D	8	(9)	1
3	Henri Louste		02/12/92	D		(5)	
33	Muller	BRA	15/11/90	D	15	(2)	
14	Matias Ojala		28/02/95	M	23	(7)	
1	Juhani Pennanen		19/02/93	G	20	(2)	
20	Aleksi Räihä		09/01/86	D	9	(3)	
15	Željko Savić	SRB	18/03/88	D	31		1
11	Cornelius Stewart	VIN	07/10/89	A	9	(10)	1
23	Kalle Taimi		27/01/92	D	19		1
13	Janne Turpeenniemi		17/05/89	D	17	(5)	
7	Erik Törnros	SWE	11/06/93	A	13		8
4	Filip Valenčič	SVN	07/01/92	M	9	(3)	1
21	Nicolae Vasile	ROU	29/12/95	D	4	(1)	
8	Joona Veteli		21/04/95	M	28		
35	Mikko Vilmunen		23/08/80	G	11		
24	Topias Wiena		10/05/96	A		(2)	
7	Rundell Winchester	TRI	16/12/93	A	4	(2)	

KuPS Kuopio

1923 • Savon Sanomat Areena (4,778) • kups.fi

Major honours
Finnish League (5) 1956, 1958, 1966, 1974, 1976; Finnish Cup (2) 1968, 1989

Coach: Marko Rajamäki

2016

Date		Opponent		Score	Scorers
09/04	h	Ilves	L	0-1	
14/04	h	PK-35	L	2-3	*Salami, Pennanen (p)*
18/04	a	Inter	L	1-3	*Savolainen*
24/04	h	Lahti	W	2-0	*Salami, Egwuekwe*
28/04	a	HIFK	L	2-3	*Salami, Pennanen*
04/05	h	Kemi	W	2-0	*Pennanen 2*
07/05	h	VPS	W	1-0	*Savolainen*
13/05	a	RoPS	W	1-0	*Egwuekwe*
21/05	h	SJK	D	0-0	
25/05	a	Mariehamn	W	3-0	*Diallo, Egwuekwe, Salami*
29/05	h	HJK	D	0-0	
09/06	a	Ilves	L	0-1	
12/06	a	PK-35	D	1-1	*Egwuekwe*
19/06	h	Inter	W	2-1	*Salami, Savolainen*
03/07	a	Lahti	D	0-0	
10/07	h	HIFK	W	1-0	*Salami*
16/07	a	Kemi	W	2-0	*Pennanen, Hakola*
25/07	a	VPS	L	0-3	
31/07	h	RoPS	D	1-1	*Egwuekwe*
06/08	a	SJK	L	0-1	
10/08	h	Mariehamn	W	1-0	*Salami (p)*
13/08	a	HJK	W	3-2	*Hakola, Salami, Jaiteh*
21/08	h	PK-35	W	3-0	*Diallo, Jovović, Pennanen*
28/08	a	HJK	L	0-1	
09/09	h	Mariehamn	W	2-1	*Salami 2 (1p)*
12/09	a	VPS	D	1-1	*Savolainen*
16/09	a	Lahti	D	1-1	*Salami (p)*
21/09	h	Ilves	L	1-2	*og (Milosavljević)*
28/09	a	SJK	L	0-1	
02/10	h	Inter	L	0-2	
14/10	a	RoPS	L	1-2	*Salami*
17/10	a	HIFK	W	2-0	*Salami, Pennanen*
23/10	h	Kemi	W	1-0	*Salami*

No	Name	Nat	DoB	Pos	Aps	(s)	Gls
18	Aliyu Abubakar	NGA	15/06/96	D	21	(4)	
17	Patrik Alaharjula		05/07/97	A		(3)	
19	Babacar Diallo	SEN	25/03/89	D	31		2
45	Azubuike Egwuekwe	NGA	16/07/89	D	32		5
7	Juha Hakola		27/10/87	A	22	(7)	2
12	Craig Hill	USA	27/12/87	G	9		
24	Atte Hoivala		10/02/92	D	8	(1)	
14	Tijan Jaiteh	GAM	31/12/88	M	23	(3)	1
22	Saša Jovović	MNE	06/09/86	A	10	(1)	1
1	Johannes Kreidl	AUT	07/03/96	G	24		
28	Joona Lautamaja		12/07/95	D	21	(2)	
21	Jani Mahanen		12/01/90	M		(2)	
11	Ilmari Niskanen		27/10/97	M	10	(15)	
25	Urho Nissilä		04/04/96	M	7	(19)	
26	Joonas Nissinen		24/04/97	M		(1)	
10	Paul Onobi	NGA	27/11/92	D	21	(1)	
8	Petteri Pennanen		19/09/90	M	29	(3)	7
23	Patrick Poutiainen		14/06/91	M	8	(6)	
32	Tuomas Rannankari		21/05/91	M	17	(5)	
39	Gbolahan Salami	NGA	15/04/91	A	31		14
6	Saku Savolainen		13/08/96	A	18	(13)	4
9	Mika Ääritalo		25/07/88	M	21	(9)	

FC Lahti

1996 • Kisapuisto (3,187); Lahden stadion (7,465) • fclahti.fi

Coach: Toni Korkeakunnas

2016

Date		Opponent		Score	Scorers
09/04	a	Inter	D	1-1	*Tuominen*
18/04	h	HIFK	D	2-2	*Hostikka, Tuominen*
24/04	a	KuPS	L	0-2	
28/04	h	VPS	W	4-0	*Tuominen, Kärkkäinen, Paananen, Sadat*
05/05	a	RoPS	D	0-0	
09/05	h	SJK	W	3-0	*Tatar, Tuominen, Euller*
15/05	a	Mariehamn	L	0-3	
20/05	h	HJK	L	1-2	*Hauhia*
25/05	a	Ilves	L	0-2	
28/05	h	PK-35	W	2-1	*Kärkkäinen, Tuominen (p)*
09/06	h	Inter	W	1-0	*Kuningas*
12/06	a	Kemi	L	1-2	*Länsitalo*
18/06	a	HIFK	D	2-2	*Tuominen, Multanen*
29/06	h	Kemi	W	1-0	*Euller*
03/07	h	KuPS	D	0-0	
08/07	a	VPS	L	0-1	
17/07	h	RoPS	L	1-2	*Länsitalo*
23/07	a	SJK	L	1-4	*Rafael*
31/07	h	Mariehamn	D	1-1	*Hostikka*
07/08	a	HJK	D	2-2	*og (Rexhepi), Tuominen*
10/08	h	Ilves	W	3-2	*Tatar, Hauhia, Bonilha*
13/08	a	PK-35	D	1-1	*Vasyutin*
21/08	h	Inter	L	1-2	*Sesay*
27/08	a	RoPS	L	0-3	
09/09	h	PK-35	W	2-0	*Tuominen, Hostikka*
12/09	a	HJK	W	4-1	*Multanen, Tuominen (p), Paananen, Kärkkäinen*
16/09	h	KuPS	D	1-1	*Tanska*
21/09	a	Kemi	W	4-2	*Multanen 3, Tuominen*
26/09	h	HIFK	D	0-0	
02/10	h	Ilves	D	0-0	
14/10	a	SJK	D	2-2	*Kuningas, Osipov*
17/10	h	Mariehamn	L	0-2	
23/10	a	VPS	W	1-0	*Hostikka*

No	Name	Nat	DoB	Pos	Aps	(s)	Gls
13	Paavo Ahola		13/01/98	D		(2)	
5	Bonilha	BRA	26/01/96	M	9	(10)	1
10	Euller	BRA	30/01/95	M	7	(10)	2
3	Mikko Hauhia		03/09/84	D	33		2
16	Santeri Hostikka		30/09/97	A	28	(1)	4
25	Mikko Kuningas		10/07/97	M	16	(9)	2
6	Pyry Kärkkäinen		10/11/86	D	28		3
31	Jussi Länsitalo		30/06/90	A	10	(11)	2
1	Tomi Maanoja		12/09/86	G	11	(1)	
30	Miikka Mujunen		14/08/96	G	3		
17	Kalle Multanen		07/04/89	A	12	(13)	5
18	Pavel Osipov	RUS	28/01/96	M	8	(4)	1
19	Aleksi Paananen		25/01/93	M	33		2
12	Santeri Pakkanen		07/05/98	G	7		
9	Rafael	BRA	01/08/78	A	7	(9)	1
21	Fareed Sadat	AFG	10/11/98	A	4	(11)	1
15	Hassan Sesay	SLE	22/10/87	M	22	(2)	1
11	Drilon Shala		20/03/87	A	3	(3)	
90	Ivan Solovyov	RUS	29/03/93	A	11	(1)	
8	Duarte Tammilehto		15/02/90	M	27	(2)	
2	Jani Tanska		29/07/88	D	28		1
20	Boris Tatar	MNE	17/03/93	D	15	(6)	2
14	Jasse Tuominen		12/11/95	M	27		10
78	Aleksandr Vasyutin	RUS	04/03/95	G	12		1
24	Paavo Voutilainen		25/02/99	D	2	(1)	

FINLAND

IFK Mariehamn

1919 • Wiklöf Holding Arena (1,635) • ifkfotboll.ax

Major honours
Finnish League (1) 2016; Finnish Cup (1) 2015

Coach: Peter Lundberg & Kari Virtanen

2016

02/04	a	HJK	L	0-2	
09/04	h	RoPS	W	1-0	*Orgill*
14/04	a	SJK	W	1-0	*Orgill*
17/04	a	Kemi	W	2-1	*Diego Assis, Orgill*
24/04	h	HJK	D	0-0	
29/04	a	Ilves	W	1-0	*Dafaa*
04/05	h	PK-35	D	0-0	
09/05	a	Inter	W	2-0	*Orgill 2*
15/05	h	Lahti	W	3-0	*Span, Lyyski, Orgill*
20/05	a	HIFK	W	1-0	*Diego Assis*
25/05	h	KuPS	L	0-3	
29/05	h	VPS	D	2-2	*Diego Assis, Sid*
09/06	a	RoPS	D	0-0	
12/06	h	SJK	W	1-0	*Diego Assis*
19/06	h	Kemi	W	2-0	*Orgill, Kangaskolkka*
10/07	h	Ilves	W	3-1	*Kangaskolkka (p), Lyyski, Ibrahim*
17/07	a	PK-35	W	2-0	*Sparrdal Mantilla, Lyyski*
25/07	h	Inter	D	0-0	
31/07	a	Lahti	D	1-1	*Ekhalie*
07/08	h	HIFK	L	2-5	*Orgill 2*
10/08	a	KuPS	L	0-1	
14/08	a	VPS	W	2-0	*Kojola, Mäkinen*
21/08	h	HIFK	W	1-0	*Kangaskolkka (p)*
28/08	h	VPS	D	0-0	
09/09	a	KuPS	L	1-2	*Kangaskolkka*
12/09	h	Kemi	W	1-0	*Span*
17/09	a	SJK	L	0-1	
21/09	h	Inter	D	1-1	*Orgill*
25/09	a	RoPS	D	1-1	*Diego Assis*
02/10	h	PK-35	W	4-2	*Kangaskolkka, Orgill, Ibrahim, Lyyski*
14/10	a	HJK	D	1-1	*Kangaskolkka*
17/10	a	Lahti	W	2-0	*Orgill, Lyyski*
23/10	h	Ilves	W	2-1	*Friberg da Cruz, Diego Assis*

No	Name	Nat	DoB	Pos	Aps	(s)	Gls
20	Anthony Dafaa	KEN	26/06/88	M	17		1
25	Diego Assis	BRA	14/09/87	M	24	(8)	6
15	Amos Ekhalie	KEN	08/07/88	M	19	(12)	1
55	Bobbie Friberg da Cruz	SWE	16/02/82	D	28	(2)	1
2	Albin Granlund		01/09/89	D	20	(1)	
11	Josef Ibrahim	SWE	13/03/91	M	4	(11)	2
33	Aleksei Kangaskolkka		29/10/88	A	22	(7)	6
3	Kristian Kojola		12/09/86	D	33		1
8	Jani Lyyski		16/03/83	D	31		5
26	Joel Mattsson		17/03/99	M		(1)	
18	Thomas Mäkinen		30/01/97	M	4	(16)	1
5	Dever Orgill	JAM	08/03/90	A	27	(1)	12
14	Gabriel Petrovic	SWE	25/05/84	M	28		
17	Robin Sid		21/09/94	M	13	(10)	1
9	Brian Span	USA	23/02/92	A	27	(4)	2
4	Philip Sparrdal Mantilla	SWE	11/08/93	D	27	(2)	1
1	Walter Viitala		09/01/92	G	33		
7	Tommy Wirtanen		19/01/83	D	6	(6)	

PK-35 Vantaa

1935 • Myyrmäen jalkapallostadion (4,600) • pk35vantaa.fi

Coach: Shefki Kuqi;
(28/07/16) Pasi Pihamaa

2016

02/04	h	RoPS	L	3-4	*Kuqi 2, Ristola*
09/04	h	HIFK	L	0-2	
14/04	a	KuPS	W	3-2	*Ristola, og (Diallo), Míguez (p)*
17/04	h	VPS	L	0-2	
24/04	a	RoPS	L	0-1	
29/04	h	SJK	D	0-0	
04/05	a	Mariehamn	D	0-0	
07/05	h	HJK	L	1-2	*Ristola*
13/05	a	Ilves	L	0-2	
21/05	h	Kemi	D	2-2	*Míguez, Kuqi*
25/05	h	Inter	W	3-1	*Kuqi (p), Ristola, Mombilo*
28/05	a	Lahti	L	1-2	*Kuqi*
09/06	a	HIFK	W	2-1	*Lucas Kaufmann, Kuqi*
12/06	h	KuPS	D	1-1	*Raimi*
08/07	a	SJK	L	2-3	*Kuqi (p), Äijälä*
13/07	a	VPS	L	1-2	*Äijälä*
17/07	h	Mariehamn	L	0-2	
24/07	a	HJK	L	2-4	*Ömer, Kuqi*
02/08	h	Ilves	D	1-1	*Rasimus*
06/08	a	Kemi	L	1-2	*Ristola*
10/08	a	Inter	D	2-2	*Ristola, Lucas Kaufmann*
13/08	h	Lahti	D	1-1	*Mombilo*
21/08	a	KuPS	L	0-3	
24/08	a	HJK	L	0-2	
26/08	h	Kemi	L	0-1	
09/09	a	Lahti	L	0-2	
12/09	h	Ilves	L	1-3	*Väisänen*
16/09	a	RoPS	L	0-1	
20/09	h	HIFK	L	0-2	
02/10	a	Mariehamn	L	2-4	*Ömer, Kastrati*
14/10	h	VPS	L	1-2	*Ömer*
17/10	a	SJK	L	0-5	
23/10	h	Inter	W	2-1	*Xhaferi, Ömer*

No	Name	Nat	DoB	Pos	Aps	(s)	Gls
21	Nosh A Lody		17/07/89	D	4	(1)	
2	Altin Ademaj		04/01/96	D	11	(1)	
80	Ahmed Said Ahmed		04/07/98	D	8	(3)	
8	Mnwas Awari		11/01/96	M	3	(4)	
6	Carlos Caloi	ESP	11/02/87	M	2	(2)	
38	Pablo Couñago	ESP	09/08/79	M	3	(6)	
7	Yerai Couñago	ESP	11/01/91	M	10		
14	Bob Diasonama		13/03/96	D	2	(3)	
22	Lucas García	ARG	13/01/88	M	8	(1)	
58	Reza Heidari		18/04/96	M	9	(9)	
55	Marcus Heimonen		11/10/93	M	15	(9)	
5	Riku Heinonen		05/06/94	D	9	(4)	
7	Abaas Ismail		19/05/98	A	2	(4)	
15	Karim Jouini		29/02/96	A	6	(2)	
11	Kastriot Kastrati		02/10/93	M	2	(2)	1
18	Omar Khary		12/05/95	M	6	(3)	
1	Daniel Kollár		29/03/94	G	26	(1)	
99	Njazi Kuqi		25/03/83	A	12		8
33	Fernando Liñán	ESP	31/07/86	M	7		
15	Lucas Kaufmann	BRA	26/03/91	M	21	(3)	2
3	Kosta Manev		07/04/93	D	9		
8	Mateo Míguez	ESP	11/05/87	M	9		2
17	Kevin Mombilo		06/05/93	A	17	(4)	2
19	Calvin N'Sombo		24/06/97	M	1	(1)	
6	Ojembe Olatuga	NGA	24/01/88	D	9	(2)	
20	Otto Pitkänen		09/07/97	D	6		
4	Kim Raimi		25/02/85	D	9	(1)	1
35	Daniel Rantanen		11/05/98	M	1	(6)	
16	Konsta Rasimus		15/12/90	D	30		1
19	Aleksi Ristola		06/11/89	M	20	(4)	6
28	Driton Shala		26/05/97	A	5	(4)	
13	Samu Volotinen		26/08/98	G	7	(2)	
3	Leo Väisänen		23/07/97	D	9		1
10	Ymer Xhaferi	KOS	06/11/85	M	29	(1)	1
11	Ilari Äijälä		30/09/86	D	20		2
9	Masar Ömer		12/06/93	A	16	(12)	4

RoPS Rovaniemi

1950 • Keskuskenttä (3,000) • rops.fi

Major honours
Finnish Cup (2) 1986, 2013

Coach: Juha Malinen

2016

02/04	a	PK-35	W	4-3	*Heikkilä, Taylor, Saxman, Kokko*
09/04	a	Mariehamn	L	0-1	
14/04	h	HJK	D	2-2	*Kokko, John*
24/04	h	PK-35	W	1-0	*Kokko*
28/04	a	Inter	W	2-1	*Taylor, Kokko*
05/05	h	Lahti	D	0-0	
09/05	a	HIFK	D	1-1	*Saxman*
13/05	h	KuPS	L	0-1	
22/05	a	VPS	L	0-1	
28/05	h	SJK	L	2-3	*Taylor, Osei*
09/06	h	Mariehamn	D	0-0	
12/06	a	HJK	D	1-1	*John*
18/06	h	Ilves	W	1-0	*Taylor*
23/06	a	Kemi	W	2-0	*Muinonen, Mravec*
10/07	h	Inter	W	2-1	*Kokko 2*
17/07	a	Lahti	W	2-1	*Taylor, Mäkitalo*
24/07	h	HIFK	W	1-0	*Taylor (p)*
31/07	a	KuPS	D	1-1	*Kokko*
07/08	h	VPS	W	2-0	*Taylor, Kokko*
10/08	h	Kemi	W	5-0	*Taylor 3 (2p), Kokko, Mravec*
13/08	a	SJK	L	1-3	*Muinonen*
20/08	a	Kemi	L	1-3	*Prosa*
24/08	a	Ilves	D	1-1	*og (Matrone)*
27/08	h	Lahti	W	3-0	*Nganbe Nganbe 2, Saine*
09/09	a	Ilves	L	1-2	*Lahdenmäki*
12/09	h	SJK	D	1-1	*Taylor (p)*
16/09	h	PK-35	W	1-0	*Pirinen (p)*
21/09	a	HJK	L	1-2	*Muinonen*
25/09	h	Mariehamn	D	1-1	*Saksela*
02/10	a	VPS	L	0-1	
14/10	h	KuPS	W	2-1	*Prosa, Lahdenmäki*
17/10	a	Inter	D	1-1	*Saksela*
23/10	h	HIFK	D	0-0	

No	Name	Nat	DoB	Pos	Aps	(s)	Gls
77	José Pedrosa Galán	ESP	02/02/86	M	4	(2)	
21	Aapo Heikkilä		13/04/94	M	5	(14)	1
18	Juho Hyvärinen		27/03/00	M		(1)	
47	Juuso Hämäläinen		08/12/93	D	28		
86	Abdou Jammeh	GAM	13/02/86	D	31		
85	Will John	USA	13/06/85	A	15	(12)	2
13	Lassi Järvenpää		28/10/96	D	6		
2	Akseli Kalermo		17/03/97	D	4	(2)	
11	Aleksandr Kokko		04/06/87	A	14	(1)	9
3	Jarkko Lahdenmäki		16/04/91	D	21	(4)	2
15	Jarkko Luiro		22/03/98	A		(1)	
23	Michal Mravec	SVK	10/06/87	M	11	(6)	2
14	Eetu Muinonen		05/04/86	M	15	(9)	3
7	Mika Mäkitalo		12/06/85	M	22	(4)	1
10	Jean Fridolin Nganbe Nganbe	CMR	11/05/88	A	17	(8)	2
4	Antti Okkonen		06/06/82	M	15	(1)	
19	Ransford Osei	GHA	05/12/90	A	4	(12)	1
6	Juha Pirinen		22/10/91	D	30	(1)	1
99	Albert Prosa	EST	01/10/90	A	7	(3)	2
25	Antonio Reguero	ESP	04/07/82	G	19		
22	Ricardo	BRA	18/02/93	G	14		
17	Mamut Saine	GAM	31/12/93	M	7	(10)	1
5	Janne Saksela		14/03/93	D	30		2
16	Ville Saxman		15/11/89	D	14	(3)	2
8	Robert Taylor		21/10/94	M	30	(1)	11

SJK Seinäjoki

2007 • OmaSp Stadion (5,817) • sjk2007.fi

Major honours
Finnish League (1) 2015; Finnish Cup (1) 2016

Coach: Simo Valakari

2016					
12/04	a	Kemi	L	0-3	*(w/o; original result 2-0 Vasara, Riski)*
14/04	h	Mariehamn	L	0-1	
18/04	a	HJK	L	1-2	*Ngueukam*
24/04	h	Ilves	L	0-2	
29/04	a	PK-35	D	0-0	
05/05	h	Inter	W	1-0	*Riski*
09/05	a	Lahti	L	0-3	
14/05	h	HIFK	W	2-1	*Riski, Kink*
21/05	a	KuPS	D	0-0	
25/05	h	VPS	W	1-0	*Riski*
28/05	a	RoPS	W	3-2	*Riski, Ngueukam, Méïté*
09/06	h	Kemi	W	1-0	*Vasara*
12/06	a	Mariehamn	L	0-1	
18/06	h	HJK	L	2-3	*Penninkangas, Hradecky*
28/06	a	Inter	W	3-1	*Hurme, Riski 2*
02/07	a	Ilves	L	1-2	*Kink*
08/07	h	PK-35	W	3-2	*Izuegbu, Riski, Vasara*
23/07	h	Lahti	W	4-1	*Vasara, Riski 2 (1p), Rahimi*
30/07	a	HIFK	D	1-1	*Ngueukam*
06/08	h	KuPS	W	1-0	*Hetemaj*
10/08	a	VPS	L	1-2	*Lehtinen*
13/08	h	RoPS	W	3-1	*Dorman, Vasara 2*
20/08	h	Ilves	W	4-0	*Riski 3, Vasara*
27/08	a	HIFK	L	1-3	*Riski*
09/09	h	Inter	W	1-0	*Ions*
12/09	a	RoPS	D	1-1	*Ions*
17/09	h	Mariehamn	W	1-0	*Vasara*
21/09	a	VPS	W	2-1	*Ions, Ngueukam*
28/09	h	KuPS	W	1-0	*Riski*
01/10	a	Kemi	W	3-1	*Riski, Hradecky, Vasara*
14/10	h	Lahti	D	2-2	*Penninkangas, Ions*
17/10	h	PK-35	W	5-0	*Riski (p), Hradecky 2, Klinga, Ions*
23/10	a	HJK	D	0-0	

No	Name	Nat	DoB	Pos	Aps	(s)	Gls
5	Henri Aalto		20/04/89	D	22	(1)	
33	Mihkel Aksalu	EST	07/11/84	G	31		
4	Richard Dorman	WAL	14/06/88	D	8	(5)	1
10	Alexei Eremenko		24/03/83	M	3	(2)	
58	Mehmet Hetemaj		08/12/87	M	16	(1)	1
6	Matej Hradecky		17/04/95	M	28	(4)	4
18	Jarkko Hurme		04/06/86	D	25	(1)	1
10	Billy Ions	ENG	11/03/94	M	9	(1)	5
3	Abonima Izuegbu	NGA	27/11/94	D	3		1
2	El-Hadji Gana Kane	SEN	11/04/95	D	8		
16	Tarmo Kink	EST	06/10/85	M	8	(4)	2
15	Matti Klinga		10/12/94	M	21	(6)	1
1	Jere Koponen		23/05/92	G	2		
8	Johannes Laaksonen		13/12/90	M	16	(8)	
14	Toni Lehtinen		05/05/84	A	1	(7)	1
35	Abdoulaye Méïté	CIV	06/10/80	D	18		1
24	Aimar Moratalla	ESP	11/01/87	D	7	(2)	
11	Ariel Ngueukam	CMR	15/11/88	A	23	(9)	4
3	Juhani Ojala		19/06/89	D	9		
17	Teemu Penninkangas		24/07/92	A	25	(1)	2
19	Youness Rahimi		13/02/95	A	2	(13)	1
13	Roope Riski		16/08/91	A	33		17
26	Jesse Sarajärvi		20/05/95	M	1	(5)	
7	Timo Tahvanainen		26/06/86	M	3	(7)	
21	Marc Vales	AND	04/04/90	D	12	(1)	
9	Jussi Vasara		14/05/87	M	29	(1)	9

VPS Vaasa

1924 • Elisa Stadion (6,000) • vepsu.fi

Major honours
Finnish League (2) 1945, 1948

Coach: Petri Vuorinen

2016					
08/04	a	HJK	L	1-3	*Hertsi*
17/04	a	PK-35	W	2-0	*Hertsi (p), Soiri*
24/04	h	Inter	D	0-0	
28/04	a	Lahti	L	0-4	
04/05	h	HIFK	W	3-1	*Peth, Clennon, Soiri*
07/05	a	KuPS	L	0-1	
13/05	h	Kemi	L	0-1	
22/05	h	RoPS	W	1-0	*Soiri*
25/05	a	SJK	L	0-1	
29/05	a	Mariehamn	D	2-2	*Soiri (p), Tamminen*
09/06	h	HJK	W	3-0	*Morrissey, Lahti, Clennon*
12/06	a	Ilves	L	0-1	
28/06	h	Ilves	W	2-0	*Clennon, Soiri*
04/07	a	Inter	W	2-0	*Clennon, Morrissey*
08/07	h	Lahti	W	1-0	*Soiri (p)*
13/07	h	PK-35	W	2-1	*Strandvall, Soiri*
18/07	a	HIFK	W	1-0	*Vahtera*
25/07	h	KuPS	W	3-0	*Soiri, Voutilainen, Strandvall*
30/07	a	Kemi	D	0-0	
07/08	a	RoPS	L	0-2	
10/08	h	SJK	W	2-1	*Morrissey 2*
14/08	h	Mariehamn	L	0-2	
21/08	h	HJK	D	0-0	
28/08	a	Mariehamn	D	0-0	
09/09	a	HIFK	W	1-0	*Vahtera*
12/09	h	KuPS	D	1-1	*Levänen*
16/09	a	Ilves	D	0-0	
21/09	h	SJK	L	1-2	*Boxall*
26/09	a	Inter	D	1-1	*Vahtera*
02/10	h	RoPS	W	1-0	*Soiri*
14/10	a	PK-35	W	2-1	*Soiri, Lähde*
17/10	a	Kemi	W	4-1	*Strandvall (p), Voutilainen, Vahtera, Morrissey*
23/10	h	Lahti	L	0-1	

No	Name	Nat	DoB	Pos	Aps	(s)	Gls
13	Samu Alanko		16/05/98	A		(1)	
19	Nikko Boxall	NZL	24/02/92	M	28		1
18	Andre Clennon	JAM	15/08/89	A	23	(8)	4
4	Jesper Engström		24/04/92	M	15	(1)	
22	Loorents Hertsi		13/11/92	M	20	(5)	2
1	Evgeni Kobozev	RUS	11/01/90	G	33		
3	Ville Koskimaa		21/05/83	D	26	(2)	
16	Aatu Laatikainen		13/01/97	M	23		
2	Timi Lahti		28/06/90	D	16	(7)	1
8	Veli Lampi		18/07/84	D	17	(4)	
15	Jonas Levänen		12/01/94	D	15	(6)	1
9	Juho Lähde		11/02/91	M	23	(1)	1
10	Steven Morrissey	JAM	25/07/86	A	18	(9)	5
14	Kevin Peth		26/04/93	D	11	(10)	1
11	Pyry Soiri		22/09/94	M	27	(3)	10
28	Sebastian Strandvall		16/09/86	M	16	(4)	3
7	Eero Tamminen		19/05/95	M	5	(13)	1
17	Joonas Vahtera		06/01/96	M	21	(7)	4
5	Mikko Viitikko		18/04/95	D	14		
6	Jerry Voutilainen		29/03/95	D	12	(13)	2

Top goalscorers

17	Roope Riski (SJK)
16	Alfredo Morelos (HJK)
	Njazi Kuqi (PK-35/Inter)
14	Gbolahan Salami (KuPS)
13	Billy Ions (Kemi/SJK)
12	Dever Orgill (Mariehamn)
11	Robert Taylor (RoPS)
10	Jasse Tuominen (Lahti)
	Pyry Soiri (VPS)
9	Lauri Ala-Myllymäki (Ilves)
	Aleksandr Kokko (RoPS)
	Jussi Vasara (SJK)

Promoted club

JJK Jyväskylä

1992 • Harjun stadion (4,500) • jjk.fi

Coach: Juha Pasoja

Second level final table 2016

		Pld	W	D	L	F	A	Pts
1	JJK Jyväskylä	27	16	4	7	49	38	52
2	TPS Turku	27	16	3	8	60	38	51
3	FF Jaro	27	12	8	7	47	33	44
4	AC Oulu	27	12	7	8	50	31	43
5	KPV Kokkola	27	11	6	10	40	43	39
6	GrIFK Grankulla	27	11	3	13	33	43	36
7	Valkeakosken Haka	27	8	8	11	42	46	32
8	EIF Ekenäs	27	10	1	16	36	53	31
9	FC KTP Kotka	27	6	10	11	47	50	28
10	FC Jazz Pori	27	4	8	15	35	64	20

Promotion/Relegation play-offs

(26/10/16 & 29/10/16)
TPS 0-0 Inter
Inter 2-0 TPS
(Inter 2-0)

DOMESTIC CUP

Suomen Cup 2016

FOURTH ROUND

(05/03/16)
NuPS 0-6 HIFK
AC Oulu 0-3 Jaro
P-Iirot 5-1 Härmä

(06/03/16)
Tampere United 0-4 TPS *(aet)*
ToTe 0-3 JäPS

(08/03/16)
EPS 2-2 Honka Akatemia *(aet; 1-3 on pens)*

(11/03/16)
JIPPO 3-1 PeKa
Korso/United 0-5 JJK

(12/03/16)
Espoo 0-3 Jazz
JBK 1-5 AC Kajaani
Kontu 1-4 KäPa
MPS/Atletico Malmi 1-0 Gnistan
OTP 1-2 Närpes Kraft
RiPS 0-8 Lahti Akatemia
SalPa 0-2 Ilves
Wolves 0-2 MuSa
Åland 1-4 Inter

(13/03/16)
EsPa 3-6 Haka *(aet)*
GBK 1-3 PS Kemi
LoPa 0-5 Honka
Vesa 0-6 Legirus Inter

(18/03/16)
KTP 1-2 PK-35 *(aet)*
MP 0-3 KuPS

(19/03/16)
Kiisto 2-2 JS Hercules *(aet; 3-5 on pens)*
TP-47 0-3 KPV
TPV 1-0 EIF

FIFTH ROUND

(19/03/16)
Honka Akatemia 1-3 HJK
Jaro 0-2 VPS

(20/03/16)
AC Kajaani 4-0 P-Iirot

(22/03/16)
KäPa 0-2 Inter

(23/03/16)
Honka 4-4 TPS *(aet; 6-5 on pens)*

(24/03/16)
JJK 4-1 JIPPO

(26/03/16)
Legirus Inter 1-3 Mariehamn *(aet)*
PK-35 2-1 HIFK *(aet)*

(29/03/16)
JS Hercules 0-8 RoPS

(30/03/16)
Lahti Akatemia 2-4 JäPS *(aet)*

(01/04/16)
Haka 0-0 Ilves *(aet; 5-4 on pens)*
MPS/Atletico Malmi 0-6 Lahti

(02/04/16)
Jazz 2-1 Närpes Kraft
MuSa 0-5 KPV

(05/04/16)
PS Kemi 1-1 SJK *(aet; 4-5 on pens)*
TPV 2-3 KuPS *(aet)*

SIXTH ROUND

(19/04/16)
JJK 2-2 Jazz *(aet; 1-3 on pens)*
KPV 1-2 Honka *(aet)*

(20/04/16)
Haka 4-1 RoPS

(21/04/16)
Inter 0-4 PK-35
JäPS 0-1 KuPS
AC Kajaani 1-5 HJK *(aet)*
Mariehamn 1-2 Lahti *(aet)*
VPS 1-2 SJK

QUARTER-FINALS

(15/06/16)
Haka 2-1 Honka *(Rantanen 33, Järvi 58; Jean Carlo 76)*

Jazz 0-1 Lahti *(Sadat 82)*

KuPS 1-4 HJK *(Salami 79; Kolehmainen 39, Morelos 53, 73, 85p)*

PK-35 1-3 SJK *(Kuqi 21; Penninkangas 17, Riski 24, Ngueukam 90+2)*

SEMI-FINALS

(23/06/16)
Haka 1-6 SJK *(Dudu 67; Tahvanainen 13, Ngueukam 26, Riski 33, Hradecky 54, Rahimi 75, Klinga 88)*

Lahti 0-3 HJK *(Morelos 33, Malolo 62, Tanaka 79)*

FINAL

(24/09/16)
Ratinan stadion, Tampere
SJK SEINÄJOKI 1 *(Riski 74)*
HJK HELSINKI 1 *(Morelos 49)*
(aet; 7-6 on pens)
Referee: *Järvinen*
SJK: *Aksalu, Moratalla, Vales, Ojala, Hurme, Hetemaj, Hradecky (Laaksonen 75), Vasara, Klinga (Penninkangas 46), Ngueukam, Riski (Lehtinen 106)*
HJK: *Dähne, Jalasto, Peiponen (Forssell 100), Kolehmainen (Dahlström 75), Taiwo (Tatomirović 91), Sorsa, Rafinha, Annan, Oduamadi, Pelvas, Morelos*

A year after claiming their first league title, SJK secured a maiden Finnish Cup triumph with a penalty shoot-out win against HJK

FRANCE

Fédération Française de Football (FFF)

Address	87 boulevard de Grenelle FR-75738 Paris, Cedex 15	**President**	Noël Le Graët
		General secretary	Laura Georges
Tel	+33 1 4431 7300	**Media officer**	Philippe Tournon
Fax	+33 1 4431 7373	**Year of formation**	1919
E-mail	competitions. internationales@fff.fr	**National stadium**	Stade de France, Saint-Denis (81,338)
Website	fff.fr		

LIGUE 1 CLUBS

 1 **Angers SCO**

 2 **SC Bastia**

 3 **FC Girondins de Bordeaux**

 4 **SM Caen**

 5 **Dijon FCO**

 6 **EA Guingamp**

 7 **LOSC Lille**

 8 **FC Lorient**

 9 **Olympique Lyonnais**

 10 **Olympique de Marseille**

 11 **FC Metz**

 12 **AS Monaco FC**

 13 **Montpellier Hérault SC**

 14 **AS Nancy-Lorraine**

 15 **FC Nantes**

 16 **OGC Nice**

 17 **Paris Saint-Germain**

 18 **Stade Rennais FC**

 19 **AS Saint-Étienne**

 20 **Toulouse FC**

PROMOTED CLUBS

 21 **RC Strasbourg Alsace**

 22 **Amiens SC**

 23 **ES Troyes AC**

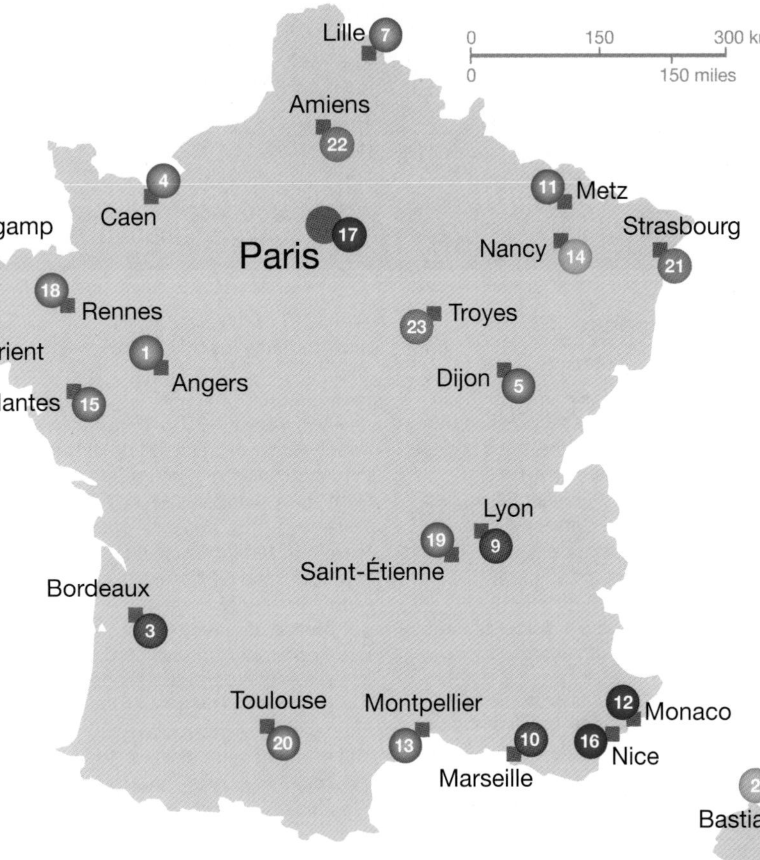

KEY

- UEFA Champions League
- UEFA Europa League
- Promoted
- Relegated

Majestic Monaco turn on the style

Paris Saint-Germain's four-year reign as French champions was unexpectedly brought to a halt in 2016/17 as a swashbuckling young Monaco side, astutely led by Portuguese coach Leonardo Jardim, tore up the script with a brilliant, goal-laden Ligue 1 title triumph.

Paris eclipsed Monaco in both domestic cup competitions, retaining the League Cup and Coupe de France, but it was the club from the Principality that outshone and outlasted them in Europe, reaching the UEFA Champions League semi-finals, while Lyon also made it through to the last four of the UEFA Europa League.

Thrilling title triumph for principality club

Paris lose out in league but retain domestic cups

Eventful European campaign for Ligue 1 teams

Domestic league

PSG's domination of French football in 2015/16 was so ruthless and emphatic that the possibility of a challenge to their hegemony seemed remote, but a change of coach, with Sevilla's Unai Emery coming in to replace Laurent Blanc, plus the departure of the talismanic Zlatan Ibrahimović to Manchester United, rocked the blue-and-red boat sufficiently to enable Monaco, third in 2015/16 but heavily reinforced with a cluster of exciting new summer signings, to turn it over.

The first wave to thud into PSG's bows arrived in the third week of the season when Monaco hosted the champions at the Stade Louis II and convincingly beat them 3-1. Jardim had strengthened his defence by bringing in Polish international centre-back Kamil Glik (from Torino) and full-backs Djibril Sidibé (Lille) and Benjamin Mendy (Marseille). The recall of striker Radamel Falcao from a forgettable loan spell in England would also prove to be a telling move, but in the early weeks of the campaign the ex-Premier League striker hogging the headlines was Mario Balotelli. The capricious Italian hit the ground running at new club Nice, scoring twice on his debut in a 3-2 win against Marseille before grabbing another double as his team routed Monaco 4-0 in the Riviera derby.

With PSG and Monaco both subsequently losing in Toulouse, it was Nice, to widespread amazement, who took charge of the title race. Having finished fourth in 2015/16 but then lost coach Claude Puel and two of their most influential players, Hatem Ben Arfa (to Paris) and Nampalys Mendy (to Leicester), little was expected of the team now led by Swiss coach Lucien Favre, but the ex-Borussia Mönchengladbach boss, like Balotelli, got off to a sensational start and from late September through to Christmas, Nice were the confident leaders of Ligue 1. Just a single defeat – 1-0 at Caen – stained the team's record during a first half of the season in which they pocketed 44 points – two more than Monaco and five more than Paris. The lead over the champions would have been greater still had two goals from prolific PSG striker Edinson Cavani not rescued a draw for his team at the Parc des Princes after Favre's men had audaciously gone 2-0 up.

Nice's lengthy sojourn at the Ligue 1 summit ended just one game into the New Year, however, when they drew 0-0 at home to Metz while Monaco, who had recorded a club-record 7-0 victory away to the same opponents, grabbed another eye-catching away win at Marseille (4-1). Jardim's juggernaut was now fully into its stride, and when the Monégasques followed up a 1-1 draw at the Parc des Princes – salvaged by Bernardo Silva's superb late equaliser – with a thumping 3-0 home win over Nice – featuring a Falcao double – they headed into their final 15 games with a three-point cushion over both rivals.

With the exception of an unlikely 1-1 draw at Corsican strugglers Bastia, Monaco won every one of those matches. Despite continued involvement in Europe, their form never wavered. As the wins and goals piled up, with multi-talented 18-year-old striker Kylian Mbappé becoming increasingly influential alongside Falcao in attack, the realisation dawned that this was a team of special talents that would go down as arguably the best, certainly the most exciting, in Monaco's history.

With Cavani continuing to score for fun, Paris matched Monaco victory for victory during the spring, but Emery's team were never able to take over at the top and when Nice, who had gone unbeaten in 11 matches, beat the title holders 3-1 at home on the last day of April, the coast was clear for Monaco to freewheel to glory, a 2-0 victory over Saint-Étienne on the Wednesday evening of the season's final week clinching the club's eighth French title and first for 17 years.

Monaco's final figures were seriously impressive. Thirty wins and only three defeats gave them 95 points – just one shy of PSG's record total in 2015/16 – while they notched 107 goals, 63 of them at the Stade Louis II, where they were victorious in 17 of their 19 matches. Jardim's Dream Team attacked in every game and were a joy to behold. Megastar-in-waiting Mbappé was the cream of an extraordinary young crop, with Sidibé and Mendy outstanding as overlapping full-backs, Jemerson a rock in defence, Tiémoué Bakayoko and Fabinho all-purposeful in midfield and Bernardo Silva and Thomas Lemar relentlessly clever and creative in support of the attack. Revitalised captain Falcao was back to his world-class best, scoring 21 goals, while goalkeeper Danijel Subašić, centre-back Glik and midfielder João Moutinho all added important international experience and knowhow.

PSG finished eight points in arrears. Undefeated at home and victorious 14 times on the road, their record would have been good enough to win the title in most seasons, but the stardust of previous campaigns was sprinkled less liberally. Cavani had a magnificent season, scoring 35 goals to win the golden boot by a landslide, and there was sustained excellence also from midfield terrier Marco Verratti and skipper Thiago Silva, but new signings Ben Arfa, Jesé and Grzegorz Krychowiak all struggled, which had the effect of overburdening some of the regulars, most of whom starred only fitfully and seldom in the big games against Monaco and Nice, none of which were won.

Nice did superbly to finish third and earn a first crack at UEFA Champions League football. Although they failed to sustain a season-long title challenge, eventually rolling home 17 points adrift of Monaco, they lost only four times and revealed a couple of outstanding midfielders in Wylan Cyprien and Ivory Coast international Jean Michaël Seri. Balotelli ended up with 16 goals, which earned him a new contract, while Favre's stock as a master strategist scaled new heights.

The rise of Monaco and Nice left 2015/16 runners-up Lyon in fourth place, a surfeit of defeats in their new Parc OL home hampering their bid to qualify for a third successive UEFA Champions League campaign. Striker Alexandre Lacazette was their leading light, scoring 28 goals at the apex of an attack skilfully supported by Corentin Tolisso and fit-again Nabil Fekir. While Lyon stayed loyal to Bruno Génésio, Marseille profited from a mid-season change of coach, with ex-Roma boss Rudi Garcia masterminding a revival at the Stade Vélodrome that resulted in a fifth-place finish and a return to Europe. OM closed the season on an 11-match unbeaten run – an outstanding response to their heaviest home league defeat since 1953, when PSG routed them 5-1 in front of a record attendance of 65,252. Marseille goalkeeper Yohann Pelé won the Ligue 1 golden glove by keeping 18 clean sheets, while English Premier League rejects Bafétimbi Gomis and Florian Thauvin revived their reputations with goal tallies of 20 and 15, respectively.

Paris striker Edinson Cavani heads home one of his 35 Ligue 1 goals in a 2-2 draw against Nice at the Parc des Princes

Jocelyn Gourvennec's Bordeaux completed the top six, leaving eighth-placed Saint-Étienne outside the European bracket for the first time in five seasons. There was disappointment too for Lille, down in 11th, while an intense battle to avoid relegation left Bastia and newly-promoted Nancy in the relegation zone, with Lorient later falling through the trapdoor as well after they lost their play-off against Troyes. The final day of the Ligue 2 season was extremely tense, with no fewer than six teams, separated by just three points, all harbouring hopes of going up. Remarkably, all six won, including Amiens, whose winning goal at Reims came deep into added time, earning the club a second successive promotion and a first elevation to France's top flight. Strasbourg topped the table to return to Ligue 1 after a nine-year absence, but Lens, Brest and Nîmes all just missed out.

Domestic cups

The Ligue 1 trophy might have left the capital for pastures new, but PSG won both domestic knockout competitions for the third year in a row. Indeed, the League Cup win was their fourth on the trot and record seventh in all, while victory in the Coupe de France enabled the club to become the most successful in that competition too, their 11th triumph taking them above Marseille in the all-time roll of honour.

There was a change of venue for the League Cup final as the Parc OL stood in for the Stade de France, the fixture being taken outside the capital for the very first time. Theoretically the alternative travel arrangements should have favoured

Monaco, but the night belonged to PSG, who scored early, through January signing Julian Draxler, before rendering Lemar's brilliant equaliser redundant with further goals from Ángel Di María and the inevitable Cavani (two).

The final of the Coupe de France, the season's traditional curtain-closer, remained at its usual venue in the northern Parisian suburb of Saint-Denis, and it ended with another PSG trophy-lift. Victory for Emery's side, however, was achieved under duress, with first-time finalists and rank outsiders Angers holding them to a stalemate until the first minute of added time, when Senegalese defender Issa Cissokho put through his own net. It was a heartbreaking climax for Stéphane Moulin's brave battlers but far from an undeserved victory for a largely dominant PSG side who, in winning 1-0, went through their entire six-match programme without conceding a goal, walloping Monaco 5-0 en route.

Europe

After four successive quarter-final exits from the UEFA Champions League, PSG failed even to make it that far in 2016/17. A momentous 4-0 first-leg victory over Barcelona in the round of 16 should have guaranteed a safe passage through to the last eight, but brilliantly though they played at the Parc des Princes, Emery's team fell apart in the return at the Camp Nou, conceding three late goals – albeit one of them a soft penalty – to lose 6-1 and enter the history books in ignominy as the first team to surrender a four-goal first-leg advantage in a UEFA Champions League knockout tie.

Monaco, who had begun their European campaign at the third qualifying round stage of the same competition, maintained French interest in the latter stages by coming out on top of an enthralling 12-goal tie with Manchester City – their second English victim, after Tottenham Hotspur in the group stage. Mbappé, who scored in each leg against City, struck three more goals as Borussia Dortmund were ousted 6-3 on aggregate in the quarter-finals, but he and his team-mates had no answer to the class of Juventus in the last four.

Lyon also reached the semi-finals of the UEFA Europa League, having finished third in a UEFA Champions League group headed by Juve. A record-breaking 11-2 aggregate win over AZ Alkmaar preceded three edge-of-the-seat thrillers against Roma, Beşiktaş and Ajax, but after winning the first two, Lacazette and co could not quite turn around the semi-final after losing the first leg 4-1 in Amsterdam. Local rivals Saint-Étienne's UEFA Europa League run was ended in the round of 32 by Manchester United, the team that would beat Ajax in the final, whereas Nice underperformed in the group stage and Lille were unexpectedly eliminated in the third qualifying round by Qäbälä of Azerbaijan.

Ousmane Dembélé points the way forward for France after scoring the winning goal in a 3-2 friendly victory against England

National team

The season after UEFA EURO 2016 and the agonising extra-time defeat to Portugal in the Stade de France final was a generally positive one for Didier Deschamps' side. However, there was yet another painful sting in the tail for Les Bleus and their followers to endure as a sensational stoppage-time winner from Sweden in their sixth FIFA World Cup qualifier not only ended France's unbeaten run in Group A but enabled their conquerors to replace them, on goal difference, at the top of the table. A victory at the Friends Arena – which looked on the cards when Olivier Giroud scored his sixth goal in three international starts with a spectacular 27th-minute volley – would have all but secured France's place in Russia, but the defeat left the group wide open, with much to play for in their final four fixtures.

The depth of French talent now available to Deschamps is remarkable, with top-class players like Lacazette barely able to get a game. Evidence of this came in the final friendly of the season, when defender Samuel Umtiti, Sidibé and 20-year-old Ousmane Dembélé all scored their first international goals in an impressive Paul Pogba-inspired 3-2 victory at home to England. Sidibé was one of five Monaco players who received their first senior caps for France during the season, with Lemar, Mendy, Mbappé and Bakayoko all following suit. Assuming that Les Bleus make it to Russia, there is every chance that they could return home with the same trophy that Deschamps lifted as the team's captain on home soil 20 years earlier.

DOMESTIC SEASON AT A GLANCE

Ligue 1 2016/17 final table

			Home					Away					Total					
		Pld	W	D	L	F	A	W	D	L	F	A	W	D	L	F	A	Pts
1	**AS Monaco FC**	**38**	**17**	**1**	**1**	**63**	**13**	**13**	**4**	**2**	**44**	**18**	**30**	**5**	**3**	**107**	**31**	**95**
2	Paris Saint-Germain	38	13	6	0	42	7	14	0	5	41	20	27	6	5	83	27	87
3	OGC Nice	38	14	4	1	39	16	8	8	3	24	20	22	12	4	63	36	78
4	Olympique Lyonnais	38	12	1	6	46	26	9	3	7	31	22	21	4	13	77	48	67
5	Olympique de Marseille	38	13	4	2	33	13	4	7	8	24	28	17	11	10	57	41	62
6	FC Girondins de Bordeaux	38	9	6	4	27	19	6	8	5	26	24	15	14	9	53	43	59
7	FC Nantes	38	8	4	7	19	24	6	5	8	21	30	14	9	15	40	54	51
8	AS Saint-Étienne	38	7	9	3	24	18	5	5	9	17	24	12	14	12	41	42	50
9	Stade Rennais FC	38	10	6	3	26	15	2	8	9	10	27	12	14	12	36	42	50
10	EA Guingamp	38	12	3	4	28	13	2	5	12	18	40	14	8	16	46	53	50
11	LOSC Lille	38	7	3	9	24	24	6	4	9	16	23	13	7	18	40	47	46
12	Angers SCO	38	8	5	6	23	17	5	2	12	17	32	13	7	18	40	49	46
13	Toulouse FC	38	8	6	5	28	18	2	8	9	9	23	10	14	14	37	41	44
14	FC Metz	38	7	7	5	27	34	4	3	12	12	38	11	10	17	39	72	43
15	Montpellier Hérault SC	38	8	5	6	28	22	2	4	13	20	44	10	9	19	48	66	39
16	Dijon FCO	38	7	6	6	27	21	1	7	11	19	37	8	13	17	46	58	37
17	SM Caen	38	7	2	10	21	37	3	5	11	15	28	10	7	21	36	65	37
18	FC Lorient	38	7	4	8	25	29	3	2	14	19	41	10	6	22	44	70	36
19	AS Nancy-Lorraine	38	7	3	9	21	23	2	5	12	8	29	9	8	21	29	52	35
20	SC Bastia	38	5	9	5	17	14	3	1	15	12	40	8	10	20	29	54	34

European qualification 2017/18

Champion: AS Monaco FC (group stage)

Cup winner: Paris Saint-Germain (group stage)

OGC Nice (third qualifying round)

Olympique Lyonnais (group stage)

Olympique de Marseille (third qualifying round)

FC Girondins de Bordeaux (third qualifying round)

Top scorer Edinson Cavani (Paris), 35 goals
Relegated clubs SC Bastia, AS Nancy-Lorraine, FC Lorient
Promoted clubs RC Strasbourg Alsace, Amiens SC, ES Troyes AC
Cup final Paris Saint-Germain 1-0 Angers SCO
League Cup final Paris Saint-Germain 4-1 AS Monaco FC

Player of the season

Edinson Cavani
(Paris Saint-Germain)

Cavani's fourth season in Paris was his first as the team's principal source of goals. The departure of Zlatan Ibrahimović enabled the strapping Uruguayan striker to step out of the Swede's shadows and return to his customary centre-forward role. He responded by scoring 49 times in all competitions, only missing out on a round half-century (in as many appearances) when, for once, he failed to find the net in the final of the Coupe de France. His 35 league goals enabled him to win the golden boot, and he also succeeded Ibrahimović as the official Ligue 1 player of the year.

Newcomer of the season

Kylian Mbappé
(AS Monaco FC)

The 'new Thierry Henry' was the inevitable label attached to Mbappé as the jet-heeled teenager soared to prominence both in Ligue 1 and the UEFA Champions League, playing a leading role in Monaco's French title triumph and run to the semi-finals of Europe's flagship club competition. A European Under-19 champion with France in July 2016, his first senior cap arrived eight months later at a time when he was firmly establishing himself as one of the game's most dazzling young prospects with a succession of glorious goalscoring displays for Monaco.

Team of the season

(4-3-3)

Coach: Jardim *(Monaco)*

FRANCE

NATIONAL TEAM

International honours
FIFA World Cup (1) 1998
UEFA European Championship (2) 1984, 2000
FIFA Confederations Cup (2) 2001, 2003

International tournament appearances
FIFA World Cup (13) 1930, 1938 (2nd round), 1954, 1958 (3rd), 1966, 1978, 1982 (4th), 1986 (3rd), 1998 (Winners), 2002, 2006 (runners-up), 2010, 2014 (qtr-finals)
UEFA European Championship (9) 1960 (4th), 1984 (Winners), 1992, 1996 (semi-finals), 2000 (Winners), 2004 (qtr-finals), 2008, 2012 (qtr-finals), 2016 (runners-up)

Top five all-time caps
Lilian Thuram (142); Thierry Henry (123); Marcel Desailly (116); Zinédine Zidane (108); Patrick Vieira (107)

Top five all-time goals
Thierry Henry (51); Michel Platini (41); David Trezeguet (34); Zinédine Zidane (31); Just Fontaine & Jean-Pierre Papin (30)

Results 2016/17

Date	Opponent	H/A	Venue	Result	Score	Scorers
01/09/16	Italy	A	Bari	W	3-1	*Martial (17), Giroud (28), Kurzawa (81)*
06/09/16	Belarus (WCQ)	A	Borisov	D	0-0	
07/10/16	Bulgaria (WCQ)	H	Saint-Denis	W	4-1	*Gameiro (23, 59), Payet (26), Griezmann (38)*
10/10/16	Netherlands (WCQ)	A	Amsterdam	W	1-0	*Pogba (30)*
11/11/16	Sweden (WCQ)	H	Saint-Denis	W	2-1	*Pogba (58), Payet (65)*
15/11/16	Ivory Coast	H	Lens	D	0-0	
25/03/17	Luxembourg (WCQ)	A	Luxembourg	W	3-1	*Giroud (28, 77), Griezmann (37p)*
28/03/17	Spain	H	Saint-Denis	L	0-2	
02/06/17	Paraguay	H	Rennes	W	5-0	*Giroud (9, 13, 69), Sissoko (76), Griezmann (77)*
09/06/17	Sweden (WCQ)	A	Solna	L	1-2	*Giroud (37)*
13/06/17	England	H	Saint-Denis	W	3-2	*Umtiti (22), Sidibé (43), Dembélé (78)*

Appearances 2016/17

Coach: Didier Deschamps	15/10/68		Ita	BLR	BUL	NED	SWE	Civ	LUX	Esp	Par	SWE	Eng	Caps	Goals
Steve Mandanda	28/03/88	Crystal Palace (ENG)	G	G										24	-
Djibril Sidibé	29/07/92	Monaco	D	D	s27	D	D	D69	D62		D	D	D90	10	1
Raphaël Varane	25/04/93	Real Madrid (ESP)	D	D	D	D	D	D46				D	D 47*	37	2
Laurent Koscielny	10/09/85	Arsenal (ENG)	D83	D	D	D	D	s46	D	D	D	D	s52	47	1
Layvin Kurzawa	04/09/92	Paris	D92	D	D	D				D				7	1
Paul Pogba	15/03/93	Man. United (ENG)	M	M	M	M	M	M46			M46	M	M	47	8
N'Golo Kanté	29/03/91	Chelsea (ENG)	M	M		s93	s88	M	M	M	s46		M	17	1
Blaise Matuidi	09/04/87	Paris	M63		M	M	M		M83		M	M		58	8
Antoine Griezmann	21/03/91	Atlético (ESP)	A63	M	M83	M93	M88		M	A	M80	M75		43	16
Olivier Giroud	30/09/86	Arsenal (ENG)	A46	A83			A	s63	A	s65	A73	A	A52	64	27
Anthony Martial	05/12/95	Man. United (ENG)	A46	M57		s67								15	1
André-Pierre Gignac	05/12/85	Tigres (MEX)	s46		s72	s79								36	7
Dimitri Payet	29/03/87	West Ham (ENG) /Marseille	s46	s57	M	M67	M	A	M78		M46	M76		35	8
Ousmane Dembélé	15/05/97	Dortmund (GER)	s63	s69				A46	M	s80	M46		M	7	1
Moussa Sissoko	16/08/89	Tottenham (ENG)	s63	M69	M	M	M	s46			s46	M		52	2
Samuel Umtiti	14/11/93	Barcelona (ESP)	s83						D	D	D		D	8	1
Lucas Digne	20/07/93	Barcelona (ESP)	s92					D			s67		s21	17	-
Kevin Gameiro	09/05/87	Atlético (ESP)		s83	A72	A79		A63		A80				13	3
Hugo Lloris	26/12/86	Tottenham (ENG)			G	G	G		G	G	G	G	G	90	-
Bacary Sagna	14/02/83	Man City (ENG)			D27									65	-
Nabil Fekir	18/07/93	Lyon			s83			s46						7	1
Patrice Evra	15/05/81	Juventus (ITA)					D							81	-
Benoît Costil	03/07/87	Rennes						G						1	-
Adil Rami	27/12/85	Sevilla (ESP)						D						33	1
Adrien Rabiot	03/04/95	Paris						M78	s83	M46				3	-
Sébastien Corchia	01/11/90	LOSC						s69						1	-
Thomas Lemar	12/11/95	Monaco						s78		s80	s46	s76	M	5	-
Benjamin Mendy	17/07/94	Monaco							D		D67	D	D21	4	-
Christophe Jallet	31/10/83	Lyon							s62	D			s90	14	1
Kylian Mbappé	20/12/98	Monaco							s78	A65		s75	A	4	-
Corentin Tolisso	03/08/94	Lyon								M80				1	-
Tiémoué Bakayoko	17/08/94	Monaco								s46				1	-
Alexandre Lacazette	28/05/91	Lyon									s73			11	1
Florian Thauvin	26/01/93	Marseille									s80			1	-

EUROPE

Paris Saint-Germain

Group A
Match 1 - Arsenal FC (ENG)
H 1-1 *Cavani (1)*
Areola, Thiago Silva, Krychowiak (Pastore 79), Marquinhos, Verratti, Cavani, Di María, Matuidi, Maxwell, Aurier (Meunier 84), Rabiot (Thiago Motta 73). Coach: Unai Emery (ESP)
Red card: Verratti 90+4
Match 2 - PFC Ludogorets Razgrad (BUL)
A 3-1 *Matuidi (41), Cavani (56, 60)*
Areola, Thiago Silva, Marquinhos, Verratti (Krychowiak 80), Lucas, Thiago Motta, Cavani (Augustin 90+1), Di María (Ikoné 88), Matuidi, Maxwell, Aurier. Coach: Unai Emery (ESP)
Match 3 - FC Basel 1893 (SUI)
H 3-0 *Di María (40), Lucas (62), Cavani (90+3p)*
Areola, Thiago Silva, Marquinhos, Verratti, Lucas (Ben Arfa 81), Cavani, Di María (Jesé 86), Matuidi (Krychowiak 83), Aurier, Kurzawa, Rabiot. Coach: Unai Emery (ESP)
Match 4 - FC Basel 1893 (SUI)
A 2-1 *Matuidi (43), Meunier (90)*
Areola, Thiago Silva (Krychowiak 46), Marquinhos, Verratti, Lucas (Jesé 83), Thiago Motta, Cavani, Di María, Meunier, Matuidi (Rabiot 77), Kurzawa. Coach: Unai Emery (ESP)
Match 5 - Arsenal FC (ENG)
A 2-2 *Cavani (18), Iwobi (77og)*
Areola, Thiago Silva, Krychowiak (Ben Arfa 67), Marquinhos, Verratti, Lucas (Jesé 89), Thiago Motta, Cavani, Meunier, Matuidi, Maxwell. Coach: Unai Emery (ESP)
Match 6 - PFC Ludogorets Razgrad (BUL)
H 2-2 *Cavani (61), Di María (90+2)*
Areola, Thiago Silva, Marquinhos, Lucas (Jesé 85), Thiago Motta, Cavani, Di María, Meunier (Aurier 88), Matuidi, Maxwell (Kurzawa 80), Ben Arfa. Coach: Unai Emery (ESP)

Round of 16 - FC Barcelona (ESP)
H 4-0 *Di María (18, 55), Draxler (40), Cavani (72)*
Trapp, Kimpembe, Marquinhos, Verratti (Nkunku 69), Cavani, Di María (Lucas 61), Meunier, Matuidi, Kurzawa, Draxler (Pastore 86), Rabiot. Coach: Unai Emery (ESP)
A 1-6 *Cavani (62)*
Trapp, Thiago Silva, Marquinhos, Verratti, Lucas (Di María 55), Cavani, Meunier (Krychowiak 90+3), Matuidi, Kurzawa, Draxler (Aurier 75), Rabiot. Coach: Unai Emery (ESP)

Olympique Lyonnais

Group H
Match 1 - GNK Dinamo Zagreb (CRO)
H 3-0 *Tolisso (13), Ferri (49), Cornet (57)*
Anthony Lopes, Yanga-Mbiwa, N'Koulou, Tolisso (Ghezzal 78), Ferri, Darder, Morel, Rafael, Gonalons (Tousart 32), Cornet (Kalulu 72), Rybus. Coach: Bruno Génésio (FRA)
Match 2 - Sevilla FC (ESP)
A 0-1
Anthony Lopes, Yanga-Mbiwa (Valbuena 70), N'Koulou, Tolisso, Darder, Morel, Fekir (Kalulu 70), Gonalons, Gaspar (Ghezzal 79), Cornet, Rybus. Coach: Bruno Génésio (FRA)
Match 3 - Juventus (ITA)
H 0-1
Anthony Lopes, Yanga-Mbiwa (Ghezzal 82), N'Koulou, Diakhaby, Tolisso, Lacazette (Cornet 72), Darder (Ferri 64), Morel, Fekir, Rafael, Gonalons. Coach: Bruno Génésio (FRA)
Match 4 - Juventus (ITA)
A 1-1 *Tolisso (85)*
Anthony Lopes, Mammana, Diakhaby, Tolisso, Lacazette, Ghezzal, Morel, Fekir (Darder 77), Rafael, Gonalons, Rybus (Cornet 70). Coach: Bruno Génésio (FRA)
Match 5 - GNK Dinamo Zagreb (CRO)
A 1-0 *Lacazette (72)*
Anthony Lopes, Yanga-Mbiwa, N'Koulou, Lacazette, Ferri, Darder (Tolisso 66), Morel, Rafael, Gonalons, Cornet (Fekir 66), Valbuena (Rybus 88). Coach: Bruno Génésio (FRA)
Match 6 - Sevilla FC (ESP)
H 0-0
Anthony Lopes, Yanga-Mbiwa, Diakhaby, Tolisso (Grenier 78), Lacazette, Ghezzal (Fekir 65), Darder (Cornet 72), Morel, Rafael, Gonalons, Valbuena. Coach: Bruno Génésio (FRA)

Round of 32 - AZ Alkmaar (NED)
A 4-1 *Tousart (26), Lacazette (45+2, 57), Ferri (90+5)*
Anthony Lopes, Mammana, Diakhaby, Tolisso, Lacazette (Cornet 65), Jallet, Darder (Aouar 84), Fekir, Gonalons, Tousart (Ferri 67), Rybus. Coach: Bruno Génésio (FRA)
H 7-1 *Fekir (5, 27, 78), Cornet (17), Darder (34), Aouar (87), Diakhaby (89)*
Anthony Lopes, Yanga-Mbiwa, Diakhaby, Ghezzal (Lacazette 77), Ferri, Jallet, Darder, Fekir, Rafael, Cornet (Aouar 63), Tousart (Tolisso 81). Coach: Bruno Génésio (FRA)

Round of 16 - AS Roma (ITA)
H 4-2 *Diakhaby (8), Tolisso (47), Fekir (74), Lacazette (90+2)*
Anthony Lopes, Mammana (Fekir 71), Diakhaby, Tolisso, Lacazette, Ghezzal (Cornet 75), Morel, Rafael (Jallet 46), Gonalons, Valbuena, Tousart. Coach: Bruno Génésio (FRA)
A 1-2 *Diakhaby (16)*
Anthony Lopes, Mammana (Yanga-Mbiwa 78), Diakhaby, Tolisso, Lacazette (Fekir 84), Jallet, Morel, Gonalons, Cornet, Valbuena (Rafael 90+1), Tousart. Coach: Bruno Génésio (FRA)

Quarter-finals - Beşiktaş JK (TUR)
H 2-1 *Tolisso (83), Morel (85)*
Anthony Lopes, Mammana, Diakhaby, Tolisso, Lacazette, Ghezzal (Cornet 52), Morel, Fekir, Rafael (Jallet 52), Valbuena, Tousart. Coach: Bruno Génésio (FRA)
A 1-2 (aet; 7-6 on pens) *Lacazette (34)*
Anthony Lopes, N'Koulou, Diakhaby, Tolisso, Lacazette (Ghezzal 91), Jallet, Morel (Rybus 120+1), Gonalons, Cornet (Fekir 77), Valbuena, Tousart. Coach: Bruno Génésio (FRA)

Semi-finals - AFC Ajax (NED)
A 1-4 *Valbuena (66)*
Anthony Lopes, N'Koulou, Diakhaby, Tolisso, Jallet (Rafael 69), Morel, Fekir, Gonalons, Cornet (Lacazette 76), Valbuena, Tousart (Ghezzal 58). Coach: Bruno Génésio (FRA)
H 3-1 *Lacazette (45p, 45+1), Ghezzal (81)*
Anthony Lopes, N'Koulou, Diakhaby, Tolisso, Lacazette, Morel (Rybus 75), Fekir, Rafael, Gonalons, Cornet, Valbuena (Ghezzal 77). Coach: Bruno Génésio (FRA)

AS Monaco FC

Third qualifying round - Fenerbahçe SK (TUR)
A 1-2 *Falcao (42)*
De Sanctis (Badiashile 13), Fabinho, Jemerson, Dirar (Bernardo Silva 76), Falcao, Bakayoko, Germain (Ivan Cavaleiro 86), Sidibé, Mendy, Raggi, Lemar. Coach: Leonardo Jardim (POR)
H 3-1 *Germain (2, 65), Falcao (18p)*
Subašić, Fabinho, Jemerson, Dirar, Falcao (Carrillo 44), Bakayoko, Germain (Glik 90+2), Sidibé, Mendy, Raggi, Lemar (Bernardo Silva 81). Coach: Leonardo Jardim (POR)

Play-offs - Villarreal CF (ESP)
A 2-1 *Fabinho (3p), Bernardo Silva (72)*
Subašić, Fabinho, Jemerson, Dirar, Bernardo Silva (João Moutinho 81), Bakayoko, Germain (Carrillo 69), Mendy, Raggi, Glik, Lemar. Coach: Leonardo Jardim (POR)
Red card: Mendy 86
H 1-0 *Fabinho (90+1p)*
Subašić, Fabinho, Jemerson, Dirar, Bernardo Silva, Bakayoko, Germain (Carrillo 81), Sidibé, Raggi, Glik, Lemar (João Moutinho 68). Coach: Leonardo Jardim (POR)

Group E
Match 1 - Tottenham Hotspur FC (ENG)
A 2-1 *Bernardo Silva (15), Lemar (31)*
Subašić, Fabinho, Jemerson, Dirar (Lemar 5), João Moutinho, Falcao (Germain 81), Bernardo Silva, Bakayoko, Sidibé, Raggi, Glik. Coach: Leonardo Jardim (POR)
Match 2 - Bayer 04 Leverkusen (GER)
H 1-1 *Glik (90+4)*
Subašić, Fabinho, Jemerson, João Moutinho, Bernardo Silva (Boschilia 81), Bakayoko (Mbappé 77), Germain (Carrillo 73), Sidibé, Raggi, Glik, Lemar. Coach: Leonardo Jardim (POR)
Match 3 - PFC CSKA Moskva (RUS)
A 1-1 *Bernardo Silva (87)*
Subašić, Fabinho, Jemerson, João Moutinho (Carrillo 41), Bernardo Silva, Bakayoko (Mbappé 83), Germain, Sidibé, Raggi (Mendy 69), Glik, Lemar. Coach: Leonardo Jardim (POR)
Match 4 - PFC CSKA Moskva (RUS)
H 3-0 *Germain (13), Falcao (29, 41)*
Subašić, Fabinho, Jemerson (Raggi 89), Falcao (Carrillo 74), Bernardo Silva, Bakayoko, Germain (Mbappé 85), Sidibé, Mendy, Glik, Lemar. Coach: Leonardo Jardim (POR)
Match 5 - Tottenham Hotspur FC (ENG)
H 2-1 *Sidibé (48), Lemar (53)*
Subašić, Fabinho, Jemerson, Falcao (Raggi 89), Bernardo Silva, Bakayoko, Germain (Carrillo 77), Sidibé, Mendy, Glik, Lemar (João Moutinho 81). Coach: Leonardo Jardim (POR)

Match 6 - Bayer 04 Leverkusen (GER)
A 0-3
De Sanctis, Jemerson, Dirar, João Moutinho, Carrillo (Lemar 79), Raggi, Boschilia (Traoré 67), Jean (Germain 76), Diallo, N'Doram, Touré. Coach: Leonardo Jardim (POR)

Round of 16 - Manchester City FC (ENG)
A 3-5 *Falcao (32, 61), Mbappé (40)*
Subašić, Fabinho, Falcao, Bernardo Silva (João Moutinho 84), Bakayoko (Dirar 88), Sidibé, Mendy, Raggi, Glik, Lemar, Mbappé (Germain 79). Coach: Leonardo Jardim (POR)
H 3-1 *Mbappé (8), Fabinho (29), Bakayoko (77)*
Subašić, Fabinho, Jemerson, Bernardo Silva, Bakayoko, Germain (Dirar 90+1), Sidibé, Mendy, Raggi (Touré 70), Lemar, Mbappé (João Moutinho 81). Coach: Leonardo Jardim (POR)

Quarter-finals - Borussia Dortmund (GER)
A 3-2 *Mbappé (19, 79), Bender (35og)*
Subašić, Fabinho, Jemerson, João Moutinho, Falcao (Germain 85), Bernardo Silva (Dirar 66), Raggi, Glik, Lemar, Mbappé, Touré. Coach: Leonardo Jardim (POR)
H 3-1 *Mbappé (3), Falcao (17), Germain (81)*
Subašić, Jemerson, João Moutinho, Falcao (Dirar 67), Bernardo Silva (Raggi 90), Bakayoko, Mendy, Glik, Lemar, Mbappé (Germain 81), Touré. Coach: Leonardo Jardim (POR)

Semi-finals - Juventus (ITA)
H 0-2
Subašić, Fabinho, Jemerson, Dirar, Falcao, Bernardo Silva (Touré 82), Bakayoko (João Moutinho 66), Sidibé, Glik, Lemar (Germain 67), Mbappé. Coach: Leonardo Jardim (POR)
A 1-2 *Mbappé (69)*
Subašić, Jemerson, João Moutinho, Falcao, Bernardo Silva (Lemar 69), Bakayoko (Germain 78), Sidibé, Mendy (Fabinho 54), Raggi, Glik, Mbappé. Coach: Leonardo Jardim (POR)

OGC Nice

EUROPA LEAGUE

Group I
Match 1 - FC Schalke 04 (GER)
H 0-1
Cardinale, Baysse, Seri, Balotelli, Pléa, Ricardo, Cyprien, Koziello (Bodmer 67), Dalbert (Belhanda 81), Dante, Sarr. Coach: Lucien Favre (SUI)
Match 2 - FC Krasnodar (RUS)
A 2-5 *Balotelli (43), Cyprien (71)*
Cardinale, Baysse, Belhanda, Seri, Balotelli (Pléa 46), Eysseric, Ricardo, Koziello (Walter 79), Dalbert (Cyprien 66), Dante, Sarr. Coach: Lucien Favre (SUI)
Match 3 - FC Salzburg (AUT)
A 1-0 *Pléa (13)*
Cardinale, Baysse, Eysseric, Pléa, Walter, Ricardo, Bodmer (Seri 73), Koziello (Cyprien 74), Dalbert (Belhanda 76), Dante, Sarr. Coach: Lucien Favre (SUI)
Match 4 - FC Salzburg (AUT)
H 0-2
Cardinale, Souquet, Belhanda, Seri (Walter 76), Balotelli, Pléa (Eysseric 71), Ricardo, Cyprien (Donis 78), Koziello, Dante, Sarr. Coach: Lucien Favre (SUI)

Match 5 - FC Schalke 04 (GER)
A 0-2
Cardinale, Souquet, Belhanda (Eysseric 65), Walter (Marcel 69), Ricardo (Pléa 66), Donis, Bodmer, Koziello, Boscagli, Dalbert, Dante. Coach: Lucien Favre (SUI)
Match 6 - FC Krasnodar (RUS)
H 2-1 *Bosetti (64p), Le Marchand (77)*
Benítez, Souquet (Rafetraniaina 74), Lusamba, Balotelli (Bosetti 46), Le Marchand, Donis (Mahou 68), Bodmer, Boscagli, Marcel, Burner, Perraud. Coach: Lucien Favre (SUI)

LOSC Lille

EUROPA LEAGUE

Third qualifying round – Qäbälä FK (AZE)
H 1-1 *Ryan Mendes (47)*
Enyeama, Corchia, Civelli, Obbadi (Benzia 27), Amalfitano, Bauthéac, Palmieri, Rony Lopes, Ryan Mendes (Bissouma 76), Mavuba (Amadou 62), Baša. Coach: Frédéric Antonetti (FRA)
A 0-1
Enyeama, Corchia, Civelli, Amadou, Obbadi (Sankharé 64), Amalfitano (Benzia 73), Bauthéac (Ryan Mendes 64), Palmieri, Rony Lopes, Éder, Soumaoro. Coach: Frédéric Antonetti (FRA)

AS Saint-Étienne

EUROPA LEAGUE

Third qualifying round - AEK Athens FC (GRE)
H 0-0
Ruffier, Théophile-Catherine, Polomat, Pajot (Dabo 69), Roux, Tannane (Berič 64), Selnæs, Lemoine, Pogba, Hamouma (Monnet-Paquet 86), Perrin. Coach: Christophe Galtier (FRA)
A 1-0 *Berič (23)*
Ruffier, Théophile-Catherine, Polomat, Dabo (Pajot 30), Tannane, Selnæs, Lemoine (Monnet-Paquet 79), Pogba, Hamouma (Roux 84), Perrin, Berič. Coach: Christophe Galtier (FRA)

Play-offs - Beitar Jerusalem FC (ISR)
A 2-1 *Lemoine (15), Rueda (30og)*
Ruffier, Théophile-Catherine, Polomat, Pajot, Selnæs, Lemoine, Pogba, Hamouma (Roux 46), Monnet-Paquet, Perrin, Berič (Tannane 78). Coach: Christophe Galtier (FRA)
H 0-0
Ruffier, Théophile-Catherine, Roux (Pajot 86), Selnæs, Lemoine, Pogba, Monnet-Paquet (Tannane 53), Perrin, Malcuit, Berič, Saint-Louis (Moulin 45). Coach: Christophe Galtier (FRA)
Red card: Ruffier 44

Group C
Match 1 - 1. FSV Mainz 05 (GER)
A 1-1 *Berič (88)*
Moulin, Théophile-Catherine, Dabo (Tannane 57), Saivet (Søderlund 80), Selnæs, Lemoine (Veretout 67), Pogba, Hamouma, Perrin, Malcuit, Berič. Coach: Christophe Galtier (FRA)
Match 2 - RSC Anderlecht (BEL)
H 1-1 *Roux (90+4)*
Moulin, Lacroix, Pajot (Søderlund 76), Clément (Corgnet 86), Dabo (Tannane 77), Roux, Veretout, Hamouma, Monnet-Paquet, Malcuit, Karamoko. Coach: Christophe Galtier (FRA)
Match 3 - Gabala SC (AZE)
H 1-0 *Ricardinho (70og)*
Moulin, Théophile-Catherine, Roux, Tannane (Berič 62), Saivet (Pajot 90+2), M'Bengue, Veretout, Selnæs, Pogba, Monnet-Paquet, Perrin. Coach: René Lobello (FRA)
Match 4 - Gabala SC (AZE)
A 2-1 *Tannane (45+1), Berič (53)*
Ruffier, Tannane (Roux 84), Saivet (Pajot 74), M'Bengue, Veretout, Selnæs, Pogba, Monnet-Paquet, Perrin, Malcuit, Berič (Søderlund 62). Coach: Christophe Galtier (FRA)
Match 5 - 1. FSV Mainz 05 (GER)
H 0-0
Ruffier, Théophile-Catherine, Polomat, Roux (Pajot 83), Tannane, Saivet, Veretout (Lacroix 90+2), Selnæs, Pogba, Monnet-Paquet (Nordin 59), Perrin. Coach: Christophe Galtier (FRA)
Match 6 - RSC Anderlecht (BEL)
A 3-2 *Søderlund (62, 67), Monnet-Paquet (74)*
Ruffier, Théophile-Catherine, Polomat, Lacroix, Dabo, Saivet (Pajot 63), Pogba, Monnet-Paquet, Søderlund (Tannane 76), Malcuit, Nordin (Hamouma 63). Coach: Christophe Galtier (FRA)

Round of 32 - Manchester United FC (ENG)
A 0-3
Ruffier, Théophile-Catherine, Pajot (Selnæs 72), Saivet, Veretout, Pogba (Berič 79), Hamouma, Monnet-Paquet, Perrin, Malcuit, Jorginho (Roux 65). Coach: Christophe Galtier (FRA)
H 0-1
Ruffier, Théophile-Catherine, Pajot, Saivet (Jorginho 53), Veretout (Lemoine 68), Pogba, Hamouma, Monnet-Paquet, Perrin, Malcuit, Berič (Roux 59). Coach: Christophe Galtier (FRA)

DOMESTIC LEAGUE CLUB-BY-CLUB

Angers SCO

1919 • Stade Jean Bouin (15,603) • angers-sco.fr

Coach: Stéphane Moulin

2016

13/08 a Montpellier L 0-1
20/08 h Nice L 0-1
27/08 a Metz L 0-2
10/09 h Dijon W 3-1 *Diedhiou, N'Doye, Toko Ekambi*
17/09 a Bordeaux W 1-0 *Toko Ekambi*
21/09 h Caen W 2-1 *Ketkeophomphone, og (Da Silva)*
24/09 a Monaco L 1-2 *Diedhiou*
02/10 h Marseille D 1-1 *Capelle*
15/10 a Bastia W 2-1 *Diedhiou 2*
22/10 h Toulouse D 0-0
29/10 a Guingamp L 0-1
05/11 h LOSC W 1-0 *Diedhiou*
19/11 a Rennes D 1-1 *Pépé*
27/11 h St-Étienne L 1-2 *Pépé*
30/11 a Paris L 0-2
03/12 h Lorient D 2-2 *Diedhiou (p), N'Doye*
10/12 a Nancy L 0-2
16/12 h Nantes L 0-2
21/12 a Lyon L 0-2

2017

14/01 h Bordeaux D 1-1 *Traoré*
22/01 a St-Étienne L 1-2 *Pavlović*
28/01 h Metz W 2-1 *Tait, Pépé*
05/02 a Toulouse L 0-4
08/02 h Rennes D 0-0
11/02 a LOSC W 2-1 *Capelle, Thomas*
18/02 h Nancy W 1-0 *J Bamba*
25/02 h Bastia W 3-0 *Toko Ekambi 2, Bourillon*
04/03 a Caen W 3-2 *Toko Ekambi, N'Doye, Mangani (p)*
10/03 a Marseille L 0-3
18/03 h Guingamp W 3-0 *J Bamba, Mangani, Diedhiou*
02/04 a Nantes L 1-2 *Diedhiou*
08/04 h Monaco L 0-1
14/04 h Paris L 0-2
22/04 a Dijon L 2-3 *Mangani (p), Toko Ekambi*
28/04 h Lyon L 1-2 *N'Doye*
06/05 a Lorient D 1-1 *Manceau*
14/05 a Nice W 2-0 *N'Doye, Toko Ekambi*
20/05 h Montpellier W 2-0 *J Bamba, Tait*

No	Name	Nat	DoB	Pos	Aps	(s)	Gls
3	Yoann Andreu		03/05/89	D	16		
25	Abdoulaye Bamba	CIV	25/04/90	D	7	(1)	
22	Jonathan Bamba		26/03/96	A	9	(7)	3
2	Kévin Bérigaud		09/05/88	A	4	(9)	
6	Grégory Bourillon		01/07/84	D	4	(1)	1
15	Pierrick Capelle		15/04/87	M	20	(12)	2
28	Issa Cissokho	SEN	23/02/85	D	13		
9	Famara Diedhiou	SEN	15/12/92	A	28	(3)	8
27	Férébory Doré	CGO	21/01/89	A	1	(9)	
14	Billy Ketkeophomphone		24/03/90	A	4	(1)	1
30	Alexandre Letellier		11/12/90	G	6		
29	Vincent Manceau		10/07/89	D	32	(1)	1
5	Thomas Mangani		29/04/87	M	33	(1)	3
21	Pablo Martinez		21/02/89	D	6	(3)	
16	Mathieu Michel		04/09/91	G	23		
17	Cheikh N'Doye	SEN	29/03/86	M	32	(1)	5
11	Dickson Nwakaeme	NGA	21/04/86	A		(6)	
4	Mateo Pavlović	CRO	09/06/90	D	9	(3)	1
18	Nicolas Pépé		29/09/95	M	11	(22)	3
1	Denis Petrič	SVN	24/05/88	G	9		
23	Jamel Saihi	TUN	27/01/87	M	3	(2)	
18	Baptiste Santamaria		09/03/95	M	35	(3)	
10	Gilles Sunu		30/03/91	A	8	(14)	
26	Mehdi Tahrat	ALG	24/01/90	M	3	(4)	
20	Flavien Tait		02/02/93	M	5	(6)	2
24	Romain Thomas		12/06/88	D	36		1
7	Karl Toko Ekambi	CMR	14/09/90	M	29	(2)	7
8	Ismaël Traoré	CIV	18/08/86	D	32		1
12	Yoane Wissa		03/09/96	A		(2)	

SC Bastia

1905 • Armand-Cesari (16,078) • sc-bastia.corsica

Major honours
French Cup (1) 1981

Coach: François Ciccolini; (27/02/17) Rui Almeida (POR)

2016

12/08 h Paris L 0-1
20/08 a Lorient W 3-0 *Saint-Maximin, Crivelli 2*
27/08 a Caen L 0-2
10/09 h Toulouse W 2-1 *Diallo, Bengtsson*
18/09 a St-Étienne L 0-1
21/09 h Nancy D 0-0
24/09 h Guingamp W 1-0 *Crivelli*
01/10 a Nantes L 0-1
15/10 h Angers L 1-2 *Bifouma*
22/10 a LOSC L 1-2 *Diallo*
29/10 h Dijon D 0-0
05/11 a Lyon L 1-2 *Crivelli*
19/11 h Montpellier D 1-1 *og (Skhiri)*
27/11 a Nice D 1-1 *Crivelli*
30/11 h Bordeaux D 1-1 *Bifouma*
03/12 a Monaco L 0-5
10/12 h Metz W 2-0 *Danic, Saint-Maximin*
17/12 a Rennes W 2-1 *Crivelli, Danic*
21/12 h Marseille L 1-2 *Djiku*

2017

14/01 a Nancy L 0-1
20/01 h Nice D 1-1 *Oniangué*
28/01 h Caen D 1-1 *Saint-Maximin*
04/02 a Montpellier L 1-2 *Crivelli*
11/02 a Toulouse L 1-4 *Oniangué*
17/02 h Monaco D 1-1 *Diallo*
25/02 a Angers L 0-3
01/03 h Nantes D 2-2 *Danic, Oniangué*
04/03 h St-Étienne D 0-0
11/03 a Guingamp L 0-5
17/03 a Metz L 0-1
01/04 h LOSC L 0-1
08/04 a Dijon W 2-1 *Crivelli, Cahuzac*
16/04 h Lyon L 0-0 *(w/o; original match abandoned at halftime, awarded as goalless defeat)*
22/04 a Bordeaux L 0-2
29/04 h Rennes W 1-0 *Crivelli*
06/05 a Paris L 0-5
14/05 h Lorient W 2-0 *Crivelli, Danic*
20/05 a Marseille L 0-1

No	Name	Nat	DoB	Pos	Aps	(s)	Gls
33	Geoffrey Acheampong	GHA	28/01/97	M		(2)	
20	Pierre Bengtsson	SWE	12/04/88	D	29	(1)	1
13	Thievy Bifouma	CGO	13/05/92	A	9	(5)	2
22	Farid Boulaya		25/02/93	M	1	(1)	
7	Jerson Cabral	NED	03/01/91	A		(6)	
14	Yannick Cahuzac		18/01/85	M	29		1
30	Paul Charruau		12/07/93	G		(1)	
29	Gilles Cioni		14/06/84	D	23	(2)	
25	Lassana Coulibaly	MLI	10/04/96	M	25	(5)	
27	Enzo Crivelli		06/02/95	A	24		10
8	Gaël Danic		19/11/81	M	19	(10)	4
2	Sadio Diallo	GUI	28/12/90	M	20	(8)	3
23	Alexander Djiku		09/08/94	D	21	(2)	1
4	Abdelhamid El Kaoutari	MAR	17/03/90	D	16	(2)	
13	Abdoulaye Keita	MLI	05/01/94	D	14	(7)	
16	Jean-Louis Leca		21/09/85	G	34		
28	Florian Marange		03/03/86	D	16	(3)	
18	Mehdi Mostefa	ALG	30/08/83	M	26	(5)	
11	Lenny Nangis		24/03/94	A	12	(18)	
19	Axel Ngando		13/07/93	M	10	(10)	
15	Prince Oniangué	CGO	04/11/88	M	13	(1)	3
17	Mathieu Peybernes		21/10/90	D	19		
9	Florian Raspentino		06/06/89	A	3	(6)	
17	Lindsay Rose		08/02/92	D	7	(2)	
6	Allan Saint-Maximin		12/03/97	A	30	(4)	3
3	Nicolas Saint-Ruf		24/10/92	D	4	(1)	
5	Sébastien Squillaci		11/08/80	D	10		
30	Alexis Thébaux		17/03/85	G	1		
30	Thomas Vincensini		12/09/93	G	3		

FC Girondins de Bordeaux

1881 • Matmut Atlantique (41,908) • girondins.com

Major honours
French League (6) 1950, 1984, 1985, 1987, 1999, 2009; French Cup (4) 1941, 1986, 1987, 2013; League Cup (3) 2002, 2007, 2009

Coach: Jocelyn Gourvennec

2016

13/08 h St-Étienne W 3-2 *Laborde, Rolán, Malcom*
20/08 a Toulouse L 1-4 *Kiese Thelin*
28/08 h Nantes W 1-0 *Rolán*
10/09 a Lyon W 3-1 *Malcom, Sertic, Ménez*
17/09 h Angers L 0-1
21/09 a Metz W 3-0 *Malcom, Laborde, Kiese Thelin (p)*
24/09 h Caen D 0-0
01/10 a Paris L 0-2
16/10 a Rennes D 1-1 *Pallois*
22/10 h Nancy D 1-1 *Ménez*
30/10 a Marseille D 0-0
05/11 h Lorient W 2-1 *Kamano, Rolán*
20/11 a Guingamp D 1-1 *Lewczuk*
26/11 h Dijon W 3-2 *Rolán, Kamano 2*
30/11 a Bastia D 1-1 *Laborde*
03/12 h LOSC L 0-1
10/12 h Monaco L 0-4
17/12 a Montpellier L 0-4
21/12 h Nice D 0-0

2017

14/01 a Angers D 1-1 *og (Santamaria)*
21/01 h Toulouse W 1-0 *Vada*
28/01 a Nancy W 2-0 *og (Cuffaut), Malcom*
04/02 h Rennes D 1-1 *Ménez*
07/02 a Caen W 4-0 *Rolán, Kamano 2, Plašil*
10/02 h Paris L 0-3
19/02 h Guingamp W 3-0 *Kamano, Pallois, Laborde*
25/02 a LOSC W 3-2 *Vada, Ounas 2*
03/03 h Lyon D 1-1 *Vada*
11/03 a Monaco L 1-2 *Rolán*
18/03 h Montpellier W 5-1 *Rolán 2, Sankharé, Vada (p), Malcom*
02/04 a Nice L 1-2 *Laborde*
08/04 h Metz W 3-0 *Malcom, Vada 2 (1p)*
16/04 a Nantes W 1-0 *Sankharé*
22/04 h Bastia W 2-0 *Malcom, Sankharé*
30/04 a Dijon D 0-0
05/05 a St-Étienne D 2-2 *Ounas (p), Laborde*
14/05 h Marseille D 1-1 *Rolán*
20/05 a Lorient D 1-1 *Sankharé*

No	Name	Nat	DoB	Pos	Aps	(s)	Gls
10	Mauro Arambarri	URU	30/09/95	M		(4)	
16	Cédric Carrasso		30/12/81	G	24		
3	Diego Contento	GER	01/05/90	D	24	(1)	
2	Milan Gajić	SRB	28/01/96	D	11	(3)	
26	Frédéric Guilbert		24/12/94	D	2	(1)	
4	Vukašin Jovanović	SRB	17/05/96	D	8		
11	François Kamano	GUI	01/05/96	A	17	(13)	6
12	Isaac Kiese Thelin	SWE	24/06/92	A	2	(5)	2
20	Gaëtan Laborde		03/05/94	A	21	(15)	6
6	Igor Lewczuk	POL	30/05/85	D	25		1
25	Malcom	BRA	26/02/97	M	33	(4)	7
7	Jérémy Ménez		07/05/87	A	17	(9)	3
22	Adam Ounas		11/11/96	M	11	(15)	3
5	Nicolas Pallois		19/09/87	D	31		2
21	Théo Pellenard		04/03/94	D	5	(1)	
18	Jaroslav Plašil	CZE	05/01/82	M	26	(11)	1
29	Maxime Poundjé		16/08/92	D	7		
30	Jérôme Prior		08/08/95	G	14		
9	Diego Rolán	URU	24/03/93	A	19	(10)	9
20	Youssouf Sabaly		05/03/93	D	30		
13	Younousse Sankharé	SEN	10/09/89	M	15	(1)	4
8	Grégory Sertic		05/08/89	M	15	(2)	1
14	Jérémy Toulalan		10/09/83	M	30		
13	Thomas Touré	CIV	27/12/93	M	5	(1)	
7	Abdou Traoré	MLI	17/01/88	M		(6)	
23	Valentin Vada	ARG	06/03/96	M	25	(3)	6
33	Zaydou Youssouf		11/07/99	M	1	(1)	

FRANCE

SM Caen

1913 • Michel d'Ornano (21,068) • smcaen.fr

Coach: Patrice Garande

2016

13/08	h	Lorient	W	3-2	*Rodelin, Santini 2*
19/08	a	Lyon	L	0-2	
27/08	h	Bastia	W	2-0	*Féret, Bazile*
11/09	a	Rennes	L	0-2	
16/09	h	Paris	L	0-6	
21/09	a	Angers	L	1-2	*Karamoh*
24/09	a	Bordeaux	D	0-0	
01/10	h	Toulouse	W	1-0	*Santini (p)*
15/10	a	Montpellier	L	2-3	*Yahia, Santini*
23/10	h	St-Étienne	L	0-2	
29/10	a	Nancy	L	0-2	
06/11	h	Nice	W	1-0	*Santini (p)*
20/11	a	Marseille	L	0-1	
26/11	h	Guingamp	D	1-1	*Rodelin*
29/11	a	LOSC	L	2-4	*Féret, Rodelin*
02/12	h	Dijon	D	3-3	*Santini 2, Karamoh*
18/12	h	Metz	W	3-0	*Karamoh, Santini, Sané*
21/12	a	Monaco	L	1-2	*Bazile*

2017

15/01	h	Lyon	W	3-2	*og (Cornet), Santini 2 (1p)*
18/01	a	Nantes	L	0-1	
28/01	a	Bastia	D	1-1	*Rodelin (p)*
04/02	a	Guingamp	W	1-0	*Karamoh*
07/02	h	Bordeaux	L	0-4	
11/02	a	Dijon	L	0-2	
18/02	h	LOSC	L	0-1	
21/02	h	Nancy	W	1-0	*Rodelin*
26/02	a	St-Étienne	W	1-0	*Rodelin*
04/03	h	Angers	L	2-3	*Rodelin, Santini*
10/03	a	Nice	D	2-2	*Santini, Karamoh*
19/03	h	Monaco	L	0-3	
02/04	a	Lorient	L	0-1	
08/04	h	Montpellier	L	0-2	
15/04	a	Metz	D	2-2	*Santini, Rodelin*
22/04	h	Nantes	L	0-2	
30/04	h	Marseille	L	1-5	*Santini*
06/05	a	Toulouse	W	1-0	*Santini*
14/05	h	Rennes	L	0-1	
20/05	a	Paris	D	1-1	*Rodelin*

No	Name	Nat	DoB	Pos	Aps	(s)	Gls
18	Jordan Adéoti	BEN	12/03/89	D	23	(4)	
20	Hervé Bazile	HAI	18/03/90	A	7	(12)	2
13	Syam Ben Youssef	TUN	31/03/89	D	14	(3)	
11	Vincent Bessat		08/11/85	D	31	(6)	
28	Damien Da Silva		17/05/88	D	36		
23	Mouhamadou Dabo		28/11/86	D	2		
6	Jonathan Delaplace		20/03/86	M	31	(2)	
4	Ismaël Diomandé	CIV	28/08/92	M	7	(5)	
40	Mathieu Dreyer		20/03/89	G	2		
25	Julien Féret		05/07/82	M	35		2
29	Romain Genevois	HAI	28/10/87	D	10	(3)	
24	Frédéric Guilbert		24/12/94	D	23		
15	Emmanuel Imorou	BEN	16/09/88	D	8	(1)	
7	Yann Karamoh		08/07/98	M	25	(10)	5
19	Jordan Leborgne		29/09/95	D	2	(4)	
14	Jeff Louis	HAI	08/08/92	M	3	(2)	
17	Jean-Victor Makengo		12/06/98	M	9	(8)	
10	Steed Malbranque		06/01/80	M	3	(10)	
32	Exaucé N'Gassaki N'Dongo	CGO	30/01/97	A		(1)	
30	Pascal Reulet		14/01/94	G	2	(1)	
12	Ronny Rodelin		18/11/89	M	31	(6)	9
22	Pape Sané	SEN	30/12/91	A	3	(10)	1
26	Ivan Santini	CRO	21/05/89	A	34		15
2	Nicolas Seube		11/08/79	M	13	(7)	
32	Jordan Tell		10/06/97	A		(5)	
1	Rémy Vercoutre		26/06/80	G	34		
5	Alaeddine Yahia	TUN	26/09/81	D	30	(1)	1

Dijon FCO

1998 • Gaston Gérard (10,578) • dfco.fr

Coach: Olivier Dall'Oglio

2016

13/08	h	Nantes	L	0-1	
20/08	a	LOSC	L	0-1	
27/08	h	Lyon	W	4-2	*Samaritano (p), Júlio Tavares, Bahamboula, Lees-Melou*
10/09	a	Angers	L	1-3	*Samaritano*
17/09	h	Metz	D	0-0	
20/09	a	Paris	L	0-3	
24/09	h	Rennes	W	3-0	*Diony 2, Marié*
01/10	h	Montpellier	D	3-3	*Diony, og (Vanden Borre), Rivière*
16/10	a	St-Étienne	D	1-1	*Lees-Melou*
22/10	h	Lorient	W	1-0	*Lotiès*
29/10	a	Bastia	D	0-0	
05/11	h	Guingamp	D	3-3	*Varrault, Diony, Júlio Tavares*
19/11	a	Nancy	L	0-1	
26/11	a	Bordeaux	L	2-3	*Abeid, Júlio Tavares*
29/11	h	Monaco	D	1-1	*Samaritano*
02/12	a	Caen	D	3-3	*Lees-Melou, Diony, og (Bessat)*
10/12	h	Marseille	L	1-2	*Abeid*
18/12	a	Nice	L	1-2	*Júlio Tavares (p)*
21/12	h	Toulouse	W	2-0	*Júlio Tavares (p), Lees-Melou*

2017

14/01	a	Montpellier	D	1-1	*Júlio Tavares*
21/01	h	LOSC	D	0-0	
28/01	a	Lorient	W	3-2	*Diony, Lotiès, Lees-Melou*
04/02	h	Paris	L	1-3	*Júlio Tavares*
08/02	a	Metz	L	1-2	*Varrault*
11/02	h	Caen	W	2-0	*Abeid, Diony*
19/02	a	Lyon	L	2-4	*Júlio Tavares, Diony*
24/02	a	Nantes	L	1-3	*og (Dubois)*
04/03	h	Nice	L	0-1	
11/03	a	Rennes	D	1-1	*Júlio Tavares*
19/03	h	St-Étienne	L	0-1	
01/04	a	Marseille	D	1-1	*og (Sertic)*
08/04	h	Bastia	L	1-2	*Lees-Melou*
15/04	a	Monaco	L	1-2	*Varrault*
22/04	h	Angers	W	3-2	*Diony 2, Lees-Melou*
30/04	h	Bordeaux	D	0-0	
06/05	a	Guingamp	L	0-4	
14/05	h	Nancy	W	2-0	*Samaritano, Diony*
20/05	a	Toulouse	D	0-0	

No	Name	Nat	DoB	Pos	Aps	(s)	Gls
21	Yunis Abdelhamid	MAR	28/09/87	D	15	(3)	
17	Mehdi Abeid	ALG	06/08/92	M	27	(1)	3
20	Roman Amalfitano		27/08/89	M	15	(11)	
29	Dylan Bahamboula		22/05/95	M	4	(7)	1
15	Florent Balmont		02/02/80	M	21	(4)	
10	Jérémie Bela		08/04/93	M	2	(11)	
3	Anthony Belmonte		16/10/95	M	3	(2)	
5	Quentin Bernard		07/07/89	D	6	(1)	
25	Arnold Bouka Moutou	CGO	28/11/88	D	8	(1)	
26	Fouad Chafik	MAR	16/10/86	D	27		
9	Loïs Diony		20/12/92	A	31	(4)	11
22	Johan Gastien		25/01/88	M	8	(7)	
5	Oussama Haddadi	TUN	28/01/92	D	12	(1)	
11	Júlio Tavares	CPV	19/11/88	A	31	(4)	9
22	Kwon Chang-hoon	KOR	30/06/94	M	2	(6)	
2	Ádám Lang	HUN	17/01/93	D	18	(1)	
8	Pierre Lees-Melou		25/05/93	M	30	(2)	7
1	Benjamin Leroy		07/04/89	G	1		
4	Jordan Lotiès		05/08/84	D	23	(1)	2
14	Jordan Marié		29/09/91	M	17	(7)	1
13	Marvin Martin		10/01/88	M	4	(7)	
30	Baptiste Reynet		28/10/90	G	37		
7	Yohann Rivière		18/08/84	A	1	(13)	1
19	Valentin Rosier		19/08/96	D	3		
23	Vincent Rüfli	SUI	22/01/88	D	17	(2)	
18	Frédéric Samaritano		23/03/86	M	23	(8)	4
27	Cédric Varrault		30/01/80	D	32		3

EA Guingamp

1912 • Roudourou (18,197) • eaguingamp.com

Major honours

French Cup (2) 2009, 2014

Coach: Antoine Kombouaré

2016

12/08	a	Monaco	D	2-2	*Diallo, Privat*
21/08	h	Marseille	W	2-1	*Salibur, Sorbon*
27/08	a	Nancy	W	2-0	*Diallo, Giresse*
10/09	h	Montpellier	D	1-1	*Coco*
17/09	a	Toulouse	L	1-2	*Briand (p)*
21/09	h	Lorient	W	1-0	*Briand (p)*
24/09	a	Bastia	L	0-1	
30/09	a	Rennes	L	0-1	
15/10	h	LOSC	W	1-0	*Privat*
22/10	a	Lyon	W	3-1	*Salibur, Coco 2*
29/10	h	Angers	W	1-0	*De Pauw*
05/11	a	Dijon	D	3-3	*Coco, Mendy, De Pauw*
20/11	h	Bordeaux	D	1-1	*Briand*
26/11	a	Caen	D	1-1	*De Pauw*
30/11	h	Nice	L	0-1	
03/12	h	Nantes	W	2-0	*Briand, Salibur*
11/12	a	St-Étienne	L	0-1	
17/12	h	Paris	W	2-1	*Salibur, De Pauw*
21/12	a	Metz	D	2-2	*Briand 2*

2017

14/01	a	Lorient	L	1-3	*Salibur*
21/01	h	Rennes	D	1-1	*Diallo*
29/01	a	Nice	L	1-3	*Briand*
04/02	h	Caen	L	0-1	
08/02	a	Marseille	L	0-2	
11/02	h	Lyon	W	2-1	*Diallo, Benezet*
19/02	a	Bordeaux	L	0-3	
25/02	h	Monaco	L	1-2	*Didot*
04/03	a	Montpellier	D	1-1	*Briand*
11/03	h	Bastia	W	5-0	*Salibur, Deaux, Briand, Blas, Mendy*
18/03	a	Angers	L	0-3	
31/03	h	Nancy	W	1-0	*Privat*
09/04	a	Paris	L	0-4	
15/04	h	Toulouse	W	2-1	*Briand (p), Mendy*
22/04	a	LOSC	L	0-3	
29/04	h	St-Étienne	L	0-2	
06/05	h	Dijon	W	4-0	*Briand 2, Salibur 2 (1p)*
14/05	a	Nantes	L	1-4	*Deaux*
20/05	h	Metz	W	1-0	*Diallo*

No	Name	Nat	DoB	Pos	Aps	(s)	Gls
4	Benjamin Angoua	CIV	28/11/86	D	6	(1)	
10	Nicolas Benezet		24/02/91	M	3	(2)	1
21	Ludovic Blas		31/12/97	M	10	(14)	1
27	Mathieu Bodmer		22/11/82	M	8	(2)	
23	Jimmy Briand		02/08/85	A	32	(2)	12
24	Marcus Coco		24/06/96	M	31	(3)	4
12	Nill De Pauw	BEL	06/01/90	M	3	(25)	4
8	Lucas Deaux		26/12/88	M	35	(3)	2
5	Moustapha Diallo	SEN	14/05/86	M	22	(4)	5
17	Étienne Didot		24/07/83	M	26	(2)	1
3	Fernando Marçal	BRA	19/02/89	D	31		
26	Thibault Giresse		25/05/81	M	4	(9)	1
16	Théo Guivarch		17/11/95	G		(1)	
2	Jordan Ikoko	COD	03/02/94	D	25	(2)	
1	Karl-Johan Johnsson	SWE	28/01/90	G	37		
29	Christophe Kerbrat		02/08/86	D	35		
7	Dorian Lévêque		22/11/89	D	2		
32	Alexis Mané		30/04/97	D		(4)	
22	Jonathan Martins Pereira		30/01/86	D	12	(1)	
9	Alexandre Mendy		20/03/94	A	5	(17)	3
11	Sloan Privat		24/07/89	A	12	(8)	3
19	Yannis Salibur		21/01/91	M	34	(1)	8
30	Romain Salin		29/07/84	G	1		
6	Baïssama Sankoh	GUI	20/03/92	D	11	(6)	
15	Jérémy Sorbon		05/08/83	D	33		1

LOSC Lille

1944 • Pierre-Mauroy (49,000) • losc.fr

Major honours
French League (3) 1946, 1954, 2011; French Cup (6) 1946, 1947, 1948, 1953, 1955, 2011

Coach: Frédéric Antonetti; (22/11/16) (Patrick Collot); (14/02/17) Franck Passi

2016

Date		Opponent		Score	Scorers
13/08	a	Metz	L	2-3	*Rony Lopes 2*
20/08	h	Dijon	W	1-0	*Sankharé*
27/08	a	Nice	D	1-1	*Béria*
10/09	h	Monaco	L	1-4	*Palmieri*
17/09	a	Lorient	L	0-1	
20/09	h	Toulouse	L	1-2	*Baša*
25/09	a	St-Étienne	L	1-3	*Civelli*
01/10	h	Nancy	W	1-0	*Éder (p)*
15/10	a	Guingamp	L	0-1	
22/10	h	Bastia	W	2-1	*Corchia, Éder*
28/10	h	Paris	L	0-1	
05/11	a	Angers	L	0-1	
18/11	h	Lyon	L	0-1	
26/11	a	Nantes	D	0-0	
29/11	h	Caen	W	4-2	*Éder, Sliti, De Préville, Rony Lopes*
03/12	a	Bordeaux	W	1-0	*De Préville*
10/12	h	Montpellier	W	2-1	*De Préville, Sankharé*
18/12	a	Marseille	L	0-2	
21/12	h	Rennes	D	1-1	*Éder*

2017

Date		Opponent		Score	Scorers
13/01	h	St-Étienne	D	1-1	*De Préville*
21/01	a	Dijon	D	0-0	
28/01	a	Lyon	W	2-1	*Benzia 2 (1p)*
04/02	h	Lorient	L	0-1	
07/02	a	Paris	L	1-2	*De Préville*
11/02	h	Angers	L	1-2	*Bissouma*
18/02	a	Caen	W	1-0	*El Ghazi*
25/02	h	Bordeaux	L	2-3	*De Préville (p), Éder*
05/03	a	Toulouse	D	1-1	*Benzia*
11/03	a	Nancy	W	2-1	*De Préville (p), Rony Lopes*
17/03	h	Marseille	D	0-0	
01/04	a	Bastia	W	1-0	*De Préville*
07/04	h	Nice	L	1-2	*Amadou*
15/04	a	Rennes	L	0-2	
22/04	h	Guingamp	W	3-0	*De Préville 2 (1p), Éder*
29/04	a	Montpellier	W	3-0	*De Préville (p), Xeka, Terrier*
06/05	h	Metz	L	0-2	
14/05	a	Monaco	L	0-4	
20/05	h	Nantes	W	3-0	*De Préville 3 (1p)*

No	Name	Nat	DoB	Pos	Aps	(s)	Gls
22	Júnior Alonso	PAR	09/02/93	D	10	(2)	
6	Ibrahim Amadou	CMR	06/04/93	M	34	(1)	1
31	Morgan Amalfitano		20/03/85	M	8	(9)	
26	Farès Bahlouli		08/04/95	M	1	(2)	
25	Marko Baša	MNE	29/12/82	D	23		1
11	Éric Bauthéac		24/08/87	M	9	(4)	
9	Yassine Benzia	ALG	08/09/94	M	21	(4)	3
18	Franck Béria		23/05/83	D	27	(1)	1
21	Yves Bissouma	MLI	30/08/96	M	5	(18)	1
5	Renato Civelli	ARG	14/10/83	D	12	(1)	1
2	Sébastien Corchia		01/11/90	D	38		1
12	Nicolas De Préville		08/01/91	A	23	(7)	14
19	Éder	POR	22/12/87	A	28	(3)	6
7	Anwar El Ghazi	NED	03/05/95	A	7	(5)	1
1	Vincent Enyeama	NGA	29/08/82	G	33		
4	Gabriel	BRA	19/12/97	D		(1)	
10	Ricardo Kishna	NED	04/01/95	M	5	(6)	
3	Youssouf Koné	MLI	05/07/95	D	2		
16	Mike Maignan		03/07/95	G	5	(1)	
24	Rio Mavuba		08/03/84	M	14	(4)	
34	Hamza Mendyl	MAR	21/10/97	D		(1)	
8	Mounir Obbadi	MAR	04/04/83	M	5		
27	Julian Palmieri		17/12/86	D	16	(6)	1
17	Rony Lopes	POR	28/12/95	M	22	(3)	4
20	Ryan Mendes	CPV	08/01/90	A	2	(5)	
4	Younousse Sankharé	SEN	10/09/89	M	17	(3)	2
27	Naïm Sliti	TUN	27/07/92	M	10	(7)	1
23	Adama Soumaoro		18/06/92	D	26	(1)	
13	Stoppila Sunzu	ZAM	22/06/89	D	1	(3)	
33	Martin Terrier		04/03/97	M	1	(10)	1
8	Xeka	POR	10/11/94	M	13		1

FC Lorient

1926 • Le Moustoir-Yves-Allainmat (17,755) • fclweb.fr

Major honours
French Cup (1) 2002

Coach: Sylvain Ripoll; (08/11/16) Bernard Casoni

2016

Date		Opponent		Score	Scorers
13/08	a	Caen	L	2-3	*Moukandjo 2 (1p)*
20/08	h	Bastia	L	0-3	
26/08	a	Marseille	L	0-2	
10/09	h	Nancy	L	0-2	
17/09	h	LOSC	W	1-0	*Moukandjo (p)*
21/09	a	Guingamp	L	0-1	
24/09	h	Lyon	W	1-0	*Cabot*
02/10	a	Nice	L	1-2	*Moukandjo*
15/10	h	Nantes	L	1-2	*Hamel*
22/10	a	Dijon	L	0-1	
29/10	h	Montpellier	D	2-2	*Touré, Marveaux*
05/11	a	Bordeaux	L	1-2	*og (Prior)*
18/11	h	Monaco	L	0-3	
26/11	a	Metz	D	3-3	*Waris, Moukandjo 2 (1p)*
29/11	h	Rennes	W	2-1	*Ciani, Waris*
03/12	a	Angers	D	2-2	*Marveaux, Waris*
10/12	a	Toulouse	L	2-3	*Moukandjo, Waris*
17/12	h	St-Étienne	W	2-1	*Philippoteaux, Cabot*
21/12	a	Paris	L	0-5	

2017

Date		Opponent		Score	Scorers
14/01	h	Guingamp	W	3-1	*Waris 2, Cabot*
22/01	a	Monaco	L	0-4	
28/01	h	Dijon	L	2-3	*Marveaux, Waris (p)*
04/02	a	LOSC	W	1-0	*Aliadière*
08/02	h	Toulouse	D	1-1	*Marveaux*
12/02	a	St-Étienne	L	0-4	
18/02	h	Nice	L	0-1	
25/02	a	Rennes	L	0-1	
05/03	h	Marseille	L	1-4	*Moukandjo*
12/03	h	Paris	L	1-2	*Ciani*
18/03	a	Nancy	W	3-2	*Moukandjo, Lautoa, Mvuemba*
02/04	h	Caen	W	1-0	*Moukandjo*
08/04	a	Lyon	W	4-1	*Waris, Marveaux, Moukandjo 2*
15/04	a	Montpellier	L	0-2	
22/04	h	Metz	W	5-1	*Ciani, Waris, Cabot 2, Moukandjo*
29/04	a	Nantes	L	0-1	
06/05	h	Angers	D	1-1	*Philippoteaux*
14/05	a	Bastia	L	0-2	
20/05	h	Bordeaux	D	1-1	*Le Goff*

No	Name	Nat	DoB	Pos	Aps	(s)	Gls
14	Jérémie Aliadière		30/03/83	A	6	(7)	1
28	Maxime Barthelmé		08/09/88	M	3	(6)	
6	François Bellugou		25/04/87	M	16	(9)	
26	Issam Ben Khemis	TUN	10/01/96	M		(2)	
27	Jimmy Cabot		18/04/94	M	11	(14)	5
8	Cafú	POR	26/02/93	M	15	(3)	
13	Michael Ciani		06/04/84	D	25		3
16	Paul Delecroix		14/10/88	G	6		
23	Moryké Fofana	CIV	23/11/91	M	4	(3)	
4	Mátteo Guendouzi		14/04/99	M	4	(4)	
33	Pierre-Yves Hamel		19/03/94	A		(3)	1
22	Benjamin Jeannot		22/01/92	A	4	(12)	
34	Erwin Koffi		10/01/95	D	11	(1)	
24	Wesley Lautoa		25/08/87	D	18	(3)	1
4	Vincent Le Goff		15/09/89	D	37	(1)	1
40	Benjamin Lecomte		26/04/91	G	32		
36	Mohamed Mara	GUI	16/12/96	M	7	(2)	
19	Sylvain Marveaux		15/04/86	M	24		5
17	Walid Mesloub	ALG	04/09/85	M	11	(9)	
20	Steven Moreira		13/08/94	D	28		
12	Benjamin Moukandjo	CMR	12/11/88	A	24	(1)	13
7	Arnold Mvuemba		28/01/85	M	31	(1)	1
7	Didier N'Dong	GAB	17/06/94	M	2		
15	Mathieu Peybernes		21/10/90	D	18		
19	Romain Philippoteaux		02/03/88	M	18	(12)	2
2	Lindsay Rose		08/02/92	D	3		
11	Faiz Selemani		14/11/93	D		(3)	
5	Zargo Touré	SEN	11/10/89	D	21	(2)	1
23	Alhassan Wakaso	GHA	07/01/92	M	8	(5)	
9	Majeed Waris	GHA	19/09/91	A	31	(4)	9

Olympique Lyonnais

1950 • Parc OL (59,186) • olweb.fr

Major honours
French League (7) 2002, 2003, 2004, 2005, 2006, 2007, 2008; French Cup (5) 1964, 1967, 1973, 2008, 2012; League Cup (1) 2001

Coach: Bruno Génésio

2016

Date		Opponent		Score	Scorers
14/08	a	Nancy	W	3-0	*Lacazette 3*
19/08	h	Caen	W	2-0	*Lacazette 2 (2p)*
27/08	a	Dijon	L	2-4	*Tolisso, Lacazette*
10/09	h	Bordeaux	L	1-3	*Kalulu*
18/09	a	Marseille	D	0-0	
21/09	h	Montpellier	W	5-1	*Fekir 2 (1p), Tolisso 2, Cornet*
24/09	a	Lorient	L	0-1	
02/10	h	St-Étienne	W	2-0	*Darder, Ghezzal*
14/10	a	Nice	L	0-2	
22/10	h	Guingamp	L	1-3	*Lacazette (p)*
29/10	a	Toulouse	W	2-1	*Lacazette 2 (1p)*
05/11	h	Bastia	W	2-1	*Lacazette (p), og (Bengtsson)*
18/11	a	LOSC	W	1-0	*Cornet*
27/11	h	Paris	L	1-2	*Valbuena*
30/11	a	Nantes	W	6-0	*Tolisso, Lacazette (p), Gonalons, Valbuena, Diakhaby, Fekir*
11/12	h	Rennes	W	1-0	*Valbuena*
18/12	a	Monaco	W	3-1	*Ghezzal, Valbuena, Lacazette*
21/12	h	Angers	W	2-0	*Lacazette, Fekir*

2017

Date		Opponent		Score	Scorers
15/01	a	Caen	L	2-3	*Lacazette 2 (1p)*
22/01	h	Marseille	W	3-1	*Valbuena, Lacazette 2*
28/01	h	LOSC	L	1-2	*Lacazette (p)*
05/02	a	St-Étienne	L	0-2	
08/02	h	Nancy	W	4-0	*Valbuena, Fekir, Lacazette (p), Depay*
11/02	a	Guingamp	L	1-2	*Lacazette*
19/02	h	Dijon	W	4-2	*Tolisso 2, Lacazette (p), Fekir*
26/02	h	Metz	W	5-0	*Depay 2, og (Iván Balliu), Lacazette, Valbuena*
03/03	a	Bordeaux	D	1-1	*Mammana*
12/03	h	Toulouse	W	4-0	*Jallet, Cornet, Depay 2*
19/03	a	Paris	L	1-2	*Lacazette*
02/04	a	Rennes	D	1-1	*Cornet*
05/04	a	Metz	W	3-0	*Lacazette, Ferri, Tolisso*
08/04	h	Lorient	L	1-4	*Tolisso*
16/04	a	Bastia	W	0-0	*(w/o; original match abandoned at halftime, awarded as goalless win)*
23/04	h	Monaco	L	1-2	*Tousart*
28/04	a	Angers	W	2-1	*Valbuena, Fekir*
07/05	h	Nantes	W	3-2	*Fekir (p), Cornet 2*
14/05	a	Montpellier	W	3-1	*Fekir, Lacazette 2*
20/05	h	Nice	D	3-3	*og (Le Marchand), Lacazette 2*

No	Name	Nat	DoB	Pos	Aps	(s)	Gls
1	Anthony Lopes	POR	01/10/90	G	37		
25	Houssem Aouar		30/06/98	M	1	(2)	
27	Maxwel Cornet	CIV	27/09/96	A	19	(14)	6
14	Sergi Darder	ESP	22/12/93	M	15	(8)	1
9	Memphis Depay	NED	13/02/94	M	13	(4)	5
5	Mouctar Diakhaby		19/12/96	D	22		1
18	Nabil Fekir		18/07/93	M	28	(4)	9
12	Jordan Ferri		12/03/92	M	11	(17)	1
23	Jordy Gaspar		23/04/97	D	2		
11	Rachid Ghezzal	ALG	09/05/92	M	15	(11)	2
21	Maxime Gonalons		10/03/89	M	29	(1)	1
30	Mathieu Gorgelin		05/08/90	G	1		
7	Clément Grenier		07/01/91	M		(4)	
13	Christophe Jallet		31/10/83	D	12	(1)	1
26	Aldo Kalulu		21/01/96	A	1	(3)	1
24	Olivier Kemen		20/07/96	M		(2)	
10	Alexandre Lacazette		28/05/91	A	28	(2)	28
4	Emanuel Mammana	ARG	10/02/96	D	17		1
19	Jean-Philippe Mateta		28/06/97	A	1	(1)	
15	Jérémy Morel		02/04/84	D	29		
3	Nicolas N'Koulou	CMR	27/03/90	D	13		
20	Rafael	POR	09/07/90	D	25	(2)	
31	Maciej Rybus	POL	19/08/89	D	14	(5)	
8	Corentin Tolisso		03/08/94	M	29	(2)	8
29	Lucas Tousart		29/04/97	M	17	(5)	1
28	Mathieu Valbuena		28/09/84	M	15	(15)	8
2	Mapou Yanga-Mbiwa		15/05/89	D	24	(1)	

FRANCE

Olympique de Marseille

1899 • Vélodrome (65,960) • om.net

Major honours
UEFA Champions League (1) 1993; French League (9) 1937, 1948, 1971, 1972, 1989, 1990, 1991, 1992, 2010; French Cup (10) 1924, 1926, 1927, 1935, 1938, 1943, 1969, 1972, 1976, 1989; League Cup (3) 2010, 2011, 2012

Coach: (Franck Passi); (21/10/16) Rudi García

2016

14/08	h	Toulouse	D	0-0	
21/08	a	Guingamp	L	1-2	*Thauvin*
26/08	h	Lorient	W	2-0	*Cabella, Gomis*
11/09	a	Nice	L	2-3	*Thauvin, Gomis (p)*
18/09	h	Lyon	D	0-0	
21/09	a	Rennes	L	2-3	*Gomis 2 (1p)*
25/09	h	Nantes	W	2-1	*N'Jie, Gomis (p)*
02/10	a	Angers	D	1-1	*Thauvin*
16/10	h	Metz	W	1-0	*Gomis*
23/10	a	Paris	D	0-0	
30/10	h	Bordeaux	D	0-0	
04/11	a	Montpellier	L	1-3	*og (Pionnier)*
20/11	h	Caen	W	1-0	*Rolando*
26/11	a	Monaco	L	0-4	
30/11	a	St-Étienne	D	0-0	
04/12	h	Nancy	W	3-0	*Thauvin, Gomis, N'Jie*
10/12	a	Dijon	W	2-1	*Lopez, Gomis*
18/12	h	LOSC	W	2-0	*Gomis, Thauvin*
21/12	a	Bastia	W	2-1	*Gomis, N'Jie*

2017

15/01	h	Monaco	L	1-4	*Rolando*
22/01	a	Lyon	L	1-3	*Dória*
27/01	h	Montpellier	W	5-1	*Gomis 3, Rolando, Thauvin (p)*
03/02	a	Metz	L	0-1	
08/02	h	Guingamp	W	2-0	*Gomis, Payet*
12/02	a	Nantes	L	2-3	*Gomis 2*
18/02	h	Rennes	W	2-0	*N'Jie, Thauvin*
26/02	h	Paris	L	1-5	*Fanni*
05/03	a	Lorient	W	4-1	*Rolando, Payet, Thauvin, Sanson*
10/03	h	Angers	W	3-0	*Thauvin 2, Cabella*
17/03	a	LOSC	D	0-0	
01/04	h	Dijon	D	1-1	*Payet*
09/04	a	Toulouse	D	0-0	
16/04	h	St-Étienne	W	4-0	*Thauvin 2, Gomis, Payet*
21/04	a	Nancy	D	0-0	
30/04	a	Caen	W	5-1	*Thauvin 3, Lopez 2*
07/05	h	Nice	W	2-1	*Gomis, Evra*
14/05	a	Bordeaux	D	1-1	*Gomis*
20/05	h	Bastia	W	1-0	*Gomis*

No	Name	Nat	DoB	Pos	Aps	(s)	Gls
11	Romain Alessandrini		03/04/89	M	3	(3)	
12	Henri Bedimo		04/06/84	D	13	(3)	
7	Rémy Cabella		08/03/90	M	17	(12)	2
5	Abou Diaby		11/03/86	M	2		
10	Lassana Diarra		10/03/85	M	8	(3)	
3	Dória	BRA	08/11/94	D	14	(9)	1
21	Patrice Evra		15/05/81	D	11		1
24	Rod Fanni		06/12/81	D	27	(1)	1
18	Bafétimbi Gomis		06/08/85	A	30	(1)	20
15	Tomáš Hubočan	SVK	17/09/85	D	11	(2)	
20	Saîf-Eddine Khaoui	TUN	27/04/95	M	1	(8)	
22	Aaron Leya Iseka	BEL	15/11/97	A	3	(5)	
27	Maxime Lopez		04/12/97	M	26	(4)	3
23	Zinédine Machach		05/01/96	M	4	(6)	
14	Clinton N'Jie	CMR	15/08/93	A	11	(11)	4
11	Dimitri Payet		29/03/87	M	14	(1)	4
16	Yohann Pelé		04/11/82	G	38		
28	Antoine Rabillard		22/09/95	A		(2)	
4	Karim Rekik	NED	02/12/94	D	8	(2)	
6	Rolando	POR	31/08/85	D	29	(1)	4
2	Hiroki Sakai	JPN	12/04/90	D	34	(1)	
8	Morgan Sanson		18/08/94	M	15	(2)	1
17	Bouna Sarr		31/01/92	M	9	(17)	
13	Grégory Sertic		05/08/89	M	7	(1)	
26	Florian Thauvin		26/01/93	M	36	(2)	15
19	William Vainqueur		19/11/88	M	29		
29	André Zambo Anguissa	CMR	16/11/95	M	18	(15)	

FC Metz

1932 • Saint-Symphorien (25,636) • fcmetz.com

Major honours
French Cup (2) 1984, 1988; League Cup (1) 1996

Coach: Philippe Hinschberger

2016

13/08	h	LOSC	W	3-2	*Mevlüt 2 (1p), Jouffre (p)*
21/08	a	Paris	L	0-3	
27/08	h	Angers	W	2-0	*Falette, Milán*
11/09	a	Nantes	W	3-0	*Mevlüt 3 (1p)*
17/09	a	Dijon	D	0-0	
21/09	h	Bordeaux	L	0-3	
24/09	a	Montpellier	W	1-0	*Mevlüt (p)*
01/10	h	Monaco	L	0-7	
16/10	a	Marseille	L	0-1	
23/10	h	Nice	L	2-4	*Mandjeck, Diallo*
30/10	a	Rennes	L	0-1	
06/11	h	St-Étienne	D	0-0	
19/11	a	Toulouse	W	2-1	*Jouffre (p), Mandjeck*
26/11	h	Lorient	D	3-3	*Falette, Vion 2*
30/11	a	Nancy	L	0-4	
10/12	a	Bastia	L	0-2	
18/12	a	Caen	L	0-3	
21/12	h	Guingamp	D	2-2	*Nguette, Hein*

2017

15/01	a	Nice	D	0-0	
21/01	h	Montpellier	W	2-0	*Diabaté 2*
28/01	a	Angers	L	1-2	*og (Traoré)*
03/02	h	Marseille	W	1-0	*Jouffre*
08/02	h	Dijon	W	2-1	*Sarr, Diabaté (p)*
11/02	a	Monaco	L	0-5	
18/02	h	Nantes	D	1-1	*Diabaté (p)*
26/02	a	Lyon	L	0-5	
04/03	h	Rennes	D	1-1	*Diabaté*
12/03	a	St-Étienne	D	2-2	*Sarr, Falette*
17/03	h	Bastia	W	1-0	*og (Cioni)*
05/04	h	Lyon	L	0-3	
08/04	a	Bordeaux	L	0-3	
15/04	h	Caen	D	2-2	*Sarr, Diabaté*
18/04	h	Paris	L	2-3	*Jouffre, Diabaté*
22/04	a	Lorient	L	1-5	*Diabaté (p)*
29/04	h	Nancy	W	2-1	*Sarr, Nguette*
06/05	a	LOSC	W	2-0	*Mandjeck, Cohade*
14/05	h	Toulouse	D	1-1	*Sarr*
20/05	a	Guingamp	L	0-1	

No	Name	Nat	DoB	Pos	Aps	(s)	Gls
32	Benoît Assou-Ekoto	CMR	24/03/84	D	16	(2)	
33	Nicolas Basin		22/07/98	D		(1)	
4	Milan Biševac	SRB	31/08/83	D	21		
24	Renaud Cohade		29/09/84	M	32	(1)	1
18	Cheick Diabaté	MLI	25/04/88	A	12	(2)	8
2	Fallou Diagne	SEN	14/08/89	M	12		
17	Habib Diallo	SEN	18/06/95	A	7	(12)	1
1	Thomas Didillon		28/11/95	G	32		
10	Cheick Doukouré	CIV	11/09/92	M	27	(2)	
6	Simon Falette		19/02/92	D	35		3
7	Gauthier Hein		07/08/96	M	6	(7)	1
25	Iván Balliu	ESP	01/01/92	D	26	(1)	
8	Yann Jouffre		23/07/84	M	14	(6)	4
16	Eiji Kawashima	JPN	20/03/83	G	5		
22	Kevin Lejeune		22/01/85	M	8	(6)	
14	Georges Mandjeck	CMR	09/12/88	M	27	(2)	3
34	Boris Mathis		15/08/97	A		(2)	
33	Youssef Maziz		24/06/98	M		(1)	
9	Mevlüt Erdinç	TUR	25/02/87	A	15	(9)	6
5	Guido Milán	ARG	03/07/87	D	18	(4)	1
19	Florent Mollet		19/11/91	M	9	(16)	
11	Opa Nguette	SEN	08/07/94	M	26	(7)	2
30	David Oberhauser		29/11/91	G	1		
23	Chris Philipps	LUX	08/03/94	M	9	(2)	
3	Jonathan Rivierez		15/05/89	D	14	(2)	
26	Ismaïla Sarr	SEN	25/02/98	M	20	(11)	5
31	Moussa Seydi	SEN	21/08/96	M		(1)	
13	Franck Signorino		19/09/81	D	17		
29	Vincent Thill	LUX	04/02/00	A		(1)	
12	Matthieu Udol		20/03/96	D	3		
15	Thibaut Vion		11/12/93	A	6	(7)	2

AS Monaco FC

1919 • Louis-II (18,174) • asmonaco.com

Major honours
French League (8) 1961, 1963, 1978, 1982, 1988, 1997, 2000, 2017; French Cup (5) 1960, 1963, 1980, 1985, 1991; League Cup (1) 2003

Coach: Leonardo Jardim (POR)

2016

12/08	h	Guingamp	D	2-2	*Fabinho (p), Bernardo Silva*
20/08	a	Nantes	W	1-0	*Boschilia*
28/08	h	Paris	W	3-1	*João Moutinho, Fabinho (p), og (Aurier)*
10/09	a	LOSC	W	4-1	*Sidibé, Traoré, Fabinho, Glik*
17/09	h	Rennes	W	3-0	*Falcao, Lemar 2*
21/09	a	Nice	L	0-4	
24/09	h	Angers	W	2-1	*Glik, og (Nwakaeme)*
01/10	a	Metz	W	7-0	*Lemar, Germain, Bernardo Silva, Fabinho (p), Carrillo 2, Boschilia*
14/10	a	Toulouse	L	1-3	*Germain*
21/10	h	Montpellier	W	6-2	*Falcao (p), Mbappé, Jemerson, Germain, Lemar, Traoré*
29/10	a	St-Étienne	D	1-1	*Glik*
05/11	h	Nancy	W	6-0	*Falcao 2 (1p), Mbappé, Carrillo 2, Fabinho (p)*
18/11	a	Lorient	W	3-0	*Falcao, Lemar, Boschilia*
26/11	h	Marseille	W	4-0	*Boschilia, Germain 2, Carrillo*
29/11	a	Dijon	D	1-1	*Carrillo*
03/12	h	Bastia	W	5-0	*Mbappé, Lemar, Falcao 2, Carrillo*
10/12	a	Bordeaux	W	4-0	*Sidibé, Falcao 3 (1p)*
18/12	h	Lyon	L	1-3	*Bakayoko*
21/12	h	Caen	W	2-1	*Falcao (p), Bakayoko*

2017

15/01	a	Marseille	W	4-1	*Lemar, Falcao, Bernardo Silva 2*
22/01	h	Lorient	W	4-0	*Boschilia 2, Germain 2*
29/01	a	Paris	D	1-1	*Bernardo Silva*
04/02	h	Nice	W	3-0	*Germain, Falcao 2*
07/02	a	Montpellier	W	2-1	*Glik, Mbappé*
11/02	h	Metz	W	5-0	*Mbappé 3, Falcao 2*
17/02	a	Bastia	D	1-1	*Bernardo Silva*
25/02	a	Guingamp	W	2-1	*Glik, Fabinho (p)*
05/03	h	Nantes	W	4-0	*Mbappé 2, Germain, Fabinho (p)*
11/03	h	Bordeaux	W	2-1	*Mbappé, João Moutinho*
19/03	a	Caen	W	3-0	*Mbappé 2, Fabinho (p)*
08/04	a	Angers	W	1-0	*Falcao*
15/04	h	Dijon	W	2-1	*Dirar, Falcao*
23/04	a	Lyon	W	2-1	*Falcao, Mbappé*
29/04	h	Toulouse	W	3-1	*Glik, Mbappé, Lemar*
06/05	a	Nancy	W	3-0	*og (Badila), Bernardo Silva, Lemar*
14/05	h	LOSC	W	4-0	*Falcao 2, Bernardo Silva, og (Alonso)*
17/05	h	St-Étienne	W	2-0	*Mbappé, Germain*
20/05	a	Rennes	W	3-2	*Fabinho, Jemerson, Jorge*

No	Name	Nat	DoB	Pos	Aps	(s)	Gls
40	Loïc Badiashile		05/02/98	G		(1)	
14	Tiémoué Bakayoko		17/08/94	M	25	(7)	2
10	Bernardo Silva	POR	10/08/94	M	33	(4)	8
26	Boschilia	BRA	05/03/96	M	5	(6)	6
33	Irvin Cardona		08/08/97	A		(3)	
11	Guido Carrillo	ARG	25/05/91	A	5	(14)	7
16	MorganDe Sanctis	ITA	26/03/77	G	1		
34	Abdou Diallo		04/05/96	D	4	(1)	
7	Nabil Dirar	MAR	25/02/86	M	8	(10)	1
2	Fabinho	BRA	23/10/93	M	33	(4)	9
9	Radamel Falcao	COL	10/02/86	A	22	(7)	21
18	Valère Germain		17/04/90	A	28	(9)	10
25	Kamil Glik	POL	03/02/88	D	35		6
17	Ivan Cavaleiro	POR	18/10/93	A	1	(1)	
28	Corentin Jean		15/07/95	A	1	(1)	
5	Jemerson	BRA	24/08/92	D	34		2
8	João Moutinho	POR	08/09/86	M	19	(12)	2
6	Jorge	BRA	28/03/96	D	1	(1)	1
27	Thomas Lemar		12/11/95	M	28	(6)	9
29	Kylian Mbappé		20/12/98	A	17	(12)	15
23	Benjamin Mendy		17/07/94	D	24	(1)	
35	Kévin N'Doram		22/01/96	M	3	(2)	
24	Andrea Raggi	ITA	24/06/84	D	12	(3)	
19	Djibril Sidibé		29/07/92	D	25	(3)	2
1	Danijel Subašić	CRO	27/10/84	G	36		
30	Seydou Sy	SEN	12/12/95	G	1		
32	Marcel Tisserand	COD	10/01/93	D	1		
38	Almamy Touré	MLI	28/04/96	D	12	(3)	
20	Adama Traoré	MLI	28/06/95	M	4	(1)	2

Montpellier Hérault SC

1974 • La Mosson (28,500) • mhscfoot.com

Major honours
French League (1) 2012; French Cup (1) 1990

Coach: Frédéric Hantz;
(31/01/17) Jean-Louis Gasset

2016

Date		Opponent		Score	Scorers
13/08	h	Angers	W	1-0	*Boudebouz*
21/08	a	St-Étienne	L	1-3	*Mounié*
27/08	h	Rennes	D	1-1	*Congré*
10/09	a	Guingamp	D	1-1	*M Sanson*
18/09	h	Nice	D	1-1	*Boudebouz (p)*
21/09	a	Lyon	L	1-5	*M Sanson*
24/09	h	Metz	L	0-1	
01/10	a	Dijon	D	3-3	*Ninga 3*
15/10	h	Caen	W	3-2	*Ninga 2, Mounié*
21/10	a	Monaco	L	2-6	*Boudebouz 2 (1p)*
29/10	a	Lorient	D	2-2	*Camara, M Sanson*
04/11	h	Marseille	W	3-1	*Boudebouz 2, Mounié*
19/11	a	Bastia	D	1-1	*Mounié*
26/11	h	Nancy	D	0-0	
30/11	a	Toulouse	L	0-1	
03/12	h	Paris	W	3-0	*Lasne, Skhiri, Boudebouz*
10/12	a	LOSC	L	1-2	*Mounié*
17/12	h	Bordeaux	W	4-0	*Lasne, Sessègnon, Mounié, Sylla*
21/12	a	Nantes	L	0-1	

2017

Date		Opponent		Score	Scorers
14/01	h	Dijon	D	1-1	*Roussillon*
21/01	a	Metz	L	0-2	
27/01	a	Marseille	L	1-5	*Boudebouz*
04/02	h	Bastia	W	2-1	*Mounié 2*
07/02	h	Monaco	L	1-2	*Hilton*
11/02	a	Nancy	W	3-0	*Mbenza 2, Mounié*
19/02	h	St-Étienne	W	2-1	*Lasne, Mounié*
24/02	a	Nice	L	1-2	*Mounié*
04/03	h	Guingamp	D	1-1	*Mounié*
11/03	h	Nantes	L	2-3	*Mounié, Boudebouz*
18/03	a	Bordeaux	L	1-5	*Boudebouz (p)*
02/04	h	Toulouse	L	0-1	
08/04	a	Caen	W	2-0	*Sessègnon, Ikoné*
15/04	h	Lorient	W	2-0	*Boudebouz, Mbenza*
22/04	a	Paris	L	0-2	
29/04	h	LOSC	L	0-3	
07/05	a	Rennes	L	0-1	
14/05	h	Lyon	L	1-3	*Mounié*
20/05	a	Angers	L	0-2	

No	Name	Nat	DoB	Pos	Aps	(s)	Gls
11	Kévin Bérigaud		09/05/88	A	6	(7)	
10	Ryad Boudebouz	ALG	19/02/90	M	33		11
19	Souleymane Camara	SEN	22/12/82	A	10	(17)	1
3	Daniel Congré		05/04/85	D	21	(3)	1
25	Mathieu Deplagne		01/10/91	D	14	(5)	
20	Keagan Dolly	RSA	22/01/93	M	5	(6)	
4	Hilton	BRA	13/09/77	D	32		1
11	Jonathan Ikoné		02/05/88	M	7	(7)	1
16	Geoffrey Jourdren		04/02/86	G	13		
7	Paul Lasne		16/01/89	M	16	(8)	3
33	Alexandre Llovet		26/11/97	A		(2)	
6	Joris Marveaux		15/08/82	D	4	(4)	
18	Isaac Mbenza	BEL	08/03/96	M	12	(3)	3
27	Cédric Mongongu	COD	22/06/89	D		(3)	
15	Steve Mounié	BEN	29/09/94	A	32	(3)	14
23	Nordi Mukiele		01/11/97	D	16	(1)	
2	Mamadou N'Diaye	SEN	28/05/95	D	1	(2)	
29	Casimir Ninga	CHA	17/05/93	A	6	(3)	5
33	Bryan Passi		05/08/97	D	1	(2)	
1	Laurent Pionnier		24/05/82	G	25		
33	Morgan Poaty		15/07/97	D	1	(2)	
12	Lukáš Pokorný	CZE	05/07/93	D	12	(1)	
21	William Rémy		04/04/91	D	8	(7)	
24	Jérôme Roussillon		06/01/93	D	31	(1)	1
23	Jamel Saihi	TUN	27/01/87	M		(2)	
18	Nicolas Saint-Ruf		24/11/92	D	7		
22	Killian Sanson		07/06/97	M		(1)	
8	Morgan Sanson		18/08/94	M	20		3
28	Stéphane Sessègnon	BEN	01/06/84	M	26	(1)	2
13	Ellyes Skhiri		10/05/95	M	37		1
5	Yacouba Sylla	MLI	29/11/90	M	13	(6)	1
20	Anthony Vanden Borre	BEL	24/10/87	D	9	(1)	

AS Nancy-Lorraine

1967 • Marcel-Picot (20,087) • asnl.net

Major honours
French Cup (1) 1978; League Cup (1) 2006

Coach: Pablo Correa (URU)

2016

Date		Opponent		Score	Scorers
14/08	h	Lyon	L	0-3	
20/08	a	Rennes	L	0-2	
27/08	h	Guingamp	L	0-2	
10/09	a	Lorient	W	2-0	*Aït Bennasser, Dalé*
17/09	h	Nantes	D	1-1	*Puyo*
21/09	a	Bastia	D	0-0	
25/09	h	Nice	L	0-1	
01/10	a	LOSC	L	0-1	
15/10	h	Paris	L	1-2	*Diarra*
22/10	a	Bordeaux	D	1-1	*Koura*
29/10	h	Caen	W	2-0	*Mandanne, Diarra*
05/11	a	Monaco	L	0-6	
19/11	h	Dijon	W	1-0	*Badila*
26/11	a	Montpellier	D	0-0	
30/11	h	Metz	W	4-0	*Pedretti, Cuffaut, Dia, Aït Bennasser*
04/12	a	Marseille	L	0-3	
10/12	h	Angers	W	2-0	*Dia, Puyo*
17/12	a	Toulouse	D	1-1	*Aït Bennasser*
21/12	a	St-Étienne	D	0-0	

2017

Date		Opponent		Score	Scorers
14/01	h	Bastia	W	1-0	*Dia*
28/01	h	Bordeaux	L	0-2	
05/02	a	Nantes	W	2-0	*Dia, Cétout*
08/02	a	Lyon	L	0-4	
11/02	h	Montpellier	L	0-3	
18/02	a	Angers	L	0-1	
21/02	a	Caen	L	0-1	
25/02	h	Toulouse	D	0-0	
04/03	a	Paris	L	0-1	
11/03	h	LOSC	L	1-2	*Dia*
18/03	h	Lorient	L	2-3	*Faitout Maouassa, Dia (p)*
31/03	a	Guingamp	L	0-1	
08/04	h	Rennes	W	3-0	*Dalé, Dia 2*
15/04	a	Nice	L	1-3	*Dalé*
21/04	h	Marseille	D	0-0	
29/04	a	Metz	L	1-2	*Faitout Maouassa*
06/05	h	Monaco	L	0-3	
14/05	a	Dijon	L	0-2	
20/05	h	St-Étienne	W	3-1	*Busin, Diagne, Faitout Maouassa*

No	Name	Nat	DoB	Pos	Aps	(s)	Gls
6	Youssef Aït Bennasser	MAR	07/06/96	M	23	(3)	3
3	Tobias Badila		12/05/93	D	24	(2)	1
33	Amine Bassi		27/11/97	M	1		
27	Alexis Busin		07/09/95	A	2	(4)	1
24	Erick Cabaco	URU	19/04/95	D	18	(2)	
28	Julien Cétout		02/01/88	D	27	(1)	1
1	Sergei Chernik	BLR	20/07/88	G	15	(2)	
20	Michaël Chrétien	MAR	10/07/84	D	13		
11	Karim Coulibaly		03/06/93	M	6	(3)	
14	Jouffrey Cuffaut		15/03/88	D	29	(1)	1
9	Maurice-Junior Dalé		12/07/85	A	16	(9)	3
10	Issiar Dia	SEN	08/06/87	M	22	(9)	8
4	Modou Diagne		03/01/94	D	21	(1)	1
5	Alou Diarra		15/07/81	M	16	(2)	2
17	Christ-Emmanuel Faitout Maouassa		06/07/98	D	13	(1)	3
18	Diallo Guidileye	MTN	30/12/89	M	18	(6)	
15	Youssouf Hadji	MAR	07/02/80	A	14	(12)	
23	Anthony Koura		06/05/93	A	8	(7)	1
2	Clément Lenglet		17/06/95	D	18		
12	Christophe Mandanne		07/02/85	A	9	(11)	1
8	Vincent Marchetti		04/07/97	M	10	(7)	
26	Vincent Muratori		03/08/97	D	17		
16	Guy Roland N'Dy Assembé	CMR	28/02/86	G	23		
13	Serge N'Guessan	CIV	31/07/94	M	6	(3)	
25	Benoit Pedretti		12/11/80	M	21	(5)	1
19	Loïc Puyo		19/12/88	M	15	(7)	2
7	Anthony Robic		05/03/86	M	13	(11)	

FC Nantes

1943 • La Beaujoire-Louis Fontenau (37,555) • fcnantes.com

Major honours
French League (8) 1965, 1966, 1973, 1977, 1980, 1983, 1995, 2001; French Cup (3) 1979, 1999, 2000

Coach: René Girard;
(01/12/16) (Philippe Mao);
(08/12/16) Sérgio Conceição (POR)

2016

Date		Opponent		Score	Scorers
13/08	a	Dijon	W	1-0	*Thomsen*
20/08	h	Monaco	L	0-1	
28/08	a	Bordeaux	L	0-1	
11/09	h	Metz	L	0-3	
17/09	a	Nancy	D	1-1	*Stępiński*
21/09	h	St-Étienne	D	0-0	
25/09	a	Marseille	L	1-2	*Sala*
01/10	h	Bastia	W	1-0	*Stępiński*
15/10	a	Lorient	W	2-1	*Bammou, Gillet*
22/10	h	Rennes	L	1-2	*Sala*
30/10	a	Nice	L	1-4	*Sala*
05/11	h	Toulouse	D	1-1	*Stępiński*
19/11	a	Paris	L	0-2	
26/11	h	LOSC	D	0-0	
30/11	h	Lyon	L	0-6	
03/12	a	Guingamp	L	0-2	
16/12	a	Angers	W	2-0	*Gillet, Harit*
21/12	h	Montpellier	W	1-0	*Lucas Lima (p)*

2017

Date		Opponent		Score	Scorers
14/01	a	Toulouse	W	1-0	*Sala*
18/01	h	Caen	W	1-0	*Sala*
21/01	h	Paris	L	0-2	
28/01	a	Rennes	D	1-1	*Iloki*
05/02	h	Nancy	L	0-2	
12/02	h	Marseille	W	3-2	*Diego Carlos, Stępiński, Thomasson*
18/02	a	Metz	D	1-1	*Rongier*
24/02	h	Dijon	W	3-1	*Bammou, Sala (p), Pardo*
01/03	a	Bastia	D	2-2	*Sala, Diego Carlos*
05/03	a	Monaco	L	0-4	
11/03	a	Montpellier	W	3-2	*Nakoulma 2, Sala*
18/03	h	Nice	D	1-1	*Sala*
02/04	h	Angers	W	2-1	*Nakoulma 2*
09/04	a	St-Étienne	D	1-1	*Nakoulma*
16/04	h	Bordeaux	L	0-1	
22/04	a	Caen	W	2-0	*Bammou 2*
29/04	h	Lorient	W	1-0	*Sala*
07/05	a	Lyon	L	2-3	*Rongier, Gillet*
14/05	h	Guingamp	W	4-1	*Thomasson, Sala 2, Nakoulma*
20/05	a	LOSC	L	0-3	

No	Name	Nat	DoB	Pos	Aps	(s)	Gls
24	Alexis Alégué	CMR	23/12/96	A		(2)	
2	Fernando Aristegueita	VEN	09/04/92	A		(5)	
10	Yacine Bammou	MAR	11/09/91	A	18	(14)	4
3	Diego Carlos	BRA	15/03/93	D	34		2
26	Koffi Djidji	CIV	30/11/92	D	28		
15	Léo Dubois		14/09/94	D	35	(1)	
30	Maxime Dupé		04/03/93	G	15		
27	Guillaume Gillet	BEL	09/03/84	M	38		3
14	Amine Harit		18/06/97	M	23	(7)	1
7	Jules Iloki		14/01/92	M	15	(8)	1
11	Alexander Kacaniklic	SWE	13/08/91	M	7	(10)	
25	Enock Kwateng		09/04/97	D	4	(3)	
6	Lucas Lima	BRA	10/10/91	D	38		1
13	Wilfried Moimbé		18/10/88	D	1	(7)	
22	Préjuce Nakoulma	BFA	21/04/87	A	10	(1)	6
20	Felipe Pardo	COL	17/08/90	M	6	(7)	1
1	Rémy Riou		06/08/87	G	23		
28	Valentin Rongier		07/12/94	M	26	(5)	2
22	Emiliano Sala	ARG	31/10/90	A	29	(5)	12
23	Sérgio Oliveira	POR	02/06/92	M		(6)	
9	Kolbeinn Sigthórsson	ISL	14/03/90	A	2		
18	Mariusz Stępiński	POL	12/05/95	A	16	(5)	4
8	Adrien Thomasson		10/12/93	M	21	(8)	2
23	Nicolaj Thomsen	DEN	08/05/93	M	9	(4)	1
19	Abdoulaye Touré		03/03/94	M	3	(9)	
4	Oswaldo Vizcarrondo	VEN	31/05/84	D	14	(6)	
17	Anthony Walongwa	COD	15/10/93	D	3		

FRANCE

OGC Nice

1904 • Allianz Riviera (27,478) • ogcnice.com

Major honours
French League (4) 1951, 1952, 1956, 1959; French Cup (3) 1952, 1954, 1997

Coach: Lucien Favre (SUI)

2016

14/08	h	Rennes	W	1-0	*Sarr*
20/08	a	Angers	W	1-0	*Pléa*
27/08	h	LOSC	D	1-1	*Koziello*
11/09	h	Marseille	W	3-2	*Balotelli 2 (1p), Cyprien*
18/09	a	Montpellier	D	1-1	*Belhanda*
21/09	h	Monaco	W	4-0	*Baysse, Balotelli 2, Pléa*
25/09	a	Nancy	W	1-0	*Pléa*
02/10	h	Lorient	W	2-1	*Ricardo, Balotelli*
14/10	h	Lyon	W	2-0	*Baysse, Seri*
23/10	a	Metz	W	4-2	*Pléa 3 (1p), Cyprien*
30/10	h	Nantes	W	4-1	*Cyprien 2, Balotelli, Pléa*
06/11	a	Caen	L	0-1	
20/11	a	St-Étienne	W	1-0	*Eysseric*
27/11	h	Bastia	D	1-1	*Pléa*
30/11	a	Guingamp	W	1-0	*Belhanda*
04/12	h	Toulouse	W	3-0	*Pléa, Belhanda, Seri*
11/12	a	Paris	D	2-2	*Cyprien, Pléa*
18/12	h	Dijon	W	2-1	*Balotelli 2 (1p)*
21/12	a	Bordeaux	D	0-0	

2017

15/01	h	Metz	D	0-0	
20/01	a	Bastia	D	1-1	*Souquet*
29/01	h	Guingamp	W	3-1	*Pléa, Seri, Balotelli*
04/02	a	Monaco	L	0-3	
08/02	h	St-Étienne	W	1-0	*Cyprien*
12/02	a	Rennes	D	2-2	*Donis, Eysseric*
18/02	a	Lorient	W	1-0	*Cyprien*
24/02	h	Montpellier	W	2-1	*Le Bihan 2*
04/03	a	Dijon	W	1-0	*Cyprien*
10/03	h	Caen	D	2-2	*Balotelli, Donis*
18/03	a	Nantes	D	1-1	*Seri*
02/04	h	Bordeaux	W	2-1	*Balotelli (p), Eysseric*
07/04	a	LOSC	W	2-1	*Balotelli 2*
15/04	h	Nancy	W	3-1	*Le Bihan, Seri 2 (1p)*
23/04	a	Toulouse	D	1-1	*Eysseric*
30/04	h	Paris	W	3-1	*Balotelli, Ricardo, Donis*
07/05	a	Marseille	L	1-2	*Balotelli*
14/05	h	Angers	L	0-2	
20/05	a	Lyon	D	3-3	*Donis 2, Seri (p)*

No	Name	Nat	DoB	Pos	Aps	(s)	Gls
9	Mario Balotelli	ITA	12/08/90	A	20	(3)	15
4	Paul Baysse		18/05/88	D	20	(2)	2
5	Younès Belhanda	MAR	25/02/90	M	28	(3)	3
40	Walter Benítez	ARG	19/01/93	G	2	(1)	
24	Mathieu Bodmer		22/11/82	M	7	(5)	
28	Olivier Boscagli		18/11/97	D		(1)	
15	Patrick Burner		11/04/96	M	3	(1)	
30	Yoan Cardinale		27/03/94	G	36		
25	Wylan Cyprien		28/01/95	M	26	(2)	8
29	Dalbert	BRA	08/09/93	D	34		
31	Dante	BRA	18/10/83	D	33		
22	Anastasios Donis	GRE	29/08/96	A	3	(15)	5
13	Valentin Eysseric		25/03/92	M	23	(6)	4
26	Vincent Koziello		28/10/95	M	19	(8)	1
10	Mickaël Le Bihan		16/05/90	M	2	(8)	3
20	Maxime Le Marchand		11/10/89	D	8	(2)	
8	Arnaud Lusamba		04/01/97	M	3	(3)	
34	Hicham Mahou		02/07/99	A		(1)	
33	Vincent Marcel		09/04/97	M	3	(3)	
24	Mounir Obbadi	MAR	04/04/83	M	3	(3)	
14	Alassane Pléa		10/03/93	A	22	(3)	11
21	Ricardo	POR	06/10/93	D	23	(1)	2
34	Malang Sarr		23/01/99	D	25	(2)	1
6	Jean Michaël Seri	CIV	19/07/91	M	34		7
2	Arnaud Souquet		12/02/92	D	26		1
11	Bassem Srarfi	TUN	25/06/97	M		(5)	
18	Rémi Walter		26/04/95	M	15	(7)	

Paris Saint-Germain

1970 • Parc des Princes (47,929) • psg.fr

Major honours
UEFA Cup Winners' Cup (1) 1996; French League (6) 1986, 1994, 2013, 2014, 2015, 2016; French Cup (11) 1982, 1983, 1993, 1995, 1998, 2004, 2006, 2010, 2015, 2016, 2017; League Cup (7) 1995, 1998, 2008, 2014, 2015, 2016, 2017

Coach: Unai Emery (ESP)

2016

12/08	a	Bastia	W	1-0	*Kurzawa*
21/08	h	Metz	W	3-0	*Lucas, Kurzawa, Verratti*
28/08	a	Monaco	L	1-3	*Cavani*
09/09	h	St-Étienne	D	1-1	*Lucas (p)*
16/09	a	Caen	W	6-0	*Cavani 4 (1p), Lucas, Augustin*
20/09	h	Dijon	W	3-0	*og (Lang), Cavani (p), Lucas*
23/09	a	Toulouse	L	0-2	
01/10	h	Bordeaux	W	2-0	*Cavani 2*
15/10	a	Nancy	W	2-1	*Lucas, Cavani*
23/10	h	Marseille	D	0-0	
28/10	a	LOSC	W	1-0	*Cavani*
06/11	h	Rennes	W	4-0	*og (Fernandes), Cavani, Rabiot, Verratti*
19/11	h	Nantes	W	2-0	*Di María, Jesé (p)*
27/11	a	Lyon	W	2-1	*Cavani 2 (1p)*
30/11	h	Angers	W	2-0	*Thiago Silva, Cavani (p)*
03/12	a	Montpellier	L	0-3	
11/12	h	Nice	D	2-2	*Cavani 2*
17/12	a	Guingamp	L	1-2	*Cavani*
21/12	h	Lorient	W	5-0	*Meunier, og (Touré), Thiago Silva, Cavani (p), Lucas*

2017

14/01	a	Rennes	W	1-0	*Draxler*
21/01	a	Nantes	W	2-0	*Cavani 2*
29/01	h	Monaco	D	1-1	*Cavani (p)*
04/02	a	Dijon	W	3-1	*Lucas, Thiago Silva, Cavani*
07/02	h	LOSC	W	2-1	*Cavani, Lucas*
10/02	a	Bordeaux	W	3-0	*Cavani 2, Di María*
19/02	h	Toulouse	D	0-0	
26/02	a	Marseille	W	5-1	*Marquinhos, Cavani, Lucas, Draxler, Matuidi*
04/03	h	Nancy	W	1-0	*Cavani (p)*
12/03	a	Lorient	W	2-1	*og (Jeannot), Nkunku*
19/03	h	Lyon	W	2-1	*Rabiot, Draxler*
09/04	h	Guingamp	W	4-0	*Di María, Cavani 2, Matuidi*
14/04	a	Angers	W	2-0	*Di María 2*
18/04	a	Metz	W	3-2	*Cavani, Matuidi 2*
22/04	h	Montpellier	W	2-0	*Cavani, Di María*
30/04	a	Nice	L	1-3	*Marquinhos*
06/05	h	Bastia	W	5-0	*Lucas, Verratti, Cavani 2, Marquinhos*
14/05	a	St-Étienne	W	5-0	*Cavani 2, Lucas 2, Draxler*
20/05	h	Caen	D	1-1	*Rabiot*

No	Name	Nat	DoB	Pos	Aps	(s)	Gls
16	Alphonse Areola		27/02/93	G	14	(1)	
29	Jean-Kévin Augustin		16/06/97	A	1	(9)	1
19	Serge Aurier	CIV	24/12/92	D	21	(1)	
21	Hatem Ben Arfa		07/03/87	M	5	(18)	
34	Lorenzo Callegari		27/02/98	M		(1)	
9	Edinson Cavani	URU	14/02/87	A	35	(1)	35
32	David Luiz	BRA	22/04/87	D	3		
11	Ángel Di María	ARG	14/02/88	M	24	(5)	6
23	Julian Draxler	GER	20/09/93	M	12	(5)	4
15	Gonçalo Guedes	POR	29/11/96	M	1	(6)	
36	Jonathan Ikoné		02/05/98	M	2	(2)	
22	Jesé	ESP	26/02/93	A	1	(8)	1
3	Presnel Kimpembe		13/08/95	D	19		
4	Grzegorz Krychowiak	POL	29/01/90	M	7	(4)	
20	Layvin Kurzawa		04/09/92	D	18		2
18	Giovani Lo Celso	ARG	09/04/96	M	1	(3)	
7	Lucas	BRA	13/08/92	M	29	(8)	12
5	Marquinhos	BRA	14/05/94	D	27	(2)	3
14	Blaise Matuidi		09/04/87	M	26	(8)	4
17	Maxwell	BRA	27/08/81	D	19	(1)	
12	Thomas Meunier	BEL	12/09/91	D	18	(4)	1
24	Christopher Nkunku		14/11/97	M	5	(3)	1
10	Javier Pastore	ARG	20/06/89	M	9	(6)	
25	Adrien Rabiot		03/04/95	M	20	(7)	3
8	Thiago Motta	ITA	28/08/82	M	25	(5)	
2	Thiago Silva	BRA	22/09/84	D	27		3
1	Kevin Trapp	GER	08/07/90	G	24		
6	Marco Verratti	ITA	05/11/92	M	25	(3)	3

Stade Rennais FC

1901 • Roazhon Park (29,269) • staderennais.com

Major honours
French Cup (2) 1965, 1971

Coach: Christian Gourcuff

2016

14/08	a	Nice	L	0-1	
20/08	h	Nancy	W	2-0	*Gourcuff, Sio*
27/08	a	Montpellier	D	1-1	*Diakhaby*
11/09	h	Caen	W	2-0	*Saïd, Prcić*
17/09	a	Monaco	L	0-3	
21/09	h	Marseille	W	3-2	*Sio, Grosicki (p), Hunou*
24/09	a	Dijon	L	0-3	
30/09	h	Guingamp	W	1-0	*Diakhaby*
16/10	h	Bordeaux	D	1-1	*og (Contento)*
22/10	a	Nantes	W	2-1	*Grosicki 2*
30/10	h	Metz	W	1-0	*Saïd*
06/11	a	Paris	L	0-4	
19/11	h	Angers	D	1-1	*Sio*
25/11	h	Toulouse	W	1-0	*Gourcuff*
29/11	a	Lorient	L	1-2	*Sio*
04/12	h	St-Étienne	W	2-0	*Ntep, Grosicki*
11/12	a	Lyon	L	0-1	
17/12	h	Bastia	L	1-2	*Sio*
21/12	a	LOSC	D	1-1	*Ntep*

2017

14/01	h	Paris	L	0-1	
21/01	a	Guingamp	D	1-1	*Gourcuff*
28/01	h	Nantes	D	1-1	*Gnagnon*
04/02	a	Bordeaux	D	1-1	*Gourcuff*
08/02	a	Angers	D	0-0	
12/02	h	Nice	D	2-2	*Amalfitano, Sio*
18/02	a	Marseille	L	0-2	
25/02	h	Lorient	W	1-0	*Sio*
04/03	a	Metz	D	1-1	*Saïd*
11/03	h	Dijon	D	1-1	*Saïd*
18/03	a	Toulouse	D	0-0	
02/04	h	Lyon	D	1-1	*Mubele*
08/04	a	Nancy	L	0-3	
15/04	h	LOSC	W	2-0	*Mubele, Sio*
23/04	a	St-Étienne	D	1-1	*Mexer*
29/04	a	Bastia	L	0-1	
07/05	h	Montpellier	W	1-0	*Mubele*
14/05	a	Caen	W	1-0	*Sio*
20/05	h	Monaco	L	2-3	*Diakhaby 2 (1p)*

No	Name	Nat	DoB	Pos	Aps	(s)	Gls
25	Afonso Figueiredo	POR	06/01/93	D	2	(3)	
18	Morgan Amalfitano		20/03/85	M	6		1
21	Benjamin André		03/08/90	M	36		
22	Sylvain Armand		01/08/80	D		(1)	
24	Ludovic Baal		24/05/86	D	33		
15	Rami Bensebaini	ALG	16/04/95	D	22	(3)	
19	Dimitri Cavaré		05/02/95	D	1	(1)	
8	Clément Chantôme		11/09/87	M	6	(1)	
1	Benoît Costil		03/07/87	G	38		
29	Romain Danzé		03/07/86	D	34	(1)	
31	Adama Diakhaby		05/07/96	M	3	(22)	4
9	Kermit Erasmus	RSA	08/07/90	A	1	(7)	
6	Gelson Fernandes	SUI	02/09/86	M	21	(6)	
32	Joris Gnagnon	CIV	13/01/97	D	27		1
28	Yoann Gourcuff		11/07/86	M	27		4
10	Kamil Grosicki	POL	08/06/88	M	9	(7)	4
23	Adrien Hunou		19/01/94	M	11	(11)	1
35	Nicolas Janvier		11/08/98	M	1	(3)	
14	Aldo Kalulu		21/01/96	A	5	(5)	
33	James Lea Siliki		12/06/96	M		(1)	
17	Ermir Lenjani	ALB	05/08/89	D		(2)	
4	Mexer	MOZ	08/12/88	D	21	(3)	1
12	Steven Moreira		13/08/94	D	1		
7	Firmin Mubele	COD	17/04/94	A	13	(2)	3
7	Paul-Georges Ntep		29/07/92	M	14	(1)	2
18	Pedro Henrique	BRA	16/06/90	A	4	(9)	
5	Pedro Mendes	POR	01/10/90	D	19		
26	Sanjin Prcić	BIH	20/11/93	M	21	(3)	1
11	Wesley Saïd		19/04/95	M	9	(16)	4
13	Giovanni Sio	CIV	31/03/89	A	32	(2)	9
2	Mehdi Zeffane	ALG	19/05/92	D	1		

AS Saint-Étienne

1919 • Geoffroy-Guichard (42,000) • asse.fr

Major honours
French League (10) 1957, 1964, 1967, 1968, 1969, 1970, 1974, 1975, 1976, 1981; French Cup (6) 1962, 1968, 1970, 1974, 1975, 1977; League Cup (1) 2013

Coach: Christophe Galtier

2016					
13/08	a	Bordeaux	L	2-3	*Hamouma, Søderlund*
21/08	h	Montpellier	W	3-1	*Monnet-Paquet, Saint-Louis, Berič*
28/08	h	Toulouse	D	0-0	
09/09	a	Paris	D	1-1	*Berič*
18/09	h	Bastia	W	1-0	*Hamouma (p)*
21/09	a	Nantes	D	0-0	
25/09	h	LOSC	W	3-1	*Berič, Nordin, Roux*
02/10	a	Lyon	L	0-2	
16/10	h	Dijon	D	1-1	*Roux (p)*
23/10	a	Caen	W	2-0	*Saivet, Veretout*
29/10	h	Monaco	D	1-1	*Perrin*
06/11	a	Metz	D	0-0	
20/11	h	Nice	L	0-1	
27/11	a	Angers	W	2-1	*Pogba, Tannane*
30/11	h	Marseille	D	0-0	
04/12	a	Rennes	L	0-2	
11/12	h	Guingamp	W	1-0	*Hamouma*
17/12	a	Lorient	L	1-2	*Pajot*
21/12	h	Nancy	D	0-0	
2017					
13/01	a	LOSC	D	1-1	*Hamouma*
22/01	h	Angers	W	2-1	*og (A Bamba), Perrin*
29/01	a	Toulouse	W	3-0	*Roux 2 (2p), Monnet-Paquet*
05/02	h	Lyon	W	2-0	*Monnet-Paquet, Hamouma*
08/02	a	Nice	L	0-1	
12/02	h	Lorient	W	4-0	*Perrin, Veretout, Hamouma, Jorginho*
19/02	a	Montpellier	L	1-2	*Monnet-Paquet*
26/02	h	Caen	L	0-1	
04/03	a	Bastia	D	0-0	
12/03	h	Metz	D	2-2	*Berič, Perrin*
19/03	a	Dijon	W	1-0	*Veretout*
09/04	h	Nantes	D	1-1	*Corgnet*
16/04	a	Marseille	L	0-4	
23/04	h	Rennes	D	1-1	*Berič*
29/04	a	Guingamp	W	2-0	*Pajot, Hamouma (p)*
05/05	h	Bordeaux	D	2-2	*Berič, Pajot*
14/05	h	Paris	L	0-5	
17/05	a	Monaco	L	0-2	
20/05	a	Nancy	L	1-3	*Nordin*

No	Name	Nat	DoB	Pos	Aps	(s)	Gls
27	Robert Berič	SVN	17/06/91	A	18	(4)	6
6	Jérémy Clément		26/08/84	M	3	(2)	
8	Benjamin Corgnet		06/04/87	M	3	(7)	1
7	Bryan Dabo		18/02/92	M	8	(6)	
34	Lamine Ghezali		06/07/99	A		(1)	
21	Romain Hamouma		29/03/87	M	22	(7)	7
26	Jorginho	POR	21/09/95	M	3	(2)	1
32	Benjamin Karamoko	CIV	17/05/95	D	1		
32	Hamidou Keyta		17/12/94	M	2	(2)	
4	Léo Lacroix	SUI	27/02/92	D	18	(2)	
18	Fabien Lemoine		16/03/87	M	9	(7)	
12	Cheick M'Bengue	SEN	23/07/88	D	15		
32	Habib Maïga	CIV	01/01/96	M	4	(1)	
1	Anthony Maissonial		23/03/98	G	1	(1)	
25	Kévin Malcuit		31/07/91	D	23	(2)	
22	Kévin Monnet-Paquet		19/08/88	A	27	(7)	4
30	Jessy Moulin		13/01/86	G	6		
35	Mickaël Nade		04/03/99	D	1		
31	Arnaud Nordin		17/06/98	M	5	(10)	2
5	Vincent Pajot		19/08/90	M	15	(6)	3
24	Loïc Perrin		07/08/85	D	26	(1)	4
33	Ronaël Pierre-Gabriel		13/06/98	D	11	(3)	
19	Florentin Pogba	GUI	19/08/90	D	16	(1)	1
3	Pierre-Yves Polomat		27/12/93	D	6	(5)	
31	Kenny Rocha Santos	CPV	03/01/00	M	1	(2)	
9	Nolan Roux		01/03/88	A	12	(9)	4
16	Stéphane Ruffier		27/09/86	G	31		
31	Dylan Saint-Louis		26/04/95	A	1		1
11	Henri Saivet	SEN	26/10/90	M	21	(6)	1
17	Ole Kristian Selnæs	NOR	07/07/94	M	23	(3)	
23	Alexander Søderlund	NOR	03/08/87	A	8	(9)	1
10	Oussama Tannane	MAR	23/03/94	M	14	(3)	1
2	Kévin Théophile-Catherine		28/10/89	D	30	(1)	
14	Jordan Veretout		01/03/93	M	34	(1)	3

Toulouse FC

1970 • Stadium Municipal (20,907) • tfc.info

Coach: Pascal Dupraz

2016					
14/08	a	Marseille	D	0-0	
20/08	h	Bordeaux	W	4-1	*Diop, Jullien, Braithwaite 2*
28/08	a	St-Étienne	D	0-0	
10/09	a	Bastia	L	1-2	*Braithwaite*
17/09	h	Guingamp	W	2-1	*Braithwaite (p), Durmaz*
20/09	a	LOSC	W	2-1	*Toivonen 2*
23/09	h	Paris	W	2-0	*Bodiger (p), Durmaz*
01/10	a	Caen	L	0-1	
14/10	h	Monaco	W	3-1	*Trejo, Braithwaite 2*
22/10	a	Angers	D	0-0	
29/10	h	Lyon	L	1-2	*Jullien*
05/11	a	Nantes	D	1-1	*Braithwaite (p)*
19/11	h	Metz	L	1-2	*Edouard*
25/11	a	Rennes	L	0-1	
30/11	h	Montpellier	W	1-0	*Sylla*
04/12	a	Nice	L	0-3	
10/12	h	Lorient	W	3-2	*Toivonen 3*
17/12	h	Nancy	D	1-1	*Jullien*
21/12	a	Dijon	L	0-2	
2017					
14/01	h	Nantes	L	0-1	
21/01	a	Bordeaux	L	0-1	
29/01	h	St-Étienne	L	0-3	
05/02	h	Angers	W	4-0	*Delort, Braithwaite (p), Trejo, Toivonen*
08/02	a	Lorient	D	1-1	*Delort*
11/02	h	Bastia	W	4-1	*Delort, Braithwaite 2 (1p), Diop*
19/02	a	Paris	D	0-0	
25/02	a	Nancy	D	0-0	
05/03	h	LOSC	D	1-1	*Jullien*
12/03	a	Lyon	L	0-4	
18/03	h	Rennes	D	0-0	
02/04	a	Montpellier	W	1-0	*Delort*
09/04	h	Marseille	D	0-0	
15/04	a	Guingamp	L	1-2	*Delort (p)*
23/04	h	Nice	D	1-1	*Jean*
29/04	a	Monaco	L	1-3	*Toivonen*
06/05	h	Caen	L	0-1	
14/05	a	Metz	D	1-1	*Braithwaite*
20/05	h	Dijon	D	0-0	

No	Name	Nat	DoB	Pos	Aps	(s)	Gls
7	Jean-Daniel Akpa-Akpro	CIV	11/10/92	M		(2)	
2	Kelvin Amian		08/02/98	D	20	(2)	
27	Alexis Blin		16/09/96	M	26		
23	Yann Bodiger		09/02/95	M	23	(6)	1
9	Martin Braithwaite	DEN	05/06/91	A	33	(1)	11
32	Mathieu Cafaro		25/03/97	M		(4)	
39	Andy Delort		09/10/91	A	15		5
33	Quentin Depehi		06/06/97	A		(1)	
5	Issa Diop		09/07/97	D	30		2
4	Tongo Doumbia	MLI	06/08/89	M	5	(5)	
21	Jimmy Durmaz	SWE	22/03/89	M	17	(10)	2
18	Odsonne Edouard		16/01/98	A	4	(12)	1
1	Mauro Goicoechea	URU	27/03/88	G	2		
15	Corentin Jean		15/07/95	A	16		1
6	Christopher Jullien		22/03/93	D	35		4
40	Alban Lafont		23/01/99	G	36		
8	Dodi Lukebakio	COD	24/09/97	M		(5)	
34	Clément Michelin		11/05/97	D	6	(2)	
29	François Moubandje	SUI	21/06/90	D	34		
3	Yrondu Musavu-King	GAB	08/01/92	D	3		
24	Pavle Ninkov	SRB	20/04/85	D		(9)	
25	Jessy Pi		24/09/93	M	3	(12)	
17	Ibrahim Sangaré	CIV	02/12/97	M	3	(2)	
14	François Sirieix		07/10/80	M		(4)	
19	Somália	BRA	28/09/88	M	18	(10)	
12	Issiaga Sylla	GUI	01/01/94	M	21	(6)	1
11	Ola Toivonen	SWE	03/07/86	A	19	(16)	7
18	Óscar Trejo	ARG	26/04/88	M	27	(2)	2
22	Dušan Veškovac	SRB	16/03/86	D	1		
20	Steeve Yago	BFA	16/12/92	D	21	(1)	

Top goalscorers

35	Edinson Cavani (Paris)
28	Alexandre Lacazette (Lyon)
21	Radamel Falcao (Monaco)
20	Bafétimbi Gomis (Marseille)
15	Ivan Santini (Caen)
	Florian Thauvin (Marseille)
	Kylian Mbappé (Monaco)
	Mario Balotelli (Nice)
14	Nicolas De Préville (LOSC)
	Steve Mounié (Montpellier)

Promoted clubs

RC Strasbourg Alsace

1906 • La Meinau (29,320) • rcstrasbourgalsace.fr

Major honours
French League (1) 1979; French Cup (3) 1951, 1966, 2001; League Cup (2) 1997, 2005

Coach: Thierry Laurey

Amiens SC

1901 • La Licorne (12,097) • amiensfootball.com

Coach: Christophe Pélissier

ES Troyes AC

1986 • L'Aube (20,400) • estac.fr

Coach: Jean-Louis Garcia

Second level final table 2016/17

		Pld	W	D	L	F	A	Pts
1	RC Strasbourg Alsace	38	19	10	9	63	47	67
2	Amiens SC	38	19	9	10	56	38	66
3	ES Troyes AC	38	19	9	10	59	43	66
4	RC Lens	38	18	11	9	59	40	65
5	Stade Brestois 29	38	19	8	11	58	44	65
6	Nîmes Olympique	38	17	13	8	58	40	64
7	Stade de Reims	38	14	13	11	42	39	55
8	Le Havre AC	38	14	12	12	39	31	54
9	Gazélec FC Ajaccio	38	13	12	13	47	51	51
10	Chamois Niortais FC	38	12	13	13	45	57	49
11	AC Ajaccio	38	13	9	16	47	58	48
12	Clermont Foot Auvergne	38	11	13	14	46	48	46
13	FC Sochaux-Montbéliard	38	11	13	14	38	43	46
14	Valenciennes FC	38	10	15	13	44	44	45
15	Football Bourg-en-Bresse Péronnas 01	38	11	11	16	49	58	44
16	Tours FC	38	10	13	15	55	60	43
17	AJ Auxerre	38	11	10	17	28	40	43
18	US Orléans	38	11	9	18	41	54	38
19	Red Star FC	38	8	12	18	36	56	36
20	Stade Lavallois MFC	38	5	15	18	33	52	30

NB US Orléans – 4 pts deducted.

Promotion play-offs

(25/05/17 & 28/05/17)
Troyes 2-1 Lorient
Lorient 0-0 Troyes
(Troyes 2-1)

DOMESTIC CUPS

Coupe de France 2016/17

1/32 FINALS

(06/01/17)
Avranches 3-1 Laval
Les Herbiers 4-3 GFC Ajaccio
Monaco 2-1 AC Ajaccio

(07/01/17)
Bergerac 2-2 Rodeo *(aet; 3-2 on pens)*
Besançon 0-3 Nancy
Blagnac 0-1 Niort
Blois 1-2 Nantes
Grenoble 1-2 Fréjus-St-Raphaël
Guingamp 2-1 Le Havre
Hauts Lyonnais 0-0 CA Bastia *(aet; 3-4 on pens)*
Le Poiré sur Vie 3-1 Viry Châtillon
LOSC 4-1 Excelsior
Louhans-Cuiseaux 0-2 Dijon
Paris SG 7-0 SC Bastia
Quevilly Rouen 3-2 Drancy JA
Sarreguemines 2-1 Reims
Strasbourg 4-2 Épinal *(aet)*

(08/01/17)
Auxerre 4-2 Troyes *(aet)*
Biarritz 0-6 Rennes
Châteauroux 4-1 Pau
Clermont 0-1 Bordeaux
Croix Football IC 1-4 St-Étienne
Granville 1-2 Angers
Istres 1-3 Consolat Marseille *(aet)*
Lens 2-0 Metz
Lorient 2-1 Nice
Lyon 5-0 Montpellier
Sainte Geneviève 0-3 Caen
Toulouse 1-2 Marseille *(aet)*

(14/01/17)
Lunéville 0-2 Chambly
Prix-lès-Mézières 2-1 Feignies-Aulnoye

(18/01/17)
Fleury 91 2-0 Brest

1/16 FINALS

(31/01/17)
Bergerac 2-0 Lens
Bordeaux 2-1 Dijon
Châteauroux 2-3 Lorient *(aet)*
Le Poiré sur Vie 0-1 Strasbourg
LOSC 1-0 Nantes
Marseille 2-1 Lyon *(aet)*
Quevilly Rouen 3-0 Consolat Marseille
Sarreguemines 0-3 Niort

(01/02/17)
Angers 3-1 Caen
Auxerre 3-0 St-Étienne *(aet)*
Avranches 1-0 Fleury 91
CA Bastia 2-0 Nancy
Chambly 4-5 Monaco *(aet)*
Fréjus-St-Raphaël 1-0 Prix-lès-Mézières
Les Herbiers 1-2 Guingamp *(aet)*
Rennes 0-4 Paris SG

1/8 FINALS

(28/02/17)
Bordeaux 2-1 Lorient
CA Bastia 0-1 Angers
Fréjus-St-Raphaël 2-0 Auxerre

(01/03/17)
Avranches 1-1 Strasbourg *(aet, 6-5 on pens)*
Marseille 3-4 Monaco *(aet)*
Niort 0-2 Paris SG
Quevilly Rouen 1-2 Guingamp

(02/03/17)
Bergerac 1-2 LOSC

QUARTER-FINALS

(04/04/17)
Fréjus-St-Raphaël 0-1 Guingamp *(Mendy 50)*

Monaco 2-1 LOSC *(Germain 35, 45; El Ghazi 90+3)*

(05/04/17)
Angers 2-1 Bordeaux *(Bérigaud 8, N'Doye 67; Sankharé 18)*

Avranches 0-4 Paris SG *(Ben Arfa 35, 53, Lucas 56, Pastore 82)*

SEMI-FINALS

(25/04/17)
Angers 2-0 Guingamp *(Mangani 38, Toko Ekambi 90+2)*

(26/04/17)
Paris SG 5-0 Monaco *(Draxler 26, Cavani 31, Mbaé 50og, Matuidi 52, Marquinhos 90)*

FINAL

(27/05/17)
Stade de France, Saint-Denis
PARIS SAINT-GERMAIN 1 *(Cissokho 90+1og)*
ANGERS SCO 0
Referee: *Bastien*
PARIS: *Areola, Aurier, Marquinhos, Thiago Silva, Maxwell, Verratti, Thiago Motta, Matuidi, Di María, Cavani, Draxler (Pastore 72)*
ANGERS: *Letellier, Cissokho, Traoré, Thomas, Manceau, Santamaria (Bérigaud 90+2), Pépé (Tait 84), N'Doye, Mangani, Toko Ekambi, Diedhiou (J Bamba 63)*

Coupe de la Ligue 2016/17

QUARTER-FINALS

(10/01/17)
Nantes 0-2 Nancy *(Dalé 31, Cuffaut 45+3)*

Sochaux 1-1 Monaco *(Andriatsima 16; João Moutinho 83) (aet; 3-4 on pens)*

(11/01/17)
Bordeaux 3-2 Guingamp *(Kamano 16, Laborde 36, 65; Privat 11, Benezet 88)*

Paris SG 2-0 Metz *(Thiago Silva 27, 72)*

SEMI-FINALS

(24/01/17)
Bordeaux 1-4 Paris SG *(Rolán 32; Di María 19, 81, Cavani 60, 74)*

(25/01/17)
Monaco 1-0 Nancy *(Falcao 45+2)*

FINAL

(01/04/17)
Parc OL, Lyon
PARIS SAINT-GERMAIN 4 *(Draxler 4, Di María 44, Cavani 54, 90)*
AS MONACO FC 1 *(Lemar 27)*
Referee: *Schneider*
PARIS: *Trapp, Aurier, Thiago Silva, Kimpembe, Kurzawa, Verratti (Matuidi 81), Thiago Motta (Lucas 86), Rabiot, Di María, Cavani, Draxler (Pastore 55)*
MONACO: *Subašić, Sidibé (Touré 90+3), Glik, Jemerson, Mendy, Bernardo Silva, João Moutinho, Bakayoko, Lemar (Cardona 77), Germain (Dirar 62), Mbappé*

Paris Saint-Germain's Coupe de France win completed a hat-trick of domestic cup doubles

GEORGIA

Georgian Football Federation (GFF)

Address 76a Chavchavadze Ave.
GE-0179 Tbilisi
Tel +995 32 291 2670
Fax +995 32 291 5995
E-mail gff@gff.ge
Website gff.ge

President Levan Kobiashvili
General secretary David Mujiri
Media officer Otar Giorgadze
Year of formation 1990
National stadium Boris Paichadze Dinamo Arena, Tbilisi (53,233)

KEY

- UEFA Champions League
- UEFA Europa League
- Relegated

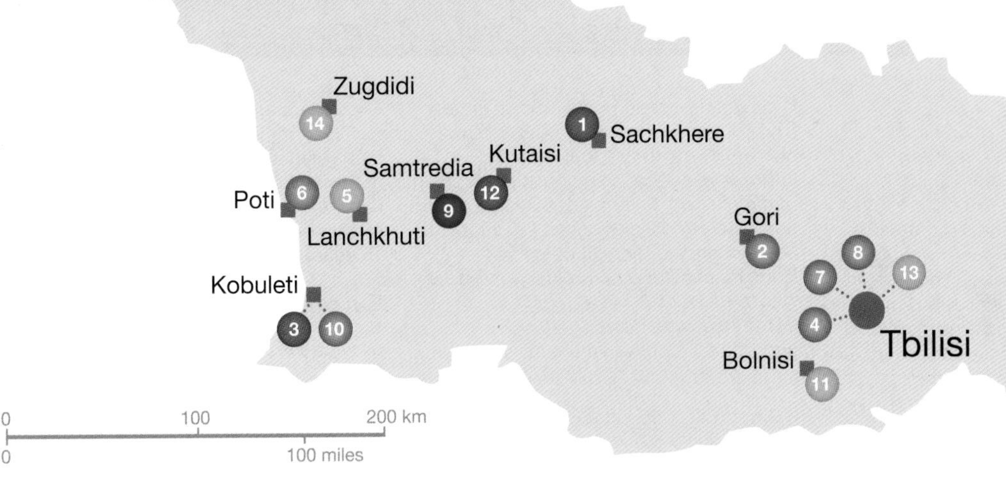

UMAGLESI LIGA CLUBS

  1 **FC Chikhura Sachkhere**

  2 **FC Dila Gori**

  3 **FC Dinamo Batumi**

  4 **FC Dinamo Tbilisi**

 5 **FC Guria Lanchkhuti**

  6 **FC Kolkheti Poti**

  7 **FC Locomotive Tbilisi**

  8 **FC Saburtalo Tbilisi**

  9 **FC Samtredia**

 10 **FC Shukura Kobuleti**

  11 **FC Sioni Bolnisi**

  12 **FC Torpedo Kutaisi**

  13 **FC Tskhinvali**

  14 **FC Zugdidi**

Smooth transition for Samtredia

A switch to a spring-to-autumn schedule entailed a brief transitional Georgian championship in the autumn of 2016, and it produced an unlikely outcome as two provincial clubs who had never previously been crowned national champions, Samtredia and Chikhura Sachkhere, won their respective groups to reach the play-off final.

It was Samtredia, runners-up in 2015/16, who emerged triumphant, 4-2 on aggregate, as defending champions Dinamo Tbilisi surprisingly failed to qualify for Europe. Their lengthy run of success in the Georgian Cup was also ended by eventual winners Torpedo Kutaisi.

Provincials win short stop-gap championship

Chikhura beaten in two-legged title play-off

Torpedo Kutaisi take domestic cup honours

Domestic league

In order to pave the way for the revamped league structure in 2017, headed by a ten-team top flight entitled the Erovnuli Liga, 14 clubs did battle from August to December in what would be the final Umaglesi Liga. They were split – by 2015/16 classification – into two seven-team groups (Red and White), with each club playing the others in their section twice before the end-of-season play-offs, the main event of which was the home-and-away championship decider between the two group winners.

Samtredia were strongly fancied to win the Red Group, and they duly delivered, remaining unbeaten until they had clinched their place in the final with two games to spare, the goals of 22-year-old striker Budu Zivzivadze, who topped the scoring charts with 11 goals, ensuring a steady run of positive results for Gia Tsetsadze's side. Dinamo Tbilisi, meanwhile, were expected to dominate the White Group, but when Chikhura beat them 2-1 in Tbilisi, it not only led to the sacking of Dinamo's 2015/16 double-winning coach Juraj Jarábek, but also enabled their conquerors to take control of the section. They eventually finished six points clear to book their place in the title showdown with Samtredia.

Led by long-serving coach Soso Pruidze, Chikhura had won all six away fixtures, but they were unable to keep that impressive sequence going in the first leg of the play-off, a Zivzivadze double giving hosts Samtredia a precious 2-0 win. The second leg, staged eight days at the Boris Paichadze Dinamo Arena in Tbilisi, was to be bossed once again by Samtredia, who made it 4-0 on aggregate before Chikhura salvaged some pride with a couple of late replies.

If Samtredia's first title was a turn-up for the books, so too was the result of the UEFA Europa League qualification play-off final the previous day, with Dinamo Tbilisi losing 1-0 to Red Group runners-up Dinamo Batumi and thus missing out on Europe for only the second time since independence. The relegation play-offs proved fatal for Guria Lanchkhuti and Sioni Bolnisi, who joined Zugdidi and Tskhinvali in the new ten-club second tier (Erovnuli Liga 2). No clubs were promoted in their place.

Domestic cup

Torpedo Kutaisi finished eight points behind Dinamo Tbilisi in the White Group, failing to score in their two encounters, but they sprung a surprise in the Georgian Cup semi-finals when they triumphed 3-2 in the capital to eliminate the club that had won the four previous editions of the competition.

The other semi also produced an upset as Chikhura lost 3-0 to Merani Martvili, a club relegated from the top division six months earlier. Order, however, was restored in the final as Torpedo reclaimed the trophy for the first time in 15 years with a 2-1 victory in Zestafoni.

Europe

Only one European tie was won by a Georgian club in 2016/17. All three UEFA Europa League participants had bitten the dust before Dinamo Tbilisi saw off the Armenians of Alashkert in the second qualifying round of the UEFA Champions League. Subsequent ties against Dinamo Zagreb and PAOK, however, proved too tough for the Georgian champions, who failed to score in any of the four matches.

National team

There were no wins recorded by Georgia in their first six 2018 FIFA World Cup qualifiers, a bleak balance sheet under new Slovakian coach Vladimír Weiss displaying three draws and three defeats. The team's most impressive performance came in a 1-1 draw away to Wales, where playmaker Jano Ananidze virtually ran the show. The 24-year-old was one of several Georgian players to lift club silverware abroad in 2016/17, his Russian title win with Spartak Moskva arguably the most prestigious.

DOMESTIC SEASON AT A GLANCE

Umaglesi Liga 2016 final tables

Red Group	Pld	Home W	Home D	Home L	Home F	Home A	Away W	Away D	Away L	Away F	Away A	Total W	Total D	Total L	Total F	Total A	Pts
1 FC Samtredia	12	4	1	1	11	4	4	2	0	16	5	8	3	1	27	9	27
2 FC Dinamo Batumi	12	2	2	2	9	4	3	3	0	11	1	5	5	2	20	5	20
3 FC Saburtalo Tbilisi	12	3	3	0	14	6	2	1	3	3	6	5	4	3	17	12	19
4 FC Kolkheti Poti	12	3	0	3	5	9	3	0	3	5	9	6	0	6	10	18	18
5 FC Dila Gori	12	3	2	1	8	4	2	0	4	5	8	5	2	5	13	12	17
6 FC Sioni Bolnisi	12	2	0	4	7	11	1	2	3	6	8	3	2	7	13	19	11
7 FC Zugdidi	12	2	0	4	2	11	0	0	6	3	19	2	0	10	5	30	6

White Group	Pld	Home W	Home D	Home L	Home F	Home A	Away W	Away D	Away L	Away F	Away A	Total W	Total D	Total L	Total F	Total A	Pts
1 FC Chikhura Sachkhere	12	3	2	1	11	7	6	0	0	16	4	9	2	1	27	11	29
2 FC Dinamo Tbilisi	12	2	3	1	9	3	4	2	0	8	2	6	5	1	17	5	23
3 FC Torpedo Kutaisi	12	3	1	2	11	5	1	2	3	5	7	4	3	5	16	12	15
4 FC Locomotive Tbilisi	12	2	3	1	6	6	2	0	4	5	12	4	3	5	11	18	15
5 FC Shukura Kobuleti	12	2	0	4	7	10	0	6	0	3	3	2	6	4	10	13	12
6 FC Guria Lanchkhuti	12	2	2	2	3	5	1	0	5	5	16	3	2	7	8	21	11
7 FC Tskhinvali	12	1	1	4	7	11	1	2	3	5	10	2	3	7	12	21	9

Championship Play-offs

(03/12/16 & 11/12/16)
Erosi Manjgaladze, Samtredia
FC SAMTREDIA 2 *(Zivzivadze 18, 40)*
FC CHIKHURA SACHKHERE 0
Referee: *Silagava*
SAMTREDIA: *Migineishvili, Gogiashvili, Sandokhadze, Mchedlishvili, Shergelashvili, Datunaishvili, Rajamashvili (Mtivlishvili 90+5), Manjgaladze (Tsnobiladze 90+5), Arabuli, Zivzivadze, Jikia (Gamkrelidze 86)*
CHIKHURA: *Hamzić, Kashia, Rekhviashvili, Grigalashvili, Gorgiashvili, Ganugrava (Lekvtadze 46), Dobrovolski, Koripadze, Lobjanidze (Gabedava 87), Tatanashvili (Mumladze 46), Sardalishvili*

Boris Paichadze Dinamo Arena, Tbilisi
FC CHIKHURA SACHKHERE 2 *(Dekanoidze 82, Lobjanidze 90p)*
FC SAMTREDIA 2 *(Arubuli 42p, Datunaishvili 59)*
Referee: *Silagava*
CHIKHURA: *Hamzić, Kashia, Rekhviashvili, Kakubava, Grigalashvili, Ganugrava (Dekanoidze 46), Lekvtadze, Koripadze, Lobjanidze, Mumladze (Gabedava 46), Sardalishvili*
SAMTREDIA: *Migineishvili, Gogiashvili, Sandokhadze (Imedashvili 77), Mchedlishvili, Shergelashvili, Datunaishvili, Rajamashvili (Gamkrelidze 65), Manjgaladze, Arabuli (Markozashvili 73), Zivzivadze, Jikia*

(Samtredia 4-2)

European qualification 2017/18

Champion: FC Samtredia (second qualifying round)

Cup winner: FC Torpedo Kutaisi (first qualifying round)

FC Chikhura Sachkhere (first qualifying round)
FC Dinamo Batumi (first qualifying round)

Top scorer	Budu Zivzivadze (Samtredia), 11 goals
Relegated clubs	FC Zugdidi, FC Tskhinvali, FC Sioni Bolnisi, FC Guria Lanchkhuti
Promoted clubs	none
Cup final	FC Torpedo Kutaisi 2-1 FC Merani Martvili

Player of the season

Budu Zivzivadze
(FC Samtredia)

A scorer of 16 goals in 29 appearances for Samtredia during the 2015/16 Umaglesi Liga campaign, Kutaisi-born Zivzivadze upped his strike rate in the transitional autumn championship, scoring 11 times in 12 starts to top the league's golden boot rankings before netting the two goals that brought his club a decisive 2-0 lead in the first leg of the title play-off against Chikhura. He was rewarded two-fold for his efforts in early 2017, making his national team debut for Georgia against Uzbekistan and earning a transfer to Danish Superliga club Esbjerg.

Newcomer of the season

Otar Kiteishvili
(FC Dinamo Tbilisi)

Although he had played his part for Dinamo Tbilisi in their 2015/16 double-winning campaign, it was during the second half of 2016 that Kiteishvili's talent really came to the fore, the 20-year-old midfielder repeatedly impressing for the club in Europe – not least with a goal on his UEFA Champions League bow in a qualifying victory over Alashkert – then in the transitional Umaglesi Liga campaign, where by common consent he was Dinamo's standout performer. A first cap for the senior Georgian national side duly followed in January 2017.

Team of the season

(4-4-2)

Coach: Tsetsadze *(Samtredia)*

GEORGIA

NATIONAL TEAM

Top five all-time caps
Levan Kobiashvili (100); Zurab Khizanishvili (93); Kakha Kaladze (83); Giorgi Nemsadze (69); Aleksandre Iashvili (67)

Top five all-time goals
Shota Arveladze (26); Temur Ketsbaia (17); Aleksandre Iashvili (15); Giorgi Demetradze & Levan Kobiashvili (12)

Results 2016/17

05/09/16	Austria (WCQ)	H	Tbilisi	L	1-2	*Ananidze (78)*
06/10/16	Republic of Ireland (WCQ)	A	Dublin	L	0-1	
09/10/16	Wales (WCQ)	A	Cardiff	D	1-1	*Okriashvili (57)*
12/11/16	Moldova (WCQ)	H	Tbilisi	D	1-1	*Kazaishvili (16)*
23/01/17	Uzbekistan	N	Dubai (UAE)	D	2-2	*Shonia (69), S Lobjanidze (77)*
25/01/17	Jordan	N	Dubai (UAE)	L	0-1	
24/03/17	Serbia (WCQ)	H	Tbilisi	L	1-3	*Kacharava (6)*
28/03/17	Latvia	H	Tbilisi	W	5-0	*Ananidze (18p, 77), Kvilitaia (33, 66), Arabidze (89)*
07/06/17	St Kitts & Nevis	H	Tbilisi	W	3-0	*Arabidze (50, 72p), Dvalishvili (81)*
11/06/17	Moldova (WCQ)	A	Chisinau	D	2-2	*Merebashvili (65), Kazaishvili (70)*

Appearances 2016/17

Coach: Vladimír Weiss (SVK)	22/09/64		AUT	IRL	WAL	MDA	Uzb	Jor	SRB	Lva	Skn	MDA	Caps	Goals
Giorgi Loria	27/01/86	Krylya Sovetov (RUS)	G	G	G	G			G				39	-
Ucha Lobjanidze	23/02/87	Dinamo Tbilisi /Atyrau (KAZ)	D84				D	D63		D		D35	54	1
Solomon Kverkvelia	06/02/92	Rubin (RUS) /Lokomotiv Moskva (RUS)	D	D	D	D			D		s73	D	23	-
Aleksandre Amisulashvili	20/08/82	Dinamo Tbilisi	D76										50	4
Giorgi Navalovski	28/06/86	Veria (GRE) /Neftçi (AZE)	D	D89	D	D			D	D78	D77	D	23	-
Murtaz Daushvili	01/05/89	Diósgyőr (HUN)	M	M93	M	M					s46	M46	34	-
Guram Kashia	04/07/87	Vitesse (NED)	M	D	D	D			D	D	D	D	55	1
Jambul Jigauri	08/07/92	Dinamo Tbilisi /Vardar (MKD)	M		s91				s90	A63			6	-
Jano Ananidze	10/10/92	Spartak Moskva (RUS)	M	M73	M93				M	M83			36	6
Valeri Kazaishvili	29/01/93	Legia (POL)	M	M	M	M80			M83	s83	M67	s46	25	5
Vladimer Dvalishvili	20/04/86	Dinamo Tbilisi /Atyrau (KAZ)	A63		s75	s71	s70	A		A63	s67	A65	42	6
Davit Skhirtladze	16/03/93	Silkeborg (DEN)	s63	s73		s80							3	-
Tornike Okriashvili	12/02/92	unattached /Krasnodar (RUS)	s76	M	M91	M							34	8
Giorgi Chanturia	11/04/93	Ural (RUS)	s84			M							14	2
Otar Kakabadze	27/06/95	Gimnàstic ((ESP) /Esbjerg (DEN)		D	D	D			D70		D73		9	-
Valerian Gvilia	24/05/94	BATE (BLR)		M	M	M71			M90	M36			5	-
Levan Mchedlidze	24/03/90	Empoli (ITA)		A	A75								31	3
Aleksandre Kobakhidze	11/02/87	Vorskla (UKR) /Göztepe (TUR)		s89						s63			35	3
Nika Kacharava	13/01/94	Ethnikos Achnas (CYP)		s93	s93				A	s78	A67	A	7	1
Giorgi Kvilitaia	01/10/93	Rapid Wien (AUT)				A64			s83	A78			6	2
Jaba Kankava	18/03/86	Reims (FRA)				s64			M		M	M	66	7
Roin Kvaskhvadze	31/05/89	Torpedo Kutaisi					G						6	-
David Khocholava	08/02/93	Chornomorets (UKR)					D	D		D			3	-
Giorgi Rekhviashvili	22/02/88	Locomotive Tbilisi					D						1	-
Lasha Shergelashvili	17/01/92	Rīgas FS (LVA)					D89	D88			s77		3	-
Saba Lobjanidze	18/12/94	Dinamo Tbilisi					M82	M79					2	1
Teimuraz Shonia	28/05/90	Dinamo Batumi					M84	M85					2	1
Otar Kiteishvili	26/03/96	Dinamo Tbilisi					M89	M		s36			3	-
Bachana Arabuli	05/01/94	Dinamo Tbilisi					M57	s46			A46		3	-
Beka Tugushi	24/01/89	Torpedo Kutaisi					M70	M82					2	-
Budu Zivzivadze	10/03/94	Samtredia					A	A46					2	-
Lasha Parunashvili	14/02/93	Dinamo Tbilisi					s57						1	-
Giorgi Kharaishvili	29/07/96	Saburtalo					s82	s85					2	-
Oleg Mamasakhlisi	25/11/95	Torpedo Kutaisi					s84	s82					2	-
Jemal Tabidze	18/03/96	Gent (BEL) /Ural (RUS)					s89	D		s78	D	D	5	-
Giorgi Papunashvili	02/09/95	Dinamo Tbilisi					s89						4	-
Omar Migineishvili	02/06/84	Samtredia						G					2	-
Tornike Grigalashvili	28/01/93	Chikhura						s63					1	-
Giorgi Kimadze	11/02/92	Torpedo Kutaisi						s79					1	-
Giorgi Ganugrava	21/02/88	Chikhura						s88					10	-
Nika Kvekveskiri	29/05/92	Qäbälä (AZE)							M	M	M46	s35	9	-
Giorgi Arabidze	04/03/98	Shakhtar Donetsk (UKR)							s70	s63	s46	M	4	3
Giorgi Makaridze	31/03/90	Moreirense (POR)								G	G	G	8	-
Giorgi Merebashvili	15/08/86	Wisła Płock (POL)									M	s65	20	1
Elguja Lobjanidze	17/09/92	Orenburg (RUS)									s67		1	-

EUROPE

FC Dinamo Tbilisi

Second qualifying round - Alashkert FC (ARM)
H 2-0 *Kiteishvili (55), Kvilitaia (69p)*
Scribe, Lobjanidze (Kiteishvili 49), Amisulashvili, Chanturishvili, Dvalishvili (Coureur 83), Kvilitaia (Papunashvili 76), Parunashvili, Rene, Jigauri, Špičić, Velev. Coach: Juraj Jarábek (SVK)
A 1-1 *Jigauri (21)*
Scribe, Lobjanidze, Amisulashvili, Chanturishvili (Coureur 84), Dvalishvili, Kvilitaia (Tsintsadze 62), Kiteishvili (Papunashvili 68), Parunashvili, Rene, Jigauri, Chelidze. Coach: Juraj Jarábek (SVK)

Third qualifying round - GNK Dinamo Zagreb (CRO)
A 0-2
Scribe, Lobjanidze, Amisulashvili, Chanturishvili, Dvalishvili (Tsintsadze 78), Papunashvili (Coureur 56), Kiteishvili (Gelashvili 46), Parunashvili, Rene, Jigauri, Chelidze. Coach: Juraj Jarábek (SVK)
H 0-1
Scribe, Lobjanidze, Amisulashvili, Chanturishvili, Dvalishvili, Papunashvili (Mikel Álvaro 72), Parunashvili, Coureur (Gelashvili 46), Rene, Jigauri, Špičić (Kiteishvili 46). Coach: Juraj Jarábek (SVK)

Play-offs - PAOK FC (GRE)
H 0-3
Scribe, Lobjanidze (Tevzadze 58), Amisulashvili, Tsintsadze (Mikel Álvaro 70), Chanturishvili, Papunashvili (Dvalishvili 63), Kiteishvili, Parunashvili, Rene, Jigauri, Chelidze. Coach: Juraj Jarábek (SVK)
A 0-2
Scribe, Lobjanidze, Amisulashvili, Tsintsadze (Velev 74), Dvalishvili (Mikeltadze 77), Papunashvili, Kiteishvili (Chanturishvili 62), Parunashvili, Mikel Álvaro, Rene, Špičić. Coach: Juraj Jarábek (SVK)

FC Samtredia

First qualifying round – Qäbälä FK (AZE)
A 1-5 *Shergelashvili (59)*
Migineishvili, Gogiashvili, Sandokhadze, Manjgaladze (Tsnobiladze 71), Rajamashvili, Arabuli, Zivzivadze (Markozashvili 59), Jikia (Gamkrelidze 46), Shergelashvili, Mchedlishvili, Datunaishvili. Coach: Gia Tsetsadze (GEO)
H 2-1 *Zivzivadze (14p), Shergelashvili (90+2)*
Migineishvili, Gogiashvili, Sandokhadze, Arabuli, Zivzivadze, Tsnobiladze (Rajamashvili 75), Shergelashvili, Mchedlishvili, Datunaishvili, Gorgiashvili (Manjgaladze 46), Gamkrelidze (Jikia 63). Coach: Gia Tsetsadze (GEO)

FC Dila Gori

First qualifying round - FC Shirak (ARM)
H 1-0 *Modebadze (36)*
Mujrishvili, Samkharadze, Razmadze, Tsikaridze (Kikabidze 68), Nonikashvili (Katamadze 89), Modebadze, Kvirkvelia, Eristavi (Sabadze 79), Gongadze, Dolidze, Karkuzashvili. Coach: Ucha Sosiashvili (GEO)
A 0-1 (aet; 1-4 on pens)
Mujrishvili, Samkharadze, Razmadze, Tsikaridze (Sharikadze 72), Japaridze (Kikabidze 91), Modebadze, Kvirkvelia, Eristavi (Nonikashvili 68), Gongadze, Dolidze, Karkuzashvili. Coach: Ucha Sosiashvili (GEO)

FC Chikhura Sachkhere

First qualifying round - FC Zimbru Chisinau (MDA)
A 1-0 *Tatanashvili (39)*
Hamzić, Grigalashvili, Ganugrava, Lobjanidze (Lekvtadze 66), Gabedava (Dobrovolski 57), Tatanashvili, Kakubava, Ivanishvili (Dekanoidze 90+2), Chikvaidze, Kashia, Rekhviashvili. Coach: Soso Pruidze (GEO)
Red card: Ganugrava 61
H 2-3 *Ivanishvili (13), Kakubava (55)*
Hamzić, Grigalashvili, Lobjanidze (Dekanoidze 78), Koripadze, Tatanashvili (Mumladze 90+1), Kakubava, Ivanishvili (Lekvtadze 71), Chikvaidze, Dobrovolski, Kashia, Rekhviashvili. Coach: Soso Pruidze (GEO)

DOMESTIC LEAGUE CLUB-BY-CLUB

FC Chikhura Sachkhere

1938 • Central (750) • fcchikhura.ge

Coach: Soso Pruidze

2016

Date		Opponent		Score	Scorers
07/08	h	Dinamo Tbilisi	D	0-0	
13/08	a	Shukura	W	3-1	*Lobjanidze, Tatanashvili, Mumladze*
20/08	h	Locomotive	W	3-2	*Grigalashvili, Lobjanidze 2*
27/08	a	Torpedo	W	3-0	*Lobjanidze 2, Dekanoidze*
17/09	h	Guria	L	1-2	*Lobjanidze*
25/09	a	Tskhinvali	W	2-1	*Tatanashvili, Gorgiashvili*
01/10	a	Dinamo Tbilisi	W	2-1	*Lekvtadze, Ivanishvili*
15/10	h	Shukura	D	1-1	*Dobrovolski*
23/10	a	Locomotive	W	4-1	*Gorgiashvili, Ganugrava, Lobjanidze 2 (1p)*
29/10	h	Torpedo	W	2-1	*Gorgiashvili, Chikvaidze*
18/11	a	Guria	W	2-0	*Mumladze, Kakubava*
26/11	h	Tskhinvali	W	4-1	*Gabedava, Tatanashvili 2, Gorgiashvili*

Name	Nat	DoB	Pos	Aps	(s)	Gls
Lasha Chikvaidze		04/10/89	D	8	(1)	1
Besik Dekanoidze		01/03/92	M	2	(5)	1
Denis Dobrovolski		10/10/85	M	10	(1)	1
Giorgi Gabedava		03/10/89	A	4	(4)	1
Giorgi Ganugrava		21/02/88	M	12		1
Tornike Gorgiashvili		27/04/88	M	7	(4)	4
Tornike Grigalashvili		28/01/93	D	12		1
Lasha Gvalia		06/10/91	M		(3)	
Dino Hamzić	BIH	22/01/88	G	11		
Giorgi Ivanishvili		18/10/89	M	7		1
Levan Kakubava		15/10/90	D	2	(2)	1
Shota Kashia		22/10/84	D	11		
Giorgi Koripadze		03/10/89	M	5	(1)	
Irakli Lekvtadze		30/08/91	M	7	(3)	1
Saba Lobjanidze		18/12/94	M	9	(1)	8
Tornike Mumladze		23/07/92	A	4	(1)	2
Giorgi Rekhviashvili		22/02/88	D	9	(1)	
Mikheil Sardalishvili		17/09/92	M	5	(4)	
Konstantine Sepiashvili		19/03/86	G	1		
Dimitri Tatanashvili		19/10/83	A	6	(4)	4

FC Dila Gori

1949 • Tengiz Burjanadze (4,483) • fcdila.ge

Major honours

Georgian League (1) 2015; Georgian Cup (1) 2012

Coach: Ucha Sosiashvili

Date		Opponent		Score	Scorers
14/08	h	Zugdidi	W	4-1	*Modebadze, Nonikashvili, Tsikaridze, Chakhvashvili*
20/08	a	Dinamo Batumi	L	1-3	*Eristavi*
27/08	h	Sioni	W	2-1	*Gongadze, Gamtsemlidze*
11/09	a	Saburtalo	L	1-2	*Gamtsemlidze*
17/09	h	Samtredia	L	1-2	*Gamtsemlidze*
25/09	a	Kolkheti	W	1-0	*Kowa*
16/10	a	Zugdidi	L	0-1	
22/10	h	Dinamo Batumi	D	0-0	
30/10	a	Sioni	L	0-2	
05/11	h	Saburtalo	D	0-0	
19/11	a	Samtredia	W	2-0	*og (Manjgaladze), Eliauri*
26/11	h	Kolkheti	W	1-0	*Kapanadze*

Name	Nat	DoB	Pos	Aps	(s)	Gls
Giorgi Begashvili		12/02/91	G	4		
Thibault Biassadila	CGO	02/02/95	A	2	(3)	
Ioseb Chakhvashvili		03/08/93	A		(8)	1
Nika Eliauri		13/02/97	M	2		1
Giorgi Eristavi		04/02/94	M	6	(2)	1
Romaric Etou	CGO	25/01/95	D	8	(2)	
Aleksandre Gamtsemlidze		24/10/97	M	7	(3)	3
Giorgi Gavashelishvili		31/10/89	D	1	(1)	
Nikoloz Gelashvili		05/08/85	A	3	(2)	
Teimuraz Gongadze		08/09/85	D	11		1
Akaki Janelidze		23/09/91	M		(1)	
Nika Kalandarishvil		09/09/98	A	1	(1)	
David Kapanadze		09/03/97	A	1	(1)	1
Givi Karkuzashvili		20/09/86	D		(1)	
Koffi Dan Kowa	GHA	17/09/89	D	6		1
Giorgi Kurmashvili		12/11/97	D		(1)	
Aleksandre Kvakhadze		17/08/84	D	7		
Ilia Lomidze		04/11/89	D	3	(2)	
Vaja Matiashvili		22/03/94	A		(1)	
Yaniv Mizrahi	ISR	30/08/95	M	1	(2)	
Irakli Modebadze		04/10/84	A	7		1
Mikheil Mujrishvili		30/04/84	G	8		
Levan Nonikashvili		05/04/95	M	11		1
Giorgi Papava		16/02/93	M	1		
Luka Razmadze		30/12/83	M	7		
Lasha Salukvadze		21/12/81	D	9		
Giga Samkharadze		28/04/95	M	11		
Rati Tsatskrialashvili		11/10/93	M	4	(2)	
Tengiz Tsikaridze		21/12/95	M	11		1

FC Dinamo Batumi

1923 • Chele Arena, Kobuleti (3,800) • dinamobatumi.com

Major honours

Georgian Cup (1) 1998

Coach: Levan Khomeriki

2016

Date		Opponent		Score	Scorers
07/08	h	Samtredia	D	1-1	*Shonia*
14/08	a	Kolkheti	W	5-0	*Shonia, Lobjanidze, Marjanović, og (Gedenidze), Tevdoradze (p)*
20/08	h	Dila	W	3-1	*Shonia 2, Kvantaliani*
27/08	a	Zugdidi	W	2-0	*Shonia, Kvantaliani*
17/09	h	Sioni	D	0-0	
24/09	a	Saburtalo	D	0-0	
02/10	a	Samtredia	D	1-1	*Kvantaliani*
15/10	h	Kolkheti	L	0-1	
22/10	a	Dila	D	0-0	
30/10	h	Zugdidi	W	5-0	*Kvantaliani, Gegechkori 2 (1p), Lobjanidze, Gogitidze*
20/11	a	Sioni	W	3-0	*Lobjanidze 3*
26/11	h	Saburtalo	L	0-1	

Name	Nat	DoB	Pos	Aps	(s)	Gls
Beka Chkuaseli		12/10/96	A		(7)	
Bakhtiyar Gabdollin	KAZ	27/04/95	A		(1)	
Levan Gegechkori		05/06/94	M	10	(1)	2
Gela Gogitidze		25/11/90	M	11		1
Mikhail Gorelishvili	RUS	29/05/93	A	3	(3)	
Giorgi Kavtaradze		01/01/89	M	10		
Nika Kvantaliani		06/02/98	A	4	(6)	4
David Kvirkvelia		27/06/80	D	9		
Elguja Lobjanidze		17/09/92	A	9	(3)	5
Lazar Marjanović	SRB	08/09/89	A	6	(1)	1
Nika Mgeladze		20/12/85	D	3	(1)	
Papuna Poniava		10/03/94	M	7	(2)	
Teimuraz Shonia		28/05/90	M	11		5
Anzor Sukhiashvili		27/10/88	D	12		
Tornike Tarkhnishvili		30/06/90	M	11		
Valerian Tevdoradze		11/10/93	A	2	(8)	1
Anatoliy Timofeev	UKR	19/04/92	G	12		
Archil Tvildiani		31/01/93	D	11		
Beka Varshanidze		01/11/93	M	1	(3)	

FC Dinamo Tbilisi

1925 • Boris Paichadze Dinamo Arena (53,233) • fcdinamo.ge

Major honours
UEFA Cup Winners Cup (1) 1981; USSR League (2) 1964, 1978; Georgian League (16) 1990, 1991, 1992, 1993, 1994, 1995, 1996, 1997, 1998, 1999, 2003, 2005, 2008, 2013, 2014, 2016 (spring); USSR Cup (2) 1976, 1979; Georgian Cup (13) 1992, 1993, 1994, 1995, 1996, 1997, 2003, 2004, 2009, 2013, 2014, 2015, 2016 (spring)

Coach: Juraj Jarábek (SVK); (10/10/16) (Tamaz Samkharadze); (25/10/16) Vyacheslav Hrozniy (UKR)

2016

Date		Opponent	Res	Score	Scorers
07/08	a	Chikhura	D	0-0	
13/08	h	Guria	W	3-0	*Papunashvili, Chanturishvili, Jigauri*
21/08	a	Tskhinvali	W	4-2	*Tsintsadze (p), Kiteishvili, Rene, Papunashvili*
11/09	h	Shukura	D	1-1	*Amisulashvili*
17/09	a	Locomotive	D	0-0	
25/09	h	Torpedo	D	0-0	
01/10	h	Chikhura	L	1-2	*Dvalishvili*
15/10	a	Guria	W	2-0	*Dvalishvili, Chelidze*
23/10	h	Tskhinvali	D	0-0	
06/11	a	Shukura	W	1-0	*Chelidze*
18/11	h	Locomotive	W	4-0	*Papunashvili, Chanturishvili, Mikeltadze, Jigauri*
26/11	a	Torpedo	W	1-0	*Zaria*

Name	Nat	DoB	Pos	Aps	(s)	Gls
Aleksandre Amisulashvili		20/08/82	D	8		1
Giorgi Chakvetadze		29/08/99	M		(5)	
Vakhtang Chanturishvili		05/08/93	M	7	(2)	2
Zaza Chelidze		12/01/87	D	6	(1)	2
Mathias Coureur	FRA	22/03/88	A	1	(1)	
Vladimer Dvalishvili		20/04/86	A	7		2
Jambul Jigauri		08/07/92	M	9	(2)	2
Akaki Khubutia		17/03/86	D	4		
Tornike Kirkitadze		23/07/96	M	1		
Otar Kiteishvili		26/03/96	M	10	(1)	1
David Kobouri		24/01/98	D	1		
Giorgi Kutsia		27/10/99	M		(1)	
Enver Liluashvili		04/11/97	A		(2)	
Ucha Lobjanidze		23/02/87	D	9		
Luka Lochoshvili		29/05/98	D	2		
Giorgi Lomaia		08/08/79	G	4		
Mikel Álvaro	ESP	20/12/82	M	3		
Beka Mikeltadze		26/11/97	A	4	(4)	1
Nika Ninua		22/06/99	D	1	(2)	
Giorgi Papunashvili		02/09/95	M	10		3
Lasha Parunashvili		14/02/93	M	6	(4)	
Rene	BRA	21/04/92	D	9		1
Nukri Revishvili		02/03/87	G	4		
Anthony Scribe	FRA	01/01/88	G	4		
Matija Špičić	CRO	24/02/88	D	3		
Giorgi Tevzadze		25/08/96	D	3	(5)	
Mate Tsintsadze		07/01/95	M	11		1
Stefan Velev	BUL	02/05/89	M	3	(3)	
Giorgi Zaria		14/07/97	A	2	(4)	1

FC Guria Lanchkhuti

1924 • Evgrapi Shevardnadze (4,500) • no website

Major honours
Georgian Cup (1) 1990

Coach: Teimuraz Makharadze; (22/08/16) Oleh Leshchinskiy (UKR); (21/11/16) Zaza Inashvili

2016

Date		Opponent	Res	Score	Scorers
07/08	h	Tskhinvali	D	0-0	
13/08	a	Dinamo Tbilisi	L	0-3	
20/08	h	Shukura	D	0-0	
27/08	a	Locomotive	L	1-2	*Diniz*
10/09	h	Torpedo	W	2-1	*Morozenko, Chaduneli*
17/09	a	Chikhura	W	2-1	*Murashov 2 (1p)*
01/10	a	Tskhinvali	L	1-2	*Diniz*
15/10	h	Dinamo Tbilisi	L	0-2	
22/10	a	Shukura	L	1-3	*Kirkitadze*
29/10	h	Locomotive	W	1-0	*Murashov*
06/11	a	Torpedo	L	0-5	
18/11	h	Chikhura	L	0-2	

Name	Nat	DoB	Pos	Aps	(s)	Gls
Berika Barbakadze		04/01/96	M		(1)	
Gia Chaduneli		15/05/95	D	11		1
Chiaber Chechelashvili		10/10/95	M	10	(2)	
Giorgi Chedia		28/08/88	A	7	(2)	
Giga Cheishvili		17/09/93	D	9		
Nika Diasamidze		02/09/94	M	1	(4)	
Diniz	BRA	07/03/88	A	10	(2)	2
Filipe	BRA	09/02/91	D	6	(4)	
Zurab Gelashvili		09/04/96	D	1	(1)	
Robert Imerlishvili		24/07/93	G	12		
Luka Imnadze		26/08/97	A	1	(6)	
Paterson Kaboré	BFA	05/05/90	D	3	(3)	
David Kirkitadze		03/09/92	M	9		1
David Megrelishvili		25/05/91	D	11		
Yevhen Morozenko	UKR	16/12/91	M	11	(1)	1
Yevhen Murashov	UKR	09/05/95	A	8		3
Luka Nozadze		25/12/96	D	11		
Tornike Stepniashvili		10/11/92	M	3	(5)	
Zurab Tevzadze		28/08/94	D	3	(1)	
Bidzina Tsintsadze		04/06/89	D	4		
Yuri	BRA	02/06/98	M	1		

FC Kolkheti Poti

1913 • Park Arena (2,800); Chele Arena, Kobuleti (3,800) • no website

Coach: Gela Sanaia

2016

Date		Opponent	Res	Score	Scorers
07/08	a	Zugdidi	W	1-0	*Gogonaia (p)*
14/08	h	Dinamo Batumi	L	0-5	
20/08	a	Sioni	W	2-0	*Ramaldanov, Kilasonia*
27/08	h	Saburtalo	W	1-0	*Bolkvadze (p)*
11/09	a	Samtredia	L	0-2	
25/09	h	Dila	L	0-1	
02/10	h	Zugdidi	W	2-0	*Ozarkiv, Jgamaia*
15/10	a	Dinamo Batumi	W	1-0	*Korobka*
23/10	h	Sioni	W	1-0	*Korobka*
29/10	a	Saburtalo	L	1-6	*Ramaldanov*
05/11	h	Samtredia	L	1-3	*Lukava (p)*
26/11	a	Dila	L	0-1	

Name	Nat	DoB	Pos	Aps	(s)	Gls
David Bolkvadze		05/06/80	M	8		1
Aliko Chakvetadze		28/03/95	D	8	(3)	
Lasha Dzagania		14/01/88	G	1		
Bichiko Gedenidze		21/11/91	M	2	(3)	
Omar Gogonaia		24/01/90	D	6		1
Vitaliy Ivanko	UKR	09/04/92	A	4	(2)	
Lasha Jgamaia		30/10/95	M	4	(5)	1
Tamaz Jishkariani		13/03/93	M	9	(2)	
Levan Kakulia		28/05/92	M	4	(3)	
Tsotne Keburia		24/02/95	D	8	(3)	
Shota Kerdzevadze		20/03/93	M	10		
Giorgi Kilasonia		21/05/86	D	10		1
Bachuki Kokaia		28/10/99	D	2		
Volodymyr Korobka	UKR	22/07/89	A	9		2
Aleksandre Kvaratskhelia		21/01/94	A		(1)	
Guram Lukava		14/04/95	M	4	(5)	1
Giorgi Nikabadze		10/01/91	A	10	(1)	
Ihor Ozarkiv	UKR	22/01/92	M	10		1
Rasim Ramaldanov	AZE	24/01/86	D	12		2
Tamaz Shalikashvili		21/05/99	M		(4)	
Gabriel Tebidze		10/11/94	G	11		

GEORGIA

FC Locomotive Tbilisi

1936 • Mikheil Meskhi (24,939) • fcloco.ge

Major honours
Georgian Cup (3) 2000, 2002, 2005

Coach: Gerard Zaragoza (ESP); (25/10/16) Giorgi Devdariani

2016

13/08	h Torpedo	D 0-0	
20/08	a Chikhura	L 2-3	*Chagelishvili, Khidesheli*
27/08	h Guria	W 2-1	*Diasamidze, og (Tsintsadze)*
10/09	a Tskhinvali	W 2-1	*Diasamidze 2*
17/09	h Dinamo Tbilisi	D 0-0	
25/09	a Shukura	W 1-0	*Kikabidze*
15/10	a Torpedo	L 0-3	
23/10	h Chikhura	L 1-4	*Vatsadze*
29/10	a Guria	L 0-1	
06/11	h Tskhinvali	W 2-0	*Diasamidze 2*
18/11	a Dinamo Tbilisi	L 0-4	
26/11	h Shukura	D 1-1	*Ardazishvili*

Name	Nat	DoB	Pos	Aps	(s)	Gls
Rati Ardazishvili		27/01/98	M	4	(1)	1
Irakli Bugridze		03/01/98	A	3		
David Chagelishvili		10/01/87	A	8	(1)	1
Nika Chanturia		19/01/95	D	1		
Revaz Chiteishvili		30/01/94	D	5	(1)	
Giorgi Diasamidze		20/02/92	M	11	(1)	5
Giorgi Gabadze		02/03/95	D	9	(1)	
Mamia Gavashelishvili		08/01/95	A		(3)	
Giorgi Getiashvili		07/03/90	D	7	(1)	
Giorgi Khidesheli		23/01/88	D	10		1
Luka Kikabidze		21/01/95	M	2	(3)	1
Vaja Kikava		28/12/95	M	4	(3)	
Giorgi Kiknadze		27/09/97	M		(5)	
Irakli Klimiashvili		30/05/88	M	11		
Giorgi Kukhianidze		01/07/92	M	10		
Boris Makharadze		08/11/90	M	7		
Omar Patarkatsishvili		05/02/96	D	1	(1)	
Giorgi Popkhadze		25/09/86	D	7	(1)	
David Samurkasovi		05/02/98	M	2	(4)	
Nugzar Spanderashvili		16/01/99	A		(1)	
Revaz Tevdoradze		14/02/88	G	12		
Bachana Tskhadadze		23/10/87	A	2	(2)	
David Ubilava		27/01/94	D	9		
Mate Vatsadze		17/12/88	A	1	(3)	1
Luka Zarandia		17/02/96	A	6	(4)	

FC Saburtalo Tbilisi

1999 • Mikheil Meskhi (24,939); Mikheil Meskhi reserve pitch (2,000) • fcsaburtalo.ge

Coach: Pablo Franco (ESP); (12/10/16) Giorgi Chiabrishvili

2016

07/08	a Sioni	W 2-1	*Juanfri, Alwyn*
20/08	h Samtredia	D 2-2	*Kharaishvili (p), Bidzinashvili*
27/08	a Kolkheti	L 0-1	
11/09	h Dila	W 2-1	*Juanfri, Margvelashvili*
18/09	a Zugdidi	L 0-1	
24/09	h Dinamo Batumi	D 0-0	
02/10	h Sioni	D 1-1	*Kharaishvili (p)*
23/10	a Samtredia	L 0-3	
29/10	h Kolkheti	W 6-1	*Goncalves, Kharaishvili 2 (1p), Pantsulaia 3*
05/11	a Dila	D 0-0	
20/11	h Zugdidi	W 3-1	*Goncalves, Kharaishvili, Santi Jara*
26/11	a Dinamo Batumi	W 1-0	*Santi Jara*

Name	Nat	DoB	Pos	Aps	(s)	Gls
Sandro Altunashvili		14/01/97	M	5	(1)	
Tera Alwyn	KEN	18/01/97	M	11		1
Irakli Bidzinashvili		27/02/97	M	1	(1)	1
Giorgi Bukhaidze		09/12/91	A		(6)	
José Carrasco	ESP	18/01/88	D	8	(1)	
Grigol Chabradze		20/04/96	D	9	(1)	
Vagner Goncalves	FRA	27/04/96	A	7	(3)	2
Otar Goshadze		13/01/97	G	6		
Tedore Grigalashvili		12/05/93	D	8		
Nodar Iashvili		24/01/93	D	12		
Juanfri	ESP	01/10/89	A	7	(2)	2
Giorgi Kharaishvili		29/07/96	M	12		5
Giorgi Kokhreidze		18/11/98	M		(8)	
Beka Kurdadze		24/01/97	G	6		
Vladimer Mamuchashvili		28/08/97	M	4	(4)	
Gagi Margvelashvili		30/10/96	D	11		1
Tsotne Nadaraia		21/02/97	D	3		
Giorgi Pantsulaia		06/01/94	A	8	(3)	3
Irakli Rukhadze		28/10/96	M	1	(2)	
Santi Jara	ESP	02/02/91	A	11		2
Andro Sopromadze		25/03/93	M	2	(3)	
Rati Tsatskrialashvili		11/10/93	M		(1)	

FC Samtredia

1936 • Erosi Manjgaladze (3,000) • fcsamtredia.com

Major honours
Georgian League (1) 2016 (autumn)

Coach: Gia Tsetsadze

2016

07/08	a Dinamo Batumi	D 1-1	*Zivzivadze*
14/08	h Sioni	W 4-1	*Arabuli, Zivzivadze 2, Gamkrelidze*
20/08	a Saburtalo	D 2-2	*Rajamashvili, Shergelashvili*
11/09	h Kolkheti	W 2-0	*Zivzivadze, Datunaishvili*
17/09	a Dila	W 2-1	*Arabuli, Manjgaladze*
25/09	h Zugdidi	W 1-0	*Shergelashvili*
02/10	h Dinamo Batumi	D 1-1	*Zivzivadze*
15/10	a Sioni	W 3-0	*Rajamashvili, Zivzivadze, Arabuli*
23/10	h Saburtalo	W 3-0	*Jikia, Arabuli, Zivzivadze*
05/11	a Kolkheti	W 3-1	*Zivzivadze 2, Rajamashvili*
19/11	h Dila	L 0-2	
26/11	a Zugdidi	W 5-0	*Zivzivadze 2, Arabuli 2, Gogiashvili*

Name	Nat	DoB	Pos	Aps	(s)	Gls
Giorgi Akhaladze		26/07/97	M	1	(1)	
Bachana Arabuli		05/01/94	A	11	(1)	6
Giorgi Datunaishvili		09/02/85	M	11		1
Giorgi Gamkrelidze	UKR	30/09/87	M	3	(7)	1
Jemal Gogiashvili		06/05/88	D	10	(1)	1
David Imedashvili		15/12/84	D	1	(2)	
David Jikia		10/01/95	A	3	(9)	1
Zaur Khabeishvili		11/08/98	A		(1)	
Giuly Manjgaladze	UKR	09/09/92	M	11		1
Teimuraz Markozashvili		09/08/94	M	5	(4)	
Giorgi Mchedlishvili		18/01/92	D	7	(2)	
Kakhaber Meshveliani		14/04/92	G	1		
Omar Migineishvili		02/06/84	G	11		
David Mtivlishvili		26/10/94	D	5	(2)	
Akaki Ninua		17/02/99	M		(1)	
David Rajamashvili		28/10/88	M	12		3
Nika Sandokhadze		20/02/94	D	11		
Lasha Shergelashvili		17/01/92	D	11		2
Bachana Tskhadadze		23/10/87	A	1		
Dachi Tsnobiladze		28/01/94	D	5	(5)	
Budu Zivzivadze		10/03/94	A	12		11

FC Shukura Kobuleti

1936 • Chele Arena (3,800) • no website

Coach: Teimuraz Shalamberidze; (15/09/16) Avtandil Namgaladze; (21/10/16) Gia Guruli

2016

Date		Opponent	Res	Score	Scorers
07/08	a	Torpedo	D	0-0	
13/08	h	Chikhura	L	1-3	*Beriashvili*
20/08	a	Guria	D	0-0	
27/08	h	Tskhinvali	L	1-3	*Kutalia*
11/09	a	Dinamo Tbilisi	D	1-1	*Guruli*
25/09	h	Locomotive	L	0-1	
01/10	h	Torpedo	W	2-1	*Kutalia 2*
05/10	a	Chikhura	D	1-1	*Shalamberidze*
22/10	h	Guria	W	3-1	*Shalamberidze, Komakhidze, Chanukvadze*
30/10	a	Tskhinvali	D	0-0	
06/11	h	Dinamo Tbilisi	L	0-1	
26/11	a	Locomotive	D	1-1	*Shalamberidze*

Name	Nat	DoB	Pos	Aps	(s)	Gls
Guram Adamadze		31/08/88	D	6		
Levan Ananidze		03/07/96	M		(1)	
Zurab Arziani	RUS	19/10/87	M	9		
Giorgi Beriashvili		10/09/86	A	6	(2)	1
Avtandil Brachuli		02/04/92	D		(1)	
Roman Chachua		01/01/97	D	10	(1)	
Giorgi Chanukvadze		07/03/95	M	1	(2)	1
Giorgi Chelebadze		01/01/92	M	4	(1)	
Irakli Chezhiya	RUS	22/05/92	D	9	(1)	
Azamat Dzhioev	RUS	06/01/91	G	12		
Aleksandre Guruli		09/11/85	M	8	(1)	1
Lasha Japaridze		16/04/85	D	8		
Jefinho	BRA	23/02/89	A	6	(1)	
Giorgi Kalandadze		02/07/96	D		(1)	
Irakli Komakhidze		26/03/97	M	10	(1)	1
Godwin Konyeha	NGA	22/06/92	M	2	(4)	
Levan Kutalia		19/07/89	M	9	(1)	3
Zurab Malania		07/10/96	D	2	(3)	
Giga Mamulashvili	RUS	02/10/91	M	4	(5)	
Bakar Mirtskhulava		24/05/92	D	11		
Lasha Omanidze		01/03/94	A	1	(5)	
Levan Sabadze		17/03/92	M	6		
Koba Shalamberidze		15/10/84	M	8	(2)	3

FC Sioni Bolnisi

1936 • Tamaz Stepania (3,500) • fcsionibolnisi.com

Major honours
Georgian League (1) 2006

Coach: Armaz Jeladze

2016

Date		Opponent	Res	Score	Scorers
07/08	h	Saburtalo	L	1-2	*Volkovi*
14/08	a	Samtredia	L	1-4	*Volkovi (p)*
17/08	h	Kolkheti	L	0-2	
27/08	a	Dila	L	1-2	*Dzaria*
10/09	h	Zugdidi	W	4-1	*Dzaria, Sushkin, Kobakhidze, Janelidze*
17/09	a	Dinamo Batumi	D	0-0	
02/10	a	Saburtalo	D	1-1	*Volkovi*
15/10	h	Samtredia	L	0-3	
23/10	a	Kolkheti	L	0-1	
30/10	h	Dila	W	2-0	*Volkovi (p), Sikharulidze*
06/11	a	Zugdidi	W	3-0	*Volkovi 2 (1p), Janelidze*
20/11	h	Dinamo Batumi	L	0-3	

Name	Nat	DoB	Pos	Aps	(s)	Gls
Iakob Apkhazava		30/04/91	A		(1)	
Nika Daushvili		16/10/89	G	8		
Irakli Dzaria		01/12/88	M	7	(1)	2
Giorgi Gaprindashvili		06/05/95	M	10		
Guram Giorbelidze		25/02/96	M	4	(4)	
Olexandr Ilyushchenkov	UKR	23/03/90	G	2		
Jader	BRA	18/01/90	M	4	(3)	
Giorgi Janelidze		25/09/89	M	11		2
Mindaugas Kalonas	LTU	28/02/84	M		(1)	
Lasha Kasradze		28/07/89	D	12		
David Khurtsilava		09/03/88	D	6		
Otar Kobakhidze		29/02/96	A	6	(4)	1
Zviad Lobjanidze		19/04/90	M		(5)	
Soslan Naniev	RUS	08/12/89	G	2		
Dachi Popkhadze		27/01/84	D	9		
Lasha Shindagoridze		30/01/93	M	1	(2)	
Irakli Sikharulidze		18/07/90	A	6	(4)	1
Vyacheslav Sushkin	RUS	11/02/91	A	5	(2)	1
David Svanidze		14/10/79	D	7		
Lasha Totadze		24/08/88	D	11		
Jaba Ugulava		08/04/92	A	1	(6)	
Giorgi Vasadze		14/06/89	M	9	(1)	
Denys Vasilyev	UKR	08/05/87	D	1		
David Volkovi		03/06/95	A	10	(2)	6

FC Torpedo Kutaisi

1946 • Ramaz Shengelia (11,880) • fctorpedo.ge

Major honours
Georgian League (3) 2000, 2001, 2002; Georgian Cup (3) 1999, 2001, 2016 (autumn)

Coach: Koba Jorjikashvili; (16/09/16) Kakhaber Chkhetiani

2016

Date		Opponent	Res	Score	Scorers
07/08	h	Shukura	D	0-0	
13/08	a	Locomotive	D	0-0	
27/08	h	Chikhura	L	0-3	
10/09	a	Guria	L	1-2	*Kvernadze*
17/09	h	Tskhinvali	W	3-1	*Tugushi, Guruli, Kapanadze*
25/09	a	Dinamo Tbilisi	D	0-0	
01/10	a	Shukura	L	1-2	*Mamasakhlisi (p)*
15/10	h	Locomotive	W	3-0	*Mamasakhlisi 2 (2p), og (Getiashvili)*
29/10	a	Chikhura	L	1-2	*Mamasakhlisi (p)*
06/11	h	Guria	W	5-0	*Mamasakhlisi (p), Tugushi, Babunashvili, Kapanadze 2*
18/11	a	Tskhinvali	W	2-1	*Tugushi, Kapanadze*
26/11	h	Dinamo Tbilisi	L	0-1	

Name	Nat	DoB	Pos	Aps	(s)	Gls
Shota Babunashvili		17/11/80	M	11	(1)	1
Aleksi Benashvili		20/03/89	D	1	(3)	
Tengiz Bregvadze		15/03/95	M	1	(1)	
Shalva Burjanadze		29/10/98	D	1		
Anri Chichinadze		05/10/97	D	8		
Jurgen Colin	NED	20/01/81	D	4		
Grigol Dolidze		25/10/82	M	11		
Avtandil Endeladze		17/09/94	M	3	(4)	
Giorgi Guruli		31/07/88	D	12		1
Tornike Kapanadze		04/06/92	A	6	(6)	4
Giorgi Kimadze		11/02/92	D	10	(1)	
Lasha Kuchukhidze		14/03/92	A		(2)	
Vakhtang Kvaratskhelia		30/03/88	A		(3)	
Roin Kvaskhvadze		31/05/89	G	11		
Otar Kvernadze		10/09/93	A	6	(5)	1
Maksime Kvilitaia		17/09/85	G	1		
Oleg Mamasakhlisi		25/11/95	M	8		5
Tsotne Meskhi		31/05/96	M		(1)	
Giorgi Nergadze		20/08/82	M	2	(2)	
Guga Palavandishvili		14/08/93	M	11		
Shalva Purtskhvanidze		22/09/97	M		(1)	
Gabriel Sagrishvili		17/06/98	A	2	(6)	
Vaja Tabatadze		01/02/91	D	12		
Vano Tsilosani		09/11/95	A		(2)	
Beka Tugushi		24/01/89	M	11		3

GEORGIA

FC Tskhinvali

1936 • Mikheil Meskhi reserve pitch, Tbilisi (2,000) • no website
Coach: Kakhi Kacharava

2016					
07/08	a	Guria	D	0-0	
21/08	h	Dinamo Tbilisi	L	2-4	*Dvali, Tomashvili*
27/08	a	Shukura	W	3-1	*Dvali 2 (1p), Makharoblidze*
10/09	h	Locomotive	L	1-2	*Dvali*
17/09	a	Torpedo	L	1-3	*Kakhelishvili*
25/09	h	Chikhura	L	1-2	*Dvali (p)*
01/10	h	Guria	W	2-1	*Dvali 2 (1p)*
23/10	a	Dinamo Tbilisi	D	0-0	
30/10	h	Shukura	D	0-0	
06/11	a	Locomotive	L	0-2	
18/11	h	Torpedo	L	1-2	*Kardava*
26/11	a	Chikhura	L	1-4	*Makatsaria*

Name	Nat	DoB	Pos	Aps	(s)	Gls
Vasiko Bachiashvili		04/11/92	D	12		
Jaba Dvali		08/02/85	A	11		7
Nikoloz Gabrichidze		16/09/97	M	2	(4)	
Moris Gelashvili		11/11/97	D		(4)	
Giorgi Kachkachishvili		08/08/90	D	6	(3)	
Giorgi Kakhelishvili		22/05/87	A	12		1
Bakar Kardava		04/10/94	M	12		1
Jaba Kasrelishvili		18/02/99	D		(1)	
Lasha Kochladze		22/08/95	M	10		
David Maisashvili		18/02/89	D	12		
Tamaz Makatsaria		03/10/95	A		(11)	1
Bidzina Makharoblidze		10/10/92	M	11		1
Giorgi Nadiradze		14/03/92	G	12		
Grigol Pirtskhalava		27/02/97	M		(3)	
Lasha Shindagoridze		30/01/93	M	3	(6)	
Erekle Sultanishvili		11/07/94	M	12		
Gulverd Tomashvili		13/10/88	D	6	(3)	1
Giorgi Tsertsvadze		15/11/94	D	11		

FC Zugdidi

1918 • Central, Zeda Etseri (1,800) • fczugdidi.ge
Coach: Otar Gabelia;
(22/08/16) Volodymyr Lyutiy (UKR);
(11/10/16) Levan Mikadze

2016					
07/08	h	Kolkheti	L	0-1	
14/08	a	Dila	L	1-4	*Lashkhia*
27/08	h	Dinamo Batumi	L	0-2	
10/09	a	Sioni	L	1-4	*Narmania*
18/09	h	Saburtalo	W	1-0	*Narmania*
25/09	a	Samtredia	L	0-1	
02/10	a	Kolkheti	L	0-2	
16/10	h	Dila	W	1-0	*Tutberidze*
30/10	a	Dinamo Batumi	L	0-5	
06/11	h	Sioni	L	0-3	
20/11	a	Saburtalo	L	1-3	*Zozulya*
26/11	h	Samtredia	L	0-5	

Name	Nat	DoB	Pos	Aps	(s)	Gls
Badri Akubardia	UKR	11/01/93	D	5	(1)	
Nikoloz Apakidze		04/04/92	D	10		
Fousseni Bamba	CIV	19/04/90	M	2		
Giga Bechvaia		29/08/86	M	7	(3)	
Khvicha Bukia		22/01/98	M		(1)	
Edgar Caparrós	ESP	19/03/97	M	2		
Giorgi Chankotadze		06/05/91	M	1	(1)	
Paata Chanturia		13/02/94	D		(4)	
Tengiz Chikviladze		12/08/83	D	2		
Raphael Chukwurah	NGA	17/05/92	D	5	(1)	
Aziz Deen-Conteh	SLE	14/01/93	D	4		
Olexandr Ermachenko	UKR	29/01/93	A	4	(5)	
Glvi Ioseliani		25/10/90	M	7		
Otar Javashvili		17/08/93	D		(1)	
Giorgi Kantaria		27/04/97	D	4	(1)	
David Kokhia		22/04/93	M	2	(1)	
Lasha Kukava		12/01/92	M		(3)	
Nika Lashkhia		28/01/97	M	3	(2)	1
Serhiy Litovchenko	UKR	04/10/87	G	9		
Saba Lomia		07/07/90	A	1	(1)	
Shota Lomia		13/02/84	M	1		
Goderdzi Machaidze		17/07/92	D	2	(2)	
Nika Narmania		15/08/94	D	1	(4)	2
Guram Samushia		05/09/94	M	11		
Yuriy Shevel	UKR	29/01/88	A	3	(1)	
Zviad Sikharulia		01/08/92	M	6	(2)	
Rudolf Sukhomlynov	UKR	11/03/93	D	7		
Valiko Tkemaladze		14/11/87	M	12		
Levan Tsurtsumia		28/01/89	M	5		
Dimitri Tutberidze		22/03/97	M	3	(2)	1
Tornike Zarkua		01/09/90	G	3		
Dmytro Zozulya	UKR	29/06/88	D	10		1

Top goalscorers

11	Budu Zivzivadze (Samtredia)
8	Saba Lobjanidze (Chikhura)
7	Jaba Dvali (Tskhinvali)
6	Bachana Arabuli (Samtredia)
	David Volkovi (Sioni)
5	Elguja Lobjanidze (Dinamo Batumi)
	Teimuraz Shonia (Dinamo Batumi)
	Giorgi Diasamidze (Locomotive)
	Giorgi Kharaishvili (Saburtalo)
	Oleg Mamasakhlisi (Torpedo)

Second level

Second level final tables 2016

Red Group		Pld	W	D	L	F	A	Pts
1	FC WIT Georgia	16	11	3	2	34	14	36
2	FC Gagra	16	9	4	3	29	21	28
3	FC Borjomi	16	8	1	7	22	17	22
4	FC Skuri Tsalenjikha	16	6	3	7	32	24	21
5	FC Sulori Vani	16	7	3	6	20	21	21
6	FC Chiatura	16	7	2	7	15	21	20
7	FC Sapovnela Terjola	16	5	4	7	14	18	19
8	FC Odishi 1919 Zugdidi	16	7	1	8	31	32	16
9	FC Gardabani	16	1	1	14	13	42	4

NB FC Odishi 1919 Zugdidi – 6 pts deducted; FC Gagra, FC Borjomi, FC Sulori Vani & FC Chiatura – 3 pts deducted.

White Group		Pld	W	D	L	F	A	Pts
1	FC Rustavi	16	12	2	2	40	15	32
2	FC Samgurali Tskhaltubo	16	10	2	4	29	24	32
3	FC Meshakhte Tkibuli	16	9	2	5	25	12	29
4	FC Merani Martvili	16	9	5	2	31	11	26
5	FC Kolkheti Khobi	16	5	6	5	20	24	21
6	FC Liakhvi Tskhinvali	16	2	4	10	16	39	4
7	FC Mark Stars Tbilisi	16	1	3	12	15	34	3
8	FC Imereti Khoni	16	4	3	9	20	29	0
9	FC Chkherimela Kharagauli	16	1	3	12	13	45	0

NB FC Rustavi, FC Merani Martvili & FC Liakhvi Tskhinvali – 6 points deducted; FC Mark Stars Tbilisi – 3 pts deducted; FC Imereti Khoni & FC Chkherimela Kharagauli excluded with zero points after 16 of the 18 rounds - their remaining two matches were awarded as 0-3 defeats.

No promotion to 2017 top division (Erovnuli Liga).

UEFA Europa League qualification play-offs

SEMI-FINALS

(30/11/16 & 04/12/16)
Saburtalo 0-0 Dinamo Tbilisi
Dinamo Tbilisi 1-0 Saburtalo *(Zaria 25)*
(Dinamo Tbilisi 1-0)

Torpedo Kutaisi 2-1 Dinamo Batumi *(Babunashvili 29p, Kimadze 65; Shonia 72)*
Dinamo Batumi 1-0 Torpedo Kutaisi *(Kavtaradze 8)*
(2-2; Dinamo Batumi on away goal)

FINAL

(10/12/16)
Dinamo Batumi 1-0 Dinamo Tbilisi *(Shonia 16)*

Relegation play-offs

(01/12/16 & 06/12/16)
Sioni 4-3 Shukura *(Svanidze 16, Sikharulidze 45, 85, Vasadze 72; Komakhidze 9, Konyeha 18, Shalamberidze 84)*
Shukura 2-0 Sioni *(Guruli 40, Jefinho 90)*
(Shukura 5-4)

Guria 0-2 Dila *(Kowa 56, Etou 82)*
Dila 0-0 Guria
(Dila 2-0)

DOMESTIC CUP

Sakartvelos Tasi 2016

SECOND ROUND

(23/08/16)
Chiatura 0-3 Kolkheti Poti
Chkherimela 2-1 Saburtalo
Gagra 1-2 Guria
Imereti 1-2 Sioni
Liakhvi Tskhinvali 2-0 Shukura
Merani Martvili 2-0 Dinamo Batumi
Samgurali 1-4 Torpedo
Sulori 1-0 Zugdidi
WIT Georgia 0-1 Locomotive Tbilisi

(24/08/16)
Borjomi 4-0 Sapovnela
Kolkheti Khobi 2-0 Tskhinvali
Odishi 1919 3-2 Gardabani *(aet)*

Byes – Chikhura, Dila, Dinamo Tbilisi, Samtredia

THIRD ROUND

(21/09/16)
Borjomi 0-3 Dinamo Tbilisi
Chkherimela 0-3 Samtredia
Kolkheti Khobi 1-3 Chikhura
Liakhvi Tskhinvali 0-3 Locomotive Tbilisi
Merani Martvili 1-1 Dila *(aet; 4-3 on pens)*
Odishi 1919 3-4 Torpedo
Sioni 0-1 Kolkheti Poti
Sulori 3-1 Guria

QUARTER-FINALS

(19/10/16)
Chikhura 0-0 Samtredia *(aet; 5-3 on pens)*

Dinamo Tbilisi 3-1 Locomotive Tbilisi *(Kiteishvili 25, 38, 90+2; Chagelishvili 81)*

Merani Martvili 1-0 Kolkheti Poti *(Shulaia 100) (aet)*

Sulori 0-1 Torpedo *(Kvernadze 84)*

SEMI-FINALS

(02/11/16)
Dinamo Tbilisi 2-3 Torpedo *(Jigauri 30, 62; Tabatadze 19, Kimadze 47, Dolidze 63)*

Merani Martvili 3-0 Chikhura *(Kantaria 34, Tskarozia 53p, Tsotsonava 90)*

FINAL

(22/11/16)
David Abashidze, Zestafoni
FC TORPEDO KUTAISI 2 *(Guruli 16, Tugushi 36)*
FC MERANI MARTVILI 1 *(Sabanadze 54)*
Referee: *Vadachkoria*
TORPEDO: *Kvaskhvadze, Tabatadze, Guruli, Chichinadze, Kimadze, Mamasakhlisi, Palavandishvili, Babunashvili (Sagrishvili 72), Dolidze (Benashvili 86), Tugushi, Kapanadze (Nergadze 80)*
MERANI: *Kupatadze, Meliava (Tsotsonava 90), Orbeladze, Tsimakuridze, Giorgadze, Teidi, Jikia (Kantaria 46), Chaladze, Tskarozia (Gegia 72), Sabanadze, Shulaia*

Torpedo Kutaisi ended a 15-year wait for their third Georgian Cup win

GERMANY

Deutscher Fussball-Bund (DFB)

Address	Otto-Fleck-Schneise 6 Postfach 710265 DE-60492 Frankfurt am Main
Tel	+49 69 67 880
Fax	+49 69 67 88266
E-mail	info@dfb.de
Website	dfb.de

President	Reinhard Grindel
General secretary	Friedrich Curtius
Media officer	Ralf Köttker
Year of formation	1900

BUNDESLIGA CLUBS

 1 **FC Augsburg**

 2 **Bayer 04 Leverkusen**

 3 **FC Bayern München**

 4 **Borussia Dortmund**

 5 **VfL Borussia Mönchengladbach**

 6 **SV Darmstadt 98**

 7 **Eintracht Frankfurt**

 8 **SC Freiburg**

 9 **Hamburger SV**

 10 **Hertha BSC Berlin**

 11 **TSG 1899 Hoffenheim**

  12 **FC Ingolstadt 04**

 13 **1. FC Köln**

 14 **RB Leipzig**

 15 **1. FSV Mainz 05**

 16 **FC Schalke 04**

  17 **SV Werder Bremen**

   18 **VfL Wolfsburg**

Hamburg
Bremen
Wolfsburg
Hannover (Hanover)
Berlin
Gelsenkirchen
Dortmund
Mönchengladbach
Leverkusen
Köln (Cologne)
Leipzig
Frankfurt
Mainz
Darmstadt
Sinsheim-Hoffenheim
Ingolstadt
Stuttgart
Augsburg
Freiburg
München (Munich)

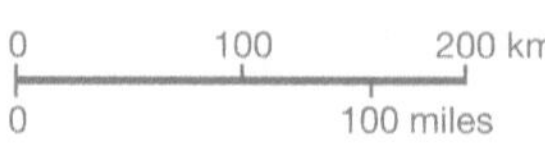

KEY

- UEFA Champions League
- UEFA Europa League
- Promoted
- Relegated

PROMOTED CLUBS

 19 **VfB Stuttgart**

 20 **Hannover 96**

Bayern breeze to fifth straight title

FC Bayern München's stranglehold on the Bundesliga title tightened still further in 2016/17 as they became champions of Germany for an unprecedented fifth season in a row, new coach Carlo Ancelotti simply carrying on where the departed Pep Guardiola had left off.

Borussia Dortmund won the DFB-Pokal, having eliminated Bayern in the semi-finals, but it was newly-promoted RB Leipzig who put up the strongest challenge to the Bavarian giants in the league. Joachim Löw's national side enjoyed a memorable season, victory in the FIFA Confederations Cup coming shortly after the Under-21 team became European champions in Poland.

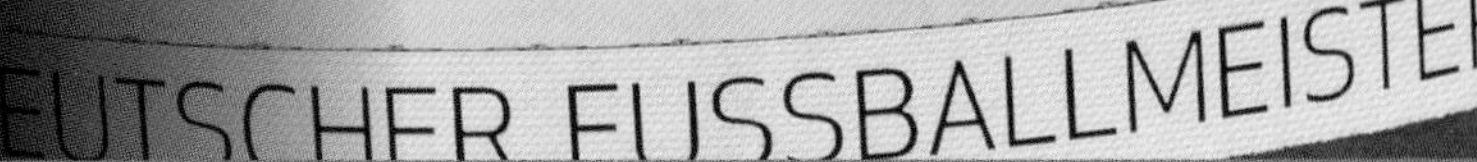

Ancelotti keeps Bundesliga shield in Munich

Leipzig and Hoffenheim come of age

Successful season for national selections

Domestic league

After three seasons of domestic dominance under Guardiola, Bayern called on the vast experience of Ancelotti to keep the team at the pinnacle of the German game. The Italian's arrival was not accompanied by a wave of transfer activity, with only two major new signings, defender Mats Hummels and young Portuguese midfielder Renato Sanches, being brought in, but the Bayern squad was already fit-to-bursting with top-class players and they entered the 2016/17 Bundesliga, like virtually every other campaign before it, as firm favourites to take the title.

A 2-0 win over Thomas Tuchel's newly-strengthened Dortmund side in the German Super Cup got Ancelotti's reign off to a good start – as did the 6-0 victory in the Allianz Arena, featuring a hat-trick from ever-prolific Polish striker Robert Lewandowski, with which Bayern opened the 54th Bundesliga season. Maximum points were taken from the team's first five matches, and Ancelotti was just one game short of equalling a Bundesliga record when his side were held 1-1 at home by 1. FC Köln on the first day of October.

If Bayern's bright start was no surprise, few foresaw that Leipzig, the first club from the territory of the former East Germany to appear in the Bundesliga since 2009, would be the team to lead the resistance against them. The newly promoted club's unconventional and rapid rise had not been to the taste of every German football follower, but Ralph Hasenhüttl's side were young, energetic and exciting to watch, and although they drew three of their first five games, they beat Dortmund 1-0 in their opening home fixture and from late September through to early December reeled off eight successive victories to not just challenge Bayern but actually overtake them at the top of the table.

Leipzig's residence at the summit, however, was to be short-lived, starting on 18 November – when Bayern lost 1-0 at Dortmund (their first defeat of the season) and Hasenhüttl's men came from behind to win 3-2 at Bayer Leverkusen – and ending on 10 December – when they lost for the first time, 1-0 at bottom club Ingolstadt, and Bayern battered Wolfsburg 5-0 in Munich. The two front-runners were level on points when they met at the Allianz Arena in the last game before the winter break. It was an eagerly anticipated contest, but its outcome was decided by half-time with Bayern three goals to the good and Leipzig down to ten men following the sending-off of their in-form Swedish playmaker Emil Forsberg.

While the autumn had not seen the best of Bayern, prompting some critics to question Ancelotti's methods despite the club's three-point lead, they came into their own in the spring, and with Leipzig finding the pressure of the chase too hot to handle, losing four times in February and March, an intriguing duel soon turned into a one-team procession to the title. Spearheaded up front by Lewandowski, and with Arjen Robben, Arturo Vidal and Thiago offering excellent support, Bayern began to take teams apart, hammering Hamburg 8-0 and Augsburg 6-0. Their Hummels-marshalled defence was nigh-on unbreachable, too, and it took a brilliant strike from Hoffenheim's Andrej Kramarić to end a run of five clean sheets – and also to inflict a first defeat on Ancelotti's men in 16 matches.

By then, however, Bayern were too far out in front to be concerned. They responded by beating an erratic Dortmund side 4-1 at home and three weeks later clinched their record-extending 27th German title – and 26th in the Bundesliga – with another impressive demonstration of their superiority, winning 6-0 at Wolfsburg. Even then the show wasn't over as they somehow won their final away fixture, 5-4 at Leipzig, after entering added time 4-3 down.

Bayern ended up 15 points clear, winning 25 of their 34 matches, scoring a whopping 89 goals and conceding just 22. Leipzig did well to hang on to second place. Indeed, that excruciating loss at home to Bayern was their only defeat in the last two months of the campaign. Qualifying for the UEFA Champions League was a massive achievement for the club, who, despite their general unpopularity, provided some splendid entertainment, with Forsberg, Guinean midfield warrior Naby Keïta, Austrian international Marcel Sabitzer and 21-goal, 21-year-old striker Timo Werner all taking their careers to a new level.

Another tale of the unexpected was provided by Hoffenheim and their brilliant, innovative, ultra-cool 29-year-old coach Julian Nagelsmann. While a preponderance of draws prevented them from immersing themselves in the title race, they were the last Bundesliga team to be beaten, completing half a season before Leipzig finally felled them in late January. Not once did they lose at home, and in 15-goal striker Kramarić, centre-back Niklas Süle, goalkeeper Oliver Baumann and midfield duo Sebastian Rudy and Kerem Demirbay they boasted players who consistently delivered the goods on a weekly basis. A place in the 2017/18 UEFA Champions League play-offs was the least they deserved, and but for a 2-1 defeat at Dortmund in their penultimate away fixture direct access to the group stage would almost certainly have been their prize.

Six wins in their last ten games enabled Dortmund to edge ahead of Hoffenheim and claim third place. A squad stuffed with gifted attacking midfielders – Mario Götze, André Schürrle, Emre Mor and Ousmane Dembélé had all arrived during the summer to compensate for the departure of Henrikh Mkhitaryan and İlkay Gündoğan to Manchester – at times appeared unbalanced, but Tuchel's team boasted the Bundesliga's most prolific marksman in Pierre-Emerick Aubameyang, and his 31 goals – one more than Lewandowski – ensured that the Black-and-Yellows made it on to the Bundesliga podium.

The top four teams ended up some way distant of the pack, which meant that Köln, who managed only 12 wins, Hertha Berlin and newly-promoted Freiburg, who both lost as many games as they won, all qualified for the UEFA Europa League. Köln had 25-goal French striker Anthony Modeste to thank for restoring European football to the Cathedral City for the first time in a quarter of a century, while Hertha and Freiburg were grateful that several of the Bundesliga's more powerful units – Schalke, Bayer Leverkusen and Borussia Mönchengladbach, top-five finishers all in 2015/16 – had a season to forget.

Leverkusen's drop from third place to 12th was the most dramatic, with coach Roger Schmidt losing his job after a humbling 6-2 defeat at Dortmund in early March. Gladbach gave Andre Schubert the boot just before Christmas, turning instead to Dieter Hecking, himself dismissed by Wolfsburg in October after an atrocious start that would send the 2015/16 UEFA Champions League quarter-finalists spiralling into trouble at the wrong end of the table and eventually lead to their belated salvation when they defeated Eintracht Braunschweig in the promotion/relegation play-off.

Wolfsburg were forced into that pressure-packed fixture after losing their final league game 2-1 to a late winning goal from fellow strugglers Hamburg, who therefore once again preserved their record of being the only ever-present Bundesliga club. Northern rivals Werder Bremen also looked to be in big trouble in mid-February, but a storming run of 11 games without defeat (including nine victories) lifted them all the way from 16th to eighth. Striker Max Kruse found the net ten times during that run, including a four-goal haul away to Ingolstadt, who, like Darmstadt, could not survive a second successive season in the top flight and were relegated. The two automatic promotion spots were filled by the two clubs that had gone down 12 months earlier – Stuttgart and Hannover.

Domestic cup

After three successive defeats in the German Cup final, Dortmund made it fourth time lucky at Berlin's Olympiastadion, Tuchel's team prevailing 2-1 against Eintracht Frankfurt in what would prove to be the coach's last game in charge. Victory brought Dortmund their first major trophy for five years – since their double-winning success under Jürgen Klopp in 2011/12 – and their fourth DFB-Pokal in all.

While Frankfurt, who had endured a miserable time in the league since the turn of the year, put up stout resistance, equalising Dembélé's exquisite early strike through Croatian striker Ante Rebić, they were undone midway through the second half by an Aubameyang penalty – converted in audacious 'Panenka' style – and thus missed out on both a first trophy for 29 years and a place in Europe. It was ironic that Niko Kovač's team should be downed by a penalty as they had won three shoot-outs

Pierre-Emerick Aubameyang fires past Hamburg goalkeeper René Adler – one of the Dortmund striker's chart-topping 31 Bundesliga goals in 2016/17

en route to the final, the third of them in the semi-finals against Mönchengladbach, which came a day after Dortmund had produced arguably their finest display of the season to come from behind and beat Bayern 3-2 in Munich, thus denying the holders the possibility of a fourth double in five years.

Europe

Bayern reached the UEFA Champions League semi-finals in all three seasons of Guardiola's reign, but their first European campaign under competition specialist Ancelotti came unstuck a round earlier as Real Madrid ended the Bavarians' record run of 16 successive home wins with a 2-1 victory in the Allianz Arena before overcoming them 4-2 after extra time in the Bernabéu. Bayern, who had finished second in their group to the other Madrid side, Atlético, before thrashing Arsenal 10-2 on aggregate in the round of 16, were entitled to feel hard done by as a couple of contentious decisions went against them, but it was the fourth season running that they had been eliminated by a Spanish club, a curiosity that was fast becoming a curse.

Dortmund also reached the last eight, having topped their group – ahead of Real Madrid – thanks to a record haul of 21 goals, two thirds of which were scored against Legia Warszawa. An Aubameyang hat-trick swept them past Benfica after a first-leg loss in Lisbon, but their quarter-final against Monaco was scarred by a bomb attack on the team bus as it set off to the stadium for the first leg in Dortmund. Although only one player was injured – defender Marc Bartra broke his arm – there was lasting psychological damage to the squad, and defeats in both legs were perhaps an unavoidable consequence.

Leverkusen finished second to Monaco in their group, having beaten Tottenham Hotspur 1-0 at Wembley, but lost to Atlético in the round of 16, while Mönchengladbach finished third in their section and staged an extraordinary Lars Stindl-led comeback against Fiorentina in Tuscany before their UEFA Europa League journey was cut short on the away-goals rule by Schalke. Markus Weinzierl's side never led in that all-Bundesliga tie, but they were 3-2 up on aggregate against ten-man Ajax in extra time of their quarter-final second leg before conceding two goals that put the lid on Germany's European challenge for another season.

Lars Stindl (No13) is congratulated by team-mates Timo Werner (11) and Sebastian Rudy (21) after scoring Germany's winning goal against Chile in the Confederations Cup final

National team

While the country's clubs generally disappointed on foreign fields, Germany's national selections enjoyed a season bordering on perfection. In the main event, the 2018 FIFA World Cup qualifying campaign, Löw's defending champions won all of their first six matches, scoring 27 goals and conceding just one, to take complete control of Group C. For the last of those fixtures, a 7-0 win against San Marino in Nuremberg, the coach, who had extended his contract to 2020 in October, rested the vast majority of his World Cup winners, and it was the same largely second-string squad that he took to the FIFA Confederations Cup in Russia.

It proved to be a smart move. Not only did a number of fringe players such as Süle, Werner, Rudy, Stindl and Schalke's Leon Goretzka gain invaluable experience alongside regular first-teamers like Joshua Kimmich, Jonas Hector and skipper Julian Draxler, but they performed so well that Germany actually lifted the trophy. They won four of their five games, the only draw coming in the group stage against a Chile side they would later defeat, albeit with a degree of fortune, in the St Petersburg final, Stindl's 20th-minute tap-in proving to be the only goal of a game in which the German defence was forced to work overtime by the lively South American champions.

A first Confederations Cup triumph came just two days after Germany's second victory in the UEFA European Under-21 Championship, Stefan Kuntz's young charges also triumphing 1-0 in the final, thanks to Mitchell Weiser's 40th-minute header, against a Spain side that had gone into the Krakow showdown as strong favourites.

With a year to go until their World Cup defence, German fans could not have wished for more. With so many quality players to choose from, all of whom now know what it takes to win big tournaments, Germany will surely be the team to beat in Russia. A record-equalling fifth World Cup victory would appear to be theirs for the taking.

DOMESTIC SEASON AT A GLANCE

Bundesliga 2016/17 final table

			Home					Away					Total					
		Pld	W	D	L	F	A	W	D	L	F	A	W	D	L	F	A	Pts
1	**FC Bayern München**	**34**	**13**	**4**	**0**	**55**	**9**	**12**	**3**	**2**	**34**	**13**	**25**	**7**	**2**	**89**	**22**	**82**
2	RB Leipzig	34	12	2	3	35	16	8	5	4	31	23	20	7	7	66	39	67
3	Borussia Dortmund	34	13	4	0	41	12	5	6	6	31	28	18	10	6	72	40	64
4	TSG 1899 Hoffenheim	34	11	6	0	35	14	5	8	4	29	23	16	14	4	64	37	62
5	1. FC Köln	34	9	6	2	29	17	3	7	7	22	25	12	13	9	51	42	49
6	Hertha BSC Berlin	34	12	1	4	28	19	3	3	11	15	28	15	4	15	43	47	49
7	SC Freiburg	34	10	2	5	23	24	4	4	9	19	36	14	6	14	42	60	48
8	SV Werder Bremen	34	8	1	8	28	24	5	5	7	33	40	13	6	15	61	64	45
9	VfL Borussia Mönchengladbach	34	7	5	5	26	18	5	4	8	19	31	12	9	13	45	49	45
10	FC Schalke 04	34	8	5	4	29	15	3	5	9	16	25	11	10	13	45	40	43
11	Eintracht Frankfurt	34	7	7	3	24	18	4	2	11	12	25	11	9	14	36	43	42
12	Bayer 04 Leverkusen	34	5	6	6	27	28	6	2	9	26	27	11	8	15	53	55	41
13	FC Augsburg	34	5	6	6	22	25	4	5	8	13	26	9	11	14	35	51	38
14	Hamburger SV	34	8	4	5	21	25	2	4	11	12	36	10	8	16	33	61	38
15	1. FSV Mainz 05	34	7	4	6	30	26	3	3	11	14	29	10	7	17	44	55	37
16	VfL Wolfsburg	34	5	3	9	15	25	5	4	8	19	27	10	7	17	34	52	37
17	FC Ingolstadt 04	34	4	5	8	21	30	4	3	10	15	27	8	8	18	36	57	32
18	SV Darmstadt 98	34	6	3	8	18	25	1	1	15	10	38	7	4	23	28	63	25

European qualification 2017/18

Champion: FC Bayern München (group stage)
RB Leipzig (group stage)
Cup winner: Borussia Dortmund (group stage)
TSG 1899 Hoffenheim (play-offs)

1. FC Köln (group stage)
Hertha BSC Berlin (group stage)
SC Freiburg (third qualifying round)

Top scorer Pierre-Emerick Aubameyang (Dortmund), 31 goals
Relegated clubs SV Darmstadt 98, FC Ingolstadt 04
Promoted clubs VfB Stuttgart, Hannover 96
Cup final Borussia Dortmund 2-1 Eintracht Frankfurt

Player of the season

Pierre-Emerick Aubameyang
(Borussia Dortmund)

A fabulous 2015/16 season for Dortmund was followed by an even better one for Aubameyang as the rangy Gabonese striker struck 40 goals in all competitions – one more than the previous term – to confirm his standing as one of the game's most accomplished attacking talents. He pipped Bayern's Robert Lewandowski to the Bundesliga's *Torschützenkönig* prize with two goals in the final game to lift his tally to 31 – the largest winning total for 40 years – before crowning his magnificent season by scoring the winner in the German Cup final.

Newcomer of the season

Kai Havertz
(Bayer 04 Leverkusen)

Germany's victories in the FIFA Confederations Cup and UEFA European Under-21 Championship showcased the extraordinary pool of young talent available both now and in the immediate future to national team coach Joachim Löw. One player destined to make an impact for his country further down the line is Havertz. An elegant left-footed playmaker in the mould of Mesut Özil, he became, at 17 years of age, Leverkusen's youngest Bundesliga player and scorer after breaking through in 2016/17. Two goals against Hertha on the final day confirmed a special talent.

Team of the season

(3-2-3-2)

Coach: Nagelsmann *(Hoffenheim)*

NATIONAL TEAM

International honours*
FIFA World Cup (4) 1954, 1974, 1990, 2014
UEFA European Championship (3) 1972, 1980, 1996
FIFA Confederations Cup (1) 2017

International tournament appearances*
FIFA World Cup (18) 1934 (3rd), 1938, 1954 (Winners), 1958 (4th), 1962 (qtr-finals), 1966 (runners-up), 1970 (3rd), 1974 (Winners), 1978 (2nd phase), 1982 (runners-up), 1986 (runners-up), 1990 (Winners), 1994 (qtr-finals), 1998 (qtr-finals), 2002 (runners-up), 2006 (3rd), 2010 (3rd), 2014 (Winners)
UEFA European Championship (12) 1972 (Winners), 1976 (runners-up), 1980 (Winners), 1984, 1988 (semi-finals), 1992 (runners-up), 1996 (Winners), 2000, 2004, 2008 (runners-up), 2012 (semi-finals), 2016 (semi-finals)

Top five all-time caps
Lothar Matthäus (150); Miroslav Klose (137); **Lukas Podolski** (130); **Bastian Schweinsteiger** (121); Philipp Lahm (113)

Top five all-time goals
Miroslav Klose (71); Gerd Müller (68); **Lukas Podolski** (49); Jürgen Klinsmann & Rudi Völler (47)

(before 1992 as West Germany)*

Results 2016/17

31/08/16	Finland	H	Monchengladbach	W	2-0	*Meyer (55), Özil (77)*
04/09/16	Norway (WCQ)	A	Oslo	W	3-0	*Müller (15, 60), Kimmich (45)*
08/10/16	Czech Republic (WCQ)	H	Hamburg	W	3-0	*Müller (13, 65), Kroos (49)*
11/10/16	Northern Ireland (WCQ)	H	Hanover	W	2-0	*Draxler (13), Khedira (17)*
11/11/16	San Marino (WCQ)	A	Serravalle	W	8-0	*Khedira (7), Gnabry (9, 58, 76), Hector (32, 65), Stefanelli (82og), Volland (85)*
15/11/16	Italy	A	Milan	D	0-0	
22/03/17	England	H	Dortmund	W	1-0	*Podolski (69)*
26/03/17	Azerbaijan (WCQ)	A	Baku	W	4-1	*Schürrle (19, 81), Müller (36), Gomez (45)*
06/06/17	Denmark	A	Brondby	D	1-1	*Kimmich (88)*
10/06/17	San Marino (WCQ)	H	Nuremberg	W	7-0	*Draxler (11), Wagner (16, 29, 85), Younes (38), Mustafi (47), Brandt (72)*
19/06/17	Australia (CC)	N	Sochi (RUS)	W	3-2	*Stindl (5), Draxler (44p), Goretzka (48)*
22/06/17	Chile (CC)	N	Kazan (RUS)	D	1-1	*Stindl (41)*
25/06/17	Cameroon (CC)	N	Sochi (RUS)	W	3-1	*Demirbay (48), Werner (66, 81)*
29/06/17	Mexico (CC)	N	Sochi (RUS)	W	4-1	*Goretzka (6, 8), Werner (59), Younes (90+1)*
02/07/17	Chile (CC)	N	St Petersburg (RUS)	W	1-0	*Stindl (20)*

Appearances 2016/17

Coach: Joachim Löw	03/02/60		Fin	NOR	CZE	NIR	SMR	Ita	Eng	AZE	Den	SMR	AUS	CHI	CMR	MEX	CHI	Caps	Goals
Marc-André ter Stegen	30/04/92	Barcelona (ESP)	G46				G		G			G		G	G	G	G	14	-
Joshua Kimmich	08/02/95	Bayern	D	D	D	D	D	M	D	D	M	D	D	M	M	D	M	20	2
Shkodran Mustafi	17/04/92	Arsenal (ENG)	D			s69		D				D	D	D			D	19	2
Niklas Süle	03/09/95	Hoffenheim	D58								D		s63	D	D		s92	6	-
Bastian Schweinsteiger	01/08/84	Man. United (ENG)	M68															121	24
Karim Bellarabi	08/04/90	Leverkusen	M															11	1
Max Meyer	18/09/95	Schalke	M	s84			s71											4	1
Jonas Hector	27/05/90	Köln	M63	D	D68	D81	D		D	D	M88	D55	M	M		M	M	33	3
Julian Brandt	02/05/96	Leverkusen	A78	s72	s80				M59		s67	M	M63		s77	s78		10	1
Kevin Volland	30/07/92	Leverkusen	A			s81	s71	s60										10	1
Mario Götze	03/06/92	Dortmund	A	A72	A	A	M71	s70										62	17
Bernd Leno	04/03/92	Leverkusen	s46					G		G			G					5	-
Jonathan Tah	11/02/96	Leverkusen	s58					s46										3	-
Mesut Özil	15/10/88	Arsenal (ENG)	s63	M	M	M46				s61								84	21
Julian Weigl	08/09/95	Dortmund	s68	s84				M70	M66									5	-
Thomas Müller	13/09/89	Bayern	s78	M	M	M	M	A60	s77	M								85	37
Manuel Neuer	27/03/86	Bayern		G	G	G												74	-
Benedikt Höwedes	29/02/88	Schalke		D	s68			D		D								44	2
Mats Hummels	16/12/88	Bayern		D	D	D	D	D46	D	D								57	4
Sami Khedira	04/04/87	Juventus (ITA)		M84	M	M	M77			M								70	7
Toni Kroos	04/01/90	Real Madrid (ESP)		M	M76	M			M	M89								76	12
Julian Draxler	20/09/93	Wolfsburg /Paris (FRA)		M84	M80	M				M84	M	M76	M	M	M80	M81	M	35	5
Jérôme Boateng	03/09/88	Bayern			D	D69												67	1
İlkay Gündoğan	24/10/90	Man. City (ENG)			s76	s46	M	M										20	4
Benjamin Henrichs	23/02/97	Leverkusen					D								s74	M		3	-
Serge Gnabry	14/07/95	Bremen					M	s60										2	3
Mario Gomez	10/07/85	Wolfsburg					A71			A61								70	30
Leon Goretzka	06/02/95	Schalke					s77	M60			M76	M	M	M		M67	M92	9	3
Sebastian Rudy	28/02/90	Hoffenheim						M	s84	s89	M59		M	M	M74	M	M	20	-
Yannick Gerhardt	13/03/94	Wolfsburg						M										1	-
Antonio Rüdiger	03/03/93	Roma (ITA)							D		D		D		D	D	D	17	-
Leroy Sané	11/01/96	Man. City (ENG)							M	s84								6	-
Lukas Podolski	04/06/85	Galatasaray (TUR)							A84									130	49
Timo Werner	06/03/96	RB Leipzig							A77			s55	s57		A	A	A79	6	3
André Schürrle	06/11/90	Dortmund							s59	M								57	22
Emre Can	12/01/94	Liverpool (ENG)							s66		s59	M	s78	M	M	s67	s79	15	-
Kevin Trapp	08/07/90	Paris (FRA)									G							1	-
Matthias Ginter	19/01/94	Dortmund									D66			D	D	D	D	14	-
Lars Stindl	26/08/88	Mönchengladbach									A	A55	A78	A		M78	M	6	3
Sandro Wagner	29/11/87	Hoffenheim									A67	A	A57					3	3
Amin Younes	06/08/93	Ajax (NED)									s66	M			s80	s81		4	2
Kerem Demirbay	03/07/93	Hoffenheim									s76				M77			2	1
Marvin Plattenhardt	26/01/92	Hertha									s88	s55			M			3	-
Diego Demme	21/11/91	RB Leipzig										s76						1	-

EUROPE

FC Bayern München

CHAMPIONS LEAGUE

Group D

Match 1 - FC Rostov (RUS)
H 5-0 *Lewandowski (28p), Müller (45+2), Kimmich (53, 60), Bernat (90)*
Neuer, Hummels (Bernat 51), Thiago (Renato Sanches 71), Javi Martínez, Lewandowski, Douglas Costa (Ribéry 64), Rafinha, Vidal, Müller, Alaba, Kimmich. Coach: Carlo Ancelotti (ITA)

Match 2 - Club Atlético de Madrid (ESP)
A 0-1
Neuer, Thiago (Kimmich 66), Ribéry, Javi Martínez, Lewandowski, Xabi Alonso, Boateng (Hummels 62), Lahm, Vidal, Müller (Robben 59), Alaba. Coach: Carlo Ancelotti (ITA)

Match 3 - PSV Eindhoven (NED)
H 4-1 *Müller (13), Kimmich (21), Lewandowski (59), Robben (84)*
Neuer, Hummels, Thiago, Lewandowski, Robben (Renato Sanches 87), Xabi Alonso, Boateng, Lahm, Müller (Douglas Costa 71), Alaba, Kimmich (Javi Martínez 85). Coach: Carlo Ancelotti (ITA)

Match 4 - PSV Eindhoven (NED)
A 2-1 *Lewandowski (34p, 74)*
Neuer, Hummels, Lewandowski, Robben (Douglas Costa 64), Xabi Alonso, Boateng, Lahm, Vidal, Müller (Renato Sanches 85), Alaba, Kimmich (Coman 64). Coach: Carlo Ancelotti (ITA)

Match 5 - FC Rostov (RUS)
A 2-3 *Douglas Costa (35), Bernat (52)*
Ulreich, Thiago, Ribéry, Lewandowski, Douglas Costa, Rafinha, Boateng (Hummels 58), Bernat, Lahm, Badstuber, Renato Sanches (Müller 73). Coach: Carlo Ancelotti (ITA)

Match 6 - Club Atlético de Madrid (ESP)
H 1-0 *Lewandowski (28)*
Neuer, Hummels, Thiago, Lewandowski (Müller 80), Robben (Kimmich 83), Douglas Costa (Javi Martínez 87), Rafinha, Bernat, Vidal, Alaba, Renato Sanches. Coach: Carlo Ancelotti (ITA)

Round of 16 - Arsenal FC (ENG)
H 5-1 *Robben (11), Lewandowski (53), Thiago (56, 63), Müller (88)*
Neuer, Hummels, Thiago, Javi Martínez, Lewandowski (Müller 86), Robben (Rafinha 88), Douglas Costa (Kimmich 84), Xabi Alonso, Lahm, Vidal, Alaba. Coach: Carlo Ancelotti (ITA)
A 5-1 *Lewandowski (55p), Robben (68), Douglas Costa (78), Vidal (80, 85)*
Neuer, Hummels, Thiago (Renato Sanches 79), Ribéry (Kimmich 79), Javi Martínez, Lewandowski, Robben (Douglas Costa 71), Rafinha, Xabi Alonso, Vidal, Alaba. Coach: Carlo Ancelotti (ITA)

Quarter-finals - Real Madrid CF (ESP)
H 1-2 *Vidal (25)*
Neuer, Thiago, Ribéry (Douglas Costa 66), Javi Martínez, Robben, Xabi Alonso (Bernat 64), Boateng, Lahm, Vidal, Müller (Coman 81), Alaba. Coach: Carlo Ancelotti (ITA)
Red card: Javi Martínez 61
A 2-4 (aet) *Lewandowski (53p), Sergio Ramos (78og)*
Neuer, Hummels, Thiago, Ribéry (Douglas Costa 71), Lewandowski (Kimmich 88), Robben, Xabi Alonso (Müller 75), Boateng, Lahm, Vidal, Alaba. Coach: Carlo Ancelotti (ITA)
Red card: Vidal 84

Borussia Dortmund

CHAMPIONS LEAGUE

Group F

Match 1 - Legia Warszawa (POL)
A 6-0 *Götze (7), Papastathopoulos (15), Bartra (17), Raphaël Guerreiro (51), Castro (76), Aubameyang (87)*
Bürki, Bartra, Dembélé (Emre Mor 75), Götze (Castro 75), Raphaël Guerreiro, Aubameyang, Pulisic, Papastathopoulos, Piszczek, Schmelzer, Weigl (Ginter 79). Coach: Thomas Tuchel (GER)

Match 2 - Real Madrid CF (ESP)
H 2-2 *Aubameyang (43), Schürrle (87)*
Bürki, Dembélé (Pulisic 73), Götze (Schürrle 58), Raphaël Guerreiro (Emre Mor 77), Aubameyang, Papastathopoulos, Piszczek, Castro, Ginter, Schmelzer, Weigl. Coach: Thomas Tuchel (GER)

Match 3 - Sporting Clube de Portugal (POR)
A 2-1 *Aubameyang (9), Weigl (43)*
Bürki, Bartra (Piszczek 68), Dembélé, Götze, Aubameyang, Pulisic, Kagawa, Papastathopoulos, Ginter (Rode 71), Passlack (Burnic 90+2), Weigl. Coach: Thomas Tuchel (GER)

Match 4 - Sporting Clube de Portugal (POR)
H 1-0 *Ramos (12)*
Bürki, Bartra, Dembélé (Schürrle 46), Götze (Rode 69), Raphaël Guerreiro, Ramos, Pulisic, Papastathopoulos, Castro (Piszczek 69), Ginter, Weigl. Coach: Thomas Tuchel (GER)

Match 5 - Legia Warszawa (POL)
H 8-4 *Kagawa (17, 18), Nuri Şahin (20), Dembélé (29), Reus (32, 52), Passlack (81), Rzeźniczak (90+2og)*
Weidenfeller, Bartra (Durm 62), Dembélé (Schürrle 72), Nuri Şahin (Aubameyang 70), Reus, Rode, Pulisic, Kagawa, Castro, Ginter, Passlack. Coach: Thomas Tuchel (GER)

Match 6 - Real Madrid CF (ESP)
A 2-2 *Aubameyang (60), Reus (88)*
Weidenfeller, Bartra, Dembélé, Aubameyang, Schürrle (Reus 61), Pulisic (Emre Mor 61), Papastathopoulos, Piszczek, Castro (Rode 80), Schmelzer, Weigl. Coach: Thomas Tuchel (GER)

Round of 16 - SL Benfica (POR)
A 0-1
Bürki, Bartra, Dembélé, Reus (Pulisic 82), Raphaël Guerreiro (Castro 82), Aubameyang (Schürrle 62), Papastathopoulos, Piszczek, Schmelzer, Weigl, Durm. Coach: Thomas Tuchel (GER)
H 4-0 *Aubameyang (4, 61, 85), Pulisic (59)*
Bürki, Bartra, Dembélé (Kagawa 81), Aubameyang (Schürrle 86), Pulisic, Papastathopoulos (Ginter 88), Piszczek, Castro, Schmelzer, Weigl, Durm. Coach: Thomas Tuchel (GER)

Quarter-finals - AS Monaco FC (FRA)
H 2-3 *Dembélé (57), Kagawa (84)*
Bürki, Bender (Nuri Şahin 46), Dembélé, Raphaël Guerreiro, Aubameyang, Kagawa, Papastathopoulos, Piszczek, Ginter, Schmelzer (Pulisic 46), Weigl. Coach: Thomas Tuchel (GER)
A 1-3 *Reus (48)*
Bürki, Nuri Şahin (Schmelzer 46), Reus, Raphaël Guerreiro (Pulisic 72), Aubameyang, Kagawa, Papastathopoulos, Piszczek, Ginter, Weigl, Durm (Dembélé 27). Coach: Thomas Tuchel (GER)

Bayer 04 Leverkusen

CHAMPIONS LEAGUE

Group E

Match 1 - PFC CSKA Moskva (RUS)
H 2-2 *Mehmedi (9), Hakan Çalhanoğlu (15)*
Leno, Tah, Hernández (Pohjanpalo 46), Bender (Volland 51), Hakan Çalhanoğlu (Aránguiz 46), Mehmedi, Wendell, Brandt, Ömer Toprak, Henrichs, Kampl. Coach: Roger Schmidt (GER)

Match 2 - AS Monaco FC (FRA)
A 1-1 *Hernández (74)*
Leno, Tah, Hernández (Baumgartlinger 90), Bender, Hakan Çalhanoğlu, Brandt (Kiessling 63), Aránguiz, Ömer Toprak, Volland (Mehmedi 73), Henrichs, Kampl. Coach: Roger Schmidt (GER)

Match 3 - Tottenham Hotspur FC (ENG)
H 0-0
Leno, Tah, Hernández (Brandt 85), Bender (Jedvaj 74), Hakan Çalhanoğlu (Baumgartlinger 46), Kiessling, Mehmedi, Aránguiz, Ömer Toprak, Henrichs, Kampl. Coach: Roger Schmidt (GER)

Match 4 - Tottenham Hotspur FC (ENG)
A 1-0 *Kampl (65)*
Leno, Tah, Hernández, Mehmedi, Baumgartlinger, Wendell, Brandt (Hakan Çalhanoğlu 70), Aránguiz (Havertz 86), Ömer Toprak, Henrichs, Kampl (Volland 85). Coach: Roger Schmidt (GER)

Match 5 - PFC CSKA Moskva (RUS)
A 1-1 *Volland (16)*
Leno, Tah, Hernández (Baumgartlinger 81), Hakan Çalhanoğlu, Jedvaj, Brandt (Havertz 70), Aránguiz, Ömer Toprak, Volland, Henrichs, Kampl (Mehmedi 90). Coach: Roger Schmidt (GER)

Match 6 - AS Monaco FC (FRA)
H 3-0 *Yurchenko (30), Brandt (48), De Sanctis (82og)*
Özcan, Dragovic, Hernández, Hakan Çalhanoğlu (Aránguiz 67), Kiessling, Baumgartlinger, Jedvaj, Wendell, Brandt (Kruse 71), Da Costa, Yurchenko (Henrichs 76). Coach: Roger Schmidt (GER)

Round of 16 - Club Atlético de Madrid (ESP)
H 2-4 *Bellarabi (48), Savić (68og)*
Leno, Dragovic, Hernández, Wendell, Brandt (Bailey 87), Aránguiz, Ömer Toprak, Havertz (Volland 56), Bellarabi (Pohjanpalo 66), Henrichs, Kampl. Coach: Roger Schmidt (GER)
A 0-0
Leno, Dragovic, Hernández (Mehmedi 81), Hilbert, Baumgartlinger, Jedvaj, Wendell, Brandt (Bailey 78), Volland (Aránguiz 88), Bellarabi, Kampl. Coach: Tayfun Korkut (TUR)

VfL Borussia Mönchengladbach

Play-offs - BSC Young Boys (SUI)
A 3-1 *Raffael (11), Hahn (67), Rochat (69og)*
Sommer, Christensen, Strobl, Kramer, Hazard (Hahn 66), Raffael, Stindl (Johnson 81), Traoré (Vestergaard 79), Wendt, Jantschke, Elvedi. Coach: André Schubert (GER)
H 6-1 *Hazard (9, 64, 84), Raffael (33, 40, 77)*
Sommer, Christensen, Strobl (Vestergaard 53), Kramer (Dahoud 59), Herrmann, Hazard, Raffael, Stindl, Johnson, Jantschke (Korb 72), Elvedi. Coach: André Schubert (GER)

Group C
Match 1 - Manchester City FC (ENG)
A 0-4
Sommer, Christensen, Strobl, Kramer (Korb 38), Dahoud, Raffael, Stindl (Traoré 81), Wendt, Johnson, Hahn (Hazard 59), Elvedi. Coach: André Schubert (GER)
Match 2 - FC Barcelona (ESP)
H 1-2 *Hazard (34)*
Sommer, Christensen, Kramer, Dahoud, Hazard (Herrmann 80), Raffael (Johnson 48), Stindl (Hahn 83), Traoré, Wendt, Korb, Elvedi. Coach: André Schubert (GER)
Match 3 - Celtic FC (SCO)
A 2-0 *Stindl (57), Hahn (77)*
Sommer, Vestergaard, Strobl, Kramer, Stindl, Traoré (Schulz 86), Wendt, Hofmann, Korb, Hahn (Herrmann 90), Elvedi. Coach: André Schubert (GER)
Match 4 - Celtic FC (SCO)
H 1-1 *Stindl (32)*
Sommer, Vestergaard, Strobl (Jantschke 77), Kramer, Hazard (Herrmann 69), Stindl (Raffael 81), Wendt, Johnson, Korb, Hahn, Elvedi. Coach: André Schubert (GER)
Red card: Korb 75
Match 5 - Manchester City FC (ENG)
H 1-1 *Raffael (23)*
Sommer, Christensen, Strobl, Dahoud (Vestergaard 60), Raffael (Hahn 84), Stindl, Traoré (Hofmann 41), Wendt, Johnson, Jantschke, Elvedi. Coach: André Schubert (GER)
Red card: Stindl 51
Match 6 - FC Barcelona (ESP)
A 0-4
Sommer, Christensen, Vestergaard, Strobl, Dahoud (Kramer 59), Hazard (Raffael 72), Schulz (Johnson 59), Jantschke, Korb, Hahn, Elvedi. Coach: André Schubert (GER)

Round of 32 - ACF Fiorentina (ITA)
H 0-1
Sommer, Christensen, Vestergaard, Kramer, Herrmann (Hahn 77), Dahoud, Hazard, Stindl, Wendt, Johnson (Korb 77), Jantschke (Drmic 64). Coach: Dieter Hecking (GER)
A 4-2 *Stindl (44p, 47, 55), Christensen (60)*
Sommer, Christensen, Vestergaard, Kramer, Herrmann, Dahoud (Strobl 80), Hazard (Drmic 27), Stindl, Wendt, Hofmann (Johnson 73), Jantschke. Coach: Dieter Hecking (GER)

Round of 16 - FC Schalke 04 (GER)
A 1-1 *Hofmann (15)*
Sommer, Kolodziejczak, Vestergaard, Strobl, Dahoud, Raffael (Herrmann 79), Stindl, Wendt, Johnson (Hahn 65), Hofmann (Schulz 84), Jantschke. Coach: Dieter Hecking (GER)
H 2-2 *Christensen (26), Dahoud (45+2)*
Sommer, Christensen, Vestergaard, Kramer (Strobl 46), Herrmann, Dahoud, Drmic (Hahn 83), Raffael, Wendt, Johnson (Hofmann 16), Jantschke. Coach: Dieter Hecking (GER)

FC Schalke 04

Group I
Match 1 - OGC Nice (FRA)
A 1-0 *Rahman (75)*
Fährmann, Höwedes, Goretzka (Kolašinac 90+1), Bentaleb, Choupo-Moting, Rahman, Stambouli (Meyer 58), Schöpf (Konoplyanka 53), Naldo, Nastasić, Embolo. Coach: Markus Weinzierl (GER)
Match 2 - FC Salzburg (AUT)
H 3-1 *Goretzka (15), Ćaleta-Car (47og), Höwedes (58)*
Fährmann, Höwedes, Geis, Kolašinac (Rahman 80), Meyer (Stambouli 89), Goretzka (Konoplyanka 67), Bentaleb, Schöpf, Naldo, Nastasić, Embolo. Coach: Markus Weinzierl (GER)
Match 3 - FC Krasnodar (RUS)
A 1-0 *Konoplyanka (11)*
Fährmann, Júnior Caiçara, Höwedes, Meyer (Huntelaar 77), Di Santo (Kehrer 90+3), Konoplyanka (Schöpf 67), Rahman, Aogo, Stambouli, Naldo, Nastasić. Coach: Markus Weinzierl (GER)
Match 4 - FC Krasnodar (RUS)
H 2-0 *Júnior Caiçara (25), Bentaleb (28)*
Fährmann, Júnior Caiçara, Höwedes, Bentaleb (Goretzka 58), Konoplyanka (Schöpf 82), Choupo-Moting, Rahman (Kolašinac 69), Aogo, Stambouli, Naldo, Nastasić. Coach: Markus Weinzierl (GER)
Match 5 - OGC Nice (FRA)
H 2-0 *Konoplyanka (14), Aogo (80p)*
Fährmann, Júnior Caiçara, Meyer (Reese 46), Konoplyanka (Bentaleb 61; Avdijaj 81), Rahman, Aogo, Stambouli, Kehrer, Riether, Naldo, Tekpetey. Coach: Markus Weinzierl (GER)
Red card: Tekpetey 90+3
Match 6 - FC Salzburg (AUT)
A 0-2
Giefer, Júnior Caiçara, Höwedes, Konoplyanka (Sam 75), Rahman, Aogo, Reese (Schöpf 58), Stambouli, Kehrer, Riether (Uchida 83), Avdijaj. Coach: Markus Weinzierl (GER)

Round of 32 - PAOK FC (GRE)
A 3-0 *Burgstaller (27), Meyer (81), Huntelaar (89)*
Fährmann, Caligiuri (Konoplyanka 79), Höwedes, Kolašinac, Meyer, Goretzka, Stambouli, Burgstaller (Huntelaar 84), Schöpf (Kehrer 46), Naldo, Nastasić. Coach: Markus Weinzierl (GER)
H 1-1 *Schöpf (23)*
Fährmann, Höwedes, Geis, Kolašinac, Meyer, Bentaleb (Kehrer 84), Choupo-Moting (Goretzka 56), Schöpf, Huntelaar, Naldo (Badstuber 72), Nastasić. Coach: Markus Weinzierl (GER)

Round of 16 - VfL Borussia Mönchengladbach (GER)
H 1-1 *Burgstaller (25)*
Fährmann, Caligiuri, Höwedes, Geis, Kolašinac, Goretzka, Stambouli (Bentaleb 55), Burgstaller (Di Santo 84), Kehrer, Schöpf (Choupo-Moting 72), Nastasić. Coach: Markus Weinzierl (GER)
A 2-2 *Goretzka (54), Bentaleb (68p)*
Fährmann, Caligiuri (Schöpf 88), Höwedes, Geis (Meyer 46), Kolašinac, Goretzka, Bentaleb (Stambouli 79), Choupo-Moting, Burgstaller, Kehrer, Nastasić. Coach: Markus Weinzierl (GER)

Quarter-finals - AFC Ajax (NED)
A 0-2
Fährmann, Caligiuri (Konoplyanka 83), Höwedes, Meyer (Stambouli 59), Goretzka, Bentaleb, Aogo, Burgstaller, Kehrer, Schöpf (Huntelaar 71), Nastasić. Coach: Markus Weinzierl (GER)
H 3-2 (aet) *Goretzka (53), Burgstaller (56), Caligiuri (101)*
Fährmann, Caligiuri, Höwedes, Kolašinac, Meyer, Goretzka (Geis 84), Bentaleb, Stambouli (Huntelaar 53), Burgstaller, Riether (Avdijaj 112), Nastasić. Coach: Markus Weinzierl (GER)

1. FSV Mainz 05

Group C
Match 1 - AS Saint-Étienne (FRA)
H 1-1 *Bungert (57)*
Lössl, Donati, Muto (Córdoba 69), Yunus Mallı, Bell, Bussmann, Gbamin, Bungert, Clemens (Öztunali 84), De Blasis, Serdar (Frei 72). Coach: Martin Schmidt (SUI)
Match 2 – Qäbälä FK (AZE)
A 3-2 *Muto (41), Córdoba (68), Öztunali (78)*
Lössl, José Rodríguez (Córdoba 67), Muto (Serdar 84), Yunus Mallı, Bell, Brosinski, Frei, Bussmann, Clemens (Öztunali 67), De Blasis, Hack. Coach: Martin Schmidt (SUI)
Match 3 - RSC Anderlecht (BEL)
H 1-1 *Yunus Mallı (10p)*
Lössl, Donati, Yunus Mallı, Córdoba, Bell, Onisiwo (Öztunali 80), Bussmann, Gbamin, Bungert, De Blasis (Jairo Samperio 76), Serdar (Brosinski 59). Coach: Martin Schmidt (SUI)
Match 4 - RSC Anderlecht (BEL)
A 1-6 *De Blasis (15)*
Lössl, Donati (Öztunali 79), Balogun, Yunus Mallı, Córdoba, Bell, Brosinski, Onisiwo, Gbamin, De Blasis, Serdar (Jairo Samperio 67). Coach: Martin Schmidt (SUI)

Match 5 - AS Saint-Étienne (FRA)
A 0-0
Lössl, Balogun, Öztunali, Yunus Mallı, Córdoba, Bell, Brosinski, Onisiwo, André Ramalho (Frei 65), Bussmann (Jairo Samperio 83), Gbamin (Seydel 83). Coach: Martin Schmidt (SUI)
Match 6 - Qäbälä FK (AZE)
H 2-0 *Hack (30), De Blasis (40)*
Huth, Donati, Córdoba (Seydel 81), Bell, Jairo Samperio, Frei, André Ramalho, Bussmann, Gbamin (Yunus Mallı 69), De Blasis (Holtmann 86), Hack. Coach: Martin Schmidt (SUI)

Hertha BSC Berlin

Third qualifying round - Brøndby IF (DEN)
H 1-0 *Ibišević (28)*
Jarstein, Pekarík, Skjelbred, Darida, Kalou (Haraguchi 73), Langkamp, Ibišević (Schieber 87), Plattenhardt, Weiser, Brooks, Lustenberger (Stark 90). Coach: Pál Dárdai (HUN)
A 1-3 *Ibišević (30)*
Kraft, Pekarík (Stocker 84), Skjelbred (Stark 62), Darida, Kalou, Langkamp, Ibišević, Plattenhardt, Weiser, Brooks, Lustenberger (Allagui 62). Coach: Pál Dárdai (HUN)

DOMESTIC LEAGUE CLUB-BY-CLUB

FC Augsburg

1907 • WKK-Arena (30,660) • fcaugsburg.de
Coach: Dirk Schuster;
(14/12/16) Manuel Baum

2016

27/08	h	Wolfsburg	L 0-2	
11/09	a	Bremen	W 2-1	*Gouweleeuw, Stafylidis*
18/09	h	Mainz	L 1-3	*Stafylidis*
21/09	a	Leverkusen	D 0-0	
24/09	h	Darmstadt	W 1-0	*Finnbogason*
30/09	a	Leipzig	L 1-2	*Ji*
15/10	h	Schalke	D 1-1	*Baier*
22/10	a	Freiburg	L 1-2	*Halil*
29/10	h	Bayern	L 1-3	*Koo*
05/11	a	Ingolstadt	W 2-0	*Bobadilla, Halil*
19/11	h	Hertha	D 0-0	
26/11	a	Köln	D 0-0	
04/12	h	Frankfurt	D 1-1	*Ji*
10/12	a	Hamburg	L 0-1	
17/12	h	Mönchengladbach	W 1-0	*Hinteregger*
20/12	a	Dortmund	D 1-1	*Ji*

2017

21/01	h	Hoffenheim	L 0-2	
28/01	a	Wolfsburg	W 2-1	*Halil, Kohr*
05/02	h	Bremen	W 3-2	*Schmid, Koo, Bobadilla*
10/02	a	Mainz	L 0-2	
17/02	h	Leverkusen	L 1-3	*Kohr*
25/02	a	Darmstadt	W 2-1	*Verhaegh (p), Bobadilla*
03/03	h	Leipzig	D 2-2	*Stafylidis, Hinteregger*
12/03	a	Schalke	L 0-3	
18/03	h	Freiburg	D 1-1	*Stafylidis*
01/04	a	Bayern	L 0-6	
05/04	h	Ingolstadt	L 2-3	*Verhaegh (p), Halil*
09/04	a	Hertha	L 0-2	
15/04	h	Köln	W 2-1	*Hinteregger, Verhaegh (p)*
22/04	a	Frankfurt	L 1-3	*Gouweleeuw*
30/04	h	Hamburg	W 4-0	*Halil 2, Max, Bobadilla*
06/05	a	Mönchengladbach	D 1-1	*Finnbogason*
13/05	h	Dortmund	D 1-1	*Finnbogason*
20/05	a	Hoffenheim	D 0-0	

No	Name	Nat	DoB	Pos	Aps	(s)	Gls
10	Daniel Baier		18/05/84	M	27		1
25	Raúl Bobadilla	PAR	18/06/87	A	13	(5)	4
30	Caiuby	BRA	14/07/88	M	2	(3)	
18	Jan-Ingwer Callsen-Bracker		23/09/84	D		(1)	
38	Kevin Danso	AUT	19/09/98	A	7		
8	Markus Feulner		12/02/82	M		(1)	
27	Alfred Finnbogason	ISL	01/02/89	A	13		3
32	Raphael Framberger		06/09/95	D	2	(1)	
6	Jeffrey Gouweleeuw	NED	10/07/91	D	18		2
33	Julian Günther-Schmidt		13/09/94	A		(4)	
7	Halil Altıntop	TUR	08/12/82	M	17	(14)	6
36	Martin Hinteregger	AUT	07/09/92	D	31		3
35	Marwin Hitz	SUI	18/09/87	G	32		
16	Christoph Janker		14/02/85	D	12	(3)	
22	Ji Dong-won	KOR	28/05/91	A	24	(10)	3
20	Gojko Kačar	SRB	26/01/87	M	11	(11)	
21	Dominik Kohr		31/01/94	M	21	(5)	2
19	Koo Ja-cheol	KOR	27/02/89	M	22	(1)	2
5	Moritz Leitner		08/12/92	M	2	(4)	
1	Andreas Luthe		10/03/87	G	2		
31	Philipp Max		30/09/93	D	20	(5)	1
14	Jan Morávek	CZE	01/11/89	M	10	(3)	
40	Tim Rieder		03/09/93	D	2	(3)	
11	Jonathan Schmid	FRA	22/06/90	M	20	(5)	1
3	Kostas Stafylidis	GRE	02/12/93	D	26	(1)	4
28	Georg Teigl	AUT	09/02/91	M	4	(14)	
39	Takashi Usami	JPN	06/05/92	M	5	(6)	
2	Paul Verhaegh	NED	01/09/83	D	31		3

Bayer 04 Leverkusen

1904 • BayArena (30,210) • bayer04.de
Major honours
UEFA Cup (1) 1988; German Cup (1) 1993
Coach: Roger Schmidt;
(06/03/17) Tayfun Korkut (TUR)

2016

27/08	a	Mönchengladbach	L 1-2	*Pohjanpalo*
10/09	h	Hamburg	W 3-1	*Pohjanpalo 3*
17/09	a	Frankfurt	L 1-2	*Hernández*
21/09	h	Augsburg	D 0-0	
24/09	a	Mainz	W 3-2	*Hernández 3*
01/10	h	Dortmund	W 2-0	*Mehmedi, Hernández*
15/10	a	Bremen	L 1-2	*Hakan*
22/10	h	Hoffenheim	L 0-3	
29/10	a	Wolfsburg	W 2-1	*Mehmedi, Jedvaj*
05/11	h	Darmstadt	W 3-2	*Hakan, Brandt, Aránguiz*
18/11	h	Leipzig	L 2-3	*Kampl, Brandt*
26/11	a	Bayern	L 1-2	*Hakan*
03/12	h	Freiburg	D 1-1	*Hakan*
11/12	a	Schalke	W 1-0	*Kiessling*
18/12	h	Ingolstadt	L 1-2	*Mehmedi*
21/12	a	Köln	D 1-1	*Wendell*

2017

22/01	h	Hertha	W 3-1	*Ömer, Hakan 2 (1p)*
28/01	h	Mönchengladbach	L 2-3	*Tah, Hernández*
03/02	a	Hamburg	L 0-1	
11/02	h	Frankfurt	W 3-0	*Hernández 2, Volland*
17/02	a	Augsburg	W 3-1	*Bellarabi, Hernández 2*
25/02	h	Mainz	L 0-2	
04/03	a	Dortmund	L 2-6	*Volland, Wendell*
10/03	h	Bremen	D 1-1	*Volland*
18/03	a	Hoffenheim	L 0-1	
02/04	h	Wolfsburg	D 3-3	*Bellarabi, Volland, Havertz*
05/04	a	Darmstadt	W 2-0	*Brandt, Volland*
08/04	a	Leipzig	L 0-1	
15/04	h	Bayern	D 0-0	
23/04	a	Freiburg	L 1-2	*Volland (p)*
28/04	h	Schalke	L 1-4	*Kiessling*
06/05	a	Ingolstadt	D 1-1	*Havertz*
13/05	h	Köln	D 2-2	*Kiessling, Pohjanpalo*
20/05	a	Hertha	W 6-2	*Hernández, Havertz 2, Kiessling, Aránguiz (p), Pohjanpalo*

No	Name	Nat	DoB	Pos	Aps	(s)	Gls
20	Charles Aránguiz	CHI	17/04/89	M	22	(4)	2
9	Leon Bailey	JAM	09/08/97	A		(8)	
15	Julian Baumgartlinger	AUT	02/01/88	M	19	(3)	
38	Karim Bellarabi		08/04/90	M	14	(2)	2
8	Lars Bender		27/04/89	M	9		
19	Julian Brandt		02/05/96	M	25	(7)	3
23	Danny Da Costa		13/07/93	D	1	(2)	
6	Aleksandar Dragovic	AUT	06/03/91	D	15	(4)	
10	Hakan Çalhanoğlu	TUR	08/02/94	M	14	(1)	6
29	Kai Havertz		11/06/99	M	15	(9)	4
39	Benjamin Henrichs		23/02/97	D	27	(2)	
7	Javier Hernández	MEX	01/06/88	A	20	(6)	11
13	Roberto Hilbert		16/10/84	D	7		
16	Tin Jedvaj	CRO	28/11/95	D	16	(2)	1
44	Kevin Kampl	SVN	09/10/90	M	28	(2)	1
11	Stefan Kiessling		25/01/84	A	6	(14)	4
1	Bernd Leno		04/03/92	G	34		
14	Admir Mehmedi	SUI	16/03/91	A	16	(6)	3
21	Ömer Toprak	TUR	21/07/89	D	25		1
17	Joel Pohjanpalo	FIN	13/09/94	A	1	(10)	6
4	Jonathan Tah		11/02/96	D	16	(3)	1
31	Kevin Volland		30/07/92	A	16	(7)	6
18	Wendell	BRA	20/07/93	D	27	(5)	2
35	Vladlen Yurchenko	UKR	22/01/94	M	1	(2)	

FC Bayern München

1900 • Allianz Arena (75,024) • fcbayern.com

Major honours
European Champion Clubs' Cup/UEFA Champions League (5) 1974, 1975, 1976, 2001, 2013; UEFA Cup Winners' Cup (1) 1967; UEFA Cup (1) 1996; UEFA Super Cup (1) 2013; European/South American Cup (2) 1976, 2001; FIFA Club World Cup (1) 2013; German League (27) 1932, 1969, 1972, 1973, 1974, 1980, 1981, 1985, 1986, 1987, 1989, 1990, 1994, 1997, 1999, 2000, 2001, 2003, 2005, 2006, 2008, 2010, 2013, 2014, 2015, 2016, 2017; German Cup (18) 1957, 1966, 1967, 1969, 1971, 1982, 1984, 1986, 1998, 2000, 2003, 2005, 2006, 2008, 2010, 2013, 2014, 2016

Coach: Carlo Ancelotti (ITA)

2016

Date		Opponent		Score	Scorers
26/08	h	Bremen	W	6-0	*Xabi Alonso, Lewandowski 3 (1p), Lahm, Ribéry*
09/09	a	Schalke	W	2-0	*Lewandowski, Kimmich*
17/09	h	Ingolstadt	W	3-1	*Lewandowski, Xabi Alonso, Rafinha*
21/09	h	Hertha	W	3-0	*Ribéry, Thiago, Robben*
24/09	a	Hamburg	W	1-0	*Kimmich*
01/10	h	Köln	D	1-1	*Kimmich*
15/10	a	Frankfurt	D	2-2	*Robben, Kimmich*
22/10	h	Mönchengladbach	W	2-0	*Vidal, Douglas Costa*
29/10	a	Augsburg	W	3-1	*Lewandowski 2, Robben*
05/11	h	Hoffenheim	D	1-1	*og (Zuber)*
19/11	a	Dortmund	L	0-1	
26/11	h	Leverkusen	W	2-1	*Thiago, Hummels*
02/12	a	Mainz	W	3-1	*Lewandowski 2, Robben*
10/12	h	Wolfsburg	W	5-0	*Robben, Lewandowski 2, Müller, Douglas Costa*
18/12	a	Darmstadt	W	1-0	*Douglas Costa*
21/12	h	Leipzig	W	3-0	*Thiago, Xabi Alonso, Lewandowski (p)*

2017

Date		Opponent		Score	Scorers
20/01	a	Freiburg	W	2-1	*Lewandowski 2*
28/01	a	Bremen	W	2-1	*Robben, Alaba*
04/02	h	Schalke	D	1-1	*Lewandowski*
11/02	a	Ingolstadt	W	2-0	*Vidal, Robben*
18/02	a	Hertha	D	1-1	*Lewandowski*
25/02	h	Hamburg	W	8-0	*Vidal, Lewandowski 3 (1p), Alaba, Coman 2, Robben*
04/03	a	Köln	W	3-0	*Javi Martínez, Bernat, Ribéry*
11/03	h	Frankfurt	W	3-0	*Lewandowski 2, Douglas Costa*
19/03	a	Mönchengladbach	W	1-0	*Müller*
01/04	h	Augsburg	W	6-0	*Lewandowski 3, Müller 2, Thiago*
04/04	a	Hoffenheim	L	0-1	
08/04	h	Dortmund	W	4-1	*Ribéry, Lewandowski 2 (1p), Robben*
15/04	a	Leverkusen	D	0-0	
22/04	h	Mainz	D	2-2	*Robben, Thiago*
29/04	a	Wolfsburg	W	6-0	*Alaba, Lewandowski 2, Robben, Müller, Kimmich*
06/05	h	Darmstadt	W	1-0	*Bernat*
13/05	a	Leipzig	W	5-4	*Lewandowski 2 (1p), Thiago, Alaba, Robben*
20/05	h	Freiburg	W	4-1	*Robben, Vidal, Ribéry, Kimmich*

No	Name	Nat	DoB	Pos	Aps	(s)	Gls
27	David Alaba	AUT	24/06/92	D	29	(3)	4
28	Holger Badstuber		13/03/89	D		(1)	
18	Juan Bernat	ESP	01/03/93	D	13	(5)	2
17	Jérôme Boateng		03/09/88	D	10	(3)	
29	Kingsley Coman	FRA	13/06/96	M	10	(9)	2
11	Douglas Costa	BRA	14/09/90	M	14	(9)	4
5	Mats Hummels		16/12/88	D	24	(3)	1
8	Javi Martínez	ESP	02/09/88	D	25		1
32	Joshua Kimmich		08/02/95	M	15	(12)	6
21	Philipp Lahm		11/11/83	D	24	(2)	1
9	Robert Lewandowski	POL	21/08/88	A	31	(2)	30
25	Thomas Müller		13/09/89	A	25	(4)	5
1	Manuel Neuer		27/03/86	G	26		
13	Rafinha	BRA	07/09/85	D	10	(10)	1
35	Renato Sanches	POR	18/08/97	M	6	(11)	
7	Franck Ribéry	FRA	07/04/83	M	14	(8)	5
10	Arjen Robben	NED	23/01/84	M	21	(5)	13
22	Tom Starke		18/03/81	G	3		
6	Thiago Alcántara	ESP	11/04/91	M	26	(1)	6
26	Sven Ulreich		03/08/88	G	5		
23	Arturo Vidal	CHI	22/05/87	M	21	(6)	4
14	Xabi Alonso	ESP	25/11/81	M	22	(5)	3

Borussia Dortmund

1909 • Signal-Iduna-Park (81,360) • bvb.de

Major honours
UEFA Champions League (1) 1997; UEFA Cup Winners' Cup (1) 1966; European/South American Cup (1) 1997; German League (8) 1956, 1957, 1963, 1995, 1996, 2002, 2011, 2012; German Cup (4) 1965, 1989, 2012, 2017

Coach: Thomas Tuchel

2016

Date		Opponent		Score	Scorers
27/08	h	Mainz	W	2-1	*Aubameyang 2 (1p)*
10/09	a	Leipzig	L	0-1	
17/09	h	Darmstadt	W	6-0	*Castro 2, Ramos, Pulisic, Rode, Emre*
20/09	a	Wolfsburg	W	5-1	*Raphaël Guerreiro, Aubameyang 2, Dembélé, Piszczek*
23/09	h	Freiburg	W	3-1	*Aubameyang, Piszczek, Raphaël Guerreiro*
01/10	a	Leverkusen	L	0-2	
14/10	h	Hertha	D	1-1	*Aubameyang*
22/10	a	Ingolstadt	D	3-3	*Aubameyang, Ramos, Pulisic*
29/10	h	Schalke	D	0-0	
05/11	a	Hamburg	W	5-2	*Aubameyang 4, Dembélé*
19/11	h	Bayern	W	1-0	*Aubameyang*
26/11	a	Frankfurt	L	1-2	*Aubameyang*
03/12	h	Mönchengladbach	W	4-1	*Aubameyang 2, Piszczek, Dembélé*
10/12	a	Köln	D	1-1	*Reus*
16/12	a	Hoffenheim	D	2-2	*Götze, Aubameyang*
20/12	h	Augsburg	D	1-1	*Dembélé*

2017

Date		Opponent		Score	Scorers
21/01	a	Bremen	W	2-1	*Schürrle, Piszczek*
29/01	a	Mainz	D	1-1	*Reus*
04/02	h	Leipzig	W	1-0	*Aubameyang*
11/02	a	Darmstadt	L	1-2	*Raphaël Guerreiro*
18/02	h	Wolfsburg	W	3-0	*og (Bruma), Piszczek, Dembélé*
25/02	a	Freiburg	W	3-0	*Papastathopoulos, Aubameyang 2*
04/03	h	Leverkusen	W	6-2	*Dembélé, Aubameyang 2, Pulisic, Schürrle (p), Raphaël Guerreiro*
11/03	a	Hertha	L	1-2	*Aubameyang*
17/03	h	Ingolstadt	W	1-0	*Aubameyang*
01/04	a	Schalke	D	1-1	*Aubameyang*
04/04	h	Hamburg	W	3-0	*Castro, Kagawa, Aubameyang*
08/04	a	Bayern	L	1-4	*Raphaël Guerreiro*
15/04	h	Frankfurt	W	3-1	*Reus, Papastathopoulos, Aubameyang*
22/04	a	Mönchengladbach	W	3-2	*Reus (p), Aubameyang, Raphaël Guerreiro*
29/04	h	Köln	D	0-0	
06/05	h	Hoffenheim	W	2-1	*Reus, Aubameyang*
13/05	a	Augsburg	D	1-1	*Aubameyang*
20/05	h	Bremen	W	4-3	*Reus 2 (1p), Aubameyang 2 (1p)*

No	Name	Nat	DoB	Pos	Aps	(s)	Gls
17	Pierre-Emerick Aubameyang	GAB	18/06/89	A	31	(1)	31
5	Marc Bartra	ESP	15/01/91	D	18	(1)	
6	Sven Bender		27/04/89	M	3	(3)	
38	Roman Bürki	SUI	14/11/90	G	27		
32	Dzenis Burnic		22/05/98	M	1		
27	Gonzalo Castro		11/06/87	M	23	(5)	3
7	Ousmane Dembélé	FRA	15/05/97	M	22	(10)	6
37	Erik Durm		12/05/92	D	10	(3)	
9	Emre Mor	TUR	24/07/97	M	5	(7)	1
28	Matthias Ginter		19/01/94	D	26	(3)	
10	Mario Götze		03/06/92	M	9	(2)	1
23	Shinji Kagawa	JPN	17/03/89	M	13	(8)	1
24	Mikel Merino	ESP	22/06/96	M	2	(6)	
8	Nuri Şahin	TUR	05/09/88	M	4	(1)	
25	Sokratis Papastathopoulos	GRE	09/06/88	D	26		2
3	Park Joo-ho	KOR	16/01/87	D	1	(1)	
30	Felix Passlack		29/05/98	D	6	(4)	
26	Łukasz Piszczek	POL	03/06/85	D	23	(2)	5
22	Christian Pulisic	USA	18/09/98	M	15	(14)	3
20	Adrián Ramos	COL	22/01/86	A	4	(3)	2
13	Raphaël Guerreiro	POR	22/12/93	M	17	(7)	6
11	Marco Reus		31/05/89	M	16	(1)	7
18	Sebastian Rode		11/10/90	M	5	(9)	1
29	Marcel Schmelzer		22/01/88	D	25	(1)	
21	André Schürrle		06/11/90	M	8	(7)	2
1	Roman Weidenfeller		06/08/80	G	7		
33	Julian Weigl		08/09/95	M	27	(3)	

GERMANY

VfL Borussia Mönchengladbach

1900 • Borussia-Park (54,014) • borussia.de

Major honours

UEFA Cup (2) 1975, 1979; German League (5) 1970, 1971, 1975, 1976, 1977; German Cup (3) 1960, 1973, 1995

Coach: André Schubert; (22/12/16) Dieter Hecking

2016

Date		Opponent		Score	Scorers
27/08	h	Leverkusen	W	2-1	*Hahn, Stindl*
10/09	a	Freiburg	L	1-3	*Hazard*
17/09	h	Bremen	W	4-1	*Hazard 2, Raffael 2 (1p)*
21/09	a	Leipzig	D	1-1	*Johnson*
24/09	h	Ingolstadt	W	2-0	*Stindl, Wendt*
02/10	a	Schalke	L	0-4	
15/10	h	Hamburg	D	0-0	
22/10	a	Bayern	L	0-2	
28/10	h	Frankfurt	D	0-0	
04/11	a	Hertha	L	0-3	
19/11	h	Köln	L	1-2	*Stindl*
26/11	h	Hoffenheim	D	1-1	*Dahoud*
03/12	a	Dortmund	L	1-4	*Raffael*
11/12	h	Mainz	W	1-0	*Christensen*
17/12	a	Augsburg	L	0-1	
20/12	h	Wolfsburg	L	1-2	*Hazard*

2017

Date		Opponent		Score	Scorers
21/01	a	Darmstadt	D	0-0	
28/01	a	Leverkusen	W	3-2	*Stindl 2, Raffael*
04/02	h	Freiburg	W	3-0	*Stindl, Raffael, Herrmann*
11/02	a	Bremen	W	1-0	*Hazard*
19/02	h	Leipzig	L	1-2	*Vestergaard*
26/02	a	Ingolstadt	W	2-0	*Stindl, Hahn*
04/03	h	Schalke	W	4-2	*Johnson 2, Wendt, Raffael*
12/03	a	Hamburg	L	1-2	*Christensen*
19/03	h	Bayern	L	0-1	
01/04	a	Frankfurt	D	0-0	
05/04	h	Hertha	W	1-0	*Bénes*
08/04	a	Köln	W	3-2	*Vestergaard, Traoré, Stindl*
15/04	a	Hoffenheim	L	3-5	*Vestergaard, Stindl, Dahoud*
22/04	h	Dortmund	L	2-3	*Stindl, og (Schmelzer)*
29/04	a	Mainz	W	2-1	*Stindl, Schulz*
06/05	h	Augsburg	D	1-1	*Hahn*
13/05	a	Wolfsburg	D	1-1	*Vestergaard*
20/05	h	Darmstadt	D	2-2	*Hazard, Raffael*

No	Name	Nat	DoB	Pos	Aps	(s)	Gls
22	László Bénes	SVK	09/09/97	M	3	(5)	1
3	Andreas Christensen	DEN	10/04/96	D	31		2
8	Mahmoud Dahoud		01/01/96	M	26	(2)	2
9	Josip Drmic	SUI	08/08/92	A	2	(10)	
30	Nico Elvedi	SUI	30/09/96	D	23	(2)	
28	André Hahn		13/08/90	M	18	(12)	3
10	Thorgan Hazard	BEL	29/03/93	M	18	(5)	6
7	Patrick Herrmann		12/02/91	M	9	(9)	1
23	Jonas Hofmann		14/07/92	M	16	(5)	
24	Tony Jantschke		07/04/90	D	17	(5)	
19	Fabian Johnson	USA	11/12/87	M	12	(9)	3
25	Timothée Kolodziejczak	FRA	01/10/91	D		(1)	
27	Julian Korb		21/03/92	D	7	(5)	
6	Christoph Kramer		19/02/91	M	23	(1)	
11	Raffael	BRA	28/03/85	A	18	(2)	7
14	Nico Schulz		01/04/93	M	4	(8)	1
44	Ba-Muaka Simakala		28/01/97	A		(1)	
1	Yann Sommer	SUI	17/12/88	G	34		
20	Djibril Sow	SUI	06/02/97	M		(1)	
13	Lars Stindl		26/08/88	A	29	(1)	11
5	Tobias Strobl		12/05/90	M	18	(5)	
16	Ibrahima Traoré	GUI	21/04/88	M	9	(5)	1
4	Jannik Vestergaard	DEN	03/08/92	D	29	(5)	4
17	Oscar Wendt	SWE	24/10/85	D	28		2

SV Darmstadt 98

1898 • Jonathan-Heimes-Stadion am Böllenfalltor (17,468) • sv98.de

Coach: Norbert Meier; (05/12/16) (Ramon Berndroth); (27/12/16) Torsten Frings

2016

Date		Opponent		Score	Scorers
27/08	a	Köln	L	0-2	
10/09	h	Frankfurt	W	1-0	*Sirigu*
17/09	a	Dortmund	L	0-6	
20/09	h	Hoffenheim	D	1-1	*Oliynyk*
24/09	a	Augsburg	L	0-1	
01/10	h	Bremen	D	2-2	*Čolak 2 (1p)*
16/10	a	Mainz	L	1-2	*Gondorf (p)*
22/10	h	Wolfsburg	W	3-1	*Ben-Hatira, Kleinheisler, Sirigu*
29/10	h	Leipzig	L	0-2	
05/11	a	Leverkusen	L	2-3	*Čolak, Vrančić*
19/11	h	Ingolstadt	L	0-1	
27/11	a	Schalke	L	1-3	*Heller*
04/12	h	Hamburg	L	0-2	
10/12	a	Freiburg	L	0-1	
18/12	h	Bayern	L	0-1	
21/12	a	Hertha	L	0-2	

2017

Date		Opponent		Score	Scorers
21/01	h	Mönchengladbach	D	0-0	
28/01	h	Köln	L	1-6	*Sam (p)*
05/02	a	Frankfurt	L	0-2	
11/02	h	Dortmund	W	2-1	*Boyd, Čolak*
18/02	a	Hoffenheim	L	0-2	
25/02	h	Augsburg	L	1-2	*Heller*
04/03	a	Bremen	L	0-2	
11/03	h	Mainz	W	2-1	*Aytaç, Sam (p)*
18/03	a	Wolfsburg	L	0-1	
01/04	a	Leipzig	L	0-4	
05/04	h	Leverkusen	L	0-2	
09/04	a	Ingolstadt	L	2-3	*Vrančić 2 (1p)*
16/04	h	Schalke	W	2-1	*Vrančić, Gondorf*
22/04	a	Hamburg	W	2-1	*Aytaç, Platte*
29/04	h	Freiburg	W	3-0	*Platte, Gondorf, Schipplock*
06/05	a	Bayern	L	0-1	
13/05	h	Hertha	L	0-2	
20/05	a	Mönchengladbach	D	2-2	*Schipplock, Heller*

No	Name	Nat	DoB	Pos	Aps	(s)	Gls
4	Aytaç Sulu	TUR	11/12/85	D	27		2
26	Patrick Banggaard	DEN	04/04/94	D	9		
28	Änis Ben-Hatira	TUN	18/07/88	M	8	(3)	1
14	Roman Bezjak	SVN	21/02/89	A	7	(4)	
15	Terrence Boyd	USA	16/02/91	A	5	(2)	1
16	Antonio Čolak	CRO	17/09/93	A	12	(10)	4
1	Daniel Fernandes	POR	13/11/92	G	6	(1)	
31	Michael Esser		22/11/87	G	28		
7	Artem Fedetskiy	UKR	26/04/85	D	13	(3)	
8	Jérôme Gondorf		26/06/88	M	29		3
5	Benjamin Gorka		15/04/84	D		(1)	
2	Leon Guwara		28/06/96	D	11	(6)	
34	Hamit Altıntop	TUR	08/12/82	M	15	(1)	
20	Marcel Heller		12/02/86	M	31	(1)	3
21	Immanuel Höhn		23/12/91	D	12		
32	Fabian Holland		11/07/90	D	25	(1)	
23	Florian Jungwirth		27/01/89	M	12	(4)	
36	Wilson Kamavuaka	COD	29/03/90	M	6	(2)	
30	László Kleinheisler	HUN	08/04/94	M	10	(2)	1
3	Alexander Milosevic	SWE	30/01/92	D	18		
18	Peter Niemeyer		22/11/83	M	13	(2)	
11	Victor Obinna	NGA	25/03/87	A		(2)	
22	Denys Oliynyk	UKR	16/06/87	M		(4)	1
19	Felix Platte		11/02/96	A	6	(3)	2
10	Jan Rosenthal		07/04/86	M	10	(9)	
33	Sidney Sam		31/01/88	M	11	(2)	2
39	Sven Schipplock		08/11/88	A	12	(11)	2
17	Sandro Sirigu		07/10/88	D	17	(13)	2
13	Markus Steinhöfer		07/03/86	D	3	(4)	
9	Dominik Stroh-Engel		27/11/85	A		(4)	
6	Mario Vrančić	BIH	23/05/89	M	18	(5)	4
40	Silas Zehnder		30/06/99	A		(1)	

Eintracht Frankfurt

1899 • Commerzbank-Arena (51,500) • eintracht.de

Major honours

UEFA Cup (1) 1980; German League (1) 1959; German Cup (4) 1974, 1975, 1981, 1988

Coach: Niko Kovač (CRO)

2016

Date		Opponent		Score	Scorers
27/08	h	Schalke	W	1-0	*Meier*
10/09	a	Darmstadt	L	0-1	
17/09	h	Leverkusen	W	2-1	*Meier, Fabián*
20/09	a	Ingolstadt	W	2-0	*Abraham, Oczipka*
24/09	h	Hertha	D	3-3	*Fabián, Meier, Hector*
01/10	a	Freiburg	L	0-1	
15/10	h	Bayern	D	2-2	*Huszti, Fabián*
21/10	a	Hamburg	W	3-0	*og (Holtby), Tarashaj, Seferovic*
28/10	a	Mönchengladbach	D	0-0	
05/11	h	Köln	W	1-0	*Gaćinović*
20/11	a	Bremen	W	2-1	*Meier, Barkok*
26/11	h	Dortmund	W	2-1	*Huszti, Seferovic*
04/11	a	Augsburg	D	1-1	*Hrgota*
09/12	h	Hoffenheim	D	0-0	
17/12	a	Wolfsburg	L	0-1	
20/12	h	Mainz	W	3-0	*Hrgota 2, Barkok*

2017

Date		Opponent		Score	Scorers
21/01	a	Leipzig	L	0-3	
27/01	a	Schalke	W	1-0	*Meier*
05/02	h	Darmstadt	W	2-0	*Hasebe (p), Rebić*
11/02	a	Leverkusen	L	0-3	
18/02	h	Ingolstadt	L	0-2	
25/02	a	Hertha	L	0-2	
05/03	h	Freiburg	L	1-2	*Hrgota*
11/03	a	Bayern	L	0-3	
18/03	h	Hamburg	D	0-0	
01/04	h	Mönchengladbach	D	0-0	
04/04	a	Köln	L	0-1	
07/04	h	Bremen	D	2-2	*Gaćinović, Fabián (p)*
15/04	a	Dortmund	L	1-3	*Fabián*
22/04	h	Augsburg	W	3-1	*Fabián 2, Rebić*
30/04	a	Hoffenheim	L	0-1	
06/05	h	Wolfsburg	L	0-2	
13/05	a	Mainz	L	2-4	*Hrgota, Seferovic*
20/05	h	Leipzig	D	2-2	*Jesús Vallejo, Blum*

No	Name	Nat	DoB	Pos	Aps	(s)	Gls
19	David Abraham	ARG	15/07/86	D	30		1
28	Aymen Barkok		21/05/98	M	6	(12)	2
18	Max Besuschkow		31/05/97	M	1	(2)	
7	Danny Blum		07/01/91	M	3	(11)	1
22	Timothy Chandler	USA	29/03/90	D	31	(1)	
10	Marco Fabián	MEX	21/07/89	M	23	(1)	7
11	Mijat Gaćinović	SRB	08/02/95	M	26	(2)	2
20	Makoto Hasebe	JPN	18/01/84	M	21	(1)	1
15	Michael Hector	JAM	19/07/92	D	14	(8)	1
1	Lukas Hradecky	FIN	24/11/89	G	33		
31	Branimir Hrgota	SWE	12/01/93	A	22	(6)	5
8	Szabolcs Huszti	HUN	18/04/83	M	14	(1)	2
5	Jesús Vallejo	ESP	05/01/97	D	22	(3)	1
13	Heinz Lindner	AUT	17/07/90	G	1	(1)	
39	Omar Mascarell	ESP	02/02/93	M	27	(1)	
14	Alexander Meier		17/01/83	A	15	(6)	5
6	Bastian Oczipka		12/01/89	D	33		1
29	Anderson Ordóñez	ECU	29/01/94	D	3	(1)	
17	Ante Rebić	CRO	21/09/93	A	16	(8)	2
4	Marco Russ		04/08/85	D	3	(1)	
9	Haris Seferovic	SUI	22/02/92	A	11	(14)	3
21	Marc Stendera		10/12/95	M	2		
30	Shani Tarashaj	SUI	07/02/95	A	1	(12)	1
33	Taleb Tawatha	ISR	21/06/92	D	8	(6)	
3	Guillermo Varela	URU	24/03/93	D	6	(1)	
24	Marius Wolf		27/05/95	A	2	(1)	

SC Freiburg

1904 • Schwarzwald-Stadion (24,000) • scfreiburg.com

Coach: Christian Streich

2016					
28/08	a	Hertha	L	1-2	*Höfler*
10/09	h	Mönchengladbach	W	3-1	*Philipp 2, Petersen (p)*
16/09	a	Köln	L	0-3	
20/09	h	Hamburg	W	1-0	*Petersen*
23/09	a	Dortmund	L	1-3	*Philipp*
01/10	h	Frankfurt	W	1-0	*Grifo*
15/10	a	Hoffenheim	L	1-2	*Niederlechner*
22/10	h	Augsburg	W	2-1	*Philipp, Petersen*
29/10	a	Bremen	W	3-1	*Philipp, Grifo (p), Abrashi*
05/11	h	Wolfsburg	L	0-3	
19/11	a	Mainz	L	2-4	*Grifo, Petersen*
25/11	h	Leipzig	L	1-4	*Niederlechner*
03/12	a	Leverkusen	D	1-1	*Haberer*
10/12	h	Darmstadt	W	1-0	*Petersen (p)*
17/12	a	Schalke	D	1-1	*Niederlechner*
21/12	a	Ingolstadt	W	2-1	*Niederlechner 2 (1p)*
2017					
20/01	h	Bayern	L	1-2	*Haberer*
29/01	h	Hertha	W	2-1	*Haberer, Petersen*
04/02	a	Mönchengladbach	L	0-3	
12/02	h	Köln	W	2-1	*Grifo, Philipp*
18/02	a	Hamburg	D	2-2	*Philipp, Grifo*
25/02	h	Dortmund	L	0-3	
05/03	a	Frankfurt	W	2-1	*Niederlechner 2*
11/03	h	Hoffenheim	D	1-1	*Philipp*
18/03	a	Augsburg	D	1-1	*Niederlechner (p)*
01/04	h	Bremen	L	2-5	*Petersen, Grifo*
05/04	a	Wolfsburg	W	1-0	*Niederlechner*
08/04	h	Mainz	W	1-0	*Petersen*
15/04	a	Leipzig	L	0-4	
23/04	h	Leverkusen	W	2-1	*Petersen, Stenzel*
29/04	a	Darmstadt	L	0-3	
07/05	h	Schalke	W	2-0	*Niederlechner 2 (1p)*
13/05	h	Ingolstadt	D	1-1	*Philipp*
20/05	a	Bayern	L	1-4	*Petersen*

No	Name	Nat	DoB	Pos	Aps	(s)	Gls
6	Amir Abrashi	ALB	27/03/90	M	16	(4)	1
4	Çağlar Söyüncü	TUR	23/05/96	D	24		
25	Jonas Föhrenbach		26/01/96	D	1	(2)	
8	Mike Frantz		14/10/86	M	29	(1)	
32	Vicenzo Grifo	ITA	07/04/93	M	27	(3)	6
31	Karim Guédé	SVK	07/01/85	A	3	(2)	
5	Manuel Gulde		12/02/91	D	19	(1)	
30	Christian Günter		28/02/93	D	30	(1)	
19	Janik Haberer		02/04/94	M	22	(10)	3
27	Nicolas Höfler		09/03/90	M	26	(2)	1
2	Aleksandar Ignjovski	SRB	27/01/91	D	12	(7)	
20	Marc-Oliver Kempf		28/01/95	D	12	(1)	
17	Lukas Kübler		30/08/92	D	14	(2)	
22	Jonas Meffert		04/09/94	M	1		
16	Mats Møller Dæhli	NOR	02/03/95	M		(2)	
7	Florian Niederlechner		24/10/90	A	29	(5)	11
24	Georg Niedermeier		26/02/96	D		(6)	
14	Håvard Nielsen	NOR	15/07/93	A		(4)	
11	Onur Bulut	TUR	16/04/94	M	12	(9)	
18	Nils Petersen		06/12/88	A	7	(26)	10
26	Maximilian Philipp		01/03/94	A	23	(2)	9
23	Julian Schuster		15/04/85	M	9	(4)	
1	Alexander Schwolow		02/06/92	G	34		
15	Pascal Stenzel		20/03/96	D	14	(5)	1
3	Marc Torrejón	ESP	18/02/86	D	10	(2)	

Hamburger SV

1887 • Volksparkstadion (57,000) • hsv.de

Major honours

European Champion Clubs' Cup (1) 1983; UEFA Cup Winners' Cup (1) 1977; German League (6) 1923, 1928, 1960, 1979, 1982, 1983; German Cup (3) 1963, 1976, 1987

Coach: Bruno Labbadia; (26/09/16) Markus Gisdol

2016					
27/08	h	Ingolstadt	D	1-1	*Wood*
10/09	a	Leverkusen	L	1-3	*Wood*
17/09	h	Leipzig	L	0-4	
20/09	a	Freiburg	L	0-1	
24/09	h	Bayern	L	0-1	
01/10	a	Hertha	L	0-2	
15/10	a	Mönchengladbach	D	0-0	
21/10	h	Frankfurt	L	0-3	
30/10	a	Köln	L	0-3	
07/11	h	Dortmund	L	2-5	*Müller 2*
20/11	a	Hoffenheim	D	2-2	*Kostić, Müller*
26/11	h	Bremen	D	2-2	*Gregoritsch 2*
04/12	a	Darmstadt	W	2-0	*Gregoritsch, Ostrzolek*
10/12	h	Augsburg	W	1-0	*Kostić*
17/12	a	Mainz	L	1-3	*Wood*
20/12	h	Schalke	W	2-1	*Müller, Wood*
2017					
21/01	a	Wolfsburg	L	0-1	
28/01	a	Ingolstadt	L	1-3	*Sakai*
03/02	h	Leverkusen	W	1-0	*Papadopoulos*
11/02	a	Leipzig	W	3-0	*Papadopoulos, Walace, Hunt*
18/02	h	Freiburg	D	2-2	*Hunt, Gregoritsch*
25/02	a	Bayern	L	0-8	
05/03	h	Hertha	W	1-0	*Ekdal*
12/03	h	Mönchengladbach	W	2-1	*Kostić, Wood*
18/03	a	Frankfurt	D	0-0	
01/04	h	Köln	W	2-1	*Müller, Holtby*
04/04	a	Dortmund	L	0-3	
08/04	h	Hoffenheim	W	2-1	*Hunt 2*
16/04	a	Bremen	L	1-2	*Gregoritsch*
22/04	h	Darmstadt	L	1-2	*og (Holland)*
30/04	a	Augsburg	L	0-4	
07/05	h	Mainz	D	0-0	
13/05	a	Schalke	D	1-1	*Lasogga*
20/05	h	Wolfsburg	W	2-1	*Kostić, Waldschmidt*

No	Name	Nat	DoB	Pos	Aps	(s)	Gls
1	René Adler		15/01/85	G	19		
21	Nabil Bahoui	SWE	05/02/91	M	1		
3	Cléber	BRA	05/12/90	D	5		
2	Dennis Diekmeier		20/10/89	D	21	(3)	
5	Johan Djourou	SUI	18/01/87	D	12	(2)	
6	Douglas Santos	BRA	22/03/94	D	19	(1)	
20	Albin Ekdal	SWE	28/07/89	M	13	(8)	1
39	Ashton Götz		16/07/93	D	1		
11	Michael Gregoritsch	AUT	18/04/94	A	14	(16)	5
23	Alen Halilović	CRO	18/06/96	M	1	(5)	
8	Lewis Holtby		18/09/90	M	29		1
14	Aaron Hunt		04/09/86	M	14	(8)	4
26	Vasilije Janjicic	SUI	12/11/98	M	2	(2)	
18	Bakery Jatta	GAM	06/06/98	A	1	(5)	
28	Gideon Jung		12/09/94	M	26	(3)	
17	Filip Kostić	SRB	01/11/92	M	29	(2)	4
10	Pierre-Michel Lasogga		15/12/91	A	5	(15)	1
31	Christian Mathenia		31/03/92	G	14		
13	Mërgim Mavraj	ALB	09/06/86	D	14		
12	Tom Mickel		19/04/89	G	1		
27	Nicolai Müller		25/09/87	M	22	(3)	5
22	Matthias Ostrzolek		05/06/90	D	23	(1)	1
9	Kyriakos Papadopoulos	GRE	23/02/92	D	15		2
34	Finn Porath		23/02/97	M		(1)	
24	Gotoku Sakai	JPN	14/03/91	D	29	(4)	1
4	Emir Spahić	BIH	18/08/80	D	9	(2)	
12	Walace	BRA	04/04/95	M	9		1
15	Luca Waldschmidt		19/05/96	A	3	(11)	1
7	Bobby Wood	USA	15/11/92	A	23	(5)	5

Hertha BSC Berlin

1892 • Olympiastadion (74,649) • herthabsc.de

Major honours

German League (2) 1930, 1931

Coach: Pál Dárdai (HUN)

2016					
28/08	h	Freiburg	W	2-1	*Darida, Schieber*
10/09	a	Ingolstadt	W	2-0	*Ibišević, Schieber*
18/09	h	Schalke	W	2-0	*Weiser, Stocker*
21/09	a	Bayern	L	0-3	
24/09	a	Frankfurt	D	3-3	*Ibišević 2 (1p), Esswein*
01/10	h	Hamburg	W	2-0	*Ibišević 2 (1p)*
14/10	a	Dortmund	D	1-1	*Stocker*
22/10	h	Köln	W	2-1	*Ibišević, Stark*
30/10	a	Hoffenheim	L	0-1	
04/11	h	Mönchengladbach	W	3-0	*Kalou 3*
19/11	a	Augsburg	D	0-0	
27/11	h	Mainz	W	2-1	*Ibišević 2*
03/12	a	Wolfsburg	W	3-2	*Plattenhardt, Esswein, Kalou (p)*
10/12	h	Bremen	L	0-1	
17/12	a	Leipzig	L	0-2	
21/12	h	Darmstadt	W	2-0	*Plattenhardt, Kalou*
2017					
22/01	a	Leverkusen	L	1-3	*Stocker*
29/01	a	Freiburg	L	1-2	*Schieber*
04/02	h	Ingolstadt	W	1-0	*Haraguchi*
11/02	a	Schalke	L	0-2	
18/02	h	Bayern	D	1-1	*Ibišević*
25/02	h	Frankfurt	W	2-0	*Ibišević, Darida*
05/03	a	Hamburg	L	0-1	
11/03	h	Dortmund	W	2-1	*Kalou, Plattenhardt*
18/03	a	Köln	L	2-4	*Ibišević (p), Brooks*
31/03	h	Hoffenheim	L	1-3	*Pekarík*
05/04	a	Mönchengladbach	L	0-1	
09/04	h	Augsburg	W	2-0	*Brooks, Stocker*
15/04	a	Mainz	L	0-1	
22/04	h	Wolfsburg	W	1-0	*Ibišević*
29/04	a	Bremen	L	0-2	
06/05	h	Leipzig	L	1-4	*og (Khedira)*
13/05	a	Darmstadt	W	2-0	*Kalou, Torunarigha*
20/05	h	Leverkusen	L	2-6	*Weiser, Allagui (p)*

No	Name	Nat	DoB	Pos	Aps	(s)	Gls
11	Sami Allagui	TUN	28/05/86	A		(12)	1
20	Allan	BRA	03/03/97	M	8	(7)	
27	Florian Baak		18/03/99	D		(2)	
25	John Brooks	USA	28/01/93	D	24		2
6	Vladimír Darida	CZE	08/08/90	M	21	(4)	2
10	Ondrej Duda	SVK	05/12/94	M		(3)	
7	Alexander Esswein		25/03/90	M	15	(14)	2
24	Genki Haraguchi	JPN	09/05/91	M	23	(8)	1
13	Jens Hegeler		22/01/88	M	2	(4)	
19	Vedad Ibišević	BIH	06/08/84	A	32		12
22	Rune Almenning Jarstein	NOR	29/09/84	G	34		
30	Julius Kade		20/05/99	M		(1)	
8	Salomon Kalou	CIV	05/08/85	A	25	(1)	7
18	Sinan Kurt		23/07/96	M		(2)	
15	Sebastian Langkamp		15/01/88	D	26	(1)	
28	Fabian Lustenberger	SUI	02/05/88	M	17	(2)	
33	Arne Maier		08/01/99	M		(1)	
34	Maximilian Mittelstädt		18/03/97	D	5	(7)	
2	Peter Pekarík	SVK	30/10/86	D	30	(1)	1
21	Marvin Plattenhardt		26/01/92	D	27		3
16	Julian Schieber		13/02/89	A	2	(16)	3
3	Per Ciljan Skjelbred	NOR	16/06/87	M	25	(1)	
5	Niklas Stark		14/04/95	D	27		1
14	Valentin Stocker	SUI	12/04/89	M	14	(3)	4
40	Jordan Torunarigha		07/08/97	D	5	(3)	1
23	Mitchell Weiser		21/04/94	D	12	(5)	2

GERMANY

TSG 1899 Hoffenheim

1899 • Wirsol Rhein-Neckar-Arena (30,150) • achtzehn99.de

Coach: Julian Nagelsmann

Date		Opponent		Score	Scorers
2016					
28/08	h	Leipzig	D	2-2	*Rupp, Uth*
11/09	a	Mainz	D	4-4	*Wagner, Uth 2, Szalai*
17/09	h	Wolfsburg	D	0-0	
20/09	a	Darmstadt	D	1-1	*Kramarić*
25/09	h	Schalke	W	2-1	*Kramarić, Rupp*
01/10	a	Ingolstadt	W	2-1	*Wagner, Demirbay*
15/10	h	Freiburg	W	2-1	*Wagner, Kramarić (p)*
22/10	a	Leverkusen	W	3-0	*Demirbay, Wagner, Zuber*
30/10	h	Hertha	W	1-0	*Süle*
05/11	a	Bayern	D	1-1	*Demirbay*
20/11	h	Hamburg	D	2-2	*Wagner, Zuber*
26/11	a	Mönchengladbach	D	1-1	*Amiri*
03/12	h	Köln	W	4-0	*Wagner 2, Toljan, Uth*
09/12	a	Frankfurt	D	0-0	
16/12	h	Dortmund	D	2-2	*Uth, Wagner*
21/12	h	Bremen	D	1-1	*Wagner*
2017					
21/01	a	Augsburg	W	2-0	*Wagner, Kramarić*
28/01	a	Leipzig	L	1-2	*Amiri*
04/02	h	Mainz	W	4-0	*Uth, Terrazzino, Szalai 2*
12/02	a	Wolfsburg	L	1-2	*Zuber*
18/02	h	Darmstadt	W	2-0	*Kramarić 2 (1p)*
26/02	a	Schalke	D	1-1	*Rudy*
04/03	h	Ingolstadt	W	5-2	*Rudy, Szalai 2, Kramarić, Hübner*
11/03	a	Freiburg	D	1-1	*Kramarić*
18/03	h	Leverkusen	W	1-0	*Wagner*
31/03	a	Hertha	W	3-1	*Kramarić 2 (1p), Süle*
04/04	h	Bayern	W	1-0	*Kramarić*
08/04	a	Hamburg	L	1-2	*Kramarić (p)*
15/04	h	Mönchengladbach	W	5-3	*Szalai 2, Demirbay 2, Uth*
21/04	a	Köln	D	1-1	*Demirbay*
30/04	h	Frankfurt	W	1-0	*Hübner*
06/05	a	Dortmund	L	1-2	*Kramarić (p)*
13/05	a	Bremen	W	5-3	*Szalai, Kramarić 2, Zuber, Bičakčić*
20/05	h	Augsburg	D	0-0	

No	Name	Nat	DoB	Pos	Aps	(s)	Gls
18	Nadiem Amiri		27/10/96	M	20	(13)	2
34	Barış Atik	TUR	09/01/95	A		(3)	
1	Oliver Baumann		02/06/90	G	34		
4	Ermin Bičakčić	BIH	24/01/90	D	11	(7)	1
13	Kerem Demirbay		03/07/93	M	27	(1)	6
21	Benjamin Hübner		04/07/89	D	25		2
3	Pavel Kadeřábek	CZE	25/04/92	D	22	(1)	
27	Andrej Kramarić	CRO	19/06/91	A	28	(6)	15
30	Philipp Ochs		17/04/97	M	2	(1)	
8	Eugen Polanski	POL	17/03/86	M	7	(7)	
6	Sebastian Rudy		28/02/90	M	32		2
7	Lukas Rupp		08/01/91	M	8	(6)	2
5	Fabian Schär	SUI	20/12/91	D	3	(3)	
16	Pirmin Schwegler	SUI	09/03/87	M	2	(8)	
25	Niklas Süle		03/09/95	D	33		2
28	Ádám Szalai	HUN	09/12/87	A	7	(15)	8
23	Marco Terrazzino		15/04/91	A	4	(5)	1
15	Jeremy Toljan		08/08/94	D	14	(6)	1
19	Mark Uth		24/08/91	A	12	(10)	7
9	Eduardo Vargas	CHI	20/11/89	A		(5)	
22	Kevin Vogt		23/09/91	D	30	(1)	
14	Sandro Wagner		29/11/87	A	30	(1)	11
17	Steven Zuber	SUI	17/08/91	M	23	(1)	4

FC Ingolstadt 04

2004 • Audi-Sportpark (15,200) • fcingolstadt.de

Coach: Markus Kauczinski; (12/11/16) Maik Walpurgis

Date		Opponent		Score	Scorers
2016					
27/08	a	Hamburg	D	1-1	*Hinterseer*
10/09	h	Hertha	L	0-2	
17/09	a	Bayern	L	1-3	*Lezcano*
20/09	h	Frankfurt	L	0-2	
24/09	a	Mönchengladbach	L	0-2	
01/10	h	Hoffenheim	L	1-2	*Hinterseer (p)*
15/10	a	Köln	L	1-2	*Hinterseer (p)*
22/10	h	Dortmund	D	3-3	*Cohen, Lezcano 2*
29/10	a	Mainz	L	0-2	
05/11	h	Augsburg	L	0-2	
19/11	a	Darmstadt	W	1-0	*Hartmann*
26/11	h	Wolfsburg	D	1-1	*Jung*
03/12	a	Bremen	L	1-2	*Suttner*
10/12	h	Leipzig	W	1-0	*Roger*
18/12	a	Leverkusen	W	2-1	*Morales, Cohen*
21/12	h	Freiburg	L	1-2	*Suttner*
2017					
21/01	a	Schalke	L	0-1	
28/01	h	Hamburg	W	3-1	*Gross, Suttner, Cohen (p)*
04/02	a	Hertha	L	0-1	
11/02	h	Bayern	L	0-2	
18/02	a	Frankfurt	W	2-0	*Brégerie, Gross (p)*
26/02	h	Mönchengladbach	L	0-2	
04/03	a	Hoffenheim	L	2-5	*Cohen, og (Süle)*
11/03	h	Köln	D	2-2	*Lezcano, Brégerie*
17/03	a	Dortmund	L	0-1	
02/04	h	Mainz	W	2-1	*Brégerie, Hadergjonaj*
05/04	a	Augsburg	W	3-2	*Kittel, Cohen 2*
09/04	h	Darmstadt	W	3-2	*Gross, Cohen, Suttner*
15/04	a	Wolfsburg	L	0-3	
22/04	h	Bremen	L	2-4	*Lezcano, Gross (p)*
29/04	a	Leipzig	D	0-0	
06/05	h	Leverkusen	D	1-1	*Kittel*
13/05	a	Freiburg	D	1-1	*Lezcano*
20/05	h	Schalke	D	1-1	*Gross (p)*

No	Name	Nat	DoB	Pos	Aps	(s)	Gls
18	Romain Brégerie	FRA	09/08/86	D	17		3
19	Max Christiansen		25/09/96	M	4	(7)	
36	Almog Cohen	ISR	01/09/88	M	29	(2)	7
10	Pascal Gross		15/06/91	M	31	(2)	5
33	Florent Hadergjonaj	SUI	31/07/94	D	25		1
35	Martin Hansen	DEN	15/06/90	G	23		
9	Moritz Hartmann		20/06/86	A	12	(2)	1
16	Lukas Hinterseer	AUT	28/03/91	A	8	(20)	3
3	Anthony Jung		03/11/91	M	8	(8)	1
21	Sonny Kittel		06/01/93	M	7	(13)	2
7	Matthew Leckie	AUS	04/02/91	A	25	(5)	
13	Robert Leipertz		01/02/93	A		(6)	
28	Tobias Levels		22/11/86	D	8	(2)	
14	Stefan Lex		27/11/89	A	2	(11)	
11	Darío Lezcano	PAR	30/06/90	A	27	(6)	6
34	Marvin Matip	CMR	25/09/85	D	33		
6	Alfredo Morales	USA	12/05/90	M	20	(7)	1
31	Maurice Multhaup		15/12/96	M		(1)	
1	Ørjan Håskjold Nyland	NOR	10/09/90	G	11	(1)	
8	Roger	BRA	10/08/85	M	26	(4)	1
29	Markus Suttner	AUT	16/04/87	D	31		4
32	Marcel Tisserand	COD	10/01/93	D	27	(1)	

1. FC Köln

1948 • RheinEnergieStadion (50,000) • fc-koeln.de

Major honours

German League (3) 1962, 1964, 1978; German Cup (4) 1968, 1977, 1978, 1983

Coach: Peter Stöger (AUT)

Date		Opponent		Score	Scorers
2016					
27/08	h	Darmstadt	W	2-0	*Risse, Modeste*
10/09	a	Wolfsburg	D	0-0	
16/09	h	Freiburg	W	3-0	*Modeste 2, Bittencourt*
21/09	a	Schalke	W	3-1	*Osako, Modeste, Zoller*
25/09	h	Leipzig	D	1-1	*Osako*
01/10	a	Bayern	D	1-1	*Modeste*
15/10	h	Ingolstadt	W	2-1	*Modeste 2 (1p)*
22/10	a	Hertha	L	1-2	*Modeste*
30/10	h	Hamburg	W	3-0	*Modeste 3*
05/11	a	Frankfurt	L	0-1	
19/11	a	Mönchengladbach	W	2-1	*Modeste, Risse*
26/11	h	Augsburg	D	0-0	
03/12	a	Hoffenheim	L	0-4	
10/12	h	Dortmund	D	1-1	*Rudņevs*
17/12	a	Bremen	D	1-1	*Rudņevs*
21/12	h	Leverkusen	D	1-1	*Modeste*
2017					
22/01	a	Mainz	D	0-0	
28/01	a	Darmstadt	W	6-1	*og (Aytaç), Osako 2, Modeste, Jojić, Rudņevs*
04/02	h	Wolfsburg	W	1-0	*Modeste (p)*
12/02	a	Freiburg	L	1-2	*Modeste*
19/02	h	Schalke	D	1-1	*Modeste*
25/02	a	Leipzig	L	1-3	*Osako*
04/03	h	Bayern	L	0-3	
11/03	a	Ingolstadt	D	2-2	*Modeste 2 (1p)*
18/03	h	Hertha	W	4-2	*Osako, Modeste 3*
01/04	a	Hamburg	L	1-2	*Jojić*
04/04	h	Frankfurt	W	1-0	*Jojić*
08/04	h	Mönchengladbach	L	2-3	*Clemens, Modeste*
15/04	a	Augsburg	L	1-2	*og (Max)*
21/04	h	Hoffenheim	D	1-1	*Bittencourt*
29/04	a	Dortmund	D	0-0	
05/05	h	Bremen	W	4-3	*Modeste 2, Bittencourt, Zoller*
13/05	a	Leverkusen	D	2-2	*Jojić, Klünter*
20/05	h	Mainz	W	2-0	*Hector, Osako*

No	Name	Nat	DoB	Pos	Aps	(s)	Gls
21	Leonardo Bittencourt		19/12/93	M	12	(4)	3
17	Christian Clemens		04/08/91	M	10	(2)	1
19	Sehrou Guirassy	FRA	12/03/96	A		(6)	
30	Marcel Hartel		19/01/96	M		(2)	
14	Jonas Hector		27/05/90	D	33		1
3	Dominique Heintz		15/08/93	D	30	(2)	
6	Marco Höger		16/09/89	M	24	(6)	
1	Timo Horn		12/05/93	G	20		
8	Miloš Jojić	SRB	19/03/92	M	13	(6)	4
18	Thomas Kessler		20/01/86	G	13		
24	Lukas Klünter		26/05/95	D	8		1
33	Matthias Lehmann		28/05/83	M	21		
5	Dominic Maroh	SVN	04/03/87	D	8	(4)	
15	Mërgim Mavraj	ALB	09/06/86	D	16		
25	Filip Mladenović	SRB	15/08/91	D		(2)	
27	Anthony Modeste	FRA	14/04/88	A	34		25
35	Sven Müller		16/02/96	G	1		
16	Paweł Olkowski	POL	13/02/90	D	12	(2)	
13	Yuya Osako	JPN	18/05/90	A	27	(3)	7
20	Salih Özcan		11/01/98	M	3	(10)	
34	Konstantin Rausch		15/03/90	M	23	(5)	
7	Marcel Risse		17/12/89	M	13		2
9	Artjoms Rudņevs	LVA	13/01/88	A	6	(12)	3
4	Frederik Sørensen	DEN	14/04/92	D	30	(1)	
2	Neven Subotić	SRB	10/12/88	D	9	(3)	
11	Simon Zoller		26/06/91	A	8	(18)	2

RB Leipzig

2009 • Red Bull Arena (42,959) • dierotenbullen.com

Coach: Ralph Hasenhüttl (AUT)

2016					
28/08	a	Hoffenheim	D	2-2	*Kaiser, Sabitzer*
10/09	h	Dortmund	W	1-0	*Keïta*
17/09	a	Hamburg	W	4-0	*Forsberg (p), Werner 2, Selke*
21/09	h	Mönchengladbach	D	1-1	*Werner*
25/09	a	Köln	D	1-1	*Burke*
30/09	h	Augsburg	W	2-1	*Forsberg, Poulsen*
16/10	a	Wolfsburg	W	1-0	*Forsberg*
23/10	h	Bremen	W	3-1	*Keïta 2, Selke*
29/10	a	Darmstadt	W	2-0	*Sabitzer 2*
06/11	h	Mainz	W	3-1	*Werner 2, Forsberg*
18/11	a	Leverkusen	W	3-2	*og (Baumgartlinger), Forsberg, Orban*
25/11	a	Freiburg	W	4-1	*Keïta, Werner 2, Sabitzer*
03/12	h	Schalke	W	2-1	*Werner (p), og (Kolašinac)*
10/12	a	Ingolstadt	L	0-1	
17/12	h	Hertha	W	2-0	*Werner, Orban*
21/12	a	Bayern	L	0-3	
2017					
21/01	h	Frankfurt	W	3-0	*Compper, Werner, og (Jesús Vallejo)*
28/01	h	Hoffenheim	W	2-1	*Werner, Sabitzer*
04/02	a	Dortmund	L	0-1	
11/02	h	Hamburg	L	0-3	
19/02	a	Mönchengladbach	W	2-1	*Forsberg, Werner*
25/02	h	Köln	W	3-1	*Forsberg, og (Maroh), Werner*
03/03	a	Augsburg	D	2-2	*Werner, Compper*
11/03	h	Wolfsburg	L	0-1	
18/03	a	Bremen	L	0-3	
01/04	h	Darmstadt	W	4-0	*Keïta 2, Forsberg, Orban*
05/04	a	Mainz	W	3-2	*Sabitzer, Werner, Keïta*
08/04	h	Leverkusen	W	1-0	*Poulsen*
15/04	h	Freiburg	W	4-0	*Poulsen, Werner, Keïta, Demme*
23/04	a	Schalke	D	1-1	*Werner*
29/04	h	Ingolstadt	D	0-0	
06/05	a	Hertha	W	4-1	*Werner 2, Selke 2*
13/05	h	Bayern	L	4-5	*Sabitzer, Werner 2 (1p), Poulsen*
20/05	a	Frankfurt	D	2-2	*Sabitzer, Poulsen*

No	Name	Nat	DoB	Pos	Aps	(s)	Gls
3	Bernardo	BRA	14/05/95	D	21	(1)	
17	Massimo Bruno	BEL	17/09/93	M		(1)	
19	Oliver Burke	SCO	07/04/97	M	5	(20)	1
1	Fabio Coltorti	SUI	03/12/80	G	1		
33	Marvin Compper		14/06/85	D	25		2
31	Diego Demme		21/11/91	M	32		1
10	Emil Forsberg	SWE	23/10/91	M	27	(3)	8
32	Péter Gulácsi	HUN	06/05/90	G	33		
23	Marcel Halstenberg		27/09/91	D	30		
13	Stefan Ilsanker	AUT	18/05/89	M	29	(4)	
24	Dominik Kaiser		16/09/88	M	7	(18)	1
8	Naby Keïta	GUI	10/02/95	M	29	(2)	8
6	Rani Khedira		27/01/94	M	1	(9)	
16	Lukas Klostermann		03/06/96	D	1		
4	Willi Orban		03/11/92	D	28		3
38	Federico Palacios Martínez		09/04/95	M		(2)	
5	Kyriakos Papadopoulos	GRE	23/02/92	D		(1)	
9	Yussuf Poulsen	DEN	15/06/94	A	25	(4)	5
7	Marcel Sabitzer	AUT	17/03/94	M	31	(1)	8
20	Benno Schmitz		17/11/94	D	11	(5)	
27	Davie Selke		20/01/95	A	2	(19)	4
17	Dayot Upamecano	FRA	27/11/98	D	8	(4)	
11	Timo Werner		06/03/96	A	28	(3)	21

1. FSV Mainz 05

1905 • Opel Arena (34,000) • mainz05.de

Coach: Martin Schmidt (SUI)

2016					
27/08	a	Dortmund	L	1-2	*Muto*
11/09	h	Hoffenheim	D	4-4	*De Blasis 2, Córdoba, Öztunali*
18/09	a	Augsburg	W	3-1	*Córdoba, Yunus, Muto*
21/09	a	Bremen	W	2-1	*Yunus, De Blasis*
24/09	h	Leverkusen	L	2-3	*Yunus, Bell*
02/10	a	Wolfsburg	D	0-0	
16/10	h	Darmstadt	W	2-1	*De Blasis, Yunus (p)*
23/10	a	Schalke	L	0-3	
29/10	h	Ingolstadt	W	2-0	*Yunus (p), Öztunali*
06/11	a	Leipzig	L	1-3	*Bell*
19/11	h	Freiburg	W	4-2	*Bungert, Yunus (p), Bell, Onisiwo*
27/11	a	Hertha	L	1-2	*Seydel*
02/12	h	Bayern	L	1-3	*Córdoba*
11/12	a	Mönchengladbach	L	0-1	
17/12	h	Hamburg	W	3-1	*Latza 3*
20/12	a	Frankfurt	L	0-3	
2017					
22/01	h	Köln	D	0-0	
29/01	h	Dortmund	D	1-1	*Latza*
04/02	a	Hoffenheim	L	0-4	
10/02	h	Augsburg	W	2-0	*Öztunali, Jairo Samperio (p)*
18/02	h	Bremen	L	0-2	
25/02	a	Leverkusen	W	2-0	*Bell, Öztunali*
04/03	h	Wolfsburg	D	1-1	*Córdoba*
11/03	a	Darmstadt	L	1-2	*Quaison*
19/03	h	Schalke	L	0-1	
02/04	a	Ingolstadt	L	1-2	*Öztunali*
05/04	h	Leipzig	L	2-3	*Jairo Samperio (p), Muto*
08/04	a	Freiburg	L	0-1	
15/04	h	Hertha	W	1-0	*og (Brooks)*
22/04	a	Bayern	D	2-2	*Bojan, Brosinski (p)*
29/04	h	Mönchengladbach	L	1-2	*Muto*
07/05	a	Hamburg	D	0-0	
13/05	h	Frankfurt	W	4-2	*Córdoba, Bell, Muto, De Blasis (p)*
20/05	a	Köln	L	0-2	

No	Name	Nat	DoB	Pos	Aps	(s)	Gls
22	André Ramalho	BRA	16/02/92	D	12	(6)	
3	Leon Balogun	NGA	28/06/88	D	13	(4)	
16	Stefan Bell		24/08/91	D	30	(1)	5
10	Bojan Krkić	ESP	28/08/90	A	8	(3)	1
41	Mounir Bouziane	FRA	05/02/91	A		(1)	
18	Daniel Brosinski		17/07/88	D	27	(2)	1
26	Niko Bungert		24/10/86	D	9	(1)	1
24	Gaëtan Bussmann	FRA	02/02/91	D	12	(2)	
27	Christian Clemens		04/08/91	M	2	(1)	
15	Jhon Córdoba	COL	11/05/93	A	27	(2)	5
32	Pablo De Blasis	ARG	04/02/88	M	17	(14)	5
2	Giulio Donati	ITA	05/02/90	D	31	(1)	
20	Fabian Frei	SUI	08/01/89	M	19	(4)	
25	Jean-Philippe Gbamin	CIV	25/09/95	M	21	(4)	
42	Alexander Hack		08/09/93	D	13	(2)	
38	Gerrit Holtmann		25/03/95	M	1	(4)	
33	Jannik Huth		15/04/94	G	7		
17	Jairo Samperio	ESP	11/07/93	M	11	(6)	2
5	José Rodríguez	ESP	16/12/94	M		(2)	
6	Danny Latza		07/12/89	M	18	(3)	4
1	Jonas Lössl	DEN	01/02/89	G	27		
9	Yoshinori Muto	JPN	15/07/92	A	10	(9)	5
21	Karim Onisiwo	AUT	17/03/92	M	10	(6)	1
8	Levin Öztunali		15/03/96	M	23	(7)	5
7	Robin Quaison	SWE	09/10/93	M	6	(5)	1
45	Suat Serdar		11/04/97	M	4	(4)	
36	Aaron Seydel		07/02/96	A	1	(5)	1
11	Yunus Mallı	TUR	24/02/92	M	15	(1)	6

FC Schalke 04

1904 • Veltins-Arena (62,271) • schalke04.de

Major honours
UEFA Cup (1) 1997; German League (7) 1934, 1935, 1937, 1939, 1940, 1942, 1958; German Cup (5) 1937, 1972, 2001, 2002, 2011

Coach: Markus Weinzierl

2016					
27/08	a	Frankfurt	L	0-1	
09/09	h	Bayern	L	0-2	
18/09	a	Hertha	L	0-2	
21/09	h	Köln	L	1-3	*Huntelaar*
25/09	a	Hoffenheim	L	1-2	*Choupo-Moting*
02/10	h	Mönchengladbach	W	4-0	*Choupo-Moting (p), Embolo 2, Goretzka*
15/10	a	Augsburg	D	1-1	*Bentaleb*
23/10	h	Mainz	W	3-0	*Bentaleb 2, Meyer*
29/10	a	Dortmund	D	0-0	
06/11	h	Bremen	W	3-1	*Schöpf 2, Bentaleb*
19/11	a	Wolfsburg	W	1-0	*Goretzka*
27/11	h	Darmstadt	W	3-1	*Kolašinac, Choupo-Moting, Schöpf*
03/12	a	Leipzig	L	1-2	*Kolašinac*
11/12	h	Leverkusen	L	0-1	
17/12	h	Freiburg	D	1-1	*Konoplyanka*
20/12	a	Hamburg	L	1-2	*Avdijaj*
2017					
21/01	h	Ingolstadt	W	1-0	*Burgstaller*
27/01	h	Frankfurt	L	0-1	
04/02	a	Bayern	D	1-1	*Naldo*
11/02	h	Hertha	W	2-0	*Burgstaller, Goretzka*
19/02	a	Köln	D	1-1	*Schöpf*
26/02	h	Hoffenheim	D	1-1	*Schöpf*
04/03	a	Mönchengladbach	L	2-4	*Bentaleb (p), Goretzka*
12/03	h	Augsburg	W	3-0	*Burgstaller 2, Caligiuri*
19/03	a	Mainz	W	1-0	*Kolašinac*
01/04	h	Dortmund	D	1-1	*Kehrer*
04/04	a	Bremen	L	0-3	
08/04	h	Wolfsburg	W	4-1	*Burgstaller 2, Goretzka, Caligiuri*
16/04	a	Darmstadt	L	1-2	*Coke*
23/04	h	Leipzig	D	1-1	*Huntelaar*
28/04	a	Leverkusen	W	4-1	*Burgstaller 2, Höwedes, Schöpf*
07/05	a	Freiburg	L	0-2	
13/05	h	Hamburg	D	1-1	*Burgstaller*
20/05	a	Ingolstadt	D	1-1	*Avdijaj*

No	Name	Nat	DoB	Pos	Aps	(s)	Gls
15	Dennis Aogo		14/01/87	D	3	(4)	
33	Donis Avdijaj	KOS	25/08/96	A	2	(7)	2
24	Holger Badstuber		13/03/89	D	10		
10	Nabil Bentaleb	ALG	24/11/94	M	28	(4)	5
19	Guido Burgstaller	AUT	29/04/89	A	17	(1)	9
18	Daniel Caligiuri	ITA	15/01/88	M	14	(2)	2
13	Eric Maxim Choupo-Moting	CMR	23/03/89	A	19	(4)	3
23	Coke	ESP	26/04/87	D	7	(1)	1
9	Franco Di Santo	ARG	07/04/89	A	3	(9)	
36	Breel Embolo	SUI	14/02/97	A	4	(3)	2
1	Ralf Fährmann		27/09/88	G	34		
5	Johannes Geis		17/08/93	M	17	(1)	
8	Leon Goretzka		06/02/95	M	30		5
4	Benedikt Höwedes		29/02/88	D	31		1
25	Klaas-Jan Huntelaar	NED	12/08/83	A	7	(9)	2
3	Júnior Caiçara	BRA	27/04/89	D	1	(2)	
20	Thilo Kehrer		21/09/96	D	12	(4)	1
6	Sead Kolašinac	BIH	20/06/93	D	24	(1)	3
11	Yevhen Konoplyanka	UKR	22/09/89	M	5	(12)	1
2	Weston McKennie	USA	28/08/98	M		(1)	
7	Max Meyer		18/09/95	M	18	(9)	1
29	Naldo	BRA	10/09/82	D	19		1
31	Matija Nastasić	SRB	28/03/93	D	21	(1)	
14	Abdul Baba Rahman	GHA	02/07/94	D	7	(6)	
16	Fabian Reese		29/11/97	A	1	(2)	
27	Sascha Riether		23/03/83	D	3	(2)	
21	Alessandro Schöpf	AUT	07/02/94	M	22	(6)	6
17	Benjamin Stambouli	FRA	13/08/90	M	15	(8)	
32	Bernard Tekpetey	GHA	03/09/97	A		(2)	

GERMANY

SV Werder Bremen

1899 • Weserstadion (42,100) • werder.de

Major honours
UEFA Cup Winners' Cup (1) 1992; German League (4) 1965, 1988, 1993, 2004; German Cup (6) 1961, 1991, 1994, 1999, 2004, 2009

Coach: Viktor Skrypnyk (UKR);
(18/09/16) Alexander Nouri

Date		Opponent		Score	Scorers
2016					
26/08	a	Bayern	L	0-6	
11/09	h	Augsburg	L	1-2	*Jóhannsson (p)*
17/09	a	Mönchengladbach	L	1-4	*Gnabry*
21/09	h	Mainz	L	1-2	*Hajrović*
24/09	h	Wolfsburg	W	2-1	*Thy, Gebre Selassie*
01/10	a	Darmstadt	D	2-2	*Sané, Gnabry*
15/10	h	Leverkusen	W	2-1	*Junuzovic, Manneh*
23/10	a	Leipzig	L	1-3	*Gnabry*
29/10	h	Freiburg	L	1-3	*S García*
06/11	a	Schalke	L	1-3	*Gnabry (p)*
20/11	h	Frankfurt	L	1-2	*Grillitsch*
26/11	a	Hamburg	D	2-2	*Bartels, Gnabry*
03/12	h	Ingolstadt	W	2-1	*Kruse, Bartels*
10/12	a	Hertha	W	1-0	*Kruse*
17/12	h	Köln	D	1-1	*Gnabry*
21/12	a	Hoffenheim	D	1-1	*Gnabry*
2017					
21/01	h	Dortmund	L	1-2	*Bartels*
28/01	h	Bayern	L	1-2	*Kruse*
05/02	a	Augsburg	L	2-3	*Gebre Selassie, Kruse (p)*
11/02	h	Mönchengladbach	L	0-1	
18/02	a	Mainz	W	2-0	*Gnabry, Delaney*
24/02	a	Wolfsburg	W	2-1	*Gnabry 2*
04/03	h	Darmstadt	W	2-0	*Kruse 2 (1p)*
10/03	a	Leverkusen	D	1-1	*Pizarro*
18/03	h	Leipzig	W	3-0	*Junuzovic, Grillitsch, Kainz*
01/04	a	Freiburg	W	5-2	*Kruse, Delaney 3, Bartels*
04/04	h	Schalke	W	3-0	*Gebre Selassie, Kruse (p), Eggestein*
07/04	a	Frankfurt	D	2-2	*Junuzovic, Bartels*
16/04	h	Hamburg	W	2-1	*Kruse, Kainz*
22/04	a	Ingolstadt	W	4-2	*Kruse 4 (1p)*
29/04	h	Hertha	W	2-0	*Bartels, Kruse*
05/05	a	Köln	L	3-4	*Bartels, Gebre Selassie, Gnabry*
13/05	h	Hoffenheim	L	3-5	*Gebre Selassie, Bargfrede, Bauer*
20/05	a	Dortmund	L	3-4	*Junuzovic, Bartels, Kruse*

No	Name	Nat	DoB	Pos	Aps	(s)	Gls
44	Philipp Bargfrede		03/03/89	M	4	(7)	1
22	Fin Bartels		07/02/87	M	23	(8)	8
4	Robert Bauer		09/04/95	D	25	(2)	1
3	Luca Caldirola	ITA	01/02/91	D	5		
6	Thomas Delaney	DEN	03/09/91	M	11	(2)	4
21	Fallou Diagne	SEN	14/08/89	D	2		
33	Jaroslav Drobný	CZE	18/10/79	G	10		
35	Maximilian Eggestein		08/12/96	M	8	(7)	1
8	Clemens Fritz		07/12/80	M	17	(1)	
39	Lukas Fröde		23/01/95	M		(3)	
2	Santiago García	ARG	08/07/88	D	16	(3)	1
20	Ulisses Garcia	SUI	11/01/96	D	3	(4)	
23	Theodor Gebre Selassie	CZE	24/12/86	D	26	(4)	5
29	Serge Gnabry		14/07/95	M	23	(4)	11
27	Florian Grillitsch	AUT	07/08/95	M	21	(2)	2
15	Izet Hajrović	BIH	04/08/91	M	6	(4)	1
9	Aron Jóhannsson	USA	10/11/90	A	2	(7)	1
16	Zlatko Junuzovic	AUT	26/09/87	M	28	(2)	4
7	Florian Kainz	AUT	24/10/92	M	1	(13)	2
10	Max Kruse		19/03/88	A	23		15
47	Ousman Manneh	GAM	10/03/97	A	6		1
18	Niklas Moisander	FIN	29/09/85	D	29	(1)	
25	Thanos Petsos	GRE	05/06/91	M	2	(1)	
14	Claudio Pizarro	PER	03/10/78	A	10	(9)	1
26	Lamine Sané	SEN	22/03/87	D	27		1
38	Niklas Schmidt		01/03/98	M		(1)	
37	Janek Sternberg		19/10/92	D		(2)	
11	Lennart Thy		25/02/92	A		(6)	1
13	Miloš Veljković	SRB	26/09/95	D	20	(6)	
42	Felix Wiedwald		15/03/90	G	24	(1)	
5	Sambou Yatabaré	MLI	02/03/89	M	2		

VfL Wolfsburg

1945 • Volkswagen-Arena (30,000) • vfl-wolfsburg.de

Major honours
German League (1) 2009; German Cup (1) 2015

Coach: Dieter Hecking;
(17/10/16) Valérien Ismaël (FRA);
(27/02/17) Andries Jonker (NED)

Date		Opponent		Score	Scorers
2016					
27/08	a	Augsburg	W	2-0	*Didavi, Rodríguez*
10/09	h	Köln	D	0-0	
17/09	a	Hoffenheim	D	0-0	
20/09	h	Dortmund	L	1-5	*Didavi*
24/09	a	Bremen	L	1-2	*og (Bauer)*
02/10	h	Mainz	D	0-0	
16/10	h	Leipzig	L	0-1	
22/10	a	Darmstadt	L	1-3	*Gomez*
29/10	h	Leverkusen	L	1-2	*Arnold*
05/11	a	Freiburg	W	3-0	*Gomez 2, Rodríguez (p)*
19/11	h	Schalke	L	0-1	
26/11	a	Ingolstadt	D	1-1	*Caligiuri*
03/12	h	Hertha	L	2-3	*Borja Mayoral, Seguin*
10/12	a	Bayern	L	0-5	
17/12	h	Frankfurt	W	1-0	*Bruma*
20/12	a	Mönchengladbach	W	2-1	*Caligiuri, Gomez*
2017					
21/01	h	Hamburg	W	1-0	*Gomez*
28/01	h	Augsburg	L	1-2	*Gomez*
04/02	a	Köln	L	0-1	
12/02	h	Hoffenheim	W	2-1	*Arnold, Didavi*
18/02	a	Dortmund	L	0-3	
24/02	h	Bremen	L	1-2	*Borja Mayoral*
04/03	a	Mainz	D	1-1	*Gomez*
11/03	a	Leipzig	W	1-0	*Gomez*
18/03	h	Darmstadt	W	1-0	*Gomez*
02/04	a	Leverkusen	D	3-3	*Gomez 3 (1p)*
05/04	h	Freiburg	L	0-1	
08/04	a	Schalke	L	1-4	*Gomez (p)*
15/04	h	Ingolstadt	W	3-0	*og (Suttner), Yunus, Gomez*
22/04	a	Hertha	L	0-1	
29/04	h	Bayern	L	0-6	
06/05	a	Frankfurt	W	2-0	*Didavi, Gomez*
13/05	h	Mönchengladbach	D	1-1	*Gomez*
20/05	a	Hamburg	L	1-2	*Knoche*

No	Name	Nat	DoB	Pos	Aps	(s)	Gls
27	Maximilian Arnold		27/05/94	M	28	(4)	2
6	Riechedly Bazoer	NED	12/10/96	M	12		
1	Diego Benaglio	SUI	08/09/83	G	14		
14	Jakub Błaszczykowski	POL	14/12/85	M	20	(8)	
17	Borja Mayoral	ESP	05/04/97	A	3	(16)	2
25	Josip Brekalo	CRO	23/06/98	M		(4)	
5	Jeffrey Bruma	NED	13/11/91	D	20		1
16	Bruno Henrique	BRA	30/12/90	A	1	(6)	
7	Daniel Caligiuri	ITA	15/01/88	M	13	(3)	2
28	Koen Casteels	BEL	25/06/92	G	20		
11	Daniel Didavi		21/02/90	M	11	(7)	4
12	Bas Dost	NED	31/05/89	A	1		
10	Julian Draxler		20/09/93	M	12	(1)	
13	Yannick Gerhardt		13/03/94	D	25	(2)	
33	Mario Gomez		10/07/85	A	32	(1)	16
23	Josuha Guilavogui	FRA	19/09/90	M	17	(2)	
41	Hendrik Hansen		04/11/94	D		(1)	
21	Jannes Horn		06/02/97	D	10	(3)	
24	Sebastian Jung		22/06/90	D	4		
31	Robin Knoche		22/05/92	D	21	(29)	1
22	Luiz Gustavo	BRA	23/07/87	M	26	(1)	
26	Justin Möbius		21/04/97	M		(2)	
9	Paul-Georges Ntep	FRA	29/07/92	M	5	(5)	
18	Victor Osimhen	NGA	29/12/98	A		(2)	
34	Ricardo Rodríguez	SUI	25/08/92	D	23	(1)	2
4	Marcel Schäfer		07/06/84	D	2	(2)	
30	Paul Seguin		29/03/95	M	15	(7)	1
15	Christian Träsch		01/09/87	D	7	(4)	
8	Vieirinha	POR	24/01/86	M	13	(8)	
2	Philipp Wollscheid		06/03/89	D	6	(1)	
10	Yunus Mallı	TUR	24/02/92	M	13	(3)	1

Top goalscorers

31	Pierre-Emerick Aubameyang (Dortmund)
30	Robert Lewandowski (Bayern)
25	Anthony Modeste (Köln)
21	Timo Werner (Leipzig)
16	Mario Gomez (Wolfsburg)
15	Andrej Kramarić (Hoffenheim) Max Kruse (Bremen)
13	Arjen Robben (Bayern)
12	Vedad Ibišević (Hertha)
11	Javier Hernández (Leverkusen) Lars Stindl (Mönchengladbach) Florian Niederlechner (Freiburg) Sandro Wagner (Hoffenheim) Serge Gnabry (Bremen)

Promoted clubs

VfB Stuttgart

1893 • Mercedes-Benz-Arena (60,441) • vfb.de

Major honours
German League (5) 1950, 1952, 1984, 1992, 2007; German Cup (3) 1954, 1958, 1997

Coach: Jos Luhukay (NED);
(15/09/16) (Olaf Janssen);
(20/09/16) Hannes Wolf

Hannover 96

1896 • HDI Arena (49,000) • hannover96.de

Major honours
German League (2) 1938, 1954; German Cup (1) 1992

Coach: Daniel Stendel;
(20/03/17) André Breitenreiter

Second level final table 2016/17

		Pld	W	D	L	F	A	Pts
1	VfB Stuttgart	34	21	6	7	63	37	69
2	Hannover 96	34	19	10	5	51	32	67
3	TSV Eintracht Braunschweig	34	19	9	6	50	36	66
4	1. FC Union Berlin	34	18	6	10	51	39	60
5	SG Dynamo Dresden	34	13	11	10	53	46	50
6	1. FC Heidenheim	34	12	10	12	43	39	46
7	FC St Pauli	34	12	9	13	39	35	45
8	SpVgg Greuther Fürth	34	12	9	13	33	40	45
9	VfL Bochum	34	10	14	10	42	47	44
10	SV Sandhausen	34	10	12	12	41	36	42
11	Fortuna Düsseldorf	34	10	12	12	37	39	42
12	1. FC Nürnberg	34	12	6	16	46	52	42
13	1. FC Kaiserslautern	34	10	11	13	29	33	41
14	FC Erzgebirge Aue	34	10	9	15	37	52	39
15	DSC Arminia Bielefeld	34	8	13	13	50	54	37
16	TSV 1860 München	34	10	6	18	37	47	36
17	Würzburger Kickers	34	7	13	14	32	41	34
18	Karlsruher SC	34	5	10	19	27	56	25

Promotion/Relegation play-offs

(25/05/17 & 29/05/17)
Wolfsburg 1-0 Braunschweig
Braunschweig 0-1 Wolfsburg
(Wolfsburg 2-0)

DOMESTIC CUP

DFB-Pokal 2016/17

FIRST ROUND

(19/08/16)
Jena 0-5 Bayern
Lübeck 0-3 St Pauli
Ravensburg 0-2 Augsburg

(20/08/16)
1860 München 2-1 Karlsruhe
Babelsberg 0-4 Freiburg
BFC Preussen 0-7 1. FC Köln
Drochtersen 0-1 Mönchengladbach
Dynamo Dresden 2-2 RB Leipzig *(aet; 5-4 on pens)*
FSV Frankfurt 1-2 Wolfsburg
Halle 4-3 Kaiserslautern *(aet)*
Homburg 0-3 Stuttgart
Rostock 0-3 Düsseldorf
Rot-Weiss Essen 2-2 Bielefeld *(aet; 4-5 on pens)*
Viktoria Köln 1-1 Nürnberg *(aet; 5-6 on pens)*
Villingen 1-4 Schalke
Würzburg 1-0 Braunschweig *(aet)*

(21/08/16)
Aue 0-0 Ingolstadt *(aet; 7-8 on pens)*
Bremer SV 0-7 Darmstadt
Duisburg 1-2 Union Berlin *(aet)*
Egestorf 0-6 Hoffenheim
Hauenstein 1-2 Leverkusen
Lotte 2-1 Werder Bremen
Magdeburg 1-1 Eintracht Frankfurt *(aet; 3-4 on pens)*
Norderstedt 1-4 Greuther Fürth
Regensburg 1-1 Hertha BSC *(aet; 3-5 on pens)*
Unterhaching 3-3 Mainz *(aet; 2-4 on pens)*
Walldorf 4-3 Bochum *(aet)*
Wattenscheid 1-2 Heidenheim

(22/08/16)
Offenbach 2-3 Hannover *(aet)*
Paderborn 1-2 Sandhausen
Trier 0-3 Dortmund
Zwickau 0-1 Hamburg

SECOND ROUND

(25/10/16)
Dynamo Dresden 0-1 Bielefeld
Eintracht Frankfurt 0-0 Ingolstadt *(aet; 4-1 on pens)*
Freiburg 3-3 Sandhausen *(aet; 3-4 on pens)*
Halle 0-4 Hamburg
Lotte 2-2 Leverkusen *(aet; 4-3 on pens)*
Mönchengladbach 2-0 Stuttgart
St Pauli 0-2 Hertha BSC
Würzburg 0-0 1860 München *(aet; 3-4 on pens)*

(26/10/16)
Bayern 3-1 Augsburg
Dortmund 1-1 Union Berlin *(aet; 3-0 on pens)*
Greuther Fürth 2-1 Mainz
Hannover 6-1 Düsseldorf
Heidenheim 0-1 Wolfsburg
1. FC Köln 2-1 Hoffenheim *(aet)*
Nürnberg 2-3 Schalke
Walldorf 1-0 Darmstadt

THIRD ROUND

(07/02/17)
Bayern 1-0 Wolfsburg
Greuther Fürth 0-2 Mönchengladbach
Hamburg 2-0 1. FC Köln
Walldorf 0-0 Bielefeld *(aet; 4-5 on pens)*

(08/02/17)
Dortmund 1-1 Hertha BSC *(aet; 3-2 on pens)*
Hannover 1-2 Eintracht Frankfurt
Lotte 2-0 1860 München
Sandhausen 1-4 Schalke

QUARTER-FINALS

(28/02/17)
Eintracht Frankfurt 1-0 Bielefeld *(Blum 6)*

(01/03/17)
Bayern 3-0 Schalke *(Lewandowski 3, 29, Thiago 16)*

Hamburg 1-2 Mönchengladbach *(Wood 90; Stindl 53p, Raffael 61p)*

(14/03/17)
Lotte 0-3 Dortmund *(Pulisic 57, Schürrle 66, Schmelzer 83)*

SEMI-FINALS

(25/04/17)
Bayern 2-3 Dortmund *(Javi Martínez 28, Hummels 41; Reus 19, Aubameyang 69, Dembélé 74)*

(26/04/17)
Mönchengladbach 1-1 Eintracht Frankfurt *(Hofmann 45; Tawatha 15) (aet; 6-7 on pens)*

FINAL

(27/05/17)
Olympiastadion, Berlin
BORUSSIA DORTMUND 2 *(Dembélé 8, Aubameyang 67p)*
EINTRACHT FRANKFURT 1 *(Rebić 29)*
Referee: *Aytekin*
DORTMUND: *Bürki, Bartra (Durm 76), Papastathopoulos, Schmelzer (Castro 46), Piszczek, Ginter, Raphaël Guerreiro, Dembélé, Kagawa, Aubameyang, Reus (Pulisic 46)*
EINTRACHT FRANKFURT: *Hradecky, Hector, Abraham, Jesús Vallejo, Chandler (Meier 72), Medojević (Tawatha 56), Gaćinović, Oczipka, Fabián (Blum 79), Rebić, Seferovic*

Dortmund's German Cup win was the club's first trophy success in five years

GIBRALTAR

Gibraltar Football Association (GFA)

Address	PO Box 513 2nd Floor, 62/64 Irish town GX11 1AA Gibraltar
Tel	+350 200 42 941
Fax	+350 200 42 211
E-mail	info@gibraltarfa.com
Website	gibraltarfa.com

President	Michael Llamas
General secretary	Dennis Beiso
Media officer	Steven Gonzalez
Year of formation	1895
National stadium	Victoria Stadium (5,000)

PREMIER DIVISION CLUBS

 1 **Europa FC**

 2 **Europa Point FC**

 3 **Gibraltar United FC**

 4 **Glacis United FC**

 5 **Lincoln FC**

 6 **Lions Gibraltar FC**

 7 **Lynx FC**

 8 **Manchester 62 FC**

 9 **Mons Calpe SC**

 10 **St Joseph's FC**

PROMOTED CLUB

 11 **Gibraltar Phoenix FC**

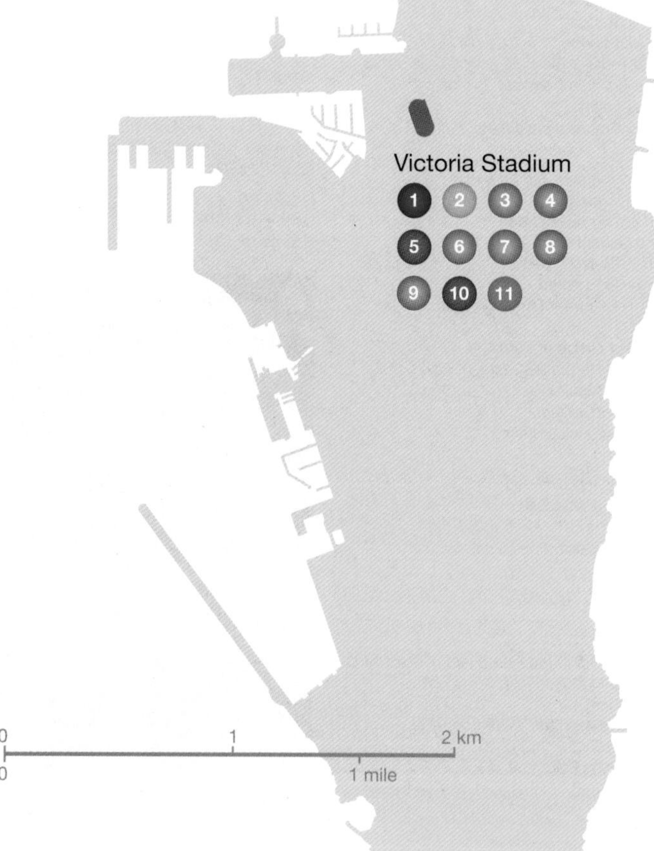

KEY

- UEFA Champions League
- UEFA Europa League
- Promoted
- Relegated

Europa FC end Lincoln's reign

The end to Lincoln FC's long reign as Gibraltar champions finally occurred in 2016/17 as Europa FC, runners-up the season before, seized their chance after an eight month-long dogfight, a final-day 2-0 win against Glacis United enabling them to finish a point ahead of their rivals.

The Red Imps' 14-year run of Premier League triumphs thus came to an end, and a week later they were forced to bow to Europa's superiority once again when they were beaten 3-0 in a one-sided Rock Cup final.

League and cup double for Green-and-Blacks

Red Imps miss out on 15th successive title

National team still without a qualifying point

Domestic league

Europa had not been crowned champions of Gibraltar since 1952, but having matched Lincoln in their three head-to-head encounters in 2015/16 (the season after the club had changed its name from College Europa FC), there was a certain pre-season optimism in the camp. New league rules meant that they had to supplement their squad of Spaniards with some native Gibraltarians, and they landed a prize catch with the recruitment of Gibraltar international midfielder Liam Walker from Lincoln.

Walker it was, perhaps inevitably, who struck the winning goal as Europa defeated Lincoln 1-0 in the first head-to-head encounter in late October. It would be the only points dropped by the perennial champions in their first 17 matches. Europa managed to stay in front, however, until the second top-of-the-table clash in mid-January, their only faux pas until then being a 1-1 draw against St Joseph's.

Another win for Juan José Gallardo's side would have taken them five points clear, but victory went instead to Julio César Ribas's Lincoln, 3-1, and the following week they celebrated by crushing newly-promoted Europa Point FC (no relation) 15-0. At the end of February, however, it was Lincoln's turn to be held by St Joseph's (who would go on to finish third and thus take the third European spot available to Andorra in 2017/18), and when they drew again, 3-3 against Glacis in early April, Europa, who had stitched together eight wins on the trot, were back in front with a two-point lead.

The third direct clash came next, and Lincoln won it, handing out a comprehensive 4-1 beating to their rivals to leapfrog them back into top spot. With five games left, the show appeared to be over, but there would be another dramatic twist to the tale as in the penultimate round the Red Imps surrendered another two points, astonishingly held 2-2 by the other newly-promoted side, Mons Calpe. Europa now had only to defeat Glacis on the final day and the title would be theirs. Goals from Walker and the prolific Kike Gómez, with his 30th of the campaign, did the job, prompting widespread jubilation at the final whistle.

Domestic cup

It was perhaps a reflection of the mood in both camps at the time that Europa bossed the Rock Cup final to complete the double eight days later. Lincoln didn't help themselves by having defender Bernardo Lopes red-carded after just 12 minutes. Alejandro Rodríguez opened the scoring for the champions seven minutes later and the irrepressible Gómez finished Lincoln off with two further goals after the interval. The Red Imps finished the game with only eight men, symbolic of the team's fall from grace at the end of a deeply disappointing domestic season.

Europe

The Premier League campaign was preceded by some eventful European action, with Lincoln and Europe both unexpectedly winning their opening ties, against Flora Tallinn and FC Pyunik respectively, and Lincoln then causing one of the biggest shocks in UEFA Champions League qualifying history by beating Glasgow giants Celtic 1-0 at the Victoria Stadium. No matter that they lost the return at Celtic Park 3-0; that prized scalp will always be theirs to savour.

National team

There was nothing comparable to celebrate for the Gibraltar national side – and their legion of Lincoln players – during the country's first FIFA World Cup qualifying adventure, at least not in the first six matches, which, like the ten UEFA EURO 2016 qualifiers before them, all ended in defeat. On the positive side, Jeff Wood's team did manage to find an equalising goal in three of those games, but that first qualifying point remained agonisingly elusive.

DOMESTIC SEASON AT A GLANCE

Premier Division 2016/17 final table

		Pld	W	D	L	F	A	Pts
1	**Europa FC**	**27**	**24**	**1**	**2**	**93**	**18**	**73**
2	Lincoln FC	27	23	3	1	100	16	72
3	St Joseph's FC	27	16	6	5	53	18	54
4	Glacis United FC	27	12	8	7	42	34	44
5	Mons Calpe SC	27	13	3	11	44	35	42
6	Lynx FC	27	8	4	15	34	45	28
7	Gibraltar United FC	27	4	9	14	20	43	21
8	Lions Gibraltar FC	27	4	9	14	17	54	21
9	Manchester 62 FC	27	4	5	18	27	60	17
10	Europa Point FC	27	2	2	23	13	120	8

European qualification 2017/18

Champion/Cup winner: Europa FC (first qualifying round)

Lincoln FC (first qualifying round)
St Joseph's FC (first qualifying round)

Top scorer	Kike Gómez (Europa), 30 goals
Relegated club	Europa Point FC
Promoted club	Gibraltar Phoenix FC
Cup final	Europa FC 3-0 Lincoln FC

Player of the season

Liam Walker
(Europa FC)

Walker's transfer from Lincoln to Europa was pivotal in the Premier League power shift that earned the midfielder a third double in as many seasons. He scored 15 league goals plus another special strike for Gibraltar in their opening World Cup qualifier against Greece.

Newcomer of the season

Kike Gómez
(Europa FC)

A replacement for Pedro Carrión in Europa's attack, the 23-year-old Spaniard succeeded him as the Premier League golden boot winner, scoring 30 goals. He found the net in two thirds of Europa's league games and also bagged a brace in the cup final win over Lincoln.

Team of the season
(4-3-3)

Coach: Gallardo *(Europa)*

DOMESTIC CUP

Rock Cup 2016/17

SECOND ROUND

(10/02/17)
Boca Juniors Gibraltar 1-8 Lynx

(11/02/17)
Manchester 62 2-0 Gibraltar United
Mons Calpe 0-1 St Joseph's

(12/02/17)
Glacis 1-3 Europa
Lincoln 12-0 Hound Dogs

(13/02/17)
College 1975 0-3 Europa Point

(14/02/17)
Cannons 1-3 Lions Gibraltar

(15/02/17)
Leo 0-6 Gibraltar Phoenix

QUARTER-FINALS

(10/03/17)
Lincoln 3-0 Manchester 62 *(Calderón 52, L Casciaro 71, Bardon 87)*

(11/03/17)
Europa 2-0 Europa Point *(Gómez 76, Walker 87)*
Gibraltar Phoenix 2-0 Lions Gibraltar *(Rubio 49, Cortés 86)*

(12/03/17)
Lynx 0-0 St Joseph's *(2-4 on pens)*

SEMI-FINALS

(25/04/17)
Lincoln 1-0 St Joseph's *(J Chipolina 41p)*

(26/04/17)
Gibraltar Phoenix 0-2 Europa *(González 57, Rodríguez 79)*

FINAL

(28/05/17)
Victoria Stadium, Gibraltar
EUROPA FC 3 *(Rodríguez 19, Gómez 57, 68)*
LINCOLN FC 0
Referee: *Barcelo*
EUROPA: *Muñoz, Ayew (A García 79), Belfortti, Merino, Toscano, Walker, Moya, Rodríguez (González 71), Yahaya, Roldán (Garro 75), Gómez*
LINCOLN: *Navas, Garcia, Bernardo Lopes, R Chipolina, J Chipolina, Calderón (R Casciaro 46), Patiño, K Casciaro (Clinton 72), Bardon (Etchemaite 66), Martínez, L Casciaro*
Red cards: *Bernardo Lopes (12), Etchematie (83), R Casciaro (84)*

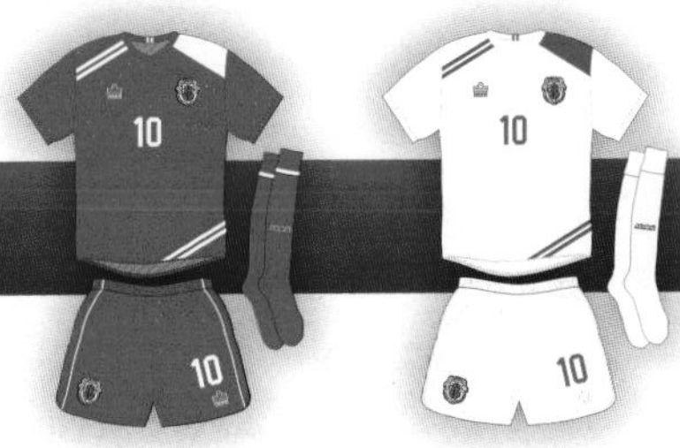

NATIONAL TEAM

Top five all-time caps
Joseph Chipolina (25); **Liam Walker** (24); **Kyle Casciaro** & **Roy Chipolina** (23); **Ryan Casciaro** (22)

Top five all-time goals
Lee Casciaro & **Jake Gosling** (2); **Kyle Casciaro**, **Roy Chipolina**, **Anthony Hernandez** & **Liam Walker** (1)

Results 2016/17

01/09/16	Portugal	A	Porto	L	0-5	
06/09/16	Greece (WCQ)	H	Faro (POR)	L	1-4	*Walker (26)*
07/10/16	Estonia (WCQ)	A	Tallinn	L	0-4	
10/10/16	Belgium (WCQ)	H	Faro (POR)	L	0-6	
13/11/16	Cyprus (WCQ)	A	Nicosia	L	1-3	*L Casciaro (51)*
25/03/17	Bosnia & Herzegovina (WCQ)	A	Zenica	L	0-5	
09/06/17	Cyprus (WCQ)	H	Faro (POR)	L	1-2	*Hernandez (30)*

Appearances 2016/17

Coach: Jeff Wood (ENG)	**04/02/54**		**Por**	**GRE**	**EST**	**BEL**	**CYP**	**BIH**	**CYP**	**Caps**	**Goals**
Jordan Perez	13/11/86	St Joseph's	G46	G	G					17	-
Jean-Carlos Garcia	05/07/92	Lincoln	D	D	D	M	D	D	D	20	-
Scott Wiseman	09/10/85	Scunthorpe (ENG)	D	D		D				10	-
Roy Chipolina	20/01/83	Lincoln	D	D	D	D		D	D	23	1
Ryan Casciaro	11/05/84	Lincoln	D	D	D	D	D		M81	22	-
Jayce Mascarenhas-Olivero	02/07/98	unattached /Abingdon United (ENG)	D		D	M	D 80*		D	7	-
Anthony Bardon	19/01/93	Lincoln	M25		M	s80	M68	s75	M90	15	-
Aaron Payas	24/05/85	Manchester 62	M63		s58	s46		D		12	-
Liam Walker	13/04/88	Europa	M88	M	M	M80	M	M	M	24	1
Joseph Chipolina	14/12/87	Lincoln	M75	D	D89	D	M	D	D	25	-
Kyle Casciaro	02/12/87	Lincoln	A63	s71	s89	M86	M74	M87	s90	23	1
Anthony Hernandez	03/02/95	Gibraltar United	s25	M			s68	M	M	8	1
Jamie Robba	26/10/91	Torquay (ENG)	s46							8	-
Jamie Bosio	24/09/91	Gibraltar United	s63	M71	M58	M46				9	-
Michael Yome	29/08/94	unattached /Canterbury (ENG)	s63	s85		s86				7	-
Robert Guiling	14/10/80	Lynx	s75					M75		11	-
Erin Barnett	02/09/96	Gibraltar United	s88				D		D	8	-
Jamie Coombes	27/05/96	unattached /Undy (WAL)		M85	s65				s81	6	-
Lee Casciaro	29/09/81	Lincoln		A	A	A	M	A	A	16	2
Adam Priestley	14/08/90	Alfreton (ENG)			M65		s85			13	-
Deren Ibrahim	09/03/91	Dartford (ENG)				G	G	G	G	4	-
George Cabrera	14/12/88	Lincoln					A85			6	-
Sykes Garro	26/02/93	Europa					s74			1	-
Kenneth Chipolina	08/04/94	Lincoln						D53		1	-
Jason Pusey	18/02/89	Gibraltar United						s53		1	-
John Paul Duarte	13/12/86	St Joseph's						s87		10	-

EUROPE

Lincoln FC

First qualifying round - FC Flora Tallinn (EST)

A 1-2 *J Chipolina (57)*

Navas, Garcia, J Chipolina, Bardon (Calderón 63), R Casciaro, Bernardo Lopes, L Casciaro (Peña 63), K Casciaro, R Chipolina, Patiño, Walker. Coach: Julio César Ribas (URU)

H 2-0 *J Chipolina (15p), Calderón (79)*

Navas, Garcia, J Chipolina, Bardon (Calderón 71), R Casciaro, Bernardo Lopes, L Casciaro (Cabrera 64), K Casciaro, R Chipolina, Patiño (K Chipolina 78), Walker. Coach: Julio César Ribas (URU)

Second qualifying round - Celtic FC (SCO)

H 1-0 *L Casciaro (48)*

Navas, Garcia, J Chipolina, R Casciaro, Bernardo Lopes, L Casciaro (Cabrera 74), K Casciaro, R Chipolina, Calderón, Patiño (K Chipolina 90+4), Walker (Bardon 86). Coach: Julio César Ribas (URU)

A 0-3

Navas, Garcia, J Chipolina, R Casciaro, Bernardo Lopes, L Casciaro (Cabrera 90), K Casciaro, R Chipolina, Calderón (Bardon 89), Patiño, Walker (Livramento 89). Coach: Julio César Ribas (URU)

Europa FC

First qualifying round - FC Pyunik (ARM)

H 2-0 *Carrión (32), Félix López (39)*

Muñoz, Moya, A García (González 58), Félix López, Carrión (Copi 76), Toscano, Roldán, Rodríguez (Villodres 66), Vázquez, Belfortti, Merino. Coach: Juan José Gallardo (ESP)

A 1-2 *González (10)*

Muñoz, Moya (González 4; Copi 75), A García, Félix López, Carrión (Villodres 61), Toscano, Roldán, Rodríguez, Vázquez, Belfortti, Merino. Coach: Juan José Gallardo (ESP)

Second qualifying round - AIK (SWE)

A 0-1

Muñoz, Moya, A García (Piñero 89), Carrión (González 66), Toscano, Roldán, Rodríguez (Copi 75), Yahaya, Vázquez, Belfortti, Merino. Coach: Juan José Gallardo (ESP)

H 0-1

Muñoz, Moya, A García (Copi 67), Carrión, Toscano, Roldán, Rodríguez (González 39), Yahaya, Vázquez, Belfortti, Merino. Coach: Juan José Gallardo (ESP)

DOMESTIC LEAGUE CLUB-BY-CLUB

Stadium

Victoria Stadium (5,000)

Europa FC

1925 • europafc.gi

Major honours

Gibraltar League (7) 1929, 1930, 1932, 1933, 1938, 1952, 2017; Gibraltar Cup (6) 1938, 1946, 1950, 1951, 1952, 2017

Coach: Juan José Gallardo (ESP)

Date	Opponent		Score	Scorers
2016				
24/09	Lions Gibraltar	W	2-1	*Walker, Garro*
02/10	Europa Point	W	2-1	*Gómez, Rodríguez*
17/10	Manchester 62	W	4-0	*Gómez 2, Walker, Trofimenko*
22/10	Lincoln	W	1-0	*Walker*
29/10	Mons Calpe	W	3-0	*Gómez 2, Yahaya*
05/11	St Joseph's	D	1-1	*Roldán*
18/11	Lynx	W	7-0	*Belfortti, Gómez 4, Roldán, Romero*
27/11	Gibraltar United	W	3-0	*Gómez 2, Walker*
05/12	Glacis	W	2-0	*Gómez, Walker*
12/12	Lions Gibraltar	W	7-0	*Gómez 2, Walker 2, Roldán, González 2*
17/12	Europa Point	W	4-1	*Romero, Roldán 2, González*
2017				
07/01	Manchester 62	W	8-0	*Rodríguez 2, Roldán 2, Romero, González 2, Gilbert*
14/01	Lincoln	L	1-3	*Yahaya*
22/01	Mons Calpe	W	2-0	*Belfortti, Gómez*
28/01	St Joseph's	W	4-1	*Gómez 3, Roldán*
05/02	Lynx	W	3-1	*Walker, Roldán, Adams*
20/02	Gibraltar United	W	1-0	*Gómez*
25/02	Glacis	W	4-3	*Walker, Yahaya, Gómez 2*
03/03	Lions Gibraltar	W	1-0	*Walker*
19/03	Europa Point	W	13-1	*Gómez 2, Roldán 2, Walker 3, Rodríguez 4, Garro, Ayew*
03/04	Manchester 62	W	4-0	*Gómez, González, Walker, Rodríguez*
08/04	Lincoln	L	1-4	*Gómez*
21/04	Mons Calpe	W	3-0	*Gómez 2, Belfortti*
30/04	St Joseph's	W	2-1	*Gómez, Roldán*
05/05	Lynx	W	1-0	*González*
12/05	Gibraltar United	W	7-0	*Toscano, Moya, González, Rodríguez, Roldán 2, Gómez*
21/05	Glacis	W	2-0	*Walker, Gómez*

No	Name	Nat	DoB	Pos	Aps	(s)	Gls
35	James Adams	FRA	05/01/98	M		(1)	1
3	Ibrahim Ayew	GHA	16/04/88	D	23	(1)	1
22	Martín Belfortti	ARG	07/04/81	D	19	(2)	3
4	Lance Cabezutto		03/03/93	D		(5)	
13	Matthew Cafer	ENG	27/09/94	G		(1)	
26	José Manuel Camara	ESP	25/01/93	G	10		
16	José Manuel Gallego	ESP	09/06/00	M		(3)	
11	Antonio García	ESP	07/08/91	D	12	(2)	
21	Javier García	ESP	21/05/89	D	9		
7	Sykes Garro		26/02/93	M	7	(8)	2
30	Sean Gilbert		14/11/92	M		(3)	1
9	Kike Gómez	ESP	04/05/94	A	24	(1)	30
19	José Miguel González	ESP	10/05/92	A	17	(7)	8
27	Carl Machin		29/07/93	D		(1)	
41	Alberto Merino	ESP	02/05/75	D	27		
6	Iván Moya	ESP	16/09/87	M	20	(1)	1
1	Javier Muñoz	ESP	27/01/82	G	17		
2	Karim Piñero		30/04/92	D	6	(5)	
8	Alejandro Rodríguez	ESP	07/10/86	M	20	(4)	9
17	Guillermo Roldán	ESP	23/06/81	A	25		14
18	Yeray Romero	ESP	14/01/99	A	3	(10)	3
14	Jesús Toscano	ESP	13/12/90	D	20	(1)	1
5	Kirill Trofimenko	RUS	19/12/96	A		(1)	1
10	Liam Walker		13/04/88	M	26		15
20	Mustapha Yahaya	GHA	01/01/94	M	12	(9)	3

Europa Point FC

2014 • europapointfc.com

Coach: George Jermy (ENG); (15/12/16) Daniel Rodríguez Amaya (ESP)

Date	Opponent		Score	Scorers
2016				
21/09	Glacis	L	1-3	*Askew*
02/10	Europa	L	1-2	*Luca*
15/10	Lions Gibraltar	D	1-1	*Arana*
23/10	Manchester 62	W	2-1	*Junco, Arora*
28/10	Lincoln	L	0-4	
06/11	Mons Calpe	L	1-4	*Askew*
19/11	St Joseph's	L	0-6	
28/11	Lynx	L	0-3	*(w/o; original result 1-2 Eve)*
03/12	Gibraltar United	L	0-3	*(w/o)*
11/12	Glacis	L	0-5	
17/12	Europa	L	1-4	*Albert*
2017				
06/01	Lions Gibraltar	L	0-2	
13/01	Manchester 62	L	0-4	
23/01	Lincoln	L	0-15	
28/01	Mons Calpe	L	0-2	
03/02	St Joseph's	L	0-3	
18/02	Lynx	L	0-3	
25/02	Gibraltar United	W	1-0	*Britto (p)*
04/03	Glacis	L	1-6	*Golpe*
19/03	Europa	L	1-13	*Golpe*
01/04	Lions Gibraltar	L	0-1	
20/04	Lincoln	L	0-9	
24/04	Manchester 62	L	0-6	
29/04	Mons Calpe	L	1-6	*Melgani*
06/05	St Joseph's	L	0-9	
15/05	Lynx	L	0-3	
22/05	Gibraltar United	D	2-2	*Golpe, Britto*

No	Name	Nat	DoB	Pos	Aps	(s)	Gls
9	Marek Albert	USA	18/12/90	A	7	(2)	1
17	Anderson Pinto	POR	11/02/94	A	1	(2)	
8	José María Arana	ESP	26/04/91	D	8		1
4	Pedro Ardanaz	ESP	07/04/95	D	2	(1)	
15	Uday Arora	CAN	15/11/96	D	1	(3)	1
11	Dakota Askew	ENG	26/06/97	M	7	(1)	2
25	Isaac Attias		31/10/98	D		(4)	
20	Jesús Ayala	ARG	29/06/96	D	10		
13	Kaylan Borda		13/08/96	G	1	(1)	
3	Ethan Britto		30/11/00	D	13		2
10	Juan José Cabrera	ESP	03/01/00	A	6	(4)	
2	Rubén Cádiz	ESP	19/07/95	D	8		
15	Leonardo Cano	ARG	15/03/98	M	9		
16	Kivan Castle		21/02/90	A	14	(2)	
17	Murray Cox	ENG	23/01/94	D	5		
12	Miguel Ángel Cruz	ESP	10/02/95	M	3	(3)	
24	Habib Dannoun	FRA	27/08/91	M	4	(4)	
18	Tjay De Barr		13/03/00	A	8	(3)	
7	José Alberto Durán	ESP	26/11/91	M	5	(7)	
12	Roxan Equebat	FRA	29/01/92	M	1	(2)	
6	Sean Eve	ENG	04/08/97	D	10		1
17	Adrián García	ESP	01/02/92	A	1		
14	Adrián Golpe	ESP	23/01/97	A	13		3
12	Paul Grech		08/12/86	D	9	(1)	
1	Jaylan Hankins		17/11/00	G	12		
4	George Jermy	ENG	12/01/88	M	5		
11	Jorge Junco	ESP	14/04/94	A	7		1
3	Halim Khali	FRA	10/07/95	D	6	(1)	
14	Adam Luca	ITA	09/02/90	A	5	(1)	1
10	Charles-Francois Mallmann	FRA	24/05/86	M	2	(2)	
8	Cristian Márquez	ESP	08/12/95	M	6	(1)	
7	Luis McCoy		02/09/94	M	6	(4)	
22	Nicholas Melgani	ARG	07/08/88	D	9		1
18	Carlos Méndez	ESP	23/06/87	D	9		
15	Liam Muscat		03/01/94	M	2	(2)	
15	Daniel Rogers		18/04/91	D	4	(3)	
6	Iván Ruiz	ESP	10/03/95	D	12		
11	Kevin Ruiz	ESP	06/06/94	A	12	(2)	
4	Aaron Scott	ENG	01/07/97	D	6	(1)	
2	Adam Spinks	ENG	20/10/95	D	9	(1)	
1	William Sykes	CAN	09/02/96	G	13		
19	Jaron Vinet		19/12/97	D	12		
16	Gareth Williams	ENG	16/12/81	M	3		

Gibraltar United FC

1943 • gibraltarunitedfc.com

Major honours

Gibraltar League (11) 1947, 1948, 1949, 1950, 1951, 1954, 1960, 1962, 1964, 1965, 2002; Gibraltar Cup (4) 1947, 1999, 2000, 2001

Coach: Manolo Sánchez Núñez (ESP)

Date	Opponent		Result	Scorers
2016				
22/09	Manchester 62	D	2-2	*Montovio 2 (1p)*
30/09	Lincoln	L	0-2	
15/10	Mons Calpe	L	1-3	*Bosio*
22/10	St Joseph's	L	0-1	
30/10	Lynx	W	1-0	*Montovio*
04/11	Lions Gibraltar	D	0-0	
20/11	Glacis	L	0-2	
27/11	Europa	L	0-3	
03/12	Europa Point	W	3-0	*(w/o)*
09/12	Manchester 62	W	3-1	*Montovio, Podesta 2*
17/12	Lincoln	L	0-2	
2017				
08/01	Mons Calpe	D	2-2	*Bothen, Anthony Hernandez*
15/01	St Joseph's	L	1-4	*Anthony Hernandez*
21/01	Lynx	L	0-1	
30/01	Lions Gibraltar	D	1-1	*Montovio (p)*
04/02	Glacis	D	0-0	
20/02	Europa	L	0-1	
25/02	Europa Point	L	0-1	
04/03	Manchester 62	L	0-3	
17/03	Lincoln	L	0-1	
01/04	Mons Calpe	L	1-2	*Bosio*
09/04	St Joseph's	D	0-0	
21/04	Lynx	D	1-1	*Bosio*
29/04	Lions Gibraltar	D	0-0	
06/05	Glacis	W	2-1	*Anthony Hernandez, Andrew Hernandez*
12/05	Europa	L	0-7	
22/05	Europa Point	D	2-2	*Montovio, Anthony Hernandez*

No	Name	Nat	DoB	Pos	Aps	(s)	Gls
21	Erin Barnett		02/09/96	D	21	(2)	
24	Jamie Bosio		24/09/91	M	21	(1)	3
20	Max Bothen		27/04/91	M	2	(3)	1
11	Jared Buhagiar		20/10/92	D	2		
22	James Currer		29/06/92	A	5	(8)	
16	Naoufal El Andaloussi		07/03/91	M	1	(2)	
1	Kyle Goldwin		24/04/85	G	22		
11	Paul Grech		08/12/86	D	1	(1)	
9	Evan Green		13/03/93	M	8	(9)	
8	Andrew Hernandez		10/01/99	M	22	(2)	1
4	Anthony Hernandez		03/02/95	M	22	(2)	4
7	Robert Montovio		03/08/84	A	17	(4)	6
15	Aymen Mouelhi	TUN	14/09/86	D	23	(1)	
12	Tyron Oton		28/05/00	G		(1)	
6	Dexter Panzavechia		30/12/90	M	14	(2)	
3	Ashley Perez		22/02/89	D	19	(1)	
3	Ashley Perez		22/02/89	G	3		
14	Paul Podesta		27/07/90	A	11	(5)	2
19	Brad Power		29/10/92	D	14		
5	Jason Pusey		18/02/89	D	23		
2	Duane Robba		19/06/75	M		(1)	
26	Ashley Rodriguez		13/11/89	M	18	(3)	
17	Kaylan Rumbo		12/12/90	M	7	(11)	
2	Carl Thomas		06/07/88	D	3		
23	Jesse Victory		02/04/96	M	6	(6)	
13	Daniel Wink		10/12/81	G	1		

Glacis United FC

1965 • no website

Major honours

Gibraltar League (17) 1966, 1967, 1968, 1969, 1970, 1971, 1972, 1973, 1974, 1976, 1981, 1982, 1983, 1985 (shared), 1989, 1997, 2000; Gibraltar Cup (4) 1975, 1981, 1982, 1998

Coach: Manuel Jiménez Pérez (ESP)

Date	Opponent		Result	Scorers
2016				
21/09	Europa Point	W	3-1	*Cano 2, Carrasco*
28/09	Manchester 62	W	1-0	*Carrasco*
16/10	Lincoln	L	0-7	
21/10	Mons Calpe	W	3-0	*(w/o; original result 0-0)*
31/10	St Joseph's	D	1-1	*Llaves*
05/11	Lynx	W	2-0	*A Sánchez, Carrasco*
20/11	Gibraltar United	W	2-0	*Carrasco 2*
26/11	Lions Gibraltar	D	1-1	*Llaves*
05/12	Europa	L	0-2	
11/12	Europa Point	W	5-0	*Llaves 3, Pereyra, Carrasco*
19/12	Manchester 62	W	3-0	*Carrasco, Bado, Llaves*
2017				
07/01	Lincoln	L	0-5	
16/01	Mons Calpe	W	3-1	*Carrasco, Llaves, Pérez*
21/01	St Joseph's	L	0-2	
27/01	Lynx	D	1-1	*Cano*
04/02	Gibraltar United	D	0-0	
19/02	Lions Gibraltar	W	1-0	*Cano*
25/02	Europa	L	3-4	*Castro, Carrasco, S García*
04/03	Europa Point	W	6-1	*S García 3, Pérez 2, Carrasco*
16/03	Manchester 62	D	1-1	*Vera*
02/04	Lincoln	D	3-3	*Llaves, Carrasco, Buhagiar*
09/04	Mons Calpe	W	1-0	*Llaves*
18/04	St Joseph's	D	0-0	
30/04	Lynx	W	1-0	*S García*
06/05	Gibraltar United	L	1-2	*Tirado*
13/05	Lions Gibraltar	D	0-0	
21/05	Europa	L	0-2	

No	Name	Nat	DoB	Pos	Aps	(s)	Gls
10	Julio Bado		03/06/83	M	22	(1)	1
17	Jared Buhagiar		20/10/92	D	4	(8)	1
6	Francisco Cano	ESP	01/03/91	D	25		4
24	Salvador Carrasco	ESP	24/03/86	M	18	(4)	11
16	Adrián Castro	ESP	17/12/90	M	10	(2)	1
33	José Luis Chico Ferrer	ESP	18/06/96	M	2	(3)	
31	Javier Fernández	ESP	08/06/95	M	1	(12)	
11	Javi García	ESP	16/08/86	M	3	(4)	
27	Salvador García	ESP	17/02/87	A	8	(4)	5
1	Borja González	ESP	30/06/88	G	25	(1)	
25	José Miguel González	ESP	08/04/93	G	2		
14	Juan Manuel González	ESP	02/05/91	M	10		
3	Daniel Guerrero	ESP	08/07/83	D	22		
9	Juan Manuel Llaves	ESP	03/11/84	A	22	(3)	9
21	Carlos Méndez	ESP	23/06/87	D	2	(2)	
30	Yves Nyami	FRA	24/08/85	M		(4)	
8	Leandro Pereyra	ARG	27/02/85	M	21		1
18	Juan José Pérez	ESP	21/09/90	D	16	(2)	3
26	Andrew Rodriguez		18/07/92	M		(2)	
2	Juan José Ruesca	ESP	24/11/90	D	17	(2)	
7	Ander Sánchez	ESP	22/02/91	D	20	(2)	1
27	José Miguel Sánchez	ESP	02/07/91	M	3	(3)	
12	Carl Thomas		06/07/88	D	3	(8)	
23	Miguel Ángel Tirado	ESP	01/10/84	D	20	(1)	1
4	Adrián Vera	ESP	21/02/90	M	21	(3)	1

Lincoln FC

1976 • lincolnredimpsfc.com

Major honours

Gibraltar League (22) 1985 (shared), 1986, 1990, 1991, 1992, 1993, 1994, 2001, 2003, 2004, 2005, 2006, 2007, 2008, 2009, 2010, 2011, 2012, 2013, 2014, 2015, 2016; Gibraltar Cup (17) 1986, 1989, 1990, 1993, 1994, 2002, 2004, 2005, 2006, 2007, 2008, 2009, 2010, 2011, 2014, 2015, 2016

Coach: Julio César Ribas (URU)

Date	Opponent		Result	Scorers
2016				
24/09	Lynx	W	5-0	*J Chipolina 3, K Casciaro, R Chipolina*
30/09	Gibraltar United	W	2-0	*J Chipolina, Cabrera*
16/10	Glacis	W	7-0	*L Casciaro, Bardon 3, J Chipolina (p), Cabrera, Guirado*
22/10	Europa	L	0-1	
28/10	Europa Point	W	4-0	*L Casciaro 3, Cabrera*
03/11	Manchester 62	W	6-1	*Garcia 2, J Chipolina, Cabrera 2, Clinton*
21/11	Lions Gibraltar	W	4-1	*Garcia, J Chipolina, R Casciaro, L Casciaro*
26/11	Mons Calpe	W	4-1	*Patiño, Colman, J Chipolina, L Casciaro*
02/12	St Joseph's	W	2-1	*Garcia, Guirado*
10/12	Lynx	W	2-1	*J Chipolina (p), L Casciaro*
17/12	Gibraltar United	W	2-0	*Guirado, Clinton*
2017				
07/01	Glacis	W	5-0	*Cabrera 2, Bardon 2, Clinton*
14/01	Europa	W	3-1	*L Casciaro 2, Calderón*
23/01	Europa Point	W	15-0	*K Chipolina, Calderón, Garcia, R Casciaro, L Casciaro, Cabrera 3, K Casciaro, Etchemaite 4, og (Sykes), Martínez*
29/01	Manchester 62	W	2-0	*R Chipolina, J Chipolina*
04/02	Lions Gibraltar	W	5-0	*R Chipolina, J Chipolina, L Casciaro, Etchemaite 2*
17/02	Mons Calpe	W	2-1	*Bernardo Lopes, K Casciaro*
27/02	St Joseph's	D	2-2	*J Chipolina, Bardon*
05/03	Lynx	W	1-0	*R Chipolina*
17/03	Gibraltar United	W	1-0	*K Casciaro*
02/04	Glacis	D	3-3	*J Chipolina (p), Clinton, K Casciaro*
08/04	Europa	W	4-1	*J Chipolina 2, Cabrera, Bardon*
20/04	Europa Point	W	9-0	*Bernardo Lopes, Clinton 3, Cabrera 2, L Casciaro, Etchemaite 2*
02/05	Manchester 62	W	3-0	*Bernardo Lopes, L Casciaro, J Chipolina*
08/05	Lions Gibraltar	W	4-0	*J Chipolina, Etchemaite 2, Bernardo Lopes*
13/05	Mons Calpe	D	2-2	*Patiño 2*
20/05	St Joseph's	W	1-0	*K Casciaro*

No	Name	Nat	DoB	Pos	Aps	(s)	Gls
8	Anthony Bardon		19/01/93	M	26		7
6	Bernardo Lopes	POR	30/07/93	D	27		4
11	George Cabrera		14/12/88	A	14	(6)	13
19	Antonio Calderón	ESP	31/03/84	M	21	(5)	2
10	Kyle Casciaro		02/12/87	M	20	(4)	6
7	Lee Casciaro		29/09/81	A	23	(2)	13
5	Ryan Casciaro		11/05/84	D	18	(3)	2
3	Joseph Chipolina		14/12/87	D	25		17
8	Kenneth Chipolina		08/04/94	D	13	(7)	1
14	Roy Chipolina		20/01/83	D	16		4
17	Leon Clinton		19/07/98	A	3	(16)	7
16	Christhian Colman	URU	26/02/93	D	7	(2)	1
28	Tjay De Barr		13/03/00	A		(1)	
21	Tulio Etchemaite	ARG	10/07/87	A	3	(6)	10
2	Jean-Carlos Garcia		05/07/92	D	27		5
9	Angel Guirado	PHI	29/09/84	A	2	(8)	3
89	Diego Martínez	ESP	20/03/89	M	8	(6)	1
1	Raúl Navas	ESP	03/05/78	G	27		
20	Yeray Patiño	ESP	19/05/91	M	17	(3)	3
34	Federico Tobler	URU	15/02/92	D		(1)	
12	Dean Torrilla		30/07/94	M		(5)	

GIBRALTAR

Lions Gibraltar FC

1966 • lionsgibraltarfc.com

Coach: Rafael Bado (ESP)

Date	Opponent			Scorers
2016				
24/09	Europa	L	1-2	*Gilroy*
29/09	St Joseph's	L	0-3	
15/10	Europa Point	D	1-1	*Gilroy (p)*
24/10	Lynx	D	1-1	*N Santos*
29/10	Manchester 62	L	1-5	*Moreno*
04/11	Gibraltar United	D	0-0	
21/11	Lincoln	L	1-4	*Jeremy Lopez*
26/11	Glacis	D	1-1	*Gilroy*
04/12	Mons Calpe	L	0-1	
12/12	Europa	L	0-7	
18/12	St Joseph's	L	0-2	
2017				
06/01	Europa Point	W	2-0	*Castro, N Santos*
14/01	Lynx	L	2-7	*Breakspear, Gilroy*
20/01	Manchester 62	D	1-1	*Fernández*
30/01	Gibraltar United	D	1-1	*González*
04/02	Lincoln	L	0-5	
19/02	Glacis	L	0-1	
24/02	Mons Calpe	D	1-1	*I Pérez*
03/03	Europa	L	0-1	
18/03	St Joseph's	L	0-3	
01/04	Europa Point	W	1-0	*Gilroy*
10/04	Lynx	W	2-1	*Castro, F Santos*
19/04	Manchester 62	W	1-0	*F Santos (p)*
29/04	Gibraltar United	D	0-0	
08/05	Lincoln	L	0-4	
13/05	Glacis	D	0-0	
19/05	Mons Calpe	L	0-2	

No	Name	Nat	DoB	Pos	Aps	(s)	Gls
26	Rafael Bado		30/12/84	M	1	(2)	
5	Jesse Ballester		30/06/93	M	2	(5)	
1	Louie Barnfather Marfe		07/10/92	G	7		
50	Dennis Bautista		03/08/00	M	1	(5)	
6	Shea Breakspear		22/11/91	D	22	(1)	1
1	Francisco Cáceres	ESP	24/08/93	G	1		
15	Alberto Castro	ESP	23/03/90	M	12		2
2	Tarik Chrayeh		05/11/86	D	2	(1)	
22	Jayce Consigliero		01/08/97	M	21	(4)	
27	Ayoub El Himdi		30/09/00	A		(1)	
5	Ismael Fernández	ESP	13/10/86	D	10		1
32	Samuel Gilroy	ESP	27/06/93	M	23		5
23	Alberto González	ESP	11/02/85	M	8	(2)	1
39	Hamza Gouicimhoussein	FRA	14/01/00	M		(2)	
18	Al Greene		05/05/78	A	19	(2)	
24	Thomas Hastings		23/09/92	D	17	(4)	
7	Jeremy Lopez		09/07/89	M	10	(1)	1
21	Jonay López	ESP	17/01/91	M	11	(2)	
32	Johann Mills		14/08/00	M		(1)	
17	Juan Morales	ESP	11/07/89	M	8	(3)	
21	Enrique Moreno	ESP	09/01/92	M	8		1
10	Lee Muscat		23/09/88	A		(1)	
33	Liam Neale		01/12/96	G	4		
30	Lennard Neame		30/01/00	D		(1)	
43	James Parkinson		21/05/00	D	3	(3)	
27	Richie Parral		23/03/99	M		(2)	
20	Ignacio Pérez	ESP	19/09/90	D	7	(4)	1
3	Kailan Perez		22/08/88	D	23		
44	Javan Robertson		19/06/00	D	2	(4)	
14	Ian Rodriguez		20/07/88	M	2	(2)	
25	Imanol Romero	ARG	17/03/90	D	1	(4)	
4	Justin Rovegno		17/07/89	D	3	(3)	
16	Francisco Santos	ESP	22/05/84	M	6	(5)	2
14	Nathan Santos		11/10/88	A	23	(3)	2
13	Adam Szpilczynski	ESP	19/11/84	G	15		
9	Graeme Torrilla		03/09/97	M	24	(2)	
15	Reed Wilson	ENG	30/07/97	D	1	(4)	

Lynx FC

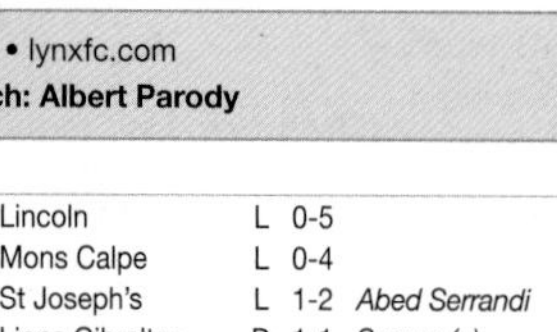

2007 • lynxfc.com

Coach: Albert Parody

Date	Opponent			Scorers
2016				
24/09	Lincoln	L	0-5	
02/10	Mons Calpe	L	0-4	
14/10	St Joseph's	L	1-2	*Abed Serrandi*
24/10	Lions Gibraltar	D	1-1	*Segura (p)*
30/10	Gibraltar United	L	0-1	
05/11	Glacis	L	0-2	
18/11	Europa	L	0-7	
28/11	Europa Point	W	3-0	*(w/o; original result 2-1 Soussi, Segura)*
03/12	Manchester 62	D	2-2	*Segura (p), og (Pacheco)*
10/12	Lincoln	L	1-2	*Abed Serrandi*
16/12	Mons Calpe	L	0-2	
2017				
09/01	St Joseph's	L	1-3	*Segura (p)*
14/01	Lions Gibraltar	W	7-2	*O'Dwyer, Mitchell 4, Soussi, Segura*
21/01	Gibraltar United	W	1-0	*Mitchell*
27/01	Glacis	D	1-1	*og (Ruesca)*
05/02	Europa	L	1-3	*Kamara*
18/02	Europa Point	W	3-0	*Segura 2, Kamara*
26/02	Manchester 62	W	4-0	*Mitchell, O'Dwyer, Guiling, Olmos*
05/03	Lincoln	L	0-1	
18/03	Mons Calpe	W	2-0	*Kamara 2*
31/03	St Joseph's	L	0-2	
10/04	Lions Gibraltar	L	1-2	*Pereira*
22/04	Gibraltar United	D	1-1	*Kamara*
30/04	Glacis	L	0-1	
05/05	Europa	L	0-1	
15/05	Europa Point	W	3-0	*Segura, O'Dwyer, Hassan*
20/05	Manchester 62	W	1-0	*Hassan*

No	Name	Nat	DoB	Pos	Aps	(s)	Gls
23	Yacine Abed Serrandi	FRA	07/03/96	M	16	(7)	2
10	Aleksa Aleksić	SRB	20/02/95	A	1		
3	Jerry Asamoah	BEL	13/08/93	D	2	(1)	
22	Tyronne Avellano		01/05/00	M	1		
8	Derek Ceballos	ESP	18/04/95	M	5	(1)	
11	Joshua Cuby		25/05/92	M	6	(3)	
5	Ryan Dean		18/07/98	D		(2)	
3	Luke Evans	ENG	23/10/99	D	2	(3)	
1	Danny Fernandez	FRA	29/05/96	G	12		
12	German García	ARG	18/02/96	M	3	(2)	
30	Ivans Glushco	LVA	25/09/84	M	10	(5)	
20	Gabriel Gonzalez		16/07/91	A	14	(5)	
9	Robert Guiling		14/10/80	M	19	(2)	1
77	Unai Gutiérrez	ESP	15/02/91	M	13	(2)	
22	Mattias Hall	SWE	03/02/88	D	7	(2)	
7	Mohamed Hassan	EGY	25/11/89	M	11	(12)	2
10	Sean Hendrick		29/01/86	D	1		
8	Sheku Kamara	SWE	23/04/91	A	5	(3)	5
88	Leonardo da Silva	BRA	14/01/88	D	4	(2)	
2	Charlie Mitchell	ENG	11/11/97	D	20		6
88	Elkin Mosquera	COL	24/11/88	M	14		
6	Youcef Mziou	FRA	11/07/96	M	3		
10	William O'Dwyer	ROU	30/07/90	M	15	(1)	3
4	Lucas Olmos	ESP	17/03/96	D	26		1
19	Ismael Ouattara	FRA	19/04/96	M	18	(1)	
8	Ismael Panel	ESP	22/07/84	M		(1)	
8	Javan Parody		06/04/88	D		(1)	
14	Mariano Pereira	ESP	27/03/90	M	8	(13)	1
12	Robert Rae	ENG	30/05/99	G	7	(1)	
1	Richard Rico	ESP	05/05/95	G	6		
5	Rodrigo Costa	BRA	12/05/88	D	9		
77	Raúl Segura	ESP	11/04/91	M	26		8
66	Steven Soussi		30/07/92	M	11	(5)	2
13	Salvador Tellez	ESP	01/04/93	G	2		

Manchester 62 FC

1962 • man62fc.com

Major honours

Gibraltar League (7) 1975, 1977, 1979, 1980, 1984, 1995, 1999; Gibraltar Cup (4) 1977, 1980, 1997, 2003

Coach: Gabino Rodríguez (ESP); (19/12/16) Carlos Inarejos (ESP); (21/03/17) Kiko Prieto (ESP)

Date	Opponent			Scorers
2016				
21/09	Gibraltar United	D	2-2	*Mejías, Toncheff*
28/09	Glacis	L	0-1	
17/10	Europa	L	0-4	
23/10	Europa Point	L	1-2	*Toncheff*
29/10	Lions Gibraltar	W	5-1	*Lopez 2, og (Gilroy), Toncheff 2*
03/11	Lincoln	L	1-6	*C Díaz*
19/11	Mons Calpe	L	0-3	
25/11	St Joseph's	L	0-1	
03/12	Lynx	D	2-2	*Domínguez, Payas*
09/12	Gibraltar United	L	1-3	*Toncheff*
19/12	Glacis	L	0-3	
2017				
07/01	Europa	L	0-8	
13/01	Europa Point	W	4-0	*Durán, Junco, Payas, Poggio*
20/01	Lions Gibraltar	D	1-1	*Payas*
29/01	Lincoln	L	0-2	
06/02	Mons Calpe	L	0-2	
18/02	St Joseph's	L	0-2	
26/02	Lynx	L	0-4	
04/03	Gibraltar United	W	3-0	*Navarro 2, Payas*
16/03	Glacis	D	1-1	*Mejías*
03/04	Europa	L	0-4	
19/04	Lions Gibraltar	L	0-1	
24/04	Europa Point	W	6-0	*Payas 2, Tra 2, Durán, Lopez*
02/05	Lincoln	L	0-3	
07/05	Mons Calpe	L	0-3	
14/05	St Joseph's	D	0-0	
20/05	Lynx	L	0-1	

No	Name	Nat	DoB	Pos	Aps	(s)	Gls
91	José María Arana	ESP	26/04/91	D	5		
36	Stefan Bonavia		10/03/00	M	1		
1	Matthew Cafer	ENG	27/09/94	G	8		
6	Mark Casciaro		11/07/84	M	6	(1)	
4	Francisco Chacón	ESP	29/03/94	D	23	(1)	
19	Liam Clarke		04/12/87	M	1		
46	Liam Crisp		23/09/99	D	11	(3)	
69	José Antonio Cruz	ESP	03/08/99	M	6		
21	Antonio Díaz	ESP	28/09/85	M	2	(1)	
19	Carlos Díaz	PAR	28/04/97	A	3	(8)	1
23	José Antonio Domínguez	ESP	23/01/92	D	23		1
12	Aarón Durán	ESP	26/01/94	D	23	(2)	2
74	Kieron Garcia		04/08/98	M	8	(9)	
39	Miguel Ángel García	ESP	25/05/97	M	1	(1)	
12	Raúl Gillen Durán	ESP	23/06/95	D	1	(5)	
22	Philip Gillingwater Pedersen		16/01/99	D	1	(4)	
13	Raúl Hernández	ESP	09/11/98	G	3		
14	Thomas Isola		17/01/96	M	1	(1)	
28	Antonio Jiménez	ESP	28/02/96	D	14		
25	Jorge Junco	ESP	14/04/94	A	6	(1)	1
92	Makan Keita	FRA	01/04/95	G	4		
7	Andrew Lopez		15/04/84	M	16	(4)	3
21	Jonas Luque	ESP	07/04/96	D	7	(3)	
80	Juan Mateo	ESP	24/12/80	G	12	(1)	
15	Neil Medina		15/04/87	D	4		
4	Francisco Mejías	ESP	05/05/87	M	6	(1)	2
17	Álvaro Navarro	ESP	14/04/91	A	21	(3)	2
5	Diego Pacheco	ESP	06/09/96	D	17	(2)	
8	Aaron Payas		24/05/85	M	19	(4)	6
2	Bernardo Perea	ESP	07/04/81	D	2	(1)	
9	Brian Perez		16/09/86	M	1		
99	Karl Poggio		08/06/99	M	4	(7)	1
26	Ian Rodriguez		20/07/88	M		(1)	
10	Cristian Toncheff	ARG	25/03/82	A	9		5
18	Marc-Alain Tra	FRA	17/10/95	A	12		2
20	Antonio Urenda	ESP	27/12/95	M	16	(4)	

Mons Calpe SC

2013 • monscalpesc.com

Coach: William (BRA); (16/01/17) Terrence Jolley; (17/03/17) Mauro Ardizzone (ITA)

2016			
23/09	St Joseph's	W 2-0	*Pereira, Di Piedi*
02/10	Lynx	W 4-0	*Pereira 3, Vela*
15/10	Gibraltar United	W 3-1	*Otero, Di Piedi, Cascio*
21/10	Glacis	L 0-3	*(w/o; original result 0-0)*
29/10	Europa	L 0-3	
06/11	Europa Point	W 4-1	*Colace, Camacho, Di Piedi, Pereira*
19/11	Manchester 62	W 3-0	*Di Piedi, Colace, Pereira*
26/11	Lincoln	L 1-4	*Di Piedi*
04/12	Lions Gibraltar	W 1-0	*Otero*
10/12	St Joseph's	L 0-2	
16/12	Lynx	W 2-0	*Colace 2*
2017			
08/01	Gibraltar United	D 2-2	*Cascio 2*
16/01	Glacis	L 1-3	*Otero*
22/01	Europa	L 0-2	
28/01	Europa Point	W 2-0	*Cascio, André Santos*
06/02	Manchester 62	W 2-0	*Camacho, Pereira*
17/02	Lincoln	L 1-2	*Pereira*
24/02	Lions Gibraltar	D 1-1	*Serra*
06/03	St Joseph's	L 0-1	
18/03	Lynx	L 0-2	
01/04	Gibraltar United	W 2-1	*Pereira, Di Piedi*
09/04	Glacis	L 0-1	
21/04	Europa	L 0-3	
29/04	Europa Point	W 6-1	*Cascio 2, Filipe Aguiar, Zúñiga, Di Piedi, Trentin*
07/05	Manchester 62	W 3-0	*Pereira, Cascio 2 (1p)*
13/05	Lincoln	D 2-2	*Pereira, Cascio*
19/05	Lions Gibraltar	W 2-0	*Di Piedi, Colace*

No	Name	Nat	DoB	Pos	Aps	(s)	Gls
41	Marek Albert	USA	18/12/90	A	2		
2	André Santos	BRA	19/02/92	D	26		1
18	Tyronne Avellano		01/05/00	M	1	(2)	
23	Adam Aziz	ENG	01/12/88	M		(1)	
22	Manuel Camacho	ESP	07/02/93	M	22	(2)	2
10	Facundo Cascio	ITA	02/08/97	A	16	(7)	9
29	Hugo Colace	ARG	16/01/84	M	20		5
8	Max Cottrell		15/09/99	M	12	(7)	
40	Nick Dembele	ENG	19/05/97	M		(1)	
33	Michele Di Piedi	ITA	04/12/80	M	19	(1)	8
42	Naoufal El Andaloussi		07/03/91	M	1	(3)	
5	Filipe Aguiar	POR	04/01/91	D	7	(4)	1
1	Christian Fraiz	ESP	22/02/88	G	22		
32	Jeremy Funes	FRA	23/06/90	M		(1)	
30	Sacha Funes	ITA	15/08/84	M	2	(4)	
13	Lucio Hernando	ESP	05/10/94	G	5		
19	Ethan Jolley		29/03/97	D	21	(3)	
20	Marcos Meireles	POR	04/12/89	M		(2)	
38	Lython Marquez		06/02/95	A		(1)	
11	Gabriele Novello	ITA	18/08/98	A	1	(3)	
3	José Luis Otero	ESP	03/02/96	D	16		3
7	Alan Parker		15/05/96	M	7	(6)	
16	Jaydan Parody		08/05/98	D		(1)	
9	Juan Pablo Pereira	ESP	02/07/87	A	20	(2)	11
25	Reece Placid	ENG	13/11/95	A		(3)	
6	Renan Bernardes	BRA	21/03/92	M	26	(1)	
21	Tyson Ruiz		10/03/88	M	19	(1)	
12	Tomas Scaldaferro	ITA	21/03/97	D	2	(2)	
31	Alfons Serra	ESP	10/12/90	M	4		1
14	Giovanni Trentin	ITA	26/09/98	A		(4)	1
4	Leonardo Vela	ITA	05/02/82	D	15	(3)	1
43	Francisco Zúñiga	ESP	22/12/90	D	11	(1)	1

St Joseph's FC

1912 • stjosephsfcgib.com

Major honours

Gibraltar League (1) 1996; Gibraltar Cup (9) 1979, 1983, 1984, 1985, 1987, 1992, 1996, 2012, 2013

Coach: Alfonso Cortijo Cabrera (ESP); (19/12/16) Raúl Procopio (ESP)

2016			
23/09	Mons Calpe	L 0-2	
29/09	Lions Gibraltar	W 3-0	*Reyes, López, Gómez*
14/10	Lynx	W 2-1	*Robles, Reyes*
22/10	Gibraltar United	W 1-0	*Romero*
31/10	Glacis	D 1-1	*Cano*
05/11	Europa	D 1-1	*Lobato*
19/11	Europa Point	W 6-0	*Montes, Reyes 2, López, Cano, Villalba*
25/11	Manchester 62	W 1-0	*Duarte*
02/12	Lincoln	L 1-2	*Reyes*
10/12	Mons Calpe	W 2-0	*Gómez, Reyes*
18/12	Lions Gibraltar	W 2-0	*Montes, López*
2017			
09/01	Lynx	W 3-1	*Duarte 2, López*
15/01	Gibraltar United	W 4-1	*og (Andrew Hernandez), Reyes 2, Duarte*
21/01	Glacis	W 2-0	*Romero, Duarte*
28/01	Europa	L 1-4	*Duarte*
03/02	Europa Point	W 3-0	*Caballero, Duarte 2*
18/02	Manchester 62	W 2-0	*Duarte, Alegre*
27/02	Lincoln	D 2-2	*og (Patiño), Romero*
06/03	Mons Calpe	W 1-0	*Duarte*
18/03	Lions Gibraltar	W 3-0	*og (Breakspear), Yeps Roda, Lobato*
31/03	Lynx	W 2-0	*Villalba, Robles*
09/04	Gibraltar United	D 0-0	
18/04	Glacis	D 0-0	
30/04	Europa	L 1-2	*Alegre*
06/05	Europa Point	W 9-0	*Gómez, Alegre 2, Duarte 5, og (I Ruiz)*
15/05	Manchester 62	D 0-0	
20/05	Lincoln	L 0-1	

No	Name	Nat	DoB	Pos	Aps	(s)	Gls
31	Salvador Alegre	ESP	04/05/91	A	5	(3)	4
19	Samuel Aragón	ESP	08/04/98	D	10		
30	Josemi Caballero	ESP	28/11/88	M	10	(1)	1
22	Jesús Cano	ESP	25/11/94	A	6	(10)	2
3	Jesús Cantizano	ESP	01/01/89	D	26	(1)	
9	John Paul Duarte		13/12/86	A	14	(6)	15
25	José Antonio Ferrer	ESP	16/10/95	M	2	(8)	
13	José García	ESP	03/09/82	G	12		
8	Alberto Gil	ESP	08/01/87	M	23	(3)	
28	Borja Gómez	ESP	13/08/92	M	21	(3)	3
6	Iván Lobato	ESP	28/05/91	D	20	(1)	2
10	Javier López	ESP	13/11/87	A	23	(1)	4
16	Francisco Márquez	ESP	09/04/84	M		(1)	
5	Esteban Montes	ESP	03/04/88	D	21	(1)	2
16	Michael Negrette		14/09/98	M		(4)	
1	Jordan Perez		13/11/86	G	8		
17	Cecil Prescott		10/05/99	A	3	(3)	
11	Shelby Printemps	HAI	10/08/90	A	1		
14	Juan Francisco Puertas	ESP	15/08/88	M		(1)	
7	José Luis Reyes	ESP	05/10/81	A	21	(2)	8
1	Jamie Robba		26/10/91	G	7		
2	Jaime Robles	ESP	23/04/93	D	20	(2)	2
15	Carlos Rodríguez	ESP	28/12/87	M	5	(3)	
12	José Luis Romero	ESP	19/07/92	A	16	(7)	3
14	Juan Manuel Santiago	ESP	27/06/91	M		(1)	
18	Jamie Serra		30/10/98	D	1	(2)	
21	Juan Carlos Villalba	ESP	01/05/89	A	19	(7)	2
11	Jorge Yeps Roda	ESP	25/02/89	A	3	(10)	1

Top goalscorers

30	Kike Gómez (Europa)
17	Joseph Chipolina (Lincoln)
15	Liam Walker (Europa)
	John Paul Duarte (St Joseph's)
14	Guillermo Roldán (Europa)
13	George Cabrera (Lincoln)
	Lee Casciaro (Lincoln)
11	Salvador Carrasco (Glacis)
	Juan Pablo Pereira (Mons Calpe)
10	Tulio Etchemaite (Lincoln)

Promoted club

Gibraltar Phoenix FC

2011 • no website

Coach: Alberto Ferri (ESP)

Second level final table 2016/17

		Pld	W	D	L	F	A	Pts
1	Gibraltar Phoenix FC	16	14	0	2	82	10	42
2	FC Bruno's Magpies	16	12	3	1	63	12	39
3	FC Boca Juniors Gibraltar	16	10	2	4	32	21	32
4	Cannons FC	16	7	3	6	33	29	24
5	Leo FC	16	6	1	9	28	52	19
6	FC Olympique Gibraltar 13	16	5	2	9	28	35	17
7	College 1975 FC	16	5	1	10	24	40	16
8	Angels FC	16	4	1	11	17	66	13
9	FC Hound Dogs	16	2	1	13	9	51	7

Promotion/Relegation play-off

(30/05/17)

Manchester 62 3-1 Bruno's Magpies

GREECE

Elliniki Podosfairiki Omospondia (EPO)

Address	Goudi Park PO Box 14161 GR-11510 Athens
Tel	+30 210 930 6000
Fax	+30 210 935 9666
E-mail	epo@epo.gr
Website	epo.gr

President	vacant
General secretary	Alexandros Dedes
Media officer	Michalis Tsapidis
Year of formation	1926
National stadium	Georgios Karaiskakis, Piraeus (32,130)

SUPERLEAGUE CLUBS

1 **AEK Athens FC**

2 **Asteras Tripolis FC**

3 **Atromitos FC**

4 **Iraklis FC**

5 **Kerkyra FC**

6 **AE Larissa FC**

7 **Levadiakos FC**

8 **Olympiacos FC**

9 **Panathinaikos FC**

10 **Panetolikos GFS**

11 **Panionios GSS**

12 **PAOK FC**

13 **PAS Giannina FC**

14 **Platanias FC**

15 **Veria FC**

16 **Xanthi FC**

KEY

- UEFA Champions League
- UEFA Europa League
- Promoted
- Relegated

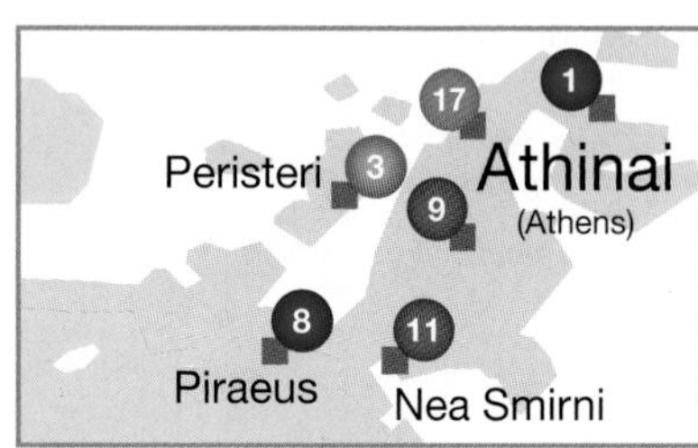

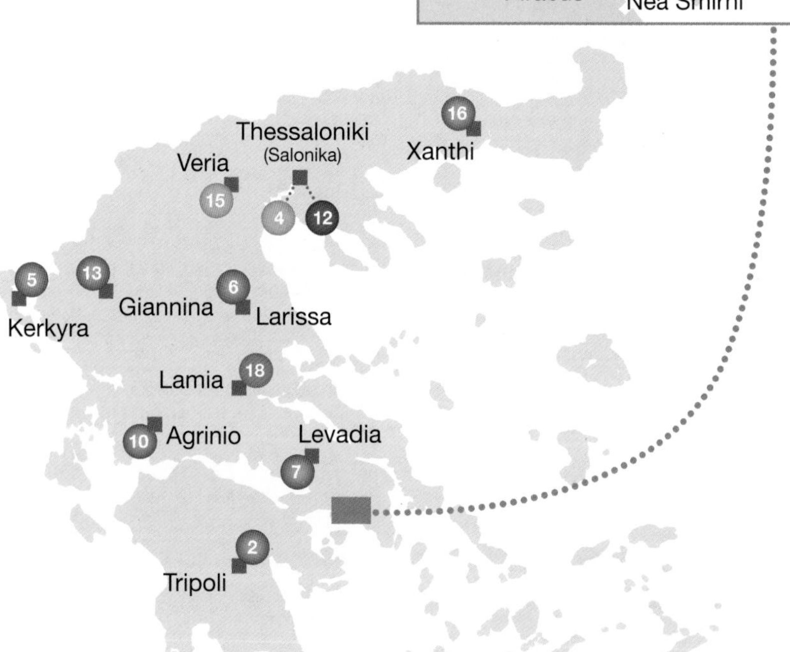

PROMOTED CLUBS

17 **Apollon Smyrnis FC**

18 **PAS Lamia 1964**

Olympiacos ride out the storm

The Greek Superleague title was won for the seventh successive season by Olympiacos. For most of the campaign the Piraeus club were their usual untouchable selves, but a dramatic early-spring slump temporarily derailed them before the familiar figure of Takis Lemonis – in his third spell as coach – got them safely back on track.

PAOK won the Greek Cup for the first time in 14 years. The Salonika club also finished second in the Superleague but lost out to AEK Athens for the second UEFA Champions League place after a dramatic climax to the play-offs.

Seventh successive title for Piraeus giants

Lemonis steers team home after mini-collapse

AEK win play-offs but lose cup final to PAOK

Domestic league

There was a change of coach at Olympiacos before the league got under way, with Víctor Sánchez, the successor to Marco Silva, being sacked in August after an unscheduled UEFA Champions League exit and replaced by former Portugal boss Paulo Bento. An unexpected defeat at newly-promoted Larissa raised further concerns, but those were rapidly dismissed as the Red-and-Whites went on a familiar autumn rampage, successive home wins against AEK (3-0), PAOK (2-1) and Panathinaikos (3-0) propelling them on a long unbeaten run that lasted four months and put them 13 points clear with ten games remaining.

Then, all of a sudden, the wheels stopped turning. A 1-0 defeat in a stormy encounter at AEK was one thing, but when that was followed by another, against closest pursuers Panionios in their own Georgios Karaiskakis stadium – where they had not lost in the league since December 2014 – the crisis talk began in earnest. A tricky away fixture at PAOK followed and, sure enough, Olympiacos lost that too. It was the first time in 21 years that they had suffered three consecutive league defeats, and it cost Bento his job.

Caretaker boss Vasilios Vouzas stood in, but after an edgy, rot-stopping home win against Atromitos, a visit to Panathinaikos brought yet another defeat, with Superleague top scorer Marcus Berg grabbing the only goal. It was then that the call went out for Lemonis – an Olympiacos stalwart who had coached the club to four previous titles. With five games left, the defending champions still led by six points but they could ill-afford any more nasty surprises. Four wins and a draw duly prevented the unthinkable, a thumping 5-0 victory at home to PAS Giannina securing the club's 44th title in the penultimate round.

Vladimir Ivić's PAOK won their last six games to finish second and carry a two-point advantage into the UEFA Champions League qualification play-offs. But they lost their opening game 1-0 at home to Manolo Jiménez's AEK, and that would eventually prove decisive when they were also beaten at home by Marinos Ouzounidis's Panathinaikos on the final day – with a 90th-minute winner – that enabled AEK, 2-1 winners at Vladan Milojević's Panionios, to finish top by a point.

Domestic cup

A few weeks earlier PAOK had been the team celebrating after a late Pedro Henrique goal beat holders AEK 2-1 in a Greek Cup final delayed for 30 minutes because of pre-match fan violence in Volos. PAOK had not won the trophy since 2003. Indeed it was only their fifth victory in 18 final appearances, their 13 defeats constituting an unenviable competition record.

Europe

Olympiacos were the last Greek team standing in Europe, but theirs was an unexceptional campaign. Although they racked up 14 matches, they won only five and were surprisingly found wanting against the champions of both Israel and Cyprus before bowing out of the UEFA Europa League to the best team in Turkey. PAOK reached the round of 32 in the same competition, but there was more group stage gloom for Panathinaikos, winless in their six matches for the second successive year.

National team

After a disastrous UEFA EURO 2016 qualifying campaign, spirits were raised ahead of the 2018 FIFA World Cup preliminaries when Greece, now under the charge of German coach Michael Skibbe, beat the Netherlands for the very first time in an Eindhoven friendly. With confidence restored, Skibbe's men won their opening three qualifiers – against Gibraltar, Cyprus and Estonia – then commendably drew the next three, holding Bosnia & Herzegovina twice (firstly at home with a stunning stoppage-time strike from Georgios Tzavellas) and group leaders Belgium 1-1 in Brussels thanks to in-form Benfica striker Kostas Mitroglou's third goal of the campaign.

DOMESTIC SEASON AT A GLANCE

Superleague 2016/17 final table

		Pld	Home W	D	L	F	A	Away W	D	L	F	A	Total W	D	L	F	A	Pts
1	**Olympiacos FC**	**30**	**13**	**1**	**1**	**39**	**6**	**8**	**3**	**4**	**18**	**10**	**21**	**4**	**5**	**57**	**16**	**67**
2	PAOK FC	30	12	1	2	33	9	8	3	4	19	10	20	4	6	52	19	61
3	Panathinaikos FC	30	12	2	1	28	4	4	7	4	17	15	16	9	5	45	19	57
4	AEK Athens FC	30	9	5	1	36	7	5	6	4	18	16	14	11	5	54	23	53
5	Panionios GSS	30	8	4	3	19	12	7	3	5	16	11	15	7	8	35	23	52
6	Xanthi FC	30	8	5	2	19	8	5	4	6	15	17	13	9	8	34	25	48
7	Platanias FC	30	8	4	3	24	17	3	5	7	10	21	11	9	10	34	38	42
8	Atromitos FC	30	6	2	7	14	16	5	4	6	15	22	11	6	13	29	38	39
9	PAS Giannina FC	30	5	6	4	16	10	3	6	6	14	27	8	12	10	30	37	36
10	Kerkyra FC	30	6	4	5	12	15	2	4	9	10	28	8	8	14	22	43	32
11	Panetolikos GFS	30	7	2	6	21	16	1	5	9	8	24	8	7	15	29	40	31
12	Asteras Tripolis FC	30	4	7	4	17	18	2	3	10	17	31	6	10	14	34	49	28
13	AE Larissa FC	30	6	5	4	16	16	0	5	10	7	26	6	10	14	23	42	28
14	Levadiakos FC	30	5	5	5	19	21	1	3	11	8	28	6	8	16	27	49	26
15	Iraklis FC	30	3	8	4	16	17	3	3	9	12	22	6	11	13	28	39	26
16	Veria FC	30	4	5	6	17	18	1	2	12	6	38	5	7	18	23	56	22

NB Iraklis FC & PAOK FC – 3 pts deducted.

European qualification 2017/18

Champion: Olympiacos FC (third qualifying round)
AEK Athens FC (third qualifying round)

Cup winner: PAOK FC (third qualifying round)
Panathinaikos FC (third qualifying round)
Panionios GSS (second qualifying round)

Top scorer Marcus Berg (Panathinaikos), 22 goals
Relegated clubs Veria FC, Iraklis FC
Promoted clubs Apollon Smyrnis FC, PAS Lamia 1964
Cup final PAOK FC 2-1 AEK Athens FC

Player of the season

Luka Milivojević
(Olympiacos FC)

It was no coincidence that Olympiacos's form crashed shortly after Milivojević left the club at the end of January to join Crystal Palace. The Serbian international was the glue that held the team together, the central orchestrator in midfield and also an accurate deliverer of set-pieces. His six goals all contributed to victories, including the winning strikes at home to PAOK and away to Veria on his farewell appearance. An ever-present starter for Serbia in their opening six (unbeaten) FIFA World Cup qualifiers, he also helped rescue new club Palace from relegation.

Newcomer of the season

Panagiotis Retsos
(Olympiacos FC)

Like many big European clubs nowadays, Olympiacos tend to look abroad for new players rather than to their own academy, but in 2016/17 the Piraeus club unearthed a jewel from their youth set-up as Retsos was promoted from the club's youth team and proved such a huge hit that he not only earned a regular berth in the first XI but also captained the team, aged 18, in a Greek Cup tie against Atromitos. Mostly used at left-back but equally comfortable in the centre of defence, his meteoric rise has already been noted by – yes – a number of big European clubs.

Team of the season

(4-1-3-2)

Coach: Milojević *(Panionios)*

NATIONAL TEAM

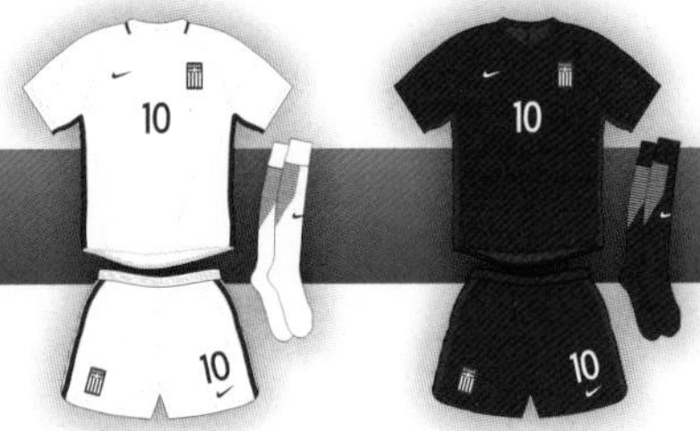

International honours
UEFA European Championship (1) 2004

International tournament appearances
FIFA World Cup (3) 1994, 2010, 2014 (2nd round)
UEFA European Championship (4) 1980, 2004 (Winners), 2008, 2012 (qtr-finals)

Top five all-time caps
Georgios Karagounis (139); Theodoros Zagorakis (120); Kostas Katsouranis (116); Angelos Basinas (100); Efstratios Apostolakis (96)

Top five all-time goals
Nikolaos Anastopoulos (29); Angelos Charisteas (25); Theofanis Gekas (24); Dimitrios Saravakos (22); Dimitrios "Mimis" Papaioannou (21)

Results 2016/17

Date	Opponent		Venue	Res	Score	Scorers
01/09/16	Netherlands	A	Eindhoven	W	2-1	*Mitroglou (29), Gianniotas (74)*
06/09/16	Gibraltar (WCQ)	A	Faro (POR)	W	4-1	*Mitroglou (10), Wiseman (44og), Fortounis (45), Torosidis (45+2)*
07/10/16	Cyprus (WCQ)	H	Piraeus	W	2-0	*Mitroglou (12), Mantalos (42)*
10/10/16	Estonia (WCQ)	A	Tallinn	W	2-0	*Torosidis (2), Stafylidis (61)*
09/11/16	Belarus	H	Piraeus	L	0-1	
13/11/16	Bosnia & Herzegovina (WCQ)	H	Piraeus	D	1-1	*Tzavellas (90+5)*
25/03/17	Belgium (WCQ)	A	Brussels	D	1-1	*Mitroglou (46)*
09/06/17	Bosnia & Herzegovina (WCQ)	A	Zenica	D	0-0	

Appearances 2016/17

Coach: Michael Skibbe (GER)	04/08/65		Ned	GIB	CYP	EST	Blr	BIH	BEL	BIH	Caps	Goals
Orestis Karnezis	11/07/85	Udinese (ITA)	G46	G	G	G		G		G	42	-
Vasilios Torosidis	10/06/85	Bologna (ITA)	D46	D	D	D18	s86	D	D	D	91	9
Kostas Manolas	14/06/91	Roma (ITA)	D46	D	D	D			D	D	29	-
Sokratis Papastathopoulos	09/06/88	Dortmund (GER)	D	D	D	D6	s46	D	D	D	73	2
Georgios Tzavellas	26/11/87	PAOK /Alanyaspor (TUR)	D	D	D88		s74	D	D 95*		24	2
Petros Mantalos	31/08/91	AEK Athens	M83	M62	M	M	M46	M87	M84	M91	15	2
Ioannis Maniatis	12/10/86	Olympiacos /Atromitos	M	M71	M	M86	D46	M61		s94	47	1
Andreas Samaris	13/06/89	Benfica (POR)	M	M			M46	M	M		28	1
Kostas Fortounis	16/10/92	Olympiacos	M55	M	M		s68	M	M67	M94	26	3
José Holebas	27/06/84	Watford (ENG)	M46		s77						38	1
Kostas Mitroglou	12/03/88	Benfica (POR)	A	A73	A	A		A	A92	A	54	13
Anastasios Bakasetas	28/06/93	AEK Athens	s46	M	M77	M				M50	7	-
Stefanos Kapino	18/03/94	Olympiacos	s46						G		9	-
Kyriakos Papadopoulos	23/02/92	RB Leipzig (GER)	s46		s70	M	D86	D 78*			25	4
Kostas Stafylidis	02/12/93	Augsburg (GER)	s46		M70	D	D74	M	M	D	17	2
Ioannis Gianniotas	29/04/93	APOEL (CYP)	s55	s62			M68	s61			6	1
Nikolaos Karelis	24/02/92	Genk (BEL)	s83		s88	M	M	s87			17	2
Alexandros Tziolis	13/02/85	PAOK /Hearts (SCO)		s71		s86	M		s67	M	64	1
Apostolos Vellios	08/01/92	Nottingham Forest (ENG)		s73			A		s92		6	-
Panagiotis Tachtsidis	15/02/91	Cagliari (ITA)				s6	s46		M 65*		20	1
Marios Oikonomou	06/10/92	Bologna (ITA)				s18	D				5	-
Panagiotis Glykos	10/10/86	PAOK					G				5	-
Dimitrios Diamantakos	05/03/93	Karlsruhe (GER)					s46				4	-
Zeca	31/08/88	Panathinaikos							s84	M	2	-
Anastasios Donis	29/08/96	Nice (FRA)								s50	1	-
Dimitrios Kourbelis	02/11/93	Panathinaikos								s91	1	-

EUROPE

Olympiacos FC

Third qualifying round - Hapoel Beer-Sheva FC (ISR)
H 0-0
Kapino, Maniatis (Bouhalakis 63), Botía, Milivojević, Fortounis, Durmaz (Domínguez 58), Siovas (Manuel da Costa 40), De la Bella, Diogo Figueiras, Sebá, Ideye. Coach: Víctor Sánchez (ESP)
A 0-1
Kapino, Botía (Pulido 82), Milivojević, Manuel da Costa, Fortounis, Bouhalakis, Domínguez (Masuaku 60), Cambiasso, De la Bella, Diogo Figueiras (Maniatis 51), Ideye. Coach: Víctor Sánchez (ESP)

Play-offs - FC Arouca (POR)
A 1-0 *Sebá (27)*
Kapino, Botía, Milivojević, Manuel da Costa, Domínguez (Androutsos 72), Cambiasso, De la Bella, Diogo Figueiras, Pardo (Zdjelar 90), Sebá (Durmaz 88), Ideye. Coach: Paulo Bento (POR)
H 2-1 (aet) *Domínguez (94), Ideye (113)*
Kapino, Botía, Milivojević, Manuel da Costa, Fortounis (André Martins 72), Cambiasso (Domínguez 91), De la Bella, Retsos, Pardo (Manthatis 99), Sebá, Ideye. Coach: Paulo Bento (POR)

Group B
Match 1 - BSC Young Boys (SUI)
A 1-0 *Cambiasso (42)*
Leali, Botía, Milivojević, Manuel da Costa, Marin (André Martins 63), Elyounoussi (Romao 90+3), Cambiasso, De la Bella, Diogo Figueiras, Sebá, Ideye (Cardozo 82). Coach: Paulo Bento (POR)
Match 2 - APOEL FC (CYP)
H 0-1
Leali, Botía, Milivojević, Manuel da Costa, Fortounis (Elyounoussi 64), Marin (Cardozo 78), Cambiasso (André Martins 79), De la Bella, Diogo Figueiras, Sebá, Ideye. Coach: Paulo Bento (POR)
Match 3 - FC Astana (KAZ)
H 4-1 *Diogo Figueiras (25), Elyounoussi (33), Sebá (34, 65)*
Leali, Botía, Milivojević (Cambiasso 73), Manuel da Costa, Fortounis (Bouhalakis 79), Cardozo, Elyounoussi (Manthatis 69), André Martins, Retsos, Diogo Figueiras, Sebá. Coach: Paulo Bento (POR)
Match 4 - FC Astana (KAZ)
A 1-1 *Sebá (30)*
Leali, Botía, Bouhalakis, Cardozo, Elabdellaoui, Cambiasso (Romao 81), André Martins (Androutsos 90+1), Bruno Viana, Retsos, Manthatis (Elyounoussi 64), Sebá. Coach: Paulo Bento (POR)
Match 5 - BSC Young Boys (SUI)
H 1-1 *Fortounis (48)*
Leali, Botía, Milivojević, Manuel da Costa, Fortounis, Elyounoussi (Manthatis 84), André Martins, Retsos, Diogo Figueiras, Sebá, Ideye. Coach: Paulo Bento (POR)
Match 6 - APOEL FC (CYP)
A 0-2
Leali, Romao, Manuel da Costa, Fortounis (Domínguez 76), Elyounoussi, De la Bella (Manthatis 76), André Martins (Androutsos 66), Bruno Viana, Diogo Figueiras, Sebá, Ideye. Coach: Paulo Bento (POR)

Round of 32 - Osmanlıspor (TUR)
H 0-0
Leali, Botía, Fortounis (Manthatis 72), Cardozo (Romao 76), Cissokho, André Martins (Ansarifard 87), Androutsos, Bruno Viana, Retsos, Diogo Figueiras, Sebá. Coach: Paulo Bento (POR)
Red card: Bruno Viana 73
A 3-0 *Ansarifard (47, 86), Elyounoussi (70)*
Leali, Botía, Manuel da Costa, Fortounis (Romao 85), Ansarifard , Elyounoussi (Manthatis 81), Cissokho, André Martins (Androutsos 65), Retsos, Diogo Figueiras, Sebá. Coach: Paulo Bento (POR)

Round of 16 - Beşiktaş JK (TUR)
H 1-1 *Cambiasso (36)*
Leali, Botía (Manuel da Costa 64), Romao, Fortounis (Marin 73), Ansarifard , Elyounoussi, Cambiasso (André Martins 70), Cissokho, Retsos, Manthatis, Diogo Figueiras. Coach: Vasilios Vouzas (GRE)
A 1-4 *Elyounoussi (31)*
Leali, Romao (André Martins 76), Manuel da Costa, Fortounis, Ansarifard , Elyounoussi, Cambiasso (Marin 68), Cissokho, Retsos, Manthatis (Sebá 56), Diogo Figueiras. Coach: Vasilios Vouzas (GRE)

PAOK FC

Third qualifying round - AFC Ajax (NED)
A 1-1 *Djalma (27)*
Glykos, Léo Matos, Leovac, Charisis (Tziolis 69), Djalma, Crespo, Cimirot, Mendes Rodrigues (Mystakidis 83), Shakhov, Tzavellas, Athanasiadis (Koulouris 90+1). Coach: Vladimir Ivić (SRB)
H 1-2 *Athanasiadis (4)*
Glykos, Léo Matos, Leovac, Charisis (Biseswar 84), Djalma, Crespo, Cimirot, Mendes Rodrigues (Mystakidis 70), Shakhov (Koulouris 89), Tzavellas, Athanasiadis. Coach: Vladimir Ivić (SRB)

Play-offs - FC Dinamo Tbilisi (GEO)
A 3-0 *Léo Matos (20), Crespo (71), Pereyra (83)*
Glykos, Léo Matos, Leovac, Charisis (Cañas 46), Djalma (Pereyra 81), Crespo, Cimirot, Mendes Rodrigues, Shakhov (Biseswar 68), Tzavellas, Athanasiadis. Coach: Vladimir Ivić (SRB)
H 2-0 *Mendes Rodrigues (5), Tzavellas (45)*
Glykos, Léo Matos, Leovac (Kitsiou 65), Djalma, Pereyra, Crespo (Varela 76), Cimirot, Mendes Rodrigues, Shakhov (Biseswar 57), Tzavellas, Cañas. Coach: Vladimir Ivić (SRB)

Group J
Match 1 - ACF Fiorentina (ITA)
H 0-0
Glykos, Léo Matos, Leovac, Djalma (Crespo 58), Cimirot, Mendes Rodrigues, Tzavellas, Athanasiadis (Thiam 79), Varela, Pelkas (Shakhov 57), Cañas. Coach: Vladimir Ivić (SRB)
Match 2 - FC Slovan Liberec (CZE)
A 2-1 *Athanasiadis (10p, 82)*
Glykos, Léo Matos, Leovac, Djalma (Mystakidis 59), Cimirot, Mendes Rodrigues, Shakhov (Thiam 73), Tzavellas, Athanasiadis (Crespo 86), Varela, Cañas. Coach: Vladimir Ivić (SRB)
Match 3 - Qarabağ FK (AZE)
A 0-2
Glykos, Léo Matos, Leovac, Thiam (Pereyra 66), Djalma (Koulouris 76), Crespo, Cimirot, Mendes Rodrigues, Shakhov, Varela, Cañas (Biseswar 59). Coach: Vladimir Ivić (SRB)
Match 4 - Qarabağ FK (AZE)
H 0-1
Glykos, Léo Matos, Leovac, Cimirot (Shakhov 81), Biseswar (Thiam 73), Mendes Rodrigues, Mystakidis (Pereyra 61), Tzavellas, Athanasiadis, Varela, Cañas. Coach: Vladimir Ivić (SRB)
Match 5 - ACF Fiorentina (ITA)
A 3-2 *Shakhov (5), Djalma (26), Mendes Rodrigues (90+3)*
Brkić, Léo Matos, Leovac, Djalma (Pelkas 71), Crespo, Cimirot, Koulouris (Thiam 61), Mendes Rodrigues, Shakhov (Mystakidis 83), Varela, Cañas. Coach: Vladimir Ivić (SRB)
Match 6 - FC Slovan Liberec (CZE)
H 2-0 *Mendes Rodrigues (29), Pelkas (67)*
Glykos, Léo Matos, Leovac (Malezas 82), Djalma, Crespo, Cimirot, Mendes Rodrigues, Athanasiadis (Koulouris 71), Varela, Pelkas (Shakhov 80), Cañas. Coach: Vladimir Ivić (SRB)

Round of 32 - FC Schalke 04 (GER)
H 0-3
Glykos, Léo Matos, Leovac, Malezas, Crespo, Cimirot, Biseswar (Pedro Henrique 77), Mystakidis (Djalma 55), Shakhov, Athanasiadis (Warda 85), Varela. Coach: Vladimir Ivić (SRB)
A 1-1 *Nastasić (25og)*
Glykos, Djalma Campos (Pelkas 78), Malezas, Crespo, Cimirot, Koulouris, Mystakidis (Pedro Henrique 63), Shakhov, Pougouras, Kitsiou, Warda (Biseswar 69). Coach: Vladimir Ivić (SRB)

AEK Athens FC

Third qualifying round - AS Saint-Étienne (FRA)
A 0-0
Anestis, Hélder Barbosa, André Simões, Vargas (Galanopoulos 67), Rodrigo Galo, Pekhart (Bakasetas 46), Johansson, Chygrynskiy, Mantalos (Platellas 82), Dídac Vilà, Kolovetsios. Coach: Temur Ketsbaia (GEO)
H 0-1
Anestis, Lambropoulos, Hélder Barbosa (Aravidis 61), André Simões (Hugo Almeida 67), Vargas (Platellas 53), Rodrigo Galo, Chygrynskiy, Mantalos, Dídac Vilà, Kolovetsios, Bakasetas. Coach: Temur Ketsbaia (GEO)

DOMESTIC LEAGUE CLUB-BY-CLUB

Panathinaikos FC

EUROPA LEAGUE

Third qualifying round - AIK (SWE)

H 1-0 *Rodrigo Moledo (79)*

Steele, Koutroumbis (Villafáñez 46), Ibarbo (Lod 89), Berg, Zeca, Wakaso (Leto 71), Hult, Ledesma, Mesto, Rodrigo Moledo, Ivanov. Coach: Andrea Stramaccioni (ITA)

A 2-0 *Ibarbo (46), Berg (73)*

Steele, Koutroumbis, Ibarbo (Leto 70), Berg, Zeca, Lod (Villafáñez 84), Wakaso, Ledesma (Nano 67), Mesto, Rodrigo Moledo, Ivanov. Coach: Andrea Stramaccioni (ITA)

Play-offs - Brøndby IF (DEN)

H 3-0 *Berg (45+2, 82), Ledesma (54p)*

Steele, Koutroumbis (Leto 58), Ibarbo, Berg (Rinaldi 86), Zeca, Wakaso (Villafáñez 74), Hult, Ledesma, Mesto, Rodrigo Moledo, Ivanov. Coach: Andrea Stramaccioni (ITA)

A 1-1 *Ivanov (66)*

Steele, Koutroumbis, Ibarbo (Leto 46), Berg, Zeca, Wakaso, Hult (Villafáñez 85), Ledesma (Lod 59), Mesto, Rodrigo Moledo, Ivanov. Coach: Andrea Stramaccioni (ITA)

Group G

Match 1 - AFC Ajax (NED)

H 1-2 *Berg (5)*

Steele, Koutroumbis (Villafáñez 68), Berg, Zeca, Lod (Samba 73), Wakaso, Hult, Ledesma (Leto 65), Mesto, Rodrigo Moledo, Ivanov. Coach: Andrea Stramaccioni (ITA)

Red cards: Ivanov 69, Wakaso 90+2

Match 2 - RC Celta de Vigo (ESP)

A 0-2

Steele, Koutroumbis (M'Poku 88), Samba, Ibarbo, Berg, Zeca, Lod, Villafáñez, Ledesma, Rodrigo Moledo, Coulibaly. Coach: Andrea Stramaccioni (ITA)

Match 3 - R. Standard de Liège (BEL)

A 2-2 *Ibarbo (12, 36)*

Steele, Koutroumbis, Samba (Ivanov 46), Ibarbo, Zeca (M'Poku 78), Leto (Lod 74), Villafáñez, Hult, Ledesma, Rodrigo Moledo, Coulibaly. Coach: Andrea Stramaccioni (ITA)

Match 4 - R. Standard de Liège (BEL)

H 0-3

Steele, Chouchoumis, Koutroumbis, Ibarbo (Rinaldi 86), Berg (Leto 30), Lod, Mesto (Hatzigiovannis 77), Rodrigo Moledo, M'Poku, Ivanov, Coulibaly. Coach: Andrea Stramaccioni (ITA)

Red card: M'Poku 77

Match 5 - AFC Ajax (NED)

A 0-2

Steele, Koutroumbis, Samba (Ivanov 57), Ibarbo (Rinaldi 75), Zeca, Lod, Villafáñez (Ledesma 62), Wakaso, Hult, Rodrigo Moledo, Coulibaly. Coach: Andrea Stramaccioni (ITA)

Match 6 - RC Celta de Vigo (ESP)

H 0-2

Steele, Chouchoumis, Zeca, Lod (Koutroumbis 83), Villafáñez (Leto 70), Rinaldi (Ibarbo 60), Wakaso, Mesto, Rodrigo Moledo, M'Poku, Ivanov. Coach: Marinos Ouzounidis (GRE)

PAS Giannina FC

EUROPA LEAGUE

Second qualifying round - Odds BK (NOR)

H 3-0 Mihail (7), *Fonsi (31), Noé Acosta (68)*

Pashalakis, Lila, Berios, Mihail, Giakos (Donis 80), Tzimopoulos, Noé Acosta (Skondras 90+2), Ferfelis (Pedro Conde 77), Fonsi, Karanikas, Kozoronis. Coach: Ioannis Petrakis (GRE)

A 1-3 (aet) *Koutris (98)*

Pashalakis, Lila, Berios, Mihail, Giakos (Maboulou 79), Tzimopoulos, Noé Acosta, Ferfelis (Koutris 66), Fonsi, Karanikas, Kozoronis (Donis 94). Coach: Ioannis Petrakis (GRE)

Third qualifying round - AZ Alkmaar (NED)

A 0-1

Pashalakis, Lila, Berios, Mihail, Giakos (Donis 74), Tzimopoulos, Noé Acosta, Ferfelis (Maboulou 50), Fonsi, Karanikas, Kozoronis (Koutris 61). Coach: Ioannis Petrakis (GRE)

H 1-2 *Pedro Conde (9)*

Pashalakis, Lila, Berios, Mihail, Giakos (Maboulou 51), Tzimopoulos (Skondras 46), Pedro Conde, Noé Acosta, Fonsi, Karanikas, Kozoronis (Donis 78). Coach: Ioannis Petrakis (GRE)

AEK Athens FC

1924 • OACA Spyro Louis (74,767) • aekfc.gr

Major honours

Greek League (11) 1939, 1940, 1963, 1968, 1971, 1978, 1979, 1989, 1992, 1993, 1994; Greek Cup (15) 1932, 1939, 1949, 1950, 1956, 1964, 1966, 1978, 1983, 1996, 1997, 2000, 2002, 2011, 2016

Coach: Temur Ketsbaia (GEO); (18/10/16) José Morais (POR); (19/01/17) Manolo Jiménez (ESP)

Date		Opponent		Score	Scorers
2016					
11/09	h	Xanthi	W	4-1	*Hugo Almeida 2, Mantalos, Dídac Vilà*
17/09	a	Veria	W	2-0	*Bakasetas, Vargas*
26/09	h	Iraklis	D	0-0	
02/10	a	Olympiacos	L	0-3	
17/10	a	Larissa	W	2-1	*Platellas 2*
22/10	h	Panionios	D	0-0	
30/10	a	PAOK	L	0-1	
05/11	h	Atromitos	D	2-2	*Mantalos, Patito Rodríguez*
26/11	h	Platanias	W	3-0	*Mantalos 2, Aravidis*
03/12	a	Kerkyra	D	1-1	*Lambropoulos*
10/12	h	Levadiakos	W	4-0	*André Simões, Pekhart, Galanopoulos, Patito Rodríguez*
19/12	h	Giannina	D	1-1	*Pekhart*
2017					
04/01	h	Panetolikos	D	0-0	
07/01	a	Asteras	L	2-3	*Pekhart 2*
15/01	a	Panathinaikos	D	0-0	
18/01	a	Panetolikos	L	2-3	*Hugo Almeida, Galanopoulos*
22/01	h	Asteras	W	2-0	*Pekhart, Mantalos*
28/01	a	Xanthi	D	0-0	
05/02	h	Veria	W	6-0	*Christodoulopoulos 2, Lambropoulos, Mantalos, og (Tomás), Vranješ*
13/02	a	Iraklis	D	2-2	*Vargas, Christodoulopoulos*
19/02	h	Olympiacos	W	1-0	*Ajdarevic*
26/02	h	Larissa	W	3-0	*Pekhart, Chygrynskiy, Hugo Almeida*
06/03	a	Panionios	D	1-1	*Araujo*
12/03	h	PAOK	W	3-0	*Araujo 2, Aravidis*
18/03	a	Atromitos	W	1-0	*Mantalos*
02/04	h	Panathinaikos	L	2-3	*Christodoulopoulos (p), Pekhart*
06/04	a	Platanias	W	2-0	*Vinícius, Aravidis*
09/04	h	Kerkyra	W	5-0	*Bakasetas 2, Pekhart 2, Dídac Vilà*
23/04	a	Levadiakos	W	2-0	*Araujo, og (Moulopoulos)*
30/04	a	Giannina	D	1-1	*Patito Rodríguez*

No	Name	Nat	DoB	Pos	Aps	(s)	Gls
6	Astrit Ajdarevic	SWE	17/04/90	M	12	(3)	1
8	André Simões	POR	16/12/89	M	20	(2)	1
22	Ioannis Anestis		09/03/91	G	10		
11	Sergio Araujo	ARG	28/01/92	A	7	(2)	4
21	Christos Aravidis		13/03/87	A	8	(5)	3
27	Mihail Bakakis		18/03/91	D	5	(4)	
28	Anastasios Bakasetas		28/06/93	A	11	(7)	3
1	Vasilios Barkas		30/05/94	G	20		
7	Lazaros Christodoulopoulos		19/12/86	M	13	(11)	4
19	Dmytro Chygrynskiy	UKR	07/11/86	D	9	(1)	1
3	Juan Díaz	URU	28/10/87	D	1		
23	Dídac Vilà	ESP	09/06/89	D	26		2
25	Konstantinos Galanopoulos		28/12/97	M	6	(7)	2
9	Hugo Almeida	POR	23/05/84	A	9	(7)	4
18	Jakob Johansson	SWE	21/06/90	M	25	(3)	
26	Dimitrios Kolovetsios		16/10/91	D	19	(1)	
5	Vasilios Lambropoulos		31/03/90	D	21	(2)	2
6	Joleon Lescott	ENG	16/08/82	D	4		
20	Petros Mantalos		31/08/91	M	25	(1)	7
29	Patito Rodríguez	ARG	04/05/90	M	16	(6)	3
14	Tomáš Pekhart	CZE	26/05/89	A	14	(9)	9
11	Evangelos Platellas		01/12/88	M	2	(3)	2
12	Rodrigo Galo	BRA	19/09/86	D	23		
30	Elias Tselios		06/10/97	A		(2)	
10	Ronald Vargas	VEN	02/12/86	M	9	(7)	2
17	Vinícius	BRA	07/03/93	D	3	(3)	1
4	Ognjen Vranješ	BIH	24/10/89	D	12		1

GREECE

Asteras Tripolis FC

1931 • Theodoros Kolokotronis (7,493) • asterastripolis.gr

Coach: Ioakim Havos; (27/09/16) Dimitrios Eleftheropoulos; (19/02/17) (Apostolos Haralambidis); (09/03/17) Staikos Vergetis

2016

10/09 a Panionios L 0-3
19/09 h PAOK L 1-2 *Ioannidis (p)*
25/09 a Atromitos L 0-1
02/10 a Panathinaikos L 1-3 *Ioannidis (p)*
15/10 h Platanias W 2-0 *og (Vanderson), Kaltsas*
22/10 a Kerkyra L 0-2
30/10 h Levadiakos W 1-0 *Fernández*
05/11 a Giannina W 2-1 *Fariña, Mazza*
26/11 h Larissa D 1-1 *Ioannidis (p)*
04/12 a Xanthi L 1-3 *Ioannidis*
10/12 h Veria D 0-0
18/12 a Iraklis D 1-1 *Bertos*

2017

04/01 a Olympiacos L 1-2 *Mazza (p)*
07/01 h AEK W 3-2 *Stanisavljević, Igor Carioca, Tsoukalas*
15/01 h Panetolikos W 4-1 *Stanisavljević 2, Mazza (p), Tsoukalas*
18/01 h Olympiacos D 0-0
22/01 a AEK L 0-2
28/01 h Panionios D 1-1 *Mazza (p)*
05/02 a PAOK L 2-3 *Manias 2*
11/02 h Atromitos L 0-1
18/02 h Panathinaikos L 0-5
25/02 a Platanias L 0-3
05/03 h Kerkyra L 1-2 *Mazza*
13/03 a Levadiakos D 1-1 *Manias*
19/03 h Giannina D 1-1 *Manias*
02/04 a Panetolikos D 1-1 *Mazza*
05/04 a Larissa W 4-1 *Manias 3 (1p), Mazza (p)*
09/04 h Xanthi D 0-0
23/04 a Veria L 3-4 *Manias 3*
30/04 h Iraklis D 2-2 *Kyriakopoulos, Gondo (p)*

No	Name	Nat	DoB	Pos	Aps	(s)	Gls
30	Georgios Athanasiadis		07/04/93	G	3		
29	Ioannis Bastianos		29/04/98	M	1	(1)	
4	Emmanouil Bertos		13/05/89	D	21		1
9	Cristian Chávez	ARG	16/06/86	M		(1)	
21	Elini Dimoutsos		18/06/88	M	16	(4)	
90	Antonio Donnarumma	ITA	07/07/90	G	21		
2	Dudú	BRA	14/03/89	M		(1)	
35	Elias Evangelou		18/05/97	D	2	(1)	
20	Luis Fariña	ARG	20/04/91	M	17	(7)	1
11	Nicolás Fernández	ARG	17/11/86	M	6	(2)	1
3	Vitali Gaiduchik	BLR	12/07/89	D	4	(1)	
18	Konstantinos Giannoulis		09/12/87	D	28		
6	Cedric Gondo	CIV	25/11/96	A	2	(5)	1
54	Rachid Hamdani	MAR	08/04/85	D	17	(8)	
17	Walter Iglesias	ARG	18/04/85	M	14	(5)	
96	Igor Carioca	BRA	21/08/96	D	13	(2)	1
10	Nikolaos Ioannidis		26/04/94	A	13	(13)	4
23	Nikolaos Kaltsas		03/05/90	M	18	(4)	1
1	Tomáš Košický	SVK	11/03/86	G	6		
27	Ioannis Kotsiras		16/12/92	M	3	(5)	
8	Dimitrios Kourbelis		02/11/93	M	4		
77	Georgios Kyriakopoulos		05/02/96	D	3	(5)	1
11	Mihail Manias		20/02/90	A	18		10
7	Pablo Mazza	ARG	21/12/87	M	21	(6)	7
4	Sonhy Sefil	FRA	16/06/94	D	5		
33	Yevhen Selin	UKR	09/05/88	D	18		
31	Aleksandar Stanisavljević	SRB	11/06/89	M	8	(8)	3
5	Konstantinos Triantafyllopoulos		03/04/93	D	4	(1)	
19	Kosmas Tsilianidis		09/05/94	A	15	(7)	
13	Stavros Tsoukalas		23/05/88	M	28	(1)	2
69	Lionel Zouma	FRA	10/09/93	D	1		

Atromitos FC

1923 • Dimotiko Peristeriou (9,000) • atromitosfc.gr

Coach: Traianos Dellas; (19/09/16) (Georgios Korakakis); (06/02/17) Ricardo Sá Pinto (POR)

2016

11/09 a Giannina L 0-3
18/09 h Panetolikos L 0-2
25/09 h Asteras W 1-0 *Umbides*
03/10 a Xanthi D 0-0
16/10 h Veria W 1-0 *Tonso*
23/10 a Iraklis W 2-1 *Umbides (p), Tonso*
29/10 h Olympiacos L 0-1
05/11 a AEK D 2-2 *Le Tallec, Umbides*
28/11 a PAOK W 4-3 *Le Tallec, Umbides (p), Papadopoulos, Tonso*
04/12 a Larissa W 2-1 *Limnios, Le Tallec*
11/12 h Panathinaikos L 0-1
17/12 a Platanias L 0-3

2017

04/01 a Kerkyra D 1-1 *Le Tallec*
07/01 h Levadiakos W 2-0 *Tonso 2*
15/01 h Panionios L 1-2 *Umbides (p)*
18/01 h Kerkyra L 1-4 *Fitanidis*
22/01 a Levadiakos D 1-1 *Le Tallec*
29/01 h Giannina D 1-1 *Le Tallec*
04/02 a Panetolikos L 0-2
11/02 a Asteras W 1-0 *Dauda*
18/02 h Xanthi W 2-1 *Platellas, Tonso*
27/02 a Veria W 1-0 *Diguiny*
05/03 h Iraklis W 1-0 *Vasiliou*
12/03 a Olympiacos L 0-2
18/03 h AEK L 0-1
02/04 a Panionios L 1-2 *Diguiny*
05/04 h PAOK L 0-2
09/04 h Larissa D 0-0
23/04 a Panathinaikos L 0-1
30/04 h Platanias W 4-1 *Dauda, Diguiny 2, og (Fouflia)*

No	Name	Nat	DoB	Pos	Aps	(s)	Gls
5	Dmitri Baga	BLR	04/01/90	M	21	(5)	
25	Mihail Bastakos		27/07/96	M		(1)	
3	Mariano Bíttolo	ARG	24/04/90	D	11	(2)	
27	Abiola Dauda	NGA	03/02/88	A	8	(4)	2
14	Nicolas Diguiny	FRA	31/05/88	M	7	(3)	4
7	Eduardo Brito	BRA	21/09/82	M	6	(9)	
6	Sokratis Fitanidis		25/05/84	D	25		1
35	Andrei Gorbunov	BLR	25/05/83	G	29		
31	Spiridon Gougoudis		17/04/89	M	1		
32	Dimitrios Grontis		21/08/94	M	1		
30	Alexandros Katranis		04/05/98	D	16	(1)	
15	Paul Keita	SEN	26/06/92	M	9	(3)	
2	Ioannis Kontoes		24/05/86	D	9	(5)	
21	Pavlos Kyriakidis		03/09/91	M	9	(4)	
19	Kyriakos Kyvrakidis		21/07/92	D	22		
24	Nikolaos Lazaridis		12/07/79	D	18		
9	Anthony Le Tallec	FRA	03/10/84	A	18	(8)	6
29	Dimitrios Limnios		27/05/98	M	17	(8)	1
22	Ioannis Maniatis		12/10/86	M	9	(2)	
28	Spyridon Natsos		09/06/98	M		(1)	
3	Athanasios Panteliadis		06/09/87	D	3		
11	Dimitrios Papadopoulos		20/10/81	A	4	(6)	1
17	Evangelos Platellas		01/12/88	M	11	(5)	1
18	Miloš Stojčev	MNE	19/01/87	M	5	(2)	
33	Christos Theodorakis		17/09/96	G	1		
10	Martín Tonso	ARG	19/10/89	M	23	(4)	6
11	Dimitrios Tsatsopoulos		12/04/96	A		(1)	
8	Javier Umbides	ARG	09/02/82	M	25	(2)	5
20	Thomas Vasiliou		28/07/94	M	8	(9)	1
13	Georgios Zisopoulos		23/05/84	D	14	(4)	

Iraklis FC

1908 • Kaftanzoglio (29,080) • fciraklis.gr

Major honours
Greek Cup (1) 1976

Coach: Nikos Papadopoulos; (18/10/16) (Ioannis Amanatidis); (01/11/16) Savvas Pantelidis

2016

12/09 a Larissa D 2-2 *Lambrou, Leozinho*
18/09 h Olympiacos L 1-2 *Perrone*
26/09 a AEK D 0-0
01/10 h Panionios L 1-2 *Leozinho*
16/10 a PAOK L 0-1
23/10 h Atromitos L 1-2 *Loukinas*
30/10 a Panathinaikos L 0-2
07/11 h Platanias D 1-1 *Kyriakidis*
27/11 a Levadiakos L 0-3
05/12 h Giannina W 2-1 *Perrone, Angelopoulos*
11/12 a Panetolikos L 0-2
18/12 h Asteras D 1-1 *Kyriakidis*

2017

03/01 h Xanthi L 0-1
18/01 a Xanthi L 1-3 *Passas*
21/01 h Veria D 1-1 *Stamou*
25/01 a Veria W 2-0 *Grontis, Leozinho (p)*
28/01 h Larissa D 1-1 *og (Rentzas)*
01/02 h Kerkyra D 0-0
05/02 a Olympiacos L 0-3
13/02 h AEK D 2-2 *Perrone, Monteiro*
19/02 a Panionios L 0-1
26/02 h PAOK D 1-1 *Bastakos*
05/03 a Atromitos L 0-1
11/03 h Panathinaikos D 1-1 *og (Thelander)*
20/03 a Platanias L 0-1
02/04 a Kerkyra W 3-0 *Leozinho, Donis, Kouros*
05/04 h Levadiakos W 1-0 *Donis*
09/04 a Giannina W 2-1 *Bastakos, Donis*
23/04 h Panetolikos W 2-1 *Perrone, Bastakos*
30/04 a Asteras D 2-2 *Ziabaris, Donis*

No	Name	Nat	DoB	Pos	Aps	(s)	Gls
23	Vasilios Amarantidis		02/04/97	A		(1)	
14	Vasilios Angelopoulos		12/02/97	M	9	(10)	1
4	Leonidas Argiropoulos		29/05/90	D	12		
94	Argyrios Barettas		06/05/94	A		(1)	
22	Sebastián Bartolini	ARG	01/02/82	D	11		
22	Mihail Bastakos		27/07/96	M	2	(8)	3
18	Christos Donis		09/10/94	M	15		4
40	Serafeim Giannikoglou		25/03/93	G	2		
21	Dimitrios Grontis		21/08/94	M	8	(7)	1
1	Huanderson	BRA	03/08/83	G	26		
19	Antonios Iliadis		27/07/93	A		(3)	
8	Eleftherios Intzoglou		03/03/87	M	24	(2)	
2	Vasilios Karagounis		18/01/94	D	3	(8)	
55	Alexandros Kouros		21/08/93	M	27		1
26	Panagiotis Kynigopoulos		24/09/96	M		(6)	
19	Pavlos Kyriakidis		03/09/91	M	11		2
80	Lazaros Lambrou		19/12/97	A	7	(3)	1
10	Leozinho	BRA	12/12/85	M	22	(5)	4
25	Ioannis Loukinas		20/09/91	A	5	(8)	1
27	Monteiro	POR	15/08/88	M	25	(1)	1
11	Ioannis Passas		07/10/90	M	13	(13)	1
30	Dušan Perniš	SVK	28/11/84	G	2		
9	Emanuel Perrone	ARG	14/06/83	A	21	(2)	4
16	Albert Roussos		22/02/96	D	14	(2)	
3	Georgios Saramantas		29/01/92	D	25	(2)	
5	Dimitrios Stamou		27/04/91	D	18		1
4	Ioannis Tsotras		30/04/96	D		(1)	
6	Adam Tzanetopoulos		10/02/95	D	17		
42	Dimitrios Vosnakidis		14/02/94	D	1	(2)	
33	Nikolaos Ziabaris		18/02/91	D	10	(3)	1

Kerkyra FC

1968 • Ethniko Athlitiko Kentro (EAK) Kerkyras (2,685) • aokkerkyra.gr

Coach: Mihail-Rizos Grigoriou; (10/04/17) (Kostas Christoforakis)

Date		Opponent		Score	Scorers
2016					
10/09	h	Platanias	L	0-1	
18/09	h	Larissa	W	2-0	*Ellong, Epstein*
25/09	a	Levadiakos	L	1-2	*Arnarellis*
01/10	h	Giannina	L	0-1	
15/10	a	Panetolikos	L	0-4	
22/10	h	Asteras	W	2-0	*Thuram 2*
29/10	a	Xanthi	D	0-0	
06/11	h	Veria	W	2-0	*og (Iván Malón), Thuram*
27/11	a	Olympiacos	D	0-0	
03/12	h	AEK	D	1-1	*Thuram*
11/12	a	Panionios	L	0-1	
17/12	h	PAOK	L	0-5	
2017					
04/01	h	Atromitos	D	1-1	*Kontos*
09/01	a	Panathinaikos	L	0-1	
18/01	a	Atromitos	W	4-1	*Epstein, og (Lazaridis), Ellong, Georgakopoulos*
22/01	h	Panathinaikos	D	1-1	*Epstein*
29/01	a	Platanias	L	1-2	*Thuram*
01/02	a	Iraklis	D	0-0	
04/02	a	Larissa	D	1-1	*Nikić*
12/02	h	Levadiakos	W	1-0	*Gomes*
18/02	a	Giannina	L	0-1	
25/02	h	Panetolikos	D	0-0	
05/03	a	Asteras	W	2-1	*Thuram 2*
12/03	h	Xanthi	W	1-0	*Diogo*
18/03	a	Veria	L	0-4	
02/04	h	Iraklis	L	0-3	
05/04	h	Olympiacos	L	0-2	
09/04	a	AEK	L	0-5	
23/04	h	Panionios	W	1-0	*Epstein*
30/04	a	PAOK	L	1-5	*Pamlidis*

No	Name	Nat	DoB	Pos	Aps	(s)	Gls
92	Moise Adilehou	FRA	01/11/95	D	1	(3)	
21	Kyriakos Andreopoulos		18/01/94	M	9	(6)	
1	Ioannis Arabatzis		28/05/84	G	3		
9	Alexandros Arnarellis		01/10/91	A		(1)	1
3	Vladimir Dimitrovski	MKD	30/11/88	D	13	(4)	
29	Kevin Diogo	FRA	08/07/91	M	7		1
18	Viera Ellong	EQG	14/06/87	M	9	(9)	2
26	Denis Epstein	GER	02/07/86	M	21	(5)	4
20	Efthimios Gamagas		26/09/95	A		(1)	
77	Konstantinos Georgakopoulos		03/01/94	A	2	(11)	1
7	Fotios Georgiou		19/07/85	M	15	(5)	
11	Mathieu Gomes	FRA	06/03/85	D	17	(7)	1
55	Christos Gromitsaris		10/02/91	D	1	(1)	
23	Efstratios Hintzidis		13/12/87	D		(1)	
24	Ioannis Ioannou		09/04/84	D	25	(1)	
30	Jordão Diogo	STP	12/11/85	D	15	(1)	
2	Paul Keita	SEN	26/06/92	M	4	(1)	
19	Alexandros Kontos		12/09/86	M	16	(10)	1
13	Fotios Koutzavasilis		11/03/89	G	27		
4	David Nazim	NGA	07/11/96	M	1	(1)	
83	Branislav Nikić	BIH	15/08/83	M	15	(6)	1
9	Ifeanyi Onyilo	NGA	31/10/90	A	1	(2)	
14	Georgios Pamlidis		13/11/93	M	1	(5)	1
22	Stefanos Siondis		04/09/87	M	28		
17	Spiridon Spinoulas		08/04/86	D	21	(1)	
50	Thuram	BRA	01/02/91	A	24		7
80	Dimitrios Trepeklis		17/01/98	D		(1)	
6	Marios Tzanoulinos		15/04/96	D		(1)	
5	Anastasios Venetis		24/03/80	D	20		
33	Ioannis Zaradoukas		12/12/85	D	15	(2)	
7	Panagiotis Zorbas		21/04/87	M	19	(3)	

AE Larissa FC

1964 • AEL FC Arena (16,118) • aelfc.gr

Major honours
Greek League (1) 1988; Greek Cup (2) 1985, 2007

Coach: Angelos Anastasiadis; (01/11/16) Sakis Tsiolis; (22/03/17) (Theodoros Voutyritsas); (03/04/17) André Paus (NED)

Date		Opponent		Score	Scorers
2016					
12/09	h	Iraklis	D	2-2	*Avraam 2*
18/09	a	Kerkyra	L	0-2	
25/09	h	Olympiacos	W	1-0	*Golias*
01/10	a	Levadiakos	D	1-1	*Dodô*
17/10	h	AEK	L	1-2	*Nazlidis*
23/10	a	Giannina	L	0-4	
29/10	h	Panionios	W	2-0	*Varela (p), Nazlidis*
06/11	a	Panetolikos	L	1-2	*Nazlidis*
26/11	a	Asteras	D	1-1	*Nazlidis (p)*
04/12	h	Atromitos	L	1-2	*Maroukakis*
10/12	a	Xanthi	L	0-1	
18/12	h	Panathinaikos	D	0-0	
2017					
04/01	h	Veria	W	2-1	*Gállego, Nazlidis (p)*
08/01	a	Platanias	L	2-3	*Nazlidis 2 (1p)*
18/01	a	Veria	D	1-1	*Ikaunieks*
22/01	h	Platanias	D	0-0	
28/01	a	Iraklis	D	1-1	*Rentzas*
01/02	h	PAOK	L	0-2	
04/02	h	Kerkyra	D	1-1	*Nazlidis*
11/02	a	Olympiacos	L	0-2	
20/02	h	Levadiakos	W	2-1	*Aganović, Rentzas*
26/02	a	AEK	L	0-3	
04/03	h	Giannina	D	1-1	*Jovanović*
11/03	a	Panionios	L	0-1	
18/03	h	Panetolikos	W	1-0	*Farkaš*
02/04	a	PAOK	L	0-2	
05/04	h	Asteras	L	1-4	*Nazlidis*
09/04	a	Atromitos	D	0-0	
23/04	h	Xanthi	W	1-0	*Anastasopoulos*
17/04	a	Panathinaikos	L	0-2	

No	Name	Nat	DoB	Pos	Aps	(s)	Gls
20	Adnan Aganović	CRO	03/10/87	M	8		1
4	Nikolaos Anastasopoulos		01/02/93	M	13	(4)	1
64	Fatjon Andoni	ALB	19/06/91	M	24	(1)	
11	Andreas Avraam	CYP	06/06/87	M	18	(5)	2
99	Alejandro Chacopino	ESP	05/11/88	A	3	(4)	
32	Matías Degra	ARG	18/06/83	G	1		
77	Miloš Deletić	SRB	13/10/93	M	20	(6)	
54	Dodô	BRA	16/10/87	A	8	(1)	1
96	James Evmorfidis		18/01/96	M		(2)	
26	Pavol Farkaš	SVK	27/03/85	D	27		1
97	Pablo Gállego	ESP	01/10/93	M	2	(4)	1
16	Nikolaos Golias		29/07/93	D	17	(3)	1
13	Francisco Pol Hurtado	VEN	17/09/87	M	3	(1)	
24	Jānis Ikaunieks	LVA	16/02/95	M	8	(2)	1
5	Borislav Jovanović	SRB	16/08/86	D	14	(2)	1
19	Dimitrios Kapos		28/08/93	A	4	(8)	
31	Zaharias Kavousakis		11/01/89	G	4		
23	Owusu-Ansah Kontor	GHA	24/08/93	D	14	(5)	
8	Vasilios Koutsianikoulis		09/08/88	M		(7)	
37	Andreas Lambropoulos		30/07/88	A	1	(6)	
9	Mattheos Maroukakis		04/01/90	A	2	(3)	1
12	Lehlogonolo Masalesa	RSA	21/03/92	M	13	(1)	
21	Ioannis Masouras		24/08/96	M		(2)	
6	Emmanouil Moniakis		09/11/88	D	12	(1)	
7	Thomas Nazlidis		23/10/87	A	29		9
92	Ioannis Potouridis		27/02/92	M	4	(2)	
44	Amit Quluzadä	AZE	20/11/92	M	1	(3)	
18	Vasilios Rentzas		16/04/92	D	23	(2)	2
9	Diego Reyes	HON	13/01/90	A	1	(3)	
35	Dimitrios Souliotis		23/07/95	D	1		
25	Konstantinos Theodoropoulos		27/03/90	G	8	(1)	
15	Steven Thicot	FRA	14/02/87	D	6	(2)	
10	Nicolás Varela	URU	19/01/91	M	14	(5)	1
67	Gennadios Xenodochov		30/05/88	G	17		
30	Ximo Navarro	ESP	12/09/88	M	10	(3)	

Levadiakos FC

1961 • Dimotiko Livadias (6,200) • levadiakosfc.gr

Coach: Ratko Dostanić (SRB); (12/01/17) Ioannis Christopoulos; (07/04/17) (Dimitrios Farantos)

Date		Opponent		Score	Scorers
2016					
10/09	h	Panathinaikos	L	0-3	
17/09	a	Platanias	L	2-3	*Karachalios, Giakoumakis*
25/09	h	Kerkyra	W	2-1	*Toni Silva, Mantzios*
01/10	h	Larissa	D	1-1	*Toni Silva*
23/10	h	Panetolikos	W	2-1	*Giakoumakis, Toni Silva*
30/10	a	Asteras	L	0-1	
05/11	h	Xanthi	D	1-1	*Ouon*
23/11	a	Giannina	D	0-0	
27/11	h	Iraklis	W	3-0	*Giakoumakis, Toni Silva, Mantzios*
04/12	a	Olympiacos	L	0-4	
10/12	a	AEK	L	0-4	
18/12	h	Panionios	L	1-4	*Giakoumakis*
2017					
03/01	h	PAOK	L	0-1	
07/01	a	Atromitos	L	0-2	
14/01	a	Veria	L	0-2	
19/01	a	PAOK	L	0-3	
22/01	h	Atromitos	D	1-1	*Youssouf*
29/01	a	Panathinaikos	D	0-0	
06/02	h	Platanias	L	1-2	*Toni Silva (p)*
12/02	a	Kerkyra	L	0-1	
20/02	a	Larissa	L	1-2	*Kaltsas*
26/02	h	Giannina	W	2-1	*Vasiliou, Carlos Milhazes (p)*
04/03	a	Panetolikos	L	0-2	
13/03	h	Asteras	D	1-1	*Vasiliou*
19/03	a	Xanthi	D	2-2	*Vasiliou, Toni Silva*
01/04	h	Veria	W	3-1	*Carlos Milhazes (p), Vasiliou, Giakoumakis*
05/04	a	Iraklis	L	0-1	
09/04	h	Olympiacos	D	1-1	*Vasiliou*
23/04	h	AEK	L	0-2	
30/04	a	Panionios	W	3-1	*Karaboué, Mendy, Giakoumakis*

No	Name	Nat	DoB	Pos	Aps	(s)	Gls
14	Chakhir Belghazouani	MAR	06/10/86	M	3	(2)	
55	Carlos Milhazes	POR	17/03/81	D	24	(1)	2
86	Chumbinho	BRA	21/09/86	M	5	(3)	
5	Gary Coulibaly	FRA	30/03/86	M	21	(3)	
20	Petros Giakoumakis		03/07/92	M	19	(8)	6
27	Nikolaos V Kaltsas		28/06/89	M	15	(9)	1
7	Mattheos Kapsaskis		12/08/96	M	2	(6)	
88	Lossémy Karaboué	CIV	18/03/88	M	12	(6)	1
21	Zisis Karachalios		10/01/96	D	10	(4)	1
18	Qazim Laçi	ALB	19/01/96	M	5	(5)	
16	Antonios Magas		28/02/94	D		(2)	
6	Dimitrios Maheras		16/08/90	M	15	(5)	
9	Evangelos Mantzios		22/04/83	A	18		2
23	Jackson Mendy	SEN	25/05/87	D	18	(3)	1
28	Theodoros Moshonas		03/12/90	G	2	(1)	
81	Athanasios Moulopoulos		09/06/85	D	21	(1)	
1	Stanislav Namasco	MDA	10/11/86	G	28		
15	Ibrahima Niasse	SEN	18/04/88	M	8	(1)	
29	Edwin Ouon	RWA	26/01/81	D	28		1
77	Konstantinos Pappas		30/11/91	M	1	(1)	
97	Leonard Senka	ALB	26/02/97	M		(3)	
17	Toni Silva	GNB	15/09/93	M	22	(1)	6
12	Marius Topi		19/10/95	D		(2)	
2	Theodoros Tripotseris		04/03/86	D	16	(2)	
11	Stilianos Vasiliou		29/04/91	A	9	(12)	5
44	Praxitelis Vouros		05/05/95	D	9	(1)	
39	Mohamed Youssouf	COM	26/03/88	M	5	(4)	1
8	Zézinho	GNB	23/09/92	M	14	(3)	

GREECE

Olympiacos FC

1925 • Georgios Karaiskakis (32,130) • olympiacos.org

Major honours
Greek League (44) 1931, 1933, 1934, 1936, 1937, 1938, 1947, 1948, 1951, 1954, 1955, 1956, 1957, 1958, 1959, 1966, 1967, 1973, 1974, 1975, 1980, 1981, 1982, 1983, 1987, 1997, 1998, 1999, 2000, 2001, 2002, 2003, 2005, 2006, 2007, 2008, 2009, 2011, 2012, 2013, 2014, 2015, 2016, 2017; Greek Cup (27) 1947, 1951, 1952, 1953, 1954, 1957, 1958, 1959, 1960, 1961, 1963, 1965, 1968, 1971, 1973, 1975, 1981, 1990, 1992, 1999, 2005, 2006, 2008, 2009, 2012, 2013, 2015

Coach: Víctor Sánchez (ESP); (11/08/16) Paulo Bento (POR); (06/03/17) (Vasilios Vouzas); (23/03/17) Takis Lemonis

2016

11/09	h	Veria	W	6-1	*Ideye 3, Sebá, Elyounoussi, Milivojević*
18/09	a	Iraklis	W	2-1	*Domínguez (p), Ideye*
25/09	a	Larissa	L	0-1	
02/10	h	AEK	W	3-0	*Ideye, André Martins, Fortounis*
15/10	a	Panionios	W	2-0	*Botía, Milivojević*
23/10	h	PAOK	W	2-1	*og (Varela), Milivojević*
29/10	a	Atromitos	W	1-0	*Ideye*
06/11	h	Panathinaikos	W	3-0	*Botía, Elyounoussi, Ideye*
27/11	h	Kerkyra	D	0-0	
04/12	h	Levadiakos	W	4-0	*Ideye 2, Milivojević, Fortounis*
12/12	a	Giannina	W	2-0	*Cardozo, Sebá*
18/12	h	Panetolikos	W	3-1	*Sebá, Cardozo, Diogo Figueiras*
2017					
04/01	h	Asteras	W	2-1	*Fortounis, Marin*
08/01	a	Xanthi	W	2-0	*Ideye, Milivojević*
14/01	a	Platanias	D	2-2	*Ideye 2*
18/01	a	Asteras	D	0-0	
21/01	h	Xanthi	W	2-0	*og (Svarnas), Manthatis*
29/01	a	Veria	W	2-1	*Fortounis, Milivojević*
05/02	h	Iraklis	W	3-0	*Bruno Viana, Elyounoussi, Fortounis*
11/02	h	Larissa	W	2-0	*Androutsos, Ideye*
19/02	a	AEK	L	0-1	
26/02	h	Panionios	L	0-1	
05/03	a	PAOK	L	0-2	
12/03	h	Atromitos	W	2-0	*Manuel da Costa, og (Fitanidis)*
19/03	a	Panathinaikos	L	0-1	
01/04	h	Platanias	W	2-1	*Marin, Romao*
05/04	a	Kerkyra	W	2-0	*Fortounis, Marin*
09/04	a	Levadiakos	D	1-1	*Cardozo*
23/04	h	Giannina	W	5-0	*Marin, Manuel da Costa, De la Bella 2, Domínguez (p)*
30/04	a	Panetolikos	W	2-0	*Domínguez, Elyounoussi*

No	Name	Nat	DoB	Pos	Aps	(s)	Gls
28	André Martins	POR	21/01/90	M	19	(5)	1
32	Athanasios Androutsos		06/05/97	M	8	(9)	1
17	Karim Ansarifard	IRN	03/04/90	A	5	(4)	
3	Alberto Botía	ESP	27/01/89	D	20		2
8	Andreas Bouhalakis		05/04/93	M	2	(6)	
36	Bruno Viana	BRA	05/02/95	D	14	(3)	1
19	Esteban Cambiasso	ARG	18/08/80	M	6	(8)	
9	Óscar Cardozo	PAR	20/05/83	A	9	(13)	3
22	Aly Cissokho	FRA	15/09/87	D	3		
24	Alberto de la Bella	ESP	02/12/85	D	20		2
77	Diogo Figueiras	POR	07/01/91	D	24		1
10	Alejandro Domínguez	ARG	10/06/81	M	5	(6)	3
14	Omar Elabdellaoui	NOR	05/12/91	D	1	(1)	
18	Tarik Elyounoussi	NOR	23/02/88	M	18	(5)	4
7	Kostas Fortounis		16/10/92	M	23	(2)	6
21	Gonçalo Paciência	POR	01/08/94	A		(1)	
99	Brown Ideye	NGA	10/10/88	A	16	(4)	13
27	Stefanos Kapino		18/03/94	G	18		
31	Nicola Leali	ITA	17/02/93	G	12	(1)	
52	Georgios Manthatis		11/05/97	M	3	(8)	1
6	Manuel da Costa	MAR	06/05/86	D	17		2
11	Marko Marin	GER	13/03/89	M	11	(3)	4
5	Luka Milivojević	SRB	07/04/91	M	17		6
43	Dimitrios Nikolaou		13/08/98	D	2		
90	Felipe Pardo	COL	17/08/90	A	2	(5)	
44	Juan Carlos Paredes	ECU	08/07/87	D	4		
45	Panagiotis Retsos		09/08/98	D	14	(4)	
4	Alaixys Romao	TOG	18/01/84	M	10	(1)	1
92	Sebá	BRA	08/06/92	M	26		3
20	Konstantinos Tsimikas		12/05/96	D	1		

Panathinaikos FC

1908 • Apostolos Nikolaidis (16,003) • pao.gr

Major honours
Greek League (20) 1930, 1949, 1953, 1960, 1961, 1962, 1964, 1965, 1969, 1970, 1972, 1977, 1984, 1986, 1990, 1991, 1995, 1996, 2004, 2010; Greek Cup (18) 1940, 1948, 1955, 1967, 1969, 1977, 1982, 1984, 1986, 1988, 1989, 1991, 1993, 1994, 1995, 2004, 2010, 2014

Coach: Andrea Stramaccioni (ITA); (01/12/16) Marinos Ouzounidis

2016

10/09	a	Levadiakos	W	3-0	*Ledesma (p), Wakaso, Leto*
18/09	h	Giannina	W	4-0	*Berg 2, Lod, Leto*
24/09	a	Panetolikos	D	0-0	
02/10	h	Asteras	W	3-1	*Berg, Ledesma 2 (2p)*
16/10	h	Xanthi	L	1-2	*Leto*
24/10	a	Veria	D	1-1	*Berg*
30/10	h	Iraklis	W	2-0	*Leto, M'Poku*
06/11	a	Olympiacos	L	0-3	
27/11	a	Panionios	D	1-1	*Villafáñez*
04/12	h	PAOK	W	1-0	*Lod*
11/12	a	Atromitos	W	1-0	*Berg*
18/12	a	Larissa	D	0-0	
2017					
05/01	a	Platanias	L	0-1	
09/01	h	Kerkyra	W	1-0	*Leto*
15/01	h	AEK	D	0-0	
19/01	h	Platanias	W	2-1	*Berg 2 (1p)*
22/01	a	Kerkyra	D	1-1	*Berg*
29/01	h	Levadiakos	D	0-0	
04/02	a	Giannina	D	1-1	*Berg*
12/02	h	Panetolikos	W	4-0	*Berg 3, Lod*
18/02	a	Asteras	W	5-0	*Klonaridis, Berg, Rodrigo Moledo, M'Poku, Boumale*
25/02	a	Xanthi	L	0-1	
04/03	h	Veria	W	5-0	*Berg 3 (2p), Klonaridis, Villafáñez*
11/03	a	Iraklis	D	1-1	*Berg (p)*
19/03	h	Olympiacos	W	1-0	*Berg*
02/04	a	AEK	W	3-2	*Klonaridis, Berg 2*
06/04	h	Panionios	W	1-0	*Berg (p)*
09/04	a	PAOK	L	0-3	
23/04	h	Atromitos	W	1-0	*Molins*
30/04	h	Larissa	W	2-0	*Leto, Berg*

No	Name	Nat	DoB	Pos	Aps	(s)	Gls
9	Marcus Berg	SWE	17/08/86	A	28		22
7	Olivier Boumale	CMR	17/09/89	M	8	(7)	1
3	Diamantis Chouchoumis		17/07/94	D	5	(1)	
78	Ousmane Coulibaly	MLI	09/07/89	D	17		
41	Stefanos Evangelou		12/05/98	D	7		
39	Anastasios Hatzigiovannis		31/05/97	M	1	(4)	
23	Niklas Hult	SWE	13/02/90	M	23	(1)	
8	Víctor Ibarbo	COL	19/05/90	A	7	(1)	
51	Ivan Ivanov	BUL	25/02/88	D	7		
14	Viktor Klonaridis	BEL	28/07/92	A	10		3
21	Dimitrios Kourbelis		02/11/93	M	14	(1)	
4	Georgios Koutroumbis		10/02/91	D	22		
24	Cristian Ledesma	ITA	24/09/82	M	6		3
11	Sebastián Leto	ARG	30/08/86	M	7	(11)	6
17	Robin Lod	FIN	17/04/93	M	20	(6)	3
40	Paul-José M'Poku	COD	19/04/92	M	12	(10)	2
12	Nikolaos Marinakis		12/09/93	D	5	(2)	
27	Giandomenico Mesto	ITA	25/05/82	D	11	(1)	
38	Theodoros Mingos		06/02/98	M		(1)	
8	Guillermo Molins	SWE	26/09/88	A	1	(3)	1
5	Nuno Reis	POR	31/01/91	M	4	(11)	
49	Sotirios Pispas		08/01/98	A		(2)	
20	Lautaro Rinaldi	ARG	30/12/93	A		(8)	
31	Rodrigo Moledo	BRA	27/10/87	D	16	(3)	1
6	Christopher Samba	CGO	28/03/84	D	2		
34	Paschalis Staikos		08/02/96	M		(1)	
15	Luke Steele	ENG	24/09/84	G	9		
25	Rasmus Thelander	DEN	09/07/91	D	7	(1)	
19	Lucas Villafáñez	ARG	04/10/91	M	24	(3)	2
99	Odysseas Vlahodimos	GER	26/04/94	G	21		
71	Panagiotis Vlahodimos		11/10/91	M	5	(9)	
22	Wakaso Mubarak	GHA	25/07/90	M	8		1
10	Zeca		31/08/88	M	23		

Panetolikos GFS

1926 • Panetolikou (6,000) • panetolikos.gr

Coach: Ioannis Matzourakis; (17/01/17) (Ioannis Dalakouras); (22/01/17) Ioakim Havos

2016

Date		Opponent		Score	Scorers
11/09	a	PAOK	L	1-2	*Warda*
18/09	a	Atromitos	W	2-0	*Miguel Rodrigues, Warda*
24/09	h	Panathinaikos	D	0-0	
02/10	a	Platanias	D	0-0	
15/10	h	Kerkyra	W	4-0	*Tomané, Marcos Paulo 2, Farley Rosa*
23/10	a	Levadiakos	L	1-2	*Markovski (p)*
31/10	h	Giannina	L	1-2	*Ferreyra*
06/11	h	Larissa	W	2-1	*Warda, Markovski*
27/11	h	Xanthi	L	2-3	*Warda (p), Luís Rocha*
03/12	a	Veria	D	1-1	*Makos*
11/12	h	Iraklis	W	2-0	*Clésio, Markovski*
18/12	a	Olympiacos	L	1-3	*Kousas*

2017

Date		Opponent		Score	Scorers
04/01	a	AEK	D	0-0	
08/01	h	Panionios	L	0-2	
15/01	a	Asteras	L	1-4	*Muñoz*
18/01	h	AEK	W	3-2	*Markovski (p), Makos 2*
21/01	a	Panionios	L	0-2	
29/01	h	PAOK	L	0-1	
04/02	h	Atromitos	W	2-0	*Markovski, Muñoz*
12/02	a	Panathinaikos	L	0-4	
19/02	h	Platanias	L	1-2	*Álvaro Rey*
25/02	a	Kerkyra	D	0-0	
04/03	h	Levadiakos	W	2-0	*Papadopoulos, Markovski*
11/03	a	Giannina	D	0-0	
18/03	a	Larissa	L	0-1	
02/04	h	Asteras	D	1-1	*Álvaro Rey*
05/04	a	Xanthi	L	0-3	
09/04	h	Veria	W	1-0	*Farley Rosa*
23/04	a	Iraklis	L	1-2	*Farley Rosa*
30/04	h	Olympiacos	L	0-2	

No	Name	Nat	DoB	Pos	Aps	(s)	Gls
16	Álvaro Rey	ESP	11/07/89	M	8	(1)	2
6	Federico Bravo	ARG	05/10/93	M	6	(3)	
10	Clésio	MOZ	11/10/94	A	21	(4)	1
30	Diego Lopes	BRA	03/05/94	M	11	(3)	
8	Farley Rosa	BRA	14/01/94	M	12	(7)	3
11	Osmar Ferreyra	ARG	09/01/83	M	9	(2)	1
29	Elias Gianniotis		05/04/97	M		(2)	
44	Dimitrios Hantakias		04/01/95	D	16	(1)	
36	Wilson Kamavuaka	COD	29/03/90	D	2	(5)	
5	Georgios Kousas		12/08/82	D	29		1
2	Dimitrios Koutromanos		25/02/87	D	5	(12)	
82	Dimitrios Kyriakidis		24/06/86	G	30		
27	Emmanuel Ledesma	ITA	24/05/88	M	3	(6)	
20	Luís Rocha	POR	27/06/93	D	14	(8)	1
14	Grigorios Makos		18/01/87	M	24	(1)	3
3	Alexandros Malis		19/03/97	D		(1)	
17	Marcos Paulo	BRA	13/07/88	M	27		2
15	Marko Markovski	SRB	26/05/86	A	17	(8)	6
22	Georgios Migas		07/04/94	D	21		
4	Miguel Rodrigues	POR	16/03/93	D	14	(1)	1
7	Fabián Muñoz	ARG	03/11/91	A	7	(12)	2
11	Dimitrios Papadopoulos		20/10/81	A	4	(5)	1
12	Anastasios Papazoglou		24/09/88	D	4	(1)	
28	Stefanos Papoutsogiannopoulos		10/08/94	M		(2)	
9	Tomané	POR	23/10/92	A	10	(1)	1
19	Anastasios Tsokanis		02/05/91	D	22	(1)	
23	Georgios Vakrakos		18/10/97	M	1		
96	Efstathios Vasiloudis		23/02/96	A	1	(3)	
74	Amr Warda	EGY	17/09/93	M	12		4

Panionios GSS

1890 • Panionios GSS (16,800) • panioniosfc.gr

Major honours
Greek Cup (2) 1979, 1998

Coach: Marinos Ouzounidis; (11/08/16) Vladan Milojević (SRB)

2016

Date		Opponent		Score	Scorers
10/09	h	Asteras	W	3-0	*Fountas 2, Ansarifard*
17/09	a	Xanthi	W	2-0	*Shojaei, Risvanis*
24/09	h	Veria	L	1-2	*N'Gog*
01/10	a	Iraklis	W	2-1	*Shojaei, Ansarifard*
15/10	h	Olympiacos	L	0-2	
22/10	a	AEK	D	0-0	
29/10	a	Larissa	L	0-2	
06/11	h	PAOK	W	1-0	*Ansarifard*
27/11	h	Panathinaikos	D	1-1	*Ansarifard*
03/12	a	Platanias	D	1-1	*Ben Nabouhane*
11/12	h	Kerkyra	W	1-0	*Tasoulis*
18/12	a	Levadiakos	W	4-1	*Risvanis, Korbos, Shojaei, Ben Nabouhane*

2017

Date		Opponent		Score	Scorers
05/01	h	Giannina	D	1-1	*Ansarifard*
08/01	a	Panetolikos	W	2-0	*Shojaei, Masouras*
15/01	a	Atromitos	W	2-1	*Ben Nabouhane, Savvidis*
18/01	a	Giannina	L	0-1	
21/01	h	Panetolikos	W	2-0	*Risvanis, Katharios*
28/01	a	Asteras	D	1-1	*Tapoko*
05/02	h	Xanthi	W	2-0	*Korbos, Ben Nabouhane*
11/02	a	Veria	W	1-0	*Ben Nabouhane*
19/02	h	Iraklis	W	1-0	*Ben Nabouhane*
26/02	a	Olympiacos	W	1-0	*Masouras*
06/03	h	AEK	D	1-1	*Masouras*
11/03	h	Larissa	W	1-0	*Ben Nabouhane*
19/03	a	PAOK	L	0-1	
02/04	h	Atromitos	W	2-1	*Masouras, Ben Nabouhane*
06/04	a	Panathinaikos	L	0-1	
09/04	h	Platanias	D	1-1	*Ben Nabouhane (p)*
23/04	a	Kerkyra	L	0-1	
30/04	h	Levadiakos	L	1-3	*Tapoko*

No	Name	Nat	DoB	Pos	Aps	(s)	Gls
10	Karim Ansarifard	IRN	03/04/90	A	14	(5)	5
15	Marios Antoniades	CYP	14/05/90	D	8	(2)	
20	Leonidas Argiropoulos		29/05/90	D		(1)	
8	Panagiotis Ballas		06/09/93	M		(1)	
73	Georgios Bantis		30/04/85	G	2		
31	El Fardou Ben Nabouhane	COM	10/06/89	M	27	(1)	9
9	Taxiarhis Fountas		04/09/95	M	19		2
22	Andreas Gianniotis		18/12/92	G	28		
13	Jérôme Guihoata	CMR	07/10/94	D	11	(4)	
6	Evangelos Ikonomou		18/07/87	D	25		
64	Nikolaos Katharios		07/10/94	M	2	(9)	1
7	Panagiotis Korbos		11/09/86	M	29		2
11	Lazaros Lambrou		19/12/97	A		(10)	
52	Aidin Mahmutović	BIH	06/04/86	A	2	(7)	
19	Georgios Masouras		01/01/94	M	19	(9)	4
5	Stefanos Mouktaris	CYP	10/07/94	D	2		
24	David N'Gog	FRA	01/04/89	A	2	(11)	1
93	Michael Olaitan	NGA	01/01/93	A		(6)	
4	Vasilios Patsatzoglou		14/04/94	D		(1)	
2	Vasilios Pliatsikas		14/04/88	D	1		
44	Spiridon Risvanis		03/01/94	D	24		3
88	Kyriakos Savvidis		20/06/95	M	6	(13)	1
77	Masoud Shojaei	IRN	09/06/84	M	25		4
21	Emmanouil Siopis		14/05/94	M	28		
72	Kevin Tapoko	FRA	13/04/94	M	2	(7)	2
3	Christos Tasoulis		03/05/91	D	22	(1)	1
37	Valentinos Vlahos		14/01/92	D	26		
23	Gerasimos Voukelatos		29/03/98	A		(1)	
69	Samed Yeşil	GER	25/05/94	A	6	(3)	

PAOK FC

1926 • Toumbas (31,060) • paokfc.gr

Major honours
Greek League (2) 1976, 1985; Greek Cup (5) 1972, 1974, 2001, 2003, 2017

Coach: Vladimir Ivić (SRB)

2016

Date		Opponent		Score	Scorers
11/09	h	Panetolikos	W	2-1	*Biseswar, Mendes Rodrigues*
19/09	a	Asteras	W	2-1	*Koulouris 2*
25/09	h	Xanthi	D	0-0	
02/10	a	Veria	D	0-0	
16/10	h	Iraklis	W	1-0	*Mendes Rodrigues*
23/10	a	Olympiacos	L	1-2	*Varela*
30/10	h	AEK	W	1-0	*Léo Matos*
06/11	a	Panionios	L	0-1	
28/11	h	Atromitos	L	3-4	*Mendes Rodrigues, Koulouris, Mystakidis*
04/12	a	Panathinaikos	L	0-1	
11/12	h	Platanias	W	3-0	*Léo Matos 2, og (Banana)*
17/12	a	Kerkyra	W	5-0	*og (Andreopoulos), Biseswar, Djalma 2, Léo Matos*

2017

Date		Opponent		Score	Scorers
03/01	a	Levadiakos	W	1-0	*Pelkas*
08/01	h	Giannina	L	0-1	
19/01	h	Levadiakos	W	3-0	*Léo Matos, Pereyra 2*
23/01	a	Giannina	W	1-0	*Leovac*
29/01	a	Panetolikos	W	1-0	*Mystakidis*
01/02	a	Larissa	W	2-0	*Mystakidis, Léo Matos*
05/02	h	Asteras	W	3-2	*Shakhov, Prijović, Pedro Henrique*
12/02	a	Xanthi	D	0-0	
19/02	h	Veria	W	4-0	*Pedro Henrique, Prijović 2 (1p), Pelkas*
26/02	a	Iraklis	D	1-1	*Prijović*
05/03	h	Olympiacos	W	2-0	*Shakhov, Prijović*
12/03	a	AEK	L	0-3	
19/03	h	Panionios	W	1-0	*Pelkas*
02/04	h	Larissa	W	2-0	*Cañas, Kitsiou*
05/04	a	Atromitos	W	2-0	*Biseswar, Koulouris*
09/04	h	Panathinaikos	W	3-0	*Pedro Henrique, Leovac, Shakhov*
23/04	a	Platanias	W	3-1	*Warda, Djalma, Shakhov*
30/04	h	Kerkyra	W	5-1	*Kaçe, Koulouris, Biseswar (p), Warda, Prijović*

No	Name	Nat	DoB	Pos	Aps	(s)	Gls
33	Stefanos Athanasiadis		24/12/88	A	15	(6)	
21	Diego Biseswar	NED	08/03/88	M	19	(5)	4
23	Željko Brkić	SRB	09/07/86	G	4	(1)	
87	José Cañas	ESP	27/05/87	M	20	(2)	1
8	Charilaos Charisis		12/01/95	M	4	(5)	
16	Gojko Cimirot	BIH	19/12/92	M	24	(2)	
15	José Ángel Crespo	ESP	09/02/87	D	25	(1)	
41	Panagiotis Deligiannidis		29/08/96	M	2		
10	Djalma	ANG	30/05/87	A	21	(3)	3
71	Panagiotis Glykos		10/10/86	G	26		
26	Ergys Kaçe	ALB	08/07/93	M	3	(3)	1
70	Stilianos Kitsiou		28/09/93	D	5	(6)	1
20	Efthimios Koulouris		06/03/96	A	11	(5)	5
3	Léo Matos	BRA	02/04/86	D	26	(1)	6
4	Marin Leovac	CRO	07/08/88	D	21	(4)	2
13	Stilianos Malezas		11/03/85	D	15	(7)	
24	Garry Mendes Rodrigues	CPV	27/11/90	M	11	(1)	3
27	Ioannis Mystakidis		07/12/94	A	7	(10)	3
11	Pedro Henrique	BRA	16/06/90	M	8	(2)	3
77	Dimitrios Pelkas		26/10/93	M	5	(6)	3
14	Facundo Pereyra	ARG	03/09/87	M	2	(6)	2
44	Achilleas Pougouras		13/12/95	D	1	(1)	
9	Aleksandar Prijović	SRB	21/04/90	A	4	(5)	6
28	Yevhen Shakhov	UKR	30/11/90	M	17	(4)	4
99	Marios Siampanis		28/09/99	G		(2)	
7	Mame Baba Thiam	SEN	09/10/92	A		(1)	
31	Georgios Tzavellas		26/11/87	D	5		
43	Fernando Varela	CPV	26/11/87	D	22	(1)	1
74	Amr Warda	EGY	17/09/93	M	7	(1)	2

GREECE

PAS Giannina FC

1966 • Oi Zosimades (7,652) • pasgiannina.gr
Coach: Ioannis Petrakis

Date		Opponent		Score	Scorers
2016					
11/09	h	Atromitos	W	3-0	*Noé Acosta (p), Pedro Conde 2*
18/09	a	Panathinaikos	L	0-4	
24/09	h	Platanias	D	0-0	
01/10	a	Kerkyra	W	1-0	*Higor Vidal*
23/10	h	Larissa	W	4-0	*Pedro Conde 3, Giakos*
31/10	a	Panetolikos	W	2-1	*Maboulou 2*
05/11	h	Asteras	L	1-2	*Jairo*
23/11	h	Levadiakos	D	0-0	
26/11	h	Veria	W	2-0	*Pedro Conde, Kozoronis*
05/12	a	Iraklis	L	1-2	*Kozoronis*
12/12	h	Olympiacos	L	0-2	
19/12	a	AEK	D	1-1	*Maboulou*
2017					
05/01	a	Panionios	D	1-1	*Tzimopoulos*
08/01	a	PAOK	W	1-0	*Tzimopoulos*
15/01	a	Xanthi	L	0-2	
18/01	h	Panionios	W	1-0	*Mihail*
23/01	h	PAOK	L	0-1	
29/01	a	Atromitos	D	1-1	*Pedro Conde*
04/02	h	Panathinaikos	D	1-1	*Pedro Conde*
12/02	a	Platanias	D	3-3	*Pedro Conde 2, Tzimopoulos*
18/02	h	Kerkyra	W	1-0	*Pedro Conde (p)*
26/02	a	Levadiakos	L	1-2	*Pedro Conde*
04/03	a	Larissa	D	1-1	*Pedro Conde*
11/03	h	Panetolikos	D	0-0	
19/03	a	Asteras	D	1-1	*Jairo*
01/04	h	Xanthi	D	1-1	*Jairo*
05/04	a	Veria	L	0-3	
09/04	h	Iraklis	L	1-2	*Higor Vidal*
23/04	a	Olympiacos	L	0-5	
30/04	h	AEK	D	1-1	*Lila*

No	Name	Nat	DoB	Pos	Aps	(s)	Gls
4	Theodoros Berios		21/03/89	D	20	(2)	
2	Mihail Boukouvalas		14/01/88	D	14	(4)	
18	Christos Donis		09/10/94	M		(3)	
14	Dimitrios Ferfelis		05/04/93	A		(1)	
17	Fonsi	ESP	22/01/86	D	14	(8)	
5	Iraklis Garoufalias		01/05/93	M	7	(8)	
7	Evripidis Giakos		09/04/91	M	20	(7)	1
33	Higor Vidal	BRA	26/09/96	M	4	(11)	2
10	Jairo	BRA	06/05/92	A	21	(5)	3
20	Nikolaos Karanikas		04/03/92	D	15	(3)	
34	Nikolaos Korovesis		10/08/91	M	2	(5)	
23	Leonardo Koutris		23/07/95	M	22	(6)	
22	Chrisovalantis Kozoronis		03/08/92	M	24	(5)	2
3	Andi Lila	ALB	12/02/86	D	18		1
93	Christopher Maboulou	FRA	19/03/90	A	13	(9)	3
42	Konstantinos Mavropanos		11/12/97	D	2		
6	Alexios Mihail		18/08/86	D	26		1
88	Alexandros Nikolias		23/07/94	M	2	(1)	
11	Noé Acosta	ESP	10/12/83	M	21	(3)	1
1	Alexandros Pashalakis		28/07/89	G	20		
9	Pedro Conde	ESP	26/07/88	A	21	(4)	13
12	Konstantinos Peristeridis		24/01/91	G	10	(1)	
44	Apostolos Skondras		29/12/88	D	11	(2)	
8	Themistoklis Tzimopoulos	NZL	20/11/85	D	23		3

Platanias FC

1931 • Dimotiko Perivolion (3,700) • fcplatanias.gr
Coach: Georgios Parashos

Date		Opponent		Score	Scorers
2016					
10/09	a	Kerkyra	W	1-0	*Giakoumakis*
17/09	h	Levadiakos	W	3-2	*Manousos 2, Giakoumakis*
24/09	a	Giannina	D	0-0	
02/10	h	Panetolikos	D	0-0	
15/10	a	Asteras	L	0-2	
22/10	h	Xanthi	L	0-1	
30/10	a	Veria	D	0-0	
07/11	a	Iraklis	D	1-1	*Apostolopoulos*
26/11	a	AEK	L	0-3	
03/12	h	Panionios	D	1-1	*Manousos*
11/12	a	PAOK	L	0-3	
17/12	h	Atromitos	W	3-0	*Karipidis, Giakoumakis 2*
2017					
05/01	h	Panathinaikos	W	1-0	*Banana*
08/01	h	Larissa	W	3-2	*Munafo, Pryndeta, Manousos*
14/01	h	Olympiacos	D	2-2	*Giakoumakis, Manousos (p)*
19/01	a	Panathinaikos	L	1-2	*Giakoumakis*
22/01	a	Larissa	D	0-0	
29/01	h	Kerkyra	W	2-1	*Vanderson, Manousos (p)*
06/02	a	Levadiakos	W	2-1	*Mendrinos, Signevich*
12/02	h	Giannina	D	3-3	*Giakoumakis, Kargas, Signevich*
19/02	a	Panetolikos	W	2-1	*Manousos (p), Karipidis*
25/02	h	Asteras	W	3-0	*Giakoumakis 2, Munafo*
05/03	a	Xanthi	L	0-1	
12/03	h	Veria	W	1-0	*Munafo*
20/03	h	Iraklis	W	1-0	*Giakoumakis*
01/04	a	Olympiacos	L	1-2	*Manousos (p)*
06/04	h	AEK	L	0-2	
09/04	a	Panionios	D	1-1	*Giakoumakis*
23/04	h	PAOK	L	1-3	*Mendrinos*
30/04	a	Atromitos	L	1-4	*Kargas*

No	Name	Nat	DoB	Pos	Aps	(s)	Gls
77	Alexandros Apostolopoulos		07/11/91	M	12	(7)	1
22	Yaya Banana	CMR	29/07/91	D	25		1
90	Dídac Devesa	ESP	30/12/90	M	11	(9)	
99	Haris Dilaver	BIH	06/02/90	A		(3)	
26	Athanasios Dinas		12/11/89	M		(11)	
2	Saado Fouflia	PLE	23/11/97	D		(1)	
11	Georgios Giakoumakis		09/12/94	A	26		11
6	Ognjen Gnjatić	BIH	16/10/91	M	11		
20	Fanourios Goundoulakis		13/07/83	M	5	(13)	
3	Ioannis Kargas		09/12/94	D	16	(4)	2
5	Christos Karipidis		02/12/82	D	24		2
92	Antonios Kokkalas		16/02/92	G	5		
9	Georgios Manousos		03/12/87	A	26		8
55	Stilianos Marangos		04/05/89	D	2	(5)	
7	Konstantinos Mendrinos		28/05/85	M	18	(7)	2
8	Juan Munafo	ARG	20/03/83	M	26	(1)	3
39	Ioannis Papanikolaou		18/11/98	M	1	(1)	
34	Vitaliy Pryndeta	UKR	02/02/93	D	12	(2)	1
23	Raúl Llorente	ESP	02/04/86	D	10	(6)	
10	Nikolai Signevich	BLR	20/02/92	A	11	(5)	2
98	Dimitrios Skouloudakis		01/10/98	M		(1)	
32	Dimitrios Sotiriou		13/09/87	G	25		
4	Filip Stanisavljević	SRB	20/05/87	M	12	(8)	
25	Ioannis Stathis		20/05/87	D	23	(3)	
10	Athanasios Tsourakis		12/05/90	A	2	(2)	
27	Vanderson	BRA	27/09/84	D	27		1
97	Renato Ziko	ALB	16/11/97	M		(1)	

Veria FC

1960 • Dimotikon Verias (7,000) • veriafc.gr
Coach: Alexandros Vosniadis; (23/09/16) (Apostolos Terzis); (25/09/16) Thomas Grafas; (27/01/17) (Apostolos Terzis); (14/02/17) Ratko Dostanić (SRB); (26/04/17) (Apostolos Terzis)

Date		Opponent		Score	Scorers
2016					
11/09	a	Olympiacos	L	1-6	*Kapetanos*
17/09	h	AEK	L	0-2	
24/09	a	Panionios	W	2-1	*Vitti 2*
02/10	h	PAOK	D	0-0	
16/10	a	Atromitos	L	0-1	
24/10	h	Panathinaikos	D	1-1	*Balafas*
30/10	h	Platanias	D	0-0	
06/11	a	Kerkyra	L	0-2	
26/11	a	Giannina	L	0-2	
03/12	h	Panetolikos	D	1-1	*Sarpong*
10/12	a	Asteras	D	0-0	
17/12	h	Xanthi	L	0-4	
2017					
04/01	a	Larissa	L	1-2	*Toni Calvo*
14/01	h	Levadiakos	W	2-0	*Miljević, Kapetanos*
18/01	h	Larissa	D	1-1	*Sarpong*
21/01	a	Iraklis	D	1-1	*Linardos*
25/01	h	Iraklis	L	0-2	
29/01	h	Olympiacos	L	1-2	*Sarpong*
05/02	a	AEK	L	0-6	
11/02	h	Panionios	L	0-1	
19/02	a	PAOK	L	0-4	
27/02	h	Atromitos	L	0-1	
04/03	a	Panathinaikos	L	0-5	
12/03	a	Platanias	L	0-1	
18/03	h	Kerkyra	W	4-0	*Balafas, Stojčev, Kapetanos, Kali*
01/04	a	Levadiakos	L	1-3	*Kapetanos*
05/04	h	Giannina	W	3-0	*Kapetanos, Sarpong, Soulé*
09/04	a	Panetolikos	L	0-1	
23/04	h	Asteras	W	4-3	*Linardos 2, Kapetanos, Sarpong*
30/04	a	Xanthi	L	0-3	

No	Name	Nat	DoB	Pos	Aps	(s)	Gls
15	Gael Andonyan	ARM	07/02/95	D	8	(2)	
26	Terry Antonis	AUS	15/11/92	M		(1)	
10	Pedro Arce	MEX	25/11/91	M	17	(4)	
3	Mark Asigba	GHA	07/07/90	D	20	(2)	
25	Sotirios Balafas		19/08/86	M	23	(1)	2
75	Tijani Belaid	TUN	06/09/87	M	1	(7)	
95	Ioannis Charontakis		07/08/95	D	7	(3)	
24	Alexandros Doris		10/07/98	M	1		
88	Yacine Hadji	ALG	09/03/93	M	1		
18	Iván Malón	ESP	26/08/86	D	18		
55	Jonathan López	ESP	16/04/81	G	22		
21	Cyril Kali	FRA	21/04/84	D	26		1
1	Georgios Kantimiris		19/09/82	G	7	(1)	
9	Pantelis Kapetanos		08/06/83	A	24		6
99	Vasilios Konstantinidis		21/04/86	A	1	(3)	
22	Panagiotis Linardos		08/07/91	M	14	(2)	3
5	Stilianos Marangos		04/05/89	D	6		
96	Dimitrios Mavrias		03/10/96	M		(3)	
20	Dimitrios Melikiotis		10/07/96	A	4	(3)	
4	Christos Melissis		01/12/82	D	3	(4)	
11	Kristijan Miljević	SRB	15/07/92	M	5	(8)	1
88	Giorgi Navalovski	GEO	28/06/86	D	5	(2)	
77	Mihalandreas Niktaris		30/12/99	M	1		
19	Ioannis Papadopoulos		09/03/89	M	2	(5)	
71	Emmanouil Papasterianos		15/08/87	M	1	(3)	
16	Sofoklis Radis		21/02/98	D	1		
12	Alexandros Safarikas		26/08/99	G	1		
17	Jeffrey Sarpong	NED	03/08/88	M	23	(1)	5
14	Sisi	ESP	22/04/86	M	9	(2)	
6	Mohamadou Sissoko	FRA	08/08/88	D	9	(4)	
14	Halifa Soulé	COM	12/11/90	M	2	(3)	1
20	Miloš Stojčev	MNE	19/01/87	M	11	(1)	1
8	Antonio Tomás	ESP	13/01/85	M	12	(3)	
7	Toni Calvo	ESP	28/03/87	M	13	(6)	1
66	Christos Tzioras		05/10/88	A		(1)	
2	Stavros Vasilantonopoulos		28/01/92	D	25	(3)	
28	Pablo Vitti	ARG	09/07/85	A	7	(5)	2
23	Ioakim Zyngeridis		20/09/99	A		(1)	

Xanthi FC

1967 • Xanthi Arena (7,500) • xanthifc.gr
Coach: Răzvan Lucescu (ROU)

Date		Opponent	Res		Scorers
2016					
11/09	a	AEK	L	1-4	*Younès*
17/09	h	Panionios	L	0-2	
25/09	a	PAOK	D	0-0	
03/10	h	Atromitos	D	0-0	
16/10	a	Panathinaikos	W	2-1	*De Lucas, Vasilakakis*
22/10	a	Platanias	W	1-0	*Younès*
29/10	h	Kerkyra	D	0-0	
05/11	a	Levadiakos	D	1-1	*Younès*
27/11	a	Panetolikos	W	3-2	*Triadis, Lazić, Younès (p)*
04/12	h	Asteras	W	3-1	*Vasilakakis, Younès, Lazić*
10/12	h	Larissa	W	1-0	*Vasilakakis*
17/12	a	Veria	W	4-0	*Lisgaras, Younès 3 (2p)*
2017					
03/01	a	Iraklis	W	1-0	*Younès*
08/01	h	Olympiacos	L	0-2	
15/01	h	Giannina	W	2-0	*Soltani, Younès*
18/01	h	Iraklis	W	3-1	*Younès 2 (1p), Triadis*
21/01	a	Olympiacos	L	0-2	
28/01	h	AEK	D	0-0	
05/02	a	Panionios	L	0-2	
12/02	h	PAOK	D	0-0	
18/02	a	Atromitos	L	1-2	*Younès (p)*
25/02	h	Panathinaikos	W	1-0	*Vasilakakis*
05/03	h	Platanias	W	1-0	*Younès*
12/03	a	Kerkyra	L	0-1	
19/03	h	Levadiakos	D	2-2	*Younès (p), Lazić*
01/04	a	Giannina	D	1-1	*Vasilakakis*
05/04	h	Panetolikos	W	3-0	*Younès 2 (1p), Vasilakakis*
09/04	a	Asteras	D	0-0	
23/04	a	Larissa	L	0-1	
30/04	h	Veria	W	3-0	*Younès 2 (1p), Soltani*

No	Name	Nat	DoB	Pos	Aps	(s)	Gls
5	Dimosthenis Baxevanidis		14/04/88	D	20	(1)	
66	Khassa Camara	MTN	22/10/92	M	18	(3)	
15	Okan Chatziterzoglou		05/03/96	D	7	(3)	
6	Pablo De Lucas	ESP	20/09/86	M	26	(2)	1
21	Konstantinos Fliskas		22/12/80	D	20	(3)	
4	Aristotelis Karasalidis		03/05/91	D	19	(1)	
8	Konstantinos Kostas		29/05/97	M		(2)	
22	Djordje Lazić	SRB	18/06/83	M	18	(8)	3
31	Christos Lisgaras		12/02/86	D	22	(1)	1
11	Adrián Lucero	ARG	16/08/84	M	23	(3)	
12	Alfredo Mejía	HON	03/04/90	M	3	(6)	
23	Daniel Nieto	ESP	04/05/91	M	5	(7)	
26	Lazaros Orfanidis		10/03/95	M	2	(1)	
24	Petros Orfanidis		23/03/96	M	1	(5)	
2	Athanasios Papageorgiou		09/05/87	D	3	(2)	
71	Emmanouil Papasterianos		15/08/87	M		(2)	
25	Marcos Pizzelli	ARM	03/10/84	M	2	(8)	
19	Antonios Ranos		15/06/93	A	3	(13)	
10	Karim Soltani	ALG	29/08/84	A	14	(6)	2
33	Stratos Svarnas		11/11/97	D	2		
27	Salimo Sylla	FRA	25/01/94	D	5	(1)	
7	Panagiotis Triadis		09/09/92	M	16	(8)	2
16	Theodoros Vasilakakis		20/07/88	M	26	(2)	6
17	Wallace	BRA	29/10/86	D	19		
9	Hamza Younès	TUN	16/04/86	A	26	(1)	19
20	Živko Živković	SRB	14/04/89	G	30		

Top goalscorers

22	Marcus Berg (Panathinaikos)
19	Hamza Younès (Xanthi)
13	Brown Ideye (Olympiacos)
	Pedro Conde (Giannina)
11	Georgios Giakoumakis (Platanias)
10	Mihail Manias (Asteras)
9	Tomáš Pekhart (AEK)
	Thomas Nazlidis (Larissa)
	El Fardou Ben Nabouhane (Panionios)
8	Georgios Manousos (Platanias)

Promoted clubs

Apollon Smyrnis FC

1891 • Georgios Kamaras (14,000) • fcapollon.gr
Coach: Dimitrios Spanos; (29/12/16) Apostolos Mantzios

PAS Lamia 1964

1964 • Dimotiko Lamias (5,500) • lamia1964.gr
Coach: Charalambos Tennes

Second level final table 2016/17

		Pld	W	D	L	F	A	Pts
1	Apollon Smyrnis FC	34	25	8	1	61	14	83
2	PAS Lamia 1964	34	25	5	4	55	11	80
3	Aris Thessaloniki FC	34	23	8	3	58	17	77
4	OFI Crete FC	34	22	6	6	68	20	72
5	AO Trikala FC	34	22	5	7	65	19	71
6	Agrotikos Asteras FC	34	16	4	14	49	35	52
7	Panserraikos FC	34	12	8	14	38	44	44
8	Panegialios FC	34	11	11	12	33	28	44
9	Sparti FC	34	12	9	13	38	42	42
10	Aiginiakos Aiginiou FC	34	11	8	15	44	52	41
11	PGS Kissamikos FC	34	11	7	16	29	38	40
12	Anagennisis Karditsas FC	34	10	9	15	26	38	39
13	AO Chania FC	34	11	5	18	37	60	38
14	Acharnaikos FC	34	11	5	18	38	51	36
15	Kallithea FC	34	9	6	19	42	49	33
16	Panelefsiniakos FC	34	6	10	18	21	56	28
17	Kalloni FC	34	4	7	23	21	75	7
18	Panthrakikos FC	34	3	3	28	7	81	-6

NB Panthrakikos FC – 18 pts deducted; Kalloni FC – 12 pts deducted; Sparti FC – 3 pts deducted; Acharnaikos FC – 2 pts deducted.

UEFA Champions League qualification play-offs 2016/17

(14/05/17)
Panionios 1-1 Panathinaikos *(Masouras 56; Berg 38)*
PAOK 0-1 AEK *(Dídac Vilà 10)*

(17/05/17)
AEK 0-1 Panionios *(Yeşil 7)*
Panathinaikos 0-3 PAOK *(w/o; original match abandoned after 54 mins at 1-0 Berg 9)*

(21/05/17)
AEK 1-0 Panathinaikos *(Christodoulopoulos 85)*
PAOK 1-0 Panionios *(Prijović 75)*

(24/05/17)
Panathinaikos 1-0 AEK *(Leto 62p)*
Panionios 0-1 PAOK *(Risvanis 14og)*

(28/05/17)
AEK 1-0 PAOK *(Bakasetas 42)*
Panathinaikos 1-0 Panionios *(Lod 17)*

(31/05/17)
Panionios 1-2 AEK *(Masouras 21; Mantalos 34, Araujo 81)*
PAOK 2-3 Panathinaikos *(Biseswar 20, Pedro Henrique 68; Klonaridis 27, Lod 79, Molins 90)*

		Home					Away					Total					
	Pld	W	D	L	F	A	W	D	L	F	A	W	D	L	F	A	Pts
2 AEK FC	6	2	0	1	2	1	2	0	1	3	2	4	0	2	5	3	12
3 PAOK FC	6	1	0	2	3	4	2	0	1	4	1	3	0	3	7	5	11
4 Panathinaikos FC	6	2	0	1	2	3	1	1	1	4	4	3	1	2	6	7	7
5 Panionios GSS	6	0	1	2	2	4	1	0	2	1	2	1	1	4	3	6	4

NB Points carried forward from Superleague – PAOK 2 pts; AEK, Panathinaikos & Panionios 0 pts; Panathinaikos FC – 3 pts deducted.

DOMESTIC CUP

Kypello Ellados 2016/17

SECOND ROUND

Group 1

(26/10/16)
PAOK 2-0 Larissa

(27/10/16)
Panelefsiniakos 0-5 Trikala

(30/11/16)
Larissa 2-1 Panelefsiniakos

(01/12/16)
Trikala 0-0 PAOK

(14/12/16)
Panelefsiniakos 0-7 PAOK
Trikala 1-0 Larissa

Final standings
1 PAOK 7 pts; 2 Trikala 7 pts *(qualified);*
3 Larissa 3 pts; 4 Panelefsiniakos 0 pts *(eliminated)*

Group 2

(26/10/16)
Olympiacos 3-0 Platanias

(27/10/16)
Sparti 4-0 Chania

(29/11/16)
Platanias 1-0 Sparti

(01/12/16)
Chania 0-4 Olympiacos

(14/12/16)
Chania 1-2 Platanias

(15/12/16)
Sparti 0-1 Olympiacos

Final standings
1 Olympiacos 9 pts; 2 Platanias 6 pts *(qualified);*
3 Sparti 3 pts; 4 Chania 0 pts *(eliminated)*

Group 3

(25/10/16)
Apollon Smyrnis 1-0 OFI

(27/10/16)
Panathinaikos 0-0 Iraklis

(30/11/16)
Iraklis 3-0 Apollon Smyrnis
OFI 2-1 Panathinaikos

(15/12/16)
Apollon Smyrnis 3-4 Panathinaikos
OFI 2-1 Iraklis

Final standings
1 OFI 6 pts; 2 4 Panathinaikos 4 pts *(qualified);*
3 Iraklis 4 pts; 4 Apollon Smyrnis 3 pts *(eliminated)*

Group 4

(25/10/16)
Kalloni 1-2 Agrotikos Asteras

(26/10/16)
Giannina 1-0 Xanthi

(29/11/16)
Agrotikos Asteras 0-1 Giannina

(01/12/16)
Xanthi 3-1 Kalloni

(13/12/16)
Agrotikos Asteras 1-1 Xanthi

(15/12/16)
Kalloni 1-3 Giannina

Final standings
1 Giannina 9 pts; 2 Xanthi 4 pts *(qualified);*
3 Agrotikos Asteras 4 pts; 4 Kalloni 0 pts
(eliminated)

Group 5

(25/10/16)
Aiginiakos Aiginiou 0-3 Aris

(27/10/16)
Asteras Tripolis 1-0 Veria

(29/11/16)
Aris 3-3 Asteras Tripolis
Veria 0-1 Aiginiakos Aiginiou

(13/12/16)
Aiginiakos Aiginiou 1-4 Asteras Tripolis
Aris 0-0 Veria

Final standings
1 Asteras Tripolis 7 pts; 2 Aris 5 pts *(qualified);*
3 Aiginiakos Aiginiou 3 pts; 4 Veria 1 pt *(eliminated)*

Group 6

(25/10/16)
AEK 4-0 Kerkyra

(27/10/16)
Lamia 1-0 Anagennisis Karditsas

(29/11/16)
Anagennisis Karditsas 2-2 AEK

(30/11/16)
Kerkyra 2-2 Lamia

(14/12/16)
Anagennisis Karditsas 0-6 Kerkyra
Lamia 0-0 AEK

Final standings
1 AEK 5 pts; 2 Lamia 5 pts *(qualified);*
3 Kerkyra 4 pts; 4 Anagennisis Karditsas 1 pt
(eliminated)

Group 7

(25/10/16)
Panthrakikos 3-0 Kallithea

(26/10/16)
Atromitos 1-0 Panetolikos

(30/11/16)
Panetolikos 1-0 Panthrakikos

(01/12/16)
Kallithea 1-0 Atromitos

(14/12/16)
Kallithea 1-5 Panetolikos
Panthrakikos 0-3 Atromitos

Final standings
1 Atromitos 6 pts; 2 Panetolikos 6 pts *(qualified);*
3 Panthrakikos 3 pts; 4 Kallithea 3 pts *(eliminated)*

Group 8

(26/10/16)
Panionios 0-0 Levadiakos

(27/10/16)
Panserraikos 0-2 Kissamikos

(01/12/16)
Levadiakos 3-1 Panserraikos

(07/12/16)
Kissamikos 3-0 Panionios

(13/12/16)
Kissamikos 1-1 Levadiakos

(15/12/16)
Panserraikos 0-3 Panionios

Final standings
1 Kissamikos 7 pts; 2 Levadiakos 5 pts *(qualified);*
3 Panionios 4pts; 4 Panserraikos 0 pts *(eliminated)*

THIRD ROUND

(10/01/17 & 25/01/17)
Trikala 0-2, 0-1 Asteras Tripolis *(0-3)*

(11/01/17 & 26/01/17)
Panetolikos 0-2, 1-4 PAOK *(1-6)*

(12/01/17 & 01/02/17)
Panathinaikos 3-0, 4-0 Kissamikos *(7-0)*

(24/01/17 & 31/01/17)
Xanthi 1-0, 1-2 OFI *(2-2; Xanthi on away goal)*

(25/01/17 & 01/02/17)
Lamia 2-2, 0-2 Atromitos *(2-4)*
Levadiakos 0-1, 0-6 AEK *(0-7)*

(25/01/17 & 02/02/17)
Aris 1-1, 0-2 Olympiacos *(1-3)*

(26/01/17 & 01/02/17)
Platanias 1-0, 2-1 Giannina *(aet; 3-1)*

QUARTER-FINALS

(08/02/17 & 01/03/17)
Panathinaikos 4-0 Asteras Tripolis *(Nuno Reis 6, Klonaridis 31, Villafáñez 61, M'Poku 68p)*
Asteras Tripolis 0-1 Panathinaikos *(Marinakis 90)*
(Panathinaikos 5-0)

(08/02/17 & 02/03/17)
Olympiacos 0-0 Atromitos
Atromitos 1-2 Olympiacos *(Dauda 46; Romao 63, Fortounis 71)*
(Olympiacos 2-1)

(09/02/17 & 01/03/17)
Platanias 0-0 AEK
AEK 3-0 Platanias *(Christodoulopoulos 13p, Araujo 28, Johansson 59)*
(AEK 3-0)

(09/02/17 & 02/03/17)
Xanthi 1-2 PAOK *(Lazić 52; Mystakidis 20, Prijović 63)*
PAOK 0-1 Xanthi *(Younès 64)*
(2-2; PAOK on away goals)

SEMI-FINALS

(12/04/17 & 27/04/17)
Panathinaikos 2-0 PAOK *(Rodrigo Moledo 21, Leto 83)*
PAOK 4-0 Panathinaikos *(Pelkas 14, Léo Matos 48, Shakhov 73, Prijović 83)*
(PAOK 4-2)

(13/04/17 & 26/04/17)
Olympiacos 1-2 AEK *(Diogo Figueiras 13; Araujo 6, Patito Rodríguez 64)*
AEK 0-1 Olympiacos *(Romao 82)*
(2-2; AEK on away goals)

FINAL

(06/05/17)
Panthessaliko,Volos
PAOK FC 2 *(Biseswar 24, Pedro Henrique 81)*
AEK ATHENS FC 1 *(Christodoulopoulos 26)*
Referee: *Kominis*
PAOK: *Glykos, Léo Matos, Varela, Crespo, Leovac, Cañas, Cimirot (Malezas 86), Shakhov, Djalma (Pedro Henrique 73), Biseswar (Kitsiou 89), Prijović*
AEK: *Anestis, Rodrigo Galo, Vranješ, Chygrynskiy, Dídac Vilà, Johansson, André Simões (Hugo Almeida 83), Christodoulopoulos (Vargas 86), Mantalos, Patito Rodríguez (Galanopoulos 68), Araujo*

HUNGARY

Magyar Labdarúgó Szövetség (MLSZ)

Address	Kánai út 2.D HU-1112 Budapest
Tel	+36 1 577 9500
Fax	+36 1 577 9503
E-mail	mlsz@mlsz.hu
Website	mlsz.hu

President	Sándor Csányi
General secretary	Márton Vági
Head of communications	Márton Dinnyés
Year of formation	1901

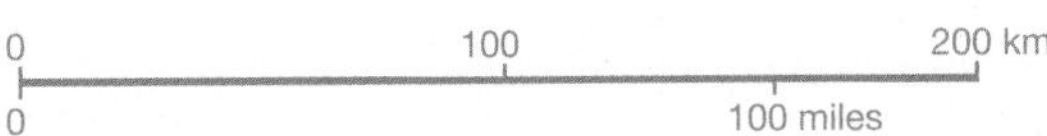

Miskolc 3

Sopron 9

Gyirmót 5

2 Debrecen

Paks 8

NB I CLUBS

1 Budapest Honvéd FC

2 Debreceni VSC

3 Diósgyőri VTK

4 Ferencvárosi TC

5 Gyirmót FC Győr

6 Mezőkövesd Zsóry SE

7 MTK Budapest

8 Paksi FC

9 Szombathelyi Haladás

10 Újpest FC

11 Vasas FC

12 Videoton FC

PROMOTED CLUBS

13 Puskás Akadémia FC

14 Balmazújvárosi FC

KEY

- UEFA Champions League
- UEFA Europa League
- Promoted
- Relegated

Honvéd hold their nerve

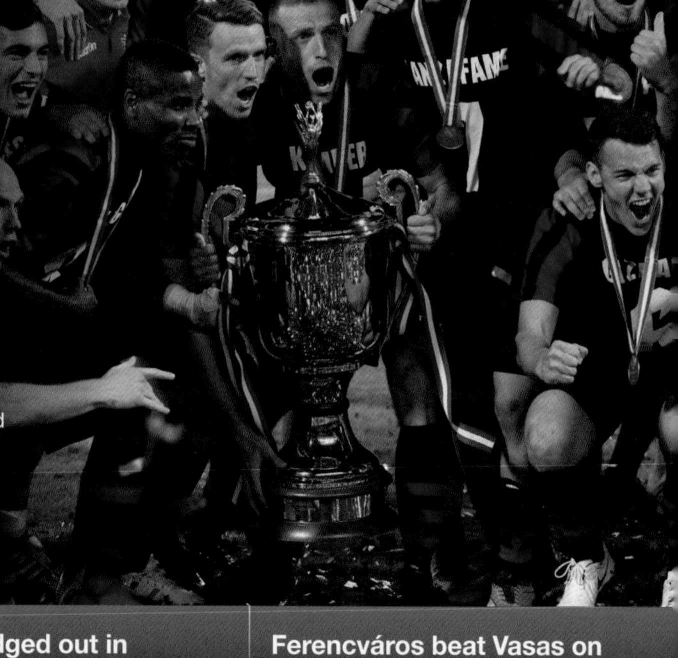

After Ferencváros the previous season, another Budapest giant of yesteryear, Honvéd, ended a long wait to be recrowned champions of Hungary, Italian coach Marco Rossi leading the Red-and-Blacks to their first league title in 24 years after they emerged triumphant from a winner-takes-all last-day showdown with Videoton.

A single goal from the NB I's top scorer, Márton Eppel, decided the sell-out contest at the Bozsik stadium in Honvéd's favour. Four days later Ferencváros defeated another club from the capital, Vasas, on penalties to retain the Hungarian Cup.

Budapest club capture first league title for 24 years

Videoton edged out in final-day showdown

Ferencváros beat Vasas on penalties to retain cup

Domestic league

A mere eighth in 2015/16, Rossi's first full season at the helm, Honvéd had few pretensions about challenging for a prize they had not won since 1992/93, and for most of the autumn they were well off the pace as Vasas, even more surprisingly, led the way. A late-autumn surge, however, improved their position and by the winter break, with 19 of the 33 matches played, they were level on points with both Vasas and Videoton, two teams also under the command of foreign coaches in, respectively, German Michael Oenning and Norwegian Henning Berg.

Vasas fell away in the spring, and with Thomas Doll's Ferencváros struggling for consistency, the race for the NB I title developed into a direct duel between Honvéd and Videoton. The 2014/15 champions made a potentially decisive move when they trounced their rivals 3-0 at the Pancho Aréna in round 22 to take a one-point lead. With six home games to play in the final third of the season as opposed to five for Honvéd (a legacy of the two teams' final placings the season before), Videoton appeared to have the edge.

In the event, the lead changed hands as many as three times thereafter, and when both clubs won four games on the trot to stay level on points ahead of their last-day head-to-head in Budapest, it meant that Honvéd were in pole position on account of their greater number of victories. Had goal difference or head-to-head records been the decisive factor, Videoton would have led, but the local rule favoured Honvéd. Rossi's men therefore only needed a draw in front of an excited capacity crowd of 8,516 in south-east Budapest, but thanks to a close-range strike on the hour from Eppel – the 25-year-old striker's 16th goal of the season – their long-awaited 14th national title was appropriately sealed with a victory.

While Honvéd rejoiced, another famous Budapest club, MTK, despaired as they failed to get the win they needed at Paks to avoid relegation, the dreaded 'most victories' rule enabling Diósgyőr to stay up at the expense of a club that had begun the season in Europe. Newly-promoted Gyirmót Győr had long been doomed to the drop, while there was an immediate return in the opposite direction for Puskás Akadémia FC, accompanied up by NB I newcomers Balmazújváros.

Domestic cup

Ferencváros knocked Honvéd out of the cup and went on to reach the final, where their opponents were Vasas, who had not won the trophy since 1986. Alas for Oenning and his players, that would remain unchanged after a 1-1 draw and a penalty shoot-out in which Fradi's five takers all found the target but one of Vasas's, Macedonian defender Kire Ristevski, did not. It was Ferencváros's record-extending 23rd cup win and their third in a row.

Europe

Doll's side might have ended the season with a shoot-out victory in the Groupama Aréna, but they began it with a spot-kick defeat at the same venue, resulting in elimination from the UEFA Champions League second qualifying round by late Albanian entrants Partizani. No Hungarian team made it to the UEFA Europa League play-offs. Videoton lasted longest before coming to grief in extra time against FC Midtjylland.

National team

Just a year on from the uplifting experience of UEFA EURO 2016, Hungarian football was back in the doldrums after Bernd Storck's national team suffered the shock of losing a FIFA World Cup qualifier to Andorra. The German coach nobly offered his resignation afterwards, but although that was Hungary's fourth successive defeat without a goal and effectively signalled the end of the team's qualifying hopes, the Hungarian FA declined it, asking him instead to see out the rest of the campaign.

DOMESTIC SEASON AT A GLANCE

NB I 2016/17 final table

			Home					Away					Total					
		Pld	W	D	L	F	A	W	D	L	F	A	W	D	L	F	A	Pts
1	**Budapest Honvéd FC**	**33**	**12**	**2**	**2**	**26**	**9**	**8**	**3**	**6**	**29**	**21**	**20**	**5**	**8**	**55**	**30**	**65**
2	Videoton FC	33	12	2	3	45	14	6	6	4	20	14	18	8	7	65	28	62
3	Vasas FC	33	7	4	5	28	21	8	3	6	22	19	15	7	11	50	40	52
4	Ferencvárosi TC	33	8	6	3	35	21	6	4	6	19	23	14	10	9	54	44	52
5	Paksi FC	33	6	9	1	21	9	5	3	9	20	28	11	12	10	41	37	45
6	Szombathelyi Haladás	33	8	5	4	25	16	4	2	10	17	30	12	7	14	42	46	43
7	Újpest FC	33	4	8	5	24	26	6	4	6	23	25	10	12	11	47	51	42
8	Debreceni VSC	33	6	5	6	22	19	5	3	8	20	27	11	8	14	42	46	41
9	Mezőkövesd Zsóry SE	33	8	2	6	25	24	2	8	7	14	30	10	10	13	39	54	40
10	Diósgyőri VTK	33	8	3	5	26	23	2	4	11	13	35	10	7	16	39	58	37
11	MTK Budapest	33	6	5	6	14	15	2	8	6	12	21	8	13	12	26	36	37
12	Gyirmót FC Győr	33	3	3	10	10	23	2	6	9	11	28	5	9	19	21	51	24

European qualification 2017/18

Champion: Budapest Honvéd FC (second qualifying round)

Cup winner: Ferencvárosi TC (first qualifying round)

Videoton FC (first qualifying round)
Vasas FC (first qualifying round)

Top scorer Márton Eppel (Honvéd), 16 goals
Relegated clubs Gyirmót FC Győr, MTK Budapest
Promoted clubs Puskás Akadémia FC, Balmazújvárosi FC
Cup final Ferencvárosi TC 1-1 Vasas FC *(aet; 5-4 on pens)*

Player of the season

Danko Lazović
(Videoton FC)

It is not often that a prominent former foreign international player tries his luck in the Hungarian league, but that was what Lazović, the 47-cap ex-Serbia star who represented his country at the 2010 FIFA World Cup, decided to do in the summer of 2016. It proved a worthwhile experience, too, because the former PSV Eindhoven and Zenit winger not only excelled for Videoton but came within a whisker of helping the club win the title. That honour went instead to Honvéd, the team he scored two goals against in a memorable 3-0 win in March.

Newcomer of the season

Donát Zsótér
(Budapest Honvéd FC)

There was a sweet irony in Honvéd's Hungarian title win for 21-year-old attacking midfielder Zsótér as the team they defeated on the final day, Videoton, were the club that groomed but rejected him. The Hungarian youth international was actually on loan to Honvéd from Belgian club Sint-Truidense in 2016/17 and he certainly enjoyed the experience more than the previous season, which had seen his loan club Puskás Akadémia relegated, important goals from him against Újpest, Ferencváros and Paks helping Honvéd on the path to paradise.

Team of the season

(3-3-2-2)

Coach: Rossi *(Honvéd)*

HUNGARY

NATIONAL TEAM

International tournament appearances

FIFA World Cup (9) 1934 (2nd round), 1938 (runners-up), 1954 (runners-up), 1958, 1962 (qtr-finals), 1966 (qtr finals), 1978, 1982, 1986
UEFA European Championship (3) 1964 (3rd), 1972 (4th), 2016 (round of 16)

Top five all-time caps

Gábor Király (108); József Bozsik (101); **Zoltán Gera** (97); **Roland Juhász** (95); László Fazekas (92)

Top five all-time goals

Ferenc Puskás (84); Sándor Kocsis (75); Imre Schlosser (59); Lajos Tichy (51); György Sárosi (42)

Results 2016/17

06/09/16	Faroe Islands (WCQ)	A	Torshavn	D	0-0	
07/10/16	Switzerland (WCQ)	H	Budapest	L	2-3	*Szalai (53, 71)*
10/10/16	Latvia (WCQ)	A	Riga	W	2-0	*Gyurcsó (10), Szalai (77)*
13/11/16	Andorra (WCQ)	H	Budapest	W	4-0	*Gera (34), Lang (43), Gyurcsó (73), Szalai (88)*
15/11/16	Sweden	H	Budapest	L	0-2	
25/03/17	Portugal (WCQ)	A	Lisbon	L	0-3	
05/06/17	Russia	H	Budapest	L	0-3	
09/06/17	Andorra (WCQ)	A	Andorra la Vella	L	0-1	

Appearances 2016/17

Coach: Bernd Storck (GER)	25/01/63		FRO	SUI	LVA	AND	Swe	POR	Rus	AND	Caps	Goals
Péter Gulácsi	06/05/90	RB Leipzig (GER)	G	G	G	G		G	G	G	10	-
Attila Fiola	17/02/90	Videoton	D	D			D69				19	-
Richárd Guzmics	16/04/87	Wisła Kraków (POL)	D	D	D	D					22	1
Ádám Lang	17/01/93	Dijon (FRA)	D	D		D		D46	D	D56	21	1
Tamás Kádár	14/03/90	Lech (POL)	D	D	D		D					
		/Dynamo Kyiv (UKR)						D	D46		39	-
Ádám Nagy	17/06/95	Bologna (ITA)	M	M	M	M		M	M	M	18	-
Krisztián Németh	05/01/89	Al-Gharafa (QAT)	M70	s76		s81	M				30	3
László Kleinheisler	08/04/94	Darmstadt (GER)	M80	M76	s46	M74						
		/Ferencváros							s70	M	13	1
Ákos Elek	21/07/88	Diósgyőr	M				M				42	1
Balázs Dzsudzsák	23/12/86	Al-Wahda (UAE)	M	M	M	M		M	M70	M	89	20
Tamás Priskin	27/09/86	Slovan Bratislava (SVK)	A27				A58				60	17
Ádám Szalai	09/12/87	Hoffenheim (GER)	s27	A87	A	A		A			41	13
Nemanja Nikolić	31/12/87	Legia (POL)	s70	s87	A46						23	3
Zoltán Stieber	16/10/88	Kaiserslautern (GER)	s80	M		s74	M		M75	M21	21	3
Zoltán Gera	22/04/79	Ferencváros		M	M83	M81		M85			97	26
Barnabás Bese	06/05/94	Le Havre (FRA)			D	D		D	D	D	7	-
Mihály Korhut	01/12/88	H. Beer Sheva (ISR)			D	D		D			9	-
Ádám Gyurcsó	06/03/91	Pogoń (POL)			M	M81		M69	s75	M71	18	3
Máté Vida	08/03/96	Vasas			s83		M46				3	-
Dániel Böde	24/10/86	Ferencváros				s84	s58				16	4
Gábor Király	01/04/76	Haladás					G28				108	-
Roland Juhász	01/07/83	Videoton					D46				95	6
Ádám Pintér	12/06/88	Ferencváros					D					
		/Greuther Fürth (GER)						s85			26	-
Gergő Lovrencsics	01/09/88	Ferencváros					M78	s46			16	1
Balázs Megyeri	31/03/90	Greuther Fürth (GER)					s28				1	-
Zsombor Berecz	13/12/95	Vasas					s46				1	-
Szilveszter Hangya	02/01/94	Vasas					s46		D46		2	-
Endre Botka	25/08/94	Honvéd					s69				1	-
Dominik Nagy	08/05/95	Ferencváros					s78					
		/Legia (POL)								s21	2	-
Paulo Vinícius	21/02/90	Videoton						D	s46	D	3	-
Zsolt Kalmár	09/06/95	Brøndby (DEN)						s69	M46		9	-
Dávid Márkvárt	20/09/94	Puskás Akadémia							M		1	-
Márton Eppel	26/10/91	Honvéd							A70	A	2	-
Márk Kleisz	02/07/98	Vasas							s46		1	-
Roland Sallai	22/05/97	Palermo (ITA)							s46	s71	3	-
Norbert Balogh	21/02/96	Palermo (ITA)							s70	s56	2	-
Bence Tóth	25/05/98	Puskás Akadémia								D	1	-

EUROPE

Ferencvárosi TC

CHAMPIONS LEAGUE

Second qualifying round - FK Partizani (ALB)

A 1-1 *Böde (71)*

Dibusz, Lovrencsics, Radó (Šesták 66), Nagy (Trinks 88), Leandro, Pintér, Gera, Djuricin (Böde 66), Nalepa, Dilaver, Ramirez. Coach: Thomas Doll (GER)

H 1-1 (aet; 1-3 on pens) *Gera (14p)*

Dibusz, Hüsing, Lovrencsics, Böde, Leandro, Pintér (Nagy 46), Gera, Trinks (Djuricin 66), Dilaver, Ramirez, Varga (Šesták 46). Coach: Thomas Doll (GER)

Videoton FC

EUROPA LEAGUE

First qualifying round - FC Zaria Balti (MDA)

H 3-0 *Géresi (18), Feczesin (88, 90+4)*

Kovácsik, Paulo Vinícius, Fejes, Nego, Pátkai, Bódi, Szolnoki, Barczi (Feczesin 72), Simon, Géresi (Kovács 84), Suljić. Coach: Henning Berg (NOR)

A 0-2

Kovácsik, Paulo Vinícius, Nego, Filipe Oliveira (Fejes 87), Lang, Stopira, Bódi (Feczesin 67), Szolnoki, Simon, Géresi, Suljić. Coach: Henning Berg (NOR)

Second qualifying round - FK Čukarički (SRB)

H 2-0 *Bódi (58), Suljić (90+2)*

Kovácsik, Paulo Vinícius, Nego, Pátkai, Lang, Stopira, Bódi, Szolnoki, Barczi (Filipe Oliveira 81), Géresi (Feczesin 84), Suljić. Coach: Henning Berg (NOR)

Red card: Nego 80

A 1-1 *Géresi (76)*

Kovácsik, Paulo Vinícius, Pátkai, Lang, Stopira, Bódi, Szolnoki, Barczi, Simon (Filipe Oliveira 79), Géresi (Feczesin 79), Suljić. Coach: Henning Berg (NOR)

Third qualifying round - FC Midtjylland (DEN)

H 0-1

Kovácsik, Paulo Vinícius, Lazović (Feczesin 46), Nego, Pátkai, Lang, Stopira, Bódi (Filipe Oliveira 61), Szolnoki, Géresi (Barczi 83), Suljić. Coach: Henning Berg (NOR)

A 1-1 (aet) *Kovács (75)*

Kovácsik, Paulo Vinícius, Kovács (Suljić 91), Nego, Pátkai, Lang, Stopira (Bódi 12), Juhász, Szolnoki, Barczi, Géresi (Feczesin 67). Coach: Henning Berg (NOR)

Red card: Paulo Vinícius 47

Debreceni VSC

EUROPA LEAGUE

First qualifying round - SP La Fiorita (SMR)

A 5-0 *Szakály (5, 83), Tisza (34, 49), Kulcsár (89)*

Radošević, Holman, Tisza (Sekulić 68), Ferenczi, N Mészáros, Brković, K Mészáros (Djelmić 58), Varga, Szakály, Jovanović, Castillion (Kulcsár 46). Coach: Elemér Kondás (HUN)

H 2-0 *Tisza (41), Holman (51)*

Radošević, Szatmári, Holman (Sekulić 67), Tisza, Djelmić (K Mészáros 46), Brković, Varga, Szakály (Ferenczi 61), Korhut, Jovanović, Castillion. Coach: Elemér Kondás (HUN)

Second qualifying round - FC Torpedo Zhodino (BLR)

H 1-2 *Tisza (2)*

Radošević, Holman (Ferenczi 82), Tisza, N Mészáros, Brković, K Mészáros (Djelmić 63), Varga, Szakály, Korhut, Jovanović, Castillion (Takács 57). Coach: Elemér Kondás (HUN)

A 0-1

Radošević, Holman (Horváth 59), Tisza, N Mészáros, Sekulić, Brković, Varga, Szakály (Ferenczi 65), Korhut, Jovanović, Castillion (Takács 57). Coach: Elemér Kondás (HUN)

MTK Budapest

EUROPA LEAGUE

First qualifying round - FC Aktobe (KAZ)

A 1-1 *Torghelle (30)*

Hegedűs, Baki, Grgić, Nikač (Deutsch 90+1), L Szatmári (Borbély 88), Torghelle, Kanta, Vadnai, Poór, Gera, Vass. Coach: Vaszilisz Teodoru (HUN)

H 2-0 *Nikač (7), Bese (84)*

Hegedűs, Baki, Grgić, Nikač (Hrepka 83), L Szatmári (Borbély 62), Torghelle, Bese, Kanta (Jakab 90), Poór, Gera, Vass. Coach: Vaszilisz Teodoru (HUN)

Second qualifying round – Qäbälä FK (AZE)

H 1-2 *Torghelle (70)*

Hegedűs, Baki, Grgić, Nikač (Varga 65), Torghelle, Bese, Kanta, Poór, Borbély (L Szatmári 74), Gera (Jakab 78), Vass. Coach: Vaszilisz Teodoru (HUN)

A 0-2

Hegedűs, Baki, Grgić, Nikač (Hrepka 52), L Szatmári, Torghelle, Bese (Varga 77), Kanta (Borbély 72), Vadnai, Poór, Vass. Coach: Vaszilisz Teodoru (HUN)

DOMESTIC LEAGUE CLUB-BY-CLUB

Budapest Honvéd FC

1909 • Bozsik József (13,500) • honvedfc.hu

Major honours

Hungarian League (14) 1950, 1950 (autumn), 1952, 1954, 1955, 1980, 1984, 1985, 1986, 1988, 1989, 1991, 1993, 2017; Hungarian Cup (7) 1926, 1964, 1985, 1989, 1996, 2007, 2009

Coach: Marco Rossi (ITA)

Date		Opponent		Score	Scorers
2016					
16/07	a	Újpest	W	2-0	*Hidi, Eppel*
23/07	h	Ferencváros	L	0-1	
30/07	a	Haladás	D	1-1	*og (Bošnjak)*
06/08	a	Diósgyőr	W	3-0	*Eppel 2 (2p), Koszta*
13/08	h	Paks	W	3-1	*Eppel 2 (2p), Vasiljević*
17/08	a	Vasas	L	0-2	
21/08	h	Gyirmót	D	0-0	
10/09	a	Mezőkövesd	L	1-3	*Hidi*
17/09	h	MTK	W	5-0	*Prosser, Lanzafame, Koszta, D Bobál, Nagy*
20/09	a	Debrecen	W	1-0	*Lanzafame*
24/09	h	Videoton	L	1-2	*Lanzafame*
15/10	h	Újpest	D	1-1	*Lanzafame*
22/10	a	Ferencváros	L	2-3	*Kamber, Lanzafame (p)*
29/10	h	Haladás	W	2-1	*Lanzafame (p), Prosser*
05/11	h	Diósgyőr	W	2-0	*Lanzafame (p), Koszta*
19/11	a	Paks	D	1-1	*og (Szabó)*
26/11	h	Vasas	W	2-1	*Prosser, Eppel*
03/12	a	Gyirmót	W	4-0	*Prosser, Holender, Kamber, Hidi*
10/12	h	Mezőkövesd	W	1-0	*Eppel*
2017					
18/02	a	MTK	W	2-1	*Lanzafame, Eppel (p)*
25/02	h	Debrecen	W	1-0	*Eppel*
04/03	a	Videoton	L	0-3	
11/03	a	Újpest	D	1-1	*Zsótér*
01/04	h	Ferencváros	W	2-1	*Zsótér, Eppel*
08/04	a	Haladás	W	1-0	*Eppel*
11/04	a	Diósgyőr	L	0-2	
15/04	h	Paks	W	2-0	*Eppel, Zsótér*
22/04	a	Vasas	L	0-1	
29/04	h	Gyirmót	W	1-0	*Lanzafame*
06/05	a	Mezőkövesd	W	5-1	*Kamber, Lanzafame 2, D Bobál, Eppel*
13/05	h	MTK	W	2-1	*Holender, og (Korozmán)*
20/05	a	Debrecen	W	5-2	*Koszta 3, Eppel 2*
27/05	h	Videoton	W	1-0	*Eppel*

No	Name	Nat	DoB	Pos	Aps	(s)	Gls
92	Zsolt Balázs		11/08/88	M	1	(8)	
36	Botond Baráth		21/04/92	D	17	(5)	
2	Dávid Bobál		31/08/95	D	22	(2)	2
5	Gergely Bobál		31/08/95	A	1	(1)	
21	Endre Botka		25/04/94	D	17		
9	Márton Eppel		26/10/91	A	24	(3)	16
6	Dániel Gazdag		02/03/96	M	31	(1)	
99	Dávid Gróf		17/04/89	G	25		
38	Ádám Hajdu		16/01/93	D	11	(2)	
26	Patrik Hidi		27/11/90	M	27	(1)	3
57	Filip Holender	SRB	27/07/94	M	19	(8)	2
18	András Horváth		03/02/88	G	8		
8	George Ikenne	NGA	29/10/91	M	19	(2)	
11	Kadima Kabangu	COD	15/06/93	A		(5)	
24	Djordje Kamber	SRB	20/11/83	D	32		3
19	Márk Koszta		26/09/96	M	23	(8)	6
20	Dániel Kovács		14/06/96	A		(1)	
86	Zsolt Laczkó		18/12/86	M	3		
7	Davide Lanzafame	ITA	09/02/87	A	25		11
25	Ivan Lovrić	CRO	11/07/85	D	26	(2)	
77	Gergő Nagy		07/01/93	M	12	(7)	1
30	Raul Palmes	ROU	18/06/96	D		(1)	
17	Dániel Prosser		15/06/94	M	7	(4)	4
21	Bálint Tömösvári		14/06/98	A		(3)	
66	Dušan Vasiljević	SRB	07/05/82	M	1	(14)	1
7	Richárd Vernes		24/02/92	M	1	(5)	
89	Balázs Villám		02/06/89	D		(5)	
23	Donát Zsótér		06/01/96	M	11	(11)	3

Debreceni VSC

1902 • Nagyerdei (20,000) • dvsc.hu

Major honours
Hungarian League (7) 2005, 2006, 2007, 2009, 2010, 2012, 2014; Hungarian Cup (6) 1999, 2001, 2008, 2010, 2012, 2013

Coach: Elemér Kondás; (27/07/16) (András Herczeg); (08/08/16) Leonel Pontes (POR) ; (22/05/17) (András Herczeg)

Date		Opponent	Res	Score	Scorers
2016					
17/07	h	Paks	D	1-1	*Takács*
24/07	a	Vasas	L	1-3	*Ferenczi*
31/07	h	Gyirmót	W	4-0	*Horváth, Korhut, Tisza, Takács*
07/08	a	Mezőkövesd	W	1-0	*Kuti*
13/08	h	MTK	D	1-1	*Castillion*
17/08	h	Haladás	L	0-1	
21/08	a	Videoton	L	1-5	*Ferenczi*
10/09	h	Újpest	W	2-1	*Holman, Horváth*
17/09	a	Ferencváros	L	1-3	*Bobko*
20/09	h	Honvéd	L	0-1	
24/09	a	Diósgyőr	W	3-1	*Holman, Szakály, Tőzsér*
15/10	a	Paks	D	1-1	*Vittek*
22/10	h	Vasas	L	1-2	*Holman*
29/10	a	Gyirmót	W	2-1	*Vittek, Holman*
05/11	h	Mezőkövesd	D	0-0	
19/11	a	MTK	D	1-1	*Holman*
26/11	a	Haladás	L	0-1	
03/12	h	Videoton	L	0-1	
10/12	a	Újpest	L	0-2	
2017					
18/02	h	Ferencváros	D	0-0	
25/02	a	Honvéd	L	0-1	
04/03	h	Diósgyőr	W	3-0	*Osváth, Ferenczi, Feltscher*
11/03	h	Paks	L	1-3	*Tőzsér*
01/04	a	Vasas	W	3-2	*Tőzsér, og (Burmeister), Könyves*
08/04	h	Gyirmót	W	2-1	*Brković, N Mészáros*
12/04	a	Mezőkövesd	L	1-2	*Tőzsér*
15/04	h	MTK	D	0-0	
22/04	h	Haladás	W	4-2	*Handžić, Holman 2, Könyves*
29/04	a	Videoton	L	2-3	*Könyves, Handžić*
06/05	h	Újpest	W	1-0	*og (Heris)*
13/05	a	Ferencváros	D	0-0	
20/05	h	Honvéd	L	2-5	*Jovanović, Suk*
27/05	a	Diósgyőr	W	3-1	*Jovanović, Szatmári, Könyves*

No	Name	Nat	DoB	Pos	Aps	(s)	Gls
37	Szabolcs Barna		27/04/96	D		(1)	
23	Dániel Bereczki		02/06/95	A		(4)	
70	Ivan Bobko	UKR	10/12/90	M	8	(2)	1
25	Dušan Brković	SRB	20/01/89	D	30		1
91	Geoffrey Castillion	NED	25/05/91	A		(7)	1
44	Branislav Danilović	SRB	24/06/88	G	29		
16	Ognjen Djelmić	BIH	18/08/88	M	5	(4)	
22	Frank Feltscher	VEN	17/05/88	M	10	(2)	1
11	János Ferenczi		03/04/91	D	19	(5)	3
4	Ioan Filip	ROU	20/05/89	M	23	(2)	
90	Haris Handžić	BIH	20/06/90	A	7	(5)	2
10	Dávid Holman		17/03/93	M	23	(3)	7
88	Zsolt Horváth		19/05/88	M	10	(8)	2
77	Aleksandar Jovanović	BIH	26/10/84	M	29	(1)	2
42	Norbert Könyves	SRB	10/06/89	M	12	(5)	4
69	Mihály Korhut		01/12/88	D	6		1
66	Nándor Kóródi		15/08/99	A		(1)	
70	Tamás Kulcsár		13/10/82	A	5	(1)	
14	Krisztián Kuti		04/12/92	D	5		1
21	Bence Ludánszki		25/10/90	D	1	(1)	
19	Justin Mengolo	CMR	24/06/93	M	1	(4)	
27	Karol Mészáros	SVK	25/07/93	M	4	(5)	
17	Norbert Mészáros		19/08/80	D	23	(2)	1
70	Kevin Nagy		11/09/95	M		(1)	
28	Zoltán Nagy		25/10/85	D	4	(2)	
18	Derick Ogbu	NGA	19/03/90	A	2	(3)	
2	Attila Osváth		10/12/95	D	13	(1)	1
24	Danilo Sekulić	SRB	18/04/90	M	10	(9)	
91	Suk Hyun-jun	KOR	29/06/91	A	6	(7)	1
55	Péter Szakály		17/08/86	M	10	(2)	1
3	Csaba Szatmári		14/06/94	D	12	(1)	1
5	Péter Szilvási		20/07/94	D	1		
20	Tamás Takács		20/02/91	A	5	(6)	2
10	Tibor Tisza		10/11/84	A	4	(2)	1
8	Dániel Tőzsér		12/05/85	M	24		4
33	József Varga		06/06/88	M	4		
87	István Verpecz		04/02/87	G	4	(1)	
33	Róbert Vittek	SVK	01/04/82	A	7	(1)	2
15	Dániel Völgyi		07/06/87	D	7		

Diósgyőri VTK

1910 • DVTK-Borsodi (12,000); Nagyerdei, Debrecen (20,000); Városi, Mezőkövesd (5,200) • dvtk.eu

Major honours
Hungarian Cup (2) 1977, 1980

Coach: Ferenc Horváth; (02/03/17) (Zoltán Vitelki); (13/03/17) Tamás Bódog

Date		Opponent	Res	Score	Scorers
2016					
17/07	a	Videoton	W	2-1	*Bognár 2*
23/07	h	Újpest	W	2-1	*Oláh, Bognár*
30/07	a	Ferencváros	L	2-6	*Diego Vela, Tamás*
06/08	h	Honvéd	L	0-3	
13/08	a	Haladás	L	1-3	*Lipták*
17/08	a	Paks	L	1-2	*Nikházi*
21/08	h	Vasas	D	1-1	*Bacsa*
10/09	a	Gyirmót	L	0-1	
17/09	h	Mezőkövesd	D	1-1	*Novothny*
21/09	a	MTK	L	0-1	
24/09	h	Debrecen	L	1-3	*Novothny (p)*
15/10	h	Videoton	W	2-0	*Novothny, Elek*
22/10	a	Újpest	D	4-4	*Diego Vela, Bognár (p), Lipták, Jagodinskis*
29/10	h	Ferencváros	L	2-3	*Novothny, Nono*
05/11	a	Honvéd	L	0-2	
19/11	h	Haladás	W	2-1	*Lipták, Ugrai*
26/11	h	Paks	W	2-0	*Lipták, Ugrai*
03/12	a	Vasas	L	0-3	
10/12	h	Gyirmót	W	1-0	*Diego Vela*
2017					
18/02	a	Mezőkövesd	L	0-3	
25/02	h	MTK	L	2-3	*og (Myke), Fülöp*
04/03	a	Debrecen	L	0-3	
11/03	a	Videoton	L	0-2	
01/04	h	Újpest	W	3-1	*Makrai, Ugrai (p), Karan*
08/04	a	Ferencváros	D	1-1	*Tamás*
11/04	h	Honvéd	W	2-0	*Karan, Diego Vela*
15/04	a	Haladás	L	0-2	
22/04	a	Paks	W	1-0	*Ugrai*
29/04	h	Vasas	W	2-1	*Szarka, Makrai*
06/05	a	Gyirmót	D	1-1	*Makrai*
13/05	h	Mezőkövesd	D	2-2	*Makrai, Busai*
20/05	a	MTK	D	0-0	
27/05	h	Debrecen	L	1-3	*Ugrai*

No	Name	Nat	DoB	Pos	Aps	(s)	Gls
99	Botond Antal		22/08/91	G	15		
9	Patrik Bacsa		03/06/92	A	8	(10)	1
10	István Bognár		06/05/91	M	14	(4)	4
14	Gábriel Boros		26/09/97	M		(1)	
1	Erik Bukrán		06/12/96	G	1		
20	Attila Busai		21/01/89	M	7	(4)	1
23	Murtaz Daushvili	GEO	01/05/89	M	20	(6)	
6	Diego Vela	ESP	27/11/91	M	26	(5)	4
25	Ákos Elek		21/07/88	M	18		1
94	Gábor Eperjesi		12/01/94	D	20	(1)	
24	István Fülöp	ROU	18/05/90	M	3	(9)	1
50	Georges Griffiths	CIV	24/02/90	A	2	(6)	
2	Vitālijs Jagodinskis	LVA	28/02/92	D	11	(2)	1
48	Dejan Karan	SRB	13/08/88	D	11		2
17	Miklós Kitl		01/06/97	M	3	(3)	
88	Pál Lázár		11/03/88	D	12		
5	Zoltán Lipták		10/12/84	D	28		4
12	Patrik Lőrincz		01/12/97	D	1		
3	Marcell Mahalek		26/08/94	D	3		
7	Gábor Makrai		26/06/96	A	13	(6)	4
15	Patrick Mevoungou	CMR	15/02/86	M	9		
19	Tibor Nagy		14/08/91	D	1	(1)	
33	Milán Nemes		27/09/96	D	15		
29	Milán Németh		29/05/88	D	5	(1)	
20	Márk Nikházi		02/02/89	M	5	(7)	1
30	Nono	ESP	30/03/93	M	18	(5)	1
86	Soma Novothny		16/06/94	A	20	(3)	4
7	Dražen Okuka	SRB	05/03/86	D	3	(1)	
8	Bálint Oláh		02/12/94	M	7	(2)	1
22	Ivan Radoš	CRO	21/02/84	G	17		
11	Balázs Szabó		16/04/98	A		(4)	
98	Dávid Szalóczy		31/07/98	M	1		
27	Ákos Szarka	SVK	24/11/90	A	11	(2)	1
4	Márk Tamás		28/10/93	D	21		2
74	Patrik Ternován		10/06/97	A	3	(2)	
87	Róbert Tucsa		17/03/98	A		(2)	
70	Roland Ugrai		13/11/92	A	11	(7)	5

Ferencvárosi TC

1899 • Groupama Aréna (22,000) • fradi.hu

Major honours
Inter Cities Fairs Cup (1) 1965; Hungarian League (29) 1903, 1905, 1907, 1909, 1910, 1911, 1912, 1913, 1926, 1927, 1928, 1932, 1934, 1938, 1940, 1941, 1949, 1963, 1964, 1967, 1968, 1976, 1981, 1992, 1995, 1996, 2001, 2004, 2016; Hungarian Cup (23) 1913, 1922, 1927, 1928, 1933, 1935, 1942, 1943, 1944, 1958, 1972, 1974, 1976, 1978, 1991, 1993, 1994, 1995, 2003, 2004, 2015, 2016, 2017

Coach: Thomas Doll (GER)

Date		Opponent	Res	Score	Scorers
2016					
16/07	h	Haladás	W	3-1	*Trinks, Böde 2*
23/07	a	Honvéd	W	1-0	*Böde*
30/07	h	Diósgyőr	W	6-2	*Trinks, Leandro, Djuricin 2, Dilaver, Gera*
06/08	a	Paks	D	0-0	
13/08	h	Vasas	L	1-2	*Trinks*
17/08	a	Gyirmót	W	1-0	*Böde*
21/08	h	Mezőkövesd	D	2-2	*Djuricin, Nagy*
10/09	a	MTK	L	1-2	*Ryu*
17/09	h	Debrecen	W	3-1	*Böde 2, Dilaver*
21/09	a	Videoton	D	1-1	*Djuricin*
24/09	h	Újpest	D	3-3	*Djuricin, Leandro, og (Pávkovics)*
15/10	a	Haladás	L	0-2	
22/10	h	Honvéd	W	3-2	*Böde, Hajnal, Djuricin*
29/10	a	Diósgyőr	W	3-2	*og (Jagodinskis), Busai, Nalepa*
05/11	h	Paks	L	1-2	*Busai*
19/11	a	Vasas	D	2-2	*Djuricin, Gera (p)*
26/11	h	Gyirmót	W	2-0	*og (Présinger), Djuricin*
03/12	a	Mezőkövesd	L	0-2	
10/12	h	MTK	D	1-1	*og (Baki)*
2017					
18/02	a	Debrecen	D	0-0	
25/02	h	Videoton	D	0-0	
04/03	a	Újpest	W	1-0	*Gera*
11/03	h	Haladás	W	3-1	*Moutari, Gera (p), Böde*
01/04	a	Honvéd	L	1-2	*Moutari*
08/04	h	Diósgyőr	D	1-1	*Varga*
12/04	a	Paks	L	1-3	*Böde*
15/04	h	Vasas	L	1-2	*Sternberg*
22/04	a	Gyirmót	W	3-2	*Gera 3 (1p)*
29/04	h	Mezőkövesd	W	3-1	*Böde 2, Gera*
06/05	a	MTK	W	3-1	*Varga, Lovrencsics, Moutari*
13/05	h	Debrecen	D	0-0	
20/05	a	Videoton	L	1-4	*og (Nego)*
27/05	h	Újpest	W	2-0	*Hajnal (p), Varga*

No	Name	Nat	DoB	Pos	Aps	(s)	Gls
13	Dániel Böde		24/10/86	A	25	(4)	11
11	István Bognár		06/05/91	M	6	(2)	
21	Endre Botka		25/04/94	D	6	(4)	
22	Attila Busai		21/01/89	M	2	(4)	2
21	Kornél Csernik		02/07/98	M	1	(7)	
30	Vladan Čukić	SRB	27/06/80	M	6	(9)	
90	Dénes Dibusz		19/11/90	G	28		
66	Emir Dilaver	AUT	07/05/91	D	29	(1)	2
23	Marco Djuricin	AUT	12/12/92	A	17	(8)	8
20	Zoltán Gera		22/04/79	M	29		8
19	Gábor Gyömbér		27/02/88	M	3	(9)	
15	Tamás Hajnal		15/03/81	M	17	(2)	2
31	Ádám Holczer		28/03/88	G	5		
5	Oliver Hüsing	GER	17/02/93	D	15	(4)	
6	László Kleinheisler		08/04/94	M	7	(3)	
19	Julian Koch	GER	11/11/90	M	5	(1)	
3	Norbert Kundrák		18/05/99	A	1	(1)	
16	Leandro		19/03/82	D	24	(1)	2
8	Gergő Lovrencsics		01/09/88	M	22	(6)	1
40	Amadou Moutari	NIG	19/01/94	M	14		3
14	Dominik Nagy		08/05/95	M	14	(4)	1
27	Michał Nalepa	POL	22/01/93	D	19	(2)	1
17	Ádám Pintér		12/06/88	D	8	(3)	
10	András Radó		09/09/93	M	5	(8)	
77	Cristian Ramírez	ECU	08/12/94	D	14		
18	Ryu Seong-woo	KOR	17/12/93	M	6	(5)	1
11	Stanislav Šesták	SVK	16/12/82	A	1	(5)	
37	Janek Sternberg	GER	19/10/92	D	11		1
35	Florian Trinks	GER	11/03/92	M	10		3
97	Roland Varga		23/01/90	M	13	(4)	3

Gyirmót FC Győr

1993 • Alcufer (4,500) • gyirmotfc.hu

Coach: István Urbányi

Date		Opponent			Scorers
2016					
16/07	a	Mezőkövesd	D	2-2	*Lengyel, Vass*
24/07	h	MTK	D	0-0	
31/07	a	Debrecen	L	0-4	
07/08	h	Videoton	L	0-4	
13/08	a	Újpest	L	1-3	*Máté*
17/08	h	Ferencváros	L	0-1	
21/08	a	Honvéd	D	0-0	
10/09	h	Diósgyőr	W	1-0	*Sallói*
17/09	a	Paks	D	0-0	
21/09	h	Vasas	W	1-0	*Filkor*
24/09	a	Haladás	W	1-0	*Sallói*
15/10	h	Mezőkövesd	L	0-1	
22/10	a	MTK	L	0-1	
29/10	h	Debrecen	L	1-2	*Madarász*
05/11	a	Videoton	L	0-4	
19/11	h	Újpest	L	1-2	*Bojović*
26/11	a	Ferencváros	L	0-2	
03/12	h	Honvéd	L	0-4	
10/12	a	Diósgyőr	L	0-1	
2017					
18/02	h	Paks	D	0-0	
25/02	a	Vasas	D	1-1	*Novák*
04/03	h	Haladás	L	1-2	*Radeljić*
11/03	a	Mezőkövesd	D	1-1	*Bojović*
01/04	h	MTK	W	1-0	*András Simon*
08/04	a	Debrecen	L	1-2	*András Simon*
12/04	h	Videoton	L	0-1	
15/04	a	Újpest	D	2-2	*Bojović, Novák*
22/04	h	Ferencváros	L	2-3	*Novák, Tamás*
29/04	a	Honvéd	L	0-1	
06/05	h	Diósgyőr	D	1-1	*Radeljić*
13/05	a	Paks	L	0-3	
20/05	h	Vasas	L	1-2	*Csiki*
27/05	a	Haladás	W	2-1	*Szegi, Máté*

No	Name	Nat	DoB	Pos	Aps	(s)	Gls
32	Sebastian Achim	ROU	02/06/86	D	19	(1)	
69	Olexiy Antonov	UKR	08/05/86	A	4	(1)	
6	Béla Balogh		30/12/84	D	7		
10	Bebeto	SEN	31/12/91	A	6		
7	Gergő Beliczky		03/07/90	A	1	(1)	
25	Mijuško Bojović	MNE	09/08/88	D	22		3
31	Gábor Bori		16/01/84	M	14	(1)	
14	Ádám Borkai		13/01/95	M		(1)	
88	Norbert Csiki		21/05/91	M	15	(8)	1
7	Zoltán Farkas		11/08/95	A		(2)	
18	Attila Filkor		12/07/88	M	16		1
14	Bence Gyurján		21/02/92	M		(5)	
22	Adrián Horváth		20/11/87	M	1	(1)	
70	András Jancsó		22/04/96	D	11		
91	Máté Kiss		30/04/91	M	32		
29	Kristián Kolčák	SVK	30/01/90	D	10	(1)	
97	Zsolt Kovács		06/09/97	A		(1)	
90	Patrik Lázár		24/08/90	D	6		
23	Dániel Lengyel		01/03/89	D	7		1
8	Márk Madarász		24/11/95	M	13	(14)	1
21	János Máté		19/05/90	A	3	(8)	2
20	Olivér Nagy		30/01/89	M	3	(6)	
13	Sándor Nagy		01/01/88	D	4	(2)	
71	Sándor Nagy	UKR	02/09/85	G	9		
28	Csanád Novák		24/09/94	A	12	(6)	3
93	Roland Paku		24/06/93	M	11	(4)	
11	Ádám Présinger		26/01/89	D	20	(1)	
18	Anto Radeljić	BIH	31/12/90	D	12		2
12	Edvárd Rusák		06/04/94	G	2		
30	Dániel Sallói		19/07/96	A	12	(1)	2
1	Zsolt Sebők		03/04/79	G	22	(1)	
46	Ádám Simon		30/03/90	M	10		
17	András Simon		30/03/90	A	17	(5)	2
10	Attila Simon		04/02/83	A	2	(4)	
16	Tibor Szabó		26/07/96	M		(1)	
67	Gergő Szalánszki		29/09/98	M	1	(2)	
85	Vince Szegi		01/07/97	M	7	(7)	1
13	Adrián Szekeres		21/04/89	D	1		
6	Krisztián Tamás		18/04/95	D	7		1
34	Volodymyr Tanchyk	UKR	17/10/91	M	1	(2)	
9	Norbert Tóth		04/02/83	A		(6)	
19	Patrik Vass		17/01/93	M	19	(1)	1
27	Szilárd Veres	ROU	27/01/96	M	1	(2)	
15	Dániel Völgyi		07/06/87	D	3	(1)	

Mezőkövesd Zsóry SE

1975 • Városi (5,200) • mezokovesdzsory.hu

Coach: Attila Pintér;
(27/12/16) Tomislav Sivić (SRB) ;
(02/05/17) Mikuláš Radványi (SVK)

Date		Opponent			Scorers
2016					
16/07	h	Gyirmót	D	2-2	*Střeštík 2*
23/07	a	Haladás	D	1-1	*Gohér*
31/07	a	MTK	W	1-0	*Kink*
07/08	h	Debrecen	L	0-1	
13/08	a	Videoton	L	0-2	
17/08	h	Újpest	L	0-2	
21/08	a	Ferencváros	D	2-2	*Hudák, Bačelić-Grgić*
10/09	h	Honvéd	W	3-1	*Bačelić-Grgić, Střeštík, Egerszegi*
17/09	a	Diósgyőr	D	1-1	*Egerszegi*
21/09	h	Paks	L	1-3	*Fröhlich*
24/09	a	Vasas	L	0-4	
15/10	a	Gyirmót	W	1-0	*Diallo*
22/10	h	Haladás	W	3-0	*Diallo 2, Molnár*
29/10	h	MTK	W	1-0	*Gohér*
05/11	a	Debrecen	D	0-0	
19/11	h	Videoton	W	2-1	*Kink, Střeštík*
26/11	a	Újpest	D	1-1	*Pauljević*
03/12	h	Ferencváros	W	2-0	*Molnár, Bačelić-Grgić (p)*
10/12	a	Honvéd	L	0-1	
2017					
18/02	h	Diósgyőr	W	3-0	*Balogh, Bačelić-Grgić, Molnár*
25/02	a	Paks	L	0-5	
04/03	h	Vasas	L	0-2	
11/03	h	Gyirmót	D	1-1	*Molnár*
01/04	a	Haladás	L	2-4	*Molnár, Baracskai*
08/04	a	MTK	L	0-2	
12/04	h	Debrecen	W	2-1	*Veselinović, Baracskai*
15/04	a	Videoton	D	1-1	*Molnár*
22/04	h	Újpest	L	1-3	*Bačelić-Grgić*
29/04	a	Ferencváros	L	1-3	*Molnár*
06/05	h	Honvéd	L	1-5	*Kink*
13/05	a	Diósgyőr	D	2-2	*Molnár, Sós*
20/05	h	Paks	W	3-2	*Bačelić-Grgić, Diallo, Gohér*
27/05	a	Vasas	D	1-1	*Vági*

No	Name	Nat	DoB	Pos	Aps	(s)	Gls
28	Stipe Bačelić-Grgić	CRO	16/02/88	M	18	(10)	6
4	Béla Balogh		30/12/84	D	3		1
8	Roland Baracskai		11/04/92	A		(11)	2
21	Aleksandar Damcevski	MKD	21/11/92	D	2	(1)	
13	Szilárd Devecseri		13/02/90	D	10	(3)	
9	Ulysse Diallo	MLI	26/10/92	A	9	(6)	4
23	Marko Dinjar	CRO	21/05/86	D	2	(1)	
1	Dávid Dombó		26/02/93	G	9		
17	Tamás Egerszegi		02/08/91	M	25	(2)	2
2	Dániel Farkas	SRB	13/01/93	D	5	(2)	
3	Dominik Fótyik	SVK	16/09/90	D	10	(1)	
10	Roland Fröhlich		08/08/88	A	2	(3)	1
6	Gergő Gohér		16/06/87	D	22		3
24	Dávid Hegedűs		06/06/85	M	3	(5)	
39	David Hudák	SVK	21/03/93	D	30		1
19	Tarmo Kink	EST	06/10/85	M	21	(4)	3
5	Patrick Mevoungou	CMR	15/02/86	M	12		
33	Gábor Molnár		16/05/94	M	24	(3)	8
20	Mihai Nicorec	ROU	28/03/86	M	4	(3)	
11	Márk Orosz		24/10/89	M	1	(4)	
49	Branko Pauljević	SRB	12/06/89	M	13	(12)	1
99	Bence Sós		10/05/94	M	12	(8)	1
15	Marek Střeštík	CZE	01/02/87	M	30	(2)	4
20	Peter Šulek	SVK	21/09/88	M	1	(1)	
88	Tamás Szeles		07/12/93	D	19	(1)	
7	Bence Tóth		27/07/89	M	14	(7)	
90	Tomáš Tujvel	SVK	19/09/83	G	24		
29	András Vági		25/12/88	D	31		1
14	Lazar Veselinović	SRB	04/08/86	A	6	(1)	1
77	Jan Vošahlík	CZE	08/03/89	M	1	(5)	

MTK Budapest

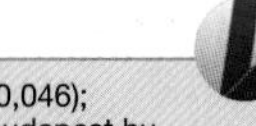

1888 • Dunaferr, Dunaújváros (10,046); Hidegkuti Nándor (5,322) • mtkbudapest.hu

Major honours
Hungarian League (23) 1904, 1908, 1914, 1917, 1918, 1919, 1920, 1921, 1922, 1923, 1924, 1925, 1929, 1936, 1937, 1951, 1953, 1958, 1987, 1997, 1999, 2003, 2008; Hungarian Cup (12) 1910, 1911, 1912, 1914, 1923, 1925, 1932, 1952, 1968, 1997, 1998, 2000

Coach: Vaszilisz Teodoru
(20/12/16) Zsolt Tamási

Date		Opponent			Scorers
2016					
17/07	h	Vasas	L	0-1	
24/07	a	Gyirmót	D	0-0	
31/07	h	Mezőkövesd	L	0-1	
07/08	h	Haladás	L	0-2	
13/08	a	Debrecen	D	1-1	*Vogyicska*
16/08	h	Videoton	W	1-0	*Torghelle*
21/08	a	Újpest	D	0-0	
10/09	h	Ferencváros	W	2-1	*Gera, Torghelle (p)*
17/09	a	Honvéd	L	0-5	
21/09	h	Diósgyőr	W	1-0	*Poór*
24/09	a	Paks	D	0-0	
15/10	a	Vasas	L	2-3	*Vadnai, Torghelle*
22/10	h	Gyirmót	W	1-0	*Torghelle*
29/10	a	Mezőkövesd	L	0-1	
05/11	a	Haladás	D	1-1	*Torghelle*
19/11	h	Debrecen	D	1-1	*Kanta (p)*
26/11	a	Videoton	L	0-2	
03/12	h	Újpest	D	1-1	*Poór*
10/12	a	Ferencváros	D	1-1	*Torghelle*
2017					
18/02	h	Honvéd	L	1-2	*Torghelle (p)*
25/02	a	Diósgyőr	W	3-2	*Gera, Kolomoyets, Kanta*
04/03	h	Paks	L	1-2	*Kanta (p)*
11/03	h	Vasas	W	1-0	*Myke*
01/04	a	Gyirmót	L	0-1	
08/04	h	Mezőkövesd	W	2-0	*Torghelle, Baki*
12/04	h	Haladás	D	0-0	
15/04	a	Debrecen	D	0-0	
22/04	h	Videoton	D	1-1	*Kolomoyets*
29/04	a	Újpest	W	2-1	*Torghelle (p), Hrepka*
06/05	h	Ferencváros	L	1-3	*Myke*
13/05	a	Honvéd	L	1-2	*Myke*
20/05	h	Diósgyőr	D	0-0	
27/05	a	Paks	D	1-1	*Hrepka*

No	Name	Nat	DoB	Pos	Aps	(s)	Gls
4	Ákos Baki		24/08/94	D	22	(5)	1
18	Barnabás Bese		06/05/94	D	1		
30	Bálint Borbély		30/11/89	M	16	(3)	
11	Dániel Gera		29/08/95	M	12	(5)	2
5	Mato Grgić	CRO	27/09/87	D	14		
1	Lajos Hegedűs		19/12/87	G	7		
13	Ádám Hrepka		15/04/87	A	7	(6)	2
12	Dávid Jakab		21/05/93	M	1	(3)	
19	József Kanta		24/03/84	M	32		3
61	Máté Katona		22/06/97	M	11	(11)	
26	Yuriy Kolomoyets	UKR	22/03/90	A	10	(2)	2
60	Kevin Korozmán		02/03/97	M	13	(6)	
10	Leandro Martínez	ITA	15/10/89	A	1	(5)	
7	Myke	BRA	30/10/92	M	17	(4)	3
9	Darko Nikač	MNE	15/09/90	A	2	(4)	
89	Márk Nikházi		02/02/89	M	1	(5)	
6	Dražen Okuka	SRB	05/03/86	D	13	(5)	
1	Danijel Petković	MNE	25/05/93	G	26		
24	Patrik Poór		25/11/93	D	33		2
65	András Schäfer		13/04/99	M		(2)	
64	Ádám Szabó		04/04/96	M		(1)	
58	István Szatmári		27/05/97	A	4	(6)	
25	Lóránd Szatmári		03/10/88	M	1	(3)	
62	Ronald Takács		26/01/98	M		(4)	
14	Sándor Torghelle		05/05/82	A	25	(1)	9
23	Dániel Vadnai		19/02/88	D	29		1
27	Szabolcs Varga		17/03/95	A		(8)	
38	Ádám Vass		09/08/88	M	31		
8	Bálint Vogyicska		27/02/98	M	20	(4)	1
21	Dragan Vukmir	SRB	02/08/78	D	14		

HUNGARY

Paksi FC

1952 • Városi (5,000) • paksifc.hu

Coach: Aurél Csertői

2016

17/07 a Debrecen D 1-1 *Bartha*
24/07 h Videoton D 1-1 *Gévay*
30/07 a Újpest L 0-1
06/08 h Ferencváros D 0-0
13/08 a Honvéd L 1-3 *Hahn*
17/08 h Diósgyőr W 2-1 *Bartha, Bertus*
21/08 a Haladás L 1-3 *Koltai (p)*
10/09 a Vasas L 0-1
17/09 h Gyirmót D 0-0
21/09 a Mezőkövesd W 3-1 *Haraszti, Bartha, Hahn*
24/09 h MTK D 0-0
15/10 h Debrecen D 1-1 *Bartha*
22/10 a Videoton L 1-5 *Hahn*
29/10 h Újpest D 1-1 *Szakály*
05/11 a Ferencváros W 2-1 *Hahn, Koltai*
19/11 h Honvéd D 1-1 *Szabó*
26/11 a Diósgyőr L 0-2
03/12 h Haladás W 2-1 *Koltai (p), Szakály*
10/12 h Vasas W 1-0 *Hahn*

2017

18/02 a Gyirmót D 0-0
25/02 h Mezőkövesd W 5-0 *Szabó, Gévay, Kulcsár, Papp, Bartha*
04/03 a MTK W 2-1 *Vernes (p), Szabó*
11/03 a Debrecen W 3-1 *Haraszti, Kulcsár, Bartha*
01/04 h Videoton D 0-0
08/04 a Újpest D 1-1 *Bartha (p)*
12/04 h Ferencváros W 3-1 *Bartha, Haraszti, Hajdu*
15/04 a Honvéd L 0-2
22/04 h Diósgyőr L 0-1
29/04 a Haladás L 0-2
06/05 a Vasas W 3-0 *Lenzsér, Bartha, Hahn*
13/05 h Gyirmót W 3-0 *Bartha, Szakály 2*
20/05 a Mezőkövesd L 2-3 *Kulcsár, Bertus (p)*
27/05 h MTK D 1-1 *Bartha*

No	Name	Nat	DoB	Pos	Aps	(s)	Gls
92	Zsolt Balázs		11/08/88	A		(1)	
7	Tamás Báló		12/01/84	D	14	(2)	
39	László Bartha		09/02/87	M	20	(7)	11
26	Lajos Bertus		26/09/90	M	30	(2)	2
94	Bence Daru		05/06/94	A		(4)	
22	Áron Fejős		17/04/97	M		(2)	
5	Zsolt Gévay		19/11/87	D	31		2
9	János Hahn		15/05/95	A	20	(10)	6
38	Ádám Hajdu		16/01/93	D	9	(2)	1
10	Zsolt Haraszti		04/11/91	M	23	(1)	3
98	Richárd Jelena		08/01/98	A		(14)	
8	Tamás Kecskés		15/01/86	M	21	(5)	
71	Szabolcs Kemenes		18/05/86	G	16		
19	Barna Kesztyűs		04/09/93	M		(3)	
29	Tamás Koltai		30/04/87	M	16	(10)	3
6	Gábor Kovács		04/09/87	D	2	(1)	
27	Róbert Kővári		23/11/95	A		(1)	
77	Dávid Kulcsár		25/02/88	D	30		3
86	Zsolt Laczkó		18/12/86	M	4	(7)	
96	Bence Lenzsér		09/06/96	D	23	(1)	1
1	Péter Molnár	SVK	14/12/83	G	15		
21	Kristóf Papp		04/05/93	M	31		1
30	János Szabó		11/07/89	D	19		3
17	Dénes Szakály		15/03/88	M	16	(8)	4
40	András Szalai		03/02/98	D	3	(2)	
25	György Székely		02/06/95	G	2		
70	Richárd Vernes		24/02/92	A	7	(9)	1
20	Péter Zachán		12/12/97	D	11	(1)	

Szombathelyi Haladás

1919 • Káposztás utcai, Sopron (6,000) • haladas.hu

Coach: Géza Mészöly

2016

16/07 a Ferencváros L 1-3 *Iszlai (p)*
23/07 h Mezőkövesd D 1-1 *Rácz*
30/07 h Honvéd D 1-1 *og (Hajdu)*
07/08 a MTK W 2-0 *Hegedűs, Williams*
13/08 h Diósgyőr W 3-1 *Williams, Németh, Rácz*
17/08 a Debrecen W 1-0 *Williams*
21/08 h Paks W 3-1 *Gaál, Williams, og (Gévay)*
10/09 a Videoton L 0-3
17/09 h Vasas W 1-0 *Iszlai*
21/09 a Újpest D 1-1 *Wils*
24/09 h Gyirmót L 0-1
15/10 h Ferencváros W 2-0 *Gaál, Iszlai*
22/10 a Mezőkövesd L 0-3
29/10 a Honvéd L 1-2 *Gaál*
05/11 h MTK D 1-1 *Gaál*
19/11 a Diósgyőr L 1-2 *Gaál*
26/11 h Debrecen W 1-0 *Ars*
03/12 a Paks L 1-2 *Gaál*
10/12 h Videoton D 1-1 *Gaál*

2017

25/02 h Újpest L 0-2
04/03 a Gyirmót W 2-1 *Halmosi, Kovács*
11/03 a Ferencváros L 1-3 *Jancsó*
16/03 a Vasas W 3-2 *Williams 2, Kovács*
01/04 h Mezőkövesd W 4-2 *Wils, Iszlai (p), Kovács, Williams*
08/04 h Honvéd L 0-1
12/04 a MTK D 0-0
15/04 h Diósgyőr W 2-0 *Jancsó, Williams*
22/04 a Debrecen L 2-4 *Williams, Tóth*
29/04 h Paks W 2-0 *Jancsó, Iszlai*
06/05 a Videoton L 0-2
13/05 h Vasas D 2-2 *Iszlai (p), Schimmer*
20/05 a Újpest L 1-2 *Williams*
27/05 h Gyirmót L 1-2 *Williams (p)*

No	Name	Nat	DoB	Pos	Aps	(s)	Gls
24	Zsolt Angyal		24/03/94	D	1	(1)	
9	Sjoerd Ars	NED	15/04/84	A	7	(7)	1
8	Funsho Bamgboye	NGA	09/01/99	A		(3)	
35	Predrag Bošnjak		13/11/85	D	28	(1)	
33	Szilárd Devecseri		13/02/90	D	11		
20	Gergő Dombi		25/01/99	A		(7)	
	Ezequiel	ESP	12/01/91	M	1		
14	Bálint Gaál		14/07/91	M	12	(2)	7
9	Zsolt Gajdos		04/02/93	A		(2)	
44	Márton Gyurján		01/12/95	G	4		
79	Péter Halmosi		25/09/79	M	24	(5)	1
68	János Hegedűs		04/10/96	D	16		1
83	Sándor Hidvégi		09/04/83	D	1	(1)	
15	Bence Iszlai		29/05/90	M	30		6
26	Márk Jagodics		12/04/92	D	19	(1)	
70	András Jancsó		22/04/96	D	13		3
1	Gábor Király		01/04/76	G	19		
12	Bence Kiss		01/07/99	M	6	(5)	
21	Tamás Kiss		24/11/00	A		(4)	
27	Lóránt Kovács	ROU	06/06/93	M	22	(5)	3
10	Karol Mészáros	SVK	25/07/93	M	6	(3)	
31	Márió Németh		01/05/95	M	9	(2)	1
88	Sjoerd Overgoor	NED	06/09/88	M	4	(3)	
13	Kristóf Polgár		28/11/96	D	24	(4)	
16	Barnabás Rácz		26/04/96	M	32	(1)	2
66	Dániel Rózsa		24/11/84	G	10	(2)	
23	Szabolcs Schimmer		24/02/84	D	7	(8)	1
28	Dániel Szőke		06/01/98	M		(1)	
98	Máté Tóth		20/06/98	M	4	(19)	1
11	David Williams	AUS	26/02/88	A	21	(4)	11
6	Stef Wils	BEL	08/02/82	D	32		2
17	András Winkler		09/11/00	A		(1)	

Újpest FC

1885 • Illovszky Rudolf (18,000); Széktói, Kecskemét (6,500); Szusza Ferenc (13,500) • ujpestfc.hu

Major honours

Hungarian League (20) 1930, 1931, 1933, 1935, 1939, 1945, 1946, 1947, 1960, 1969, 1970, 1971, 1972, 1973, 1974, 1975, 1978, 1979, 1990, 1998; Hungarian Cup (9) 1969, 1970, 1975, 1982, 1983, 1987, 1992, 2002, 2014

Coach: Nebojša Vignjević (SRB)

2016

16/07 h Honvéd L 0-2
23/07 a Diósgyőr L 1-2 *Andrić (p)*
30/07 h Paks W 1-0 *Lázok*
06/08 a Vasas W 1-0 *Bardi*
13/08 h Gyirmót W 3-1 *Bardi 2, Balázs*
17/08 a Mezőkövesd W 2-0 *Andrić, Diarra*
21/08 h MTK D 0-0
10/09 a Debrecen L 1-2 *og (Sekulić)*
17/09 h Videoton L 3-4 *Windecker, Diarra, Bardi*
21/09 h Haladás D 1-1 *og (Wils)*
24/09 a Ferencváros D 3-3 *Diarra, Balogh 2 (1p)*
15/10 a Honvéd D 1-1 *Lázok*
22/10 h Diósgyőr D 4-4 *Lázok, Cseke 2, Bardi*
29/10 a Paks D 1-1 *Balázs*
05/11 h Vasas D 2-2 *Windecker, Bardi*
19/11 a Gyirmót W 2-1 *Lázok, Windecker*
26/11 h Mezőkövesd D 1-1 *Andrić (p)*
03/12 a MTK D 1-1 *Bardi*
10/12 h Debrecen W 2-0 *Andrić, Bardi*

2017

18/02 a Videoton L 1-5 *Perović*
25/02 a Haladás W 2-0 *Perović, Szűcs*
04/03 h Ferencváros L 0-1
11/03 h Honvéd D 1-1 *Angelov*
01/04 a Diósgyőr L 1-3 *Lázok*
08/04 h Paks D 1-1 *Heris*
11/04 a Vasas W 3-2 *Heris, Balogh, Mohl*
15/04 h Gyirmót D 2-2 *Diarra, Bardi*
22/04 a Mezőkövesd W 3-1 *Andrić, Bardi, Balázs*
29/04 h MTK L 1-2 *Bardi (p)*
06/05 a Debrecen L 0-1
13/05 h Videoton L 0-3
20/05 h Haladás W 2-1 *Balogh, Bardi*
27/05 a Ferencváros L 0-2

No	Name	Nat	DoB	Pos	Aps	(s)	Gls
19	Nemanja Andrić	SRB	13/06/87	M	23	(6)	5
17	Viktor Angelov	MKD	27/03/94	A	7	(7)	1
1	Szabolcs Balajcza		14/07/79	G	17		
21	Benjámin Balázs		26/04/90	M	23	(8)	3
8	Balázs Balogh		11/06/90	M	25	(1)	4
23	Dávid Banai		09/05/94	G	15	(1)	
7	Enis Bardi	MKD	02/07/95	M	24	(5)	12
5	Benjámin Cseke		22/07/94	M	22	(7)	2
20	Souleymane Diarra	MLI	30/01/95	M	26	(1)	4
10	Kylian Hazard	BEL	05/08/95	M	2	(3)	
3	Jonathan Heris	BEL	03/09/90	D	17	(3)	2
4	Dávid Kálnoki Kis		06/08/91	D	19	(1)	
15	Ákos Kecskés		04/01/96	D	20	(2)	
32	Zoltán Kovács		29/10/84	G	1		
28	János Lázok		04/10/84	A	13	(11)	5
13	Dávid Mohl		28/04/85	D	32		1
14	Gábor Nagy		16/10/85	M		(5)	
2	Tibor Nagy		14/08/91	D	13	(2)	
27	Bence Pávkovics		27/03/97	D	14	(8)	
11	Mihailo Perović	MNE	23/01/97	A	4	(8)	2
18	Bojan Sanković	MNE	21/11/93	M	12	(4)	
29	Kristóf Szűcs		03/01/97	D	6	(2)	1
24	Patrik Tóth		31/07/96	A		(5)	
6	József Windecker		02/12/92	M	28	(5)	3

Vasas FC

1911 • Illovszky Rudolf (18,000); Bozsik József (13,500); Szusza Ferenc (13,500) • vasasfc.hu

Major honours
Hungarian League (6) 1957, 1961, 1962, 1965, 1966, 1977; Hungarian Cup (4) 1955, 1973, 1981, 1986

Coach: Michael Oenning (GER)

Date		Opponent	Res		Scorers
2016					
17/07	a	MTK	W	1-0	*Ádám (p)*
24/07	h	Debrecen	W	3-1	*Ádám, Vaskó 2*
31/07	a	Videoton	W	2-1	*Korcsmár, Pavlov*
06/08	h	Újpest	L	0-1	
13/08	a	Ferencváros	W	2-1	*Vaskó, Pavlov*
17/08	h	Honvéd	W	2-0	*Berecz, Remili*
21/08	a	Diósgyőr	D	1-1	*Ádám*
10/09	h	Paks	W	1-0	*Kulcsár*
17/09	a	Haladás	L	0-1	
21/09	a	Gyirmót	L	0-1	
24/09	h	Mezőkövesd	W	4-0	*Ádám 2 (1p), Berecz, Vida*
15/10	h	MTK	W	3-2	*Ádám (p), Mahir 2*
22/10	a	Debrecen	W	2-1	*Murka, Mahir*
29/10	h	Videoton	D	1-1	*Remili*
05/11	a	Újpest	D	2-2	*Mahir, Korcsmár*
19/11	h	Ferencváros	D	2-2	*Ferenczi 2 (1p)*
26/11	a	Honvéd	L	1-2	*Pavlov*
03/12	h	Diósgyőr	W	3-0	*og (Németh), Vaskó, Berecz*
10/12	a	Paks	L	0-1	
2017					
25/02	h	Gyirmót	D	1-1	*Király*
04/03	a	Mezőkövesd	W	2-0	*Ristevski, Berecz*
11/03	a	MTK	L	0-1	
16/03	h	Haladás	L	2-3	*Ristevski, Mahir*
01/04	h	Debrecen	L	2-3	*Ádám (p), Vaskó*
08/04	a	Videoton	W	2-1	*Remili, Murka*
11/04	h	Újpest	L	2-3	*Gaál, Király*
15/04	a	Ferencváros	W	2-1	*Berecz, Mahir*
22/04	h	Honvéd	W	1-0	*Burmeister*
29/04	a	Diósgyőr	L	1-2	*Burmeister*
06/05	h	Paks	L	0-3	
13/05	a	Haladás	D	2-2	*Burmeister, Gaál*
20/05	a	Gyirmót	W	2-1	*Kulcsár, Berecz*
27/05	h	Mezőkövesd	D	1-1	*Vaskó*

No	Name	Nat	DoB	Pos	Aps	(s)	Gls
8	Martin Ádám		06/11/94	A	22	(2)	7
13	Zsombor Berecz		13/12/95	M	32		6
19	Felix Burmeister	GER	09/03/90	D	24	(3)	3
77	Péter Czvitkovics		10/02/83	M	1	(4)	
89	András Debreceni		21/04/89	D	12	(4)	
39	István Ferenczi		14/09/77	A		(6)	2
30	Bálint Gaál		14/07/91	A	8	(5)	2
7	Szilveszter Hangya		02/01/94	M	30		
3	Manjrekar James	CAN	05/08/93	M	5	(6)	
12	Botond Király		26/10/94	M		(10)	2
20	Márk Kleisz		02/07/98	M	12	(8)	
42	Norbert Könyves	SRB	10/06/89	A		(1)	
21	Zsolt Korcsmár		09/01/89	D	23		2
70	Tamás Kulcsár		13/10/82	A	4	(8)	2
66	Mahir Sağlık	TUR	18/01/83	A	19	(6)	6
27	Benedek Murka		10/09/97	M	14	(6)	2
1	Gergely Nagy		27/05/94	G	29		
99	Csanád Novák		24/09/94	A		(4)	
2	Attila Osváth		10/12/95	D		(3)	
17	Yevhen Pavlov	UKR	12/03/91	A	13	(7)	3
33	Vukašin Poleksić	MNE	30/08/82	G	4		
10	Mohamed Remili		31/05/85	M	29	(1)	3
4	Kire Ristevski	MKD	22/10/90	D	31		2
6	Donát Szivacski		18/01/97	M	14	(1)	
28	Tamás Vaskó		20/02/84	D	14	(10)	6
23	Máté Vida		08/03/96	M	23	(2)	1

Videoton FC

1941 • Pancho Aréna, Felcsut (3,816) • vidi.hu

Major honours
Hungarian League (2) 2011, 2015; Hungarian Cup (1) 2006

Coach: Henning Berg (NOR)

Date		Opponent	Res		Scorers
2016					
17/07	h	Diósgyőr	L	1-2	*Feczesin*
24/07	a	Paks	D	1-1	*Feczesin*
31/07	h	Vasas	L	1-2	*Paulo Vinícius*
07/08	a	Gyirmót	W	4-0	*Juhász, Lazović, Pátkai, Feczesin*
13/08	h	Mezőkövesd	W	2-0	*Pátkai, Lazović*
16/08	a	MTK	L	0-1	
21/08	h	Debrecen	W	5-1	*Lang 2, Feczesin 2, Géresi*
10/09	h	Haladás	W	3-0	*Stopira, Feczesin, Géresi*
17/09	a	Újpest	W	4-3	*Lazović, Géresi, Stopira, Pátkai*
21/09	h	Ferencváros	D	1-1	*Šćepović (p)*
24/09	a	Honvéd	W	2-1	*Juhász, Géresi*
15/10	a	Diósgyőr	L	0-2	
22/10	h	Paks	W	5-1	*Šćepović 2, Géresi, Hadžić, Lazović*
29/10	a	Vasas	D	1-1	*Lazović*
05/11	h	Gyirmót	W	4-0	*Feczesin 2, Šćepović 2*
19/11	a	Mezőkövesd	L	1-2	*Šćepović*
26/11	h	MTK	W	2-0	*Lazović 2*
03/12	a	Debrecen	W	1-0	*Hadžić*
10/12	a	Haladás	D	1-1	*Šćepović*
2017					
18/02	h	Újpest	W	5-1	*Hadžić, Šćepović 2, Suljić, Stopira*
25/02	a	Ferencváros	D	0-0	
04/03	h	Honvéd	W	3-0	*Lazović 2, Šćepović (p)*
11/03	h	Diósgyőr	W	2-0	*Paulo Vinícius, og (Jagodinskis)*
01/04	a	Paks	D	0-0	
08/04	h	Vasas	L	1-2	*og (Burmeister)*
12/04	a	Gyirmót	W	1-0	*Šćepović (p)*
15/04	h	Mezőkövesd	D	1-1	*Suljić*
22/04	a	MTK	D	1-1	*Marić*
29/04	h	Debrecen	W	3-2	*og (N Mészáros), Šćepović, Hadžić*
06/05	h	Haladás	W	2-0	*Nego, Géresi*
13/05	a	Újpest	W	3-0	*Nego, Stopira, Šćepović*
20/05	h	Ferencváros	W	4-1	*Lazović, Stopira, og (Koch), Marić*
27/05	a	Honvéd	L	0-1	

No	Name	Nat	DoB	Pos	Aps	(s)	Gls
31	Dávid Barczi		01/02/89	M	2	(3)	
27	Ádám Bódi		18/10/90	M	4	(7)	
9	Róbert Feczesin		22/02/86	A	11	(7)	8
6	András Fejes		26/08/88	D	3	(1)	
16	Filipe Oliveira	POR	27/05/84	M	4	(1)	
5	Attila Fiola		17/02/90	D	15	(2)	
49	Krisztián Géresi		14/06/94	M	15	(15)	6
88	Anel Hadžić	BIH	16/08/89	M	18	(2)	4
23	Roland Juhász		01/07/83	D	30		2
10	István Kovács		27/03/92	M	2	(10)	
74	Ádám Kovácsik		04/04/91	G	33		
18	Ádám Lang		17/01/93	D	7		2
7	Danko Lazović	SRB	17/05/83	M	29	(1)	10
9	Mirko Marić	CRO	16/05/95	A	3	(9)	2
11	Loïc Nego	FRA	15/01/91	D	32		2
17	Máté Pátkai		06/03/88	M	28	(3)	3
3	Paulo Vinícius		21/02/90	D	32		2
44	Marko Šćepović	SRB	23/05/91	A	23	(1)	13
15	Viktor Sejben		04/06/96	M		(1)	
46	Ádám Simon		30/03/90	M	1		
22	Stopira	CPV	20/05/88	D	23	(1)	5
99	Asmir Suljić	BIH	11/09/91	M	14	(4)	2
30	Roland Szolnoki		21/01/92	D	19	(2)	
33	József Varga		06/06/88	M	15	(2)	

Top goalscorers

16	Márton Eppel (Honvéd)
13	Marko Šćepović (Videoton)
12	Enis Bardi (Újpest)
11	Davide Lanzafame (Honvéd) Dániel Böde (Ferencváros) László Bartha (Paks) David Williams (Haladás)
10	Danko Lazović (Videoton)
9	Sándor Torghelle (MTK) Bálint Gaál (Haladás/Vasas)

Promoted clubs

Puskás Akadémia FC

2012 • Pancho Aréna (3,816) • pfla.hu

Coach: István Szijjártó; (02/11/16) István Vincze; (22/12/16) Attila Pintér

Balmazújvárosi FC

2011 • Városi Sportpálya (2,435) • balmazfoci.hu

Coach: Tamás Feczkó

Second level final table 2016/17

		Pld	W	D	L	F	A	Pts
1	Puskás Akadémia FC	38	22	11	5	67	39	77
2	Balmazújvárosi FC	38	22	7	9	49	34	73
3	Kisvárda SE	38	20	9	9	55	30	69
4	Soroksár SC	38	19	10	9	63	40	67
5	Békéscsaba 1912 Előre	38	19	8	11	55	34	65
6	Vác FC	38	16	11	11	45	38	59
7	Zalaegerszegi TE	38	14	13	11	56	49	55
8	Dorogi FC	38	15	9	14	46	35	54
9	Mosonmagyaróvári TE	38	14	12	12	48	40	54
10	Szolnoki MÁV FC	38	14	10	14	49	50	52
11	Szeged 2011	38	12	15	11	39	29	51
12	Nyíregyháza Spartacus FC	38	14	8	16	48	50	50
13	Soproni VSE	38	11	16	11	37	38	49
14	BFC Siófok	38	13	9	16	43	51	48
15	Budaörsi SC	38	13	8	17	48	56	47
16	Csákvári TK	38	8	16	14	44	57	40
17	Ceglédi VSE	38	10	9	19	42	55	39
18	Kozármisleny SE	38	10	7	21	33	61	37
19	Cigánd SE	38	7	11	20	27	64	29
20	SZEOL SC	38	4	7	27	20	64	19

NB Cigánd SE – 3 pts deducted.

DOMESTIC CUP

Magyar Kupa 2016/17

FIRST ROUND

(14/09/16)
BKV Előre 0-1 Ferencváros
Eger 1-3 Diósgyőr
ETO FC Győr 1-0 Debrecen
Felsőzsolca 0-4 Újpest
Füzesgyarmat 0-2 Haladás
Ménfőcsanak 1-1 Ajka *(aet; 3-1 on pens)*
Mórahalom 1-7 Honvéd
Oroszlány 0-4 MTK
Pécsi MFC 0-4 Videoton
Rakamaz 0-2 Mezőkövesd
Szekszárd 0-1 Paks
Testvériség 0-4 Vasas
Zalakomár 0-7 Gyirmót

(21/09/16)
Andráshida 0-3 Balmazújváros
Bácsalmás 3-1 Diósd
Baktalórántháza 4-4 Cigánd *(aet; 5-4 on pens)*
Balassagyarmat 2-1 Hajdúböszörmény
Balatonfüred 0-3 Tiszakécske
Balatonlelle 0-2 Budaörs
Balkány 1-2 Budafok
Berettyóújfalu 0-4 Salgótarján
Berkenye 2-3 Jászberény
Cered 2-5 Csorna
Csepel 0-1 Cegléd
Dabas-Gyón 0-3 Komárom
Építők 0-6 Békéscsaba
ESMTK 1-3 Vác
Gyulai Termál 1-1 Tiszaújváros *(aet; 6-5 on pens)*
Hévíz 0-1 Szeged 2011
Hódmezővásárhely 2-0 Kisvárda
Inter CDF 1-2 Mosonmagyaróvár
Iváncsa 0-3 Nyíregyháza
Kazincbarcika 1-2 Soproni VSE
Kecskemét 7-0 Babócsa
Komló 1-2 Csákvár
Kondoros 0-4 Rákóczi
Körmend 3-2 Szajol
Koroncó 3-0 Bonyhád
Mád 5-0 Edelény
Makó 2-2 Sárvár *(aet; 4-2 on pens)*
Marcali 3-3 Pénzügyőr *(aet; 4-3 on pens)*
Méhkerék 0-2 Putnok
Monor 1-7 Szolnoki MÁV
Mór 3-2 Dabas
Nagykanizsa 1-1 Celldömölk *(aet; 3-4 on pens)*
Nagykáta 1-2 Szigetszentmiklós *(aet)*
Nyúl 2-4 Rákosmenti KSK
Olajmunkás 0-1 Dunaharaszti
Pétervására 1-6 Soroksár
REAC 2-0 Siófok
Sárrétudvari 0-2 Dunaújváros PASE
Sellye 2-5 Szentlőrinc
Siklós 2-3 SZEOL
Szentantalfa 1-1 Király SZE *(aet; 9-10 on pens)*
Taksony 0-6 Érd
Tállya 4-0 III. Kerületi TVE
Tatabánya 0-3 Dorog
Tatai AC 0-5 Puskás Akadémia
Tevel 0-9 Zalaegerszeg
Tiszasziget 4-1 Szászvár
Törökszentmiklós 0-1 Hatvan *(aet)*
Tura 2-1 Nyírbátor
Várpalota 1-6 Bicske
Veszprém 0-3 Kozármisleny

SECOND ROUND

(25/10/16)
Csákvár 1-1 Békéscsaba *(aet; 6-5 on pens)*
Dunaújváros PASE 2-3 Szolnoki MÁV
Ménfőcsanak 0-1 Soroksár

(26/10/16)
Bácsalmás 1-2 Celldömölk
Baktalórántháza 1-1 Gyula *(aet; 4-3 on pens)*
Balassagyarmat 1-3 MTK
Balmazújváros 3-2 Paks
Bicske 2-1 Szigetszentmiklós
Budafok 2-1 Szeged 2011
Csorna 2-7 Vasas
Érd 3-3 Budaörs *(aet; 4-1 on pens)*
ETO FC Győr 7-1 Komárom
Hatvan 3-2 Jászberény
Hódmezővásárhely 0-4 Dorog
Kecskemét 5-0 Dunaharaszti
Király SZE 0-4 REAC
Körmend 2-5 Szentlőrinc
Koroncó 0-9 Ferencváros
Kozármisleny 3-2 Nyíregyháza
Mád 0-4 Újpest
Makó 1-6 Videoton
Marcali 0-13 Mezőkövesd
Mór 0-3 Puskás Akadémia
Mosonmagyaróvár 2-3 Gyirmót
Rákosmenti KSK 1-6 Honvéd
Salgótarján 0-1 Diósgyőr
SZEOL 1-3 Soproni VSE
Tállya 1-3 Cegléd
Tiszakécske 0-1 Zalaegerszeg
Tiszasziget 0-1 Rákóczi *(aet)*
Tura 1-2 Putnok
Vác 0-3 Haladás

THIRD ROUND

(29/11/16)
ETO FC Győr 2-3 Vasas
REAC 1-3 Mezőkövesd

(30/11/16)
Baktalórántháza 1-2 Szolnok
Balmazújváros 1-2 Zalaegerszeg
Bicske 0-2 Cegléd
Budafok 2-1 Videoton
Celldömölk 0-1 Szentlőrinc
Dorog 1-0 MTK
Érd 3-3 Haladás *(aet; 5-3 on pens)*
Hatvan 1-2 Csákvár
Kecskemét 0-2 Gyirmót
Kozármisleny 1-1 Újpest *(aet; 2-4 on pens)*
Ménfőcsanak 0-5 Honvéd
Puskás Akadémia 1-2 Ferencváros *(aet)*
Putnok 1-4 Diósgyőr
Rákóczi 0-1 Soproni VSE

FOURTH ROUND

(11/02/17 & 28/02/17)
Dorog 1-2, 0-4 Vasas *(1-6)*

(11/02/17 & 01/03/17)
Csákvár 2-1, 0-2 Soproni VSE *(2-3)*
Érd 2-1, 0-2 Budafok *(2-3)*
Ferencváros 2-1, 2-0 Honvéd *(4-1)*
Mezőkövesd 0-0, 1-1 Gyirmót *(1-1; Mezőkövesd on away goal)*
Zalaegerszeg 1-4, 0-2 Újpest *(1-6)*

(14/02/17 & 01/03/17)
Cegléd 0-1, 0-2 Diósgyőr *(0-3)*
Szentlőrinc 0-2, 0-3 Szolnoki MÁV *(0-5)*

QUARTER-FINALS

(28/03/17 & 05/04/17)
Mezőkövesd 3-1 Szolnoki MÁV *(Kenderes 2og, Vági 25, Veselinović 30; Tóth 45)*
Szolnoki MÁV 3-4 Mezőkövesd *(Hajba 5, Pantović 47, Berdó 74; Diallo 26, Baracskai 72, Střeštík 77, Molnár 84)*
(Mezőkövesd 7-4)

(29/03/17 & 04/04/17)
Ferencváros 2-1 Diósgyőr *(Böde 65, Moutari 90+2; Ugrai 13p)*
Diósgyőr 0-0 Ferencváros
(Ferencváros 2-1)

(29/03/17 & 05/04/17)
Budafok 1-2 Soproni VSE *(Pölöskei 90+3; Kapacina 29p, Erdélyi 78)*
Soproni VSE 0-2 Budafok *(Kovács 8, Csizmadia 45)*
(Budafok 3-2)

Újpest 1-2 Vasas *(Lázok 5; James 62, Remili 82)*
Vasas 0-1 Újpest *(Andrić 45)*
(2-2; Vasas on away goals)

SEMI-FINALS

(26/04/17 & 17/05/17)
Ferencváros 8-0 Budafok *(Bognár 13, 40, Böde 26, 55, Varga 38, Moutari 44, Djuricin 56, 58)*
Budafok 2-4 Ferencváros *(Csizmadia 25, Kovács 49; Kundrák 21, 33, Hajnal 30p, Moutari 71)*
(Ferencváros 12-2)

Vasas 2-0 Mezőkövesd *(Berecz 45p, Kulcsár 49)*
Mezőkövesd 0-5 Vasas *(Berecz 4, Kulcsár 28, Mahir 68, Ádám 71, Hangya 86)*
(Vasas 7-0)

FINAL

(31/05/17)
Groupama Aréna, Budapest
FERENCVÁROSI TC 1 *(Varga 26)*
VASAS FC 1 *(Kulcsár 47)*
(aet; 5-4 on pens)
Referee: *Solymosi*
FERENCVÁROS: *Dibusz, Dilaver, Nalepa, Leandro, Lovrencsics (Csernik 90+5), Gera (Čukić 69), Hajnal (Sternberg 80), Varga, Kleinheisler, Moutari, Radó*
VASAS: *Nagy, Vaskó, Burmeister (Korcsmár 46), Ristevski, Kleisz, Berecz, Vida, Hangya (Murka 57), Remili, Kulcsár (Gaál 96), Mahir*

ICELAND

Knattspyrnusamband Íslands (KSÍ)

Address	Laugardal IS-104 Reykjavík
Tel	+354 510 2900
Fax	+354 568 9793
E-mail	ksi@ksi.is
Website	ksi.is

President	Gudni Bergsson
Media officer	Óskar Örn Guðbrandsson
Year of formation	1947
National stadium	Laugardalsvöllur, Reykjavik (9,800)

KEY

UEFA Champions League

UEFA Europa League

Promoted

Relegated

ÚRVALSDEILD CLUBS

 1 **Breidablik**

 2 **FH Hafnarfjördur**

 3 **Fjölnir**

 4 **Fylkir**

 5 **ÍA Akranes**

 6 **ÍBV Vestmannaeyjar**

 7 **KR Reykjavík**

 8 **Stjarnan**

 9 **Thróttur Reykjavík**

 10 **Valur Reykjavík**

 11 **Víkingur Ólafsvík**

 12 **Víkingur Reykjavík**

PROMOTED CLUBS

  13 **KA Akureyri**

  14 **Grindavík**

FH freewheel to eighth title

The dominant force in Icelandic football during the first two decades of the 21st century, FH claimed the Úrvalsdeild title for the eighth time in 13 years and the fifth under long-serving coach Heimir Gudjónsson. It was not the most spectacular of their triumphs, but no other team could live with their consistency.

Valur also retained the trophy they had won in 2015, beating ÍBV 2-0 in the cup final. They could only manage fifth place in the league, with Stjarnan and KR finishing second and third, respectively, after they both closed the campaign with impressive winning streaks.

Hafnarfjordur club successfully defend trophy

Valur keep hold of Icelandic Cup

National team keep World Cup dream alive

Domestic league

FH were the Úrvalsdeild's top-scoring team in 2015 with 47 goals, but in 2016 they could muster just 32 in their 22 matches, never scoring more than three in any fixture and with seven-goal 36-year-old Atli Vidar Björnsson their leading marksman. Against that, however, Gudjónsson's team were solid as a rock at the back, where ex-Manchester City and Motherwell goalkeeper Gunnar Nielsen, a Faroe Islands international, proved a vital acquisition after joining at the start of the season from Stjarnan. He and his team conceded just 17 goals and a mere seven away from home.

Tough to beat, FH lost only twice before the title was secured on 19 September when Breidablik were held 1-1 at home to ÍBV. Both of those defeats were against KR, but the country's record champions were unable to profit fully from the six points they took from the champions, a woeful June, in which they lost all three matches, effectively scuppering their hopes of a 27th title and resulting in the dismissal of coach Bjarni Gudjónsson.

Stjarnan were second to FH at the halfway point of the season, but the team that won the title in such dramatic fashion in 2014 were far too erratic to mount a sustained challenge. Their victories and defeats came in clusters, and it was only thanks to a powerful surge at the end that they managed to race through the peloton and grab the runners-up spot.

In contrast, FH's form seldom fluctuated. They went ten matches unbeaten between the two 1-0 defeats by KR and followed up the second of those, at home in Kaplakriki, with a run of four wins and two draws that was enough to carry them unchallenged to the title, with Breidablik, the last team to have a mathematical chance of catching them, eventually dropping all the way down to sixth.

The relegation zone looked set to ensnare the two teams that had just come up, but while Thróttur could not escape, Víkingur Ólafsvík saved themselves with victories in their last two games, the first of them against newly crowned champions FH, to send Fylkir down instead. KA and Grindavík were promoted, the former, from the northern port of Akureyri, ensuring costlier travel bills for the top-flight clubs in 2017.

Domestic cup

Modestly impressive in the league, where 13-goal Kristinn Freyr Sigurdsson was the leading attraction, Valur enjoyed another exceptional season in the cup, retaining the trophy for the first time since the early 1990s. The Reykjavik Reds had midfielder Sigurdur Egil Lárusson to thank for two early goals in the Laugardalsvöllur that ended ÍBV's hopes of a first trophy since their 1998 double.

Europe

The Icelandic national side's exploits in France during the summer of 2016 had no knock-on effect for the country's clubs in Europe, with only one of the four teams, KR, winning a tie. The concession of 13 goals in five home matches hastened the Úrvalsdeild contingent's collective downfall, and it was on away goals that FH were eliminated by Dundalk in the second qualifying round of the UEFA Champions League – the first time in five years that Heimir Gudjónsson's men had lost their opening European tie.

National team

A late winning goal from Hördur Magnússon at home to previously undefeated section leaders Croatia in June enabled Iceland and their fans to hold on firmly to the dream of reaching the 2018 FIFA World Cup finals in Russia. That 1-0 win enabled Heimir Hallgrímsson's side to maintain their perfect home record, draw level on points with their opponents and keep both Turkey and Ukraine at arm's length in an increasingly gripping four-way tussle for the top two places in Group I.

DOMESTIC SEASON AT A GLANCE

Úrvalsdeild 2016 final table

			Home					Away					Total					
		Pld	W	D	L	F	A	W	D	L	F	A	W	D	L	F	A	Pts
1	**FH Hafnarfjördur**	**22**	**5**	**5**	**1**	**16**	**10**	**7**	**2**	**2**	**16**	**7**	**12**	**7**	**3**	**32**	**17**	**43**
2	Stjarnan	22	7	1	3	26	13	5	2	4	17	18	12	3	7	43	31	39
3	KR Reykjavík	22	6	4	1	16	8	5	1	5	13	12	11	5	6	29	20	38
4	Fjölnir	22	6	2	3	21	11	5	2	4	21	14	11	4	7	42	25	37
5	Valur Reykjavík	22	8	0	3	24	9	2	5	4	17	19	10	5	7	41	28	35
6	Breidablik	22	4	3	4	9	10	6	2	3	18	10	10	5	7	27	20	35
7	Víkingur Reykjavík	22	7	2	2	20	12	2	3	6	9	20	9	5	8	29	32	32
8	ÍA Akranes	22	7	1	3	17	9	3	0	8	11	24	10	1	11	28	33	31
9	ÍBV Vestmannaeyjar	22	3	3	5	14	14	3	2	6	9	13	6	5	11	23	27	23
10	Víkingur Ólafsvík	22	4	2	5	14	15	1	4	6	9	23	5	6	11	23	38	21
11	Fylkir	22	2	3	6	14	24	2	4	5	11	16	4	7	11	25	40	19
12	Thróttur Reykjavík	22	2	3	6	11	24	1	2	8	8	26	3	5	14	19	50	14

European qualification 2017/18

Champion: FH Hafnarfjördur (second qualifying round)

Cup winner: Valur Reykjavík (first qualifying round)

Stjarnan (first qualifying round)
KR Reykjavík (first qualifying round)

Top scorer Gardar Gunnlaugsson (ÍA), 14 goals
Relegated clubs Thróttur Reykjavík, Fylkir
Promoted clubs KA Akureyri, Grindavík
Cup final Valur Reykjavík 2-0 ÍBV Vestmannaeyjar

Player of the season

Kristinn Freyr Sigurdsson
(Valur Reykjavík)

A Valur player since 2012, Sigurdsson had scored a total of 11 goals in his first four Úrvalsdeild campaigns with the club. He more than doubled that number in 2016, striking 13 times to finish second in the golden boot standings – one behind ÍA's Gardar Gunnlaugsson. He took first place, however, in the players' player of the year vote and was also a winner for the second year running in the Icelandic Cup. To cap off a memorable year, the 25-year-old joined Swedish Allsvenskan club GIF Sundsvall in the winter.

Newcomer of the season

Óttar Magnús Karlsson
(Víkingur Reykjavík)

A young striker of exceptional promise, Karlsson returned to his homeland in 2016 after finding the competition too hot to handle at the Ajax academy, and at 19 he turned out to be the top-scoring star of a Víkingur Reykjavík side that won more games than they lost in finishing a respectable seventh in the Úrvalsdeild. An Icelandic youth and Under-21 international, he was voted young player of the year before leaving his homeland once again to embark on a new chapter to his career in Norway with Molde.

Team of the season
(3-5-2)

Coach: Gudjónsson *(FH)*

ICELAND

NATIONAL TEAM

International tournament appearances

UEFA European Championship (1) 2016 (qtr-finals)

Top five all-time caps

Rúnar Kristinsson (104); Hermann Hreidarsson (89); Eidur Smári Gudjohnsen (88); Gudni Bergsson (80); Brynjar Björn Gunnarsson & Birkir Kristinsson (74)

Top five all-time goals

Eidur Smári Gudjohnsen (26); Kolbeinn Sigthórsson (22); Ríkhardur Jónsson (17); **Gylfi Thór Sigurdsson** (15); Ríkhardur Dadason & Arnór Gudjohnsen (14)

Results 2016/17

05/09/16	Ukraine (WCQ)	A	Kyiv	D	1-1	*A Finnbogason (41)*
06/10/16	Finland (WCQ)	H	Reykjavik	W	3-2	*Árnason (37), A Finnbogason (90+1), R Sigurdsson (90+6)*
09/10/16	Turkey (WCQ)	H	Reykjavik	W	2-0	*T Bjarnason (42), A Finnbogason (44)*
12/11/16	Croatia (WCQ)	A	Zagreb	L	0-2	
15/11/16	Malta	A	Ta' Qali	W	2-0	*Traustason (47), Ingason (75)*
10/01/17	China	A	Nanning	W	2-0	*Kjartan Finnbogason (64), A Sigurdarson (88)*
15/01/17	Chile	N	Nanning (CHN)	L	0-1	
08/02/17	Mexico	N	Las Vegas (USA)	L	0-1	
24/03/17	Kosovo (WCQ)	A	Shkoder (ALB)	W	2-1	*B Sigurdarson (25), G Sigurdsson (35p)*
28/03/17	Republic of Ireland	A	Dublin	W	1-0	*Magnússon (22)*
11/06/17	Croatia (WCQ)	H	Reykjavik	W	1-0	*Magnússon (90)*

Appearances 2016/17

Coach: Heimir Hallgrímsson	**10/06/67**		**UKR**	**FIN**	**TUR**	**CRO**	**Mlt**	**Chn**	**Chi**	**Mex**	**KOS**	**Irl**	**CRO**	**Caps**	**Goals**
Hannes Thór Halldórsson	27/04/84	Randers (DEN)	G		G	G		G			G		G	44	-
Birkir Már Sævarsson	11/11/84	Hammarby (SWE)	D	D89	D	D	D80	D	D90		D	D85	D	72	1
Kári Árnason	13/10/82	Malmö (SWE) /Omonia (CYP)	D	D	D	D		D	D		D		D	60	3
Ragnar Sigurdsson	19/06/86	Fulham (ENG)	D	D	D	D	s80				D	D52	D91	69	3
Ari Freyr Skúlason	14/05/87	Lokeren (BEL)	D42	D	D		D				D	s88		49	-
Jóhann Berg Gudmundsson	27/10/90	Burnley (ENG)	M84	M	M	M	s58						M	58	5
Aron Einar Gunnarsson	22/04/89	Cardiff (ENG)	M	M		M	s70				M	M	M	71	2
Gylfi Thór Sigurdsson	08/09/89	Swansea (ENG)	M	M	M	A					M		M	50	15
Birkir Bjarnason	27/05/88	Basel (SUI) /Aston Villa (ENG)	M75	M	M	M	s58						M81	58	8
Jón Dadi Bödvarsson	25/05/92	Wolverhampton (ENG)	A		A61	A75	s70				s69	A		32	2
Alfred Finnbogason	01/02/89	Augsburg (GER)	A	A	A67								A77	41	11
Hördur Björgvin Magnússon	11/02/93	Bristol City (ENG)	s42		s85	D						D	D	10	2
Arnór Ingvi Traustason	30/04/93	Rapid Wien (AUT)	s75			s75	M				M72			13	5
Emil Hallfredsson	29/06/84	Udinese (ITA)	s84								M		M	58	1
Ögmundur Kristinsson	19/06/89	Hammarby (SWE)		G					G			G		14	-
Björn Bergmann Sigurdarson	26/02/91	Molde (NOR)		A75	s61			A90	A		A86		s77	7	1
Vidar Örn Kjartansson	11/03/90	M. Tel-Aviv (ISR)		s75	s67	s75	A70				A69			14	1
Theódór Elmar Bjarnason	04/03/87	AGF (DEN)		s89	M85	M75	s80	M76	M78					36	1
Ingvar Jónsson	18/10/89	Sandefjord (NOR)					G							6	-
Sverrir Ingi Ingason	05/08/93	Lokeren (BEL) /Granada (ESP)					D					D	s91	11	3
Hólmar Örn Eyjólfsson	06/08/90	Rosenborg (NOR) /M. Haifa (ISR)					D80					s52		6	-
Arnór Smárason	07/09/88	Hammarby (SWE)					M58	M59	s81			s79		22	2
Rúnar Már Sigurjónsson	18/06/90	Grasshoppers (SUI)					M58							12	1
Ólafur Ingi Skúlason	01/04/83	Karabükspor (TUR)					M70				s86	M79		29	1
Elías Már Ómarsson	18/01/95	Göteborg (SWE)					A	A90	s56			s66		9	-
Jón Gudni Fjóluson	10/04/89	Norrköping (SWE)						D	D					10	-
Kristinn Jónsson	04/08/90	Sarpsborg (NOR) /Sogndal (NOR)						D59	D66	s78				8	-
Gudlaugur Victor Pálsson	30/04/91	Esbjerg (DEN)						M	M81					6	-
Björn Daníel Sverrisson	29/05/90	AGF (DEN)						M73	M66					8	-
Kjartan Henry Finnbogason	09/07/86	Horsens (DEN)						s59	A			A72		7	1
Bödvar Bödvarsson	09/04/95	FH						s59	s90	D78				3	-
Aron Sigurdarson	08/10/93	Tromsø (NOR)						s73	s66	M78		M66		5	2
Óttar Magnús Karlsson	21/02/97	Molde (NOR)						s76	s78			s72		3	-
Albert Gudmundsson	15/06/97	PSV (NED)						s90						1	-
Orri Sigurdur Ómarsson	18/02/95	Valur						s90		D				2	-
Sigurdur Egill Lárusson	22/01/92	Valur							M56	M				2	-
Vidar Ari Jónsson	10/03/94	Fjölnir /Brann (NOR)							s66	D86		s85		3	-
Frederik Schram	19/01/95	Roskilde (DEN)								G				1	-
Hallgrímur Jónasson	04/05/86	Lyngby (DEN)								D				16	3
Kristinn Freyr Sigurdsson	25/12/91	Sundsvall (SWE)								M67				1	-
Davíd Thór Vidarsson	24/04/84	FH								M				9	-
Aron Elís Thrándarson	10/11/94	Aalesund (NOR)								M78				2	-
Kristján Flóki Finnbogason	12/01/95	FH								A55				1	-
Oliver Sigurjónsson	03/03/95	Breidablik								s55				2	-
Tryggvi Hrafn Haraldsson	30/09/96	ÍA								s67				1	-
Kristinn Steindórsson	29/04/90	Sundsvall (SWE)								s78				3	2
Árni Vilhjálmsson	09/05/94	Jönköping (SWE)								s78				1	-
Adam Örn Arnarson	27/08/95	Aalesund (NOR)								s86				1	-
Rúrik Gíslason	25/02/88	Nürnberg (GER)									s72	M88	s81	40	3

EUROPE

FH Hafnarfjördur

CHAMPIONS LEAGUE

Second qualifying round - Dundalk FC (IRL)

A 1-1 *Lennon (77)*

Nielsen, Ólafsson, Lennon, Pálsson, Valdimarsson, D Vidarsson (P Vidarsson 87), Gudnason (Hewson 79), B Vidarsson, Doumbia, Bödvarsson, Hendrickx. Coach: Heimir Gudjónsson (ISL)

H 2-2 *Hewson (19), Finnbogason (78)*

Nielsen, Ólafsson, Hewson (Björnsson 77), Lennon, Pálsson (P Vidarsson 66), Valdimarsson, D Vidarsson, B Vidarsson (Finnbogason 66), Doumbia, Bödvarsson, Hendrickx. Coach: Heimir Gudjónsson (ISL)

Valur Reykjavík

EUROPA LEAGUE

First qualifying round - Brøndby IF (DEN)

H 1-4 *Ingvarsson (90+2)*

Einarsson, Lýdsson (Ingvarsson 66), H Sigurdsson (Sturluson 77), Halldórsson (Toft 73), K Sigurdsson, Lárusson, Hansen, Christiansen, Ómarsson, Eiríksson, A Stefánsson. Coach: Ólafur Jóhannesson (ISL)

A 0-6

Kale, Lýdsson, H Sigurdsson, Halldórsson, K Sigurdsson (Ingvarsson 76), Lárusson (Bergsson 77), Hansen (Toft 60), Christiansen, Ómarsson, Eiríksson, A Stefánsson. Coach: Ólafur Jóhannesson (ISL)

Breidablik

EUROPA LEAGUE

First qualifying round - FK Jelgava (LVA)

H 2-3 *Daniel Bamberg (13), O Sigurjónsson (90+6)*

Gunnleifsson, O Sigurjónsson, Muminovic, Helgason, Atlason (Eyjólfsson 62), Ólafsson, Glenn (Leifsson 62), Hreinsson, Daniel Bamberg, Sampsted, Yeoman (Hlynsson 78). Coach: Arnar Grétarsson (ISL)

A 2-2 *Hreinsson (31), Daniel Bamberg (33p)*

Gunnleifsson, O Sigurjónsson, Muminovic, Helgason, Atlason, Eyjólfsson (Glenn 83), Ólafsson, Hreinsson, Daniel Bamberg (Hlynsson 77), Adalsteinsson, Yeoman (A Sigurjónsson 77). Coach: Arnar Grétarsson (ISL)

KR Reykjavík

EUROPA LEAGUE

First qualifying round - Glenavon FC (NIR)

H 2-1 *Pálmason (40), Fridjónsson (78p)*

Magnússon, Beck, Præst, Gunnarsson, Fridgeirsson (Jósepsson 82), Margeirsson, Pálmason, Andersen (Fridjónsson 72), Sigurdsson, Chopart, Hauksson (Fazlagic 87). Coach: Willum Thór Thórsson (ISL)

A 6-0 *Chopart (6, 29), Fridjónsson (53p), Andersen (68), Hauksson (78), Fazlagic (80)*

Magnússon, Beck, Præst (Michaelsson 80), Gunnarsson, Margeirsson, Fridjónsson (Andersen 56), Pálmason, Sigurdsson, Chopart (Fazlagic 58), Jósepsson, Hauksson. Coach: Willum Thór Thórsson (ISL)

Second qualifying round - Grasshopper Club Zürich (SUI)

H 3-3 *Andersen (46, 50), Hauksson (77p)*

Magnússon, Beck, Præst, Gunnarsson, Margeirsson, Fridjónsson (Andersen 46), Pálmason (Fazlagic 76), Sigurdsson, Chopart, Jósepsson, Hauksson (Tryggvason 90+1). Coach: Willum Thór Thórsson (ISL)

A 1-2 *Andersen (52)*

Magnússon, Beck, Præst (Fazlagic 72), Gunnarsson, Margeirsson, Pálmason, Andersen, Sigurdsson, Chopart, Jósepsson, Hauksson (Tryggvason 81). Coach: Willum Thór Thórsson (ISL)

DOMESTIC LEAGUE CLUB-BY-CLUB

Breidablik

1950 • Kópavogsvöllur (3,009) • breidablik.is

Major honours

Icelandic League (1) 2010; Icelandic Cup (1) 2009

Coach: Arnar Grétarsson

2016

Date		Opponent		Score	Scorers
01/05	h	Víkingur Ólafsvík	L	1-2	*Yeoman*
08/05	a	Fylkir	W	2-1	*Atlason, Muminovic*
13/05	h	Víkingur Reykjavík	W	1-0	*A Sigurjónsson*
17/05	a	Thróttur	L	0-2	
22/05	h	KR	W	1-0	*Gunnlaugsson*
30/05	a	Stjarnan	W	3-1	*Daniel Bamberg, A Sigurjónsson, Atlason*
05/06	h	FH	L	0-1	
15/06	a	ÍBV	W	2-0	*Hreinsson, og (Carrillo)*
24/06	h	Valur	D	0-0	
11/07	h	ÍA	L	0-1	
17/07	a	Fjölnir	W	3-0	*Daniel Bamberg, Eyjólfsson, Yeoman*
24/07	a	Víkingur Ólafsvík	W	2-0	*Vilhjálmsson, Atlason*
03/08	h	Fylkir	D	1-1	*Muminovic*
08/08	a	Víkingur Reykjavík	L	1-3	*Vilhjálmsson*
15/08	h	Thróttur	W	2-0	*Vilhjálmsson, O Sigurjónsson*
21/08	a	KR	D	1-1	*Daniel Bamberg (p)*
27/08	h	Stjarnan	W	2-1	*Atlason, Gunnlaugsson*
11/09	a	FH	D	1-1	*Vilhjálmsson*
15/09	a	Valur	W	3-0	*Vilhjálmsson 2, Eyjólfsson*
19/09	h	ÍBV	D	1-1	*Gunnlaugsson*
25/09	a	ÍA	L	0-1	
01/10	h	Fjölnir	L	0-3	

No	Name	Nat	DoB	Pos	Aps	(s)	Gls
29	Arnór Sveinn Adalsteinsson		26/01/86	D	10		
6	Kári Ársælsson		02/07/85	D		(1)	
8	Arnthór Ari Atlason		12/10/93	M	22		4
23	Daniel Bamberg	BRA	23/04/84	A	22		3
33	Gísli Eyjólfsson		31/05/94	A	12	(3)	2
31	Gudmundur Fridriksson		06/02/94	D	1		
17	Jonathan Glenn	TRI	27/08/87	A	6	(8)	
7	Höskuldur Gunnlaugsson		26/09/94	A	5	(14)	3
1	Gunnleifur Gunnleifsson		14/07/75	G	22		
5	Elfar Freyr Helgason		27/07/89	D	22		
16	Ágúst Edvald Hlynsson		28/03/00	M		(4)	
22	Ellert Hreinsson		12/10/86	A	6	(9)	1
13	Sólon Breki Leifsson		20/06/98	A		(1)	
21	Viktor Örn Margeirsson		22/07/94	D	2	(7)	
4	Damir Muminovic		13/05/90	D	20		2
15	Davíd Kristján Ólafsson		15/05/95	D	18	(2)	
26	Alfons Sampsted		06/04/98	D	15	(2)	
28	Alexander Helgi Sigurdarson		08/04/96	M		(1)	
10	Atli Sigurjónsson		01/07/91	M	4	(10)	2
3	Oliver Sigurjónsson		03/03/95	M	18		1
18	Gudmundur Atli Steinthórsson		24/06/87	A	3	(3)	
9	Árni Vilhjálmsson		09/05/94	A	12		6
19	Willum Thór Willumsson		23/10/98	M		(1)	
30	Andri Rafn Yeoman		18/04/92	M	22		2

ICELAND

FH Hafnarfjördur

1929 • Kaplakriki (6,450) • fh.is

Major honours
Icelandic League (8) 2004, 2005, 2006, 2008, 2009, 2012, 2015, 2016; Icelandic Cup (2) 2007, 2010

Coach: Heimir Gudjónsson

2016

Date		Opponent		Score	Scorers
01/05	a	Thróttur	W	3-0	*Lennon, Björnsson, Gudnason*
08/05	h	ÍA	W	2-1	*B Vidarsson, Björnsson*
12/05	a	KR	L	0-1	
16/05	h	Fjölnir	W	2-0	*og (Jónsson), Lennon*
23/05	a	Stjarnan	D	1-1	*Pálsson*
30/05	h	Víkingur Ólafsvík	D	1-1	*Lennon*
05/06	a	Breidablik	W	1-0	*Pálsson*
16/06	a	Valur	W	1-0	*Pálsson*
24/06	h	Fylkir	W	1-0	*Lennon*
09/07	h	Víkingur Reykjavík	D	2-2	*Finnbogason, Björnsson*
16/07	a	ÍBV	D	1-1	*Serwy*
24/07	h	Thróttur	W	2-0	*Valdimarsson, Lennon*
03/08	a	ÍA	W	3-1	*Björnsson 2, Serwy*
08/08	h	KR	L	0-1	
15/08	a	Fjölnir	W	1-0	*Pálsson*
22/08	h	Stjarnan	W	3-2	*Björnsson, Doumbia, og (D Laxdal)*
28/08	a	Víkingur Ólafsvík	W	2-0	*Björnsson, Pálsson*
11/09	h	Breidablik	D	1-1	*Finnbogason*
15/09	a	Fylkir	W	3-2	*Doumbia, Finnbogason, D Vidarsson*
18/09	h	Valur	D	1-1	*Finnbogason*
25/09	a	Víkingur Reykjavík	L	0-1	
01/10	h	ÍBV	D	1-1	*Lennon (p)*

No	Name	Nat	DoB	Pos	Aps	(s)	Gls
19	Kaj Leo í Bartalsstovu	FRO	23/06/91	M	2	(5)	
17	Atli Vidar Björnsson		04/01/80	A	9	(8)	7
21	Bödvar Bödvarsson		09/04/95	D	19	(1)	
20	Kassim Doumbia	MLI	18/06/90	D	20		2
18	Kristján Flóki Finnbogason		12/01/95	A	8	(11)	4
23	Brynjar Ásgeir Gudmundsson		22/06/92	D	6	(4)	
11	Atli Gudnason		28/09/84	A	14	(4)	1
14	Grétar Snær Gunnarsson		08/01/97	D		(1)	
26	Jonathan Hendrickx	BEL	25/12/93	D	19		
6	Sam Hewson	ENG	28/11/88	M	10	(2)	
7	Steven Lennon	SCO	20/01/88	A	16	(4)	6
16	Sonni Nattestad	FRO	05/08/94	D		(1)	
1	Gunnar Nielsen	FRO	07/10/86	G	22		
5	Bergsveinn Ólafsson		09/09/92	D	20		
8	Emil Pálsson		10/06/93	M	18	(2)	5
22	Jérémy Serwy	BEL	04/06/91	A	7	(6)	2
9	Thórarinn Ingi Valdimarsson		23/04/90	M	16	(3)	1
13	Bjarni Thór Vidarsson		05/03/88	M	12	(8)	1
10	Davíd Thór Vidarsson		24/04/84	M	20		1
5	Pétur Vidarsson		25/11/87	D	4	(3)	

Fjölnir

1988 • Extra-völlurinn (1,300) • fjolnir.is

Coach: Ágúst Thór Gylfason

2016

Date		Opponent		Score	Scorers
01/05	a	Valur	W	2-1	*T Gudjónsson 2 (1p)*
07/05	h	ÍBV	W	2-0	*Lund 2*
12/05	a	ÍA	L	0-1	
16/05	a	FH	L	0-2	
22/05	h	Víkingur Ólafsvík	W	5-1	*Lund, Gunnar Már Gudmundsson, Jónsson, H Gudmundsson, Solberg*
30/05	a	Fylkir	D	2-2	*Lund, Salquist*
05/06	h	Víkingur Reykjavík	W	2-1	*T Gudjónsson, Jugović*
15/06	h	KR	W	3-1	*Lund, og (Gunnarsson), Solberg*
24/06	a	Thróttur	W	5-0	*B Ingason 2, Lund, T Gudjónsson 2 (1p)*
11/07	a	Stjarnan	L	1-2	*Lund*
17/07	h	Breidablik	L	0-3	
24/07	h	Valur	D	2-2	*Gunnar Már Gudmundsson, B Ingason*
03/08	a	ÍBV	W	2-0	*Salquist, T Gudjónsson*
07/08	h	ÍA	W	4-0	*Gunnar Már Gudmundsson, Solberg, Gudmundur Karl Gudmundsson, og (A Gudjónsson)*
15/08	h	FH	L	0-1	
21/08	a	Víkingur Ólafsvík	D	2-2	*Solberg 2*
28/08	h	Fylkir	D	1-1	*Óskarsson*
10/09	a	Víkingur Reykjavík	W	2-1	*Lund 2*
15/09	h	Thróttur	W	2-0	*Óskarsson, T Gudjónsson (p)*
18/09	a	KR	L	2-3	*Gunnar Már Gudmundsson, Óskarsson*
25/09	h	Stjarnan	L	0-1	
01/10	a	Breidablik	W	3-0	*H Gudmundsson, Óskarsson, og (Muminovic)*

No	Name	Nat	DoB	Pos	Aps	(s)	Gls
16	Gudmundur Bödvar Gudjónsson		03/08/89	M	1	(5)	
9	Thórir Gudjónsson		07/04/91	A	17	(2)	7
29	Gudmundur Karl Gudmundsson		30/03/91	M	15	(5)	1
4	Gunnar Már Gudmundsson		15/12/83	M	18	(4)	4
28	Hans Viktor Gudmundsson		09/09/96	D	13	(6)	2
1	Steinar Örn Gunnarsson		11/02/91	G	4		
20	Birnir Snær Ingason		04/12/96	A	6	(9)	3
12	Thórdur Ingason		30/03/88	G	18		
3	Daniel Ivanovski	MKD	27/06/83	D	9	(1)	
11	Ægir Jarl Jónasson		08/03/98	A		(14)	
7	Vidar Ari Jónsson		10/03/94	D	21		1
8	Igor Jugović	CRO	23/01/89	M	22		1
10	Martin Lund	DEN	04/08/91	A	20	(2)	9
27	Ingimundur Óskarsson		04/02/86	A	7	(3)	4
5	Tobias Salquist	DEN	18/05/95	D	21		2
21	Ingibergur Kort Sigurdsson		27/04/98	A		(1)	
22	Ólafur Páll Snorrason		22/04/82	M	16	(2)	
18	Marcus Solberg	DEN	17/02/95	A	13	(9)	5
2	Mario Tadejević	CRO	28/08/89	D	21		
6	Atli Már Thorbergsson		13/03/92	D		(1)	

Fylkir

1967 • Floridana-völlurinn (1,892) • fylkir.com

Major honours
Icelandic Cup (2) 2001, 2002

Coach: Hermann Hreidarsson

2016

Date		Opponent		Score	Scorers
02/05	a	Stjarnan	L	0-2	
08/05	h	Breidablik	L	1-2	*Ingason*
12/05	a	Valur	L	0-2	
16/05	h	ÍBV	L	0-3	
21/05	a	ÍA	D	1-1	*Ingason*
30/05	h	Fjölnir	D	2-2	*Ingason, Jóhannsson*
05/06	a	Víkingur Ólafsvík	L	0-1	
24/06	a	FH	L	0-1	
28/06	h	Víkingur Reykjavík	W	1-0	*Seoane*
11/07	a	Thróttur	W	4-1	*Thorvardarson 2, Jóhannesson, Ingimundarson*
17/07	h	KR	L	1-4	*Radovniković*
24/07	h	Stjarnan	L	1-2	*Jóhannesson*
03/08	a	Breidablik	D	1-1	*Ásmundsson*
07/08	h	Valur	D	2-2	*Ingason, Jóhannsson*
18/08	a	ÍBV	W	2-1	*Ingason 2*
22/08	h	ÍA	L	0-3	
28/08	a	Fjölnir	D	1-1	*Álvaro Montejo*
11/09	h	Víkingur Ólafsvík	W	2-1	*Seoane, Bergsson (p)*
15/09	h	FH	L	2-3	*Sveinsson, Ingason*
18/09	a	Víkingur Reykjavík	D	2-2	*Jóhannsson, Gudmundsson*
25/09	h	Thróttur	D	2-2	*Jóhannsson, Sveinsson*
01/10	a	KR	L	0-3	

No	Name	Nat	DoB	Pos	Aps	(s)	Gls
20	Álvaro Montejo	ESP	12/12/90	A	3	(4)	1
29	Axel Andri Antonsson		29/09/98	M		(5)	
17	Ásgeir Örn Arnthórsson		02/05/90	M	8	(4)	
3	Ásgeir Börkur Ásgeirsson		16/04/87	M	9	(2)	
22	Emil Ásmundsson		08/01/95	M	12	(4)	1
7	Arnar Bragi Bergsson		30/04/93	M	5	(2)	1
24	Elís Rafn Björnsson		13/10/92	M	5	(4)	
18	Styrmir Erlendsson		13/12/93	M	1	(1)	
5	Ásgeir Eythórsson		29/04/93	D	16		
6	Oddur Ingi Gudmundsson		28/01/89	M	11	(2)	1
14	Albert Brynjar Ingason		16/01/86	A	21	(1)	7
25	Valdimar Thór Ingimundarson		28/04/99	A	1	(2)	1
10	Andrés Már Jóhannesson		21/12/88	M	18	(2)	2
15	Gardar Jóhannsson		01/04/80	A	12	(7)	4
23	Andri Thór Jónsson		24/02/91	D	15	(2)	
28	Sonni Nattestad	FRO	05/08/94	D	8		
21	Dadi Ólafsson		05/01/94	D	1	(1)	
1	Ólafur Íshólm Ólafsson		08/05/95	G	13	(1)	
7	Ingimundur Níels Óskarsson		04/02/86	A	2	(2)	
12	Marko Pridigar	SVN	18/05/85	G	6		
4	Tonči Radovniković	CRO	27/10/88	D	21		1
8	José Seoane	ESP	16/03/89	A	13	(7)	2
9	Ragnar Bragi Sveinsson		18/12/94	A	15	(2)	2
16	Tómas Jod Thorsteinsson		08/12/88	D	16	(1)	
11	Vídir Thorvardarson		07/07/92	A	7	(6)	2
12	Lewis Ward	ENG	05/03/97	G	3		

ÍA Akranes

1946 • Nordurálsvöllur (5,550) • ia.is

Major honours
Icelandic League (18) 1951, 1953, 1954, 1957, 1958, 1960, 1970, 1974, 1975, 1977, 1983, 1984, 1992, 1993, 1994, 1995, 1996, 2001; Icelandic Cup (9) 1978, 1982, 1983, 1984, 1986, 1993, 1996, 2000, 2003

Coach: Gunnlaugur Jónsson

2016

Date		Opponent		Score	Scorers
01/05	a	ÍBV	L	0-4	
08/05	a	FH	L	1-2	*Ákason*
12/05	h	Fjölnir	W	1-0	*Gunnlaugsson*
16/05	a	Víkingur Ólafsvík	L	0-3	
21/05	h	Fylkir	D	1-1	*Gunnlaugsson*
29/05	a	Víkingur Reykjavík	L	2-3	*Ákason, Gunnlaugsson*
05/06	h	Thróttur	L	0-1	
23/06	a	KR	W	2-1	*Gunnlaugsson 2 (1p)*
29/06	h	Stjarnan	W	4-2	*Gunnlaugsson 3 (1p), Lough*
11/07	a	Breidablik	W	1-0	*Gunnlaugsson*
17/07	h	Valur	W	2-1	*og (H Sigurdsson), Gunnlaugsson*
24/07	h	ÍBV	W	2-0	*Gunnlaugsson, Björnsson*
03/08	h	FH	L	1-3	*T Thórdarson*
07/08	a	Fjölnir	L	0-4	
15/08	h	Víkingur Ólafsvík	W	3-0	*T Thórdarson, Gunnlaugsson, A Gudjónsson*
22/08	a	Fylkir	W	3-0	*Hafsteinsson, Lough, Gunnlaugsson*
28/08	h	Víkingur Reykjavík	W	2-0	*Gunnlaugsson, Haraldsson*
11/09	a	Thróttur	L	1-3	*Ákason*
15/09	h	KR	L	0-1	
19/09	a	Stjarnan	L	1-3	*og (Árnason)*
25/09	h	Breidablik	W	1-0	*G Gudjónsson*
01/10	a	Valur	L	0-1	

No	Name	Nat	DoB	Pos	Aps	(s)	Gls
10	Jón Vilhelm Ákason		20/11/86	M	7	(7)	3
25	Andri Geir Alexandersson		16/06/90	D		(2)	
5	Ármann Smári Björnsson		07/01/81	D	18		1
8	Hallur Flosason		01/05/93	M	13	(1)	
11	Arnar Már Gudjónsson		20/02/87	M	16	(1)	1
29	Gudmundur Bödvar Gudjónsson		03/08/89	M	6	(1)	1
4	Arnór Snær Gudmundsson		20/04/93	D	15		
9	Gardar Gunnlaugsson		25/04/83	A	22		14
20	Gylfi Veigar Gylfason		12/04/93	D	10	(4)	
18	Albert Hafsteinsson		05/06/96	M	12	(5)	1
17	Tryggvi Hrafn Haraldsson		30/09/96	A	13	(3)	1
7	Martin Hummervoll	NOR	13/03/96	A	4		
19	Eggert Kári Karlsson		14/05/91	M	4	(5)	
28	Aron Ingi Kristinsson		17/06/98	D	4	(3)	
27	Darren Lough	ENG	23/09/89	D	19		2
23	Ásgeir Marteinsson		07/07/94	A	6	(6)	
12	Árni Snær Ólafsson		16/08/91	G	22		
15	Hafthór Pétursson		25/09/97	D	3		
21	Arnór Sigurdsson		15/05/99	M		(6)	
31	Stefán Teitur Thórdarson		16/10/98	A	1	(3)	
16	Thórdur Thorsteinn Thórdarson		22/02/95	D	17	(2)	2
22	Steinar Thorsteinsson		06/12/97	A	3	(10)	
14	Ólafur Valur Valdimarsson		13/12/90	M	13	(3)	
6	Iain Williamson	SCO	12/01/88	M	14	(3)	

ÍBV Vestmannaeyjar

1903 • Hásteinsvöllur (3,000) • ibv.is

Major honours
Icelandic League (3) 1979, 1997, 1998; Icelandic Cup (4) 1968, 1972, 1981, 1998

Coach: Bjarni Jóhannsson;
(20/08/16) (Ian Jeffs (ENG) & Alfred Jóhannsson)

2016

Date		Opponent		Score	Scorers
01/05	h	ÍA	W	4-0	*Smidt, A Bjarnason, Sindri Snær Magnússon, Vernam*
07/05	a	Fjölnir	L	0-2	
12/05	h	Víkingur Ólafsvík	D	1-1	*Benónýsson*
16/05	a	Fylkir	W	3-0	*Maigaard, Sindri Snær Magnússon, Benónýsson*
22/05	h	Víkingur Reykjavík	L	0-3	
29/05	a	Thróttur	W	1-0	*Maigaard*
04/06	h	KR	W	1-0	*Gunnarsson*
15/06	h	Breidablik	L	0-2	
23/06	a	Stjarnan	L	0-1	
11/07	a	Valur	L	1-2	*Smidt*
16/07	h	FH	D	1-1	*og (Ólafsson)*
24/07	a	ÍA	L	0-2	
03/08	h	Fjölnir	L	0-2	
07/08	a	Víkingur Ólafsvík	W	1-0	*Thorvaldsson*
18/08	h	Fylkir	L	1-2	*Vignisson*
22/08	a	Víkingur Reykjavík	L	1-2	*Smidt*
28/08	h	Thróttur	D	1-1	*Vignisson*
10/09	a	KR	L	0-2	
16/09	h	Stjarnan	L	1-2	*A Bjarnason*
19/09	a	Breidablik	D	1-1	*Briem*
25/09	h	Valur	W	4-0	*Briem, A Bjarnason 3*
01/10	a	FH	D	1-1	*Griffin*

No	Name	Nat	DoB	Pos	Aps	(s)	Gls
18	Søren Andreasen	DEN	13/03/96	A	3	(5)	
14	Jonathan Barden	ENG	09/11/92	D	16	(1)	
17	Sigurdur Grétar Benónýsson		27/08/96	A	8		2
7	Aron Bjarnason		14/10/95	A	20	(1)	5
23	Benedikt Októ Bjarnason		03/04/95	D	1	(4)	
4	Hafsteinn Briem		28/02/91	D	20		2
22	Derby Carrillo	SLV	19/09/87	G	17		
26	Felix Örn Fridriksson		16/03/99	D	7	(4)	
21	Halldór Páll Geirsson		21/07/94	G	5		
15	Devon Már Griffin		23/04/97	D	2	(3)	1
10	Bjarni Gunnarsson		29/01/93	A		(7)	1
31	Gudmundur Steinn Hafsteinsson		14/06/89	A		(1)	
8	Jón Ingason		21/09/95	D	18	(2)	
30	Ian Jeffs	ENG	12/10/82	M		(4)	
2	Sigurdur Arnar Magnússon		30/06/99	A		(2)	
11	Sindri Snær Magnússon		18/02/92	M	11		2
9	Mikkel Maigaard	DEN	20/09/95	M	16	(4)	2
32	Andri Ólafsson		26/06/85	M	11	(1)	
5	Avni Pepa	KOS	14/11/88	D	17	(1)	
6	Pablo Punyed	SLV	18/04/90	M	19	(1)	
20	Mees Siers	NED	06/10/87	M	15	(3)	
19	Simon Smidt	DEN	26/10/90	A	16	(3)	3
34	Gunnar Heidar Thorvaldsson		01/04/82	A	6	(3)	1
33	Charles Vernam	ENG	08/10/96	A	7	(2)	1
27	Elvar Ingi Vignisson		23/01/95	A	7	(9)	2

KR Reykjavík

1899 • Alvogen-völlurinn (2,801) • kr.is

Major honours
Icelandic League (26) 1912, 1919, 1926, 1927, 1928, 1929, 1931, 1932, 1934, 1941, 1948, 1949, 1950, 1952, 1955, 1959, 1961, 1963, 1965, 1968, 1999, 2000, 2002, 2003, 2011, 2013; Icelandic Cup (14) 1960, 1961, 1962, 1963, 1964, 1966, 1967, 1994, 1995, 1999, 2008, 2011, 2012, 2014

Coach: Bjarni Gudjónsson;
(26/06/16) Willum Thór Thórsson

2016

Date		Opponent		Score	Scorers
02/05	h	Víkingur Reykjavík	D	0-0	
08/05	a	Thróttur	D	2-2	*Hauksson (p), Chopart*
12/05	h	FH	W	1-0	*Pálmason*
17/05	h	Stjarnan	D	1-1	*Sigurdsson*
22/05	a	Breidablik	L	0-1	
29/05	h	Valur	W	2-1	*Hauksson, Fazlagic*
04/06	a	ÍBV	L	0-1	
15/06	a	Fjölnir	L	1-3	*Præst*
23/06	h	ÍA	L	1-2	*Chopart*
10/07	h	Víkingur Ólafsvík	D	0-0	
17/07	a	Fylkir	W	4-1	*Andersen, Jósepsson, Hauksson 2*
25/07	a	Víkingur Reykjavík	L	0-1	
03/08	h	Thróttur	W	2-1	*Chopart, Hansen*
08/08	a	FH	W	1-0	*Chopart*
15/08	a	Stjarnan	W	3-1	*og (J Laxdal), Chopart, Hauksson (p)*
21/08	h	Breidablik	D	1-1	*Andersen*
28/08	a	Valur	L	0-2	
10/09	h	ÍBV	W	2-0	*Andersen, Hauksson*
15/09	a	ÍA	W	1-0	*Andersen*
18/09	h	Fjölnir	W	3-2	*Chopart, Hauksson, Andersen*
25/09	a	Víkingur Ólafsvík	W	1-0	*Pálmason*
01/10	h	Fylkir	W	3-0	*Fazlagic, Andersen, Hauksson*

No	Name	Nat	DoB	Pos	Aps	(s)	Gls
11	Morten Beck Andersen	DEN	02/01/88	A	13	(8)	6
21	Atli Hrafn Andrason		04/01/99	A	1	(2)	
2	Morten Beck	DEN	06/12/94	D	22		
17	Kennie Chopart	DEN	01/06/90	A	18	(2)	6
20	Denis Fazlagic	DEN	07/06/92	M	14	(8)	2
7	Skúli Jón Fridgeirsson		30/07/88	D	13	(4)	
9	Hólmbert Aron Fridjónsson		19/04/93	A	6	(4)	
6	Gunnar Thór Gunnarsson		04/10/85	D	22		
19	Jeppe Hansen	DEN	10/02/89	A	5	(5)	1
22	Óskar Örn Hauksson		22/08/84	A	22		8
18	Aron Bjarki Jósepsson		21/11/89	D	10	(5)	1
1	Stefán Logi Magnússon		05/09/80	G	22		
8	Finnur Orri Margeirsson		08/03/91	M	20	(1)	
24	Valtýr Már Michaelsson		21/08/98	M	2	(1)	
10	Pálmi Rafn Pálmason		09/11/84	M	19	(1)	2
4	Michael Præst	DEN	25/07/86	M	13	(3)	1
30	Axel Sigurdarson		18/04/98	A		(2)	
16	Indridi Sigurdsson		12/10/81	D	20		1
3	Ástbjörn Thórdarson		26/07/99	D		(1)	
27	Gudmundur Andri Tryggvason		04/11/99	A		(4)	

ICELAND

Stjarnan

1960 • Samsung-völlur (1,400) • stjarnan.is

Major honours
Icelandic League (1) 2014

Coach: Rúnar Páll Sigmundsson

2016

Date		Opponent		Score	Scorers
02/05	h	Fylkir	W	2-0	*Gunnarsson 2*
08/05	a	Víkingur Reykjavík	W	2-1	*Sigurdsson, Björnsson*
12/05	h	Thróttur	W	6-0	*Baldvinsson 2, Gunnarsson, Æ Jóhannesson, Hansen 2*
17/05	a	KR	D	1-1	*Sigurdsson*
23/05	h	FH	D	1-1	*Halldórsson*
30/05	h	Breidablik	L	1-3	*A Björgvinsson*
05/06	a	Valur	L	0-2	
23/06	h	ÍBV	W	1-0	*A Björgvinsson*
29/06	a	ÍA	L	2-4	*Halldórsson, Gudjónsson*
11/07	h	Fjölnir	W	2-1	*Björnsson 2*
17/07	a	Víkingur Ólafsvík	W	3-2	*Sigurdsson, Sigurdarson, A Björgvinsson*
24/07	a	Fylkir	W	2-1	*Halldórsson 2*
04/08	h	Víkingur Reykjavík	W	3-0	*Halldórsson, Baldvinsson, og (Perković)*
08/08	a	Thróttur	D	1-1	*Halldórsson (p)*
15/08	h	KR	L	1-3	*D Laxdal*
22/08	a	FH	L	2-3	*Fridjónsson 2*
27/08	a	Breidablik	L	1-2	*Björnsson*
11/09	h	Valur	L	2-3	*Æ Jóhannesson, Halldórsson*
16/09	a	ÍBV	W	2-1	*Baldvinsson 2*
19/09	h	ÍA	W	3-1	*Hédinsson, Björnsson, Sigurdsson*
25/09	a	Fjölnir	W	1-0	*D Laxdal*
01/10	h	Víkingur Ólafsvík	W	4-1	*Æ Jóhannesson, Gunnarsson 2, A Björgvinsson*

No	Name	Nat	DoB	Pos	Aps	(s)	Gls
14	Hördur Árnason		19/05/89	D	20	(2)	
7	Gudjón Baldvinsson		15/02/86	A	19		5
11	Arnar Már Björgvinsson		10/02/90	A	6	(10)	4
25	Hördur Fannar Björgvinsson		26/06/97	G	2		
23	Halldór Orri Björnsson		02/03/87	A	19	(3)	5
17	Ólafur Karl Finsen		30/03/92	A		(1)	
19	Hólmbert Aron Fridjónsson		19/04/93	A	5	(4)	2
2	Brynjar Gauti Gudjónsson		27/02/92	D	17		1
10	Veigar Páll Gunnarsson		21/03/80	M	3	(14)	5
15	Hilmar Árni Halldórsson		14/02/92	M	17	(3)	7
19	Jeppe Hansen	DEN	10/02/89	A	2	(5)	2
20	Eyjólfur Hédinsson		01/01/85	M	14	(2)	1
25	Sveinn Jóhannesson		22/01/95	G	1		
16	Ævar Ingi Jóhannesson		31/01/95	A	15	(6)	3
1	Duwayne Kerr	JAM	16/01/87	G	14		
22	Thórhallur Kári Knútsson		16/05/95	A		(1)	
26	Kristófer Konrádsson		31/03/98	A		(1)	
9	Daníel Laxdal		22/09/86	D	17		2
33	Jóhann Laxdal		27/01/90	D	10	(2)	
6	Thorri Geir Rúnarsson		24/04/95	M	7	(3)	
5	Grétar Sigurdarson		09/10/82	D	14	(1)	1
8	Baldur Sigurdsson		24/04/85	M	14	(4)	4
13	Gudjón Orri Sigurjónsson		01/12/92	G	5		
12	Heidar Ægisson		10/08/95	D	21		

Thróttur Reykjavík

1949 • Thróttarvöllur (2,341) • trottur.is

Coach: Gregg Ryder (ENG)

2016

Date		Opponent		Score	Scorers
01/05	h	FH	L	0-3	
08/05	h	KR	D	2-2	*Acoff, Atlason*
12/05	a	Stjarnan	L	0-6	
17/05	h	Breidablik	W	2-0	*Acoff, Pálmason*
22/05	a	Valur	L	1-4	*Thiago Borges*
29/05	h	ÍBV	L	0-1	
05/06	a	ÍA	W	1-0	*Albertsson*
24/06	h	Fjölnir	L	0-5	
28/06	a	Víkingur Ólafsvík	L	2-3	*Jónasson, Pálmason*
11/07	h	Fylkir	L	1-4	*Thiago Borges*
18/07	a	Víkingur Reykjavík	L	0-2	
24/07	a	FH	L	0-2	
03/08	a	KR	L	1-2	*Stefánsson*
08/08	h	Stjarnan	D	1-1	*Sørensen*
15/08	a	Breidablik	L	0-2	
22/08	h	Valur	L	0-4	
28/08	a	ÍBV	D	1-1	*Albertsson*
11/09	h	ÍA	W	3-1	*Sørensen, Jónasson 2*
15/09	a	Fjölnir	L	0-2	
19/09	h	Víkingur Ólafsvík	D	1-1	*Pálmason*
25/09	a	Fylkir	D	2-2	*Björnsson, Fridriksson*
01/10	h	Víkingur Reykjavík	L	1-2	*Stefánsson*

No	Name	Nat	DoB	Pos	Aps	(s)	Gls
11	Dion Acoff	USA	23/09/91	A	19	(1)	2
22	Aron Thórdur Albertsson		27/06/96	D	5	(5)	2
15	Davíd Thór Ásbjörnsson		24/02/92	D	4	(3)	
8	Hilmar Ástthórsson		31/03/91	D	1		
9	Emil Atlason		22/07/93	A	3		1
19	Karl Brynjar Björnsson		11/04/85	D	19		1
2	Callum Brittain	ENG	12/03/98	D	6		
18	Gudmundur Fridriksson		06/02/94	D	9		1
23	Aron Lloyd Green		05/01/93	D	8	(2)	
3	Hallur Hallsson		10/03/80	M	12	(2)	
25	Aron Dagur Heidarsson		06/03/99	A	1	(1)	
20	Viktor Unnar Illugason		25/01/90	A	6	(8)	
10	Brynjar Jónasson		14/09/94	A	12	(4)	3
29	Kristian Larsen	DEN	10/01/96	D	5		
21	Tonny Mawejje	UGA	15/12/86	M	10	(3)	
18	Dean Morgan	MSR	03/10/83	A	1	(4)	
16	Finnur Ólafsson		30/01/84	M	8	(3)	
26	Júlíus Óskar Ólafsson		10/02/99	A		(1)	
6	Vilhjálmur Pálmason		01/11/91	A	15	(6)	3
1	Arnar Darri Pétursson		16/03/91	G	12		
5	Aron Ýmir Pétursson		30/01/90	D	5		
17	Ragnar Pétursson		18/03/94	M	11	(3)	
30	Trausti Sigurbjörnsson		25/09/90	G	10		
8	Christian Sørensen	DEN	06/08/92	M	12		2
13	Björgvin Stefánsson		20/12/94	A	6	(4)	2
2	Baldvin Sturluson		09/04/89	D	9	(1)	
14	Sebastian Svärd	DEN	15/01/83	D	7	(1)	
27	Thiago Borges	BRA	22/10/88	M	12	(8)	2
25	Kabongo Tshimanga	ENG	22/07/97	A	2	(4)	
4	Hreinn Ingi Örnólfsson		22/09/93	D	12	(2)	

Valur Reykjavík

1911 • Valsvöllur (2,465) • valur.is

Major honours
Icelandic League (20) 1930, 1933, 1935, 1936, 1937, 1938, 1940, 1942, 1943, 1944, 1945, 1956, 1966, 1967, 1976, 1978, 1980, 1985, 1987, 2007; Icelandic Cup (11) 1965, 1974, 1976, 1977, 1988, 1990, 1991, 1992, 2005, 2015, 2016

Coach: Ólafur Jóhannesson

2016

Date		Opponent		Score	Scorers
01/05	h	Fjölnir	L	1-2	*Lýdsson*
08/05	a	Víkingur Ólafsvík	L	1-2	*Toft*
12/05	h	Fylkir	W	2-0	*Lýdsson, H Sigurdsson*
17/05	a	Víkingur Reykjavík	D	2-2	*K Sigurdsson, H Sigurdsson*
22/05	h	Thróttur	W	4-1	*Hansen, Lýdsson, Lárusson, K Sigurdsson*
29/05	a	KR	L	1-2	*H Sigurdsson*
05/06	h	Stjarnan	W	2-0	*Hansen, og (Rúnarsson)*
16/06	h	FH	L	0-1	
24/06	a	Breidablik	D	0-0	
11/07	h	ÍBV	W	2-1	*Lýdsson, Halldórsson*
17/07	a	ÍA	L	1-2	*Adolphsson*
24/07	a	Fjölnir	D	2-2	*K Sigurdsson, Halldórsson*
03/08	h	Víkingur Ólafsvík	W	3-1	*Lárusson, K Sigurdsson 2 (1p)*
07/08	a	Fylkir	D	2-2	*Halldórsson, K Sigurdsson*
18/08	h	Víkingur Reykjavík	W	7-0	*K Sigurdsson 2, Halldórsson 2, Lárusson 2, og (Í Jónsson)*
22/08	a	Thróttur	W	4-0	*K Sigurdsson 2, Adolphsson, Halldórsson*
28/08	h	KR	W	2-0	*K Sigurdsson 2 (1p)*
11/09	a	Stjarnan	W	3-2	*Lárusson, Albech 2*
15/09	h	Breidablik	L	0-3	
18/09	a	FH	D	1-1	*K Sigurdsson (p)*
25/09	a	ÍBV	L	0-4	
01/10	h	ÍA	W	1-0	*Lárusson*

No	Name	Nat	DoB	Pos	Aps	(s)	Gls
17	Andri Adolphsson		01/12/92	A	12	(5)	2
2	Andreas Albech	DEN	20/10/91	D	12		2
6	Dadi Bergsson		11/03/95	A	2	(8)	
15	Sindri Björnsson		29/03/95	M	4	(4)	
13	Rasmus Christiansen	DEN	06/10/89	D	21		
25	Anton Ari Einarsson		25/08/94	G	20		
21	Bjarni Ólafur Eiríksson		28/03/82	D	20		
1	Jón Freyr Eythórsson		31/05/99	G		(1)	
3	Kristian Gaarde	DEN	10/06/89	M	12		
24	Sveinn Aron Gudjohnsen		12/05/98	A	1	(5)	
8	Kristinn Ingi Halldórsson		08/04/89	A	16	(3)	6
12	Nikolaj Hansen	DEN	15/03/93	A	5	(2)	2
4	Einar Karl Ingvarsson		08/10/93	M		(6)	
1	Ingvar Thór Kale		08/12/83	G	2		
11	Sigurdur Egill Lárusson		22/01/92	M	21		6
5	Gudjón Pétur Lýdsson		28/12/87	M	14	(8)	4
20	Orri Sigurdur Ómarsson		18/02/95	D	21		
7	Haukur Páll Sigurdsson		05/08/87	M	17		3
10	Kristinn Freyr Sigurdsson		25/12/91	M	20	(1)	13
23	Andri Fannar Stefánsson		22/04/91	D	14	(1)	
22	Björgvin Stefánsson		20/12/94	A		(6)	
19	Baldvin Sturluson		09/04/89	M		(1)	
9	Rolf Toft	DEN	04/08/92	A	8	(9)	1

Víkingur Ólafsvík

1928 • Ólafsvíkurvöllur (1,300) • no website
Coach: Ejub Purisevic

2016				
01/05	a	Breidablik	W 2-1	*Ragnarsson, Turudija*
08/05	h	Valur	W 2-1	*Tokić 2*
12/05	a	ÍBV	D 1-1	*Tokić (p)*
16/05	h	ÍA	W 3-0	*William, Tokić, Aleix Egea*
22/05	a	Fjölnir	L 1-5	*Tokić*
30/05	a	FH	D 1-1	*Tokić*
05/06	h	Fylkir	W 1-0	*Pálsson*
24/06	a	Víkingur Reykjavík	L 0-2	
28/06	h	Thróttur	W 3-2	*Tokić, Hjaltalín, Aleix Egea*
10/07	a	KR	D 0-0	
17/07	h	Stjarnan	L 2-3	*Tokić, Ragnarsson*
24/07	h	Breidablik	L 0-2	
03/08	a	Valur	L 1-3	*Nordenberg*
07/08	h	ÍBV	L 0-1	
15/08	a	ÍA	L 0-3	
21/08	h	Fjölnir	D 2-2	*Turudija, Ragnarsson*
28/08	h	FH	L 0-2	
11/09	a	Fylkir	L 1-2	*Faye*
15/09	h	Víkingur Reykjavík	D 1-1	*Turudija*
19/09	a	Thróttur	D 1-1	*Faye*
25/09	h	KR	L 0-1	
01/10	a	Stjarnan	L 1-4	*Tokić (p)*

No	Name	Nat	DoB	Pos	Aps	(s)	Gls
2	Aleix Egea	ESP	25/12/87	D	18		2
6	Óttar Ásbjörnsson		24/05/96	M		(5)	
13	Emir Dokara	BIH	11/09/86	D	16	(1)	
9	Kristófer James Eggertsson		24/02/88	A		(1)	
11	Gísli Eyjólfsson		31/05/94	M	2	(1)	
19	Pape Mamadou Faye		06/03/91	A	10	(10)	2
21	Fannar Hilmarsson		17/04/88	A		(1)	
18	Alfred Már Hjaltalín		26/06/94	A	19	(3)	1
1	Einar Hjörleifsson		22/10/77	G	2	(1)	
4	Egill Jónsson		15/02/91	M	20		
12	Thórhallur Kári Knútsson		16/05/95	M	7	(3)	
12	Denis Kramar	SVN	07/11/91	D	8		
7	Tomasz Luba	POL	18/11/86	D	16		
30	Cristian Martínez	ESP	02/05/89	G	20		
15	Pontus Nordenberg	SWE	16/02/95	D	22		1
5	Björn Pálsson		28/12/86	D	9	(9)	1
9	Kristinn Magnús Pétursson		09/02/96	M		(3)	
10	Thorsteinn Már Ragnarsson		19/04/90	M	17	(2)	3
22	Vignir Snær Stefánsson		26/10/96	A		(3)	
11	Martin Svensson	DEN	10/08/89	A	9	(1)	
17	Hrvoje Tokić	CRO	17/06/90	A	19	(2)	9
24	Kenan Turudija	BIH	24/06/90	M	13	(2)	3
8	William	BRA	31/08/87	A	14	(7)	1
3	Farid Zato	TOG	23/04/92	M	1	(5)	

Víkingur Reykjavík

1908 • Víkingsvöllur (1,449) • vikingur.is
Major honours
Icelandic League (5) 1920, 1924, 1981, 1982, 1991; Icelandic Cup (1) 1971
Coach: Milos Milojevic

2016				
02/05	a	KR	D 0-0	
08/05	h	Stjarnan	L 1-2	*Hilmarsson*
13/05	a	Breidablik	L 0-1	
17/05	h	Valur	D 2-2	*Hilmarsson, Karlsson*
22/05	a	ÍBV	W 3-0	*Kristinsson, Martin, V Jónsson*
29/05	h	ÍA	W 3-2	*Tufegdžić, Karlsson, Í Jónsson*
05/06	a	Fjölnir	L 1-2	*Hilmarsson*
24/06	h	Víkingur Ólafsvík	W 2-0	*Martin 2 (1p)*
28/06	a	Fylkir	L 0-1	
09/07	a	FH	D 2-2	*Martin, Karlsson*
18/07	h	Thróttur	W 2-0	*Karlsson, Martin*
25/07	h	KR	W 1-0	*Tufegdžić*
04/08	a	Stjarnan	L 0-3	
08/08	h	Breidablik	W 3-1	*Karlsson 3*
18/08	a	Valur	L 0-7	
22/08	h	ÍBV	W 2-1	*Tufegdžić 2*
28/08	a	ÍA	L 0-2	
10/09	h	Fjölnir	L 1-2	*Runólfsson*
15/09	a	Víkingur Ólafsvík	D 1-1	*Hilmarsson*
18/09	h	Fylkir	D 2-2	*Tufegdžić, Fuček*
25/09	h	FH	W 1-0	*Hilmarsson*
01/10	a	Thróttur	W 2-1	*Kristinsson, Í Jónsson*

No	Name	Nat	DoB	Pos	Aps	(s)	Gls
19	Erlingur Agnarsson		05/03/98	M	3	(3)	
13	Viktor Örlygur Andrason		05/02/00	A		(3)	
8	Viktor Bjarki Arnarsson		22/01/83	M	8	(2)	
27	Davíd Örn Atlason		18/08/94	D	11	(3)	
15	Andri Rúnar Bjarnason		12/11/90	A		(1)	
17	Josip Fuček	CRO	26/02/85	A	2	(5)	1
5	Tómas Gudmundsson		10/02/92	D		(2)	
7	Alex Freyr Hilmarsson		26/07/93	M	15	(6)	5
16	Stefán Bjarni Hjaltested		14/06/97	M		(1)	
12	Kristófer Karl Jensson		19/02/96	G	1	(1)	
3	Ívar Örn Jónsson		02/02/94	D	21		2
9	Viktor Jónsson		23/06/94	A	6	(12)	1
23	Óttar Magnús Karlsson		21/02/97	A	13	(7)	7
21	Arnthór Ingi Kristinsson		15/03/90	M	16	(2)	2
22	Alan Lowing	SCO	07/01/88	D	21		
10	Gary Martin	ENG	10/10/90	A	13		5
1	Róbert Örn Óskarsson		27/03/87	G	21		
20	Stefán Thór Pálsson		31/05/95	M	4	(2)	
27	Marko Perković	CRO	30/08/91	D	7	(1)	
14	Bjarni Páll Runólfsson		10/09/96	M	5	(2)	1
6	Halldór Smári Sigurdsson		04/10/88	D	16	(3)	
11	Dofri Snorrason		21/07/90	M	22		
17	Martin Svensson		10/08/89	M	2	(1)	
4	Igor Tasković	SRB	04/01/82	M	18	(2)	
25	Vladimir Tufegdžić	SRB	12/06/91	A	17	(1)	5
13	Iain Williamson	SCO	12/01/88	M		(1)	

Top goalscorers

14	Gardar Gunnlaugsson (ÍA)
13	Kristinn Freyr Sigurdsson (Valur)
9	Martin Lund (Fjölnir) Hrvoje Tokić (Víkingur Ólafsvík)
8	Óskar Örn Hauksson (KR)
7	Atli Vidar Björnsson (FH) Thórir Gudjónsson (Fjölnir) Albert Brynjar Ingason (Fylkir) Hilmar Árni Halldórsson (Stjarnan) Óttar Magnús Karlsson (Víkingur Reykjavík)

Promoted clubs

KA Akureyri

1928 • Akureyrarvöllur (1,645) • ka.is
Major honours
Icelandic League (1) 1989
Coach: Srdjan Tufegdžić (SRB)

Grindavík

1935 • Grindavíkurvöllur (1,750) • umfg.is
Coach: Óli Stefán Flóventsson

Second level final table 2016

		Pld	W	D	L	F	A	Pts
1	KA Akureyri	22	16	3	3	42	16	51
2	Grindavík	22	12	6	4	50	21	42
3	Keflavík	22	8	11	3	31	20	35
4	Thór Akureyri	22	10	3	9	34	38	33
5	Haukar	22	9	4	9	31	35	31
6	Fram Reykjavík	22	8	6	8	25	29	30
7	Leiknir Reykjavík	22	8	5	9	21	28	29
8	Selfoss	22	6	10	6	28	25	28
9	HK Kópavogur	22	5	7	10	32	45	22
10	Leiknir Fáskrúdsfjördur	22	6	3	13	32	45	21
11	Huginn	22	5	6	11	20	34	21
12	Fjardabyggd	22	3	8	11	26	36	17

DOMESTIC CUP

Bikarkeppnin 2016

THIRD ROUND

(24/05/16)
Fram 2-0 HK
Grótta 6-1 Augnablik
Leiknir Reykjavík 3-2 KFG
Reynir 1-2 Vestri *(aet)*

(25/05/16)
Fjölnir 0-1 Valur
Grindavík 1-0 KA
Haukar 1-2 Víkingur Reykjavík
ÍA 1-0 KV
ÍBV 2-0 Huginn
Keflavík 1-2 Fylkir
KR 1-2 Selfoss *(aet)*
Thróttur Reykjavík 3-1 Völsungur
Vídir 2-0 Sindri *(aet)*

(26/05/16)
FH 9-0 KF
Kría 0-3 Breidablik
Stjarnan 2-2 Víkingur Ólafsvík *(aet; 7-6 on pens)*

FOURTH ROUND

(08/06/16)
FH 4-1 Leiknir Reykjavík
Grindavík 0-2 Fylkir
Thróttur Reykjavík 4-0 Grótta
Vestri 2-3 Fram

(09/06/16)
ÍA 1-2 Breidablik *(aet)*
Selfoss 4-3 Vídir *(aet)*
Stjarnan 0-2 ÍBV
Víkingur Reykjavík 2-3 Valur *(aet)*

QUARTER-FINALS

(03/07/16)
Breidablik 2-3 ÍBV *(Eyjólfsson 43, Adalsteinsson 47; Briem 50, Smidt 54, 59)*
Valur 5-0 Fylkir *(Toft 4, Hansen 20, 37, K Sigurdsson 71, 74)*

(04/07/16)
Thróttur Reykjavík 0-3 FH *(Valdimarsson 21, 48, Finnbogason 54)*

(05/07/16)
Fram 0-2 Selfoss *(Martinez 9p, Jónsson 74og)*

SEMI-FINALS

(27/07/16)
Selfoss 1-2 Valur *(Mack 90; K Sigurdsson 49, Halldórsson 81)*

(28/07/16)
ÍBV 1-0 FH *(Smidt 40)*

FINAL

(13/08/16)
Laugardalsvöllur, Reykjavik
VALUR REYKJAVÍK 2 *(Lárusson 8, 21)*
ÍBV VESTMANNAEYJAR 0
Referee: *Árnason*
VALUR: *Einarsson, Albech (A Stefánsson 90), Christiansen, Ómarsson, Eiríksson, H Sigurdsson, K Sigurdsson (Lýdsson 83), Gaarde, Lárusson, Adolphsson (Toft 75), Halldórsson*
ÍBV: *Carrillo, Barden, Briem, Pepa (Ingason 11), Fridriksson (Vignisson 83), Siers, Punyed, Maigaard, Andreasen (A Bjarnason 69), Thorvaldsson, Smidt*

Valur made a successful defence of the Icelandic Cup, defeating ÍBV 2-0 in the final

ISRAEL

Israel Football Association (IFA)

Address	Ramat Gan Stadium 299 Aba Hillel Street PO Box 3591 Il-52134 Ramat Gan
Tel	+972 3 617 1500
Fax	+972 3 570 2044
E-Mail	info@football.org.il
Website	football.org.il

President	Ofer Eini
Chief executive	Rotem Kamer
Media officer	Shlomi Barzel
Year of formation	1928

LIGAT HA'AL CLUBS

1 **FC Ashdod**

2 **Beitar Jerusalem FC**

3 **Bnei Sakhnin FC**

4 **Bnei Yehuda Tel-Aviv FC**

5 **Hapoel Ashkelon FC**

6 **Hapoel Beer Sheva FC**

7 **Hapoel Haifa FC**

8 **Hapoel Kfar-Saba FC**

9 **Hapoel Kiryat Shmona FC**

10 **Hapoel Ra'anana FC**

11 **Hapoel Tel-Aviv FC**

12 **Maccabi Haifa FC**

13 **Maccabi Petach-Tikva FC**

14 **Maccabi Tel-Aviv FC**

PROMOTED CLUBS

15 **Maccabi Netanya FC**

16 **Hapoel Akko FC**

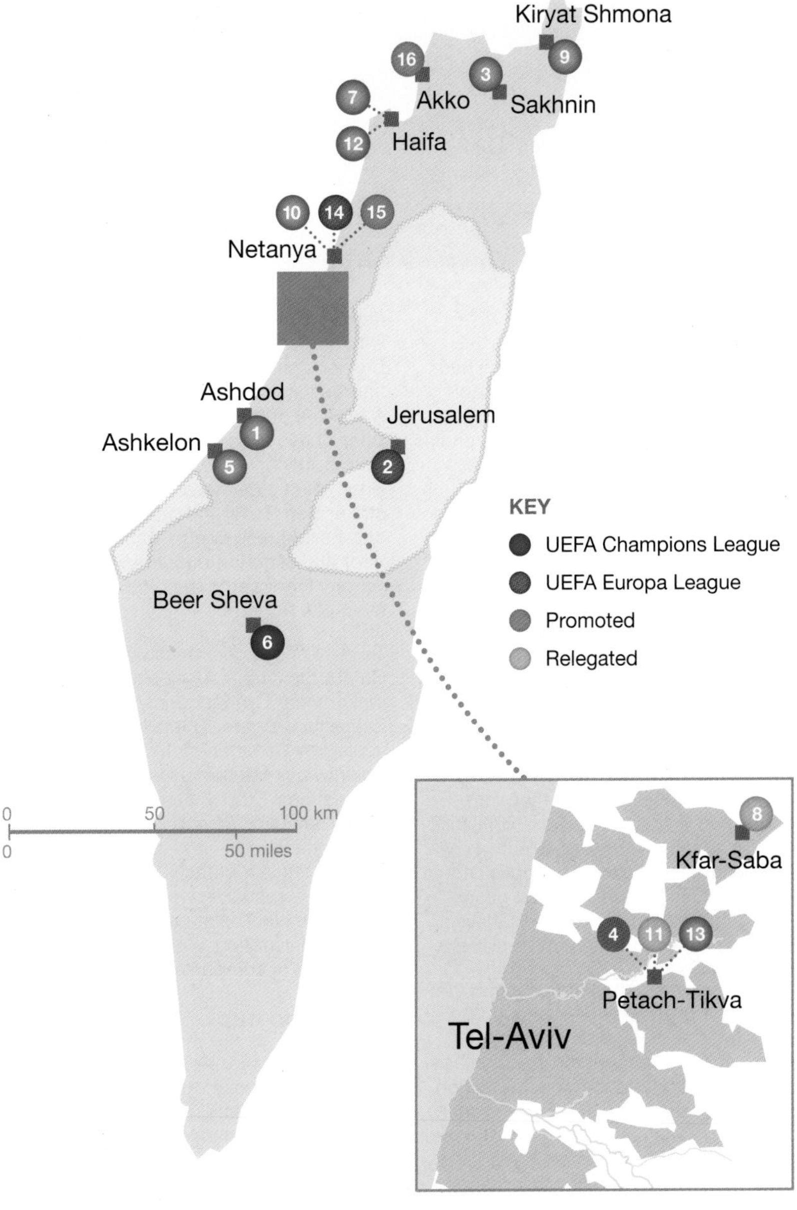

Kiryat Shmona 9
16 Akko
3 Sakhnin
7 12 Haifa
10 14 15 Netanya
Ashdod 1
Ashkelon 5
Jerusalem 2
Beer Sheva 6
8 Kfar-Saba
4 11 13 Petach-Tikva
Tel-Aviv

0 50 100 km
0 50 miles

KEY
- UEFA Champions League
- UEFA Europa League
- Promoted
- Relegated

Hapoel Beer Sheva have what it takes

They waited 40 years to recapture the Israeli league title, and then another one came along straight away. Hapoel Beer Sheva successfully defended their Ligat Ha'al crown in 2016/17, charismatic young coach Barak Bakhar again masterminding the team's success as they finished the season powerfully to see off lone challengers Maccabi Tel-Aviv.

As in 2015/16, Tel-Aviv finished runners-up in both domestic competitions, city rivals Bnei Yehuda surprising them with a penalty shoot-out win after a goalless State Cup final.

Successful title defence for Barak Bakhar's team

Timely ten-game winning streak proves decisive

Bnei Yehuda beat Maccabi Tel-Aviv in cup final

Domestic league

Beer Sheva's 2015/16 title triumph had been a close-run thing, with Maccabi Tel-Aviv pressing them hard throughout, but the Yellows, who had lost their prolific marksman Eran Zahavi to the Chinese Super League, were only able to challenge periodically in 2016/17. While they blew hot and cold, the defending champions were seldom off the boil. Bakhar's men took charge by stringing together nine successive wins in the autumn, and although they faltered momentarily around the turn of the year, there was always the sense that they had the talent and wherewithal to keep Tel-Aviv at bay.

Tel-Aviv sacked coach Shota Arveladze in January and suddenly hit top form under, firstly, sports director Jordi Cruijff (son of Johan), who stood in as caretaker, then replacement boss Lito Vidigal. When the league's first phase ended, after 26 matches, Beer Sheva's lead was down to a mere three points.

Now, however, with their European campaign over, Beer Sheva found an extra gear. Already on a three-match winning run entering the play-off phase, they duly extended that to ten, beating Tel-Aviv 1-0 at home and then, to seal the title in style, 2-1 away, giving them an 11-point lead with three games remaining. The final margin of victory rose to 13 as Beer Sheva finished up with 85 points – two more than the previous season – and by far the best figures for both attack and defence. A mixture of Israelis and foreigners, Beer Sheva's leading performers came from both camps, with defender Ben Biton, midfielder Maor Melikson and striker Ben Sahar the best of the locals and Portuguese centre-back Miguel Vítor and Nigerian duo John Ogu and Antony Nwakaeme the pick of the overseas brigade.

Tel-Aviv once again boasted the Ligat Ha'al's top scorer, 19-goal Icelandic striker Vidar Örn Kjartansson succeeding Zahavi in that role. The tally of 14 goals scored by Sahar and Nwakaeme for Beer Sheva was matched by Israeli international Etay Shechter for Beitar Jerusalem, who finished strongly to snatch third spot – and a European place – from Maccabi Petach-Tikva. Hapoel Tel-Aviv, meanwhile, were relegated as a result of a nine-point penalty for going into administration, with Hapoel Kfar-Saba accompanying them down.

Domestic cup

Bnei Yehuda were never far away from the relegation zone but found the strength to not only reach the final of the State Cup but also lift the trophy for the first time since 1981. As in that final against Hapoel Tel-Aviv, they needed penalties to prevail, a dramatic shoot-out turning one way then the other, with Maccabi Tel-Aviv's veteran Israeli internatonal Yossi Benayoun missing the spot kick that would have won the trophy before Bnei Yehuda substitute Stav Finish converted the one that actually did.

Europe

The top two in the league both enjoyed long and productive runs in Europe, Beer Sheva getting the better of Olympiacos in the UEFA Champions League qualifiers and then sensationally doing the double over Internazionale en route to the knockout phase of the UEFA Europa League, while Tel-Aviv achieved the rare feat of reaching the UEFA Europa League group stage from the starting point of the first qualifying round.

National team

Israel's route to the 2018 FIFA World Cup finals was effectively barred once they were drawn in the same qualifying group as Italy and Spain. An opening home defeat to the Azzurri confirmed the enormity of new coach Elisha Levi's task, and although his team won their next three games to raise a glimmer of hope, a 4-1 defeat in Spain and a 3-0 loss in Haifa against Albania – in which Benayoun collected his record 99th cap – put any lingering optimism to rest.

DOMESTIC SEASON AT A GLANCE

Ligat Ha'al 2016/17 final table

			Home					Away					Total					
		Pld	W	D	L	F	A	W	D	L	F	A	W	D	L	F	A	Pts
1	**Hapoel Beer Sheva FC**	**36**	**16**	**2**	**0**	**46**	**7**	**10**	**5**	**3**	**27**	**11**	**26**	**7**	**3**	**73**	**18**	**85**
2	Maccabi Tel-Aviv FC	36	12	3	3	33	11	10	3	5	28	17	22	6	8	61	28	72
3	Beitar Jerusalem FC	36	8	7	3	24	15	8	5	5	29	21	16	12	8	53	36	60
4	Maccabi Petach-Tikva FC	36	7	6	5	22	16	8	5	5	20	18	15	11	10	42	34	56
5	Bnei Sakhnin FC	36	7	4	7	17	23	6	5	7	15	23	13	9	14	32	46	48
6	Maccabi Haifa FC	36	6	4	8	19	20	6	5	7	15	21	12	9	15	34	41	45
7	Hapoel Kiryat Shmona FC	33	6	2	9	23	24	4	7	5	21	24	10	9	14	44	48	39
8	Hapoel Haifa FC	33	5	5	7	21	23	5	2	9	18	23	10	7	16	39	46	37
9	FC Ashdod	33	3	10	4	15	16	4	5	7	7	16	7	15	11	22	32	36
10	Hapoel Ra'anana FC	33	4	4	9	7	22	5	5	6	15	18	9	9	15	22	40	36
11	Bnei Yehuda Tel-Aviv FC	33	4	6	6	12	19	4	5	8	14	20	8	11	14	26	39	35
12	Hapoel Ashkelon FC	33	4	6	6	11	17	3	5	9	13	25	7	11	15	24	42	32
13	Hapoel Kfar-Saba FC	33	4	4	8	12	21	3	6	8	11	19	7	10	16	23	40	31
14	Hapoel Tel-Aviv FC	33	4	7	5	15	13	4	7	6	14	21	8	14	11	29	34	29

NB League splits into top six and bottom eight after 26 games, after which the clubs play exclusively against teams in their group; Hapoel Tel-Aviv FC – 9 pts deducted.

European qualification 2017/18

Champion: Hapoel Beer Sheva FC (second qualifying round)

Cup winner: Bnei Yehuda Tel-Aviv FC (second qualifying round)

Maccabi Tel-Aviv FC (first qualifying round)
Beitar Jerusalem FC (first qualifying round)

Top scorer Vidar Örn Kjartansson (M. Tel-Aviv), 19 goals
Relegated clubs Hapoel Tel-Aviv FC, Hapoel Kfar-Saba FC
Promoted clubs Maccabi Netanya FC, Hapoel Akko FC
Cup final Bnei Yehuda Tel-Aviv FC 0-0 Maccabi Tel-Aviv FC *(aet; 4-3 on pens)*

Player of the season

Miguel Vítor
(Hapoel Beer Sheva FC)

Recruited by Beer Sheva from Greek club PAOK in the summer of 2016, Miguel Vitor became the linchpin of the club's defence, earning rave reviews from both press and public almost from day one. Beer Sheva were rocked when the Portuguese centre-back missed three months in mid-season through injury, but when he returned to action in March, everything clicked again at the back and the defending champions soared away to another title. Despite his lengthy lay-off, the ex-Benfica man was officially named Ligat Ha'al player of the season.

Newcomer of the season

Omri Glazer
(Maccabi Haifa FC)

The 2016/17 season will not be remembered with any fondness by Maccabi Haifa fans as the club messed up a decent start by surrendering their State Cup crown early and dropping to sixth place in the league. However, one fairly large crumb of comfort was the emergence of their new goalkeeper. Signed from Hapoel Ra'anana as a replacement for experienced Serbian international Vladimir Stojković, at just 20 years of age, Glazer took to the task superbly, earning a couple of call-ups for Israel as understudy to Hapoel Beer Sheva's Dudu Goresh.

Team of the season

(4-3-3)

Coach: Bakhar *(H. Beer Sheva)*

ISRAEL

NATIONAL TEAM

International tournament appearances
FIFA World Cup (1) 1970

Top five all-time caps
Yossi Benayoun (99); Arik Benado (94); **Tal Ben Haim I** (92); Alon Harazi (89); Amir Schelach (85)

Top five all-time goals
Mordechay Shpiegler (33); **Yossi Benayoun** & Yehushua Feigenboim (24); Ronen Harazi (23); Nahum Stelmach (22)

Results 2016/17

05/09/16	Italy (WCQ)	H	Haifa	L	1-3	*Ben Haim II (35p)*
06/10/16	FYR Macedonia (WCQ)	A	Skopje	W	2-1	*Hemed (25), Ben Haim II (43)*
09/10/16	Liechtenstein (WCQ)	H	Jerusalem	W	2-1	*Hemed (4, 16)*
12/11/16	Albania (WCQ)	A	Elbasan	W	3-0	*Zahavi (18p), Einbinder (66), Atar (83)*
24/03/17	Spain (WCQ)	A	Gijon	L	1-4	*Refaelov (76)*
06/06/17	Moldova	H	Netanya	D	1-1	*Sahar (90+5p)*
11/06/17	Albania (WCQ)	H	Haifa	L	0-3	

Appearances 2016/17

Coach: Elisha Levi	18/11/57		ITA	MKD	LIE	ALB	ESP	Mda	ALB	Caps	Goals
Dudu Goresh	01/02/80	H. Beer Sheva	G	G	G	G		G	G	7	-
Ben Biton	03/01/91	H. Beer Sheva	D							2	-
Eitan Tibi	16/11/87	M. Tel-Aviv	D50	D 94*		D	D19	s46	D	32	-
Shir Tzedek	22/08/89	H. Beer Sheva	D	D	D	D	D	D	D	12	-
Ofir Davidzada	05/05/91	Gent (BEL)	D	D						7	-
Beram Kayal	02/05/88	Brighton (ENG)	M					s46		33	1
Nir Biton	30/10/91	Celtic (SCO)	M57	M						20	2
Sheran Yeini	08/12/86	Vitesse (NED)	M							18	-
Eran Zahavi	25/07/87	Guangzhou R&F (CHN)	A	A	A	A	A	A63	A	38	6
Tomer Hemed	02/05/87	Brighton (ENG)	A	A75	A75	s70	s64			27	15
Tal Ben Haim II	05/08/89	M. Tel-Aviv	A62	A68	A81	A75	M64			24	5
Rami Gershon	12/08/88	Gent (BEL)	s50		D	D	D			26	2
Omer Atzili	27/07/93	Granada (ESP)	s57		s63					2	-
Roi Kehat	12/05/92	M. Haifa	s62		s75					5	-
Eli Dasa	03/12/92	M. Tel-Aviv		D	D	D	D	D46	D	9	-
Almog Cohen	01/09/88	Ingolstadt (GER)		M	M	M	M	M46	M	20	-
Eyal Golasa	07/10/91	M. Tel-Aviv		M72	M			M61	M53	11	-
Maor Buzaglo	14/01/88	H. Beer Sheva		s68	M63	s64				23	1
Dan Einbinder	16/02/89	Beitar Jerusalem		s72		M70	M60			3	1
Ahmed Abed	30/03/90	H. Kiryat Shmona		s75						1	-
Omri Ben Harush	07/03/90	M. Tel-Aviv			D					15	-
Munas Dabbur	14/05/92	Salzburg (AUT)			s81					7	1
Bebras Natcho	18/02/88	CSKA Moskva (RUS)				M	M	M	M	46	1
Ben Sahar	10/08/89	H. Beer Sheva				A64		A	A67	41	7
Eliran Atar	17/02/87	M. Haifa				s75				4	1
Ofir Marciano	07/10/89	Hibernian (SCO)					G			11	-
Lior Refaelov	26/04/86	Club Brugge (BEL)					M	M68	M57	38	6
Taleb Tawatha	21/06/92	Eintracht Frankfurt (GER)					s19	D	D	8	-
David Keltjens	11/06/95	Beitar Jerusalem					s60	s46		2	-
Tal Ben Haim I	31/03/82	M. Tel-Aviv						D46		92	1
Yossi Benayoun	05/05/80	M. Tel-Aviv						s61	s67	99	24
Etay Shechter	22/02/87	Beitar Jerusalem						s63	s53	26	4
Idan Vered	01/01/89	Beitar Jerusalem						s68	s57	2	-

EUROPE

Hapoel Beer Sheva FC

Second qualifying round - FC Sheriff (MDA)
H 3-2 *Ogu (43), Barda (52p), Radi (90p)*
Goresh, Biton (Radi 64), Nwakaeme, Barda, Buzaglo (Ohayon 90+1), Hoban (Sahar 70), Davidzada, Taha, Melikson, William, Ogu. Coach: Barak Bakhar (ISR)
A 0-0
Goresh, Biton, Miguel Vítor, Radi (Shabtai 74), Nwakaeme, Hoban, Davidzada, Sahar (Barda 61), Melikson (Buzaglo 90+2), William, Ogu. Coach: Barak Bakhar (ISR)
Red card: Hoban 90+4

Third qualifying round - Olympiacos FC (GRE)
A 0-0
Goresh, Biton, Miguel Vítor, Nwakaeme (Shabtai 90+2), Barda (Sahar 69), Davidzada, Broun, Taha, Melikson (Radi 76), William, Ogu. Coach: Barak Bakhar (ISR)
H 1-0 *Tzedek (79)*
Goresh, Biton, Miguel Vítor, Tzedek, Nwakaeme, Barda (Lúcio Maranhão 61), Hoban, Davidzada, Broun (Radi 66), Melikson (Taha 83), Ogu. Coach: Barak Bakhar (ISR)

Play-offs - Celtic FC (SCO)
A 2-5 *Lúcio Maranhão (55), Melikson (57)*
Goresh, Biton, Tzedek, Radi (Broun 85), Nwakaeme, Hoban (Buzaglo 79), Davidzada, Taha, Lúcio Maranhão (Sahar 69), Melikson, Ogu. Coach: Barak Bakhar (ISR)
H 2-0 *Sahar (21), Hoban (48)*
Goresh, Biton, Miguel Vítor (Shabtai 75), Tzedek, Radi, Nwakaeme, Hoban, Davidzada, Lúcio Maranhão (Sahar 19), Melikson (Buzaglo 34), Ogu. Coach: Barak Bakhar (ISR)

Group K
Match 1 - FC Internazionale Milano (ITA)
A 2-0 *Miguel Vítor (54), Buzaglo (69)*
Goresh, Biton, Miguel Vítor, Tzedek, Nwakaeme, Buzaglo (Sahar 77), Hoban, Taha, Lúcio Maranhão (Melikson 67), Ogu, Korhut (Turgeman 85). Coach: Barak Bakhar (ISR)
Match 2 - Southampton FC (ENG)
H 0-0
Goresh, Biton, Miguel Vítor, Tzedek, Radi (Hoban 80), Nwakaeme, Taha, Lúcio Maranhão (Sahar 62), Melikson (Buzaglo 70), Ogu, Korhut. Coach: Barak Bakhar (ISR)
Match 3 - AC Sparta Praha (CZE)
H 0-1
Goresh, Biton, Miguel Vítor, Tzedek, Radi (Buzaglo 68), Nwakaeme, Hoban (Sahar 73), Lúcio Maranhão (Ghadir 82), Melikson, Ogu, Korhut. Coach: Barak Bakhar (ISR)
Match 4 - AC Sparta Praha (CZE)
A 0-2
Goresh, Biton, Miguel Vítor (Shabtai 46), Tzedek, Radi, Buzaglo (Ghadir 62), Hoban, Taha, Lúcio Maranhão (Sahar 73), Melikson, Korhut. Coach: Barak Bakhar (ISR)
Match 5 - FC Internazionale Milano (ITA)
H 3-2 *Lúcio Maranhão (58), Nwakaeme (71p), Sahar (90+3)*
Goresh, Biton, Miguel Vítor, Tzedek, Nwakaeme, Buzaglo, Hoban (Ghadir 81), Taha (Radi 36), Lúcio Maranhão (Sahar 75), Ogu, Korhut. Coach: Barak Bakhar (ISR)
Match 6 - Southampton FC (ENG)
A 1-1 *Buzaglo (79)*
Goresh, Biton, Miguel Vítor, Tzedek, Radi, Nwakaeme, Buzaglo, Hoban (Ghadir 56), Sahar (Lúcio Maranhão 68), Ogu, Korhut (Shabtai 77). Coach: Barak Bakhar (ISR)

Round of 32 - Beşiktaş JK (TUR)
H 1-3 *Barda (44)*
Goresh, Biton, Turgeman, Tzedek , Radi, Nwakaeme, Barda (Sahar 79), Hoban (Ohana 67), Melikson (Ghadir 58), William, Ogu. Coach: Barak Bakhar (ISR)
A 1-2 *Nwakaeme (64)*
Goresh, Turgeman, Tzedek , Ghadir (Melikson 64), Nwakaeme, Hoban, Sahar (Barda 70), Broun (Buzaglo 57), Ohayon, William, Ogu. Coach: Barak Bakhar (ISR)

Maccabi Haifa FC

Second qualifying round - Nõmme Kalju FC (EST)
H 1-1 *Vermouth (70)*
Levita, Valiente, Abu Abaid, Kagelmacher (Gozlan 65), Obraniak, Rukavytsya, Vermouth, Menachem, Mugrabi (Raiyan 78), Meshumar (Habashi 84), Lavi. Coach: Ronny Levi (ISR)
A 1-1 (aet; 3-5 on pens) *Rukavytsya (34p)*
Levita, Valiente, Abu Abaid, Kagelmacher, Obraniak, Rukavytsya, Vermouth (Zenati 89), Menachem, Mugrabi (Gozlan 77), Meshumar (Keinan 71), Lavi. Coach: Ronny Levi (ISR)

Maccabi Tel-Aviv FC

First qualifying round - ND Gorica (SVN)
H 3-0 *Igiebor (13, 69), Orlando Sá (45)*
Rajković, Medunjanin, Alberman, Ben Haim (II) (Ben Basat 78), Micha, Tibi, Ben Harush (Rikan 82), Carlos García, Igiebor, D Peretz, Orlando Sá (Itzhaki 70). Coach: Shota Arveladze (GEO)
A 1-0 *Benayoun (10)*
Rajković, Medunjanin, Alberman, Micha (Ben Haim (II) 71), Tibi (Filipenko 64), Ben Harush, Ben Haim (I), Igiebor, D Peretz, Benayoun, Orlando Sá (Ben Basat 46). Coach: Shota Arveladze (GEO)

Second qualifying round - FC Kairat Almaty (KAZ)
A 1-1 *Benayoun (90+1)*
Rajković, Medunjanin (Golasa 90), Alberman, Ben Haim (II) (Benayoun 73), Micha, Tibi, Rikan, Ben Haim (I), Igiebor (Itzhaki 86), D Peretz, Orlando Sá. Coach: Shota Arveladze (GEO)
H 2-1 *Ben Haim (II) (5), Alberman (86)*
Rajković, Medunjanin (Filipenko 90), Alberman, Ben Haim (II) (Benayoun 75), Micha, Tibi, Rikan, Ben Haim (I), Igiebor, D Peretz (Dasa 69), Orlando Sá. Coach: Shota Arveladze (GEO)

Third qualifying round - CS Pandurii Târgu Jiu (ROU)
A 3-1 *Ben Haim (II) (7), Igiebor (49), Micha (77)*
Rajković, Medunjanin (E Peretz 68), Alberman, Ben Haim (II), Micha, Tibi, Filipenko, Rikan, Igiebor (Itzhaki 79), D Peretz, Orlando Sá (Ben Basat 75). Coach: Shota Arveladze (GEO)
H 2-1 *Igiebor (24), Scarione (80)*
Rajković, Dasa, Medunjanin, Alberman (Scarione 59), Micha, Tibi, Filipenko, Rikan, Igiebor, Benayoun (Ben Basat 82), Orlando Sá (Itzhaki 72). Coach: Shota Arveladze (GEO)

Play-offs - HNK Hajduk Split (CRO)
H 2-1 *Alberman (9), Scarione (77)*
Rajković, Medunjanin, Scarione (Benayoun 84), Alberman (Ben Basat 68), Ben Haim (II), Micha, Tibi, Filipenko, Rikan, Igiebor, D Peretz (Dasa 63). Coach: Shota Arveladze (GEO)
A 1-2 (aet; 4-3 on pens) *Scarione (52)*
Rajković, Dasa, Medunjanin, Scarione, Ben Basat (Rikan 106), Micha (Itzhaki 114), Tibi, Ben Harush, Ben Haim (I), Igiebor, Benayoun (Orlando Sá 81). Coach: Shota Arveladze (GEO)

Group D
Match 1 - FC Zenit (RUS)
H 3-4 *Medunjanin (26, 70), Kjartansson (50)*
Rajković, Dasa, Medunjanin, Alberman, Ben Haim (II) (D Peretz 85), Ben Harush, Filipenko, Kjartansson (Ben Basat 74), Ben Haim (I), Igiebor, Benayoun (Micha 79). Coach: Shota Arveladze (GEO)
Red card: Dasa 81
Match 2 - Dundalk FC (IRL)
A 0-1
Rajković, Medunjanin, Scarione, Alberman (Itzhaki 75), Ben Haim (II) (Benayoun 81), Tibi, Ben Harush, Kjartansson, Ben Haim (I), Igiebor (Micha 59), D Peretz. Coach: Shota Arveladze (GEO)
Match 3 - AZ Alkmaar (NED)
A 2-1 *Scarione (24), Golasa (82)*
Rajković, Dasa, Medunjanin, Scarione (Filipenko 84), Alberman (Igiebor 79), Ben Haim (II) (Micha 69), Tibi, Ben Harush, Golasa, Kjartansson, Ben Haim (I). Coach: Shota Arveladze (GEO)
Match 4 - AZ Alkmaar (NED)
H 0-0
Rajković, Dasa, Medunjanin, Scarione, Alberman, Ben Haim (II), Micha (Benayoun 81), Tibi, Ben Harush (Rikan 71), Kjartansson (Igiebor 72), Ben Haim (I). Coach: Shota Arveladze (GEO)
Match 5 - FC Zenit (RUS)
A 0-2
Rajković, Dasa, Medunjanin (E Peretz 82), Scarione (Benayoun 46), Ben Basat, Ben Haim (II) (Yehezkel 46), Tibi, Ben Harush, Filipenko, Golasa, Igiebor. Coach: Shota Arveladze (GEO)
Match 6 - Dundalk FC (IRL)
H 2-1 *Ben Haim (II) (21p), Micha (38)*
Rajković, Dasa, Medunjanin, Ben Haim (II) (Ben Basat 88), Micha, Tibi, Ben Harush, Golasa (Alberman 82), Kjartansson, Ben Haim (I), Igiebor (Benayoun 84). Coach: Shota Arveladze (GEO)

DOMESTIC LEAGUE CLUB-BY-CLUB

Beitar Jerusalem FC

First qualifying round - FK Sloboda Tuzla (BIH)

A 0-0

Kleiman, Jesús Rueda, Mori, Atzili, Shechter (Brihon 80), Einbinder, Claudemir, Valpoort (Nachmani 89), Moyal (L Cohen 66), Mishan, Magbo. Coach: Ran Ben-Shimon (ISR)

H 1-0 Atzili (66p)

Kleiman, Jesús Rueda, Mori, Atzili, Shechter (Keltjens 78), Einbinder, Claudemir, Valpoort (Brihon 72), Moyal (L Cohen 85), Mishan, Magbo. Coach: Ran Ben-Shimon (ISR)

Second qualifying round - AC Omonia (CYP)

H 1-0 *Abuhazira (71)*

Kleiman, Keltjens, Mori, Kachila, Atzili, Vered (Moyal 72), Einbinder, Claudemir, Valpoort (Shechter 85), Brihon (Abuhazira 64), Magbo. Coach: Ran Ben-Shimon (ISR)

A 2-3 *Atzili (17, 45p)*

Kleiman, Keltjens, Jesús Rueda, Mori, Atzili, Shechter (Abuhazira 78), Einbinder, Claudemir, Valpoort (Vered 58), Moyal (Rali 64), Magbo. Coach: Ran Ben-Shimon (ISR)

Third qualifying round - FK Jelgava (LVA)

A 1-1 *Vered (25)*

Kleiman, Jesús Rueda, Mori, Atzili, Vered, Shechter (Heister 80), Einbinder, Claudemir, L Cohen (Abuhazira 73), Rali (Benish 69), Magbo. Coach: Ran Ben-Shimon (ISR)

H 3-0 *Atzili (16p), Shechter (29), Heister (47)*

Kleiman, Jesús Rueda, Mori, Atzili, Vered (Abuhazira 76), Shechter, Einbinder, Claudemir, L Cohen (Keltjens 66), Heister (Magbo 57), Rali. Coach: Ran Ben-Shimon (ISR)

Play-offs - AS Saint-Étienne (FRA)

H 1-2 *Vered (8)*

Kleiman, Jesús Rueda, Mori, Atzili, Vered (Keltjens 82), Shechter (Audel 82), Einbinder, Claudemir, L Cohen (Abuhazira 59), Heister, Rali. Coach: Ran Ben-Shimon (ISR)

A 0-0

Kleiman, Keltjens (Atzili 46), Jesús Rueda, Mori, Vered, Shechter, Einbinder, Claudemir, L Cohen (Audel 69), Heister, Rali (Benish 59). Coach: Ran Ben-Shimon (ISR)

FC Ashdod

1999 • Yud-Alef (8,200) • no website

Coach: Ronny Awat
(14/02/17) Ran Ben-Shimon

2016

20/08	a	H. Kiryat Shmona	L	0-1	
28/08	h	M. Tel-Aviv	L	1-2	*Kinda*
11/09	a	H. Ashkelon	D	0-0	
17/09	h	H. Haifa	L	1-3	*Biton*
24/09	a	H. Kfar-Saba	L	0-1	
01/10	h	Bnei Yehuda	D	2-2	*Zrihan, Azriel*
22/10	h	Beitar	D	0-0	
29/10	a	H. Ra'anana	D	0-0	
05/11	h	H. Tel-Aviv	W	1-0	*Zrihan*
19/11	a	Bnei Sakhnin	W	1-0	*Moshel*
26/11	h	M. Haifa	D	1-1	*David*
03/12	a	H. Beer Sheva	L	0-5	
11/12	h	M. Petach-Tikva	D	2-2	*Azriel, Bagarić*
17/12	h	H. Kiryat Shmona	D	0-0	
24/12	a	M. Tel-Aviv	L	0-1	

2017

01/01	h	H. Ashkelon	W	1-0	*Biton*
11/01	a	H. Haifa	W	1-0	*David*
14/01	h	H. Kfar-Saba	D	0-0	
22/01	a	Bnei Yehuda	L	0-2	
28/01	a	Beitar	D	1-1	*David*
05/02	h	H. Ra'anana	L	0-1	
12/02	a	H. Tel-Aviv	L	0-2	
18/02	h	Bnei Sakhnin	D	1-1	*Inbrum*
25/02	a	M. Haifa	W	1-0	*Inbrum*
04/03	h	H. Beer Sheva	L	0-1	
11/03	a	M. Petach-Tikva	W	1-0	*Biton*
20/03	h	H. Kfar-Saba	D	0-0	
03/04	a	H. Ashkelon	D	0-0	
09/04	h	H. Kiryat Shmona	D	1-1	*Siroshtein*
22/04	a	H. Haifa	D	1-1	*Inbrum*
29/04	h	H. Tel-Aviv	W	2-0	*Mond, Inbrum*
06/05	h	H. Ra'anana	D	2-2	*Davidov 2*
13/05	a	Bnei Yehuda	L	1-2	*David*

No	Name	Nat	DoB	Pos	Aps	(s)	Gls
12	Itzhak Asefa		19/11/98	A	1	(1)	
7	Chen Azriel		26/06/88	A	20	(8)	2
32	Dražen Bagarić	CRO	12/11/92	A	4	(8)	1
5	Nir Barda		25/01/96	D	11	(2)	
25	Georgi Bataev	RUS	15/02/97	M	2	(1)	
11	Roei Beckel		07/10/87	M	18	(7)	
23	Ben Ben Yair		23/12/92	A	1	(8)	
15	Tom Ben Zaken		29/10/94	D	26		
19	Dan Biton		20/07/95	M	22	(7)	3
2	Karlo Bručić	CRO	17/04/92	D	28		
14	Dean David		14/03/96	A	19	(9)	4
24	Ido Davidov		23/11/94	M	2	(3)	2
9	Dolly Menga	ANG	02/05/93	A	8	(5)	
4	Hatem Elhamed		18/03/91	D	27		
26	Nino Galović	CRO	06/07/92	D	6		
22	Yoav Gerafi		29/08/93	G	31		
6	Stanislav Goldberg	EST	30/10/92	M		(3)	
33	Sandro Gotal	AUT	09/09/91	A		(4)	
99	Or Inbrum		12/01/96	M	20	(7)	4
21	Saša Ivković	SRB	13/05/93	M	2		
8	Gadi Kinda		23/03/94	M	14	(2)	1
10	Lúcio Maranhão	BRA	28/09/88	A	9	(4)	
1	Roei Mishpati		23/11/92	G	2		
17	Tom Mond		06/07/91	M	21		1
18	Benzi Moshel		31/07/93	A	18	(6)	1
3	Nivaldo	BRA	23/06/80	D	6	(2)	
9	Michael Ohana		04/10/95	A	1	(1)	
77	Moshe Ohayon		24/05/83	M	5	(8)	
20,28	Miki Siroshtein		24/04/89	D	26		1
16	Adir Tubul		03/06/79	D	1	(1)	
10	Niv Zrihan		24/05/94	A	12	(2)	2

Beitar Jerusalem FC

1936 • Teddy (34,000) • beitarfc.co.il

Major honours

Israeli League (6) 1987, 1993, 1997, 1998, 2007, 2008; Israeli Cup (7) 1976, 1979, 1985, 1986, 1989, 2008, 2009

Coach: Ran Ben-Shimon
(06/02/17) Sharon Mimer

2016

21/08	a	M. Petach-Tikva	D	2-2	*L Cohen, Vered*
28/08	h	H. Kiryat Shmona	D	2-2	*Abuhazira, L Cohen*
11/09	a	M. Tel-Aviv	D	2-2	*Vered, Abuhazira*
17/09	h	H. Ashkelon	W	3-0	*Vered, Jesús Rueda, Abuhazira*
24/09	a	H. Haifa	L	0-4	
01/10	h	H. Kfar-Saba	W	1-0	*Jesús Rueda*
22/10	a	Ashdod	D	0-0	
31/10	h	Bnei Yehuda	D	2-2	*Shechter, Vered*
05/11	h	H. Ra'anana	W	1-0	*Jesús Rueda*
21/11	h	H. Tel-Aviv	D	1-1	*Shechter*
28/11	h	Bnei Sakhnin	L	0-1	
05/12	a	M. Haifa	W	2-0	*L Cohen 2*
12/12	h	H. Beer Sheva	L	1-3	*Claudemir*
17/12	h	M. Petach-Tikva	D	1-1	*Jesús Rueda*
24/12	a	H. Kiryat Shmona	L	0-2	

2017

02/01	h	M. Tel-Aviv	W	1-0	*Shechter (p)*
10/01	a	H. Ashkelon	D	1-1	*Shechter (p)*
15/01	h	H. Haifa	W	1-0	*Einbinder*
22/01	a	H. Kfar-Saba	W	2-0	*Vered, Zaguri*
28/01	h	Ashdod	D	1-1	*Shechter (p)*
04/02	a	Bnei Yehuda	D	1-1	*Shechter*
11/02	a	H. Ra'anana	W	4-0	*Keltjens, Einbinder, Ezra, Vered*
20/02	a	H. Tel-Aviv	W	2-1	*Jesús Rueda, Shechter*
26/02	a	Bnei Sakhnin	W	2-0	*Shechter, Vered*
06/03	h	M. Haifa	L	0-1	
13/03	a	H. Beer Sheva	L	1-2	*Shechter*
18/03	a	M. Petach-Tikva	W	1-0	*Einbinder*
01/04	a	M. Haifa	L	2-3	*Ezra, Shechter (p)*
08/04	h	Bnei Sakhnin	W	3-0	*Shechter (p), Sabo, Vered*
17/04	a	H. Beer Sheva	L	0-2	
22/04	h	M. Tel-Aviv	D	1-1	*Vered*
26/04	h	M. Petach-Tikva	W	2-1	*Jesús Rueda, Vered*
29/04	h	M. Haifa	W	2-0	*Vered, Einbinder*
06/05	a	Bnei Sakhnin	W	5-1	*Shechter 2, Sabo (p), Keltjens, Brihon*
15/05	h	H. Beer Sheva	D	1-1	*Brihon*
20/05	a	M. Tel-Aviv	W	2-0	*Sabo, Shechter*

No	Name	Nat	DoB	Pos	Aps	(s)	Gls
7,19	Shimon Abuhazira		10/10/86	A	6	(9)	3
20	Johan Audel	FRA	12/12/83	M	8	(6)	
26	Shlomi Avisidris		14/05/89	A	2	(8)	
15	Tal Benish		26/10/89	D	3	(1)	
30,77	Yakov Brihon		06/07/93	A	5	(15)	2
14	Claudemir	BRA	17/08/84	M	31	(5)	1
12	Avishay Cohen		19/06/95	A		(8)	
17	Lidor Cohen		16/12/92	M	10	(7)	4
2	Antoine Conte	FRA	29/01/94	D	13	(1)	
16	Hezi Dilmoni		07/05/89	D	5	(3)	
11	Dan Einbinder		16/02/89	M	33	(1)	4
18	Hen Ezra		19/01/89	M	12	(3)	2
23	Marcel Heister	GER	29/07/92	D	29		
4	Jesús Rueda	ESP	19/02/87	D	33		6
6	Tal Kachila		26/06/92	D	4		
3	David Keltjens		11/06/95	D	33	(1)	2
1	Boris Kleiman		26/10/90	G	36		
77	Uri Magbo		12/09/87	D	3		
5	Dan Mori		08/11/88	D	28	(1)	
21	Kobi Moyal		12/06/87	M	2	(11)	
27	Oz Rali		22/12/87	M	10	(4)	
52	Eric Sabo	SVK	22/11/91	M	27	(4)	3
9	Etay Shechter		22/02/87	A	31	(3)	14
8	Idan Vered		01/01/89	A	30	(4)	11
7	Israel Zaguri		29/01/90	M	2	(11)	1

Bnei Sakhnin FC

1991 • Doha (8,500) • no website

Major honours
Israeli Cup (1) 2004

Coach: Yossi Abuksis

2016
20/08 a Bnei Yehuda D 1-1 *Georginho*
27/08 h M. Haifa W 1-0 *Georginho*
10/09 a H. Beer Sheva L 0-3
18/09 h M. Petach-Tikva L 0-1
21/09 h M. Tel-Aviv L 0-3
24/09 a H. Kiryat Shmona D 2-2 *Shemesh, Georginho*
22/10 a H. Ashkelon W 1-0 *Avidor*
29/10 h H. Haifa W 2-1 *Avidor, Nworuh*
07/11 a H. Kfar-Saba L 1-2 *Safuri*
19/11 h Ashdod L 0-1
28/11 a Beitar W 1-0 *Safuri*
04/12 h H. Ra'anana D 1-1 *Abraham Paz (p)*
10/12 a H. Tel-Aviv D 1-1 *Abraham Paz*
17/12 h Bnei Yehuda D 1-1 *Abraham Paz*
26/12 a M. Haifa W 2-1 *Safuri, Georginho*

2017
01/01 h H. Beer Sheva D 0-0
10/01 a M. Petach-Tikva D 1-1 *Abraham Paz*
16/01 h H. Kiryat Shmona W 5-2 *Avidor 3, Osman, Abraham Paz*
22/01 a M. Tel-Aviv L 1-2 *Georginho*
29/01 h H. Ashkelon W 1-0 *Shemesh*
04/02 a H. Haifa W 1-0 *Shemesh*
12/02 h H. Kfar-Saba W 1-0 *Shemesh*
18/02 a Ashdod D 1-1 *Shemesh*
26/02 h Beitar L 0-2
04/03 a H. Ra'anana W 1-0 *Mugrabi*
11/03 h H. Tel-Aviv D 0-0
18/03 a M. Tel-Aviv L 0-3
02/04 h M. Petach-Tikva W 1-0 *Lax*
08/04 a Beitar L 0-3
15/04 a M. Haifa W 1-0 *Avidor*
22/04 h H. Beer Sheva L 1-3 *Avidor*
25/04 h M. Tel-Aviv L 1-3 *Osman*
29/04 a M. Petach-Tikva L 0-1
06/05 h Beitar L 1-5 *Shemesh*
13/05 h M. Haifa W 1-0 *Mugrabi*
20/05 a H. Beer Sheva L 0-2

No	Name	Nat	DoB	Pos	Aps	(s)	Gls
5	Abraham Paz	ESP	29/06/79	D	29		5
11	Yuval Avidor		19/10/86	A	25	(11)	7
23	Muhamad Badarna		15/11/95	A		(3)	
9	Lassina Dao	CIV	20/12/96	M	1	(4)	
4	Sari Falach		22/11/91	D	33		
14	Ihab Ganaem		11/06/96	M	2	(3)	
2	Maroun Gantus		15/06/96	D	11	(1)	
52	Georginho	BRA	25/03/91	M	28	(2)	5
99	Osama Halaila		06/04/98	A		(2)	
15	Haled Halaula		16/12/82	M	22	(5)	
23	Ataa Jaber		03/10/94	M	4	(2)	
22	Mahmoud Kannadli		11/08/88	G	33		
12	Nir Lax		10/08/94	M	15	(10)	1
66,26	Firas Mugrabi		24/07/91	M	19	(1)	2
77	Siraj Nasser		02/09/90	M	16	(13)	
9	Jude Nworuh	NGA	09/06/89	A	10	(2)	1
18	Ali Osman		08/02/87	M	27	(1)	2
1	Asaf Raz		21/02/87	G	3		
27	Rodrigo Antônio	BRA	27/07/87	M	5	(9)	
10	Ramzi Safuri		21/10/95	A	23	(9)	3
6	Tambi Sages		21/10/94	M	34		
13,27	Ihab Shami		18/09/93	D	1	(3)	
24	Idan Shemesh		06/08/90	A	9	(16)	6
31	Ahmad Tzabih		11/01/97	M	1		
25	Wanderson	BRA	13/09/91	D	36		
7	Mohamed Zbedat		15/11/91	D	9	(10)	

Bnei Yehuda Tel-Aviv FC

1936 • HaMoshava, Petach-Tikva (11,500) • no website

Major honours
Israeli League (1) 1990; Israeli Cup (3) 1968, 1981, 2017

Coach: Arik Benado
(30/10/16) Yaakov Asyag
(29/11/16) (Eilon Shwager)
(15/12/16) Nissan Yehezkel
(04/05/17) (Kfir Edri)

2016
20/08 h Bnei Sakhnin D 1-1 *Turgeman*
27/08 a H. Haifa L 0-1
10/09 h M. Haifa D 1-1 *Avital*
17/09 a H. Kfar-Saba W 1-0 *Turgeman*
25/09 h H. Beer Sheva L 0-3
01/10 a Ashdod D 2-2 *Jovanović, Cohen*
22/10 h M. Petach-Tikva L 1-4 *Turgeman*
31/10 a Beitar D 2-2 *Buzaglo, Jovanović*
05/11 h H. Kiryat Shmona L 0-1
20/11 a H. Ra'anana L 0-1
27/11 h M. Tel-Aviv W 1-0 *Buzaglo*
04/12 h H. Tel-Aviv L 0-1
10/12 a H. Ashkelon L 0-1
17/12 a Bnei Sakhnin D 1-1 *og (Georginho)*
24/12 h H. Haifa D 1-1 *Buzaglo*
31/12 a M. Haifa D 1-1 *Cohen*

2017
11/01 h H. Kfar-Saba D 1-1 *Cohen*
14/01 a H. Beer Sheva L 1-2 *og (Biton)*
22/01 h Ashdod W 2-0 *Turgeman, Buzaglo*
28/01 a M. Petach-Tikva L 0-2
04/02 h Beitar D 1-1 *Valskis*
11/02 a H. Kiryat Shmona W 1-0 *Valskis*
18/02 h H. Ra'anana L 0-2
25/02 a M. Tel-Aviv L 0-2
04/03 a H. Tel-Aviv W 2-1 *Galván, Cohen*
12/03 h H. Ashkelon D 0-0
19/03 a H. Ra'anana W 2-0 *Valskis 2*
01/04 a H. Tel-Aviv L 0-2
08/04 h H. Kfar-Saba W 1-0 *Galván*
22/04 a H. Ashkelon L 0-1
27/04 h H. Kiryat Shmona L 0-2
06/05 a H. Haifa D 1-1 *Mršić (p)*
13/05 h Ashdod W 2-1 *Kandil, Finish*

No	Name	Nat	DoB	Pos	Aps	(s)	Gls
10	Hasan Abu Zaid		04/02/91	M	9	(1)	
9	Amir Agaiev		10/02/92	M		(6)	
34	Shahar Amsalem		26/03/99	G		(1)	
27	Daniel Avital		01/01/97	A	6	(13)	1
17	Itzhak Azoz		30/11/85	D	23	(2)	
25	Paz Ben Ari		10/12/96	M	2	(2)	
70	Sahar Benbenisti		26/11/91	M	1	(6)	
19	Liel Biton		19/03/98	D	1		
18	Aviad Bourla		13/12/93	M	1		
77	Almog Buzaglo		08/12/92	M	29	(3)	4
15	Yonatan Cohen		29/06/96	A	21	(6)	4
30	Stav Finish		26/03/92	M	7	(9)	1
6,11	Dovev Gabay		01/04/87	A	7	(4)	
20	Pedro Galván	ARG	18/08/85	M	9	(6)	2
13	Sean Goldberg		13/06/95	D	29	(3)	
10	Roy Gordana		06/04/90	M	11	(2)	
26	Eli Harush		29/08/95	A		(4)	
14	Tijan Jaiteh	GAM	31/12/88	M	12		
31	Marko Jovanović	SRB	26/03/88	D	24	(1)	2
6	Tal Kachila		26/06/92	D	11		
23	Maor Kandil		27/11/93	D	19	(1)	1
22	Nikita Khaykin		11/07/95	G	2		
9,55	Shay Konstantini		27/06/96	A	2	(3)	
51	Nikola Mitrović	SRB	02/01/87	M	14	(2)	
5	Antonio Mršić	CRO	05/06/87	M	23	(5)	1
88,16	Yarden Shua		16/06/99	A		(2)	
4	Xavier Tomas	FRA	04/01/86	D	11		
33	Dinko Trebotić	CRO	30/07/90	M	4	(3)	
7	Alon Turgeman		09/06/91	A	29	(2)	4
3	Ben Tzairi		17/05/92	D	13	(7)	
21	Nerijus Valskis	LTU	04/08/87	M	12	(2)	4
1	Emilijus Zubas	LTU	10/07/90	G	31		

Hapoel Ashkelon FC

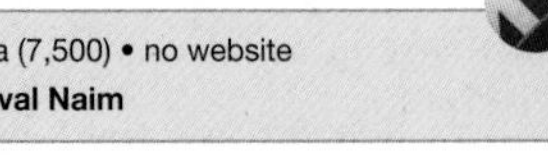

1955 • Sela (7,500) • no website

Coach: Yuval Naim

2016
20/08 h H. Haifa W 3-2 *Lingane 3*
29/08 a H. Kfar-Saba D 1-1 *Suissa*
11/09 h Ashdod D 0-0
17/09 a Beitar L 0-3
24/09 h H. Ra'anana D 0-0
01/10 a H. Tel-Aviv L 0-2
22/10 h Bnei Sakhnin L 0-1
29/10 a M. Haifa L 0-5
06/11 h H. Beer Sheva L 1-5 *Dao*
19/11 a M. Petach-Tikva D 1-1 *Galván*
26/11 a H. Kiryat Shmona L 1-4 *Dao*
03/12 a M. Tel-Aviv D 0-0
10/12 h Bnei Yehuda W 1-0 *Dao*
18/12 a H. Haifa L 1-3 *Lingane*
24/12 h H. Kfar-Saba D 0-0

2017
01/01 a Ashdod L 0-1
10/01 h Beitar D 1-1 *Suissa*
14/01 a H. Ra'anana W 2-0 *og (Mbola), Mesika*
21/01 h H. Tel-Aviv L 0-1
29/01 a Bnei Sakhnin L 0-1
06/02 h M. Haifa L 0-2
11/02 a H. Beer Sheva L 1-2 *Ivančić*
19/02 h M. Petach-Tikva L 0-1
25/02 h H. Kiryat Shmona D 1-1 *Manga*
05/03 h M. Tel-Aviv L 1-2 *Ivančić*
12/03 a Bnei Yehuda D 0-0
18/03 a H. Haifa W 4-1 *Manga, Hozez, Lingane 2*
03/04 h Ashdod D 0-0
08/04 a H. Ra'anana W 2-0 *Ivančić, Meir*
22/04 h Bnei Yehuda W 1-0 *Jovanović*
29/04 a H. Kfar-Saba L 0-1
06/05 a H. Tel-Aviv D 0-0
13/05 h H. Kiryat Shmona W 2-1 *Hadad, Abuhazira*

No	Name	Nat	DoB	Pos	Aps	(s)	Gls
24	Moshe Abuhazira		24/12/92	D	12	(11)	1
30	Bamidele Aiyenugba	NGA	20/11/83	G	33		
8	Ben Azubel		19/09/93	A	2		
21	Yakov Ben Hemo		09/04/89	M	11	(4)	
23	Amir Ben Shimon		14/12/93	M	8	(3)	
9	Asi Buzaglo		03/12/82	M	7	(6)	
99	Lassina Dao	CIV	20/12/96	M	9		3
10	Baruch Dego		26/03/81	M	9	(8)	
20	Pedro Galván	ARG	18/08/85	M	6	(2)	1
16	Rudi Hadad		05/02/85	M	19	(3)	1
17	Matan Hozez		12/08/96	A	11	(10)	1
20	Josip Ivančić	CRO	29/03/91	A	12		3
3	Haim Izrin		22/12/87	D	18		
28	Branislav Jovanović	SRB	21/09/85	M	15	(1)	1
37	Issoumaila Lingane	CIV	15/03/91	M	19	(4)	6
18	Moshe Lugasi		04/02/91	D	22	(5)	
33	Tal Machluf		31/08/91	M	17	(2)	
25	Avi Malka		29/07/87	D	28	(1)	
11	David Manga	CTA	03/02/89	A	11	(2)	2
91	Raz Meir		30/11/96	M	20	(6)	1
14	Reef Mesika		15/06/89	M	11	(10)	1
42	Snir Mishan		13/11/88	D	18	(3)	
5	Andriy Mishchenko	UKR	07/04/91	D	16		
11	Nevo Mizrachi		26/07/87	M	2	(6)	
6	Mirko Oremuš	CRO	06/09/88	M	19		
7	Tomer Suissa		21/12/88	A	8	(10)	2

ISRAEL

Hapoel Beer Sheva FC

1949 • Turner (16,100) • hapoelb7.co.il

Major honours
Israeli League (4) 1975, 1976, 2016, 2017; Israeli Cup (1) 1997

Coach: Barak Bakhar

Date		Opponent	Res	Score	Scorers
2016					
20/08	h	H. Ra'anana	W	2-1	*Sahar, Radi*
27/08	a	H. Tel-Aviv	D	0-0	
10/09	h	Bnei Sakhnin	W	3-0	*Nwakaeme 2, Lúcio Maranhão*
19/09	a	M. Haifa	L	1-2	*Buzaglo*
25/09	a	Bnei Yehuda	W	3-0	*Nwakaeme 2, Lúcio Maranhão*
15/10	h	M. Petach-Tikva	W	5-0	*Lúcio Maranhão, Nwakaeme (p), Ohana, Miguel Vítor 2*
24/10	a	H. Kiryat Shmona	W	2-0	*Sahar 2*
30/10	h	M. Tel-Aviv	W	2-0	*Sahar, Buzaglo*
06/11	a	H. Ashkelon	W	5-1	*Sahar 2 (1p), Ohana, Biton, Ghadir*
19/11	h	H. Haifa	W	5-1	*Ohana, Sahar (p), Nwakaeme, Radi, Ghadir*
27/11	a	H. Kfar-Saba	W	2-0	*Buzaglo, Nwakaeme*
03/12	h	Ashdod	W	5-0	*Radi 2, og (Bručić), Buzaglo (p), Nwakaeme*
12/12	a	Beitar	W	3-1	*Nwakaeme, Buzaglo 2 (1p)*
18/12	a	H. Ra'anana	L	0-1	
25/12	h	H. Tel-Aviv	D	1-1	*Sahar*
2017					
01/01	a	Bnei Sakhnin	D	0-0	
10/01	h	M. Haifa	W	2-0	*Nwakaeme, Sahar (p)*
14/01	h	Bnei Yehuda	W	2-1	*Melikson, Sahar*
21/01	a	M. Petach-Tikva	D	1-1	*Buzaglo*
28/01	h	H. Kiryat Shmona	W	2-0	*Nwakaeme, Radi*
04/02	a	M. Tel-Aviv	L	0-1	
11/02	h	H. Ashkelon	W	2-1	*Barda 2*
19/02	a	H. Haifa	D	0-0	
27/02	h	H. Kfar-Saba	W	3-0	*Melikson, Barda, Ohana*
04/03	a	Ashdod	W	1-0	*Melikson*
13/03	h	Beitar	W	2-1	*Zrihan 2*
19/03	h	M. Haifa	W	4-0	*Hoban, Ohana, Sahar (p), Radi*
01/04	h	M. Tel-Aviv	W	1-0	*Sahar (p)*
09/04	a	M. Petach-Tikva	W	2-1	*Nwakaeme, Sahar*
17/04	h	Beitar	W	2-0	*Radi, Barda*
22/04	h	Bnei Sakhnin	W	3-1	*Barda, Nwakaeme, Radi*
25/04	a	M. Haifa	W	1-0	*Nwakaeme*
29/04	a	M. Tel-Aviv	W	2-1	*Melikson, Ogu*
08/05	h	M. Petach-Tikva	D	1-1	*Ghadir*
15/05	a	Beitar	D	1-1	*Sahar*
20/05	h	Bnei Sakhnin	W	2-0	*Hoban (p), Melikson*

No	Name	Nat	DoB	Pos	Aps	(s)	Gls
10	Elyaniv Barda		15/12/82	A	7	(12)	5
2	Ben Biton		03/01/91	D	32	(1)	1
15	Vladimir Broun		06/05/89	M	8	(8)	
11	Maor Buzaglo		14/01/88	M	20	(7)	7
21	Or Dadia		12/07/97	D	1	(1)	
29	Yonatan Elias		16/03/98	A		(1)	
13	Yoel Ganon		07/01/97	D	1		
16,8	Mohammad Ghadir		21/01/91	A	4	(10)	3
1	Dudu Goresh		01/02/80	G	21		
55	Guy Haimov		09/03/86	G	15		
12	Ovidiu Hoban	ROU	27/12/82	M	19	(5)	2
69	Mihály Korhut	HUN	01/12/88	D	22		
22	Lúcio Maranhão	BRA	28/09/88	A	3	(8)	3
24	Maor Melikson		30/10/84	M	23	(2)	5
4	Miguel Vítor	POR	30/06/89	D	19	(1)	2
36	Gal Navon		11/12/96	G		(1)	
9	Anthony Nwakaeme	NGA	21/03/89	A	29	(5)	14
30	John Ogu	NGA	20/04/88	M	30		1
18	Michael Ohana		04/10/95	A	16	(14)	5
17	Matan Ohayon		25/02/86	D	5	(3)	
7	Mahran Radi		01/07/82	M	28	(6)	8
14	Ben Sahar		10/08/89	A	25	(7)	14
21	Yuval Shabtai		18/12/86	M	2		
16	Itamar Shaviro		17/06/98	A		(1)	
20	Loai Taha		26/11/89	D	12	(3)	
3	Ben Turgeman		09/01/89	D	13	(1)	
5	Shir Tzedek		22/08/89	D	33		
25	William	BRA	07/02/85	D	4	(3)	
19	Niv Zrihan		24/05/94	A	4	(4)	2

Hapoel Haifa FC

1924 • Sammy Ofer (30,820) • hapoel-haifa.org.il

Major honours
Israeli League (1) 1999; Israeli Cup (3) 1963, 1966, 1974

Coach: Eli Cohen;
(15/12/16) Dani Golan
(25/03/17) (Nir Klinger)
(02/04/17) Meir Ben Margi

Date		Opponent	Res	Score	Scorers
2016					
20/08	a	H. Ashkelon	L	2-3	*Elbaz, Adilson*
27/08	h	Bnei Yehuda	W	1-0	*Falkoschenko*
10/09	h	H. Kfar-Saba	L	1-2	*Maman*
17/09	a	Ashdod	W	3-1	*Al Lala, Júlio César, Adilson*
24/09	h	Beitar	W	4-0	*Adilson 2, Jazvić, Arbeitman*
01/10	a	H. Ra'anana	L	0-2	
22/10	h	H. Tel-Aviv	L	0-2	
29/10	a	Bnei Sakhnin	L	1-2	*Kapiloto*
05/11	h	M. Haifa	D	0-0	
19/11	a	H. Beer Sheva	L	1-5	*Maman*
26/11	h	M. Petach-Tikva	W	2-1	*Júlio César, Maman*
03/12	a	H. Kiryat Shmona	L	0-2	
11/12	h	M. Tel-Aviv	L	2-4	*Al Lala, Maman*
18/12	h	H. Ashkelon	W	3-1	*Al Lala 2, Arbeitman*
24/12	a	Bnei Yehuda	D	1-1	*Arbeitman*
31/12	a	H. Kfar-Saba	W	2-1	*Falkoschenko, Maman*
2017					
11/01	h	Ashdod	L	0-1	
15/01	a	Beitar	L	0-1	
21/01	h	H. Ra'anana	W	1-0	*Al Lala*
29/01	a	H. Tel-Aviv	D	0-0	
04/02	h	Bnei Sakhnin	L	0-1	
11/02	a	M. Haifa	W	3-0	*Al Lala 2, Arbeitman*
19/02	h	H. Beer Sheva	D	0-0	
26/02	a	M. Petach-Tikva	L	1-3	*Maman*
04/03	h	H. Kiryat Shmona	L	1-2	*Al Lala*
12/03	a	M. Tel-Aviv	L	0-1	
18/03	h	H. Ashkelon	L	1-4	*Ben Basat*
01/04	a	H. Kiryat Shmona	W	2-0	*Arbeitman, Sardal*
08/04	h	H. Tel-Aviv	D	3-3	*Adilson, Falkoschenko, Al Lala*
22/04	h	Ashdod	D	1-1	*Ben Basat*
27/04	a	H. Ra'anana	W	2-0	*Falkoschenko, og (Babayev)*
06/05	h	Bnei Yehuda	D	1-1	*Malul*
13/05	a	H. Kfar-Saba	L	0-1	

No	Name	Nat	DoB	Pos	Aps	(s)	Gls
31	Adilson	BRA	27/09/92	M	25	(6)	5
11	Maaran Al Lala		07/03/82	A	20	(10)	9
19	Shlomi Arbeitman		14/05/85	A	10	(15)	5
9	Eden Ben Basat		08/09/86	A	15		2
16	Bruno Pinheiro	POR	21/08/87	D	23	(2)	
26	Yossi Dora		25/08/91	M	2		
4	Eli Elbaz		21/01/92	A		(1)	1
23	Rotem Fadida		04/01/97	G		(1)	
20	Saar Fadida		04/01/97	A	2	(5)	
77,7	Maxim Falkoschenko		04/01/96	A	19	(9)	4
5	Ofek Fishler		24/08/96	D	4	(4)	
10	Idan Golan		29/02/96	M	1	(15)	
9	Filip Jazvić	CRO	22/10/90	A	9	(4)	1
86	Júlio César	BRA	04/01/88	M	21	(2)	2
55	Nissim Kapiloto		01/10/89	D	32		1
8	Hisham Kiwan		17/05/87	M	5	(8)	
1	Rubi Levkovich		31/08/88	G	6	(1)	
4	Dor Malul		30/04/89	D	30		1
15	Hanan Maman		28/08/89	M	26	(5)	6
3	Haim Megrelashvili		04/07/82	D	15	(8)	
42	Dor Peretz		17/05/95	M	13	(1)	
21	Oshri Roash		25/07/88	D	10	(1)	
24	Liran Sardal		02/07/94	M	29	(2)	1
18	Shmuel Scheimann		03/11/87	D	16		
28	Ido Vayer		10/10/96	M		(1)	
22	Piet Velthuizen	NED	03/11/86	G	27		
6	Miki Yazao		01/01/91	M	3		

Hapoel Kfar-Saba FC

1928 • Levita (5,800) • hapoel-kfs.org.il

Major honours
Israeli League (1) 1982; Israeli Cup (3) 1975, 1980, 1990

Coach: Sharon Mimer;
(25/01/17) Eli Cohen
(13/04/17) Felix Naim

Date		Opponent	Res	Score	Scorers
2016					
21/08	a	M. Tel-Aviv	L	1-3	*Tchibota*
29/08	h	H. Ashkelon	D	1-1	*Elbaz*
10/09	a	H. Haifa	W	2-1	*Tchibota, Elbaz*
17/09	h	Bnei Yehuda	L	0-1	
24/09	h	Ashdod	W	1-0	*Ayele*
01/10	a	Beitar	L	0-1	
22/10	h	H. Ra'anana	L	1-2	*Tchibota*
29/10	a	H. Tel-Aviv	D	1-1	*Matović*
07/11	h	Bnei Sakhnin	W	2-1	*I Cohen, Tchibota*
19/11	a	M. Haifa	L	0-2	
27/11	h	H. Beer Sheva	L	0-2	
03/12	a	M. Petach-Tikva	D	0-0	
10/12	h	H. Kiryat Shmona	D	2-2	*Diogo Kachuba (p), Itzhak*
17/12	h	M. Tel-Aviv	D	1-1	*Elbaz*
24/12	a	H. Ashkelon	D	0-0	
31/12	h	H. Haifa	L	1-2	*R Cohen*
2017					
11/01	a	Bnei Yehuda	D	1-1	*Elbaz*
14/01	a	Ashdod	D	0-0	
22/01	h	Beitar	L	0-2	
28/01	a	H. Ra'anana	L	0-1	
05/02	h	H. Tel-Aviv	D	0-0	
12/02	a	Bnei Sakhnin	L	0-1	
18/02	h	M. Haifa	L	0-2	
27/02	a	H. Beer Sheva	L	0-3	
05/03	h	M. Petach-Tikva	L	1-3	*Itzhak (p)*
11/03	a	H. Kiryat Shmona	W	2-1	*Omoregie, Elbaz*
20/03	a	Ashdod	D	0-0	
02/04	h	H. Ra'anana	L	0-2	
08/04	a	Bnei Yehuda	L	0-1	
24/04	a	H. Tel-Aviv	L	0-2	
29/04	h	H. Ashkelon	W	1-0	*Elbaz*
06/05	a	H. Kiryat Shmona	W	4-1	*Elbaz 2, Ayele, Tchibota*
13/05	h	H. Haifa	W	1-0	*Elbaz*

No	Name	Nat	DoB	Pos	Aps	(s)	Gls
11	Tal Ayele		25/05/89	A	23	(4)	2
16	Tal Benish		26/10/89	D	14	(4)	
41	Sahar Braun		06/10/94	M	17	(1)	
7	Bruno Fernandes	BRA	02/03/89	A	6	(1)	
3	Itzhak Cohen		22/04/83	D	32		1
15	Raz Cohen		11/11/94	M	22	(6)	1
26	Hezi Dilmoni		07/05/89	D	14		
8	Diogo Kachuba	BRA	16/02/90	M	19	(4)	1
14	Eli Elbaz		21/01/92	A	23	(7)	9
20	Semi Elyakim		30/03/87	M	6	(1)	
18	Amar Fadida		17/07/90	M	9	(16)	
17	Ben Grabli		08/04/94	M		(1)	
23	Guy Hadida		23/07/95	M	2	(9)	
21	Ran Itzhak		09/10/87	M	10	(15)	2
1	Ran Kadosh		04/10/85	G	33		
4	Ben Khawaz		19/07/91	D		(4)	
30	Lior Levy		26/10/87	D	27		
22	Tomer Levy		25/05/93	M	4	(4)	
81	Dušan Matović	SRB	08/07/83	D	32		1
10	Sunny Omoregie	NGA	02/01/89	M	4	(4)	1
9	Slobodan Simović	SRB	22/05/89	M	26	(3)	
88	Maksim Skavysh	BLR	13/11/89	A	1	(7)	
10	Slaviša Stojanović	SRB	27/01/89	A	4	(6)	
13	Mavis Tchibota	CGO	07/05/96	A	27	(2)	5
17	Yuval Ya'akubovitch		13/02/95	M	8	(1)	

Hapoel Kiryat Shmona FC

2000 • Municipal (5,300) • iturank8.co.il

Major honours
Israeli League (1) 2012; Israeli Cup (1) 2014

Coach: Moti Ivanir
(31/10/16) Beni Ben-Zaken
(26/11/16) Tomer Kashtan

Date		Opponent		Score	Scorers
2016					
20/08	h	Ashdod	W	1-0	*Abed (p)*
28/08	a	Beitar	D	2-2	*og (Benish), Brossou*
10/09	h	H. Ra'anana	D	0-0	
17/09	a	H. Tel-Aviv	D	3-3	*og (Simić), N'Douassel, S Azulay (II)*
24/09	h	Bnei Sakhnin	D	2-2	*S Azulay (I), Abed*
01/10	a	M. Haifa	D	0-0	
24/10	h	H. Beer Sheva	L	0-2	
30/10	a	M. Petach-Tikva	L	1-2	*Heitor*
05/11	a	Bnei Yehuda	W	1-0	*S Azulay (I)*
20/11	h	M. Tel-Aviv	L	1-2	*N'Douassel*
26/11	h	H. Ashkelon	W	4-1	*S Azulay (II), S Azulay (I), Shamir, Abed (p)*
03/12	h	H. Haifa	W	2-0	*S Azulay (II), Abed*
10/12	a	H. Kfar-Saba	D	2-2	*Mauricio, Davidov*
17/12	a	Ashdod	D	0-0	
24/12	h	Beitar	W	2-0	*Abed, Mauricio*
31/12	a	H. Ra'anana	W	3-0	*N'Douassel, S Azulay (II), S Azulay (I)*
2017					
12/01	h	H. Tel-Aviv	W	2-1	*Kriaf, Abed*
16/01	a	Bnei Sakhnin	L	2-5	*S Azulay (I), Abed*
21/01	h	M. Haifa	W	3-0	*Kriaf, S Azulay (I), S Azulay (II)*
28/01	a	H. Beer Sheva	L	0-2	
04/02	h	M. Petach-Tikva	L	0-1	
11/02	h	Bnei Yehuda	L	0-1	
18/02	a	M. Tel-Aviv	L	0-3	
25/02	a	H. Ashkelon	D	1-1	*Gozlan*
04/03	a	H. Haifa	W	2-1	*Gozlan 2*
11/03	h	H. Kfar-Saba	L	1-2	*Elkayam*
18/03	h	H. Tel-Aviv	L	2-3	*Shamir, Hazoharoi*
01/04	h	H. Haifa	L	0-2	
09/04	a	Ashdod	D	1-1	*Gozlan*
22/04	h	H. Ra'anana	L	2-3	*S Azulay (II), Gozlan*
27/04	a	Bnei Yehuda	W	2-0	*Abed, Gozlan*
06/05	h	H. Kfar-Saba	L	1-4	*S Azulay (II) (p)*
13/05	a	H. Ashkelon	L	1-2	*Elkayam*

No	Name	Nat	DoB	Pos	Aps	(s)	Gls
7	Ahmed Abed		30/03/90	M	22	(6)	8
5	Nazar Abu Ktifan		23/11/98	D	4		
11	Shlomi Azulay (I)		18/10/89	A	22	(8)	6
5,8	Shlomi Azulay (II)		30/03/90	M	24	(4)	7
15	Eli Balilti		23/02/94	M	1	(1)	
12	Oren Biton		16/06/94	D	27	(1)	
28	Didier Brossou	CIV	23/12/89	M	24	(4)	1
25	Eden Dahan		01/08/96	M		(1)	
8	Ido Davidov		23/11/94	M	2	(5)	1
14	Oded Elkayam		09/02/88	D	17	(5)	2
19	Joseph Gande		10/03/97	A		(3)	
21	Shoval Gozlan		25/04/94	A	9	(4)	6
19	Rotem Hatuel		12/04/98	A		(1)	
23	Yogev Hazoharoi		20/10/91	D	17	(3)	1
4	Heitor	BRA	09/11/89	D	6	(1)	1
17	Bar Hilel		05/05/96	M	6		
3	Kassio	BRA	11/02/87	D	19	(1)	
10	Ofir Kriaf		17/03/91	M	18	(8)	2
22	Omer Lakao		07/02/98	M	2		
15	Anas Mahamid		26/04/98	M	2	(1)	
26	Dean Maimoni		04/05/90	D	23	(2)	
9,97	Mauricio	BRA	31/12/92	A	17	(8)	2
29	Ezechiel N'Douassel	CHA	22/04/88	A	6	(5)	3
2	Idan Nachmias		17/03/97	D		(1)	
6	Amir Nassar		24/11/96	M	17	(5)	
1	Itamar Nitzan		23/06/87	G	28		
27	Jacob Njoku	NGA	10/03/97	A	4	(6)	
21	Rafael Jatai	BRA	18/05/89	M	5		
18	Eden Shamir		25/06/95	M	20	(4)	2
24	Ofir Takiyar		15/10/95	M		(1)	
16	Amar Tchalisher		22/01/93	D	16	(8)	
45	Mehdi Zoabi		15/07/95	G	5		

Hapoel Ra'anana FC

1972 • Winner, Netanya (13,800) • hapoel-raanana.co.il

Coach: Haim Silvas

Date		Opponent		Score	Scorers
2016					
20/08	a	H. Beer Sheva	L	1-2	*Mihelič (p)*
27/08	h	M. Petach-Tikva	L	0-1	
10/09	a	H. Kiryat Shmona	D	0-0	
18/09	h	M. Tel-Aviv	L	0-3	
24/09	a	H. Ashkelon	D	0-0	
01/10	h	H. Haifa	W	2-0	*Vahaba, Shaker*
22/10	a	H. Kfar-Saba	W	2-1	*Shaker 2*
29/10	h	Ashdod	D	0-0	
05/11	a	Beitar	L	0-1	
20/11	h	Bnei Yehuda	W	1-0	*Hugy*
26/11	h	H. Tel-Aviv	D	0-0	
04/12	a	Bnei Sakhnin	D	1-1	*Levy*
10/12	h	M. Haifa	D	1-1	*Babayev*
18/12	h	H. Beer Sheva	W	1-0	*Shaker*
25/12	a	M. Petach-Tikva	L	0-2	
31/12	h	H. Kiryat Shmona	L	0-3	
2017					
11/01	a	M. Tel-Aviv	L	1-4	*Shaker*
14/01	h	H. Ashkelon	L	0-2	
21/01	a	H. Haifa	L	0-1	
28/01	h	H. Kfar-Saba	W	1-0	*Shaker*
05/02	a	Ashdod	W	1-0	*Abuhazira (p)*
11/02	h	Beitar	L	0-4	
18/02	a	Bnei Yehuda	W	2-0	*Shabtai, Kalibat*
25/02	a	H. Tel-Aviv	D	0-0	
04/03	h	Bnei Sakhnin	L	0-1	
11/03	a	M. Haifa	L	0-2	
19/03	h	Bnei Yehuda	L	0-2	
02/04	a	H. Kfar-Saba	W	2-0	*Kalibat, Hugy*
08/04	h	H. Ashkelon	L	0-2	
22/04	A	H. Kiryat Shmona	W	3-2	*Abuhazira 2, Shoker*
27/04	h	H. Haifa	L	0-2	
06/05	a	Ashdod	D	2-2	*og (Siroshtein), Hugy*
13/05	h	H. Tel-Aviv	D	1-1	*Shoker*

No	Name	Nat	DoB	Pos	Aps	(s)	Gls
18	Shimon Abuhazira		10/10/86	A	15		3
18	Gal Arel		09/07/89	M	2	(3)	
7	Eli Babayev		01/11/90	M	20	(4)	1
10	Barak Badash		30/08/92	A	1		
19	Ben Binyamin		17/12/85	M	32		
12	Omer Cohen		15/09/96	D		(1)	
30	Yarden Cohen		26/03/97	M	7	(2)	
15	El'ad Gabai		15/11/85	D	18	(2)	
4	Ayad Habashi		10/05/95	D	4		
14	Shahar Hirsh		13/02/93	M	2	(4)	
9	Dor Hugy		10/07/95	A	14	(9)	3
11	Mohammed Kalibat		15/06/90	A	10	(2)	2
11	Aleksandr Karnitski	BLR	14/02/89	M	11	(3)	
10	Rogers Kola	ZAM	04/06/89	A	9	(5)	
26	Aharon Lemel		03/02/87	G	2		
21	Ido Levy		31/07/90	D	32		1
24	Conlyde Luchanga	ZAM	11/03/97	A		(6)	
23	Emmanuel Mbola	ZAM	10/05/93	D	28	(1)	
5	Liran Michaeli		16/04/99	D	1		
82	Rene Mihelič	SVN	05/07/88	M	15	(3)	1
5	Adi Nimni		27/08/91	D	16	(6)	
77	Zama Rambuwane	RSA	24/01/97	M	2	(5)	
6	Yuval Shabtai		18/12/86	M	12	(2)	1
16	Mohammad Shaker		14/11/96	M	22	(7)	6
8	Snir Shoker		08/05/89	M		(8)	2
55	Roei Shukrani		26/06/90	M	23	(6)	
66	Yuval Teitelman		16/02/97	A	3	(13)	
11	Fwayo Tembo	ZAM	20/05/89	A		(2)	
1	Assaf Tzur		25/08/98	G	2		
32	Ben Vahaba		27/03/92	D	31	(1)	1
22	Arie Yanko		21/12/91	G	29		

Hapoel Tel-Aviv FC

1923 • HaMoshava, Petach-Tikva (11,500) • hapoelta-fc.co.il

Major honours
Israeli League (13) 1934, 1935, 1938, 1940, 1944, 1957, 1966, 1969, 1981, 1986, 1988, 2000, 2010; Israeli Cup (15) 1928 (shared), 1934, 1937, 1938, 1939, 1961, 1972, 1983, 1999, 2000, 2006, 2007, 2010, 2011, 2012

Coach: Eli Gutman;
(21/09/16) Guy Luzon;
(17/01/17) Menachem Koretski

Date		Opponent		Score	Scorers
2016					
22/08	a	M. Haifa	L	0-1	
27/08	h	H. Beer Sheva	D	0-0	
12/09	a	M. Petach-Tikva	L	0-2	
17/09	h	H. Kiryat Shmona	D	3-3	*Altman, Schoenfeld, Šovšić*
25/09	a	M. Tel-Aviv	L	0-5	
01/10	h	H. Ashkelon	W	2-0	*Gutliv, Altman*
22/10	a	H. Haifa	W	2-0	*Altman, Gutliv*
29/10	h	H. Kfar-Saba	D	1-1	*Bumba*
05/11	a	Ashdod	L	0-1	
21/11	a	Beitar	D	1-1	*Altman (p)*
26/11	a	H. Ra'anana	D	0-0	
04/12	a	Bnei Yehuda	W	1-0	*Ezra*
10/12	h	Bnei Sakhnin	D	1-1	*Ezra*
19/12	h	M. Haifa	L	0-2	
25/12	a	H. Beer Sheva	D	1-1	*Altman (p)*
31/12	h	M. Petach-Tikva	L	0-1	
2017					
12/01	a	H. Kiryat Shmona	L	1-2	*Schoenfeld*
16/01	h	M. Tel-Aviv	L	0-1	
21/01	a	H. Ashkelon	W	1-0	*Werta*
29/01	h	H. Haifa	D	0-0	
05/02	a	H. Kfar-Saba	D	0-0	
12/02	h	Ashdod	W	2-0	*Hirsh, N'Douassel*
20/02	h	Beitar	L	1-2	*Reichert*
25/02	h	H. Ra'anana	D	0-0	
04/03	h	Bnei Yehuda	L	1-2	*Altman*
11/3	a	Bnei Sakhnin	D	0-0	
18/03	a	H. Kiryat Shmona	W	3-2	*Barshatzki 2, Chibuike*
01/04	h	Bnei Yehuda	W	2-0	*Tamuz, Chibuike*
08/04	h	H. Haifa	D	3-3	*Altman, Chibuike, Hirsh*
24/04	h	H. Kfar-Saba	W	2-0	*Gande, Gutliv*
29/04	a	Ashdod	L	0-2	
06/05	h	H. Ashkelon	D	0-0	
13/05	a	H. Ra'anana	D	1-1	*Gutliv*

No	Name	Nat	DoB	Pos	Aps	(s)	Gls
8	Hasan Abu Zaid		04/02/91	M	12	(2)	
10	Omri Altman		23/03/94	M	29	(2)	7
16	Wiyam Amasha		08/08/85	A		(2)	
21	Moti Barshatzki		06/09/96	M	11		2
11	Sahar Benbenisti		26/11/91	M	6	(4)	
18	Amit Biton		24/07/96	D	12	(1)	
17	Dudu Biton		01/03/88	A	1	(8)	
7	Claudiu Bumba	ROU	05/01/94	M	3	(1)	1
16	John Chibuike	NGA	10/10/88	A	8	(3)	3
29	Roy Dayan		14/05/97	M		(1)	
4	Orel Dgani		08/01/89	D	27		
29	Dolly Menga	ANG	02/05/93	A	11	(3)	
24	Shay Elias		25/02/99	D	4	(5)	
8	Hen Ezra		19/01/89	M	10	(3)	2
12,30	Joseph Gande		10/03/97	A	1	(7)	1
25	Nicolás Gorobsov	ARG	25/11/89	M	3	(2)	
6	Edi Gutliv		16/08/92	D	19		4
1	Ariel Harush		08/02/88	G	32		
22	Tzlil Hatuka		06/02/89	G	1		
30	Eden Hershkovich		23/08/97	M	1	(1)	
19	Shahar Hirsh		13/02/93	M	7	(7)	2
35	Yonatan Levy		25/08/99	M		(1)	
21	Anas Mahamid		26/04/98	M		(3)	
27	Eyal Meshumar		10/08/83	D	10	(1)	
80	Ezechiel N'Douassel	CHA	22/04/88	A	4	(1)	1
23	Nemanja Nikolić	MNE	01/01/88	M	7		
7	Or Ostvind		18/12/87	M	1	(1)	
9	Ben Reichert		04/03/94	M	20	(8)	1
15	Ibrahim Safuri		23/06/97	M		(2)	
18	Shmuel Scheimann		03/11/87	D	13		
12	Aaron Schoenfeld	USA	17/04/90	A	11		2
31	Michael Seaton	JAM	01/05/96	A		(1)	
20	Gal Shish		28/01/89	D	24	(1)	
27	Raz Shlomo		13/08/99	D	1	(1)	
3	Itzik Shoolmaister		31/10/97	D	4	(4)	
5	Marko Simić	MNE	16/06/87	D	6		
14	Damir Šovšić	BIH	05/02/90	M	8	(4)	1
5	Deslay Tagania		12/05/97	D	1		
99	Toto Tamuz		01/04/88	A	6	(3)	1
2	Ofer Werta		23/05/90	D	17	(3)	1
26	Avihai Yadin		26/10/86	M	24	(1)	
16	Sagiv Yehezkel		31/03/95	A	1	(1)	
11	Israel Zaguri		29/01/90	M	7	(3)	

ISRAEL

Maccabi Haifa FC

1913 • Sammy Ofer (30,820) • mhaifafc.com

Major honours
Israeli League (12) 1984, 1985, 1989, 1991, 1994, 2001, 2002, 2004, 2005, 2006, 2009, 2011; Israeli Cup (6) 1962, 1991, 1993, 1995, 1998, 2016

Coach: Ronny Levi;
(09/08/16) René Meulensteen (NED)
(14/02/17) Guy Luzon

Date		Opponent		Score	Scorers
2016					
22/08	h	H. Tel-Aviv	W	1-0	Plet
27/08	a	Bnei Sakhnin	L	0-1	
10/09	a	Bnei Yehuda	D	1-1	*Rukavytsya (p)*
19/09	h	H. Beer Sheva	W	2-1	*Rukavytsya (p), Plet*
26/09	a	M. Petach-Tikva	D	2-2	*Kehat, Gozlan*
01/10	h	H. Kiryat Shmona	D	0-0	
24/10	a	M. Tel-Aviv	W	2-0	*Atar, Kagelmacher*
29/10	h	H. Ashkelon	W	5-0	*Menachem, Plet, Atar 2 (1p), Vermouth (p)*
05/11	a	H. Haifa	D	0-0	
19/11	h	H. Kfar-Saba	W	2-0	*Atar, Menachem*
26/11	a	Ashdod	D	1-1	*Kehat*
05/12	h	Beitar	L	0-2	
10/12	a	H. Ra'anana	D	1-1	*Atar*
19/12	a	H. Tel-Aviv	W	2-0	*Atar (p), Vermouth*
26/12	h	Bnei Sakhnin	L	1-2	*Keinan*
31/12	h	Bnei Yehuda	D	1-1	*Vermouth*
2017					
10/01	a	H. Beer Sheva	L	0-2	
14/01	h	M. Petach-Tikva	L	0-2	
21/01	a	H. Kiryat Shmona	L	0-3	
30/01	h	M. Tel-Aviv	D	2-2	*Damari, Kehat*
06/02	a	H. Ashkelon	W	2-0	*Damari, Atar (p)*
11/02	h	H. Haifa	L	0-3	
18/02	a	H. Kfar-Saba	W	2-0	*Keinan 2*
25/02	h	Ashdod	L	0-1	
06/03	a	Beitar	W	1-0	*Vermouth*
11/03	h	H. Ra'anana	W	2-0	*Vermouth 2 (2p)*
19/03	a	H. Beer Sheva	L	0-4	
01/04	h	Beitar	W	3-2	*Awad, Rukavytsya 2*
09/04	a	M. Tel-Aviv	L	0-3	
15/04	h	Bnei Sakhnin	L	0-1	
22/04	a	M. Petach-Tikva	W	1-0	*Keinan*
25/04	h	H. Beer Sheva	L	0-1	
29/04	a	Beitar	L	0-2	
07/05	h	M. Tel-Aviv	L	0-2	
13/05	a	Bnei Sakhnin	L	0-1	
20/05	h	M. Petach-Tikva	D	0-0	

No	Name	Nat	DoB	Pos	Aps	(s)	Gls
5	Iyad Abu Abaid		31/12/94	D	8	(2)	
36	Mohammad Abu Fani		27/04/98	M	1	(1)	
8	Enis Alushi	KOS	22/12/85	M	10	(2)	
16	Eliran Atar		17/02/87	A	19	(5)	7
29	Muhamad Awad		09/06/97	A	5	(6)	1
9	Fitim Azemi	NOR	25/06/92	A	3	(5)	
3	Shay Ben David		19/07/97	D	12	(2)	
28	Yaniv Brik		28/05/95	M	8	(4)	
10	Omer Damari		24/03/89	A	7	(2)	2
15	Hólmar Örn Eyjólfsson	ISL	06/08/90	D	16		
55	Omri Glazer		11/03/96	G	26		
17	Shoval Gozlan		25/04/94	A		(11)	1
34	Yahav Gurfinkel		27/06/98	D		(3)	
2	Ayad Habashi		10/05/95	D	3	(2)	
23	Ataa Jaber		03/10/94	M	2	(1)	
6	Gary Kagelmacher	URU	21/04/88	D	34		1
19	Roi Kehat		12/05/92	M	28	(4)	3
21	Dekel Keinan		15/09/84	D	30		4
31	Neta Lavi		25/08/96	M	26	(5)	
40	Yonatan Levi		02/01/98	D	2		
1	Ohad Levita		17/02/86	G	10		
7	Sun Menachem		07/09/93	M	19	(4)	2
26	Firas Mugrabi		24/07/91	M	5	(6)	
3	Mario Musa	CRO	06/07/90	D	11		
9	Glynor Plet	NED	30/01/87	A	7	(6)	3
11	Ismail Raiyan		24/04/94	A	7	(10)	
13	Nikita Rukavytsya	AUS	22/06/87	A	15	(6)	4
25	Kamil Vacek	CZE	18/05/87	M	24	(5)	
4	Marc Valiente	ESP	29/03/87	D	17	(2)	
35	Eitan Velblum		27/02/97	M	4	(3)	
14	Gil Vermouth		05/08/85	M	29	(3)	6
32	Amit Zenati		02/04/97	A	8	(7)	

Maccabi Petach-Tikva FC

1912 • HaMoshava (11,500) • m-pt.co.il

Major honours
Israeli Cup (2) 1935, 1952

Coach: Kobi Refua

Date		Opponent		Score	Scorers
2016					
21/08	h	Beitar	D	2-2	*Kalibat, Kanyuk*
27/08	a	H. Ra'anana	W	1-0	*Tzairi*
12/09	h	H. Tel-Aviv	W	2-0	*Kanyuk 2*
18/09	a	Bnei Sakhnin	W	1-0	*Roman*
26/09	h	M. Haifa	D	2-2	*Elo, Tzairi*
15/10	a	H. Beer Sheva	L	0-5	
22/10	a	Bnei Yehuda	W	4-1	*Kanyuk, Roman 2, Kalibat*
30/10	h	H. Kiryat Shmona	W	2-1	*Melamed 2*
06/11	a	M. Tel-Aviv	D	0-0	
19/11	h	H. Ashkelon	D	1-1	*Roman*
26/11	a	H. Haifa	L	1-2	*Tzairi*
03/12	h	H. Kfar-Saba	D	0-0	
11/12	a	Ashdod	D	2-2	*Kanyuk 2*
17/12	a	Beitar	D	1-1	*Roman*
25/12	h	H. Ra'anana	W	2-0	*Melamed, Roman*
31/12	a	H. Tel-Aviv	W	1-0	*Kanyuk*
2017					
10/01	h	Bnei Sakhnin	D	1-1	*Melamed*
14/01	a	M. Haifa	W	2-0	*Adamović, Melamed*
21/01	h	H. Beer Sheva	D	1-1	*Magbo*
28/01	h	Bnei Yehuda	W	2-0	*Roman, Solomon*
04/02	a	H. Kiryat Shmona	W	1-0	*Gabay*
13/02	h	M. Tel-Aviv	L	0-1	
19/02	a	H. Ashkelon	W	1-0	*Tzairi*
26/02	h	H. Haifa	W	3-1	*Melamed, Kanyuk, Romário (p)*
05/03	a	H. Kfar-Saba	W	3-1	*Melamed 2, Kanyuk*
11/03	h	Ashdod	L	0-1	
18/03	h	Beitar	L	0-1	
02/04	a	Bnei Sakhnin	L	0-1	
09/04	h	H. Beer Sheva	L	1-2	*Kanyuk (p)*
15/04	a	M. Tel-Aviv	L	0-2	
22/04	h	M. Haifa	L	0-1	
26/04	a	Beitar	L	1-2	*Melamed*
29/04	h	Bnei Sakhnin	W	1-0	*Tzairi*
08/05	a	H. Beer Sheva	D	1-1	*Cohen*
14/05	h	M. Tel-Aviv	W	2-1	*Solomon, Cohen*
20/05	a	M. Haifa	D	0-0	

No	Name	Nat	DoB	Pos	Aps	(s)	Gls
22	Nenad Adamović	SRB	12/01/89	M	11	(10)	1
30	Aitor Monroy	ESP	08/10/87	M	6	(18)	
2	Allyson	BRA	23/10/90	D	31		
82	Dani Amos		02/02/87	G	34		
28	Avihu Azar		06/05/97	A		(1)	
44	Thai Baribo		15/01/98	A		(4)	
10	Lidor Cohen		16/12/92	M	9	(2)	2
5	Carlos Cuéllar	ESP	23/08/81	D	28	(2)	
3	Omer Danino		17/02/95	D	18	(3)	
18	Dor Elo		26/09/93	D	32	(1)	1
9	Dovev Gabay		01/04/87	A	3	(7)	1
1	Yossi Ginzburg		11/10/91	G	2		
7	Hagai Goldenberg		15/09/90	D	7	(8)	
10	Mohammed Kalibat		15/06/90	A	12	(5)	2
26	Gidi Kanyuk		11/02/93	M	33	(2)	10
78	Gal Levi		09/02/94	M	5	(3)	
23	Omri Luzon		07/01/99	D		(1)	
77	Uri Magbo		12/09/87	D	11	(2)	1
14	Shmuel Malul		03/04/93	D	1	(1)	
20	Guy Melamed		21/12/92	A	26	(2)	9
11	Naor Paser		18/10/85	D	23	(2)	
9	Oz Peretz		19/04/94	A	1	(2)	
17	Mihai Roman	ROU	31/05/92	A	29	(6)	7
52	Romário	BRA	16/01/89	M	33		1
6	Liran Rotman		07/06/96	M	1	(5)	
19	Manor Solomon		24/07/99	A	7	(16)	2
55	Liroy Tzairi		02/03/89	M	33		5

Maccabi Tel-Aviv FC

1906 • Winner, Netanya (13,800) • maccabi-tlv.co.il

Major honours
Israeli League (21) 1936, 1937, 1942, 1947, 1950, 1952, 1954, 1956, 1958, 1968, 1970, 1972, 1977, 1979, 1992, 1995, 1996, 2003, 2013, 2014, 2015; Israeli Cup (23) 1929, 1930, 1933, 1941, 1946, 1947, 1954, 1955, 1958, 1959, 1964, 1965, 1967, 1970, 1977, 1987, 1988, 1994, 1996, 2001, 2002, 2005, 2015

Coach: Shota Arveladze (GEO);
(04/01/17) (Jordi Cruijff (NED));
(14/02/17) Lito Vidigal (ANG)

Date		Opponent		Score	Scorers
2016					
21/08	h	H. Kfar-Saba	W	3-1	*Ben Basat, T Ben Haim (II) 2 (1p)*
28/08	a	Ashdod	W	2-1	*Scarione, T Ben Haim (II) (p)*
11/09	h	Beitar	D	2-2	*Igiebor, T Ben Haim (II) (p)*
18/09	a	H. Ra'anana	W	3-0	*T Ben Haim (II) 2, Rikan*
21/09	a	Bnei Sakhnin	W	3-0	*Scarione 2 (1p), Kjartansson*
25/09	h	H. Tel-Aviv	W	5-0	*Igiebor, T Ben Haim (II) 2, Kjartansson 2*
24/10	h	M. Haifa	L	0-2	
30/10	a	H. Beer Sheva	L	0-2	
06/11	h	M. Petach-Tikva	D	0-0	
20/11	a	H. Kiryat Shmona	W	2-1	*Kjartansson 2*
27/11	a	Bnei Yehuda	L	0-1	
03/12	h	H. Ashkelon	D	0-0	
11/12	a	H. Haifa	W	4-2	*Micha, og (Fishler), Alberman, Kjartansson*
17/12	a	H. Kfar-Saba	D	1-1	*Itzhaki*
24/12	h	Ashdod	W	1-0	*Itzhaki*
2017					
02/01	a	Beitar	L	0-1	
11/01	h	H. Ra'anana	W	4-1	*Benayoun, Itzhaki, T Ben Haim (II) (p), Kjartansson*
16/01	a	H. Tel-Aviv	W	1-0	*Kjartansson*
22/01	h	Bnei Sakhnin	W	2-1	*Scarione 2*
30/01	a	M. Haifa	D	2-2	*Kjartansson 2*
04/02	h	H. Beer Sheva	W	1-0	*Kjartansson*
13/02	a	M. Petach-Tikva	W	1-0	*Itzhaki*
18/02	h	H. Kiryat Shmona	W	3-0	*Kjartansson 3*
25/02	h	Bnei Yehuda	W	2-0	*Itzhaki, Kjartansson*
05/03	a	H. Ashkelon	W	2-1	*T Ben Haim (II), Rikan*
12/03	h	H. Haifa	W	1-0	*og (Peretz)*
18/03	h	Bnei Sakhnin	W	3-0	*Itzhaki, Rúben Micael, T Ben Haim (II)*
01/04	a	H. Beer Sheva	L	0-1	
09/04	h	M. Haifa	W	3-0	*T Ben Haim (II) 2, Micha*
15/04	h	M. Petach-Tikva	W	2-0	*og (Amos), T Ben Haim (II)*
22/04	a	Beitar	D	1-1	*T Ben Haim (II)*
25/04	a	Bnei Sakhnin	W	3-1	*Golasa, Kjartansson 2*
29/04	h	H. Beer Sheva	L	1-2	*Kjartansson*
07/05	a	M. Haifa	W	2-0	*Kjartansson, Rikan*
14/05	a	M. Petach-Tikva	L	1-2	*Rikan*
20/05	h	Beitar	L	0-2	

No	Name	Nat	DoB	Pos	Aps	(s)	Gls
6	Gal Alberman		17/04/83	M	26	(5)	1
9	Eden Ben Basat		08/09/86	A	1	(9)	1
26	Tal Ben Haim (I)		31/03/82	D	30	(1)	
11	Tal Ben Haim (II)		05/08/89	A	28	(1)	15
20	Omri Ben Harush		07/03/90	D	11	(1)	
51	Yossi Benayoun		05/05/80	M	14	(13)	1
2	Eli Dasa		03/12/92	D	31		
21	Yegor Filipenko	BLR	10/04/88	D	15	(2)	
23	Eyal Golasa		07/10/91	M	17	(4)	1
40	Emmanuel Nosa Igiebor	NGA	09/11/90	M	10	(6)	2
10	Barak Itzhaki		25/09/84	A	16	(10)	6
24,9	Vidar Örn Kjartansson	ISL	11/03/90	A	30	(3)	19
1	Daniel Lifshitz		24/04/88	G	1		
29	Marcelo	BRA	29/05/94	M		(3)	
4,26	Haris Medunjanin	BIH	08/03/85	M	15	(3)	
15	Dor Micha		02/03/92	M	23	(8)	2
14,42	Dor Peretz		17/05/95	M	1	(3)	
45	Eliel Peretz		18/11/96	M	3	(6)	
95	Predrag Rajković	SRB	31/10/95	G	35		
4	Ramon	BRA	03/05/95	D	1	(2)	
22	Avi Rikan		10/09/88	D	13	(2)	4
14	Rúben Micael	POR	19/08/86	M	11	(4)	1
5	Ezequiel Scarione	ARG	14/07/85	M	11	(8)	5
25	Aaron Schoenfeld	USA	17/04/90	A	2	(8)	
3	Yuval Shpungin		03/04/87	D	4	(1)	
18	Eitan Tibi		16/11/87	D	25		
17	Sagiv Yehezkel		21/03/95	A	7	(5)	
13	Sheran Yeini		08/12/86	M	15	(1)	

Top goalscorers

19 Vidar Örn Kjartansson (M. Tel-Aviv)

15 Tal Ben Haim (II) (M. Tel-Aviv)

14 Etay Shechter (Beitar)
Anthony Nwakaeme (H. Beer Sheva)
Ben Sahar (H. Beer Sheva)

11 Idan Vered (Beitar)

10 Eli Elbaz (H. Haifa/H. Kfar-Saba)
Gidi Kanyuk (M. Petach-Tikva)

9 Maaran Al Lala (H. Haifa)
Guy Melamed (M. Petach-Tikva)

Promoted clubs

Maccabi Netanya FC

1934 • Winner (13,800) • fcmn.co.il

Major honours
Israeli League (5) 1971, 1974, 1978, 1980, 1983; Israeli Cup (1) 1978

Coach: Slobodan Drapich

Hapoel Akko FC

1946 • Toto (5,000) • no website

Coach: Shlomi Dora

Second level final table 2016/17

		Pld	W	D	L	F	A	Pts
1	Maccabi Netanya FC	37	22	13	2	80	41	70
2	Hapoel Akko FC	37	17	11	9	58	41	62
3	Beitar Tel-Aviv Ramla FC	37	16	11	10	67	39	59
4	Hapoel Ramat Gan FC	37	15	10	12	53	46	55
5	Hapoel Katamon Jerusalem FC	37	15	8	14	55	56	53
6	Hapoel Petach-Tikva FC	37	14	11	12	55	51	52
7	Hapoel Bnei Lod FC	37	13	8	16	49	62	47
8	Maccabi Ahi Nazareth FC	37	10	15	12	45	52	45
9	Hapoel Ironi Nir Ramat HaSharon FC	37	12	11	14	38	42	47
10	Hapoel Ironi Rishon-LeZion FC	37	11	13	13	38	39	46
11	Hapoel Afula FC	37	9	18	10	55	59	45
12	Ironi Nesher FC	37	9	16	12	26	35	43
13	Maccabi Herzliya FC	37	10	13	14	45	55	43
14	Hapoel Nazareth Illit FC	37	9	13	15	32	53	40
15	Hapoel Jerusalem FC	37	9	11	17	29	44	38
16	Maccabi Shearayim FC	37	8	12	17	40	50	36

NB League splits into top and bottom halves after 30 games, after which the clubs play exclusively against teams in their group; Maccabi Netanya FC – 9 pts deducted; Hapoel Petach-Tikva FC – 1 pt deducted.

DOMESTIC CUP

G'Viaa Hamedina (State Cup) 2016/17

EIGHTH ROUND

(05/01/17)
H. Akko 3-3 Bnei Yehuda *(aet; 3-4 on pens)*
H. Ashkelon 5-2 M. Jaffa
H. Beer Sheva 2-0 M. Zur-Shalom
H. Haifa 6-1 H. Kfar-Kasem
H. Ra'anana 4-1 M. Ahi Nazareth
M. Shaarayim 1-3 Bnei Sakhnin

(06/01/17)
Beitar Tel-Aviv Ramla 2-1 H. Nazareth Illit
H. Hod Hasharon 0-1 H. Kiryat Shmona *(aet)*
H. Iksal 1-3 Ashdod *(aet)*
H. Jerusalem 3-2 H. Afula
M. Netanya 1-2 H. Rishon LeZion *(aet)*
M. Kiryat Ata 0-3 H. Ramat Gan

(07/01/17)
Beitar Jerusalem 3-0 H. Kfar-Saba
H. Bnei Lod 0-3 M. Tel-Aviv
M. Haifa 0-2 M. Petach-Tikva

(08/01/17)
H. Tel-Aviv 1-0 H. Ramat HaSharon

NINTH ROUND

(24/01/17)
H. Beer Sheva 0-1 H. Kiryat Shmona
H. Haifa 3-0 H. Rishon LeZion
H. Jerusalem 0-0 H. Ramat Gan *(aet; 3-4 on pens)*
H. Tel-Aviv 0-2 M. Petach-Tikva

(25/01/17)
Ashdod 1-1 Beitar Tel-Aviv Ramla *(aet; 5-4 on pens)*
Beitar Jerusalem 2-1 Bnei Sakhnin
H. Ashkelon 0-4 Bnei Yehuda
H. Ra'anana 1-1 M. Tel-Aviv *(aet; 2-4 on pens)*

QUARTER-FINALS

(07/02/17 & 01/03/17)
Beitar Jerusalem 2-0 H. Kiryat Shmona *(Shechter 21p, 56)*
H. Kiryat Shmona 1-0 Beitar Jerusalem *(Mauricio 22)*
(Beitar Jerusalem 2-1)

(08/02/17 & 28/02/17)
Ashdod 1-4 Bnei Yehuda *(Lúcio Maranhão 25; Kachila 9, Cohen 60, Buzaglo 76, Galván 88)*
Bnei Yehuda 2-0 Ashdod *(Kachila 49, Cohen 89)*
(Bnei Yehuda 6-1)

(08/02/17 & 01/03/17)
H. Haifa 1-1 H. Ramat Gan *(Ben Basat 75; Rosh 78)*
H. Ramat Gan 2-1 H. Haifa *(Halaila 77, Cohen 85; Al Lala 90)*
(H. Ramat Gan 3-2)

(08/02/17 & 01/03/17)
M. Petach-Tikva 0-1 M. Tel-Aviv *(T Ben Haim (II) 76)*
M. Tel-Aviv 2-1 M. Petach-Tikva *(Kjartansson 50, Scarione 90p; Melamed 55)*
(M. Tel-Aviv 3-1)

SEMI-FINALS

(04/05/17)
Bnei Yehuda 1-0 H. Ramat Gan *(Cohen 22)*

(05/05/17)
Beitar Jerusalem 1-2 M. Tel-Aviv *(Ezra 90; Schoenfeld 18, Micha 60)*

FINAL

(25/05/17)
Teddy, Jerusalem
BNEI YEHUDA TEL-AVIV FC 0
MACCABI TEL-AVIV FC 0
(aet; 4-3 on pens)
Referee: *Hachmon*
BNEI YEHUDA: *Zubas, Jovanović, Kachila, Goldberg, Kandil (Azoz 77), Jaiteh, Gordana, Mršić (Finish 112), Valskis, Turgeman (Buzaglo 84), Cohen*
M. TEL-AVIV: *Rajković, Dasa, Tibi, T Ben Haim (I), Yeini, Golasa, Alberman, Rúben Micael (Rikan 84), Micha (Benayoun 100), T Ben Haim (II) (Scarione 108), Kjartansson*

Bnei Yehuda edged out local rivals Maccabi Tel-Aviv on penalties to win the Israeli State Cup for the third time

ITALY

Federazione Italiana Giuoco Calcio (FIGC)

Address	Via Gregorio Allegri 14 CP 2450 IT-00198 Roma
Tel	+39 0684 912 553
Fax	+39 0625 496 455
E-mail	figc.segreteria@figc.it
Website	figc.it

President	Carlo Tavecchio
General secretary	Michele Uva
Media officer	Paolo Corbi
Year of formation	1898

SERIE A CLUBS

1 **Atalanta BC**

2 **Bologna FC**

3 **Cagliari Calcio**

4 **AC Chievo Verona**

5 **FC Crotone**

6 **Empoli FC**

7 **ACF Fiorentina**

8 **Genoa CFC**

9 **FC Internazionale Milano**

10 **Juventus FC**

11 **SS Lazio**

12 **AC Milan**

13 **SSC Napoli**

14 **US Città di Palermo**

15 **Pescara Calcio**

16 **AS Roma**

17 **UC Sampdoria**

18 **US Sassuolo Calcio**

19 **Torino FC**

20 **Udinese Calcio**

PROMOTED CLUBS

21 **SPAL**

22 **Hellas Verona FC**

23 **Benevento Calcio**

Bergamo (1, 12) · Udine (20) · Milano (Milan) (9, 12) · Verona (4, 22) · Torino (Turin) (10, 19) · Reggio Emilia (18) · Ferrara (21) · Genova (Genoa) (8, 17) · Bologna (2) · Empoli (6) · Firenze (Florence) (7) · Pescara (15) · Roma (Rome) (11, 16) · Napoli (Naples) (13) · Benevento (23) · Cagliari (3) · Crotone (5) · Palermo (14)

KEY
- UEFA Champions League
- UEFA Europa League
- Promoted
- Relegated

0 200 400 km
0 200 miles

Comfort and joy for Juventus

Massimiliano Allegri's third season as Juventus coach ended with a third consecutive Serie A/Coppa Italia double as the Turin giants' domination of Italian football continued.

Roma and Napoli scored freely and kept the Old Lady on her toes throughout the league campaign, but a record-breaking sixth successive scudetto was never truly in doubt. Lazio also came out second best in the cup final, but the coveted title of European champions eluded the Bianconeri once again as Real Madrid defeated them 4-1 in the UEFA Champions League final.

Third domestic double in a row for Allegri's team

Bianconeri also reach UEFA Champions League final

Roma pip Napoli to runners-up spot as Totti bows out

Domestic league

Juventus had been forced to come from behind to win the 2015/16 Serie A title after a bad start, but in 2016/17 there was no need for any such heroics. Allegri's team were always fully in control of their destiny. They pitched camp at the top of the table in the early weeks and made it their home for the next eight months, always keeping their challengers at a safe distance. The key to their success was a formidable record in Turin, where the only visiting team to avoid defeat were city rivals Torino – and that in the penultimate home fixture of the season, bringing to an end their hosts' astonishing run of 33 successive Serie A wins in the Juventus Stadium.

Juve were defeated five times on their travels – at Internazionale, Milan, Genoa, Fiorentina and Roma – but on every occasion they bounced back, not just with a home win but also a victory in their next away fixture. They never looked rattled, never lost their belief or hunger, and even when Allegri opted to alter the team's formation, the transition was seamless. The coach knew he had players who could adapt, and they did not let him down.

With midfield general Paul Pogba having been sold to Manchester United for a world-record fee, Juventus re-stocked their squad with a cluster of new signings including, poignantly, two of their southern rivals' most influential players – striker Gonzalo Higuaín from Napoli and midfielder Miralem Pjanić from Roma. Both enjoyed excellent first seasons in Turin, slotting into the side with effortless ease. Higuaín scored the winner on the opening day at home to Fiorentina and never looked back, ending up with 24 Serie A goals, most of them vitally important such as the deciders at home to both Napoli (2-1) and Roma (1-0). He also scored nine goals in eight games after the turn of the year at a time when Juventus, free from European distractions, pressed on the accelerator and sped ahead of their pursuers.

Higuaín's arrival at the apex of the attack lessened the goalscoring impact of Paulo Dybala and Mario Mandžukić, but the Argentinian and the Croatian still played a major role in the team's success, albeit in more of a supporting role. German international Sami Khedira enjoyed an excellent injury-free season in the centre of midfield alongside Pjanić, while the Juventus defence was as solid and dependable as ever, with veteran goalkeeper Gianluigi Buffon, who made his 600th appearance for the club midway through the season, continuing to perform wonders behind the now-legendary 'BBC' rearguard of Andrea Barzagli, Leonardo Bonucci and Giorgio Chiellini. Brazilian full-backs/wing-backs Dani Alves and Alex Sandro also prospered, while Colombian winger Juan Cuadrado was often the ace up Allegri's sleeve.

The 33rd scudetto in Juventus's history was wrapped up on the penultimate weekend – four days after the Coppa Italia final – with a routine 3-0 win over Crotone, Mandžukić, Dybala and Alex Sandro scoring the goals. They could have secured it a week earlier had they not succumbed to a 3-1 defeat by Roma at the Stadio Olimpico. That result proved crucial to the Giallorossi, although less in terms of keeping their title hopes alive than in protecting their second place, with its direct access to the UEFA Champions League group stage, from the threat of Napoli.

That contest for the runners-up spot would provide a riveting climax, with Roma's Diego Perotti scoring a 90th-minute goal against Genoa on the final day to win the game 3-2 and maintain his team's one-point lead over a Napoli side that simultaneously won 4-2 at Sampdoria. It was a fitting finale for Roma's 40-year-old talisman Francesco Totti, who paid an emotional farewell to a packed Stadio Olimpico after the final whistle, ending his one-club playing career with the remarkable figures of 786 Roma appearances and 307 goals, including at least one in 23 consecutive seasons.

Roma's star striker in 2016/17 was Edin Džeko, who topped the Serie A scoring charts with 29 goals. The Bosnia & Herzegovina captain was a constant menace to defences all season with his height, power and finishing prowess. The only two teams that prevented him from scoring against them were champions Juventus and city rivals Lazio. Egyptian winger Mohamed Salah and Belgian midfield powerhouse Radja Nainggolan also enjoyed productive seasons, helping Roma to accumulate 90 goals in total – 13 more than Juve, but four fewer than Napoli.

Despite the loss of Higuaín, Maurizio Sarri's team remained committed to attack. Like Luciano Spalletti's Roma, they were a joy to watch, home and away, and although their only tangible reward for a scintillating season was a ticket to the UEFA Champions League play-offs, they drew widespread admiration for the open, uninhibited style of their play. Even the long-term injury sustained by Higuaín's replacement, Arkadiusz Milik, proved no hindrance. Instead, Sarri sent Belgian midfielder-cum-winger Dries Mertens up front and he responded by scoring in virtually every game he started, missing out on the capocannoniere crown by just one goal. He was one of four Napoli scorers to reach double figures, Lorenzo Insigne, José Callejón and long-serving skipper Marek Hamšík rustling up 44 goals between them.

The only team Napoli failed to score against were Atalanta, who defeated them 1-0 at home and 2-0 away. New coach Gian Piero Gasperini was on the verge of the sack when the Bergamo club lost four of their opening five games, but the ex-Genoa and Inter boss not only survived but went on to mastermind a magnificent campaign, the Black-and-Blues rising from 13th in 2015/16 to finish with a club-record tally of 72 points in a barely believable fourth place – ahead of, among others, both heavyweight clubs from nearby Milan – and return to European competition, in the UEFA Europa League, for the first time since 1990/91. Young Italian defenders Andrea Conti and Mattia Caldara – who scored both goals in Naples – enjoyed magnificent

Gonzalo Higuaín scores for Juventus against Empoli – one of 24 goals the ex-Napoli striker registered for his new club in their triumphant Serie A campaign

breakthrough campaigns alongside brilliant young Ivory Coast midfielder Franck Kessié, while Argentinian skipper/schemer Alejandro 'Papu' Gómez was the team's chief inspiration in attack, helping himself to 16 goals and his team-mates to another ten.

Lazio, led by Simone Inzaghi, finished fifth, with newly acquired Italian international striker Ciro Immobile scoring 23 goals, while Vincenzo Montella's Milan returned to Europe after a three-year absence by claiming sixth spot. Although they were the only team to keep a clean sheet against Juventus – thanks to ever-present 18-year-old goalkeeper Gianluigi Donnarumma – it was another season of water-treading for the once-mighty Rossoneri. That looked set to change, however, following a €740m takeover from a Chinese consortium that brought Silvio Berlusconi's 31-year ownership of the club to an end.

One place and one point below Milan were Inter. When they thrashed Atalanta 7-1 at San Siro in mid-March – a rare off day for Gasperini's team – that end-of-season scenario looked highly unlikely, but they picked up just two points from their next eight matches, which meant that Stefano Pioli became the second Nerazzurri coach to be sacked during the season, ex-Ajax boss Frank de Boer – a summer replacement for Roberto Mancini – having lasted just 85 days when he was dismissed in the autumn. Mauro Icardi's 24 goals were not sufficiently supported elsewhere to gain Inter a European place, and it was the same story at Torino, for whom new Italy striker Andrea Belotti struck 26 times, including an eight-minute hat-trick at home to Palermo.

Eighth-placed Fiorentina lost only once at home, to Empoli, but that was not enough to help their Tuscan neighbours stay in Serie A. They were relegated on the final day, a 2-1 defeat away to Palermo – already condemned to the drop alongside bottom club Pescara – combining with a 3-1 victory for Crotone at home to Lazio to send them down. Crotone, in Serie A for the first time, looked certain to make their stay a

brief one before staging one of the most astonishing relegation escapes Italy's top division had ever witnessed. With two months of the season remaining the Calabrians had just three wins and a paltry 14 points to their name. Their last nine fixtures, however, yielded six wins and 20 points, their only defeat during that spell being Juventus's title-clinching 3-0 victory in Turin.

Serie A had another top-flight newcomer to greet in 2017/18 as Benevento emerged victorious from Serie B's end-of-season play-offs, defeating Spezia, Perugia and Carpi to join automatically-promoted SPAL – themselves back among the elite after a 49-year absence – and Hellas Verona, who returned to the top level after just a single season away.

Domestic cup

The only club to have won the Coppa Italia ten or more times, Juventus wrote another piece of competition history in 2016/17 as they became the first to lift the trophy three years in a row. It had been successfully defended eight times previously but never in two consecutive seasons. Allegri's team did not have an easy path to Rome, having to draw on all their reserves to beat Atalanta (3-2), Milan (2-1) and Napoli (5-4 on aggregate), but the final against Lazio, who had knocked out Genoa, Inter and – in an epic semi-final – Roma, brought a relatively straightforward victory, two early goals from defenders Bonucci and Dani Alves allowing Juve to play the rest of the game in protective mode as their well-drilled defence withstood all that Lazio, seeking a seventh Coppa win, could throw at them.

Europe

Italy's champions and cup winners also turned on the style in Europe, reaching their second UEFA Champions League final in three years. But, as in 2015 and on five other occasions before that, Juve's quest to become kings of the continent fell just short, Real Madrid outplaying them in the second half of the final and deservedly winning 4-1. Losing so emphatically, indeed losing at all, was hard for Juventus and their fans to stomach. They arrived in Cardiff unbeaten in their 12 matches, having conceded just three goals. For the first five games of the knockout phase, including two against their 2015 final conquerors Barcelona, Buffon and his defenders were unbreached. Monaco were also masterfully cast aside in the semi-finals, 4-1 on aggregate, after two awesome displays. In south Wales, however, the dream died, Mandžukić's brilliant equalising goal being consigned to the footnotes as Cristiano Ronaldo and co ran amok in a one-sided second period.

Napoli were also eliminated by Madrid, 6-2 on aggregate in the round of 16, while Roma's European interest was restricted to the UEFA Europa League after they calamitously lost 3-0 at home to FC Porto – later eliminated by Juve – in the second leg of their UEFA Champions League play-off. With a seemingly disinterested Inter and European debutants Sassuolo both departing at the group stage, and Fiorentina exiting unexpectedly after a rousing Borussia Mönchengladbach comeback in the round of 32, Roma were Italy's last team standing in the UEFA Europa League. But after a wonderful 4-0 win at Villarreal, in which Džeko became the competition's joint-top scorer with his second hat-trick of the campaign, the Giallorossi lost out to Lyon in the last 16. Those would be the last European engagements of coach Spalletti's second spell with Roma as he left for Inter at the end of the season, to be replaced by Sassuolo's Eusebio Di Francesco.

National team

With Antonio Conte having resumed his club career in England at Chelsea, Italy had a new coach to lead them into battle for the 2018 FIFA World Cup qualifying campaign – ex-Torino boss Giampiero Ventura, at 69 the oldest of all the 54 European coaches seeking to steer their teams to Russia. Defeated in his first game, a friendly against France in Bari (1-3), the new man would not lose any of his next ten, which included six European Qualifiers. Five of those delivered maximum points, while the other, at home to Spain, ended 1-1 – a set of results that prolonged the Azzurri's undefeated run in World Cup and UEFA European Championship qualifying games to a remarkable 56, but left them second behind Spain on goal difference with a visit to the group leaders still to come.

Ventura gave caps to 50 players, 24 of them having never previously been selected, including Donnarumma, who became Italy's youngest debutant for over a century and the country's youngest ever goalkeeper. At the other end of the age scale, 39-year-old Buffon won his 168th cap in a March qualifier against Albania, which not only established a European record but also came on the occasion of his 1,000th appearance as a senior professional.

Ciro Immobile (No11) heads in his fifth goal of the 2018 World Cup qualifying campaign, against Albania in Palermo, as his Italy strike partner Andrea Belotti looks on

DOMESTIC SEASON AT A GLANCE

Serie A 2016/17 final table

		Pld	Home W	Home D	Home L	Home F	Home A	Away W	Away D	Away L	Away F	Away A	Total W	Total D	Total L	Total F	Total A	Pts
1	**Juventus FC**	**38**	**18**	**1**	**0**	**48**	**9**	**11**	**3**	**5**	**29**	**18**	**29**	**4**	**5**	**77**	**27**	**91**
2	AS Roma	38	16	1	2	50	18	12	2	5	40	20	28	3	7	90	38	87
3	SSC Napoli	38	13	4	2	44	19	13	4	2	50	20	26	8	4	94	39	86
4	Atalanta BC	38	12	4	3	31	18	9	5	5	31	23	21	9	8	62	41	72
5	SS Lazio	38	12	2	5	40	23	9	5	5	34	28	21	7	10	74	51	70
6	AC Milan	38	12	2	5	32	20	6	7	6	25	25	18	9	11	57	45	63
7	FC Internazionale Milano	38	11	3	5	44	22	8	2	9	28	27	19	5	14	72	49	62
8	ACF Fiorentina	38	10	8	1	34	23	6	4	9	29	34	16	12	10	63	57	60
9	Torino FC	38	9	8	2	43	31	4	6	9	28	35	13	14	11	71	66	53
10	UC Sampdoria	38	8	6	5	28	23	4	6	9	21	32	12	12	14	49	55	48
11	Cagliari Calcio	38	11	3	5	38	34	3	2	14	17	42	14	5	19	55	76	47
12	US Sassuolo Calcio	38	7	3	9	27	28	6	4	9	31	35	13	7	18	58	63	46
13	Udinese Calcio	38	8	5	6	30	23	4	4	11	17	33	12	9	17	47	56	45
14	AC Chievo Verona	38	6	5	8	25	30	6	2	11	18	31	12	7	19	43	61	43
15	Bologna FC	38	8	2	9	24	25	3	6	10	16	33	11	8	19	40	58	41
16	Genoa CFC	38	6	7	6	24	24	3	2	14	14	40	9	9	20	38	64	36
17	FC Crotone	38	6	4	9	21	25	3	3	13	13	33	9	7	22	34	58	34
18	Empoli FC	38	5	4	10	16	29	3	4	12	13	32	8	8	22	29	61	32
19	US Città di Palermo	38	4	3	12	13	30	2	5	12	20	47	6	8	24	33	77	26
20	Pescara Calcio	38	2	5	12	19	38	1	4	14	18	43	3	9	26	37	81	18

European qualification 2017/18

Champion/Cup winner: Juventus FC (group stage)
AS Roma (group stage)
SSC Napoli (play-offs)

Atalanta BC (group stage)
SS Lazio (group stage)
AC Milan (third qualifying round)

Top scorer	Edin Džeko (Roma), 29 goals
Relegated clubs	Pescara Calcio, US Città di Palermo, Empoli FC
Promoted clubs	SPAL, Hellas Verona FC, Benevento Calcio
Cup final	Juventus FC 2-0 SS Lazio

Player of the season

Dries Mertens
(SSC Napoli)

Mertens' fourth season at Napoli revealed a side to the Belgian international that had largely been kept under wraps. Pressed into service as an emergency striker following the sale of Gonzalo Higuaín and a serious injury to new signing Arkadiusz Milik, he showed in his 30th year that he could not just operate in the role but fill it with great distinction. Eight goals in three games just before Christmas sparked a fantastic run of form that propelled Napoli to a succession of victories and the player himself to second place in the end-of-term Serie A scorers' charts with 28 goals.

Newcomer of the season

Franck Kessié
(Atalanta BC)

Back from a loan spell in Serie B with Cesena where he was transformed from a central defender into an all-action midfielder, Kessié scored twice on his Serie A debut for Atalanta and proceeded to draw plaudits and praise whenever and wherever he played. A high-energy all-rounder who did not turn 20 until midway through the season, the young Ivorian played a leading role in the Bergamo club's remarkable rise up to fourth place in Serie A. His impressive form inevitably drew the attention of Italy's bigger clubs and in the summer he moved to AC Milan.

Team of the season
(4-3-1-2)

Coach: Allegri *(Juventus)*

NATIONAL TEAM

International honours
FIFA World Cup (4) 1934, 1938, 1982, 2006
UEFA European Championship (1) 1968

International tournament appearances
FIFA World Cup (18) 1934 (Winners), 1938 (Winners), 1950, 1954, 1962, 1966, 1970 (runners-up), 1974, 1978 (4th), 1982 (Winners), 1986 (2nd round), 1990 (3rd), 1994 (runners-up), 1998 (qtr-finals), 2002 (2nd round), 2006 (Winners), 2010, 2014
UEFA European Championship (9) 1968 (Winners), 1980 (4th), 1988 (semi-finals), 1996, 2000 (runners-up), 2004, 2008 (qtr-finals), 2012 (runners-up), 2016 (qtr-finals)

Top five all-time caps
Gianluigi Buffon (169); Fabio Cannavaro (136); Paolo Maldini (126); Andrea Pirlo (116); **Daniele De Rossi** (114)

Top five all-time goals
Luigi Riva (35); Giuseppe Meazza (33); Silvio Piola (30); Roberto Baggio & Alessandro Del Piero (27)

Results 2016/17

01/09/16	France	H	Bari	L	1-3	*Pellè (21)*
05/09/16	Israel (WCQ)	A	Haifa	W	3-1	*Pellè (14), Candreva (31p), Immobile (83)*
06/10/16	Spain (WCQ)	H	Turin	D	1-1	*De Rossi (82p)*
09/10/16	FYR Macedonia (WCQ)	A	Skopje	W	3-2	*Belotti (24), Immobile (75, 90+2)*
12/11/16	Liechtenstein (WCQ)	A	Vaduz	W	4-0	*Belotti (11, 44), Immobile (12), Candreva (32)*
15/11/16	Germany	H	Milan	D	0-0	
24/03/17	Albania (WCQ)	H	Palermo	W	2-0	*De Rossi (12p), Immobile (80)*
28/03/17	Netherlands	A	Amsterdam	W	2-1	*Éder (11), Bonucci (32)*
31/05/17	San Marino	H	Empoli	W	8-0	*Lapadula (10, 19, 49), Ferrari (13), Petagna (16), Caldara (48), Politano (58), Bonini (65og)*
06/06/17	Uruguay	N	Nice (FRA)	W	3-0	*Giménez (7og), Éder (82), De Rossi (90+2p)*
11/06/17	Liechtenstein (WCQ)	H	Udine	W	5-0	*Insigne (35), Belotti (52), Éder (74), Bernardeschi (83), Gabbiadini (90+1)*

Appearances 2016/17

Coach: Giampiero Ventura	**14/01/48**		**Fra**	**ISR**	**ESP**	**MKD**	**LIE**	**Ger**	**ALB**	**Ned**	**Smr**	**Uru**	**LIE**	**Caps**	**Goals**
Gianluigi Buffon	28/01/78	Juventus	G46	G	G	G	G	G46	G				G	169	-
Andrea Barzagli	08/05/81	Juventus	D46	D	D	D			D			D78	D	68	-
Davide Astori	07/01/87	Fiorentina	D					s46						13	1
Giorgio Chiellini	14/08/84	Juventus	D	D 55*								s78	D	92	7
Antonio Candreva	28/02/87	Internazionale	M	M67		M	M74		M			M58	M60	47	6
Marco Parolo	25/01/85	Lazio	M	M	M76	s64		M		M				30	-
Daniele De Rossi	24/07/83	Roma	M46		M		M	M	M	M37		M	M	114	21
Giacomo Bonaventura	22/08/89	Milan	M66	M63	s30	M64	M67							8	-
Mattia De Sciglio	20/10/92	Milan	M58		M	M	D		D					31	-
Graziano Pellè	15/07/85	Shandong Luneng (CHN)	A	A	A59									20	9
Éder	15/11/86	Internazionale	A75	A70	A	s84	s74	A68		A69		s46	s67	23	6
Gianluigi Donnarumma	25/02/99	Milan	s46					s46		G		G		4	-
Riccardo Montolivo	18/01/85	Milan	s46		M30							s18		65	2
Daniele Rugani	29/07/94	Juventus	s46					D		D				3	-
Alessandro Florenzi	11/03/91	Roma	s58	s67	M									24	2
Marco Verratti	05/11/92	Paris (FRA)	s66	M		M	M		M	M90				21	1
Andrea Belotti	20/12/93	Torino	s75		s76	A84	A	A88	A	s53		A46	A75	9	4
Leonardo Bonucci	01/05/87	Juventus		D	D	D	D	D	D	D		D		70	5
Luca Antonelli	11/02/87	Milan		M										13	-
Angelo Ogbonna	23/05/88	West Ham (ENG)		s63										13	-
Ciro Immobile	20/02/90	Lazio		s70	s59	A	A81	A89	A	A53		A82	A67	24	6
Alessio Romagnoli	12/01/95	Milan			D	D	D	D46		D				5	-
Federico Bernardeschi	16/02/94	Fiorentina				M64		s68				s58	s60	9	1
Nicola Sansone	10/09/91	Villarreal (ESP)				s64		s88						3	-
Davide Zappacosta	11/06/92	Torino					D	M	D	M62				4	-
Lorenzo Insigne	04/06/91	Napoli					s67		M			M64	M	16	3
Simone Zaza	25/06/91	West Ham (ENG)					s81	s89						16	1
Matteo Darmian	02/12/89	Man. United (ENG)						M		M89		D	D	30	1
Roberto Gagliardini	07/04/94	Internazionale								s37	M46			2	-
Leonardo Spinazzola	25/03/93	Atalanta								s62		D	D	3	-
Andrea Petagna	30/06/95	Atalanta								s69	A46			2	1
Danilo D'Ambrosio	09/09/88	Internazionale								s89	D			2	-
Simone Verdi	12/07/92	Bologna								s90				1	-
Simone Scuffet	31/05/96	Udinese									G			1	-
Andrea Conti	02/03/94	Atalanta									D70			1	-
Mattia Caldara	05/05/94	Atalanta									D			1	1
Gianmarco Ferrari	15/05/92	Crotone									D			1	1
Daniele Baselli	12/03/92	Torino									M46			1	-
Federico Chiesa	25/10/97	Fiorentina									A62			1	-
Gianluca Lapadula	07/02/90	Milan									A			1	3
Domenico Berardi	01/08/94	Sassuolo									A46			1	-
Lorenzo Pelligrini	19/06/96	Sassuolo									s46		M	2	-
Danilo Cataldi	06/08/94	Genoa									s46			1	-
Matteo Politano	03/08/93	Sassuolo									s46			1	1
Diego Falcinelli	26/06/91	Crotone									s46			1	-
Gianluca Caprari	30/07/93	Pescara									s62			1	-
Cristiano Biraghi	01/09/92	Pescara									s70			1	-
Claudio Marchisio	19/01/86	Juventus										M18		55	5
Stephan El Shaarawy	27/10/92	Roma										s64		21	3
Manolo Gabbiadini	26/11/91	Southampton (ENG)										s82	s75	8	2

EUROPE

Juventus FC

Group H
Match 1 - Sevilla FC (ESP)
H 0-0
Buffon, Chiellini, Khedira, Higuaín, Barzagli, Lemina, Bonucci, Dybala (Pjaca 86), Asamoah (Pjanić 68), Dani Alves, Evra (Alex Sandro 68). Coach: Massimiliano Allegri (ITA)
Match 2 - GNK Dinamo Zagreb (CRO)
A 4-0 *Pjanić (24), Higuaín (31), Dybala (57), Dani Alves (85)*
Buffon, Chiellini, Pjanić (Cuadrado 46), Khedira, Higuaín (Mandžukić 71), Hernanes, Barzagli (Pjaca 68), Bonucci, Dybala, Dani Alves, Evra. Coach: Massimiliano Allegri (ITA)
Match 3 - Olympique Lyonnais (FRA)
A 1-0 *Cuadrado (76)*
Buffon, Pjanić, Khedira (Sturaro 75), Higuaín, Alex Sandro, Barzagli, Lemina, Bonucci, Dybala (Cuadrado 69), Dani Alves (Benatia 84), Evra. Coach: Massimiliano Allegri (ITA)
Red card: Lemina 54
Match 4 - Olympique Lyonnais (FRA)
H 1-1 *Higuaín (13p)*
Buffon, Pjanić (Alex Sandro 68), Khedira, Marchisio, Higuaín (Cuadrado 83), Barzagli, Mandžukić, Bonucci (Benatia 68), Dani Alves, Sturaro, Evra. Coach: Massimiliano Allegri (ITA)
Match 5 - Sevilla FC (ESP)
A 3-1 *Marchisio (45+2p), Bonucci (84), Mandžukić (90+4)*
Buffon, Pjanić (Kean 84), Khedira, Cuadrado (Chiellini 87), Marchisio, Alex Sandro, Mandžukić, Bonucci, Dani Alves, Rugani, Evra (Sturaro 72). Coach: Massimiliano Allegri (ITA)
Match 6 - GNK Dinamo Zagreb (CRO)
H 2-0 *Higuaín (52), Rugani (73)*
Neto, Benatia, Pjanić (Dybala 80), Cuadrado, Marchisio (Sturaro 74), Higuaín, Mandžukić (Hernanes 85), Lemina, Asamoah, Rugani, Evra. Coach: Massimiliano Allegri (ITA)

Round of 16 - FC Porto (POR)
A 2-0 *Pjaca (72), Dani Alves (74)*
Buffon, Chiellini, Pjanić, Khedira, Cuadrado (Pjaca 67), Higuaín, Alex Sandro, Barzagli, Mandžukić, Dybala (Marchisio 86), Lichtsteiner (Dani Alves 73). Coach: Massimiliano Allegri (ITA)
H 1-0 *Dybala (42p)*
Buffon, Benatia (Barzagli 60), Khedira, Cuadrado (Pjaca 46), Marchisio, Higuaín, Alex Sandro, Mandžukić, Bonucci, Dybala (Rincón 78), Dani Alves. Coach: Massimiliano Allegri (ITA)

Quarter-finals - FC Barcelona (ESP)
H 3-0 *Dybala (7, 22), Chiellini (55)*
Buffon, Chiellini, Pjanić (Barzagli 89), Khedira, Cuadrado (Lemina 73), Higuaín, Alex Sandro, Mandžukić, Bonucci, Dybala (Rincón 81), Dani Alves. Coach: Massimiliano Allegri (ITA)
A 0-0
Buffon, Chiellini, Pjanić, Khedira, Cuadrado (Lemina 84), Higuaín (Asamoah 88), Alex Sandro, Mandžukić, Bonucci, Dybala (Barzagli 75), Dani Alves. Coach: Massimiliano Allegri (ITA)

Semi-finals - AS Monaco FC (FRA)
A 2-0 *Higuaín (29, 59)*
Buffon, Chiellini, Pjanić (Lemina 89), Marchisio (Rincón 81), Higuaín (Cuadrado 77), Alex Sandro, Barzagli, Mandžukić, Bonucci, Dybala, Dani Alves. Coach: Massimiliano Allegri (ITA)
H 2-1 *Mandžukić (33), Dani Alves (44)*
Buffon, Chiellini, Pjanić, Khedira (Marchisio 10), Higuaín, Alex Sandro, Barzagli (Benatia 85), Mandžukić, Bonucci, Dybala (Cuadrado 54), Dani Alves. Coach: Massimiliano Allegri (ITA)

Final - Real Madrid CF (ESP)
N 1-4 *Mandžukić (27)*
Buffon, Chiellini, Pjanić (Marchisio 71), Khedira, Higuaín, Alex Sandro, Barzagli (Cuadrado 66), Mandžukić, Bonucci, Dybala (Lemina 78), Dani Alves. Coach: Massimiliano Allegri (ITA)
Red card: Cuadrado 84

SSC Napoli

Group B
Match 1 - FC Dynamo Kyiv (UKR)
A 2-1 *Milik (36, 45+2)*
Reina, Hysaj, Allan, Callejón, Jorginho, Mertens (Insigne 73), Hamšík (Zieliński 62), Koulibaly, Ghoulam, Albiol, Milik (Gabbiadini 82). Coach: Maurizio Sarri (ITA)
Match 2 - SL Benfica (POR)
H 4-2 *Hamšík (20), Mertens (51, 58), Milik (54p)*
Reina, Hysaj, Allan, Callejón (Insigne 70), Jorginho, Mertens (Giaccherini 82), Hamšík, Koulibaly, Ghoulam, Albiol (Maksimović 11), Milik. Coach: Maurizio Sarri (ITA)
Match 3 - Beşiktaş JK (TUR)
H 2-3 *Mertens (30), Gabbiadini (69p)*
Reina, Callejón, Jorginho (Diawara 70), Maggio, Mertens, Hamšík, Zieliński (Allan 82), Chiricheş, Insigne (Gabbiadini 65), Koulibaly, Ghoulam. Coach: Maurizio Sarri (ITA)
Match 4 - Beşiktaş JK (TUR)
A 1-1 *Hamšík (82)*
Reina, Hysaj, Allan (Zieliński 81), Callejón, Jorginho (Diawara 79), Hamšík, Maksimović, Gabbiadini (Mertens 63), Insigne, Koulibaly, Ghoulam. Coach: Maurizio Sarri (ITA)
Match 5 - FC Dynamo Kyiv (UKR)
H 0-0
Reina, Hysaj, Callejón, Mertens (Giaccherini 86), Hamšík, Zieliński (Allan 78), Insigne (Gabbiadini 66), Koulibaly, Ghoulam, Albiol, Diawara. Coach: Maurizio Sarri (ITA)
Match 6 - SL Benfica (POR)
A 2-1 *Callejón (60), Mertens (79)*
Reina, Hysaj, Allan, Callejón, Hamšík (Zieliński 72), Gabbiadini (Mertens 57), Insigne (Rog 80), Koulibaly, Ghoulam, Albiol, Diawara. Coach: Maurizio Sarri (ITA)

Round of 16 - Real Madrid CF (ESP)
A 1-3 *Insigne (8)*
Reina, Hysaj, Callejón, Mertens, Hamšík (Milik 83), Zieliński (Allan 75), Insigne, Koulibaly, Ghoulam, Albiol, Diawara. Coach: Maurizio Sarri (ITA)
H 1-3 *Mertens (24)*
Reina, Hysaj, Allan (Rog 56), Callejón, Mertens, Hamšík (Zieliński 75), Insigne (Milik 70), Koulibaly, Ghoulam, Albiol, Diawara. Coach: Maurizio Sarri (ITA)

AS Roma

Play-offs - FC Porto (POR)
A 1-1 *Felipe (21og)*
Alisson, Juan, Nainggolan, Strootman, Perotti (Emerson 44), Džeko, Salah (Fazio 77), Vermaelen, De Rossi, Florenzi (Paredes 85), Manolas. Coach: Luciano Spalletti (ITA)
Red card: Vermaelen 41
H 0-3
Szczęsny, Juan, Nainggolan, Paredes (Emerson 42), Strootman, Perotti (Gerson 86), Džeko (Iturbe 59), Salah, Bruno Peres, De Rossi, Manolas. Coach: Luciano Spalletti (ITA)
Red cards: De Rossi 39, Emerson 50

Group E
Match 1 - FC Viktoria Plzeň (CZE)
A 1-1 *Perotti (4p)*
Alisson, Juan, Nainggolan, Paredes, Iturbe (Florenzi 71), Perotti, Bruno Peres, Fazio, Gerson (Džeko 46), Manolas, El Shaarawy (Totti 72). Coach: Luciano Spalletti (ITA)
Match 2 - FC Astra Giurgiu (ROU)
H 4-0 *Strootman (15), Fazio (45+2), Fabrício (47og), Salah (55)*
Alisson, Juan, Paredes, Strootman (Gerson 69), Iturbe, Perotti, Totti, Salah (Nainggolan 57), Bruno Peres (Florenzi 63), Fazio, Manolas. Coach: Luciano Spalletti (ITA)
Match 3 - FK Austria Wien (AUT)
H 3-3 *El Shaarawy (19, 34), Florenzi (69)*
Alisson, Juan, Nainggolan, Paredes, Iturbe (Džeko 81), Totti, Fazio, Florenzi (Emerson 76), Gerson, Manolas, El Shaarawy (Salah 65). Coach: Luciano Spalletti (ITA)
Match 4 - FK Austria Wien (AUT)
A 4-2 *Džeko (5, 65), De Rossi (18), Nainggolan (78)*
Alisson, Rüdiger, Juan, Nainggolan, Paredes, Strootman, Perotti (Iturbe 84), Džeko, Bruno Peres, De Rossi, El Shaarawy (Gerson 70). Coach: Luciano Spalletti (ITA)
Match 5 - FC Viktoria Plzeň (CZE)
H 4-1 *Džeko (11, 61, 88), Matějů (82og)*
Alisson, Rüdiger, Nainggolan, Paredes, Strootman (Gerson 89), Iturbe (Perotti 63), Džeko, Salah (De Rossi 83), Bruno Peres, Fazio, Emerson. Coach: Luciano Spalletti (ITA)
Match 6 - FC Astra Giurgiu (ROU)
A 0-0
Alisson, Juan, Strootman (Nainggolan 70), Iturbe, Totti, Bruno Peres, Vermaelen, Seck, Gerson, Emerson (Marchizza 89), El Shaarawy (Džeko 70). Coach: Luciano Spalletti (ITA)

Round of 32 - Villarreal CF (ESP)
A 4-0 *Emerson (32), Džeko (65, 79, 86)*
Alisson, Rüdiger (Juan 71), Nainggolan (Paredes 90), Strootman, Džeko, Bruno Peres, De Rossi, Fazio, Emerson, Manolas, El Shaarawy (Salah 62). Coach: Luciano Spalletti (ITA)
H 0-1
Alisson, Juan, Paredes, Perotti, Totti, Bruno Peres (Fazio 84), Vermaelen, De Rossi (Nainggolan 76), Mário Rui, Manolas (Rüdiger 46), El Shaarawy. Coach: Luciano Spalletti (ITA)
Red card: Rüdiger 81

Round of 16 - Olympique Lyonnais (FRA)
A 2-4 *Salah (20), Fazio (33)*
Alisson, Juan, Nainggolan (Perotti 85), Strootman, Džeko (El Shaarawy 90+3), Salah, Bruno Peres, De Rossi (Paredes 82), Fazio, Emerson, Manolas. Coach: Luciano Spalletti (ITA)
H 2-1 *Strootman (17), Tousart (60og)*
Alisson, Rüdiger, Nainggolan, Strootman, Džeko, Salah, Bruno Peres (El Shaarawy 59), De Rossi (Totti 84), Fazio, Mário Rui (Perotti 76), Manolas. Coach: Luciano Spalletti (ITA)

FC Internazionale Milano

Group K
Match 1 - Hapoel Beer-Sheva FC (ISR)
H 0-2
Handanovič, Felipe Melo (Icardi 73), Palacio, Biabiany (Candreva 58), Ranocchia, Medel, Éder, Murillo, D'Ambrosio, Nagatomo, Brozović (Éver Banega 46). Coach: Frank de Boer (NED)
Match 2 - AC Sparta Praha (CZE)
A 1-3 *Palacio (71)*
Handanovič, Felipe Melo, Palacio, Ranocchia, Éver Banega, Éder, Murillo, Gnoukouri (Icardi 70), D'Ambrosio (Ansaldi 56), Candreva (Perišić 63), Miangue. Coach: Frank de Boer (NED)
Red card: Ranocchia 75
Match 3 - Southampton FC (ENG)
H 1-0 *Candreva (67)*
Handanovič, Icardi, Medel, Santon, Éder (Perišić 86), Murillo, Miranda, Gnoukouri, Nagatomo (D'Ambrosio 90+1), Brozović, Candreva (Ansaldi 80). Coach: Frank de Boer (NED)
Red card: Brozović 77
Match 4 - Southampton FC (ENG)
A 1-2 *Icardi (33)*
Handanovič, Icardi, Ranocchia, Medel (Éder 74), Éver Banega, Miranda, Gnoukouri (Felipe Melo 82), D'Ambrosio, Perišić, Nagatomo, Candreva (Biabiany 89). Coach: Stefano Vecchi (ITA)
Match 5 - Hapoel Beer-Sheva FC (ISR)
A 2-3 *Icardi (13), Brozović (25)*
Handanovič, Felipe Melo (Gnoukouri 62), Icardi, Éver Banega (Carrizo 70), Éder (Perišić 60), Murillo, Miranda, D'Ambrosio, Nagatomo, Brozović, Candreva. Coach: Stefano Pioli (ITA)
Red card: Handanovič 69
Match 6 - AC Sparta Praha (CZE)
H 2-1 *Éder (23, 90)*
Carrizo, Andreolli, Felipe Melo, Palacio (Perišić 46), Biabiany, Ranocchia, Ansaldi, Éder, Murillo, Miangue, Pinamonti (Bakayoko 80). Coach: Stefano Pioli (ITA)

ACF Fiorentina

Group J
Match 1 - PAOK FC (GRE)
A 0-0
Tătăruşanu, Gonzalo Rodríguez, Badelj, Kalinić, Astori, Olivera, Salcedo (Bernardeschi 74), Borja Valero, Babacar (Tello 76), Tomović, Iličič (Sánchez 63). Coach: Paulo Sousa (POR)
Match 2 - Qarabağ FK (AZE)
H 5-1 *Babacar (39, 45+2), Kalinić (43), Zárate (63, 78)*
Tătăruşanu, De Maio, Sánchez (Vecino 46), Kalinić (Zárate 61), Bernardeschi (Chiesa 61), Olivera, Tello, Salcedo, Cristóforo, Babacar, Tomović. Coach: Paulo Sousa (POR)
Match 3 - FC Slovan Liberec (CZE)
A 3-1 *Kalinić (8, 23), Babacar (70)*
Tătăruşanu, Gonzalo Rodríguez, Badelj, Vecino, Kalinić (Tello 53), Astori, Olivera, Cristóforo (Bernardeschi 62), Borja Valero, Babacar (Sánchez 79), Tomović. Coach: Paulo Sousa (POR)
Match 4 - FC Slovan Liberec (CZE)
H 3-0 *Iličič (30p), Kalinić (43), Cristóforo (73)*
Tătăruşanu, Gonzalo Rodríguez, De Maio, Sánchez, Kalinić (Bernardeschi 86), Cristóforo, Borja Valero (Babacar 79), Chiesa, Milić, Tomović, Iličič (Vecino 69). Coach: Paulo Sousa (POR)
Match 5 - PAOK FC (GRE)
H 2-3 *Bernardeschi (33), Babacar (50)*
Lezzerini, Gonzalo Rodríguez, Badelj, Vecino, Bernardeschi, Astori, Tello (Iličič 83), Cristóforo (Sánchez 66), Babacar, Milić (Chiesa 51), Tomović. Coach: Paulo Sousa (POR)
Match 6 - Qarabağ FK (AZE)
A 2-1 *Vecino (60), Chiesa (76)*
Tătăruşanu, Gonzalo Rodríguez, Badelj, Vecino, Bernardeschi (Sánchez 83), Astori, Olivera, Cristóforo (Borja Valero 61), Chiesa, Babacar (Kalinić 51), Tomović. Coach: Paulo Sousa (POR)
Red card: Chiesa 84

Round of 32 - VfL Borussia Mönchengladbach (GER)
A 1-0 *Bernardeschi (44)*
Tătăruşanu, Gonzalo Rodríguez, Badelj, Sánchez, Vecino, Kalinić (Babacar 77), Bernardeschi (Cristóforo 64), Astori, Olivera, Tello (Tomović 86), Borja Valero. Coach: Paulo Sousa (POR)
H 2-4 *Kalinić (16), Borja Valero (29)*
Tătăruşanu, Gonzalo Rodríguez, Badelj (Babacar 63), Sánchez, Vecino, Kalinić, Bernardeschi (Iličič 63), Astori, Olivera, Borja Valero, Chiesa. Coach: Paulo Sousa (POR)

US Sassuolo Calcio

Third qualifying round - FC Luzern (SUI)
A 1-1 *Berardi (42p)*
Consigli, Magnanelli, Biondini, Sansone (Politano 72), Defrel (Falcinelli 81), Peluso, Acerbi, Gazzola, Berardi (Mazzitelli 90), Cannavaro, Duncan. Coach: Eusebio Di Francesco (ITA)
H 3-0 *Berardi (19, 39p), Defrel (64)*
Consigli, Magnanelli, Biondini (Sensi 72), Sansone, Defrel (Falcinelli 82), Peluso, Acerbi, Gazzola, Berardi (Politano 72), Cannavaro, Duncan. Coach: Eusebio Di Francesco (ITA)

Play-offs - FK Crvena zvezda (SRB)
H 3-0 *Berardi (17), Politano (41), Defrel (69)*
Consigli, Magnanelli, Biondini, Defrel (Trotta 76), Peluso, Acerbi, Politano (Sensi 84), Gazzola, Berardi (Falcinelli 69), Cannavaro, Duncan. Coach: Eusebio Di Francesco (ITA)
A 1-1 *Berardi (28)*
Consigli, Magnanelli, Biondini, Matri (Trotta 83), Peluso, Acerbi, Politano (Falcinelli 62), Pol Lirola, Berardi (Letschert 72), Cannavaro, Duncan. Coach: Eusebio Di Francesco (ITA)

Group F
Match 1 - Athletic Club (ESP)
H 3-0 *Pol Lirola (60), Defrel (75), Politano (82)*
Consigli, Magnanelli, Biondini, Defrel (Matri 83), Acerbi, Politano, Pol Lirola, Mazzitelli (Duncan 73), Ricci (Ragusa 54), Cannavaro, Letschert. Coach: Eusebio Di Francesco (ITA)
Match 2 - KRC Genk (BEL)
A 1-3 *Politano (65)*
Consigli, Magnanelli, Pellegrini (Mazzitelli 66), Biondini (Ragusa 59), Defrel, Peluso, Acerbi, Politano, Pol Lirola, Ricci (Caputo 79), Letschert. Coach: Eusebio Di Francesco (ITA)
Match 3 - SK Rapid Wien (AUT)
A 1-1 *Schrammel (66og)*
Consigli, Magnanelli, Antei, Pellegrini, Matri (Ricci 78), Peluso, Acerbi, Politano (Adjapong 87), Pol Lirola, Mazzitelli, Ragusa (Defrel 58). Coach: Eusebio Di Francesco (ITA)
Match 4 - SK Rapid Wien (AUT)
H 2-2 *Defrel (34), Pellegrini (45+2)*
Consigli, Pellegrini, Biondini, Matri (Politano 65), Defrel (Franchini 90+1), Peluso, Acerbi, Pol Lirola, Gazzola, Ragusa (Ricci 81), Adjapong. Coach: Eusebio Di Francesco (ITA)
Match 5 - Athletic Club (ESP)
A 2-3 *Balenziaga (2og), Ragusa (83)*
Consigli, Magnanelli, Pellegrini (Missiroli 70), Biondini (Matri 71), Defrel (Politano 77), Acerbi, Pol Lirola, Gazzola, Ricci, Cannavaro, Ragusa. Coach: Eusebio Di Francesco (ITA)
Match 6 - KRC Genk (BEL)
H 0-2
Pegolo, Antei, Missiroli (Pellegrini 46), Matri, Acerbi, Pol Lirola, Mazzitelli, Cannavaro, Caputo (Magnanelli 74), Ragusa (Ricci 46), Adjapong. Coach: Eusebio Di Francesco (ITA)

DOMESTIC LEAGUE CLUB-BY-CLUB

Atalanta BC

1907 • Atleti Azzurri d'Italia (26,542) • atalanta.it

Major honours
Italian Cup (1) 1963

Coach: Gian Piero Gasperini

Date		Opponent		Score	Scorers
2016					
21/08	h	Lazio	L	3-4	*Kessié 2, Petagna*
28/08	a	Sampdoria	L	1-2	*Kessié*
11/09	h	Torino	W	2-1	*Masiello, Kessié (p)*
18/09	a	Cagliari	L	0-3	
21/09	h	Palermo	L	0-1	
26/09	a	Crotone	W	3-1	*Petagna, Kurtič, Gómez*
02/10	h	Napoli	W	1-0	*Petagna*
16/10	a	Fiorentina	D	0-0	
23/10	h	Internazionale	W	2-1	*Masiello, Pinilla (p)*
26/10	a	Pescara	W	1-0	*Caldara*
30/10	h	Genoa	W	3-0	*Kurtič 2, Gómez*
06/11	a	Sassuolo	W	3-0	*Gómez, Caldara, Conti*
20/11	h	Roma	W	2-1	*Caldara, Kessié (p)*
27/11	a	Bologna	W	2-0	*Masiello, Kurtič*
03/12	a	Juventus	L	1-3	*Freuler*
11/12	h	Udinese	L	1-3	*Kurtič*
17/12	a	Milan	D	0-0	
20/12	h	Empoli	W	2-1	*Kessié, D'Alessandro*
2017					
08/01	a	Chievo	W	4-1	*Gómez 2, Conti, Freuler*
15/01	a	Lazio	L	1-2	*Petagna*
22/01	h	Sampdoria	W	1-0	*Gómez (p)*
29/01	a	Torino	D	1-1	*Petagna*
05/02	h	Cagliari	W	2-0	*Gómez 2*
12/02	a	Palermo	W	3-1	*Conti, Gómez, Cristante*
18/02	h	Crotone	W	1-0	*Conti*
25/02	a	Napoli	W	2-0	*Caldara 2*
05/03	h	Fiorentina	D	0-0	
12/03	a	Internazionale	L	1-7	*Freuler*
19/03	h	Pescara	W	3-0	*Gómez 2, Grassi*
02/04	a	Genoa	W	5-0	*Conti, Gómez 3 (1p), Caldara*
08/04	h	Sassuolo	D	1-1	*Cristante*
15/04	a	Roma	D	1-1	*Kurtič*
22/04	h	Bologna	W	3-2	*Conti, Freuler, Caldara*
28/04	h	Juventus	D	2-2	*Conti, Freuler*
07/05	a	Udinese	D	1-1	*Cristante*
13/05	h	Milan	D	1-1	*Conti*
21/05	a	Empoli	W	1-0	*Gómez*
27/05	h	Chievo	W	1-0	*Gómez*

No	Name	Nat	DoB	Pos	Aps	(s)	Gls
95	Alessandro Bastoni		13/04/99	D	1	(2)	
1	Etrit Berisha	ALB	10/03/89	G	26		
52	Bryan Cabezas	ECU	20/03/97	M		(1)	
13	Mattia Caldara		05/05/94	D	30		7
17	Carlos Carmona	CHI	21/02/87	M	2		
24	Andrea Conti		02/03/94	D	31	(2)	8
4	Bryan Cristante		03/03/95	M	7	(5)	3
7	Marco D'Alessandro		17/02/91	M	4	(20)	1
93	Boukary Dramé	SEN	22/07/85	D	8	(2)	
11	Remo Freuler	SUI	15/04/92	M	29	(4)	5
13	Roberto Gagliardini		07/04/94	M	8	(5)	
91	Pierluigi Gollini		18/03/95	G	4		
10	Alejandro Gómez	ARG	15/02/88	M	37		16
88	Alberto Grassi		07/03/95	M	4	(14)	1
33	Hans Hateboer	NED	09/01/94	D	3	(3)	
19	Franck Kessié	CIV	19/12/96	M	25	(5)	6
25	Abdoulay Konko	FRA	09/03/84	D	7	(3)	
27	Jasmin Kurtič	SVN	10/01/89	M	35	(2)	6
5	Andrea Masiello		05/02/86	D	34	(1)	3
94	Filippo Melegoni		18/02/99	M	1		
8	Giulio Migliaccio		23/06/81	M		(3)	
87	Anthony Mounier	FRA	27/09/87	M		(5)	
43	Alberto Paloschi		04/01/90	A	4	(9)	
9	Aleksandar Pešić	SRB	21/05/92	A		(6)	
29	Andrea Petagna		30/06/95	A	31	(3)	5
51	Mauricio Pinilla	CHI	04/02/84	A	2	(2)	1
3	Rafael Tolói	BRA	10/10/90	D	31	(1)	
77	Cristian Raimondi		30/04/81	M	4	(4)	
37	Leonardo Spinazzola		25/03/93	M	28	(2)	
57	Marco Sportiello		10/05/92	G	8		
2	Guglielmo Stendardo		06/05/81	D		(1)	
6	Ervin Zukanović	BIH	11/02/87	D	14	(5)	

Bologna FC

1909 • Renato Dall'Ara (39,444) • bolognafc.it

Major honours
Italian League (7) 1925, 1929, 1936, 1937, 1939, 1941, 1964; Italian Cup (2) 1970, 1974

Coach: Roberto Donadoni

Date		Opponent		Score	Scorers
2016					
21/08	h	Crotone	W	1-0	*Destro*
28/08	a	Torino	L	1-5	*Taïder*
11/09	h	Cagliari	W	2-1	*Verdi, Di Francesco*
17/09	a	Napoli	L	1-3	*Verdi*
21/09	h	Sampdoria	W	2-0	*Verdi, Destro*
25/09	a	Internazionale	D	1-1	*Destro*
02/10	h	Genoa	L	0-1	
16/10	a	Lazio	D	1-1	*Helander*
23/10	h	Sassuolo	D	1-1	*Verdi*
26/10	a	Chievo	D	1-1	*Pulgar*
29/10	h	Fiorentina	L	0-1	
06/11	a	Roma	L	0-3	
20/11	h	Palermo	W	3-1	*Destro, Dzemaili, Viviani*
27/11	h	Atalanta	L	0-2	
05/12	a	Udinese	L	0-1	
11/12	h	Empoli	D	0-0	
18/12	a	Pescara	W	3-0	*Masina, Dzemaili, Krejčí (p)*
2017					
08/01	a	Juventus	L	0-3	
14/01	a	Crotone	W	1-0	*Dzemaili*
22/01	h	Torino	W	2-0	*Dzemaili 2*
29/01	a	Cagliari	D	1-1	*Destro*
04/02	h	Napoli	L	1-7	*Torosidis*
08/02	h	Milan	L	0-1	
12/02	a	Sampdoria	L	1-3	*Dzemaili*
19/02	h	Internazionale	L	0-1	
26/02	a	Genoa	D	1-1	*Viviani*
05/03	h	Lazio	L	0-2	
12/03	a	Sassuolo	W	1-0	*Destro*
19/03	h	Chievo	W	4-1	*Verdi, Dzemaili 2, Di Francesco*
02/04	a	Fiorentina	L	0-1	
09/04	h	Roma	L	0-3	
15/04	a	Palermo	D	0-0	
22/04	a	Atalanta	L	2-3	*Destro, Di Francesco*
30/04	h	Udinese	W	4-0	*Destro 2, Taïder, og (Danilo)*
07/05	a	Empoli	L	1-3	*Verdi*
14/05	h	Pescara	W	3-1	*Destro 2, Di Francesco*
21/05	a	Milan	L	0-3	
27/05	h	Juventus	L	1-2	*Taïder*

No	Name	Nat	DoB	Pos	Aps	(s)	Gls
10	Mattia Destro		20/03/91	A	28	(2)	11
14	Federico Di Francesco		14/06/94	M	11	(13)	4
17	Godfred Donsah	GHA	07/06/96	M	10	(3)	
31	Blerim Dzemaili	SUI	12/04/86	M	29	(2)	8
24	Alex Ferrari		01/07/94	D	1		
26	Sergio Floccari		12/11/81	A	3	(2)	
28	Daniele Gastaldello		25/06/83	D	24		
18	Filip Helander	SWE	22/04/93	D	9	(2)	1
1	Júnior Costa	BRA	12/11/83	G	17	(1)	
4	Emil Krafth	SWE	02/08/94	D	16	(10)	
11	Ladislav Krejčí	CZE	05/07/92	M	33	(4)	1
20	Domenico Maietta		03/08/82	D	29		
25	Adam Masina		02/01/94	D	28	(4)	1
15	Ibrahima Mbaye	SEN	19/11/94	D	11	(5)	
83	Antonio Mirante		08/07/83	G	21		
3	Archimede Morleo		26/09/83	D		(1)	
7	Anthony Mounier	FRA	27/09/87	M	4	(2)	
16	Ádám Nagy	HUN	17/06/95	M	22	(3)	
2	Marios Oikonomou	GRE	06/10/92	D	12	(6)	
30	Orji Okwonkwo	NGA	19/01/98	A	1	(8)	
32	Bruno Petković	CRO	16/09/94	A	4	(8)	
5	Erick Pulgar	CHI	15/01/94	M	17	(10)	1
22	Luca Rizzo		24/04/92	M	4	(8)	
8	Saphir Taïder	ALG	29/02/92	M	22	(2)	3
35	Vasilios Torosidis	GRE	10/06/85	D	23	(5)	1
19	Sadiq Umar	NGA	02/02/97	A	1	(6)	
9	Simone Verdi		12/07/92	M	25	(3)	6
6	Federico Viviani		24/03/92	M	13	(4)	2

Cagliari Calcio

1920 • Sant'Elia (16,000) • cagliaricalcio.com

Major honours
Italian League (1) 1970

Coach: Massimo Rastelli

Date		Opponent		Score	Scorers
2016					
21/08	a	Genoa	L	1-3	*Borriello*
28/08	h	Roma	D	2-2	*Borriello, Sau*
11/09	a	Bologna	L	1-2	*Bruno Alves*
18/09	h	Atalanta	W	3-0	*Borriello 2, Sau*
21/09	a	Juventus	L	0-4	
26/09	h	Sampdoria	W	2-1	*João Pedro, Melchiorri*
02/10	h	Crotone	W	2-1	*Di Gennaro, Padoin*
16/10	a	Internazionale	W	2-1	*Melchiorri, og (Handanovič)*
23/10	h	Fiorentina	L	3-5	*Di Gennaro, Capuano, Borriello*
26/10	a	Lazio	L	1-4	*og (Wallace)*
31/10	h	Palermo	W	2-1	*Dessena 2*
05/11	a	Torino	L	1-5	*Melchiorri*
19/11	a	Chievo	L	0-1	
27/11	h	Udinese	W	2-1	*Diego Farias (p), Sau*
04/12	a	Pescara	D	1-1	*Borriello*
11/12	h	Napoli	L	0-5	
17/12	a	Empoli	L	0-2	
22/12	h	Sassuolo	W	4-3	*Sau, Borriello, Diego Farias 2*
2017					
08/01	a	Milan	L	0-1	
15/01	h	Genoa	W	4-1	*Borriello 2, João Pedro, Diego Farias (p)*
22/01	a	Roma	L	0-1	
29/01	h	Bologna	D	1-1	*Borriello*
05/02	a	Atalanta	L	0-2	
12/02	h	Juventus	L	0-2	
19/02	a	Sampdoria	D	1-1	*Isla*
26/02	a	Crotone	W	2-1	*João Pedro, Borriello*
05/03	h	Internazionale	L	1-5	*Borriello*
12/03	a	Fiorentina	L	0-1	
19/03	h	Lazio	D	0-0	
02/04	a	Palermo	W	3-1	*Ionita 2, Borriello*
09/04	h	Torino	L	2-3	*Borriello (p), Han*
15/04	h	Chievo	W	4-0	*Borriello, Sau, João Pedro 2*
23/04	a	Udinese	L	1-2	*Borriello*
30/04	h	Pescara	W	1-0	*João Pedro (p)*
06/05	a	Napoli	L	1-3	*Diego Farias*
14/05	h	Empoli	W	3-2	*Sau, Diego Farias 2*
21/05	a	Sassuolo	L	2-6	*Sau, Ionita*
28/05	h	Milan	W	2-1	*João Pedro, Pisacane*

No	Name	Nat	DoB	Pos	Aps	(s)	Gls
18	Nicolò Barella		07/02/97	M	22	(6)	
33	Roberto Biancu		19/01/00	M		(1)	
26	Luca Bittante		14/08/93	D	3	(2)	
22	Marco Borriello		18/06/82	A	30	(6)	16
2	Bruno Alves	POR	27/11/81	D	36		1
24	Marco Capuano		14/10/91	D	8	(4)	1
23	Luca Ceppitelli		11/08/89	D	19		
13	Roberto Colombo		24/08/75	G		(1)	
26	Luca Crosta		23/02/98	G	1		
27	Alessandro Deiola		01/08/95	M	3	(1)	
4	Daniele Dessena		10/05/87	M	16	(2)	2
8	Davide Di Gennaro		16/06/88	M	17	(3)	2
17	Diego Farias	BRA	10/05/90	M	12	(8)	7
16	Paolo Faragò		12/02/93	M	1	(8)	
28	Gabriel	BRA	27/09/92	G	3		
32	Niccolò Giannetti		12/05/91	A	1	(10)	
32	Han Kwang-song	PRK	21/07/98	A		(5)	1
32	Víctor Ibarbo	COL	19/05/90	A		(3)	
21	Artur Ionita	MDA	17/08/90	M	14	(4)	3
3	Mauricio Isla	CHI	12/06/88	D	32	(2)	1
10	João Pedro	BRA	09/03/92	M	17	(5)	7
9	Federico Melchiorri		06/01/87	A	4	(6)	3
12	Senna Miangue	BEL	05/02/97	D		(4)	
16	Gianni Munari		24/06/83	M	3	(8)	
29	Nicola Murru		16/12/94	D	26		
20	Simone Padoin		18/03/84	M	25	(6)	1
33	Marko Pajač	CRO	11/05/93	M		(1)	
19	Fabio Pisacane		28/01/86	D	29		1
1	Rafael	BRA	03/03/82	G	19	(2)	
35	Bartosz Salamon	POL	01/05/91	D	9	(6)	
25	Marco Sau		03/11/87	A	29	(5)	7
38	Federico Serra		09/12/97	M		(1)	
30	Marco Storari		07/01/77	G	15		
77	Panagiotis Tachtsidis	GRE	15/02/91	M	24	(2)	

AC Chievo Verona

1929 • Marc'Antonio Bentegodi (39,211) • chievoverona.it

Coach: Rolando Maran

2016

21/08 h Internazionale W 2-0 *Birsa 2*
28/08 a Fiorentina L 0-1
11/09 h Lazio D 1-1 *Gamberini*
18/09 a Udinese W 2-1 *Castro, Cacciatore*
21/09 h Sassuolo W 2-1 *Rigoni, Castro*
24/09 a Napoli L 0-2
01/10 a Pescara W 2-0 *Meggiorini, Inglese*
16/10 h Milan L 1-3 *Birsa*
23/10 a Empoli D 0-0
26/10 h Bologna D 1-1 *og (Mbaye)*
30/10 a Crotone L 0-2
06/11 h Juventus L 1-2 *Pellissier (p)*
19/11 h Cagliari W 1-0 *Gobbi*
26/11 a Torino L 1-2 *Inglese*
05/12 h Genoa D 0-0
11/12 a Palermo W 2-0 *Birsa, Pellissier*
18/12 h Sampdoria W 2-1 *Meggiorini, Pellissier (p)*
22/12 a Roma L 1-3 *De Guzmán*

2017

08/01 h Atalanta L 1-4 *Pellissier*
14/01 a Internazionale L 1-3 *Pellissier*
21/01 h Fiorentina L 0-3
28/01 a Lazio W 1-0 *Inglese*
05/02 h Udinese D 0-0
12/02 a Sassuolo W 3-1 *Inglese 3*
19/02 h Napoli L 1-3 *Meggiorini*
26/02 h Pescara W 2-0 *Birsa, Castro*
04/03 a Milan L 1-3 *De Guzmán (p)*
12/03 h Empoli W 4-0 *Inglese, Pellissier, Birsa, Cesar*
19/03 a Bologna L 1-4 *Castro*
02/04 h Crotone L 1-2 *Pellissier*
08/04 a Juventus L 0-2
15/04 a Cagliari L 0-4
23/04 h Torino L 1-3 Pellissier
30/04 a Genoa W 2-1 *Bastien, Birsa*
07/05 h Palermo D 1-1 *Pellissier (p)*
14/05 a Sampdoria D 1-1 *Inglese*
20/05 h Roma L 3-5 *Castro, Inglese 2*
27/05 a Atalanta L 0-1

No	Name	Nat	DoB	Pos	Aps	(s)	Gls
28	Samuel Bastien	BEL	26/09/96	M	8	(4)	1
23	Valter Birsa	SVN	07/08/86	M	34	(1)	7
29	Fabrizio Cacciatore		08/10/86	D	29		1
19	Lucas Castro	ARG	09/04/89	M	33		5
12	Boštjan Cesar	SVN	09/07/82	D	16	(1)	1
36	Filippo Costa		21/05/95	D		(1)	
3	Dario Dainelli		09/06/79	D	25	(1)	
1	Jonathan de Guzmán	NED	13/09/87	M	15	(12)	2
97	Fabio Depaoli		24/04/97	M	5	(1)	
83	Antonio Floro Flores		18/06/83	A	6	(6)	
21	Nicolas Frey	FRA	06/03/84	D	13	(2)	
7	Serge Gakpé	TOG	07/05/87	A	1	(7)	
5	Alessandro Gamberini		27/08/81	D	20		1
18	Massimo Gobbi		31/10/80	D	30		1
56	Perparim Hetemaj	FIN	12/12/86	M	21	(2)	
45	Roberto Inglese		12/11/91	A	22	(12)	10
13	Mariano Izco	ARG	13/03/83	M	12	(13)	
95	Lamin Jallow	GAM	18/12/95	M		(2)	
80	Sofian Kiyine	BEL	02/10/97	M		(7)	
69	Riccardo Meggiorini		04/09/85	A	20	(7)	3
27	Vittorio Parigini		25/03/96	A		(3)	
31	Sergio Pellissier		12/04/79	A	18	(12)	9
8	Ivan Radovanović	SRB	29/08/88	M	32	(3)	
4	Nicola Rigoni		12/11/90	M	5	(7)	1
20	Gennaro Sardo		08/05/79	D		(1)	
90	Andrea Seculin		14/07/90	G	4		
70	Stefano Sorrentino		28/03/79	G	34		
2	Nicolás Spolli	ARG	20/02/83	D	15	(6)	
55	Emanuel Vignato		24/08/00	M		(2)	

FC Crotone

1923 • Ezio Scida (9,631) • fccrotone.it

Coach: Davide Nicola

2016

21/08 a Bologna L 0-1
28/08 h Genoa L 1-3 *Palladino*
12/09 h Empoli L 1-2 *Sampirisi*
18/09 h Palermo D 1-1 *Trotta*
21/09 a Roma L 0-4
26/09 h Atalanta L 1-3 *Nwankwo*
02/10 a Cagliari L 1-2 *Stoian*
16/10 a Sassuolo L 1-2 *Falcinelli*
23/10 h Napoli L 1-2 *Rosi*
26/10 a Fiorentina D 1-1 *Falcinelli*
30/10 h Chievo W 2-0 *Trotta (p), Falcinelli*
06/11 a Internazionale L 0-3
20/11 h Torino L 0-2
27/11 h Sampdoria D 1-1 *Falcinelli*
04/12 a Milan L 1-2 *Falcinelli*
10/12 h Pescara W 2-1 *Palladino (p), Ferrari*
18/12 a Udinese L 0-2

2017

08/01 a Lazio L 0-1
14/01 h Bologna L 0-1
22/01 a Genoa D 2-2 *Ceccherini, Ferrari*
29/01 h Empoli W 4-1 *Stoian, Falcinelli 3 (1p)*
05/02 a Palermo L 0-1
08/02 h Juventus L 0-2
12/02 h Roma L 0-2
18/02 a Atalanta L 0-1
26/02 h Cagliari L 1-2 *Stoian*
05/03 h Sassuolo D 0-0
12/03 a Napoli L 0-3
19/03 h Fiorentina L 0-1
02/04 a Chievo W 2-1 *Ferrari, Falcinelli*
09/04 h Internazionale W 2-1 *Falcinelli 2 (1p)*
15/04 a Torino D 1-1 *Nwankwo*
23/04 a Sampdoria W 2-1 *Falcinelli, Nwankwo*
30/04 h Milan D 1-1 *Trotta*
07/05 a Pescara W 1-0 *Tonev*
14/05 h Udinese W 1-0 *Rohdén*
21/05 a Juventus L 0-3
28/05 h Lazio W 3-1 *Nalini 2, Falcinelli*

No	Name	Nat	DoB	Pos	Aps	(s)	Gls
27	Boadu Acosty		10/09/91	M	3	(8)	
18	Andrea Barberis		11/12/93	M	23	(3)	
92	Giuseppe Borello		28/04/99	A		(1)	
28	Leonardo Capezzi		28/03/95	M	18	(7)	
17	Federico Ceccherini		11/05/92	D	35		1
3	Claiton	BRA	07/09/84	D	9	(1)	
1	Alex Cordaz		01/01/83	G	36		
8	Lorenzo Crisetig		20/01/93	M	29	(3)	
21	Giuseppe Cuomo		02/02/98	D		(1)	
10	Pietro De Giorgio		16/02/83	A		(1)	
11	Nunzio Di Roberto		21/09/85	A		(1)	
23	Noë Dussenne	BEL	07/04/92	D	4	(4)	
11	Diego Falcinelli		26/06/91	A	35		13
77	Nicolò Fazzi		02/03/95	A		(1)	
13	Gianmarco Ferrari		15/02/92	D	37		3
5	Marco Festa		06/06/92	G	2	(1)	
14	Eddy Gnahoré	FRA	14/11/93	M		(1)	
20	Andrej Kotnik	SVN	04/08/95	M		(2)	
87	Bruno Martella		14/08/92	D	26	(3)	
15	Djamel Mesbah	ALG	09/10/84	D	8	(2)	
9	Andrea Nalini		20/06/90	A	7	(10)	2
99	Simy Nwankwo	NGA	07/05/92	A	4	(17)	3
7	Raffaele Palladino		17/04/84	A	16	(3)	2
6	Marcus Rohdén	SWE	11/05/91	M	30	(4)	1
22	Aleandro Rosi		17/05/87	D	30	(1)	1
20	Aniello Salzano		20/07/91	M	6	(1)	
31	Mario Sampirisi		31/10/92	D	11	(12)	1
12	Adrian Stoian	ROU	11/02/91	M	17	(10)	3
92	Ćazim Suljić	BIH	29/10/96	M		(2)	
24	Alexander Tonev	BUL	03/02/90	M	9	(4)	1
29	Marcello Trotta		29/09/92	A	23	(6)	3

Empoli FC

1920 • Carlo Castellani (21,113) • empolicalcio.it

Coach: Giovanni Martusciello

2016

21/08 h Sampdoria L 0-1
28/08 a Udinese L 0-2
12/09 h Crotone W 2-1 *Bellusci, Costa*
18/09 a Torino D 0-0
21/09 h Internazionale L 0-2
25/09 a Lazio L 0-2
02/10 h Juventus L 0-3
16/10 a Genoa D 0-0
23/10 h Chievo D 0-0
26/10 a Napoli L 0-2
30/10 h Roma D 0-0
06/11 a Pescara W 4-0 *Maccarone 2, Pucciarelli, Saponara*
20/11 h Fiorentina L 0-4
26/11 h Milan L 1-4 *Saponara*
04/12 a Sassuolo L 0-3
11/12 a Bologna D 0-0
17/12 h Cagliari W 2-0 *Mchedlidze 2*
20/12 a Atalanta L 1-2 *Mchedlidze*

2017

07/01 h Palermo W 1-0 *Maccarone (p)*
15/01 a Sampdoria D 0-0
22/01 h Udinese W 1-0 *Mchedlidze*
29/01 a Crotone L 1-4 *Mchedlidze*
05/02 h Torino D 1-1 *Pucciarelli*
12/02 a Internazionale L 0-2
18/02 h Lazio L 1-2 *Krunić*
25/02 a Juventus L 0-2
05/03 h Genoa L 0-2
12/03 a Chievo L 0-4
19/03 h Napoli L 2-3 *El Kaddouri, Maccarone (p)*
01/04 a Roma L 0-2
08/04 h Pescara D 1-1 *El Kaddouri*
15/04 a Fiorentina W 2-1 *El Kaddouri, Pasqual (p)*
23/04 a Milan W 2-1 *Mchedlidze, Thiam*
30/04 h Sassuolo L 1-3 *Pucciarelli (p)*
07/05 h Bologna W 3-1 *Croce, Pasqual, Costa*
14/05 a Cagliari L 2-3 *Zajc, Maccarone*
21/05 h Atalanta L 0-1
28/05 a Palermo L 1-2 *Krunić*

No	Name	Nat	DoB	Pos	Aps	(s)	Gls
19	Federico Barba		01/09/93	D	9	(2)	
6	Giuseppe Bellusci		21/08/89	D	33		1
77	Marcel Büchel	LIE	18/03/91	M	10	(5)	
24	Uroš Ćosić	SRB	24/10/92	D	8	(6)	
15	Andrea Costa		01/02/86	D	25	(1)	2
11	Daniele Croce		09/09/82	M	32	(3)	1
4	Federico Dimarco		10/11/97	D	6	(6)	
8	Assane Dioussé	SEN	20/09/97	M	26	(7)	
10	Omar El Kaddouri	MAR	21/08/90	M	15		3
18	Alberto Gilardino		05/07/82	A	5	(9)	
25	Arnel Jakupovic	AUT	29/05/98	A		(1)	
33	Rade Krunić	BIH	07/10/93	M	29	(3)	2
2	Vincent Laurini	FRA	10/06/89	D	24		
7	Massimo Maccarone		06/09/79	A	17	(11)	5
17	Raffaele Maiello		10/07/91	M	1		
89	Guido Marilungo		09/08/89	A	11	(9)	
31	Matheus	BRA	25/02/98	M		(1)	
5	José Mauri		16/05/96	M	10	(4)	
9	Levan Mchedlidze	GEO	24/03/90	A	11	(4)	6
21	Manuel Pasqual		13/03/82	D	32		2
23	Alberto Pelagotti		09/03/89	G	3		
20	Manuel Pucciarelli		17/06/91	A	25	(7)	3
10	Riccardo Saponara		21/12/91	M	18		2
28	Łukasz Skorupski	POL	05/05/91	G	35		
88	Andrés Tello	COL	06/09/96	M	8	(10)	
27	Mame Baba Thiam	SEN	09/10/92	A	9	(6)	1
13	Frederic Veseli	ALB	20/11/92	D	11	(6)	
17	Miha Zajc	SVN	01/07/94	M	1	(4)	1
3	Marco Zambelli		22/08/85	D	4	(6)	

ITALY

ACF Fiorentina

1926 • Artemio Franchi (43,147) • violachannel.tv

Major honours
UEFA Cup Winners' Cup (1) 1961; Italian League (2) 1956, 1969; Italian Cup (6) 1940, 1961, 1966, 1975, 1996, 2001

Coach: Paulo Sousa (POR)

Date		Opponent		Score	Scorers
2016					
20/08	a	Juventus	L	1-2	*Kalinić*
28/08	h	Chievo	W	1-0	*Sánchez*
18/09	h	Roma	W	1-0	*Badelj*
21/09	a	Udinese	D	2-2	*Babacar, Bernardeschi (p)*
25/09	h	Milan	D	0-0	
02/10	a	Torino	L	1-2	*Babacar*
16/10	h	Atalanta	D	0-0	
23/10	a	Cagliari	W	5-3	*Kalinić 3, Bernardeschi 2*
26/10	h	Crotone	D	1-1	*Astori*
29/10	a	Bologna	W	1-0	*Kalinić (p)*
06/11	h	Sampdoria	D	1-1	*Bernardeschi*
20/11	a	Empoli	W	4-0	*Bernardeschi 2, Iličič 2 (1p)*
28/11	a	Internazionale	L	2-4	*Kalinić, Iličič*
04/12	h	Palermo	W	2-1	*Bernardeschi (p), Babacar*
12/12	h	Sassuolo	W	2-1	*Kalinić 2*
15/12	a	Genoa	L	0-1	
18/12	a	Lazio	L	1-3	*Zárate*
22/12	h	Napoli	D	3-3	*Bernardeschi 2, Zárate*
2017					
15/01	h	Juventus	W	2-1	*Kalinić, Badelj*
21/01	a	Chievo	W	3-0	*Tello, Babacar (p), Chiesa*
29/01	h	Genoa	D	3-3	*Iličič, Chiesa, Kalinić*
01/02	a	Pescara	W	2-1	*Tello 2*
07/02	a	Roma	L	0-4	
11/02	h	Udinese	W	3-0	*Borja Valero, Babacar, Bernardeschi (p)*
19/02	a	Milan	L	1-2	*Kalinić*
27/02	h	Torino	D	2-2	*Saponara, Kalinić*
05/03	a	Atalanta	D	0-0	
12/03	h	Cagliari	W	1-0	*Kalinić*
19/03	a	Crotone	W	1-0	*Kalinić*
02/04	h	Bologna	W	1-0	*Babacar*
09/04	a	Sampdoria	D	2-2	*Gonzalo Rodríguez, Babacar*
15/04	h	Empoli	L	1-2	*Tello*
22/04	h	Internazionale	W	5-4	*Vecino 2, Astori, Babacar 2*
30/04	a	Palermo	L	0-2	
07/05	a	Sassuolo	D	2-2	*Chiesa, Bernardeschi*
13/05	h	Lazio	W	3-2	*Babacar, Kalinić, og (Lombardi)*
20/05	a	Napoli	L	1-4	*Iličič*
28/05	h	Pescara	D	2-2	*Saponara, Vecino*

No	Name	Nat	DoB	Pos	Aps	(s)	Gls
28	Marcos Alonso	ESP	28/12/90	D	2		
13	Davide Astori		07/01/87	D	33		2
30	Khouma Babacar	SEN	17/03/93	A	13	(9)	10
5	Milan Badelj	CRO	25/02/89	M	29	(4)	2
10	Federico Bernardeschi		16/02/94	M	27	(5)	11
20	Borja Valero	ESP	12/01/85	M	30	(1)	1
25	Federico Chiesa		25/10/97	M	17	(10)	3
19	Sebastián Cristóforo	URU	23/08/93	M	7	(12)	
4	Sebastian De Maio	FRA	05/03/87	D	6		
17	Kevin Diks	NED	06/10/96	D		(2)	
97	Bartłomiej Drągowski	POL	19/08/97	G	1		
2	Gonzalo Rodríguez	ARG	10/04/84	D	26		1
24	Ianis Hagi	ROU	22/10/98	M		(2)	
72	Josip Iličič	SVN	29/01/88	M	23	(6)	5
9	Nikola Kalinić	CRO	05/01/88	A	26	(6)	15
1	Luca Lezzerini		24/03/95	G		(1)	
31	Hrvoje Milić	CRO	10/05/89	D	16	(1)	
32	Jan Mlakar	SVN	23/10/98	A		(1)	
15	Maximiliano Olivera	URU	05/03/92	D	13	(5)	
26	Joshua Perez	USA	21/01/98	A		(1)	
22	Giuseppe Rossi		01/02/87	A		(1)	
18	Carlos Salcedo	MEX	29/09/93	D	15	(3)	
6	Carlos Sánchez	COL	06/02/86	M	23	(8)	1
21	Riccardo Saponara		21/12/91	M	4	(7)	2
57	Marco Sportiello		10/05/92	G	2		
12	Ciprian Tătăruşanu	ROU	09/02/86	G	35		
16	Cristian Tello	ESP	11/08/91	M	22	(14)	4
40	Nenad Tomović	SRB	30/08/87	D	21	(4)	
8	Matías Vecino	URU	24/08/91	M	26	(5)	3
7	Mauro Zárate	ARG	18/03/87	A	1	(6)	2

Genoa CFC

1893 • Luigi Ferraris (36,599) • genoacfc.it

Major honours
Italian League (9) 1898, 1899, 1900, 1902, 1903, 1904, 1915, 1923, 1924; Italian Cup (1) 1937

Coach: Ivan Jurić (CRO); (20/02/17) Andrea Mandorlini; (10/04/17) Ivan Jurić (CRO)

Date		Opponent		Score	Scorers
2016					
21/08	h	Cagliari	W	3-1	*Ntcham, Laxalt, Rigoni*
28/08	a	Crotone	W	3-1	*Gakpé, Pavoletti 2*
18/09	a	Sassuolo	L	0-2	
21/09	h	Napoli	D	0-0	
25/09	h	Pescara	D	1-1	*Simeone*
02/10	a	Bologna	W	1-0	*Simeone*
16/10	h	Empoli	D	0-0	
22/10	a	Sampdoria	L	1-2	*Rigoni*
25/10	h	Milan	W	3-0	*Ninković, og (Kucka), Pavoletti*
30/10	a	Atalanta	L	0-3	
06/11	h	Udinese	D	1-1	*Ocampos*
20/11	a	Lazio	L	1-3	*Ocampos*
27/11	h	Juventus	W	3-1	*Simeone 2, og (Alex Sandro)*
05/12	a	Chievo	D	0-0	
11/12	a	Internazionale	L	0-2	
15/12	h	Fiorentina	W	1-0	*Lazović*
18/12	h	Palermo	L	3-4	*Simeone 2, Ninković*
22/12	a	Torino	L	0-1	
2017					
08/01	h	Roma	L	0-1	
15/01	a	Cagliari	L	1-4	*Simeone*
22/01	h	Crotone	D	2-2	*Simeone, Ocampos (p)*
29/01	a	Fiorentina	D	3-3	*Simeone 2 (1p), Hiljemark*
05/02	h	Sassuolo	L	0-1	
10/02	a	Napoli	L	0-2	
19/02	a	Pescara	L	0-5	
26/02	h	Bologna	D	1-1	*Ntcham*
05/03	a	Empoli	W	2-0	*Ntcham, Hiljemark*
11/03	h	Sampdoria	L	0-1	
18/03	a	Milan	L	0-1	
02/04	h	Atalanta	L	0-5	
09/04	a	Udinese	L	0-3	
15/04	h	Lazio	D	2-2	*Simeone, Pandev*
23/04	a	Juventus	L	0-4	
30/04	h	Chievo	L	1-2	*Pandev*
07/05	h	Internazionale	W	1-0	*Pandev*
14/05	a	Palermo	L	0-1	
21/05	h	Torino	W	2-1	*Rigoni, Simeone*
28/05	a	Roma	L	2-3	*Pellegri, Lazović*

No	Name	Nat	DoB	Pos	Aps	(s)	Gls
16	Andrea Beghetto		11/10/94	M	1	(2)	
14	Davide Biraschi		02/07/94	D	4	(3)	
8	Nicolás Burdisso	ARG	12/04/81	D	35		
94	Danilo Cataldi		06/08/94	M	10	(3)	
4	Isaac Cofie	GHA	20/09/91	M	11	(4)	
2	Edenílson	BRA	18/12/89	M	9	(7)	
29	Riccardo Fiamozzi		18/05/93	D	1	(3)	
13	Serge Gakpé	TOG	07/05/87	A	2	(5)	1
3	Santiago Gentiletti	ARG	09/01/85	D	15		
15	Oscar Hiljemark	SWE	28/06/92	M	10	(4)	2
5	Armando Izzo		02/03/92	D	29		
23	Eugenio Lamanna		07/08/89	G	20	(1)	
93	Diego Laxalt	URU	07/02/93	M	36		1
22	Darko Lazović	SRB	15/09/90	M	30	(3)	2
15	Giovanni Marchese		17/10/84	D		(1)	
44	Miguel Veloso	POR	11/05/86	M	22	(1)	
32	Leonardo Morosini		13/10/95	M	1	(3)	
24	Ezequiel Muñoz	ARG	08/10/90	D	25	(6)	
99	Nikola Ninković	SRB	19/12/94	M	5	(12)	2
10	Olivier Ntcham	FRA	09/02/96	M	10	(10)	3
11	Lucas Ocampos	ARG	11/07/94	M	12	(2)	3
21	Lucas Orbán	ARG	03/02/89	D	8	(3)	
11	Raffaele Palladino		17/04/84	A	9	(3)	
27	Goran Pandev	MKD	27/07/83	A	6	(14)	3
19	Leonardo Pavoletti		26/11/88	A	7	(2)	3
64	Pietro Pellegri		17/03/01	A	1	(2)	1
1	Mattia Perin		10/11/92	G	16		
51	Mauricio Pinilla	CHI	04/02/84	A	6	(6)	
30	Luca Rigoni		07/12/84	M	29	(2)	3
88	Tomás Rincón	COL	13/01/88	M	16		
83	Rubinho	BRA	04/08/82	G	2		
9	Giovanni Simeone	ARG	05/07/95	A	29	(6)	12
17	Adel Taarabt	MAR	24/05/89	M	1	(5)	

FC Internazionale Milano

1908 • Giuseppe Meazza (80,018) • inter.it

Major honours
European Champion Clubs' Cup/UEFA Champions League (3) 1964, 1965, 2010; UEFA Cup (3) 1991, 1994, 1998; European/South American Cup (2) 1964, 1965; FIFA Club World Cup (1) 2010; Italian League (18) 1910, 1920, 1930, 1938, 1940, 1953, 1954, 1963, 1965, 1966, 1971, 1980, 1989, 2006, 2007, 2008, 2009, 2010; Italian Cup (7) 1939, 1978, 1982, 2005, 2006, 2010, 2011

Coach: Frank de Boer (NED); (01/11/16) (Stefano Vecchi); (08/11/16) Stefano Pioli; (10/05/17) (Stefano Vecchi)

Date		Opponent		Score	Scorers
2016					
21/08	a	Chievo	L	0-2	
28/08	h	Palermo	D	1-1	*Icardi*
11/09	a	Pescara	W	2-1	*Icardi 2*
18/09	h	Juventus	W	2-1	*Icardi, Perišić*
21/09	a	Empoli	W	2-0	*Icardi 2*
25/09	h	Bologna	D	1-1	*Perišić*
02/10	a	Roma	L	1-2	*Éver Banega*
16/10	h	Cagliari	L	1-2	*João Mário*
23/10	a	Atalanta	L	1-2	*Éder*
26/10	h	Torino	W	2-1	*Icardi 2*
30/10	a	Sampdoria	L	0-1	
06/11	h	Crotone	W	3-0	*Perišić, Icardi 2 (1p)*
20/11	a	Milan	D	2-2	*Candreva, Perišić*
28/11	h	Fiorentina	W	4-2	*Brozović, Candreva, Icardi 2*
02/12	a	Napoli	L	0-3	
11/12	h	Genoa	W	2-0	*Brozović 2*
18/12	a	Sassuolo	W	1-0	*Candreva*
21/12	h	Lazio	W	3-0	*Éver Banega, Icardi 2*
2017					
08/01	a	Udinese	W	2-1	*Perišić 2*
14/01	h	Chievo	W	3-1	*Icardi, Perišić, Éder*
22/01	a	Palermo	W	1-0	*João Mário*
28/01	h	Pescara	W	3-0	*D'Ambrosio, João Mário, Éder*
05/02	a	Juventus	L	0-1	
12/02	h	Empoli	W	2-0	*Éder, Candreva*
19/02	a	Bologna	W	1-0	*Gabriel*
26/02	h	Roma	L	1-3	*Icardi*
05/03	a	Cagliari	W	5-1	*Perišić 2, Éver Banega, Icardi (p), Gagliardini*
12/03	h	Atalanta	W	7-1	*Icardi 3 (1p), Éver Banega 3, Gagliardini*
18/03	a	Torino	D	2-2	*Kondogbia, Candreva*
03/04	h	Sampdoria	L	1-2	*D'Ambrosio*
09/04	a	Crotone	L	1-2	*D'Ambrosio*
15/04	h	Milan	D	2-2	*Candreva, Icardi*
22/04	a	Fiorentina	L	4-5	*Perišić, Icardi 3*
30/04	h	Napoli	L	0-1	
07/05	a	Genoa	L	0-1	
14/05	h	Sassuolo	L	1-2	*Éder*
21/05	a	Lazio	W	3-1	*Andreolli, og (Hoedt), Éder*
28/05	h	Udinese	W	5-2	*Éder 2, Perišić, Brozović, og (Angella)*

No	Name	Nat	DoB	Pos	Aps	(s)	Gls
2	Marco Andreolli		10/06/86	D	4	(2)	1
15	Cristian Ansaldi	ARG	20/09/86	D	17	(4)	
11	Jonathan Biabiany	FRA	28/04/88	A		(1)	
77	Marcelo Brozović	CRO	16/11/92	M	20	(3)	4
87	Antonio Candreva		28/02/87	M	36	(2)	6
30	Juan Pablo Carrizo	ARG	06/05/84	G	1		
33	Danilo D'Ambrosio		09/09/88	D	32		3
23	Éder		15/11/86	A	13	(20)	8
19	Éver Banega	ARG	29/06/88	M	20	(8)	6
5	Felipe Melo	BRA	26/06/83	M	1	(4)	
96	Gabriel	BRA	30/08/96	A		(9)	1
5	Roberto Gagliardini		07/04/94	M	18		2
27	Assane Gnoukouri	CIV	28/09/96	M		(4)	
1	Samir Handanovič	SVN	14/07/84	G	37		
9	Mauro Icardi	ARG	19/02/93	A	34		24
6	João Mário	POR	19/01/93	M	22	(8)	3
10	Stevan Jovetić	MNE	02/11/89	A		(5)	
7	Geoffrey Kondogbia	FRA	15/02/93	M	20	(4)	1
17	Gary Medel	CHI	03/08/87	M	26		
95	Senna Miangue	BEL	05/02/97	D	1	(2)	
25	Miranda	BRA	07/09/84	D	32		
24	Jeison Murillo	COL	27/05/92	D	23	(4)	
55	Yuto Nagatomo	JPN	12/09/86	D	11	(5)	
8	Rodrigo Palacio	ARG	05/02/82	A	3	(12)	
44	Ivan Perišić	CRO	02/02/89	M	31	(5)	11
99	Andrea Pinamonti		19/05/99	A		(2)	
13	Andrea Ranocchia		16/02/88	D	5		
20	Trent Sainsbury	AUS	05/01/92	D		(1)	
21	Davide Santon		02/01/91	D	11	(3)	

Juventus FC

1897 • Juventus Stadium (41,254) • juventus.com

Major honours
European Champion Clubs' Cup/UEFA Champions League (2) 1985, 1996; UEFA Cup Winners' Cup (1) 1984; UEFA Cup (3) 1977, 1990, 1993; UEFA Super Cup (2) 1984, 1997; European/South American Cup (2) 1985, 1996; Italian League (33) 1905, 1926, 1931, 1932, 1933, 1934, 1935, 1950, 1952, 1958, 1960, 1961, 1967, 1972, 1973, 1975, 1977, 1978, 1981, 1982, 1984, 1986, 1995, 1997, 1998, 2002, 2003, 2012, 2013, 2014, 2015, 2016, 2017; Italian Cup (12) 1938, 1942, 1959, 1960, 1965, 1979, 1983, 1990, 1995, 2015, 2016, 2017

Coach: Massimiliano Allegri

Date		Opponent		Score	Scorers
2016					
20/08	h	Fiorentina	W	2-1	*Khedira, Higuaín*
27/08	a	Lazio	W	1-0	*Khedira*
10/09	h	Sassuolo	W	3-1	*Higuaín 2, Pjanić*
18/09	a	Internazionale	L	1-2	*Lichtsteiner*
21/09	h	Cagliari	W	4-0	*Rugani, Higuaín, Dani Alves, og (Ceppitelli)*
24/09	a	Palermo	W	1-0	*og (Goldaniga)*
02/10	a	Empoli	W	3-0	*Dybala, Higuaín 2*
15/10	h	Udinese	W	2-1	*Dybala 2 (1p)*
22/10	a	Milan	L	0-1	
26/10	h	Sampdoria	W	4-1	*Mandžukić, Chiellini 2, Pjanić*
29/10	h	Napoli	W	2-1	*Bonucci, Higuaín*
06/11	a	Chievo	W	2-1	*Mandžukić, Pjanić*
19/11	h	Pescara	W	3-0	*Khedira, Mandžukić, Hernanes*
27/11	a	Genoa	L	1-3	*Pjanić*
03/12	h	Atalanta	W	3-1	*Alex Sandro, Rugani, Mandžukić*
11/12	a	Torino	W	3-1	*Higuaín 2, Pjanić*
17/12	h	Roma	W	1-0	*Higuaín*
2017					
08/01	h	Bologna	W	3-0	*Higuaín 2, Dybala (p)*
15/01	a	Fiorentina	L	1-2	*Higuaín*
22/01	h	Lazio	W	2-0	*Dybala, Higuaín*
29/01	a	Sassuolo	W	2-0	*Higuaín, Khedira*
05/02	h	Internazionale	W	1-0	*Cuadrado*
08/02	a	Crotone	W	2-0	*Mandžukić, Higuaín*
12/02	a	Cagliari	W	2-0	*Higuaín 2*
17/02	h	Palermo	W	4-1	*Marchisio, Dybala 2, Higuaín*
25/02	h	Empoli	W	2-0	*og (Skorupski), Alex Sandro*
05/03	a	Udinese	D	1-1	*Bonucci*
10/03	h	Milan	W	2-1	*Benatia, Dybala (p)*
19/03	a	Sampdoria	W	1-0	*Cuadrado*
02/04	a	Napoli	D	1-1	*Khedira*
08/04	h	Chievo	W	2-0	*Higuaín 2*
15/04	a	Pescara	W	2-0	*Higuaín 2*
23/04	h	Genoa	W	4-0	*og (Muñoz), Dybala, Mandžukić, Bonucci*
28/04	a	Atalanta	D	2-2	*og (Spinazzola), Dani Alves*
06/05	h	Torino	D	1-1	*Higuaín*
14/05	a	Roma	L	1-3	*Lemina*
21/05	h	Crotone	W	3-0	*Mandžukić, Dybala, Alex Sandro*
27/05	a	Bologna	W	2-1	*Dybala, Kean*

No	Name	Nat	DoB	Pos	Aps	(s)	Gls
12	Alex Sandro	BRA	26/01/91	D	25	(2)	3
22	Kwadwo Asamoah	GHA	09/12/88	M	16	(2)	
32	Emil Audero		18/01/97	G	1		
15	Andrea Barzagli		08/05/81	D	17	(6)	
4	Medhi Benatia	MAR	17/04/87	D	14	(1)	1
19	Leonardo Bonucci		01/05/87	D	26	(3)	3
1	Gianluigi Buffon		28/01/78	G	30		
3	Giorgio Chiellini		14/08/84	D	20	(1)	2
7	Juan Cuadrado	COL	26/05/88	M	21	(9)	2
23	Dani Alves	BRA	06/05/83	D	15	(4)	2
21	Paulo Dybala	ARG	15/11/93	A	26	(5)	11
33	Patrice Evra	FRA	15/05/81	D	3	(3)	
11	Hernanes	BRA	29/05/85	M	8	(2)	1
9	Gonzalo Higuaín	ARG	10/12/87	A	32	(6)	24
34	Moise Kean		28/02/00	A		(3)	1
6	Sami Khedira	GER	04/04/87	M	31		5
18	Mario Lemina	GAB	01/09/93	M	8	(11)	1
26	Stephan Lichtsteiner	SUI	16/01/84	D	22	(4)	1
38	Rolando Mandragora		29/06/97	M		(1)	
17	Mario Mandžukić	CRO	21/05/86	A	28	(6)	7
8	Claudio Marchisio		19/01/86	M	15	(3)	1
25	Neto	BRA	19/07/89	G	7	(1)	
20	Marko Pjaca	CRO	06/05/95	M	3	(11)	
5	Miralem Pjanić	BIH	02/04/90	M	25	(5)	5
28	Tomás Rincón	COL	13/01/88	M	2	(11)	
24	Daniele Rugani		29/07/94	D	11	(4)	2
27	Stefano Sturaro		09/03/93	M	12	(9)	

SS Lazio

1900 • Olimpico (70,634) • sslazio.it

Major honours
UEFA Cup Winners' Cup (1) 1999; UEFA Super Cup (1) 1999; Italian League (2) 1974, 2000; Italian Cup (6) 1958, 1998, 2000, 2004, 2009, 2013

Coach: Simone Inzaghi

Date		Opponent		Score	Scorers
2016					
21/08	a	Atalanta	W	4-3	*Immobile, Hoedt, Lombardi, Cataldi*
27/08	h	Juventus	L	0-1	
11/09	a	Chievo	D	1-1	*De Vrij*
17/09	h	Pescara	W	3-0	*Milinković-Savić, Radu, Immobile*
20/09	a	Milan	L	0-2	
25/09	h	Empoli	W	2-0	*Baldé, Lulić*
01/10	a	Udinese	W	3-0	*Immobile 2, Baldé*
16/10	h	Bologna	D	1-1	*Immobile (p)*
23/10	a	Torino	D	2-2	*Immobile, Murgia*
26/10	h	Cagliari	W	4-1	*Baldé, Immobile 2 (1p), Felipe Anderson*
30/10	h	Sassuolo	W	2-1	*Lulić, Immobile*
05/11	a	Napoli	D	1-1	*Baldé*
20/11	h	Genoa	W	3-1	*Felipe Anderson, Biglia (p), Wallace*
27/11	a	Palermo	W	1-0	*Milinković-Savić*
04/12	h	Roma	L	0-2	
10/12	a	Sampdoria	W	2-1	*Milinković-Savić, Parolo*
18/12	h	Fiorentina	W	3-1	*Baldé, Biglia (p), Radu*
21/12	a	Internazionale	L	0-3	
2017					
08/01	h	Crotone	W	1-0	*Immobile*
15/01	a	Atalanta	W	2-1	*Milinković-Savić, Immobile (p)*
22/01	a	Juventus	L	0-2	
28/01	h	Chievo	L	0-1	
05/02	a	Pescara	W	6-2	*Parolo 4, Baldé, Immobile*
13/02	h	Milan	D	1-1	*Biglia (p)*
18/02	a	Empoli	W	2-1	*Immobile, Baldé*
26/02	h	Udinese	W	1-0	*Immobile (p)*
05/03	a	Bologna	W	2-0	*Immobile 2*
13/03	h	Torino	W	3-1	*Immobile, Baldé, Felipe Anderson*
19/03	a	Cagliari	D	0-0	
01/04	a	Sassuolo	W	2-1	*Immobile, og (Consigli)*
09/04	h	Napoli	L	0-3	
15/04	a	Genoa	D	2-2	*Biglia, Luis Alberto*
23/04	h	Palermo	W	6-2	*Immobile 2, Baldé 3 (1p), Crecco*
30/04	a	Roma	W	3-1	*Baldé 2, Basta*
07/05	h	Sampdoria	W	7-3	*Baldé, Immobile 2 (1p), Hoedt, Felipe Anderson (p), De Vrij, Lulić*
13/05	a	Fiorentina	L	2-3	*Baldé, Murgia*
21/05	h	Internazionale	L	1-3	*Baldé (p)*
28/05	a	Crotone	L	1-3	*Immobile (p)*

No	Name	Nat	DoB	Pos	Aps	(s)	Gls
14	Keita Baldé	SEN	08/03/95	A	21	(10)	16
8	Dušan Basta	SRB	18/08/84	D	24	(3)	1
15	Bastos	ANG	27/03/91	D	10	(1)	
20	Lucas Biglia	ARG	30/01/86	M	28	(1)	4
5	Danilo Cataldi		06/08/94	M	5	(6)	1
11	Luca Crecco		06/09/95	M		(3)	1
3	Stefan de Vrij	NED	05/02/92	D	27		2
9	Filip Djordjević	SRB	28/09/87	A	4	(13)	
10	Felipe Anderson	BRA	15/04/93	M	33	(3)	4
2	Wesley Hoedt	NED	06/03/94	D	21	(2)	2
17	Ciro Immobile		20/02/90	A	35	(1)	23
7	Ricardo Kishna	NED	04/01/95	A	2	(3)	
23	Moritz Leitner	GER	08/12/92	M		(2)	
25	Cristiano Lombardi		19/08/95	A	3	(15)	1
18	Luis Alberto	ESP	28/09/92	M	4	(5)	1
6	Jordan Lukaku	BEL	25/07/94	D	8	(8)	
19	Senad Lulić	BIH	18/01/86	M	29	(2)	3
22	Federico Marchetti		07/02/83	G	17		
21	Sergej Milinković-Savić	SRB	27/02/95	M	31	(3)	4
96	Alessandro Murgia		09/08/96	M	4	(10)	2
16	Marco Parolo		25/01/85	M	34		5
4	Patric	ESP	17/04/93	D	10	(9)	
44	Franjo Prce	CRO	07/01/96	D		(1)	
26	Ştefan Radu	ROU	22/10/86	D	29		2
97	Alessandro Rossi		03/01/97	A		(3)	
43	Giorgio Spizzichino		10/08/99	D		(1)	
1	Thomas Strakosha	ALB	19/03/95	G	20	(1)	
71	Mamadou Tounkara	SEN	19/01/96	A		(1)	
55	Ivan Vargić	CRO	15/03/87	G	1		
13	Wallace	BRA	14/10/94	D	18	(7)	1

AC Milan

1899 • Giuseppe Meazza (80,018) • acmilan.com

Major honours
European Champion Clubs' Cup/UEFA Champions League (7) 1963, 1969, 1989, 1990, 1994, 2003, 2007; UEFA Cup Winners' Cup (2) 1968, 1973; UEFA Super Cup (5) 1989, 1990, 1995, 2003, 2007; European/South American Cup (3) 1969, 1989, 1990; FIFA Club World Cup (1) 2007; Italian League (18) 1901, 1906, 1907, 1951, 1955, 1957, 1959, 1962, 1968, 1979, 1988, 1992, 1993, 1994, 1996, 1999, 2004, 2011; Italian Cup (5) 1967, 1972, 1973, 1977, 2003

Coach: Vincenzo Montella

Date		Opponent		Score	Scorers
2016					
21/08	h	Torino	W	3-2	*Bacca 3 (1p)*
27/08	a	Napoli	L	2-4	*Niang, Suso*
11/09	h	Udinese	L	0-1	
16/09	a	Sampdoria	W	1-0	*Bacca*
20/09	h	Lazio	W	2-0	*Bacca, Niang (p)*
25/09	a	Fiorentina	D	0-0	
02/10	h	Sassuolo	W	4-3	*Bonaventura, Bacca (p), Locatelli, Paletta*
16/10	a	Chievo	W	3-1	*Kucka, Niang, og (Dainelli)*
22/10	h	Juventus	W	1-0	*Locatelli*
25/10	a	Genoa	L	0-3	
30/10	h	Pescara	W	1-0	*Bonaventura*
06/11	a	Palermo	W	2-1	*Suso, Lapadula*
20/11	h	Internazionale	D	2-2	*Suso 2*
26/11	a	Empoli	W	4-1	*Lapadula 2, Suso, og (Costa)*
04/12	h	Crotone	W	2-1	*Pašalić, Lapadula*
12/12	a	Roma	L	0-1	
17/12	h	Atalanta	D	0-0	
2017					
08/01	h	Cagliari	W	1-0	*Bacca*
16/01	a	Torino	D	2-2	*Bertolacci, Bacca (p)*
21/01	h	Napoli	L	1-2	*Kucka*
29/01	a	Udinese	L	1-2	*Bonaventura*
05/02	h	Sampdoria	L	0-1	
08/02	a	Bologna	W	1-0	*Pašalić*
13/02	a	Lazio	D	1-1	*Suso*
19/02	h	Fiorentina	W	2-1	*Kucka, Deulofeu*
26/02	a	Sassuolo	W	1-0	*Bacca (p)*
04/03	h	Chievo	W	3-1	*Bacca 2, Lapadula (p)*
10/03	a	Juventus	L	1-2	*Bacca*
18/03	h	Genoa	W	1-0	*Fernández*
02/04	a	Pescara	D	1-1	*Pašalić*
09/04	h	Palermo	W	4-0	*Suso, Pašalić, Bacca, Deulofeu*
15/04	a	Internazionale	D	2-2	*Romagnoli, Zapata*
23/04	h	Empoli	L	1-2	*Lapadula*
30/04	a	Crotone	D	1-1	*Paletta*
07/05	h	Roma	L	1-4	*Pašalić*
13/05	a	Atalanta	D	1-1	*Deulofeu*
21/05	h	Bologna	W	3-0	*Deulofeu, Honda, Lapadula*
28/05	a	Cagliari	L	1-2	*Lapadula (p)*

No	Name	Nat	DoB	Pos	Aps	(s)	Gls
20	Ignazio Abate		12/11/86	D	22	(1)	
31	Luca Antonelli		11/02/87	D	3	(4)	
70	Carlos Bacca	COL	08/09/86	A	26	(6)	13
91	Andrea Bertolacci		11/01/91	M	9	(6)	1
5	Giacomo Bonaventura		22/08/89	M	19		3
96	Davide Calabria		06/12/96	D	11	(1)	
63	Patrick Cutrone		02/01/98	A		(1)	
2	Mattia De Sciglio		20/10/92	D	23	(2)	
7	Gerard Deulofeu	ESP	13/03/94	A	16	(1)	4
99	Gianluigi Donnarumma		25/02/99	G	38		
14	Matías Fernández	CHI	15/05/86	M	8	(5)	1
15	Gustavo Gómez	PAR	06/05/93	D	11	(7)	
10	Keisuke Honda	JPN	13/06/86	M	2	(6)	1
33	Juraj Kucka	SVK	26/02/87	M	23	(7)	3
9	Gianluca Lapadula		07/02/90	A	12	(15)	8
73	Manuel Locatelli		08/01/98	M	17	(8)	2
7	Luiz Adriano	BRA	12/04/87	A	1	(6)	
18	Riccardo Montolivo		18/01/85	M	9		
11	M'Baye Niang	FRA	19/12/94	A	13	(5)	3
11	Lucas Ocampos	ARG	11/07/94	M	4	(8)	
29	Gabriel Paletta		15/02/86	D	30		2
80	Mario Pašalić	CRO	09/02/95	M	20	(4)	5
16	Andrea Poli		29/09/89	M	3	(10)	
13	Alessio Romagnoli		12/01/95	D	27		1
23	José Sosa	ARG	19/06/85	M	15	(3)	
8	Suso	ESP	19/11/93	A	33	(1)	7
21	Leonel Vangioni	ARG	05/05/87	D	11	(4)	
17	Cristián Zapata	COL	30/09/86	D	12	(3)	1

ITALY

SSC Napoli

1926 • San Paolo (60,240) • sscnapoli.it

Major honours

UEFA Cup (1) 1989; Italian League (2) 1987, 1990; Italian Cup (5) 1962, 1976, 1987, 2012, 2014

Coach: Maurizio Sarri

Date		Opponent			Scorers
2016					
21/08	a	Pescara	D	2-2	*Mertens 2*
27/08	h	Milan	W	4-2	*Milik 2, Callejón 2*
10/09	a	Palermo	W	3-0	*Hamšík, Callejón 2*
17/09	h	Bologna	W	3-1	*Callejón, Milik 2*
21/09	a	Genoa	D	0-0	
24/09	h	Chievo	W	2-0	*Gabbiadini, Hamšík*
02/10	a	Atalanta	L	0-1	
15/10	h	Roma	L	1-3	*Koulibaly*
23/10	a	Crotone	W	2-1	*Callejón, Maksimović*
26/10	h	Empoli	W	2-0	*Mertens, Chiricheş*
29/10	a	Juventus	L	1-2	*Callejón*
05/11	h	Lazio	D	1-1	*Hamšík*
19/11	a	Udinese	W	2-1	*Insigne 2*
28/11	h	Sassuolo	D	1-1	*Insigne*
02/12	h	Internazionale	W	3-0	*Zieliński, Hamšík, Insigne*
11/12	a	Cagliari	W	5-0	*Mertens 3, Hamšík, Zieliński*
18/12	h	Torino	W	5-3	*Mertens 4 (1p), Chiricheş*
22/12	a	Fiorentina	D	3-3	*Insigne, Mertens, Gabbiadini (p)*
2017					
07/01	h	Sampdoria	W	2-1	*Gabbiadini, Tonelli*
15/01	h	Pescara	W	3-1	*Tonelli, Hamšík, Mertens*
21/01	a	Milan	W	2-1	*Insigne, Callejón*
29/01	h	Palermo	D	1-1	*Mertens*
04/02	a	Bologna	W	7-1	*Hamšík 3, Insigne, Mertens 3*
10/02	h	Genoa	W	2-0	*Zieliński, Giaccherini*
19/02	a	Chievo	W	3-1	*Insigne, Hamšík, Zieliński*
25/02	h	Atalanta	L	0-2	
04/03	a	Roma	W	2-1	*Mertens 2*
12/03	h	Crotone	W	3-0	*Insigne 2 (1p), Mertens (p)*
19/03	a	Empoli	W	3-2	*Insigne 2 (1p), Mertens*
02/04	h	Juventus	D	1-1	*Hamšík*
09/04	a	Lazio	W	3-0	*Callejón, Insigne 2*
15/04	h	Udinese	W	3-0	*Mertens, Allan, Callejón*
23/04	a	Sassuolo	D	2-2	*Mertens, Milik*
30/04	a	Internazionale	W	1-0	*Callejón*
06/05	h	Cagliari	W	3-1	*Mertens 2, Insigne*
14/05	a	Torino	W	5-0	*Callejón 2, Insigne, Mertens, Zieliński*
20/05	h	Fiorentina	W	4-1	*Koulibaly, Insigne, Mertens 2*
28/05	a	Sampdoria	W	4-2	*Mertens, Insigne, Hamšík, Callejón*

No	Name	Nat	DoB	Pos	Aps	(s)	Gls
33	Raúl Albiol	ESP	04/09/85	D	25	(1)	
5	Allan	BRA	08/01/91	M	19	(10)	1
7	José Callejón	ESP	11/02/87	M	37		14
21	Vlad Chiricheş	ROU	14/11/89	D	13	(1)	2
42	Amadou Diawara	GUI	17/07/97	M	10	(8)	
77	Omar El Kaddouri	MAR	21/08/90	M		(5)	
23	Manolo Gabbiadini		26/11/91	A	7	(6)	3
31	Faouzi Ghoulam	ALG	01/02/91	D	26	(3)	
4	Emanuele Giaccherini		05/05/85	M	1	(15)	1
17	Marek Hamšík	SVK	27/07/87	M	37	(1)	12
2	Elseid Hysaj	ALB	20/02/94	D	34	(1)	
24	Lorenzo Insigne		04/06/91	A	35	(2)	18
8	Jorginho		20/12/91	M	27		
26	Kalidou Koulibaly	SEN	20/06/91	D	28		2
11	Christian Maggio		11/02/82	D	4	(3)	
19	Nikola Maksimović	SRB	25/11/91	D	7	(1)	1
14	Dries Mertens	BEL	06/05/87	A	28	(7)	28
99	Arkadiusz Milik	POL	28/02/94	A	4	(13)	5
32	Leonardo Pavoletti		26/11/88	A	2	(4)	
1	Rafael Cabral	BRA	20/05/90	G	1		
25	Pepe Reina	ESP	31/08/82	G	37		
30	Marko Rog	CRO	19/07/95	M	2	(13)	
3	Ivan Strinić	CRO	17/07/87	D	12		
62	Lorenzo Tonelli		17/01/90	D	3		2
6	Mirko Valdifiori		21/04/86	M	1		
20	Piotr Zieliński	POL	20/05/94	M	18	(18)	5

US Città di Palermo

1900 • Renzo Barbera (36,349) • palermocalcio.it

Coach: Davide Ballardini; (06/09/16) Roberto De Zerbi; (30/11/16) Eugenio Corini; (26/01/17) Diego López (URU); (11/04/17) (Diego Bortoluzzi)

Date		Opponent			Scorers
2016					
21/08	h	Sassuolo	L	0-1	
28/08	a	Internazionale	D	1-1	*Rispoli*
10/09	h	Napoli	L	0-3	
18/09	a	Crotone	D	1-1	*Nestorovski*
21/09	a	Atalanta	W	1-0	*Nestorovski*
24/09	h	Juventus	L	0-1	
02/10	a	Sampdoria	D	1-1	*Nestorovski*
17/10	h	Torino	L	1-4	*Chochev*
23/10	a	Roma	L	1-4	*Quaison*
27/10	h	Udinese	L	1-3	*Nestorovski*
31/10	a	Cagliari	L	1-2	*Nestorovski*
06/11	h	Milan	L	1-2	*Nestorovski*
20/11	a	Bologna	L	1-3	*Nestorovski*
27/11	h	Lazio	L	0-1	
04/12	a	Fiorentina	L	1-2	*Jajalo*
11/12	h	Chievo	L	0-2	
18/12	a	Genoa	W	4-3	*Quaison, Goldaniga, Rispoli, Trajkovski*
22/12	h	Pescara	D	1-1	*Quaison*
2017					
07/01	a	Empoli	L	0-1	
15/01	a	Sassuolo	L	1-4	*Quaison*
22/01	h	Internazionale	L	0-1	
29/01	a	Napoli	D	1-1	*Nestorovski*
05/02	h	Crotone	W	1-0	*Nestorovski*
12/02	h	Atalanta	L	1-3	*Chochev*
17/02	a	Juventus	L	1-4	*Chochev*
26/02	h	Sampdoria	D	1-1	*Nestorovski (p)*
05/03	a	Torino	L	1-3	*Rispoli*
12/03	h	Roma	L	0-3	
19/03	a	Udinese	L	1-4	*Sallai*
02/04	h	Cagliari	L	1-3	*González*
09/04	a	Milan	L	0-4	
15/04	h	Bologna	D	0-0	
23/04	a	Lazio	L	2-6	*Rispoli 2*
30/04	h	Fiorentina	W	2-0	*Diamanti, Aleesami*
07/05	a	Chievo	D	1-1	*Goldaniga*
14/05	h	Genoa	W	1-0	*Rispoli*
22/05	a	Pescara	L	0-2	
28/05	h	Empoli	W	2-1	*Nestorovski, Bruno Henrique*

No	Name	Nat	DoB	Pos	Aps	(s)	Gls
19	Haitam Aleesami	NOR	31/07/91	D	29	(2)	1
4	Siniša Andjelkovič	SVN	13/02/86	D	21	(1)	
22	Norbert Balogh	HUN	21/02/96	A	6	(10)	
27	Accursio Bentivegna		21/06/96	A	2	(1)	
24	Ouasim Bouy	NED	11/06/93	M		(2)	
25	Bruno Henrique	BRA	21/10/89	M	24	(9)	1
18	Ivaylo Chochev	BUL	18/02/93	M	25	(5)	3
15	Thiago Cionek	POL	21/04/86	D	26	(3)	
23	Alessandro Diamanti		02/05/83	A	18	(13)	1
11	Carlos Embaló	GNB	25/11/94	M	8	(4)	
68	Andrea Fulignati		31/10/94	G	9		
14	Alessandro Gazzi		28/01/83	M	22	(3)	
6	Edoardo Goldaniga		02/11/93	D	26	(2)	2
12	Giancarlo González	CRC	08/02/88	D	18	(3)	1
10	Oscar Hiljemark	SWE	28/06/92	M	12	(3)	
28	Mato Jajalo	BIH	25/05/88	M	22	(4)	1
98	Simone Lo Faso		18/02/98	M	1	(9)	
89	Michel Morganella	SUI	17/05/89	D	7	(4)	
30	Ilija Nestorovski	MKD	12/03/90	A	34	(3)	11
97	Giuseppe Pezzella		29/11/97	D	9	(1)	
1	Josip Posavec	CRO	10/03/96	G	29		
21	Robin Quaison	SWE	09/10/93	M	11	(6)	4
5	Slobodan Rajković	SRB	03/02/89	D	4		
3	Andrea Rispoli		29/09/88	D	30	(2)	6
61	Gennaro Ruggiero		04/02/00	M	2		
20	Roland Sallai	HUN	22/05/97	A	11	(10)	1
9	Stefan Silva	SWE	11/03/90	A		(1)	
44	Toni Šunjić	BIH	15/12/88	D	2	(5)	
8	Aleksandar Trajkovski	MKD	05/09/92	A	5	(6)	1
2	Roberto Vitiello		08/05/83	D	5		

Pescara Calcio

1936 • Adriatico (20,476) • pescaracalcio.com

Coach: Massimo Oddo; (17/02/17) Zdeněk Zeman (CZE)

Date		Opponent			Scorers
2016					
21/08	h	Napoli	D	2-2	*Benali, Caprari*
28/08	a	Sassuolo	W	3-0	*(w/o; original result 1-2 Manaj)*
11/09	h	Internazionale	L	1-2	*Bahebeck*
17/09	a	Lazio	L	0-3	
21/09	h	Torino	D	0-0	
25/09	a	Genoa	D	1-1	*Manaj*
01/10	h	Chievo	L	0-2	
15/10	h	Sampdoria	D	1-1	*Campagnaro*
23/10	a	Udinese	L	1-3	*Aquilani*
26/10	h	Atalanta	L	0-1	
30/10	a	Milan	L	0-1	
06/11	h	Empoli	L	0-4	
19/11	a	Juventus	L	0-3	
27/11	a	Roma	L	2-3	*Memushaj, Caprari*
04/12	h	Cagliari	D	1-1	*Caprari*
10/12	a	Crotone	L	1-2	*Campagnaro*
18/12	h	Bologna	L	0-3	
22/12	a	Palermo	D	1-1	*Biraghi (p)*
2017					
15/01	a	Napoli	L	1-3	*Caprari (p)*
22/01	h	Sassuolo	L	1-3	*Bahebeck*
28/01	a	Internazionale	L	0-3	
01/02	h	Fiorentina	L	1-2	*Caprari*
05/02	h	Lazio	L	2-6	*Benali, Brugman*
12/02	a	Torino	L	3-5	*og (Ajeti), Benali 2*
19/02	h	Genoa	W	5-0	*og (Orbán), Caprari 2, Benali, Cerri*
26/02	a	Chievo	L	0-2	
04/03	a	Sampdoria	L	1-3	*Cerri*
12/03	h	Udinese	L	1-3	*Muntari*
19/03	a	Atalanta	L	0-3	
02/04	h	Milan	D	1-1	*og (Paletta)*
08/04	a	Empoli	D	1-1	*Caprari*
15/04	h	Juventus	L	0-2	
24/04	h	Roma	L	1-4	*Benali*
30/04	a	Cagliari	L	0-1	
07/05	h	Crotone	L	0-1	
14/05	a	Bologna	L	1-3	*Bahebeck*
22/05	h	Palermo	W	2-0	*Murić, Mitriță*
28/05	a	Fiorentina	D	2-2	*Caprari, Bahebeck*

No	Name	Nat	DoB	Pos	Aps	(s)	Gls
20	Alberto Aquilani		07/07/84	M	6	(3)	1
15	Jean-Christophe Bahebeck	FRA	01/05/93	A	11	(4)	4
10	Ahmad Benali	LBY	07/02/92	M	31	(2)	6
3	Cristiano Biraghi		01/09/92	D	33	(2)	1
31	Albano Bizzarri	ARG	09/11/77	G	29		
83	Cesare Bovo		14/01/83	D	9	(1)	
16	Gastón Brugman	URU	07/09/92	M	22	(5)	1
5	Alessandro Bruno		04/07/83	M	10	(5)	
14	Hugo Campagnaro	ARG	27/06/80	D	18	(1)	2
17	Gianluca Caprari		30/07/93	A	34	(1)	9
20	Alberto Cerri		16/04/96	A	7	(6)	2
35	Andrea Coda		25/04/85	D	12	(1)	
33	Mamadou Coulibaly	SEN	03/02/99	M	6	(3)	
2	Alessandro Crescenzi		25/09/91	D	14	(7)	
6	Bryan Cristante		03/03/95	M	10	(6)	
36	Adrián Cubas	ARG	11/05/96	M		(1)	
1	Vincenzo Fiorillo		13/01/90	G	9		
44	Michele Fornasier		22/08/93	D	16	(6)	
19	Alberto Gilardino		05/07/82	A	1	(2)	
37	Norbert Gyömbér	SVK	03/07/92	D	10		
9	Grigoris Kastanos	CYP	30/01/98	A	3	(5)	
9	Rey Manaj	ALB	24/02/97	A	4	(8)	2
8	Ledian Memushaj	ALB	07/12/86	M	35	(1)	1
93	Hrvoje Miličević	CRO	30/04/93	D	1	(2)	
28	Alexandru Mitriță	ROU	08/02/95	M	4	(11)	1
13	Sulley Ali Muntari	GHA	27/08/84	M	7	(2)	1
30	Robert Murić	CRO	12/03/96	A	2	(3)	1
21	Simone Pepe		30/08/83	A	3	(9)	
27	Stefano Pettinari		27/01/92	A	2	(4)	
86	Guglielmo Stendardo		06/05/81	D	9		
7	Valerio Verre		11/01/94	M	23	(5)	
26	Davide Vitturini		21/02/97	D	2	(1)	
11	Francesco Zampano		30/09/93	D	32	(2)	
13	Dario Župarić	CRO	03/05/92	D	3	(4)	

AS Roma

1927 • Olimpico (70,634) • asroma.com

Major honours
Inter Cities Fairs Cup (1) 1961; Italian League (3) 1942, 1983, 2001; Italian Cup (9) 1964, 1969, 1980, 1981, 1984, 1986, 1991, 2007, 2008

Coach: Luciano Spalletti

Date		Opponent		Score	Scorers
2016					
20/08	h	Udinese	W	4-0	*Perotti 2 (2p), Džeko, Salah*
28/08	a	Cagliari	D	2-2	*Perotti (p), Strootman*
11/09	h	Sampdoria	W	3-2	*Salah, Džeko, Totti (p)*
18/09	a	Fiorentina	L	0-1	
21/09	h	Crotone	W	4-0	*El Shaarawy, Salah, Džeko 2*
25/09	a	Torino	L	1-3	*Totti (p)*
02/10	h	Internazionale	W	2-1	*Džeko, og (Icardi)*
15/10	a	Napoli	W	3-1	*Džeko 2, Salah*
23/10	h	Palermo	W	4-1	*Salah, Paredes, Džeko, El Shaarawy*
26/10	a	Sassuolo	W	3-1	*Džeko 2 (1p), Nainggolan*
30/10	a	Empoli	D	0-0	
06/11	h	Bologna	W	3-0	*Salah 3*
20/11	a	Atalanta	L	1-2	*Perotti (p)*
27/11	h	Pescara	W	3-2	*Džeko 2, Perotti (p)*
04/12	a	Lazio	W	2-0	*Strootman, Nainggolan*
12/12	h	Milan	W	1-0	*Nainggolan*
17/12	a	Juventus	L	0-1	
22/12	h	Chievo	W	3-1	*El Shaarawy, Džeko, Perotti (p)*
2017					
08/01	a	Genoa	W	1-0	*og (Izzo)*
15/01	a	Udinese	W	1-0	*Nainggolan*
22/01	h	Cagliari	W	1-0	*Džeko*
29/01	a	Sampdoria	L	2-3	*Bruno Peres, Džeko*
07/02	h	Fiorentina	W	4-0	*Džeko 2, Fazio, Nainggolan*
12/02	a	Crotone	W	2-0	*Nainggolan, Džeko*
19/02	h	Torino	W	4-1	*Džeko, Salah, Paredes, Nainggolan*
26/02	a	Internazionale	W	3-1	*Nainggolan 2, Perotti (p)*
04/03	h	Napoli	L	1-2	*Strootman*
12/03	a	Palermo	W	3-0	*El Shaarawy, Džeko, Bruno Peres*
19/03	h	Sassuolo	W	3-1	*Paredes, Salah, Džeko*
01/04	h	Empoli	W	2-0	*Džeko 2*
09/04	a	Bologna	W	3-0	*Fazio, Salah, Džeko*
15/04	h	Atalanta	D	1-1	*Džeko*
24/04	a	Pescara	W	4-1	*Strootman, Nainggolan, Salah 2*
30/04	h	Lazio	L	1-3	*De Rossi (p)*
07/05	a	Milan	W	4-1	*Džeko 2, El Shaarawy, De Rossi (p)*
14/05	h	Juventus	W	3-1	*De Rossi, El Shaarawy, Nainggolan*
20/05	a	Chievo	W	5-3	*El Shaarawy 2, Salah 2, Džeko*
28/05	h	Genoa	W	3-2	*Džeko, De Rossi, Perotti*

No	Name	Nat	DoB	Pos	Aps	(s)	Gls
13	Bruno Peres	BRA	01/03/90	D	24	(6)	2
16	Daniele De Rossi		24/07/83	M	27	(4)	4
9	Edin Džeko	BIH	17/03/86	A	33	(4)	29
92	Stephan El Shaarawy		27/10/92	A	19	(13)	8
33	Emerson	BRA	03/08/94	D	23	(2)	
20	Federico Fazio	ARG	17/03/87	D	35	(2)	2
24	Alessandro Florenzi		11/03/91	D	8	(1)	
30	Gerson	BRA	20/05/97	M	2	(2)	
7	Clément Grenier	FRA	07/01/91	M	1	(5)	
7	Juan Manuel Iturbe	PAR	04/06/93	A		(5)	
3	Juan	BRA	10/06/91	D	13	(7)	
44	Kostas Manolas	GRE	14/06/91	D	32	(1)	
22	Mário Rui	POR	27/05/91	D	3	(2)	
4	Radja Nainggolan	BEL	04/05/88	M	35	(2)	11
5	Leandro Paredes	ARG	29/06/94	M	15	(12)	3
8	Diego Perotti	ARG	26/07/88	M	20	(12)	8
2	Antonio Rüdiger	GER	03/03/93	D	25	(1)	
11	Mohamed Salah	EGY	15/06/92	A	29	(2)	15
6	Kevin Strootman	NED	13/02/90	M	31	(2)	4
1	Wojciech Szczęsny	POL	18/04/90	G	38		
10	Francesco Totti		27/09/76	A	1	(17)	2
15	Thomas Vermaelen	BEL	14/11/85	D	4	(5)	

UC Sampdoria

1946 • Luigi Ferraris (36,599) • sampdoria.it

Major honours
UEFA Cup Winners' Cup (1) 1990; Italian League (1) 1991; Italian Cup (4) 1985, 1988, 1989, 1994

Coach: Marco Giampaolo

Date		Opponent		Score	Scorers
2016					
21/08	a	Empoli	W	1-0	*Muriel*
28/08	h	Atalanta	W	2-1	*Quagliarella (p), Barreto*
11/09	a	Roma	L	2-3	*Muriel, Quagliarella*
16/09	h	Milan	L	0-1	
21/09	a	Bologna	L	0-2	
26/09	a	Cagliari	L	1-2	*Bruno Fernandes*
02/10	h	Palermo	D	1-1	*Bruno Fernandes*
15/10	a	Pescara	D	1-1	*og (Campagnaro)*
22/10	h	Genoa	W	2-1	*Muriel, og (Izzo)*
26/10	a	Juventus	L	1-4	*Schick*
30/10	h	Internazionale	W	1-0	*Quagliarella*
06/11	a	Fiorentina	D	1-1	*Muriel*
20/11	h	Sassuolo	W	3-2	*Quagliarella, Muriel 2 (1p)*
27/11	a	Crotone	D	1-1	*Bruno Fernandes*
04/12	h	Torino	W	2-0	*Barreto, Schick*
10/12	h	Lazio	L	1-2	*Schick*
18/12	a	Chievo	L	1-2	*Schick*
22/12	h	Udinese	D	0-0	
2017					
07/01	a	Napoli	L	1-2	*og (Hysaj)*
15/01	h	Empoli	D	0-0	
22/01	a	Atalanta	L	0-1	
29/01	h	Roma	W	3-2	*Praet, Schick, Muriel*
05/02	a	Milan	W	1-0	*Muriel (p)*
12/02	h	Bologna	W	3-1	*Muriel (p), Schick, og (Mbaye)*
19/02	h	Cagliari	D	1-1	*Quagliarella*
26/02	a	Palermo	D	1-1	*Quagliarella*
04/03	h	Pescara	W	3-1	*Bruno Fernandes, Quagliarella, Schick*
11/03	a	Genoa	W	1-0	*Muriel*
19/03	h	Juventus	L	0-1	
03/04	a	Internazionale	W	2-1	*Schick, Quagliarella (p)*
09/04	h	Fiorentina	D	2-2	*Bruno Fernandes, Álvarez*
15/04	a	Sassuolo	L	1-2	*Schick*
23/04	h	Crotone	L	1-2	*Schick*
29/04	a	Torino	D	1-1	*Schick*
07/05	a	Lazio	L	3-7	*Linetty, Quagliarella 2 (1p)*
14/05	h	Chievo	D	1-1	*Quagliarella*
21/05	a	Udinese	D	1-1	*Muriel (p)*
28/05	h	Napoli	L	2-4	*Quagliarella, Álvarez*

No	Name	Nat	DoB	Pos	Aps	(s)	Gls
11	Ricardo Álvarez	ARG	12/04/88	M	11	(10)	2
8	Édgar Barreto	PAR	15/07/84	M	32		2
24	Bartosz Bereszyński	POL	12/07/92	D	11	(2)	
10	Bruno Fernandes	POR	08/09/94	M	22	(11)	5
47	Ante Budimir	CRO	22/07/91	A	2	(9)	
21	Luca Cigarini		20/06/86	M	3	(1)	
23	Filip Djuričić	SRB	30/01/92	M	3	(16)	
5	Dodô	BRA	06/02/92	D	4	(3)	
6	Mirko Eramo		12/07/89	M		(1)	
16	Karol Linetty	POL	02/02/95	M	27	(8)	1
9	Luis Muriel	COL	16/04/91	A	25	(6)	11
17	Angelo Palombo		25/09/81	M	2	(2)	
20	Daniel Pavlović	BIH	22/04/88	D	8	(1)	
13	Pedro Pereira	POR	22/01/98	D	8	(4)	
18	Dennis Praet	BEL	14/05/94	M	19	(13)	1
1	Christian Puggioni		17/01/81	G	21		
27	Fabio Quagliarella		31/01/83	A	35	(2)	12
19	Vasco Regini		09/09/90	D	30	(4)	
22	Jacopo Sala		05/12/91	D	19	(1)	
14	Patrik Schick	CZE	24/01/96	A	14	(18)	11
26	Matías Silvestre	ARG	25/09/84	D	36		
37	Milan Škriniar	SVK	11/02/95	D	34	(1)	
34	Lucas Torreira	URU	11/02/96	M	35		
2	Emiliano Viviano		01/12/85	G	17		

US Sassuolo Calcio

1920 • Città del Tricolore, Reggio Emilia (21,584) • sassuolocalcio.it

Coach: Eusebio Di Francesco

Date		Opponent		Score	Scorers
2016					
21/08	a	Palermo	W	1-0	*Berardi (p)*
28/08	h	Pescara	L	0-3	*(w/o; original result 2-1 Defrel, Berardi)*
10/09	a	Juventus	L	1-3	*Antei*
18/09	h	Genoa	W	2-0	*Politano (p), Defrel*
21/09	a	Chievo	L	1-2	*Defrel*
25/09	h	Udinese	W	1-0	*Defrel*
02/10	a	Milan	L	3-4	*Politano, Acerbi, Pellegrini*
16/10	h	Crotone	W	2-1	*Sensi, Iemmello*
23/10	a	Bologna	D	1-1	*Matri*
26/10	h	Roma	L	1-3	*Cannavaro*
30/10	a	Lazio	L	1-2	*Defrel*
06/11	h	Atalanta	L	0-3	
20/11	a	Sampdoria	L	2-3	*Ricci, Ragusa*
28/11	a	Napoli	D	1-1	*Defrel*
04/12	h	Empoli	W	3-0	*Pellegrini (p), Ricci (p), Ragusa*
12/12	a	Fiorentina	L	1-2	*Acerbi*
18/12	h	Internazionale	L	0-1	
22/12	a	Cagliari	L	3-4	*Adjapong, Pellegrini, Acerbi (p)*
2017					
08/01	h	Torino	D	0-0	
15/01	h	Palermo	W	4-1	*Matri 2, Ragusa, Politano*
22/01	a	Pescara	W	3-1	*Matri 2, Pellegrini*
29/01	h	Juventus	L	0-2	
05/02	a	Genoa	W	1-0	*Pellegrini*
12/02	h	Chievo	L	1-3	*Matri*
19/02	a	Udinese	W	2-1	*Defrel 2*
26/02	h	Milan	L	0-1	
05/03	a	Crotone	D	0-0	
12/03	h	Bologna	L	0-1	
19/03	a	Roma	L	1-3	*Defrel*
01/04	h	Lazio	L	1-2	*Berardi (p)*
08/04	a	Atalanta	D	1-1	*Pellegrini*
15/04	h	Sampdoria	W	2-1	*Ragusa, Acerbi*
23/04	h	Napoli	D	2-2	*Berardi, Mazzitelli*
30/04	a	Empoli	W	3-1	*Peluso, Matri, Duncan*
07/05	h	Fiorentina	D	2-2	*Politano (p), Iemmello*
14/05	a	Internazionale	W	2-1	*Iemmello 2*
21/05	h	Cagliari	W	6-2	*Magnanelli, Berardi, Politano, og (Borriello), Iemmello (p), Matri*
28/05	a	Torino	L	3-5	*Defrel 3 (1p)*

No	Name	Nat	DoB	Pos	Aps	(s)	Gls
15	Francesco Acerbi		10/02/88	D	38		4
98	Claud Adjapong		06/05/98	M	6	(3)	1
5	Luca Antei		19/04/92	D	11	(4)	1
21	Alberto Aquilani		07/07/84	M	14	(2)	
25	Domenico Berardi		01/08/94	A	20	(1)	5
8	Davide Biondini		24/01/83	M	9	(5)	
28	Paolo Cannavaro		26/06/81	D	16	(2)	1
47	Andrea Consigli		27/01/87	G	37		
11	Grégoire Defrel	FRA	17/06/91	A	23	(6)	12
39	Cristian Dell'Orco		10/02/94	D	9		
32	Alfred Duncan	GHA	10/03/93	M	14	(7)	1
9	Diego Falcinelli		26/06/91	A		(1)	
23	Marcello Gazzola		03/04/85	D	16		
9	Pietro Iemmello		06/03/92	A	3	(14)	5
55	Timo Letschert	NED	25/05/93	D	9		
4	Francesco Magnanelli		12/11/84	M	14	(1)	1
10	Alessandro Matri		19/08/84	A	16	(15)	8
22	Luca Mazzitelli		15/11/95	M	12	(5)	1
7	Simone Missiroli		23/05/86	M	9	(4)	
79	Gianluca Pegolo		25/03/81	G	1		
6	Lorenzo Pellegrini		19/06/96	M	24	(4)	6
13	Federico Peluso		20/01/84	D	33	(1)	1
20	Pol Lirola	ESP	13/08/97	D	17	(5)	
16	Matteo Politano		03/08/93	A	25	(7)	5
90	Antonino Ragusa		27/03/90	A	16	(9)	4
27	Federico Ricci		27/05/94	A	10	(14)	2
12	Stefano Sensi		05/08/95	M	14	(2)	1
26	Emanuele Terranova		14/04/87	D	2	(1)	

Torino FC

1906 • Olimpico Grande Torino (27,958) • torinofc.it

Major honours
Italian League (7) 1928, 1943, 1946, 1947, 1948, 1949, 1976; Italian Cup (5) 1936, 1943, 1968, 1971, 1993

Coach: Siniša Mihajlović (SRB)

Date		Opponent		Score	Scorers
2016					
21/08	a	Milan	L	2-3	*Belotti, Baselli*
28/08	h	Bologna	W	5-1	*Belotti 3, Martínez, Baselli*
11/09	a	Atalanta	L	1-2	*Iago Falqué*
18/09	h	Empoli	D	0-0	
21/09	a	Pescara	D	0-0	
25/09	h	Roma	W	3-1	*Belotti, Iago Falqué 2 (1p)*
02/10	h	Fiorentina	W	2-1	*Iago Falqué, Benassi*
17/10	a	Palermo	W	4-1	*Ljajić 2, Benassi, Baselli*
23/10	h	Lazio	D	2-2	*Iago Falqué, Ljajić (p)*
26/10	a	Internazionale	L	1-2	*Belotti*
31/10	a	Udinese	D	2-2	*Benassi, Ljajić*
05/11	h	Cagliari	W	5-1	*Belotti 2 (1p), Ljajić, Benassi, Baselli*
20/11	a	Crotone	W	2-0	*Belotti 2*
26/11	h	Chievo	W	2-1	*Iago Falqué 2*
04/12	a	Sampdoria	L	0-2	
11/12	h	Juventus	L	1-3	*Belotti*
18/12	a	Napoli	L	3-5	*Belotti, Rossettini, Iago Falqué (p)*
22/12	h	Genoa	W	1-0	*Belotti*
2017					
08/01	a	Sassuolo	D	0-0	
16/01	h	Milan	D	2-2	*Belotti, Benassi*
22/01	a	Bologna	L	0-2	
29/01	h	Atalanta	D	1-1	*Iago Falqué*
05/02	a	Empoli	D	1-1	*Belotti*
12/02	h	Pescara	W	5-3	*Iago Falqué, Ajeti, Belotti 2, Ljajić*
19/02	a	Roma	L	1-4	*Maxi López*
27/02	a	Fiorentina	D	2-2	*Belotti 2*
05/03	h	Palermo	W	3-1	*Belotti 3*
13/03	a	Lazio	L	1-3	*Maxi López*
18/03	h	Internazionale	D	2-2	*Baselli, Acquah*
02/04	h	Udinese	D	2-2	*Moretti, Belotti*
09/04	a	Cagliari	W	3-2	*Ljajić, Belotti, Acquah*
15/04	h	Crotone	D	1-1	*Belotti (p)*
23/04	a	Chievo	W	3-1	*Ljajić, Zappacosta, Iago Falqué*
29/04	h	Sampdoria	D	1-1	*Iturbe*
06/05	a	Juventus	D	1-1	*Ljajić*
14/05	h	Napoli	L	0-5	
21/05	a	Genoa	L	1-2	*Ljajić*
28/05	h	Sassuolo	W	5-3	*Boyé, Baselli, De Silvestri, Iago Falqué, Belotti*

No	Name	Nat	DoB	Pos	Aps	(s)	Gls
6	Afriyie Acquah	GHA	05/01/92	M	13	(7)	2
93	Arlind Ajeti	ALB	25/09/93	D	3	(1)	1
30	Mattia Aramu		14/05/95	A	1		
23	Antonio Barreca		18/03/95	D	25	(3)	
8	Daniele Baselli		12/03/92	M	28	(9)	6
9	Andrea Belotti		20/12/93	A	34	(1)	26
15	Marco Benassi		08/09/94	M	24	(4)	5
5	Cesare Bovo		14/01/83	D	4		
31	Lucas Boyé	ARG	28/02/96	A	14	(16)	1
5	Carlão	BRA	19/01/86	D	4		
26	Danilo Avelar	BRA	09/06/89	D	3		
29	Lorenzo De Silvestri		23/05/88	D	15	(1)	1
16	Samuel Gustafsson	SWE	11/01/95	M	1	(4)	
21	Joe Hart	ENG	19/04/87	G	36		
14	Iago Falqué	ESP	04/01/90	M	31	(4)	12
19	Juan Manuel Iturbe	PAR	04/06/93	A	4	(12)	1
4	Leandro Castán	BRA	05/11/86	D	13	(1)	
10	Adem Ljajić	SRB	29/09/91	M	30	(3)	10
25	Saša Lukić	SRB	13/08/96	M	7	(7)	
17	Josef Martínez	VEN	19/05/93	A	4	(7)	1
11	Maxi López	ARG	03/04/84	A	2	(14)	2
3	Cristian Molinaro		30/07/83	D	9	(1)	
24	Emiliano Moretti		11/06/81	D	23		1
22	Joel Obi	NGA	22/05/91	M	9	(11)	
1	Daniele Padelli		25/10/85	G	2		
13	Luca Rossettini		09/05/85	D	29	(1)	1
18	Mirko Valdifiori		21/04/86	M	22	(2)	
20	Giuseppe Vives		14/07/80	M	3		
7	Davide Zappacosta		11/06/92	D	25	(4)	1

Udinese Calcio

1896 • Dacia Arena (25,144) • udinese.it

Coach: Giuseppe Iachini; (04/10/16) Luigi Delneri

Date		Opponent		Score	Scorers
2016					
20/08	a	Roma	L	0-4	
28/08	h	Empoli	W	2-0	*Felipe, Perica*
11/09	a	Milan	W	1-0	*Perica*
18/09	h	Chievo	L	1-2	*Zapata*
21/09	h	Fiorentina	D	2-2	*Zapata, Danilo*
25/09	a	Sassuolo	L	0-1	
01/10	h	Lazio	L	0-3	
15/10	a	Juventus	L	1-2	*Jankto*
23/10	h	Pescara	W	3-1	*Théréau 2 (1p), Zapata (p)*
27/10	a	Palermo	W	3-1	*Théréau, Fofana 2*
31/10	h	Torino	D	2-2	*Théréau, Zapata*
06/11	a	Genoa	D	1-1	*Théréau*
19/11	h	Napoli	L	1-2	*Perica*
27/11	a	Cagliari	L	1-2	*Fofana*
05/12	h	Bologna	W	1-0	*Danilo*
11/12	a	Atalanta	W	3-1	*Zapata, Fofana, Théréau*
18/12	h	Crotone	W	2-0	*Théréau 2*
22/12	a	Sampdoria	D	0-0	
2017					
08/01	h	Internazionale	L	1-2	*Jankto*
15/01	h	Roma	L	0-1	
22/01	a	Empoli	L	0-1	
29/01	h	Milan	W	2-1	*Théréau, De Paul*
05/02	a	Chievo	D	0-0	
11/02	a	Fiorentina	L	0-3	
19/02	h	Sassuolo	L	1-2	*Fofana*
26/02	a	Lazio	L	0-1	
05/03	h	Juventus	D	1-1	*Zapata*
12/03	a	Pescara	W	3-1	*Zapata, Jankto, Théréau*
19/03	h	Palermo	W	4-1	*Théréau, Zapata, De Paul, Jankto*
02/04	a	Torino	D	2-2	*Jankto, Perica*
09/04	h	Genoa	W	3-0	*De Paul 2, Zapata*
15/04	a	Napoli	L	0-3	
23/04	h	Cagliari	W	2-1	*Perica, Angella*
30/04	a	Bologna	L	0-4	
07/05	h	Atalanta	D	1-1	*Perica*
14/05	a	Crotone	L	0-1	
21/05	h	Sampdoria	D	1-1	*Théréau*
28/05	a	Internazionale	L	2-5	*Balić, Zapata*

No	Name	Nat	DoB	Pos	Aps	(s)	Gls
53	Ali Adnan	IRQ	19/12/93	D	8	(6)	
8	Emmanuel Agyemang-Badu	GHA	02/12/90	M	20	(9)	
4	Gabriele Angella		28/04/89	D	10	(4)	1
7	Pablo Armero	COL	02/11/86	D	2		
99	Andrija Balić	CRO	11/08/97	M	3	(1)	1
5	Danilo	BRA	10/05/84	D	36		2
10	Rodrigo de Paul	ARG	24/05/94	M	32	(2)	4
96	Ewandro	BRA	15/03/96	A		(5)	
37	Davide Faraoni		25/10/91	D	4	(1)	
30	Felipe	BRA	31/07/84	D	31	(1)	1
6	Seko Fofana	CIV	07/05/95	M	21	(1)	5
34	Gabriel Silva	BRA	13/05/91	D	2	(3)	
23	Emil Hallfredsson	ISL	29/06/84	M	23	(5)	
75	Thomas Heurtaux	FRA	03/07/88	D	6	(6)	
14	Jakub Jankto	CZE	19/01/96	M	24	(5)	5
1	Orestis Karnezis	GRE	11/07/85	G	33		
33	Panagiotis Kone	GRE	26/07/87	M	3	(2)	
26	Sven Kums	BEL	26/02/88	M	20	(9)	
20	Francesco Lodi		23/03/84	M		(1)	
95	Lucas Evangelista	BRA	06/05/95	M	2	(4)	
11	Adalberto Peñaranda	VEN	31/05/97	A	1	(5)	
18	Stipe Perica	CRO	07/07/95	A	5	(22)	6
19	Ryder Matos	BRA	27/02/93	A	4	(16)	
3	Samir	BRA	05/12/94	D	21		
22	Simone Scuffet		31/05/96	G	5	(1)	
77	Cyril Théréau	FRA	24/04/83	A	31	(2)	12
2	Molla Wagué	MLI	21/02/91	D	6		
27	Silvan Widmer	SUI	05/03/93	D	28		
9	Duván Zapata	COL	01/04/91	A	37	(1)	10

Top goalscorers

29	Edin Džeko (Roma)
28	Dries Mertens (Napoli)
26	Andrea Belotti (Torino)
24	Mauro Icardi (Internazionale)
	Gonzalo Higuaín (Juventus)
23	Ciro Immobile (Lazio)
18	Lorenzo Insigne (Napoli)
16	Alejandro Gómez (Atalanta)
	Marco Borriello (Cagliari)
	Keita Baldé (Lazio)

Promoted clubs

SPAL

1907 • Paolo Mazza (8,500) • spalferrara.it
Coach: Leonardo Semplici

Hellas Verona FC

1903 • Marc'Antonio Bentegodi (39,211) • hellasverona.it
Major honours
Italian League (1) 1985
Coach: Fabio Pecchia

Benevento Calcio

1929 • Ciro Vigorito (12,847) • beneventocalcio.club
Coach: Marco Baroni

Second level final table 2016/17

		Pld	W	D	L	F	A	Pts
1	SPAL	42	22	12	8	66	39	78
2	Hellas Verona FC	42	20	14	8	64	40	74
3	Frosinone Calcio	42	21	11	10	57	42	74
4	AC Perugia	42	15	20	7	54	40	65
5	Benevento Calcio	42	18	12	12	56	42	65
6	AS Cittadella	42	19	6	17	60	54	63
7	Carpi FC 1909	42	16	14	12	41	40	62
8	Spezia Calcio	42	15	15	12	38	34	60
9	Novara Calcio	42	15	11	16	48	50	56
10	US Salernitana 1919	42	13	15	14	44	44	54
11	Virtus Entella	42	13	15	14	54	51	54
12	FC Bari 1908	42	13	14	15	39	44	53
13	AC Cesena	42	12	17	13	51	48	53
14	Brescia Calcio	42	11	17	14	49	58	50
15	Ascoli FC	42	10	19	13	44	49	49
16	FC Pro Vercelli 1892	42	10	19	13	35	45	49
17	AS Avellino	42	13	13	16	40	55	49
18	Ternana Calcio	42	13	10	19	42	53	49
19	Trapani Calcio	42	10	14	18	45	55	44
20	Vicenza Calcio	42	9	14	19	33	52	41
21	AC Pisa 1909	42	6	21	15	23	36	35
22	Latina Calcio	42	6	21	15	38	50	32

NB Latina Calcio – 7 pts deducted; AC Pisa 1909 – 4 pts deducted; AS Avellino – 3 pts deducted; Benevento Calcio – 1 pt deducted.

Promotion/Relegation play-offs

(22/05/17)
Cittadella 1-2 Carpi

(25/05/17)
Benevento 2-1 Spezia

(26/05/17 & 29/05/17)
Carpi 0-0 Frosinone
Frosinone 0-1 Carpi
(Carpi 1-0)

(27/05/17 & 30/05/17)
Benevento 1-0 Perugia
Perugia 1-1 Benevento
(Benevento 2-1)

(04/06/17 & 08/06/17)
Carpi 0-0 Benevento
Benevento 1-0 Carpi
(Benevento 1-0)

DOMESTIC CUP

Coppa Italia 2016/17

THIRD ROUND

(12/08/16)
Bologna 2-0 Trapani
Genoa 3-2 Lecce
Palermo 1-0 Bari *(aet)*
(13/08/16)
Atalanta 3-0 Cremonese
Cesena 2-0 Ternana
Chievo 3-0 Virtus Entella
Empoli 2-0 Vicenza
Novara 1-0 Latina *(aet)*
Perugia 2-1 Carpi
Pescara 2-0 Frosinone
Torino 4-1 Pro Vercelli
Udinese 2-3 Spezia

(14/08/16)
Salernitana 1-1 Pisa *(aet; 3-4 on pens)*
Sampdoria 3-0 Bassano Virtus
Verona 2-1 Crotone

(15/08/16)
Cagliari 5-1 SPAL

FOURTH ROUND

(29/11/16)
Chievo 3-0 Novara
Empoli 1-2 Cesena *(aet)*
Torino 4-0 Pisa *(aet)*

(30/11/16)
Atalanta 3-0 Pescara
Palermo 0-0 Spezia *(aet; 4-5 on pens)*
Sampdoria 3-0 Cagliari

(01/12/16)
Bologna 4-0 Verona
Genoa 4-3 Perugia *(aet)*

FIFTH ROUND

(10/01/17)
Napoli 3-1 Spezia

(11/01/17)
Fiorentina 1-0 Chievo
Juventus 3-2 Atalanta

(12/01/17)
Milan 2-1 Torino

(17/01/17)
Internazionale 3-2 Bologna *(aet)*

(18/01/17)
Lazio 4-2 Genoa
Sassuolo 1-2 Cesena

(19/01/17)
Roma 4-0 Sampdoria

QUARTER-FINALS

(24/01/17)
Napoli 1-0 Fiorentina *(Callejón 71)*

(25/01/17)
Juventus 2-1 Milan *(Dybala 10, Pjanić 21; Bacca 53)*

(31/01/17)
Internazionale 1-2 Lazio *(Brozović 84; Felipe Anderson 20, Biglia 56p)*

(01/02/17)
Roma 2-1 Cesena *(Džeko 68, Totti 90p; Garritano 73)*

SEMI-FINALS

(28/02/17 & 05/04/17)
Juventus 3-1 Napoli *(Dybala 47p, 69p, Higuaín 64; Callejón 36)*
Napoli 3-2 Juventus *(Hamšík 53, Mertens 61, Insigne 67; Higuaín 32, 58)*
(Juventus 5-4)

(01/03/17 & 04/04/17)
Lazio 2-0 Roma *(Milinković-Savić 29, Immobile 78)*
Roma 3-2 Lazio *(El Shaarawy 43, Salah 66, 90; Milinković-Savić 37, Immobile 56)*
(Lazio 4-3)

FINAL

(17/05/17)
Stadio Olimpico, Rome
JUVENTUS FC 2 *(Dani Alves 12, Bonucci 25)*
SS LAZIO 0
Referee: *Tagliavento*
JUVENTUS: *Neto, Barzagli, Bonucci, Chiellini, Dani Alves, Marchisio, Rincón, Alex Sandro, Dybala (Lemina 79), Mandžukić, Higuaín*
LAZIO: *Strakosha, Bastos (Felipe Anderson 53), De Vrij (Luis Alberto 69), Wallace, Basta, Parolo (Radu 21), Biglia, Milinković-Savić, Lulić, Baldé, Immobile*

Juventus made it a hat-trick of Coppa Italia successes with a 2-0 win over Lazio in Rome

KAZAKHSTAN

Kazakhstannin Futbol Federatsiyasi (KFF)

Address	29 Syganak street 9th floor KZ-010000 Astana
Tel	+7 7172 790780
Fax	+7 7172 790788
E-mail	info@kff.kz
Website	kff.kz

President	Seilda Baishakov
General secretary	Kanysh Aubakirov
Media officer	Yerbol Kairov
Year of formation	1992
National stadium	Astana Arena, Astana (30,200)

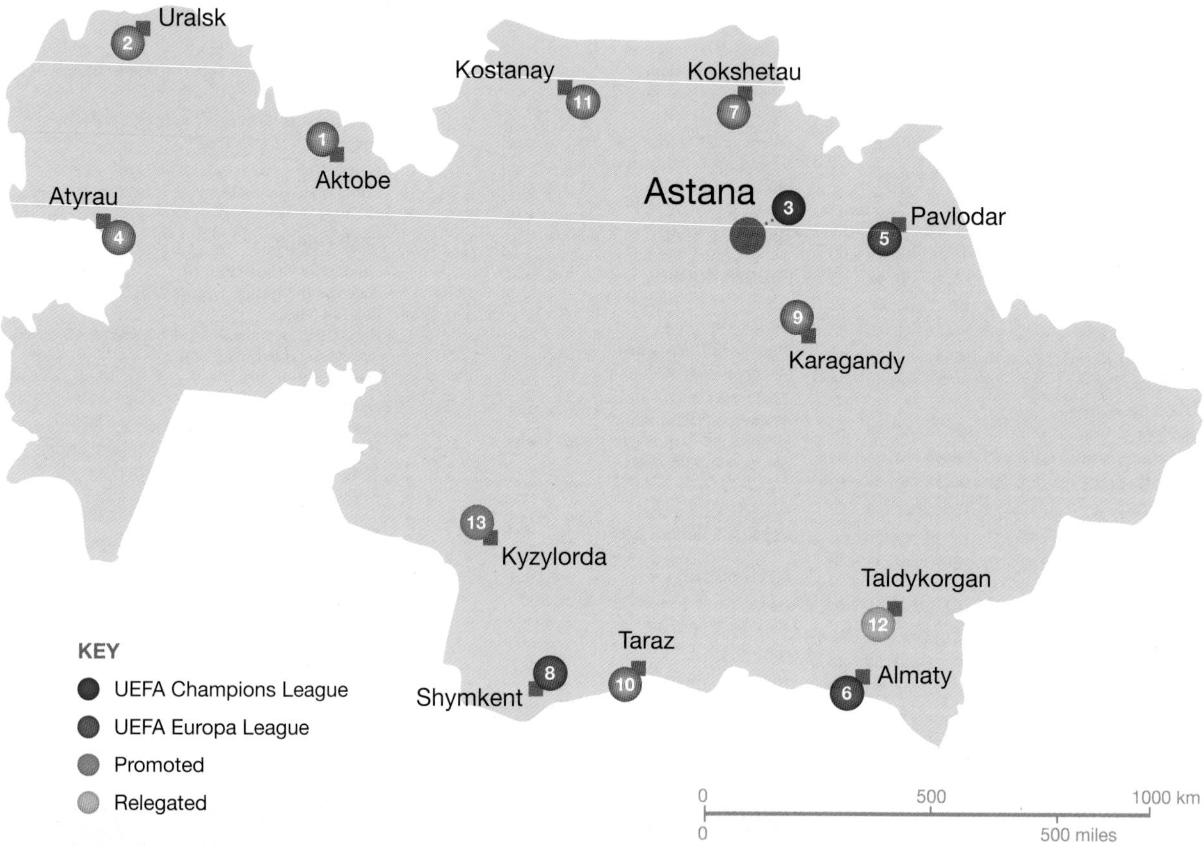

Uralsk
Kostanay
Kokshetau
Aktobe
Atyrau
Astana
Pavlodar
Karagandy
Kyzylorda
Taldykorgan
Taraz
Shymkent
Almaty

KEY

- UEFA Champions League
- UEFA Europa League
- Promoted
- Relegated

0 500 1000 km
0 500 miles

PREMIER LEAGUE CLUBS

1 **FC Aktobe**

2 **FC Akzhayik Uralsk**

3 **FC Astana**

4 **FC Atyrau**

5 **FC Irtysh Pavlodar**

6 **FC Kairat Almaty**

7 **FC Okzhetpes Kokshetau**

8 **FC Ordabasy Shymkent**

9 **FC Shakhter Karagandy**

10 **FC Taraz**

11 **FC Tobol Kostanay**

12 **FC Zhetysu Taldykorgan**

PROMOTED CLUB

13 **FC Kaysar Kyzylorda**

All systems go for Astana

For the second season running the battle for the Kazakh Premier League title turned into a private contest between FC Astana and Kairat Almaty. Once again it was the former, led by ex-Bulgaria coach Stanimir Stoilov, who claimed first prize, edging home with the help of a tweak to the division's two-tiered structure.

Astana's third successive league title was accompanied by victory in the Kazakh Cup, which ended Kairat's bid for a trophy hat-trick while enabling the winners to capture their first domestic double.

Capital club claim first domestic double

Kairat edged out in league and cup

Gerard Gohou retains golden boot

Domestic league

In taking the 2015 title, Astana had benefited from the rule that permitted them to round up their half-point to a full one at the 22-game split, eventually finishing a point ahead of Kairat despite the two teams' identical number of wins, draws and defeats over the full campaign. It was consequently decided to alter the format for 2016, with all points won in the first phase (rather than half of them) being carried over to the play-offs.

Alas for Kairat, the new system, like the old one, was to favour their championship rivals. Had the 2015 format been retained, Kairat would – on a purely mathematical basis – have won the title they had been chasing for a dozen years, with a one-point advantage over Astana. As it transpired, though, they ended up two in arrears, the defending champions successfully exploiting the seven-point lead they held at the split and, despite losing home and away to Kairat in the play-offs, going on to complete their title hat-trick with a match to spare.

A 0-0 draw in their game in hand, away to Okzhetpes Kokshetau, carried Astana home. It was appropriate that a clean sheet, rather than a goal fest, got them over the line, for it was one of 17 that they registered over the campaign, during which they conceded just 21 goals.

Goalkeeper Nenad Erić received excellent protection from his defence, notably Dmitri Shomko, Yuri Logvinenko and Bosnian import Marin Aničić, while at the other end the goals were generally spread around, with several players chipping in at important times.

Kairat had much the greater firepower, finding the net 75 times compared to Astana's 47. Ivorian striker Gerard Gohou topped the league's goal charts for the second season in a row, with the same tally of 22, while playmaker Baurzhan Islamkhan added 17 and new signing Andrei Arshavin, the ex-Zenit, Arsenal and Russia star, scored eight.

It was an early-season change of coach, with Georgian Kakhaber Tskhadadze replacing Russian Aleksandr Borodyuk, which fuelled Kairat's title charge. Unbeaten at home and victorious three times out of four against Astana, their main failing was an inability to beat Ordabasy Shymkent, who, as in 2015, ended up fourth – a place behind Irtysh Pavlodar, who, like Astana, were skilfully led by a Bulgarian coach in Dimitar Dimitrov.

Domestic cup

Kairat had defeated Astana 2-1 in the 2015 Kazakh Cup final at the Astana Arena, but in the 2016 rematch, in Kairat's home stadium, the pendulum swung in the other direction, with Astana prevailing thanks to a solitary goal scored just after half-time by Junior Kabananga, the very man who had broken Kairat hearts a year earlier with his late league title-winning strike against Aktobe on the final day.

Europe

Astana maintained a high profile in Europe by reaching the group stage of the UEFA Europa League a year after they had enjoyed equally lengthy participation in the UEFA Champions League. Furthermore, Stoilov's charges again went through their six home fixtures undefeated. It would have been a much briefer European adventure, however, had Aničić not scored a crucial stoppage-time winner against Žalgiris Vilnius in their opening tie.

National team

Despite his short, troubled spell at Kairat, Borodyuk was appointed as the new head coach of Kazakhstan in February 2017, replacing Talgat Baysufinov, but, as at Kairat, he failed to win any of his first three games. Indeed, he lost them all, including two European Qualifiers against Armenia and Denmark, which left the team stranded at the foot of their FIFA World Cup qualifying group with just two points – claimed in autumn draws at the Astana Arena against Poland (2-2) and Romania (0-0).

DOMESTIC SEASON AT A GLANCE

Premier League 2016 final table

		Pld	Home W	Home D	Home L	Home F	Home A	Away W	Away D	Away L	Away F	Away A	Total W	Total D	Total L	Total F	Total A	Pts
1	**FC Astana**	**32**	**14**	**1**	**1**	**27**	**9**	**9**	**3**	**4**	**20**	**12**	**23**	**4**	**5**	**47**	**21**	**73**
2	FC Kairat Almaty	32	13	3	0	42	12	9	2	5	33	18	22	5	5	75	30	71
3	FC Irtysh Pavlodar	32	8	4	4	29	17	6	3	7	23	19	14	7	11	52	36	49
4	FC Ordabasy Shymkent	32	9	3	4	24	19	4	6	6	17	25	13	9	10	41	44	48
5	FC Okzhetpes Kokshetau	32	7	4	5	24	18	6	2	8	18	26	13	6	13	42	44	45
6	FC Aktobe	32	6	5	5	21	22	3	4	9	16	30	9	9	14	37	52	36
7	FC Tobol Kostanay	32	8	2	6	23	17	4	3	9	17	23	12	5	15	40	40	41
8	FC Atyrau	32	8	5	3	20	11	2	4	10	15	28	10	9	13	35	39	39
9	FC Shakhter Karagandy	32	6	3	7	16	17	4	3	9	9	23	10	6	16	25	40	36
10	FC Akzhayik Uralsk	32	6	1	9	14	28	5	1	10	13	22	11	2	19	27	50	35
11	FC Taraz	32	8	2	6	21	20	2	3	11	12	22	10	5	17	33	42	35
12	FC Zhetysu Taldykorgan	32	5	4	7	18	22	3	3	10	19	31	8	7	17	37	53	31

NB League splits into top and bottom halves after 22 games, after which the clubs play exclusively against teams in their group. Points obtained during the regular season are carried forward in full.

European qualification 2017/18

Champion/Cup Winner: FC Astana (second qualifying round)

FC Kairat Almaty (first qualifying round)
FC Irtysh Pavlodar (first qualifying round)
FC Ordabasy Shymkent (first qualifying round)

Top scorer	Gerard Gohou (Kairat), 22 goals
Relegated club	FC Zhetysu Taldykorgan
Promoted club	FC Kaysar Kyzylorda
Cup final	FC Astana 1-0 FC Kairat Almaty

Player of the season

Baurzhan Islamkhan
(FC Kairat Almaty)

Unlike his first two seasons with Kairat, which ended with domestic cup triumphs, Islamkhan did not win a trophy, but from an individual perspective the skilful playmaker made significant career progress, scoring 17 league goals and captaining the team to within a whisker of the title. He also skippered the Kazakhstan national side, making a sufficient number of positive displays – a red card for an errant elbow against Denmark notwithstanding - to suggest that he might break the mould of the current squad and try his luck abroad.

Newcomer of the season

Didar Zhalmukan
(FC Aktobe)

First exposed to international competition in the qualifying competition for the 2017 UEFA European Under-21 Championship, during which he represented Kazakhstan five times, Zhalmukan scored on his European club debut for Aktobe – a penalty against MTK Budapest – and shone repeatedly in the Premier League. Indeed, the diminutive young dribbler's second full season at that level improved on his first to such a degree that his third would be spent at champions Astana, who used their pulling power to recruit him on the eve of the 2017 campaign.

Team of the season
(3-4-2-1)

Coach: Stoilov *(Astana)*

NATIONAL TEAM

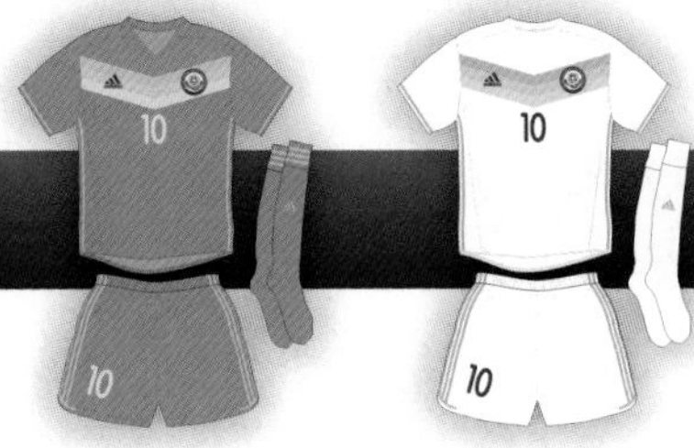

Top five all-time caps

Samat Smakov (76); Ruslan Baltiyev (73); Nurbol Zhumaskaliyev (58); Andrei Karpovich (55); **David Loria** (43)

Top five all-time goals

Ruslan Baltiyev (13); Viktor Zubarev (12); Dmitri Byakov & **Sergei Khizhnichenko** (8); Nurbol Zhumaskaliyev (7)

Results 2016/17

30/08/16	Kyrgyzstan	A	Bishkek	L	0-2	
04/09/16	Poland (WCQ)	H	Astana	D	2-2	*Khizhnichenko (51, 58)*
08/10/16	Montenegro (WCQ)	A	Podgorica	L	0-5	
11/10/16	Romania (WCQ)	H	Astana	D	0-0	
11/11/16	Denmark (WCQ)	A	Copenhagen	L	1-4	*Suyumbayev (17)*
22/03/17	Cyprus	A	Larnaca	L	1-3	*Nuserbayev (29)*
26/03/17	Armenia (WCQ)	A	Yerevan	L	0-2	
10/06/17	Denmark (WCQ)	H	Almaty	L	1-3	*Kuat (76)*

Appearances 2016/17

Coach: Talgat Baysufinov /(27/02/17) Aleksandr Borodyuk (RUS)	**04/09/68 30/11/62**		**Kgz**	**POL**	**MNE**	**ROU**	**DEN**	**Cyp**	**ARM**	**DEN**	**Caps**	**Goals**
David Loria	31/10/81	Irtysh	G46						G	G	43	-
Abzal Beysebekov	30/11/92	Astana	D	D	D	D		D	D	s56	12	-
Sergei Maliy	05/06/90	Astana /Tobol	D	D	D	D	D	D	D 64*		22	-
Eldos Akhmetov	01/06/90	Irtysh /Kairat	D	D61		D	D			D	8	-
Viktor Dmitrenko	04/04/91	Tobol	D57						s82		16	1
Gafurzhan Suyumbayev	19/08/90	Kairat	D66				D	D	D	D	17	1
Maksat Bayzhanov	06/08/84	Shakhter /Kaisar	M76	M69		M66	M		s87		28	1
Samat Smakov	08/12/78	Ordabasy	M60			M					76	2
Baurzhan Islamkhan	23/02/93	Kairat	M46	M79	M64		M70	M64	M87	M 43*	28	2
Islambek Kuat	12/01/93	Kairat	M	M	M76	M86		M72	M82	M	13	3
Sergei Khizhnichenko	17/07/91	Tobol	A46	A	A85	A82	A60				42	8
Zhasulan Moldakaraev	07/05/87	Okzhetpes	s46				s60				2	-
Azat Nurgaliyev	30/06/86	Astana /Ordabasy	s46	s69	M	s66		M89	M	M56	36	3
Stas Pokatilov	08/12/92	Kairat	s46	G	G	G	G	G			14	-
Aleksandr Kislitsyn	08/03/86	Okzhetpes	s57	D	D						25	-
Askhat Tagybergen	09/08/90	Astana /Tobol	s60	s79	s76	s86		M	M		14	-
Dmitri Shomko	19/03/90	Astana	s66	D	D	D	D	D	D	D67	32	2
Roman Murtazayev	10/09/93	Irtysh /Astana	s76		s85	s82	s70	s89			6	-
Serikzhan Muzhikov	17/06/89	Astana		M	s64	M	M81		s79	M	14	-
Renat Abdulin	14/04/82	Ordabasy		s61							30	2
Yuri Logvinenko	22/07/88	Astana			D	D	D			D	41	4
Almir Mukhutdinov	09/06/85	Tobol			M		M				3	-
Yerkebulan Tunggyshbayev	14/01/95	Ordabasy					s81	M67	M79	s74	4	-
Tanat Nuserbayev	01/01/87	Ordabasy						A90	A	A74	28	3
Georgi Zhukov	19/11/94	Kairat						s64		M	4	-
Dmitri Miroshnichenko	26/02/92	Tobol						s67			6	-
Aleksei Shchetkin	21/05/91	Tobol						s72			19	1
Grigori Sartakov	19/08/94	Tobol						s90			1	-
Yan Vorogovskiy	07/08/96	Kairat								s67	1	-

EUROPE

FC Astana

CHAMPIONS LEAGUE

Second qualifying round - FK Žalgiris Vilnius (LTU)
A 0-0
Erić, Aničić, Maksimović, Muzhikov, Ibraimi (Tagybergen 80), Shitov, Nuserbayev (Kabananga 72), Twumasi (Despotović 90+2), Logvinenko, Shomko, Cañas. Coach: Stanimir Stoilov (BUL)
H 2-1 *Aničić (31, 90+2)*
Erić, Aničić, Maksimović, Ibraimi (Despotović 72), Shitov, Nuserbayev (Muzhikov 55), Twumasi (Beysebekov 90+4), Logvinenko, Kabananga, Shomko, Cañas. Coach: Stanimir Stoilov (BUL)

Third qualifying round - Celtic FC (SCO)
H 1-1 *Logvinenko (19)*
Erić, Aničić, Maksimović, Nurgaliyev (Muzhikov 62), Shitov, Beysebekov (Ibraimi 84), Twumasi, Logvinenko, Kabananga (Despotović 86), Shomko, Cañas. Coach: Stanimir Stoilov (BUL)
A 1-2 *Ibraimi (62)*
Erić, Aničić, Muzhikov (Despotović 90+3), Nurgaliyev (Ibraimi 57), Shitov, Beysebekov, Twumasi, Logvinenko, Kabananga, Shomko, Cañas. Coach: Stanimir Stoilov (BUL)
Red cards: Shitov 90+1, Shomko 90+2

EUROPA LEAGUE

Play-offs - FC BATE Borisov (BLR)
H 2-0 *Kabananga (70), Nurgaliyev (80)*
Erić, Aničić, Maksimović, Muzhikov, Ibraimi (Nurgaliyev 63), Beysebekov, Twumasi (Tagybergen 89), Maliy, Logvinenko, Kabananga (Despotović 84), Cañas. Coach: Stanimir Stoilov (BUL)
A 2-2 *Maksimović (50), Twumasi (76)*
Mokin, Aničić, Maksimović, Muzhikov (Tagybergen 85), Nurgaliyev (Beysebekov 46), Shitov, Twumasi, Logvinenko (Maliy 46), Kabananga, Shomko, Cañas. Coach: Stanimir Stoilov (BUL)

Group B
Match 1 - APOEL FC (CYP)
A 1-2 *Maksimović (45+1)*
Erić, Aničić, Maksimović, Muzhikov (Tagybergen 77), Despotović (Twumasi 57), Shitov, Beysebekov, Maliy, Kabananga (Nuserbayev 70), Shomko, Cañas. Coach: Stanimir Stoilov (BUL)
Match 2 - BSC Young Boys (SUI)
H 0-0
Erić, Aničić, Maksimović, Muzhikov (Nurgaliyev 84), Despotović (Nuserbayev 74), Shitov, Beysebekov, Maliy, Kabananga (Tagybergen 84), Shomko, Cañas. Coach: Stanimir Stoilov (BUL)
Match 3 - Olympiacos FC (GRE)
A 1-4 *Kabananga (54)*
Erić, Aničić, Tagybergen (Muzhikov 63), Beysebekov, Nuserbayev (Shitov 59), Twumasi, Maliy, Logvinenko, Kabananga (Despotović 72), Shomko, Cañas. Coach: Stanimir Stoilov (BUL)
Red card: Cañas 58
Match 4 - Olympiacos FC (GRE)
H 1-1 *Despotović (8)*
Erić, Maksimović, Muzhikov, Despotović (Kulbekov 82), Shitov, Beysebekov, Twumasi (Najaryan 90+3), Maliy, Logvinenko, Kabananga, Shomko. Coach: Stanimir Stoilov (BUL)
Match 5 - APOEL FC (CYP)
H 2-1 *Aničić (59), Despotović (84)*
Erić, Aničić, Maksimović, Muzhikov (Nurgaliyev 81), Despotović, Shitov (Nuserbayev 77), Beysebekov, Logvinenko, Kabananga (Maliy 90+4), Shomko, Cañas. Coach: Stanimir Stoilov (BUL)
Match 6 - BSC Young Boys (SUI)
A 0-3
Erić, Maksimović, Muzhikov (Zhunusov 87), Despotović (Najaryan 77), Shitov, Beysebekov, Twumasi, Logvinenko (Maliy 55), Kabananga, Shomko, Cañas. Coach: Stanimir Stoilov (BUL)

FC Kairat Almaty

EUROPA LEAGUE

First qualifying round - KF Teuta (ALB)
A 1-0 *Arshavin (70)*
Plotnikov, Tesák, Marković, Bakaev, Islamkhan, Isael (Kuat 80), Gohou (Tawamba 90+2), Kuantayev, Lunin, Arshavin (Acevedo 78), Tymoshchuk. Coach: Kakhaber Tskhadadze (GEO)
H 5-0 *Gohou (27, 61), Bakaev (45+2), Tawamba (72), Turysbek (79)*
Plotnikov, Vorogovskiy, Marković, Kuat, Bakaev, Islamkhan (Acevedo 66), Isael, Gohou (Tawamba 69), Lunin, Arshavin (Turysbek 76), Tymoshchuk. Coach: Kakhaber Tskhadadze (GEO)

Second qualifying round - Maccabi Tel-Aviv FC (ISR)
H 1-1 *Arshavin (29)*
Plotnikov, Marković, Bakaev, Islamkhan, Isael, Gohou (Tawamba 83), Kuantayev, Lunin, Suyumbayev, Arshavin (Kuat 77), Tymoshchuk. Coach: Kakhaber Tskhadadze (GEO)
Red card: Islamkhan 90+3
A 1-2 *Gohou (64)*
Plotnikov, Marković, Bakaev, Isael (Tawamba 88), Gohou, César Arzo (Kuantayev 80), Lunin, Suyumbayev, Arshavin, Acevedo (Kuat 46), Tymoshchuk. Coach: Kakhaber Tskhadadze (GEO)

FC Aktobe

EUROPA LEAGUE

First qualifying round - MTK Budapest (HUN)
H 1-1 *Zhalmukan (44p)*
Otarbayev, Sitdikov, Kouadja, Kairov, Kryukov, Zhalmukan (Shestakov 83), Tsveiba, Mitošević, Bocharov, Dao (Golubov 62), Sorokin. Coach: Yuri Utkulbaev (RUS)
A 0-2
Otarbayev, Sitdikov, Kouadja, Kairov, Kryukov, Zhalmukan, Tsveiba, Mitošević, Bocharov, Dao (Golubov 57; Abdukarimov 81), Sorokin. Coach: Yuri Utkulbaev (RUS)

FC Ordabasy Shymkent

EUROPA LEAGUE

First qualifying round - FK Čukarički (SRB)
A 0-3
Boychenko, Mukhtarov, Chatto (Beysenov 86), Kasalica (Kozhabayev 84), Tolebek (Geynrikh 59), Tunggyshbayev, Diakhate, Abdulin, Gogua, Adyrbekov, Simčević. Coach: Bakhtiyar Baiseitov (KAZ)
Red card: Mukhtarov 29
H 3-3 *Geynrikh (45+2), Tunggyshbayev (67), Erlanov (90+3)*
Boychenko, Chatto, Kaykibasov (Kasalica 46), Trajković, Tolebek, Tunggyshbayev (Beysenov 78), Diakhate (Gogua 46), Erlanov, Geynrikh, Adyrbekov, Simčević. Coach: Bakhtiyar Baiseitov (KAZ)

DOMESTIC LEAGUE CLUB-BY-CLUB

FC Aktobe

1967 • Koblandy Batyr (12,729) • fc-aktobe.kz

Major honours
Kazakhstan League (5) 2005, 2007, 2008, 2009, 2013; Kazakhstan Cup (1) 2008

Coach: Yuri Utkulbaev (RUS)

2016

Date		Opponent		Score	Scorers
13/03	a	Ordabasy	L	1-3	*Davlyatov*
19/03	a	Taraz	D	1-1	*Smakov (p)*
03/04	a	Astana	L	0-1	
09/04	h	Zhetysu	W	3-2	*Smakov, Bocharov, Zhangylyshbay*
13/04	a	Tobol	W	2-1	*Kakimov, Bocharov*
17/04	h	Irtysh	D	1-1	*Smakov (p)*
23/04	a	Kairat	L	0-3	
01/05	h	Okzhetpes	W	1-0	*Smakov (p)*
05/05	a	Akzhayik	D	0-0	
09/05	h	Atyrau	W	1-0	*Zhalmukan (p)*
14/05	a	Shakhter	W	2-0	*Zhalmukan, Zhangylyshbay*
21/05	h	Taraz	D	2-2	*Smakov (p), Zhalmukan*
29/05	h	Astana	L	0-1	
02/06	a	Zhetysu	D	1-1	*Tsveiba*
11/06	h	Tobol	L	0-1	
15/06	a	Irtysh	L	1-4	*Zhalmukan*
19/06	h	Kairat	L	2-6	*Shestakov, Zhalmukan (p)*
24/06	a	Okzhetpes	L	1-4	*Golubov*
03/07	h	Akzhayik	W	1-0	*Bocharov*
10/07	a	Atyrau	D	1-1	*Bocharov*
17/07	h	Shakhter	W	2-0	*Dao, Shchetkin*
24/07	h	Ordabasy	D	0-0	
13/08	h	Ordabasy	D	4-4	*Shchetkin 2, Kakimov, Kryukov*
20/08	a	Kairat	L	1-3	*Shchetkin*
26/08	h	Irtysh	W	1-0	*Bocharov*
12/09	a	Okzhetpes	W	3-0	*Bocharov, Shchetkin 2*
18/09	h	Astana	L	1-2	*Sorokin*
25/09	h	Kairat	L	0-1	
01/10	a	Irtysh	L	1-5	*Bocharov*
16/10	h	Okzhetpes	D	2-2	*og (Abylgazy), Zhalmukan*
23/10	a	Astana	L	0-1	
29/10	a	Ordabasy	L	1-2	*Kakimov*

No	Name	Nat	DoB	Pos	Aps	(s)	Gls
37	Abylkhan Abdukarimov		07/04/98	M		(5)	
95	Abat Aimbetov		07/08/95	A	1	(1)	
21	Egor Azovskiy		10/01/85	D	11	(6)	
69	Nikita Bocharov	RUS	12/06/92	M	31		7
87	Igor Boychuk		04/06/97	M	4	(5)	
77	Lassina Dao	CIV	20/12/96	A	2	(3)	1
11	Bobir Davlyatov	UZB	01/03/96	M	11	(2)	1
85	Dmitri Golubov	RUS	24/06/85	A	1	(1)	1
5	Bagdat Kairov		27/04/93	D	21		
47	Aslanbek Kakimov		02/10/93	M	16	(5)	3
3	Kouassi Kouadja	CIV	22/06/95	D	27	(2)	
6	Viktor Kryukov		30/06/90	D	21	(4)	1
19	Sergei Lisenkov		17/06/91	A	1		
12	Ilya Mikhalyov	UKR	31/07/90	A	7	(1)	
33	Vuk Mitošević	SRB	12/02/91	M	11	(2)	
72	Nemanya Nikolić	MNE	19/10/92	A		(5)	
32	Samat Otarbayev		18/02/90	G	28		
35	Stanislav Pavlov		30/05/94	G	2	(2)	
24	Mikhail Petrolay	RUS	19/08/94	M	12		
88	Aleksei Shchetkin		21/05/91	A	7	(1)	6
22	Kirill Shestakov		14/11/85	M	19	(8)	1
2	Marat Sitdikov	RUS	23/07/91	D	32		
81	Anton Skvortsov		30/11/99	M		(1)	
8	Samat Smakov		08/12/78	M	11	(1)	5
80	Egor Sorokin	RUS	04/11/95	D	28	(1)	1
99	Murat Tleshev		12/04/80	A		(6)	
9	Abylaykhan Totay		16/02/92	M	2	(1)	
42	Igor Trofimets		20/08/96	G	2		
14	Sandro Tsveiba	RUS	05/09/93	M	16	(12)	1
10	Didar Zhalmukan		22/05/96	A	19	(9)	6
18	Tokhtar Zhangylyshbay		25/05/93	A	7	(5)	2
25	Sayat Zhumagali		25/04/95	D	2	(1)	
17	Nurbol Zhumashev		09/07/94	D		(2)	

FC Akzhayik Uralsk

1968 • Pyotr Atoyan (8,320) • fc-akzhayik.kz

Coach: Talgat Baysufinov; (23/07/16) Vakhid Masudov

2016

Date		Opponent		Score	Scorers
13/03	a	Tobol	L	0-1	
19/03	h	Irtysh	L	0-3	
03/04	h	Kairat	W	2-1	*Coronel (p), Valiullin*
09/04	h	Okzhetpes	L	0-2	
13/04	a	Taraz	W	1-0	*Begalyn*
17/04	a	Atyrau	L	0-2	
23/04	h	Shakhter	L	0-1	
01/05	a	Ordabasy	L	0-1	
05/05	h	Aktobe	D	0-0	
10/05	a	Astana	L	0-2	
15/05	h	Zhetysu	L	1-2	*Khromtsov*
21/05	a	Irtysh	D	0-0	
29/05	a	Kairat	L	2-3	*Valiullin, Khromtsov*
02/06	a	Okzhetpes	L	2-4	*Antipov, Begalyn*
11/06	h	Taraz	W	2-1	*Coronel 2 (1p)*
15/06	h	Atyrau	L	0-4	
19/06	a	Shakhter	L	1-3	*Lečić*
24/06	h	Ordabasy	L	0-1	
03/07	a	Aktobe	L	0-1	
08/07	h	Astana	L	1-5	*Govedarica*
16/07	a	Zhetysu	L	0-2	
24/07	h	Tobol	L	0-5	
14/08	h	Zhetysu	W	1-0	*Lečić (p)*
21/08	a	Shakhter	W	1-0	*Coronel (p)*
26/08	h	Taraz	W	2-0	*Dudchenko, Lečić*
10/09	h	Tobol	W	1-0	*Lečić*
17/09	a	Atyrau	W	2-1	*Dudchenko 2*
24/09	h	Shakhter	L	1-2	*Lečić*
01/10	a	Taraz	L	1-2	*Shakhmetov*
16/10	a	Tobol	W	1-0	*Coronel*
22/10	h	Atyrau	W	3-1	*Dudchenko, Coronel 2*
29/10	a	Zhetysu	W	2-0	*Sergienko, Coronel*

No	Name	Nat	DoB	Pos	Aps	(s)	Gls
77	Eldar Abdrakhmanov		16/01/87	D	22	(1)	
5	Ivan Antipov		14/01/96	M	2	(8)	1
87	Roman Bagautdinov		20/09/87	G	7		
24	Kuanysh Begalyn		05/09/92	A	5	(8)	2
16	Freddy Coronel	PAR	25/04/89	M	32		8
40	Kostyantyn Dudchenko	UKR	08/07/86	A	16	(1)	4
55	Predrag Govedarica	SRB	21/10/84	M	29		1
11	Sergei Gridin		20/05/87	A	3	(2)	
1	Nurbolat Kalmenov		15/09/90	G	10		
18	Ruslan Khairov		18/01/90	M	3	(3)	
20	Oleg Khromtsov		30/05/83	A	11	(4)	2
6	Saša Kolunija	SRB	09/06/87	D	20		
28	Zakhar Korobov		18/05/88	D	4		
12	Miroslav Lečić	SRB	20/04/85	A	16		5
97	Evgeni Levin		12/07/92	D	1		
8	Aleksei Maltsev		25/10/86	A	5	(7)	
83	Danilo Nikolić	SRB	29/07/83	D	15	(1)	
29	Kairat Nurdauletov		06/11/82	D		(1)	
29	Mike Odibe	NGA	23/07/88	D	10		
14	Baurzhan Omarov		03/08/90	D	16	(7)	
32	Srdjan Ostojić	BIH	10/01/83	G	5		
11	Rakhimzhan Rozybakiev		02/01/91	D	11	(6)	
97	Matías Rubio	CHI	08/08/88	M	3	(4)	
13	Miram Sapanov		12/03/86	D	20	(5)	
7	Izym Sarsekenov		30/03/93	M	1		
33	Eduard Sergienko		18/02/83	M	26	(3)	1
44	Marat Shakhmetov		06/02/89	M	1	(5)	1
17	Sergei Shevtsov		29/10/90	M	5	(5)	
88	Anton Shurygin		03/12/88	M	13	(6)	
26	Yerkin Tapalov		03/09/93	D	7	(2)	
32	Denis Tolebayev		07/02/87	G	10		
20	Abylaykhan Totay		16/02/92	M		(2)	
9	Ruslan Valiullin		09/09/94	M	23	(7)	2
23	Nikolai Zabrodin		23/07/90	M		(3)	

FC Astana

2009 • Astana Arena (30,200) • fca.kz

Major honours
Kazakhstan League (3) 2014, 2015, 2016; Kazakhstan Cup (3) 2010, 2012, 2016

Coach: Stanimir Stoilov (BUL)

2016

Date		Opponent		Score	Scorers
12/03	h	Shakhter	W	2-1	*Despotović, Nuserbayev*
20/03	a	Ordabasy	W	3-1	*Despotović, og (Simčević), Aničić*
03/04	h	Aktobe	W	1-0	*Twumasi*
09/04	h	Taraz	W	2-1	*Nuserbayev, Shomko*
13/04	a	Zhetysu	W	1-0	*Logvinenko*
17/04	h	Tobol	W	1-0	*Haruna*
23/04	a	Irtysh	D	2-2	*Despotović, Muzhikov*
01/05	h	Kairat	W	1-0	*Maksimović*
05/05	a	Okzhetpes	W	1-0	*Despotović*
10/05	h	Akzhayik	W	2-0	*Nuserbayev, Twumasi*
15/05	a	Atyrau	L	0-1	
21/05	h	Ordabasy	W	3-1	*Aničić, Cañas, Nuserbayev*
29/05	a	Aktobe	W	1-0	*Maksimović*
02/06	a	Taraz	W	2-0	*Despotović, Muzhikov*
11/06	h	Zhetysu	W	1-0	*Nuserbayev*
15/06	a	Tobol	W	2-1	*Maksimović, Tagybergen*
19/06	h	Irtysh	D	1-1	*Nuserbayev*
23/06	a	Kairat	L	0-1	
05/07	h	Okzhetpes	W	1-0	*Kabananga*
08/07	a	Akzhayik	W	5-1	*Nurgaliyev 2, Kabananga, Tagybergen, Muzhikov*
16/07	h	Atyrau	W	2-1	*Nurgaliyev 2*
07/08	a	Shakhter	L	0-2	
12/08	h	Irtysh	W	3-0	*Logvinenko, Kabananga, Despotović*
21/08	h	Ordabasy	W	2-0	*Nurgaliyev (p), Twumasi*
10/09	h	Kairat	L	1-4	*Despotović*
18/09	a	Aktobe	W	2-1	*Kabananga, Aničić*
25/09	a	Ordabasy	W	1-0	*Kabananga*
02/10	h	Okzhetpes	W	3-0	*Twumasi 2, Nurgaliyev*
16/10	a	Kairat	L	0-2	
23/10	h	Aktobe	W	1-0	*Despotović*
26/10	a	Okzhetpes	D	0-0	
29/10	a	Irtysh	D	0-0	

No	Name	Nat	DoB	Pos	Aps	(s)	Gls
16	Besart Abdurahimi	MKD	31/07/90	M	1	(3)	
95	Amanbol Aliyev		10/07/95	D	1		
5	Marin Aničić	BIH	17/08/89	D	27		3
15	Abzal Beysebekov		30/11/92	D	18	(4)	
88	Roger Cañas	COL	27/03/90	M	30	(1)	1
10	Djordje Despotović	SRB	04/03/92	A	21	(10)	8
1	Nenad Erić		26/05/82	G	30		
4	Mark Gurman		09/02/89	D	2	(4)	
20	Lukman Haruna	NGA	12/04/90	M	6	(4)	1
9	Agim Ibraimi	MKD	29/08/88	M	4	(2)	
30	Junior Kabananga	COD	04/04/89	A	9	(4)	5
37	Amir Kalabayev		13/11/96	M	1		
28	Birzhan Kulbekov		22/04/94	D	1	(1)	
27	Yuri Logvinenko		22/07/88	D	23	(2)	2
6	Nemanja Maksimović	SRB	26/01/95	M	28	(3)	3
25	Sergei Maliy		05/06/90	D	7		
35	Aleksandr Mokin		19/06/81	G	2		
7	Serikzhan Muzhikov		17/06/89	M	26	(1)	3
12	Gevorg Najaryan		06/01/98	M	1		
13	Azat Nurgaliyev		30/06/86	M	10	(1)	6
17	Tanat Nuserbayev		01/01/87	A	18	(7)	6
44	Evgeni Postnikov		16/04/86	D	16		
11	Aleksei Shchetkin		21/05/91	A		(15)	
14	Igor Shitov	BLR	24/10/86	D	7	(2)	
77	Dmitri Shomko		19/03/90	D	28	(1)	1
8	Askhat Tagybergen		09/08/90	M	9	(17)	2
18	Patrick Twumasi	GHA	09/05/94	A	24	(4)	5
71	Madi Zhakipbayev		21/03/00	M	1	(1)	
31	Abay Zhunusov		15/03/95	M	1	(1)	

KAZAKHSTAN

FC Atyrau

1980 • Munayshi (8,900) • rfcatyrau.kz

Major honours
Kazakhstan Cup (1) 2009

Coach: Vladimir Nikitenko; (11/05/16) (Yuri Konkov); (06/06/16) Stoycho Mladenov (BUL)

2016

Date		Opponent		Score	Scorers
12/03	a	Zhetysu	D	1-1	*Konysbayev*
03/04	a	Irtysh	L	0-3	
09/04	h	Kairat	L	0-1	
13/04	a	Okzhetpes	L	0-2	
17/04	h	Akzhayik	W	2-0	*Shabalin, Trytko*
23/04	a	Taraz	D	0-0	
01/05	a	Shakhter	D	0-0	
05/05	h	Ordabasy	D	2-2	*Trytko 2*
09/05	a	Aktobe	L	0-1	
15/05	h	Astana	W	1-0	*Sarapov*
21/05	a	Tobol	W	2-1	*Damcevski, Makas*
29/05	h	Irtysh	L	0-1	
02/06	a	Kairat	L	2-5	*Arzhanov, Curtean*
11/06	h	Okzhetpes	W	2-1	*Shabalin, Trytko*
15/06	a	Akzhayik	W	4-0	*Korobkin, Arzhanov, Sharpar, Curtean*
19/06	h	Taraz	W	1-0	*Damcevski*
25/06	h	Shakhter	D	0-0	
29/06	h	Tobol	D	0-0	
03/07	a	Ordabasy	L	1-2	*Korobkin*
10/07	h	Aktobe	D	1-1	*Arzhanov*
16/07	a	Astana	L	1-2	*Arzhanov*
24/07	h	Zhetysu	W	1-0	*Trytko*
14/08	a	Tobol	D	0-0	
21/08	a	Taraz	L	0-1	
26/08	h	Zhetysu	D	3-3	*Arzhanov 2, Trytko*
10/09	a	Shakhter	L	0-3	
17/09	h	Akzhayik	L	1-2	*Curtean*
25/09	h	Taraz	W	1-0	*Curtean*
01/10	a	Zhetysu	L	3-4	*Fedin, Trytko, Arzhanov*
16/10	h	Shakhter	W	2-0	*Arzhanov, Shabalin*
22/10	a	Akzhayik	L	1-3	*Sharpar*
29/10	h	Tobol	W	3-0	*Sharpar (p), og (Kassai), Essame*

No	Name	Nat	DoB	Pos	Aps	(s)	Gls
9	Volodymyr Arzhanov	UKR	29/11/85	M	31	(1)	8
2	Aldan Baltaev		15/01/89	D	6	(3)	
8	Valentin Chureev		29/08/86	D	11	(5)	
30	Alexandru Curtean	ROU	27/03/87	M	26	(3)	4
21	Aleksandar Damcevski	MKD	21/11/92	D	20	(1)	2
12	Ruslan Esatov		31/10/84	D	15	(3)	
7	Guy Stéphane Essame	CMR	25/11/84	M	27	(1)	1
96	Maksim Fedin		08/06/96	M	4	(9)	1
17	Ulan Konysbayev		28/05/89	M	12	(1)	1
19	Valeri Korobkin		02/07/84	M	23	(2)	2
28	Vladislav Kuzmin		03/07/87	D	16	(4)	
33	Abdel Lamanje	CMR	27/07/90	D	31	(1)	
13	Aleksandr Makas	BLR	08/10/91	A	7	(17)	1
5	Aleksei Marov		02/10/95	M	1	(4)	
3	Aleksei Muldarov		24/04/84	D	27	(1)	
34	Zhasur Narzikulov		13/04/84	G	32		
35	Ramil Nurmukhametov		21/12/87	G		(1)	
6	Altynbek Sarapov		26/04/95	M	13	(8)	1
10	Pavel Shabalin		23/10/88	M	17	(8)	3
11	Vyacheslav Sharpar	UKR	02/06/87	M	13	(7)	3
26	Przemysław Trytko	POL	26/08/87	A	20	(8)	7
14	Nauryzbek Zhagorov		01/03/98	M		(2)	

FC Irtysh Pavlodar

1965 • Tsentralny (11,828) • fcirtysh.kz

Major honours
Kazakhstan League (5) 1993, 1997, 1999, 2002, 2003; Kazakhstan Cup (1) 1998

Coach: Dimitar Dimitrov (BUL)

2016

Date		Opponent		Score	Scorers
13/03	h	Okzhetpes	W	1-0	*Maliy*
19/03	a	Akzhayik	W	3-0	*Akhmetov, Jallow, Murtazayev*
03/04	h	Atyrau	W	3-0	*Murtazayev, Maliy, Gogua*
09/04	a	Shakhter	W	2-0	*Freidgeimas, Kerla*
13/04	h	Ordabasy	W	2-0	*Murtazayev, Gogua (p)*
17/04	a	Aktobe	D	1-1	*Gogua (p)*
23/04	h	Astana	D	2-2	*Akhmetov, Carlos Fonseca*
01/05	a	Zhetysu	W	3-0	*Murtazayev 2, Herrera*
05/05	h	Tobol	W	3-1	*Fall, Murtazayev, Gogua (p)*
09/05	h	Taraz	W	2-1	*Murtazayev, Fall*
15/05	a	Kairat	L	0-1	
21/05	h	Akzhayik	D	0-0	
29/05	a	Atyrau	W	1-0	*Murtazayev*
02/06	h	Shakhter	D	0-0	
11/06	a	Ordabasy	L	0-2	
15/06	h	Aktobe	W	4-1	*Herrera, Murtazayev (p), Akhmetov, Jallow*
19/06	a	Astana	D	1-1	*Kerla*
25/06	h	Zhetysu	W	3-1	*Jallow, Herrera, Murtazayev*
03/07	a	Tobol	L	2-3	*Jirsák, Grigalashvili*
09/07	a	Taraz	L	0-1	
17/07	h	Kairat	L	2-3	*Kerla, Murtazayev (p)*
24/07	a	Okzhetpes	W	2-0	*Murtazayev, Geteriev*
12/08	a	Astana	L	0-3	
20/08	h	Okzhetpes	L	0-2	
26/08	a	Aktobe	L	0-1	
11/09	h	Ordabasy	L	1-2	*Murtazayev*
17/09	a	Kairat	L	1-2	*Grigalashvili*
25/09	a	Okzhetpes	W	4-1	*Carlos Fonseca, Murtazayev 2, Geteriev*
01/10	h	Aktobe	W	5-1	*Grigalashvili, Carlos Fonseca 2, Murtazayev 2*
16/10	a	Ordabasy	D	3-3	*Murtazayev (p), Carlos Fonseca, Akhmetov*
23/10	h	Kairat	L	1-3	*Carlos Fonseca*
29/10	h	Astana	D	0-0	

No	Name	Nat	DoB	Pos	Aps	(s)	Gls
2	Eldos Akhmetov		01/06/90	D	23		4
5	Pirali Aliyev		13/01/84	M	10	(10)	
13	Alibek Ayaganov		13/01/92	M	3	(8)	
40	Carlos Fonseca	POR	23/08/87	M	28		6
8	Damir Dautov		03/03/90	D	9		
25	Ruslan Esimov		28/04/90	D	18	(1)	
9	Baye Djiby Fall	SEN	20/04/85	A	12	(13)	2
4	Georgas Freidgeimas	LTU	10/08/87	D	29		1
33	Kazbek Geteriev		30/06/85	M	23	(4)	2
7	Gogita Gogua	GEO	04/09/83	M	11	(1)	4
11	Shota Grigalashvili	GEO	21/06/86	M	9	(4)	3
10	Ignacio Herrera	CHI	30/10/87	A	13	(15)	3
99	Ousman Jallow	GAM	21/10/88	A	21		3
20	Tomáš Jirsák	CZE	29/06/84	M	27		1
15	Semir Kerla	BIH	26/09/87	D	23	(1)	3
5	Aleksandr Kislitsyn		08/03/86	D	2	(1)	
17	Vitali Li		13/03/94	A	3	(7)	
1	David Loria		31/10/81	G	24		
27	Sergei Maliy		05/06/90	D	14		2
45	Roman Murtazayev		10/09/93	M	30	(2)	18
57	Artem Popov		17/01/98	M	1	(5)	
19	Grigori Sartakov		19/08/94	D	11	(4)	
20	Anton Tsirin		10/08/87	G	8		
77	Vladimir Vomenko		22/05/95	M		(4)	

FC Kairat Almaty

1954 • Tsentralny (23,804) • fckairat.kz

Major honours
Kazakhstan League (2) 1992, 2004; Kazakhstan Cup (7) 1992, 1996, 2000, 2001 (autumn), 2003, 2014, 2015

Coach: Aleksandr Borodyuk (RUS); (07/04/16) Kakhaber Tskhadadze (GEO)

2016

Date		Opponent		Score	Scorers
12/03	a	Taraz	L	1-2	*Li*
19/03	a	Okzhetpes	D	1-1	*Gohou*
03/04	a	Akzhayik	L	1-2	*Li*
09/04	a	Atyrau	W	1-0	*Gohou*
13/04	h	Shakhter	D	0-0	
17/04	a	Ordabasy	L	0-1	
23/04	h	Aktobe	W	3-0	*Marković, Arshavin, Tymoshchuk*
01/05	a	Astana	L	0-1	
05/05	h	Zhetysu	W	2-0	*og (Tyrysbek), Tawamba*
10/05	a	Tobol	W	2-1	*Gohou 2*
15/05	h	Irtysh	W	1-0	*Isael*
21/05	h	Okzhetpes	W	6-0	*Arshavin 2, Islamkhan 2 (1p), Gohou 2*
29/05	h	Akzhayik	W	3-2	*Islamkhan (p), Gohou, Tawamba*
02/06	h	Atyrau	W	5-2	*Islamkhan 2, Isael, Arshavin, Gohou*
11/06	a	Shakhter	W	5-0	*Isael, Gohou, Darabayev, Islamkhan 2 (1p)*
15/06	h	Ordabasy	D	2-2	*Gohou, Marković*
19/06	a	Aktobe	W	6-2	*Tesák, Islamkhan, Gohou 2, Arshavin, Isael*
23/06	h	Astana	W	1-0	*Gohou*
03/07	a	Zhetysu	D	1-1	*Gohou*
10/07	h	Tobol	W	3-2	*Islamkhan, Kuat, Isael*
17/07	a	Irtysh	W	3-2	*Islamkhan (p), Tawamba 2*
24/07	h	Taraz	W	3-1	*Islamkhan, Arshavin, Gohou*
13/08	a	Okzhetpes	W	3-1	*Islamkhan (p), Isael, Acevedo*
20/08	h	Aktobe	W	3-1	*Islamkhan (p), Suyumbayev, Gohou*
26/08	a	Ordabasy	L	1-2	*Kuat*
10/09	a	Astana	W	4-1	*Acevedo, Islamkhan, Gohou, Arshavin*
17/09	h	Irtysh	W	2-1	*Gohou, Islamkhan*
25/09	a	Aktobe	W	1-0	*Arshavin*
01/10	h	Ordabasy	D	1-1	*Gohou*
16/10	h	Astana	W	2-0	*César Arzo, Kuat*
23/10	a	Irtysh	W	3-1	*Gohou 2, Islamkhan*
29/10	h	Okzhetpes	W	5-0	*Gohou, Isael, Islamkhan, Kuat, Suyumbayev*

No	Name	Nat	DoB	Pos	Aps	(s)	Gls
30	Gerson Acevedo	CHI	05/04/88	M	6	(5)	2
28	Andrei Arshavin	RUS	29/05/81	M	25	(3)	8
8	Mikhail Bakaev		05/08/87	M	25	(4)	
4	Bruno Soares	BRA	21/08/88	D	2		
14	César Arzo	ESP	21/01/86	D	12		1
21	Nurlan Dairov		26/06/95	D	1	(2)	
17	Aslan Darabayev		21/01/89	M	6	(10)	1
11	Gerard Gohou	CIV	29/12/88	A	26	(3)	22
10	Isael	BRA	13/05/88	M	27	(2)	7
9	Baurzhan Islamkhan		23/02/93	M	30	(1)	17
13	Yermek Kuantayev		13/10/90	D	14	(2)	
7	Islambek Kuat		12/01/93	M	20	(7)	4
18	Vitali Li		13/03/94	A	2	(9)	2
19	Stanislav Lunin		02/05/93	D	15	(6)	
6	Žarko Marković	SRB	28/01/87	D	28		2
1	Vladimir Plotnikov		03/04/86	G	23	(1)	
27	Stas Pokatilov		08/12/92	G	8		
22	Madiyar Raimbek		15/08/95	A		(1)	
2	Timur Rudoselskiy		21/12/94	D	18	(4)	
16	Andrei Sidelnikov		08/03/80	G	1		
15	Sito Riera	ESP	05/01/87	A	1	(1)	
23	Gafurzhan Suyumbayev		19/08/90	D	13		2
20	Leandre Tawamba	CMR	20/12/89	A	6	(16)	4
5	Lukáš Tesák	SVK	08/03/85	D	18		1
15	Baurzhan Turysbek		15/10/91	M		(9)	
44	Anatoliy Tymoshchuk	UKR	30/03/79	M	24		1
3	Yan Vorogovskiy		07/08/96	D	1	(5)	

FC Okzhetpes Kokshetau

1957 • Okzhetpes (4,158) • okzhetpes.kz

Coach: Vladimir Mukhanov (RUS)

2016

Date		Opponent		Score	Scorers
13/03	a	Irtysh	L	0-1	
19/03	h	Kairat	D	1-1	*Buleshev*
03/04	a	Taraz	W	3-1	*Buleshev (p), Chichulin, N'Ganbe*
09/04	a	Akzhayik	W	2-0	*Buleshev, Ristović*
13/04	h	Atyrau	W	2-0	*Khairullin, Moldakaraev*
17/04	a	Shakhter	W	1-0	*Chizhov*
23/04	h	Ordabasy	W	2-0	*Chizhov, Moldakaraev*
01/05	a	Aktobe	L	0-1	
05/05	h	Astana	L	0-1	
10/05	a	Zhetysu	W	4-1	*Khairullin 2, N'Ganbe, Moldakaraev*
15/05	h	Tobol	D	1-1	*N'Ganbe*
21/05	a	Kairat	L	0-6	
29/05	h	Taraz	D	0-0	
02/06	h	Akzhayik	W	4-2	*N'Ganbe 2, Ristović, Khairullin*
11/06	a	Atyrau	L	1-2	*N'Ganbe*
15/06	h	Shakhter	W	3-0	*Moldakaraev 2 (1p), Chertov*
19/06	a	Ordabasy	D	2-2	*Buleshev, Yurin*
24/06	h	Aktobe	W	4-1	*Khairullin 2, Kislitsyn, Buleshev*
05/07	a	Astana	L	0-1	
10/07	h	Zhetysu	W	2-0	*Buleshev, Moldakaraev*
16/07	a	Tobol	W	1-0	*Yurin*
24/07	h	Irtysh	L	0-2	
13/08	h	Kairat	L	1-3	*Canales*
20/08	a	Irtysh	W	2-0	*Canales, Khairullin*
12/09	h	Aktobe	L	0-3	
17/09	a	Ordabasy	L	0-1	
25/09	h	Irtysh	L	1-4	*Khairullin (p)*
02/10	a	Astana	L	0-3	
16/10	a	Aktobe	D	2-2	*N'Ganbe 2*
23/10	h	Ordabasy	W	3-0	*N'Ganbe, Ristović, Zhumakhanov*
26/10	h	Astana	D	0-0	
29/10	a	Kairat	L	0-5	

No	Name	Nat	DoB	Pos	Aps	(s)	Gls
56	Sultan Abylgazy		22/02/97	A	1	(3)	
33	Aleksandr Alkhazov	RUS	27/05/84	A	1	(3)	
24	Dzhurakhon Babakhanov		31/10/91	G	3		
5	Anatoli Bogdanov		07/08/81	M	3	(1)	
10	Alibek Buleshev		09/04/81	A	10	(13)	6
32	Nicolás Canales	CHI	27/06/85	A	5	(6)	2
88	Daniil Chertov	RUS	15/11/90	D	18	(2)	1
66	Anton Chichulin		27/10/84	D	21		1
77	Olexandr Chizhov	UKR	10/08/86	D	26		2
19	Marat Khairullin		26/04/84	M	27		8
4	Aleksandr Kislitsyn		08/03/86	D	8	(1)	1
10	Zhakyp Kozhamberdy		26/02/92	M	15	(7)	
15	Anton Kuksin		03/07/95	D	16	(7)	
6	Ilnur Mangutkin		16/09/86	D	24		
17	Zhasulan Moldakaraev		07/05/87	A	25	(6)	6
88	Serge Bando N'Ganbe	CMR	11/05/88	M	22	(6)	9
29	Joseph Nane	CMR	12/03/87	M	30		
16	Risto Ristović	SRB	05/05/88	M	12	(13)	3
1	Saša Stamenković	SRB	05/01/85	G	29		
23	Miras Tuliev		30/08/94	D	5	(1)	
11	Vitali Volkov	RUS	22/03/81	M	27	(4)	
14	Igor Yurin		03/07/82	M	19	(6)	2
43	Yerlan Zhaguparov		16/09/95	M		(1)	
7	Sanat Zhumakhanov		30/01/88	M	5	(11)	1

FC Ordabasy Shymkent

2000 • Kazhimukan Munaitpasov (20,000) • fcordabasy.kz

Major honours

Kazakhstan Cup (1) 2011

Coach: Bakhtiyar Baiseitov

2016

Date		Opponent		Score	Scorers
13/03	h	Aktobe	W	3-1	*Nurgaliyev 2, Junuzović*
20/03	h	Astana	L	1-3	*Junuzović*
03/04	a	Zhetysu	W	2-1	*Junuzović, Nurgaliyev*
09/04	h	Tobol	D	2-2	*Tolebek, Diakhate*
13/04	a	Irtysh	L	0-2	
17/04	h	Kairat	W	1-0	*Kasalica*
23/04	a	Okzhetpes	L	0-2	
01/05	h	Akzhayik	W	1-0	*Tazhimbetov*
05/05	a	Atyrau	D	2-2	*Kasalica, og (Narzikulov)*
09/05	h	Shakhter	W	2-0	*Nurgaliyev (p), Tunggyshbayev*
14/05	a	Taraz	W	2-1	*Kasalica 2*
21/05	a	Astana	L	1-3	*Simčević*
29/05	h	Zhetysu	L	0-1	
02/06	a	Tobol	L	0-1	
11/06	h	Irtysh	W	2-0	*Nurgaliyev 2 (1p)*
15/06	a	Kairat	D	2-2	*Tolebek, Simčević*
19/06	h	Okzhetpes	D	2-2	*Diakhate, Suyumbayev*
24/06	a	Akzhayik	W	1-0	*Suyumbayev*
03/07	h	Atyrau	W	2-1	*Gogua (p), Tunggyshbayev*
10/07	a	Shakhter	D	0-0	
17/07	h	Taraz	L	0-3	
24/07	a	Aktobe	D	0-0	
13/08	a	Aktobe	D	4-4	*Martsvaladze, Geynrikh 3 (2p)*
21/08	a	Astana	L	0-2	
26/08	h	Kairat	W	2-1	*Geynrikh, Martsvaladze*
11/09	a	Irtysh	W	2-1	*Geynrikh 2 (1p)*
17/09	h	Okzhetpes	W	1-0	*Geynrikh*
25/09	h	Astana	L	0-1	
01/10	a	Kairat	D	1-1	*Tunggyshbayev*
16/10	h	Irtysh	D	3-3	*Geynrikh 2 (2p), Diakhate*
23/10	a	Okzhetpes	L	0-3	
29/10	h	Aktobe	W	2-1	*Tolebek, Geynrikh (p)*

No	Name	Nat	DoB	Pos	Aps	(s)	Gls
23	Renat Abdulin		14/04/82	D	26	(1)	
77	Talgat Adyrbekov		26/01/89	D	6	(6)	
10	Kairat Ashirbekov		21/10/82	M	6	(5)	
1	Almat Bekbayev		14/07/84	G	16		
8	Bekzat Beysenov		18/02/87	M	1	(13)	
29	Sergei Boychenko		27/09/77	G	16		
6	Dominic Chatto	NGA	07/12/85	M	25	(4)	
22	Abdoulaye Diakhate	SEN	16/01/88	M	31		3
32	Temirlan Erlanov		09/07/93	D	2	(1)	
50	Aleksandr Geynrikh	UZB	06/10/84	M	14	(6)	10
7	Gogita Gogua	GEO	04/09/83	M	14	(2)	1
14	Farhadbek Irismetov		10/08/81	D	2	(3)	
28	Edin Junuzović	CRO	28/04/86	A	8	(3)	3
9	Filip Kasalica	MNE	17/12/88	A	19	(7)	4
2	Bakdaulet Kozhabayev		19/06/92	D	13	(9)	
88	Otar Martsvaladze	GEO	14/07/84	A	7	(3)	2
4	Mukhtar Mukhtarov		01/01/86	D	11	(3)	
7	Azat Nurgaliyev		30/06/86	M	17		6
87	Aleksandar Simčević	SRB	15/02/87	D	27	(2)	2
18	Samat Smakov		08/12/78	M	8		
5	Gafurzhan Suyumbayev		19/08/90	D	15		2
18	Daurenbek Tazhimbetov		02/07/85	A		(7)	1
17	Mardan Tolebek		18/12/90	M	19	(9)	3
15	Branislav Trajković	SRB	29/08/89	D	24		
89	Miloš Trifunović	SRB	15/10/84	A	1	(3)	
21	Yerkebulan Tunggyshbayev		14/01/95	M	24	(4)	3

FC Shakhter Karagandy

1958 • Shakhter (19,500) • shahter.kz

Major honours

Kazakhstan League (2) 2011, 2012; Kazakhstan Cup (1) 2013

Coach: Jozef Vukušič (SVK); (04/08/16) Aleksei Yeryomenko (RUS)

2016

Date		Opponent		Score	Scorers
12/03	a	Astana	L	1-2	*Ubbink*
20/03	h	Zhetysu	D	0-0	
03/04	a	Tobol	L	0-3	
09/04	h	Irtysh	L	0-2	
13/04	a	Kairat	D	0-0	
17/04	h	Okzhetpes	L	0-1	
23/04	a	Akzhayik	W	1-0	*Finonchenko*
01/05	h	Atyrau	D	0-0	
05/05	a	Taraz	W	2-1	*Skorykh, Finonchenko*
09/05	a	Ordabasy	L	0-2	
14/05	h	Aktobe	L	0-2	
21/05	a	Zhetysu	L	0-2	
29/05	h	Tobol	W	1-0	*Bayzhanov*
02/06	a	Irtysh	D	0-0	
11/06	h	Kairat	L	0-5	
15/06	a	Okzhetpes	L	0-3	
19/06	h	Akzhayik	W	3-1	*Vasiljević, Ubbink 2*
25/06	a	Atyrau	D	0-0	
02/07	h	Taraz	L	0-1	
10/07	h	Ordabasy	D	0-0	
17/07	a	Aktobe	L	0-2	
07/08	h	Astana	W	2-0	*Vasiljević, Goriachiy*
14/08	h	Taraz	W	1-0	*Ubbink*
21/08	h	Akzhayik	L	0-1	
26/08	a	Tobol	L	0-2	
10/09	h	Atyrau	W	3-0	*Zošák, Skorykh, Tattybaev*
18/09	a	Zhetysu	W	2-1	*Szöke, Goriachiy*
24/09	a	Akzhayik	W	2-1	*Goriachiy, Szöke*
01/10	h	Tobol	L	2-3	*Simonovski 2*
16/10	a	Atyrau	L	0-2	
22/10	h	Zhetysu	W	4-1	*Szöke, Bayzhanov 2, Ubbink*
29/10	a	Taraz	L	1-2	*Ubbink*

No	Name	Nat	DoB	Pos	Aps	(s)	Gls
5	Robert Arzumanyan	ARM	24/07/85	D	8		
1	Yaroslav Baginski		03/10/87	G	14		
11	Maksat Bayzhanov		06/08/84	M	32		3
15	Grigori Dubkov		22/11/90	D	2	(3)	
14	Andrei Finonchenko		21/06/82	A	11	(4)	2
4	Mikhail Gabyshev		02/01/90	D	15	(2)	
77	Evgeni Goriachiy		02/02/91	D	10	(9)	3
24	Olexiy Kurilov	UKR	24/04/88	D	4		
17	Aybar Nuribekov		29/08/92	A	12	(10)	
98	Oralkhan Omirtayev		16/07/98	A		(5)	
34	Igor Pikalkin		19/03/92	D	21	(4)	
71	Vyatceslav Putintsev		25/09/97	A		(2)	
20	Ivan Sadovnichi	BLR	11/05/87	D	30		
89	Filip Serečin	SVK	04/10/89	A	3	(1)	
30	Igor Shatskiy		11/05/89	G	16	(1)	
24	Marko Simonovski	MKD	02/01/92	A	7	(3)	2
84	Sergei Skorykh		25/05/84	M	26	(4)	2
27	Július Szöke	SVK	01/08/95	M	29		3
19	Evgeni Tarasov		16/04/85	D	17	(3)	
9	Aydos Tattybaev		26/04/90	A	4	(15)	1
25	Sergei Tkachuk		15/02/92	G	2		
7	Desley Ubbink	NED	15/06/93	M	29	(1)	6
3	Nikola Vasiljević	BIH	19/12/83	D	16		2
88	Vladislav Vassiljev		10/04/97	A		(2)	
16	Sergei Vetrov		11/11/94	A	4	(6)	
97	Moshtagh Yaghoubi	FIN	08/11/94	M	5	(6)	
44	Kuanysh Yermekov		14/04/94	M	11	(5)	
10	Erfan Zeneli	FIN	28/12/86	M	10	(4)	
18	Štefan Zošák	SVK	03/04/84	M	14		1

KAZAKHSTAN

FC Taraz

1960 • Tsentralny (12,527) • fctaraz.kz

Major honours
Kazakhstan League (1) 1996; Kazakhstan Cup (1) 2004

Coach: Nurmat Mirzabayev; (15/05/16) Yuriy Maksymov (UKR)

2016					
12/03	h	Kairat	W	2-1	*Zenkovich, Danilyuk*
19/03	h	Aktobe	D	1-1	*Zenkovich*
03/04	h	Okzhetpes	L	1-3	*Shakhmetov*
09/04	a	Astana	L	1-2	*Zenkovich*
13/04	h	Akzhayik	L	0-1	
17/04	a	Zhetysu	L	1-2	*Mané*
23/04	h	Atyrau	D	0-0	
01/05	a	Tobol	L	0-1	
05/05	h	Shakhter	L	1-2	*Baytana*
09/05	a	Irtysh	L	1-2	*Mané*
14/05	h	Ordabasy	L	1-2	*Mané*
21/05	a	Aktobe	D	2-2	*V Yevstigneev, Mané*
29/05	a	Okzhetpes	D	0-0	
02/06	h	Astana	L	0-2	
11/06	a	Akzhayik	L	1-2	*Aliyev*
15/06	h	Zhetysu	L	2-3	*Mané, Mera*
19/06	a	Atyrau	L	0-1	
25/06	h	Tobol	W	2-0	*Tazhimbetov, Mané*
02/07	a	Shakhter	W	1-0	*Mané*
09/07	h	Irtysh	W	1-0	*Mera*
17/07	a	Ordabasy	W	3-0	*Yakovlev, Suley 2*
24/07	a	Kairat	L	1-3	*Tazhimbetov*
14/08	a	Shakhter	L	0-1	
21/08	h	Atyrau	W	1-0	*Mané*
26/08	a	Akzhayik	L	0-2	
10/09	h	Zhetysu	W	3-2	*Mané 3 (1p)*
18/09	a	Tobol	L	1-3	*Yakovlev*
25/09	a	Atyrau	L	0-1	
01/10	h	Akzhayik	W	2-1	*Mané (p), Suley*
16/10	a	Zhetysu	D	0-0	
22/10	h	Tobol	W	2-1	*Mané, Mera*
29/10	h	Shakhter	W	2-1	*Erghashev, Kirov*

No	Name	Nat	DoB	Pos	Aps	(s)	Gls
44	Adilet Abdenabi		04/02/96	M		(2)	
88	Olexandr Aliyev	UKR	03/02/85	M	3	(6)	1
21	Maksat Amirkhanov		10/02/92	D	9	(6)	
14	Berik Aytbaev		26/06/91	D	6	(5)	
11	Sherkhan Bauyrzhan		28/08/92	M		(3)	
2	Daniyar Bayaliev		30/01/93	D	12	(3)	
10	Baurzhan Baytana		06/06/92	M	11	(4)	1
25	Taras Danilyuk	UKR	29/01/84	D	28	(3)	1
84	Davron Erghashev	TJK	19/03/88	M	14		1
5	Jovan Golić	SRB	18/09/86	M	2		
1	Aleksandr Grigorenko		06/02/85	G	30		
85	Anton Grigoryev	RUS	13/12/85	M	14	(1)	
23	Kurmet Karaman		02/08/95	D	6	(2)	
13	Kanat Karimolla		06/02/95	M		(2)	
15	Ardak Karpyk		01/04/92	M	1	(2)	
99	Aleksandr Kirov		04/06/84	D	13		1
80	Kiril Korotkevich		12/06/92	G	2	(1)	
11	Malick Mané	SEN	14/10/88	M	30		13
12	Ioan Mera	ROU	05/01/87	D	24	(1)	3
17	Oleg Nedashkovsky		09/09/87	M	3	(2)	
22	Madiyar Nuraly		20/01/95	D	9	(8)	
75	Olexandr Pishchur	UKR	26/01/81	A	9	(2)	
21	Bakhytzhan Rymtaev		01/02/95	M	1	(4)	
6	Marat Shakhmetov		06/02/89	M	11	(4)	1
7	Alisher Suley		01/11/95	M	20	(9)	3
3	Abzal Taubay		18/02/95	M	10	(9)	
71	Daurenbek Tazhimbetov		02/07/85	A	15		2
4	Ilya Vorotnikov		01/02/86	D	27	(1)	
67	Andriy Yakovlev	UKR	20/02/89	M	14	(2)	2
19	Dmitri Yevstigneev		27/11/86	D	14	(5)	
8	Vitali Yevstigneev		08/05/85	M	8	(4)	1
78	Igor Zenkovich	BLR	17/09/87	A	6		3

FC Tobol Kostanay

1967 • Tsentralny (8,050) • fc-tobol.kz

Major honours
Kazakhstan League (1) 2010; Kazakhstan Cup (1) 2007

Coach: Dmitriy Ogay; (30/04/16) Oleg Lotov; (30/05/16) Omari Tetradze (RUS)

2016					
13/03	h	Akzhayik	W	1-0	*Dudchenko*
03/04	h	Shakhter	W	3-0	*Yavorskiy, Simkovic, Khizhnichenko*
09/04	a	Ordabasy	D	2-2	Simkovic, Zhumaskaliyev
13/04	h	Aktobe	L	1-2	*Dudchenko*
17/04	a	Astana	L	0-1	
23/04	h	Zhetysu	D	2-2	*Dzhalilov 2*
01/05	h	Taraz	W	1-0	*N'Diaye*
05/05	a	Irtysh	L	1-3	*Zhumaskaliyev*
10/05	h	Kairat	L	1-2	*Simkovic (p)*
15/05	a	Okzhetpes	D	1-1	*Khizhnichenko*
21/05	h	Atyrau	L	1-2	*Zhumaskaliyev*
29/05	a	Shakhter	L	0-1	
02/06	h	Ordabasy	W	1-0	*Khizhnichenko*
11/06	a	Aktobe	W	1-0	*Yavorskiy*
15/06	h	Astana	L	1-2	*Levin*
19/06	a	Zhetysu	W	1-0	*Simkovic (p)*
25/06	a	Taraz	L	0-2	
29/06	a	Atyrau	D	0-0	
03/07	h	Irtysh	W	3-2	*Žulpa, Simkovic (p), Asildarov (p)*
10/07	a	Kairat	L	2-3	*Žulpa, Khizhnichenko*
16/07	h	Okzhetpes	L	0-1	
24/07	a	Akzhayik	W	5-0	*Savic 2, Žulpa, Zhumaskaliyev, Khizhnichenko*
14/08	h	Atyrau	D	0-0	
21/08	a	Zhetysu	L	0-2	
26/08	h	Shakhter	W	2-0	*Khizhnichenko 2*
10/09	a	Akzhayik	L	0-1	
18/09	h	Taraz	W	3-1	*Glavina, Simkovic (p), Asildarov*
24/09	h	Zhetysu	W	3-2	*Simkovic (p), Khizhnichenko 2*
01/10	a	Shakhter	W	3-2	*Khizhnichenko, Simkovic, Deac*
16/10	h	Akzhayik	L	0-1	
22/10	a	Taraz	L	1-2	*Deac*
29/10	a	Atyrau	L	0-3	

No	Name	Nat	DoB	Pos	Aps	(s)	Gls
10	Shamil Asildarov	RUS	18/05/83	A	8	(10)	2
2	Rafkat Aslan		02/02/94	D	1		
30	Sultan Busurmanov		10/05/96	G	1		
22	Ciprian Deac	ROU	16/02/86	M	29	(2)	2
8	Viktor Dmitrenko		04/04/91	D	16	(2)	
7	Timur Dosmagambetov		01/05/89	M	9	(14)	
14	Kostyantyn Dudchenko	UKR	08/07/86	A	3	(8)	2
11	Raul Dzhalilov		20/07/94	M	7	(12)	2
50	Temirlan Elmurzayev		03/01/96	A		(2)	
3	Denis Glavina	CRO	03/03/86	D	26	(1)	1
18	Mark Gurman		09/02/89	D	13	(1)	
4	Fernander Kassaï	CTA	01/07/87	D	25		
91	Sergei Khizhnichenko		17/07/91	A	20	(8)	10
19	Nurtas Kurgulin		20/09/86	D	2	(3)	
4	Evgeni Levin		12/07/92	M	2	(2)	1
85	Vladimir Loginovski		08/10/85	G	24		
17	Dmitri Miroshnichenko		26/02/92	D	29	(1)	
77	Almir Mukhutdinov		09/06/85	M	21	(2)	
25	Alassane N'Diaye	FRA	25/02/90	M	3	(7)	1
35	Aleksandr Petukhov		11/01/85	G	7		
6	Rakhimzhan Rozybakiev		02/01/91	M	2	(1)	
20	Dusan Savic	MKD	01/01/85	A	8	(1)	2
81	Tomas Simkovic	AUT	16/04/87	M	25	(3)	8
23	Serhiy Yavorskiy	UKR	05/07/89	D	26	(2)	2
37	Aleksandr Zhukov		04/11/97	D		(1)	
9	Nurbol Zhumaskaliyev		11/05/81	M	24	(3)	4
5	Artūras Žulpa	LTU	10/06/90	M	21	(2)	3

FC Zhetysu Taldykorgan

1981 • Zhetysu (5,550) • fc-zhetisu.kz

Coach: Almas Kulshinbaev

2016					
12/03	h	Atyrau	D	1-1	*Tyrysbek*
20/03	a	Shakhter	D	0-0	
03/04	h	Ordabasy	L	1-2	*Kadio*
09/04	a	Aktobe	L	2-3	*Klein, Savic*
13/04	h	Astana	L	0-1	
17/04	h	Taraz	W	2-1	*Savic, Simonovski*
23/04	a	Tobol	D	2-2	*Savic, Tyrysbek*
01/05	h	Irtysh	L	0-3	
05/05	a	Kairat	L	0-2	
10/05	h	Okzhetpes	L	1-4	*Simonovski*
15/05	a	Akzhayik	W	2-1	*Simonovski, Savic (p)*
21/05	h	Shakhter	W	2-0	*Savic, Kalinin*
29/05	a	Ordabasy	W	1-0	*Savic*
02/06	h	Aktobe	D	1-1	*Amirseitov*
11/06	a	Astana	L	0-1	
15/06	a	Taraz	W	3-2	*Savic 3*
19/06	h	Tobol	L	0-1	
25/06	a	Irtysh	L	1-3	*Borovskiy*
03/07	h	Kairat	D	1-1	*Savic*
10/07	a	Okzhetpes	L	0-2	
16/07	h	Akzhayik	W	2-0	*Djalović, Kadio*
24/07	a	Atyrau	L	0-1	
14/08	a	Akzhayik	L	0-1	
21/08	h	Tobol	W	2-0	*Beglaryan, Kasyanov*
26/08	a	Atyrau	D	3-3	*Djermanovič, Djalović, Beglaryan*
10/09	a	Taraz	L	2-3	*Borovskiy, Zhangylyshbay*
18/09	h	Shakhter	L	1-2	*Djermanovič*
24/09	a	Tobol	L	2-3	*Djermanovič, Borovskiy*
01/10	h	Atyrau	W	4-3	*Kasyanov, Djermanovič 2, Zhangylyshbay*
16/10	h	Taraz	D	0-0	
22/10	a	Shakhter	L	1-4	*Azovskiy*
29/10	h	Akzhayik	L	0-2	

No	Name	Nat	DoB	Pos	Aps	(s)	Gls
2	Timerlan Adilkhanov		28/03/94	D	12	(4)	
13	Ilyas Amirseitov		22/10/89	D	27	(2)	1
18	Maksim Azovskiy		04/06/86	D	12	(6)	1
23	Adyl Balgabaev		13/07/95	M		(2)	
15	Ruslan Barzukayev		05/12/87	M		(1)	
14	Narek Beglaryan	ARM	01/09/85	A	8	(3)	2
11	Vadim Borovskiy		30/10/86	M	12	(5)	3
87	Boti Demel	CIV	03/03/89	A	2	(3)	
86	Marko Djalović	SRB	19/05/86	D	28		2
9	Dejan Djermanovič	SVN	17/06/88	A	10	(2)	5
3	Didier Kadio	CIV	05/04/90	D	21		2
22	Ilya Kalinin		03/02/92	M	21	(11)	1
88	Artem Kasyanov	UKR	20/04/83	M	15	(2)	2
6	Mikhail Kharun-Zade		02/02/96	M	1	(4)	
44	Martin Klein	CZE	02/07/84	D	30		1
14	Gjorgi Mojsov	MKD	27/05/85	M	8	(6)	
23	Askhat Mynbaev		21/02/91	D		(2)	
17	Dias Mynbaev		06/12/95	D		(5)	
19	Daniyar Nurzhumaev		19/06/96	M		(1)	
20	Andrei Pasechenko		09/08/87	G	13		
7	Filip Rudik	BLR	22/03/87	M	7		
8	Serik Sagyndykov		09/01/84	M	16	(7)	
10	Dusan Savic	MKD	01/01/85	A	19		10
27	Andrei Shabaev		15/02/87	D	20	(1)	
1	Andrei Shabanov		17/11/86	G	19		
13	Berik Shaikhov		20/02/94	M	11	(1)	
24	Marko Simonovski	MKD	02/01/92	A	12	(5)	3
9	Baurzhan Tyrysbek		15/10/91	M	15	(2)	2
90	Mamadou Wague	FRA	19/08/90	D	10	(3)	
10	Tokhtar Zhangylyshbay		25/05/93	A	3	(9)	2

Top goalscorers

22 Gerard Gohou (Kairat)
18 Roman Murtazayev (Irtysh)
17 Baurzhan Islamkhan (Kairat)
13 Malick Mané (Taraz)
12 Azat Nurgaliyev (Ordabasy/Astana)
Dusan Savic (Zhetysu/Tobol)
10 Aleksandr Geynrikh (Ordabasy)
Sergei Khizhnichenko (Tobol)
9 Serge Bando N'Ganbe (Okzhetpes)
8 Freddy Coronel (Akzhayik)
Djordje Despotović (Astana)
Volodymyr Arzhanov (Atyrau)
Andrei Arshavin (Kairat)
Marat Khairullin (Okzhetpes)
Tomas Simkovic (Tobol)

Promoted club

FC Kaysar Kyzylorda

1968 • Ghani Muratbayev (7,000) • fckaysar.kz
Major honours
Kazakhstan Cup (1) 1999
Coach: Sultan Abildayev

Second level final table 2016

		Pld	W	D	L	F	A	Pts
1	FC Kaysar Kyzylorda	28	20	7	1	49	9	67
2	FC Altai Semey	28	17	7	4	49	17	58
3	FC Kyzylzhar Petropavlovsk SK	28	14	9	5	45	25	51
4	FC Kaspiy Aktau	28	12	7	9	38	29	43
5	FC Makhtaaral Zhetysay	28	11	8	9	31	31	41
6	FC Ekibastuz	28	8	6	14	17	27	30
7	FC Kyran Shymkent	24	11	1	12	31	26	34
8	FC Shakhter-Bolat Temirtau	24	5	4	15	23	37	19
9	FC Baykonur Kyzylorda	24	4	2	18	17	54	14
10	FC Bayterek Astana	24	4	1	19	17	62	13

NB League splits into top six and bottom four after 18 games, after which the clubs play exclusively against teams in their group.

Promotion/Relegation play-off

(05/11/16)
Taraz 0-3 Altai

NB FC Altai Semey were subsequently denied licence for 2017 Premier League.

DOMESTIC CUP

Kubok Kazakhstana 2016

THIRD ROUND

(26/04/16)
Astana 1-0 Kaspiy

(27/04/16)
Aktobe 0-1 Zhetysu
Akzhayik 0-1 Irtysh
Atyrau 1-0 Altai Semey
Kairat 4-0 Shakhter
Okzhetpes 2-1 Taraz
Ordabasy 2-0 Kaysar
Tobol 0-0 Kyzylzhar *(aet; 2-4 on pens)*

QUARTER-FINALS

(25/05/16)
Atyrau 1-1 Ordabasy *(Arzhanov 71; Abdulin 90) (aet; 4-1 on pens)*

Kyzylzhar 2-3 Astana *(Burtsev 69, Stupić 80; Despotović 33, 65, Tagybergen 73)*

Okzhetpes 1-2 Irtysh *(Chertov 49; Carlos Fonseca 41, Fall 73)*

Zhetysu 0-2 Kairat *(Lunin 4, Djalović 14og)*

SEMI-FINALS

(21/09/16 & 05/11/16)
Kairat 1-0 Atyrau *(Kuat 72)*
Atyrau 0-3 Kairat *(Suyumbayev 2, Arshavin 65, Acevedo 90+2)*
(Kairat 4-0)

(21/09/16 & 06/11/16)
Irtysh 1-2 Astana *(Murtazayev 33; Tagybergen 23, Nuserbayev 37)*
Astana 5-3 Irtysh *(Despotović 19, Kabananga 35, 62, Maliy 84, Cañas 90+2; Smailov 37, 48, Carlos Fonseca 45)*
(Astana 7-4)

FINAL

(19/11/16)
Tsentralny, Almaty
FC ASTANA 1 *(Kabananga 47)*
FC KAIRAT ALMATY 0
Referee: *Duzmambetov*
ASTANA: *Mokin, Shitov, Logvinenko, Aničić, Shomko, Beysebekov, Maksimović, Cañas, Twumasi (Despotović 64), Kabananga (Maliy 87), Muzhikov (Nuserbayev 82)*
KAIRAT: *Pokatilov, Kuat, César Arzo, Marković, Suyumbayev, Bakaev, Tymoshchuk, Isael, Islamkhan, Arshavin, Gohou*

FC Astana secured a first domestic double with a 1-0 victory in the cup final against Kairat

KOSOVO

Federata e Futbollit e Kosovës (FFK)

Address	Rruga 28 Nëntori XK-10000 Prishtina
Tel	+381 38 226 223
Fax	+381 38 226 225
E-mail	ffk-kosova@hotmail.com
Website	ffk-kosova.com

President	Fadil Vokrri
General secretary	Eroll Salihu
Media officer	Fazil Berisha
Year of formation	1946

SUPERLIGA CLUBS

 1 **KF Besa**

 2 **KF Drenica**

 3 **FC Drita**

 4 **KF Ferizaj**

 5 **KF Feronikeli**

 6 **KF Gjilani**

 7 **KF Hajvalia**

 8 **KF Liria**

 9 **KF Llapi**

 10 **FC Prishtina**

 11 **KF Trepça**

 12 **KF Trepça'89**

PROMOTED CLUBS

 13 **KF Flamurtari**

 14 **FC Vëllaznimi**

 15 **KF Vllaznia**

KEY

- UEFA Champions League
- UEFA Europa League
- Promoted
- Relegated

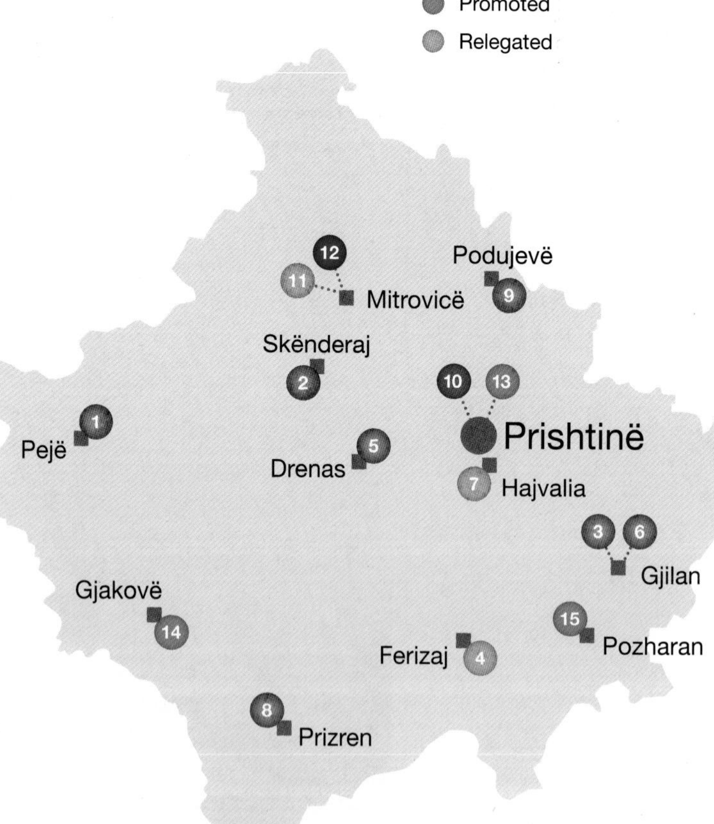

Historic triumph for Trepça'89

The admission of the Football Federation of Kosovo to UEFA in May 2016 brought new meaning to the country's domestic Superliga, and the honour of becoming the first team to win the league and gain access to the UEFA Champions League went to FK Trepça'89.

The club from Mitrovica had never previously won the title, but they led virtually throughout the 2016/17 season, a posse of pursuers never quite getting close enough to put them under undue pressure. The Kosovan Cup was won by sixth-placed Besa, who beat Llapi on penalties in the final.

First league title for team from Mitrovica

European entry also for runners-up Prishtina

National team make debut in competitive arena

Domestic league

Defending champions Feronikeli were seeking a hat-trick of Superliga successes, but they started poorly, losing their opening two fixtures, and although they recovered to beat Trepça'89 4-1, those would be the only points dropped by their opponents in the first 11 matches. Inspired by the prolific goalscoring of 18-year-old Nigerian striker Otto John, Trepça'89 soared to the top of the table and, despite valiant runs at them from record ten-time champions Prishtina, Llapi and – belatedly – Feronikeli, they remained unmoved for the rest of the campaign.

Three points clear at the winter break, Trepça'89 strengthened their position in the spring, winning their first six games, including a vital 1-0 success against Prishtina, in which John scored the only goal. There was no stopping the leaders now, and although they were on to their third coach of the season in Zekerlja Ramadani, their team was settled and overflowing with confidence. With three matches still to play, they made mathematically certain of their maiden title with a 2-0 win at Besa.

Dead-rubber defeats against Prishtina and Feronikeli in their last two games served only to distort the final figures. The truth was that Trepça'89 had been a class apart in terms of both consistency and their ability to score goals, John finishing with a personal contribution of 27 to the team's final total of 72 – 26 more than Prishtina, whose strong finish earned them second place and, ultimately, the honour of being Kosovo's first representative in the UEFA Europa League. The club from the capital boasted the league's best defence – assisted by two veteran Albanian internationals, Armend Dallku and Debatik Curri.

Llapi, who finished third, were the only one of the 12 Superliga clubs to employ the same coach from start to finish, Tahir Batatina claiming that distinction. 2015/16 runners-up Hajvalia only used two but that was one more than the number of victories they registered. Trepça were the other team relegated automatically, with Ferizaj also falling through the trapdoor after a penalty shoot-out defeat in their play-off.

Domestic cup

The narrative of the 2016/17 Kosovan Cup was dominated by penalties. Trepça'89 were knocked out by local rivals and near-namesakes Trepça when they lost a shoot-out in the quarter-finals, and in the final Besa, who thrashed Trepça 6-0 in the second leg of the semis, also prevailed against Llapi on spot kicks after both goals in regulation play had come from penalties. Defeat meant no first major trophy for Llapi, whereas victory earned Besa their third cup win after previous successes in 2005 and 2011.

National team

Although there were no Superliga clubs in European club action during 2016/17, a late spot was found for the Kosovo national team in the 2018 FIFA World Cup qualifying campaign. It would begin brightly with a 1-1 draw in Finland – in which midfielder Valon Berisha, who had won 20 senior caps for Norway before opting to switch international allegiance, became the first player to score for Kosovo in a competitive international – but be followed by five defeats. The country's first three home qualifiers all took place in the northern Albanian town of Shkoder, the first of them resulting in a 6-0 mauling by Croatia.

Coach Albert Bunjaku selected 26 players for World Cup duty and not one of them belonged to a Kosovan club. Indeed, they were scattered far and wide, from Australia to Iceland, with Germany the most popular country of residence. Berisha, voted Kosovan player of the year in January, was the team's most productive export, winning the Austrian double with Salzburg, while Milot Rashica, another ever-present World Cup starter, lifted the Dutch Cup with Vitesse.

DOMESTIC SEASON AT A GLANCE

Superliga 2016/17 final table

			Home					Away					Total					
		Pld	W	D	L	F	A	W	D	L	F	A	W	D	L	F	A	Pts
1	**KF Trepça'89**	**33**	**13**	**3**	**1**	**43**	**11**	**11**	**2**	**3**	**29**	**13**	**24**	**5**	**4**	**72**	**24**	**77**
2	FC Prishtina	33	13	1	3	28	9	9	5	2	18	9	22	6	5	46	18	72
3	KF Llapi	33	14	2	1	29	8	7	3	6	15	22	21	5	7	44	30	68
4	KF Feronikeli	33	11	2	4	36	14	9	3	4	25	13	20	5	8	61	27	65
5	KF Gjilani	33	8	4	5	19	10	5	5	6	17	18	13	9	11	36	28	48
6	KF Besa	33	8	4	5	23	16	5	4	7	19	23	13	8	12	42	39	47
7	KF Drenica	33	7	6	3	23	14	3	4	10	14	33	10	10	13	37	47	40
8	KF Liria	33	8	4	4	30	14	2	3	12	11	25	10	7	16	41	39	37
9	FC Drita	33	5	4	7	13	15	4	4	9	8	19	9	8	16	21	34	35
10	KF Ferizaj	33	4	6	6	16	17	2	7	8	8	19	6	13	14	24	36	31
11	KF Trepça	33	2	4	10	16	29	3	4	10	21	35	5	8	20	37	64	23
12	KF Hajvalia	33	0	4	12	8	32	1	0	16	4	55	1	4	28	12	87	7

European qualification 2017/18

Champion: KF Trepça'89 (first qualifying round)

FC Prishtina (first qualifying round)

NB Cup winner KF Besa did not receive a licence to compete in Europe.

Top scorer Otto John (Trepça'89), 27 goals
Relegated clubs KF Hajvalia, KF Trepça, KF Ferizaj
Promoted clubs KF Flamurtari, FC Vëllaznimi, KF Vllaznia
Cup final KF Besa 1-1 KF Llapi *(aet; 4-2 on pens)*

Player of the season

Bledar Hajdini
(KF Trepça'89)

There were a number of candidates for the Kosovan Superliga's player of the season in 2016/17, the majority of them inevitably belonging to champions Trepça'89. The man who eventually scooped the prize was the club's German-born 22-year-old goalkeeper. Hajdini was an ever-present contributor to the Mitrovica club's runaway title triumph and also the only player from the league to be regularly selected for Kosovo's national squad – albeit as third-choice 'keeper behind captain Samir Ujkani and his understudy Adis Nurković.

Newcomer of the season

Florent Hasani
(KF Trepça'89)

A raw member of the Trepça'89 side that finished third in the 2015/16 Kosovan Superliga, 20-year-old Hasani was one of the outstanding performers in the 2016/17 title-winning side. Involved in all 33 games, 27 of them in the starting XI, the young attacking midfielder flourished from start to finish of a breakthrough campaign that ended with him scoring 16 goals – a figure second only to his young Nigerian team-mate Otto John in the final golden boot standings. A Kosovo Under-21 international, he is expected to graduate to senior level sooner rather than later.

Team of the season

(4-1-4-1)

Coach: **Sejdiu** *(Besa)*

NATIONAL TEAM

Top five all-time caps

Fanol Perdedaj & **Samir Ujkani** (11); **Enis Alushi** & **Bernard Berisha** (8); **Hekuran Kryeziu**, **Leart Paqarada** & **Alban Pnishi** (7)

Top five all-time goals

Albert Bunjaku (3); Mergim Brahimi & Elbasan Rashani (2); **Valon Berisha**, Imran Bunjaku, **Bersant Celina**, **Atdhe Nuhiu** & **Amir Rrahmani** (1)

Results 2016/17

05/09/16	Finland (WCQ)	A	Turku	D	1-1	*V Berisha (60p)*
06/10/16	Croatia (WCQ)	H	Shkoder (ALB)	L	0-6	
09/10/16	Ukraine (WCQ)	A	Krakow (POL)	L	0-3	
12/11/16	Turkey (WCQ)	A	Antalya	L	0-2	
24/03/17	Iceland (WCQ)	H	Shkoder (ALB)	L	1-2	*Nuhiu (52)*
11/06/17	Turkey (WCQ)	H	Shkoder (ALB)	L	1-4	*Rrahmani (22)*

Appearances 2016/17

Coach: Albert Bunjaku	**18/06/71**		**FIN**	**CRO**	**UKR**	**TUR**	**ISL**	**TUR**	**Caps**	**Goals**
Samir Ujkani	05/07/88	Pisa (ITA)	G	G	G	G	G	G53	11	-
Fanol Perdedaj	16/07/91	1860 München (GER)	D	D	D77	D	D74		11	-
Amir Rrahmani	24/02/94	Lokomotiva Zagreb (CRO)	D		D	D	D	D	6	1
Alban Pnishi	20/10/90	Grasshoppers (SUI)	D	D	D	D	D	D	7	-
Leart Paqarada	08/11/94	Sandhausen (GER)	D	D	D				7	-
Hekuran Kryeziu	12/02/93	Luzern (SUI)	M	M	M		M	M	7	-
Milot Rashica	28/06/96	Vitesse (NED)	M	M	M66	M	M64	s74	6	-
Valon Berisha	07/02/93	Salzburg (AUT)	M93	M	M	M	M	M	6	1
Enis Alushi	22/12/85	Nürnberg (GER) /M. Haifa (ISR)	M			M		M	8	-
Bernard Berisha	24/10/91	Anji (RUS) /Terek (RUS)	M81	M58	s54		s83	s53 84*	8	-
Albert Bunjaku	29/11/83	St Gallen (SUI)	A66	s68					6	3
Bersant Celina	09/09/96	Twente (NED)	s66	A68			s64		6	1
Besar Halimi	12/12/94	Mainz (GER)	s81	s58					5	-
Alban Meha	25/04/86	Konyaspor (TUR)	s93		M54				2	-
Avni Pepa	14/11/88	ÍBV (ISL)		D					5	-
Arber Zeneli	25/02/95	Heerenveen (NED)		M77	s66	M		M53	4	-
Herolind Shala	01/02/92	Kasımpaşa (TUR)		s77	M	M	M		4	-
Vedat Muriqi	24/04/94	Gençlerbirliği (TUR)			A	A			2	-
Valmir Sulejmani	01/02/96	Hannover (GER)			s77				3	-
Benjamin Kololli	15/05/92	Lausanne (SUI)				D	D		2	-
Besart Berisha	29/07/85	Melbourne Victory (AUS)					M83		1	-
Atdhe Nuhiu	29/07/89	Sheffield Wednesday (ENG)					A	A	2	1
Donis Avdijaj	25/08/96	Schalke (GER)					s74	M74	2	-
Fidan Aliti	03/10/93	Slaven Koprivnica (CRO)						D	1	-
Mërgim Vojvoda	01/02/95	Mouscron (BEL)						D	1	-
Adis Nurković	28/04/86	Travnik (BIH)						s53	1	-

DOMESTIC LEAGUE CLUB-BY-CLUB

KF Besa

1923 • Shahin Haxhizeka (8,500) • no website

Major honours
Kosovan League (3) 2005, 2006, 2007;
Kosovan Cup (3) 2005, 2011, 2017

Coach: Gani Sejdiu;
(02/04/17) Astrit Imami

2016

20/08	a	Feronikeli	W	2-1	*Shabani 2*
28/08	h	Ferizaj	W	2-0	*og (Mirsad Idrizi), Elshani*
07/09	a	Drenica	D	1-1	*Elshani*
11/09	h	Prishtina	D	1-1	*Elshani*
18/09	a	Trepça	D	1-1	*Elshani*
25/09	h	Drita	W	2-0	*Elshani, Shabani*
29/09	a	Llapi	L	2-3	*Elshani 2*
12/10	h	Liria	W	2-0	*Emini, Karahoda*
15/10	a	Hajvalia	D	0-0	
23/10	a	Trepça'89	L	1-2	*Emini*
30/10	h	Gjilani	D	0-0	
02/11	h	Feronikeli	D	1-1	*Prekazi*
06/11	a	Ferizaj	W	1-0	*Karahoda*
16/11	h	Drenica	W	2-1	*Shabani, Miftaraj*
19/11	a	Prishtina	L	0-2	
27/11	h	Trepça	L	1-2	*Miftaraj (p)*
01/12	a	Drita	D	1-1	*Miftaraj*

2017

25/02	h	Llapi	W	1-0	*Shabani*
05/03	a	Liria	W	1-0	*Emini*
08/03	h	Hajvalia	W	4-0	*Karahoda, Fisnik Papuqi 2 (1p), Emini*
12/03	h	Trepça'89	L	2-3	*og (Izmaku), Elshani*
19/03	a	Gjilani	W	1-0	*Shabani*
02/04	h	Trepça	L	1-3	*Fisnik Papuqi (p)*
05/04	a	Hajvalia	W	6-1	*Elshani 3, Shabani 2, Emini*
09/04	h	Gjilani	D	1-1	*Miftaraj (p)*
16/04	h	Liria	W	1-0	*Fisnik Papuqi (p)*
23/04	a	Llapi	L	0-2	
30/04	h	Prishtina	L	1-2	*Rexha*
06/05	a	Feronikeli	L	1-4	*Karahoda*
09/05	h	Trepça'89	L	0-2	
14/05	a	Drenica	L	1-3	*Shabani*
20/05	h	Ferizaj	W	1-0	*Emini (p)*
28/05	a	Drita	L	0-2	

No	Name	Nat	DoB	Pos	Aps	(s)	Gls
27	Liridon Balaj		15/08/99	A	3		
11	Arben Beqiri		02/06/88	G	7	(1)	
13	Albert Dabiqaj		10/07/96	M	15	(11)	
10	Qemail Elshani		28/06/91	A	22	(7)	11
26	Leart Emini		24/11/92	A	21	(8)	6
8	Dukagjin Gashi		07/10/85	M	13	(1)	
36	Lirim Gashi		24/05/98	M	2		
31	Vildan Gutiq		15/03/99	D	1	(1)	
38	Elvis Hysenaj		25/04/99	D	1	(1)	
29	Shpat Ismajli		10/11/95	A	5	(3)	
16	Fatih Karahoda		07/04/87	A	12	(12)	4
9	Fetim Kasapi		13/05/83	M	9	(6)	
18	Genis Kastrioti		30/11/97	D	7	(1)	
1	Granit Kolshi		17/08/90	G	25		
40	Ardi Krasniqi		20/11/99	D	2		
24	Demokrat Maloku		08/11/97	A	7	(1)	
2	Gentian Mazrekaj		20/02/95	D		(2)	
3	Diar Miftaraj		20/10/90	M	24	(3)	4
7	Perparim Osmani		27/09/88	D	24	(4)	
20	Shkelqim Pacolli		28/02/94	A	12	(1)	
4	Fisnik Papuqi		01/07/83	D	23	(1)	4
12	Florent Papuqi		18/02/88	D	8		
33	Fatlum Pishtani		17/05/98	D	1	(1)	
23	Arber Prekazi		21/10/89	D	28		1
15	Florent Qorraj		14/01/95	A	19	(9)	
21	Kastriot Rexha		27/09/88	A	4	(1)	1
35	Fatmir Rexhaj		25/05/96	D	4		
5	Adonis Ruhani		11/04/94	D	5	(1)	
6	Xhevdet Shabani		10/10/86	M	23	(6)	9
22	Donat Sheqerolli		26/01/95	M	14	(2)	
34	Andi Thaqi		13/04/96	G		(1)	
19	Edmond Turku		06/01/89	D	16	(1)	
37	Enis Velia		13/07/84	G	1		
39	Shpat Vokshi		12/01/98	A	1		
30	Argjend Xhafa		24/10/99	M	4		

KF Drenica

1958 • Bajram Aliu (6,000) • no website

Coach: Afrim Jashari;
(25/02/17) Fadil Rama

2016

20/08	h	Liria	W	2-1	*Arifaj 2*
28/08	a	Hajvalia	W	1-0	*Osmani*
07/09	h	Besa	D	1-1	*Meziu*
10/09	a	Gjilani	L	0-2	
17/09	h	Feronikeli	L	1-2	*Dajaku*
25/09	a	Ferizaj	W	3-2	*Arifaj 3*
28/09	h	Trepça'89	L	2-3	*Arifaj 2*
12/10	h	Prishtina	D	0-0	
16/10	a	Trepça	D	0-0	
22/10	h	Drita	D	1-1	*Arifaj*
30/10	a	Llapi	L	0-1	
02/11	a	Liria	D	1-1	*Arifaj*
05/11	h	Hajvalia	W	1-0	*Caka*
16/11	a	Besa	L	1-2	*Rexhaj*
19/11	h	Gjilani	D	1-1	*Abazi*
25/11	a	Feronikeli	L	0-1	
30/11	h	Ferizaj	D	1-1	*Merlaku*

2017

26/02	a	Trepça'89	L	0-4	
03/03	a	Prishtina	L	0-6	
08/03	h	Trepça	W	1-0	*Uka*
12/03	a	Drita	L	1-2	*Arifaj*
18/03	h	Llapi	W	2-0	*Dajaku, K Lushtaku*
01/04	a	Feronikeli	W	3-1	*K Lushtaku 2, Abazi*
06/04	h	Trepça'89	D	0-0	
09/04	a	Liria	D	0-0	
16/04	a	Ferizaj	D	1-1	*K Lushtaku*
23/04	h	Drita	W	2-0	*Arifaj, Uka*
30/04	a	Trepça	L	1-2	*Uka*
06/05	h	Hajvalia	W	4-0	*Arifaj 2, Dajaku, K Lushtaku*
10/05	a	Gjilani	L	1-4	*K Lushtaku*
14/05	h	Besa	W	3-1	*K Lushtaku, Dajaku (p), Arifaj*
20/05	a	Llapi	L	1-4	*Uka*
28/05	h	Prishtina	L	1-3	*Geci (p)*

No	Name	Nat	DoB	Pos	Aps	(s)	Gls
16	Armend Abazi		17/08/94	A	18	(1)	2
14	Granit Arifaj		29/11/90	A	21	(10)	14
4	Granit Avdyli		11/07/89	D	1	(1)	
9	Liridon Behrami		12/11/87	D	2		
17	Azem Bejta		03/08/90	D	28	(2)	
27	Drilon Bekteshi		27/12/94	D	3	(1)	
19	Ismet Caka		05/01/86	D	28	(2)	1
22	Taulant Dajaku		09/01/87	M	29	(1)	4
24	Besfot Dervishaj		24/09/99	M	3	(11)	
5	Dukagjin Gashi		07/10/85	M	13	(1)	
15	Sami Geci		20/03/75	D	28	(2)	1
20	Adnan Haxhaj		16/09/88	D	8		
2	Fetah Ibrahimi		06/07/85	D	18	(1)	
7	Qendrim Krasniqi		19/12/91	A	17	(8)	
11	Kreshnik Lushtaku		20/07/94	A	12	(1)	7
18	Shkelzen Lushtaku		24/06/90	D	18	(1)	
10	Altin Merlaku		07/03/93	A	5	(9)	1
25	Osman Meziu		05/09/99	A	8	(6)	1
28	Muharrem Musa		25/06/94	D	3		
21	Kreshnik Nebihu		09/01/97	M	8	(7)	
23	Drilon Osmani		19/07/94	M	14	(8)	1
6	Mergim Rexhaj		28/08/93	D	15	(2)	1
26	Burim Sadiku		15/05/88	G	19	(3)	
33	Liridon Syla		21/02/87	A	7	(2)	
8	Hysen Tahiri		28/09/92	A	13	(8)	
12	Kreshnik Uka		07/01/95	A	10	(8)	4
1	Arion Ymeri		30/03/95	G	14		

FC Drita

1947 • City Stadium (7,000) • dritafc.com

Major honours
Kosovan League (1) 2003; Kosovan Cup (1) 2001

Coach: Sedat Pajaziti;
(25/09/16) (Amir Allagić (BIH));
(22/10/16) Ismet Munishi;
(09/04/17) Milaim Zuzaku

2016

21/08	a	Trepça	W	1-0	*Kryeziu*
28/08	a	Trepça'89	L	0-1	
07/09	h	Llapi	L	0-1	
11/09	a	Liria	L	1-3	*Glavevski*
18/09	h	Hajvalia	L	0-1	
25/09	a	Besa	L	0-2	
30/09	h	Gjilani	L	0-1	
11/10	a	Feronikeli	L	0-1	
16/10	h	Ferizaj	D	0-0	
22/10	a	Drenica	D	1-1	*Kryeziu*
30/10	h	Prishtina	L	0-1	
02/11	h	Trepça	D	2-2	*Osmani, Maliqi*
06/11	h	Trepça'89	D	0-0	
16/11	a	Llapi	L	0-1	
20/11	h	Liria	W	1-0	*Gilberto*
26/11	a	Hajvalia	W	1-0	*Edenilson*
01/12	h	Besa	D	1-1	*Gilberto*

2017

26/02	a	Gjilani	D	1-1	*Livoreka*
05/03	h	Feronikeli	L	0-1	
08/03	a	Ferizaj	L	0-1	
12/03	h	Drenica	W	2-1	*Zeneli, Livoreka*
18/03	a	Prishtina	W	1-0	*Kryeziu*
02/04	a	Llapi	L	0-2	
05/04	h	Prishtina	L	1-3	*Shillova*
08/04	a	Feronikeli	D	0-0	
16/04	h	Trepça'89	L	0-2	
23/04	a	Drenica	L	0-2	
30/04	h	Ferizaj	W	2-1	*D Haliti, Livoreka*
07/05	a	Liria	L	0-3	*(w/o; match abandoned after 90 mins at 0-1)*
10/05	a	Trepça	D	1-1	*Kuka*
14/05	h	Hajvalia	W	2-0	*Zeneli, Gashi*
20/05	a	Gjilani	W	1-0	*Livoreka*
28/05	h	Besa	W	2-0	*Zeneli, Kryeziu (p)*

No	Name	Nat	DoB	Pos	Aps	(s)	Gls
5	Hasib Ajdari		06/07/93	M	6	(3)	
27	Granit Aliu		10/06/94	D	1		
18	Durim Baxhaku		29/03/94	D	8	(3)	
14	Florim Berisha		10/09/87	M	23	(4)	
46	Martin Blazevski	MKD	13/05/92	M	4	(1)	
20	Florent Byqmeti		14/05/96	D	5		
4	Alban Dragusha		11/12/81	D	21	(2)	
38	Edenilson	BRA	13/09/87	M	2	(2)	1
30	Gezim Gashi		01/10/85	D	11	(1)	1
34	Dren Gasi		29/11/94	M	6	(1)	
40	Gilberto	BRA	11/07/87	A	7	(1)	2
28	Blagojce Glavevski	MKD	06/04/88	M	3	(1)	1
47	Betim Halimi		28/02/96	G	12	(1)	
29	Denis Haliti		21/01/87	D	7	(1)	1
16	Taulant Haliti		16/02/94	D	11		
13	Erdin Hashani		26/02/82	D	26	(1)	
48	Premtim Isufi		30/06/98	M	1	(1)	
32	Armend Kastrati		28/03/87	M	2	(2)	
25	Regi Kastrati		25/02/95	D	1		
24	Leotrim Kryeziu		25/01/99	A	15	(11)	4
11	Viktor Kuka		25/06/90	D	28		1
1	Artan Latifi		05/04/83	G	19		
36	Perparim Livoreka		24/06/87	A	5	(4)	4
15	Bergin Maliqi		12/04/89	A	15	(9)	1
9	Alban Mavriqi		07/07/89	A	10	(5)	
7	Almedin Murati		19/02/95	A	10	(2)	
26	Nderim Nedzipi	MKD	22/05/84	M	7	(5)	
8	Petrit Osmani		12/10/90	A	13	(3)	1
6	Arbnor Ramadani		03/06/94	M	16	(7)	
19	Dorart Ramadani		02/10/89	G	2		
19	Dorart Ramadani		02/10/89	M	1		
17	Alban Rexhepi		15/12/95	A	22	(6)	
33	Qendrim Sejdiu		03/10/87	D	8	(3)	
31	Alban Shillova		13/08/92	A	10	(1)	1
2	Alban Tusuni		18/12/92	D	13	(1)	
12	Semir Zeneli		08/03/89	A	12	(11)	3

KF Ferizaj

1923 • Ismet Shabani (4,000) • no website

Coach: Agron Selmani; (18/09/16) Arsim Abazi; (26/02/17) Argjend Beqiri (MKD); (23/04/17) Fatos Vishi

Date		Opponent		Score	Scorers
2016					
21/08	h	Hajvalia	W	4-0	*Salihu 4*
28/08	a	Besa	L	0-2	
07/09	h	Gjilani	L	1-2	*Bushi*
11/09	a	Feronikeli	L	1-2	*Sadriu*
18/09	h	Trepça'89	L	0-1	
25/09	h	Drenica	L	2-3	*Kuka, B Shabani (p)*
29/09	a	Prishtina	L	0-1	
12/10	h	Trepça	D	2-2	*Salihu, Mirsad Idrizi*
16/10	a	Drita	D	0-0	
22/10	h	Llapi	D	0-0	
30/10	a	Liria	L	0-3	
02/11	a	Hajvalia	D	0-0	
06/11	h	Besa	L	0-1	
16/11	a	Gjilani	W	1-0	*Selmani*
20/11	h	Feronikeli	W	2-0	*Thaqi, og (Livoreka)*
27/11	a	Trepça'89	L	1-4	*Salihu*
30/11	a	Drenica	D	1-1	*Salihu*
2017					
25/02	h	Prishtina	D	0-0	
04/03	a	Trepça	D	1-1	*Behluli*
08/03	h	Drita	W	1-0	*Behluli*
11/03	a	Llapi	D	0-0	
19/03	h	Liria	D	0-0	
31/03	a	Prishtina	L	0-1	
05/04	h	Feronikeli	L	0-4	
09/04	a	Trepça'89	D	0-0	
16/04	h	Drenica	D	1-1	*Behluli*
23/04	a	Liria	D	1-1	*Ristovski*
30/04	a	Drita	L	1-2	*Ristovski*
07/05	h	Trepça	W	2-1	*Ristovski, Babaj*
10/05	a	Hajvalia	W	1-0	*Thaqi*
14/05	h	Gjilani	D	0-0	
20/05	a	Besa	L	0-1	
28/05	h	Llapi	L	1-2	*Salihu*

No	Name	Nat	DoB	Pos	Aps	(s)	Gls
37	Murat Adili		22/09/92	M	9	(2)	
24	Florent Ahmeti		21/08/95	M	5	(1)	
25	Shpetim Babaj		09/12/81	M	10	(2)	1
6	Behar Bardhi		24/03/93	D	25	(4)	
9	Maliq Behluli		27/08/94	M	11	(3)	3
28	Argjend Bekteshi		23/11/96	D	5	(1)	
10	Muhabi Bushi		21/07/88	A	12	(12)	1
27	Fisnik Halimi		19/03/88	D	17	(5)	
40	Gentonis Haliti		01/09/98	M	1		
3	Mensur Idrizi		30/01/87	M	3	(1)	
17	Mirsad Idrizi		07/05/85	M	25	(1)	1
4	Agron Istrefi		29/08/78	M	17	(1)	
21	Rinor Jashari			M	3		
7	Enis Kuka		05/06/94	M	17	(9)	1
14	Ismail Marevci		18/10/95	D	1		
36	Dardan Miftari		02/12/83	G	5		
15	Florent Papuqi		01/07/83	D	13		
18	Albion Pira		25/06/94	A	6	(1)	
1	Leotrim Rexhepi		16/04/94	G	28	(1)	
39	Milan Ristovski	MKD	01/03/89	M	11	(4)	3
23	Edon Sadriu		25/05/97	A	20	(13)	1
11	Shkembim Salihu		07/09/89	A	20	(7)	8
8	Ardian Selimi		26/08/94	M	1	(1)	
22	Jasir Selmani		24/01/91	A	10	(1)	1
5	Burim Shabani		02/03/86	D	14	(4)	1
38	Fitim Shabani		24/01/95	M	1	(1)	
12	Labinot Shabani		07/09/89	M	15	(7)	
19	Lavdrim Skenderi		17/01/94	A	7	(5)	
16	Qerim Tershana		13/01/92	D	29		
26	Elbasan Thaqi		16/08/91	M	21	(5)	2
2	Blendion Troni		24/06/96	D	1		

KF Feronikeli

1974 • Rexhep Rexhepi (5,000) • no website

Major honours
Kosovan League (2) 2015, 2016; Kosovan Cup (2) 2014, 2015

Coach: Afrim Tovërlani; (06/05/17) Ramiz Dervishi

Date		Opponent		Score	Scorers
2016					
20/08	h	Besa	L	1-2	*Maliqi (p)*
28/08	a	Gjilani	L	1-2	*Krasniqi*
08/09	h	Trepça'89	W	4-1	*Zhdrella, Kurtishaj, Hoti, Maliqi*
11/09	h	Ferizaj	W	2-1	*Hoti, Kurtishaj*
17/09	a	Drenica	W	2-1	*Zeka, Maliqi*
24/09	h	Prishtina	L	0-1	
28/09	a	Trepça	W	1-0	*og (Kutllovci)*
11/10	h	Drita	W	1-0	*Milicaj*
16/10	a	Llapi	W	3-0	*(w/o; match abandoned after 56 mins at 3-0 Hoti, Kurtishaj 2)*
22/10	h	Liria	W	1-0	*Shabani*
28/10	a	Hajvalia	W	3-2	*Zhdrella, Kurtishaj, Hoti*
02/11	a	Besa	D	1-1	*Maliqi (p)*
05/11	h	Gjilani	W	1-0	*Livoreka*
16/11	a	Trepça'89	D	0-0	
20/11	a	Ferizaj	L	0-2	
25/11	h	Drenica	W	1-0	*Zeka*
30/11	a	Prishtina	D	0-0	
2017					
25/02	h	Trepça	W	5-1	*Osmani, Hoti 2, Milicaj, Hoxha*
05/03	a	Drita	W	1-0	*Milicaj*
08/03	h	Llapi	W	1-0	*Shabani*
12/03	a	Liria	W	3-1	*Hoti, Prokshi, Zeka*
17/03	h	Hajvalia	W	6-1	*Hoti, Hoxha, Milicaj 2, Camara, Gërbeshi (p)*
01/04	h	Drenica	L	1-3	*Zhdrella*
05/04	a	Ferizaj	W	4-0	*Osmani 2, Zhdrella, Kurtishaj*
08/04	h	Drita	D	0-0	
15/04	a	Trepça	W	3-1	*Camara 2, Osmani*
21/04	h	Hajvalia	W	6-0	*Shabani 3, Osmani, Zhdrella, Hoxha*
29/04	a	Gjilani	L	0-1	
06/05	h	Besa	W	4-1	*Osmani, Prokshi, Zeka, Hoxha*
10/05	a	Llapi	L	0-2	
14/05	h	Prishtina	L	1-2	*Maliqi (p)*
20/05	h	Liria	D	1-1	*Maliqi (p)*
28/05	a	Trepça'89	W	3-0	*Hoti, Camara, Zeka*

No	Name	Nat	DoB	Pos	Aps	(s)	Gls
21	Argjend Bardhi		28/04/95	M	16	(3)	
29	Abu Camara	LBR	04/01/97	A	2	(9)	4
13	Mirlind Demaku		12/10/94	A	3		
16	Lulzim Doshlaku		28/01/91	D	19	(1)	
12	Asdren Gashi		12/05/97	M		(2)	
3	Fidan Gërbeshi		19/05/85	D	31	(1)	1
25	Ahmet Halit		01/10/88	D	27		
14	Mendurim Hoti		23/02/96	A	14	(13)	9
30	Yll Hoxha		26/12/87	A	13	(1)	4
27	Labinot Jashanica		16/04/97	A		(1)	
22	Besnik Krasniqi		01/02/90	D	11	(1)	1
9	Blenard Kurtishaj		03/09/93	A	19	(3)	6
4	Ardian Limani		18/11/93	D	25	(4)	
10	Perparim Livoreka		24/06/87	A	10		1
18	Drin Lladrovci		08/01/88	D		(4)	
17	Behar Maliqi		22/09/86	M	21	(4)	6
23	Faton Maloku		14/06/91	G	16		
7	Mark Milicaj		15/01/87	A	17	(10)	5
1	Flamur Neziri		22/05/87	G	14		
11	Labinot Osmani		15/08/85	A	10	(5)	6
20	Diar Prokshi		27/08/98	M		(17)	2
24	Burim Qorri		29/03/92	M	7		
19	Bujar Shabani		11/10/90	M	27	(2)	5
15	Haxhi Shala		17/05/93	D	22	(3)	
5	Astrit Thaqi		20/04/93	D	4	(1)	
26	Jacek Deniz Troshupa		10/04/93	G	3		
8	Mevlan Zeka		24/05/94	A	15	(8)	5
6	Mentor Zhdrella		06/10/90	M	17	(3)	5

KF Gjilani

1995 • City Stadium (7,000) • no website

Major honours
Kosovan Cup (1) 2000

Coach: Arbnor Morina

Date		Opponent		Score	Scorers
2016					
20/08	h	Trepça'89	L	1-2	*Eminhaziri (p)*
28/08	h	Feronikeli	W	2-1	*Eminhaziri, Haxhimusa*
07/09	a	Ferizaj	W	2-1	*Eminhaziri, Haxhimusa*
10/09	h	Drenica	W	2-0	*B Ahmeti, Haxhimusa*
16/09	a	Prishtina	L	0-1	
25/09	h	Trepça	D	0-0	
30/09	a	Drita	W	1-0	*Kastrati*
12/10	h	Llapi	L	0-1	
15/10	a	Liria	L	0-1	
23/10	h	Hajvalia	W	1-0	*og (Sejdiu)*
30/10	a	Besa	D	0-0	
02/11	a	Trepça'89	D	1-1	*Kosumi*
05/11	a	Feronikeli	L	0-1	
16/11	h	Ferizaj	L	0-1	
19/11	a	Drenica	D	1-1	*Eminhaziri*
25/11	h	Prishtina	W	1-0	*Haxhimusa*
30/11	a	Trepça	W	2-0	*Mustafa, Shabani*
2017					
26/02	h	Drita	D	1-1	*Haxhimusa*
04/03	a	Llapi	L	0-1	
08/03	h	Liria	D	0-0	
11/03	a	Hajvalia	W	2-1	*B Ahmeti, Hyseni*
19/03	h	Besa	L	0-1	
02/04	h	Hajvalia	W	3-0	*Eminhaziri, Haxhimusa 2*
06/04	h	Liria	W	2-0	*Eminhaziri 2*
09/04	a	Besa	D	1-1	*Haxhimusa*
15/04	h	Llapi	D	1-1	*Mustafa*
22/04	a	Prishtina	L	0-1	
29/04	h	Feronikeli	W	1-0	*Rusi*
05/05	a	Trepça'89	L	2-5	*Eminhaziri (p), Shabani*
10/05	h	Drenica	W	4-1	*Haxhimusa 4*
14/05	a	Ferizaj	D	0-0	
20/05	h	Drita	L	0-1	
26/05	a	Trepça	W	5-3	*Hyseni, Morina 2, Kosumi, Rusi*

No	Name	Nat	DoB	Pos	Aps	(s)	Gls
10	Azem Ahmeti		19/01/84	M	19	(2)	
34	Berat Ahmeti		26/01/95	M	16	(9)	2
25	Roland Ajeti		01/10/99	M	1	(1)	
36	Altin Aliu		11/11/99	A	5	(8)	
21	Festim Aliu		20/10/98	D	4	(3)	
27	Leotrim Bekteshi		24/04/92	D	28		
17	Leart Bilalli		16/06/99	A	1	(4)	
19	Ilir Blakqori		01/02/93	D	25	(1)	
8	Isa Eminhaziri		09/09/87	A	18	(6)	8
16	Dren Gashi		25/01/94	M	11	(3)	
24	Betim Haxhimusa		14/04/92	M	17	(8)	12
13	Ergon Hyseni		18/01/94	D	18		2
26	Vllaznim Jashari		28/09/91	M	12		
32	Jorge Emanuel	POR	05/06/95	A	6		
31	Donat Kaqiu		20/09/93	G	16		
3	Ylber Kastrati		09/04/87	D	24	(3)	1
7	Salih Kosumi		21/11/92	D	13	(3)	2
35	Yll Maliqi		13/01/92	M	1		
1	Faton Maloku		14/06/91	G	17		
9	Besart Morina		24/02/93	M	7	(1)	2
6	Zgjim Mustafa		21/11/94	M	20	(7)	2
22	Kreshnik Nebihu		18/06/96	M	2	(8)	
18	Gezim Rusi		29/11/94	A	21	(1)	2
23	Egzon Shabani		07/08/89	M	13	(12)	2
20	Valton Sherifi		14/03/97	A	1	(8)	
5	Arbios Thaqi		13/10/93	M	19	(6)	
2	Armend Thaqi		10/10/92	D	28	(1)	

KOSOVO

KF Hajvalia

1999 • Kizhnicë (1,000) • no website

Coach: Sunaj Keçi;
(05/11/16) Emin Bajrami

Date		Opponent		Score	Scorers
2016					
20/08	a	Ferizaj	L	0-4	
28/08	h	Drenica	L	0-1	
07/09	a	Prishtina	L	0-3	
10/09	h	Trepça	D	1-1	*Daku*
18/09	a	Drita	W	1-0	*Babaj*
24/09	h	Llapi	L	0-2	
28/09	a	Liria	L	0-3	
12/10	a	Trepça'89	L	0-1	
15/10	h	Besa	D	0-0	
23/10	a	Gjilani	L	0-1	
28/10	h	Feronikeli	L	2-3	*og (Maliqi), E Halimi*
02/11	h	Ferizaj	D	0-0	
05/11	a	Drenica	L	0-1	
15/11	h	Prishtina	D	0-0	
20/11	a	Trepça	L	0-3	
25/11	h	Drita	L	0-1	
01/12	a	Llapi	L	1-3	*I Bytyqi*
2017					
25/02	h	Liria	L	2-4	*Kqiku, Vitia*
03/03	h	Trepça'89	L	0-4	
08/03	a	Besa	L	0-4	
11/03	h	Gjilani	L	1-2	*Pajaziti*
17/03	a	Feronikeli	L	1-6	*Kqiku (p)*
02/04	a	Gjilani	L	0-3	
05/04	h	Besa	L	1-6	*Morina*
09/04	a	Llapi	L	0-2	
14/04	h	Prishtina	L	0-1	
21/04	a	Feronikeli	L	0-6	
28/04	h	Trepça'89	L	0-3	
06/05	a	Drenica	L	0-4	
10/05	h	Ferizaj	L	0-1	
14/05	a	Drita	L	0-2	
20/05	h	Trepça	L	1-3	*Kqiku*
28/05	a	Liria	L	1-9	*Rezniqi*

No	Name	Nat	DoB	Pos	Aps	(s)	Gls
36	Malsor Ajeti		15/09/98	M	14	(5)	
30	Mentor Ajeti		27/04/00	D	4	(1)	
31	Valon Avdullahu		01/05/95	D	9	(2)	
61	Lirim Avdulli			A	2		
9	Shpetim Babaj		09/12/81	M	14		1
59	Fatlind Basha			D	2		
5	Mentor Borovci		02/08/98	G	4		
21	Idriz Bytyqi			M	3		1
39	Masar Bytyqi		12/02/98	D	9	(2)	
27	Valon Bytyqi		23/06/90	D	7	(2)	
22	Mirlind Daku		01/01/98	A	10	(4)	1
53	Flamur Dulahu		22/09/95	D	3	(1)	
11	Burim Fejzullahu		18/01/94	A	3	(3)	
46	Arber Fona		18/08/97	D	4	(2)	
3	Elbasan Gashi		22/05/92	M	9	(2)	
37	Flamur Gashi		28/11/96	D		(2)	
17	Gezim Gashi		01/10/85	M	8	(2)	
25	Fillim Guraziu		15/01/84	D	5	(5)	
1	Armend Halili		22/06/97	M	8		
13	Betim Halimi		28/02/96	G	14		
4	Etrit Halimi		06/05/94	G	11		1
44	Lulzon Halit		02/04/97	A	6	(2)	
8	Victor Hamedi	CGO	22/01/97	A	2	(1)	
51	Rinor Havolli		02/11/91	A	4		
12	Endrit Humolli		28/02/95	A	2		
57	Argjend Ibrahimi			D	2		
26	Armend Kastrati		24/03/87	A	1	(2)	
14	Jon Katanolli		16/10/95	M	1		
24	Shqiperim Kelmendi		07/06/93	A	5	(7)	
58	Albinot Kosumi			D	6		
32	Edison Kqiku		16/01/99	M	19	(4)	3
16	Shpend Krasniqi		17/07/90	D	12		
55	Drilon Leci		03/10/87	D	8	(3)	
33	Lucas Martins	BRA	23/01/96	M	3		
6	Endrit Maloku		25/12/93	D	11	(1)	
2	Matheus	BRA	25/07/95	A	1		
35	Armend Misini		17/07/98	A	10	(2)	
23	Vilson Morina		16/03/98	M	9	(4)	1
54	Muhamet Pajaziti		16/07/97	A	8	(5)	1
19	Yll Prekopuca		10/08/89	A	11	(2)	
29	Çlirim Ramadani		22/06/98	M	6	(1)	
50	Blert Rashiti		19/12/95	D	15		
45	Fahri Rashiti		19/05/96	A	4	(1)	
10	Mal Rezniqi		01/09/98	M	11	(3)	1
43	Toni Salihu		13/07/99	A	11	(1)	
20	Qendrim Sejdiu		03/10/87	M	8	(5)	
40	Kushtrim Sogojeva		07/04/98	M	10		
38	Driton Suleviq		23/10/97	D	1	(2)	
42	Shpat Tabaku		19/06/94	D	14	(1)	
56	Granit Uka			A	2		
7	Ekber Vitia		27/10/96	M	11	(4)	1
60	Egzon Vrajolli		23/02/97	M	2		
18	Aid Zeqiri		24/02/90	G	4	(4)	

KF Liria

1930 • Përparim Thaçi (4,000) • liriafc.com

Major honours
Kosovan League (1) 1995; Kosovan Cup (3) 1995, 2007, 2010

Coach: Ramiz Krasniqi;
(30/10/16) (Genc Tamniku);
(20/11/16) Blerim Zherka;
(31/03/17) Bekim Bakaj

Date		Opponent		Score	Scorers
2016					
20/08	a	Drenica	L	1-2	*Fetahaj*
27/08	h	Prishtina	L	1-2	*Berisha*
07/09	a	Trepça	W	4-1	*B Memaj, Berisha, Fetahaj, D Gashi*
11/09	h	Drita	W	3-1	*Korenica, B Memaj, Shillova*
18/09	a	Llapi	L	0-2	
23/09	a	Trepça'89	L	0-2	
28/09	h	Hajvalia	W	3-0	*Mustafa, Q Gashi 2*
12/10	a	Besa	L	0-2	
15/10	h	Gjilani	W	1-0	*Berisha (p)*
22/10	a	Feronikeli	L	0-1	
30/10	h	Ferizaj	W	3-0	*Mustafa, Fetahaj, Chibueze*
02/11	h	Drenica	D	1-1	*Shillova*
06/11	a	Prishtina	L	0-1	
16/11	h	Trepça	W	1-0	*Berisha*
20/11	a	Drita	L	0-1	
27/11	h	Llapi	D	0-0	
30/11	h	Trepça'89	L	0-3	
2017					
25/02	a	Hajvalia	W	4-2	*Fetahaj 3, Chibueze*
05/03	h	Besa	L	0-1	
08/03	a	Gjilani	D	0-0	
12/03	h	Feronikeli	L	1-3	*Chibueze*
19/03	a	Ferizaj	D	0-0	
02/04	a	Trepça'89	L	0-2	
06/04	a	Gjilani	L	0-2	
09/04	h	Drenica	D	0-0	
16/04	a	Besa	L	0-1	
23/04	h	Ferizaj	D	1-1	*Guraziu (p)*
29/04	a	Llapi	L	0-2	
07/05	h	Drita	W	3-0	*(w/o; match abandoned after 90 mins at 1-0 Guraziu (p))*
10/05	a	Prishtina	L	1-3	*Chibueze*
14/05	h	Trepça	W	3-1	*Korenica, Guraziu, Fetahaj*
20/05	a	Feronikeli	D	1-1	*Mustafa*
28/05	h	Hajvalia	W	9-1	*Likaj, Fetahaj 5, Kastrati, A Memaj, Osmani*

No	Name	Nat	DoB	Pos	Aps	(s)	Gls
36	Burhan Aliji		29/09/98	M	7	(4)	
33	Richard Asare	GHA	08/03/95	D	11	(1)	
5	Visar Berisha		07/12/86	D	14	(1)	4
42	Armend Blakqori		08/06/90	G	3		
38	Valon Bytyqi		23/06/90	D	2		
35	Henry Chibueze	NGA	15/11/92	A	17	(5)	4
32	Joel Deji	NGA	23/11/92	M	4		
15	Behar Dina		18/04/95	D	20	(5)	
10	Liridon Fetahaj		21/09/91	A	26	(4)	12
11	Durim Gashi		14/06/91	A	9	(2)	1
40	Elbasan Gashi			D	5		
19	Qendrim Gashi		27/03/93	A	15	(5)	2
20	Ron Gashi		06/06/98	M	15	(3)	
3	Ibrahim Gavazaj		22/07/98	D	1	(1)	
22	Robert Gjeraj		12/04/85	D	26	(2)	
41	Fillim Guraziu		15/01/84	A	5	(1)	3
14	Adnan Haxhaj		16/09/88	D	10	(1)	
12	Valmir Haziraj		17/08/85	G	11		
21	Besart Islamaj		22/01/93	D	21	(3)	
39	Bledion Kastrati		01/01/95	D	1		1
8	Meriton Korenica		15/12/96	M	10	(8)	2
7	Ramadan Kryeziu		25/07/90	M	4	(1)	
27	Arber Likaj		03/04/97	A	7	(1)	1
18	Albin Memaj		09/11/96	A	10	(4)	1
17	Blendi Memaj		02/01/95	M	13	(16)	2
34	Karim Muhamed	GHA	25/11/95	M	3	(1)	
24	Ilir Mustafa		07/08/96	M	28	(3)	3
37	Florent Osmani		28/05/88	A	7	(7)	1
23	Fisnik Ramadanaj		24/03/91	D	18	(1)	
4	Vigan Rexhaj		06/05/93	M	11	(8)	
1	Armend Ruxhi		30/12/85	G	19		
9	Alban Shillova		13/08/92	A	10	(2)	2

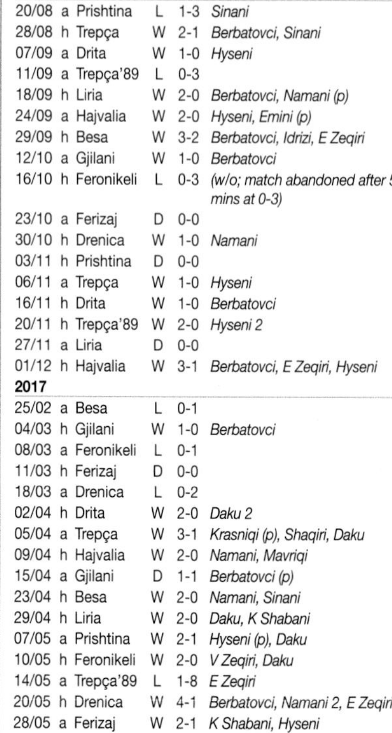

KF Llapi

1932 • Zahir Pajaziti (3,000) • no website

Coach: Tahir Batatina

Date		Opponent		Score	Scorers
2016					
20/08	a	Prishtina	L	1-3	*Sinani*
28/08	h	Trepça	W	2-1	*Berbatovci, Sinani*
07/09	a	Drita	W	1-0	*Hyseni*
11/09	a	Trepça'89	L	0-3	
18/09	h	Liria	W	2-0	*Berbatovci, Namani (p)*
24/09	a	Hajvalia	W	2-0	*Hyseni, Emini (p)*
29/09	h	Besa	W	3-2	*Berbatovci, Idrizi, E Zeqiri*
12/10	a	Gjilani	W	1-0	*Berbatovci*
16/10	h	Feronikeli	L	0-3	*(w/o; match abandoned after 56 mins at 0-3)*
23/10	a	Ferizaj	D	0-0	
30/10	h	Drenica	W	1-0	*Namani*
03/11	h	Prishtina	D	0-0	
06/11	a	Trepça	W	1-0	*Hyseni*
16/11	h	Drita	W	1-0	*Berbatovci*
20/11	h	Trepça'89	W	2-0	*Hyseni 2*
27/11	a	Liria	D	0-0	
01/12	h	Hajvalia	W	3-1	*Berbatovci, E Zeqiri, Hyseni*
2017					
25/02	a	Besa	L	0-1	
04/03	h	Gjilani	W	1-0	*Berbatovci*
08/03	a	Feronikeli	L	0-1	
11/03	h	Ferizaj	D	0-0	
18/03	a	Drenica	L	0-2	
02/04	h	Drita	W	2-0	*Daku 2*
05/04	a	Trepça	W	3-1	*Krasniqi (p), Shaqiri, Daku*
09/04	h	Hajvalia	W	2-0	*Namani, Mavriqi*
15/04	a	Gjilani	D	1-1	*Berbatovci (p)*
23/04	h	Besa	W	2-0	*Namani, Sinani*
29/04	h	Liria	W	2-0	*Daku, K Shabani*
07/05	a	Prishtina	W	2-1	*Hyseni (p), Daku*
10/05	h	Feronikeli	W	2-0	*V Zeqiri, Daku*
14/05	a	Trepça'89	L	1-8	*E Zeqiri*
20/05	h	Drenica	W	4-1	*Berbatovci, Namani 2, E Zeqiri*
28/05	a	Ferizaj	W	2-1	*K Shabani, Hyseni*

No	Name	Nat	DoB	Pos	Aps	(s)	Gls
13	Afrim Ademi		19/05/89	G	6		
12	Ilir Avdyli		20/05/90	G	27		
11	Florim Berbatovci		29/08/89	A	17	(12)	9
19	Mirlind Daku		01/01/98	A	9	(5)	6
22	Qendrim Dautaj		07/01/91	M	2	(2)	
7	Getoar Dragusha		31/03/93	D	8	(4)	
34	Benjamin Emini		10/07/92	A	8	(2)	1
30	Nikola Georgievski	MKD	17/08/95	D		(1)	
39	Ardian Gjata			M	1		
40	Rrahman Hoti			D	1		
9	Berat Hyseni		26/10/86	A	17	(7)	8
4	Bujar Idrizi		11/12/92	D	27		1
5	Dardan Jashari		28/03/90	D	27	(2)	
3	Leutrim Kadriu		01/04/94	D	23	(3)	
8	Fuat Karabegu		01/02/97	M	12	(12)	
27	Festim Krasniqi		12/07/91	A	11	(8)	1
18	Arleison Martínez	COL	26/08/94	A	1		
17	Alban Mavriqi		07/07/89	A	8	(1)	1
21	Nazif Mulaku		29/08/89	A	3	(2)	
20	Ardian Musliu		05/07/97	A	4	(1)	
16	Hamdi Namani		16/10/95	M	27	(3)	6
31	Ardian Potera		07/04/96	A	1		
29	Egzon Qerimi		10/11/93	M	2		
23	Lumbardh Salihu		18/11/92	M	4	(1)	
41	Alban Shabani			M	1		
24	Kushtrim Shabani		08/02/97	M	12	(6)	2
15	Filonit Shaqiri		25/05/93	M	18	(3)	1
14	Egzon Sinani		07/06/94	D	25	(1)	3
2	Rron Statovci		18/01/97	D	12	(8)	
38	Visar Zeneli		23/09/93	A	7		
25	Arbnor Zeqiri		02/08/96	M	6		
10	Edon Zeqiri		04/06/90	M	23	(3)	4
26	Valon Zeqiri		28/08/95	A	13	(8)	1

FC Prishtina

1922 • City Stadium (16,200) • prishtinafc.com

Major honours
Kosovan League (10) 1992, 1996, 1997, 2000, 2001, 2004, 2008, 2009, 2012, 2013; Kosovan Cup (4) 1994, 2006, 2013, 2016

Coach: Kushtrim Munishi; (24/09/16) Lutz Lindemann (GER); (31/03/17) Arsim Thaçi

2016

Date		Opponent		Score	Scorers
20/08	h	Llapi	W	3-1	*Kelmendi, Januzi, Makenda*
28/08	a	Liria	W	2-1	*Krasniqi 2*
07/09	h	Hajvalia	W	3-0	*Osmani, Leci, Januzi*
11/09	a	Besa	D	1-1	*Basit*
16/09	h	Gjilani	W	1-0	*Kukaj*
24/09	a	Feronikeli	W	1-0	*Curri*
29/09	h	Ferizaj	W	1-0	*Curri*
12/10	a	Drenica	D	0-0	
16/10	h	Trepça'89	L	0-2	
22/10	h	Trepça	W	2-1	*Dallku, Kukaj*
30/10	a	Drita	W	1-0	*Makenda*
03/11	a	Llapi	D	0-0	
06/11	h	Liria	W	1-0	*Osmani*
15/11	a	Hajvalia	D	0-0	
19/11	h	Besa	W	2-0	*Pevqeli, Krasniqi*
26/11	a	Gjilani	L	0-1	
30/11	h	Feronikeli	D	0-0	

2017

Date		Opponent		Score	Scorers
25/02	a	Ferizaj	D	0-0	
03/03	h	Drenica	W	6-0	*Basit 2, Boshnjaku, Begolli, Neziri, Kelmendi*
07/03	a	Trepça'89	L	0-1	
11/03	a	Trepça	W	2-1	*Leci, Makenda*
18/03	h	Drita	L	0-1	
31/03	h	Ferizaj	W	1-0	*Makenda*
05/04	a	Drita	W	3-1	*Basit 3*
08/04	h	Trepça	W	2-1	*Leci (p), Pevqeli*
14/04	a	Hajvalia	W	1-0	*Pevqeli*
22/04	h	Gjilani	W	1-0	*Basit*
29/04	a	Besa	W	2-1	*Basit 2*
07/05	h	Llapi	L	1-2	*Basit*
10/05	h	Liria	W	3-1	*Makenda 2, Basit*
14/05	a	Feronikeli	W	2-1	*Basit, Makenda*
20/05	h	Trepça'89	W	1-0	*Makenda*
28/05	a	Drenica	W	3-1	*Makenda 2, Basit*

No	Name	Nat	DoB	Pos	Aps	(s)	Gls
20	Blendi Baftiu		17/02/98	M	5	(2)	
21	Khalid Abdul Basit	GHA	10/08/96	A	18	(11)	13
13	Gentrit Begolli		21/02/92	A	14	(4)	1
9	Visar Bekaj		24/05/97	G	6		
4	Lorik Boshnjaku		07/07/95	M	20	(4)	1
3	Debatik Curri	ALB	28/12/83	M	20	(8)	2
2	Armend Dallku	ALB	16/06/83	D	28	(1)	1
15	Gentrit Dumani		13/07/93	D	15	(1)	
31	Atdhe Grajqevci		22/11/98	M	1		
12	Genc Hamiti		21/09/93	M	18	(5)	
26	Arber Hoxha		06/10/98	A	8	(1)	
22	Ahmed Januzi	ALB	08/07/88	A	9	(9)	2
6	Shend Kelmendi		21/09/94	M	9	(11)	2
5	Endrit Krasniqi		26/10/94	M	13	(8)	3
18	Liridon Kukaj		22/06/83	D	19	(1)	2
10	Liridon Leci		11/02/85	D	25		3
32	Kreshnik Lushtaku		20/07/94	A	9	(1)	
11	Gauthier Makenda	CMR	20/07/97	A	22	(7)	10
19	Lorik Maxhuni		02/07/92	D	26		
16	Miloš Milović	MNE	22/12/95	D	2		
1	Alban Muqiqi		10/11/95	G	27	(1)	
30	Mergim Neziri		30/04/93	A	18	(2)	1
7	Labinot Osmani		15/08/85	A	12	(4)	2
27	Mergim Pevqeli		25/11/93	A	13	(13)	3
8	Bleon Sekiraqa		17/10/00	A	4		
25	Agon Xhaka		09/06/97	D	2		

KF Trepça

1932 • Adem Jashari (16,000) • no website

Major honours
Kosovan League (1) 2010

Coach: Nazmi Rama; (11/09/16) Fidaim Haxhiu

2016

Date		Opponent		Score	Scorers
20/08	h	Drita	L	0-1	
28/08	a	Llapi	L	1-2	*Baliqi*
07/09	h	Liria	L	1-4	*Hyseni*
10/09	a	Hajvalia	D	1-1	*Hyseni*
18/09	h	Besa	D	1-1	*Hyseni*
25/09	a	Gjilani	D	0-0	
28/09	h	Feronikeli	L	0-1	
12/10	a	Ferizaj	D	2-2	*Hyseni, Avdyli*
16/10	h	Drenica	D	0-0	
22/10	a	Prishtina	L	1-2	*Ardian Muja*
29/10	h	Trepça'89	L	1-3	*Baliqi*
02/11	a	Drita	D	2-2	*Ardian Muja, Kurta*
06/11	h	Llapi	L	0-1	
16/11	a	Liria	L	0-1	
19/11	h	Hajvalia	W	3-0	*Berisha, Hyseni 2*
27/11	a	Besa	W	2-1	*Mustafa, Shabani*
30/11	h	Gjilani	L	0-2	

2017

Date		Opponent		Score	Scorers
25/02	a	Feronikeli	L	1-5	*Zabërgja*
04/03	h	Ferizaj	D	1-1	*Zuqaku*
08/03	a	Drenica	L	0-1	
11/03	h	Prishtina	L	1-2	*Zabërgja*
19/03	a	Trepça'89	L	1-6	*Zabërgja*
02/04	a	Besa	W	3-1	*Arbnor Muja, Sahiti, Ergyn Ahmeti*
05/04	h	Llapi	L	1-3	*Zabërgja*
08/04	a	Prishtina	L	1-2	*Prishtina (p)*
26/04	h	Feronikeli	L	1-3	*Zabërgja*
23/04	a	Trepça'89	L	1-3	*Ergyn Ahmeti*
30/04	h	Drenica	W	2-1	*Zabërgja, Ergyn Ahmeti*
07/05	a	Ferizaj	L	1-2	*Hajdini*
10/05	h	Drita	D	1-1	*Ergyn Ahmeti*
14/05	a	Liria	L	1-3	*Hajdini*
20/05	a	Hajvalia	W	3-1	*D Voca 2, Krasniqi*
28/05	h	Gjilani	L	3-5	*Arbnor Muja 2, Sahiti*

No	Name	Nat	DoB	Pos	Aps	(s)	Gls
30	Edis Ahmeti		22/05/93	A	2		
13	Ergyn Ahmeti		21/12/95	M	22	(4)	4
46	Genc Asllani		26/05/96	M	2		
9	Florent Avdyli		10/07/93	M	15	(6)	1
8	Emin Baliqi		02/06/83	M	8	(5)	2
3	Blerim Berisha		14/08/84	D	15	(3)	1
16	Shpetim Fetahu		01/07/82	M	7	(3)	
50	Theo Fodjo	CMR	04/04/92	G	5		
23	Ermal Gashi		16/01/96	G	4		
14	Edmond Hajdari		17/09/95	D	9		
35	Pleurat Hajdini		21/01/95	M	9	(1)	2
33	Hasan Hyseni		14/04/97	A	8	(7)	6
10	Albert Kajtazi		23/08/96	D	1		
41	Milot Kamberi		05/08/97	D	19	(3)	
37	Jon Katanolli		16/10/95	D	8	(2)	
48	Arianit Krasniqi			M	2	(1)	1
25	Ervin Kurta		23/03/95	A	8		1
4	Kujtim Kutllovci		06/01/85	D	24		
51	Geart Latifi			M	2		
1	Enis Manxholli		14/07/86	G	16		
28	Arbnor Muja		09/12/97	A	12	(10)	3
5	Ardian Muja		09/12/97	A	10	(6)	2
11	Arben Mustafa		18/04/94	M	9	(5)	1
49	Afrim Mziu		09/11/82	A	3		
21	Ardian Neziri		04/06/96	M	6	(4)	
38	Yll Prekopuca		10/07/89	M	8	(1)	
19	Amir Prishtina		22/01/94	D	18	(6)	1
15	Egzon Qerimi		10/11/93	M	3	(1)	
39	Bujar Rama		31/12/91	M	2	(1)	
47	Samir Sahiti		15/08/88	M	23	(4)	2
52	Besart Selimi		27/10/92	D		(1)	
29	Veton Shabani		05/05/90	M	11	(3)	1
18	Petrit Tahiri		06/02/93	G	8		
45	Drilon Teheci		26/12/97	D	2		
2	Din Voca		22/01/91	D	1	(2)	2
17	Liridon Voca		04/12/93	M	27	(2)	
34	Ferdinand Wilson	GHA	03/06/96	M	1	(1)	
24	Burim Xhemajli		09/09/90	M	15	(2)	
6	Enis Zabërgja		22/06/84	A	13	(7)	6
7	Bajram Zuqaku		26/07/89	A	5	(2)	1

KF Trepça'89

1989 • Riza Lushta (7,000) • no website

Major honours
Kosovan League (1) 2017; Kosovan Cup (1) 2012

Coach: Bekim Shotani; (07/09/16) Veton Çitaku; (03/03/17) Zekerija Ramadani (MKD)

2016

Date		Opponent		Score	Scorers
20/08	a	Gjilani	W	2-1	*John, Hasani*
28/08	h	Drita	W	1-0	*Idrizi (p)*
08/09	a	Feronikeli	L	1-4	*John*
11/09	h	Llapi	W	3-0	*Hasani, Hajdari 2*
18/09	a	Ferizaj	W	1-0	*Potoku*
23/09	h	Liria	W	2-0	*Idrizi, John*
28/09	a	Drenica	W	3-2	*John, Hajdari 2*
12/10	h	Hajvalia	W	1-0	*John*
16/10	a	Prishtina	W	2-0	*John 2*
23/10	h	Besa	W	2-1	*John, Hasani (p)*
29/10	a	Trepça	W	3-1	*Idrizi (p), Boniface, Hasani*
02/11	h	Gjilani	D	1-1	*D Mustafa*
06/11	a	Drita	D	0-0	
16/11	h	Feronikeli	D	0-0	
20/11	a	Llapi	L	0-2	
27/11	h	Ferizaj	W	4-1	*Hajdari, John 2, Hasani*
30/11	a	Liria	W	3-0	*John 2, Hasani*

2017

Date		Opponent		Score	Scorers
26/02	h	Drenica	W	4-0	*Islami, Hasani, Hajdari 2*
03/03	a	Hajvalia	W	4-0	*John 2, Hasani, Hyseni*
07/03	h	Prishtina	W	1-0	*John*
12/03	a	Besa	W	3-2	*John 2, Hasani (p)*
19/03	h	Trepça	W	6-1	*Hajdari, Idrizi, John, Hasani 2, Broja*
02/04	h	Liria	W	2-0	*John 2*
06/04	a	Drenica	D	0-0	
09/04	h	Ferizaj	D	0-0	
16/04	a	Drita	W	2-0	*Idrizi (p), John*
23/04	h	Trepça	W	3-1	*Broja, Idrizi, Jashari*
28/04	a	Hajvalia	W	3-0	*Hasani, John, Hajdari*
05/05	h	Gjilani	W	5-2	*Hasani 2, Lladrovci, John, Islami*
09/05	a	Besa	W	2-0	*John, Jashari*
14/05	h	Llapi	W	8-1	*Potoku, John 3, Hasani 2, Hyseni, Hajdari*
20/05	a	Prishtina	L	0-1	
28/05	h	Feronikeli	L	0-3	

No	Name	Nat	DoB	Pos	Aps	(s)	Gls
20	Genc Asllani		06/05/96	M	1		
28	Mathew Boniface	NGA	05/10/94	A	7	(2)	1
30	Rron Broja		09/04/96	M	12	(4)	2
10	Fiton Hajdari		19/09/91	M	22	(9)	10
1	Bledar Hajdini		19/06/95	G	32	(1)	
8	Pleurat Hajdini		21/01/95	A	1		
7	Florent Hasani		30/03/97	M	27	(6)	16
37	Hasan Hyseni		14/04/97	M	7	(2)	2
9	Shpetim Idrizi		12/11/81	M	12	(18)	6
21	Perparim Islami		01/05/93	D	31	(1)	2
23	Ilir Izmaku		17/05/83	D	28	(1)	
15	Muharrem Jashari		21/02/98	M	22	(7)	2
3	Otto John	NGA	25/01/98	A	14	(19)	27
26	Lapidar Lladrovci		15/12/90	D	4	(6)	1
17	Ylber Maloku		04/01/96	M	23	(8)	
12	Enis Manxholli		14/07/86	G	1		
35	Marco de Paula	BRA	31/05/98	M	1		
6	Daut Maxhuni		09/12/90	D	6	(3)	
27	Argjend Mustafa		22/10/93	M	9	(3)	
14	Diar Mustafa		07/11/93	M	17	(9)	1
18	Rrahim Nimani		17/03/99	M	6		
4	Edon Pasoma		21/08/92	D	18	(1)	
16	Albert Peci		06/06/97	D	2		
19	Diar Pepiqi		13/02/97	M	2		
13	Arbër Potoku		18/09/94	D	31		2
38	Kaba Sambou	GAM	20/04/96	D	10	(1)	
25	Leotrim Troshupa		12/08/92	A	17		

KOSOVO

Top goalscorers

27	Otto John (Trepça'89)
16	Florent Hasani (Trepça'89)
14	Granit Arifaj (Drenica)
13	Khalid Abdul Basit (Prishtina)
12	Betim Haxhimusa (Gjilani) Liridon Fetahaj (Liria)
11	Qemail Elshani (Besa)
10	Gauthier Makenda (Prishtina) Fiton Hajdari (Trepça'89)
9	Xhevdet Shabani (Besa) Mendurim Hoti (Feronikeli) Florim Berbatovci (Llapi)

Promoted clubs

KF Flamurtari

1968 • Flamurtari (2,000) • no website
Coach: Samuel Nikaj (ALB)

FC Vëllaznimi

1927 • Zahir Pajaziti (3,000) • no website
Coach: Arsim Gojani

KF Vllaznia

1973 • Ibrahim Kurteshi (1,000) • no website
Coach: Sallah Sherifi

Second level final table 2016/17

		Pld	W	D	L	F	A	Pts
1	KF Flamurtari	30	21	5	4	44	12	68
2	FC Vëllaznimi	30	21	5	4	60	27	68
3	KF Vllaznia	30	15	7	8	43	25	52
4	KF Dukagjini	30	15	7	8	50	28	52
5	KF 2 Korriku	30	12	11	7	48	33	47
6	KF Vushtrria	30	13	6	11	42	32	45
7	KF Fushë Kosova	30	12	6	12	34	28	42
8	KF Vitia	30	10	11	9	38	38	41
9	KF KEK-u	30	11	7	12	35	38	40
10	KF Ballkani	30	9	8	13	32	45	35
11	KF Ramiz Sadiku	30	10	5	15	34	51	35
12	KF Kosova Prishtinë	30	10	4	16	44	58	34
13	KF Ulpiana	30	8	8	14	34	52	32
14	KF Rahoveci	30	8	6	16	22	39	30
15	KF Istogu	30	6	7	17	37	52	25
16	KF Deçani	30	4	7	19	26	65	19

Promotion/Relegation play-offs

(03/06/17)
Vllaznia 1-1 Ferizaj *(aet; 3-2 on pens)*

(04/06/17)
Drita 2-1 Dukagjini

DOMESTIC CUP

Kupa e Kosovës 2016/17

FOURTH ROUND

(18/02/17)
Drenica 3-0 KEK-u
Ferizaj 1-0 Gjilani
Feronikeli 2-2 Llapi *(aet; 2-4 on pens)*
Hajvalia 0-4 Trepça'89

(19/02/17)
Besa 3-1 Drita *(aet)*
Liria 2-0 Bashkimi
Vëllaznimi 0-1 Prishtina

(21/02/17)
Flamurtari 0-0 Trepça *(aet; 4-5 on pens)*

QUARTER-FINALS

(15/03/17)
Besa 1-0 Prishtina *(Dumani 35og)*

Drenica 1-0 Ferizaj *(Dajaku 44p)*

Llapi 4-3 Liria *(Krasniqi 38p, Hyseni 39, 93, Karabegu 65; B Memaj 45, Chibueze 56, 58) (aet)*

(16/03/17)
Trepça 2-2 Trepça'89 *(Sahiti 51, Ergyn Ahmeti 78; Hajdari 88, Hyseni 90+1) (aet; 4-3 on pens)*

SEMI-FINALS

(29/03/17 & 19/04/17)
Drenica 0-0 Llapi
Llapi 4-1 Drenica *(Berbatovci 18, 60, Namani 48, 69; Abazi 90+1)*
(Llapi 4-1)

Trepça 2-2 Besa *(Hajdini 39, Qerimi 79; Elshani 8, Qorraj 63)*
Besa 6-0 Trepça *(Shabani 3, 31, Sheqerolli 37, 64, Karahoda 70, Rexha 78)*
(Besa 8-2)

FINAL

(31/05/17)
Riza Lushta, Mitrovice
KF BESA 1 *(Miftaraj 29p)*
KF LLAPI 1 *(Krasniqi 49p)*
(aet; 4-2 on pens)
Referee: *Nuza*
BESA: *Beqiri, Fisnik Papuqi, Turku, Prekazi, Osmani, Emini, Elshani, Miftaraj, Dabiqaj, Shabani (Qorraj 41), Karahoda (Rexha 57)*
LLAPI: *Avdyli, Idrizi, Jashari, Sinani, Kadriu, Namani, E Zeqiri, Karabegu (Hyseni 80), Berbatovci, V Zeqiri, Daku (K Shabani 98)*

Besa lift the Kosovan Cup for the third time

LATVIA

Latvijas Futbola Federācija (LFF)

Address	Olympic Sports Centre Grostonas Street 6b LV-1013 Rīga
Tel	+371 67 292988
Fax	+371 67 315604
E-mail	futbols@lff.lv
Website	lff.lv

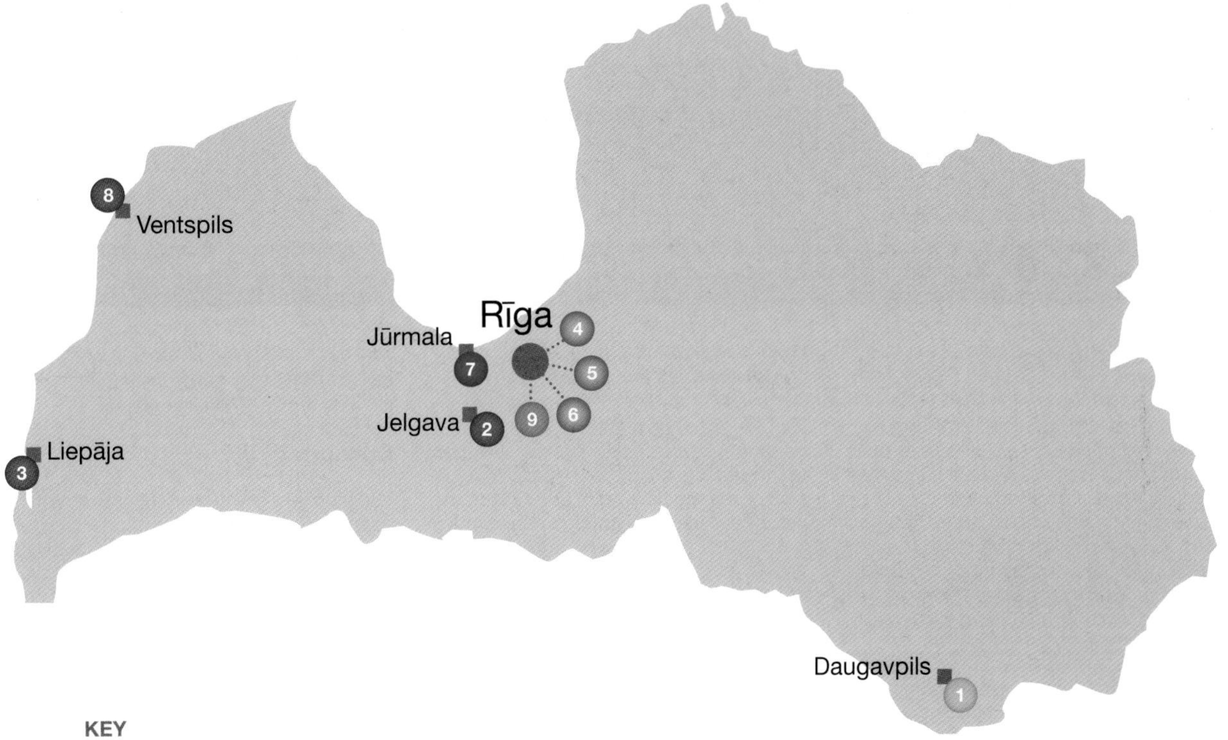

President	Guntis Indriksons
General secretary	Jānis Mežeckis
Media officer	Viktors Sopirins
Year of formation	1921
National stadium	Skonto, Riga (9,500)

Ventspils 8
Rīga 4 5 6 9
Jūrmala 7
Jelgava 2
Liepāja 3
Daugavpils 1

KEY
- UEFA Champions League
- UEFA Europa League
- Promoted
- Relegated

0 50 100 km
0 50 miles

VIRSLĪGA CLUBS

1 **BFC Daugavpils**

2 **FK Jelgava**

3 **FK Liepāja**

4 **FS METTA**

5 **Riga FC**

6 **Rīgas FS**

7 **FK Spartaks Jūrmala**

8 **FK Ventspils**

PROMOTED CLUB

9 **SK Babīte**

Spartaks take centre stage

There was a new addition to the Virslīga roll of honour – in the year of the competition's 25th anniversary – as Spartaks Jūrmala upset the odds to become the fourth different Latvian champions in five seasons.

It was the first Virslīga campaign to be staged without financially-stricken Skonto FC, winners of the first 13 editions, and Spartaks dominated throughout until a late slump almost let in FK Ventspils, who went on to win the Latvian Cup the following spring.

Jurmala outfit secure first Virslīga title

Ventspils win cup final in penalty shoot-out

Starkovs replaces Pahars as national team coach

Domestic league

Spartaks had never managed to finish higher than fifth in their four previous seasons among Latvia's elite, with their debut season in 2012 the only time they had ended up in the top half of the table. A woeful ending to the 2015 campaign, with seven of their last eight fixtures resulting in defeat, prompted a change of coach, Belarusian Oleg Kubarev returning to the club he had led in the first half of the 2013 campaign.

Aided by some astute new signings, including a trio of his compatriots – defender Sergei Pushnyakov, midfielder Sergei Kozeka and striker Dmitri Platonov – Kubarev started his second spell in style, overseeing five wins in the opening six games. Things got even better in mid-campaign when Kubarev's youthful charges reeled off ten wins in 12 matches to assume a seemingly unbreachable position at the top of the table.

At the end of August, with eight games left, Spartaks boasted a commanding ten-point lead over Ventspils. But then, suddenly, the tide turned. Spartaks failed to win any of their next five games while their rivals, with four wins and a draw over the same stretch, including a 1-0 victory in Jurmala, now found themselves a point clear at the top. However, no sooner were Paul Ashworth's side in front than they fell behind again, and when they followed a home defeat against third-placed Jelgava with another 2-1 loss at lowly METTA – despite veteran striker Ģirts Karlsons' golden boot-winning 17th goal of the season – Spartaks took advantage, beating METTA 2-0 at home before sealing their maiden title with a 2-0 win at Virslīga newcomers Rīgas FS thanks to a header from midfielder Andrejs Kiriļins and a late second goal from Russian import Evgeni Kozlov.

Spartaks were champions despite losing a quarter of their matches. BFC Daugavpils lost three times as many, though, and were doomed to relegation long before the season's end. METTA saved their top-flight status with a play-off win, meaning that only runaway 1. līga winners SK Babīte (26 wins from 28 matches) won promotion, thereby reaching the top flight for the first time.

Domestic cup

After squandering the opportunity to win a seventh league title, Ventspils made partial amends by lifting a seventh Latvian Cup, the 2016/17 competition concluding like four of the previous eight with a penalty shoot-out. New merger club Riga FC were their victims in the final, going down 6-5 on spot-kicks after a see-saw encounter that had brought a goal apiece for each side in both normal and extra time. Ventspils' victory confirmed that it was not a campaign for upsets, with all eight quarter-final spots having been filled by the 2016 Virslīga clubs.

Europe

The highlight of a generally uneventful summer for Latvian clubs on the European front was a 3-0 home (and aggregate) win for Jelgava against Slovan Bratislava in the second qualifying round of the UEFA Europa League. Spartaks' elimination in the previous round was particularly poignant for Kubarev and co as they fell to Belarusian opposition in Dinamo Minsk.

National team

Latvia began their 2018 FIFA World Cup qualifying campaign with a 1-0 win in Andorra courtesy of striker Valērijs Šabala's tenth international goal. However, that was as good as it got, and by the end of the season, somewhat surprisingly, Latvia found themselves a point below the minnows from the Pyrenees at the foot of the Group B table, having lost five games in a row. Marians Pahars stood down after a 5-0 friendly defeat by Georgia in March, paving the way for the return – for a third spell in charge – of the country's most revered and successful coach, Aleksandrs Starkovs.

DOMESTIC SEASON AT A GLANCE

Virslīga 2016 final table

			Home					Away					Total					
		Pld	W	D	L	F	A	W	D	L	F	A	W	D	L	F	A	Pts
1	**FK Spartaks Jūrmala**	**28**	**9**	**2**	**3**	**26**	**9**	**8**	**2**	**4**	**20**	**13**	**17**	**4**	**7**	**46**	**22**	**55**
2	FK Jelgava	28	11	0	3	28	11	5	3	6	9	13	16	3	9	37	24	51
3	FK Ventspils	28	8	3	3	20	9	7	3	4	27	19	15	6	7	47	28	51
4	FK Liepāja	28	6	2	6	23	19	6	4	4	15	12	12	6	10	38	31	42
5	Riga FC	28	6	6	2	15	8	2	6	6	13	16	8	12	8	28	24	36
6	Rīgas FS	28	6	4	4	14	13	3	4	7	8	18	9	8	11	22	31	35
7	FS METTA	28	5	5	4	18	16	3	1	10	14	31	8	6	14	32	47	30
8	BFC Daugavpils	28	2	3	9	8	26	0	2	12	5	30	2	5	21	13	56	11

European qualification 2017/18

Champion: FK Spartaks Jūrmala (second qualifying round)

Cup winner: FK Ventspils (first qualifying round)

FK Jelgava (first qualifying round)
FK Liepāja (first qualifying round)

Top scorer Ģirts Karlsons (Ventspils), 17 goals
Relegated club BFC Daugavpils
Promoted club SK Babīte
Cup final FK Ventspils 2-2 Riga FC *(aet; 6-5 on pens)*

Player of the season

Gļebs Kļuškins
(FK Jelgava)

A regular place in midfield for the Latvian national team during the 2018 FIFA World Cup qualifying campaign was the reward for Kļuškins after a stellar 2016 season in the Virslīga for another maroon-shirted team, Jelgava. The blond-haired 24-year-old saved his best form for the closing weeks, scoring both goals in a 2-0 win over league leaders Spartaks Jūrmala and the winner in a 2-1 victory away to Ventspils that helped his club claim the league runners-up spot for the first time. He ended the season as Jelgava's joint top scorer with seven goals.

Newcomer of the season

Jevgeņijs Kazačoks
(FK Spartaks Jūrmala)

Kazačoks began his first full season as a Spartaks regular by striking the winning goal on the opening day against defending champions FK Liepāja. It proved to be the sign of things to come for both player and club, with the 21-year-old attacking midfielder proving to be one of his team's principal assets as they went on to win the Virslīga title. He ended up with ten goals for the season and earned promotion from the Latvian Under-21s to the senior side the following year, making his debut against Portugal in Aleksandrs Starkovs' first match back in charge.

Team of the season

(4-2-3-1)

Coach: Kubarev *(Spartaks)*

LATVIA

NATIONAL TEAM

International tournament appearances
UEFA European Championship (1) 2004

Top five all-time caps
Vitālijs Astafjevs (167); Andrejs Rubins (117); Juris Laizāns (108); Imants Bleidelis (106); Mihails Zemļinskis (105)

Top five all-time goals
Māris Verpakovskis (29); Ēriks Pētersons (21); Vitālijs Astafjevs (16); Juris Laizāns & Marians Pahars (15)

Results 2016/17

02/09/16	Luxembourg	H	Riga	W	3-1	*D Ikaunieks (3), Zjuzins (46, 51)*
06/09/16	Andorra (WCQ)	A	Andorra la Vella	W	1-0	*Šabala (48)*
07/10/16	Faroe Islands (WCQ)	H	Riga	L	0-2	
10/10/16	Hungary (WCQ)	H	Riga	L	0-2	
13/11/16	Portugal (WCQ)	A	Faro	L	1-4	*Zjuzins (67)*
25/03/17	Switzerland (WCQ)	A	Geneva	L	0-1	
28/03/17	Georgia	A	Tbilisi	L	0-5	
09/06/17	Portugal (WCQ)	H	Riga	L	0-3	
12/06/17	Estonia	H	Riga	L	1-2	*D Ikaunieks (22)*

Appearances 2016/17

Coach: Marians Pahars /(19/04/17) Aleksandrs Starkovs	**05/08/76 26/07/55**		Lux	AND	FRO	HUN	POR	SUI	Geo	POR	Est	Caps	Goals
Andris Vaņins	30/04/80	Zürich (SUI)	G	G	G	G	G	G	G46	G		82	-
Vladislavs Gabovs	13/07/87	Korona (POL)	D	D	D	D	M	s56				31	-
Igors Tarasovs	16/10/88	Giresunspor (TUR)	D68			M	M					18	-
Kaspars Gorkšs	06/11/81	Liepāja /Riga	D	D	D	D	D	D	D	D	D	86	5
Vitālijs Maksimenko	08/12/90	Mattersburg (AUT)	D	D	D	D	D		D	D	s46	31	1
Dāvis Ikaunieks	07/01/94	Jihlava (CZE)	M54	M63	s76	M	M59	M69	M	M68	M46	11	2
Artūrs Zjuzins	18/06/91	Tambov (RUS)	M75	M74	s72	s57	s59					36	7
Artis Lazdiņš	03/05/86	Jelgava	M	M45				M77	s81			29	-
Aleksejs Višņakovs	03/02/84	Rīgas FS	M67	M	M	M57	s79	M56	M46			75	9
Valērijs Šabala	12/10/94	Dunajská Streda (SVK) /Riga	A54	A	A	A		A	s46	A	A65	34	10
Artjoms Rudņevs	13/01/88	Köln (GER)	A84				A87					38	2
Jānis Ikaunieks	16/02/95	Metz (FRA) /Larissa (GRE)	s54	M		s68			M		s76	16	2
Cristián Torres	18/06/85	Liepāja	s54	s63								2	-
Artūrs Karašausks	29/01/92	Wil (SUI)	s67	s74		s77						13	-
Vitālijs Jagodinskis	28/02/92	unattached /Diósgyőr (HUN)	s68	D	D	D	D	D	D46	D	D46	17	-
Oļegs Laizāns	28/03/87	Riga	s75	s45	M	M77	M	M	M81	M	M58	42	-
Sergejs Vorobjovs	09/10/95	Riga	s84									3	-
Gļebs Kļuškins	01/10/92	Jelgava			M72	M68	M79	M	M65	M62	s58	8	-
Ivans Lukjanovs	24/01/87	Fakel (RUS)			M76				s65			17	-
Vladislavs Gutkovskis	02/04/95	Nieciecza (POL)			A64		s87	s77			s46	4	-
Ģirts Karlsons	07/06/81	Ventspils			s64				A46			51	9
Gints Freimanis	09/05/85	Jelgava					D	D				8	-
Aleksandrs Solovjovs	25/02/88	Rīgas FS						D	D	D	D	4	-
Deniss Rakels	20/08/92	Reading (ENG)						s69	s46	s68		17	-
Mārcis Ošs	25/07/91	Jelgava							s46			1	-
Pāvels Šteinbors	21/09/85	Arka (POL)							s46		G	3	-
Ņikita Koļesovs	25/09/96	Ventspils								D	D	2	-
Jevgeņijs Kazačoks	12/08/95	Spartaks Jūrmala								M72	M58	2	-
Dāvis Indrāns	06/06/95	METTA								s62	M76	2	-
Edgars Vardanjans	09/05/93	Spartaks Jūrmala								s72	s58	2	-
Vladimirs Kamešs	28/10/88	Enisey (RUS)									M	14	1
Roberts Uldriķis	03/04/98	Rīgas FS									s65	1	-

EUROPE

FK Liepāja

Second qualifying round - FC Salzburg (AUT)

A 0-1

Doroševs, Kļava, Strumia (Gucs 27), Gorkšs, Kārkliņš, Torres (Afanasjevs 70), Brtan, Ivanovs, Mickevičs (Kurtišs 61), Kamešs, Kluk. Coach: Viktors Dobrecovs (LVA)

H 0-2

Doroševs, Kļava, Gorkšs, Gucs (Mickevičs 71), Kārkliņš, Torres, Grebis (Gauračs 65), Brtan, Ivanovs, Kamešs (Afanasjevs 57), Kluk. Coach: Viktors Dobrecovs (LVA)

FK Jelgava

First qualifying round - Breidablik (ISL)

A 3-2 *Kļuškins (10), Redjko (33), Grigaravičius (44)*

Ikstens, Smirnovs, Freimanis, Nakano, Redjko, Bogdaškins (Malašenoks 90), Turkovs (Silich 70), Diallo, Grigaravičius (Sorokins 78), Kļuškins, Lazdiņš. Coach: Saulius Širmelis (LTU)

H 2-2 *Turkovs (15), Diallo (70)*

Ikstens, Smirnovs (Savčenkovs 46), Freimanis, Nakano, Redjko, Bogdaškins, Turkovs (Kovaļovs 84), Diallo, Grigaravičius, Kļuškins, Lazdiņš. Coach: Saulius Širmelis (LTU)

Second qualifying round - ŠK Slovan Bratislava (SVK)

A 0-0

Ikstens, Savčenkovs, Freimanis, Nakano (Sorokins 82), Redjko, Bogdaškins, Turkovs (Malašenoks 72), Diallo, Grigaravičius (Kovaļovs 62), Kļuškins, Lazdiņš. Coach: Saulius Širmelis (LTU)

H 3-0 *Kļuškins (27p), Bogdaškins (48), Malašenoks (85)*

Ikstens, Savčenkovs, Freimanis, Nakano, Redjko, Bogdaškins, Malašenoks (Smirnovs 90+1), Diallo, Grigaravičius (Kovaļovs 82), Kļuškins (Osipovs 64), Lazdiņš. Coach: Saulius Širmelis (LTU)

Red card: Diallo 89

Third qualifying round - Beitar Jerusalem FC (ISR)

H 1-1 *Smirnovs (70)*

Ikstens, Savčenkovs, Smirnovs, Freimanis, Nakano, Redjko (Osipovs 28), Bogdaškins, Malašenoks, Grigaravičius (Kovaļovs 71), Kļuškins (Perepļotkins 55), Lazdiņš. Coach: Saulius Širmelis (LTU)

A 0-3

Ikstens, Savčenkovs, Smirnovs, Freimanis, Nakano, Bogdaškins, Perepļotkins (Kovaļovs 54), Osipovs, Grigaravičius (Labanovskis 71), Kļuškins (Malašenoks 63), Lazdiņš. Coach: Saulius Širmelis (LTU)

FK Ventspils

First qualifying round - Víkingur (FRO)

H 2-0 *Karlsons (5, 37)*

Uvarenko, Siņeļnikovs, Paulius, Tīdenbergs, Alekseev (Mujeci 46), Koļesovs, Karlsons (Svārups 90+2), Rečickis, Boranijašević, Rugins, Jemeļins. Coach: Paul Ashworth (ENG)

A 2-0 *Jemeļins (57p), Karlsons (90+2)*

Uvarenko, Siņeļnikovs (Žigajevs 64), Paulius, Tīdenbergs, Alekseev (Obuobi 76), Koļesovs, Karlsons, Rečickis (Alfa 63), Boranijašević, Rugins, Jemeļins. Coach: Paul Ashworth (ENG)

Second qualifying round - Aberdeen FC (SCO)

A 0-3

Uvarenko, Siņeļnikovs, Paulius, Tīdenbergs (Žuļevs 81), Alekseev (Svārups 87), Koļesovs, Karlsons, Rečickis, Boranijašević, Rugins, Jemeļins. Coach: Paul Ashworth (ENG)

H 0-1

Uvarenko, Obuobi, Siņeļnikovs (Tīdenbergs 65), Paulius, Alekseev (Svārups 81), Koļesovs, Karlsons, Rečickis (Alfa 86), Boranijašević, Rugins, Jemeļins. Coach: Paul Ashworth (ENG)

FK Spartaks Jūrmala

First qualifying round - FC Dinamo Minsk (BLR)

A 1-2 *Ulimbaševs (80)*

Kurakins, Kazačoks, Adeyemo, Kozlov, Yaghoubi, Pushnyakov, Kozeka, Kozlovs, Mihadjuks, Platonov (Ulimbaševs 35), Šlampe. Coach: Oleg Kubarev (BLR)

H 0-2

Kurakins, Ulimbaševs (Stuglis 71), Kazačoks, Adeyemo (Platonov 81), Kozlov, Yaghoubi, Pushnyakov, Kozeka, Kozlovs (Korzāns 66), Mihadjuks, Šlampe. Coach: Oleg Kubarev (BLR)

DOMESTIC LEAGUE CLUB-BY-CLUB

BFC Daugavpils

2009 • Celtnieks (4,070) • no website

Coach: Sergejs Pogodins

2016

Date		Opponent		Score	Scorers
13/03	a	METTA	L	1-2	*Ryzhevski*
19/03	a	Spartaks	L	0-3	
03/04	h	Rīgas FS	W	1-0	*og (Isajevs)*
16/04	h	Ventspils	L	0-5	
23/04	h	Riga	L	0-2	
30/04	a	Jelgava	L	1-3	*Ryzhevski*
09/05	h	Liepāja	L	0-3	
15/05	h	METTA	L	0-1	
27/05	h	Spartaks	L	0-2	
12/06	a	Rīgas FS	D	0-0	
18/06	a	Ventspils	L	0-3	
26/06	a	Riga	L	0-2	
08/07	a	Liepāja	L	0-1	
23/07	a	METTA	D	2-2	*Krot 2*
30/07	a	Spartaks	L	1-4	*Alexeev*
08/08	h	Rīgas FS	L	0-1	
13/08	a	Ventspils	L	0-2	
20/08	h	Riga	D	2-2	*Krot, Klimaševičs*
24/08	h	Jelgava	D	0-0	
28/08	a	Jelgava	L	0-2	
10/09	h	Liepāja	L	0-1	
18/09	h	METTA	D	3-3	*Krot (p), Ryzhevski, Shebanov*
24/09	h	Spartaks	W	2-1	*Ryzhevski, Shebanov*
01/10	a	Rīgas FS	L	0-2	
16/10	h	Ventspils	L	0-4	
23/10	a	Riga	L	0-3	
29/10	h	Jelgava	L	0-1	
05/11	a	Liepāja	L	0-1	

No	Name	Nat	DoB	Pos	Aps	(s)	Gls
19	Mirabdulla Abbasov	AZE	27/04/95	M	4	(3)	
25	Serghei Alexeev	MDA	31/05/86	A	5	(2)	1
10	Moez Aloulou	TUN	30/06/88	M	7		
4	Deniss Bezuščonoks		20/08/96	D	17		
29	Jānis Bovins		23/06/93	M		(1)	
1	Pavels Davidovs		30/12/80	G	4		
28	Marks Deružinskis		23/10/97	M	7	(4)	
20	Ņikita Dobratulins		20/07/95	M	5	(5)	
21	Vitālijs Dubrovskis		21/06/96	M	1	(4)	
3	Papa Abdoulaye Faly	USA	12/11/91	D	8	(2)	
9,39	Vladislavs Fjodorovs		27/09/96	M	21		
8	Oleg Inkin	RUS	06/03/90	M	1	(1)	
18	Dmitrijs Klimaševičs		16/04/95	D	22		1
10	Kaspars Kokins		26/04/00	A	2	(5)	
30,99	Deniss Kozlovs		29/04/99	A		(5)	
19	Sergei Krot	BLR	27/06/80	A	6	(7)	4
28	Cedric Krou	FRA	25/07/91	D	5		
25	Roman Kulikov	CZE	05/10/95	D	7	(1)	
4,5	Pāvels Liholetovs		04/07/97	D	11		
4	Dmitrijs Litvinskis		17/08/99	D	7	(1)	
30	Miguel Cid	POR	21/05/92	M	9		
17	Anastasijs Mordatenko		24/08/96	M	5	(1)	
22,1	Jevģēnijs Nerugals		26/02/89	G	17		
20,8	Haralds Pakers		11/12/99	D		(1)	
99	John Prince	NGA	08/01/98	A		(1)	
8	Orxan Qurbanlı	AZE	12/07/95	M	5	(3)	
20	Denis Rassulov	MDA	02/01/90	D	5	(1)	
23	Pavel Ryzhevski	BLR	03/03/81	A	14	(7)	4
8	Aleksei Shebanov	RUS	01/06/93	M	12	(1)	2
20	Raivis Skrebels		26/09/99	M	3	(3)	
25	Armands Snarskis		29/11/99	D	1	(1)	
11	Jurijs Sokolovs		12/09/83	D	22	(1)	
27	Sergei Tsvetinski	BLR	22/02/84	D	13		
8	Aivars Ugarenko		05/06/97	M		(4)	
21	Edgars Urbāns		15/09/99	M	1	(2)	
5	Edgars Vērdiņš		29/03/93	M	20	(2)	
1	Aleksandrs Vlasovs		07/05/86	G	7		
25	Vladimirs Volkovs		10/08/84	M	25	(2)	
99	Ričards Žaldovskis		05/06/99	A	1	(6)	
29	Vitālijs Ziļs		19/08/87	A	8	(2)	

LATVIA

FK Jelgava

2004 • Zemgales Olimpiskā centra (2,560) • fkjelgava.lv

Major honours
Latvian Cup (4) 2010, 2014, 2015, 2016

Coach: Vitālijs Astafjevs; (17/05/16) Dāvis Caune; (07/06/16) Saulius Širmelis (LTU)

2016					
12/03	h	Rīgas FS	W	4-0	*Savčenkovs, Lazdiņš, Silich, Kauber*
20/03	a	Riga	D	1-1	*Turkovs*
04/04	h	Liepāja	L	0-1	
16/04	a	Spartaks	L	0-3	
22/04	a	Ventspils	L	0-1	
30/04	h	Daugavpils	W	3-1	*Klimovich 2, Smirnovs*
08/05	a	METTA	L	0-3	
14/05	a	Rīgas FS	L	0-1	
28/05	h	Riga	W	2-1	*Turkovs, Kovaļovs*
11/06	a	Liepāja	W	1-0	*Bogdaškins*
18/06	h	Spartaks	L	0-1	
22/06	h	Ventspils	W	4-3	*Grigaravičius, Bogdaškins, Kļuškins, Kovaļovs (p)*
10/07	h	METTA	W	2-0	*Grigaravičius, Kovaļovs*
25/07	h	Rīgas FS	W	2-0	*Diallo, Osipovs*
08/08	h	Liepāja	W	3-2	*Grigaravičius, Laukžemis, Kovaļovs*
13/08	a	Spartaks	D	0-0	
20/08	h	Ventspils	W	2-0	*Bogdaškins, Kļuškins*
24/08	a	Daugavpils	D	0-0	
28/08	h	Daugavpils	W	2-0	*Kļuškins, Kovaļovs*
10/09	a	METTA	W	1-0	*Nakano*
16/09	a	Rīgas FS	L	0-1	
25/09	h	Riga	W	1-0	*Perepļotkins*
30/09	a	Liepāja	W	3-1	*Laukžemis, Perepļotkins, Kļuškins*
16/10	h	Spartaks	W	2-0	*Kļuškins 2*
19/10	a	Riga	L	0-1	
22/10	a	Ventspils	W	2-1	*Nakano, Kļuškins*
29/10	a	Daugavpils	W	1-0	*Kovaļovs*
05/11	h	METTA	L	1-2	*Kovaļovs*

No	Name	Nat	DoB	Pos	Aps	(s)	Gls
10	Boriss Bogdaškins		21/02/90	M	19	(5)	3
19	Aleksejs Davidenkovs		27/06/98	A		(1)	
15	Abdoulaye Diallo	SEN	21/10/92	D	17	(3)	1
5	Gints Freimanis		09/05/85	D	25		
20	Mindaugas Grigaravičius	LTU	15/07/92	M	14	(3)	3
1	Kaspars Ikstens		05/06/88	G	28		
29	Kevin Kauber	EST	23/03/95	A	3	(6)	1
21	Vladislav Klimovich	BLR	12/06/96	A	8	(2)	2
23	Gļebs Kļuškins		01/10/92	M	20	(2)	7
8	Andrejs Kovaļovs		23/03/89	M	22	(4)	7
19	Karolis Laukžemis	LTU	11/03/92	A	14	(1)	2
28	Artis Lazdiņš		03/05/86	M	20		1
17	Viktors Litvinskis		07/02/96	D	6	(1)	
12	Oļegs Malašenoks		27/04/86	A	1	(19)	
6	Ryotaro Nakano	JPN	13/06/88	M	20	(4)	2
17	Artjoms Osipovs		08/01/89	D	10	(2)	1
25	Mārcis Ošs		25/07/91	D	10		
14	Andrejs Perepļotkins		27/12/84	A	8	(7)	2
7	Valerijs Redjko		10/03/83	D	15	(3)	
3	Igors Savčenkovs		03/11/82	D	14		1
9	Kyrylo Silich	UKR	03/08/90	M	8	(4)	1
4	Vitālijs Smirnovs		28/06/86	D	12		1
2	Vladislavs Sorokins		10/05/97	D	7	(2)	
11	Daniils Turkovs		17/02/88	A	7	(6)	2
27	Verners Zalaks		05/04/97	A		(1)	

FK Liepāja

2014 • Daugava (5,008); Daugava artificial (2,000) • fkliepaja.lv

Major honours
Latvian League (1) 2015

Coach: Viktors Dobrecovs

2016					
11/03	h	Spartaks	L	1-2	*Ikaunieks*
20/03	a	Ventspils	D	2-2	*Kļava 2*
04/04	a	Jelgava	W	1-0	*Ikaunieks*
17/04	a	METTA	W	2-0	*Kļava (p), Kamešs*
24/04	a	Rīgas FS	L	0-1	
30/04	h	Riga	W	3-0	*Ikaunieks, Gauračs 2*
09/05	a	Daugavpils	W	3-0	*Kļava, Gauračs, Ikaunieks*
14/05	a	Spartaks	W	1-0	*Grebis*
26/05	a	Ventspils	L	0-2	
11/06	h	Jelgava	L	0-1	
17/06	h	METTA	W	3-0	*Kamešs 2, Dobrecovs*
26/06	h	Rīgas FS	W	3-1	*Ikaunieks, Kamešs, Gauračs*
01/07	a	Riga	D	0-0	
08/07	h	Daugavpils	W	1-0	*Kārkliņš*
24/07	h	Spartaks	W	4-3	*Kamešs, Brtan, Grebis 2*
30/07	h	Ventspils	L	2-3	*Mickevičs, Kurtišs*
08/08	a	Jelgava	L	2-3	*Kurtišs, Kārkliņš*
13/08	h	METTA	L	2-3	*Mickevičs, Kurtišs*
19/08	a	Rīgas FS	D	1-1	*Brtan*
26/08	a	Riga	W	1-0	*Torres*
10/09	a	Daugavpils	W	1-0	*Kļava (p)*
17/09	a	Spartaks	D	0-0	
23/09	h	Ventspils	D	0-0	
30/09	h	Jelgava	L	1-3	*Tomić*
15/10	a	METTA	L	1-3	*Kurtišs*
21/10	h	Rīgas FS	L	0-1	
29/10	h	Riga	D	2-2	*Kļava, Dobrecovs*
05/11	h	Daugavpils	W	1-0	*Kurtišs*

No	Name	Nat	DoB	Pos	Aps	(s)	Gls
19	Valerijs Afanasjevs		20/09/82	M	21	(4)	
8	Ņikita Bērenfelds		07/06/95	D	10	(3)	
24	Marko Brtan	CRO	07/04/91	M	13		2
91	Devids Dobrecovs		26/02/97	M	2	(6)	2
12	Pāvels Doroševs		09/10/80	G	26		
6	Ubong Francis	NGA	02/05/95	D	1		
10	Edgars Gauračs		10/03/88	A	7	(5)	4
13	Kaspars Gorkšs		06/11/81	D	13		
23	Kristaps Grebis		31/12/80	A	12	(7)	3
17	Toms Gucs		28/04/92	M	11	(10)	
4	Krists Kristers Gulbis		15/01/97	D	1		
7	Dmitrijs Hmizs		31/07/92	M		(2)	
9	Dāvis Ikaunieks		07/01/94	A	12		5
26	Deniss Ivanovs		31/08/97	D	19	(1)	
33	Vladimirs Kamešs		28/10/88	D	14		5
18	Krišs Kārkliņš		31/01/96	M	17	(8)	2
3	Oskars Kļava		08/08/83	D	23	(1)	6
40	Dino Kluk	CRO	13/05/91	D	13		
11	Marks Kurtišs		26/01/98	A	10	(14)	5
27	Romāns Mickevičs		29/03/93	M	17	(10)	2
24	Pāvels Mihadjuks		27/05/80	D	3	(1)	
14	Endijs Šlampe		24/07/94	D	4	(1)	
32	Gļebs Sopots		18/08/96	G	1		
5	Leonel Strumia	ARG	29/09/92	M	25		
9	Dario Tomić	BIH	23/06/87	D	9		1
20	Cristián Torres		18/06/85	M	18	(8)	1
15	Antons Tumanovs		16/04/97	D	5	(2)	
1	Krišjānis Zviedris		25/01/97	G	1		

FS METTA

2006 • Hanzas vidusskolas laukums (2,000) • fsmetta.lv

Coach: Andris Riherts

2016					
13/03	h	Daugavpils	W	2-1	*G Kalniņš 2*
19/03	a	Rīgas FS	L	2-3	*og (Dzelme), Vardanjans*
02/04	h	Riga	W	1-0	*Bāliņš*
17/04	h	Liepāja	L	0-2	
23/04	h	Spartaks	L	0-1	
30/04	a	Ventspils	L	0-2	
08/05	h	Jelgava	W	3-0	*Ashrifie, G Kalniņš, Stuglis*
15/05	a	Daugavpils	W	1-0	*og (Klimaševičs)*
28/05	h	Rīgas FS	D	1-1	*Abdullahi*
11/06	a	Riga	L	1-2	*Ashrifie*
17/06	a	Liepāja	L	0-3	
25/06	a	Spartaks	L	1-4	*Indrāns*
10/07	a	Jelgava	L	0-2	
23/07	h	Daugavpils	D	2-2	*Uldriķis 2*
01/08	a	Rīgas FS	L	0-3	
06/08	h	Riga	D	1-1	*Stuglis (p)*
13/08	a	Liepāja	W	3-2	*G Kalniņš, Šibass, Uldriķis*
19/08	h	Spartaks	L	1-3	*Uldriķis*
24/08	h	Ventspils	D	1-1	*G Kalniņš*
28/08	a	Ventspils	L	0-2	
10/09	h	Jelgava	L	0-1	
18/09	a	Daugavpils	D	3-3	*Uldriķis, Abdullahi, Stuglis (p)*
24/09	h	Rīgas FS	D	1-1	*Miyazaki*
01/10	a	Riga	L	1-2	*Vardanjans (p)*
15/10	h	Liepāja	W	3-1	*Emsis, Abbas, Abdullahi*
22/10	a	Spartaks	L	0-2	
29/10	h	Ventspils	W	2-1	*Uldriķis, Vardanjans*
05/11	a	Jelgava	W	2-1	*Abdullahi, Miyazaki*

No	Name	Nat	DoB	Pos	Aps	(s)	Gls
20	Usman Abbas	NGA	10/07/98	D	14		1
14	Adamu Abdullahi	NGA	01/01/94	A	22	(2)	4
25	Abraham Ashrifie	GHA	20/08/95	D	25		2
3	Dāvids Bagdasarjans		04/09/94	D	2	(2)	
21	Hassan Bala	NGA	08/08/96	D	2	(1)	
20	Klavs Bāliņš		09/02/96	D	4	(1)	1
6	Eduards Emsis		23/02/96	M	23		1
11	Konstantīns Fjodorovs		28/04/96	A	1	(7)	
9	Mindaugas Grigaravičius	LTU	15/07/92	M	11		
1	Dmitrijs Grigorjevs		13/05/92	G	23		
26	Roberts Ralfs Gudēns		19/01/96	D	3		
5	Dāvis Indrāns		06/06/95	M	18	(3)	1
19	Gatis Kalniņš		12/08/81	A	23	(3)	5
16	Krists Kalniņš		22/05/98	M		(1)	
2	Matīss Miezis		11/09/95	D		(2)	
18	Takumi Miyazaki	JPN	08/08/97	M	6	(3)	2
11	Artjoms Osipovs		08/01/89	M	2	(5)	
24	Dāvis Ošs		03/12/94	G	5		
18	Ēriks Punculs		18/01/94	A	5	(3)	
4	Kirils Ševeļovs		02/06/90	D	15		
15	Rendijs Šibass		01/05/97	D	19	(5)	1
45	Dāvis Sandis Strods		24/04/96	D	24		
88	Ingars Sarmis Stuglis		12/02/96	M	10	(5)	3
17	Artūrs Švalbe		27/03/95	A	7	(7)	
9	Akihiro Takada	JPN	15/02/96	A		(1)	
10	Roberts Uldriķis		03/04/98	M	17	(5)	6
7	Edgars Vardanjans		09/05/93	M	23	(2)	3
16	Sergejs Vasiļjevs		13/06/96	M		(4)	
8	Takato Yamazaki	JPN	15/05/95	M	4	(3)	

Riga FC

2015 • Skonto (9,500) • no website

Coach: Kirill Kurbatov (RUS); (11/04/16) Dmitri Khomukha (RUS); (12/08/16) Vladimir Volchek (RUS)

2016

Date		Opponent	Res	Score	Scorers
12/03	a	Ventspils	D	1-1	*Saito*
20/03	h	Jelgava	D	1-1	*Saito*
02/04	a	METTA	L	0-1	
17/04	h	Rīgas FS	D	0-0	
23/04	a	Daugavpils	W	2-0	*Vorobjovs 2*
30/04	a	Liepāja	L	0-3	
08/05	h	Spartaks	D	0-0	
13/05	h	Ventspils	D	1-1	*Savaļnieks*
28/05	a	Jelgava	L	1-2	*Vorobjovs (p)*
11/06	h	METTA	W	2-1	*Vorobjovs, Saito*
19/06	a	Rīgas FS	D	1-1	*Apiņš*
26/06	h	Daugavpils	W	2-0	*Sergeev, Apiņš*
01/07	h	Liepāja	D	0-0	
10/07	a	Spartaks	L	0-1	
24/07	h	Ventspils	L	1-2	*Knyazev*
06/08	a	METTA	D	1-1	*Timofejevs*
14/08	h	Rīgas FS	W	1-0	*Savaļnieks*
20/08	a	Daugavpils	D	2-2	*Punculs, Saito*
26/08	h	Liepāja	L	0-1	
11/09	h	Spartaks	D	1-1	*Saito*
17/09	a	Ventspils	L	0-1	
25/09	a	Jelgava	L	0-1	
01/10	h	METTA	W	2-1	*Savaļnieks, Vaštšuk*
16/10	a	Rīgas FS	D	0-0	
19/10	h	Jelgava	W	1-0	*Vaštšuk*
23/10	h	Daugavpils	W	3-0	*Savaļnieks, Bancé, Vaštšuk*
29/10	a	Liepāja	D	2-2	*Sherenkov, Savaļnieks*
05/11	a	Spartaks	W	3-0	*(w/o)*

No	Name	Nat	DoB	Pos	Aps	(s)	Gls
11	Verners Apiņš		14/04/92	A	8	(13)	2
70	Klāvs Bāliņš		09/02/96	D		(1)	
9	Aristide Bancé	BFA	19/09/84	A	4	(4)	1
23	Vitālijs Barinovs		04/05/93	D	18	(2)	
34	Antonijs Černomordijs		26/09/96	D	10	(1)	
5	Dmitrijs Daņilovs		25/01/91	D	4	(4)	
35	Ivan Enin	RUS	06/02/94	M	13	(2)	
33	Pavlo Fedosov	UKR	14/08/96	M		(4)	
6	Reinis Flaksis		03/04/94	M	2	(5)	
17	Dmitrijs Halvitovs		03/04/86	D		(1)	
15	Nikita Juhnevičs		28/05/97	M	1	(1)	
33	John Kamara	SLE	05/12/88	M	24	(2)	
1	Denis Kniga	RUS	14/04/92	G	3		
4	Ivan Knyazev	RUS	05/11/92	D	18		1
34	Sergejs Kožans		16/02/86	D	2		
14	Oļegs Laizāns		28/03/87	M	25		
72	Ihor Lytovka	UKR	05/06/88	G	21		
22	Takeo Ogawa	JPN	17/09/92	M		(3)	
12	Roberts Ozols		10/09/95	G	3		
8	Armands Pētersons		05/12/90	M	20	(4)	
18	Ēriks Punculs		18/01/94	M	15		1
17	Alekss Regža		16/07/94	M		(4)	
21	Iļja Šadčins		02/07/94	M	5	(2)	
77	Yosuke Saito	JPN	07/04/88	A	12	(3)	5
10	Roberts Savaļnieks		04/02/93	M	19	(3)	5
77	Ivan Sergeev	RUS	11/05/95	M	5	(2)	1
7	Evgeni Sherenkov	RUS	27/01/91	M	13	(8)	1
5	Sergei Shumeyko	RUS	17/02/93	D	8	(2)	
32	Oļegs Timofejevs		28/11/88	D	27		1
6	Bogdan Vaštšuk	EST	04/10/95	M	4	(1)	3
17,70	Sergejs Vorobjovs		09/10/95	M	13	(6)	4

Rīgas FS

1962 • Arkādija (1,000); Hanzas vidusskolas laukums (2,000) • fkrfs.lv

Coach: Jurijs Popkovs; (07/04/16) Jurijs Ševļakovs; (27/05/16) Oleg Vasilenko (RUS); (17/07/16) Jurijs Ševļakovs

2016

Date		Opponent	Res	Score	Scorers
12/03	a	Jelgava	L	0-4	
19/03	h	METTA	W	3-2	*Njie, Jurkovskis 2*
03/04	a	Daugavpils	L	0-1	
17/04	a	Riga	D	0-0	
24/04	h	Liepāja	W	1-0	*Ivanovs*
30/04	a	Spartaks	L	0-2	
08/05	h	Ventspils	L	1-2	*Kozlovs*
14/05	h	Jelgava	W	1-0	*Jurkovskis*
28/05	a	METTA	D	1-1	*Kazubovičius*
12/06	h	Daugavpils	D	0-0	
19/06	h	Riga	D	1-1	*Jurkovskis*
26/06	a	Liepāja	L	1-3	*Jurkovskis*
10/07	a	Ventspils	W	1-0	*Kaļiņins*
25/07	a	Jelgava	L	0-2	
01/08	h	METTA	W	3-0	*Kozlovs, Višņakovs, og (Strods)*
08/08	a	Daugavpils	W	1-0	*Sorokins*
14/08	a	Riga	L	0-1	
19/08	h	Liepāja	D	1-1	*Diakvnishvili*
24/08	h	Spartaks	L	0-2	
28/08	a	Spartaks	L	1-2	*Kozlovs (p)*
10/09	h	Ventspils	L	0-3	
16/09	h	Jelgava	W	1-0	*Kozlovs (p)*
24/09	a	METTA	D	1-1	*Jurkovskis*
01/10	h	Daugavpils	W	2-0	*Višņakovs, Kozlovs*
16/10	h	Riga	D	0-0	
21/10	a	Liepāja	W	1-0	*Diakvnishvili*
29/10	h	Spartaks	L	0-2	
05/11	a	Ventspils	D	1-1	*Njie*

No	Name	Nat	DoB	Pos	Aps	(s)	Gls
14	Igors Arhipovs-Prokofjevs		23/03/97	D	1		
19	Vsevolod Čamkins		20/12/94	A		(3)	
22	Aleksejs Davidenkovs		27/06/98	A		(2)	
20	Giorgi Diakvnishvili	GEO	21/11/87	M	9	(5)	2
24	Kristaps Dzelme		30/01/90	G	2		
19	Reinis Flaksis		03/04/94	M	5	(2)	
6	Aleksejs Grjaznov		01/10/97	M	7	(1)	
7	Daņiils Hvoiņickis		08/04/98	A	3	(8)	
26	Vjačeslavs Isajevs		27/08/93	D	23		
22	Ņikita Ivanovs		25/03/96	A	1	(8)	1
9	Edgars Jermolajevs		16/06/92	M	4	(4)	
13	Raivis Andris Jurkovskis		09/12/96	M	27		6
8	Ņikita Kaļiņins		26/11/95	D	19	(2)	1
21	Darius Kazubovičius	LTU	19/02/95	A	14	(6)	1
11	Ņikita Kovaļonoks		02/07/95	D		(6)	
17	Igors Kozlovs		26/03/87	M	25		5
4	Ritus Krjauklis		23/04/86	D	27		
44	Andris Krušatins		01/09/96	M	8	(2)	
23	Kristaps Liepa		14/03/98	M	6	(1)	
3	Viktors Litvinskis		07/02/96	D	4	(2)	
1	Germans Māliņš		12/10/87	G	26		
35	Ensa Njie	GAM	01/09/91	A	23	(1)	2
15	Nika Piliev	RUS	21/03/91	D	20	(1)	
3	Vitaliy Polyanskiy	UKR	30/11/88	D	3		
18	Marko Regža		20/01/99	A		(2)	
31	Vlads Rimkus		28/05/93	M		(5)	
20	Aleksejs Rosoha		01/08/94	A	1	(1)	
2	Romans Rožkovskis		03/12/90	D	5	(2)	
81	Iļja Šadčins		02/07/94	M		(3)	
5	Endijs Šlampe		24/07/94	D	7	(1)	
2	Vladislavs Sorokins		10/05/97	D	13	(1)	1
10	Aleksejs Višņakovs		03/02/84	M	25	(1)	2

FK Spartaks Jūrmala

2007 • Slokas Stadionā (2,800) • spartaksjurmala.com

Major honours
Latvian League (1) 2016

Coach: Oleg Kubarev (BLR)

2016

Date		Opponent	Res	Score	Scorers
11/03	a	Liepāja	W	2-1	*Platonov, Kazačoks*
19/03	h	Daugavpils	W	3-0	*Stuglis 2, Platonov (p)*
02/04	a	Ventspils	L	1-2	*Platonov*
16/04	h	Jelgava	W	3-0	*Kozlovs, Platonov, Kozlov*
23/04	a	METTA	W	1-0	*Platonov*
30/04	h	Rīgas FS	W	2-0	*Kiriļins, Kazačoks*
08/05	a	Riga	D	0-0	
14/05	h	Liepāja	L	0-1	
27/05	a	Daugavpils	W	2-0	*Khairullin, Stuglis*
10/06	h	Ventspils	W	5-1	*Kozlov, Kazačoks 2 (1p), Kozlovs 2*
18/06	a	Jelgava	W	1-0	*Kozlovs*
25/06	h	METTA	W	4-1	*Kazačoks 3, Platonov*
10/07	h	Riga	W	1-0	*Kazačoks*
24/07	a	Liepāja	L	3-4	*Bogdan, Korzāns, Kazačoks*
30/07	h	Daugavpils	W	4-1	*Gauračs 2, Platonov, Kozeka*
05/08	a	Ventspils	W	1-0	*Platonov*
13/08	h	Jelgava	D	0-0	
19/08	a	METTA	W	3-1	*Platonov, Kozlov 2*
24/08	a	Rīgas FS	W	2-0	*Platonov, Gauračs*
28/08	h	Rīgas FS	W	2-1	*Bogdan, Platonov*
11/09	a	Riga	D	1-1	*Ulimbaševs*
17/09	h	Liepāja	D	0-0	
24/09	a	Daugavpils	L	1-2	*Platonov*
01/10	h	Ventspils	L	0-1	
16/10	a	Jelgava	L	0-2	
22/10	h	METTA	W	2-0	*Korzāns, Kazačoks*
29/10	a	Rīgas FS	W	2-0	*Kiriļins, Kozlov*
05/11	h	Riga	L	0-3	*(w/o)*

No	Name	Nat	DoB	Pos	Aps	(s)	Gls
9	Ridwaru Adeyemo	CIV	01/11/94	A	6	(2)	
17	Romāns Bespalovs		18/10/88	M		(3)	
2	Constantin Bogdan	MDA	29/12/93	D	13		2
3	Nauris Bulvītis		15/03/87	D	11		
5	Felipe Fumaça	BRA	08/07/93	M	5	(1)	
10	Edgars Gauračs		10/03/88	A	10	(3)	3
5	Aleksandrs Gubins		16/05/88	D	9	(2)	
2	Tomislav Havojić	CRO	10/04/89	M		(1)	
19	Artis Jaudzems		04/04/95	A		(3)	
21	Nikolai Kashevski	BLR	05/10/80	D	3	(2)	
8	Jevgeņijs Kazačoks		12/08/95	M	25	(1)	10
13	Rinat Khairullin	KAZ	19/02/94	M	2	(4)	1
17	Andrejs Kiriļins		03/11/95	M	12	(9)	2
25	Ričards Korzāns		03/05/97	A	5	(4)	2
4	Sergejs Kožans		16/02/86	D	7		
20	Sergei Kozeka	BLR	17/09/86	M	26	(1)	1
6	Evgeni Kozlov	RUS	04/02/95	M	19	(7)	5
21	Vladislavs Kozlovs		30/11/87	M	17	(5)	4
35	Vladislavs Kurakins		09/07/96	G	26		
22	Pavels Mihadjuks		27/05/80	D	13		
3,32	Pāvels Pilats		04/02/97	M		(1)	
23	Dmitri Platonov	BLR	07/02/86	A	19	(2)	12
18	Sergei Pushnyakov	BLR	08/02/93	D	23	(2)	
18	Aigars Putraševičs		31/05/88	A	1		
99,77	Marius Rapalis	LTU	22/03/83	G	1		
32	Ingus Šlampe		31/01/89	D	18		
11	Elvis Stuglis		04/07/93	A	4	(15)	3
7	Deniss Ulimbaševs		12/03/92	M	16	(7)	1
9	Moshtagh Yaghoubi	FIN	08/11/94	M	6		

LATVIA

FK Ventspils

1997 • OSC Ventspils (3,044) • fkventspils.lv

Major honours
Latvian League (6) 2006, 2007, 2008, 2011, 2013, 2014; Latvian Cup (7) 2003, 2004, 2005, 2007, 2011, 2013, 2017

Coach: Paul Ashworth (ENG)

2016

12/03	h	Riga	D	1-1	*Tīdenbergs*
20/03	h	Liepāja	D	2-2	*Tīdenbergs 2*
02/04	h	Spartaks	W	2-1	*Karlsons 2*
16/04	a	Daugavpils	W	5-0	*Siņeļņikovs, Koļesovs, Boranijašević, Karlsons, Alfa*
22/04	h	Jelgava	W	1-0	*Karlsons*
30/04	h	METTA	W	2-0	*Karlsons 2*
08/05	a	Rīgas FS	W	2-1	*Svārups, Karlsons*
13/05	a	Riga	D	1-1	*Karlsons*
26/05	h	Liepāja	W	2-0	*Siņeļņikovs, Karlsons*
10/06	a	Spartaks	L	1-5	*og (Šlampe)*
18/06	h	Daugavpils	W	3-0	*Jemeļins (p), Tīdenbergs, Svārups*
22/06	a	Jelgava	L	3-4	*Siņeļņikovs, Karlsons, Tīdenbergs (p)*
10/07	h	Rīgas FS	L	0-1	
24/07	a	Riga	W	2-1	*Alekseev, Tīdenbergs*
30/07	a	Liepāja	W	3-2	*Siņeļņikovs, Tīdenbergs (p), Rugins*
05/08	h	Spartaks	L	0-1	
13/08	h	Daugavpils	W	2-0	*Karlsons, Alekseev*
20/08	a	Jelgava	L	0-2	
24/08	a	METTA	D	1-1	*Siņeļņikovs*
28/08	h	METTA	W	2-0	*Karlsons, Alekseev*
10/09	a	Rīgas FS	W	3-0	*Karlsons 2, Alekseev*
17/09	h	Riga	W	1-0	*Paulius*
23/09	a	Liepāja	D	0-0	
01/10	a	Spartaks	W	1-0	*Svārups*
16/10	a	Daugavpils	W	4-0	*Obuobi, Karlsons 2 (1p), Postnikov*
22/10	h	Jelgava	L	1-2	*Tīdenbergs (p)*
29/10	a	METTA	L	1-2	*Karlsons*
05/11	h	Rīgas FS	D	1-1	*Alekseev*

No	Name	Nat	DoB	Pos	Aps	(s)	Gls
5	Adebayo Adigun	NGA	15/11/90	D		(2)	
15	Aleksei Alekseev	RUS	12/06/88	M	13	(1)	5
11	Abdullahi Alfa	NGA	29/07/96	M	9	(10)	1
22	Nikola Boranijašević	SRB	31/05/89	D	26		1
26	Antons Jemeļins		19/02/84	D	12	(1)	1
20	Ģirts Karlsons		07/06/81	A	26		17
19	Ņikita Koļesovs		25/09/96	D	26		1
10	Ndue Mujeci	ALB	24/02/93	A	7	(3)	
18	Vladimirs Mukins		28/01/93	M	1	(2)	
4	Rashid Obuobi	GHA	18/12/94	D	9		1
9	Simonas Paulius	LTU	12/05/91	M	24	(1)	1
16	Andrejs Pavlovs		22/02/79	G	11	(1)	
44	Evgeni Postnikov	KAZ	16/04/86	D	9		1
13	Valentīns Raļkevičs		08/03/91	G	2		
21	Vitālijs Rečickis		08/09/86	M	20	(4)	
25	Ritvars Rugins		17/10/89	D	21	(5)	1
4,8	Alans Siņeļņikovs		14/05/90	M	23	(4)	5
24	Artjoms Solomatovs		09/08/94	D	1		
23	Kaspars Svārups		28/01/94	A	4	(14)	3
14	Eduards Tīdenbergs		18/12/94	M	22	(6)	8
1	Maksims Uvarenko		17/01/87	G	15		
7	Jurijs Žigajevs		14/11/85	M	13	(10)	
3	Vadims Žuļevs		01/03/88	D	14		

Top goalscorers

17	Ģirts Karlsons (Ventspils)
12	Dmitri Platonov (Spartaks)
10	Jevgeņijs Kazačoks (Spartaks)
8	Eduards Tīdenbergs (Ventspils)
7	Gļebs Kļuškins (Jelgava)
	Andrejs Kovaļovs (Jelgava)
	Edgars Gauračs (Liepāja/Spartaks)
6	Oskars Kļava (Liepāja)
	Roberts Uldriķis (METTA)
	Raivis Andris Jurkovskis (Rīgas FS)

Promoted club

SK Babīte

2001 • Piņķu stadions (1,000) • no website

Coach: Mihails Miholaps

Second level final table 2016

		Pld	W	D	L	F	A	Pts
1	SK Babīte	28	26	0	2	102	25	78
2	AFA Olaine/ SK Super Nova	28	20	2	6	74	21	62
3	FK Auda	28	20	1	7	78	42	61
4	Valmiera Glass FK/BSS	28	19	0	9	81	29	57
5	Rēzeknes FA/BJSS	28	18	1	9	103	47	55
6	FK Tukums 2000 TSS	28	16	2	10	100	59	50
7	FK Smiltene/BJSS	28	15	3	10	74	47	48
8	Skonto FC	28	16	2	10	71	40	42
9	RTU FC	28	13	3	12	59	46	42
10	FK Staiceles Bebri	28	10	2	16	48	73	32
11	JDFS Alberts	28	9	2	17	32	61	29
12	FK Ogre	28	7	1	20	37	70	22
13	Preiļu BJSS	28	5	1	22	28	91	16
14	FK Jēkabpils/JSC	28	4	2	22	32	138	14
15	JFK Saldus	28	1	0	27	13	143	3

NB Skonto FC – 8 pts deducted.

Promotion/Relegation play-offs

(09/11/16 & 13/11/16)
Olaine/Super Nova 1-1 METTA
METTA 1-0 Olaine/Super Nova
(METTA 2-1)

DOMESTIC CUP

Latvijas Kauss 2016/17

1/8 FINALS

(16/07/16)
Caramba Rīga 2-5 Liepāja
Tukums 2000 TSS 0-1 BFC Daugavpils

(17/07/16)
Babīte 0-2 METTA
Jēkabpils/JSC 0-10 Spartaks
Skonto 0-2 Jelgava *(aet)*
Staiceles Bebri 0-4 Riga

(18/07/16)
Ogre 0-7 Rīgas FS

(25/09/16)
Rēzeknes FA/BJSS 0-2 Ventspils

QUARTER-FINALS

(08/04/17)
Ventspils 3-0 Liepāja *(Vaskov 5, Aiyegun 26, Rugins 42)*
Spartaks 1-0 Jelgava *(Platonov 90+1)*

(09/04/17)
METTA 0-1 Rīgas FS *(Uldriķis 60)*
Riga 3-0 BFC Daugavpils *(Appaev 14, Kovaļovs 52, Pētersons 79)*

SEMI-FINALS

(26/04/17 & 03/05/17)
Riga 2-0 Spartaks *(Šabala 8, Mihelič 62p)*
Spartaks 1-2 Riga *(Vardanjans 5; Kovaļovs 46, Šabala 71)*
(Riga 4-1)

Rīgas FS 1-1 Ventspils *(Uldriķis 85; Rode 90og)*
Ventspils 1-0 Rīgas FS *(Akinyemi 90+1)*
(Ventspils 2-1)

FINAL

(17/05/17)
Skonto, Riga
FK VENTSPILS 2 *(Aiyegun 54, Vaskov 114)*
RIGA FC 2 *(Šabala 62, Punculs 102)*
(aet; 6-5 on pens)
Referee: *Treimanis*
VENTSPILS: *Pavlovs, Žuļevs, Jemeļins, Koļesovs, Rugins (Alekseev 84), Tīdenbergs, Vaskov, Rečickis, Paulius (Žigajevs 104), Aiyegun, Akinyemi (Karlsons 69)*
RIGA: *Kurakins, Timofejevs, Smirnovs, Gorkšs, Kurakins, Enin, Kovaļovs (Černomordijs 112), Laizāns, Mihelič (Appaev 46), Šabala, Punculs*

Ventspils celebrate a seventh Latvian Cup win

LIECHTENSTEIN

Liechtensteiner Fussballverband (LFV)

Address	Landstrasse 149 FL-9494 Schaan
Tel	+423 237 4747
Fax	+423 237 4748
E-mail	info@lfv.li
Website	lfv.li

President	Hugo Quaderer
General secretary	Philipp Patsch
Media officer	Sandra Schwendener
Year of formation	1934
National stadium	Rheinpark, Vaduz (6,127)

CLUBS

1 **FC Balzers**

2 **USV Eschen/Mauren**

3 **FC Ruggell**

4 **FC Schaan**

5 **FC Triesen**

6 **FC Triesenberg**

7 **FC Vaduz**

Ruggell
Mauren
Eschen
Schaan
Vaduz
Triesenberg
Triesen
Balzers

KEY

UEFA Europa League

Bittersweet season for FC Vaduz

FC Vaduz extended their world-record number of domestic cup wins to 45 as they overcame USV Eschen/Mauren 5-1 in the final, but it was also a season to forget for the club as they suffered relegation from the Swiss Super League, 20 defeats in 36 matches ending their three-year sojourn.

Long-serving coach Giorgio Contini did not see out the campaign, although he began it by steering Vaduz to victory in their opening European tie for the third summer in succession. It was a season of disappointment, however, for Liechtenstein's national side, defeated in all of their FIFA World Cup qualifiers.

World-record 45th cup win captured with ease

Relegation ends three-year stay in Swiss Super League

Peter Jehle becomes national record cap-holder

Vaduz were obliged to play only three matches in defence of the Liechtenstein Cup, and they won all of them with alarming ease. Having thrashed Schaan with a record 11-0 win in the 2015 final, they opened up with a repeat scoreline against Ruggell. Six months later, when the semi-finals came around, with German Roland Vrabec having replaced Contini, the team's appetite for goals was even more voracious and they hammered Triesen 18-0, with two players, Aldin Turkes and Stjepan Kukuruzović, bagging five and four goals respectively.

The final against Eschen/Mauren – the only club other than Vaduz to have won the trophy in two decades – was less one-sided, although even the disadvantage of playing in their opponents' stadium could not prevent Vaduz from running out clear 5-1 winners, Turkes contributing another hat-trick.

Moreno Costanzo was Vaduz's main man in Europe, scoring four goals against FK Sileks and FC Midtjylland, while the individual plaudits at national team level belonged mostly to Vaduz goalkeeper Peter Jehle, who was named 2016 Liechtenstein footballer of the year and started all of the opening six 2018 FIFA World Cup qualifiers to overtake Mario Frick as Liechtenstein's most-capped player, his landmark 126th cap coming in a 5-0 defeat by Italy.

DOMESTIC CUP

FL1 Aktiv Cup 2016/17

FIRST ROUND

(17/08/16)
Schaan III 1-4 Eschen/Mauren III

(23/08/16)
Schaan Azzurri 1-2 Ruggell

(24/08/16)
Eschen/Mauren II 3-0 Triesenberg II

(07/09/16)
Triesen II 1-5 Balzers

SECOND ROUND

(27/09/16)
Eschen/Mauren II 0-3 Balzers

(28/09/16)
Balzers III 0-2 Ruggell
Eschen/Mauren III 0-7 Triesenberg

(04/10/16)
Ruggell II 0-1 Triesen

QUARTER-FINALS

(25/10/16)
Balzers 0-4 Eschen/Mauren
Ruggell 0-11 Vaduz
Triesenberg 3-1 Schaan

(26/10/16)
Balzers II 0-2 Triesen

SEMI-FINALS

(05/04/17)
Triesenberg 2-4 Eschen/Mauren *(Tiefenthaler 27, Barandun 75; Pola 18, 82, Kieber 45, Bärtsch 70)*

(11/04/17)
Triesen 0-18 Vaduz *(Burgmeier 6, 90p, Turkes 13, 33, 35, 38p, 46, Frick 19og, Bühler 27, Muntwiler 45, Kukuruzović 51, 61, 67, 78, Mathys 69, 87, Brunner 73, Zárate 81)*

FINAL

(24/05/17)
Sportpark, Eschen
FC VADUZ 5 *(Turkes 1, 26, 51, Muntwiler 43, Kukuruzović 56)*
USV ESCHEN/MAUREN 1 *(Pola 30)*
Referee: *Amhof*
VADUZ: *Siegrist, Borgmann, Konrad, Bühler, Göppel (Grippo 74), Kukuruzović, Muntwiler (Stanko 58), Ciccone, Turkes (Felfel 69), Mathys, Zárate*
ESCHEN/MAUREN: *Antic, Sele (Baumann 72), Trajkovic (Willi 77), Thöni, Martinovic, Kieber, Coppola, Fässler (Quintans 58), Knuth, Pola, Bärtsch*

NATIONAL TEAM

Top five all-time caps
Peter Jehle (126); Mario Frick (125); Martin Stocklasa (113); **Franz Burgmeier** (107); Thomas Beck (92)

Top five all-time goals
Mario Frick (16); **Franz Burgmeier** (9); Thomas Beck, **Michele Polverino** & Martin Stocklasa (5)

Results 2016/17

31/08/16	Denmark	A	Horsens	L	0-5	
05/09/16	Spain (WCQ)	A	Leon	L	0-8	
06/10/16	Albania (WCQ)	H	Vaduz	L	0-2	
09/10/16	Israel (WCQ)	A	Jerusalem	L	1-2	*Göppel (49)*
12/11/16	Italy (WCQ)	H	Vaduz	L	0-4	
24/03/17	FYR Macedonia (WCQ)	H	Vaduz	L	0-3	
07/06/17	Finland	A	Turku	D	1-1	*Hasler (62)*
11/06/17	Italy (WCQ)	A	Udine	L	0-5	

Appearances 2016/17

Coach: René Pauritsch (AUT)	04/02/64		Den	ESP	ALB	ISR	ITA	MKD	Fin	ITA	Caps	Goals
Peter Jehle	22/01/82	Vaduz	G46	G	G	G	G	G		G	126	-
Martin Rechsteiner	15/02/89	Balzers	D	D71	s46	D	D	D78	D81	D	34	-
Michele Polverino	26/09/84	Rapperswil-Jona (SUI) /Balzers	D46	D	D46		D		M	M87	60	5
Daniel Kaufmann	22/12/90	Chiasso (SUI)	D	D	D	D	D				41	1
Franz Burgmeier	07/04/82	Vaduz	D	M	M	M81	M	D	M46	M68	107	9
Sandro Wieser	03/02/93	Reading (ENG)	M79	M	M	D	M				38	1
Nicolas Hasler	04/05/91	Vaduz	M	A	M	M		M	M	M	46	2
Andreas Christen	29/08/89	Eschen/Mauren	M54			M	M				27	-
Martin Büchel	19/02/87	Unterföhring (GER)	M	M83		M	M	M83	M	M	67	2
Dennis Salanovic	26/02/96	Rapperswil-Jona (SUI)	M46	M77	M73	s88	A	M87	M70	M59	21	-
Marcel Büchel	18/03/91	Empoli (ITA)	A56	M	M	M88	M	M			10	-
Benjamin Büchel	04/07/89	Oxford (ENG)	s46						G		12	-
Simon Kühne	30/04/94	Eschen/Mauren	s46		s73	s81					16	-
Maximilian Göppel	31/08/97	Vaduz	s46	D	D	D		D	D	D	8	1
Sandro Wolfinger	24/08/91	Wolfratshausen (GER)	s54	s77				s78	s46	s68	16	1
Daniel Brändle	23/01/92	St Andrews (MLT)	s56					s87	s46	s59	15	-
Robin Gubser	17/04/91	Balzers	s79	s83	A59	A75		D	D	D	27	1
Seyhan Yildiz	30/04/89	Balzers		s71							23	-
Yves Oehri	15/03/87	YF Juventus (SUI)			D		D		s61		53	-
Yanik Frick	27/05/98	Altach (AUT)			s59	s75		A	A61	A	5	-
Andreas Malin	31/01/94	Dornbirn (AUT)						D	D46	D	4	-
Aron Sele	02/09/96	Balzers						s83			2	-
Philippe Erne	14/12/86	Balzers							s70		25	1
Mathias Sele	28/05/92	Eschen/Mauren							s81		4	-
Ivan Quintans	15/10/89	Eschen/Mauren								s87	22	-

EUROPE

FC Vaduz

First qualifying round - FK Sileks (MKD)
H 3-1 *Costanzo (36, 45+2), Grippo (90+5)*
Jehle, Grippo, Ciccone, Zárate (Mathys 70), Costanzo, Borgmann, Brunner, Kukuruzović, Muntwiler (Hasler 76), Bühler, Janjatovic (Avdijaj 63). Coach: Giorgio Contini (SUI)

A 2-1 *Costanzo (89p), Messaoud (90+3)*
Siegrist, Grippo, Ciccone, Zárate (Messaoud 82), Costanzo, Mathys (Schürpf 72), Hasler (Avdijaj 62), Borgmann, Brunner, Kukuruzović, Bühler. Coach: Giorgio Contini (SUI)

Second qualifying round - FC Midtjylland (DEN)
A 0-3
Jehle, Grippo, Ciccone, Zárate (Avdijaj 80), Costanzo, Mathys (Messaoud 65), Borgmann, Brunner (Pfründer 80), Kukuruzović, Muntwiler, Bühler. Coach: Giorgio Contini (SUI)
H 2-2 *Brunner (83), Costanzo (86p)*
Siegrist, Pfründer, Grippo, Strohmaier, Ciccone, Zárate (Brunner 65), Costanzo, Mathys (Burgmeier 80), Borgmann, Kukuruzović (Hasler 65), Muntwiler. Coach: Giorgio Contini (SUI)

European qualification 2017/18

Cup winner: FC Vaduz (first qualifying round)

LITHUANIA

Lietuvos futbolo federacija (LFF)

Address Stadiono g. 2
LT-02106 Vilnius
Tel +370 5 2638741
Fax +370 5 2638740
E-mail info@lff.lt
Website lff.lt

President vacant
General secretary Nerijus Dunauskas
Media officer Vaiva Zizaitė
Year of formation 1922
National stadium LFF Stadium, Vilnius (5,067)

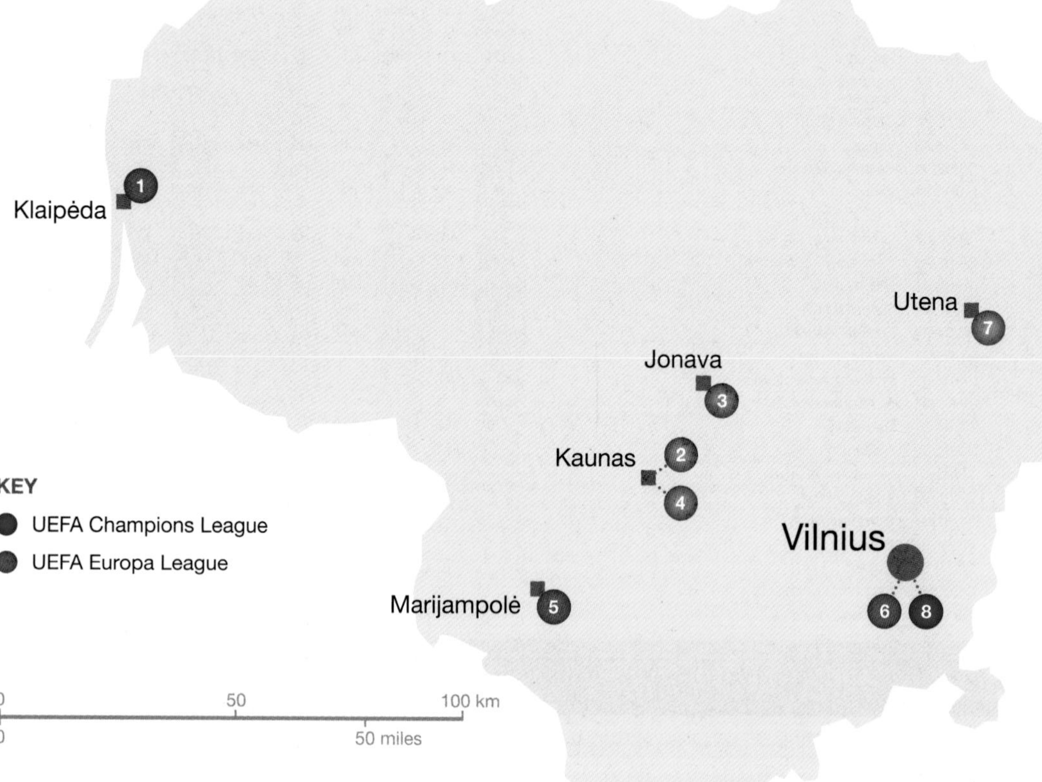

A LYGA CLUBS

 1 **FK Atlantas**

 2 **FK Kauno Žalgiris**

 3 **FK Lietava**
NB Renamed FK Jonava for 2017 season

 4 **FC Stumbras**

 5 **FK Sūduva**

 6 **FK Trakai**

 7 **FK Utenis**

 8 **FK Žalgiris Vilnius**

Žalgiris continue to conquer

For the fourth year in a row FK Žalgiris Vilnius made a clean sweep of Lithuania's major domestic silverware. Indeed, they had three trophies, rather than the customary two, to show off in 2016 with a double triumph in the Lithuanian Cup adding to more A Lyga glory.

Although they won the league in some comfort at the finish, Žalgiris were second best during the first half of the campaign to FK Trakai before speeding clear with a succession of victories during the summer months to reassert their authority and claim a seventh title since independence.

Fourth A Lyga title on the trot for Vilnius club

Second cup win in 2016 completes trophy treble

Trakai retain league runners-up spot

Domestic league

With just eight clubs kicking off the 2016 A Lyga – as opposed to ten the previous campaign – and not one of them other than Žalgiris having ever won the title, it was pretty obvious which team started out as favourites. Four straight wins reinforced the view that Valdas Dambrauskas's Green Machine would go on to stage another one-sided title procession, but three successive away defeats – against the teams that had occupied places two, three and four in 2015, namely Trakai, Atlantas and Sūduva – changed the landscape completely.

Trakai, led again by their five-time A Lyga-winning coach (with FK Ekranas), Valdas Urbonas, recovered from an opening-day defeat at Žalgiris to win seven games in a row and unseat the champions from top spot in the table. Indeed, they remained in pole position up to the halfway point in the season, when, after stuttering to three defeats in four games – and consequently dismissing Urbonas – they fell victim to a thunderous show of strength from their rivals, who, with newly acquired Serbian striker Andrija Kaludjerović hitting the ground running, romped to nine successive wins.

Žalgiris were 16 games undefeated when Atlantas beat them 1-0 in Vilnius on the first day of October. Four weeks later, Žalgiris hosted the same opponents and this time prevailed 2-0 to make their title triumph a mathematical certainty with three matches still to play. Despite featuring for only half a season Kaludjerović finished up as the league's top marksman with 20 goals, scoring at an average of more than one a game to demote Trakai's 17-goal Lithuanian international, Nerijus Valskis, into second place. Another new foreign signing, Senegalese defender Pape Mamadou Mbodj, also enjoyed an outstanding ever-present debut season in green and white, while homegrown Mantas Kuklys and Vytautas Lukša were Žalgiris's main men in midfield.

Trakai, Sūduva and Atlantas all finished in the top four for the second year running to requalify for the UEFA Europa League, and, as in 2015, there was another sizeable gap between the leading quartet and the rest. FK Kauno Žalgiris, who finished fifth the previous season in their former guise as FK Spyris, ended up bottom, but with second tier champions FK Šilas declining promotion, they retained their A Lyga status – as did seventh-placed Utenis, who edged their play-off against Palanga on away goals.

Domestic cup

A rescheduling of the Lithuanian Cup meant that there were two finals in 2016, the first of them staged in May, the second in late September. One-nil winners after extra time over Trakai in the first of them, Žalgiris had another tough game in the autumn showpiece against Sūduva in Klaipeda, semi-final hero Kaludjerović opening the scoring before a late Kuklys penalty sealed victory and at the same time led to a protesting Sūduva ending the game with just eight men. It was Žalgiris's sixth successive cup final success – all against different opponents and all in different venues.

Europe

Lithuania suffered a European whitewash in 2016, with Žalgiris, Trakai, Atlantas and Sūduva all falling at the first hurdle of their respective competitions.

National team

In contrast to the country's clubs, Edgaras Jankauskas's national side made a promising start to their 2018 FIFA World Cup qualifying campaign, captain Fedor Černych scoring in each of the first three matches that would have brought a maximum nine points, rather than just five, had it not been for late equalisers conceded against Slovenia in Vilnius and Scotland in Glasgow. However, the team's next three qualifiers – two against Slovakia and one against England at Wembley – all ended in defeat, quashing any early optimism about a potential challenge for a play-off place.

DOMESTIC SEASON AT A GLANCE

A Lyga 2016 final table

		Pld	Home W	D	L	F	A	Away W	D	L	F	A	Total W	D	L	F	A	Pts
1	**FK Žalgiris Vilnius**	**33**	**13**	**2**	**2**	**39**	**16**	**11**	**2**	**3**	**35**	**13**	**24**	**4**	**5**	**74**	**29**	**76**
2	FK Trakai	33	11	3	3	31	15	9	4	3	24	11	20	7	6	55	26	67
3	FK Sūduva	33	11	3	3	28	13	6	4	6	27	28	17	7	9	55	41	58
4	FK Atlantas	33	9	4	3	22	11	7	4	6	20	21	16	8	9	42	32	56
5	FC Stumbras	33	4	5	7	24	33	4	4	9	19	30	8	9	16	43	63	33
6	FK Lietava	33	4	5	7	18	28	4	3	10	17	30	8	8	17	35	58	32
7	FK Utenis	28	3	2	9	12	23	1	2	11	12	24	4	4	20	24	47	16
8	FK Kauno Žalgiris	28	1	4	9	10	28	1	5	8	13	27	2	9	17	23	55	15

NB After 28 rounds the top six teams play five additional matches; FK Kauno Žalgiris subsequently permitted to remain in A Lyga.

European qualification 2017/18

Champion/Cup winner: FK Žalgiris Vilnius (second qualifying round)

FK Trakai (first qualifying round)
FK Sūduva (first qualifying round)
FK Atlantas (first qualifying round)

Top scorer Andrija Kaludjerović (Žalgiris), 20 goals
Relegated clubs none
Promoted clubs none
Cup final FK Žalgiris Vilnius 2-0 FK Sūduva

Player of the season

Mantas Kuklys
(FK Žalgiris Vilnius)

A key member of Žalgiris's 2016 A Lyga-title winning team, Kuklys enjoyed the best of his five seasons with the club, fortifying his standing as the most accomplished all-round midfielder in the country. A dependable, two-footed schemer, he prompted many of Žalgiris's attacks from his central berth and chipped in with five league goals plus the late penalty in the Lithuanian Cup final that sealed his team's 2-0 win over Sūduva. Furthermore, the 30-year-old appeared from the start in every one of Lithuania's seven international matches in 2016/17.

Newcomer of the season

Eligijus Jankauskas
(FK Utenis/FK Sūduva)

A Lithuanian international at every age group from Under-17 to U21, Jankauskas made the grade at A Lyga level in 2016 and put in so many eye-catching performances in the first half of the season for Utenis that he was transferred in mid-campaign to Sūduva. The progression did not stop there, and although he was only a substitute for the cup final against Žalgiris, the young winger ended the season strongly enough to earn himself a winter transfer abroad to Slovakian league leaders – and eventual champions – MŠK Žilina.

Team of the season
(4-4-2)

Coach: Dambrauskas *(Žalgiris)*

NATIONAL TEAM

Top five all-time caps

Andrius Skerla (84); Deividas Šemberas (82); Saulius Mikoliūnas (75); Tomas Danilevičius (71); Žydrūnas Karčemarskas (66)

Top five all-time goals

Tomas Danilevičius (19); Antanas Lingis (12); Edgaras Jankauskas & Robertas Poškus (10); Virginijus Baltušnikas (9)

Results 2016/17

04/09/16	Slovenia (WCQ)	H	Vilnius	D	2-2	*Černych (32), Slivka (34)*
08/10/16	Scotland (WCQ)	A	Glasgow	D	1-1	*Černych (59)*
11/10/16	Malta (WCQ)	H	Vilnius	W	2-0	*Černych (76), Novikovas (84p)*
11/11/16	Slovakia (WCQ)	A	Trnava	L	0-4	
22/03/17	Czech Republic	A	Usti nad Labem	L	0-3	
26/03/17	England (WCQ)	A	London	L	0-2	
10/06/17	Slovakia (WCQ)	H	Vilnius	L	1-2	*Novikovas (90+3)*

Appearances 2016/17

Coach: Edgaras Jankauskas	12/03/75		SVN	SCO	MLT	SVK	Cze	ENG	SVK	Caps	Goals
Ernestas Šetkus	25/05/85	Den Haag (NED)	G	G	G	G	G46	G		14	-
Egidijus Vaitkūnas	08/08/88	Žalgiris	D	D	D	D	D46	D		32	-
Georgas Freidgeimas	10/08/87	Irtysh (KAZ)	D	D	D	D				28	-
Edvinas Girdvainis	17/01/93	Piast (POL)	D	D		D				7	-
Vaidas Slavickas	26/02/86	Sūduva	D	D64			D46	D	D	15	-
Mantas Kuklys	10/06/87	Žalgiris	M	M	M79	M	M46	M	M	22	-
Artūras Žulpa	10/06/90	Tobol (KAZ)	M	M66	M	M33	s60	M		23	-
Fedor Černych	21/05/91	Jagiellonia (POL)	M70	M	M	M	s60	M	M	33	8
Vykintas Slivka	29/04/95	Den Bosch (NED) /Ascoli (ITA)	M79	M	M	M	M60	M87	M75	19	1
Arvydas Novikovas	18/12/90	Bochum (GER) /Jagiellonia (POL)	M	M	M87	M	s60	M54	M	37	5
Nerijus Valskis	04/08/87	Trakai /Bnei Yehuda (ISR)	A85	A85	A62	A87	s60	A74	A72	14	1
Mindaugas Grigaravičius	15/07/92	Jelgava (LVA)	s70	s85	s87		M60	s54		5	-
Karolis Chvedukas	21/04/91	Split (CRO)	s79	s66	s79	s33				18	-
Deivydas Matulevičius	08/04/89	Botoşani (ROU) /Mouscron (BEL)	s85		s62		A60	s74	s72	33	5
Vytautas Andriuškevičius	08/10/90	Portland Timbers (USA)		s64	D	D				26	-
Tomas Mikuckis	13/01/83	SKA-Khabarovsk (RUS)			D		s60			18	-
Manfredas Ruzgis	05/01/97	Köln (GER)				s87				1	-
Arūnas Klimavičius	05/10/82	Trakai					D60			43	3
Linas Klimavičius	10/04/89	Žalgiris					D60	D	D	12	-
Vytautas Lukša	14/08/84	Žalgiris					M60			27	-
Simonas Paulius	12/05/91	Ventspils (LVA)					M60	s87		4	-
Emilijus Zubas	10/07/90	Bnei Yehuda (ISR)					s46		G	11	-
Rolandas Baravykas	23/08/95	Žalgiris					s46			4	-
Valdemar Borovskij	02/05/84	Trakai					s46		D	18	-
Ovidijus Verbickas	04/07/93	Sūduva					s46			2	-
Tadas Kijanskas	06/09/85	Brno (CZE)					s60	D	D	46	1
Tautvydas Eliošius	03/11/91	Jonava					s60			2	-
Darvydas Šernas	22/07/84	Žalgiris							M	36	5
Martynas Dapkus	16/02/93	Jonava							s75	2	-

EUROPE

FK Žalgiris Vilnius

Second qualifying round - FC Astana (KAZ)
H 0-0
Klevinskas, Klimavičius, Slijngard, Mbodj, Blagojević, Vaitkūnas, Lukša, Mikoliūnas (Elivelto 64), Pilibaitis (Ljujić 59), Kuklys, Kaludjerović. Coach: Valdas Dambrauskas (LTU)
A 1-2 *Elivelto (57)*
Klevinskas, Klimavičius, Slijngard, Mbodj, Blagojević, Vaitkūnas, Lukša, Mikoliūnas (Atajić 54), Elivelto (Ljujić 77), Kuklys, Kaludjerović (Žaliukas 85). Coach: Valdas Dambrauskas (LTU)

FK Atlantas

First qualifying round - HJK Helsinki (FIN)
H 0-2
Valinčius, Gedminas (Kazlauskas 67), Šimkus (Bartkus 67), Beneta, Sylla, Baravykas, Epifanov, Gnedojus, Maksimov, Verbickas, Dmitriev (Papšys 77). Coach: Konstantin Sarsania (RUS)
A 1-1 *Papšys (76)*
Adamonis, Gašpuitis, Bartkus (Kazlauskas 67), Rakauskas (Papšys 39), Beneta, Sylla, Baravykas, Epifanov, Maksimov, Verbickas, Dmitriev (Šimkus 54). Coach: Konstantin Sarsania (RUS)

FK Trakai

First qualifying round - Nõmme Kalju FC (EST)
H 2-1 *Valskis (69), Arshakyan (78)*
Rapalis, Vorobjovas, Česnauskis, Rekish (Kochanauskas 76), Arshakyan, Januševskij, Šilėnas, Zasavitschi, Valskis (Masenzovas 86), Gurenko (Vitukynas 79), Bychenok. Coach: Valdas Urbonas (LTU)
A 1-4 *Arshakyan (14)*
Rapalis, Vorobjovas, Česnauskis, Rekish, Arshakyan, Vitukynas, Januševskij, Šilėnas, Zasavitschi, Gurenko (Kochanauskas 87), Bychenok. Coach: Valdas Urbonas (LTU)

FK Sūduva

First qualifying round - FC Midtjylland (DEN)
A 0-1
Kardum, Leimonas, Švrljuga, Kecap, E Jankauskas (Antanavičius 90+2), Slavickas, Jamak, A Jankauskas, Pavlović, Jablan, Laukžemis (Janušauskas 51). Coach: Aleksandar Veselinović (SRB)
H 0-1
Kardum, Leimonas, Radzinevičius (Veliulis 62), Švrljuga, Kecap, Janušauskas, Slavickas, Jamak (E Jankauskas 46), A Jankauskas, Pavlović (Laukžemis 89), Jablan. Coach: Aleksandar Veselinović (SRB)

DOMESTIC LEAGUE CLUB-BY-CLUB

FK Atlantas

1962 • Centrinis (4,428); Centrinis Artificial (1,000) • atlantas.lt
Major honours
Lithuanian Cup (2) 2001, 2003 (spring)
Coach: Konstantin Sarsania (RUS)

2016

Date		Opponent	Res	Score	Scorers
05/03	h	Stumbras	W	2-0	*Papšys, Sylla*
09/03	a	Sūduva	L	0-1	
16/03	h	Utenis	W	1-0	*Maksimov*
20/03	a	Lietava	W	1-0	*Sylla*
02/04	h	Kauno Ž	W	3-1	*Maksimov 2, Sylla*
06/04	h	Žalgiris	W	2-1	*Maksimov, Gnedojus*
17/04	a	Trakai	L	0-2	
21/04	a	Stumbras	W	3-2	*Kazlauskas, Maksimov, Razulis*
27/04	h	Sūduva	L	1-2	*Maksimov (p)*
05/05	a	Utenis	W	2-0	*Gnedojus, Sylla*
08/05	h	Lietava	W	2-0	*Verbickas, Sylla*
17/05	a	Kauno Ž	W	2-0	*Sylla 2*
21/05	a	Žalgiris	L	0-1	
09/06	h	Trakai	D	2-2	*Maksimov, Gedminas*
15/06	h	Stumbras	W	2-0	*Gedminas, Dmitriev*
24/06	a	Sūduva	D	3-3	*Gedminas, Dmitriev, Sylla*
12/07	h	Utenis	W	2-0	*Verbickas, Šimkus*
19/07	a	Lietava	W	2-1	*Gašpuitis, Verbickas*
27/07	h	Kauno Ž	D	1-1	*Maksimov*
02/08	h	Žalgiris	L	0-1	
10/08	a	Trakai	L	0-3	
16/08	a	Stumbras	W	2-0	*Bartkus, Rakauskas*
24/08	h	Sūduva	W	2-1	*Gnedojus, Sylla*
08/09	a	Utenis	D	1-1	*Papšys (p)*
15/09	h	Lietava	D	0-0	
21/09	a	Kauno Ž	D	1-1	*Kazlauskas*
01/10	a	Žalgiris	W	1-0	*Verbickas*
16/10	h	Trakai	L	0-1	
21/10	h	Trakai	D	0-0	
30/10	a	Žalgiris	L	0-2	
06/11	h	Lietava	W	2-1	*Verbickas, Maksimov*
20/11	a	Sūduva	L	1-3	*Maksimov*
26/11	a	Stumbras	D	1-1	*Verbickas*

No	Name	Nat	DoB	Pos	Aps	(s)	Gls
31	Marius Adamonis		13/05/97	G	6		
23	Rolandas Baravykas		23/08/95	D	26		
6	Andrius Bartkus		21/01/86	M	22	(2)	1
17	Markas Beneta		08/07/93	D	27	(1)	
77	Jonas Bičkus		04/02/00	A	2	(4)	
99	Oleg Dmitriev	RUS	18/11/95	M	20	(5)	2
25	Aleksei Epifanov	RUS	21/07/83	D	22	(1)	
14	Pascal Feindouno	GUI	27/02/81	M		(3)	
28	Rokas Filipavičius		22/12/99	M		(1)	
3	Vytas Gašpuitis		04/03/94	D	20	(2)	1
10	Rokas Gedminas		13/04/93	M	8	(10)	3
30	Kazimieras Gnedojus		28/02/86	D	22	(2)	3
18	Andrius Jokšas		12/01/79	D	6	(7)	
9	Donatas Kazlauskas		31/03/94	M	23	(8)	2
7	Maksim Maksimov	RUS	04/11/95	A	23	(8)	10
20	Dovydas Norvilas		05/04/93	M	14	(1)	
93	Andrei Panyukov	RUS	25/09/94	A		(2)	
70	Marius Papšys		13/05/89	M	17	(10)	2
8	Skirmantas Rakauskas		07/01/96	M	1	(7)	1
21	Justas Raziūnas		23/01/95	D	6	(2)	
7	Evaldas Razulis		03/04/86	A		(6)	1
19	Abdoul Karim Sylla	NED	23/01/92	A	25	(1)	9
24	Vincentas Šarkauskas		11/08/99	G	1	(1)	
11	Domantas Šimkus		10/02/96	M	15	(11)	1
1	Povilas Valinčius		16/05/89	G	26		
74	Ovidijus Verbickas		04/07/93	M	31		6

FK Kauno Žalgiris

2005 • S.Dariaus ir S.Girėno (9,180); NFA (500) • zalgiris.lt

Coach: Laimis Bičkauskas

2016

Date		Opponent		Score	Scorers
05/03	a	Utenis	W	3-2	*Šilkaitis, Krušnauskas 2*
13/03	h	Trakai	L	0-2	
17/03	a	Lietava	D	2-2	*Krušnauskas, Kalonas*
21/03	h	Stumbras	L	1-2	*Bučma*
02/04	a	Atlantas	L	1-3	*Mushnikov*
10/04	h	Sūduva	D	2-2	*Gvildys, og (Činikas)*
16/04	a	Žalgiris	L	0-3	
22/04	h	Utenis	L	1-3	*Velička*
28/04	a	Trakai	D	0-0	
04/05	h	Lietava	L	1-5	*Mushnikov (p)*
11/05	a	Stumbras	D	0-0	
17/05	h	Atlantas	L	0-2	
21/05	a	Sūduva	L	0-1	
09/06	h	Žalgiris	D	1-1	*Širvys*
14/06	a	Utenis	L	1-2	*Gvildys*
21/06	h	Trakai	L	0-4	
13/07	a	Lietava	L	2-3	*Velička, Neverdauskas*
20/07	h	Stumbras	W	2-1	*Šilkaitis, Gavrilovas*
27/07	a	Atlantas	D	1-1	*Bučma*
04/08	h	Sūduva	L	0-1	
11/08	a	Žalgiris	L	1-3	*Sikorskis*
18/08	h	Utenis	D	1-1	*Dedura*
25/08	a	Trakai	L	0-3	
08/09	h	Lietava	L	0-1	
14/09	a	Stumbras	D	2-2	*Velička, Stulga*
21/09	h	Atlantas	D	1-1	*Mikelionis*
01/10	a	Sūduva	L	0-2	
16/10	h	Žalgiris	L	0-2	

No	Name	Nat	DoB	Pos	Aps	(s)	Gls
26	Bruno Amorim	BRA	16/01/93	M	7		
8	Tomas Bučma		27/01/94	M	23	(1)	2
77	Andrei Chukhlei	BLR	02/10/87	M	7		
77	Paulius Daukša		09/09/93	D	15		
28	Davi Moreira	BRA	26/09/96	M		(1)	
20	Ignas Dedura		01/06/78	D	18	(1)	1
25	Mantas Fridrikas		13/09/88	D	14		
6	Matas Gavrilovas		22/11/95	M	8	(3)	1
7	Karolis Gvildys		13/05/94	M	23	(1)	2
27	Darius Jankauskas		27/04/92	M	5	(3)	
10	Mindaugas Kalonas		28/02/84	M	3	(2)	1
18	Edvinas Kloniūnas		28/06/98	M	14	(2)	
9	Rokas Krušnauskas		04/11/95	A	12	(3)	3
29	Audrius Kšanavičius		14/01/77	M		(1)	
23	Andrei Lyasyuk	BLR	14/04/84	A	6	(3)	
42	Povilas Malakas		08/10/98	M		(1)	
19	Ernestas Mickevičius		11/11/96	M	2	(6)	
1	Deividas Mikelionis		08/05/95	G	24		1
3	Marius Miškinis		19/02/92	D	15	(5)	
22	Leonid Mushnikov	RUS	30/12/92	M	20	(4)	2
38	Kasparas Neverdauskas		03/05/97	M		(4)	1
14	Benas Olencevičius		07/08/95	M		(9)	
4	Ernestas Pilypas		17/05/90	D	26		
23	Lukas Sendžikas		28/11/92	M	16		
13	Rokas Sikorskis		13/04/95	M	7	(8)	1
33	Modestas Stonys		17/01/80	G	4		
10	Donatas Stulga		22/08/95	M	2	(12)	1
15	Karolis Šilkaitis		02/06/96	D	18	(1)	2
21	Darius Šinkūnas		13/10/92	D		(1)	
36	Pijus Širvys		01/04/98	M		(2)	1
17	Andrius Velička		05/04/79	A	19	(4)	3

FK Lietava

1991 • Centrinis (1,000); NFA, Kaunas (500) • fklietava.lt

Coach: Robertas Poškus

2016

Date		Opponent		Score	Scorers
06/03	h	Sūduva	D	1-1	*Šušnjar*
13/03	a	Utenis	W	1-0	*Galkevičius*
17/03	h	Kauno Ž	D	2-2	*Galkevičius (p), Borovskij*
20/03	h	Atlantas	L	0-1	
02/04	a	Žalgiris	D	2-2	*Galkevičius (p), Salamanavičius*
10/04	h	Trakai	L	0-1	
16/04	a	Stumbras	L	0-2	
20/04	a	Sūduva	L	0-3	
26/04	h	Utenis	W	1-0	*Paškevičius*
04/05	a	Kauno Ž	W	5-1	*og (Pilypas), Stonkus 2, Paškevičius, Salamanavičius*
08/05	a	Atlantas	L	0-2	
18/05	h	Žalgiris	L	0-1	
22/05	a	Trakai	L	0-3	
08/06	h	Stumbras	D	2-2	*Salamanavičius, Tadas Eliošius*
16/06	h	Sūduva	D	1-1	*Salamanavičius*
22/06	a	Utenis	L	1-3	*Stonkus*
14/07	h	Kauno Ž	W	3-2	*Stonkus, Borovskij, Ganusauskas*
19/07	h	Atlantas	L	1-2	*Galkevičius (p)*
27/07	a	Žalgiris	L	1-4	*Tadas Eliošius*
03/08	h	Trakai	D	1-1	*Tadas Eliošius*
11/08	a	Stumbras	L	1-2	*Salamanavičius*
17/08	a	Sūduva	D	0-0	
25/08	h	Utenis	W	1-0	*Stonkus*
08/09	a	Kauno Ž	W	1-0	*Galkevičius*
15/09	a	Atlantas	D	0-0	
20/09	h	Žalgiris	L	0-4	
02/10	a	Trakai	W	2-0	*Salamanavičius, Tadas Eliošius*
16/10	h	Stumbras	L	1-4	*Tadas Eliošius*
22/10	h	Žalgiris	L	1-4	*Galkevičius*
29/10	a	Stumbras	L	1-3	*Galkevičius*
06/11	a	Atlantas	L	1-2	*Krušnauskas*
20/11	a	Trakai	L	1-3	*Stonkus*
26/11	h	Sūduva	W	3-2	*Stonkus, Tadas Eliošius 2*

No	Name	Nat	DoB	Pos	Aps	(s)	Gls
5	Julius Aleksandravičius		13/01/95	D	21		
33	Dmytro Babenko	UKR	28/06/78	G	7	(1)	
2	Valdemaras Borovskij		02/05/84	D	33		2
77	Ivan Carandasov	MDA	21/01/91	M	9		
22	Vladislav Chernyakov	UKR	15/03/97	M		(2)	
3	Martynas Dūda		23/01/93	D	20	(3)	
90	Tadas Eliošius		01/03/90	M	30	(1)	7
91	Tautvydas Eliošius		03/11/91	M	11	(1)	
88	Dominykas Galkevičius		16/10/86	M	25	(2)	7
99	Marius Ganusauskas		13/05/94	A	6	(22)	1
96	Rokas Krušnauskas		04/11/95	A	3	(11)	1
1	Giedrius Kvedaras		09/07/91	G	26	(1)	
8	Edgaras Makarovas		10/01/98	M		(3)	
20	Lukas Miščiukas		08/10/94	M	13	(5)	
9	Savio Nsereko	GER	27/07/89	A	10	(3)	
21	Arnas Paškevičius		28/06/96	M	23	(5)	2
94	Artūras Ročys		07/10/94	M	26	(1)	
10	Tomas Salamanavičius		31/03/93	M	29	(4)	6
96	Benas Spietinis		15/02/96	D	3		
11	Laurynas Stonkus		18/01/92	A	18	(6)	7
6	Aleksandar Šušnjar	SRB	19/08/95	D	14		1
7	Eisvinas Utyra		14/09/90	M	17	(6)	
13	Gytis Vasylius		12/08/99	D	2	(3)	
53	Edgaras Žarskis		04/05/94	D	17		

FC Stumbras

2013 • S.Dariaus ir S.Girėno (9,180); NFA (500) • fcstumbras.lt

Coach: Darius Gvildys; (20/06/16) Mariano Barreto (POR)

2016

Date		Opponent		Score	Scorers
05/03	a	Atlantas	L	0-2	
12/03	h	Žalgiris	L	3-6	*Račkus, Eriba, Zaleckis*
17/03	a	Trakai	L	2-3	*Snapkauskas, Janonis*
21/03	a	Kauno Ž	W	2-1	*Snapkauskas, Rimkevičius*
03/04	h	Sūduva	L	2-3	*og (Kardum), Flores*
09/04	a	Utenis	L	0-1	
16/04	h	Lietava	W	2-0	*Eduardo Farias, Mačiulis*
21/04	h	Atlantas	L	2-3	*og (Verbickas), Eriba*
27/04	a	Žalgiris	L	0-2	
03/05	h	Trakai	D	0-0	
11/05	h	Kauno Ž	D	0-0	
18/05	a	Sūduva	W	1-0	*Eduardo Farias*
22/05	h	Utenis	W	3-1	*Russo 2, Mačiulis*
08/06	a	Lietava	D	2-2	*Russo, Upstas*
15/06	a	Atlantas	L	0-2	
24/06	h	Žalgiris	L	0-5	
14/07	a	Trakai	W	2-0	*Kore, Upstas*
20/07	a	Kauno Ž	L	1-2	*Russo (p)*
26/07	h	Sūduva	L	2-3	*Vėževičius 2*
03/08	a	Utenis	D	0-0	
11/08	h	Lietava	W	2-1	*Vėževičius, Sadauskas*
16/08	h	Atlantas	L	0-2	
24/08	a	Žalgiris	L	1-3	*Cristian*
07/09	h	Trakai	L	1-4	*Snapkauskas*
14/09	h	Kauno Ž	D	2-2	*Vėževičius, Basit*
20/09	a	Sūduva	L	0-2	
02/10	h	Utenis	D	1-1	*Cristian*
16/10	a	Lietava	W	4-1	*Cristian 2, Vėževičius, og (Miščiukas)*
22/10	a	Sūduva	L	1-6	*Konikas*
29/10	h	Lietava	W	3-1	*Basit, Konikas, Sissoko*
06/11	a	Trakai	D	1-1	*Basit*
18/11	a	Žalgiris	D	2-2	*Armanavičius, Sissoko*
26/11	h	Atlantas	D	1-1	*Vėževičius*

No	Name	Nat	DoB	Pos	Aps	(s)	Gls
1	Evan Aleksandrov Ridley	AUS	19/06/94	G	5		
8	Vilius Armanavičius		08/05/95	M	25		1
4	Lukas Artimavičius		12/08/94	D	15		
14	Sofoniyas Asres	ETH	30/05/98	M		(2)	
21	Lukas Baranauskas		26/11/93	A	4	(2)	
29	Ainas Bareikis		30/09/96	M	17	(3)	
25	Abdul Basit	GHA	10/12/90	M	24		3
22	Romualdas Blaževičius		06/04/97	M		(3)	
27	Alpha Camara	GUI	15/08/94	M		(1)	
37	Cristian	BRA	01/12/93	M	7	(6)	4
55	Lukas Čerkauskas		12/03/94	D	7	(1)	
3	Douglas Brenner	BRA	02/09/95	D	1		
36	Eduardo Farias	BRA	04/06/90	A	6	(1)	2
15	Kennedy Eriba	NGA	21/12/90	M	3	(15)	2
66	Maksim Ermakov	RUS	21/04/95	M	5	(1)	
81	Éverson Pequi	BRA	08/02/85	A	1	(1)	
14	Francisco Flores	CRC	02/04/88	D	9		1
10	Klaidas Janonis		13/05/97	M	14		1
28	Jardel Nazaré	POR	16/05/95	D	13		
21	Donatas Konikas		21/04/98	A	1	(4)	2
77	Alexandre Kore	FRA	11/12/91	A	12	(1)	1
36	Pavel Kotov	RUS	21/06/95	D	5	(1)	
23	Nerijus Mačiulis		01/04/85	M	16	(5)	2
26	Andrea Muto	ITA	26/11/97	D	3		
45	Nauris Petkevičius		19/02/00	M	5	(6)	
5	Audrius Račkus		27/12/88	D	11		1
30	Matas Radžiukynas		05/04/99	A	4	(4)	
44	Rafael Broetto	BRA	18/08/90	G	17		
11	Artūras Rimkevičius		14/04/83	A		(3)	1
16	Giorgio Russo	ITA	03/02/89	M	21	(4)	4
18	Rimvydas Sadauskas		21/07/96	D	30	(1)	1
12	Aleksandr Sikorski	RUS	01/06/95	G	11		
38	Oumar Sissoko	MLI	20/06/96	M		(6)	2
7	Erikas Skripnikas		07/01/95	M	4	(4)	
20	Tomas Snapkauskas		12/06/92	D	26	(1)	3
9	Klaudijus Upstas		30/10/94	M	9	(16)	2
33	Robertas Vėževičius		05/01/86	M	24	(1)	6
13	Hayato Wakino	JPN	10/04/93	M	1	(4)	
99	Martynas Zaleckis		30/01/96	D	6		1
24	Vytautas Žemaitis		24/01/96	D	1		

LITHUANIA

FK Sūduva

1968 • ARVI (6,250); ARVI Arena (2,500) • fksuduva.lt

Major honours
Lithuanian Cup (2) 2006, 2009

Coach: Aleksandar Veselinović (SRB); (08/09/16) Vladimir Cheburin (KAZ)

2016

Date		Opponent		Score	Scorers
06/03	a	Lietava	D	1-1	*Radzinevičius*
09/03	h	Atlantas	W	1-0	*Jablan*
16/03	a	Žalgiris	L	2-3	*Pavlović, Laukžemis*
20/03	h	Trakai	L	0-2	
03/04	a	Stumbras	W	3-2	*Kecap, Pavlović, Radzinevičius*
10/04	a	Kauno Ž	D	2-2	*Švrljuga, Kecap*
17/04	h	Utenis	W	2-1	*Pavlović, Veliulis*
20/04	h	Lietava	W	3-0	*Radzinevičius, Chvedukas, A Jankauskas*
27/04	a	Atlantas	W	2-1	*Radzinevičius, Janušauskas*
04/05	h	Žalgiris	W	1-0	*Veliulis*
07/05	a	Trakai	L	1-3	*Kecap*
18/05	h	Stumbras	L	0-1	
21/05	h	Kauno Ž	W	1-0	*Kecap*
08/06	a	Utenis	W	4-0	*Kecap, Laukžemis, Radzinevičius, Šoblinskas*
16/06	a	Lietava	D	1-1	*Kecap*
24/06	h	Atlantas	D	3-3	*Pavlović, og (Epifanov), Radzinevičius*
20/07	h	Trakai	W	1-0	*Radzinevičius*
26/07	a	Stumbras	W	3-2	*Radzinevičius 2, E Jankauskas*
04/08	a	Kauno Ž	W	1-0	*Veliulis*
10/08	h	Utenis	W	2-1	*Janušauskas, Radzinevičius*
17/08	h	Lietava	D	0-0	
24/08	a	Atlantas	L	1-2	*Kecap*
28/08	a	Žalgiris	L	1-4	*Radzinevičius*
07/09	h	Žalgiris	D	0-0	
14/09	a	Trakai	L	0-2	
20/09	h	Stumbras	W	2-0	*Leimonas, Veliulis*
01/10	h	Kauno Ž	W	2-0	*Pavlović, E Jankauskas*
16/10	a	Utenis	W	2-1	*Veliulis, Pavlović*
22/10	h	Stumbras	W	6-1	*Pavlović 2, Janušauskas, Švrljuga 2, Veliulis*
29/10	a	Trakai	D	1-1	*Činikas*
05/11	h	Žalgiris	L	1-3	*Radzinevičius*
20/11	h	Atlantas	W	3-1	*Radzinevičius, Veliulis 2*
26/11	a	Lietava	L	2-3	*Veliulis, Radzinevičius*

No	Name	Nat	DoB	Pos	Aps	(s)	Gls
40	Leonid Akulinin	UKR	07/03/93	A	2	(4)	
98	Domantas Antanavičius		18/11/98	M	1	(12)	
2	Valentin Baranovskij		15/10/86	M	5	(9)	
13	Karolis Chvedukas		21/04/91	M	7	(2)	1
3	Marius Činikas		17/05/86	D	19	(9)	1
5	Darius Isoda		27/07/94	D	12		
85	Miljan Jablan	SRB	30/01/85	D	21		1
24	Nermin Jamak	BIH	25/08/86	M	29	(1)	
33	Algis Jankauskas		27/09/82	D	31	(1)	1
3	Eligijus Jankauskas		22/06/98	M	10	(8)	2
16	Paulius Janušauskas		28/02/89	M	23	(9)	3
8	Gabrielius Judickas		04/07/95	M	1	(1)	
45	Ivan Kardum	CRO	18/07/87	G	31		
14	Admir Kecap	SRB	25/11/87	M	26	(2)	7
92	Karolis Laukžemis		11/03/92	A	6	(10)	2
6	Povilas Leimonas		16/11/87	M	16		1
28	Martynas Matuzas		28/08/89	G	2		
77	Predrag Pavlović	SRB	19/06/86	M	20	(8)	8
10	Tomas Radzinevičius		05/06/81	A	23	(6)	14
19	Vaidas Slavickas		26/02/86	D	27		
88	Marius Šoblinskas		23/08/87	M		(8)	1
11	Andro Švrljuga	CRO	24/10/85	D	22		3
7	Ernestas Veliulis		22/08/92	M	29	(3)	9

FK Trakai

2005 • LFF, Vilnius (5,067) • fkt.lt

Coach: Valdas Urbonas; (29/07/16) Albert Rybak (BLR); (26/08/16) Serhiy Kovalets (UKR)

2016

Date		Opponent		Score	Scorers
02/03	a	Žalgiris	L	0-2	
13/03	a	Kauno Ž	W	2-0	*Dapkus, Valskis*
17/03	h	Stumbras	W	3-2	*Valskis 2, Arshakyan*
20/03	a	Sūduva	W	2-0	*Gurenko, Valskis*
30/03	h	Utenis	W	1-0	*Mamaev*
10/04	a	Lietava	W	1-0	*Rekish*
17/04	h	Atlantas	W	2-0	*Arshakyan, Gurenko*
20/04	h	Žalgiris	W	1-0	*Arshakyan*
28/04	h	Kauno Ž	D	0-0	
03/05	a	Stumbras	D	0-0	
07/05	h	Sūduva	W	3-1	*Januševskij, Vitukynas, Arshakyan*
19/05	a	Utenis	W	2-0	*Valskis 2*
22/05	h	Lietava	W	3-0	*Klimavičius, Vitukynas, Gurenko*
09/06	a	Atlantas	D	2-2	*Gurenko, Arshakyan (p)*
15/06	a	Žalgiris	L	1-3	*Rekish*
21/06	a	Kauno Ž	W	4-0	*og (Fridrikas), Gurenko, Valskis, Arshakyan*
14/07	h	Stumbras	L	0-2	
20/07	a	Sūduva	L	0-1	
28/07	h	Utenis	W	4-3	*Arshakyan 3 (1p), Bychenok*
03/08	a	Lietava	D	1-1	*Valskis*
10/08	h	Atlantas	W	3-0	*Bychenok, Gurenko, Valskis*
17/08	h	Žalgiris	L	1-2	*Valskis (p)*
25/08	h	Kauno Ž	W	3-0	*Dorley, Valskis, Zasavitschi*
07/09	a	Stumbras	W	4-1	*Valskis 2 (1p), Zasavitschi, Masenzovas*
14/09	h	Sūduva	W	2-0	*Valskis, Zasavitschi*
19/09	a	Utenis	W	1-0	*Shyshka*
02/10	h	Lietava	L	0-2	
16/10	a	Atlantas	W	1-0	*Klimavičius*
21/10	a	Atlantas	D	0-0	
29/10	h	Sūduva	D	1-1	*Dorley*
06/11	h	Stumbras	D	1-1	*Valskis (p)*
20/11	h	Lietava	W	3-1	*Dorley, Labukas, Januševskij*
26/11	a	Žalgiris	W	3-1	*Valskis 2, Zasavitschi*

No	Name	Nat	DoB	Pos	Aps	(s)	Gls
10	David Arshakyan	ARM	16/08/94	A	18		9
2	Mattia Broli	ITA	04/05/94	D		(3)	
77	Aleksandr Bychenok	BLR	30/05/85	M	31		2
7	Deividas Česnauskis		30/06/81	D	30	(1)	
23	Martynas Dapkus		16/02/93	M	7	(4)	1
11	Oscar Dorley	LBR	19/07/98	M	12	(1)	3
37	Matas Gudaitis		28/06/00	A		(2)	
22	Artem Gurenko	BLR	18/06/94	M	28	(4)	6
15	Justinas Januševskij		26/03/94	D	23	(3)	2
32	Simonas Jurgilas		14/10/98	D		(1)	
5	Andrius Kazakevičius		28/03/91	D		(2)	
2	Arūnas Klimavičius		05/10/82	D	30		2
18	Lukas Kochanauskas		27/02/90	A	1	(6)	
37	Pavel Kruk	BLR	03/02/92	D	5	(2)	
10	Tadas Labukas		10/01/84	A	6	(3)	1
19	Mantas Leonavičius		19/01/94	D	2	(2)	
79	Yuri Mamaev	RUS	03/02/84	M	5	(4)	1
30	Rokas Masenzovas		02/08/94	M	1	(9)	1
33	Georgios Pelagias	CYP	10/05/85	D	6	(2)	
13	Ignas Plūkas		08/02/93	G	17		
1	Marius Rapalis		22/03/83	G	16		
9	Dmitri Rekish	BLR	14/09/88	M	9	(3)	2
23	Mykhailo Shyshka	UKR	05/07/94	M	12	(1)	1
96	Donatas Šėgžda		16/01/96	A	1	(6)	
21	Vaidotas Šilėnas		16/07/85	D	16		
27	Nerijus Valskis		04/08/87	M	29		17
14	Titas Vitukynas		23/10/94	M	3	(15)	2
4	Modestas Vorobjovas		30/12/95	M	12	(15)	
22	Alma Wakili	NGA	02/09/96	D	13		
24	Evgheny Zasavitschi	MDA	24/11/92	M	30	(2)	4

FK Utenis

1933 • Utenis (3,000); Visaginas Artificial (200) • utenosutenis.lt

Coach: Mindaugas Čepas; (09/05/16) Oleh Boychyshyn (UKR)

2016

Date		Opponent		Score	Scorers
05/03	h	Kauno Ž	L	2-3	*Jankauskas, Moroz*
13/03	h	Lietava	L	0-1	
16/03	a	Atlantas	L	0-1	
19/03	h	Žalgiris	L	0-1	
30/03	a	Trakai	L	0-1	
09/04	h	Stumbras	W	1-0	*Jankauskas*
17/04	a	Sūduva	L	1-2	*Zagurskas*
22/04	a	Kauno Ž	W	3-1	*Moroz, Jankauskas, Mastianica*
26/04	a	Lietava	L	0-1	
05/05	h	Atlantas	L	0-2	
08/05	a	Žalgiris	L	0-2	
19/05	h	Trakai	L	0-2	
22/05	a	Stumbras	L	1-3	*Moroz*
08/06	h	Sūduva	L	0-4	
14/06	h	Kauno Ž	W	2-1	*Freidgeimas (p), K Levšin*
22/06	h	Lietava	W	3-1	*Mastianica, Polyanskiy, Freidgeimas (p)*
12/07	a	Atlantas	L	0-2	
23/07	h	Žalgiris	L	2-4	*K Levšin, Vereshchak*
28/07	a	Trakai	L	3-4	*Vereshchak, K Levšin, Polyanskiy*
03/08	h	Stumbras	D	0-0	
10/08	a	Sūduva	L	1-2	*Vereshchak*
18/08	a	Kauno Ž	D	1-1	*Romanovskij*
25/08	a	Lietava	L	0-1	
08/09	h	Atlantas	D	1-1	*Vereshchak*
15/09	a	Žalgiris	L	1-2	*Romanovskij*
19/09	h	Trakai	L	0-1	
02/10	a	Stumbras	D	1-1	*Zagurskas*
16/10	h	Sūduva	L	1-2	*Moroz*

No	Name	Nat	DoB	Pos	Aps	(s)	Gls
4	Lukas Artimavičius		12/08/94	D	14	(1)	
4	Mikhail Bashilov	RUS	12/01/93	D	7		
11	Arsenij Buinickij		10/10/85	A	6	(10)	
23	Tomas Dombrauskis		24/09/96	M	18	(2)	
20	Yuriy Flyak	UKR	24/04/94	D	2		
3	Robertas Freidgeimas		21/02/89	D	23	(1)	2
17	Eligijus Jankauskas		22/06/98	M	13	(1)	3
6	Valentin Jeriomenko		19/02/89	M	17	(1)	
8	Mykolas Krasnovskis		08/07/94	M	8	(6)	
12	Pavel Leus		15/09/78	G	3	(1)	
29	Aleksandr Levšin		14/08/99	D		(6)	
30	Kiril Levšin		08/09/96	A	8	(8)	3
8	Ivan Lukanyuk	UKR	06/02/93	A	1	(4)	
10	Edgaras Mastianica		26/10/88	M	16		2
28	Takuya Matsunaga	JPN	10/06/90	M	4	(1)	
7	Jevgenij Moroz		20/01/90	M	22	(5)	4
77	Vitaliy Myrniy	UKR	03/04/92	G	8		
1	Lukas Paukštė		25/09/98	G	5		
16	Gabrielius Petuchovas		20/04/00	M		(2)	
15	Vitaliy Polyanskiy	UKR	30/11/88	M	13		2
9	Ihor Poruchynskiy	UKR	20/10/94	M	8	(10)	
33	Nikola Prebiračević	SRB	23/01/87	D	1		
19	Daniel Romanovskij		19/06/96	M	13		2
5	Benas Spietinis		15/02/96	D	5	(1)	
2	Aurimas Tručinskas		25/10/94	M	23		
36	Mindaugas Ubelka		08/07/99	A		(2)	
5	Lukas Valvonis		06/07/97	D	7	(1)	
21	Arminas Vaskėla		12/08/90	M	16	(3)	
10	Yuriy Vereshchak	UKR	04/04/94	A	11		4
13	Gabrielius Zagurskas		13/05/92	D	24		2
18	Lukas Žukauskas		18/05/93	G	12		

FK Žalgiris Vilnius

1947 • LFF (5,067); Sportima Arena (3,157) • fkzalgiris.lt

Major honours
Lithuanian League (7) 1991, 1992, 1999, 2013, 2014, 2015, 2016; Lithuanian Cup (11) 1991, 1993, 1994, 1997, 2003 (autumn), 2012, 2013, 2014, 2015, 2016 (spring), 2016 (autumn)

Coach: Valdas Dambrauskas

2016					
02/03	h	Trakai	W	2-0	*Atajić 2*
12/03	a	Stumbras	W	6-3	*Vaitkūnas, Atajić 2, Pilibaitis, Kuklys, Elivelto*
16/03	h	Sūduva	W	3-2	*Mbodj, Mikoliūnas, Kuklys (p)*
19/03	a	Utenis	W	1-0	*Elton*
02/04	h	Lietava	D	2-2	*Žaliūkas, Mbodj*
06/04	a	Atlantas	L	1-2	*Mbodj*
16/04	h	Kauno Ž	W	3-0	*Pilibaitis (p), Stankevičius, Lucas Gaúcho*
20/04	a	Trakai	L	0-1	
27/04	h	Stumbras	W	2-0	*Kuklys (p), Lukša*
04/05	a	Sūduva	L	0-1	
08/05	h	Utenis	W	2-0	*Matoš, Lukša*
18/05	a	Lietava	W	1-0	*Klimavičius*
21/05	h	Atlantas	W	1-0	*Mbodj*
09/06	a	Kauno Ž	D	1-1	*Lasickas*
15/06	h	Trakai	W	3-1	*Pilibaitis 2, Ljujić*
24/06	a	Stumbras	W	5-0	*Vaitkūnas, Pilibaitis 2, Matoš, Kaludjerović*
23/07	a	Utenis	W	4-2	*Kaludjerović 3, Pilibaitis*
27/07	h	Lietava	W	4-1	*Kaludjerović 3, Mbodj*
02/08	a	Atlantas	W	1-0	*Kaludjerović*
11/08	h	Kauno Ž	W	3-1	*Pilibaitis, Atajić, Kaludjerović*
17/08	a	Trakai	W	2-1	*Kaludjerović 2*
24/08	h	Stumbras	W	3-1	*Ljujić, Mbodj, Lukša*
28/08	h	Sūduva	W	4-1	*Kaludjerović, Lukša, Elivelto, Matoš*
07/09	a	Sūduva	D	0-0	
15/09	h	Utenis	W	2-1	*Elivelto, Kuklys*
20/09	a	Lietava	W	4-0	*Mikoliūnas, Atajić 3*
01/10	h	Atlantas	L	0-1	
16/10	a	Kauno Ž	W	2-0	*Mikoliūnas, Pilibaitis*
22/10	a	Lietava	W	4-1	*Kaludjerović 3, Lukša*
30/10	h	Atlantas	W	2-0	*Ljujić, og (Raziūnas)*
05/11	a	Sūduva	W	3-1	*Kaludjerović 2, Kuklys*
18/11	h	Stumbras	D	2-2	*Kaludjerović 2*
26/11	h	Trakai	L	1-3	*Kaludjerović*

No	Name	Nat	DoB	Pos	Aps	(s)	Gls
33	Bahrudin Atajić	BIH	16/11/93	A	16	(8)	8
20	Dominykas Barauskas		18/04/97	D	2	(2)	
7	Slavko Blagojević	CRO	21/03/87	M	12	(2)	
17	Tautvydas Eliošius		03/11/91	M	3	(3)	
80	Elivelto	BRA	02/01/92	M	15	(9)	3
7	Elton	BRA	20/07/89	M	6	(2)	1
9	Jorge Chula	POR	13/02/90	M	2	(5)	
99	Andrija Kaludjerović	SRB	05/07/87	A	18	(1)	20
65	Saulius Klevinskas		02/04/84	G	14		
2	Linas Klimavičius		10/04/89	D	26	(2)	1
18	Aldas Korsakas		21/05/96	D	2		
88	Mantas Kuklys		10/06/87	M	29	(2)	5
22	Justas Lasickas		06/10/97	M	6	(10)	1
27	Matija Ljujić	SRB	28/10/93	M	11	(4)	3
10	Lucas Gaúcho	BRA	13/06/91	A		(3)	1
21	Vytautas Lukša		14/08/84	M	28	(3)	5
4	Marin Matoš	CRO	26/01/89	M	12	(10)	3
6	Pape Mamadou Mbodj	SEN	12/03/93	D	33		6
31	Saulius Mikoliūnas		02/05/84	M	19	(8)	3
28	Julius Momkus		28/02/98	A		(2)	
77	Linas Pilibaitis		05/04/85	M	20	(10)	9
13	Daniel Romanovskij		19/06/96	M	1	(4)	
71	Jonas Skinderis		04/04/97	M		(1)	
5	Donovan Slijngard	NED	28/08/87	D	30		
11	Simonas Stankevičius		03/10/95	A	5	(3)	1
8	Egidijus Vaitkūnas		08/08/88	D	27	(1)	2
1	Armantas Vitkauskas		23/03/89	G	19		
26	Marius Žaliūkas		10/11/83	D	7	(4)	1

Top goalscorers

20	Andrija Kaludjerović (Žalgiris)
17	Nerijus Valskis (Trakai)
14	Tomas Radzinevičius (Sūduva)
10	Maksim Maksimov (Atlantas)
9	Abdoul Karim Sylla (Atlantas)
	Ernestas Veliulis (Sūduva)
	David Arshakyan (Trakai)
	Linas Pilibaitis (Žalgiris)
8	Predrag Pavlović (Sūduva)
	Bahrudin Atajić (Žalgiris)

Second level

Second level final table 2016

		Pld	W	D	L	F	A	Pts
1	FK Šilas	30	23	3	4	95	25	72
2	FK Palanga	30	21	7	2	96	29	70
3	FK Vilniaus Vytis	30	19	3	8	102	34	60
4	FK Nevėžis	30	17	9	4	76	38	60
5	FK Panevėžys	30	17	8	5	68	35	59
6	FK Banga	30	15	7	8	62	31	52
7	FK Džiugas	30	15	3	12	51	44	48
8	FK Žalgiris Vilnius B	30	14	3	13	62	61	45
9	DFK Dainava	30	13	4	13	57	46	43
10	FK Hegelmann Litauen	30	13	3	14	55	56	42
11	FK Trakai-2	30	9	3	18	44	59	30
12	FK Šilutė	30	8	6	16	38	60	30
13	FK Kražantė	30	8	4	18	47	86	28
14	FK Lokomotyvas	30	6	5	19	42	86	23
15	FBK Kaunas	30	4	1	25	25	134	13
16	FK Minija	30	3	1	26	27	123	10

Promotion/Relegation play-offs

(29/10/16 & 06/11/16)
Palanga 2-3 Utenis
Utenis 0-1 Palanga
(3-3; Utenis on away goals)

NB FK Šilas subsequently declined promotion to 2017 A Lyga.

DOMESTIC CUP

LFF Taurė 2016

THIRD ROUND

(08/06/16)
Navigatoriai 1-3 Rotalis

(11/06/16)
Ateitis 0-7 Atlantas
DFK Dainava 3-5 Džiugas
Eurostandartas 2-4 Radviliškis *(aet)*
FA Dainava 1-6 Palanga
Lygis 0-2 Trakai
Sveikata 0-1 Panevėžys

(12/06/16)
Kruša 1-3 Švyturys
Lietava 0-0 Sūduva *(aet; 5-6 on pens)*
Lokomotyvas 2-3 Banga
Nevėžis 2-0 Utenis

(16/06/16)
Adiada 2-1 Saulininkas
Babrungas 2-1 Šilutė

(18/06/16)
Kauno Ž 0-6 Žalgiris
Versmė 0-5 Koralas

(19/06/16)
Granitas 0-2 Stumbras

FOURTH ROUND

(29/06/16)
Koralas 0-1 Džiugas *(aet)*

(05/07/16)
Adiada 2-2 Radviliškis *(aet; 4-5 on pens)*
Švyturys 2-1 Babrungas

(06/08/16)
Banga 1-2 Nevėžis
Palanga 0-4 Žalgiris
Panevėžys 0-2 Stumbras
Rotalis 0-4 Atlantas

(07/08/16)
Sūduva 4-0 Trakai *(aet)*

QUARTER-FINALS

(20/08/16)
Džiugas 1-2 Atlantas *(Viktoravičius 83; Papšys 43, 90+3)*

Nevėžis 0-3 Stumbras *(Rukuiža 45og, Vėževičius 59, 61)*

Radviliškis 0-7 Žalgiris *(Matoš 3, Jorge Chula 10, Elivelto 20, 77, Momkus 23, 31, Mikoliūnas 44)*

Švyturys 1-10 Sūduva *(Matulevičius 37; Radzinevičius 15, 25, 30, 42, Janušauskas 17, Veliulis 20, 35, Bielkauskas 55og, Kardokas 79, Pavlović 88)*

SEMI-FINALS

(10/09/16)
Stumbras 0-2 Sūduva *(Janušauskas 43, Baranovskij 64)*

(11/09/16)
Atlantas 1-2 Žalgiris *(Gašpuitis 19; Mikoliūnas 10, Kaludjerović 90+2)*

FINAL

(25/09/16)
Centrinis, Klaipeda
FK ŽALGIRIS VILNIUS 2 *(Kaludjerović 64, Kuklys 90+3p)*
FK SŪDUVA 0
Referee: *Slyva*
ŽALGIRIS: *Vitkauskas, Slijngard, Klimavičius, Mbodj, Vaitkūnas, Mikoliūnas (Elivelto 86), Blagojević, Kuklys, Lukša, Atajić (Ljujić 59), Kaludjerović (Pilibaitis 90+1)*
SŪDUVA: *Kardum, A Jankauskas, Činikas, Isoda, Slavickas, Švrljuga (Akulinin 72), Leimonas, Pavlović (Kecap 81), Janušauskas, Veliulis (E Jankauskas 68), Radzinevičius*
Red cards: *A Jankauskas (90), Činikas (90+3), Slavickas (90+3)*

LUXEMBOURG

Fédération Luxembourgeoise de Football (FLF)

Address	BP5, Rue de Limpach LU-3901 Mondercange
Tel	+352 488 665 1
Fax	+352 488 665 82
E-mail	flf@football.lu
Website	football.lu

President	Paul Philipp
General secretary	Joël Wolff
Media officer	Marc Diederich
Year of formation	1908
National stadium	Josy Barthel, Luxembourg (8,022)

NATIONAL DIVISION CLUBS

 1 **FC Differdange 03**

 2 **F91 Dudelange**

 3 **CS Fola Esch**

 4 **FC RM Hamm Benfica**

 5 **FC Jeunesse Canach**

 6 **AS Jeunesse Esch**

 7 **UN Käerjéng 97**

 8 **US Mondorf-les-Bains**

 9 **FC Progrès Niederkorn**

 10 **Racing FC Union Lëtzebuerg**

 11 **US Rumelange**

 12 **FC UNA Strassen**

 13 **FC Union Titus Pétange**

 14 **FC Victoria Rosport**

PROMOTED CLUBS

 15 **US Esch**

 16 **FC Rodange 91**

 17 **US Hostert**

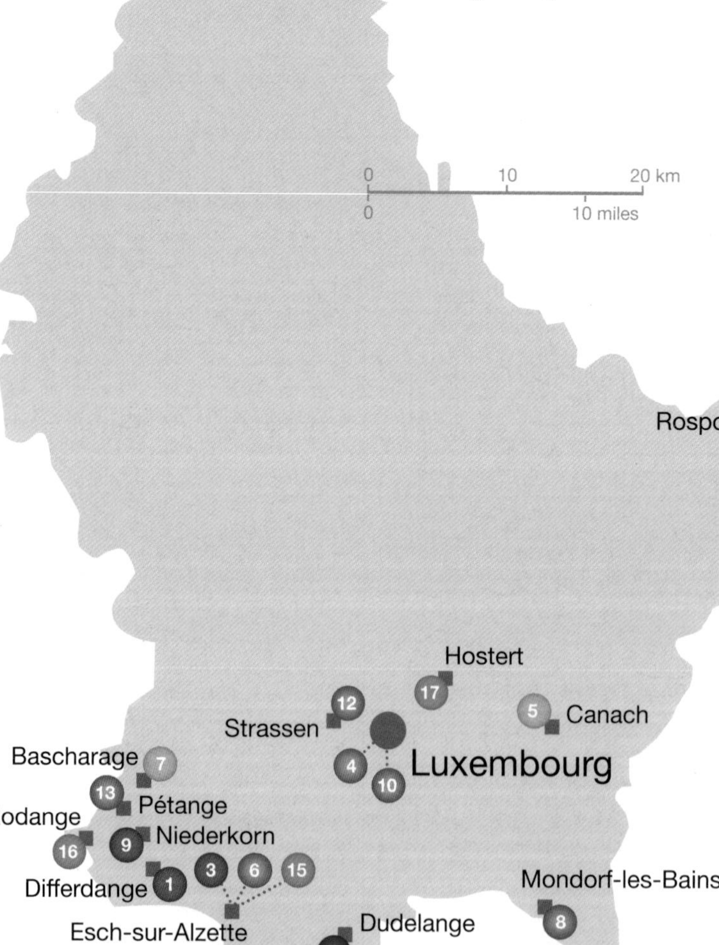

Dudelange double up

For the second season in succession, the National Division of Luxembourg was won by F91 Dudelange on goal difference. After Fola Esch had been narrowly squeezed out the previous season, it was FC Differdange 03's turn to become frustrated runners-up in 2016/17.

The title race went to the wire, but retaining the Luxembourg Cup was a relatively stress-free experience for a Dudelange side led by new German coach Dino Toppmöller, son of Klaus, the man who led Bayer Leverkusen to the 2002 UEFA Champions League final.

Border club successfully defend league and cup

Differdange denied first title on goal difference

Aurélien Joachim hits four World Cup goals

Domestic league

Recruited from Hamm Benfica to replace Dudelange coaching legend Michel Leflochmoan, Toppmöller bore the weight of expectation at his new club well. His team made an impressive start and maintained their form for the duration of the 26-match campaign. Their problem was that Differdange, with a new coach themselves in Frenchman Pascal Carzaniga, did exactly the same.

Even Jeff Strasser's Fola, the 2012/13 and 2014/15 champions, could not keep pace with the top two and they were beaten just twice all season – once by Differdange in the autumn, once by Dudelange in the spring. With Luxembourg international David Turpel spearheading a deadly Dudelange attack and the ever-reliable Omar Er Rafik continuing to score liberally for Differdange, victories became a weekly routine for both teams. The main difference was Dudelange's superior defence, shored up by long-serving goalkeeper Jonathan Joubert, who would win his tenth title with the club.

Joubert and his team-mates would have to wait until the final whistle of the final game, a 2-0 win at Jeunesse Canach, before the silverware was secure. Although they were level on points with Differdange going into that match, their goal difference was so superior that realistically only the acquisition of three points was necessary. Goals just before and after the interval, from Luxembourg internationals Daniel Da Mota and Turpel respectively, did the job, bringing the club their 13th national title, all of them won since the turn of the century.

Differdange had never been crowned champions of Luxembourg, and although they beat Dudelange on head-to-head, drawing 0-0 at home and winning 1-0 away (the champions' sole defeat), their title hopes effectively died when, with a two-point lead and just four games remaining, they were held 1-1 by Fola. That draw, coupled with their only defeat of the campaign, a shock 1-0 reverse at Jeunesse Esch in February, proved fatal.

Fola finished nine points off the pace in third, with Progrès Niederkorn another 12 points back in fourth – a position that carried the bonus of a place in the UEFA Europa League. Record champions Jeunesse Esch won just seven games and finished only six points clear of a relegation zone that ensnared Käerjéng, Rumelange and – after a play-off – Jeunesse Canach.

Domestic cup

Dudelange's seventh cup success in 14 years was sealed by a 4-1 win over a Fola side seeking their first victory in the competition since 1955. Three goals in the final quarter ended Fola's hopes and served as an impressive response from Dudelange to the first goal they had conceded in the competition. Four clean sheets and 17 goals had transported them to the final, the highlight a 3-0 victory away to Differdange in the last eight.

Europe

Not for the first time, Luxembourg's four European representatives all bit the dust on entry. On the positive side, there were no heavy defeats and Er Rafik lifted his remarkable tally of European goals to 13 in five seasons as Differdange drew 1-1 at home to Cliftonville.

National team

Luxembourg were unfortunate to be on the wrong end of a seven-goal thriller in their opening 2018 FIFA World Cup qualifier, away to Bulgaria. Aurélien Joachim scored twice to put his team 2-1 up at one stage of that 4-3 defeat and the striker would go on to double his tally for the competition with two further strikes, the first earning a 1-1 draw against Belarus in Borisov, the second bringing Luxembourg level from the penalty spot in a 3-1 defeat at home to France. One point from six matches was probably less than Luxembourg deserved, but Luc Holtz's team did cheer up their supporters by beating Albania 2-1 in a June friendly.

DOMESTIC SEASON AT A GLANCE

National Division 2016/17 final table

			Home					Away					Total					
		Pld	W	D	L	F	A	W	D	L	F	A	W	D	L	F	A	Pts
1	**F91 Dudelange**	**26**	**12**	**0**	**1**	**41**	**7**	**8**	**5**	**0**	**27**	**7**	**20**	**5**	**1**	**68**	**14**	**65**
2	FC Differdange 03	26	12	1	0	41	9	8	4	1	24	12	20	5	1	65	21	65
3	CS Fola Esch	26	8	5	0	38	16	8	3	2	31	18	16	8	2	69	34	56
4	FC Progrès Niederkorn	26	5	3	5	26	19	8	2	3	31	19	13	5	8	57	38	44
5	FC UNA Strassen	26	5	2	6	20	25	6	2	5	19	22	11	4	11	39	47	37
6	FC Union Titus Pétange	26	4	4	5	18	18	6	1	6	20	15	10	5	11	38	33	35
7	US Mondorf-les-Bains	26	6	2	5	15	17	3	1	9	14	28	9	3	14	29	45	30
8	AS Jeunesse Esch	26	4	4	5	17	21	3	4	6	21	28	7	8	11	38	49	29
9	FC Victoria Rosport	26	4	3	6	20	25	4	1	8	18	29	8	4	14	38	54	28
10	Racing FC Union Lëtzebuerg	26	5	1	7	18	22	3	2	8	20	30	8	3	15	38	52	27
11	FC RM Hamm Benfica	26	3	3	7	13	21	4	2	7	16	26	7	5	14	29	47	26
12	FC Jeunesse Canach	26	4	2	7	18	27	1	6	6	12	27	5	8	13	30	54	23
13	US Rumelange	26	4	5	4	17	19	1	3	9	12	34	5	8	13	29	53	23
14	UN Käerjéng 97	26	4	1	8	23	33	3	0	10	14	30	7	1	18	37	63	22

European qualification 2017/18

Champion/Cup winner: F91 Dudelange (second qualifying round)

FC Differdange 03 (first qualifying round)
CS Fola Esch (first qualifying round)
FC Progrès Niederkorn (first qualifying round)

Top scorer Omar Er Rafik (Differdange), 26 goals
Relegated clubs UN Käerjéng 97, US Rumelange, FC Jeunesse Canach
Promoted clubs US Esch, FC Rodange 91, US Hostert
Cup final F91 Dudelange 4-1 CS Fola Esch

Player of the season

Omar Er Rafik
(FC Differdange 03)

A 31-year-old Frenchman of Moroccan ancestry, Er Rafik has built up a reputation in Luxembourg as one of the deadliest goalscorers around. Celebrated above all for his ability to find the net in European qualifying ties, he supplemented a 13th UEFA Europa League goal in the summer of 2016 by winning the National Division golden boot for the second time (after 2011/12, his debut season with Differdange). His final tally of 26 goals, boosted by five against Victoria Rosport on the final day, was the highest in Luxembourg's top flight for eight years.

Newcomer of the season

Dirk Carlson
(FC Union Titus Pétange)

Used only once as a substitute by Racing Union Lëtzebuerg in 2015/16, Carlson switched to Union Titus and became, at just 18 years of age, the linchpin of the team's defence, starting 21 National Division encounters and helping the newly-promoted club to an unexpected sixth-place finish. Quick to appreciate the youngster's potential, Luxembourg coach Luc Holtz introduced him to the national side, although the experience was not all sweetness and light as he left the field in tears after being red-carded in a FIFA World Cup qualifier against Belarus.

Team of the season

(3-4-3)

Coach: Toppmöller *(Dudelange)*

NATIONAL TEAM

Top five all-time caps
Jeff Strasser (98); **Mario Mutsch** (94); René Peters (93); Eric Hoffmann (89); Carlo Weis (88)

Top five all-time goals
Léon Mart (16); Gusty Kemp (15); Camille Libar (14); Nicolas Kettel (13); **Aurélien Joachim** & François Müller (12)

Results 2016/17

02/09/16	Latvia	A	Riga	L	1-3	*Da Mota (46)*
06/09/16	Bulgaria (WCQ)	A	Sofia	L	3-4	*Joachim (60, 62), Bohnert (90+1)*
07/10/16	Sweden (WCQ)	H	Luxembourg	L	0-1	
10/10/16	Belarus (WCQ)	A	Borisov	D	1-1	*Joachim (85)*
13/11/16	Netherlands (WCQ)	H	Luxembourg	L	1-3	*Chanot (44p)*
25/03/17	France (WCQ)	H	Luxembourg	L	1-3	*Joachim (34p)*
28/03/17	Cape Verde Islands	H	Hesperange	L	0-2	
04/06/17	Albania	H	Luxembourg	W	2-1	*Turpel (63), Malget (74)*
09/06/17	Netherlands (WCQ)	A	Rotterdam	L	0-5	

Appearances 2016/17

Coach: Luc Holtz	**14/06/69**		**Lva**	**BUL**	**SWE**	**BLR**	**NED**	**FRA**	**Cpv**	**Alb**	**NED**	**Caps**	**Goals**
Jonathan Joubert	12/09/79	Dudelange	G	G								86	-
Laurent Jans	05/08/92	Waasland-Beveren (BEL)	D	D	D	D	D26	D	D	D	D	40	-
Christopher Martins	19/02/97	Lyon (FRA)	D72	D	D	D35		D	D73	M	M	21	-
Kevin Malget	15/01/91	Dudelange	D	D	D 82*		D	D	D	D	D	20	1
Dirk Carlson	01/04/98	Union Titus	D72		D	D 44*			D30			4	-
Mario Mutsch	03/09/84	St Gallen (SUI)	M84	M	M	M	M	M62	M			94	4
Lars Gerson	05/02/90	Sundsvall (SWE)	M	M				M	M68	s82	s54	60	4
Chris Philipps	08/03/94	Metz (FRA)	M55	M84	M	M	M	M	M46	D53		40	-
Daniel Da Mota	11/09/85	Dudelange	M	M68	s66	M	M75	M81	s46			77	5
Vincent Thill	04/02/00	Metz (FRA)	M85	M59	M66	M46	s82			M73	M54	9	1
David Turpel	19/10/92	Dudelange	A60	s59	s66	s72	A		A46	A90	A	28	2
Florian Bohnert	09/11/97	Schalke (GER)	s55	s68	M	M72	M	s62	M30	M61	s85	10	1
Maurice Deville	31/07/92	FSV Frankfurt (GER)	s60	s84	M66				s68	s73		34	3
Mathias Jänisch	27/08/90	Differdange	s72			s46	s26			s86		47	1
Tom Laterza	09/05/92	Fola	s72									34	-
Eric Veiga	18/02/97	Braunschweig (GER)	s84			s35						2	-
Sébastien Thill	29/12/93	Progrès	s85							s61	M	9	1
Maxime Chanot	21/11/89	New York City (USA)		D			D	D			D25	25	2
Aurélien Joachim	10/08/86	Lierse (BEL)		A	A	A		A	A			67	12
Anthony Moris	29/04/90	Mechelen (BEL)			G	G		G21				8	-
Ricardo Delgado	22/02/94	Jeunesse Esch				D				s53	s25	10	-
Ralph Schon	20/01/90	UNA Strassen					G	s21	G	G	G	5	-
Enes Mahmutovic	22/05/97	Fola					D		s30	D86	D	4	-
Stefano Bensi	11/08/88	Fola					A82	A	s46	A82	A	42	4
Kevin Kerger	17/11/94	UNA Strassen					s75					1	-
Gerson Rodrigues	20/06/95	Fola						s81	s30	M	M85	4	-
Tim Hall	15/04/97	Elversberg (GER)							s73			1	-
Jan Ostrowski	14/04/99	Eintracht Frankfurt (GER)								s90		1	-

EUROPE

F91 Dudelange

Second qualifying round - Qarabağ FK (AZE)

A 0-2

Joubert, Schnell, Pokar (N'Diaye 56), Da Mota, Dikaba, Stolz, Nakache (Stélvio 81), Prempeh, Mélisse, Malget (Moreira 67), Turpel. Coach: Dino Toppmöller (GER)

H 1-1 *N'Diaye (71)*

Joubert, Moreira, Schnell, Da Mota (Laurentié 80), Dikaba, Stolz, Nakache (Pokar 66), Prempeh, Mélisse, Turpel, N'Diaye (Ibrahimović 86). Coach: Dino Toppmöller (GER)

FC Differdange 03

First qualifying round - Cliftonville FC (NIR)

H 1-1 *Er Rafik (38)*

Weber, Rodrigues, Siebenaler (Bukvic 71), May, Pedro Ribeiro (Sinani 67), Er Rafik, Yéyé (Lascak 81), Vandenbroeck, Jänisch, Franzoni, Luisi. Coach: Pascal Carzaniga (FRA)

A 0-2

Weber, Rodrigues, Siebenaler, May, Pedro Ribeiro (Luisi 78), Er Rafik, Sinani (Lascak 49), Caron, Yéyé, Vandenbroeck, Franzoni. Coach: Pascal Carzaniga (FRA)

Red card: Siebenaler 57

CS Fola Esch

First qualifying round - Aberdeen FC (SCO)

A 1-3 *Klein (70)*

Hym, Martino, Bernard (Sacras 70), Muharemović, Dallevedove, Françoise, Hadji, Laterza (Rodrigues 67), Kirch (Mahmutovic 82), Bensi, Klein. Coach: Jeff Strasser (LUX)

H 1-0 *Hadji (45)*

Hym, Bernard, Muharemović (Lopes 87), Dallevedove, Françoise (Camerling 78), Hadji, Laterza, Kirch, Klapp (Rodrigues 71), Bensi, Klein. Coach: Jeff Strasser (LUX)

AS Jeunesse Esch

First qualifying round - Saint Patrick's Athletic FC (IRL)

A 0-1

Oberweis, Ontiveros (Deidda 80), Todorovic, Portier, Corral (Sardaryan 24), Mertinitz, Stumpf, Peters, Pinna, Delgado, Lapierre. Coach: Carlo Weis (LUX)

H 2-1 *Stumpf (22, 87)*

Oberweis, Ontiveros (Deidda 88), Todorovic, Portier, Kühne, Mertinitz, Stumpf, Peters, Pinna, Delgado, Lapierre (Sardaryan 80). Coach: Carlo Weis (LUX)

Red card: Portier 90+3

DOMESTIC LEAGUE CLUB-BY-CLUB

FC Differdange 03

2003 • Parc des Sports (1,800) • fcd03.lu

Major honours

Luxembourg Cup (4) 2010, 2011, 2014, 2015

Coach: Pascal Carzaniga (FRA)

2016					
07/08	a	Rosport	D	1-1	*Vandenbroeck*
12/08	h	Progrès	W	2-0	*Er Rafik, Caron*
21/08	a	UNA Strassen	D	4-4	*Vandenbroeck, Er Rafik 2, Jänisch (p)*
28/08	h	Jeunesse Esch	W	3-1	*Almeida, Bastos, Pedro Ribeiro*
11/09	a	Jeunesse Canach	W	1-0	*Yéyé*
24/09	h	Union Titus	W	1-0	*Vandenbroeck (p)*
01/10	a	Hamm Benfica	W	3-1	*og (Veiga), Er Rafik 2*
16/10	h	Racing Union	W	3-2	*Sinani 3 (1p)*
23/10	h	Dudelange	D	0-0	
05/11	a	Rumelange	D	0-0	
27/11	h	Fola	W	2-0	*Almeida, Er Rafik*
04/12	a	Käerjéng	W	5-3	*Caron, Er Rafik 3, Almeida*
11/12	h	Mondorf-les-Bains	W	6-0	*Er Rafik 2, Caron 2, Almeida, Bettmer*
2017					
11/02	a	Progrès	W	2-1	*Er Rafik 2 (1p)*
19/02	h	UNA Strassen	W	4-1	*Vandenbroeck, Almeida, Hamzaoui 2*
26/02	a	Jeunesse Esch	L	0-1	
05/03	h	Jeunesse Canach	W	5-1	*Er Rafik, Siebenaler, Caron, Hamzaoui (p), og (Kalú)*
12/03	a	Union Titus	W	1-0	*Er Rafik*
18/03	h	Hamm Benfica	W	1-0	*Vandenbroeck*
02/04	a	Racing Union	W	2-0	*og (Jackson), Holter*
09/04	a	Dudelange	W	1-0	*Er Rafik*
23/04	h	Rumelange	W	2-0	*Bastos, Bettmer (p)*
30/04	a	Fola	D	1-1	*Hamzaoui*
07/05	h	Käerjéng	W	6-2	*Caron, Er Rafik 3, Hamzaoui, May*
14/05	a	Mondorf-les-Bains	W	3-0	*Hamzaoui, Er Rafik 2*
21/05	h	Rosport	W	6-2	*Er Rafik 5 (1p), Hamzaoui*

Name	Nat	DoB	Pos	Aps	(s)	Gls
Gonçalo Almeida		26/11/90	M	14	(3)	5
Yannick Bastos		30/05/93	M	11	(8)	2
Gilles Bettmer		31/03/89	M	11	(8)	2
Ante Bukvic		14/11/87	D		(1)	
Gauthier Caron	FRA	27/12/89	A	16	(3)	6
Omar Er Rafik	FRA	07/01/86	A	22	(3)	26
David Fleurival	FRA	19/02/84	M	26		
Geoffrey Franzoni	FRA	18/02/91	D	21	(1)	
Mounir Hamzaoui	TUN	09/12/87	M	11	(2)	7
Dwayn Holter		15/06/95	M	14	(4)	1
Mathias Jänisch		27/08/90	D	18		1
Jeff Lascak		13/02/94	M	2	(4)	
Antonio Luisi		07/10/94	M	7	(7)	
Andy May		02/09/89	M	5	(9)	1
Jérémy Méligner	FRA	11/06/91	M	1	(6)	
Pedro Ribeiro	POR	07/01/89	M	3	(1)	1
André Rodrigues		06/12/87	D	11	(4)	
Arnaud Schaab	FRA	03/09/90	G	3		
Tom Siebenaler		28/09/90	D	26		1
Dejvid Sinani		02/04/93	M	7	(4)	3
David Vandenbroeck	BEL	12/07/85	D	26		5
Julien Weber	FRA	12/10/85	G	23	(1)	
Jordan Yéyé	FRA	02/11/88	M	8	(8)	1

F91 Dudelange

1991 • Jos Nosbaum (4,500) • f91.lu

Major honours
Luxembourg League (13) 2000, 2001, 2002, 2005, 2006, 2007, 2008, 2009, 2011, 2012, 2014, 2016, 2017; Luxembourg Cup (7) 2004, 2006, 2007, 2009, 2012, 2016, 2017

Coach: Dino Toppmöller (GER)

Date		Opponent		Score	Scorers
2016					
06/08	h	Jeunesse Canach	W	6-1	*Turpel 2, Pokar, Stolz, N'Diaye, Moreira*
14/08	h	Käerjéng	W	1-0	*Stolz*
21/08	a	Union Titus	D	1-1	*Malget*
28/08	h	Mondorf-les-Bains	W	1-0	*Da Mota*
11/09	a	Hamm Benfica	W	3-0	*Prempeh, Turpel, Stolz*
25/09	h	Rosport	W	3-0	*Ibrahimović 2, Laurentié*
01/10	a	Racing Union	W	2-1	*Moreira, Turpel*
16/10	h	Progrès	W	4-0	*Stolz, Turpel 2, Ibrahimović*
23/10	a	Differdange	D	0-0	
05/11	h	UNA Strassen	W	3-0	*Turpel 2, Benzouien*
27/11	a	Rumelange	W	3-0	*Turpel, Pokar, og (Thior)*
04/12	h	Jeunesse Esch	W	5-1	*Stolz, Pokar (p), Turpel 2, Ibrahimović*
10/12	a	Fola	D	2-2	*Schnell, Turpel*
2017					
12/02	a	Käerjéng	D	1-1	*Benzouien*
19/02	h	Union Titus	W	3-0	*Pokar (p), Turpel (p), og (D Skenderovic)*
25/02	a	Mondorf-les-Bains	D	1-1	*Mélisse*
05/03	h	Hamm Benfica	W	3-0	*Stolz, Schnell, Da Mota*
12/03	a	Rosport	W	4-0	*Stolz 3, Turpel*
18/03	h	Racing Union	W	4-0	*Pedro, Da Mota 2, Malget*
02/04	a	Progrès	W	2-1	*Turpel, Pokar*
09/04	h	Differdange	L	0-1	
23/04	a	UNA Strassen	W	3-0	*Pokar, Turpel, Dikaba*
30/04	h	Rumelange	W	3-2	*Stolz, Turpel, Ibrahimović*
07/05	a	Jeunesse Esch	W	3-0	*Turpel 2 (1p), Stolz*
14/05	h	Fola	W	5-2	*Stolz, Turpel (p), Stélvio, Da Mota, Pokar*
21/05	a	Jeunesse Canach	W	2-0	*Da Mota, Turpel (p)*

Name	Nat	DoB	Pos	Aps	(s)	Gls
Yassine Ben Ajiba	MAR	01/11/84	M	1	(1)	
Sofian Benzouien	BEL	11/08/86	M		(4)	2
Ricardo Couto Pinto		14/01/96	M	1	(8)	
Daniel Da Mota		11/09/85	M	19	(3)	6
Dylan Deligny	FRA	05/08/93	M		(1)	
Rodrigue Dikaba	COD	28/10/85	M	25		1
Joé Frising		13/01/94	G	1		
Sanel Ibrahimović	BIH	24/11/87	A	10	(15)	5
Edisson Jordanov	BUL	08/06/93	M	6	(4)	
Jonathan Joubert		12/09/79	G	25		
Alexandre Laurentié	FRA	19/11/89	D	15	(3)	1
Kevin Malget		15/01/91	D	13	(3)	2
Bryan Mélisse	FRA	25/03/89	D	14	(2)	1
Clayton de Sousa Moreira		24/02/88	D	14	(3)	2
Momar N'Diaye	SEN	13/07/87	A	3	(9)	1
Kevin Nakache	FRA	05/04/89	M	1	(5)	
Joël Pedro		10/04/92	M	11	(4)	1
Mario Pokar	GER	18/01/90	M	22	(2)	7
Jerry Prempeh	FRA	29/12/88	D	21	(1)	1
Julien Quercia	FRA	17/08/86	A		(1)	
Tom Schnell		08/10/85	D	23		2
Stélvio	ANG	24/01/89	M	15	(4)	1
Dominik Stolz	GER	04/05/90	M	24	(1)	12
David Turpel		19/10/92	A	22	(3)	21

CS Fola Esch

1906 • Emile Mayrisch (6,000) • csfola.lu

Major honours
Luxembourg League (7) 1918, 1920, 1922, 1924, 1930, 2013, 2015; Luxembourg Cup (3) 1923, 1924, 1955

Coach: Jeff Strasser

Date		Opponent		Score	Scorers
2016					
07/08	a	Käerjéng	W	4-0	*Hadji 3, og (Bourgeois)*
15/08	h	Mondorf-les-Bains	W	1-0	*Dallevedove*
21/08	a	Rosport	W	3-1	*Hadji 2, Klein*
26/08	h	Progrès	D	1-1	*Rodrigues*
11/09	a	UNA Strassen	W	3-1	*Muharemović, Hadji, Lopes*
25/09	h	Jeunesse Esch	D	2-2	*Rodrigues, Laterza*
01/10	a	Jeunesse Canach	W	4-3	*Muharemović, Hadji (p), Laterza, Dallevedove*
16/10	h	Union Titus	W	3-1	*Ronny, Hadji 2*
23/10	a	Hamm Benfica	D	1-1	*Klapp*
05/11	h	Racing Union	W	4-1	*Hadji 2, Dallevedove, Françoise (p)*
27/11	a	Differdange	L	0-2	
04/12	h	Rumelange	W	7-1	*Rodrigues 2, Hadji 2, Camerling 2, Bechtold*
10/12	h	Dudelange	D	2-2	*Camerling, Rodrigues*
2017					
12/02	a	Mondorf-les-Bains	W	3-1	*Françoise 2 (1p), Laterza*
19/02	h	Rosport	W	3-1	*Françoise, Sacras, Hadji*
25/02	a	Progrès	D	2-2	*Hadji, Françoise*
05/03	h	UNA Strassen	W	5-0	*Kirch, Françoise, Hadji 3*
12/03	a	Jeunesse Esch	W	3-0	*Françoise, Hadji (p), Rodrigues*
18/03	h	Jeunesse Canach	D	2-2	*Hadji (p), Klapp*
02/04	a	Union Titus	D	1-1	*Françoise*
09/04	h	Hamm Benfica	W	3-2	*Françoise, Rodrigues, Camerling*
23/04	a	Racing Union	W	2-0	*Klapp, Rodrigues*
30/04	h	Differdange	D	1-1	*Françoise*
07/05	a	Rumelange	W	3-1	*Françoise (p), Rodrigues, Bensi*
14/05	a	Dudelange	L	2-5	*Bensi, Camerling*
21/05	h	Käerjéng	W	4-2	*Bensi, Françoise 2 (1p), Lopes*

Name	Nat	DoB	Pos	Aps	(s)	Gls
Michel Bechtold		01/07/95	M	3	(5)	1
Stefano Bensi		11/08/88	A	9	(6)	3
Billy Bernard		09/04/91	D	20	(2)	
Emanuel Cabral		02/08/96	G	1		
Basile Camerling	FRA	19/04/87	A	2	(7)	5
Alexander Cvetković	SRB	29/11/96	M	2	(12)	
Jakob Dallevedove	GER	21/11/87	M	21	(4)	3
Emmanuel Françoise	FRA	07/06/82	M	17	(2)	13
Samir Hadji	FRA	12/09/89	A	21		20
Thomas Hym	FRA	29/08/87	G	25		
Mehdi Kirch	FRA	27/01/90	D	22	(3)	1
Ryan Klapp		10/01/93	M	25	(1)	3
Julien Klein	FRA	07/04/87	D	18		1
Kevin Lacroix	FRA	13/10/84	D	1	(1)	
Tom Laterza		09/05/92	D	9	(5)	3
Stefan Lopes		24/09/98	A	2	(11)	2
Enes Mahmutovic		22/05/97	D	21	(1)	
Veldin Muharemović	BIH	06/12/84	M	17	(4)	2
Gerson Rodrigues		20/06/95	M	13	(7)	9
Ronny	CPV	07/12/78	M	22	(4)	1
Cédric Sacras		28/09/96	D	15	(1)	1

FC RM Hamm Benfica

2004 • Terrain de Football Cents (2,800) • no website

Coach: Daniel Santos

Date		Opponent		Score	Scorers
2016					
07/08	a	UNA Strassen	W	5-0	*Tino Barbosa 3, Paulo Arantes, Runser*
15/08	h	Jeunesse Esch	L	1-3	*Runser*
21/08	a	Jeunesse Canach	L	1-4	*Teixeira Pinto*
28/08	h	Union Titus	L	0-1	
11/09	h	Dudelange	L	0-3	
25/09	a	Racing Union	L	1-2	*Runser*
01/10	h	Differdange	L	1-3	*Tino Barbosa*
16/10	a	Rumelange	D	0-0	
23/10	h	Fola	D	1-1	*Tino Barbosa (p)*
06/11	a	Käerjéng	L	0-6	
27/11	h	Mondorf-les-Bains	W	2-0	*Teixeira Pinto, Tino Barbosa*
04/12	a	Rosport	W	1-0	*Tino Barbosa*
11/12	h	Progrès	L	0-3	
2017					
12/02	a	Jeunesse Esch	D	1-1	*Tino Barbosa*
19/02	h	Jeunesse Canach	W	2-0	*Paulo Arantes, Tino Barbosa (p)*
25/02	a	Union Titus	W	2-1	*Tino Barbosa 2*
05/03	a	Dudelange	L	0-3	
12/03	h	Racing Union	L	2-3	*Tino Barbosa, João Martins*
18/03	a	Differdange	L	0-1	
02/04	h	Rumelange	D	0-0	
09/04	a	Fola	L	2-3	*João Martins, Tino Barbosa*
23/04	h	Käerjéng	L	1-2	*Tino Barbosa*
30/04	a	Mondorf-les-Bains	W	2-1	*André Ferreira, Teixeira Pinto*
07/05	h	Rosport	W	2-1	*og (Heinz), João Martins*
14/05	a	Progrès	L	1-4	*Tino Barbosa*
21/05	h	UNA Strassen	D	1-1	*Tino Barbosa (p)*

Name	Nat	DoB	Pos	Aps	(s)	Gls
André Ferreira	POR	16/05/96	M	7	(5)	1
Ioannis Balabanos	GRE	02/11/95	M		(3)	
Joris Belgacem	FRA	20/06/94	M	12	(3)	
Ahmed Cherif	ALG	09/09/93	M		(8)	
Chris Clement		29/12/91	G	4		
Milton Da Fonseca		31/01/97	M		(1)	
Joël Da Mata		04/09/95	D	7	(5)	
Dany Rodrigues	POR	10/02/94	G	7		
Nicolas Desgranges		19/06/96	D	7	(6)	
Eurico Gomes	POR	26/08/87	M	24		
João Martins	ANG	20/06/82	A	6	(5)	3
Arsène Menèssou	BEN	03/12/87	M	22		
Arthur Michaux	FRA	06/06/94	M	9	(5)	
Randy Nzita	COD	20/09/86	D	16		
Alexandros Papadopoulos	GRE	02/03/97	D	7	(5)	
Paulo Arantes	POR	15/11/86	D	26		2
Piero Rizzi		18/05/96	D	11	(1)	
Benjamin Runser	FRA	04/09/91	A	16	(1)	3
Mike Schneider		01/02/95	D	23		
Patrik Teixeira Pinto		10/05/96	M	23	(1)	3
Tiago Alves	POR	15/05/81	G	15		
Tino Barbosa	POR	06/05/92	M	25		16
Famory Touré		19/05/97	M	2	(6)	
David Veiga		12/06/91	D	17		

LUXEMBOURG

FC Jeunesse Canach

1957 • Stade Rue de Lenningen (1,000) • fccanach.lu

Coach: Oséias Ferreira (POR); (26/10/16) Patrick Maurer

Date		Opponent		Score	Scorers
2016					
06/08	a	Dudelange	L	1-6	*Maquart*
15/08	a	Union Titus	D	0-0	
21/08	h	Hamm Benfica	W	4-1	*Sy Seck, Rodrigão Ribeiro 2, Marco Semedo*
28/08	a	Racing Union	L	0-1	
11/09	h	Differdange	L	0-1	
25/09	a	Rumelange	D	1-1	*Bonet*
01/10	h	Fola	L	3-4	*Pedro Ferro 2, Sy Seck*
16/10	a	Käerjéng	L	1-3	*Lefranc*
23/10	h	Mondorf-les-Bains	D	1-1	*Dervisevic*
06/11	a	Rosport	D	0-0	
27/11	h	Progrès	L	0-5	
04/12	a	UNA Strassen	W	2-0	*Pedro Ferro (p), Bonet (p)*
11/12	h	Jeunesse Esch	D	1-1	*Pedro Ferro*
2017					
12/02	h	Union Titus	L	0-4	
19/02	a	Hamm Benfica	L	0-2	
25/02	h	Racing Union	W	3-2	*Pedro Ferro 2, Lefranc*
05/03	a	Differdange	L	1-5	*Pedro Ferro*
12/03	h	Rumelange	W	3-1	*Pedro Ferro, Maquart, Mukendi*
18/03	a	Fola	D	2-2	*Maquart, Pedro Ferro*
02/04	h	Käerjéng	W	2-0	*Dervisevic, Maurer*
09/04	a	Mondorf-les-Bains	L	0-3	
23/04	h	Rosport	L	0-2	
28/04	a	Progrès	D	2-2	*Pedro Ferro 2 (1p)*
07/05	h	UNA Strassen	L	1-3	*Gbale*
14/05	a	Jeunesse Esch	D	2-2	*Gbale, Lefranc*
21/05	h	Dudelange	L	0-2	

Name	Nat	DoB	Pos	Aps	(s)	Gls
Baptista	GNB	26/10/82	A		(3)	
Donovan Bonet	FRA	18/03/89	M	9	(3)	2
Cadabra	CPV	26/06/84	G	26		
Claudio Delgado	POR	08/09/86	D	1		
Aldi Dervisevic		19/08/89	M	24	(1)	2
Dimitri	BRA	18/06/79	D	19		
Eriton Sousa	BRA	21/11/83	A	2		
Fernando Gomes	BRA	27/12/93	D	4	(1)	
Jeff Flies		02/02/97	M		(4)	
Dally Gbale	CIV	01/01/87	A	4	(8)	2
Laurent Hoeser		20/10/86	D	4		
Jorge Ribeiro	POR	24/10/92	M	5	(1)	
Kalú	CPV	08/09/84	M	11	(1)	
Christian Kouamou	CMR	06/05/88	M	18	(2)	
Kevin Lefranc	FRA	01/03/86	A	13	(6)	3
Thibault Maquart	BEL	31/08/92	M	23		3
Marco Semedo	POR	08/10/87	D	26		1
Adrian Mărunţelu	ROU	07/07/96	M	2		
Tom Maurer		25/09/97	M	8	(10)	1
Olivier Mukendi	BEL	08/06/91	A	8	(6)	1
Mickaël Negi	FRA	22/03/84	D	19	(1)	
Pedro Ferro	POR	21/07/87	A	17	(4)	11
Tun Rauen		19/01/95	D	4	(7)	
Rodrigão Ribeiro	BRA	18/07/78	D	6	(1)	2
Babacar Sy Seck	SEN	02/01/94	A	14	(7)	2
David Teixeira Caçador		17/12/86	D	9	(2)	
Christophe Thiel		25/12/96	M	10	(6)	
Valdino Borges	CPV	01/10/80	M		(1)	

AS Jeunesse Esch

1907 • Stade de la Frontière (7,000) • jeunesse-esch.lu

Major honours
Luxembourg League (28) 1921, 1937, 1951, 1954, 1958, 1959, 1960, 1963, 1967, 1968, 1970, 1973, 1974, 1975, 1976, 1977, 1980, 1983, 1985, 1987, 1988, 1995, 1996, 1997, 1998, 1999, 2004, 2010; Luxembourg Cup (13) 1935, 1937, 1946, 1954, 1973, 1974, 1976, 1981, 1988, 1997, 1999, 2000, 2013

Coach: Carlo Weis; (06/03/17) Marc Thomé

Date		Opponent		Score	Scorers
2016					
08/08	h	Union Titus	W	2-1	*Corral, Peters (p)*
15/08	a	Hamm Benfica	W	3-1	*Stumpf 3 (1p)*
21/08	h	Racing Union	L	1-2	*Papadopoulos*
28/08	a	Differdange	L	1-3	*Stumpf*
12/09	h	Rumelange	W	3-0	*Corral, Sardaryan, Stumpf*
25/09	a	Fola	D	2-2	*Lapierre, Ontiveros*
01/10	h	Käerjéng	W	3-1	*Stumpf 2, Kühne*
16/10	a	Mondorf-les-Bains	L	0-1	
23/10	h	Rosport	D	2-2	*Stumpf 2*
05/11	a	Progrès	D	1-1	*Kühne*
27/11	h	UNA Strassen	D	1-1	*Deidda*
04/12	a	Dudelange	L	1-5	*og (Joubert)*
11/12	a	Jeunesse Canach	D	1-1	*Corral*
2017					
12/02	h	Hamm Benfica	D	1-1	*Peters*
19/02	a	Racing Union	W	2-1	*Stumpf, Kyereh*
26/02	h	Differdange	W	1-0	*Stumpf*
05/03	a	Rumelange	L	2-3	*Stumpf, og (Pauly)*
12/03	h	Fola	L	0-3	
19/03	a	Käerjéng	W	4-1	*Kyereh, De Sousa 2, Pinna*
02/04	h	Mondorf-les-Bains	L	1-3	*Stumpf*
09/04	a	Rosport	L	1-2	*Todorovic*
23/04	h	Progrès	L	0-2	
01/05	a	UNA Strassen	D	1-1	*Kühne*
07/05	h	Dudelange	L	0-3	
14/05	h	Jeunesse Canach	D	2-2	*Manzetti, Delgado*
21/05	a	Union Titus	L	2-6	*Lapierre, Pinna*

Name	Nat	DoB	Pos	Aps	(s)	Gls
Ken Corral		08/05/92	M	19	(6)	3
David De Sousa		15/07/95	M	17	(1)	2
Andrea Deidda		15/12/93	A	9	(8)	1
Ricardo Delgado		22/02/94	D	24	(1)	1
Frank Devas		06/03/94	G	3		
Johannes Kühne	GER	02/05/88	M	20		3
Frederick Kyereh	GER	18/10/93	M	8	(4)	2
Emmanuel Lapierre	FRA	05/08/93	D	19	(1)	2
Mario Manzetti		03/03/99	A	1	(3)	1
Marvin Martins		17/02/95	D	18	(4)	
Robin Mertinitz	GER	19/04/90	M	12	(2)	
Tom Nilles		01/03/92	A		(1)	
Marc Oberweis		06/11/82	G	23		
Martin Ontiveros	USA	06/12/91	M	8		1
Thomas Papadopoulos	GRE	11/12/93	A		(8)	1
René Peters		15/06/81	M	18	(3)	2
Giancarlo Pinna	ITA	31/03/89	D	16	(6)	2
Adrien Portier	FRA	02/02/88	D	14		
Ashot Sardaryan	ARM	23/03/92	M	8	(10)	1
Brandon Soares Rosa		15/08/98	D	3	(1)	
Patrick Stumpf	GER	11/04/88	A	22	(2)	13
Milos Todorovic		18/08/95	D	24		1

UN Käerjéng 97

1997 • Käerjénger Dribbel (2,000) • un-kaerjeng.lu

Coach: Angelo Fiorucci (ITA); (09/11/16) Dan Theis

Date		Opponent		Score	Scorers
2016					
07/08	h	Fola	L	0-4	
14/08	a	Dudelange	L	0-1	
21/08	a	Mondorf-les-Bains	L	1-2	*Dutot*
28/08	h	Rosport	L	2-3	*Teixeira Soares, Brix*
12/09	a	Progrès	W	2-0	*Barbosa, Bourgeois*
25/09	h	UNA Strassen	L	0-2	
01/10	a	Jeunesse Esch	L	1-3	*Barbosa (p)*
16/10	h	Jeunesse Canach	W	3-1	*Heinz, Teixeira Soares, Alunni*
06/11	h	Hamm Benfica	W	6-0	*Guérenne, Alunni 2, Teixeira Soares, Bourgeois, Barbosa*
20/11	a	Union Titus	L	1-3	*Fernandes*
27/11	a	Racing Union	L	0-3	
04/12	h	Differdange	L	3-5	*Heinz, Teixeira Soares, Alunni*
11/12	a	Rumelange	L	1-2	*Barbosa (p)*
2017					
12/02	h	Dudelange	D	1-1	*og (Stélvio)*
19/02	h	Mondorf-les-Bains	W	1-0	*Barbosa*
25/02	a	Rosport	W	2-1	*Alunni, Dublin*
05/03	h	Progrès	L	2-4	*Guérenne 2*
12/03	a	UNA Strassen	L	0-2	
19/03	h	Jeunesse Esch	L	1-4	*Alunni*
02/04	a	Jeunesse Canach	L	0-2	
09/04	h	Union Titus	L	0-3	
23/04	a	Hamm Benfica	W	2-1	*Barbosa, Alunni*
30/04	h	Racing Union	L	0-3	
07/05	a	Differdange	L	2-6	*Cassan, Alunni*
14/05	h	Rumelange	W	4-3	*Dublin, Bourgeois (p), Alunni, Hess*
21/05	a	Fola	L	2-4	*Dublin, Cassan*

Name	Nat	DoB	Pos	Aps	(s)	Gls
Alessandro Alunni		19/12/91	M	20	(4)	9
Michael Barbosa	POR	31/10/84	M	12	(9)	6
Bryan Barbosa Manata		07/07/98	A	1	(1)	
Nabil Benhamza	FRA	22/08/88	M	24		
Thibaut Bourgeois	FRA	05/01/90	A	12	(8)	3
Jérôme Brix		22/09/92	D	9	(8)	1
Olivier Cassan	FRA	01/06/84	M	13		2
Kevin D'Anzico		14/08/00	A		(2)	
Hugo Da Silva	POR	14/07/88	M	1	(4)	
Yannis Dublin		19/03/88	M	23	(2)	3
Alexis Dutot	FRA	14/03/92	D	23		1
Noé Ewert		24/02/97	D	22	(3)	
Nicolas Fernandes	FRA	07/01/88	D	21		1
Bryan Fortes Gomes		31/08/98	D	5	(4)	
Julien Guérenne	BEL	31/10/86	A	17	(1)	3
Fabien Heinz		30/07/98	M	9	(8)	2
Pit Hess		17/01/92	D	24		1
Anel Hodžić	BIH	03/03/92	A	3	(4)	
Luca Ivesic		07/04/95	G	9		
Sifeddine Khemici Jérôme	FRA	30/04/93	A	7	(4)	
Marcolino Rodrigues		27/03/89	D	4	(3)	
Tom Ottelé		20/01/98	G	5		
Sergio Teixeira Soares		03/01/92	M	10	(10)	4
Jérôme Winckel		20/12/85	G	12	(1)	

US Mondorf-les-Bains

1915 • John Grün (3,500) • usmondorf.lu

Coach: Arno Bonvini

2016

Date		Opponent		Score	Scorers
07/08	h	Rumelange	D	0-0	
15/08	a	Fola	L	0-1	
21/08	h	Käerjéng	W	2-1	*Nabli, Scanzano*
28/08	a	Dudelange	L	0-1	
11/09	a	Rosport	W	3-1	*Cabral 2, Ketlas*
25/09	h	Progrès	W	2-0	*Yao, Cabral*
29/09	a	UNA Strassen	L	1-3	*Cabral*
16/10	h	Jeunesse Esch	W	1-0	*Haddadji*
23/10	a	Jeunesse Canach	D	1-1	*Thonon (p)*
05/11	h	Union Titus	L	0-2	
27/11	a	Hamm Benfica	L	0-2	
04/12	h	Racing Union	W	2-1	*Mutuale, Ketlas*
11/12	a	Differdange	L	0-6	

2017

Date		Opponent		Score	Scorers
12/02	h	Fola	L	1-3	*Ketlas*
19/02	a	Käerjéng	L	0-1	
25/02	h	Dudelange	D	1-1	*Cabral*
05/03	h	Rosport	W	2-1	*Mutuale, Cabral*
12/03	a	Progrès	W	2-1	*Selimovic, Cabral*
18/03	h	UNA Strassen	L	0-3	
02/04	a	Jeunesse Esch	W	3-1	*Soares, Ketlas, Yao*
09/04	h	Jeunesse Canach	W	3-0	*Cabral, Yao, D'Alessandro*
23/04	a	Union Titus	L	1-2	*Ketlas (p)*
30/04	h	Hamm Benfica	L	1-2	*Thonon*
06/05	a	Racing Union	L	1-3	*Nabli*
14/05	h	Differdange	L	0-3	
21/05	a	Rumelange	L	2-5	*Ketlas, Selimovic*

Name	Nat	DoB	Pos	Aps	(s)	Gls
Ahmed Benhemine	FRA	15/01/87	D	20	(3)	
Cabral	POR	30/09/87	A	23	(1)	8
Dušan Crnomut	SRB	22/05/96	M	1		
Fabio D'Alessandro		28/06/96	A	10	(7)	1
Christophe De Sousa		16/01/92	D	10		
Ilies Haddadji	FRA	09/04/90	M	10	(5)	1
Sven Kalisa		14/03/97	D		(5)	
Samir Ketlas	FRA	14/03/87	M	20	(2)	6
Olivier Marques		21/03/92	M	9	(9)	
Glenn Marques da Costa		10/06/94	G	1		
Michael Monteiro		11/12/91	D	17	(4)	
Yamukile Mutuale	FRA	25/08/87	D	18	(1)	2
Mohamed Nabli	TUN	27/05/85	M	25		2
Ahmed Rani	FRA	20/08/87	M	8	(7)	
Jerson Ribeiro	NED	09/03/88	M	1	(3)	
Rick Risch		30/06/95	M		(1)	
Alessandro Scanzano		14/03/96	A	11	(8)	1
Fahret Selimovic		26/09/93	M	7	(2)	2
Alex Semedo		22/08/89	D	22		
Cédric Soares		19/10/95	M	11	(5)	1
Thibaut Thonon	FRA	05/02/87	M	24	(1)	2
Christophe Wilwert		24/01/88	G		(1)	
Patrick Worré		01/10/84	G	25		
Fabrice Yao	FRA	29/12/95	A	13	(7)	3

FC Progrès Niederkorn

1919 • Jos Haupert (4,000) • progres.lu

Major honours
Luxembourg League (3) 1953, 1978, 1981;
Luxembourg Cup (4) 1933, 1945, 1977, 1978

Coach: Fabien Tissot (FRA);
(29/11/16) Paolo Amodio

2016

Date		Opponent		Score	Scorers
07/08	h	Racing Union	W	2-1	*Ramdedović, og (M'Boup)*
12/08	a	Differdange	L	0-2	
19/08	h	Rumelange	W	4-0	*Laurent 2, Bouzid, Lafon*
26/08	a	Fola	D	1-1	*S Thill*
12/09	h	Käerjéng	L	0-2	
25/09	a	Mondorf-les-Bains	L	0-2	
29/09	h	Rosport	W	3-1	*Menaï, Laurent, S Thill*
16/10	a	Dudelange	L	0-4	
23/10	a	UNA Strassen	W	3-1	*Laurent 3*
05/11	h	Jeunesse Esch	D	1-1	*Laurent*
27/11	a	Jeunesse Canach	W	5-0	*Bouzid, Lafon, Laurent 2, O Thill (p)*
11/12	a	Hamm Benfica	W	3-0	*Laurent, Garos, Menaï*
14/12	h	Union Titus	L	0-2	

2017

Date		Opponent		Score	Scorers
11/02	h	Differdange	L	1-2	*Laurent*
19/02	a	Rumelange	W	3-1	*Watzka, S Thill 2*
25/02	h	Fola	D	2-2	*O Thill, Garos*
05/03	a	Käerjéng	W	4-2	*Barbaro, Watzka, O Thill, S Thill*
12/03	h	Mondorf-les-Bains	L	1-2	*O Thill*
18/03	a	Rosport	D	2-2	*O Thill, Bors*
02/04	h	Dudelange	L	1-2	*S Thill*
09/04	h	UNA Strassen	W	5-1	*Laurent 4, Menaï*
23/04	a	Jeunesse Esch	W	2-0	*Laurent, Lafon*
28/04	h	Jeunesse Canach	D	2-2	*Ferino, Laurent*
07/05	a	Union Titus	W	3-0	*Lafon, Laurent, Borges Magalhaes*
14/05	h	Hamm Benfica	W	4-1	*O Thill (p), Watzka, Laurent 2 (1p)*
21/05	a	Racing Union	W	5-4	*Laurent 4 (1p), S Thill*

Name	Nat	DoB	Pos	Aps	(s)	Gls
Valerio Barbaro		16/02/98	M	3	(9)	1
Jo Barnabo		20/11/98	M	1	(1)	
Ricardo Borges Magalhaes		28/05/99	M		(9)	1
David Bors	GER	13/04/95	A	4	(3)	1
Ismaël Bouzid	ALG	21/07/83	D	16		2
Olivier Cassan	FRA	01/06/84	M	2	(3)	
David Soares	POR	20/02/91	D	17	(3)	
Marco De Sousa		17/08/96	M	3	(5)	
Samuel Dog	FRA	13/02/85	D	2	(1)	
Adrien Ferino	FRA	19/06/92	D	24		1
Alessandro Fiorani		16/02/89	D	15	(1)	
Sébastien Flauss	FRA	29/12/89	G	25		
Mickaël Garos	FRA	10/05/88	M	21	(3)	2
Igor Perreira	POR	06/07/87	M		(1)	
João Machado	POR	09/04/99	G	1	(1)	
Alexis Lafon	FRA	26/01/86	M	19	(2)	4
Rémi Laurent	FRA	15/04/87	A	23	(3)	24
Tim Lehnen		17/06/86	D	1	(5)	
Tony Mastrangelo		01/09/94	D	18	(4)	
Hakim Menaï	FRA	27/03/86	A	13	(5)	3
Valentin Poinsignon	FRA	23/03/94	M	10	(7)	
Dzenid Ramdedović	MNE	25/02/92	M	13	(5)	1
Olivier Thill		17/12/96	M	22	(3)	6
Sébastien Thill		29/12/93	M	25	(1)	7
Maximilian Watzka	GER	25/05/86	M	8	(3)	3

Racing FC Union Lëtzebuerg

2005 • Stade Achille Hammerel (5,864) • no website

Coach: Samy Smaily (FRA);
(01/03/17) Philippe Ciancanelli;
(20/03/17) Jacques Muller

2016

Date		Opponent		Score	Scorers
07/08	a	Progrès	L	1-2	*Bahloul*
14/08	h	UNA Strassen	W	1-0	*Osmanović*
21/08	a	Jeunesse Esch	W	2-1	*Hennetier, Shala*
28/08	h	Jeunesse Canach	W	1-0	*Bernardelli*
11/09	a	Union Titus	D	1-1	*Jahier*
25/09	h	Hamm Benfica	W	2-1	*Skrijelj, Jahier*
01/10	h	Dudelange	L	1-2	*Jahier*
16/10	a	Differdange	L	2-3	*Jahier (p), Sinani*
23/10	h	Rumelange	D	1-1	*Osmanović*
05/11	a	Fola	L	1-4	*Jahier*
27/11	h	Käerjéng	W	3-0	*Jahier 2, Osmanović*
04/12	a	Mondorf-les-Bains	L	1-2	*Sinani*
11/12	h	Rosport	L	1-2	*Jahier*

2017

Date		Opponent		Score	Scorers
12/02	a	UNA Strassen	L	0-3	
19/02	h	Jeunesse Esch	L	1-2	*Skrijelj*
25/02	a	Jeunesse Canach	L	2-3	*Hennetier, Sinani*
05/03	h	Union Titus	L	0-4	
12/03	a	Hamm Benfica	W	3-2	*Osmanović, Lehnen, Sinani*
18/03	a	Dudelange	L	0-4	
02/04	h	Differdange	L	0-2	
09/04	a	Rumelange	D	1-1	*Jahier*
23/04	h	Fola	L	0-2	
30/05	a	Käerjéng	W	3-0	*Jahier, Shala, Sinani*
06/05	h	Mondorf-les-Bains	W	3-1	*Jahier 2 (1p), Sinani*
14/05	a	Rosport	L	3-4	*Jahier 2 (1p), Shala*
21/05	h	Progrès	L	4-5	*Nouidra, Shala 2, Bellini*

Name	Nat	DoB	Pos	Aps	(s)	Gls
Rodolph Amessan	CIV	27/09/90	A	4	(2)	
Yanis Bahloul	FRA	12/06/94	M	4	(13)	1
Seid Behram	BIH	12/07/98	M	2	(4)	
Johan Bellini	FRA	02/06/83	M	8	(3)	1
Gauthier Bernardelli	FRA	28/08/91	D	16	(3)	1
Fine Bop	SEN	12/10/89	M	4	(4)	
Yannick Dias da Graca		13/07/96	D	5	(2)	
Ricardo Diomisio		23/01/98	A	16	(2)	
Glenn Gomes Borges		16/05/95	A	1	(8)	
Jason Goncalves		01/11/95	G	2		
Steve Guedes		24/11/94	D	1		
Jonathan Hennetier	FRA	06/11/91	D	19		2
Giuliano Jackson		23/09/94	D	9	(2)	
Julien Jahier	FRA	28/11/80	A	19	(3)	14
Kevin Lacroix	FRA	13/10/84	D	3		
Tim Lehnen		17/06/86	D	10		1
Pape M'Boup	SEN	13/08/87	D	16	(2)	
Dylan Meireles		24/12/87	D	12	(2)	
Tarek Nouidra	FRA	09/05/87	M	23		1
Edis Osmanović	BIH	30/06/88	M	20	(3)	4
Lucas Pignatone	FRA	23/07/95	M	2	(2)	
Romain Ruffier	FRA	04/10/89	G	24		
Nikola Schreiner		01/09/95	D	13	(8)	
Kai Schwitz		23/05/97	M		(1)	
Florik Shala		19/07/97	M	7	(8)	5
Danel Sinani		05/04/97	M	23	(1)	6
Admir Skrijelj		03/06/92	M	23	(2)	2

LUXEMBOURG

US Rumelange

1908 • Stade Municipal (2,950) • usrumelange.lu

Major honours
Luxembourg Cup (2) 1968, 1975

Coach: Christian Joachim

2016

07/08	a	Mondorf-les-Bains	D	0-0	
13/08	h	Rosport	W	3-1	*Thior, Diallo, Sahin*
19/08	a	Progrès	L	0-4	
27/08	h	UNA Strassen	L	0-2	
12/09	a	Jeunesse Esch	L	0-3	
25/09	h	Jeunesse Canach	D	1-1	*Bryan Gomes*
29/09	a	Union Titus	W	2-1	*Inácio Cabral, Diallo*
16/10	h	Hamm Benfica	D	0-0	
23/10	a	Racing Union	D	1-1	*Diallo (p)*
05/11	h	Differdange	D	0-0	
27/11	h	Dudelange	L	0-3	
04/12	a	Fola	L	1-7	*Bryan Gomes*
11/12	h	Käerjéng	W	2-1	*Diallo, Sahin*

2017

12/02	a	Rosport	L	2-4	*Diallo 2 (1p)*
19/02	h	Progrès	L	1-3	*Inácio Cabral*
25/02	a	UNA Strassen	L	0-2	
05/03	h	Jeunesse Esch	W	3-2	*Donval, Mokrani, Diallo*
12/03	a	Jeunesse Canach	L	1-3	*Mokrani*
18/03	h	Union Titus	D	0-0	
02/04	a	Hamm Benfica	D	0-0	
09/04	h	Racing Union	D	1-1	*Dragovic (p)*
23/04	a	Differdange	L	0-2	
30/04	a	Dudelange	L	2-3	*Bryan Gomes, Dragovic (p)*
07/05	h	Fola	L	1-3	*Diallo*
14/05	a	Käerjéng	L	3-4	*Diallo 2, Inácio Cabral*
21/05	h	Mondorf-les-Bains	W	5-2	*Donval, Fostier, Thior 2, Diallo*

Name	Nat	DoB	Pos	Aps	(s)	Gls
Dany Albuquerque		14/10/98	M	13	(2)	
André Rodrigues Vaz	POR	16/10/87	M		(3)	
Bryan Gomes	POR	05/12/93	M	13	(10)	3
Jules Diallo	FRA	08/03/93	A	24	(2)	11
Etienne Donval	FRA	04/04/95	D	24		2
Nenad Dragovic		04/06/94	M	22	(2)	2
Julien Fostier	FRA	27/08/90	M	22	(1)	1
Inácio Cabral	POR	15/11/83	D	23		3
Tom Ivesic		17/07/99	A		(2)	
Johnny Santos	POR	06/06/94	M		(1)	
Kevin Majerus		30/09/85	A	1	(3)	
Idir Mokrani	ALG	23/01/91	A	9	(1)	2
Omar Muhovic		14/11/97	M		(6)	
Jeff Pauly		01/03/93	G	2		
Christophe Pazos	ESP	19/05/90	M	13	(2)	
Jonathan Proietti		17/07/82	M	1	(5)	
Raphaël Rodrigues		16/02/89	D	24	(1)	
Fatih Sahin	FRA	18/01/85	A	25	(1)	2
Charly Schinker		05/11/87	G	24		
Eric Schmit		29/10/99	M	2	(10)	
Mateusz Siebert	POL	04/04/89	D	19		
Kerim Skenderović	MNE	26/06/97	A		(5)	
François Thior	FRA	11/02/85	M	25		3

FC UNA Strassen

1922 • Complexe Sportif Jean Wirtz (2,000) • fcuna-strassen.lu

Coach: Patrick Grettnich

2016

07/08	h	Hamm Benfica	L	0-5	
14/08	a	Racing Union	L	0-1	
21/08	h	Differdange	D	4-4	*Gilson Delgado 2, Ruppert 2 (1p)*
27/08	a	Rumelange	W	2-0	*Jager, Jocelino Silva*
11/09	h	Fola	L	1-3	*E Agovic*
25/09	a	Käerjéng	W	2-0	*Hoffmann, Gilson Delgado*
29/09	h	Mondorf-les-Bains	W	3-1	*Ruppert (p), E Agovic, Jager*
16/10	a	Rosport	W	2-1	*Jager, E Agovic*
23/10	h	Progrès	L	1-3	*Ruppert*
05/11	a	Dudelange	L	0-3	
27/11	a	Jeunesse Esch	D	1-1	*Jager*
04/12	h	Jeunesse Canach	L	0-2	
11/12	a	Union Titus	W	3-0	*Alverdi, Kerger, Ruppert*

2017

12/02	h	Racing Union	W	3-0	*Jager, E Agovic, Mondon-Konan*
19/02	a	Differdange	L	1-4	*Jager*
25/02	h	Rumelange	W	2-0	*Lourenco 2*
05/03	a	Fola	L	0-5	
12/03	h	Käerjéng	W	2-0	*Jager, E Agovic*
18/03	a	Mondorf-les-Bains	W	3-0	*E Agovic, Jager 2*
02/04	h	Rosport	L	0-2	
09/04	a	Progrès	L	1-5	*Jager*
23/04	h	Dudelange	L	0-3	
01/05	h	Jeunesse Esch	D	1-1	*Jocelino Silva*
07/05	a	Jeunesse Canach	W	3-1	*Jager 3*
14/05	h	Union Titus	W	3-1	*E Agovic, Jager 2*
21/05	a	Hamm Benfica	D	1-1	*E Agovic*

Name	Nat	DoB	Pos	Aps	(s)	Gls
Denis Agovic		12/07/93	M	23	(1)	
Edis Agovic		12/07/93	M	23	(3)	8
Sam Alverdi		23/08/97	M	10	(5)	1
Dan Collette		02/04/85	D	10	(7)	
Kevin De Wilde	BEL	30/12/85	G	1		
Gilson Delgado	CPV	19/10/92	M	18	(6)	3
Ben Guettai		11/05/96	M		(1)	
Eric Hoffmann		21/06/84	D	23		1
Edvin Huremovic		15/10/92	M	1		
Mickaël Jager	FRA	13/01/89	A	22	(1)	15
Jocelino Silva	POR	29/08/89	D	22		2
Kevin Kerger		17/11/94	D	19	(3)	1
Julien Lacour	FRA	24/03/92	M	9	(2)	
Kevin Lourenco		12/05/92	M	8	(8)	2
Donovan Maury	BEL	08/05/81	D	10	(2)	
Lex Menster		13/10/91	G	2		
Patrice Mondon-Konan	CIV	17/03/83	D	19		1
Ricardo Monteiro		28/10/94	M	1	(5)	
Ben Payal		08/09/88	M	13	(8)	
Christopher Rondel	FRA	15/01/90	M	1	(5)	
Kevin Ruppert		16/08/91	A	17	(5)	5
Ralph Schon		20/01/90	G	23	(1)	
Taimo Vaz Djassi	POR	09/03/88	M	11	(4)	

FC Union Titus Pétange

2015 • Stade Municipal (2,400) • uniontituspetange.lu

Coach: Paolo Amodio;
(01/10/16) (Carlos Fangueiro) (POR);
(19/10/16) Manuel Correia (POR)

2016

08/08	a	Jeunesse Esch	L	1-2	*Bossi*
15/08	h	Jeunesse Canach	D	0-0	
21/08	h	Dudelange	D	1-1	*Artur Abreu*
28/08	a	Hamm Benfica	W	1-0	*Nonnweiler*
11/09	h	Racing Union	D	1-1	*Matias*
24/09	a	Differdange	L	0-1	
29/09	h	Rumelange	L	1-2	*Smigalović*
16/10	a	Fola	L	1-3	*Cissé*
05/11	a	Mondorf-les-Bains	W	2-0	*Artur Abreu 2*
20/11	h	Käerjéng	W	3-1	*Baier, Bossi (p), Artur Abreu*
27/11	h	Rosport	W	2-0	*Artur Abreu 2 (1p)*
11/12	h	UNA Strassen	L	0-3	
14/12	a	Progrès	W	2-0	*Artur Abreu 2 (1p)*

2017

12/02	a	Jeunesse Canach	W	4-0	*Bojić, Artur Abreu 2 (1p), Baier*
19/02	a	Dudelange	L	0-3	
25/02	h	Hamm Benfica	L	1-2	*Handžić*
05/03	a	Racing Union	W	4-0	*Arthuro, Bojić 2, Handžić*
12/03	h	Differdange	L	0-1	
18/03	a	Rumelange	D	0-0	
02/04	h	Fola	D	1-1	*Cissé*
09/04	a	Käerjéng	W	3-0	*Cissé, Zwick (p), Artur Abreu*
23/04	h	Mondorf-les-Bains	W	2-1	*Zwick (p), Bojić*
30/04	a	Rosport	L	1-3	*Silaj*
07/05	h	Progrès	L	0-3	
14/05	a	UNA Strassen	L	1-3	*Cissé*
21/05	h	Jeunesse Esch	W	6-2	*D Skenderovic, Gashi, Artur Abreu, Lahyani, Cissé 2*

Name	Nat	DoB	Pos	Aps	(s)	Gls
Andrea Amodio		13/07/97	G	10	(1)	
Benjamin Arnold	GER	25/09/95	D	2	(4)	
Arthuro	BRA	27/08/82	A	5	(3)	1
Artur Abreu	POR	11/08/94	M	24	(1)	12
Tobias Baier	GER	18/11/88	A	11	(8)	2
Filip Bojić	CRO	05/10/92	M	12		4
Paul Bossi		22/07/91	M	13	(4)	2
Dirk Carlson		01/04/98	D	21		
Isaac Cissé	CIV	02/03/94	A	12	(10)	6
Samuel Correia		29/09/97	M	1	(1)	
Šemsudin Džanić	BIH	12/07/92	A	5	(2)	
Filipe Ribeiro	POR	27/04/86	M	1	(5)	
Eliot Gashi		15/04/95	M	1	(10)	1
Kenan Handžić	BIH	23/01/91	M	20	(4)	2
Michel Kettenmeyer		07/02/89	M	7	(2)	
Khalid Lahyani	GER	24/02/93	M	16	(5)	1
Yann Matias		12/11/96	D	18		1
Miguel Palha	POR	26/02/95	G	16		
Yannick Nonnweiler	GER	23/08/94	A	6	(4)	1
Christian Silaj	GER	07/04/92	M	25		1
Aldin Skenderovic		28/06/97	D	23		
Delvin Skenderovic		23/01/94	D	7	(5)	1
Almir Smigalović	BIH	06/05/90	A	3	(3)	1
Glodi Zingha		04/11/93	D	15	(2)	
Dominik Zwick	GER	26/01/89	D	12	(2)	2

FC Victoria Rosport

1928 • VictoriArena (1,500) • no website
Coach: Patrick Zöllner (GER); (07/03/17) René Roller

2016				
07/08	h	Differdange	D 1-1	*Steinbach*
13/08	a	Rumelange	L 1-3	*Karapetyan*
21/08	h	Fola	L 1-3	*Gaspar*
28/08	a	Käerjéng	W 3-2	*Karapetyan 2, Steinbach*
11/09	h	Mondorf-les-Bains	L 1-3	*Karapetyan*
25/09	a	Dudelange	L 0-3	
29/09	a	Progrès	L 1-3	*Pedro dos Santos*
16/10	h	UNA Strassen	L 1-2	*B Vogel*
23/10	a	Jeunesse Esch	D 2-2	*Steinbach, Dücker*
06/11	h	Jeunesse Canach	D 0-0	
27/11	a	Union Titus	L 0-2	
04/12	h	Hamm Benfica	L 0-1	
11/12	a	Racing Union	W 2-1	*Karapetyan 2*
2017				
12/02	h	Rumelange	W 4-2	*Karapetyan 3 (1p), Weirich*
19/02	a	Fola	L 1-3	*Karapetyan*
25/02	h	Käerjéng	L 1-2	*Karapetyan*
05/03	a	Mondorf-les-Bains	L 1-2	*Karapetyan (p)*
12/03	h	Dudelange	L 0-4	
18/03	h	Progrès	D 2-2	*Weirich, Valente*
02/04	a	UNA Strassen	W 2-0	*Kasel, Steinbach*
09/04	h	Jeunesse Esch	W 2-1	*Karapetyan, Weirich*
23/04	a	Jeunesse Canach	W 2-0	*Kasel, Weirich*
30/04	h	Union Titus	W 3-1	*Weirich 2, Valente*
07/05	a	Hamm Benfica	L 1-2	*Karapetyan*
14/05	h	Racing Union	W 4-3	*Kasel, Karapetyan 3 (1p)*
21/05	a	Differdange	L 2-6	*Karapetyan 2*

Name	Nat	DoB	Pos	Aps	(s)	Gls
Christian Adams	GER	22/08/88	M	8	(6)	
Niklas Bürger	GER	07/10/92	G	25		
Raphaël De Sousa		05/06/93	M	24		
Nicolas Dücker	GER	05/02/90	D	18	(6)	1
Raphael Duhr	GER	04/08/93	M		(1)	
Gilles Feltes		06/12/95	D	14	(11)	
Gabriel Gaspar		20/07/90	M	16	(2)	1
Timo Heinz	GER	06/03/91	M	21	(4)	
Isaías Cardoso	POR	15/12/88	A	1	(4)	
Alexander Karapetyan	ARM	23/12/87	A	22	(2)	19
Patrik Kasel	GER	04/04/86	A	22	(4)	3
Kevin Marques		16/01/98	M	5	(12)	
Pedro dos Santos	POR	21/11/90	M	14	(4)	1
Artur Poloshenko	GER	06/01/87	M	8	(6)	
Alex Pott		21/10/88	A		(2)	
Johannes Steinbach	GER	02/07/92	D	26		4
Ramiro Valente		26/01/89	M	7	(2)	2
Ben Vogel		22/12/94	D	23		1
Dylan Vogel		29/10/98	G	1		
Florian Weirich	GER	23/09/90	M	15	(3)	6
Philippe Werdel		12/05/90	D	16	(5)	

Top goalscorers

26	Omar Er Rafik (Differdange)
24	Rémi Laurent (Progrès)
21	David Turpel (Dudelange)
20	Samir Hadji (Fola)
19	Alexander Karapetyan (Rosport)
16	Tino Barbosa (Hamm Benfica)
15	Mickaël Jager (UNA Strassen)
14	Julien Jahier (Racing Union)
13	Emmanuel Françoise (Fola)
	Patrick Stumpf (Jeunesse Esch)

Promoted clubs

US Esch

1913 • Zone d'activité Lankhelz (1,100) • no website
Coach: Pedro Resende (POR)

FC Rodange 91

1991 • Stade Jos Philippart (3,400) • fcr91.lu
Coach: Seraphin Ribeiro (POR)

US Hostert

1946 • Stade Jos Becker (1,500) • ushostert.lu
Coach: Henri Bossi

Second level final table 2016/17

		Pld	W	D	L	F	A	Pts
1	US Esch	26	18	4	4	57	31	58
2	FC Rodange 91	26	17	4	5	61	40	55
3	US Hostert	26	15	5	6	64	31	50
4	FC Etzella Ettelbruck	26	14	6	6	56	30	48
5	FC Swift Hesper	26	13	3	10	49	41	42
6	FC Wiltz 71	26	12	6	8	41	34	42
7	US Sandweiler	26	11	5	10	47	45	38
8	FC Mamer 32	26	10	6	10	40	43	36
9	FF Norden 02	26	10	4	12	41	44	34
10	FC Union Mertert-Wasserbillig	26	10	4	12	41	53	34
11	CS Grevenmacher	26	8	3	15	31	36	27
12	FC Mondercange	26	8	3	15	31	54	27
13	FC Atert Bissen	26	4	6	16	29	55	18
14	FC Avenir Beggen	26	1	3	22	23	74	6

Promotion/Relegation play-off

(25/05/17)
Hostert 2-2 Jeunesse Canach *(aet; 4-2 on pens)*

DOMESTIC CUP

Coupe de Luxembourg 2016/17

FIFTH ROUND

(28/10/16)
Steinsel 1-2 Lorentzweiler *(aet)*

(29/10/16)
Grevenmacher 3-1 Jeunesse Canach *(aet)*
Koerich/Simmern 0-3 Wiltz
Lintgen 2-3 Mondercange
Medernach 0-4 Etzella

(30/10/16)
Differdange 2-0 Jeunesse Esch
Dudelange 6-0 Union Titus
Hostert 2-1 Progrès
Feulen 0-2 Swift
Hosingen 0-4 Rodange
Käerjéng 0-1 Hamm Benfica
Kehlen 0-2 Rumelange *(aet)*
Mondorf-les-Bains 1-3 Rosport
Norden 1-4 Racing Union
Sandweiler 0-1 Fola
US Esch 4-2 UNA Strassen

SIXTH ROUND

(19/11/16)
Lorentzweiler 0-4 Racing Union

(20/11/16)
Etzella 2-1 Rumelange *(aet)*
Grevenmacher 0-1 Differdange
Hostert 3-5 Fola
Rodange 3-1 Mondercange *(aet)*
Rosport 5-1 Hamm Benfica
US Esch 2-1 Swift *(aet)*
Wiltz 0-5 Dudelange

QUARTER-FINALS

(15/04/17)
Etzella 0-2 Racing Union *(Jahier 23, 85)*
Fola 2-0 Rosport *(Françoise 43p, Rodrigues 89)*
Differdange 0-3 Dudelange *(Ibrahimović 41, Stélvio 67, Turpel 89)*

(17/04/17)
Rodange 2-3 US Esch *(Hornuss 15, 60; Dias Da Graca 22, Nuno Martins 32, Viana 92p) (aet)*

SEMI-FINALS

(26/04/17)
Fola 4-0 Racing Union *(Rodrigues 5, Dallevedove 40, Bensi 78, 90)*

(27/04/17)
US Esch 0-3 Dudelange *(Turpel 19, Stolz 60, 62)*

FINAL

(28/05/17)
Stade Josy Barthel, Luxembourg
F91 DUDELANGE 4 *(Jordanov 39, Stolz 72, Turpel 81, Ibrahimović 88)*
CS FOLA ESCH 1 *(Rodrigues 51)*
Referee: *Tropeano*
DUDELANGE: *Joubert, Moreira (Malget 59), Prempeh, Schnell, Mélisse, Dikaba, Pokar (Stélvio 81), Jordanov (Ibrahimović 71), Stolz, Da Mota, Turpel*
FOLA: *Cabral, Mahmutovic, Klein, Bernard (Lopes 81), Kirch, Klapp (Rodrigues 46), Muharemović, Ronny (Camerling 79), Dallevedove, Françoise, Bensi*

Former Yugoslav Republic of

MACEDONIA

Fudbalska Federacija na Makedonija (FFM)

Address	Bul. ASNOM bb MK-1000 Skopje
Tel	+389 23 129 291
Fax	+389 23 165 448
E-mail	zarko.ignjatovski @ffm.com.mk
Website	ffm.com.mk

President	Ilco Gjorgioski
General secretary	Filip Popovski
Media officer	Zlatko Andonovski
Year of formation	1948
National stadium	Telekom Arena, Skopje (33,460)

PRVA LIGA CLUBS

1 **FK Bregalnica Stip**

2 **FK Makedonija**

3 **FK Pelister**

4 **FK Pobeda**

5 **FK Rabotnicki**

6 **KF Renova**

7 **KF Shkëndija**

8 **FK Shkupi**

9 **FK Sileks**

10 **FK Vardar**

PROMOTED CLUBS

11 **FK Akademija Pandev**

12 **FK Skopje**

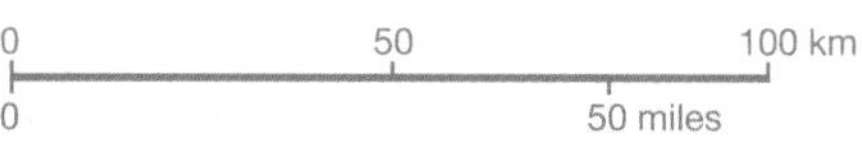

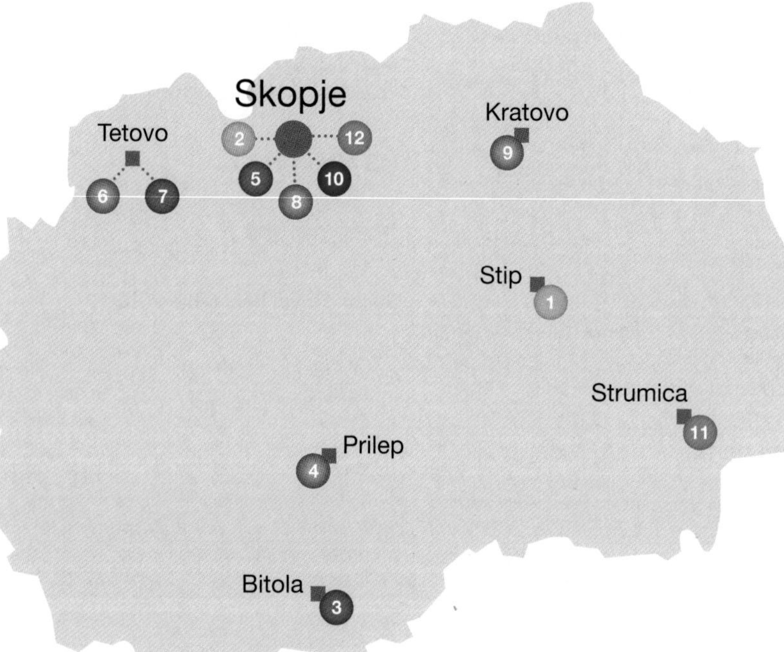

KEY

- UEFA Champions League
- UEFA Europa League
- Promoted
- Relegated

Tenth title for Vardar

Although there was a new format introduced to the Prva Liga in 2016/17, the title race was almost a re-run of the previous season, with FK Vardar, led again by coach Goce Sedloski, retaining their title in relative comfort ahead of KF Shkëndija while the other eight teams were nowhere to be seen.

One of those also-rans did, however, win the Macedonian Cup as fourth-placed Pelister edged out holders Shkëndija on penalties after a goalless final to take the trophy for the second time after a 16-year wait.

Skopje club complete Prva Liga hat-trick

Pelister capture Macedonian Cup for second time

Shkëndija finish runners-up in league and cup

Domestic league

Vardar's bid to win three league titles in a row for the first time since the mid-1990s began with positive intent as Sedloski's side carried forward their strong form from the end of the previous campaign, beating their fellow Red-and-Blacks Shkëndija home and away and eventually stretching their unbeaten run in the Prva Liga to 20 matches before Skopje rivals Rabotnicki ground it to a halt with a 3-0 victory in late November. At the winter break, with 18 of the 36 fixtures played, Vardar were on top of the table but only by four points from a resurgent Shkëndija side powered by the goals of resident marksmen Ferhan Hasani and Besart Ibraimi, who jointly topped the scorer charts with ten goals apiece.

Shkëndija's biggest test came two games into the spring campaign when, with new German coach Thomas Brdaric in charge, they revisited the leaders in the newly-named Telekom Arena. A win would have reignited the title race, but Vardar were too good for them again, a brace from Brazilian schemer Juan Felipe helping the defending champions to a 3-1 win that, to all intents and purposes, gave the club from the capital a free run to the title. Shkëndija would finally defeat Vardar in the clubs' fourth head-to-head encounter, but by then it was academic.

Seven successive wins, in which leading scorers Jonathan Balotelli and Dejan Blazevski hit top form, had put Sedloski's team out of reach, and on 7 May, with four games to spare, they sealed their record-extending tenth title in style with their biggest win of the season, 6-0 at home to relegation-bound Makedonija.

Vardar's final margin of victory was 13 points, while Shkëndija finished 16 clear of third-placed Rabotnicki. The champions ended up with the best attack (75 goals) and defence (24), while Ibraimi – once on the books of German club Schalke – topped the individual scoring list for the second season in a row, with 20 goals. Makedonija were duly relegated alongside Bregalnica Stip, with Shkupi rescuing their top-flight status in a play-off. The two teams promoted were FK Skopje and newcomers Akademija Pandev, the club founded and owned by FYR Macedonia's record goalscorer Goran Pandev and based in his home town of Strumica.

Domestic cup

Strumica was the venue for the 2017 Macedonian Cup final, the city's Mladost stadium hosting the fixture for the first time in 15 years. Unfortunately, it was the stage for only the second goalless final in the competition's 25-year history, but those among the 6,000 spectators rooting for Pelister were not complaining at the end of the fixture's sixth penalty shoot-out as the team from Bitola triumphed 4-3, with much-travelled veteran striker Blaze Ilijoski converting the winning spot kick.

Europe

The tone for Shkëndija's nearly-but-not-quite season was set in the summer of 2016 as the club's quest to play in the group stage of a European competition for the first time extended from the first qualifying round of the UEFA Europa League to the play-offs, where, after narrowly losing the first leg 2-1 away to Gent, they fell apart in Skopje, going down 4-0. All of FYR Macedonia's other three European entrants exited after just two matches.

National team

Three points were all that new FYR Macedonia head coach Igor Angelovski had to show for his team's efforts in their opening six 2018 FIFA World Cup qualifying matches, but there was encouragement to be had from narrow home defeats against Italy (2-3) and Spain (1-2) as well as the four goals scored by striker Ilija Nestrovski, who also enjoyed a fine first season in Serie A – despite his club Palermo's relegation.

DOMESTIC SEASON AT A GLANCE

Prva Liga 2016/17 final table

			Home					Away					Total					
		Pld	W	D	L	F	A	W	D	L	F	A	W	D	L	F	A	Pts
1	**FK Vardar**	**36**	**14**	**4**	**0**	**44**	**8**	**11**	**4**	**3**	**31**	**16**	**25**	**8**	**3**	**75**	**24**	**83**
2	KF Shkëndija	36	11	5	2	40	16	9	5	4	31	23	20	10	6	71	39	70
3	FK Rabotnicki	36	9	5	4	27	18	5	7	6	22	23	14	12	10	49	41	54
4	FK Pelister	36	11	2	5	25	10	3	8	7	19	25	14	10	12	44	35	52
5	KF Renova	36	9	7	2	27	16	4	6	8	15	21	13	13	10	42	37	52
6	FK Sileks	36	9	5	4	26	20	2	9	7	15	23	11	14	11	41	43	47
7	FK Pobeda	36	6	7	5	17	19	4	4	10	17	31	10	11	15	34	50	41
8	FK Shkupi	36	5	9	4	19	17	3	4	11	8	22	8	13	15	27	39	37
9	FK Bregalnica Stip	36	4	7	7	25	25	0	5	13	14	44	4	12	20	39	69	24
10	FK Makedonija	36	2	6	10	18	40	2	5	11	17	40	4	11	21	35	80	23

European qualification 2017/18

Champion: FK Vardar (second qualifying round)

Cup winner: FK Pelister (first qualifying round)
KF Shkëndija (first qualifying round)
FK Rabotnicki (first qualifying round)

Top scorer	Besart Ibraimi (Shkëndija), 20 goals
Relegated clubs	FK Makedonija, FK Bregalnica Stip
Promoted clubs	FK Akademija Pandev, FK Skopje
Cup final	FK Pelister 0-0 KF Shkëndija *(aet; 4-3 on pens)*

Player of the season

Juan Felipe
(FK Vardar)

For the second season running the most influential and eye-catching player for Vardar – and in the Prva Liga as a whole – was their Brazilian schemer Juan Felipe. The 29-year-old was everything he had been in 2015/16 and a bit more besides, making the play and chipping in with some crucial goals, nine in total including five in the four games straddling the winter break. Once again, he started more games for Vardar than anyone else – 33 out of 36 – and formed a particularly productive bond with new signing and fellow Brazilian Jonathan Balotelli.

Newcomer of the season

Eljif Elmas
(FK Rabotnicki)

The youngest of all the 276 players present at the 2017 UEFA U21 European Championship finals, 17-year-old Elmas came on as a substitute in all three of FYR Macedonia's matches and did enough to suggest that his country have unearthed a special talent. After a marvellous breakthrough season with Rabotnicki, in which he played in virtually every game and scored six goals, the extravagantly gifted young midfielder was handed his first senior cap in a World Cup qualifier against Spain before joining up with his U21 team-mates in Poland.

Team of the season

(3-4-2-1)

Coach: Sedloski *(Vardar)*

NATIONAL TEAM

Top five all-time caps

Goce Sedloski (100); **Goran Pandev** (87); Velice Sumulikoski (84); Artim Sakiri (72); Igor Mitreski (70)

Top five all-time goals

Goran Pandev (29); Georgi Hristov (16); Artim Sakiri (15); Goran Maznov (10); Ilco Naumoski (9)

Results 2016/17

05&06/09/16	Albania (WCQ)	A	Shkoder	L	1-2	*Alioski (51)*
06/10/16	Israel (WCQ)	H	Skopje	L	1-2	*Nestorovski (63)*
09/10/16	Italy (WCQ)	H	Skopje	L	2-3	*Nestorovski (57), Hasani (59)*
12/11/16	Spain (WCQ)	A	Granada	L	0-4	
24/03/17	Liechtenstein (WCQ)	A	Vaduz	W	3-0	*Nikolov (43), Nestorovski (68, 73)*
28/03/17	Belarus	H	Skopje	W	3-0	*Spirovski (40), Pandev (61, 69)*
05/06/17	Turkey	H	Skopje	D	0-0	
11/06/17	Spain (WCQ)	H	Skopje	L	1-2	*Ristovski (66)*

Appearances 2016/17

Coach: Igor Angelovski	**02/06/76**		**ALB**	**ISR**	**ITA**	**ESP**	**LIE**	**Blr**	**Tur**	**ESP**	**Caps**	**Goals**
Kostadin Zahov	08/11/87	Shkëndija	G								1	-
Stefan Ristovski	12/02/92	Rijeka (CRO)	D	D	D	M	D	D	D81	M	33	1
Daniel Mojsov	25/12/87	AEK Larnaca (CYP)	D89	D	D	D		D	D	D85	39	-
Vance Sikov	19/07/85	Neftçi (AZE) /Rabotnicki	D	D51	D		D	D	D	D	56	4
Kire Ristevski	22/10/90	Vasas (HUN)	D	D	D	D	D	D	D	D	19	-
Leonard Zhuta	09/08/92	Rijeka (CRO)	D	D	D46	s60					15	-
Ferhan Hasani	18/06/90	Shkëndija	M74	M	M84	M87			M63		28	2
Ostoja Stjepanovic	17/01/85	Śląsk (POL)	M61					M83	M	M46	18	-
Stefan Spirovski	23/08/90	Vardar	M	s46	M	M60	M85	M78	M90	M	16	1
Goran Pandev	27/07/83	Genoa (ITA)	M	M76	M	A	A	A73	A71	A	87	29
Ezgjan Alioski	12/02/92	Lugano (SUI)	A	M	M	M		M83	A	D	13	1
Milovan Petrovic	23/01/90	Osijek (CRO)	s61	M46	s68						9	-
Nikola Gjorgjev	22/08/97	Grasshoppers (SUI)	s74			s87	s85				5	-
Besart Ibraimi	17/12/86	Shkëndija	s89	s51	s46	s82	M64	s83	s83		15	-
Martin Bogatinov	26/04/86	Ethnikos Achnas (CYP)		G	G						18	-
Ilija Nestorovski	12/03/90	Palermo (ITA)		A	A68	A82	A	A78	A83	A	15	5
Adis Jahovic	18/03/87	Göztepe (TUR)		s76							15	3
Dusko Trajcevski	01/11/90	Rabotnicki			s84			s73	s90		5	-
Stole Dimitrievski	25/12/93	Gimnàstic (ESP)				G	G	G	G	G	11	-
Darko Velkovski	21/06/95	Vardar				D	D				5	-
Enis Bardi	02/07/95	Újpest (HUN)				M					6	-
Ivan Trickovski	18/04/87	AEK Larnaca (CYP)					M78	s56	s71	s85	45	4
Boban Nikolov	28/07/94	Vardar					M				3	1
Aleksandar Trajkovski	05/09/92	Palermo (ITA)					s64	M56	s63	s74	35	8
David Babunski	01/03/94	Yokohama F Marinos (JPN)					s78				9	-
Muzafer Ejupi	16/09/88	Osijek (CRO)						s78			2	-
Kristijan Tosevski	06/05/94	Pelister						s78	s81	D74	3	-
Darko Churlinov	11/07/00	Köln (GER)						s83			1	-
Eljif Elmas	24/09/99	Rabotnicki								s46	1	-

EUROPE

FK Vardar

Second qualifying round - GNK Dinamo Zagreb (CRO)

H 1-2 *Hambardzumyan (54)*

Pacovski, Popov, Mijušković, Grncarov, Spirovski, Kojašević, Asani (Obregón 71), Gligorov (Velkovski 46), Hambardzumyan, Juan Felipe, Petkovski (Jonathan Balotelli 46). Coach: Goce Sedloski (MKD)

A 2-3 *Velkovski (39, 63)*

Aleksovski, Grncarov, Spirovski, Kojašević, Asani (Nikolov 67), Velkovski (Petkovski 71), Hambardzumyan, Novak, Glishic, Juan Felipe, Jonathan Balotelli (Obregón 75). Coach: Goce Sedloski (MKD)

Play-offs - KAA Gent (BEL)

A 1-2 *Ibraimi (9)*

Zahov, Bejtulai, Alimi (Taipi 82), Cuculi, Ibraimi (Imeri 90+2), Hasani, Stênio Júnior, Demiri, Polozani, Todorovski, Vujcic. Coach: Bruno Akrapović (BIH)

H 0-4

Zahov, Bejtulai, Alimi (Totre 74), Cuculi, Ibraimi, Hasani, Stênio Júnior (Victor Juffo 66), Demiri, Taipi (Radeski 40), Polozani, Todorovski. Coach: Bruno Akrapović (BIH)

KF Shkëndija

First qualifying round - MKS Cracovia Kraków (POL)

H 2-0 *Ibraimi (41), Stênio Júnior (68)*

Zahov, Bejtulai, Alimi (Polozani 73), Cuculi, Ibraimi, Hasani (Victor Juffo 87), Radeski, Stênio Júnior (Taipi 84), Demiri, Todorovski, Vujcic. Coach: Bruno Akrapović (BIH)

A 2-1 *Ibraimi (13), Hasani (90+3)*

Zahov, Bejtulai, Alimi (Polozani 71), Cuculi, Ibraimi (Victor Juffo 88), Hasani, Radeski (Taipi 83), Stênio Júnior, Demiri, Todorovski, Vujcic. Coach: Bruno Akrapović (BIH)

Second qualifying round - Neftçi PFK (AZE)

A 0-0

Zahov, Bejtulai, Alimi, Cuculi, Ibraimi (Polozani 90+2), Hasani, Radeski, Stênio Júnior, Demiri, Todorovski, Vujcic. Coach: Bruno Akrapović (BIH)

H 1-0 *Ibraimi (31)*

Zahov, Bejtulai, Alimi (Victor Juffo 90+4), Cuculi, Ibraimi (Polozani 87), Hasani (Taipi 90+2), Radeski, Stênio Júnior, Demiri, Todorovski, Vujcic. Coach: Bruno Akrapović (BIH)

Third qualifying round - FK Mladá Boleslav (CZE)

H 2-0 *Stênio Júnior (69), Hasani (75)*

Zahov, Bejtulai, Alimi (Victor Juffo 66), Cuculi, Ibraimi (Imeri 81), Hasani, Radeski (Taipi 46), Stênio Júnior, Demiri, Todorovski, Vujcic. Coach: Bruno Akrapović (BIH)

A 0-1

Zahov, Bejtulai, Alimi (Polozani 54), Cuculi, Ibraimi, Hasani, Radeski (Taipi 75), Stênio Júnior (Bojku 85), Demiri, Todorovski, Vujcic. Coach: Bruno Akrapović (BIH)

FK Sileks

First qualifying round - FC Vaduz (LIE)

A 1-3 *Mickov (86)*

Vujanac, Ivanov, Gucev, Acevski (Kalanoski 61), Tanushev (Stojchevski 90+2), G Gligorov, Panovski, Timovski (Filipovski 52), Dzonov, Mickov, Nedeljković. Coach: Gordan Zdravkov (MKD)

H 1-2 *Mickov (30)*

Vujanac, Filipovski (Biljali 72), Ivanov, Gucev, Tanushev, G Gligorov, Panovski (Georgiev 83), Kalanoski (Acevski 56), Dzonov, Mickov, Nedeljković. Coach: Gordan Zdravkov (MKD)

FK Rabotnicki

First qualifying round - FK Budućnost Podgorica (MNE)

H 1-1 *Elmas (80)*

Siskovski, Najdovski, Mitrev, S Sahiti, Najdenov (Elmas 62), Siljanovski, Markoski (Herrera 76), Galić (Duranski 54), Altiparmakovski, Trajcevski, Cikarski. Coach: Tomislav Franc (MKD)

A 0-1

Siskovski, Najdovski, Mitrev, Herrera (Elmas 55), S Sahiti, Duranski (Galić 75), Najdenov, Siljanovski (Tomaš 46), Altiparmakovski, Trajcevski, Cikarski. Coach: Tomislav Franc (MKD)

Red card: Najdovski 17

DOMESTIC LEAGUE CLUB-BY-CLUB

FK Bregalnica Stip

1921 • City, Stip (6,000); Nikola Mantov, Kocani (5,000) • no website

Coach: Igor Stojanov;
(03/11/16) Zdravko Cvetanoski;
(14/03/17) Nikola Kuzmanov

2016					
07/08	h	Renova	D	1-1	*Zdravkov*
14/08	a	Pelister	L	0-3	
21/08	h	Sileks	L	0-2	
27/08	a	Vardar	L	1-5	*Velinov*
11/09	h	Shkëndija	D	1-1	*Velinov*
18/09	a	Pobeda	D	0-0	
25/09	h	Shkupi	W	1-0	*Zdravkov*
28/09	h	Makedonija	L	1-2	*Velinov*
01/10	a	Rabotnicki	D	1-1	*Zdravkov*
16/10	a	Renova	L	0-1	
23/10	h	Pelister	D	0-0	
30/10	a	Sileks	L	0-1	
05/11	h	Vardar	L	0-1	
16/11	a	Shkëndija	L	2-5	*Zdravkov 2 (1p)*
20/11	h	Pobeda	L	2-3	*Muratović, Iliev*
27/11	a	Shkupi	D	1-1	*Leskaroski*
30/11	a	Makedonija	D	2-2	*Velinov, Temelkov*
04/12	h	Rabotnicki	D	0-0	
2017					
19/02	h	Renova	L	0-1	
25/02	a	Pelister	L	1-2	*Dalceski*
05/03	h	Sileks	D	3-3	*Georgiev, Naumov, Stojanov*
12/03	a	Vardar	L	0-2	
18/03	h	Shkëndija	L	1-3	*Zdravkov*
02/04	a	Pobeda	D	0-0	
05/04	h	Shkupi	W	3-0	*Naumov 2, Zdravkov (p)*
09/04	h	Makedonija	W	1-0	*Georgiev*
15/04	a	Rabotnicki	L	1-3	*Iliev*
23/04	a	Renova	L	0-4	
26/04	h	Pelister	D	1-1	*og (Mecinovic)*
30/04	a	Sileks	L	2-3	*Georgiev, Naumov*
03/05	h	Vardar	D	3-3	*Zdravkov 2 (2p), Naumov*
07/05	a	Shkëndija	L	0-3	
14/05	h	Pobeda	L	1-2	*Miovski*
21/05	a	Shkupi	L	0-3	
28/05	a	Makedonija	L	3-5	*Temelkov, Naumov, Miovski*
31/05	h	Rabotnicki	W	6-2	*Georgiev 3, Zdravkov 2, Velkovski*

Name	Nat	DoB	Pos	Aps	(s)	Gls
Florin Achim	ROU	16/07/91	M	9	(3)	
Dejan Apostolovski		06/08/90	G		(1)	
Robert Căruță	ROU	24/01/96	M	2	(4)	
Aleksandar Dalceski		18/04/91	M	17	(3)	1
Martin Davkov		18/12/98	G		(1)	
Diego Neres	BRA	08/03/90	A	1	(4)	
Boban Georgiev		26/01/97	M	22	(7)	6
Saso Gjoreski		18/09/82	D	22	(1)	
Aleksandar Ilić	BIH	08/04/94	A	1	(5)	
Lazar Iliev		23/05/87	A	8	(13)	2
Miroslav Jovanovski		13/05/91	M	14	(1)	
Matija Kobetić	CRO	08/11/84	G	30		
Stefan Kocev		23/02/94	D	23	(6)	
Tomi Kostadinov	BUL	15/03/91	M	6	(6)	
Stefan Kostov		31/10/96	D	22	(2)	
Dejan Leskaroski		17/10/85	D	11	(1)	1
Bojan Miovski		24/06/99	A	2	(5)	2
Stefan Misev		11/03/96	M		(1)	
Ivan Mitrov		24/10/88	M	4	(3)	
Vedran Muratović	CRO	04/10/83	A	4	(5)	1
Angel Nacev		10/10/89	A		(1)	
Riste Naumov		14/04/81	A	10	(7)	6
Tomica Petrov		16/07/90	D	11		
Marko Randjelović	SRB	16/08/84	D	15		
Borjan Ristovski		20/02/92	G	6		
Stefan Ristovski		22/12/92	D	33	(1)	
Bojan Spirkoski		22/04/95	A		(2)	
Darko Stojanov		11/02/90	D	16		1
Aleksandar Temelkov		06/10/87	M	18	(7)	2
Stojanco Velinov		03/09/89	A	17		4
Slavce Velkovski		05/07/87	M	20	(10)	1
Marko Vučetić	SRB	24/06/86	M	18		
Goran Zdravkov		11/11/80	M	34	(2)	11

FK Makedonija

1932 • Gjorce Petrov (3,000) • no website

Major honours
Macedonian League (1) 2009; Macedonian Cup (1) 2006

Coach: Bobi Stojkovski; (18/09/16) Ivan Cakarov; (01/01/17) Jovica Knežević (SRB)

2016					
10/08	h	Rabotnicki	L	0-4	
14/08	a	Renova	L	0-1	
21/08	h	Pelister	D	2-2	*Cvetanoski 2*
27/08	a	Sileks	D	1-1	*Jakimoski*
11/09	h	Vardar	L	0-4	
18/09	a	Shkëndija	L	0-3	
25/09	h	Pobeda	D	1-1	*Kostovski*
28/09	a	Bregalnica	W	2-1	*Jasharovski 2*
02/10	h	Shkupi	L	0-1	
15/10	a	Rabotnicki	L	1-2	*Jasharovski*
23/10	h	Renova	W	3-1	*T Stojkovski, Jasharovski 2 (1p)*
30/10	a	Pelister	L	0-1	
05/11	h	Sileks	D	1-1	*Kostovski*
16/11	a	Vardar	L	1-4	*Serafimovski*
20/11	h	Shkëndija	L	0-4	
27/11	a	Pobeda	D	0-0	
30/11	h	Bregalnica	D	2-2	*Jasharovski, Jakimoski*
04/12	a	Shkupi	W	2-0	*Jasharovski, Jakimoski*
2017					
19/02	h	Rabotnicki	L	0-3	
26/02	a	Renova	D	2-2	*Jonuzi, K Stojkovski*
05/03	h	Pelister	L	1-2	*Jonuzi*
12/03	a	Sileks	L	2-4	*Alomerovic 2*
18/03	h	Vardar	L	0-5	
02/04	a	Shkëndija	L	1-5	*Ivanoski*
05/04	h	Pobeda	D	0-0	
09/04	a	Bregalnica	L	0-1	
15/04	h	Shkupi	D	0-0	
22/04	a	Rabotnicki	D	1-1	*Jonuzi*
26/04	h	Renova	L	1-3	*Jonuzi*
30/04	a	Pelister	L	1-3	*Alomerovic*
03/05	h	Sileks	L	0-1	
07/05	a	Vardar	L	0-6	
14/05	h	Shkëndija	L	2-3	*K Stojkovski, Zdravkovski (p)*
21/05	a	Pobeda	L	2-4	*Jasharovski, K Stojkovski*
28/05	h	Bregalnica	W	5-3	*Jakimoski, Jasharovski 3, Hadzhija*
31/05	a	Shkupi	D	1-1	*Jasharovski*

Name	Nat	DoB	Pos	Aps	(s)	Gls
Sabahudin Alomerovic		29/06/97	D	22	(6)	3
Bobi Celeski		10/06/97	G	13		
Konstantin Cheshmedzhiev		29/01/96	D	26	(2)	
Matej Cvetanoski		18/08/97	M	24	(8)	2
Hristijan Denkovski		15/04/94	M	2	(1)	
Toni Dzhangarovski		17/06/85	D	21	(1)	
Ersin Fetahi		01/08/96	D	5	(1)	
Diassana Guy	MLI	01/01/99	A	1	(2)	
Destan Hadzhija		02/08/93	A	4	(13)	1
Darko Ilovski		14/09/92	D	15	(1)	
Jane Ivanoski		15/07/88	M	12	(2)	1
Mihajlo Jakimoski		16/04/96	M	14	(8)	4
Alen Jasharovski		06/11/91	A	25	(7)	12
Valmir Jonuzi		23/05/94	M	5	(8)	4
Tigran Kandikyan	ARM	11/03/93	G	21		
Diassana Khalifa	MLI	12/03/97	M	2		
Kristijan Kostovski		15/12/95	A	17	(8)	2
Stefan Lazarevikj		18/02/97	M	1	(6)	
Lucão	BRA	22/09/95	A	4	(7)	
Todor Nikolovski		23/10/96	M	7	(6)	
Denis Ramadan		27/11/89	D	18		
Milan Ristovski		01/03/89	A	7	(1)	
Mark Rizoski		22/01/97	M		(3)	
Viktor Serafimovski		24/10/95	M	25	(3)	1
Stefan Stojanovski		23/05/93	D	4	(2)	
Kristijan Stojkovski		17/09/91	A	31	(3)	3
Trajce Stojkovski		23/02/89	D	26	(1)	1
Dejan Tanturovski		12/08/92	M	9	(1)	
Dimitar Trajkovski		09/08/99	M		(1)	
Goran Trajkovski		20/05/97	G	2		
Burak Zairi		27/01/95	A		(1)	
Davor Zdravkovski		20/03/98	M	33		1

FK Pelister

1945 • Tumbe Kafe (8,000); Biljanini Izvori, Ohrid (3,000) • fkpelister.mk

Major honours
Macedonian Cup (2) 2001, 2017

Coach: Naum Ljamcevski; (14/10/16) Naci Şensoy (TUR)

2016					
07/08	a	Pobeda	W	2-0	*Lucas, Bujcevski*
14/08	h	Bregalnica	W	3-0	*Ljamchevski, Markovski, Petrov*
21/08	a	Makedonija	D	2-2	*Ljamchevski, Lucas*
27/08	h	Rabotnicki	W	3-0	*Bujcevski, Ljamchevski, Fernando Augusto*
11/09	a	Renova	L	0-2	
17/09	a	Shkupi	L	1-2	*Lucas*
25/09	h	Sileks	D	0-0	
28/09	a	Vardar	D	1-1	*Lucas*
02/10	h	Shkëndija	L	1-2	*Lucas*
16/10	h	Pobeda	W	2-0	*Bujcevski, Lucas*
23/10	a	Bregalnica	D	0-0	
30/10	h	Makedonija	W	1-0	*Bujcevski*
05/11	a	Rabotnicki	W	1-0	*Lucas*
16/11	h	Renova	W	1-0	*Kovachev*
20/11	h	Shkupi	W	2-0	*Trifunovski, Bozinovski*
27/11	a	Sileks	D	0-0	
30/11	h	Vardar	L	0-1	
04/12	a	Shkëndija	L	0-1	
2017					
19/02	a	Pobeda	D	2-2	*Bojović, Ilijoski (p)*
25/02	h	Bregalnica	W	2-1	*Ilijoski, Fernando Silva*
05/03	a	Makedonija	W	2-1	*Lucas, Fernando Silva*
12/03	h	Rabotnicki	L	0-1	
18/03	a	Renova	L	1-2	*Lucas*
02/04	a	Shkupi	L	0-1	
05/04	h	Sileks	D	0-0	
09/04	a	Vardar	L	1-3	*Kovachev (p)*
15/04	h	Shkëndija	L	0-1	
23/04	h	Pobeda	W	1-0	*Trifunovski*
26/04	a	Bregalnica	D	1-1	*Lucas*
30/04	h	Makedonija	W	3-1	*Markoski, Kovachev, Ilijoski*
03/05	a	Rabotnicki	D	1-1	*Petrov*
07/05	h	Renova	W	3-0	*Fernando Silva, Ilijoski 2*
14/05	h	Shkupi	W	1-0	*Fernando Silva*
21/05	a	Sileks	D	3-3	*Lucas, Bujcevski, Ilijoski*
28/05	h	Vardar	L	2-3	*Ilijoski (p), Bujcevski*
31/05	a	Shkëndija	L	1-3	*Ilijoski*

Name	Nat	DoB	Pos	Aps	(s)	Gls
Darko Atanasovski		17/07/94	G	1		
Martin Blazevski		13/05/92	M	1	(3)	
Radenko Bojović	SRB	26/12/80	D	18	(1)	1
Toshe Boshevski		05/02/98	M		(1)	
Bobi Bozinovski		24/02/81	M	8	(17)	1
Antonio Bujcevski		24/01/90	A	15	(10)	6
Benjamin Demir		16/05/96	M	3		
Hristijan Denkovski		15/04/94	M	1	(1)	
Fernando Augusto	BRA	25/07/93	D	24	(4)	1
Fernando Silva	BRA	18/05/91	M	11	(6)	4
Dimitar Iliev	BUL	27/07/86	M	29	(2)	
Blaze Ilijoski		09/07/84	A	15	(1)	8
Blagojce Konjarski		18/02/89	M	1	(3)	
Martin Kovachev	BUL	12/03/83	D	26	(1)	3
Petar Ljamchevski		08/08/91	M	11	(3)	3
Lucas	BRA	07/04/94	M	24	(5)	11
Riste Markoski		30/04/86	M	25	(5)	1
Blagojce Markovski		13/10/87	A	1	(7)	1
Jasmin Mecinovic		22/10/90	D	7		
Filip Milenkovski		07/01/90	D	14	(3)	
Martin Mirchevski		11/02/97	M	7	(1)	
Filip Mishevski		01/11/91	D	9	(1)	
Goran Pashovski		15/02/80	G	20		
Filip Petrov		23/02/89	A	7	(5)	2
Hristijan Petrovski		23/02/99	G	2		
Ilce Petrovski		22/07/89	G	13	(2)	
Jovan Popzlatanov		06/07/96	M	24	(1)	
Metodija Stepanovski		26/05/83	D	8		
Goce Todorovski		13/09/82	M	11	(5)	
Kristijan Toshevski		06/05/94	D	34		
Ive Trifunovski		04/07/90	A	20	(14)	2
Milen Vasilev	BUL	17/05/88	M	6	(5)	
Boban Zdravevski		24/07/99	A		(1)	

FK Pobeda

2010 • Mogila (2,000); Tumbe Kafe, Bitola (8,000); Biljanini Izvori, Ohrid (3,000); Mladost, Strumica (6,370) • no website

Coach: Darko Krsteski; (27/09/16) Zoran Sterjovski

2016					
07/08	h	Pelister	L	0-2	
14/08	a	Sileks	L	1-2	*Geshoski*
21/08	h	Vardar	L	0-1	
28/08	a	Shkëndija	L	1-3	*Sharkoski (p)*
11/09	h	Shkupi	W	2-1	*og (Bajrami), Cvetanovski*
18/09	h	Bregalnica	D	0-0	
25/09	a	Makedonija	D	1-1	*Krsteski*
28/09	h	Rabotnicki	W	2-1	*Sharkoski, Geshoski*
02/10	a	Renova	D	1-1	*og (Musliu)*
16/10	a	Pelister	L	0-2	
23/10	h	Sileks	D	1-1	*Cvetanovski*
30/10	a	Vardar	L	1-2	*Geshoski*
05/11	h	Shkëndija	L	1-2	*Sharkoski*
16/11	a	Shkupi	D	1-1	*Sharkoski*
20/11	a	Bregalnica	W	3-2	*Sharkoski 2, Geshoski*
27/11	h	Makedonija	D	0-0	
30/11	a	Rabotnicki	L	1-3	*Sharkoski*
04/12	h	Renova	L	0-2	
2017					
19/02	h	Pelister	D	2-2	*Geshoski (p), Krsteski*
26/02	a	Sileks	L	0-2	
05/03	h	Vardar	W	2-1	*Cvetanovski 2*
12/03	a	Shkëndija	L	0-4	
18/03	h	Shkupi	D	1-1	*og (Zendeli)*
02/04	h	Bregalnica	D	0-0	
05/04	a	Makedonija	D	0-0	
09/04	h	Rabotnicki	D	0-0	
15/04	a	Renova	L	0-1	
23/04	a	Pelister	L	0-1	
26/04	h	Sileks	W	1-0	*J Naumoski (p)*
30/04	a	Vardar	L	0-4	
03/05	h	Shkëndija	W	1-0	*Stanić*
07/05	a	Shkupi	W	2-1	*Geshoski, Cvetanovski*
14/05	a	Bregalnica	W	2-1	*Geshoski (p), Stanić*
21/05	h	Makedonija	W	4-2	*Ristevski, Ilijovski, Cvetanovski, Mustafov*
28/05	a	Rabotnicki	W	3-0	*Geshoski, Stanić, Sharkoski*
31/05	h	Renova	L	0-3	

Name	Nat	DoB	Pos	Aps	(s)	Gls
Kemal Alomerovic		08/12/80	A	1		
Dejan Cvetanovski		15/05/90	A	24	(4)	6
Denis Dimitrioski		21/03/88	D	1		
Zvezdan Djordjilović	SRB	12/05/94	D	6	(3)	
Stojance Dunimagloski		29/09/91	M	3	(9)	
Blagoja Geshoski		28/04/81	A	32	(2)	8
Bojan Gjorgjievski		25/01/92	D	16	(1)	
Darko Ilieski		14/10/95	D	30	(1)	
Riste Ilijovski		27/09/94	M	13	(10)	1
Daniel Karcheski		07/03/92	M	25	(7)	
Valentin Koleski		18/11/90	D	12	(1)	
Blagojce Konjarski		18/02/89	M	2		
Daniel Koteski		24/04/90	D	2	(1)	
Daniel Kotevski		16/08/99	G	1		
Aleksandar Krsteski		03/09/83	D	24		2
Vanche Manchevski		03/09/82	G	11	(1)	
Toni Meglenski		22/05/81	M	6	(5)	
Burhan Mustafov		02/03/94	M	17	(9)	1
Filip Najdoski		13/09/92	M	26		
Jordanco Naumoski		15/02/95	M	29	(2)	1
Mario Naumoski		31/08/00	M	1	(2)	
Aleksandar Nedanoski		12/10/96	A	2	(6)	
Hristijan Petreski		08/01/93	M	3	(2)	
Petar Petroski		06/06/99	M	1		
Ramon	BRA	18/03/93	A		(2)	
Aleksandar Ristevski		21/08/89	D	31		1
Nikolche Sharkoski		08/03/94	M	24	(6)	8
Bojan Spirkoski		22/04/95	A		(2)	
Miroslav Stanić	SRB	11/12/93	M	11	(6)	3
Daniel Taleski		27/07/91	D	5		
Davor Taleski		19/05/95	G	23		
Nikola Tosheski		26/01/95	G	1		
Luka Trajkoski		08/02/00	D	6	(5)	
Milan Vojvodić	SRB	20/01/94	M	7	(7)	
Dejan Zdraveski		10/11/92	M		(6)	

FK Rabotnicki

1937 • Telekom Arena (33,460); Gjorce Petrov (3,000); Boris Trajkovski (3,000) • fkrabotnicki.com

Major honours
Macedonian League (4) 2005, 2006, 2008, 2014; Macedonian Cup (4) 2008, 2009, 2014, 2015

Coach: Tomislav Franc;
(19/07/16) Viktor Trenevski

2016

10/08 a Makedonija W 4-0 *Najdenov (p), Elmas 2, Kudijan*
14/08 h Shkupi W 1-0 *Najdovski*
21/08 h Renova W 1-0 *Markoski*
27/08 a Pelister L 0-3
10/09 h Sileks W 3-1 *Elmas, Markoski, Duranski*
18/09 a Vardar L 0-1
24/09 h Shkëndija L 1-3 *Sadiki*
28/09 a Pobeda L 1-2 *Najdenov*
01/10 h Bregalnica D 1-1 *Siljanovski*
15/10 h Makedonija W 2-1 *Markoski, Najdenov*
23/10 h Shkupi W 3-1 *Trajcevski, Ivanovski, S Sahiti*
30/10 a Renova D 1-1 *Elmas*
05/11 h Pelister L 0-1
16/11 a Sileks L 1-2 *Duranski*
20/11 h Vardar W 3-0 *S Sahiti, Duranski, Ivanovski (p)*
27/11 a Shkëndija D 2-2 *Ivanovski (p), Markoski*
30/11 h Pobeda W 3-1 *Siljanovski, Najdenov, Herrera*
04/12 a Bregalnica D 0-0

2017

19/02 a Makedonija W 3-0 *S Sahiti, Ivanovski 2 (2p)*
26/02 a Shkupi D 1-1 *S Sahiti*
04/03 h Renova D 0-0
12/03 a Pelister W 1-0 *Elmas*
18/03 h Sileks W 2-0 *Siljanovski, S Sahiti*
02/04 a Vardar L 0-2
05/04 h Shkëndija W 1-0 *Trajcevski*
09/04 a Pobeda D 0-0
15/04 h Bregalnica W 3-1 *Trajcevski, S Sahiti 2*
22/04 h Makedonija D 1-1 *Elmas*
27/04 h Shkupi L 0-1
30/04 a Renova D 1-1 *og (Miskovski)*
03/05 h Pelister D 1-1 *Duranski*
07/05 a Sileks W 2-0 *Ivanovski, Vuković*
14/05 h Vardar D 2-2 *Sadiki, Siljanovski*
21/05 a Shkëndija D 2-2 *Markoski, Vuković*
28/05 h Pobeda L 0-3
31/05 a Bregalnica L 2-6 *Demir, Ivanovski*

Name	Nat	DoB	Pos	Aps	(s)	Gls
Kristijan Ackovski		15/02/98	M	2	(1)	
Ridvan Adeshina	NGA	18/11/97	A	2	(4)	
Daniel Bozinovski		09/07/89	G	13		
Alexander Cordoba	COL	25/10/98	D	2	(7)	
Benjamin Demir		16/05/96	D	3	(7)	1
Filip Duranski		17/07/91	M	20	(11)	4
Eljif Elmas		24/09/99	M	31	(2)	6
Ivan Galić	CRO	09/01/95	A		(1)	
Sebastián Herrera	COL	23/01/95	D	28	(1)	1
Filip Ivanovski		01/05/85	A	30	(4)	7
Andrej Kudijan		04/09/97	A	1	(3)	1
Kire Markoski		20/02/95	M	16	(7)	5
Dejan Mitrev		20/07/88	D	27	(3)	
Bojan Najdenov		27/01/91	M	27	(3)	4
Leon Najdovski		17/10/94	D	15	(5)	1
Filip Naumchevski		26/10/92	M	8	(9)	
Momčilo Rašo	MNE	06/02/97	D	21	(1)	
Milan Ristovski		08/04/98	M		(5)	
Nehar Sadiki		16/03/98	D	8	(1)	2
Emir Sahiti	ALB	29/11/98	M	10	(6)	
Suad Sahiti	ALB	06/02/95	M	19	(3)	7
Pajazit Saliu		27/04/93	A		(1)	
Vance Sikov		19/07/86	D	15		
Goran Siljanovski		01/07/90	D	30		4
Damjan Siskovski		18/03/95	G	23		
Mario Stankovski		06/09/99	A	2	(1)	
Viktor Stojkovski		03/07/98	M	2		
Mile Todorov		20/08/99	M		(2)	
Luka Tomaš	CRO	31/01/92	D	2	(4)	
Dusko Trajcevski		01/11/90	M	28		3
Ivan Vuković	MNE	09/02/87	A	11	(6)	2

KF Renova

2003 • Ecolog Arena (15,000) • kfrenova.com

Major honours
Macedonian League (1) 2010; Macedonian Cup (1) 2012

Coach: Catip Osmani

2016

07/08 a Bregalnica D 1-1 *Musliu*
14/08 h Makedonija W 1-0 *Adili*
21/08 a Rabotnicki L 0-1
27/08 a Shkupi D 0-0
11/09 h Pelister W 2-0 *Gafuri, Selmani*
18/09 a Sileks D 0-0
25/09 h Vardar D 0-0
28/09 a Shkëndija D 1-1 *Musliu*
02/10 h Pobeda D 1-1 *Abdula*
16/10 h Bregalnica W 1-0 *Nuhiu (p)*
23/10 a Makedonija L 1-3 *Gafuri*
30/10 h Rabotnicki D 1-1 *Selmani*
05/11 h Shkupi W 1-0 *Ramadani*
16/11 a Pelister L 0-1
20/11 h Sileks D 2-2 *Ramadani, Nuhiu (p)*
27/11 a Vardar L 0-1
30/11 h Shkëndija L 1-2 *Gafuri*
04/12 a Pobeda W 2-0 *Gafuri 2*

2017

19/02 a Bregalnica W 1-0 *Useini*
26/02 h Makedonija D 2-2 *Velinov 2*
04/03 a Rabotnicki D 0-0
12/03 a Shkupi L 2-3 *Sadiki, Jusufi*
18/03 h Pelister W 2-1 *Gafuri, Velinov*
02/04 a Sileks L 0-3
05/04 h Vardar L 0-1
09/04 a Shkëndija D 1-1 *Velinov*
15/04 h Pobeda W 1-0 *Gafuri*
23/04 h Bregalnica W 4-0 *Miskovski, Velinov, Nafiu 2 (1p)*
26/04 a Makedonija W 3-1 *Musliu 2, Velinov*
30/04 h Rabotnicki D 1-1 *Nafiu*
03/05 h Shkupi W 2-1 *Petkovski, Nafiu*
07/05 a Pelister L 0-3
14/05 h Sileks W 1-0 *Velinov*
21/05 a Vardar L 0-2
28/05 h Shkëndija D 4-4 *Nuhiu (p), Selmani, Gafuri, Useini*
31/05 a Pobeda W 3-0 *Selmani 2, Neziri (p)*

Name	Nat	DoB	Pos	Aps	(s)	Gls
Dzhelil Abdula		25/09/91	D	20		1
Murat Adili		22/09/92	A	2	(7)	1
Arlind Bajrami		05/11/95	M	2		
Saimir Fetai		04/04/89	D	10	(12)	
Ardjen Gafuri		01/02/89	M	33	(1)	8
Eglant Haxho	ALB	10/11/88	G	35		
Liridon Iljazi		13/07/96	D	3	(4)	
Platin Imeri		27/09/94	M	1	(4)	
Vulnet Islami		14/11/95	G		(1)	
Fatjon Jusufi		06/03/97	M	19	(4)	1
Agron Memedi		05/12/80	D	6		
Nenad Miskovski		19/12/86	D	34		1
Visar Musliu		13/11/94	D	33		4
Saljadin Mustafi		13/04/93	G	1		
Valmir Nafiu		23/04/94	A	14	(13)	4
Medzhit Neziri		02/09/90	D	31		1
Fisnik Nuhiu		26/01/83	M	31		3
Filip Petkovski		24/05/90	M	5	(10)	1
Emran Ramadani		29/01/92	M	9	(16)	2
Burim Sadiki		05/08/89	M	22	(6)	1
Meriton Saliji		15/01/96	M	1	(1)	
Remzifaik Selmani		05/05/97	A	24	(4)	5
Bunjamin Shabani		30/01/91	M	7	(6)	
Ljavdrim Skenderi		17/01/94	A		(10)	
Muhamed Useini		21/11/88	M	29		2
Bashkim Velija		01/08/93	D	11	(3)	
Stojanco Velinov		03/09/89	A	13		7

KF Shkëndija

1979 • Ecolog Arena (15,000) • kfshkendija.com

Major honours
Macedonian League (1) 2011; Macedonian Cup (1) 2016

Coach: Bruno Akrapović (BIH);
(27/10/16) Jeton Bekjiri;
(07/01/17) Thomas Brdaric (GER);
(09/05/17) Erhan Selimi

2016

08/08 h Sileks W 2-1 *Victor Juffo, Ibraimi*
14/08 a Vardar L 0-3
28/08 h Pobeda W 3-1 *Hasani (p), Alimi, Imeri*
11/09 a Bregalnica D 1-1 *Todorovski*
18/09 h Makedonija W 3-0 *Hasani 2, og (Dzhangarovski)*
24/09 a Rabotnicki W 3-1 *Ibraimi 2, Victor Juffo*
28/09 h Renova D 1-1 *Stênio Júnior*
02/10 a Pelister W 2-1 *Hasani, Stênio Júnior*
16/10 a Sileks W 3-1 *Stênio Júnior, Ibraimi 2*
23/10 h Vardar L 0-2
26/10 h Shkupi L 0-1
30/10 a Shkupi D 0-0
05/11 a Pobeda W 2-1 *Stênio Júnior, Ibraimi*
16/11 h Bregalnica W 5-2 *Ibraimi 3, Alimi, Hasani*
20/11 a Makedonija W 4-0 *Ibraimi, Hasani 2, Polozani*
27/11 h Rabotnicki D 2-2 *Hasani 2*
30/11 a Renova W 2-1 *Alimi, Hasani*
04/12 h Pelister W 1-0 *Alimi*

2017

19/02 h Sileks W 2-0 *Hasani, Medjedovic*
26/02 a Vardar L 1-3 *Ibraimi*
05/03 h Shkupi D 0-0
12/03 h Pobeda W 4-0 *Medjedovic, Vujcic, Ibraimi, Stênio Júnior*
18/03 a Bregalnica W 3-1 *Ibraimi, Abdurahimi, Alimi*
02/04 h Makedonija W 5-1 *Medjedovic 3, Ibraimi 2 (1p)*
05/04 a Rabotnicki L 0-1
09/04 h Renova D 1-1 *Ibraimi*
15/04 a Pelister W 1-0 *Radeski*
23/04 a Sileks D 1-1 *Stênio Júnior*
26/04 h Vardar W 3-1 *Medjedovic, Ibraimi 2*
30/04 a Shkupi D 1-1 *Hasani*
03/05 a Pobeda L 0-1
07/05 h Bregalnica W 3-0 *Ibraimi, Abdurahimi, Radeski*
14/05 a Makedonija W 3-2 *Abdurahimi, Alimi, Radeski*
21/05 h Rabotnicki D 2-2 *Radeski 2*
28/05 a Renova D 4-4 *Ibraimi, Radeski 3*
31/05 h Pelister W 3-1 *Asani 2, Victor Juffo*

Name	Nat	DoB	Pos	Aps	(s)	Gls
Besart Abdurahimi		31/07/90	A	11	(4)	3
Riad Agushi		02/03/98	M		(1)	
Armend Alimi		11/12/87	M	25	(6)	6
Shpend Asani		14/11/96	M	1	(3)	2
Egzon Bejtulai		07/01/94	D	14	(3)	
Besmir Bojku		03/01/95	A	2	(14)	
Ivan Čeliković	CRO	10/04/89	D	13		
Iljaz Chiljafi		28/02/98	M		(1)	
Jure Čolak	CRO	21/08/89	D	14		
Ardian Cuculi		19/07/87	D	28		
Besir Demiri		01/08/94	M	2		
Enis Fazlagikj		27/03/00	M	1	(2)	
Federico Haberkorn	ARG	18/08/94	A		(7)	
Ferhan Hasani		18/06/90	M	23	(4)	12
Besart Ibraimi		17/12/86	A	30		20
Demir Imeri		27/10/95	A	3	(4)	1
Marko Jovanovski		24/07/88	G	17		
Ard Kasami		03/01/98	D		(1)	
Bashkim Ljama		22/08/96	A		(1)	
Dino Medjedovic	AUT	13/06/89	A	12	(2)	6
Gonzalo Menéndez	ARG	16/12/92	D	6	(1)	
Mevlan Murati		05/03/94	D	13	(1)	
Besir Nuhii		26/09/94	G	1		
Elian Parrino	ARG	03/09/88	D	2		
Artim Polozani		25/06/82	D	19	(5)	1
Marjan Radeski		10/02/95	M	9	(15)	8
Shefit Shefiti		19/02/98	M	1	(3)	
Stênio Júnior	BRA	10/06/91	A	26	(4)	6
Sciprim Taipi		19/02/97	M	4	(2)	
Blagoja Todorovski		11/06/85	D	29	(1)	1
Ennur Totre		29/10/96	M	25	(6)	
Victor Juffo	BRA	24/02/93	M	8	(8)	3
Stephan Vujcic	GER	03/01/86	M	30		1
Kostadin Zahov		08/11/87	G	18		
Arbin Zejnulai		15/02/99	M	9	(5)	

FK Shkupi

2012 • Cair (6,000) • fcshkupi.com

Coach: Visar Ganiu;
(01/01/17) Ardijan Nuhiji

2016

07/08 a Vardar D 1-1 *Adili*
14/08 h Rabotnicki L 0-1
27/08 h Renova D 0-0
11/09 a Pobeda L 1-2 *Bajrami*
17/09 h Pelister W 2-1 *Iseni, Lazarevski*
25/09 a Bregalnica L 0-1
28/09 h Sileks D 1-1 *Osmani*
02/10 a Makedonija W 1-0 *Traoré*
16/10 h Vardar D 0-0
23/10 a Rabotnicki L 1-3 *Lambin*
26/10 a Shkëndija W 1-0 *Adem*
30/10 h Shkëndija D 0-0
05/11 a Renova L 0-1
16/11 h Pobeda D 1-1 *Zuka*
20/11 a Pelister L 0-2
27/11 h Bregalnica D 1-1 *Osmani*
30/11 a Sileks L 0-1
04/12 h Makedonija L 0-2

2017

19/02 a Vardar L 0-3
26/02 h Rabotnicki D 1-1 *Lazarevski*
05/03 a Shkëndija D 0-0
12/03 h Renova W 3-2 *J Asani 2, Iseni*
18/03 a Pobeda D 1-1 *Lazarevski*
02/04 h Pelister W 1-0 *Bajrami*
05/04 a Bregalnica L 0-3
09/04 h Sileks W 3-1 *Adem, Mbella, B Shabani*
15/04 a Makedonija D 0-0
23/04 h Vardar L 0-2
27/04 a Rabotnicki W 1-0 *Iseni*
30/04 h Shkëndija D 1-1 *J Asani*
03/05 a Renova L 1-2 *B Shabani*
07/05 h Pobeda L 1-2 *Mbella*
14/05 a Pelister L 0-1
21/05 h Bregalnica W 3-0 *Bajrami, J Asani, Janevski*
28/05 a Sileks L 0-1
31/05 h Makedonija D 1-1 *Avdulai*

Name	Nat	DoB	Pos	Aps	(s)	Gls
Ermadin Adem		07/07/90	M	27	(3)	2
Mevlan Adili		30/03/94	D	17		1
Fatmir Arif		17/06/93	D	4	(14)	
Bujamin Asani		10/08/88	D	32		
Jasir Asani		19/05/95	M	13	(1)	4
Bejtula Avdulai		10/09/98	D	1		1
Muharem Bajrami		29/11/85	M	33		3
Sedat Berisha		03/09/89	D	18		
Husein Demiri		06/09/95	A	10	(7)	
Agon Elezi		01/03/01	M	2		
Filip Gligorov		31/07/93	D	2	(4)	
Nikola Ilic	GER	27/01/94	A	1		
Besar Iseni		18/01/97	M	31	(1)	3
Fati Ismailji		29/08/97	M	4	(10)	
Filip Janevski		08/03/94	M	9	(18)	1
Fati Jusufi		10/09/98	A	1		
Florian Kadriu		29/08/96	M	18	(12)	
Besart Krivanjeva		28/02/96	D	10		
Khalil Lambin	CIV	03/08/92	A	4	(8)	1
Dimitrija Lazarevski		23/09/82	D	22		3
Edis Maliqi		04/05/95	D	30	(1)	
Dzhavid Mamuti		07/12/98	D		(1)	
Emmanuel Mbella	FRA	18/06/92	A	10	(2)	2
Burhan Mustafa		22/07/90	G	2		
Florent Osmani		28/05/88	M	16	(2)	2
Besir Ramadani		09/06/00	M	2		
Altin Sefo		27/08/00	M	1	(1)	
Bunjamin Shabani		30/01/91	M	10	(4)	2
Samir Shabani		08/06/87	D		(1)	
Aliou Traoré	FRA	02/09/90	M	14		1
Suat Zendeli		24/02/81	G	34		
Fisnik Zuka		03/09/95	M	18	(12)	1

FK Sileks

1965 • Sileks (5,000) • no website

Major honours
Macedonian League (3) 1996, 1997, 1998; Macedonian Cup (2) 1994, 1997

Coach: Momcilo Mitevski;
(25/10/16) Zikica Tasevski

2016

08/08 a Shkëndija L 1-2 *Nedeljković (p)*
14/08 h Pobeda W 2-1 *Tanushev, Nedeljković (p)*
21/08 a Bregalnica W 2-0 *Nedeljković (p), Timovski*
27/08 h Makedonija D 1-1 *Nedeljković*
10/09 a Rabotnicki L 1-3 *Nedeljković*
18/09 h Renova D 0-0
25/09 a Pelister D 0-0
28/09 a Shkupi D 1-1 *Gucev*
02/10 h Vardar L 1-3 *Acevski*
16/10 h Shkëndija L 1-3 *Nedeljković*
23/10 a Pobeda D 1-1 *Jonuzi*
30/10 h Bregalnica W 1-0 *Nedeljković*
05/11 a Makedonija D 1-1 *Panovski*
16/11 h Rabotnicki W 2-1 *Acevski, Iljazi*
20/11 a Renova D 2-2 *G Gligorov, Filipovski*
27/11 h Pelister D 0-0
30/11 h Shkupi W 1-0 *Nedeljković*
04/12 a Vardar D 1-1 *Filipovski*

2017

19/02 a Shkëndija L 0-2
26/02 h Pobeda W 2-0 *Kalanoski, Nedeljković*
05/03 a Bregalnica D 3-3 *Nedeljković, Kalanoski (p), Timov*
12/03 h Makedonija W 4-2 *Tanushev, Nedeljković, Kalanoski, Filipovski*
18/03 a Rabotnicki L 0-2
02/04 h Renova W 3-0 *Panovski, Kalanoski, Nedeljković*
05/04 a Pelister D 0-0
09/04 a Shkupi L 1-3 *Kalanoski*
15/04 h Vardar L 0-1
23/04 h Shkëndija D 1-1 *Filipovski*
26/04 a Pobeda L 0-1
30/04 h Bregalnica W 3-2 *Filipović, G Gligorov, Dodev*
03/05 a Makedonija W 1-0 *Panovski*
07/05 h Rabotnicki L 0-2
14/05 a Renova L 0-1
21/05 h Pelister D 3-3 *Kastratović, G Gligorov (p), og (Mishevski)*
28/05 h Shkupi W 1-0 *Nedeljković*
31/05 a Vardar D 0-0

Name	Nat	DoB	Pos	Aps	(s)	Gls
Andrej Acevski		05/06/91	M	15	(15)	2
Lutfi Biljali	SVN	14/04/92	A		(2)	
Darko Dodev		16/01/98	A	2	(10)	1
Gjorgje Dzonov		20/09/91	D	3	(1)	
Igor Filipović	SRB	17/04/92	D	17		1
Kristijan Filipovski		02/10/96	M	33	(1)	4
Filip Gligorov		31/07/93	D	14	(2)	
Gligor Gligorov		15/03/87	M	31	(1)	3
Blagoj Gucev		22/03/90	M	27	(4)	1
Liridon Iljazi		13/07/96	D	2	(9)	1
Nemanja Ivanov	SRB	06/10/94	D	18		
Valmir Jonuzi		23/05/94	M	2	(3)	1
Antonio Kalanoski		25/04/94	M	19	(9)	5
Jovan Kastratović	SRB	22/01/93	A	4	(5)	1
Mitko Mavrov		08/04/91	M	9	(1)	
Marjan Mickov		10/02/87	D	23	(6)	
Milan Mitrović	SRB	27/02/91	G	11		
Dušan Mladenović	SRB	18/09/95	D	2	(6)	
Gjorgi Mojsov		27/05/85	M	4	(5)	
Igor Nedeljković	SRB	24/09/91	A	33		13
Todor Nikolovski		23/10/96	M	2	(4)	
Aleksandar Panovski		30/06/88	M	23	(4)	3
Stojan Stojchevski		30/10/92	D	21	(4)	
Gjorgi Tanushev		07/01/91	M	31	(3)	2
Filip Timov		22/05/92	A	5	(3)	1
Angel Timovski		13/11/94	D	20	(8)	1
Darijo Trajanovski		06/08/97	A		(2)	
Nikola Vujanac	SRB	22/06/91	G	25		

FK Vardar

1947 • Telekom Arena (33,460) • fkvardar.mk

Major honours
Macedonian League (10) 1993, 1994, 1995, 2002, 2003, 2012, 2013, 2015, 2016, 2017; Yugoslav Cup (1) 1961; Macedonian Cup (5) 1993, 1995, 1998, 1999, 2007

Coach: Goce Sedloski

2016

07/08 h Shkupi D 1-1 *Jonathan Balotelli*
14/08 h Shkëndija W 3-0 *Gligorov, Jonathan Balotelli, Kojašević*
21/08 a Pobeda W 1-0 *Juan Felipe*
27/08 h Bregalnica W 5-1 *Jonathan Balotelli 3, Kojašević, Mijušković*
11/09 a Makedonija W 4-0 *Grncarov, Jonathan Balotelli, Nikolov, Gligorov*
18/09 h Rabotnicki W 1-0 *Nikolov*
25/09 a Renova D 0-0
28/09 h Pelister D 1-1 *Kojašević*
02/10 a Sileks W 3-1 *Spirovski, Juan Felipe (p), Kojašević*
16/10 a Shkupi D 0-0
23/10 a Shkëndija W 2-0 *Spirovski, Nikolov*
30/10 h Pobeda W 2-1 *Asani, Kojašević*
05/11 a Bregalnica W 1-0 *Novak*
16/11 h Makedonija W 4-1 *Nikolov, Blazevski, Kojašević, Asani*
20/11 a Rabotnicki L 0-3
27/11 h Renova W 1-0 *Blazevski*
30/11 a Pelister W 1-0 *Juan Felipe*
04/12 h Sileks D 1-1 *Juan Felipe*

2017

19/02 h Shkupi W 3-0 *og (Krivanjeva), Juan Felipe, Blazevski*
26/02 h Shkëndija W 3-1 *Barseghyan, Juan Felipe 2 (1p)*
05/03 a Pobeda L 1-2 *Grncarov*
12/03 h Bregalnica W 2-0 *Blazevski, Petkovski*
18/03 a Makedonija W 5-0 *Popov, Hambardzumyan, Barseghyan, Blazevski, Spirovski*
02/04 h Rabotnicki W 2-0 *Kojašević, Nikolov*
05/04 a Renova W 1-0 *Blazevski*
09/04 h Pelister W 3-1 *Jonathan Balotelli, Spirovski, Barseghyan*
15/04 a Sileks W 1-0 *Blazevski*
23/04 a Shkupi W 2-0 *Jonathan Balotelli, Barseghyan*
26/04 a Shkëndija L 1-3 *Jonathan Balotelli*
30/04 h Pobeda W 4-0 *Juan Felipe, Blazevski, Jigauri, Kojašević*
03/05 a Bregalnica D 3-3 *Velkovski, Blazevski (p), Jigauri*
07/05 h Makedonija W 6-0 *Blazevski 2 (1p), Nikolov, Kojašević, Barseghyan, Jonathan Balotelli*
14/05 a Rabotnicki D 2-2 *Jigauri, Barseghyan*
21/05 h Renova W 2-0 *Barseghyan, Jonathan Balotelli*
28/05 a Pelister W 3-2 *Nikolov, Petkovski, Juan Felipe*
31/05 h Sileks D 0-0

Name	Nat	DoB	Pos	Aps	(s)	Gls
Igor Aleksovski		24/02/95	G	5		
Jasir Asani		19/05/95	M	3	(10)	2
Tigran Barseghyan	ARM	22/09/93	M	15	(1)	7
Dejan Blazevski		06/12/85	M	17	(9)	11
Vladica Brdarovski		07/02/90	D	27	(3)	
Besir Demiri		01/08/94	D	14	(2)	
Filip Gacevski		17/08/90	G	31		
Nikola Gligorov		15/08/83	M	26	(7)	2
Darko Glishic		23/09/91	D	6	(3)	
Boban Grncarov		12/08/82	D	27		2
Vlatko Grozdanoski		30/01/83	M	4	(7)	
Hovhannes Hambardzumyan	ARM	04/10/90	D	8	(4)	1
Jambul Jigauri	GEO	08/07/92	M	7	(8)	3
Jonathan Balotelli	BRA	20/04/89	A	25	(4)	11
Juan Felipe	BRA	05/12/87	M	33		9
Damir Kojašević	MNE	03/06/87	M	21	(5)	9
Bojan Kolevski		20/07/00	A		(3)	
Blagojce Ljamcevski		07/04/87	D	9	(4)	
Nemanja Mijušković	MNE	04/03/92	D	2	(2)	1
Boban Nikolov		28/07/94	M	21	(13)	7
Yevheniy Novak	UKR	01/02/89	D	27		1
Jhon Obregón	COL	08/02/90	A	1	(1)	
Petar Petkovski		03/01/97	M	11	(8)	2
Goran Popov		02/10/84	D	8	(1)	1
Stefan Spirovski		23/08/90	M	21	(8)	4
Filip Stojcevski		04/02/99	M	1		
Todor Todoroski		26/02/99	D		(3)	
Darko Velkovski		21/06/95	M	26	(2)	1

Top goalscorers

20	Besart Ibraimi (Shkëndija)
13	Igor Nedeljković (Sileks)
12	Alen Jasharovski (Makedonija) Ferhan Hasani (Shkëndija)
11	Goran Zdravkov (Bregalnica) Stojanco Velinov (Bregalnica/Renova) Lucas (Pelister) Dejan Blazevski (Vardar) Jonathan Balotelli (Vardar)
9	Juan Felipe (Vardar) Damir Kojašević (Vardar)

Promoted clubs

FK Akademija Pandev

2010 • Mladost, Strumica (6,370) • fkakademijapandev.mk
Coach: Risto Panov

FK Skopje

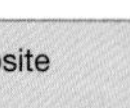

1960 • Zelezarnica (3,000) • no website
Coach: Igor Ivanovski

Second level final table 2016/17

		Pld	W	D	L	F	A	Pts
1	FK Akademija Pandev	27	21	3	3	69	24	66
2	FK Skopje	27	16	6	5	43	26	54
3	FK Novaci	27	13	6	8	39	27	45
4	FK Turnovo	27	9	9	9	37	29	36
5	FK Gorno Lisice	27	10	5	12	29	30	35
6	FK Vëllazërimi	27	8	8	11	33	36	32
7	FK Teteks	27	7	7	13	16	29	28
8	GFK Tikves	27	9	1	17	25	53	28
9	FK Metalurg Skopje	27	7	5	15	27	50	26
10	FK Vardar Negotino	27	5	10	12	17	31	25

Promotion/Relegation play-offs

(04/06/17 & 07/06/17)
Shkupi 4-1 Novaci
Novaci 1-3 Shkupi
(Shkupi 7-2)

DOMESTIC CUP

Kup na Makedonija 2016/17

FIRST ROUND

(16/08/16)
Sateska Volino 0-3 Metalurg

(17/08/16)
Akademija Pandev 5-0 Makedonija
Belasica 2-2 Pelister *(1-3 on pens)*
Caklani 1-6 Rabotnicki
Fortuna 0-3 Pobeda *(w/o)*
Gorno Lisice 1-3 Renova
Kozuf Miravci 0-3 Vëllazërimi *(w/o)*
Ljuboten 0-6 Turnovo
Males 0-1 Sileks
Novaci 2-1 Skopje
Vardar Negotino 0-2 Shkupi
Vlaznimi 0-1 Teteks

(24/08/16)
Skënderbeu 0-9 Vardar Skopje

(31/08/16)
Golemo Konjari 0-11 Shkëndija

Byes - Bregalnica Stip & Mladost Carev Dvor

SECOND ROUND

(21/09/16 & 12/10/16)
Akademija Pandev 0-1, 1-3 Shkupi *(1-4)*
Bregalnica Stip 4-0, 2-1 Teteks *(6-1)*
Metalurg *w/o* Mladost Carev Dvor
Novaci 1-2, 0-5 Pobeda *(1-7)*
Sileks 2-1, 3-3 Turnovo *(5-4)*

(21/09/16 & 19/10/16)
Pelister 2-0, 1-3 Renova *(3-3; Pelister on away goal)*
Rabotnicki 0-2, 0-0 Shkëndija *(0-2)*
Vëllazërimi 1-3, 0-2 Vardar Skopje *(1-5)*

QUARTER-FINALS

(23/11/16 & 07/12/16)
Metalurg 1-4 Vardar Skopje *(Fidanovski 89; Asani 9, Nikolov 26, Popov 29, Petkovski 45)*
Vardar Skopje 4-1 Metalurg *(Nikolov 27, Jonathan Balotelli 51, 87, 89; Fidanovski 68)*
(Vardar 8-2)

Pelister 1-0 Sileks *(Bozinovski 78)*
Sileks 1-2 Pelister *(G Gligorov 76; Markoski 45, Bozinovski 66)*
(Pelister 3-1)

Pobeda 2-2 Bregalnica Stip *(Ristevski 17, Geshoski 77p; Zdravkov 42, Velinov 49)*
Bregalnica Stip 3-0 Pobeda *(Jovanovski 21, Georgiev 69, Zdravkov 90+2)*
(Bregalnica Stip 5-2)

Shkupi 0-0 Shkëndija
Shkëndija 4-0 Shkupi *(Ibraimi 12, 45p, 61, Stênio Júnior 25)*
(Shkëndija 4-0)

SEMI-FINALS

(01/03/17 & 19/04/17)
Bregalnica Stip 2-2 Pelister *(Zdravkov 8, Kostadinov 70; Ilijoski 38p, Bojović 67)*
Pelister 1-0 Bregalnica Stip *(Lucas 80)*
(Pelister 3-2)

Vardar Skopje 1-3 Shkëndija *(Juan Felipe 51; Ibraimi 25, 45, Hasani 75)*
Shkëndija 0-1 Vardar Skopje *(Velkovski 60)*
(Shkëndija 3-2)

FINAL

(17/05/17)
Mladost, Strumica
FK PELISTER 0
KF SHKËNDIJA 0
(aet; 4-3 on pens)
Referee: *Stavrev*
PELISTER: *H Petrovski (I Petrovski 1), Toshevski, Kovachev, Bojović, Milenkovski, Iliev, Markoski (Todorovski 117), Fernando Silva, Bozinovski (Lucas 64), Petrov, Ilijoski*
SHKËNDIJA: *Zahov, Todorovski, Čolak (Polozani 109), Cuculi, Čeliković, Totre (Alimi 46), Vujcic, Radeski, Hasani, Stênio Júnior (Abdurahimi 106), Ibraimi*

Pelister overcame holders Shkëndija on penalties to win the Macedonian Cup final

MALTA

Malta Football Association (MFA)

Address	Millennium Stand, Floor 2 National Stadium MT-Ta' Qali ATD 4000
Tel	+356 21 232 581
Fax	+356 21 245 136
E-mail	info@mfa.com.mt
Website	mfa.com.mt

President	Norman Darmanin Demajo
General secretary	Angelo Chetcuti
Communications officer	Kevin Azzopardi
Year of formation	1900
National stadium	Ta' Qali National Stadium, Ta' Qali (17,797)

KEY

- UEFA Champions League
- UEFA Europa League
- Promoted
- Relegated

PREMIER LEAGUE CLUBS

 1 **Balzan FC**

 2 **Birkirkara FC**

 3 **Floriana FC**

 4 **Gżira United FC**

 5 **Hamrun Spartans FC**

 6 **Hibernians FC**

 7 **Mosta FC**

 8 **Pembroke Athleta FC**

 9 **St Andrews FC**

 10 **Sliema Wanderers FC**

 11 **Tarxien Rainbows FC**

 12 **Valletta FC**

PROMOTED CLUBS

 13 **Lija Athletic FC**

 14 **Senglea Athletic FC**

 15 **Naxxar Lions FC**

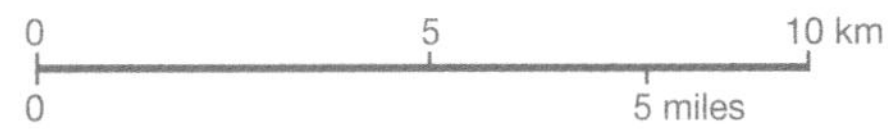

Happy ending for Hibernians

Reunited with their English coach Mark Miller, Hibernians came out on top of a season-long scrap with surprise pace-setters Balzan and defending champions Valletta to win the Maltese Premier League for the second time in three years and the 12th time in all.

Floriana collected the other major domestic silverware on offer as they lifted the FA Trophy for the 20th time after defeating holders and historical arch-rivals Sliema Wanderers 2-0 in the final.

Mark Miller leads Paola club to 12th league title

Early front-runners Balzan fail to last the pace

Floriana upset Sliema Wanderers in FA Trophy final

Domestic league

There was a slight modification to the Premier League format in 2016/17, with the 12 teams, as before, facing each other three times but without a two-phase structure and a 22-match cut-off where points tallies were halved. This time every point counted in full from start to finish and Hibernians would end up with 71 of them, seven more than Balzan, thanks to victories in two thirds of their games and a consistency of performance that none of their challengers could match.

Miller, a long-time resident on the Mediterranean island who had led Hibs to their tenth league crown in the second of his two previous spells, thus made a triumphant return to a club in some turmoil following the departure of 2014/15 title-winning Serbian coach Branko Nišević. Crucially, the bulk of the Brazilian brigade that had prospered under Nišević remained in situ, and they would again prove hugely influential, with Rodolfo Soares and Marcelo Dias shining in defence, Jackson running the midfield and Jorginho leading the attack. There were also some major contributions from the team's Maltese contingent, with Bjorn Kristensen the league's most consistent performer and 16-goal Jurgen Degabriele its nascent star.

Balzan reaffirmed their status as the coming force in the Premier League, Oliver Spiteri's side topping the table for much of the campaign but never stringing enough wins together to shake off their rivals and then, when the pressure intensified, losing to Valletta, Hibernians and Birkirkara in quick succession to surrender the initiative and slip out of the race. Balzan's bid for a first major trophy – and Valletta's title defence – ended on the last day of April when Hibs defeated St Andrews 3-1 with goals from Kristensen, Jackson and Jorginho. There was, however, a consolation prize for Balzan in the shape of the Premier League golden boot, which went to their 23-goal Montenegrin marksman Bojan Kaljević.

Valletta dropped to fourth place after losing their last three games but still qualified for the UEFA Europa League as Birkirkara, who snatched third spot from them thanks to an 11-game unbeaten run, were refused a licence to compete in Europe.

Domestic cup

Floriana finished only fifth in the league, but under ex-Birkirkara boss Giovanni Tedesco they ended the season on an exhilarating high by winning the FA Trophy. Although final opponents Sliema Wanderers, the holders, had beaten Floriana in all three league encounters and were on a ten-game undefeated run, the Ta' Qali showdown did not go with the form book, Floriana scoring once early and once late to claim a 2-0 win and therefore move to within one of Sliema's all-time record of 21 victories in the competition.

Europe

Unable to enter Europe in 2017/18, Birkirkara were the best of the Maltese quartet in 2016/17 (as they had also been in 2015/16), the Stripes stunning Scottish side Hearts with a 2-1 win at Tynecastle to reach the third qualifying round of the UEFA Europa League.

National team

The Maltese national side could not stage a repeat of Birkirkara's exploit when they opened up their 2018 FIFA World Cup campaign at home to Scotland – despite being level at half-time thanks to a wonderful diving header from Balzan striker Alfred Effiong. Malta lost the game 5-1 and had a man sent off – the first of four red cards incurred by Pietro Ghedin's side in their opening five qualifiers. A 2-0 defeat away to Slovenia in June left the team still awaiting their first point of the competition. The previous encounter with Slovenia, at Ta' Qali in November, had seen Michael Mifsud overtake David Carabott as Malta's most-capped international to add to his long-held distinction of being the country's all-time top goalscorer.

DOMESTIC SEASON AT A GLANCE

Premier League 2016/17 final table

		Pld	W	D	L	F	A	Pts
1	**Hibernians FC**	**33**	**22**	**5**	**6**	**64**	**31**	**71**
2	Balzan FC	33	19	7	7	66	40	64
3	Birkirkara FC	33	18	8	7	64	30	62
4	Valletta FC	33	16	11	6	51	29	59
5	Floriana FC	33	15	9	9	51	37	54
6	Sliema Wanderers FC	33	15	7	11	47	37	52
7	St Andrews FC	33	9	10	14	45	51	37
8	Gżira United FC	33	10	7	16	43	51	37
9	Tarxien Rainbows FC	33	8	11	14	38	48	35
10	Hamrun Spartans FC	33	9	6	18	44	61	33
11	Mosta FC	33	7	5	21	29	71	21
12	Pembroke Athleta FC	33	4	6	23	28	84	18

NB Mosta FC – 5 pts deducted.

European qualification 2017/18

Champion: Hibernians FC (first qualifying round)

Cup winner: Floriana FC (first qualifying round)

Balzan FC (first qualifying round)
Valletta FC (first qualifying round)

Top scorer Bojan Kaljević (Balzan), 23 goals
Relegated club Pembroke Athleta FC
Promoted clubs Lija Athletic FC, Senglea Athletic FC, Naxxar Lions FC
Cup final Floriana FC 2-0 Sliema Wanderers FC

Player of the season

Bjorn Kristensen
(Hibernians FC)

His Danish name reflects the nationality of his father, but Kristensen is Maltese by birth and a loyal stalwart to Hibernians. The 24-year-old midfielder's seventh successive season at the Paola club was unquestionably his finest and resulted not just in a Premier League title triumph but also with individual recognition on two fronts as both the Malta FA and the local players' association voted him their player of the year. In addition to his excellence at club level, he was called up regularly by Malta boss Pietro Ghedin and started three FIFA World Cup qualifiers.

Newcomer of the season

Jurgen Degabriele
(Hibernians FC)

Deployed only as a supersub when Hibernians won the league title under Branko Nišević in 2014/15, 20-year-old Degabriele was one of the first names on new boss Mark Miller's teamsheet in 2016/17, and he rewarded the Englishman's faith in his abilities by scoring 16 goals to propel the team to more Premier League glory. A Maltese youth and Under-21 international who can operate either as a left-winger or central striker, he crowned his breakthrough season with a hat-trick in Hibs' title-celebration 6-1 win against Tarxien Rainbows.

Team of the season
(4-4-2)

Coach: Miller *(Hibernians)*

NATIONAL TEAM

Top five all-time caps

Michael Mifsud (125); David Carabott (121); Gilbert Agius (120); Carmel Busuttil (111); Joe Brincat (103)

Top five all-time goals

Michael Mifsud (40); Carmel Busuttil (23); David Carabott (12); Gilbert Agius & Hubert Suda (8)

Results 2016/17

31/08/16	Estonia	A	Parnu	D	1-1	*Effiong (59)*
04/09/16	Scotland (WCQ)	H	Ta' Qali	L	1-5	*Effiong (14)*
08/10/16	England (WCQ)	A	London	L	0-2	
11/10/16	Lithuania (WCQ)	A	Vilnius	L	0-2	
11/11/16	Slovenia (WCQ)	H	Ta' Qali	L	0-1	
15/11/16	Iceland	H	Ta' Qali	L	0-2	
26/03/17	Slovakia (WCQ)	H	Ta' Qali	L	1-3	*Farrugia (14)*
06/06/17	Ukraine	N	Graz (AUT)	W	1-0	*Z Muscat (14)*
10/06/17	Slovenia (WCQ)	A	Ljubljana	L	0-2	

Appearances 2016/17

Coach: Pietro Ghedin (ITA)	21/11/52		Est	SCO	ENG	LTU	SVN	Isl	SVK	Ukr	SVN	Caps	Goals
Andrew Hogg	02/03/85	Hibernians	G	G	G	G	G	G	G	G46	G	54	-
Joseph Zerafa	31/05/88	Birkirkara	D	D		D	D	D77	D	s57		15	-
Andrei Agius	12/08/86	Hibernians	D	D	D	D	D	D		D	D	66	1
Steve Borg	15/05/88	Valletta	D61	D	D	D	s68	D		D92	D89	27	-
Jonathan Caruana	24/07/86	Valletta	D	D 59*		D 82*						39	2
Clayton Failla	08/01/86	Hibernians	D46					D57		D57	D	53	2
Paul Fenech	20/12/86	Balzan	M84	M	M	M85			M			39	1
Gareth Sciberras	29/03/83	Birkirkara	M	M	M	M	M	M78	M			52	-
Luke Gambin	16/03/93	Barnet (ENG)	M	M 91*			M	M85					
		/Luton (ENG)							M73	s60	s46	9	-
André Schembri	27/05/86	Boavista (POR)	M85	M66	M86	M83	M	M65	M91	M60	M62	81	3
Alfred Effiong	29/11/84	Balzan	A74	A89	A76	s80		A54		A70	A	18	4
Ryan Camilleri	22/05/88	Valletta	s46	s79	D		D68		D81	s46		33	-
Zach Muscat	22/08/93	Arezzo (ITA)	s61		D	D	D		D	D46	D	22	1
Michael Mifsud	17/04/81	Valletta	s74	s89	s76	A	A77	s54		s70	s62	125	40
Roderick Briffa	24/08/81	Valletta	s84	s66								93	1
Bjorn Kristensen	05/04/93	Hibernians	s85		M	M80		s78	s73	M67	M46	21	-
Ryan Scicluna	30/07/93	Birkirkara		D79				s77				6	-
Alex Muscat	14/12/84	Sliema			D					D92	D	35	-
Rowen Muscat	05/06/91	Birkirkara			s86	s83	M	M				29	-
Steve Pisani	07/08/92	Floriana				s85		s85		M	M	8	-
Sam Magri	30/03/94	Dover (ENG)					D	D	D	s92	s89	5	-
Jean-Paul Farrugia	21/03/92	Sliema					s77	s65	A 79*			7	1
Ryan Camenzuli	08/09/94	Floriana						s57				4	-
Cain Attard	10/09/94	Birkirkara							D			2	-
Clifford Gatt Baldacchino	09/02/88	Gżira							s81			5	-
Luke Montebello	13/08/95	Valletta							s91			1	-
Ryan Fenech	20/04/86	Balzan								M82	M	44	1
Henry Bonello	13/10/88	Birkirkara								s46		5	-
Dale Camilleri	17/10/92	St Andrews								s67		1	-
Johann Bezzina	30/05/94	Hibernians								s82		1	-
Myles Beerman	13/03/99	Rangers (SCO)								s92		1	-

EUROPE

Valletta FC

First qualifying round - B36 Tórshavn (FRO)

H 1-0 *Falcone (69)*

Bonello, Caruana, Azzopardi, Gill, Briffa, Falcone (Mifsud 87), Cremona (Malano 57), Pani, Aguirre, Jhonnattann (J Borg 80), Romeu. Coach: Paul Zammit (MLT)

A 1-2 *Falcone (24)*

Bonello, Caruana, Azzopardi, Gill, Malano (Cremona 79), Briffa, Falcone, Pani, Aguirre (J Borg 90+3), Jhonnattann (Mifsud 88), Romeu. Coach: Paul Zammit (MLT)

Second qualifying round - FK Crvena zvezda (SRB)

H 1-2 *Falcone (15)*

Bonello, Caruana, Azzopardi (Umeh 83), S Borg, Gill, Briffa (Cremona 78), Falcone (Malano 40), Pani, Aguirre, Jhonnattann, Romeu. Coach: Paul Zammit (MLT)

A 1-2 *Caruana (11)*

Bartolo, Caruana, Azzopardi (Umeh 79), S Borg, Gill, Mifsud, Briffa (Cremona 90+3), Pani, Aguirre, Jhonnattann, Romeu (Malano 72). Coach: Paul Zammit (MLT)

Hibernians FC

First qualifying round - FC Spartak Trnava (SVK)

A 0-3

Haber, Pearson, Jackson, Rodolfo Soares, Marcelo Dias, Cohen, Failla, Varea (Farrugia 76), Mbele (Renan 62), Bezzina (Mbong 88), Agius. Coach: Mark Miller (ENG)

H 0-3

Haber, Pearson, Jackson, Rodolfo Soares, Marcelo Dias, Kristensen, Failla (Mbong 72), Varea (Degabriele 80), Renan, Agius (Mbele 30), Jorginho. Coach: Mark Miller (ENG)

Birkirkara FC

First qualifying round - NK Široki Brijeg (BIH)

A 1-1 *Attard (15)*

Koprić, Bubalović, Sciberras, Emerson, Camenzuli (Bajada 57), Dimitrov, Plut, Zerafa (Guillaumier 63), Scicluna (Zárate 76), Attard, Jović. Coach: Dražen Besek (CRO)

H 2-0 *Dimitrov (29), Marković (76og)*

Koprić, Bubalović, Sciberras, Emerson, Dimitrov (Zárate 75), Plut, Bajada, Zerafa, Scicluna (Guillaumier 65), Attard, Jović (Camenzuli 78). Coach: Dražen Besek (CRO)

Second qualifying round - Heart of Midlothian FC (SCO)

H 0-0

Koprić, Bubalović, Sciberras, Emerson, Dimitrov (Zárate 90+3), Plut, Bajada (Temile 81), Zerafa, Scicluna (Marotti 90+2), Attard, Guillaumier. Coach: Dražen Besek (CRO)

A 2-1 *Bubalović (55), Herrera (67)*

Koprić, Herrera, Bubalović, Sciberras, Emerson, Dimitrov (Guillaumier 73), Plut, Bajada (Jović 66), Zerafa, Scicluna (Camenzuli 90+2), Attard. Coach: Dražen Besek (CRO)

Third qualifying round - FC Krasnodar (RUS)

H 0-3

Koprić, Bubalović, Sciberras, Emerson, Dimitrov (Guillaumier 83), Djordjević (Andjelković 62), Plut, Bajada (Temile 62), Zerafa, Scicluna, Attard. Coach: Dražen Besek (CRO)

Red card: Scicluna 87

A 1-3 *Jović (61)*

Koprić, Herrera, Bubalović, Sciberras, Emerson (Temile 46), Dimitrov (Djordjević 77), Plut, Bajada (Jović 46), Zerafa, Attard, Andjelković. Coach: Dražen Besek (CRO)

Balzan FC

First qualifying round - Neftçi PFK (AZE)

H 0-2

Janjušević, P Fenech, Manevski (Micallef 65), Grima (Arab 81), Bezzina, Brincat (Grioli 74), Effiong, Dê, Serrano, Bruno Oliveira, Kaljević. Coach: Oliver Spiteri (MLT)

A 2-1 *Micallef (51, 67)*

Cassar, Grioli, P Fenech, Manevski (Micallef 46), Grima (Brincat 82), Bezzina, Effiong, Dê, Serrano, Bruno Oliveira, Kaljević. Coach: Oliver Spiteri (MLT)

DOMESTIC LEAGUE CLUB-BY-CLUB

Stadiums

Ta' Qali National Stadium (17,797)
Hibernians Ground (2,000)
Victor Tedesco Stadium (2,000)
MFA Centenary Stadium (2,000)

Balzan FC

1937 • balzanfc.com
Coach: Oliver Spiteri

Date	Opponent		Score	Scorers
2016				
20/08	Mosta	W	3-2	*Agius, Effiong, Kaljević (p)*
26/08	Pembroke	W	2-1	*Kaljević 2*
10/09	Floriana	W	1-0	*Micallef (p)*
17/09	Valletta	D	2-2	*Kaljević, Nafti*
22/09	Hibernians	W	2-0	*Kaljević (p), Effiong*
26/09	Gżira	W	3-1	*P Fenech, Kaljević, Picciollo*
30/09	St Andrews	W	3-0	*Nafti, P Fenech, Kaljević (p)*
16/10	Birkirkara	L	0-3	
22/10	Hamrun	W	3-1	*Alan, Kaljević, Effiong*
29/10	Tarxien	D	2-2	*Alan, Nafti*
04/11	Sliema	D	1-1	*Kaljević*
19/11	Mosta	W	1-0	*Kaljević*
26/11	Pembroke	W	4-0	*Kaljević 3 (1p), Arab*
04/12	Floriana	L	1-3	*og (Ruiz)*
11/12	Valletta	D	2-2	*Kaljević, Picciollo*
17/12	Hibernians	W	2-1	*Picciollo, og (Jackson)*
2017				
08/01	Gżira	W	2-1	*Picciollo 2*
15/01	Birkirkara	D	1-1	*Kaljević (p)*
21/01	St Andrews	W	1-0	*Dê*
28/01	Tarxien	D	2-2	*Nafti, P Fenech*
04/02	Hamrun	W	1-0	*Alan*
12/02	Sliema	L	1-2	*Kaljević*
24/02	Mosta	W	7-1	*Effiong, Kaljević 2, Picciollo, Alan, Micallef 2*
05/03	Pembroke	W	5-2	*Alan 3, Kaljević, Picciollo*
12/03	Floriana	W	2-0	*Serrano, Dê*
17/03	Valletta	L	0-1	
02/04	Hibernians	L	1-3	*Effiong*
05/04	Gżira	W	3-1	*Nafti, Micallef (p), Kaljević*
08/04	Birkirkara	L	1-3	*Kaljević*
15/04	St Andrews	W	2-1	*Kaljević, Serrano*
22/04	Tarxien	W	3-0	*Micallef, Alan, Effiong*
29/04	Hamrun	D	1-1	*Kaljević*
05/05	Sliema	L	1-2	*Effiong*

Name	Nat	DoB	Pos	Aps	(s)	Gls
Terence Agius		15/01/94	M	9	(13)	1
Alan	BRA	09/12/87	M	20	(3)	8
Samir Arab		25/03/94	D	18	(4)	1
Steve Bezzina		05/01/87	D	21	(2)	
Clive Brincat		31/05/83	M	16	(5)	
Bruno Oliveira	BRA	20/04/85	D	26		
Gary Camilleri		05/08/99	D		(1)	
Christian Cassar		22/03/92	G	12		
Sean Cipriott		10/09/97	D	3	(3)	
Dê	BRA	09/04/86	M	15	(4)	2
Alfred Effiong		29/11/84	A	22	(6)	7
Paul Fenech		20/12/86	M	15	(3)	3
Ryan Fenech		20/04/86	M	24	(2)	
Dylan Grima		18/07/90	M	19	(4)	
Justin Grioli		20/09/87	D	8	(3)	
Ivan Janjušević	MNE	11/07/86	G	21	(7)	
Bojan Kaljević	MNE	25/01/86	A	30	(2)	23
Paul Lapira		05/02/98	A	1	(3)	
Miloš Lepović	SRB	03/10/87	M	3	(3)	
Lydon Micallef		16/05/92	A	13	(16)	5
Abdelkarim Nafti	TUN	03/08/81	M	17	(9)	5
Matteo Picciollo	ITA	15/10/92	A	21	(7)	7
Elkin Serrano	COL	17/03/84	D	29		2
Jamie Zerafa		02/03/98	M		(1)	

MALTA

Birkirkara FC

1950 • birkirkarafc.com

Major honours
Maltese League (4) 2000, 2006, 2010, 2013; Maltese Cup (5) 2002, 2003, 2005, 2008, 2015

Coach: Dražen Besek (CRO); (07/12/16) Nikola Jaroš (CRO)

2016				
19/08	St Andrews	W	4-0	*Dimitrov, Herrera, Scicluna, Brincat*
26/08	Tarxien	W	4-0	*Plut, Dimitrov, Temile, Sciberras*
11/09	Hamrun	W	2-1	*Attard, Brincat*
18/09	Sliema	L	1-2	*Temile*
22/09	Mosta	W	2-0	*Dimitrov, Temile*
26/09	Pembroke	L	1-2	*Temile*
30/09	Valletta	D	1-1	*Attard*
16/10	Balzan	W	3-0	*Plut 2, og (Bezzina)*
22/10	Gżira	W	7-1	*Plut, Dimitrov 2, Scicluna, Sciberras, Temile, Guillaumier*
30/10	Hibernians	L	0-1	
04/11	Floriana	D	1-1	*Plut*
19/11	St Andrews	D	1-1	*Desira Buttigieg*
26/11	Tarxien	W	3-1	*Plut (p), Dimitrov, og (Tabone)*
04/12	Hamrun	L	0-2	
11/12	Sliema	L	1-2	*Bubalović*
2017				
04/01	Mosta	W	2-0	*Plut, Jović*
08/01	Pembroke	W	2-0	*Dimitrov, Herrera*
15/01	Balzan	D	1-1	*Andjelković*
21/01	Valletta	L	0-1	
29/01	Hibernians	W	2-1	*Plut, Vukanac*
05/02	Gżira	W	2-1	*Herrera, Andjelković*
11/02	Floriana	L	1-2	*Plut*
25/02	St Andrews	D	2-2	*Alba (p), Malán*
04/03	Tarxien	W	1-0	*Alba*
12/03	Hamrun	W	3-0	*Malán, Bubalović, Dimitrov*
18/03	Sliema	D	1-1	*Dimitrov*
01/04	Mosta	W	3-0	*og (T Farrugia), Alba, Dimitrov*
04/04	Pembroke	W	2-0	*Alba, Malán*
08/04	Balzan	W	3-1	*Dimitrov, Malán (p), Plut*
15/04	Valletta	D	3-3	*Vukanac, Bubalović, Herrera (p)*
23/04	Hibernians	W	2-0	*Plut, Vukanac*
30/04	Gżira	D	1-1	*Plut*
05/05	Floriana	W	2-1	*Alba, Plut*

Name	Nat	DoB	Pos	Aps	(s)	Gls
Edmond Agius		23/02/87	M	4	(8)	
Ini Etim Akpan	NGA	03/08/84	G	1		
Miguel Alba	ARG	14/08/88	A	11	(1)	5
Mislav Andjelković	CRO	22/04/88	M	29		2
Cain Attard		10/09/94	D	29	(1)	2
Shaun Bajada		19/08/83	M	3	(10)	
Henry Bonello		13/10/88	G	17		
Steve Bonnici		02/02/89	D	1	(8)	
James Brincat		03/12/96	D	3	(13)	2
Christian Bubalović	CRO	09/08/91	D	22		3
Matteo Desira Buttigieg		07/08/93	A	2	(8)	1
Srdjan Dimitrov	SRB	28/07/92	M	29	(1)	11
Dejan Djordjević	SRB	20/09/92	M	3		
Matthew Guillaumier		30/11/96	M	10	(11)	1
Edward Herrera		14/11/86	D	12	(7)	4
Predrag Jović	SRB	29/05/87	D	15	(3)	1
Miroslav Koprić	CRO	23/12/84	G	15		
Gonzalo Malán	URU	08/04/88	A	12	(1)	4
Gary Muir	SCO	15/12/85	D	3		
Rowen Muscat		05/06/91	M	5	(4)	
Jhon Obregón	COL	08/02/90	A		(2)	
Vito Plut	SVN	08/07/88	A	25	(3)	13
Gareth Sciberras		29/03/83	M	30	(1)	2
Ryan Scicluna		30/07/93	M	11	(13)	2
Franc Temile	NGA	15/07/90	M	15		5
Nikola Vukanac	SRB	14/01/86	D	29		3
Joseph Zerafa		31/05/88	D	27	(2)	

Floriana FC

1894 • florianafc.org

Major honours
Maltese League (25) 1910, 1912, 1913, 1921, 1922, 1925, 1927, 1928, 1929, 1931, 1935, 1937, 1950, 1951, 1952, 1953, 1955, 1958, 1962, 1968, 1970, 1973, 1975, 1977, 1993; Maltese Cup (20) 1938, 1945, 1947, 1949, 1950, 1953, 1954, 1955, 1957, 1958, 1961, 1966, 1967, 1972, 1976, 1981, 1993, 1994, 2011, 2017

Coach: Giovanni Tedesco (ITA)

2016				
20/08	Pembroke	W	2-1	*Fontanella, og (B Muscat)*
27/08	St Andrews	W	3-1	*Fontanella, S Pisani, Samb*
10/09	Balzan	L	0-1	
17/09	Tarxien	L	0-1	
21/09	Valletta	W	2-0	*Samb, Fontanella*
26/09	Hamrun	D	1-1	*Chiesa*
01/10	Sliema	L	1-3	*Fontanella*
15/10	Hibernians	D	0-0	
22/10	Mosta	W	1-0	*Chiesa*
28/10	Gżira	W	1-0	*Chiesa (p)*
04/11	Birkirkara	D	1-1	*Chiesa*
20/11	Pembroke	W	2-1	*Varela, Samb*
25/11	St Andrews	W	4-1	*Varela 2 (1p), Chiesa 2 (1p)*
04/12	Balzan	W	3-1	*Varela, Samb, S Pisani*
10/12	Tarxien	D	1-1	*Fontanella*
17/12	Valletta	D	0-0	
2017				
07/01	Hamrun	W	5-1	*Samb, Fontanella, Chiesa (p), Ruiz 2*
15/01	Hibernians	D	2-2	*Chiesa, Varela*
22/01	Sliema	L	1-3	*Fontanella (p)*
29/01	Gżira	L	3-4	*Varela, Camenzuli, Fontanella*
04/02	Mosta	W	4-0	*Varela, Nayar (p), Vella, Camenzuli*
11/02	Birkirkara	W	2-1	*Fontanella 2*
25/02	Pembroke	W	2-0	*Varela, Ruiz*
04/02	St Andrews	D	0-0	
12/03	Balzan	L	0-2	
18/03	Tarxien	W	1-0	*Fontanella*
02/04	Valletta	D	1-1	*Camenzuli*
05/04	Hamrun	W	2-1	*Cini, Fontanella (p)*
09/04	Hibernians	L	2-3	*Varela, Fontanella*
17/04	Sliema	L	0-3	
22/04	Gżira	D	1-1	*Monticelli*
29/04	Mosta	W	2-0	*Camenzuli, Fontanella*
05/05	Birkirkara	L	1-2	*Pepe*

Name	Nat	DoB	Pos	Aps	(s)	Gls
Darrell Baldacchino		28/02/96	D		(1)	
Clyde Borg		20/03/92	M	19	(9)	
Denilson Borg Castaldi		28/10/99	M		(1)	
Ryan Camenzuli		08/09/94	M	22	(7)	4
Zack Camilleri		10/12/99	M		(2)	
Nicolás Chiesa	ARG	26/05/80	M	29		8
Alexander Cini		28/10/91	D	25	(4)	1
Lomar Cutajar		19/10/99	M		(1)	
Brooke Farrugia		17/07/93	M		(8)	
Mario Fontanella	ITA	28/06/89	A	24	(5)	14
Matthew Grech		19/02/96	G	7	(2)	
Gustavo	BRA	24/04/98	A	1	(5)	
Justin Haber		09/06/81	G	26		
Antonio Monticelli	ITA	25/05/89	M	18	(4)	1
Sebastián Nayar	ARG	10/05/88	M	11		1
Enrico Pepe	ITA	12/11/89	D	27		1
Duncan Pisani		25/05/88	D	2		
Jurgen Pisani		03/09/92	D	23	(1)	
Steve Pisani		07/08/92	M	20	(8)	2
Enzo Ruiz	ARG	20/06/89	D	29		3
Amadou Samb	SEN	22/04/88	A	20	(3)	5
Andre Scicluna		22/09/98	D	15	(7)	
Ignacio Varela	ARG	20/07/90	A	24	(2)	9
Maurizio Vella	ITA	10/05/91	A	21	(2)	1
Mattia Zarb		15/03/00	M		(1)	

Gżira United FC

1947 • no website

Major honours
Maltese Cup (1) 1973

Coach: Branko Nišević (SRB); (15/11/16) Darren Abdilla

2016				
19/08	Tarxien	D	1-1	*Tony*
27/08	Hamrun	D	1-1	*Tony*
10/09	Sliema	W	1-0	*Robert*
17/09	Mosta	L	1-2	*Gatt Baldacchino*
22/09	Pembroke	W	3-0	*Tonna, Liliu, Corbalan*
26/09	Balzan	L	1-3	*Joceano Baiano*
30/09	Hibernians	D	1-1	*Liliu*
15/10	Valletta	L	1-3	*Tony*
22/10	Birkirkara	L	1-7	*Moises Pérez*
28/10	Floriana	L	0-1	
05/11	St Andrews	L	0-1	
19/11	Tarxien	L	0-1	
25/11	Hamrun	L	0-2	
04/12	Sliema	L	0-1	
10/12	Mosta	W	3-0	*Rafael Ledesma, Corbalan, Diamouténé*
18/12	Pembroke	D	0-0	
2017				
08/01	Balzan	L	1-2	*Correa*
14/01	Valletta	L	0-1	
22/01	Hibernians	L	0-3	
29/01	Floriana	W	4-3	*Adeshina, I Azzopardi, Corbalan, Zomé*
05/02	Birkirkara	L	1-2	*Cohen (p)*
11/02	St Andrews	W	3-2	*Zomé, Cohen (p), Corbalan*
25/02	Tarxien	W	1-0	*Moises Pérez*
04/03	Hamrun	W	3-1	*Zomé, Reyna, Jacob Borg*
11/03	Sliema	L	0-1	
17/03	Mosta	W	4-1	*Scerri, Conti, Reyna 2 (1p)*
01/04	Pembroke	W	5-1	*Conti, Cohen (p), Reyna 3*
05/04	Balzan	L	1-3	*Scerri*
08/04	Valletta	D	1-1	*Conti*
15/04	Hibernians	L	0-2	
22/04	Floriana	D	1-1	*Corbalan*
30/04	Birkirkara	D	1-1	*Adeshina*
04/05	St Andrews	W	3-2	*Cohen, Adeshina, Amaira*

Name	Nat	DoB	Pos	Aps	(s)	Gls
Ige Adeshina		01/08/86	A	13	(3)	3
Emerson Amaira		01/10/86	M		(7)	1
Ian Azzopardi		12/08/82	D	12	(1)	1
Jamie Azzopardi		01/09/97	G	2		
Mauro Boerchio	ITA	16/08/89	G	8		
Jonathan Bondin		11/10/82	D	19	(2)	
Jacob Borg		02/05/91	D	22	(7)	1
Jurgen Borg		08/08/94	G	20		
Andrew Cohen		13/05/81	M	10		4
Gianmarco Conti	ITA	01/02/92	M	30		3
Juan Corbalan		03/03/97	M	27	(2)	5
Ricardo Correa	URU	20/07/94	M	5		1
Anthony Curmi		20/11/82	G	3		
James D'Agostino		19/02/98	D		(1)	
Souleymane Diamouténé	MLI	30/01/83	D	27		1
Dyson Falzon		09/03/86	M	2	(7)	
Clifford Gatt Baldacchino		09/02/88	D	21	(3)	1
Kyle Gerada		05/01/91	G		(1)	
Salvatore Grixti		26/06/96	M		(1)	
Mamadou Jallow	GAM	30/03/92	A	5		
Joceano Baiano	BRA	12/09/90	A	4	(2)	1
Liliu	BRA	30/03/90	A	2	(2)	2
Moises Pérez	ESP	13/07/88	M	28		2
John Nwoba	NGA	18/08/89	A		(12)	
Karl Pulo		30/07/89	M	7	(13)	
Rafael Ledesma	BRA	31/12/82	M	12	(1)	1
Carlos Reyna	ARG	11/06/94	A	7	(6)	6
Robert	BRA	27/02/81	A	5	(1)	1
Zachary Scerri		08/03/96	M	24	(5)	2
Yanis Tonna		07/02/92	D	9	(5)	1
Tony	BRA	11/05/90	D	21	(4)	3
Andre White		01/01/91	D	7	(8)	
Louis Zomé	CMR	06/04/88	A	11	(1)	3

Hamrun Spartans FC

1907 • hamrunspartans.com

Major honours
Maltese League (7) 1914, 1918, 1947, 1983, 1987, 1988, 1991; Maltese Cup (6) 1983, 1984, 1987, 1988, 1989, 1992

Coach: Steve D'Amato; (10/11/16) (Jonathan Holland); (23/12/16) Jacques Scerri

Date	Opponent		Score	Scorers
2016				
19/08	Hibernians	W	3-1	*J Grech, Mifsud Triganza 2*
27/08	Gżira	D	1-1	*Jorginho*
11/09	Birkirkara	L	1-2	*Garba*
18/09	St Andrews	W	3-1	*Giusti, Garba 2*
22/09	Tarxien	L	1-2	*Mifsud Triganza*
26/09	Floriana	D	1-1	*J Grech (p)*
30/09	Mosta	W	5-2	*Garba 2, Jorginho, J Grech 2 (1p)*
15/10	Sliema	L	0-3	
22/10	Balzan	L	1-3	*Vergara*
29/10	Pembroke	W	2-1	*J Grech, Mifsud Triganza*
05/11	Valletta	L	0-3	
20/11	Hibernians	L	1-4	*J Grech*
25/11	Gżira	W	2-0	*Jorginho, J Grech*
04/12	Birkirkara	W	2-0	*Giusti 2*
10/12	St Andrews	L	1-3	*J Grech*
18/12	Tarxien	L	2-3	*Giusti 2*
2017				
07/01	Floriana	L	1-5	*Patrick Jean*
14/01	Sliema	W	2-1	*J Grech (p), og (Potezica)*
22/01	Mosta	W	3-0	*J Grech 2, Paiber*
28/01	Pembroke	L	0-1	
04/02	Balzan	L	0-1	
12/02	Valletta	L	0-2	
25/02	Hibernians	D	3-3	*Paiber (p), Leandro Motta, Giusti*
04/03	Gżira	L	1-3	*Chircop*
12/03	Birkirkara	L	0-3	
17/03	St Andrews	D	1-1	*K Micallef*
01/04	Tarxien	D	1-1	*J Grech*
05/04	Floriana	L	1-2	*K Micallef*
09/04	Sliema	L	0-2	
17/04	Mosta	L	1-2	*Giusti*
22/04	Pembroke	L	1-2	*Giusti*
29/04	Balzan	D	1-1	*Manset*
05/05	Valletta	W	2-1	*Giusti, Manset*

Name	Nat	DoB	Pos	Aps	(s)	Gls
Christian Anigbogu	NGA	05/05/90	D	3		
Siraj Arab		25/03/94	A	5	(8)	
Glenn Azzopardi		08/08/93	D	9	(1)	
Kambala Batusila	CGO	03/05/95	G	2	(3)	
Mark Anthony Borg		14/06/82	D	8	(1)	
David Cassar		24/11/87	G	24		
Philip Chircop		02/10/89	D	17	(3)	1
Trevor Cilia		01/02/83	A		(5)	
Daniel Debono		20/06/99	M		(3)	
Darren Falzon		08/05/92	A		(8)	
Matthew Farrugia		17/04/81	G	3	(2)	
Haruna Garba	NGA	17/01/94	A	6		5
Massimiliano Giusti	ITA	29/12/95	M	21	(7)	9
Jake Grech		18/11/97	M	30	(2)	12
Luke Grech		06/01/94	D	25		
Jorginho	BRA	25/01/91	M	19	(2)	3
Leandro Motta	BRA	14/01/92	A	23	(5)	1
Christian Maldini	ITA	14/06/96	D	5		
Mathieu Manset	FRA	05/08/89	A	6	(5)	2
Karl Micallef		08/09/96	D	13	(1)	2
Manolito Micallef		16/11/83	M	14	(2)	
Jean Pierre Mifsud Triganza		20/11/81	A	8	(4)	4
Igor Mišan	SRB	05/05/90	M	13		
Saturday Nanapere	NGA	22/10/91	A	20	(12)	
Brandon Paiber		05/06/95	M	6	(4)	2
Patrick Jean	BRA	17/10/88	A	12	(4)	1
Rodney Refalo		08/01/95	M		(4)	
Bradley Schembri		10/08/98	A		(1)	
Luke Sciberras		15/09/89	A	28		
Sergio Raphael	BRA	23/10/92	D	26	(1)	
Miguel Simiana		16/07/99	M		(1)	
Ryan Spiteri		02/02/95	M	2		
Fredrick Tabone		08/11/88	G	4	(1)	
Luis Vergara	COL	31/08/90	D	11	(2)	1

Hibernians FC

1922 • hiberniansfc.org

Major honours
Maltese League (12) 1961, 1967, 1969, 1979, 1981, 1982, 1994, 1995, 2002, 2009, 2015, 2017; Maltese Cup (10) 1962, 1970, 1971, 1980, 1982, 1998, 2006, 2007, 2012, 2013

Coach: Mark Miller (ENG)

Date	Opponent		Score	Scorers
2016				
19/08	Hamrun	L	1-3	*og (Patrick Jean)*
26/08	Sliema	W	1-0	*Failla (p)*
10/09	Mosta	W	3-1	*Failla (p), Kristensen, Degabriele*
17/09	Pembroke	W	2-1	*Varea, Kristensen*
22/09	Balzan	L	0-2	
25/09	Valletta	W	2-0	*Rodolfo Soares, Degabriele*
30/09	Gżira	D	1-1	*Degabriele*
15/10	Floriana	D	0-0	
23/10	St Andrews	W	1-0	*Jackson*
30/10	Birkirkara	W	1-0	*Failla (p)*
05/11	Tarxien	W	2-1	*Jackson, Jorginho*
20/11	Hamrun	W	4-1	*Degabriele, Kristensen, Failla (p), Cohen (p)*
26/11	Sliema	W	3-1	*Degabriele, Jorginho, Bezzina*
04/12	Mosta	W	2-0	*Degabriele (p), Pearson*
10/12	Pembroke	D	1-1	*Degabriele (p)*
17/12	Balzan	L	1-2	*Jorginho*
2017				
08/01	Valletta	W	1-0	*Jackson*
15/01	Floriana	D	2-2	*Jorginho, Rodolfo Soares*
22/01	Gżira	W	3-0	*Jorginho, Jallow 2*
29/01	Birkirkara	L	1-2	*Degabriele*
04/02	St Andrews	W	2-1	*Degabriele, Rodolfo Soares*
11/02	Tarxien	W	1-0	*Gilmar*
25/02	Hamrun	D	3-3	*Degabriele 2, Gilmar*
04/03	Sliema	W	2-1	*Degabriele, Kristensen*
11/03	Mosta	W	4-0	*Gilmar 2, Jorginho, Kristensen*
17/03	Pembroke	W	3-0	*Jorginho, Degabriele, Boljević*
02/04	Balzan	W	3-1	*Failla, Bezzina, Jorginho*
05/04	Valletta	L	0-1	
09/04	Floriana	W	3-2	*Failla, Jackson, Agius*
15/04	Gżira	W	2-0	*Jorginho, Gilmar*
23/04	Birkirkara	L	0-2	
30/04	St Andrews	W	3-1	*Kristensen, Jackson, Jorginho*
06/05	Tarxien	W	6-1	*Degabriele 3, Jorginho, Jackson, Gilmar*

Name	Nat	DoB	Pos	Aps	(s)	Gls
Andrei Agius		12/08/86	D	32		1
Johann Bezzina		30/05/94	M	23	(6)	2
Dejan Boljević	MNE	30/05/90	D	8	(3)	1
Rudi Briffa		21/08/96	G	1	(1)	
Andrew Cohen		13/05/81	M	5	(10)	1
Jurgen Degabriele		10/10/96	A	29	(4)	16
Clayton Failla		08/01/86	M	25	(2)	6
Gilmar	BRA	26/03/90	M	10	(3)	6
Andrew Hogg		02/03/85	G	32		
Jackson	BRA	09/07/82	M	32		6
Mamadou Jallow	GAM	30/03/92	A	4	(5)	2
Jorginho	BRA	04/12/85	A	23	(1)	11
Bjorn Kristensen		05/04/93	M	31		6
Marcelo Dias	BRA	29/09/85	D	31		
Diosdado Mbele	EQG	08/04/97	D	1		
Joseph Essien Mbong		15/07/97	A	14	(3)	
Montell Moore	ENG	23/12/95	A	2	(9)	
Kyle O'Brien	USA	27/05/90	M	1	(1)	
Jonathan Pearson		13/01/87	D	2	(2)	1
Renan	BRA	28/11/88	M	10	(6)	
Rodolfo Soares	BRA	25/05/85	D	32		3
Rui da Gracia	EQG	28/05/85	D	1		
Michael Shaddock	USA	10/09/91	A	1	(1)	
Timothy Tabone Desira		15/07/95	D	5	(3)	
Juan Manuel Varea	ARG	23/03/86	A	2	(10)	1
Dunstan Vella		27/04/96	D	5	(17)	
Connor Zammit		26/09/98	D	1		

Mosta FC

1935 • no website

Coach: Edmund Lufi; (02/10/16) Ivan Zammit; (14/12/16) (Jojo Bajada); (03/01/17) Zsolt Hornyák (SVK); (28/03/17) Johann Scicluna

Date	Opponent		Score	Scorers
2016				
20/08	Balzan	L	2-3	*Vlček, Oseghale (p)*
26/08	Valletta	L	0-1	
10/09	Hibernians	L	1-3	*Priso (p)*
17/09	Gżira	W	2-1	*Priso, Oseghale*
22/09	Birkirkara	L	0-2	
26/09	St Andrews	W	1-0	*Reid*
30/09	Hamrun	L	2-5	*Reid 2*
15/10	Tarxien	D	1-1	*Priso*
22/10	Floriana	L	0-1	
30/10	Sliema	D	1-1	*Priso*
05/11	Pembroke	L	0-3	
19/11	Balzan	L	0-1	
26/11	Valletta	D	0-0	
04/12	Hibernians	L	0-2	
10/12	Gżira	L	0-3	
2017				
04/01	Birkirkara	L	0-2	
07/01	St Andrews	D	1-1	*Oseghale*
14/01	Tarxien	L	0-2	
22/01	Hamrun	L	0-3	
28/01	Sliema	W	2-1	*Priso, Brincat*
04/02	Floriana	L	0-4	
11/02	Pembroke	W	3-0	*(w/o; original result 0-5)*
24/02	Balzan	L	1-7	*Oseghale*
05/03	Valletta	L	0-4	
11/03	Hibernians	L	0-4	
17/03	Gżira	L	1-4	*T Farrugia*
01/04	Birkirkara	L	0-3	
05/04	St Andrews	L	1-2	*Pedrinho (p)*
09/04	Tarxien	W	3-1	*Priso 2, Fenech*
17/04	Hamrun	W	2-1	*Fenech, Priso*
22/04	Sliema	D	1-1	*Mifsud Triganza*
29/04	Floriana	L	0-2	
05/05	Pembroke	W	4-2	*Priso, Pedrinho 3 (1p)*

Name	Nat	DoB	Pos	Aps	(s)	Gls
Josué Ahoure	FRA	18/07/93	A	2		
Kevaughn Atkinson	JAM	11/11/95	A	5	(1)	
Manuel Bartolo		26/08/83	G	8		
Gabriel Bezak	SVK	24/04/93	A	11	(1)	
Antoine Borg		04/04/94	M		(4)	
Zachary Brincat		24/06/98	A	11	(1)	1
Calvin Camilleri		02/01/00	M		(1)	
Adrian Caruana		15/07/93	M	17	(5)	
Yenz Cini		04/01/94	G	21		
Dany Djoufack	CMR	07/03/95	D	14		
Jonas Ekani	CMR	13/10/92	D	7	(1)	
Enmy Peña	DOM	17/09/92	M		(1)	
Nicholas Farrugia		18/02/00	M		(3)	
Tyrone Farrugia		22/02/89	D	10		1
David Fenech		17/06/88	M	14		2
Kyle Frendo		30/06/95	M	18	(10)	
Neil Frendo		04/01/99	M	5	(9)	
Luke Galea		21/01/97	M		(1)	
Kyle Gatt		18/04/99	A		(5)	
Tristan Grant	CAN	31/01/92	D	8		
Jurgen Grech		28/04/99	D	1	(3)	
Ryan Grech		03/04/85	M	1		
Cédric Hengbart	FRA	13/07/80	D	7		
Heron	BRA	19/04/90	D	5	(1)	
Kemmu Jackson	JAM	11/07/95	M	6	(2)	
Kurt Magro		04/06/86	M	26		
Ricardo Martin	JAM	04/06/88	D	3	(1)	
Luca Martinelli	ITA	20/12/88	D	7	(3)	
Chevaughn McLaren	JAM	04/05/94	M	3		
Bradley Meledje	FRA	17/07/93	A	1	(1)	
Jean Pierre Mifsud Triganza		20/11/81	A	10	(1)	1
Erik Mikeš	SVK	05/06/97	M	1	(1)	
Edin Murga	ITA	21/12/94	A	2	(1)	
David Nworah	NGA	18/10/94	M	1		
Chinatu Onwudinjo	NGA	28/08/92	D	19	(2)	
Victor Oseghale	NGA	12/08/95	A	15	(1)	4
Chinedu Oweregbulam	NGA	07/09/92	D	2		
Raylon Paisley	JAM	13/12/93	A	3		
Pedrinho	BRA	04/08/86	M	11		4
Njongo Priso	CMR	24/12/88	A	24		9
Kemar Reid	JAM	15/08/94	M	7	(2)	3
Jaroslav Repa	SVK	29/08/95	D	8		
Cesar Romero	USA	02/08/89	A	4	(1)	
Mário Tóth	SVK	06/04/95	D	15		
Sheldon Vassallo		11/06/97	D		(1)	
Andreas Vella		14/10/98	G	4		
Emerson Vella		09/09/91	D	7	(4)	
Martin Vlček	SVK	05/02/96	A	9	(2)	1
Dexter Xuereb		21/09/97	D	10	(11)	

MALTA

Pembroke Athleta FC

1962 • no website

Coach: Winston Muscat; (19/10/16) Artim Sakiri (MKD)

Date	Opponent			Scorers
2016				
20/08	Floriana	L	1-2	*Montebello*
26/08	Balzan	L	1-2	*og (Bezzina)*
10/09	Valletta	L	1-5	*Scozzese*
17/09	Hibernians	L	1-2	*og (Agius)*
22/09	Gżira	L	0-3	
26/09	Birkirkara	W	2-1	*Borg, Bernardo*
01/10	Tarxien	D	2-2	*Asani, Levnajić*
16/10	St Andrews	L	1-4	*Bernardo*
23/10	Sliema	L	0-1	
29/10	Hamrun	L	1-2	*Manevski*
05/11	Mosta	W	3-0	*og (E Vella), og (Martinelli), Micallef*
20/11	Floriana	L	1-2	*Borg*
26/11	Balzan	L	0-4	
03/12	Valletta	L	0-3	
10/12	Hibernians	D	1-1	*Barbetti (p)*
18/12	Gżira	D	0-0	
2017				
08/01	Birkirkara	L	0-2	
14/01	St Andrews	D	2-2	*Dhrami, Račić*
22/01	Tarxien	L	1-7	*Jawad*
28/01	Hamrun	W	1-0	*Falzon*
04/02	Sliema	D	1-1	*Kooh-Sohna*
11/02	Mosta	L	0-3	*(w/o; original result 5-0 Radovniković, Scozzese, Račić (p), Falzon, Borg)*
25/02	Floriana	L	0-2	
05/03	Balzan	L	2-5	*Nagaoka, Falzon*
11/03	Valletta	L	0-4	
17/03	Hibernians	L	0-3	
01/04	Gżira	L	1-5	*Račić*
04/04	Birkirkara	L	0-2	
09/04	St Andrews	L	0-6	
15/04	Tarxien	D	1-1	*Račić (p)*
22/04	Hamrun	W	2-1	*Jawad, Račić*
29/04	Sliema	L	0-2	
05/05	Mosta	L	2-4	*Račić, Kooh-Sohna*

Name	Nat	DoB	Pos	Aps	(s)	Gls
Craig Abdilla		17/03/99	G		(1)	
Ugochukwu Akuto	NGA	03/01/97	M	5	(2)	
Siraj Arab		25/03/94	A	15		
Dzelil Asani	MKD	12/09/95	D	12	(2)	1
Miguel Attard		10/03/95	A	20	(4)	
Paltemio Barbetti	ITA	25/10/89	M	20		1
Bernardo	BRA	07/11/88	A	9	(5)	2
Adrian Borg		20/05/89	D	23	(1)	3
Owen Bugeja		20/02/90	D	9	(2)	
Matthew Buhagiar		25/08/95	D		(1)	
Matthew Cremona Calleja		14/09/94	G	23	(1)	
Arbër Dhrami	ALB	23/06/88	A	5		1
Sunday Eboh	NGA	30/09/81	M	10	(5)	
Darren Falzon		08/05/92	A	13	(3)	3
Brooke Farrugia		17/07/93	M	3	(4)	
David Fenech		17/06/88	M		(4)	
Tyron Fenech		20/10/95	M	4	(8)	
Clifford Gauci		08/04/92	A	6	(1)	
Panagiotis Giannopoulos	GRE	21/07/94	M	4		
Neil Grech		24/06/96	M	3		
Zachary Grech		21/07/99	D		(7)	
Daniane Jawad	MAR	14/04/86	D	11		2
Raphael Kooh-Sohna	CMR	22/04/90	A	9		2
Zoran Levnajić	CRO	04/04/87	M	28		1
Olexandr Maksymov	UKR	13/02/85	M	6	(2)	
Borce Manevski	MKD	05/07/85	M	8	(3)	1
Mateus Regis	BRA	27/07/94	M	5	(3)	
Manolito Micallef		16/11/83	M	13		1
James Mifsud		13/07/96	M		(3)	
Luke Montebello		13/08/95	A	3	(1)	1
Brandon Muscat		03/11/94	M	11		
Mario Muscat		18/08/76	G	4		
Emmanuel Naatey	GHA	26/12/97	D	4	(1)	
Go Nagaoka	JPN	23/05/84	M	6		1
Joseph Okonkwo	NGA	29/09/86	A	1		
Nevin Portelli		16/09/99	M		(1)	
Christian Pouga	CMR	19/06/86	A	2		
Stevan Račić	SRB	17/01/84	A	14		6
Tonči Radovniković	CRO	27/10/88	D	11		1
Argyris Roppas	GRE	07/02/86	G	5		
Iraklis Roppas	GRE	02/01/84	M	10		
Filippo Scozzese	ITA	08/12/88	D	19	(3)	2
Shola Shodiya	NGA	17/06/91	A	8	(1)	
Fredrick Tabone		08/11/88	G	1		

St Andrews FC

1968 • no website

Coach: Jose Borg; (08/10/16) Danilo Dončić (SRB)

Date	Opponent			Scorers
2016				
19/08	Birkirkara	L	0-4	
27/08	Floriana	L	1-3	*McKay*
11/09	Tarxien	W	1-0	*Nwoko*
18/09	Hamrun	L	1-3	*Farrugia (p)*
21/09	Sliema	W	3-0	*Darmanin, Farrugia (p), Enmy Peña*
26/09	Mosta	L	0-1	
30/09	Balzan	L	0-3	
16/10	Pembroke	W	4-1	*Farrugia 2 (2p), Kastrevec, Walker*
23/10	Hibernians	L	0-1	
28/10	Valletta	D	0-0	
05/11	Gżira	W	1-0	*McKay*
19/11	Birkirkara	D	1-1	*Enmy Peña*
25/11	Floriana	L	1-4	*Kešinović*
03/12	Tarxien	D	1-1	*Enmy Peña*
10/12	Hamrun	W	3-1	*Johnson, Kešinović, Paz*
18/12	Sliema	D	1-1	*Johnson*
2017				
07/01	Mosta	D	1-1	*Kastrevec*
14/01	Pembroke	D	2-2	*Paz 2*
21/01	Balzan	L	0-1	
28/01	Valletta	D	1-1	*Kastrevec*
04/02	Hibernians	L	1-2	*Paz*
11/02	Gżira	L	2-3	*Friggieri, Paz (p)*
25/02	Birkirkara	D	2-2	*Nwoko 2*
04/03	Floriana	D	0-0	
11/03	Tarxien	W	1-0	*Johnson*
17/03	Hamrun	D	1-1	*Enmy Peña*
01/04	Sliema	L	1-4	*Kastrevec*
05/04	Mosta	W	2-1	*Nwoko, Camilleri*
09/04	Pembroke	W	6-0	*Paz (p), Camilleri, Farrugia, Friggieri, Choi, Walker*
15/04	Balzan	L	1-2	*Farrugia (p)*
22/04	Valletta	W	3-1	*Friggieri, Enmy Peña, Farrugia*
30/04	Hibernians	L	1-3	*Belacević*
04/05	Gżira	L	2-3	*Kastrevec, Walker*

Name	Nat	DoB	Pos	Aps	(s)	Gls
Ante Bakmaz	CRO	07/03/92	D	7	(1)	
Nenad Belacević	SRB	26/12/93	M	11	(11)	1
Daniel Brändle	LIE	23/01/92	M	6	(5)	
Dale Camilleri		17/10/92	M	24	(5)	2
Choi Bong-won	KOR	16/05/94	D	29	(1)	1
Ryan Darmanin		12/12/85	A	3	(16)	1
Enmy Peña	DOM	17/09/92	M	27		5
Joseph Farrugia		26/07/81	M	31		7
Duncan Formosa		30/06/00	G	1		
Aidan Jake Friggieri		28/04/98	A	13	(1)	3
Jake Galea		15/04/96	G	31		
Liam Grech		03/02/97	M		(3)	
Michael Johnson		11/05/94	D	30		3
Žiga Kastrevec	SVN	25/02/94	A	29	(1)	5
Karlo Kešinović	CRO	12/12/89	D	31		2
Godwin McKay		20/07/95	A	12	(10)	2
Kyrian Nwoko		09/07/97	M	25	(6)	4
Iván Paz	ARG	25/01/96	A	27	(4)	6
Ryan Sammut		06/04/92	M		(1)	
Alex Satariano		25/10/01	A		(1)	
Dean Sciberras		28/03/97	G	1		
Mark Scicluna		24/02/97	D		(1)	
Felix Udoh	NGA	28/12/93	D	25	(5)	
Nicki Vella Petroni		10/09/91	M		(1)	
Jacob Walker		31/07/97	A		(24)	3

Sliema Wanderers FC

1909 • no website

Major honours
Maltese League (26) 1920, 1923, 1924, 1926, 1930, 1933, 1934, 1936, 1938, 1939, 1940, 1949, 1954, 1956, 1957, 1964, 1965, 1966, 1971, 1972, 1976, 1989, 1996, 2003, 2004, 2005; Maltese Cup (21) 1935, 1936, 1937, 1940, 1946, 1948, 1951, 1952, 1956, 1959, 1963, 1965, 1968, 1969, 1974, 1979, 1990, 2000, 2004, 2009, 2016

Coach: John Buttigieg

Date	Opponent			Scorers
2016				
19/08	Valletta	L	1-2	*Muchardi*
26/08	Hibernians	L	0-1	
10/09	Gżira	L	0-1	
18/09	Birkirkara	W	2-1	*A Muscat (p), Salomon*
21/09	St Andrews	L	0-3	
25/09	Tarxien	W	2-1	*Salomon, Potezica*
01/10	Floriana	W	3-1	*Farrugia, Salomon, Potezica*
15/10	Hamrun	W	3-0	*A Muscat (p), Farrugia, og (Maldini)*
23/10	Pembroke	W	1-0	*Mandinho*
30/10	Mosta	D	1-1	*Salomon*
04/11	Balzan	D	1-1	*Muchardi*
19/11	Valletta	L	1-2	*Scerri*
26/11	Hibernians	L	1-3	*Denni (p)*
04/12	Gżira	W	1-0	*Farrugia*
11/12	Birkirkara	W	2-1	*Farrugia 2*
18/12	St Andrews	D	1-1	*Denni*
2017				
08/01	Tarxien	L	0-1	
14/01	Hamrun	L	1-2	*Denni (p)*
22/01	Floriana	W	3-1	*Scerri, Farrugia, Denni (p)*
28/01	Mosta	L	1-2	*A Muscat (p)*
04/02	Pembroke	D	1-1	*Temile*
12/02	Balzan	W	2-1	*Farrugia, Spiteri*
24/02	Valletta	L	1-3	*Scerri*
04/03	Hibernians	L	1-2	*A Muscat (p)*
11/03	Gżira	W	1-0	*Aquilina*
18/03	Birkirkara	D	1-1	*Denni*
01/04	St Andrews	W	4-1	*A Muscat, Farrugia 2, Muchardi*
04/04	Tarxien	D	1-1	*Salomon*
09/04	Hamrun	W	2-0	*Muchardi, Correa*
17/04	Floriana	W	3-0	*Scerri, Temile, Farrugia*
23/04	Mosta	D	1-1	*Correa*
29/04	Pembroke	W	2-0	*Bianciardi, Farrugia*
05/05	Balzan	W	2-1	*Denni, Aquilina*

Name	Nat	DoB	Pos	Aps	(s)	Gls
Gabriel Aquilina		07/12/95	M	15	(10)	2
Stefano Bianciardi	ITA	15/03/85	D	23		1
Luca Brincat		04/07/97	D	7	(1)	
Ricardo Correa	URU	20/07/94	M	13		2
Denni	BRA	21/08/82	A	22	(2)	6
Jean-Paul Farrugia		21/03/92	A	26	(6)	11
Aidan Jake Friggieri		28/04/98	A	2	(3)	
Miloš Galin	BIH	22/04/90	A	6	(3)	
Leonardo Incorvaia	ARG	26/06/92	D	3	(1)	
Mandinho	BRA	28/01/84	M	4	(8)	1
John Mintoff		23/08/88	M	22	(6)	
Matías Muchardi	ARG	09/02/88	M	22	(3)	4
Gary Muir	SCO	15/12/85	D	16		
Alex Muscat		14/12/84	D	29		5
Beppe Muscat		13/04/89	D	3	(1)	
Jonathan Pearson		13/01/87	D	11		
Marko Potezica	SRB	05/12/85	M	10	(3)	2
Clive Psaila		28/05/96	M	1		
Roger	BRA	03/01/94	D	12		
Michel Salomon	BEN	01/10/88	A	14	(10)	5
Michele Sansone		02/07/98	M	1	(9)	
Giuseppe Saraò	ITA	01/01/88	G	18		
Mark Scerri		16/01/90	M	26		4
Kurt Shaw		01/08/99	M		(1)	
Ryan Spiteri		02/02/95	M	10	(14)	1
Franc Temile	NGA	15/07/90	M	14	(1)	2
Peter Xuereb		07/05/92	M	18	(6)	
Glenn Zammit		08/05/87	G	15	(1)	

Tarxien Rainbows FC

1944 • no website

Coach: Jacques Scerri; (18/11/16) (Ryan Pulis); (26/11/16) (Brian Testaferrata) (01/12/16) Jesmond Zerafa; (04/04/17) (Tristan Caruana)

Date	Opponent		Score	Scorers
2016				
19/08	Gżira	D	1-1	*Dani Ponce*
26/08	Birkirkara	L	0-4	
11/09	St Andrews	L	0-1	
17/09	Floriana	W	1-0	*Prendes*
22/09	Hamrun	W	2-1	*Lecão, Dani Ponce*
25/09	Sliema	L	1-2	*Baker*
01/10	Pembroke	D	2-2	*Baker, Dani Ponce*
15/10	Mosta	D	1-1	*Nilsson*
22/10	Valletta	L	0-1	
29/10	Balzan	D	2-2	*Nilsson 2*
05/11	Hibernians	L	1-2	*T Caruana (p)*
19/11	Gżira	W	1-0	*Galea*
26/11	Birkirkara	L	1-3	*T Caruana*
03/12	St Andrews	D	1-1	*Galea*
10/12	Floriana	D	1-1	*T Caruana*
18/12	Hamrun	W	3-2	*Galea, Tabone, og (Chircop)*
2017				
08/01	Sliema	W	1-0	*Lecão*
14/01	Mosta	W	2-0	*Nilsson, Zerafa*
22/01	Pembroke	W	7-1	*Dani Ponce 2, Nilsson 2, Lecão 2, Francés*
28/01	Balzan	D	2-2	*Galea, Nilsson*
05/02	Valletta	D	1-1	*Nilsson*
11/02	Hibernians	L	0-1	
25/02	Gżira	L	0-1	
04/03	Birkirkara	L	0-1	
11/03	St Andrews	L	0-1	
18/03	Floriana	L	0-1	
01/04	Hamrun	D	1-1	*Nilsson*
04/04	Sliema	D	1-1	*Emerson*
09/04	Mosta	L	1-3	*og (Ekani)*
15/04	Pembroke	D	1-1	*Azzopardi (p)*
22/04	Balzan	L	0-3	
29/04	Valletta	W	2-0	*Nilsson, Baker*
06/05	Hibernians	L	1-6	*Nilsson (p)*

Name	Nat	DoB	Pos	Aps	(s)	Gls
Andrew Agius		01/06/91	D	7	(9)	
Ayrton Azzopardi		12/09/93	M	10	(8)	1
Ebiabowei Baker	NGA	30/01/94	D	26		3
Bradley Barbara		18/06/00	M	1		
Kurt Borg		29/08/95	M		(1)	
Sacha Borg		26/04/93	D	19	(6)	
Matthew Brincat		07/01/97	M	4	(5)	
Lyon Caruana		16/01/97	M		(1)	
Triston Caruana		15/09/91	M	28	(1)	3
Andrea Cassar		19/12/92	G	18		
Dani Ponce	ESP	16/05/91	D	28	(1)	5
Matthew Degiorgio		16/10/97	A		(1)	
Eloy	EQG	16/03/85	D	1	(3)	
Emerson	BRA	24/02/91	M	24	(2)	1
Claudio Francés	ARG	26/06/92	M	8	(3)	1
Julian Galea		09/02/89	M	12	(13)	4
Lecão	BRA	17/01/93	A	30	(1)	4
Dylan Micallef		30/06/94	M	6	(18)	
Alexander Nilsson	SWE	23/10/92	A	28	(2)	11
Pedrinho	BRA	18/06/93	M	3		
Sergio Prendes	ESP	15/07/86	A	22	(3)	1
Rogélio Ávila	BRA	07/07/87	A	1	(1)	
Philippe Schranz		14/07/96	G	15		
Matthew Sladden		12/12/99	A	1	(1)	
Matthew Tabone		29/04/92	D	22		1
Luke Zahra		07/05/95	M		(1)	
Kurt Zammit		26/02/96	D	25	(4)	
Daniel Zerafa		08/04/94	D	24		1

Valletta FC

1943 • vallettafc.net

Major honours

Maltese League (23) 1915, 1932, 1945, 1946, 1948, 1959, 1960, 1963, 1974, 1978, 1980, 1984, 1990, 1992, 1997, 1998, 1999, 2001, 2008, 2011, 2012, 2014, 2016; Maltese Cup (13) 1960, 1964, 1975, 1977, 1978, 1991, 1995, 1996, 1997, 1999, 2001, 2010, 2014

Coach: Paul Zammit

Date	Opponent		Score	Scorers
2016				
19/08	Sliema	W	2-1	*Cremona, Briffa*
26/08	Mosta	W	1-0	*Jhonnattann (p)*
10/09	Pembroke	W	5-1	*Falcone 2, Romeu, Azzopardi, Jhonnattann*
17/09	Balzan	D	2-2	*Aguirre, Umeh*
21/09	Floriana	L	0-2	
25/09	Hibernians	L	0-2	
30/09	Birkirkara	D	1-1	*Jhonnattann*
15/10	Gżira	W	3-1	*Jhonnattann, Falcone (p), J Borg*
22/10	Tarxien	W	1-0	*Mifsud*
28/10	St Andrews	D	0-0	
05/11	Hamrun	W	3-0	*Jhonnattann 2 (1p), Aguirre*
19/11	Sliema	W	2-1	*Falcone, Cremona*
26/11	Mosta	D	0-0	
03/12	Pembroke	W	3-0	*Mifsud, Malano, Aguirre*
11/12	Balzan	D	2-2	*Falcone, Jhonnattann*
17/12	Floriana	D	0-0	
2017				
08/01	Hibernians	L	0-1	
14/01	Gżira	W	1-0	*Montebello*
21/01	Birkirkara	W	1-0	*Malano*
28/01	St Andrews	D	1-1	*Radzinevičius*
05/02	Tarxien	D	1-1	*Aguirre*
12/02	Hamrun	W	2-0	*Umeh, Malano*
24/02	Sliema	W	3-1	*Velasco 2, Umeh*
05/03	Mosta	W	4-0	*Velasco 2, Montebello 2*
11/03	Pembroke	W	4-0	*Montebello, Valesco, Umeh, Mifsud*
17/03	Balzan	W	1-0	*Romeu*
02/04	Floriana	D	1-1	*Mifsud*
05/04	Hibernians	W	1-0	*S Borg*
08/04	Gżira	D	1-1	*Montebello*
15/04	Birkirkara	D	3-3	*Malano, Velasco 2*
22/04	St Andrews	L	1-3	*Velasco*
29/04	Tarxien	L	0-2	
05/05	Hamrun	L	1-2	*Velasco*

Name	Nat	DoB	Pos	Aps	(s)	Gls
Leandro Aguirre	ARG	08/02/89	D	30		4
Ian Azzopardi		12/08/82	D	2	(3)	1
Dziugas Bartkus	LTU	07/11/89	G	25		
Henry Bonello		13/10/88	G	7		
Jean Pierre Borg		08/01/98	D	16	(11)	1
Steve Borg		15/05/88	D	27		1
Roderick Briffa		24/08/81	M	5	(4)	1
Maverick Buhagiar		28/07/98	G		(1)	
Ryan Camilleri		22/05/88	D	25	(1)	
Jonathan Caruana		24/07/86	D	28		
Llywelyn Cremona		07/05/95	A	11	(16)	2
Shaun Dimech		08/08/01	M		(2)	
Federico Falcone	ARG	21/12/90	A	12		5
Russell Fenech		07/02/98	A		(7)	
Juan Cruz Gill	ARG	18/07/83	D	6	(1)	
Jhonnattann	BRA	27/07/89	M	18		7
Santiago Malano	ARG	29/01/87	A	26	(2)	4
Michael Mifsud		17/04/81	A	13	(10)	4
Luke Montebello		13/08/95	A	9	(10)	5
Rowen Muscat		05/06/91	M	7		
Claudio Pani	ITA	11/03/86	M	26		
Nicholas Pulis		28/01/98	D		(3)	
Tomas Radzinevičius	LTU	05/06/81	A	4	(1)	1
Romeu	BRA	10/04/90	M	20	(6)	2
Jurgen Suda		24/09/96	A		(3)	
Uchenna Umeh	NGA	10/10/91	A	19	(5)	4
Valdo Alhinho	ANG	17/12/88	M	16		
Maximiliano Velasco	ARG	19/06/90	A	10	(1)	9
Nicholas Vella		27/08/89	G	1		

Top goalscorers

23	Bojan Kaljević (Balzan)
16	Jurgen Degabriele (Hibernians)
14	Mario Fontanella (Floriana)
13	Vito Plut (Birkirkara)
12	Jake Grech (Hamrun)
11	Srdjan Dimitrov (Birkirkara) Jorginho (Hibernians) Jean-Paul Farrugia (Sliema) Alexander Nilsson (Tarxien)
9	Ignacio Varela (Floriana) Massimiliano Giusti (Hamrun) Njongo Priso (Mosta) Maximiliano Velasco (Valletta)

MALTA

Promoted clubs

Lija Athletic FC

1949 • no website
Coach: Joseph Galea

Senglea Athletic FC

1943 • no website
Coach: Pablo Doffo (ARG)
(22/12/16) Steve D'Amato

Naxxar Lions FC

1920 • no website
Coach: Vince Carbonaro

Second level final table 2016/17

		Pld	W	D	L	F	A	Pts
1	Lija Athletic FC	26	16	6	4	63	34	54
2	Senglea Athletic FC	26	16	5	5	57	21	53
3	Naxxar Lions FC	26	16	3	7	57	37	51
4	Qormi FC	26	13	7	6	36	26	46
5	Mqabba FC	26	13	5	8	39	32	44
6	Pietà Hotspurs FC	26	13	2	11	48	38	41
7	Vittoriosa Stars FC	26	12	4	10	50	37	40
8	Sirens FC	26	10	4	12	40	44	34
9	Melita FC	26	8	7	11	29	39	31
10	Żebbuġ Rangers FC	26	8	6	12	40	47	30
11	Rabat Ajax FC	26	7	6	13	33	54	27
12	Marsa FC	26	7	4	15	35	49	25
13	Gharghur FC	26	4	6	16	30	65	18
14	Fgura United FC	26	3	7	16	20	54	16

Promotion/Relegation play-off

(12/05/17)
Mosta 3-1 Qormi

DOMESTIC CUP

FA Trophy 2016/17

THIRD ROUND

(29/11/16)
St Andrews 3-0 Birkirkara
Senglea 3-2 Hibernians *(aet)*

(30/11/16)
Marsa 3-2 Xewkija *(aet)*
Pietà 0-2 Lija
Sliema 3-2 Mosta

(07/12/16)
Victoria Wanderers 5-0 Mgarr

(13/12/16)
Floriana 5-0 Birzebbuga
Gharghur 0-6 Tarxien
Siggiewi 0-2 Mqabba
Swieqi 0-1 Qrendi

(14/12/16)
Balzan 3-1 Żebbuġ
Sirens 1-2 Pembroke
Valletta 1-0 San Gwann
Victoria Hotspurs 2-3 Ghajnsielem
Vittoriosa 3-2 Gżira

(11/01/17)
Nadur 0-2 Hamrun

FOURTH ROUND

(17/01/17)
Lija 0-3 Tarxien
Vittoriosa 1-2 Senglea *(aet)*

(18/01/17)
Balzan 1-0 Valletta
Floriana 4-1 Ghajnsielem
Hamrun 1-0 Mqabba
Marsa 1-2 Pembroke
Sliema 5-0 Qrendi
Victoria Wanderers 1-0 St Andrews

QUARTER-FINALS

(18/02/17)
Senglea 0-0 Sliema *(aet; 2-3 on pens)*

(19/02/17)
Balzan 1-2 Tarxien *(Baker 42og; T Caruana 51p, Arab 114og) (aet)*

Floriana 2-0 Hamrun *(Fontanella 21, Pepe 25)*

Victoria Wanderers 2-0 Pembroke *(Attard 28og, Djordjević 48)*

SEMI-FINALS

(13/05/17)
Tarxien 0-3 Sliema *(Denni 23, Incorvaia 38, Scerri 63)*

Victoria Wanderers 1-3 Floriana *(Giarrizo 45; S Pisani 23, 71p, Vella 53)*

FINAL

(20/05/17)
National Stadium, Ta' Qali
FLORIANA FC 2 *(Ruiz 4, Borg 90+3)*
SLIEMA WANDERERS FC 0
Referee: *Tonna*
FLORIANA: *Haber, Scicluna, Pepe, Ruiz, Camenzuli, Nayar, Chiesa (Borg 86), S Pisani, Vella (Cini 71), Varela, Fontanella*
SLIEMA: *Saraò, A Muscat, Bianciardi, Pearson, Incorvaia (Xuereb 67), Muchardi (Spiteri 81), Scerri, Correa, Temile, Denni (Mintoff 32), Farrugia*

Floriana claimed the FA Trophy for the 20th time with a 2-0 victory over 21-time record winners Sliema Wanderers in the final

MOLDOVA

Federatia Moldoveneasca de Fotbal (FMF)

Address	Str. Tricolorului 39 MD-2012 Chisinau
Tel	+373 22 210 413
Fax	+373 22 210 432
E-mail	fmf@fmf.md
Website	fmf.md

President	Pavel Cebanu
General secretary	Nicolai Cebotari
Media officer	Victor Daghi
Year of formation	1990
National stadium	Zimbru, Chisinau (10,500)

DIVIZIA NATIONALA CLUBS

 1 **FC Academia Chisinau**

 2 **FC Dacia Chisinau**

 3 **FC Dinamo-Auto**

 4 **FC Milsami Orhei**

 5 **CS Petrocub**

 6 **FC Saxan**

 7 **FC Sheriff**

 8 **CSF Speranta**

 9 **FC Ungheni**

 10 **FC Zaria Balti**

 11 **FC Zimbru Chisinau**

PROMOTED CLUBS

 12 **FC Sfintul Gheorghe**

 13 **FC Spicul Chiscareni**

KEY

- UEFA Champions League
- UEFA Europa League
- Promoted
- Relegated

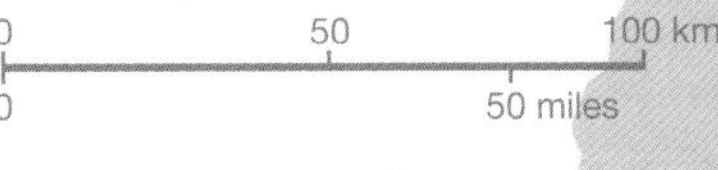

Sheriff strike it rich again

For the third season in a row, points alone could not deliver a clear winner of Moldova's Divizia Nationala, and for the second successive campaign an additional 'Golden Game' was required to reveal the champions. As in 2015/16, it was FC Sheriff who emerged victorious, with FC Dacia once again the unlucky losers.

A penalty shoot-out win enabled Sheriff to lift the league trophy for the 15th time in 17 years and also seal their seventh domestic double, the first part having been completed five days earlier with a record-equalling 5-0 win against Zaria Balti in the Moldovan Cup final.

Tiraspol side retain title in repeat play-off triumph

Dacia denied again after spot-kick ordeal

Double sealed with 5-0 win over Zaria in cup final

Domestic league

Although Sheriff and Dacia were ultimately obliged to go into overtime in their bid for championship glory, they were not the only two teams involved in an enthralling, unpredictable title race, with Zaria and 2014/15 champions Milsami Orhei also having a large say. Twists and turns abounded, as did changes at the top of the table. Each of the four contenders dropped points against each other, Dacia winning twice and losing once against Sheriff, who in turn took six points off Milsami, who did likewise against Zaria, two-time victors against Dacia.

Milsami did their best work in the autumn, winning 11 and drawing one of their 12 matches leading up to the mid-season shutdown, at which stage they held a two-point lead over Sheriff with a game in hand. Dacia, in contrast, were the kings of the spring, their third coach of the season, ex-Moldova striker Viorel Frunza, making a sensational start to his new career by leading the club to 12 wins in 13 games. Zaria's best sequence was a nine-match winning streak straddling the winter break, whereas Sheriff, under Italian coach Roberto Bordin, an early-season replacement for Frenchman Bruno Irles, were generally the most consistent team of the four and also by far the most prolific in attack.

Goal difference, however, was not a significant factor in Divizia Nationala classification. Head-to-head records had decided the 2014/15 title in Milsami's favour but that was because three teams finished level on points. When just two were locked together at the top, the tie-breaker was a championship play-off on neutral soil. A second such fixture in as many seasons was confirmed when the top two prevailed on the final day, Sheriff with ease, 6-0 against bottom club FC Ungheni, who were therefore relegated, while Dacia edged past the other strugglers, FC Saxan, 3-2. Milsami also beat Zaria 2-0, but only to finish third.

The Golden Match, in Chisinau's Zimbru stadium, was as tightly contested as the campaign in general, with Sheriff taking the lead in the first half, Dacia equalising in the second and no further goals ensuing in extra time. A title-winning hero was needed in the penalty shoot-out and Sheriff provided an unlikely one in veteran third-choice goalkeeper Serghei Juric, who saved two kicks. Joy for Sheriff brought despair for Dacia, empty-handed again despite accumulating the same amount of points as the champions for the third year in a row.

Domestic cup

Sheriff had not won the double for seven years but their 15th league title was preceded by a ninth victory in the Moldovan Cup. Zaria, the holders, kept them at bay until half-time, but four goals in the first 15 minutes of the second period – two apiece from Vitalie Damascan and Cyrille Bayala – settled the outcome, with the final scoreline of 5-0 matching the highest winning margin in the fixture.

Europe

Sheriff's domestic double made up for a rapid exit from Europe – a fate shared by both Zaria and Dacia. The only tie won by a Moldovan club came courtesy of an added-time strike by Zimbru's Brazilian defender Emerson that earned his team an away-goals success against Georgian club Chikhura Sachkhere.

National team

Two draws against Georgia – 1-1 in Tbilisi, 2-2 in Chisinau – provided the Moldovan national team with the only points from their opening six 2018 FIFA World Cup qualifiers. Heavy defeats by Wales and Serbia got the campaign off on the wrong foot, and by the end of term, despite Sheriff striker Radu Ginsari's third goal in as many games, the sad fact was that Moldova's only victories in three years of international football had come in friendlies against Andorra and San Marino.

DOMESTIC SEASON AT A GLANCE

Divizia Nationala 2016/17 final table

			Home					Away					Total					
		Pld	W	D	L	F	A	W	D	L	F	A	W	D	L	F	A	Pts
1=	FC Dacia Chisinau	30	11	2	2	30	8	11	1	3	24	7	22	3	5	54	15	69
	FC Sheriff	**30**	**12**	**0**	**3**	**44**	**7**	**10**	**3**	**2**	**27**	**8**	**22**	**3**	**5**	**71**	**15**	**69**
3	FC Milsami Orhei	30	13	1	1	35	7	9	1	5	22	13	22	2	6	57	20	68
4	FC Zaria Balti	30	10	2	3	29	10	10	3	2	27	11	20	5	5	56	21	65
5	FC Zimbru Chisinau	30	8	3	4	19	8	5	4	6	13	21	13	7	10	32	29	46
6	CS Petrocub	30	5	5	5	19	18	3	5	7	12	20	8	10	12	31	38	34
7	CSF Speranta	30	4	3	8	11	13	3	5	7	13	22	7	8	15	24	35	29
8	FC Academia Chisinau	30	4	2	9	12	25	4	1	10	9	27	8	3	19	21	52	27
9	FC Dinamo-Auto	30	3	5	7	14	24	2	3	10	17	34	5	8	17	31	58	23
10	FC Saxan	30	5	3	7	19	24	0	1	14	4	33	5	4	21	23	57	19
11	FC Ungheni	30	2	3	10	12	31	2	2	11	7	48	4	5	21	19	79	17

Championship play-off

(30/05/17)
Zimbru, Chisinau
FC SHERIFF 1 *(Damascan 37)*
FC DACIA CHISINAU 1 *(Posmac 73)*
(aet; 3-0 on pens)
Referee: *Banari*
SHERIFF: *Juric, Jardan (Rozgoniuc 55), Savić, Dionatan, Sušić, Yahaya (Joálisson 118), Bayala, Ginsari (Oancea 91), Badibanga (Jabbie 63), Ricardinho, Damascan*
DACIA: *Railean, Seoane, Mamah, Posmac, Gavrilenko (Diarra 71), Palavandishvili, Pascenco (Sarmov 60), Zastavniy, Bejan (Jalba 79), Kablash (Cojocaru 55), Isa*

European qualification 2017/18

Champion/Cup winner: FC Sheriff (second qualifying round)

FC Dacia Chisinau (first qualifying round)
FC Milsami Orhei (first qualifying round)
FC Zaria Balti (first qualifying round)

Top scorer Ricardinho (Sheriff), 15 goals
Relegated clubs FC Ungheni, FC Saxan (withdrew), FC Academia Chisinau (withdrew)
Promoted clubs FC Sfintul Gheorghe, FC Spicul Chiscareni
Cup final FC Sheriff 5-0 FC Zaria Balti

Player of the season

Ricardinho
(FC Sheriff)

Sheriff boasted the most potent attack in the 2016/17 Divizia Nationala, scoring 71 goals – 17 more than their play-off opponents Dacia. Directly responsible for a considerable percentage of that haul was the team's Brazilian star, Ricardinho. The 27-year-old's fourth season in Tiraspol brought him a second golden boot (after 2014/15), and in addition to scoring 15 goals – three more than his Croatian team-mate Josip Brezovac - he also topped the assists chart with 14. In the summer he left for Belgrade to join Serbian heavyweights FK Crvena zvezda.

Newcomer of the season

Vitalie Damascan
(FC Zimbru Chisinau/ FC Sheriff)

Transferred from Zimbru to Sheriff in the winter break, 18-year-old Damascan made an astonishing impact. The dynamic young striker's first goal for his new club came against his old one, in a crucial 1-0 victory, and after scoring three more in the regular league campaign, he bagged a brace in the cup final victory over Zaria before putting Sheriff 1-0 up in the championship play-off against Dacia. An Under-21 international already, his natural eye for goal and nerveless big-game temperament could turn out to be invaluable assets to the senior Moldova side.

Team of the season
(4-3-2-1)

Coach: Bordin *(Sheriff)*

MOLDOVA

NATIONAL TEAM

Top five all-time caps
Alexandru Epureanu & **Victor Golovatenco** (79); Radu Rebeja (74); Serghey Clescenco (69); Ivan Testimitanu (56)

Top five all-time goals
Serghey Clescenco (11); Serghey Rogaciov (9); **Igor Bugaiov**, Serghey Dadu & Iurie Miterev (8)

Results 2016/17

05/09/16	Wales (WCQ)	A	Cardiff	L	0-4	
06/10/16	Serbia (WCQ)	H	Chisinau	L	0-3	
09/10/16	Republic of Ireland (WCQ)	H	Chisinau	L	1-3	*Bugaiov (45+1)*
12/11/16	Georgia (WCQ)	A	Tbilisi	D	1-1	*Gatcan (78)*
17/01/17	Qatar	A	Doha	D	1-1	*Cojocari (24)*
19/03/17	San Marino	A	Serravalle	W	2-0	*Posmac (26), Gatcan (72)*
24/03/17	Austria (WCQ)	A	Vienna	L	0-2	
27/03/17	Turkey	A	Eskisehir	L	1-3	*Ginsari (90+2)*
06/06/17	Israel	A	Netanya	D	1-1	*Ginsari (51)*
11/06/17	Georgia (WCQ)	H	Chisinau	D	2-2	*Ginsari (15), Dedov (36)*

Appearances 2016/17

Coach: Igor Dobrovolski (RUS)	27/08/67		WAL	SRB	IRL	GEO	Qat	Smr	AUT	Tur	Isr	GEO	Caps	Goals
Ilie Cebanu	29/12/86	Mordovia (RUS)	G	G		G							24	-
Ion Jardan	10/01/90	Zimbru /Sheriff	D			M	s46	s66					17	-
Andrian Cascaval	10/06/87	Luch-Energia (RUS)	D				s74						9	-
Alexandru Epureanu	27/09/86	İstanbul Başakşehir (TUR)	D	D		D			D	D		D	79	7
Igor Armas	14/07/87	Kuban (RUS)	D		D36								51	4
Artur Ionita	17/08/90	Cagliari (ITA)	M						s62				25	2
Alexandru Gatcan	27/03/84	Rostov (RUS)	M	M	M	M		M76	M				55	5
Evgheny Cebotari	16/10/84	Sibir (RUS)	M75	M77	s61				M	M	s66	M	53	1
Andrei Cojocari	21/01/87	Milsami	M	M	M		M	M		M	s76	s73	31	2
Alexandr Dedov	26/07/89	Milsami	M85	M63	M		M85	M83	M	M	M	M	42	3
Radu Ginsari	10/12/91	Sheriff	A75	s77			A	A	A	A	A	A	18	4
Igor Bugaiov	26/06/84	Zaria	s75	A	A	A	A56	A76	A	A56	s77	s73	52	8
Eugen Sidorenco	19/03/89	Milsami	s75	s63	s83	M70		s46		s56			34	7
Maxim Mihaliov	22/08/86	Zaria	s85	s69		M77	M75	s76	s90	M46			11	-
Petru Racu	17/07/87	Milsami		D		D41		D66	s80	D46	s68	s78	44	-
Catalin Carp	20/10/93	Viitorul (ROU) /Ufa (RUS)		D							M76	M73	13	1
Vadim Bolohan	15/08/86	Milsami		D	D	D	D	D84	D90	D	D68		21	-
Gheorghe Andronic	25/09/91	Milsami		M69	M83	s77		s76					10	1
Nicolae Calancea	29/08/86	U Craiova (ROU)			G								18	-
Vitalie Bordian	11/08/84	Sheriff			D	M	D74				D	D	45	1
Veaceslav Posmac	07/11/90	Dacia			D	D		D	D	s46	D	D	19	2
Evgheny Zasavitschi	24/11/92	Trakai (LTU)			M61								1	-
Victor Golovatenco	28/04/84	Zaria			s36	s41	D	D	D80	D			79	3
Alexandru Antoniuc	23/05/89	Milsami				s70		M46	M62	s46	M90	M	29	3
Alexei Coselev	19/11/93	Sheriff					G46	G					3	-
Vladislav Ivanov	07/05/90	Sheriff /Dinamo-Auto					M46	s83					7	-
Dinu Graur	27/12/94	Milsami					M56				s90		2	-
Serghei Pascenco	18/12/82	Zaria					s46			G	s46		19	-
Maxim Antoniuc	15/01/91	Academia					s56						9	-
Artiom Zabun	23/04/96	Victoria Bardar					s56						1	-
Sergiu Platica	05/06/91	Speranta					s75						1	-
Igor Andronic	11/03/88	Speranta					s85						3	-
Maxim Potirniche	13/06/89	Sheriff						s84					7	-
Stanislav Namasco	10/11/86	Levadiakos (GRE)							G		G46	G	45	-
Igor Tigirlas	24/02/84	Zaria									D	D78	23	1
Gheorghe Anton	27/01/93	Zimbru									M66		1	-
Eugen Cociuc	11/05/93	Žilina (SVK)									M77	M73	4	-

EUROPE

FC Sheriff

Second qualifying round - Hapoel Beer Sheva FC (ISR)

A 2-3 *Ivančić (22), Brezovec (64)*

Mitrev, Aliti, Ginsari (Metoua 31), Ivančić (Subotic 74), Ricardinho, Yahaya, Škvorc, Brezovec, Sušić, Kvržić, Savić (Dupovac 46). Coach: Bruno Irles (FRA)

Red card: Aliti 26

H 0-0

Mitrev, Ginsari, Ivančić, Metoua, Škvorc, Brezovec, Subotic (Ricardinho 57), Oancea (Puntus 82), Sušić, Kvržić, Savić. Coach: Bruno Irles (FRA)

FC Dacia Chisinau

First qualifying round - Käpäz PFK (AZE)

A 0-0

Celeadnic, Slinkin, Bulgaru, Posmac, Valeev (Gavrilenko 40), Bugaiov (Mani 61), Bejan (Bugneac 83), Kozhanov, Cociuc, Mamah, Feshchuk. Coach: Oleg Bejenari (MDA)

H 0-1

Celeadnic, Slinkin, Bulgaru, Posmac, Bejan (Bugneac 72), Kozhanov (Bugaiov 77), Mani (Valeev 67), Cociuc, Gavrilenko, Mamah, Feshchuk. Coach: Oleg Bejenari (MDA)

FC Zaria Balti

First qualifying round - Videoton FC (HUN)

A 0-3

Pascenco, Golovatenco, Onica (Rata 81), Novicov, Erhan, Picusceac, Ovsiannicov (Boghiu 69), Tigirlas, Mihaliov, Gómez, Grosu (Suvorov 72). Coach: Vlad Goian (MDA)

Red cards: Picusceac 53, Suvorov 90+2

H 2-0 *Mihaliov (9), Ovsiannicov (29)*

Paşcenco, Golovatenco, Onica, Novicov, Erhan, Ovsiannicov, Tigirlas, Boghiu, Mihaliov, Gómez, Grosu. Coach: Vlad Goian (MDA)

FC Zimbru Chisinau

First qualifying round - FC Chikhura Sachkhere (GEO)

H 0-1

Rusu, Diego Lima (Zagaevschi 46), Anton, Spataru (Daniel Jalo 86), Amâncio Fortes, Luan, Alex Bruno, Emerson, Jardan, Izaldo, Coulibaly (Erick 81). Coach: Flavius Stoican (ROU)

Red card: Anton 36

A 3-2 *Emerson (45+2, 90+3), Jardan (61)*

Rusu, Spataru, Amâncio Fortes (Burghiu 88), Erick (Zagaevschi 80), Luan, Alex Bruno, I Damascan, Emerson, Jardan, Izaldo, Coulibaly (Diego Lima 39). Coach: Flavius Stoican (ROU)

Second qualifying round - Osmanlıspor (TUR)

H 2-2 *Zagaevschi (24), I Damascan (62)*

Rusu, Diego Lima (Burghiu 74), Amâncio Fortes (Rusnac 90), Zagaevschi, Erick, Luan, Alex Bruno, Hugo Moreira, I Damascan (Izaldo 85), Emerson, Jardan. Coach: Flavius Stoican (ROU)

A 0-5

Rusu, Diego Lima, Amâncio Fortes, Zagaevschi (Anton 57), Erick (Spataru 46; Daniel Jalo 76), Luan, Alex Bruno, Hugo Moreira, I Damascan, Emerson, Jardan. Coach: Flavius Stoican (ROU)

DOMESTIC LEAGUE CLUB-BY-CLUB

FC Academia Chisinau

2006 • Joma Arena (1,200); Satesc, Ghidighici (1,500) • academia.md

Coach: Viorel Frunza; (12/02/17) Sergei Secu

2016

24/07	h	Ungheni	W	4-1	*Birdan, Cricimari 2, Slivca*
30/07	a	Saxan	L	0-1	
06/08	h	Zimbru	L	0-2	
13/08	a	Dacia	L	0-2	
20/08	h	Milsami	L	0-4	
11/09	a	Speranta	W	1-0	*Vremea*
17/09	h	Sheriff	L	0-1	
25/09	a	Petrocub	W	1-0	*Apostol*
30/09	h	Zaria	L	0-2	
16/10	a	Dinamo-Auto	L	1-3	*Vremea*
21/10	a	Ungheni	W	2-1	*Jalba, Apostol*
29/10	h	Saxan	W	1-0	*Vremea*
05/11	a	Zimbru	L	0-2	
19/11	h	Dacia	L	0-1	
25/11	a	Milsami	L	0-2	
04/12	h	Speranta	W	3-1	*Jalba 2, Kurzenev*
10/12	a	Sheriff	L	0-1	

2017

24/02	h	Petrocub	W	2-1	*O Andronic, Burlaca*
28/02	a	Zaria	L	0-6	
06/03	h	Dinamo-Auto	L	1-2	*O Andronic*
12/03	h	Dinamo-Auto	D	1-1	*O Andronic*
17/03	a	Saxan	L	0-1	
31/03	h	Ungheni	L	0-1	
05/04	a	Milsami	L	2-3	*O Andronic, Polyutkin*
09/04	h	Zaria	L	0-4	
14/04	a	Sheriff	W	2-1	*Rosca, Vremea*
30/04	a	Zimbru	L	0-4	
03/05	h	Dacia	L	0-4	
12/05	h	Petrocub	D	0-0	
21/05	a	Speranta	D	0-0	

No	Name	Nat	DoB	Pos	Aps	(s)	Gls
12	Oleg Andronic		06/02/89	A	18	(6)	4
7	Valeriu Andronic		21/12/82	M	8	(1)	
9	Maxim Antoniuc		15/01/91	A	6	(6)	
17	Mihai Apostol		21/01/97	M	22	(1)	2
12	Cristian Avram		27/07/94	G	25		
8	Valentin Birdan		13/05/95	M	15	(1)	1
14	Ivan Burlaca		12/06/98	D	7	(6)	1
11	Ivan Carandasov		21/01/91	M	5	(3)	
7	Dan Cater		28/02/96	A	6	(3)	
13	Eugen Celeadnic		09/10/90	D	17	(1)	
26	Petru Costin		08/07/97	D	13		
10	Vadim Cricimari	RUS	22/08/88	D	6	(3)	2
9	Daniel Danu		28/12/97	A	2	(5)	
23	Oleg Dinga		31/01/98	G	3	(1)	
1	Maxim Frunza		06/01/96	G	2	(1)	
7	Sergiu Istrati		07/08/88	A	2		
2	Cristin Jalba		02/07/97	M	13	(1)	3
7	Aleksei Kurzenev	RUS	09/01/95	A	5		1
28	Ion Moroz		07/02/94	M	1	(5)	
17	Petru Ojog		17/07/90	M	3		
28	Valeriu Osipenco		27/07/96	M	6	(3)	
9	Alexandru Parfeni		14/07/96	M	2	(4)	
27	Viktor Patrashko	RUS	26/09/98	D	14		
20	Dan Pisla		14/06/86	D	6	(5)	
27	Anton Polyutkin	RUS	02/02/93	D	8	(1)	1
4	Dumitru Privalov		26/11/97	A	7		
3	Mihai Rosca		26/03/95	D	23		1
5	Ion Sandu		09/03/93	D	2		
13	Eugeniu Slivca		13/07/89	M	7	(3)	1
6	Vasile Soltan		09/12/92	M	9	(1)	
18	Vasile Stefu		26/07/00	A	3	(7)	
6	Corneliu Tibuleac		23/08/96	M	20	(1)	
8	Iaser Turcan		07/01/98	D	12	(1)	
16	Mihai Turcan		20/08/89	A	5	(4)	
19	Dan Ursu		10/10/97	M		(5)	
18	Nikita Vorona	RUS	08/07/95	A	8		
20	Alexandru Vremea		03/11/91	M	19	(3)	4

MOLDOVA

FC Dacia Chisinau

1999 • Moldova, Speia (8,550); Joma Arena (1,200) • fcdacia.md

Major honours
Moldovan League (1) 2011

Coach: Oleg Bejenari; (15/08/16) Igors Kļosovs (LVA); (13/02/17) Viorel Frunza

Date		Opponent		Score	Scorers
2016					
25/07	h	Zimbru	L	0-1	
06/08	a	Milsami	L	0-1	
13/08	h	Academia	W	2-0	*Palagnyuk, Feshchuk*
20/08	a	Speranta	W	2-1	*Cojocaru, Slinkin*
10/09	a	Petrocub	W	4-0	*Isa, Sarmov, Kablash, Bursuc*
17/09	h	Zaria	L	1-2	*og (Golovatenco)*
21/09	h	Sheriff	W	3-0	*Feshchuk 2, Cojocaru*
25/09	a	Dinamo-Auto	W	3-0	*Feshchuk (p), Bursuc, Palagnyuk*
01/10	h	Ungheni	W	3-0	*Feshchuk 3*
15/10	a	Saxan	W	2-0	*Sarmov (p), Isa*
21/10	a	Zimbru	W	1-0	*Bejan*
05/11	h	Milsami	D	1-1	*Karaneychev*
19/11	a	Academia	W	1-0	*Posmac (p)*
26/11	h	Speranta	W	1-0	*Isa*
30/11	a	Sheriff	L	0-1	
04/12	h	Petrocub	D	1-1	*Bejan*
10/12	a	Zaria	L	0-1	
2017					
25/02	h	Dinamo-Auto	W	4-1	*Bejan, Sarmov, Kablash 2*
01/03	a	Ungheni	W	2-1	*Pascenco, og (Popovici)*
05/03	h	Saxan	W	2-0	*Sarmov, Mudrac*
11/03	h	Ungheni	W	3-0	*Kablash 2, Sarmov (p)*
16/03	a	Milsami	D	0-0	
01/04	h	Zaria	W	1-0	*Isa*
05/04	a	Sheriff	W	1-0	*Cojocaru*
14/04	h	Zimbru	W	3-1	*Bejan, Bulgaru, Seoane*
30/04	h	Petrocub	W	1-0	*Diarra*
03/05	a	Academia	W	4-0	*Ilescu, Gavrilenko, Diarra 2*
07/05	a	Speranta	W	1-0	*Cojocaru*
12/05	h	Dinamo-Auto	W	4-1	*Diarra 2, Ilescu, Cojocaru*
21/05	a	Saxan	W	3-2	*Sarmov 2, Isa*

No	Name	Nat	DoB	Pos	Aps	(s)	Gls
10	Alexandru Bejan		07/05/96	M	18	(2)	4
8	Maxim Bucataru		27/05/92	M	4	(8)	
4	Simeon Bulgaru		26/05/85	D	24		1
14	Andrei Bursuc		23/05/97	M	3	(4)	2
1	Dumitru Celeadnic		23/04/92	G	1	(1)	
17	Eugeniu Cociuc		11/05/93	M	3		
20	Maxim Cojocaru		13/01/98	D	10	(17)	5
3	Petru Costin		08/07/97	D		(2)	
17	Cheick Diarra	FRA	23/06/93	A	3	(4)	5
28	Maxym Feshchuk	UKR	25/11/85	A	12	(1)	7
19	Maxym Gavrilenko	UKR	18/08/91	M	9	(2)	1
15	Denis Ilescu		20/01/87	D	3	(2)	2
11	Ismail Isa	BUL	26/06/89	A	14	(4)	5
28	Cristian Jalba		02/09/97	M	6	(1)	
3	Vasile Jardan		20/07/93	D	4	(3)	
9	Olexandr Kablash	UKR	05/09/89	M	17	(9)	5
22	Georgi Karaneychev	BUL	09/06/88	A	3	(7)	1
24	Abdul-Gafar Mamah	TOG	24/08/85	D	27		
15	Sapol Mani	TOG	05/06/91	M	5	(3)	
8	Andrei Marandici		14/12/98	D		(6)	
3	Sandu Mateescu		29/12/98	M		(3)	
23	Victor Mudrac		03/03/94	D	6	(6)	1
26	Zaurbek Olisaev	RUS	02/02/94	A	2	(1)	
7	Vasyl Palagnyuk	UKR	07/03/91	A	5	(5)	2
14	Guga Palavandishvili	GEO	14/08/93	M	7		
7	Alexandr Pascenco		28/05/89	M	11	(1)	1
5	Veaceslav Posmac		07/11/90	D	25		1
19	Dorian Railean		13/10/93	G	29		
18	Oleg Roganov	RUS	26/04/95	M	8	(3)	
8	Georgi Sarmov	BUL	07/09/85	M	23		7
13	Diego Seoane	ESP	26/04/88	D	10		1
13	Ruslan Shaukhvalov	RUS	31/12/96	M		(1)	
2	Andriy Slinkin	UKR	19/02/91	D	11	(1)	1
29	Iaser Turcan		07/01/98	D	1	(1)	
25	Dmytro Yusov	UKR	11/05/93	M	2	(4)	
21	Volodymyr Zastavniy	UKR	02/09/90	D	24	(2)	

FC Dinamo-Auto

2009 • Dinamo-Auto, Tirnauca (1,300); Teren Sintetic, Tirnauca (1,000) • dinamo-auto.com

Coach: Nicolai Mandricenco; (27/08/16) (Nicolai Rudac); (27/09/16) Iury Groshev

Date		Opponent		Score	Scorers
2016					
23/07	a	Speranta	D	0-0	
30/07	h	Sheriff	L	0-1	
05/08	a	Petrocub	L	1-3	*Tofan*
14/08	h	Zaria	L	1-3	*A Popovici*
27/08	a	Ungheni	L	1-2	*Truhanov (p)*
10/09	h	Saxan	W	1-0	*Bobrov*
17/09	a	Zimbru	L	0-1	
25/09	h	Dacia	L	0-3	
30/09	a	Milsami	L	1-4	*Diarra*
15/10	h	Academia	W	3-1	*Casian (p), Onofrei, Diarra*
21/10	h	Speranta	L	1-4	*Volosin*
30/10	a	Sheriff	L	0-3	
04/11	h	Petrocub	L	0-1	
20/11	a	Zaria	L	1-2	*Diarra*
29/11	h	Ungheni	D	2-2	*Mudrac, Onofrei*
03/12	a	Saxan	W	3-0	*Diarra (p), Onofrei 2*
10/12	h	Zimbru	D	1-1	*og (Cararus)*
2017					
25/02	a	Dacia	L	1-4	*Rassulov*
01/03	h	Milsami	L	0-4	
06/03	a	Academia	W	2-1	*Bursuc, Bugneac*
12/03	a	Academia	D	1-1	*Bursuc*
16/03	h	Petrocub	D	2-2	*Truhanov (p), Onofrei*
31/03	a	Speranta	L	1-4	*Onofrei*
09/04	h	Saxan	W	2-0	*Mandricenco, Onofrei*
14/04	a	Ungheni	D	2-2	*Ivanov, Onofrei*
30/04	a	Zaria	L	2-3	*Mandricenco, Jardan*
03/05	h	Milsami	L	0-1	
07/05	h	Sheriff	D	0-0	
12/05	a	Dacia	L	1-4	*Ivanov*
21/05	h	Zimbru	D	1-1	*Borovschi*

No	Name	Nat	DoB	Pos	Aps	(s)	Gls
19	Andrian Apostol		19/01/92	M	1	(2)	
23	Valentin Birdan		13/05/95	M	7	(2)	
22	Serghei Bobrov		07/09/91	A	10	(3)	1
19	Eugeniu Borovschi		16/04/94	A	3	(4)	1
25	Andrei Bugneac		30/03/88	A	10	(1)	1
8	Andrei Bursuc		23/05/97	M	10	(3)	2
7	Alexei Casian		01/10/87	D	28	(1)	1
17	Anatol Cheptine		20/05/90	M	3	(3)	
14	Vadim Cricimari	RUS	22/08/88	D	1		
9	Cheick Diarra	FRA	23/06/93	A	11		4
20	Serghei Gheorghiev		29/10/91	M	9		
2	Vladislav Ivanov		07/05/90	A	4	(4)	2
24	Vasile Jardan		20/07/93	D	9	(1)	1
9	Constantin Mandricenco		19/02/91	A	8	(1)	2
1	Ghenadie Mosneaga		25/04/85	G	23		
4	Victor Mudrac		03/03/94	M	12	(1)	1
4	Victor Negara		14/07/91	D	15	(5)	
22	Gheorghe Nicologlo		02/01/91	M	2	(2)	
18	Octavian Onofrei		16/05/91	A	11	(15)	8
15	Igor Poiarcov		26/07/90	M		(1)	
23	Dumitru Popescu		11/04/95	A	2	(2)	
11	Alexandr Popovici		09/04/77	A	21	(3)	1
5	Dmitri Popovici		05/08/83	D	27	(1)	
15	Vladimir Rassulov		11/11/92	M	23	(2)	1
6	Alexandr Scripcenco		13/01/91	D	24	(1)	
24	Stanislav Sinkovskii		16/04/94	M		(5)	
9	Valeriu Tiron		08/04/93	M	10	(1)	
19	Alexandru Tofan		19/08/87	M	4	(1)	1
10	Victor Truhanov		30/01/91	M	18	(2)	2
17	Andrei Turculet		14/07/96	D		(5)	
14	Vladislav Vatav		24/04/97	A	11	(5)	
8	Dmitri Volosin		26/07/94	M	6	(6)	1
1	Alexandr Zveagintsev		26/07/87	G	7	(1)	

FC Milsami Orhei

2005 • Municipal (3,000); CPSN, Vadul lui Voda (1,000) • milsami.md

Major honours
Moldovan League (1) 2015; Moldovan Cup (1) 2012

Coach: Andrian Sosnovschi

Date		Opponent		Score	Scorers
2016					
23/07	h	Saxan	W	2-0	*Sidorenco, Rakhmanov*
31/07	a	Zimbru	L	0-1	
06/08	h	Dacia	W	1-0	*Sidorenco*
20/08	a	Academia	W	4-0	*Zhigulev, Banović, Cojocari, Zenko*
10/09	a	Sheriff	L	0-2	
16/09	h	Petrocub	W	5-0	*Banović, Cojocari, Andronic 2, Belous*
21/09	h	Speranta	W	4-0	*Dedov, Andronic, Banović, Racu (p)*
25/09	a	Zaria	W	2-0	*Andronic, Belous*
30/09	h	Dinamo-Auto	W	4-1	*Racu 2 (1p), Zenko 2*
16/10	h	Ungheni	W	4-0	*Sidorenco, Rakhmanov, Banović, Zhigulev*
21/10	a	Saxan	W	1-0	*Zhigulev*
30/10	h	Zimbru	W	1-0	*Zenko*
05/11	a	Dacia	D	1-1	*Banović*
25/11	h	Academia	W	2-0	*Bello 2*
30/11	a	Speranta	W	2-0	*Belous, Andronic*
04/12	h	Sheriff	W	2-1	*Andronic, og (Rebenja)*
09/12	a	Petrocub	W	2-0	*Antoniuc, Banović*
2017					
24/02	h	Zaria	L	1-2	*Boiciuc*
01/03	a	Dinamo-Auto	W	4-0	*Boiciuc, Dedov, Balashov, Belous*
05/03	a	Ungheni	W	2-0	*Balashov, Boiciuc*
11/03	a	Sheriff	L	0-5	
16/03	h	Dacia	D	0-0	
01/04	a	Zimbru	L	0-1	
05/04	h	Academia	W	3-2	*Banović, Balashov 2*
09/04	a	Petrocub	L	1-3	*Boiciuc*
14/04	h	Speranta	W	1-0	*Racu*
30/04	h	Saxan	W	3-1	*Dedov, Boiciuc, Belous*
03/05	a	Dinamo-Auto	W	1-0	*Racu (p)*
08/05	a	Ungheni	W	2-0	*Belous 2*
21/05	h	Zaria	W	2-0	*Racu, Boiciuc*

No	Name	Nat	DoB	Pos	Aps	(s)	Gls
10	Gheorghe Andronic		25/09/91	M	19	(5)	6
16	Alexandru Antoniuc		23/05/89	M	10	(6)	1
19	Vitaliy Balashov	UKR	07/02/91	A	7	(3)	4
24	Igor Banović	CRO	12/05/87	M	26	(2)	7
14	Karlo Belak	CRO	22/04/91	M	3	(1)	
27	Yero Bello	NGA	11/12/87	A	5	(6)	2
26	Ilya Belous	RUS	01/01/95	A	9	(15)	7
6	Constantin Bogdan		29/12/93	D	6	(2)	
18	Alexandr Boiciuc		21/08/97	A	10	(3)	6
23	Vadim Bolohan		15/08/86	D	23		
11	Daniel Ciobanu		17/07/98	A		(1)	
15	Octavian Ciuntu		14/06/95	M		(1)	
17	Andrei Cojocari		21/01/87	M	20		2
7	Alexandr Dedov		26/07/89	M	24	(2)	3
6	Diego	BRA	03/02/89	D	6	(3)	
9	Alexandr Dulghier		03/01/95	M		(3)	
22	Dinu Graur		27/12/94	M	14	(9)	
3	Dan Gustiuc		05/03/97	D	4	(6)	
20	Sven Jajčinović	CRO	04/03/93	M	9	(15)	
4	Serhiy Melnyk	UKR	04/09/88	D	13	(10)	
1	Radu Mitu		04/11/94	G	30		
14	Aleksandr Morgunov	RUS	04/06/95	M	6	(2)	
55	Nejc Potokar	SVN	02/12/88	D	4	(1)	
5	Petru Racu		17/07/87	D	26		6
2	Artem Rakhmanov	BLR	10/07/90	D	14	(3)	2
2	Adil Rhaili	MAR	25/04/91	D		(1)	
8	Eugen Sidorenco		19/03/89	M	18	(5)	3
28	Nikolai Zenko	BLR	11/03/89	A	13	(7)	4
9	Ilya Zhigulev	RUS	01/02/96	M	11	(1)	3

CS Petrocub

Municipal (2,672); Baza Zimbru (2,142)

Coach: Eduard Blanuta; (23/02/17) Iurie Osipenco

Date		Opponent	Result	Scorers
2016				
30/07	a	Zaria	D 0-0	
05/08	h	Dinamo-Auto	W 3-1	*Burghiu, Ambros, D Taras*
13/08	a	Ungheni	W 2-0	*Slivca, V Macritschii*
21/08	h	Saxan	W 2-1	*V Macritschii, D Taras*
10/09	h	Dacia	L 0-4	
16/09	a	Milsami	L 0-5	
21/09	a	Zimbru	D 0-0	
25/09	h	Academia	L 0-1	
30/09	a	Speranta	L 0-1	
16/10	h	Sheriff	D 0-0	
30/10	h	Zaria	D 2-2	*Calugher, Slivca*
04/11	a	Dinamo-Auto	W 1-0	*Ambros*
19/11	h	Ungheni	W 5-0	*Popovici 2, A Rusu, Patras, og (Marjin)*
25/11	a	Saxan	L 0-2	
30/11	h	Zimbru	L 1-2	*V Macritschii*
04/12	a	Dacia	D 1-1	*Burghiu*
09/12	h	Milsami	L 0-2	
2017				
24/02	a	Academia	L 1-2	*Dima*
28/02	h	Speranta	D 1-1	*Dima*
04/03	a	Sheriff	L 0-4	
16/03	a	Dinamo-Auto	D 2-2	*Calugher, Patras*
20/03	h	Speranta	D 0-0	
31/03	h	Saxan	W 1-0	*Osipenco*
04/04	a	Ungheni	W 4-0	*Patras 2 (1p), Dima, V Rusu*
09/04	h	Milsami	W 3-1	*Plamadeala, A Rusu, Ursu*
15/04	a	Zaria	L 1-2	*Patras*
30/04	a	Dacia	L 0-1	
03/05	h	Sheriff	L 0-2	
07/05	h	Zimbru	D 1-1	*Plamadeala*
12/05	a	Academia	D 0-0	

No	Name	Nat	DoB	Pos	Aps	(s)	Gls
9	Vladimir Ambros		30/12/93	A	18		2
23	Maxim Antoniuc		15/01/91	A	8	(3)	
6	Kennedy Bahgob	CMR	04/06/98	M	3		
13	Vadim Bejenari		16/05/97	M	1	(9)	
15	Alexandr Belevschi		21/03/95	D	9	(2)	
19	Nicolai Borta		19/06/97	M	3	(6)	
94	Victor Buga		26/06/94	G	10		
3	Stefan Burghiu		28/03/91	D	14		2
1	Vasilii Buza		01/03/92	G	17		
17	Vadim Calugher		07/09/95	M	21	(4)	2
16	David Chemschi		12/05/95	D	22	(7)	
4	Eduard Ciornii		21/01/00	D		(1)	
20	Vladimir Cojocaru		18/04/88	M	1	(4)	
24	Alexandru Dem		06/06/98	M	1	(2)	
13	Igor Dima		11/02/93	A	10	(3)	3
20	Donalio Douanla	CMR	24/09/97	M	2	(1)	
6	Maxim Focsa		21/04/92	D	16		
33	Denis Gutul		15/08/99	G		(1)	
23	Andrei Macritschii		13/02/96	A	7	(3)	
9	Valerii Macritschii		13/02/96	D	14	(2)	3
1	Lionel Ndjomo	CMR	20/09/93	G	3		
2	Jacques Ndzomo	CMR	23/08/93	M	3		
3	Henry Onguene	CMR	25/07/93	M	2	(1)	
19	Valeriu Osipenco		27/07/96	M	9	(1)	1
8	Artur Patras		01/10/88	M	18	(3)	5
15	Vitalie Plamadeala		21/05/85	M	10	(2)	2
22	Dorin Popovici		01/07/96	M	5	(3)	2
7	Cristian Prozorovschi		21/04/94	M	3	(14)	
5	Arcadie Rusu		28/06/93	D	20	(6)	2
14	Vasile Rusu		28/06/85	D	26	(1)	1
11	Vladislav Slivca		10/09/98	D	23	(5)	2
21	Cristian Taras		26/09/98	M		(2)	
10	Dan Taras		13/02/94	M	25	(2)	2
18	Andrei Trifan		11/02/96	M	3	(9)	
9	Ion Ursu		19/08/94	A	3	(6)	1

FC Saxan

2010 • Ceadir-Lunga municipal (2,000) • fc-saxan.com

Coach: Oleg Fistican; (06/01/17) Ivan Tabanov

Date		Opponent	Result	Scorers
2016				
23/07	a	Milsami	L 0-2	
30/07	h	Academia	W 1-0	*Pislaru (p)*
05/08	a	Speranta	L 1-2	*P Fofana*
13/08	a	Sheriff	L 0-3	
21/08	a	Petrocub	L 1-2	*Sandu (p)*
10/09	a	Dinamo-Auto	L 0-1	
16/09	h	Ungheni	D 2-2	*M Fofana, Sandu*
01/10	a	Zimbru	L 0-2	
15/10	h	Dacia	L 0-2	
21/10	h	Milsami	L 0-1	
29/10	a	Academia	L 0-1	
04/11	h	Zaria	L 1-4	*Konan*
09/11	h	Speranta	D 2-2	*Puntus, Calmis*
20/11	h	Sheriff	L 1-5	*P Fofana*
25/11	h	Petrocub	W 2-0	*M Fofana, Puntus*
29/11	a	Zaria	L 0-2	
03/12	h	Dinamo-Auto	L 0-3	
09/12	a	Ungheni	L 0-3	
2017				
01/03	h	Zimbru	W 3-0	*Eza 2, Muyiwa*
05/03	a	Dacia	L 0-2	
11/03	a	Zimbru	D 0-0	
17/03	h	Academia	W 1-0	*Sangare*
31/03	a	Petrocub	L 0-1	
04/04	h	Speranta	L 0-1	
09/04	a	Dinamo-Auto	L 0-2	
30/04	a	Milsami	L 1-3	*Calaras*
03/05	h	Ungheni	W 3-0	*Calaras, Eza, Konan*
07/05	h	Zaria	D 1-1	*Eza*
12/05	a	Sheriff	L 1-7	*Shumchin*
21/05	h	Dacia	L 2-3	*Eza (p), og (Mamah)*

No	Name	Nat	DoB	Pos	Aps	(s)	Gls
77	Mohammed Aliyu	NGA	12/02/93	D	9	(1)	
34	Bendé Bende	CIV	17/08/95	M	6	(4)	
10	Dumitru Calaras		13/10/95	A	10		2
14	Constantin Calmis		19/08/95	D	15	(2)	1
22	Evgheny Cimpoes		29/06/98	A		(2)	
1	Andrei Colibaba		04/06/94	G	28		
21	Veaceslav Dobrioglo		17/12/90	D	5		
15	Samuel Duah	GHA	13/10/96	M	3		
88	Wilfried Eza	CIV	28/12/96	A	15	(1)	5
5	Mamadou Fofana	CIV	21/05/95	M	12	(7)	2
30	Philippe Fofana	CIV	18/07/96	A	8	(18)	2
8	Michael Gnolou	CIV	05/01/98	M	19	(2)	
20	Gafur Gulberdiyev	TKM	23/08/95	D	17	(2)	
19	Vladimir Haritov		05/01/95	M	18	(9)	
21	Nichita Horozov		25/02/96	M	1	(14)	
5	Salif Inoua	CMR	11/04/95	D	2		
7	Christ Konan	CIV	20/07/97	A	19	(3)	2
15	Ibrahim Koné	CIV	30/01/95	M	15	(2)	
25	Gnohoré Krizo	CIV	20/06/97	M	6	(1)	
88	Guram Maghaldadze	GEO	02/02/84	M		(1)	
17	Andrei Mincev		30/09/98	M	3	(3)	
15	Olabiran Muyiwa	NGA	07/09/98	A	10		1
23	Ion Pislaru		02/02/95	M	4	(1)	1
7	Artiom Puntus		31/05/95	A	8	(3)	2
11	Constantin Sandu		15/09/93	M	11	(3)	2
24	Idrissa Sangare	CIV	27/05/96	D	27		1
9	Roman Shumchin		11/03/93	M	10	(1)	1
23	Ismaila Soro	CIV	07/05/98	M	21	(1)	
1	Serghei Tanasoglo		08/10/94	G	1	(2)	
19	Mihail Tiscul		25/02/97	D	12		
17	Andrei Topciu		18/11/97	M	1	(4)	
25	David Traoré	CIV	01/01/97	M	5		
23	Ion Ursu		19/08/94	A	8	(10)	
12	Igor Vitev		09/03/88	G	1	(1)	

FC Sheriff

1997 • Sheriff Main (13,300); Sheriff Small (8,000); Sheriff Indoor (3,500) • fc-sheriff.com

Major honours
Moldovan League (15) 2001, 2002, 2003, 2004, 2005, 2006, 2007, 2008, 2009, 2010, 2012, 2013, 2014, 2016, 2017; Moldovan Cup (9) 1999, 2001, 2002, 2006, 2008, 2009, 2010, 2015, 2017

Coach: Bruno Irles (FRA); (04/10/16) Roberto Bordin (ITA)

Date		Opponent	Result	Scorers
2016				
23/07	h	Zaria	L 1-2	*Kvrzić*
30/07	a	Dinamo-Auto	W 1-0	*Rebenja*
06/08	h	Ungheni	W 7-0	*Savić, Rebenja, Brezovec (p), Kvrzić 2, Iurcu, Jabbie*
14/08	h	Saxan	W 3-0	*Brezovec 2, Subotic*
20/08	h	Zimbru	W 3-0	*og (Anton), Sušić, Kvrzić*
10/09	h	Milsami	W 2-0	*Brezovec (p), Škvorc*
17/09	a	Academia	W 1-0	*og (Jalba)*
21/09	a	Dacia	L 0-3	
25/09	h	Speranta	W 2-0	*Subotic, Balima*
16/10	a	Petrocub	D 0-0	
21/10	a	Zaria	D 0-0	
30/10	h	Dinamo-Auto	W 3-0	*Brezovec, Ricardinho (p), Subotic*
05/11	a	Ungheni	W 2-1	*Ricardinho, Rebenja*
20/11	a	Saxan	W 5-1	*Brezovec 2 (1p), Kvrzić, Rebenja, Svinarenco*
26/11	a	Zimbru	W 4-1	*Brezovec (p), Ricardinho 2, Ginsari*
30/11	h	Dacia	W 1-0	*Ginsari*
04/12	a	Milsami	L 1-2	*Ivančić*
10/12	h	Academia	W 1-0	*Brezovec*
2017				
24/02	a	Speranta	W 2-0	*Oancea, Brezovec*
04/03	h	Petrocub	W 4-0	*Bayala, Ricardinho 2, Brezovec*
11/03	h	Milsami	W 5-0	*Brezovec, Badibanga, Savić, Bayala, Ginsari*
16/03	a	Zaria	W 2-0	*Oancea, Ricardinho*
05/04	h	Dacia	L 0-1	
09/04	a	Zimbru	W 1-0	*Damascan*
14/04	h	Academia	L 1-2	*Ricardinho*
30/04	h	Speranta	W 4-1	*Ricardinho 3, Bayala*
03/05	a	Petrocub	W 2-0	*Bayala, Ricardinho*
07/05	a	Dinamo-Auto	D 0-0	
12/05	h	Saxan	W 7-1	*Savić, Ginsari, Bayala, Damascan 2, Joálisson 2*
21/05	a	Ungheni	W 6-0	*Damascan, Ricardinho 3, og (Negru), Bayala*

No	Name	Nat	DoB	Pos	Aps	(s)	Gls
3	Fidan Aliti	ALB	03/10/93	D	1		
9	Vladimir Ambros		30/12/93	M	2	(3)	
39	Ziguy Badibanga	BEL	26/11/91	M	6	(2)	1
14	Wilfried Balima	BFA	20/03/85	D	17	(6)	1
20	Cyrille Bayala	BFA	24/05/96	M	16	(6)	6
37	Vitalie Bordian		11/08/84	D	17	(2)	
30	Josip Brezovec	CRO	12/03/86	M	28		12
33	Mihail Caimacov		22/07/98	M		(2)	
28	Alexei Coselev		19/11/93	G	22		
99	Vitalie Damascan		24/01/99	A	2	(3)	4
23	Dionatan	SVK	24/07/92	D	5	(4)	
8	Radu Ginsari		10/12/91	M	14	(8)	4
89	Maxim Iurcu		01/02/93	A	1	(3)	1
11	Josip Ivančić	CRO	29/03/91	A	2	(7)	1
17	Vladislav Ivanov		07/05/90	A	4	(6)	
4	Khalifa Jabbie	SLE	20/01/93	M	13	(6)	1
3	Ion Jardan		10/01/90	D	8		
7	Joálisson	BRA	31/03/91	A		(4)	2
25	Serghei Juric		03/03/84	G	4		
18	Ibrahim Koné	CIV	30/01/95	M		(2)	
88	Zoran Kvrzić	BIH	07/08/88	M	18	(8)	5
15	Marcel Metoua	CIV	15/11/88	D	3	(2)	
1	Bozhidar Mitrev	BUL	31/03/87	G	4		
30	Evgheni Oancea		05/01/96	M	10	(2)	2
21	Maxim Potirniche		13/06/89	D	16	(1)	
23	Artiom Puntus		31/05/95	A		(1)	
88	Eugeniu Rebenja		05/03/95	A	11	(6)	4
11	Ricardinho	BRA	04/09/89	M	22	(4)	15
17	Artiom Rozgoniuc		01/10/95	M	1	(1)	
90	Vujadin Savić	SRB	01/07/90	D	14	(1)	3
26	Dino Škvorc	CRO	02/02/90	D	16		1
31	Danijel Subotic	SUI	31/01/89	A	5	(4)	3
55	Mateo Sušić	BIH	18/11/90	D	19	(1)	1
19	Serghei Svinarenco		18/09/96	D	2	(2)	1
34	Ivan Urvantev		02/05/97	A	7	(14)	
6	Victor	BRA	28/05/94	D	5	(2)	
24	Seidu Yahaya	GHA	31/12/89	M	15	(3)	

MOLDOVA

CSF Speranta

1991 • Nisporeni municipal (2,000) • no website

Coach: Cristian Efros

Date		Opponent		Score	Scorers
2016					
23/07	h	Dinamo-Auto	D	0-0	
31/07	a	Ungheni	D	0-0	
05/08	h	Saxan	W	2-1	*Platica, Pavlov*
14/08	a	Zimbru	L	0-2	
20/08	h	Dacia	L	1-2	*Platica*
11/09	h	Academia	L	0-1	
21/09	a	Milsami	L	0-4	
25/09	a	Sheriff	L	0-2	
30/09	h	Petrocub	W	1-0	*Lupusor*
16/10	a	Zaria	W	2-0	*Plamadeala, Igwe (p)*
21/10	a	Dinamo-Auto	W	4-1	*Dragan 2, Platica, Igwe*
29/10	h	Ungheni	W	3-0	*Lupusor, Igwe, Platica*
09/11	a	Saxan	D	2-2	*Plamadeala, Platica*
19/11	h	Zimbru	L	0-1	
26/11	a	Dacia	L	0-1	
30/11	h	Milsami	L	0-2	
04/12	a	Academia	L	1-3	*Dragan*
2017					
24/02	h	Sheriff	L	0-2	
28/02	a	Petrocub	D	1-1	*Platica*
04/03	h	Zaria	L	0-1	
20/03	a	Petrocub	D	0-0	
31/03	h	Dinamo-Auto	W	4-1	*Platica 2, D Andronic (p), Pisla*
04/04	a	Saxan	W	1-0	*Dragan*
08/04	h	Ungheni	L	0-1	
14/04	a	Milsami	L	0-1	
30/04	a	Sheriff	L	1-4	*Platica*
03/05	h	Zaria	D	0-0	
07/05	h	Dacia	L	0-1	
12/05	a	Zimbru	D	1-1	*Pisla*
21/05	h	Academia	D	0-0	

No	Name	Nat	DoB	Pos	Aps	(s)	Gls
18	David Andronic		09/07/95	M	19	(5)	1
20	Igor Andronic		11/03/88	D	14	(1)	
10	Oleg Andronic		06/02/89	A		(5)	
13	Ion Arabadji		31/07/84	D	8		
10	Vladimir Bogdanović	SRB	05/10/86	M	10		
5	Mihail Bolun		16/05/89	D	18	(3)	
31	Vasulii Buza		01/03/92	G	8		
3	Constantin Calmis		19/08/95	D	9	(1)	
15	Dan Cater		28/02/96	A		(2)	
78	Alexandru Chirilov		28/01/78	G	1		
27	Andrei Ciofu		31/05/84	M	9	(3)	
10	Serghei Ciuico		02/02/83	A		(2)	
2	Ichaka Diarra	MLI	18/01/95	D	1	(2)	
13	Igor Dima		11/02/93	A	5	(4)	
14	Serghei Diulgher		21/03/91	D	12		
23	Ion Dragan		14/06/94	A	12	(13)	4
22	Stefan Efros		08/05/90	D	28		
11	Irakli Goginashvili	GEO	29/03/94	M	2	(2)	
12	Andrei Gubanov	RUS	15/01/94	M	8	(7)	
19	Heron	BRA	19/04/90	D	4	(1)	
19	Ion Ibrean		21/03/98	A	2	(8)	
4	Akinjide Idowu	NGA	09/09/96	M	8	(1)	
11	Kastan Igwe	NGA	01/03/92	A	4	(4)	3
11	Maxim Iurcu		01/02/93	A	8	(2)	
9	Ahmed Kadiri	NGA	13/09/92	M	5	(4)	
25	Kelvin	BRA	14/03/95	G	2		
17	Oleg Lupusor		14/09/94	M	17	(6)	2
8	Vladimir Macritchii		13/02/96	D	9		
2	Vasile Marjin		15/07/97	D	1		
3	Vitalie Negru		15/01/87	M	9	(3)	
9	Mihail Negura		29/08/94	M	1	(4)	
33	Mihail Paius		06/02/83	G	5		
8	Ion Pavlov		29/08/91	M	5	(7)	1
20	Dan Pisla		14/06/86	M	6	(6)	2
7	Vitalie Plamadeala		21/05/85	M	8	(2)	2
21	Sergiu Platica		05/06/91	A	24	(6)	9
7	Viorel Primac		23/01/85	M	6	(3)	
14	Artiom Rozgoniuc		01/10/95	M	16		
15	Constantin Sandu		15/09/93	M	10	(2)	
24	Nicolai Tiverenco		30/03/96	D	2	(1)	
33	Nicolae Turcan		09/12/89	G	14		

FC Ungheni

2012 • Nisporeni municipal, Nisporeni (2,000) • cfungheni.com

Coach: Vadim Boret; (13/11/16) Nicolai Turcan; (01/02/17) Igor Ursachi

Date		Opponent		Score	Scorers
2016					
24/07	a	Academia	L	1-4	*Avram*
31/07	h	Speranta	D	0-0	
06/08	a	Sheriff	L	0-7	
13/08	h	Petrocub	L	0-2	
21/08	a	Zaria	L	0-3	
27/08	h	Dinamo-Auto	W	2-1	*Primac, Gusan*
16/09	a	Saxan	D	2-2	*Primac 2*
25/09	h	Zimbru	D	1-1	*Primac*
01/10	a	Dacia	L	0-3	
16/10	a	Milsami	L	0-4	
21/10	h	Academia	L	1-2	*C Arama*
29/10	a	Speranta	L	0-3	
05/11	h	Sheriff	L	1-2	*Lacusta*
19/11	a	Petrocub	L	0-5	
25/11	h	Zaria	L	0-3	
29/11	a	Dinamo-Auto	D	2-2	*Primac 2*
09/12	h	Saxan	W	3-0	*Hamed, Arabadji, Primac*
2017					
25/02	a	Zimbru	L	0-4	
01/03	h	Dacia	L	1-2	*Gusan (p)*
05/03	h	Milsami	L	0-2	
11/03	a	Dacia	L	0-3	
16/03	h	Zimbru	L	1-2	*Gusan*
31/03	a	Academia	W	1-0	*Leuca (p)*
04/04	h	Petrocub	L	0-4	
08/04	a	Speranta	W	1-0	*Gusan (p)*
14/04	h	Dinamo-Auto	D	2-2	*Leuca, Pavlov*
03/05	a	Saxan	L	0-3	
07/05	h	Milsami	L	0-2	
12/05	a	Zaria	L	0-5	
21/05	h	Sheriff	L	0-6	

No	Name	Nat	DoB	Pos	Aps	(s)	Gls
12	Eugeniu Afanasiev		12/02/92	G	3		
4	Igor Andronic		11/03/88	D	8		
21	Cristian Apostolachi		13/09/00	G		(1)	
5	Ion Arabadji		31/07/84	D	15		1
16	Chiril Arama		28/07/97	A	2	(8)	1
9	Vadim Arama		09/07/87	M	2	(7)	
6	Eduard Avram		05/01/90	M	15	(2)	1
19	Olexandr Bezimov	UKR	08/02/84	A	13	(3)	
17	Maxim Bucataru		27/05/92	M	11	(1)	
15	Alexandru Cheltuiala		05/02/83	D	5		
24	Irakli Chomakhashvili	GEO	26/04/95	M	19	(3)	
24	Serghei Ciuico		02/02/83	A	11	(1)	
2	Oleg Clonin		04/02/88	M	3	(1)	
3	Florin Cojocaru		27/11/97	M		(5)	
4	Andrei Cusnir		12/11/97	D	6	(4)	
22	Victor Dolbus		01/01/96	A	6	(4)	
21	Pavel Galac		06/09/95	G	9	(1)	
2	Vladimir Ghenaitis		30/03/95	D	15	(1)	
16	Ion Ghimp		11/09/96	D	4	(3)	
7	Roman Gusan		23/12/85	M	22		4
29	Adabi Hamed	IRN	06/04/92	M	5	(8)	1
12	Stanislav Ivanov		22/04/96	G	13		
18	Denis Janu		18/05/95	M	14	(1)	
11	Nikola Kovačević	SRB	22/04/93	A	1	(1)	
11	Ion Lacusta		24/02/95	A	7	(4)	1
23	Petru Leuca		19/07/90	A	11		2
7	Veaceslav Lisa		24/03/93	A	4		
7	Stanislav Luca		28/06/86	A	5		
7	Dmitri Maneacov		06/03/92	A	6		
15	Gheorghe Mardari		03/10/97	D	8	(3)	
17	Vasile Marjin		15/07/97	M	2	(4)	
8	Andrei Miron		03/12/76	D	4	(5)	
21	Serghei Mutu		19/07/87	G	3	(1)	
3	Vitalie Negru		15/01/87	M	9	(3)	
8	Ion Pavlov		29/08/91	M	9	(4)	1
61	Umberto Pisani	ITA	11/01/95	G	1	(2)	
10	Dorin Popovici		01/07/96	M	7	(3)	
16	Petru Postoronca		09/12/91	M	4	(2)	
10	Viorel Primac		23/01/85	M	14	(2)	7
6	Pavel Pulucciu		29/04/94	M	6	(2)	
14	Radu Rogac		07/06/95	D	9		
5	Iurie Tarasov		29/11/94	D	11	(1)	
22	Octavian Vatavu		29/04/91	D	5	(3)	
22	Octavian Vatavu		29/04/91	G	1		
19	Pietro Viggiani	ITA	29/10/91	A	2	(6)	

FC Zaria Balti

1984 • Municipal (5,953); Teren Sintetic (2,000) • fczaria.md

Major honours
Moldovan Cup (1) 2016

Coach: Vlad Goian

Date		Opponent		Score	Scorers
2016					
23/07	a	Sheriff	W	2-1	*Novicov, Bugaiov*
30/07	h	Petrocub	D	0-0	
14/08	a	Dinamo-Auto	W	3-1	*Tigirlas, Bugaiov, Picusceac*
21/08	h	Ungheni	W	3-0	*Golovatenco, Bugaiov, Rata*
11/09	h	Zimbru	W	3-0	*Mihaliov, Boghiu, Ovsiannicov*
17/09	a	Dacia	W	2-1	*Gómez, Mihaliov*
25/09	h	Milsami	L	0-2	
30/09	a	Academia	W	2-0	*Mihaliov, Picusceac*
16/10	h	Speranta	L	0-2	
21/10	h	Sheriff	D	0-0	
30/10	a	Petrocub	D	2-2	*Onica, Novicov*
04/11	a	Saxan	W	4-1	*Suvorov, Tigirlas, Ermak, Grosu*
20/11	h	Dinamo-Auto	W	2-1	*Tigirlas 2*
25/11	a	Ungheni	W	3-0	*Boghiu 2 (1p), Grosu*
29/11	h	Saxan	W	2-0	*Mihaliov, Boghiu*
04/12	a	Zimbru	W	1-0	*Golovatenco*
10/12	h	Dacia	W	1-0	*Novicov*
2017					
24/02	a	Milsami	W	2-1	*Golovatenco, Bugaiov*
28/02	h	Academia	W	6-0	*Bugaiov, Mihaliov 2, Tigirlas, Ovsiannicov, Gulceac*
04/03	a	Speranta	W	1-0	*Bugaiov*
16/03	h	Sheriff	L	0-2	
01/04	a	Dacia	L	0-1	
05/04	h	Zimbru	W	2-0	*Golovatenco, Boghiu*
09/04	a	Academia	W	4-0	*Rata 2, Bugaiov (p), Suvorov (p)*
15/04	h	Petrocub	W	2-1	*Grosu, Novicov*
30/04	h	Dinamo-Auto	W	3-2	*Bugaiov, Tigirlas, Rata*
03/05	a	Speranta	D	0-0	
07/05	a	Saxan	D	1-1	*Onica*
12/05	h	Ungheni	W	5-0	*Novicov, Mihaliov, Boghiu, og (Tarasov), Morin*
21/05	a	Milsami	L	0-2	

No	Name	Nat	DoB	Pos	Aps	(s)	Gls
11	Gheorghe Boghiu		26/10/81	A	11	(13)	6
21	Igor Bugaiov		26/06/84	A	21	(7)	8
3	Ion Burlacu		03/02/95	D	16		
3	Ion Cararus		25/06/96	M	5	(1)	
15	Cristian Dros		15/04/98	M	1		
6	Iulian Erhan		01/07/86	D	10	(2)	
20	Oleh Ermak	UKR	09/03/86	D	10		1
2	Victor Golovatenco		28/04/84	D	27	(1)	4
22	Rubén Gómez	ARG	26/01/84	M	14	(2)	1
88	Alexandru S Grosu		16/05/86	A	16	(6)	3
18	Vadim Gulceac		06/08/98	M	8	(4)	1
26	Artem Khachaturov	ARM	18/06/92	D	3		
1	Vladimir Livsit		23/03/84	G	9		
19	Maxim Mihaliov		22/08/86	M	25	(2)	7
7	Alvarado Morin	MEX	04/10/88	A	1	(6)	1
5	Andrei Novicov		24/04/86	D	20	(1)	5
4	Alexandru Onica		29/07/84	M	25	(1)	2
9	Gheorghe Ovsiannicov		12/10/85	A	10	(18)	2
33	Serghei Pascenco		18/12/82	G	21		
7	Igor Picusceac		27/03/83	A	4	(6)	2
27	Denis Rassulov		02/01/90	D	3	(1)	
8	Vadim Rata		05/05/93	M	19	(6)	4
2	Andriy Slinkin	UKR	19/02/91	D	10		
16	Alexandr Suvorov		02/02/87	M	11	(8)	2
10	Igor Tigirlas		24/02/84	D	20	(7)	6
26	Tihomir Trifonov	BUL	25/11/86	D	10		

FC Zimbru Chisinau

1947 • Zimbru (10,500); Baza Zimbru (2,142) • zimbru.md

Major honours
Moldovan League (8) 1992, 1993, 1994, 1995, 1996, 1998, 1999, 2000; Moldovan Cup (6) 1997, 1998, 2003, 2004, 2007, 2014

Coach: Flavius Stoican (ROU); (23/09/16) Veaceslav Rusnac; (01/02/17) Ştefan Stoica (ROU)

Date		Opponent		Score	Scorers
2016					
23/07	a	Dacia	W	1-0	*Amâncio Fortes*
31/07	h	Milsami	W	1-0	*Alex Bruno*
06/08	a	Academia	W	2-0	*Amâncio Fortes, I Damascan (p)*
14/08	h	Speranta	W	2-0	*Diego Lima, Hugo Neto*
20/08	a	Sheriff	L	0-3	
11/09	a	Zaria	L	0-3	
17/09	h	Dinamo-Auto	W	1-0	*Alex Bruno (p)*
21/09	h	Petrocub	D	0-0	
25/09	a	Ungheni	D	1-1	*Spataru*
01/10	h	Saxan	W	2-0	*Jardan 2*
21/10	h	Dacia	L	0-1	
30/10	a	Milsami	L	0-1	
05/11	h	Academia	W	2-0	*Hugo Neto, Anton*
19/11	a	Speranta	W	1-0	*Jean Theodoro*
26/11	h	Sheriff	L	1-4	*Rusnac*
30/11	a	Petrocub	W	2-1	*Jean Theodoro, V Damascan*
04/12	h	Zaria	L	0-1	
10/12	a	Dinamo-Auto	D	1-1	*Zagaevschi*
2017					
25/02	h	Ungheni	W	4-0	*Hugo Neto, Stina, Jean Theodoro, Iurasco*
01/03	a	Saxan	L	0-3	
11/03	h	Saxan	D	0-0	
16/03	a	Ungheni	W	2-1	*I Damascan, Jean Theodoro*
01/04	h	Milsami	W	1-0	*Milinceanu*
05/04	a	Zaria	L	0-2	
09/04	h	Sheriff	L	0-1	
15/04	a	Dacia	L	1-3	*Jean Theodoro*
30/04	h	Academia	W	4-0	*Prepelita, Stina, Hugo Neto, Anton*
07/05	a	Petrocub	D	1-1	*Hugo Neto*
12/05	h	Speranta	D	1-1	*Hugo Neto*
21/05	a	Dinamo-Auto	D	1-1	*Staris*

No	Name	Nat	DoB	Pos	Aps	(s)	Gls
70	Shady Ahdy	EGY	27/07/93	A	3	(3)	
30	Alex Bruno	BRA	07/10/93	M	8		2
77	Amâncio Fortes	POR	18/04/90	M	8		2
8	Gheorghe Anton		27/01/93	M	23	(1)	2
4	Igor Arhiri		17/02/97	D	12	(4)	
30	Vadim Bejenari		16/05/97	M	3	(1)	
15	Alexandru Belevschi		21/03/95	D	2	(2)	
23	Ion Cararus		25/06/96	M	6	(2)	
3	Calin Chirilov		20/07/98	D		(1)	
3	Artur Craciun		29/06/98	D	7	(3)	
77	Ilie Damascan		12/10/95	A	12	(8)	2
99	Vitalie Damascan		24/01/99	A	6	(7)	1
7	Diego Lima	BRA	30/09/88	M	6	(2)	1
83	Emerson	BRA	22/07/83	D	4		
21	Erick	BRA	24/03/88	M	1	(4)	
23	Denis Furtuna		13/10/99	D		(1)	
35	Hugo Moreira	POR	30/10/90	D	28	(1)	
10	Hugo Neto	POR	07/03/97	A	8	(13)	6
73	Nichita Iurasco		17/05/99	A		(2)	1
93	Izaldo	BRA	03/06/93	D	2		
90	Ion Jardan		10/01/90	D	16		2
9	Jean Theodoro	BRA	25/02/93	M	16	(4)	5
2	Artem Khachaturov	ARM	18/06/92	D	8	(1)	
26	Luan	BRA	17/09/88	D	17		
9	Lucas Gonçalves	BRA	14/09/91	A	5	(2)	
21	Nicolae Milinceanu		01/08/92	A	8		1
6	Ovye Monday	NGA	14/08/92	D	13	(1)	
20	Cristian Nagornii		17/06/98	M	2	(3)	
97	Anatolie Prepelita		06/08/97	D	10	(2)	1
22	Andrei Rusnac		22/09/96	A	12	(3)	1
23	Denis Rusu		02/08/90	G	23		
11	Pavel Secrier		11/01/91	M	5	(3)	
94	Dan Spataru		24/05/94	M	10	(2)	1
5	Alexandru Staris		04/01/95	D	11	(3)	1
98	Victor Stina		20/03/98	M	7	(15)	2
23	Dmitri Telegin	RUS	02/02/92	D	5		
1	Emil Timbur		21/07/97	G	7		
73	Bogdan Vasile	ROU	02/02/95	M	7		
17	Veaceslav Zagaevschi		04/04/96	M	9	(16)	1

Top goalscorers

15	Ricardinho (Sheriff)
12	Josip Brezovec (Sheriff)
9	Cheick Diarra (Dinamo-Auto/Dacia) Sergiu Platica (Speranta)
8	Octavian Onofrei (Dinamo-Auto) Igor Bugaiov (Zaria)
7	Maxym Feshchuk (Dacia) Georgi Sarmov (Dacia) Igor Banović (Milsami) Ilya Belous (Milsami) Viorel Primac (Ungheni) Maxim Mihaliov (Zaria)

Promoted clubs

FC Sfintul Gheorghe

2003 • Suruceni (1,500) • no website

Coach: Vadim Boret

FC Spicul Chiscareni

2014 • Spicul (1,000); Singerei (1,500) • no website

Coach: Denis Calincov

Second level final table 2016/17

		Pld	W	D	L	F	A	Pts
1	FC Sheriff-2	28	22	2	4	94	19	68
2	FC Sfintul Gheorghe	28	21	3	4	79	23	66
3	FC Spicul Chiscareni	28	21	3	4	62	22	66
4	FC Victoria Bardar	28	20	4	4	78	26	64
5	FC Zimbru-2 Chisinau	28	13	5	10	57	38	44
6	CF Sparta Selemet	28	13	2	13	51	61	41
7	FC Singerei	28	13	1	14	48	53	40
8	FC Edinet	28	11	3	14	55	57	36
9	FC Iskra	28	10	5	13	39	50	35
10	FC Dacia-2 Buiucani	28	10	4	14	39	45	34
11	Real Succes Lilcora FC	28	9	2	17	37	54	29
12	CF Gagauziya-Oguzsport	28	9	2	17	51	74	29
13	FC Codru Lozova	28	8	3	17	48	81	27
14	CF Intersport-Aroma	28	6	4	18	20	50	22
15	FC Prut Leova	28	2	1	25	19	124	7

NB FC Sheriff-2 ineligible for promotion.

DOMESTIC CUP

Cupa Moldovei 2016/17

SECOND ROUND

(20/09/16)
Iskra 0-5 Saxan
Prut 0-3 Sparta
Sfintul Gheorghe 1-0 Ungheni
Victoria 0-2 Spicul

(21/09/16)
Academia 6-0 Edinet
Anina 2-2 Intersport-Aroma *(aet; 3-1 on pens)*
Codru 1-0 Intersport

1/8 FINALS

(25/10/16)
Dinamo-Auto 3-2 Sfintul Gheorghe
Gagauziya-Oguzsport 1-8 Zaria
Milsami 4-0 Academia
Sheriff 13-0 Codru
Speranta 0-1 Saxan
Spicul 0-3 Petrocub

(26/10/16)
Sparta 1-4 Dacia
Zimbru 10-0 Anina

QUARTER-FINALS

(26/04/17)
Dacia 1-1 Zaria *(Isa 117; Boghiu 95) (aet; 2-4 on pens)*

Dinamo-Auto 0-4 Zimbru *(Anton 13, 87, Milinceanu 31, Jean Theodoro 58)*

Milsami 0-1 Sheriff *(Ginsari 62)*

Petrocub 3-0 Saxan *(Dima 22, Ursu 82, D Taras 86)*

SEMI-FINALS

(16/05/17)
Petrocub 1-1 Sheriff *(Calugher 11; Savić 39) (aet; 4-5 on pens)*

Zaria 1-0 Zimbru *(Suvorov 115) (aet)*

FINAL

(25/05/17)
Zimbru, Chisinau
FC SHERIFF 5 *(Damascan 48, 59, Bayala 54, 56, Joálisson 89)*
FC ZARIA BALTI 0
Referee: *Alper Ulusoy (TUR)*
SHERIFF: *Juric, Balima (Jardan 52), Savić, Potirniche, Sušić, Yahaya, Bayala (Joálisson 78), Ginsari, Badibanga (Dionatan 70), Ricardinho, Damascan (Jabbie 60)*
ZARIA: *Pascenco, Tigirlas, Golovatenco, Novicov, Slinkin, Rata, Onica, Suvorov (Gómez 65), Mihaliov (Gulceac 80), Ermak (Boghiu 51), Ovsiannicov*

MONTENEGRO

Futbalski savez Crne Gore (FSCG)

Address	Ulica “19. decembra” 13 ME-81000 Podgorica
Tel	+382 20 445 600
Fax	+382 20 445 601
E-mail	info@fscg.me
Website	fscg.me

President	Dejan Savićević
General secretary	Momir Djurdjevac
Media officer	Branko Latinović
Year of formation	1931
National stadium	Pod Goricom, Podgorica (12,000)

PRVA LIGA CLUBS

  1 **FK Bokelj**

 2 **FK Budućnost Podgorica**

 3 **FK Dečić**

 4 **OFK Grbalj**

 5 **FK Iskra**

 6 **FK Jedinstvo Bijelo Polje**

 7 **FK Lovćen**

 8 **FK Mladost Podgorica**

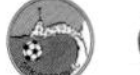 9 **OFK Petrovac**

 10 **FK Rudar Pljevlja**

 11 **FK Sutjeska**

 12 **FK Zeta**

PROMOTED CLUB

 13 **FK Kom**

KEY

- UEFA Champions League
- UEFA Europa League
- Promoted
- Relegated

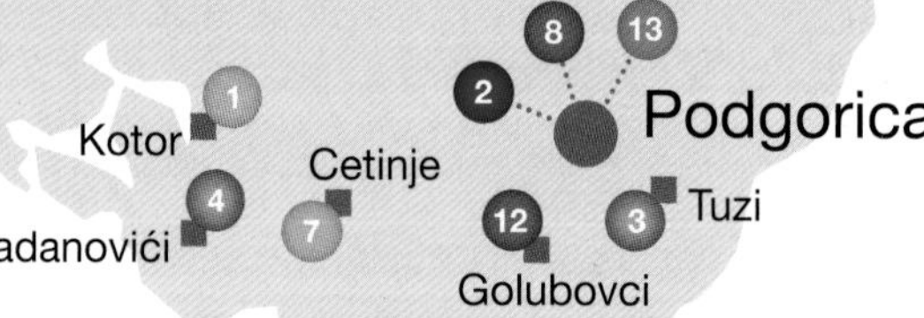

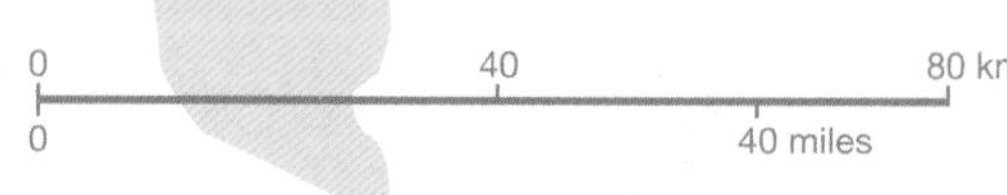

Budućnost survive spring collapse

There was an extraordinary narrative to the 2016/17 Prva Liga. After a brilliant autumn that gave them a huge lead, Budućnost Podgorica's form completely deserted them in the spring. They eventually sneaked home thanks to their superior record in a three-way head-to-head with defending champions Mladost Podgorica and FK Zeta after all three clubs had finished level on points.

Zeta would have been champions but for a six-point deduction, and Sutjeska Nikšić also spurned an opportunity to finish top – though they consoled themselves by claiming a maiden victory in the Montenegrin Cup.

Podgorica club cling on to claim record third title

Zeta and Mladost edged out in three-way head-to-head

Sutjeska beat Grbalj to win Montenegrin Cup

Domestic league

For two and a half months over the winter it appeared that nothing could prevent Budućnost from going on to win a record third Prva Liga title. Miodrag Vukotić's all-Montenegrin side sat 11 points clear of second-placed Mladost having dropped points in only four of their first 17 matches. Powered by the goals of Milivoje Raičević, Goran Vujović and 34-year-old former international Radomir Djalović, the country's best-supported club looked nailed-on for their first league triumph in five years.

Four points from their first two games after the break gave no indication of the astonishing meltdown that was to follow. A 1-0 defeat up north at Rudar Pljevlja – the only team to have beaten them in the autumn – should not have caused undue concern, but it was to trigger a shocking decline that gradually eroded Budućnost's lead and, remarkably, revived a moribund title race.

Defeats became almost a weekly occurrence for Vukotić's struggling front-runners, but luckily for them the buffer they had built up in the first half of the season allowed them to hold on to their position, and with Mladost also finding victories difficult to come by, the pressure was not as intense as it might have been. Budućnost were also helped by the fact that Zeta were burdened with two separate three-point deductions for disciplinary breaches.

Zeta would hit peak form under new coach Dušan Vlaisavljević in the run-in, posting seven successive wins, including victories over Mladost, Budućnost and, before that, ever-improving Sutjeska, but it was not enough to force them ahead of Budućnost. Sutjeska, for their part, blew their chances with a 1-0 defeat at Iskra in the penultimate round, while the nine points out of nine that Mladost took from their last three fixtures, including three from an abandoned Podgorica derby against the leaders, brought parity with Budućnost but not outright victory.

Budućnost finally pulled themselves together to win their final game, 4-1 at home to relegated Jedinstvo Bijelo Polje, and that proved enough for them to avoid a 'Hare and the Tortoise'-like conclusion to the story. Although their final total of 57 points was matched by Zeta and Mladost, the ten they had taken from the six meetings with their two rivals compared favourably with Zeta's eight and Mladost's seven and therefore, by the skin of their teeth, the wire-to-wire leaders were the Prva Liga champions. It was Budućnost's third title, which enabled them to move ahead of two-time winners Rudar, Sutjeska and Mogren Budva in the league's 11-year roll of honour.

Domestic cup

Sutjeska, the only ever back-to-back Montenegrin champions, had never won the country's domestic cup. Indeed, their only appearance in the final had come in the inaugural competition of 2006/07, when they lost to Rudar. A decade on, though, they were back as winners, Miljan Vlaisavljević's 72nd-minute strike deciding a tightly-contested duel with OFK Grbalj that was interrupted for several minutes after the goal because of security concerns.

Europe

Budućnost were the only one of Montenegro's four clubs to survive their opening European tie. After edging past Rabotnicki of FYR Macedonia, they almost pulled off a famous comeback against Genk, only be defeated on penalties in Podgorica by a team that would go on to reach the UEFA Europa League quarter-finals.

National team

Stevan Jovetić was the six-goal star of Montenegro's 2018 FIFA World Cup qualifying campaign, the Sevilla striker's brilliant hat-trick in a 4-1 home win over Armenia in June – which lifted his record tally of goals to 23 in 46 appearances – placing the team in a more than satisfactory position with four matches to go as they targeted a runners-up spot behind runaway Group E leaders Poland.

DOMESTIC SEASON AT A GLANCE

Prva Liga 2016/17 final table

			Home					Away					Total					
		Pld	W	D	L	F	A	W	D	L	F	A	W	D	L	F	A	Pts
1	**FK Budućnost Podgorica**	**33**	**12**	**1**	**4**	**36**	**15**	**5**	**5**	**6**	**16**	**13**	**17**	**6**	**10**	**52**	**28**	**57**
2	FK Zeta	33	12	3	2	22	5	7	3	6	16	12	19	6	8	38	17	57
3	FK Mladost Podgorica	33	10	3	4	33	15	6	6	4	13	7	16	9	8	46	22	57
4	FK Sutjeska	33	8	8	1	22	10	7	2	7	21	15	15	10	8	43	25	55
5	FK Dečić	33	10	3	4	20	15	4	5	7	7	17	14	8	11	27	32	50
6	FK Iskra	33	8	2	6	13	14	6	5	6	16	18	14	7	12	29	32	49
7	OFK Grbalj	33	8	5	4	18	13	3	8	5	10	12	11	13	9	28	25	46
8	FK Rudar Pljevlja	33	8	6	2	20	7	3	3	11	15	24	11	9	13	35	31	42
9	OFK Petrovac	33	7	3	6	18	19	4	3	10	12	31	11	6	16	30	50	39
10	FK Bokelj	33	5	7	4	14	11	3	5	9	14	23	8	12	13	28	34	36
11	FK Lovćen	33	6	4	6	14	12	4	3	10	11	24	10	7	16	25	36	34
12	FK Jedinstvo Bijelo Polje	33	2	4	10	10	25	1	1	15	10	44	3	5	25	20	69	14

NB FK Zeta – 6 pts deducted; FK Lovćen – 3 pts deducted.

European qualification 2017/18

Champion: FK Budućnost Podgorica (second qualifying round)

Cup winner: FK Sutjeska (first qualifying round)

FK Zeta (first qualifying round)
FK Mladost Podgorica (first qualifying round)

Top scorer Zoran Petrović (Mladost), 14 goals
Relegated clubs FK Jedinstvo Bijelo Polje, FK Lovćen, FK Bokelj
Promoted club FK Kom
Cup final FK Sutjeska 1-0 OFK Grbalj

Player of the season

Igor Vujačić
(FK Zeta)

While champions Budućnost boasted the most potent attack in the 2016/17 Prva Liga, the best defence belonged to runners-up Zeta. With Montenegro's first-choice goalkeeper, Mladen Božović, at the rear, that was no great surprise, but it was one of the men in front of him, 22-year-old Vujačić, who took at least equal share of the credit for the team's spectacular figures of just 17 goals conceded in 33 games and 19 clean sheets. The ex-Under-21 international belied his age with a series of mature displays that showcased both his strength and his grace under pressure.

Newcomer of the season

Nikola Krstović
(FK Zeta)

The best team on the field in the 2016/17 Prva Liga were Zeta, who won 19 matches to Budućnost's 17 and lost eight to the champions' ten, but disciplinary measures denied them a second league title. A consolation for the team's fans, however, came in the shape of 17-year-old striker Krstović, who displayed enormous potential by scoring seven goals in the spring, including winning strikes against Rudar, Sutjeska, Mladost and Budućnost, to reignite the club's title challenge. Despite his limited game time, the youngster would end up as the club's joint-top scorer.

Team of the season

(4-3-3)

Coach: Vlaisavljević *(Zeta)*

 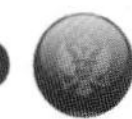

NATIONAL TEAM

Top five all-time caps
Elsad Zverotić (59); **Fatos Bećiraj** (47); **Stevan Jovetić** & **Mirko Vučinić** (46); Simon Vukčević (45)

Top five all-time goals
Stevan Jovetić (23); **Mirko Vučinić** (17); **Fatos Bećiraj** & Dejan Damjanović (8); Radomir Djalović (7)

Results 2016/17

04/09/16	Romania (WCQ)	A	Cluj-Napoca	D	1-1	*Jovetić (87)*
08/10/16	Kazakhstan (WCQ)	H	Podgorica	W	5-0	*Tomašević (24), Vukčević (59), Jovetić (64), Bećiraj (73), Savić (78)*
11/10/16	Denmark (WCQ)	A	Copenhagen	W	1-0	*Bećiraj (31)*
11/11/16	Armenia (WCQ)	A	Yerevan	L	2-3	*Kojašević (36), Jovetić (38)*
26/03/17	Poland (WCQ)	H	Podgorica	L	1-2	*Mugoša (63)*
04/06/17	Iran	H	Podgorica	L	1-2	*Jovetić (32)*
10/06/17	Armenia (WCQ)	H	Podgorica	W	4-1	*Bećiraj (2), Jovetić (28, 54, 82)*

Appearances 2016/17

Coach: Ljubiša Tumbaković (SRB)	02/09/52		ROU	KAZ	DEN	ARM	POL	Irn	ARM	Caps	Goals
Mladen Božović	01/08/84	Zeta	G	G	G	G	G			42	-
Žarko Tomašević	22/02/90	Oostende (BEL)	D	D	D			D46	D75	22	3
Stefan Savić	08/01/91	Atlético (ESP)	D	D	D	D	D	D46	D	43	4
Marko Simić	16/06/87	H. Tel-Aviv (ISR) /Rostov (RUS)	D	D	D70			D	D	22	-
Marko Bakić	01/11/93	Braga (POR)	D68	s83						11	-
Adam Marušić	17/10/92	Oostende (BEL)	M	D	D	D	D92		D	15	-
Marko Vešović	28/08/91	Rijeka (CRO)	M80	M	M90	M86	M			12	-
Nikola Vukčević	13/12/91	Braga (POR)	M	M68	M	M63	M		M71	22	1
Aleksandar Šćekić	12/12/91	Gençlerbirliği (TUR)	M	M83	M	M	M86		s71	8	-
Stevan Jovetić	02/11/89	Internazionale (ITA) /Sevilla (ESP)	A	A	A	A		A64	A	46	23
Fatos Bećiraj	05/05/88	Dinamo Moskva (RUS)	A92	A76	A	A	A	A46	A	47	8
Stefan Mugoša	26/02/92	1860 München (GER) /Karlsruhe (GER)	s68			s86	A	s64		14	1
Damir Kojašević	03/06/87	Vardar (MKD)	s80	M	M63	M74	M81	s63		6	1
Nemanja Nikolić	01/01/88	H. Tel-Aviv (ISR)	s92	s68						12	-
Filip Raičević	02/07/93	Vicenza (ITA)		s76						3	-
Vladimir Jovović	26/10/94	Napredak (SRB) /Spartak Subotica (SRB)			s63	s74		M71	M84	10	-
Aleksandar Šofranac	21/10/90	Rijeka (CRO)			s70		D			4	-
Nemanja Mijušković	04/03/92	Vardar (MKD)			s90					2	-
Marko Baša	29/12/82	LOSC (FRA)				D		s46		39	2
Filip Stojković	22/01/93	1860 München (GER)				D	D	s46		4	-
Elsad Zverotić	31/10/86	Sion (SUI)				s63				59	5
Mirko Ivanić	13/09/93	BATE (BLR)					s81			1	-
Luka Djordjević	09/07/94	Zenit (RUS)					s86	s71		6	1
Mirko Vučinić	01/10/83	Al-Jazira (UAE)					s92	s46		46	17
Danijel Petković	25/05/93	MTK (HUN)						G	G	3	-
Emrah Klimenta	13/02/91	Sacramento (USA)						D	s75	3	-
Nebojša Kosović	24/02/95	Partizan (SRB)						M	M	3	-
Marko Janković	09/07/95	Partizan (SRB)						M63	M	3	-
Vukan Savićević	29/01/94	Slovan (SVK)						M		1	-
Sead Hakšabanović	04/05/99	Halmstad (SWE)							s84	1	-

EUROPE

FK Mladost Podgorica

Second qualifying round - PFC Ludogorets Razgrad (BUL)

A 0-2

Ljuljanović, Boris Z Kopitović, Raičević, Vlaisavljević, Boris G Kopitović (Lazarević 46), Burzanović (Stijepović 90+1), Djurišić, Novović, Petrović (Bukorac 71), Igumanović, Lakić. Coach: Nikola Rakojević (MNE)

H 0-3

Ljuljanović, Boris Z Kopitović, Raičević (Petričević 83), Vlaisavljević, Burzanović, Djurišić, Novović, Igumanović (Petrović 60), Lakić, Bukorac, Lazarević (Stijepović 75). Coach: Nikola Rakojević (MNE)

FK Budućnost Podgorica

First qualifying round - FK Rabotnicki (MKD)

A 1-1 *Janketić (36)*

Dragojević, Vukčević, Vušurović, Seratlić (Raičević 57), Mitrović, Raičković (Marković 87), Pejaković, Hočko, Mirković, Janketić (Camaj 64), Djalović. Coach: Miodrag Vukotić (MNE)

H 1-0 *Radunović (18p)*

Dragojević, Radunović, Vukčević, Vušurović, Mitrović, Raičković (Marković 82), Raspopović, Pejaković (Seratlić 73), Hočko, Mirković (Janketić 77), Djalović. Coach: Miodrag Vukotić (MNE)

Second qualifying round - KRC Genk (BEL)

A 0-2

Dragojević, Radunović, Vukčević, Vušurović (Camaj 85), Mitrović, Raičković (Janketić 60), Raspopović, Pejaković (Seratlić 75), Hočko, Mirković, Djalović. Coach: Miodrag Vukotić (MNE)

H 2-0 (aet; 2-4 on pens) *Djalović (1), Raičković (40)*

Dragojević, Radunović, Vukčević, Vušurović, Mitrović, Vujović (Raičević 92), Raičković (Hočko 64), Raspopović, Mirković, Janketić (Pejaković 53), Djalović. Coach: Miodrag Vukotić (MNE)

FK Rudar Pljevlja

First qualifying round - FK Kukësi (ALB)

A 1-1 *Radanović (71p)*

Radanović, Noma (Marković 90+4), Alić, Soppo, Ivanović (Reljić 90), Nestorović, Radišić, Božović (Jovanović 78), Brnović, Živković, Vlahović. Coach: Dragan Radojičić (MNE)

H 0-1

Radanović, Noma (Jovanović 73), Alić, Soppo (Marković 81), Ivanović, Nestorović, Radišić (Vuković 86), Božović, Brnović, Živković, Vlahović. Coach: Dragan Radojičić (MNE)

FK Bokelj

First qualifying round - FK Vojvodina (SRB)

H 1-1 *Djenić (5)*

Mijatović, Mladenović, Bogdanović, Zlatičanin, Ognjanović, Tomić (Kotorac 64), M Todorović, Djenić, Vučinić (Maraš 72), Macanović, Pepić (Pajović 76). Coach: Slobodan Drašković (MNE)

A 0-5

Mijatović, Mladenović, Bogdanović, Zlatičanin, Ognjanović, Tomić (Nikezić 64), M Todorović, Djenić, Vučinić, Macanović (Kotorac 52), Pepić (Maraš 52). Coach: Slobodan Drašković (MNE)

Red card: Vučinić 90+2

DOMESTIC LEAGUE CLUB-BY-CLUB

FK Bokelj

1922 • Pod Vrmcem (5,000) • no website

Coach: Slobodan Drašković; (14/04/17) Milorad Malovrazić

2016

06/08	h	Grbalj	D	0-0	
13/08	h	Zeta	L	0-1	
20/08	a	Sutjeska	L	0-2	
24/08	h	Rudar	W	2-1	*Macanović, Nikezić*
27/08	a	Dečić	W	3-1	*Nikezić, Macanović, Vučinić*
10/09	h	Budućnost	D	2-2	*Nikezić, Kotorac*
17/09	a	Iskra	L	0-1	
24/09	h	Petrovac	W	3-0	*Pajović, Ognjanović 2 (2p)*
01/10	a	Jedinstvo	L	0-1	
15/10	h	Lovćen	D	0-0	
22/10	a	Mladost	L	1-3	*Vučinić*
29/10	a	Grbalj	D	0-0	
05/11	a	Zeta	L	0-1	
16/11	h	Sutjeska	L	1-2	*Vučinić*
19/11	a	Rudar	L	0-2	
26/11	h	Dečić	D	1-1	*Vučinić*
03/12	a	Budućnost	L	0-3	

2017

21/02	h	Iskra	L	0-1	
26/02	a	Petrovac	D	1-1	*Denković*
04/03	h	Jedinstvo	W	2-1	*Macanović, Pržica*
11/03	a	Lovćen	L	0-2	
18/03	h	Mladost	W	1-0	*Denković*
28/03	h	Mladost	D	0-0	
01/04	a	Budućnost	D	2-2	*Macanović, Kotorac*
08/04	h	Lovćen	L	0-1	
15/04	a	Jedinstvo	W	3-1	*Macanović, Pajović, Zlatičanin*
22/04	a	Iskra	D	0-0	
30/04	h	Rudar	D	0-0	
06/05	a	Petrovac	W	3-1	*Nikezić, Tomić, Denković*
10/05	h	Grbalj	D	0-0	
13/05	a	Sutjeska	D	1-1	*Denković*
20/05	h	Dečić	W	2-1	*Pajović, Macanović*
27/05	a	Zeta	L	0-1	

Name	Nat	DoB	Pos	Aps	(s)	Gls
Marko Avramović	SRB	02/04/87	D	2	(8)	
Miloš Banićević		23/01/98	D		(1)	
Javier Bayk	ARG	02/02/94	M	13	(10)	
Ilija Bogdanović		14/03/92	M	6	(1)	
Nikola Braunović		21/07/97	D		(1)	
Stefan Denković		16/06/91	A	14	(1)	4
Predrag Kašćelan		30/06/90	D	11	(3)	
Dejan Kotorac		31/05/96	M	22	(4)	2
Aleksandar Macanović		16/04/93	M	32	(1)	6
Luka Maraš		24/05/96	M	21	(7)	
Ivan Mijušković		17/02/88	D	15		
Miloš Nikezić		02/03/87	A	10	(9)	4
Dejan Ognjanović		21/06/78	D	24		2
Lazar Pajović		10/11/95	D	18	(6)	3
Jovan Perović		28/12/89	G	29		
Dejan Pržica		19/01/91	M	8	(15)	1
Miloš Radunović		07/06/90	D	31		
Andrija Simunović		21/03/91	M	30		
Rion Taki	JPN	06/06/92	A	4	(4)	
Ilija Todorović		22/02/92	G	4	(1)	
Mirko Todorović	SRB	22/08/85	D	14		
Danilo Tomić		23/06/86	M	31		1
Jovan Vučinić		20/01/92	A	9	(7)	4
Marko Vujović		23/07/85	M	1	(7)	
Miroslav Zlatičanin	SRB	26/05/85	M	14	(8)	1

FK Budućnost Podgorica

1925 • Pod Goricom (12,000) • no website

Major honours
Montenegrin League (3) 2008, 2012, 2017; Montenegrin Cup (1) 2013

Coach: Miodrag Vukotić

Date		Opponent	Result	Scorers
2016				
06/08	h	Iskra	W 2-0	*Raičević, Camaj*
13/08	a	Petrovac	W 2-0	*Djalović, Raspopović*
20/08	h	Jedinstvo	W 2-0	*Vujović 2*
24/08	a	Lovćen	W 2-0	*Djalović 2*
28/08	h	Mladost	W 1-0	*Djalović*
10/09	a	Bokelj	D 2-2	*Mirković, Radunović (p)*
18/09	h	Zeta	W 1-0	*Raičević*
25/09	a	Sutjeska	D 1-1	*Vušurović*
02/10	h	Rudar	L 0-2	
15/10	a	Dečić	W 2-1	*Vukčević, Pejaković*
22/10	h	Grbalj	W 2-0	*Raičević, Vujović*
29/10	a	Iskra	W 3-0	*Radunović (p), Raičević, Vušurović*
05/11	h	Petrovac	W 5-0	*Radunović (p), Vujović 2, Raičević, Janketić*
16/11	a	Jedinstvo	D 0-0	
19/11	h	Lovćen	W 5-0	*Raičević 2, Radunović, Vujović, Djalović*
26/11	a	Mladost	W 2-1	*Djalović 2*
03/12	h	Bokelj	W 3-0	*Raičević 2, Vujović*
2017				
22/02	a	Zeta	D 1-1	*Hočko*
26/02	h	Sutjeska	W 4-2	*Vušurović, Vujović, Djalović, Nikač*
04/03	a	Rudar	L 0-1	
11/03	h	Dečić	L 0-1	
18/03	a	Grbalj	D 1-1	*Vušurović*
28/03	a	Lovćen	L 0-1	
01/04	h	Bokelj	D 2-2	*Djalović, Nikač*
08/04	a	Iskra	L 0-1	
15/04	h	Rudar	W 3-2	*Vujović 2 (1p), Djalović*
22/04	a	Petrovac	L 0-1	
30/04	h	Grbalj	L 0-2	
06/05	a	Sutjeska	L 0-1	
10/05	h	Dečić	W 2-0	*Vušurović, Vujović*
13/05	a	Zeta	L 0-1	
20/05	h	Mladost	L 0-3	*(w/o; original match abandoned after 79 mins at 0-1)*
27/05	h	Jedinstvo	W 4-1	*Djalović, Hočko, Vujović, Nikač*

Name	Nat	DoB	Pos	Aps	(s)	Gls
Balša Banović		26/01/98	M	4	(1)	
Driton Camaj		07/03/97	A	3	(21)	1
Radomir Djalović		29/10/82	A	32		11
Miloš Dragojević		03/02/89	G	33		
Deni Hočko		22/04/94	M	17	(8)	2
Velizar Janketić		15/11/96	M	2	(15)	1
Danilo Marković		15/07/98	M	9	(3)	
Luka Mirković		01/11/90	M	23	(6)	1
Filip Mitrović		17/11/93	D	18	(1)	
Darko Nikač		15/09/90	A	3	(11)	3
Ivan Pejaković		22/08/92	M	22	(9)	1
Risto Radunović		04/05/92	D	23	(1)	4
Milivoje Raičević		21/07/93	M	17	(4)	9
Miloš Raičković		02/12/93	M	25	(3)	
Momčilo Raspopović		18/03/94	D	32		1
Balša Sekulić		10/06/98	A	1	(4)	
Ermin Seratlić		21/08/90	A	4	(2)	
Janko Simović		02/04/87	D	10	(1)	
Vasilije Terzić		12/05/99	M		(1)	
Goran Vujović		03/05/87	A	32		12
Nikola Vukčević		22/03/84	D	27		1
Milan Vušurović		18/04/95	M	26	(6)	5

FK Dečić

1926 • Tuško polje (3,000) • no website

Coach: Milija Savović; (05/09/16) Edis Mulalić (BIH)

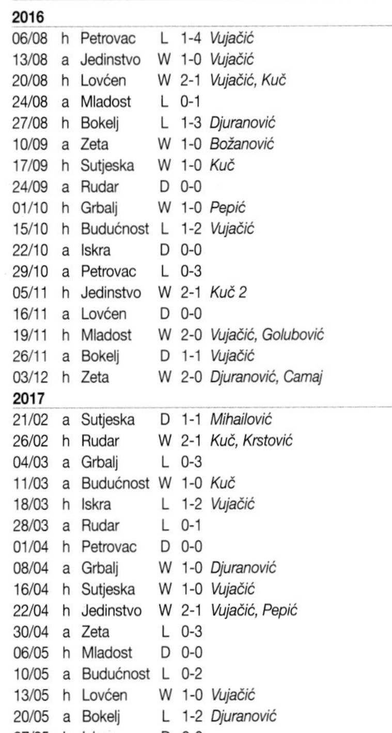

Date		Opponent	Result	Scorers
2016				
06/08	h	Petrovac	L 1-4	*Vujačić*
13/08	a	Jedinstvo	W 1-0	*Vujačić*
20/08	h	Lovćen	W 2-1	*Vujačić, Kuč*
24/08	a	Mladost	L 0-1	
27/08	h	Bokelj	L 1-3	*Djuranović*
10/09	a	Zeta	W 1-0	*Božanović*
17/09	h	Sutjeska	W 1-0	*Kuč*
24/09	a	Rudar	D 0-0	
01/10	h	Grbalj	W 1-0	*Pepić*
15/10	h	Budućnost	L 1-2	*Vujačić*
22/10	a	Iskra	D 0-0	
29/10	a	Petrovac	L 0-3	
05/11	h	Jedinstvo	W 2-1	*Kuč 2*
16/11	a	Lovćen	D 0-0	
19/11	h	Mladost	W 2-0	*Vujačić, Golubović*
26/11	a	Bokelj	D 1-1	*Vujačić*
03/12	h	Zeta	W 2-0	*Djuranović, Camaj*
2017				
21/02	a	Sutjeska	D 1-1	*Mihailović*
26/02	h	Rudar	W 2-1	*Kuč, Krstović*
04/03	a	Grbalj	L 0-3	
11/03	a	Budućnost	W 1-0	*Kuč*
18/03	h	Iskra	L 1-2	*Vujačić*
28/03	a	Rudar	L 0-1	
01/04	h	Petrovac	D 0-0	
08/04	a	Grbalj	W 1-0	*Djuranović*
16/04	h	Sutjeska	W 1-0	*Vujačić*
22/04	h	Jedinstvo	W 2-1	*Vujačić, Pepić*
30/04	a	Zeta	L 0-3	
06/05	h	Mladost	D 0-0	
10/05	a	Budućnost	L 0-2	
13/05	h	Lovćen	W 1-0	*Vujačić*
20/05	a	Bokelj	L 1-2	*Djuranović*
27/05	h	Iskra	D 0-0	

Name	Nat	DoB	Pos	Aps	(s)	Gls
Dražen Andjušić		19/01/93	M	1	(16)	
Matija Božanović		13/04/94	M	30		1
Ilir Camaj		24/06/96	M		(15)	1
Dalibor Djukić		19/09/86	M	22	(3)	
Uroš Djuranović		01/02/94	A	29		4
Sava Gardašević		27/01/93	A	1	(5)	
Radivoje Golubović		22/04/90	D	8	(13)	1
Modjieb Jamali	AFG	30/04/91	M	3	(5)	
Andjelko Jovanović		18/11/99	M		(4)	
Aldin Kalač		07/07/94	A		(1)	
Demir Krkanović		19/07/96	M		(5)	
Koča Krstović		27/03/95	A	3	(7)	1
Edvin Kuč		27/10/93	A	30	(1)	6
Nikola Mihailović		15/09/84	D	29		1
Milan Mijatović		26/07/87	G	32		
Ivan Mijušković		17/02/88	D	10	(2)	
Dušan Nestorović	SRB	26/06/86	D	15		
Daniel Kamy Ntankeu	FRA	08/03/96	D	10	(1)	
Nijazim Padović		19/11/87	D	21		
Rijad Pepić		12/07/90	M	31		2
Nikola Prebiračević	SRB	23/01/87	D	10	(1)	
Filip Rosandić		27/03/97	G	1		
Petar Spasić	SRB	18/01/92	D	8	(1)	
Idriz Toskić		12/10/95	M	12	(9)	
Amel Tuzović		31/03/95	M	23	(2)	
Leon Ujkaj		03/03/97	M	2	(1)	
Vule Vujačić		20/03/88	A	32		10
Kristijan Vulaj		25/06/98	M		(4)	

OFK Grbalj

1970 • Donja Sutvara (1,500) • ofkgrbalj.me

Coach: Dragoljub Djuretić

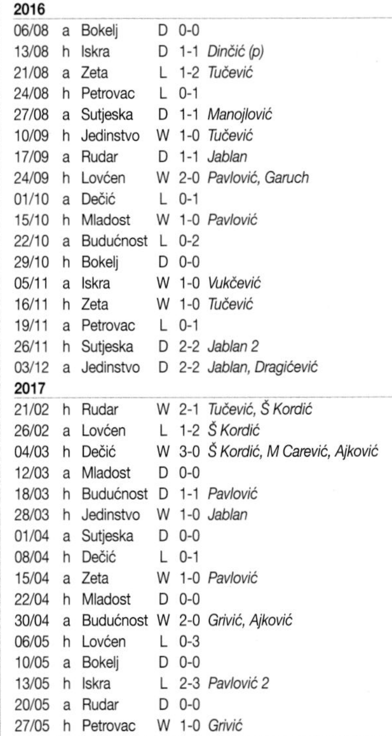

Date		Opponent	Result	Scorers
2016				
06/08	a	Bokelj	D 0-0	
13/08	h	Iskra	D 1-1	*Dinčić (p)*
21/08	a	Zeta	L 1-2	*Tučević*
24/08	h	Petrovac	L 0-1	
27/08	a	Sutjeska	D 1-1	*Manojlović*
10/09	h	Jedinstvo	W 1-0	*Tučević*
17/09	a	Rudar	D 1-1	*Jablan*
24/09	h	Lovćen	W 2-0	*Pavlović, Garuch*
01/10	a	Dečić	L 0-1	
15/10	h	Mladost	W 1-0	*Pavlović*
22/10	a	Budućnost	L 0-2	
29/10	h	Bokelj	D 0-0	
05/11	a	Iskra	W 1-0	*Vukčević*
16/11	h	Zeta	W 1-0	*Tučević*
19/11	a	Petrovac	L 0-1	
26/11	h	Sutjeska	D 2-2	*Jablan 2*
03/12	a	Jedinstvo	D 2-2	*Jablan, Dragićević*
2017				
21/02	h	Rudar	W 2-1	*Tučević, Š Kordić*
26/02	a	Lovćen	L 1-2	*Š Kordić*
04/03	h	Dečić	W 3-0	*Š Kordić, M Carević, Ajković*
12/03	a	Mladost	D 0-0	
18/03	h	Budućnost	D 1-1	*Pavlović*
28/03	h	Jedinstvo	W 1-0	*Jablan*
01/04	a	Sutjeska	D 0-0	
08/04	h	Dečić	L 0-1	
15/04	a	Zeta	W 1-0	*Pavlović*
22/04	h	Mladost	D 0-0	
30/04	a	Budućnost	W 2-0	*Grivić, Ajković*
06/05	h	Lovćen	L 0-3	
10/05	a	Bokelj	D 0-0	
13/05	h	Iskra	L 2-3	*Pavlović 2*
20/05	a	Rudar	D 0-0	
27/05	h	Petrovac	W 1-0	*Grivić*

Name	Nat	DoB	Pos	Aps	(s)	Gls
Srdjan Ajković		15/10/91	M	10	(5)	2
Danilo Bakić		28/10/95	M	1	(2)	
Lazar Carević		16/03/99	G	31		
Milan Carević		05/10/93	D	32		1
Nikola Čelebić		04/07/89	D	13	(1)	
Vuk Damjanović		20/04/96	A	1	(2)	
Slobodan Dinčić	SRB	07/08/82	A	5	(5)	1
Zdravko Dragićević		17/06/86	A	19	(7)	1
Marcin Garuch	POL	14/09/88	M	26		1
Dragan Grivić		12/02/96	D	24	(1)	2
Marko Ilinčić		06/11/95	A	2	(6)	
Ivan Jablan		18/07/79	A	14	(13)	5
Marko Kaljević		09/06/94	M		(1)	
Vladan Karadžić		04/02/95	M	1	(1)	
Šaleta Kordić		19/04/93	A	13	(2)	3
Vladan Kordić		22/06/98	M		(5)	
Bojan Lazarević		09/09/93	M	15	(1)	
Milenko Malović	SRB	23/08/94	D	4	(4)	
Ćetko Manojlović		03/01/91	D	13	(5)	1
Nemanja Nedić		06/04/95	M	23	(1)	
Marko Nikolić	SRB	09/06/89	M	28		
Vojin Pavlović		09/11/93	M	28	(3)	6
Stefan Spasojević		23/08/93	G	2		
Ilija Tučević		18/10/95	D	13	(6)	4
Jovan Vujović		20/01/96	M	1	(3)	
Djordje Vukčević		18/08/96	D	18	(4)	1
Ilija Vukotić		07/01/99	M	4	(5)	
Milan Zorica	SRB	07/01/92	M	22	(8)	

MONTENEGRO

FK Iskra

1919 • Braće Velašević (2,000) • no website

Coach: Radislav Dragićević; (28/12/16) Mirsad Omerhodžić (CRO)

Date		Opponent		Score	Scorers
2016					
06/08	a	Budućnost	L	0-2	
13/08	a	Grbalj	D	1-1	*Krstović*
20/08	h	Petrovac	W	1-0	*Kovačević*
24/08	a	Jedinstvo	W	2-1	*Petrović, Bulajić*
27/08	h	Lovćen	W	1-0	*Kovačević*
10/09	a	Mladost	D	0-0	
17/09	h	Bokelj	W	1-0	*Drinčić*
24/09	a	Zeta	L	1-3	*Kalezić*
01/10	h	Sutjeska	L	0-3	
15/10	a	Rudar	D	0-0	
22/10	h	Dečić	D	0-0	
29/10	h	Budućnost	L	0-3	
05/11	h	Grbalj	L	0-1	
16/11	a	Petrovac	L	1-2	*Kalezić*
19/11	h	Jedinstvo	L	1-2	*Šćepanović (p)*
26/11	a	Lovćen	L	0-1	
04/12	h	Mladost	L	1-3	*Petrović*
2017					
21/02	a	Bokelj	W	1-0	*Paunović*
26/02	h	Zeta	L	0-2	
04/03	a	Sutjeska	L	1-2	*Paunović (p)*
11/03	h	Rudar	W	1-0	*Paunović (p)*
18/03	a	Dečić	W	2-1	*Paunović, Muhović*
28/03	h	Zeta	W	1-0	*Paunović*
01/04	a	Mladost	W	2-1	*Paunović 2*
08/04	h	Budućnost	W	1-0	*Muhović*
15/04	a	Lovćen	D	0-0	
22/04	h	Bokelj	D	0-0	
30/04	a	Jedinstvo	W	2-0	*Paunović, Bošnjak*
06/05	a	Rudar	L	0-2	
10/05	h	Petrovac	W	4-0	*Muhović, Burzanović, Bošnjak, Perutović*
13/05	a	Grbalj	W	3-2	*Bošnjak, Petrović, Paunović*
20/05	h	Sutjeska	W	1-0	*Muhović*
27/05	a	Dečić	D	0-0	

Name	Nat	DoB	Pos	Aps	(s)	Gls
Semir Agović		27/02/92	M	3	(5)	
Haris Banda		14/05/93	M	1		
Srdjan Blažić		26/11/82	G	25		
Armin Bošnjak		20/04/94	D	31	(1)	3
Balša Božović		01/05/87	M	2	(2)	
Boris Bulajić		27/04/88	M	27	(4)	1
Goran Burzanović		04/08/84	M	8	(18)	1
Miloš Drinčić		14/02/99	D	29		1
Adis Hadžanović	BIH	02/01/93	D	12	(1)	
Sead Hadžibulić	BIH	30/01/83	M	2	(2)	
Miroje Jovanović		10/03/87	M	15		
Miloš Kalezić		09/08/93	M	11	(2)	2
Andrija Kaludjerović		14/06/90	M	2	(3)	
Nemanja Kosović		15/05/93	D	1	(2)	
Danko Kovačević		10/07/91	A	13	(2)	2
Željko Krstović		15/10/89	M	30		1
Boris Lakićević		24/10/88	G	8		
Anton Memčević		23/08/98	M		(3)	
Dušan Mladenović	SRB	13/10/90	D	13		
Jasmin Muhović		02/04/89	M	8	(6)	4
Baćo Nikolić		19/01/86	M	7	(5)	
Milivoje Novović		29/02/84	D	4	(7)	
Rodoljub Paunović	SRB	20/06/85	A	14		9
Luka Pavićević		02/02/99	A		(1)	
Luka Pejović		30/07/85	D	14		
Blažo Perutović		08/12/83	A	7	(19)	1
Mihailo Petrović		12/12/89	D	27	(1)	3
Ilija Radunović		01/08/93	A	18	(1)	
Irfan Šahman		05/10/93	D	11	(1)	
Vladimir Savićević		27/11/89	M	8	(7)	
Marko Šćepanović		08/08/82	A	12	(5)	1

FK Jedinstvo Bijelo Polje

1922 • Gradski (4,000) • no website

Coach: Sava Kovačević; (20/09/16) Slavoljub Bubanja; (16/01/17) Goran Jovanović

Date		Opponent		Score	Scorers
2016					
06/08	a	Rudar	L	0-5	
13/08	h	Dečić	L	0-1	
20/08	a	Budućnost	L	0-2	
24/08	h	Iskra	L	1-2	*Baošić*
27/08	a	Petrovac	D	0-0	
10/09	a	Grbalj	L	0-1	
17/09	h	Lovćen	L	0-2	
24/09	a	Mladost	L	0-5	
01/10	h	Bokelj	W	1-0	*Hajrović*
15/10	a	Zeta	L	0-1	
22/10	h	Sutjeska	D	0-0	
29/10	h	Rudar	D	0-0	
05/11	a	Dečić	L	1-2	*Nikolić*
16/11	h	Budućnost	D	0-0	
19/11	a	Iskra	W	2-1	*Nikolić, Hajrović*
26/11	h	Petrovac	L	1-3	*Šahman*
03/12	h	Grbalj	D	2-2	*Šahman, Nikolić*
2017					
21/02	a	Lovćen	L	0-2	
27/02	h	Mladost	L	0-1	
04/03	a	Bokelj	L	1-2	*Boričić*
11/03	h	Zeta	L	0-3	
18/03	a	Sutjeska	L	2-3	*Boričić, Drašković*
28/03	a	Grbalj	L	0-1	
01/04	h	Lovćen	L	0-1	
08/04	a	Sutjeska	L	0-4	
15/04	h	Bokelj	L	1-3	*Hajrović*
22/04	a	Dečić	L	1-2	*Nakahara*
30/04	h	Iskra	L	0-2	
06/05	a	Zeta	L	0-3	
10/05	h	Rudar	L	1-4	*Hajrović*
13/05	a	Mladost	L	2-6	*Pavićević 2*
20/05	h	Petrovac	W	3-1	*Kriještorac, Nakahara, Hajrović*
27/05	a	Budućnost	L	1-4	*Idrizović*

Name	Nat	DoB	Pos	Aps	(s)	Gls
Jovan Baošić		07/07/95	D	27		1
Dino Bećirović		14/12/89	M		(5)	
Vladimir Boričić		09/01/85	M	13		2
Marko Bugarin		16/08/99	D	1	(1)	
Djordjije Ćetković		03/01/83	M	1		
Almedin Ćorović		11/03/99	M		(3)	
Stefan Djordjević		16/11/90	A	4	(7)	
Ljubomir Djurović	SRB	19/06/89	G	22		
Milanko Drašković		10/07/83	D	16		1
Meldin Drešković		26/03/98	D	2	(2)	
Momčilo Dulović		25/05/82	D	9	(2)	
Nemanja Gojačanin		29/04/93	D	11		
Vladan Gordić		27/07/90	D	29	(1)	
Orhan Hajrović		16/05/96	M	25	(4)	5
Aldin Hasanović		17/09/98	M		(1)	
Mirza Idrizović		10/12/97	M	4	(5)	1
Miloš Joksimović		12/10/93	G	3		
Armin Kalić		18/08/95	M	14	(1)	
Emin Kasumović		07/02/92	A	3	(3)	
Rinat Khairullin	KAZ	19/02/94	M	2	(3)	
Yuta Kikuchi	JPN	14/05/94	M	7	(4)	
Rašid Kolić		28/03/99	M	1	(4)	
Miljan Kovačević		24/07/99	M	2	(5)	
Eniks Kriještorac		17/01/99	A	13	(5)	1
Slobodan Lakićević		12/01/88	D	15		
Lazar Lalošević		07/05/95	A	7	(5)	
Vuko Marković		08/09/94	M	1	(6)	
Dragan Masoničić		01/11/88	G	4		
Adis Muzurović		25/04/97	M	15	(1)	
Shoya Nakahara	JPN	06/06/94	M	15		2
Dragan Nikolić		20/01/93	M	9	(3)	3
Jovan Pajović		28/08/96	D	5	(2)	
Lazar Pavićević		16/05/98	M	3		2
Marko Raičević		31/05/88	M	24	(4)	
Luka Rakonjac		17/07/97	G	4	(1)	
Marko Rakonjac		25/05/00	M		(6)	
Dženan Ramović		11/05/98	D	1	(3)	
Irfan Šahman		05/10/93	M	17	(2)	2
Filip Šćekić		28/12/99	D	8	(1)	
Luka Tiodorović		21/01/86	M	16		
Danilo Vuković		01/04/89	D	10	(2)	

FK Lovćen

1913 • Obilića Poljana (5,000) • fklovcen.me

Major honours
Montenegrin Cup (1) 2014

Coach: Milorad Malovrazić; (18/09/16) Dragan Kanatlarovski (MKD)

Date		Opponent		Score	Scorers
2016					
07/08	a	Sutjeska	L	0-1	
13/08	h	Rudar	D	0-0	
20/08	a	Dečić	L	1-2	*Vujanović*
24/08	h	Budućnost	L	0-2	
27/08	a	Iskra	L	0-1	
10/09	h	Petrovac	L	0-1	
17/09	a	Jedinstvo	W	2-0	*Jabučanin, Pepić*
24/09	a	Grbalj	L	0-2	
01/10	h	Mladost	D	0-0	
15/10	a	Bokelj	D	0-0	
22/10	h	Zeta	L	0-1	
29/10	h	Sutjeska	L	0-2	
05/11	a	Rudar	D	1-1	*Pepić*
16/11	h	Dečić	D	0-0	
19/11	a	Budućnost	L	0-5	
26/11	h	Iskra	W	1-0	*Djurović*
03/12	a	Petrovac	L	0-1	
2017					
21/02	h	Jedinstvo	W	2-0	*Djurović, Montenegro*
27/02	h	Grbalj	W	2-1	*Djurović (p), og (Pavlović)*
04/03	a	Mladost	D	0-0	
11/03	h	Bokelj	W	2-0	*Gemistos, Montenegro*
18/03	a	Zeta	L	0-1	
28/03	h	Budućnost	W	1-0	*Djurović (p)*
01/04	a	Jedinstvo	W	1-0	*Ž Marković*
08/04	a	Bokelj	W	1-0	*Djurović (p)*
15/04	h	Iskra	D	0-0	
22/04	a	Rudar	L	0-2	
30/04	h	Petrovac	W	6-0	*Lopičić, Nikolić, Djurović 2, Montenegro, Gemistos*
06/05	a	Grbalj	W	3-0	*Djurović, Gemistos, Martinović*
10/05	h	Sutjeska	L	0-2	
13/05	a	Dečić	L	0-1	
20/05	h	Zeta	L	0-3	
27/05	a	Mladost	L	2-7	*Djurović, Gemistos*

Name	Nat	DoB	Pos	Aps	(s)	Gls
Draško Adžić		22/08/96	M	3	(2)	
Marc-Anthony Aouad Ayaman	AUS	10/02/95	G	1		
Ivan Batrićević		23/06/97	M		(1)	
Dejan Bogdanović		08/08/90	M	17	(4)	
Božidar Bujiša		15/05/99	M	6	(10)	
Dominique Correa	SEN	04/09/92	D	13	(1)	
Mitar Ćuković		06/04/95	D	13	(1)	
Aladin Djakovac	BIH	22/05/92	M	10	(1)	
Marko Djurović		22/05/91	A	23	(6)	9
Boris Došljak		04/06/89	M	3	(3)	
Flamarion	BRA	30/07/96	M	1	(4)	
Georgios Gemistos	GRE	19/12/94	A	13	(3)	4
Bojan Golubović		28/11/85	D	10	(1)	
Joko Jabučanin		06/07/97	M	5	(8)	1
Petar Jovović		31/01/91	A		(3)	
Srdja Kosović		02/05/92	M	9	(2)	
Srdjan Lopičić		20/11/83	M	14	(1)	1
Igor Marković		05/11/95	D	13	(1)	
Stevan Marković		31/01/88	D	8	(1)	
Željko Marković		25/01/96	M	10	(9)	1
Ilija Martinović		31/01/94	D	13	(4)	1
Julian Montenegro	ARG	23/03/89	M	16		3
Baćo Nikolić		19/01/86	M	11	(2)	1
Vuk Orlandić		05/01/97	D	2	(1)	
Miloš Pejaković		16/08/95	M	17	(7)	
Dejan Pepić		27/07/93	M	10	(1)	2
Mićo Perović		04/07/93	G	27		
Danijel Petković		25/05/93	G	5		
Ivan Racković		13/09/94	M	14		
Vasilije Radenović		10/05/94	D	1	(1)	
Radisav Sekulić		27/09/85	A	2	(6)	
Dušan Stevanović	SRB	22/06/96	D	8	(1)	
Vladan Tatar		28/01/84	D	32		
Luka Vujanović		17/07/94	M	13	(4)	1
Filip Vujović		18/10/97	M	1	(1)	
Ivan Vuković		09/02/87	A	14		
Hiroaki Yamamoto	JPN	12/04/91	M	5	(1)	

FK Mladost Podgorica

1950 • Stari Aerodrom (1,000) • fkmladost.me

Major honours
Montenegrin League (1) 2016; Montenegrin Cup (1) 2015

Coach: Nikola Rakojević;
(01/01/17) Goran Perišić;
(02/04/2017) Dejan Vukićević

2016

07/08	a	Zeta	D	0-0	
13/08	h	Sutjeska	W	2-1	*Petrović, Djurišić*
20/08	a	Rudar	W	1-0	*Adrović*
24/08	h	Dečić	W	1-0	*Burzanović*
28/08	a	Budućnost	L	0-1	
10/09	h	Iskra	D	0-0	
17/09	a	Petrovac	W	3-0	*og (Kovačević), Adrović, Novović*
24/09	h	Jedinstvo	W	5-0	*Adrović 3, Petrović 2*
01/10	a	Lovćen	D	0-0	
15/10	a	Grbalj	L	0-1	
22/10	h	Bokelj	W	3-1	*Boris G Kopitović, Petrović, Vlaisavljević*
29/10	h	Zeta	W	1-0	*Bukorac*
05/11	a	Sutjeska	D	1-1	*Vlaisavljević*
16/11	h	Rudar	W	2-1	*Boris G Kopitović, Adrović*
19/11	a	Dečić	L	0-2	
26/11	h	Budućnost	L	1-2	*Boris Z Kopitović*
04/12	a	Iskra	W	3-1	*Adrović 2, Petrović*

2017

21/02	h	Petrovac	W	1-0	*Boris G Kopitović*
27/02	a	Jedinstvo	W	1-0	*Boris G Kapitović*
04/03	h	Lovćen	D	0-0	
12/03	h	Grbalj	D	0-0	
18/03	a	Bokelj	L	0-1	
28/03	a	Bokelj	D	0-0	
01/04	h	Iskra	L	1-2	*Lakić*
08/04	a	Rudar	W	1-0	*Burzanović*
15/04	h	Petrovac	W	2-0	*Boris G Kapitović, Petrović*
22/04	a	Grbalj	D	0-0	
30/04	h	Sutjeska	L	1-3	*Petrović*
06/05	a	Dečić	D	0-0	
10/05	h	Zeta	L	0-1	
13/05	h	Jedinstvo	W	6-2	*Petrović 3, Boris G Kapitović, Raičević, Jablan*
20/05	a	Budućnost	W	3-0	*(w/o; original match abandoned after 79 mins at 1-0 Novović)*
27/05	h	Lovćen	W	7-2	*Petrović 4, Raičević, Knežević, Boris G Kapitović*

Name	Nat	DoB	Pos	Aps	(s)	Gls
Admir Adrović		08/05/88	A	14		8
Stefan Bukorac	SRB	15/02/91	M	26	(3)	1
Marko Burzanović		13/01/98	M	20	(8)	2
Milan Djurišić		11/04/87	M	31	(1)	1
Blažo Igumanović		19/01/86	D	7	(8)	
Ivan Ivanović		14/09/89	M	11	(3)	
Miljan Jablan	SRB	30/01/85	D	9	(1)	1
Andrija Kaludjerović		29/10/93	M	13	(4)	
Ivan Knežević		22/02/86	A	4	(10)	1
Boris G Kopitović		27/04/95	A	13	(11)	7
Boris Z Kopitović		17/09/94	D	14		1
Miloš Lakić		21/12/85	D	28		1
Bojan Lazarević		09/09/93	M	3	(6)	
Damir Ljuljanović		23/02/92	G	28		
Vuk Martinović		19/09/89	D	27	(1)	
Ivan Novović		26/04/89	D	27	(3)	2
Masashi Otani	JPN	14/06/94	M	1	(3)	
Luka Petričević		06/07/92	M	7	(9)	
Zoran Petrović		14/07/97	A	23	(7)	14
Vuk Radović		28/02/93	G	5		
Miloš B Radulović		06/08/90	D	18	(3)	
Mirko Raičević		22/03/82	M	25	(3)	2
Marko Roganović		21/06/96	D	2	(1)	
Ognjen Stijepović		22/10/99	M		(6)	
Miljan Vlaisavljević		16/04/91	A	7	(4)	2

OFK Petrovac

1969 • Pod Malim brdom (1,630) • no website

Major honours
Montenegrin Cup (1) 2009

Coach: Aleksandar Nedović

2016

06/08	a	Dečić	W	4-1	*Radulović (p), Vujačić 2, Mikijelj*
13/08	h	Budućnost	L	0-2	
20/08	a	Iskra	L	0-1	
24/08	a	Grbalj	W	1-0	*Marković*
28/08	h	Jedinstvo	D	0-0	
10/09	a	Lovćen	W	1-0	*Rudović*
17/09	h	Mladost	L	0-3	
24/09	a	Bokelj	L	0-3	
01/10	h	Zeta	D	1-1	*Ragipović*
15/10	a	Sutjeska	D	0-0	
22/10	h	Rudar	L	1-2	*Vujačić*
29/10	h	Dečić	W	3-0	*Vujačić, Rudović, Kacić*
05/11	a	Budućnost	L	0-5	
16/11	h	Iskra	W	2-1	*Radulović (p), Kacić*
19/11	h	Grbalj	W	1-0	*Rudović*
26/11	a	Jedinstvo	W	3-1	*Kacić, Vujačić, Rudović*
03/12	h	Lovćen	W	1-0	*Mikijelj*

2017

21/02	a	Mladost	L	0-1	
26/02	h	Bokelj	D	1-1	*Vujović*
04/03	a	Zeta	D	0-0	
11/03	h	Sutjeska	L	0-3	
18/03	a	Rudar	L	2-3	*Vučinić, Rudović*
28/03	h	Sutjeska	L	0-1	
01/04	a	Dečić	D	0-0	
08/04	h	Zeta	W	3-1	*Pepić, Košuta, Rudović*
15/04	a	Mladost	D	0-2	
22/04	h	Budućnost	W	1-0	*Burzanović*
30/04	a	Lovćen	L	0-6	
06/05	h	Bokelj	L	1-3	*Burzanović*
10/05	a	Iskra	L	0-4	
13/05	h	Rudar	W	3-1	*Burzanović, Boričić, Korniychuk*
20/05	a	Jedinstvo	L	1-3	*Vujović*
27/05	a	Grbalj	L	0-1	

Name	Nat	DoB	Pos	Aps	(s)	Gls
Balša Boričić		07/01/97	M	14	(13)	1
Nikola Bulatović		19/05/96	M	1	(3)	
Vladan Burzan		12/04/98	M		(2)	
Igor Burzanović		25/08/85	M	9	(4)	3
Aleksandar Čolić	SRB	25/09/88	D	22	(2)	
Andjeo Drobnjak		31/07/95	M		(6)	
Ivan Gazivoda		20/04/94	D	2	(6)	
Benjamin Kacić		28/06/91	M	29	(2)	3
Filip Kalačević		12/03/94	M		(3)	
Anatoliy Korniychuk	UKR	10/10/90	M	2	(5)	1
Damir Košuta		09/06/95	M	20	(7)	1
Miloš Kovačević		31/03/91	D	11	(2)	
Marko Marković		05/09/87	M	27	(3)	1
Lazar Martinović		03/07/89	D	1	(6)	
Luka Medigović		03/04/95	M	1	(3)	
Zoran Mikijelj		13/12/91	D	30		2
Vuk Orlandić		05/01/97	M	5	(4)	
Dejan Pepić		27/07/93	M	9	(4)	1
Stefan Popović		11/01/93	G	8	(2)	
Stefan Radovanović	SRB	19/02/92	D	9	(1)	
Mileta Radulović		29/01/81	G	25		2
Kenan Ragipović	SRB	16/09/82	M	18	(1)	1
Blažo Rajović		26/03/86	D	16		
Andjelo Rudović		03/05/96	A	19	(7)	6
Nikola Savović		30/09/94	M	4	(2)	
Miloš Stevović		14/09/89	M	5		
Mihailo Tomković		10/06/91	D	13		
Darko Vučić		28/08/91	A	9		
Jovan Vučinić		20/01/92	A	14	(1)	1
Aleksandar Vujačić		19/03/90	A	16		5
Nenad Vujović		02/01/89	D	24	(1)	2

FK Rudar Pljevlja

1920 • Pod Golubinjom (8,500) • fkrudarpljevlja.com

Major honours
Montenegrin League (2) 2010, 2015; Montenegrin Cup (4) 2007, 2010, 2011, 2016

Coach: Dragan Radojičić;
(28/08/16) Mirko Marić;
(22/02/17) Milan Lešnjak (SRB);
(20/04/17) Radislav Dragićević

2016

06/08	h	Jedinstvo	W	5-0	*Vuković, Marković 2, Vlahović 2*
13/08	a	Lovćen	D	0-0	
20/08	h	Mladost	L	0-1	
24/08	a	Bokelj	L	1-2	*Marković*
27/08	h	Zeta	D	1-1	*Vuković*
11/09	a	Sutjeska	L	0-1	
17/09	h	Grbalj	D	1-1	*Melunović*
24/09	h	Dečić	D	0-0	
02/10	a	Budućnost	W	2-0	*Noma, Brnović*
15/10	h	Iskra	D	0-0	
22/10	a	Petrovac	W	2-1	*Yamamoto 2*
29/10	a	Jedinstvo	D	0-0	
05/11	h	Lovćen	D	1-1	*Noma*
16/11	a	Mladost	L	1-2	*Zečević*
19/11	h	Bokelj	W	2-0	*Melunović 2*
26/11	a	Zeta	L	0-3	
03/12	h	Sutjeska	W	1-0	*Brnović*

2017

21/02	a	Grbalj	L	1-2	*Zečević*
26/02	a	Dečić	L	1-2	*Zečević*
04/03	h	Budućnost	W	1-0	*Zečević*
11/03	a	Iskra	L	0-1	
18/03	h	Petrovac	W	3-2	*Vuković 2, Kalić*
28/03	h	Dečić	W	1-0	*Vuković*
01/04	a	Zeta	L	0-1	
08/04	h	Mladost	L	0-1	
15/04	a	Budućnost	L	2-3	*Melunović 2*
22/04	h	Lovćen	W	2-0	*Vuković, Melunović*
30/04	a	Bokelj	D	0-0	
06/05	h	Iskra	W	2-0	*og (Krstović), Golubović*
10/05	a	Jedinstvo	W	4-1	*Melunović, Božović, Radišić, Janković*
13/05	a	Petrovac	L	1-3	*Janković*
20/05	h	Grbalj	D	0-0	
27/05	a	Sutjeska	L	0-2	

Name	Nat	DoB	Pos	Aps	(s)	Gls
Ermin Alić		23/02/92	D	24	(2)	
Draško Božović		30/06/88	M	15		1
Predrag Brnović		22/10/86	M	27	(4)	2
Arben Buqaj	CRO	19/10/91	A	1	(3)	
Nikola Gačević		14/05/87	M	3	(11)	
Milija Golubović		25/04/86	D	17	(10)	1
Ivan Ivanović		14/09/89	A	13	(2)	
Branislav Janković		08/02/92	M	14	(1)	2
Miroje Jovanović		10/03/87	M	5	(7)	
Armin Kalić		18/08/95	M	1	(3)	1
Danko Kovačević		10/07/91	M	1	(1)	
Slobodan Lakićević		12/01/88	D	11		
Ivan Marković	SRB	23/12/91	A	9	(1)	3
Alen Melunović	BIH	26/01/90	A	16	(5)	7
Dušan Nestorović	SRB	26/06/86	D	7		
Shodai Nishikava	JPN	21/09/93	M	1	(3)	
Ryota Noma	JPN	15/11/92	M	12	(2)	2
Miloš Radanović		05/11/80	G	33		
Mirko Radišić		01/09/90	D	24	(1)	1
Stevan Reljić		31/03/86	D	23		
Alphonse Soppo	CMR	15/05/85	M	22	(5)	
Željko Tomašević		05/04/88	D	13	(3)	
Mihailo Tomković		10/06/91	D	1	(1)	
Nedjeljko Vlahović		15/01/84	M	5		2
Marko Vuković		20/03/96	A	20	(8)	6
Sho Yamamoto	JPN	12/11/96	A	12	(3)	2
Miloš Zečević		28/01/99	M	12	(13)	4
Radule Živković		22/10/90	D	21	(3)	

MONTENEGRO

FK Sutjeska

1927 • Kraj Bistrice (10,800) • fksutjeska.me

Major honours

Montenegrin League (2) 2013, 2014; Montenegrin Cup (1) 2017

Coach: Nebojša Jovović;
(28/02/17) Nikola Rakojević

Date		Opponent		Score	Scorers
2016					
07/08	h	Lovćen	W	1-0	*Vuković*
13/08	a	Mladost	L	1-2	*Jildemar*
20/08	h	Bokelj	W	2-0	*J Nikolić, B Božović*
24/08	a	Zeta	L	0-1	
27/08	h	Grbalj	D	1-1	*Bakrač*
11/09	h	Rudar	W	1-0	*J Nikolić (p)*
17/09	a	Dečić	L	0-1	
25/09	h	Budućnost	D	1-1	*B Božović*
01/10	a	Iskra	W	3-0	*B Božović, Vuković 2*
15/10	h	Petrovac	D	0-0	
22/10	a	Jedinstvo	D	0-0	
29/10	a	Lovćen	W	2-0	*Vuković, Vujović*
05/11	h	Mladost	D	1-1	*Zarubica*
16/11	a	Bokelj	W	2-1	*J Nikolić (p), Shimura*
19/11	h	Zeta	D	0-0	
26/11	a	Grbalj	D	2-2	*B Božović, Zarubica*
03/12	a	Rudar	L	0-1	
2017					
21/02	h	Dečić	D	1-1	*Kovačević*
26/02	a	Budućnost	L	2-4	*Ivanović 2*
04/03	h	Iskra	W	2-1	*Kovačević, og (Krstović)*
11/03	a	Petrovac	W	3-0	*Kovačević, Ivanović, B Božović*
18/03	h	Jedinstvo	W	3-2	*Kovačević, Zarubica, Ivanović*
28/03	a	Petrovac	W	1-0	*Vlaisavljević*
01/04	h	Grbalj	D	0-0	
08/04	h	Jedinstvo	W	4-0	*Ivanović 2, B Božović 2*
15/04	a	Dečić	L	0-1	
22/04	h	Zeta	L	1-2	*Ivanović*
30/04	a	Mladost	W	3-1	*Ivanović, B Božović 2*
06/05	h	Budućnost	W	1-0	*B Božović*
10/05	a	Lovćen	W	2-0	*Zarubica, B Božović*
13/05	h	Bokelj	D	1-1	*Bakrač*
20/05	a	Iskra	L	0-1	
27/05	h	Rudar	W	2-0	*Bošković (p), Marko Vučić*

Name	Nat	DoB	Pos	Aps	(s)	Gls
Miloš Bakrač		25/02/92	D	31	(1)	2
Ivan Bošković		01/01/82	A	5	(7)	1
Bojan Božović		03/02/85	A	22	(7)	11
Draško Božović		30/06/88	M	9	(4)	
Vladan Bubanja		21/02/99	D		(2)	
Igor Ćuković		06/06/93	D	8		
Slavko Damjanović		02/11/92	D	25		
Masanobu Egawa	JPN	29/08/96	D	4	(3)	
Vladan Giljen		07/12/89	G	31		
Igor Ivanović		09/09/90	M	26		8
Jildemar	BRA	05/01/89	A	9	(7)	1
Stevan Kovačević	SRB	09/01/88	M	20	(5)	4
Suad Ličina		08/02/95	G	2		
Stefan Lončar		19/02/96	M	9	(2)	
Jovan Nikolić		21/07/91	M	17		3
Nemanja Nikolić		18/05/97	M		(1)	
Igor Poček		23/12/94	D		(10)	
Noburu Shimura	JPN	11/03/93	M	30	(1)	1
Nikola Stijepović		02/11/93	D	19	(6)	
Miljan Vlaisavljević		16/04/91	M	14	(1)	1
Marko Vučić		30/12/96	D	12	(8)	1
Miloš Vučić		26/08/95	M	19	(5)	
Matija Vujović		09/06/95	M	1	(9)	1
Veljko Vuković	SRB	14/07/89	A	27		4
Dejan Zarubica		11/04/93	A	19	(9)	4
Igor Zonjić		16/10/91	D	4	(5)	

FK Zeta

1927 • Trešnjica (5,000) • fkzeta.net

Major honours

Montenegrin League (1) 2007

Coach: Dejan Vukićević;
(06/01/17) Dušan Vlaisavljević

Date		Opponent		Score	Scorers
2016					
07/08	h	Mladost	D	0-0	
13/08	a	Bokelj	W	1-0	*Klikovac*
20/08	h	Grbalj	W	2-1	*Klikovac, Kordić*
24/08	h	Sutjeska	W	1-0	*Kordić*
27/08	a	Rudar	D	1-1	*Kordić*
10/09	h	Dečić	L	0-1	
18/09	a	Budućnost	L	0-1	
24/09	h	Iskra	W	3-1	*Rogošić, Krkotić 2*
01/10	a	Petrovac	D	1-1	*Ljuljdjuraj*
15/10	h	Jedinstvo	W	1-0	*Ljuljdjuraj*
22/10	a	Lovćen	W	1-0	*Krkotić*
29/10	a	Mladost	L	0-1	
05/11	h	Bokelj	W	1-0	*Vujačić*
16/11	a	Grbalj	L	0-1	
19/11	a	Sutjeska	D	0-0	
26/11	h	Rudar	W	3-0	*Ljuljdjuraj, Krkotić (p), Kukuličić*
03/12	a	Dečić	L	0-2	
2017					
22/02	h	Budućnost	D	1-1	*Kukuličić*
26/02	a	Iskra	W	2-0	*Kukuličić, Ljuljdjuraj*
05/03	h	Petrovac	D	0-0	
11/03	a	Jedinstvo	W	3-0	*N Krstović 2, Kalezić*
18/03	h	Lovćen	W	1-0	*Ljuljdjuraj*
28/03	a	Iskra	L	0-1	
01/04	h	Rudar	W	1-0	*N Krstović*
08/04	a	Petrovac	L	1-3	*Ljuljdjuraj*
15/04	h	Grbalj	L	0-1	
22/04	a	Sutjeska	W	2-1	*N Sekulić, N Krstović*
30/04	h	Dečić	W	3-0	*Adžović (p), N Krstović, D Pešukić*
06/05	h	Jedinstvo	W	3-0	*Cavnić, B Božović, Rogošić*
10/05	a	Mladost	W	1-0	*N Krstović*
13/05	h	Budućnost	W	1-0	*N Krstović*
20/05	a	Lovćen	W	3-0	*Kalezić 2, B Božović*
27/05	h	Bokelj	W	1-0	*Ljuljdjuraj*

Name	Nat	DoB	Pos	Aps	(s)	Gls
Aldin Adžović		16/06/94	M	29		1
Bojan Aligrudić		08/02/95	D	16	(6)	
Balša Božović		01/05/87	M	2	(8)	2
Mladen Božović		01/08/84	G	32		
Bruno Paiva	BRA	13/01/91	M	3	(6)	
Nemanja Cavnić		05/09/95	D	31		1
Zvonko Ceklić		11/04/99	D	1		
Božidar Djukić		25/09/97	D	7	(2)	
Vasko Kalezić		14/03/94	M	8	(5)	3
Luka Klikovac		01/06/93	M	10		2
Šaleta Kordić		19/04/93	A	11	(4)	3
Miloš Krkotić		29/09/87	M	15		4
Nikola Krstović		05/04/00	A	10	(9)	7
Pavle Krstović		18/04/99	A		(6)	
Srdjan Krstović		05/08/00	M		(1)	
Filip Kukuličić		13/02/96	A	23	(8)	3
Pjeter Ljuljdjuraj		29/06/92	M	30		7
Goran Milojko		05/01/94	M	30		
Marko Novović		24/11/96	G	1	(1)	
Deni Pavlović	SRB	01/09/93	M	2		
Danilo Pešukić		20/09/00	M		(7)	1
Periša Pešukić		07/12/97	D	6		
Miloš Popović		05/12/96	M		(7)	
Miloš Radulović		23/02/90	D	9	(1)	
Vladislav Rogošić		21/09/94	M	10	(13)	2
Nemanja Sekulić		29/03/94	D	26	(1)	1
Radisav Sekulić		27/09/85	A		(1)	
Igor Vujačić		08/08/94	D	28		1
Stefan Vukčević		11/04/97	M	17	(9)	
Stevan Živković	SRB	18/10/89	M	6	(3)	

Top goalscorers

14	Zoran Petrović (Mladost)
12	Goran Vujović (Budućnost)
11	Radomir Djalović (Budućnost)
	Bojan Božović (Sutjeska)
10	Vule Vujačić (Dečić)
9	Milivoje Raičević (Budućnost)
	Rodoljub Paunović (Iskra)
	Marko Djurović (Lovćen)
8	Admir Adrović (Mladost)
	Igor Ivanović (Sutjeska)

Promoted club

FK Kom

1958 • Zlatica (1,200) • no website
Coach: Nenad Vukčević

Second level final table 2016/17

		Pld	W	D	L	F	A	Pts
1	FK Kom	30	18	8	4	67	21	62
2	FK Ibar	30	18	6	6	42	16	60
3	FK Otrant-Olympic	30	15	7	8	32	22	51
4	FK Mornar	30	13	10	7	37	21	49
5	FK Jezero	30	12	8	10	34	26	44
6	FK Berane	30	12	8	10	46	43	41
7	FK Cetinje	30	11	6	13	27	35	39
8	OFK Igalo	30	10	4	16	30	43	34
9	FK Čelik	30	9	4	17	26	47	27
10	FK Radnički	30	6	6	18	31	68	24
11	FK Bratstvo	30	4	7	19	27	57	19
12	FK Grafičar	0	0	0	0	0	0	-5

NB FK Grafičar withdrew after round 15 – all their matches were annulled; FK Grafičar – 5 pts deducted; FK Čelik – 4 pts deducted; FK Berane – 3 pts deducted; FK Otrant-Olympic – 1 pt deducted.

Promotion/Relegation play-offs

(31/05/17 & 04/06/17)
Otrant-Olympic 1-0 Rudar
Rudar 3-0 Otrant-Olympic
(Rudar 3-1)

Petrovac 4-0 Ibar
Ibar 1-1 Petrovac
(Petrovac 5-1)

DOMESTIC CUP

Kup Crne Gore 2016/17

FIRST ROUND

(20/09/16)
Sloga 0-6 Lovćen

(21/09/16)
Bokelj 2-0 Mornar
Bratstvo 0-3 Grbalj
Brskovo 1-1 Gorštak *(4-2 on pens)*
Hajduk 0-8 Mladost Podgorica
Ibar 1-3 Iskra
Igalo 0-4 Dečić
Jedinstvo 0-0 Čelik *(4-2 on pens)*
Jezero 0-4 Zeta
Mladost Lješkopolje 0-0 Cetinje *(4-2 on pens)*
Otrant-Olympic 1-1 Berane *(3-4 on pens)*
Petnjica 0-2 Kom
Petrovac 3-0 Grafičar
Sutjeska 5-0 Radnički

Byes – Budućnost, Rudar

SECOND ROUND

(28/09/16 & 26/10/16)
Bokelj 1-0, 2-0 Berane *(3-0)*
Brskovo 2-4, 0-1 Lovćen *(2-5)*
Grbalj 3-1, 1-2 Mladost Podgorica *(4-3)*
Iskra 4-1, 1-1 Mladost Lješkopolje *(5-2)*
Kom 1-5, 0-1 Budućnost *(1-6)*
Petrovac 3-0, 0-2 Jedinstvo (3-2)
Rudar 0-0, 1-1 Dečić *(1-1; Rudar on away goal)*
Zeta 0-1, 2-2 Sutjeska *(2-3)*

QUARTER-FINALS

(02/11/16 & 30/11/16)
Budućnost 2-1 Grbalj *(Djalović 25, 42; Dinčić 74)*
Grbalj 1-0 Budućnost *(Pavlović 88)*
(2-2; Grbalj on away goal)

Iskra 1-0 Lovćen *(Šćepanović 45p)*
Lovćen 1-2 Iskra *(Djurović 67; Perutović 10, Krstović 53)*
(Iskra 3-1)

Petrovac 1-0 Sutjeska *(Vujačić 9)*
Sutjeska 1-0 Petrovac *(B Božović 78)*
(1-1; Sutjeska 4-3 on pens)

Rudar 1-1 Bokelj *(Golubović 3; Vujović 62)*
Bokelj 0-1 Rudar *(Alić 52)*
(Rudar 2-1)

SEMI-FINALS

(12/04/17 & 26/04/17)
Iskra 0-5 Sutjeska *(Vlaisavljević 3, 23, Kovačević 37, Ivanović 54, Zarubica 67)*
Sutjeska 4-3 Iskra *(Shimura 29, Poček 49, Zarubica 59, Bošković 90; Perutović 5, Savićević 44, Memčević 80)*
(Sutjeska 9-3)

Rudar 1-1 Grbalj *(Božović 5; Nedić 78)*
Grbalj 1-0 Rudar *(Zorica 89)*
(Grbalj 2-1)

FINAL

(31/05/17)
Pod Goricom, Podgorica
FK SUTJESKA 1 *(Vlaisavljević 72)*
OFK GRBALJ 0
Referee: *Milačić*
SUTJESKA: *Giljen, Bakrač, Stijepović, Damjanović, Kovačević (Poček 88), Vlaisavljević, Miloš Vučić, Lončar, Shimura, Bošković (Zarubica 82), Vuković*
GRBALJ: *L Carević, M Carević, Manojlović (Vukčević 77), Grivić, Ajković (Vukotić 46), Lazarević, Nikolić, Zorica (Jablan 80), Pavlović, Nedić, Š Kordić*

Sutjeska defeated Grbalj 1-0 in the Montenegrin Cup final to claim the trophy for the first time

NETHERLANDS

Koninklijke Nederlandse Voetbalbond (KNVB)

Address	Woudenbergseweg 56-58 Postbus 515 NL-3700 AM Zeist
Tel	+31 343 499 201
Fax	+31 343 499 189
E-mail	concern@knvb.nl
Website	knvb.nl

President	Michael van Praag
General secretary	Bert van Oostveen
Media officer	Bas Ticheler
Year of formation	1889

EREDIVISIE CLUBS

 1 **ADO Den Haag**

 2 **AFC Ajax**

 3 **AZ Alkmaar**

 4 **SBV Excelsior**

 5 **Feyenoord**

 6 **Go Ahead Eagles**

 7 **FC Groningen**

 8 **sc Heerenveen**

 9 **Heracles Almelo**

 10 **NEC Nijmegen**

 11 **PEC Zwolle**

 12 **PSV Eindhoven**

 13 **Roda JC**

 14 **Sparta Rotterdam**

 15 **FC Twente**

 16 **FC Utrecht**

 17 **Vitesse**

 18 **Willem II**

PROMOTED CLUBS

 19 **VVV-Venlo**

 20 **NAC Breda**

KEY

- UEFA Champions League
- UEFA Europa League
- Promoted
- Relegated

Fabulous Feyenoord front-run to victory

Rotterdam was a city in celebration on 14 May 2017 as Feyenoord clinched their first Eredivisie title of the 21st century, ending an 18-year wait to be crowned Dutch champions. Giovanni van Bronckhorst's passionately supported team occupied top spot all season but were pressed all the way by arch-rivals Ajax.

The Amsterdam club also finished runners-up in the UEFA Europa League, while Vitesse claimed a long-awaited first major honour with victory in the Dutch Cup. At national team level, Danny Blind was sacked as Bondscoach and replaced – for a third spell – by Dick Advocaat.

Eredivisie title returns to Rotterdam after 18 years

Runners-up Ajax reach UEFA Europa League final

Vitesse win Dutch Cup to claim first major trophy

Domestic league

A brilliant display of front-running made 2016/17 a season to treasure for Feyenoord. They beat FC Groningen 5-0 away on the opening day and, imbued with confidence, set off on a nine-month campaign that would feature a multitude of memorable performances as well as a relentless resolve to succeed that continuously kept at bay both Ajax and the champions of the previous two seasons, PSV Eindhoven.

Outpointing both Ajax and PSV was never going to be easy, but Feyenoord gave themselves every chance by winning their first nine matches. The evident highlight was a 1-0 victory in Eindhoven, thanks to a late goal from Brazilian defender Eric Botteghin, but each of those early victories suggested that Feyenoord were the real deal – well-drilled, determined and laden with in-form players, foremost among them Danish striker Nicolai Jørgensen, newly signed from FC København.

Feyenoord's victory march was halted by a 1-1 home draw against Ajax, although veteran skipper Dirk Kuyt's 85th-minute equaliser ensured that the locals remained in good spirits. That was not the case after the next two results – a home draw with Hereenveen and 1-0 defeat at newly-promoted Go Ahead Eagles – but just as the pressure on Van Bronckhorst, a Dutch Cup-winning coach the season before, began to intensify, the former Netherlands captain reaffirmed his leadership skills by steering the team on a fabulous ten-match winning run during the winter months. That sequence concluded with another huge win against Phillip Cocu's PSV – a team undefeated since their earlier home reverse against Feyenoord but now, effectively, out of the race for the title.

Ajax, under new coach Peter Bosz, were also going well, but when the spring international break came around, they still had a six-point deficit to make up on the irrepressible Rotterdammers, their next visitors in Amsterdam. It was a game Ajax had to win, and win it they did, a first-minute goal from Danish schemer Lasse Schöne – at 30 the veteran of an extremely young team – setting them up for a 2-1 victory that reduced the gap to three points.

Feyenoord's response was emphatic – an 8-0 win against Go Ahead Eagles – but further dropped points at PEC Zwolle (2-2) meant that with three games to go their lead was down to just a single point. Two Jørgensen goals – his 20th and 21st of the season, enough to win the golden boot – gave Feyenoord victory in Arnhem against Vitesse, and when PSV beat Ajax 1-0 later that day in Eindhoven, the title race appeared to be over.

One win in their last two fixtures would see Feyenoord home. The first of them was away to Excelsior – traditionally Feyenoord's feeder club rather than a Rotterdam rival but in this instance a team at the wrong end of the table equally desperate for points. Furthermore, Excelsior were a team in form, and they confirmed that against the champions-in-waiting, three goals in ten second-half minutes bringing a thumping 3-0 win that would ensure their safety while potentially plunging their opponents into a sea of self-doubt.

With Ajax easily beating Go Ahead Eagles, Feyenoord's lead was back to one point. Victory on the final day against mid-table Heracles Almelo in De Kuip – where they had surrendered just four points all season – was now imperative. Cometh the hour, cometh the man. Captain Kuyt, controversially dropped to the bench against Excelsior, was recalled to the starting XI, and the 36-year-old gave the performance of his life to lead Feyenoord to glory, opening the scoring in the first minute, adding a second goal not long afterwards and, to a background of joyous delirium, completing his hat-trick from the penalty spot six minutes from time. Heracles got a goal back late on but it didn't matter. The title was Feyenoord's.

Kuyt, the hero of the day, promptly announced his retirement. Winning his first Eredivisie title in the way that he did was the perfect climax to a wonderful career. It was a triumph to savour, too, for everyone else associated with the club, not least coach Van Bronckhorst and a whole phalanx of players, from Brad Jones in goal and ever-present Botteghin at the back to midfield fulcrum Karim El Ahmadi and the dynamic front three of Jens Toornstra, Jørgensen and Eljero Elia.

Ajax had chased well but, as in 2015/16, missed out on the final day. They were not quite as prolific as Feyenoord, but 79 goals and 81 points both amounted to decent returns and the tradition of the club was kept vibrantly alive by Bosz as he fielded an assortment of outstanding youngsters. Danish debutant Kasper Dolberg, with his 16 goals, was the standout figure but there were honourable mentions too for Colombian centre-back Davinson Sánchez, Cameroonian goalkeeper André Onana and tricky wingers Hakim Ziyech and Amin Younes.

PSV lost fewer matches than both Feyenoord and Ajax – just two, both against the champions – but were undone by a proliferation of draws. Almost every one of Cocu's outfield players scored, but Gastón Pereiro was alone in reaching double figures, on ten. The spark of the previous two seasons was not quite there, and although PSV finished 14 points above fourth-placed FC Utrecht, the teams' European reward was identical – a place in the third qualifying round of the UEFA Europa League. Utrecht had to put in some overtime to claim that prize, a thrilling second-leg comeback in their play-off final against AZ Alkmaar ending in a triumphant penalty shoot-out.

The promotion/relegation play-offs produced one winner apiece from the Eredivisie – 17th-placed Roda JC – and the Eerste Divisie – fifth-placed NAC Breda – as NEC Nijmegen went down alongside automatically relegated Go Ahead Eagles, while the sole promotion spot was claimed by VVV-Venlo.

Domestic cup

Back at first club Vitesse after spells abroad in Portugal, England, France and Spain, Ricky van Wolfswinkel had an excellent season in the Eredivisie, scoring 20 goals, but the 28-year-old striker's piece de resistance came in the final of the KNVB-Beker, when he scored twice late on against AZ to give the Arnhem club the first major trophy in their 125-year history. Henk Fräser's side had earlier eliminated Feyenoord in the quarter-finals; neither PSV nor Ajax made it even that far, their respective conquerors Sparta and Cambuur both progressing to the last four.

Vitesse striker Ricky van Wolfswinkel stoops to head past AZ goalkeeper Tim Krul and score the first of his two goals in the Dutch Cup final

Europe

Ajax reached their first European final for 21 years, seven home wins out of seven powering them to a UEFA Europa League showdown in Stockholm with Manchester United. However, on the big night they were well beaten by José Mourinho's side, going down 2-0 in what would be Bosz's final game, the Ajax coach leaving to replace Thomas Tuchel at Borussia Dortmund. United's opening match in the competition had been a 1-0 defeat at Feyenoord, but the Rotterdammers won only once more and failed to get out of their group. AZ did make it to the round of 32 but might have wished they hadn't when Lyon thrashed them 11-2 on aggregate.

In the UEFA Champions League, PSV's bid to reach the knockout phase for the second straight year never got going and they failed to win a game. Victory at home to Rostov on matchday six would have secured springtime UEFA Europa League football, but the Russian team that had previously pulverised Ajax in the play-offs, winning 5-2 overall, held out for a 0-0 draw, leaving Cocu's side with a measly two points.

National team

The Netherlands' shock failure to reach UEFA EURO 2016 demanded a rapid recovery in the 2018 FIFA World Cup qualifying campaign, but a home defeat by France and a dispiriting 2-0 loss in Bulgaria left the Oranje in such a precarious position that coach Blind was jettisoned after less than two years in the job, his only victories in matches that mattered having come against Kazakhstan, Belarus and Luxembourg.

The tough task of reviving the team's fortunes was handed to the avuncular, experienced Advocaat – for the third time in his career, after spells from 1992-94 and 2002-04 – and, after being appointed in early May then seeing out his contract at Fenerbahçe, Blind's erstwhile assistant oversaw a 5-0 home win over Luxembourg in his first game, Wesley Sneijder scoring one of the goals on his record 131st appearance. With four qualifiers left and a three-point deficit to make up on both Sweden and France, Advocaat and his players had a steep mountain to climb if they were to reach the finals of a competition in which they had finished second in 2010 and third in 2014.

DOMESTIC SEASON AT A GLANCE

Eredivisie 2016/17 final table

			Home					Away					Total					
		Pld	W	D	L	F	A	W	D	L	F	A	W	D	L	F	A	Pts
1	**Feyenoord**	**34**	**15**	**2**	**0**	**56**	**11**	**11**	**2**	**4**	**30**	**14**	**26**	**4**	**4**	**86**	**25**	**82**
2	AFC Ajax	34	14	2	1	48	12	11	4	2	31	11	25	6	3	79	23	81
3	PSV Eindhoven	34	13	3	1	35	9	9	7	1	33	14	22	10	2	68	23	76
4	FC Utrecht	34	10	3	4	28	17	8	5	4	26	21	18	8	8	54	38	62
5	Vitesse	34	9	2	6	31	21	6	4	7	20	19	15	6	13	51	40	51
6	AZ Alkmaar	34	5	9	3	31	25	7	4	6	25	27	12	13	9	56	52	49
7	FC Twente	34	8	4	5	28	22	4	5	8	20	28	12	9	13	48	50	45
8	FC Groningen	34	5	8	4	25	24	5	5	7	30	27	10	13	11	55	51	43
9	sc Heerenveen	34	8	5	4	26	16	4	2	11	28	37	12	7	15	54	53	43
10	Heracles Almelo	34	8	3	6	32	21	4	4	9	21	34	12	7	15	53	55	43
11	ADO Den Haag	34	7	3	7	22	21	4	2	11	15	38	11	5	18	37	59	38
12	SBV Excelsior	34	6	5	6	27	25	3	5	9	16	35	9	10	15	43	60	37
13	Willem II	34	5	5	7	17	22	4	4	9	12	22	9	9	16	29	44	36
14	PEC Zwolle	34	5	5	7	19	28	4	3	10	20	39	9	8	17	39	67	35
15	Sparta Rotterdam	34	6	4	7	24	24	3	3	11	18	37	9	7	18	42	61	34
16	NEC Nijmegen	34	6	4	7	21	26	3	3	11	11	33	9	7	18	32	59	34
17	Roda JC	34	6	5	6	17	18	1	7	9	9	33	7	12	15	26	51	33
18	Go Ahead Eagles	34	4	1	12	20	35	2	4	11	12	38	6	5	23	32	73	23

European qualification 2017/18

Champion: Feyenoord (group stage)
AFC Ajax (third qualifying round)

Cup winner: Vitesse (group stage)
PSV Eindhoven (third qualifying round)
FC Utrecht (third qualifying round)

Top scorer Nicolai Jørgensen (Feyenoord), 21 goals
Relegated clubs Go Ahead Eagles, NEC Nijmegen
Promoted clubs VVV-Venlo, NAC Breda
Cup final Vitesse 2-0 AZ Alkmaar

Player of the season

Karim El Ahmadi
(Feyenoord)

A two-year spell in the English Premier League with Aston Villa did not quite go to plan for El Ahmadi, but after the Enschede-born Moroccan international returned to former club Feyenoord in 2014, his fortunes rose and in 2016/17 he played the finest football of his career to inspire the Rotterdam club to their title triumph. The 32-year-old was the prime mover and shaker at the heart of the Feyenoord midfield, orchestrating the team's play and chipping in with five goals as he added Eredivisie glory to his Dutch Cup winner's medal from the season before.

Newcomer of the season

Kasper Dolberg
(AFC Ajax)

There had been much talk in Amsterdam about the special talent of the tall, blond Danish youth international in the Ajax academy, and when he was handed his first-team opportunity by new coach Peter Bosz in 2016/17 the 19-year-old seized it with a firm grip, scoring in the Eredivisie and UEFA Europa League at the rate of a goal every other game and topping the scorers' charts for Ajax in both competitions. With sharp, instinctive finishing allied to natural flair, fluid movement and icy composure, Dolberg appears destined for the very top of his profession.

Team of the season

(3-4-3)

Coach: Van Bronckhorst *(Feyenoord)*

NETHERLANDS

NATIONAL TEAM

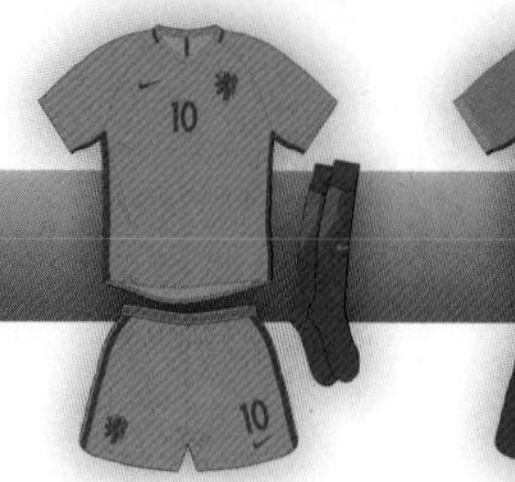

International honours
UEFA European Championship (1) 1988

International tournament appearances
FIFA World Cup (10) 1934, 1938, 1974 (runners-up), 1978 (runners-up), 1990 (2nd round), 1994 (qtr-finals), 1998 (4th), 2006 (2nd round), 2010 (runners-up), 2014 (3rd)
UEFA European Championship (9) 1976 (3rd), 1980, 1988 (Winners), 1992 (semi-finals), 1996 (qtr-finals), 2000 (semi-finals), 2004 (semi-finals), 2008 (qtr-finals), 2012

Top five all-time caps
Wesley Sneijder (131); Edwin van der Sar (130); Frank de Boer (112); Rafael van der Vaart (109); Giovanni van Bronckhorst (106)

Top five all-time goals
Robin van Persie (50); Klaas-Jan Huntelaar (42); Patrick Kluivert (40); Dennis Bergkamp (37); Ruud van Nistelrooy & Faas Wilkes (35)

Results 2016/17

01/09/16	Greece	H	Eindhoven	L	1-2	*Wijnaldum (14)*
06/09/16	Sweden (WCQ)	A	Solna	D	1-1	*Sneijder (67)*
07/10/16	Belarus (WCQ)	H	Rotterdam	W	4-1	*Promes (15, 31), Klaassen (56), Janssen (64)*
10/10/16	France (WCQ)	H	Amsterdam	L	0-1	
09/11/16	Belgium	H	Amsterdam	D	1-1	*Klaassen (38p)*
13/11/16	Luxembourg (WCQ)	A	Luxembourg	W	3-1	*Robben (36), Depay (58, 84)*
25/03/17	Bulgaria (WCQ)	A	Sofia	L	0-2	
28/03/17	Italy	H	Amsterdam	L	1-2	*Romagnoli (10og)*
31/05/17	Morocco	A	Agadir	W	2-1	*Promes (22), Janssen (68)*
04/06/17	Ivory Coast	H	Rotterdam	W	5-0	*Veltman (13, 36), Robben (32p), Klaassen (69), Janssen (75)*
09/06/17	Luxembourg (WCQ)	H	Rotterdam	W	5-0	*Robben (21), Sneijder (34), Wijnaldum (62), Promes (70), Janssen (84p)*

Appearances 2016/17

Coach: Danny Blind /(26/03/17) (Fred Grim) /(09/05/17) Dick Advocaat	**01/08/61 17/08/65 27/09/47**		**Gre**	**SWE**	**BLR**	**FRA**	**Bel**	**LUX**	**BUL**	**Ita**	**Mar**	**Civ**	**LUX**	**Caps**	**Goals**
Jeroen Zoet	06/01/91	PSV	G	G					G	G	G			9	-
Joël Veltman	15/01/92	Ajax	D				D				D	D	D	17	2
Jeffrey Bruma	13/11/91	Wolfsburg (GER)	D	D	D	D	D	D						25	1
Daley Blind	09/03/90	Man. United (ENG)	D	D	D	D	D	D	D	D82		D	D	46	2
Jetro Willems	30/03/94	PSV	D80			s84								22	-
Georginio Wijnaldum	11/11/90	Liverpool (ENG)	M72	M66	M	M62	M89	M	M46	M77		s64	M	40	8
Wesley Sneijder	09/06/84	Galatasaray (TUR)	M65	A	A46		A75	A46	s46	s82	s72	s70	M82	131	31
Kevin Strootman	13/02/90	Roma (ITA)	M65	M	M79	M			M	M46		M84	M	36	3
Steven Berghuis	19/12/91	Feyenoord	A	s78				s46		s88	A46	s77		9	-
Vincent Janssen	15/06/94	Tottenham (ENG)	A	A	A83	A	A27				A72	A77	A	13	7
Quincy Promes	04/01/92	Spartak Moskva (RUS)	A72	A78	A	A16			A68	A88	M	s78	s66	21	4
Jorrit Hendrix	06/02/95	PSV	s65											1	-
Davy Pröpper	02/09/91	PSV	s65		s46	M84						M64		5	-
Davy Klaassen	21/02/93	Ajax	s72	M	M	M	M46	M	M	M82		M70		14	4
Luciano Narsingh	13/09/90	PSV	s72											19	4
Bas Dost	31/05/89	Sporting (POR)	s80	s66	s83	s62	s27	A	A		s72	s77		15	1
Daryl Janmaat	22/07/89	Watford (ENG)		D										28	-
Virgil van Dijk	08/07/91	Southampton (ENG)		D	D	D	D	D						12	-
Maarten Stekelenburg	22/09/82	Everton (ENG)			G	G	G	G						58	-
Rick Karsdorp	11/02/95	Feyenoord			D	D			D					3	-
Jordy Clasie	27/06/91	Southampton (ENG)			s79		s15							17	-
Memphis Depay	13/02/94	Man. United (ENG) /Lyon (FRA)				s16	s67	s46		A	A74	A77	A66	31	5
Stijn Schaars	11/01/84	Heerenveen					M15							24	-
Jeremain Lens	24/11/87	Fenerbahçe (TUR)					A67			A			s73	34	8
Joshua Brenet	20/03/94	PSV					s46	D						2	-
Tonny Vilhena de Trindade	03/01/95	Feyenoord					s75			s46	M			4	-
Bart Ramselaar	29/06/96	PSV					s89	M88				s84		3	-
Arjen Robben	23/01/84	Bayern (GER)						A46	A			A78	A73	92	33
Marten de Roon	29/03/91	Middlesbrough (ENG)						s88			s46			2	-
Matthijs de Ligt	12/08/99	Ajax							D46		D 70*			2	-
Bruno Martins Indi	08/02/92	Stoke (ENG)							D	D		D		34	2
Wesley Hoedt	06/03/94	Lazio (ITA)							s46	D	D		D	4	-
Luuk de Jong	27/08/90	PSV							s68					13	3
Kenny Tete	09/10/95	Ajax								D		D		6	-
Jens Toornstra	04/04/89	Feyenoord								s77	M72			4	-
Nick Viergever	03/08/89	Ajax								s82	s74			3	-
Nathan Aké	18/02/95	Chelsea (ENG)									D		s82	2	-
Jasper Cillessen	22/04/89	Barcelona (ESP)										G	G	32	-
Stefan de Vrij	05/02/92	Lazio (ITA)											D	31	3

EUROPE

PSV Eindhoven

Group D
Match 1 - Club Atlético de Madrid (ESP)
H 0-1
Zoet, Isimat-Mirin, Moreno, Schwaab (Pereiro 80), Pröpper, Hendrix (Ramselaar 67), L de Jong, Narsingh (Bergwijn 80), Willems, Guardado, Brenet. Coach: Phillip Cocu (NED)
Match 2 - FC Rostov (RUS)
A 2-2 *Pröpper (14), L de Jong (45+1)*
Zoet, Isimat-Mirin, Moreno, Arias, Schwaab, Pröpper, Hendrix (Bergwijn 63), L de Jong, Narsingh (S de Jong 73), Willems, Guardado. Coach: Phillip Cocu (NED)
Match 3 - FC Bayern München (GER)
A 1-4 *Narsingh (41)*
Zoet, Moreno, Schwaab (Zinchenko 85), Pröpper, Pereiro (Bergwijn 77), L de Jong, S de Jong, Narsingh, Willems, Guardado (Isimat-Mirin 61), Brenet. Coach: Phillip Cocu (NED)
Match 4 - FC Bayern München (GER)
H 1-2 *Arias (14)*
Pasveer, Isimat-Mirin, Moreno, Arias, Schwaab, Pröpper, Pereiro (Bergwijn 67), L de Jong, Willems (Brenet 46), Guardado, Ramselaar (Zinchenko 74). Coach: Phillip Cocu (NED)
Match 5 - Club Atlético de Madrid (ESP)
A 0-2
Zoet, Isimat-Mirin, Moreno, Arias, Schwaab, Pröpper (Lundqvist 84), Pereiro, Willems (De Wijs 46), Ramselaar, Zinchenko, Bergwijn (Narsingh 61). Coach: Phillip Cocu (NED)
Match 6 - FC Rostov (RUS)
H 0-0
Zoet, Isimat-Mirin (Narsingh 77), Moreno, Arias (Pereiro 62), Schwaab, Pröpper, L de Jong, Brenet, Ramselaar, Zinchenko (S de Jong 62), Bergwijn. Coach: Phillip Cocu (NED)

AFC Ajax

Third qualifying round - PAOK FC (GRE)
H 1-1 *Dolberg (58)*
Cillessen, Tete, Veltman, Riedewald, El Ghazi (Černý 88), Klaassen, Cassierra (Younes 58), Dolberg, Viergever, Van de Beek (Schöne 77), Dijks. Coach: Peter Bosz (NED)
A 2-1 *Klaassen (45+1p, 88)*
Cillessen, Tete, Veltman, Riedewald, Klaassen, Westermann, Cassierra, Dolberg (El Ghazi 63), Viergever, Gudelj, Dijks. Coach: Peter Bosz (NED)

Play-offs - FC Rostov (RUS)
H 1-1 *Klaassen (38p)*
Cillessen, Veltman, Riedewald, Sánchez, Bazoer, El Ghazi, Traoré (Dolberg 82), Klaassen, Younes (Cassierra 68), Gudelj, Dijks. Coach: Peter Bosz (NED)
A 1-4 *Klaassen (84p)*
Cillessen, Tete, Veltman, Riedewald, Bazoer (Dolberg 58), El Ghazi (Schöne 46), Traoré, Klaassen, Younes (Cassierra 77), Viergever, Gudelj. Coach: Peter Bosz (NED)

Group G
Match 1 - Panathinaikos FC (GRE)
A 2-1 *Traoré (33), Riedewald (67)*
Onana, Veltman, Riedewald, Sánchez, Traoré (Dolberg 73), Klaassen (Schöne 89), Younes (Sinkgraven 86), Ziyech, Viergever, Gudelj, Dijks. Coach: Peter Bosz (NED)
Red card: Ziyech 79
Match 2 - R. Standard de Liège (BEL)
H 1-0 *Dolberg (28)*
Onana, Veltman, Sánchez, Sinkgraven, Traoré, Klaassen, Younes (El Ghazi 85), Schöne (Riedewald 62), Dolberg (Cassierra 69), Viergever, Gudelj. Coach: Peter Bosz (NED)
Match 3 - RC Celta de Vigo (ESP)
A 2-2 *Ziyech (22), Younes (71)*
Onana, Veltman, Sánchez, Sinkgraven, Traoré, Klaassen, Younes (Cassierra 77), Ziyech (Bazoer 77), Dolberg, Viergever, Gudelj. Coach: Peter Bosz (NED)
Match 4 - RC Celta de Vigo (ESP)
H 3-2 *Dolberg (41), Ziyech (68), Younes (71)*
Onana, Veltman, Riedewald, Sánchez, Sinkgraven, Traoré, Klaassen, Younes, Schöne, Ziyech (Gudelj 77), Dolberg (Cassierra 83). Coach: Peter Bosz (NED)
Match 5 - Panathinaikos FC (GRE)
H 2-0 *Schöne (40), Tete (50)*
Onana, Tete, Younes (Clement 62), Westermann, Černý, Cassierra, Schöne (De Jong 68), Van de Beek, Nouri, Dijks, De Ligt. Coach: Peter Bosz (NED)
Match 6 - R. Standard de Liège (BEL)
A 1-1 *El Ghazi (27)*
Boer, Tete, Riedewald, El Ghazi, Klaassen, Younes (Dolberg 66), Cassierra, Van de Beek, Nouri (Ziyech 79), Dijks, De Ligt. Coach: Peter Bosz (NED)

Round of 32 - Legia Warszawa (POL)
A 0-0
Onana, Tete, Sánchez, Sinkgraven, Traoré (Kluivert 73; Westermann 86), Klaassen, Younes, Schöne, Ziyech (Van de Beek 81), Dolberg, Viergever. Coach: Peter Bosz (NED)
Red card: Tete 84
H 1-0 *Viergever (49)*
Onana, Veltman, Riedewald, Sánchez, Traoré, Klaassen, Younes, Schöne, Ziyech, Dolberg (Nouri 81), Viergever. Coach: Peter Bosz (NED)

Round of 16 - FC København (DEN)
A 1-2 *Dolberg (32)*
Onana, Tete, Sinkgraven, Traoré (David Neres 77), Klaassen, Younes, Schöne, Dolberg, Viergever, Van de Beek (Ziyech 77), De Ligt. Coach: Peter Bosz (NED)
H 2-0 Traoré (23), Dolberg (45+2p)
Onana, Veltman (Tete 20), Sánchez, Traoré (Kluivert 81), Younes, Schöne, Ziyech, Dolberg, Viergever, Van de Beek (De Jong 75), De Ligt. Coach: Peter Bosz (NED)

Quarter-finals - FC Schalke 04 (GER)
H 2-0 *Klaassen (23p, 52)*
Onana, Veltman, Sánchez, Sinkgraven (De Ligt 46), Traoré, Klaassen, Younes, Ziyech, Viergever, Van de Beek (De Jong 87), Kluivert (David Neres 74). Coach: Peter Bosz (NED)
A 2-3 (aet) *Viergever (111), Younes (120)*
Onana, Veltman, Sánchez, Traoré (Tete 82), Klaassen, Younes, Schöne (Van de Beek 74), Ziyech, Viergever, De Ligt, Kluivert (Dolberg 61). Coach: Peter Bosz (NED)
Red card: Veltman 80

Semi-finals - Olympique Lyonnais (FRA)
H 4-1 *Traoré (25, 71), Dolberg (34), Younes (49)*
Onana, Tete, Riedewald, Sánchez, Traoré, Klaassen, Younes (Kluivert 79), Schöne (Van de Beek 71), Ziyech, Dolberg (David Neres 88), De Ligt. Coach: Peter Bosz (NED)
A 1-3 *Dolberg (27)*
Onana, Veltman (Tete 64), Sánchez, Traoré, Klaassen, Younes (Kluivert 82), Schöne (Van de Beek 58), Ziyech, Dolberg, Viergever, De Ligt. Coach: Peter Bosz (NED)
Red card: Viergever 84

Final - Manchester United FC (ENG)
N 0-2
Onana, Veltman, Riedewald (De Jong 82), Sánchez, Traoré, Klaassen, Younes, Schöne (Van de Beek 70), Ziyech, Dolberg (David Neres 62), De Ligt. Coach: Peter Bosz (NED)

Feyenoord

Group A
Match 1 - Manchester United FC (ENG)
H 1-0 *Trindade de Vilhena (79)*
Jones, Karsdorp (Nieuwkoop 90+1), Kongolo, Van der Heijden, Kuyt, El Ahmadi, Jørgensen, Trindade de Vilhena, Berghuis (Bilal Başacıkoğlu 68), Toornstra, Botteghin. Coach: Giovanni van Bronckhorst (NED)
Match 2 - Fenerbahçe SK (TUR)
A 0-1
Jones, Karsdorp, Kongolo, Van der Heijden, Kuyt, El Ahmadi, Jørgensen, Trindade de Vilhena, Berghuis (Bilal Başacıkoğlu 57), Toornstra, Botteghin (Kramer 82). Coach: Giovanni van Bronckhorst (NED)
Match 3 - FC Zorya Luhansk (UKR)
H 1-0 *Jørgensen (55)*
Jones, Karsdorp, Kongolo, Van der Heijden, El Ahmadi, Jørgensen (Kramer 81), Trindade de Vilhena, Bilal Başacıkoğlu, Tapia, Toornstra, Botteghin. Coach: Giovanni van Bronckhorst (NED)
Match 4 - FC Zorya Luhansk (UKR)
A 1-1 *Jørgensen (15)*
Jones, Karsdorp, Kongolo, Vejinovic, Van der Heijden, Kuyt (Bilal Başacıkoğlu 70), Jørgensen (Nelom 46), Elia, Tapia, Toornstra (Nieuwkoop 81), Botteghin. Coach: Giovanni van Bronckhorst (NED)
Red card: Botteghin 43
Match 5 - Manchester United FC (ENG)
A 0-4
Jones, Karsdorp, Van der Heijden, Kuyt (Berghuis 61), Jørgensen (Kramer 73), Trindade de Vilhena, Elia, Nelom, Tapia, Toornstra (Bilal Başacıkoğlu 78), Dammers. Coach: Giovanni van Bronckhorst (NED)

Match 6 - Fenerbahçe SK (TUR)
H 0-1
Jones, Karsdorp, Van der Heijden, Kuyt, El Ahmadi, Jørgensen, Trindade de Vilhena (Kramer 75), Elia, Nelom, Toornstra (Bilal Başacıkoğlu 46), Botteghin. Coach: Giovanni van Bronckhorst (NED)

AZ Alkmaar

Third qualifying round - PAS Giannina FC (GRE)
H 1-0 *Luckassen (36)*
Rochet, Johansson, Vlaar, Haps, Jahanbakhsh (Garcia 63), Van Overeem (Seuntjens 87), Weghorst (Friday 63), Henriksen, Dos Santos, Luckassen, Wuytens. Coach: John van den Brom (NED)
A 2-1 *Dos Santos (29), Luckassen (36)*
Rochet, Van Eijden, Vlaar, Haps, Jahanbakhsh, Van Overeem (Til 71), Weghorst, Henriksen, Dos Santos (Garcia 79), Luckassen, Wuytens. Coach: John van den Brom (NED)

Play-offs - FK Vojvodina (SRB)
A 3-0 *Wuytens (32, 83), Friday (45+2)*
Rochet, Johansson, Van Eijden, Vlaar, Haps, Jahanbakhsh, Henriksen, Luckassen, Friday (Weghorst 79), Garcia (Dos Santos 74), Wuytens (Til 86). Coach: John van den Brom (NED)
H 0-0
Rochet, Johansson, Van Eijden, Vlaar, Haps, Jahanbakhsh (Van Overeem 76), Henriksen, Luckassen, Friday (Weghorst 70), Garcia (Dos Santos 65), Wuytens. Coach: John van den Brom (NED)

Group D
Match 1 - Dundalk FC (IRL)
H 1-1 *Wuytens (61)*
Rochet, Johansson, Van Eijden, Vlaar, Haps, Jahanbakhsh (Bel Hassani 75), Van Overeem, Dos Santos, Luckassen, Friday (Weghorst 55), Wuytens (Rienstra 65). Coach: John van den Brom (NED)
Match 2 - FC Zenit (RUS)
A 0-5
Rochet, Van Eijden, Vlaar (Rienstra 57), Haps, Van Overeem, Weghorst (Seuntjens 27), Dos Santos (Bel Hassani 73), Luckassen, Friday, Lewis, Wuytens. Coach: John van den Brom (NED)
Match 3 - Maccabi Tel-Aviv FC (ISR)
H 1-2 *Mühren (72)*
Rochet, Johansson, Van Eijden, Haps, Rienstra (Til 57), Van Overeem (Garcia 61), Bel Hassani, Mühren, Luckassen (Weghorst 84), Friday, Wuytens. Coach: John van den Brom (NED)
Match 4 - Maccabi Tel-Aviv FC (ISR)
A 0-0
Rochet, Johansson, Van Eijden (Mühren 55), Vlaar, Haps, Rienstra, Weghorst (Friday 77), Bel Hassani (Dos Santos 61), Luckassen, Garcia, Wuytens. Coach: John van den Brom (NED)
Match 5 - Dundalk FC (IRL)
A 1-0 *Weghorst (9)*
Rochet, Johansson, Vlaar, Haps, Rienstra, Jahanbakhsh (Dos Santos 75), Weghorst (Friday 87), Tankovic (Ouwejan 79), Seuntjens, Luckassen, Wuytens. Coach: John van den Brom (NED)
Match 6 - FC Zenit (RUS)
H 3-2 *Rienstra (7), Haps (43), Tankovic (68)*
Rochet, Johansson, Haps, Rienstra, Weghorst, Tankovic (Dos Santos 69), Bel Hassani (Jahanbakhsh 69), Seuntjens (Van Overeem 73), Mühren, Luckassen, Wuytens. Coach: John van den Brom (NED)

Round of 32 - Olympique Lyonnais (FRA)
H 1-4 *Jahanbakhsh (68p)*
Krul, Van Eijden, Haps, Rienstra, Jahanbakhsh, Weghorst (Friday 65), Tankovic (Garcia 65), Bel Hassani, Seuntjens (Van Overeem 74), Luckassen, Wuytens. Coach: John van den Brom (NED)
A 1-7 *Garcia (26)*
Krul, Johansson, Vlaar (Van Eijden 46), Haps, Rienstra, Jahanbakhsh (Seuntjens 71), Bel Hassani, Luckassen, Friday (Weghorst 77), Garcia, Wuytens. Coach: John van den Brom (NED)

Heracles Almelo

Third qualifying round - FC Arouca (POR)
H 1-1 *Gladon (53)*
Castro, Breukers, Te Wierik (Pröpper 74), Bel Hassani, Gladon, Bruns, Pelupessy, Navrátil (Darri 81), Kuwas, Zomer, Gosens. Coach: John Stegeman (NED)
A 0-0
Castro, Breukers, Te Wierik, Bel Hassani, Gladon, Bruns (Pröpper 82), Pelupessy, Navrátil, Kuwas (Van Mieghem 61), Zomer (Hoogma 46), Gosens. Coach: John Stegeman (NED)

DOMESTIC LEAGUE CLUB-BY-CLUB

ADO Den Haag

1905 • Kyocera (15,000) • adodenhaag.nl
Major honours
Dutch League (2) 1942, 1943; Dutch Cup (2) 1968, 1975
Coach: Željko Petrović (MNE); (08/02/17) Alfons Groenendijk

Date		Opponent		Score	Scorers
2016					
06/08	h	Go Ahead Eagles	W	3-0	*Havenaar 2 (1p), Ebuehi*
13/08	a	Vitesse	W	2-1	*Kastaneer 2*
19/08	a	Excelsior	W	2-1	*Kastaneer, Beugelsdijk*
28/08	h	Heracles	D	1-1	*Havenaar*
11/09	a	Feyenoord	L	1-3	*Marengo*
17/09	a	Twente	L	1-4	*Jansen*
24/09	h	Heerenveen	L	0-3	
30/09	a	Zwolle	L	1-2	*Trybull*
16/10	h	Ajax	L	0-2	
22/10	a	Roda	D	1-1	*Duplan*
30/10	h	AZ	L	0-1	
05/11	h	Willem II	W	1-0	*Beugelsdijk*
19/11	a	Groningen	L	1-2	*Duplan*
26/11	a	PSV	L	1-3	*Beugelsdijk (p)*
04/12	h	Utrecht	L	0-2	
10/12	a	NEC	L	0-3	
18/12	h	Sparta	W	1-0	*Becker*
2017					
14/01	a	Heerenveen	L	0-2	
21/01	h	Zwolle	L	1-2	*Kastaneer*
29/01	a	Ajax	L	0-3	
03/02	h	Vitesse	L	0-2	
11/02	a	Go Ahead Eagles	L	1-3	*El Khayati (p)*
19/02	h	Feyenoord	L	0-1	
24/02	h	Twente	D	1-1	*Schaken*
05/03	a	Utrecht	D	1-1	*Malone*
11/03	h	NEC	W	1-0	*Havenaar*
19/03	a	AZ	L	0-4	
02/04	h	Roda	W	4-1	*Becker, El Khayati (p), Havenaar, Fernandez*
05/04	a	Willem II	W	2-1	*El Khayati, Havenaar*
08/04	h	Groningen	W	4-3	*Bakker, Malone 2, Havenaar*
15/04	h	PSV	D	1-1	*Havenaar*
23/04	a	Sparta	W	1-0	*El Khayati*
07/05	a	Heracles	L	0-4	
14/05	h	Excelsior	W	4-1	*Becker, Havenaar, El Khayati, Kanon*

No	Name	Nat	DoB	Pos	Aps	(s)	Gls
31	Chovanie Amatkarijo		20/05/99	A		(1)	
34	Hennos Asmelash		01/07/99	D		(2)	
17	Danny Bakker		16/01/95	M	19		1
77	Sheraldo Becker		09/02/95	A	18	(11)	3
4	Tom Beugelsdijk		07/08/90	D	26	(2)	3
27	Trevor David		28/01/97	D	3		
21	Édouard Duplan	FRA	13/05/83	M	29	(4)	2
28	Tyronne Ebuehi		16/12/95	D	27	(2)	1
23	Abdenasser El Khayati		07/02/89	M	9	(3)	5
6	Achraf El Mahdioui		24/05/96	M	8	(5)	
19	Guyon Fernandez		18/04/86	A	6	(7)	1
14	Donny Gorter		15/06/88	M	5	(5)	
9	Mike Havenaar	JPN	20/05/87	A	22	(7)	9
23	Hector Hevel		15/05/96	M	5	(1)	
7	Kevin Jansen		08/04/92	M	6	(5)	1
5	Wilfried Kanon	CIV	06/07/93	D	27	(1)	1
33	Gervane Kastaneer		09/06/96	A	12	(2)	4
2	Dion Malone		13/02/89	M	13		3
11	Ludcinio Marengo		14/09/91	A	3	(11)	1
8	Aaron Meijers		28/10/87	D	19		
3	Thomas Meissner	GER	26/03/91	D	27	(1)	
13	José San Román	ARG	17/07/88	D	11	(1)	
20	Ruben Schaken		03/04/82	M	19	(5)	1
30	Jerdy Schouten		12/01/97	A		(2)	
1	Ernestas Šetkus	LTU	25/05/85	G	22		
12	Tom Trybull	GER	09/03/93	M	22		1
19	Dennis van der Heijden		17/02/97	A	2	(14)	
11	Randy Wolters		06/04/90	A	2	(10)	
22	Robert Zwinkels		04/05/83	G	12		

AFC Ajax

1900 • Amsterdam ArenA (51,638) • ajax.nl

Major honours
European Champion Clubs' Cup/UEFA Champions League (4) 1971, 1972, 1973, 1995; UEFA Cup Winners' Cup (1) 1987; UEFA Cup (1) 1992; UEFA Super Cup (3) 1972, 1974, 1995; European/South American Cup (2) 1972, 1995; Dutch League (33) 1918, 1919, 1931, 1932, 1934, 1937, 1939, 1947, 1957, 1960, 1966, 1967, 1968, 1970, 1972, 1973, 1977, 1979, 1980, 1982, 1983, 1985, 1990, 1994, 1995, 1996, 1998, 2002, 2004, 2011, 2012, 2013, 2014; Dutch Cup (18) 1917, 1943, 1961, 1967, 1970, 1971, 1972, 1979, 1983, 1986, 1987, 1993, 1998, 1999, 2002, 2006, 2007, 2010

Coach: Peter Bosz

Date		Opponent		Score	Scorers
2016					
07/08	a	Sparta	W	3-1	*Klaassen, Sinkgraven, Cassierra*
13/08	h	Roda	D	2-2	*Dolberg 2*
20/08	h	Willem II	L	1-2	*Klaassen*
28/08	a	Go Ahead Eagles	W	3-0	*Klaassen 2 (1p), Gudelj*
11/09	h	Vitesse	W	1-0	*Viergever*
18/09	a	Heracles	W	2-0	*Klaassen, Gudelj*
24/09	h	Zwolle	W	5-1	*Sánchez 2, Dolberg 2, Traoré*
02/10	h	Utrecht	W	3-2	*og (Leeuwin), Schöne (p), Ziyech*
16/10	a	Den Haag	W	2-0	*Klaassen, Traoré*
23/10	a	Feyenoord	D	1-1	*Dolberg*
29/10	h	Excelsior	W	1-0	*Ziyech*
06/11	a	AZ	D	2-2	*Traoré, Klaassen*
20/11	h	NEC	W	5-0	*Dolberg 3, Traoré, Schöne*
27/11	a	Heerenveen	W	1-0	*Klaassen*
04/12	h	Groningen	W	2-0	*Sánchez, Ziyech (p)*
11/12	a	Twente	L	0-1	
18/12	h	PSV	D	1-1	*Klaassen*
2017					
15/01	a	Zwolle	W	3-1	*Schöne (p), Ziyech 2*
22/01	a	Utrecht	W	1-0	*Schöne*
29/01	h	Den Haag	W	3-0	*Ziyech, Schöne, Dolberg*
05/02	a	Roda	W	2-0	*Klaassen, Younes*
12/02	h	Sparta	W	2-0	*Traoré, Dolberg*
19/02	a	Vitesse	W	1-0	*Klaassen*
26/02	h	Heracles	W	4-1	*Dolberg, De Ligt, Sánchez, Traoré*
05/03	a	Groningen	D	1-1	*Klaassen*
12/03	h	Twente	W	3-0	*Younes, Dolberg 2*
19/03	a	Excelsior	D	1-1	*Kluivert*
02/04	h	Feyenoord	W	2-1	*Schöne, David Neres*
05/04	h	AZ	W	4-1	*Traoré, Sánchez, Schöne (p), Younes*
08/04	a	NEC	W	5-1	*og (Golla), David Neres, Traoré 2, Ziyech*
16/04	h	Heerenveen	W	5-1	*Viergever, De Ligt, Klaassen, Dolberg (p), David Neres*
23/04	a	PSV	L	0-1	
07/05	h	Go Ahead Eagles	W	4-0	*Kluivert, Dolberg, De Jong, Cassierra*
14/05	a	Willem II	W	3-1	*Dolberg, Sánchez, Klaassen*

No	Name	Nat	DoB	Pos	Aps	(s)	Gls
6	Riechedly Bazoer		12/10/96	M	3	(2)	
19	Mateo Cassierra	COL	13/04/97	A	1	(16)	2
17	Václav Černý	CZE	17/10/97	A	2	(3)	
1	Jasper Cillessen		22/04/89	G	2		
44	Pelle Clement		19/05/96	A		(1)	
7	David Neres	BRA	03/03/97	A	5	(3)	3
21	Frenkie de Jong		12/05/97	M	1	(3)	1
36	Matthijs de Ligt		12/08/99	D	6	(5)	2
35	Mitchell Dijks		09/02/93	D	8	(4)	
25	Kasper Dolberg	DEN	06/10/97	A	26	(3)	16
7	Anwar El Ghazi		03/05/95	A	7	(5)	
27	Nemanja Gudelj	SRB	16/11/91	M	5	(1)	2
10	Davy Klaassen		21/02/93	M	33		14
45	Justin Kluivert		05/05/99	A	7	(7)	2
34	Abdelhak Nouri		02/04/97	M	1	(8)	
24	André Onana	CMR	02/04/96	G	32		
4	Jaïro Riedewald		09/09/96	D	11	(5)	
5	Davinson Sánchez	COL	12/06/96	D	32		6
20	Lasse Schöne	DEN	27/05/86	M	26	(1)	7
8	Daley Sinkgraven		04/07/95	M	21	(3)	1
2	Kenny Tete		09/10/95	D	5		
9	Bertrand Traoré	BFA	06/09/95	A	22	(2)	9
30	Donny van de Beek		18/04/97	M	4	(15)	
3	Joël Veltman		15/01/92	D	30		
26	Nick Viergever		03/08/89	D	27	(2)	2
16	Heiko Westermann	GER	14/08/83	D	1	(3)	
11	Amin Younes	GER	06/08/93	M	28	(1)	3
42	Deyovaisio Zeefuik		11/03/98	D		(1)	
22	Hakim Ziyech	MAR	19/03/93	M	28		7

AZ Alkmaar

1967 • AFAS (17,150) • az.nl

Major honours
Dutch League (2) 1981, 2009; Dutch Cup (4) 1978, 1981, 1982, 2013

Coach: John van den Brom

Date		Opponent		Score	Scorers
2016					
07/08	h	Heerenveen	D	2-2	*Henriksen, Weghorst (p)*
14/08	a	PSV	L	0-1	
21/08	a	Utrecht	W	2-1	*Henriksen, Jahanbakhsh*
28/08	h	NEC	W	2-0	*Dos Santos, Jahanbakhsh*
10/09	h	Willem II	W	2-0	*Jahanbakhsh, Garcia*
18/09	a	Zwolle	W	2-0	*Weghorst, Til*
24/09	h	Go Ahead Eagles	D	2-2	*Weghorst 2 (1p)*
02/10	a	Sparta	D	1-1	*Til*
15/10	h	Vitesse	D	2-2	*Mühren 2*
23/10	a	Groningen	L	0-2	
30/10	a	Den Haag	W	1-0	*Mühren*
06/11	h	Ajax	D	2-2	*Weghorst 2*
20/11	a	Roda	D	1-1	*Weghorst*
27/11	h	Heracles	W	5-1	*Mühren 2, Weghorst, Dos Santos, Jahanbakhsh*
03/12	a	Excelsior	D	3-3	*Mühren, Tankovic, Wuytens*
11/12	h	Feyenoord	L	0-4	
17/12	a	Twente	W	2-1	*Weghorst, og (Bijen)*
2017					
13/01	a	Go Ahead Eagles	W	3-1	*Weghorst, Jahanbakhsh 2 (1p)*
21/01	h	Sparta	D	1-1	*Luckassen*
29/01	a	Vitesse	L	1-2	*og (Kashia)*
04/02	h	PSV	L	2-4	*Friday 2*
12/02	a	Heerenveen	W	2-1	*Tankovic, Bel Hassani*
19/02	a	Willem II	D	1-1	*Luckassen*
26/02	h	Zwolle	D	1-1	*Friday*
05/03	h	Excelsior	D	1-1	*og (Hahn)*
12/03	a	Feyenoord	L	2-5	*Luckassen, Weghorst*
19/03	h	Den Haag	W	4-0	*Dos Santos 2, Van Overeem, Friday*
01/04	h	Groningen	D	0-0	
05/04	a	Ajax	L	1-4	*Weghorst*
09/04	h	Roda	D	1-1	*Jahanbakhsh*
14/04	a	Heracles	W	2-1	*Weghorst, Jahanbakhsh*
22/04	h	Twente	W	2-1	*og (Bijen), Friday*
07/05	a	NEC	L	1-2	*Jahanbakhsh*
14/05	h	Utrecht	L	2-3	*Van Eijden, Jahanbakhsh*

No	Name	Nat	DoB	Pos	Aps	(s)	Gls
8	Iliass Bel Hassani		16/09/92	M	14	(11)	1
19	Dabney dos Santos		31/07/96	M	18	(9)	4
27	Fred Friday	NGA	22/05/95	A	10	(11)	5
28	Levi Garcia	TRI	20/11/97	M	8	(9)	1
5	Ridgeciano Haps		12/06/93	D	30		
12	Pantelis Hatzidiakos	GRE	18/01/97	D	2		
26	Jeremy Helmer		03/07/97	M		(2)	
10	Markus Henriksen	NOR	25/07/92	M	3		2
7	Alireza Jahanbakhsh	IRN	11/08/93	A	25	(4)	10
2	Mattias Johansson	SWE	16/02/92	D	22	(3)	
24	Tim Krul		03/04/88	G	14		
29	Fernando Lewis		31/01/93	D	2	(1)	
23	Derrick Luckassen		03/07/95	M	31		3
21	Robert Mühren		18/05/89	M	8	(4)	6
22	Thomas Ouwejan		30/06/96	D	3	(3)	
6	Ben Rienstra		05/06/90	M	18	(4)	
1	Sergio Rochet	URU	23/03/93	G	20		
20	Mats Seuntjens		17/04/92	M	15	(6)	
34	Calvin Stengs		18/12/98	A		(1)	
17	Jonas Svensson	NOR	06/03/93	D	8		
11	Muamer Tankovic	SWE	22/02/95	A	8	(5)	2
15	Guus Til		22/12/97	M	3	(7)	2
3	Rens van Eijden		03/03/88	D	22		1
8	Joris van Overeem		01/06/94	M	16	(7)	1
4	Ron Vlaar		16/02/85	D	20	(1)	
9	Wout Weghorst		07/08/92	A	24	(6)	13
35	Owen Wijndal		28/11/99	D	1		
30	Stijn Wuytens	BEL	08/10/89	M	29		1

SBV Excelsior

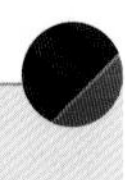

1902 • Woudestein (3,531) • sbvexcelsior.nl

Coach: Mitchell van der Gaag

Date		Opponent		Score	Scorers
2016					
06/08	a	Twente	W	2-1	*Vermeulen, Owusu*
13/08	h	Groningen	W	2-0	*Mattheij, Vermeulen*
19/08	h	Den Haag	L	1-2	*Mattheij*
27/08	a	Feyenoord	L	1-4	*Elbers*
10/09	h	Heracles	W	3-1	*Karami, Koolwijk, Fredy*
17/09	a	Willem II	D	1-1	*Faik*
24/09	h	PSV	L	1-3	*Bruins (p)*
01/10	a	Go Ahead Eagles	L	0-3	
16/10	h	Roda	L	0-1	
21/10	h	Zwolle	L	0-2	
29/10	a	Ajax	L	0-1	
06/11	a	Utrecht	L	1-2	*Elbers*
19/11	h	Sparta	W	3-2	*Elbers, Fredy, Hasselbaink (p)*
26/11	a	Vitesse	D	2-2	*Faik 2*
03/12	h	AZ	D	3-3	*Elbers, Hasselbaink (p), Faik*
10/12	a	Heerenveen	L	1-2	*Hasselbaink (p)*
18/12	h	NEC	D	2-2	*Elbers, Karami*
2017					
14/01	a	PSV	L	0-2	
22/01	h	Go Ahead Eagles	D	1-1	*Hasselbaink*
28/01	a	Roda	L	0-4	
04/02	a	Groningen	D	1-1	*Hadouir*
12/02	h	Twente	D	1-1	*Hasselbaink*
18/02	a	Heracles	L	0-4	
25/02	h	Willem II	L	0-2	
05/03	a	AZ	D	1-1	*Van Duinen*
11/03	h	Heerenveen	W	4-1	*Elbers, Mattheij, Massop, Hasselbaink*
19/03	h	Ajax	D	1-1	*og (Tete)*
01/04	a	Zwolle	D	1-1	*Bruins*
04/04	h	Utrecht	L	1-3	*Van Duinen*
07/04	a	Sparta	W	3-2	*Hasselbaink 2, Elbers*
15/04	h	Vitesse	W	1-0	*Hasselbaink*
22/04	a	NEC	W	1-0	*Van Duinen*
07/05	h	Feyenoord	W	3-0	*Hasselbaink, Elbers, Koolwijk*
14/05	a	Den Haag	L	1-4	*Jeffry Fortes*

No	Name	Nat	DoB	Pos	Aps	(s)	Gls
44	Arghus	BRA	19/01/88	D		(1)	
14	Cedric Badjeck	CMR	25/01/95	A		(2)	
20	Elso Brito		02/04/94	D		(1)	
10	Luigi Bruins		09/03/87	M	18	(6)	2
30	Jordy de Wijs		08/01/95	D	15		
4	Henrico Drost		21/01/87	D	19	(2)	
11	Stanley Elbers		14/05/92	A	25	(5)	8
24	Hicham Faik		19/03/92	M	17	(5)	4
17	Fredy	ANG	27/03/90	A	31	(1)	2
6	Anouar Hadouir		14/09/82	M	1	(18)	1
25	Warner Hahn		15/06/92	G	17		
34	Dogucan Haspolat		11/02/00	M		(1)	
7	Nigel Hasselbaink		21/11/90	A	24	(8)	10
12	Jeffry Fortes	CPV	22/03/89	M	15	(5)	1
2	Khalid Karami		29/12/89	D	33		2
8	Ryan Koolwijk		08/08/85	M	28	(4)	2
5	Bas Kuipers		17/08/94	D	20	(2)	
23	Milan Massop		01/12/93	D	13	(2)	1
15	Jurgen Mattheij		01/04/93	D	31		3
22	Tom Muyters	BEL	05/12/84	G	17		
9	Terell Ondaan		09/09/93	M	9	(16)	
3	Leeroy Owusu		13/08/96	D	5		1
21	Danilo Pantić	SRB	26/10/96	M	3	(6)	
29	Mike van Duinen		06/11/91	A	14	(8)	3
18	Kevin Vermeulen		20/11/94	M	19	(6)	2

NETHERLANDS

Feyenoord

1908 • De Kuip (51,137) • feyenoord.nl

Major honours
European Champion Clubs' Cup (1) 1970; UEFA Cup (2) 1974, 2002; European/South American Cup (1) 1970; Dutch League (15) 1924, 1928, 1936, 1938, 1940, 1961, 1962, 1965, 1969, 1971, 1974, 1984, 1993, 1999, 2017; Dutch Cup (12) 1930, 1935, 1965, 1969, 1980, 1984, 1991, 1992, 1994, 1995, 2008, 2016

Coach: Giovanni van Bronckhorst

2016

Date		Opponent		Score	Scorers
07/08	a	Groningen	W	5-0	*Trindade de Vilhena, Elia 3, Jørgensen*
14/08	h	Twente	W	2-0	*Toornstra, Jørgensen*
21/08	a	Heracles	W	1-0	*El Ahmadi*
27/08	h	Excelsior	W	4-1	*Kuyt 2, Berghuis, Toornstra*
11/09	h	Den Haag	W	3-1	*Kuyt, Jørgensen, El Ahmadi*
18/09	a	PSV	W	1-0	*Botteghin*
25/09	h	Roda	W	5-0	*Jørgensen 2, El Ahmadi, Toornstra, Kongolo*
02/10	a	Willem II	W	2-0	*Jørgensen, Tapia*
16/10	a	NEC	W	2-1	*Jørgensen, Kramer*
23/10	h	Ajax	D	1-1	*Kuyt*
30/10	h	Heerenveen	D	2-2	*Jørgensen, Karsdorp*
06/11	a	Go Ahead Eagles	L	0-1	
20/11	h	Zwolle	W	3-0	*Kuyt, El Ahmadi, Toornstra*
27/11	a	Utrecht	D	3-3	*Kuyt, Jørgensen, Kramer*
04/12	h	Sparta	W	6-1	*Trindade de Vilhena, Toornstra, Jørgensen 2, Botteghin, Elia*
11/12	a	AZ	W	4-0	*Berghuis, Van der Heijden, Jørgensen, Trindade de Vilhena*
17/12	h	Vitesse	W	3-1	*Elia, Berghuis 2*

2017

Date		Opponent		Score	Scorers
15/01	a	Roda	W	2-0	*Kuyt, Elia*
21/01	h	Willem II	W	1-0	*Toornstra*
29/01	h	NEC	W	4-0	*Berghuis, Elia, Jørgensen 2*
05/02	a	Twente	W	2-0	*Botteghin, Jørgensen*
11/02	h	Groningen	W	2-0	*Toornstra 2*
19/02	a	Den Haag	W	1-0	*El Ahmadi*
26/02	h	PSV	W	2-1	*Toornstra, og (Zoet)*
05/03	a	Sparta	L	0-1	
12/03	h	AZ	W	5-2	*Jørgensen 3 (1p), Toornstra, Kuyt*
19/03	a	Heerenveen	W	2-1	*Jørgensen, Trindade de Vilhena*
02/04	a	Ajax	L	1-2	*Kramer*
05/04	h	Go Ahead Eagles	W	8-0	*Toornstra 3, Elia, Kuyt, Van der Heijden, Botteghin, Kramer*
09/04	a	Zwolle	D	2-2	*Berghuis 2*
16/04	h	Utrecht	W	2-0	*Toornstra, Elia*
23/04	a	Vitesse	W	2-0	*Jørgensen 2*
07/05	a	Excelsior	L	0-3	
14/05	h	Heracles	W	3-1	*Kuyt 3 (1p)*

No	Name	Nat	DoB	Pos	Aps	(s)	Gls
19	Steven Berghuis		19/12/91	A	25	(5)	7
14	Bilal Başaçıkoğlu	TUR	26/03/95	A	5	(19)	
33	Eric Botteghin	BRA	31/08/87	D	34		4
8	Karim El Ahmadi	MAR	27/01/85	M	30		5
40	Mohamed El Hankouri		01/07/97	M		(1)	
11	Eljero Elia		13/02/87	A	21	(3)	9
27	Simon Gustafsson	SWE	11/01/95	M		(2)	
38	Gustavo Hamer		24/06/97	M		(2)	
36	Emil Hansson	NOR	15/06/98	M		(2)	
30	Pär Hansson	SWE	22/06/86	G	1		
25	Brad Jones	AUS	19/03/82	G	32		
9	Nicolai Jørgensen	DEN	15/01/91	A	32		21
2	Rick Karsdorp		11/02/95	D	29	(1)	1
4	Terence Kongolo		14/02/94	D	22	(1)	1
29	Michiel Kramer		03/12/88	A	1	(16)	4
7	Dirk Kuyt		22/07/80	M	27	(4)	12
18	Miguel Nelom		22/09/90	D	12	(4)	
26	Bart Nieuwkoop		07/03/96	D	6	(7)	
20	Renato Tapia	PER	28/07/95	M	1	(7)	1
28	Jens Toornstra		04/04/89	A	31	(3)	14
10	Tonny Trindade de Vilhena		03/01/95	M	29		4
6	Jan-Arie van der Heijden		03/03/88	D	29	(2)	2
5	Marko Vejinovic		03/02/90	M	1	(1)	
1	Kenneth Vermeer		10/01/86	G	1		
15	Lucas Woudenberg		25/04/94	D	5	(3)	

Go Ahead Eagles

1902 • Adelaarshorst (6,750) • ga-eagles.nl

Major honours
Dutch League (4) 1917, 1922, 1930, 1933

Coach: Hans de Koning;
(25/03/17) Robert Maaskant

2016

Date		Opponent		Score	Scorers
06/08	a	Den Haag	L	0-3	
14/08	h	NEC	D	2-2	*Duits, Ojamaa*
21/08	a	Sparta	L	0-1	
28/08	h	Ajax	L	0-3	
11/09	h	Roda	W	2-0	*Brands (p), Maatsen*
17/09	a	Vitesse	L	0-2	
24/09	a	AZ	D	2-2	*Duits, Hendriks*
01/10	h	Excelsior	W	3-0	*Duits, Hendriks 2 (2p)*
15/10	a	Utrecht	L	0-3	
22/10	h	Twente	L	0-2	
30/10	a	Zwolle	L	1-3	*Fischer*
06/11	h	Feyenoord	W	1-0	*Antonia*
19/11	a	Heracles	L	1-2	*Antonia*
25/11	h	Willem II	L	0-1	
03/12	h	Heerenveen	L	1-3	*Maatsen*
10/12	a	PSV	L	0-1	
18/12	a	Groningen	D	1-1	*Antonia*

2017

Date		Opponent		Score	Scorers
13/01	h	AZ	L	1-3	*Antonia (p)*
22/01	a	Excelsior	D	1-1	*Chirivella*
28/01	h	Utrecht	L	0-1	
04/02	a	NEC	W	2-1	*Manu, Antonia*
11/02	h	Den Haag	W	3-1	*Hendriks 2, Ritzmaier*
17/02	a	Roda	L	0-1	
26/02	h	Vitesse	L	1-3	*Crowley*
03/03	a	Heerenveen	D	2-2	*Hendriks, De Kogel*
11/03	h	PSV	L	1-3	*Manu*
19/03	h	Zwolle	L	1-3	*Chirivella*
02/04	a	Twente	W	2-1	*Hendriks, Ritzmaier*
05/04	a	Feyenoord	L	0-8	
08/04	h	Heracles	L	1-4	*Crowley*
16/04	a	Willem II	L	0-2	
22/04	h	Groningen	L	2-3	*Hendriks, Maatsen*
07/05	a	Ajax	L	0-4	
14/05	h	Sparta	L	1-3	*Maatsen*

No	Name	Nat	DoB	Pos	Aps	(s)	Gls
35	Rochdi Achenteh	MAR	07/03/88	D	13	(3)	
77	Jarchinio Antonia		27/12/90	A	27	(2)	5
21	Kevin Brands		28/03/88	A	8	(3)	1
7	Sinan Bytyqi	KOS	15/01/95	M	2	(2)	
29	Pedro Chirivella	ESP	23/05/97	M	17		2
7	Dan Crowley	ENG	03/08/97	M	15	(1)	2
26	Tom Daemen		17/06/85	M		(3)	
9	Leon de Kogel		13/11/91	A	10	(11)	1
6	Sander Duits		29/08/83	M	29	(1)	3
3	Sander Fischer		03/09/88	D	33		1
32	Joey Groenbast		04/05/95	D	26	(5)	
47	Mohamed Hamdaoui		10/06/93	A		(1)	
19	Sam Hendriks		25/01/95	A	17	(9)	8
2	Lars Lambooij		16/04/88	D	6		
17	Sébastien Locigno	BEL	02/09/95	D	10	(5)	
14	Darren Maatsen		30/01/91	M	12	(13)	4
27	Patrick Maneschijn		04/01/97	A		(1)	
28	Elvis Manu		13/08/93	A	14		2
11	Ludcinio Marengo		14/09/91	A	1	(5)	
23	Norichio Nieveld		25/04/89	D	6	(7)	
22	Henrik Ojamaa	EST	20/05/91	A	3	(3)	1
5	Lum Rexhepi	KOS	03/08/92	D		(2)	
24	Marcel Ritzmaier	AUT	22/04/93	M	28		2
4	Xandro Schenk		28/04/93	D	32		
8	Joey Suk		08/07/89	M	9	(7)	
5	Kenny Teijsse		19/07/92	D	2	(11)	
20	Teije ten Den		29/04/93	A		(1)	
15	Robin van der Meer		21/02/95	D	3		
21	Givan Werkhoven		27/09/97	A		(1)	
11	Randy Wolters		06/04/90	A	17	(3)	
1	Theo Zwarthoed		19/11/82	G	34		

FC Groningen

1971 • Noordlease (22,329) • fcgroningen.nl

Major honours
Dutch Cup (1) 2015

Coach: Ernest Faber

2016

Date		Opponent		Score	Scorers
07/08	h	Feyenoord	L	0-5	
13/08	a	Excelsior	L	0-2	
21/08	h	Twente	L	3-4	*Mahi, Idrissi, Hoesen*
28/08	a	PSV	D	0-0	
11/09	h	Sparta	D	1-1	*Mahi*
16/09	a	Utrecht	W	5-1	*Idrissi 2, Hoesen 2, Van Weert*
24/09	h	Heracles	D	0-0	
01/10	a	Vitesse	L	1-2	*Hoesen (p)*
15/10	h	Heerenveen	L	0-3	
23/10	h	AZ	W	2-0	*Linssen, Van Weert*
29/10	a	Willem II	L	1-2	*Mahi*
05/11	a	NEC	D	1-1	*Van Weert*
19/11	h	Den Haag	W	2-1	*Hateboer, Van Weert*
26/11	a	Zwolle	W	4-0	*Tibbling, Van Weert, Rusnák, Mahi*
04/12	a	Ajax	L	0-2	
09/12	h	Roda	W	2-0	*Mahi, Sørloth*
18/12	h	Go Ahead Eagles	D	1-1	*Mahi*

2017

Date		Opponent		Score	Scorers
14/01	a	Heracles	W	4-1	*Mahi 2, Payne, Sørloth*
21/01	h	Vitesse	D	1-1	*og (Leerdam)*
29/01	a	Heerenveen	D	0-0	
04/02	h	Excelsior	D	1-1	*Mahi (p)*
11/02	a	Feyenoord	L	0-2	
19/02	a	Sparta	D	2-2	*Yttergård Jenssen, Mahi*
25/02	h	Utrecht	L	2-3	*Linssen 2*
05/03	h	Ajax	D	1-1	*Linssen*
12/03	a	Roda	L	1-3	*Linssen*
18/03	h	Willem II	D	1-1	*Yttergård Jenssen*
01/04	a	AZ	D	0-0	
05/04	h	NEC	W	2-0	*Mahi, Bacuna*
08/04	a	Den Haag	L	3-4	*Mahi (p), Linssen 2*
16/04	h	Zwolle	W	5-1	*Linssen 2, Mahi 2, Hrustic*
22/04	a	Go Ahead Eagles	W	3-2	*Mahi 2, Drost*
07/05	h	PSV	D	1-1	*Mahi*
14/05	a	Twente	W	5-3	*Linssen, Idrissi 2, og (Thesker), Sørloth*

No	Name	Nat	DoB	Pos	Aps	(s)	Gls
7	Jarchinio Antonia		27/12/90	A	3		
12	Juninho Bacuna		07/08/97	M	21	(3)	1
35	Glenn Bijl		13/07/95	M	1		
2	Jason Davidson	AUS	29/06/91	D	20		
17	Jesper Drost		11/01/93	M	11	(6)	1
33	Hans Hateboer		09/01/94	D	19		1
24	Tom Hiariej		25/07/88	M	19	(4)	
9	Danny Hoesen		15/01/91	A	6	(4)	4
36	Ajdin Hrustic	AUS	05/07/96	M		(5)	1
45	Oussama Idrissi		26/02/96	M	15	(12)	5
3	Kasper Larsen	DEN	25/01/93	D	22		
11	Bryan Linssen		08/10/90	A	23	(5)	10
23	Hedwiges Maduro		13/02/85	M	2	(2)	
14	Mimoun Mahi		13/03/94	M	30	(2)	17
5	Samir Memišević	BIH	13/08/93	D	20	(5)	
1	Sergio Padt		06/06/90	G	34		
25	Desevio Payne	USA	30/11/95	D	5	(1)	1
6	Etiënne Reijnen		05/04/87	D	23	(4)	
10	Albert Rusnák	SVK	07/07/94	M	10	(3)	1
13	Alexander Sørloth	NOR	05/12/95	A	6	(19)	3
22	Simon Tibbling	SWE	07/09/94	M	22	(4)	1
21	Martijn van der Laan		29/07/88	D		(2)	
20	Yoëll van Nieff		17/06/93	D	18	(5)	
19	Tom van Weert		07/06/90	A	11	(4)	5
8	Ruben Yttergård Jenssen	NOR	04/05/88	M	33		2

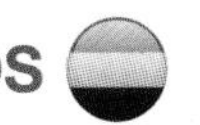

sc Heerenveen

1920 • Abe Lenstra (26,100) • sc-heerenveen.nl

Major honours
Dutch Cup (1) 2009

Coach: Jürgen Streppel

Date		Opponent		Score	Scorers
2016					
07/08	a	AZ	D	2-2	*Zeneli, Schaars*
12/08	h	Utrecht	D	2-2	*Slagveer, Ghoochannejhad*
20/08	a	NEC	L	1-2	*Van Amersfoort*
27/08	h	Zwolle	W	1-0	*Larsson*
10/09	h	Twente	W	3-1	*Ghoochannejhad 2, Larsson*
17/09	a	Roda	W	3-0	*Larsson, Veerman, Zeneli*
24/09	a	Den Haag	W	3-0	*og (Kanon), Zeneli, Veerman*
01/10	h	PSV	D	1-1	*Zeneli*
15/10	a	Groningen	W	3-0	*Zeneli, Larsson, Ghoochannejhad*
23/10	h	Heracles	W	3-1	*Marzo, Larsson, St Juste*
30/10	a	Feyenoord	D	2-2	*Ghoochannejhad, Zeneli*
04/11	a	Sparta	L	1-3	*St Juste*
19/11	h	Vitesse	D	1-1	*Veerman*
27/11	h	Ajax	L	0-1	
03/12	a	Go Ahead Eagles	W	3-1	*Ghoochannejhad 2, Kobayashi*
10/12	h	Excelsior	W	2-1	*Larsson 2*
16/12	a	Willem II	L	1-2	*og (Heerkens)*
2017					
14/01	h	Den Haag	W	2-0	*Ghoochannejhad 2*
22/01	a	PSV	L	3-4	*Ghoochannejhad 3*
29/01	h	Groningen	D	0-0	
05/02	a	Utrecht	L	0-1	
12/02	h	AZ	L	1-2	*Ghoochannejhad*
18/02	a	Twente	L	0-1	
25/02	h	Roda	W	3-0	*Schmidt, Veerman, Ghoochannejhad (p)*
03/03	h	Go Ahead Eagles	D	2-2	*Veerman, Slagveer*
11/03	a	Excelsior	L	1-4	*Slagveer*
19/03	h	Feyenoord	L	1-2	*Ghoochannejhad (p)*
01/04	a	Heracles	L	1-4	*Ghoochannejhad (p)*
04/04	h	Sparta	W	3-0	*Van Amersfoort, Van Aken, Ghoochannejhad*
08/04	a	Vitesse	L	2-4	*Slagveer, Larsson*
16/04	a	Ajax	L	1-5	*Ghoochannejhad*
21/04	h	Willem II	W	1-0	*Larsson*
07/05	a	Zwolle	L	1-2	*Ghoochannejhad*
14/05	h	NEC	L	0-2	

No	Name	Nat	DoB	Pos	Aps	(s)	Gls
5	Lucas Bijker		04/03/93	D	33		
22	Caner Cavlan		05/02/92	D	1	(6)	
24	Shay Facey	ENG	07/01/95	D	1	(2)	
22	Wout Faes	BEL	03/04/98	D	6	(1)	
9	Reza Ghoochannejhad	IRN	20/09/87	A	34		19
25	Willem Huizing		01/02/95	D		(1)	
21	Yuki Kobayashi	JPN	24/04/92	M	30		1
11	Sam Larsson	SWE	10/04/93	A	29	(2)	9
2	Stefano Marzo	BEL	22/03/91	D	33		1
1	Erwin Mulder		03/03/89	G	34		
18	Younes Namli	DEN	20/06/94	M	9	(9)	
17	Martin Ødegaard	NOR	17/12/98	M	8	(6)	
6	Stijn Schaars		11/01/84	M	17	(3)	1
12	Doke Schmidt		07/04/92	D	8	(3)	1
7	Luciano Slagveer		05/10/93	A	10	(17)	4
16	Jerry St Juste		19/10/96	D	27		2
10	Simon Thern	SWE	18/09/92	M		(4)	
8	Morten Thorsby	NOR	05/05/96	M	14	(9)	
4	Joost van Aken		13/05/94	D	26		1
19	Pelle van Amersfoort		01/04/96	M	26	(5)	2
20	Henk Veerman		30/06/93	A		(23)	5
37	Michel Vlap		02/06/97	M		(1)	
13	Arber Zeneli	KOS	25/02/95	A	28	(4)	6

Heracles Almelo

1903 • Polman (8,500) • heracles.nl

Major honours
Dutch League (2) 1927, 1941

Coach: John Stegeman

Date		Opponent		Score	Scorers
2016					
07/08	a	Roda	D	1-1	*Navrátil*
14/08	h	Willem II	W	3-1	*Bel Hassani, Gladon 2*
21/08	h	Feyenoord	L	0-1	
28/08	a	Den Haag	D	1-1	*Gosens*
10/09	a	Excelsior	L	1-3	*Vermeij*
18/09	h	Ajax	L	0-2	
24/09	a	Groningen	D	0-0	
02/10	h	Twente	D	1-1	*Armenteros*
15/10	a	PSV	D	1-1	*Armenteros*
23/10	a	Heerenveen	L	1-3	*Kuwas*
29/10	h	Sparta	D	2-2	*Darri, Kuwas*
06/11	a	Vitesse	W	2-1	*Darri, Armenteros (p)*
19/11	h	Go Ahead Eagles	W	2-1	*Armenteros 2*
27/11	a	AZ	L	1-5	*Armenteros (p)*
02/12	h	NEC	W	2-0	*Duarte, Armenteros*
11/12	a	Utrecht	L	0-2	
18/12	h	Zwolle	W	3-0	*Armenteros (p), Vermeij, Van Mieghem*
2017					
14/01	h	Groningen	L	1-4	*Van Mieghem*
20/01	a	Twente	L	0-1	
28/01	h	PSV	L	1-2	*Armenteros*
04/02	a	Willem II	W	3-1	*Van Ooijen, Peterson, Gosens*
11/02	h	Roda	D	2-2	*Armenteros 2*
18/02	h	Excelsior	W	4-0	*Kuwas, Bruns, Te Wierik, Peterson*
26/02	a	Ajax	L	1-4	*Armenteros*
05/03	a	NEC	L	1-3	*Armenteros (p)*
11/03	h	Utrecht	W	2-1	*Kuwas, Bruns*
18/03	a	Sparta	L	1-3	*Pelupessy*
01/04	h	Heerenveen	W	4-1	*Niemeijer, Armenteros, Kuwas, Peterson*
05/04	h	Vitesse	L	0-1	
08/04	a	Go Ahead Eagles	W	4-1	*Bruns (p), Armenteros 2 (1p), Peterson*
14/04	h	AZ	L	1-2	*Kuwas*
22/04	a	Zwolle	W	2-1	*Armenteros 2*
07/05	h	Den Haag	W	4-0	*Niemeijer 2, Armenteros, Bruns*
14/05	a	Feyenoord	L	1-3	*Van Ooijen*

No	Name	Nat	DoB	Pos	Aps	(s)	Gls
24	Gor Agbalyan	ARM	25/04/97	M		(1)	
9	Samuel Armenteros	SWE	27/05/90	A	28	(1)	19
8	Iliass Bel Hassani		19/09/92	M	4		1
2	Tim Breukers		04/11/87	D	24	(1)	
10	Thomas Bruns		07/01/92	M	31	(1)	4
1	Bram Castro	BEL	30/09/82	G	34		
7	Brahim Darri		14/09/94	A	14	(15)	2
12	Wout Droste		20/05/89	D	10	(3)	
8	Lerin Duarte		11/08/90	M	15	(3)	1
25	Renze Fij		26/09/92	G		(1)	
23	Mark-Jan Fledderus		14/12/82	D	1	(3)	
9	Paul Gladon		18/03/92	A	3		2
21	Robin Gosens	GER	05/07/94	D	27	(1)	2
27	Justin Hoogma		11/06/98	D	34		
17	Brandley Kuwas		19/09/92	A	27	(6)	6
15	Jaroslav Navrátil	CZE	30/12/91	A	12	(14)	1
29	Reuven Niemeijer		27/03/95	M	7	(4)	3
14	Joey Pelupessy		15/05/93	M	34		1
18	Kristoffer Peterson	SWE	28/11/94	A	13	(2)	4
4	Robin Pröpper		23/09/93	D	14	(4)	
3	Mike te Wierik		08/06/92	D	29		1
26	Sander Thomas		26/06/97	M		(2)	
30	Tim van de Berg		23/11/97	D		(1)	
22	Daryl van Mieghem		05/12/89	A	4	(5)	2
20	Peter van Ooijen		16/02/92	M	5	(10)	2
19	Vincent Vermeij		09/08/94	A	3	(11)	2
6	Dario Vujičević	CRO	01/04/90	M	1	(1)	

NEC Nijmegen

1900 • Goffert (12,500) • nec-nijmegen.nl

Coach: Peter Hyballa (GER); (24/04/17 Ron de Groot)

Date		Opponent		Score	Scorers
2016					
05/08	h	Zwolle	D	1-1	*Ofosu*
14/08	a	Go Ahead Eagles	D	2-2	*Mayi 2*
20/08	h	Heerenveen	W	2-1	*Dumić, Ofosu*
28/08	a	AZ	L	0-2	
10/09	h	PSV	L	0-4	
18/09	a	Sparta	L	0-2	
25/09	h	Willem II	D	0-0	
01/10	a	Roda	W	1-0	*Mayi*
16/10	h	Feyenoord	L	1-2	*Rayhi*
23/10	h	Vitesse	D	1-1	*Dumić*
30/10	a	Utrecht	D	1-1	*Kadioglu*
05/11	h	Groningen	D	1-1	*Kadioglu*
20/11	a	Ajax	L	0-5	
26/11	h	Twente	W	3-2	*Grot 2, Dumić*
02/12	a	Heracles	L	0-2	
10/12	h	Den Haag	W	3-0	*Mayi, og (Ebuehi), Rayhi*
18/12	a	Excelsior	D	2-2	*Grot, Dumić*
2017					
15/01	a	Willem II	W	1-0	*Grot*
22/01	h	Roda	W	2-0	*Breinburg 2 (2p)*
29/01	a	Feyenoord	L	0-4	
04/02	h	Go Ahead Eagles	L	1-2	*Grot*
10/02	a	Zwolle	L	0-2	
18/02	a	PSV	L	1-3	*Messaoud*
25/02	h	Sparta	L	0-1	
05/03	h	Heracles	W	3-1	*Von Haacke, Heinloth, og (Hoogma)*
11/03	a	Den Haag	L	0-1	
18/03	h	Utrecht	L	0-3	
02/04	a	Vitesse	L	1-2	*Kadioglu*
05/04	a	Groningen	L	0-2	
08/04	h	Ajax	L	1-5	*Kadioglu*
15/04	a	Twente	L	0-3	
22/04	h	Excelsior	L	0-1	
07/05	h	AZ	W	2-1	*Von Haacke, Awoniyi*
14/05	a	Heerenveen	W	2-0	*Groeneveld, Awoniyi*

No	Name	Nat	DoB	Pos	Aps	(s)	Gls
9	Taiwo Awoniyi	NGA	12/08/97	A	9	(9)	2
34	Gregor Breinburg	ARU	16/09/91	M	33		2
28	Lorenzo Burnet		11/01/91	D	7	(2)	
15	Robin Buwalda		17/08/94	D	12	(6)	
1	Joris Delle	FRA	29/03/90	G	34		
3	Dario Dumić	BIH	30/01/92	D	34		4
6	Mikael Dyrestam	SWE	10/12/91	D	15	(2)	
24	André Fomitschow	GER	07/09/90	D	23	(2)	
27	Fabian Gmeiner	AUT	27/01/97	D		(1)	
4	Wojciech Golla	POL	12/01/92	D	33		
47	Arnaut Groeneveld		31/01/97	M	5	(7)	1
17	Jay-Roy Grot		13/03/98	A	17	(3)	5
2	Michael Heinloth	GER	09/02/92	D	17	(5)	1
8	Janio Bikel	POR	28/06/95	M	26	(3)	
16	Ferdi Kadioglu		07/10/99	M	9	(18)	4
11	Jordan Larsson	SWE	27/06/97	A	4	(4)	
37	Jeffrey Leiwakabessy		23/02/81	D		(1)	
7	Sam Lundholm	SWE	01/07/94	A		(4)	
10	Stefan Mauk	AUS	12/10/95	M	1	(1)	
18	Kévin Mayi	FRA	14/01/93	A	21	(5)	4
21	Ali Messaoud		13/04/91	M	8	(5)	1
14	Reagy Ofosu	GER	20/09/91	M	9	(7)	2
21	Quincy Owusu-Abeyie	GHA	15/04/86	A	6	(6)	
20	Mohammed Rayhi		01/07/94	M	21	(5)	2
11	Joey Sleegers		20/07/94	M		(1)	
30	Frank Sturing		29/05/97	D	3		
19	Julian von Haacke	GER	14/02/94	M	27	(3)	2

PEC Zwolle

1910 • MAC³PARK (12,500) • peczwolle.nl

Major honours
Dutch Cup (1) 2014

Coach: Ron Jans

Date		Opponent		Score	Scorers
2016					
05/08	a	NEC	D	1-1	*Menig*
13/08	h	Sparta	L	0-3	
20/08	h	PSV	L	0-4	
27/08	a	Heerenveen	L	0-1	
10/09	h	Utrecht	D	1-1	*Ehizibue*
18/09	h	AZ	L	0-2	
24/09	a	Ajax	L	1-5	*Brama*
30/09	h	Den Haag	W	2-1	*Mokhtar 2*
16/10	a	Twente	D	2-2	*Mokhtar, Warmerdam*
21/10	a	Excelsior	W	2-0	*Menig, Warmerdam*
30/10	h	Go Ahead Eagles	W	3-1	*Menig, Saymak, Holla*
05/11	h	Roda	D	0-0	
20/11	a	Feyenoord	L	0-3	
26/11	h	Groningen	L	0-4	
03/12	a	Vitesse	L	1-3	*Schenkeveld*
10/12	h	Willem II	D	0-0	
18/12	a	Heracles	L	0-3	
2017					
15/01	h	Ajax	L	1-3	*Brock-Madsen*
21/01	a	Den Haag	W	2-1	*Ehizibue, Brock-Madsen*
29/01	h	Twente	L	1-2	*Menig*
05/02	a	Sparta	W	3-2	*Menig, Brock-Madsen, Israelsson*
10/02	h	NEC	W	2-0	*Brock-Madsen, Menig*
18/02	a	Utrecht	L	1-3	*Brock-Madsen*
26/02	a	AZ	D	1-1	*Thomas*
04/03	h	Vitesse	W	3-1	*Saymak, Brock-Madsen, Holla*
12/03	a	Willem II	L	0-2	
19/03	a	Go Ahead Eagles	W	3-1	*Menig, Warmerdam, Van Polen (p)*
01/04	h	Excelsior	D	1-1	*Warmerdam*
06/04	a	Roda	L	1-2	*Mokhtar*
09/04	h	Feyenoord	D	2-2	*Menig, Van Polen*
16/04	a	Groningen	L	1-5	*Brock-Madsen*
22/04	h	Heracles	L	1-2	*Van de Pavert*
07/05	h	Heerenveen	W	2-1	*Holla, Menig*
14/05	a	PSV	L	1-4	*Van de Pavert*

No	Name	Nat	DoB	Pos	Aps	(s)	Gls
9	Anass Achahbar		13/01/94	A	8	(11)	
15	Ouasim Bouy		11/06/93	M	13		
14	Wout Brama		21/08/86	M	14		1
44	Nicolai Brock-Madsen	DEN	09/01/93	A	20	(3)	7
46	Max de Boom		17/02/96	M		(1)	
20	Kingsley Ehizibue		25/05/95	M	24	(5)	2
18	Gustavo	BRA	05/04/96	M	3		
23	Danny Holla		31/12/87	M	24	(1)	3
14	Erik Israelsson	SWE	25/02/89	M	1	(4)	1
33	Athanasios Karagounis	GRE	25/09/91	M		(5)	
17	Josef Kvída	CZE	23/01/97	D	2		
4	Dirk Marcellis		13/04/88	D	29		
8	Wouter Marinus		18/02/95	M	6	(6)	
98	Hachim Mastour	MAR	15/06/98	A	1	(4)	
11	Queensy Menig		19/08/95	A	29	(2)	9
7	Youness Mokhtar	MAR	29/08/91	A	14	(10)	4
10	Stefan Nijland		10/08/88	A	1	(12)	
35	Hervin Ongenda	FRA	24/06/95	A		(3)	
13	Philippe Sandler		10/02/97	D	4	(2)	
6	Mustafa Saymak		11/02/93	M	23	(3)	2
22	Bart Schenkeveld		28/08/91	D	12	(8)	1
30	Ryan Thomas	NZL	20/12/94	M	24	(7)	1
3	Ted van de Pavert		06/01/92	D	20	(3)	2
1	Mickey van der Hart		13/06/94	G	34		
2	Bram van Polen		11/10/85	D	31		2
31	Bas van Wijnen		31/07/97	M		(1)	
5	Calvin Verdonk		26/04/97	D	14	(3)	
21	Django Warmerdam		02/09/95	M	23	(3)	4

PSV Eindhoven

1913 • Philips (35,000) • psv.nl

Major honours
European Champion Clubs' Cup (1) 1988; UEFA Cup (1) 1978; Dutch League (23) 1929, 1935, 1951, 1963, 1975, 1976, 1978, 1986, 1987, 1988, 1989, 1991, 1992, 1997, 2000, 2001, 2003, 2005, 2006, 2007, 2008, 2015, 2016; Dutch Cup (9) 1950, 1974, 1976, 1988, 1989, 1990, 1996, 2005, 2012

Coach: Phillip Cocu

Date		Opponent		Score	Scorers
2016					
06/08	a	Utrecht	W	2-1	*Pröpper, Pereiro*
14/08	h	AZ	W	1-0	*Moreno*
20/08	a	Zwolle	W	4-0	*Isimat-Mirin, Hendrix, L de Jong, Bergwijn*
28/08	h	Groningen	D	0-0	
10/09	a	NEC	W	4-0	*Ramselaar, Pereiro, Brenet, L de Jong*
18/09	h	Feyenoord	L	0-1	
24/09	a	Excelsior	W	3-1	*Narsingh, L de Jong, Pröpper*
01/10	a	Heerenveen	D	1-1	*og (St Juste)*
15/10	h	Heracles	D	1-1	*Pereiro*
22/10	h	Sparta	W	1-0	*Ramselaar*
29/10	a	Vitesse	W	2-0	*Pereiro 2*
05/11	h	Twente	D	1-1	*Moreno*
19/11	a	Willem II	D	0-0	
26/11	h	Den Haag	W	3-1	*Pereiro (p), og (Beugelsdijk), L de Jong*
03/12	a	Roda	D	0-0	
10/12	h	Go Ahead Eagles	W	1-0	*S de Jong*
18/12	a	Ajax	D	1-1	*S de Jong*
2017					
14/01	h	Excelsior	W	2-0	*Van Ginkel, Pröpper*
22/01	h	Heerenveen	W	4-3	*Pröpper, Pereiro, Van Ginkel, Moreno*
28/01	a	Heracles	W	2-1	*Ramselaar, Pröpper*
04/02	a	AZ	W	4-2	*Willems 2, Pereiro, L de Jong*
12/02	h	Utrecht	W	3-0	*L de Jong, Bergwijn, Van Ginkel*
18/02	h	NEC	W	3-1	*Van Ginkel (p), Ramselaar, L de Jong*
26/02	a	Feyenoord	L	1-2	*Pereiro*
04/03	h	Roda	W	4-0	*Moreno 2, S de Jong 2 (1p)*
11/03	a	Go Ahead Eagles	W	3-1	*S de Jong (p), L de Jong, Guardado*
18/03	h	Vitesse	W	1-0	*S de Jong*
01/04	a	Sparta	W	2-0	*Locadia, Van Ginkel*
06/04	a	Twente	D	2-2	*Locadia, Moreno*
09/04	h	Willem II	W	5-0	*Isimat-Mirin, Van Ginkel 2, Pereiro, Guardado*
15/04	a	Den Haag	D	1-1	*Pröpper*
23/04	h	Ajax	W	1-0	*Locadia*
07/05	a	Groningen	D	1-1	*Lammers*
14/05	h	Zwolle	W	4-1	*Moreno, Arias, Lammers, Ramselaar*

No	Name	Nat	DoB	Pos	Aps	(s)	Gls
4	Santiago Arias	COL	13/01/92	D	28		1
27	Steven Bergwijn		08/10/97	A	8	(17)	2
20	Joshua Brenet		20/03/94	D	13	(7)	1
9	Luuk de Jong		27/08/90	A	31	(1)	8
10	Siem de Jong		28/01/89	M	10	(9)	6
18	Andrés Guardado	MEX	28/09/86	M	27		2
8	Jorrit Hendrix		06/02/95	M	8	(11)	1
2	Nicolas Isimat-Mirin	FRA	15/11/91	D	27	(1)	2
17	Florian Jozefzoon		09/02/91	A		(5)	
50	Sam Lammers		30/04/97	A	1	(4)	2
19	Jürgen Locadia		07/11/93	A	9	(4)	3
38	Ramon Lundqvist	SWE	10/05/97	M		(2)	
3	Héctor Moreno	MEX	17/01/88	D	32		7
11	Luciano Narsingh		13/09/90	A	9	(6)	1
22	Remko Pasveer		08/11/83	G	3		
7	Gastón Pereiro	URU	11/06/95	M	26	(4)	10
6	Davy Pröpper		02/09/91	M	33	(1)	6
23	Bart Ramselaar		29/06/96	M	22	(5)	5
5	Daniel Schwaab	GER	23/08/88	D	13	(10)	
28	Marco van Ginkel		01/12/92	M	15		7
15	Jetro Willems		30/03/94	D	24	(1)	2
25	Olexandr Zinchenko	UKR	15/12/96	M	4	(8)	
1	Jeroen Zoet		06/01/91	G	31		

Roda JC

1962 • Parkstad Limburg (18,936) • rodajc.nl

Major honours
Dutch Cup (2) 1997, 2000

Coach: Yannis Anastasiou (GRE)

Date		Opponent		Score	Scorers
2016					
07/08	h	Heracles	D	1-1	*Auassar*
13/08	a	Ajax	D	2-2	*Auassar, Van Hyfte*
20/08	h	Vitesse	L	0-1	
27/08	a	Willem II	D	0-0	
11/09	a	Go Ahead Eagles	L	0-2	
17/09	h	Heerenveen	L	0-3	
25/09	a	Feyenoord	L	0-5	
01/10	h	NEC	L	0-1	
16/10	a	Excelsior	W	1-0	*Boysen*
22/10	h	Den Haag	D	1-1	*Paulissen*
28/10	a	Twente	D	0-0	
05/11	a	Zwolle	D	0-0	
20/11	h	AZ	D	1-1	*Ajagun*
27/11	a	Sparta	D	2-2	*Kum, Mytidis*
03/12	h	PSV	D	0-0	
09/12	a	Groningen	L	0-2	
17/12	h	Utrecht	D	0-0	
2017					
15/01	h	Feyenoord	L	0-2	
22/01	a	NEC	L	0-2	
28/01	h	Excelsior	W	4-0	*Schahin, Paulissen 2, Papazoglou*
05/02	h	Ajax	L	0-2	
11/02	a	Heracles	D	2-2	*Paulissen, Van Hyfte*
17/02	h	Go Ahead Eagles	W	1-0	*Kum*
25/02	a	Heerenveen	L	0-3	
04/03	a	PSV	L	0-4	
12/03	h	Groningen	W	3-1	*Ajagun, Kum, Schahin*
17/03	h	Twente	L	0-3	
02/04	a	Den Haag	L	1-4	*El Makrini*
06/04	h	Zwolle	W	2-1	*Van Velzen, Rosheuvel*
09/04	a	AZ	D	1-1	*Werker*
15/04	h	Sparta	W	3-1	*Ajagun 2, Rosheuvel*
23/04	a	Utrecht	L	0-1	
07/05	h	Willem II	W	1-0	*Ajagun*
14/05	a	Vitesse	L	0-3	

No	Name	Nat	DoB	Pos	Aps	(s)	Gls
14	Abdul Ajagun	NGA	10/02/93	M	30	(1)	5
27	Frederic Ananou	GER	20/09/97	D	17	(1)	
8	Adil Auassar		06/10/86	M	24	(5)	2
11	Beni Badibanga	BEL	19/02/96	A	1	(5)	
29	Tim Blättler		04/09/94	A		(1)	
21	David Boysen	DEN	30/04/91	M	11	(2)	1
4	Roel Brouwers		28/11/81	D	3	(2)	
23	Simon Church	WAL	10/12/88	A	4		
10	Daniel De Silva	AUS	06/03/97	M	4	(4)	
32	Célestin Djim	BEL	14/05/95	A		(2)	
30	Mohamed El Makrini		06/07/87	M	9	(2)	1
4	Ognjen Gnjatić	BIH	16/10/91	M	5	(3)	
3	Christian Kum		13/09/85	D	30	(1)	3
16	Marcos Gullón	ESP	20/02/89	M	13	(2)	
2	Martin Milec	SVN	20/09/91	D	24	(1)	
11	Nestoras Mytidis	CYP	01/06/91	A	8	(8)	1
24	Farshad Noor		02/10/94	M	6	(8)	
25	Sakis Papazoglou	GRE	30/03/88	A	2	(9)	1
19	Mitchel Paulissen		21/04/93	M	16	(15)	4
21	Simeon Raykov	BUL	06/06/87	A	1	(1)	
17	Mikhail Rosheuvel		10/08/90	A	25	(7)	2
6	Nathan Rutjes		01/12/83	M	5		
9	Dani Schahin	GER	09/07/89	A	13	(5)	2
31	Danny Stassar		19/09/97	D		(1)	
7	Tom Van Hyfte	BEL	28/04/86	M	28	(3)	2
1	Benjamin van Leer		09/04/92	G	34		
5	Ard van Peppen		26/06/85	D	32		
15	Gyliano van Velzen		14/04/94	A	9	(3)	1
44	Bryan Verboom	BEL	30/01/92	D	1	(3)	
20	Daryl Werker		27/06/94	D	19	(4)	1

Sparta Rotterdam

1888 • Het Kasteel (11,000) • sparta-rotterdam.nl

Major honours
Dutch League (6) 1909, 1911, 1912, 1913, 1915, 1959; Dutch Cup (3) 1958, 1962, 1966

Coach: Alex Pastoor

Date		Opponent		Score	Scorers
2016					
07/08	h	Ajax	L	1-3	*Sanusi*
13/08	a	Zwolle	W	3-0	*Brogno 2, Goodwin*
21/08	h	Go Ahead Eagles	W	1-0	*Brogno (p)*
27/08	a	Twente	L	1-3	*Brogno (p)*
11/09	a	Groningen	D	1-1	*El Azzouzi*
18/09	h	NEC	W	2-0	*Verhaar, El Azzouzi*
25/09	a	Utrecht	L	0-2	
02/10	h	AZ	D	1-1	*Breuer*
15/10	h	Willem II	D	2-2	*Goodwin, Verhaar*
22/10	a	PSV	L	0-1	
29/10	a	Heracles	D	2-2	*El Azzouzi, Brogno*
04/11	h	Heerenveen	W	3-1	*Spierings, El Azzouzi, Goodwin*
19/11	a	Excelsior	L	2-3	*Brogno, Dumfries*
27/11	h	Roda	D	2-2	*Brogno, Dougall*
04/12	a	Feyenoord	L	1-6	*Verhaar*
11/12	h	Vitesse	L	0-1	
18/12	a	Den Haag	L	0-1	
2017					
14/01	h	Utrecht	L	1-2	*Iván Calero*
21/01	a	AZ	D	1-1	*Pogba*
27/01	a	Willem II	L	2-3	*El Azzouzi, Verhaar*
05/02	h	Zwolle	L	2-3	*Pogba 2*
12/02	a	Ajax	L	0-2	
19/02	h	Groningen	D	2-2	*Van Moorsel, Iván Calero*
25/02	a	NEC	W	1-0	*Van Moorsel*
05/03	h	Feyenoord	W	1-0	*Pogba*
10/03	a	Vitesse	L	0-5	
18/03	h	Heracles	W	3-1	*Sanusi, Pusic 2*
01/04	h	PSV	L	0-2	
04/04	a	Heerenveen	L	0-3	
07/04	h	Excelsior	L	2-3	*og (Koolwijk), Pusic*
15/04	a	Roda	L	1-3	*Verhaar*
23/04	h	Den Haag	L	0-1	
07/05	h	Twente	W	1-0	*Pusic*
14/05	a	Go Ahead Eagles	W	3-1	*Pusic 2, Goodwin*

Name	Nat	DoB	Pos	Aps	(s)	Gls
Ragnar Ache		28/07/98	A		(1)	
Ilias Alhaft		23/02/97	A	3	(1)	
Roland Bergkamp		03/04/91	A		(2)	
Michel Breuer		25/05/80	D	32		1
Loris Brogno	BEL	18/09/92	A	18	(4)	7
Jerson Cabral		03/01/91	A	12	(1)	
Cyril Chevreuil	FRA	13/01/90	A		(2)	
Mart Dijkstra		10/08/90	M	31		
Kenneth Dougall	AUS	07/05/93	M	14	(6)	1
Denzel Dumfries		18/04/96	D	30	(1)	1
Zakaria El Azzouzi		07/05/96	A	19	(2)	5
Sherel Floranus		23/08/98	D	21	(3)	
Craig Goodwin	AUS	16/12/91	A	12	(15)	4
Iván Calero	ESP	21/04/95	A	7	(1)	2
Rick Ketting		15/01/96	D	1		
Roy Kortsmit		26/08/92	G	33		
David Mendes da Silva		04/08/82	M	7	(2)	
Florian Pinteaux	FRA	04/02/92	D	9	(2)	
Mathias Pogba	GUI	19/08/90	A	2	(12)	4
Martin Pusic	AUT	24/10/87	A	10	(4)	6
Janne Saksela	FIN	14/03/93	D	2	(3)	
Ryan Sanusi	BEL	05/01/92	M	19	(2)	2
Stijn Spierings		12/03/96	M	21	(2)	1
Finn Stokkers		18/04/96	A		(5)	
Rick van Drongelen		20/12/98	D	31		
Paco van Moorsel		15/12/89	M	13	(8)	2
Thomas Verhaar		08/03/88	A	16	(10)	5
Michael Verrips		03/12/96	G	1		
Bart Vriends		09/05/91	D	10	(8)	

NB Sparta Rotterdam did not use squad numbers.

FC Twente

1965 • De Grolsch Veste (24,244) • fctwente.nl

Major honours
Dutch League (1) 2010; Dutch Cup (3) 1977, 2001, 2011

Coach: René Hake

Date		Opponent		Score	Scorers
2016					
06/08	h	Excelsior	L	1-2	*Oosterwijk*
14/08	a	Feyenoord	L	0-2	
21/08	a	Groningen	W	4-3	*Enes 3, Oosterwijk*
27/08	h	Sparta	W	3-1	*Ziyech 2, Yeboah*
10/09	a	Heerenveen	L	1-3	*Celina*
17/09	h	Den Haag	W	4-1	*Enes 2, Celina, Mokotjo*
25/09	h	Vitesse	W	2-1	*Enes, Celina*
02/10	a	Heracles	D	1-1	*Klich (p)*
16/10	h	Zwolle	D	2-2	*Klich (p), Enes*
22/10	a	Go Ahead Eagles	W	2-0	*Yeboah, Celina*
28/10	h	Roda	D	0-0	
05/11	a	PSV	D	1-1	*Enes*
20/11	h	Utrecht	D	1-1	*Ter Avest*
26/11	a	NEC	L	2-3	*Enes, og (Dyrestam)*
04/12	a	Willem II	D	0-0	
11/12	h	Ajax	W	1-0	*Klich (p)*
17/12	h	AZ	L	1-2	*Enes*
2017					
15/01	a	Vitesse	L	1-3	*Klich (p)*
20/01	h	Heracles	W	1-0	*Andersen*
29/01	a	Zwolle	W	2-1	*Seys, Assaidi*
05/02	h	Feyenoord	L	0-2	
12/02	a	Excelsior	D	1-1	*Jensen*
18/02	h	Heerenveen	W	1-0	*Klich (p)*
24/02	a	Den Haag	D	1-1	*Enes*
04/03	h	Willem II	W	2-1	*og (Lachman), Enes*
12/03	a	Ajax	L	0-3	
17/03	a	Roda	W	3-0	*Jensen 2, Enes*
02/04	h	Go Ahead Eagles	L	1-2	*Enes*
06/04	h	PSV	D	2-2	*Enes, Celina*
09/04	a	Utrecht	L	0-3	
15/04	h	NEC	W	3-0	*Enes 2, Jensen*
22/04	a	AZ	L	1-2	*Andersen*
07/05	a	Sparta	L	0-1	
14/05	h	Groningen	L	3-5	*George, Klich (p), Enes*

No	Name	Nat	DoB	Pos	Aps	(s)	Gls
3	Joachim Andersen	DEN	31/05/96	D	21	(1)	2
8	Oussama Assaidi	MAR	15/08/88	M	3	(2)	1
25	Peet Bijen		28/01/95	D	23	(3)	
9	Torgeir Børven	NOR	03/12/91	A		(1)	
27	Enis Bunjaki	GER	17/10/97	A		(3)	
10	Bersant Celina	KOS	09/09/96	M	26	(1)	5
7	Chinedu Ede	GER	05/02/87	M	13	(6)	
17	Enes Ünal	TUR	10/05/97	A	31	(1)	18
30	Dylan George		27/06/98	A	2	(6)	1
12	Tim Hölscher	GER	21/01/95	M		(5)	
4	Jos Hooiveld		22/04/83	D	1	(6)	
19	Fredrik Jensen	FIN	09/09/97	M	18	(7)	4
4	Georgios Katsikas	GRE	14/06/90	D		(4)	
43	Mateusz Klich	POL	13/06/90	M	29		6
1	Nick Marsman		01/10/90	G	34		
22	Kamohelo Mokotjo	RSA	11/03/91	M	32	(1)	1
24	Jari Oosterwijk		03/03/95	A	3	(9)	2
11	Dylan Seys	BEL	26/09/96	M	8	(9)	1
2	Hidde ter Avest		20/05/97	D	31		1
5	Stefan Thesker	GER	11/04/91	D	28	(1)	
6	Dejan Trajkovski	SVN	14/04/92	D	16	(6)	
23	Jelle van der Heyden		31/08/95	M	6	(4)	
28	Jeroen van der Lely		22/03/96	D	25	(2)	
14	Yaw Yeboah	GHA	28/03/97	M	20	(6)	2
10	Hakim Ziyech	MAR	19/03/93	M	4		2

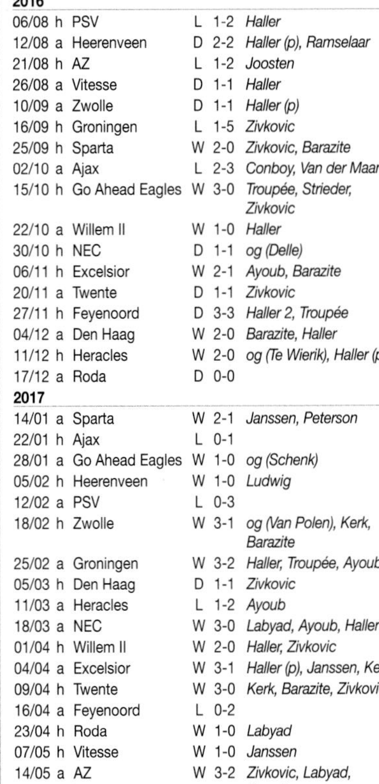

FC Utrecht

1970 • Galgenwaard (24,500) • fcutrecht.nl

Major honours
Dutch Cup (3) 1985, 2003, 2004

Coach: Erik ten Hag

Date		Opponent		Score	Scorers
2016					
06/08	h	PSV	L	1-2	*Haller*
12/08	a	Heerenveen	D	2-2	*Haller (p), Ramselaar*
21/08	h	AZ	L	1-2	*Joosten*
26/08	a	Vitesse	D	1-1	*Haller*
10/09	a	Zwolle	D	1-1	*Haller (p)*
16/09	h	Groningen	L	1-5	*Zivkovic*
25/09	h	Sparta	W	2-0	*Zivkovic, Barazite*
02/10	a	Ajax	L	2-3	*Conboy, Van der Maarel*
15/10	h	Go Ahead Eagles	W	3-0	*Troupée, Strieder, Zivkovic*
22/10	a	Willem II	W	1-0	*Haller*
30/10	h	NEC	D	1-1	*og (Delle)*
06/11	h	Excelsior	W	2-1	*Ayoub, Barazite*
20/11	a	Twente	D	1-1	*Zivkovic*
27/11	h	Feyenoord	D	3-3	*Haller 2, Troupée*
04/12	a	Den Haag	W	2-0	*Barazite, Haller*
11/12	h	Heracles	W	2-0	*og (Te Wierik), Haller (p)*
17/12	a	Roda	D	0-0	
2017					
14/01	a	Sparta	W	2-1	*Janssen, Peterson*
22/01	h	Ajax	L	0-1	
28/01	a	Go Ahead Eagles	W	1-0	*og (Schenk)*
05/02	h	Heerenveen	W	1-0	*Ludwig*
12/02	a	PSV	L	0-3	
18/02	h	Zwolle	W	3-1	*og (Van Polen), Kerk, Barazite*
25/02	a	Groningen	W	3-2	*Haller, Troupée, Ayoub*
05/03	h	Den Haag	D	1-1	*Zivkovic*
11/03	a	Heracles	L	1-2	*Ayoub*
18/03	a	NEC	W	3-0	*Labyad, Ayoub, Haller*
01/04	h	Willem II	W	2-0	*Haller, Zivkovic*
04/04	a	Excelsior	W	3-1	*Haller (p), Janssen, Kerk*
09/04	h	Twente	W	3-0	*Kerk, Barazite, Zivkovic*
16/04	a	Feyenoord	L	0-2	
23/04	h	Roda	W	1-0	*Labyad*
07/05	h	Vitesse	W	1-0	*Janssen*
14/05	a	AZ	W	3-2	*Zivkovic, Labyad, Barazite*

No	Name	Nat	DoB	Pos	Aps	(s)	Gls
25	Sofyan Amrabat	MAR	21/08/96	M	29	(2)	
6	Yassine Ayoub	MAR	06/03/94	M	31	(1)	4
10	Nacer Barazite		27/05/90	M	20	(7)	6
28	Edson Braafheid		08/04/83	D	1	(4)	
23	Wout Brama		21/08/86	M	13	(1)	
5	Kevin Conboy	DEN	15/10/87	D	14	(3)	1
22	Sébastien Haller	FRA	22/06/94	A	32		13
12	Jeff Hardeveld		27/02/95	D	2	(2)	
8	Willem Janssen		04/07/86	D	31	(1)	3
16	David Jensen	DEN	25/03/92	G	19	(1)	
24	Patrick Joosten		14/04/96	A	6	(7)	1
27	Gyrano Kerk		02/12/95	A	12	(3)	3
17	Sean Klaiber		31/07/94	D	6	(4)	
14	Menno Koch		02/07/94	D	2	(2)	
19	Zakaria Labyad	MAR	09/03/93	M	7	(7)	3
3	Ramon Leeuwin		01/09/87	D	31	(1)	
11	Andreas Ludwig	GER	11/09/90	M	5	(13)	1
53	Tafari Moore	ENG	05/07/97	D		(1)	
21	Kristoffer Peterson	SWE	28/11/94	A		(3)	1
23	Bart Ramselaar		29/06/96	M	2		1
26	Darren Rosheuvel		15/05/94	M	1	(1)	
18	Rubio Rubin	USA	01/03/96	A	3		
1	Robbin Ruiter		25/03/87	G	15		
7	Rico Strieder	GER	06/07/92	M	16		1
20	Giovanni Troupée		20/03/98	D	26	(3)	3
2	Mark van der Maarel		12/08/89	D	13	(8)	1
15	Robin van der Meer		21/02/95	D	18	(1)	
54	Nick Venema		09/04/99	A		(3)	
9	Richairo Zivkovic		05/09/96	A	19	(12)	8

NETHERLANDS

Vitesse

1892 • GelreDome (26,600) • vitesse.nl

Major honours
Dutch Cup (1) 2017

Coach: Henk Fräser

Date		Opponent	Res	Score	Scorers
2016					
06/08	a	Willem II	W	4-1	*Van Wolfswinkel, Kazaishvili, Nathan 2*
13/08	h	Den Haag	L	1-2	*Van Wolfswinkel*
20/08	a	Roda	W	1-0	*Baker*
26/08	h	Utrecht	D	1-1	*Van Wolfswinkel*
11/09	a	Ajax	L	0-1	
17/09	h	Go Ahead Eagles	W	2-0	*Van Wolfswinkel (p), Baker*
25/09	a	Twente	L	1-2	*Baker*
01/10	h	Groningen	W	2-1	*Baker, Leerdam*
15/10	a	AZ	D	2-2	*Baker, Van Wolfswinkel (p)*
23/10	a	NEC	D	1-1	*Foor*
29/10	h	PSV	L	0-2	
06/11	h	Heracles	L	1-2	*Van Wolfswinkel*
19/11	a	Heerenveen	D	1-1	*Baker*
26/11	h	Excelsior	D	2-2	*Van Wolfswinkel (p), Tighadouini*
03/12	h	Zwolle	W	3-1	*Baker (p), Zhang, Nathan*
11/12	a	Sparta	W	1-0	*Van Wolfswinkel*
17/12	a	Feyenoord	L	1-3	*Tighadouini*
2017					
15/01	h	Twente	W	3-1	*Baker, Van Wolfswinkel, Rashica*
21/01	a	Groningen	D	1-1	*Foor*
29/01	h	AZ	W	2-1	*Baker, Nathan*
03/02	a	Den Haag	W	2-0	*Tighadouini, Van Wolfswinkel*
11/02	h	Willem II	L	0-2	
19/02	h	Ajax	L	0-1	
26/02	a	Go Ahead Eagles	W	3-1	*Van Wolfswinkel, Foor, Rashica*
04/03	a	Zwolle	L	1-3	*Van Wolfswinkel*
10/03	h	Sparta	W	5-0	*Van Wolfswinkel, Foor, Kruiswijk, Nakamba, Kashia*
18/03	a	PSV	L	0-1	
02/04	h	NEC	W	2-1	*Van Wolfswinkel 2 (1p)*
05/04	a	Heracles	W	1-0	*Foor*
08/04	h	Heerenveen	W	4-2	*Foor, Van Wolfswinkel 3*
15/04	a	Excelsior	L	0-1	
23/04	h	Feyenoord	L	0-2	
07/05	a	Utrecht	L	0-1	
14/05	h	Roda	W	3-0	*Van Wolfswinkel 2, Baker*

No	Name	Nat	DoB	Pos	Aps	(s)	Gls
8	Mukhtar Ali	ENG	30/10/97	M		(6)	
34	Lewis Baker	ENG	25/04/95	M	33		10
28	Alexander Büttner		11/02/89	D	2	(8)	
41	Julian Calor		27/01/97	M	1		
14	Abiola Dauda	NGA	03/02/88	A		(1)	
17	Kevin Diks		06/10/96	D	11		
43	Lassana Faye		15/06/98	D	1	(1)	
25	Navarone Foor		04/02/92	M	26	(3)	6
37	Guram Kashia	GEO	04/07/87	D	34		1
10	Valeri Kazaishvili	GEO	29/01/93	A	2	(1)	1
30	Arshak Koryan	RUS	17/06/95	A	1	(2)	
6	Arnold Kruiswijk		02/11/84	D	24	(3)	1
5	Kelvin Leerdam		24/06/90	D	25	(3)	1
19	Matt Miazga	USA	19/07/95	D	15	(8)	
18	Marvelous Nakamba	ZIM	19/01/94	M	31		1
11	Nathan	BRA	13/03/96	A	19	(8)	4
20	Mohammed Osman		01/01/94	M		(3)	
8	Kosuke Ota	JPN	23/07/87	D	7	(3)	
7	Milot Rashica	KOS	28/06/96	A	31	(2)	2
1	Eloy Room	CUW	06/02/89	G	33		
10	Adnane Tighadouini	MAR	30/11/92	A	17	(8)	3
23	Michael Tørnes	DEN	08/01/86	G	1	(1)	
16	Mitchell van Bergen		27/08/99	A	2	(15)	
3	Maikel van der Werff		22/04/89	D	16	(1)	
13	Ricky van Wolfswinkel		27/01/89	A	32		20
21	Sheran Yeini	ISR	08/12/86	M	8	(2)	
9	Zhang Yuning	CHN	05/01/97	A	2	(14)	1

Willem II

1896 • Koning Willem II (14,700) • willem-ii.nl

Major honours
Dutch League (3) 1916, 1952, 1955; Dutch Cup (2) 1944, 1963

Coach: Erwin van der Looi

Date		Opponent	Res	Score	Scorers
2016					
06/08	h	Vitesse	L	1-4	*Fran Sol*
14/08	a	Heracles	L	1-3	*Falkenburg*
20/08	a	Ajax	W	2-1	*Falkenburg, Fran Sol*
27/08	h	Roda	D	0-0	
10/09	a	AZ	L	0-2	
17/09	h	Excelsior	D	1-1	*Fran Sol*
25/09	a	NEC	D	0-0	
02/10	h	Feyenoord	L	0-2	
15/10	a	Sparta	D	2-2	*Fran Sol 2*
22/10	h	Utrecht	L	0-1	
29/10	h	Groningen	W	2-1	*Haye, Ogbeche*
05/11	a	Den Haag	L	0-1	
19/11	h	PSV	D	0-0	
25/11	a	Go Ahead Eagles	W	1-0	*Schuurman*
04/12	h	Twente	D	0-0	
10/12	a	Zwolle	D	0-0	
16/12	h	Heerenveen	W	2-1	*Fran Sol 2*
2017					
15/01	h	NEC	L	0-1	
21/01	a	Feyenoord	L	0-1	
27/01	h	Sparta	W	3-2	*Fran Sol, Lachman, Haye*
04/02	h	Heracles	L	1-3	*Fran Sol (p)*
11/02	a	Vitesse	W	2-0	*Koppers, Oularé*
19/02	h	AZ	D	1-1	*Falkenburg*
25/02	a	Excelsior	W	2-0	*Koppers, Falkenburg*
04/03	a	Twente	L	1-2	*Croux*
12/03	h	Zwolle	W	2-0	*Falkenburg, Haye*
18/03	a	Groningen	D	1-1	*Oularé*
01/04	a	Utrecht	L	0-2	
05/04	h	Den Haag	L	1-2	*Oularé*
09/04	a	PSV	L	0-5	
16/04	h	Go Ahead Eagles	W	2-0	*Fran Sol, Schuurman*
21/04	a	Heerenveen	L	0-1	
07/05	a	Roda	L	0-1	
14/05	h	Ajax	L	1-3	*Schuurman*

No	Name	Nat	DoB	Pos	Aps	(s)	Gls
28	Asumah Abubakar	POR	10/05/97	A	5	(10)	
11	Bruno Andrade	BRA	02/03/89	A	4	(5)	
30	Andreas Calcan	ROU	09/04/94	M	2	(9)	
14	Jordy Croux	BEL	15/01/94	M	23	(6)	1
10	Erik Falkenburg		05/05/88	M	24	(4)	5
9	Fran Sol	ESP	13/03/92	A	25	(5)	10
8	Thom Haye		09/02/95	M	26	(6)	3
3	Freek Heerkens		13/09/89	D	11	(4)	
24	Guus Joppen		14/11/89	D	9	(2)	
20	Anouar Kali	MAR	03/06/91	M	26	(2)	
45	Thomas Kok		15/05/98	M	1		
5	Dico Koppers		31/01/92	D	11	(6)	2
29	Darryl Lachman	CUW	11/11/89	D	32		1
1	Kostas Lamprou	GRE	18/09/91	G	34		
25	Elmo Lieftink		03/02/94	M	8	(7)	
22	Bartholomew Ogbeche	NGA	01/10/84	A	2	(12)	1
6	Funso Ojo	BEL	28/08/91	M	28		
58	Obbi Oularé	BEL	08/01/96	A	10	(1)	3
4	Jordens Peters		03/05/87	D	31		
16	Vajebah Sakor	NOR	14/04/96	M		(1)	
7	Jari Schuurman		22/02/97	M	5	(6)	3
26	Katuku Tshimanga	COD	06/11/88	D	21	(1)	
46	Pele van Anholt		23/04/91	D	22	(1)	
17	Branco van den Boomen		21/07/95	M	6	(2)	
15	Dries Wuytens	BEL	18/03/91	D	8	(7)	

Top goalscorers

21	Nicolai Jørgensen (Feyenoord)
20	Ricky van Wolfswinkel (Vitesse)
19	Reza Ghoochannejhad (Heerenveen) Samuel Armenteros (Heracles)
18	Enes Ünal (Twente)
17	Mimoun Mahi (Groningen)
16	Kasper Dolberg (Ajax)
14	Davy Klaassen (Ajax) Jens Toornstra (Feyenoord)
13	Wout Weghorst (AZ) Sébastien Haller (Utrecht)

UEFA Europa League qualification play-offs

FIRST ROUND

(17/05/17 & 20/05/17)
Heerenveen 1-3 Utrecht *(Ødegaard 61; Amrabat 15, Ayoub 20, Haller 72)*
Utrecht 2-1 Heerenveen *(Leeuwin 30, Zivkovic 38; Ghoochannejhad 61p)*
(Utrecht 5-2)

Groningen 1-4 AZ *(Drost 68; Jahanbakhsh 45, Weghorst 66, 90, Stengs 74)*
AZ 4-1 Groningen *(Weghorst 9, Van Overeem 54, 82, Stengs 62; Linssen 37)*
(AZ 8-2)

SECOND ROUND

(25/05/17 & 28/05/17)
AZ 3-0 Utrecht *(Van Overeem 17, Ayoub 32og, Weghorst 65)*
Utrecht 3-0 AZ *(Janssen 13, Haller 28, Kerk 82)* *(aet)*
(3-3; Utrecht 4-3 on pens)

Promoted clubs

VVV-Venlo

1903 • De Koel (8,000) • vvv-venlo.nl
Coach: Maurice Steijn

NAC Breda

1912 • Rat Verlegh (19,000) • nac.nl
Major honours
Dutch League (1) 1921; Dutch Cup (1) 1973
Coach: Marinus Dijkhuizen; (01/01/17) Stijn Vreven

Second level final table 2016/17

		Pld	W	D	L	F	A	Pts
1	VVV-Venlo (*2,*3)	38	25	5	8	75	35	80
2	Jong Ajax	38	23	7	8	93	54	76
3	SC Cambuur (*4)	38	22	5	11	78	42	71
4	Jong PSV (*1)	38	20	9	9	66	35	69
5	NAC Breda	38	19	7	12	65	50	64
6	FC Volendam	38	17	11	10	63	44	62
7	MVV Maastricht	38	15	14	9	55	45	59
8	Almere City FC	38	17	8	13	74	66	59
9	FC Emmen	38	14	13	11	50	40	55
10	RKC Waalwijk	38	15	9	14	62	70	54
11	FC Eindhoven	38	15	8	15	64	71	53
12	De Graafschap	38	15	5	18	70	63	50
13	Helmond Sport	38	14	7	17	51	67	49
14	FC Den Bosch	38	12	9	17	48	67	45
15	FC Oss	38	12	5	21	67	95	41
16	Telstar	38	10	10	18	46	64	40
17	Fortuna Sittard	38	13	9	16	54	67	39
18	Jong FC Utrecht	38	10	7	21	50	71	37
19	FC Dordrecht	38	5	9	24	42	72	24
20	Achilles '29	38	5	7	26	37	92	19

NB (*) period champions; Helmond Sport qualified for play-offs as second-placed club in period 2 to VVV-Venlo, who had already qualified as second-placed club in period 1, won by ineligible Jong PSV. Fortuna Sittard - 9 pts deducted; Achilles '29 - 3 pts deducted.

Promotion/Relegation play-offs

FIRST ROUND

(08/05/17 & 12/05/17)
Helmond Sport 4-2 Almere City
Almere City 0-2 Helmond Sport
(Helmond Sport 6-2)

RKC 1-5 Emmen
Emmen 0-1RKC
(Emmen 5-2)

SECOND ROUND

(18/05/17 & 21/05/17)
Emmen 1-3 NEC
NEC 1-0 Emmen
(NEC 4-1)

Helmond Sport 0-1 Roda
Roda 1-1 Helmond Sport
(Roda 2-1)

MVV 1-1 Cambuur
Cambuur 1-2 MVV
(MVV 3-2)

Volendam 2-2 NAC
NAC 2-0 Volendam
(NAC 4-2)

THIRD ROUND

(25/05/17 & 28/05/17)
NAC 1-0 NEC
NEC 1-4 NAC
(NAC 5-1)

MVV 0-0 Roda
Roda 1-0 MVV
(Roda 1-0)

DOMESTIC CUP

KNVB-Beker 2016/17

FIRST ROUND

(20/09/16)
Barendrecht 0-1 Excelsior
Capelle 0-4 Groningen
Den Bosch 2-3 Eindhoven
EVV 0-3 RKC
Heerenveen 5-1 De Graafschap *(aet)*
HHC 2-2 Jodan Boys *(aet; 6-7 on pens)*
IJsselmeervogels 3-1 Achilles 29
JVC 1-3 Telstar
Kozakken Boys 3-0 Helmond Sport
NAC 0-2 VVV
Rijnsburgse Boys 0-2 Almere City
Rijnvogels 0-1 Cambuur
Scheveningen 1-2 Emmen
Volendam 3-3 MVV *(aet; 5-4 on pens)*

(21/09/16)
Achilles Veen 1-4 VVSB
Ajax 5-0 Willem II
De Treffers 0-3 ASWH
Dongen 1-3 Go Ahead Eagles
DVS 33 1-4 Zwolle
Excelsior Maassluis 1-3 Heracles *(aet)*
HFC 6-1 OJC
Katwijk 2-1 Harkemase Boys
Lienden 1-4 AZ
NEC 1-1 Den Haag *(aet; 3-5 on pens)*
PSV 4-0 Roda
Spakenburg 2-1 Fortuna Sittard
Sparta 3-1 Dordrecht
UNA 1-0 Huizen

(22/09/16)
De Dijk 2-7 Vitesse
HSC 21 1-5 TEC
Feyenoord 4-1 Oss
Twente 1-3 Utrecht

SECOND ROUND

(25/10/16)
Den Haag 2-1 Telstar
Go Ahead Eagles 1-2 Jodan Boys
Spakenburg 2-3 ASWH *(aet)*
Sparta 3-1 PSV
TEC 0-4 Cambuur
Volendam 2-1 Almere City *(aet)*
VVSB 3-0 Katwijk

(26/10/16)
AZ 1-0 Emmen
Feyenoord 4-0 Excelsior
Heracles 5-0 UNA
IJsselmeervogels 3-1 HFC
Kozakken Boys 1-6 Ajax
Utrecht 1-0 Groningen
Vitesse 4-1 RKC

(27/10/16)
Eindhoven 1-2 Heerenveen
Zwolle 2-1 VVV

THIRD ROUND

(13/12/16)
IJsselmeervogels 0-1 Heerenveen
Volendam 4-1 VVSB

(14/12/16)
AZ 2-0 ASWH
Feyenoord 5-1 Den Haag
Vitesse 4-0 Jodan Boys
Zwolle 1-2 Utrecht

(15/12/16)
Cambuur 2-1 Ajax
Heracles 0-3 Sparta

QUARTER-FINALS

(24/01/17)
Volendam 1-1 Sparta *(Steltenpool 110; Verhaar 108) (aet; 5-6 on pens)*

(25/01/17)
AZ 1-0 Heerenveen *(Luckassen 71)*
Utrecht 2-2 Cambuur *(Leeuwin 29, Troupée 89; Bakker 47p, Barto 67) (aet; 6-7 on pens)*

(26/01/17)
Vitesse 2-0 Feyenoord *(Kashia 56, Tighadouini 61)*

SEMI-FINALS

(01/03/17)
Sparta 1-2 Vitesse *(Kashia 75og; Baker 13, 73)*

(02/03/17)
AZ 0-0 Cambuur *(aet; 3-2 on pens)*

FINAL

(30/04/17)
De Kuip, Rotterdam
VITESSE 2 *(Van Wolfswinkel 81, 88)*
AZ ALKMAAR 0
Referee: *Makkelie*
VITESSE: *Room, Leerdam (Diks 84), Kashia, Miazga, Kruiswijk, Nakamba, Foor (Van der Werff 90+1), Baker, Rashica, Van Wolfswinkel, Nathan (Tighadouini 73)*
AZ: *Krul, Svensson, Van Eijden (Friday 83), Vlaar, Haps, Luckassen, Van Overeem (Seuntjens 67), Wuytens, Jahanbakhsh, Weghorst, Dos Santos (Bel Hassani 79)*

Vitesse lift their long-awaited first major trophy

NORTHERN IRELAND

Irish Football Association (IFA)

Address	National Football Stadium Donegal Avenue GB-Belfast BT12 5LW
Tel	+44 2890 669 458
Fax	+44 2890 667 620
E-mail	info@irishfa.com
Website	irishfa.com

President	David Martin
General secretary	Patrick Nelson
Media officer	Neil Brittain
Year of formation	1880
National stadium	Windsor Park, Belfast (18,600)

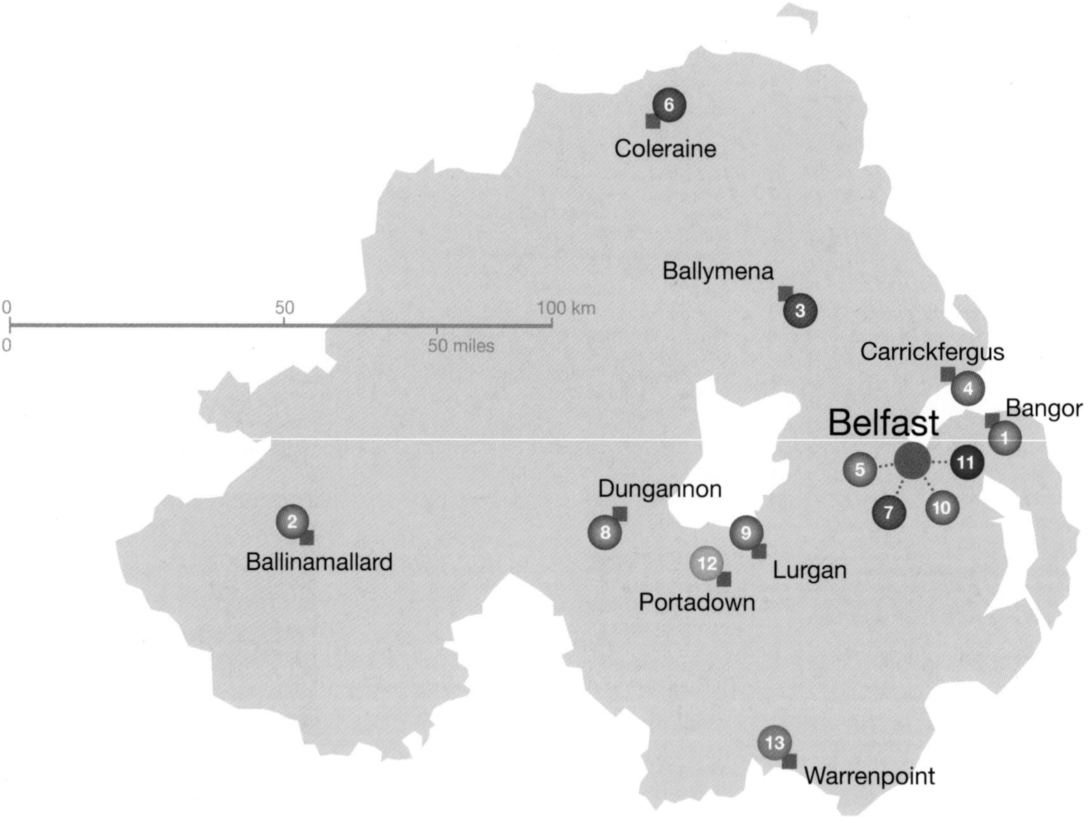

0 50 100 km
0 50 miles

Coleraine
Ballymena
Carrickfergus
Belfast
Bangor
Dungannon
Ballinamallard
Lurgan
Portadown
Warrenpoint

PREMIERSHIP CLUBS

  1 **Ards FC**

  2 **Ballinamallard United FC**

  3 **Ballymena United FC**

  4 **Carrick Rangers FC**

  5 **Cliftonville FC**

 6 **Coleraine FC**

  7 **Crusaders FC**

  8 **Dungannon Swifts FC**

  9 **Glenavon FC**

  10 **Glentoran FC**

 11 **Linfield FC**

 12 **Portadown FC**

PROMOTED CLUB

  13 **Warrenpoint Town FC**

KEY

- UEFA Champions League
- UEFA Europa League
- Promoted
- Relegated

Linfield end trophy drought

Without a major trophy for five years, Linfield returned to their customary position at the pinnacle of Northern Irish football by winning the double of Premiership and Irish Cup. Their 52nd league triumph was won on the final day after defending champions Crusaders had let slip a nine-point lead.

Northern Ireland's record goalscorer David Healy thus won both of the province's most important competitions in his first full campaign as Linfield manager. It was also a memorable season for Michael O'Neill as he guided the national team to a promising position in their FIFA World Cup qualifying group.

League and cup double for David Healy's Blues

Holders Crusaders surrender big lead with late slump

National team make waves in World Cup qualifiers

Domestic league

Crusaders, led by long-serving coach Stephen Baxter, spent most of the season with their eyes trained on the prize of a Premiership hat-trick. Defeated only once before Christmas, they looked well set for further success. Their one problem was that they could not get the better of Linfield. Two goalless draws against their Belfast rivals preceded a New Year's Eve defeat at home, and although Baxter's boys made an excellent start to 2017, building up a nine-point lead with nine games to go, Linfield would not surrender the fight.

All Healy's side could do was keep winning and hope that Crusaders slipped up. That is precisely what happened, with the teams' fourth league meeting of the campaign, at Windsor Park on 8 April, pivotal to that outcome. Linfield won it 1-0 with a goal from Aaron Burns, and suddenly the gap was down to just a single point. The Blues had not topped the table all season, but when the Crues were beaten 3-0 at Ballymena in the penultimate round – their third defeat in five games – the two title rivals finally swapped places.

Now in pole position and with a run of eight successive victories behind them, Linfield made the short trip to Cliftonville knowing that, with a two-point lead and a vastly superior goal difference, a draw was all they needed to end their five-year drought. At half-time that scenario was far from certain as their hosts led 1-0, but cometh the hour, cometh the man, and after 15 minutes of the second period Linfield were in total control of the game thanks to a hat-trick from leading marksman Andrew Waterworth. Furthermore, Cliftonville were down to ten men. Crusaders would simultaneously beat Glenavon 6-1, but their chance to make history had gone. A year earlier Crusaders had won 3-1 at Cliftonville to clinch the Premiership crown; now it was Linfield's turn.

It was a comeback triumph to rank with any of Linfield's previous 51 Irish League wins, but the bitterest of pills to swallow for Crusaders. They did, however, finish a full 22 points ahead of third-placed Coleraine, who were joined in the UEFA Europa League by play-off winners – and first-time League Cup winners – Ballymena United. Portadown's first season in 30 years without manager Ronnie McFall was a disaster. Burdened throughout with a 12-point penalty for faulty player registration, they never looked like clawing back the deficit and were duly relegated – to be replaced by the the previous season's fallers, Warrenpoint Town.

Domestic cup

Another Waterworth hat-trick gave Linfield victory over Coleraine in the season-closing Irish Cup final, the 3-0 win at Windsor Park ensuring that for the seventh successive time the Blues' league title had been accompanied by victory in the country's most important knockout competition. It was the 24th domestic double in the club's illustrious history.

Europe

There was little to shout about for Northern Ireland's European contingent as Linfield lost the cross-border clash with Cork City and four of the five games played on home soil ended in defeat, the sole exception being Cliftonville's 2-0 win against Differdange that enabled them to win the tie.

National team

With six of their ten 2018 FIFA World Cup qualifiers completed, the general consensus was that Northern Ireland could hardly have fared any better as they sought to reach back-to-back major tournaments for the first time. Two wins over Azerbaijan, one apiece against Norway and San Marino, an opening goalless draw in the Czech Republic, plus a respectable 2-0 away defeat to trophy-holders Germany were all positively received, leaving O'Neill's men in a strong position to reach the play-offs.

DOMESTIC SEASON AT A GLANCE

Premiership 2016/17 final table

			Home					Away					Total					
		Pld	W	D	L	F	A	W	D	L	F	A	W	D	L	F	A	Pts
1	**Linfield FC**	**38**	**11**	**5**	**2**	**39**	**10**	**16**	**3**	**1**	**48**	**14**	**27**	**8**	**3**	**87**	**24**	**89**
2	Crusaders FC	38	15	2	1	49	17	12	4	4	34	19	27	6	5	83	36	87
3	Coleraine FC	38	11	8	2	40	23	7	3	7	16	19	18	11	9	56	42	65
4	Ballymena United FC	38	12	2	6	49	34	6	3	9	26	39	18	5	15	75	73	59
5	Cliftonville FC	38	12	3	5	28	19	5	4	9	27	31	17	7	14	55	50	58
6	Glenavon FC	38	9	4	5	33	17	4	9	7	22	38	13	13	12	55	55	52
7	Dungannon Swifts FC	38	7	6	6	38	29	7	4	8	29	30	14	10	14	67	59	52
8	Ards FC	38	8	3	8	34	35	5	5	9	27	35	13	8	17	61	70	47
9	Glentoran FC	38	5	6	8	18	22	7	4	8	27	31	12	10	16	45	53	46
10	Ballinamallard United FC	38	7	1	12	26	31	3	4	11	19	41	10	5	23	45	72	35
11	Carrick Rangers FC	38	2	6	10	17	34	3	1	16	14	45	5	7	26	31	79	22
12	Portadown FC	38	6	1	11	16	30	1	3	16	12	45	7	4	27	28	75	13

NB League splits into top and bottom halves after 33 games, after which the clubs play exclusively against teams in their group; Portadown FC – 12 pts deducted.

European qualification 2017/18

Champion/Cup winner: Linfield FC (first qualifying round)

Crusaders FC (first qualifying round)
Coleraine FC (first qualifying round)
Ballymena United FC (first qualifying round)

Top scorer Andrew Mitchell (Dungannon), 25 goals
Relegated club Portadown FC
Promoted club Warrenpoint Town FC
Cup final Linfield FC 3-0 Coleraine FC

Player of the season

Roy Carroll
(Linfield FC)

After two decades and more of plying his trade outside Northern Ireland – with the exception of home internationals at Windsor Park – Carroll decided at the age of 38 to rejoin forces with his former national team colleague David Healy and sign a short-term contract with Linfield. The move turned out to be a masterstroke as the veteran goalkeeper helped the Blues to their first league and cup wins in five years. Revelling in the experience, the ex-Manchester United player made a number of telling saves as Linfield conceded just 24 goals in their 38 league matches.

Newcomer of the season

Cathair Friel
(Ballymena United FC)

Recruited at the age of 23 from third-tier Limavady United, where he had scored 46 goals in 2015/16, Friel arrived in the Premiership full of confidence, but few foresaw quite how well he would adapt to life at the top level. Impressive from day one under the wily stewardship of ex-Linfield boss David Jeffrey at Ballymena, he fired the club to fourth place with 17 goals, then saved his best until last with a decisive double in the post-season play-off final win against Glenavon that earned the Sky Blues a berth in the 2017/18 UEFA Europa League.

Team of the season

(4-4-2)

Coach: Healy *(Linfield)*

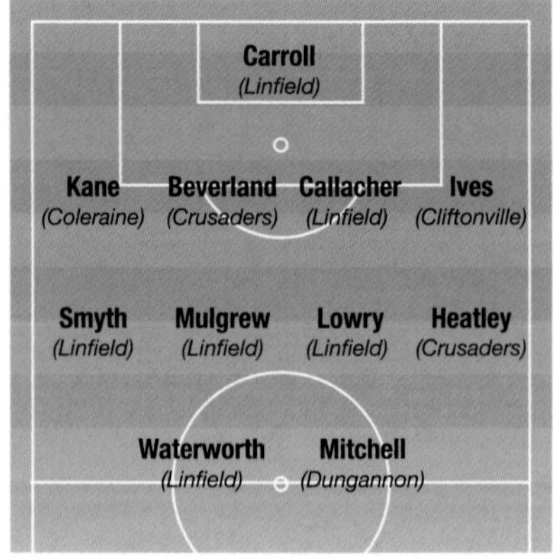

NATIONAL TEAM

International tournament appearances
FIFA World Cup (3) 1958 (qtr-finals), 1982 (2nd phase), 1986
UEFA European Championship (1) 2016 (round of 16)

Top five all-time caps
Pat Jennings (119); **Aaron Hughes** (106); **Steven Davis** & David Healy (95); Mal Donaghy (91)

Top five all-time goals
David Healy (36); **Kyle Lafferty** (20); Colin Clarke & Billy Gillespie (13); Gerry Armstrong, Joe Bambrick, Iain Dowie & Jimmy Quinn (12)

Results 2016/17

04/09/16	Czech Republic (WCQ)	A	Prague	D	0-0	
08/10/16	San Marino (WCQ)	H	Belfast	W	4-0	*Davis (26p), Lafferty (79, 90+4), Ward (85)*
11/10/16	Germany (WCQ	A	Hanover	L	0-2	
11/11/16	Azerbaijan (WCQ)	H	Belfast	W	4-0	*Lafferty (27), McAuley (40), McLaughlin (66), Brunt (83)*
15/11/16	Croatia	H	Belfast	L	0-3	
26/03/17	Norway (WCQ)	H	Belfast	W	2-0	*Ward (2), Washington (33)*
02/06/17	New Zealand	H	Belfast	W	1-0	*Boyce (6)*
10/06/17	Azerbaijan (WCQ)	A	Baku	W	1-0	*Dallas (90+2)*

Appearances 2016/17

Coach: Michael O'Neill	**05/07/69**		**CZE**	**SMR**	**GER**	**AZE**	**Cro**	**NOR**	**Nzl**	**AZE**	**Caps**	**Goals**
Michael McGovern	12/07/84	Norwich (ENG	G	G	G	G		G	G84	G	22	-
Conor McLaughlin	26/07/91	Fleetwood (ENG)	D	D77		D	s46	D	M	D	26	1
Gareth McAuley	05/12/79	West Brom (ENG)	D	D	D	D	D46	D		D25	72	9
Jonny Evans	03/01/88	West Brom (ENG)	D	D	D	D	D	D	D	D	61	1
Shane Ferguson	12/07/91	Millwall (ENG)	D66	D	D	M73			s46		31	1
Jamie Ward	12/05/86	Burton (ENG) /Nottingham Forest (ENG)	M74	M	M61			M80			30	4
Paddy McNair	27/04/95	Sunderland (ENG)	M	s77	s73	s81	M				16	-
Oliver Norwood	12/04/91	Brighton (ENG)	M	M	M73	M	M	M	M	M	46	-
Steven Davis	01/01/85	Southampton (ENG)	M	M	M	M	s46	M	s46	M	95	9
Stuart Dallas	19/04/91	Leeds (ENG)	M	M65				D88	M74	D	22	2
Kyle Lafferty	16/09/87	Norwich (ENG)	A59	s72	s76	A61	s56	s85	s46	s77	62	20
Josh Magennis	15/08/90	Charlton (ENG)	s59	A72	A76	M	M56		A83	A	29	1
Lee Hodson	02/10/91	Rangers (SCO)	s66		D		D			s86	20	-
Niall McGinn	20/07/87	Aberdeen (SCO)	s74	M	s61	s73	M62	s80		s25 /86	52	3
Conor Washington	18/05/92	QPR (ENG)		s65				A85			10	3
Aaron Hughes	08/11/79	Kerala Blasters (IND) /Hearts (SCO)			D				D	D	106	1
Corry Evans	30/07/90	Blackburn (ENG)			M	M81					39	1
Chris Brunt	14/12/84	West Brom (ENG)				D	D46	M	M46	M	59	2
Will Grigg	03/07/91	Wigan (ENG)				s61	s68				10	1
Alan Mannus	19/05/82	St Johnstone (SCO)					G				9	-
Matty Lund	21/11/90	Rochdale (ENG)					M46	s88	M46		3	-
Liam Boyce	08/04/91	Ross County (SCO)					A68		A46	A77	10	1
Ryan McGivern	08/01/90	Shrewsbury (ENG)					s46				24	-
Paul Paton	18/04/87	St Johnstone (SCO)					s62		s74		4	-
Craig Cathcart	06/02/89	Watford (ENG)						D			33	2
Tom Flanagan	21/10/91	Burton (ENG)							D		1	-
Shay McCartan	18/05/94	Accrington (ENG)							s83		1	-
Roy Carroll	30/09/77	Linfield							s84		45	-

EUROPE

Crusaders FC

CHAMPIONS LEAGUE

Second qualifying round - FC København (DEN)

H 0-3

O'Neill, Burns, Beverland, Coates, Caddell (Mitchell 61), McClean, Owens, Snoddy (Gault 74), Clarke (Cushley 53), Heatley, Whyte. Coach: Stephen Baxter (NIR)

A 0-6

O'Neill, Burns, Beverland, Gault (Snoddy 68), Lowry (Owens 60), Mitchell, Carvill, Cushley (Heatley 57), Caddell, Forsythe, McClean. Coach: Stephen Baxter (NIR)

Glenavon FC

EUROPA LEAGUE

First qualifying round - KR Reykjavík (ISL)

A 1-2 *Kelly (14)*

Tuffey, Kelly, Lindsay (Doyle 56), Marshall, Cooper, Bradley, Hall, Patton, Sykes, Moorhouse (Hamilton 71), Martyn (Kilmartin 82). Coach: Gary Hamilton (NIR)

H 0-6

Tuffey, Hamilton (Moorhouse 64), Kelly, Marshall, Cooper, Bradley, Hall (O'Mahony 79), Patton, Sykes, Doyle, Martyn (Kilmartin 71). Coach: Gary Hamilton (NIR)

Linfield FC

EUROPA LEAGUE

First qualifying round - Cork City FC (IRL)

H 0-1

Carroll, Stafford, Haughey, Waterworth, Lowry, Millar (R Clarke 84), Mulgrew (Kee 56), Glendinning, Quinn, Gaynor, Smyth (Burns 72). Coach: David Healy (NIR)

A 1-1 *Stafford (52)*

Carroll, Stafford, Haughey, Waterworth, Lowry, Millar (Burns 78), M Clarke (McLellan 88), Mulgrew, Quinn, Gaynor, Smyth. Coach: David Healy (NIR)

Cliftonville FC

EUROPA LEAGUE

First qualifying round - FC Differdange 03 (LUX)

A 1-1 *Lavery (89)*

Mooney, Ives, Bonner, McGuinness, Curran (Murray 85), Knowles, M Donnelly (Lavery 67), Hughes (McDaid 56), Catney, Winchester, J Donnelly. Coach: Gerard Lyttle (NIR)

H 2-0 *McDaid (2), J Donnelly (75)*

Mooney, Ives (Lavery 66), Bonner, McGuinness, Curran, McDaid (Hughes 84), M Donnelly, Catney, Winchester (Knowles 73), J Donnelly, Cosgrove. Coach: Gerard Lyttle (NIR)

Second qualifying round - AEK Larnaca FC (CYP)

H 2-3 *McGuinness (18), J Donnelly (50)*

Mooney, Ives, Bonner, McGuinness, Curran, Knowles, McDaid (Hughes 74), M Donnelly (Lavery 82), Winchester (Garrett 88), J Donnelly, Cosgrove. Coach: Gerard Lyttle (NIR)

A 0-2

Mooney, McGovern, Ives, Bonner, Curran (Murray 75), Knowles, McDaid (Ramsey 15), Catney, Winchester (Garrett 55), J Donnelly, Cosgrove. Coach: Gerard Lyttle (NIR)

Red card: Bonner 11

DOMESTIC LEAGUE CLUB-BY-CLUB

Ards FC

1900 • Clandeboye Park, Bangor (1,895) • ardsfc.co.uk

Major honours
Irish League (1) 1958; Irish Cup (4) 1927, 1952, 1969, 1974

Manager: Niall Currie; (12/12/16) Colin Nixon

Date		Opponent		Score	Scorers
2016					
06/08	h	Cliftonville	D	2-2	*Ruddy (p), McKinney*
10/08	a	Dungannon	W	2-1	*Keke, Cherry*
13/08	h	Portadown	W	1-0	*McComb*
20/08	a	Ballymena	W	4-3	*S McMullan, Friars, McKinney, Tommons*
26/08	a	Glenavon	L	0-1	
03/09	h	Crusaders	L	0-1	
10/09	h	Glentoran	W	2-0	*Taylor, Arthurs*
16/09	a	Ballinamallard	L	1-2	*McKinney*
24/09	a	Linfield	L	0-4	
01/10	h	Carrick	W	3-1	*Ruddy (p), Friars, McComb*
08/10	h	Coleraine	L	1-2	*McKinney*
15/10	a	Cliftonville	L	0-2	
22/10	h	Dungannon	D	3-3	*Ruddy (p), McAllister, McComb*
29/10	a	Portadown	W	3-0	*(w/o; original result 1-3 Ruddy (p))*
05/11	h	Ballymena	L	2-4	*McAllister, McMillen*
12/11	h	Glenavon	L	0-1	
19/11	a	Crusaders	L	0-1	
26/11	a	Glentoran	L	0-1	
02/12	h	Ballinamallard	D	3-3	*McMillen, Friars, Ruddy (p)*
10/12	h	Linfield	L	0-2	
17/12	a	Coleraine	D	1-1	*McAllister*
26/12	a	Carrick	D	1-1	*Friars*
31/12	h	Ballymena	W	4-2	*McComb, Cherry, Friars, Liggett*
2017					
03/01	h	Crusaders	L	2-4	*McMillen (p), McComb*
14/01	a	Cliftonville	L	1-2	*Ruddy (p)*
20/01	h	Glentoran	L	1-3	*Bradley*
28/01	a	Coleraine	L	1-3	*Ruddy (p)*
04/02	h	Carrick	L	0-4	
11/02	a	Portadown	W	3-0	*Cherry, Arthurs, Shevlin*
25/02	a	Dungannon	D	3-3	*Keke 2, Liggett*
10/03	h	Ballinamallard	W	2-0	*Ruddy (p), Keke*
18/03	a	Linfield	L	1-5	*Keke*
25/03	h	Glenavon	W	1-0	*Ruddy*
08/04	h	Dungannon	W	4-1	*Ruddy (p), Shevlin 2, Keke*
15/04	a	Carrick	D	2-2	*Keke 2*
18/04	h	Portadown	W	3-2	*McAllister, Shevlin, Keke*
21/04	a	Ballinamallard	W	3-2	*Shevlin, Cherry, Ruddy*
29/04	a	Glentoran	D	1-1	*Cherry*

No	Name	Nat	DoB	Pos	Aps	(s)	Gls
8	Ross Arthurs		13/10/89	M	9	(16)	2
41	Kevin Bradley		29/04/92	D	5	(1)	1
14	Francis Brennan		11/08/91	M	9	(1)	
21	Calum Byers		28/07/97	D	6	(2)	
44	Rory Carson		31/12/90	A	1		
20	Kyle Cherry		13/05/93	M	28	(2)	5
43	Josh Doherty		15/03/96	M	8		
40	Jamie Douglas		04/07/92	A	7	(2)	
25	Emmett Friars		14/09/85	D	32		5
2	Greg Hall		11/09/89	D	29		
18	Aaron Hogg		14/01/88	G	37		
12	Jordan Hughes		27/01/91	A	1	(12)	
19	Guillaume Keke	FRA	13/03/91	A	25	(7)	9
32	Joshua Kelly		08/03/99	M	1	(2)	
9	Gary Liggett		28/09/87	A	3	(14)	2
15	Adam McAleenan		13/07/00	D	1		
11	David McAllister		01/09/94	M	31	(3)	4
1	Liam McAuley		06/10/89	G	1		
17	Carl McComb		14/08/92	A	13	(18)	5
6	David McCullough		24/04/87	M	26	(1)	
10	Joe McKinney		02/01/94	A	21		4
7	Craig McMillen		19/07/87	M	28	(1)	3
27	Gerard McMullan		04/11/95	M		(3)	
4	Stuart McMullan		30/05/89	D	11	(2)	1
26	Jonah Mitchell		23/06/99	A		(2)	
22	Jamie Rea		23/06/97	D	1	(2)	
3	Michael Ruddy		05/08/93	D	31	(2)	11
42	Matthew Shevlin		07/12/98	A	6	(4)	5
5	Johnny Taylor		30/06/88	D	28		1
16	Gareth Tommons		18/05/89	M	19	(8)	1

Ballinamallard United FC

1975 • Ferney Park (2,000) • ballinamallardfc.co.uk

Manager: Gavin Dykes (IRL)

Date		Opponent		Score	Scorers
2016					
06/08	h	Linfield	L	1-2	*McConnell*
10/08	a	Portadown	L	1-2	*McGinty*
13/08	h	Ballymena	L	0-1	
20/08	a	Carrick	D	3-3	*Lecky 2, Mayse*
27/08	h	Cliftonville	L	1-2	*Lecky*
03/09	h	Coleraine	L	0-3	
10/09	a	Glenavon	W	1-0	*Lecky (p)*
16/09	h	Ards	W	2-1	*McKenna, Morris*
24/09	a	Crusaders	L	1-5	*Mayse*
01/10	h	Dungannon	W	2-0	*McKenna, Lecky (p)*
08/10	a	Glentoran	D	1-1	*Lecky*
15/10	a	Linfield	L	0-4	
22/10	h	Portadown	L	1-2	*McGinty*
29/10	a	Ballymena	L	0-4	
04/11	h	Carrick	L	1-3	*Mayse*
12/11	a	Cliftonville	L	0-1	
19/11	a	Coleraine	L	1-3	*McGinty*
02/12	a	Ards	D	3-3	*Lecky 3*
10/12	h	Crusaders	L	0-1	
17/12	h	Glentoran	W	2-1	*Mayse, McIlwaine*
26/12	a	Dungannon	L	2-3	*McCartney, McIlwaine*
30/12	h	Portadown	W	1-0	*Lecky*
2017					
03/01	a	Dungannon	D	2-2	*Lecky (p), Owens*
13/01	a	Carrick	W	2-1	*McIlwaine 2*
17/01	h	Glenavon	D	1-1	*McIlwaine*
21/01	h	Coleraine	L	1-2	*Taheny*
28/01	a	Glentoran	W	1-0	*Mayse*
11/02	h	Cliftonville	W	1-0	*Mayse*
17/02	a	Glenavon	L	0-3	
25/02	h	Ballymena	L	1-2	*McGinty*
10/03	a	Ards	L	0-2	
20/03	a	Crusaders	L	1-3	*McGinty*
25/03	h	Linfield	L	1-2	*Curran*
08/04	h	Glentoran	W	3-0	*Mayse, McLaughlin, McGinty*
14/04	a	Portadown	L	0-1	
18/04	h	Dungannon	L	1-4	*Mullen*
21/04	h	Ards	L	2-3	*Armstrong, McLaughlin*
29/04	h	Carrick	W	4-1	*Mayse 2 (1p), Curran, Morris*

No	Name	Nat	DoB	Pos	Aps	(s)	Gls
9	Gary Armstrong	IRL	29/01/86	A	7	(7)	1
30	Richard Brush	ENG	26/11/84	G	13		
26	Jordan Cadden		11/11/97	M		(1)	
23	Cameron Crawford		05/04/94	G	6		
14	Christopher Crilly		03/03/84	D		(1)	
28	Ryan Curran	IRL	23/02/95	M	8	(2)	2
12	John Currie		10/09/93	M	2	(2)	
25	David Elliott		08/09/95	D	19	(2)	
5	Steve Feeney	IRL	16/05/84	D	13	(3)	
16	Liam Flatley	IRL	21/11/96	A	2	(1)	
24	Callum Frempong		22/06/98	A	6	(7)	
20	Stuart Hutchinson		10/05/91	M	9		
10	Johnny Lafferty		02/01/87	M	27	(3)	
17	Adam Lecky		03/05/91	M	21		11
19	Ryan Mayse		07/12/93	A	31	(5)	9
6	Shane McCabe		21/12/81	M	28		
25	Ben McCann		22/10/83	A	5	(2)	
11	Jason McCartney	IRL	06/09/86	M	31	(3)	1
15	Ryan McConnell	IRL	03/10/95	D	27		1
13	Stefan McCusker		01/12/89	G	2		
7	Shane McGinty	IRL	14/04/94	M	33	(2)	6
1	James McGrath		19/04/88	G	17	(1)	
21	Joshua McIlwaine		13/11/94	A	9	(14)	5
8	James McKenna		20/07/84	M	22	(2)	2
3	Colm McLaughlin	IRL	01/08/93	D	16		2
2	Liam McMenamin		10/04/89	D	18	(2)	
18	Ryan Morris		04/09/97	A	14	(10)	2
16	Warner Mullen		16/09/85	M	1	(7)	1
22	Niall Owens		28/03/00	M	4	(19)	1
4	Ross Taheny	IRL	20/05/97	D	27	(3)	1

Ballymena United FC

1928 • Ballymena Showgrounds (4,390) • ballymenaunitedfc.com

Major honours
Irish Cup (5) 1940, 1958, 1981, 1984, 1989

Manager: David Jeffrey

Date		Opponent		Score	Scorers
2016					
06/08	a	Crusaders	L	0-6	
10/08	h	Glenavon	D	3-3	*Owens 2, Friel*
13/08	a	Ballinamallard	W	1-0	*T Kane (p)*
20/08	h	Ards	L	3-4	*Jenkins, Friel, Loughran*
26/08	a	Carrick	W	4-1	*Jenkins, Friel, McMurray, McCloskey*
03/09	a	Dungannon	D	2-2	*McCloskey, Friel*
10/09	h	Cliftonville	W	3-2	*T Kane 2 (2p), Friel*
17/09	a	Portadown	W	2-0	*Owens, McMurray*
24/09	h	Glentoran	W	4-1	*Jenkins, Faulkner, T Kane 2 (2p)*
01/10	a	Coleraine	D	2-2	*Friel 2*
15/10	h	Crusaders	W	2-1	*T Kane (p), og (Coates)*
22/10	a	Glenavon	L	0-5	
29/10	h	Ballinamallard	W	4-0	*McMurray 2, Gage, Friel*
05/11	a	Ards	W	4-2	*T Kane (p), Friel 3*
08/11	h	Linfield	L	1-4	*T Kane*
12/11	h	Carrick	W	2-0	*Owens, Faulkner*
19/11	h	Dungannon	L	1-4	*Millar*
26/11	a	Cliftonville	L	0-2	
03/12	h	Portadown	W	2-0	*McCaffrey 2*
10/12	a	Glentoran	W	3-2	*McCaffrey, T Kane, McMurray*
17/12	a	Linfield	L	1-2	*T Kane (p)*
26/12	h	Coleraine	W	2-0	*Friel, T Kane*
31/12	a	Ards	L	2-4	*og (Hogg), McMurray*
2017					
03/01	h	Glenavon	L	3-4	*McCaffrey 2, Gage*
14/01	h	Dungannon	W	3-2	*Owens, T Kane (p), Loughran*
21/01	a	Linfield	L	0-2	
28/01	h	Carrick	W	3-1	*Friel 2, McMurray*
11/02	a	Crusaders	L	1-2	*T Kane*
25/02	a	Ballinamallard	W	2-1	*McMurray, McCloskey*
11/03	h	Portadown	W	3-0	*Kerr, Flynn, T Kane (p)*
18/03	h	Glentoran	L	2-4	*Flynn, McCloskey*
21/03	h	Coleraine	D	1-1	*McMurray*
25/03	a	Cliftonville	L	1-2	*McMurray*
08/04	a	Glenavon	L	0-3	
15/04	h	Linfield	L	0-2	
18/04	h	Cliftonville	W	4-1	*Owens, McMurray 2, Friel*
22/04	h	Crusaders	W	3-0	*McCloskey, Friel 2*
29/04	a	Coleraine	D	1-1	*Balmer*

No	Name	Nat	DoB	Pos	Aps	(s)	Gls
28	Tim Allen	AUS	05/04/92	G	6		
91	Kofi Balmer		19/09/00	D	1		1
18	Alan Blayney		09/10/81	G	10		
22	Kevin Braniff		04/03/83	A	5	(2)	
21	Jim Ervin		05/06/85	D	37		
12	Willie Faulkner		18/01/90	A	21	(7)	2
5	Jonny Flynn		18/11/89	D	17	(1)	2
14	Cathair Friel		25/05/93	A	32	(2)	17
6	Denver Gage		03/05/87	D	6		2
1	Ross Glendinning		18/05/93	G	21		
9	Darren Henderson		25/01/86	A	1	(8)	
10	Allan Jenkins	SCO	07/10/81	M	29	(8)	3
37	Jason Johnston		23/07/96	A		(1)	
15	Eoin Kane		10/01/96	M	1	(7)	
2	Tony Kane		29/08/87	D	31	(1)	14
30	Michael Kerr		06/03/98	D	6	(1)	1
34	Caolan Loughran		09/01/95	D	19	(1)	2
20	Neil Lowry		09/08/93	A	3	(7)	
25	Kyle Mackie		28/10/94	M		(2)	
3	Stephen McBride		06/04/83	D	1		
29	Francis McCaffrey		22/04/93	M	12	(4)	5
38	Ben McCauley		02/05/98	G	1	(1)	
11	Conor McCloskey		29/01/92	M	14	(11)	5
39	Adam McCracken		21/11/98	D	8		
26	Joe McKinney		02/01/94	A	9	(2)	
27	Jonathan McMurray		19/09/94	A	30	(3)	12
23	Leroy Millar		01/09/95	M	26	(4)	1
4	Kyle Owens		09/07/92	D	34		6
16	Matthew Shevlin		07/12/98	A		(4)	
28	Michael Smyth		01/07/92	M	1		
8	Gavin Taggart		15/11/84	M	5	(3)	
7	Gary Thompson		26/05/90	A	14	(2)	
17	Daniel Wallace		21/10/94	D	17		

Carrick Rangers FC

1939 • Taylors Avenue (6,000) • carrickrangers.co.uk

Major honours
Irish Cup (1) 1976

Manager: Kieran Harding; (13/10/16) Aaron Callaghan (IRL)

Date		Opponent		Score	Scorers
2016					
06/08	a	Glenavon	L	0-4	
10/08	h	Crusaders	L	1-4	*T Murray*
13/08	a	Glentoran	W	1-0	*Miguel Chines*
20/08	h	Ballinamallard	D	3-3	*McKeown, Miguel Chines, T Murray*
26/08	h	Ballymena	L	1-4	*Hanley*
03/09	a	Portadown	L	0-4	
10/09	a	Coleraine	L	0-2	
17/09	h	Linfield	L	0-2	
24/09	h	Dungannon	L	0-3	
01/10	a	Ards	L	1-3	*M Murray (p)*
08/10	a	Cliftonville	L	0-1	
15/10	h	Glenavon	D	0-0	
22/10	a	Crusaders	L	1-3	*McNicholl*
29/10	h	Glentoran	L	1-2	*McNally*
04/11	a	Ballinamallard	W	3-1	*McNicholl 2, M Murray (p)*
12/11	a	Ballymena	L	0-2	
19/11	h	Portadown	D	1-1	*Salley*
26/11	h	Coleraine	W	2-0	*Kelly 2*
03/12	a	Linfield	L	0-3	
10/12	a	Dungannon	L	1-3	*McCullough*
17/12	h	Cliftonville	L	0-3	
26/12	h	Ards	D	1-1	*Kelly*
31/12	a	Coleraine	L	0-2	
2017					
03/01	a	Cliftonville	D	0-0	
13/01	h	Ballinamallard	L	1-2	*og (Mayse)*
21/01	h	Dungannon	L	0-1	
28/01	a	Ballymena	L	1-3	*McNally*
04/02	a	Ards	W	4-0	*McAllister, Noble, O'Brien, M Murray (p)*
11/02	h	Linfield	L	0-2	
25/02	h	Glenavon	D	0-0	
11/03	a	Crusaders	L	0-3	
18/03	h	Portadown	W	3-2	*og (Hazley), M Murray, T Murray*
24/03	a	Glentoran	L	0-1	
08/04	a	Portadown	L	1-2	*M Murray (p)*
15/04	h	Ards	D	2-2	*M Murray, McNally*
18/04	h	Glentoran	L	1-2	*T Murray*
22/04	a	Dungannon	L	0-4	
29/04	a	Ballinamallard	L	1-4	*Kelly*

No	Name	Nat	DoB	Pos	Aps	(s)	Gls
23	Tyler Briers		30/07/88	G	2		
27	Lee Chapman		19/11/94	D	16	(3)	
15	Mark Clarke		23/08/89	M	10	(1)	
9	Thomas Elder		01/05/88	A	3	(5)	
17	Elliott English		20/02/95	A		(3)	
2	Seanna Foster		29/01/97	D	11	(2)	
31	Sean Green		02/06/99	A		(2)	
14	Nathan Hanley		18/07/90	D	19	(2)	1
5	Daniel Kelly		06/01/93	A	19	(4)	4
24	Daniel Larmour		03/09/98	A	1	(1)	
10	Gary Lavery		04/05/97	A	5	(9)	
40	Eamon McAllister		19/11/87	M	6	(2)	1
7	Brian McCaul		06/08/90	M	6	(2)	
41	Nathan McConnell		31/07/82	A	1	(4)	
11	Steven McCullough		30/08/94	D	36		1
19	Conor McFall	CAN	03/01/93	M	1		
3	Gareth McKeown		14/07/83	D	12		1
6	Paddy McNally		20/08/94	D	31	(1)	3
18	Tiarnan McNicholl		26/05/95	A	16	(4)	3
37	Kyle McVey		07/07/86	D	8	(1)	
9	Miguel Chines	POR	04/09/79	A	3	(3)	2
16	Ryan Morrell		15/06/96	G	1		
13	Chris Morrow		20/09/85	M	15	(13)	
25	Martin Murray		18/08/93	M	21	(3)	6
20	Thomas Murray		23/03/95	M	27	(4)	4
35	Toyeeb Mustapha	NGA	26/08/95	M	2	(3)	
1	Brian Neeson		28/06/89	G	34		
34	Sean Noble	IRL	20/03/96	M	10	(3)	1
29	Declan O'Brien	IRL	16/06/79	A	8	(1)	1
36	Sam O'Connor	IRL	22/12/95	A	4		
3	Stephen Quigley	IRL	13/01/85	D	3	(1)	
12	Francis Rice		09/06/96	A	14	(6)	
19	Adam Salley		07/02/97	A	17	(2)	1
33	Aaron Smyth		25/08/87	D	10	(1)	
23	Simon Steele		06/02/87	G	1		
4	Mark Surgenor		19/12/85	D	26	(1)	
8	Glenn Taggart		02/11/80	M	11	(7)	
26	Tyler Waide		09/09/96	A		(4)	
22	Jonathan Wilson		07/11/96	M	8	(3)	

NORTHERN IRELAND

Cliftonville FC

1879 • Solitude (5,442) • cliftonvillefc.net

Major honours
Irish League (5) 1906 (shared), 1910, 1998, 2013, 2014; Irish Cup (8) 1883, 1888, 1897, 1900, 1901, 1907, 1909, 1979

Manager: Gerard Lyttle; (24/03/17) Tommy Breslin

Date		Opponent			Scorers
2016					
06/08	a	Ards	D	2-2	*Ives, J Donnelly*
10/08	h	Glentoran	W	2-0	*Curran, McDaid*
13/08	a	Glenavon	L	2-3	*J Donnelly 2*
20/08	h	Dungannon	L	1-2	*Bonner*
27/08	a	Ballinamallard	W	2-1	*Murray, og (McConnell)*
10/09	a	Ballymena	L	2-3	*McDaid, Lavery*
17/09	h	Coleraine	W	1-0	*Hughes*
24/09	a	Portadown	W	3-0	*McGuinness, McDaid, Garrett*
01/10	a	Crusaders	L	3-4	*Hughes, J Donnelly, Harkin*
08/10	h	Carrick	W	1-0	*McDaid*
15/10	h	Ards	W	2-0	*Hughes, McGuinness*
18/10	h	Linfield	W	2-1	*Knowles (p), J Donnelly*
22/10	a	Glentoran	L	1-2	*J Donnelly*
29/10	h	Glenavon	W	3-0	*McGuinness, Harkin, McDaid*
05/11	a	Dungannon	D	1-1	*Curran*
12/11	h	Ballinamallard	W	1-0	*McDaid*
19/11	a	Linfield	W	2-1	*Hughes, Lavery*
26/11	h	Ballymena	W	2-0	*Knowles, Winchester*
02/12	a	Coleraine	W	1-0	*Garrett*
10/12	h	Portadown	W	1-0	*og (Breen)*
17/12	a	Carrick	W	3-0	*McDaid, Garrett 2 (1p)*
26/12	h	Crusaders	L	0-4	
30/12	a	Glenavon	D	2-2	*McDaid, Garrett*
2017					
03/01	h	Carrick	D	0-0	
14/01	h	Ards	W	2-1	*McDaid, Ives*
21/01	a	Crusaders	L	0-1	
28/01	h	Portadown	W	3-0	*Winchester, J Donnelly, Curran*
11/02	a	Ballinamallard	L	0-1	
17/02	h	Glentoran	D	1-1	*Hughes*
25/02	h	Coleraine	D	0-0	
13/03	a	Linfield	L	0-2	
19/03	a	Dungannon	D	2-2	*Haire, Hughes*
25/03	h	Ballymena	W	2-1	*J Donnelly 2*
08/04	a	Coleraine	L	0-2	
15/04	h	Crusaders	L	2-3	*Ives 2*
18/04	a	Ballymena	L	1-4	*Garrett*
22/04	h	Glenavon	L	1-3	*M Donnelly*
29/04	h	Linfield	L	1-3	*Hughes*

No	Name	Nat	DoB	Pos	Aps	(s)	Gls
4	Caoimhin Bonner		15/01/93	D	9	(4)	1
12	Peter Burke	IRL	03/03/96	G	24	(1)	
17	Ryan Catney		17/02/87	M	11	(7)	
23	Tomas Cosgrove		11/12/92	D	38		
7	Chris Curran		05/01/91	M	26	(7)	3
25	Aaron Donnelly		27/03/00	A	2		
29	Gary Donnelly		14/11/97	D	1	(2)	
21	Jay Donnelly		10/04/95	A	24	(4)	9
11	Martin Donnelly		28/08/88	M	26	(7)	1
32	Paul Finnegan	IRL	18/06/96	D	9	(1)	
10	Stephen Garrett		13/04/87	A	19	(14)	6
35	Aaron Haire		27/11/90	A	4	(3)	1
16	Ruairi Harkin	IRL	11/10/89	M	13	(1)	2
14	Daniel Hughes		03/05/92	A	24	(2)	7
3	Levi Ives		28/06/97	D	35		4
8	James Knowles		06/04/93	M	18		2
22	Ross Lavery		29/07/96	M	5	(19)	2
9	David McDaid		03/12/90	A	14	(12)	9
2	Jamie McGovern		29/05/89	D	29	(1)	
6	Jason McGuinness	IRL	08/08/82	D	27		3
24	Tiarnan McNicholl		26/05/95	A		(2)	
1	Jason Mooney		26/02/89	G	14		
19	Darren Murray		24/10/91	A	1	(2)	1
34	Kym Nelson		18/07/95	M	11		
5	Chris Ramsey		25/05/90	D	6		
30	Daniel Reynolds		24/03/99	A		(7)	
15	Eamon Seydak		25/02/86	D	2	(1)	
18	Jude Winchester		13/04/93	M	26	(6)	2

Coleraine FC

1927 • The Showgrounds (3,960) • colerainefc.com

Major honours
Irish League (1) 1974; Irish Cup (5) 1965, 1972, 1975, 1977, 2003

Manager: Oran Kearney

Date		Opponent			Scorers
2016					
06/08	h	Portadown	W	3-0	*(w/o)*
10/08	a	Linfield	D	1-1	*McLaughlin*
13/08	a	Dungannon	L	0-4	
20/08	h	Crusaders	D	1-1	*Ogilby*
26/08	h	Glentoran	W	4-1	*McCafferty (p), McCauley, McLaughlin 2*
03/09	a	Ballinamallard	W	3-0	*Parkhill, McGonigle 2*
10/09	h	Carrick	W	2-0	*McLaughlin, McCauley*
17/09	a	Cliftonville	L	0-1	
24/09	h	Glenavon	D	2-2	*McGonigle, Allan*
01/10	h	Ballymena	D	2-2	*Allan 2*
08/10	a	Ards	W	2-1	*McCauley, McGonigle*
15/10	a	Portadown	W	1-0	*Lyons*
22/10	h	Linfield	D	1-1	*McLaughlin*
28/10	h	Dungannon	D	2-2	*McCafferty (p), Lyons*
05/11	a	Crusaders	L	0-1	
12/11	a	Glentoran	W	1-0	*McGonigle*
19/11	h	Ballinamallard	W	3-1	*Allan, McLaughlin, McCafferty (p)*
26/11	a	Carrick	L	0-2	
02/12	h	Cliftonville	L	0-1	
10/12	a	Glenavon	L	0-1	
17/12	h	Ards	D	1-1	*Lyons*
26/12	a	Ballymena	L	0-2	
31/12	h	Carrick	W	2-0	*McGonigle 2*
2017					
03/01	a	Linfield	W	1-0	*Allan*
14/01	h	Portadown	W	4-2	*Lyons 2, McCafferty, McCauley*
21/01	a	Ballinamallard	W	2-1	*McGonigle 2*
28/01	h	Ards	W	3-1	*Parkhill, McGonigle, McLaughlin*
11/02	h	Dungannon	W	2-1	*McCauley (p), McLaughlin*
25/02	a	Cliftonville	D	0-0	
11/03	h	Glentoran	W	2-0	*Bradley (p), McGonigle*
18/03	a	Glenavon	W	2-1	*McGonigle 2*
21/03	a	Ballymena	D	1-1	*Bradley*
25/03	h	Crusaders	W	1-0	*Bradley (p)*
08/04	h	Cliftonville	W	2-0	*McCauley 2*
15/04	h	Glenavon	D	1-1	*McCauley*
18/04	a	Crusaders	L	2-3	*McLaughlin, McGonigle*
22/04	h	Linfield	L	1-5	*McLaughlin*
29/04	h	Ballymena	D	1-1	*McGonigle*

No	Name	Nat	DoB	Pos	Aps	(s)	Gls
23	Jordan Allan	SCO	07/02/95	M	14	(16)	5
22	Eoin Bradley		30/12/83	A	10		3
11	Rodney Brown		13/08/95	M	19		
20	Michael Doherty		19/10/83	G	1		
5	Stephen Douglas		27/09/77	D	27	(2)	
17	Mark Edgar		17/02/97	D	5		
4	Ciaron Harkin		15/01/96	M	12		
4	Ruaidhri Higgins		23/10/84	M	1	(5)	
1	Chris Johns		13/05/95	G	36		
2	Lyndon Kane		15/02/97	D	28		
12	David Kee		09/08/88	M	26	(1)	
4	Luke Kennedy		20/03/99	D	1		
15	Glenn Law		25/03/87	M		(1)	
14	Bradley Lyons		26/05/97	M	24		5
8	Neil McCafferty	IRL	19/07/84	M	20	(7)	4
15	Saul McCaughan		03/02/95	A		(2)	
7	Darren McCauley		21/02/91	M	35	(1)	8
13	Gareth McConaghie		05/05/88	D	23	(1)	
19	Jamie McGonigle		05/03/96	A	27	(7)	15
9	James McLaughlin		06/03/80	A	14	(13)	10
18	Sammy Morrow		03/03/85	A		(2)	
3	Adam Mullan		24/10/95	D	25	(3)	
6	David Ogilby		02/06/84	D	22	(5)	1
16	Ian Parkhill		07/04/90	M	31	(3)	2
10	Gary Twigg	SCO	19/03/84	A	4	(2)	
2	Calum Whiteside		16/07/88	D	1		
26	Ryan Whiteside		07/04/99	M	1		

Crusaders FC

1898 • Seaview (3,330) • crusadersfc.com

Major honours
Irish League (6) 1973, 1976, 1995, 1997, 2015, 2016; Irish Cup (3) 1967, 1968, 2009

Manager: Stephen Baxter

Date		Opponent			Scorers
2016					
06/08	h	Ballymena	W	6-0	*Heatley 2, Owens 3 (1p), Whyte*
10/08	a	Carrick	W	4-1	*og (McCullough), Cushley, Heatley, Lowry*
13/08	h	Linfield	D	0-0	
20/08	a	Coleraine	D	1-1	*og (Douglas)*
27/08	h	Portadown	W	2-1	*Beverland, Coates*
03/09	a	Ards	W	1-0	*Owens*
10/09	h	Dungannon	W	3-1	*Whyte (p), Heatley 2*
17/09	a	Glentoran	W	3-1	*Coates, Owens, Caddell*
24/09	h	Ballinamallard	W	5-1	*Heatley, Owens, McClean, Whyte 2*
01/10	h	Cliftonville	W	4-3	*Owens 2, Cushley 2*
15/10	a	Ballymena	L	1-2	*og (Ervin)*
22/10	h	Carrick	W	3-1	*Heatley 3*
29/10	a	Linfield	D	0-0	
05/11	h	Coleraine	W	1-0	*Owens*
08/11	a	Glenavon	D	3-3	*Heatley 2, Owens*
12/11	a	Portadown	W	1-0	*Whyte (p)*
19/11	h	Ards	W	1-0	*Cushley*
26/11	a	Dungannon	W	1-0	*Cushley*
03/12	h	Glentoran	D	2-2	*Whyte (p), Clarke*
10/12	a	Ballinamallard	W	1-0	*Forsythe*
17/12	h	Glenavon	W	3-1	*Caddell, Whyte, Owens*
26/12	a	Cliftonville	W	4-0	*Owens, Beverland, Whyte, Caddell*
31/12	h	Linfield	L	1-2	*Owens*
2017					
03/01	a	Ards	W	4-2	*Heatley 2, Caddell, og (Friars)*
14/01	a	Glentoran	W	3-0	*Caddell, Whyte, Heatley*
21/01	h	Cliftonville	W	1-0	*Carvill*
28/01	a	Glenavon	W	1-0	*Caddell*
11/02	h	Ballymena	W	2-1	*Whyte, Cushley*
17/02	a	Dungannon	W	2-1	*Heatley, Coates*
25/02	a	Portadown	D	1-1	*Owens*
11/03	h	Carrick	W	3-0	*Lowry, Owens, Burns*
20/03	h	Ballinamallard	W	3-1	*Owens, Heatley 2*
25/03	a	Coleraine	L	0-1	
08/04	a	Linfield	L	0-1	
15/04	a	Cliftonville	W	3-2	*Carvill, Owens 2*
18/04	h	Coleraine	W	3-2	*Owens, Heatley 2*
22/04	a	Ballymena	L	0-3	
29/04	h	Glenavon	W	6-1	*Carvill 2, Heatley 2, Owens, Snoddy*

No	Name	Nat	DoB	Pos	Aps	(s)	Gls
3	Howard Beverland		30/03/90	D	36		2
34	Rodney Brown		13/08/95	M	1	(1)	
2	Billy Joe Burns		28/04/89	D	38		1
12	Declan Caddell		13/04/88	M	28	(4)	6
10	Michael Carvill		03/04/88	M	26	(9)	4
20	Richard Clarke		28/11/85	M	8	(15)	1
6	Colin Coates		26/10/85	D	18		3
11	David Cushley		22/07/89	M	9	(21)	6
16	Michael Dougherty		05/09/79	G	1		
14	Jordan Forsythe		11/02/91	M	33	(3)	1
4	Michael Gault		15/04/83	M	19	(4)	
22	Paul Heatley		30/06/87	M	35		21
15	Ross Holden		27/11/97	A		(1)	
21	Alan Keane	IRL	23/09/84	D	10		
7	Philip Lowry		15/07/89	M	8	(11)	2
9	Márcio Soares	POR	07/04/96	A		(2)	
17	Craig McClean		06/07/85	D	34	(1)	1
8	Andrew Mitchell		06/04/92	D	6	(10)	
1	Sean O'Neill		11/04/88	G	37		
18	Jordan Owens		09/07/89	A	37		20
19	Matthew Snoddy		02/06/93	M		(5)	1
35	Mikel Suárez	ESP	28/09/86	A		(7)	
23	Gavin Whyte		31/01/96	A	34		10

 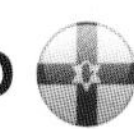

Dungannon Swifts FC

1949 • Stangmore Park (2,154) • dungannonswifts.co.uk

Manager: Rodney McAree

Date		Opponent	Result		Scorers
2016					
06/08	a	Glentoran	L	0-1	
10/08	h	Ards	L	1-2	*Burns*
13/08	h	Coleraine	W	4-0	*Teggart, Harpur 2, Clucas*
20/08	a	Cliftonville	W	2-1	*Mitchell 2*
27/08	a	Linfield	D	1-1	*Lowe*
03/09	h	Ballymena	D	2-2	*Mitchell 2*
10/09	a	Crusaders	L	1-3	*Clucas*
17/09	h	Glenavon	D	1-1	*Armstrong*
24/09	a	Carrick	W	3-0	*Lavery, Mitchell 2*
01/10	a	Ballinamallard	L	0-2	
08/10	h	Portadown	W	6-0	*Wilson, Armstrong, Burke, Fitzpatrick, Hegarty, Mitchell*
15/10	h	Glentoran	L	0-1	
22/10	a	Ards	D	3-3	*Mitchell, Burke 2*
28/10	a	Coleraine	D	2-2	*Mitchell (p), Hegarty*
05/11	h	Cliftonville	D	1-1	*Mitchell*
12/11	h	Linfield	L	0-4	
19/11	a	Ballymena	W	4-1	*Mitchell 2, O'Rourke, og (Owens)*
26/11	h	Crusaders	L	0-1	
02/12	a	Glenavon	W	1-0	*Mitchell*
10/12	h	Carrick	W	3-1	*Teggart, Harpur, Mitchell*
17/12	a	Portadown	L	0-2	
26/12	h	Ballinamallard	W	3-2	*Mitchell 2 (1p), McElroy*
31/12	a	Glentoran	D	2-2	*Mitchell 2*
2017					
03/01	h	Ballinamallard	D	2-2	*Glackin, Wilson*
14/01	a	Ballymena	L	2-3	*Lowe, Mitchell*
21/01	a	Carrick	W	1-0	*og (O'Connor)*
28/01	h	Linfield	L	1-4	*Teggart*
11/02	a	Coleraine	L	1-2	*Harpur (p)*
17/02	h	Crusaders	L	1-2	*Burke*
25/02	h	Ards	D	3-3	*Wilson, Mitchell, Burke*
11/03	a	Glenavon	L	0-2	
18/03	h	Cliftonville	D	2-2	*Mitchell 2*
25/03	a	Portadown	W	1-0	*McMahon*
08/04	a	Ards	L	1-4	*Hegarty*
15/04	h	Glentoran	W	2-1	*Hegarty, Glackin*
18/04	a	Ballinamallard	W	4-1	*Harpur, Mitchell 2, Wilson*
22/04	h	Carrick	W	4-0	*Mitchell, Harpur 2, Brennan*
29/04	h	Portadown	W	2-0	*Fitzpatrick, Hegarty*

No	Name	Nat	DoB	Pos	Aps	(s)	Gls
18	Stuart Addis		05/07/79	G	6	(1)	
5	David Armstrong		23/01/87	D	34	(1)	2
2	Francis Brennan		11/08/91	M	6		1
19	Cormac Burke		11/11/93	M	19	(9)	5
14	Andrew Burns		29/05/92	D	26	(1)	1
27	Rhys Campbell		01/07/99	A		(1)	
16	Seanan Clucas		08/11/92	M	18	(6)	2
1	Andy Coleman		13/06/85	G	32		
22	Caolin Coyle		23/04/00	D	1		
17	Jamie Douglas		04/07/92	A		(3)	
6	Terry Fitzpatrick		23/03/82	D	6	(14)	2
7	Jamie Glackin		16/02/95	M	34	(1)	2
10	Ryan Harpur		01/12/88	M	31	(2)	7
8	Matt Hazley		25/02/87	M	1	(4)	
3	Chris Hegarty		13/08/92	D	29	(2)	5
23	Stefan Lavery		20/07/93	A	4	(17)	1
24	Tommy Lockhart		20/12/93	A	4	(4)	
15	Kris Lowe		06/01/96	M	19	(8)	2
25	Ruairi McDonald		11/03/97	M		(2)	
20	Paul McElroy		07/07/94	A	15	(8)	1
29	Peter McMahon	ENG	20/04/89	M	11	(9)	1
9	Andrew Mitchell		25/01/94	A	34	(1)	25
12	Jarlath O'Rourke		13/02/95	D	34	(1)	1
31	Thomas Roscoe		12/09/99	M		(1)	
11	Alan Teggart		24/11/86	M	22	(9)	3
4	Douglas Wilson		03/03/93	D	32	(1)	4
28	Ronan Young		23/03/98	D		(1)	

Glenavon FC

1889 • Mourneview Park (4,160) • glenavonfc.com

Major honours
Irish League (3) 1952, 1957, 1960; Irish Cup (7) 1957, 1959, 1961, 1992, 1997, 2014, 2016

Manager: Gary Hamilton

Date		Opponent	Result		Scorers
2016					
06/08	h	Carrick	W	4-0	*Marshall 2, Cooper, Patton*
10/08	a	Ballymena	D	3-3	*Bates (p), Moorhouse, Martyn*
13/08	h	Cliftonville	W	3-2	*Cooper, og (Mooney), Moorhouse*
20/08	a	Linfield	L	0-4	
26/08	h	Ards	W	1-0	*og (McAllister)*
10/09	h	Ballinamallard	L	0-1	
13/09	a	Glentoran	D	2-2	*Bradley, Cooper*
17/09	a	Dungannon	D	1-1	*Bradley*
24/09	a	Coleraine	D	2-2	*Bradley, Braniff*
01/10	h	Portadown	W	1-0	*Braniff*
15/10	a	Carrick	D	0-0	
22/10	h	Ballymena	W	5-0	*Bradley 2, Martyn, og (Ervin), Moorhouse*
29/10	a	Cliftonville	L	0-3	
05/11	h	Linfield	D	2-2	*McCourt, Moorhouse*
08/11	h	Crusaders	D	3-3	*Elebert 2, Marshall*
12/11	a	Ards	W	1-0	*Moorhouse*
19/11	h	Glentoran	D	1-1	*Cooper*
02/12	h	Dungannon	L	0-1	
10/12	h	Coleraine	W	1-0	*Marshall*
17/12	a	Crusaders	L	1-3	*Patton*
26/12	a	Portadown	L	0-3	*(w/o; original result 2-2 Martyn, Sykes)*
30/12	h	Cliftonville	D	2-2	*Bates, McGrory*
2017					
03/01	a	Ballymena	W	4-3	*Moorhouse 3, Martyn*
14/01	h	Linfield	L	1-2	*McGrory (p)*
17/01	a	Ballinamallard	D	1-1	*Hamilton*
21/01	a	Portadown	W	2-1	*Gray, Moorhouse*
28/01	h	Crusaders	L	0-1	
11/02	a	Glentoran	D	0-0	
17/02	h	Ballinamallard	W	3-0	*Hall, Sykes, Moorhouse*
25/02	a	Carrick	D	0-0	
11/03	h	Dungannon	W	2-0	*Elebert, Gray*
18/03	h	Coleraine	L	1-2	*Cooper*
25/03	a	Ards	L	0-1	
08/04	h	Ballymena	W	3-0	*Jenkins 2, Moorhouse*
15/04	a	Coleraine	D	1-1	*Singleton*
18/04	a	Linfield	L	0-3	
22/04	a	Cliftonville	W	3-1	*Hall 2, McGrory*
29/04	a	Crusaders	L	1-6	*Norton*

No	Name	Nat	DoB	Pos	Aps	(s)	Gls
28	Guy Bates	ENG	31/10/85	A	16	(6)	2
10	Eoin Bradley		30/12/83	A	15	(1)	5
22	Kevin Braniff		04/03/83	A	5	(5)	2
26	Bobby Burns		07/09/99	D		(1)	
5	Aaron Canning		07/03/92	D	7	(1)	
9	Joel Cooper		29/02/96	M	25	(7)	5
16	Andrew Doyle		28/10/90	D	12	(3)	
25	David Elebert	IRL	21/03/96	D	14		3
34	James Gray		26/06/92	A	9	(5)	2
11	Andy Hall		19/09/89	M	20	(5)	3
2	Gary Hamilton		06/10/80	A		(15)	1
32	Jordan Jenkins		28/02/00	A	4	(2)	2
4	Simon Kelly		04/07/84	D	15	(1)	
7	Andy Kilmartin		08/01/83	M	19	(3)	
6	Kris Lindsay		05/02/84	D	20	(3)	
15	Caolan Marron		04/07/98	D	17	(2)	
8	Rhys Marshall		16/01/95	D	31		4
24	Ciaran Martyn	IRL	25/03/80	M	19	(2)	4
23	Paddy McCourt		16/12/83	M	10	(2)	1
17	Andrew McGrory		15/12/91	M	22	(3)	3
20	Gregory Moorhouse	IRL	10/07/94	A	21	(8)	11
3	Kyle Neill		30/03/78	D	7	(4)	
37	Robbie Norton		16/04/98	A	1	(3)	1
19	Declan O'Brien	IRL	16/06/79	A	2	(4)	
12	Mark Patton		21/06/89	M	14	(8)	2
77	Renato	BRA	07/02/89	A	3	(3)	
27	James Singleton		22/08/95	D	21	(2)	1
14	Mark Sykes		04/08/97	M	27	(4)	2
18	James Taylor		12/05/84	G	2		
1	Jonny Tuffey		20/01/87	G	36		
22	Chris Turner		03/01/87	M	4		
13	Conall Young		19/02/99	D		(1)	

Glentoran FC

1882 • The Oval (9,400) • glentoran.com

Major honours
Irish League (23) 1894, 1897, 1905, 1912, 1913, 1921, 1925, 1931, 1951, 1953, 1964, 1967, 1968, 1970, 1972, 1977, 1981, 1988, 1992, 1999, 2003, 2005, 2009; Irish Cup (22) 1914, 1917, 1921, 1932, 1933, 1935, 1951, 1966, 1973, 1983, 1985, 1986, 1987, 1988, 1990, 1996, 1998, 2000, 2001, 2004, 2013, 2015

Manager: Alan Kernaghan (IRL); (29/09/16) Gary Haveron

Date		Opponent	Result		Scorers
2016					
06/08	h	Dungannon	W	1-0	*Caldwell*
10/08	a	Cliftonville	L	0-2	
13/08	h	Carrick	L	0-1	
20/08	a	Portadown	W	1-0	*K Nelson*
26/08	a	Coleraine	L	1-4	*Smith*
10/09	a	Ards	L	0-2	
13/09	h	Glenavon	D	2-2	*Smith, Gordon*
17/09	h	Crusaders	L	1-3	*Smith*
24/09	a	Ballymena	L	1-4	*Allen*
01/10	h	Linfield	L	1-2	*Addis*
08/10	h	Ballinamallard	D	1-1	*Caldwell*
15/10	a	Dungannon	W	1-0	*Smith (p)*
22/10	h	Cliftonville	W	2-1	*Nacho Novo, Gordon*
29/10	a	Carrick	W	2-1	*Gordon, Allen*
05/11	h	Portadown	D	0-0	
12/11	h	Coleraine	L	0-1	
19/11	a	Glenavon	D	1-1	*Magee*
26/11	h	Ards	W	1-0	*Allen*
03/12	a	Crusaders	D	2-2	*Allen 2*
10/12	h	Ballymena	L	2-3	*og (McCracken), McAlorum*
17/12	a	Ballinamallard	L	1-2	*Magee*
26/12	a	Linfield	D	1-1	*Harmon*
31/12	h	Dungannon	D	2-2	*Allen, Ferrin*
2017					
03/01	a	Portadown	W	5-0	*Allen 2, Nacho Novo, Lavery, Smith*
14/01	h	Crusaders	L	0-3	
20/01	a	Ards	W	3-1	*O'Flynn 2, Allen*
28/01	h	Ballinamallard	L	0-1	
11/02	h	Glenavon	D	0-0	
17/02	a	Cliftonville	D	1-1	*Allen*
25/02	h	Linfield	L	0-1	
11/03	a	Coleraine	L	0-2	
18/03	a	Ballymena	W	4-2	*Allen 3 (1p), Gordon*
24/03	h	Carrick	W	1-0	*Nacho Novo*
08/04	a	Ballinamallard	L	0-3	
15/04	a	Dungannon	L	1-2	*og (Brennan)*
18/04	a	Carrick	W	2-1	*Smith, Allen*
22/04	h	Portadown	W	3-0	*Allen 2, Foley*
29/04	h	Ards	D	1-1	*Foley*

No	Name	Nat	DoB	Pos	Aps	(s)	Gls
19	Jonny Addis		27/09/92	M	34	(2)	1
9	Curtis Allen		22/02/88	A	32	(1)	16
5	Calum Birney		19/04/93	D	19	(1)	
34	Curtis Black		16/05/93	A		(1)	
20	Patrick Cafolla		06/03/98	M		(3)	
8	Ciaran Caldwell		10/10/89	M	20	(4)	2
34	Conall Delaney		08/02/98	A	6		
24	James Ferrin		23/09/89	M	21	(5)	1
14	Eric Foley	IRL	30/01/90	M	25	(1)	2
22	Steven Gordon		27/07/93	D	15	(7)	4
12	Karl Hamill		06/08/98	D	1	(1)	
15	Aaron Harmon		05/11/89	A	27	(3)	1
32	Salou Jallow		03/07/98	A	3		
3	Marcus Kane		08/12/91	D	15	(3)	
11	Chris Lavery		20/01/91	M	29	(2)	1
29	Alexandru Leu	MDA	04/05/91	D	2	(1)	
6	Jay Magee		04/05/88	D	29	(1)	2
16	Stephen McAlorum		11/06/86	M	12	(3)	1
17	Tiarnan McAuley		18/03/88	M	11	(2)	
1	Elliott Morris		04/05/81	G	35		
10	Nacho Novo	ESP	26/03/79	A	9	(14)	3
18	Dwayne Nelson		05/09/84	G	3		
34	Kym Nelson		18/07/95	M	5	(5)	1
27	Stephen O'Flynn	IRL	27/04/82	A	6	(8)	2
35	Paul O'Neill		07/01/00	A		(1)	
23	Ross Redman		23/11/89	D	35	(1)	
25	Jonathan Smith		12/07/97	A	17	(17)	6
4	Aaron Smyth		25/08/87	D	4		
4	Tre Sterling		16/02/99	A	2	(2)	
31	Ethan Warnock		15/02/01	D	1		

NORTHERN IRELAND

Linfield FC

1886 • Windsor Park (18,600) • linfieldfc.com

Major honours
Irish League (52) 1891, 1892, 1893, 1895, 1898, 1902, 1904, 1907, 1908, 1909, 1911, 1914, 1922, 1923, 1930, 1932, 1934, 1935, 1949, 1950, 1954, 1955, 1956, 1959, 1961, 1962, 1966, 1969, 1971, 1975, 1978, 1979, 1980, 1982, 1983, 1984, 1985, 1986, 1987, 1989, 1993, 1994, 2000, 2001, 2004, 2006, 2007, 2008, 2010, 2011, 2012, 2017; Irish Cup (43) 1891, 1892, 1893, 1895, 1898, 1899, 1902, 1904, 1912, 1913, 1915, 1916, 1919, 1922, 1923, 1930, 1931, 1934, 1936, 1939, 1942, 1945, 1946, 1948, 1950, 1953, 1960, 1962, 1963, 1970, 1978, 1980, 1982, 1994, 1995, 2002, 2006, 2007, 2008, 2010, 2011, 2012, 2017

Manager: David Healy

Date		Opponent		Score	Scorers
2016					
06/08	a	Ballinamallard	W	2-1	*Lowry, Millar*
10/08	h	Coleraine	D	1-1	*Burns*
13/08	a	Crusaders	D	0-0	
20/08	h	Glenavon	W	4-0	*Carson, Burns 2, Ward*
27/08	h	Dungannon	D	1-1	*Haughey*
10/09	h	Portadown	W	4-1	*Gaynor, Stafford, Smyth, Burns*
17/09	a	Carrick	W	2-0	*Gaynor, Burns*
24/09	h	Ards	W	4-0	*Burns, Lowry, Millar, og (Friars)*
01/10	a	Glentoran	W	2-1	*og (Kane), Callacher*
15/10	h	Ballinamallard	W	4-0	*Waterworth, Clingan, Haughey, Smyth*
18/10	a	Cliftonville	L	1-2	*Smyth*
22/10	a	Coleraine	D	1-1	*Waterworth*
29/10	h	Crusaders	D	0-0	
05/11	a	Glenavon	D	2-2	*Waterworth, Smyth*
08/11	a	Ballymena	W	4-1	*Waterworth, Lowry, Haughey, Mulgrew*
12/11	a	Dungannon	W	4-0	*Callacher, Mulgrew, Quinn, Gaynor*
19/11	h	Cliftonville	L	1-2	*Waterworth*
26/11	a	Portadown	W	5-0	*Lowry, Smyth, Millar, Stafford, Mulgrew*
03/12	h	Carrick	W	3-0	*Waterworth 2, Stafford*
10/12	a	Ards	W	2-0	*Callacher 2*
17/12	h	Ballymena	W	2-1	*Callacher, Stafford*
26/12	h	Glentoran	D	1-1	*Haughey*
31/12	a	Crusaders	W	2-1	*Burns, Waterworth*
2017					
03/01	h	Coleraine	L	0-1	
14/01	a	Glenavon	W	2-1	*Burns, Waterworth*
21/01	h	Ballymena	W	2-0	*Stafford, Waterworth*
28/01	a	Dungannon	W	4-1	*Haughey, Waterworth, Stewart, Callacher*
11/02	a	Carrick	W	2-0	*Lowry (p), Smyth*
17/02	h	Portadown	D	1-1	*Carson*
25/02	a	Glentoran	W	1-0	*Waterworth*
13/03	h	Cliftonville	W	2-0	*Lowry (p), Waterworth*
18/03	h	Ards	W	5-1	*Stewart, Millar, Waterworth, Lowry, Burns*
25/03	a	Ballinamallard	W	2-1	*Burns, Lowry*
08/04	h	Crusaders	W	1-0	*Burns*
15/04	a	Ballymena	W	2-0	*Callacher, Waterworth*
18/04	h	Glenavon	W	3-0	*Burns, Haughey, Smyth*
22/04	a	Coleraine	W	5-1	*Burns 2, Smyth, Waterworth 2*
29/04	a	Cliftonville	W	3-1	*Waterworth 3 (1p)*

No	Name	Nat	DoB	Pos	Aps	(s)	Gls
21	Kevin Amuneke	NGA	10/05/86	A		(2)	
9	Kris Bright	NZL	05/09/86	A		(6)	
14	Aaron Burns		29/05/92	M	16	(15)	14
6	Jimmy Callacher		11/06/91	D	38		7
1	Roy Carroll		30/09/77	G	35		
24	Josh Carson		03/06/93	M	3	(10)	2
18	Chris Casement		12/01/88	D	20	(7)	
16	Matthew Clarke		03/03/94	D	25	(1)	
32	Ross Clarke		17/05/93	M	3	(4)	
4	Sammy Clingan		13/01/84	M	11		1
35	Gareth Deane		14/06/94	G	2		
20	Stephen Fallon		03/03/97	M	3	(4)	
27	Jonathan Frazer		30/05/96	A	2	(2)	
34	Ross Gaynor	IRL	09/09/87	M	16	(8)	3
23	Reece Glendinning		09/06/95	D	1		
5	Mark Haughey		23/01/91	D	32		6
8	Stephen Lowry		14/10/86	M	28	(1)	8
10	Michael McLellan		22/01/93	A		(1)	
12	Kirk Millar		07/07/92	M	20	(14)	4
40	Alex Moore		27/08/98	G	1		
22	Jamie Mulgrew		05/06/86	M	29		3
31	Niall Quinn		02/08/93	D	28	(1)	1
35	Paul Smyth		10/09/97	M	22	(7)	8
2	Mark Stafford		20/08/87	D	25	(2)	5
3	Cameron Stewart		11/03/97	A	5	(6)	2
19	Ryan Strain		12/02/00	A		(1)	
15	Sean Ward		12/01/84	D	17	(7)	1
7	Andrew Waterworth		11/04/86	A	36	(2)	20

Portadown FC

1924 • Shamrock Park (15,800) • portadownfc.co.uk

Major honours
Irish League (4) 1990, 1991, 1996, 2002; Irish Cup (3) 1991, 1999, 2005

Manager: Pat McGibbon; (20/10/16) (Vinny Arkins (IRL)); (05/12/16) Niall Currie

Date		Opponent		Score	Scorers
2016					
06/08	a	Coleraine	L	0-3	*(w/o)*
10/08	h	Ballinamallard	W	2-1	*Breen, McAllister*
13/08	a	Ards	L	0-1	
20/08	h	Glentoran	L	0-1	
27/08	a	Crusaders	L	1-2	*og (Beverland)*
03/09	h	Carrick	W	4-0	*S Hughes, Byrne, Haire, Garrett*
10/09	a	Linfield	L	1-4	*Garrett*
17/09	h	Ballymena	L	0-2	
24/09	h	Cliftonville	L	0-3	
01/10	a	Glenavon	L	0-1	
08/10	a	Dungannon	L	0-6	
15/10	h	Coleraine	L	0-1	
22/10	a	Ballinamallard	W	2-1	*Henderson (p), S Hughes*
29/10	h	Ards	L	0-3	*(w/o; original result 3-1 Garrett, S Hughes, Shannon (p))*
05/11	a	Glentoran	D	0-0	
12/11	h	Crusaders	L	0-1	
19/11	a	Carrick	D	1-1	*Kirwan*
26/11	h	Linfield	L	0-5	
03/12	a	Ballymena	L	0-2	
10/12	a	Cliftonville	L	0-1	
17/12	h	Dungannon	W	2-0	*McAllister, S Hughes*
26/12	h	Glenavon	W	3-0	*(w/o; original result 2-2 Carson, Haire)*
30/12	a	Ballinamallard	L	0-1	
2017					
03/01	h	Glentoran	L	0-5	
14/01	a	Coleraine	L	2-4	*Foley, Byrne*
21/01	h	Glenavon	L	1-2	*Henderson (p)*
28/01	a	Cliftonville	L	0-3	
11/02	h	Ards	L	0-3	
17/02	a	Linfield	D	1-1	*Foley*
25/02	h	Crusaders	D	1-1	*Márcio Soares*
11/03	a	Ballymena	L	0-3	
18/03	a	Carrick	L	2-3	*Márcio Soares 2*
25/03	h	Dungannon	L	0-1	
08/04	h	Carrick	W	2-1	*Henderson (p), L Wilson*
15/04	h	Ballinamallard	W	1-0	*Larkin*
18/04	a	Ards	L	2-3	*Breen, C Ferris (p)*
22/04	a	Glentoran	L	0-3	
29/04	a	Dungannon	L	0-2	

No	Name	Nat	DoB	Pos	Aps	(s)	Gls
6	Gary Breen	IRL	17/03/89	D	23	(1)	2
33	Adam Brown		16/01/98	D	1	(2)	
26	Alan Byrne	IRL	21/07/83	D	18	(1)	2
21	Mark Carson		09/11/92	M	22	(2)	1
37	Shane Dolan	IRL	06/02/88	M		(1)	
1	Jack Duffin		02/03/92	G	5	(1)	
16	Callum Ferris		05/07/01	A	1	(7)	1
22	Nathaniel Ferris		03/12/98	A	2	(10)	
19	Adam Foley	IRL	11/12/89	M	8	(1)	2
30	Jamie Gardiner		02/05/88	A	1	(4)	
20	Robert Garrett		05/05/88	M	35		3
35	Aaron Haire		27/11/90	A	18	(4)	2
8	Matthew Hazley		30/12/87	M	11		
7	Niall Henderson		07/02/88	M	29		3
17	Jackson Holmes		31/08/99	A	1	(5)	
31	Liam Hughes		19/08/01	G		(1)	
9	Stephen Hughes		18/11/86	A	25	(2)	4
15	Eoin Kirwan	IRL	09/07/96	M	4	(12)	1
28	Ross Larkin		08/03/99	A	9		1
3	Jordan Lyttle		14/05/96	D	5		
22	Nedas Maciulaitis	LTU	06/08/99	M	1	(3)	
8	Sean Mackle	SCO	10/04/88	M	12	(4)	
16	Márcio Soares	POR	07/04/96	A	9	(5)	3
10	Mark McAllister		26/04/88	A	10	(3)	2
14	Chris McGaughey		13/01/92	G	26		
12	Shea McGerrigan		26/09/88	M	8		
23	Scott Megaw		18/12/99	A	1	(1)	
1	David Miskelly		03/09/79	G	6		
11	Tim Mouncey		27/04/82	M	3	(1)	
25	Tiarnan Mulvenna	IRL	10/12/88	A	3	(3)	
4	Keith O'Hara		03/02/81	D	24		
5	Ken Oman	IRL	29/07/82	D	13		
17	Matthew Parker		24/05/95	D	16	(3)	
24	Jake Richardson		18/08/96	D	1	(1)	
3	Adam Rodgers		30/04/91	D	8		
12	Matthew Rooney		18/02/90	A		(3)	
2	Brendan Shannon		27/09/88	D	34		1
18	Sam Simpson	IRL	16/04/94	M	5	(8)	
35	Luke Wilson		15/02/00	M	5	(1)	1
27	Zac Wilson		21/09/99	A	3	(3)	
30	Mikey Withers		23/05/94	A	1	(4)	

Top goalscorers

25	Andrew Mitchell (Dungannon)
21	Paul Heatley (Crusaders)
20	Jordan Owens (Crusaders) Andrew Waterworth (Linfield)
17	Cathair Friel (Ballymena)
16	Curtis Allen (Glentoran)
15	Jamie McGonigle (Coleraine)
14	Tony Kane (Ballymena) Aaron Burns (Linfield)
12	Jonathan McMurray (Ballymena)

UEFA Europa League qualification play-offs

SEMI-FINAL

(08/05/17)

Ballymena 5-2 Dungannon *(T Kane 3, 40p, McKinney 36, McMurray 72, Owens 82; Lowe 64, Glackin 75)*

Cliftonville 3-5 Glenavon *(Winchester 7, Curran 33, J Donnelly 42; Marshall 3, Moorhouse 40, Singleton 49, Gray 69, McGrory 72p)*

FINAL

(12/05/17)

Ballymena 2-1 Glenavon *(Friel 53, 80; Marshall 67)*

Promoted club

Warrenpoint Town FC

1987 • Milltown (1,280) • warrenpointtownfc.co.uk

Manager: Barry Gray; (12/11/16) Matthew Tipton (WAL)

Second level final table 2016/17

		Pld	W	D	L	F	A	Pts
1	Warrenpoint Town FC	32	22	6	4	78	35	72
2	Institute FC	32	16	9	7	64	39	57
3	Ballyclare Comrades FC	32	15	6	11	64	56	51
4	PSNI FC	32	13	10	9	49	44	49
5	Dergview FC	32	12	6	14	67	55	42
6	Loughgall FC	32	12	3	17	54	59	3
7	Harland & Wolff Welders FC	32	15	6	11	52	41	51
8	Knockbreda FC	32	14	4	14	56	52	46
9	Larne FC	32	11	7	14	52	51	40
10	Lurgan Celtic FC	32	12	3	17	56	71	39
11	Armagh City FC	32	9	7	16	41	55	34
12	Annagh United FC	32	4	7	21	32	107	19

NB League splits into top and bottom halves after 22 games, after which the clubs play exclusively against teams in their group.

Promotion/Relegation play-offs

(02/05/17 & 05/05/17)
Ballyclare 1-0 Institute
Institute 3-1 Ballyclare
(Institute 3-2)

(09/05/17 & 12/05/17)
Institute 1-1 Carrick
Carrick 4-1 Institute
(Carrick 5-2)

DOMESTIC CUP

Irish Cup 2016/17

FIFTH ROUND

(07/01/17)
Annagh United 0-2 Tobermore United
Armagh 2-1 Trojans
Ballyclare 2-4 Institute
Ballymena 1-1 Cliftonville *(aet; 4-3 on pens)*
Coleraine 5-1 Carrick
Crusaders 2-0 Ards
Dungannon 3-0 Dergview
Glenavon 4-1 Portstewart
Glentoran 1-2 Linfield *(aet)*
Harland & Wolff Welders 1-0 Lurgan Celtic
Knockbreda 1-2 Crewe United
Larne 1-2 Portadown
Loughgall 3-0 Fivemiletown United
PSNI 2-1 Lisburn Distillery
Richhill 1-4 Dollingstown
Warrenpoint 0-0 Ballinamallard *(aet; 5-4 on pens)*

SIXTH ROUND

(04/02/17)
Armagh 0-2 Glenavon
Coleraine 1-0 Tobermore
Crusaders 2-0 PSNI
Dungannon 4-1 Dollinsgtown
Harland & Wolff Welders 1-3 Ballymena *(aet)*
Institute 0-2 Linfield
Loughgall 1-2 Portadown
Warrenpoint 5-0 Crewe United

QUARTER-FINALS

(04/03/17)
Ballymena 0-4 Coleraine *(McGonigle 12, 71, Bradley 45+1, 54)*

Crusaders 0-2 Linfield *(Lowry 74p, Quinn 90)*

Dungannon 2-1 Warrenpoint *(Dane 72og, Wilson 93; Traynor 53) (aet)*

Portadown 0-5 Glenavon *(Martyn 42, Cooper 59, 67, Singleton 78, Sykes 81)*

SEMI-FINALS

(01/04/17)
Coleraine 2-1 Glenavon *(Lyons 48, McLaughlin 89; Singleton 69)*

Linfield 1-0 Dungannon *(Lowry 89)*

FINAL

(06/05/17)
Windsor Park, Belfast
LINFIELD FC 3 *(Waterworth 29, 33, 87)*
COLERAINE FC 0
Referee: *Kennedy*
LINFIELD: *Carroll, Haughey, Callacher, Stafford, R Clarke, Smyth (Casement 89), Lowry, Mulgrew, Quinn, Burns (Stewart 82), Waterworth*
COLERAINE: *Johns, Kane, Ogilby, McConaghie, Mullan, Lyons, McCauley, McLaughlin (Parkhill 57), McGonigle (Allan 82), Harkin, Bradley*

Linfield completed the double with a comprehensive Irish Cup final win against Coleraine

NORWAY

Norges Fotballforbund (NFF)

Address	Serviceboks 1 Ullevaal stadion NO-0840 Oslo
Tel	+47 210 29300
Fax	+47 210 29301
E-mail	nff@fotball.no
Website	fotball.no

President	Terje Svendsen
General secretary	Pål Bjerketvedt
Media officer	Yngve Haavik
Year of formation	1902
National stadium	Ullevaal, Oslo (27,182)

TIPPELIGAEN CLUBS

 1 **Aalesunds FK**

 2 **FK Bodø/Glimt**

3 **SK Brann**

4 **FK Haugesund**

5 **Lillestrøm SK**

 6 **Molde FK**

 7 **Odds BK**

 8 **Rosenborg BK**

 9 **Sarpsborg 08 FF**

 10 **Sogndal Fotball**

 11 **Stabæk Fotball**

 12 **IK Start**

 13 **Strømsgodset IF**

 14 **Tromsø IL**

 15 **Viking FK**

 16 **Vålerenga Fotball**

PROMOTED CLUBS

17 **Kristiansund BK**

 18 **Sandefjord Fotball**

Tromsø 14

2 Bodø

KEY

- UEFA Champions League
- UEFA Europa League
- Promoted
- Relegated

Repeat double for rampant Rosenborg

Back to their omnipotent best in 2015, Rosenborg staged an encore in 2016, dominating the Norwegian domestic scene again on both fronts to retain the Tippeligaen title and the Norwegian Cup – both with relative ease.

Coach Kåre Ingebrigtsen thus made it two doubles in as many full seasons in charge of the Trondheim club where he won eight league titles as a player. There was satisfaction also down the coast in Bergen, where Lars Arne Nilsen's Brann finished runners-up in their first season back among the elite after promotion.

League and cup successfully defended by Trondheim club

Tippeligaen title won with 26-game unbeaten run

National team appoint Swedish coach Lagerbäck

Domestic league

Rosenborg lost their opening game of the season, 1-0 at Odds BK, but there would be no more league defeats for the defending champions until 225 days later, when Odd again got the better of them, winning 2-1, this time at the Lerkendal stadium, where Rosenborg had never lost a league game under Ingebrigtsen and claimed three points in every one of their previous encounters in 2016.

By then, however, the club's 24th national title was already secure, that stunning 26-match unbeaten run having catapulted the defending champions into a big lead that had become unassailable a month earlier when they won 3-1 at local rivals Molde. By the end of term Rosenborg had precisely the same number of points (69), wins (21), draws (6) and defeats (3) as they had registered in 2015. Their goal output was down, but against that they conceded slighty fewer and had a greater margin of victory, their 15-point advantage comparing favourably with the 12-point gap of a year earlier.

Many key players from the 2015 campaign remained, with Danish schemer Mike Jensen, right-back Jonas Svensson, goalkeeper André Hansen and midfielder Fredrik Midtsjø foremost among those making decisive contributions to another runaway triumph. The most impressive newcomer was Danish striker Christian Gytkjær, who, after three consistent seasons with Haugesund, raised the bar for Rosenborg, scoring 19 goals to carry off the Tippeligaen golden boot, the award won the previous season by the man he replaced, Alexander Søderlund.

No Brann player scored more than six goals, but thanks to Nilsen's excellent tutelage, a strong team spirit and an enthusiastic home support (their average gate of 12,380 was second only in the league to Rosenborg's 17,585), the team that had finished runners-up in Norway's second tier in 2015 claimed the same position in the top flight 12 months later. Second place had been filled for most of the campaign by Odd, who claimed UEFA Europa League qualification for the third season running, with fourth-placed Haugesund joining them after a string of results went their way on the final day – and a fortnight later in the Ullevaal.

Domestic cup

Rosenborg completed their double with the biggest win in the Norwegian Cup final for 26 years – a 4-0 trouncing of second-tier Kongsvinger, who would also lose their promotion play-off a week later. The traditional full house in the national stadium (26,912) witnessed a splendid hat-trick from Norwegian international Pål André Helland as Rosenborg cantered to an 11th victory in a competition they were on the verge of exiting in the quarter-final against Tromsø until a late Gytkjær equaliser.

Europe

It was a quiet season in Europe for Norwegian clubs, with only 14 matches played by the four Tippeligaen representatives – a third as many as in 2015/16, when both Molde and Rosenborg were involved until December. This time interest ended in August, when Rosenborg, who had begun the summer with a thrilling victory over Swedish champions Norrköping, bowed out in the UEFA Europa League play-offs to Austria Wien.

National team

A forgettable season for Norwegian teams abroad was compounded by an underwhelming effort from the national side in their FIFA World Cup qualifying section, which yielded just four points from six games, three of them from a nervous home win over San Marino. Per-Mathias Høgmo stood down in November after losing nine of his last 13 matches, and although Scandinavian national team specialist Lars Lagerbäck was recruited to replace him, there was no immediate improvement from a side short of quality and experience, with not one player in the squad having earned 50 caps or scored ten international goals.

DOMESTIC SEASON AT A GLANCE

Tippeligaen 2016 final table

			Home					Away					Total					
		Pld	W	D	L	F	A	W	D	L	F	A	W	D	L	F	A	Pts
1	**Rosenborg BK**	**30**	**14**	**0**	**1**	**42**	**11**	**7**	**6**	**2**	**23**	**14**	**21**	**6**	**3**	**65**	**25**	**69**
2	SK Brann	30	11	3	1	24	6	5	3	7	18	21	16	6	8	42	27	54
3	Odds BK	30	8	3	4	24	16	7	3	5	20	19	15	6	9	44	35	51
4	FK Haugesund	30	8	6	1	31	18	4	4	7	16	25	12	10	8	47	43	46
5	Molde FK	30	8	4	3	29	16	5	2	8	19	26	13	6	11	48	42	45
6	Sarpsborg 08 FF	30	7	5	3	18	10	5	4	6	17	27	12	9	9	35	37	45
7	Strømsgodset IF	30	9	5	1	30	15	3	3	9	14	25	12	8	10	44	40	44
8	Viking FK	30	5	4	6	16	17	7	3	5	17	18	12	7	11	33	35	43
9	Aalesunds FK	30	6	5	4	27	21	6	1	8	19	30	12	6	12	46	51	42
10	Vålerenga Fotball	30	5	5	5	20	14	5	3	7	21	25	10	8	12	41	39	38
11	Sogndal Fotball	30	4	7	4	20	19	4	5	6	13	18	8	12	10	33	37	36
12	Lillestrøm SK	30	5	4	6	24	22	3	6	6	21	28	8	10	12	45	50	34
13	Tromsø IL	30	6	3	6	20	20	3	4	8	16	26	9	7	14	36	46	34
14	Stabæk Fotball	30	5	1	9	15	18	3	6	6	20	24	8	7	15	35	42	31
15	FK Bodø/Glimt	30	5	3	7	19	22	3	3	9	17	23	8	6	16	36	45	30
16	IK Start	30	2	4	9	15	34	0	6	9	8	25	2	10	18	23	59	16

European qualification 2017/18

Champion/Cup winner: Rosenborg BK (second qualifying round)

SK Brann (second qualifying round)
Odds BK (first qualifying round)
FK Haugesund (first qualifying round)

Top scorer Christian Gytkjær (Rosenborg), 19 goals
Relegated clubs IK Start, FK Bodø/Glimt
Promoted clubs Kristiansund BK, Sandefjord Fotball
Cup final Rosenborg BK 4-0 Kongsvinger IL

Player of the season

Mike Jensen
(Rosenborg BK)

The plaudits continued to rain down on Rosenborg's Danish conductor-in-chief as he masterminded the club's second successive league and cup double, his influence on the team's performances every bit as profound as in 2015. Jensen's assist count was down, but his goal output was up as he found the net eight times in the Tippeligaen – second only at the club to his 19-goal compatriot Christian Gytkjær, with whom he developed an excellent understanding. Most significantly, he scored twice in the 3-1 win at Molde that clinched the league title.

Newcomer of the season

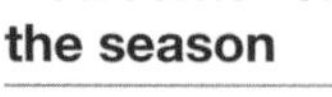

Sander Berge
(Vålerenga Fotball)

A giant defensive midfielder, Berge had started only half a dozen Tippeligaen matches before the 2016 campaign got under way, but as the season progressed he became an increasingly important figure for Vålerenga. Foreign scouts got wind of his talent and in January, still only 18, he signed a four-year deal with Genk, where he replaced Leicester City-bound Wilfred Ndidi and helped his new club into the UEFA Europa League quarter-finals. He also won his first senior cap for Norway, against Northern Ireland, in Lars Lagerbäck's first game in charge.

Team of the season
(4-4-2)

Coach: Nilsen *(Brann)*

NATIONAL TEAM

International tournament appearances
FIFA World Cup (3) 1938, 1994, 1998 (2nd round)
UEFA European Championship (1) 2000

Top five all-time caps
John Arne Riise (110); Thorbjørn Svenssen (104); Henning Berg (100); Erik Thorstvedt (97); John Carew & Brede Hangeland (91)

Top five all-time goals
Jørgen Juve (33); Einar Gundersen (26); Harald Hennum (25); John Carew (24); Tore André Flo & Ole Gunnar Solskjær (23)

Results 2016/17

31/08/16	Belarus	H	Oslo	L	0-1	
04/09/16	Germany (WCQ)	H	Oslo	L	0-3	
08/10/16	Azerbaijan (WCQ)	A	Baku	L	0-1	
11/10/16	San Marino (WCQ)	H	Oslo	W	4-1	*D Simoncini (12og), Diomandé (77), Samuelsen (82), King (83)*
11/11/16	Czech Republic (WCQ)	A	Prague	L	1-2	*King (87)*
26/03/17	Northern Ireland (WCQ)	A	Belfast	L	0-2	
10/06/17	Czech Republic (WCQ)	H	Oslo	D	1-1	*Søderlund (55p)*
13/06/17	Sweden	H	Oslo	D	1-1	*M Elyounoussi (44)*

Appearances 2016/17

Coach: Per-Mathias Høgmo /(01/02/17) Lars Lagerbäck (SWE)	**01/12/59 16/07/48**		**Blr**	**GER**	**AZE**	**SMR**	**CZE**	**NIR**	**CZE**	**Swe**	**Caps**	**Goals**
Ørjan Håskjold Nyland	10/09/90	Ingolstadt (GER)	G							G	24	-
Jonas Svensson	06/03/93	Rosenborg /AZ (NED)	D	D	D	D			D	D	8	-
Even Hovland	14/02/89	Nürnberg (GER)	D	D	D	D	D	D		D	24	-
Stefan Strandberg	25/07/90	Hannover (GER)	D		D	D					10	-
Haitam Aleesami	31/07/91	Palermo (ITA)	D88	D	D	D	D		D	s83	14	-
Veton Berisha	13/04/94	Greuther Fürth (GER)	M62	M							4	1
Magnus Wolff Eikrem	08/08/90	Malmö (SWE)	M68								17	-
Ole Kristian Selnæs	07/07/94	St-Étienne (FRA)	M46	s61	M	M				s46	10	-
Stefan Johansen	08/01/91	Fulham (ENG)	M	M67	s84		M	M75	M		35	3
Jo Inge Berget	11/09/90	Malmö (SWE)	M62		s71	M73	M71		M61		17	2
Joshua King	15/01/92	Bournemouth (ENG)	A46	A72	A61	A	A	A			28	7
Alexander Sørloth	05/12/95	Groningen (NED)	s46	s72	s61	s73					7	1
Alexander Tettey	04/04/86	Norwich (ENG)	s46	M		M67	M				34	3
Adama Diomandé	14/02/90	Hull (ENG)	s62	M	M	s46	s61	s63			11	1
Martin Samuelsen	17/04/97	Blackburn (ENG)	s62			s67					3	1
Martin Linnes	20/09/91	Galatasaray (TUR)	s68								15	-
Jørgen Skjelvik	05/07/91	Rosenborg	s88					D			4	-
Rune Almenning Jarstein	29/09/84	Hertha (GER)		G	G	G	G	G	G		46	-
Håvard Nordtveit	21/06/90	West Ham (ENG)		D				M	D	D46	32	2
Markus Henriksen	25/07/92	Hull (ENG)		M61	A	A46	A61				31	2
Ruben Yttergård Jenssen	04/05/88	Groningen (NED)		s67							39	-
Pål André Helland	04/01/90	Rosenborg			M71						6	1
Per Ciljan Skjelbred	16/06/87	Hertha (GER)			M84	M	M51				43	1
Omar Elabdellaoui	05/12/91	Olympiacos (GRE) /Hull (ENG)					D	D			24	-
Vegard Forren	16/02/88	Molde					D				33	1
Mats Møller Dæhli	02/03/95	Freiburg (GER) /St Pauli (GER)					s51	s53	s61	M83	16	1
Tarik Elyounoussi	23/02/88	Olympiacos (GRE)					s71	M53	A	s56	43	9
Gustav Valsvik	26/05/93	Braunschweig (GER)						D	s33	s46	3	-
Mohamed Elyounoussi	04/08/94	Basel (SUI)						M	M	M	8	1
Alexander Søderlund	03/08/87	St-Étienne (FRA)						A63	A71	A46	29	2
Sander Berge	14/02/98	Genk (BEL)						s75	M	M46	3	-
Tore Reginiussen	10/04/86	Rosenborg							D33		22	2
Bjørn Johnsen	06/11/91	Hearts (SCO)							s71	A56	2	-
Per-Egil Flo	18/01/89	Slavia Praha (CZE)								D	5	-
Anders Trondsen	30/03/95	Sarpsborg								M	2	-
Ohi Omoijuanfo	10/01/94	Stabæk								s46	1	-

EUROPE

Rosenborg BK

Second qualifying round - IFK Norrköping (SWE)
H 3-1 *Eyjólfsson (48), Helland (62), De Lanlay (65)*
Londak, Svensson, Reginiussen, Eyjólfsson, Jensen, Konradsen, Gytkjær (Vilhjálmsson 80), De Lanlay (Gersbach 86), Skjelvik, Midtsjø (Thórarinsson 88), Helland. Coach: Kåre Ingebrigtsen (NOR)
A 2-3 *Gytkjær (36p), De Lanlay (55)*
Londak, Svensson, Reginiussen, Eyjólfsson, Jensen, Konradsen, Gytkjær (Bjørdal 90+5), De Lanlay (Thórarinsson 84), Skjelvik, Midtsjø (Vilhjálmsson 67), Helland. Coach: Kåre Ingebrigtsen (NOR)

Third qualifying round - APOEL FC (CYP)
H 2-1 *Gytkjær (23), Skjelvik (45+1)*
Kwarasey, Svensson, Reginiussen, Eyjólfsson, Jensen, Konradsen, Gytkjær, De Lanlay (Bakenga 75), Skjelvik, Midtsjø (Vilhjálmsson 79), Helland. Coach: Kåre Ingebrigtsen (NOR)
A 0-3
Kwarasey, Svensson, Reginiussen, Eyjólfsson, Jensen (Bjørdal 87), Konradsen, Gytkjær, De Lanlay, Skjelvik, Midtsjø (Vilhjálmsson 76), Helland (Rashani 81). Coach: Kåre Ingebrigtsen (NOR)

Play-offs - FK Austria Wien (AUT)
A 1-2 *Reginiussen (90+1)*
Kwarasey, Svensson, Reginiussen, Eyjólfsson, Jensen, Konradsen, Gytkjær, Skjelvik (Rashani 71), Gersbach, Midtsjø (Vilhjálmsson 77), Helland. Coach: Kåre Ingebrigtsen (NOR)
H 1-2 *Gytkjær (59p)*
Kwarasey, Svensson, Reginiussen, Eyjólfsson, Jensen, Konradsen, Gytkjær, Rashani, Skjelvik (Gersbach 70), Midtsjø, Helland (Vilhjálmsson 24). Coach: Kåre Ingebrigtsen (NOR)

Strømsgodset IF

Second qualifying round - SønderjyskE (DEN)
A 1-2 *Pedersen (16)*
Bugge Pettersen, Hamoud, Madsen, Pedersen, Kastrati (Parr 75), Francisco Júnior, Abu, Adjei-Boateng, Vilsvik, Valsvik, Keita. Coach: Björn Petter Ingebretsen (NOR)
H 2-2 (aet) *Keita (17, 45+2)*
Bugge Pettersen, Hamoud, Madsen, Storflor (Kastrati 66), Pedersen, Francisco Júnior (Vaagan Moen 72), Abu, Adjei-Boateng, Vilsvik, Valsvik, Keita (Parr 96). Coach: Björn Petter Ingebretsen (NOR)

Stabæk Fotball

First qualifying round - Connah's Quay FC (WAL)
A 0-0
Sandhu (Mandé 30), Skjønsberg, Næss, Asante, Grossman, Gorozia, Njie (Mehmeti 65), Moe, Issah, Meling, Omoijuanfo. Coach: Billy McKinlay (SCO)
H 0-1
Mandé, Skjønsberg (Haugstad 72), Næss, Asante, Grossman, Gorozia (Mehmeti 54), Njie, Moe (Eghan 66), Issah, Meling, Omoijuanfo. Coach: Billy McKinlay (SCO)
Red card: Issah 51

Odds BK

First qualifying round - IFK Mariehamn (FIN)
H 2-0 *Grøgaard (63), Occéan (86)*
Rossbach, Ruud, Grøgaard (Jensen 75), Berg (Zekhnini 55), Halvorsen, Johansen (Occéan 55), Nordkvelle, Nilsen, Hagen, Eriksen, Akabueze. Coach: Dag-Eilev Fagermo (NOR)
A 1-1 *Akabueze (78)*
Rossbach, Ruud, Berg, Halvorsen, Johansen, Zekhnini (Akabueze 71), Semb Berge (Bergan 86), Nilsen, Jensen (Occéan 82), Hagen, Eriksen. Coach: Dag-Eilev Fagermo (NOR)

Second qualifying round - PAS Giannina FC (GRE)
A 0-3
Rossbach, Ruud, Grøgaard, Berg (Jensen 46), Halvorsen, Johansen, Nordkvelle (Bergan 86), Nilsen (Haugen 73), Hagen, Eriksen, Akabueze. Coach: Dag-Eilev Fagermo (NOR)
H 3-1 (aet) *Nordkvelle (55p), Akabueze (57), Ruud (89)*
Rossbach, Ruud, Grøgaard, Samuelsen (Berg 63), Johansen, Zekhnini, Nordkvelle (Messoudi 84), Semb Berge, Jensen (Nilsen 101), Hagen, Akabueze. Coach: Dag-Eilev Fagermo (NOR)

DOMESTIC LEAGUE CLUB-BY-CLUB

Aalesunds FK

1914 • Color Line (10,778) • aafk.no

Major honours
Norwegian Cup (2) 2009, 2011

Coach: Trond Fredriksen

2016

11/03	h	Stabæk	W	1-0	*Larsen*
19/03	a	Haugesund	L	0-3	
03/04	h	Brann	L	1-2	*Larsen*
10/04	a	Rosenborg	L	0-1	
17/04	h	Viking	L	1-2	*Boli*
21/04	a	Lillestrøm	D	1-1	*Boli*
24/04	h	Tromsø	W	6-0	*Abdellaoue 3, Boli, Hoff, Thrándarson*
30/04	a	Molde	L	0-1	
08/05	h	Sogndal	L	1-4	*Abdellaoue*
12/05	a	Sarpsborg	L	0-1	
16/05	h	Start	D	1-1	*Skagestad*
22/05	a	Bodø/Glimt	W	1-0	*O Lie*
29/05	h	Vålerenga	D	2-2	*Gyasi 2*
04/07	a	Strømsgodset	L	2-4	*Abdellaoue, Larsen*
10/07	a	Odd	L	1-4	*Gyasi*
16/07	h	Rosenborg	D	1-1	*Skagestad*
22/07	a	Brann	L	0-6	
31/07	h	Lillestrøm	W	2-0	*Kirkeskov, Boli*
05/08	a	Tromsø	W	2-1	*og (Antonsen), Abdellaoue*
14/08	h	Molde	L	0-2	
21/08	a	Stabæk	L	0-3	
26/08	h	Sarpsborg	D	2-2	*Fet, Boli*
09/09	a	Start	W	4-1	*B Riise, Thrándarson, Fet, Boli*
18/09	h	Strømsgodset	W	4-2	*Gyasi, Carlsen, Abdellaoue, B Riise*
25/09	a	Vålerenga	W	1-0	*Abdellaoue*
02/10	h	Odd	W	1-0	*Gyasi*
15/10	h	Bodø/Glimt	W	1-0	*Boli*
21/10	a	Viking	W	3-2	*Abdellaoue 2 (1p), Kirkeskov*
30/10	h	Haugesund	D	3-3	*Abdellaoue 2 (1p), Larsen*
06/11	a	Sogndal	W	4-2	*Abdellaoue, Thrándarson, Gyasi, og (Teniste)*

No	Name	Nat	DoB	Pos	Aps	(s)	Gls
30	Mustafa Abdellaoue		01/08/88	A	22	(7)	13
22	Adam Örn Arnarson	ISL	27/08/95	D	24	(2)	
7	Franck Boli	CIV	07/12/93	A	26	(1)	7
8	Fredrik Carlsen		01/12/89	M	19	(5)	1
24	Lars Cramer		25/05/91	G	2		
40	Sondre Brunstad Fet		17/01/97	M	2	(14)	2
3	Daníel Leo Grétarsson	ISL	02/10/95	D	7	(5)	
14	Edwin Gyasi	NED	01/07/91	M	18	(8)	6
18	Vebjørn Hoff		13/02/96	M	20	(7)	1
19	Flamur Kastrati	KOS	14/11/91	A	2	(1)	
2	Mikkel Kirkeskov	DEN	05/09/91	D	29		2
10	Peter Orry Larsen		25/02/89	M	22	(3)	4
1	Andreas Lie		31/08/87	G	28		
5	Oddbjørn Lie		31/08/87	D	25	(1)	1
15	Marlinho	BRA	24/03/94	M	1	(11)	
20	Thomas Martinussen		05/02/95	M		(1)	
4	Tero Mäntylä	FIN	18/04/91	D		(3)	
21	Bjørn Helge Riise		21/06/83	M	24		2
6	John Arne Riise		24/09/80	M	7	(3)	
23	Edvard Skagestad		06/07/88	D	19	(5)	2
11	Aron Elís Thrándarson	ISL	10/11/94	M	23	(6)	3
6	Vito Wormgoor	NED	16/11/88	D	10	(1)	

FK Bodø/Glimt

1916 • Aspmyra (7,564) • glimt.no

Major honours
Norwegian Cup (2) 1975, 1993

Coach: Aasmund Bjørkan

2016

13/03	h	Sogndal	W	2-0	*Jonassen, Jevtović*
20/03	a	Lillestrøm	D	1-1	*Jevtović*
03/04	h	Stabæk	W	3-1	*Azemi, Jevtović, Bjørnbak*
10/04	a	Brann	L	0-1	
17/04	h	Molde	L	1-2	*Furebotn*
20/04	h	Haugesund	L	3-4	*Olsen, Azemi 2 (1p)*
23/04	a	Strømsgodset	L	0-2	
02/05	h	Sarpsborg	L	0-2	
08/05	a	Odd	L	1-2	*Jevtović*
11/05	h	Vålerenga	D	0-0	
16/05	a	Tromsø	W	2-1	*Jevtović 2*
22/05	h	Aalesund	L	0-1	
29/05	a	Viking	L	0-2	
02/07	h	Rosenborg	D	0-0	
08/07	a	Start	W	4-1	*Olsen, Furebotn, Azemi, Hauge (p)*
17/07	h	Odd	W	2-1	*Olsen, Azemi*
24/07	a	Sogndal	D	2-2	*Olsen 2*
31/07	h	Tromsø	L	0-3	
06/08	a	Molde	L	2-3	*Berg, Olsen*
11/08	h	Lillestrøm	D	1-1	*Azemi*
19/08	a	Vålerenga	D	1-1	*Azemi*
28/08	h	Start	W	2-0	*Azemi, Halvorsen*
11/09	a	Sarpsborg	W	2-1	*Halvorsen, Manzon*
18/09	h	Brann	L	1-3	*Azemi*
26/09	a	Stabæk	L	0-1	
30/09	h	Strømsgodset	W	4-2	*Halvorsen (p), Azemi, Bjørnbak, Mockenhaupt*
15/10	a	Aalesund	L	0-1	
23/10	a	Haugesund	L	1-2	*Halvorsen*
30/10	h	Viking	L	0-2	
06/11	a	Rosenborg	L	1-2	*Azemi*

No	Name	Nat	DoB	Pos	Aps	(s)	Gls
7	Fitim Azemi		25/06/92	A	29		11
10	Ruslan Babenko	UKR	08/07/92	M	14	(5)	
27	Patrick Berg		24/11/97	M	12	(6)	1
24	Fredrik Bjørkan		21/08/98	D	2	(7)	
4	Martin Bjørnbak		22/03/92	D	30		2
21	Daniel Edvardsen		31/08/91	D	16	(5)	
8	Henrik Furebotn		11/02/86	M	13	(3)	2
25	Hannes Thór Haldórsson	ISL	27/04/84	G	14		
8	Ole Jørgen Halvorsen		02/10/87	A	9	(1)	4
28	William Hanssen		10/05/98	A		(1)	
31	Jens Petter Hauge		12/10/99	A	2	(18)	1
5	Thomas Jacobsen		16/09/83	D	28		
9	Alexander Jakobsen	DEN	18/03/94	M	10		
11	Milan Jevtović	SRB	13/06/93	A	17	(3)	6
3	Emil Jonassen		17/02/93	D	20	(2)	1
6	Anders Karlsen		15/02/90	M	4	(5)	
16	Morten Konradsen		03/05/96	M	1	(11)	
22	Vadim Manzon	RUS	05/12/94	A	2	(8)	1
6	Sascha Mockenhaupt	GER	10/09/91	D	10		1
18	Brede Moe		15/12/91	D	17		
17	Mathias Normann		28/05/96	M	26	(1)	
30	Trond Olsen		05/02/84	A	29	(1)	6
19	Joachim Osvold		23/09/94	A		(1)	
23	Serhiy Pohoriliy	UKR	28/07/86	G	7		
14	Ulrik Saltnes		10/11/92	M	7	(5)	
1	Simon Thomas	CAN	12/04/90	G	9		
9	Martin Wiig		22/08/83	A	2	(5)	

SK Brann

1908 • Brann (17,686) • brann.no

Major honours
Norwegian League (3) 1962, 1963, 2007; Norwegian Cup (6) 1923, 1925, 1972, 1976, 1982, 2004

Coach: Lars Arne Nilsen

2016

13/03	a	Strømsgodset	D	2-2	*Huseklepp, Orlov*
20/03	h	Odd	D	0-0	
03/04	a	Aalesund	W	2-1	*Johansen, Karadas*
10/04	h	Bodø/Glimt	W	1-0	*Orlov*
16/04	a	Rosenborg	L	0-3	
20/04	a	Viking	W	1-0	*Haugen*
23/04	h	Sogndal	W	2-0	*Acosta, Haugen*
01/05	a	Tromsø	L	0-1	
07/05	h	Start	W	1-0	*Skålevik*
11/05	a	Lillestrøm	L	0-1	
16/05	h	Stabæk	W	1-0	*Nilsen*
21/05	a	Molde	L	0-2	
29/05	h	Haugesund	W	1-0	*Skålevik*
03/07	a	Sarpsborg	L	0-1	
09/07	h	Vålerenga	W	4-1	*Barmen, og (S Larsen), Skålevik, Huseklepp*
17/07	a	Stabæk	D	1-1	*Karadas*
22/07	h	Aalesund	W	6-0	*Acosta, og (Skagestad), Nilsen, Huseklepp, Karadas 2*
31/07	a	Odd	W	3-1	*Demidov, Haugen 2*
07/08	h	Strømsgodset	W	1-0	*Vega*
13/08	a	Vålerenga	L	2-3	*Barmen, Nilsen*
21/08	h	Rosenborg	D	1-1	*Orlov*
27/08	a	Haugesund	L	2-3	*Barmen, Skålevik*
10/09	h	Viking	D	0-0	
18/09	a	Bodø/Glimt	W	3-1	*Barmen 2, Orlov*
25/09	h	Tromsø	W	1-0	*Vega*
01/10	a	Sogndal	D	0-0	
16/10	h	Lillestrøm	L	1-2	*Karadas*
22/10	h	Molde	W	2-1	*Skålevik 2*
30/10	a	Start	W	2-1	*Huseklepp, Haugen*
06/11	h	Sarpsborg	W	2-1	*Orlov, Sørensen*

No	Name	Nat	DoB	Pos	Aps	(s)	Gls
15	Bismar Acosta	CRC	19/12/86	D	20		2
29	Kristoffer Barmen		19/08/93	M	24	(1)	5
25	Daniel Braaten		20/05/82	A	25		
22	Torgeir Børven		03/12/91	A	2	(2)	
6	Vadim Demidov		10/10/86	D	26		1
5	Jonas Grønner		11/04/94	D	12	(3)	
26	Dani Hatakka	FIN	12/03/94	D	1		
8	Fredrik Haugen		13/06/92	M	23	(4)	5
1	Alex Horwath	USA	27/03/87	G	3		
13	Erik Huseklepp		05/09/84	A	9	(17)	4
22	Mads Hvilsom	DEN	23/08/92	A	7	(3)	
16	Remi Johansen		04/09/90	M	3	(7)	1
18	Azar Karadas		09/08/81	D	2	(22)	5
21	Ruben Kristiansen		20/02/88	D	28		
7	Kristoffer Larsen		19/01/92	M		(5)	
24	Piotr Leciejewski	POL	23/03/85	G	27		
23	Sivert Heltne Nilsen		02/10/91	M	28		3
33	Amin Nouri		10/01/90	D	30		
10	Jakob Orlov	SWE	15/03/86	A	22	(2)	5
9	Kasper Skaanes		19/03/95	M	9	(7)	
11	Steffen Lie Skålevik		31/03/93	A	8	(10)	6
35	Halldor Stenevik		02/02/00	M		(2)	
17	Gilli Sørensen	FRO	11/08/92	D	6	(1)	1
19	Deyver Vega	CRC	19/09/92	M	15	(3)	2

FK Haugesund

1993 • Haugesund (8,993) • fkh.no

Coach: Mark Dempsey (ENG); (15/07/16) Eirik Horneland

2016

13/03	a	Sarpsborg	W	1-0	*Karikari*
19/03	h	Aalesund	W	3-0	*Troost-Ekong, Tronstad, Karikari*
03/04	a	Strømsgodset	L	0-2	
08/04	a	Sogndal	L	0-1	
15/04	h	Lillestrøm	D	2-2	*Mæland, Agdestein*
20/04	a	Bodø/Glimt	W	4-3	*Agdestein 2, Kiss (p), Stølås*
25/04	h	Stabæk	W	3-1	*Miljeteig, Tronstad, Kiss*
01/05	a	Viking	L	2-3	*Agdestein 2*
08/05	h	Molde	D	3-3	*Andreassen, Kiss 2 (1p)*
11/05	h	Odd	W	3-1	*Agdestein, Hajradinović 2*
16/05	a	Vålerenga	W	1-0	*Ibrahim*
22/05	h	Rosenborg	D	1-1	*Ibrahim*
29/05	a	Brann	L	0-1	
02/07	h	Start	W	2-1	*Skjerve, Miljeteig*
09/07	a	Tromsø	D	2-2	*Miljeteig, Agdestein*
16/07	h	Viking	W	4-1	*Agdestein, Stølås 2, Abdi*
23/07	a	Rosenborg	L	0-6	
31/07	h	Sogndal	L	0-1	
07/08	a	Stabæk	W	1-0	*Agdestein*
14/08	h	Tromsø	W	2-1	*Stølås, Haraldseid*
20/08	a	Lillestrøm	D	1-1	*Myrestam*
27/08	h	Brann	W	3-2	*Hajradinović (p), Troost-Ekong, Haraldseid*
11/09	a	Molde	D	0-0	
16/09	h	Vålerenga	D	1-1	*Stølås*
25/09	a	Start	L	0-1	
02/10	h	Sarpsborg	D	1-1	*Kiss (p)*
16/10	a	Odd	L	1-2	*Skjerve*
23/10	h	Bodø/Glimt	W	2-1	*Troost-Ekong, Kiss*
30/10	a	Aalesund	D	3-3	*Agdestein, Skjerve, Hajradinović*
06/11	h	Strømsgodset	D	1-1	*Abdi*

No	Name	Nat	DoB	Pos	Aps	(s)	Gls
7	Liban Abdi		05/10/88	A	7	(7)	2
14	Torbjørn Agdestein		18/09/91	A	25	(5)	10
11	Tor Arne Andreassen		16/03/83	M	6	(5)	1
15	Izuchukwu Anthony	NGA	03/11/97	D	11	(3)	
26	Sverre Bjørkkjær		12/07/96	D	1	(1)	
1	Per Kristian Bråtveit		15/02/96	G	23		
23	Haris Hajradinović	BIH	18/02/94	M	21	(6)	4
19	Kristoffer Haraldseid		17/01/94	D	25		2
17	Shuaibu Ibrahim	NGA	19/12/96	A	8	(9)	2
20	Kwame Karikari	GHA	21/01/92	A	2	(11)	2
6	Filip Kiss	SVK	13/10/90	M	27		6
29	Robert Kling		01/05/97	M	1	(5)	
16	Derrick Mensah	GHA	28/05/95	M	2	(2)	
10	Roy Miljeteig		12/06/88	A	12	(6)	3
21	Erling Myklebust		28/05/96	A		(5)	
3	David Myrestam	SWE	04/04/87	D	29	(1)	1
13	Eirik Mæland		15/02/89	M	16	(2)	1
12	Helge Sandvik		05/02/90	G	7		
18	Vegard Skjerve		22/05/88	D	26		3
22	Alexander Stølås		30/04/89	M	26	(2)	5
8	Sondre Tronstad		26/08/95	M	19	(4)	2
5	William Troost-Ekong	NGA	01/09/93	D	24		3
55	Nemanja Tubić	SRB	18/04/84	D	12		

Lillestrøm SK

1917 • Åråsen (11,637) • lsk.no

Major honours
Norwegian League (5) 1959, 1976, 1977, 1986, 1989; Norwegian Cup (5) 1977, 1978, 1981, 1985, 2007

Coach: Rúnar Kristinsson (ISL); (19/09/16) (Arne Erlandsen)

2016

13/03	a	Start	D	1-1	*M Martin*
20/03	h	Bodø/Glimt	D	1-1	*M Martin*
01/04	a	Molde	L	2-4	*Friday, Knudtzon*
09/04	h	Sarpsborg	W	4-0	*Friday 2, Mikalsen, Rindarøy*
15/04	a	Haugesund	D	2-2	*Mikalsen, Friday*
21/04	h	Aalesund	D	1-1	*Friday*
24/04	a	Odd	W	3-1	*Ofkir, Jradi, Friday*
30/04	h	Vålerenga	W	2-0	*Friday, Jradi*
07/05	a	Strømsgodset	L	1-3	*Friday*
11/05	h	Brann	W	1-0	*Knudtzon*
16/05	a	Rosenborg	L	1-2	*Kippe*
22/05	h	Viking	L	1-2	*M Martin (p)*
29/05	a	Sogndal	D	2-2	*M Martin, Jradi*
01/07	h	Tromsø	L	2-4	*M Martin, Jradi*
10/07	h	Stabæk	L	1-2	*Kolstad*
17/07	a	Sarpsborg	L	0-3	
24/07	h	Strømsgodset	W	2-0	*Lundemo, Mikalsen*
31/07	a	Aalesund	L	0-2	
06/08	h	Rosenborg	L	3-4	*Knudtzon, M Martin, Ofkir*
11/08	a	Bodø/Glimt	D	1-1	*Ofkir*
20/08	h	Haugesund	D	1-1	*G Martin*
28/08	a	Viking	D	2-2	*Knudtzon, Lundemo*
11/09	h	Odd	L	2-4	*G Martin, Mikalsen*
17/09	a	Tromsø	L	1-2	*Malec*
25/09	h	Sogndal	L	1-2	*Mathew*
01/10	a	Stabæk	W	2-1	*Sinyan, G Martin*
16/10	a	Brann	W	2-1	*Mathew, Knudtzon*
23/10	h	Start	D	1-1	*Malec*
30/10	a	Vålerenga	D	1-1	*G Martin*
06/11	h	Molde	W	1-0	*M Martin*

No	Name	Nat	DoB	Pos	Aps	(s)	Gls
4	Marius Amundsen		30/11/91	D	29		
1	Haraldur Björnsson	ISL	11/01/89	G	1		
15	Erik Brenden		07/01/94	M		(6)	
12	Jacob Faye-Lund		15/09/94	G	4		
23	Fred Friday	NGA	22/05/95	A	14		8
41	Pål Vestly Heigre		15/03/95	G	2		
18	Bonke Innocent	NGA	20/01/96	M	23	(1)	
22	Michael Jakobsen	DEN	02/01/86	D	9	(4)	
7	Bassel Jradi	LIB	06/07/93	M	26		4
13	Frode Kippe		17/01/78	D	19	(3)	1
11	Erling Knudtzon		15/12/88	A	25	(2)	5
17	Jørgen Kolstad		31/08/95	M	7	(8)	1
10	Marius Lundemo		11/04/94	M	18	(1)	2
23	Tomáš Malec	SVK	05/01/93	A	8	(4)	2
19	Gary Martin	ENG	10/10/90	A	7	(3)	4
8	Malaury Martin	FRA	25/08/88	M	25	(5)	7
6	Ifeanyi Mathew	NGA	20/01/97	M	6	(2)	2
3	Simen Kind Mikalsen		04/05/93	D	27		4
20	Mohamed Ofkir		04/08/96	M	13	(10)	3
77	Arnold Origi	KEN	15/11/83	G	23		
5	Ole Martin Rindarøy		16/05/95	D	9	(10)	1
26	Sheriff Sinyan		19/07/96	M	4	(6)	1
16	Håkon Skogseid		14/01/88	D	28		
9	Árni Vilhjálmsson	ISL	09/05/94	A	3	(4)	

Molde FK

1911 • Aker (11,249) • moldefk.no

Major honours
Norwegian League (3) 2011, 2012, 2014; Norwegian Cup (4) 1994, 2005, 2013, 2014

Coach: Ole Gunnar Solskjær

2016

13/03	h	Tromsø	D	1-1	*Aursnes*
20/03	a	Stabæk	W	2-1	*Elyounoussi 2*
01/04	h	Lillestrøm	W	4-2	*Moström, S Svendsen, Singh, Gudjohnsen (p)*
10/04	a	Start	D	1-1	*Strand*
17/04	a	Bodø/Glimt	W	2-1	*Amang, Flo*
21/04	h	Vålerenga	W	4-0	*S Svendsen, og (Jääger), Strand, Toivio*
24/04	a	Sarpsborg	L	0-4	
30/04	h	Aalesund	W	1-0	*Gulbrandsen*
08/05	a	Haugesund	D	3-3	*Hestad, Strand, Gulbrandsen*
11/05	h	Strømsgodset	W	4-2	*Gulbrandsen, Elyounoussi 2, Amang*
16/05	a	Odd	L	0-2	
21/05	h	Brann	W	2-0	*Aursnes (p), Gulbrandsen*
28/05	a	Rosenborg	L	1-3	*Elyounoussi*
03/07	h	Viking	L	0-1	
09/07	a	Sogndal	L	3-4	*Toivio, Singh 2*
17/07	h	Start	D	2-2	*S Svendsen, Toivio*
23/07	h	Sarpsborg	L	0-1	
01/08	a	Vålerenga	L	0-3	
06/08	h	Bodø/Glimt	W	3-2	*Aursnes, Brustad, S Svendsen*
14/08	a	Aalesund	W	2-0	*Brustad, Hestad*
21/08	h	Odd	W	4-2	*Sigurdarson 2, T Svendsen, Singh*
27/08	a	Strømsgodset	W	2-0	Singh (p), Sigurdarson
11/09	h	Haugesund	D	0-0	
17/09	a	Viking	L	0-1	
24/09	h	Rosenborg	L	1-3	*Sigurdarson*
02/10	a	Tromsø	W	2-0	*Hestad, og (Antonsen)*
16/10	h	Sogndal	D	0-0	
22/10	a	Brann	L	1-2	*Strand*
30/10	h	Stabæk	W	3-0	*Gatt, Flo, Toivio*
06/11	a	Lillestrøm	L	0-1	

No	Name	Nat	DoB	Pos	Aps	(s)	Gls
21	Agnaldo	BRA	11/03/94	M	1	(6)	
20	Thomas Amang	CMR	09/02/98	A	3	(19)	2
17	Fredrik Aursnes		10/12/95	M	21	(2)	3
27	Mushaga Bakenga		08/08/92	A	2		
33	Fredrik Brustad		22/06/89	A	6	(3)	2
3	Amidou Diop	SEN	25/02/92	M	2	(6)	
30	Pape Paté Diouf	SEN	04/04/86	A	2		
24	Mohamed Elyounoussi		04/08/94	A	11	(1)	5
15	Per-Egil Flo		18/01/89	D	21		2
25	Vegard Forren		16/02/88	D	22	(1)	
4	Ruben Gabrielsen		10/03/92	D	28	(1)	
2	Joshua Gatt	USA	29/08/91	A	5	(1)	1
28	Stian Gregersen		17/05/95	M	4	(3)	
22	Eidur Smári Gudjohnsen	ISL	15/09/78	A	7	(6)	1
8	Fredrik Gulbrandsen		10/09/92	A	6	(3)	4
19	Eirik Hestad		26/06/95	M	17	(4)	3
1	Ethan Horvath	USA	09/06/95	G	22		
26	Andreas Linde	SWE	24/07/93	G	8	(1)	
9	Mattias Moström	SWE	25/02/83	M	17	(3)	1
22	Christoffer Remmer	DEN	16/02/93	D	9		
23	Knut Olav Rindarøy		17/07/85	D	10	(1)	
53	Martin Ove Roseth		10/07/98	D		(1)	
8	Babacar Sarr	SEN	15/02/91	M	13		
10	Björn Bergmann Sigurdarson	ISL	26/02/91	A	10	(1)	4
7	Harmeet Singh		12/11/90	M	23	(3)	5
32	Isak Ssewankambo	SWE	27/02/96	D	7	(2)	
14	Petter Strand		24/08/94	M	25	(3)	4
11	Sander Svendsen		06/08/97	A	14	(11)	4
52	Tobias Svendsen		31/08/99	M		(4)	1
5	Joona Toivio	FIN	10/03/88	D	14	(3)	4

Odds BK

1894 • Skagerak Arena (11,938) • odd.no

Major honours
Norwegian Cup (12) 1903, 1904, 1905, 1906, 1913, 1915, 1919, 1922, 1924, 1926, 1931, 2000

Coach: Dag-Eilev Fagermo

2016

Date	H/A	Opponent	Res	Score	Scorers
12/03	h	Rosenborg	W	1-0	*Nordkvelle*
20/03	a	Brann	D	0-0	
03/04	h	Tromsø	D	0-0	
10/04	a	Viking	W	2-0	*Akabueze, Zekhnini*
17/04	h	Start	W	3-0	*Nordkvelle, Semb Berge 2*
20/04	a	Sogndal	W	1-0	*Samuelsen (p)*
24/04	h	Lillestrøm	L	1-3	*Nilsen*
01/05	a	Stabæk	W	2-1	*Nordkvelle, Akabueze*
08/05	h	Bodø/Glimt	W	2-1	*Occéan 2*
11/05	a	Haugesund	L	1-3	*Semb Berge*
16/05	h	Molde	W	2-0	*Occéan, Zekhnini*
20/05	a	Sarpsborg	D	0-0	
29/05	h	Strømsgodset	W	2-1	*Nordkvelle (p), Akabueze*
03/07	a	Vålerenga	W	1-0	*Zekhnini*
10/07	h	Aalesund	W	4-1	*Occéan 2, Akabueze, Zekhnini*
17/07	a	Bodø/Glimt	L	1-2	*Ruud*
24/07	h	Viking	D	2-2	*Semb Berge, Occéan*
31/07	h	Brann	L	1-3	*Occéan*
07/08	a	Start	W	2-1	*Akabueze, Occéan*
14/08	h	Sarpsborg	D	0-0	
21/08	a	Molde	L	2-4	*Hagen, Akabueze*
28/08	h	Vålerenga	L	1-2	*Ruud*
11/09	a	Lillestrøm	W	4-2	*Ruud 3, Haugen*
18/09	h	Stabæk	L	0-1	
25/09	a	Strømsgodset	D	1-1	*Akabueze*
02/10	a	Aalesund	L	0-1	
16/10	h	Haugesund	W	2-1	*Occéan, Nordkvelle (p)*
23/10	a	Rosenborg	W	2-1	*Nordkvelle, Semb Berge*
30/10	h	Sogndal	W	3-1	*Nordkvelle, Mladenovic, Zekhnini*
06/11	a	Tromsø	L	1-3	*Occéan*

No	Name	Nat	DoB	Pos	Aps	(s)	Gls
26	Chukwuma Akabueze	NGA	06/05/89	A	26	(4)	7
6	Oliver Berg		28/08/89	M	19	(4)	
4	Vegard Bergan		20/02/95	D	2	(3)	
23	Lars-Kristian Eriksen		28/06/83	D	6	(3)	
3	Ardian Gashi		20/06/81	M		(2)	
5	Thomas Grøgaard		08/02/94	D	23	(3)	
21	Steffen Hagen		08/03/86	D	30		1
7	Ole Jørgen Halvorsen		02/10/87	A	5	(11)	
15	Sigurd Haugen		17/07/97	A		(3)	1
20	Fredrik Oldrup Jensen		18/05/93	M	28		
9	Henrik Kjelsrud Johansen		22/03/93	A	1	(9)	
19	Zakaria Messoudi	CAN	30/10/93	A		(2)	
13	Stefan Mladenovic		03/04/94	M		(11)	1
18	Joakim Våge Nilsen		24/04/91	M	9	(13)	1
14	Fredrik Nordkvelle		13/09/85	M	26	(3)	7
10	Olivier Occéan	CAN	23/10/81	A	27	(1)	10
24	Riku Riski	FIN	16/08/89	A	12	(2)	
1	Sondre Rossbach		07/02/96	G	30		
2	Espen Ruud		26/02/84	D	29		5
8	Jone Samuelsen		06/07/84	M	13	(2)	1
16	Fredrik Semb Berge		06/02/90	D	24		5
11	Rafik Zekhnini		12/01/98	A	20	(2)	5

Rosenborg BK

1917 • Lerkendal (21,405) • rbk.no

Major honours
Norwegian League (24) 1967, 1969, 1971, 1985, 1988, 1990, 1992, 1993, 1994, 1995, 1996, 1997, 1998, 1999, 2000, 2001, 2002, 2003, 2004, 2006, 2009, 2010, 2015, 2016; Norwegian Cup (11) 1960, 1964, 1971, 1988, 1990, 1992, 1995, 1999, 2003, 2015, 2016

Coach: Kåre Ingebrigtsen

2016

Date	H/A	Opponent	Res	Score	Scorers
12/03	a	Odd	L	0-1	
19/03	h	Strømsgodset	W	1-0	*Gytkjær*
02/04	a	Vålerenga	W	2-0	*De Lanlay, Jensen*
10/04	h	Aalesund	W	1-0	*Reginiussen*
16/04	h	Brann	W	3-0	*Vilhjálmsson, De Lanlay, Jensen (p)*
21/04	a	Tromsø	W	2-1	*Jensen, Konradsen*
24/04	h	Viking	W	4-0	*Eyjólfsson, Jensen, Thórarinsson, Gytkjær*
01/05	a	Sogndal	D	1-1	*Konradsen*
08/05	h	Stabæk	W	3-1	*Midtsjø 2, Gytkjær*
12/05	a	Start	W	2-0	*Vilhjálmsson 2*
16/05	h	Lillestrøm	W	2-1	*Gytkjær, Konradsen*
22/05	a	Haugesund	D	1-1	*Konradsen*
28/05	h	Molde	W	3-1	*Helland, Gytkjær 2*
02/07	a	Bodø/Glimt	D	0-0	
09/07	h	Sarpsborg	W	5-2	*Helland 2, Gytkjær (p), Jensen, Rashani*
16/07	a	Aalesund	D	1-1	*Rashani*
23/07	h	Haugesund	W	6-0	*Gytkjær, og (Stølås), Vilhjálmsson 2, Bakenga 2*
06/08	a	Lillestrøm	W	4-3	*Gytkjær 3, Midtsjø*
11/08	a	Viking	W	2-0	*Gytkjær 2*
14/08	h	Sogndal	W	3-1	*Midtsjø, Bakenga, Svensson*
21/08	a	Brann	D	1-1	*Gytkjær*
28/08	h	Tromsø	W	3-1	*Gytkjær 2, Rashani*
11/09	a	Stabæk	W	2-0	*Bakenga, Jensen*
18/09	h	Start	W	2-0	*Gytkjær, Reitan (p)*
24/09	a	Molde	W	3-1	*Jensen 2, Gytkjær*
02/10	h	Vålerenga	W	3-1	*Reitan, Helland, Bakenga*
15/10	a	Sarpsborg	D	2-2	*Reginiussen, Gytkjær*
23/10	h	Odd	L	1-2	*Bakenga*
30/10	a	Strømsgodset	L	0-2	
06/11	h	Bodø/Glimt	W	2-1	*Bakenga, Eyjólfsson*

No	Name	Nat	DoB	Pos	Aps	(s)	Gls
27	Mushaga Bakenga		08/08/92	A	5	(4)	7
14	Johan Lædre Bjørdal		05/05/86	D	9	(3)	
11	Yann-Erik de Lanlay		14/05/92	A	16	(1)	2
5	Hólmar Örn Eyjólfsson	ISL	06/08/90	D	25	(2)	2
20	Alex Gersbach	AUS	08/05/97	D	14	(5)	
9	Christian Gytkjær	DEN	06/05/90	A	24	(4)	19
1	André Hansen		17/12/89	G	19		
23	Pål André Helland		04/01/90	A	16	(4)	4
7	Mike Jensen	DEN	19/02/88	M	27	(1)	8
8	Anders Konradsen		18/07/90	M	24	(2)	4
24	Adam Larsen Kwarasey	GHA	12/12/87	G	9		
30	Pavel Londak	EST	14/05/80	G	2	(1)	
21	Fredrik Midtsjø		11/08/93	M	26	(2)	4
15	Elbasan Rashani	KOS	09/05/93	A	10	(9)	3
4	Tore Reginiussen		10/04/86	D	18	(1)	2
32	Erlend Dahl Reitan		11/09/97	D	3		2
9	Riku Riski	FIN	16/08/89	A		(3)	
16	Jørgen Skjelvik		05/07/91	D	24	(2)	
22	Sivert Solli		27/07/97	M		(1)	
18	Magnus Stamnestrø		18/04/92	M	2	(11)	
2	Jonas Svensson		06/03/93	D	25	(1)	1
28	Gudmundur Thórarinsson	ISL	15/04/92	M	15	(9)	1
10	Matthías Vilhjálmsson	ISL	30/01/87	A	17	(12)	5

Sarpsborg 08 FF

2008 • Sarpsborg (5,137) • sarpsborg08.no

Coach: Geir Bakke

2016

Date	H/A	Opponent	Res	Score	Scorers
13/03	h	Haugesund	L	0-1	
20/03	a	Viking	D	0-0	
03/04	h	Sogndal	D	0-0	
09/04	a	Lillestrøm	L	0-4	
17/04	h	Stabæk	D	1-1	*Groven*
21/04	a	Start	W	4-1	*Tokstad 3, Mortensen*
24/04	h	Molde	W	4-0	*Kirkevold 2 (1p), Rosted, Hovda*
02/05	a	Bodø/Glimt	W	2-0	*Thomassen, Ernemann*
08/05	a	Vålerenga	L	0-3	
12/05	h	Aalesund	W	1-0	*Trondsen*
16/05	a	Strømsgodset	L	0-4	
20/05	h	Odd	D	0-0	
28/05	a	Tromsø	W	2-1	*Ernemann 2 (2p)*
03/07	h	Brann	W	1-0	*Kirkevold*
09/07	a	Rosenborg	L	2-5	*Kirkevold, Rosted*
17/07	h	Lillestrøm	W	3-0	*Lindberg, Nielsen 2*
23/07	a	Molde	W	1-0	*Tokstad*
29/07	h	Start	W	1-0	*Lindberg*
07/08	h	Vålerenga	L	0-2	
14/08	a	Odd	D	0-0	
21/08	h	Strømsgodset	W	1-0	*Kirkevold*
26/08	a	Aalesund	D	2-2	*Mortensen, Kirkevold*
11/09	h	Bodø/Glimt	L	1-2	*Heintz*
18/09	a	Sogndal	L	0-3	
24/09	h	Viking	W	1-0	*Ugwuadu*
02/10	a	Haugesund	D	1-1	*Ernemann*
15/10	h	Rosenborg	D	2-2	*Lindberg, Tveita*
22/10	a	Stabæk	W	2-1	*Sundli, Mortensen*
30/10	h	Tromsø	D	2-2	*Mortensen, Rosted*
06/11	a	SK Brann	L	1-2	*Mortensen*

No	Name	Nat	DoB	Pos	Aps	(s)	Gls
4	Kjetil Berge		05/06/81	D	8		
85	Alexy Bosetti	FRA	23/04/93	A		(2)	
17	Steffen Ernemann	DEN	26/04/82	M	19	(6)	4
23	Jakob Glesnes		25/03/94	D	13	(1)	
29	Alexander Groven		02/01/92	D	18	(4)	1
42	Magnus Hart		20/04/96	M		(1)	
13	Ole Heieren Hansen		26/02/87	D	12	(2)	
14	Tobias Heintz		13/07/98	A	1	(2)	1
18	Tor Øyvind Hovda		24/09/89	M	7	(10)	1
19	Kristinn Jónsson	ISL	04/08/90	D	6	(3)	
7	Pål Alexander Kirkevold		10/11/90	A	22	(6)	6
21	Anders Kristiansen		17/03/90	G	17		
10	Jonas Lindberg	SWE	24/03/89	A	19	(2)	3
24	Amani Mbedule		19/09/96	A	2	(3)	
69	Patrick Mortensen	DEN	13/07/89	A	21	(5)	5
5	Matti Lund Nielsen	DEN	08/05/88	M	23	(5)	2
23	Kristoffer Normann Hansen		01/01/94	A		(4)	
15	Sigurd Rosted		22/07/94	D	21	(2)	3
4	Morten Sundli		31/03/90	D	1	(4)	1
16	Joachim Thomassen		04/05/88	D	28		1
3	Henri Toivomäki	FIN	21/02/91	D	9	(3)	
11	Kristoffer Tokstad		05/07/91	M	19	(1)	4
6	Anders Trondsen		30/03/95	M	20	(2)	1
22	Jon-Helge Tveita		27/01/92	A	15	(14)	1
8	Onyekachi Hope Ugwuadu	NGA	05/05/97	A	2	(5)	1
1	Arild Østbø		19/04/91	G	13		
20	Anders Østli		08/01/83	D	14	(1)	

NORWAY

Sogndal Fotball

1926 • Fosshaugane Campus (5,622) • sogndalfotball.no

Coach: Eirik Bakke

2016					
13/03	a	Bodø/Glimt	L	0-2	
20/03	h	Vålerenga	W	1-0	*Ramsland*
03/04	a	Sarpsborg	D	0-0	
08/04	h	Haugesund	W	1-0	*Otoo*
16/04	a	Strømsgodset	L	1-2	*Utvik*
20/04	h	Odd	L	0-1	
23/04	a	Brann	L	0-2	
01/05	h	Rosenborg	D	1-1	*Sarr*
08/05	a	Aalesund	W	4-1	*Sveen, og (Kirkeskov), Ramsland, Koomson*
12/05	h	Tromsø	D	0-0	
16/05	a	Viking	D	0-0	
22/05	h	Start	D	2-2	*Psyché 2*
29/05	h	Lillestrøm	D	2-2	*Sarr, Opseth*
03/07	a	Stabæk	W	1-0	*Otoo*
09/07	h	Molde	W	4-3	*Patronen, Kjemhus 2, Sveen*
15/07	a	Vålerenga	D	1-1	*Sveen*
24/07	h	Bodø/Glimt	D	2-2	*Opseth, Sveen*
31/07	a	Haugesund	W	1-0	*Sveen*
07/08	h	Viking	L	1-2	*Otoo*
14/08	a	Rosenborg	L	1-3	*og (Svensson)*
21/08	a	Start	D	1-1	*Furebotn*
28/08	h	Stabæk	D	1-1	*Ramsland*
11/09	a	Tromsø	L	0-2	
18/09	h	Sarpsborg	W	3-0	*Ramsland, Sveen, Koomson*
25/09	a	Lillestrøm	W	2-1	*Koomson (p), Sveen*
01/10	h	Brann	D	0-0	
16/10	a	Molde	D	0-0	
23/10	h	Strømsgodset	L	0-1	
30/10	a	Odd	L	1-3	*Raitala*
06/11	h	Aalesund	L	2-4	*Psyché, Ramsland*

No	Name	Nat	DoB	Pos	Aps	(s)	Gls
27	Eirik Birkelund		13/01/94	M	21	(5)	
7	Rune Bolseth		14/07/80	M	16	(9)	
34	Simen Brekkhus		06/05/97	M	1	(3)	
1	Mathias Dyngeland		07/10/95	G	30		
8	Fredrik Flo		10/10/96	A		(1)	
6	Henrik Furebotn		11/02/86	M	13		1
5	Victor Grodås		09/12/91	D		(1)	
25	Ruben Holsæter		20/04/91	M		(10)	
28	Johan Hove		07/09/00	M		(3)	
22	Lars Christian Kjemhus		03/03/94	M	19	(5)	2
10	Gilbert Koomson	GHA	09/09/94	M	27	(1)	3
16	Vegard Leikvoll Moberg		23/01/91	M	2	(4)	
20	Kristian Opseth		06/01/90	A	2	(16)	2
18	Mahatma Otoo	GHA	06/02/92	A	9	(11)	3
4	Hannu Patronen	FIN	23/05/84	D	19	(4)	1
26	Magnus Pedersen	DEN	23/11/96	D	4	(3)	
17	Christophe Psyché	FRA	28/07/88	D	27	(2)	3
15	Jukka Raitala	FIN	15/09/88	D	28		1
11	Martin Ramsland		02/04/93	A	27	(1)	5
16	Babacar Sarr	SEN	15/02/91	M	15		2
19	Ole Amund Sveen		05/01/90	M	27	(1)	7
2	Taijo Teniste	EST	31/01/88	D	27		
3	Bjørn Inge Utvik		28/02/96	D	16	(4)	1
23	Edin Øy		20/05/97	M		(1)	

Stabæk Fotball

1912 • Nadderud (4,938) • stabak.no

Major honours
Norwegian League (1) 2008; Norwegian Cup (1) 1998

Coach: Billy McKinlay (SCO); (08/07/16) Antoni Ordinas (ESP)

2016					
11/03	a	Aalesund	L	0-1	
20/03	h	Molde	L	1-2	*Meling*
03/04	a	Bodø/Glimt	L	1-3	*Omoijuanfo*
09/04	h	Vålerenga	W	2-1	*Kassi, Gorozia*
17/04	a	Sarpsborg	D	1-1	*Mehmeti*
20/04	h	Strømsgodset	L	0-1	
25/04	a	Haugesund	L	1-3	*Kassi*
01/05	h	Odd	L	1-2	*Mehmeti*
08/05	a	Rosenborg	L	1-3	*Kassi*
12/05	h	Viking	W	1-0	*Asante*
16/05	a	Brann	L	0-1	
21/05	h	Tromsø	L	0-3	
29/05	a	Start	W	5-0	*Omoijuanfo, Gorozia, Njie 2, Meling*
03/07	h	Sogndal	L	0-1	
10/07	a	Lillestrøm	W	2-1	*Njie, Mehmeti*
17/07	h	Brann	D	1-1	*Issah*
24/07	a	Tromsø	D	2-2	*og (Wangberg), Mehmeti*
31/07	a	Strømsgodset	D	2-2	*Gorozia, og (Vilsvik)*
07/08	h	Haugesund	L	0-1	
14/08	a	Viking	D	2-2	*Asante, Meling*
21/08	h	Aalesund	W	3-0	*Grossman, Keita, Kassi*
28/08	a	Sogndal	D	1-1	*Meling*
11/09	h	Rosenborg	L	0-2	
18/09	a	Odd	W	1-0	*Keita*
26/09	h	Bodø/Glimt	W	1-0	*Hanche-Olsen*
01/10	h	Lillestrøm	L	1-2	*Pedersen*
16/10	a	Vålerenga	D	1-1	*Keita (p)*
22/10	h	Sarpsborg	L	1-2	*Njie*
30/10	a	Molde	L	0-3	
06/11	h	Start	W	3-0	*Omoijuanfo 2, Alanzinho*

No	Name	Nat	DoB	Pos	Aps	(s)	Gls
30	Markus Aanesland		18/04/98	M		(1)	
32	Alanzinho	BRA	22/02/83	M	5	(3)	1
7	Ernest Asante	GHA	06/11/88	M	20		2
17	Alex Davey	SCO	24/11/94	D	4	(1)	
19	Shadrach Eghan	GHA	04/07/94	M		(4)	
7	Mynor Escoe	CRC	06/04/91	A	4	(2)	
9	Giorgi Gorozia	GEO	26/03/95	M	14	(9)	3
21	Daniel Granli		01/05/94	D	13	(4)	
8	Cole Grossman	USA	10/04/89	M	23		1
16	Andreas Hanche-Olsen		17/01/97	D	11	(2)	1
13	Eirik Haugstad		17/01/94	M		(9)	
20	Kamal Issah	GHA	29/08/92	M	17		1
28	Luc Kassi	CIV	20/08/94	M	21	(2)	4
77	Muhamed Keita		02/09/90	A	9		3
1	Sayouba Mandé	CIV	15/06/93	G	29		
10	Agon Mehmeti	ALB	20/11/89	A	17	(7)	4
50	Marcus Mehnert		28/10/97	A	1	(1)	
25	Birger Meling		17/12/94	D	27	(1)	4
18	Jeppe Moe		03/08/95	D	12	(5)	
4	Marcus Nilsson	SWE	26/02/88	D	13		
11	Moussa Njie		02/10/95	A	22	(6)	4
4	Nicolai Næss		18/01/93	D	16		
99	Ohi Omoijuanfo		10/01/94	A	15	(13)	4
98	Sebastian Pedersen		08/06/99	A	1	(4)	1
60	Edvard Race		22/05/97	D	5	(2)	
22	Gurpreet Singh Sandhu	IND	03/02/92	G	1		
3	Morten Morisbak Skjønsberg		12/02/83	D	30		
40	Marius Østvold		04/11/97	M		(1)	

IK Start

1905 • Sparebanken Sør Arena (14,448) • ikstart.no

Major honours
Norwegian League (2) 1978, 1980

Coach: Steinar Pedersen

2016					
13/03	h	Lillestrøm	D	1-1	*Heikkilä*
18/03	a	Tromsø	D	0-0	
02/04	h	Viking	L	0-1	
10/04	h	Molde	D	1-1	*Rasmussen*
17/04	a	Odd	L	0-3	
21/04	h	Sarpsborg	L	1-4	*Heikkilä*
24/04	a	Vålerenga	L	0-2	
01/05	h	Strømsgodset	D	2-2	*Sandnes, Salvesen*
07/05	a	Brann	L	0-1	
12/05	h	Rosenborg	L	0-2	
16/05	a	Aalesund	D	1-1	*Nwakali*
22/05	a	Sogndal	D	2-2	*De John, Hoff*
29/05	h	Stabæk	L	0-5	
02/07	a	Haugesund	L	1-2	*Rasmussen*
08/07	h	Bodø/Glimt	L	1-4	*Nwakali*
17/07	a	Molde	D	2-2	*Børufsen, Kristjánsson*
24/07	h	Vålerenga	L	2-4	*Børufsen 2*
29/07	a	Sarpsborg	L	0-1	
07/08	h	Odd	L	1-2	*Johnson (p)*
14/08	a	Strømsgodset	D	1-1	*Salvesen*
21/08	h	Sogndal	D	1-1	*Salvesen*
28/08	a	Bodø/Glimt	L	0-2	
09/09	h	Aalesund	L	1-4	*Nwakali*
18/09	a	Rosenborg	L	0-2	
25/09	h	Haugesund	W	1-0	*Sigurdsen*
02/10	a	Viking	L	0-2	
16/10	h	Tromsø	W	2-1	*Segberg, Salvesen*
23/10	a	Lillestrøm	D	1-1	*Antwi*
30/10	h	Brann	L	1-2	*Sandnes*
06/11	a	Stabæk	L	0-3	

No	Name	Nat	DoB	Pos	Aps	(s)	Gls
9	Daniel Aase		22/06/89	A	5	(5)	
6	Kristoffer Ajer		17/04/98	M	11		
33	Dennis Antwi	GHA	12/01/93	A	10	(1)	1
18	Jibril Bojang		13/09/94	M	4	(5)	
14	Espen Børufsen		04/03/88	M	27		3
4	Alex De John	USA	10/05/91	D	17	(2)	1
3	Tapio Heikkilä	FIN	08/04/90	D	30		2
8	Espen Hoff		20/11/81	A	9	(7)	1
16	Andreas Hollingen		03/10/94	M	12	(3)	
11	Uduak Idemokon	NGA	01/12/94	A	3		
19	Austin Ikenna	NGA	15/08/93	A	2	(1)	
10	Dulee Johnson	LBR	07/11/84	M	7	(1)	1
17	Gudmundur Kristjánsson	ISL	01/03/89	M	14	(8)	1
7	Chidiebere Nwakali	NGA	26/12/96	M	21	(1)	3
1	Håkon André Opdal		11/06/82	G	30		
32	Mathias Rasmussen		25/11/97	M	11	(4)	2
15	Henrik Robstad		12/05/91	D	30		
22	Lars-Jørgen Salvesen		19/02/96	A	13	(13)	4
5	Robert Sandnes		29/12/91	D	8	(14)	2
23	Erlend Segberg		12/04/97	M	9	(1)	1
30	Lasse Sigurdsen		01/06/97	A	4	(12)	1
2	Jens Kristian Skogmo		16/07/87	D	19	(1)	
28	Rolf Daniel Vikstøl		22/02/89	D	20	(1)	
27	Eirik Wichne		12/05/97	M	14	(6)	

Strømsgodset IF

1907 • Marienlyst (8,935) • godset.no

Major honours
Norwegian League (2) 1970, 2013; Norwegian Cup (5) 1969, 1970, 1973, 1991, 2010

Coach: Bjørn Petter Ingebretsen; (13/10/16) (Håkon Wibe-Lund); (18/10/16) Tor Ole Skullerud

2016

Date		Opponent		Score	Scorers
13/03	h	Brann	D	2-2	*Storflor, Høiland*
19/03	a	Rosenborg	L	0-1	
03/04	h	Haugesund	W	2-0	*Adjei-Boateng, Ovenstad*
10/04	a	Tromsø	L	0-2	
16/04	h	Sogndal	W	2-1	*Pedersen 2*
20/04	a	Stabæk	W	1-0	*Vilsvik (p)*
23/04	h	Bodø/Glimt	W	2-0	*Pedersen (p), Kastrati*
01/05	a	Start	D	2-2	*Storflor, Nguen*
07/05	h	Lillestrøm	W	3-1	*Pedersen, Nguen, Høiland*
11/05	a	Molde	L	2-4	*Vaagan Moen, Kastrati*
16/05	h	Sarpsborg	W	4-0	*Parr, Valsvik, Storflor, Pedersen*
22/05	h	Vålerenga	W	3-2	*Keita, Vilsvik, Vaagan Moen*
29/05	a	Odd	L	1-2	*Nguen*
04/07	h	Aalesund	W	4-2	*Keita, og (Kirkeskov), Vilsvik, Kastrati*
09/07	a	Viking	W	1-0	*Keita*
17/07	h	Tromsø	W	1-0	*Keita*
24/07	a	Lillestrøm	L	0-2	
31/07	h	Stabæk	D	2-2	*Adjei-Boateng, Pedersen*
07/08	a	Brann	L	0-1	
14/08	h	Start	D	1-1	*Pedersen (p)*
21/08	a	Sarpsborg	L	0-1	
27/08	h	Molde	L	0-2	
10/09	a	Vålerenga	D	1-1	*Andersen*
18/09	a	Aalesund	L	2-4	*Tokstad, Pedersen (p)*
25/09	h	Odd	D	1-1	*Adjei-Boateng*
30/09	a	Bodø/Glimt	L	2-4	*Høiland 2*
14/10	h	Viking	D	1-1	*Andersen*
23/10	a	Sogndal	W	1-0	*Andersen*
30/10	h	Rosenborg	W	2-0	*Parr, Storflor*
06/11	a	Haugesund	D	1-1	*og (Kiss)*

No	Name	Nat	DoB	Pos	Aps	(s)	Gls
20	Mohammed Abu	GHA	14/11/91	M	27		
22	Bismark Adjei-Boateng	GHA	10/05/94	M	25	(4)	3
34	Abdul-Basit Agouda		26/05/99	A		(1)	
23	Eirik Ulland Andersen		21/09/92	A	7	(1)	3
1	Espen Bugge Pettersen		10/05/80	G	30		
19	Francisco Júnior	GNB	18/01/92	M	16	(4)	
21	Mathias Berg Gjerstrøm		30/06/97	M	1	(5)	
5	Jakob Glesnes		25/03/94	D	11		
2	Mounir Hamoud		01/02/85	D	17	(1)	
66	Kristoffer Hoven		10/08/96	A		(2)	
28	Marius Høibråten		23/01/95	D	14	(2)	
7	Tommy Høiland		11/04/89	A	10	(12)	4
15	Flamur Kastrati	KOS	14/11/91	A	3	(8)	3
77	Muhamed Keita		02/09/90	A	9	(4)	4
4	Kim André Madsen		12/03/89	D	18		
93	Tokmac Nguen		20/10/93	A	11	(3)	3
11	Martin Rønning Ovenstad		18/04/94	M	12	(5)	1
3	Jonathan Parr		21/10/88	D	24	(2)	2
10	Marcus Pedersen		08/06/90	A	14	(5)	8
9	Øyvind Storflor		18/12/79	A	19	(5)	4
23	Thomas Sørum		17/11/82	A	1	(3)	
15	Kristoffer Tokstad		05/07/91	M	9		1
8	Petter Vaagan Moen		05/02/84	M	7	(13)	2
71	Gustav Valsvik		26/05/93	D	17		1
26	Lars-Christopher Vilsvik		18/10/88	D	28	(1)	3

Tromsø IL

1920 • Alfheim (6,801) • til.no

Major honours
Norwegian Cup (2) 1986, 1996

Coach: Bård Flovik

2016

Date		Opponent		Score	Scorers
13/03	a	Molde	D	1-1	*Sigurdarson*
18/03	h	Start	D	0-0	
03/04	a	Odd	D	0-0	
10/04	h	Strømsgodset	W	2-0	*Espejord, Moussa*
17/04	a	Vålerenga	L	0-4	
21/04	h	Rosenborg	L	1-2	*Moussa*
24/04	a	Aalesund	L	0-6	
01/05	h	Brann	W	1-0	*Moussa*
07/05	a	Viking	L	0-2	
12/05	a	Sogndal	D	0-0	
16/05	h	Bodø/Glimt	L	1-2	*Olsen*
21/05	a	Stabæk	W	3-0	*Gjesdal, Olsen, Wangberg*
28/05	h	Sarpsborg	L	1-2	*Olsen*
01/07	a	Lillestrøm	W	4-2	*Olsen, Ingebrigtsen, Moussa (p), Andersen*
09/07	h	Haugesund	D	2-2	*Ingebrigtsen, Gundersen*
17/07	a	Strømsgodset	L	0-1	
24/07	h	Stabæk	D	2-2	*Antonsen, Ingebrigtsen*
31/07	a	Bodø/Glimt	W	3-0	*Espejord, Sigurdarson, Gundersen*
05/08	h	Aalesund	L	1-2	*Espejord*
14/08	a	Haugesund	L	1-2	*Gundersen*
21/08	h	Viking	W	2-1	*Åsen, Andersen*
28/08	a	Rosenborg	L	1-3	*Espejord*
11/09	h	Sogndal	W	2-0	*Wangberg, Yttergård Jenssen*
17/09	h	Lillestrøm	W	2-1	*Åsen, Olsen*
25/09	a	Brann	L	0-1	
02/10	h	Molde	L	0-2	
16/10	a	Start	L	1-2	*Olsen*
23/10	h	Vålerenga	L	0-3	
30/10	a	Sarpsborg	D	2-2	*Olsen 2*
06/11	h	Odd	W	3-1	*Sigurdarson, Moussa, Espejord*

No	Name	Nat	DoB	Pos	Aps	(s)	Gls
15	Magnus Andersen		28/05/86	M	27	(1)	2
3	Kent-Are Antonsen		12/02/95	D	20	(4)	1
30	Runar Espejord		26/02/96	A	15	(7)	5
7	Morten Gamst Pedersen		08/09/81	M	4	(4)	
4	Henrik Gjesdal		19/07/93	D	5	(4)	1
26	Jostein Gundersen		02/04/96	D	11	(6)	3
24	Mikael Ingebrigtsen		21/07/96	A	15	(9)	3
11	Jonas Johansen		22/03/85	M	9	(5)	
20	Christer Johnsgård		17/02/87	A		(2)	
1	Gudmund Kongshavn		23/01/91	G	14		
6	Christian Landu Landu		25/01/92	M	26	(2)	
12	Filip Lončarić	CRO	17/09/86	G	16		
27	Fredrik Michalsen		15/09/96	M	2	(4)	
9	Sofien Moussa	TUN	06/02/88	A	12	(8)	5
25	Lasse Nilsen		21/02/95	D	5	(6)	
14	Hans Nordbye		16/01/87	D	24	(2)	
10	Thomas Lehne Olsen		29/06/91	A	24	(6)	8
17	Aron Sigurdarson	ISL	08/10/93	A	12	(12)	3
22	Simen Wangberg		06/05/91	D	23	(3)	2
8	Ulrik Yttergård Jenssen		17/07/96	M	11	(1)	1
5	Magnar Ødegaard		11/05/93	D	27		
23	Gjermund Åsen		22/05/91	M	28	(1)	2

Viking FK

1899 • Viking (16,300) • viking-fk.no

Major honours
Norwegian League (8) 1958, 1972, 1973, 1974, 1975, 1979, 1982, 1991; Norwegian Cup (5) 1953, 1959, 1979, 1989, 2001

Coach: Kjell Jonevret (SWE)

2016

Date		Opponent		Score	Scorers
14/03	a	Vålerenga	W	2-0	*Sverrisson, Bringaker*
20/03	h	Sarpsborg	D	0-0	
02/04	a	Start	W	1-0	*Abdullahi*
10/04	h	Odd	L	0-2	
17/04	a	Aalesund	W	2-1	*Bringaker, Abdullahi*
20/04	h	Brann	L	0-1	
24/04	a	Rosenborg	L	0-4	
01/05	h	Haugesund	W	3-2	*Bringaker, Abdullahi 2*
07/05	h	Tromsø	W	2-0	*Sverrisson, Adegbenro*
12/05	a	Stabæk	L	0-1	
16/05	h	Sogndal	D	0-0	
22/05	a	Lillestrøm	W	2-1	*Abdullahi, Adegbenro*
29/05	h	Bodø/Glimt	W	2-0	*Sverrisson, Kronberg*
03/07	a	Molde	W	1-0	*Bringaker*
09/07	h	Strømsgodset	L	0-1	
16/07	a	Haugesund	L	1-4	*Haukås*
24/07	a	Odd	D	2-2	*Ibrahim, Pedersen*
07/08	a	Sogndal	W	2-1	*Sverrisson, Adegbenro*
11/08	h	Rosenborg	L	0-2	
14/08	h	Stabæk	D	2-2	*Aasheim, Pedersen*
21/08	a	Tromsø	L	1-2	*Pedersen*
28/08	h	Lillestrøm	D	2-2	*Danielsen, Ryerson*
10/09	a	Brann	D	0-0	
17/09	h	Molde	W	1-0	*Pedersen*
24/09	a	Sarpsborg	L	0-1	
02/10	h	Start	W	2-0	*og (Heikkilä), Jørgensen*
14/10	a	Strømsgodset	D	1-1	*Ibrahim*
21/10	h	Aalesund	L	2-3	*Pedersen, Bringaker*
30/10	a	Bodø/Glimt	W	2-0	*Sale, Danielsen (p)*
06/11	h	Vålerenga	L	0-2	

No	Name	Nat	DoB	Pos	Aps	(s)	Gls
20	Tor André Aasheim		06/03/96	A	10	(4)	1
8	Suleiman Abdullahi	NGA	10/12/96	A	13		5
7	Samuel Adegbenro	NGA	03/12/95	A	27	(1)	3
1	Iven Austbø		22/02/85	G	30		
27	Mathias Bringaker		30/01/97	A	8	(16)	5
11	Zymer Bytyqi		14/09/96	M	7	(11)	
14	André Danielsen		20/01/85	D	29		2
8	Chris Dawson	WAL	02/09/94	M	5	(4)	
28	Kristoffer Haugen		21/02/94	D	26		
19	Michael Haukås		21/11/86	M	12	(12)	1
16	Abdisalam Ibrahim		01/05/91	M	25		2
4	Joackim Jørgensen		20/09/88	M	20	(3)	1
22	Claes Kronberg	DEN	19/04/87	D	25	(3)	1
2	Rasmus Martinsen		14/04/96	D		(1)	
6	Karol Mets	EST	16/05/93	D	29		
30	Stian Michalsen		28/03/97	M		(1)	
9	Patrick Pedersen	DEN	25/11/91	A	18	(10)	5
18	Julian Ryerson		17/11/97	D	12	(6)	1
25	Usman Sale	NGA	27/08/95	M	2	(7)	1
5	Anthony Soares	USA	28/11/88	D	12		
13	Per-Magnus Steiring		07/02/97	D	1	(2)	
10	Björn Daníel Sverrisson	ISL	29/05/90	M	19	(1)	4
17	Aniekpeno Udo	NGA	11/11/96	A		(3)	

NORWAY

Vålerenga Fotball

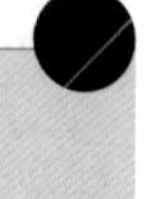

1913 • Ullevaal (27,200) • vif-fotball.no

Major honours

Norwegian League (5) 1965, 1981, 1983, 1984, 2005; Norwegian Cup (4) 1980, 1997, 2002, 2008

Coach: Kjetil Rekdal

2016					
14/03	h	Viking	L	0-2	
20/03	a	Sogndal	L	0-1	
02/04	h	Rosenborg	L	0-2	
09/04	a	Stabæk	L	1-2	*Brown*
17/04	h	Tromsø	W	4-0	*Brown, Holm (p), Zahid, Lindkvist*
21/04	a	Molde	L	0-4	
24/04	h	Start	W	2-0	*Brown 2*
30/04	a	Lillestrøm	L	0-2	
08/05	h	Sarpsborg	W	3-0	*Jääger, Brown, Ómarsson*
11/05	a	Bodø/Glimt	D	0-0	
16/05	h	Haugesund	L	0-1	
22/05	a	Strømsgodset	L	2-3	*Brown, og (Abu)*
29/05	a	Aalesund	D	2-2	*Ómarsson, Wæhler*
03/07	h	Odd	L	0-1	
09/07	a	Brann	L	1-4	*Abdellaoue*
15/07	h	Sogndal	D	1-1	*Zahid*
24/07	a	Start	W	4-2	*Tollås, Zahid, Grindheim, Johansen*
01/08	h	Molde	W	3-0	*Abdellaoue, S Larsen, Zahid*
07/08	a	Sarpsborg	W	2-0	*Lindkvist, Abdellaoue*
13/08	h	Brann	W	3-2	*Zahid 2, Juklerød*
19/08	h	Bodø/Glimt	D	1-1	*Juklerød*
28/08	a	Odd	W	2-1	*Abdellaoue 2*
10/09	h	Strømsgodset	D	1-1	*Juklerød*
16/09	a	Haugesund	D	1-1	*Zahid*
25/09	h	Aalesund	L	0-1	
02/10	a	Rosenborg	L	1-3	*og (Reginiussen)*
16/10	h	Stabæk	D	1-1	*Lindkvist*
23/10	a	Tromsø	W	3-0	*Johansen, Tollås, Zahid*
30/10	h	Lillestrøm	D	1-1	*Sakor*
06/11	a	Viking	W	2-0	*Abdellaoue, Grødem*

No	Name	Nat	DoB	Pos	Aps	(s)	Gls
25	Mohammed Abdellaoue		23/10/85	A	15	(3)	6
39	Ernest Agyiri	GHA	06/03/98	A	1		
8	Jesper Arvidsson	SWE	01/01/85	D	5	(1)	
23	Sander Berge		14/02/98	M	23	(2)	
26	Deshorn Brown	JAM	22/12/90	A	13	(1)	6
17	Niklas Castro		08/01/96	A	4	(5)	
28	Thomas Elsebutangen		29/03/98	A		(2)	
30	Aslak Falch		25/05/92	G	13		
19	Christian Grindheim		17/07/83	M	26	(2)	1
29	Magnus Grødem		14/08/98	A	1		1
7	Daniel Fredheim Holm		30/07/85	M	13	(7)	1
20	Henrik Kjelsrud Johansen		22/03/93	A	5	(9)	2
21	Simen Juklerød		18/05/94	M	14	(5)	3
3	Enar Jääger	EST	18/11/84	D	11		1
18	Rino Falk Larsen		14/02/96	M		(3)	
6	Simon Larsen		01/06/88	D	26		1
8	Magnus Lekven		13/01/88	M	6	(4)	
9	Rasmus Lindkvist	SWE	16/05/90	D	25	(2)	3
5	Robert Lundström	SWE	01/11/89	D	16	(4)	
15	Markus Nakkim		21/07/96	D	6		
33	Anders Nedrebø		19/08/88	M	1	(4)	
22	Elías Már Ómarsson	ISL	18/01/95	A	5	(8)	2
16	Vajebah Sakor		14/04/96	M	13	(8)	1
1	Marcus Sandberg	SWE	07/11/90	G	17		
43	Mathusan Sandrakumar		21/02/98	D		(1)	
14	Herman Stengel		26/08/95	M	11	(14)	
4	Jonatan Tollås		01/07/90	D	11		2
24	Kjetil Wæhler		16/03/76	D	21		1
10	Ghayas Zahid		18/11/94	M	28		8

Top goalscorers

19	Christian Gytkjær (Rosenborg)
13	Mustafa Abdellaoue (Aalesund)
11	Fitim Azemi (Bodø/Glimt)
10	Torbjørn Agdestein (Haugesund)
	Olivier Occéan (Odd)
8	Fred Friday (Lillestrøm)
	Mike Jensen (Rosenborg)
	Marcus Pedersen (Strømsgodset)
	Thomas Lehne Olsen (Tromsø)
	Ghayas Zahid (Vålerenga)

Promoted clubs

Kristiansund BK

2003 • Kristiansund Stadion (3,000) • kristiansundbk.no

Coach: Christian Michelsen

Sandefjord Fotball

1998 • Komplett.no Arena (5,982) • sandefjordfotball.no

Coach: Lars Bohinen

Second level final table 2016

		Pld	W	D	L	F	A	Pts
1	Kristiansund BK	30	19	5	6	47	30	62
2	Sandefjord Fotball	30	18	5	7	54	35	59
3	FK Jerv	30	15	8	7	47	34	53
4	Sandnes Ulf	30	15	6	9	55	28	51
5	Kongsvinger IL	30	14	7	9	56	42	49
6	Mjøndalen IF	30	13	10	7	49	38	49
7	Strømmen IF	30	13	8	9	46	45	47
8	Levanger FK	30	13	6	11	52	46	45
9	Ranheim IL	30	11	6	13	45	48	39
10	Åsane Fotball	30	10	8	12	36	37	38
11	Fredrikstad FK	30	8	9	13	34	48	33
12	Ullensaker/Kisa IL	30	8	8	14	47	50	32
13	Bryne FK	30	7	9	14	33	48	30
14	IL Hødd Fotball	30	8	6	16	31	57	30
15	KFUM Oslo	30	6	8	16	31	48	26
16	Raufoss Fotball	30	6	3	21	33	62	21

Promotion/Relegation play-offs

(05/11/16)
Sandnes Ulf 0-2 Kongsvinger

(19/11/16)
Jerv 2-1 Mjøndalen
NB First half played on 05/11/16

(26/11/16)
Jerv 2-1 Kongsvinger

(30/11/16 & 04/12/16)
Jerv 1-0 Stabæk
Stabæk 2-0 Jerv
(Stabæk 2-1)

DOMESTIC CUP

Norgesmesterskapet 2016

FIRST ROUND

(12/04/16)
Aurskog-Høland 1-4 Lillestrøm
Stord 1-8 Haugesund

(13/04/16)
Brattvåg 2-1 Florø *(aet)*
Brumunddal 1-6 Ullensaker/Kisa
Charlottenlund 3-4 Levanger *(aet)*
Eidsvold Turn 0-0 HamKam *(aet; 3-2 on pens)*
Elverum 2-1 Tynset
Flisa 0-1 Kongsvinger
Fløya 0-6 Bodø/Glimt
Fram Larvik 3-0 Fløy
Frøyland 0-1 Egersund
Funnefoss/Vormsund 2-3 Asker
Fyllingen 1-1 Varegg *(aet; 2-4 on pens)*
Førde 0-0 Brann *(aet; 5-4 on pens)*
Gjøvik-Lyn 3-0 Raufoss
Godøy 1-6 Hødd
Halsen 0-8 Sandefjord
Harstad 0-1 Mjølner
Herd 2-2 Kristiansund BK *(aet; 4-2 on pens)*
Junkeren 0-1 Tromsdalen
KIL/Hemne 1-2 Nardo
Kolstad 0-2 Byåsen
Kongsberg 1-8 Strømsgodset
Korsvoll 1-4 Stabæk
Kvik Halden 3-1 Ullern
Kristiansund FK 0-6 Molde
Kråkerøy 0-2 KFUM Oslo
Lillehammer 3-2 Nybergsund *(aet)*
Lyn 0-7 Tromsø
Løten 1-4 Vålerenga
Nesodden 0-6 Moss
Notodden 3-1 Lørenskog
Os 2-4 Lysekloster *(aet)*
Riska 2-3 Bryne
Salangen 0-1 Finnsnes
Sandnessjøen 0-1 Mo
Senja 1-1 Skjervøy *(aet; 10-9 on pens)*
Skeid 1-3 Strømmen
Sola 1-3 Vidar
Sotra 1-3 Fana
Sparta Sarpsborg 2-0 Follo
Spjelkavik 0-1 Aalesund
Stjørdals-Blink 3-3 Strindheim *(aet; 4-3 on pens)*
Tertnes 0-5 Åsane
Tollnes 0-5 Odd
Trygg/Lade 0-2 Ranheim
Tønsberg 5-2 Oppsal
Valdres 1-5 Sogndal
Vardeneset 1-5 Viking
Vestfossen 2-4 Bærum
Vestsiden-Askøy 2-4 Nest-Sotra
Vigør 1-2 Jerv *(aet)*
Ørn Horten 0-3 Kjelsås
Østsiden 2-3 Fredrikstad *(aet)*
Åfjord 0-3 Rosenborg
Åkra 0-3 Vard Haugesund
Ås 0-5 Sarpsborg

(14/04/16)
Arendal 2-3 Vindbjart *(aet)*
Donn 0-8 Start
Grorud 4-2 Pors Grenland *(aet)*
Holmen 1-4 Mjøndalen
Hønefoss 1-0 Frigg Oslo
Kirkenes 2-5 Alta *(aet)*
Madla 1-2 Sandnes Ulf

SECOND ROUND

(26/04/16)
Eidsvold Turn 0-1 Strømsgodset

(27/04/16)
Asker 2-2 Mjøndalen *(aet; 4-3 on pens)*
Brattvåg 1-0 Hødd
Byåsen 1-5 Rosenborg
Bærum 2-0 Ullensaker/Kisa
Elverum 0-1 Kongsvinger
Egersund 0-2 Sandnes Ulf
Fana 1-3 Nest-Sotra
Fram Larvik 0-3 Start
Gjøvik-Lyn 2-3 KFUM Oslo
Grorud 2-3 Molde
Herd 3-4 Aalesund *(aet)*
Hønefoss 1-3 Vålerenga
Kjelsås 0-1 Sandefjord
Lillehammer 0-2 Lillestrøm
Lysekloster 3-6 Åsane *(aet)*
Mjølner 0-2 Tromsø
Mo 0-6 Bodø/Glimt
Moss 1-2 Fredrikstad
Nardo 2-1 Ranheim
Stjørdals-Blink 1-0 Levanger
Strømmen 3-1 Notodden
Tønsberg 0-6 Odd
Vard Haugesund 0-3 Viking
Vidar 2-2 Bryne *(aet; 5-4 on pens)*
Vindbjart 2-0 Jerv

(28/04/16)
Alta 3-1 Finnsnes *(aet)*
Førde 0-1 Sogndal
Kvik Halden 0-3 Sarpsborg
Sparta Sarpsborg 1-7 Stabæk
Tromsdalen 5-3 Senja
Varegg 2-4 Haugesund

THIRD ROUND

(03/05/16)
Brattvåg 1-1 Aalesund *(aet; 5-4 on pens)*

(04/05/16)
Asker 2-3 Odd
Bærum 0-3 Stabæk
KFUM Oslo 0-2 Vålerenga
Kongsvinger 1-1 Strømmen *(aet; 4-3 on pens)*
Nardo 1-4 Rosenborg
Nest-Sotra 1-0 Sogndal
Sandefjord 1-0 Lillestrøm
Sandnes Ulf 3-1 Start
Stjørdals-Blink 2-1 Molde
Tromsdalen 2-3 Tromsø
Vidar 2-1 Viking
Vindbjart 1-2 Strømsgodset
Åsane 1-4 Haugesund

(05/05/16)
Alta 1-4 Bodø/Glimt
Fredrikstad 1-3 Sarpsborg

FOURTH ROUND

(25/05/16)
Bodø/Glimt 3-3 Haugesund *(aet; 7-6 on pens)*
Kongsvinger 1-0 Brattvåg
Rosenborg 3-1 Nest-Sotra
Sandefjord 2-1 Sandnes Ulf
Sarpsborg 3-0 Stjørdals-Blink
Strømsgodset 1-0 Stabæk
Tromsø 3-2 Odd *(aet)*
Vålerenga 3-1 Vidar

QUARTER-FINALS

(21/09/16)
Bodø/Glimt 4-0 Sarpsborg *(Manzon 5, 43, Berg 77, Osvold 90+1)*

Tromsø 1-1 Rosenborg *(Olsen 53; Gytkjær 90+1) (aet; 3-5 on pens)*

(22/09/16)
Kongsvinger 2-1 Sandefjord *(Ellingsen 8, C Hansen 70og; Larsen 58)*

Strømsgodset 2-0 Vålerenga *(Pedersen 45+2, 50p)*

SEMI-FINALS

(26/10/16)
Rosenborg 2-0 Bodø/Glimt *(Midtsjø 22, Skjelvik 90+2)*

(27/10/16)
Strømsgodset 1-2 Kongsvinger *(Tokstad 64; Pålerud 55, Røyrane 73)*

FINAL

(20/11/16)
Ullevaal stadion, Oslo
ROSENBORG BK 4 *(Helland 12, 63, 65, Reginiussen 50)*
KONGSVINGER IL 0
Referee: *Hansen*
ROSENBORG: *Hansen, Svensson, Reginiussen, Eyjólfsson, Skjelvik, Jensen, Konradsen, Midtsjø (Vilhjálmsson 80), Helland (Gersbach 82), Gytkjær, Bakenga (Rashani 70)*
KONGSVINGER: *Fredrikson, Pålerud, Ovlien, Suslov (Nystuen 72), Richardsen, Ellingsen, Holter (Wennberg 68), Røyrane, Hélio Pinto, Güven (Niang 66), Maikel*

Rosenborg completed the double with a comfortable 4-0 win over second-tier Kongsvinger in the cup final

POLAND

Polski Związek Piłki Nożnej (PZPN)

Address Bitwy Warszawskiej 1920 r.7
PL-02 366 Warszawa
Tel +48 22 551 2300
Fax +48 22 551 2240
E-mail pzpn@pzpn.pl
Website pzpn.pl

President Zbigniew Boniek
General secretary Maciej Sawicki
Media officer Janusz Basałaj
Year of formation 1919
National stadium PGE Narodowy, Warsaw (58,145)

EKSTRAKLASA CLUBS

 1 Arka Gdynia

 2 MKS Cracovia Kraków

 3 GKS Górnik Łęczna

 4 Jagiellonia Białystok

 5 Korona Kielce

 6 KKS Lech Poznań

 7 KS Lechia Gdańsk

 8 Legia Warszawa

 9 KS Nieciecza

 10 GKS Piast Gliwice

 11 MKS Pogoń Szczecin

 12 Ruch Chorzów

 13 WKS Śląsk Wrocław

 14 Wisła Kraków

 15 Wisła Płock

16 Zagłębie Lubin

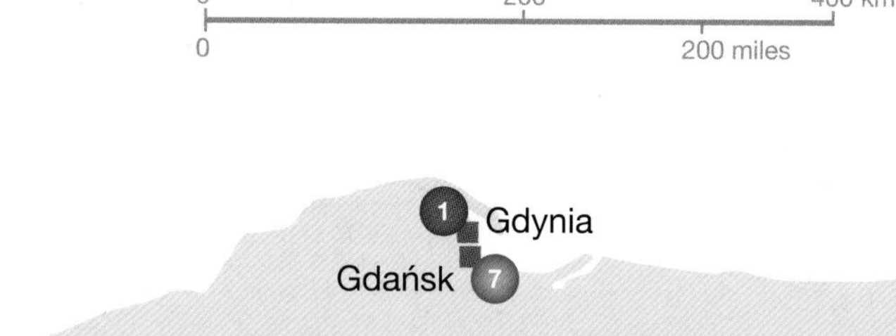

 17 Sandecja Nowy Sącz

 18 Górnik Zabrze

KEY

- UEFA Champions League
- UEFA Europa League
- Promoted
- Relegated

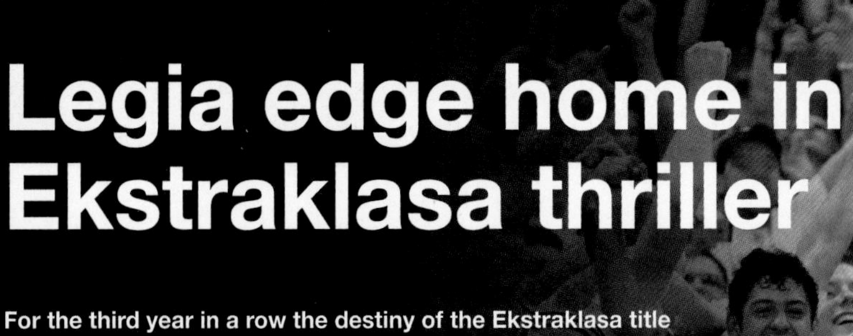

Legia edge home in Ekstraklasa thriller

For the third year in a row the destiny of the Ekstraklasa title race was undecided until the final day. In 2016/17, however, the tension was greater than ever as no fewer than four teams went into their 37th and last fixture still in with a chance of being crowned champions of Poland.

It was Legia Warszawa, the defending champions, who eventually emerged triumphant, leaving Jagiellonia Białystok, Lech Poznań and Lechia Gdańsk to rue their missed opportunity. Lech's disappointment was compounded by a third successive Polish Cup final defeat, going down 2-1 after extra time to Arka Gdynia.

Comeback triumph gives Warsaw giants their 12th title

Four teams all in contention on gripping final day

Lewandowski fires national side towards Russia

Domestic league

Legia's road to a successful title defence was anything but straightforward. The appointment of Albanian coach Besnik Hasi proved ill-starred, with the ex-Anderlecht boss being sacked as early as mid-September following a run of just two wins in nine league games, which left the champions in an unthinkable 14th place. The ship was soon steadied by replacement coach Jacek Magiera, and by the winter break Legia had rocketed into third spot – just four points adrift of unlikely joint leaders Jagiellonia and Lechia.

Piotr Nowak's Lechia beat Michał Probierz's Jagiellonia 3-0 in the first match after the break, but the team from the Baltic port lost three games in a row to allow Jagiellonia to return to top spot, where they remained until the 30-game split. With points duly halved (and rounded upwards), Probierz's side were one point in front of a resurgent Legia, two ahead of Lech and three in advance of Lechia.

The last seven matchdays were high on intrigue. Jagiellonia continued to hold sway for the first three of them, but when Lechia routed the leaders 4-0 in Gdansk, it was Legia's turn to go top for the first time. Despite the mid-term departure of strikers Nemanja Nikolić and Aleksandar Prijović, Magiera's side had continued to score freely, but it was now that their defence, marshalled by Polish international Michał Pazdań, came to the fore. Clean sheets were kept in each of the team's final six fixtures, accounting for 14 precious points.

The two 0-0 draws in that sequence proved especially valuable, the first, at Jagiellonia, keeping Legia on top, the second, at home to Lechia, securing the title. Had Legia lost to Lechia, or Jagiellonia not been simultaneously held 2-2 at home by Lech, there would have been a new name on the Ekstraklasa trophy. Instead, Legia's was inscribed for the fourth time in five seasons and 12th in all. With no defeats in nine games against their three rivals, it was a triumph beyond dispute.

Jagiellonia, Lech and Legia all finished two points in arrears, and head-to-head records classified them in that order, which was tough on Lechia as they missed out on Europe. More sorrowful still were Ruch Chorzów, who finished last and were relegated, with fellow record Polish champions Górnik Zabrze moving in the opposite direction after just a year away.

Domestic cup

The Polish Cup final took place a month before the Ekstraklasa ended, and there was a dramatic conclusion to that competition too as Lech, defeated by Legia in the previous two finals, came to grief again, losing 2-1 to outsiders Arka after three goals were scored in the second period of extra time.

Europe

Hasi's stay at Legia might have been brief, but he did take the club into the group stage of the UEFA Champions League for the first time in 21 years. An opening 6-0 home defeat by Borussia Dortmund nonetheless hastened his exit, and after an 8-4 loss in the return fixture it was no mean feat for the Polish champions to recover and beat Sporting CP to prolong their European journey in the UEFA Europa League.

National team

Robert Lewandowski scored 11 goals in Poland's first six 2018 FIFA World Cup qualifiers, including hat-tricks against Denmark and Romania, to take Adam Nawałka's team to the brink of the finals in Russia. With 16 points in the bag – six more than their closest pursuers – it seemed inconceivable that Poland would not finish on top of Group E. The Bayern München striker ended the season with 46 international goals – just two short of Włodzimierz Lubański's national record – having found the net in a remarkable 11 successive European Qualifiers.

DOMESTIC SEASON AT A GLANCE

Ekstraklasa 2016/17 final table

		Pld	Home W	D	L	F	A	Away W	D	L	F	A	Total W	D	L	F	A	Pts
1	**Legia Warszawa**	**37**	**8**	**8**	**3**	**32**	**15**	**13**	**2**	**3**	**38**	**16**	**21**	**10**	**6**	**70**	**31**	**44**
2	Jagiellonia Białystok	37	11	4	4	36	17	10	4	4	28	22	21	8	8	64	39	42
3	KKS Lech Poznań	37	12	4	3	29	12	8	5	5	33	17	20	9	8	62	29	42
4	KS Lechia Gdańsk	37	15	2	2	44	16	5	6	7	13	21	20	8	9	57	37	42
5	Korona Kielce	37	11	2	5	33	20	3	3	13	14	45	14	5	18	47	65	28
6	Wisła Kraków	37	11	3	4	33	18	3	3	13	21	39	14	6	17	54	57	26
7	MKS Pogoń Szczecin	37	8	7	3	35	21	3	6	10	16	33	11	13	13	51	54	25
8	KS Nieciecza	37	6	5	7	18	21	7	2	10	17	34	13	7	17	35	55	25
9	Zagłębie Lubin	37	6	6	7	28	27	8	5	5	23	18	14	11	12	51	45	34
10	GKS Piast Gliwice	37	8	5	5	27	26	4	5	10	18	28	12	10	15	45	54	31
11	WKS Śląsk Wrocław	37	6	6	7	28	27	6	4	8	21	25	12	10	15	49	52	29
12	Wisła Płock	37	7	5	7	26	27	5	6	7	23	30	12	11	14	49	57	28
13	Arka Gdynia	37	6	5	8	26	27	4	4	10	18	33	10	9	18	44	60	24
14	MKS Cracovia Kraków	37	7	6	5	28	18	1	9	9	17	34	8	15	14	45	52	24
15	GKS Górnik Łęczna	37	6	3	9	24	26	3	7	9	23	37	9	10	18	47	63	22
16	Ruch Chorzów	37	5	4	9	20	27	5	4	10	22	35	10	8	19	42	62	19

NB League splits into top and bottom halves after 30 games, after which the clubs play exclusively against teams in their group. Points obtained during the regular season are halved (and rounded upwards); Ruch Chorzów – 4 pts deducted.

European qualification 2017/18

Champion: Legia Warszawa (second qualifying round)

Cup winner: Arka Gdynia (third qualifying round)

Jagiellonia Białystok (first qualifying round)
KKS Lech Poznań (first qualifying round)

Top scorer Marcin Robak (Lech) & Marco Paixão (Lechia), 18 goals
Relegated clubs Ruch Chorzów, GKS Górnik Łęczna
Promoted clubs Sandecja Nowy Sącz, Górnik Zabrze
Cup final Arka Gdynia 2-1 KKS Lech Poznań (aet)

Player of the season

Vadis Odjidja-Ofoe
(Legia Warszawa)

After a disappointing spell in England with Norwich City, ex-Club Brugge midfielder Odjidja-Ofoe left in 2016 to join Legia. It was to be a smart move, for not only did the 28-year-old rediscover his best form, he also went on to win the first major honour of his career. With four goals and 14 assists, he was the Polish champions' most prominent performer, his alliance with Frenchman Thibault Moulin serving the club well both in attack and defence. His first season in Warsaw, however, was to be his last as he joined Greek champions Olympiacos in the summer.

Newcomer of the season

Jarosław Niezgoda
(Ruch Chorzów)

Some prolific goalscoring for lower-league outfit Wisła Puławy earned Niezgoda a 2016 transfer to Legia Warszawa, but after just one Ekstraklasa appearance he was sent out on loan to Ruch. Four goals in as many games during the autumn raised awareness of the 21-year-old's talent and by the middle of March he had augmented his tally to double figures. Unfortunately, as his goals dried up, so did Ruch's and the 14-time champions were relegated. He ended the season playing on home soil for Poland at the 2017 UEFA European Under-21 Championship.

Team of the season
(4-4-2)

Coach: Bartoszek *(Korona)*

NATIONAL TEAM

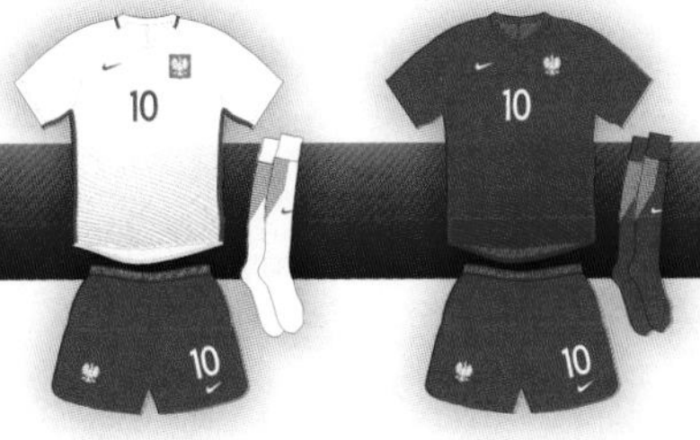

International tournament appearances

FIFA World Cup (7) 1938, 1974 (3rd), 1978 (2nd phase), 1982 (3rd), 1986 (2nd round), 2002, 2006

UEFA European Championship (3) 2008, 2012, 2016 (qtr-finals)

Top five all-time caps

Michał Żewłakow (102); Grzegorz Lato (100); Kazimierz Deyna (97); Jacek Bąk & Jacek Krzynówek (96)

Top five all-time goals

Włodzimierz Lubański (48); **Robert Lewandowski** (46); Grzegorz Lato (45); Kazimierz Deyna (41); Ernest Pol (39)

Results 2016/17

04/09/16	Kazakhstan (WCQ)	A	Astana	D	2-2	*Kapustka (9), Lewandowski (35p)*
08/10/16	Denmark (WCQ)	H	Warsaw	W	3-2	*Lewandowski (20, 36p, 48)*
11/10/16	Armenia (WCQ)	H	Warsaw	W	2-1	*Mkoyan (48og), Lewandowski (90+5)*
11/11/16	Romania (WCQ)	A	Bucharest	W	3-0	*Grosicki (11), Lewandowski (82, 90+1p)*
14/11/16	Slovenia	H	Wroclaw	D	1-1	*Teodorczyk (79)*
26/03/17	Montenegro (WCQ)	A	Podgorica	W	2-1	*Lewandowski (40), Piszczek (82)*
10/06/17	Romania (WCQ)	H	Warsaw	W	3-1	*Lewandowski (29p, 57, 62p)*

Appearances 2016/17

Coach: Adam Nawałka	23/10/57		KAZ	DEN	ARM	ROU	Svn	MNE	ROU	Caps	Goals
Łukasz Fabiański	18/04/85	Swansea (ENG)	G	G	G	G		G		39	-
Łukasz Piszczek	03/06/85	Dortmund (GER)	D	D		D		D	D	55	3
Kamil Glik	03/02/88	Monaco (FRA)	D	D	D	D		D		51	3
Bartosz Salamon	01/05/91	Cagliari (ITA)	D							9	-
Maciej Rybus	19/08/89	Lyon (FRA)	D	s74	M					44	2
Jakub Błaszczykowski	14/12/85	Wolfsburg (GER)	M	M89	D	M	s66	M	M	91	18
Grzegorz Krychowiak	29/01/90	Paris (FRA)	M	M	M	M	M46		s44	45	2
Piotr Zieliński	20/05/94	Napoli (ITA)	M	M	M	M80	s61	M	M81	23	3
Arkadiusz Milik	28/02/94	Napoli (ITA)	M	M46					s72	34	11
Bartosz Kapustka	23/12/96	Leicester (ENG)	M83		s70		M71			14	3
Robert Lewandowski	21/08/88	Bayern (GER)	A	A	A	A		A	A	87	46
Karol Linetty	02/02/95	Sampdoria (ITA)	s83	s46		M70		M78	M72	15	1
Thiago Cionek	21/04/86	Palermo (ITA)		D	D		D	s92	D	12	-
Artur Jędrzejczyk	04/11/87	Krasnodar (RUS) /Legia		D	D34	D	D	D	D	30	3
Kamil Grosicki	08/06/88	Rennes (FRA) /Hull (ENG)		M74	M70	M89	s71	M95	M	50	9
Sławomir Peszko	19/02/85	Lechia		s89		s89		s95		43	2
Łukasz Teodorczyk	03/06/91	Anderlecht (BEL)			A85	s80	A	s78	s81	13	4
Paweł Wszołek	30/04/92	QPR (ENG)			s34		M66			10	2
Kamil Wilczek	14/01/88	Brøndby (DEN)			s85		s46			2	-
Michał Pazdan	21/09/87	Legia				D	D	D	D	26	-
Krzysztof Mączyński	23/05/87	Wisła Kraków				s70	M83	M92	M44	24	1
Artur Boruc	20/02/80	Bournemouth (ENG)					G46			64	-
Bartosz Bereszyński	12/07/92	Legia					D			3	-
Jacek Góralski	21/09/92	Jagiellonia					M61			1	-
Wojciech Szczęsny	18/04/90	Roma (ITA)					s46		G	29	-
Damian Dąbrowski	27/08/92	Cracovia					s83			1	-

POLAND

EUROPE

Legia Warszawa

Second qualifying round - HŠK Zrinjski (BIH)
A 1-1 *Nikolić (49)*
Malarz (Cierzniak 46), Jodłowiec, Lewczuk, Guilherme, Duda (Alexandrov 60), Nikolić (Prijović 76), Hloušek, Kucharczyk, Rzeźniczak, Broź, Moulin. Coach: Besnik Hasi (ALB)
H 2-0 *Nikolić (28p, 62)*
Malarz, Pazdan, Jodłowiec, Lewczuk, Guilherme (Hämäläinen 15), Nikolić (Kopczyński 75), Hloušek, Kucharczyk (Brzyski 84), Broź, Moulin, Alexandrov. Coach: Besnik Hasi (ALB)

Third qualifying round - FK AS Trenčín (SVK)
A 1-0 *Nikolić (69)*
Malarz, Pazdan, Jodłowiec (Hämäläinen 85), Lewczuk, Nikolić (Prijović 75), Kopczyński, Brzyski, Kucharczyk, Bereszyński, Moulin, Alexandrov (Broź 89). Coach: Besnik Hasi (ALB)
H 0-0
Malarz, Pazdan, Jodłowiec, Lewczuk, Langil (Alexandrov 69), Nikolić (Prijović 78), Hloušek, Kopczyński, Kucharczyk, Bereszyński (Broź 56), Moulin. Coach: Besnik Hasi (ALB)

Play-offs - Dundalk FC (IRL)
A 2-0 *Nikolić (56p), Prijović (90+4)*
Malarz, Pazdan, Jodłowiec, Lewczuk, Langil (Alexandrov 88), Odjidja-Ofoe (Kopczyński 76), Nikolić (Prijović 83), Hloušek, Kucharczyk, Broź, Moulin. Coach: Besnik Hasi (ALB)
H 1-1 *Kucharczyk (90+2)*
Malarz, Pazdan, Jodłowiec, Lewczuk, Langil (Guilherme 65), Odjidja-Ofoe, Nikolić (Bereszyński 71), Hloušek, Kucharczyk, Broź, Moulin (Prijović 90+3). Coach: Besnik Hasi (ALB)
Red card: Hloušek 67

Group F
Match 1 - Borussia Dortmund (GER)
H 0-6
Malarz, Jodłowiec, Czerwiński, Dąbrowski, Guilherme, Langil, Odjidja-Ofoe, Kazaishvili (Alexandrov 66), Bereszyński, Moulin (Radović 76), Prijović (Nikolić 63). Coach: Besnik Hasi (ALB)
Match 2 - Sporting Clube de Portugal (POR)
A 0-2
Malarz, Jodłowiec, Czerwiński, Guilherme, Langil (Alexandrov 46), Nikolić (Odjidja-Ofoe 60), Hloušek, Bereszyński, Rzeźniczak, Radović, Moulin (Kopczyński 86). Coach: Jacek Magiera (POL)
Match 3 - Real Madrid CF (ESP)
A 1-5 *Radović (22p)*
Malarz, Jodłowiec, Czerwiński, Guilherme (Kazaishvili 74), Odjidja-Ofoe, Hloušek, Kucharczyk, Bereszyński, Rzeźniczak, Radović (Nikolić 74), Moulin (Kopczyński 81). Coach: Jacek Magiera (POL)
Match 4 - Real Madrid CF (ESP)
H 3-3 *Odjidja-Ofoe (40), Radović (58), Moulin (83)*
Malarz, Pazdan, Guilherme, Odjidja-Ofoe (Jodłowiec 86), Nikolić (Kucharczyk 69), Hloušek, Kopczyński, Bereszyński, Rzeźniczak, Radović (Prijović 77), Moulin. Coach: Jacek Magiera (POL)
Match 5 - Borussia Dortmund (GER)
A 4-8 *Prijović (10, 24), Kucharczyk (57), Nikolić (83)*
Cierzniak, Pazdan, Czerwiński, Guilherme (Jodłowiec 55), Odjidja-Ofoe (Nikolić 75), Kopczyński, Kucharczyk, Bereszyński, Rzeźniczak, Radović, Prijović (Wieteska 69). Coach: Jacek Magiera (POL)
Match 6 - Sporting Clube de Portugal (POR)
H 1-0 *Guilherme (30)*
Malarz, Pazdan, Guilherme (Kucharczyk 62), Odjidja-Ofoe, Hloušek, Kopczyński, Bereszyński, Rzeźniczak, Radović (Dąbrowski 90+4), Moulin, Prijović (Hämäläinen 86). Coach: Jacek Magiera (POL)

Round of 32 - AFC Ajax (NED)
H 0-0
Malarz, Pazdan, Jodłowiec, Dąbrowski, Odjidja-Ofoe (Hämäläinen 82), Kazaishvili (Guilherme 59), Hloušek, Kopczyński, Necid (Kucharczyk 58), Broź, Radović. Coach: Jacek Magiera (POL)
A 0-1
Malarz, Pazdan, Jodłowiec (Moulin 57), Dąbrowski, Guilherme (Necid 73), Odjidja-Ofoe, Kazaishvili, Hloušek, Kopczyński (Chima 82), Kucharczyk, Broź. Coach: Jacek Magiera (POL)

GKS Piast Gliwice

Second qualifying round - IFK Göteborg (SWE)
H 0-3
Szmatuła, Mráz, Pietrowski, Murawski, Barišić (Mak 72), Živec, Mokwa (Masłowski 46), Szeliga (Jankowski 61), Bukata, Hebert, Girdvainis. Coach: Radoslav Látal (CZE)
A 0-0
Rusov, Flis (Szeliga 69), Jankowski (Barišić 81), Moskwik, Masłowski (Murawski 73), Mak, Gerard Badía, Mokwa, Sedlar, Bukata, Korun. Coach: Jiří Neček (CZE)

Zagłębie Lubin

First qualifying round - PFC Slavia Sofia (BUL)
A 0-1
Poláček, Dąbrowski, Čotra, Todorovski, Woźniak, Janoszka (Janus 74), Kubicki, K Piątek (Papadopulos 68), L Piątek, Guldan, Vlasko (Rakowski 83). Coach: Piotr Stokowiec (POL)
H 3-0 *Guldan (20), L Piątek (64), Dąbrowski (81)*
Poláček, Dąbrowski, Čotra, Todorovski, Woźniak, Janoszka (Tosik 85), Kubicki, K Piątek (Papadopulos 77), L Piątek, Guldan, Vlasko (Rakowski 61). Coach: Piotr Stokowiec (POL)

Second qualifying round - FK Partizan (SRB)
A 0-0
Poláček, Dąbrowski, Čotra, Todorovski (Tosik 73), Woźniak, Janoszka (Vlasko 82), Rakowski (K Piątek 66), Kubicki, Papadopulos, L Piątek, Guldan. Coach: Piotr Stokowiec (POL)
Red card: Papadopulos 56
H 0-0 (aet; 4-3 on pens)
Poláček, Dąbrowski, Čotra, Todorovski, Woźniak, Janoszka (Janus 74), Rakowski (Vlasko 61), Kubicki, K Piątek (Tosik 101), L Piątek, Guldan. Coach: Piotr Stokowiec (POL)

Third qualifying round - SønderjyskE (DEN)
H 1-2 *Janoszka (45+2)*
Poláček, Dąbrowski, Čotra, Todorovski, Woźniak, Janoszka (Janus 73), Kubicki, K Piątek (Papadopulos 79), L Piątek, Guldan, Vlasko (Starzyński 46). Coach: Piotr Stokowiec (POL)
A 1-1 *Guldan (22)*
Poláček, Dąbrowski, Čotra, Todorovski, Janus (Janoszka 67), Starzyński, Kubicki, K Piątek (Papadopulos 72), L Piątek, Guldan, Vlasko (Tosik 85). Coach: Piotr Stokowiec (POL)

MKS Cracovia Kraków

First qualifying round - KF Shkëndija (MKD)
A 0-2
Sandomierski, Litauszki, Bejan, Wójcicki, Vestenický (Wdowiak 61), Cetnarski (Čovilo 61), Dąbrowski, Wołąkiewicz (Karachanakov 77), Deleu, Budziński, Jendrišek. Coach: Jacek Zieliński (POL)
H 1-2 *Demiri (68og)*
Sandomierski, Čovilo, Wójcicki, Vestenický (Wdowiak 46), Dąbrowski (Cetnarski 46), Wołąkiewicz, Polczak, Deleu, Budziński, Jendrišek, Karachanakov (Steblecki 50). Coach: Jacek Zieliński (POL)

DOMESTIC LEAGUE CLUB-BY-CLUB

Arka Gdynia

1929 • Miejski (15,139) • arka.gdynia.pl

Major honours
Polish Cup (2) 1979, 2017

Coach: Grzegorz Niciński; (10/04/17) Leszek Ojrzyński

Date		Opponent	Res	Score	Scorers
2016					
18/07	a	Nieciecza	L	0-2	
22/07	h	Wisła Kraków	W	3-0	*Kakoko, Zjawiński, Marcus Vinícius*
29/07	h	Ruch	W	3-0	*Zjawiński, Božok, Siemaszko*
05/08	a	Jagiellonia	L	1-4	*Sołdecki*
13/08	h	Śląsk	W	2-0	*Marcus Vinícius (p), Siemaszko*
20/08	a	Legia	W	3-1	*Marcus Vinícius, Marciniak 2*
27/08	h	Zagłębie	D	1-1	*Božok*
10/09	a	Korona	L	0-1	
19/09	h	Cracovia	W	1-0	*Marcus Vinícius*
25/09	a	Lech	D	0-0	
01/10	h	Piast	L	1-2	*Marcus Vinícius (p)*
15/10	a	Górnik	D	0-0	
21/10	h	Pogoń	L	0-3	
30/10	h	Lechia	D	1-1	*Błąd*
04/11	a	Wisła Płock	D	0-0	
20/11	h	Niecieczа	L	1-3	*Marcus Vinícius (p)*
26/11	a	Wisła Kraków	L	1-5	*Warcholak*
05/12	a	Ruch	W	2-1	*Marcjanik, Marcus Vinícius (p)*
12/12	h	Jagiellonia	L	2-3	*Łukasiewicz, Siemaszko*
18/12	a	Śląsk	W	2-0	*Siemaszko, Marcjanik*
2017					
11/02	h	Legia	L	0-1	
20/02	a	Zagłębie	L	0-1	
24/02	h	Korona	W	4-1	*Formella, Szwoch (p), Siemaszko, Hofbauer*
04/03	a	Cracovia	D	1-1	*Trytko*
10/03	h	Lech	L	1-4	*Siemaszko*
18/03	a	Piast	L	2-3	*Szwoch (p), Siemaszko*
01/04	h	Górnik	L	2-4	*Formella, Barišić*
08/04	a	Pogoń	L	1-5	*Trytko*
17/04	a	Lechia	L	1-2	*Hofbauer*
22/04	h	Wisła Płock	D	1-1	*Siemaszko*
28/04	h	Piast	D	1-1	*Szwoch (p)*
08/05	a	Cracovia	L	0-2	
12/05	h	Górnik	W	1-0	*Siemaszko*
16/05	h	Wisła Płock	L	0-1	
19/05	a	Śląsk	L	1-4	*Sołdecki*
27/05	h	Ruch	D	1-1	*Siemaszko*
02/06	a	Zagłębie	W	3-1	*Siemaszko, Formella, Warcholak*

No	Name	Nat	DoB	Pos	Aps	(s)	Gls
9	Paweł Abbott		05/05/82	A	5	(6)	
90	Josip Barišić	CRO	14/11/86	A	2	(3)	1
7	Adrian Błąd		16/04/91	M	3	(11)	1
19	Miroslav Božok	SVK	19/10/84	M	23	(7)	2
77	Dariusz Formella		21/10/95	M	12	(5)	3
20	Dominik Hofbauer	AUT	19/09/90	M	22	(3)	2
13	Konrad Jałocha		09/05/91	G	28		
21	Yannick Kakoko	GER	26/01/90	M	24	(1)	1
6	Antoni Łukasiewicz		26/06/83	M	24	(2)	1
17	Adam Marciniak		28/09/88	D	24	(6)	2
29	Michał Marcjanik		15/12/94	D	30		2
8	Marcus Vinícius	BRA	29/03/84	M	26	(4)	7
14	Michał Nalepa		24/03/95	M		(10)	
11	Rafał Siemaszko		11/09/86	A	12	(18)	11
3	Krzysztof Sobieraj		25/08/81	D	22		
2	Tadeusz Socha		15/02/88	D	17	(1)	
4	Dawid Sołdecki		29/04/87	D	20		2
1	Pāvels Šteinbors	LVA	21/09/85	G	9		
32	Przemysław Stolc		03/07/94	D	4	(2)	
10	Mateusz Szwoch		19/03/93	M	32	(4)	3
26	Przemysław Trytko		26/08/87	A	5	(6)	2
23	Marcin Warcholak		08/08/89	D	25	(1)	2
25	Paweł Wojkowski		27/08/94	M	3	(1)	
18	Rashid Yussuff	ENG	23/09/89	M	1	(11)	
45	Luka Zarandia	GEO	17/02/96	M	1	(6)	
33	Damian Zbozień		25/04/89	D	20	(1)	
22	Dariusz Zjawiński		19/08/86	A	13	(2)	2

MKS Cracovia Kraków

1906 • im. Józefa Piłsudskiego (15,016) • cracovia.pl

Major honours
Polish League (5) 1921, 1930, 1932, 1937, 1948

Coach: Jacek Zieliński

Date		Opponent	Res	Score	Scorers
2016					
17/07	h	Piast	W	5-1	*Čovilo 2, Szczepaniak, Deleu, Budziński*
24/07	a	Niecieczа	L	2-3	*Jendrišek, Dąbrowski*
31/07	a	Górnik	D	0-0	
05/08	h	Wisła Kraków	W	2-1	*Budziński, Szczepaniak*
12/08	a	Lech	L	1-2	*Čovilo*
20/08	h	Ruch	D	1-1	*Čovilo*
27/08	a	Pogoń	D	1-1	*Szczepaniak*
09/09	h	Lechia	L	0-1	
19/09	a	Arka	L	0-1	
24/09	a	Zagłębie	D	1-1	*Budziński*
02/10	h	Korona	W	6-0	*Szczepaniak, Piątek 2, Budziński, Čovilo, Wdowiak*
14/10	h	Wisła Płock	W	1-0	*Wójcicki*
22/10	a	Śląsk	D	2-2	*Čovilo, Dąbrowski (p)*
30/10	h	Jagiellonia	L	1-3	*Cetnarski (p)*
06/11	a	Legia	L	0-2	
18/11	a	Piast	D	2-2	*Čovilo, Budziński*
25/11	h	Niecieczа	L	1-3	*Szczepaniak*
04/12	h	Górnik	D	1-1	*Piątek*
10/12	a	Wisła Kraków	D	1-1	*Piątek*
17/12	h	Lech	D	1-1	*Budziński*
2017					
10/02	a	Ruch	W	1-0	*Piątek*
19/02	h	Pogoń	D	1-1	*Piątek*
25/02	a	Lechia	L	2-4	*Piątek 2*
04/03	h	Arka	D	1-1	*Mihalík*
13/03	h	Zagłębie	D	1-1	*Budziński*
19/03	a	Korona	L	0-3	
01/04	a	Wisła Płock	L	1-4	*Steblecki*
07/04	h	Śląsk	W	1-0	*Polczak*
15/04	a	Jagiellonia	D	0-0	
22/04	h	Legia	L	1-2	*Dąbrowski (p)*
01/05	a	Zagłębie	D	2-2	*Szczepaniak, Piątek*
08/05	h	Arka	W	2-0	*Piątek, Dąbrowski (p)*
13/05	a	Wisła Płock	D	1-1	*Steblecki*
16/05	a	Górnik	L	0-3	
19/05	h	Ruch	W	2-0	*Steblecki, Piątek*
27/05	a	Śląsk	L	0-2	
02/06	h	Piast	L	0-1	

No	Name	Nat	DoB	Pos	Aps	(s)	Gls
18	Hubert Adamczyk		23/02/98	M	2	(2)	
6	Florin Bejan	ROU	28/03/91	D	1		
2	Tomasz Brzyski		10/01/82	D	18	(3)	
27	Marcin Budziński		06/07/90	M	32	(1)	7
10	Mateusz Cetnarski		06/07/88	M	17	(10)	1
5	Miroslav Čovilo	SRB	06/05/86	M	21		7
28	Jakub Čunta	SVK	28/08/96	D	1	(1)	
14	Damian Dąbrowski		27/08/92	M	30	(1)	4
26	Deleu	BRA	01/03/84	D	21	(3)	1
87	Diego	BUL	21/05/92	D	10	(2)	
8	Milan Dimun	SVK	19/09/96	M	2	(4)	
44	Paweł Jaroszyński		02/10/94	D	9	(3)	
62	Erik Jendrišek	SVK	26/10/86	A	20	(11)	1
13	Radosław Kanach		03/04/99	M	5		
67	Bartosz Kapustka		23/12/96	M		(2)	
4	Róbert Litauszki	HUN	15/03/90	D	2	(1)	
22	Piotr Malarczyk		01/08/91	D	19	(1)	
23	Jaroslav Mihalík	SVK	27/07/94	M	4	(6)	1
33	Kamil Pestka		22/08/98	D		(1)	
99	Krzysztof Piątek		01/07/95	A	21	(6)	11
24	Piotr Polczak		25/08/86	D	24	(4)	1
29	Grzegorz Sandomierski		05/09/89	G	36		
17	Sebastian Steblecki		16/01/92	M	13	(13)	3
19	Krystian Stępniowski		05/12/92	G	1		
20	Mateusz Szczepaniak		23/01/91	M	29	(5)	6
9	Tomáš Vestenický	SVK	06/04/96	A	6	(16)	
96	Mateusz Wdowiak		28/08/96	M	2	(11)	1
21	Hubert Wołąkiewicz		21/10/85	D	29		
7	Jakub Wójcicki		09/07/88	D	32		1

GKS Górnik Łęczna

1979 • Arena Lublin, Lublin (15,500) • gornik.leczna.pl

Coach: Andrzej Rybarski; (02/12/16) (Sławomir Nazaruk); (15/12/16) Franciszek Smuda

Date		Opponent	Res	Score	Scorers
2016					
16/07	a	Ruch	L	1-2	*og (Skaba)*
25/07	h	Lechia	L	1-2	*og (Milinković-Savić)*
31/07	h	Cracovia	D	0-0	
06/08	a	Niecieczа	L	1-2	*Szmatiuk*
13/08	h	Legia	W	1-0	*Ubiparip*
21/08	a	Zagłębie	D	0-0	
27/08	h	Jagiellonia	L	0-2	
10/09	a	Piast	D	3-3	*Piesio, Javi Hernández 2*
17/09	h	Korona	W	4-0	*Bonin 2, Śpiączka, Juriša*
24/09	a	Pogoń	D	1-1	*Śpiączka*
30/09	h	Lech	L	1-2	*Grzelczak*
15/10	h	Arka	D	0-0	
22/10	a	Wisła Płock	W	2-1	*Piesio, Drewniak*
29/10	h	Śląsk	L	0-3	
06/11	a	Wisła Kraków	L	2-3	*Danielewicz, Drewniak (p)*
19/11	h	Ruch	L	0-4	
28/11	a	Lechia	L	0-3	
04/12	a	Cracovia	D	1-1	*og (Čovilo)*
10/12	h	Niecieczа	W	3-0	*Sasin, Drewniak (p), Grzelczak*
18/12	a	Legia	L	0-5	
2017					
17/02	a	Jagiellonia	L	0-5	
26/02	h	Piast	W	1-0	*Grzelczak*
03/03	a	Korona	L	1-2	*Śpiączka*
07/03	h	Zagłębie	L	0-1	
12/03	h	Pogoń	D	2-2	*Bonin, Śpiączka*
19/03	a	Lech	D	0-0	
01/04	a	Arka	W	4-2	*Javi Hernández, Bonin, Śpiączka, Drewniak*
08/04	h	Wisła Płock	L	2-3	*Pitry, Grzelczak*
15/04	a	Śląsk	D	2-2	*Drewniak, Javi Hernández*
22/04	h	Wisła Kraków	W	3-1	*Śpiączka 2, Bonin*
29/04	a	Śląsk	W	2-0	*Śpiączka, Bonin*
06/05	h	Wisła Płock	L	2-3	*Grzelczak, Ubiparip*
12/05	a	Arka	L	0-1	
16/05	h	Cracovia	W	3-0	*Leandro, Dźwigała, Śpiączka*
20/05	a	Piast	L	1-2	*Dźwigała*
27/05	h	Zagłębie	L	1-3	*Gérson*
02/06	a	Ruch	D	2-2	*Śpiączka, Grzelczak*

No	Name	Nat	DoB	Pos	Aps	(s)	Gls
37	Stefan Askovski	MKD	24/02/92	D		(1)	
13	Josimar Atoche	PER	29/09/89	M	8	(1)	
93	Łukasz Bogusławski		11/02/93	D	2	(2)	
15	Grzegorz Bonin		02/12/83	M	36		6
77	Krzysztof Danielewicz		26/07/91	M	12	(5)	1
25	Szymon Drewniak		11/07/93	M	26	(3)	5
12	Nika Dzalamidze	GEO	06/01/92	M	7	(4)	
16	Adam Dźwigała		25/09/95	M	12		2
4	Gérson	BRA	07/01/92	D	24		1
9	Piotr Grzelczak		02/03/88	A	19	(13)	6
21	Dariusz Jarecki		23/03/81	D	3	(3)	
10	Javi Hernández	ESP	06/06/89	M	20	(8)	4
11	Slaven Juriša	CRO	28/01/92	M	1	(3)	1
3	Aleksander Komor		24/06/94	D	17	(1)	
2	Leandro	BRA	29/12/83	D	34		1
1	Wojciech Małecki		11/10/90	G	12		
14	Gabriel Matei	ROU	26/02/90	D	14	(1)	
22	Łukasz Mierzejewski		31/08/82	D	1	(1)	
8	Grzegorz Piesio		17/07/88	M	16	(12)	2
45	Przemysław Pitry		11/09/81	A	16	(7)	1
20	Kamil Poźniak		11/12/89	M		(1)	
17	Radosław Pruchnik		11/10/86	D	9		
79	Sergiusz Prusak		01/05/79	G	25		
6	Paweł Sasin		02/10/83	D	25	(4)	1
23	Maciej Szmatiuk		09/05/80	D	18	(2)	1
18	Bartosz Śpiączka		19/08/91	A	25	(7)	10
5	Łukasz Tymiński		08/11/90	M	16	(6)	
19	Vojo Ubiparip	SRB	10/05/88	A	6	(11)	2
7	Dragomir Vukobratović	SRB	12/05/88	M	3	(2)	

POLAND

Jagiellonia Białystok

1920 • Miejski (22,432) • jagiellonia.pl

Major honours
Polish Cup (1) 2010

Coach: Michał Probierz

Date	Opponent	Result	Scorers
2016			
16/07 a	Legia	D 1-1	*Černych*
23/07 h	Ruch	W 4-1	*Grzyb, Górski, Vassiljev, Świderski*
29/07 a	Lech	W 2-0	*Vassiljev 2 (1p)*
05/08 h	Arka	W 4-1	*Vassiljev 2 (1p), Černych 2*
15/08 a	Wisła Płock	L 0-1	
21/08 h	Lechia	L 0-1	
27/08 a	Górnik	W 2-0	*Černych, Romanchuk*
11/09 h	Wisła Kraków	W 2-1	*Khomchenovskiy, Vassiljev*
16/09 a	Śląsk	W 4-0	*Frankowski 2, Vassiljev, Romanchuk*
25/09 a	Korona	W 2-1	*Frankowski, Runje*
02/10 h	Pogoń	D 0-0	
16/10 a	Nieciecza	D 0-0	
23/10 h	Zagłębie	L 1-2	*Góralski*
30/10 a	Cracovia	W 3-1	*Vassiljev (p), Černych, Frankowski*
05/11 h	Piast	W 2-0	*Romanchuk, Frankowski*
18/11 h	Legia	L 1-4	*Romanchuk*
26/11 a	Ruch	W 2-1	*Černych, Vassiljev*
04/12 h	Lech	W 2-1	*Świderski, Černych*
12/12 a	Arka	W 3-2	*Černych, Guti, Vassiljev*
17/12 h	Wisła Płock	L 1-2	*Černych*
2017			
12/02 a	Lechia	L 0-3	
17/02 h	Górnik	W 5-0	*Khomchenovskiy, Vassiljev 2 (1p), Romanchuk, Černych*
25/02 a	Wisła Kraków	L 1-3	*Szymański*
05/03 h	Śląsk	W 4-1	*Frankowski 2, Vassiljev, Góralski*
11/03 h	Korona	W 4-1	*Frankowski, og (Borjan), Černych 2*
18/03 a	Pogoń	D 0-0	
02/04 h	Nieciecza	W 1-0	*Sheridan (p)*
07/04 a	Zagłębie	W 4-3	*Sheridan 2 (1p), Runje, Novikovas*
15/04 h	Cracovia	D 0-0	
22/04 a	Piast	W 1-0	*Sheridan*
30/04 h	Pogoń	W 1-0	*Sheridan*
05/05 a	Korona	D 1-1	*Novikovas*
13/05 h	Wisła Kraków	W 2-0	*Sheridan, Khomchenovskiy*
17/05 a	Lechia	L 0-4	
21/05 h	Legia	D 0-0	
28/05 a	Nieciecza	W 2-1	*Sheridan 2*
04/06 h	Lech	D 2-2	*Góralski, Novikovas*

No	Name	Nat	DoB	Pos	Aps	(s)	Gls
8	Łukasz Burliga		10/05/88	D	18	(3)	
10	Fedor Černych	LTU	21/05/91	A	34		12
21	Przemysław Frankowski		12/04/95	M	31	(4)	8
2	Ziggy Gordon	SCO	23/04/93	D	8	(1)	
4	Jacek Góralski		21/09/92	M	29		3
18	Maciej Górski		01/03/90	A	2	(8)	1
22	Rafał Grzyb		16/01/83	M	28	(4)	1
16	Guti	BRA	29/06/91	D	34		1
25	Marián Kelemen	SVK	07/12/79	G	36		
7	Dmytro Khomchenovskiy	UKR	16/04/90	M	15	(13)	3
27	Patryk Klimala		05/08/98	A		(3)	
11	Karol Mackiewicz		01/06/92	M	5	(3)	
13	Przemysław Mystkowski		25/04/98	A		(12)	
9	Arvydas Novikovas	LTU	18/12/90	M	7	(8)	3
6	Taras Romanchuk	UKR	14/11/91	M	28	(5)	5
17	Ivan Runje	CRO	09/10/90	D	32		2
18	Cillian Sheridan	IRL	23/02/89	A	14		8
3	Jonatan Straus		30/06/94	D	4	(1)	
23	Damian Szymański		16/06/95	M	3	(12)	1
20	Dawid Szymonowicz		07/07/95	D	5	(1)	
28	Karol Świderski		23/01/97	A	8	(18)	2
77	Piotr Tomasik		31/10/87	D	32	(1)	
5	Konstantin Vassiljev	EST	16/08/84	M	29	(3)	13
14	Marek Wasiluk		03/06/87	D	4	(2)	
96	Damian Węglarz		21/03/96	G	1		

Korona Kielce

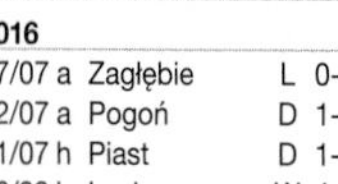

1973 • Miejski Arena Kielc (15,550) • korona-kielce.pl

Coach: Tomasz Wilman; (25/10/16) (Sławomir Grzesik); (10/11/16) Maciej Bartoszek

Date	Opponent	Result	Scorers
2016			
17/07 a	Zagłębie	L 0-4	
22/07 a	Pogoń	D 1-1	*Pylypchuk*
31/07 h	Piast	D 1-1	*Sekulski*
06/08 h	Lech	W 4-1	*Sekulski 2 (1p), Palanca, Grzelak*
12/08 a	Lechia	L 2-3	*Możdżeń, Diaw*
22/08 h	Wisła Kraków	W 1-0	*Kiełb*
26/08 a	Wisła Płock	W 2-1	*Sekulski, Dejmek*
10/09 h	Arka	W 1-0	*Sekulski*
17/09 a	Górnik	L 0-4	
25/09 h	Jagiellonia	L 1-2	*Palanca*
02/10 a	Cracovia	L 0-6	
17/10 h	Śląsk	L 1-2	*Dani Abalo*
24/10 a	Ruch	L 0-4	
28/10 h	Legia	L 2-4	*Palanca (p), Grzelak*
05/11 a	Nieciecza	W 3-1	*Dejmek, Pylypchuk, Aankour*
21/11 h	Zagłębie	W 2-1	*Palanca 2*
26/11 h	Pogoń	W 4-1	*Marković 2, Aankour 2*
03/12 a	Piast	L 0-1	
11/12 a	Lech	L 0-1	
17/12 h	Lechia	W 2-0	*Kiełb 2*
2017			
11/02 a	Wisła Kraków	L 0-2	
18/02 h	Wisła Płock	W 4-2	*Mitsanski, Kiełb 2 (2p), Palanca*
24/02 a	Arka	L 1-4	*Mitsanski*
03/03 h	Górnik	W 2-1	*Kiełb 2 (1p)*
11/03 a	Jagiellonia	L 1-4	*Mitsanski*
19/03 h	Cracovia	W 3-0	*Żubrowski, Górski, Kiełb*
31/03 a	Śląsk	L 0-3	
10/04 h	Ruch	W 1-0	*og (Grodzicki)*
17/04 a	Legia	D 0-0	
22/04 h	Nieciecza	L 0-1	
28/04 a	Lech	L 2-3	*Możdżeń, Kiełb (p)*
05/05 h	Jagiellonia	D 1-1	*Pylypchuk*
14/05 a	Lechia	D 0-0	
17/05 h	Wisła Kraków	W 3-2	*Dejmek, Możdżeń, Kiełb (p)*
22/05 a	Nieciecza	W 2-0	*Możdżeń, Rymaniak*
28/05 h	Legia	L 0-1	
04/06 a	Pogoń	L 0-3	

No	Name	Nat	DoB	Pos	Aps	(s)	Gls
10	Nabil Aankour	MAR	09/08/93	M	27	(2)	3
4	Adrian Bednarski		05/10/94	D		(1)	
82	Milan Borjan	CAN	23/10/87	G	14		
7	Marcin Cebula		06/12/95	M	10	(13)	
9	Dani Abalo	ESP	29/09/87	M	9	(12)	1
32	Radek Dejmek	CZE	02/02/88	D	32		3
23	El Hadji Diaw	SEN	31/12/94	D	15	(1)	1
28	Vladislavs Gabovs	LVA	13/07/87	D	12	(5)	
33	Maciej Gostomski		27/09/88	G	8		
16	Maciej Górski		01/03/90	A	4	(7)	1
27	Rafał Grzelak		07/08/88	D	31		2
19	Ken Kallaste	EST	31/08/88	D	24		
15	Jacek Kiełb		10/01/88	M	24	(5)	10
55	Jakub Kotarzewski		22/01/94	M	1	(7)	
99	Bartosz Kwiecień		07/05/94	D	9		
1	Zbigniew Małkowski		19/01/78	G	7		
6	Vanja Marković	SRB	20/06/94	M	14	(16)	2
20	Iliyan Mitsanski	BUL	20/12/85	A	8		3
88	Michał Mokrzycki		29/12/97	M		(1)	
8	Mateusz Możdżeń		14/03/91	M	35	(1)	4
37	Jakub Mrozik		21/06/93	M	4	(5)	
17	Miguel Palanca	ESP	18/12/87	M	27	(6)	6
30	Michal Peškovič	SVK	08/02/82	G	8		
90	Piotr Poński		10/04/98	A		(1)	
77	Michał Przybyła		01/07/94	A	4	(8)	
5	Serhiy Pylypchuk	UKR	26/11/84	M	19	(7)	3
26	Bartosz Rymaniak		13/11/89	D	32		1
44	Łukasz Sekulski		03/11/90	A	10		5
93	Michał Smolarczyk		11/09/93	A	1	(1)	
13	Dmitri Verkhovtsov	BLR	10/10/86	D	6		
11	Tomasz Zając		14/07/95	M		(6)	
14	Jakub Żubrowski		21/03/92	M	12	(1)	1

KKS Lech Poznań

1922 • INEA (42,837) • lechpoznan.pl

Major honours
Polish League (7) 1983, 1984, 1990, 1992, 1993, 2010, 2015; Polish Cup (5) 1982, 1984, 1988, 2004, 2009

Coach: Jan Urban; (30/08/16) Nenad Bjelica (CRO)

Date	Opponent	Result	Scorers
2016			
15/07 a	Śląsk	D 0-0	
24/07 h	Zagłębie	L 0-2	
29/07 h	Jagiellonia	L 0-2	
06/08 a	Korona	L 1-4	*Robak*
12/08 h	Cracovia	W 2-1	*Bednarek, Robak*
19/08 a	Nieciecza	D 0-0	
28/08 h	Piast	W 2-0	*Formella, Gajos*
11/09 h	Pogoń	W 3-1	*Robak 2 (1p), Tetteh*
18/09 a	Lechia	L 1-2	*Robak*
25/09 h	Arka	D 0-0	
30/09 a	Górnik	W 2-1	*Gajos, Makuszewski*
16/10 h	Wisła Kraków	D 1-1	*Jevtic*
22/10 a	Legia	L 1-2	*Robak (p)*
29/10 h	Wisła Płock	W 2-0	*Kownacki, Robak (p)*
04/11 a	Ruch	W 5-0	*Jevtic, Kownacki, Majewski, Robak (p), Pawłowski*
20/11 h	Śląsk	W 3-0	*Jevtic, Robak 2 (1p)*
25/11 a	Zagłębie	W 3-0	*Arajuuri, Jevtic, Kownacki*
04/12 a	Jagiellonia	L 1-2	*Arajuuri*
11/12 h	Korona	W 1-0	*Kownacki*
17/12 a	Cracovia	D 1-1	*Nielsen*
2017			
10/02 h	Nieciecza	W 3-0	*Kownacki (p), Robak (p), Jevtic (p)*
18/02 a	Piast	W 3-0	*Majewski 2, Kownacki*
24/02 a	Pogoń	W 3-0	*Kownacki 2, Robak*
05/03 h	Lechia	W 1-0	*Majewski*
10/03 a	Arka	W 4-1	*Gajos, Jevtic, Kownacki, Robak*
19/03 h	Górnik	D 0-0	
31/03 a	Wisła Kraków	D 0-0	
09/04 h	Legia	L 1-2	*Kędziora*
15/04 a	Wisła Płock	W 3-0	*Robak 2, Majewski*
22/04 h	Ruch	W 3-0	*og (Surma), Gajos, Jevtic*
28/04 h	Korona	W 3-2	*Jevtic, Robak 2 (2p)*
07/05 a	Nieciecza	W 3-0	*Răduț, og (Gutkovskis), Majewski*
14/05 h	Pogoń	W 2-0	*Robak, Trałka*
17/05 a	Legia	L 0-2	
21/05 h	Lechia	D 0-0	
28/05 h	Wisła Kraków	W 2-1	*Majewski, Makuszewski*
04/06 a	Jagiellonia	D 2-2	*Majewski, Trałka*

No	Name	Nat	DoB	Pos	Aps	(s)	Gls
23	Paulus Arajuuri	FIN	15/06/88	D	12		2
35	Jan Bednarek		12/04/96	D	27		1
19	Nicki Bille Nielsen	DEN	07/02/88	A	3	(5)	
1	Jasmin Burić	BIH	18/02/87	G	7		
20	Dariusz Formella		21/10/95	A	3	(8)	1
14	Maciej Gajos		19/03/91	M	29	(5)	4
2	Robert Gumny		04/06/98	D	5	(1)	
10	Darko Jevtic	SUI	08/02/93	M	24	(7)	8
29	Kamil Jóźwiak		22/04/98	M		(6)	
5	Tamás Kádár	HUN	14/03/90	D	16	(1)	
4	Tomasz Kędziora		11/06/94	D	36		1
22	Volodymyr Kostevych	UKR	23/10/92	D	17		
24	Dawid Kownacki		14/03/97	M	16	(11)	9
86	Radosław Majewski		15/12/86	M	31	(6)	8
17	Maciej Makuszewski		29/09/89	M	26	(7)	2
3	Lasse Nielsen	DEN	03/03/87	D	14	(5)	1
8	Szymon Pawłowski		04/11/86	M	16	(6)	1
27	Tymoteusz Puchacz		23/01/99	D		(1)	
30	Matúš Putnocký	SVK	01/11/84	G	30		
18	Mihai Răduț	ROU	18/03/90	M	4	(9)	1
11	Marcin Robak		29/11/82	A	21	(16)	18
55	Abdul Aziz Tetteh	GHA	25/05/90	M	20	(6)	1
8	Paweł Tomczyk		04/05/98	A		(4)	
6	Łukasz Trałka		11/05/84	M	29	(5)	2
28	Marcin Wasielewski		23/08/94	M	1	(1)	
26	Maciej Wilusz		25/09/88	D	20		

KS Lechia Gdańsk

1945 • PGE Arena Gdańsk (43,165) • lechia.pl

Major honours
Polish Cup (1) 1983

Coach: Piotr Nowak

Date	H/A	Opponent	Res	Score	Scorers
2016					
15/07	a	Wisła Płock	L	1-2	*Marco Paixão*
25/07	a	Górnik	W	2-1	*Krasić, Kuświk*
30/07	h	Wisła Kraków	W	3-1	*Flávio Paixão 2, Marco Paixão*
06/08	a	Śląsk	D	0-0	
12/08	h	Korona	W	3-2	*Kuświk 2, og (Dejmek)*
21/08	a	Jagiellonia	W	1-0	*Kovačević*
28/08	h	Nieciecza	L	1-2	*Flávio Paixão*
09/09	a	Cracovia	W	1-0	*Marco Paixão*
18/09	h	Lech	W	2-1	*Marco Paixão, og (Wilusz)*
24/09	h	Ruch	W	2-1	*Peszko, Flávio Paixão*
01/10	a	Legia	L	0-3	
15/10	a	Zagłębie	W	2-1	*Janicki, Kuświk*
23/10	h	Piast	W	3-2	*Peszko, Flávio Paixão 2 (1p)*
30/10	a	Arka	D	1-1	*Marco Paixão*
05/11	h	Pogoń	D	1-1	*Wolski*
19/11	h	Wisła Płock	W	2-1	*Kuświk 2*
28/11	h	Górnik	W	3-0	*Marco Paixão, Wolski, Haraslín*
03/12	a	Wisła Kraków	L	0-3	
09/12	h	Śląsk	W	3-0	*Flávio Paixão 2, Kuświk*
17/12	a	Korona	L	0-2	
2017					
12/02	h	Jagiellonia	W	3-0	*Marco Paixão 2, Flávio Paixão (p)*
17/02	a	Nieciecza	D	1-1	*Peszko*
25/02	h	Cracovia	W	4-2	*Borysiuk, Flávio Paixão (p), Kuświk, Wojtkowiak*
05/03	a	Lech	L	0-1	
11/03	a	Ruch	L	1-2	*Marco Paixão*
19/03	h	Legia	L	1-2	*Maloča*
02/04	h	Zagłębie	W	1-0	*Marco Paixão*
09/04	a	Piast	D	1-1	*Maloča*
17/04	h	Arka	W	2-1	*Marco Paixão, og (Marcjanik)*
22/04	a	Pogoń	L	1-3	*Krasić*
29/04	h	Nieciecza	W	2-0	*Haraslín, Marco Paixão*
06/05	a	Wisła Kraków	W	1-0	*og (Załuska)*
14/05	h	Korona	D	0-0	
17/05	h	Jagiellonia	W	4-0	*Marco Paixão 3 (2p), Haraslín*
21/05	a	Lech	D	0-0	
28/05	h	Pogoń	W	4-0	*Marco Paixão 3 (1p), Wiśniewski*
04/06	a	Legia	D	0-0	

No	Name	Nat	DoB	Pos	Aps	(s)	Gls
24	Mateusz Bąk		24/02/83	G		(1)	
16	Ariel Borysiuk		29/07/91	M	14		1
20	Michał Chrapek		03/04/92	M	12	(6)	
28	Flávio Paixão	POR	19/09/84	M	24	(9)	10
38	Milen Gamakov	BUL	12/04/94	M	4		
35	Gérson	BRA	07/01/92	D	1		
17	Lukáš Haraslín	SVK	26/05/96	M	11	(15)	3
2	Rafał Janicki		05/07/92	D	26	(2)	1
30	João Nunes	POR	19/11/95	D	17	(6)	
4	Aleksandar Kovačević	SRB	09/01/92	M	3	(2)	1
7	Miloš Krasić	SRB	01/11/84	M	34		2
1	Dušan Kuciak	SVK	21/05/85	G	17		
11	Grzegorz Kuświk		23/05/87	A	20	(13)	8
9	Michał Mak		14/11/91	M		(5)	
22	Mario Maloča	CRO	04/05/89	D	31		2
19	Marco Paixão	POR	19/09/84	A	27	(8)	18
10	Sebastian Mila		10/07/82	M	2	(6)	
32	Vanja Milinković-Savić	SRB	20/02/97	G	18		
13	Bartłomiej Pawłowski		13/11/92	M	1	(5)	
21	Sławomir Peszko		19/02/85	M	28	(1)	3
77	Damian Podleśny		18/05/95	G	2		
6	Simeon Slavchev	BUL	25/09/93	M	17	(6)	
41	Paweł Stolarski		28/01/96	D	12	(12)	
99	Gino van Kessel	CUW	09/03/93	A	2	(1)	
5	Steven Vitoria	CAN	11/01/87	D	5	(3)	
3	Jakub Wawrzyniak		07/07/83	D	35		
14	Piotr Wiśniewski		11/08/82	M		(4)	1
23	Grzegorz Wojtkowiak		26/01/84	D	12	(4)	1
27	Rafał Wolski		10/11/92	M	32	(2)	2

Legia Warszawa

1916 • Wojska Polskiego im. Marszałka Józefa Piłsudskiego (31,284) • legia.com

Major honours
Polish League (12) 1955, 1956, 1969, 1970, 1994, 1995, 2002, 2006, 2013, 2014, 2016, 2017; Polish Cup (18) 1955, 1956, 1964, 1966, 1973, 1980, 1981, 1989, 1990, 1994, 1995, 1997, 2008, 2011, 2012, 2013, 2015, 2016

Coach: Besnik Hasi (ALB);
(19/09/16) (Aleksandar Vuković (SRB));
(24/09/16) Jacek Magiera

Date	H/A	Opponent	Res	Score	Scorers
2016					
16/07	h	Jagiellonia	D	1-1	*Alexandrov*
23/07	h	Śląsk	D	0-0	
30/07	a	Wisła Płock	W	3-2	*Prijović, Kucharczyk, Lewczuk*
07/08	h	Piast	D	0-0	
13/08	a	Górnik	L	0-1	
20/08	h	Arka	L	1-3	*Hämäläinen*
28/08	a	Ruch	W	2-0	*Nikolić, og (Grodzicki)*
10/09	a	Nieciecza	L	1-2	*Nikolić*
18/09	h	Zagłębie	L	2-3	*Czerwiński, Langil*
23/09	a	Wisła Kraków	D	0-0	
01/10	h	Lechia	W	3-0	*Guilherme 2, Nikolić*
14/10	a	Pogoń	L	2-3	*Radović 2*
22/10	h	Lech	W	2-1	*Nikolić, Hämäläinen*
28/10	a	Korona	W	4-2	*Guilherme, Nikolić, og (Rymaniak), Prijović*
06/11	h	Cracovia	W	2-0	*Nikolić, Radović*
18/11	a	Jagiellonia	W	4-1	*Guilherme, Odjidja-Ofoe, Prijović, Kucharczyk*
27/11	a	Śląsk	W	4-0	*Radović, og (Filipe Gonçalves), Prijović 2*
02/12	h	Wisła Płock	D	2-2	*Nikolić, Hämäläinen*
11/12	a	Piast	W	5-1	*Radović 2, Nikolić 2, Odjidja-Ofoe*
18/12	h	Górnik	W	5-0	*Nikolić 3, Radović, Hämäläinen*
2017					
11/02	a	Arka	W	1-0	*Jodłowiec*
19/02	h	Ruch	L	1-3	*Radović*
26/02	h	Nieciecza	D	1-1	*Radović*
03/03	a	Zagłębie	W	3-1	*Moulin, Dąbrowski, Szymański*
12/03	h	Wisła Kraków	W	1-0	*Radović*
19/03	a	Lechia	W	2-1	*Kucharczyk 2*
01/04	h	Pogoń	W	2-0	*Kucharczyk, Odidja-Ofoe*
09/04	a	Lech	W	2-1	*Dąbrowski, Hämäläinen*
17/04	h	Korona	D	0-0	
22/04	a	Cracovia	W	2-1	*Nagy, Necid*
30/04	h	Wisła Kraków	D	1-1	*Jędrzejczyk*
07/05	a	Pogoń	W	2-0	*Nagy, Moulin*
14/05	h	Nieciecza	W	6-0	*Hämäläinen 2, Radović, Nagy, Guilherme (p), Kazaishvili*
17/05	h	Lech	W	2-0	*Odjidja-Ofoe, Kucharczyk*
21/05	a	Jagiellonia	D	0-0	
28/05	a	Korona	W	1-0	*Nagy*
04/06	h	Lechia	D	0-0	

No	Name	Nat	DoB	Pos	Aps	(s)	Gls
77	Mihail Alexandrov	BUL	11/06/89	M	3	(4)	1
19	Bartosz Bereszyński		12/07/92	D	11		
28	Łukasz Broź		17/12/85	D	11	(2)	
17	Tomasz Brzyski		10/01/82	D	2	(1)	
27	Daniel Chima	NGA	04/04/91	A		(2)	
33	Radosław Cierzniak		24/04/83	G	1		
4	Jakub Czerwiński		06/08/91	D	7	(1)	1
5	Maciej Dąbrowski		20/04/87	D	18		2
8	Ondrej Duda	SVK	05/12/94	M		(1)	
6	Guilherme	BRA	21/05/91	M	26	(3)	5
22	Kasper Hämäläinen	FIN	08/08/86	M	14	(17)	7
14	Adam Hloušek	CZE	20/12/88	D	31		
55	Artur Jędrzejczyk		04/11/87	D	16		1
3	Tomasz Jodłowiec		08/09/85	M	12	(10)	1
9	Valeri Kazaishvili	GEO	29/01/93	M	3	(9)	1
15	Michał Kopczyński		15/06/92	M	25	(6)	
13	Jakub Kosecki		29/08/90	M	1	(1)	
18	Michał Kucharczyk		20/03/91	M	10	(11)	6
7	Steeven Langil	FRA	04/03/88	M	3	(3)	1
4	Igor Lewczuk		30/05/85	D	5		1
1	Arkadiusz Malarz		19/06/80	G	36		
57	Konrad Michalak		19/09/97	M		(1)	
75	Thibault Moulin	FRA	13/01/90	M	30	(2)	2
21	Dominik Nagy	HUN	08/05/95	M	7	(5)	4
24	Tomáš Necid	CZE	13/08/89	A	5	(1)	1
20	Jarosław Niezgoda		15/03/95	A	1		
11	Nemanja Nikolić	HUN	31/12/87	A	15	(4)	12
8	Vadis Odjidja-Ofoe	BEL	21/02/89	M	29	(2)	4
2	Michał Pazdan		21/09/87	D	28		
99	Aleksandar Prijović	SRB	21/04/90	A	9	(5)	5
32	Miroslav Radović	SRB	16/01/84	M	29		11
25	Jakub Rzeźniczak		26/10/86	D	16	(3)	
53	Sebastian Szymański		10/05/99	M	1	(9)	1
23	Stojan Vranješ	BIH	11/10/86	M	1		
52	Mateusz Wieteska		11/02/97	D	1	(1)	

KS Nieciecza

1922 • Bruk-Bet (4,666) • termalica.brukbet.com

Coach: Czesław Michniewicz;
(22/03/17) (Marcin Węglewski)

Date	H/A	Opponent	Res	Score	Scorers
2016					
18/07	h	Arka	W	2-0	*Gutkovskis, Štefánik*
24/07	h	Cracovia	W	3-2	*Gutkovskis, Kupczak, og (Litauszki)*
31/07	a	Zagłębie	L	0-2	
06/08	h	Górnik	W	2-1	*Jovanović (p), Juhar*
13/08	a	Pogoń	L	0-5	
19/08	h	Lech	D	0-0	
28/08	a	Lechia	W	2-1	*Gutkovskis 2*
10/09	h	Legia	W	2-1	*Jovanović (p), Kędziora (p)*
16/09	a	Ruch	W	1-0	*Gutkovskis*
23/09	h	Wisła Płock	D	0-0	
02/10	a	Śląsk	W	2-1	*Kędziora (p), Osyra*
16/10	h	Jagiellonia	D	0-0	
21/10	a	Wisła Kraków	L	0-2	
28/10	a	Piast	L	1-2	*Mišák*
05/11	h	Korona	L	1-3	*Jovanović*
20/11	a	Arka	W	3-1	*Babiarz, Gutkovskis, Guba*
25/11	a	Cracovia	W	3-1	*Mišák 2, Osyra*
02/12	h	Zagłębie	L	0-1	
10/12	a	Górnik	L	0-3	
16/12	h	Pogoń	W	2-0	*Mišák, Štefánik*
2017					
10/02	a	Lech	L	0-3	
17/02	h	Lechia	D	1-1	*Gutkovskis (p)*
26/02	a	Legia	D	1-1	*Štefánik*
04/03	h	Ruch	D	0-0	
11/03	a	Wisła Płock	L	0-1	
17/03	h	Śląsk	L	1-2	*Putivtsev*
02/04	a	Jagiellonia	L	0-1	
08/04	h	Wisła Kraków	L	2-3	*Mišák, Putivtsev*
17/04	h	Piast	W	1-0	*D Nowak*
22/04	a	Korona	W	1-0	*D Nowak*
29/04	a	Lechia	L	0-2	
07/05	h	Lech	L	0-3	
14/05	a	Legia	L	0-6	
17/05	a	Pogoń	D	1-1	*Gutkovskis*
22/05	h	Korona	L	0-2	
28/05	h	Jagiellonia	L	1-2	*Jovanović*
04/06	a	Wisła Kraków	W	2-1	*Kędziora, Mikovič*

No	Name	Nat	DoB	Pos	Aps	(s)	Gls
6	Bartłomiej Babiarz		03/02/89	M	29	(4)	1
1	Krzysztof Baran		12/02/90	G	1		
8	Patryk Fryc		24/02/93	D	29	(3)	
10	Roman Gergel	SVK	22/02/88	M	14	(7)	
19	Dávid Guba	SVK	29/06/91	M	13	(8)	1
22	Guilherme	BRA	01/04/90	D	24	(1)	
21	Vladislavs Gutkovskis	LVA	02/04/95	A	24	(7)	8
28	Vlastimir Jovanović	BIH	03/04/85	M	29		4
99	Martin Juhar	SVK	09/03/88	M	3	(6)	1
24	Wojciech Kędziora		20/12/80	A	7	(17)	3
23	Szczepan Kogut		11/07/96	M		(1)	
88	Volodymyr Koval	UKR	06/03/92	A		(5)	
25	Mateusz Kupczak		20/02/92	M	35		1
16	Martin Mikovič	SVK	12/09/90	M	6	(3)	1
11	Patrik Mišák	SVK	29/03/91	M	23	(7)	5
20	Dawid Nowak		30/11/84	A	7	(10)	2
27	Piotr Nowak		06/03/98	M		(1)	
15	Kornel Osyra		07/02/93	D	31		2
33	Krystian Peda		05/09/97	M	1	(3)	
80	Krzysztof Pilarz		09/11/80	G	27	(1)	
17	Dalibor Pleva	SVK	02/04/84	D	17	(4)	
77	Artem Putivtsev	UKR	29/08/88	D	34		2
9	Bartłomiej Smuczyński		25/08/95	M		(3)	
18	Pavol Staňo	SVK	29/09/77	D	1	(2)	
7	Samuel Štefánik	SVK	16/11/91	M	26	(7)	3
96	Przemysław Szarek		22/04/96	D	10	(1)	
12	Dariusz Trela		05/12/89	G	9		
14	Jakub Wróbel		30/07/93	M	1	(4)	
5	Sebastian Ziajka		15/12/82	D	6	(2)	

POLAND

GKS Piast Gliwice

1945 • Miejski (10,037) • piast-gliwice.eu

Coach: Radoslav Látal (CZE); (15/07/16) (Jiří Neček (CZE)); (01/09/16) Radoslav Látal (CZE); (03/03/17) Dariusz Wdowczyk

2016

17/07 a	Cracovia	L 1-5	*Szeliga*
24/07 h	Wisła Płock	W 2-1	*Živec, Mráz*
31/07 a	Korona	D 1-1	*Szeliga*
07/08 a	Legia	D 0-0	
14/08 h	Zagłębie	D 0-0	
20/08 h	Pogoń	L 0-2	
28/08 a	Lech	L 0-2	
10/09 h	Górnik	D 3-3	*Pietrowski, Murawski (p), Jankowski*
17/09 a	Wisła Kraków	L 0-1	
26/09 h	Śląsk	D 1-1	*Hebert*
01/10 a	Arka	W 2-1	*Gerard Badía, Hebert*
15/10 h	Ruch	W 2-1	*Mokwa, Sedlar*
23/10 a	Lechia	L 2-3	*Korun, Živec*
28/10 h	Nieciecza	W 2-1	*Masłowski, Barišić*
05/11 a	Jagiellonia	L 0-2	
18/11 h	Cracovia	D 2-2	*Gerard Badía, Gotal (p)*
27/11 a	Wisła Płock	D 0-0	
03/12 h	Korona	W 1-0	*Gerard Badía*
11/12 h	Legia	L 1-5	*Sapała*
19/12 a	Zagłębie	L 1-2	*Jankowski*

2017

13/02 a	Pogoń	L 1-2	*Papadopulos*
18/02 h	Lech	L 0-3	
26/02 a	Górnik	L 0-1	
04/03 h	Wisła Kraków	L 1-2	*Gerard Badía*
10/03 a	Śląsk	W 4-3	*Gerard Badía 3, Korun*
18/03 h	Arka	W 3-2	*Bukata, Jankowski, Gerard Badía*
03/04 a	Ruch	D 0-0	
09/04 h	Lechia	D 1-1	*Sedlar*
17/04 a	Nieciecza	L 0-1	
22/04 h	Jagiellonia	L 0-1	
28/04 a	Arka	D 1-1	*Jankowski*
06/05 h	Śląsk	W 2-0	*Murawski, Živec*
12/05 a	Zagłębie	L 1-3	*Papadopulos*
16/05 a	Ruch	W 3-0	*og (Oleksy), Gerard Badía, Hebert*
20/05 h	Górnik	W 2-1	*Gojko, Sedlar*
27/05 h	Wisła Płock	W 4-0	*Živec, Jankowski 2, Bukata*
02/06 a	Cracovia	W 1-0	*Jankowski*

No	Name	Nat	DoB	Pos	Aps	(s)	Gls
10	Josip Barišić	CRO	14/11/86	A	6	(7)	1
82	Martin Bukata	SVK	02/10/93	M	17	(9)	2
45	Lukáš Čmelik	SVK	13/04/96	M		(2)	
16	Patryk Dziczek		25/03/98	D	1	(1)	
4	Marcin Flis		10/02/94	M	4		
21	Gerard Badía	ESP	18/10/89	M	26	(6)	9
93	Edvinas Girdvainis	LTU	17/01/93	D	7	(3)	
3	Denis Gojko		16/02/98	M	2	(4)	1
99	Sandro Gotal	AUT	09/09/91	A	1	(3)	1
91	Hebert	BRA	23/05/91	D	29	(1)	3
7	Maciej Jankowski		04/01/90	A	19	(7)	7
88	Uroš Korun	SVN	25/05/87	D	26	(2)	2
18	Łukasz Krakowczyk		21/02/98	A		(1)	
19	Mateusz Mak		14/11/91	M		(1)	
15	Michał Masłowski		19/12/89	M	19	(11)	1
22	Tomasz Mokwa		10/02/93	D	16	(3)	1
11	Paweł Moskwik		08/06/92	D	7	(7)	
17	Adam Mójta		30/06/86	D	6	(3)	
2	Patrik Mráz	SVK	01/02/87	D	25	(3)	1
9	Radosław Murawski		22/04/94	M	33		2
27	Michal Papadopulos	CZE	14/04/85	A	11	(4)	2
5	Marcin Pietrowski		01/03/88	D	31	(2)	1
31	Dobrivoj Rusov	SVK	13/01/93	G	3	(1)	
77	Igor Sapała		11/10/95	M		(2)	1
25	Aleksandar Sedlar	SRB	13/12/91	D	29	(2)	3
44	Łukasz Sekulski		03/11/90	A	8	(4)	
26	Bartosz Szeliga		10/01/93	M	20	(6)	2
1	Jakub Szmatuła		22/03/81	G	34		
23	Stojan Vranješ	BIH	11/10/86	M	8	(2)	
12	Saša Živec	SVN	02/04/91	M	19	(12)	4

MKS Pogoń Szczecin

1948 • im. Floriana Krygiera (15,717) • pogonszczecin.pl

Coach: Kazimierz Moskal

2016

16/07 a	Wisła Kraków	L 1-2	*Fojut*
22/07 h	Korona	D 1-1	*Kort*
01/08 h	Śląsk	L 0-2	
07/08 a	Zagłębie	D 1-1	*Drygas*
13/08 h	Nieciecza	W 5-0	*Matras, Murawski 2, Ricardo Nunes, Drygas*
20/08 a	Piast	W 2-0	*Kitano, Drygas*
27/08 h	Cracovia	D 1-1	*Kort*
11/09 a	Lech	L 1-3	*Zwoliński*
17/09 a	Wisła Płock	L 0-2	
24/09 h	Górnik	D 1-1	*Murawski*
02/10 a	Jagiellonia	D 0-0	
14/10 h	Legia	W 3-2	*Frączczak 2 (1p), Murawski*
21/10 a	Arka	W 3-0	*Frączczak 2, Matras*
29/10 h	Ruch	W 2-1	*Delev 2*
05/11 a	Lechia	D 1-1	*Frączczak (p)*
19/11 h	Wisła Kraków	W 6-2	*Gyurcsó 4, Matras, Ricardo Nunes*
26/11 a	Korona	L 1-4	*Matras*
03/12 a	Śląsk	D 1-1	*Frączczak (p)*
09/12 h	Zagłębie	D 1-1	*Frączczak*
16/12 a	Nieciecza	L 0-2	

2017

13/02 h	Piast	W 2-1	*Murawski, Gyurcsó*
19/02 a	Cracovia	D 1-1	*Frączczak*
24/02 h	Lech	L 0-3	
06/03 h	Wisła Płock	D 1-1	*Fojut*
12/03 a	Górnik	D 2-2	*Matras, Delev*
18/03 h	Jagiellonia	D 0-0	
01/04 a	Legia	L 0-2	
08/04 h	Arka	W 5-1	*Frączczak 2, Delev, Râpă, og (Marcjanik)*
15/04 a	Ruch	W 2-1	*Kort, Frączczak*
22/04 h	Lechia	W 3-1	*Frączczak, Kort 2*
30/04 a	Jagiellonia	L 0-1	
07/05 h	Legia	L 0-2	
14/05 a	Lech	L 0-2	
17/05 h	Nieciecza	D 1-1	*Kort*
20/05 a	Wisła Kraków	L 0-4	
28/05 a	Lechia	L 0-4	
04/06 h	Korona	W 3-0	*Murawski 2, Obst*

No	Name	Nat	DoB	Pos	Aps	(s)	Gls
27	Takafumi Akahoshi	JPN	27/05/86	M	7	(2)	
4	Jakub Czerwiński		06/08/91	D	7		
11	Spas Delev	BUL	22/09/89	M	27	(3)	4
14	Kamil Drygas		07/09/91	M	26	(6)	3
3	Jarosław Fojut		17/10/87	D	31		2
9	Adam Frączczak		07/08/87	A	29	(2)	12
7	Ádám Gyurcsó	HUN	06/03/91	M	34	(1)	5
12	Adrian Henger		18/05/96	G	4		
18	Seiya Kitano	JPN	02/08/97	A	7	(11)	1
10	Dawid Kort		29/04/95	M	13	(11)	6
55	Sebastian Kowalczyk		22/08/98	M	1	(4)	
66	Dawid Kudła		21/03/92	G	13		
33	Mateusz Lewandowski		18/03/93	D	9	(5)	
29	Marcin Listkowski		10/02/98	A	10	(7)	
23	Mateusz Matras		23/01/91	M	31	(2)	5
15	Hubert Matynia		04/11/95	D	4	(9)	
6	Rafał Murawski		09/10/81	M	29	(1)	7
17	Nadir Çiftçi	TUR	12/02/92	A	3	(5)	
24	David Niepsuj		16/08/95	D	12		
32	Robert Obst		06/07/95	M	1	(6)	1
19	Jakub Piotrowski		04/10/97	M	2	(2)	
2	Cornel Râpă	ROU	16/01/90	D	24		1
77	Ricardo Nunes	RSA	18/06/86	D	27	(5)	2
21	Sebastian Rudol		21/02/95	D	24	(6)	
1	Jakub Słowik		31/08/91	G	20		
8	Mate Tsintsadze	GEO	07/01/95	M	7	(3)	
93	Łukasz Zwoliński		24/02/93	A	5	(15)	1

Ruch Chorzów

1920 • Miejski (9,300) • ruchchorzow.com.pl

Major honours
Polish League (14) 1933, 1934, 1935, 1936, 1938, 1951, 1952, 1953, 1960, 1968, 1974, 1975, 1979, 1989; Polish Cup (3) 1951, 1974, 1996

Coach: Waldemar Fornalik; (24/04/17) Krzysztof Warzycha

2016

16/07 h	Górnik	W 2-1	*Arak, Stępiński*
23/07 a	Jagiellonia	L 1-4	*Lipski*
29/07 a	Arka	L 0-3	
08/08 h	Wisła Płock	D 2-2	*Stępiński, Grodzicki (p)*
14/08 a	Wisła Kraków	W 2-1	*Stępiński, Oleksy*
20/08 a	Cracovia	D 1-1	*Arak*
28/08 h	Legia	L 0-2	
12/09 a	Śląsk	W 2-1	*Ćwielong 2*
16/09 h	Nieciecza	L 0-1	
24/09 a	Lechia	L 1-2	*Grodzicki (p)*
30/09 h	Zagłębie	L 1-2	*Niezgoda*
15/10 a	Piast	L 1-2	*Niezgoda*
24/10 h	Korona	W 4-0	*Niezgoda, Moneta, Ćwielong, Oleksy*
29/10 a	Pogoń	L 1-2	*Niezgoda*
04/11 h	Lech	L 0-5	
19/11 a	Górnik	W 4-0	*Ćwielong, Pazio, Niezgoda, Arak*
26/11 h	Jagiellonia	L 1-2	*Ćwielong (p)*
05/12 h	Arka	L 1-2	*Lipski*
10/12 a	Wisła Płock	L 3-4	*Niezgoda, Lipski 2*
16/12 h	Wisła Kraków	W 1-0	*Niezgoda*

2017

10/02 h	Cracovia	L 0-1	
19/02 a	Legia	W 3-1	*Lipski, Urbańczyk, Niezgoda*
27/02 h	Śląsk	W 2-0	*Przybecki, Grodzicki (p)*
04/03 a	Nieciecza	D 0-0	
11/03 h	Lechia	W 2-1	*Lipski, Niezgoda*
18/03 a	Zagłębie	W 1-0	*Niezgoda*
03/04 h	Piast	D 0-0	
10/04 a	Korona	L 0-1	
15/04 h	Pogoń	L 1-2	*Nowak*
22/04 a	Lech	L 0-3	
29/04 a	Wisła Płock	D 1-1	*Arak*
05/05 h	Zagłębie	D 1-1	*Moneta*
13/05 a	Śląsk	L 0-6	
16/05 h	Piast	L 0-3	
19/05 a	Cracovia	L 0-2	
27/05 a	Arka	D 1-1	*Moneta*
02/06 h	Górnik	D 2-2	*Koj, Višņakovs*

No	Name	Nat	DoB	Pos	Aps	(s)	Gls
9	Jakub Arak		02/04/95	A	9	(24)	4
72	Przemysław Bargiel		26/03/00	M		(1)	
2	Mateusz Cichocki		31/01/92	D	5	(2)	
20	Piotr Ćwielong		23/04/86	M	18	(2)	5
38	Milen Gamakov	BUL	12/04/94	M		(2)	
51	Rafał Grodzicki		28/10/83	D	30		3
22	Łukasz Hanzel		16/09/86	M	3	(1)	
39	Michał Helik		09/09/95	D	20		
33	Libor Hrdlička	SVK	02/01/86	G	25		
14	Michał Koj		28/07/93	D	16	(1)	1
15	Martin Konczkowski		14/09/93	D	36		
5	Marcin Kowalczyk		09/04/85	D	23	(1)	
1	Kamil Lech		15/09/94	G	9		
10	Patryk Lipski		12/06/94	M	25	(4)	6
27	Kamil Mazek		22/07/94	M	13	(5)	
13	Łukasz Moneta		13/05/94	M	24	(7)	3
11	Jarosław Niezgoda		15/03/95	A	22	(5)	10
37	Bartosz Nowak		25/08/93	M	9	(8)	1
23	Paweł Oleksy		01/04/91	D	14	(5)	2
21	Adam Pazio		27/09/92	D	5	(4)	1
16	Miłosz Przybecki		02/01/91	M	18	(7)	1
84	Wojciech Skaba		09/04/84	G	3		
6	Kamil Słoma		20/08/98	M		(1)	
18	Mariusz Stępiński		12/05/95	A	3	(2)	3
4	Łukasz Surma		28/06/77	M	35		
66	Miłosz Trojak		05/05/94	D	2	(10)	
17	Maciej Urbańczyk		02/04/95	M	33		1
90	Eduards Višņakovs	LVA	10/05/90	A	6	(9)	1
8	Michał Walski		27/02/97	M	1	(4)	

WKS Śląsk Wrocław

1947 • Miejski (42,771) • slaskwroclaw.pl

Major honours
Polish League (2) 1977, 2012; Polish Cup (2) 1976, 1987

Coach: Mariusz Rumak; (05/01/17) Jan Urban

2016

Date		Opponent	Result	Scorers
15/07	h	Lech	D 0-0	
23/07	a	Legia	D 0-0	
01/08	a	Pogoń	W 2-0	*Kokoszka, Filipe Gonçalves*
06/08	h	Lechia	D 0-0	
13/08	a	Arka	L 0-2	
19/08	h	Wisła Płock	D 0-0	
26/08	a	Wisła Kraków	W 5-1	*Biliński, Marioka 2, Filipe Gonçalves, Stjepanovic (p)*
12/09	h	Ruch	L 1-2	*Marioka (p)*
16/09	h	Jagiellonia	L 0-4	
26/09	a	Piast	D 1-1	*Biliński (p)*
02/10	h	Nieciecza	L 1-2	*og (Fryc)*
17/10	a	Korona	W 2-1	*Dankowski, Kokoszka*
22/10	h	Cracovia	D 2-2	*Grajciar 2*
29/10	a	Górnik	W 3-0	*Marioka, Biliński, Grajciar*
06/11	h	Zagłębie	W 2-1	*Dvali, Alvarinho*
20/11	a	Lech	L 0-3	
27/11	h	Legia	L 0-4	
03/12	h	Pogoń	D 1-1	*Celeban*
09/12	a	Lechia	L 0-3	
18/12	h	Arka	L 0-2	

2017

Date		Opponent	Result	Scorers
12/02	a	Wisła Płock	D 1-1	*Pich*
18/02	h	Wisła Kraków	W 1-0	*Joan Román*
27/02	a	Ruch	L 0-2	
05/03	a	Jagiellonia	L 1-4	*Pich*
10/03	h	Piast	L 3-4	*Kovačević, Pich 2*
17/03	a	Nieciecza	W 2-1	*Pich, Kokoszka*
31/03	h	Korona	W 3-0	*Marioka (p), og (Dejmek), Biliński (p)*
07/04	a	Cracovia	L 0-1	
15/04	h	Górnik	D 2-2	*Biliński, Pich*
22/04	a	Zagłębie	D 1-1	*Celeban*
29/04	h	Górnik	L 0-2	
06/05	a	Piast	L 0-2	
13/05	h	Ruch	W 6-0	*Biliński 3, Marioka 2, Celeban*
16/05	a	Zagłębie	L 0-2	
19/05	h	Arka	W 4-1	*Pawelec, Pich, Biliński, Engels*
27/05	h	Cracovia	W 2-0	*Biliński, Marioka*
02/06	a	Wisła Płock	W 3-0	*Engels 2, Biliński*

No	Name	Nat	DoB	Pos	Aps	(s)	Gls
14	Alvarinho	POR	03/09/90	M	19	(4)	1
5	Augusto	POR	30/08/87	D	17	(3)	
19	Kamil Biliński		23/01/88	A	22	(10)	11
12	Dominik Budziński		02/06/92	G	2	(1)	
3	Piotr Celeban		25/06/85	D	37		3
30	Kamil Dankowski		22/07/96	D	28	(3)	1
21	Lasha Dvali	GEO	14/05/95	D	19		1
9	Mario Engels	GER	22/10/93	M	6	(11)	3
6	Filipe Gonçalves	POR	12/08/84	M	15	(1)	2
8	András Gosztonyi	HUN	07/11/90	M		(1)	
29	Peter Grajciar	SVK	17/09/83	M	7	(6)	3
27	Mariusz Idzik		01/04/97	A	1	(6)	
7	Joan Román	ESP	18/05/93	M	8	(4)	1
1	Ľuboš Kamenár	SVK	17/06/87	G	9		
20	Adam Kokoszka		06/10/86	D	30		3
8	Aleksandar Kovačević	SRB	09/01/92	M	16		1
28	Mateusz Lewandowski		18/03/93	D	10	(3)	
26	Daniel Łuczak		12/07/96	M		(1)	
35	Adrian Łuszczarz		22/08/99	M		(2)	
18	Łukasz Madej		14/04/82	M	22	(5)	
10	Ryota Marioka	JPN	12/04/91	M	32	(4)	8
11	Bence Mervó	HUN	05/03/95	A	6	(5)	
17	Mariusz Pawelec		14/04/86	D	21		1
33	Mariusz Pawełek		17/03/81	G	26		
16	Róbert Pich	SVK	12/11/88	M	17		7
22	Sito Riera	ESP	05/01/87	A	13	(9)	
32	Ostoja Stjepanovic	MKD	17/01/85	M	15	(12)	1
23	Paweł Zieliński		17/07/90	D	3	(3)	
11	Łukasz Zwoliński		24/02/93	A	6	(7)	

Wisła Kraków

1906 • Miejski im. Henryka Reymana (33,326) • wisla.krakow.pl

Major honours
Polish League (13) 1927, 1928, 1949, 1950, 1978, 1999, 2001, 2003, 2004, 2005, 2008, 2009, 2011; Polish Cup (4) 1926, 1967, 2002, 2003

Coach: Dariusz Wdowczyk; (10/11/16) (Kazimierz Kmiecik); (03/01/17) Kiko Ramírez (ESP)

2016

Date		Opponent	Result	Scorers
16/07	h	Pogoń	W 2-1	*Brożek, Pietrzak*
22/07	a	Arka	L 0-3	
30/07	a	Lechia	L 1-3	*Boguski*
05/08	a	Cracovia	L 1-2	*Małecki*
14/08	h	Ruch	L 1-2	*Zachara*
22/08	a	Korona	L 0-1	
26/08	h	Śląsk	L 1-5	*Mójta (p)*
11/09	a	Jagiellonia	L 1-2	*Małecki*
17/09	h	Piast	W 1-0	*Małecki*
23/09	h	Legia	D 0-0	
01/10	a	Wisła Płock	W 3-2	*Zachara, Guzmics, Małecki*
16/10	a	Lech	D 1-1	*Brożek*
21/10	h	Nieciecza	W 2-0	*Ondrášek 2 (1p)*
31/10	a	Zagłębie	D 2-2	*Brlek, Bartosz*
06/11	h	Górnik	W 3-2	*Boguski 3*
19/11	a	Pogoń	L 2-6	*Bartosz, Mójta*
26/11	h	Arka	W 5-1	*Boguski 3, Brlek, Brożek*
03/12	h	Lechia	W 3-0	*Głowacki, Boguski, Zachara*
10/12	h	Cracovia	D 1-1	*Brlek*
16/12	a	Ruch	L 0-1	

2017

Date		Opponent	Result	Scorers
11/02	h	Korona	W 2-0	*Małecki, Brożek*
18/02	a	Śląsk	L 0-1	
25/02	h	Jagiellonia	W 3-1	*Brożek, Małecki, Boguski*
04/03	a	Piast	W 2-1	*Ondrášek, Brlek*
12/03	a	Legia	L 0-1	
17/03	h	Wisła Płock	W 3-2	*Brlek, Štilić, Bartosz*
31/03	h	Lech	D 0-0	
08/04	a	Nieciecza	W 3-2	*og (Putivtsev), Brlek, Zachara*
17/04	h	Zagłębie	W 1-0	*Małecki*
22/04	a	Górnik	L 1-3	*Głowacki*
30/04	a	Legia	D 1-1	*Brlek (p)*
06/05	h	Lechia	L 0-1	
13/05	a	Jagiellonia	L 0-2	
17/05	a	Korona	L 2-3	*Brlek, Mączyński*
20/05	h	Pogoń	W 4-0	*Małecki, Brożek, González, Boguski*
28/05	a	Lech	L 1-2	*Boguski*
04/06	h	Nieciecza	L 1-2	*Boguski*

No	Name	Nat	DoB	Pos	Aps	(s)	Gls
5	Jakub Bartkowski		07/11/91	D	1	(1)	
17	Jakub Bartosz		13/08/96	D	6	(15)	3
9	Rafał Boguski		09/06/84	M	33	(3)	12
21	Peter Brlek	CRO	29/01/94	M	24	(7)	8
23	Paweł Brożek		21/04/83	A	25	(6)	6
19	Tomasz Cywka		27/06/88	D	20	(5)	
13	Krzysztof Drzazga		20/06/95	A	3	(2)	
6	Arkadiusz Głowacki		13/03/79	D	26	(1)	2
32	Iván González	ESP	15/02/88	D	16		1
26	Richárd Guzmics	HUN	16/04/87	D	11		1
5	Boban Jovič	SVN	25/06/91	D	12	(1)	
47	Kacper Laskoś		05/01/00	M		(1)	
7	Pol Llonch	ESP	07/10/92	M	14	(2)	
29	Krzysztof Mączyński		23/05/87	M	30	(1)	1
88	Patryk Małecki		01/08/88	M	35		8
1	Michał Miśkiewicz		20/01/89	G	9		
15	Adam Mójta		30/06/86	D	7	(3)	2
14	Zdeněk Ondrášek	CZE	22/12/88	A	15	(9)	3
2	Rafał Pietrzak		30/01/92	D	4	(5)	1
10	Denis Popovič	SVN	15/10/89	M	15	(1)	
40	Przemysław Porębski		30/06/98	M		(1)	
4	Maciej Sadlok		29/06/89	D	29		
11	Wojciech Słomka		04/11/98	M		(1)	
33	Matija Špičić	CRO	24/02/88	D	6		
18	Semir Štilić	BIH	08/10/87	M	7	(7)	1
8	Alan Uryga		19/02/94	D	17	(3)	
10	Éver Valencia	ECU	23/01/97	M		(2)	
93	Hugo Vidémont	FRA	19/02/93	M	2	(6)	
20	Mateusz Zachara		27/03/90	A	12	(15)	4
24	Łukasz Załuska		16/06/82	G	28		
3	Piotr Żemło		10/07/95	D		(2)	

Wisła Płock

1947 • im. Kazimierza Górskiego (12,800) • wisla-plock.pl

Major honours
Polish Cup (1) 2006

Coach: Marcin Kaczmarek

2016

Date		Opponent	Result	Scorers
15/07	h	Lechia	W 2-1	*Szymiński, Furman (p)*
24/07	a	Piast	L 1-2	*Reca*
30/07	h	Legia	L 2-3	*Božić, Szymiński*
08/08	a	Ruch	D 2-2	*Kanté, Merebashvili*
15/08	h	Jagiellonia	W 1-0	*Iliev*
19/08	a	Śląsk	D 0-0	
26/08	h	Korona	L 1-2	*Iliev*
09/09	a	Zagłębie	W 2-1	*Merebashvili, Kun*
17/09	h	Pogoń	W 2-0	*Kanté 2*
23/09	a	Nieciecza	D 0-0	
01/10	h	Wisła Kraków	L 2-3	*Furman (p), Merebashvili*
14/10	a	Cracovia	L 0-1	
22/10	h	Górnik	L 1-2	*Kanté*
29/10	a	Lech	L 0-2	
04/11	h	Arka	D 0-0	
19/11	a	Lechia	L 1-2	*Merebashvili*
27/11	h	Piast	D 0-0	
02/12	a	Legia	D 2-2	*Furman, Sylwestrzak*
10/12	h	Ruch	W 4-3	*Wlazło 3 (1p), Reca*
17/12	a	Jagiellonia	W 2-1	*Wlazło, Sylwestrzak*

2017

Date		Opponent	Result	Scorers
12/02	h	Śląsk	D 1-1	*Kanté*
18/02	a	Korona	L 2-4	*Merebashvili, Kanté*
25/02	h	Zagłębie	W 2-1	*Kanté, Merebashvili*
06/03	a	Pogoń	D 1-1	*Szymiński*
11/03	h	Nieciecza	W 1-0	*og (Szarek)*
17/03	a	Wisła Kraków	L 2-3	*Krivets, Piątkowski*
01/04	h	Cracovia	W 4-1	*Krivets, Wlazło (p), Piątkowski 2*
08/04	a	Górnik	W 3-2	*og (Sasin), Byrtek, Iliev*
15/04	h	Lech	L 0-3	
22/04	a	Arka	D 1-1	*Kanté (p)*
29/04	h	Ruch	D 1-1	*Kanté (p)*
06/05	a	Górnik	W 3-2	*Wlazło (p), Kanté, Reca*
13/05	h	Cracovia	D 1-1	*Wlazło (p)*
16/05	a	Arka	W 1-0	*Reca*
20/05	h	Zagłębie	L 1-2	*Sylwestrzak*
27/05	a	Piast	L 0-4	
02/06	h	Śląsk	L 0-3	

No	Name	Nat	DoB	Pos	Aps	(s)	Gls
24	Tomislav Božić	CRO	01/11/87	D	20	(1)	1
17	Damian Byrtek		07/03/91	D	17	(3)	1
19	Emil Drozdowicz		05/07/86	A		(8)	
8	Dominik Furman		06/07/92	M	32		3
27	Vitaliy Hemeha	UKR	10/01/94	M	3	(5)	
41	Dimitar Iliev	BUL	25/09/88	M	16	(13)	3
29	José Kanté	GUI	27/09/90	A	25	(7)	10
87	Seweryn Kiełpin		18/12/87	G	30		
97	Dawid Kieplin		10/07/97	M	1	(1)	
30	Sergei Krivets	BLR	08/06/86	M	16	(7)	2
1	Mateusz Kryczka		20/07/92	G	7		
22	Dominik Kun		22/06/93	M	11	(8)	1
11	Mikołaj Lebedyński		14/10/90	A	2	(1)	
10	Giorgi Merebashvili	GEO	15/08/86	M	30	(2)	6
3	Marcin Mielczarski		24/05/98	D		(1)	
23	Piotr Mroziński		24/08/92	M		(1)	
27	Mateusz Piątkowski		22/11/84	A	10	(7)	3
7	Damian Piotrowski		09/01/87	M	2	(6)	
98	Krystian Popiela		19/01/98	A		(2)	
9	Arkadiusz Reca		17/06/95	M	19	(13)	4
21	Maksymilian Rogalski		24/06/83	M	28	(2)	
5	Bartłomiej Sielewski		09/08/84	D	6	(3)	
6	Harmeet Singh	NOR	12/11/90	M	1		
20	Cezary Stefańczyk		21/02/84	D	26	(1)	
95	Patryk Stępiński		16/01/95	D	29	(4)	
2	Kamil Sylwestrzak		16/07/88	D	18	(2)	3
25	Przemysław Szymiński		24/06/94	D	32	(2)	3
94	Seweryn Truskolaski		29/01/94	M	1		
18	Piotr Wlazło		03/06/89	M	25	(7)	7

Zagłębie Lubin

1945 • Zagłębia (16,100) • zaglebie.com

Major honours
Polish League (2) 1991, 2007

Coach: Piotr Stokowiec

2016				
17/07	h	Korona	W 4-0	*L Piątek, Janus (p), Dąbrowski, K Piątek*
24/07	a	Lech	W 2-0	*Papadopulos, Starzyński*
31/07	h	Nieciecza	W 2-0	*Janus, Starzyński*
07/08	h	Pogoń	D 1-1	*Janoszka*
14/08	a	Piast	D 0-0	
21/08	h	Górnik	D 0-0	
27/08	a	Arka	D 1-1	*og (Marcjanik)*
09/09	h	Wisła Płock	L 1-2	*Guldan*
18/09	a	Legia	W 3-2	*Jach, Janus (p), og (Pazdan)*
24/09	h	Cracovia	D 1-1	*Janoszka*
30/09	a	Ruch	W 2-1	*Janoszka, Janus (p)*
15/10	h	Lechia	L 1-2	*Nešpor*
23/10	a	Jagiellonia	W 2-1	*Nešpor, Woźniak*
31/10	h	Wisła Kraków	D 2-2	*Woźniak 2*
06/11	a	Śląsk	L 1-2	*og (Dankowski)*
21/11	a	Korona	L 1-2	*L Piątek*
25/11	h	Lech	L 0-3	
02/12	a	Nieciecza	W 1-0	*Buksa*
09/12	a	Pogoń	D 1-1	*Buksa*
19/12	h	Piast	W 2-1	*Woźniak 2*
2017				
20/02	h	Arka	W 1-0	*Starzyński (p)*
25/02	a	Wisła Płock	L 1-2	*Nešpor*
03/03	h	Legia	L 1-3	*Woźniak*
07/03	a	Górnik	W 1-0	*Starzyński*
13/03	a	Cracovia	D 1-1	*Starzyński*
18/03	h	Ruch	L 0-1	
02/04	a	Lechia	L 0-1	
07/04	h	Jagiellonia	L 3-4	*Woźniak, L Piątek, Janoszka*
17/04	a	Wisła Kraków	L 0-1	
22/04	h	Śląsk	D 1-1	*Woźniak*
01/05	h	Cracovia	D 2-2	*Guldan, Nešpor*
05/05	a	Ruch	D 1-1	*Tosik*
12/05	h	Piast	W 3-1	*Starzyński, Mazek, Woźniak*
16/05	h	Śląsk	W 2-0	*Starzyński, L Piątek*
20/05	a	Wisła Płock	W 2-1	*Tosik, Buksa*
27/05	a	Górnik	W 3-1	*Tosik, og (Małecki), Kubicki*
02/06	h	Arka	L 1-3	*og (Marcjanik)*

No	Name	Nat	DoB	Pos	Aps	(s)	Gls
21	Adam Buksa		12/07/96	A	10	(12)	3
3	Djordje Čotra	SRB	13/09/84	D	20	(1)	
2	Maciej Dąbrowski		20/04/87	D	3		1
23	Daniel Dziwniel		19/08/92	D	15	(2)	
12	Konrad Forenc		17/07/92	G	3		
33	Ľubomír Guldan	SVK	30/01/83	D	31		2
5	Jarosław Jach		17/02/94	D	23		1
19	Filip Jagiełło		08/08/97	M	9	(8)	
14	Łukasz Janoszka		18/03/87	M	27	(7)	4
7	Krzysztof Janus		25/03/86	M	21	(5)	4
27	Dominik Jończy		17/05/97	D	4		
20	Jarosław Kubicki		07/08/95	M	32	(2)	1
77	Sebastian Madera		30/05/85	D	8	(3)	
22	Zbigniew Małkowski		19/01/78	G	1		
27	Kamil Mazek		22/07/94	M	5	(5)	1
25	Patryk Mucha		11/09/97	M		(1)	
13	Martin Nešpor	CZE	05/06/90	A	16	(9)	4
27	Michal Papadopulos	CZE	14/04/85	A	12	(4)	1
88	Deimantas Petravičius	LTU	02/09/95	M		(1)	
26	Krzysztof Piątek		01/07/95	A	1	(4)	1
28	Łukasz Piątek		21/09/85	M	30	(3)	4
1	Martin Polaček	SVK	02/04/90	G	33		
17	Adrian Rakowski		07/10/90	M	6	(11)	
11	Artur Siemaszko		06/01/97	A		(3)	
18	Filip Starzyński		27/05/91	M	19	(6)	7
4	Aleksandar Todorovski	MKD	26/02/84	D	21	(1)	
24	Jakub Tosik		21/05/87	D	29	(3)	3
90	Ján Vlasko	SVK	11/01/90	M	6	(8)	
9	Arkadiusz Woźniak		01/06/90	M	22	(10)	9
16	Paweł Żyra		07/04/98	M		(1)	

Top goalscorers

Marcin Robak

Marco Paixão

18	Marcin Robak (Lech)
	Marco Paixão (Lechia)
13	Konstantin Vassiljev (Jagiellonia)
12	Fedor Černych (Jagiellonia)
	Nemanja Nikolić (Legia)
	Adam Frączczak (Pogoń)
	Rafał Boguski (Wisła Kraków)
	Krzysztof Piątek (Zagłębie/Cracovia)
11	Rafał Siemaszko (Arka)
	Miroslav Radović (Legia)
	Kamil Biliński (Śląsk)

Promoted clubs

Sandecja Nowy Sącz

1910 • im. Ojca Władysława Augustynka (5,000) • sandecja.com.pl

Coach: Radosław Mroczkowski

Górnik Zabrze

1948 • Arena Zabrze (24,563) • gornikzabrze.pl

Major honours
Polish League (14) 1957, 1959, 1961, 1963, 1964, 1965, 1966, 1967, 1971, 1972, 1985, 1986, 1987, 1988; Polish Cup (6) 1965, 1968, 1969, 1970, 1971, 1972

Coach: Marcin Brosz

Second level final table 2016/17

		Pld	W	D	L	F	A	Pts
1	Sandecja Nowy Sącz	34	18	7	9	50	29	61
2	Górnik Zabrze	34	17	7	10	53	34	58
3	Zagłębie Sosnowiec	34	16	9	9	53	44	57
4	Miedź Legnica	34	16	9	9	49	27	57
5	Chojniczanka Chojnice	34	13	17	4	54	48	56
6	GKS Olimpia Grudziądz	34	17	5	12	48	35	56
7	GKS Katowice	34	15	9	10	47	32	54
8	TS Podbeskidzie Bielsko-Biała	34	14	11	9	40	39	53
9	Wigry Suwałki	34	15	7	12	51	45	52
10	Stal Mielec	34	12	9	13	39	42	45
11	MKP Pogoń Siedlce	34	13	5	16	34	46	44
12	Chrobry Głogów	34	12	7	15	50	50	43
13	Stomil Olsztyn	34	9	13	12	48	50	37
14	GKS Tychy	34	10	7	17	42	52	37
15	MKS Bytovia Bytów	34	8	11	15	38	47	35
16	Wisła Puławy	34	7	12	15	33	49	33
17	Znicz Pruszków	34	8	6	20	35	64	30
18	MKS Kluczbork	34	4	13	17	35	66	25

NB Stomil Olsztyn - 3 pts deducted.

DOMESTIC CUP

Puchar Polski 2016/17

FIRST ROUND

(22/07/16)
Radomiak Radom 1-0 GKS Katowice
ROW 1964 Rybnik 1-3 Stomil Olsztyn

(23/07/16)
Błękitni Stargard Szczeciński 1-2 Bytovia Bytów
GKS Bełchatów 1-1 Miedź Legnica *(aet; 6-7 on pens)*
Kotwica Kołobrzeg 2-3 Chojniczanka Chojnice
Kalisz 1-0 Polonia Bytom
Legionovia Leginowo 0-3 Zagłębie Sosnowiec
Olimpia Zambrów 2-1 GKS Tychy
Ostrowiec Świętokrzyski 2-1 Pogoń Siedlce *(aet)*
Raków Częstochowa 2-2 Chrobry Głogów *(aet; 6-5 on pens)*
Siarka Tarnobrzeg 2-4 Sandecja Nowy Sącz *(aet)*
Świt Nowy Dwór Mazowiecki 0-1 Wigry Suwałki
Wda Świecie 1-2 Puszcza Niepołomice *(aet)*

(26/07/16)
Rominta Gołdap 1-4 Arka Gdynia

(27/07/16)
Stal Mielec 4-3 Wisła Płock

SECOND ROUND

(09/08/16)
Cracovia Kraków 0-1 Jagiellonia Białystok
Olimpia Zambrów 0-1 Arka Gdynia
Ostrowiec Świętokrzyski 3-2 Raków Częstochowa
Miedź Legnica 2-3 Górnik Łęczna
Podbeskidzie Bielsko-Biała 0-3 Lech Poznań
Puszcza Niepołomice 1-1 Korona Kielce *(aet; 3-2 on pens)*
Wigry Suwałki 2-1 Nieciecza
Zagłębie Sosnowiec 3-4 Wisła Kraków *(aet)*

(10/08/16)
Bytovia Bytów 1-0 Zagłębie Lubin
Chojniczanka Chojnice 2-0 Stal Mlelec
GKS Jastrzębie 2-1 Radomiak Radom
Górnik Zabrze 3-2 Legia Warszawa *(aet)*
KKS 1925 Kailsz 0-4 Pogoń Szczecin
Sandecja Nowy Sącz 1-2 Śląsk Wrocław *(aet)*

(11/08/16)
Stomil Olsztyn 0-0 Ruch Chorzów *(aet; 6-7 on pens)*

(24/08/16)
Piast Gliwice 0-0 Lechia Gdańsk *(aet; 3-5 on pens)*

THIRD ROUND

(20/09/16)
GKS Jastrzębie 1-1 Górnik Łęczna *(aet; 7-6 on pens)*
Górnik Zabrze 0-2 Wigry Suwałki

(21/09/16)
Puszcza Niepołomice 1-1 Lechia Gdańsk *(aet; 4-2 on pens)*
Ruch Chorzów 0-3 Lech Poznań

(22/09/16)
Bytovia Bytów 3-0 Śląsk Wrocław
Ostrowiec Świętokrzyski 1-2 Arka Gdynia

(27/09/16)
Chojniczanka Chojnice 1-2 Wisła Kraków

(28/09/16)
Pogoń Szczecin 4-1 Jagiellonia Białystok

QUARTER-FINALS

(25/10/16 & 29/11/16)
Bytovia Bytów 2-1 Arka Gdynia *(Surdykowski 29, Bąk 82; Abbott 85)*
Arka Gdynia 1-0 Bytovia Bytów *(Hofbauer 76)*
(2-2; Arka Gdynia on away goal)

(25/10/16 & 30/11/16)
GKS Jastrzębie 1-2 Wigry Suwałki *(Caniboł 45p; Zapolnik 12, Adamek 76)*
Wigry Suwałki 1-1 GKS Jastrzębie *(Wroński 34; Tront 46)*
(Wigry Suwałki 3-2)

Lech Poznań 1-1 Wisła Kraków *(Kownacki 78; Brożek 48)*
Wisła Kraków 2-4 Lech Poznań *(Brlek 51, Małecki 66; Robak 21p, Makuszewski28, Jevtic 39, Majewski 82)*
(Lech Poznań 5-3)

(26/10/16 & 29/11/16)
Puszcza Niepołomice 1-2 Pogoń Szczecin *(Orłowski 84; Ricardo Nunes 21, Frączczak 56)*
Pogoń Szczecin 2-0 Puszcza Niepołomice *(Drygas 10, Frączczak 54)*
(Pogoń Szczecin 4-1)

SEMI-FINALS

(28/02/17 & 04/04/17)
Wigry Suwałki 0-3 Arka Gdynia *(Szwoch 37p, Siemaszko 68, Formella 90)*
Arka Gdynia 2-4 Wigry Suwałki *(Szwoch 50p, Hofbauer 64; Kądzior 21, 79, Zapolnik 45p, Omar Santana 52)*
(Arka Gdynia 5-4)

(01/03/17 & 05/04/17)
Lech Poznań 3-0 Pogoń Szczecin *(Pawłowski 32, Kownacki 53, Nielsen 66)*
Pogoń Szczecin 0-1 Lech Poznań *(Robak 41)*
(Lech Poznań 4-0)

FINAL

(02/05/17)
PGE Narodowy, Warsaw
ARKA GDYNIA 2 *(Siemaszko 107, Zarandia 111)*
KKS LECH POZNAŃ 1 *(Tralka 119)*
(aet)
Referee: *Musiał*
ARKA: *Šteinbors, Socha, Marcjanik, Sobieraj, Warcholak, Łukasiewicz, Marciniak, Marcus Vinícius (Siemaszko 55), Szwoch, Božok (Hofbauer 83), Trytko (Zarandia 71)*
LECH: *Burić, Kędziora, Bednarek, Nielsen (Răduţ 110), Kostevych, Tralka, Gajos, Jevtic (Pawłowski 85), Majewski, Kownacki (Makuszewski 74), Robak*

Arka Gdynia lift the Polish Cup for the first time in 38 years

PORTUGAL

Federação Portuguesa de Futebol (FPF)

Address	Avenida das Seleções PT-1495-433 Cruz Quebrada – Dafundo	**President**	Fernando Gomes
Tel	+351 21 325 2700	**General secretary**	Tiago Craveiro
Fax	+351 21 325 2780	**Media officer**	Onofre Costa
E-mail	ceo@fpf.pt	**Year of formation**	1914
Website	fpf.pt		

PRIMEIRA LIGA CLUBS

1. FC Arouca
2. Os Belenenses
3. SL Benfica
4. Boavista FC
5. SC Braga
6. GD Chaves
7. Estoril Praia
8. CD Feirense
9. CS Marítimo
10. Moreirense FC
11. CD Nacional
12. FC Paços de Ferreira
13. FC Porto
14. Rio Ave FC
15. Sporting Clube de Portugal
16. CD Tondela
17. Vitória FC (Setúbal)
18. Vitória SC (Guimarães)

PROMOTED CLUBS

19. Portimonense SC
20. CD Aves

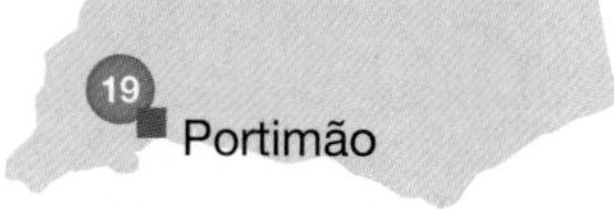

Benfica make fresh history

Benfica's 36th Portuguese title was a little bit more special than all of those that had preceded it as it was the first time that the illustrious Lisbon club had ever been crowned champions of their country for a fourth successive year.

Landmark Liga success was also accompanied by a 26th victory in the Taça de Portugal, enabling Benfica not only to take their all-time tally of wins in the competition to ten more than both FC Porto and Sporting CP but also to complete an 11th domestic double.

Lisbon giants win landmark fourth straight title

Cup win completes club's 11th domestic double

International goals keep flowing for Cristiano Ronaldo

Domestic league

Victory in the 2015/16 Primeira Liga had enabled Benfica to register the sixth title hat-trick in their history, but on every previous occasion that they had endeavoured to make it four in a row – in 1938/39, 1965/66, 1969/70, 1973/74 and 1977/78 – they had been foiled either by Sporting (twice) or Porto (three times). Furthermore, both of their rivals had achieved the four-in-a-row feat, with Porto setting an all-time record for consecutive triumphs when they won the competition five seasons running in the late 1990s.

The task for coach Rui Vitória and his players in 2016/17 was not made any easier by the loss of several key players, either through transfers – Nicolas Gaitán and Renato Sanches having left for Atlético Madrid and Bayern München, respectively – or injuries – Brazilian duo Jardel and Jonas both being laid low for extended periods. Fortunately, though, Benfica found excellent replacements, most of them from within their existing squad, with long-serving skipper Luisão and fit-again Eduardo Salvio enjoying a renaissance and youngsters such as central defender Victor Lindelöf, full-back Nélson Semedo and goalkeeper Ederson all rising superbly to the challenge alongside ever-consistent midfield string-puller Pizzi. Twenty-year-old winger Gonçalo Guedes was another to shine before he too departed, for Paris Saint-Germain, in January.

While there was some concern about a reduction in quality, there was never any doubt about the resolve of Rui Vitória's side, and they started their title defence strongly, winning eight of their opening nine fixtures before salvaging a crucial 1-1 draw at Porto with a stoppage-time equaliser from defender Lisandro López. A first defeat, at Marítimo, was quickly offset by a 2-1 home win over Sporting, and at the festive break Benfica held a four-point lead over Porto.

The pressure from Porto intensified after the turn of the year as Nuno Espírito Santo's side, boosted by the arrival of Brazilian striker Francisco Soares – aka Tiquinho – from Vitória Guimarães, reeled off nine successive wins, including a 2-1 success at home to Sporting that all but removed their opponents from the title race. By the time the two remaining contenders came face to face, at the Estádio da Luz on 1 April, Benfica's lead over Porto was down to a solitary point. A penalty from the recuperated, in-form Jonas gave the home side an early advantage, but a sweet 49th-minute strike from Maxi Pereira, Porto's ex-Benfica full-back, earned the visitors a 1-1 draw that kept the race wide open with seven games to play.

Benfica's toughest test in the run-in was away at Sporting, but a stunning free-kick from Swedish defender Lindelöf secured a 1-1 draw that, combined with an absence of slip-ups elsewhere and some unlikely points surrendered by Porto, enabled the Eagles to stay perched at the top of the Primeira Liga tree. Title No36 was confirmed in fitting style with their biggest win of the season, 5-0 against Guimarães, in front of a capacity crowd of 64,591 joyful spectators.

Five draws in seven games for Porto over the closing stretch had simplified Benfica's task, and a last-day defeat at Moreirense, which thus ended Porto's 30-match unbeaten streak, left the champions with a six-point victory margin – the same gap that separated Porto from third-placed Sporting. Benfica's final tally of 82 points was six down on 2015/16, Rui Vitória's debut season in charge, and the goal figure was greatly reduced from 88 to 72, but all that mattered was first place and that historic fourth successive title.

Despite an improvement on the previous season's third place, Porto viewed the season as one of failure and parted company with Nuno Espírito Santo, bringing in former player Sérgio Conceição from Nantes as his replacement. Another summer departure was that of the season's revelation,

21-year-old striker André Silva to AC Milan. He top-scored for Porto with 16 goals – the same number as Benfica's leading marksman, Kostas Mitroglou – but dwarfing everyone else in the golden boot charts was Sporting's prolific Dutchman Bas Dost, who, in his debut season, racked up 34 goals, exactly half his club's total.

Given that Sporting managed to hold on to three of their four UEFA EURO 2016 winners – Rui Patrício, William Carvalho and Adrien Silva staying while only João Mário left, to Internazionale – the Lions' second season under ex-Benfica boss Jorge Jesus had to go down as one of underachievement. They lost six league games – three times as many as both Benfica and Porto – and suffered from inconsistency plus the lack of a killer instinct in the big games.

Despite the sale of Francisco Soares, Guimarães were comfortable fourth-place finishers, new coach Pedro Martins lifting the club six places higher than in 2015/16. Marítimo's rise was even more pronounced, leaping from 13th spot to sixth – one place below Braga – and therefore bringing European football to Madeira in 2017/18. Their fellow islanders Nacional, by contrast, endured a miserable campaign, finishing bottom with just 21 points.

The issue of the second relegated side remained unresolved until the final day, when Moreirense and Tondela won, leaving Arouca, fifth-place finishers and European qualifiers a year before, in the dreaded 17th position after they lost 4-2 at Estoril – a result that sent them down on goal difference. The coach who had taken Arouca up four seasons earlier, Vítor Oliveira, continued his astonishing sequence of second division success, 2016/17 promotion with Portimonense being the fifth consecutive year in which he had led a different club into the top flight – after Arouca, Moreirense, União Madeira and Chaves.

Domestic cup

Moreirense caused quite a stir by lifting the League Cup in January, beating Braga 1-0 in the final after eliminating holders Benfica 3-1 in the semis, but the country's premier domestic knockout trophy, the Taça de Portugal, was adorned once again with red ribbons as Benfica closed their historic season in fitting style with another victory over Guimarães. There was no repeat 5-0 rout, but goals from Raúl Jiménez and Salvio sufficed to secure a 2-1 win against the 2012/13 winners at Lisbon's Estádio Nacional. Arguably the team of the competition, however, were Chaves, who knocked out both Porto and Sporting before narrowly losing to Guimarães in the semi-final.

Europe

Portuguese clubs made little European impact in 2016/17, with not one of the six entrants reaching the quarter-finals of either competition. There was no Primeira Liga presence in the UEFA Europa League knockout phase for the first time, while none of the Big Three distinguished themselves in the UEFA Champions League, Sporting exiting before Christmas while group runners-up Benfica and Porto both succumbed in the round of 16.

Arguably the best performance of the season was Porto's 3-0 win at Roma in the UEFA Champions League play-off, which booked the club a record-equalling 21st group stage participation, but they finished second to Leicester City in their group and had a man sent off early in each of their two round of 16 defeats by Juventus. Benfica also lost twice to Italian opposition, sneaking through their group behind Napoli with just eight points, and despite beating Borussia Dortmund, one of Sporting's group stage conquerors, 1-0 at home – in skipper Luisão's 500th game for the club – a second successive quarter-final was denied them after a 4-0 hammering in the return.

National team

With Cristiano Ronaldo still recovering from the injury he sustained in the UEFA EURO 2016 final against France, Portugal lost their first competitive game as European champions when Switzerland defeated them 2-0 in Basel. It was a major setback to the team's bid for 2018 FIFA World Cup qualification, but with their captain back on board Fernando Santos's side duly amassed the 15 points expected of them in their next five games. Andorra, the Faroe Islands, Latvia (twice) and Hungary were all seen off with ease as Portugal rattled in 22 goals, with Ronaldo scoring half of them and his new strike partner André Silva helping himself to half a dozen.

Ronaldo added two more goals at the FIFA Confederations Cup – including the winner against host nation Russia – to reach the staggering total of 75 for his country, which left only another Real Madrid legend, Ferenc Puskás (84 goals), ahead of him in the all-time European list. Portugal could not make it two major trophies in successive summers, however, as they were eliminated on penalties when all three Portuguese spot-kick takers failed to find the net after a goalless semi-final in Kazan against Chile.

Cristiano Ronaldo (left) heads home the second of his four goals in Portugal's 6-0 victory at home to Andorra

DOMESTIC SEASON AT A GLANCE

Primeira Liga 2016/17 final table

			Home					Away					Total					
		Pld	W	D	L	F	A	W	D	L	F	A	W	D	L	F	A	Pts
1	**SL Benfica**	**34**	**14**	**3**	**0**	**49**	**9**	**11**	**4**	**2**	**23**	**9**	**25**	**7**	**2**	**72**	**18**	**82**
2	FC Porto	34	14	3	0	44	9	8	7	2	27	10	22	10	2	71	19	76
3	Sporting Clube de Portugal	34	12	3	2	37	14	9	4	4	31	22	21	7	6	68	36	70
4	Vitória SC	34	8	5	4	27	20	10	3	4	23	19	18	8	8	50	39	62
5	SC Braga	34	10	4	3	37	18	5	5	7	14	18	15	9	10	51	36	54
6	CS Marítimo	34	10	5	2	25	12	3	6	8	9	20	13	11	10	34	32	50
7	Rio Ave FC	34	8	4	5	23	18	6	3	8	18	21	14	7	13	41	39	49
8	CD Feirense	34	7	2	8	15	23	7	4	6	16	22	14	6	14	31	45	48
9	Boavista FC	34	5	6	6	18	15	5	7	5	15	21	10	13	11	33	36	43
10	Estoril Praia	34	6	2	9	18	21	4	6	7	18	21	10	8	16	36	42	38
11	GD Chaves	34	6	8	3	19	15	2	6	9	16	27	8	14	12	35	42	38
12	Vitória FC	34	7	3	7	16	15	3	5	9	14	24	10	8	16	30	39	38
13	FC Paços de Ferreira	34	6	8	3	15	11	2	4	11	17	34	8	12	14	32	45	36
14	Os Belenenses	34	4	6	7	14	19	5	3	9	13	26	9	9	16	27	45	36
15	Moreirense FC	34	4	7	6	18	20	4	2	11	15	28	8	9	17	33	48	33
16	CD Tondela	34	7	3	7	19	20	1	5	11	10	32	8	8	18	29	52	32
17	FC Arouca	34	6	2	9	18	23	3	3	11	15	34	9	5	20	33	57	32
18	CD Nacional	34	2	6	9	11	23	2	3	12	11	35	4	9	21	22	58	21

European qualification 2017/18

Champion/Cup winner: SL Benfica (group stage)
FC Porto (group stage)
Sporting Clube de Portugal (play-offs)

Vitória SC (group stage)
SC Braga (third qualifying round)
CS Marítimo (third qualifying round)

Top scorer Bas Dost (Sporting), 34 goals
Relegated clubs CD Nacional, FC Arouca
Promoted clubs Portimonense SC, CD Aves
Cup final SL Benfica 2-1 Vitória SC

Player of the season

Bas Dost
(Sporting Clube de Portugal)

The departure of their 2015/16 top scorer, 27-goal Algerian striker Islam Slimani, to English champions Leicester left a void in the Sporting attack, but it did not take long to fill. Dost, newly arrived from Wolfsburg, hit the ground running, scoring four goals in his first three games, and never let up. The lanky Dutch striker's form in the second half of the season was especially explosive, including a four-goal haul at Tondela and three subsequent hat-tricks, including one in the unique setting of Braga's Estádio Municipal, where Sporting came from behind to win 3-2. In contrast, no player in Benfica's title-winning squad scored a hat-trick all season.

Newcomer of the season

André Silva
(FC Porto)

A Portuguese youth international of some pedigree, André Silva was barely used in the Porto first team until Nuno Espírito Santo gave the young striker his full blessing to lead the Dragons' line in 2016/17. No sooner was he tearing Primeira Liga defences to shreds with his clever movement and sharp finishing than he was doing the same for the senior Portugal side, scoring four goals on his first two starts including a hat-trick in the Faroe Islands. By the end of the season the 21-year-old would be Porto's top scorer, a regular for his country and in possession of a five-year contract with AC Milan after joining the Italian giants for €38m.

Team of the season

(4-3-2-1)

Coach: Rui Vitória *(Benfica)*

PORTUGAL

NATIONAL TEAM

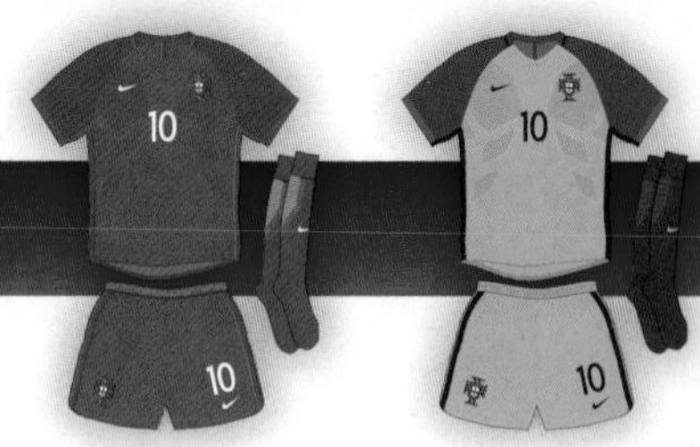

International honours

UEFA European Championship (1) 2016

International tournament appearances

FIFA World Cup (6) 1966 (3rd), 1986, 2002, 2006 (4th), 2010 (2nd round), 2014
UEFA European Championship (7) 1984 (semi-finals), 1996 (qtr-finals), 2000 (semi-finals), 2004 (runners-up), 2008 (qtr-finals), 2012 (semi-finals), 2016 (Winners)

Top five all-time caps

Cristiano Ronaldo (143); Luís Figo (127); **Nani** (112); Fernando Couto (110); **João Moutinho** (102)

Top five all-time goals

Cristiano Ronaldo (75); Pauleta (47); Eusébio (41); Luís Figo (32); Nuno Gomes (29)

Results 2016/17

01/09/16	Gibraltar	H	Porto	W	5-0	*Nani (27, 55), João Cancelo (73), Bernardo Silva (76), Pepe (79)*
06/09/16	Switzerland (WCQ)	A	Basel	L	0-2	
07/10/16	Andorra (WCQ)	H	Aveiro	W	6-0	*Cristiano Ronaldo (2, 4, 47, 68), João Cancelo (44), André Silva (86)*
10/10/16	Faroe Islands (WCQ)	A	Torshavn	W	6-0	*André Silva (12, 22, 37), Cristiano Ronaldo (65), João Moutinho (90+1), João Cancelo (90+3)*
13/11/16	Latvia (WCQ)	H	Faro	W	4-1	*Cristiano Ronaldo (28p, 85), William Carvalho (70), Bruno Alves (90+2)*
25/03/17	Hungary (WCQ)	H	Lisbon	W	3-0	*André Silva (32), Cristiano Ronaldo (36, 65)*
28/03/17	Sweden	H	Funchal	L	2-3	*Cristiano Ronaldo (18), Granqvist (34og)*
03/06/17	Cyprus	H	Estoril	W	4-0	*João Moutinho (3, 42), Pizzi (63), André Silva (70)*
09/06/17	Latvia (WCQ)	A	Riga	W	3-0	*Cristiano Ronaldo (41, 63), André Silva (67)*
18/06/17	Mexico (CC)	N	Kazan (RUS)	D	2-2	*Ricardo Quaresma (34), Cédric (86)*
21/06/17	Russia (CC)	A	Moscow	W	1-0	*Cristiano Ronaldo (8)*
24/06/17	New Zealand (CC)	N	St Petersburg (RUS)	W	4-0	*Cristiano Ronaldo (33p), Bernardo Silva (37), André Silva (80), Nani (90+1)*
28/06/17	Chile (CC)	N	Kazan (RUS)	D	0-0	*(aet; 0-3 on pens)*
02/07/17	Mexico (CC)	N	Moscow (RUS)	W	2-1	*Pepe (90+1), Adrien Silva (104p) (aet)*

Appearances 2016/17

Coach: Fernando Santos	10/10/54		Gib	SUI	AND	FRO	LVA	HUN	Swe	Cyp	LVA	MEX	RUS	NZL	CHI	MEX	Caps	Goals
Eduardo	19/09/82	Chelsea (ENG)	G														36	-
João Cancelo	27/05/94	Valencia (ESP)	D		D	D	D		D								5	3
Pepe	26/02/83	Real Madrid (ESP)	D	D	D72	D		D				D	D	D		D	86	5
Bruno Alves	27/11/81	Cagliari (ITA)	D				D		D		D		D	D	D		93	11
Raphaël Guerreiro	22/12/93	Dortmund (GER)	D63	D	D52		D	D			D	D	D65				20	2
João Moutinho	08/09/86	Monaco (FRA)	M62	M68	M	s81		s83	M46	M46	M	M58		M	s102	M82	102	7
William Carvalho	07/04/92	Sporting	M46	M46		M	M	M	s46	s46	M	M	M		M	s91	37	1
João Mário	19/01/93	Internazionale (ITA)	M63	s46	s66	M81	M71	M83		M46							25	-
Ricardo Quaresma	26/09/83	Beşiktaş (TUR)	A46	s68	A	A67	s65	A	s59		s57	M82		M83	s83	s70	69	9
Éder	22/12/87	LOSC (FRA)	A46	A46		s79			s46								33	4
Nani	17/11/86	Valencia (ESP)	A	A			A65			A60	s80	A58		s67	s76	A70	112	24
Adrien Silva	15/03/89	Sporting	s46	M						s46		s58	M83		M102	s82	20	1
André Silva	06/11/95	Porto	s46	s46	A	A79	A	A67		A	A80	s82	A78	A	A76	A	13	8
Bernardo Silva	10/08/94	Monaco (FRA)	s46	A	M			s67	A46	M46			M	M46	M83		15	2
Rafa Silva	17/05/93	Benfica	s62														10	-
André Gomes	30/07/93	Barcelona (ESP)	s63		M66	M	M87	M86	s79	s46	M	M	M		M116	s82	25	-
Eliseu	01/10/83	Benfica	s63						D46	D			s65	D	D	D	25	1
Rui Patrício	15/02/88	Sporting		G	G	G	G	G		G	G	G	G	G	G	G	64	-
Cédric	31/08/91	Southampton (ENG)		D				D		D67	D71	D	D		D		22	1
José Fonte	22/12/83	Southampton (ENG) /West Ham (ENG)		D	D	D	D	D		D	D	D			D		25	-
Cristiano Ronaldo	05/02/85	Real Madrid (ESP)			A	A	A	A	A59		A	A	A	A67	A		143	75
Antunes	01/04/87	Dynamo Kyiv (UKR)			s52	D											11	-
Gelson Martins	11/05/95	Sporting			s72	s67	s71		A79	s46	M57	s58	s78	s83	s116	M	11	-
Renato Sanches	18/08/97	Bayern (GER)					s87		M								13	1
Pizzi	06/10/89	Benfica						s86	s46	s60				s46		M91	9	2
Marafona	08/05/87	Braga							G								1	-
Luís Neto	26/05/88	Zenit (RUS)							D	D						D	14	-
Danilo Pereira	09/09/91	Porto							M46	M46			s83	M		M82	22	1
Nélson Semedo	16/11/93	Benfica							s46	s67	s71			D		D 106*	6	-

EUROPE

SL Benfica

CHAMPIONS LEAGUE

Group B
Match 1 - Beşiktaş JK (TUR)
H 1-1 *Cervi (12)*
Ederson, Lisandro López, Álex Grimaldo, Fejsa (Celis 89), André Horta, Lindelöf, Salvio, Gonçalo Guedes, Pizzi, Cervi (Samaris 70), Nélson Semedo. Coach: Rui Vitória (POR)
Match 2 - SSC Napoli (ITA)
A 2-4 *Gonçalo Guedes (70), Salvio (86)*
Júlio César, Lisandro López, Álex Grimaldo, Fejsa (José Gomes 82), André Horta (Salvio 56), Mitroglou, Lindelöf, Carrillo (Gonçalo Guedes 67), Pizzi, André Almeida, Nélson Semedo. Coach: Rui Vitória (POR)
Match 3 - FC Dynamo Kyiv (UKR)
A 2-0 *Salvio (9p), Cervi (55)*
Ederson, Álex Grimaldo, Luisão, Fejsa, Mitroglou (Jiménez 71), Lindelöf, Salvio, Gonçalo Guedes (Eliseu 90), Pizzi, Cervi (Celis 83), Nélson Semedo. Coach: Rui Vitória (POR)
Match 4 - FC Dynamo Kyiv (UKR)
H 1-0 *Salvio (45+2p)*
Ederson, Álex Grimaldo, Luisão, Fejsa (Samaris 59), Mitroglou (Jiménez 70), Lindelöf, Salvio, Gonçalo Guedes (André Almeida 87), Pizzi, Cervi, Nélson Semedo. Coach: Rui Vitória (POR)
Match 5 - Beşiktaş JK (TUR)
A 3-3 *Gonçalo Guedes (10), Nélson Semedo (25), Fejsa (31)*
Ederson, Luisão, Fejsa, Mitroglou (Jiménez 86), Lindelöf, Salvio, Eliseu, Gonçalo Guedes (Samaris 75), Pizzi, Cervi (Rafa Silva 64), Nélson Semedo. Coach: Rui Vitória (POR)
Match 6 - SSC Napoli (ITA)
H 1-2 *Jiménez (87)*
Ederson, Luisão, Fejsa, Jiménez, Lindelöf, Salvio (Mitroglou 80), Gonçalo Guedes (Rafa Silva 57), Pizzi, Cervi (Carrillo 68), André Almeida, Nélson Semedo. Coach: Rui Vitória (POR)

Round of 16 - Borussia Dortmund (GER)
H 1-0 *Mitroglou (48)*
Ederson, Luisão, Fejsa, Mitroglou (Jiménez 75), Lindelöf, Carrillo (Filipe Augusto 46), Salvio, Eliseu, Pizzi, Rafa Silva (Cervi 67), Nélson Semedo. Coach: Rui Vitória (POR)
A 0-4
Ederson, Luisão, Samaris (A Živković 74), Mitroglou, Lindelöf, Salvio (Jonas 64), Eliseu, Pizzi, Cervi (Jiménez 82), André Almeida, Nélson Semedo. Coach: Rui Vitória (POR)

Sporting Clube de Portugal

CHAMPIONS LEAGUE

Group F
Match 1 - Real Madrid CF (ESP)
A 1-2 *Bruno César (48)*
Rui Patrício, B Ruiz (Campbell 90+2), Bruno César, Coates, William Carvalho, João Pereira, Adrien Silva (Elías 73), Dost, Zeegelaar, Rúben Semedo, Gelson Martins (Marković 70). Coach: Jorge Jesus (POR)
Match 2 - Legia Warszawa (POL)
H 2-0 *B Ruiz (28), Dost (37)*
Rui Patrício, Jefferson, B Ruiz (Petrović 87), Bruno César (Marković 67), Coates, William Carvalho, João Pereira, Adrien Silva, Dost, Rúben Semedo, Gelson Martins (Campbell 76). Coach: Jorge Jesus (POR)
Match 3 - Borussia Dortmund (GER)
H 1-2 *Bruno César (67)*
Rui Patrício, Schelotto, Marković (Campbell 65), B Ruiz (André 79), Coates, William Carvalho, Elías (Bruno César 60), Dost, Zeegelaar, Rúben Semedo, Gelson Martins. Coach: Jorge Jesus (POR)
Match 4 - Borussia Dortmund (GER)
A 0-1
Rui Patrício, Schelotto, B Ruiz (Marković 78), Bruno César (Adrien Silva 58), Coates, William Carvalho, Paulo Oliveira, Castaignos (Dost 46), Zeegelaar, Rúben Semedo, Gelson Martins. Coach: Jorge Jesus (POR)
Match 5 - Real Madrid CF (ESP)
H 1-2 *Adrien Silva (80p)*
Rui Patrício, B Ruiz (Schelotto 67), Bruno César (Campbell 62), Coates, William Carvalho, João Pereira, Adrien Silva, Dost (André 76), Zeegelaar, Rúben Semedo, Gelson Martins. Coach: Jorge Jesus (POR)
Red card: João Pereira 64
Match 6 - Legia Warszawa (POL)
A 0-1
Rui Patrício, Marković (B Ruiz 58), Bruno César, Coates, William Carvalho, Paulo Oliveira (Ricardo Esgaio 58), Adrien Silva, Dost, Zeegelaar (André 68), Rúben Semedo, Gelson Martins. Coach: Jorge Jesus (POR)
Red card: William Carvalho 85

FC Porto

CHAMPIONS LEAGUE

Play-offs - AS Roma (ITA)
H 1-1 *André Silva (61p)*
Casillas, Maxi Pereira, Marcano, André Silva, Adrián López (Corona 75), Alex Telles, Herrera, André André (Layún 66), Danilo Pereira, Otávio (Evandro 85), Felipe. Coach: Nuno Espírito Santo (POR)
A 3-0 *Felipe (8), Layún (73), Corona (75)*
Casillas, Maxi Pereira (Layún 45+2), Marcano, André Silva (Adrián López 66), Alex Telles, Herrera, Corona, André André, Danilo Pereira, Otávio (Sérgio Oliveira 57), Felipe. Coach: Nuno Espírito Santo (POR)

Group G
Match 1 - FC København (DEN)
H 1-1 *Otávio (13)*
Casillas, Marcano, André Silva, Alex Telles, Herrera (Brahimi 70), Corona (Depoitre 62), Layún, Danilo Pereira, Otávio (Diogo Jota 82), Felipe, Óliver Torres. Coach: Nuno Espírito Santo (POR)
Match 2 - Leicester City FC (ENG)
A 0-1
Casillas, Marcano, André Silva, Adrián López (Diogo Jota 63), Alex Telles, André André (Herrera 63), Layún, Danilo Pereira, Otávio, Felipe, Óliver Torres (Corona 77). Coach: Nuno Espírito Santo (POR)
Match 3 - Club Brugge KV (BEL)
A 2-1 *Layún (68), André Silva (90+3p)*
Casillas, Marcano, André Silva, Alex Telles, Herrera (Brahimi 59), Diogo Jota (Corona 60), Layún, Danilo Pereira, Otávio (André André 72), Felipe, Óliver Torres. Coach: Nuno Espírito Santo (POR)
Match 4 - Club Brugge KV (BEL)
H 1-0 *André Silva (37)*
Casillas, Maxi Pereira, Marcano, André Silva, Alex Telles, Herrera (Rúben Neves 62), Diogo Jota (Corona 71), Danilo Pereira, Otávio (Layún 79), Felipe, Óliver Torres. Coach: Nuno Espírito Santo (POR)
Match 5 - FC København (DEN)
A 0-0
Casillas, Maxi Pereira, Marcano, André Silva, Alex Telles, Corona (Varela 88), Diogo Jota, Danilo Pereira, Otávio (Evandro 84), Felipe, Óliver Torres. Coach: Nuno Espírito Santo (POR)
Match 6 - Leicester City FC (ENG)
H 5-0 *André Silva (6, 64p), Corona (26), Brahimi (44), Diogo Jota (77)*
Casillas, Maxi Pereira, Marcano, Brahimi, André Silva (Rui Pedro 78), Alex Telles, Corona (Herrera 76), Diogo Jota, Danilo Pereira (Rúben Neves 76), Felipe, Óliver Torres. Coach: Nuno Espírito Santo (POR)

Round of 16 - Juventus (ITA)
H 0-2
Casillas, Maxi Pereira, Marcano, Rúben Neves (Corona 61), Brahimi (Diogo Jota 73), André Silva (Layún 30), Alex Telles, Herrera, Danilo Pereira, Felipe, Francisco Soares. Coach: Nuno Espírito Santo (POR)
Red card: Alex Telles 27
A 0-1
Casillas, Maxi Pereira, Marcano, Brahimi (Diogo Jota 67), André Silva (Boly 46), André André, Layún, Danilo Pereira, Felipe, Francisco Soares, Óliver Torres (Otávio 70). Coach: Nuno Espírito Santo (POR)
Red card: Maxi Pereira 40

DOMESTIC LEAGUE CLUB-BY-CLUB

SC Braga

Group H

Match 1 - KAA Gent (BEL)

H 1-1 *André Pinto (24)*

Matheus, Rosić, André Pinto, Wilson Eduardo (Alan 84), Bakić (Vukčević 73), Hassan, Baiano, Pedro Santos (Stojiljković 76), Pedro Tiba, Mauro, Marcelo Goiano. Coach: José Peseiro (POR)

Match 2 - FC Shakhtar Donetsk (UKR)

A 0-2

Marafona, Rosić, Wilson Eduardo (Martínez 67), Hassan, Baiano, Ricardo Horta (Stojiljković 57), Pedro Santos (Bakić 67), Vukčević, Artur Jorge, Mauro, Marcelo Goiano. Coach: José Peseiro (POR)

Match 3 - Konyaspor (TUR)

A 1-1 *Hassan (55)*

Matheus, Velázquez, Rosić, Wilson Eduardo (Ricardo Horta 67), Hassan (Stojiljković 75), Baiano, Pedro Santos, Alan (Rui Fonte 75), Vukčević, Mauro, Marcelo Goiano. Coach: José Peseiro (POR)

Match 4 - Konyaspor (TUR)

H 3-1 *Velázquez (34), Wilson Eduardo (45+1), Ricardo Horta (90+7)*

Matheus, Velázquez (Alan 73), Rosić, Wilson Eduardo (Pedro Santos 70), Hassan, Baiano, Rui Fonte (Pedro Tiba 43), Ricardo Horta, Vukčević, Mauro, Marcelo Goiano. Coach: José Peseiro (POR)

Red card: Mauro 38

Match 5 - KAA Gent (BEL)

A 2-2 *Stojiljković (14), Hassan (36)*

Matheus, Rosić, André Pinto (Artur Jorge 65), Wilson Eduardo, Hassan (Rui Fonte 76), Baiano, Stojiljković, Ricardo Horta (Pedro Santos 89), Pedro Tiba, Vukčević, Marcelo Goiano. Coach: José Peseiro (POR)

Match 6 - FC Shakhtar Donetsk (UKR)

H 2-4 *Stojiljković (43), Vukčević (89)*

Marafona, Rosić, André Pinto, Wilson Eduardo (Benítez 66), Baiano, Rui Fonte (Hassan 58), Stojiljković (Alan 70), Ricardo Horta, Pedro Tiba, Vukčević, Marcelo Goiano. Coach: José Peseiro (POR)

FC Arouca

Third qualifying round - Heracles Almelo (NED)

A 1-1 *González (90+1)*

Rafael Bracalli, Hugo Basto, Artur (Nuno Valente 50), Adilson Goiano (André Santos 55), Mateus, Gegé, Jubal, Nelsinho, Nuno Coelho, Zequinha (Rafael Crivellaro 88), González. Coach: Lito Vidigal (ANG)

H 0-0

Rafael Bracalli, Hugo Basto, Anderson Luís, Nuno Valente (Adilson Goiano 90+1), Mateus, Gegé, André Santos (De Jesús 78), Jubal, Nuno Coelho, Zequinha, González (Rafael Crivellaro 69). Coach: Manuel Gomes (POR)

Play-offs - Olympiacos FC (GRE)

H 0-1

Rafael Bracalli, Hugo Basto, Anderson Luís, Artur (André Santos 68), Adilson Goiano (Rafael Crivellaro 75), Nuno Valente, Mateus, Thiago Carleto (De Jesús 59), Jubal, Nuno Coelho, González. Coach: Lito Vidigal (ANG)

A 1-2 (aet) *Gegé (80)*

Rafael Bracalli, Hugo Basto, Velázquez, Artur (Nuno Valente 90+4), De Jesús, Gegé (Bruno Lopes 112), André Santos, Jubal, Rafael Crivellaro, Zequinha (Mateus 77), González. Coach: Lito Vidigal (ANG)

Rio Ave FC

Third qualifying round - SK Slavia Praha (CZE)

A 0-0

Cássio, Eliseu Cassamá, Krovinović (Guedes 69), João Novais, Roderick, Wakaso, Gil Dias, Marcelo, Rafa Soares, Rúben Ribeiro (Tarantini 82), Yazalde (Héldon 59). Coach: Capucho (POR)

H 1-1 *Rúben Ribeiro (57)*

Cássio, Eliseu Cassamá, Krovinović (Pedrinho 46), João Novais (Héldon 61), Roderick, Wakaso, Gil Dias, Marcelo, Rafa Soares, Rúben Ribeiro, Yazalde (Tarantini 46). Coach: Capucho (POR)

Red card: Eliseu Cassamá 45+1

FC Arouca

1951 • Municipal de Arouca (5,100) • fcarouca.eu

Coach: Lito Vidigal (ANG); (11/02/17) Manuel Machado; (21/03/17) Jorge Leitão

2016					
14/08	a	Boavista	L	0-2	
21/08	h	Nacional	W	2-0	*Rafael Crivellaro, Zequinha*
28/08	a	Setúbal	L	0-2	
09/09	h	Benfica	L	1-2	*González*
18/09	h	Chaves	L	0-1	
26/09	a	Belenenses	D	1-1	*Kuca*
02/10	h	Braga	D	1-1	*González*
22/10	a	Porto	L	0-3	
30/10	h	Marítimo	W	1-0	*González*
06/11	a	Sporting	L	0-3	
27/11	h	Paços Ferreira	W	1-0	*Jorginho*
04/12	a	Feirense	W	2-0	*Nelsinho, González*
12/12	h	Rio Ave	L	0-2	
17/12	a	Moreirense	W	4-1	*Jorginho 3, Mateus*
23/12	h	Guimarães	L	0-1	
2017					
08/01	a	Tondela	W	2-1	*González, Jorginho*
13/01	h	Estoril	W	2-1	*Adilson Goiano, Kuca*
21/01	h	Boavista	L	1-2	*Tómané*
28/01	a	Nacional	D	1-1	*Nuno Coelho*
05/02	h	Setúbal	W	2-1	*Kuca 2*
10/02	a	Benfica	L	0-3	
18/02	a	Chaves	L	0-2	
27/02	h	Belenenses	L	1-2	*Tómané*
04/03	a	Braga	L	1-3	*Mateus*
10/03	h	Porto	L	0-4	
19/03	a	Marítimo	L	1-3	*Sami*
02/04	h	Sporting	L	1-2	*Mateus*
08/04	a	Paços Ferreira	D	1-1	*André Santos*
15/04	h	Feirense	W	2-0	*Kuca 2 (1p)*
21/04	a	Rio Ave	L	0-3	
30/04	h	Moreirense	D	2-2	*Tómané, Rafael Crivellaro*
07/05	a	Guimarães	L	0-1	
13/05	h	Tondela	L	1-2	*Rafael Crivellaro*
21/05	a	Estoril	L	2-4	*Adilson Goiano 2*

No	Name	Nat	DoB	Pos	Aps	(s)	Gls
8	Adilson Goiano	BRA	09/02/88	M	24	(3)	3
5	Anderson Luís	BRA	31/07/88	D	31		
26	André Santos		02/03/89	M	28	(2)	1
7	Artur		18/02/84	M	23	(4)	
99	Bruno Lopes	BRA	19/05/95	A		(4)	
9	Marlon de Jesús	ECU	04/09/91	A	4	(5)	
14	Gegé	CPV	24/02/88	D	4	(4)	
42	Gilson Costa		24/09/96	M		(2)	
95	Walter González	PAR	21/06/95	A	14	(19)	5
3	Hugo Basto		14/05/93	D	12	(5)	
11	Jorginho		21/09/95	A	9	(1)	5
33	Jubal	BRA	29/08/93	D	32		
77	Karl	BRA	07/04/93	M		(2)	
21	Keirrison	BRA	03/12/88	A		(2)	
17	Kuca	CPV	02/08/89	A	10	(14)	6
12	Mateus	ANG	19/06/84	A	28	(4)	3
55	Nelsinho	BRA	01/01/88	D	16		1
66	Nuno Coelho		23/11/87	M	27	(1)	1
50	Nuno Valente		22/11/91	M	13	(10)	
1	Rafael Bracalli	BRA	05/05/81	G	19		
50	Rafael Crivellaro	BRA	18/02/89	M	13	(11)	3
13	Rui Sacramento		31/01/85	G	3		
11	Sami	GNB	18/12/88	A	4	(2)	1
20	Sancidino Silva		05/03/94	A		(5)	
38	Sinan Bolat	TUR	03/09/88	G	12	(1)	
16	Thiago Carleto	BRA	24/03/89	D	2		
16	Tómané		23/10/92	A	15	(2)	3
15	Jeffre Vargas	VEN	12/01/95	D	1		
4	José Manuel Velázquez	VEN	08/09/90	D	15	(2)	
6	Vítor	BRA	01/07/94	D	8		
87	Zequinha		07/01/87	A	7		1

Os Belenenses

1919 • Restelo (19,856) • osbelenenses.com

Major honours
Portuguese League (1) 1946; Portuguese Cup (3) 1942, 1960, 1989

Coach: Julio Velázquez (ESP); (06/10/16) Quim Machado; (18/04/17) Domingos Paciência

Date		Opponent		Score	Scorers
2016					
14/08	a	Setúbal	L	0-2	
19/08	h	Boavista	D	0-0	
27/08	a	Tondela	W	1-0	*Fábio Sturgeon*
10/09	h	Nacional	W	2-1	*Abel Camará, og (Bonilla)*
17/09	a	Guimarães	D	1-1	*João Palhinha*
26/09	h	Arouca	D	1-1	*Abel Camará*
01/10	a	Chaves	L	1-3	*Domingos Duarte*
23/10	h	Benfica	L	0-2	
30/10	a	Braga	L	1-2	*Tiago Caeiro*
05/11	a	Feirense	W	1-0	*Fábio Sturgeon*
26/11	h	Porto	D	0-0	
04/12	a	Estoril	D	1-1	*Abel Camará*
10/12	h	Marítimo	W	1-0	*Gerso*
16/12	a	Paços Ferreira	L	0-1	
22/12	h	Sporting	L	0-1	
2017					
09/01	a	Moreirense	L	0-1	
15/01	h	Rio Ave	W	1-0	*Gonçalo Silva*
22/01	h	Setúbal	L	1-2	*Tiago Caeiro*
27/01	a	Boavista	W	1-0	*João Diogo*
05/02	h	Tondela	D	0-0	
12/02	a	Nacional	D	1-1	*Juanto*
19/02	h	Guimarães	D	1-1	*Miguel Rosa*
27/02	a	Arouca	W	2-1	*Maurides 2*
05/03	h	Chaves	W	2-1	*Maurides, Tiago Caeiro*
13/03	a	Benfica	L	0-4	
18/03	h	Braga	L	1-2	*Maurides (p)*
02/04	h	Feirense	L	1-2	*Juanto*
08/04	a	Porto	L	0-3	
14/04	h	Estoril	L	1-3	*Maurides*
22/04	a	Marítimo	L	0-3	
30/04	h	Paços Ferreira	L	1-2	*Maurides*
07/05	a	Sporting	W	3-1	*Abel Camará (p), Dinis Almeida, Gonçalo Silva*
12/05	h	Moreirense	D	1-1	*João Diogo*
20/05	a	Rio Ave	L	0-2	

No	Name	Nat	DoB	Pos	Aps	(s)	Gls
30	Abel Camará	GNB	06/01/90	A	27	(1)	4
8	André Sousa		09/07/90	M	22	(9)	
95	Komnen Andrić	SRB	01/07/95	A	3	(5)	
21	Benny		04/01/97	M	2	(4)	
11	Betinho		21/07/93	A		(2)	
99	Cristiano		19/11/90	G	14		
4	Dinis Almeida		28/06/95	D	5	(1)	1
70	Diogo Viana		22/02/90	A	3	(3)	
14	Domingos Duarte		10/03/95	D	28		1
5	Edgar Ié		01/05/94	D	12		
92	Fábio Nunes		24/07/92	M	4	(9)	
71	Fábio Sturgeon		04/02/94	M	14	(3)	2
10	Gerso		23/02/91	M	9	(5)	1
28	Gonçalo Brandão		09/10/86	D	11	(1)	
37	Gonçalo Silva		04/06/91	D	21	(1)	2
29	Florent Hanin	FRA	04/02/90	D	34		
2	João Diogo		28/02/88	D	31		2
66	João Palhinha		09/07/95	M	13		1
12	Joel Pereira		28/06/96	G	8		
23	Juanto	ESP	11/02/92	A	11	(5)	2
27	Luís Silva		29/09/92	M		(6)	
16	Maurides	BRA	10/03/94	A	10	(2)	6
76	Mica Pinto		04/06/93	D	1	(5)	
7	Miguel Rosa		13/01/89	M	18	(8)	1
6	Oriol Rosell	ESP	07/07/92	M	9	(5)	
77	Rúben Pinto		24/04/92	M	2		
9	Tiago Caeiro		29/03/84	A	1	(17)	3
24	Ventura		14/01/88	G	12		
25	Vítor Gomes		25/12/87	M	25	(3)	
23	Hassan Yebda	ALG	14/05/84	M	15	(3)	
18	Robert Åhman Persson	SWE	26/03/87	M	9	(3)	

SL Benfica

1904 • Sport Lisboa e Benfica (65,647) • slbenfica.pt

Major honours
European Champion Clubs' Cup (2) 1961, 1962; Portuguese League (36) 1936, 1937, 1938, 1942, 1943, 1945, 1950, 1955, 1957, 1960, 1961, 1963, 1964, 1965, 1967, 1968, 1969, 1971, 1972, 1973, 1975, 1976, 1977, 1981, 1983, 1984, 1987, 1989, 1991, 1994, 2005, 2010, 2014, 2015, 2016, 2017; Portuguese Cup (26) 1940, 1943, 1944, 1949, 1951, 1952, 1953, 1955, 1957, 1959, 1962, 1964, 1969, 1970, 1972, 1980, 1981, 1983, 1985, 1986, 1987, 1993, 1996, 2004, 2014, 2017

Coach: Rui Vitória

Date		Opponent		Score	Scorers
2016					
13/08	a	Tondela	W	2-0	*Lisandro López, André Horta*
21/08	h	Setúbal	D	1-1	*Jiménez (p)*
27/08	a	Nacional	W	3-1	*og (Ghazal), Carrillo, Jiménez*
09/09	a	Arouca	W	2-1	*Nélson Semedo, Lisandro López*
19/09	h	Braga	W	3-1	*Mitroglou 2, Pizzi*
24/09	a	Chaves	W	2-0	*Mitroglou, Pizzi*
02/10	h	Feirense	W	4-0	*og (Luís Aurélio), Salvio, Cervi, Álex Grimaldo*
23/10	a	Belenenses	W	2-0	*Mitroglou, Álex Grimaldo*
28/10	h	Paços Ferreira	W	3-0	*Gonçalo Guedes, Salvio, Pizzi*
06/11	a	Porto	D	1-1	*Lisandro López*
27/11	h	Moreirense	W	3-0	*Pizzi 2, Jiménez*
02/12	a	Marítimo	L	1-2	*Gonçalo Guedes*
11/12	h	Sporting	W	2-1	*Salvio, Jiménez*
17/12	a	Estoril	W	1-0	*Jiménez (p)*
21/12	h	Rio Ave	W	2-0	*Mitroglou, Pizzi*
2017					
07/01	a	Guimarães	W	2-0	*Jonas, Mitroglou*
17/01	h	Boavista	D	3-3	*Mitroglou, Jonas (p), og (Fábio Espinho)*
22/01	h	Tondela	W	4-0	*Pizzi 2, Rafa Silva, Jonas (p)*
30/01	a	Setúbal	L	0-1	
05/02	h	Nacional	W	3-0	*Jonas 2, Mitroglou*
10/02	h	Arouca	W	3-0	*Mitroglou 2, Carrillo*
19/02	a	Braga	W	1-0	*Mitroglou*
24/02	h	Chaves	W	3-1	*Mitroglou 2, Rafa Silva*
04/03	a	Feirense	W	1-0	*Pizzi*
13/03	h	Belenenses	W	4-0	*André Almeida, Mitroglou, Salvio, Jonas*
18/03	a	Paços Ferreira	D	0-0	
01/04	h	Porto	D	1-1	*Jonas (p)*
09/04	a	Moreirense	W	1-0	*Mitroglou*
14/04	h	Marítimo	W	3-0	*og (Luís Martins), Jonas 2*
22/04	a	Sporting	D	1-1	*Lindelöf*
29/04	h	Estoril	W	2-1	*Jonas 2 (1p)*
07/05	a	Rio Ave	W	1-0	*Jiménez*
13/05	h	Guimarães	W	5-0	*Cervi, Jiménez, Pizzi, Jonas 2 (1p)*
20/05	a	Boavista	D	2-2	*Mitroglou, Kalaica*

No	Name	Nat	DoB	Pos	Aps	(s)	Gls
3	Álex Grimaldo	ESP	20/09/95	D	14		2
34	André Almeida		10/09/90	M	10	(4)	1
8	André Horta		07/11/96	M	7	(3)	1
15	André Carrillo	PER	04/06/91	A	3	(17)	2
28	Guillermo Celis	COL	08/05/93	M		(3)	
22	Franco Cervi	ARG	26/05/94	M	16	(10)	2
37	Danilo	BRA	28/02/96	M		(2)	
1	Ederson	BRA	17/08/93	G	27		
19	Eliseu		01/10/83	D	12	(3)	
5	Ljubomir Fejsa	SRB	14/08/88	M	25		
6	Filipe Augusto	BRA	12/08/93	M	1	(8)	
20	Gonçalo Guedes		29/11/96	A	14	(2)	2
33	Jardel	BRA	29/03/86	D	1		
9	Raúl Jiménez	MEX	05/05/91	A	6	(13)	7
10	Jonas	BRA	01/04/84	A	15	(4)	13
70	José Gomes		08/04/99	A		(3)	
35	Luka Jović	SRB	23/12/97	M		(1)	
12	Júlio César	BRA	03/09/79	G	7	(1)	
16	Branimir Kalaica	CRO	01/06/98	D	1		1
14	Victor Lindelöf	SWE	17/07/94	D	32	(1)	1
2	Lisandro López	ARG	01/09/89	D	6	(2)	3
4	Luisão	BRA	13/02/81	D	28		
38	Marcelo Hermes	BRA	02/01/95	D	1		
11	Kostas Mitroglou	GRE	12/03/88	A	26	(2)	16
50	Nélson Semedo		16/11/93	D	31		1
13	Paulo Lopes		29/06/78	G		(1)	
23	Pedro Pereira		22/01/88	D	1		
21	Pizzi		06/10/89	M	33		10
27	Rafa Silva		17/05/93	M	12	(8)	2
18	Eduardo Salvio	ARG	13/07/90	M	26	(3)	4
7	Andreas Samaris	GRE	13/06/89	M	9	(9)	
17	Andrija Živković	SRB	11/07/96	M	10	(5)	

Boavista FC

1903 • Bessa (30,000) • boavistafc.pt

Major honours
Portuguese League (1) 2001; Portuguese Cup (5) 1975, 1976, 1979, 1992, 1997

Coach: Erwin Sánchez (BOL); (11/10/16) Miguel Leal

Date		Opponent		Score	Scorers
2016					
14/08	h	Arouca	W	2-0	*Mandiang, Lucas*
19/08	a	Belenenses	D	0-0	
28/08	h	Chaves	D	2-2	*Schembri, Fábio Espinho*
11/09	a	Braga	L	0-3	
18/09	h	Feirense	L	1-2	*Bukia*
23/09	a	Porto	L	1-3	*Nuno Henrique*
02/10	h	Moreirense	W	2-0	*Lucas, Mandiang*
21/10	a	Marítimo	D	1-1	*Carraça*
29/10	h	Estoril	D	0-0	
05/11	a	Rio Ave	W	2-1	*Renato Santos, Nuno Henrique*
26/11	h	Sporting	L	0-1	
05/12	a	Paços Ferreira	L	1-2	*Renato Santos*
10/12	h	Guimarães	L	1-2	*Philipe Sampaio*
18/12	a	Tondela	D	1-1	*Anderson Carvalho*
22/12	a	Nacional	W	2-0	*Mahmudov, Renato Santos*
2017					
08/01	h	Setúbal	W	1-0	*Fábio Espinho*
14/01	a	Benfica	D	3-3	*Iuri Medeiros, Lucas, Schembri*
21/01	a	Arouca	W	2-1	*Mandiang, Iuri Medeiros*
27/01	h	Belenenses	L	0-1	
04/02	a	Chaves	D	0-0	
12/02	h	Braga	D	1-1	*Fábio Espinho*
18/02	a	Feirense	W	1-0	*Bulos*
26/02	h	Porto	L	0-1	
03/03	a	Moreirense	D	0-0	
12/03	h	Marítimo	W	3-0	*Iuri Medeiros 2, Bulos*
17/03	a	Estoril	D	0-0	
01/04	h	Rio Ave	L	0-1	
08/04	a	Sporting	L	0-4	
14/04	h	Paços Ferreira	D	0-0	
23/04	a	Guimarães	L	0-2	
29/04	h	Tondela	W	1-0	*Iuri Medeiros*
06/05	h	Nacional	D	2-2	*Iuri Medeiros, Fábio Espinho (p)*
15/05	a	Setúbal	W	1-0	*Iuri Medeiros*
20/05	h	Benfica	D	2-2	*Renato Santos, Schembri*

No	Name	Nat	DoB	Pos	Aps	(s)	Gls
1	Kamran Ağayev	AZE	09/02/86	G	12		
26	Aidi Fulangxisi	CHN	17/12/90	D	1	(1)	
27	Anderson Carvalho	BRA	20/05/90	M	23	(5)	1
6	Anderson Correia	BRA	06/05/91	D	3	(1)	
25	Mamadou Ba	SEN	08/05/85	G	1		
95	André Bukia	COD	03/03/95	M	7	(9)	1
19	Ivan Bulos	PER	20/05/93	A	9	(3)	2
22	Carlos Santos		31/03/89	D	3	(5)	
17	Carraça		01/03/93	M	17	(9)	1
9	Idelino Colubali	GNB	01/01/94	A		(5)	
70	Digas		31/12/92	A	1	(6)	
20	Edu Machado		26/04/90	D	22	(2)	
32	Erivelto	BRA	01/10/88	A	1	(7)	
10	Fábio Espinho		18/08/85	M	29	(1)	4
45	Iuri Medeiros		10/07/94	M	26	(1)	7
3	Lucas	BRA	05/11/90	D	31		3
15	Emin Mahmudov	AZE	27/04/92	M	3	(9)	1
42	Idrissa Mandiang	SEN	27/12/84	M	28		3
11	David Mbala	COD	19/04/93	M		(3)	
61	Mickaël Meira		25/01/94	G	4		
12	Mika		08/03/91	G	3		
23	Nuno Henrique		19/10/86	D	10	(2)	2
94	Philipe Sampaio	BRA	11/11/94	D	23	(2)	1
7	Renato Santos		05/10/91	M	29	(3)	4
16	Rochinha		03/05/95	M	1	(7)	
88	Samu		21/04/86	M	1	(4)	
30	André Schembri	MLT	27/05/86	A	23	(7)	3
5	Talocha		30/08/89	D	32		
8	Tengarrinha		17/02/89	M	5	(5)	
28	Tiago Mesquita		23/11/90	D	12	(3)	
33	Vagner	BRA	06/06/86	G	14		

PORTUGAL

SC Braga

1921 • Municipal de Braga (30,286) • scbraga.pt

Major honours
Portuguese Cup (2) 1966, 2016

Coach: José Peseiro; (15/12/16) (Abel Ferreira); (19/12/16) Jorge Simão; (26/04/17) Abel Ferreira

2016

14/08	a	Guimarães	W	1-0	*Pedro Santos*
22/08	h	Rio Ave	D	1-1	*Stojiljković*
27/08	a	Estoril	W	3-1	*Pedro Santos, Wilson Eduardo, André Pinto*
11/09	h	Boavista	W	3-0	*Hassan, Pedro Santos (p), Wilson Eduardo*
19/09	a	Benfica	L	1-3	*Rosić*
24/09	h	Setúbal	W	2-1	*Alan (p), Wilson Eduardo*
02/10	a	Arouca	D	1-1	*Pedro Santos*
24/10	h	Chaves	W	1-0	*Pedro Santos (p)*
30/10	h	Belenenses	W	2-1	*Ricardo Horta 2*
06/11	a	Marítimo	L	0-1	
28/11	h	Feirense	W	6-2	*Rui Fonte 2, Hassan, Wilson Eduardo 2, Ricardo Horta*
06/12	a	Porto	L	0-1	
11/12	h	Paços Ferreira	W	3-0	*Rui Fonte 2, Ricardo Horta*
18/12	a	Sporting	W	1-0	*Wilson Eduardo*
22/12	h	Moreirense	W	2-1	*André Pinto, Ricardo Ferreira*

2017

07/01	a	Nacional	D	0-0	
16/01	h	Tondela	W	2-0	*Rui Fonte 2*
22/01	h	Guimarães	L	1-2	*Stojiljković*
02/02	a	Rio Ave	L	0-1	
06/02	h	Estoril	D	1-1	*Rosić*
12/02	a	Boavista	D	1-1	*Stojiljković*
19/02	h	Benfica	L	0-1	
26/02	a	Setúbal	D	1-1	*Fede Cartabia*
04/03	h	Arouca	W	3-1	*Rui Fonte 2, Battaglia*
11/03	a	Chaves	D	0-0	
18/03	a	Belenenses	W	2-1	*og (Hanin), Rui Fonte*
02/04	h	Marítimo	D	3-3	*Baiano, Fede Cartabia, Rui Fonte*
07/04	a	Feirense	W	1-0	*Fede Cartabia*
15/04	h	Porto	D	1-1	*Pedro Santos*
23/04	a	Paços Ferreira	L	1-3	*Rodrigo Pinho*
30/04	h	Sporting	L	2-3	*Ricardo Horta, Rui Fonte*
05/05	a	Moreirense	L	1-2	*Ricardo Horta*
14/05	h	Nacional	W	4-0	*og (César), Stojiljković 2, Pedro Neto*
21/05	a	Tondela	L	0-2	

No	Name	Nat	DoB	Pos	Aps	(s)	Gls
30	Alan	BRA	19/09/79	M	8	(14)	1
6	André Pinto		05/10/89	D	10		2
44	Artur Jorge		14/08/94	D	16	(4)	
15	Baiano	BRA	23/02/87	D	25	(1)	1
8	Marko Bakić	MNE	01/11/93	M		(6)	
5	Rodrigo Battaglia	ARG	12/07/91	M	16		1
26	Óscar Benítez	ARG	14/01/93	A	1	(1)	
5	Willy Boly	FRA	03/02/91	D	3		
43	Bruno Wilson		27/12/96	D	1		
9	Crislan	BRA	13/03/92	A	1		
16	Djavan	BRA	31/12/87	D	13	(3)	
20	Douglas Coutinho	BRA	08/02/94	A		(1)	
11	Fede Cartabia	ARG	20/01/93	M	7	(4)	3
84	Gamboa		31/08/96	M	6	(1)	
20	Ahmed Hassan	EGY	05/03/93	A	10	(4)	2
28	Marafona		08/05/87	G	29		
87	Marcelo Goiano	BRA	13/10/87	D	22	(4)	
10	Tomás Martínez	ARG	07/03/95	M	1	(2)	
92	Matheus	BRA	29/03/92	G	5	(1)	
63	Mauro	BRA	31/10/90	M	9		
22	Paulinho		13/07/91	D	8		
71	Pedro Neto		09/03/00	A		(2)	1
23	Pedro Santos		22/04/88	M	25	(2)	6
25	Pedro Tiba		31/08/88	M	2	(7)	
18	Rafa Silva		17/05/93	M	1		
14	Rafael Assis	BRA	31/10/90	M	7		
24	Ricardo Ferreira		25/11/92	D	12	(1)	1
21	Ricardo Horta		15/09/94	M	22	(10)	6
13	Rodrigo Pinho	BRA	30/05/91	A	1	(9)	1
3	Lazar Rosić	SRB	29/06/93	D	20	(3)	2
17	Rui Fonte		23/04/90	A	24	(2)	11
19	Nikola Stojiljković	SRB	17/08/92	A	15	(9)	5
2	Emiliano Velázquez	URU	30/04/94	D	6		
35	Nikola Vukčević	MNE	13/12/91	M	21	(4)	
6	Wilson Eduardo		08/07/90	M	15	(3)	6
75	Xadas		02/12/97	M	1	(3)	
80	Xeka		10/11/94	M	11		

GD Chaves

1949 • Municipal Eng Manuel Branco Teixeira (9,000) • gdchaves.pt

Coach: Jorge Simão; (20/12/16) Ricardo Soares

2016

20/08	h	Tondela	D	1-1	*João Mário*
28/08	a	Boavista	D	2-2	*Elhouni, Perdigão*
04/09	a	Nacional	W	1-0	*Bruno Braga*
11/09	h	Setúbal	D	0-0	
18/09	a	Arouca	W	1-0	*Perdigão*
24/09	h	Benfica	L	0-2	
01/10	h	Belenenses	W	3-1	*Bruno Braga, Battaglia, Willian*
24/10	a	Braga	L	0-1	
31/10	h	Feirense	D	1-1	*Battaglia*
05/11	a	Paços Ferreira	D	1-1	*Battaglia*
26/11	h	Marítimo	D	0-0	
04/12	a	Guimarães	D	1-1	*João Patrão*
10/12	h	Moreirense	W	2-1	*Willian, Rafael Lopes*
19/12	a	Porto	L	1-2	*Rafael Lopes*
22/12	h	Estoril	W	1-0	*Fábio Martins*

2017

08/01	a	Rio Ave	D	2-2	*Fábio Martins, Rafael Lopes*
14/01	h	Sporting	D	2-2	*Rafael Lopes, Fábio Martins*
23/01	h	Nacional	W	2-0	*Bruno Braga, Davidson*
28/01	a	Tondela	L	0-2	
04/02	h	Boavista	D	0-0	
11/02	a	Setúbal	D	0-0	
18/02	h	Arouca	W	2-0	*Renan Bressan, Fábio Martins*
24/02	a	Benfica	L	1-3	*Renan Bressan*
05/03	a	Belenenses	L	1-2	*Pedro Tiba*
11/03	h	Braga	D	0-0	
19/03	a	Feirense	L	2-3	*Renan Bressan, Fábio Martins*
31/03	h	Paços Ferreira	W	1-0	*og (Gegé)*
10/04	a	Marítimo	L	1-2	*Perdigão*
15/04	h	Guimarães	L	2-3	*Rafael Lopes, Willian*
24/04	a	Moreirense	D	0-0	
29/04	h	Porto	L	0-2	
08/05	a	Estoril	L	1-2	*Renan Bressan*
14/05	h	Rio Ave	D	2-2	*Fábio Martins, Pedro Tiba*
21/05	a	Sporting	L	1-4	*Willian*

No	Name	Nat	DoB	Pos	Aps	(s)	Gls
1	António Filipe		14/04/85	G	10		
16	Rodrigo Battaglia	ARG	12/07/91	M	14		3
25	Bruno Braga		17/06/83	M	31	(1)	3
26	Carlos Ponck	CPV	13/01/95	D	25	(2)	
91	Davidson	BRA	05/06/91	M	6	(9)	1
17	Hamdou Elhouni	LBY	12/02/94	M	3	(9)	1
23	Emanuel Novo		26/08/92	G		(1)	
47	Fábio Martins		24/07/93	M	27	(2)	6
4	Fábio Santos		22/05/88	D	3	(3)	
18	Alioune Fall	SEN	24/12/94	A		(7)	
33	Felipe Lopes	BRA	07/08/87	D	6		
7	João Mário	GNB	11/10/93	A	4	(5)	1
8	João Patrão		22/01/90	M	7	(12)	1
44	Leandro Freire	BRA	21/08/89	D	18		
11	Luís Alberto	BRA	17/11/83	M		(1)	
21	Nélson Lenho		22/03/84	D	34		
14	Nuno André Coelho		07/01/86	D	12	(1)	
2	Paulinho		13/07/91	D	14		
24	Pedro Queirós		08/08/84	D	13	(1)	
15	Pedro Tiba		31/08/88	M	13	(1)	2
10	Perdigão	BRA	17/07/91	M	28	(3)	3
5	Nemanja Petrović	SRB	17/04/92	D		(1)	
6	Rafael Assis	BRA	31/10/90	M	17		
29	Rafael Batatinha	BRA	09/02/90	A	2	(8)	
9	Rafael Lopes		28/07/91	A	22	(7)	5
12	Renan Bressan	BLR	03/01/88	M	14	(1)	4
13	Ricardo		06/07/82	G	24		
20	Rodrigo	BRA	26/12/92	D	7		
92	Victor Massaia	BRA	09/02/92	D	6	(3)	
3	Simon Vukčević	MNE	29/01/86	M	1	(10)	
99	Willian	BRA	07/12/91	A	13	(10)	4

Estoril Praia

1939 • António Coimbra da Mota (5,015) • estorilpraia.pt

Coach: Fabiano Soares (BRA); (15/12/16) Pedro Gómez Carmona (ESP); (08/03/17) Pedro Emanuel

2016

15/08	h	Feirense	L	0-2	
20/08	a	Porto	L	0-1	
27/08	h	Braga	L	1-3	*Alisson*
11/09	a	Paços Ferreira	D	0-0	
17/09	h	Moreirense	W	2-0	*Matheus Índio 2*
23/09	a	Sporting	L	2-4	*Bruno Gomes 2*
01/10	a	Rio Ave	W	2-1	*Matheus Índio, Diogo Amado*
23/10	h	Guimarães	L	0-2	
29/10	a	Boavista	D	0-0	
05/11	h	Tondela	W	2-0	*Gustavo Tocantins 2*
26/11	a	Nacional	W	1-0	*og (Ghazal)*
04/12	h	Belenenses	D	1-1	*Bazelyuk*
09/12	a	Setúbal	L	0-2	
17/12	h	Benfica	L	0-1	
22/12	a	Chaves	L	0-1	

2017

07/01	h	Marítimo	L	0-1	
13/01	a	Arouca	L	1-2	*João Basso*
22/01	a	Feirense	L	0-1	
22/01	h	Porto	L	1-2	*Dankler*
06/02	a	Braga	D	1-1	*Kléber*
11/02	h	Paços Ferreira	W	2-1	*Licá, og (Pedro Monteiro)*
18/02	a	Moreirense	D	1-1	*og (Pedro Rebocho)*
25/02	h	Sporting	L	0-2	
06/03	h	Rio Ave	L	0-2	
12/03	a	Guimarães	D	3-3	*Kléber, Matheus Índio, Mattheus*
17/03	h	Boavista	D	0-0	
01/04	a	Tondela	W	2-0	*Kléber 2*
09/04	h	Nacional	L	0-1	
14/04	a	Belenenses	W	3-1	*Kléber, Allano Lima, Carlinhos*
22/04	h	Setúbal	W	3-0	*Kléber (p), Carlinhos, Eduardo*
29/04	a	Benfica	L	1-2	*Kléber*
08/05	h	Chaves	W	2-1	*André Claro, Mattheus*
14/05	a	Marítimo	D	1-1	*Kléber*
21/05	h	Arouca	W	4-2	*André Claro (p), Carlinhos, Bruno Gomes, Gustavo Tocantins*

No	Name	Nat	DoB	Pos	Aps	(s)	Gls
6	Afonso Taira		17/06/92	M	19	(1)	
3	Ailton	BRA	16/03/95	D	14	(4)	
18	Alisson	BRA	07/04/96	A	7	(3)	1
95	Allano Lima	BRA	24/04/95	A	9	(1)	1
22	André Claro		31/03/91	A	5	(4)	2
71	Konstantin Bazelyuk	RUS	12/04/93	A	4	(7)	1
9	Bruno Gomes	BRA	19/07/96	A	9	(14)	3
76	Carlinhos	BRA	22/06/94	M	10	(1)	3
33	Dankler	BRA	24/01/92	D	22	(6)	1
15	Oumar Diakhité	SEN	09/12/93	D	11	(3)	
25	Diogo Amado		21/01/90	M	28	(1)	1
8	Eduardo	BRA	07/06/93	M	22	(5)	1
13	Anderson Esiti	NGA	24/05/94	M	2		
11	Felipe Augusto	BRA	06/03/92	A	3	(5)	
28	Gonçalo Brandão		09/10/86	D	6		
14	Gustavo Tocantins	BRA	11/01/96	A	8	(17)	3
2	João Afonso		28/05/90	D	27		
4	João Basso	BRA	13/01/97	D		(2)	1
5	Joel Ferreira		10/01/92	D	26	(1)	
10	Kléber	BRA	02/05/90	A	18	(8)	8
88	Licá		08/09/88	A	11	(2)	1
23	Lucas Farias	BRA	18/08/94	D	7	(2)	
96	Luís Ribeiro		19/04/92	G	5		
7	Mano		09/04/87	D	18	(2)	
20	Matheus Índio	BRA	28/02/96	M	20	(6)	4
27	Mattheus	BRA	07/07/94	M	25	(1)	2
31	Moreira		20/03/82	G	28		
12	Paulo Henrique	BRA	13/03/89	A	2		
21	Thiago Cardoso	BRA	04/08/91	D	5	(1)	
1	Thierry Graça	CPV	27/01/95	G	1		
19	Dmytro Yarchuk	UKR	23/03/94	M	2	(5)	

CD Feirense

1918 • Marcelino de Castro (5,400) • cdfeirense.pt

Coach: José Mota; (20/12/16) Nuno Manta

Date		Opponent			Scorers
2016					
15/08	a	Estoril	W	2-0	*Platiny, Karamanos*
21/08	h	Moreirense	L	0-3	
28/08	a	Rio Ave	L	0-1	
12/09	h	Tondela	W	2-1	*Karamanos 2*
18/09	a	Boavista	W	2-1	*Tiago Silva, Vítor Bruno*
24/09	h	Nacional	L	0-3	
02/10	a	Benfica	L	0-4	
22/10	h	Setúbal	D	1-1	*Ícaro*
31/10	a	Chaves	D	1-1	*Karamanos*
05/11	h	Belenenses	L	0-1	
28/11	a	Braga	L	2-6	*og (Rosić), Platiny*
04/12	h	Arouca	L	0-2	
11/12	h	Porto	L	0-4	
19/12	a	Marítimo	L	0-2	
22/12	h	Paços Ferreira	W	2-0	*Fabinho (p), Platiny (p)*
2017					
08/01	a	Sporting	L	1-2	*Platiny*
14/01	h	Guimarães	D	0-0	
22/01	h	Estoril	W	1-0	*Platiny*
02/02	a	Moreirense	D	1-1	*Fabinho*
06/02	h	Rio Ave	W	2-1	*Platiny, Karamanos*
11/02	a	Tondela	W	1-0	*Tiago Silva (p)*
18/02	h	Boavista	L	0-1	
26/02	a	Nacional	D	0-0	
04/03	h	Benfica	L	0-1	
11/03	a	Setúbal	W	2-1	*og (Venâncio), Luís Machado*
19/03	h	Chaves	W	3-2	*Tiago Silva, Luís Machado, Etebo*
02/04	a	Belenenses	W	2-1	*Edson Farias, Etebo (p)*
07/04	h	Braga	L	0-1	
15/04	a	Arouca	L	0-2	
23/04	a	Porto	D	0-0	
30/04	h	Marítimo	W	2-1	*Karamanos, Tiago Silva (p)*
06/05	a	Paços Ferreira	W	1-0	*Ícaro*
15/05	h	Sporting	W	2-1	*Tiago Silva 2 (1p)*
20/05	a	Guimarães	W	1-0	*Tchuameni*

No	Name	Nat	DoB	Pos	Aps	(s)	Gls
28	Jean Sony Alcénat	HAI	23/01/86	D	14	(7)	
5	Babanco	CPV	27/07/85	D	8	(7)	
17	Cris		17/01/84	M	24	(4)	
40	Iduitua David	NGA	17/03/97	A		(1)	
12	Edson Farias	BRA	12/01/92	A	7	(4)	1
95	Oghenekaro Etebo	NGA	09/11/95	M	21	(2)	2
10	Fabinho		21/12/94	M	12	(12)	2
32	Flávio		12/05/94	D	20	(2)	
25	Guima		11/03/86	A		(2)	
77	Hugo Seco		17/06/88	A		(5)	
2	Ícaro	BRA	16/04/89	D	21	(3)	2
3	Alex Kakuba	UGA	12/06/91	D	5	(1)	
9	Anastasios Karamanos	GRE	21/09/90	A	26	(6)	6
30	Luís Aurélio		17/08/88	M	26	(5)	
7	Luís Machado		04/11/92	M	22	(6)	2
13	Luís Rocha		12/08/86	D	17	(1)	
37	Paulo Monteiro		21/01/85	D	9	(4)	
1	Peçanha	BRA	11/01/90	G	9		
22	Pelé		29/09/91	M		(1)	
99	Platiny	BRA	02/10/90	A	11	(11)	6
18	Ricardo Dias		25/02/91	M	13	(4)	
35	Sérgio Barge		04/01/84	D	23	(1)	
6	Sérgio Semedo	CPV	23/03/88	M	11	(1)	
21	Hervé Tchami	CMR	20/02/88	A		(1)	
45	William Tchuameni	CMR	25/12/96	A	1	(2)	1
8	Tiago Silva		02/06/93	M	19	(8)	6
91	Vaná	BRA	25/04/91	G	25		
90	Vítor Bruno		13/01/90	D	30		1
29	Wellington	BRA	05/10/87	A		(1)	

CS Marítimo

1910 • Marítimo (10,932) • csmaritimo.org.pt

Coach: Paulo César Gusmão (BRA); (22/09/16) Daniel Ramos

Date		Opponent			Scorers
2016					
13/08	a	Sporting	L	0-2	
20/08	h	Guimarães	L	0-2	
28/08	a	Moreirense	W	1-0	*Fransérgio*
11/09	h	Rio Ave	L	0-1	
16/09	a	Nacional	L	0-2	
25/09	h	Tondela	W	2-0	*Éber Bessa, Dyego Sousa*
02/10	a	Setúbal	W	1-0	*Dyego Sousa*
21/10	h	Boavista	D	1-1	*Dyego Sousa (p)*
30/10	a	Arouca	L	0-1	
06/11	h	Braga	W	1-0	*Edgar Costa*
26/11	a	Chaves	D	0-0	
02/12	h	Benfica	W	2-1	*Ghazaryan, Maurício*
12/12	a	Belenenses	L	0-1	
15/12	a	Porto	L	1-2	*Djoussé*
19/12	h	Feirense	W	2-0	*Maurício 2*
2017					
07/01	a	Estoril	W	1-0	*Raúl Silva*
15/01	h	Paços Ferreira	W	3-1	*Dyego Sousa 2 (1p), Raúl Silva*
21/01	h	Sporting	D	2-2	*Éber Bessa, Raúl Silva*
28/01	a	Guimarães	D	0-0	
06/02	h	Moreirense	W	1-0	*Fransérgio*
13/02	a	Rio Ave	D	0-0	
20/02	h	Nacional	D	0-0	
25/02	a	Tondela	D	1-1	*Raúl Silva*
05/03	h	Setúbal	W	1-0	*Fransérgio*
12/03	a	Boavista	L	0-3	
19/03	h	Arouca	W	3-1	*Zainadine Júnior, Keita, Fransérgio*
02/04	a	Braga	D	3-3	*Keita, Erdem 2*
10/04	h	Chaves	W	2-1	*Keita, António Xavier*
14/04	a	Benfica	L	0-3	
22/04	h	Belenenses	W	3-0	*Raúl Silva 2, Patrick*
30/04	a	Feirense	L	1-2	*og (Flávio)*
06/05	h	Porto	D	1-1	*Djoussé*
14/05	h	Estoril	D	1-1	*Raúl Silva*
20/05	a	Paços Ferreira	D	0-0	

No	Name	Nat	DoB	Pos	Aps	(s)	Gls
7	Alex Soares	BRA	01/03/91	M	16	(8)	
99	Amido Baldé	GNB	16/05/91	A		(2)	
50	António Xavier		06/07/92	A	17	(12)	1
90	Baba Diawara	SEN	05/01/88	A	3	(6)	
77	Brito	CPV	16/11/87	A	8	(12)	
28	Carlos Daniel		11/07/94	A		(1)	
94	Charles	BRA	04/02/94	G	18		
4	Deyvison	BRA	18/10/88	D	10	(6)	
5	Dirceu	BRA	05/01/88	D	2		
20	Donald Djoussé	CMR	18/03/90	A	5	(10)	2
9	Dyego Sousa	BRA	14/09/89	A	13	(2)	5
11	Éber Bessa	BRA	23/03/92	M	20	(7)	2
12	Edgar Costa		14/04/87	A	24	(3)	1
6	Erdem Şen	TUR	05/01/89	M	27		2
40	Esquerdinha	BRA	16/11/90	M	1	(5)	
45	Fábio China		07/07/92	D	12		
35	Fransérgio	BRA	18/10/90	M	30		4
10	Gevorg Ghazaryan	ARM	05/04/88	M	16	(7)	1
32	Gottardi	BRA	15/10/85	G	16		
15	Jean Cléber	BRA	29/04/90	M	7	(6)	
8	Alhassane Keita	GUI	16/04/92	A	10	(1)	3
14	Luís Martins		10/06/92	D	13		
3	Maurício	BRA	06/02/92	D	28		3
17	Gevaro Nepomuceno	CUW	10/11/92	A	1	(4)	
91	Patrick	BRA	22/01/91	D	29	(1)	1
2	Pedro Coronas		19/09/90	D	5	(2)	
34	Raúl Silva	BRA	04/11/89	D	29		7
8	Samuel Santos	BRA	25/04/90	D	3	(3)	
5	Zainadine Júnior	MOZ	24/06/88	D	11	(4)	1

Moreirense FC

1938 • Comendador Joaquim Almeida Freitas (6,151) • moreirensefc.pt

Coach: Pepa; (22/11/16) (Leandro Mendes); (28/11/16) Augusto Inácio; (20/03/17) Petit

Date		Opponent			Scorers
2016					
13/08	h	Paços Ferreira	D	1-1	*Ença Fati*
21/08	a	Feirense	W	3-0	*Roberto, Marcelo Oliveira, Francisco Geraldes*
28/08	h	Marítimo	L	0-1	
10/09	a	Sporting	L	0-3	
17/09	a	Estoril	L	0-2	
25/09	h	Guimarães	L	0-1	
02/10	a	Boavista	L	0-2	
23/10	h	Rio Ave	D	1-1	*Cauê*
29/10	a	Tondela	W	2-1	*Daniel Podence, Boateng*
06/11	h	Setúbal	L	1-2	*Boateng*
27/11	a	Benfica	L	0-3	
04/12	h	Nacional	W	3-1	*André Micael, Daniel Podence 2*
10/12	a	Chaves	L	1-2	*Boateng*
17/12	h	Arouca	L	1-4	*Boateng*
22/12	a	Braga	L	1-2	*Dramé*
2017					
09/01	h	Belenenses	W	1-0	*Ramírez*
15/01	a	Porto	L	0-3	
20/01	a	Paços Ferreira	W	2-0	*Roberto, Daniel Podence*
02/02	h	Feirense	D	1-1	*Roberto*
06/02	a	Marítimo	L	0-1	
12/02	h	Sporting	L	2-3	*og (Bruno César), Cauê (p)*
18/02	h	Estoril	D	1-1	*Modou Sougou*
24/02	a	Guimarães	L	0-1	
03/03	h	Boavista	D	0-0	
12/03	a	Rio Ave	L	2-3	*Alex, Roberto*
18/03	h	Tondela	D	1-1	*Modou Sougou*
02/04	a	Setúbal	L	0-2	
09/04	h	Benfica	L	0-1	
17/04	a	Nacional	W	1-0	*Ramírez*
24/04	h	Chaves	D	0-0	
30/04	a	Arouca	D	2-2	*Boateng 2*
05/05	h	Braga	W	2-1	*Nildo, Alan Schons*
12/05	a	Belenenses	D	1-1	*Nildo*
21/05	h	Porto	W	3-1	*Boateng, Fréderic Maciel, Alex*

No	Name	Nat	DoB	Pos	Aps	(s)	Gls
7	Alan Schons	BRA	24/05/93	M	11	(9)	1
10	Alex		27/08/91	A	7	(7)	2
3	André Micael		04/02/89	D	19		1
30	Ary Papel	ANG	03/03/94	A		(1)	
29	Emmanuel Boateng	GHA	23/05/96	A	16	(10)	7
18	Cauê	BRA	24/05/89	M	32	(1)	2
56	Daniel Podence		21/10/95	A	14		4
44	Diego Galo	BRA	14/01/84	D	31		
14	Diego Ivo	BRA	06/04/89	D	10		
93	Ousmane Dramé	FRA	25/08/92	A	21	(3)	1
17	Ença Fati		11/08/93	M		(6)	1
65	Fernando Alexandre	BRA	02/08/85	M	6		
8	Francisco Geraldes		18/04/95	M	15	(1)	1
67	Fréderic Maciel		15/03/94	A	1	(16)	1
6	Jander	BRA	08/07/88	D	7	(4)	
1	Giorgi Makaridze	GEO	31/03/90	G	33		
26	Marcelo Oliveira	BRA	05/09/81	D	8		1
28	Modou Sougou	SEN	18/12/84	A	4	(9)	2
91	Neto	BRA	02/09/91	M	22	(1)	
16	Nildo	BRA	01/05/86	M	20	(10)	2
11	Ernest Ohemeng	GHA	17/01/96	A		(1)	
5	Pedro Rebocho		23/01/95	D	29		
99	Pedro Taborda		22/06/78	G	1		
21	David Ramírez	CRC	28/05/93	A	6	(15)	2
9	Roberto		28/11/88	A	17	(5)	4
95	Pierre Sagna	FRA	21/08/90	D	29	(1)	
90	Bakary Saré	BFA	05/04/90	M	9	(3)	
2	Tiago Almeida	CPV	13/09/90	D	5	(6)	
20	Tiago Morgado		28/07/93	M		(2)	
42	Wallyson	BRA	16/02/94	M	1		

PORTUGAL

CD Nacional

1910 • Madeira (5,132) • cdnacional.pt

Coach: Manuel Machado; (30/12/16) Predrag Jokanović (SRB); (21/03/17) João de Deus

Date		Opponent		Score	Scorers
2016					
21/08	a	Arouca	L	0-2	
27/08	h	Benfica	L	1-3	*Tobias Figueiredo*
04/09	h	Chaves	L	0-1	
10/09	a	Belenenses	L	1-2	*Bonilla*
16/09	h	Marítimo	W	2-0	*Salvador Agra, og (Fábio China)*
24/09	a	Feirense	W	3-0	*Hamzaoui 3*
01/10	h	Porto	L	0-4	
21/10	a	Paços Ferreira	D	1-1	*Tiago Rodrigues*
28/10	h	Sporting	D	0-0	
04/11	a	Guimarães	L	1-2	*Hamzaoui*
26/11	h	Estoril	L	0-1	
04/12	a	Moreirense	L	1-3	*Salvador Agra (p)*
11/12	h	Tondela	W	3-2	*og (Kaká) 2, César*
18/12	a	Rio Ave	L	1-2	*Willyan*
22/12	h	Boavista	L	0-2	
2017					
07/01	h	Braga	D	0-0	
14/01	a	Setúbal	L	0-1	
23/01	a	Chaves	L	0-2	
28/01	h	Arouca	D	1-1	*Salvador Agra (p)*
05/02	a	Benfica	L	0-3	
12/02	h	Belenenses	D	1-1	*Aristeguieta*
20/02	a	Marítimo	D	0-0	
26/02	h	Feirense	D	0-0	
04/03	a	Porto	L	0-7	
13/03	h	Paços Ferreira	D	1-1	*Cádiz*
18/03	a	Sporting	L	0-2	
31/03	h	Guimarães	L	1-2	*Zizo*
09/04	a	Estoril	W	1-0	*Zizo*
17/04	h	Moreirense	L	0-1	
22/04	a	Tondela	L	0-2	
29/04	h	Rio Ave	L	0-2	
06/05	a	Boavista	D	2-2	*Mezga, Hamzaoui*
14/05	a	Braga	L	0-4	
20/05	h	Setúbal	L	1-2	*Zequinha (p)*

No	Name	Nat	DoB	Pos	Aps	(s)	Gls
31	Adriano	BRA	12/03/83	G	15		
27	Fernando Aristeguieta	VEN	09/04/92	A	11	(2)	1
11	Nelson Bonilla	SLV	11/09/90	A	3	(11)	1
18	Jhonder Cádiz	VEN	29/07/95	A	4	(7)	1
3	César	BRA	28/12/92	D	27		1
25	Filipe Gonçalves		12/08/84	M	14	(2)	
2	Víctor García	VEN	11/06/94	D	22		
6	Ali Ghazal	EGY	01/02/92	M	12	(2)	
9	Okacha Hamzaoui	ALG	29/11/90	A	14	(6)	5
19	Jota		07/03/93	M	8	(6)	
66	Geraldo Matsimbe	MOZ	22/10/92	M		(1)	
55	Mauro Cerqueira		20/08/92	D	3	(1)	
88	Dejan Mezga	CRO	16/07/85	M	5	(1)	1
22	Nuno Campos		13/06/93	D	9	(1)	
5	Nuno Sequeira		19/08/90	D	29		
23	Ricardo Gomes	CPV	18/12/91	M	13	(11)	
21	Roniel	BRA	02/06/94	A	1	(4)	
33	Rui Correia		23/08/90	D	24		
1	Rui Silva		07/02/94	G	18		
7	Salvador Agra		11/11/91	A	28	(3)	3
10	Tiago Rodrigues		21/01/92	M	21	(1)	1
4	Tobias Figueiredo		02/02/94	D	20	(2)	1
12	Vítor Bento		09/08/92	G	1	(1)	
20	Vítor Gonçalves		29/03/92	M	6	(14)	
8	Washington	BRA	20/01/89	M	28	(2)	
28	Willyan	BRA	17/02/84	M	14	(8)	1
17	Witi	MOZ	26/08/96	M	7	(5)	
87	Zequinha		07/01/87	A	9	(3)	1
40	Zizo	EGY	10/01/95	M	8	(5)	2

FC Paços de Ferreira

1950 • Mata Real (5,172) • fcpf.pt

Coach: Carlos Pinho; (28/11/16) Vasco Seabra

Date		Opponent		Score	Scorers
2016					
13/08	a	Moreirense	D	1-1	*Welthon*
20/08	h	Sporting	L	0-1	
26/08	a	Guimarães	L	3-5	*Andrézinho, Pedrinho 2 (1p)*
11/09	h	Estoril	D	0-0	
17/09	a	Setúbal	W	4-1	*Ricardo Valente 2, Welthon 2*
25/09	h	Rio Ave	W	2-1	*Mateus Silva, Osei*
30/09	a	Tondela	L	1-2	*Miguel Vieira*
21/10	h	Nacional	D	1-1	*Ricardo Valente*
28/10	a	Benfica	L	0-3	
05/11	h	Chaves	D	1-1	*Pedrinho*
27/11	a	Arouca	L	0-1	
05/12	h	Boavista	W	2-1	*Marco Baixinho, Welthon*
11/12	a	Braga	L	0-3	
16/12	h	Belenenses	W	1-0	*Welthon*
22/12	a	Feirense	L	0-2	
2017					
07/01	h	Porto	D	0-0	
15/01	a	Marítimo	L	1-3	*Welthon*
20/01	h	Moreirense	L	0-2	
28/01	a	Sporting	L	2-4	*Welthon 2*
03/02	h	Guimarães	W	2-0	*Pedrinho, Welthon*
11/02	a	Estoril	L	1-2	*Osei*
19/02	h	Setúbal	W	2-1	*Welthon 2*
25/02	a	Rio Ave	D	0-0	
05/03	h	Tondela	D	0-0	
13/03	a	Nacional	D	1-1	*Pedrinho*
18/03	h	Benfica	D	0-0	
31/03	a	Chaves	L	0-1	
08/04	h	Arouca	D	1-1	*Ricardo Valente*
14/04	a	Boavista	D	0-0	
23/04	h	Braga	W	3-1	*Luiz Phellype 2 (1p), Andrézinho*
30/04	a	Belenenses	W	2-1	*Luiz Phellype (p), Vasco Rocha*
06/05	h	Feirense	L	0-1	
14/05	a	Porto	L	1-4	*Andrézinho*
20/05	h	Marítimo	D	0-0	

No	Name	Nat	DoB	Pos	Aps	(s)	Gls
36	André Sousa		16/07/97	M		(1)	
20	Andrézinho		06/08/95	M	14	(7)	3
6	Bruno Santos		07/02/93	D	28	(1)	
8	Christian	BRA	14/06/89	M	6	(5)	
9	Cícero	GNB	08/05/86	A		(13)	
11	Diego Medeiros	BRA	28/03/93	M	12	(3)	
30	Filipe Ferreira		27/09/90	D	23		
26	Filipe Melo		03/11/89	M	13	(3)	
33	Francisco Afonso		24/04/97	D	2	(1)	
14	Gegé	CPV	24/02/88	D	14		
17	Gleison	BRA	23/06/95	A	4	(5)	
23	Ivo Rodrigues		30/03/95	M	17	(9)	
13	João Gois		05/05/90	D	8	(2)	
21	Leandro Silva		04/05/94	M	5	(2)	
28	Luiz Phellype	BRA	27/09/93	A	6	(7)	3
2	Marco Baixinho		11/07/89	D	23		1
86	Mário Felgueiras		12/12/86	G	7		
15	Mateus Silva	BRA	30/08/91	M	17	(4)	1
22	Miguel Vieira		08/10/90	D	13	(1)	1
10	Minhoca		29/04/89	M	6	(8)	
16	Barnes Osei	GHA	08/01/95	M	15	(8)	2
12	Pedrinho		20/12/92	M	28	(3)	5
3	Pedro Monteiro		30/01/94	D	9		
1	Rafael Defendi	BRA	22/12/83	G	27		
19	Ricardo	CPV	19/08/80	D	14		
91	Ricardo Valente		03/04/91	M	15	(12)	4
18	Tony Taylor	PAN	13/07/89	M		(2)	
29	Vasco Rocha		29/01/89	M	20	(2)	1
7	Welthon	BRA	21/06/92	A	28		11

FC Porto

1893 • Dragão (50,476) • fcporto.pt

Major honours

European Champion Clubs' Cup/UEFA Champions League (2) 1987, 2004; UEFA Cup (1) 2003; UEFA Europa League (1) 2011; UEFA Super Cup (1) 1987; European/South American Cup (2) 1987, 2004; Portuguese League (27) 1935, 1939, 1940, 1956, 1959, 1978, 1979, 1985, 1986, 1988, 1990, 1992, 1993, 1995, 1996, 1997, 1998, 1999, 2003, 2004, 2006, 2007, 2008, 2009, 2011, 2012, 2013; Portuguese Cup (16) 1956, 1958, 1968, 1977, 1984, 1988, 1991, 1994, 1998, 2000, 2001, 2003, 2006, 2009, 2010, 2011

Coach: Nuno Espírito Santo

Date		Opponent		Score	Scorers
2016					
12/08	a	Rio Ave	W	3-1	*Corona, Herrera, André Silva*
20/08	h	Estoril	W	1-0	*André Silva*
28/08	a	Sporting	L	1-2	*Felipe*
10/09	h	Guimarães	W	3-0	*Marcano, Óliver Torres, og (João Aurélio)*
18/09	a	Tondela	D	0-0	
23/09	h	Boavista	W	3-1	*André Silva 2 (1p), Alex Telles*
01/10	a	Nacional	W	4-0	*Diogo Jota 3, André Silva*
22/10	h	Arouca	W	3-0	*André Silva 2, Brahimi*
29/10	a	Setúbal	D	0-0	
06/11	h	Benfica	D	1-1	*Diogo Jota*
26/11	a	Belenenses	D	0-0	
03/12	h	Braga	W	1-0	*Rui Pedro*
11/12	a	Feirense	W	4-0	*André Silva 2 (1p), Brahimi, Marcano*
15/12	h	Marítimo	W	2-1	*Brahimi, André Silva*
19/12	h	Chaves	W	2-1	*Depoitre, Danilo Pereira*
2017					
07/01	a	Paços Ferreira	D	0-0	
15/01	h	Moreirense	W	3-0	*Óliver Torres, André Silva, Marcano*
21/01	h	Rio Ave	W	4-2	*Felipe, Marcano, Danilo Pereira, Rui Pedro*
28/01	a	Estoril	W	2-1	*André Silva (p), Corona*
04/02	h	Sporting	W	2-1	*Francisco Soares 2*
11/02	a	Guimarães	W	2-0	*Francisco Soares, Diogo Jota*
17/02	h	Tondela	W	4-0	*André Silva (p), Rúben Neves, Francisco Soares, Diogo Jota*
26/02	a	Boavista	W	1-0	*Francisco Soares*
04/03	h	Nacional	W	7-0	*Óliver Torres, Brahimi, André Silva 2, Francisco Soares 2, Layún*
10/03	a	Arouca	W	4-0	*Danilo Pereira, Francisco Soares 2, Diogo Jota*
19/03	h	Setúbal	D	1-1	*Corona*
01/04	a	Benfica	D	1-1	*Maxi Pereira*
08/04	h	Belenenses	W	3-0	*Danilo Pereira, Francisco Soares, Brahimi (p)*
15/04	a	Braga	D	1-1	*Francisco Soares*
23/04	h	Feirense	D	0-0	
29/04	a	Chaves	W	2-0	*Francisco Soares, André André*
06/05	a	Marítimo	D	1-1	*Otávio*
14/05	h	Paços Ferreira	W	4-1	*Herrera, Brahimi (p), Diogo Jota, André Silva (p)*
21/05	a	Moreirense	L	1-3	*Maxi Pereira*

No	Name.	Nat	DoB	Pos	Aps	(s)	Gls
11	Adrián López	ESP	08/01/88	A	1	(4)	
13	Alex Telles	BRA	15/12/92	D	32		1
20	André André		26/08/89	M	19	(6)	1
10	André Silva		06/11/95	A	28	(4)	16
4	Willy Boly	FRA	03/02/91	D	4		
8	Yacine Brahimi	ALG	08/02/90	M	16	(6)	6
1	Iker Casillas	ESP	20/05/81	G	33		
17	Jesús Corona	MEX	06/01/93	A	20	(9)	3
22	Danilo Pereira		09/09/91	M	27	(1)	4
9	Laurent Depoitre	BEL	07/12/88	A	2	(5)	1
19	Diogo Jota		04/12/96	A	15	(12)	8
28	Felipe	BRA	16/05/89	D	32		2
52	Fernando Fonseca		14/03/97	D	1		
29	Francisco Soares	BRA	07/01/91	A	15		12
16	Héctor Herrera	MEX	19/04/90	M	14	(9)	2
18	João Carlos Teixeira		18/01/93	M		(8)	
12	José Sá		17/01/93	G	1		
23	Kelvin	BRA	01/06/93	A		(1)	
21	Miguel Layún	MEX	25/06/88	D	12	(4)	1
5	Iván Marcano	ESP	23/06/87	D	32		4
2	Maxi Pereira	URU	08/06/84	D	23	(1)	2
30	Óliver Torres	ESP	10/11/94	M	24	(5)	3
25	Otávio	BRA	09/02/95	M	16	(7)	1
6	Rúben Neves		13/03/97	M	6	(7)	1
59	Rui Pedro		20/03/98	A		(9)	2
3	Sérgio Oliveira		02/06/92	M		(1)	
7	Silvestre Varela		02/02/85	A	1	(3)	

Rio Ave FC

1939 • Rio Ave (12,815) • rioavefc.pt

Coach: Capucho;
(14/11/16) Luís Castro

Date		Opponent		Score	Scorers
2016					
12/08	h	Porto	L	1-3	*Marcelo*
22/08	a	Braga	D	1-1	*Pedro Moreira*
28/08	h	Feirense	W	1-0	*Rafa Soares*
11/09	a	Marítimo	W	1-0	*Guedes*
18/09	h	Sporting	W	3-1	*Tarantini, Guedes, Gil Dias*
25/09	a	Paços Ferreira	L	1-2	*Wakaso*
01/10	h	Estoril	L	1-2	*Krovinović*
23/10	a	Moreirense	D	1-1	*Roderick (p)*
30/10	h	Guimarães	L	0-3	
05/11	h	Boavista	L	1-2	*Gil Dias*
25/11	a	Setúbal	W	1-0	*Filipe Augusto*
03/12	h	Tondela	W	3-1	*Yazalde, Gil Dias, Filipe Augusto*
12/12	a	Arouca	W	2-0	*og (Nelsinho), Ronan*
18/12	h	Nacional	W	2-1	*og (Ghazal), Krovinović*
21/12	a	Benfica	L	0-2	
2016					
08/01	h	Chaves	D	2-2	*Tarantini, Guedes*
15/01	a	Belenenses	L	0-1	
21/01	a	Porto	L	2-4	*Guedes, Roderick (p)*
02/02	h	Braga	W	1-0	*Rafa Soares*
06/02	a	Feirense	L	1-2	*Gonçalo Paciência*
13/02	h	Marítimo	D	0-0	
18/02	a	Sporting	L	0-1	
25/02	h	Paços Ferreira	D	0-0	
06/03	a	Estoril	W	2-0	*Guedes, Gil Dias*
12/03	h	Moreirense	W	3-2	*Gil Dias, Rafa Soares, Guedes*
19/03	a	Guimarães	L	0-3	
01/04	a	Boavista	W	1-0	*Traoré*
09/04	h	Setúbal	D	0-0	
15/04	a	Tondela	L	1-2	*Krovinović*
21/04	h	Arouca	W	3-0	*og (Jubal), Krovinović, Tarantini*
29/04	a	Nacional	W	2-0	*Tarantini, Krovinović*
07/05	h	Benfica	L	0-1	
14/05	a	Chaves	D	2-2	*Guedes, Tarantini*
20/05	h	Belenenses	W	2-0	*Guedes, Gil Dias*

No	Name	Nat	DoB	Pos	Aps	(s)	Gls
14	André Vilas Boas		04/06/83	D	1		
13	Bruno Teles	BRA	01/05/86	D		(1)	
1	Cássio	BRA	12/08/90	G	33		
75	Tafsir Chérif	GUI	19/06/95	A		(1)	
2	Eliseu Cassamá		06/02/94	D	5	(2)	
5	Filipe Augusto	BRA	12/08/93	M	6	(2)	2
31	Gil Dias		28/09/96	M	30	(4)	6
9	Gonçalo Paciência		01/08/94	A	5	(10)	1
7	Guedes		07/05/87	A	23	(8)	8
24	Héldon	CPV	14/11/88	M	24	(3)	
11	Jaime Pinto		28/08/97	M		(1)	
20	João Novais		10/07/93	M	2	(9)	
17	William Kizito	UGA	20/12/93	A	1	(8)	
10	Filip Krovinović	CRO	29/08/95	M	18	(8)	5
12	Lionn	BRA	29/01/89	D	13	(2)	
46	Marcelo	BRA	27/07/89	D	31		1
4	Nélson Monte		30/07/95	D	8	(1)	
26	Pedrinho		06/03/85	D	13	(2)	
6	Pedro Moreira		15/03/89	M	7	(6)	1
22	Radosav Petrović	SRB	08/03/89	M	13		
55	Rafa Soares		09/05/95	D	32		3
25	Roderick		30/03/91	D	33		2
19	Ronan	BRA	22/04/95	A	1	(10)	1
70	Rúben Ribeiro		01/08/87	M	27	(4)	
71	Rui Vieira		13/11/91	G	1	(1)	
8	Tarantini		07/10/83	M	30	(2)	5
23	Adama Traoré	MLI	28/06/95	M		(7)	1
30	Alhassan Wakaso	GHA	07/01/92	M	13	(1)	1
88	Yazalde		10/09/88	A	4	(9)	1

Sporting Clube de Portugal

1906 • José Alvalade (50,466) • sporting.pt

Major honours
UEFA Cup Winners' Cup (1) 1964; Portuguese League (18) 1941, 1944, 1947, 1948, 1949, 1951, 1952, 1953, 1954, 1958, 1962, 1966, 1970, 1974, 1980, 1982, 2000, 2002; Portuguese Cup (16) 1941, 1945, 1946, 1948, 1954, 1963, 1971, 1973, 1974, 1978, 1982, 1995, 2002, 2007, 2008, 2015

Coach: Jorge Jesus

Date		Opponent		Score	Scorers
2016					
13/08	h	Marítimo	W	2-0	*Coates, B Ruiz*
20/08	a	Paços Ferreira	W	1-0	*Adrien Silva*
28/08	h	Porto	W	2-1	*Slimani, Gelson Martins*
10/09	h	Moreirense	W	3-0	*Gelson Martins, Campbell, Dost*
18/09	a	Rio Ave	L	1-3	*Dost*
23/09	h	Estoril	W	4-2	*Dost 2, Coates, André*
01/10	a	Guimarães	D	3-3	*Marković, Coates, Elías*
22/10	h	Tondela	D	1-1	*Campbell*
28/10	a	Nacional	D	0-0	
06/11	h	Arouca	W	3-0	*Dost 2, Campbell*
26/11	a	Boavista	W	1-0	*Dost*
03/12	h	Setúbal	W	2-0	*William Carvalho, Bruno César*
11/12	a	Benfica	L	1-2	*Dost*
18/12	h	Braga	L	0-1	
22/12	a	Belenenses	W	1-0	*Dost*
2017					
08/01	h	Feirense	W	2-1	*Dost 2*
14/01	a	Chaves	D	2-2	*Dost 2*
21/01	a	Marítimo	D	2-2	*Dost, Gelson Martins*
28/01	h	Paços Ferreira	W	4-2	*Adrien Silva (p), Dost 2, Gelson Martins*
04/02	a	Porto	L	1-2	*A Ruiz*
12/02	a	Moreirense	W	3-2	*A Ruiz, Dost, Adrien Silva*
18/02	h	Rio Ave	W	1-0	*A Ruiz*
25/02	a	Estoril	W	2-0	*B Ruiz, Dost (p)*
05/03	h	Guimarães	D	1-1	*A Ruiz*
11/03	a	Tondela	W	4-1	*Dost 4*
18/03	h	Nacional	W	2-0	*Dost 2*
02/04	a	Arouca	W	2-1	*A Ruiz, Bruno César*
08/04	h	Boavista	W	4-0	*A Ruiz, Dost 3 (1p)*
14/04	a	Setúbal	W	3-0	*Gelson Martins, William Carvalho, Dost*
22/04	h	Benfica	D	1-1	*Adrien Silva (p)*
30/04	a	Braga	W	3-2	*Dost 3*
07/05	h	Belenenses	L	1-3	*Bruno César*
13/05	a	Feirense	L	1-2	*Gelson Martins*
21/05	h	Chaves	W	4-1	*Dost 3, Matheus Pereira*

No	Name	Nat	DoB	Pos	Aps	(s)	Gls
23	Adrien Silva		15/03/89	M	26	(1)	4
16	André	BRA	27/09/90	A	2	(5)	1
34	Beto		01/05/82	G	3		
11	Bruno César	BRA	03/11/88	M	22	(9)	3
30	Bruno Paulista	BRA	21/08/95	M		(3)	
7	Joel Campbell	CRC	26/06/92	A	7	(12)	3
36	Carlos Mané		11/03/94	A		(2)	
20	Luc Castaignos	NED	27/09/92	A		(6)	
13	Sebastián Coates	URU	07/10/90	D	33		3
56	Daniel Podence		21/10/95	A	4	(9)	
28	Bas Dost	NED	31/05/89	A	30	(1)	34
19	Douglas	BRA	12/01/88	D	1	(1)	
22	Elías	BRA	16/05/85	M	1	(7)	1
18	Francisco Geraldes		18/04/95	M		(4)	
57	Gelson Dala	ANG	13/07/96	A		(1)	
77	Gelson Martins		11/05/95	M	32		6
4	Jefferson	BRA	05/07/88	D	8	(2)	
6	João Mário		19/01/93	M	1		
66	João Palhinha		09/07/95	M	4	(7)	
21	João Pereira		25/02/84	D	8	(1)	
3	Lazar Marković	SRB	02/03/94	M	2	(4)	1
73	Matheus Pereira	BRA	05/05/96	A	5	(2)	1
15	Paulo Oliveira		08/01/92	D	10	(3)	
47	Ricardo Esgaio		16/05/93	D	5	(3)	
35	Rúben Semedo		04/04/94	D	24		
1	Rui Patrício		15/02/88	G	31		
99	Alan Ruiz	ARG	19/08/93	A	19	(4)	6
10	Bryan Ruiz	CRC	18/08/85	M	23	(9)	2
2	Ezequiel Schelotto	ITA	23/05/89	D	22	(1)	
9	Islam Slimani	ALG	18/06/88	A	2		1
14	William Carvalho		07/04/92	M	31	(1)	2
31	Marvin Zeegelaar	NED	12/08/90	D	18	(2)	

CD Tondela

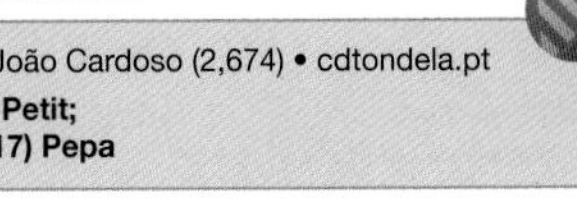

1933 • João Cardoso (2,674) • cdtondela.pt

Coach: Petit;
(10/01/17) Pepa

Date		Opponent		Score	Scorers
2016					
13/08	h	Benfica	L	0-2	
20/08	a	Chaves	D	1-1	*Murillo*
27/08	h	Belenenses	L	0-1	
12/09	a	Feirense	L	1-2	*Candé*
18/09	h	Porto	D	0-0	
25/09	a	Marítimo	L	0-2	
30/09	h	Paços Ferreira	W	2-1	*Moreno, Murillo*
22/10	a	Sporting	D	1-1	*Murillo*
29/10	h	Moreirense	L	1-2	*Wagner*
05/11	a	Estoril	L	0-2	
27/11	h	Guimarães	W	2-1	*Wagner 2*
03/12	a	Rio Ave	L	1-3	*Bruno Monteiro*
11/12	a	Nacional	L	2-3	*Wagner, Miguel Cardoso*
18/12	h	Boavista	D	1-1	*Lystsov*
23/12	a	Setúbal	L	0-3	
2017					
08/01	h	Arouca	L	1-2	*Pité*
16/01	a	Braga	L	0-2	
22/01	a	Benfica	L	0-4	
28/01	h	Chaves	W	2-0	*Osorio, Heliardo*
05/02	a	Belenenses	D	0-0	
11/02	h	Feirense	L	0-1	
17/02	a	Porto	L	0-4	
25/02	h	Marítimo	D	1-1	*Murillo*
05/03	a	Paços Ferreira	D	0-0	
11/03	h	Sporting	L	1-4	*Murillo*
18/03	a	Moreirense	D	1-1	*Kaká*
01/04	h	Estoril	L	0-2	
09/04	a	Guimarães	L	1-2	*Jaílson (p)*
15/04	h	Rio Ave	W	2-1	*og (Marcelo), Osorio*
22/04	h	Nacional	W	2-0	*Jaílson (p), Osorio*
29/04	a	Boavista	L	0-1	
07/05	h	Setúbal	W	2-1	*Murilo, Jaílson (p)*
13/05	a	Arouca	W	2-1	*Pedro Nuno 2*
21/05	h	Braga	W	2-0	*Heliardo, Kaká*

No	Name	Nat	DoB	Pos	Aps	(s)	Gls
18	Amido Baldé	GNB	16/05/91	A		(2)	
9	Batista	BRA	16/06/95	A		(4)	
27	Bruno Monteiro		05/10/84	M	13	(7)	1
24	Mamadu Candé	GNB	28/08/91	D	12		1
7	Claude Gonçalves		09/04/94	M	24	(4)	
1	Cláudio Ramos		16/11/91	G	33		
9	Júnior Correia	GNB	22/10/96	A		(7)	
18	Crislan	BRA	13/03/92	A	7	(3)	
22	David Bruno		14/02/92	D	20		
92	Fábio Nunes		24/07/92	D	1	(1)	
14	Fernando Ferreira		20/11/86	M	17	(5)	
6	Dylan Flores	CRC	30/05/93	M	1	(8)	
41	Hélder Tavares		26/12/89	M	22	(3)	
99	Heliardo	BRA	14/12/91	A	12	(4)	2
13	Jaílson	BRA	21/01/91	D	24		3
10	João Jaquité	GNB	22/02/86	M	1		
4	Kaká	BRA	16/05/81	D	24	(1)	2
79	Vitali Lystsov	RUS	11/07/95	D	4	(2)	1
11	Miguel Cardoso		19/06/94	A	25	(5)	1
16	Erick Moreno	COL	24/11/91	A	10	(3)	1
15	Jhon Murillo	VEN	04/06/95	A	27	(4)	5
77	Murilo	BRA	12/05/96	A	7	(14)	1
24	Yordan Osorio	VEN	10/05/94	D	14	(1)	3
17	Pedro Nuno		13/01/95	M	14	(2)	2
3	Pica		08/04/86	D	11	(2)	
20	Pité		22/08/94	D	3	(9)	1
44	Rafael Amorim	BRA	30/07/87	D	16	(1)	
12	Ricardo Janota		10/03/87	G	1		
90	Ruca		11/09/90	D	7	(1)	
93	Alassane També	MLI	26/01/92	D	1	(4)	
28	Wagner	BRA	03/04/87	M	23	(5)	4

Vitória FC (Setúbal)

1910 • Bonfim (18,694) • vfc.pt

Major honours
Portuguese Cup (3) 1965, 1967, 2005

Coach: José Couceiro

2016				
14/08	h	Belenenses	W 2-0	*André Claro (p), Venâncio*
21/08	a	Benfica	D 1-1	*Venâncio*
28/08	h	Arouca	W 2-0	*João Amaral, André Claro*
11/09	a	Chaves	D 0-0	
17/09	h	Paços Ferreira	L 1-4	*Vasco Fernandes*
24/09	a	Braga	L 1-2	*André Claro*
02/10	h	Marítimo	L 0-1	
22/10	a	Feirense	D 1-1	*Fábio Pacheco*
29/10	h	Porto	D 0-0	
06/11	a	Moreirense	W 2-1	*André Claro, João Amaral*
25/11	h	Rio Ave	L 0-1	
03/12	a	Sporting	L 0-2	
09/12	h	Estoril	W 2-0	*João Amaral, Edinho*
18/12	a	Guimarães	L 1-3	*Edinho*
23/12	h	Tondela	W 3-0	*og (Pica) 2, João Amaral*
2017				
08/01	a	Boavista	L 0-1	
14/01	h	Nacional	W 1-0	*Venâncio*
22/01	a	Belenenses	W 2-1	*Edinho 2*
30/01	h	Benfica	W 1-0	*José Manuel*
05/02	a	Arouca	L 1-2	*Edinho (p)*
11/02	h	Chaves	D 0-0	
19/02	a	Paços Ferreira	L 1-2	*Meyong (p)*
26/02	h	Braga	D 1-1	*Costinha*
05/03	a	Marítimo	L 0-1	
11/03	h	Feirense	L 1-2	*Vasco Fernandes*
19/03	a	Porto	D 1-1	*João Carvalho*
02/04	h	Moreirense	W 2-0	*João Amaral, Edinho*
09/04	a	Rio Ave	D 0-0	
14/04	h	Sporting	L 0-3	
22/04	a	Estoril	L 0-3	
28/04	h	Guimarães	L 0-2	
07/05	a	Tondela	L 1-2	*Edinho*
15/05	h	Boavista	L 0-1	
20/05	a	Nacional	W 2-1	*Edinho, José Manuel*

No	Name	Nat	DoB	Pos	Aps	(s)	Gls
14	Mikel Agu	NGA	27/05/93	M	25	(2)	
18	André Claro		31/03/91	A	12	(4)	4
22	André Geraldes		02/05/91	D	14		
27	André Pedrosa		12/04/97	M		(2)	
12	Bruno Varela		04/11/94	G	29		
11	Costinha		28/05/92	M	32		1
36	Edinho		07/07/82	A	18	(8)	8
4	Fábio Cardoso		19/04/94	D	21	(2)	
6	Fábio Pacheco		26/05/88	M	15	(2)	1
44	Ryan Gauld	SCO	16/12/95	M	4	(1)	
7	Arnold Issoko	COD	06/04/92	A	8	(16)	
24	João Amaral		07/09/91	M	28	(5)	5
30	João Carvalho		09/03/97	M	13	(2)	1
70	José Manuel		23/10/90	M	15	(13)	2
42	Luís Felipe	BRA	08/04/91	D	1	(1)	
19	Albert Meyong	CMR	19/10/80	A	3	(9)	1
8	Nenê Bonilha	BRA	17/02/92	M	11	(6)	
21	Nuno Pinto		06/08/86	D	31		
10	Nuno Santos		13/02/95	M	19	(7)	
2	Pedro Pinto		08/11/94	D	6	(1)	
88	Pedro Trigueira		04/01/88	G	5	(1)	
90	Ruca		11/09/90	D	1		
17	Thiago Santana	BRA	04/02/93	A	5	(13)	
23	Vasco Costa		08/08/91	A	2	(6)	
13	Vasco Fernandes		12/11/86	D	30	(1)	2
3	Venâncio		04/02/93	D	26		3

Vitória SC (Guimarães)

1922 • D. Afonso Henriques (30,146) • vitoriasc.pt

Major honours
Portuguese Cup (1) 2013

Coach: Pedro Martins

2016				
14/08	h	Braga	L 0-1	
20/08	a	Marítimo	W 2-0	*Rafinha, Marega*
26/08	h	Paços Ferreira	W 5-3	*Marega 2, og (Mateus Silva), Hurtado, Francisco Soares (p)*
10/09	a	Porto	L 0-3	
17/09	h	Belenenses	D 1-1	*Marega*
25/09	a	Moreirense	W 1-0	*Marega*
01/10	h	Sporting	D 3-3	*Marega 2 (1p), Francisco Soares*
23/10	a	Estoril	W 2-0	*Francisco Soares, Rafinha*
30/10	a	Rio Ave	W 3-0	*Marega 3 (1p)*
04/11	h	Nacional	W 2-1	*Francisco Soares 2 (1p)*
27/11	a	Tondela	L 1-2	*Francisco Soares*
04/12	h	Chaves	D 1-1	*Hernâni*
10/12	a	Boavista	W 2-1	*Texeira, Hurtado*
18/12	h	Setúbal	W 3-1	*João Pedro, Rafinha, Hernâni*
23/12	a	Arouca	W 1-0	*Hernâni*
2017				
07/01	h	Benfica	L 0-2	
14/01	a	Feirense	D 0-0	
22/01	a	Braga	W 2-1	*Josué Sá, Francisco Soares*
28/01	h	Marítimo	D 0-0	
03/02	a	Paços Ferreira	L 0-2	
11/02	h	Porto	L 0-2	
19/02	a	Belenenses	D 1-1	*Hernâni*
24/02	h	Moreirense	W 1-0	*Hurtado*
05/03	a	Sporting	D 1-1	*Marega*
12/03	h	Estoril	D 3-3	*Rafael Miranda, Marega, Rafael Martins*
19/03	h	Rio Ave	W 3-0	*Rafael Martins, Hernâni, Texeira*
31/03	a	Nacional	W 2-1	*Rafael Miranda, Texeira*
09/04	h	Tondela	W 2-1	*Texeira, Hurtado*
15/04	a	Chaves	W 3-2	*Texeira, Hernâni, Hurtado*
23/04	h	Boavista	W 2-0	*Hurtado, Hernâni*
28/04	a	Setúbal	W 2-0	*Hernâni, Rafinha*
07/05	h	Arouca	W 1-0	*Marega*
13/05	a	Benfica	L 0-5	
20/05	h	Feirense	L 0-1	

No	Name	Nat	DoB	Pos	Aps	(s)	Gls
11	Alex		27/08/91	A		(2)	
78	Alex Pinto		08/07/98	D		(1)	
45	Alex Silva		16/03/97	A	1	(3)	
43	Joseph Amoah	GHA	26/06/94	M		(2)	
76	Bruno Gaspar		21/04/93	D	26	(2)	
37	Bruno Mendes	BRA	02/08/94	M		(1)	
93	Guillermo Celis	COL	08/05/93	M	7	(6)	
1	Douglas	BRA	09/03/83	G	30		
71	Fábio Sturgeon		04/02/94	A	4	(4)	
18	Francisco Soares	BRA	07/01/91	A	16		7
26	Prince Gouano	FRA	24/12/93	D	5	(4)	
9	Hernâni		20/08/91	M	21	(6)	8
16	Paolo Hurtado	PER	27/07/90	M	29	(2)	6
20	João Aurélio		17/08/88	D	16	(9)	
58	João Pedro		03/04/93	M	17		1
23	João Vigário		20/11/95	A		(1)	
3	Josué Sá		17/06/92	D	30		1
53	Ghislain Konan	CIV	27/12/95	D	20		
21	Moussa Marega	MLI	14/04/91	A	23	(2)	13
13	Bernard Mensah	GHA	17/10/94	M	7	(14)	
56	Miguel Silva		07/04/95	G	4		
6	Moreno		19/08/81	D	1	(3)	
2	Pedro Henrique	BRA	18/12/92	D	33		
99	Rafael Martins	BRA	17/03/89	A	6	(3)	2
5	Rafael Miranda	BRA	11/08/84	M	17	(2)	2
81	Rafinha	BRA	14/02/96	M	18	(4)	4
7	Ricardo Valente		03/04/91	M	1		
41	Rúben Ferreira		17/02/90	D	14	(1)	
49	Rui Areias		22/11/93	A		(1)	
17	Falaye Sacko	MLI	01/05/95	D	1		
91	David Texeira	URU	27/02/91	A	10	(9)	5
10	Tozé		14/01/93	M	2	(9)	
8	Bongani Zungu	RSA	09/02/92	M	15	(1)	

Top goalscorers

34	Bas Dost (Sporting)
19	Francisco Soares (Guimarães/Porto)
16	Kostas Mitroglou (Benfica) André Silva (Porto)
13	Jonas (Benfica) Moussa Marega (Guimarães)
11	Rui Fonte (Braga) Welthon (Paços Ferreira)
10	Pizzi (Benfica)
8	Kléber (Estoril) Diogo Jota (Porto) Guedes (Rio Ave) Edinho (Setúbal) Hernâni (Guimarães)

Promoted clubs

Portimonense SC

1914 • Municipal de Portimão (4,807) • portimonense.pt

Coach: Vítor Oliveira

CD Aves

1930 • CD Aves (4,291) • cdaves.pt

Coach: Ivo Vieira;
(18/02/17) José Mota

Second level final table 2016/17

		Pld	W	D	L	F	A	Pts
1	Portimonense SC	42	25	8	9	70	39	83
2	CD Aves	42	23	12	7	63	38	81
3	CF União da Madeira	42	17	13	12	52	43	64
4	SL Benfica B	42	18	9	15	56	58	63
5	Penafiel FC	42	18	9	15	56	55	63
6	A. Académica de Coimbra	42	17	11	14	42	35	62
7	SC Braga B	42	16	14	12	64	50	62
8	SC Covilhã	42	15	17	10	51	41	62
9	Varzim SC	42	17	10	15	45	48	61
10	CD Santa Clara	42	16	12	14	44	42	60
11	Vitória SC B	42	18	6	18	54	50	60
12	FC Porto B	42	16	12	14	52	49	60
13	Gil Vicente FC	42	13	17	12	47	49	56
14	Sporting Clube de Portugal B	42	15	10	17	64	62	55
15	FC Famalicão	42	14	11	17	47	50	53
16	CD Cova da Piedade	42	14	11	17	45	60	53
17	Académico de Viseu FC	42	13	13	16	49	54	52
18	Leixões SC	42	10	16	16	44	48	46
19	FC Vizela	42	9	19	14	39	49	46
20	AD Fafe	42	11	12	19	52	65	45
21	SC Freamunde	42	9	13	20	39	52	40
22	SC Olhanense	42	7	7	28	45	83	28

DOMESTIC CUP

Taça de Portugal 2016/17

THIRD ROUND

(13/10/16)
Famalicão 0-1 Sporting

(14/10/16)
1 de Dezembro 1-2 Benfica
Covilhã 1-0 Freamunde *(aet)*

(15/10/16)
AD Oliveirense 1-3 Braga
Aves 1-2 Paços Ferreira *(aet)*
Fátima 1-2 Olhanense
Gafanha 0-3 Porto
Penafiel 1-0 Amarante *(aet)*
União Leiria 0-2 Boavista

(16/10/16)
Académica 2-0 Belenenses
Alcanenense 1-2 Feirense
Aljustrelense 1-0 Limianos
Caldas 0-1 Estoril
Cinfães 0-1 Benfica Castelo Branco
Estarreja 1-3 Nacional
Gil Vicente 0-0 Casa Pia *(aet; 4-1 on pens)*
Merelinense 2-2 Leixões *(aet; 6-7 on pens)*
Mortágua 0-1 Cova Piedade
Naval 0-4 Marítimo
Oriental 2-0 Barreirense
Praiense 3-1 Farense
Real 1-0 Arouca
Sanjoanense 2-1 Lusitano VRSA
Santa Clara 1-1 Rio Ave *(aet; 4-2 on pens)*
Santa Iria 1-2 Guimarães
Sernache 0-1 Vilafranquense
Sertanense 0-4 Tondela
Torreense 2-0 Académico Viseu
Trofense 0-0 Setúbal *(aet; 2-4 on pens)*
União Madeira 0-1 Chaves
Varzim 3-0 Águeda
Vizela 1-0 Moreirense

FOURTH ROUND

(13/11/16)
Varzim 0-1 Covilhã

(17/11/16)
Sporting 5-1 Praiense

(18/11/16)
Chaves 0-0 Porto *(aet; 3-2 on pens)*

(19/11/16)
Benfica 6-0 Marítimo
Estoril 2-0 Cova Piedade
Feirense 0-0 Académica *(aet; 4-5 on pens)*
Sanjoanense 1-0 Gil Vicente

(20/11/16)
Aljustrelense 1-2 Tondela
Benfica Castelo Branco 0-2 Setúbal
Boavista 1-2 Guimarães *(aet)*
Braga 2-1 Santa Clara
Oriental 1-2 Leixões *(aet)*
Real 2-0 Olhanense
Torreense 1-0 Nacional
Vilafranquense 1-0 Paços Ferreira
Vizela 0-1 Penafiel

FIFTH ROUND

(14/12/16)
Académica 1-0 Penafiel
Braga 1-2 Covilhã
Estoril 4-2 Sanjoanense *(aet)*
Leixões 2-1 Tondela
Real 0-3 Benfica
Setúbal 0-1 Sporting
Torreense 2-3 Chaves

(15/12/16)
Guimarães 1-0 Vilafranquense

QUARTER-FINALS

(17/01/17)
Chaves 1-0 Sporting *(Carlos Ponck 87)*
Estoril 2-1 Académica *(Alisson 30, Kléber 85; Traquina 58)*

(18/01/17)
Benfica 6-2 Leixões *(Pizzi 21, André Almeida 31, Jonas 38, Mitroglou 60p, 71, 90; Rafael Porcellis 44, 67)*
Covilhã 0-1 Guimarães *(Hernâni 79)*

SEMI-FINALS

(28/02/17 & 05/04/17)
Estoril 1-2 Benfica *(Kléber 41p; Mitroglou 36, 90)*
Benfica 3-3 Estoril *(Carrillo 33, Živković 54, Jonas 62; Bruno Gomes 31, 78, Carlinhos 46)*
(Benfica 5-4)

(01/03/17 & 04/04/17)
Guimarães 2-0 Chaves *(Hernâni 10, 77)*
Chaves 3-1 Guimarães *(Perdigão 1, Renan Bressan 33, Nuno André Coelho 63; Marega 65)*
(3-3; Guimarães on away goal)

FINAL

(28/05/17)
Estádio Nacional, Lisbon
SL BENFICA 2 *(Jiménez 48, Salvio 53)*
VITÓRIA SC 1 *(Zungu 78)*
Referee: *Hugo Miguel*
BENFICA: *Ederson, Nélson Semedo, Luisão, Lindelöf, Álex Grimaldo, Fejsa (Samaris 24), Salvio, Cervi (Rafa Silva 82), Pizzi, Jiménez, Jonas (Filipe Augusto 90)*
GUIMARÃES: *Miguel Silva, Bruno Gaspar, Josué Sá, Pedro Henrique, Konan (Texeira 57), Zungu, Rafael Miranda, Hurtado (Celis 45), Hernâni (Fábio Sturgeon 63), Rafinha, Marega*

A 2-1 victory over Vitória Guimarães sealed a 26th Portuguese Cup triumph for Benfica

REPUBLIC OF IRELAND

Cumann Peile na héireann/Football Association of Ireland (FAI)

Address	National Sports Campus Abbotstown IE-Dublin 15
Tel	+353 1 8999500
Fax	+353 1 8999502
E-mail	info@fai.ie
Website	fai.ie

President	Tony Fitzgerald
Chief executive	John Delaney
Media officer	Ian Mallon
Year of formation	1921
National stadium	Aviva Stadium, Dublin (51,700)

PREMIER DIVISION CLUBS

 1 **Bohemian FC**

 2 **Bray Wanderers FC**

 3 **Cork City FC**

 4 **Derry City FC**

 5 **Dundalk FC**

 6 **Finn Harps FC**

 7 **Galway United FC**

 8 **Longford Town FC**

 9 **Saint Patrick's Athletic FC**

 10 **Shamrock Rovers FC**

 11 **Sligo Rovers FC**

 12 **Wexford Youths FC**

PROMOTED CLUBS

 13 **Limerick FC**

 14 **Drogheda United FC**

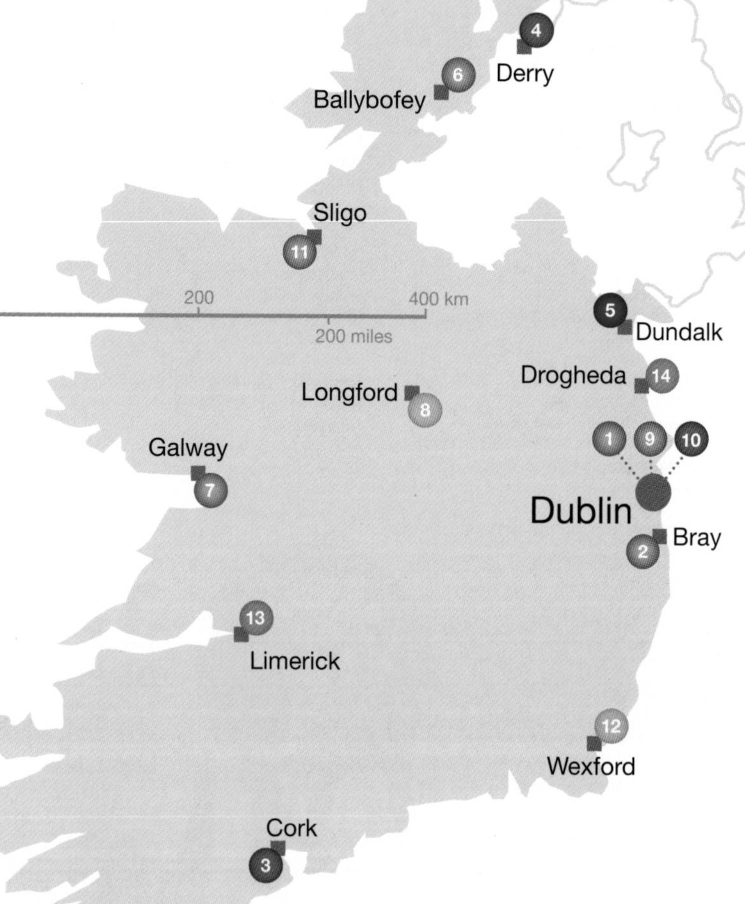

KEY

- UEFA Champions League
- UEFA Europa League
- Promoted
- Relegated

Title hat-trick for Dundalk

Dundalk made it three Premier Division titles in a row in 2016, withstanding another concerted challenge from Cork City, who finished runners-up for the third season running but denied the champions back-to-back doubles by defeating them with a last-gasp winning goal in the FAI Cup final.

Stephen Kenny's side held firm in the league despite a fixture overload generated by a historic run in continental competition as they reached the UEFA Europa League group stage, where they did the Republic of Ireland proud.

Stephen Kenny's team dominate again

Cork deny champions double with late cup final strike

Landmark European campaign for Lilywhites

Domestic league

Having retained the league title for the first time in 2015, Dundalk promptly did it again 12 months later. Kenny, who took charge at a difficult time for the club in November 2012, was once again the key figure in their triumph, the 46-year-old Dubliner managing his resources through a challenging schedule with quiet, controlled efficiency.

It was evident early on that Dundalk and Cork would be the pace-setters once again. John Caulfield's side laid down a marker when they defeated the defending champions 1-0 at Oriel Park with a penalty from new signing Sean Maguire – a fringe player at Dundalk in 2015. However, that home defeat proved to be a mere blip for Kenny's team, which, virtually unchanged from the previous campaign bar top-scoring midfielder Richie Towell, who had crossed the Irish Sea to join Brighton, plundered 28 points from the next 30.

Another 1-0 defeat by Cork, who had put together an impressive run of their own, kept the title race alive, and the two teams largely matched each other result for result until the third head-to-head, in early October, by which stage Dundalk's lead was down to a single point following a shock 3-0 home defeat by Sligo Rovers. The pressure was on, but, spurred on by 4,126 locals, Dundalk made it third time lucky, winning 2-1, the decisive second goal coming from star midfielder Daryl Horgan. Three wins later, the last of them at home to Bohemians, where skipper Andy Boyle and fellow defender Brian Gartland found the target, the title hat-trick was complete.

Seven points was the margin of victory at the finish, with Dundalk's exceptional away form proving a crucial advantage over a Cork side who, though prolific at Turner's Cross, managed just seven wins on the road – compared to the champions' 13. Those included a 5-0 victory across the border at Derry City, who finished third to qualify for the UEFA Europa League alongside Shamrock Rovers, the only club from Dublin to finish in the top half of the table.

Domestic cup

The country's top two came face to face in the FAI Cup final for the second year in a row, and once again the game went into extra time after 90 goalless minutes. On this occasion, though, the trophy went to Cork, with Maguire, who topped the Premier Division charts with 18 goals, adding to his hat-trick in the quarter-finals and double in the semis with a perfectly-timed and wildly-celebrated 120th-minute winner.

Europe

Thanks to a tremendous 3-0 victory over BATE Borisov, Dundalk became the first Irish club to compete in the UEFA Champions League play-offs then only the second to reach the UEFA Europa League group stage – after Shamrock Rovers five years earlier – and the first to register a draw, then a victory as they took four points from their opening two fixtures, holding AZ Alkmaar 1-1 away and defeating Maccabi Tel-Aviv 1-0 at the Tallaght Stadium in Dublin, which became their home from home in Group D. They lost their last four matches (including two against group winners Zenit), but in each case only by a one-goal margin, having put Irish club football firmly on the European map.

National team

Six matches into their 2018 FIFA World Cup qualifying campaign, the Republic of Ireland retained high hopes of qualifying for Russia and a third major tournament in four attempts. Undefeated Martin O'Neill's men sat second only to group leaders Serbia on goal difference but with a four-point buffer over third place. The highlight was a 1-0 victory in Austria, the low point a horrific injury to skipper Séamus Coleman, who broke his leg in the 0-0 draw at home to Wales.

DOMESTIC SEASON AT A GLANCE

Premier Division 2016 final table

			Home					Away					Total					
		Pld	W	D	L	F	A	W	D	L	F	A	W	D	L	F	A	Pts
1	**Dundalk FC**	**33**	**12**	**2**	**2**	**31**	**16**	**13**	**0**	**4**	**42**	**12**	**25**	**2**	**6**	**73**	**28**	**77**
2	Cork City FC	33	14	2	1	46	11	7	5	4	19	12	21	7	5	65	23	70
3	Derry City FC	33	9	5	2	23	15	8	6	3	25	14	17	11	5	48	29	62
4	Shamrock Rovers FC	33	8	4	4	22	14	8	3	6	24	20	16	7	10	46	34	55
5	Sligo Rovers FC	33	8	7	2	22	9	5	3	8	20	26	13	10	10	42	35	49
6	Bray Wanderers FC	33	9	3	5	28	19	4	4	8	11	21	13	7	13	39	40	46
7	Saint Patrick's Athletic FC	33	7	3	7	30	23	6	3	7	15	18	13	6	14	45	41	45
8	Bohemian FC	33	8	3	5	21	17	4	2	11	9	20	12	5	16	30	37	41
9	Galway United FC	33	7	4	5	21	21	3	4	10	23	33	10	8	15	44	54	38
10	Finn Harps FC	33	7	2	8	13	23	1	6	9	10	26	8	8	17	23	49	32
11	Wexford Youths FC	33	4	3	10	15	25	2	2	12	16	45	6	5	22	31	70	23
12	Longford Town FC	33	0	4	12	11	35	2	4	11	14	36	2	8	23	25	71	14

European qualification 2017/18

Champion: Dundalk FC (second qualifying round)

Cup winner: Cork City FC (first qualifying round)
Derry City FC (first qualifying round)
Shamrock Rovers FC (first qualifying round)

Top scorer Sean Maguire (Cork), 18 goals
Relegated clubs Longford Town FC, Wexford Youths FC
Promoted clubs Limerick FC, Drogheda United FC
Cup final Cork City FC 1-0 Dundalk FC

Player of the season

Daryl Horgan
(Dundalk FC)

A third Premier Division winner's medal in his three seasons at Dundalk was accompanied by individual recognition as Horgan scooped the PFAI Player of the Year prize. It was an honour the stocky, skilful Galway-born winger fully merited at the end of a year in which he struck ten goals in the Lilywhites' league success and also featured prominently in the club's epic European run. He left Oriel Park in the winter to join English Championship club Preston and was awarded his first senior cap for Ireland in a Dublin friendly against Iceland a few months later.

Newcomer of the season

Sean Maguire
(Cork City FC)

Barely used by Dundalk in 2015, Maguire moved south to join rivals Cork and promptly blossomed into the most lethal striker in the Premier Division. Two goals on his City debut against Bohemians set the tone, and by the end of term he had added 16 more to become the league's top marksman – just ahead of Derry's Rory Patterson and Dundalk's David McMillan. The 22-year-old sharpshooter saved his best for last, however, scoring a dramatic 120th-minute winner in the FAI Cup final against Dundalk to give Cork their third victory in the competition.

Team of the season

(4-4-2)

Coach: Kenny *(Dundalk)*

NATIONAL TEAM

International tournament appearances

FIFA World Cup (3) 1990 (qtr-finals), 1994 (2nd round), 2002 (2nd round)
UEFA European Championship (3) 1988, 2012, 2016 (round of 16)

Top five all-time caps

Robbie Keane (146); Shay Given (134); **John O'Shea** (117); Kevin Kilbane (110); Stephen Staunton (102)

Top five all-time goals

Robbie Keane (68); Niall Quinn (21); Frank Stapleton (20); John Aldridge, Tony Cascarino & Don Givens (19)

Results 2016/17

31/08/16	Oman	H	Dublin	W	4-0	*Brady (8), Keane (30), Walters (34, 63)*
05/09/16	Serbia (WCQ)	A	Belgrade	D	2-2	*Hendrick (3), Murphy (81)*
06/10/16	Georgia (WCQ)	H	Dublin	W	1-0	*Coleman (56)*
09/10/16	Moldova (WCQ)	A	Chisinau	W	3-1	*S Long (2), McClean (69, 76)*
12/11/16	Austria (WCQ)	A	Vienna	W	1-0	*McClean (48)*
24/03/17	Wales (WCQ)	H	Dublin	D	0-0	
28/03/17	Iceland	H	Dublin	L	0-1	
01/06/17	Mexico	N	East Rutherford (USA)	L	1-3	*Gleeson (77)*
04/06/17	Uruguay	H	Dublin	W	3-1	*Walters (27), Christie (51), McClean (77)*
11/06/17	Austria (WCQ)	H	Dublin	D	1-1	*Walters (85)*

Appearances 2016/17

Coach: Martin O'Neill (NIR)	**01/03/52**		**Oma**	**SRB**	**GEO**	**MDA**	**AUT**	**WAL**	**Isl**	**Mex**	**Uru**	**AUT**	**Caps**	**Goals**
Keiren Westwood	23/10/84	Sheffield Wednesday (ENG)	G46						G		s46		21	-
Cyrus Christie	30/09/92	Derby (ENG)	D					s72	D	M73	D	D	11	2
Marc Wilson	17/08/87	Bournemouth (ENG)	D										25	1
Ciaran Clark	26/09/89	Newcastle (ENG)	D	s91	D	D	D						24	2
Robbie Brady	14/01/92	Norwich (ENG) /Burnley (ENG)	D46	M	M79		D		D		M	M	34	7
Stephen Quinn	01/04/86	Reading (ENG)	M65	s70									18	-
Glenn Whelan	13/01/84	Stoke (ENG)	M46	M	s79	M	M24	M			M46	M77	81	2
Harry Arter	28/12/89	Bournemouth (ENG)	M				M				M	M71	6	-
Jonathan Walters	20/09/83	Stoke (ENG)	M	M	M	M	A	M			A61	A	49	14
Robbie Keane	08/07/80	LA Galaxy (USA)	A57										146	68
Shane Long	22/01/87	Southampton (ENG)	A46	A91	A94	A63		A	s71				73	17
Jeff Hendrick	31/01/92	Burnley (ENG)	s46	M75	M		M	M	M62		M74	M	33	1
James McClean	22/04/89	West Brom (ENG)	s46	M	M	M	M85	M	M71	M	s74	M	52	9
Darren Randolph	12/05/87	West Ham (ENG)	s46	G	G	G	G	G		G	G46	G	22	-
Stephen Ward	20/08/85	Burnley (ENG)	s46	D70	D	D		D			D	D56	43	3
Wes Hoolahan	20/05/82	Norwich (ENG)	s57			M86	M78			s64	s46	s71	40	3
Callum O'Dowda	23/04/95	Bristol City (ENG)	s65			s63			s72	M			5	-
Séamus Coleman	11/10/88	Everton (ENG)		D	D	D	D	D72					43	1
John O'Shea	30/04/81	Sunderland (ENG)		D	s94			D					117	3
Richard Keogh	11/08/86	Derby (ENG)		D				D		D			17	1
Daryl Murphy	15/03/83	Newcastle (ENG)		s75						A64	s61	s56	26	1
Shane Duffy	01/01/92	Brighton (ENG)			D	D	D			D	D61	D	11	-
James McCarthy	12/11/90	Everton (ENG)			M	M80							41	-
David Meyler	29/05/89	Hull (ENG)				s80	s24	M79					19	-
Eunan O'Kane	10/07/90	Leeds (ENG)				s86			s62	s64			7	-
David McGoldrick	29/11/87	Ipswich (ENG)					s78			A			6	-
Aiden McGeady	04/04/86	Preston (ENG)					s85	s79	M72		s60	s77	90	5
John Egan	20/10/92	Brentford (ENG)							D62	D64			2	-
Alex Pearce	09/11/88	Derby (ENG)							D		s61		9	2
Conor Hourihane	02/02/91	Aston Villa (ENG)							M62	M64			2	-
Jonny Hayes	09/07/87	Aberdeen (SCO)							M62		M60		4	-
Kevin Doyle	18/09/83	Colorado Rapids (USA)							A				63	14
Andy Boyle	07/03/91	Preston (ENG)							s62				1	-
Stephen Gleeson	03/08/88	Birmingham (ENG)							s62	s73			4	1
Daryl Horgan	10/08/92	Preston (ENG)							s62	M73			2	-
Kevin Long	18/08/90	Burnley (ENG)								s64	D	D	3	-
Alan Browne	15/04/95	Preston (ENG)								s73			1	-

EUROPE

Dundalk FC

CHAMPIONS LEAGUE

Second qualifying round - FH Hafnarfjördur (ISL)
H 1-1 *McMillan (66)*
Rogers, Gannon, Gartland (Barrett 43), Boyle, O'Donnell, Horgan, Mountney (Benson 81), McMillan (Kilduff 78), Finn, McEleney, Massey. Coach: Stephen Kenny (IRL)
A 2-2 *McMillan (52, 62)*
Rogers, Gannon, Boyle, O'Donnell, Horgan, Mountney (Benson 46), McMillan (Kilduff 82), Finn, McEleney (Shields 79), Massey, Barrett. Coach: Stephen Kenny (IRL)

Third qualifying round - FC BATE Borisov (BLR)
A 0-1
Rogers, Gannon, Boyle, O'Donnell, Horgan, McMillan (Kilduff 78), Finn, McEleney (Shields 46), Massey, Barrett, Benson (Mountney 46). Coach: Stephen Kenny (IRL)
H 3-0 *McMillan (44, 59), Benson (90)*
Rogers, Gannon, Boyle, Shields, O'Donnell, Horgan (Kilduff 90+2), Mountney, McMillan (Benson 78), Finn (McEleney 32), Massey, Barrett. Coach: Stephen Kenny (IRL)

Play-offs - Legia Warszawa (POL)
H 0-2
Rogers, Gannon, Boyle, Shields (Benson 77), O'Donnell, Horgan, Mountney (Finn 64), McMillan (Kilduff 80), McEleney, Massey, Barrett. Coach: Stephen Kenny (IRL)
A 1-1 *Benson (19)*
Rogers, Gannon, Boyle, Shields (Meenan 83), Horgan, McMillan, Finn, McEleney (M O'Connor 88), Massey, Barrett, Benson. Coach: Stephen Kenny (IRL)

Group D
Match 1 - AZ Alkmaar (NED)
A 1-1 *Kilduff (89)*
Rogers, Gannon, Gartland, Boyle, O'Donnell, Horgan, Mountney (Benson 77), McMillan (Shields 75), Finn, McEleney (Kilduff 84), Massey. Coach: Stephen Kenny (IRL)
Red card: O'Donnell 71
Match 2 - Maccabi Tel-Aviv FC (ISR)
H 1-0 *Kilduff (72)*
Rogers, Gannon, Gartland, Boyle, Shields, Horgan, McMillan (Kilduff 64), Finn, McEleney (Mountney 75), Massey, Benson (Shiels 85). Coach: Stephen Kenny (IRL)
Match 3 - FC Zenit (RUS)
H 1-2 *Benson (52)*
Sava, Gannon, Gartland, Boyle, Shields (Shiels 86), Horgan, McMillan (Kilduff 72), Finn, McEleney, Massey, Benson (Mountney 79). Coach: Stephen Kenny (IRL)
Match 4 - FC Zenit (RUS)
A 1-2 *Horgan (52)*
Rogers, Gannon, Gartland, Boyle, Shields, Horgan, Mountney (O'Donnell 46), McMillan (Kilduff 65), Finn, McEleney (Shiels 83), Massey. Coach: Stephen Kenny (IRL)
Match 5 - AZ Alkmaar (NED)
H 0-1
Rogers, Gannon, Gartland, Boyle, O'Donnell (Mountney 42), Horgan, Finn, McEleney (Shiels 80), Massey, Kilduff (McMillan 77), Benson. Coach: Stephen Kenny (IRL)
Match 6 - Maccabi Tel-Aviv FC (ISR)
A 1-2 *Dasa (27og)*
Rogers, Gannon (O'Donnell 68), Gartland (Barrett 46), Boyle, Shields, Horgan, McMillan, Finn, McEleney (Kilduff 80), Massey, Benson. Coach: Stephen Kenny (IRL)

Cork City FC

EUROPA LEAGUE

First qualifying round - Linfield FC (NIR)
A 1-0 *Maguire (63p)*
McNulty, Bennett, Bolger, Beattie, Dooley, O'Connor, G Morrissey, Sheppard (D Morrissey 45+2), Browne, Maguire (Healy 90), Buckley (O'Sullivan 60). Coach: John Caulfield (IRL)
H 1-1 *Maguire (49p)*
McNulty, Bennett, Holohan (D Morrissey 56), Beattie, Dooley, O'Connor, G Morrissey, McSweeney (O'Sullivan 56), Browne, Maguire, Buckley (Healy 65). Coach: John Caulfield (IRL)

Second qualifying round - BK Häcken (SWE)
A 1-1 *Maguire (64p)*
McNulty, Bennett, Bolger, Beattie (Sheppard 75), Dooley, O'Connor, G Morrissey, McSweeney, Browne, Maguire (Healy 90+2), Buckley (O'Sullivan 85). Coach: John Caulfield (IRL)
H 1-0 *O'Connor (26)*
McNulty, Bennett, Bolger, Beattie, Dooley, O'Connor, G Morrissey (Holohan 79), McSweeney, Browne, Maguire (O'Sullivan 90), Buckley. Coach: John Caulfield (IRL)

Third qualifying round - KRC Genk (BEL)
A 0-1
McNulty, Bennett, Bolger, Beattie (D Morrissey 83), Dooley, O'Connor, G Morrissey, McSweeney, Browne, Maguire (O'Sullivan 86), Buckley. Coach: John Caulfield (IRL)
H 1-2 *Bennett (63)*
McNulty, Bennett, Bolger, Beattie, Dooley, O'Connor, G Morrissey (O'Sullivan 46), McSweeney (D Morrissey 46), Browne, Maguire (Sheppard 56), Buckley. Coach: John Caulfield (IRL)

Shamrock Rovers FC

EUROPA LEAGUE

First qualifying round - RoPS Rovaniemi (FIN)
H 0-2
Hyland, Cornwall, O'Connor, Miele, K Brennan (McCabe 75), Shaw, G Brennan (D Clarke 56), Cregg, Madden, Heaney, McPhail (Boyd 86). Coach: Pat Fenlon (IRL)
A 1-1 *McCabe (22p)*
Hyland, Cornwall, McCabe, Miele (T Clarke 67), K Brennan, Shaw (Dobbs 74), G Brennan, Cregg, Madden, D Clarke (Boyd 74), Heaney. Coach: Stephen Bradley (IRL)

Saint Patrick's Athletic FC

EUROPA LEAGUE

First qualifying round - AS Jeunesse Esch (LUX)
H 1-0 *Fagan (10)*
Clarke, O'Brien, Bermingham, D Dennehy, Hoare, Cawley, Byrne (Timlin 60), Treacy, Fagan, G Kelly, B Dennehy. Coach: Liam Buckley (IRL)
A 1-2 *B Dennehy (73)*
Clarke, O'Brien, Bermingham, D Dennehy, Hoare, Cawley, Byrne, Treacy (Verdon 82), Fagan, Timlin (G Kelly 79), B Dennehy. Coach: Liam Buckley (IRL)

Second qualifying round - FC Dinamo Minsk (BLR)
A 1-1 *Fagan (54)*
Clarke, O'Brien, Bermingham, D Dennehy, Hoare, Byrne, Treacy (Cawley 72), Fagan (Corcoran 79), Timlin (Verdon 79), G Kelly, B Dennehy. Coach: Liam Buckley (IRL)
H 0-1
Clarke, O'Brien, Bermingham, D Dennehy, Hoare, Byrne (Corcoran 90), Treacy, Fagan, Timlin (McGrath 62), G Kelly (Cawley 69), B Dennehy. Coach: Liam Buckley (IRL)

DOMESTIC LEAGUE CLUB-BY-CLUB

Bohemian FC

1890 • Dalymount Park (4,500) • bohemianfc.com

Major honours
League of Ireland (11) 1924, 1928, 1930, 1934, 1936, 1975, 1978, 2001, 2003 (spring), 2008, 2009; Irish Cup (1) 1908; FAI Cup (7) 1928, 1935, 1970, 1976, 1992, 2001, 2008

Manager: Keith Long

2016

Date		Opponent	Res	Score	Scorers
04/03	a	Cork	L	0-2	
11/03	h	Sligo	W	1-0	*K Byrne*
14/03	a	St Patrick's	L	0-3	
18/03	h	Wexford	D	3-3	*Quigley 2 (1p), P Kavanagh*
26/03	a	Galway	L	0-1	
01/04	h	Longford	W	2-0	*Buckley, Ben Mohamed*
09/04	a	Bray	W	2-0	*D Byrne, Ben Mohamed*
15/04	h	Shamrock Rovers	L	0-4	
22/04	a	Derry	L	0-1	
29/04	h	Dundalk	L	0-2	
06/05	a	Finn Harps	D	0-0	
10/05	h	Cork	L	0-1	
14/05	a	Sligo	L	0-1	
29/05	h	St Patrick's	W	5-1	*Lopes, Akinade, Kelly 2, K Byrne (p)*
03/06	a	Wexford	W	1-0	*Akinade*
24/06	h	Galway	D	1-1	*Akinade*
02/07	a	Longford	W	1-0	*K Byrne*
08/07	h	Bray	D	0-0	
15/07	a	Shamrock Rovers	L	1-3	*K Byrne*
22/07	h	Derry	L	0-1	
05/08	h	Finn Harps	W	2-0	*Kelly, Akinade*
12/08	a	Cork	D	0-0	
15/08	h	Sligo	W	3-2	*Akinade, K Byrne, Best*
26/08	a	St Patrick's	W	1-0	*K Byrne*
02/09	h	Dundalk	L	1-2	*K Byrne*
16/09	a	Galway	L	0-2	
19/09	h	Wexford	W	1-0	*K Byrne*
23/09	h	Longford	W	1-0	*K Byrne*
30/09	a	Bray	L	1-2	*Buckley*
07/10	h	Shamrock Rovers	W	1-0	*Lopes*
14/10	a	Derry	L	1-2	*K Byrne*
23/10	a	Dundalk	L	1-2	*Quigley (p)*
28/10	a	Finn Harps	L	0-1	

No	Name	Nat	DoB	Pos	Aps	(s)	Gls
24	Ismahil Akinade	NGA	17/06/92	A	16	(2)	5
16	Ayman Ben Mohamed	TUN	08/12/94	M	10	(7)	2
12	Stephen Best		15/03/97	D	5	(1)	1
8	Keith Buckley		17/06/92	M	29	(2)	2
6	Dan Byrne		07/05/93	D	19	(7)	1
10	Kurtis Byrne		09/04/90	A	25	(6)	10
22	Dean Casey		15/12/97	D		(2)	
17	Marco Chindea	ROU	18/04/94	A		(3)	
1	Dean Delany		15/09/80	G	23	(1)	
18	Adam Evans		03/05/94	A		(2)	
3	Lorcan Fitzgerald		03/01/89	D	25	(2)	
21	Dylan Hayes		09/04/95	D	10	(2)	
23	James Kavanagh		12/01/93	D		(2)	
14	Patrick Kavanagh		29/12/85	M	28	(2)	1
11	Jake Kelly		18/06/90	M	12	(11)	3
4	Roberto Lopes		17/06/92	M	31		2
18	Ian Morris		27/02/87	M	7	(3)	
15	Dave Mulcahy		28/01/78	M	12	(2)	
17	Anthony Murphy		01/08/82	M	4	(2)	
16	Dean O'Halloran		02/01/96	M	7	(3)	
2	Derek Pender		02/10/84	D	30		
5	Derek Prendergast		17/10/84	D	27	(1)	
9	Mark Quigley		27/10/85	A	11	(15)	3
30	Shane Supple		04/05/87	G	10		
7	Eoin Wearen		02/10/92	M	22	(6)	

Bray Wanderers FC

1942 • Carlisle Grounds (3,000) • braywanderersfc.ie

Major honours
FAI Cup (2) 1990, 1999

Manager: Harry Kenny

2016

Date		Opponent	Res	Score	Scorers
05/03	h	Dundalk	L	1-3	*Salmon*
11/03	a	Galway	L	0-4	
14/03	h	Derry	L	0-3	
19/03	a	Longford	D	1-1	*Kelly*
26/03	h	Sligo	W	4-0	*Brennan 2, Moore, Lewis*
01/04	a	Wexford	L	0-2	
09/04	h	Bohemians	L	0-2	
15/04	a	Finn Harps	L	0-1	
23/04	h	St Patrick's	W	1-0	*Pender*
29/04	a	Shamrock Rovers	L	0-2	
07/05	h	Cork	L	0-2	
10/05	a	Dundalk	L	0-1	
14/05	h	Galway	L	1-2	*Lewis*
29/05	a	Derry	L	0-2	
03/06	h	Longford	D	0-0	
24/06	a	Sligo	D	0-0	
02/07	h	Wexford	W	3-0	*Kelly, Lewis, Moore*
08/07	a	Bohemians	D	0-0	
16/07	h	Finn Harps	W	1-0	*Kenna*
29/07	h	Shamrock Rovers	D	1-1	*Connolly*
10/08	h	Dundalk	W	2-1	*Salmon, Moore*
19/08	a	Galway	W	2-0	*Connolly, Lyons*
27/08	h	Derry	D	2-2	*Connolly 2*
30/08	a	Cork	L	0-4	
06/09	a	St Patrick's	W	2-1	*Pender, Douglas*
10/09	a	Longford	W	2-0	*Pender, Noone*
17/09	h	Sligo	W	4-0	*Pender, Noone, Lewis, Harding*
23/09	a	Wexford	W	3-1	*Salmon, Pender, Lynch*
30/09	h	Bohemians	W	2-1	*Pender, Sullivan*
07/10	a	Finn Harps	L	1-2	*Kelly*
14/10	h	St Patrick's	W	2-1	*Pender, McNally*
21/10	a	Shamrock Rovers	D	0-0	
28/10	h	Cork	W	4-1	*Marks, Connolly, Sullivan, Pender*

No	Name	Nat	DoB	Pos	Aps	(s)	Gls
7	Ryan Brennan		11/11/91	M	20	(2)	2
6	Alan Byrne		21/07/83	D	3	(3)	
1	Peter Cherrie	SCO	01/10/83	G	33		
21	Tim Clancy		08/06/84	D	13		
16	Dylan Connolly		02/05/95	M	28	(3)	5
21	Robbie Creevy		24/08/89	M	12		
2	Hugh Douglas		22/06/93	D	28	(2)	1
20	Paul Finnegan		18/06/96	D	2	(2)	
24	Sean Harding		17/09/88	D	14	(3)	1
15	Alan Kehoe		12/04/96	D	2	(4)	
9	Dean Kelly		18/09/85	A	10	(7)	3
4	Conor Kenna		21/11/84	D	31		1
18	Andrew Lewis	ENG	09/04/95	A	14	(7)	4
19	Kevin Lynch		21/03/92	D	14	(1)	1
27	Chris Lyons		08/05/93	A	1	(6)	1
11	Jason Marks		02/05/89	M	17	(9)	1
23	Gareth McDonagh		27/02/96	M	6	(12)	
5	Alan McNally		15/09/82	D	18	(2)	1
10	Karl Moore		09/11/88	M	31		3
3	Curtis Murphy		12/07/96	D	3	(1)	
15	Sean Noble		20/03/96	M		(2)	
22	Darragh Noone		28/04/97	M	8	(8)	2
17	Ger Pender		22/05/94	A	19	(11)	8
8	Mark Salmon		31/10/88	M	22	(4)	3
3	John Sullivan		06/01/91	M	14		2

Cork City FC

1984 • Turner's Cross (7,365) • corkcityfc.ie

Major honours
League of Ireland (2) 1993, 2005; FAI Cup (3) 1998, 2007, 2016

Manager: John Caulfield

2016

Date		Opponent	Res	Score	Scorers
04/03	h	Bohemians	W	2-0	*Maguire 2*
11/03	a	Derry	L	0-1	
14/03	h	Longford	W	6-0	*Beattie 3, Maguire, D Morrissey 2*
18/03	a	Dundalk	W	1-0	*Maguire (p)*
02/04	a	Sligo	D	0-0	
08/04	h	Wexford	D	1-1	*O'Sullivan*
15/04	a	Galway	D	2-2	*Dooley, O'Connell*
22/04	h	Finn Harps	W	3-1	*G Morrissey, Maguire, Sheppard*
25/04	h	Shamrock Rovers	W	2-0	*Beattie, Sheppard*
29/04	h	St Patrick's	W	1-0	*Sheppard*
07/05	a	Bray	W	2-0	*Maguire, Sheppard*
10/05	a	Bohemians	W	1-0	*Buckley*
13/05	h	Derry	W	2-1	*D Morrissey, Browne*
29/05	a	Longford	W	3-0	*Maguire, O'Sullivan, Dooley*
03/06	h	Dundalk	W	1-0	*Dooley*
24/06	a	Shamrock Rovers	D	0-0	
10/07	a	Wexford	W	1-0	*Buckley*
08/08	h	Sligo	L	1-2	*Maguire (p)*
12/08	h	Bohemians	D	0-0	
15/08	a	Derry	D	0-0	
26/08	h	Longford	W	5-2	*Bennett, Maguire 2 (1p), Sheppard 2*
30/08	h	Bray	W	4-0	*G Morrissey, Holohan, Browne, Maguire (p)*
16/09	h	Shamrock Rovers	W	3-0	*Maguire, Bolger (p), Buckley*
19/09	a	Finn Harps	W	1-0	*Maguire (p)*
24/09	a	Sligo	D	0-0	
27/09	h	Galway	W	5-3	*Mulcahy 2, Maguire, Buckley, O'Connor*
08/10	a	Galway	W	5-0	*Maguire 2, Dooley, Buckley, Ogbene*
11/10	a	Dundalk	L	1-2	*O'Sullivan*
14/10	h	Finn Harps	W	2-0	*O'Connor, Dooley*
17/10	a	St Patrick's	L	1-3	*Bennett*
21/10	h	St Patrick's	W	3-1	*O'Sullivan, Maguire, Beattie*
24/10	h	Wexford	W	5-0	*Ogbene 2, Maguire, McCarthy, Holohan*
28/10	a	Bray	L	1-4	*Sheppard*

No	Name	Nat	DoB	Pos	Aps	(s)	Gls
10	Steven Beattie		20/08/88	M	26	(3)	5
3	Alan Bennett		04/10/81	D	27		2
6	Greg Bolger		09/09/88	M	27		1
22	Kenny Browne		07/08/86	D	26		2
26	Garry Buckley		19/08/93	M	20	(4)	5
29	Cian Coleman		01/01/97	M		(2)	
11	Stephen Dooley		19/10/91	M	24	(2)	5
4	John Dunleavy		03/07/91	D	13		
7	Colin Healy		14/03/80	M	6	(13)	
8	Gavan Holohan		15/12/91	M	17	(3)	2
2	John Kavanagh		22/11/87	D	2	(1)	
24	Sean Maguire		01/05/94	A	28	(2)	18
21	Conor McCarthy		11/04/98	D	2		1
1	Mark McNulty		13/10/80	G	33		
18	Michael McSweeney		17/06/88	D	10	(4)	
9	Danny Morrissey		13/12/93	A	4	(13)	3
16	Gearóid Morrissey		17/11/91	M	23	(1)	2
15	Dave Mulcahy		28/01/78	M	7	(6)	2
5	Eoghan O'Connell		13/08/95	D	7		1
14	Kevin O'Connor		07/05/95	D	28		2
23	Mark O'Sullivan		01/02/83	A	5	(22)	4
20	Chiedozie Ogbene		01/05/97	M	2	(6)	3
19	Karl Sheppard		14/02/91	A	23	(5)	7
27	Ian Turner		19/04/89	M	3	(11)	

REPUBLIC OF IRELAND

Derry City FC

1928 • The Brandywell (7,700) • derrycityfc.net

Major honours
Irish League (1) 1965; League of Ireland (2) 1989, 1997; Irish Cup (3) 1949, 1954, 1964; FAI Cup (5) 1989, 1995, 2002 (autumn), 2006, 2012

Manager: Kenny Shiels (NIR)

2016

Date		Opponent		Score	Scorers
04/03	a	Finn Harps	L	1-2	*Patterson*
11/03	h	Cork	W	1-0	*Curtis*
14/03	a	Bray	W	3-0	*Barry, Patterson 2*
18/03	h	Galway	W	2-1	*Boyle 2*
26/03	a	Wexford	W	2-1	*McCormack, Patterson*
01/04	a	Dundalk	D	1-1	*McNamee*
08/04	h	Shamrock Rovers	W	3-0	*Curtis, Monaghan, Patterson (p)*
16/04	a	Longford	D	1-1	*McClean*
22/04	h	Bohemians	W	1-0	*Patterson*
29/04	h	Sligo	L	0-2	
06/05	a	St Patrick's	W	1-0	*McNamee*
10/05	h	Finn Harps	D	2-2	*Daniels, Patterson*
13/05	a	Cork	L	1-2	*Vemmelund*
29/05	h	Bray	W	2-0	*Daniels, Boyle*
03/06	a	Galway	D	0-0	
24/06	h	Wexford	W	1-0	*Boyle*
01/07	h	Dundalk	L	0-5	
15/07	h	Longford	W	4-0	*McEneff, Schubert, McNamee, Patterson*
22/07	a	Bohemians	W	1-0	*Patterson*
29/07	a	Sligo	D	0-0	
05/08	h	St Patrick's	D	1-1	*Patterson*
12/08	a	Finn Harps	W	5-0	*McEneff 2 (2p), Boyle, Schubert, Ward*
15/08	h	Cork	D	0-0	
27/08	a	Bray	D	2-2	*Patterson, McEneff (p)*
30/08	a	Shamrock Rovers	W	1-0	*Patterson*
02/09	h	Galway	D	0-0	
16/09	a	Wexford	D	0-0	
23/09	a	Dundalk	L	1-3	*Schubert*
27/09	h	Shamrock Rovers	D	2-2	*Curtis 2*
08/10	a	Longford	W	3-2	*McNamee, Patterson 2*
14/10	h	Bohemians	W	2-1	*McEneff (p), Patterson*
21/10	h	Sligo	W	2-1	*McEneff, McNamee*
28/10	a	St Patrick's	W	2-0	*Patterson 2 (1p)*

No	Name	Nat	DoB	Pos	Aps	(s)	Gls
9	Jordan Allan	SCO	20/10/95	A	1	(4)	
30	Aaron Barry		24/11/94	D	17		1
16	Nathan Boyle	NIR	14/04/94	A	10	(19)	5
21	Cristian Castells	ESP	19/10/84	D	3		
27	Ronan Curtis	NIR	29/03/96	M	19	(5)	4
12	Joshua Daniels	NIR	22/02/96	M	8	(12)	2
23	Ben Doherty	NIR	24/03/97	M	3	(6)	
1	Gerard Doherty		24/08/81	G	32		
26	Ryan Doherty	NIR	15/04/96	A		(2)	
32	Rory Holden	NIR	23/08/97	A	1	(3)	
3	Dean Jarvis	NIR	01/06/92	D	28	(2)	
33	Maximilian Karner	AUT	30/01/90	D	4	(1)	
5	Ryan McBride		15/12/89	D	20		
22	Patrick McClean		22/11/96	D	7	(5)	1
6	Conor McCormack		18/05/90	M	29	(2)	1
25	Conor McDermott	NIR	18/09/97	M	16	(5)	
4	Aaron McEneff	NIR	09/07/95	M	27	(2)	6
14	Gareth McGlynn		29/10/82	M	6		
7	Barry McNamee		17/02/92	M	30		5
8	Harry Monaghan	SCO	24/03/93	M	13	(5)	1
11	Rory Patterson	NIR	16/07/84	A	32		17
20	Shaun Patton		22/08/95	G	1		
29	Lukas Schubert	AUT	25/06/89	M	14	(1)	3
2	Niclas Vemmelund	DEN	02/10/92	D	32		1
10	Keith Ward		12/10/90	M	10	(9)	1
32	Scot Whiteside	NIR	16/06/97	D		(2)	

Dundalk FC

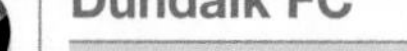

1903 • Oriel Park (4,500) • dundalkfc.com

Major honours
League of Ireland (12) 1933, 1963, 1967, 1976, 1979, 1982, 1988, 1991, 1995, 2014, 2015, 2016; FAI Cup (10) 1942, 1949, 1952, 1958, 1977, 1979, 1981, 1988, 2002 (spring), 2015

Manager: Stephen Kenny

2016

Date		Opponent		Score	Scorers
05/03	a	Bray	W	3-1	*Kilduff 2, Finn*
11/03	h	Finn Harps	W	3-0	*Barrett, McEleney, og (Curran)*
14/03	a	Wexford	W	2-1	*McMillan, Kilduff*
18/03	h	Cork	L	0-1	
24/03	a	St Patrick's	W	4-0	*O'Donnell, McMillan, Horgan, Gartland*
01/04	h	Derry	D	1-1	*McMillan*
09/04	a	Longford	W	4-0	*Finn 3 (1p), Gartland*
15/04	h	Sligo	W	1-0	*Finn (p)*
22/04	a	Shamrock Rovers	W	2-0	*og (Webster), Finn*
29/04	a	Bohemians	W	2-0	*Horgan 2*
06/05	h	Galway	W	2-1	*McMillan 2*
10/05	h	Bray	W	1-0	*Boyle*
13/05	a	Finn Harps	W	7-0	*Benson 2, Horgan, Finn, McMillan, Boyle, Barrett*
29/05	h	Wexford	W	3-2	*Horgan, Meenan, McEleney*
03/06	a	Cork	L	0-1	
24/06	h	St Patrick's	W	2-0	*Kilduff, Finn*
01/07	a	Derry	W	5-0	*McMillan 3, Massey, Horgan*
05/07	h	Longford	W	4-3	*McMillan 3, Kilduff*
05/08	a	Galway	L	0-1	
10/08	a	Bray	L	1-2	*Horgan*
26/08	a	Wexford	W	1-0	*McMillan*
02/09	a	Bohemians	W	2-1	*Gartland, Mountney*
06/09	a	Sligo	W	1-0	*McMillan*
12/09	h	Finn Harps	W	2-0	*McEleney, Horgan*
20/09	h	Shamrock Rovers	D	1-1	*Gartland*
23/09	h	Derry	W	3-1	*Mountney, Gartland, McMillan*
08/10	h	Sligo	L	0-3	
11/10	h	Cork	W	2-1	*og (McNulty), Horgan*
14/10	a	Shamrock Rovers	W	3-0	*Gartland, Massey, Kilduff*
17/10	a	Longford	W	3-0	*Massey, McMillan, Horgan*
23/10	h	Bohemians	W	2-1	*Boyle, Gartland*
25/10	a	St Patrick's	L	2-5	*Shiels, M O'Connor*
28/10	h	Galway	W	4-1	*Shiels 2, Barrett, Kilduff*

No	Name	Nat	DoB	Pos	Aps	(s)	Gls
15	Paddy Barrett		22/07/93	D	9	(7)	3
18	Robbie Benson		07/05/92	M	12	(12)	2
4	Andy Boyle		07/03/91	D	32		3
31	Keith Dalton		10/09/97	D	1		
10	Ronan Finn		21/12/87	M	28	(1)	8
2	Sean Gannon		11/07/91	D	26		
3	Brian Gartland		04/11/86	D	27	(2)	7
12	Shane Grimes		09/03/87	D	3	(1)	
7	Daryl Horgan		10/08/92	M	31		10
24	Alan Keane		23/09/84	D	5		
16	Ciaran Kilduff		29/09/88	A	9	(11)	7
14	Dane Massey		17/04/88	D	30		3
11	Patrick McEleney	NIR	26/09/92	M	17	(6)	3
9	David McMillan		14/12/88	A	26	(5)	16
21	Darren Meenan	NIR	16/11/86	M	10	(14)	1
8	John Mountney		22/02/93	M	21	(9)	2
20	Ciaran O'Connor		04/07/96	A	1	(4)	
26	Michael O'Connor		31/07/98	M	1	(2)	1
6	Stephen O'Donnell		15/01/86	M	21	(2)	1
17	Georgie Poynton		08/09/97	M	1	(3)	
1	Gary Rogers		25/09/81	G	29		
22	Gabriel Sava	ITA	15/10/86	G	4		
5	Chris Shields		27/12/90	M	17	(8)	
19	Dean Shiels	NIR	01/02/85	M	2	(7)	3
28	Carlton Ubaezuono		22/04/98	D		(1)	

Finn Harps FC

1954 • Finn Park (3,000) • finnharps.com

Major honours
FAI Cup (1) 1974

Manager: Ollie Horgan

2016

Date		Opponent		Score	Scorers
04/03	h	Derry	W	2-1	*Scully, Curran*
11/03	a	Dundalk	L	0-3	
14/03	h	Shamrock Rovers	L	0-1	
19/03	a	Sligo	D	1-1	*McNulty*
26/03	h	Longford	W	1-0	*Curran (p)*
08/04	a	Galway	L	0-1	
11/04	h	St Patrick's	L	1-2	*McHugh (p)*
15/04	h	Bray	W	1-0	*Scully*
22/04	a	Cork	L	1-3	*Curran*
29/04	a	Wexford	D	1-1	*Curran (p)*
06/05	h	Bohemians	D	0-0	
10/05	a	Derry	D	2-2	*Curran, Houston*
13/05	h	Dundalk	L	0-7	
17/05	a	St Patrick's	L	0-4	
29/05	a	Shamrock Rovers	D	1-1	*Scully*
03/06	h	Sligo	W	3-0	*Houston 2, Curran*
24/06	a	Longford	W	2-0	*J Mailey, McNamee*
08/07	h	Galway	W	1-0	*Houston*
16/07	a	Bray	L	0-1	
29/07	h	Wexford	L	0-1	
05/08	a	Bohemians	L	0-2	
12/08	h	Derry	L	0-5	
26/08	h	Shamrock Rovers	L	0-2	
12/09	a	Dundalk	L	0-2	
19/09	h	Cork	L	0-1	
16/09	h	Longford	L	0-1	
01/10	a	Galway	L	2-3	*Keating, Hanlon*
04/10	a	Sligo	D	0-0	
07/10	h	Bray	W	2-1	*Houston 2*
11/10	h	St Patrick's	D	1-1	*Houston*
14/10	a	Cork	L	0-2	
21/10	a	Wexford	D	0-0	
28/10	h	Bohemians	W	1-0	*Curran*

No	Name	Nat	DoB	Pos	Aps	(s)	Gls
17	BJ Banda	RSA	01/06/98	A	2	(5)	
22	Ethan Boyle		01/04/97	M	24	(3)	
73	Richard Brush	ENG	26/11/84	G	19		
3	Ciaran Coll		19/08/91	D	29		
4	Keith Cowan		23/08/85	D	27		
31	Mark Coyle		13/02/97	M		(1)	
12	Matthew Crossan		23/09/86	D		(2)	
9	Ryan Curran		13/10/93	A	26	(4)	7
24	Liam Flatley		21/11/96	M	1	(8)	
8	Raymond Foy		10/03/93	M	4	(8)	
7	Michael Funston		13/05/85	M	11	(13)	
1	Ciaran Gallagher		01/04/92	G	14	(1)	
18	Adam Hanlon		03/06/92	M	24	(4)	1
6	Gareth Harkin		19/12/87	M	24	(1)	
16	Sean Houston		29/10/89	M	26	(1)	7
30	Ruairi Keating		16/07/95	A	8	(3)	1
19	Josh Mailey		10/01/91	D	10	(3)	1
5	Packie Mailey		18/04/88	D	25	(1)	
15	Ryan McConnell		03/10/95	D		(1)	
10	Kevin McHugh		19/01/80	A	1	(17)	1
14	Thomas McMonagle		19/10/91	D	9		
11	Tony McNamee		16/08/93	M	18	(8)	1
2	Damien McNulty	NIR	10/02/91	D	24		1
39	Barry Molloy		28/11/83	M	19	(1)	
28	Daire O'Baoill		29/10/97	D		(1)	
20	Dave Scully		20/01/85	M	18	(9)	3

Galway United FC

2013 • Eamonn Deacy Park (5,000) • galwayunitedfc.ie

Manager: Tommy Dunne; (30/09/16) (Leo Tierney)

2016

Date		Opponent		Score	Scorers
04/03	a	St Patrick's	W	3-1	*Faherty, Sullivan, Curran*
11/03	h	Bray	W	4-0	*Devaney, og (Finnegan), Faherty, Keating*
14/03	a	Sligo	D	1-1	*Keating*
18/03	a	Derry	L	1-2	*Devaney*
26/03	h	Bohemians	W	1-0	*Faherty*
01/04	a	Shamrock Rovers	L	0-2	
08/04	h	Finn Harps	W	1-0	*Faherty*
15/04	h	Cork	D	2-2	*Faherty, Shanahan*
22/04	a	Wexford	W	2-0	*Faherty 2*
29/04	h	Longford	D	2-2	*Faherty, Curran*
06/05	a	Dundalk	L	1-2	*Foley*
10/05	h	St Patrick's	L	0-3	
14/05	a	Bray	W	2-1	*Foley, Ludden*
29/05	h	Sligo	L	1-2	*Shanahan*
03/06	h	Derry	D	0-0	
24/06	a	Bohemians	D	1-1	*Connolly*
08/07	a	Finn Harps	L	0-1	
22/07	h	Wexford	W	4-2	*Shanahan, Faherty 2, Connolly*
30/07	a	Longford	D	1-1	*Sinnott*
05/08	h	Dundalk	W	1-0	*Faherty*
12/08	a	St Patrick's	L	0-1	
19/08	h	Bray	L	0-2	
27/08	a	Sligo	L	1-2	*Shanahan*
02/09	a	Derry	D	0-0	
06/09	h	Shamrock Rovers	L	0-1	
16/09	h	Bohemians	W	2-0	*Aganovic, Devaney*
23/09	a	Shamrock Rovers	L	2-4	*Connolly 2*
27/09	a	Cork	L	3-5	*Cantwell, Devaney 2*
01/10	h	Finn Harps	W	3-2	*Faherty, Curran, C Horgan*
08/10	h	Cork	L	0-5	
14/10	a	Wexford	L	4-5	*Devaney 2, og (Friel), Melody*
21/10	h	Longford	D	0-0	
28/10	a	Dundalk	L	1-4	*Connolly*

No	Name	Nat	DoB	Pos	Aps	(s)	Gls
37	Armin Aganovic	SWE	06/04/94	D	18		1
4	Alex Byrne		08/03/95	M	13	(4)	
5	Kilian Cantwell		24/05/95	D	17	(8)	1
10	Ryan Connolly		13/01/92	M	29		5
18	Padraic Cunningham		13/11/96	A	6	(11)	
9	Enda Curran		11/06/92	A	14	(10)	3
14	Kevin Devaney		26/09/90	M	22	(4)	7
24	Jesse Devers		11/01/97	M		(4)	
11	Vinny Faherty		13/06/87	A	29	(4)	12
57	Stephen Folan		14/01/92	D	23	(1)	
22	Eric Foley		30/01/90	M	2	(4)	2
2	Colm Horgan		02/07/94	D	31		1
16	Kevin Horgan		26/04/97	G	3		
8	José García	ESP	08/07/91	M	1	(4)	
30	Ruairi Keating		16/07/95	A	7	(7)	2
3	Marc Ludden		28/02/90	D	16	(3)	1
15	Conor Melody		15/03/97	M	8	(9)	1
25	Sam Ramsbottom	ENG	03/04/96	G	5		
17	Gary Shanahan		15/02/93	M	27	(6)	4
6	Paul Sinnott		24/07/86	M	28	(1)	1
8	John Sullivan		06/01/91	D	15		1
7	Stephen Walsh		29/08/90	D	24		
1	Conor Winn		26/02/92	G	25		

Longford Town FC

1924 • City Calling Stadium (4,500) • ltfc.ie

Major honours
FAI Cup (2) 2003, 2004

Manager: Tony Cousins; (13/08/16) (Gary Cronin); (21/08/16) Alan Mathews

2016

Date		Opponent		Score	Scorers
04/03	a	Wexford	W	2-0	*O'Connor, O'Hanlon*
11/03	h	St Patrick's	L	0-1	
14/03	a	Cork	L	0-6	
19/03	h	Bray	D	1-1	*O'Sullivan*
26/03	a	Finn Harps	L	0-1	
01/04	a	Bohemians	L	0-2	
09/04	h	Dundalk	L	0-4	
16/04	h	Derry	D	1-1	*O'Sullivan*
23/04	a	Sligo	L	0-3	
29/04	a	Galway	D	2-2	*O'Hanlon, og (Winn)*
07/05	h	Shamrock Rovers	L	0-2	
10/05	h	Wexford	L	2-4	*O'Sullivan, og (G Delaney)*
13/05	a	St Patrick's	D	3-3	*Gannon, Powell, O'Sullivan (p)*
29/05	h	Cork	L	0-3	
03/06	a	Bray	D	0-0	
24/06	h	Finn Harps	L	0-2	
02/07	h	Bohemians	L	0-1	
05/07	a	Dundalk	L	3-4	*Duffy, Haverty, Gorman*
15/07	a	Derry	L	0-4	
23/07	h	Sligo	D	2-2	*Gorman, Dsane*
30/07	h	Galway	D	1-1	*Simon*
05/08	a	Shamrock Rovers	L	1-2	*O'Sullivan*
12/08	a	Wexford	L	0-2	
15/08	h	St Patrick's	L	0-1	
26/08	a	Cork	L	2-5	*McGlynn 2*
10/09	h	Bray	L	0-2	
16/09	a	Finn Harps	W	1-0	*O'Connor*
23/09	a	Bohemians	L	0-1	
08/10	h	Derry	L	2-3	*O'Sullivan 2 (1p)*
14/10	a	Sligo	L	0-1	
17/10	h	Dundalk	L	0-3	
21/10	a	Galway	D	0-0	
28/10	h	Shamrock Rovers	L	2-4	*Hughes, O'Sullivan*

No	Name	Nat	DoB	Pos	Aps	(s)	Gls
17	Keith Beirne		28/03/97	D		(1)	
25	Karl Chambers		07/06/96	A		(4)	
30	Ryan Coulter		08/02/89	G	12		
9	Don Cowan		16/11/89	A	15	(6)	
7	Kealan Dillon		21/02/94	M	21	(7)	
22	Eddie Dsane	ENG	05/02/97	A	11	(2)	1
16	Lee Duffy		07/10/91	A	6	(5)	1
20	Pat Flynn		13/01/85	D	20	(2)	
21	Philip Gannon		11/10/96	M	27	(5)	1
24	Rhys Gorman		24/01/94	M	11	(4)	2
4	Noel Haverty		24/02/89	D	17	(2)	1
6	Mark Hughes		30/11/89	M	21	(2)	1
14	Gaius Makouta	FRA	25/07/97	M	1	(6)	
8	Peter McGlynn		02/09/89	D	19	(4)	2
14	John McKeown		28/02/94	M	2	(4)	
18	Ian Molloy		27/11/96	G	2	(1)	
10	Cody Mulhall		25/08/96	A		(1)	
2	Jamie Mulhall		29/01/96	D	19	(5)	
17	Yann Mvita	FRA	11/05/96	D	13		
12	Tristan Noack-Hofmann		08/10/98	D	6	(1)	
11	Kevin O'Connor		19/10/85	M	23	(3)	2
10	Josh O'Hanlon		25/09/95	A	10	(6)	2
5	Daniel O'Reilly		11/04/95	D	6	(2)	
15	David O'Sullivan		04/10/87	A	24	(7)	8
3	Conor Powell		26/08/87	D	27		1
22	Mark Rossiter		27/05/83	D	9		
19	Kaleem Simon		08/07/96	M	22	(7)	1
1	Paul Skinner		03/02/89	G	19		

Saint Patrick's Athletic FC

1929 • Richmond Park (4,000) • stpatsfc.com

Major honours
League of Ireland (8) 1952, 1955, 1956, 1990, 1996, 1998, 1999, 2013; FAI Cup (3) 1959, 1961, 2014

Manager: Liam Buckley

2016

Date		Opponent		Score	Scorers
04/03	h	Galway	L	1-3	*Fagan*
11/03	a	Longford	W	1-0	*Fagan*
14/03	h	Bohemians	W	3-0	*Timlin, Fagan, B Dennehy*
18/03	a	Shamrock Rovers	W	2-0	*B Dennehy, Fagan*
24/03	h	Dundalk	L	0-4	
08/04	h	Sligo	D	1-1	*Fagan*
11/04	a	Finn Harps	W	2-1	*og (P Mailey), Timlin*
15/04	h	Wexford	W	4-0	*Timlin, Fagan, Byrne 2*
23/04	a	Bray	L	0-1	
29/04	a	Cork	L	0-1	
06/05	h	Derry	L	0-1	
10/05	a	Galway	W	3-0	*Hoare, B Dennehy, Byrne*
13/05	h	Longford	D	3-3	*Verdon, Byrne, McGrath*
17/05	h	Finn Harps	W	4-0	*Timlin 2, Byrne, B Dennehy*
29/05	a	Bohemians	L	1-5	*Bermingham*
03/06	h	Shamrock Rovers	L	0-2	
24/06	a	Dundalk	L	0-2	
09/07	a	Sligo	L	0-1	
01/08	a	Wexford	W	1-0	*Bermingham*
05/08	a	Derry	D	1-1	*Treacy*
12/08	h	Galway	W	1-0	*Fagan*
15/08	a	Longford	W	1-0	*Timlin*
26/08	h	Bohemians	L	0-1	
02/09	a	Shamrock Rovers	D	0-0	
06/09	h	Bray	L	1-2	*G Kelly*
27/09	h	Sligo	D	0-0	
07/10	h	Wexford	W	4-1	*Byrne 2 (1p), Fagan, G Kelly*
11/10	a	Finn Harps	D	1-1	*Timlin*
14/10	a	Bray	L	1-2	*McGrath*
17/10	h	Cork	W	3-1	*Fagan, Verdon, Byrne (p)*
21/10	a	Cork	L	1-3	*Byrne*
25/10	h	Dundalk	W	5-2	*Fagan, Byrne 2, Bermingham, Lunney*
28/10	h	Derry	L	0-2	

No	Name	Nat	DoB	Pos	Aps	(s)	Gls
22	Michael Barker		16/08/93	D	14	(2)	
3	Ian Bermingham		16/06/89	D	31		3
7	Conán Byrne		10/07/85	M	26	(6)	11
6	David Cawley		19/09/91	M	16	(2)	
1	Brendan Clarke		17/09/85	G	29		
10	Daniel Corcoran		13/02/89	A	2	(13)	
20	Billy Dennehy		17/02/87	M	23	(4)	4
4	Darren Dennehy		21/09/88	D	23	(1)	
12	Lee Desmond		22/01/95	D	16	(1)	
9	Christy Fagan		11/05/89	A	26	(1)	10
13	Rory Feely		03/01/97	M	10	(3)	
5	Sean Hoare		15/03/94	D	20	(1)	1
25	Patrick Jennings		24/09/79	G	1		
26	Ciaran Kelly		04/07/98	D		(1)	
14	Graham Kelly		31/10/91	M	26	(3)	2
24	Steven Kinsella		22/08/88	M	5	(5)	
30	Jonathan Lunney		02/02/98	D	2	(1)	1
21	Darragh Markey		23/05/97	M		(7)	
15	Shane McEleney		31/01/91	D	10	(1)	
17	Dylan McGlade		22/04/95	M		(5)	
19	Jamie McGrath		30/09/96	M	17	(6)	2
23	Jason McGuinness		08/08/82	D		(1)	
2	Ger O'Brien		02/07/84	D	26	(1)	
16	Conor O'Malley		01/08/94	G	3		
11	Fuad Sule		20/01/97	M		(1)	
11	Mark Timlin		07/11/94	M	21	(5)	7
8	Keith Treacy		13/09/88	M	7	(7)	1
18	Sam Verdon		03/09/95	A	9	(9)	2

REPUBLIC OF IRELAND

Shamrock Rovers FC

1901 • Tallaght Stadium (6,500) • shamrockrovers.ie

Major honours
League of Ireland (17) 1923, 1925, 1927, 1932, 1938, 1939, 1954, 1957, 1959, 1964, 1984, 1985, 1986, 1987, 1994, 2010, 2011; FAI Cup (24) 1925, 1929, 1930, 1931, 1932, 1933, 1936, 1940, 1944, 1945, 1948, 1955, 1956, 1962, 1964, 1965, 1966, 1967, 1968, 1969, 1978, 1985, 1986, 1987

Manager: Pat Fenlon; (03/07/16) (Stephen Bradley)

2016					
05/03	a	Sligo	W	2-0	*Miele, North*
11/03	h	Wexford	W	2-0	*North, McCabe (p)*
14/03	a	Finn Harps	W	1-0	*McCabe (p)*
18/03	h	St Patrick's	L	0-2	
01/04	h	Galway	W	2-0	*Miele, T Clarke*
08/04	a	Derry	L	0-3	
15/04	a	Bohemians	W	4-0	*McCabe, Miele 2, G Brennan*
22/04	h	Dundalk	L	0-2	
25/04	a	Cork	L	0-2	
29/04	h	Bray	W	2-0	*K Brennan, D Clarke*
07/05	a	Longford	W	2-0	*og (J Mulhall), North*
10/05	h	Sligo	W	3-0	*McCabe 2 (1p), Shaw*
13/05	a	Wexford	L	0-2	
29/05	h	Finn Harps	D	1-1	*Shaw*
03/06	a	St Patrick's	W	2-0	*Miele, Shaw*
24/06	h	Cork	D	0-0	
15/07	h	Bohemians	W	3-1	*D Clarke, Shaw, Boyd*
29/07	a	Bray	D	1-1	*McCabe (p)*
05/08	h	Longford	W	2-1	*Miele, Heaney*
12/08	a	Sligo	L	2-3	*Boyd, Dobbs*
15/08	h	Wexford	W	3-1	*McCabe, Miele, Boyd*
26/08	a	Finn Harps	W	2-0	*Boyd, D Clarke*
30/08	h	Derry	L	0-1	
02/09	h	St Patrick's	D	0-0	
06/09	a	Galway	W	1-0	*Shaw*
16/09	a	Cork	L	0-3	
20/09	a	Dundalk	D	1-1	*Shaw*
23/09	h	Galway	W	4-2	*Boyd, og (Ramsbottom), Heaney, McCabe*
27/09	a	Derry	D	2-2	*McCabe, McPhail*
07/10	a	Bohemians	L	0-1	
14/10	h	Dundalk	L	0-3	
21/10	h	Bray	D	0-0	
28/10	a	Longford	W	4-2	*McCabe (p), Dobbs, Miele 2*

No	Name	Nat	DoB	Pos	Aps	(s)	Gls
6	Maxime Blanchard	FRA	27/09/86	D	9		
8	Aaron Bolger		02/02/00	M	1	(2)	
22	Sean Boyd		20/06/98	A	13	(6)	5
15	Gavin Brennan		23/01/88	D	16	(1)	1
11	Killian Brennan		31/01/84	M	17	(2)	1
3	Luke Byrne		08/07/93	D	1		
18	Dean Clarke		29/03/93	A	23	(6)	3
20	Trevor Clarke		26/03/98	M	14	(12)	1
2	Rob Cornwall		16/10/94	D	21		
16	Patrick Cregg		21/02/86	M	22	(7)	
26	Aaron Dobbs		06/01/99	A	4	(8)	2
29	James Doona		15/01/98	M	2	(5)	
8	Michael Drennan		02/02/94	A	8		
21	Shane Hanney		19/02/98	D	5	(1)	
23	Sean Heaney		27/01/96	D	15		2
25	Craig Hyland		08/09/90	G	14		
3	Luke Kiely		09/06/99	M		(3)	
17	Simon Madden		01/05/88	D	33		
7	Gary McCabe		01/08/88	M	24	(4)	10
37	Stephen McPhail		09/12/79	M	12	(4)	1
10	Brandon Miele		28/08/94	M	28	(2)	9
1	Barry Murphy		08/06/85	G	19	(1)	
9	Danny North		07/09/87	A	5	(7)	3
5	David O'Connor		24/08/91	D	17	(1)	
14	Gary Shaw		10/05/92	A	21	(6)	6
4	David Webster		08/09/89	D	19	(2)	

Sligo Rovers FC

1928 • The Showgrounds (5,500) • sligorovers.com

Major honours
League of Ireland (3) 1937, 1977, 2012; FAI Cup (5) 1983, 1994, 2010, 2011, 2013

Manager: Dave Robertson (ENG)

2016					
05/03	h	Shamrock Rovers	L	0-2	
11/03	a	Bohemians	L	0-1	
14/03	h	Galway	D	1-1	*Martin*
19/03	h	Finn Harps	D	1-1	*Lyons*
26/03	a	Bray	L	0-4	
02/04	h	Cork	D	0-0	
08/04	a	St Patrick's	D	1-1	*Boylan*
15/04	a	Dundalk	L	0-1	
23/04	h	Longford	W	3-0	*Richards, Cretaro, og (Noack-Hofmann)*
29/04	a	Derry	W	2-0	*Cretaro, Keohane*
07/05	h	Wexford	W	4-1	*Cretaro, Richards, Martin, Gordon*
10/05	a	Shamrock Rovers	L	0-3	
14/05	h	Bohemians	W	1-0	*Martin*
29/05	a	Galway	W	2-1	*Sadlier 2*
03/06	a	Finn Harps	L	0-3	
24/06	h	Bray	D	0-0	
09/07	h	St Patrick's	W	1-0	*Cretaro*
23/07	a	Longford	D	2-2	*Cretaro, Roberts*
29/07	h	Derry	D	0-0	
05/08	a	Wexford	W	5-0	*Cretaro, Kearns, Campion, Sadlier 2*
08/08	a	Cork	W	2-1	*Sadlier, Cretaro*
12/08	h	Shamrock Rovers	W	3-2	*Campion, Russell, Cretaro*
15/08	a	Bohemians	L	2-3	*Sadlier, Martin*
27/08	h	Galway	W	2-1	*Cretaro, Campion*
06/09	h	Dundalk	L	0-1	
17/09	a	Bray	L	0-4	
24/09	h	Cork	D	0-0	
27/09	a	St Patrick's	D	0-0	
04/10	h	Finn Harps	D	0-0	
08/10	a	Dundalk	W	3-0	*Campion, Roberts, Cretaro*
14/10	h	Longford	W	1-0	*Sadlier*
21/10	a	Derry	L	1-2	*McCann*
28/10	h	Wexford	W	5-0	*Sadlier 2, Kearns, Keohane, Place*

No	Name	Nat	DoB	Pos	Aps	(s)	Gls
2	Tobi Adebayo-Rowling	ENG	16/11/96	D	32		
14	Gary Boylan		24/04/96	D	24	(3)	1
7	Achille Campion	FRA	10/03/90	A	10	(1)	4
5	Tim Clancy		08/06/84	D	5	(2)	
10	Raffaele Cretaro		15/10/81	A	20	(5)	10
3	Regan Donelon		17/04/96	D	19	(1)	
21	Paul Doyle		10/04/98	M		(1)	
28	Jaanai Gordon	ENG	07/12/95	A	5	(7)	1
28	Mark Hannon		07/02/98	M		(1)	
19	Daniel Kearns		26/08/91	M	10	(4)	2
17	Jimmy Keohane		22/01/91	M	31		2
4	Michael Leahy		30/04/89	D	24	(2)	
7	Chris Lyons		08/05/93	A	3	(3)	1
27	Liam Martin		23/01/94	M	28	(2)	4
6	Patrick McCann	USA	06/10/90	M	10		1
16	Ciaran Nugent	USA	27/10/91	G	8		
44	Gavin Peers		10/11/85	D	17	(1)	
24	Mikey Place		09/04/98	M		(7)	1
12	Jordan Richards	ENG	06/07/97	D	12	(3)	2
9	Philip Roberts		07/04/94	A	9	(10)	2
8	Craig Roddan	ENG	22/04/93	M	28		
18	John Russell		18/05/85	M	20	(7)	1
11	Kieran Sadlier		14/09/94	M	23	(6)	9
1	Michael Schlingermann		23/06/91	G	25		

Wexford Youths FC

2007 • Ferrycarrig Park (2,500) • wexfordyouthsfc.ie

Manager: Shane Keegan

2016					
04/03	h	Longford	L	0-2	
11/03	a	Shamrock Rovers	L	0-2	
14/03	h	Dundalk	L	1-2	*Last*
18/03	a	Bohemians	D	3-3	*Furlong (p), Kenny, G Delaney*
26/03	h	Derry	L	1-2	*Furlong*
01/04	h	Bray	W	2-0	*Murphy 2*
08/04	a	Cork	D	1-1	*Molloy*
15/04	a	St Patrick's	L	0-4	
22/04	h	Galway	L	0-2	
29/04	h	Finn Harps	D	1-1	*Mulligan*
07/05	a	Sligo	L	1-4	*Furlong*
10/05	a	Longford	W	4-2	*R Delaney, Kenny, Mulligan, Murphy*
13/05	h	Shamrock Rovers	W	2-0	*Mulligan, Kenny*
29/05	a	Dundalk	L	2-3	*Murphy, Molloy*
03/06	h	Bohemians	L	0-1	
24/06	a	Derry	L	0-1	
02/07	a	Bray	L	0-3	
10/07	h	Cork	L	0-1	
22/07	a	Galway	L	2-4	*Dunne, Mulligan*
29/07	a	Finn Harps	W	1-0	*G Delaney*
01/08	h	St Patrick's	L	0-1	
05/08	h	Sligo	L	0-5	
12/08	h	Longford	W	2-0	*Bonner, Murphy (p)*
15/08	a	Shamrock Rovers	L	1-3	*Furlong (p)*
26/08	h	Dundalk	L	0-1	
16/09	h	Derry	D	0-0	
19/09	a	Bohemians	L	0-1	
23/09	h	Bray	L	1-3	*Dempsey*
07/10	a	St Patrick's	L	1-4	*Bonner*
14/10	h	Galway	W	5-4	*Keenan, Furlong 2, Whittle, O'Connor*
21/10	h	Finn Harps	D	0-0	
24/10	a	Cork	L	0-5	
28/10	a	Sligo	L	0-5	

No	Name	Nat	DoB	Pos	Aps	(s)	Gls
17	Jonny Bonner		09/07/91	M	25	(3)	2
15	Paul Brennan		30/06/97	A	1		
22	Corey Chambers		11/01/98	G		(1)	
6	Lee Chin		08/10/92	D	5		
4	Gary Delaney		11/05/94	D	23	(2)	2
3	Ryan Delaney		06/09/96	D	14	(1)	1
25	Shane Dempsey		19/05/89	M	5	(7)	1
1	Graham Doyle		30/05/78	G	33		
21	Shane Dunne		04/04/93	M	12	(9)	1
18	Conor English		15/09/95	A		(1)	
14	Aidan Friel	NIR	15/01/91	D	22	(4)	
9	Danny Furlong		06/11/89	A	23	(2)	6
7	Dean George		28/05/98	A	1		
5	Lee Grace		01/12/92	D	21		
8	Peter Higgins		04/05/87	M	3	(4)	
10	Aidan Keenan		09/08/83	M	6	(6)	1
12	Chris Kenny		04/05/90	D	24	(5)	3
26	Stephen Last		05/10/91	D	19	(3)	1
23	Danny Ledwith		17/08/91	M	9	(7)	
2	Craig McCabe		14/05/93	D	27	(2)	
29	Owen McCormack		03/03/98	D	1	(1)	
11	Eric Molloy		12/12/92	M	20	(3)	2
7	Andy Mulligan		07/07/93	M	19	(8)	4
20	Paul Murphy		19/03/91	A	27	(1)	5
27	Andrew O'Connor		02/07/95	D	5	(1)	1
16	Conor O'Keeffe		19/09/93	D	6	(3)	
13	John Peare		12/10/94	M		(1)	
28	Eoin Porter		10/06/99	A	4	(2)	
18	Vincent Quinlan		09/05/99	M	3		
29	Conor Sutton		03/10/97	M	1		
6	Craig Wall		17/03/91	M	1	(4)	
19	Conor Whittle		28/04/95	D	3	(5)	1

Top goalscorers

18	Sean Maguire (Cork)
17	Rory Patterson (Derry)
16	David McMillan (Dundalk)
12	Vinny Faherty (Galway)
11	Conán Byrne (St Patrick's)
10	Kurtis Byrne (Bohemians) Daryl Horgan (Dundalk) Christy Fagan (St Patrick's) Gary McCabe (Shamrock Rovers) Raffaele Cretaro (Sligo)

Promoted clubs

Limerick FC

1937 • Markets Field (5,000) • limerickfc.ie

Major honours
League of Ireland (2) 1960, 1980; FAI Cup (2) 1971, 1982

Manager: Martin Russell

Drogheda United FC

1919 • United Park (2,500) • droghedaunited.ie

Major honours
League of Ireland (1) 2007; FAI Cup (1) 2005

Manager: Pete Mahon

Second level final table 2016

	Pld	W	D	L	F	A	Pts
1 Limerick FC	28	24	3	1	86	26	75
2 Drogheda United FC	28	15	7	6	42	29	52
3 Cobh Ramblers FC	28	15	5	8	40	33	50
4 University College Dublin AFC	28	14	6	8	57	40	48
5 Waterford United FC	28	10	3	15	43	65	33
6 Shelbourne FC	28	9	3	16	36	40	30
7 Cabinteely FC	28	4	4	20	19	54	16
8 Athlone Town AFC	28	3	5	20	26	62	14

Promotion/Relegation play-offs

(22/10/16 & 28/10/16)
Cobh 0-2 Drogheda
Drogheda 1-2 Cobh
(Drogheda 3-2)

(31/10/16 & 04/11/16)
Wexford 2-0 Drogheda
Drogheda 3-0 Wexford
(Drogheda 3-2)

DOMESTIC CUP

FAI Cup 2016

SECOND ROUND

(20/05/16)
Bohemians 2-0 Galway
Cork 4-0 St Peter's
Derry 1-1 Drogheda
Dundalk 2-0 Shelbourne
Firhouse 0-3 Wexford
Shamrock Rovers 4-0 Midleton
UCD 4-3 Bray
Waterford 0-2 Longford

(21/05/16)
Athlone 0-0 Letterkenny
Bluebell 2-5 Limerick
Cobh 2-1 Cherry Orchard
Finn Harps 0-1 Crumlin
Ringmahon 2-1 Glebe North
Sligo 3-0 Cabinteely
St Patrick's 8-0 Pike

(22/05/16)
Janesboro 2-1 Sheriff

Replays

(24/05/16)
Drogheda 1-2 Derry
Letterkenny 0-1 Athlone *(aet)*

THIRD ROUND

(19/08/16)
Athlone 0-5 Shamrock Rovers
Bohemians 0-2 Derry
St Patrick's 2-0 Limerick
Wexford 2-1 Sligo

(20/08/16)
Longford 1-4 Cork
Ringmahon 1-4 Cobh
UCD 3-1 Janesboro

(30/08/16)
Crumlin 0-5 Dundalk

QUARTER-FINALS

(09/09/16)
Shamrock Rovers 0-5 Cork *(Maguire 4, 46, 50, Buckley 12, Sheppard 33)*
UCD 0-1 Dundalk *(Kilduff 66)*
Wexford 1-3 Derry *(Molloy 6; Patterson 45, Schubert 47, McNamee 85)*

(10/09/16)
St Patrick's 3-2 Cobh *(Fagan 15, McGrath 21, B Dennehy 37; Ellis 49p, Lehane 61)*

SEMI-FINALS

(02/10/16)
Dundalk 2-2 Derry *(Shiels 21, Kilduff 45+2; Patterson 65, Curtis 86)*
St Patrick's 1-3 Cork *(Fagan 38; Bennett 23, Maguire 49, 77)*

Replay

(04/10/16)
Derry 1-2 Dundalk *(Curtis 4; Kilduff 36p, Finn 67)*

FINAL

(06/11/16)
Aviva Stadium, Dublin
CORK CITY FC 1 *(Maguire 120)*
DUNDALK FC 0
(aet)
Referee: *Rogers*
CORK: *McNulty, Beattie, Bennett, Browne, O'Connor, Bolger (O'Sullivan 96), G Morrissey (Healy 100), Buckley, Dooley, Sheppard (Ogbene 78), Maguire*
DUNDALK: *Rogers, Gannon, Gartland, Boyle, Massey, O'Donnell, Shields (Mountney 55), McEleney (Shiels 76), Finn, Horgan, McMillan (Kilduff 79)*

Cork City struck late to defeat champions Dundalk in the FAI Cup final

ROMANIA

Federaţia Română de Fotbal (FRF)

Address Casa Fotbalului
Str. Vasile Şerbănică nr. 12
Sektor 2
RO-022186 Bucureşti
Tel +40 21 325 0678
Fax +40 21 325 0679
E-mail frf@frf.ro
Website frf.ro

President Răzvan Burleanu
General secretary Radu Traian Visan
Media officer Gabriel Berceanu
Year of formation 1909
National stadium Arena Naţională, Bucharest (55,634)

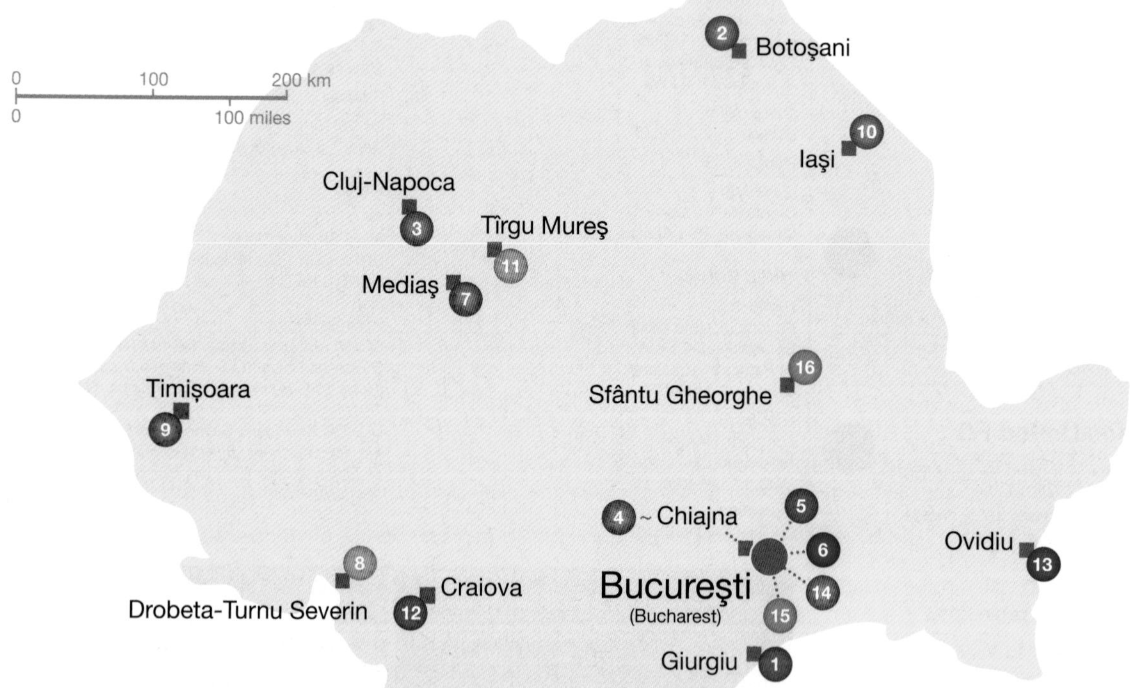

LIGA I CLUBS

 1 FC Astra Giurgiu

 2 FC Botoşani

 3 CFR 1907 Cluj

 4 CS Concordia Chiajna

 5 FC Dinamo Bucureşti

 6 FCSB

 7 CS Gaz Metan Mediaş

  8 CS Pandurii Târgu Jiu

 9 ACS Poli Timişoara

 10 CSM Politehnica Iaşi

 11 ASA Tîrgu Mureş

 12 CS U Craiova

 13 FC Viitorul

 14 FC Voluntari

PROMOTED CLUBS

  15 CS Juventus Bucureşti

 16 Sepsi OSK Sfântu Gheorghe

KEY

- UEFA Champions League
- UEFA Europa League
- Promoted
- Relegated

Victory for FC Viitorul

It was a case of 'V' for victory in 2016/17 as Romanian football welcomed two new clubs to its winner's circle – FC Viitorul, who claimed their first Liga I title, and FC Voluntari, who triumphed in the Romanian Cup.

Viitorul, owned and coached by the country's greatest ever footballer, Gheorghe Hagi, ended the two-phase league with the same number of points as FCSB, the club that began the season as Steaua Bucureşti before they were legally obliged at the end of March to change their famous name to a set of initials.

Gheorghe Hagi's club upset the odds to take title

Runners-up Steaua renamed FCSB

Voluntari beat Astra on penalties to win cup final

Domestic league

With Marius Şumudică's defending champions Astra Giurgiu getting off to a terrible start and effectively removing themselves from title contention before mid-September, opportunity knocked for Laurenţiu Reghecampf's Steaua (as they then still were) to regain the trophy they had won in the three seasons preceding Astra's triumph. A bright start lifted them to the top of the table and they remained there until Hagi's young Viitorul side racked up five successive victories to enter the winter break with a two-point lead.

Gaz Metan Mediaş were challenging hard at that point thanks to their free-scoring Albanian striker Azdren Llullaku, but he left in mid-term for Kazakh champions FC Astana, and although he would remain top of the golden boot listings at season's end with his 16 goals, Gaz Metan's challenge without him faded to such an extent that they failed even to reach the championship play-offs. As the first phase concluded Viitorul were still in front, but after the points had been halved, their lead was down to just two.

A 3-1 win over Steaua in what would be the club's last fixture under that name – following a successful legal challenge from Romania's Ministry of Defence – increased Viitorul's advantage, but a four-game dry spell enabled FCSB to retake control, only to cede their advantage in a 2-1 defeat at arch-rivals Dinamo. The top two clubs were now level on points, and because Viitorul had won and drawn the teams' two play-off encounters, they were in the driving seat. Hagi's 'kids' (average age just over 22) needed six points from their final two fixtures to guarantee the title, and a couple of nail-biting 1-0 wins – the first at U Craiova, the second in Ovidiu at home to CFR Cluj – did the trick.

FCSB matched the champions' points haul and had a superior head-to-head record over the entire season, having defeated Viitorul twice in the first phase, but in the final reckoning it was only the two games in the play-offs that mattered. Dinamo, impressive in the play-offs, moved up from sixth to third to end a five-year absence from Europe, while ineligibility elsewhere enabled U Craiova and Astra to take the other two UEFA Europa League spots.

Domestic cup

FC Voluntari were, like CFR Cluj, unable to obtain a European licence, but the club formed only in 2010 did have a first major trophy to treasure as they overcame Astra 5-3 on penalties to win the Romanian Cup final after the match in Ploiesti had finished 1-1. It was a first success also for Voluntari's recently-installed coach, ex-Romania striker Claudiu Niculescu.

Europe

Astra were Romania's star turn in Europe – not in the UEFA Champions League but the UEFA Europa League, from which they eliminated West Ham United in the qualifying phase for the second year running, after a 1-0 victory in London, before progressing to the round of 32 thanks to further wins on the road against Viktoria Plzeň and Austria Wien. They won none of their six home fixtures, although there were no heavy defeats like Steaua's in the UEFA Champions League play-offs, when Manchester City thumped them 5-0 in the Arena Naţională.

National team

Romania went into the 2018 FIFA World Cup qualifiers with a new coach, but it was an unsatisfactory debut season for Christoph Daum, the esteemed 63-year-old German who had been out of the game for over two years. A 5-0 win in Armenia suggested better times ahead after a stoppage-time penalty miss had denied Romania an opening win against Montenegro, but three games without a goal followed, and when the team's drought ended, away to Poland, they were already en route to a second comprehensive defeat by the group leaders.

DOMESTIC SEASON AT A GLANCE

Liga I 2016/17 final tables

Championship play-offs

		Pld	Home W	D	L	F	A	Away W	D	L	F	A	Total W	D	L	F	A	Pts
1	**FC Viitorul**	**10**	**3**	**1**	**1**	**7**	**4**	**2**	**2**	**1**	**5**	**4**	**5**	**3**	**2**	**12**	**8**	**44**
2	FCSB	10	4	1	0	11	2	2	1	2	4	5	6	2	2	15	7	44
3	FC Dinamo Bucureşti	10	3	2	0	7	3	2	2	1	8	5	5	4	1	15	8	40
4	CFR 1907 Cluj	10	1	2	2	3	8	2	0	3	5	6	3	2	5	8	14	33
5	CS U Craiova	10	0	1	4	4	11	2	2	1	4	3	2	3	5	8	14	31
6	FC Astra Giurgiu	10	0	1	4	2	6	1	1	3	8	11	1	2	7	10	17	27

First phase

		Pld	Home W	D	L	F	A	Away W	D	L	F	A	Total W	D	L	F	A	Pts
1	FC Viitorul	26	10	2	1	27	10	6	1	6	12	12	16	3	7	39	22	51
2	FC Steaua Bucureşti	26	6	5	2	16	10	7	3	3	18	12	13	8	5	34	22	47
3	FC Astra Giurgiu	26	7	2	4	17	13	6	3	4	15	15	13	5	8	32	28	44
4	CFR 1907 Cluj	26	7	5	1	21	6	7	2	4	21	17	14	7	5	42	23	43
5	CS U Craiova	26	10	1	2	23	9	3	3	7	13	17	13	4	9	36	26	43
6	FC Dinamo Bucureşti	26	8	2	3	23	13	4	3	6	17	20	12	5	9	40	33	41
7	CS Gaz Metan Mediaş	26	6	4	3	20	14	4	5	4	16	13	10	9	7	36	27	39
8	FC Botoşani	26	6	3	4	18	14	3	2	8	12	17	9	5	12	30	31	32
9	FC Voluntari	26	5	2	6	17	15	3	4	6	13	22	8	6	12	30	37	30
10	CSM Politehnica Iaşi	26	5	2	6	16	16	3	3	7	12	15	8	5	13	28	31	29
11	CS Concordia Chiajna	26	3	3	7	8	18	3	4	6	9	14	6	7	13	17	32	25
12	CS Pandurii Târgu Jiu	26	3	5	5	12	17	3	2	8	12	25	6	7	13	24	42	19
13	ACS Poli Timişoara	26	5	3	5	14	18	2	4	7	11	24	7	7	12	25	42	14
14	ASA Tîrgu Mureş	26	3	3	7	10	18	2	3	8	10	19	5	6	15	20	37	12

NB League splits into top six and bottom eight after 26 games, after which the clubs play exclusively against teams in their group.
Points obtained during the regular season are halved (and rounded upwards); ACS Poli Timişoara – 14 pts deducted; ASA Tîrgu Mureş – 9 pts deducted; CFR 1907 Cluj & CS Pandurii Tîrgu Jiu – 6 pts deducted; FC Steaua Bucureşti were renamed as FCSB on 30/03/17.

European qualification 2017/18

Champion: FC Viitorul (third qualifying round)

FCSB (third qualifying round)

FC Dinamo Bucureşti (third qualifying round)
CS U Craiova (third qualifying round)
FC Astra Giurgiu (second qualifying round)

NB Cup winner FC Voluntari did not receive a licence.

Top scorer Azdren Llullaku (Gaz Metan), 16 goals
Relegated clubs ASA Tîrgu Mureş, CS Pandurii Târgu Jiu
Promoted clubs CS Juventus Bucureşti, Sepsi OSK Sfântu Gheorghe
Cup final FC Voluntari 1-1 FC Astra Giurgiu *(aet; 5-3 on pens)*

Player of the season

Denis Alibec
(FC Astra Giurgiu/FCSB)

A Romanian champion with Astra in 2015/16, Alibec came within a whisker of emulating the feat with FCSB 12 months later. The powerful left-footed striker was not his usual self with Astra in the first half of the season – although he did score some notable goals during the club's UEFA Europa League run – but after transferring to the club where he once played as a junior, he was back to his formidable best, his eight goals in 14 starts reigniting an attack that had struggled to fire during the autumn.

Newcomer of the season

Florinel Coman
(FC Viitorul)

A prominent graduate of Gheorghe Hagi's academy, Coman became a first-team regular for Viitorul in 2016/17, the Romanian youth international helping the Black Sea club to an unexpected title triumph with half a dozen goals, the last of them in an all-important 1-0 win at Universitatea Craiova. The 19-year-old was also responsible for winning the penalty, converted by team-mate Gabriel Iancu, that decided the outcome of Viitorul's title-clinching last-day win against CFR Cluj. The future looks full of promise for the sprightly, skilful left-winger.

Team of the season
(4-4-2)

Coach: Hagi *(Viitorul)*

NATIONAL TEAM

International tournament appearances

FIFA World Cup (7) 1930, 1934, 1938, 1970, 1990 (2nd round), 1994 (qtr-finals), 1998 (2nd round)
UEFA European Championship (5) 1984, 1996, 2000 (qtr-finals), 2008, 2016

Top five all-time caps

Dorinel Munteanu (134); Gheorghe Hagi (124); Gheorghe Popescu (115); Răzvan Raţ (113); László Bölöni (102)

Top five all-time goals

Gheorghe Hagi & Adrian Mutu (35); Iuliu Bodola (30); Ciprian Marica & Viorel Moldovan (25)

Results 2016/17

04/09/16	Montenegro (WCQ)	H	Cluj-Napoca	D	1-1	*Popa (85)*
08/10/16	Armenia (WCQ)	A	Yerevan	W	5-0	*Stancu (4p), Popa (10), Marin (12), Stanciu (29), Chipciu (60)*
11/10/16	Kazakhstan (WCQ)	A	Astana	D	0-0	
11/11/16	Poland (WCQ)	H	Bucharest	L	0-3	
15/11/16	Russia	A	Grozny	L	0-1	
26/03/17	Denmark (WCQ)	H	Cluj-Napoca	D	0-0	
10/06/17	Poland (WCQ)	A	Warsaw	L	1-3	*Stancu (77)*
13/06/17	Chile	H	Cluj-Napoca	W	3-2	*Stancu (31), Stanciu (60), Băluţă (83)*

Appearances 2016/17

Coach: Christoph Daum (GER)	24/10/53		MNE	ARM	KAZ	POL	Rus	DEN	POL	Chi	Caps	Goals
Costel Pantilimon	01/02/87	Watford (ENG)	G				G			G	25	-
Romario Benzar	26/03/92	Viitorul	D	D	D	D		M	D	D46	7	-
Cosmin Moţi	03/12/84	Ludogorets (BUL)	D		s26						10	-
Dragoş Grigore	07/09/86	Al-Sailiya (QAT)	D	D	D26	D	D91				28	-
Steliano Filip	15/05/94	Dinamo Bucureşti	D				s66				7	-
Ovidiu Hoban	27/12/82	H. Beer Sheva (ISR)	M	M	M	M46					27	1
Cristian Săpunaru	05/04/84	Astra	M	D	D		D	D	D		22	-
Eric Bicfalvi	05/02/88	Tom (RUS) /Ural (RUS)	M76	s82						s86	4	-
Bogdan Stancu	28/06/87	Gençlerbirliği (TUR) /Bursaspor (TUR)	M90	A57	A	A	M92		M	M66	51	14
Nicolae Stanciu	07/05/93	Anderlecht (BEL)	M	M82	M	M82		M	s60	M86	14	6
Florin Andone	11/04/93	Deportivo (ESP)	A70		s84	s46	A		A	A46	15	1
Gabriel Torje	22/11/89	Terek (RUS)	s70								55	12
Adrian Popa	24/07/88	FCSB	s76	M	M84	M46	s83				21	3
Claudiu Keşerü	02/12/86	Ludogorets (BUL)	s90	s57		s82		A63			18	5
Ciprian Tătăruşanu	09/02/86	Fiorentina (ITA)		G	G	G		G	G		45	-
Iasmin Latovlevici	11/05/86	Karabükspor (TUR)		D			D66	M76	D60		13	-
Răzvan Marin	23/05/96	Viitorul /Standard Liège (BEL)		M	M	M	M	M	M79	M46	7	1
Alexandru Chipciu	18/05/89	Anderlecht (BEL)		M67	M46	M		A85	M60		29	4
Dorin Rotariu	29/07/95	Dinamo Bucureşti /Club Brugge (BEL)		s67			M	s76		s46	4	-
Alin Toşca	14/03/92	FCSB /Betis (ESP)			D	D		D	D	D	7	-
Gabriel Enache	18/08/90	FCSB			s46		D				5	-
Vlad Chiricheş	14/11/89	Napoli (ITA)				D		D	D	D	48	-
Andrei Prepeliţă	08/12/85	Rostov (RUS)				s46	M				14	-
Gheorghe Grozav	29/09/90	Terek (RUS)					M83		s60	s46	21	3
Bogdan Ţîru	15/03/94	Viitorul					s91			s70	2	-
Dragoş Nedelcu	16/02/97	Viitorul					s92				1	-
Mihai Pintilii	09/11/84	FCSB						M	M	M	37	1
Denis Alibec	05/01/91	FCSB						s63			7	1
Andrei Ivan	04/01/97	U Craiova						s85		s46	5	-
Sergiu Hanca	04/04/92	Dinamo Bucureşti							s79	M	2	-
Cristian Ganea	24/05/92	Viitorul								D70	1	-
Alexandru Băluţă	13/09/93	U Craiova								s66	1	1

EUROPE

FC Astra Giurgiu

Third qualifying round - FC København (DEN)
H 1-1 *Filipe Teixeira (7)*
Lung, Geraldo Alves, Fabrício, Seto (William 72), Júnior Morais, Lovin, Niculae (Florea 90+2), Fernando Boldrin, Boudjemaa (Săpunaru 60), Vangjeli, Filipe Teixeira. Coach: Cristian Petre (ROU)
A 0-3
Lung, Geraldo Alves, Fabrício, Júnior Morais, Lovin, Niculae (Florea 76), Săpunaru (Seto 76), Fernando Boldrin, Boudjemaa (William 57), Stan, Filipe Teixeira. Coach: Cristian Petre (ROU)

Play-offs - West Ham United FC (ENG)
H 1-1 *Alibec (83)*
Lung, Geraldo Alves, Fabrício, Seto, Júnior Morais, Lovin, Niculae, Săpunaru, Ioniță (Florea 85), Vangjeli (Alibec 58), Filipe Teixeira (Balaure 90+4). Coach: Marius Șumudică (ROU)
A 1-0 *Filipe Teixeira (45)*
Lung, Geraldo Alves, Fabrício, Seto, Alibec, Júnior Morais, Lovin (Florea 88), Niculae (Oroș 57), Săpunaru, Ioniță (Stan 75), Filipe Teixeira. Coach: Marius Șumudică (ROU)

Group E
Match 1 - FK Austria Wien (AUT)
H 2-3 *Alibec (18), Săpunaru (74)*
Lung, Geraldo Alves, Fabrício, Alibec, Budescu, Júnior Morais, Lovin (Nicoară 46), Niculae (Seto 46), Săpunaru, Boudjemaa (Florea 76), Filipe Teixeira. Coach: Marius Șumudică (ROU)
Match 2 - AS Roma (ITA)
A 0-4
Lung, Geraldo Alves, Fabrício, Lazic (Niculae 61), Alibec, Seto, Júnior Morais, Nicoară (Budescu 61), Mansaly (Lovin 46), Săpunaru, Filipe Teixeira. Coach: Marius Șumudică (ROU)
Match 3 - FC Viktoria Plzeň (CZE)
A 2-1 *Alibec (41), Hořava (64og)*
Lung, Geraldo Alves, Fabrício, Lazic, Alibec (Florea 90+1), Seto, Budescu (Ioniță 84), Júnior Morais, Mansaly, Lovin (Oroș 90+3), Săpunaru. Coach: Marius Șumudică (ROU)
Match 4 - FC Viktoria Plzeň (CZE)
H 1-1 *Stan (19)*
Lung, Geraldo Alves, Seto, Budescu (Niculae 75), Júnior Morais, Oroș, Mansaly, Lovin (Nicoară 55), Săpunaru, Stan, Filipe Teixeira (Ioniță 88). Coach: Marius Șumudică (ROU)
Match 5 - FK Austria Wien (AUT)
A 2-1 *Florea (79), Budescu (88p)*
Lung, Geraldo Alves, Alibec, Seto, Budescu (Nicoară 90+3), Júnior Morais, Oroș (Florea 61), Mansaly (Lovin 71), Săpunaru, Stan, Filipe Teixeira. Coach: Marius Șumudică (ROU)
Match 6 - AS Roma (ITA)
H 0-0
Lung, Fabrício (Florea 72), Alibec (Niculae 90), Seto, Budescu (Mansaly 88), Oroș, Nicoară, Lovin, Săpunaru, Stan, Filipe Teixeira. Coach: Marius Șumudică (ROU)

Round of 32 - KRC Genk (BEL)
H 2-2 *Budescu (43), Seto (90)*
Lung, Geraldo Alves, Fabrício, Seto, Budescu, Júnior Morais, Niculae (Buș 63; Nicoară 80), Săpunaru, Ioniță (Florea 64), Stan, Filipe Teixeira. Coach: Marius Șumudică (ROU)
A 0-1
Lung, Geraldo Alves, Seto (Ioniță 82), Budescu, Júnior Morais, Mansaly, Lovin (Florea 67), Niculae (Buș 70), Săpunaru, Stan, Filipe Teixeira. Coach: Marius Șumudică (ROU)

FC Steaua București

Third qualifying round - AC Sparta Praha (CZE)
A 1-1 *Stanciu (75)*
Niță, Tamaș, Pintilii, Tudorie (Popa 55), Stanciu, Toșca, Golubović, Momčilović, Aganović (Muniru 62), Achim (D Popescu 89), Enache. Coach: Laurențiu Reghecampf (ROU)
H 2-0 *Stanciu (31, 63)*
Niță, Tamaș, Hamroun, Pintilii, Stanciu (Aganović 81), Toșca, Golubović (Tudorie 88), Momčilović, Achim (Muniru 64), Enache, Popa. Coach: Laurențiu Reghecampf (ROU)

Play-offs - Manchester City FC (ENG)
H 0-5
Niță, Tamaș, Hamroun, Stanciu, Muniru (O Popescu 67), Toșca, Golubović (Tudorie 46), Momčilović, Achim (Bourceanu 46), Enache, Popa. Coach: Laurențiu Reghecampf (ROU)
A 0-1
Cojocaru, Mitrea, Tamaș, Hamroun, Tudorie, Muniru (Achim 62), Momčilović, Aganović (Stanciu 53), O Popescu (Popa 53), Enache, Bourceanu. Coach: Laurențiu Reghecampf (ROU)

Group L
Match 1 - Osmanlıspor (TUR)
A 0-2
Niță, Tamaș, Toșca, Golubović (Mitrea 46), Aganović, Moke, Fernando Boldrin (Tănase 61), William (Jakoliš 67), Enache, Bourceanu, Popa. Coach: Laurențiu Reghecampf (ROU)
Red card: Enache 45+2
Match 2 - Villarreal CF (ESP)
H 1-1 *Muniru (19)*
Niță, Tamaș, Muniru, Toșca, Golubović (Tănase 77), Momčilović, Moke, Fernando Boldrin, William (O Popescu 89), Bourceanu, Popa (Jakoliš 77). Coach: Laurențiu Reghecampf (ROU)
Match 3 - FC Zürich (SUI)
H 1-1 *Golubović (63)*
Niță, Tamaș, Muniru (Jakoliš 83), Toșca, Golubović (Tudorie 79), Momčilović, O Popescu, Fernando Boldrin, William, Bourceanu, Popa. Coach: Laurențiu Reghecampf (ROU)
Match 4 - FC Zürich (SUI)
A 0-0
Niță, Tamaș, Muniru (Tudorie 84), Toșca, Golubović (Achim 72), Momčilović, Moke, Fernando Boldrin, William, Bourceanu (Aganović 63), Popa. Coach: Laurențiu Reghecampf (ROU)
Match 5 - Osmanlıspor (TUR)
H 2-1 *Momčilović (68), Tamaș (86)*
Niță, Tamaș, Pintilii (Bourceanu 46), Muniru (Achim 63), Toșca, Momčilović, Moke, Fernando Boldrin, William, Enache (Golubović 46), Popa. Coach: Laurențiu Reghecampf (ROU)
Match 6 - Villarreal CF (ESP)
A 1-2 *Achim (55)*
Niță, Tamaș, Pintilii (Achim 54), Toșca, Momčilović, Moke, Fernando Boldrin (O Popescu 76), William, Enache (Golubović 46), Bourceanu, Popa. Coach: Laurențiu Reghecampf (ROU)
Red card: Tamaș 79

CS Pandurii Târgu Jiu

Third qualifying round - Maccabi Tel-Aviv FC (ISR)
H 1-3 *Herea (30)*
Stanca, Bunoza, Vasiljević, Voiculeț, Hora, Herea (Munteanu 62), Ungurușan, Grecu, Mrzljak (Obodo 62), Pleașcă (Trifu 80), Răuță. Coach: Petre Grigoraș (ROU)
A 1-2 *Pleașcă (57)*
Lazar, Bunoza, Buijs (Trifu 71), Munteanu (Voiculeț 46), Vasiljević, Herea, Pițian, Mrzljak, Pleașcă, Pârcălabu (Grecu 79), Răuță. Coach: Petre Grigoraș (ROU)

FC Viitorul

Third qualifying round - KAA Gent (BEL)
A 0-5
Rîmniceanu, Filip (Hodorogea 46), Benzar, Tănase, Iancu (Nedelcu 46), Țîru, Marin, Ganea, Chițu, Purece, Carp (Casap 70). Coach: Gheorghe Hagi (ROU)
H 0-0
Buzbuchi, Rădoi, Casap (Marin 65), Rusu (Tănase 46), Iancu (Dumitrescu 77), Dani López, Nedelcu, Brandán, Hodorogea, Carp, Nimely. Coach: Gheorghe Hagi (ROU)

DOMESTIC LEAGUE CLUB-BY-CLUB

CSM Politehnica Iaşi

Second qualifying round - HNK Hajduk Split (CRO)

H 2-2 *Cristea (19), Piccioni (23)*

Grahovac, Mihalache, Gheorghe, Cristea, Piccioni (Roman 83), Voicu, Bőle, Mitić, Frăsinescu, Ţigănaşu (Martin 78), Ciucur (Ciucă 64). Coach: Nicolò Napoli (ITA)

A 1-2 *Ciucur (26)*

Grahovac, Mihalache, Gheorghe (Creţu 76), Cristea (Roman 81), Piccioni, Voicu, Bőle, Mitić, Frăsinescu, Ţigănaşu, Ciucur (Martin 62). Coach: Nicolò Napoli (ITA)

FC Astra Giurgiu

1921 • Marin Anastasovici (8,057) • afcastragiurgiu.ro

Major honours
Romanian League (1) 2016; Romanian Cup (1) 2014

Coach: Marius Şumudică

2016

Date		Opponent		Score	Scorers
23/07	h	Dinamo	L	1-4	*Fernando Boldrin (p)*
31/07	a	Pandurii	D	0-0	
06/08	h	U Craiova	L	1-2	*Niculae*
13/08	h	Poli Timişoara	W	3-1	*Săpunaru 2 (2p), Niculae*
21/08	a	CFR Cluj	L	1-5	*Niculae*
28/08	h	Voluntari	D	1-1	*Budescu*
11/09	a	Steaua	L	0-1	
19/09	h	Gaz Metan	L	0-2	
22/09	a	Tîrgu Mureş	W	2-0	*Alibec, Florea*
26/09	h	Politehnica Iaşi	W	1-0	*Budescu (p)*
02/10	a	Viitorul	L	0-1	
15/10	h	Concordia	D	1-1	*Niculae*
24/10	a	Botoşani	D	0-0	
29/10	a	Dinamo	D	2-2	*Săpunaru, Nicoară (p)*
06/11	h	Pandurii	W	2-0	*Filipe Teixeira, Ioniţă*
20/11	a	U Craiova	W	1-0	*Săpunaru (p)*
27/11	a	Poli Timişoara	L	0-2	
01/12	h	CFR Cluj	L	1-2	*Alibec*
04/12	a	Voluntari	W	2-1	*Budescu, Filipe Teixeira*
11/12	h	Steaua	W	1-0	*Budescu*
19/12	a	Gaz Metan	W	1-0	*Alibec*

2017

Date		Opponent		Score	Scorers
03/02	h	Tîrgu Mureş	W	1-0	*Seto*
19/02	h	Viitorul	W	1-0	*Filipe Teixeira*
27/02	a	Concordia	W	3-1	*Fabrício, Florea, Budescu*
02/03	a	Politehnica Iaşi	W	3-2	*Niculae, Săpunaru (p), Filipe Teixeira*
06/03	h	Botoşani	W	3-0	*Budescu, Belu-Iordache, Buş*
11/03	h	U Craiova	D	0-0	
17/03	a	CFR Cluj	L	2-3	*Ioniţă, Săpunaru*
03/04	h	Viitorul	L	1-2	*Florea*
06/04	a	FCSB	L	0-3	
10/04	h	Dinamo	L	1-2	*Săpunaru*
15/04	a	U Craiova	W	3-1	*Ioniţă, Buş, Săpunaru*
22/04	h	CFR Cluj	L	0-1	
29/04	a	Viitorul	L	2-3	*Niculae, Geraldo Alves*
08/05	h	FCSB	L	0-1	
13/05	a	Dinamo	D	1-1	*Ioniţă*

No	Name	Nat	DoB	Pos	Aps	(s)	Gls
7	Denis Alibec		05/01/91	A	12	(1)	3
96	Silviu Balaure		06/02/96	M	2	(12)	
7	Claudiu Belu-Iordache		07/11/93	D	2	(3)	1
24	Damien Boudjemaa	FRA	07/06/85	M		(3)	
10	Constantin Budescu		19/02/89	M	24	(3)	6
9	Sergiu Buş		02/11/92	A	5	(4)	2
4	Fabrício	BRA	20/02/90	D	23		1
23	Fernando Boldrin	BRA	23/02/89	M	3		1
80	Filipe Teixeira	POR	02/10/80	M	25	(3)	4
11	Daniel Florea		17/04/88	A	6	(21)	3
12	George Gavrilaş		15/12/90	G	3		
2	Geraldo Alves	POR	08/11/80	D	14	(5)	1
98	Valentin Gheorghe		14/02/97	D		(2)	
23	Plamen Iliev	BUL	30/11/91	G	6	(2)	
31	Alexandru Ioniţă		14/12/94	M	29	(2)	4
13	Júnior Morais	BRA	22/07/86	D	28	(1)	
25	Romario Kortzorg	NED	25/08/89	A	6	(3)	
5	Vlatko Lazic	NED	01/05/89	D	1		
20	Florin Lovin		11/02/82	M	22	(4)	
1	Silviu Lung		04/06/89	G	27		
19	Boubacar Mansaly	SEN	04/02/88	M	12	(7)	
14	Romario Moise		21/09/95	M	4	(5)	
19	Viorel Nicoară		27/09/87	M	8	(7)	1
21	Daniel Niculae		06/10/82	A	16	(6)	6
15	Cristian Oroş		15/10/84	D	18	(1)	
71	Andrei Piţian		16/11/95	M	4	(2)	
44	Ricardo Alves	POR	09/05/91	D	2	(2)	
22	Cristian Săpunaru		05/04/84	D	30	(2)	8
8	Takayuki Seto	JPN	05/02/86	M	31	(2)	1
77	Alexandru Stan		07/02/89	D	26	(2)	
32	Kristi Vangjeli	ALB	05/09/85	D	4	(1)	
91	William	BRA	15/12/91	M	3		

FC Botoşani

2001 • Municipal (7,782) • fcbotosani.ro

Coach: Leontin Grozavu

2016

Date		Opponent		Score	Scorers
30/07	h	CFR Cluj	W	3-1	*Matulevičius, I Fülöp, Muşat*
05/08	a	Voluntari	L	2-4	*I Fülöp 2*
12/08	h	Steaua	L	0-2	
18/08	a	Poli Timişoara	W	5-0	*I Fülöp 2, Golofca, Astafei, L Fülöp (p)*
22/08	a	Gaz Metan	D	0-0	
29/08	h	Tîrgu Mureş	W	4-2	*Bordeianu, Golofca, Matulevičius 2*
11/09	a	Politehnica Iaşi	W	1-0	*I Fülöp*
16/09	h	Viitorul	L	1-2	*I Fülöp*
21/09	a	Concordia	W	2-0	*Golofca, Vaşvari*
24/09	a	U Craiova	L	0-1	
01/10	h	Dinamo	W	2-1	*Elek, Vaşvari (p)*
15/10	a	Pandurii	L	1-2	*Târnovan*
24/10	h	Astra	D	0-0	
31/10	h	Poli Timişoara	W	2-0	*Willie 2*
07/11	a	CFR Cluj	L	0-1	
18/11	h	Voluntari	L	0-1	
27/11	a	Steaua	D	0-0	
30/11	h	Gaz Metan	D	0-0	
04/12	a	Tîrgu Mureş	L	0-2	
10/12	h	Politehnica Iaşi	L	1-3	*Burcă*
19/12	a	Viitorul	L	1-3	*Roman*

2017

Date		Opponent		Score	Scorers
05/02	h	Concordia	D	1-1	*Buş*
11/02	h	U Craiova	W	1-0	*Kuku*
20/02	a	Dinamo	L	0-1	
26/02	h	Pandurii	W	3-1	*Roman, Kuku, Golofca*
06/03	a	Astra	L	0-3	
10/03	h	Poli Timişoara	L	1-2	*Miron*
19/03	a	Gaz Metan	D	0-0	
31/03	h	Tîrgu Mureş	W	2-0	*Golofca, Vaşvari (p)*
05/04	h	Voluntari	W	3-0	*Golofca, Vaşvari (p), L Fülöp*
08/04	a	Politehnica Iaşi	L	1-2	*Golofca*
14/04	h	Concordia	D	1-1	*Târnovan*
21/04	a	Pandurii	D	1-1	*Vaşvari (p)*
01/05	a	Poli Timişoara	D	1-1	*Golofca*
07/05	h	Gaz Metan	D	0-0	
15/05	a	Tîrgu Mureş	W	2-0	*Roman 2*
21/05	a	Voluntari	L	0-1	
25/05	h	Politehnica Iaşi	L	0-1	
29/05	a	Concordia	L	1-2	*Herghelegiu (p)*
04/06	h	Pandurii	W	2-1	*Golofca, L Fülöp*

No	Name	Nat	DoB	Pos	Aps	(s)	Gls
12	Cătălin Albuţ		23/05/81	G	5		
7	Victoraş Astafei		06/07/87	M	17	(2)	1
37	Cătălin Bordeianu		18/11/91	M	24	(4)	1
3	Andrei Burcă		15/04/93	D	26	(1)	1
7	Laurenţiu Buş		27/08/87	M	9	(6)	1
6	Alin Cârstocea		16/01/92	M	6	(1)	
1	Alberto Cobrea		01/11/90	G	15		
17	Stelian Cucu		15/09/89	M	20	(3)	
88	Radoslav Dimitrov	BUL	12/08/88	D	15		
29	Robert Elek		13/06/88	A	8	(8)	1
95	Endrick	BRA	07/03/95	M	3	(3)	
24	Istvan Fülöp		18/05/90	A	12		7
80	Lorand Fülöp		24/07/97	M	6	(10)	3
9	Cătălin Golofca		21/04/90	M	24	(10)	9
20	Răzvan Greu		16/03/95	M	3	(4)	
21	Andrei Herghelegiu		21/03/92	A	12	(16)	1
16	Alexandru Ichim		16/01/89	D	3	(2)	
1	Plamen Iliev	BUL	30/11/91	G	20		
8	Claudiu Juncănaru		18/02/96	M	1	(2)	
14	Benjamin Kuku	NGA	08/03/95	A	10	(5)	2
77	Deivydas Matulevičius	LTU	08/04/89	A	8	(5)	3
4	Andrei Miron		28/05/94	D	28	(3)	1
11	Olimpiu Moruţan		25/04/99	M	8	(11)	
30	Nicolae Muşat		04/12/86	D	30		1
19	Andrei Patache		29/10/87	D	11	(1)	
5	Florin Plămadă		30/04/92	D	10	(4)	
93	Sergiu Popovici		23/03/93	M	11	(3)	
28	Mihai Roman		16/10/84	M	25	(5)	4
15	Alexandru Târnovan		27/07/95	M	2	(4)	2
16	Răzvan Tincu		15/07/87	D	13		
18	Bogdan Unguruşan		20/02/83	D	13		
10	Gabriel Vaşvari		13/11/86	M	32	(4)	5
23	Willie	BRA	15/05/93	M	10	(2)	2

ROMANIA

CFR 1907 Cluj

1907 • Dr Constantin Rădulescu (23,500) • cfr1907.ro

Major honours
Romanian League (3) 2008, 2010, 2012; Romanian Cup (4) 2008, 2009, 2010, 2016

Coach: Vasile Miriuță (HUN)

2016

24/07 h Concordia W 2-0 *Cristian López, Guima*
30/07 a Botoșani L 1-3 *Jakoliš*
08/08 h Dinamo D 0-0
14/08 a Pandurii D 1-1 *Cristian López*
21/08 h Astra W 5-1 *Cristian López 2 (2p), Tiago Lopes, Petrucci 2 (1p)*
27/08 a Poli Timișoara D 1-1 *Bud*
10/09 h U Craiova D 0-0
17/09 h Voluntari W 5-0 *Bud 3, Omrani, Gomelt*
22/09 a Steaua W 2-1 *Bud 2*
26/09 h Gaz Metan D 1-1 *Filipe Nascimento (p)*
30/09 a Tîrgu Mureș W 3-1 *Filipe Nascimento, Mureșan, Omrani*
14/10 h Politehnica Iași W 1-0 *Filipe Nascimento*
21/10 a Viitorul L 1-2 *Bud*
28/10 a Concordia W 2-1 *Bud, Omrani*
07/11 h Botoșani W 1-0 *Larie*
21/11 a Dinamo W 2-0 *Juan Carlos, Šorša*
28/11 h Pandurii L 0-1
01/12 a Astra W 2-1 *Bud, Filipe Nascimento (p)*
05/12 h Poli Timișoara D 2-2 *Filipe Nascimento 2 (2p)*
09/12 a U Craiova L 1-2 *Bud*
17/12 a Voluntari L 1-2 *Bud*

2017

05/02 h Steaua D 1-1 *Deac*
11/02 a Gaz Metan W 2-1 *Omrani, Păun-Alexandru*
17/02 h Tîrgu Mureș W 2-0 *Šorša, Păun-Alexandru*
27/02 a Politehnica Iași W 2-1 *Larie, Peteleu*
05/03 h Viitorul W 1-0 *Deac*
12/03 a Steaua L 0-2
17/03 h Astra W 3-2 *Păun-Alexandru, Deac, Omrani*
01/04 a U Craiova W 4-1 *Deac 2, Păun-Alexandru, Gomelt*
05/04 a Dinamo L 0-2
09/04 h Viitorul D 0-0
17/04 h FCSB D 0-0
22/04 a Astra W 1-0 *Deac*
30/04 h U Craiova L 0-3
06/05 h Dinamo L 0-3
13/05 a Viitorul L 0-1

No	Name	Nat	DoB	Pos	Aps	(s)	Gls
18	Liviu Antal		02/06/89	M		(7)	
26	Cristian Bud		26/06/85	A	22	(6)	11
45	Camora	POR	21/09/86	D	23	(1)	
20	Alexandru Chiriță		24/06/96	M	4	(3)	
11	Cristian López	ESP	24/07/89	A	6		4
99	Ciprian Deac		16/02/86	M	14		6
2	Cornel Ene		21/07/93	D		(4)	
8	Filipe Nascimento	POR	07/01/95	M	21	(4)	6
10	Tomislav Gomelt	CRO	07/01/95	M	14	(5)	2
9	Guima	POR	11/03/86	A		(2)	1
57	Laszlo Hodgyai		18/01/92	A		(2)	
4	Răzvan Horj		17/12/95	D	20	(6)	
17	Antonio Jakoliš	CRO	28/02/92	M	5		1
25	Juan Carlos	ESP	15/03/91	M	20	(4)	1
6	Ionuț Larie		16/01/87	D	36		2
28	Traian Marc		16/01/83	G	12		
1	Mihai Mincă		08/10/84	G	20		
30	Andrei Mureșan		01/08/85	D	18	(5)	1
93	Alexandru Neagu		26/01/93	M		(3)	
21	Sergiu Negruț		01/04/93	A		(5)	
19	Bryan Nouvier	FRA	21/06/95	M	26	(6)	
9	Billel Omrani	FRA	02/06/93	A	18	(10)	5
7	Adrian Păun-Alexandru		01/04/95	M	22	(7)	4
77	Andrei Peteleu		20/08/92	D	17	(5)	1
10	Davide Petrucci	ITA	05/10/91	M	6		2
11	Dan Roman		22/12/85	A	1	(7)	
31	Laurențiu Rus		07/05/85	M	22	(3)	
29	Cosmin Sîrbu		29/03/96	A	1	(2)	
17	Tomislav Šorša	CRO	11/05/89	M	12	(8)	2
14	Andrei Tânc		03/07/85	D	1	(2)	
22	Tiago Lopes	POR	04/01/89	D	31	(1)	1
12	Cosmin Vâtcă		12/05/82	G	4		

CS Concordia Chiajna

1957 • Concordia (4,600) • csconcordia.ro

Coach: Emil Săndoi; (06/11/16) (Emil Ursu); (23/12/16) Dan Alexa

2016

24/07 a CFR Cluj L 0-2
01/08 h Voluntari L 0-4
06/08 a Steaua L 0-1
13/08 h Gaz Metan W 1-0 *Grădinaru*
20/08 a Tîrgu Mureș W 1-0 *Koenders*
26/08 h Politehnica Iași D 0-0
12/09 a Viitorul L 1-2 *Pena*
18/09 a U Craiova D 1-1 *Constantinescu*
21/09 h Botoșani L 0-2
24/09 a Dinamo W 1-0 *Cristescu*
03/10 h Pandurii D 0-0
15/10 a Astra D 1-1 *Cristescu (p)*
21/10 h Poli Timișoara L 0-2
28/10 h CFR Cluj L 1-2 *Roșu (p)*
05/11 a Voluntari L 0-1
19/11 h Steaua W 1-0 *Roșu*
26/11 a Gaz Metan L 1-3 *Ciobanu*
29/11 h Tîrgu Mureș L 1-2 *Ciobanu*
02/12 a Politehnica Iași L 0-1
12/12 h Viitorul L 1-2 *Cristescu*
16/12 h U Craiova D 0-0

2017

05/02 a Botoșani D 1-1 *Herea*
13/02 h Dinamo W 2-1 *Costin, Cristescu*
19/02 a Pandurii W 1-0 *Costin*
27/02 h Astra L 1-3 *Serediuc*
04/03 a Poli Timișoara D 1-1 *Albu*
11/03 a Politehnica Iași L 1-3 *Alexandru*
18/03 a Tîrgu Mureș L 1-2 *Alexandru*
31/03 h Pandurii L 0-1
04/04 a Poli Timișoara D 0-0
10/04 h Gaz Metan D 1-1 *Dobrosavlevici*
14/04 a Botoșani D 1-1 *Munteanu*
21/04 h Voluntari L 0-2
28/04 h Politehnica Iași D 0-0
05/05 h Tîrgu Mureș W 2-0 *Grădinaru, Cristescu*
10/05 h Poli Timișoara W 3-1 *Pena, Albu, Feussi*
15/05 a Pandurii L 2-3 *Herea, Munteanu*
23/05 a Gaz Metan D 0-3
29/05 h Botoșani W 2-1 *Cristescu, Munteanu*
04/06 a Voluntari W 1-0 *Grădinaru*

No	Name	Nat	DoB	Pos	Aps	(s)	Gls
3	Cristian Albu		17/08/93	D	33	(2)	2
9	Alessandro Celin	BRA	11/09/89	A		(6)	
9	Valentin Alexandru		17/09/91	A	2	(5)	2
29	Lucian Asanache		25/09/94	D		(3)	
34	Cristian Bălgrădean		21/03/88	G	35		
2	Ștefan Bărboianu		24/01/88	D	16	(2)	
6	Florin Bejan		28/03/91	D	7	(1)	
99	Bruno Madeira	POR	17/09/84	M	3		
21	Bogdan Bucurică		11/02/86	D	20		
91	Alin Buleică		12/09/91	M	8	(4)	
11	Cristian Ciobanu		03/07/94	M	10	(5)	2
20	Marian Constantinescu		08/08/81	A	6	(5)	1
19	Raul Costin		29/01/85	M	30	(2)	2
33	Adrian Cristea		30/11/83	M	1	(4)	
18	Marian Cristescu		17/03/85	M	29	(7)	6
97	Octavian Deaconu		13/05/97	M	7		
24	Alin Dobrosavlevici		24/10/94	D	15	(2)	1
1	Virgil Drăghia		31/07/90	G	5		
26	Patrice Feussi	CMR	03/10/86	D	18	(2)	1
94	Nicușor Fota		01/12/96	D	6	(1)	
95	Răzvan Grădinaru		23/08/95	M	29	(5)	3
10	Ovidiu Herea		26/03/85	M	13	(6)	2
46	Milano Koenders	NED	31/07/86	D	15	(3)	1
15	Iulian Mamele		17/02/85	D	6		
5	Cristian Melinte		09/05/88	D	24	(2)	
77	Valentin Munteanu		24/10/89	M	3	(12)	3
16	Cristi Novacek		08/02/96	M		(1)	
30	Marius Pena		02/05/85	A	24	(9)	2
80	Dan Popescu		20/02/88	D	9		
96	Robert Răducanu		05/09/96	A	9	(5)	
17	Florin Răsdan		13/04/95	M	7	(4)	
14	Daniel Rogoveanu		30/07/95	M		(1)	
10	Neluț Roșu		05/07/93	M	15	(5)	2
7	Tiberiu Serediuc		02/07/92	M	22	(11)	1
4	Răzvan Tincu		15/07/87	D	13	(2)	

FC Dinamo București

1948 • Dinamo (15,400); Arena Națională (55,634) • fcdinamo.ro

Major honours
Romanian League (18) 1955, 1962, 1963, 1964, 1965, 1971, 1973, 1975, 1977, 1982, 1983, 1984, 1990, 1992, 2000 ,2002, 2004, 2007; Romanian Cup (13) 1959, 1964, 1968, 1982, 1984, 1986, 1990, 2000, 2001, 2003, 2004, 2005, 2012

Coach: Ioan Andone; (15/02/17) Cosmin Contra

2016

23/07 a Astra W 4-1 *Gnohéré 3 (2p), Lazăr*
30/07 h Poli Timișoara W 2-1 *Rotariu 2*
08/08 a CFR Cluj D 0-0
15/08 h Voluntari W 3-1 *Gnohéré, Filip, Lazăr*
20/08 a Steaua D 1-1 *Rotariu*
26/08 h Gaz Metan D 1-1 *Lazăr*
12/09 a Tîrgu Mureș L 1-2 *Rotariu*
17/09 h Politehnica Iași W 3-1 *Marić, Lazăr, Nemec*
20/09 a Viitorul D 1-1 *Lazăr*
24/09 h Concordia L 0-1
01/10 a Botoșani L 1-2 *Rotariu*
17/10 a U Craiova L 1-2 *Hanca*
22/10 h Pandurii W 4-0 *og (Lazăr), Lazăr 2, Palić*
29/10 h Astra D 2-2 *Nemec, Hanca*
05/11 a Poli Timișoara W 2-1 *Nedelcearu, Marić*
21/11 h CFR Cluj L 0-2
26/11 a Voluntari W 2-1 *Gnohéré (p), Rotariu*
30/11 h Steaua W 3-1 *Hanca (p), Nedelcearu, Nemec*
05/12 a Gaz Metan L 0-4
10/12 h Tîrgu Mureș W 1-0 *Nemec*
18/12 a Politehnica Iași L 1-3 *Nedelcearu*

2017

04/02 h Viitorul L 1-2 *Nistor*
13/02 a Concordia L 1-2 *Nemec*
20/02 h Botoșani W 1-0 *Hanca*
25/02 h U Craiova W 2-1 *Nemec 2*
05/03 a Pandurii W 2-0 *Nemec, Nistor*
13/03 a Viitorul D 0-0
19/03 h U Craiova D 0-0
02/04 a FCSB L 1-2 *Nemec*
05/04 h CFR Cluj W 2-0 *Nemec, Rivaldinho*
10/04 a Astra Giurgiu W 2-1 *Rivaldinho, Bumba*
16/04 h Viitorul W 2-1 *Hanca 2*
22/04 a U Craiova D 2-2 *Romera, Nistor*
01/05 h FCSB W 2-1 *Hanca 2 (2p)*
06/05 a CFR Cluj W 3-0 *Filip, Hanca, Bumba*
13/05 h Astra Giurgiu D 1-1 *Nemec*

No	Name	Nat	DoB	Pos	Aps	(s)	Gls
28	Paul Anton		10/05/91	D	1		
8	Thaer Bawab	JOR	01/03/85	A	2	(10)	
1	Laurențiu Brănescu		30/03/94	G	17		
31	Claudiu Bumba		05/01/94	M	6	(3)	2
6	Azer Bušuladžić	BIH	12/11/91	M	29	(4)	
24	Luca Ceccarelli	ITA	24/03/83	D	5	(2)	
1	Vytautas Černiauskas	LTU	12/03/89	G	5		
3	Laurențiu Corbu		10/05/94	D	1		
15	Claude Dielna	FRA	14/12/87	D	10		
4	Alin Dudea		06/06/97	D	1	(3)	
7	Steliano Filip		15/05/94	D	30	(1)	2
10	Harlem Gnohéré	FRA	21/02/88	A	10	(4)	5
44	Sergiu Hanca		04/04/92	M	29	(4)	9
8	Valentin Lazăr		21/08/89	M	19		7
18	May Mahlangu	RSA	01/05/89	M	12	(10)	
28	Luka Marić	CRO	25/04/87	D	15	(2)	2
17	Miha Mevlja	SVN	12/06/90	M	6		
5	Ionuț Nedelcearu		25/04/96	D	33		3
17	Adam Nemec	SVK	02/09/85	A	25	(3)	11
15	Dan Nistor		05/06/88	M	24	(5)	3
16	Maximiliano Oliva	ARG	04/03/90	D	6	(5)	
96	Vlad Olteanu		21/03/96	M	1	(3)	
20	Antun Palić	CRO	25/06/88	M	30	(1)	1
26	Jaime Penedo	PAN	26/09/81	G	14		
19	Patrick Petre		09/05/97	M	3	(11)	
13	Daniel Popa		14/07/95	A		(11)	
2	Mihai Popescu		07/05/93	D	8	(3)	
9	Rivaldinho	BRA	29/04/95	A	5	(6)	2
29	José Romera	ESP	08/09/87	D	31	(1)	1
9	Dorin Rotariu		29/07/95	A	16	(5)	6
21	Danu Spătaru	MDA	24/05/94	M		(2)	
23	Ionuț Șerban		07/08/95	M	2	(3)	
30	Andrei Tîrcoveanu		22/05/97	M		(1)	

FCSB

1947 • Arena Naţională (55,634) • steauafc.com

Major honours*
European Champion Clubs' Cup (1) 1986;
UEFA Super Cup (1) 1986;
Romanian League (26) 1951, 1952, 1953, 1956, 1960, 1961, 1968, 1976, 1978, 1985, 1986, 1987, 1988, 1989, 1993, 1994, 1995, 1996, 1997, 1998, 2001, 2005, 2006, 2013, 2014, 2015;
Romanian Cup (23) 1949, 1950, 1951, 1952, 1955, 1962, 1966, 1967, 1969, 1970, 1971, 1976, 1979, 1985, 1987, 1988, 1989, 1992, 1996, 1997, 1999, 2011, 2015

Coach: Laurenţiu Reghecampf

Date		Opponent		Score	Scorers
2016					
31/07	a	Viitorul	W	3-1	*Tudorie, Popa, Stanciu*
06/08	h	Concordia	W	1-0	*Achim*
12/08	a	Botoşani	W	2-0	*Hamroun, Tănase*
20/08	h	Dinamo	D	1-1	*William*
27/08	a	Pandurii	W	1-0	*Fernando Boldrin*
31/08	h	Politehnica Iaşi	D	1-1	*Vîlceanu*
11/09	h	Astra	W	1-0	*Fernando Boldrin*
18/09	a	Poli Timişoara	W	1-0	*Tănase*
22/09	h	CFR Cluj	L	1-2	*Tănase*
25/09	a	Voluntari	W	3-2	*Popa, Fernando Boldrin, Momčilović*
02/10	h	U Craiova	W	2-1	*William, Fernando Boldrin*
16/10	h	Gaz Metan	L	0-1	
23/10	a	Tîrgu Mureş	D	1-1	*Moke*
30/10	a	Politehnica Iaşi	W	2-0	*Tamaş, Man*
06/11	h	Viitorul	W	2-0	*Fernando Boldrin (p), Momčilović*
19/11	a	Concordia	L	0-1	
27/11	h	Botoşani	D	0-0	
30/11	a	Dinamo	L	1-3	*Fernando Boldrin (p)*
04/12	h	Pandurii	W	3-1	*Enache 2 (1p), Pintilii*
11/12	a	Astra	L	0-1	
17/12	h	Poli Timişoara	W	1-0	*Popa*
2017					
05/02	a	CFR Cluj	D	1-1	*Alibec*
12/02	h	Voluntari	D	2-2	*Fernando Boldrin, Gnohéré (p)*
18/02	a	U Craiova	W	2-1	*Pintilii, Enache*
26/02	a	Gaz Metan	D	1-1	*Alibec*
04/03	h	Tîrgu Mureş	D	1-1	*Gnohéré*
12/03	h	CFR Cluj	W	2-0	*Gnohéré, O Popescu*
18/03	a	Viitorul	L	1-3	*Alibec*
02/04	h	Dinamo	W	2-1	*Alibec, Fernando Boldrin*
06/04	h	Astra	W	3-0	*Alibec 2, Tănase*
09/04	a	U Craiova	W	1-0	*Gnohéré*
17/04	a	CFR Cluj	D	0-0	
24/04	h	Viitorul	D	1-1	*Pintilii*
01/05	a	Dinamo	L	1-2	*Pleaşcă*
08/05	a	Astra	W	1-0	*Gnohéré*
13/05	h	U Craiova	W	3-0	*Alibec 2, Jakoliš*

No	Name	Nat	DoB	Pos	Aps	(s)	Gls
20	Vlad Achim		07/04/89	M	10	(9)	1
19	Adnan Aganović	CRO	03/10/87	M	6	(3)	
7	Denis Alibec		05/01/91	A	14		8
14	Mihai Bălaşa		14/01/95	D	13	(1)	
31	Theodor Botă		24/05/97	A	1		
55	Alexandru Bourceanu		24/04/85	M	11	(7)	
12	Valentin Cojocaru		01/10/95	G	2		
44	Gabriel Enache		18/08/90	D	22	(7)	3
25	Rareş Enceanu		05/08/94	M		(2)	
23	Fernando Boldrin	BRA	23/02/89	M	24	(6)	8
31	Harlem Gnohéré	FRA	21/02/88	A	3	(11)	5
14	Bojan Golubović	SRB	22/08/83	A	9	(1)	
5	Jugurtha Hamroun	ALG	27/01/89	M	3	(2)	1
17	Antonio Jakoliš	CRO	28/02/92	M	12	(7)	1
7	Dennis Man		26/08/98	M	1	(5)	1
17	Mario Mihai		16/02/99	M		(1)	
18	Vlad Mihalcea		28/10/98	M		(1)	
3	Bogdan Mitrea		29/09/87	D	5		
21	Wilfred Moke	COD	12/02/88	D	24	(3)	1
15	Marko Momčilović	SRB	11/06/87	D	31	(1)	2
11	Sulley Muniru	GHA	25/10/92	M	16	(4)	
1	Florin Niţă		03/07/87	G	29		
26	Cristian Onţel		05/04/98	M		(1)	
6,5	Mihai Pintilii		09/11/84	M	18	(3)	3
13	Marian Pleaşcă		06/02/90	D	7		1
77	Adrian Popa		24/07/88	M	15	(4)	3
24	Dan Popescu		20/02/88	D	2		
23	Ovidiu Popescu		27/02/94	M	21	(6)	1
10	Nicolae Stanciu		07/05/93	M	3	(2)	1
33	Eduard Stăncioiu		03/03/81	G	5		
4	Gabriel Tamaş		09/11/83	D	25	(3)	1
7	Florin Tănase		30/12/94	M	18	(4)	4
13	Alin Toşca		14/03/92	D	15	(1)	
9	Alexandru Tudorie		19/03/96	A	3	(4)	1
16	Robert Vîlceanu		29/03/97	M	1		1
29	William	BRA	15/12/91	M	27	(5)	2

** The right to these honours are the subject of an ongoing legal dispute.*

CS Gaz Metan Mediaş

1945 • Gaz Metan (7,814) • gaz-metan-medias.ro

Coach: Cristian Pustai

Date		Opponent		Score	Scorers
2016					
23/07	h	Tîrgu Mureş	W	2-1	*Llullaku, Axente*
29/07	a	Politehnica Iaşi	L	1-3	*Axente*
07/08	h	Viitorul	W	2-1	*Munteanu, Llullaku*
13/08	a	Concordia	L	0-1	
22/08	h	Botoşani	D	0-0	
26/08	a	Dinamo	D	1-1	*Llullaku*
09/09	h	Pandurii	L	1-3	*Llullaku (p)*
19/09	a	Astra	W	2-0	*Llullaku 2*
22/09	h	Poli Timişoara	D	1-1	*Llullaku*
26/09	a	CFR Cluj	D	1-1	*Llullaku*
01/10	h	Voluntari	W	1-0	*Axente*
16/10	a	Steaua	W	1-0	*Munteanu*
22/10	h	U Craiova	D	2-2	*Llullaku 2*
30/10	a	Tîrgu Mureş	W	3-1	*Llullaku 2, Eric*
04/11	h	Politehnica Iaşi	W	2-1	*Axente, Trtovac*
21/11	a	Viitorul	D	1-1	*Llullaku*
26/11	h	Concordia	W	3-1	*Axente 2, Llullaku*
30/11	a	Botoşani	D	0-0	
05/12	h	Dinamo	W	4-0	*Llullaku 2 (2p), Axente 2*
10/12	a	Pandurii	W	5-2	*Munteanu 3, Axente, Bic*
19/12	h	Astra	L	0-1	
2017					
06/02	a	Poli Timişoara	D	1-1	*Buziuc*
11/02	h	CFR Cluj	L	1-2	*Sikorski*
18/02	a	Voluntari	L	0-1	
26/02	h	Steaua	D	1-1	*Sikorski*
05/03	a	U Craiova	L	0-1	
13/03	h	Tîrgu Mureş	W	2-0	*Munteanu, Sikorski*
19/03	h	Botoşani	D	0-0	
02/04	a	Voluntari	D	2-2	*Buziuc, Cristea*
05/04	h	Politehnica Iaşi	L	0-2	
10/04	a	Concordia	D	1-1	*Trtovac*
16/04	h	Pandurii	W	3-1	*Munteanu, Eric, Sikorski*
20/04	a	Poli Timişoara	L	0-1	
29/04	a	Tîrgu Mureş	D	0-0	
07/05	a	Botoşani	D	0-0	
12/05	h	Voluntari	W	4-1	*Eric 2, Buziuc 2*
19/05	a	Politehnica Iaşi	L	0-1	
23/05	h	Concordia	W	3-0	*Curtean (p), Trif, Olaru (p)*
26/05	a	Pandurii	D	0-0	
04/06	h	Poli Timişoara	D	2-2	*Eric 2*

No	Name	Nat	DoB	Pos	Aps	(s)	Gls
20	Mircea Axente		14/03/87	A	14	(4)	9
94	Ovidiu Bic		23/02/94	M	27	(5)	1
8	Ionuţ Buzean		18/09/82	D	20	(9)	
21	Alexandru Buziuc		15/03/94	A	13	(9)	4
89	Valentin Creţu		02/01/89	D	36		
15	Iulian Cristea		17/07/94	M	19	(9)	1
7	Alexandru Curtean		27/03/87	M	6	(5)	1
28	Cristan Danci		15/07/88	M	15	(9)	
10	Eric	BRA	05/12/85	M	30	(4)	6
9	Cristian Gavra		03/04/93	A	5	(5)	
1	Alexandru Greab		16/05/92	G	19		
35	Akaki Khubutia	GEO	17/03/86	D	4		
7	Azdren Llullaku	ALB	15/02/88	M	20		16
27	Sabin Lupu		14/03/93	A	4	(9)	
22	Alexandru Munteanu		31/10/87	M	29	(8)	7
17	Darius Olaru		03/03/98	A	2	(8)	1
5	Bernand Onanga Itoua	COD	07/09/88	D	3	(2)	
2	Ciprian Petre		10/12/80	M	7	(13)	
12	Răzvan Pleşca		25/11/82	G	21		
80	Roberto Romeo	ITA	27/04/90	D	11	(9)	
24	Dario Rugašević	CRO	29/01/91	D	25		
33	Daniel Sikorski	AUT	02/11/87	A	13	(2)	4
6	Aleksandar Šušnjar	SRB	19/08/95	D	18		
6	Aymen Tahar	ALG	02/10/89	M	8	(4)	
19	Răzvan Trif		09/10/97	D		(2)	1
3	Jasmin Trtovac	SRB	27/12/86	D	38	(1)	2
90	Alexandru Zaharia		25/05/90	M		(1)	
16	Radu Zaharia		25/01/89	D	33		

CS Pandurii Târgu Jiu

1962 • Municipal, Drobeta-Turnu Severin (19,128) • panduriics.ro

Coach: Petre Grigoraş; (11/01/17) Flavius Stoican

Date		Opponent		Score	Scorers
2016					
22/07	h	U Craiova	W	2-1	*Herea, Hora*
31/07	h	Astra	D	0-0	
07/08	a	Poli Timişoara	W	3-1	*Ţucudean, Obodo (p), Munteanu*
14/08	h	CFR Cluj	D	1-1	*Mrzljak*
21/08	a	Voluntari	D	0-0	
27/08	h	Steaua	L	0-1	
09/09	a	Gaz Metan	W	3-1	*Ţucudean 2, Mrzljak*
16/09	h	Tîrgu Mureş	W	1-0	*og (Belu-Iordache)*
20/09	a	Politehnica Iaşi	L	2-3	*Alexandru 2*
23/09	h	Viitorul	L	0-1	
03/10	a	Concordia	D	0-0	
15/10	h	Botoşani	W	2-1	*Herea (p), Ţucudean*
22/10	a	Dinamo	L	0-4	
29/10	a	U Craiova	L	1-2	*Ţucudean*
06/11	a	Astra	L	0-2	
18/11	h	Poli Timişoara	D	2-2	*Antal 2*
28/11	a	CFR Cluj	W	1-0	*Pleaşcă*
01/12	h	Voluntari	D	1-1	*Sânmărtean*
04/12	a	Steaua	L	1-3	*Herea*
10/12	h	Gaz Metan	L	2-5	*Sânmărtean, og (Rugašević)*
18/12	a	Tîrgu Mureş	L	0-3	*(w/o; original result 0-2)*
2017					
03/02	h	Politehnica Iaşi	D	1-1	*Negruţ*
13/02	a	Viitorul	L	0-3	
19/02	h	Concordia	L	0-1	
26/02	a	Botoşani	L	1-3	*Negruţ*
05/03	h	Dinamo	L	0-2	
12/03	a	Voluntari	D	1-1	*Surugiu*
20/03	h	Politehnica Iaşi	D	0-0	
31/03	a	Concordia	W	1-0	*Firţulescu*
04/04	a	Tîrgu Mureş	D	0-0	
07/04	h	Poli Timişoara	L	1-3	*Hlistei*
16/04	a	Gaz Metan	L	1-3	*Negruţ (p)*
21/04	h	Botoşani	D	1-1	*Păcurar (p)*
30/04	h	Voluntari	L	1-3	*Surugiu*
08/05	a	Politehnica Iaşi	L	0-3	
15/05	h	Concordia	W	3-2	*Batin 2, Hamed*
19/05	h	Tîrgu Mureş	W	1-0	*Erico*
23/05	a	Poli Timişoara	W	1-0	*Păcurar*
26/05	h	Gaz Metan	D	0-0	
04/06	a	Botoşani	L	1-2	*Ilie*

No	Name	Nat	DoB	Pos	Aps	(s)	Gls
19	Valentin Alexandru		17/09/91	A	5	(4)	2
9	Liviu Antal		02/06/89	M	12	(1)	2
70	Armiche		12/06/88	M		(1)	
13	Paul Batin		29/06/87	A	3	(2)	2
4	Denis Brînzan		26/11/96	D	2	(3)	
4	Jordy Buijs	NED	28/12/88	D	7		
3	Gordan Bunoza	BIH	05/02/88	D	6	(3)	
24	Sorin Buşu		08/07/89	D	18		
89	Ionuţ Cioinac		14/01/91	M	14		
70	Andrei David		03/04/99	D	1		
18	Bogdan Dănăricu		20/01/95	M		(1)	
99	Gabriel Dodoi		27/09/98	A	1	(4)	
5	Cornel Ene		21/07/93	D	16		
21	Erico	BRA	20/07/89	D	6	(1)	1
10	Dragoş Firţulescu		15/05/89	M	14	(3)	1
23	Constantin Grecu		08/06/88	D	15		
27	Yasin Hamed		12/09/99	M	2	(14)	1
30	Ovidiu Herea		26/03/85	M	17	(2)	3
20	Cătălin Hlistei		24/08/94	M	18	(5)	1
9	Ioan Hora		21/08/88	A	2		1
6	Florin Ilie		18/06/92	D	13	(2)	1
29	Jeffrey Ket	NED	06/04/93	M	4		
1	David Lazăr		08/08/91	G	11		
9	Daniel Mărgărit		30/08/96	A	1	(1)	
24	Filip Mrzljak	CRO	16/04/93	M	11	(1)	2
5	Valentin Munteanu		24/10/89	M	5	(8)	1
17	Ciprian Negoiţă		28/04/92	D	10	(2)	
99	Sergiu Negruţ		01/04/93	A	15	(3)	3
3	Samson Nwabueze	NGA	20/04/88	D	10	(3)	
99	Christian Obodo	NGA	11/05/84	M	8	(1)	1
7	Paul Păcurar		05/03/91	M	10	(3)	2
26	Adelin Pârcălabu		01/05/96	A	8	(11)	
7	George Pirtea		24/07/96	M	1	(1)	
17	Andrei Piţian		16/11/95	M	9	(5)	
25	Marian Pleaşcă		06/02/90	D	13		1
12	Daniel Popescu		25/08/93	G	2	(1)	
1	Laurenţiu Popescu		18/01/97	G	9		
52	Alexandru Răuţă		17/06/92	M	11	(5)	
8	Lucian Sănmărtean		13/03/80	M	16	(1)	2
16	Cristian Sârghi		23/11/86	D		(1)	
25	Ionel Stana		02/12/82	M	12	(1)	
33	Răzvan Stanca		18/01/80	G	18		
70	Olivian Surugiu		23/06/90	M	13	(1)	2
52	Ionuţ Tătaru		05/10/89	D	3	(1)	
77	Rodemis Trifu		08/10/95	M	4	(12)	
27	Angelotti Trocan		07/10/95	M	1	(1)	
3	Laurenţiu Tudor		17/08/97	D	1		
29	Marius Ţucudean		30/04/91	A	12	(3)	5
18	Bogdan Unguruşan		20/02/83	D	11	(1)	
6	Nikola Vasiljević	SRB	30/06/91	D	16		
8	Claudiu Voiculeţ		08/08/95	M	12	(3)	
8	Ionuţ Zaina		25/01/94	M	11	(1)	

ACS Poli Timişoara

1921 • Dan Păltinişanu (32,972) • acspoli.ro

Major honours
Romanian Cup (2) 1958, 1980

Coach: Ionuţ Popa

Date		Opponent		Score	Scorers
2016					
30/07	a	Dinamo	L	1-2	*Scutaru*
07/08	h	Pandurii	L	1-3	*Elek*
13/08	a	Astra	L	1-3	*Croitoru*
18/08	h	Botoşani	L	0-5	
22/08	h	U Craiova	W	3-2	*Artean 2 (2p), Bărbuţ*
27/08	h	CFR Cluj	D	1-1	*Cânu*
10/09	a	Voluntari	L	1-4	*Pedro Henrique*
18/09	h	Steaua	L	0-1	
22/09	a	Gaz Metan	D	1-1	*Popovici*
25/09	h	Tîrgu Mureş	L	0-1	
30/09	a	Politehnica Iaşi	W	1-0	*Drăghici*
17/10	h	Viitorul	W	1-0	*Cârstocea (p)*
21/10	a	Concordia	W	2-0	*Drăghici, og (Albu)*
31/10	a	Botoşani	L	0-2	
05/11	h	Dinamo	L	1-2	*Doman (p)*
18/11	a	Pandurii	D	2-2	*Popovici, Doman (p)*
27/11	h	Astra	W	2-0	*Şeroni, Pedro Henrique*
30/11	a	U Craiova	L	0-2	
05/12	a	CFR Cluj	D	2-2	*Drăghici 2*
09/12	h	Voluntari	W	1-0	*Doman (p)*
17/12	a	Steaua	L	0-1	
2017					
06/02	h	Gaz Metan	D	1-1	*Doman*
10/02	a	Tîrgu Mureş	D	0-0	
20/02	h	Politehnica Iaşi	W	2-1	*Pedro Henrique, Šoljić*
25/02	a	Viitorul	L	0-5	
04/03	h	Concordia	D	1-1	*Şeroni*
10/03	a	Botoşani	W	2-1	*Croitoru, Şeroni (p)*
20/03	h	Voluntari	W	1-0	*Popovici*
01/04	a	Politehnica Iaşi	L	0-1	
04/04	h	Concordia	D	0-0	
07/04	a	Pandurii	W	3-1	*Pedro Henrique, Bărbuţ, Cânu*
15/04	a	Tîrgu Mureş	D	0-0	
20/04	h	Gaz Metan	W	1-0	*Străuţ*
01/05	h	Botoşani	D	1-1	*Cânu*
05/05	a	Voluntari	L	1-2	*Pedro Henrique*
10/05	a	Concordia	L	1-3	*Mailat*
14/05	h	Politehnica Iaşi	D	1-1	*Fuček*
23/05	h	Pandurii	L	0-1	
28/05	h	Tîrgu Mureş	W	3-1	*Popovici 2, Mailat*
04/06	a	Gaz Metan	D	2-2	*Popovici, Mailat*

No	Name	Nat	DoB	Pos	Aps	(s)	Gls
18	Andrei Artean		14/08/93	M	38		2
7	Cristian Bărbuţ		22/04/95	M	34		2
26	Cosmin Bîrnoi		17/08/97	D		(5)	
15	Cristian Bocşan		31/01/95	D	23	(5)	
23	Gabriel Cânu		18/01/81	D	28		3
14	Alin Cârstocea		16/01/92	M	9	(7)	1
8	Marius Croitoru		02/10/80	M	33	(2)	2
33	Vasile Curileac		18/02/84	G	5		
10	Cătălin Doman		30/01/88	M	16	(4)	4
85	Octavian Drăghici		26/11/85	A	14	(9)	4
19	Robert Elek		13/06/88	A	4	(1)	1
11	Josip Fuček	CRO	26/02/85	A	14	(1)	1
19	Alin Ignea		28/04/89	M		(2)	
4	Fernando Llorente	ESP	18/09/90	M	12	(1)	
12	Sebastian Mailat		12/12/97	M	4	(19)	3
3	George Neagu		24/04/85	D	11	(10)	
22	Leopold Novak	CRO	03/12/90	D	19		
91	Pedro Henrique	BRA	28/03/91	A	10	(7)	5
5	Adrian Poparadu		13/10/87	M	7	(4)	
9	Adrian Popovici		06/09/88	M	18	(16)	6
24	Iulian Roşu		30/05/94	M	2	(5)	
83	Andrei Săntean		16/06/99	A		(2)	
13	Cristian Scutaru		13/04/87	D	23	(1)	1
16	Josip Šoljić	CRO	18/06/87	M	17		1
16	Deian Sorescu		29/08/97	M	1	(4)	
25	Cătălin Straton		09/10/89	G	35		
32	Bogdan Străuţ		28/04/86	D	31	(1)	1
30	Alin Şeroni		26/03/87	D	23	(8)	3
94	Daniel Vădrariu		25/06/90	M	6	(2)	
11	Cătălin Vraciu		21/01/89	A	3	(2)	

CSM Politehnica Iaşi

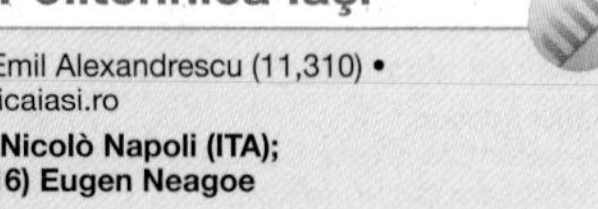

2010 • Emil Alexandrescu (11,310) • politehnicaiasi.ro

Coach: Nicolò Napoli (ITA); (08/10/16) Eugen Neagoe

Date		Opponent		Score	Scorers
2016					
29/07	h	Gaz Metan	W	3-1	*Ţigănaşu, Bőle, Cristea*
05/08	a	Tîrgu Mureş	W	3-0	*Bőle, Cristea, Târşă*
15/08	a	U Craiova	L	0-2	
19/08	h	Viitorul	D	0-0	
26/08	a	Concordia	D	0-0	
31/08	a	Steaua	D	1-1	*Bőle*
11/09	h	Botoşani	L	0-1	
17/09	a	Dinamo	L	1-3	*Piccioni*
20/09	h	Pandurii	W	3-2	*Ciucur, Boiciuc, Piccioni*
26/09	a	Astra	L	0-1	
30/09	h	Poli Timişoara	L	0-1	
14/10	a	CFR Cluj	L	0-1	
23/10	h	Voluntari	L	1-2	*Piccioni*
30/10	h	Steaua	L	0-2	
04/11	a	Gaz Metan	L	1-2	*Mihalache*
19/11	h	Tîrgu Mureş	D	0-0	
25/11	h	U Craiova	W	2-1	*Ciucur, Bőle (p)*
29/11	a	Viitorul	L	0-1	
02/12	h	Concordia	W	1-0	*Cristea*
10/12	a	Botoşani	W	3-1	*Bőle 2, Cristea (p)*
18/12	h	Dinamo	W	3-1	*Cristea (p), Ştefănescu, Gheorghe*
2017					
03/02	a	Pandurii	D	1-1	*Gheorghe*
20/02	a	Poli Timişoara	L	1-2	*Cristea (p)*
27/02	h	CFR Cluj	L	1-2	*Cristea*
02/03	h	Astra	L	2-3	*Ştefănescu, Cristea (p)*
06/03	a	Voluntari	W	1-0	*Golubović*
11/03	h	Concordia	W	3-1	*Cristea 2, Golubović*
20/03	a	Pandurii	D	0-0	
01/04	h	Poli Timişoara	W	1-0	*Bőle*
05/04	a	Gaz Metan	W	2-0	*Gheorghe (p), Ştefănescu*
08/04	h	Botoşani	W	2-1	*Ştefănescu, Boşoi*
17/04	a	Voluntari	D	0-0	
24/04	h	Tîrgu Mureş	D	0-0	
28/04	a	Concordia	D	0-0	
08/05	h	Pandurii	W	3-0	*Golubović 2, og (Cioinac)*
14/05	a	Poli Timişoara	D	1-1	*Bőle*
19/05	h	Gaz Metan	W	1-0	*Bőle*
25/05	a	Botoşani	W	1-0	*Cristea*
31/05	h	Voluntari	D	1-1	*Golubović*
05/06	a	Tîrgu Mureş	D	1-1	*Moldovan*

No	Name	Nat	DoB	Pos	Aps	(s)	Gls
44	Mario Asăvoaei		02/10/98	M		(1)	
5	Narcis Bădic		15/07/91	M	3	(4)	
9	Alexandru Boiciuc	MDA	21/08/97	A	6	(5)	1
21	Lukács Bőle	HUN	27/03/90	M	32		9
8	Gabriel Boşoi		11/08/87	D	20	(3)	1
1	Alessandro Caparco	ITA	07/09/83	G	10	(2)	
13	Marius Chelaru		02/03/97	M	1	(3)	
19	Mădălin Ciucă		04/11/82	D	13	(1)	
90	Alexandru Ciucur		01/03/90	M	18	(13)	2
6	Alexandru Creţu		24/04/92	D	11		
10	Andrei Cristea		15/05/84	A	29	(6)	11
18	Vlad Danale		29/01/98	A		(3)	
23	Cosmin Frăsinescu		10/02/85	D	37		
7	Vasile Gheorghe		05/09/85	M	28	(8)	3
14	Bojan Golubović	SRB	22/08/83	A	14	(4)	5
12	Branko Grahovac	BIH	08/07/83	G	30		
27	Mădălin Martin		21/06/92	M		(2)	
4	Marius Mihalache		14/12/84	D	30	(1)	1
22	Milan Mitić	SRB	22/01/84	M	25	(9)	
91	Adrian Moldovan		16/03/99	A	3	(4)	1
11	Ionuţ Panţîru		22/03/96	D	4	(8)	
11	Gianmarco Piccioni	ITA	18/07/91	A	8	(8)	3
6	Alexandru Răuţă		17/06/92	M	15	(1)	
24	Dan Roman		22/12/85	A		(4)	
44	Ante Sarić	CRO	17/06/92	D	2	(2)	
16	Daisuke Sato	PHI	20/09/94	D	18	(6)	
27	Sténio	CPV	06/05/88	M	2	(1)	
88	Cătălin Ştefănescu		30/11/94	M	25	(5)	4
29	Marian Târşă		16/04/98	M	5	(2)	1
30	Alexandru Ţigănaşu		12/06/90	D	29	(7)	1
20	Ionuţ Voicu		02/08/84	D	22	(2)	

ASA Tîrgu Mureş

2008 • Trans-Sil (8,200) • asatirgumures.ro

Coach: Dario Bonetti (ITA); (07/08/16) Dan Alexa; (28/12/16) Ilie Stan; (24/03/17) Ionuț Chirilă; (12/04/17) (Darius Miclea); (18/04/17) Ionel Ganea

2016

Date		Opponent		Score	Scorers
23/07	a	Gaz Metan	L	1-2	*Candrea*
01/08	a	U Craiova	L	1-2	*Zicu*
05/08	h	Politehnica Iași	L	0-3	
14/08	a	Viitorul	L	1-3	*Ioniță*
20/08	h	Concordia	L	0-1	
29/08	a	Botoșani	L	2-4	*Zicu, Matei*
12/09	h	Dinamo	W	2-1	*Zicu 2*
16/09	a	Pandurii	L	0-1	
22/09	h	Astra	L	0-2	
25/09	a	Poli Timișoara	W	1-0	*Rus*
30/09	h	CFR Cluj	L	1-3	*Zicu*
16/10	a	Voluntari	D	1-1	*Morar*
23/10	h	Steaua	D	1-1	*Kuku*
30/10	h	Gaz Metan	L	1-3	*Morar*
05/11	h	U Craiova	L	0-2	
19/11	a	Politehnica Iași	D	0-0	
25/11	h	Viitorul	L	0-2	
29/11	a	Concordia	W	2-1	*Ciolacu, Matei*
04/12	h	Botoșani	W	2-0	*Kuku, Morar*
10/12	a	Dinamo	L	0-1	
18/12	h	Pandurii	W	3-0	*(w/o; original result 2-0 Mureșan, Morar)*

2017

Date		Opponent		Score	Scorers
03/02	a	Astra	L	0-1	
10/02	h	Poli Timișoara	D	0-0	
17/02	a	CFR Cluj	L	0-2	
24/02	h	Voluntari	D	0-0	
04/03	a	Steaua	D	1-1	*Constantin (p)*
13/03	a	Gaz Metan	L	0-2	
18/03	h	Concordia	W	2-1	*Mureșan (p), Ciolacu*
31/03	a	Botoșani	L	0-2	
04/04	h	Pandurii	D	0-0	
08/04	a	Voluntari	L	1-2	*Gorobsov (p)*
15/04	h	Poli Timișoara	D	0-0	
24/04	a	Politehnica Iași	D	0-0	
29/04	h	Gaz Metan	D	0-0	
05/05	a	Concordia	L	0-2	
15/05	h	Botoșani	L	0-2	
19/05	a	Pandurii	L	0-1	
24/05	h	Voluntari	L	0-2	
28/05	a	Poli Timișoara	L	1-3	*Nicoliță*
05/06	h	Politehnica Iași	D	1-1	*Nicoliță*

No	Name	Nat	DoB	Pos	Aps	(s)	Gls
91	Florent André	FRA	06/06/91	A	5	(1)	
8	Cristian Balgiu		03/08/94	M	6	(3)	
11	Marius Bâtfoi		19/05/90	A	9		
8	Claudiu Belu-Iordache		07/11/93	D	11		
12	Mirel Bolboașă		11/07/89	G	1		
30	Adrian Borza		18/02/85	M	3		
5	Sebastian Bucur		10/12/96	D	2	(2)	
13	Robert Candrea		03/02/95	M	20	(6)	1
2	Carlos Cherteș		26/07/99	M	3		
9	Andrei Ciolacu		09/08/92	M	12	(14)	2
23	Marius Constantin		25/10/84	D	24		1
4	Andrei Cordoş		06/06/88	D	18		
20	Raul Costin		29/01/85	M	3		
78	Octavian Deaconu		13/05/97	M	2	(6)	
7	Emil Dică		17/07/82	M	13	(8)	
24	Alin Dobrosavljevic		24/10/94	D	18		
24	Răzvan Dulap		16/10/95	D	2	(2)	
96	Norbert Feketics		13/06/96	M	3	(5)	
14	Viorel Ferfelea		26/04/85	M	8	(7)	
19	Nicolas Gorobsov	ARG	25/11/89	M	10	(1)	1
21	Yasin Hamed		12/09/99	D	1	(2)	
96	Raul Iliescu		02/09/98	M		(1)	
19	Alexandru Ioniță		05/08/89	M	2	(4)	1
31	Yuval Jacobovich	ISR	09/11/92	M	7	(2)	
11	Benjamin Kuku	NGA	08/03/95	A	12	(8)	2
78	Valentin Lemnaru		24/06/84	A		(7)	
14	Gabriel Matei		26/02/90	D	18		2
37	Gaston Mendy	SEN	22/11/85	D	25	(2)	
33	Pedro Mingote	POR	02/08/80	G	14		
95	Bogdan Moga		14/05/95	G	2		
77	Vlad Morar		01/08/93	A	11	(2)	4
6	Gabriel Mureșan		18/03/82	M	23		2
70	Alon Netzer	ISR	02/06/93	D	4	(2)	
16	Bănel Nicoliță		07/01/85	M	19		2
33	Eduard Pap		01/07/94	G	17		
70	Vasile Petra		12/01/94	M	5	(4)	
89	Tiberiu Petriș		20/06/94	M	4	(6)	
4	Konstantinos Rougalas	GRE	13/10/93	D	10		
31	Ciprian Rus		01/03/91	A	13	(9)	1
21	Marvin Schieb		27/07/96	A	3	(3)	
20	Andrei Sin		26/10/91	A	9	(2)	
33	Eduard Stăncioiu		03/03/81	G	5		
18	Răzvan Stoica		19/01/95	A	3	(2)	
31	Romeo Surdu		12/01/84	M	12	(1)	
99	Andrei Tornyai		30/11/99	M		(1)	
94	Alexandru Tudose		03/04/87	D	7		
94	Octavian Ursu		15/11/94	M	3	(1)	
31	Javier Velayos	ESP	06/04/87	D	18		
1	Adrian Viciu		14/01/91	G	1		
10	Ianis Zicu		23/10/83	M	19	(1)	5

CS U Craiova

2013 • Extensiv (6,071); Municipal, Drobeta-Turnu Severin (19,128); Nicolae Dobrin, Pitesti (15,170) • csuc.ro

Coach: Gheorghe Mulțescu

2016

Date		Opponent		Score	Scorers
22/07	a	Pandurii	L	1-2	*Vătăjelu (p)*
01/08	h	Tîrgu Mureș	W	2-1	*Nuno Rocha, Măzărache*
06/08	a	Astra	W	2-1	*Nuno Rocha, Măzărache*
15/08	h	Politehnica Iași	W	2-0	*Kay, Ivan*
22/08	a	Poli Timișoara	L	2-3	*Zlatinski (p), Nuno Rocha*
28/08	h	Viitorul	W	2-1	*Bancu, Măzărache*
10/09	a	CFR Cluj	D	0-0	
18/09	h	Concordia	D	1-1	*Măzărache*
21/09	a	Voluntari	W	1-0	*Ivan*
24/09	h	Botoșani	W	1-0	*Băluță*
02/10	a	Steaua	L	1-2	*Vătăjelu*
17/10	h	Dinamo	W	2-1	*Ivan, Briceag*
22/10	a	Gaz Metan	D	2-2	*og (Romeo), Ivan*
29/10	h	Pandurii	W	2-1	*Măzărache, Ivan*
05/11	a	Tîrgu Mureș	W	2-0	*Popov, Zlatinski (p)*
20/11	h	Astra	L	0-1	
25/11	a	Politehnica Iași	L	1-2	*Băluță*
30/11	h	Poli Timișoara	W	2-0	*Nuno Rocha, Gustavo*
03/12	a	Viitorul	L	0-2	
09/12	h	CFR Cluj	W	2-1	*Zlatinski (p), Gustavo*
16/12	a	Concordia	D	0-0	

2017

Date		Opponent		Score	Scorers
04/02	h	Voluntari	W	5-0	*Nuno Rocha, Bancu, Băluță 2, Ivan*
11/02	a	Botoșani	L	0-1	
18/02	h	Steaua	L	1-2	*Zlatinski (p)*
25/02	a	Dinamo	L	1-2	*Gustavo*
05/03	h	Gaz Metan	W	1-0	*Bancu*
11/03	a	Astra	D	0-0	
19/03	a	Dinamo	D	0-0	
01/04	h	CFR Cluj	L	1-4	*Gustavo (p)*
06/04	a	Viitorul	W	1-0	*Mateiu*
09/04	h	FCSB	L	0-1	
15/04	h	Astra	L	1-3	*Gustavo (p)*
22/04	h	Dinamo	D	2-2	*Ivan, Zlatinski*
30/04	a	CFR Cluj	W	3-0	*Ivan 2, Zlatinski*
07/05	h	Viitorul	L	0-1	
13/05	a	FCSB	L	0-3	

No	Name	Nat	DoB	Pos	Aps	(s)	Gls
3	Stephane Acka	CIV	11/10/90	D	22		
11	Nicușor Bancu		18/09/92	M	26	(9)	3
5	Alexandre Barthe	FRA	05/03/86	D	8	(1)	
22	Alexandru Băluță		13/09/93	M	30	(1)	4
37	Nicolae Bîrzan		12/09/99	D		(2)	
7	Marius Briceag		06/04/92	D	23		1
31	Bogdan Bucurică		11/02/86	D	4	(1)	
36	Andrei Burlacu		12/01/97	M		(2)	
12	Nicolai Calancea	MDA	29/08/86	G	32		
30	Radoslav Dimitrov	BUL	12/08/88	D	14		
19	Andrei Dumitraș		23/01/88	D	3	(6)	
21	Nusmir Fajić	BIH	12/01/87	A	2	(3)	
10	Gustavo	BRA	14/11/91	M	13	(11)	5
9	Andrei Ivan		04/01/97	M	32	(1)	9
21	Nusmir Jazvić	BIH	12/01/87	A	3	(5)	
4	Kay	CPV	05/01/88	D	12	(1)	1
6	Renato Kelić	CRO	31/03/91	D	15	(6)	
28	Mádson	BRA	09/05/91	M	5	(3)	
46	Alin Manea		09/01/97	M	2	(2)	
16	Jovan Markovic		23/03/01	A		(3)	
8	Alexandru Mateiu		10/12/89	M	15	(4)	1
27	Simion Măzărache		10/01/93	A	20	(10)	5
15	Nuno Rocha	CPV	25/03/92	M	22	(2)	5
80	Pedro Mingote	POR	02/08/80	G	3		
20	Robert Petre		27/04/97	M	1	(5)	
25	Alexandru Popescu		06/01/98	A	1		
18	Apostol Popov	BUL	22/12/82	D	21	(1)	1
29	Rambé	CPV	04/10/89	A	4	(9)	
54	Vladimir Screciu		13/01/00	M	9	(4)	
55	Olivian Surugiu		23/06/90	M		(5)	
5	Bogdan Vătăjelu		24/04/93	D	21		2
52	Daniel Vlad		15/04/99	G	1		
2	Ștefan Vlădoiu		28/12/98	D		(1)	
23	Hristo Zlatinski	BUL	22/01/85	M	32	(3)	6

FC Viitorul

2009 • Viitorul, Ovidiu (4,500) • academiahagi.tv

Major honours
Romanian League (1) 2017

Coach: Gheorghe Hagi

2016

Date		Opponent		Score	Scorers
22/07	a	Voluntari	W	1-0	*Iancu*
31/07	h	Steaua	L	1-3	*Chițu*
07/08	a	Gaz Metan	L	1-2	*Țîru*
14/08	h	Tîrgu Mureș	W	3-1	*Chițu, Coman, Purece*
19/08	a	Politehnica Iași	D	0-0	
28/08	a	U Craiova	L	1-2	*Casap*
12/09	h	Concordia	W	2-1	*Chițu 2*
16/09	a	Botoșani	W	2-1	*Chițu, Nimely*
20/09	h	Dinamo	D	1-1	*Nimely*
23/09	a	Pandurii	W	1-0	*Nedelcu*
02/10	h	Astra	W	1-0	*Marin*
17/10	a	Poli Timișoara	L	0-1	
21/10	h	CFR Cluj	W	2-1	*Iancu, Chițu (p)*
31/10	h	Voluntari	W	2-1	*Marin (p), Boli*
06/11	a	Steaua	L	0-2	
21/11	h	Gaz Metan	D	1-1	*Nimely*
25/11	a	Tîrgu Mureș	W	2-0	*Marin (p), Boli*
29/11	h	Politehnica Iași	W	1-0	*Nimely*
03/12	h	U Craiova	W	2-0	*Chițu, Hodorogea*
12/12	a	Concordia	W	2-1	*Benzar, Purece*
19/12	h	Botoșani	W	3-1	*Iancu (p), Chițu, Marin*

2017

Date		Opponent		Score	Scorers
04/02	a	Dinamo	W	2-1	*Boli, Coman*
13/02	h	Pandurii	W	3-0	*Iancu, Chițu (p), Coman*
19/02	a	Astra	L	0-1	
25/02	h	Poli Timișoara	W	5-0	*Morar 3, Chițu, Coman*
05/03	a	CFR Cluj	L	0-1	
13/03	h	Dinamo	D	0-0	
18/03	h	Steaua	W	3-1	*Coman, Morar, Casap*
03/04	a	Astra	W	2-1	*Chițu, og (Săpunaru)*
06/04	h	U Craiova	L	0-1	
09/04	a	CFR Cluj	D	0-0	
16/04	a	Dinamo	L	1-2	*Țucudean*
24/04	a	FCSB	D	1-1	*Țucudean*
29/04	h	Astra	W	3-2	*Morar, Țucudean 2*
07/05	a	U Craiova	W	1-0	*Coman*
13/05	h	CFR Cluj	W	1-0	*Iancu (p)*

No	Name	Nat	DoB	Pos	Aps	(s)	Gls
6	Romario Benzar		26/03/92	D	34		1
21	Kevin Boli	FRA	21/06/91	D	33		3
19	Pablo Brandán	ARG	05/03/83	M	13	(1)	
31	Alexandru Buzbuchi		31/10/93	G	8		
93	Catalin Carp	MDA	20/10/93	D	9	(5)	
8	Carlo Casap		29/12/98	M	5	(10)	2
25	Aurelian Chițu		25/03/91	A	34	(2)	11
23	Alexandru Cicâldău		08/07/97	M	1	(5)	
13	Florin Cioablă		23/04/96	M		(1)	
24	Andrei Ciobanu		18/01/98	A		(2)	
98	Florinel Coman		10/04/98	A	18	(10)	6
11	Dani López	ESP	31/03/92	M	8	(4)	
17	Doru Dumitrescu		25/05/98	M	1	(4)	
4	Ioan Filip		20/05/89	M	2	(2)	
22	Cristian Ganea		24/05/92	D	25	(1)	
29	Robert Hodorogea		24/03/95	D	10	(7)	1
10	Gabriel Iancu		15/04/94	M	15	(9)	5
18	Răzvan Marin		23/05/96	M	20		4
14	Bogdan Mitache		01/01/94	D	1	(1)	
19	Sebastian Mladen		11/12/91	D	1	(1)	
11	Vlad Morar		01/08/93	A	9	(5)	5
16	Dragoș Nedelcu		16/02/97	M	22	(6)	1
99	Alex Nimely	LBR	11/05/91	A	10	(8)	4
30	Florin Purece		06/11/91	M	23	(7)	2
3	Sorin Rădoi		30/06/85	D	2	(5)	
12	Victor Rîmniceanu		11/04/90	G	28		
93	Neluț Roșu		05/07/93	M	13	(1)	
97	Alexandru Stoica		30/06/97	A	1	(4)	
7	Florin Tănase		30/12/94	M	3		
15	Bogdan Țîru		15/03/94	D	33		1
20	George Țucudean		03/04/91	A	4	(2)	4
28	Ionuț Vână		20/02/95	M	10	(5)	

FC Voluntari

2010 • Anghel Iordănescu (4,600) • voluntarifc.ro

Major honours
Romanian Cup (1) 2017

Coach: Florin Marin; (10/03/17) Dinu Todoran; (03/04/17) Claudiu Niculescu

2016					
22/07	h	Viitorul	L	0-1	
01/08	a	Concordia	W	4-0	*Novac, Căpățână, Ivanovici, Bălan*
05/08	h	Botoșani	W	4-2	*Spahija, Ivanovici 2, Novac*
15/08	a	Dinamo	L	1-3	*Ivanovici*
21/08	h	Pandurii	D	0-0	
28/08	a	Astra	D	1-1	*Marinescu*
10/09	h	Poli Timișoara	W	4-1	*Marinescu, Popadiuc, Cernat 2 (1p)*
17/09	a	CFR Cluj	L	0-5	
21/09	h	U Craiova	L	0-1	
25/09	h	Steaua	L	2-3	*Ivanovici, Bălan*
01/10	a	Gaz Metan	L	0-1	
16/10	h	Tîrgu Mureș	D	1-1	*Bălan*
23/10	a	Politehnica Iași	W	2-1	*Bălan, Căpățână*
31/10	a	Viitorul	L	1-2	*Cernat (p)*
05/11	h	Concordia	W	1-0	*Cernat*
18/11	a	Botoșani	W	1-0	*Bălan*
26/11	h	Dinamo	L	1-2	*Bălan*
01/12	a	Pandurii	D	1-1	*Balaur*
04/12	h	Astra	L	1-2	*Ivanovici*
09/12	a	Poli Timișoara	L	0-1	
17/12	h	CFR Cluj	W	2-1	*Marinescu (p), Spahija*
2017					
04/02	a	U Craiova	L	0-5	
12/02	a	Steaua	D	2-2	*Ivanovici, Cernat*
18/02	h	Gaz Metan	W	1-0	*Ivanovici*
24/02	a	Tîrgu Mureș	D	0-0	
06/03	h	Politehnica Iași	L	0-1	
12/03	h	Pandurii	D	1-1	*Deac*
20/03	a	Poli Timișoara	L	0-1	
02/04	h	Gaz Metan	D	2-2	*Voduț, Marinescu*
05/04	a	Botoșani	L	0-3	
08/04	h	Tîrgu Mureș	W	2-1	*Bălan, Căpățână*
17/04	h	Politehnica Iași	D	0-0	
21/04	a	Concordia	W	2-0	*Bălan 2*
30/04	a	Pandurii	W	3-1	*Cazan, Popadiuc, Cernat*
05/05	h	Poli Timișoara	W	2-1	*Balaur, Popadiuc*
12/05	a	Gaz Metan	L	1-4	*og (Buzean)*
21/05	h	Botoșani	W	1-0	*Cernat (p)*
24/05	a	Tîrgu Mureș	W	2-0	*Căpățână, Mihai*
31/05	a	Politehnica Iași	D	1-1	*Deac*
04/06	h	Concordia	L	0-1	

No	Name	Nat	DoB	Pos	Aps	(s)	Gls
2	Cosmin Achim		19/09/95	D	3		
87	Florin Acsinte		10/04/87	D	28		
28	Ionuț Balaur		06/06/89	D	27	(2)	2
22	Dragoș Balauru		11/11/89	G	20		
90	Adrian Bălan		14/03/90	A	18	(11)	9
23	Mircea Bornescu		03/05/80	G	16		
25	Lucian Cazan		25/12/89	D	17	(1)	1
11	Mihai Căpățână		16/12/95	M	21	(15)	4
10	Florin Cernat		10/03/80	M	35		7
12	Alexandru Coman		16/10/91	D	13	(2)	
30	Costin Curelea		11/07/84	A	5	(10)	
26	Gabriel Deac		26/04/95	M	5	(14)	2
45	Venelin Filipov	BUL	20/08/90	D	21	(4)	
1	George Gavrilaș		15/12/90	G	4		
14	Andrei Ionescu		29/03/88	M	1	(2)	
7	Petre Ivanovici		02/03/90	M	30	(6)	8
15	Costin Lazăr		24/04/81	M	20		
4	Mircea Leașă		22/02/99	D	1	(1)	
14	Andrei Lungu		29/01/89	M	1	(10)	
24	Vasile Maftei		01/01/81	D	28		
20	Laurențiu Marinescu		25/08/84	M	30	(7)	4
95	Vasile Mihai		29/11/95	M		(1)	1
21	Wilfred Moke	COD	12/02/88	M	6		
8	Daniel Novac		26/09/87	M	30	(4)	2
59	Doru Popadiuc		18/02/95	M	22	(9)	3
44	Hrvoje Spahija	CRO	23/03/88	D	23	(2)	2
6	Sorin Tăbăcariu		23/07/94	M	8	(7)	
17	Marius Tudorică		12/11/93	M		(2)	
9	Mihai Voduț		28/07/94	A	7	(7)	1

Top goalscorers

16	Azdren Llullaku (Gaz Metan)
11	Denis Alibec (Astra/FCSB)
	Cristian Bud (CFR Cluj)
	Adam Nemec (Dinamo)
	Andrei Cristea (Politehnica Iași)
	Aurelian Chițu (Viitorul)
10	Harlem Gnohéré (Dinamo/FCSB)
9	Fernando Boldrin (Astra/FCSB)
	Cătălin Golofca (Botoșani)
	Sergiu Hanca (Dinamo)
	Mircea Axente (Gaz Metan)
	Lukács Bőle (Politehnica Iași)
	Vlad Morar (Tîrgu Mureș/Viitorul)
	Andrei Ivan (U Craiova)
	Adrian Bălan (Voluntari)

Relegation play-offs 2016/17

			Home					Away					Total					
		Pld	W	D	L	F	A	W	D	L	F	A	W	D	L	F	A	Pts
1	CSM Politehnica Iași	14	5	2	0	11	3	2	5	0	5	2	7	7	0	16	5	43
2	CS Gaz Metan Mediaș	14	4	2	1	14	6	0	5	2	3	5	4	7	3	17	11	39
3	FC Voluntari	14	3	3	1	8	6	3	1	3	9	10	6	4	4	17	16	37
4	FC Botoșani	14	3	2	2	9	5	1	3	3	6	7	4	5	5	15	12	33
5	CS Concordia Chiajna	14	3	2	2	8	6	1	2	4	6	12	4	4	6	14	18	29
6	ACS Poli Timișoara	14	3	3	1	7	4	2	2	3	9	10	5	5	4	16	14	27
7	CS Pandurii Târgu Jiu	14	2	3	2	7	9	2	2	3	5	9	4	5	5	12	18	27
8	ASA Tîrgu Mureș	14	1	4	2	3	6	0	1	6	2	12	1	5	8	5	18	14

Promoted clubs

CS Juventus Bucureşti

1992 • Juventus (2,500) • no website

Coach: Marin Barbu; (01/01/17) Daniel Opriţa

Sepsi OSK Sfântu Gheorghe

2011 • Municipal (5,000) • fcceahlaul.ro

Coach: László Polgár; (01/01/17) Sándor Nagy

Second level final tables 2016/17

		Pld	W	D	L	F	A	Pts
1	CS Juventus Bucureşti	34	27	3	4	77	18	84
2	Sepsi OSK Sfântu Gheorghe	34	21	8	5	62	29	71
3	UTA Bătrâna Doamnă	34	20	6	8	64	32	66
4	CS Mioveni	34	17	8	9	51	30	59
5	FC Chindia Târgovişte	34	18	4	12	57	37	58
6	FC Braşov	34	15	11	8	49	35	56
7	FC Dunărea 2005 Călăraşi	34	16	8	10	52	40	56
8	CS Afumaţi	34	17	5	12	56	36	56
9	FC Olimpia 2010 Satu Mare	34	16	6	12	53	34	54
10	CS Luceafărul Oradea	34	14	5	15	48	38	47
11	ASC Dacia Unirea Brăila	34	14	4	16	37	56	46
12	ACS Foresta Suceava	34	12	5	17	49	69	41
13	CS Baloteşti	34	11	7	16	44	56	40
14	FC Academica Clinceni	34	11	6	17	47	69	39
15	SS Politehnica Timişoara	34	10	8	16	48	59	38
16	CSM Metalul Reşiţa	34	6	3	25	35	77	21
17	CSM Râmnicu Vâlcea	33	4	6	23	16	67	18
18	CS Unirea Tărlungeni	33	2	5	26	15	78	1
19	ACS Berceni	0	0	0	0	0	0	0
20	CS Şoimii Pâncota	0	0	0	0	0	0	0

NB CS Şoimii Pâncota were excluded after round 13 and ACS Berceni withdrew after round 15 – all of their matches were annulled; CSM Râmnicu Vâlcea & CS Unirea Tărlungeni withdrew after round 21 – their matches from round 18 onwards were awarded as 0-3 defeats; CS Unirea Tărlungeni – 10 pts deducted.

Promotion play-offs

(12/06/17 & 15/06/17)
Poli Timişoara 2-1 Bătrâna Doamnă
Bătrâna Doamnă 1-3 Poli Timişoara
(Poli Timişoara 5-2)

DOMESTIC CUP

Cupa României 2016/17

FIRST ROUND

(25/10/16)
Metalosport Galaţi 0-1 Luceafărul
Râmnicu Vâlcea 0-1 CFR Cluj
Sepsi 0-1 U Craiova *(aet)*
SS Poli Timişoara 0-3 Pandurii

(26/10/16)
Academica 1-5 Voluntari
Cetate 1-7 Gaz Metan
Chindia 0-2 ACS Poli Timişoara
Dacia Unirea 1-0 Concordia
Dinamo II 1-2 Dinamo
Metalurgistul Cugir 0-2 Politehnica Iaşi
Olimpia 1-3 Mioveni
Unirea Tărlungeni 0-5 Tîrgu Mureş

(27/10/16)
Afumaţi 1-0 Botoşani
Baloteşti 0-4 Viitorul
Foresta 1-2 Steaua
Nuova Mama Mia 0-1 Astra

SECOND ROUND

(13/12/16)
Afumaţi 0-3 ACS Poli Timişoara
CFR Cluj 2-0 Politehnica Iaşi
Dacia Unirea 0-2 U Craiova

(14/12/16)
Mioveni 1-1 Steaua *(aet; 5-4 on pens)*
Voluntari 3-0 Tîrgu Mureş

(15/12/16)
Gaz Metan 1-3 Dinamo
Luceafărul 1-3 Astra
Viitorul 3-0 Pandurii

QUARTER-FINALS

(28/03/17)
ACS Poli Timişoara 0-0 CFR Cluj *(aet; 6-5 on pens)*

(29/03/17)
Mioveni 1-2 Voluntari *(Neagoe 35; Cernat 13, Deac 90+1)*
U Craiova 0-0 Dinamo *(aet; 6-5 on pens)*

(30/03/17)
Viitorul 1-3 Astra *(Morar 61; Seto 40, Budescu 44p, Florea 85)*

SEMI-FINALS

(25/04/17 & 17/05/17)
Astra 4-1 ACS Poli Timişoara *(Budescu 4p, 52p, Săpunaru 36, Ioniţă 76; Popovici 9)*
ACS Poli Timişoara 0-3 Astra *(Budescu 40, Buş 49, Nicoară 83)*
(Astra 7-1)

(27/04/17 & 18/05/17)
U Craiova 0-1 Voluntari *(Marinescu 89p)*
Voluntari 0-0 U Craiova
(Voluntari 1-0)

FINAL

(27/05/17)
Ilie Oană, Ploiesti
FC VOLUNTARI 1 *(Marinescu 83p)*
FC ASTRA GIURGIU 1 *(Ioniţă 36)*
(aet; 5-3 on pens)
Referee: *Kovacs*
VOLUNTARI: *Balauru, Maftei, Balaur, Cazan (Achim 63), Acsinte, Novac (Voduţ 76), Lazăr, Căpăţână, Marinescu, Popadiuc (Ivanovici 46), Bălan*
ASTRA: *Lung, Stan, Săpunaru, Fabrício, Júnior Morais, Lovin (Piţian 79), Seto, Ioniţă, Budescu, Filipe Teixeira (Nicoară 62), Buş (Florea 75)*

Voluntari won the Romanian Cup after a penalty shoot-out success in the final against Astra

RUSSIA

Russian Football Union (RFS)

Address	Ulitsa Narodnaya 7 RU-115172 Moskva
Tel	+7 495 926 1300
Fax	+7 495 201 1303
E-mail	info@rfs.ru
Website	rfs.ru

President	Vitali Mutko
General secretary	Aleksandr Alaev
Media officer	Igor Vladimirov
Year of formation	1912

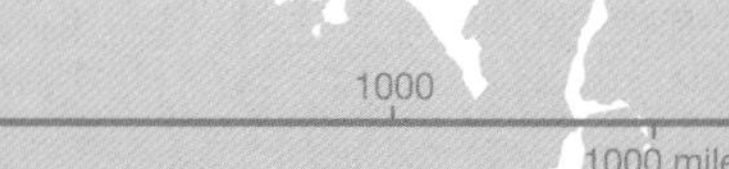

PREMIER-LIGA CLUBS

 1 **FC Amkar Perm**

 2 **FC Anji**

 3 **PFC Arsenal Tula**

 4 **PFC CSKA Moskva**

 5 **FC Krasnodar**

 6 **PFC Krylya Sovetov Samara**

 7 **FC Lokomotiv Moskva**

 8 **FC Orenburg**

 9 **FC Rostov**

 10 **FC Rubin**

 11 **FC Spartak Moskva**

 12 **FC Terek Grozny**
NB Renamed FC Akhmat Grozny for 2017/18 season

 13 **FC Tom Tomsk**

 14 **FC Ufa**

 15 **FC Ural Sverdlovsk Oblast**

 16 **FC Zenit**

PROMOTED CLUBS

  17 **FC Dinamo Moskva**

  18 **FC Tosno**

 19 **FC SKA-Khabarovsk**

Spartak reignite their flame

Spartak Moskva's bid to become Russian champions for the tenth time finally ended after a 16-year wait in 2016/17 as relatively unknown Italian coach Massimo Carrera steered the country's best-supported club to the Premier-Liga title.

Recent champions CSKA Moskva and FC Zenit both ended the season empty-handed as Lokomotiv matched CSKA's record of seven Russian Cup wins, while fans of the Russian national team found little reason for optimism a year in advance of the 2018 FIFA World Cup.

First league title in 16 years for popular Moscow club

Lokomotiv land record-equalling seventh Russian Cup

National side fail to convince in World Cup rehearsal

Domestic league

Spartak began the 2016/17 season in turmoil, with coach Dmitri Alenichev stepping down after just one league game following a shock early exit from Europe, but they ended it in triumph as Carrera, a former Juventus and Italy defender who had only just arrived at the club as Alenichev's assistant, took on the senior position and masterminded the Red-and-Whites' return to the Premier-Liga pinnacle for the first time since 2001.

Spartak had won nine of the first ten Russian titles, from 1992-2001, but, despite remaining the most popular team in the land, had been usurped in the decade and a half since their last league triumph by CSKA and Zenit. Another battle royale between that pair was anticipated in 2016/17, but with Carrera at the controls Spartak led the table virtually from start to finish, their consistency of performance eroding the challenge from both Moscow and St Petersburg and enabling them to clinch the title with three games to spare.

At the winter break Spartak held a five-point lead over Zenit, now coached by long-time Shakhtar Donetsk boss Mircea Lucescu. Defending champions CSKA were a further three points back, which, combined with disappointment in Europe, led to their coach of seven years, Leonid Slutski, announcing his resignation. The Army Men would lose only once under Slutski's replacement, Viktor Goncharenko (summoned from FC Ufa), but that would be in a crucial match at home to Spartak, the 2-1 defeat all but dashing their hopes of a fourth title in five years.

Zenit's bid to regain the title had also effectively ground to a halt after a 2-1 defeat by Spartak a fortnight earlier, and it was when Lucescu's men lost again, 1-0 against Terek Grozny in their majestic new Krestovsky stadium on 7 May, that Spartak's long-awaited title triumph was officially confirmed, Carrera's team having beaten Tom Tomsk 1-0 at home the previous day to open up a ten-point lead at the top.

The champions ended the season with 22 victories in their 30 matches, which was four more than both CSKA and Zenit. No fewer than 11 of those wins were achieved with a 1-0 scoreline, which spoke volumes not only about the solidity of the Spartak defence but also about the team's ability to defend slender leads. Those were qualities their coach had acquired both as a Serie A defender and an assistant coach to Antonio Conte with Juventus and Italy, and Spartak were more than delighted to be able to accommodate them.

That Spartak scored just 46 goals – and never more than three in any game on Carrera's watch – was neither here nor there. They functioned effectively as a unit and won the matches that mattered, including 14 of their 15 at home. Every other team in the division was beaten at least once, with CSKA being conquered in both derbies for the first time since 1999, the 3-1 home win in October attracting a season-high attendance of 44,884 to the Otkrytiye Arena. Key personnel included Russian international midfielders Denis Glushakov and Roman Zobnin, new Brazilian signing Fernando and ace Dutch attacker Quincy Promes, who provided 12 goals and ten assists.

Spartak's title win secured access to the 2017/18 UEFA Champions League group stage, and it was CSKA who claimed the second spot, in the third qualifying round, after they convincingly won their last four matches to edge Zenit into third place by a point. While CSKA boasted the Premier-Liga's best defence, conceding just 15 goals and keeping 20 clean sheets, Zenit were the only team in a low-scoring league to find the net 50 times, with totemic centre-forward Artem Dzyuba striking 13 of those goals and classy Brazilian newcomer Giuliano adding another eight. Coach Lucescu decided nevertheless that after 12 seasons with Shakhtar, one would suffice at Zenit, so he left – to be replaced by Carrera's compatriot, ex-Manchester City manager Roberto Mancini.

FC Krasnodar finished fourth for the second season in a row, thanks once again to the golden boot-winning contribution of their Russian international striker Fedor Smolov, who scored 18 goals. They finished one point ahead of both Terek and 2015/16 runners-up FC Rostov, the latter's hopes of a repeat performance helped by a second successive season without a home defeat but hindered by away-day blues and a penchant for goalless draws, of which they registered nine, including five in a row during the early spring. Tom, Krylya Sovetov Samara and Arsenal Tula were all relegated, which meant another three teams came up – Dinamo Moskva, after just one season away, FC Tosno and, after a play-off, SKA-Khabarovsk from Russia's far east, 6140km distant from Moscow as the crow flies or, for the more adventurous, 8370km away by road.

Domestic cup

Veteran ex-Russia coach Yuri Semin returned for a fourth spell at Lokomotiv Moskva in August 2016, replacing Igor Cherevchenko, and although he could lift the Railwaymen no higher than eighth in the Premier-Liga, he guided them to victory in the Russian Cup for the fifth time. It was Lokomotiv's seventh triumph in total, equalling the record number that CSKA had set in 2013, and it came about thanks to a stormy 2-0 victory over Ural Sverdlovsk Oblast in Sochi, the match finishing in a brawl that resulted in both teams being reduced to nine men.

Late goals from Russian internationals Igor Denisov and Aleksei Miranchuk earned Semin's team the victory they sought over a Ural side that had reached their first final thanks to a couple of penalty shoot-out wins over Amkar Perm and Krasnodar in previous rounds. For Spartak, CSKA and holders Zenit, on the other hand, the competition ended much earlier than anticipated, with Carrera's team biting the dust half a world away in Khabarovsk.

Europe

For the fourth year in a row CSKA competed in the UEFA Champions League group stage but finished bottom of their section, with goalkeeper Igor Akinfeev yet again starting and finishing all six games and failing to keep a clean sheet. CSKA's efforts were eclipsed by competition debutants Rostov, who eliminated experienced European campaigners Anderlecht and Ajax in the qualifying phase before beating Bayern München 3-2 at home and drawing 0-0 at PSV Eindhoven to finish third in their group and transfer to the UEFA Europa League, where they overpowered Sparta Praha before narrowly succumbing to eventual winners Manchester United in the round of 16.

Christian Noboa (No16) sets off on a celebratory run after scoring a free-kick to help his Rostov side beat Bayern München 3-2 in the UEFA Champions League

Spartak crashed horribly to AEK Larnaca in the UEFA Europa League third qualifying round, prompting Alenichev's resignation, but Krasnodar, led by ex-Internazionale midfielder Igor Shalimov, knocked out Nice, Salzburg and Fenerbahçe before coming to grief against Celta Vigo in the round of 16. In the process they outlasted Zenit, who won their first five group games and possessed the competition's joint-top scorer in eight-goal Giuliano but conceded a fatal late goal at home to Anderlecht in the second leg of the round of 32.

National team

As hosts of the 2018 FIFA World Cup, Russia also got to stage the 2017 FIFA Confederations Cup, but while the eight-team competition, staged at four World Cup stadiums – in Moscow, St Petersburg, Kazan and Sochi – proved to be an administrative success, it confirmed the fears of many locals that the Russian national team had made few, if any, strides forward since their inglorious early exit from UEFA EURO 2016.

With Slutski having stepped down after the team's misadventure in France, the onus was on new coach Stanislav Cherchesov, appointed in August 2016, to build a World Cup-worthy national side in less than two years. Halfway into that task the ex-goalkeeper's balance sheet of 12 games, four wins, three draws and five defeats did not inspire optimism – especially as four of the defeats came on home soil, including their second and third group games at the Confederations Cup, against Portugal and Mexico respectively, which, despite an opening 2-0 win against New Zealand, ended the hosts' interest in the competition.

A similar outcome at the World Cup would be disastrous, but on the evidence of the team's June 2017 fixtures, Russia's wholly home-based squad is handicapped by a shortage of true international quality. Goalkeeper Akinfeev – who earned his 100th cap against Portugal – has the pedigree, but only Glushakov, Smolov and midfielder Aleksandr Samedov – who transferred from Lokomotiv to Spartak in mid-season – performed consistently well at the Confederations Cup. Many more will need to do so if Russia are to fulfil their objective and make a nation proud and happy in the summer of 2018.

DOMESTIC SEASON AT A GLANCE

Premier-Liga 2016/17 final table

			Home					Away					Total					
		Pld	W	D	L	F	A	W	D	L	F	A	W	D	L	F	A	Pts
1	**FC Spartak Moskva**	**30**	**14**	**0**	**1**	**26**	**6**	**8**	**3**	**4**	**20**	**21**	**22**	**3**	**5**	**46**	**27**	**69**
2	PFC CSKA Moskva	30	9	5	1	31	6	9	3	3	16	9	18	8	4	47	15	62
3	FC Zenit	30	11	3	1	28	9	7	4	4	22	10	18	7	5	50	19	61
4	FC Krasnodar	30	8	6	1	26	11	4	7	4	14	11	12	13	5	40	22	49
5	FC Terek Grozny	30	8	2	5	22	16	6	4	5	16	19	14	6	10	38	35	48
6	FC Rostov	30	11	4	0	24	4	2	5	8	12	14	13	9	8	36	18	48
7	FC Ufa	30	6	4	5	12	14	6	3	6	10	11	12	7	11	22	25	43
8	FC Lokomotiv Moskva	30	4	7	4	20	14	6	5	4	19	13	10	12	8	39	27	42
9	FC Rubin	30	6	4	5	15	12	4	4	7	15	22	10	8	12	30	34	38
10	FC Amkar Perm	30	7	4	4	13	9	1	7	7	12	20	8	11	11	25	29	35
11	FC Ural Sverdlovsk Oblast	30	6	2	7	13	16	2	4	9	11	28	8	6	16	24	44	30
12	FC Anji	30	3	6	6	14	18	4	3	8	10	20	7	9	14	24	38	30
13	FC Orenburg	30	6	5	4	16	11	1	4	10	9	25	7	9	14	25	36	30
14	PFC Arsenal Tula	30	7	4	4	13	11	0	3	12	5	29	7	7	16	18	40	28
15	PFC Krylya Sovetov Samara	30	3	7	5	19	20	3	3	9	12	19	6	10	14	31	39	28
16	FC Tom Tomsk	30	3	2	10	10	33	0	3	12	7	31	3	5	22	17	64	14

European qualification 2017/18

Champion: FC Spartak Moskva (group stage)
PFC CSKA Moskva (third qualifying round)

Cup winner: FC Lokomotiv Moskva (group stage)
FC Zenit (third qualifying round)
FC Krasnodar (third qualifying round)

Top scorer Fedor Smolov (Krasnodar), 18 goals
Relegated clubs FC Tom Tomsk, PFC Krylya Sovetov Samara, FC Orenburg
Promoted clubs FC Dinamo Moskva, FC Tosno, FC SKA-Khabarovsk
Cup final FC Lokomotiv Moskva 2-0 FC Ural Sverdlovsk Oblast

Player of the season

Denis Glushakov
(FC Spartak Moskva)

A Spartak player since 2013, when he joined from city rivals Lokomotiv, Glushakov's fourth season at the club was unquestionably his best, a catalogue of dogged and dominant midfield displays from the 30-year-old epitomising the team's victorious return to Premier-Liga prominence. Generally renowned for his defensive and destructive capabilities, the Russian international became bolder in attack under new Spartak coach Massimo Carrera and scored eight league goals, including vital strikes in both big games against Muscovite rivals CSKA.

Newcomer of the season

Fedor Chalov
(PFC CSKA Moskva)

Short of a consistent marksman up front, CSKA increasingly turned to academy prospect Chalov as the 2016/17 season progressed, and they were rewarded with half a dozen goals from the vibrant 19-year-old striker. The Russian youth international was especially prominent during the closing weeks when CSKA won their last four games to secure the Premier-Liga runners-up spot and qualification for the 2017/18 UEFA Champions League. Under contract with CSKA until 2020, his talent has already reportedly been flagged up for further appraisal by a number of foreign scouts.

Team of the season
(4-4-2)

Coach: **Carrera** *(Spartak)*

NATIONAL TEAM

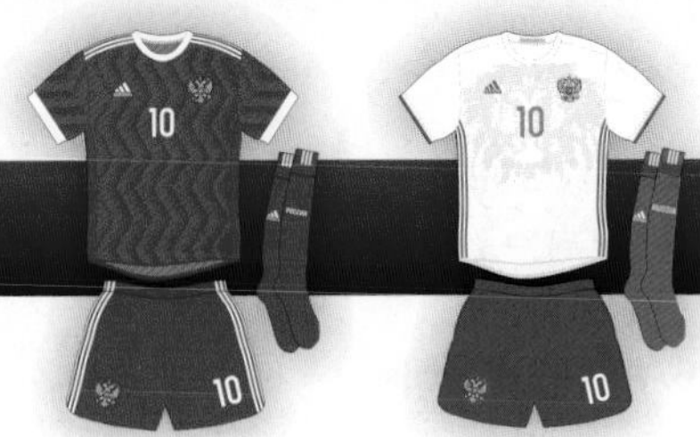

International honours*
UEFA European Championship (1) 1960

International tournament appearances*
FIFA World Cup (10) 1958 (qtr-finals), 1962 (qtr-finals), 1966 (4th), 1970 (qtr-finals), 1982 (2nd phase), 1986 (2nd round), 1990, 1994, 2002, 2014
UEFA European Championship (11) 1960 (Winners), 1964 (runners-up), 1968 (4th), 1972 (runners-up), 1988 (runners-up), 1992, 1996, 2004, 2008 (semi-finals), 2012, 2016

Top five all-time caps
Sergei Ignashevich (120); Viktor Onopko (113); Oleh Blokhin (112); **Igor Akinfeev** & **Vasili Berezutski** (101)

Top five all-time goals
Oleh Blokhin (42); Aleksandr Kerzhakov (30); Oleh Protasov (29); Vladimir Beschastnykh & Valentin Ivanov (26)

(before 1992 as USSR; 1992 as CIS)*

Results 2016/17

31/08/16	Turkey	A	Antalya	D	0-0	
06/09/16	Ghana	H	Moscow	W	1-0	*Smolov (20)*
09/10/16	Costa Rica	H	Krasnodar	L	3-4	*Samedov (31), Dzyuba (48, 61)*
10/11/16	Qatar	A	Doha	L	1-2	*Samedov (5p)*
15/11/16	Romania	H	Grozny	W	1-0	*Ozdoev (90+3)*
24/03/17	Ivory Coast	H	Krasnodar	L	0-2	
28/03/17	Belgium	H	Sochi	D	3-3	*Vasin (3), Miranchuk (74), Bukharov (90+2)*
05/06/17	Hungary	A	Budapest	W	3-0	*Smolov (20), Eppel (40og), Poloz (89)*
09/06/17	Chile	H	Moscow	D	1-1	*Vasin (67)*
17/06/17	New Zealand (CC)	H	St Petersburg	W	2-0	*Boxall (31og), Smolov (69)*
21/06/17	Portugal (CC)	H	Moscow	L	0-1	
24/06/17	Mexico (CC)	H	Kazan	L	1-2	*Samedov (25)*

Appearances 2016/17

Coach: Stanislav Cherchesov	02/09/63		Tur	Gha	Crc	Qat	Rou	Civ	Bel	Hun	Chi	NZL	POR	MEX	Caps	Goals
Igor Akinfeev	08/04/86	CSKA Moskva	G	G		G58	G	G	G	G	G	G	G	G	101	-
Ivan Novoseltsev	25/08/91	Zenit	D				s84								5	-
Vasili Berezutski	20/06/82	CSKA Moskva	D	D	D										101	5
Fedor Kudryashov	05/04/87	Rostov	D67	s79		D	D84	D	D	D	D81	D	D83	D	11	-
Aleksandr Samedov	19/07/84	Lokomotiv Moskva /Spartak Moskva	M	M69	M88	M85	M	M	M	M75	M	M	M	M	42	6
Magomed Ozdoev	05/11/92	Rubin /Terek	M79	s64	s88		s46		s17 /72						11	1
Aleksei Miranchuk	17/10/95	Lokomotiv Moskva	M55	s58			M61	s80	s72	s84	M60	s90			10	2
Dmitri Tarasov	18/03/87	Lokomotiv Moskva	M61							s88		s77			6	1
Oleg Shatov	29/07/90	Zenit	M	s82	M56										28	2
Yuri Zhirkov	20/08/83	Zenit	M	M82	s81		M46	M71		M88	s73	M	M	M 68*	78	2
Fedor Smolov	09/02/90	Krasnodar	A79	A88						A84	A86	A90	A	A78	24	8
Aleksandr Yerokhin	13/10/89	Rostov	s55		M81	M53	s68	M	M76	s33	s66	M77	s46	M70	11	-
Yuri Gazinski	20/07/89	Krasnodar	s61	M64	M	s53		s78							5	-
Roman Neustädter	18/02/88	Fenerbahçe (TUR)	s67						D						5	-
Maksim Kanunnikov	14/07/91	Rubin	s79	s69	s89			s75	A46					s78	12	-
Roman Zobnin	11/02/94	Spartak Moskva	s79	M	M	M	M	M	M	M33					9	-
Roman Shishkin	27/01/87	Lokomotiv Moskva /Krasnodar		D		s46				s81	D		M46		16	-
Andrei Semyonov	24/03/89	Terek		D			D	D							6	-
Sergei Petrov	02/01/91	Krasnodar		D79	D										2	-
Alan Dzagoev	17/06/90	CSKA Moskva		M58					M17						51	9
Dmitri Poloz	12/07/91	Rostov		s88	s56	A46	s61	A80	A62	s63	s60	A64	s68	s64	13	1
Soslan Dzhanaev	13/03/87	Rostov			G										1	-
Ilya Kutepov	29/07/93	Spartak Moskva			D	D	D	D							4	-
Igor Smolnikov	08/08/88	Zenit			D					s75	D66			s70	21	-
Artem Dzyuba	22/08/88	Zenit			A89										22	11
Viktor Vasin	06/10/88	Ufa /CSKA Moskva				D			D	D	D	D	D	D	9	2
Denis Glushakov	27/01/87	Spartak Moskva				M	M		s76	M	M	M	M	M	54	5
Dmitri Kombarov	22/01/87	Spartak Moskva				M81		s71	M		D73		M68		45	2
Aleksandr Kokorin	19/03/91	Zenit				A	A								44	12
Stanislav Kritsyuk	01/12/90	Krasnodar				s58									2	-
Kirill Panchenko	16/10/89	Dinamo Moskva				s81									1	-
Pavel Mogilevets	25/01/93	Zenit				s85	M68								3	-
Aleksandr Golovin	30/05/96	CSKA Moskva						M78	s62	M	M	M	M	M	15	2
Aleksandr Bukharov	12/03/85	Rostov						A75	s46	A63	s86	s64	s83	A64	9	1
Georgi Dzhikia	21/11/93	Spartak Moskva								D81		D	D	D	4	-
Ruslan Kambolov	01/01/90	Rubin									s81				2	-

EUROPE

PFC CSKA Moskva

Group E
Match 1 - Bayer 04 Leverkusen (GER)
A 2-2 *Dzagoev (36), Eremenko (38)*
Akinfeev, Mário Fernandes, Wernbloom, Ignashevich, Traoré (Strandberg 73), Dzagoev, Ionov (Milanov 78), Golovin (A Berezutski 90+2), V Berezutski, Eremenko, Schennikov. Coach: Leonid Slutski (RUS)
Match 2 - Tottenham Hotspur FC (ENG)
H 0-1
Akinfeev, Mário Fernandes, Wernbloom, Ignashevich, Tošić (Natcho 72), Milanov, Traoré, Golovin, V Berezutski (A Berezutski 46), Eremenko, Schennikov. Coach: Leonid Slutski (RUS)
Match 3 - AS Monaco FC (FRA)
H 1-1 *Traoré (34)*
Akinfeev, Mário Fernandes, Wernbloom, Ignashevich, Tošić (Gordyushenko 75), Traoré (Strandberg 84), Ionov (Milanov 46), Golovin, V Berezutski, Schennikov, Natcho. Coach: Leonid Slutski (RUS)
Match 4 - AS Monaco FC (FRA)
A 0-3
Akinfeev, Mário Fernandes, Wernbloom, Ignashevich, A Berezutski, Tošić (Milanov 71), Ionov, Golovin, Strandberg (Traoré 63), Schennikov (Nababkin 90), Natcho. Coach: Leonid Slutski (RUS)
Match 5 - Bayer 04 Leverkusen (GER)
H 1-1 *Natcho (76p)*
Akinfeev, Mário Fernandes, Wernbloom, A Berezutski, Milanov, Dzagoev (Traoré 83), Golovin, V Berezutski, Schennikov, Chalov (Strandberg 90), Natcho. Coach: Leonid Slutski (RUS)
Match 6 - Tottenham Hotspur FC (ENG)
A 1-3 *Dzagoev (33)*
Akinfeev, A Berezutski, Tošić (Gordyushenko 71), Milanov, Traoré (Strandberg 79), Dzagoev, Nababkin, Golovin (Chalov 46), V Berezutski, Schennikov, Natcho. Coach: Leonid Slutski (RUS)

FC Rostov

Third qualifying round - RSC Anderlecht (BEL)
H 2-2 *Ezatolahi (16), Poloz (60p)*
Dzhanaev, Kalachev, Ezatolahi (Terentyev 82), Poloz (Kireev 74), Bukharov (Azmoun 56), Bastos, Noboa, Novoseltsev, Kudryashov, César Navas, Gatcan. Coach: Kurban Berdyev (RUS)
A 2-0 *Noboa (28), Azmoun (47)*
Dzhanaev, Kalachev, Terentyev, Bukharov (Ezatolahi 73), Bastos, Noboa, Azmoun (Poloz 57; Yerokhin 90+2), Novoseltsev, Kudryashov, César Navas, Gatcan. Coach: Kurban Berdyev (RUS)

Play-offs - AFC Ajax (NED)
A 1-1 *Noboa (13)*
Dzhanaev, Kalachev, Terentyev, Poloz (Bayramyan 87), Bukharov (Azmoun 57), Noboa, Novoseltsev, Kudryashov, César Navas, Gatcan, Yerokhin (Ezatolahi 67). Coach: Dmitri Kirichenko (RUS)
H 4-1 *Azmoun (34), Yerokhin (52), Noboa (60), Poloz (66)*
Dzhanaev, Kalachev, Terentyev, Poloz (Doumbia 87), Noboa, Azmoun (Bukharov 73), Novoseltsev, Kudryashov, César Navas, Gatcan, Yerokhin (Ezatolahi 79). Coach: Dmitri Kirichenko (RUS)
Red card: Kudryashov 83

Group D
Match 1 - FC Bayern München (GER)
A 0-5
Dzhanaev, Kalachev, Granat, Terentyev, Poloz (Doumbia 46), Noboa, Azmoun (Prepeliţă 64), Mevlja, César Navas, Gatcan, Yerokhin. Coach: Ivan Daniliants (AUT)
Match 2 - PSV Eindhoven (NED)
H 2-2 *Poloz (8, 37)*
Dzhanaev, Kalachev, Granat, Terentyev, Poloz (Prepeliţă 90), Noboa, Azmoun (Doumbia 77), Mevlja, César Navas, Gatcan, Yerokhin. Coach: Ivan Daniliants (AUT)
Match 3 - Club Atlético de Madrid (ESP)
H 0-1
Dzhanaev, Granat, Poloz (Doumbia 77), Kireev, Noboa, Azmoun (Prepeliţă 75), Mevlja, Kudryashov, César Navas, Gatcan, Yerokhin. Coach: Ivan Daniliants (AUT)
Match 4 - Club Atlético de Madrid (ESP)
A 1-2 *Azmoun (30)*
Dzhanaev, Kalachev (Terentyev 73), Granat, Poloz, Noboa, Azmoun (Doumbia 70), Mevlja, Kudryashov, César Navas, Gatcan, Yerokhin (Prepeliţă 45+3). Coach: Ivan Daniliants (AUT)
Match 5 - FC Bayern München (GER)
H 3-2 *Azmoun (44), Poloz (50p), Noboa (67)*
Dzhanaev, Kalachev (Terentyev 87), Granat, Poloz (Ezatolahi 90+3), Noboa, Azmoun (Grigoryev 82), Mevlja, Kudryashov, César Navas, Gatcan, Yerokhin. Coach: Ivan Daniliants (AUT)
Match 6 - PSV Eindhoven (NED)
A 0-0
Dzhanaev, Kalachev (Terentyev 80), Granat, Poloz (Bukharov 89), Noboa, Azmoun (Ezatolahi 90), Mevlja, Kudryashov, César Navas, Gatcan, Yerokhin. Coach: Ivan Daniliants (AUT)

Round of 32 - AC Sparta Praha (CZE)
H 4-0 *Mevlja (15), Poloz (38), Noboa (40), Azmoun (68)*
Medvedev, Kalachev, Granat, Poloz (Dević 74), Bukharov (Azmoun 67), Noboa, Mevlja, Kudryashov, César Navas, Gatcan, Yerokhin (Prepeliţă 83). Coach: Ivan Daniliants (AUT)
A 1-1 *Poloz (13)*
Medvedev, Kalachev, Granat (Terentyev 70), Poloz, Bukharov (Azmoun 46), Noboa, Mevlja, Kudryashov, César Navas, Gatcan (Prepeliţă 46), Yerokhin. Coach: Ivan Daniliants (AUT)

Round of 16 - Manchester United FC (ENG)
H 1-1 *Bukharov (53)*
Medvedev, Kalachev, Granat (Terentyev 18), Poloz, Bukharov (Azmoun 74), Noboa, Mevlja, Kudryashov, César Navas, Gatcan, Yerokhin. Coach: Ivan Daniliants (AUT)
A 0-1
Medvedev, Terentyev, Poloz, Noboa, Bayramyan (Kireev 81), Azmoun (Bukharov 61), Mevlja, Prepeliţă (Dević 79), Kudryashov, César Navas, Yerokhin. Coach: Ivan Daniliants (AUT)

FC Zenit

Group D
Match 1 - Maccabi Tel-Aviv FC (ISR)
A 4-3 *Kokorin (77), Maurício (84), Giuliano (86), Djordjević (90+2)*
Lodygin, Criscito, Giuliano, Kokorin, A Kerzhakov (Djordjević 61), Luís Neto, Smolnikov, Javi García (Maurício 71), Witsel, Mak, Zhirkov (Novoseltsev 90+4). Coach: Mircea Lucescu (ROU)
Match 2 - AZ Alkmaar (NED)
H 5-0 *Kokorin (26, 59), Giuliano (48), Criscito (66p), Shatov (80)*
Lodygin, Criscito, Lombaerts, Giuliano, Kokorin, Luís Neto, Smolnikov, Javi García (Maurício 63), Dzyuba (Shatov 63), Witsel, Mak (Djordjević 67). Coach: Mircea Lucescu (ROU)
Match 3 - Dundalk FC (IRL)
A 2-1 *Mak (71), Giuliano (77)*
Lodygin, Anyukov, Criscito, Lombaerts, Giuliano, Luís Neto, Shatov (Kokorin 61), Javi García (Maurício 71), Dzyuba, Witsel, Mak (Djordjević 78). Coach: Mircea Lucescu (ROU)
Match 4 - Dundalk FC (IRL)
H 2-1 *Giuliano (42, 78)*
M Kerzhakov, Anyukov, Criscito, Lombaerts (Zhirkov 89), Giuliano, Maurício, Kokorin, A Kerzhakov (Djordjević 90+2), Luís Neto, Shatov (Mak 68), Witsel. Coach: Mircea Lucescu (ROU)
Match 5 - Maccabi Tel-Aviv FC (ISR)
H 2-0 *Kokorin (44), A Kerzhakov (90+1)*
Lodygin, Novoseltsev, Criscito, Giuliano, Kokorin (A Kerzhakov 66), Luís Neto, Javi García, Witsel, Mak, Djordjević (Dzyuba 46), Zhirkov (Lombaerts 75). Coach: Mircea Lucescu (ROU)
Match 6 - AZ Alkmaar (NED)
A 2-3 *Giuliano (58), Wuytens (80og)*
Lodygin, Anyukov, Novoseltsev, Lombaerts, Giuliano, Javi García (Yusupov 60), Dzyuba, Witsel, Mak, Djordjević (Kokorin 46), Zhirkov. Coach: Mircea Lucescu (ROU)

Round of 32 - RSC Anderlecht (BEL)
A 0-2
Lodygin, Criscito, Giuliano (Yusupov 80), Kokorin (Danny 71), Luís Neto, Shatov (Mak 65), Javi García, Dzyuba, Hernâni, Ivanović, Zhirkov. Coach: Mircea Lucescu (ROU)
H 3-1 *Giuliano (24, 78), Dzyuba (72)*
Lodygin, Anyukov, Criscito, Giuliano, Maurício, Kokorin, Danny (Mak 89), Luís Neto, Javi García, Dzyuba, Zhirkov. Coach: Mircea Lucescu (ROU)

FC Krasnodar

Third qualifying round - Birkirkara FC (MLT)
A 3-0 *Granqvist (45+1), Smolov (75p), Laborde (89)*
Kritsyuk, Izmailov, Strandberg, Torbinski, Granqvist, Gazinski, Ari (Wanderson 76), Akhmedov (Joãozinho 83), Pereyra (Laborde 64), Jędrzejczyk, Smolov. Coach: Oleg Kononov (RUS)
H 3-1 *Kouassi (15), Joãozinho (37), Laborde (38)*
Sinitsin, Strandberg, Martynovich, Torbinski (Pereyra 79), Wanderson, Bystrov, Laborde (Ari 40), Joãozinho, Kouassi, Kaboré (Gazinski 69), Petrov. Coach: Oleg Kononov (RUS)

Play-offs - FK Partizani (ALB)
H 4-0 *Joãozinho (18p), Smolov (27), Jędrzejczyk (45), Krasniqi (73og)*
Kritsyuk, Martynovich, Granqvist, Ari, Akhmedov (Kouassi 66), Kaleshin, Joãozinho, Pereyra (Gazinski 61), Jędrzejczyk, Kaboré, Smolov (Torbinski 76). Coach: Oleg Kononov (RUS)
A 0-0
Sinitsin, Martynovich, Torbinski, Granqvist, Ari (Vorobyev 64), Podberyozkin (Jędrzejczyk 46), Bystrov, Joãozinho, Pereyra (Akhmedov 46), Kouassi, Petrov. Coach: Oleg Kononov (RUS)

Group I
Match 1 - FC Salzburg (AUT)
A 1-0 *Joãozinho (37)*
Kritsyuk, Naldo, Granqvist, Akhmedov (Gazinski 62), Podberyozkin (Laborde 60), Joãozinho (Kaleshin 74), Kouassi, Jędrzejczyk, Kaboré, Smolov, Petrov. Coach: Igor Shalimov (RUS)
Red card: Petrov 71
Match 2 - OGC Nice (FRA)
H 5-2 *Smolov (22), Joãozinho (33, 65p), Ari (86, 90+3)*
Kritsyuk, Naldo, Torbinski, Granqvist, Akhmedov (Gazinski 59), Podberyozkin (Laborde 74), Joãozinho, Kouassi, Jędrzejczyk, Kaboré, Smolov (Ari 29). Coach: Igor Shalimov (RUS)
Match 3 - FC Schalke 04 (GER)
H 0-1
Kritsyuk, Martynovich, Granqvist, Ari, Akhmedov (Mamaev 74), Podberyozkin (Laborde 67), Joãozinho, Kouassi (Gazinski 55), Jędrzejczyk, Kaboré, Petrov. Coach: Igor Shalimov (RUS)
Match 4 - FC Schalke 04 (GER)
A 0-2
Kritsyuk, Naldo, Granqvist, Akhmedov (Izmailov 62), Podberyozkin (Laborde 12), Joãozinho, Pereyra, Kouassi, Jędrzejczyk (Kaleshin 75), Kaboré, Petrov. Coach: Igor Shalimov (RUS)
Match 5 - FC Salzburg (AUT)
H 1-1 *Smolov (85)*
Kritsyuk, Naldo, Torbinski, Granqvist, Akhmedov , Kaleshin, Joãozinho (Izmailov 73), Pereyra (Laborde 58), Kouassi (Gazinski 46), Kaboré, Smolov. Coach: Igor Shalimov (RUS)
Match 6 - OGC Nice (FRA)
A 1-2 *Smolov (52)*
Sinitsin, Naldo, Martynovich, Torbinski (Kaleshin 65), Granqvist, Gazinski, Akhmedov , Joãozinho, Kouassi, Jędrzejczyk, Smolov. Coach: Igor Shalimov (RUS)
Red card: Granqvist 61

Round of 32 - Fenerbahçe SK (TUR)
H 1-0 *Claesson (4)*
Kritsyuk, Naldo, Martynovich, Gazinski, Podberyozkin (Pereyra 69), Ramírez, Wanderson (Laborde 65), Claesson, Kaleshin, Kaboré, Smolov. Coach: Igor Shalimov (RUS)
A 1-1 *Smolov (7)*
Kritsyuk, Naldo, Granqvist, Gazinski, Podberyozkin (Pereyra 79), Ramírez, Wanderson (Laborde 64), Claesson, Kaleshin, Kaboré, Smolov. Coach: Igor Shalimov (RUS)

Round of 16 - RC Celta de Vigo (ESP)
A 1-2 *Claesson (56)*
Kritsyuk, Naldo, Martynovich, Granqvist, Gazinski, Podberyozkin (Mamaev 75), Ramírez, Wanderson (Laborde 78), Zhigulev (Torbinski 83), Claesson, Pereyra. Coach: Igor Shalimov (RUS)
H 0-2
Sinitsin, Naldo, Martynovich, Granqvist, Gazinski, Podberyozkin (Mamaev 46), Wanderson, Claesson (Joãozinho 60), Pereyra (Laborde 70), Kaboré, Petrov. Coach: Igor Shalimov (RUS)
Red card: Kaboré 86

FC Spartak Moskva

Third qualifying round - AEK Larnaca FC (CYP)
A 1-1 *Ananidze (38)*
Rebrov, Ananidze (Melkadze 72), Glushakov, Zé Luís, Promes, Bocchetti, Kutepov, Kombarov, Eschenko, Zobnin, Popov (Zuev 59). Coach: Dmitri Alenichev (RUS)
H 0-1
Rebrov, Ananidze (Glushakov 46), Zé Luís, Promes, Fernando, Bocchetti, Kutepov, Kombarov, Makeev, Eschenko (Melgarejo 90), Zobnin (Rômulo 68). Coach: Dmitri Alenichev (RUS)

DOMESTIC LEAGUE CLUB-BY-CLUB

FC Amkar Perm

1994 • Zvezda (19,500) • fc-amkar.org
Coach: Gadzhi Gadzhiev

2016

01/08	a	Rubin	D	0-0	
07/08	h	Anji	W	2-0	*Anene, Zaitsev*
15/08	a	Orenburg	D	0-0	
21/08	h	Ural	W	1-0	*Bodul*
27/08	a	Zenit	L	0-3	
10/09	h	Tom	W	1-0	*Salugin*
17/09	a	Terek	W	3-1	*Miljković, Zaitsev, Gol (p)*
26/09	h	Krylya Sovetov	D	0-0	
02/10	a	Ufa	D	1-1	*og (Stotski)*
15/10	h	Lokomotiv	D	0-0	
23/10	a	Krasnodar	L	0-1	
29/10	h	Rostov	W	1-0	*Kostyukov*
06/11	a	CSKA	D	2-2	*Dzhikia, Kostyukov*
20/11	a	Spartak	L	0-1	
26/11	h	Arsenal	W	1-0	*Prokofiev*
01/12	a	Anji	L	1-3	*Bodul*
05/12	h	Orenburg	W	3-0	*og (Žunić), Idowu, Gigolaev*

2017

05/03	a	Ural	L	0-1	
12/03	h	Zenit	W	1-0	*Gigolaev*
18/03	a	Tom	L	0-1	
02/04	h	Terek	D	1-1	*Gigolaev*
08/04	a	Krylya Sovetov	D	2-2	*Gol, Zanev (p)*
15/04	h	Ufa	D	1-1	*Bodul*
22/04	a	Lokomotiv	D	3-3	*Bodul 2 (1p), Prokofiev*
27/04	h	Krasnodar	L	0-2	
30/04	a	Rostov	L	0-1	
06/05	h	CSKA	L	0-2	
13/05	h	Spartak	L	0-1	
17/05	a	Arsenal	D	0-0	
21/05	h	Rubin	L	1-2	*Jovičić*

No	Name	Nat	DoB	Pos	Aps	(s)	Gls
11	Chuma Anene	NOR	14/05/93	A	7	(3)	1
16	Sergei Balanovich	BLR	29/08/87	M	13	(9)	
9	Darko Bodul	CRO	11/01/89	A	22	(2)	5
23	Ivan Cherenchikov		25/08/84	D	1		
6	Sekou Conde	GUI	09/06/93	D	16		
14	Georgi Dzhikia		21/11/93	D	16		1
17	Aleksei Gasilin		01/03/96	A	6	(7)	
13	Roland Gigolaev		04/01/90	M	16	(4)	3
5	Janusz Gol	POL	11/11/85	M	26		2
19	Brian Oladapo Idowu		18/05/92	D	25	(1)	1
33	Branko Jovičić	SRB	18/03/93	M	8	(12)	1
15	Dmitri Khomich		14/09/84	G	13		
25	David Khurtsidze		04/07/93	M	1	(3)	
20	Pavel Komolov		10/03/89	M	22	(6)	
27	Mikhail Kostyukov		09/08/91	M	10	(9)	2
2	Aleksandar Miljković	SRB	26/02/90	D	23	(2)	1
8	Fegor Ogude	NGA	29/07/87	M	17	(1)	
28	Stanislav Prokofiev		15/02/87	A	8	(5)	2
22	Aleksandr Salugin		23/10/88	A	3	(14)	1
57	Aleksandr Selikhov		07/04/94	G	17		
10	Alikhan Shavaev		05/01/93	M	4	(1)	
7	Anton Shynder	UKR	13/06/87	A	4	(4)	
4	Nikolai Zaitsev		01/06/89	D	23	(4)	2
3	Petar Zanev	BUL	18/10/85	D	29		1

FC Anji

1991 • Anji-Arena (26,400) • fc-anji.ru

Coach: Pavel Vrba (CZE); (06/01/17) Aleksandr Grigoryan

2016

Date		Opponent		Score	Scorers
30/07	h	CSKA	D	0-0	
07/08	a	Amkar	L	0-2	
14/08	h	Arsenal	W	1-0	*Mayevski*
19/08	a	Rubin	W	2-1	*Budkivskiy, Ebecilio*
28/08	h	Spartak	L	0-2	
10/09	a	Orenburg	D	0-0	
17/09	a	Ural	W	1-0	*Obertan*
25/09	h	Zenit	D	2-2	*Berisha (p), Boli*
01/10	a	Krylya Sovetov	L	1-2	*Berisha*
17/10	h	Terek	D	0-0	
22/10	a	Tom	W	3-0	*Iličević 2, Berisha*
30/10	h	Krasnodar	D	0-0	
05/11	a	Lokomotiv	L	0-4	
19/11	h	Ufa	L	0-1	
27/11	a	Rostov	L	0-2	
01/12	h	Amkar	W	3-1	*Budkivskiy 2, Boli (p)*
05/12	a	Arsenal	L	0-1	

2017

Date		Opponent		Score	Scorers
06/03	h	Rubin	L	0-1	
12/03	a	Spartak	L	0-1	
17/03	h	Orenburg	W	1-0	*Prudnikov*
31/03	h	Ural	L	2-3	*Prudnikov, Khubulov*
08/04	a	Zenit	D	1-1	*Yakovlev*
15/04	h	Krylya Sovetov	L	1-3	*Khubulov (p)*
22/04	a	Terek	W	1-0	*Brown Forbes*
27/04	h	Tom	D	3-3	*Khubulov 3 (3p)*
01/05	a	Krasnodar	D	0-0	
08/05	h	Lokomotiv	D	0-0	
14/05	a	Ufa	L	1-2	*Budkivskiy*
17/05	h	Rostov	L	1-2	*Prudnikov*
21/05	a	CSKA	L	0-4	

No	Name	Nat	DoB	Pos	Aps	(s)	Gls
9	Shamil Asildarov		18/05/83	A	2	(4)	
21	Maksim Batov		05/06/92	M	1	(1)	
31	Aleksandr Belenov		13/09/86	G	17		
77	Bernard Berisha	KOS	24/10/91	A	12	(5)	3
94	Yannick Boli	FRA	13/01/88	A	4	(7)	2
94	Felicio Brown Forbes	CRC	28/08/91	M	4	(1)	1
92	Sergei Bryzgalov		15/11/92	D	4	(3)	
28	Pylyp Budkivskiy	UKR	10/03/92	A	21	(8)	4
19	Pavel Dolgov		16/08/96	A	2	(3)	
14	Aslan Dudiev		15/06/90	D	1	(2)	
6	Lorenzo Ebecilio	NED	24/09/91	M	9	(4)	1
6	Saeid Ezatolahi	IRN	01/10/96	M	3	(7)	
5	Ali Gadzhibekov		06/08/89	D	8	(2)	
30	Shamil Gasanov		30/07/93	M	17	(2)	
88	Anvar Gazimagomedov		11/05/88	M	1	(5)	
17	Svyatoslav Georgievski		26/08/95	M	7	(3)	
77	Ayaz Guliev		27/11/96	M	10	(1)	
10	Ivo Iličević	CRO	14/11/86	M	10	(2)	2
10	Adlan Katsaev		20/02/88	M	9	(1)	
37	Batraz Khadartsev		23/05/93	M	2	(2)	
8	Arsen Khubulov		13/12/90	M	7	(3)	5
4	Darko Lazić	SRB	19/07/94	D	11		
18	Ivan Mayevski	BLR	05/05/88	M	13	(1)	1
4	Jonathan Mensah	GHA	13/07/90	D	6	(3)	
6	Karlen Mkrtchyan	ARM	25/11/88	M	1	(1)	
40	Amadou Moutari	NIG	19/01/94	M	1	(3)	
57	Magomed Musalov		09/02/94	D	27	(2)	
11	Gabriel Obertan	FRA	26/02/89	M	6	(2)	1
24	Sergei Parshivlyuk		18/03/89	D	19		
45	Thomas Phibel	FRA	21/05/86	D	13		
99	Aleksandr Prudnikov		26/02/89	A	5	(5)	3
15	Dmytro Shcherbak	UKR	08/12/96	M		(1)	
2	Guram Tetrashvili		02/08/88	M	10		
77	Georgi Tigiev		20/06/95	D	12	(2)	
26	Xandão	BRA	23/02/88	D	5		
91	Pavel Yakovlev		07/04/91	M	11	(3)	1
90	Cédric Yamberé	FRA	06/11/90	D	11	(1)	
1	David Yurchenko		27/03/86	G	13		
5	Aleksandr Zhirov		24/01/91	D	15		

PFC Arsenal Tula

1946 • Arsenal (20,074) • arsenaltula.ru

Coach: Sergei Pavlov; (06/10/16) Sergei Kiriakov

2016

Date		Opponent		Score	Scorers
31/07	a	Spartak	L	0-4	
06/08	h	Rubin	W	1-0	*Shevchenko*
14/08	a	Anji	L	0-1	
22/08	h	Orenburg	D	0-0	
28/08	a	Ural	D	1-1	*Vlasov*
11/09	h	Zenit	L	0-5	
17/09	a	Tom	L	0-1	
25/09	h	Terek	D	0-0	
01/10	a	Lokomotiv	D	1-1	*Brown Forbes*
16/10	h	Krasnodar	D	0-0	
21/10	a	Krylya Sovetov	D	1-1	*Brown Forbes*
30/10	h	Ufa	L	0-2	
06/11	a	Rostov	L	1-4	*Burmistrov*
18/11	h	CSKA	L	0-1	
26/11	a	Amkar	L	0-1	
30/11	a	Rubin	L	0-1	
05/12	h	Anji	W	1-0	*Belyayev*

2017

Date		Opponent		Score	Scorers
04/03	a	Orenburg	L	0-3	
10/03	h	Ural	W	2-0	*Rasic 2 (1p)*
19/03	a	Zenit	L	0-2	
01/04	h	Tom	W	3-0	*Aleksandrov, Doumbia, Kombarov*
08/04	a	Terek	L	1-3	*Rasic*
16/04	h	Lokomotiv	L	0-3	
23/04	a	Krasnodar	L	0-2	
26/04	h	Krylya Sovetov	W	2-0	*Grigalava, Rasic*
30/04	a	Ufa	L	0-1	
06/05	h	Rostov	W	1-0	*Burmistrov*
12/05	a	CSKA	L	0-3	
17/05	h	Amkar	D	0-0	
21/05	h	Spartak	W	3-0	*Rasic 2, Maksimov*

No	Name	Nat	DoB	Pos	Aps	(s)	Gls
17	Guram Adzhoyev		27/02/95	M		(1)	
4	Dmitri Aidov		10/04/82	D	2	(1)	
98	Mihail Aleksandrov	BUL	11/06/87	M	12		1
11	Hyzyr Appaev		27/01/90	A	3	(10)	
6	Maksim Belyayev		30/09/91	D	26	(1)	1
7	Kantemir Berkhamov		07/08/88	M	10	(1)	
62	Alexandru Bourceanu	ROU	24/04/85	M	13		
94	Felicio Brown Forbes	CRC	28/08/91	M	14		2
79	Danila Buranov		11/02/96	M		(2)	
18	Nikita Burmistrov		06/07/89	A	19	(1)	2
71	Aleksandr Denisov		23/02/89	D	8	(2)	
26	Moussa Doumbia	MLI	15/08/94	M	11	(1)	1
77	Aleksandr Filtsov		02/01/90	G	3		
20	Emmanuel Frimpong	GHA	10/01/92	M	1	(1)	
25	Vladimir Gabulov		19/10/83	G	13		
1	Roman Gerus		14/09/80	G	3		
32	Andrei Gorbanets		24/08/85	M	3	(2)	
39	Igor Gorbatenko		13/02/89	M	15	(8)	
29	Aleksandr Gorbatyuk		21/04/85	D	16		
61	Gia Grigalava	GEO	05/08/89	D	3	(1)	1
5	Anri Hagush		23/09/86	D	9	(2)	
16	Ivan Ivanov	BUL	25/02/88	D	5		
9	Kirill Kombarov		22/01/87	M	12		1
36	Mikhail Levashov		04/10/91	G	11	(1)	
78	Ilya Maksimov		02/02/87	M	12	(1)	1
23	Ruslan Mukhametshin		29/10/81	A	5	(4)	
19	Federico Rasic	ARG	24/03/92	A	8	(4)	6
28	Vladislav Ryzhkov		28/07/90	M	3	(5)	
2	Aleksandr Sheshukov		15/04/83	M	7	(1)	
63	Igor Shevchenko		02/02/85	A	10	(8)	1
24	Dmitri Smirnov		13/08/80	M		(2)	
99	Dmitri Starodub		19/05/95	M	1		
20	Vadim Steklov		24/03/85	M	17	(2)	
13	Stophira Sunzu	ZAM	22/06/89	D	13		
22	Lukáš Tesák	SVK	08/03/85	D	12		
21	Jherson Vergara	COL	26/05/94	D	17	(1)	
34	Oleg Vlasov		10/12/84	M	8	(12)	1
2	Ivani Yershov		22/05/79	D	5		

PFC CSKA Moskva

1911 • VEB Arena (30,000) • pfc-cska.com

Major honours

UEFA Cup (1) 2005; USSR League (7) 1946, 1947, 1948, 1950, 1951, 1970, 1991; Russian League (6) 2003, 2005, 2006, 2013, 2014, 2016; USSR Cup (5) 1945, 1948, 1951, 1955, 1991; Russian Cup (7) 2002, 2005, 2006, 2008, 2009, 2011, 2013

Coach: Leonid Slutski; (12/12/16) Viktor Goncharenko (BLR)

2016

Date		Opponent		Score	Scorers
30/07	a	Anji	D	0-0	
07/08	a	Orenburg	W	1-0	*Eremenko*
13/08	a	Ural	W	1-0	*Milanov*
20/08	a	Zenit	D	1-1	*Eremenko*
27/08	a	Tom	W	1-0	*Eremenko*
10/09	h	Terek	W	3-0	*Traoré 2, Strandberg*
18/09	a	Krylya Sovetov	W	2-1	*Golovin, Ignashevich*
24/09	h	Krasnodar	D	1-1	*Traoré*
02/10	a	Rostov	L	0-2	
14/10	h	Ufa	W	1-0	*V Berezutski*
23/10	a	Lokomotiv	L	0-1	
29/10	a	Spartak	L	1-3	*Strandberg*
06/11	h	Amkar	D	2-2	*Ignashevich (p), Tošić*
18/11	a	Arsenal	W	1-0	*Milanov*
26/11	h	Rubin	D	0-0	
30/11	h	Orenburg	W	2-0	*Natcho (p), Ignashevich*
03/12	h	Ural	W	4-0	*Traoré 2, Natcho (p), Chalov*

2017

Date		Opponent		Score	Scorers
04/03	h	Zenit	D	0-0	
11/03	h	Tom	W	4-0	*Vitinho, Dzagoev, Ionov 2*
19/03	a	Terek	W	1-0	*Ionov*
02/04	h	Krylya Sovetov	W	2-1	*Golovin, Natcho*
09/04	a	Krasnodar	D	1-1	*Wernbloom*
15/04	h	Rostov	D	0-0	
21/04	a	Ufa	W	2-0	*Vitinho, Chalov*
26/04	h	Lokomotiv	W	4-0	*Dzagoev, Vitinho, Golovin, Natcho*
30/04	h	Spartak	L	1-2	*A Berezutski*
06/05	a	Amkar	W	2-0	*Chalov, Natcho*
12/05	h	Arsenal	W	3-0	*Natcho (p), Chalov 2*
17/05	a	Rubin	W	2-0	*Vitinho, Dzagoev*
21/05	h	Anji	W	4-0	*Ignashevich (p), Vitinho 2, Chalov*

No	Name	Nat	DoB	Pos	Aps	(s)	Gls
35	Igor Akinfeev		08/04/86	G	29		
6	Aleksei Berezutski		20/06/82	D	13	(5)	1
24	Vasili Berezutski		20/06/82	D	27		1
63	Fedor Chalov		10/04/98	A	8	(7)	6
1	Sergei Chepchugov		15/07/85	G	1		
10	Alan Dzagoev		17/06/90	M	11	(4)	3
25	Roman Eremenko	FIN	19/03/87	M	9		3
17	Aleksandr Golovin		30/05/96	M	29	(1)	3
72	Astemir Gordyushenko		30/03/97	M	1	(2)	
4	Sergei Ignashevich		14/07/79	D	21	(3)	4
11	Aleksei Ionov		18/02/89	A	17	(7)	3
89	Konstantin Kuchaev		18/03/98	M		(2)	
2	Mário Fernandes		19/09/90	D	30		
8	Georgi Milanov	BUL	19/02/92	M	9	(9)	2
14	Kirill Nababkin		08/09/86	D	3	(4)	
66	Bebras Natcho	ISR	18/02/88	M	18	(8)	6
99	Aaron Olanare	NGA	04/06/94	A	2	(5)	
42	Georgi Schennikov		27/04/91	D	23	(2)	
97	Carlos Strandberg	SWE	14/04/96	A	1	(7)	2
7	Zoran Tošić	SRB	28/04/87	M	16	(8)	1
9	Lacina Traoré	CIV	20/08/90	A	11	(3)	5
5	Viktor Vasin		06/10/88	D	12	(1)	
20	Vitinho	BRA	09/10/93	A	12	(1)	6
3	Pontus Wernbloom	SWE	25/06/86	M	27		1
75	Timur Zhamaletdinov		21/05/97	A		(4)	

RUSSIA

FC Krasnodar

2008 • Kuban (35,200); Krasnodar (34,291) • fckrasnodar.ru

Coach: Oleg Kononov (BLR); (13/09/16) Igor Shalimov

2016

Date		Opponent	Res	Score	Scorers
01/08	h	Tom	W	3-0	*Smolov 2, Ari*
08/08	h	Terek	W	4-0	*Smolov 2, Ari, Wanderson*
13/08	a	Krylya Sovetov	D	1-1	*Smolov*
21/08	a	Spartak	L	0-2	
28/08	h	Lokomotiv	L	1-2	*Smolov (p)*
11/09	a	Ufa	D	0-0	
18/09	h	Rostov	W	2-1	*Naldo, Smolov (p)*
24/09	a	CSKA	D	1-1	*Smolov*
02/10	h	Rubin	W	1-0	*Ari*
16/10	a	Arsenal	D	0-0	
23/10	h	Amkar	W	1-0	*Gazinski*
30/10	a	Anji	D	0-0	
06/11	h	Orenburg	D	3-3	*Pereyra, Ari, Martynovich*
20/11	h	Ural	W	3-0	*Gazinski, Smolov, Joãozinho*
27/11	h	Zenit	W	2-1	*Izmailov, Okriashvili*
01/12	a	Terek	L	1-2	*og (Ángel)*
05/12	h	Krylya Sovetov	D	1-1	*Smolov*

2017

Date		Opponent	Res	Score	Scorers
05/03	h	Spartak	D	2-2	*og (Taşçı), Smolov (p)*
13/03	a	Lokomotiv	W	2-1	*Mamaev, Wanderson*
19/03	h	Ufa	D	0-0	
03/04	a	Rostov	D	0-0	
09/04	h	CSKA	D	1-1	*Smolov (p)*
15/04	a	Rubin	W	1-0	*Smolov*
23/04	h	Arsenal	W	2-0	*Kaboré, Smolov*
27/04	a	Amkar	W	2-0	*Smolov, Wanderson*
01/05	h	Anji	D	0-0	
07/05	a	Orenburg	L	0-1	
13/05	a	Ural	D	1-1	*Claesson*
17/05	a	Zenit	L	0-1	
21/05	a	Tom	W	5-1	*Smolov 3, Pereyra, Naldo*

No	Name	Nat	DoB	Pos	Aps	(s)	Gls
10	Odil Akhmedov	UZB	25/11/87	M	8	(6)	
9	Ari	BRA	11/12/85	A	11		4
18	Vladimir Bystrov		31/01/84	M	2	(6)	
16	Viktor Claesson	SWE	02/01/92	M	13		1
8	Yuri Gazinski		20/07/89	M	28	(1)	2
6	Andreas Granqvist	SWE	16/04/85	D	29		
2	Marat Izmailov		21/09/82	M	6	(1)	1
55	Artur Jędrzejczyk	POL	04/11/87	D	12	(1)	
22	Joãozinho	BRA	25/12/88	M	9	(12)	1
77	Charles Kaboré	BFA	09/02/88	M	21	(1)	1
17	Vitali Kaleshin		03/10/80	D	17		
88	Eboué Kouassi	CIV	13/12/97	M	7	(2)	
1	Stanislav Kritsyuk		01/12/90	G	20		
21	Ricardo Laborde	COL	16/02/88	M	3	(10)	
7	Pavel Mamaev		17/09/88	M	7	(5)	1
4	Aleksandr Martynovich	BLR	26/08/87	D	14		1
3	Naldo	BRA	25/08/88	D	14		2
70	Tornike Okriashvili	GEO	12/02/92	M	2	(9)	1
33	Mauricio Pereyra	URU	15/03/90	M	16	(5)	2
98	Sergei Petrov		02/01/91	D	15	(2)	
11	Vyacheslav Podberyozkin		21/06/92	M	8	(6)	
12	Cristian Ramírez	ECU	12/08/94	D	10	(1)	
30	Roman Shishkin		27/01/87	D	5	(1)	
17	Ragnar Sigurdsson	ISL	19/06/86	D	3		
88	Andrei Sinitsin		23/06/88	G	10	(2)	
90	Fedor Smolov		09/02/90	A	21	(1)	18
4	Stefan Strandberg	NOR	25/07/90	D	1		
5	Dmitri Torbinski		28/04/84	M	6	(6)	
14	Wanderson	BRA	18/02/86	A	8	(5)	3
15	Ilya Zhigulev		01/02/96	M	4	(3)	

PFC Krylya Sovetov Samara

1942 • Metallurg (33,001) • kc-camapa.ru

Coach: Franky Vercauteren (BEL); (03/11/16) Vadim Skripchenko (BLR)

2016

Date		Opponent	Res	Score	Scorers
31/07	a	Terek	L	0-1	
08/08	a	Spartak	L	0-1	
13/08	h	Krasnodar	D	1-1	*Rodić*
21/08	a	Lokomotiv	D	0-0	
26/08	h	Ufa	L	0-1	
09/09	a	Rostov	L	1-2	*og (Yerokhin)*
18/09	h	CSKA	L	1-2	*Yatchenko*
26/09	a	Amkar	D	0-0	
01/10	h	Anji	W	2-1	*Mollo, Tkachyov*
15/10	a	Rubin	L	0-3	
21/10	h	Arsenal	D	1-1	*Mollo (p)*
31/10	a	Orenburg	L	0-1	
05/11	h	Ural	D	2-2	*Kornilenko 2*
20/11	a	Zenit	L	1-3	*Pasquato*
27/11	h	Tom	W	3-0	*Kornilenko, Mollo 2*
01/12	h	Spartak	W	4-0	*Mollo (p), Tkachyov, Pasquato, Kornilenko*
05/12	a	Krasnodar	D	1-1	*Kornilenko*

2017

Date		Opponent	Res	Score	Scorers
05/03	h	Lokomotiv	L	0-3	
11/03	a	Ufa	L	0-1	
19/03	h	Rostov	D	0-0	
02/04	a	CSKA	L	1-2	*Pasquato*
08/04	h	Amkar	D	2-2	*Bruno, Kornilenko*
13/04	a	Anji	W	3-1	*Kornilenko, Zotov, Pasquato*
23/04	h	Rubin	D	0-0	
26/04	a	Arsenal	L	0-2	
01/05	h	Orenburg	D	1-1	*Yatchenko*
08/05	a	Ural	W	3-1	*Bruno 2, Pasquato*
13/05	h	Zenit	L	1-3	*og (Ivanović)*
17/05	a	Tom	W	2-0	*Bruno, Kornilenko*
21/05	h	Terek	L	1-3	*Bruno (p)*

No	Name	Nat	DoB	Pos	Aps	(s)	Gls
2	Evgeni Bashkirov		06/07/91	M	18	(4)	
19	Sheldon Bateau	TRI	21/01/91	D	17	(3)	
40	Sergei Bozhin		12/09/94	D	10	(5)	
29	Gianni Bruno	BEL	19/08/91	A	14	(3)	5
7	Alan Chochiyev		07/09/91	M	9	(8)	
5	Ali Gadzhibekov		06/08/89	D	3		
69	Yegor Golenkov		07/07/99	A		(1)	
16	Artem Gromov	UKR	14/01/90	M	2	(1)	
11	Aleksandr Hleb	BLR	01/05/81	M	4	(3)	
18	Adis Jahovic	MKD	18/03/87	A	4	(1)	
55	Aleksei Kontsedalov		24/07/90	D	9		
13	Evgeni Konyukhov		21/11/86	G	5		
8	Sergei Kornilenko	BLR	14/06/83	A	19	(7)	8
28	Pavel Kudryashov		27/11/96	A		(1)	
17	Giorgi Loria	GEO	27/01/86	G	25		
3	Timofei Margasov		12/06/92	D	3	(2)	
10	Jerry Mbakogu	NGA	01/10/92	A	4	(3)	
20	Srdjan Mijailović	SRB	10/11/93	M	11	(2)	
24	Yohan Mollo	FRA	18/07/89	M	12		5
6	Nadson	BRA	18/10/84	D	27	(1)	
10	Cristian Pasquato	ITA	10/07/89	A	19	(7)	5
33	Milan Rodić	SRB	02/04/91	D	14	(1)	1
9	Berat Sadik	FIN	14/09/86	A		(6)	
4	Ivan Taranov		22/06/86	D	19	(2)	
77	Sergei Tkachyov		19/05/89	M	12	(8)	2
30	Ibragim Tsallagov		12/12/90	M	17		
98	Ilya Viznovich		10/02/98	A		(2)	
3	Dmitri Yatchenko		25/08/86	D	28		2
21	Vyacheslav Zinkov		26/05/93	M	7	(6)	
31	Georgi Zotov		12/01/90	D	10		1
27	Aleksandr Zuev		26/06/96	M	8	(3)	

FC Lokomotiv Moskva

1923 • Lokomotiv (28,800) • fclm.ru

Major honours
Russian League (2) 2002, 2004; USSR Cup (2) 1936, 1957; Russian Cup (7) 1996, 1997, 2000, 2001, 2007, 2015, 2017

Coach: Igor Cherevchenko; (10/08/16) (Oleg Pashinin); (26/08/16) Yuri Semin

2016

Date		Opponent	Res	Score	Scorers
30/07	a	Zenit	D	0-0	
07/08	h	Tom	D	2-2	*Škuletić (p), Samedov (p)*
14/08	a	Terek	D	1-1	*Škuletić*
21/08	h	Krylya Sovetov	D	0-0	
28/08	a	Krasnodar	W	2-1	*Samedov, Henty (p)*
11/09	a	Spartak	L	0-1	
17/09	h	Ufa	L	0-1	
24/09	a	Rostov	L	0-1	
01/10	h	Arsenal	D	1-1	*Samedov (p)*
15/10	a	Amkar	D	0-0	
23/10	h	CSKA	W	1-0	*Maicon*
31/10	a	Rubin	L	0-2	
05/11	h	Anji	W	4-0	*Maicon 2, Manuel Fernandes, Samedov (p)*
19/11	a	Orenburg	D	1-1	*Kasaev*
26/11	h	Ural	D	1-1	*Pejčinović*
01/12	a	Tom	W	6-1	*Kolomeytsev 2, Manuel Fernandes, I Denisov, Maicon, Ignatyev*
04/12	h	Terek	W	2-0	*Aleksei Miranchuk, Manuel Fernandes*

2017

Date		Opponent	Res	Score	Scorers
05/03	a	Krylya Sovetov	W	3-0	*Ari 2, Aleksei Miranchuk*
13/03	h	Krasnodar	L	1-2	*Ignatyev*
18/03	h	Spartak	D	1-1	*Ari*
01/04	a	Ufa	W	1-0	*Farfán*
09/04	h	Rostov	D	0-0	
16/04	a	Arsenal	W	3-0	*Manuel Fernandes, Maicon (p), Ari*
22/04	h	Amkar	D	3-3	*Aleksei Miranchuk, Tarasov, Manuel Fernandes (p)*
26/04	a	CSKA	L	0-4	
29/04	h	Rubin	L	0-1	
08/05	a	Anji	D	0-0	
13/05	h	Orenburg	W	4-0	*Ari 2, Mikhalik, Manuel Fernandes*
17/05	a	Ural	W	2-1	*Pejčinović, Manuel Fernandes (p)*
21/05	h	Zenit	L	0-2	

No	Name	Nat	DoB	Pos	Aps	(s)	Gls
81	Ilya Abayev		02/08/81	G	1		
90	Ari	BRA	11/12/85	A	9		6
36	Dmitri Barinov		11/09/96	M	6	(6)	
14	Vedran Ćorluka	CRO	05/02/86	D	18	(1)	
27	Igor Denisov		17/05/84	M	23		1
29	Vitali Denisov	UZB	23/02/87	D	24		
8	Jefferson Farfán	PER	26/10/84	A	4	(2)	1
57	Artem Galadzhan		22/05/98	A		(4)	
1	Guilherme		12/12/85	G	29		
11	Ezekiel Henty	NGA	13/05/93	A	3	(3)	1
20	Vladislav Ignatyev		20/01/87	M	10	(6)	2
11	Alan Kasaev		08/04/86	M	10	(8)	1
18	Aleksandr Kolomeytsev		21/02/89	M	9	(10)	2
33	Solomon Kverkvelia	GEO	06/02/92	D	12		
10	Dmitri Loskov		12/02/74	M	1		
7	Maicon	BRA	18/02/90	M	16	(8)	5
4	Manuel Fernandes	POR	05/02/86	M	21	(1)	7
3	Timofei Margasov		12/06/92	D	1	(1)	
17	Taras Mikhalik	UKR	28/10/83	D	18	(6)	1
59	Aleksei Miranchuk		17/10/95	M	27	(2)	3
60	Anton Miranchuk		17/10/95	M	1	(2)	
88	Delvin N'Dinga	CGO	14/03/88	A	6	(3)	
5	Nemanja Pejčinović	SRB	04/11/87	D	25	(2)	2
9	Igor Portnyagin		07/01/89	A	2	(2)	
28	Boris Rotenberg	FIN	19/05/86	D		(2)	
19	Aleksandr Samedov		19/07/84	M	14	(1)	4
30	Roman Shishkin		27/01/87	D	9	(2)	
32	Petar Škuletić	SRB	29/06/90	A	5	(5)	2
23	Dmitri Tarasov		18/03/87	M	12		1
55	Renat Yanbaev		07/04/84	D	14	(2)	

FC Orenburg

1976 • Gazovik (7,500) • fcorenburg.ru

Coach: Robert Yevdokimov

Date		Opponent	Result	Scorers
2016				
30/07	a	Rostov	L 0-1	
07/08	h	CSKA	L 0-1	
15/08	h	Amkar	D 0-0	
22/08	a	Arsenal	D 0-0	
27/08	h	Rubin	D 1-1	*Efremov*
10/09	h	Anji	D 0-0	
16/09	h	Spartak	L 1-3	*Georgiev*
25/09	h	Ural	L 0-1	
01/10	a	Terek	L 1-2	*Georgiev (p)*
16/10	h	Tom	W 3-1	*Nekhaichik 3*
24/10	a	Zenit	L 0-1	
31/10	h	Krylya Sovetov	W 1-0	*Delkin*
06/11	a	Krasnodar	D 3-3	*Breyev, Poluyakhtov 2*
19/11	h	Lokomotiv	D 1-1	*Nekhaichik*
25/11	a	Ufa	L 0-1	
30/11	a	CSKA	L 0-2	
05/12	a	Amkar	L 0-3	
2017				
04/03	h	Arsenal	W 3-0	*Georgiev 2 (1p), Vorobyov*
11/03	a	Rubin	D 0-0	
17/03	a	Anji	L 0-1	
03/04	a	Spartak	L 2-3	*Popovič, Ďuriš*
06/04	a	Ural	L 0-2	
16/04	h	Terek	W 2-1	*Popovič, og (Pliev)*
23/04	a	Tom	W 2-1	*Oyewole, Georgiev*
26/04	h	Zenit	L 0-1	
01/05	a	Krylya Sovetov	D 1-1	*Georgiev*
07/05	h	Krasnodar	W 1-0	*Lobjanidze*
13/05	a	Lokomotiv	L 0-4	
17/05	h	Ufa	D 1-1	*Afonin*
21/05	h	Rostov	W 2-0	*Vorobyov, Breyev*

No	Name	Nat	DoB	Pos	Aps	(s)	Gls
33	Dmitri Abakumov		08/07/89	G	6		
29	Vadim Afonin	UZB	29/09/87	M	26		1
15	Dmitri Andreev		26/09/80	D	19	(2)	
6	Yacouba Bamba	CIV	30/11/91	M	7	(3)	
21	Maksim Batov		05/06/92	M		(5)	
27	Maksim Bordachev	BLR	18/06/86	D	1		
23	Sergei Breyev		22/04/87	M	4	(7)	2
90	Artem Delkin		02/08/90	A	8	(6)	1
50	Stanislav Dragun	BLR	04/06/88	M	8	(3)	
16	Michal Ďuriš	SVK	01/06/88	A	10	(1)	1
17	Dmitri Efremov		01/04/95	M	10	(10)	1
40	Blagoy Georgiev	BUL	21/12/81	M	21		6
48	Maksim Grigoryev		06/07/90	M	10		
30	Aleksandr Gutor	BLR	18/04/89	G	12		
34	Aleksandr Katsalapov		05/04/86	D	5	(3)	
41	Mikhail Kerzhakov		28/01/87	G	5		
24	Igor Koronov		06/04/86	M	12	(5)	
45	Elguja Lobjanidze	GEO	17/09/92	A	4	(7)	1
12	Andrei Malykh		24/08/88	D	26		
14	Ivan Markelov		17/04/88	A		(4)	
13	Pavel Nekhaichik	BLR	15/07/88	M	12	(4)	4
58	Adessoye Oyewole		18/09/82	D	27		1
9	Vladimir Parnyakov		30/01/84	M	8	(1)	
2	Vladimir Poluyakhtov		15/12/81	D	25		2
20	Aleksei Pomerko		03/05/90	M	10	(3)	
32	Denis Popovič	SVN	15/10/89	M	3	(3)	2
99	Aleksandr Prudnikov		26/02/89	A	2	(1)	
1	Aleksandr Rudenko		04/03/93	G	7		
10	Anzor Sanaya		22/05/89	A	6	(11)	
8	Marat Shogenov		26/08/84	M	1	(5)	
3	Mikhail Sivakov	BLR	16/01/88	D	12		
26	Farhod Vasiev	TJK	14/04/90	D	1		
5	Roman Vorobyov		24/03/84	M	20	(4)	2
4	Ivica Žunić	CRO	11/09/88	D	2		

FC Rostov

1930 • Olimp-2 (17,023) • fc-rostov.ru

Major honours
Russian Cup (1) 2014

Coach: Kurban Berdyev; (06/08/16) (Dmitri Kirichenko); (09/09/16) Ivan Daniliants (AUT)

Date		Opponent	Result	Scorers
2016				
30/07	h	Orenburg	W 1-0	*Novoseltsev*
07/08	h	Ural	D 0-0	
12/08	a	Zenit	L 2-3	*Poloz 2*
20/08	h	Tom	W 3-0	*Novoseltsev, Ezatolahi, Yerokhin*
28/08	a	Terek	L 1-2	*Novoseltsev*
09/09	h	Krylya Sovetov	W 2-1	*Bukharov, Prepeliță*
18/09	a	Krasnodar	L 1-2	*César Navas*
24/09	h	Lokomotiv	W 1-0	*Poloz*
02/10	h	CSKA	W 2-0	*Gatcan, Noboa*
15/10	a	Spartak	L 0-1	
22/10	a	Ufa	D 0-0	
29/10	a	Amkar	L 0-1	
06/11	h	Arsenal	W 4-1	*Yerokhin 2, Azmoun, Poloz*
18/11	a	Rubin	D 0-0	
27/11	h	Anji	W 2-0	*Azmoun, Gatcan*
30/11	a	Ural	L 0-1	
03/12	h	Zenit	D 0-0	
2017				
03/03	a	Tom	W 6-0	*Bukharov 2, Dević, Yerokhin, Azmoun 2*
12/03	h	Terek	D 0-0	
19/03	a	Krylya Sovetov	D 0-0	
03/04	h	Krasnodar	D 0-0	
09/04	a	Lokomotiv	D 0-0	
15/04	a	CSKA	D 0-0	
22/04	h	Spartak	W 3-0	*Bukharov 2, Gatcan*
25/04	h	Ufa	W 1-0	*Poloz*
30/04	h	Amkar	W 1-0	*Bukharov*
06/05	a	Arsenal	L 0-1	
14/05	h	Rubin	W 4-2	*Azmoun 2, Poloz, Noboa*
17/05	a	Anji	W 2-1	*Azmoun, Poloz*
21/05	a	Orenburg	L 0-2	

No	Name	Nat	DoB	Pos	Aps	(s)	Gls
20	Sardar Azmoun	IRN	01/01/95	A	20	(7)	7
15	Bastos	ANG	27/03/91	D	2	(1)	
19	Khoren Bayramyan		07/01/92	M	14	(6)	
11	Aleksandr Bukharov		12/03/85	A	11	(7)	6
44	César Navas	ESP	14/02/80	D	24		1
33	Marko Dević	UKR	27/10/83	A	1	(5)	1
26	Moussa Doumbia	MLI	15/08/94	M	2	(4)	
35	Soslan Dzhanaev		13/03/87	G	13		
6	Saeid Ezatolahi	IRN	01/10/96	M	5	(5)	1
84	Alexandru Gatcan	MDA	27/03/84	M	24		3
4	Vladimir Granat		22/05/87	D	11	(1)	
48	Maksim Grigoryev		06/07/90	M	3	(3)	
3	Papa Gueye	SEN	07/06/84	D	4		
2	Timofei Kalachev	BLR	01/05/81	M	22	(3)	
8	Igor Kireev		17/02/92	M	8	(3)	
69	Nikita Kovalyov		31/03/96	M		(1)	
30	Fedor Kudryashov		05/04/87	D	24		
77	Nikita Medvedev		17/12/94	G	17		
23	Miha Mevlja	SVN	12/06/90	D	21		
18	Pavel Mogilevets		25/01/93	M		(7)	
16	Christian Noboa	ECU	08/04/85	M	26		2
3	Ivan Novoseltsev		25/08/91	D	5		3
7	Dmitri Poloz		12/07/91	A	22	(4)	7
28	Andrei Prepeliță	ROU	08/12/85	M	8	(9)	1
22	Marko Simić	MNE	16/06/87	D	5	(2)	
77	Dmitri Skopintsev		02/03/97	D		(1)	
5	Denis Terentyev		13/08/92	D	17	(7)	
71	Dmitri Veber		10/09/99	M		(1)	
33	Valeri Yaroshenko		08/05/97	M		(1)	
89	Aleksandr Yerokhin		13/10/89	M	21	(4)	4

FC Rubin

1958 • Kazan-Arena (45,379); Central (27,756) • rubin-kazan.ru

Major honours
Russian League (2) 2008, 2009; Russian Cup (1) 2012

Coach: Javier Gracia (ESP)

Date		Opponent	Result	Scorers
2016				
01/08	h	Amkar	D 0-0	
06/08	a	Arsenal	L 0-1	
13/08	h	Spartak	D 1-1	*Dević*
19/08	h	Anji	L 1-2	*Kanunnikov*
27/08	a	Orenburg	D 1-1	*Kanunnikov*
12/09	h	Ural	W 3-1	*og (Novikov), Tkachuk, Lestienne*
19/09	a	Zenit	L 1-4	*Jonathas*
26/09	h	Tom	W 2-1	*Jonathas, Kambolov*
02/10	a	Krasnodar	L 0-1	
15/10	h	Krylya Sovetov	W 3-0	*Kanunnikov, Rubén Rochina, Jonathas*
22/10	a	Terek	L 1-3	*Jonathas*
31/10	h	Lokomotiv	W 2-0	*Kanunnikov, Jonathas*
05/11	a	Ufa	W 3-2	*Jonathas (p), Rubén Rochina, Nabiullin*
18/11	h	Rostov	D 0-0	
26/11	a	CSKA	D 0-0	
30/11	h	Arsenal	W 1-0	*Jonathas*
05/12	a	Spartak	L 1-2	*Jonathas*
2017				
06/03	a	Anji	W 1-0	*Kanunnikov*
11/03	h	Orenburg	D 0-0	
18/03	a	Ural	L 0-1	
02/04	h	Zenit	L 0-2	
10/04	a	Tom	D 2-2	*Lestienne 2 (1p)*
15/04	h	Krasnodar	L 0-1	
23/04	a	Krylya Sovetov	D 0-0	
26/04	h	Terek	L 0-1	
29/04	a	Lokomotiv	W 1-0	*Tkachuk*
07/05	h	Ufa	W 2-1	*Caktaš 2 (1p)*
14/05	a	Rostov	L 2-4	*M'Vila, Kanunnikov*
17/05	h	CSKA	L 0-2	
21/05	a	Amkar	W 2-1	*Jonathas, Kanunnikov*

No	Name	Nat	DoB	Pos	Aps	(s)	Gls
85	Ilzat Akhmetov		31/12/97	M	9	(3)	
23	Moritz Bauer	SUI	25/01/92	D	19	(2)	
13	Emil Bergström	SWE	19/05/93	D	3	(1)	
67	Taras Burlak		22/02/90	D	21	(1)	
20	Mijo Caktaš	CRO	08/05/92	M	13	(4)	2
11	Marko Dević	UKR	27/10/83	A	1	(7)	1
61	Gökdeniz Karadeniz	TUR	11/01/80	M	4	(5)	
22	Jonathas	BRA	06/03/89	A	23	(3)	9
88	Ruslan Kambolov		01/01/90	D	16	(3)	1
9	Maksim Kanunnikov		14/07/91	A	22		7
2	Oleg Kuzmin		09/05/81	D	5		
10	Maxime Lestienne	BEL	17/06/92	A	5	(8)	3
4	Yann M'Vila	FRA	29/06/90	M	19	(2)	1
70	Georgi Makhatadze		26/03/98	M		(3)	
3	Elmir Nabiullin		08/03/95	D	24		1
91	Yuri Nesterenko		12/06/91	G	1		
27	Magomed Ozdoev		05/11/92	M	7	(3)	
9	Igor Portnyagin		07/01/89	A	1	(1)	
21	Rubén Rochina	ESP	23/03/91	A	16	(7)	2
1	Sergei Ryzhikov		19/09/80	G	29		
77	Samuel	ESP	13/07/90	M	7	(6)	
6	Sergio Sánchez	ESP	03/04/86	D	19	(1)	
8	Alexandre Song	CMR	09/09/87	M	12	(4)	
31	Denis Tkachuk		02/07/89	M	17	(5)	2
49	Vitali Ustinov		03/05/91	D	5	(2)	
25	Carlos Zambrano	PER	10/07/89	D	20	(1)	
96	Rifat Zhemaletdinov		20/09/96	A	12	(11)	

RUSSIA

FC Spartak Moskva

1922 • Otkrytiye Arena (45,360) • spartak.com

Major honours
USSR League (12) 1936 (autumn), 1938, 1939, 1952, 1953, 1956, 1958, 1962, 1969, 1979, 1987, 1989; Russian League (10) 1992, 1993, 1994, 1996, 1997, 1998, 1999, 2000, 2001, 2017; USSR Cup (10) 1938, 1939, 1946, 1947, 1950, 1958, 1963, 1965, 1971, 1992; Russian Cup (3) 1994, 1998, 2003

Coach: Dmitri Alenichev; (05/08/16) Massimo Carrera (ITA)

Date		Opponent		Score	Scorers
2016					
31/07	h	Arsenal	W	4-0	*Ananidze 2, Promes 2*
08/08	h	Krylya Sovetov	W	1-0	*Eschenko*
13/08	a	Rubin	D	1-1	*Popov*
21/08	h	Krasnodar	W	2-0	*Zé Luís 2*
28/08	a	Anji	W	2-0	*Ananidze, Promes*
11/09	h	Lokomotiv	W	1-0	*Popov*
16/09	a	Orenburg	W	3-1	*Ananidze, Promes 2*
25/09	h	Ufa	L	0-1	
02/10	a	Zenit	L	2-4	*Bocchetti, Zé Luís*
15/10	h	Rostov	W	1-0	*Glushakov*
22/10	a	Ural	W	1-0	*Melgarejo*
29/10	h	CSKA	W	3-1	*Glushakov, Zé Luís 2*
05/11	a	Tom	W	1-0	*Fernando*
20/11	h	Amkar	W	1-0	*Glushakov*
26/11	a	Terek	W	1-0	*Maurício*
01/12	a	Krylya Sovetov	L	0-4	
05/12	h	Rubin	W	2-1	*Promes, Glushakov*
2017					
05/03	a	Krasnodar	D	2-2	*Fernando, Luiz Adriano*
12/03	h	Anji	W	1-0	*Samedov*
18/03	a	Lokomotiv	D	1-1	*Promes*
03/04	h	Orenburg	W	3-2	*Zobnin 2, Promes*
09/04	a	Ufa	W	3-1	*Glushakov, Promes (p), Melgarejo*
16/04	h	Zenit	W	2-1	*Promes, Samedov*
22/04	a	Rostov	L	0-3	
25/04	h	Ural	W	1-0	*Fernando*
30/04	a	CSKA	W	2-1	*Luiz Adriano, Glushakov*
06/05	h	Tom	W	1-0	*Promes (p)*
13/05	a	Amkar	W	1-0	*Samedov*
17/05	h	Terek	W	3-0	*Glushakov 2, Promes*
21/05	a	Arsenal	L	0-3	

No	Name	Nat	DoB	Pos	Aps	(s)	Gls
7	Jano Ananidze	GEO	10/10/92	M	13	(9)	4
16	Salvatore Bocchetti	ITA	30/11/86	D	14	(1)	1
69	Denis Davydov		22/03/95	A	1	(3)	
14	Georgi Dzhikia		21/11/93	D	8		
38	Andrei Eschenko		09/02/84	D	21	(4)	1
11	Fernando	BRA	03/03/92	M	27	(1)	3
8	Denis Glushakov		27/01/87	M	24	(1)	8
23	Dmitri Kombarov		22/01/87	D	26	(1)	
18	Ilya Kutepov		29/07/93	D	24		
64	Denis Kutin		05/10/93	D		(2)	
52	Igor Leontiev		18/03/94	M	1		
12	Luiz Adriano	BRA	12/04/87	A	6	(2)	2
34	Evgeni Makeev		24/07/89	D	1	(1)	
33	Maurício	BRA	20/09/88	D	9	(1)	1
25	Lorenzo Melgarejo	PAR	10/08/90	M	7	(14)	2
1	Sergei Pesyakov		16/12/88	G	1		
71	Ivelin Popov	BUL	26/10/87	M	17	(5)	2
10	Quincy Promes	NED	04/01/92	A	25	(1)	12
45	Aleksandr Putsko		24/02/93	D		(1)	
32	Artem Rebrov		04/03/84	G	28		
5	Rômulo	BRA	19/09/90	M	3	(5)	
19	Aleksandr Samedov		19/07/84	M	7	(3)	3
21	Sergei Selikhov		07/04/94	G	1		
35	Serdar Taşçı	GER	24/04/87	D	17	(1)	
17	Georgi Tigiev		20/06/95	D	3	(1)	
40	Artem Timofeev		12/01/94	M		(5)	
9	Zé Luís	CPV	24/01/91	A	17	(4)	5
47	Roman Zobnin		11/02/94	M	28	(1)	2
17	Aleksandr Zuev		26/06/96	M	1	(5)	

FC Terek Grozny

1946 • Ahmat-Arena (30,597) • fc-terek.ru

Major honours
Russian Cup (1) 2004

Coach: Rashid Rakhimov

Date		Opponent		Score	Scorers
2016					
31/07	h	Krylya Sovetov	W	1-0	*Grozav (p)*
08/08	a	Krasnodar	L	0-4	
14/08	h	Lokomotiv	D	1-1	*Ivanov*
20/08	a	Ufa	W	3-1	*Balaj, Sadaev, Grozav*
28/08	h	Rostov	W	2-1	*Balaj, Ángel*
10/09	a	CSKA	L	0-3	
17/09	h	Amkar	L	1-3	*Rodolfo*
25/09	a	Arsenal	D	0-0	
01/10	h	Orenburg	W	2-1	*Balaj, Lebedenko*
17/10	a	Anji	D	0-0	
22/10	h	Rubin	W	3-1	*Balaj, Grozav (p), Roshi*
30/10	a	Ural	W	4-1	*Balaj 2, og (Dinga), Mbengue*
06/11	h	Zenit	W	2-1	*Balaj 2*
21/11	h	Tom	D	0-0	
26/11	h	Spartak	L	0-1	
01/12	h	Krasnodar	W	2-1	*Píriz, Grozav*
04/12	a	Lokomotiv	L	0-2	
2017					
05/03	h	Ufa	L	0-1	
12/03	a	Rostov	D	0-0	
19/03	h	CSKA	L	0-1	
02/04	a	Amkar	D	1-1	*Mitrishev*
08/04	h	Arsenal	W	3-1	*Mitrishev 2, Berisha*
16/04	a	Orenburg	L	1-2	*Grozav*
22/04	h	Anji	L	0-1	
26/04	a	Rubin	W	1-0	*Mbengue*
29/04	h	Ural	W	5-2	*Mbengue 2, Sadaev, Lebedenko, Mohammadi*
07/05	a	Zenit	W	1-0	*Mbengue*
14/05	a	Tom	W	2-1	*Lebedenko, Mbengue*
17/05	a	Spartak	L	0-3	
21/05	a	Krylya Sovetov	W	3-1	*Mbengue, Mohammadi, Balaj*

No	Name	Nat	DoB	Pos	Aps	(s)	Gls
6	Adílson	BRA	16/01/87	M	2	(1)	
4	Wilker Ángel	VEN	18/03/93	D	25	(1)	1
18	Bekim Balaj	ALB	11/01/91	A	22	(4)	9
77	Bernard Berisha	KOS	24/10/91	A	3	(5)	1
92	Sergei Bryzgalov		15/11/92	D	2	(2)	
16	Evgeni Gorodov		13/12/85	G	28		
10	Gheorghe Grozav	ROU	29/09/90	M	16	(4)	5
33	Vitali Gudiev		22/04/95	G	1		
3	Norbert Gyömbér	SVK	03/07/92	D	6	(1)	
1	Yaroslav Hodzyur	UKR	06/03/85	G	1		
19	Oleg Ivanov		04/08/86	M	17	(3)	1
14	Daler Kuzyaev		15/01/93	M	27		
55	Igor Lebedenko		27/05/83	A	9	(8)	3
17	Ablaye Mbengue	SEN	19/05/92	A	8	(14)	7
22	Reziuan Mirzov		22/06/93	M	2	(6)	
95	Magomed Mitrishev		10/09/92	A	16	(7)	3
13	Milad Mohammadi	IRN	29/09/93	D	23	(1)	2
27	Magomed Ozdoev		05/11/92	M	4	(2)	
8	Pedro Ken	BRA	20/03/87	M	1		
23	Facundo Píriz	URU	27/03/90	M	24	(2)	1
5	Zaurbek Pliev		27/09/91	D	9	(1)	
2	Rodolfo	BRA	23/10/82	D	12	(5)	1
21	Odhise Roshi	ALB	22/05/91	M	12	(7)	1
9	Zaur Sadaev		06/11/89	A		(7)	2
15	Andrei Semyonov		24/03/89	D	28		
20	Gabriel Torje	ROU	22/11/89	M	4	(6)	
40	Rizvan Utsiyev		07/02/88	D	28		

FC Tom Tomsk

1957 • Trud (10,028) • fctomtomsk.ru

Coach: Valeri Petrakov

Date		Opponent		Score	Scorers
2016					
01/08	a	Krasnodar	L	0-3	
07/08	a	Lokomotiv	D	2-2	*Bicfalvi, Pugin*
14/08	h	Ufa	W	1-0	*Samodin*
20/08	a	Rostov	L	0-3	
27/08	h	CSKA	L	0-1	
10/09	a	Amkar	L	0-1	
17/09	h	Arsenal	W	1-0	*Dyakov*
26/09	a	Rubin	L	1-2	*Vranješ*
01/10	h	Ural	D	1-1	*Pugin*
16/10	a	Orenburg	L	1-3	*Bicfalvi*
22/10	h	Anji	L	0-3	
30/10	a	Zenit	L	0-1	
05/11	h	Spartak	L	0-1	
21/11	a	Terek	D	0-0	
27/11	a	Krylya Sovetov	L	0-3	
01/12	h	Lokomotiv	L	1-6	*Bicfalvi*
05/12	a	Ufa	L	0-1	
2017					
03/03	h	Rostov	L	0-6	
11/03	a	CSKA	L	0-4	
18/03	h	Amkar	W	1-0	*Kuznetsov*
01/04	a	Arsenal	L	0-3	
10/04	h	Rubin	D	2-2	*Pugin, Sobolev*
16/04	a	Ural	L	0-1	
23/04	h	Orenburg	L	1-2	*Pugin*
27/04	a	Anji	D	3-3	*Sobolev, Gvineyski, Bolshunov*
01/05	h	Zenit	L	0-2	
04/05	a	Spartak	L	0-1	
11/05	h	Terek	L	1-2	*Salakhutdinov*
17/05	h	Krylya Sovetov	L	0-2	
21/05	h	Krasnodar	L	1-5	*Sobolev*

No	Name	Nat	DoB	Pos	Aps	(s)	Gls
15	Evgeni Balyaikin		19/05/88	M	11	(8)	
6	Eric Bicfalvi	ROU	05/02/88	M	14	(1)	3
88	Daniil Bolshunov		03/04/97	M	2	(8)	1
27	Maksim Bordachev	BLR	18/06/86	D	10		
96	Aleksandr Bukachev		07/03/96	D	2	(5)	
92	Valeriu Ciuperca	MDA	12/06/92	M	18		
77	Lukáš Droppa	CZE	22/04/89	M	11		
14	Aslan Dudiev		15/06/90	D	6	(2)	
5	Vitali Dyakov		31/01/89	D	14		1
7	Pavel Golyshev		07/07/87	A	16		
98	Nikita Gvineyski		28/12/98	M	7	(1)	1
28	David Jablonský	CZE	08/10/91	D	5	(1)	
69	Mark Karymov		22/06/98	D	7	(3)	
89	Olexandr Kasyan	UKR	27/01/89	M	6	(6)	
77	Anton Kochenkov		02/04/87	G	12		
9	Kirill Kombarov		22/01/87	M	14		
8	Kyrylo Kovalchuk	UKR	11/06/86	M	8	(3)	
28	Pavel Kudryashov		27/11/96	M		(7)	
10	Sergei Kuznetsov		07/05/86	M	3	(2)	1
74	Anton Makurin		12/12/94	M	3	(3)	
42	Aleksandr Melikhov		23/03/98	G	7		
84	Anton Miterev		03/05/96	D	12	(1)	
94	Aleksandr Naumenko		09/11/97	M	1	(2)	
89	Dmitri Osipov		14/02/96	D	8	(2)	
98	Kirill Pogrebnyak		27/06/92	A	1	(5)	
18	Artem Popov		30/08/92	M	20	(5)	
17	Aleksei Pugin		07/03/87	M	20	(1)	4
4	Ante Puljić	CRO	15/11/87	D	10		
65	Ruslan Salakhutdinov		01/04/96	M	2	(4)	1
8	Sergei Samodin		14/02/85	A	9	(3)	1
87	Dmitri Sasin		21/08/96	M	12		
97	Aleksandr Sobolev		07/03/97	A	13		3
1	Aleksei Solosin		11/08/87	G	11	(1)	
92	Pyotr Ten		12/07/92	D	3	(1)	
31	Maksim Tishkin		11/11/89	D	14		
4	Ognjen Vranješ	BIH	24/10/89	D	7		1
5	Aleksandr Zhirov		24/01/91	D	11		
41	Andrei Zorin		04/05/97	M		(1)	

FC Ufa

2010 • Neftyanik (15,200) • fcufa.pro

Coach: Viktor Goncharenko (BLR); (30/12/16) Sergei Semak

2016

Date		Opponent	Result	Scorers
31/07	a	Ural	L 0-2	
06/08	h	Zenit	D 0-0	
14/08	a	Tom	L 0-1	
20/08	h	Terek	L 1-3	*Fatai*
26/08	a	Krylya Sovetov	W 1-0	*Igboun*
11/09	h	Krasnodar	D 0-0	
17/09	a	Lokomotiv	W 1-0	*og (Ćorluka)*
25/09	a	Spartak	W 1-0	*Fatai*
02/10	h	Amkar	D 1-1	*Fatai*
14/10	a	CSKA	L 0-1	
22/10	h	Rostov	D 0-0	
30/10	a	Arsenal	W 2-0	*Igboun, Fatai*
05/11	h	Rubin	L 2-3	*Sysuev, Stotski*
19/11	a	Anji	W 1-0	*Vaněk*
25/11	h	Orenburg	W 1-0	*Vaněk*
30/11	a	Zenit	L 0-2	
05/12	h	Tom	W 1-0	*Sukhov*

2017

Date		Opponent	Result	Scorers
05/03	a	Terek	W 1-0	*Igboun*
11/03	h	Krylya Sovetov	W 1-0	*Paurević*
19/03	a	Krasnodar	D 0-0	
01/04	h	Lokomotiv	L 0-1	
09/04	h	Spartak	L 1-3	*Oblyakov*
15/04	a	Amkar	D 1-1	*og (Gol)*
21/04	h	CSKA	L 0-2	
25/04	a	Rostov	L 0-1	
30/04	h	Arsenal	W 1-0	*Sukhov*
07/05	a	Rubin	L 1-2	*Stotski*
14/05	h	Anji	W 2-1	*Stotski, Fatai*
17/05	a	Orenburg	D 1-1	*Sukhov*
21/05	h	Ural	W 1-0	*Fatai*

No	Name	Nat	DoB	Pos	Aps	(s)	Gls
99	Islamnur Abdulavov		07/03/94	A	4	(9)	
3	Pavel Alikin		06/03/84	D	26	(1)	
48	Andrei Batyunin		28/05/95	A		(1)	
31	Aleksandr Belenov		13/09/86	G	10		
87	Igor Bezdenezhnykh		08/08/96	M	18	(2)	
93	Catalin Carp	MDA	20/10/93	D	8	(1)	
11	Diego Carlos	BRA	15/05/88	A		(4)	
21	Kehinde Fatai	NGA	19/02/90	A	15	(7)	6
44	Sylvester Igboun	NGA	08/09/90	A	22	(2)	3
5	Bojan Jokič	SVN	17/05/86	D	9	(2)	
57	Vyacheslav Krotov		14/02/93	A	7	(15)	
99	Andrei Lunyov		13/11/91	G	9	(1)	
70	Marcinho	BRA	14/05/86	M	1	(10)	
4	Aleksei Nikitin		27/01/92	D	16		
98	Ivan Oblyakov		05/07/98	M	14	(6)	1
19	Ivan Paurević	CRO	01/07/91	M	13		1
45	Aleksandr Putsko		24/02/93	D	4	(1)	
70	Nikolai Safronidi		10/09/83	M	1	(1)	
88	Georgi Sheliya		11/12/88	G	11		
39	Dmitri Stotski		01/12/89	M	29		3
33	Aleksandr Sukhov		03/01/86	D	23	(2)	3
7	Dmitri Sysuev		13/01/88	M	11	(5)	1
20	Denis Tumasyan		24/04/85	D	7		
9	Ondřej Vaněk	CZE	05/07/90	M	12	(4)	2
5	Viktor Vasin		06/10/88	D	17		
13	Azamat Zaseev		29/04/88	M	23	(2)	
17	Dmitri Zhivoglyadov		29/05/94	D	19	(1)	
60	Vladimir Zubarev		05/01/93	M	1	(8)	

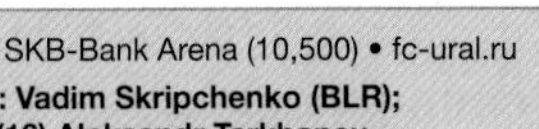

FC Ural Sverdlovsk Oblast

1930 • SKB-Bank Arena (10,500) • fc-ural.ru

Coach: Vadim Skripchenko (BLR); (03/11/16) Aleksandr Tarkhanov

2016

Date		Opponent	Result	Scorers
31/07	h	Ufa	W 2-0	*Yemelianov, Pavlyuchenko*
07/08	a	Rostov	D 0-0	
13/08	h	CSKA	L 0-1	
21/08	a	Amkar	L 0-1	
28/08	h	Arsenal	D 1-1	*Lungu*
12/09	a	Rubin	L 1-3	*Pavlyuchenko*
17/09	h	Anji	L 0-1	
25/09	a	Orenburg	W 1-0	*Pavlyuchenko*
01/10	a	Tom	D 1-1	*Fontanello*
16/10	h	Zenit	L 0-2	
22/10	h	Spartak	L 0-1	
30/10	h	Terek	L 1-4	*Chanturia (p)*
05/11	a	Krylya Sovetov	D 2-2	*Korobov, Chanturia*
20/11	a	Krasnodar	L 0-3	
26/11	a	Lokomotiv	D 1-1	*Fidler*
30/11	h	Rostov	W 1-0	*Lungu*
03/12	a	CSKA	L 0-4	

2017

Date		Opponent	Result	Scorers
05/03	h	Amkar	W 1-0	*Bicfalvi*
10/03	a	Arsenal	L 0-2	
18/03	h	Rubin	W 1-0	*Ilyin*
31/03	a	Anji	W 3-2	*Ilyin, og (Gasanov), Manucharyan*
10/04	h	Orenburg	W 2-0	*Ilyin, Lungu*
16/04	h	Tom	W 1-0	*Bicfalvi*
22/04	a	Zenit	L 0-2	
25/04	a	Spartak	L 0-1	
29/04	a	Terek	L 2-5	*Pavlyuchenko, Manucharyan*
08/05	h	Krylya Sovetov	L 1-3	*Ilyin*
13/05	h	Krasnodar	D 1-1	*og (Naldo)*
17/05	h	Lokomotiv	L 1-2	*og (Kverkvelia)*
21/05	a	Ufa	L 0-1	

No	Name	Nat	DoB	Pos	Aps	(s)	Gls
1	Dmitri Arapov		09/06/93	G	7		
4	Gregor Balažic	SVN	12/02/88	D	11		
6	Eric Bicfalvi	ROU	05/02/88	M	9		2
14	Jean-Jacques Bougouhi	CIV	12/09/92	A		(2)	
39	Giorgi Chanturia	GEO	11/04/93	A	8	(4)	2
7	Aleksandr Dantsev		14/10/84	D	26	(1)	
17	Nikolay Dimitrov	BUL	15/10/87	M	12		
5	Dominik Dinga	SRB	07/04/98	D	18	(2)	
57	Artem Fidler		14/07/83	M	23	(1)	1
29	Pablo Fontanello	ARG	26/09/84	D	16		1
32	Nikita Glushkov		23/06/94	M	1	(1)	
18	Vladimir Ilyin		20/05/92	A	12		4
2	Vladimir Khozin		03/07/89	D		(1)	
86	Mohamed Konaté	CIV	12/12/97	A		(4)	
77	Dmitri Korobov		10/06/94	M	10	(7)	1
15	Denys Kulakov	UKR	01/05/86	D	30		
80	Aleksandr Lomakin		14/02/95	M	1	(1)	
10	Chisamba Lungu	ZAM	02/10/91	A	27	(2)	3
99	Edgar Manucharyan	ARM	19/01/87	A	5	(7)	2
27	Mikhail Merkulov		26/01/94	D	6	(5)	
12	Aleksandr Novikov		12/10/84	D	15	(2)	
13	Radovan Pankov	SRB	05/08/95	D	5		
8	Aleksandr Pavlenko		20/01/85	M	12	(7)	
9	Roman Pavlyuchenko		15/12/81	A	16	(5)	4
53	Sergei Podoksyonov		29/07/97	M	3	(6)	
90	Aleksandr Scherbakov		26/06/98	A	1	(1)	
85	Sergei Serchenkov		01/01/97	M	2	(4)	
11	Aleksandr Stavpets		04/07/89	A	4	(10)	
3	Jemal Tabidze	GEO	18/03/96	D	3		
96	Andrei Timofeyev		08/02/96	G	1		
92	Roman Yemelianov		08/05/92	M	23		1
79	Artem Yusupov		29/04/97	A		(1)	
28	Nikolai Zabolotnyi		16/04/90	G	22		
25	Georgi Zhukov	KAZ	19/11/94	M	1	(3)	

FC Zenit

1925 • Petrovski (20,985); Krestovsky (68,134) • fc-zenit.ru

Major honours

UEFA Cup (1) 2008; UEFA Super Cup (1) 2008; USSR League (1) 1984; Russian League (4) 2007, 2010, 2012, 2015; USSR Cup (1) 1944; Russian Cup (3) 1999, 2010, 2016

Coach: Mircea Lucescu (ROU)

2016

Date		Opponent	Result	Scorers
30/07	h	Lokomotiv	D 0-0	
06/08	a	Ufa	D 0-0	
12/08	h	Rostov	W 3-2	*Giuliano (p), og (Ezatolahi), Djordjević*
20/08	h	CSKA	D 1-1	*Zhirkov*
27/08	h	Amkar	W 3-0	*Giuliano 2, Criscito*
11/09	a	Arsenal	W 5-0	*Kokorin, Dzyuba, Mak, Giuliano, A Kerzhakov (p)*
19/09	h	Rubin	W 4-1	*Criscito (p), Mak, Giuliano, Dzyuba*
25/09	a	Anji	D 2-2	*Dzyuba 2*
02/10	h	Spartak	W 4-2	*Criscito (p), Dzyuba, Witsel, Giuliano (p)*
16/10	a	Ural	W 2-0	*Shatov, Yusupov*
24/10	h	Orenburg	W 1-0	*Mak*
30/10	h	Tom	W 1-0	*Kokorin*
06/11	a	Terek	L 1-2	*Mak*
20/11	h	Krylya Sovetov	W 3-1	*Dzyuba 2 (1p), og (Rodić)*
27/11	a	Krasnodar	L 1-2	*Dzyuba*
30/11	h	Ufa	W 2-0	*Giuliano, Kokorin*
03/12	a	Rostov	D 0-0	

2017

Date		Opponent	Result	Scorers
04/03	a	CSKA	D 0-0	
12/03	a	Amkar	L 0-1	
19/03	h	Arsenal	W 2-0	*Criscito (p), Danny*
02/04	a	Rubin	W 2-0	*Danny, Dzyuba*
08/04	h	Anji	D 1-1	*Kokorin*
16/04	a	Spartak	L 1-2	*Dzyuba*
22/04	h	Ural	W 2-0	*Ivanović, Mollo*
26/04	a	Orenburg	W 1-0	*Giuliano (p)*
01/05	a	Tom	W 2-0	*Shatov, Danny*
07/05	h	Terek	L 0-1	
13/05	a	Krylya Sovetov	W 3-1	*Dzyuba 2, Javi García*
17/05	h	Krasnodar	W 1-0	*Dzyuba*
21/05	a	Lokomotiv	W 2-0	*Kokorin, Danny*

No	Name	Nat	DoB	Pos	Aps	(s)	Gls
2	Aleksandr Anyukov		28/09/82	D	9	(1)	
23	Evgeni Chernov		23/10/92	D	4	(2)	
4	Domenico Criscito	ITA	30/12/86	D	25		4
10	Danny	POR	07/08/83	M	12		4
77	Luka Djordjević	MNE	09/07/94	A	2	(8)	1
22	Artem Dzyuba		22/08/88	A	25	(1)	13
24	Ezequiel Garay	ARG	10/10/86	D	4		
7	Giuliano	BRA	31/05/90	M	26	(2)	8
33	Hernâni	BRA	27/03/94	M	5	(3)	
60	Branislav Ivanović	SRB	22/02/84	D	9	(1)	1
21	Javi García	ESP	08/02/87	M	22		1
11	Aleksandr Kerzhakov		27/11/82	A	1	(13)	1
41	Mikhail Kerzhakov		28/01/87	G	6		
9	Aleksandr Kokorin		19/03/91	A	25	(2)	5
1	Yuri Lodygin		26/05/90	G	14	(1)	
6	Nicolas Lombaerts	BEL	20/03/85	D	6	(2)	
13	Luís Neto	POR	26/05/88	D	22	(3)	
99	Andrei Lunyov		13/11/91	G	10		
29	Róbert Mak	SVK	08/03/91	M	9	(8)	4
8	Maurício	BRA	21/10/88	M	11	(8)	
18	Pavel Mogilevets		25/01/93	M		(1)	
24	Yohan Mollo	FRA	18/07/89	M	1	(6)	1
3	Ivan Novoseltsev		25/08/91	D	3	(2)	
17	Oleg Shatov		29/07/90	M	13	(5)	2
19	Igor Smolnikov		08/08/88	D	17		
30	Ibragim Tsallagov		12/12/90	M	7	(1)	
28	Axel Witsel	BEL	12/01/89	M	15	(1)	1
14	Artur Yusupov		01/09/89	M	7	(10)	1
81	Yuri Zhirkov		20/08/83	D	20	(1)	1

RUSSIA

Top goalscorers

18	Fedor Smolov (Krasnodar)
13	Artem Dzyuba (Zenit)
12	Quincy Promes (Spartak)
10	Ari (Krasnodar/Lokomotiv)
9	Jonathas (Rubin) Bekim Balaj (Terek)
8	Sergei Kornilenko (Krylya Sovetov) Denis Glushakov (Spartak) Giuliano (Zenit)
7	Manuel Fernandes (Lokomotiv) Aleksandr Samedov (Lokomotiv/Spartak) Sardar Azmoun (Rostov) Dmitri Poloz (Rostov) Maksim Kanunnikov (Rubin) Ablaye Mbengue (Terek)

Promoted clubs

FC Dinamo Moskva

1923 • Arena Khimki (18,636) • fcdynamo.ru

Major honours

USSR League (11) 1936 (spring), 1937, 1940, 1945, 1949, 1954, 1955, 1957, 1959, 1963, 1976 (spring); USSR Cup (6) 1937, 1953, 1967, 1970, 1977, 1984; Russian Cup (1) 1995

Coach: Yuriy Kalitvintsev (UKR)

FC Tosno

2013 • Electron Stadium, Veliki Novgorod (3,223) • fctosno.ru

Coach: Dmytro Parfenov (UKR)

FC SKA-Khabarovsk

1946 • Lenin (15,200) • fcska.ru

Coach: Aleksandr Grigoryan; (05/01/17) Andrei Gordeev; (01/05/17) (Aleksei Poddubski)

Second level final table 2016/17

		Pld	W	D	L	F	A	Pts
1	FC Dinamo Moskva	38	26	9	3	64	25	87
2	FC Tosno	38	21	12	5	63	30	75
3	FC Enisey Krasnoyarsk	38	19	6	13	54	42	63
4	FC SKA-Khabarovsk	38	15	14	9	45	33	59
5	FC Tambov	38	15	12	11	42	34	57
6	FC Spartak Moskva-2	38	15	11	12	56	43	56
7	FC Kuban Krasnodar	38	14	13	11	44	37	55
8	FC Shinnik Yaroslavl	38	15	9	14	41	39	54
9	FC Tyumen	38	14	11	13	48	43	53
10	FC Fakel Voronezh	38	14	11	13	38	40	53
11	FC Khimki	38	11	16	11	40	47	49
12	FC Volgar Astrakhan	38	12	9	17	39	49	45
13	FC Zenit-2	38	9	16	13	44	51	43
14	FC Baltika Kaliningrad	38	9	15	14	25	35	42
15	FC Sibir Novosibirsk	38	9	15	14	31	46	42
16	FC Luch-Energia Vladivostok	38	9	15	14	27	41	42
17	FC Mordovia Saransk	38	11	7	20	39	50	40
18	PFC Sokol Saratov	38	8	15	15	34	53	39
17	PFC Spartak Nalchik	38	7	17	14	26	37	38
18	FC Neftekhimik Nizhnekamsk	38	6	9	23	28	53	27

Promotion/Relegation play-offs

(25/05/17 & 28/05/17)
Enisey 2-1 Arsenal
Arsenal 1-0 Enisey
(2-2; Arsenal on away goal)

SKA-Khabarovsk 0-0 Orenburg
Orenburg 0-0 SKA-Khabarovsk *(aet)*
(0-0; SKA-Khabarovsk 5-3 on pens)

DOMESTIC CUP

Kubok Rossii 2016/17

1/16 FINALS

(21/09/16)
Chelyabinsk 0-3 Ural
Dinamo Moskva 4-0 Rostov
Energomash Belgorod 1-1 Ufa *(aet; 3-5 on pens)*
Enisey Krasnoyarsk 2-1 CSKA Moskva
Fakel Voronezh 1-1 Terek *(aet; 3-5 on pens)*
Khimki 0-3 Lokomotiv Moskva
Mordovia 1-2 Anji
Sibir Novosibirsk 1-0 Tom *(aet)*
SKA-Khabarovsk 1-0 Spartak Moskva
Spartak Nalchik 0-2 Krasnodar
Tosno 2-0 Arsenal Tula
Volga Ulyanovsk 0-0 Amkar *(aet; 3-4 on pens)*
Volgar Astrakhan 0-1 Orenburg

(22/09/16)
Chita 0-1 Rubin
Shinnik Yaroslavl 0-2 Krylya Sovetov
Tambov 0-5 Zenit

1/8 FINALS

(26/10/16)
Amkar 1-1 Ural *(aet; 2-4 on pens)*
Enisey Krasnoyarsk 2-3 Sibir Novosibirsk *(aet)*
Rubin 1-0 SKA-Khabarovsk *(aet)*
Terek 1-1 Ufa *(aet; 3-4 on pens)*
Tosno 3-2 Dinamo Moskva

(27/10/16)
Anji 4-0 Zenit
Krasnodar 3-2 Orenburg *(aet)*
Krylya Sovetov 1-3 Lokomotiv Moskva

QUARTER-FINALS

(28/02/17)
Ural 3-3 Krasnodar *(Ilyin 35, Bicfalvi 53, 65; Smolov 2, Claesson 14, 32) (aet; 4-3 on pens)*

(01/03/17)
Lokomotiv Moskva 1-0 Tosno *(Aleksei Miranchuk 19)*

Rubin 1-0 Sibir Novosibirsk *(Jonathas 88)*

Ufa 1-0 Anji *(Zaseev 64)*

SEMI-FINALS

(05/04/17)
Lokomotiv Moskva 1-0 Ufa *(Manuel Fernandes 44)*

(06/04/17)
Ural 2-1 Rubin *(Ilyin 13, Novikov 58; Jonathas 31)*

FINAL

(02/05/17)
Fisht Olympic Stadium, Sochi
FC LOKOMOTIV MOSKVA 2 *(I Denisov 76, Aleksei Miranchuk 90+1)*
FC URAL SVERDLOVSK OBLAST 0
Referee: *Nikolayev*
LOKOMOTIV MOSKVA: *Guilherme, Ignatyev, Pejčinović, Kverkvelia, V Denisov, I Denisov, Tarasov (Barinov 90+7), Maicon (Farfán 85), Aleksei Miranchuk, Manuel Fernandes, Ari*
Red cards: *Ari (90+6), Farfán (90+6)*
URAL: *Zabolotnyi, Novikov, Tabidze, Balažic, Dantsev, Dimitrov (Glushkov 88), Yemelianov (Manucharyan 79), Bicfalvi, Lungu, Ilyin, Pavlyuchenko (Fidler 46)*
Red cards: *Fidler (90+6), Manucharyan (90+6)*

SAN MARINO

Federazione Sammarinese Giuoco Calcio (FSGC)

Address	Strada di Montecchio 17 SM-47890 San Marino
Tel	+378 0549 990 515
Fax	+378 0549 992 348
E-mail	fsgc@omniway.sm
Website	fsgc.sm

President	Marco Tura
General secretary	Luigi Zafferani
Media officer	Matteo Rossi
Year of formation	1931
National stadium	San Marino Stadium, Serravalle (4,801)

CAMPIONATO SAMMARINESE CLUBS

1 **SP Cailungo**

 2 **SS Cosmos**

 3 **FC Domagnano**

 4 **SC Faetano**

 5 **FC Fiorentino**

 6 **SS Folgore**

 7 **AC Juvenes/Dogana**

 8 **SP La Fiorita**

 9 **AC Libertas**

 10 **SS Murata**

 11 **SS Pennarossa**

 12 **SS San Giovanni**

 13 **SP Tre Fiori**

 14 **SP Tre Penne**

 15 **Virtus FC**

KEY

- UEFA Champions League
- UEFA Europa League

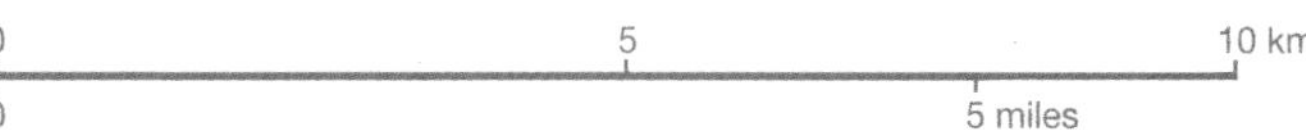

La Fiorita leave it late

The two clubs that collected San Marino's major trophies in 2015/16 were at it again 12 months later, only this time La Fiorita replaced Tre Penne as league champions while the latter succeeded the former as victors of the domestic cup.

The two teams' dominance was reinforced by their appearance in both finals, with Tre Penne striking first blood in the Coppa Titano showdown, winning 2-0, before La Fiorita turned the tables on their rivals a month later to claim a dramatic 2-1 extra-time victory in the championship play-off decider.

Dramatic turnaround in championship play-off final

Tre Penne win sixth Coppa Titano in style

Barren run in World Cup qualifiers continues

Domestic league

The Campionato Sammarinese, with its unconventional mixture of league and cup formats, is set up to provide an exciting denouement, but rarely can it have witnessed a more dramatic late twist than in 2016/17. The final in the San Marino Stadium was won by a team that trailed for practically the whole of the regular 90 minutes before fighting back to win the game in extra time.

Defending champions Tre Penne took the lead with just 20 seconds on the clock thanks to an acrobatic strike from their leading scorer in the league phase, Andrea Moretti. Several other opportunities were created and spurned by Marco Protti's side as they sought their fourth title in six years, but it looked as if that one goal would be enough to win it until the third minute of added time, when La Fiorita's San Marino international Danilo Rinaldi collected a free-kick at the far post and squeezed his shot underneath Tre Penne 'keeper Mattia Migani to take the match into extra time. Rinaldi then struck again, with a powerful header from a corner, to win the game and bring La Fiorita their fourth national title.

The team from Montegiardino, coached for the second successive season by Italian Luigi Bizzotto, might have left it late in the final, but they were worthy champions, having topped their first phase group, provided the league's leading scorer in 26-goal veteran Marco Martini, then won each of their first two play-off games without conceding a goal.

Tre Penne, on the other hand, were runners-up in their group, behind Libertas, and suffered a shock defeat in their opening play-off encounter when Juvenes/Dogana came from two goals down to score three times in the last ten minutes and beat them 3-2. That defeat meant the title holders were obliged to play four more matches, and win them all, to reach the final, which they duly did, eliminating Juvenes/Dogana in a rematch en route. Folgore, the 2014/15 double winners, lost to both finalists, but having previously defeated Libertas and, on penalties, Juvenes/Dogana, their semi-final place earned them a European spot.

Domestic cup

The first UEFA Europa League place was filled by Tre Penne in advance of the championship play-offs when they romped to victory in the Coppa Titano, becoming the fourth different winners in as many seasons. Second-half goals in the final against La Fiorita from Michele Simoncelli and Pietro Calzolari secured the club's first victory in the competition since 2000 – there had been three final defeats since then – and sixth in all. As in the league, the best team throughout took the trophy, Tre Penne having won all eight of their games on the road to the final. La Fiorita, in contrast, were beaten twice in the group stage.

Europe

Tre Penne, La Fiorita and Folgore were all well beaten in their first qualifying round ties, San Marino's trio of European representatives losing all six matches for the third summer in a row.

National team

There were understandably wild celebrations from San Marino's players and coaching staff when Mattia Stefanelli scored a brilliant goal to draw his team level with Norway in Oslo 54 minutes into the country's third 2018 FIFA World Cup qualifier. It was the team's first away goal in a World Cup fixture since April 2001. Unfortunately, though, it did not bring San Marino their first point in the competition since that 2002 series, when they drew 1-1 with Latvia, and there would be no further goals to celebrate, either, as they ended the season with 30 conceded in their opening six qualifying games, half of them to world champions Germany.

DOMESTIC SEASON AT A GLANCE

Campionato Sammarinese 2016/17 final tables

FIRST PHASE

Group A

		Pld	W	D	L	F	A	Pts
1	SP La Fiorita	20	14	2	4	51	22	44
2	Virtus FC	20	12	5	3	38	19	41
3	AC Juvenes/Dogana	20	8	7	5	27	22	31
4	FC Fiorentino	20	7	9	4	22	18	30
5	SS Cosmos	20	8	4	8	36	36	28
6	SP Tre Fiori	20	6	4	10	31	41	22
7	SC Faetano	20	4	4	12	16	33	16

Group B

		Pld	W	D	L	F	A	Pts
1	AC Libertas	21	14	5	2	37	13	47
2	SP Tre Penne	21	12	7	2	43	15	43
3	SS Folgore	21	13	4	4	53	15	43
4	FC Domagnano	21	11	3	7	44	26	36
5	SS Murata	21	6	2	13	28	50	20
6	SS Pennarossa	21	2	4	15	23	61	10
7	SP Cailungo	21	2	3	16	20	52	9
8	SS San Giovanni	21	1	5	15	15	61	8

CHAMPIONSHIP PLAY-OFFS

FIRST ROUND

(29/04/17)
Tre Penne 2-3 Juvenes/Dogana *(Simoncelli 11, Gai 58; Santini 83, Sorrentino 86, 89)*
Virtus 1-2 Folgore *(Aruci 38; Perrotta 9, Bezzi 61)*

SECOND ROUND

(03/05/17)
Folgore 0-0 Juvenes/Dogana *(aet; 3-0 on pens)*

(05/05/17)
Virtus 0-1 Tre Penne *(Fraternali 36)*
(Virtus eliminated)

THIRD ROUND

(06/05/17)
La Fiorita 1-0 Libertas *(M Martini 87)*

(09/05/17)
Juvenes/Dogana 1-3 Tre Penne *(Cuttone 24; Gai 71, Moretti 83, 90+3)*
(Juvenes/Dogana eliminated)

FOURTH ROUND

(12/05/17)
La Fiorita 2-0 Folgore *(Zafferani 103, Gasperoni 105) (aet)*

(13/05/17)
Tre Penne 2-0 Libertas *(Moretti 50, Simoncelli 84p)*
(Libertas eliminated)

SEMI-FINAL

(16/05/17)
Tre Penne 1-0 Folgore *(Moretti 88)*
(Folgore eliminated)

FINAL

(20/05/17)
San Marino Stadium, Serravalle
SP LA FIORITA 2 *(Rinaldi 90+3, 110)*
SP TRE PENNE 1 *(Moretti 1)*
(aet)
Referee: *Barbeno*
LA FIORITA: *Vivan, Gasperoni, Olivi, A Martini, Rinaldi, Lunadei (Parma 84), Cejas, Cangini (Cavalli 118), Zafferani, Mottola, M Martini (Guidi 63)*
TRE PENNE: *Migani, Cesarini (Valli 110), Fraternali, Rossi, Merendino, Gasperoni, Patregnani, Gai, Palazzi (Bonini 90), Simoncelli, Moretti (Capicchioni 65)*
Red card: *Rossi (119)*

European qualification 2017/18

Champion: SP La Fiorita (first qualifying round)

Cup winner: SP Tre Penne (first qualifying round)
SS Folgore (first qualifying round)

Top scorer Marco Martini (La Fiorita), 26 goals
Cup final SP Tre Penne 2-0 SP La Fiorita

Player of the season

Marco Martini
(SP La Fiorita)

Martini ended a long and winding playing career with a bang as, at the age of 38, he won the Campionato Sammarinese with La Fiorita and scooped the golden boot for the second successive year, his winning tally of 26 goals in 20 group stage matches being supplemented by the winner against Libertas in the play-offs. The Italian striker had previously played in his country's Serie B with Pescara and Frosinone, but it was to his hometown club of Rimini FC, in Serie D, that he returned, as assistant coach, after hanging up his boots following La Fiorita's play-off win against Tre Penne.

Newcomer of the season

Michael Battistini
(AC Juvenes/Dogana)

A versatile 20-year-old who can operate at right-back in addition to his favoured midfield role, Battistini had played for various San Marino youth selections before he made the step up to the Campionato Sammarinese in 2016/17 with Juvenes/Dogana. After starting the season on the bench, he established himself as a regular in the first XI and was instrumental in helping the team into the play-offs, where they shocked champions Tre Penne with a remarkable 3-2 win in the opening game. He won his first senior cap for San Marino in a March friendly against Moldova.

Team of the season

(4-3-3)

Coach: Bizzotto *(La Fiorita)*

NATIONAL TEAM

Top five all-time caps
Andy Selva (73); Damiano Vannucci (68); **Alessandro Della Valle** (64); **Simone Bacciocchi** (60); Aldo Simoncini (56)

Top five all-time goals
Andy Selva (8); Manuel Marani (2)

NB No other player has scored more than one goal.

Results 2016/17

04/09/16	Azerbaijan (WCQ)	H	Serravalle	L	0-1	
08/10/16	Northern Ireland (WCQ)	A	Belfast	L	0-4	
11/10/16	Norway (WCQ)	A	Oslo	L	1-4	*Stefanelli (54)*
11/11/16	Germany (WCQ)	H	Serravalle	L	0-8	
22/02/17	Andorra	H	Serravalle	L	0-2	
19/03/17	Moldova	H	Serravalle	L	0-2	
26/03/17	Czech Republic (WCQ)	H	Serravalle	L	0-6	
31/05/17	Italy	A	Empoli	L	0-8	
10/06/17	Germany (WCQ)	A	Nuremberg	L	0-7	

Appearances 2016/17

Coach: Pierangelo Manzaroli	**25/03/69**		**AZE**	**NIR**	**NOR**	**GER**	**And**	**Mda**	**CZE**	**Ita**	**GER**	**Caps**	**Goals**
Aldo Simoncini	30/08/86	Libertas	G	G	G	G	s46	G46	G	s46		56	-
Cristian Brolli	28/02/92	Folgore	D 52*		D	s83		D		D	s87	20	-
Davide Cesarini	16/02/95	Tre Penne	D	s56		D		D	D	D63	D87	10	-
Davide Simoncini	30/08/86	Libertas	D	D	D	D	D84	D	D			48	-
Mirko Palazzi	24/03/87	Tre Penne	D	D 49*		D	D	D	D		D	33	-
Marco Berardi	12/02/93	Folgore	D	D	s46	D						6	-
Filippo Berardi	18/05/97	Torino (ITA)	M73									1	-
Luca Tosi	04/11/92	Folgore & Giovane Cattolica (ITA)	M	M	M	M58	s46	M46		M55		16	-
Nicola Chiaruzzi	25/12/87	Tre Penne	M54									9	-
Adolfo Hirsch	31/01/86	Folgore	M	M56	s68	s91	s84	A67		M	s78	21	-
Matteo Vitaioli	27/10/89	Tropical Coriano (ITA)	A86	M		M91	M		M	M62		48	1
Lorenzo Gasperoni	03/01/90	Juvenes/Dogana	s54									10	-
Danilo Rinaldi	18/04/86	La Fiorita	s73		D46		s71	s46	D62	A	A78	31	1
Carlo Valentini	15/03/82	Murata	s86		M68			D46				46	-
Fabio Vitaioli	05/04/84	Tropical Coriano (ITA)	D	D	D				D			45	-
Alessandro Della Valle	08/06/82	Juvenes/Dogana		D	D		D			s55	D	64	1
Matteo Coppini	05/05/89	Amiternina (ITA)		M71								14	-
Mattia Stefanelli	12/03/93	Vis Novafeltria (ITA)		A88	A82	A	A		A84	s86		13	1
Enrico Golinucci	16/07/91	Libertas		s71			M46	s80				6	-
Tommaso Zafferani	19/02/96	La Fiorita & Fya Riccione (ITA)		s88	M	M83	M61		M	s62	M	8	-
Pier Filippo Mazza	20/08/88	Sant'Ermete (ITA)			M				s84	s71	M69	17	-
Andy Selva	23/05/76	La Fiorita			s82							73	8
Alex Gasperoni	30/06/84	Tre Penne				M						37	1
Marco Domeniconi	29/01/84	Folgore				s58	M	M83	M			20	-
Elia Benedettini	22/06/95	Novara (ITA)					G46	s46		G46	G	7	-
Alessandro D'Addario	09/09/97	Pianese (ITA)					D71					1	-
Lorenzo Lunadei	12/07/97	Fya Riccione (ITA)					M46					1	-
Alessandro Golinucci	10/10/94	Tropical Coriano (ITA)					s46			M	M	5	-
Fabio Tomassini	05/02/96	Romagna Centro (ITA)					s61	M80	s62			4	-
Michele Cervellini	14/04/88	Libertas						M	M91	M	M	32	-
Michael Battistini	08/10/96	Juvenes/Dogana						s46	s91			2	-
Marco Bernardi	02/01/94	Fiorentino						s67			s69	2	-
Maicol Berretti	01/05/89	Libertas						s83				25	-
Juri Biordi	01/01/95	Fiorentino								D86	D	4	-
Michele Cevoli	22/07/98	Savignanese (ITA)								D71		1	-
Giovanni Bonini	05/09/86	Tre Penne								s63	D	25	-

NB The San Marino amateur players are permitted to appear for more than one club at the same time.

EUROPE

SP Tre Penne

First qualifying round - The New Saints FC (WAL)

A 1-2 *Fraternali (16)*

Migani, Capicchioni, Merendino, Patregnani, Rossi, Gai, Valli (Palazzi 28), Calzolari, Censoni (Chiaruzzi 73), Fraternali, Agostinelli (Friguglietti 81). Coach: Marco Protti (SMR)

H 0-3

Migani, Capicchioni (Cesarini 72), Merendino, Patregnani, Rossi, Gasperoni (Friguglietti 79), Gai, Palazzi, Chiaruzzi (Calzolari 52), Fraternali, Agostinelli. Coach: Marco Protti (SMR)

SP La Fiorita

First qualifying round - Debreceni VSC (HUN)

H 0-5

Vivan, A Martini, Bugli, Cavalli (Parma 65), M Martini, Bollini (Mazzola 75), Rinaldi, Tommasi, Gasperoni, Cangini, Zafferani (Guidi 89). Coach: Luigi Bizzotto (ITA)

A 0-2

Vivan, Bugli, Parma (Cavalli 70), Selva (Guidi 83), M Martini, Bollini, Rinaldi, Tommasi, Gasperoni, Cangini (Righi 89), Zafferani. Coach: Luigi Bizzotto (ITA)

SS Folgore

First qualifying round - AEK Larnaca FC (CYP)

A 0-3

Montanari, Righi (Brolli 69), Nucci (Angelini 59), Muccini, Traini, Bezzi (Rossi 86), Perrotta, Genestreti, Hirsch, Quintavalla, Camillini. Coach: Luciano Mularoni (SMR)

H 1-3 *Traini (35)*

Montanari, Nucci (Rossi 72), Muccini, Traini, Bezzi, Angelini (Della Valle 87), Perrotta, Genestreti, Berardi (Brolli 67), Quintavalla, Camillini. Coach: Luciano Mularoni (SMR)

DOMESTIC LEAGUE CLUB-BY-CLUB

Stadiums

Stadio di Domagnano, Domagnano (200)
Serravalle B, Serravalle (350)
Stadio Federico Crescentini, Fiorentino (1,500)
Montecchio, Città di San Marino (500)
Stadio Ezio Conti, Dogana (350)
San Marino Stadium, Serravalle (4,801)

SP Cailungo

1974 • spcailungo.com

Coach: Giacomo Mugellesi (ITA); (25/02/17) Oscar Lasagni (ITA)

2016

11/09	Domagnano	L	1-4	*Longoni (p)*
17/09	Folgore	L	1-4	*Longoni (p)*
24/09	Libertas	L	0-2	
01/10	Pennarossa	D	1-1	*Boschi*
15/10	Tre Penne	L	0-1	
22/10	San Giovanni	L	0-1	
06/11	Murata	L	0-1	
16/11	Juvenes/Dogana	L	2-3	*Polidori, Manzari*
26/11	Fiorentino	L	0-1	
03/12	La Fiorita	L	1-5	*Manzari*
11/12	Tre Fiori	L	1-2	*Bartolini (p)*

2017

04/02	Faetano	W	3-1	*Villa, Giordani, Manzari*
11/02	Virtus	L	0-3	
19/02	Cosmos	L	0-4	
25/02	Domagnano	L	1-3	*Giordani*
05/03	Folgore	L	0-7	
12/03	Libertas	L	2-3	*Ciavatta 2*
02/04	Pennarossa	D	2-2	*N Venerucci, Ciavatta*
05/04	Tre Penne	L	0-2	
08/04	San Giovanni	D	1-1	*Zanotti*
13/04	Murata	W	4-1	*Angeli 2, Casali, og (Fariselli)*

Name	Nat	DoB	Pos	Aps	(s)	Gls
Daniele Angeli		29/07/92	D	9		2
Andrea Bartoli	ITA	10/09/76	A	6	(4)	
Luca Bartolini		11/02/84	M	19		1
Lorenzo Boschi		30/04/86	M	19		1
Andreas Bucci		07/06/89	A		(1)	
Enrico Casadei		18/02/96	D	9	(3)	
Filippo Casadei		02/07/01	G		(1)	
Massimiliano Casali		02/02/96	M	8	(5)	1
Simone Ciavatta		18/09/91	M	12	(3)	3
Daniele Donati	ITA	05/11/72	G	1		
Massimo Francioni		17/06/93	G	12		
Nicolò Giordani	ITA	12/04/96	M	10		2
Mattia Gualandi		08/04/93	D	10	(1)	
Manuel Iuzzolino	ITA	05/05/90	D	15	(1)	
Martin Longoni	ITA	25/09/91	A	8	(1)	2
Jacopo Manzari		06/03/88	A	6	(3)	3
Giovanni Marcucci		31/03/95	D	2	(2)	
Gianluca Micheloni		21/05/90	M	5	(3)	
Guido Nanni		30/09/90	D	5	(2)	
Filip Nedelkovski	MKD	03/07/97	M	1		
Nicola Polidori		12/03/91	M	5	(5)	1
Andrea Prunella	ITA	04/07/88	D	8	(1)	
Riccardo Regno	ITA	12/08/92	D	5		
Simone Santarini	ITA	17/10/91	M	8	(1)	
Nicolò Tamagnini		07/02/88	G	8		
Fabio Vecchiola	ITA	23/02/82	M	7	(3)	
Davide Venerucci		08/06/97	M	15	(1)	
Nicolò Venerucci		27/08/95	M	5	(5)	1
Alberto Villa	ITA	18/03/79	A	2		1
Luca Zafferani		06/09/97	D	5	(2)	
Michele Zanotti		05/01/88	D	6	(4)	1

SS Cosmos

1979 • no website

Major honours

San Marino League (1) 2001; San Marino Cup (4) 1980, 1981, 1995, 1999

Coach: Matteo Cecchetti (ITA); (22/11/16) Sereno Uraldi (ITA)

2016

11/09	Juvenes/Dogana	L	0-2	
18/09	Faetano	L	1-3	*Giardi*
25/09	Fiorentino	L	1-3	*Maurizi*
02/10	Virtus	W	3-1	*Marigliano, Neri (p), Celli*
16/10	Tre Fiori	W	1-0	*Negri*
05/11	La Fiorita	D	3-3	*Zaboul, Neri, Marigliano*
15/11	Tre Penne	L	2-5	*Neri, Zaboul*
20/11	Pennarossa	W	5-0	*Zaboul (p), Marigliano 2, Maurizi, Giulianelli*
27/11	Domagnano	L	1-5	*Neri (p)*
03/12	Libertas	L	0-3	
10/12	San Giovanni	W	5-1	*Neri 2 (1p), Zaboul 2, Marigliano*

2017

05/02	Murata	W	1-0	*Camillini*
11/02	Folgore	D	0-0	
19/02	Cailungo	W	4-0	*Negri, Camillini, Giulianelli, Moretti*
25/02	Juvenes/Dogana	D	1-1	*Negri*
04/03	Faetano	W	1-0	*Giardi*
11/03	Fiorentino	L	1-3	*Negri*
01/04	Virtus	D	1-1	*Guerra*
04/04	Tre Fiori	W	3-2	*Negri 2, Zaghini*
14/04	La Fiorita	L	2-3	*Camillini, og (Guidi)*

Name	Nat	DoB	Pos	Aps	(s)	Gls
Matteo Camillini	ITA	10/01/84	D	9	(2)	3
Giuseppe Casali		08/07/73	G	1		
Alex Cavalli		26/02/92	D	18	(1)	
Alberto Celli		25/06/85	M	3	(1)	1
Lorenzo Fortunato	ITA	08/01/88	D		(5)	
Matteo Giardi		14/04/97	A	1	(8)	2
Daniel Giulianelli		12/01/95	D	19	(1)	2
Fabiano Grassi	ITA	06/05/88	M	20		
Tommaso Guerra		22/08/90	M	16	(3)	1
Luca Lelli	ITA	25/09/79	G	19		
Kevin Marigliano	ITA	10/05/93	A	16		5
Francesco Maurizi	ITA	10/01/90	A	8	(2)	2
Manuel Molinari		20/08/86	D	5	(3)	
Nicola Moretti		20/04/84	D	3	(9)	1
Cristian Negri		16/01/85	A	11	(3)	6
Roberto Neri	ITA	06/08/93	A	16	(1)	6
Stefano Pari		13/12/93	A	6	(9)	
Alberto Semprini	ITA	13/02/90	D	18		
Massimo Vagnetti		25/06/79	D	1	(3)	
Mohammed Zaboul	MAR	19/02/79	A	8	(7)	5
Guido Zaghini	ITA	06/12/88	M	19		1
Kevin Zonzini		11/08/97	M	3		

SAN MARINO

FC Domagnano

1966 • no website

Major honours
San Marino League (4) 1989, 2002, 2003, 2005; San Marino Cup (8) 1972, 1988, 1990, 1992, 1996, 2001, 2002, 2003

Coach: Cristian Protti (ITA)

2016			
11/09	Cailungo	W 4-1	*Chiarabini 2, Casadei, Rossi*
17/09	San Giovanni	D 0-0	
25/09	Folgore	L 0-4	
01/10	Libertas	L 1-4	*Agostinelli*
15/10	Murata	D 2-2	*Bianchi, Chiarabini*
23/10	Tre Penne	W 4-1	*Chiarabini, Bianchi, Agostinelli, Narducci*
05/11	Pennarossa	W 5-0	*og (Broccoli), L Ceccaroli, Dolcini, Bianchi 2*
15/11	La Fiorita	L 0-3	
19/11	Fiorentino	W 2-0	*Agostinelli, Chiarabini*
27/11	Cosmos	W 5-1	*Chiarabini 3, Bianchi 2*
03/12	Tre Fiori	W 3-0	*Venerucci, Chiarabini 2 (1p)*
10/12	Faetano	W 3-0	*L Ceccaroli, Agostinelli, Locatelli*
2017			
05/02	Virtus	L 0-1	
12/02	Juvenes/Dogana	D 1-1	*Agostinelli*
25/02	Cailungo	W 3-1	*Chiarabini (p), Narducci, Agostinelli*
05/03	San Giovanni	W 3-0	*Chiarabini 2 (1p), Narducci*
11/03	Folgore	L 0-2	
02/04	Libertas	L 0-1	
05/04	Murata	W 4-2	*L Ceccaroli, Agostinelli, Rossi 2*
08/04	Tre Penne	L 0-1	
13/04	Pennarossa	W 4-1	*Chiarabini (p), Sensoli 2, L Ceccaroli*

Name	Nat	DoB	Pos	Aps	(s)	Gls
Marco Agostinelli	ITA	22/04/78	A	18	(2)	7
Alessandro Bianchi		19/07/89	A	19	(1)	6
Elia Bollini		13/10/97	M		(1)	
Federico Buldrini	ITA	18/09/83	D	14	(1)	
Michele Casadei		24/01/92	M	5	(9)	1
Luca Ceccaroli		05/07/95	M	13	(1)	4
Marco Ceccaroli		09/03/82	M	1	(2)	
Marco Cecchetti		03/02/97	M	2	(4)	
Mattia Censoni		31/03/96	D	9	(3)	
Carlo Chiarabini	ITA	27/04/76	A	17	(3)	14
Davide Dolcini		30/01/91	D	11	(5)	1
Alessio Faetanini		15/03/90	M	11	(1)	
Adriano Francioni		16/05/91	G	1		
Matteo Giannoni		25/03/88	D	11	(5)	
Luca Locatelli	ITA	16/01/78	D	21		1
Michele Moretti		01/04/85	D	1		
Giacomo Muraccini		29/09/90	G	20		
Marco Narducci		21/11/89	M	14		3
Mirko Piscaglia	ITA	06/09/83	M	4	(4)	
Nicola Ranocchini	ITA	16/09/89	M	4	(3)	
Giovanni Righi		07/03/91	A		(6)	
Paolo Rossi		05/07/94	M	19		3
Luca Sensoli		02/08/79	M	2	(7)	2
Andrea Venerucci		26/11/89	M	14	4	1

SC Faetano

1962 • faetanocalcio.sm

Major honours
San Marino League (3) 1986, 1991, 1999; San Marino Cup (3) 1993, 1994, 1998

Coach: Antonio Gespi (ITA)

2016			
18/09	Cosmos	W 3-1	*Moroni 2 (1p), Tomassoni*
23/09	Virtus	L 0-2	
02/10	Fiorentino	D 0-0	
15/10	La Fiorita	W 1-0	*Tomassoni*
21/10	Juvenes/Dogana	D 0-0	
06/11	Tre Fiori	D 1-1	*Ordonselli*
16/11	Libertas	L 1-2	*Giardi*
19/11	San Giovanni	W 2-1	*Giardi, Valentini*
26/11	Pennarossa	W 4-2	*Ordonselli 2, Bizzocchi, Giardi*
04/12	Folgore	L 0-3	
10/12	Domagnano	L 0-3	
2017			
04/02	Cailungo	L 1-3	*Moroni*
12/02	Tre Penne	D 0-0	
18/02	Murata	L 1-2	*Tomassoni*
04/03	Cosmos	L 0-1	
11/03	Virtus	L 1-2	*Ordonselli*
01/04	Fiorentino	L 0-1	
05/04	La Fiorita	L 0-2	
09/04	Juvenes/Dogana	L 1-3	*Giunchi*
14/04	Tre Fiori	L 0-4	

Name	Nat	DoB	Pos	Aps	(s)	Gls
Giacomo Barbanti	ITA	25/07/94	G	19	(1)	
Nicholas Bizzocchi	ITA	10/01/85	A	7	(6)	1
Sergio Carlucci	ITA	17/12/74	D		(2)	
Alex Della Valle		13/06/90	D	16	(1)	
Riccardo Ercolani		17/07/85	D	1	(5)	
Nicolò Ferrari	ITA	03/02/91	D	17		
Emanuele Fonte	ITA	06/08/92	D	14		
Mattia Giardi		15/12/91	M	17		3
Luca Giunchi	ITA	07/12/85	M	15		1
Marco Golfi		18/06/98	D		(2)	
Simone Guidi		14/06/00	G	1		
Massimo Moroni		17/02/90	A	11	(9)	3
Jacopo Ordonselli	ITA	07/07/94	M	16		4
Enrico Raggini	ITA	30/07/90	M	17	(1)	
Giacomo Rinaldi		23/03/90	D	20		
Matteo Rossi		09/07/86	M	1	(1)	
Samuel Toccaceli		09/11/96	M	4	(4)	
Luca Tomassoni		21/11/94	M	16		3
Marian Tubrea	ROU	21/03/88	A	3	(5)	
Simone Ugolini		28/02/91	M	16	(1)	
Massimo Vagnetti		25/06/79	D		(1)	
Vittorio Valentini		09/10/73	D	9	(4)	1

FC Fiorentino

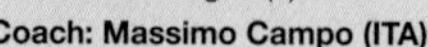

1974 • no website

Major honours
San Marino League (1) 1992

Coach: Massimo Campo (ITA)

2016			
11/09	La Fiorita	L 1-2	*Jaupi*
25/09	Cosmos	W 3-1	*Jaupi, Baizan, Vicini*
02/10	Faetano	D 0-0	
15/10	Virtus	D 0-0	
22/10	Tre Fiori	D 0-0	
06/11	Juvenes/Dogana	D 0-0	
16/11	San Giovanni	W 3-0	*Maiani, Jaupi, Vicini*
19/11	Domagnano	L 0-2	
26/11	Cailungo	W 1-0	*Jaupi*
04/12	Pennarossa	D 1-1	*M Bernardi*
10/12	Folgore	D 2-2	*Polanco (p), Vicini*
2017			
04/02	Tre Penne	D 1-1	*Jaupi*
12/02	Murata	W 2-1	*Jaupi (p), Pratelli*
18/02	Libertas	L 0-2	
25/02	La Fiorita	W 2-1	*Polanco, M Bernardi*
11/03	Cosmos	W 3-1	*og (Giulianelli), Ceccoli, Jaupi*
01/04	Faetano	W 1-0	*Polanco (p)*
04/04	Virtus	L 0-2	
09/04	Tre Fiori	D 2-2	*Vicini 2*
14/04	Juvenes/Dogana	D 0-0	

Name	Nat	DoB	Pos	Aps	(s)	Gls
Maximiliano Baizan		23/03/93	A	7	(8)	1
Andrea Bernardi		08/11/88	D	13	(1)	
Marco Bernardi		02/01/94	A	11	(6)	2
Luca Bianchi	ITA	27/02/90	G	20		
Juri Biordi		01/01/95	D	18		
Andrea Borgagni		21/10/93	M	1	(2)	
Manuel Carlini		26/05/93	D	5	(4)	
Andrea Ceccoli		22/09/93	M	8	(9)	1
Michele Giuliani		26/08/93	M	7	(7)	
Enea Jaupi	ALB	06/10/93	A	18		7
Evgeni Lipen	BLR	15/12/92	D	19		
Lorenzo Liverani		13/05/93	M	14	(4)	
Daniele Maiani		04/08/93	D	15	(3)	1
Alessandro Molinari	ITA	14/05/89	M	15	(1)	
Samuele Paoloni		18/01/97	A		(1)	
Emiliano Polanco	ITA	05/07/84	M	13	(3)	3
Massimiliano Pratelli	ITA	14/04/83	D	19		1
Emanuele Vicini	ITA	11/07/86	A	16	(3)	5
Enrico Zanotti		15/05/97	M		(1)	
Gerhard Zenunay	ALB	06/12/89	A	1	(4)	

SS Folgore

1972 • folgorecalcio.com

Major honours
San Marino League (4) 1997, 1998, 2000, 2015; San Marino Cup (1) 2015

Coach: Nicola Berardi

2016				
09/09	Murata	W	3-0	*Angelini, Della Valle, Camillini*
17/09	Cailungo	W	4-1	*Angelini 2, Brolli, Perrotta*
25/09	Domagnano	W	4-0	*Angelini 4*
02/10	San Giovanni	W	4-0	*Muccini, Hirsch, Della Valle, Rossi*
16/10	Libertas	L	1-2	*Perrotta*
22/10	Pennarossa	W	1-0	*Paradisi*
05/11	Tre Penne	L	0-1	
15/11	Tre Fiori	W	2-1	*Righi, Hirsch*
20/11	Virtus	W	2-1	*Angelini, Hirsch*
04/12	Faetano	W	3-0	*Domeniconi, Nucci, Angelini*
10/12	Fiorentino	D	2-2	*Angelini, Muccini*
2017				
04/02	Juvenes/Dogana	L	0-1	
11/02	Cosmos	D	0-0	
19/02	La Fiorita	L	1-2	*Angelini (p)*
26/02	Murata	W	5-0	*Perrotta 2, Angelini, Nucci, Guidi (p)*
05/03	Cailungo	W	7-0	*Angelini 2 (1p), Bezzi, Perrotta, og (Angeli), Aluigi (p), Nucci*
11/03	Domagnano	W	2-0	*Domeniconi, Angelini*
01/04	San Giovanni	W	6-1	*Rossi, Angelini 3 (1p), Nucci, Hirsch*
05/04	Libertas	D	1-1	*og (Cervellini)*
08/04	Pennarossa	W	3-0	*Perrotta (p), og (Gabrielli), Ballarini*
13/04	Tre Penne	D	2-2	*Angelini (p), Pacini*

Name	Nat	DoB	Pos	Aps	(s)	Gls
Riccardo Aluigi		20/07/93	M	2	(9)	1
Michael Angelini	ITA	25/11/83	A	13	(2)	19
Marco Ballarini		19/03/85	A	10		1
Marco Berardi		12/02/93	D	13	(3)	
Luca Bezzi	ITA	05/06/89	M	19	(1)	1
Davide Bicchiarelli	ITA	19/05/89	G	18		
Cristian Brolli		28/02/92	D	15	(1)	1
Filippo Burioni		02/05/98	A		(2)	
Matteo Camillini	ITA	10/01/84	M	9	(2)	1
Achille Della Valle		31/01/89	A	9	(6)	2
Marco Domeniconi		29/10/84	M	15	(2)	2
Cristofer Genestreti	ITA	30/05/84	D	12	(1)	
Tomas Guidi		04/09/92	D	2	(3)	1
Adolfo Hirsch		31/01/86	A	12	(5)	4
Simone Montanari	ITA	11/03/80	G	2		
Manuel Muccini	ITA	24/11/89	D	18	(1)	2
Andrea Nucci	ITA	06/09/86	M	16	(3)	4
Simone Pacini	ITA	08/01/81	M	4	(4)	1
Luca Paradisi	ITA	29/04/91	M	8	(2)	1
Francesco Perrotta	ITA	27/08/81	A	13	(3)	6
Luca Righi		01/04/95	D	9	(6)	1
Luca Rossi	ITA	14/04/93	M	9	(1)	2
Giuseppe Taddei		10/12/92	G	1	(1)	
Luca Tosi		04/11/92	M	2	(2)	

AC Juvenes/Dogana

2000 • no website

Major honours
San Marino Cup (2) 2009, 2011

Coach: Giampaolo Ceramicola (ITA)

2016				
10/09	Cosmos	W	2-0	*Mariotti 2*
18/09	Virtus	L	1-2	*Zafferani*
25/09	Tre Fiori	L	2-3	*Sorrentino, Mariotti*
01/10	La Fiorita	L	0-1	
21/10	Faetano	D	0-0	
06/11	Fiorentino	D	0-0	
16/11	Cailungo	W	3-2	*Santini, Sorrentino, Mantovani*
19/11	Libertas	D	0-0	
26/11	San Giovanni	W	3-1	*Mariotti, Sorrentino 2*
03/12	Murata	W	2-1	*Mariotti, Mantovani*
11/12	Tre Penne	D	0-0	
2017				
04/02	Folgore	W	1-0	*T Raschi*
12/02	Domagnano	D	1-1	*Santini*
18/02	Pennarossa	W	3-0	*Cuttone, Sorrentino (p), Michael Battistini (p)*
25/02	Cosmos	D	1-1	*Cuttone (p)*
03/03	Virtus	L	1-5	*Mariotti*
11/03	Tre Fiori	W	3-2	*Canini, Sorrentino (p), Zafferani*
02/04	La Fiorita	L	1-2	*Sorrentino*
09/04	Faetano	W	3-1	*Canini, Sorrentino 2*
14/04	Fiorentino	D	0-0	

Name	Nat	DoB	Pos	Aps	(s)	Gls
Manuel Battistini		22/07/94	D	2		
Michael Battistini		08/10/96	M	10	(1)	1
Nicola Canini		14/08/88	D	5	(9)	2
Nicolas Cavalli		22/04/94	A		(3)	
Thomas Cavalli	ITA	17/01/88	D	16	(4)	
Eugenio Colombini		16/01/92	M	2	(7)	
Alessandro Cuttone	ITA	24/03/84	M	8		2
Alessandro Della Valle		08/10/82	D	16		
Daniele Friguglietti	ITA	21/11/79	A	3	(2)	
Lorenzo Gasperoni		03/01/90	M	13	(4)	
Eros Gobbi		16/10/89	G	4		
Cristian Maccagno	ITA	05/06/83	M	14	(1)	
Mirko Mantovani	ITA	14/11/86	D	20		2
Mattia Manzaroli		03/10/91	G	16		
Giorgio Mariotti	ITA	06/05/86	A	14		6
Mattia Merlini		23/01/93	D	14		
Jacopo Raschi		28/04/98	A	1	(1)	
Thomas Raschi		11/07/96	M	6	(4)	1
Riccardo Santini	ITA	18/10/86	M	14	(2)	2
Luca Sorrentino	ITA	08/05/94	A	19		9
Daniele Villa	ITA	24/05/82	D	17		
Nicola Zafferani		06/11/91	M	5	(7)	2
Alessandro Zonzini		11/10/94	D	1	(1)	

SP La Fiorita

1967 • lafiorita.sm

Major honours
San Marino League (4) 1987, 1990, 2014, 2017; San Marino Cup (4) 1986, 2012, 2013, 2016

Coach: Luigi Bizzotto (ITA)

2016				
11/09	Fiorentino	W	2-1	*M Martini 2*
17/09	Tre Fiori	W	3-2	*Rinaldi, M Martini 2*
01/10	Juvenes/Dogana	W	1-0	*Selva (p)*
15/10	Faetano	L	0-1	
23/10	Virtus	D	1-1	*Mottola*
05/11	Cosmos	D	3-3	*og (Grassi), M Martini, Gasperoni*
15/11	Domagnano	W	3-0	*og (Locatelli), M Martini, Gasperoni*
20/11	Tre Penne	L	0-2	
27/11	Murata	W	4-0	*M Martini 2, Parma, Selva*
03/12	Cailungo	W	5-1	*og (Vecchiola), M Martini 3, Guidi*
11/12	Libertas	L	0-2	
2017				
05/02	Pennarossa	W	4-1	*M Martini 2, Selva 2*
11/02	San Giovanni	W	4-0	*Olivi, M Martini 2, Cangini*
19/02	Folgore	W	2-1	*Mottola (p), Selva*
25/02	Fiorentino	L	1-2	*M Martini*
04/03	Tre Fiori	W	6-1	*M Martini 2, Gasperoni, Mottola, Selva, Parma*
02/04	Juvenes/Dogana	W	2-1	*M Martini, Gasperoni*
05/04	Faetano	W	2-0	*A Martini, M Martini*
09/04	Virtus	W	5-1	*A Martini, M Martini 4*
14/04	Cosmos	W	3-2	*M Martini 2, Rinaldi*

Name	Nat	DoB	Pos	Aps	(s)	Gls
Francesco Beinat		16/12/96	M		(1)	
Gian Luca Bollini		24/03/80	D	9	(2)	
Davide Bugli		03/11/90	M	7	(3)	
Alessio Cangini	ITA	05/01/91	M	20		1
Nicola Cavalli		15/12/86	M	10	(8)	
Maximiliano Cejas	ARG	07/02/80	M	19		
Thomas De Biagi		03/11/90	M	1	(1)	
Emilio Benito Docente	ITA	11/12/83	A	1		
Marco Gasperoni	ITA	18/02/92	D	18		4
Alessandro Guidi		14/12/86	A	5	(9)	1
Lorenzo Lunadei		12/07/97	M	1		
Andrea Martini	ITA	24/12/81	D	19		2
Marco Martini	ITA	12/04/79	A	20		26
Alberto Mazzola	ITA	21/07/84	D	13	(1)	
Tiziano Mottola	ITA	06/07/86	M	11	(2)	3
Alan Neri		11/07/97	G	1	(1)	
Samuele Olivi	ITA	01/08/80	D	8		1
Simon Parma	ITA	20/03/83	A	4	(7)	2
Andrea Righi		10/07/97	M	3	(6)	
Danilo Rinaldi		18/04/86	A	15		2
Andy Selva		23/05/76	A	14	(1)	6
Gianluca Vivan	ITA	27/12/83	G	19		
Tommaso Zafferani		19/02/96	M	2	(2)	

SAN MARINO

AC Libertas

1928 • polisportivalibertas.com

Major honours
San Marino League (1) 1996; San Marino Cup (11) 1937, 1950, 1954, 1958, 1959, 1961, 1987, 1989, 1991, 2006, 2014

Coach: Pasquale D'Orsi (ITA)

2016

10/09	Pennarossa	W	2-1	*S Rossi, Morelli*
18/09	Tre Penne	L	0-1	
24/09	Cailungo	W	2-0	*S Rossi 2*
01/10	Domagnnao	W	4-1	*Golinucci, S Rossi 3*
16/10	Folgore	W	2-1	*Casadei, Morelli*
23/10	Murata	W	2-0	*S Rossi, Casadei*
05/11	San Giovanni	D	0-0	
16/11	Faetano	W	2-1	*og (Barbanti), Morelli (p)*
19/11	Juvenes/Dogana	D	0-0	
26/11	Virtus	L	0-2	
03/12	Cosmos	W	3-0	*S Rossi, D Simoncini, Casadei*
11/12	La Fiorita	W	2-0	*Golinucci, Morelli*

2017

04/02	Tre Fiori	W	4-0	*Morelli, Soumah, S Rossi 2*
18/02	Fiorentino	W	2-0	*Berretti, Casadei*
26/02	Pennarossa	W	3-1	*Buda, Casadei, Golinucci*
05/03	Tre Penne	D	0-0	
12/03	Cailungo	W	3-2	*Casadei, Buda 2*
02/04	Domagnano	W	1-0	*Morelli*
05/04	Folgore	D	1-1	*Casadei*
08/04	Murata	W	2-0	*Rocchi, Buda*
13/04	San Giovanni	D	2-2	*Buda, Casadei*

Name	Nat	DoB	Pos	Aps	(s)	Gls
Daniele Angeli		29/07/92	D		(2)	
Andrea Benvenuti		24/07/90	D		(3)	
Maicol Berretti		01/05/89	M	9	(5)	1
Samuele Buda	ITA	04/07/86	M	19	(1)	5
Michele Camillini	ITA	10/01/84	D	20		
Marco Casadei		20/09/85	A	20		8
Michele Cervellini		14/04/88	D	19	(1)	
Marco Cupi		27/01/99	D	3	(6)	
Mirko Giardi		11/05/95	M	1		
Enrico Golinucci		16/07/91	M	17	(3)	3
Gian Luca Morelli	ITA	13/02/85	A	19		6
Daniele Rocchi	ITA	23/06/82	D	18		1
Michele Rossi		26/01/95	D	9	(5)	
Simone Rossi	ITA	13/06/87	A	15	(1)	10
Aldo Simoncini		30/08/86	G	15		
Davide Simoncini		30/08/86	D	19		1
Abdoulaziz Soumah	ITA	22/01/96	M	20		1
Francesco Stacchini		18/01/97	D	1	(4)	
Andrea Zavoli		04/07/94	M	1	(7)	
Matteo Zavoli		06/07/96	G	6		

SS Murata

1966 • muratacalcio.com

Major honours
San Marino League (3) 2006, 2007, 2008; San Marino Cup (3) 1997, 2007, 2008

Coach: Fabrizio Costantini

2016

09/09	Folgore	L	0-3	
18/09	Pennarossa	W	3-2	*Antonioni, Valentini, Albani*
24/09	San Giovanni	W	5-2	*Bernabucci 2, Antonioni 3*
01/10	Tre Penne	D	1-1	*Agostinelli*
15/10	Domagnano	D	2-2	*Angelini, Sternini*
23/10	Libertas	L	0-2	
06/11	Cailungo	W	1-0	*Antonioni*
19/11	Tre Fiori	L	1-3	*Sternini*
27/11	La Fiorita	L	0-4	
03/12	Juvenes/Dogana	L	1-2	*N Casadei*
10/12	Virtus	L	1-2	*Agostinelli*

2017

05/02	Cosmos	L	0-1	
12/02	Fiorentino	L	1-2	*Antonioni (p)*
18/02	Faetano	W	2-1	*Antonioni, Innocenti*
26/02	Folgore	L	0-5	
04/03	Pennarossa	W	5-1	*Innocenti 2, Angelini, Valentini, og (Lazzarini)*
12/03	San Giovanni	W	2-1	*Sternini, Bagli*
01/04	Tre Penne	L	0-6	
05/04	Domagnano	L	2-4	*Antonioni, Angelini*
08/04	Libertas	L	0-2	
13/04	Cailungo	L	1-4	*Innocenti*

Name	Nat	DoB	Pos	Aps	(s)	Gls
Luca Agostinelli	ITA	05/02/89	M	9		2
Nicola Albani		15/04/81	D	17		1
Nicolò Angelini		15/03/92	A	10	(7)	3
Enrico Antonioni	ITA	08/08/82	M	20		8
Giordo Bagli	ITA	15/01/81	M	13	(1)	1
Davide Bernabucci	ITA	27/04/85	A	9		2
Andrea Borgagni		21/10/96	M	3	(2)	
Lorenzo Bugli		19/06/98	G	5		
Lorenzo Buscarini		27/05/91	D	17		
Mattia Casadei		26/01/89	D	14	(3)	
Nicola Casadei		24/01/89	M	13	(6)	1
Vincenzo Committante	ITA	06/09/80	D	5		
Thomas De Biagi		03/11/90	M	1	(1)	
Angelo Faetanini		17/01/93	D	14	(1)	
Marco Fariselli	ITA	17/05/87	D	7	(1)	
Thomas Felici		26/11/95	A	2	(6)	
Federico Gennari		28/08/92	A	3	(8)	
Marco Graziosi		26/08/89	G	16		
William Innocenti	ITA	30/04/87	A	7		4
Steven Raul James		07/07/98	G		(1)	
Alessandro Protti		28/07/81	M	2	(7)	
Michael Simoncini		01/02/87	M	10		
Francesco Sternini	ITA	29/06/87	M	16		3
Samuele Tardini	ITA	05/01/97	D	3	(6)	
Carlo Valentini		15/03/82	M	15	(2)	2

SS Pennarossa

1968 • pennarossa.com

Major honours
San Marino League (1) 2004; San Marino Cup (2) 2004, 2005

Coach: Ligor Cobo (ALB); (05/02/17) Matteo Selva

2016

10/09	Libertas	L	1-2	*Lago*
18/09	Murata	L	2-3	*N Ciacci, Aissaoui*
24/09	Tre Penne	W	2-0	*Aissaoui, N Ciacci*
01/10	Cailungo	D	1-1	*Podeschi*
16/10	San Giovanni	W	4-0	*Aissaoui 2, N Ciacci 2*
22/10	Folgore	L	0-1	
05/11	Domagnano	L	0-5	
15/11	Virtus	L	0-2	
20/11	Cosmos	L	0-5	
26/11	Faetano	L	2-4	*N Ciacci, Toccaceli*
04/12	Fiorentino	D	1-1	*Lago*

2017

05/02	La Fiorita	L	1-4	*og (Olivi)*
11/02	Tre Fiori	L	1-4	*Lago*
18/02	Juvenes/Dogana	L	0-3	
26/02	Libertas	L	1-3	*Frigueglietti*
04/03	Murata	L	1-5	*Lago*
12/03	Tre Penne	L	1-7	*Aissaoui*
02/04	Cailungo	D	2-2	*Frigueglietti, A Ciacci*
05/04	San Giovanni	D	2-2	*og (Borgelli), Frigueglietti*
08/04	Folgore	L	0-3	
13/04	Domagnano	L	1-4	*Lago*

Name	Nat	DoB	Pos	Aps	(s)	Gls
Amir Aissaoui	ITA	30/12/92	M	21		5
Marco Baldani		05/12/97	M	10	(4)	
Emanuele Bindi	ITA	23/02/99	M	6	(4)	
Andrea Boschi	ITA	19/05/98	D	15	(4)	
Denis Broccoli	ITA	08/10/88	G	19		
Nicholas Capozzi	ITA	12/12/87	A	1	(2)	
Alessandro Ciacci		15/07/96	A	8	(5)	1
Nicola Ciacci		07/07/82	A	14	(1)	5
Daniele Conti	ITA	06/06/90	D	7	(1)	
Tommaso Conti	ITA	18/06/92	M	4	(1)	
Andrea Farabegoli	ITA	01/08/76	D	17		
Daniele Frigueglietti	ITA	21/11/79	A	10		3
Alessio Gabrielli	ITA	18/02/96	D	8	(1)	
Luca Giuliani	ITA	15/02/83	G	2	(2)	
Anxhelo Isaraj	ALB	25/12/91	M	6		
Ramiro Martín Lago	ARG	14/10/87	A	16	(2)	5
Luca Lazzarini		28/05/92	D	16		
Sandro Macerata	ITA	08/10/69	D	14		
Paolo Mariotti		05/11/79	D	3	(3)	
Jai Emanuel Pacheco	ARG	22/12/90	A		(5)	
Mirco Paglialonga	ITA	19/09/93	D	18	(1)	
Alessandro Podeschi		05/04/97	M	9	(8)	1
Nicholas Stradaioli	ITA	21/01/85	M		(2)	
Glori Taraj	ITA	21/09/90	D	2	(1)	
Samuel Toccaceli		11/09/96	M	5	(4)	1

SS San Giovanni

1948 • no website

Coach: Ermanno Zonzini; (28/01/17) Ivo Crescentini (ITA)

2016

11/09	Tre Penne	L 1-4	*Renzi*
17/09	Domagnano	D 0-0	
24/09	Murata	L 2-5	*Cecchetti, Esposito*
02/10	Folgore	L 0-4	
16/10	Pennarossa	L 0-4	
22/10	Cailungo	W 1-0	*Cuttone*
05/11	Libertas	D 0-0	
16/11	Fiorentino	L 0-3	
19/11	Faetano	L 1-2	*Moroni*
26/11	Juvenes/Dogana	L 1-3	*Moroni*
04/12	Virtus	L 0-4	
10/12	Cosmos	L 1-5	*Antonelli*

2017

11/02	La Fiorita	L 0-4	
19/02	Tre Fiori	L 1-2	*og (Galassi)*
25/02	Tre Penne	L 0-5	
05/03	Domagnano	L 0-3	
12/03	Murata	L 1-2	*Karamo*
01/04	Folgore	L 1-6	*Franklin*
05/04	Pennarossa	D 2-2	*Franklin (p), Bugli*
08/04	Cailungo	D 1-1	*Henrique António*
13/04	Libertas	D 2-2	*Franklin 2*

Name	Nat	DoB	Pos	Aps	(s)	Gls
Filippo Antonelli	ITA	28/01/83	M	8		1
Marco Borgelli	ITA	19/01/81	D	14	(1)	
Matteo Bugli		10/03/83	D	15	(2)	1
Edoardo Cecchetti		14/07/93	D	17		1
Alessandro Cuttone	ITA	24/03/84	M	7		1
Alessandro Esposito		06/08/93	A	8	(7)	1
Sam Fantini		17/09/92	D	1	(3)	
Marco Fariselli	ITA	17/05/87	D	7		
Franklin	BRA	13/04/84	A	6		4
Gabriele Genghini		07/10/90	D	10	(1)	
Fabio Giardi		15/03/71	D	4	(3)	
Domenico Giordani	ITA	25/03/83	D	19		
Henrique António	BRA	19/05/82	M	6		1
Samathe Karamo	GAM	24/02/94	M	18		1
Nicolas Lazzaro	ITA	20/07/93	D		(2)	
Andrea Manzaroli		12/02/95	G	19		
Andrea Manzaroli		12/02/95	D	2		
Andrea Molari	ITA	25/04/89	A	1		
Andrea Moroni		10/10/85	A	13		2
Samuele Paoloni		18/01/97	D	8		
William Pierini		12/06/96	A	1	(5)	
Andrea Renzi	ITA	13/01/84	A	6		1
Andrea Tellinai		28/07/86	M	7		
Andrea Valentini		04/11/98	M	10	(6)	
Matteo Venerucci		16/12/80	G	2		
Matteo Venerucci		16/12/80	D		(2)	
Denis Veronesi		17/07/88	M	16	(1)	
Loris Zafferani		14/08/83	D	4	(3)	
Andrea Zanotti		05/05/92	M	2	(6)	

SP Tre Fiori

1949 • no website

Major honours
San Marino League (7) 1988, 1993, 1994, 1995, 2009, 2010, 2011; San Marino Cup (6) 1966, 1971, 1974, 1975, 1985, 2010

Coach: Altin Lisi (ALB); (26/10/16) Massimo Gori (ITA)

2016

10/09	Virtus	L 1-4	*Camilli*
17/09	La Fiorita	L 2-3	*Gabrielli, Andreini*
25/09	Juvenes/Dogana	W 3-2	*Andreini, Camilli 2*
16/10	Cosmos	L 0-1	
22/10	Fiorentino	D 0-0	
06/11	Faetano	D 1-1	*Teodorani*
15/11	Folgore	L 1-2	*Camilli (p)*
19/11	Murata	W 3-1	*Camilli 2, Verri*
27/11	Tre Penne	L 0-2	
03/12	Domagnano	L 0-3	
11/12	Cailungo	W 2-1	*Verri 2*

2017

04/02	Libertas	L 0-4	
11/02	Pennarossa	W 4-1	*og (Boschi), Badalassi, Camilli 2*
19/02	San Giovanni	W 2-1	*Camilli, Badalassi (p)*
26/02	Virtus	D 1-1	*Badalassi*
04/03	La Fiorita	L 1-6	*Camilli*
11/03	Juvenes/Dogana	L 2-3	*Camilli (p), Bencistà*
04/04	Cosmos	L 2-3	*Badalassi 2*
09/04	Fiorentino	D 2-2	*Camilli, F Matteoni*
14/04	Faetano	W 4-0	*og (Della Valle), Badalassi 2, Andreini*

Name	Nat	DoB	Pos	Aps	(s)	Gls
Federico Amici		27/03/82	A	1	(3)	
Matteo Andreini		10/11/81	D	4		3
Imre Badalassi	ITA	08/02/95	A	8		7
Alberto Balducci	ITA	16/08/93	M	5	(2)	
Daniele Bencistà	ITA	26/02/76	M	8	(1)	1
Giacomo Benedettini		07/10/82	D	2	(3)	
Massimo Camilli	ITA	18/01/95	A	17		12
Nicholas Capozzi	ITA	12/12/87	A		(1)	
Michele Carlini		25/11/97	D	1	(2)	
Michele Ceccoli		04/12/73	G	7		
Stefano Conti		18/07/70	D		(1)	
Nicola Della Valle		19/05/97	M	11	(6)	
Alessio Gabrielli	ITA	18/02/96	D	3	(2)	1
Simone Galassi	ITA	23/04/96	D	16	(1)	
Federico Maiani		25/12/92	A	7	(1)	
Filippo Matteoni		27/05/96	M	7	(3)	1
Simone Matteoni		26/04/96	M	10	(4)	
Oscar Muratori	ITA	20/02/84	M	19		
Meriglen Shosha	ALB	29/01/87	D	11		
Alex Stimac	ITA	22/06/96	G	13		
Davide Succi	ITA	07/06/90	D	13		
Andrea Tamagnini		27/09/97	M	18	(1)	
Alessandro Teodorani	ITA	09/12/71	M	16		1
Fabio Vannoni	ITA	07/10/77	M	4	(6)	
Matteo Vendemini		18/01/82	D	2	(4)	
Paolo Verri	ITA	25/05/97	A	17	(3)	3

SP Tre Penne

1956 • trepenne.sm

Major honours
San Marino League (3) 2012, 2013, 2016; San Marino Cup (6) 1967, 1970, 1982, 1983, 2000, 2017

Coach: Marco Protti

2016

11/09	San Giovanni	W 4-1	*Gai, Palazzi, Rossi, Moretti*
18/09	Libertas	W 1-0	*Gai*
24/09	Pennarossa	L 0-2	
01/10	Murata	D 1-1	*Patregnani*
15/10	Cailungo	W 1-0	*Moretti*
23/10	Domagnano	L 1-4	*Patregnani*
05/11	Folgore	W 1-0	*Gai*
15/11	Cosmos	W 5-2	*Moretti 4, Gai*
20/11	La Fiorita	W 2-0	*Simoncelli, Moretti*
27/11	Tre Fiori	W 2-0	*Lazzarini, Palazzi*
11/12	Juvenes/Dogana	D 0-0	

2017

04/02	Fiorentino	D 1-1	*Palazzi*
12/02	Faetano	D 0-0	
18/02	Virtus	D 1-1	*Gai*
25/02	San Giovanni	W 5-0	*Moretti 3, Calzolari, og (Giardi)*
05/03	Libertas	D 0-0	
12/03	Pennarossa	W 7-1	*Rossi, Moretti 3, Merendino, Simoncelli, Gai*
01/04	Murata	W 6-0	*Moretti 3, Patregnani, Gasperoni 2 (1p)*
05/04	Cailungo	W 2-0	*Patregnani, Moretti*
08/04	Domagnano	W 1-0	*Palazzi*
13/04	Folgore	D 2-2	*Patregnani, Simoncelli*

Name	Nat	DoB	Pos	Aps	(s)	Gls
Giovanni Bonini		05/09/86	D	2	(1)	
Pietro Calzolari		28/10/91	M	15	(4)	1
Lorenzo Capicchioni		27/01/89	D	11	(3)	
Davide Cesarini		16/02/95	D	15	(2)	
Nicola Chiaruzzi		25/12/87	M	4	(1)	
Matteo Colonna		10/05/90	D	2		
Stefano Fraternali	ITA	13/04/86	D	19		
Nicola Gai	ITA	06/12/87	M	16		6
Alex Gasperoni		30/06/84	M	15	(2)	2
Andrea Lazzarini	ITA	08/04/86	A	4	(7)	1
Fabio Macaluso		05/08/86	G	1	(2)	
Dario Merendino	ITA	14/11/83	D	18	(1)	1
Mattia Migani	ITA	10/03/92	G	20		
Andrea Moretti	ITA	14/01/89	A	19		17
Federico Muccioli		20/06/96	D		(1)	
Mirko Palazzi		21/03/87	A	20		4
Luca Patregnani	ITA	08/04/85	M	20		5
Andrea Rossi	ITA	20/07/87	D	15	(1)	2
Michele Simoncelli	ITA	03/03/82	A	14	(3)	3
Matteo Valli		11/09/86	A	1	(5)	
Giacomo Zafferani		16/07/96	M		(12)	

Virtus FC

1964 • no website
Coach: Floriano Sperindio

2016				
10/09	Tre Fiori	W	4-1	*Brici, Semprini 2, Aruci*
18/09	Juvenes/Dogana	W	2-1	*Innocenti, Aruci*
23/09	Faetano	W	2-0	*Aruci 2 (1p)*
02/10	Cosmos	L	1-3	*Semprini*
15/10	Fiorentino	D	0-0	
23/10	La Fiorita	D	1-1	*Sacco*
15/11	Pennarossa	W	2-0	*L Nanni, Cesari*
20/11	Folgore	L	1-2	*Aruci*
26/11	Libertas	W	2-0	*Brici, Aruci*
04/12	San Giovanni	W	4-0	*Aruci 2, Semprini, Campidelli*
10/12	Murata	W	2-1	*Aruci 2*
2017				
05/02	Domagnano	W	1-0	*Montebelli*
11/02	Cailungo	W	3-0	*Montebelli, L Nanni, Aruci*
18/02	Tre Penne	D	1-1	*Aruci*
26/02	Tre Fiori	D	1-1	*Lusini*
03/03	Juvenes/Dogana	W	5-1	*Aruci 4, Montebelli*
11/03	Faetano	W	2-1	*Aruci, Bonifazi*
01/04	Cosmos	D	1-1	*L Nanni*
04/04	Fiorentino	W	2-0	*Aruci 2 (1p)*
09/04	La Fiorita	L	1-5	*Lusini*

Name	Nat	DoB	Pos	Aps	(s)	Gls
Armando Aruci	ITA	10/07/89	A	17	(1)	19
Gian Marco Baschetti	ITA	19/04/91	A	1	(5)	
Francesco Bonfé		27/05/94	D	1	(4)	
Luca Bonifazi		12/11/82	M	15		1
Emanuele Brici	ITA	16/02/87	D	18		2
Diego Campidelli	ITA	20/07/94	D	11	(1)	1
Vittorio Cesari	ITA	11/01/92	D	14		1
Mattia Dominici	ITA	29/07/94	D	13	(2)	
William Innocenti	ITA	30/04/87	A	10	(1)	1
Massimiliano La Monaca		26/04/95	G	1		
Daniele Lusini	ITA	10/03/82	D	19		2
Luca Montebelli	ITA	22/02/95	A	9		3
Luca Nanni		30/01/95	M	17		3
Matteo Nanni		07/03/83	M	5	(12)	
Andrea Righi		16/09/97	D	5	(6)	
Stefano Sacco	ITA	10/02/91	M	12	(1)	1
Matteo Scarponi		28/09/91	M	2		
Matteo Semprini	ITA	30/03/95	M	12	(1)	4
Alex Stefanelli		26/11/89	A		(6)	
Luca Tosi		23/07/94	A	2	(8)	
Davide Vagnetti		19/07/83	M	1	(1)	
Federico Valentini		22/01/82	G	19		
Marco Zannoni	ITA	14/08/82	M	16	(3)	

Top goalscorers

(excluding Play-offs)

26 Marco Martini (La Fiorita)

19 Michael Angelini (Folgore)
Armando Aruci (Virtus)

17 Andrea Moretti (Tre Penne)

14 Carlo Chiarabini (Domagnano)

12 Massimo Camilli (Tre Fiori)

10 Simone Rossi (Libertas)

9 Luca Sorrentino (Juvenes/Dogana)

8 Marco Casadei (Libertas)
Enrico Antonioni (Murata)

DOMESTIC CUP

Coppa Titano 2016/17

FIRST PHASE

(Played in Groups)

Group A

(14/09/16)
Cosmos 0-3 Pennarossa
Libertas 0-0 Cailungo

(28/09/16)
Pennarossa 1-1 Libertas

(23/11/16)
Cailungo 1-0 Pennarossa
Libertas 2-1 Cosmos

(30/11/16)
Cailungo 2-1 Cosmos

(28/01/17)
Cosmos 0-2 Cailungo

(29/01/17)
Libertas 6-0 Pennarossa

(07/02/17)
Cailungo 0-2 Libertas

(08/02/17)
Pennarossa 4-1 Cosmos

(15/03/17)
Cosmos 0-1 Libertas
Pennarossa 3-1 Cailungo

Final standings
Libertas 14 pts *(qualified)*
Pennarossa 10 pts *(qualified)*
Cailungo 10 pts
Cosmos 0 pts

Group B

(14/09/16)
Folgore 6-1 Domagnano
Juvenes/Dogana 0-2 Fiorentino

(28/09/16)
Domagnano 1-3 Juvenes/Dogana
Fiorentino 1-4 Folgore

(22/11/16)
Domagnano 1-3 Fiorentino

(23/11/16)
Folgore 2-0 Juvenes/Dogana

(28/01/17)
Domagnano 2-1 Juvenes/Dogana

(29/01/17)
Folgore 1-0 Fiorentino

(07/02/17)
Fiorentino 2-0 Juvenes/Dogana

(08/02/17)
Domagnano 2-1 Folgore

(14/03/17)
Fiorentino 1-1 Domagnano
Juvenes/Dogana 1-2 Folgore

Final standings
Folgore 15 pts *(qualified)*
Fiorentino 10 pts *(qualified)*
Domagnano 7 pts
Juvenes/Dogana 3 pts

Group C

(14/09/16)
Faetano 4-1 San Giovanni
Tre Penne 1-0 Virtus

(27/09/16)
San Giovanni 0-4 Tre Penne

(28/09/16)
Virtus 0-2 Faetano

(23/11/16)
Tre Penne 3-0 Faetano
Virtus 3-0 San Giovanni

(28/01/17)
Faetano 2-3 Virtus
Tre Penne 3-0 San Giovanni

(07/02/17)
San Giovanni 0-2 Faetano

(08/02/17)
Virtus 0-6 Tre Penne

(15/03/17)
Faetano 1-5 Tre Penne
San Giovanni 1-0 Virtus

Final standings
Tre Penne 18 pts *(qualified)*
Faetano 9 pts *(qualified)*
Virtus 6 pts
San Giovanni 3 pts

Group D

(13/09/16)
Tre Fiori 4-2 Murata

(28/09/16)
Muirata 3-2 La Fiorita

(23/11/16)
La Fiorita 2-2 Tre Fiori

(30/11/16)
Murata 1-1 Tre Fiori

(29/01/17)
Tre Fiori 1-2 La Fiorita

(08/02/17)
La Fiorita 4-1 Murata

(01/03/17)
La Fiorita 4-1 Murata

(08/03/17)
Murata 1-2 Tre Fiori

(15/03/17)
Tre Fiori 3-2 La Fiorita

Final standings
Tre Fiori 11 pts *(qualified)*
La Fiorita 10 pts *(qualified)*
Murata 4 pts

QUARTER-FINALS

(19/04/17)
La Fiorita 3-1 Libertas *(Rinaldi 31, M Martini 63, Guidi 90+2; Casadei 14)*

Tre Fiori 3-1 Pennarossa *(Balducci 12, Teodorani 23, Camilli 65; Aissaoui 73)*

(20/04/17)
Faetano 2-1 Folgore *(Ferrari 58, 68; Angelini 82)*

Tre Penne 2-1 Fiorentino *(Gai 40, Patregnani 73; Vicini 55)*

SEMI-FINALS

(22/04/17)
Tre Fiori 0-3 La Fiorita *(Zafferani 18, Rinaldi 75, M Martini 81)*

(23/04/17)
Tre Penne 2-1 Faetano *(Gai 31, Simoncelli 47; Bizzocchi 52)*

FINAL

(26/04/17)
San Marino Stadium, Serravalle
SP TRE PENNE 2 *(Simoncelli 67, Calzolari 89)*
SP LA FIORITA 0
Referee: *Avoni*
TRE PENNE: *Migani, Cesarini, Fraternali, Rossi, Merendino (Bonini 69), Gasperoni, Patregnani, Gai, Moretti (Calzolari 84), Simoncelli, Palazzi (Capicchioni 90)*
LA FIORITA: *Vivan, A Martini, Olivi, Mazzola, Gasperoni, Cejas, Zafferani (Guidi 89), Cangini, Mottola (Parma 75), Rinaldi, M Martini (Lunadei 89)*

Tre Penne captured the Coppa Titano for the sixth time

SCOTLAND

Scottish Football Association (SFA)

Address	Hampden Park GB-Glasgow G42 9AY
Tel	+44 141 616 6000
Fax	+44 141 616 6001
E-mail	info@scottishfa.co.uk
Website	scottishfa.co.uk

President	Alan McRae
Chief executive	Stewart Regan
Media officer	Greig Mailer
Year of formation	1873
National stadium	Hampden Park, Glasgow (52,063)

PREMIERSHIP CLUBS

 1 **Aberdeen FC**

 2 **Celtic FC**

 3 **Dundee FC**

 4 **Hamilton Academical FC**

 5 **Heart of Midlothian FC**

 6 **Inverness Caledonian Thistle FC**

 7 **Kilmarnock FC**

 8 **Motherwell FC**

 9 **Partick Thistle FC**

 10 **Rangers FC**

 11 **Ross County FC**

 12 **Saint Johnstone FC**

PROMOTED CLUB

 13 **Hibernian FC**

KEY
- UEFA Champions League
- UEFA Europa League
- Promoted
- Relegated

Invincible Celtic join the legends

Although the 2016/17 Scottish season witnessed the return to the Premiership of Rangers, the Ibrox side were mere bystanders as their eternal Glaswegian rivals Celtic rewrote the history books by not just winning all three major domestic trophies but doing so without losing a game.

It was an unprecedented feat, achieved in manager Brendan Rodgers' first season and on the 50th anniversary of the club's European Cup triumph. Rodgers' team were some way short of the legendary 'Lisbon Lions' in continental terms, however, failing to win a game in their UEFA Champions League group.

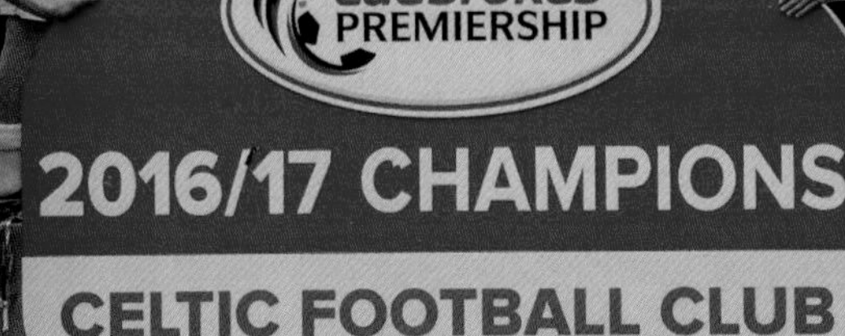

Bhoys go unbeaten through domestic programme

Rodgers lands historic treble in first season

Aberdeen take runners-up spot in all three competitions

Domestic league

Despite Rangers' first Premiership participation for five seasons, Celtic's sixth successive league title – and 48th in all – was a formality virtually from the outset. A summer recruitment drive that had focused on luring north a number of players from England reaped immediate dividends. Scott Sinclair, bought from Aston Villa, scored in the first six league games, while Moussa Dembélé, purchased from Fulham, scored the first hat-trick by a Celtic player in an Old Firm derby for 50 years as Rangers were overcome 5-1.

After a 2-2 draw in Inverness, it was victories all the way for the next six months, the Bhoys stringing 22 of them together before a 5-0 win at Hearts in early April made the inevitable a mathematical certainty. There were still eight matches left, but Celtic were on a mission and duly completed their 36-game programme without blemish, becoming the first team to go through a Scottish top-flight campaign unbeaten for 118 years.

To their record haul of 106 points Celtic added the same number of goals, with at least one scored in every game. Furthermore, only eight were conceded at home, and never more than one at a time. These were all dream figures for Rodgers and his players, many of whom enjoyed the finest season of their careers, Sinclair and Dembélé heading a list that also included midfielder Stuart Armstrong, veteran goalkeeper Craig Gordon and indefatigable skipper Scott Brown.

Derek McInnes's Aberdeen finished runners-up for the third year in a row, 30 points behind Celtic but nine ahead of Rangers, who changed manager in mid-campaign when Mark Warburton was replaced by Pedro Caixinha. An eclectic mix of youngsters and veterans, Brits and foreigners, the Gers did not have the quality to challenge Celtic, but they did qualify for Europe – as did fourth-placed St Johnstone. Inverness finished bottom by a point from Hamilton, who saved their top-flight status at Dundee United's expense in the play-offs after Hibernian, coached by ex-Celtic boss Neil Lennon, had won automatic promotion.

Domestic cups

The League Cup was advanced to the autumn, which meant that 27 November 2016 was the historic date on which Celtic claimed their 100th major trophy. They did so in style, too, beating Aberdeen 3-0 in the final. Six months to the day later, again with Aberdeen in opposition at Hampden, and again after beating Rangers in the semi-finals, Celtic completed the treble – the fourth in the club's history, after 1966/67, 1968/69 and 2000/01 – thanks to a 2-1 win secured with a dramatic added-time strike from Australian international Tom Rogic.

Europe

For all Celtic's domestic celebrations, Scotland's finest found the going considerably more arduous in Europe. They reached the UEFA Champions League group stage for the first time in three years, but only after a struggle, even losing 1-0 against the champions of Gibraltar in Rodgers' first game. A second trip to Iberia brought the club's heaviest European defeat as Barcelona trounced them 7-0 at the Camp Nou. Five matchdays later, still without a group win, their European campaign was over.

National team

Scotland's bid to end 20 years of major tournament non-participation looked unlikely to succeed as Gordon Strachan's side sat fourth in their 2018 FIFA World Cup qualifying group with just eight points. The horror of conceding a stoppage-time equaliser to England at Hampden after two late Leigh Griffiths free-kicks had given them an unlikely lead seemed destined to be the abiding memory of another frustrating campaign that started well enough, with Robert Snodgrass scoring Scotland's first World Cup hat-trick since 1969 in a 5-1 win in Malta, before veering badly off course with back-to-back 3-0 defeats away to Slovakia and England.

DOMESTIC SEASON AT A GLANCE

Premiership 2016/17 final table

			Home					Away					Total					
		Pld	W	D	L	F	A	W	D	L	F	A	W	D	L	F	A	Pts
1	**Celtic FC**	**38**	**17**	**2**	**0**	**47**	**8**	**17**	**2**	**0**	**59**	**17**	**34**	**4**	**0**	**106**	**25**	**106**
2	Aberdeen FC	38	12	3	4	34	16	12	1	6	40	19	24	4	10	74	35	76
3	Rangers FC	38	11	5	3	31	18	8	5	6	25	26	19	10	9	56	44	67
4	Saint Johnstone FC	38	8	3	8	25	25	9	4	6	25	21	17	7	14	50	46	58
5	Heart of Midlothian FC	38	9	5	5	36	20	3	5	11	19	32	12	10	16	55	52	46
6	Partick Thistle FC	38	6	5	9	21	32	4	7	7	17	22	10	12	16	38	54	42
7	Ross County FC	38	6	5	7	28	31	5	8	7	20	27	11	13	14	48	58	46
8	Kilmarnock FC	38	4	7	8	18	23	5	7	7	18	33	9	14	15	36	56	41
9	Motherwell FC	38	5	3	11	27	37	5	5	9	19	32	10	8	20	46	69	38
10	Dundee FC	38	5	5	9	19	30	5	2	12	19	32	10	7	21	38	62	37
11	Hamilton Academical FC	38	6	7	6	22	20	1	7	11	15	36	7	14	17	37	56	35
12	Inverness Caledonian Thistle FC	38	5	8	6	27	33	2	5	12	17	38	7	13	18	44	71	34

NB League splits into top and bottom halves after 33 games, with each team playing a further five matches exclusively against clubs from its half of the table.

European qualification 2017/18

Champion/Cup winner: Celtic FC (second qualifying round)

Aberdeen FC (second qualifying round)
Rangers FC (first qualifying round)
Saint Johnstone FC (first qualifying round)

Top scorer	Liam Boyce (Ross County), 23 goals
Relegated club	Inverness Caledonian Thistle FC
Promoted club	Hibernian FC
Scottish Cup final	Celtic FC 2-1 Aberdeen FC
League Cup final	Celtic FC 3-0 Aberdeen FC

Player of the season

Scott Sinclair
(Celtic FC)

Reunited at Celtic with his former Swansea City manager Brendan Rodgers, Sinclair left the disappointment of previous spells at Chelsea, Manchester City and Aston Villa in the past as he took his game to a new level in Scotland. With 21 goals, including a hat-trick in the Premiership title-clinching win at Hearts, the 27-year-old winger-cum-striker was the treble winners' top scorer in the league. He was also voted the official player of the season in Scotland by both the country's football writers and his fellow professionals.

Newcomer of the season

Moussa Dembélé
(Celtic FC)

Signed by Celtic from English Championship (second division) club Fulham on a four-year contract just before his 20th birthday, Dembélé made himself at home in Glasgow from day one and was to play a major role in the Hoops' historic treble-winning campaign. The skilful French Under-21 international amassed 32 goals for the club in all competitions – scoring five alone against Rangers plus a 24-minute hat-trick against St Johnstone – despite missing the last few weeks of the season, including the Scottish Cup final, with a hamstring injury.

Team of the season
(4-4-2)

Manager: Rodgers *(Celtic)*

NATIONAL TEAM

International tournament appearances
FIFA World Cup (8) 1954, 1958, 1974, 1978, 1982, 1986, 1990, 1998
UEFA European Championship (2) 1992, 1996

Top five all-time caps
Kenny Dalglish (102); Jim Leighton (91); **Darren Fletcher** (78); Alex McLeish (77); Paul McStay (76)

Top five all-time goals
Kenny Dalglish & Denis Law (30); Hughie Gallacher (23); Lawrie Reilly (22), Ally McCoist (19)

Results 2016/17

04/09/16	Malta (WCQ)	A	Ta' Qali	W	5-1	*Snodgrass (10, 61p, 85), C Martin (53), S Fletcher (78)*
08/10/16	Lithuania (WCQ)	H	Glasgow	D	1-1	*McArthur (89)*
11/10/16	Slovakia (WCQ)	A	Trnava	L	0-3	
11/11/16	England (WCQ)	A	London	L	0-3	
22/03/17	Canada	H	Edinburgh	D	1-1	*Naismith (35)*
26/03/17	Slovenia (WCQ)	H	Glasgow	W	1-0	*C Martin (88)*
10/06/17	England (WCQ)	H	Glasgow	D	2-2	*Griffiths (87, 90)*

Appearances 2016/17

Coach: Gordon Strachan	09/02/57		MLT	LTU	SVK	ENG	Can	SVN	ENG	Caps	Goals
David Marshall	05/03/85	Hull (ENG)	G	G	G					27	-
Callum Paterson	13/10/94	Hearts	D	D	D	s79				5	-
Russell Martin	04/01/86	Norwich (ENG)	D	D	D			D		29	-
Grant Hanley	20/11/91	Newcastle (ENG)	D	D	D	D				27	1
Andrew Robertson	11/03/94	Hull (ENG)	D	D			s46	D	M	15	1
Darren Fletcher	01/02/84	West Brom (ENG)	M	M46	M64	M	M			78	5
Barry Bannan	01/12/89	Sheffield Wednesday (ENG)	M	M	M		s46			25	-
Robert Snodgrass	07/09/87	Hull (ENG) /West Ham (ENG)	M	M	M	M82	M	M75	M67	24	6
Oliver Burke	07/04/97	RB Leipzig (GER)	M66	M57			M46			5	-
Matt Ritchie	10/09/89	Newcastle (ENG)	M86	M71	M64	s82				14	3
Chris Martin	04/11/88	Fulham (ENG)	A69	A			A62	s82	s81	13	3
James Forrest	07/07/91	Celtic	s66	s57		M		M		17	-
Steven Fletcher	26/03/87	Sheffield Wednesday (ENG)	s69		A76					30	9
Ikechi Anya	03/01/88	Derby (ENG)	s86		s64	D79	D	s75	M81	27	3
James McArthur	07/10/87	Crystal Palace (ENG)		s46	M	s66			s46	28	3
Leigh Griffiths	20/08/90	Celtic		s71	s64	A	s62	A50	A	13	2
Kieran Tierney	05/06/97	Celtic			D			D	D	4	-
John McGinn	18/10/94	Hibernian			s76		s76			3	-
Craig Gordon	31/12/82	Celtic				G		G	G	47	-
Christophe Berra	31/01/85	Ipswich (ENG)				D	D		D	36	3
Lee Wallace	01/08/87	Rangers				D	D46			10	-
James Morrison	25/05/86	West Brom (ENG)				M66		M82	M46	44	3
Scott Brown	25/06/85	Celtic				M		M	M	53	4
Allan McGregor	31/01/82	Cardiff (ENG)					G			36	-
Charlie Mulgrew	06/03/86	Blackburn (ENG)					D	D	D	27	2
Tom Cairney	20/01/91	Fulham (ENG)					M76			1	-
Steven Naismith	14/09/86	Norwich (ENG)					A62	s50		45	7
Jordan Rhodes	05/02/90	Sheffield Wednesday (ENG)					s62			14	3
Stuart Armstrong	30/03/92	Celtic						M	M	2	-
Ryan Fraser	24/02/94	Bournemouth (ENG)							s67	1	-

EUROPE

Celtic FC

Second qualifying round - Lincoln FC (GIB)
A 0-1
Gordon, Ambrose, Biton, Brown, Griffiths, Dembélé (Nadir Çiftçi 73), Christie (Forrest 57), Rogic (Armstrong 57), Janko, Sviatchenko, Tierney. Coach: Brendan Rodgers (NIR)
H 3-0 *Lustig (23), Griffiths (25), Roberts (29)*
Gordon, Brown, Griffiths, Dembélé (Nadir Çiftçi 76), Armstrong, Lustig, Roberts, Sviatchenko, McGregor, Forrest (Izaguirre 63), Tierney (Ajer 60). Coach: Brendan Rodgers (NIR)

Third qualifying round - FC Astana (KAZ)
A 1-1 *Griffiths (78)*
Gordon, Ambrose, Brown, Griffiths, Dembélé (Biton 62), Armstrong (Forrest 72), Lustig, Roberts, O'Connell, McGregor (Rogic 77), Tierney. Coach: Brendan Rodgers (NIR)
H 2-1 *Griffiths (45+2p), Dembélé (90+2p)*
Gordon, Brown, Griffiths, Armstrong (Touré 61), Janko, Lustig, Roberts (Johansen 31), O'Connell, McGregor, Forrest (Dembélé 75), Tierney. Coach: Brendan Rodgers (NIR)

Play-offs - Hapoel Beer-Sheva FC (ISR)
H 5-2 *Rogic (9), Griffiths (39, 45+1), Dembélé (73), Brown (85)*
Gordon, Touré, Brown, Griffiths, Sinclair, Rogic (Dembélé 70), Lustig (Janko 63), O'Connell, McGregor (Biton 60), Forrest, Tierney. Coach: Brendan Rodgers (NIR)
A 0-2
Gordon, Touré, Biton, Brown, Griffiths (Dembélé 57), Sinclair, Janko, Lustig, McGregor (Sviatchenko 65), Forrest (Rogic 46), Tierney. Coach: Brendan Rodgers (NIR)

Group C
Match 1 - FC Barcelona (ESP)
A 0-7
De Vries, Touré, Biton (McGregor 76), Brown, Dembélé, Sinclair, Gamboa , Lustig, Roberts (Armstrong 68), Sviatchenko (O'Connell 68), Tierney. Coach: Brendan Rodgers (NIR)
Match 2 - Manchester City FC (ENG)
H 3-3 *Dembélé (3, 47), Sterling (20og)*
Gordon, Touré, Biton (Griffiths 84), Brown, Dembélé, Sinclair, Rogic (Armstrong 57), Lustig, Sviatchenko, Forrest (Roberts 81), Tierney. Coach: Brendan Rodgers (NIR)
Match 3 - VfL Borussia Mönchengladbach (GER)
H 0-2
Gordon, Touré, Biton (McGregor 63), Brown, Dembélé, Sinclair, Rogic (Griffiths 71), Lustig, Sviatchenko, Forrest (Roberts 73), Tierney. Coach: Brendan Rodgers (NIR)
Match 4 - VfL Borussia Mönchengladbach (GER)
A 1-1 *Dembélé (76p)*
Gordon, Izaguirre, Brown, Dembélé, Sinclair, Gamboa (Henderson 85), Armstrong, Rogic (McGregor 69), Lustig, Sviatchenko, Forrest (Roberts 60). Coach: Brendan Rodgers (NIR)
Match 5 - FC Barcelona (ESP)
H 0-2
Gordon, Izaguirre, Šimunović, Brown, Dembélé, Sinclair (Forrest 46), Armstrong, Rogic (Biton 64), Lustig, Sviatchenko, McGregor (Roberts 72). Coach: Brendan Rodgers (NIR)
Match 6 - Manchester City FC (ENG)
A 1-1 Roberts (4)
Gordon, Izaguirre, Šimunović, Brown, Dembélé (Griffiths 73), Armstrong, Rogic, Lustig, Roberts, Sviatchenko, Forrest (Mackay-Steven 51). Coach: Brendan Rodgers (NIR)

Hibernian FC

Second qualifying round - Brøndby IF (DEN)
H 0-1
Virtanen, Gray, Hanlon, Bartley (Fontaine 65), McGinn, Holt, McGeouch (Keatings 65), Stevenson, Boyle (Harris 77), McGregor, Cummings. Coach: Neil Lennon (NIR)
A 1-0 (aet; 3-5 on pens) *Gray (62)*
Laidlaw, Gray (Boyle 77), Hanlon, Fontaine, Bartley (Forster 104), McGinn, Holt, McGeouch, Stevenson, McGregor, Cummings (Keatings 90+1). Coach: Garry Parker (ENG)

Aberdeen FC

First qualifying round - CS Fola Esch (LUX)
H 3-1 *Logan (68), McGinn (90+3), Rooney (90+8p)*
Lewis, Logan, Shinnie, Considine, Taylor, McLean, Flood (Rooney 55), McGinn, Hayes, Stockley, Jack. Coach: Derek McInnes (SCO)
A 0-1
Lewis, Logan, Shinnie, Considine, Taylor, McLean, Hayes, O'Connor (Reynolds 46), Pawlett (Flood 46), Stockley (Rooney 63), Jack. Coach: Derek McInnes (SCO)

Second qualifying round - FK Ventspils (LVA)
H 3-0 *Stockley (72), Rooney (76), Burns (90+2)*
Lewis, Logan, Shinnie, Considine, Taylor, Reynolds, McLean (Stockley 68), Rooney (Burns 89), McGinn, Hayes, Jack. Coach: Derek McInnes (SCO)
A 1-0 *Rooney (79)*
Lewis, Logan, Shinnie, Considine, Taylor, Reynolds, McLean, Rooney (Burns 79), McGinn (Stockley 71), Hayes (Storey 82), Jack. Coach: Derek McInnes (SCO)

Third qualifying round - NK Maribor (SVN)
H 1-1 *Hayes (88)*
Lewis, Logan, Shinnie (Burns 72), Considine, Taylor, Reynolds, Rooney, McGinn, Hayes, Stockley (McLean 72), Jack. Coach: Derek McInnes (SCO)
A 0-1
Lewis, Logan, Shinnie, Considine, Taylor, Reynolds, McLean (Storey 66), Burns (Stockley 51), Rooney, McGinn (Wright 84), Jack. Coach: Derek McInnes (SCO)
Red card: Stockley 61

Heart of Midlothian FC

First qualifying round - FCI Tallinn (EST)
H 2-1 *Buaben (28p), Kalimullin (36og)*
Hamilton, Paterson, Rherras, Alim Öztürk, Walker, Buaben (Kitchen 79), Juanma (King 65), Sutchuin Djoum, Nicholson, Souttar, Sammon. Coach: Robbie Neilson (SCO)
A 4-2 *Paterson (2), Igor Rossi (9, 52), Alim Öztürk (45+1)*
Hamilton, Paterson, Rherras, Igor Rossi, Alim Öztürk, Kitchen, Walker (Nicholson 70), Buaben (Souttar 74), Sutchuin Djoum (Juanma 89), Sammon, Smith. Coach: Robbie Neilson (SCO)

Second qualifying round - Birkirkara FC (MLT)
A 0-0
Hamilton, Paterson, Rherras, Igor Rossi, Alim Öztürk, Kitchen (Cowie 30), Walker (Nicholson 82), Buaben, Sutchuin Djoum, Sammon (Juanma 74), Smith. Coach: Robbie Neilson (SCO)
H 1-2 *Sammon (74)*
Hamilton, Paterson, Rherras, Igor Rossi (Muirhead 74), Alim Öztürk, Walker, Buaben (Cowie 81), Sutchuin Djoum, Nicholson, Sammon, Smith (Juanma 57). Coach: Robbie Neilson (SCO)

DOMESTIC LEAGUE CLUB-BY-CLUB

Aberdeen FC

1903 • Pittodrie (20,866) • afc.co.uk

Major honours
UEFA Cup Winners' Cup (1) 1983; UEFA Super Cup (1) 1983; Scottish League (4) 1955, 1980, 1984, 1985; Scottish Cup (7) 1947, 1970, 1982, 1983, 1984, 1986, 1990; Scottish League Cup (6) 1956, 1977, 1986, 1990, 1996, 2014

Manager: Derek McInnes

Date		Opponent		Score	Scorers
2016					
07/08	a	St Johnstone	D	0-0	
13/08	h	Hearts	D	0-0	
20/08	h	Partick	W	2-1	*McGinn, Storey*
27/08	a	Celtic	L	1-4	*Rooney*
10/09	h	Inverness	D	1-1	*McGinn*
18/09	a	Dundee	W	3-1	*Maddison, Stockley, McLean (p)*
25/09	h	Rangers	W	2-1	*Hayes, Maddison*
01/10	a	Kilmarnock	W	4-0	*Rooney 2 (1p), Considine, Taylor*
15/10	h	Ross County	W	4-0	*Hayes, Logan, McGinn, Stockley*
25/10	a	Hamilton	L	0-1	
29/10	h	Celtic	L	0-1	
04/11	a	Partick	W	2-1	*O'Connor, Stockley*
19/11	a	Inverness	W	3-1	*McLean 2, Rooney (p)*
03/12	a	Rangers	L	1-2	*Considine*
06/12	h	Kilmarnock	W	5-1	*Pawlett, O'Connor, Hayes 2, McGinn*
10/12	h	St Johnstone	D	0-0	
17/12	a	Ross County	L	1-2	*McGinn*
23/12	a	Motherwell	W	3-1	*Shinnie, Rooney (p), McGinn*
27/12	h	Hamilton	W	2-1	*Taylor, Rooney*
30/12	a	Hearts	W	1-0	*Hayes*
2017					
27/01	h	Dundee	W	3-0	*Jack, McGinn 2*
01/02	a	Celtic	L	0-1	
04/02	h	Partick	W	2-0	*Stockley, Christie*
15/02	h	Motherwell	W	7-2	*Hayes, Considine, Rooney 3 (1p), Christie, Pawlett*
19/02	a	Kilmarnock	W	2-1	*Stockley, Pawlett*
25/02	h	Ross County	W	1-0	*Rooney*
28/02	a	Hamilton	L	0-1	
11/03	h	Motherwell	W	1-0	*McGinn*
18/03	h	Hearts	W	2-0	*Logan, Hayes*
31/03	a	Dundee	W	7-0	*Considine 3, Rooney, McLean, Jack, McGinn*
04/04	h	Inverness	W	1-0	*og (Warren)*
09/04	h	Rangers	L	0-3	
15/04	a	St Johnstone	W	2-1	*Christie, og (Scobbie)*
29/04	h	St Johnstone	L	0-2	
07/05	a	Hearts	W	2-1	*Rooney, O'Connor*
12/05	h	Celtic	L	1-3	*Hayes*
17/05	a	Rangers	W	2-1	*Shinnie, Christie*
21/05	a	Partick	W	6-0	*Christie 2, Wright 3, Hayes*

No	Name	Nat	DoB	Pos	Aps	(s)	Gls
8	Wes Burns	WAL	23/11/94	A	7	(6)	
47	Dean Campbell		19/03/01	A		(1)	
8	Ryan Christie		28/04/95	M	7	(6)	6
4	Andrew Considine		01/04/87	D	36		6
11	Jonny Hayes	IRL	09/07/87	M	32		9
22	Ryan Jack		27/02/92	M	25		2
1	Joe Lewis	ENG	06/10/87	G	38		
2	Shay Logan	ENG	29/01/88	D	37	(1)	2
23	James Maddison	ENG	23/11/96	M	10	(4)	2
10	Niall McGinn	NIR	20/07/87	M	30	(6)	10
7	Kenny McLean		08/01/92	M	37	(1)	4
15	Anthony O'Connor	IRL	25/10/92	D	25	(7)	3
1	Peter Pawlett		18/06/91	M	6	(11)	3
6	Mark Reynolds		21/07/87	D	22	(4)	
9	Adam Rooney	IRL	21/04/88	A	32	(6)	12
27	Francis Ross		18/02/98	M		(3)	
3	Graeme Shinnie		04/08/91	M	35	(1)	2
17	Jayden Stockley	ENG	15/09/93	A	8	(19)	5
39	Miles Storey	ENG	04/01/94	A	2	(12)	1
19	Craig Storie		13/01/96	M		(2)	
5	Ash Taylor	WAL	02/09/90	D	28	(3)	2
26	Scott Wright		08/08/97	A	1	(4)	3

Celtic FC

1888 • Celtic Park (60,411) • celticfc.net

Major honours
European Champion Clubs' Cup (1) 1967;
Scottish League (48) 1893, 1894, 1896, 1898, 1905, 1906, 1907, 1908, 1909, 1910, 1914, 1915, 1916, 1917, 1919, 1922, 1926, 1936, 1938, 1954, 1966, 1967, 1968, 1969, 1970, 1971, 1972, 1973, 1974, 1977, 1979, 1981, 1982, 1986, 1988, 1998, 2001, 2002, 2004, 2006, 2007, 2008, 2012, 2013, 2014, 2015, 2016, 2017;
Scottish Cup (37) 1892, 1899, 1900, 1904, 1907, 1908, 1911, 1912, 1914, 1923, 1925, 1927, 1931, 1933, 1937, 1951, 1954, 1965, 1967, 1969, 1971, 1972, 1974, 1975, 1977, 1980, 1985, 1988, 1989, 1995, 2001, 2004, 2005, 2007, 2011, 2013, 2017;
Scottish League Cup (16) 1957, 1958, 1966, 1967, 1968, 1969, 1970, 1975, 1983, 1998, 2000, 2001, 2006, 2009, 2015, 2016

Manager: Brendan Rodgers (NIR)

Date		Opponent		Score	Scorers
2016					
07/08	a	Hearts	W	2-1	*Forrest, Sinclair*
20/08	a	St Johnstone	W	4-2	*Griffiths, Sinclair, Forrest, Christie*
27/08	h	Aberdeen	W	4-1	*Griffiths, Forrest, Sinclair (p), Rogic*
10/09	h	Rangers	W	5-1	*Dembélé 3, Sinclair, Armstrong*
18/09	a	Inverness	D	2-2	*Rogic, Sinclair*
24/09	h	Kilmarnock	W	6-1	*Dembélé 2, Forrest, Griffiths, Sinclair (p), Rogic*
01/10	a	Dundee	W	1-0	*Brown*
15/10	h	Motherwell	W	2-0	*Sinclair, Dembélé (p)*
26/10	a	Ross County	W	4-0	*Roberts, Armstrong, Sinclair, Dembélé*
29/10	a	Aberdeen	W	1-0	*Rogic*
05/11	h	Inverness	W	3-0	*Sinclair, Griffiths, Rogic*
18/11	a	Kilmarnock	W	1-0	*Armstrong*
03/12	a	Motherwell	W	4-3	*McGregor, Roberts, Armstrong, Rogic*
09/12	a	Partick	W	4-1	*Armstrong 2, Griffiths, McGregor*
13/12	h	Hamilton	W	1-0	*Griffiths*
17/12	h	Dundee	W	2-1	*Griffiths, Biton*
20/12	h	Partick	W	1-0	*Sinclair*
24/12	a	Hamilton	W	3-0	*Griffiths, Armstrong, Dembélé*
28/12	h	Ross County	W	2-0	*Sviatchenko, Armstrong*
31/12	a	Rangers	W	2-1	*Dembélé, Sinclair*
2017					
25/01	h	St Johnstone	W	1-0	*Boyata*
29/01	h	Hearts	W	4-0	*McGregor, Sinclair 2 (1p), Roberts*
01/02	h	Aberdeen	W	1-0	*Boyata*
05/02	a	St Johnstone	W	5-2	*Henderson, Dembélé 3 (1p), Sinclair*
18/02	h	Motherwell	W	2-0	*Dembélé (p), Forrest*
25/02	h	Hamilton	W	2-0	*Dembélé 2 (1p)*
01/03	a	Inverness	W	4-0	*Sinclair, Dembélé 2, Armstrong*
12/03	h	Rangers	D	1-1	*Armstrong*
19/03	a	Dundee	W	2-1	*Šimunović, Armstrong*
02/04	a	Hearts	W	5-0	*Sinclair 3 (1p), Armstrong, Roberts*
05/04	h	Partick	D	1-1	*Sinclair*
08/04	h	Kilmarnock	W	3-1	*Armstrong, Sinclair, Forrest*
16/04	a	Ross County	D	2-2	*Tierney, Roberts*
29/04	a	Rangers	W	5-1	*Sinclair (p), Griffiths, McGregor, Boyata, Lustig*
06/05	h	St Johnstone	W	4-1	*Roberts 2, Boyata, McGregor*
12/05	a	Aberdeen	W	3-1	*Boyata, Armstrong, Griffiths*
18/05	a	Partick	W	5-0	*Griffiths (p), Rogic, Roberts 2, McGregor*
21/05	h	Hearts	W	2-0	*Griffiths, Armstrong*

No	Name	Nat	DoB	Pos	Aps	(s)	Gls
76	Jack Aitchison		05/03/00	A		(2)	
14	Stuart Armstrong		30/03/92	M	25	(6)	15
6	Nir Biton	ISR	30/10/91	M	16	(10)	1
20	Dedryck Boyata	BEL	28/11/90	D	17		5
8	Scott Brown		25/06/85	M	33		1
17	Ryan Christie		28/04/95	M	3	(2)	1
24	Dorus de Vries	NED	29/12/80	G	4		
10	Moussa Dembélé	FRA	12/07/96	A	20	(9)	17
49	James Forrest		07/07/91	M	23	(5)	6
12	Cristian Gamboa	CRC	24/10/89	D	13	(4)	
1	Craig Gordon		31/12/82	G	34	(1)	
9	Leigh Griffiths		20/08/90	A	15	(8)	12
53	Liam Henderson		25/04/96	M	5	(5)	1
3	Emilio Izaguirre	HON	10/05/86	D	10	(2)	
22	Saidy Janko	SUI	22/10/95	D	1	(1)	
73	Michael Johnston		19/04/99	M	1		
8	Eboué Kouassi	CIV	13/12/97	M	1	(3)	
23	Mikael Lustig	SWE	13/12/86	D	28	(1)	1
16	Gary Mackay-Steven		31/08/90	M	4	(4)	
42	Callum McGregor		14/06/93	M	20	(11)	6
59	Calvin Miller		09/01/98	D	1		
7	Nadir Çiftçi	TUR	12/02/92	A		(1)	
34	Eoghan O'Connell	IRL	13/08/95	D	2		
56	Anthony Ralston		16/11/98	D	1		
27	Patrick Roberts	ENG	05/02/97	M	20	(12)	9
18	Tom Rogic	AUS	16/12/92	M	15	(7)	7
5	Jozo Šimunović	CRO	04/08/94	D	24	(1)	1
11	Scott Sinclair	ENG	25/03/89	M	30	(5)	21
28	Erik Sviatchenko	DEN	04/10/91	D	23	(5)	1
63	Kieran Tierney		05/06/97	D	24		1
2	Kolo Touré	CIV	19/03/81	D	5	(4)	

Dundee FC

1893 • Dens Park (11,506) • dundeefc.co.uk

Major honours
Scottish League (1) 1962; Scottish Cup (1) 1910; Scottish League Cup (3) 1952, 1953, 1974

Manager: Paul Hartley

2016

Date		Opponent		Score	Scorers
07/08	a	Ross County	W	3-1	*Loy 2 (1p), McGowan*
13/08	h	Rangers	L	1-2	*O'Hara*
19/08	h	Hamilton	D	1-1	*O'Hara*
27/08	a	Motherwell	D	0-0	
10/09	h	Kilmarnock	D	1-1	*El Bakhtaoui*
18/09	h	Aberdeen	L	1-3	*Holt*
24/09	a	Inverness	L	1-3	*Low*
01/10	h	Celtic	L	0-1	
15/10	a	Hearts	L	0-2	
23/10	a	St Johnstone	L	1-2	*Loy (p)*
26/10	h	Partick	L	0-2	
29/10	a	Hamilton	W	1-0	*McGowan*
05/11	h	Motherwell	W	2-0	*Kerr, Haber*
19/11	a	Rangers	L	0-1	
26/11	h	Inverness	W	2-1	*Wighton, Gadzhalov*
03/12	a	Kilmarnock	L	0-2	
10/12	h	Ross County	D	0-0	
17/12	a	Celtic	L	1-2	*Haber*
23/12	h	Hearts	W	3-2	*O'Dea, McGowan, Haber*
28/12	a	Partick	L	0-2	
31/12	h	St Johnstone	W	3-0	*El Bakhtaoui, Gadzhalov, og (Anderson)*

2017

Date		Opponent		Score	Scorers
27/01	a	Aberdeen	L	0-3	
04/02	a	Inverness	D	2-2	*Haber, O'Dea*
11/02	h	Kilmarnock	D	1-1	*Holt*
19/02	h	Rangers	W	2-1	*O'Hara, Holt*
25/02	a	Motherwell	W	5-1	*og (Jules), Haber 2, O'Hara, Wighton*
01/03	h	Partick	L	0-1	
11/03	a	St Johnstone	L	0-2	
19/03	h	Celtic	L	1-2	*El Bakhtaoui*
31/03	h	Aberdeen	L	0-7	
04/04	a	Ross County	L	1-2	*O'Dea (p)*
08/04	h	Hearts	L	0-1	
15/04	h	Hamilton	L	0-2	
29/04	a	Motherwell	W	3-2	*O'Hara, Haber 2*
06/05	a	Kilmarnock	W	1-0	*Haber*
13/05	h	Ross County	D	1-1	*O'Dea (p)*
17/05	h	Inverness	L	0-2	
20/05	a	Hamilton	L	0-4	

No	Name	Nat	DoB	Pos	Aps	(s)	Gls
1	Scott Bain		22/11/91	G	36		
27	Jesse Curran	AUS	16/07/96	M	1		
10	Michael Duffy	NIR	28/07/94	M	4	(4)	
20	Faissal El Bakhtaoui	FRA	08/11/92	A	15	(15)	3
16	Julen Extabeguren	ESP	07/03/91	D	14	(3)	
26	Kostadin Gadzhalov	BUL	20/07/89	D	15	(3)	2
55	Kévin Gomis	FRA	20/01/89	D	22		
21	Marcus Haber	CAN	11/01/89	A	27		9
7	Tom Hateley	ENG	12/09/89	M	26	(1)	
45	Daniel Higgins		08/04/98	D	2	(2)	
3	Kevin Holt		25/01/93	D	37		3
30	Cammy Kerr		10/09/95	D	35	(1)	1
23	Marc Klok	NED	20/04/93	M		(2)	
8	Nicky Low		06/01/92	M	2		1
9	Rory Loy		19/03/88	A	4	(9)	3
18	Paul McGowan		07/10/87	M	35	(1)	3
12	David Mitchell		04/04/90	G	2		
6	Darren O'Dea	IRL	04/02/87	D	35		4
14	Mark O'Hara		12/12/95	M	26	(2)	5
22	Henrik Ojamaa	EST	20/05/91	A	9	(5)	
17	Nick Ross		11/11/91	M	11	(8)	
19	Yordi Teijsse	NED	12/07/92	A	3	(6)	
4	James Vincent	ENG	27/09/89	M	27	(1)	
33	Craig Wighton		27/07/97	A	19	(12)	2
11	Danny Williams	ENG	25/01/88	M	11	(12)	

Hamilton Academical FC

1874 • SuperSeal Stadium (5,510) • hamiltonacciesfc.co.uk

Manager: Martin Canning

2016

Date		Opponent		Score	Scorers
06/08	a	Rangers	D	1-1	*Crawford*
13/08	h	Kilmarnock	L	1-2	*Longridge*
19/08	a	Dundee	D	1-1	*Lyon*
27/08	h	Ross County	W	1-0	*Imrie*
10/09	a	Hearts	L	1-3	*Crawford*
17/09	a	Motherwell	L	2-4	*Crawford 2*
25/09	h	St Johnstone	D	1-1	*Docherty*
01/10	h	Inverness	D	1-1	*Alexandre D'Acol*
15/10	a	Partick	D	2-2	*Donati, Brophy*
25/10	h	Aberdeen	W	1-0	*Alexandre D'Acol (p)*
29/10	h	Dundee	L	0-1	
05/11	a	Kilmarnock	D	0-0	
21/11	h	Hearts	D	3-3	*Crawford, Bingham 2*
26/11	a	Ross County	D	1-1	*Crawford*
03/12	h	Partick	D	1-1	*Alexandre D'Acol*
10/12	a	Inverness	D	1-1	*Crawford*
13/12	a	Celtic	L	0-1	
16/12	h	Rangers	L	1-2	*Imrie*
24/12	h	Celtic	L	0-3	
27/12	a	Aberdeen	L	1-2	*Imrie (p)*
31/12	h	Motherwell	D	1-1	*Alexandre D'Acol*

2017

Date		Opponent		Score	Scorers
28/01	a	St Johnstone	L	0-3	
31/01	h	Inverness	W	3-0	*Alexandre D'Acol, Gillespie, Bingham*
04/02	h	Kilmarnock	D	1-1	*Brophy*
18/02	a	Partick	L	0-2	
25/02	a	Celtic	L	0-2	
28/02	h	Aberdeen	W	1-0	*Devlin*
11/03	a	Hearts	L	0-4	
18/03	a	Rangers	L	0-4	
01/04	h	St Johnstone	W	1-0	*Alexandre D'Acol*
05/04	a	Motherwell	D	0-0	
08/04	h	Ross County	D	1-1	*Donati*
15/04	a	Dundee	W	2-0	*Alexandre D'Acol (p), Devlin*
29/04	h	Kilmarnock	L	0-2	
06/05	a	Inverness	L	1-2	*Redmond*
13/05	h	Motherwell	L	0-1	
16/05	a	Ross County	L	2-3	*Bingham, Templeton*
20/05	h	Dundee	W	4-0	*Bingham, Skondras, Imrie (p), Crawford*

No	Name	Nat	DoB	Pos	Aps	(s)	Gls
39	Blair Adams	ENG	08/09/91	D	2	(3)	
9	Alexandre D'Acol	BRA	18/07/86	A	24	(5)	7
15	Rakish Bingham	ENG	25/10/93	A	23	(7)	5
30	Steven Boyd		12/04/97	A	1	(2)	
20	Eamonn Brophy		10/03/96	A	7	(21)	2
11	Ali Crawford		03/07/91	M	31	(2)	8
28	Ross Cunningham		23/05/98	M		(2)	
4	Michael Devlin		03/10/93	D	28		2
8	Greg Docherty		10/09/96	M	23	(6)	1
21	Massimo Donati	ITA	26/03/81	M	26	(5)	2
6	Grant Gillespie		02/07/91	M	28	(3)	1
14	Alex Gogic	CYP	13/04/94	D	3	(4)	
33	Ronan Hughes		15/12/98	M		(2)	
7	Dougie Imrie		03/08/83	M	36	(1)	4
3	Antons Kurakins	LVA	01/01/90	D	1		
12	Gramoz Kurtaj	GER	30/04/91	M	5	(9)	
17	Louis Longridge		05/07/91	M	9	(7)	1
22	Darren Lyon		08/06/95	D	5	(1)	1
18	Darian MacKinnon		09/10/85	M	32	(1)	
1	Remi Matthews	ENG	10/02/94	G	17		
23	Scott McMann		06/07/96	D	21	(2)	
10	Daniel Redmond	ENG	03/02/91	M	15	(12)	1
14	Richard Roy	TRI	10/10/87	A		(1)	
89	Georgios Sarris	GRE	08/09/89	D	30		
2	Danny Seaborne	ENG	05/03/87	D	10	(1)	
3	Ioannis Skondras	GRE	21/02/90	D	11	(2)	1
46	Leonard Sowah	GER	23/08/92	D	6	(1)	
37	David Templeton		07/01/89	A	1	(2)	1
31	Ryan Tierney		30/01/98	A		(2)	
35	Robbie Thomson		07/03/93	G		(1)	
27	Shaun Want		09/02/97	D		(2)	
16	Craig Watson		13/02/95	D	2		
34	Gary Woods	ENG	01/10/90	G	21		

Heart of Midlothian FC

1874 • Tynecastle (17,480) • heartsfc.co.uk

Major honours
Scottish League (4) 1895, 1897, 1958, 1960; Scottish Cup (8) 1891, 1896, 1901, 1906, 1956, 1998, 2006, 2012; Scottish League Cup (4) 1955, 1959, 1960, 1963

Manager: Robbie Neilson; (03/12/16) (Jon Daly (IRL) & Andy Kirk (NIR)); (05/12/16) Ian Cathro

2016

Date		Opponent		Score	Scorers
07/08	h	Celtic	L	1-2	*Walker (p)*
13/08	a	Aberdeen	D	0-0	
20/08	h	Inverness	W	5-1	*Cowie 2, Sammon, Nicholson 2*
27/08	a	Partick	W	2-1	*Paterson, Watt*
10/09	h	Hamilton	W	3-1	*Walker 2 (1p), Nicholson*
17/09	a	St Johnstone	L	0-1	
24/09	h	Ross County	D	0-0	
30/09	a	Motherwell	W	3-1	*og (McManus), Paterson, Sutchuin Djoum*
15/10	h	Dundee	W	2-0	*Paterson, Johnsen*
26/10	a	Kilmarnock	L	0-2	
29/10	a	Inverness	D	3-3	*Johnsen, Rherras, Sutchuin Djoum*
05/11	h	St Johnstone	D	2-2	*Buaben, Paterson*
21/11	a	Hamilton	D	3-3	*Walker 2 (1p), Paterson*
26/11	h	Motherwell	W	3-0	*Johnsen 2, Walker*
30/11	h	Rangers	W	2-0	*Muirhead 2*
03/12	a	Ross County	D	2-2	*Sutchuin Djoum, Paterson*
10/12	a	Rangers	L	0-2	
17/12	h	Partick	D	1-1	*Johnsen*
23/12	a	Dundee	L	2-3	*Walker (p), Paterson*
27/12	h	Kilmarnock	W	4-0	*Paterson, Sutchuin Djoum, Walker 2*
30/12	h	Aberdeen	L	0-1	

2017

Date		Opponent		Score	Scorers
29/01	a	Celtic	L	0-4	
01/02	h	Rangers	W	4-1	*Nowak, Walker 2, Cowie*
04/02	a	Motherwell	W	3-0	*Tziolis, Esmaël Gonçalves 2*
18/02	h	Inverness	D	1-1	*Sutchuin Djoum*
25/02	a	Partick	L	0-2	
01/03	h	Ross County	L	0-1	
11/03	h	Hamilton	W	4-0	*Sutchuin Djoum, Esmaël Gonçalves, Walker, Martin*
18/03	a	Aberdeen	L	0-2	
02/04	h	Celtic	L	0-5	
05/04	a	St Johnstone	L	0-1	
08/04	h	Dundee	W	1-0	*Esmaël Gonçalves*
14/04	a	Kilmarnock	D	0-0	
29/04	h	Partick	D	2-2	*Esmaël Gonçalves (p), Struna*
07/05	h	Aberdeen	L	1-2	*Esmaël Gonçalves*
13/05	a	Rangers	L	1-2	*Esmaël Gonçalves*
17/05	a	St Johnstone	L	0-1	
21/05	a	Celtic	L	0-2	

No	Name	Nat	DoB	Pos	Aps	(s)	Gls
5	Alim Öztürk	TUR	17/11/92	D	2	(3)	
12	Anastasios Avlonitis	GRE	01/01/90	D	8	(1)	
22	Angus Beith		22/02/96	M		(2)	
23	Dylan Bikey	FRA	18/02/95	A		(2)	
29	Jamie Brandon		05/02/98	M	1		
8	Prince Buaben	GHA	23/04/88	M	11	(9)	1
15	Don Cowie		15/02/83	M	34		3
30	Rory Currie		20/02/98	A	1	(8)	
16	Moha El Ouriachi	MAR	13/01/96	M	3	(8)	
77	Esmaël Gonçalves	POR	25/06/91	A	15		7
1	Jack Hamilton		13/03/94	G	35		
29	Euan Henderson		29/06/00	M		(1)	
5	Aaron Hughes	NIR	08/11/79	D	8		
4	Igor Rossi	BRA	10/03/89	D	20		
20	Bjørn Johnsen	NOR	06/11/91	A	22	(12)	5
6	Perry Kitchen	USA	29/02/92	M	26	(3)	
88	Malaury Martin	FRA	25/08/88	M	5	(8)	1
23	Robbie Muirhead		08/03/96	A	6	(12)	2
11	Sam Nicholson		20/01/95	M	13	(6)	3
13	Viktor Noring	SWE	03/02/91	G	3		
19	Krystian Nowak	POL	01/04/94	D	17		1
17	Juwon Oshaniwa	NGA	14/09/90	D			
2	Callum Paterson		13/10/94	D	20		8
3	Faycal Rherras	MAR	07/04/93	D	17	(2)	1
18	Conor Sammon	IRL	06/11/86	A	9	(10)	1
24	Liam Smith		10/04/96	D	12	(8)	
14	Jon Souttar		25/09/96	D	22		
46	Lennard Sowah	GER	23/08/92	D	11		
27	Andraž Struna	SVN	23/04/89	D	13		1
10	Arnaud Sutchuin Djoum	CMR	02/05/89	M	30	(3)	6
4	Alexandros Tziolis	GRE	13/02/85	M	14	(2)	1
7	Jamie Walker		25/06/93	M	28	(6)	12
32	Tony Watt		29/12/93	A	12	(4)	1
26	Dario Zanatta	CAN	24/05/97	A		(1)	

SCOTLAND

Inverness Caledonian Thistle FC

1994 • Tulloch Caledonian Stadium (7,750) • ictfc.com

Major honours
Scottish Cup (1) 2015

Manager: Richie Foran (IRL)

2016					
06/08	a	Partick	L	0-2	
13/08	h	Ross County	L	2-3	*Boden, Draper*
20/08	a	Hearts	L	1-5	*Draper*
27/08	h	St Johnstone	W	2-1	*Draper, Meekings*
10/09	a	Aberdeen	D	1-1	*Vigurs*
18/09	h	Celtic	D	2-2	*King, Fisher*
24/09	h	Dundee	W	3-1	*Doumbouya, Tansey, Polworth*
01/10	a	Hamilton	D	1-1	*Polworth*
14/10	h	Rangers	L	0-1	
22/10	h	Kilmarnock	D	1-1	*Doumbouya*
26/10	a	Motherwell	W	3-0	*Tremarco, Doumbouya, Polworth*
29/10	h	Hearts	D	3-3	*Raven, Doumbouya, Doran*
05/11	a	Celtic	L	0-3	
19/11	h	Aberdeen	L	1-3	*Doumbouya*
26/11	a	Dundee	L	1-2	*Tremarco*
03/12	a	St Johnstone	L	0-3	
10/12	h	Hamilton	D	1-1	*Cole*
17/12	a	Kilmarnock	D	1-1	*Warren*
24/12	a	Rangers	L	0-1	
28/12	h	Motherwell	L	1-2	*Tansey*
31/12	a	Ross County	L	2-3	*Tremarco, Fisher*
2017					
28/01	h	Partick	D	0-0	
31/01	a	Hamilton	L	0-3	
04/02	h	Dundee	D	2-2	*Billy McKay (p), Tansey*
18/02	a	Hearts	D	1-1	*Tremarco*
24/02	h	Rangers	W	2-1	*Tansey, Billy McKay*
01/03	h	Celtic	L	0-4	
11/03	a	Partick	D	1-1	*Warren*
18/03	h	Ross County	D	1-1	*Tansey*
01/04	h	Kilmarnock	D	1-1	*Billy McKay*
04/04	a	Aberdeen	L	0-1	
08/04	h	St Johnstone	L	0-3	
15/04	a	Motherwell	L	2-4	*Fisher 2*
28/04	a	Ross County	L	0-4	
06/05	h	Hamilton	W	2-1	*Brad McKay, Tansey (p)*
13/05	a	Kilmarnock	L	1-2	*Fisher*
17/05	a	Dundee	W	2-0	*Billy McKay, Fisher*
20/05	h	Motherwell	W	3-2	*Tansey, Fisher 2*

No	Name	Nat	DoB	Pos	Aps	(s)	Gls
23	Henri Anier	EST	17/12/90	A	8	(5)	
19	Scott Boden	ENG	19/12/89	A	3	(10)	1
29	Larnell Cole	ENG	09/03/93	M	13	(8)	1
10	Aaron Doran	IRL	13/05/91	M	6	(11)	1
26	Lonsana Doumbouya	GUI	26/09/90	A	17	(2)	5
8	Ross Draper	ENG	20/10/88	M	35	(2)	3
9	Dean Ebbe	IRL	16/07/94	A		(3)	
1	Ryan Esson		19/03/80	G	6		
18	Alex Fisher	ENG	30/06/90	A	9	(12)	8
33	Cameron Gilchrist	ENG	29/07/97	D		(1)	
17	Lewis Horner	ENG	01/02/92	M	5	(5)	
20	Billy King		12/05/94	M	17	(9)	1
21	Louis Laing	ENG	06/03/93	D	14		
31	Cameron Mackay		09/12/96	G	1		
12	Jamie McCart		20/06/97	D	9	(2)	
13	Billy McKay	NIR	22/10/88	A	14		4
22	Brad McKay		26/03/93	D	25	(1)	1
4	Kevin McNaughton		28/08/82	D	5	(4)	
6	Josh Meekings	ENG	02/09/92	D	18		1
15	Jake Mulraney	IRL	05/04/96	M	10	(16)	
7	Liam Polworth		12/10/94	M	26	(6)	3
2	David Raven	ENG	10/03/85	D	19	(2)	1
21	Alisdair Sutherland		19/09/96	A		(1)	
16	Greg Tansey	ENG	21/11/88	M	37		7
3	Carl Tremarco	ENG	11/10/85	D	29		4
11	Iain Vigurs		07/05/88	M	28	(4)	1
5	Gary Warren	ENG	16/08/84	D	33		2
25	Owain Fon Williams	WAL	17/03/87	G	31		

Kilmarnock FC

1869 • Rugby Park (17,889) • kilmarnockfc.co.uk

Major honours
Scottish League (1) 1965; Scottish Cup (3) 1920, 1929, 1997; Scottish League Cup (1) 2012

Manager: Lee Clark (ENG); (15/02/17) (Lee McCulloch)

2016					
06/08	h	Motherwell	L	1-2	*M Smith*
13/08	a	Hamilton	W	2-1	*K Boyd, Coulibaly*
20/08	a	Ross County	L	0-2	
26/08	h	Rangers	D	1-1	*K Boyd*
10/09	a	Dundee	D	1-1	*Coulibaly*
17/09	h	Partick	D	2-2	*K Boyd, Coulibaly*
24/09	a	Celtic	L	1-6	*Coulibaly*
01/10	h	Aberdeen	L	0-4	
15/10	a	St Johnstone	W	1-0	*S Boyd*
22/10	a	Inverness	D	1-1	*Coulibaly (p)*
26/10	h	Hearts	W	2-0	*Coulibaly, S Smith*
29/10	a	Rangers	L	0-3	
05/11	h	Hamilton	D	0-0	
18/11	h	Celtic	L	0-1	
03/12	h	Dundee	W	2-0	*McKenzie, Coulibaly*
06/12	a	Aberdeen	L	1-5	*McKenzie*
10/12	a	Motherwell	D	0-0	
17/12	h	Inverness	D	1-1	*Coulibaly*
23/12	h	St Johnstone	L	0-1	
27/12	a	Hearts	L	0-4	
31/12	a	Partick	D	0-0	
2017					
28/01	h	Ross County	W	3-2	*K Boyd, Dicker, Longstaff*
04/02	a	Hamilton	D	1-1	*Longstaff*
11/02	a	Dundee	D	1-1	*K Boyd*
19/02	h	Aberdeen	L	1-2	*McKenzie*
25/02	a	St Johnstone	W	2-0	*McKenzie, Sammon*
04/03	h	Motherwell	L	1-2	*K Boyd*
11/03	a	Ross County	W	2-1	*Sammon, K Boyd*
18/03	h	Partick	D	1-1	*Sammon*
01/04	a	Inverness	D	1-1	*K Boyd (p)*
05/04	h	Rangers	D	0-0	
08/04	a	Celtic	L	1-3	*Jones*
14/04	h	Hearts	D	0-0	
29/04	a	Hamilton	W	2-0	*Sammon, Jones*
06/05	h	Dundee	L	0-1	
13/05	h	Inverness	W	2-1	*Longstaff, Jones*
16/05	a	Motherwell	L	1-3	*Frizzell*
20/05	h	Ross County	L	1-2	*Sammon (p)*

No	Name	Nat	DoB	Pos	Aps	(s)	Gls
18	Charlee Adams	ENG	16/02/95	M	4	(5)	
4	Miles Addison	ENG	07/01/89	D	8	(3)	
20	Kristoffer Ajer	NOR	17/04/98	D	16	(5)	
20	Flo Bojaj	ALB	13/04/96	A	2		
9	Kris Boyd		18/08/83	A	22	(5)	8
16	Scott Boyd		04/06/86	D	18	(1)	1
5	Will Boyle	ENG	01/09/95	D	11		
17	Jonathan Burn	ENG	01/08/95	D	6	(2)	
44	Innes Cameron		22/08/00	M		(2)	
19	Souleymane Coulibaly	CIV	26/12/94	A	18	(3)	8
8	Gary Dicker	IRL	21/07/86	M	36		1
21	Adam Frizzell		22/01/98	M	8	(7)	1
40	William Graham		23/06/99	A		(3)	
25	George Green	ENG	02/01/96	M	2	(2)	
33	Dean Hawkshaw		24/04/97	M	7	(8)	
27	Luke Hendrie	ENG	27/08/94	D	32		
11	Jordan Jones	ENG	24/10/94	M	29	(8)	3
10	Greg Kiltie		18/01/97	M	7	(4)	
18	Sean Longstaff	ENG	30/10/97	M	16		3
1	Jamie MacDonald		17/04/86	G	24		
14	Callum McFadzean	ENG	01/04/94	M	1	(3)	
7	Rory McKenzie		07/10/93	M	25	(3)	4
35	Lewis Morrison		12/03/99	M		(1)	
5	Karleigh Osborne	ENG	19/03/88	D	1		
25	Cal Roberts	ENG	14/04/97	A	4	(6)	
19	Connor Sammon	IRL	06/11/86	A	14	(1)	5
6	Martin Smith	ENG	02/10/95	M	7	(3)	1
3	Steven Smith		30/08/85	D	25	(1)	1
24	Greg Taylor		05/11/98	D	34		
12	Nathan Tyson	ENG	04/05/82	A	11	(6)	
13	Josh Umerah	ENG	01/04/97	A		(4)	
16	Mark Waddington	ENG	11/10/96	M		(1)	
2	Josh Webb	ENG	10/08/95	D		(1)	
36	Iain Wilson		15/12/98	D	16	(4)	
17	Freddie Woodman	ENG	30/10/97	G	14		

Motherwell FC

1886 • Fir Park (13,677) • motherwellfc.co.uk

Major honours
Scottish League (1) 1932; Scottish Cup (2) 1952, 1991; Scottish League Cup (1) 1951

Manager: Mark McGhee; (28/02/17) Stephen Robinson (NIR)

2016					
06/08	a	Kilmarnock	W	2-1	*Ainsworth, Johnson*
13/08	h	St Johnstone	L	1-2	*Cadden*
20/08	a	Rangers	L	1-2	*McDonald*
27/08	h	Dundee	D	0-0	
10/09	a	Ross County	D	1-1	*Moult (p)*
17/09	h	Hamilton	W	4-2	*Moult 4 (1p)*
24/09	a	Partick	D	1-1	*McDonald*
30/09	h	Hearts	L	1-3	*McFadden*
15/10	a	Celtic	L	0-2	
26/10	h	Inverness	L	0-3	
29/10	h	Ross County	W	4-1	*McDonald, og (Van der Weg), Tait, Ainsworth*
05/11	a	Dundee	L	0-2	
19/11	h	Partick	W	2-0	*Moult, McDonald*
26/11	a	Hearts	L	0-3	
03/12	h	Celtic	L	3-4	*Moult 2, Ainsworth*
10/12	h	Kilmarnock	D	0-0	
17/12	a	St Johnstone	D	1-1	*og (Clark)*
23/12	h	Aberdeen	L	1-3	*McDonald*
28/12	a	Inverness	W	2-1	*Clay, McDonald*
31/12	a	Hamilton	D	1-1	*Moult*
2017					
28/01	h	Rangers	L	0-2	
31/01	a	Ross County	W	2-1	*McDonald, Moult*
04/02	h	Hearts	L	0-3	
15/02	a	Aberdeen	L	2-7	*Bowman, Pearson*
18/02	a	Celtic	L	0-2	
25/02	h	Dundee	L	1-5	*Moult*
04/03	a	Kilmarnock	W	2-1	*McHugh, Jules*
11/03	a	Aberdeen	L	0-1	
18/03	h	St Johnstone	L	1-2	*McDonald*
01/04	a	Rangers	D	1-1	*Moult*
05/04	h	Hamilton	D	0-0	
08/04	a	Partick	L	0-1	
15/04	h	Inverness	W	4-2	*Cadden, Moult, McDonald, Campbell*
29/04	h	Dundee	L	2-3	*Moult, Cadden*
06/05	h	Ross County	L	0-1	
13/05	a	Hamilton	W	1-0	*Moult*
16/05	h	Kilmarnock	W	3-1	*McHugh, Ainsworth, Frear*
20/05	a	Inverness	L	2-3	*McFadden, Bowman (p)*

No	Name	Nat	DoB	Pos	Aps	(s)	Gls
7	Lionel Ainsworth	ENG	01/10/87	M	10	(20)	4
19	Jacob Blyth	ENG	14/08/92	A	1	(7)	
11	Ryan Bowman	ENG	30/11/91	A	11	(13)	2
12	Chris Cadden		19/09/96	M	36		3
26	Allan Campbell		04/07/98	M	6	(1)	1
15	Joe Chalmers		03/01/94	D	7	(1)	
20	Craig Clay	ENG	05/05/92	M	31	(4)	1
25	David Ferguson		24/03/96	D	7	(3)	
17	Elliott Frear	ENG	11/09/90	M	11	(4)	1
36	Shea Gordon	NIR	16/05/98	M	2	(2)	
13	Russell Griffiths	ENG	13/04/96	G	4		
3	Steven Hammell		18/02/82	D	24	(1)	
34	Jake Hastie		18/03/99	M		(3)	
4	Ben Heneghan	ENG	19/09/93	D	37		
11	Marvin Johnson	ENG	01/12/90	M	4		1
21	Zak Jules	ENG	20/02/97	D	6	(4)	1
14	Keith Lasley		21/09/79	M	25	(3)	
43	Adam Livingstone		22/02/98	D		(2)	
18	Lee Lucas	WAL	10/06/92	M	6	(4)	
27	Ross MacLean		13/03/97	M	4	(3)	
77	Scott McDonald	AUS	21/08/83	A	34	(1)	9
24	James McFadden		14/04/83	A		(6)	2
8	Carl McHugh	IRL	05/02/93	M	19		2
6	Stephen McManus		10/09/82	D	25		
30	Jack McMillan		18/12/97	D	9	(5)	
9	Louis Moult	ENG	14/05/92	A	30	(1)	15
88	Stephen Pearson		02/10/82	M	10	(1)	1
1	Craig Samson		01/04/84	G	34		
2	Richard Tait		02/12/89	D	25		1
23	Dom Thomas		14/02/86	M		(4)	

Partick Thistle FC

1876 • Firhill Stadium (10,102) • ptfc.co.uk

Major honours
Scottish Cup (1) 1921; Scottish League Cup (1) 1972

Manager: Alan Archibald

2016				
06/08	h	Inverness	W 2-0	*Amoo, Erskine*
20/08	a	Aberdeen	L 1-2	*Erskine*
27/08	h	Hearts	L 1-2	*Lindsay*
10/09	h	St Johnstone	L 0-2	
17/09	a	Kilmarnock	D 2-2	*Lawless, Lindsay*
24/09	h	Motherwell	D 1-1	*Erskine*
01/10	a	Rangers	L 0-2	
15/10	h	Hamilton	D 2-2	*Edwards, Lindsay*
22/10	h	Ross County	D 1-1	*Welsh (p)*
26/10	a	Dundee	W 2-0	*Azeez, Doolan*
29/10	a	St Johnstone	W 2-1	*Doolan, Osman*
04/11	h	Aberdeen	L 1-2	*Barton*
19/11	a	Motherwell	L 0-2	
26/11	h	Rangers	L 1-2	*Doolan*
03/12	a	Hamilton	D 1-1	*Welsh*
09/12	h	Celtic	L 1-4	*Lindsay*
17/12	a	Hearts	D 1-1	*Welsh*
20/12	a	Celtic	L 0-1	
23/12	a	Ross County	W 3-1	*Lindsay, Doolan, Erskine*
28/12	h	Dundee	W 2-0	*Booth, Doolan*
31/12	h	Kilmarnock	D 0-0	
2017				
28/01	a	Inverness	D 0-0	
01/02	h	St Johnstone	L 0-1	
04/02	a	Aberdeen	L 0-2	
18/02	h	Hamilton	W 2-0	*Doolan 2*
25/02	h	Hearts	W 2-0	*Doolan, Lindsay*
01/03	a	Dundee	W 1-0	*og (Extabeguren)*
11/03	h	Inverness	D 1-1	*Doolan*
18/03	a	Kilmarnock	D 1-1	*Erskine*
01/04	h	Ross County	W 2-1	*Doolan 2*
05/04	a	Celtic	D 1-1	*Azeez*
08/04	h	Motherwell	W 1-0	*Doolan*
15/04	a	Rangers	L 0-2	
29/04	a	Hearts	D 2-2	*Doolan, Lawless*
07/05	h	Rangers	L 1-2	*Doolan*
13/05	a	St Johnstone	L 0-1	
18/05	h	Celtic	L 0-5	
21/05	h	Aberdeen	L 0-6	

No	Name	Nat	DoB	Pos	Aps	(s)	Gls
7	David Amoo	ENG	13/04/91	M	14	(11)	1
16	Ade Azeez	ENG	08/01/94	A	19	(19)	2
13	Adam Barton	IRL	07/01/91	M	30	(1)	1
3	Callum Booth		30/05/91	D	31		1
1	Tomáš Černý	CZE	10/04/85	G	27		
15	Danny Devine	NIR	07/09/92	D	28	(2)	
9	Kris Doolan		14/09/86	A	29	(8)	14
2	Mustapha Dumbuya	SLE	07/08/87	D	8		
19	Ryan Edwards	AUS	18/11/93	M	33	(5)	1
14	Christie Elliott	ENG	26/05/91	M	26	(5)	
10	Chris Erskine		08/02/87	M	25	(11)	5
38	Ross Fleming		09/08/99	D		(1)	
23	Ziggy Gordon		23/04/93	D	12	(2)	
17	Niall Keown	IRL	05/04/95	D	14		
32	Mark Lamont		25/02/98	M		(1)	
11	Steven Lawless		12/04/91	M	24	(6)	2
5	Liam Lindsay		12/10/85	D	36		6
30	Andrew McCarthy		20/10/98	M	3	(2)	
20	Declan McDaid		22/11/95	M		(3)	
26	Neil McLaughlin		06/11/98	A		(1)	
27	Kevin Nisbet		08/03/97	A		(3)	
6	Abdul Osman	GHA	27/02/87	M	30	(1)	1
99	Mathias Pogba	GUI	19/08/90	A		(2)	
35	Mark Ridgers		09/08/90	G	1	(1)	
12	Ryan Scully		29/10/92	G	6	(1)	
35	Thorsten Stuckmann	GER	17/03/81	G	4	(1)	
4	Sean Welsh		15/03/90	M	18	(3)	3
18	David Wilson		06/09/94	M		(1)	

Rangers FC

1872 • Ibrox Stadium (50,817) • rangers.co.uk

Major honours
UEFA Cup Winners' Cup (1) 1972; Scottish League (54) 1891 (joint), 1899, 1900, 1901, 1902, 1911, 1912, 1913, 1918, 1920, 1921, 1923, 1924, 1925, 1927, 1928, 1929, 1930, 1931, 1933, 1934, 1935, 1937, 1939, 1947, 1949, 1950, 1953, 1956, 1957, 1959, 1961, 1963, 1964, 1975, 1976, 1978, 1987, 1989, 1990, 1991, 1992, 1993, 1994, 1995, 1996, 1997, 1999, 2000, 2003, 2005, 2009, 2010, 2011; Scottish Cup (33) 1894, 1897, 1898, 1903, 1928, 1930, 1932, 1934, 1935, 1936, 1948, 1949, 1950, 1953, 1960, 1962, 1963, 1964, 1966, 1973, 1976, 1978, 1979, 1981, 1992, 1993, 1996, 1999, 2000, 2002, 2003, 2008, 2009; Scottish League Cup (27) 1947, 1949, 1961, 1962, 1964, 1965, 1971, 1976, 1978, 1979, 1982, 1984, 1985, 1987, 1988, 1989, 1991, 1993, 1994, 1997, 1999, 2002, 2003, 2005, 2008, 2010, 2011.

Coach: Mark Warburton (ENG);
(10/02/17) (Graeme Murty);
(11/03/17) Pedro Caixinha (POR)

2016				
06/08	h	Hamilton	D 1-1	*Waghorn*
13/08	a	Dundee	W 2-1	*Forrester, Miller*
20/08	h	Motherwell	W 2-1	*Forrester, Miller*
26/08	a	Kilmarnock	D 1-1	*Tavernier*
10/09	a	Celtic	L 1-5	*Garner*
17/09	h	Ross County	D 0-0	
25/09	a	Aberdeen	L 1-2	*Halliday (p)*
01/10	h	Partick	W 2-0	*Kranjčar, Halliday*
14/10	a	Inverness	W 1-0	*Miller*
26/10	h	St Johnstone	D 1-1	*Garner*
29/10	h	Kilmarnock	W 3-0	*Wallace, Halliday (p), Garner*
06/11	a	Ross County	D 1-1	*Hill*
19/11	h	Dundee	W 1-0	*Forrester*
26/11	a	Partick	W 2-1	*Dodoo 2*
30/11	a	Hearts	L 0-2	
03/12	h	Aberdeen	W 2-1	*Miller, Hodson*
10/12	h	Hearts	W 2-0	*Kiernan, McKay*
16/12	a	Hamilton	W 2-1	*Waghorn 2*
24/12	h	Inverness	W 1-0	*og (Brad McKay)*
28/12	a	St Johnstone	D 1-1	*McKay*
31/12	h	Celtic	L 1-2	*Miller*
2017				
28/01	a	Motherwell	W 2-0	*Miller, Hyndman*
01/02	a	Hearts	L 1-4	*Hyndman*
04/02	h	Ross County	D 1-1	*Wallace*
18/02	a	Dundee	L 1-2	*Garner*
25/02	a	Inverness	L 1-2	*Waghorn (p)*
01/03	h	St Johnstone	W 3-2	*McKay, Waghorn, Hyndman*
12/03	a	Celtic	D 1-1	*Hill*
18/03	h	Hamilton	W 4-0	*Hyndman, Hill, Waghorn (p), Wallace*
01/04	h	Motherwell	D 1-1	*Garner*
05/04	a	Kilmarnock	D 0-0	
08/04	a	Aberdeen	W 3-0	*Miller 2, Dodoo*
15/04	h	Partick	W 2-0	*Miller, Toral*
29/04	h	Celtic	L 1-5	*Miller*
07/05	a	Partick	W 2-1	*McKay, Garner*
13/05	h	Hearts	W 2-1	*Garner, McKay*
17/05	h	Aberdeen	L 1-2	*Waghorn*
21/05	a	St Johnstone	W 2-1	*Miller, Toral*

No	Name	Nat	DoB	Pos	Aps	(s)	Gls
25	Jak Alnwick	ENG	17/06/93	G	1		
55	Jamie Barjonas		24/01/99	M	1	(3)	
8	Joey Barton	ENG	02/09/82	M	5		
27	David Bates		05/10/96	D	7		
61	Myles Beerman	MLT	13/03/99	D	6	(1)	
53	Kyle Bradley		14/02/99	D		(1)	
52	Liam Burt		01/02/99	M		(1)	
21	Matt Crooks	ENG	20/01/94	D	1	(1)	
14	Joe Dodoo	ENG	29/06/95	A	5	(15)	3
1	Wes Foderingham	ENG	14/01/91	G	37		
15	Harry Forrester	ENG	02/01/91	M	7	(14)	3
7	Joe Garner	ENG	12/04/88	A	21	(10)	7
16	Andy Halliday		11/10/91	M	24	(8)	3
3	Clint Hill	ENG	19/10/78	D	23	(1)	3
17	Lee Hodson	NIR	02/10/91	D	10	(1)	1
23	Jason Holt		19/02/93	M	28	(3)	
20	Emerson Hyndman	USA	09/04/96	M	13		4
4	Rob Kiernan	IRL	13/01/91	D	24		1
19	Niko Kranjčar	CRO	13/08/84	M	4	(5)	1
10	Barrie McKay		30/12/94	M	28	(7)	5
9	Kenny Miller		23/12/79	A	32	(5)	11
29	Michael O'Halloran		06/01/91	A	6	(1)	
18	Jordan Rossiter	ENG	24/03/97	M	3	(1)	
24	Philippe Senderos	SUI	14/02/85	D	3		
2	James Tavernier	ENG	31/10/91	D	35	(1)	1
8	Jon Toral	ESP	05/02/95	M	12		2
33	Martyn Waghorn	ENG	23/01/90	A	20	(12)	7
5	Lee Wallace		01/08/87	D	27	(3)	3
54	Aiden Wilson		02/01/99	D	2		
6	Danny Wilson		27/12/91	D	19	(2)	
11	Josh Windass	ENG	09/01/94	M	14	(7)	

SCOTLAND

Ross County FC

1929 • Global Energy Stadium (6,541) •
rosscountyfootballclub.co.uk

Major honours
Scottish League Cup (1) 2016

Manager: Jim McIntyre

Date		Opponent		Score	Scorers
2016					
06/08	h	Dundee	L	1-3	*Curran*
13/08	a	Inverness	W	3-2	*Boyce 3*
20/08	h	Kilmarnock	W	2-0	*Boyce 2*
27/08	a	Hamilton	L	0-1	
10/09	h	Motherwell	D	1-1	*Boyce*
17/09	a	Rangers	D	0-0	
24/09	a	Hearts	D	0-0	
01/10	h	St Johnstone	L	0-2	
15/10	a	Aberdeen	L	0-4	
22/10	a	Partick	D	1-1	*Burke*
26/10	h	Celtic	L	0-4	
22/10	a	Motherwell	L	1-4	*Schalk*
06/11	h	Rangers	D	1-1	*Davies*
19/11	a	St Johnstone	W	4-2	*McEveley, Routis, Curran, Boyce*
26/11	h	Hamilton	D	1-1	*Boyce*
03/12	h	Hearts	D	2-2	*McEveley, Boyce (p)*
10/12	a	Dundee	D	0-0	
17/12	h	Aberdeen	W	2-1	*Boyce, Dow*
23/12	h	Partick	L	1-3	*Boyce*
28/12	a	Celtic	L	0-2	
31/12	h	Inverness	W	3-2	*Boyce 2, Woods*
2017					
28/01	a	Kilmarnock	L	2-3	*Routis, Schalk*
31/01	h	Motherwell	L	1-2	*McEveley*
04/02	a	Rangers	D	1-1	*Schalk*
18/02	h	St Johnstone	L	1-2	*Curran*
25/02	a	Aberdeen	L	0-1	
01/03	a	Hearts	W	1-0	*Schalk*
11/03	h	Kilmarnock	L	1-2	*Boyce*
18/03	a	Inverness	D	1-1	*Schalk*
01/04	a	Partick	L	1-2	*Curran*
04/04	h	Dundee	W	2-1	*Chow, Boyce (p)*
08/04	a	Hamilton	D	1-1	*Curran*
16/04	h	Celtic	D	2-2	*Gardyne, Boyce (p)*
28/04	h	Inverness	W	4-0	*Boyce 4 (2p)*
06/05	a	Motherwell	W	1-0	*Routis*
13/05	a	Dundee	D	1-1	*Boyce*
16/05	h	Hamilton	W	3-2	*Gardyne, og (Matthews), Franks*
20/05	a	Kilmarnock	W	2-1	*Boyce 2*

No	Name	Nat	DoB	Pos	Aps	(s)	Gls
10	Liam Boyce	NIR	08/04/91	A	34		23
22	Chris Burke		02/12/83	M	4	(2)	1
12	Tim Chow	ENG	18/01/94	M	26	(4)	1
3	Erik Čikoš	SVK	31/07/88	D	5		
11	Craig Curran	ENG	23/08/89	A	26	(8)	5
15	Andrew Davies	ENG	17/12/84	D	31		1
16	Tony Dingwall		25/07/94	M	4	(10)	
58	Russell Dingwall		26/06/97	A		(1)	
9	Ryan Dow		07/06/91	A	13	(10)	1
63	Dylan Dykes		14/03/96	M		(2)	
12	Ricky Foster		31/07/85	D	1		
1	Scott Fox		28/06/87	G	35		
17	Jonathan Franks	ENG	06/04/90	A	9	(9)	1
2	Marcus Fraser		23/06/94	D	33		
7	Michael Gardyne		23/01/86	M	28	(5)	2
19	Brian Graham		23/11/87	A	1		
27	Milan Lalkovič	SVK	09/12/92	A	2	(4)	
57	Blair Malcolm		03/07/97	D	1		
31	Aaron McCarey	IRL	04/01/92	G	3	(1)	
5	Jay McEveley		11/02/85	D	19	(3)	3
44	Christopher McLaughlin		22/03/98	M		(1)	
18	Ian McShane		20/12/92	M	5	(3)	
53	Greg Morrison		19/02/98	A	1	(4)	
3	Jason Naismith		25/06/94	D	14	(2)	
6	Jim O'Brien		28/09/87	M	8	(8)	
43	Paul Quinn		07/09/86	D	19		
4	Christopher Routis	FRA	03/03/90	M	23	(7)	3
23	Alex Schalk	NED	07/08/92	A	15	(17)	5
52	Reghan Tumilty		26/02/97	M	2	(5)	
28	Kenny van der Weg	NED	19/02/91	D	27	(2)	
8	Martin Woods		01/01/86	M	29	(4)	1

Saint Johnstone FC

1884 • McDiarmid Park (10,696) •
perthstjohnstonefc.co.uk

Major honours
Scottish Cup (1) 2014

Manager: Tommy Wright (NIR)

Date		Opponent		Score	Scorers
2016					
07/08	h	Aberdeen	D	0-0	
13/08	a	Motherwell	W	2-1	*Swanson, MacLean*
20/08	h	Celtic	L	2-4	*Swanson (p), MacLean*
27/08	a	Inverness	L	1-2	*Foster*
10/09	a	Partick	W	2-0	*Anderson, MacLean*
17/09	h	Hearts	W	1-0	*Cummins*
25/09	a	Hamilton	D	1-1	*Craig*
01/10	a	Ross County	W	2-0	*Swanson (p), Kane*
15/10	h	Kilmarnock	L	0-1	
23/10	h	Dundee	W	2-1	*Anderson, Swanson (p)*
26/10	a	Rangers	D	1-1	*Alston*
29/10	h	Partick	L	1-2	*MacLean*
05/11	a	Hearts	D	2-2	*Swanson, Kane*
19/11	h	Ross County	L	2-4	*Swanson (p), MacLean*
03/12	h	Inverness	W	3-0	*Craig, Davidson, Swanson*
10/12	a	Aberdeen	D	0-0	
17/12	h	Motherwell	D	1-1	*Kane*
23/12	a	Kilmarnock	W	1-0	*Davidson*
28/12	h	Rangers	D	1-1	*MacLean*
31/12	a	Dundee	L	0-3	
2017					
25/01	a	Celtic	L	0-1	
28/01	h	Hamilton	W	3-0	*Cummins 2, Davidson*
01/02	a	Partick	W	1-0	*MacLean*
05/02	h	Celtic	L	2-5	*Watson, og (Boyata)*
18/02	a	Ross County	W	2-1	*og (McEveley), Kane*
25/02	h	Kilmarnock	L	0-2	
01/03	a	Rangers	L	2-3	*Wotherspoon, Anderson*
11/03	h	Dundee	W	2-0	*Paton, Alston*
18/03	a	Motherwell	W	2-1	*Craig 2*
01/04	a	Hamilton	L	0-1	
05/04	h	Hearts	W	1-0	*Shaughnessy*
08/04	a	Inverness	W	3-0	*MacLean, Craig (p), Cummins*
15/04	h	Aberdeen	L	1-2	*Swanson (p)*
29/04	a	Aberdeen	W	2-0	*Swanson, Thomson*
06/05	a	Celtic	L	1-4	*MacLean*
13/05	h	Partick	W	1-0	*Swanson (p)*
17/05	h	Hearts	W	1-0	*Kane*
21/05	h	Rangers	L	1-2	*Cummins*

No	Name	Nat	DoB	Pos	Aps	(s)	Gls
4	Blair Alston		23/03/92	M	25	(10)	2
6	Steven Anderson		19/12/85	D	26		3
12	Zander Clark		26/06/92	G	26		
39	Aaron Comrie		03/02/97	D		(1)	
17	Michael Coulson	ENG	04/04/88	M	7	(7)	
26	Liam Craig		27/12/86	M	27	(9)	5
29	Graham Cummins	IRL	29/12/87	A	17	(13)	5
8	Murray Davidson		07/03/88	M	19	(4)	3
24	Brian Easton		05/03/88	D	37		
19	Ricky Foster		31/07/85	D	33		1
20	Joe Gormley	NIR	26/11/89	A		(1)	
31	Greg Hurst		08/04/97	A		(1)	
25	Chris Kane		05/09/94	A	14	(11)	5
9	Steven MacLean		23/08/82	A	30	(2)	9
1	Alan Mannus	NIR	19/05/82	G	12	(2)	
15	Brad McKay		26/03/93	D	2		
7	Chris Millar		30/03/83	M	14	(3)	
18	Paul Paton	NIR	18/04/87	M	22	(6)	1
3	Tam Scobbie		31/03/88	D	14	(2)	
14	Joe Shaughnessy	IRL	06/07/92	D	38		1
15	Clive Smith	WAL	12/12/97	D	2		
11	Danny Swanson		28/12/86	M	28	(2)	10
27	Craig Thomson		10/03/95	M	2	(7)	1
22	Keith Watson		14/11/89	D	3	(1)	1
10	David Wotherspoon		16/01/90	M	20	(13)	1

Top goalscorers

23	Liam Boyce (Ross County)
21	Scott Sinclair (Celtic)
17	Moussa Dembélé (Celtic)
15	Stuart Armstrong (Celtic)
	Louis Moult (Motherwell)
14	Kris Doolan (Partick)
12	Adam Rooney (Aberdeen)
	Jamie Walker (Hearts)
	Leigh Griffiths (Celtic)
11	Kenny Miller (Rangers)

Promoted club

Hibernian FC

1875 • Easter Road (20,421) •
hibernianfc.co.uk

Major honours
Scottish League (4) 1903, 1948, 1951, 1952; Scottish Cup (3) 1887, 1902, 2016; Scottish League Cup (3) 1973, 1992, 2007

Manager: Neil Lennon (NIR)

Second level final table 2016/17

		Pld	W	D	L	F	A	Pts
1	Hibernian FC	36	19	14	3	59	25	71
2	Falkirk FC	36	16	12	8	58	40	60
3	Dundee United FC	36	15	12	9	50	42	57
4	Greenock Morton FC	36	13	13	10	44	41	52
5	Dunfermline Athletic FC	36	12	12	12	46	43	48
6	Queen of the South FC	36	11	10	15	46	52	43
7	Saint Mirren FC	36	9	12	15	52	56	39
8	Dumbarton FC	36	9	12	15	46	56	39
9	Raith Rovers FC	36	10	9	17	35	52	39
10	Ayr United FC	36	7	12	17	33	62	33

Promotion/Relegation play-offs

(06/05/17 & 12/05/17)
Morton 1-2 Dundee United
Dundee United 3-0 Morton
(Dundee United 5-1)

(16/05/17 & 19/05/17)
Dundee United 2-2 Falkirk
Falkirk 1-2 Dundee United
(Dundee United 4-3)

(25/05/17 & 28/05/17)
Dundee United 0-0 Hamilton
Hamilton 1-0 Dundee United
(Hamilton 1-0)

DOMESTIC CUPS

Scottish Cup 2016/17

FOURTH ROUND

(21/01/17)
Aberdeen 4-0 Stranraer
Alloa 2-3 Dunfermline
Ayr 0-0 Queen's Park
Bonnyrigg 1-8 Hibernian
Dundee 0-2 St Mirren
Elgin 1-2 Inverness
Kilmarnock 0-1 Hamilton
Livingston 0-1 East Fife
Morton 2-0 Falkirk
Partick 4-0 Formartine
Rangers 2-1 Motherwell
Ross County 6-2 Dundee United
St Johnstone 2-0 Stenhousemuir
Stirling Albion 2-2 Clyde

(22/01/17)
Albion Rovers 0-3 Celtic
Raith Rovers 1-1 Hearts

Replays
(24/01/17)
Queen's Park 2-2 Ayr *(aet; 4-5 on pens)*

(25/01/17)
Hearts 4-2 Raith Rovers *(aet)*

(31/01/17)
Clyde 3-2 Stirling Albion

FIFTH ROUND

(11/02/17)
Ayr 1-1 Clyde
Celtic 6-0 Inverness
Dunfermline 1-1 Hamilton
East Fife 2-3 St Mirren
Ross County 0-1 Aberdeen
St Johnstone 0-1 Partick

(12/02/17)
Hearts 0-0 Hibernian
Rangers 2-1 Morton

Replays
(14/02/17)
Clyde 1-2 Ayr *(aet)*
Hamilton 1-1 Dunfermline *(aet; 3-0 on pens)*

(22/02/17)
Hibernian 3-1 Hearts

QUARTER-FINALS

(04/03/17)
Hibernian 3-1 Ayr *(McGinn 7, Cummings 12p, Keatings 79; McGuffie 33)*

Rangers 6-0 Hamilton *(Waghorn 33p, Garner 48, 88, 90+1, Toral 77, Hill 82)*

(05/03/17)
Aberdeen 1-0 Partick *(Shinnie 43)*

Celtic 4-1 St Mirren *(Lustig 58, Sinclair 59, Dembélé 68, Griffiths 78; Davis 13)*

SEMI-FINALS

(22/04/17)
Hibernian 2-3 Aberdeen *(Holt 36, McGeouch 60; Rooney 1, Christie 25, McGregor 86og)*

(23/04/17)
Celtic 2-0 Rangers *(McGregor 11, Sinclair 51p)*

FINAL

(27/05/17)
Hampden Park, Glasgow
CELTIC FC 2 *(Armstrong 11, Rogic 90+2)*
ABERDEEN FC 1 *(Hayes 9)*
Referee: *Madden*
CELTIC: *Gordon, Lustig, Šimunović, Boyata, Tierney (Rogic 25), McGregor, Brown, Armstrong, Roberts (Sviatchenko 90+4), Sinclair, Griffiths*
ABERDEEN: *Lewis, Logan, Reynolds, Taylor, Considine, Jack (Wright 90+3), Shinnie, Hayes, McLean, McGinn (O'Connor 75), Stockley (Rooney 63)*

A last-minute winner enabled Celtic to beat Aberdeen 2-1 in the Scottish Cup final and complete the domestic season undefeated

Celtic skipper Scott Brown raises the League Cup

League Cup 2016/17

QUARTER-FINALS

(20/09/16)
Morton 2-1 Dundee United *(Quitongo 24, O'Ware 31; Van der Velden 55)*

Rangers 5-0 Queen of the South *(Holt 33, Halliday 62, Waghorn 63, 71, 83)*

(21/09/16)
Aberdeen 1-0 St Johnstone *(Rooney 90)*

Celtic 2-0 Alloa *(Forrest 83, Dembélé 90)*

SEMI-FINALS

(22/10/16)
Aberdeen 2-0 Morton *(Rooney 69, McLean 88)*

(23/10/16)
Celtic 1-0 Rangers *(Dembélé 87)*

FINAL

(27/11/16)
Hampden Park, Glasgow
CELTIC FC 3 *(Rogic 16, Forrest 37, Dembélé 64p)*
ABERDEEN FC 0
Referee: *Beaton*
CELTIC: *Gordon, Lustic, Šimunović, Sviatchenko, Izaguirre, Brown, Armstrong, Roberts (Biton 65), Rogic (McGregor 77), Forrest (Griffiths 90+1), Dembélé*
ABERDEEN: *Lewis, Logan, Taylor, O'Connor (Stockley 65), Considine, Jack, Shinnie, Hayes (McGinn 71), McLean, Maddison, Rooney (Burns 79)*

SERBIA

Fudbalski savez Srbije (FSS)

Address	Terazije 35, CP 263 RS-11000 Beograd
Tel	+381 11 323 4253
Fax	+381 11 323 3433
E-mail	office@fss.rs
Website	fss.rs

President	Slaviša Kokeza
General secretary	Jovan Šurbatović
Media officer	Milan Vuković
Year of formation	1919

SUPERLIGA CLUBS

 1 **FK Bačka**

 2 **FK Borac Čačak**

 3 **FK Crvena zvezda**

 4 **FK Čukarički**

 5 **FK Javor**

 6 **FK Metalac**

 7 **FK Mladost Lučani**

 8 **FK Napredak**

 9 **FK Novi Pazar**

 10 **FK Partizan**

 11 **FK Rad**

 12 **FK Radnički Niš**

 13 **FK Radnik Surdulica**

 14 **FK Spartak Subotica**

 15 **FK Vojvodina**

16 **FK Voždovac**

PROMOTED CLUBS

 17 **FK Mačva**

 18 **FK Zemun**

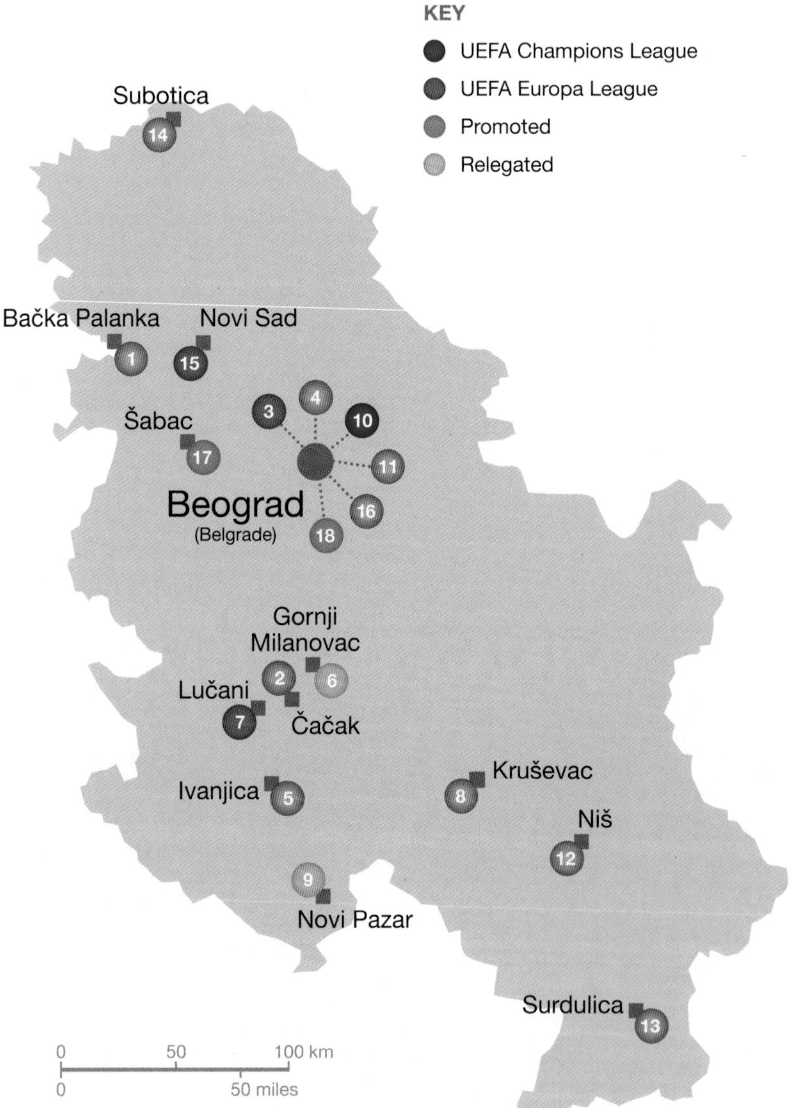

KEY

- UEFA Champions League
- UEFA Europa League
- Promoted
- Relegated

Subotica 14
Bačka Palanka 1
Novi Sad 15
Šabac 17
Beograd (Belgrade) 3 4 10 11 16 18
Gornji Milanovac 6
Čačak 2
Lučani 7
Ivanjica 5
Kruševac 8
Niš 12
Novi Pazar 9
Surdulica 13

0 50 100 km
0 50 miles

Partizan reel in their rivals

The Serbian SuperLiga title changed hands for the fourth successive year as Partizan shrugged off a poor start to stalk defending champions Crvena zvezda and eventually overtake their Belgrade rivals in the final phase of the 37-match season.

Victory enabled Partizan to match Crvena zvezda's record of 27 national league titles, and Marko Nikolić's side gained further local bragging rights by beating 'Red Star' 1-0 in the first Serbian Cup final to feature the country's top two clubs. It was Partizan's first double since 2010/11 and the sixth in their history.

Black-and-Whites storm to record-equalling 27th title

Long-time leaders Crvena zvezda falter at the finish

National team top World Cup qualifying group

Domestic league

The prospects of Partizan regaining the title looked remote when they took just one point from their opening three games. That false start signalled the end for coach Ivan Tomić, and he was replaced by 37-year-old Nikolić, who thus returned for a second spell at the club, having previously been in charge from December 2013 to March 2015. The change worked wonders. From late August onwards, supercharged by their two new strikers Uroš Djurdjević (from Palermo) and Leonardo (from FC Anji), Partizan went on a 31-match unbeaten run – 28 of them wins – that would result in one of the most unexpected, and sweetest, of all the club's title triumphs.

Partizan's recovery was remarkable, but Crvena zvezda, led still by 2015/16 title-winning boss Miodrag Božović, had only themselves to blame for allowing their arch-rivals back into contention. Even after losing the first Eternal Derby of the season, 1-0 in mid-September, the reigning champions held a six-point lead, which they protected all the way through to the end of the SuperLiga's first phase – when it was halved to a three-point advantage – as the two clubs routinely matched each other result for result, week after week, for seven months, including a 1-1 draw in the second head-to-head in early March.

Even when Partizan beat Crvena zvezda 3-1 away in the first of the play-off fixtures, Božović's side still topped the table by virtue of having accumulated more points in the first phase. Six more wins and they would keep their title, but they could only manage five, a shock 3-2 defeat at Voždovac – who would fail to win any of their other play-off fixtures – resulting in the sack for Božović and allowing Partizan to go top with three games remaining. It was a gift horse that was not looked in the mouth as Partizan stretched their winning run to 13 matches, concluding proceedings with their biggest win of the season, 5-0 at home to Mladost Lučani.

Despite that defeat, Mladost would qualify for a first crack at European football after finishing fourth. Vojvodina, as was their custom, finished third – despite the use of four coaches – while the golden boot was shared between Djurdjević and Leonardo with 24 goals apiece. That was twice as many as Crvena zvezda's leading scorer, mid-season signing Richmond Boakye, managed, although as a club the Red-and-Whites outscored the Black-and-Whites by 93 goals to 78.

Domestic cup

Only one goal mattered in the season-closing Serbian Cup final and it was scored by young Partizan defender Nikola Milenković just before half-time. It brought the club a 14th domestic cup win and a record fifth in the Serbian Cup itself, while subjecting Crvena zvezda to a first cup final defeat in a dozen years. The two teams had not met in a final since 2001, when Partizan also won 1-0 to lift the Yugoslav Cup.

Europe

Partizan's European ambitions were shelved early with a penalty shoot-out defeat by Zagłębie Lubin, whereas Crvena zvezda and Vojvodina both plotted a route to the UEFA Europa League play-offs – only to have their group stage hopes thwarted by a first-leg 3-0 defeat, against Sassuolo and AZ Alkmaar respectively.

National team

Having failed to qualify for three successive major tournaments, Serbia made significant strides towards ending that sequence as experienced coach Slavoljub Muslin guided them undefeated through their first six 2018 FIFA World Cup qualifiers. Three wins and three draws placed them at the summit of Group D on goal difference, their chief contributors being English-based duo Dušan Tadić – with four goals and a European zone-high of seven assists – and Aleksandar Marković – with five goals, including equalisers in both games against UEFA EURO 2016 semi-finalists Wales.

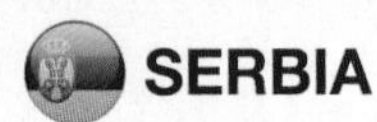

DOMESTIC SEASON AT A GLANCE

SuperLiga 2016/17 final table

		Pld	Home W	Home D	Home L	Home F	Home A	Away W	Away D	Away L	Away F	Away A	Total W	Total D	Total L	Total F	Total A	Pts
1	**FK Partizan**	**37**	**17**	**1**	**1**	**45**	**11**	**13**	**3**	**2**	**33**	**11**	**30**	**4**	**3**	**78**	**22**	**58**
2	FK Crvena zvezda	37	15	3	1	49	15	15	1	2	44	18	30	4	3	93	33	55
3	FK Vojvodina	37	14	3	2	36	11	8	3	7	22	20	22	6	9	58	31	43
4	FK Mladost Lučani	37	13	1	4	30	15	5	5	9	16	29	18	6	13	46	44	36
5	FK Radnički Niš	37	9	4	5	25	18	6	5	8	22	28	15	9	13	47	46	32
6	FK Napredak	37	11	4	4	27	13	5	4	9	17	23	16	8	13	44	36	30
7	FK Voždovac	37	7	4	7	24	23	7	2	10	17	28	14	6	17	41	51	26
8	FK Javor	37	7	4	7	19	20	4	6	9	15	30	11	10	16	34	50	22
9	FK Čukarički	37	8	4	7	28	26	7	3	8	26	23	15	7	15	54	49	32
10	FK Spartak Subotica	37	7	7	5	21	22	7	2	9	26	33	14	9	14	47	55	32
11	FK Radnik Surdulica	37	6	7	5	24	20	3	3	13	11	28	9	10	18	35	48	25
12	FK Rad	37	6	5	8	16	20	5	4	9	13	25	11	9	17	29	45	25
13	FK Bačka	37	9	1	9	21	22	2	2	14	6	24	11	3	23	27	46	23
14	FK Borac Čačak	37	5	3	10	14	20	3	4	12	15	31	8	7	22	29	51	22
15	FK Metalac	37	6	4	8	18	20	2	6	11	9	23	8	10	19	27	43	21
16	FK Novi Pazar	37	5	2	11	16	29	2	4	13	13	39	7	6	24	29	68	17

NB League splits into top and bottom halves after 30 games, after which the clubs play exclusively against teams in their group. Points obtained during the regular season are halved (and rounded upwards).

European qualification 2017/18

Champion/ Cup winner: FK Partizan (second qualifying round)

FK Crvena zvezda (first qualifying round)
FK Vojvodina (first qualifying round)
FK Mladost Lučani (first qualifying round)

Top scorer Uroš Djurdjević (Partizan) & Leonardo (Partizan), 24 goals
Relegated clubs FK Novi Pazar, FK Metalac
Promoted clubs FK Mačva, FK Zemun
Cup final FK Partizan 1-0 FK Crvena zvezda

Player of the season

Uroš Djurdjević
(FK Partizan)

Back in his homeland after an injury-stricken spell in Sicily with Palermo, Djurdjević enjoyed a wonderful debut season with Partizan, scoring 24 goals to share the SuperLiga golden boot with his Brazilian team-mate Leonardo and earn end-of-term recognition with the league's player of the season award. More importantly, his goals helped Partizan win the double. It was not only at club level that the 23-year-old striker stood out. He scored nine goals for Serbia in the 2017 UEFA Under-21 Championship qualifiers and another at the finals in Poland.

Newcomer of the season

Nikola Milenković
(FK Partizan)

A bench-warmer at the start of the 2016/17 season, Milenković became a regular in the centre of the Partizan backline following the arrival of coach Marko Nikolić. So consistent were the tall 19-year-old's displays that he was called up for international duty at Under-21 level, gaining a place in Serbia's squad for the European finals in Poland. The highlight of his dream debut season was the header he scored against Crvena zvezda to win the cup final. It was the perfect parting gift to Partizan as he had already agreed terms for a transfer to Fiorentina.

Team of the season

(4-3-3)

Coach: Nikolić *(Partizan)*

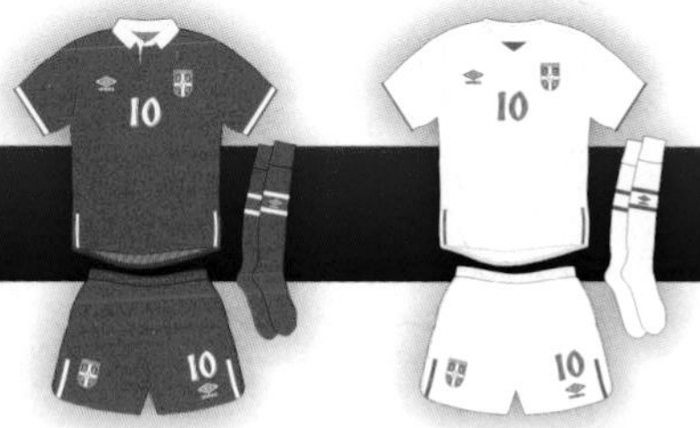

NATIONAL TEAM

International tournament appearances*
FIFA World Cup (11) 1930 (semi-finals), 1950, 1954 (qtr-finals), 1958 (qtr-finals), 1962 (4th), 1974 (2nd phase), 1982, 1990 (qtr-finals), 1998 (2nd round), 2006, 2010
UEFA European Championship (5) 1960 (runners-up), 1968 (runners-up), 1976 (4th), 1984, 2000 (qtr-finals)

Top five all-time caps
Dejan Stanković (103); Savo Milošević (102); **Branislav Ivanović** (94); Dragan Džajić (85); Dragan Stojković (84)

Top five all-time goals
Stjepan Bobek (38); Milan Galić & Savo Milošević (37); Blagoje Marjanović (36); Rajko Mitić (32)

(before 2006 as Yugoslavia; 2006 as Serbia & Montenegro.)*

Results 2016/17

05/09/16	Republic of Ireland (WCQ)	H	Belgrade	D	2-2	*Kostić (62), Tadić (69p)*
29/09/16	Qatar	A	Doha	L	0-3	
06/10/16	Moldova (WCQ)	A	Chisinau	W	3-0	*Kostić (19), Ivanović (37), Tadić (59)*
09/10/16	Austria (WCQ)	H	Belgrade	W	3-2	*A Mitrović (6, 23), Tadić (74)*
12/11/16	Wales (WCQ)	A	Cardiff	D	1-1	*A Mitrović (86)*
15/11/16	Ukraine	A	Kharkiv	L	0-2	
29/01/17	United States	A	San Diego	D	0-0	
24/03/17	Georgia (WCQ)	A	Tbilisi	W	3-1	*Tadić (45p), A Mitrović (64), Gaćinović (86)*
11/06/17	Wales (WCQ)	H	Belgrade	D	1-1	*A Mitrović (74)*

Appearances 2016/17

Coach: Slavoljub Muslin	15/06/53		IRL	Qat	MDA	AUT	WAL	Ukr	Usa	GEO	WAL	Caps	Goals
Predrag Rajković	31/10/95	M. Tel-Aviv (ISR)	G					G46				5	-
Antonio Rukavina	26/01/84	Villarreal (ESP)	D		D	D89	D			D	D	39	-
Branislav Ivanović	22/02/84	Chelsea (ENG) /Zenit (RUS)	D		D	D	D	s77		D	D	94	12
Jagoš Vuković	10/06/88	Konyaspor (TUR)	D		D69					s47	D	6	-
Matija Nastasić	28/03/93	Schalke (GER)	D		D	D	D				D	24	-
Filip Mladenović	15/08/91	Köln (GER)	D76					D				6	-
Luka Milivojević	07/04/91	Olympiacos (GRE) /Crystal Palace (ENG)	M		M	M	M			M	M63	21	-
Nemanja Gudelj	16/11/91	Ajax (NED) /Tianjin TEDA (CHN)	M		M	s77	s88	M		s71	s63	18	1
Dušan Tadić	20/11/88	Southampton (ENG)	M		M	M	M			M	M	44	12
Filip Kostić	01/11/92	Hamburg (GER)	M82		M69	M65	M70			M81	M67	15	2
Aleksandar Mitrović	16/09/94	Newcastle (ENG)	A59			A77	A88	s69		A71	A	28	9
Andrija Pavlović	16/11/93	København (DEN)	s59		A46			A46				5	-
Duško Tošić	19/01/85	Beşiktaş (TUR)	s76					D83				19	1
Aleksandar Katai	06/02/91	Alavés (ESP)	s82		s46	s65	s70	M69				6	-
Filip Kljajić	16/08/90	Partizan		G								1	-
Marko Petković	03/09/92	Crvena zvezda		D46								2	-
Nikola Milenković	12/10/97	Partizan		D46								1	-
Nikola Maraš	19/12/95	Rad		D					D			2	-
Nemanja Miletić	26/07/91	Partizan		D46					D			2	-
Nikola Stanković	18/12/93	Radnički Niš		D								1	-
Marko Poletanović	20/07/93	Crvena zvezda		M								1	-
Mihailo Ristić	31/10/95	Crvena zvezda		M46								1	-
Bogdan Mladenović	04/04/96	Rad		M46								1	-
Saša Jovanović	15/12/91	Mladost Lučani		M					M64			2	-
Ognjen Ožegović	09/06/94	Čukarički		A46								1	-
Nikola Ćirković	04/12/91	Voždovac		s46					A			2	-
Marko Gobeljić	13/09/92	Napredak		s46					D84			2	-
Vladimir Kovačević	11/11/92	Vojvodina		s46								1	-
Srdjan Plavšić	03/12/95	Crvena zvezda		s46					M81			2	-
Miloš Stanojević	20/11/93	Radnički Niš		s46								1	-
Slobodan Urošević	15/04/94	Napredak		s46								1	-
Vladimir Stojković	28/07/83	Nottingham Forest (ENG)			G	G	G			G	G	73	-
Aleksandar Kolarov	10/11/85	Man. City (ENG)			D	D				D	D	68	8
Zoran Tošić	28/04/87	CSKA Moskva (RUS)			s69			M46				76	11
Stefan Mitrović	22/05/90	Gent (BEL)			s69	D		D				11	-
Ljubomir Fejsa	14/08/88	Benfica (POR)				M						23	-
Nikola Maksimović	25/11/91	Napoli (ITA)				s89	D	s83		D		16	-
Ivan Obradović	25/07/88	Anderlecht (BEL)					D			D47		24	1
Nemanja Matić	01/08/88	Chelsea (ENG)					M			M	M	32	1
Nemanja Pejčinović	04/11/87	Lokomotiv Moskva (RUS)						D				3	-
Aleksandar Ignjovski	27/01/91	Freiburg (GER)						D77				12	-
Nemanja Radoja	06/02/93	Celta (ESP)						M				1	-
Aleksandar Jovanović	06/12/92	AGF (DEN)						s46				1	-
Lazar Marković	02/03/94	Sporting (POR)						s46				22	3
Aleksandar Pešić	21/05/92	Atalanta (ITA)						s46				1	-
Filip Manojlović	25/04/96	Crvena zvezda							G			1	-
Nemanja Ćalasan	17/03/96	Spartak Subotica							D55			1	-
Stefan Panić	20/09/92	Metalac							M			1	-
Jovan Djokić	13/08/92	Atyrau (KAZ)							M77			1	-
Aleksandar Paločević	22/08/93	Vojvodina							M64			1	-
Miloš Simonović	28/05/90	Napredak							s55			1	-
Enver Alivodić	27/12/84	Novi Pazar							s64			1	-
Marko Mrkić	20/08/96	Radnički Niš							s64			1	-
Marko Jevtović	24/07/93	Partizan							s77			1	-
Lazar Jovanović	13/07/93	Borac Čačak							s81			1	-
Marko Klisura	15/10/92	Bačka							s84			1	-
Mijat Gaćinović	08/02/95	Eintracht Frankfurt (GER)								s81		1	1
Aleksandar Prijović	21/04/90	PAOK (GRE)									s67	1	-

EUROPE

FK Crvena zvezda

Second qualifying round - Valletta FC (MLT)
A 2-1 *Katai (66), Sikimić (75)*
Kahriman, Aleksandar Luković, Le Tallec, Kanga, Katai (Ruiz 83), Cvetković, Donald, Srnić (Mouche 46), Hugo Vieira (Sikimić 65), Ibáñez, Phibel. Coach: Miodrag Božović (MNE)
H 2-1 *Donald (30), Katai (76)*
Kahriman, Le Tallec, Kanga (Ruiz 85), Katai, Mouche (Srnić 65), Cvetković, Donald, Hugo Vieira (Sikimić 71), Rendulić, Ibáñez, Phibel. Coach: Miodrag Božović (MNE)

Third qualifying round - PFC Ludogorets Razgrad (BUL)
A 2-2 *Katai (48), Kanga (66)*
Kahriman, Le Tallec, Kanga, Katai (Sikimić 88), Mouche (Ruiz 67), Cvetković, Donald, Srnić, Rendulić, Ibáñez, Phibel. Coach: Miodrag Božović (MNE)
H 2-4 (aet) *Donald (17), Ibáñez (62p)*
Kahriman, Le Tallec (Ristić 106), Kanga, Katai, Mouche (Ruiz 57), Cvetković, Donald, Srnić (Hugo Vieira 53), Rendulić, Ibáñez, Phibel. Coach: Miodrag Božović (MNE)
Red card: Kanga 46

Play-offs - US Sassuolo Calcio (ITA)
A 0-3
Kahriman, Le Tallec, Ruiz (Plavšić 57), Katai, Mouche (Srnić 71), Cvetković, Donald, Hugo Vieira (Sikimić 84), Ristić, Poletanović, Phibel. Coach: Miodrag Božović (MNE)
H 1-1 *Katai (54)*
Kahriman, Le Tallec (Rendulić 57), Ruiz (Srnić 85), Katai, Mouche (Babunski 80), Cvetković, Donald, Hugo Vieira, Ristić, Poletanović, Phibel. Coach: Miodrag Božović (MNE)

FK Partizan

Second qualifying round - Zagłębie Lubin (POL)
H 0-0
Šaranov, Vulićević, Mihajlović, Brašanac (Marjanović 75), Radović, Bogosavac, Everton Luiz, Milenković, Djurdjić (Bozhinov 69), Gogoua, Janković (A Stevanović 83). Coach: Ivan Tomić (SRB)
A 0-0 (aet; 3-4 on pens)
Šaranov, Vulićević, Mihajlović, Brašanac, Radović (Ilić 91), Bogosavac (Djuričković 120+1), Everton Luiz, Milenković, Djurdjić (Vlahović 70), Gogoua, Janković. Coach: Ivan Tomić (SRB)

FK Čukarički

First qualifying round - FC Ordabasy Shymkent (KAZ)
H 3-0 *Matić (49p, 68), Kajević (53)*
Stevanović, Lucas Piasentin, Mandić (Matić 46), B Janković (Docić 60), Fofana, Kajević, Stojković, Djurić, Živković, Lagator, Knežević (E Mašović 71). Coach: Milan Lešnjak (SRB)
A 3-3 *Mandić (10, 14), Kajević (21)*
Stevanović, Lucas Piasentin, Srnić (E Mašović 75), Mandić (Matić 59), Fofana (S Jovanovic 80), Kajević, N Janković, Djurić, Živković, Lagator, Knežević. Coach: Milan Lešnjak (SRB)

Second qualifying round - Videoton FC (HUN)
A 0-2
Stevanović, Lucas Piasentin, Docić, Mandić (S Jovanovic 56), Fofana, Kajević (Matić 46), N Janković, Djurić, Živković, Lagator, Knežević. Coach: Milan Lešnjak (SRB)
H 1-1 *Fofana (13)*
Stevanović, Docić (Radonjić 65), Fofana, Matić, A Mašović (Mandić 65), N Janković, Regan (Srnić 86), Djurić, Živković, E Mašović, Tomić. Coach: Milan Lešnjak (SRB)

FK Vojvodina

First qualifying round - FK Bokelj (MNE)
A 1-1 *Meleg (6)*
Kordić, V Kovačević, Meleg, Puškarić, S Babić (Aščerić 70), Antić, N Kovačević (Mićić 59), Malbašić, Jovančić (Paločević 59), Miletić, Trujić. Coach: Nenad Lalatović (SRB)
H 5-0 *Malbašić (9, 42), Meleg (60), Trujić (63, 87)*
Kordić, Meleg, Puškarić, Paločević (L Zličić 69), Lakićević, S Babić (Stamenić 69), Antić, Malbašić (Djurišić 68), Maksimović, Miletić, Trujić. Coach: Nenad Lalatović (SRB)

Second qualifying round - Connah's Quay FC (WAL)
H 1-0 *Paločević (86)*
Kordić, Meleg, Puškarić, Paločević, Lakićević (Jovančić 57), S Babić (Aščerić 57), Antić, Malbašić (L Zličić 82), Maksimović, Miletić, Trujić. Coach: Nenad Lalatović (SRB)
A 2-1 *Meleg (8, 49p)*
Kordić, V Kovačević, Meleg (L Zličić 82), Puškarić, Paločević, Antić, Malbašić, Maksimović, Jovančić (Mićić 68), Miletić, Trujić (Stamenić 73). Coach: Nenad Lalatović (SRB)

Third qualifying round - FC Dinamo Minsk (BLR)
H 1-1 *S Babić (29)*
Kordić, V Kovačević, Meleg, Puškarić, Paločević (L Zličić 87), S Babić, Antić, Malbašić (Trifunović 71), Maksimović, Miletić, Trujić (Jovančić 79). Coach: Nenad Lalatović (SRB)
A 2-0 *S Babić (32), Antić (81)*
Kordić, V Kovačević, Meleg (Jovančić 85), Puškarić, Paločević, S Babić (Trifunović 74), Antić, Malbašić, Maksimović, Miletić, Trujić (Mićić 84). Coach: Nenad Lalatović (SRB)

Play-offs - AZ Alkmaar (NED)
H 0-3
Kordić, V Kovačević, Meleg, Puškarić, Paločević (L Zličić 80), S Babić (Jovančić 46), Antić, Malbašić, Maksimović, Miletić, Trujić (Trifunović 63). Coach: Nenad Lalatović (SRB)
A 0-0
Kordić, Mićić, Meleg, Puškarić, Aščerić (S Babić 60), Paločević, Planić, Antić, Malbašić (Trifunović 77), Maksimović (Vukasović 71), Miletić. Coach: Nenad Lalatović (SRB)

DOMESTIC LEAGUE CLUB-BY-CLUB

FK Bačka

1945 • Slavko Maletin Vava (5,500); Karadjordje, Novi Sad (15,754) • fkbacka.com
Coach: Spasoje Jelačić; (16/11/16) Zoran Govedarica

2016

Date		Opponent	Res	Score	Scorers
24/07	h	Partizan	D	0-0	
31/07	a	Vojvodina	L	0-1	
06/08	h	Javor	L	0-1	
10/08	a	Čukarički	L	0-1	
13/08	h	Spartak	L	1-3	*Galić*
20/08	a	Rad	L	1-2	*Macanović*
27/08	h	Borac	W	1-0	*Luković*
10/09	a	Crvena zvezda	L	0-2	
17/09	h	Metalac	W	1-0	*Mojsilović*
25/09	a	Mladost	L	0-1	
02/10	h	Voždovac	W	2-1	*og (Stojanović), Ilić*
15/10	a	Radnički Niš	L	0-1	
22/10	h	Radnik	L	0-2	
30/10	a	Novi Pazar	D	1-1	*Bajić*
05/11	h	Napredak	L	1-3	*Luković*
19/11	a	Partizan	L	0-1	
26/11	h	Vojvodina	L	0-1	
30/11	a	Javor	L	0-2	
04/12	h	Čukarički	W	3-1	*Bajić (p), Trivunović, Švonja*
10/12	a	Spartak	D	0-0	
14/12	h	Rad	W	2-0	*Macanović, Bajić*
2017					
18/02	a	Borac	L	0-1	
25/02	h	Crvena zvezda	L	0-3	
04/03	a	Metalac	W	1-0	*Trivunović*
08/03	h	Mladost	W	1-0	*Balabanović*
12/03	a	Voždovac	L	0-4	
18/03	h	Radnički Niš	L	1-2	*Luković*
01/04	a	Radnik	L	0-1	
09/04	h	Novi Pazar	W	1-0	*Appiah*
13/04	a	Napredak	L	0-2	
18/04	h	Novi Pazar	W	4-0	*Čeković 2, Luković, Bajić*
23/04	a	Metalac	L	1-2	*Čeković*
29/04	h	Borac	L	0-1	
06/05	h	Čukarički	L	2-4	*Bajić (p), Balabanović*
13/05	a	Rad	W	1-0	*Balabanović*
17/05	h	Radnik	W	1-0	*Klisura*
21/05	a	Spartak	L	1-2	*Ivković*

No	Name	Nat	DoB	Pos	Aps	(s)	Gls
16	Bismark Appiah	GHA	19/01/95	A	13		1
7	Filip Bajić		18/11/93	M	25	(5)	5
15	Milorad Balabanović		18/01/90	M	19	(1)	3
8	Miroslav Bjeloš		29/10/90	M	16		
27	Darko Bošković	MNE	16/09/87	M	9	(3)	
9	Damir Čeković		19/03/90	A	16	(5)	3
25	Stefan Čupić		07/05/94	G	8		
14	Igor Djurić		22/02/85	D	14		
20	Dane Dukić		24/08/81	M		(3)	
11	Mladen Galić		09/10/87	A	9	(7)	1
4	Nemanja Ilić		27/08/92	D	29	(1)	1
18	Radovan Ivković		26/03/89	M	2	(8)	1
26	Božo Jević		12/09/86	D	1	(1)	
25	Nemanja Jevrić	MNE	30/05/97	G	5		
3	Miloš Josimov		27/09/84	D	13	(1)	
5	Marko Klisura		15/10/92	D	21	(3)	1
1	Ivan Konovalov	RUS	18/08/94	G	11		
28	Luka Luković		11/10/96	M	25	(2)	4
22	Strahinja Macanović		14/03/97	M	8	(8)	2
8	Milan Makarić		04/10/95	M	6	(6)	
25	Filip Manojlović		25/04/96	G	7		
3	Dušan Mijić		22/06/93	D	7	(3)	
24	Luka Miljević		21/01/97	D	1		
27	Zoran Milovac		29/10/88	M	8	(4)	
17	Nikola Mojsilović		03/11/91	M	10	(4)	1
26	Simon Mršić	BIH	18/06/91	A		(1)	
2	Stefan Nikolić		14/03/94	D	22	(2)	
6	Ivan Rogač		18/06/92	M	10	(3)	
13	Goran Smiljanić		31/01/90	D	11		
11	Milan Stavrić		21/05/87	A	2	(1)	
1	Miloš Stepandić		21/10/90	G	6		
17	Uroš Stepanović		21/02/93	M	3	(4)	
21	Zoran Švonja		04/10/95	M	16	(7)	1
14	Nemanja Trajković		13/06/91	D	1	(1)	
10	Veseljko Trivunović		13/01/80	M	28	(5)	2
30	Boris Varga		14/08/93	M	12	(1)	
13	Marko Vidović	MNE	03/06/88	D	5	(4)	
19	Marko Zečević		06/08/90	A	8	(14)	
99	Kristijan Župić		30/06/00	G		(1)	

FK Borac Čačak

1926 • Čačak (8,000) • boracfk.com

Coach: Ljubiša Dmitrović;
(02/11/16) Mladen Dodić;
(30/04/17) Milorad Kosanović

2016

23/07	a	Metalac	L 0-1	
30/07	h	Mladost	L 0-1	
06/08	a	Voždovac	L 0-2	
10/08	h	Radnički Niš	D 0-0	
14/08	a	Radnik	D 1-1	*Bogdanović*
20/08	h	Novi Pazar	W 2-1	*Sajčić, Drašković*
27/08	a	Bačka	L 0-1	
11/09	h	Partizan	L 0-2	
18/09	a	Vojvodina	L 1-2	*Jovanović*
25/09	h	Javor	D 1-1	*Drašković*
02/10	a	Čukarički	D 1-1	*Jovanović*
15/10	h	Spartak	D 3-3	*Zoćević, Jovanović, Thiago Galvão*
22/10	a	Rad	L 0-2	
30/10	a	Napredak	L 1-3	*Jovanović*
05/11	h	Crvena zvezda	L 0-1	
19/11	h	Metalac	L 1-2	*Thiago Galvão*
26/11	a	Mladost	L 0-3	
30/11	h	Voždovac	L 1-2	*Jovanović*
04/12	a	Radnički Niš	D 3-3	*Delić, Mihajlović 2*
10/12	h	Radnik	W 1-0	*Marčić*
14/12	a	Novi Pazar	W 2-0	*Thiago Galvão, Mihajlović*

2017

18/02	h	Bačka	W 1-0	*Jovanović*
25/02	a	Partizan	L 1-2	*Mihajlović (p)*
03/03	h	Vojvodina	L 0-1	
08/03	a	Javor Matis	L 0-2	
12/03	h	Čukarički	L 2-3	*Jovanović, Thiago Galvão*
18/03	a	Spartak	L 0-1	
01/04	h	Rad	L 0-1	
09/04	h	Napredak	L 0-1	
13/04	a	Crvena zvezda	L 0-2	
18/04	a	Rad	W 2-1	*Jovanović, Mihajlović*
22/04	h	Čukarički	L 0-1	
29/04	a	Bačka	W 1-0	*Punoševac*
06/05	h	Metalac	W 1-0	*Mihajlović*
13/05	a	Novi Pazar	L 0-2	
17/05	h	Spartak	W 1-0	*M Kostić*
21/05	a	Radnik	D 2-2	*Thiago Galvão, Mihajlović*

No	Name	Nat	DoB	Pos	Aps	(s)	Gls
1	Branimir Aleksić		24/12/90	G	20		
9	Dragoljub Andjelković		14/04/93	A	4	(8)	
23	Kennedy Asamoah	GHA	30/06/97	M	5	(1)	
8	Bacar Baldé	GNB	15/01/92	D	1	(2)	
88	Milorad Balabanović		18/01/90	M	3		
32	Vladimir Bogdanović		05/10/86	M	13	(1)	1
21	Uroš Delić		10/08/87	M	19	(5)	1
22	Dušan Djordjević		25/06/96	D	1		
19	Stefan Drašković		27/07/89	D	29	(2)	2
5	Milan Gašić		13/11/93	D	1		
17	Nikola Ignjatijević		12/12/83	D	13		
6	Nemanja Janičić		13/07/86	D	10		
73	Lazar Jovanović		13/07/93	M	32	(2)	8
3	Nenad Kočović		20/01/95	D	3	(2)	
16	Miroljub Kostić		05/06/88	D	23	(1)	1
14	Zoran Kostić		14/11/82	M	2	(2)	
6	Miloš Krstić		19/11/88	D	14	(1)	
27	Nemanja Krstić		05/08/94	M		(2)	
13	Milan Marčić		14/03/96	M	26	(6)	1
32	Marko Marinković		06/01/94	D	7	(2)	
32	Miloš Marković		10/12/86	D	6	(2)	
17	Mario Maslać		09/09/90	D	11	(1)	
30	Stefan Mihajlović		24/06/94	A	21	(9)	7
24	Saša Mišić		24/08/87	G	17	(1)	
4	Lazar Obradović		05/12/92	D	24	(2)	
80	Pavle Propadalo		24/11/94	M		(2)	
55	Bratislav Punoševac		09/07/87	A	3	(11)	1
7	Lazar Sajčić		24/09/96	A	12	(11)	1
10	Igor Savić		31/01/97	M	2	(7)	
5	Sreten Sretenović		12/01/85	D	2		
18	Nemanja Stanković		08/08/97	M	4	(12)	
28	Aleksandar Tanasin		15/11/91	D	18		
20	Thiago Galvão	BRA	24/08/89	M	30		5
34	Srdjan Vujaklija		21/03/88	A	3		
33	Boris Živanović		18/07/89	M	8	(1)	
31	Marko Zoćević		19/05/93	M	20	(10)	1

FK Crvena zvezda

1945 • Rajko Mitić (51,328) • crvenazvezdafk.com

Major honours

European Champion Clubs' Cup (1) 1991; European/South American Cup (1) 1991; Yugoslav/Serbian League (27) 1951, 1953, 1956, 1957, 1959, 1960, 1964, 1968, 1969, 1970, 1973, 1977, 1980, 1981, 1984, 1988, 1990, 1991, 1992, 1995, 2000, 2001, 2004, 2006, 2007, 2014, 2016; Yugoslav/Serbian Cup (24) 1948, 1949, 1950, 1958, 1959, 1964, 1968, 1970, 1971, 1982, 1985, 1990, 1993, 1995, 1996, 1997, 1999, 2000, 2002, 2004, 2006, 2007, 2010, 2012

Coach: Miodrag Božović (MNE);
(07/05/17) Boško Djurovski

2016

22/07	h	Napredak	D 2-2	*Plavšić, Sikimić*
29/07	h	Metalac	W 3-1	*Ruiz, Hugo Vieira, Poletanović*
06/08	a	Mladost	W 4-2	*Hugo Vieira 2, Rendulić, Poletanović*
10/08	h	Voždovac	W 3-0	*Hugo Vieira 2 (1p), Le Tallec*
14/08	a	Radnički Niš	W 3-0	*Hugo Vieira, Katai 2*
21/08	h	Radnik	W 5-0	*Aleksandar Luković (p), Orlandić 2, Srnić, Sikimić*
28/08	a	Novi Pazar	W 4-1	*Aleksandar Luković (p), Orlandić, Ruiz, Andjelković*
10/09	h	Bačka	W 2-0	*Aleksandar Luković (p), Orlandić*
17/09	a	Partizan	L 0-1	
25/09	h	Vojvodina	W 4-1	*Ruiz, Donald, Plavšić, Srnić*
02/10	a	Javor	W 4-2	*Donald, Sikimić, Le Tallec, Ristić*
16/10	h	Čukarički	W 3-1	*og (Lucas Piasentin), Sikimić, Hugo Vieira*
22/10	a	Spartak	D 1-1	*og (Radovanović)*
30/10	h	Rad	W 2-1	*Sikimić 2*
05/11	a	Borac	W 1-0	*Sikimić*
19/11	a	Napredak	W 1-0	*Ruiz*
26/11	a	Metalac	W 2-1	*Orlandić, Adžić*
01/12	h	Mladost	D 2-2	*Andjelković, Orlandić*
04/12	a	Voždovac	W 1-0	*Andjelković*
10/12	h	Radnički Niš	W 2-1	*Ruiz, Donald*
14/12	a	Radnik	W 2-1	*Andjelković (p), og (Zlatanović)*

2017

18/02	h	Novi Pazar	W 2-0	*Plavšić, Petković*
25/02	a	Bačka	W 3-0	*Boakye 2, Adžić*
04/03	h	Partizan	D 1-1	*Kanga*
08/03	a	Vojvodina	W 3-2	*Le Tallec, Boakye, og (Puškarić)*
12/03	h	Javor Matis	W 3-0	*Kanga, Plavšić, Ruiz*
19/03	a	Čukarički	W 4-3	*Boakye 2, Aleksandar Luković (p), Andjelković*
01/04	h	Spartak	W 2-1	*Vujaklija 2*
09/04	a	Rad	W 4-0	*Plavšić 2, Ristić, Petković*
13/04	h	Borac	W 2-0	*Kanga (p), Boakye*
18/04	h	Partizan	L 1-3	*Boakye*
22/04	a	Napredak	W 2-1	*Kanga (p), Plavšić*
30/04	h	Vojvodina	W 2-0	*Kanga (p), Plavšić*
06/05	a	Voždovac	L 2-3	*Aleksandar Luković (p), Poletanović*
13/05	h	Mladost	W 4-1	*Boakye, Petković, Ristić, Milić*
17/05	a	Javor Matis	W 3-0	*Kanga (p), Ristić, Boakye (p)*
21/05	h	Radnički Niš	W 4-0	*Boakye 3, Petković*

No	Name	Nat	DoB	Pos	Aps	(s)	Gls
45	Luka Adžić		17/09/98	M	1	(6)	2
33	Dušan Andjelković		15/06/82	D	24	(1)	5
18	David Babunski	MKD	01/03/94	M	3	(2)	
14	Richmond Boakye	GHA	28/01/93	A	14	(2)	12
19	Miloš Cvetković		06/01/90	D	2		
20	Mitchell Donald	NED	10/12/88	M	28	(1)	3
5	Abraham Frimpong	GHA	06/04/93	D	14		
70	Hugo Vieira	POR	25/07/88	A	6	(4)	7
95	Ivan Ilić		16/03/01	M		(1)	
95	Stefan Ilić		07/04/95	A		(1)	
1	Damir Kahriman		19/11/84	G	10		
8	Guelor Kanga	GAB	01/09/90	M	25		6
10	Aleksandar Katai		06/02/91	M	3	(1)	2
4	Damien Le Tallec	FRA	19/04/90	M	35	(1)	3
3	Aleksandar Luković		23/10/82	D	28		5
23	Andrija Luković		24/10/94	M	1	(4)	
22	Filip Manojlović		25/04/96	G	25		
16	Nemanja Milić		25/05/90	A	4	(6)	1
10	Nenad Milijaš		30/04/83	M	2	(8)	
21	Stefan Milošević		07/04/95	D	1	(1)	
11	Pablo Mouche	ARG	11/10/87	M	6	(1)	
99	Petar Orlandić	MNE	06/08/90	A	7	(4)	6
9	Milan Pavkov		09/02/94	M		(1)	
2	Marko Petković		03/09/92	D	35		4
97	Thomas Phibel	FRA	31/05/86	D	9	(1)	
17	Srdjan Plavšić		03/12/95	M	28	(5)	8
93	Marko Poletanović		20/07/93	M	20	(3)	3
6	Uroš Račić		17/03/98	M	2	(6)	
77	Zoran Rendulić		22/05/84	D	8	(2)	1
73	Mihailo Ristić		31/10/95	D	17	(9)	4
7	John Jairo Ruiz	CRC	10/01/94	M	25	(1)	6
81	Predrag Sikimić		29/08/82	A	10	(14)	7
55	Slavoljub Srnić		12/01/92	M	8	(14)	2
34	Miloš Stojanović		18/01/97	D	1		
27	Nemanja Supić	BIH	12/01/82	G	2		
98	Vanja Vučićević		22/03/98	A	1	(1)	
69	Srdjan Vujaklija		21/03/88	A	2	(6)	2

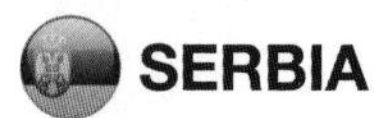

SERBIA

FK Čukarički

1926 • FK Čukarički (4,070) • fkcukaricki.rs

Major honours
Serbian Cup (1) 2015

Coach: Milan Lešnjak;
(12/09/16) (Nenad Mirosavljević);
(22/09/16) Gordan Petrić;
(26/12/16) Nenad Lalatović

2016

24/07	a	Radnički Niš	L	1-2	*Tomić*
31/07	h	Radnik	D	0-0	
06/08	a	Novi Pazar	L	0-1	
10/08	h	Bačka	W	1-0	*Radonjić*
14/08	a	Partizan	L	0-1	
21/08	h	Vojvodina	L	1-3	*Matić (p)*
27/08	a	Javor	D	0-0	
10/09	a	Napredak	L	1-2	*Fofana*
17/09	h	Spartak	L	2-4	*Jevtić, Fofana*
24/09	a	Rad	D	1-1	*Fofana*
02/10	h	Borac	D	1-1	*Docić*
16/10	a	Crvena zvezda	L	1-3	*Lucas Piasentin*
22/10	h	Metalac	W	2-1	*Docić, Lucas Piasentin*
30/10	a	Mladost	L	0-2	
05/11	h	Voždovac	W	2-1	*Docić 2 (1p)*
19/11	h	Radnički Niš	W	4-1	*Jevtić 3, Matić*
26/11	a	Radnik	D	1-1	*Fofana*
30/11	h	Novi Pazar	W	2-0	*Srnić, Ožegović*
04/12	a	Bačka	L	1-3	*Ožegović*
11/12	h	Partizan	L	1-3	*Ožegović (p)*
14/12	a	Vojvodina	L	0-2	

2017

18/02	h	Javor	W	2-1	*Ožegović, Jevtić*
25/02	h	Napredak	W	1-0	*Kajević*
04/03	a	Spartak	W	1-0	*Zorić (p)*
08/03	h	Rad	D	1-1	*Obradović*
12/03	a	Borac	W	3-2	*Obradović, Bojić 2*
19/03	h	Crvena zvezda	L	3-4	*Ožegović (p), Kajević, Jevtić*
31/03	a	Metalac	W	3-0	*Ožegović 2 (1p), Zorić*
09/04	h	Mladost	D	1-1	*Ožegović (p)*
13/04	a	Voždovac	W	3-1	*Ožegović 2, Kajević*
18/04	h	Radnik	L	1-2	*Ožegović*
22/04	a	Borac	W	1-0	*Ožegović*
30/04	h	Metalac	W	2-0	*Ožegović, Djurić*
06/05	a	Bačka	W	4-2	*S Jovanović, Kajević, Obradović 2*
13/05	h	Spartak	L	1-2	*Regan*
17/05	a	Novi Pazar	W	5-0	*Ožegović 3, Radonjić, Kajević*
21/05	h	Rad	L	0-1	

No	Name	Nat	DoB	Pos	Aps	(s)	Gls
3	Djordje Bašanović		31/07/96	D	1		
96	Miroslav Bogosavac		14/10/96	D	15		
24	Petar Bojić		04/09/91	M	12	(4)	2
89	Darko Bulatović	MNE	05/09/89	D	15	(1)	
26	Djordje Djurić		10/08/91	D	23	(2)	1
5	Marko Docić		21/04/93	M	18	(1)	4
9	Ismaël Fofana	CIV	08/09/88	A	11	(6)	4
8	Branislav Janković	MNE	08/02/92	M		(3)	
17	Nikola Janković		17/06/93	D	9		
21	Aleksandar Jevtić		30/03/85	A	14	(11)	6
22	Petar Jovanović	BIH	12/07/82	M	13		
19	Saša Jovanović		30/08/93	M	9	(12)	1
14	Asmir Kajević	MNE	15/02/90	M	23	(2)	5
77	Filip Knežević		08/11/91	M	1		
15	Boris Kopitović	MNE	17/09/94	D	7		
44	Dušan Lagator	MNE	29/03/94	M	16	(4)	
4	Lucas Piasentin	BRA	17/03/86	D	16	(1)	2
7	Staniša Mandić	MNE	27/01/95	M	6	(5)	
11	Alen Mašović		07/08/94	M	2	(5)	
55	Erhan Mašović		22/11/98	D	21	(2)	
10	Igor Matić		22/07/81	M	10	(16)	2
57	Zehrudin Mehmedović		15/03/98	M		(3)	
54	Nemanja Milojevic	GRE	23/02/98	M	3	(1)	
18	Nemanja Obradović		29/04/89	M	11	(1)	4
51	Ognjen Ožegović		09/06/94	A	23	(2)	16
71	Filip Pajović		30/07/93	G	6		
1	Nikola Petrić		11/05/91	G	30		
50	Sava Radić		04/03/98	D	5		
28	Nemanja Radonjić		15/02/96	M	10	(7)	2
20	Obeng Regan	GHA	15/08/94	M	11	(5)	1
58	Marko Šarić		28/11/98	A	2	(3)	
6	Dragoljub Srnić		12/01/92	M	23	(7)	1
12	Nemanja Stevanović		08/05/92	G	1		
23	Thiago Galvão	BRA	24/08/89	M		(1)	
66	Marko Tomić		28/10/91	M	14	(2)	1
33	Stefan Živković		01/06/90	D	16		
17	Darko Zorić	MNE	12/09/93	M	10	(1)	2

FK Javor

1912 • Ivanjica (4,000) • fkjavor.com

Coach: Miloš Veselinović;
(30/12/16) Srdjan Blagojević;
(12/04/17) Srdjan Vasiljević

2016

23/07	a	Radnik	D	2-2	*Bjedov 2*
30/07	h	Novi Pazar	D	1-1	*Gafurov*
06/08	a	Bačka	W	1-0	*Djokić*
10/08	h	Partizan	L	0-2	
14/08	a	Vojvodina	L	0-4	
20/08	a	Napredak	L	1-3	*Bjedov*
27/08	h	Čukarički	D	0-0	
10/09	a	Spartak	D	1-1	*Stojaković*
17/09	h	Rad	D	1-1	*Bjedov*
25/09	a	Borac	D	1-1	*og (Maslać)*
02/10	h	Crvena zvezda	L	2-4	*Karišik, Eliomar*
15/10	a	Metalac	D	1-1	*Eliomar*
22/10	h	Mladost	D	1-1	*Cvetković (p)*
30/10	a	Voždovac	W	2-1	*Bjedov 2*
06/11	h	Radnički Niš	W	2-0	*Bjedov, Milović*
19/11	h	Radnik	W	1-0	*Gafurov*
26/11	a	Novi Pazar	W	2-1	*Gafurov, Cvetković (p)*
30/11	h	Bačka	W	2-0	*Eliomar, Bjedov*
04/12	a	Partizan	L	0-2	
09/12	h	Vojvodina	W	2-1	*Bjedov, Milisavljević*
14/12	h	Napredak	W	1-0	*Bjedov*

2017

18/02	a	Čukarički	L	1-2	*Amanovic*
25/02	h	Spartak	L	2-3	*Christovão, Tripković*
04/03	a	Rad	D	1-1	*Cvetković (p)*
08/03	h	Borac	W	2-0	*Cvetković, Tripković*
12/03	a	Crvena zvezda	L	0-3	
18/03	h	Metalac	W	1-0	*Christovão*
01/04	a	Mladost	L	0-1	
09/04	h	Voždovac	L	0-1	
13/04	a	Radnički Niš	W	1-0	*Tripković*
18/04	a	Voždovac	D	1-1	*Tripković*
23/04	h	Mladost	L	0-1	
29/04	a	Radnički Niš	L	0-2	
05/05	h	Partizan	L	1-2	*Eliomar*
13/05	a	Napredak	L	0-3	
17/05	h	Crvena zvezda	L	0-3	
21/05	a	Vojvodina	L	0-1	

No	Name	Nat	DoB	Pos	Aps	(s)	Gls
24	Aleksa Amanovic	MKD	24/10/96	D	32		1
26	Jones Asare	GHA	10/07/97	A		(1)	
30	Darko Bjedov		28/03/89	A	20		10
13	Alexander Christovão	ANG	14/03/93	A	8	(11)	2
22	Derek Cornelius	CAN	25/11/97	D	3		
32	Ivan Cvetković		12/02/81	M	17	(2)	4
22	Aleksandar Dimitrić		24/10/96	M	4		
9	Nikola Dišić		08/07/98	A		(2)	
1	Vladan Djogatović		03/11/84	G	36		
19	Jovan Djokić		13/08/92	M	19		1
7	Eliomar	BRA	16/03/88	M	26		4
11	Husniddin Gafurov	UZB	29/07/94	M	21	(3)	3
23	Petar Glintić		09/06/92	G	1		
31	Miljan Ilić		23/04/93	M	2	(6)	
8	Jordan Jovanović		27/01/92	M	7	(7)	
16	Nikola Karaklajić		05/02/95	M	1	(4)	
3	Miloš Karišik		07/10/88	D	32		1
8	Danko Kiković		21/09/94	M	3	(4)	
14	Marko Kolaković		09/02/93	D	5	(1)	
33	Miroslav Maričić		21/01/98	M	3	(8)	
30	Milan Milanović		21/01/95	D	11	(4)	
26	Miloš Milisavljević		26/10/92	M	4	(11)	1
20	Milovan Milović		24/10/80	D	33		1
25	Vuk Mitošević		12/02/91	M	13		
19	Filip Obadović		19/08/97	M	1	(1)	
2	Filip Ristovski	MKD	03/01/95	D	7	(1)	
17	Nenad Sević		25/04/96	D	17	(13)	
25	Milan Spremo		27/04/95	M	7	(8)	
10	Igor Stojaković		27/05/80	M	6	(9)	1
15	Ismar Tandir	BIH	19/08/95	A		(4)	
21	Borislav Terzić		01/11/91	D	31		
5	Saša Tomanović		20/09/89	M	26	(5)	
18	Stefan Tripković		27/07/93	A	11	(4)	4

FK Metalac

1961 • Metalac (4,600) • fkmetalac.rs

Coach: Nenad Vanić

2016

23/07	h	Borac	W	1-0	*Otašević*
29/07	a	Crvena zvezda	L	1-3	*Mladenović*
06/08	h	Napredak	W	2-0	*Mitrović, Stojanović (p)*
10/08	h	Mladost	W	2-0	*Rovčanin, Stojanović*
14/08	a	Voždovac	D	0-0	
21/08	h	Radnički Niš	L	1-2	*Otašević*
26/08	a	Radnik	W	1-0	*Caicedo*
10/09	h	Novi Pazar	D	0-0	
17/09	a	Bačka	L	0-1	
25/09	h	Partizan	L	0-1	
02/10	a	Vojvodina	L	0-1	
15/10	h	Javor	D	1-1	*Jovanović*
22/10	a	Čukarički	L	1-2	*Jovanović*
30/10	h	Spartak	D	0-0	
05/11	a	Rad	D	1-1	*Caicedo*
19/11	a	Borac	W	2-1	*Stojanović, Jovanović*
26/11	h	Crvena zvezda	L	1-2	*Panić*
30/11	a	Napredak	L	0-1	
05/12	a	Mladost	D	1-1	*Stojanović*
10/12	h	Voždovac	L	0-2	
14/12	a	Radnički Niš	D	1-1	*Jovanović*

2017

25/02	a	Novi Pazar	D	0-0	
01/03	h	Radnik	W	3-1	*Mijić, Čumić, Jovanović*
04/03	h	Bačka	L	0-1	
08/03	a	Partizan	L	0-3	
13/03	h	Vojvodina	L	0-3	
18/03	a	Javor Matis	L	0-1	
31/03	h	Čukarički	L	0-3	
09/04	a	Spartak	D	0-0	
13/04	h	Rad	L	1-2	*Bondarenko*
18/04	a	Spartak	L	1-3	*Rovčanin*
23/04	h	Bačka	W	2-1	*Mijić (p), Tomić*
30/04	a	Čukarički	L	0-2	
06/05	a	Borac	L	0-1	
13/05	h	Radnik	D	1-1	*Panić*
17/05	a	Rad	L	0-1	
21/05	h	Novi Pazar	W	3-0	*Panić (p), Bondarenko, Nikolić*

No	Name	Nat	DoB	Pos	Aps	(s)	Gls
33	Nemanja Belić		24/04/87	G	36		
14	Taras Bondarenko	UKR	23/09/92	D	34		2
99	Walberto Caicedo	ECU	21/08/92	M	20	(1)	2
20	Nikola Čumić		20/11/98	A	10	(16)	1
6	Boško Dopudj		09/12/90	D	14	(4)	
4	Bojan Gocanin		11/10/97	M	8	(4)	
8	Aleksandar Ivanović		20/11/88	M	1	(8)	
10	Ivica Jovanović	MNE	04/12/87	A	13	(8)	5
2	Dejan Koraksić		31/12/97	D	5		
1	Ivan Kostić		24/10/95	G	1		
9	Miloš Krkotić	MNE	29/09/87	M	9	(1)	
32	Bojan Mijailović		28/08/95	M		(2)	
18	Miloš Mijić		01/11/89	M	32		2
30	Ante Mitrović	CRO	01/04/88	A	6	(8)	1
11	Nemanja Mladenović		03/03/93	M	9	(8)	1
25	Saša Nikodijević		16/07/87	D	32	(3)	
11	Marko Nikolić		10/12/97	A	4	(9)	1
15	Vladimir Otašević		08/06/86	D	27		2
3	Stefan Panić		20/09/92	M	33		3
22	Petar Pavlović		03/03/87	D	5	(4)	
7	Ersan Rovčanin		24/03/93	M	27	(6)	2
17	Srdjan Simović		17/07/85	D	32	(3)	
10	Igor Stanojević		24/10/91	M		(1)	
24	Milan Stojanović		10/05/88	M	19	(2)	4
19	Nikola Stojković		02/02/95	M	18	(4)	
16	Branislav Tomić		12/02/95	M	11	(8)	1
5	Dejan Uzelac		29/11/93	D	1	(2)	
5	Božidar Veškovac		10/01/97	D		(4)	
24	Nemanja Vukmanović		06/02/99	M		(1)	
30	Dejan Vukojević		27/04/87	A		(2)	

FK Mladost Lučani

1952 • Mladost (8,050) • fkmladostlucani.com

Coach: Nenad Milovanović

Date		Opponent	Result		Scorers
2016					
23/07	h	Rad	W	2-1	*Milosavljević, Zvrko*
30/07	a	Borac	W	1-0	*Odita*
06/08	h	Crvena zvezda	L	2-4	*Jovanović 2*
10/08	a	Metalac	L	0-2	
14/08	h	Napredak	W	1-0	*Milosavljević*
20/08	h	Voždovac	L	0-1	
27/08	a	Radnički Niš	L	0-2	
10/09	h	Radnik	W	2-0	*Bojović (p), Odita*
17/09	a	Novi Pazar	W	2-1	*Jovanović, Radivojević*
25/09	h	Bačka	W	1-0	*Bojović*
02/10	a	Partizan	L	1-3	*Bojović (p)*
16/10	h	Vojvodina	W	2-0	*Protić, Jovanović*
22/10	a	Javor	D	1-1	*Šatara*
30/10	h	Čukarički	W	2-0	*Radivojević, Bojović (p)*
05/11	a	Spartak	L	0-1	
18/11	a	Rad	W	2-1	*Bojović 2 (1p)*
26/11	h	Borac	W	3-0	*og (Maslać), Bojović 2*
01/12	a	Crvena zvezda	D	2-2	*Jovanović, Radivojević*
05/12	h	Metalac	D	1-1	*Bojović*
10/12	a	Napredak	D	0-0	
14/12	a	Voždovac	L	1-2	*Radivojević*
2017					
17/02	h	Radnički Niš	W	1-0	*Bojović (p)*
25/02	a	Radnik	D	1-1	*Nenad Gavrić*
04/03	h	Novi Pazar	L	0-1	
08/03	a	Bačka	L	0-1	
12/03	h	Partizan	L	0-2	
19/03	a	Vojvodina	W	1-0	*Odita*
01/04	h	Javor Matis	W	1-0	*Jovanović*
09/04	a	Čukarički	D	1-1	*Jovanović*
13/04	h	Spartak	W	4-1	*og (Ćalasan), Odita, Radivojević, Bojović*
18/04	h	Radnički Niš	W	3-2	*Saničanin, Golubović 2*
23/04	a	Javor Matis	W	1-0	*Bojović*
29/04	h	Voždovac	W	2-0	*Bojović, Milosavljević*
06/05	a	Vojvodina	L	1-2	*Milosavljević*
13/05	a	Crvena zvezda	L	1-4	*Tumbašević*
17/05	h	Napredak	W	3-2	*Bojović 3 (2p)*
21/05	a	Partizan	L	0-5	

No	Name	Nat	DoB	Pos	Aps	(s)	Gls
28	Nikola Andrić		23/05/92	D	15	(6)	
88	Milan Bojovic		13/04/87	A	24	(2)	16
16	Bojan Čečarić		10/10/93	A		(1)	
11	Nebojša Gavrić		27/08/91	M	3	(17)	
12	Nenad Gavrić		12/12/91	M	11	(4)	1
8	Stefan Golubović		01/08/96	M	3	(12)	2
7	Saša Jovanović		15/12/91	M	29	(2)	7
3	Tome Kitanovski	MKD	21/05/92	D		(5)	
1	Nemanja Krznarić		29/05/84	G	33		
58	Michel Mbiobe	CMR	03/02/96	A		(3)	
10	Radomir Milosavljević		30/07/92	M	32	(1)	4
44	Bogdan Milošević		17/02/89	D	24		
4	Ivan Milošević		03/11/84	D	13		
18	Emanuel Odita	NGA	14/05/83	A	22	(8)	4
77	Predrag Pavlović		19/06/86	M	2	(8)	
15	Aleksandar Pejović		28/12/90	M	32		
17	Ivan Pešić		07/07/89	D	30		
33	Radoš Protić		31/01/87	D	24	(2)	1
27	Vladimir Radivojević		04/02/86	M	33		5
13	Darko Rakočević		13/09/81	D	3	(3)	
23	Dragan Rosić		22/09/96	G	4		
5	Siniša Saničanin	BIH	24/04/95	D	13	(11)	1
93	Miloš Šatara	BIH	28/10/95	D	32	(1)	1
14	Marko Simić		07/11/93	A	2	(4)	
31	Janko Tumbasević	MNE	14/01/85	M	21	(10)	1
22	Zlatko Zečević		10/08/83	G		(1)	
9	Nikola Zvrko	MNE	07/03/95	A	2	(5)	1

FK Napredak

1946 • Mladost (10,331) • fknapredak.rs

Coach: Dragan Ivanović; (30/12/16) Vuk Rašović

Date		Opponent	Result		Scorers
2016					
22/07	a	Crvena zvezda	D	2-2	*Gobeljić, Vukanović*
31/07	h	Partizan	W	2-1	*Šljivić (p), Projić*
06/08	a	Metalac	L	0-2	
10/08	h	Vojvodina	D	0-0	
14/08	a	Mladost	L	0-1	
20/08	h	Javor	W	3-1	*Vukanović, Simonović, Urošević*
27/08	a	Voždovac	D	0-0	
10/09	h	Čukarički	W	2-1	*Urošević, Gobeljić*
16/09	a	Radnički Niš	D	1-1	*Punoševac*
25/09	h	Spartak	W	1-0	*Jovović*
02/10	a	Radnik	W	1-0	*Punoševac*
14/10	h	Rad	W	2-0	*Vukanović, Urošević*
22/10	a	Novi Pazar	W	1-0	*Gobeljić*
30/10	h	Borac	W	3-1	*N'Diaye 2, Vukanović*
05/11	a	Bačka	W	3-1	*Vukanović, N'Diaye, B Petrović*
19/11	h	Crvena zvezda	L	0-1	
25/11	a	Partizan	L	2-3	*Gobeljić, Vukanović*
30/11	h	Metalac	W	1-0	*Šarac*
04/12	a	Vojvodina	L	0-2	
10/12	h	Mladost	D	0-0	
14/12	a	Javor	L	0-1	
2017					
18/12	h	Voždovac	D	0-0	
25/02	a	Čukarički	L	0-1	
04/03	h	Radnički Niš	L	1-2	*N'Diaye*
08/03	a	Spartak	D	1-1	*Vukanović*
12/03	h	Radnik	W	2-1	*Vukanović, Šljivić*
18/03	a	Rad	W	1-0	*Vukanović*
01/04	h	Novi Pazar	W	3-0	*Vukanović, Alivodić 2*
09/04	a	Borac	W	1-0	*Kasalica*
13/04	h	Bačka	W	2-0	*og (Varga), Gobeljić*
18/04	a	Vojvodina	L	1-2	*Tubić*
22/04	h	Crvena zvezda	L	1-2	*Vukanović*
30/04	a	Partizan	L	1-3	*Kasalica*
07/05	h	Radnički Niš	L	0-2	
13/05	h	Javor Matis	W	3-0	*Šljivić (p), Urošević, N'Diaye*
17/05	a	Mladost	L	2-3	*Šljivić 2 (2p)*
21/05	h	Voždovac	D	1-1	*N'Diaye*

No	Name	Nat	DoB	Pos	Aps	(s)	Gls
22	Enver Alivodić		27/12/84	M	15	(1)	2
88	Bojan Beljić		08/05/85	M		(10)	
3	Miloš Cvetković		06/01/90	D	10		
6	Nikola Eskić	BIH	19/12/97	M	13		
6	Abraham Frimpong	GHA	06/04/93	D	12	(1)	
77	Marko Gobeljić		13/09/92	M	30	(2)	5
14	Georgije Ilić		13/05/95	A		(1)	
1	Slobodan Janković		29/08/81	G	1		
22	Vladimir Jovović	MNE	26/10/94	M		(9)	1
13	Filip Kasalica	MNE	17/12/88	A	3	(7)	2
18	Daur Kvekveskiri	RUS	07/02/98	A		(2)	
18	Nikola Leković		09/12/89	D	11		
9	Darko Lemajić		20/08/93	A		(2)	
7	Jovan Markoski		23/06/80	M	21	(4)	
4	Bojan Miladinović		24/04/82	D	21		
72	Ibrahima N'Diaye	SEN	06/01/94	A	33	(3)	6
11	Branimir Petrović		26/06/82	M	6	(7)	1
35	Nikola Petrović		10/04/88	G	36		
23	Josip Projić		23/08/87	D	19	(4)	1
13	Bratislav Punoševac		09/07/87	A	3	(9)	2
28	Dino Šarac		06/09/90	M	7	(16)	1
30	Jesse Sekidika	NGA	14/07/96	A	3	(8)	
5	Miloš Simonović		28/05/90	D	33	(1)	1
8	Nenad Šljivić		08/06/85	M	36		5
55	Nemanja Tubić		08/04/84	D	14		1
27	Slobodan Urosević		15/04/94	M	34		4
3	Boris Varga		14/08/93	D	6		
9	Nemanja Vidaković		29/09/85	A	1	(1)	
17	Aleksa Vukanović		18/06/92	M	29	(5)	11
10	Miloš Vulić		19/08/96	M	10	(13)	

FK Novi Pazar

1928 • Gradski (12,000) • fknovipazar.rs

Coach: Zoran Marić; (26/09/16) Zoran Govedarica; (16/11/16) (Izet Ljajić); (01/01/17) Nebojša Vučićević; (20/04/17) Neško Milovanović

Date		Opponent	Result		Scorers
2016					
30/07	a	Javor	D	1-1	*Tintor*
06/08	h	Čukarički	W	1-0	*Alivodić (p)*
10/08	a	Spartak	W	5-2	*Travančić 2, Dimitrijević, Alivodić 2*
14/08	h	Rad	L	0-2	
20/08	a	Borac	L	1-2	*Alivodić (p)*
28/08	h	Crvena zvezda	L	1-4	*Travančić*
10/09	a	Metalac	D	0-0	
14/09	h	Vojvodina	L	1-2	*Rušević*
17/09	h	Mladost	L	1-2	*Rušević*
25/09	a	Voždovac	L	0-2	
02/10	h	Radnički Niš	W	1-0	*Dimitrijević*
15/10	a	Radnik	L	1-3	*Alivodić*
22/10	h	Napredak	L	0-1	
30/10	h	Bačka	D	1-1	*Vusljanin (p)*
06/11	a	Partizan	L	0-4	
19/11	a	Vojvodina	L	0-3	
26/11	h	Javor	L	1-2	*Alivodić*
30/11	a	Čukarički	L	0-2	
04/12	h	Spartak	L	2-4	*Rušević 2*
10/12	a	Rad	L	0-2	
14/12	h	Borac	L	0-2	
2017					
18/02	a	Crvena zvezda	L	0-2	
25/02	h	Metalac	D	0-0	
04/03	a	Mladost	W	1-0	*Marković*
08/03	h	Voždovac	L	0-1	
12/03	a	Radnički Niš	D	2-2	*Marković, Ignjatović*
17/03	h	Radnik	W	1-0	*Krstić*
01/04	a	Napredak	L	0-3	
09/04	a	Bačka	L	0-1	
13/04	h	Partizan	L	1-3	*Marković*
18/04	a	Bačka	L	0-4	
22/04	h	Rad	W	3-0	*Marković 2 (1p), Ignjatović*
29/04	a	Spartak	L	1-2	*Plavšić*
07/05	a	Radnik	D	1-1	*Marković*
13/05	h	Borac	W	2-0	*Popović, Djoković (p)*
17/05	h	Čukarički	L	0-5	
21/05	a	Metalac	L	0-3	

No	Name	Nat	DoB	Pos	Aps	(s)	Gls
7	Enver Alivodić		27/12/84	M	19		6
30	Ibrahim Arifović	BIH	24/02/90	D	1	(2)	
22	Mehmed Avdić		15/10/88	A	4	(4)	
13	Dejan Babić		20/04/89	M	4	(4)	
33	Denis Biševac		22/09/96	D		(4)	
18	Mirsad Brunčević		11/06/94	D	7	(4)	
25	Miloš Budaković		10/07/91	G	15		
16	Bojan Čečarić		10/10/93	A	15	(2)	
32	Nikola Dimitrijević		10/05/91	M	15	(3)	2
11	Aleksandar Djoković		16/12/91	A	14	(8)	1
3	Ermin Ibrahimović		12/11/98	D		(1)	
55	Aleksandar Ignjatović		11/04/88	D	16		2
19	Ervin Kačar		23/10/91	D	3	(6)	
24	Srdja Knežević		15/04/85	D	11		
88	Miloš Krstić		07/03/87	M	10	(3)	1
17	Petar Kunić	BIH	15/07/93	A		(5)	
30	Miloš Lepović		03/10/87	M	7	(10)	
77	Slavko Marić		07/03/84	D	33		
32	Ivan Marković		23/12/91	A	16		6
88	Darko Micevski	MKD	12/04/92	M	18		
10	Stefan Milojević		29/01/89	M	9	(2)	
84	Kenan Muslimovic	AUT	13/02/97	M	4	(7)	
5	Miljan Mutavdžić		03/02/86	M	6	(8)	
21	Lazar Pajović		26/08/91	D	16	(2)	
8	Dušan Pantelić		15/03/93	M	12		
29	Nenad Perović		02/06/93	M	2	(4)	
57	Miloš Plavšić	SVK	04/04/90	A	14		1
9	Mladen Popović		29/08/88	A		(3)	1
44	Murod Rajabov	UZB	07/07/95	M	2	(1)	
9	Anes Rušević		02/12/96	A	10	(6)	4
54	Milan Savić		04/04/94	D	7	(2)	
44	Luka Sindjić		13/02/93	M	7	(2)	
4	Darko Stanojević		14/04/87	D	17		
80	Milan Svojić		09/10/85	M	5	(1)	
4	Aleksandar Tasić		06/04/88	D	9	(1)	
99	Miloš Tintor		21/08/86	D	12	(1)	1
10	Anid Travančić	BIH	07/09/93	M	14	(1)	3
2	Jovica Vasilić		08/07/90	D	23	(3)	
27	Irfan Vusljanin		07/01/86	M	8	(7)	1
1	Zlatko Zečević		10/08/83	G		(1)	
23	Mladen Živković		26/08/89	G	12		
55	Bojan Zogović	MNE	16/02/89	G	10		

SERBIA

FK Partizan

1945 • FK Partizan (30,900) • partizan.rs

Major honours
Yugoslav/Serbian League (27) 1947, 1949, 1961, 1962, 1963, 1965, 1976, 1978, 1983, 1986, 1987, 1993, 1994, 1996, 1997, 1999, 2002, 2003, 2005, 2008, 2009, 2010, 2011, 2012, 2013, 2015, 2017; Yugoslav/Serbian Cup (14) 1947, 1952, 1954, 1957, 1989, 1992, 1994, 1998, 2001, 2008, 2009, 2011, 2016, 2017

Coach: Ivan Tomić; (04/08/16) Marko Nikolić

Date		Opponent	Result	Scorers
2016				
24/07	a	Bačka	D 0-0	
31/07	a	Napredak	L 1-2	*Bozhinov*
07/08	h	Vojvodina	L 1-3	*Bozhinov*
10/08	a	Javor	W 2-0	*Radović, Mihajlović (p)*
14/08	h	Čukarički	W 1-0	*Bozhinov*
20/08	a	Spartak	L 1-2	*Leonardo*
27/08	h	Rad	W 4-0	*Bozhinov, Milenković, Leonardo, Radović*
11/09	a	Borac	W 2-0	*Miletić, Mihajlović*
17/09	h	Crvena zvezda	W 1-0	*Leonardo*
25/09	a	Metalac	W 1-0	*Leonardo*
02/10	h	Mladost	W 3-1	*Leonardo, Djurdjević, Bozhinov*
15/10	a	Voždovac	W 3-0	*Leonardo, Ostojić, Everton Luiz*
22/10	h	Radnički Niš	D 1-1	*Djurdjić*
29/10	a	Radnik	W 3-1	*Djurdjević 2, Leonardo*
06/11	h	Novi Pazar	W 4-0	*Janković, A Stevanović, Djurdjević, Djuričković*
19/11	h	Bačka	W 1-0	*Djurdjević*
25/11	h	Napredak	W 3-2	*Leonardo 2 (1p), A Stevanović*
30/11	a	Vojvodina	D 0-0	
04/12	h	Javor	W 2-0	*Djurdjević, Leonardo*
11/12	a	Čukarički	W 3-1	*Djurdjević 3*
15/12	h	Spartak	W 2-0	*Leonardo 2*
2017				
19/02	a	Rad	W 1-0	*Djurdjević*
25/02	h	Borac	W 2-1	*Kosović, Leonardo (p)*
04/03	a	Crvena zvezda	D 1-1	*Djurdjević*
08/03	h	Metalac	W 3-0	*Tawamba, Djurdjević, Djuričković*
12/03	a	Mladost	W 2-0	*Leonardo, Djurdjević*
18/03	h	Voždovac	W 4-0	*Djurdjević 2 (1p), Leonardo, Milenković*
01/04	a	Radnički Niš	W 2-0	*Djurdjević, Leonardo*
08/04	h	Radnik	W 2-1	*Janković, Djurdjević (p)*
13/04	a	Novi Pazar	W 3-1	*Djurdjević, Leonardo, Jevtović*
18/04	a	Crvena zvezda	W 3-1	*Leonardo 2, Tawamba*
22/04	h	Vojvodina	W 1-0	*Djurdjević*
30/04	h	Napredak	W 3-1	*Janković, Kosović, Leonardo*
05/05	a	Javor Matis	W 2-1	*Djurdjević 2 (1p)*
13/05	h	Voždovac	W 2-1	*Leonardo, Djurdjević (p)*
17/05	a	Radnički Niš	W 3-1	*Leonardo, Djurdjević 2*
21/05	h	Mladost	W 5-0	*Leonardo 2, Jevtović, Janković, Kosović*

No	Name	Nat	DoB	Pos	Aps	(s)	Gls
6	Gregor Balažic	SVN	12/02/88	D	15		
14	Miroslav Bogosavac		14/10/96	D	3		
86	Valeri Bozhinov	BUL	15/02/86	A	15	(5)	5
8	Darko Brašanac		12/02/92	M	2	(2)	
6	Lazar Ćirković		22/08/92	D	1		
8	Vladimir Djilas		03/03/83	A		(2)	
32	Uroš Djurdjević		02/03/94	A	28	(1)	24
40	Nikola Djurdjić		01/04/86	A	7	(6)	1
11	Petar Djuričković		20/06/91	M	2	(15)	2
25	Everton Luiz	BRA	24/05/88	M	28	(1)	1
51	Cédric Gogoua	CIV	10/07/94	D	3		
22	Saša Ilić		30/12/77	M	6	(16)	
95	Marko Janković	MNE	09/07/95	M	23	(7)	4
21	Marko Jevtović		24/07/93	M	24		2
99	Djordje Jovanović		15/02/99	A		(7)	
12	Filip Kljajić		16/08/90	G	27		
27	Nebojša Kosović	MNE	24/02/95	M	11	(5)	3
42	Leonardo	BRA	18/03/92	A	31	(3)	24
17	Saša Marjanović		13/11/87	M	4	(2)	
7	Nemanja Mihajlović		19/01/96	M	12	(13)	2
31	Nikola Milenković		12/10/97	D	32		2
26	Nemanja Miletić		26/07/91	D	32		1
13	Mohammed Mounir	LBY	08/04/92	D	2	(1)	
23	Bojan Ostojić		12/02/84	D	23	(1)	1
29	Milan Radin		25/06/91	M	3	(5)	
10	Miroslav Radović		16/01/84	M	6	(1)	2
50	Bojan Šaranov		22/10/87	G	6		
91	Alen Stevanović		07/01/91	M	11	(6)	2
85	Nemanja Stevanović		08/05/92	G	4		
3	Leandre Tawamba	CMR	20/12/89	A	10	(6)	2
9	Dušan Vlahović		28/01/00	A	1	(6)	
4	Miroslav Vulićević		29/05/85	D	35		

FK Rad

1958 • Kralj Petar I (6,000) • fkrad.rs

Coach: Aleksandar Janjić; (10/08/16) (Sladjan Nikolić); (17/08/16) Nebojša Petrović

Date		Opponent	Result	Scorers
2016				
23/07	a	Mladost	L 1-2	*Mladenović*
30/07	h	Voždovac	L 0-2	
05/08	a	Radnički Niš	L 0-3	
10/08	h	Radnik	W 1-0	*Mladenović*
14/08	a	Novi Pazar	W 2-0	*Djenić, Mladenović*
20/08	h	Bačka	W 2-1	*Veselinović, Djenić*
27/08	a	Partizan	L 0-4	
09/09	h	Vojvodina	D 0-0	
17/09	a	Javor	D 1-1	*Djenić*
24/09	h	Čukarički	D 1-1	*Maraš*
02/10	a	Spartak	W 1-0	*Lutovac*
14/10	a	Napredak	L 0-2	
22/10	h	Borac	W 2-0	*Mladenović 2*
30/10	a	Crvena zvezda	L 1-2	*Denić*
05/11	h	Metalac	D 1-1	*og (Rovčanin)*
18/11	h	Mladost	L 1-2	*Lutovac (p)*
26/11	a	Voždovac	D 0-0	
30/11	h	Radnički Niš	D 1-1	*Ćulum*
04/12	a	Radnik	L 0-1	
10/12	h	Novi Pazar	W 2-0	*Lutovac, Denić*
14/12	a	Bačka	L 0-2	
2017				
19/02	h	Partizan	L 0-1	
26/02	a	Vojvodina	L 2-3	*Lutovac, Milošev*
04/03	h	Javor Matis	D 1-1	*Bainović*
08/03	a	Čukarički	D 1-1	*Maraš*
12/03	h	Spartak	W 2-0	*Djenić 2*
18/03	h	Napredak	L 0-1	
01/04	a	Borac	W 1-0	*Rodić*
09/04	h	Crvena zvezda	L 0-4	
13/04	a	Metalac	W 2-1	*Ćulum, Milošev*
18/04	h	Borac	L 1-2	*Milošev*
22/04	a	Novi Pazar	L 0-3	
29/04	h	Radnik	L 0-2	
07/05	a	Spartak	D 0-0	
13/05	h	Bačka	L 0-1	
17/05	h	Metalac	W 1-0	*Veselinović*
21/05	a	Čukarički	W 1-0	*Guzina*

No	Name	Nat	DoB	Pos	Aps	(s)	Gls
44	Filip Bainović		23/06/96	M	10	(3)	1
55	Stevan Bates		29/11/81	D	22	(1)	
8	Milan Ćulum		28/10/84	M	22	(3)	2
11	Milorad Dabić	MNE	01/05/91	A		(5)	
1	Darko Dejanović	BIH	17/03/95	G	9		
10	Djordje Denić		01/04/96	M	17	(2)	2
32	Nikola Dimitrijević		10/05/91	M	2	(6)	
19	Dejan Djenić		02/07/86	A	19	(4)	5
16	Nikola Drinčić	MNE	07/09/84	M	13	(1)	
26	Nenad Filipović		24/04/87	G	15		
9	Boško Guzina		30/04/96	A	3		1
22	Ivica Jovanović	MNE	04/12/87	A	3	(1)	
44	Petar Jovanović	BIH	12/07/82	D	18		
18	Marko Jović		23/04/98	A	1	(4)	
7	Miloš Krstić		07/03/87	M		(4)	
6	Zoran Ljubinković		04/07/82	D	21	(6)	
17	Aleksandar Lutovac		28/06/97	M	31		4
25	Nikola Maraš		19/12/95	D	34		2
86	Miloš Marković		10/12/86	D		(1)	
27	Lazar Milošev		20/06/96	A	5	(7)	3
91	Nikola Mirković		26/07/91	G	13		
33	Bogdan Mladenović		04/04/96	M	21	(7)	5
5	Miloš Obradović		30/03/87	D	16	(1)	
21	Tomislav Pajović		15/03/86	D	12		
70	Duško Petković		24/07/90	M	6	(23)	
3	Luka Petrović		21/06/97	D		(1)	
14	Njegoš Petrović		18/07/99	M	2	(7)	
50	Miloš Radivojević		05/04/90	D	16		
20	Vladimir Rodić	MNE	07/09/93	M	15	(1)	1
20	Dejan Rusmir		28/01/80	M		(1)	
23	Nikola Šipčić		17/05/95	D	2	(1)	
88	Marko Stanojević		22/06/88	M	16	(1)	
15	Marko Stojanović		01/02/98	M	2	(3)	
77	Borko Veselinović		06/01/86	A	22	(4)	2
24	Stefan Vico	MNE	28/02/95	D	19	(9)	

FK Radnički Niš

1923 • Čair (18,151) • fkradnickinis.rs

Coach: Milan Rastavac

Date		Opponent	Result	Scorers
2016				
24/07	h	Čukarički	W 2-1	*Mrkić, Stojanović*
30/07	a	Spartak	L 1-3	*Stojanović*
05/08	h	Rad	W 3-0	*Mrkić 2, Arsić*
10/08	a	Borac	D 0-0	
14/08	h	Crvena zvezda	L 0-3	
21/08	a	Metalac	W 2-1	*Stojanović, Arsić*
27/08	h	Mladost	W 2-0	*Stojanović, Petrović*
10/09	a	Voždovac	W 4-1	*Pavkov 2, Mrkić, Arsić*
16/09	h	Napredak	D 1-1	*Arsić*
25/09	h	Radnik	W 1-0	*Mrkić*
02/10	a	Novi Pazar	L 0-1	
15/10	h	Bačka	W 1-0	*Apostolović*
22/10	a	Partizan	D 1-1	*Pavkov*
30/10	h	Vojvodina	W 1-0	*Mrkić*
06/11	a	Javor	L 0-2	
19/11	a	Čukarički	L 1-4	*Mrkić*
26/11	h	Spartak	L 0-1	
30/11	a	Rad	D 1-1	*Pavkov (p)*
04/12	h	Borac	D 3-3	*Arsić, Petrović, Mrkić*
10/12	a	Crvena zvezda	L 1-2	*Pavkov*
14/12	h	Metalac	D 1-1	*Mitrović*
2017				
17/02	a	Mladost	L 0-1	
25/02	h	Voždovac	W 2-0	*Travančić, Arsić*
04/03	a	Napredak	W 2-1	*Stojanović 2*
08/03	a	Radnik	W 2-1	*Kojić, Stojanović*
12/03	h	Novi Pazar	D 2-2	*Arsić, og (Tasić)*
18/03	a	Bačka	W 2-1	*Kojić, Arsić*
01/04	h	Partizan	L 0-2	
09/04	a	Vojvodina	D 1-1	*Mrkić (p)*
13/04	h	Javor Matis	L 0-1	
18/04	a	Mladost	L 2-3	*Arsić 2*
23/04	h	Voždovac	W 3-0	*Arsić, Aleksandar Jovanović, Apostolović*
29/04	h	Javor Matis	W 2-0	*Bulatović, Noma*
07/05	a	Napredak	W 2-0	*Noma, Kojić*
13/05	a	Vojvodina	D 0-0	
17/05	h	Partizan	L 1-3	*D Živković*
21/05	a	Crvena zvezda	L 0-4	

No	Name	Nat	DoB	Pos	Aps	(s)	Gls
70	Andreja Apostolović		16/06/96	M	6	(12)	2
11	Lazar Arsić		24/09/91	M	34	(1)	11
30	Vladimir Bajić		28/11/87	G	22		
4	Radoš Bulatović		06/05/84	D	22	(1)	1
15	Aleksandar Ignjatović		11/04/88	D	5	(3)	
99	Ramazan Isaev	RUS	17/01/98	A		(2)	
44	Dušan Ivanov		17/02/91	D		(1)	
21	Aleksa Jovanović		27/05/99	M	2	(12)	
24	Aleksandar Jovanović		17/12/85	M	25	(5)	1
26	Nemanja Kartal	MNE	17/07/94	D	1	(2)	
36	Nemanja Kojić		03/02/90	A	15	(1)	3
18	Ivan Konovalov	RUS	18/08/94	G	5		
80	Petar Krstić		03/09/97	M	5	(1)	
15	Nemanja Ljubisavljević		26/11/96	D	1		
67	Nikola Mitrović		14/12/97	M	7	(4)	1
19	Marko Mrkić		20/08/96	A	30	(5)	9
28	Ryota Noma	JPN	15/11/91	M	12	(3)	2
9	Milan Pavkov		09/02/94	A	17	(3)	5
40	Milan Perendija		05/01/86	D	11		
14	Miloš Petrović		05/05/90	D	33		2
8	Pavle Popara		20/05/87	M	7	(9)	
55	Miloš Radivojević		05/04/90	D	15		
33	Nikola Stanković		18/12/93	D	31	(1)	
23	Miloš Stanojević		20/11/93	M	14	(10)	
5	Nemanja Stevanović		13/09/98	D		(2)	
7	Saša Stojanović		21/01/83	M	26	(2)	7
16	Marko Tomić		28/10/91	M	11	(3)	
9	Anid Travančić	BIH	07/09/93	M	12	(1)	1
3	Vladimir Volkov	MNE	06/06/86	D	6		
20	Dušan Živković		31/07/96	M	6	(15)	1
6	Miloš Živković		01/12/84	D	16	(2)	
89	Bojan Zogović	MNE	16/02/89	G	10		

FK Radnik Surdulica

1926 • Gradski stadion (3,312) • fk-radnik.com

Coach: Goran Lazarević; (02/09/16) Neško Milovanović; (23/11/16) Milorad Kosanović; (04/01/17) Bratislav Živković; (21/03/17) Simo Krunić (BIH)

2016

Date		Opponent	Result	Scorers
23/07	h	Javor	D 2-2	*Pavlović, Radović*
31/07	a	Čukarički	D 0-0	
06/08	h	Spartak	W 2-1	*Mišan, Adamović*
10/08	a	Rad	L 0-1	
14/08	h	Borac	D 1-1	*Jovanović*
21/08	a	Crvena zvezda	L 0-5	
26/08	h	Metalac	L 0-1	
10/09	a	Mladost	L 0-2	
17/09	h	Voždovac	W 3-1	*Merdović, Jovanović, Vuković*
25/09	a	Radnički Niš	L 0-1	
02/10	h	Napredak	L 0-1	
15/10	h	Novi Pazar	W 3-1	*Radović, Milovanović, Nikolić*
22/10	a	Bačka	W 2-0	*Radović 2*
29/10	h	Partizan	L 1-3	*Zlatanović*
04/11	a	Vojvodina	L 0-2	
19/11	a	Javor	L 0-1	
26/11	h	Čukarički	D 1-1	*Adamović*
30/11	a	Spartak	D 1-1	*Adamović*
04/12	h	Rad	W 1-0	*Nikolić (p)*
10/12	a	Borac	L 0-1	
14/12	h	Crvena zvezda	L 1-2	*Nikolić*

2017

Date		Opponent	Result	Scorers
25/02	h	Mladost	D 1-1	*Arsenijević*
01/03	a	Metalac	L 1-3	*Stanković*
04/03	a	Voždovac	L 0-3	
08/03	h	Radnički Niš	L 1-2	*Jovanović*
12/03	a	Napredak	L 1-2	*Stanković*
17/03	a	Novi Pazar	L 0-1	
01/04	h	Bačka	W 1-0	*Trifunović (p)*
08/04	a	Partizan	L 1-2	*Arsenijević*
13/04	h	Vojvodina	D 0-0	
18/04	a	Čukarički	W 2-1	*Trifunović (p), Arsenijević*
22/04	h	Spartak	W 3-0	*Milovanović, Radović, Trifunović*
29/04	a	Rad	W 2-0	*Milovanović, Stanković*
07/05	h	Novi Pazar	D 1-1	*Trifunović*
13/05	a	Metalac	D 1-1	*og (Dopudj)*
17/05	a	Bačka	L 0-1	
21/05	h	Borac	D 2-2	*Trifunović, Zlatanović*

No	Name	Nat	DoB	Pos	Aps	(s)	Gls
8	Miloš Adamović		19/06/88	M	22	(9)	3
20	Nemanja Arsenijević		29/03/86	A	11	(2)	3
22	Ognjen Čančarević		25/09/89	G	36		
19	Ivan Djorić		07/07/95	M	8	(6)	
23	Savo Gazivoda	MNE	18/07/94	M	1	(6)	
15	Aleksandar Gojković		18/08/88	D	26		
6	Lazar Ivić		24/10/92	M	2	(2)	
16	Jovan Jovanović		02/10/85	A	5	(11)	3
6	Nikola Krčmarević		18/12/91	M	5	(2)	
10	Francis Kyeremeh	GHA	22/06/97	M	19	(4)	
4	Zlatko Liščević		08/03/91	M	3	(2)	
9	Nenad Lukić		02/09/92	A	4	(2)	
23	Luka Merdović	MNE	14/03/89	M	7		1
24	Milan Milinković		04/05/92	D	12	(2)	
3	Miloš Milovanović		09/12/87	D	26	(3)	3
20	Igor Mišan	BIH	05/05/90	M	7	(6)	1
2	Siniša Mladenović		05/02/91	D	26	(1)	
14	Uroš Nenadović		28/01/94	M	2	(5)	
9	Stefan Nikolić	MNE	16/04/90	A	11		3
13	Vladan Pavlović		24/02/84	M	21	(1)	1
17	Bratislav Pejčić		17/01/83	M	21	(5)	
25	Petar Planić		16/03/89	D	1		
11	Nikola Radović		10/07/92	M	32	(3)	5
7	Miloš Stanković		22/07/92	M	16	(12)	3
5	Danijel Stojković		14/08/90	D	3	(2)	
18	Miloš Trifunović		15/10/84	A	8		5
1	Nikola Vasiljević		24/06/96	G	1		
4	Nedeljko Vlahović	MNE	15/01/84	M	13	(4)	
14	Mladen Vukasović	MNE	22/07/92	A		(2)	
26	Slobodan Vuković		23/01/86	D	25	(1)	1
9	Nikola Žakula		18/08/92	A	8	(1)	
25	Dragan Žarković		16/04/86	D	12		
27	Igor Zlatanović		10/02/98	A	13	(14)	2

FK Spartak Subotica

1945 • Gradski (13,000); Karadjordje, Novi Sad (15,754) • fkspartak.com

Coach: Andrei Chernyshov (RUS)

2016

Date		Opponent	Result	Scorers
23/07	a	Voždovac	W 3-0	*(w/o; original result 0-0)*
30/07	h	Radnički Niš	W 3-1	*Mudrinski, Ćalasan, Ivanović*
06/08	a	Radnik	L 1-2	*Mudrinski*
10/08	h	Novi Pazar	L 2-5	*Jočić, Krmar*
13/08	a	Bačka	W 3-1	*Mudrinski, Torbica, Makarić*
20/08	h	Partizan	W 2-1	*Makarić, Milić*
28/08	a	Vojvodina	L 0-5	
10/09	h	Javor	D 1-1	*Radovanović*
17/09	a	Čukarički	W 4-2	*Milić, Torbica (p), Ivanović, Mudrinski*
25/09	a	Napredak	L 0-1	
02/10	h	Rad	L 0-1	
15/10	a	Borac	D 3-3	*Milić 2, Stojković*
22/10	h	Crvena zvezda	D 1-1	*og (Petković)*
30/10	a	Metalac	D 0-0	
05/11	h	Mladost	W 1-0	*Milić*
19/11	h	Voždovac	L 0-2	
26/11	a	Radnički Niš	W 1-0	*Milić*
30/11	h	Radnik	D 1-1	*Mudrinski*
04/12	a	Novi Pazar	W 4-2	*Mudrinski 3, Ivanović*
10/12	h	Bačka	D 0-0	
15/12	a	Partizan	L 0-2	

2017

Date		Opponent	Result	Scorers
19/02	h	Vojvodina	L 1-4	*Mudrinski*
25/02	a	Javor	W 3-2	*Kerkez, Jovović, Mudrinski (p)*
04/03	h	Čukarički	L 0-1	
08/03	h	Napredak	D 1-1	*Mudrinski*
12/03	a	Rad	L 0-2	
18/03	h	Borac	W 1-0	*Mudrinski*
01/04	a	Crvena zvezda	L 1-2	*Ivanović*
09/04	h	Metalac	D 0-0	
13/04	a	Mladost	L 1-4	*Mudrinski*
18/04	h	Metalac	W 3-1	*Stojković, Mudrinski, Ivanović*
22/04	a	Radnik	L 0-3	
29/04	h	Novi Pazar	W 2-1	*Savković, Mudrinski*
07/05	h	Rad	D 0-0	
13/05	a	Čukarički	W 2-1	*Ivanović, Mudrinski*
17/05	a	Borac	L 0-1	
21/05	h	Bačka	W 2-1	*Ivanović 2*

No	Name	Nat	DoB	Pos	Aps	(s)	Gls
28	Emil Abaz	MKD	17/01/98	A	2	(4)	
27	Nnaemeka Ajuru	NGA	28/09/86	M	11	(5)	
3	Marko Andjić		14/12/83	D	14	(3)	
13	Igor Antunic		01/01/98	M		(1)	
11	Marko Bašanović		26/09/94	D	19	(2)	
40	Nemanja Ćalasan		17/03/96	D	27	(4)	1
18	Lazar Djokić	MNE	16/05/96	D		(3)	
25	Ivan Dokić		25/03/00	G		(1)	
21	Daniel Farkaš		13/01/93	D	11	(3)	
2	Boško Gajić		29/06/96	D	2		
15	Nemanja Glavčić		19/02/97	M	23	(8)	
10	Djordje Ivanović		20/11/95	M	30	(5)	8
1	Budimir Janošević		21/10/89	G	3		
4	Branimir Jočić		30/11/94	M	5		1
1	Bojan Jović		01/04/82	G	4		
9	Vladimir Jovović	MNE	26/10/94	A	10	(2)	1
5	Dejan Kerkez		20/01/96	D	5	(2)	1
19	Nikola Kovačević		14/04/94	M	14		
21	Aljaž Krefl	SVN	20/02/94	M	9	(1)	
17	Milivoj Krmar		01/04/97	M	3	(14)	1
22	Milan Makarić		04/10/95	M	1	(2)	2
14	Predrag Medić		20/05/98	M		(1)	
16	Nemanja Milić		25/05/90	A	15	(4)	6
12	Nikola Mirković		26/07/91	G	18		
9	Andrej Mrkela		09/04/92	M	3	(1)	
7	Ognjen Mudrinski		15/11/91	A	32	(1)	16
19	Nemanja Nikolić	MNE	19/10/92	A	4	(3)	
12	Miloš Ostojić		21/04/96	G	12		
16	Marko Pantić		18/06/98	M	15		
6	Savo Pavićević	MNE	11/12/80	D	10	(2)	
26	Milan Purović	MNE	07/05/85	A	2	(8)	
66	Aleksandar Radovanović		11/11/93	D	29	(1)	1
23	Mile Savković		11/03/92	M	8	(18)	1
20	Bogdan Stamenković		19/01/98	A		(2)	
30	Arandjel Stojković		02/03/95	D	28		2
27	Dimitrije Tomović		29/04/96	D	7	(2)	
8	Vladimir Torbica		20/09/80	M	28	(5)	2
24	Zhong Haoran	CHN	15/07/94	M		(1)	
2	Vadym Zhuk	UKR	15/04/91	D	3		

FK Vojvodina

1914 • Karadjordje (15,754) • fkvojvodina.rs

Major honours
Yugoslav League (2) 1966, 1989; Serbian Cup (1) 2014

Coach: Nenad Lalatović; (23/12/16) Dragan Ivanović; (03/04/17) Aleksandar Veselinović; (23/04/17) Radoslav Batak

2016

Date		Opponent	Result	Scorers
31/07	h	Bačka	W 1-0	*Paločević*
07/08	a	Partizan	W 3-1	*Meleg, Paločević, Trifunović*
10/08	a	Napredak	D 0-0	
14/08	h	Javor	W 4-0	*Paločević, Malbašić, Meleg, Aščerić*
21/08	a	Čukarički	W 3-1	*Paločević 2, Malbašić*
28/08	h	Spartak	W 5-0	*Malbašić, Aščerić, Paločević, L Zličić 2*
09/09	a	Rad	D 0-0	
14/09	a	Novi Pazar	W 2-1	*Trifunović, og (Stanojević)*
18/09	h	Borac	W 2-1	*Jovančić, V Kovačević*
25/09	a	Crvena zvezda	L 1-4	*Malbašić*
02/10	h	Metalac	W 1-0	*Meleg*
16/10	a	Mladost	L 0-2	
21/10	h	Voždovac	W 3-1	*Malbašić, Paločević, Trujić*
30/10	a	Radnički Niš	L 0-1	
04/11	h	Radnik	W 2-0	*Aščerić, Meleg (p)*
19/11	h	Novi Pazar	W 3-0	*Paločević, Malbašić, Meleg*
26/11	a	Bačka	W 1-0	*Aščerić*
30/11	h	Partizan	D 0-0	
04/12	h	Napredak	W 2-0	*V Kovačević, L Zličić*
09/12	a	Javor	L 1-2	*Malbašić*
14/12	h	Čukarički	W 2-0	*Trujić, Malbašić*

2017

Date		Opponent	Result	Scorers
19/02	a	Spartak	W 4-1	*Meleg, S Babić, Malbašić, Maslać*
26/02	h	Rad	W 3-2	*Meleg, S Babić, Malbašić*
03/03	a	Borac	W 1-0	*Malbašić*
08/03	h	Crvena zvezda	L 2-3	*Meleg, Puškarić*
13/03	a	Metalac	W 3-0	*Malbašić 2, Paločević*
19/03	h	Mladost	L 0-1	
01/04	a	Voždovac	L 1-4	*Trujić*
09/04	h	Radnički Niš	D 1-1	*Trujić*
13/04	a	Radnik	D 0-0	
18/04	h	Napredak	W 2-1	*Malbašić, Trujić*
22/04	a	Partizan	L 0-1	
30/04	a	Crvena zvezda	L 0-2	
06/05	h	Mladost	W 2-1	*Malbašić 2 (1p)*
13/05	h	Radnički Niš	D 0-0	
17/05	a	Voždovac	W 2-0	*Jovančić, Trujić*
21/05	h	Javor Matis	W 1-0	*Spremo*

No	Name	Nat	DoB	Pos	Aps	(s)	Gls
20	Nikola Antić		04/01/94	D	35		
9	Nikola Aščerić		19/04/91	A	8	(6)	4
3	Filip Babić		27/05/95	D		(1)	
16	Siniša Babić		13/02/91	M	15	(6)	2
38	Marko Bačanin		09/07/98	A		(1)	
66	Joseph Bempah	GHA	05/09/95	M		(1)	
27	Dženan Bureković	BIH	29/05/95	D	1		
34	Mladen Devetak		12/03/99	D		(1)	
21	Stefan Djordjević	MNE	16/11/90	A		(2)	
24	Marko Djurišić		17/07/97	D		(3)	
44	Nenad Gavrić		12/12/91	M	1	(3)	
29	Dušan Jovančić		19/10/90	M	21	(4)	2
80	Filip Knežević		08/11/91	M	4	(11)	
25	Marko Kordić	MNE	22/02/95	G	21		
5	Nikola Kovačević		14/04/94	D	6	(3)	
5	Vladimir Kovačević		11/11/92	D	16		2
14	Ivan Lakićević		27/07/93	D	33		
28	Novica Maksimović		04/04/88	M	17		
22	Filip Malbašić		18/11/92	A	35		16
51	Mario Maslać		09/09/90	D	7	(1)	1
7	Dejan Meleg		01/10/94	M	32	(1)	8
4	Dušan Mićić	MNE	29/11/84	M	2	(1)	
33	Nemanja Miletić		16/01/91	D	4		
36	Mihajlo Nešković		09/02/00	A		(4)	
10	Aleksandar Paločević		22/08/93	M	30	(4)	9
15	Bogdan Planić		19/01/92	D	27	(1)	
8	Darko Puškarić		13/06/85	D	25		1
1	Emil Rockov		27/01/95	G	16		
95	Milan Spremo		27/04/95	M	2	(8)	1
31	Uroš Stamenić		14/10/96	A	2	(4)	
37	Dobrica Tegeltija	BIH	06/10/00	M		(1)	
19	Miloš Trifunović		15/10/84	A	1	(11)	2
92	Nikola Trujić		14/04/92	A	28	(4)	6
23	Marko Vukasović		10/09/90	M	15	(1)	
18	Lazar Zličić		07/02/97	M	3	(20)	3
33	Miloš Zličić		29/12/99	A		(1)	

FK Voždovac

1912 • Voždovac (5,172) • fkvozdovac.rs
Coach: Bratislav Živković; (09/11/16) Ilija Stolica

Date		Opponent	Result	Scorers
2016				
23/07	h	Spartak	L 0-3	*(w/o; original result 0-0)*
30/07	a	Rad	W 2-0	*Stojanović, Dražić*
06/08	h	Borac	W 2-0	*Georgijević 2*
10/08	a	Crvena zvezda	L 0-3	
14/08	h	Metalac	D 0-0	
20/08	a	Mladost	W 1-0	*Dražić*
27/08	h	Napredak	D 0-0	
10/09	h	Radnički Niš	L 1-4	*Lukić*
17/09	a	Radnik	L 1-3	*Petrović*
25/09	h	Novi Pazar	W 2-0	*Stojanović 2*
02/10	a	Bačka	L 1-2	*Gajić*
15/10	h	Partizan	L 0-3	
21/10	a	Vojvodina	L 1-3	*Stojanović*
30/10	h	Javor	L 1-2	*Stojanović (p)*
05/11	a	Čukarički	L 1-2	*Stojanović*
19/11	a	Spartak	W 2-0	*Stojanović (p), Zec*
26/11	h	Rad	D 0-0	
30/11	a	Borac	W 2-1	*Dražić, Lukić*
04/12	h	Crvena zvezda	L 0-1	
10/12	a	Metalac	W 2-0	*Lukić, Stojanović (p)*
14/12	h	Mladost	W 2-1	*Stojanović 2 (1p)*
2017				
18/02	a	Napredak	D 0-0	
25/02	a	Radnički Niš	L 0-2	
04/03	h	Radnik	W 3-0	*Nikolić, Marinković, Dražić*
08/03	a	Novi Pazar	W 1-0	*Filipović*
12/03	h	Bačka	W 4-0	*Pavlović, Marinković, Krasić, Zec*
18/03	a	Partizan	L 0-4	
01/04	h	Vojvodina	W 4-1	*Nikolić, Krasić, Zec, Dražić*
09/04	a	Javor Matis	W 1-0	*Dražić*
13/04	h	Čukarički	L 1-3	*Dražić*
18/04	h	Javor Matis	D 1-1	*Marković*
23/04	a	Radnički Niš	L 0-3	
29/04	a	Mladost	L 0-2	
06/05	h	Crvena zvezda	W 3-2	*og (Andjelković), Dražić, Srećković*
13/05	a	Partizan	L 1-2	*Georgijević*
17/05	h	Vojvodina	L 0-2	
21/05	a	Napredak	D 1-1	*Marković*

No	Name	Nat	DoB	Pos	Aps	(s)	Gls
14	Elmir Asani		15/09/95	M	5	(4)	
28	Jovica Blagojević		27/08/98	M	10	(1)	
16	Dejan Boljević	MNE	30/05/90	D	7	(4)	
30	Nikola Ćirković		04/12/91	M	24	(6)	
9	Stefan Dražić		14/08/92	A	29	(5)	8
29	Borko Duronjić		24/09/97	A	1	(1)	
2	Aleksandar Filipović		20/12/94	D	25	(1)	1
5	Marko Gajić		10/03/92	D	10	(4)	1
7	Dejan Georgijević		19/01/94	A	13	(12)	3
41	Saša Ivković		13/05/93	D	15	(1)	
23	Aleksandar Ješić		13/09/94	M	5	(9)	
20	Branislav Jovanović		21/09/85	M	12	(4)	
3	Ognjen Krasić		09/04/88	M	10	(1)	2
44	Nikola Lukić		14/05/90	M	11	(1)	3
13	Nenad Marinković		28/09/88	A	8	(2)	2
11	Ivan Marković		20/06/94	M	1	(2)	2
21	Miloš Mihajlov		15/12/82	D	32		
22	Marko Milošević		07/02/91	G	13		
20	Nemanja Nikolić	MNE	01/01/88	M	12	(2)	2
25	Miloš Pavlović		27/11/83	M	27		1
6	Todor Petrović	BIH	19/08/94	M	14	(10)	1
1	Zoran Popović		28/05/88	G	24		
17	Marko Putinčanin		16/12/87	D	29	(4)	
77	Bojan Puzigaća	BIH	10/05/85	D	1		
3	Slaviša Radović	BIH	08/10/93	D	3		
4	Uroš Sindjić		19/01/86	D	20	(5)	
26	Nikola Srećković		26/04/96	M	8	(9)	1
11	Jovan Stojanović		21/04/92	M	15	(4)	10
18	Filip Stuparević		30/08/00	A		(9)	
10	Djuro Zec		06/03/90	M	23	(7)	3

Top goalscorers

Uroš Djurdjević

Leonardo

24 Uroš Djurdjević (Partizan)
Leonardo (Partizan)

16 Ognjen Ožegović (Čukarički)
Milan Bojović (Mladost)
Ognjen Mudrinski (Spartak)
Filip Malbašić (Vojvodina)

12 Richmond Boakye (Crvena zvezda)

11 Aleksa Vukanović (Napredak)
Lazar Arsić (Radnički)

10 Darko Bjedov (Javor)
Jovan Stojanović (Voždovac)

Promoted clubs

FK Mačva

1919 • FK Mačva (8,000) • fkmacva.com
Coach: Predrag Rogan

FK Zemun

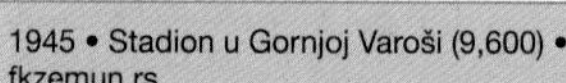

1945 • Stadion u Gornjoj Varoši (9,600) • fkzemun.rs
Coach: Milan Milanović

Second level final table 2016/17

		Pld	W	D	L	F	A	Pts
1	FK Mačva	30	19	6	5	49	26	62
2	FK Zemun	30	17	10	3	44	18	61
3	FK Sloboda Užice	30	15	9	6	43	28	54
4	FK Indjija	30	14	6	10	33	28	48
5	FK Bežanija	30	12	12	6	36	22	47
6	FK Radnički Pirot	30	12	7	11	30	31	43
7	FK Jagodina	30	12	5	13	39	35	41
8	FK Dinamo Vranje	30	10	9	11	33	43	39
9	FK Sindjelić	30	8	13	9	32	31	37
10	FK Budućnost Dobanovci	30	10	7	13	32	43	37
11	FK Proleter Novi Sad	30	9	9	12	34	40	36
12	FK ČSK Pivara	30	8	11	11	31	32	34
13	FK Kolubara	30	7	11	12	28	35	32
14	FK BSK Borča	30	9	6	15	27	39	32
15	OFK Odžaci	30	6	8	16	22	34	26
16	OFK Beograd	30	3	9	18	25	53	18

NB FK Bežanija, FK BSK Borča, FK Mačva & FK ČSK Pivara – 1 pt deducted.

DOMESTIC CUP

Kup Srbije 2016/17

FIRST ROUND

(20/09/16)
Bačka 0-3 Spartak
Rad 1-0 Dinamo

(21/09/16)
BSK Borča 1-0 Radnički Niš
Čelarevo 0-3 Crvena zvezda
Indjija 0-1 Voždovac
Kolubara 0-4 Mladost Lučani
Mladost Bački Jarak 1-4 Novi Pazar
Partizan 3-1 Napredak
Polet 0-1 Radnik
Proleter 0-1 Javor
Radan 0-5 Čukarički
Sindjelić 1-5 Jagodina
Sloboda 6-1 OFK Beograd
Vojvodina 4-0 Bežanija
Zemun 0-0 Borac *(4-5 on pens)*
Žarkovo 2-2 Metalac *(5-4 on pens)*

SECOND ROUND

(25/10/16)
Žarkovo 0-2 Partizan

(26/10/16)
Crvena zvezda 3-0 BSK Borča
Čukarički 1-0 Javor
Jagodina 1-1 Borac *(4-5 on pens)*
Mladost Lučani 1-1 Rad *(5-3 on pens)*
Novi Pazar 0-0 Vojvodina *(2-3 on pens)*
Radnik 1-2 Sloboda
Voždovac 1-0 Spartak

QUARTER-FINALS

(05/04/17)
Crvena zvezda 4-2 Mladost Lučani *(Kanga 46, Milić 52, Boakye 58, Aleksandar Luković 63p; Milosavljević 45, Bojović 70p)*

Sloboda 0-3 Čukarički *(S Jovanović 21, Kajević 45, Milojević 88)*

Vojvodina 5-2 Borac *(Malbašić 12, 71, Trujić 16, 81, S Babić 65; N Kovačević 41og, Marčić 62)*

Voždovac 1-2 Partizan *(Srećković 42; Djurdjević 80, Leonardo 90)*

SEMI-FINALS

(26/04/17 & 09/05/17)
Čukarički 1-4 Crvena zvezda *(S Jovanović 41; Le Tallec 12, Boakye 19, 39, Djurić 39og)*
Crvena zvezda 1-2 Čukarički *(Boakye 76p; Ožegović 4, Milić 54og)*
(Crvena zvezda 5-3)

(26/04/17 & 10/05/17)
Vojvodina 0-0 Partizan
Partizan 1-0 Vojvodina *(Djurdjević 45)*
(Partizan 1-0)

FINAL

(27/05/17)
FK Partizan, Belgrade
FK PARTIZAN 1 *(Milenković 42)*
FK CRVENA ZVEZDA 0
Referee: *Mažić*
PARTIZAN: *N Stevanović, Vulićević, Ostojić, Milenković, Mounir, Janković (Ilić 88), Jevtović, Kosović, Mihajlović (Djuričković 65), Leonardo (Radin 83), Djurdjević*
CRVENA ZVEZDA: *Kahriman, Petković, Le Tallec, Aleksandar Luković, Andjelković, Ristić (Milijaš 85), Donald, Plavšić (Vujaklija 69), Kanga, Srnić (Milić 60), Boakye*

SLOVAKIA

Slovenský futbalový zväz (SFZ)

Address	Trnavská 100/II SK-821 01 Bratislava
Tel	+421 2 4820 6000
Fax	+421 2 4820 6099
E-mail	office@futbalsfz.sk
Website	futbalsfz.sk

President	Ján Kováčik
General secretary	Jozef Kliment
Media officer	Monika Jurigová
Year of formation	1938

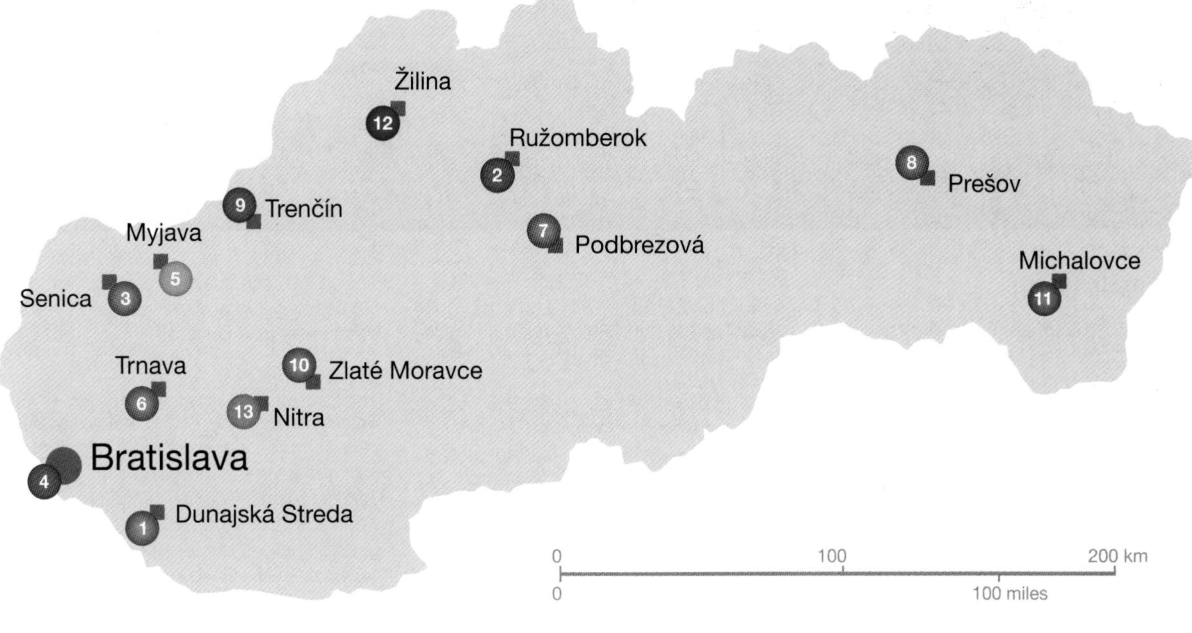

1. LIGA CLUBS

 1 **FC DAC 1904 Dunajská Streda**

 2 **MFK Ružomberok**

 3 **FK Senica**

 4 **ŠK Slovan Bratislava**

 5 **TJ Spartak Myjava**

 6 **FC Spartak Trnava**

 7 **ŽP Šport Podbrezová**
NB Renamed FK Železiarne Podbrezová for 2017/18 season

 8 **1. FC Tatran Prešov**

9 **FK AS Trenčín**

10 **FC ViOn Zlaté Moravce**

 11 **MFK Zemplín Michalovce**

 12 **MŠK Žilina**

PROMOTED CLUB

 13 **FC Nitra**

KEY

- UEFA Champions League
- UEFA Europa League
- Promoted
- Relegated

Žilina's triumph never in doubt

There was one team and one team only involved in the race for the 2016/17 Slovakian 1. Liga title. MŠK Žilina were in complete control from start to finish, running up 23 victories in a league reduced to 30 matches following the mid-season withdrawal of Spartak Myjava.

Slovan Bratislava were distant runners-up to Žilina in the league but won the Slovakian Cup, beating second-tier MFK Skalica 3-0 in the final. AS Trenčín, the double winners of the previous two seasons, only just qualified for Europe thanks to a strong finish.

Adrián Guľa's side romp home unopposed

Runners-up Slovan Bratislava win the cup

Four successive wins boost World Cup hopes

Domestic league

Trenčín's hopes of a title hat-trick were severely hampered by a summer exodus of some of their best players, including their two top scorers in 2015/16, Gino van Kessel and Matúš Bero, and three defeats in their opening four games suggested that Martin Ševela's side would struggle to contend. Confirmation of their demise came when Žilina defeated them 4-0 in late August. It was the start of a magnificent run from Adrián Guľa's side that would see them leave every other team in the division trailing helplessly in their wake.

The only team to deny Žilina all three points in the autumn months were newly-promoted Tatran Prešov, in a 1-1 draw. Otherwise it was victories all the way, and by the winter shutdown the league leaders had already racked up 50 points – or at least so they thought until their two wins against Spartak Myjava were expunged from the records following that club's withdrawal from the league just before Christmas.

Žilina's lead was large enough in any case to withstand that deduction, and although they won only one of their first four matches in the spring, allowing Slovan just a glimmer of hope, they were back on the victory trail before long, and when midfielder Michal Škvarka struck late to beat Slovan 1-0 at the Pasienky stadium on 23 April, with a month of the season still to run, Žilina's first title in five years – and seventh in all – was safely under lock and key.

By the close of the campaign Žilina's figures made impressive reading. Of the 30 matches that counted, 23 of them were won. The only points they dropped at home came on the opening day, which meant 14 successive victories in their Pod Dubňom stadium, where they scored 54 goals – as many as runners-up Slovan managed in their home and away matches combined. Žilina's aggregate goal tally was 82, with Škvarka scoring 14 of those and winger Filip Hlohovský registering 20 to end up sharing the Golden Boot with Slovan's Guinean star Seydouba Soumah.

Domestic cup

Soumah was one of Slovan's three goalscorers in the Slovakian Cup final. Milan Rundić and Aleksandar Čavrić, who, like team coach Ivan Vukomanović, both hail from Serbia, also found the net in an easy 3-0 win over a Skalica side that had caused the competition's major upset when they ousted Žilina with a pulsating 3-2 win in the quarter-finals. Skalica would narrowly miss out on promotion, too – a prize that should have gone to second division winners VSS Košice but, because of their precarious financial position, was eventually claimed by runners-up FC Nitra.

Europe

Spartak Trnava and Trenčín were Slovakia's best performers in Europe but both had their campaigns ended by painful home defeats against visitors from nearby Vienna. Trnava were eliminated in the third qualifying round on penalties after losing at home to Austria Wien, and a fortnight later Trenčín were beaten 4-0 by Rapid in a match played at Žilina's stadium, which rendered their second-leg 2-0 win in the Austrian capital redundant.

National team

Slovakia lost their opening two 2018 FIFA World Cup qualifiers, the first of them to a stoppage-time winner by England in Trnava, but recovered superbly to win each of their next four matches, scoring a dozen goals into the bargain, which placed them second in Group F – ahead of Slovenia and Scotland and just two points adrift of table-topping England with a visit to Wembley still to come. While Ján Kozák's senior side had much to smile about, so too did Pavel Hapel's Under-21s, impressive performers at the European finals just across the border in Poland, where they were desperately unlucky not to reach the semi-finals.

DOMESTIC SEASON AT A GLANCE

1. Liga 2016/17 final table

			Home					Away					Total					
		Pld	W	D	L	F	A	W	D	L	F	A	W	D	L	F	A	Pts
1	**MŠK Žilina**	**30**	**14**	**1**	**0**	**54**	**12**	**9**	**3**	**3**	**28**	**13**	**23**	**4**	**3**	**82**	**25**	**73**
2	ŠK Slovan Bratislava	30	11	2	2	29	15	7	1	7	25	19	18	3	9	54	34	57
3	MFK Ružomberok	30	11	4	1	37	15	4	3	7	18	23	15	7	8	55	38	52
4	FK AS Trenčín	30	10	3	3	35	18	4	2	8	18	30	14	5	11	53	48	47
5	ŽP Šport Podbrezová	30	6	5	4	20	16	6	4	5	14	15	12	9	9	34	31	45
6	FC Spartak Trnava	30	7	2	7	19	17	5	5	4	15	20	12	7	11	34	37	43
7	FC DAC 1904 Dunajská Streda	30	6	6	2	19	15	4	6	6	18	19	10	12	8	37	34	42
8	MFK Zemplín Michalovce	30	5	3	6	18	18	3	2	11	17	37	8	5	17	35	55	29
9	FK Senica	30	4	4	7	12	14	3	3	9	13	21	7	7	16	25	35	28
10	FC ViOn Zlaté Moravce	30	4	3	7	16	21	1	4	11	13	34	5	7	18	29	55	22
11	1. FC Tatran Prešov	30	3	5	7	11	24	0	5	10	6	39	3	10	17	17	63	19
12	TJ Spartak Myjava	0	0	0	0	0	0	0	0	0	0	0	0	0	0	0	0	0

NB TJ Spartak Myjava withdrew after round 19 - all their matches were annulled.

European qualification 2017/18

Champion: MŠK Žilina (second qualifying round)

Cup winner: ŠK Slovan Bratislava (first qualifying round)
MFK Ružomberok (first qualifying round)
FK AS Trenčín (first qualifying round)

Top scorer	Seydouba Soumah (Slovan) & Filip Hlohovský (Žilina), 20 goals
Relegated club	TJ Spartak Myjava (withdrew)
Promoted club	FC Nitra
Cup final	ŠK Slovan Bratislava 3-0 MFK Skalica

Player of the season

Filip Hlohovský
(MŠK Žilina)

Formerly with Trenčín, Slovan Bratislava and Senica, Hlohovský enjoyed by far the most fruitful season of his career with Žilina in 2016/17. It was the 29-year-old winger's goals that sparked the club's title charge, enabling them to regain the Slovakian 1. Liga crown last won in 2012. After topping the scorers' chart virtually all season, he was caught on the final day by Slovan's Seydouba Soumah, the two of them finishing with 20 goals. His second season at Žilina would be his last as he departed for South Korean second division club Seongnam FC.

Newcomer of the season

Martin Chrien
(MFK Ružomberok)

Ružomberok finished the 2016/17 1. Liga with a flourish to finish third. There was a strong Czech influence to the team, with midfielder Erik Daniel and 14-goal striker Jakub Mareš both excelling, and that also extended indirectly, during the autumn, to Chrien, a Slovakian who spent the first half of the season on loan from Viktoria Plzeň. He did so well that Plzeň recalled him in the spring. The young midfielder then starred for Slovakia at the UEFA European Under-21 finals in Poland, scoring two goals, before joining Portuguese giants Benfica in the summer.

Team of the season

(3-2-4-1)

Coach: **Guľa** *(Žilina)*

SLOVAKIA

NATIONAL TEAM

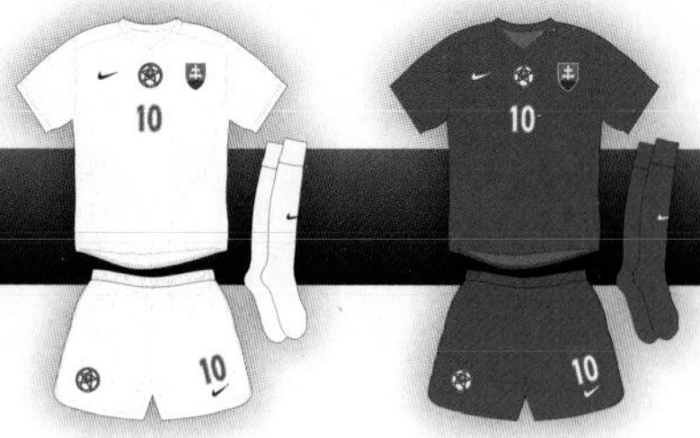

International tournament appearances

FIFA World Cup (1) 2010 (2nd round)
UEFA European Championship (1) 2016 (round of 16)

Top five all-time caps

Miroslav Karhan (107); **Marek Hamšík** (97); **Martin Škrtel** (90); **Ján Ďurica** (88); Róbert Vittek (82)

Top five all-time goals

Róbert Vittek (23); Szilárd Németh (22); **Marek Hamšík** (21); Miroslav Karhan & Marek Mintál (14)

Results 2016/17

04/09/16	England (WCQ)	H	Trnava	L	0-1	
08/10/16	Slovenia (WCQ)	A	Ljubljana	L	0-1	
11/10/16	Scotland (WCQ)	H	Trnava	W	3-0	*Mak (18, 56), Nemec (68)*
11/11/16	Lithuania (WCQ)	H	Trnava	W	4-0	*Nemec (12), Kucka (15), Škrtel (36), Hamšík (86)*
15/11/16	Austria	A	Vienna	D	0-0	
26/03/17	Malta (WCQ)	A	Ta' Qali	W	3-1	*Weiss (2), Greguš (41), Nemec (84)*
10/06/17	Lithuania (WCQ)	A	Vilnius	W	2-1	*Weiss (32), Hamšík (58)*

Appearances 2016/17

Coach: Ján Kozák	17/04/54		ENG	SVN	SCO	LTU	Aut	MLT	LTU	Caps	Goals
Matúš Kozáčik	27/12/83	Plzeň (CZE)	G	G	G	G		G		26	-
Peter Pekarík	30/10/86	Hertha (GER)	D			D		D	D	75	2
Martin Škrtel	15/12/84	Fenerbahçe (TUR)	D 57*		D	D		D	D	90	6
Ján Ďurica	10/12/81	Trabzonspor (TUR)	D	D	D	D			D	88	4
Tomáš Hubočan	17/09/85	Marseille (FRA)	D	D		D	D	D	D58	52	-
Róbert Mak	08/03/91	Zenit (RUS)	M71	A	M80	M83		M50	M77	36	9
Ján Greguš	29/01/91	København (DEN)	M	M			M46	M	M	13	1
Viktor Pečovský	24/05/83	Žilina	M55							35	1
Marek Hamšík	27/07/87	Napoli (ITA)	M	M	M87	M		s50	M	97	21
Dušan Švento	01/08/85	Slavia Praha (CZE)	M78	D79	s80	s83	M			47	1
Michal Ďuriš	01/06/88	Plzeň (CZE) /Orenburg (RUS)	A	s79	M	s77	A	s74		35	4
Norbert Gyömbér	03/07/92	Pescara (ITA) /Terek (RUS)	s55						s58	17	-
František Kubík	14/03/89	Slovan Bratislava	s71							3	-
Filip Kiss	13/10/90	Haugesund (NOR)	s78		s87		s46			11	-
Lukáš Pauschek	09/12/92	Mladá Boleslav (CZE)		D79						5	-
Kornel Saláta	24/01/85	Slovan Bratislava		D			D46			40	2
Patrik Hrošovský	22/04/92	Plzeň (CZE)		M79			M46	M		17	-
Juraj Kucka	26/02/87	Milan (ITA)		M	M	M		M74		55	6
Jakub Holúbek	12/01/91	Žilina		s79	D		D46			3	-
Erik Sabo	22/11/91	Beitar Jerusalem (ISR)		s79	D		D			12	-
Milan Škriniar	11/02/95	Sampdoria (ITA)			M	M	s46	D	M	9	-
Adam Nemec	02/09/85	Dinamo Bucureşti (ROU)			A69	A77	s85	A 91*		28	9
Marek Bakoš	15/04/83	Plzeň (CZE)			s69					14	-
Vladimír Weiss	30/11/89	Al-Gharafa (QAT)				M89	M85	M86	M	60	7
Matúš Bero	06/09/95	Trabzonspor (TUR)				s89	M			3	-
Ján Novota	29/11/83	Rapid Wien (AUT)					G46			4	-
Martin Dúbravka	15/01/89	Liberec (CZE)					s46		G	3	-
Albert Rusnák	07/07/94	Groningen (NED) /Real Salt Lake (USA)					s46	s86	s77	3	-
Stanislav Lobotka	25/11/94	Nordsjælland (DEN)					s46			1	-
Ondrej Duda	05/12/94	Hertha (GER)							A89	15	2
László Bénes	09/09/97	Mönchengladbach (GER)							s89	1	-

EUROPE

FK AS Trenčín

Second qualifying round - NK Olimpija Ljubljana (SVN)
A 4-3 *Lawrence (4), Kalu (6), Janga (20), Holúbek (32)*
Šemrinec, Skovajsa, Šulek, Lawrence (Jančo 39), Ibrahim, Janga (Udeh 89), Holúbek (Diks 78), Madu, Kalu, Bero, Kleščík. Coach: Martin Ševela (SVK)
H 2-3 *Janga (13), Bero (20)*
Šemrinec, Skovajsa, Šulek, Bala (Diks 74), Ibrahim (Rafael 90), Janga (Udeh 85), Holúbek, Madu, Kalu, Bero, Kleščík. Coach: Martin Ševela (SVK)

Third qualifying round - Legia Warszawa (POL)
H 0-1
Chovan, Šulek, Bala (Diks 79), Lawrence, Ibrahim, Janga (Prekop 85), Holúbek, Kalu, Bero, Udeh, Kleščík. Coach: Martin Ševela (SVK)
A 0-0
Chovan, Šulek, Bala, Lawrence, Janga, Holúbek, Kalu, Bero, Udeh (Rafael 90), Jančo (Prekop 77), Kleščík. Coach: Martin Ševela (SVK)

Play-offs - SK Rapid Wien (AUT)
H 0-4
Chovan, Šulek, Bala (Prekop 62), Lawrence (Ket 80), Paur, Janga, Holúbek, Kalu, Udeh, Jančo (Ibrahim 62), Kleščík. Coach: Martin Ševela (SVK)
A 2-0 *Lawrence (12), Paur (35)*
Šemrinec, Ket (Madu 64), Šulek, Bala (Prekop 79), Lawrence, Paur, Janga, Holúbek (Halgoš 84), Udeh, Jančo, Kleščík. Coach: Martin Ševela (SVK)
Red card: Jančo 53

ŠK Slovan Bratislava

First qualifying round - FK Partizani (ALB)
A 0-0
Mucha, Sekulić, Burnet, De Kamps, Lásik (Savićević 61), Zreľák, Soumah, Ligeon, Saláta, De Sa (Kubík 76), Schet. Coach: Nikodimos Papavasiliou (CYP)

NB Slovan received a bye to the second qualifying round midway through the tie when Partizani transferred to the UEFA Champions League following the expulsion of KF Skënderbeu.

Second qualifying round - FK Jelgava (LVA)
H 0-0
Mucha, Sekulić, Savićević (Pliatsikas 90+2), Burnet, De Kamps, Kubík (Lásik 87), Zreľák, Soumah, Ligeon, Saláta, Schet. Coach: Nikodimos Papavasiliou (CYP)
A 0-3
Mucha, Sekulić, Savićević (Scott 72), Burnet, De Kamps (Lásik 72), Kubík (Priskin 50), Zreľák, Soumah, Ligeon, Saláta, Schet. Coach: Nikodimos Papavasiliou (CYP)

TJ Spartak Myjava

First qualifying round - FC Admira Wacker Mödling (AUT)
A 1-1 *Kóňa (73)*
Hruška, Ostojić, Machovec, Kóňa, Mehremić, Beňo, Kolár (Sládek 64), Duga (Pekár 65), Bílovský (Marček 89), Daniel, Kukoľ. Coach: Mikuláš Radványi (SVK)
H 2-3 *Daniel (30), Pekár (89)*
Hruška, Ostojić, Machovec, Kóňa, Mehremić, Kolár, Duga (Sládek 46), Bílovský, Marček (Pekár 46), Daniel, Kukoľ (Černáček 84). Coach: Mikuláš Radványi (SVK)

FC Spartak Trnava

First qualifying round - Hibernians FC (MLT)
H 3-0 *Tambe (7, 83), Mikovič (40)*
Jakubech, Bello, Mikovič, Deket (Paukner 46), Čögley, Čonka, Godál, Schranz (Jirka 81), Halilović (Yao 71), Tambe, Greššák. Coach: Ivan Vrabec (SVK)
A 3-0 Mikovič (5), Oravec (58), Bello (90+2)
Jakubech, Bello, Mikovič, Čögley, Čonka (Kadlec 44), Godál, Schranz (Jirka 64), Halilović, Éder (Oravec 50), Tambe, Greššák. Coach: Ivan Vrabec (SVK)

Second qualifying round - FC Shirak (ARM)
A 1-1 *Jirka (87)*
Jakubech, Kadlec, Horník, Mikovič, Yao (Jirka 58), Godál, Sloboda, Schranz (Paukner 76), Halilović (Oravec 90), Éder, Greššák. Coach: Ivan Vrabec (SVK)
H 2-0 *Schranz (57), Tambe (61)*
Jakubech, Kadlec, Horník, Bello, Mikovič, Godál, Sloboda, Schranz (Košťál 87), Halilović (Paukner 80), Tambe (Jirka 76), Greššák. Coach: Ivan Vrabec (SVK)

Third qualifying round - FK Austria Wien (AUT)
A 1-0 *Tambe (46)*
Jakubech, Kadlec, Horník, Bello, Mikovič (Yao 88), Godál, Sloboda, Schranz, Halilović (Jirka 61), Tambe (Paukner 72), Greššák. Coach: Miroslav Karhan (SVK)
H 0-1 (aet; 4-5 on pens)
Jakubech, Kadlec, Horník, Bello, Mikovič, Godál, Sloboda, Schranz, Halilović (Jirka 97), Tambe (Hladík 79), Greššák. Coach: Miroslav Karhan (SVK)

DOMESTIC LEAGUE CLUB-BY-CLUB

FC DAC 1904 Dunajská Streda

1904 • DAC Aréna (6,839); NTC, Senec (3,264) • fcdac.sk

Major honours
Czechoslovakian Cup (1) 1987

Coach: Krisztián Németh; (20/10/16) Csaba László (HUN)

2016

17/07 a Žilina D 2-2 *Michalík, Vida*
24/07 a Spartak Trnava L 1-2 *Pačinda*
02/08 h Spartak Myjava L 0-1 *(match annulled)*
06/08 a Slovan L 2-3 *Štepanovský, Šabala*
13/08 h Trenčín L 2-3 *Szarka 2 (1p)*
20/08 a Michalovce L 0-1
25/08 h Senica D 0-0
10/09 a Zlaté Moravce D 1-1 *Sarr*
17/09 h Podbrezová D 0-0
24/09 a Tatran W 3-0 *Štepanovský, Kwin, Szarka*
01/10 a Ružomberok D 2-2 *Pačinda 2 (1p)*
15/10 h Žilina L 0-6
23/10 a Spartak Trnava L 0-1
29/10 a Spartak Myjava W 2-1 *Kontár, Štepanovský (match annulled)*
06/11 a Slovan L 0-1
19/11 h Trenčín W 2-0 *Živković, Ľupták*
26/11 h Michalovce W 2-1 *Sarr (p), Vida*
03/12 a Senica D 1-1 *Németh*
10/12 h Zlaté Moravce W 1-0 *Vida*

2017

18/02 a Podbrezová D 0-0
25/02 h Tatran W 5-0 *Pačinda 2, Sarr, Vida, Šafranko*
04/03 h Ružomberok D 1-1 *Šafranko*
11/03 h Žilina D 2-2 *Ljubičić, Davis (p)*
19/03 h Spartak Trnava D 0-0
08/04 h Slovan W 1-0 *Šafranko*
15/04 a Trenčín W 1-0 *Pačinda*
22/04 a Michalovce W 2-1 *Šafranko, Davis*
27/04 h Senica W 1-0 *Pačinda*
07/05 a Zlaté Moravce W 2-1 *Brašeň, Pačinda*
14/05 h Podbrezová D 2-2 *Šafranko, Vida*
19/05 a Tatran D 1-1 *Šafranko*
27/05 a Ružomberok L 0-2

No	Name	Nat	DoB	Pos	Aps	(s)	Gls
94	Esmerald Aluku	ALB	31/12/98	M	11		
21	Jakub Brašeň		02/05/89	M	13	(7)	1
23	Roland Černák		22/07/97	A	2	(7)	
31	Erick Davis	PAN	31/03/91	D	15		2
5	Tomáš Huk		22/12/94	D	28		
64	Gergö Kocsis	HUN	07/03/94	D	2	(1)	
29	Dávid Kondrlík		31/05/97	A		(1)	
80	Zoltán Kontár		07/11/93	M	7	(6)	1
14	Achile Kwin	CMR	14/01/90	D	17		1
4	Marin Ljubičić	CRO	15/06/88	M	25	(1)	1
9	Branislav Ľupták		05/06/91	M	19	(7)	1
7	Bence Mervó	HUN	05/03/95	A		(3)	
15	András Meszáros		29/03/96	A		(11)	
6	Ľubomír Michalík		13/08/83	D	15	(8)	1
17	Péter Nagy		11/12/96	M	3	(1)	
88	Zsolt Németh		01/02/91	D	7	(1)	1
8	Erik Pačinda		09/05/89	M	25	(1)	8
26	Slavomír Pagáč		07/01/97	D		(1)	
20	Yves Pambou	FRA	27/11/95	M	17	(3)	
26	Róbert Polievka		09/06/96	A	5	(6)	
94	Valērijs Šabala	LVA	12/10/94	A	7	(6)	1
7	Roman Sabler		04/09/95	A		(1)	
27	Pavol Šafranko		16/11/94	A	12		6
10	Pape Sarr	SEN	25/07/91	M	14	(7)	3
37	Ľubomír Šatka		02/12/95	D	10		
21	Matej Slávik		05/08/94	G	18		
24	Peter Štepanovský		12/01/88	M	20		3
1	Benjamín Száraz		09/03/98	G	1		
27	Ákos Szarka		24/11/90	A	8	(1)	3
3	János Szépe		15/03/96	D	1	(2)	
30	Darko Tofiloski	MKD	13/01/86	G	13		
18	Kristopher Vida	HUN	23/06/95	M	16	(13)	5
28	Marko Živković	CRO	17/05/94	D	21	(1)	1

MFK Ružomberok

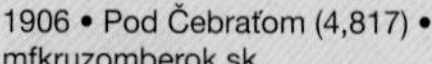

1906 • Pod Čebraťom (4,817) • mfkruzomberok.sk

Major honours
Slovakian League (1) 2006; Slovakian Cup (1) 2006

Coach: Norbert Hrnčár

2016

16/07 h Tatran W 1-0 *Chrien*
23/07 a Žilina L 2-3 *Chrien, Mareš*
31/07 h Spartak Trnava D 1-1 *Chrien*
06/08 a Spartak Myjava W 3-1 *J Maslo, P Maslo, Ďubek (match annulled)*
13/08 h Slovan W 3-2 *J Maslo, Mareš 2*
21/08 a Trenčín L 1-3 *Mareš*
27/08 h Michalovce W 4-0 *Daniel, Sapara, Nagy, Mareš*
10/09 a Senica D 1-1 *J Maslo*
17/09 h Zlaté Moravce W 6-1 *Kolčák, Daniel, Gál-Andrezly, og (Kapor), Mareš, Lačný*
24/09 a Podbrezová L 1-3 *Lačný*
01/10 h Dunajská Streda D 2-2 *Ďubek, Lačný (p)*
15/10 a Tatran L 1-2 *Kolčák*
22/10 h Žilina L 0-2
29/10 a Spartak Trnava W 1-0 *J Maslo*
05/11 h Spartak Myjava D 0-0 *(match annulled)*
20/11 a Slovan L 1-2 *Lačný*
27/11 h Trenčín D 3-3 *Chrien 2, Lačný*
10/12 h Senica W 2-1 *Mareš, Gál-Andrezly*

2017

19/02 a Zlaté Moravce D 1-1 *Faško*
26/02 h Podbrezová D 0-0
01/03 a Michalovce W 3-1 *Faško, Mareš, J Maslo*
04/03 a Dunajská Streda D 1-1 *P Maslo*
11/03 h Tatran W 5-0 *Gál-Andrezly 2, Faško 2, Gerec*
18/03 a Žilina L 1-3 *J Maslo*
02/04 h Trnava W 1-0 *Mareš*
16/04 h Slovan W 2-1 *Mareš, Lačný*
22/04 a Trenčín L 1-2 *Mareš*
26/04 h Michalovce W 3-1 *Mareš 2, Ďubek*
06/05 a Senica W 2-1 *Daniel 2*
13/05 h Zlaté Moravce W 2-1 *Ďubek (p), P Maslo*
19/05 a Podbrezová W 1-0 *Daniel*
27/05 h Dunajská Streda W 2-0 *Gál-Andrezly, Mareš*

No	Name	Nat	DoB	Pos	Aps	(s)	Gls
20	Martin Chrien		08/09/95	M	16	(1)	5
19	Matej Čurma		27/03/96	D	1		
24	Erik Daniel	CZE	04/02/92	M	30	(1)	5
26	Tomáš Ďubek		22/01/87	M	20	(7)	4
6	Michal Faško		24/08/94	M	15	(11)	4
7	Peter Gál-Andrezly		03/05/90	M	32		5
8	Tomáš Gerát		15/06/93	M		(3)	
15	Štefan Gerec		10/11/92	M		(6)	1
21	Ľuboš Hajdúch		06/03/80	G	7		
29	Kristián Kolčák		31/01/90	D	12		2
2	Dominik Kružliak		10/07/96	D	32		
18	Jakub Kudlička		10/01/99	M		(2)	
14	Šimon Kupec		11/02/96	D	25	(4)	
31	Miloš Lačný		08/03/88	A	11	(17)	6
11	Andrej Lovás		28/05/91	A		(8)	
33	Matúš Macík		19/05/93	G	25		
9	Jakub Mareš	CZE	26/01/87	A	29	(2)	14
3	Ján Maslo		05/02/86	D	28		6
17	Peter Maslo		02/02/87	D	30	(1)	3
22	Jozef Menich		15/09/94	D	4	(6)	
10	Martin Nagy		05/09/90	M	27	(2)	1
27	Marek Sapara		31/07/82	M	5	(11)	1
29	Dalibor Takáč		11/10/97	M	3	(7)	

FK Senica

1921 • OMS Arena (5,070) • fksenica.eu

Coach: Aleš Čvančara (CZE); (19/07/16) Miroslav Mentel

2016

17/07 h Slovan L 0-1
23/07 a Trenčín L 0-3
30/07 h Michalovce W 2-0 *Mráz, Guille Andrés*
06/08 a Tatran W 4-0 *Pillár, Kratochvíl, Guille Andrés, Pirulo*
13/08 a Zlaté Moravce W 1-0 *Turyna*
20/08 h Podbrezová L 0-1
25/08 a Dunajská Streda D 0-0
10/09 h Ružomberok D 1-1 *Pirulo (p)*
17/09 a Žilina L 2-4 *Mráz, Pirulo (p)*
24/09 h Spartak Trnava L 0-1
01/10 a Spartak Myjava L 0-2 *(match annulled)*
16/10 a Slovan L 0-2
22/10 h Trenčín L 1-2 *Pirulo (p)*
29/10 a Michalovce D 0-0
05/11 h Tatran D 0-0
19/11 h Zlaté Moravce L 1-3 *Pillár*
26/11 a Podbrezová L 0-2
03/12 h Dunajská Streda D 1-1 *Březina*
10/12 a Ružomberok L 1-2 *og (Kolčák)*

2017

18/02 h Žilina W 2-0 *Ranko, Turyna*
25/02 a Spartak Trnava W 1-0 *Kováč*
11/03 h Slovan L 0-1
19/03 a Trenčín D 1-1 *Brigant*
01/04 h Michalovce W 1-0 *Kratochvíl*
07/04 a Tatran L 0-1
15/04 a Zlaté Moravce L 1-2 *Blažek*
23/04 h Podbrezová D 1-1 *Kratochvíl (p)*
27/04 a Dunajská Streda L 0-1
06/05 h Ružomberok L 1-2 *Pajer*
13/05 a Žilina L 2-3 *Kováč, Kopičár*
19/05 h Spartak Trnava W 1-0 *Kováč*

No	Name	Nat	DoB	Pos	Aps	(s)	Gls
12	Ladislav Almási		06/03/99	A		(1)	
6	Boris Bališ		23/11/93	M	5	(3)	
19	Filip Blažek		11/03/98	M	13	(6)	1
21	Borja Docal	ESP	03/10/91	M	2		
6	David Březina	CZE	16/02/97	D	15	(1)	1
7	Tomáš Brigant		11/10/94	M	12		1
15	Martin Červeňák		11/01/99	D	1		
3	Alberto Delgado	ESP	04/06/91	D	16		
10	Jozef Dolný		13/05/92	M	3		
7	Alain Ebwelle	CMR	28/09/95	M	8	(9)	
9	Guille Andrés	ESP	13/10/92	A	8	(2)	2
4	Ihor Honchar	UKR	10/01/93	D	15	(2)	
20	Luboš Hušek	CZE	26/01/84	M	1	(1)	
26	Viktor Jedinák		08/02/98	A	1	(2)	
10	Adrián Kopičár		13/01/97	M	15	(3)	1
25	Jakub Kosorín		27/04/95	A	10	(2)	
25	Matej Kosorín		03/04/97	A	1	(7)	
14	Pavel Košťál	CZE	17/09/80	D	2		
28	Juraj Kotula		30/09/95	D	11		
8	Alan Kováč		22/05/93	A	9	(3)	3
5	Martin Kovaľ		10/02/99	A		(2)	
27	Miloš Kratochvíl	CZE	26/04/95	M	25		3
4	Lukáš Kučera		18/04/00	D		(1)	
20	Dominik Martišiak		09/07/00	A		(1)	
9	Viktor Miklóš		20/12/93	M	5		
11	Samuel Mráz		13/05/97	A	14	(5)	2
3	Adam Pajer	CZE	02/05/95	D	3	(5)	1
13	Pedro Astray	ESP	18/03/92	M	2	(6)	
17	Róbert Pillár		27/05/91	D	31		2
8	Pirulo	ESP	17/04/92	M	15	(2)	4
18	František Plach		08/03/92	G	4		
23	Paul Quaye	GHA	16/09/95	M	5	(7)	
21	Michal Ranko		19/02/94	D	12		1
23	Ondřej Šašinka	CZE	21/03/98	A	12		
1	Michal Šulla		15/07/91	G	27		
2	Branislav Šušolík		16/10/98	D	12		
24	Daniel Turyna	CZE	26/02/98	A	11	(13)	2
22	Peter Varga		27/01/98	M	4		
28	Weriton	BRA	28/02/92	M	11		

ŠK Slovan Bratislava

1919 • Pasienky (11,907) • skslovan.com

Major honours
UEFA Cup Winners' Cup (1) 1969; Czechoslovakian League (8) 1949, 1950, 1951, 1955, 1970, 1974, 1975, 1992; Slovakian League (12) 1940, 1941, 1942, 1944, 1994, 1995, 1996, 1999, 2009, 2011, 2013, 2014; Czechoslovakian Cup (5) 1962, 1963, 1968, 1974, 1982; Slovakian Cup (7) 1994, 1997, 1999, 2010, 2011, 2013, 2017

Coach: Nikodimos Papavasiliou (CYP); (01/08/16) Vladimír Koník; (18/08/16) Ivan Vukomanović (SRB)

2016

17/07	a	Senica	W 1-0	*Soumah*
24/07	h	Zlaté Moravce	W 3-2	*Schet, Lásik, Priskin (p)*
31/07	a	Podbrezová	L 0-2	
06/08	h	Dunajská Streda	W 3-2	*Schet 2, Soumah*
13/08	a	Ružomberok	L 2-3	*Priskin, De Kamps*
20/08	h	Žilina	W 1-0	*Soumah*
27/08	a	Spartak Trnava	D 0-0	
10/09	h	Spartak Myjava	L 1-2	*Soumah (p) (match annulled)*
17/09	h	Tatran	D 1-1	*De Kamps*
24/09	a	Trenčín	L 1-2	*De Kamps*
01/10	h	Michalovce	W 3-1	*Čavrić, Soumah (p), Vernon*
16/10	h	Senica	W 2-0	*Soumah (p), De Sa*
22/10	a	Zlaté Moravce	W 5-1	*Soumah, Savićević, og (Pintér), Oršula, Priskin*
30/10	h	Podbrezová	W 2-0	*Čavrić, Kubík*
06/11	h	Dunajská Streda	W 1-0	*Priskin*
20/11	h	Ružomberok	W 2-1	*Soumah 2 (2p)*
26/11	a	Žilina	L 1-2	*Priskin*
04/12	h	Spartak Trnava	L 0-1	
10/12	a	Spartak Myjava	D 1-1	*Oršula (match annulled)*

2017

19/02	a	Tatran	W 2-0	*Soumah 2*
25/02	h	Trenčín	W 4-3	*Soumah, Priskin 3*
05/03	h	Michalovce	W 3-1	*Priskin, Soumah, Čavrić*
11/03	a	Senica	W 1-0	*Vittek (p)*
18/03	h	Zlaté Moravce	D 1-1	*Soumah (p)*
01/04	a	Podbrezová	W 3-2	*Soumah, Priskin, Schet*
08/04	a	Dunajská Streda	L 0-1	
16/04	a	Ružomberok	L 1-2	*Soumah*
23/04	h	Žilina	L 0-1	
26/04	a	Spartak Trnava	W 3-0	*Čavrić, De Kamps, Kóňa*
12/05	h	Tatran	W 3-1	*Soumah (p), Ligeon, Rundić*
19/05	a	Trenčín	L 2-3	*Kubík, Soumah*
27/05	a	Michalovce	W 3-1	*Soumah 2, Saláta*

No	Name	Nat	DoB	Pos	Aps	(s)	Gls
27	Samuel Antálek		06/06/97	D	1		
5	Lorenzo Burnet	NED	11/01/91	D	7	(1)	
45	Aleksandar Čavrić	SRB	18/05/94	A	17	(2)	4
21	Cléber	BRA	03/06/86	M	3	(7)	
8	Uroš Damnjanović	SRB	08/02/95	A	4		
6	Joeri de Kamps	NED	10/02/92	M	21	(1)	4
77	Lesley de Sa	NED	02/04/93	M	7	(11)	1
26	Filip Ďuriš		28/03/95	A		(2)	
22	Dominik Greif		06/04/97	G	8		
9	Tomáš Kóňa		01/03/84	M	11	(2)	1
28	Juraj Kotula		30/09/95	D	11	(1)	
30	Martin Krnáč		30/01/85	G	1		
7	František Kubík		14/03/89	D	26	(3)	2
25	Adam Laczkó		02/04/97	D		(1)	
8	Richard Lásik		18/08/92	M	4		1
17	Ruben Ligeon	NED	24/05/92	D	10	(9)	1
5	Daniel Mašulovič		30/01/98	D		(1)	
82	Ján Mucha		05/12/82	G	23		
11	Filip Oršula		25/02/93	M	13	(14)	2
29	Patrik Pinte		06/01/97	A	2	(3)	
88	Vasilios Pliatsikas	GRE	14/04/88	D	4		
20	Tamás Priskin	HUN	27/09/86	A	20	(5)	10
14	Marek Rigo		15/12/97	M	6	(7)	
3	Milan Rundić	SRB	29/03/92	D	10		1
19	Kornel Saláta		24/01/85	D	31		1
4	Vukan Savićević	MNE	29/01/94	M	19	(4)	1
99	Mitchell Schet	NED	28/01/88	M	19	(2)	4
12	Granwald Scott	RSA	28/11/87	M	3	(6)	
24	Samuel Šefčík		04/11/96	M	2	(1)	
2	Boris Sekulić	SRB	21/10/91	D	22		
10	Seydouba Soumah	GUI	11/08/91	M	28	(1)	20
18	Vernon	ESP	18/11/92	D	14	(1)	1
33	Róbert Vittek		01/04/82	A	3	(5)	1
9	Adam Zreľák		05/05/94	A	2		

TJ Spartak Myjava

1920 • Myjava (2,728) • spartakmyjava.sk

Coach: Mikuláš Radványi

2016

16/07	a	Zlaté Moravce	W 2-1	*Kolár 2*
23/07	a	Podbrezová	D 0-0	
02/08	a	Dunajská Streda	W 1-0	*Duga*
06/08	h	Ružomberok	L 1-3	*Kóňa*
13/08	a	Žilina	L 0-1	
20/08	h	Spartak Trnava	D 1-1	*Sládek*
28/08	h	Tatran	W 1-0	*Kóňa*
10/09	a	Slovan	W 2-1	*Kolár 2*
17/09	h	Trenčín	W 1-0	*Kolár*
24/09	a	Michalovce	L 2-3	*Ostojić, Sládek*
01/10	h	Senica	W 2-0	*Kóňa, Kolár*
15/10	h	Zlaté Moravce	W 2-0	*Kukoľ, Machovec (p)*
22/10	h	Podbrezová	L 0-2	
29/10	h	Dunajská Streda	L 1-2	*Kolár*
05/11	a	Ružomberok	D 0-0	
20/11	h	Žilina	L 1-2	*Kukoľ*
27/11	a	Spartak Trnava	L 0-3	
03/12	a	Tatran	D 1-1	*Machovec*
10/12	h	Slovan	D 1-1	*Pekár*

NB Spartak Myjava withdrew after round 19 – all their matches were annulled.

No	Name	Nat	DoB	Pos	Aps	(s)	Gls
25	Patrik Abrahám		10/12/91	M	3	(4)	
8	Lukáš Beňo		07/11/89	D	16		
19	Frederik Bílovský		03/03/92	M	11	(2)	
17	Tomáš Brigant		11/10/94	M	11	(2)	
10	Martin Černáček		09/11/79	D	2	(5)	
22	Dávid Copko		03/07/96	M		(4)	
23	Erik Daniel	CZE	04/02/92	M		(1)	
18	Denis Duga		05/09/94	M	10	(6)	1
13	Samuel Flamík		26/05/97	M		(1)	
16	Štefan Holiš		29/06/92	A		(6)	
28	Matúš Hruška		17/09/94	G	17		
14	Ľuboš Kolár		01/09/89	A	17	(1)	7
6	Tomáš Kóňa		01/03/84	M	18		3
33	Vladimír Kukoľ		08/05/86	M	18	(1)	2
5	Jaroslav Machovec		05/09/86	D	15	(1)	2
20	Tomáš Marček		10/03/87	M	12	(4)	
7	Adi Mehremić	BIH	26/04/92	D	9	(2)	
3	Ivan Ostojić	SRB	26/06/89	D	17		1
4	Petr Pavlík	CZE	22/07/87	D	19		
9	Štefan Pekár		03/12/88	A	3	(4)	1
15	Roman Sabler		04/09/95	A	1	(5)	
29	Peter Sládek		07/07/89	A	8	(6)	2
23	Šimon Šmehýl		09/02/94	M		(1)	
1	Peter Solnička		14/06/82	G	2		

FC Spartak Trnava

1923 • Antona Malatinského (19,200); ViOn, Zlate Moravce (3,300) • spartak.sk

Major honours
Czechoslovakian League (5) 1968, 1969, 1971, 1972, 1973; Czechoslovakian Cup (4) 1967, 1971, 1975, 1986; Slovakian Cup (1) 1998

Coach: Miroslav Karhan

2016

17/07	a	Podbrezová	D 1-1	*Tambe*
26/07	h	Dunajská Streda	W 2-1	*Éder, Paukner (p)*
31/07	a	Ružomberok	D 1-1	*Jirka*
07/08	h	Žilina	L 1-2	*Sloboda*
13/08	h	Tatran	W 2-0	*Halilović, Tambe*
20/08	a	Spartak Myjava	D 1-1	*Sloboda (match annulled)*
27/08	h	Slovan	D 0-0	
10/09	a	Trenčín	D 3-3	*Sloboda, Schranz 2*
17/09	h	Michalovce	L 2-3	*Jirka, Godál (p)*
24/09	a	Senica	W 1-0	*Bello*
01/10	h	Zlaté Moravce	W 1-0	*Hladík*
15/10	h	Podbrezová	L 0-2	
23/10	h	Dunajská Streda	W 1-0	*Tambe*
29/10	h	Ružomberok	L 0-1	
06/11	a	Žilina	L 0-7	
19/11	a	Tatran	W 3-1	*Jirka, Tambe, Mikovič*
27/11	h	Spartak Myjava	W 3-0	*Halilović 2, Mikovič (match annulled)*
04/12	a	Slovan	W 1-0	*Tambe*
11/12	h	Trenčín	D 1-1	*Godál (p)*

2017

21/02	a	Michalovce	L 0-2	
25/02	h	Senica	L 0-1	
04/03	a	Zlaté Moravce	D 0-0	
12/03	a	Podbrezová	W 1-0	*Yilmaz*
19/03	a	Dunajská Streda	D 0-0	
02/04	a	Ružomberok	L 0-1	
09/04	h	Žilina	L 1-2	*Schranz*
16/04	h	Tatran	W 4-0	*Schranz, Halilović, Čonka, Tambe*
26/04	h	Slovan	L 0-3	
07/05	a	Trenčín	W 4-3	*Oravec, Jirka 3*
13/05	h	Michalovce	W 1-0	*Čonka*
19/05	a	Senica	L 0-1	
27/05	h	Zlaté Moravce	W 3-1	*Godál (p), Sloboda, Janso*

No	Name	Nat	DoB	Pos	Aps	(s)	Gls
4	Boris Bališ		23/11/93	M	1	(2)	
7	Babatunde Bello	BEN	06/10/89	M	9	(6)	1
17	Peter Čögley		11/08/88	D	16	(3)	
20	Matúš Čonka		15/10/90	D	21		2
13	Daniel Dubec		29/01/98	A		(7)	
28	Éder	BRA	10/06/88	M	3	(2)	1
77	Loïc Gagnon	FRA	21/01/91	A	5	(3)	
21	Boris Godál		27/05/87	D	25		3
34	Lukáš Greššák		23/01/89	D	27		
27	Emir Halilović	BIH	04/11/89	M	23	(2)	4
15	Ivan Hladík		30/01/93	D	19	(1)	1
5	Denis Horník		13/07/97	D	5		
1	Adam Jakubech		02/01/97	G	32		
3	Oliver Janso		08/10/93	D	20		1
33	Erik Jirka		19/09/97	M	18	(12)	6
2	Andrej Kadlec		02/02/96	D	14	(2)	
10	Kerlon	BRA	27/01/88	M		(4)	
18	Martin Košťál		23/02/96	M	4	(7)	
32	Lukáš Mihálik		10/02/97	M	5	(8)	
8	Martin Mikovič		12/09/90	M	16	(2)	2
24	Matej Oravec		30/03/98	M	10	(2)	1
11	Matúš Paukner		20/06/91	A	1	(1)	1
12	Róbert Richnák		03/05/92	M	4	(1)	
26	Ivan Schranz		13/09/93	A	12	(6)	4
23	Anton Sloboda		10/07/87	M	21	(3)	4
29	Robert Tambe	CMR	22/02/94	A	23	(4)	6
22	Martin Tóth		13/10/86	D	15	(2)	
19	Kouakou Privat Yao	CIV	30/06/91	A	1	(1)	
11	Kubilay Yilmaz	AUT	09/07/96	A	2	(7)	1

SLOVAKIA

ŽP Šport Podbrezová

1920 • ZELPO Aréna (4,061) • zpfutbal.sk

Coach: Marek Fabuľa;
(25/04/17) Karol Praženica

Date		Opponent		Score	Scorers
2016					
17/07	h	Spartak Trnava	D	1-1	*Viazanko*
23/07	h	Spartak Myjava	D	0-0	*(match annulled)*
31/07	h	Slovan	W	2-0	*Šafranko, Breznaník*
06/08	a	Trenčín	W	1-0	*Viazanko*
13/08	h	Michalovce	W	1-0	*Krivák*
20/08	a	Senica	W	1-0	*Breznaník*
27/08	h	Zlaté Moravce	D	1-1	*Podio (p)*
10/09	a	Tatran	W	2-0	*Bernadina, Podio*
17/09	a	Dunajská Streda	D	0-0	
24/09	h	Ružomberok	W	3-1	*Podio, Kochan, Vajda*
01/10	a	Žilina	L	0-1	
15/10	h	Spartak Trnava	W	2-0	*Bernadina, Viazanko*
22/10	a	Spartak Myjava	W	2-0	*Bernadina, Šafranko (match annulled)*
30/10	a	Slovan	L	0-2	
04/11	h	Trenčín	W	2-1	*Bernadina, Kuzma*
19/11	a	Michalovce	W	3-1	*Šafranko, Breznaník 2*
26/11	h	Senica	W	2-0	*Podio (p), Šafranko*
03/12	a	Zlaté Moravce	L	0-2	
10/12	h	Tatran	D	1-1	*Breznaník*
2017					
18/02	h	Dunajská Streda	D	0-0	
26/02	a	Ružomberok	D	0-0	
05/03	h	Žilina	D	2-2	*Turňa, Bernadina*
12/03	h	Spartak Trnava	L	0-1	
01/04	h	Slovan	L	2-3	*Viazanko, Kuzma*
09/04	a	Trenčín	L	0-2	
15/04	h	Michalovce	L	1-4	*Kupčík*
23/04	a	Senica	D	1-1	*Polievka*
26/04	h	Zlaté Moravce	W	2-0	*Bernadina, Mikuš*
06/05	a	Tatran	W	2-0	*Kochan (p), Viazanko*
14/05	a	Dunajská Streda	D	2-2	*Mikuš, Bernadina*
19/05	h	Ružomberok	L	0-1	
27/05	a	Žilina	L	0-4	

No	Name	Nat	DoB	Pos	Aps	(s)	Gls
90	Marius Alexe	ROU	22/02/90	M	1		
22	Endy Bernadina	NED	08/05/95	A	26	(6)	7
6	Michal Breznaník		16/12/85	M	10	(4)	5
14	Lazar Djordjević	SRB	14/07/92	D	28		
24	René Duda		06/12/96	M		(1)	
24	Adrián Kačerík		02/08/97	M		(1)	
11	Matej Kochan		21/11/92	M	19	(7)	2
4	Jaroslav Kostelný		19/04/85	D	21		
20	Ján Krivák		10/11/93	D	30		1
28	Martin Kuciak		15/03/82	G	32		
12	Ľuboš Kupčík		03/03/89	D	11	(5)	1
15	Kamil Kuzma		08/03/88	M	17	(13)	2
21	Filip Lepieš		22/12/99	M	1		
16	Adam Lipčák		19/03/97	M	1	(1)	
13	Daniel Magda		25/11/97	D	1	(1)	
7	Lukáš Migaľa		04/07/94	D	3	(13)	
33	Matúš Mikuš		08/07/91	A	7	(5)	2
17	Juraj Pančík		11/05/90	M		(4)	
16	Luka Pejović	CRO	27/07/94	M		(1)	
10	Dejan Pesevski	MKD	05/08/93	M	5	(2)	
19	Pablo Podio	ARG	07/08/89	M	32		4
17	Róbert Polievka		09/06/96	A	10	(2)	1
25	Andrej Rendla		13/10/90	A	1		
18	Pavol Šafranko		16/11/94	A	11	(7)	4
8	Peter Szczepaniak		22/10/91	M		(1)	
3	Matúš Turňa		11/05/86	D	29	(1)	1
9	Patrik Vajda		20/03/89	M	28	(1)	1
2	Miroslav Viazanko		27/10/81	M	28	(1)	5

1. FC Tatran Prešov

1898 • Tatran (5,410); NTC, Poprad (5,700) • 1fctatran.sk

Coach: Stanislav Varga;
(14/10/16) (Ján Karaffa);
(02/11/16) Miroslav Jantek

Date		Opponent		Score	Scorers
2016					
16/07	a	Ružomberok	L	0-1	
24/07	h	Michalovce	D	0-0	
30/07	a	Žilina	L	0-4	
06/08	h	Senica	L	0-4	
13/08	a	Spartak Trnava	L	0-2	
20/08	h	Zlaté Moravce	W	1-0	*D Leško*
28/08	a	Spartak Myjava	L	0-1	*(match annulled)*
10/09	h	Podbrezová	L	0-2	
17/09	a	Slovan	D	1-1	*Ashiru*
24/09	h	Dunajská Streda	L	0-3	
02/10	a	Trenčín	D	1-1	*D Leško*
15/10	h	Ružomberok	W	2-1	*Katona, Ashiru*
22/10	a	Michalovce	D	2-2	*Ashiru 2*
30/10	h	Žilina	D	1-1	*Ashiru (p)*
05/11	a	Senica	D	0-0	
19/11	h	Spartak Trnava	L	1-3	*Bartek*
26/11	a	Zlaté Moravce	L	0-3	
03/12	h	Spartak Myjava	D	1-1	*Streňo (match annulled)*
10/12	a	Podbrezová	D	1-1	*Kubus*
2017					
19/02	h	Slovan	L	0-2	
25/02	a	Dunajská Streda	L	0-5	
04/03	h	Trenčín	L	1-2	*Katona*
11/03	a	Ružomberok	L	0-5	
18/03	h	Michalovce	D	2-2	*Kubus, Trebuňák*
02/04	a	Žilina	L	0-3	
07/04	h	Senica	W	1-0	*Kubus*
16/04	a	Trnava	L	0-4	
03/05	h	Zlaté Moravce	D	1-1	*Rolinc*
06/05	h	Podbrezová	L	0-2	
12/05	a	Slovan	L	1-3	*Streňo*
19/05	h	Dunajská Streda	D	1-1	*Streňo*
27/05	a	Trenčín	L	0-4	

No	Name	Nat	DoB	Pos	Aps	(s)	Gls
18	Musefiu Ashiru	NGA	26/06/94	M	13	(1)	5
37	Jakub Bartek		01/07/92	D	23		1
30	Daniel Boloca		22/12/98	M		(1)	
2	Jozef Bujňák		27/01/94	D	8	(3)	
7	Martin Dupkala		07/05/85	M	3	(10)	
17	Ján Dzurík		18/07/93	D	32		
29	Maroš Ferenc		19/02/81	G	3		
15	Matej Grešák		31/05/99	M		(3)	
19	Emil Haladej		25/09/97	D	2	(3)	
6	Dávid Haščák		28/10/98	D		(2)	
44	Juraj Hovančík		22/11/90	M	7		
4	Patrik Jacko		26/09/92	D	18		
9	Richard Kačala		01/03/91	M	17	(5)	
10	Peter Katona		12/04/88	M	26	(5)	2
21	Dávid Keresteš		04/09/95	M	25	(3)	
33	Lukáš Kubus		15/05/88	A	14	(10)	3
11	Dávid Leško		04/06/88	A	27	(2)	2
23	Peter Leško		23/09/91	D	5		
5	Martin Luberda		18/12/91	D	5	(1)	
27	Lukáš Micherda		29/09/94	M	20	(3)	
28	Tomáš Mikluš		24/11/96	M		(2)	
1	Pavol Penksa		07/11/85	G	1		
3	Miroslav Petko		24/03/95	D	23	(1)	
14	Jakub Rolinc	CZE	12/05/92	A	14	(11)	1
24	Jozef Špyrka		30/05/99	M	1	(1)	
32	Matúš Štefančík		13/12/95	D		(1)	
16	Jakub Straka		17/06/97	M		(2)	
22	Erik Streňo		03/10/90	M	22	(2)	3
16	Jozef Talian		05/09/85	G	28		
31	Mojmír Trebuňák		30/01/93	M	8	(3)	1
8	Hector Tubonemi	NGA	05/09/88	A	7	(11)	
2	Richard Župa		27/04/98	D		(1)	

FK AS Trenčín

1992 • Na Sihoti (3,500) • astrencin.sk

Major honours
Slovakian League (2) 2015, 2016; Slovakian Cup (2) 2015, 2016

Coach: Martin Ševela

Date		Opponent		Score	Scorers
2016					
16/07	a	Michalovce	L	1-2	*Bala*
23/07	h	Senica	W	3-0	*Ibrahim, Holúbek, Kalu*
30/07	a	Zlaté Moravce	L	0-3	
06/08	h	Podbrezová	L	0-1	
13/08	a	Dunajská Streda	W	3-2	*Lawrence, Janga, Bala*
21/08	h	Ružomberok	W	3-1	*Bala 2, Janga*
28/08	a	Žilina	L	0-4	
10/09	h	Spartak Trnava	D	3-3	*Janga, Paur, Lawrence*
17/09	a	Spartak Myjava	L	0-1	*(match annulled)*
24/09	h	Slovan	W	2-1	*Janga, Paur*
02/10	h	Tatran	D	1-1	*Janga*
15/10	a	Michalovce	L	0-2	
22/10	a	Senica	W	2-1	*Janga, og (Březina)*
29/10	h	Zlaté Moravce	W	2-0	*Gabriel, Janga*
04/11	a	Podbrezová	L	1-2	*Janga*
19/11	a	Dunajská Streda	L	0-2	
27/11	a	Ružomberok	D	3-3	*Paur 2, Kvocera*
03/12	a	Žilina	L	0-3	
11/12	a	Spartak Trnava	D	1-1	*Udeh*
2017					
25/02	a	Slovan	L	3-4	*Beridze, Skovajsa, og (Vernon)*
04/03	a	Tatran	W	2-1	*Zubairu, Janga*
12/03	h	Michalovce	W	4-1	*Janga, Adekunle, Ubbink, Paur*
19/03	h	Senica	D	1-1	*Janga*
01/04	a	Zlaté Moravce	W	2-0	*Ubbink, Kvocera*
09/04	h	Podbrezová	W	2-0	*Paur, Janga*
15/04	h	Dunajská Streda	L	0-1	
22/04	h	Ružomberok	W	2-1	*Mance, Lawrence*
28/04	h	Žilina	W	2-1	*Beridze, Janga*
07/05	h	Trnava	L	3-4	*Janga, Gong, Mance*
19/05	h	Slovan	W	3-2	*Mance, Beridze, Nwofor*
27/05	h	Tatran	W	4-0	*Skovajsa, Mance, Kleščík, Beridze*

No	Name	Nat	DoB	Pos	Aps	(s)	Gls
35	Issa Adekunle	NGA	20/12/97	M	4	(2)	1
18	Aldo Baéz	ARG	05/09/88	M	4	(1)	
7	Aliko Bala	NGA	27/02/97	M	14	(3)	4
7	Giorgi Beridze	GEO	12/05/97	M	12		4
21	Matúš Bero		06/09/95	M	3		
30	Adrián Chovan		08/10/95	G	6		
19	Jamarro Diks	NED	24/06/95	A		(4)	
28	Reuben Gabriel	NGA	25/09/90	M	10	(1)	1
26	Hilary Gong	NGA	10/10/98	M		(2)	1
38	Filip Halgoš		09/03/98	M	8	(5)	
14	Jakub Holúbek		12/01/91	M	6		1
10	Rabiu Ibrahim	NGA	15/03/91	M	2	(1)	1
27	Denis Jančo		01/08/97	M	8	(3)	
11	Rangelo Janga	CUW	06/04/92	A	30	(1)	14
77	Leonard Johnson	NED	18/10/93	M		(5)	
3	Keston Julien	TRI	26/10/98	D	5		
17	Samuel Kalu	NGA	26/08/97	M	19		1
4	Jeffrey Ket	NED	06/04/93	D	8	(4)	
32	Peter Kleščík		18/09/88	D	29	(1)	1
17	Milton Klooster	NED	26/11/96	M	1	(5)	
5	Rodney Klooster	NED	26/11/96	D	6		
49	Milan Kvocera		01/01/98	M	10	(6)	2
8	Jamie Lawrence	ENG	22/08/92	D	25		3
15	Kingsley Madu	NGA	12/12/95	D	3		
77	Antonio Mance	CRO	07/08/95	A	2	(8)	4
36	Erik Mikeš		06/06/97	A		(3)	
12	Uche Nwofor	NGA	17/09/91	A	1	(11)	1
9	Jakub Paur		04/07/92	M	20		6
29	Erik Prekop		08/10/97	A	1	(11)	
33	Rafael	BRA	27/12/95	D	3		
24	Igor Šemrinec		22/11/87	G	25		
2	Lukáš Skovajsa		27/03/94	D	23		2
6	Martin Šulek		15/01/98	D	21	(3)	
10	Desley Ubbink	NED	15/06/93	M	12		2
22	Christopher Udeh	NGA	03/09/97	D	9	(5)	1
4	Abdul Zubairu	NGA	03/10/98	M	11	(1)	1

FC ViOn Zlaté Moravce

1995 • ViOn (3,300) • fcvion.sk

Major honours
Slovakian Cup (1) 2007

Coach: Peter Gergely; (06/11/16) Juraj Jarábek

2016

16/07 h Spartak Myjava L 1-2 *Kuzma (match annulled)*
24/07 a Slovan L 2-3 *Guilavogui, Bariš*
30/07 h Trenčín W 3-0 *Ranko, Válovčan, Rejdovian*
06/08 a Michalovce D 0-0
13/08 h Senica L 0-1
20/08 a Tatran L 0-1
27/08 a Podbrezová D 1-1 *Konnsimbal*
10/09 h Dunajská Streda D 1-1 *Orávik (p)*
17/09 a Ružomberok L 1-6 *Sedlák*
24/09 h Žilina L 0-2
01/10 a Spartak Trnava L 0-1
15/10 a Spartak Myjava L 0-2 *(match annulled)*
22/10 h Slovan L 1-5 *Guilavogui*
29/10 a Trenčín L 0-2
05/11 a Michalovce L 1-5 *Karlík*
19/11 a Senica W 3-1 *Bariš, Orávik (p), Mateus*
26/11 h Tatran W 3-0 *Orávik 2 (1p), Boszorád*
03/12 h Podbrezová W 2-0 *Válovčan, Orávik*
10/12 a Dunajská Streda L 0-1

2017

19/02 h Ružomberok D 1-1 *Yao*
26/02 a Žilina L 1-4 *Boszorád*
04/03 h Spartak Trnava D 0-0
18/03 a Slovan D 1-1 *Bariš*
01/04 h Trenčín L 0-2
08/04 h Michalovce L 1-2 *Kostadinov*
15/04 h Senica W 2-1 *Bariš, Kapor*
26/04 a Podbrezová L 0-2
03/05 a Tatran D 1-1 *Válovčan*
07/05 h Dunajská Streda L 1-2 *Pintér*
13/05 a Ružomberok L 1-2 *Nurković*
19/05 h Žilina L 1-4 *Válovčan*
27/05 a Spartak Trnava L 1-3 *Ewerton*

No	Name	Nat	DoB	Pos	Aps	(s)	Gls
17	Damián Bariš		09/12/94	M	29	(3)	4
4	Martin Boszorád		13/11/89	D	22	(1)	2
12	Martin Chren		02/01/84	D	12		
25	Ewerton	BRA	27/09/94	M	4	(2)	1
10	Róbert Gešnábel		24/11/91	A	10	(7)	
31	Pepe Guilavogui	GUI	02/01/93	M	10	(18)	2
21	Dominik Holec		28/07/94	G	3		
2	Adam Jamrich		07/07/98	D		(1)	
15	Milovan Kapor	CAN	05/08/91	D	24	(2)	1
23	Karol Karlík		29/06/86	D	17	(1)	1
21	Jakub Kastelovič		14/06/95	D		(2)	
12	Jesus Konnsimbal	CTA	03/03/92	A	4	(6)	1
20	Tihomir Kostadinov	MKD	04/03/96	M	17	(4)	1
30	Pavel Kováč		12/08/74	G	28		
29	Marek Kuzma		22/06/88	A	1		1
8	Ondřej Machuča	CZE	24/04/96	M	6	(2)	
40	Mateus	BRA	28/12/96	M	15		1
24	Jozef Novota		24/01/86	G	1		
13	Samir Nurković	SRB	13/06/92	A	4	(4)	1
8	Michal Obročník		04/06/91	D	12	(3)	
18	Peter Orávik		18/12/88	A	30		5
22	Miroslav Pastva		15/04/92	M	20	(4)	
42	Michal Pintér		04/02/94	D	26	(1)	1
5	Michal Ranko		19/02/94	D	11	(1)	1
37	Róbert Rejdovian		18/03/91	A	4	(8)	1
7	Miroslav Sedlák		12/03/93	M	6	(4)	1
6	Jozef Sombat		01/04/94	A	2	(3)	
13	Denis Švec		16/03/96	D	3		
11	Erik Ujlaky		13/02/92	M	5	(4)	
19	Martin Válovčan		14/05/93	A	23	(6)	4
26	Kouakou Privat Yao	CIV	30/06/91	A	3	(6)	1

MFK Zemplín Michalovce

1912 • Mestský (4,440) • mfkzemplin.sk

Coach: Anton Šoltis

2016

16/07 h Trenčín W 2-1 *Žofčák, Škutka*
24/07 a Tatran D 0-0
30/07 a Senica L 0-2
06/08 h Zlaté Moravce D 0-0
13/08 a Podbrezová L 0-1
20/08 h Dunajská Streda W 1-0 *Koscelník*
27/08 a Ružomberok L 0-4
10/09 h Žilina L 0-2
17/09 a Spartak Trnava W 3-2 *Koscelník, Škutka, Mensah*
24/09 h Spartak Myjava W 3-2 *Škutka, Podhorin, Žofčák (match annulled)*
01/10 a Slovan L 1-3 *Škutka (p)*
15/10 a Trenčín W 2-0 *Žofčák, Mensah*
22/10 h Tatran D 2-2 *Danko 2*
29/10 h Senica D 0-0
05/11 h Zlaté Moravce W 5-1 *Mensah 2, Kotora, Kunca, og (Karlík)*
19/11 h Podbrezová L 1-3 *Kunca*
26/11 a Dunajská Streda L 1-2 *Grič*
11/12 a Žilina L 1-7 *Mensah*

2017

21/02 h Spartak Trnava W 2-0 *Regáli, Žofčák*
01/03 h Ružomberok L 1-3 *og (J Maslo)*
05/03 a Slovan L 1-3 *Kushta*
12/03 a Trenčín L 1-4 *Kushta*
18/03 a Tatran D 2-2 *Koscelník, Žofčák*
01/04 a Senica L 0-1
08/04 a Zlaté Moravce W 2-1 *Serečin, Šimčák*
15/04 a Podbrezová W 4-1 *Žofčák 2 (1p), og (Viazanko), Danko*
22/04 h Dunajská Streda L 1-2 *Kushta*
26/04 a Ružomberok L 1-3 *Serečin*
06/05 h Žilina L 0-1
13/05 a Trnava L 0-1
27/05 h Slovan L 1-3 *Koscelník*

No	Name	Nat	DoB	Pos	Aps	(s)	Gls
19	Martin Bednár		22/04/99	M		(2)	
28	Pavol Bellás		28/05/97	A	1	(5)	
99	Vladislav Bragin	RUS	25/01/98	A		(3)	
15	Stanislav Danko		17/03/94	M	21	(4)	3
80	Anastasios Dimitriadis	GRE	27/02/97	M	9	(2)	
8	Jakub Grič		05/07/96	M	17	(4)	1
21	Michal Hamuľak		26/11/90	A		(1)	
37	Peter Kavka		20/11/90	D	12		
22	Matúš Kira		10/10/94	G	9		
33	Martin Kolesár		10/12/97	D	3		
9	Peter Kolesár		09/07/98	M	2	(1)	
24	Martin Koscelník		02/03/95	M	22	(3)	4
9	Ivan Kotora		27/06/91	M	9	(1)	1
17	Dominik Kunca		04/03/92	A	12	(6)	2
66	Kristjan Kushta	ALB	16/12/97	A	12	(12)	3
92	Celestine Lazarus	NGA	13/11/92	D	5		
11	Adrián Leško		26/06/95	M	3	(7)	
30	Patrik Macej	CZE	11/06/94	G	22		
7	Marcos	ESP	09/04/93	D	7		
16	Emmanuel Mensah	GHA	30/06/94	M	14		5
20	Oliver Podhorin		06/07/92	D	8	(2)	1
42	Kristi Qose	ALB	10/06/95	D	23	(2)	
14	Martin Regáli		12/10/93	A	7	(9)	1
27	Tomáš Sedlák		03/02/83	M	16	(3)	
89	Filip Serečin		04/10/89	A	7	(4)	2
2	Milan Šimčák		23/08/95	D	21	(1)	1
13	Michal Sipľak		02/02/96	D	28		
16	Dávid Škutka		25/05/88	A	13	(1)	4
98	Ilya Tereshchenko	UKR	27/05/98	A		(2)	
12	Jozef Šimon Turík		19/07/95	M	4	(6)	
23	Jozef Vajs		20/08/97	M	2	(10)	
18	Vernon	ESP	18/11/92	D	4		
10	Igor Žofčák		10/04/83	M	28		7

MŠK Žilina

1908 • Pod Dubňom (11,313) • mskzilina.sk

Major honours
Slovakian League (7) 2002, 2003, 2004, 2007, 2010, 2012, 2017; Slovakian Cup (1) 2012

Coach: Adrián Guľa

2016

17/07 h Dunajská Streda D 2-2 *Díaz, Špalek*
23/07 h Ružomberok W 3-2 *Otubanjo 2, Hlohovský*
30/07 h Tatran W 4-0 *Škvarka, Otubanjo, Špalek, Hlohovský*
07/08 a Spartak Trnava W 2-1 *Hlohovský, Otubanjo*
13/08 h Spartak Myjava W 1-0 *Vavro (match annulled)*
20/08 a Slovan L 0-1
28/08 h Trenčín W 4-0 *Hlohovský, Otubanjo, Špalek, Holúbek*
10/09 a Michalovce W 2-0 *Špalek, Kaša*
17/09 h Senica W 4-2 *Škvarka 2, Hlohovský 2*
24/09 a Zlaté Moravce W 2-0 *Otubanjo, Vavro (p)*
01/10 h Podbrezová W 1-0 *Škvarka*
15/10 a Dunajská Streda W 6-0 *Káčer, Otubanjo 2, Škvarka, Špalek, Hlohovský*
22/10 a Ružomberok W 2-0 *Hlohovský, Škvarka*
30/10 a Tatran D 1-1 *Škvarka*
06/11 h Spartak Trnava W 7-0 *Káčer, Hlohovský 2, Haskić 2, Škvarka, Jánošík*
20/11 a Spartak Myjava W 2-1 *Vavro, Škvarka (match annulled)*
26/11 h Slovan W 2-1 *Škvarka, Hlohovský*
03/12 h Trenčín W 3-0 *Haskić, Špalek, Hlohovský*
11/12 h Michalovce W 7-1 *Špalek, og (Podhorin), Haskić 2, Hlohovský 2, Kaša*

2017

18/02 a Senica L 0-2
26/02 h Zlaté Moravce W 4-1 *Káčer, Mráz, Hlohovský, Jánošík*
05/03 a Podbrezová D 2-2 *Hlohovský, og (Kochan)*
11/03 a Dunajská Streda D 2-2 *Kaša, Škvarka*
18/03 h Ružomberok W 3-1 *Mráz, Káčer, Hlohovský*
02/04 h Tatran W 3-0 *Špalek, Vavro, Şeydayev*
09/04 a Trnava W 2-1 *Škvarka, Vavro (p)*
23/04 a Slovan W 1-0 *Škvarka*
28/04 a Trenčín L 1-2 *Şeydayev*
06/05 a Michalovce W 1-0 *Şeydayev*
13/05 h Senica W 3-2 *Mazáň, Hlohovský 2 (1 p)*
19/05 a Zlaté Moravce W 4-1 *Cociuc, Škvarka, Špalek, Vavro*
27/05 h Podbrezová W 4-0 *Káčer, Şeydayev 2, Hlohovský*

No	Name	Nat	DoB	Pos	Aps	(s)	Gls
4	Momodou Ceesay	GAM	24/12/88	A		(5)	
7	Eugen Cociuc	MDA	11/05/93	M	2	(6)	1
9	Iván Díaz	ARG	23/01/93	M	32		1
16	Dávid Hancko		13/12/97	D	1	(2)	
18	Nermin Haskić	BIH	27/06/89	A	5	(4)	5
17	Joan Herrera	COL	14/04/94	D	2		
13	Filip Hlohovský		13/06/88	M	32		20
14	Jakub Holúbek		12/01/91	D	16	(2)	1
23	Eligijus Jankauskas	LTU	22/06/98	A		(1)	
8	Lukáš Jánošík		05/03/94	A	2	(11)	2
66	Miroslav Káčer		02/02/96	M	20	(9)	5
25	Filip Kaša	CZE	01/01/94	D	11	(2)	3
23	Michal Klec		05/12/95	M	1	(4)	
24	Martin Králik		03/04/95	D	27	(1)	
21	Bojan Letić	BIH	21/12/92	D	5	(1)	
45	Ernest Mabouka	CMR	16/06/88	D	29		
28	Christopher Mandiangu	GER	08/02/92	M		(4)	
30	Aleš Mandous	CZE	21/04/92	G	3		
27	Róbert Mazáň		09/02/94	D	12	(1)	1
11	Samuel Mráz		13/05/97	A	4	(7)	2
34	Yusuf Otubanjo	NGA	12/09/92	A	15	(3)	8
7	Jakub Paur		04/07/92	M	1	(2)	
12	Viktor Pečovský		24/05/83	M	10	(1)	
90	Ramil Şeydayev	AZE	15/03/96	A	7	(5)	5
20	Michal Škvarka		19/08/92	M	31		14
10	Nikolas Špalek		12/02/97	M	29	(2)	9
15	Kristián Vallo		02/06/98	M	1	(12)	
3	Denis Vavro		10/04/96	D	25		6
1	Miloš Volešák		20/04/84	G	29		

SLOVAKIA

Top goalscorers

Seydouba Soumah

Filip Hlohovský

20	Seydouba Soumah (Slovan) Filip Hlohovský (Žilina)
14	Jakub Mareš (Ružomberok) Rangelo Janga (Trenčín) Michal Škvarka (Žilina)
10	Tamás Priskin (Slovan) Pavol Šafranko (Podbrezová/ Dunajská Streda)
9	Nikolas Špalek (Žilina)
8	Erik Pačinda (Dunajská Streda) Yusuf Otubanjo (Žilina)

Promoted club

FC Nitra

1909 • Pod Zoborom (5,050) • fcnitra.com
Coach: Róbert Barborík
(01/01/17) Ivan Galád

Second level final tables 2016/17

First stage

West	Pld	W	D	L	F	A	Pts
1 MFK Skalica	22	14	5	3	38	12	47
2 ŠKF Sereď	22	14	3	5	50	23	45
3 FC ŠTK Šamorín	22	12	5	5	37	21	41
4 MŠK Žilina II	22	11	6	5	47	26	39
5 FC Nitra	22	12	3	7	45	27	39
6 FK Pohronie	22	11	3	8	29	30	36
7 FC Spartak Trnava II	22	10	5	7	39	34	35
8 AFC Nové Mesto nad Váhom	22	8	8	6	29	23	32
9 FK Dukla Banská Bystrica	22	3	5	14	19	43	14
10 ŠK Slovan Bratislava II	22	3	5	14	19	48	14
11 ŠK Svätý Jur	22	4	2	16	19	50	14
12 MŠK Fomat Martin	22	2	6	14	22	56	12

East	Pld	W	D	L	F	A	Pts
1 FC VSS Košice	18	15	2	1	28	7	47
2 FC Lokomotíva Košice	18	10	2	6	41	25	32
3 Partizán Bardejov	18	10	2	6	28	17	32
4 MFK Tatran Liptovský Mikuláš	18	9	4	5	28	17	31
5 FK Spišská Nová Ves	18	9	0	9	34	33	27
6 MFK Lokomotíva Zvolen	18	7	5	6	26	23	26
7 FK Poprad	18	6	8	4	26	17	26
8 FK Haniska	18	2	6	10	24	49	12
9 MŠK Rimavská Sobota	18	2	4	12	10	30	10
10 ŠK Odeva Lipany	18	2	3	13	11	38	9

Promotion play-offs final table

	Pld	W	D	L	F	A	Pts
1 FC VSS Košice	30	19	4	7	40	27	61
2 FC Nitra	30	18	5	7	57	32	59
3 MFK Skalica	30	17	7	6	45	19	58
4 FC ŠTK Šamorín	30	16	7	7	45	28	55
5 MŠK Žilina II	30	15	6	9	70	44	51
6 ŠKF Sereď	30	13	9	8	56	33	48
7 FC Lokomotíva Košice	30	13	8	9	56	42	47
8 Partizán Bardejov	30	14	4	12	48	39	46
9 FK Pohronie	30	14	4	12	42	44	46
10 MFK Tatran Liptovský Mikuláš	30	13	6	11	43	36	45
11 MFK Lokomotíva Zvolen	30	9	8	13	38	45	35
12 FK Spišská Nová Ves	30	9	1	20	36	67	28

NB The top six clubs from each regional group progress to the promotion play-offs, carrying forward their records against the top 10 teams in first stage. In the play-offs they play only against the qualified teams from the other regional group (home and away); FC VSS Košice withdrew from 2017/18 1. Liga; FC Nitra promoted instead.

DOMESTIC CUP

Slovenský pohár 2016/17

SECOND ROUND

(31/07/16)
Kysucké Nové Mesto 0-5 Lipany

(09/08/16)
Belá 0-3 Veľký Meder
Geca 1-3 Spartak Myjava
Plavnica 1-6 Ružomberok
Predmier 0-4 Tatran Prešov
Slovenské Ďarmoty 4-0 Haniska
Svidník 0-5 Podbrezová
Tatran Krásno 0-4 Sereď
Višňové 2-2 Tesla Stropkov *(5-4 on pens)*
Vranov 0-0 Slovan Bratislava *(2-3 on pens)*
Vrbové 0-2 Zemplín Michalovce
Zemianske Kostoľany 0-2 Púchov

(10/08/16)
Báhoň 1-1 Banská Bystrica *(4-5 on pens)*
Bešeňová 0-0 Oravské Veselé *(3-4 on pens)*
Blava 2-3 Pohronie
Borčice 7-1 Pezinok
Čaňa 0-0 Zlaté Moravce *(3-5 on pens)*
Častkovce 1-2 Boleráz
Devínska Nová Ves 1-4 Šamorín
Dlhé Klčovo 0-5 Liptovský Mikuláš
Dynamo Diviaky 0-3 VSS Košice
Fiľakovo 0-2 Vyšné Opátske
Horses Šúrovce 1-3 Svätý Jur
Hrušovany 0-1 Rohožník
Iskra Hnúšťa 2-2 Spišská Belá *(0-3 on pens)*
Jasenov 3-2 Spartak Medzev
Kolárovo 2-2 Slovan Duslo Šaľa *(2-4 on pens)*
Krompachy 2-5 Liptovská Štiavnica
Malá Ida 0-2 Sobrance
Medzibrod 1-4 Lokomotíva Košice
Nové Zámky 0-1 Veľké Ludince
Nový Život 9-1 Malacky
OFK Malženice 2-0 Dvory nad Žitavou
Oravská Poruba 2-0 Novohrad Lučenec
Pata 3-0 Slovan Most
Petržalka 1-5 Skalica
Plevník-Drienové 0-9 Trenčín
Priechod 0-6 Teplička nad Váhom
Raslavice 2-2 Veľký Horeš *(5-3 on pens)*
Rožňava 1-3 Žilina
Šaľková 2-0 Dunajská Lužná
Selce 1-4 Partizán Bardejov
Slovan Brvnište 1-1 Baník Horná Nitra *(6-5 on pens)*
Slovan Sabinov 0-1 Lokomotíva Zvolen
Slovan Šimonovany 1-1 Šurany *(4-3 on pens)*
Spišské Podhradie 1-3 Tvrdošín
Stráža 1-3 Spartak Trnava
Svit 0-2 Poprad
Tatran Horovce 1-8 Nové Mesto
Tatran Kračúnovce 1-4 Spišská Nová Ves
Tatran Ladce 1-2 Nová Baňa
Tatran VLM 0-3 Ivanka pri Dunaji
Tisovec 5-1 Máj Černová
Topoľčany 1-3 Nitra
Veľký Šariš 5-0 Kechnec
Vinica 2-0 Turčianska Štiavnička
Vydrany 1-3 Inter Bratislava
Žarnovica 1-2 Liptovský Hrádok

(16/08/16)
Beluša 0-1 Dunajská Streda
Rosina 0-5 Senica

(17/08/16)
Levoča 2-2 Strážske *(4-3 on pens)*
TEMPO Partizánske 0-2 Fomat Martin
Veľké Leváre 2-7 Gabčíkovo

(23/08/16)
Čadca 1-2 Trebišov

THIRD ROUND

(24/08/16)
Slovan Šimonovany 1-1 Inter Bratislava *(5-4 on pens)*

(31/08/16)
Pata 0-6 Zemplín Michalovce

(07/09/16)
Nový Život 3-0 Boleráz

(13/09/16)
Oravské Veselé 1-6 Slovan Bratislava
Partizán Bardejov 0-0 Ružomberok *(3-4 on pens)*

(14/09/16)
Banská Bystrica 0-1 Tatran Prešov
Borčice 0-1 Spartak Trnava
Ivánka pri Dunaji 3-4 Nové Mesto
Jasenov 0-2 Podbrezová
Levoča 1-1 Liptovská Štiavnica *(1-3 on pens)*
Liptovský Mikuláš 1-0 Lokomotíva Zvolen
OFK Malženice 2-0 Nová Baňa
Oravská Poruba 0-4 Lokomotíva Košice
Pohronie 1-3 Sereď
Raslavice 2-7 Spišská Nová Ves
Šalková 0-1 Nitra
Šamorín 0-2 Skalica
Slovan Brvnište 1-1 Rohožník *(4-2 on pens)*
Slovenské Ďarmoty 2-0 Trebišov
Sobrance 1-5 Liptovský Hrádok
Spišská Belá 1-1 Lipany *(3-4 on pens)*
Svätý Jur 1-6 Dunajská Streda
Teplička nad Váhom 1-4 Zlaté Moravce
Tisovec 2-1 Tvrdošín
Veľký Šariš 0-6 Spartak Myjava
Višňové 3-2 Vinica
Vyšné Opátske 1-5 Poprad
Žilina 3-0 VSS Košice

(21/09/16)
Gabčíkovo 1-2 Slovan Duslo Šaľa
Púchov 0-3 Trenčín
Veľké Ludince 1-1 Senica *(5-3 on pens)*
Veľký Meder 0-0 Fomat Martin *(3-1 on pens)*

FOURTH ROUND

(27/09/16)
Lipany 1-2 Žilina
Nový Život 0-3 Zemplín Michalovce
Skalica 0-0 Podbrezová *(12-11 on pens)*

(28/09/16)
Liptovská Stiavnica 0-5 Dunajská Streda
Nové Mesto 0-3 Spartak Trnava
OFK Malženice 0-1 Tatran Prešov
Sereď 3-1 Zlaté Moravce
Slovan Šimonovany 1-7 Ružomberok
Slovenské Ďarmoty 0-3 Slovan Bratislava
Tisovec 0-4 Poprad
Veľký Meder 0-1 Trenčín
Višňové 1-4 Liptovský Mikuláš

(05/10/16)
Litovský Hrádok 1-1 Lokomotíva Košice *(4-2 on pens)*
Slovan Brvnište 1-10 Nitra
Slovan Duslo Šaľa 2-5 Spartak Myjava
Veľké Ludince 2-1 Spišská Nová Ves

FIFTH ROUND

(18/10/16)
Ružomberok 0-0 Trenčín *(3-5 on pens)*
Tatran Prešov 0-3 Poprad

(19/10/16)
Liptovský Mikuláš 1-1 Liptovský Hrádok *(2-4 on pens)*
Sereď 1-1 Žilina *(3-5 on pens)*
Skalica 1-0 Spartak Myjava
Veľké Ludince 0-1 Slovan Bratislava

(22/11/16)
Zemplín Michalovce 3-2 Nitra

(30/11/16)
Dunajská Streda 1-0 Spartak Trnava

QUARTER-FINALS

(07/03/17)
Dunajská Streda 0-1 Poprad *(Šesták 4)*

(08/03/17)
Liptovský Hrádok 0-3 Zemplín Michalovce *(Dimitriadis 35, Kushta 48, Žofčák 89)*

Skalica 3-2 Žilina *(Ulrich 16, Človečko 21, Šebesta 79; Hlohovský 22, Mráz 90)*

Slovan Bratislava 3-1 Trenčín *(Priskin 12, Čavrić 59, Savićević 68; Janga 65)*

SEMI-FINALS

(04/04/17 & 11/04/17)
Zemplín Michalovce 1-2 Slovan Bratislava
(Dimitriadis 41; Priskin 5, Soumah 55)
Slovan Bratislava 1-0 Zemplín Michalovce
(Priskin 9)
(Slovan Bratislava 3-1)

(05/04/17 & 12/04/17)
Poprad 1-0 Skalica *(Šesták 56)*
Skalica 2-0 Poprad *(Hruška 8, Šebesta 69)*
(Skalica 2-1)

FINAL

(01/05/17)
NTC Poprad, Poprad
ŠK SLOVAN BRATISLAVA 3 *(Rundič 20, Čavrić 62, Soumah 76p)*
MFK SKALICA 0
Referee: *Chmura*
SLOVAN BRATISLAVA: *Greif, Sekulić, Saláta, Rundić, Kubík, Savićević (Kóňa 64), De Kamps, Šefčík (Oršula 58), Soumah, Priskin, Čavrić (Vittek 78)*
SKALICA: *Čikoš-Pavličko, Švrček, Majerník, Szöcs, Mizerák, Hlavatovič, Hruška (Vrábel 82), Pankarićan, Mészáros (Ulrich 82), Vaščák (Milunović 68), Šebesta*

Slovan Bratislava players pose with the Slovakian Cup after defeating second-tier Skalica 3-0 in the final

SLOVENIA

Nogometna zveza Slovenije (NZS)

Address	Predoslje 40 a pp 130 SI-4000 Kranj
Tel	+386 4 27 59 400
Fax	+386 4 27 59 456
E-mail	fas@nzs.si
Website	nzs.si

President	Radenko Mijatovič
General secretary	Marko Vavpetič
Media officer	Matjaž Krajnik
Year of formation	1920

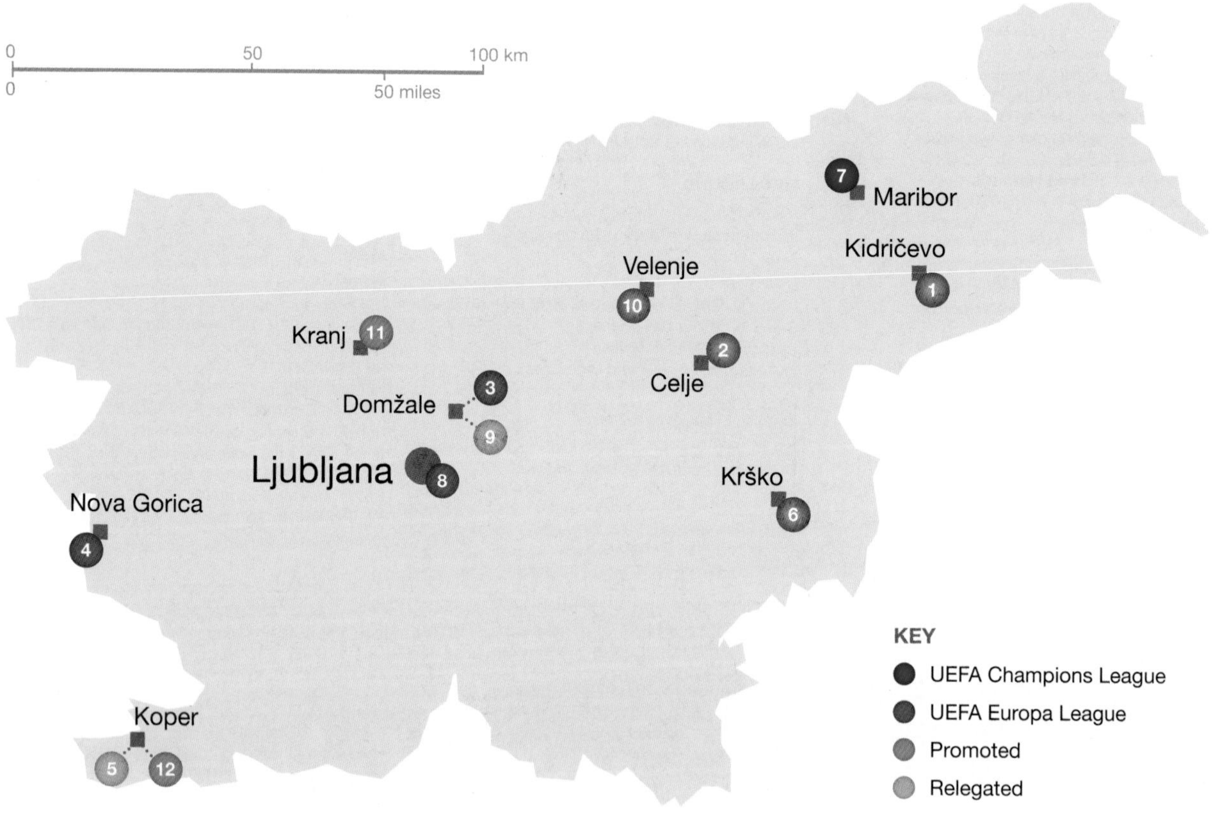

0 50 100 km
0 50 miles

Maribor (7)
Kidričevo (1)
Velenje (10)
Kranj (11)
Celje (2)
Domžale (3, 9)
Ljubljana (8)
Krško (6)
Nova Gorica (4)
Koper (5, 12)

KEY

- UEFA Champions League
- UEFA Europa League
- Promoted
- Relegated

PRVA LIGA CLUBS

  1 **NK Aluminij**

  2 **NK Celje**

  3 **NK Domžale**

  4 **ND Gorica**

  5 **FC Koper**

 6 **NK Krško**

  7 **NK Maribor**

  8 **NK Olimpija Ljubljana**

  9 **NK Radomlje**

 10 **NK Rudar Velenje**

PROMOTED CLUBS

  11 **NK Triglav**

  12 **NK Ankaran Hrvatini**

Milanič's Maribor return to power

After ceding the Slovenian Prva Liga crown to Olimpija Ljubljana in 2015/16, NK Maribor reclaimed it in some style, eventually striding clear in the spring after the reigning champions had put up a staunch title defence in the autumn.

It was Maribor's seventh league title in nine years and their fifth under coach Darko Milanič. Olimpija, for their part, used four different coaches during the season, which ended for them on an unhappy note when they were defeated 1-0 in the Slovenian Cup final by Domžale.

Record champions romp to 14th Prva Liga title

Title holders Olimpija fade away in spring

Domžale win every game in Slovenian Cup triumph

Domestic league

Milanič's return to Maribor in March 2016 had not come soon enough to prevent Olimpija from ending the club's run of five successive league titles, but the former Slovenia defender's first full season back in charge would end just like four of the five in his previous spell from 2008-13.

Maribor did not start well, but once their European commitments were over there was no stopping them. It took them a few weeks to catch Olimpija, but a 3-1 win over the title holders in Ljubljana closed the gap to a single point and by the winter break, despite a closing 3-2 defeat at Domžale – their first loss in 15 games – Maribor topped the table above Olimpija on the head-to-head rule, the two teams having collected 46 points, seven more than Domžale and 18 more than fourth-placed Gorica.

A full house of 12,000 gathered in Maribor's Ljudski vrt stadium for the top-of-the-table clash that opened the spring campaign, and the home side's 1-0 win, secured with a 51st-minute goal from the league's leading marksman at the time, Luka Zahovič (son of Slovenian all-time great Zlatko), proved to be the season's pivotal fixture. Olimpija, who had lost several key players during the break, suddenly went into freefall, while Maribor remained unbeaten over the same stretch and beyond, clinching the title with four matches to spare thanks to a 2-2 draw at home to Gorica in which veteran striker Milivoje Novakovič scored what would turn out to be the final two goals of his club career.

Maribor eased off thereafter but still secured a 13-point winning margin. Olimpija failed even to hang on to second place as Miran Srebrnič's Gorica stormed to a 13-match unbeaten run that overhauled them on the head-to-head comparison. Domžale, who matched the champions' 63-goal haul despite having no individual scorers in double figures, took fourth spot, while Rudar Velenje, the team that provided the Prva Liga's top two marksmen in 17-goal Cameroonian striker John Mary and 16-goal Croatian Dominik Glavina, finished only seventh.

Koper ended up one place above Rudar, but the Adriatic coastal club were refused a Prva Liga licence for 2017/18 and thus dropped out with bottom club Radomlje. Triglav won automatic promotion but the second division runners-up Dob declined to take the vacant second spot, so third-placed Ankaran Hrvatini, Koper's local rivals, were granted it instead.

Domestic cup

The Slovenian Cup final was staged, for the fifth successive year, in Koper's Bonifika stadium, and it was Domžale who emerged victorious, defeating Olimpija 1-0 with a 62nd-minute goal from defender Gaber Dobrovoljc, one of the club's 20 different scorers in the league. It was a triumph beyond dispute as Domžale had won all of their previous five fixtures, including both legs of the quarter-final and semi-final.

Europe

The previous summer Domžale had claimed a famous home win over West Ham United, but they lost the tie and were therefore outlasted in the UEFA Europa League by Maribor, who, after eliminating Aberdeen, were surprise play-off losers to Qäbälä despite a goal in each game from their evergreen Brazilian captain Marcos Tavares.

National team

There were mixed results for Slovenia in the 2018 FIFA World Cup qualifiers. Six goals scored in six games amounted to a meagre return, but with only half that number conceded Srečko Katanec's side accumulated 11 points, which was just three off the lead in Group F, leaving all options open ahead of the last four fixtures. The season ended on a fittingly celebratory note for Novakovič, who scored his 32nd and last international goal six minutes from the end of his final match before hanging up his boots at 38.

DOMESTIC SEASON AT A GLANCE

Prva Liga 2016/17 final table

			Home					Away					Total					
		Pld	W	D	L	F	A	W	D	L	F	A	W	D	L	F	A	Pts
1	**NK Maribor**	**36**	**14**	**2**	**2**	**33**	**9**	**7**	**8**	**3**	**30**	**21**	**21**	**10**	**5**	**63**	**30**	**73**
2	ND Gorica	36	8	7	3	26	18	8	5	5	22	21	16	12	8	48	39	60
3	NK Olimpija Ljubljana	36	9	4	5	24	18	8	5	5	25	17	17	9	10	49	35	60
4	NK Domžale	36	12	2	4	40	21	4	6	8	23	24	16	8	12	63	45	56
5	NK Celje	36	6	8	4	19	18	9	2	7	29	21	15	10	11	48	39	55
6	FC Koper	36	8	4	6	24	20	4	10	4	19	20	12	14	10	43	40	50
7	NK Rudar Velenje	36	3	9	6	21	24	7	2	9	28	29	10	11	15	49	53	41
8	NK Krško	36	4	8	6	18	19	4	7	7	21	31	8	15	13	39	50	39
9	NK Aluminij	36	7	6	5	24	24	2	5	11	14	28	9	11	16	38	52	38
10	NK Radomlje	36	0	5	13	14	49	1	5	12	9	31	1	10	25	23	80	13

NB FC Koper did not receive licence for 2017/18 Prva Liga.

European qualification 2017/18

Champion: NK Maribor (second qualifying round)

Cup winner: NK Domžale (first qualifying round)
ND Gorica (first qualifying round)
NK Olimpija Ljubljana (first qualifying round)

Top scorer John Mary (Rudar), 17 goals
Relegated clubs NK Radomlje, FC Koper (excluded)
Promoted clubs NK Triglav, NK Ankaran Hrvatini
Cup final NK Domžale 1-0 NK Olimpija Ljubljana

Player of the season

Dare Vršič
(NK Maribor)

An experienced former Slovenian international midfielder with an enviable CV boasting league title wins in Slovakia and Austria as well as his homeland, Vršič won his fourth Prva Liga winner's medal – and third in the purple and gold of Maribor – in 2016/17. The 32-year-old schemer also had the league's official player of the season award bestowed on him for the first time – due recognition for a campaign in which he provided a consistently excellent service for strikers Luka Zahovič and Milivoje Novakovič while finding the net nine times himself.

Newcomer of the season

John Mary
(NK Rudar Velenje)

A forgettable first European venture in Serbia with Vojvodina was quickly forgotten by the ex-Cameroon youth international striker as he got down to business in Slovenia with Rudar. Four goals in his first three home games soon endeared Mary to the Velenje locals, and he would find the net consistently throughout the campaign, with Rudar only once losing a match in which he scored. An interesting sideshow developed with his strike partner Dominik Glavina, with the African eventually outscoring the Croatian by one goal to win the Prva Liga golden boot.

Team of the season
(4-3-3)

Coach: Milanič *(Maribor)*

NATIONAL TEAM

International tournament appearances

FIFA World Cup (2) 2002, 2010
UEFA European Championship (1) 2000

Top five all-time caps

Boštjan Cesar (96); **Valter Birsa** (85); **Bojan Jokič** (84); Samir Handanovič (81); **Milivoje Novakovič** & Zlatko Zahovič (80)

Top five all-time goals

Zlatko Zahovič (35); **Milivoje Novakovič** (32); Sašo Udovič (16); Ermin Šiljak (14); Milenko Ačimovič (13)

Results 2016/17

04/09/16	Lithuania (WCQ)	A	Vilnius	D	2-2	*Krhin (77), Cesar (90+3)*
08/10/16	Slovakia (WCQ)	H	Ljubljana	W	1-0	*Kronaveter (74)*
11/10/16	England (WCQ)	H	Ljubljana	D	0-0	
11/11/16	Malta (WCQ)	A	Ta' Qali	W	1-0	*Verbič (47)*
14/11/16	Poland	A	Wroclaw	D	1-1	*Mevlja (24)*
26/03/17	Scotland (WCQ)	A	Glasgow	L	0-1	
10/06/17	Malta (WCQ)	H	Ljubljana	W	2-0	*Iličič (45+2), Novakovič (84)*

Appearances 2016/17

Coach: Srečko Katanec	**16/07/63**		**LTU**	**SVK**	**ENG**	**MLT**	**Pol**	**SCO**	**MLT**	**Caps**	**Goals**
Jan Oblak	07/01/93	Atlético (ESP)	G	G	G	G		G	G	14	-
Nejc Skubic	13/06/89	Konyaspor (TUR)	D			D			D89	6	-
Miral Samardžič	17/02/87	Henan Jianye (CHN) /Akhisar (TUR)	D	D	D	D	D46	D		15	-
Boštjan Cesar	09/07/82	Chievo (ITA)	D	D	D68	D		D		96	10
Bojan Jokič	17/05/86	Villarreal (ESP) /Ufa (RUS)	D	D	D			D	D	84	1
Benjamin Verbič	27/11/93	København (DEN)	M56	M	M	M	M65	s58	M	11	1
Rene Krhin	21/05/90	Granada (ESP)	M	M	M84	M	M	M	M	32	2
Valter Birsa	07/08/86	Chievo (ITA)	M	M68	M59	M71		M69		85	6
Kevin Kampl	09/10/90	Leverkusen (GER)	M					M87		25	2
Robert Berič	17/06/91	St-Étienne (FRA)	A46					s69	A64	14	1
Roman Bezjak	21/02/89	Darmstadt (GER) /Rijeka (CRO)	A	A91	M			M58	A59	17	1
Josip Iličič	29/01/88	Fiorentina (ITA)	s46	A	A	A	A53	A	A	46	3
Milivoje Novakovič	18/05/79	Maribor	s56	s68		A83			s64	80	32
Aljaž Struna	04/08/90	Carpi (ITA)		D	D			D		7	-
Jasmin Kurtič	10/01/89	Atalanta (ITA)		M72	M	M	M	M	M	40	1
Rok Kronaveter	07/12/86	Olimpija Ljubljana		s72	s59		s46			4	1
Miha Mevlja	12/06/90	Rostov (RUS)		s91	s68		D		D	5	1
Nik Omladič	21/08/89	Braunschweig (GER)			s84	s71	M	s87	s59	6	-
Dejan Trajkovski	14/04/92	Twente (NED)				D63				1	-
Boban Jovič	25/06/91	Wisła Kraków (POL)				s63	D			4	-
Andraž Šporar	27/02/94	Basel (SUI)				s83	s53			2	-
Vid Belec	06/06/90	Carpi (ITA)					G84			4	-
Gregor Sikošek	13/02/94	Koper					D			1	-
Miha Zajc	01/07/94	Olimpija Ljubljana					M46			3	-
Antonio Delamea Mlinar	10/06/91	Olimpija Ljubljana /New England Revolution (USA)					s46		D	2	-
Aleks Pihler	15/01/94	Maribor					s65			1	-
Jan Koprivec	15/07/88	Anorthosis (CYP)					s84			1	-
Matej Palčič	21/06/93	Maribor							s89	1	-

EUROPE

NK Olimpija Ljubljana

Second qualifying round - FK AS Trenčín (SVK)

H 3-4 *Velikonja (34), Zajc (43), Eleke (89)*

Šeliga, Klinar, Kelhar, Zajc, Matič, Wobay (Eleke 51), Velikonja, Kirm (Krefl 80), Novak (Ricardo Alves 75), Zarifovič, Bajrič. Coach: Rodolfo Vanoli (ITA)

A 3-2 *Kelhar (41), Eleke (45), Klinar (79)*

Šeliga, Klinar, Kelhar, Zajc, Matič, Eleke, Velikonja, Ricardo Alves (Wobay 65), Kirm (Krefl 81), Zarifovič, Bajrič. Coach: Rodolfo Vanoli (ITA)

NK Maribor

Second qualifying round - PFC Levski Sofia (BUL)

H 0-0

Handanovič, Hodžič, Janža, Šuler, Vrhovec (Vršič 46), Sallalich (Bajde 46), Marcos Tavares, Hotič, Novakovič (Omoregie 76), Kabha, Šme. Coach: Darko Milanič (SVN)

A 1-1 *Marcos Tavares (68)*

Handanovič, Hodžič, Janža, Šuler, Vrhovec (Vršič 54), Marcos Tavares, Hotič (Mertelj 76), Novakovič, Kabha, Bohar (Bajde 68), Šme. Coach: Darko Milanič (SVN)

Third qualifying round - Aberdeen FC (SCO)

A 1-1 *Novakovič (83)*

Handanovič, Janža, Šuler, Vrhovec (Pihler 68), Marcos Tavares, Hotič (Bohar 46), Novakovič, Vršič (Bajde 84), Kabha, Rodrigo Defendi, Šme. Coach: Darko Milanič (SVN)

H 1-0 *Shinnie (90+3og)*

Handanovič, Janža, Šuler, Vrhovec, Pihler (Kabha 77), Marcos Tavares, Novakovič, Vršič (Sallalich 89), Rodrigo Defendi, Bohar (Bajde 74), Šme. Coach: Darko Milanič (SVN)

Play-offs – Qäbälä FK (AZE)

A 1-3 *Marcos Tavares (17)*

Handanovič, Janža, Šuler, Vrhovec, Pihler, Marcos Tavares (Omoregie 80), Novakovič, Vršič (Bajde 72), Rodrigo Defendi, Bohar (Sallalich 72), Šme. Coach: Darko Milanič (SVN)

H 1-0 *Marcos Tavares (66)*

Handanovič, Janža, Šuler, Vrhovec (Kabha 46), Pihler (Sallalich 63), Marcos Tavares, Novakovič, Vršič, Rodrigo Defendi (Bajde 85), Bohar, Šme. Coach: Darko Milanič (SVN)

NK Domžale

First qualifying round - FC Lusitans (AND)

H 3-1 *Dobrovoljc (11), Horić (26), Črnic (43)*

Golubović, Horić, Vuk (Juninho 75), Črnic, Širok, Horvat (Repas 57), Trajkovski, Dobrovoljc, Majer, Žinko, Morel (Volarič 87). Coach: Luka Elsner (SVN)

A 2-1 *Majer (5), Morel (42)*

Golubović, Horić, Črnic, Širok, Trajkovski, Dobrovoljc (Blažič 48), Majer, Žinko (Juninho 84), Morel, Husmani (Horvat 65), Mance. Coach: Luka Elsner (SVN)

Second qualifying round - FC Shakhtyor Soligorsk (BLR)

A 1-1 *Trajkovski (52)*

Maraval, Brachi, Horić, Črnic (Repas 70), Horvat, Trajkovski, Dobrovoljc, Majer (Alvir 78), Žinko, Morel (Juninho 83), Mance. Coach: Luka Elsner (SVN)

H 2-1 *Alvir (35), Majer (69)*

Maraval, Brachi, Horić, Črnic (Repas 63), Horvat, Dobrovoljc, Balkovec, Majer (Žužek 89), Alvir, Morel, Mance (Juninho 84). Coach: Luka Elsner (SVN)

Third qualifying round - West Ham United FC (ENG)

H 2-1 *Črnic (11p, 49)*

Maraval, Brachi, Horić, Črnic (Juninho 90), Horvat, Dobrovoljc, Balkovec, Majer (Vetrih 86), Alvir, Morel (Repas 77), Mance. Coach: Luka Elsner (SVN)

A 0-3

Maraval, Brachi, Horić, Črnic, Horvat (Husmani 62), Dobrovoljc, Balkovec, Majer (Juninho 77), Alvir, Morel, Mance (Bratanovič 68). Coach: Luka Elsner (SVN)

ND Gorica

First qualifying round - Maccabi Tel-Aviv FC (ISR)

A 0-3

Sorčan, Škarabot, Gregorič, Kotnik, Kapić, Burgič (Wilson 85), Kolenc, Osuji (Nagode 70), Kavčič, Jogan, Franciosi (Arčon 58). Coach: Miran Srebrnič (SVN)

H 0-1

Sorčan, Škarabot, Gregorič, Kotnik (Grudina 71), Kapić, Burgič (Wilson 66), Kolenc, Kavčič, Marinič (Arčon 77), Boben, Nagode. Coach: Miran Srebrnič (SVN)

DOMESTIC LEAGUE CLUB-BY-CLUB

NK Aluminij

1946 • Športni park Aluminij (2,570) • nkaluminij.net

Coach: Bojan Špehonja; (03/01/17) Slobodan Grubor

2016					
17/07	a	Gorica	L	0-2	
23/07	a	Koper	L	0-1	
31/07	h	Celje	L	2-4	*Zeba, Kurež*
06/08	a	Radomlje	D	2-2	*Bizjak 2*
14/08	h	Krško	W	3-0	*Zeba, Krljanovič, Kramer*
21/08	a	Maribor	W	2-0	*Škoflek, Zeba*
28/08	h	Rudar	L	0-3	
09/09	a	Domžale	L	0-2	
18/09	h	Olimpija	L	0-3	
21/09	h	Gorica	D	0-0	
25/09	h	Koper	D	0-0	
01/10	a	Celje	L	0-1	
15/10	h	Radomlje	W	2-1	*Škoflek 2*
22/10	a	Krško	D	2-2	*Jakšić, Zeba*
30/10	h	Maribor	D	0-0	
05/11	a	Rudar	D	0-0	
20/11	h	Domžale	L	0-4	
27/11	a	Olimpija	L	0-3	
30/11	a	Gorica	L	0-3	
03/12	a	Koper	L	0-1	
10/12	h	Celje	W	2-1	Škoflek 2
2017					
25/02	a	Radomlje	W	3-0	*Zeba, Mensah, Vrbanec*
05/03	h	Krško	D	1-1	*Bizjak*
11/03	a	Maribor	L	1-4	*Bizjak*
19/03	h	Rudar	W	3-0	*Kramer, Tahiraj, Škoflek*
29/03	a	Domžale	L	1-2	*Bizjak (p)*
02/04	h	Olimpija	W	2-1	*Kramer, Škoflek*
09/04	h	Gorica	L	1-2	*Škoflek*
17/04	h	Koper	D	2-2	*Bizjak 2*
22/04	a	Celje	L	0-1	
30/04	h	Radomlje	W	3-1	*Kramer 2, Škoflek*
05/05	a	Krško	D	1-1	*Tahiraj*
14/05	h	Maribor	W	3-1	*Mesec 2, Kramer*
17/05	a	Rudar	D	2-2	*Rebernik 2*
21/05	h	Domžale	D	0-0	
27/05	a	Olimpija	L	0-1	

No	Name	Nat	DoB	Pos	Aps	(s)	Gls
11	Lovro Bizjak		12/11/93	A	21	(2)	7
16	Nejc Brodnjak		20/04/97	M		(3)	
5	Lovro Cvek	CRO	06/07/95	M	11	(3)	
19	Mateo Damiš	CRO	21/08/92	D	9	(2)	
24	Žan Florjanc		27/11/97	D		(2)	
50	Nemanja Jakšić	SRB	11/07/95	D	30		1
22	Luka Janžekovič		14/03/97	G	33		
55	Milan Kocič		16/02/90	D	32		
25	Matija Kovačić	CRO	25/02/94	G	2		
32	Alen Krajnc		01/07/95	A	1	(5)	
9	Blaž Kramer		01/06/96	A	20	(8)	6
8	Dejan Krljanovič		12/07/89	M	20		1
7	Robert Kurež		20/07/91	A	4		1
1	Kristian Lipovac		03/12/89	G	1		
99	Derrick Mensah	GHA	28/05/95	M	9		1
30	Vedran Mesec	CRO	20/02/88	A	3	(7)	2
20	Sanin Muminović	CRO	02/11/90	M	14	(1)	
7	Mateo Panadić	CRO	06/10/94	A	2	(6)	
6	Dejan Petrovič		12/01/98	M	4	(14)	
94	Toni Petrović	CRO	18/06/94	A	9	(4)	
37	Mihael Rebernik	CRO	06/08/96	A	7	(16)	2
96	Anton Rogina		05/02/96	M	10	(3)	
15	Marko Roškar		21/10/92	D		(2)	
14	Aleksandar Srdić	SRB	30/05/92	A	3	(9)	
17	Žiga Škoflek		22/07/94	M	29	(4)	9
47	Francesco Tahiraj	ALB	21/09/96	M	14	(11)	2
26	Vedran Turkalj	CRO	11/05/88	D	35		
4	Denis Vezjak		26/09/95	M	10	(2)	
10	Matic Vrbanec		28/10/96	M	35		1
23	Josip Zeba	CRO	24/04/90	D	28	(2)	5

NK Celje

1919 • Arena Petrol (13,400) • nk-celje.si

Major honours
Slovenian Cup (1) 2005

Coach: Robert Pevnik;
(06/10/16) Igor Jovičević (CRO)

Date		Opponent			Scorers
2016					
16/07	a	Olimpija	L	0-1	
22/07	h	Gorica	W	1-0	*Čirjak*
31/07	a	Aluminij	W	4-2	*Hadžić 2, Čirjak, Glavaš*
06/08	a	Koper	L	1-2	*Čirjak (p)*
12/08	h	Radomlje	D	0-0	
21/08	a	Krško	L	0-1	
28/08	h	Maribor	L	0-3	
10/09	a	Rudar	W	3-1	*Volaš 2, Čirjak*
17/09	h	Domžale	W	2-1	*Hadžić, Podlogar*
21/09	h	Olimpija	L	0-1	
24/09	a	Gorica	W	1-0	*Volaš*
01/10	h	Aluminij	W	1-0	*Podlogar*
16/10	h	Koper	D	1-1	*Rahmanović*
21/10	a	Radomlje	W	3-0	*Podlogar, Travner, Volaš*
29/10	h	Krško	L	0-3	
05/11	a	Maribor	L	0-2	
19/11	h	Rudar	W	4-0	*Volaš 2, Čirjak (p), Pungaršek*
26/11	a	Domžale	L	1-2	*Hadžić*
30/11	a	Olimpija	L	1-2	*Rahmanović*
03/12	h	Gorica	D	1-1	*Volaš*
10/12	a	Aluminij	L	1-2	*Volaš*
2017					
26/02	a	Koper	D	1-1	*Pungaršek*
04/03	h	Radomlje	W	1-0	*Volaš*
12/03	a	Krško	W	3-2	*Cvek, Belić, Rahmanović*
18/03	h	Maribor	D	1-1	*Volaš*
29/03	a	Rudar	W	2-1	*Hadžić, Podlogar*
01/04	h	Domžale	D	1-1	*Džinić*
09/04	h	Olimpija	D	1-1	*Cvijanovič*
15/04	a	Gorica	D	1-1	*Volaš*
22/04	h	Aluminij	W	1-0	*Lupeta*
30/04	h	Koper	D	2-2	*Pišek, Volaš*
06/05	a	Radomlje	W	1-0	*Podlogar*
12/05	h	Krško	L	1-2	*Volaš*
17/05	a	Maribor	W	2-0	*Cvek, og (Hodžič)*
21/05	h	Rudar	D	1-1	*Lupeta*
27/05	a	Domžale	W	4-1	*Volaš 2, Pungaršek, Belić*

No	Name	Nat	DoB	Pos	Aps	(s)	Gls
34	Tomislav Barišić	BIH	06/03/93	D	8		
24	Luka Belić	SRB	18/04/96	A	4	(2)	2
15	Amadej Brecl		06/04/97	D	7		
5	Lovro Cvek	CRO	06/07/95	M	12	(2)	2
21	Goran Cvijanovič		09/09/86	M	21	(2)	1
25	Lovre Čirjak	CRO	02/11/91	M	22	(2)	5
3	Elvedin Džinič		25/08/85	D	28	(1)	1
7	Goran Galešić	BIH	11/03/89	M		(3)	
7	Marin Glavaš	CRO	17/03/92	M	8	(3)	1
27	Damir Hadžič		01/10/84	D	24	(6)	1
11	Irfan Hadžić	BIH	15/06/93	A	9	(7)	4
6	Tilen Klemenčič		21/08/95	D	7	(5)	
29	Ihor Koshman	UKR	07/03/95	A		(1)	
12	Matic Kotnik		23/07/90	G	21		
2	Žiga Kous		27/10/92	D	13		
19	Mitja Križan		05/06/97	A		(5)	
4	Anej Lovrečič		10/05/87	M	2	(8)	
42	Lupeta	POR	24/03/93	A	3	(7)	2
17	Matic Marcius		01/02/97	A	2	(4)	
88	Danijel Miškić	CRO	11/10/93	M	2		
28	Tilen Pečnik		16/05/98	A		(1)	
32	Janez Pišek		04/05/98	M	22	(7)	1
14	Matej Podlogar		23/02/91	A	25	(6)	5
10	Rudi Požeg Vancaš		15/03/94	M	17	(9)	
23	Nino Pungaršek		01/11/95	M	29	(4)	3
8	Amar Rahmanović	BIH	13/05/94	M	11	(4)	3
33	Matjaž Rozman		03/01/87	G	15		
13	Jon Špora		22/05/97	M	6	(4)	
16	Jure Travner		28/09/85	D	32	(2)	1
30	Tadej Vidmajer		10/03/92	D	20	(3)	
9	Dalibor Volaš		27/02/87	A	26	(2)	15

NK Domžale

1921 • Športni park (3,212) • nkdomzale.si

Major honours
Slovenian League (2) 2007, 2008; Slovenian Cup (2) 2011, 2017

Coach: Luka Elsner;
(02/09/16) Simon Rožman

Date		Opponent			Scorers
2016					
17/07	h	Radomlje	W	2-0	*Vuk, Juninho*
24/07	a	Krško	D	1-1	*Vuk*
31/07	h	Maribor	D	2-2	*Juninho, Balkovec*
07/08	a	Rudar	W	2-0	*Morel (p), Juninho*
13/08	h	Koper	W	2-0	*Morel, Mance*
20/08	h	Olimpija	L	1-3	*Alvir*
26/08	a	Gorica	L	1-3	*Bratanovič*
09/09	h	Aluminij	W	2-0	*Alvir, Majer*
17/09	a	Celje	L	1-2	*Dobrovoljc*
21/09	a	Radomlje	W	5-0	*Alvir 2, Matjašič, Balkovec, Širok*
24/09	h	Krško	W	5-0	*Alvir, Repas, Vuk 2, Matjašič*
01/10	a	Maribor	L	1-3	*Horvat*
15/10	h	Rudar	W	3-1	*Repas, Vuk, Halilovič*
22/10	a	Koper	W	3-1	*Dobrovoljc 2, Horvat*
29/10	a	Olimpija	L	0-1	
05/11	h	Gorica	W	5-0	*Horvat, Alvir 3 (1p), Vuk*
20/11	a	Aluminij	W	4-0	*og (Kocič), Vuk, Mance, Dobrovoljc*
26/11	h	Celje	W	2-1	*Vetrih, Vuk*
30/11	h	Radomlje	L	0-2	
04/12	a	Krško	D	0-0	
10/12	h	Maribor	W	3-2	*Vetrih 2, Blažič*
2017					
25/02	a	Rudar	D	1-1	*Balkovec*
04/03	h	Koper	L	0-1	
12/03	h	Olimpija	W	1-0	*Repas*
18/03	a	Gorica	L	1-3	*Halilovič*
29/03	h	Aluminij	W	2-1	*Ožbolt, Balkovec*
01/04	a	Celje	D	1-1	*Firer (p)*
08/04	a	Radomlje	D	1-1	*Firer (p)*
17/04	h	Krško	W	5-3	*Firer 2, Balkovec, Majer, Vetrih*
22/04	a	Maribor	L	0-1	
28/04	h	Rudar	W	3-0	*Franjić, Repas, Majer (p)*
06/05	a	Koper	L	0-3	
13/05	a	Olimpija	L	1-3	*Bratanovič*
17/05	h	Gorica	D	1-1	*Žužek*
21/05	a	Aluminij	D	0-0	
27/05	h	Celje	L	1-4	*Ožbolt*

No	Name	Nat	DoB	Pos	Aps	(s)	Gls
77	Marko Alvir	CRO	19/04/94	M	18	(2)	8
29	Jure Balkovec		09/09/94	D	28	(2)	5
94	Veljko Batrović	MNE	05/03/94	M	6	(4)	
25	Miha Blažič		08/05/93	D	28		1
2	Álvaro Brachi	ESP	06/01/86	D	9	(2)	
92	Elvis Bratanovič		21/08/92	A	7	(14)	2
11	Matic Črnic		12/06/92	M	1	(1)	
27	Gaber Dobrovoljc		27/01/93	D	26	(2)	4
11	Rok Elsner		25/01/86	D	3	(1)	
7	Ivan Firer		19/11/84	A	11	(3)	4
30	Petar Franjić	CRO	21/05/91	M	9	(2)	1
12	Adnan Golubovič		22/07/95	G	10		
19	Denis Halilovič		02/03/86	D	10	(1)	2
23	Lucas Horvat	ARG	13/10/85	M	15	(1)	3
77	Marko Huč		01/04/98	M		(1)	
90	Zeni Husmani	MKD	28/11/90	M	16	(8)	
8	Juninho	BRA	15/03/84	M	6	(2)	3
37	Žan Majer		25/07/92	M	18	(6)	3
95	Antonio Mance	CRO	07/08/95	A	4	(6)	2
20	Kombi Mandjang	CMR	01/06/92	D	1		
11	Jure Matjašič		31/05/92	M	16	(4)	2
66	Kristjan Matoševič		05/06/97	G	1		
1	Dejan Milič		24/01/84	G	25		
87	Benjamin Morel	FRA	10/06/87	A	6	(2)	2
31	Alen Ožbolt		24/06/96	A	3	(6)	2
15	Jan Repas		19/03/97	M	25	(7)	4
33	Matija Rom		01/11/98	D	2	(1)	
17	Matija Širok		31/05/91	D	28		1
24	Dejan Trajkovski		14/04/92	D	1		
4	Amedej Vetrih		16/09/90	M	19	(6)	4
5	Luka Volarič		13/01/91	M	13	(9)	
10	Slobodan Vuk		15/09/89	A	13	(6)	8
70	Luka Žinko		23/03/83	M	11	(3)	
13	Žan Žužek		26/01/97	D	7	(6)	1

ND Gorica

1947 • Športni park (5,000) • nd-gorica.com

Major honours
Slovenian League (4) 1996, 2004, 2005, 2006; Slovenian Cup (3) 2001, 2002, 2014

Coach: Miran Srebrnič

Date		Opponent			Scorers
2016					
17/07	h	Aluminij	W	2-0	*Arčon, Kavčič*
22/07	a	Celje	L	0-1	
30/07	h	Radomlje	W	2-1	*Arčon 2*
06/08	a	Krško	L	0-1	
13/08	h	Maribor	W	2-1	*og (Šuler), Burgič*
20/08	a	Rudar	W	2-1	*Žigon, Kapić*
26/08	h	Domžale	W	3-1	*Arčon 2, Kapić*
11/09	a	Olimpija	L	0-1	
21/09	a	Aluminij	D	0-0	
24/09	h	Celje	L	0-1	
28/09	h	Koper	D	1-1	*Gregorič*
02/10	a	Radomlje	W	4-2	*Burgič 2 (2p), Nagode, Kapić (p)*
14/10	h	Krško	D	1-1	*Kotnik*
22/10	a	Maribor	L	0-1	
30/10	h	Rudar	L	1-3	*Burgič (p)*
05/11	a	Domžale	L	0-5	
19/11	h	Olimpija	D	1-1	*Burgič*
26/11	a	Koper	D	0-0	
30/11	h	Aluminij	W	3-0	*Kapić, Burgič 2 (1p)*
03/12	a	Celje	D	1-1	*Žigon*
10/12	h	Radomlje	D	1-1	*Kotnik*
2017					
26/02	a	Krško	W	2-1	*Burgič (p), Grudina*
07/03	h	Maribor	L	2-4	*Burgič 2 (1p)*
11/03	a	Rudar	W	3-1	*Filipović, Kapić, Burgič (p)*
18/03	h	Domžale	W	3-1	*Filipović, Burgič (p), Kolenc*
29/03	a	Olimpija	W	2-1	*Kapić, Žigon*
01/04	h	Koper	D	0-0	
09/04	a	Aluminij	W	2-1	*Žigon, Burgič (p)*
15/04	h	Celje	D	1-1	*Boben*
21/04	a	Radomlje	W	2-1	*Gregorič, Burgič*
29/04	h	Krško	D	0-0	
06/05	a	Maribor	D	2-2	*Žigon, Osuji*
13/05	h	Rudar	W	2-1	*Žigon, Kavčič*
17/05	a	Domžale	D	1-1	*og (Dobrovoljc)*
21/05	h	Olimpija	W	1-0	*Osuji*
27/05	a	Koper	W	1-0	*Edafe*

No	Name	Nat	DoB	Pos	Aps	(s)	Gls
11	Sandi Arčon		06/01/91	M	19	(2)	5
42	Matija Boben		26/02/94	D	24	(1)	1
10	Miran Burgič		25/09/84	A	27	(3)	14
3	Uroš Celcer		07/04/89	D	17	(2)	
29	Jani Curk		27/02/94	D	5	(2)	
9	Donatus Edafe	NGA	03/11/93	A	1	(7)	1
11	Andrija Filipović	CRO	18/04/97	A	13	(1)	2
54	Gianluca Franciosi	ITA	10/01/91	A	1	(7)	
6	Miha Gregorič		22/08/89	D	31		2
16	Rok Grudina		24/12/94	M	22	(5)	1
7	Mark Gulič		15/08/97	A		(2)	
24	Jan Humar		24/03/96	M	6	(9)	
27	Alen Jogan		24/08/85	D	19	(3)	
8	Rifet Kapić	BIH	03/07/95	M	32	(1)	6
23	Tine Kavčič		16/02/94	D	27	(1)	2
14	Jaka Kolenc		23/02/94	M	28	(3)	1
7	Andrej Kotnik		04/08/95	M	9	(8)	2
30	Leon Marinič		21/11/97	A		(6)	
96	Tilen Nagode		21/03/96	A	9	(22)	1
17	Bede Osuji	NGA	21/01/96	A	19	(10)	2
1	Grega Sorčan		05/03/96	G	36		
4	Matija Škarabot		04/02/88	D	22	(3)	
20	Dejan Žigon		30/03/89	M	29	(6)	6

SLOVENIA

FC Koper

1920 • Bonifika (5,000) • fckoper.si

Major honours
Slovenian League (1) 2010; Slovenian Cup (3) 2006, 2007, 2015

Coach: Samir Zulič; (27/09/16) (Oliver Bogatinov); (05/10/16) Igor Pamić (CRO)

2016					
17/07	a	Maribor	L	0-1	
23/07	h	Aluminij	W	1-0	*Štromajer*
30/07	a	Rudar	L	0-2	
06/08	h	Celje	W	2-1	*Ibričić 2 (1p)*
13/08	a	Domžale	L	0-2	
20/08	h	Radomlje	W	3-0	*Andrejašič, Muslimović, Pučko*
27/08	a	Olimpija	W	1-0	*Belima*
10/09	h	Krško	W	1-0	*Datković*
21/09	h	Maribor	L	1-2	*Datković*
25/09	a	Aluminij	D	0-0	
28/09	a	Gorica	D	1-1	*Ibričić*
01/10	h	Rudar	L	1-4	*Muslimović*
16/10	a	Celje	D	1-1	*Pučko*
22/10	h	Domžale	L	1-3	*Pekuson*
30/10	a	Radomlje	W	3-1	*Pekuson, Andrejašič, Ibričić (p)*
06/11	h	Olimpija	L	1-2	*Pučko*
19/11	a	Krško	D	0-0	
26/11	h	Gorica	D	0-0	
30/11	a	Maribor	L	0-4	
03/12	h	Aluminij	W	1-0	*Vekič*
10/12	a	Rudar	D	2-2	*Vekič 2*
2017					
26/02	h	Celje	D	1-1	*og (Džinič)*
04/03	a	Domžale	W	1-0	*og (Blažič)*
11/03	h	Radomlje	W	4-1	*Pranjić, Pekuson 2, Pučko*
19/03	a	Olimpija	D	1-1	*Paljk*
28/03	h	Krško	L	0-2	
01/04	a	Gorica	D	0-0	
08/04	h	Maribor	D	2-2	*Ibričić (p), Križman*
17/04	a	Aluminij	D	2-2	*Kokorović, Križman*
22/04	h	Rudar	W	1-0	*Park*
30/04	a	Celje	D	2-2	*Križman, Ibričić*
06/05	h	Domžale	W	3-0	*Hodžić, Belima 2*
12/05	a	Radomlje	W	4-0	*Križman, Pučko, Belima, Tzandaris*
16/05	h	Olimpija	D	1-1	*Hodžić*
21/05	a	Krško	D	1-1	*og (Krajcer)*
27/05	h	Gorica	L	0-1	

No	Name	Nat	DoB	Pos	Aps	(s)	Gls
12	David Adam		15/11/93	G	1	(1)	
88	Adnan Ahmetović	BIH	20/08/98	A		(1)	
2	Jan Andrejašič		16/09/95	D	16	(4)	2
1	Marijan Antolović	CRO	07/05/89	G	20		
46	Alex Bečaj		06/01/98	D		(1)	
7	Rubén Belima	EQG	11/02/92	M	19	(4)	4
34	Nick Bičič		05/01/99	G	1		
6	Jakov Biljan	CRO	02/08/95	M	12		
4	Toni Datković	CRO	06/11/93	D	30		2
15	Haris Dedič		06/07/97	D	8	(4)	
26	Šime Gregov	CRO	08/07/89	D	24		
8	Nermin Hodžić	BIH	13/07/94	M	13		2
32	Ivor Horvat	CRO	19/08/91	D	18	(4)	
17	Senijad Ibričić	BIH	26/09/85	M	29		6
5	Frane Ikić	CRO	19/06/94	D	1		
3	Jefthon	BRA	03/01/82	D	2		
99	Marin Jurina	CRO	26/11/93	A	3	(3)	
29	Ed Kevin Kokorović	CRO	04/01/95	M	20	(4)	1
23	Marko Krivičič		01/02/96	M	8	(10)	
50	Sandi Križman	CRO	17/08/89	A	10	(3)	4
9	Darko Lukanović	BIH	01/06/84	A		(3)	
13	Zlatan Muslimović	BIH	06/03/81	A	9	(5)	2
40	Igor Nenezič		23/03/84	G	1		
36	Žiga Opara		16/03/98	D	1		
45	Matic Paljk		02/10/97	D	12	(4)	1
14	Park In-hyeok	KOR	29/12/95	A	7	(4)	1
11	Courage Pekuson	GHA	02/01/95	M	18	(5)	4
22	Patrik Posavac		14/03/95	M	1	(3)	
29	Rok Požrl		14/07/98	M		(1)	
55	Danijel Pranjić	CRO	02/12/81	M	19	(1)	1
21	Matej Pučko		06/10/93	A	26	(8)	5
35	Leon Sever		09/04/98	M	1	(1)	
94	Gregor Sikošek		13/02/94	D	18		
83	Vasja Simčič		01/07/83	G	13		
5	Darnel Situ	FRA	18/03/92	D	1		
47	Martin Šroler	CRO	02/11/98	M	1		
30	Jaka Štromajer		27/07/83	A	4	(9)	1
25	Leandro Teijo	ARG	27/07/91	M	14	(1)	
9	Joël Tshibamba	COD	22/09/88	A		(1)	
33	Theofanis Tzandaris	GRE	13/06/93	M		(5)	1
10	Joel Valencia	ECU	16/11/94	M	12	(1)	
52	Luka Vekič		10/04/95	A	3	(2)	3

NK Krško

1922 • Matija Gubec (1,470) • nkkrsko.com

Coach: Tomaž Petrovič (13/03/17) Rok Zorko

2016					
16/07	a	Rudar	D	1-1	*Dangubić*
24/07	h	Domžale	D	1-1	*Bučar*
01/08	a	Olimpija	L	1-3	*Kramarič*
06/08	h	Gorica	W	1-0	*Kramarič*
14/08	a	Aluminij	L	0-3	
21/08	h	Celje	W	1-0	*Dangubić*
26/08	a	Radomlje	D	2-2	*Kramarič (p), Baskera*
10/09	a	Koper	L	0-1	
17/09	h	Maribor	L	1-2	*Šturm*
21/09	h	Rudar	W	1-0	*Dangubić*
24/09	a	Domžale	L	0-5	
02/10	h	Olimpija	L	1-2	*Mensah*
14/10	a	Gorica	D	1-1	*Dangubić*
22/10	h	Aluminij	D	2-2	*Mensah, Haljeta*
29/10	a	Celje	W	3-0	*Haljeta, Dangubić 2 (1p)*
06/11	h	Radomlje	D	1-1	*Haljeta*
19/11	h	Koper	D	0-0	
26/11	a	Maribor	L	0-4	
30/11	a	Rudar	D	2-2	*Vuklišević, Kramarič*
04/12	h	Domžale	D	0-0	
11/12	a	Olimpija	D	1-1	*Škrbić*
2017					
26/02	h	Gorica	L	1-2	*Mensah*
05/03	a	Aluminij	D	1-1	*Dangubić*
12/03	h	Celje	L	2-3	*Dangubić 2 (2p)*
18/03	a	Radomlje	W	2-0	*Mujan, Gatarić*
28/03	a	Koper	W	2-0	*Škrbić 2*
01/04	h	Maribor	D	1-1	*Dangubić (p)*
08/04	h	Rudar	L	1-2	*Gatarić*
17/04	a	Domžale	L	3-5	*Škrbić 2, Dangubić*
23/04	h	Olimpija	L	0-1	
29/04	a	Gorica	D	0-0	
05/05	h	Aluminij	D	1-1	*Dangubić*
12/05	a	Celje	W	2-1	*Mensah, Mujan*
16/05	h	Radomlje	W	2-0	*Dangubić, Mujan*
21/05	h	Koper	D	1-1	*Kramarič*
27/05	a	Maribor	L	0-1	

No	Name	Nat	DoB	Pos	Aps	(s)	Gls
77	Rok Baskera		26/05/93	A	3	(5)	1
11	David Bučar		08/02/94	A	6	(2)	1
10	Tim Čeh		13/03/94	A	12	(6)	
9	Filip Dangubić	CRO	05/05/95	A	34	(1)	13
19	Miha Drnovšek		14/01/87	M	8	(2)	
12	Marko Dušak	CRO	29/06/89	D	22	(3)	
25	Nikola Gatarić	CRO	09/03/92	M	10	(1)	2
4	Jan Gorenc		26/07/99	D	13	(1)	
22	Nermin Haljeta		07/06/97	A	6	(13)	3
65	Uroš Jovanović	SRB	03/09/98	M	1	(3)	
8	Žiga Jurečič		23/08/95	M	19		
18	Anže Kodelič		08/03/99	D	1	(1)	
8	Svetlan Kosić	SRB	15/02/95	M	4	(5)	
27	David Kovačič		27/01/99	M	12	(3)	
3	Aleš Kožar		11/10/95	D		(1)	
5	Marko Krajcer		06/06/85	D	19		
7	Martin Kramarič		14/11/97	M	25	(5)	5
14	Ibrahim Mensah	GHA	11/01/95	A	18	(9)	4
50	Ranko Moravac	SRB	25/01/95	M		(2)	
11	Tonči Mujan	CRO	19/07/95	M	11	(2)	3
19	Roko Nakić	CRO	02/09/97	M		(6)	
20	Luka Pavič		23/11/94	M	10	(5)	
45	Robert Pušaver		09/05/95	D	26	(1)	
39	Roy Rudonja		26/02/95	A	1		
44	Damir Sadiković	BIH	07/04/95	M	14	(4)	
17	Ester Sokler		04/06/99	M		(3)	
95	Miljan Škrbić	SRB	18/09/95	A	8	(4)	5
6	Jure Špiler		27/11/92	M	6	(7)	
17	Luka Štefanac	CRO	26/09/95	M	1		
23	Klemen Šturm		27/06/94	D	28	(2)	1
15	Dejan Urbanč		13/04/84	M	10	(2)	
72	Dejan Vokič		12/06/96	M	4	(5)	
16	Damjan Vuklišević		28/06/95	D	28	(1)	1
1	Marko Zalokar		18/06/90	G	36		

NK Maribor

1960 • Ljudski vrt (12,432) • nkmaribor.com

Major honours
Slovenian League (14) 1997, 1998, 1999, 2000, 2001, 2002, 2003, 2009, 2011, 2012, 2013, 2014, 2015, 2017; Slovenian Cup (9) 1992, 1994, 1997, 1999, 2004, 2010, 2012, 2013, 2016

Coach: Darko Milanič

2016					
17/07	h	Koper	W	1-0	*Vršič*
24/07	h	Rudar	W	2-0	*Omoregie 2*
31/07	a	Domžale	D	2-2	*og (Blažič), Bohar*
08/08	h	Olimpija	D	1-1	*Novakovič*
13/08	a	Gorica	L	1-2	*Bajde*
21/08	h	Aluminij	L	0-2	
28/08	a	Celje	W	3-0	*og (Pišek), Omoregie, Zahovič*
10/09	h	Radomlje	W	4-0	*Novakovič, Omoregie 2, Šuler*
17/09	a	Krško	W	2-1	*Vršič, Kabha*
21/09	a	Koper	W	2-1	*Zahovič, Marcos Tavares*
25/09	a	Rudar	D	1-1	*Novakovič*
01/10	h	Domžale	W	3-1	*Marcos Tavares 2, Zahovič*
15/10	a	Olimpija	W	3-1	*Novakovič, Pihler, Zahovič*
22/10	h	Gorica	W	1-0	*Šuler*
30/10	a	Aluminij	D	0-0	
05/11	h	Celje	W	2-0	*Zahovič, Novakovič*
20/11	a	Radomlje	W	3-0	*Šuler, Pihler 2*
26/11	h	Krško	W	4-0	*Zahovič, Vršič, Marcos Tavares, Sallalich*
30/11	h	Koper	W	4-0	*Zahovič, Marcos Tavares 2, Vršič*
03/12	h	Rudar	W	1-0	*Zahovič*
10/12	a	Domžale	L	2-3	*Zahovič 2 (1p)*
2017					
25/02	h	Olimpija	W	1-0	*Zahovič*
07/03	a	Gorica	W	4-2	*Vršič 2, Zahovič 2*
11/03	h	Aluminij	W	4-1	*Zahovič (p), Novakovič, Vršič, Marcos Tavares*
18/03	a	Celje	D	1-1	*Novakovič*
29/03	h	Radomlje	W	1-0	*Vršič*
01/04	a	Krško	D	1-1	*Vršič*
08/04	a	Koper	D	2-2	*Novakovič 2*
15/04	a	Rudar	W	1-0	*Zahovič*
22/04	h	Domžale	W	1-0	*Marcos Tavares*
29/04	a	Olimpija	D	0-0	
06/05	h	Gorica	D	2-2	*Novakovič 2*
14/05	a	Aluminij	L	1-3	*Hotič*
17/05	h	Celje	L	0-2	
21/05	a	Radomlje	D	1-1	*Marcos Tavares*
27/05	h	Krško	W	1-0	*Hotič*

No	Name	Nat	DoB	Pos	Aps	(s)	Gls
30	Valon Ahmedi	ALB	07/10/94	M	3	(2)	
20	Gregor Bajde		29/04/94	A	8	(2)	1
39	Damjan Bohar		18/10/91	M	10	(10)	1
33	Jasmin Handanovič		28/01/78	G	32		
2	Adis Hodžič		16/01/99	D	6	(1)	
10	Dino Hotič		26/07/95	M	16	(12)	2
3	Erik Janža		21/06/93	D	16		
24	Marwan Kabha	ISR	23/02/91	M	19	(1)	1
7	Žan Karničnik		18/09/94	D	1		
9	Marcos Tavares	BRA	30/03/84	A	19	(14)	9
70	Aleš Mertelj		22/03/87	M	4	(8)	
8	Dejan Mezga	CRO	16/07/85	M	2	(2)	
11	Milivoje Novakovič		18/05/79	A	20	(6)	11
69	Matko Obradović	CRO	11/05/91	G	4		
18	Sandi Ogrinec		05/06/98	M	1	(5)	
14	Sunny Omoregie	NGA	02/01/89	A	9	(5)	5
29	Matej Palčič		21/06/93	D	17		
6	Aleks Pihler		15/01/94	M	28	(3)	3
45	Robert Pušaver		09/05/95	D	1		
8	Amar Rahmanović	BIH	13/05/94	M	1		
26	Aleksander Rajčevič		17/11/86	D	10	(2)	
35	Rodrigo Defendi	BRA	17/06/86	D	25		
8	Sintayehu Sallalich	ISR	20/06/91	M	17	(5)	1
44	Denis Šme		22/03/94	D	14	(1)	
4	Marko Šuler		09/03/83	D	32		3
32	Luka Uskoković	MNE	10/04/96	D		(1)	
28	Mitja Viler		01/09/86	D	18		
5	Blaž Vrhovec		20/02/92	M	16	(11)	
22	Dare Vršič		26/09/84	M	23	(3)	9
31	Daniel Vujčič		12/04/95	M	1		
90	Luka Zahovič		15/11/95	A	23	(5)	15

NK Olimpija Ljubljana

2005 • Stožice (16,038) • nkolimpija.si

Major honours
Slovenian League (1) 2016

Coach: Rodolfo Vanoli (ITA);
(02/09/16) Luka Elsner;
(09/03/17) Marijan Pušnik
(04/04/17) Safet Hadžič

2016					
16/07	h	Celje	W	1-0	*Velikonja*
23/07	a	Radomlje	W	2-0	*Zajc, Eleke*
01/08	h	Krško	W	3-1	*Miškić, Eleke, Kelhar*
08/08	a	Maribor	D	1-1	*Zajc*
14/08	h	Rudar	L	0-2	
20/08	a	Domžale	W	3-1	*Zajc, Kronaveter, Wobay*
27/08	h	Koper	L	0-1	
11/09	h	Gorica	W	1-0	*Velikonja (p)*
18/09	a	Aluminij	W	3-0	*Eleke, Zajc, Benko*
21/09	a	Celje	W	1-0	*Zajc*
24/09	h	Radomlje	W	2-0	*Zajc, Kirm*
02/10	a	Krško	W	2-1	*og (Šturm), Velikonja*
15/10	h	Maribor	L	1-3	*Kronaveter*
23/10	a	Rudar	D	0-0	
29/10	h	Domžale	W	1-0	*Kirm*
06/11	a	Koper	W	2-1	*Benko, Kronaveter*
19/11	a	Gorica	D	1-1	*Benko*
27/11	h	Aluminij	W	3-0	*Kelhar, Miškić, Ricardo Alves*
30/11	h	Celje	W	2-1	*Benko, Ricardo Alves*
04/12	a	Radomlje	W	4-1	*og (Zukič), Kronaveter, Delamea Mlinar, Velikonja*
11/12	h	Krško	D	1-1	*Zajc*
2017					
25/02	a	Maribor	L	0-1	
05/03	h	Rudar	L	2-4	*Crețu, Benko (p)*
12/03	a	Domžale	L	0-1	
19/03	h	Koper	D	1-1	*Benko*
29/03	h	Gorica	L	1-2	*Eleke*
02/04	a	Aluminij	L	1-2	*Benko*
09/04	a	Celje	D	1-1	*Eleke*
17/04	h	Radomlje	D	1-1	*Benko*
23/04	a	Krško	W	1-0	*Abass*
29/04	h	Maribor	D	0-0	
07/05	a	Rudar	L	2-4	*Abass, Miškić*
13/05	h	Domžale	W	3-1	*Benko, Miškić, Boateng*
16/05	a	Koper	D	1-1	*Boateng*
21/05	a	Gorica	L	0-1	
27/05	h	Aluminij	W	1-0	*Benko*

No	Name	Nat	DoB	Pos	Aps	(s)	Gls
28	Issah Abass	GHA	26/09/98	M	5	(4)	2
95	Daniel Avramovski	MKD	20/02/95	M	2	(5)	
29	Dorian Babunski	MKD	29/08/96	A		(1)	
33	Kenan Bajrič		20/12/94	D	23	(1)	
77	Rok Baskera		26/05/93	M	4	(1)	
26	Leon Benko	CRO	11/11/83	A	25	(4)	10
21	Kingsley Boateng	ITA	07/04/94	M	6	(2)	2
6	Alexandru Crețu	ROU	24/04/92	M	12	(2)	1
20	Antonio Delamea Mlinar		10/06/91	D	19	(1)	1
9	Blessing Eleke	NGA	05/03/96	A	23	(7)	5
30	Branko Ilič		06/02/83	D	6		
14	Mario Jurčevič		01/06/95	M	9		
23	Nik Kapun		09/01/94	M	3	(2)	
4	Dejan Kelhar		05/04/84	D	18	(1)	2
17	Andraž Kirm		06/09/84	M	27	(4)	2
2	Denis Klinar		21/02/92	D	28	(2)	
19	Aljaž Krefl		20/02/94	D	5	(3)	
7	Rok Kronaveter		07/12/86	M	15	(2)	4
8	Darijan Matič		28/05/83	M	11	(4)	
88	Danijel Miškić	CRO	11/10/93	M	20	(4)	4
32	Nemanja Mitrovič		15/10/92	D	13		
18	Jakob Novak		04/03/98	M	3	(5)	
11	Nathan Oduwa	ENG	05/03/96	A	2	(2)	
16	Ricardo Alves	POR	25/03/93	M	12	(9)	2
1	Aleksander Šeliga		01/02/80	G	7		
44	Dino Štiglec	CRO	03/10/90	D	11	(1)	
20	David Tijanič		16/07/97	M	1	(7)	
11	Etien Velikonja		26/12/88	A	12	(9)	4
41	Nejc Vidmar		31/03/89	G	4		
13	Rok Vodišek		05/12/98	G	25		
15	Marko Vukčević	MNE	07/06/93	M	5	(7)	
10	Julius Wobay	SLE	19/05/84	A	8	(13)	1
6	Miha Zajc		01/07/94	M	19		7
27	Aris Zarifovič		02/06/88	D	13	(1)	

NK Radomlje

1972 • Športni park, Domzale (3,212) • nk-radomlje.si

Coach: Dejan Djuranovič;
(16/08/16) Janez Žilnik;
(14/11/16) (Dave McDonough (ENG))
(04/01/16) Robert Pevnik;
(19/02/17) Adnan Zildžović

2016					
17/07	a	Domžale	L	0-2	
23/07	h	Olimpija	L	0-2	
30/07	a	Gorica	L	1-2	*Nunič*
06/08	h	Aluminij	D	2-2	*Kovjenič, Gajič*
12/08	a	Celje	D	0-0	
20/08	a	Koper	L	0-3	
26/08	h	Krško	D	2-2	*Stoiljković, Barukčič (p)*
10/09	a	Maribor	L	0-4	
17/09	h	Rudar	D	2-2	*Barukčič (p), Šipek*
21/09	h	Domžale	L	0-5	
24/09	a	Olimpija	L	0-2	
02/10	h	Gorica	L	2-4	*Šipek, Nunič*
15/10	a	Aluminij	L	1-2	*Osmanaj*
21/10	h	Celje	L	0-3	
30/10	h	Koper	L	1-3	*Nunič*
06/11	a	Krško	D	1-1	*Nunič*
20/11	h	Maribor	L	0-3	
25/11	a	Rudar	L	0-2	
30/11	a	Domžale	W	2-0	*Janković, Nunič*
04/12	h	Olimpija	L	1-4	*Janković*
10/12	a	Gorica	D	1-1	*Karamatić*
2017					
25/02	h	Aluminij	L	0-3	
04/03	a	Celje	L	0-1	
11/03	a	Koper	L	1-4	*Balić*
18/03	h	Krško	L	0-2	
29/03	a	Maribor	L	0-1	
02/04	h	Rudar	L	1-5	*Jazbec*
08/04	h	Domžale	D	1-1	*Gajič*
17/04	a	Olimpija	D	1-1	*Karamatić*
21/04	h	Gorica	L	1-2	*Šipek*
30/04	a	Aluminij	L	1-3	*Cerar*
06/05	h	Celje	L	0-1	
12/05	h	Koper	L	0-4	
16/05	a	Krško	L	0-2	
21/05	h	Maribor	D	1-1	*Nunič*
27/05	a	Rudar	D	0-0	

No	Name	Nat	DoB	Pos	Aps	(s)	Gls
55	Milan Andjelkovič		01/09/81	D	13		
1	Vjekoslav Andrič		05/08/92	G	1		
18	Dorian Babunski	MKD	29/08/96	A	1	(4)	
29	Josip Balić	CRO	08/07/93	M	22	(3)	1
6	Igor Barukčič		12/11/90	M	30		2
10	Luka Cerar		26/05/93	M	33	(2)	1
5	Leo Ejup		09/09/94	D	9		
14	Luka Gajič		06/05/96	A	13	(14)	2
22	Aljaž Ivačič		29/12/93	G	35		
19	Robi Jakovljevič		07/05/93	M	12	(5)	
9	Filip Janković	SRB	17/01/95	M	15	(5)	2
44	Rok Jazbec		23/09/95	D	25	(2)	1
23	Domen Jugovar		12/12/96	D	15	(9)	
4	Tin Karamatić	CRO	01/03/93	D	26		2
5	Gregor Kosec		02/07/87	D	2		
17	Marko Kovjenič		02/02/93	M	17	(5)	1
7	Mirko Kramarić	CRO	27/01/89	D	3		
7	Amer Krcič		23/05/89	M	2	(5)	
71	Žan Kumer		16/05/96	D	10	(1)	
42	Denis Lidjan		24/09/93	D	13		
20	Grega Marinšek		19/09/96	A	8	(5)	
9	Marko Nunič		16/03/93	A	20	(14)	6
7	Liridon Osmanaj		04/01/92	A	7	(2)	1
59	Fedor Predragović	BIH	08/04/95	M	3		
15	Gal Primc		15/09/96	D	9	(6)	
39	Tadej Rems		31/07/93	D	3	(2)	
8	Mika Mario Rokavec		05/01/97	M	4	(4)	
21	Dušan Stoiljković	SRB	05/09/94	M	13	(2)	1
11	Kristijan Šipek		01/06/95	A	20	(7)	3
33	Mario Vasilj	CRO	25/01/95	A	1	(5)	
97	Miha Vidmar		16/06/97	A	1	(4)	
3	Aleksandar Zukič		05/01/91	D	10	(2)	

NK Rudar Velenje

1948 • Ob jezeru (7,000) • nkrudarvelenje.com

Major honours
Slovenian Cup (1) 1998

Coach: Slobodan Krčmarević (SRB);
(01/12/16) (Branko Čavić (SRB));
(09/01/17) Vanja Radinović (SRB)
(18/05/17) (Ramiz Smajlovič)

2015					
16/07	h	Krško	D	1-1	*Glavina*
24/07	a	Maribor	L	0-2	
30/07	h	Koper	W	2-0	*Mary 2*
07/08	h	Domžale	L	0-2	
14/08	a	Olimpija	W	2-0	*Pišek, Billong*
20/08	h	Gorica	L	1-2	*Glavina*
28/08	a	Aluminij	W	3-0	*Mary 2, Lotrič*
10/09	h	Celje	L	1-3	*Glavina*
17/09	a	Radomlje	D	2-2	*Zec, Glavina*
21/09	a	Krško	L	0-1	
25/09	h	Maribor	D	1-1	*Vručina*
01/10	a	Koper	W	4-1	*Vručina, Glavina 3*
15/10	a	Domžale	L	1-3	*Glavina*
23/10	h	Olimpija	D	0-0	
30/10	a	Gorica	W	3-1	*Lotrič, Glavina, Mary*
05/11	h	Aluminij	D	0-0	
19/11	a	Celje	L	0-4	
25/11	h	Radomlje	W	2-0	*Glavina, Grgić*
30/11	h	Krško	D	2-2	*Mary, Vručina*
03/12	a	Maribor	L	0-1	
10/12	h	Koper	D	2-2	*Mary 2*
2017					
25/02	h	Domžale	D	1-1	*Glavina*
05/03	a	Olimpija	W	4-2	*Glavina 2, Lotrič, Mary*
11/03	h	Gorica	L	1-3	*Glavina (p)*
19/03	a	Aluminij	L	0-3	
29/03	h	Celje	L	1-2	*Billong*
02/04	a	Radomlje	W	5-1	*Mary 3, S Babić, Glavina*
08/04	a	Krško	W	2-1	*Mary, Bolha*
15/04	h	Maribor	L	0-1	
22/04	a	Koper	L	0-1	
28/04	a	Domžale	L	0-3	
07/05	h	Olimpija	W	4-2	*Mary 2, Glavina, Iharoš*
13/05	a	Gorica	L	1-2	*Mary*
17/05	h	Aluminij	D	2-2	*Vručina, Zec*
21/05	a	Celje	D	1-1	*Mary*
27/05	h	Radomlje	D	0-0	

No	Name	Nat	DoB	Pos	Aps	(s)	Gls
33	Mario Babić	CRO	03/07/92	M	4		
12	Stjepan Babić	CRO	04/12/88	M	30	(1)	1
29	Jean-Claude Billong	FRA	28/12/93	D	21	(3)	2
23	Davor Bokalič		15/07/91	A	1	(10)	
19	Klemen Bolha		19/03/93	D	29		1
10	Leon Črnčič		02/03/90	M	11	(3)	
43	Sven Dodlek		28/09/95	M	1	(11)	
32	Mate Eterović	CRO	13/07/84	A	4	(6)	
14	Dominik Glavina	CRO	06/12/92	A	34		16
20	Denis Grbič		15/03/86	M	7	(3)	
45	Damir Grgić	CRO	18/05/92	D	15	(10)	1
33	Marko Iharoš	CRO	23/06/96	D	20		1
31	Senad Jahič		13/05/87	D	8		
4	David Kašnik		16/01/87	D	16	(1)	
7	Amer Krcič		23/05/89	M	3	(2)	
11	Mitja Lotrič		03/09/94	M	18	(8)	3
26	Ilya Markovskiy	UKR	06/06/97	M		(1)	
18	John Mary	CMR	09/03/93	A	25	(5)	17
3	Mateo Mužek	CRO	29/04/95	D	33		
6	Anže Pišek		06/10/96	M	12	(10)	1
13	Matej Radan		13/05/90	G	28		
1	Borivoje Ristić	SRB	19/09/83	G	8		
21	Nikola Tolimir		01/04/89	M	4	(4)	
15	Damjan Trifkovič		22/07/87	M	21	(10)	
8	Bojan Vručina	CRO	08/11/84	M	20	(11)	4
5	Darko Zec		21/02/89	D	23	(1)	2

SLOVENIA

Top goalscorers

17	John Mary (Rudar)
16	Dominik Glavina (Rudar)
15	Dalibor Volaš (Celje) Luka Zahovič (Maribor)
14	Miran Burgič (Gorica)
13	Filip Dangubić (Krško)
11	Milivoje Novakovič (Maribor)
10	Leon Benko (Olimpija)
9	Žiga Škoflek (Aluminij) Marcos Tavares (Maribor) Dare Vršič (Maribor)

Promoted clubs

NK Triglav

1920 • Stanko Mlakar (2,000) • nktriglav.si
Coach: Siniša Brkič

NK Ankaran Hrvatini

1966 • ŠRC Katerina (1,000) • nkankaran.si
Coach: Vlado Badžim

Second level final table 2016/17

		Pld	W	D	L	F	A	Pts
1	NK Triglav	25	19	4	2	64	23	61
2	NK Dob	25	16	6	3	61	26	54
3	NK Ankaran Hrvatini	25	14	4	7	45	29	46
4	NK Brežice	25	10	6	9	36	42	36
5	NK Drava Ptuj	25	9	4	12	45	55	31
6	NK Brda	25	6	8	11	27	34	26
7	NK Krka	25	7	4	14	40	42	25
8	NK Zarica Kranj	25	7	2	16	26	53	23
9	NK Veržej	25	5	6	14	21	45	21
10	NK Zavrč	9	1	2	6	13	29	5

NB NK Zavrč withdrew after round 12 – their results until round 9 stood; NK Ankaran Hrvatini subsequently promoted as NK Dob declined the place in 2017/18 Prva liga vacated by FC Koper's withdrawal.

DOMESTIC CUP

Pokal NZS 2016/17

FIRST ROUND

(17/08/16)
Beltinci 0-2 Aluminij
Bogojina 3-5 Tolmin
Dob 1-0 Triglav
Jadran Dekani 3-0 Videm
Koroška Dravograd 3-4 Krško
Krka 3-0 Brežice
Lenart 0-4 Rudar
Nafta 4-2 Zavrč *(aet)*
Postojna 0-8 Radomlje
Šmarje pri Jelšah 1-5 Koper
Turnišče 1-0 Brda
Žiri 0-5 Celje

Byes - Domžale, Gorica, Maribor, Olimpija

SECOND ROUND

(06/09/16)
Jadran Dekani 1-2 Rudar

(07/09/16)
Dob 0-1 Krka
Turnišče 0-2 Olimpija

(13/09/16)
Krško 2-2 Celje *(aet; 5-3 on pens)*
Tolmin 1-4 Domžale *(aet)*

(14/09/16)
Koper 0-0 Aluminij *(aet; 3-4 on pens)*
Radomlje 0-2 Maribor

(15/09/16)
Nafta 1-3 Gorica

QUARTER-FINALS

(18/10/16 & 26/10/16)
Olimpija 2-1 Aluminij *(Wobay 28, Velikonja 54p; Škoflek 10)*
Aluminij 1-4 Olimpija *(Srdić 56; Zajc 10, Velikonja 11, Benko 60, Kirm 78)*
(Olimpija 6-2)

Rudar 0-2 Krka *(Vukadin 56, Kambič 89)*
Krka 2-2 Rudar *(Kostanjšek 45, 57; Mary 12, Glavina 27)*
(Krka 4-2)

(19/10/16 & 25/10/16)
Krško 0-2 Domžale *(Volarič 15, 30)*
Domžale 2-1 Krško *(Bratanovič 20, Majer 58; Haljeta 90)*
(Domžale 4-1)

(19/10/16 & 26/10/16)
Gorica 1-1 Maribor *(Kotnik 58; Zahovič 44)*
Maribor 0-0 Gorica
(1-1; Maribor on away goal)

SEMI-FINALS

(04/04/17 & 11/04/17)
Domžale 2-0 Krka *(Firer 58, Batrović 83)*
Krka 0-2 Domžale *(Žužek 30, Majer 53)*
(Domžale 4-0)

(05/04/17 & 12/04/17)
Olimpija 2-1 Maribor *(Benko 81, 85; Vršič 48)*
Maribor 1-1 Olimpija *(Hotič 71; Crețu 32)*
(Olimpija 3-2)

FINAL

(31/05/17)
Bonifika, Koper
NK DOMŽALE 1 *(Dobrovoljc 62)*
NK OLIMPIJA LJUBLJANA 0
Referee: *Vinčič*
DOMŽALE: *Milič, Širok, Dobrovoljc, Blažič, Balkovec, Vetrih, Husmani, Majer, Franjić (Volarič 79), Repas (Bratanovič 87), Firer*
OLIMPIJA: *Vodišek, Klinar, Mitrovič, Zarifovič, Štiglec, Miškić, Crețu, Boateng (Wobay 50), Abass (Bajrič 61), Kirm (Oduwa 77), Benko*
Red cards: *Crețu (56), Mitrovič (90+3)*

Domžale players and staff celebrate the club's second Slovenian Cup victory

SPAIN

Real Federación Española de Fútbol (RFEF)

Address	Ramón y Cajal s/n Apartado postal 385 ES-28230 Las Rozas (Madrid)	**President**	Ángel María Villar Llona
Tel	+34 91 495 9800	**General secretary**	Esther Gascón Carbajosa
Fax	+34 91 495 9801	**Media officer**	Antonio Bustillo Abella
E-mail	rfef@rfef.es	**Year of formation**	1909
Website	rfef.es		

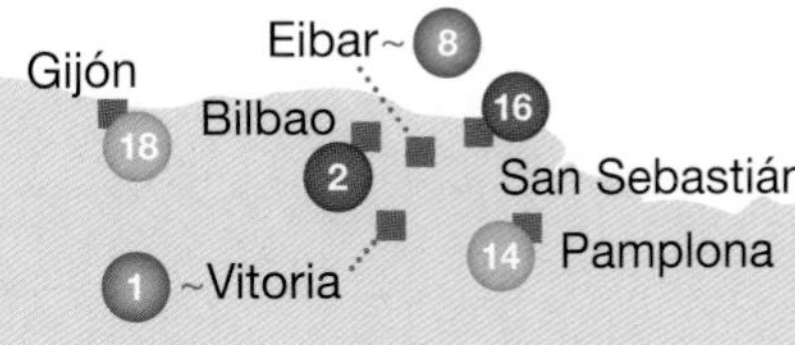

LIGA CLUBS

1 Deportivo Alavés

2 Athletic Club

3 Club Atlético de Madrid

4 FC Barcelona

5 Real Betis Balompié

6 RC Celta de Vigo

7 RC Deportivo La Coruña

8 SD Eibar

9 RCD Espanyol

10 Granada CF

11 UD Las Palmas

12 CD Leganés

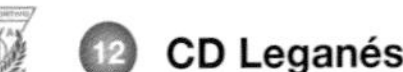
13 Málaga CF

14 CA Osasuna

15 Real Madrid CF

16 Real Sociedad de Fútbol

17 Sevilla FC

18 Real Sporting de Gijón

19 Valencia CF

20 Villarreal CF

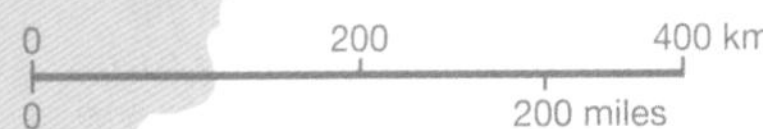

PROMOTED CLUBS

21 Levante UD

22 Girona FC

23 Getafe CF

KEY

- UEFA Champions League
- UEFA Europa League
- Promoted
- Relegated

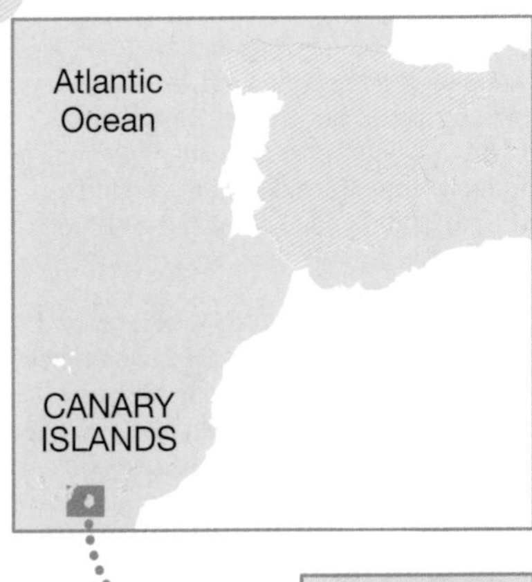

Real Madrid reclaim championship crown

As has become its custom, the outcome of the Spanish Liga title race remained unresolved until the final day of the season. For the first time in five years, however, it was won by Real Madrid, Zinédine Zidane's star-studded side thus ending the club's longest barren run since the early 1990s.

There was jubilation too for Madrid in Europe as they became the first team to make a successful defence of the UEFA Champions League. Barcelona had to content themselves with a third successive Copa del Rey triumph at the end of coach Luis Enrique's third and final season at the Camp Nou.

First Liga title in five years secured on final day

Zidane's team retain UEFA Champions League

Barcelona complete Copa del Rey hat-trick

Domestic league

Only once since Real Madrid established themselves as the superpower of Spanish and European football in the 1950s had they gone more than five years without being crowned champions of their own country (from 1980-86), so there was considerable pressure on Zidane, in his first full season as coach, and a largely unchanged squad to ensure that the 2016/17 Liga campaign was a victorious one. The quiet, unassuming Frenchman, who had led the team to UEFA Champions League glory after less than five months in the job, would hit the jackpot again, pooling his formidable resources with such skill, intelligence and audacity that Madrid became champions of both Spain and Europe in the same season for the first time since 1957/58.

The Liga triumph also broke new ground in that Madrid scored in every one of their 38 matches. No Spanish side had ever achieved that before. They racked up 106 goals in total, and 58 of those came on their travels. The great Cristiano Ronaldo, now 32 but as fit as ever, was on target 25 times. It was the lowest league tally of his eight seasons at the Bernabéu but he only started 29 matches as Zidane protected him from burn-out, ensuring that he would be in optimum condition for the club's biggest and most important games.

Two of those came in the final week of the campaign as Madrid travelled from one end of the country to the other, from Vigo to Malaga, needing four points to become champions and in the process deny Luis Enrique's Barça a hat-trick of Liga titles. Zidane's men had been level on points with their Catalan rivals for several weeks – since a brilliant last-gasp winner by Lionel Messi at the Bernabéu had decided the second Clásico of the season 3-2 in the visitors' favour. But while Barça held the head-to-head advantage, Madrid had a game in hand. That was in Galicia against a Celta side that had defeated Barcelona 4-3 at the Estadio Balaídos earlier in the season. Furthermore, Madrid's final game, in Andalusia against Málaga, was also at a stadium where Barcelona had lost, 2-0, just a few weeks earlier.

If there was pressure on Madrid, it did not show. A 10th-minute Ronaldo goal in Vigo set them on the way to a comfortable 4-1 win, with the Portuguese striker adding a second goal after the interval before Karim Benzema and Toni Kroos wrapped up the points against a Celta side reduced to ten men for the final half-hour. Now back on top of the table with a three-point lead, the Merengues headed south needing just a point in La Rosaleda against a mid-table, nothing-to-play-for Málaga team coached by Madrid legend Míchel. Once again Ronaldo struck early, this time after just 97 seconds, to put his team in control. Barcelona, meanwhile, appeared to have thrown in the towel as they went two goals down at home to Eibar, but although they recovered to win 4-2, Madrid doubled their lead early in the second half, through Benzema, and coasted to their 29th win of the season, securing the club's long-awaited and wildly-celebrated 33rd Spanish league title.

Barcelona captain Andrés Iniesta was noble enough to acknowledge that Madrid deserved their triumph, and few disagreed. They effectively led all season, playing wonderful attacking football and also showing tremendous fighting spirit that enabled them on several occasions to stage crucial comebacks and score vital late goals – not least skipper Sergio Ramos's added-time leveller in the first Clásico at the Camp Nou in early December. While Ronaldo, as usual, was the star of the show, it was very much a collective effort, with every player pulling in the same direction and serving the greater good of the team. Not one Madrid squad member started 30 games, but 20 of them played for over 1,000 minutes – which Liga statisticians reckoned had

never been done before. Rotation and rest was key to the team's success, and Madrid's strength in depth, allied to supreme talent and effective game management, made it possible for them to achieve their dream double.

In addition to scoring in every game – a feat that extended also to every other competition they played in – Madrid set a new Spanish record by going 40 matches in all competitions without defeat, beating by one the mark set by Barcelona only the season before. That run ended with a 2-1 loss at Sevilla in mid-January – three days after Madrid had broken the record at the same venue with a last-gasp 3-3 draw in the Copa del Rey. There would be two further defeats for Zidane's men – at Valencia and at home to Barcelona – but on each occasion they bounced back strongly, in the first instance coming from two goals down to win 3-2 at Villarreal and, after the Clásico calamity, running up six goals away to Deportivo La Coruña in the first of half a dozen successive victories that would transport them to the title.

In most seasons Barcelona's final tally of 90 points would have put them on top of the table. Their brilliant all-South American attacking trident of Lionel Messi, Luis Suárez and Neymar conjured up 79 goals between them – down slightly on the 90 of the previous campaign but a phenomenal haul nonetheless, enabling Barça as a team to score 116, more than ever before in a Liga campaign. Their defence was actually better than Madrid's too, conceding 37 goals to the champions' 41, but while the players who had starred in the previous two seasons of Luis Enrique's reign all generally performed to the same lofty level, there was little impact from the club's summer recruits. Samuel Umtiti established himself as a reliable central defensive partner to Gerard Piqué, but the other newcomers – André Gomes, Paco Alcácer, Lucas Digne, Jasper Cillessen and Denis Suárez – all had underwhelming debut seasons.

Atlético Madrid led the Liga table after eight matches following an unbeaten start, but three defeats in their next four fixtures, the last of them at home to Real Madrid, with Ronaldo scoring all the goals in a 3-0 win, dropped Diego Simeone's side out of title contention. Indeed, their late-autumn form was so poor that by Christmas they had plummeted to sixth place. A spring revival, however, with Antoine Griezmann sparking the attack and Diego Godín diligently marshalling the defence, lifted Atlético back up to third – albeit with a 15-point deficit on their city neighbours. It was the club's last season in the Estadio Vicente Calderón, and they signed off in style with a 3-1 victory over Athletic Club in which one of their favourite sons, Fernando Torres, scored twice. For the fourth time in Simeone's five full seasons at the helm, Atlético posted the Liga's best defensive record, while goalkeeper Jan Oblak emulated his predecessor Thibaut Courtois by winning the Zamora trophy for the second year in a row.

Sevilla were never top of the standings but they sustained a challenge to Real Madrid and Barcelona from August through to March, new boss Jorge Sampaoli kicking off with a crazy 6-4 win against Espanyol and bringing fresh impetus to a team that had lost not only their three-time UEFA Europa League-winning boss Unai Emery but also key players in Kevin Gameiro and Grzegorz Krychowiak. In the spring Sevilla's form took an abrupt turn for the worse, but four wins in their last 13 games was sufficient to keep them in the top four, with Villarreal, a resurgent Real Sociedad and their fellow Basques Athletic filling the next three spots to qualify for Europe.

Granada, Osasuna and Sporting Gijón occupied the bottom three places virtually all season, which enabled newly-promoted Leganés to defy the odds and extend their stay in the top flight for another campaign. Eibar were another side to overachieve, finishing tenth, whereas Valencia had a season to forget, ex-Italy boss Cesare Prandelli lasting just three months as the club dropped to 17th at the turn of the year before Voro steered them to safety. Their local rivals Levante won the Segunda División at a canter to secure promotion 12 months after relegation, with the Catalans of Girona accompanying them up in second place and Getafe completing the threesome after defeating Tenerife in the play-off final.

Karim Benzema (left) celebrates with captain Sergio Ramos after scoring Real Madrid's second goal in their Liga title-clinching 2-0 win at Málaga

SPAIN

Domestic cup

Alavés also had a season to remember. The 2015/16 Segunda División champions changed their coach and most of the team following promotion, and new boss Mauricio Pellegrino guided them not only to ninth place in the league but also to a first ever appearance in the Spanish Cup final, a 1-0 aggregate win over Celta in the semi-finals earning them an end-of-season date with holders Barcelona at the Calderón.

After Messi had given Barça the lead on the half-hour with his 57th goal of an another magnificently prolific season, the underdogs equalised soon afterwards with a stunning strike from Theo Hernández, but they could not hold on until half-time, Neymar and Paco Alcácer both finding the net shortly before the interval to kill the game at 3-1 and give departing coach Luis Enrique the perfect send-off. It was Barça's record-extending 29th Copa del Rey triumph and only the second time they had lifted the trophy three seasons running, the first having been way back in the early 1950s.

Europe

Real Madrid began the 2016/17 season by lifting the UEFA Super Cup thanks to a late extra-time winner from right-back Daniel Carvajal in a thrilling 3-2 victory over Sevilla. Midway through the campaign they added the FIFA Club World Cup, with Ronaldo scoring a hat-trick in another extra-time victory, 4-2 against Kashima Antlers. And in early June they rounded off one of the greatest seasons in the club's history by beating Juventus 4-1 in Cardiff to complete a successful defence of the UEFA Champions League.

Zidane's side were worthy European champions, their third victory in four seasons and 12th overall displaying the same traits that served them so well in their domestic campaign. A modest group stage, in which they remained unbeaten but finished second to Borussia Dortmund, was followed by a marvellous knockout phase, in which they beat Napoli and Bayern München home and away and ended Atlético's trophy hopes for the fourth season running before eventually sweeping Juve aside in the final. Ronaldo scored ten goals, including two hat-tricks, in the last five games, becoming the first player to score 100 in Europe, then the same number in the UEFA Champions League.

Vitolo exploits a rare Gianluigi Buffon error to put Spain 1-0 up in their World Cup qualifier against Italy in Turin

Barcelona chalked up 21 goals in their first four home games, including six against Paris Saint-Germain to complete the greatest second-leg comeback in UEFA Champions League history, but they followed a 4-0 defeat in Paris with a 3-0 defeat at Juventus and the Italian champions, unlike their French counterparts, were too canny to let slip that advantage, halting Barça's run of 15 successive European wins at the Camp Nou with a goalless draw to end the Catalans' interest at the quarter-final stage for the second successive year.

Although Villarreal lost their UEFA Champions League qualifier to Monaco, all four Liga teams in the group stage made further progress, which meant that Sevilla did not get a chance to make it four UEFA Europa League wins on the trot. Instead they were surprisingly eliminated in the round of 16 by competition debutants Leicester City, who were then knocked out in the quarter-finals by Atlético. In Sevilla's absence, Eduardo Berizzo's Celta carried the flag for Spain in the UEFA Europa League, reaching a first European semi-final before they fell agonisingly short against Manchester United.

National team

Spain's new coach Julen Lopetegui enjoyed an unbeaten first season as he steered the team to five wins and a draw in their opening six 2018 FIFA World Cup qualifiers, the only dropped points coming away to Italy. An aggregate goal tally of 21-3 enabled Spain to lead the Group G table ahead of the Azzurri, with a home fixture against their chief rivals next on the agenda, in Madrid on 2 September, when Spain would have the opportunity to extend their unbeaten run in World Cup qualifiers to 60 matches.

It was a season in which two English-based players, Diego Costa and David Silva, particularly excelled, the Chelsea striker scoring five World Cup goals and the Manchester City schemer taking his all-time tally to 32 with doubles against Belgium and Liechtenstein and Spain's opening goal in each of their first four fixtures of 2017. Sevilla midfielder Vitolo also distinguished himself with four World Cup strikes, including the all-important goal in Turin, while there were promising cameos from Saúl Ñíguez, Marco Asensio and Gerard Deulofeu, all of whom starred for the exciting Spain side that finished runners-up at the 2017 UEFA European Under-21 Championship in Poland.

DOMESTIC SEASON AT A GLANCE

Liga 2016/17 final table

		Pld	Home W	D	L	F	A	Away W	D	L	F	A	Total W	D	L	F	A	Pts
1	**Real Madrid CF**	**38**	**14**	**4**	**1**	**48**	**20**	**15**	**2**	**2**	**58**	**21**	**29**	**6**	**3**	**106**	**41**	**93**
2	FC Barcelona	38	15	3	1	64	17	13	3	3	52	20	28	6	4	116	37	90
3	Club Atlético de Madrid	38	14	2	3	40	14	9	7	3	30	13	23	9	6	70	27	78
4	Sevilla FC	38	14	4	1	39	16	7	5	7	30	33	21	9	8	69	49	72
5	Villarreal CF	38	11	4	4	35	18	8	6	5	21	15	19	10	9	56	33	67
6	Real Sociedad de Fútbol	38	10	5	4	30	24	9	2	8	29	29	19	7	12	59	53	64
7	Athletic Club	38	13	4	2	36	18	6	2	11	17	25	19	6	13	53	43	63
8	RCD Espanyol	38	8	5	6	28	24	7	6	6	21	26	15	11	12	49	50	56
9	Deportivo Alavés	38	7	8	4	19	21	7	5	7	22	22	14	13	11	41	43	55
10	SD Eibar	38	10	3	6	29	21	5	6	8	27	30	15	9	14	56	51	54
11	Málaga CF	38	10	2	7	32	25	2	8	9	17	30	12	10	16	49	55	46
12	Valencia CF	38	8	4	7	32	32	5	3	11	24	33	13	7	18	56	65	46
13	RC Celta de Vigo	38	9	2	8	30	32	4	4	11	23	37	13	6	19	53	69	45
14	UD Las Palmas	38	9	6	4	33	25	1	3	15	20	49	10	9	19	53	74	39
15	Real Betis Balompié	38	6	7	6	22	24	4	2	13	19	40	10	9	19	41	64	39
16	RC Deportivo La Coruña	38	7	5	7	27	23	1	7	11	16	38	8	12	18	43	61	36
17	CD Leganés	38	5	6	8	22	23	3	5	11	14	32	8	11	19	36	55	35
18	Real Sporting de Gijón	38	5	4	10	26	38	2	6	11	16	34	7	10	21	42	72	31
19	CA Osasuna	38	2	7	10	23	39	2	3	14	17	55	4	10	24	40	94	22
20	Granada CF	38	4	4	11	17	32	0	4	15	13	50	4	8	26	30	82	20

European qualification 2017/18

Champion: Real Madrid CF (group stage)
Cup winner: FC Barcelona (group stage)
Club Atlético de Madrid (group stage)
Sevilla FC (play-off round)

Villarreal CF (group stage)
Real Sociedad de Fútbol (group stage)
Athletic Club (third qualifying round)

Top scorer Lionel Messi (FC Barcelona), 37 goals
Relegated clubs Granada CF, CA Osasuna, Real Sporting de Gijón
Promoted clubs Levante UD, Girona FC, Getafe CF
Cup final FC Barcelona 3-1 Deportivo Alavés

Player of the season

Lionel Messi
(FC Barcelona)

Real Madrid won the 2016/17 Liga title, but once again Messi was the Spanish top division's leading individual attraction. With 37 goals in 34 games, the brilliant Barcelona striker won his fourth Pichichi award as the Liga's top scorer. Oddly there were no hat-tricks in that tally but he managed 13 doubles, one of which, against Real Madrid at the Bernabéu, secured three precious points and reopened the title race. Indeed, his second in that game, exquisitely finished with his magic wand of a left foot two minutes into added time, was his 500th goal for Barcelona.

Newcomer of the season

Marco Asensio
(Real Madrid CF)

Bought by Real Madrid in 2014 but returned on loan to his hometown club Mallorca before serving a similar spell at Espanyol, Marco Asensio finally got the chance to make his mark at the Bernabéu in 2016/17 and the elegant young left-footer duly left a deep impression. Outings in the starting XI may have been hard to come by in the company of so many superstars, but the 21-year-old's exquisite skill, technique and movement were clear for all to see. He scored three goals apiece in the Liga and UEFA Champions League, including the fourth against Juventus in Cardiff.

Team of the season

(4-2-1-3)

Coach: Zidane *(Real Madrid)*

SPAIN

NATIONAL TEAM

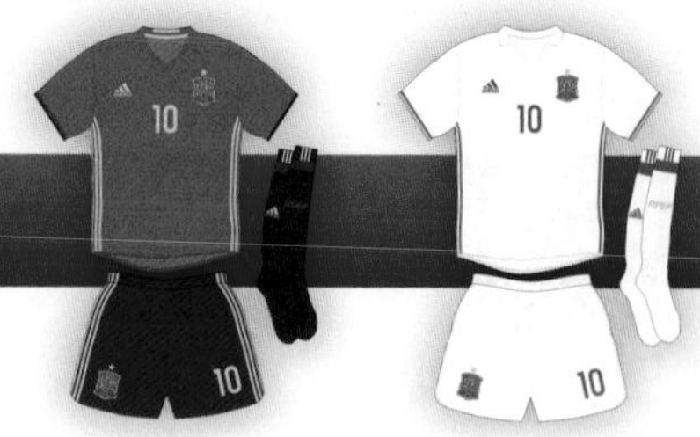

International honours
FIFA World Cup (1) 2010
UEFA European Championship (3) 1964, 2008, 2012

International tournament appearances
FIFA World Cup (14) 1934, 1950 (4th), 1962, 1966, 1978, 1982 (2nd phase), 1986 (qtr-finals), 1990 (2nd round), 1994 (qtr-finals), 1998, 2002 (qtr-finals), 2006 (2nd round), 2010 (Winners), 2014
UEFA European Championship (10) 1964 (Winners), 1980, 1984 (runners-up), 1988, 1996 (qtr-finals), 2000 (qtr-finals), 2004, 2008 (Winners), 2012 (Winners), 2016 (round of 16)

Top five all-time caps
Iker Casillas (167); **Sergio Ramos** (143); Xavi Hernández (133); Andoni Zubizarreta (126); **Andrés Iniesta** (119)

Top five all-time goals
David Villa (59); Raúl González (44); Fernando Torres (38); **David Silva** (32); Fernando Hierro (29)

Results 2016/17

01/09/16	Belgium	A	Brussels	W	2-0	*Silva (34, 62p)*
05/09/16	Liechtenstein (WCQ)	H	Leon	W	8-0	*Diego Costa (10, 66), Sergi Roberto (55), Silva (59, 90+1), Vitolo (60), Morata (82, 83)*
06/10/16	Italy (WCQ)	A	Turin	D	1-1	*Vitolo (55)*
09/10/16	Albania (WCQ)	A	Skhoder	W	2-0	*Diego Costa (55), Nolito (63)*
12/11/16	FYR Macedonia (WCQ)	H	Granada	W	4-0	*Velkovski (34og), Vitolo (63), Monreal (84), Aduriz (85)*
15/11/16	England	A	London	D	2-2	*Iago Aspas (89), Isco (90+6)*
24/03/17	Israel (WCQ)	H	Gijon	W	4-1	*Silva (13), Vitolo (45+1), Diego Costa (51), Isco (88)*
28/03/17	France	A	Saint-Denis	W	2-0	*Silva (68p), Deulofeu (77)*
07/06/17	Colombia	H	Murcia	D	2-2	*Silva (22), Morata (87)*
11/06/17	FYR Macedonia (WCQ)	A	Skopje	W	2-1	*Silva (15), Diego Costa (27)*

Appearances 2016/17

Coach: Julen Lopetegui	**28/08/66**		**Bel**	**LIE**	**ITA**	**ALB**	**MKD**	**Eng**	**ISR**	**Fra**	**Col**	**MKD**	**Caps**	**Goals**
David de Gea	07/11/90	Man. United (ENG)	G	G	G	G	G		G	G		G	21	-
Daniel Carvajal	11/01/92	Real Madrid	D85		D		D	M	D	D		D	12	-
Sergio Ramos	30/03/86	Real Madrid	D	D	D	D80			D	D		D	143	10
Gerard Piqué	02/02/87	Barcelona	D59	D	D	D			D	D	D56	D	89	5
Jordi Alba	21/03/89	Barcelona	D59	D	D22				D	D86	D46	D	54	6
Sergio Busquets	16/07/88	Barcelona	M	M	M	M	M	M78	M	M		M	97	2
Vitolo	02/11/89	Sevilla	M75	A79	A84	A60	A87	M46	A83		s76		11	4
Thiago Alcántara	11/04/91	Bayern (GER)	M	M46	s84	M	M	M56	M63	s52		M74	21	-
Koke	08/01/92	Atlético	M	M	M	M	M71	s46	s63	M74	M	s74	34	-
David Silva	08/01/86	Man. City (ENG)	M75	A	A	A	A	M64	A	s53	A46	A69	113	32
Álvaro Morata	23/10/92	Real Madrid	A27	s68	s67		A60	s64		A84	s56		20	9
Diego Costa	07/10/88	Chelsea (ENG)	s27	A68	A67	A			A			A	16	6
Marc Bartra	15/01/91	Dortmund (GER)	s59				D						12	-
César Azpilicueta	28/08/89	Chelsea (ENG)	s59					D			D		19	-
Saúl Ñíguez	21/11/94	Atlético	s75								s46	s92	3	-
Lucas Vázquez	01/07/91	Real Madrid	s75										3	-
Sergi Roberto	07/02/92	Barcelona	s85	D									3	1
Nolito	15/10/86	Man. City (ENG)		s46		s60		s78					16	6
Marco Asensio	21/01/96	Real Madrid		s79							s46		3	-
Andrés Iniesta	11/05/84	Barcelona			M	M78			M70	M52	M46	A92	119	12
Nacho	18/01/90	Real Madrid			s22		D	D		s86	D		9	-
Nacho Monreal	26/02/86	Arsenal (ENG)				D	D				s46		19	1
Isco	21/04/92	Real Madrid				s78	s71	s64	s70	A53		M	20	3
Íñigo Martínez	17/05/91	Real Sociedad				s80		D					4	-
Aritz Aduriz	11/02/81	Athletic					s60	A64					11	2
José Callejón	11/02/87	Napoli (ITA)					s87						3	-
Pepe Reina	31/08/82	Napoli (ITA)						G			G		35	-
Juan Mata	28/04/88	Man. United (ENG)						M46					41	10
Iago Aspas	01/08/87	Celta						s46	s83	s84	A56		4	1
Ander Herrera	14/08/89	Man. United (ENG)						s56		s74			2	-
Pedro Rodríguez	28/07/87	Chelsea (ENG)								A67	A76	s69	63	17
Gerard Deulofeu	13/03/94	Milan (ITA)								s67	s56		3	1
Asier Illarramendi	08/03/90	Real Sociedad									M		1	-

EUROPE

Real Madrid CF

Group F
Match 1 - Sporting Clube de Portugal (POR)
H 2-1 *Cristiano Ronaldo (89), Morata (90+4)*
Casilla, Carvajal, Sergio Ramos, Varane, Cristiano Ronaldo, Kroos (James Rodríguez 77), Benzema (Morata 68), Bale (Lucas Vázquez 67), Marcelo, Casemiro, Modrić. Coach: Zinédine Zidane (FRA)
Match 2 - Borussia Dortmund (GER)
A 2-2 *Cristiano Ronaldo (17), Varane (68)*
Navas, Carvajal, Sergio Ramos, Varane, Cristiano Ronaldo, Kroos, Benzema (Morata 88), James Rodríguez (Kovačić 69), Bale, Modrić, Danilo. Coach: Zinédine Zidane (FRA)
Match 3 - Legia Warszawa (POL)
H 5-1 *Bale (16), Jodłowiec (20og), Marco Asensio (37), Lucas Vázquez (68), Morata (84)*
Navas, Pepe, Varane, Cristiano Ronaldo, Kroos, Benzema, James Rodríguez (Lucas Vázquez 63), Bale (Morata 64), Marcelo, Marco Asensio (Kovačić 79), Danilo. Coach: Zinédine Zidane (FRA)
Match 4 - Legia Warszawa (POL)
A 3-3 *Bale (1), Benzema (35), Kovačić (85)*
Navas, Carvajal, Varane, Nacho, Cristiano Ronaldo, Kroos, Benzema (Lucas Vázquez 65), Bale, Fábio Coentrão (Marco Asensio 77), Kovačić, Morata (Díaz 85). Coach: Zinédine Zidane (FRA)
Match 5 - Sporting Clube de Portugal (POR)
A 2-1 *Varane (29), Benzema (87)*
Navas, Carvajal, Sergio Ramos, Varane, Cristiano Ronaldo, Bale (Marco Asensio 58), Marcelo (Fábio Coentrão 71), Kovačić, Lucas Vázquez, Modrić, Isco (Benzema 67). Coach: Zinédine Zidane (FRA)
Match 6 - Borussia Dortmund (GER)
H 2-2 *Benzema (28, 53)*
Navas, Carvajal, Sergio Ramos, Varane, Cristiano Ronaldo, Benzema (Morata 85), James Rodríguez, Marcelo, Casemiro, Lucas Vázquez, Modrić (Kroos 63). Coach: Zinédine Zidane (FRA)

Round of 16 - SSC Napoli (ITA)
H 3-1 *Benzema (18), Kroos (49), Casemiro (54)*
Navas, Carvajal, Sergio Ramos (Pepe 71), Varane, Cristiano Ronaldo, Kroos, Benzema (Morata 81), James Rodríguez (Lucas Vázquez 76), Marcelo, Casemiro, Modrić. Coach: Zinédine Zidane (FRA)
A 3-1 *Sergio Ramos (52), Mertens (57og), Morata (90+1)*
Navas, Carvajal, Pepe, Sergio Ramos, Cristiano Ronaldo, Kroos, Benzema (Morata 77), Bale (Lucas Vázquez 68), Marcelo, Casemiro, Modrić (Isco 80). Coach: Zinédine Zidane (FRA)

Quarter-finals - FC Bayern München (GER)
A 2-1 *Cristiano Ronaldo (47, 77)*
Navas, Carvajal, Sergio Ramos, Nacho, Ronaldo, Kroos, Benzema (James Rodríguez 83), Bale (Marco Asensio 59), Marcelo, Casemiro, Modrić (Kovačić 90+1). Coach: Zinédine Zidane (FRA)
H 4-2 (aet) *Cristiano Ronaldo (76, 105, 110), Marco Asensio (112)*
Navas, Carvajal, Sergio Ramos, Nacho, Ronaldo, Kroos (Kovačić 114), Benzema (Marco Asensio 64), Marcelo, Casemiro, Modrić, Isco (Lucas Vázquez 71). Coach: Zinédine Zidane (FRA)

Semi-finals - Club Atlético de Madrid (ESP)
H 3-0 *Cristiano Ronaldo (10, 73, 86)*
Navas, Carvajal (Nacho 46), Sergio Ramos, Varane, Cristiano Ronaldo, Kroos, Benzema (Lucas Vázquez 77), Marcelo, Casemiro, Modrić, Isco (Marco Asensio 68). Coach: Zinédine Zidane (FRA)
A 1-2 *Isco (42)*
Navas, Sergio Ramos, Varane, Cristiano Ronaldo, Kroos, Benzema (Marco Asensio 76), Marcelo, Casemiro (Lucas Vázquez 77), Modrić, Isco (Morata 88), Danilo. Coach: Zinédine Zidane (FRA)

Final - Juventus (ITA)
N 4-1 *Cristiano Ronaldo (20, 64), Casemiro (61), Marco Asensio (90)*
Navas, Carvajal, Sergio Ramos, Varane, Cristiano Ronaldo, Kroos (Morata 89), Benzema (Bale 77), Marcelo, Casemiro, Modrić, Isco (Marco Asensio 82). Coach: Zinédine Zidane (FRA)

FC Barcelona

Group C
Match 1 - Celtic FC (SCO)
H 7-0 *Messi (3, 27, 60), Neymar (50), Iniesta (59), Suárez (75, 88)*
Ter Stegen, Piqué, Rakitić (Iniesta 46), Busquets (Rafinha 61), Suárez, Messi, Neymar, Jordi Alba, Sergi Roberto, André Gomes, Umtiti. Coach: Luis Enrique (ESP)
Match 2 - VfL Borussia Mönchengladbach (GER)
A 2-1 *Arda Turan (65), Piqué (74)*
Ter Stegen, Piqué, Rakitić (Arda Turan 60), Busquets, Iniesta, Suárez, Neymar, Mascherano, Paco Alcácer (Rafinha 54), Jordi Alba, Sergi Roberto. Coach: Luis Enrique (ESP)
Match 3 - Manchester City FC (ENG)
H 4-0 *Messi (17, 61, 69), Neymar (89)*
Ter Stegen, Piqué (Mathieu 39), Rakitić, Busquets, Iniesta (André Gomes 80), Suárez, Messi, Neymar, Mascherano, Jordi Alba (Digne 10), Umtiti. Coach: Luis Enrique (ESP)
Red card: Mathieu 73
Match 4 - Manchester City FC (ENG)
A 1-3 *Messi (21)*
Ter Stegen, Rakitić (Arda Turan 61), Busquets, Suárez, Messi, Neymar, Mascherano, Digne, Sergi Roberto, André Gomes (Rafinha 76), Umtiti. Coach: Luis Enrique (ESP)
Match 5 - Celtic FC (SCO)
A 2-0 *Messi (24, 56p)*
Ter Stegen, Piqué (Marlon 72), Rakitić, Busquets, Suárez, Messi, Neymar (Arda Turan 77), Mascherano, Jordi Alba (Digne 66), Sergi Roberto, André Gomes. Coach: Luis Enrique (ESP)
Match 6 - VfL Borussia Mönchengladbach (GER)
H 4-0 *Messi (16), Arda Turan (50, 53, 67)*
Cillessen, Denis Suárez, Arda Turan (Cardona 74), Iniesta (Rafinha 61), Messi, Mascherano, Paco Alcácer, Digne, André Gomes, Aleix Vidal, Umtiti. Coach: Luis Enrique (ESP)

Round of 16 - Paris Saint-Germain (FRA)
A 0-4
Ter Stegen, Piqué, Busquets, Iniesta (Rakitić 72), Suárez, Messi, Neymar, Jordi Alba, Sergi Roberto, André Gomes (Rafinha 58), Umtiti. Coach: Luis Enrique (ESP)
H 6-1 *Suárez (3), Kurzawa (40og), Messi (50p), Neymar (88, 90+1p), Sergi Roberto (90+5)*
Ter Stegen, Piqué, Rakitić (André Gomes 84), Busquets, Iniesta (Arda Turan 65), Suárez, Messi, Neymar, Rafinha (Sergi Roberto 76), Mascherano, Umtiti. Coach: Luis Enrique (ESP)

Quarter-finals - Juventus (ITA)
A 0-3
Ter Stegen, Piqué, Rakitić, Iniesta, Suárez, Messi, Neymar, Mascherano, Sergi Roberto, Umtiti, Mathieu (André Gomes 46). Coach: Luis Enrique (ESP)
H 0-0
Ter Stegen, Piqué, Rakitić (Paco Alcácer 58), Busquets, Iniesta, Suárez, Messi, Neymar, Jordi Alba, Sergi Roberto (Mascherano 78), Umtiti. Coach: Luis Enrique (ESP)

Club Atlético de Madrid

Group D
Match 1 - PSV Eindhoven (NED)
A 1-0 *Saúl Ñíguez (43)*
Oblak, Godín, Filipe Luís, Koke, Griezmann, Saúl Ñíguez (Fernando Torres 77), Gabi, Juanfran, Gameiro (Carrasco 65), Gaitán (Tiago 61), Giménez. Coach: Diego Simeone (ARG)
Match 2 - FC Bayern München (GER)
H 1-0 *Carrasco (35)*
Oblak, Godín, Filipe Luís, Koke, Griezmann (Partey 90+2), Saúl Ñíguez, Fernando Torres (Gaitán 79), Carrasco (Gameiro 72), Gabi, Savić, Juanfran. Coach: Diego Simeone (ARG)
Match 3 - FC Rostov (RUS)
A 1-0 *Carrasco (62)*
Oblak, Godín, Filipe Luís, Koke, Griezmann (Tiago 90+1), Fernando Torres, Carrasco (Saúl Ñíguez 89), Correa (Gameiro 57), Gabi, Savić, Juanfran. Coach: Diego Simeone (ARG)
Match 4 - FC Rostov (RUS)
H 2-1 *Griezmann (28, 90+3)*
Oblak, Godín, Filipe Luís, Koke, Griezmann, Saúl Ñíguez (Gameiro 58), Fernando Torres, Carrasco (Correa 79), Gabi, Savić, Vrsaljko. Coach: Diego Simeone (ARG)
Match 5 - PSV Eindhoven (NED)
H 2-0 *Gameiro (55), Griezmann (66)*
Oblak, Godín, Filipe Luís (Juanfran 76), Tiago (Saúl Ñíguez 76), Koke, Griezmann, Carrasco, Gabi, Vrsaljko, Gameiro, Giménez. Coach: Diego Simeone (ARG)
Match 6 - FC Bayern München (GER)
A 0-1
Oblak, Godín, Koke (Partey 68), Griezmann, Saúl Ñíguez, Carrasco (Gameiro 60), Gabi, Savić, Vrsaljko, Lucas Hernández, Gaitán (Correa 60). Coach: Diego Simeone (ARG)

Round of 16 - Bayer 04 Leverkusen (GER)
A 4-2 *Saúl Ñíguez (17), Griezmann (25), Gameiro (59p), Fernando Torres (86)*
Moyá, Filipe Luís, Koke, Griezmann (Correa 78), Saúl Ñíguez, Carrasco (Fernando Torres 78), Gabi, Savić, Vrsaljko, Gameiro (Partey 71), Giménez. Coach: Diego Simeone (ARG)
H 0-0
Oblak, Godín, Koke, Griezmann, Saúl Ñíguez, Carrasco (Savić 71), Correa (Gaitán 64), Vrsaljko, Lucas Hernández, Partey, Giménez. Coach: Diego Simeone (ARG)

Quarter-finals - Leicester City FC (ENG)
H 1-0 *Griezmann (28p)*
Oblak, Godín, Filipe Luís, Koke, Griezmann, Saúl Ñíguez, Fernando Torres (Partey 75), Carrasco (Correa 65), Gabi, Savić, Juanfran. Coach: Diego Simeone (ARG)
A 1-1 *Saúl Ñíguez (26)*
Oblak, Godín, Filipe Luís (Correa 74), Koke, Griezmann, Saúl Ñíguez, Carrasco (Fernando Torres 69), Gabi, Savić, Juanfran (Lucas Hernández 55), Giménez. Coach: Diego Simeone (ARG)

Semi-finals - Real Madrid CF (ESP)
A 0-3
Oblak, Godín, Filipe Luís, Koke, Griezmann, Saúl Ñíguez (Gaitán 58), Carrasco (Correa 68), Gabi, Savić, Lucas Hernández, Gameiro (Fernando Torres 57). Coach: Diego Simeone (ARG)
H 2-1 *Saúl Ñíguez (12), Griezmann (16p)*
Oblak, Godín, Filipe Luís, Koke (Correa 76), Griezmann, Saúl Ñíguez, Fernando Torres (Gameiro 56), Carrasco, Gabi, Savić, Giménez (Partey 56). Coach: Diego Simeone (ARG)

Sevilla FC

Group H
Match 1 - Juventus (ITA)
A 0-0
Sergio Rico, Kranevitter (Mariano 78), Iborra, N'Zonzi, Sarabia (Correa 64), Sergio Escudero, Vitolo, Pareja, Vázquez (Daniel Carriço 90+1), Rami, Mercado. Coach: Jorge Sampaoli (ARG)
Match 2 - Olympique Lyonnais (FRA)
H 1-0 *Ben Yedder (53)*
Sergio Rico, Mariano, Vietto, Nasri, Ben Yedder (Sarabia 82), N'Zonzi, Sergio Escudero, Vitolo, Pareja, Vázquez (Iborra 59), Mercado (Kolodziejczak 87). Coach: Jorge Sampaoli (ARG)
Match 3 - GNK Dinamo Zagreb (CRO)
A 1-0 *Nasri (37)*
Sergio Rico, Mariano, Vietto (Ben Yedder 65), Nasri, N'Zonzi, Sergio Escudero, Vitolo, Pareja, Vázquez (Iborra 89), Rami, Mercado. Coach: Jorge Sampaoli (ARG)
Match 4 - GNK Dinamo Zagreb (CRO)
H 4-0 *Vietto (31), Sergio Escudero (66), N'Zonzi (80), Ben Yedder (87)*
Sergio Rico, Mariano, Kranevitter, Vietto, N'Zonzi, Sergio Escudero, Ganso (Kiyotake 75), Vitolo (Sarabia 75), Vázquez (Ben Yedder 61), Rami, Mercado. Coach: Jorge Sampaoli (ARG)
Match 5 - Juventus (ITA)
H 1-3 *Pareja (9)*
Sergio Rico, Mariano (Kranevitter 76), Iborra, Vietto (Sarabia 46), N'Zonzi, Sergio Escudero, Vitolo, Pareja, Vázquez, Rami, Mercado. Coach: Jorge Sampaoli (ARG)
Red card: Vázquez 36
Match 6 - Olympique Lyonnais (FRA)
A 0-0
Sergio Rico, Mariano, Iborra, Nasri (Kranevitter 87), N'Zonzi, Sarabia (Ben Yedder 65), Sergio Escudero, Vitolo, Pareja, Rami, Mercado. Coach: Jorge Sampaoli (ARG)

Round of 16 - Leicester City FC (ENG)
H 2-1 *Sarabia (25), Correa (62)*
Sergio Rico, Mariano, Nasri, Correa (Iborra 63), N'Zonzi, Jovetić, Sarabia, Sergio Escudero, Vitolo, Rami, Lenglet (Daniel Carriço 55). Coach: Jorge Sampaoli (ARG)
A 0-2
Sergio Rico, Iborra, Nasri, Ben Yedder (Correa 68), N'Zonzi, Sarabia (Jovetić 46), Sergio Escudero, Vitolo, Pareja, Rami, Mercado (Mariano 46). Coach: Jorge Sampaoli (ARG)
Red card: Nasri 74

Villarreal CF

Play-offs - AS Monaco FC (FRA)
H 1-2 *Pato (36)*
Asenjo, Mario Gaspar, José Ángel, N'Diaye, Musacchio, Pato, Trigueros, Samu Castillejo, Soriano, Bruno Soriano, Borré (Mario González 76). Coach: Fran Escribá (ESP)
A 0-1
Asenjo, Mario Gaspar, José Ángel (Jaume Costa 67), Musacchio, Víctor Ruiz, Pato, Trigueros, Samu Castillejo, Soriano (N'Diaye 80), Bruno Soriano, Borré (Suárez 75). Coach: Fran Escribá (ESP)

Group L
Match 1 - FC Zürich (SUI)
H 2-1 *Pato (28), Jonathan dos Santos (45+1)*
Andrés Fernández, José Ángel, N'Diaye, Víctor Ruiz, Cheryshev (Soriano 80), Jonathan dos Santos (Samu Castillejo 71), Pato, Álvaro González, Bruno Soriano, Rukavina, Borré (Sansone 67). Coach: Fran Escribá (ESP)
Match 2 - FC Steaua Bucureşti (ROU)
A 1-1 *Borré (9)*
Andrés Fernández, José Ángel, N'Diaye, Musacchio, Cheryshev (Soriano 73), Jonathan dos Santos, Pato (Samu Castillejo 63), Bruno Soriano, Rukavina, Bonera, Borré (Bakambu 82). Coach: Fran Escribá (ESP)
Match 3 - Osmanlıspor (TUR)
A 2-2 *N'Diaye (56), Pato (74)*
Andrés Fernández, José Ángel, N'Diaye (Sansone 82), Jonathan dos Santos (Soriano 70), Pato, Álvaro González, Samu Castillejo, Bruno Soriano, Rukavina, Bonera, Borré (Bakambu 65). Coach: Fran Escribá (ESP)
Match 4 - Osmanlıspor (TUR)
H 1-2 *Rodri Hernández (48)*
Andrés Fernández, José Ángel, Víctor Ruiz, Cheryshev (Samu Castillejo 69), Jonathan dos Santos (Sansone 80), Álvaro González, Rodri Hernández, Bakambu, Bruno Soriano, Rukavina, Borré (Pato 62). Coach: Fran Escribá (ESP)
Match 5 - FC Zürich (SUI)
A 1-1 *Bruno Soriano (14)*
Asenjo, José Ángel, Musacchio, Víctor Ruiz, Cheryshev (Samu Castillejo 70), Jonathan dos Santos, Pato (Sansone 78), Trigueros, Bakambu (Rodri Hernández 82), Bruno Soriano, Rukavina. Coach: Fran Escribá (ESP)
Match 6 - FC Steaua Bucureşti (ROU)
H 2-1 *Sansone (16), Trigueros (88)*
Asenjo, Mario Gaspar, Musacchio (Álvaro González 39), Víctor Ruiz, Jonathan dos Santos, Jaume Costa, Trigueros, Bakambu (Rodri Hernández 85), Sansone (Borré 80), Soriano, Bruno Soriano. Coach: Fran Escribá (ESP)

Round of 32 - AS Roma (ITA)
H 0-4
Asenjo, Mario Gaspar, Musacchio, Víctor Ruiz, Jonathan dos Santos, Jaume Costa, Trigueros, Bakambu (Adrián López 66), Sansone (Borré 82), Samu Castillejo (Cheryshev 67), Bruno Soriano. Coach: Fran Escribá (ESP)
A 1-0 *Borré (15)*
Andrés Fernández, José Ángel, Cheryshev (Bakambu 73), Soldado (Adrián López 66), Álvaro González, Rodri Hernández, Soriano, Bruno Soriano (Jonathan dos Santos 77), Rukavina, Bonera, Borré. Coach: Fran Escribá (ESP)

Athletic Club

Group F
Match 1 - US Sassuolo Calcio (ITA)
A 0-3
Iago Herrerín, Laporte, San José, Beñat Etxebarria, Muniain (Susaeta 54), Iñaki Williams (Aduriz 54), De Marcos, Sabín Merino, Raúl García, Balenziaga (Lekue 77), Yeray Álvarez. Coach: Ernesto Valverde (ESP)
Match 2 - SK Rapid Wien (AUT)
H 1-0 *Beñat Etxebarria (59)*
Iago Herrerín, Laporte, Beñat Etxebarria (Mikel Rico 80), Iturraspe (San José 59), Iñaki Williams, Susaeta (Muniain 59), De Marcos, Aduriz, Raúl García, Balenziaga, Yeray Álvarez. Coach: Ernesto Valverde (ESP)
Match 3 - KRC Genk (BEL)
A 0-2
Iago Herrerín, Laporte, San José (Elustondo 80), Iturraspe, Muniain, Iñaki Williams (Susaeta 80), Lekue, Aduriz, Raúl García, Balenziaga (Saborit 46), Yeray Álvarez. Coach: Ernesto Valverde (ESP)
Match 4 - KRC Genk (BEL)
H 5-3 *Aduriz (8, 24p, 44p, 74, 90+4p)*
Iago Herrerín, Laporte, Iturraspe, Muniain (Sabín Merino 83), Susaeta (Iñaki Williams 76), Mikel Rico, De Marcos, Aduriz, Raúl García (Eraso 88), Balenziaga, Yeray Álvarez. Coach: Ernesto Valverde (ESP)
Match 5 - US Sassuolo Calcio (ITA)
H 3-2 *Raúl García (10), Aduriz (58), Lekue (79)*
Iago Herrerín, Laporte, San José, Beñat Etxebarria, Muniain (Mikel Rico 71), Iñaki Williams (Bóveda 61), Lekue, Aduriz (Sabín Merino 88), Raúl García, Balenziaga, Yeray Álvarez. Coach: Ernesto Valverde (ESP)
Match 6 - SK Rapid Wien (AUT)
A 1-1 *Saborit (84)*
Gorka Iraizoz, Eraso (Susaeta 74), Muniain, Iñaki Williams, Vesga, Lekue, Etxeita, Mikel Rico (Beñat Etxebarria 64), Sabín Merino (Villalibre 77), Saborit, Yeray Álvarez. Coach: Ernesto Valverde (ESP)

Round of 32 - APOEL FC (CYP)
H 3-2 *Merkis (38og), Aduriz (61), Iñaki Williams (72)*
Gorka Iraizoz, Laporte, Beñat Etxebarria, Iturraspe (San José 57), Muniain, Iñaki Williams (Susaeta 78), De Marcos, Aduriz, Raúl García, Balenziaga (Lekue 57), Álvarez. Coach: Ernesto Valverde (ESP)
A 0-2
Gorka Iraizoz, San José, Beñat Etxebarria, Muniain, Iñaki Williams, Susaeta (Villalibre 57), Etxeita (Iturraspe 70), De Marcos (Merino 79), Raúl García, Balenziaga, Álvarez. Coach: Ernesto Valverde (ESP)
Red card: Iturraspe 90

RC Celta de Vigo

Group G

Match 1 - R. Standard de Liège (BEL)
A 1-1 *Rossi (13)*
Sergio Álvarez, David Costas, Radoja, Hernández, Sisto (Bongonda 82), Lemos, Naranjo (Wass 71), Jonny, Sergi Gómez, Cabral, Rossi (Iago Aspas 86). Coach: Eduardo Berizzo (ARG)

Match 2 - Panathinaikos FC (GRE)
H 2-0 *Guidetti (84), Wass (89)*
Sergio Álvarez, Hugo Mallo, Fontàs, Díaz, Hernández, Guidetti, Naranjo (Sisto 60), Jonny, Cabral, Señé (Wass 71), Rossi (Iago Aspas 79). Coach: Eduardo Berizzo (ARG)

Match 3 - AFC Ajax (NED)
H 2-2 *Fontàs (29), Orellana (82)*
Rubén Blanco, Fontàs, Radoja, Hernández (Wass 76), Guidetti (Rossi 73), Sisto, Lemos (Orellana 63), Sergi Gómez, Planas, Señé, Roncaglia. Coach: Eduardo Berizzo (ARG)

Match 4 - AFC Ajax (NED)
A 2-3 *Guidetti (79), Iago Aspas (86)*
Rubén Blanco, Hugo Mallo, Fontàs, Díaz, Radoja, Bongonda, Lemos (Wass 54), Sergi Gómez, Planas, Señé (Iago Aspas 72), Rossi (Guidetti 78). Coach: Eduardo Berizzo (ARG)

Match 5 - R. Standard de Liège (BEL)
H 1-1 *Iago Aspas (8)*
Rubén Blanco, Hugo Mallo, Díaz (Radoja 62), Hernández, Guidetti, Iago Aspas, Sisto, Wass (Rossi 84), Jonny (Sergi Gómez 82), Cabral, Roncaglia. Coach: Eduardo Berizzo (ARG)
Red card: Iago Aspas 90+4

Match 6 - Panathinaikos FC (GRE)
A 2-0 *Guidetti (4), Orellana (76p)*
Rubén Blanco, Hugo Mallo, Radoja, Bongonda, Hernández, Guidetti (Sergi Gómez 90), Orellana (Sisto 82), Wass (Díaz 63), Jonny, Cabral, Roncaglia. Coach: Eduardo Berizzo (ARG)

Round of 32 - FC Shakhtar Donetsk (UKR)
H 0-1
Sergio Álvarez, Hugo Mallo, Radoja (Jozabed 74), Bongonda (Sisto 58), Hernández, Guidetti (Rossi 84), Iago Aspas, Wass, Jonny, Cabral, Roncaglia. Coach: Eduardo Berizzo (ARG)
A 2-0 (aet) *Iago Aspas (90+1p), Cabral (108)*
Sergio Álvarez, Hugo Mallo, Fontàs, Hernández, Guidetti, Iago Aspas, Sisto (Rossi 85), Wass (Bongonda 80), Jonny, Cabral, Roncaglia (Jozabed 58). Coach: Eduardo Berizzo (ARG)

Round of 16 - FC Krasnodar (RUS)
H 2-1 *Wass (50), Beauvue (90)*
Sergio Álvarez, Hugo Mallo, Fontàs, Díaz, Radoja, Guidetti (Beauvue 78), Iago Aspas, Sisto, Wass (Jozabed 70), Jonny, Cabral. Coach: Eduardo Berizzo (ARG)
A 2-0 *Hugo Mallo (52), Iago Aspas (80)*
Sergio Álvarez, Hugo Mallo, Fontàs, Radoja, Hernández (Beauvue 86), Guidetti, Iago Aspas (Roncaglia 82), Sisto, Wass (Jozabed 74), Jonny, Cabral. Coach: Eduardo Berizzo (ARG)

Quarter-finals - KRC Genk (BEL)
H 3-2 *Sisto (15), Iago Aspas (18), Guidetti (38)*
Sergio Álvarez, Hugo Mallo, Fontàs, Radoja, Hernández, Guidetti (Beauvue 67), Iago Aspas, Sisto, Wass (Jozabed 78), Jonny, Cabral. Coach: Eduardo Berizzo (ARG)
A 1-1 *Sisto (63)*
Sergio Álvarez, Hugo Mallo, Fontàs, Radoja, Hernández, Guidetti (Beauvue 42; Roncaglia 91), Iago Aspas, Sisto, Wass (Jozabed 80), Jonny, Cabral. Coach: Eduardo Berizzo (ARG)

Semi-finals - Manchester United FC (ENG)
H 0-1
Sergio Álvarez, Hugo Mallo (Beauvue 90+1), Radoja, Hernández, Guidetti, Iago Aspas, Sisto, Wass (Jozabed 74), Jonny, Cabral, Roncaglia. Coach: Eduardo Berizzo (ARG)
A 1-1 *Roncaglia (85)*
Sergio Álvarez, Hugo Mallo, Radoja (Bongonda 68), Hernández, Guidetti, Iago Aspas, Sisto (Beauvue 80), Wass (Jozabed 46), Jonny, Cabral, Roncaglia. Coach: Eduardo Berizzo (ARG)
Red card: Roncaglia 88

DOMESTIC LEAGUE CLUB-BY-CLUB

Deportivo Alavés

1921 • Mendizorrotza (19,840) • deportivoalaves.com
Coach: Mauricio Pellegrino (ARG)

Date		Opponent		Score	Scorers
2016					
21/08	a	Atlético	D	1-1	*Manu García*
28/08	h	Sporting	D	0-0	
10/09	a	Barcelona	W	2-1	*Deyverson, Ibai Gómez*
19/09	h	Deportivo	D	0-0	
22/09	a	Valencia	L	1-2	*Toquero*
26/09	h	Granada	W	3-1	*Édgar Méndez, Camarasa, Deyverson*
01/10	a	Sevilla	L	1-2	*Laguardia*
16/10	h	Málaga	D	1-1	*Deyverson*
22/10	a	Real Sociedad	L	0-3	
29/10	h	Real Madrid	L	1-4	*Deyverson*
05/11	a	Osasuna	W	1-0	*Santos (p)*
20/11	h	Espanyol	L	0-1	
27/11	a	Villarreal	W	2-0	*Ibai Gómez, Camarasa*
04/12	h	Las Palmas	D	1-1	*Alexis*
11/12	a	Eibar	D	0-0	
16/12	h	Betis	W	1-0	*Deyverson*
2017					
08/01	a	Athletic	D	0-0	
15/01	a	Celta	L	0-1	
21/01	h	Leganés	D	2-2	*Laguardia, Édgar Méndez*
28/01	h	Atlético	D	0-0	
05/02	a	Sporting	W	4-2	*Sobrino, Santos (p), Édgar Méndez (p), Alexis*
11/02	h	Barcelona	L	0-6	
18/02	a	Deportivo	W	1-0	*Manu García (p)*
25/02	h	Valencia	W	2-1	*Ibai Gómez, Katai*
01/03	a	Granada	L	1-2	*Camarasa*
06/03	h	Sevilla	D	1-1	*Katai*
11/03	a	Málaga	W	2-1	*Feddal, Édgar Méndez*
18/03	h	Real Sociedad	W	1-0	*Deyverson*
02/04	a	Real Madrid	L	0-3	
05/04	h	Osasuna	L	0-1	
08/04	a	Espanyol	L	0-1	
17/04	h	Villarreal	W	2-1	*Ibai Gómez, Rodrigo Ely*
23/04	a	Las Palmas	D	1-1	*Ibai Gómez*
27/04	h	Eibar	D	0-0	
30/04	a	Betis	W	4-1	*Krstičić, Sobrino, Santos, Katai*
07/05	h	Athletic	W	1-0	*Theo Hernández*
14/05	h	Celta	W	3-1	*Manu García, Feddal, Deyverson*
20/05	a	Leganés	D	1-1	*Krstičić*

No	Name	Nat	DoB	Pos	Aps	(s)	Gls
4	Alexis		04/08/85	D	19	(5)	2
8	Víctor Camarasa		28/05/94	M	28	(3)	3
20	Deyverson	BRA	08/05/91	A	29	(3)	7
17	Édgar Méndez		30/04/91	A	18	(9)	4
14	Cristian Espinoza	ARG	03/04/95	A	1	(5)	
24	Zouhair Feddal	MAR	01/01/89	D	27		2
11	Ibai Gómez		11/11/89	A	23	(6)	5
25	Aleksandar Katai	SRB	06/02/91	M	8	(12)	3
21	Kiko Femenía		02/02/91	D	28	(3)	
23	Nenad Krstičić	SRB	03/07/90	M	9	(5)	2
5	Víctor Laguardia		05/11/89	D	24	(2)	2
6	Marcos Llorente		30/01/95	M	31	(1)	
19	Manu García		26/04/86	M	23	(2)	3
13	Adrián Ortolá		20/08/93	G	2		
1	Fernando Pacheco		18/05/92	G	36		
2	Aleksandar Pantić	SRB	11/04/92	D	1	(1)	
3	Raúl García		30/11/89	D	14	(4)	
2	Rodrigo Ely	BRA	03/11/93	D	8	(2)	1
10	Óscar Romero	PAR	04/07/92	M	4	(9)	
9	Christian Santos	VEN	24/03/88	A	8	(13)	3
7	Rubén Sobrino		01/06/92	A	5	(6)	2
15	Theo Hernández	FRA	06/10/97	D	30	(2)	1
18	Gaizka Toquero		09/08/84	M	15	(8)	1
16	Daniel Torres	COL	15/11/89	M	17	(4)	
22	Carlos Vigaray		07/09/94	D	10	(9)	

SPAIN

Athletic Club

1898 • Nuevo San Mamés (53,332) • athletic-club.eus

Major honours
Spanish League (8) 1930, 1931, 1934, 1936, 1943, 1956, 1983, 1984; Spanish Cup (23) 1903, 1904, 1910, 1911, 1914, 1915, 1916, 1921, 1923, 1930, 1931, 1932, 1933, 1943, 1944, 1945, 1950, 1955, 1956, 1958, 1969, 1973, 1984

Coach: Ernesto Valverde

2016

Date		Opponent		Score	Scorers
21/08	a	Sporting	L	1-2	*Viguera*
28/08	h	Barcelona	L	0-1	
11/09	a	Deportivo	W	1-0	*Raúl García*
18/09	h	Valencia	W	2-1	*Aduriz 2*
21/09	a	Granada	W	2-1	*Raúl García, Laporte*
24/09	h	Sevilla	W	3-1	*San José, Balenziaga, Aduriz (p)*
02/10	a	Málaga	L	1-2	*Aduriz*
16/10	h	Real Sociedad	W	3-2	*Muniain, Aduriz, Iñaki Williams*
23/10	a	Real Madrid	L	1-2	*Sabín Merino*
30/10	h	Osasuna	D	1-1	*Raúl García*
06/11	a	Espanyol	D	0-0	
20/11	h	Villarreal	W	1-0	*Raúl García*
28/11	a	Las Palmas	L	1-3	*Raúl García (p)*
04/12	h	Eibar	W	3-1	*Beñat, Iñaki Williams, Muniain*
11/12	a	Betis	L	0-1	
19/12	h	Celta	W	2-1	*Aduriz (p), San José*

2017

Date		Opponent		Score	Scorers
08/01	h	Alavés	D	0-0	
14/01	a	Leganés	D	0-0	
22/01	h	Atlético	D	2-2	*Lekue, De Marcos*
29/01	h	Sporting	W	2-1	*Muniain, Aduriz (p)*
04/02	a	Barcelona	L	0-3	
11/02	h	Deportivo	W	2-1	*Muniain, Aduriz*
19/02	a	Valencia	L	0-2	
26/02	h	Granada	W	3-1	*Susaeta, Lekue, San José*
02/03	a	Sevilla	L	0-1	
05/03	h	Málaga	W	1-0	*Raúl García (p)*
12/03	a	Real Sociedad	W	2-0	*Raúl García (p), Iñaki Williams*
18/03	h	Real Madrid	L	1-2	*Aduriz*
01/04	a	Osasuna	W	2-1	*Aduriz, Iñaki Williams*
04/04	h	Espanyol	W	2-0	*Aduriz 2 (1p)*
07/04	a	Villarreal	L	1-3	*Laporte*
14/04	h	Las Palmas	W	5-1	*San José, Muniain 2, Aduriz 2*
24/04	a	Eibar	W	1-0	*Raúl García*
27/04	h	Betis	W	2-1	*Aduriz (p), Muniain*
30/04	a	Celta	W	3-0	*Raúl García 2, Mikel Rico*
07/05	a	Alavés	L	0-1	
14/05	h	Leganés	D	1-1	*Aduriz*
21/05	a	Atlético	L	1-3	*Iñaki Williams*

No	Name	Nat	DoB	Pos	Aps	(s)	Gls
20	Aritz Aduriz		11/02/81	A	27	(5)	16
24	Mikel Balenziaga		29/02/88	D	33		1
7	Beñat Etxebarria		19/02/87	M	28	(4)	1
2	Eneko Bóveda		14/12/88	D	18	(1)	
18	Óscar De Marcos		14/04/89	D	24	(3)	1
3	Gorka Elustondo		18/03/87	M	1	(1)	
5	Javier Eraso		22/03/90	M	4	(3)	
16	Xabier Etxeita		31/10/87	D	7	(3)	
1	Gorka Iraizoz		06/03/81	G	15	(1)	
11	Iñaki Williams		15/06/94	A	31	(7)	5
8	Ander Iturraspe		08/03/89	M	12	(12)	
26	Kepa Arrizabalaga		03/10/94	G	23		
4	Aymeric Laporte	FRA	27/05/94	D	33		2
15	Iñigo Lekue		04/05/93	D	17	(8)	2
17	Mikel Rico		04/11/84	M	4	(14)	1
10	Iker Muniain		19/12/92	M	28	(7)	7
22	Raúl García		11/07/86	M	34	(2)	10
19	Sabín Merino		04/01/92	A	5	(8)	1
25	Enric Saborit		27/04/92	D	5	(4)	
6	Mikel San José		30/05/89	M	30	(5)	4
14	Markel Susaeta		14/12/87	M	11	(15)	1
12	Mikel Vesga		08/04/93	M	3	(3)	
21	Borja Viguera		26/03/87	A		(1)	1
28	Asier Villalibre		30/09/97	A		(6)	
27	Yeray Álvarez		24/01/95	D	25	(1)	

Club Atlético de Madrid

1903 • Vicente Calderón (54,851) • atleticodemadrid.com

Major honours
UEFA Cup Winners' Cup (1) 1962; UEFA Europa League (2) 2010, 2012; UEFA Super Cup (2) 2010, 2012; European/South American Cup (1) 1974; Spanish League (10) 1940, 1941, 1950, 1951, 1966, 1970, 1973, 1977, 1996, 2014; Spanish Cup (10) 1960, 1961, 1965, 1972, 1976, 1985, 1991, 1992, 1996, 2013

Coach: Diego Simeone (ARG)

2016

Date		Opponent		Score	Scorers
21/08	h	Alavés	D	1-1	*Gameiro (p)*
27/08	a	Leganés	D	0-0	
10/09	a	Celta	W	4-0	*Koke, Griezmann 2, Correa*
17/09	h	Sporting	W	5-0	*Griezmann 2, Gameiro, Fernando Torres 2 (1p)*
21/09	a	Barcelona	D	1-1	*Correa*
25/09	h	Deportivo	W	1-0	*Griezmann*
02/10	a	Valencia	W	2-0	*Griezmann, Gameiro*
15/10	h	Granada	W	7-1	*Carrasco 3, Gaitán 2, Correa, Tiago*
23/10	a	Sevilla	L	0-1	
29/10	h	Málaga	W	4-2	*Carrasco 2, Gameiro 2*
05/11	a	Real Sociedad	L	0-2	
19/11	h	Real Madrid	L	0-3	
27/11	a	Osasuna	W	3-0	*Godín, Gameiro, Carrasco*
03/12	h	Espanyol	D	0-0	
12/12	a	Villarreal	L	0-3	
17/12	h	Las Palmas	W	1-0	*Saúl Ñíguez*

2017

Date		Opponent		Score	Scorers
07/01	a	Eibar	W	2-0	*Saúl Ñíguez, Griezmann*
14/01	h	Betis	W	1-0	*Gaitán*
22/01	a	Athletic	D	2-2	*Koke, Griezmann*
28/01	a	Alavés	D	0-0	
04/02	h	Leganés	W	2-0	*Fernando Torres 2*
12/02	h	Celta	W	3-2	*Fernando Torres, Carrasco, Griezmann*
18/02	a	Sporting	W	4-1	*Carrasco, Gameiro 3*
26/02	h	Barcelona	L	1-2	*Godín*
02/03	a	Deportivo	D	1-1	*Griezmann*
05/03	h	Valencia	W	3-0	*Griezmann 2, Gameiro*
11/03	a	Granada	W	1-0	*Griezmann*
19/03	h	Sevilla	W	3-1	*Godín, Griezmann, Koke*
01/04	a	Málaga	W	2-0	*Koke, Filipe Luís*
04/04	h	Real Sociedad	W	1-0	*Filipe Luís*
08/04	a	Real Madrid	D	1-1	*Griezmann*
15/04	h	Osasuna	W	3-0	*Carrasco 2, Filipe Luís*
22/04	a	Espanyol	W	1-0	*Griezmann*
25/04	h	Villarreal	L	0-1	
29/04	a	Las Palmas	W	5-0	*Gameiro 2, Saúl Ñíguez, Partey, Fernando Torres*
06/05	h	Eibar	W	1-0	*Saúl Ñíguez*
14/05	a	Betis	D	1-1	*Savić*
21/05	h	Athletic	W	3-1	*Fernando Torres 2, Correa*

No	Name	Nat	DoB	Pos	Aps	(s)	Gls
10	Yannick Carrasco	BEL	04/09/93	M	27	(8)	10
17	Alessio Cerci	ITA	23/07/87	M		(1)	
11	Ángel Correa	ARG	09/03/95	A	10	(20)	4
12	Augusto Fernández	ARG	10/04/86	M	2	(1)	
9	Fernando Torres		20/03/84	A	13	(18)	8
3	Filipe Luís	BRA	09/08/85	D	34		3
14	Gabi		10/07/83	M	33	(1)	
23	Nicolás Gaitán	ARG	23/02/88	M	11	(11)	3
21	Kevin Gameiro	FRA	09/05/87	A	21	(9)	12
24	José María Giménez	URU	20/01/95	D	12	(5)	
2	Diego Godín	URU	16/02/86	D	30	(1)	3
7	Antoine Griezmann	FRA	21/03/91	A	36		16
20	Juanfran		09/01/85	D	21	(2)	
6	Koke		08/01/92	M	36		4
19	Lucas Hernández	FRA	14/02/96	D	13	(2)	
1	Miguel Ángel Moyá		02/04/84	G	8	(1)	
13	Jan Oblak	SVN	07/01/93	G	30		
22	Thomas Partey	GHA	13/06/93	M	6	(10)	1
8	Saúl Ñíguez		21/11/94	M	29	(4)	4
15	Stefan Savić	MNE	08/01/91	D	30	(2)	1
5	Tiago	POR	02/05/81	M	5	(7)	1
16	Šime Vrsaljko	CRO	10/01/92	D	11	(3)	

FC Barcelona

1899 • Camp Nou (98,772) • fcbarcelona.com

Major honours
European Champion Clubs' Cup/UEFA Champions League (5) 1992, 2006, 2009, 2011, 2015; UEFA Cup Winners' Cup (4) 1979, 1982, 1989, 1997; Inter Cities Fairs Cup (3) 1958, 1960, 1966; UEFA Super Cup (5) 1992, 1997, 2009, 2011, 2015; FIFA Club World Cup (3) 2009, 2011, 2015; Spanish League (24) 1929, 1945, 1948, 1949, 1952, 1953, 1959, 1960, 1974, 1985, 1991, 1992, 1993, 1994, 1998, 1999, 2005, 2006, 2009, 2010, 2011, 2013, 2015, 2016; Spanish Cup (29) 1910, 1912, 1913, 1920, 1922, 1925, 1926, 1928, 1942, 1951, 1952, 1953, 1957, 1959, 1963, 1968, 1971, 1978, 1981, 1983, 1988, 1990, 1997, 1998, 2009, 2012, 2015, 2016, 2017

Coach: Luis Enrique

2016

Date		Opponent		Score	Scorers
20/08	h	Betis	W	6-2	*Arda, Messi 2, Suárez 3*
28/08	a	Athletic	W	1-0	*Rakitić*
10/09	h	Alavés	L	1-2	*Mathieu*
17/09	a	Leganés	W	5-1	*Messi 2 (1p), Suárez, Neymar, Rafinha*
21/09	h	Atlético	D	1-1	*Rakitić*
24/09	a	Sporting	W	5-0	*Suárez, Rafinha, Neymar 2, Arda*
02/10	a	Celta	L	3-4	*Piqué 2, Neymar (p)*
15/10	h	Deportivo	W	4-0	*Rafinha 2, Suárez, Messi*
22/10	a	Valencia	W	3-2	*Messi 2 (1p), Suárez*
29/10	h	Granada	W	1-0	*Rafinha*
06/11	a	Sevilla	W	2-1	*Messi, Suárez*
19/11	h	Málaga	D	0-0	
27/11	a	Real Sociedad	D	1-1	*Messi*
03/12	h	Real Madrid	D	1-1	*Suárez*
10/12	a	Osasuna	W	3-0	*Suárez, Messi 2*
18/12	h	Espanyol	W	4-1	*Suárez 2, Jordi Alba, Messi*

2017

Date		Opponent		Score	Scorers
08/01	a	Villarreal	D	1-1	*Messi*
14/01	h	Las Palmas	W	5-0	*Suárez 2, Messi, Arda, Aleix Vidal*
22/01	a	Eibar	W	4-0	*Denis Suárez, Messi, Suárez, Neymar*
29/01	a	Betis	D	1-1	*Suárez*
04/02	h	Athletic	W	3-0	*Paco Alcácer, Messi, Aleix Vidal*
11/02	a	Alavés	W	6-0	*Suárez 2, Neymar, Messi, og (Alexis), Rakitić*
19/02	h	Leganés	W	2-1	*Messi 2 (1p)*
26/02	a	Atlético	W	2-1	*Rafinha, Messi*
01/03	h	Sporting	W	6-1	*Messi, Suárez 2, Paco Alcácer, Neymar, Rakitić*
04/03	h	Celta	W	5-0	*Messi 2, Neymar, Rakitić, Umtiti*
12/03	a	Deportivo	L	1-2	*Suárez*
19/03	h	Valencia	W	4-2	*Suárez, Messi 2 (1p), André Gomes*
02/04	a	Granada	W	4-1	*Suárez, Paco Alcácer, Rakitić, Neymar*
05/04	h	Sevilla	W	3-0	*Suárez, Messi 2*
08/04	a	Málaga	L	0-2	
15/04	h	Real Sociedad	W	3-2	*Messi 2, Paco Alcácer*
23/04	a	Real Madrid	W	3-2	*Messi 2, Rakitić*
26/04	h	Osasuna	W	7-1	*Messi 2, André Gomes 2, Paco Alcácer 2, Mascherano (p)*
29/04	a	Espanyol	W	3-0	*Suárez 2, Rakitić*
06/05	h	Villarreal	W	4-1	*Neymar, Messi 2 (1p), Suárez*
14/05	a	Las Palmas	W	4-1	*Neymar 3, Suárez*
21/05	h	Eibar	W	4-2	*og (Juncà), Suárez, Messi 2 (1p)*

No	Name	Nat	DoB	Pos	Aps	(s)	Gls
22	Aleix Vidal		21/08/89	D	5	(1)	2
28	Carles Aleñá		05/01/98	M		(3)	
21	André Gomes	POR	30/07/93	M	17	(12)	3
7	Arda Turan	TUR	30/01/87	M	14	(4)	3
13	Claudio Bravo	CHI	13/04/83	G	1		
5	Sergio Busquets		16/07/88	M	33		
13	Jasper Cillessen	NED	22/04/89	G	1		
6	Denis Suárez		06/01/94	M	12	(14)	1
19	Lucas Digne	FRA	20/07/93	D	14	(3)	
8	Andrés Iniesta		11/05/84	M	13	(10)	
18	Jordi Alba		21/03/89	D	21	(5)	1
33	Marlon	BRA	07/09/95	D	2		
14	Javier Mascherano	ARG	08/06/84	D	20	(5)	1
24	Jérémy Mathieu	FRA	29/10/83	D	12	(1)	1
10	Lionel Messi	ARG	24/06/87	A	32	(2)	37
17	Munir El Haddadi		01/09/95	A		(1)	
11	Neymar	BRA	05/02/92	A	30		13
17	Paco Alcácer		30/08/93	A	6	(13)	6
3	Gerard Piqué		02/02/87	D	25		2
12	Rafinha	BRA	12/02/93	M	14	(4)	6
4	Ivan Rakitić	CRO	10/03/88	M	26	(6)	8
20	Sergi Roberto		07/02/92	D	26	(6)	
9	Luis Suárez	URU	24/01/87	A	34	(1)	29
1	Marc-André ter Stegen	GER	30/04/92	G	36		
23	Samuel Umtiti	FRA	14/11/93	D	24	(1)	1

Real Betis Balompié

1907 • Benito Villamarín (43,500) • realbetisbalompie.es

Major honours
Spanish League (1) 1935; Spanish Cup (2) 1977, 2005

Coach: Gustavo Poyet (URU); (11/11/16) Víctor Sánchez; (10/05/17) (Alexis Trujillo)

2016

Date		Opponent		Score	Scorers
20/08	a	Barcelona	L	2-6	*Rubén Castro 2*
26/08	h	Deportivo	D	0-0	
11/09	a	Valencia	W	3-2	*Rubén Castro 2, Joaquín*
16/09	h	Granada	D	2-2	*Álex Alegría 2*
20/09	a	Sevilla	L	0-1	
23/09	h	Málaga	W	1-0	*Joaquín*
30/09	a	Real Sociedad	L	0-1	
15/10	h	Real Madrid	L	1-6	*Álvaro Cejudo*
21/10	a	Osasuna	W	2-1	*Joaquín, Gutiérrez*
30/10	h	Espanyol	L	0-1	
06/11	a	Villarreal	L	0-2	
18/11	h	Las Palmas	W	2-0	*Bruno González, Mandi*
25/11	a	Eibar	L	1-3	*Rubén Castro*
04/12	h	Celta	D	3-3	*Rubén Castro (p), Sanabria, Pezzella*
11/12	h	Athletic	W	1-0	*Rubén Castro*
16/12	a	Alavés	L	0-1	

2017

Date		Opponent		Score	Scorers
08/01	h	Leganés	W	2-0	*Rubén Castro, Piccini*
14/01	a	Atlético	L	0-1	
22/01	h	Sporting	D	0-0	
29/01	h	Barcelona	D	1-1	*Álex Alegría*
11/02	h	Valencia	D	0-0	
17/02	a	Granada	L	1-4	*Petros*
25/02	h	Sevilla	L	1-2	*Durmisi*
28/02	a	Málaga	W	2-1	*Martin, Sanabria*
03/03	h	Real Sociedad	L	2-3	*Mandi, Sanabria*
08/03	a	Deportivo	D	1-1	*Piccini*
12/03	a	Real Madrid	L	1-2	*og (Navas)*
18/03	h	Osasuna	W	2-0	*Rafa Navarro, Rubén Castro*
31/03	a	Espanyol	L	1-2	*Rubén Castro (p)*
04/04	h	Villarreal	L	0-1	
09/04	a	Las Palmas	L	1-4	*Rafa Navarro*
16/04	h	Eibar	W	2-0	*Martin, Dani Ceballos*
23/04	a	Celta	W	1-0	*Brašanac*
27/04	a	Athletic	L	1-2	*Rubén Castro*
30/04	h	Alavés	L	1-4	*Rubén Pardo*
08/05	a	Leganés	L	0-4	
14/05	h	Atlético	D	1-1	*Dani Ceballos*
20/05	a	Sporting	D	2-2	*Rubén Castro 2*

No	Name	Nat	DoB	Pos	Aps	(s)	Gls
13	Antonio Adán		13/05/87	G	37		
19	Álex Alegría		10/10/92	A	15	(10)	3
3	Álex Martínez		12/08/90	D	11	(3)	
16	Álvaro Cejudo		29/01/84	M	6	(11)	1
22	Darko Brašanac	SRB	12/02/92	M	19	(6)	1
4	Bruno González		24/05/90	D	15	(1)	1
10	Dani Ceballos		07/08/96	M	24	(6)	2
1	Dani Giménez		30/07/83	G	1		
15	Ryan Donk	NED	30/03/86	M	9	(7)	
14	Riza Durmisi	DEN	08/01/94	D	27		1
21	Fabián Ruiz		03/04/96	M	3	(1)	
6	Felipe Gutiérrez	CHI	08/10/90	M	9	(5)	1
17	Joaquín		21/07/81	A	19	(9)	3
28	José Carlos		10/05/96	D	6		
23	Aïssa Mandi	ALG	22/10/91	D	25	(1)	2
8	Jonas Martin	FRA	09/04/90	M	15	(5)	2
7	Charly Musonda	BEL	15/10/96	M	1	(7)	
11	Matías Nahuel		22/10/96	M		(10)	
5	Petros	BRA	29/05/89	M	24	(8)	1
20	Germán Pezzella	ARG	27/06/91	D	36		1
12	Cristiano Piccini	ITA	26/09/92	D	21	(2)	2
2	Rafa Navarro		23/02/94	D	14	(4)	2
24	Rubén Castro		27/06/81	A	32	(3)	13
7	Rubén Pardo		22/10/92	M	15	(1)	1
9	Antonio Sanabria	PAR	04/03/96	A	16	(6)	3
21	Alin Toşca	ROU	14/03/92	D	17		
18	Roman Zozulya	UKR	17/11/89	A	1	(5)	

RC Celta de Vigo

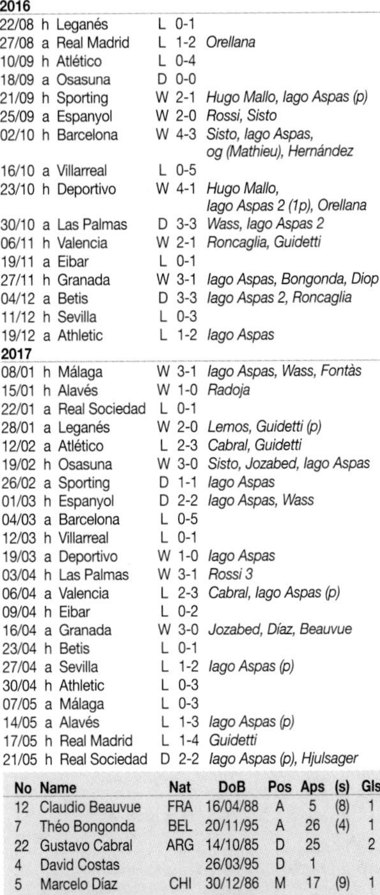

1923 • Balaídos (31,100) • celtavigo.net

Coach: Eduardo Berizzo (ARG)

2016

Date		Opponent		Score	Scorers
22/08	h	Leganés	L	0-1	
27/08	a	Real Madrid	L	1-2	*Orellana*
10/09	h	Atlético	L	0-4	
18/09	a	Osasuna	D	0-0	
21/09	h	Sporting	W	2-1	*Hugo Mallo, Iago Aspas (p)*
25/09	a	Espanyol	W	2-0	*Rossi, Sisto*
02/10	h	Barcelona	W	4-3	*Sisto, Iago Aspas, og (Mathieu), Hernández*
16/10	a	Villarreal	L	0-5	
23/10	h	Deportivo	W	4-1	*Hugo Mallo, Iago Aspas 2 (1p), Orellana*
30/10	a	Las Palmas	D	3-3	*Wass, Iago Aspas 2*
06/11	h	Valencia	W	2-1	*Roncaglia, Guidetti*
19/11	a	Eibar	L	0-1	
27/11	h	Granada	W	3-1	*Iago Aspas, Bongonda, Diop*
04/12	a	Betis	D	3-3	*Iago Aspas 2, Roncaglia*
11/12	h	Sevilla	L	0-3	
19/12	a	Athletic	L	1-2	*Iago Aspas*

2017

Date		Opponent		Score	Scorers
08/01	h	Málaga	W	3-1	*Iago Aspas, Wass, Fontàs*
15/01	h	Alavés	W	1-0	*Radoja*
22/01	a	Real Sociedad	L	0-1	
28/01	a	Leganés	W	2-0	*Lemos, Guidetti (p)*
12/02	a	Atlético	L	2-3	*Cabral, Guidetti*
19/02	h	Osasuna	W	3-0	*Sisto, Jozabed, Iago Aspas*
26/02	a	Sporting	D	1-1	*Iago Aspas*
01/03	h	Espanyol	D	2-2	*Iago Aspas, Wass*
04/03	a	Barcelona	L	0-5	
12/03	h	Villarreal	L	0-1	
19/03	a	Deportivo	W	1-0	*Iago Aspas*
03/04	h	Las Palmas	W	3-1	*Rossi 3*
06/04	a	Valencia	L	2-3	*Cabral, Iago Aspas (p)*
09/04	h	Eibar	L	0-2	
16/04	a	Granada	W	3-0	*Jozabed, Díaz, Beauvue*
23/04	h	Betis	L	0-1	
27/04	a	Sevilla	L	1-2	*Iago Aspas (p)*
30/04	h	Athletic	L	0-3	
07/05	a	Málaga	L	0-3	
14/05	a	Alavés	L	1-3	*Iago Aspas (p)*
17/05	h	Real Madrid	L	1-4	*Guidetti*
21/05	h	Real Sociedad	D	2-2	*Iago Aspas (p), Hjulsager*

No	Name	Nat	DoB	Pos	Aps	(s)	Gls
12	Claudio Beauvue	FRA	16/04/88	A	5	(8)	1
7	Théo Bongonda	BEL	20/11/95	A	26	(4)	1
22	Gustavo Cabral	ARG	14/10/85	D	25		2
4	David Costas		26/03/95	D	1		
5	Marcelo Díaz	CHI	30/12/86	M	17	(9)	1
28	Pape Cheikh Diop		08/08/97	M	5	(11)	1
3	Andreu Fontàs		14/11/89	D	17		1
9	John Guidetti	SWE	15/04/92	A	14	(9)	4
8	Pablo Hernández	ARG	24/10/86	M	20	(6)	1
17	Andrew Hjulsager	DEN	15/01/95	M	3	(4)	1
2	Hugo Mallo		22/06/91	D	22	(1)	2
10	Iago Aspas		01/08/87	A	25	(7)	19
26	Iván Villar		09/07/97	G	1		
19	Jonny		03/03/94	D	23	(7)	
16	Jozabed		08/03/91	M	12	(7)	2
15	Álvaro Lemos		30/03/93	M	5		1
14	Fabián Orellana	CHI	27/01/86	M	6	(1)	2
21	Carles Planas		04/03/91	D	11	(1)	
6	Nemanja Radoja	SRB	06/02/93	M	27	(4)	1
24	Facundo Roncaglia	ARG	10/02/87	D	30	(2)	2
25	Giuseppe Rossi	ITA	01/02/87	A	9	(9)	4
13	Rubén Blanco		25/07/95	G	11		
23	Josep Señé		10/12/91	M	8	(5)	
20	Sergi Gómez		28/03/92	D	21	(4)	
1	Sergio Álvarez		03/08/86	G	26		
11	Pione Sisto	DEN	04/02/95	M	19	(11)	3
18	Daniel Wass	DEN	31/05/89	M	29	(3)	3

RC Deportivo La Coruña

1906 • Riazor (34,600) • rcdeportivo.es

Major honours
Spanish League (1) 2000; Spanish Cup (2) 1995, 2002

Coach: Gaizka Garitano; (27/02/17) Pepe Mel

2016

Date		Opponent		Score	Scorers
19/08	h	Eibar	W	2-1	*Mosquera, Lucas Pérez (p)*
26/08	a	Betis	D	0-0	
11/09	h	Athletic	L	0-1	
19/09	a	Alavés	D	0-0	
22/09	h	Leganés	L	1-2	*Borges*
25/09	a	Atlético	L	0-1	
01/10	h	Sporting	W	2-1	*Borges, Babel*
15/10	a	Barcelona	L	0-4	
23/10	a	Celta	L	1-4	*Albentosa*
31/10	h	Valencia	D	1-1	*Emre*
05/11	a	Granada	D	1-1	*Andone*
19/11	h	Sevilla	L	2-3	*Babel, Andone*
26/11	a	Málaga	L	3-4	*Borges 2 (1p), Andone*
05/12	h	Real Sociedad	W	5-1	*Sidnei, og (Íñigo Martínez), Andone 2, Babel*
10/12	a	Real Madrid	L	2-3	*Joselu 2*
18/12	h	Osasuna	W	2-0	*Andone, Juanfran*

2017

Date		Opponent		Score	Scorers
06/01	a	Espanyol	D	1-1	*Borges*
14/01	h	Villarreal	D	0-0	
20/01	a	Las Palmas	D	1-1	*Andone*
28/01	a	Eibar	L	1-3	*Emre*
11/02	a	Athletic	L	1-2	*Emre*
18/02	h	Alavés	L	0-1	
25/02	a	Leganés	L	0-4	
02/03	h	Atlético	D	1-1	*Andone*
05/03	a	Sporting	W	1-0	*Mosquera*
08/03	h	Betis	D	1-1	*Borges (p)*
12/03	h	Barcelona	W	2-1	*Joselu, Álex Bergantiños*
19/03	h	Celta	L	0-1	
02/04	a	Valencia	L	0-3	
05/04	h	Granada	D	0-0	
08/04	a	Sevilla	L	2-4	*Kakuta 2*
15/04	h	Málaga	W	2-0	*Joselu, Mosquera*
23/04	a	Real Sociedad	L	0-1	
26/04	h	Real Madrid	L	2-6	*Andone, Joselu*
30/04	a	Osasuna	D	2-2	*Guilherme 2*
07/05	h	Espanyol	L	1-2	*Andone*
14/05	a	Villarreal	D	0-0	
20/05	h	Las Palmas	W	3-0	*Andone 2, Gil*

No	Name	Nat	DoB	Pos	Aps	(s)	Gls
6	Raúl Albentosa		07/09/88	D	26	(1)	1
4	Álex Bergantiños		07/06/85	M	6	(2)	1
10	Florin Andone	ROU	11/04/93	A	32	(5)	12
14	Alejandro Arribas		01/05/89	D	20	(3)	
23	Ryan Babel	NED	19/12/86	M	5	(6)	3
22	Celso Borges	CRC	27/05/88	M	30	(4)	6
17	Borja Valle		09/07/92	M	1	(6)	
21	Bruno Gama	POR	15/11/87	M	18	(4)	
30	Edu Expósito		01/08/96	M	1		
8	Emre Çolak	TUR	20/05/91	M	29	(4)	3
19	Fayçal Fajr	MAR	01/08/88	M	14	(10)	
3	Fernando Navarro		25/06/82	D	22	(3)	
11	Carles Gil		22/11/92	M	16	(7)	1
20	Guilherme	BRA	05/04/91	M	26	(4)	2
24	Ola John	NED	19/05/92	M	3	(8)	
7	Joselu	GER	27/03/90	M	9	(11)	5
2	Juanfran		11/09/88	D	34		1
23	Gaël Kakuta	COD	21/06/91	A	8	(2)	2
15	Laure		22/03/85	D	4	(3)	
7	Lucas Pérez		10/09/88	A	1		1
16	Luisinho	POR	05/05/85	D	20	(6)	
1	Germán Lux	ARG	07/06/82	G	25		
9	Marlos Moreno	COL	20/09/96	A	9	(10)	
5	Pedro Mosquera		21/04/88	M	17	(6)	3
28	Óscar Pinchi		17/06/96	M		(1)	
25	Davy Roef	BEL	06/02/94	G	1		
12	Sidnei	BRA	23/06/89	D	29		1
13	Przemysław Tytoń	POL	04/01/87	G	12	(1)	

SD Eibar

1940 • Ipurúa (7,083) • sdeibar.com
Coach: José Luis Mendilíbar

Date		Opponent	Result	Scorers
2016				
19/08	a	Deportivo	L 1-2	*Ramis*
27/08	h	Valencia	W 1-0	*Pedro León*
11/09	a	Granada	W 2-1	*Pedro León, Sergi Enrich*
17/09	h	Sevilla	D 1-1	*Pedro León*
20/09	a	Málaga	L 1-2	*Nano*
24/09	h	Real Sociedad	W 2-0	*og (Illarramendi), Bebé*
02/10	a	Real Madrid	D 1-1	*Fran Rico*
17/10	h	Osasuna	L 2-3	*Escalante, Sergi Enrich*
22/10	a	Espanyol	D 3-3	*Sergi Enrich, og (D Reyes), Kike García*
30/10	h	Villarreal	W 2-1	*Ramis, Pedro León*
05/11	a	Las Palmas	L 0-1	
19/11	h	Celta	W 1-0	*Fran Rico*
25/11	h	Betis	W 3-1	*Pedro León, Sergi Enrich, Kike García*
04/12	a	Athletic	L 1-3	*Sergi Enrich*
11/12	h	Alavés	D 0-0	
18/12	a	Leganés	D 1-1	*Bebé*
2017				
07/01	h	Atlético	L 0-2	
15/01	a	Sporting	W 3-2	*Adrián (p), Pedro León, Luna*
22/01	h	Barcelona	L 0-4	
28/01	h	Deportivo	W 3-1	*Adrián, Sergi Enrich, Lejeune*
04/02	a	Valencia	W 4-0	*Sergi Enrich 2, Adrián (p), Dani García*
13/02	h	Granada	W 4-0	*Adrián (p), Sergi Enrich, Ramis, Pedro León*
18/02	a	Sevilla	L 0-2	
25/02	h	Málaga	W 3-0	*Adrián 2 (1p), Sergi Enrich*
28/02	a	Real Sociedad	D 2-2	*Escalante, Pedro León*
04/03	h	Real Madrid	L 1-4	*Rubén Peña*
13/03	a	Osasuna	D 1-1	*Kike García*
18/03	h	Espanyol	D 1-1	*Kike García*
01/04	a	Villarreal	W 3-2	*Pedro León (p), Kike García, Inui*
06/04	h	Las Palmas	W 3-1	*Bebé, og (Aythami), Adrián (p)*
09/04	a	Celta	W 2-0	*Kike García, Pedro León*
16/04	a	Betis	L 0-2	
24/04	h	Athletic	L 0-1	
27/04	a	Alavés	D 0-0	
30/04	h	Leganés	W 2-0	*Kike García, Sergi Enrich*
06/05	a	Atlético	L 0-1	
14/05	h	Sporting	L 0-1	
21/05	a	Barcelona	L 2-4	*Inui 2*

No	Name	Nat	DoB	Pos	Aps	(s)	Gls
24	Adrián		25/05/88	M	19	(9)	7
18	Anaitz Arbilla		15/05/87	D	17	(5)	
30	Markel Areitio		07/09/96	G		(1)	
25	Bebé	POR	12/07/90	A	8	(12)	3
7	Ander Capa		08/02/92	D	29	(2)	
14	Dani García		24/05/90	M	36		1
5	Gonzalo Escalante	ARG	27/03/93	M	24	(6)	2
16	Fran Rico		03/08/87	M	13	(4)	2
3	Alejandro Gálvez		06/06/89	D	14	(4)	
8	Takashi Inui	JPN	02/06/88	M	26	(2)	3
25	Jota		16/06/91	M	3	(2)	
23	David Juncà		16/11/93	D	7	(2)	
17	Kike García		25/11/89	A	18	(6)	7
20	Florian Lejeune	FRA	20/05/91	D	33	(1)	1
19	Antonio Luna		17/03/91	D	24	(2)	1
15	Mauro dos Santos	ARG	07/07/89	D	8	(3)	
22	Nano		05/02/95	A	1	(5)	1
21	Pedro León		24/11/86	M	34	(2)	10
4	Iván Ramis		25/10/84	D	20	(2)	3
13	Asier Riesgo		06/10/83	G	16		
6	Christian Rivera		09/07/97	M	6	(10)	
11	Rubén Peña		18/07/91	A	9	(19)	1
9	Sergi Enrich		26/02/90	A	31	(7)	11
1	Yoel		28/08/88	G	22	(3)	

RCD Espanyol

1900 • RCDE (40,500) • rcdespanyol.com
Major honours
Spanish Cup (4) 1929, 1940, 2000, 2006
Coach: Quique Sánchez Flores

Date		Opponent	Result	Scorers
2016				
20/08	a	Sevilla	L 4-6	*Piatti, Pérez, Víctor Sánchez, Gerard Moreno*
26/08	h	Málaga	D 2-2	*Gerard Moreno 2*
09/09	a	Real Sociedad	D 1-1	*Piatti*
18/09	h	Real Madrid	L 0-2	
22/09	a	Osasuna	W 2-1	*Léo Baptistão, Gerard Moreno*
25/09	h	Celta	L 0-2	
02/10	h	Villarreal	D 0-0	
14/10	a	Las Palmas	D 0-0	
22/10	h	Eibar	D 3-3	*Pérez, Piatti, Léo Baptistão*
30/10	a	Betis	W 1-0	*D Reyes*
06/11	h	Athletic	D 0-0	
20/11	a	Alavés	W 1-0	*Gerard Moreno*
26/11	h	Leganés	W 3-0	*Gerard Moreno, Piatti 2*
03/12	a	Atlético	D 0-0	
11/12	h	Sporting	W 2-1	*Caicedo, Léo Baptistão*
18/12	a	Barcelona	L 1-4	*David López*
2017				
06/01	h	Deportivo	D 1-1	*Gerard Moreno*
15/01	a	Valencia	L 1-2	*David López*
21/01	h	Granada	W 3-1	*J Reyes, Piatti, Navarro*
29/01	h	Sevilla	W 3-1	*J Reyes (p), Navarro, Gerard Moreno*
04/02	a	Málaga	W 1-0	*Piatti*
10/02	h	Real Sociedad	L 1-2	*Pérez*
18/02	a	Real Madrid	L 0-2	
26/02	h	Osasuna	W 3-0	*Caicedo, Jurado, Gerard Moreno*
01/03	a	Celta	D 2-2	*Gerard Moreno, Piatti*
04/03	a	Villarreal	L 0-2	
10/03	h	Las Palmas	W 4-3	*David López, Gerard Moreno, Piatti (p), Jurado*
18/03	a	Eibar	D 1-1	*Jurado*
31/03	h	Betis	W 2-1	*Javi Fuego, J Reyes*
04/04	a	Athletic	L 0-2	
08/04	h	Alavés	W 1-0	*Piatti*
16/04	a	Leganés	W 1-0	*Léo Baptistão*
22/04	h	Atlético	L 0-1	
25/04	a	Sporting	D 1-1	*Gerard Moreno*
29/04	h	Barcelona	L 0-3	
07/05	a	Deportivo	W 2-1	*Léo Baptistão, Gerard Moreno*
13/05	h	Valencia	L 0-1	
19/05	a	Granada	W 2-1	*Léo Baptistão, og (Rubén Vezo)*

No	Name	Nat	DoB	Pos	Aps	(s)	Gls
29	Aarón Martín		22/04/97	D	28	(2)	
22	Álvaro González		08/01/90	D	2		
22	Álvaro Vázquez		27/04/91	A	2	(8)	
10	Felipe Caicedo	ECU	05/09/88	A	14	(13)	2
15	Michaël Ciani	FRA	06/04/84	D		(1)	
15	David López		09/10/89	D	36		3
2	Martín Demichelis	ARG	20/12/80	D	1	(1)	
13	Diego López		03/11/81	G	35		
20	Pape Diop	SEN	19/03/86	M	9	(9)	
6	Óscar Duarte	CRC	03/06/89	D	13	(2)	
3	Rubén Duarte		18/10/95	D	1	(2)	
7	Gerard Moreno		07/04/92	A	37		13
18	Javi Fuego		04/01/84	M	29	(2)	1
16	Javi López		21/01/86	D	17	(2)	
14	José Manuel Jurado		29/06/86	M	27	(4)	3
11	Léo Baptistão	BRA	26/08/92	A	16	(5)	6
30	Óscar Melendo		23/08/97	M	2	(9)	
31	Marc Navarro		02/07/95	D	10	(2)	2
17	Hernán Pérez	PAR	25/02/89	M	20	(12)	3
19	Pablo Piatti	ARG	31/03/89	M	30		10
23	Diego Reyes	MEX	19/09/92	D	32	(2)	1
9	José Antonio Reyes		01/09/83	M	10	(11)	3
1	Roberto		10/02/86	G	3	(1)	
28	Marc Roca		26/11/96	M	14	(11)	
8	Salva Sevilla		18/03/84	M	3	(3)	
5	Víctor Álvarez		14/03/93	M	2	(2)	
4	Víctor Sánchez		08/09/87	D	25	(1)	1

Granada CF

1931 • Nuevo Los Cármenes (22,500) • granadacf.es
Coach: Paco Jémez; (28/09/16) (Lluís Planagumá); (04/10/16) Lucas Alcaraz; (11/04/17) Tony Adams (ENG)

Date		Opponent	Result	Scorers
2016				
20/08	h	Villarreal	D 1-1	*Ponce*
28/08	a	Las Palmas	L 1-5	*Boga*
11/09	h	Eibar	L 1-2	*Kravets*
16/09	a	Betis	D 2-2	*Carcela-González, Bueno*
21/09	h	Athletic	L 1-2	*Carcela-González*
26/09	a	Alavés	L 1-3	*Kravets*
01/10	h	Leganés	L 0-1	
15/10	a	Atlético	L 1-7	*Cuenca*
22/10	h	Sporting	D 0-0	
29/10	a	Barcelona	L 0-1	
05/11	h	Deportivo	D 1-1	*og (Tytoń)*
20/11	a	Valencia	D 1-1	*Carcela-González*
27/11	a	Celta	L 1-3	*Kravets*
03/12	h	Sevilla	W 2-1	*Andreas Pereira, Lombán*
09/12	a	Málaga	D 1-1	*Kravets*
17/12	h	Real Sociedad	L 0-2	
2017				
07/01	a	Real Madrid	L 0-5	
15/01	h	Osasuna	D 1-1	*Kravets*
21/01	a	Espanyol	L 1-3	*Andreas Pereira*
28/01	a	Villarreal	L 0-2	
06/02	h	Las Palmas	W 1-0	*Andreas Pereira*
13/02	a	Eibar	L 0-4	
17/02	h	Betis	W 4-1	*Carcela-González, Ramos 2, Andreas Pereira*
26/02	a	Athletic	L 1-3	*Carcela-González*
01/03	h	Alavés	W 2-1	*Wakaso, Cuenca*
04/03	a	Leganés	L 0-1	
11/03	h	Atlético	L 0-1	
19/03	a	Sporting	L 1-3	*Ingason*
02/04	h	Barcelona	L 1-4	*Boga*
05/04	a	Deportivo	D 0-0	
09/04	h	Valencia	L 1-3	*Ponce*
16/04	h	Celta	L 0-3	
21/04	a	Sevilla	L 0-2	
25/04	h	Málaga	L 0-2	
29/04	a	Real Sociedad	L 1-2	*Ramos*
06/05	h	Real Madrid	L 0-4	
13/05	a	Osasuna	L 1-2	*Ramos*
19/05	h	Espanyol	L 1-2	*Andreas Pereira*

No	Name	Nat	DoB	Pos	Aps	(s)	Gls
18	Andreas Pereira	BRA	01/01/96	M	34	(1)	5
26	Victorien Angban	CIV	29/09/96	M	8	(2)	
15	Omer Atzili	ISR	27/07/93	M	3	(6)	
7	David Barral		10/05/83	A	2	(6)	
10	Jérémie Boga	CIV	03/01/97	M	14	(12)	2
23	Alberto Bueno		20/03/88	A	5	(8)	1
16	Mehdi Carcela-González	MAR	01/07/89	M	20	(2)	5
19	Isaac Cuenca		27/04/91	M	18	(7)	2
30	Juanan Entrena		19/05/96	M	1	(2)	
35	Pervis Estupiñán	ECU	21/01/98	D	2		
22	Dimitri Foulquier	FRA	23/03/93	D	21	(1)	
12	Gabriel Silva	BRA	13/05/91	D	11	(1)	
23	Héctor Hernández		23/05/91	D	11	(2)	
29	Martin Hongla	CMR	16/03/98	D	8	(2)	
25	Sverrir Ingi Ingason	ISL	05/08/93	D	17		1
28	Jean Carlos	BRA	10/05/96	A		(1)	
11	Panagiotis Kone	GRE	26/07/87	M		(2)	
24	Artem Kravets	UKR	03/06/89	A	16	(10)	5
21	Rene Krhin	SVN	21/05/90	M	11	(1)	
6	David Lombán		05/06/87	D	20	(1)	1
14	Luís Martins	POR	10/06/92	D	1	(1)	
34	Aly Malle	MLI	03/04/98	M	6	(5)	
8	Javi Márquez		11/05/86	M	4	(3)	
13	Guillermo Ochoa	MEX	13/07/85	G	38		
9	Ezequiel Ponce	ARG	29/03/97	A	10	(15)	2
7	Adrián Ramos	COL	22/01/86	A	13	(1)	4
17	Rubén Vezo	POR	25/04/94	D	17	(1)	
20	Matthieu Saunier	FRA	07/02/90	D	16		
4	Sergi Samper		20/01/95	M	13	(9)	
3	Gastón Silva	URU	05/03/94	D	19	(3)	
14	Franck Tabanou	FRA	30/01/89	D	6		
2	Tito		11/07/85	D	11	(1)	
11	Jon Miquel Toral		05/02/95	M	4	(1)	
5	Uche Agbo	NGA	04/12/95	M	28	(3)	
8	Wakaso Mubarak	GHA	25/07/90	M	10	(1)	1

UD Las Palmas

1949 • Gran Canaria (32,400) • udlaspalmas.es

Coach: Quique Setién

Date		Opponent	Res	Scorers
2016				
22/08	a	Valencia	W 4-2	*Livaja 2, Jonathan Viera (p), Boateng*
28/08	h	Granada	W 5-1	*El Zhar 2, Boateng, Momo, Araujo*
10/09	a	Sevilla	L 1-2	*Tana*
17/09	h	Málaga	W 1-0	*Momo (p)*
21/09	a	Real Sociedad	L 1-4	*Tana*
24/09	h	Real Madrid	D 2-2	*Tana, Araujo*
01/10	a	Osasuna	D 2-2	*Vicente Gómez, David García*
14/10	h	Espanyol	D 0-0	
23/10	a	Villarreal	L 1-2	*Boateng*
30/10	h	Celta	D 3-3	*Bigas, Jonathan Viera (p), Boateng*
05/11	h	Eibar	W 1-0	*Jonathan Viera (p)*
18/11	a	Betis	L 0-2	
28/11	h	Athletic	W 3-1	*Boateng, Momo, Jonathan Viera*
04/12	a	Alavés	D 1-1	*Livaja*
10/12	h	Leganés	D 1-1	*Livaja*
17/12	a	Atlético	L 0-1	
2017				
07/01	h	Sporting	W 1-0	*El Zhar*
14/01	a	Barcelona	L 0-5	
20/01	h	Deportivo	D 1-1	*García*
30/01	h	Valencia	W 3-1	*Jonathan Viera, Lemos, Boateng*
06/02	a	Granada	L 0-1	
12/02	h	Sevilla	L 0-1	
20/02	a	Málaga	L 1-2	*Lemos*
24/02	h	Real Sociedad	L 0-1	
01/03	a	Real Madrid	D 3-3	*Tana, Jonathan Viera (p), Boateng*
05/03	h	Osasuna	W 5-2	*Jesé 2, Livaja, og (Unai García), Roque Mesa*
10/03	a	Espanyol	L 3-4	*Lemos 2, García*
17/03	h	Villarreal	W 1-0	*Boateng*
03/04	a	Celta	L 1-3	*Bigas*
06/04	a	Eibar	L 1-3	*Lemos*
09/04	h	Betis	W 4-1	*Vicente Gómez, Boateng, Jonathan Viera, Jesé (p)*
14/04	a	Athletic	L 1-5	*Bigas*
23/04	h	Alavés	D 1-1	*Boateng*
26/04	a	Leganés	L 0-3	
29/04	h	Atlético	L 0-5	
06/05	a	Sporting	L 0-1	
14/05	h	Barcelona	L 1-4	*Bigas*
20/05	a	Deportivo	L 0-3	

No	Name	Nat	DoB	Pos	Aps	(s)	Gls
10	Sergio Araujo	ARG	28/01/92	A	5	(6)	2
25	Asdrúbal		13/03/91	A		(3)	
16	Aythami		02/04/86	D	8	(3)	
28	Benito Ramírez		11/07/95	M		(2)	
17	Pedro Bigas		15/05/90	D	31	(1)	4
7	Kevin-Prince Boateng	GHA	06/03/87	M	25	(3)	10
23	Dani Castellano		02/11/87	D	25	(2)	
5	David García		25/02/82	D	17	(5)	1
2	David Simón		31/12/89	D	14	(2)	
8	Nabil El Zhar	MAR	27/08/86	M	8	(4)	3
29	Erik Expósito		23/06/96	A	2		
19	Mateo García	ARG	10/09/96	M	8	(11)	2
20	Alen Halilović	CRO	18/06/96	M	6	(12)	
22	Hélder Lopes	POR	04/01/89	D	13	(2)	
14	Hernán		26/08/90	M	3	(7)	
18	Javi Castellano		02/11/87	M		(5)	
13	Javi Varas		10/09/82	G	25		
10	Jesé		26/02/93	A	13	(3)	3
21	Jonathan Viera		21/10/89	A	30	(1)	7
3	Mauricio Lemos	URU	28/12/95	D	21	(2)	5
9	Marko Livaja	CRO	26/08/93	A	16	(9)	5
1	Raúl Lizoain		27/01/91	G	13		
12	Michel	BRA	15/02/90	D	24	(1)	
11	Momo		15/07/82	M	12	(11)	3
6	Ángel Montoro		25/06/88	M	12	(5)	
15	Roque Mesa		07/06/89	M	34	(1)	1
24	Tana		20/09/90	A	25	(7)	4
20	Tyronne		24/01/91	A		(3)	
4	Vicente Gómez		31/08/88	M	28	(1)	2

CD Leganés

1928 • Butarque (10,958) • deportivoleganes.com

Coach: Asier Garitano

Date		Opponent	Res	Scorers
2016				
22/08	a	Celta	W 1-0	*Víctor Díaz*
27/08	h	Atlético	D 0-0	
11/09	a	Sporting	L 1-2	*Diego Rico*
17/09	h	Barcelona	L 1-5	*Gabriel*
22/09	a	Deportivo	W 2-1	*Luciano, Gabriel*
25/09	h	Valencia	L 1-2	*Szymanowski*
01/10	a	Granada	W 1-0	*Szymanowski*
15/10	h	Sevilla	L 2-3	*Timor, Szymanowski*
23/10	a	Málaga	L 0-4	
28/10	h	Real Sociedad	L 0-2	
06/11	a	Real Madrid	L 0-3	
21/11	h	Osasuna	W 2-0	*Ibáñez 2*
26/11	a	Espanyol	L 0-3	
03/12	h	Villarreal	D 0-0	
10/12	a	Las Palmas	D 1-1	*Guerrero (p)*
18/12	h	Eibar	D 1-1	*Guerrero*
2017				
08/01	a	Betis	L 0-2	
14/01	h	Athletic	D 0-0	
21/01	a	Alavés	D 2-2	*Guerrero, Insúa*
28/01	h	Celta	L 0-2	
04/02	a	Atlético	L 0-2	
12/02	h	Sporting	L 0-2	
19/02	a	Barcelona	L 1-2	*Unai López*
25/02	h	Deportivo	W 4-0	*Szymanowski, Mantovani, Unai López, Bueno*
28/02	a	Valencia	L 0-1	
04/03	h	Granada	W 1-0	*Machís*
11/03	a	Sevilla	D 1-1	*Gabriel*
19/03	h	Málaga	D 0-0	
01/04	a	Real Sociedad	D 1-1	*Szymanowski*
05/04	h	Real Madrid	L 2-4	*Gabriel, Luciano*
09/04	a	Osasuna	L 1-2	*Siovas*
16/04	h	Espanyol	L 0-1	
22/04	a	Villarreal	L 1-2	*Guerrero*
26/04	h	Las Palmas	W 3-0	*Luciano 2 (1p), Guerrero*
30/04	a	Eibar	L 0-2	
08/05	h	Betis	W 4-0	*Szymanowski 2 (1p), El Zhar, Gabriel*
14/05	a	Athletic	D 1-1	*Szymanowski*
20/05	h	Alavés	D 1-1	*Timor*

No	Name	Nat	DoB	Pos	Aps	(s)	Gls
4	Adrián Marín		09/01/97	D	11	(2)	
6	Alberto		31/03/89	M	14	(2)	
31	Diego Barrios		30/07/94	G		(1)	
25	Alberto Brignoli	ITA	19/08/91	G		(1)	
10	Alberto Bueno		20/03/88	A	3	(8)	1
3	Unai Bustinza		02/02/92	D	21	(1)	
1	Nereo Champagne	ARG	20/01/85	G	4		
15	Diego Rico		23/02/93	D	25		1
25	Nabil El Zhar	MAR	27/08/86	M	10	(4)	1
8	Gabriel	BRA	18/09/93	M	33	(1)	5
9	Miguel Ángel Guerrero		12/07/90	A	25	(6)	5
13	Iago Herrerín		25/01/88	G	21		
16	Robert Ibáñez		22/03/93	M	1	(4)	2
18	Pablo Insúa		09/09/93	D	20	(9)	1
14	Mamadou Koné	CIV	25/12/91	A	1	(4)	
20	Luciano	BRA	18/05/93	A	11	(14)	4
7	Darwin Machís	VEN	07/02/93	A	10	(17)	1
5	Martín Mantovani	ARG	07/07/84	D	30	(1)	1
12	Carl Medjani	ALG	15/05/85	D	7	(1)	
12	Erik Morán		25/05/91	M	11	(1)	
23	Omar Ramos		26/01/88	M	11	(4)	
21	Rubén Pérez		26/04/89	M	26	(4)	
16	Samuel		13/07/90	M	5	(6)	
22	Lluís Sastre		26/03/86	M	1		
13	Jon Ander Serantes		01/01/89	G	13		
22	Dimitrios Siovas	GRE	16/09/88	D	16		1
11	Alexander Szymanowski	ARG	13/10/88	A	24	(4)	8
24	David Timor		17/01/89	M	22	(2)	2
2	Tito		11/07/85	D	10	(1)	
19	Unai López		30/10/95	M	12	(11)	2
17	Víctor Díaz		12/06/88	D	20	(3)	1

Málaga CF

1994 • La Rosaleda (30,044) • malagacf.com

Coach: Juande Ramos; (28/12/16) Marcelo Romero (URU); (07/03/17) Míchel

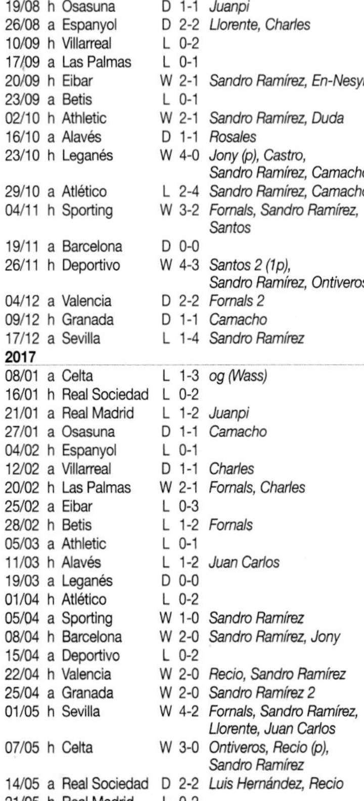

Date		Opponent	Res	Scorers
2016				
19/08	h	Osasuna	D 1-1	*Juanpi*
26/08	a	Espanyol	D 2-2	*Llorente, Charles*
10/09	h	Villarreal	L 0-2	
17/09	a	Las Palmas	L 0-1	
20/09	h	Eibar	W 2-1	*Sandro Ramírez, En-Nesyri*
23/09	a	Betis	L 0-1	
02/10	h	Athletic	W 2-1	*Sandro Ramírez, Duda*
16/10	a	Alavés	D 1-1	*Rosales*
23/10	h	Leganés	W 4-0	*Jony (p), Castro, Sandro Ramírez, Camacho*
29/10	a	Atlético	L 2-4	*Sandro Ramírez, Camacho*
04/11	h	Sporting	W 3-2	*Fornals, Sandro Ramírez, Santos*
19/11	a	Barcelona	D 0-0	
26/11	h	Deportivo	W 4-3	*Santos 2 (1p), Sandro Ramírez, Ontiveros*
04/12	a	Valencia	D 2-2	*Fornals 2*
09/12	h	Granada	D 1-1	*Camacho*
17/12	a	Sevilla	L 1-4	*Sandro Ramírez*
2017				
08/01	a	Celta	L 1-3	*og (Wass)*
16/01	h	Real Sociedad	L 0-2	
21/01	a	Real Madrid	L 1-2	*Juanpi*
27/01	a	Osasuna	D 1-1	*Camacho*
04/02	h	Espanyol	L 0-1	
12/02	a	Villarreal	D 1-1	*Charles*
20/02	h	Las Palmas	W 2-1	*Fornals, Charles*
25/02	a	Eibar	L 0-3	
28/02	h	Betis	L 1-2	*Fornals*
05/03	a	Athletic	L 0-1	
11/03	h	Alavés	L 1-2	*Juan Carlos*
19/03	a	Leganés	D 0-0	
01/04	h	Atlético	L 0-2	
05/04	a	Sporting	W 1-0	*Sandro Ramírez*
08/04	h	Barcelona	W 2-0	*Sandro Ramírez, Jony*
15/04	a	Deportivo	L 0-2	
22/04	h	Valencia	W 2-0	*Recio, Sandro Ramírez*
25/04	a	Granada	W 2-0	*Sandro Ramírez 2*
01/05	h	Sevilla	W 4-2	*Fornals, Sandro Ramírez, Llorente, Juan Carlos*
07/05	h	Celta	W 3-0	*Ontiveros, Recio (p), Sandro Ramírez*
14/05	a	Real Sociedad	D 2-2	*Luis Hernández, Recio*
21/05	h	Real Madrid	L 0-2	

No	Name	Nat	DoB	Pos	Aps	(s)	Gls
13	Denys Boyko	UKR	29/01/88	G	3		
6	Ignacio Camacho		04/05/90	M	35		4
11	Gonzalo Castro	URU	14/09/84	M	21	(8)	1
9	Charles	BRA	04/04/84	A	11	(10)	3
3	Martín Demichelis	ARG	20/12/80	D	7	(3)	
17	Duda	POR	27/06/80	M	2	(14)	1
26	Youssef En-Nesyri	MAR	01/06/97	A		(13)	1
31	Pablo Fornals		22/02/96	M	31	(1)	6
21	Jony		09/07/91	M	15	(9)	2
25	José Rodríguez		16/12/94	M	6		
7	Juan Carlos		20/03/90	D	23	(5)	2
10	Juanpi	VEN	24/01/94	M	16	(6)	2
1	Carlos Kameni	CMR	18/02/84	G	35		
20	Keko		27/12/91	M	13	(9)	
2	Bakary Koné	BFA	27/04/88	D	7		
22	Zdravko Kuzmanović	SRB	22/09/87	M	3	(1)	
5	Diego Llorente		16/08/93	D	23	(2)	2
24	Luis Hernández		14/04/89	D	19		1
29	Luis Muñoz		23/02/97	D	4	(1)	
23	Miguel Torres		28/01/86	D	18	(4)	
39	Javier Ontiveros		09/09/97	M	7	(11)	2
16	Adalberto Peñaranda	VEN	31/05/97	A	1	(2)	
14	Recio		11/10/91	M	16	(2)	3
15	Federico Ricca	URU	01/12/94	D	19	(2)	
18	Roberto Rosales	VEN	20/11/88	D	32		1
19	Sandro Ramírez		09/07/95	A	28	(2)	14
8	Michael Santos	URU	13/03/93	A	8	(6)	3
4	Mikel Villanueva	VEN	14/04/93	D	14	(1)	
3	Weligton	BRA	26/08/79	D	1		

SPAIN

CA Osasuna

1920 • El Sadar (18,761) • osasuna.es

Coach: Enrique Martín;
(08/11/16) Joaquín Caparrós;
(04/01/17) Petar Vasiljević (SRB)

Date		Opponent	Result	Scorers
2016				
19/08	a	Málaga	D 1-1	*Fran Mérida*
27/08	h	Real Sociedad	L 0-2	
10/09	a	Real Madrid	L 2-5	*Oriol Riera, David García*
18/09	h	Celta	D 0-0	
22/09	h	Espanyol	L 1-2	*Sergio León*
25/09	a	Villarreal	L 1-3	*Roberto Torres (p)*
01/10	h	Las Palmas	D 2-2	*Roberto Torres (p), Sergio León*
17/10	a	Eibar	W 3-2	*Sergio León 2, Roberto Torres*
21/10	h	Betis	L 1-2	*Roberto Torres*
30/10	a	Athletic	D 1-1	*Oriol Riera*
05/11	h	Alavés	L 0-1	
21/11	a	Leganés	L 0-2	
27/11	h	Atlético	L 0-3	
04/12	a	Sporting	L 1-3	*Miguel Flaño*
10/12	h	Barcelona	L 0-3	
18/12	a	Deportivo	L 0-2	
2017				
09/01	h	Valencia	D 3-3	*Oriol Riera, Roberto Torres, Clerc*
15/01	a	Granada	D 1-1	*Oriol Riera*
22/01	h	Sevilla	L 3-4	*Sergio León, og (Iborra), Kodro*
27/01	h	Málaga	D 1-1	*Čaušić*
05/02	a	Real Sociedad	L 2-3	*Kodro, Sergio León*
11/02	h	Real Madrid	L 1-3	*Sergio León*
19/02	a	Celta	L 0-3	
26/02	a	Espanyol	L 0-3	
01/03	h	Villarreal	L 1-4	*Roberto Torres (p)*
05/03	a	Las Palmas	L 2-5	*Kodro 2*
13/03	h	Eibar	D 1-1	*Kodro*
18/03	a	Betis	L 0-2	
01/04	h	Athletic	L 1-2	*Sergio León*
05/04	a	Alavés	W 1-0	*Álex Berenguer*
09/04	h	Leganés	W 2-1	*Sergio León 2 (1p)*
15/04	a	Atlético	L 0-3	
22/04	h	Sporting	D 2-2	*Kodro 2*
26/04	a	Barcelona	L 1-7	*Roberto Torres*
30/04	h	Deportivo	D 2-2	*Mondragón, og (Juanfran)*
07/05	a	Valencia	L 1-4	*Olavide*
13/05	h	Granada	W 2-1	*Mondragón, Kodro*
20/05	a	Sevilla	L 0-5	

No	Name	Nat	DoB	Pos	Aps	(s)	Gls
11	Álex Berenguer		04/07/95	M	22	(7)	1
27	Álvaro Fernández		13/04/98	G		(1)	
34	Aitor Buñuel		10/02/98	D	10	(5)	
8	Goran Čaušić	SRB	05/05/92	M	22	(4)	1
21	Carlos Clerc		21/02/92	D	22	(3)	1
5	David García		14/02/94	D	23	(2)	1
20	Miguel Ángel De las Cuevas		19/06/86	M	20	(8)	
23	Didier Digard	FRA	12/07/86	M	3		
14	Fausto Tienza		08/01/90	M	16	(3)	
18	Fran Mérida		04/03/90	M	9	(6)	1
16	Rafael Fuentes		05/01/90	D	16	(1)	
31	Imanol García		26/12/95	M	6	(2)	
33	Iván Márquez		09/06/94	D	4		
17	Jaime Romero		31/07/90	M	8	(11)	
24	Javi Álamo		18/08/88	D		(2)	
2	Javier Flaño		19/08/84	D	2	(2)	
30	Kike Barja		01/04/97	A		(1)	
19	Kenan Kodro	BIH	19/08/93	A	17	(11)	8
24	Raoul Loé	CMR	31/01/89	M	6	(1)	
1	Mario Fernández		30/04/88	G	7		
4	Miguel Flaño		19/08/84	D	12		1
18	Jhon Mondragón	COL	15/10/94	D	4	(1)	2
13	Nauzet Pérez		01/03/85	G	13		
6	Oier Sanjurjo		25/05/86	D	36		
35	Miguel Olavide		05/03/96	M	4	(10)	1
9	Oriol Riera		03/07/86	A	18	(4)	4
36	Antonio Otegui		07/03/98	M		(3)	
40	Luis Perea		25/08/97	M		(1)	
12	Emmanuel Rivière	FRA	03/03/90	A	8	(7)	
10	Roberto Torres		07/03/89	M	26	(6)	7
7	Sergio León		06/01/89	A	27	(6)	10
25	Salvatore Sirigu	ITA	12/01/87	G	18		
3	Tano	DOM	30/06/90	D	9	(2)	
15	Unai García		03/09/92	D	20	(2)	
22	Nikola Vujadinović	MNE	31/07/86	D	10		

Real Madrid CF

1902 • Santiago Bernabéu (81,044) • realmadrid.com

Major honours
European Champion Clubs' Cup/UEFA Champions League (12) 1956, 1957, 1958, 1959, 1960, 1966, 1998, 2000, 2002, 2014, 2016, 2017;
UEFA Cup (2) 1985, 1986;
UEFA Super Cup (3) 2002, 2014, 2016;
European/South American Cup (3) 1960, 1998, 2002; FIFA Club World Cup (2) 2014, 2016;
Spanish League (33) 1932, 1933, 1954, 1955, 1957, 1958, 1961, 1962, 1963, 1964, 1965, 1967, 1968, 1969, 1972, 1975, 1976, 1978, 1979, 1980, 1986, 1987, 1988, 1989, 1990, 1995, 1997, 2001, 2003, 2007, 2008, 2012, 2017;
Spanish Cup (19) 1905, 1906, 1907, 1908, 1917, 1934, 1936, 1946, 1947, 1962, 1970, 1974, 1975, 1980, 1982, 1989, 1993, 2011, 2014

Coach: Zinédine Zidane (FRA)

Date		Opponent	Result	Scorers
2016				
21/08	a	Real Sociedad	W 3-0	*Bale 2, Marco Asensio*
27/08	h	Celta	W 2-1	*Morata, Kroos*
10/09	h	Osasuna	W 5-2	*Cristiano Ronaldo, Danilo, Sergio Ramos, Pepe, Modrić*
18/09	a	Espanyol	W 2-0	*James Rodríguez, Benzema*
21/09	h	Villarreal	D 1-1	*Sergio Ramos*
24/09	a	Las Palmas	D 2-2	*Marco Asensio, Benzema*
02/10	h	Eibar	D 1-1	*Bale*
15/10	a	Betis	W 6-1	*Varane, Benzema, Marcelo, Isco 2, Cristiano Ronaldo*
23/10	h	Athletic	W 2-1	*Benzema, Morata*
29/10	a	Alavés	W 4-1	*Cristiano Ronaldo 3 (1p), Morata*
06/11	h	Leganés	W 3-0	*Bale 2, Morata*
19/11	a	Atlético	W 3-0	*Cristiano Ronaldo 3 (1p)*
26/11	h	Sporting	W 2-1	*Cristiano Ronaldo 2 (1p)*
03/12	a	Barcelona	D 1-1	*Sergio Ramos*
10/12	h	Deportivo	W 3-2	*Morata, Díaz, Sergio Ramos*
2017				
07/01	h	Granada	W 5-0	*Isco 2, Benzema, Cristiano Ronaldo, Casemiro*
15/01	a	Sevilla	L 1-2	*Cristiano Ronaldo (p)*
21/01	h	Málaga	W 2-1	*Sergio Ramos 2*
29/01	h	Real Sociedad	W 3-0	*Kovačić, Cristiano Ronaldo, Morata*
11/02	a	Osasuna	W 3-1	*Cristiano Ronaldo, Isco, Lucas Vázquez*
18/02	h	Espanyol	W 2-0	*Morata, Bale*
22/02	a	Valencia	L 1-2	*Cristiano Ronaldo*
26/02	a	Villarreal	W 3-2	*Bale, Cristiano Ronaldo (p), Morata*
01/03	h	Las Palmas	D 3-3	*Isco, Cristiano Ronaldo 2 (1p)*
04/03	a	Eibar	W 4-1	*Benzema 2, James Rodríguez, Marco Asensio*
12/03	h	Betis	W 2-1	*Cristiano Ronaldo, Sergio Ramos*
18/03	a	Athletic	W 2-1	*Benzema, Casemiro*
02/04	h	Alavés	W 3-0	*Benzema, Isco, Nacho*
05/04	a	Leganés	W 4-2	*James Rodríguez, Morata 3*
08/04	h	Atlético	D 1-1	*Pepe*
15/04	a	Sporting	W 3-2	*Isco 2, Morata*
23/04	h	Barcelona	L 2-3	*Casemiro, James Rodríguez*
26/04	a	Deportivo	W 6-2	*Morata, James Rodríguez 2, Lucas Vázquez, Isco, Casemiro*
29/04	h	Valencia	W 2-1	*Cristiano Ronaldo, Marcelo*
06/05	a	Granada	W 4-0	*James Rodríguez 2, Morata 2*
14/05	h	Sevilla	W 4-1	*Nacho, Cristiano Ronaldo 2, Kroos*
17/05	a	Celta	W 4-1	*Cristiano Ronaldo 2, Benzema, Kroos*
21/05	a	Málaga	W 2-0	*Cristiano Ronaldo, Benzema*

No	Name	Nat	DoB	Pos	Aps	(s)	Gls
11	Gareth Bale	WAL	16/07/89	A	17	(2)	7
9	Karim Benzema	FRA	19/12/87	A	23	(6)	11
2	Daniel Carvajal		11/01/92	D	21	(2)	
14	Casemiro	BRA	23/02/92	M	20	(5)	4
13	Kiko Casilla		02/10/86	G	11		
7	Cristiano Ronaldo	POR	05/02/85	A	29		25
23	Danilo	BRA	15/07/91	D	17		1
18	Mariano Díaz	DOM	01/08/93	A		(8)	1
15	Fábio Coentrão	POR	11/03/88	D	2	(1)	
22	Isco		21/04/92	M	18	(12)	10
10	James Rodríguez	COL	12/07/91	M	13	(9)	8
16	Mateo Kovačić	CRO	06/05/94	M	19	(8)	1
8	Toni Kroos	GER	04/01/90	M	28	(1)	3
17	Lucas Vázquez		01/07/91	M	12	(21)	2
12	Marcelo	BRA	12/05/88	D	26	(4)	2
20	Marco Asensio		21/01/96	M	11	(12)	3
19	Luka Modrić	CRO	09/09/85	M	22	(3)	1
21	Álvaro Morata		23/10/92	A	14	(12)	15
6	Nacho		18/01/90	D	24	(4)	2
1	Keylor Navas	CRC	15/12/86	G	27		
3	Pepe	POR	26/02/83	D	13		2
4	Sergio Ramos		30/03/86	D	28		7
27	Álvaro Tejero		20/07/96	D		(1)	
5	Raphaël Varane	FRA	25/04/93	D	23		1

Real Sociedad de Fútbol

1909 • Anoeta (32,076) • realsociedad.com

Major honours
Spanish League (2) 1981, 1982; Spanish Cup (2) 1909, 1987

Coach: Eusebio Sacristán

Date		Opponent	Res		Scorers
2016					
21/08	h	Real Madrid	L	0-3	
27/08	a	Osasuna	W	2-0	*Juanmi, og (Unai García)*
09/09	h	Espanyol	D	1-1	*Willian José*
18/09	a	Villarreal	L	1-2	*Yuri*
21/09	h	Las Palmas	W	4-1	*Willian José 2 (1p), Vela (p), Zurutuza*
24/09	a	Eibar	L	0-2	
30/09	h	Betis	W	1-0	*Vela*
16/10	a	Athletic	L	2-3	*Zurutuza, Íñigo Martínez*
22/10	h	Alavés	W	3-0	*Xabi Prieto, Willian José, Vela*
28/10	a	Leganés	W	2-0	*Willian José, Xabi Prieto*
05/11	h	Atlético	W	2-0	*Vela (p), Willian José (p)*
20/11	a	Sporting	W	3-1	*Xabi Prieto, Zurutuza, Íñigo Martínez*
27/11	h	Barcelona	D	1-1	*Willian José*
05/12	a	Deportivo	L	1-5	*Yuri*
10/12	h	Valencia	W	3-2	*Willian José 2, Juanmi*
17/12	a	Granada	W	2-0	*Jon Bautista, Juanmi*
2017					
07/01	h	Sevilla	L	0-4	
16/01	a	Málaga	W	2-0	*Íñigo Martínez, Juanmi*
22/01	h	Celta	W	1-0	*Juanmi*
29/01	a	Real Madrid	L	0-3	
05/02	h	Osasuna	W	3-2	*Raúl Navas, Vela, Juanmi*
10/02	a	Espanyol	W	2-1	*Vela, Illarramendi*
19/02	h	Villarreal	L	0-1	
24/02	a	Las Palmas	W	1-0	*Xabi Prieto*
28/02	h	Eibar	D	2-2	*Juanmi, Vela (p)*
03/03	a	Betis	W	3-2	*Jon Bautista, Xabi Prieto 2*
12/03	h	Athletic	L	0-2	
18/03	a	Alavés	L	0-1	
01/04	h	Leganés	D	1-1	*Juanmi*
04/04	a	Atlético	L	0-1	
10/04	h	Sporting	W	3-1	*Willian José, Juanmi, Yuri*
15/04	a	Barcelona	L	2-3	*og (Umtiti), Xabi Prieto*
23/04	h	Deportivo	W	1-0	*Willian José*
26/04	a	Valencia	W	3-2	*og (Diego Alves), Willian José (p), Oyarzábal*
29/04	h	Granada	W	2-1	*Vela, Juanmi*
05/05	a	Sevilla	D	1-1	*Vela*
14/05	h	Málaga	D	2-2	*Xabi Prieto (p), Jon Bautista*
21/05	a	Celta	D	2-2	*Oyarzábal, Juanmi*

No	Name	Nat	DoB	Pos	Aps	(s)	Gls
15	Aritz Elustondo		28/03/84	D	4	(5)	
16	Sergio Canales		16/02/91	M	7	(24)	
2	Carlos Martínez		09/04/86	D	10		
24	David Concha		20/11/96	A	1	(7)	
23	Jon Gaztañaga		28/06/91	M		(2)	
8	Esteban Granero		02/07/87	M	8	(11)	
33	Jon Guridi		28/02/95	M	1		
21	Héctor Hernández		23/05/91	D	2	(2)	
4	Asier Illarramendi		08/03/90	M	33	(1)	1
6	Íñigo Martínez		17/05/91	D	34		3
26	Jon Bautista		03/07/95	A	2	(10)	3
7	Juanmi		20/05/93	A	19	(16)	11
5	Markel Bergara		05/05/86	M	3	(3)	
3	Mikel González		24/09/85	D	8	(1)	
29	Álvaro Odriozola		14/12/95	D	15		
18	Mikel Oyarzábal		21/04/97	M	30	(8)	2
22	Raúl Navas		11/06/88	D	31	(1)	1
32	Kévin Rodrigues	POR	05/03/94	D	1	(1)	
14	Rubén Pardo		22/10/92	M	2	(1)	
1	Gerónimo Rulli	ARG	20/05/92	G	38		
11	Carlos Vela	MEX	01/03/89	M	31	(4)	9
12	Willian José	BRA	23/11/91	A	27	(1)	12
10	Xabi Prieto		29/08/83	M	32	(6)	8
19	Yuri Berchiche		10/02/90	D	35		3
20	Joseba Zaldúa		24/06/92	D	12	(2)	
27	Igor Zubeldía		30/03/97	M	3	(1)	
17	David Zurutuza		19/07/86	M	29	(2)	3

Sevilla FC

1890 • Ramón Sánchez Pizjuán (42,714) • sevillafc.es

Major honours
UEFA Cup (2) 2006, 2007; UEFA Europa League (3) 2014, 2015, 2016; UEFA Super Cup (1) 2006; Spanish League (1) 1946; Spanish Cup (5) 1935, 1939, 1948, 2007, 2010

Coach: Jorge Sampaoli (ARG)

Date		Opponent	Res		Scorers
2016					
20/08	h	Espanyol	W	6-4	*Sarabia, Vietto 2, Vázquez, Ben Yedder, Kiyotake*
28/08	a	Villarreal	D	0-0	
10/09	h	Las Palmas	W	2-1	*Sarabia (p), Carlos Fernández*
17/09	a	Eibar	D	1-1	*Vietto*
20/09	h	Betis	W	1-0	*Mercado*
24/09	a	Athletic	L	1-3	*Nasri*
01/10	h	Alavés	W	2-1	*Ben Yedder 2*
15/10	a	Leganés	W	3-2	*Vázquez, Nasri, Sarabia*
23/10	h	Atlético	W	1-0	*N'Zonzi*
29/10	a	Sporting	D	1-1	*Vietto*
06/11	h	Barcelona	L	1-2	*Vitolo*
19/11	a	Deportivo	W	3-2	*N'Zonzi, Vitolo, Mercado*
26/11	h	Valencia	W	2-1	*og (Garay), Pareja*
03/12	a	Granada	L	1-2	*Ben Yedder (p)*
11/12	a	Celta	W	3-0	*Iborra 3 (1p)*
17/12	h	Málaga	W	4-1	*Vietto 2, Ben Yedder, Vitolo*
2017					
07/01	a	Real Sociedad	W	4-0	*Ben Yedder 3, Sarabia*
15/01	h	Real Madrid	W	2-1	*og (Sergio Ramos), Jovetić*
22/01	a	Osasuna	W	4-3	*Iborra 2, Vázquez, Sarabia*
29/01	a	Espanyol	L	1-3	*Jovetić*
05/02	h	Villarreal	D	0-0	
12/02	a	Las Palmas	W	1-0	*Correa*
18/02	h	Eibar	W	2-0	*Sarabia, Vitolo*
25/02	a	Betis	W	2-1	*Mercado, Iborra*
02/03	h	Athletic	W	1-0	*Iborra*
06/03	a	Alavés	D	1-1	*Ben Yedder*
11/03	h	Leganés	D	1-1	*Jovetić*
19/03	a	Atlético	L	1-3	*Correa*
02/04	h	Sporting	D	0-0	
05/04	a	Barcelona	L	0-3	
08/04	h	Deportivo	W	4-2	*Jovetić, Sarabia, Correa, Ben Yedder*
16/04	a	Valencia	D	0-0	
21/04	h	Granada	W	2-0	*Ganso 2*
27/04	h	Celta	W	2-1	*Correa, Ben Yedder*
01/05	a	Málaga	L	2-4	*Vázquez 2*
05/05	h	Real Sociedad	D	1-1	*Sarabia*
14/05	a	Real Madrid	L	1-4	*Jovetić*
20/05	h	Osasuna	W	5-0	*Vitolo 2, Vázquez 2, Jovetić*

No	Name	Nat	DoB	Pos	Aps	(s)	Gls
12	Wissam Ben Yedder	FRA	12/08/90	A	20	(11)	11
30	Carlos Fernández		22/05/96	A	1	(2)	1
11	Joaquín Correa	ARG	13/08/94	M	15	(11)	4
6	Daniel Carriço	POR	04/08/88	D	6		
13	David Soria		04/04/93	G	1		
32	Diego González		28/01/95	D		(3)	
19	Ganso	BRA	12/10/89	M	5	(5)	2
8	Vicente Iborra		16/01/88	M	12	(19)	7
16	Stevan Jovetić	MNE	02/11/89	A	12	(9)	6
14	Hiroshi Kiyotake	JPN	12/11/89	M	3	(1)	1
5	Timothée Kolodziejczak	FRA	01/10/91	D	3	(2)	
4	Matías Kranevitter	ARG	21/05/93	M	14	(7)	
7	Michael Krohn-Dehli	DEN	06/06/83	M	2		
5	Clement Lenglet	FRA	17/06/95	D	15	(2)	
3	Mariano	BRA	23/06/86	D	29	(2)	
24	Gabriel Mercado	ARG	18/03/87	D	26	(3)	3
14	Walter Montoya	ARG	21/07/93	M	1	(3)	
10	Samir Nasri	FRA	20/06/87	M	22	(1)	2
15	Steven N'Zonzi	FRA	15/12/88	M	34	(1)	2
21	Nicolás Pareja	ARG	19/01/84	D	27		1
23	Adil Rami	FRA	27/12/85	D	21		
17	Pablo Sarabia		11/05/92	M	22	(12)	8
18	Sergio Escudero		02/09/89	D	25	(1)	
1	Sergio Rico		01/09/93	G	35		
25	Salvatore Sirigu	ITA	12/01/87	G	2		
22	Franco Vázquez	ARG	22/02/89	M	26	(4)	7
9	Luciano Vietto	ARG	05/12/93	A	14	(7)	6
20	Vitolo		02/11/89	M	25	(5)	6

Real Sporting de Gijón

1905 • El Molinón (29,000) • realsporting.com

Coach: Abelardo Fernández; (18/01/17) Rubi

Date		Opponent	Res		Scorers
2016					
21/08	h	Athletic	W	2-1	*Čop, Víctor Rodríguez*
28/08	a	Alavés	D	0-0	
11/09	h	Leganés	W	2-1	*Nacho Cases, Čop (p)*
17/09	a	Atlético	L	0-5	
21/09	a	Celta	L	1-2	*Čop (p)*
24/09	h	Barcelona	L	0-5	
01/10	a	Deportivo	L	1-2	*Sergio Álvarez*
16/10	h	Valencia	L	1-2	*Carlos Castro*
22/10	a	Granada	D	0-0	
29/10	h	Sevilla	D	1-1	*Moi Gómez*
04/11	a	Málaga	L	2-3	*Viguera, Čop*
20/11	h	Real Sociedad	L	1-3	*Čop*
26/11	a	Real Madrid	L	1-2	*Carmona*
04/12	h	Osasuna	W	3-1	*Carmona 2, Douglas*
11/12	a	Espanyol	L	1-2	*Čop*
17/12	h	Villarreal	L	1-3	*Carmona*
2017					
07/01	a	Las Palmas	L	0-1	
15/01	h	Eibar	L	2-3	*Carmona, Lillo*
22/01	a	Betis	D	0-0	
29/01	a	Athletic	L	1-2	*Čop (p)*
05/02	h	Alavés	L	2-4	*Traoré, Carlos Castro*
12/02	a	Leganés	W	2-0	*Canella, Burgui*
18/02	h	Atlético	L	1-4	*Sergio Álvarez*
26/02	h	Celta	D	1-1	*Moi Gómez (p)*
01/03	a	Barcelona	L	1-6	*Carlos Castro*
05/03	h	Deportivo	L	0-1	
11/03	a	Valencia	D	1-1	*Čop*
19/03	h	Granada	W	3-1	*Traoré, Babin, Carmona*
02/04	a	Sevilla	D	0-0	
05/04	h	Málaga	L	0-1	
10/04	a	Real Sociedad	L	1-3	*Echiéjilé*
15/04	h	Real Madrid	L	2-3	*Čop, Vesga*
22/04	a	Osasuna	D	2-2	*Canella, Carlos Castro*
25/04	h	Espanyol	D	1-1	*Víctor Rodríguez*
28/04	a	Villarreal	L	1-3	*Douglas*
06/05	h	Las Palmas	W	1-0	*Carmona*
14/05	a	Eibar	W	1-0	*Burgui*
20/05	h	Betis	D	2-2	*Douglas, Carmona*

No	Name	Nat	DoB	Pos	Aps	(s)	Gls
17	Akran Hassan Afif	QAT	18/11/96	A	2	(7)	
8	Rachid Aït-Atmane	FRA	04/02/93	M	6	(2)	
5	Fernando Amorebieta	VEN	29/03/85	D	26	(1)	
3	Jean-Sylvain Babin	MTQ	14/10/86	D	20	(2)	1
14	Burgui		29/10/93	M	21	(11)	2
15	Roberto Canella		07/02/88	D	20		2
9	Carlos Castro		01/06/95	A	10	(15)	4
19	Carlos Carmona		05/07/87	M	21	(4)	8
24	Duje Čop	CRO	01/02/90	A	27	(4)	9
1	Iván Cuéllar		27/05/84	G	36		
2	Douglas	BRA	06/08/90	D	20	(1)	3
12	Elderson Echiéjilé	NGA	20/01/88	D	2	(1)	1
18	Isma López		29/01/90	D	19	(8)	
4	Jorge Meré		17/04/97	D	31		
29	Juan Rodríguez		08/05/95	D	2	(2)	
16	Lillo		27/03/89	D	24	(1)	1
11	Alberto Lora		25/03/87	D	4	(3)	
13	Diego Mariño		09/05/90	G	2		
23	Moi Gómez		23/06/94	M	24	(2)	2
20	Dani N'Di	CMR	18/08/95	M	1	(5)	
10	Nacho Cases		22/12/87	M	16	(5)	1
26	Pablo Fernández		17/09/96	A		(2)	
31	Rubén Sánchez		25/11/94	D		(2)	
6	Sergio Álvarez		23/01/92	M	34	(2)	2
8	Lacina Traoré	CIV	20/08/90	A	5	(3)	2
22	Mikel Vesga		08/04/93	M	16	(1)	1
7	Víctor Rodríguez		23/07/89	M	15	(10)	2
25	Borja Viguera		26/03/87	A	6	(10)	1
21	Xavi Torres		21/11/86	M	8	(9)	

SPAIN

Valencia CF

1919 • Mestalla (55,000) • valenciacf.com

Major honours
UEFA Cup Winners' Cup (1) 1980; UEFA Cup (1) 2004; Inter Cities Fairs Cup (2) 1962, 1963; UEFA Super Cup (2) 1980, 2004; Spanish League (6) 1942, 1944, 1947, 1971, 2002, 2004; Spanish Cup (7) 1941, 1949, 1954, 1967, 1979, 1999, 2008

Coach: Pako Ayestarán; (21/09/16) (Voro); (28/09/16) Cesare Prandelli (ITA); (30/12/16) Voro

2016

Date		Opponent		Score	Scorers
22/08	h	Las Palmas	L	2-4	*Santi Mina 2*
27/08	a	Eibar	L	0-1	
11/09	h	Betis	L	2-3	*Rodrigo, Garay*
18/09	a	Athletic	L	1-2	*Álvaro Medrán*
22/09	h	Alavés	W	2-1	*og (Laguardia), Parejo (p)*
25/09	a	Leganés	W	2-1	*Nani, Mario Suárez*
02/10	h	Atlético	L	0-2	
16/10	a	Sporting	W	2-1	*Mario Suárez 2*
22/10	h	Barcelona	L	2-3	*Munir, Rodrigo*
31/10	a	Deportivo	D	1-1	*Rodrigo*
06/11	a	Celta	L	1-2	*Parejo (p)*
20/11	h	Granada	D	1-1	*Nani*
26/11	a	Sevilla	L	1-2	*Munir*
04/12	h	Málaga	D	2-2	*Rodrigo, Álvaro Medrán*
10/12	a	Real Sociedad	L	2-3	*Parejo (p), Bakkali*

2017

Date		Opponent		Score	Scorers
09/01	a	Osasuna	D	3-3	*Munir, og (Oriol Riera), Montoya*
15/01	h	Espanyol	W	2-1	*Montoya, Santi Mina*
21/01	a	Villarreal	W	2-0	*Carlos Soler, Santi Mina*
30/01	a	Las Palmas	L	1-3	*Santi Mina*
04/02	h	Eibar	L	0-4	
11/02	a	Betis	D	0-0	
19/02	h	Athletic	W	2-0	*Nani, Zaza*
22/02	h	Real Madrid	W	2-1	*Zaza, Orellana*
25/02	a	Alavés	L	1-2	*Carlos Soler*
28/02	h	Leganés	W	1-0	*Mangala*
05/03	a	Atlético	L	0-3	
11/03	h	Sporting	D	1-1	*Munir*
19/03	a	Barcelona	L	2-4	*Mangala, Munir*
02/04	h	Deportivo	W	3-0	*Garay, og (Albentosa), João Cancelo*
06/04	h	Celta	W	3-2	*Parejo, Munir, Carlos Soler*
09/04	a	Granada	W	3-1	*Zaza 2, Santi Mina*
16/04	h	Sevilla	D	0-0	
22/04	a	Málaga	L	0-2	
26/04	h	Real Sociedad	L	2-3	*Nani (p), Zaza*
29/04	a	Real Madrid	L	1-2	*Parejo*
07/05	h	Osasuna	W	4-1	*Garay 2, Zaza, Rodrigo*
13/05	a	Espanyol	W	1-0	*Gayá*
21/05	h	Villarreal	L	1-3	*Nani*

No	Name	Nat	DoB	Pos	Aps	(s)	Gls
23	Aymen Abdennour	TUN	06/10/89	D	9	(4)	
20	Álvaro Medrán		15/03/94	M	10	(6)	2
4	Aderlan Santos	BRA	09/04/89	D	11	(1)	
11	Zakaria Bakkali	BEL	26/01/96	M	1	(16)	1
28	Carlos Soler		02/01/97	M	19	(4)	3
1	Diego Alves	BRA	24/06/85	G	33		
16	Fede Cartabia	ARG	20/01/93	M	2	(2)	
24	Ezequiel Garay	ARG	10/10/86	D	27		4
14	José Gayá		25/05/95	D	24	(3)	1
13	Jaume Doménech		05/11/90	G	3		
2	João Cancelo	POR	27/05/94	D	27	(8)	1
26	Toni Lato		21/11/97	D	4	(4)	
5	Eliquim Mangala	FRA	13/02/91	D	30		2
7	Mario Suárez		24/02/87	M	17	(4)	3
21	Martín Montoya		14/04/91	D	26	(3)	2
9	Munir El Haddadi		01/09/95	A	22	(11)	6
5	Shkodran Mustafi	GER	17/04/92	D		(1)	
33	Nacho Gil		09/09/95	A		(2)	
17	Nani	POR	17/11/86	A	22	(3)	5
15	Fabián Orellana	CHI	27/01/86	M	13	(3)	1
9	Paco Alcácer		30/08/93	A	1		
10	Daniel Parejo		16/04/89	M	36		5
8	Enzo Pérez	ARG	22/02/86	M	26	(1)	
27	Rafa Mir		18/06/97	A		(2)	
19	Rodrigo		06/03/91	A	17	(2)	5
3	Rúben Vezo	POR	25/04/94	D	1		
25	Mathew Ryan	AUS	08/04/92	G	2		
22	Santi Mina		07/12/95	A	13	(15)	6
6	Guilherme Siqueira	BRA	28/04/86	D	7	(3)	
34	Sito Pascual		18/11/96	M		(1)	
12	Simone Zaza	ITA	25/06/91	A	15	(5)	6

Villarreal CF

1923 • La Cerámica (24,890) • villarrealcf.es

Coach: Fran Escribá

2016

Date		Opponent		Score	Scorers
20/08	a	Granada	D	1-1	*Samu Castillejo*
28/08	h	Sevilla	D	0-0	
10/09	a	Málaga	W	2-0	*Jaume Costa, Sansone*
18/09	h	Real Sociedad	W	2-1	*Sansone 2*
21/09	a	Real Madrid	D	1-1	*Bruno Soriano (p)*
25/09	h	Osasuna	W	3-1	*Pato, Bruno Soriano (p), Sansone*
02/10	a	Espanyol	D	0-0	
16/10	h	Celta	W	5-0	*Soriano 2, Bakambu, og (Wass), Trigueros*
23/10	h	Las Palmas	W	2-1	*Sansone (p), Bakambu*
30/10	a	Eibar	L	1-2	*Bruno Soriano (p)*
06/11	h	Betis	W	2-0	*Trigueros, Soriano*
20/11	a	Athletic	L	0-1	
27/11	h	Alavés	L	0-2	
03/12	a	Leganés	D	0-0	
12/12	h	Atlético	W	3-0	*Trigueros, Jonathan dos Santos, Soriano*
17/12	a	Sporting	W	3-1	*Jonathan dos Santos, Sansone, Pato*

2017

Date		Opponent		Score	Scorers
08/01	h	Barcelona	D	1-1	*Sansone*
14/01	a	Deportivo	D	0-0	
21/01	h	Valencia	L	0-2	
28/01	h	Granada	W	2-0	*Bruno Soriano, Álvaro González*
05/02	a	Sevilla	D	0-0	
12/02	h	Málaga	D	1-1	*Bruno Soriano (p)*
19/02	a	Real Sociedad	W	1-0	*Samu Castillejo*
26/02	h	Real Madrid	L	2-3	*Trigueros, Bakambu*
01/03	a	Osasuna	W	4-1	*Soriano, Soldado (p), Borré 2*
04/03	h	Espanyol	W	2-0	*Soriano, og (Diego López)*
12/03	a	Celta	W	1-0	*Soldado*
17/03	a	Las Palmas	L	0-1	
01/04	h	Eibar	L	2-3	*Soriano 2*
04/04	a	Betis	W	1-0	*Adrián López*
07/04	h	Athletic	W	3-1	*Víctor Ruiz, Bakambu, Adrián López*
17/04	a	Alavés	L	1-2	*Bakambu*
22/04	h	Leganés	W	2-1	*Bakambu 2*
25/04	a	Atlético	W	1-0	*Soriano*
28/04	h	Sporting	W	3-1	*Soldado, Bakambu 2*
06/05	a	Barcelona	L	1-4	*Bakambu*
14/05	h	Deportivo	D	0-0	
21/05	a	Valencia	W	3-1	*Soldado, Trigueros, Sansone*

No	Name	Nat	DoB	Pos	Aps	(s)	Gls
15	Adrián López		08/01/88	A	7	(7)	2
12	Álvaro González		08/01/90	D	20	(3)	1
13	Andrés Fernández		17/12/86	G	14	(1)	
1	Sergio Asenjo		28/06/89	G	24		
17	Cédric Bakambu	COD	11/04/91	A	17	(9)	10
23	Daniele Bonera	ITA	31/05/81	D	6		
24	Rafael Borré	COL	15/09/95	A	2	(15)	2
21	Bruno Soriano		12/06/84	M	33	(1)	5
27	Aitor Cantalapiedra		10/02/96	A		(1)	
7	Denis Cheryshev	RUS	26/12/90	M	2	(9)	
11	Jaume Costa		18/03/88	D	30	(1)	1
8	Jonathan dos Santos	MEX	26/04/90	M	22	(12)	2
3	José Ángel		05/09/89	D	7		
2	Mario Gaspar		24/11/90	D	36		
39	Mario González		25/02/96	M		(2)	
5	Mateo Musacchio	ARG	26/08/90	D	23		
4	Alfred N'Diaye	SEN	06/03/90	M	1	(6)	
10	Pato	BRA	02/09/89	A	11	(3)	2
35	Rodri Hernández		22/06/96	M	8	(14)	
22	Antonio Rukavina	SRB	26/01/84	D	3	(1)	
19	Samu Castillejo		18/01/95	M	24	(9)	2
18	Nicola Sansone	ITA	10/09/91	A	25	(6)	8
9	Roberto Soldado		27/05/85	A	10		4
20	Roberto Soriano	ITA	08/02/91	M	31	(2)	9
49	Leonardo Suárez	ARG	30/03/96	M		(3)	
14	Manu Trigueros		17/10/91	M	35	(2)	5
6	Víctor Ruiz		25/01/89	D	27	(1)	1

Top goalscorers

37	Lionel Messi (Barcelona)
29	Luis Suárez (Barcelona)
25	Cristiano Ronaldo (Real Madrid)
19	Iago Aspas (Celta)
16	Aritz Aduriz (Athletic)
	Antoine Griezmann (Atlético)
15	Álvaro Morata (Real Madrid)
14	Sandro Ramírez (Málaga)
13	Neymar (Barcelona)
	Rubén Castro (Betis)
	Gerard Moreno (Espanyol)

Promoted clubs

Levante UD

1939 • Ciudad de Valencia (25,500) • levanteud.com
Coach: Muñiz

Girona FC

1930 • Montilivi (9,200) • gironafc.cat
Coach: Pablo Machín

Getafe CF

1983 • Coliseum Alfonso Pérez (17,000) • getafecf.com
Coach: Juan Esnáider (ARG); (27/09/16) José Bordalás

Second level final table 2016/17

		Pld	W	D	L	F	A	Pts
1	Levante UD	42	25	9	8	57	32	84
2	Girona FC	42	20	10	12	65	45	70
3	Getafe CF	42	18	14	10	55	43	68
4	CD Tenerife	42	16	18	8	50	37	66
5	Cádiz CF	42	16	16	10	55	40	64
6	SD Huesca	42	16	15	11	53	43	63
7	Real Valladolid CF	42	18	9	15	52	47	63
8	Real Oviedo	42	17	10	15	47	47	61
9	CD Lugo	42	14	13	15	49	52	55
10	Córdoba CF	42	14	13	15	42	52	55
11	CF Reus Deportiu	42	13	16	13	31	29	55
12	Rayo Vallecano de Madrid	42	14	11	17	44	44	53
13	Sevilla Atlético Club	42	13	14	15	55	56	53
14	Club Gimnàstic de Tarragona	42	12	16	14	47	51	52
15	UD Almería	42	14	9	19	44	49	51
16	Real Zaragoza	42	12	14	16	50	52	50
17	CD Numancia de Soria	42	11	17	14	40	49	50
18	AD Alcorcón	42	13	11	18	32	43	50
19	UCAM Murcia CF	42	11	15	16	42	51	48
20	RCD Mallorca	42	9	18	15	42	50	45
21	Elche CF	42	11	10	21	49	63	43
22	CD Mirandés	42	9	14	19	40	66	41

Promotion/Relegation play-offs

(14/06/17 & 17/06/17)
Huesca 2-2 Getafe
Getafe 3-0 Huesca
(Getafe 5-2)

(15/06/17 & 18/06/17)
Cádiz 1-0 Tenerife
Tenerife 1-0 Cádiz *(aet)*
(1-1; Tenerife on higher position in regular season)

(21/06/17 & 24/06/17)
Tenerife 1-0 Getafe
Getafe 3-1 Tenerife
(Getafe 3-2)

DOMESTIC CUP

Copa del Rey 2016/17

FOURTH ROUND

(26/10/16 & 30/11/16)
Leonesa 1-7, 1-6 Real Madrid *(2-13)*

(29/11/16 & 21/12/16)
Betis 1-0, 1-3 Deportivo *(2-3)*
Leganés 1-3, 1-2 Valencia *(2-5)*
Sporting 1-2, 1-3 Eibar *(2-5)*

(29/11/16 & 22/12/16)
Alcorcón 1-1, 1-1 Espanyol *(aet; 2-2, 4-3 on pens)*

(30/11/16 & 20/12/16)
Córdoba 2-0, 4-3 Málaga *(6-3)*
Guijuelo 0-6, 1-4 Atlético *(1-10)*
Toledo 0-3, 1-1 Villarreal *(1-4)*

(30/11/16 & 21/12/16)
Formentera 1-5, 1-9 Sevilla *(2-14)*
Granada 1-0, 0-2 Osasuna *(1-2)*
Hércules 1-1, 0-7 Barcelona *(1-8)*

(30/11/16 & 22/12/16)
UCAM Murcia 0-1, 0-1 Celta *(0-2)*

(01/12/16 & 20/12/16)
Huesca 2-2, 1-2 Las Palmas *(3-4)*
Valladolid 1-3, 1-1 Real Sociedad *(2-4)*

(01/12/16 & 22/12/16)
Gimnàstic 0-3, 0-3 Alavés *(0-6)*
Racing 1-2, 0-3 Athletic *(1-5)*

FIFTH ROUND

(03/01/17 & 10/01/17)
Las Palmas 0-2, 3-2 Atlético *(3-4)*

(03/01/17 & 11/01/17)
Deportivo 2-2, 1-1 Alavés *(3-3; Alavés on away goals)*

(03/01/17 & 12/01/17)
Osasuna 0-3, 0-0 Eibar *(0-3)*
Valencia 1-4, 1-2 Celta *(2-6)*

(04/01/17 & 11/01/17)
Alcorcón 0-0, 2-1 Córdoba *(2-1)*
Real Sociedad 3-1, 1-1 Villarreal *(4-2)*

(04/01/17 & 12/01/17)
Real Madrid 3-0, 3-3 Sevilla *(6-3)*

(05/01/17 & 11/01/17)
Athletic 2-1, 1-3 Barcelona *(3-4)*

QUARTER-FINALS

(18/01/17 & 24/01/17)
Alcorcón 0-2 Alavés *(Ibai Gómez 89, 90+3)*
Alavés 0-0 Alcorcón
(Alavés 2-0)

(18/01/17 & 25/01/17)
Real Madrid 1-2 Celta *(Marcelo 69; Iago Aspas 65, Jonny 70)*
Celta 2-2 Real Madrid *(Danilo 43og, Wass 84; Cristiano Ronaldo 62, Lucas Vázquez 90)*
(Celta 4-3)

(19/01/17 & 25/01/17)
Atlético 3-0 Eibar *(Griezmann 27, Correa 60, Gameiro 67)*
Eibar 2-2 Atlético *(Sergi Enrich 72, Pedro León 79; Giménez 48, Juanfran 84)*
(Atlético 5-2)

(19/01/17 & 26/01/17)
Real Sociedad 0-1 Barcelona *(Neymar 20p)*
Barcelona 5-2 Real Sociedad *(Denis Suárez 17, 82, Messi 55p, Suárez 63, Arda Turan 80; Juanmi 62, Willian José 73)*
(Barcelona 6-2)

SEMI-FINALS

(01/02/17 & 07/02/17)
Atlético 1-2 Barcelona *(Griezmann 59; Suárez 6, Messi 33)*
Barcelona 1-1 Atlético *(Suárez 43; Gameiro 83)*
(Barcelona 3-2)

(02/02/17 & 08/02/17)
Celta 0-0 Alavés
Alavés 1-0 Celta *(Édgar Méndez 82)*
(Alavés 1-0)

FINAL

(27/05/17)
Vicente Calderón, Madrid
FC BARCELONA 3 *(Messi 30, Neymar 45, Paco Alcácer 45+3)*
DEPORTIVO ALAVÉS 1 *(Theo Hernández 33)*
Referee: *Clos Gómez*
BARCELONA: *Cillesen, Mascherano (André Gomes 11), Piqué, Umtiti, Jordi Alba, Rakitić (Aleix Vidal 83), Busquets, Iniesta, Messi, Paco Alcácer, Neymar*
ALAVÉS: *Pacheco, Kiko Femenía, Vigaray, Rodrigo Ely, Feddal, Theo Hernández (Romero 79), Édgar Méndez (Camarasa 59), Llorente, Manu García, Ibai Gómez (Sobrino 59), Deyverson*

Barcelona captured the Copa del Rey for the third year in a row

SWEDEN

Svenska Fotbollförbundet (SvFF)

Address	Evenemangsgatan 31 SE-171 23 Solna	**President**	Karl-Erik Nilsson
		General secretary	Håkan Sjöstrand
Tel	+46 8 7350900	**Media officer**	Niklas Bodell
Fax	+46 8 7350901	**Year of formation**	1904
E-Mail	svff@svenskfotboll.se	**National stadium**	Friends Arena, Solna (54,329)
Website	svenskfotboll.se		

ALLSVENSKAN CLUBS

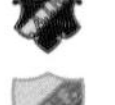  1 **AIK**

 2 **Djurgårdens IF**

 3 **IF Elfsborg**

 4 **Falkenbergs FF**

 5 **Gefle IF**

 6 **IFK Göteborg**

 7 **Hammarby Fotboll**

 8 **Helsingborgs IF**

 9 **BK Häcken**

 10 **Jönköpings Södra IF**

 11 **Kalmar FF**

 12 **Malmö FF**

 13 **IFK Norrköping**

 14 **GIF Sundsvall**

 15 **Örebro SK**

 16 **Östersunds FK**

PROMOTED CLUBS

  17 **IK Sirius FK**

 18 **AFC United**
NB Renamed AFC Eskilstuna for 2017 season

 19 **Halmstads BK**

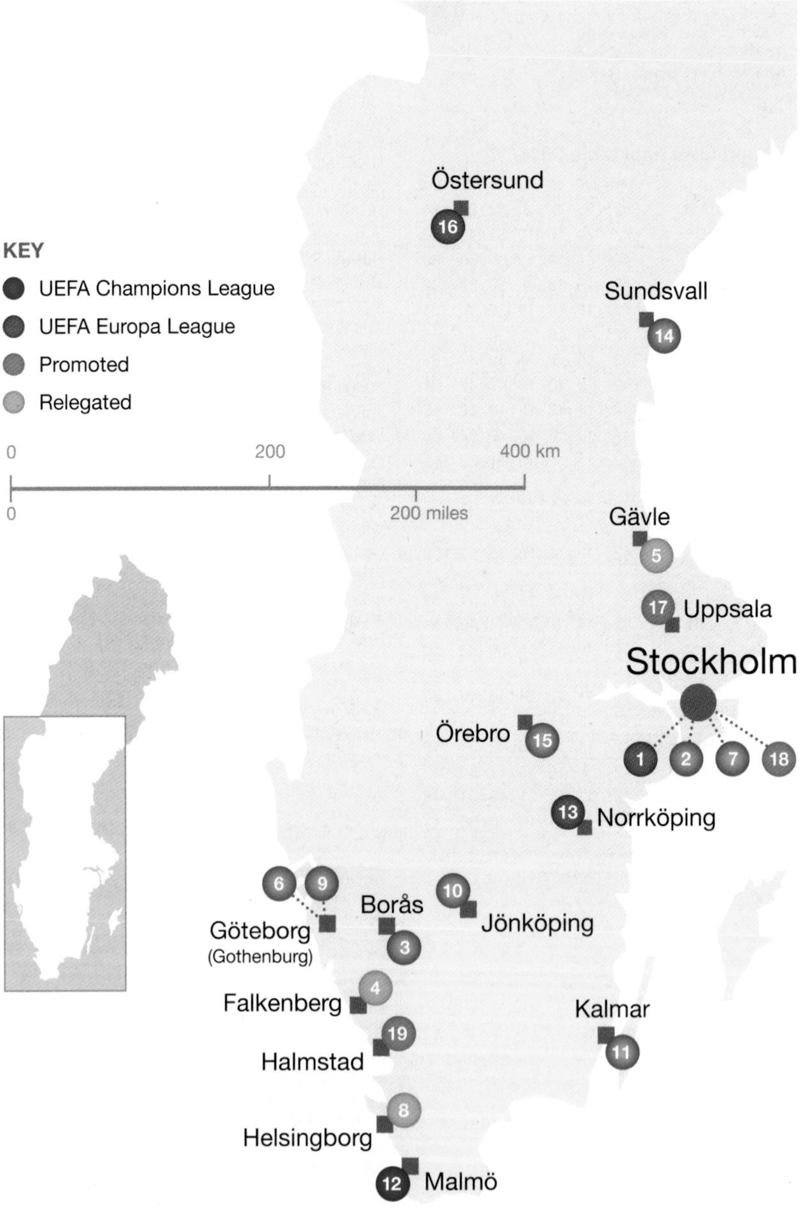

KEY
- UEFA Champions League
- UEFA Europa League
- Promoted
- Relegated

0 200 400 km
0 200 miles

Östersund 16
Sundsvall 14
Gävle 5
17 Uppsala
Stockholm 1 2 7 18
Örebro 15
13 Norrköping
6 9 Göteborg (Gothenburg)
Borås 3
10 Jönköping
Falkenberg 4
19 Halmstad
Kalmar 11
8 Helsingborg
12 Malmö

Malmö make history with record 19th title

After a difficult 2015 campaign, in which they finished fifth and failed to qualify for Europe, it was back to business as usual for Malmö FF as they claimed their third Allsvenskan crown in four seasons and in so doing became the country's record champions outright with a 19th Swedish title – one more than arch-rivals IFK Göteborg.

IFK Norrköping made a decent title defence but came up just short, as they would do also in the Swedish Cup, with 2016 Allsvenskan debutants Östersunds FK completing a flawless run in the competition by trouncing them 4-1 in the final.

Landmark league success for Light Blues

Title holders Norrköping falter at the finish

Östersund storm to shock Swedish Cup win

Domestic league

Malmö's march into the history books began with the appointment of a new coach. The choice of little-known Dane Allan Kuhn to replace experienced Norwegian Åge Hareide initially bewildered some of the locals but turned out to be an inspired choice as he masterminded a campaign in which the team won 70 per cent of their fixtures, scored 60 goals – 30 at home, 30 away – and eventually saw off the dual threat of Norrköping and AIK to clinch their record-breaking title with two games to spare.

It was almost a quarter of a century since Malmö had last been the Swedish league's most decorated club, and there was little promise of the history-making to come when Kuhn's side lost two of their first three games. But a run of nine victories in their next ten – which included a forfeit 3-0 win at Göteborg following a crowd-induced abandonment – carried them to the top of the table, and the frequent goalscoring of new Icelandic striker Vidar Örn Kjartansson plus the midfield creativity of Norwegian playmaker Magnus Wolff Eikrem ensured that they stayed there.

Norrköping maintained a commendable challenge in defence of their title despite suffering the twin mid-season blow of losing title-winning coach Jan Andersson to the Swedish national team and 2015 golden boot-winning striker Emir Kujovic to Gent. Indeed, they went on to dislodge Malmö temporarily from top spot thanks to an unbeaten 18-game run. But no sooner had hopes of another title been raised than they were summarily dashed as the team now led by Jens Gustafsson succumbed to three successive defeats, including a 6-0 submission at AIK, a result that would eventually enable their conquerors to edge them out of second place on goal difference.

Falkenberg and Gefle suffered automatic relegation, making way for the unlikely duo of Sirius and AFC United, but the big story at the bottom of the table was the relegation of Helsingborg, whose illustrious locally-born coach, Henrik Larsson, resigned on the spot after they conceded two late goals to lose their play-off against coastal rivals Halmstad.

Domestic cup

Another shock was the eighth-place finish of Allsvenskan first-timers Östersund, but the northern team led by unsung Englishman Graham Potter would have a few more surprises in store come the turn of the year as they saw off all-comers to lift the Swedish Cup. The only team to win all three of their group games, Östersund made it a maximum seven wins out of seven for the competition as a whole as they eliminated holders BK Häcken in the semi-finals before putting Norrköping to the sword in the final, staged somewhat advantageously in their own Jämtkraft Arena, and thus claiming a first major trophy.

Europe

Östersund's cup win meant no European football for Göteborg, who had been the best of Sweden's performers in 2016/17, winning three ties to reach the UEFA Europa League play-offs, where they fell to Qarabağ despite holding a 1-0 first-leg lead. Their elimination left the country without autumn involvement in Europe for the first time in six years.

National team

Life after Zlatan Ibrahimović, who retired post-UEFA EURO 2016 with a record 62 goals, was supposed to be tough for Sweden, but with new boss Andersson at the helm – in place of Erik Hamrén – and several players upping their game under his guidance, the road to Russia proved less rocky than anticipated. Furthermore, with six of their 2018 FIFA World Cup qualifying matches played, Sweden sat proudly on top of their group – courtesy of a spectacular long-range added-time winner from Ola Toivonen that enabled them to come from behind and beat previously undefeated France 2-1 at the Friends Arena in June.

DOMESTIC SEASON AT A GLANCE

Allsvenskan 2016 final table

			Home					Away					Total					
		Pld	W	D	L	F	A	W	D	L	F	A	W	D	L	F	A	Pts
1	**Malmö FF**	**30**	**12**	**1**	**2**	**30**	**9**	**9**	**2**	**4**	**30**	**17**	**21**	**3**	**6**	**60**	**26**	**66**
2	AIK	30	9	6	0	27	9	8	3	4	25	17	17	9	4	52	26	60
3	IFK Norrköping	30	11	2	2	40	17	7	4	4	19	20	18	6	6	59	37	60
4	IFK Göteborg	30	10	4	1	28	16	4	4	7	28	31	14	8	8	56	47	50
5	IF Elfsborg	30	9	4	2	35	16	4	5	6	23	22	13	9	8	58	38	48
6	Kalmar FF	30	7	4	4	25	17	5	4	6	20	23	12	8	10	45	40	44
7	Djurgårdens IF	30	8	1	6	27	22	6	0	9	21	25	14	1	15	48	47	43
8	Östersunds FK	30	9	1	5	26	18	3	5	7	18	28	12	6	12	44	46	42
9	Örebro SK	30	6	5	4	22	27	5	3	7	26	24	11	8	11	48	51	41
10	BK Häcken	30	7	2	6	38	24	4	5	6	20	21	11	7	12	58	45	40
11	Hammarby Fotboll	30	5	6	4	29	26	5	3	7	17	23	10	9	11	46	49	39
12	Jönköpings Södra IF	30	4	8	3	13	13	4	3	8	19	26	8	11	11	32	39	35
13	GIF Sundsvall	30	4	3	8	21	25	3	6	6	17	29	7	9	14	38	54	30
14	Helsingborgs IF	30	5	1	9	20	26	3	4	8	14	26	8	5	17	34	52	29
15	Gefle IF	30	2	6	7	15	26	4	3	8	19	30	6	9	15	34	56	27
16	Falkenbergs FF	30	1	2	12	13	37	1	2	12	12	47	2	4	24	25	84	10

European qualification 2017/18

Champion: Malmö FF (second qualifying round)

Cup winner: Östersunds FK (second qualifying round)
AIK (first qualifying round)
IFK Norrköping (first qualifying round)

Top scorer John Owoeri (Häcken), 17 goals
Relegated clubs Falkenbergs FF, Gefle IF, Helsingborgs IF
Promoted clubs IK Sirius FK, AFC United, Halmstads BK
Cup final Östersunds FK 4-1 IFK Norrköping

Player of the season

Andreas Johansson
(IFK Norrköping)

Norrköping were unable to repeat their 2015 Allsvenskan triumph in 2016, but it was not for the want of trying, and the man who symbolised the club's determination to hang on to their trophy was Johansson, their unflinching captain and defensive lynchpin. At 34 years of age, the once-capped Swedish international and former midfield anchorman was the league's standout performer. One of only seven outfield players to start all 30 Allsvenskan matches, it was hardly a surprise as he had missed only five league games in his previous four seasons with the club.

Newcomer of the season

Alexander Isak
(AIK)

As one door closed to the Swedish national side with the retirement of Zlatan Ibrahimović, so another one appeared to open with the emergence of Isak, an extravagantly gifted youngster who burst on to the Allsvenskan scene with local club AIK in 2016, scoring ten goals, including a double on his 17th birthday against local rivals Djurgården. The following January he became Sweden's youngest scorer of all time, at 17 years and 113 days, before joining Borussia Dortmund a week and a half later for a reported Allsvenskan record fee.

Team of the season

(4-4-2)

Coach: Potter *(Östersund)*

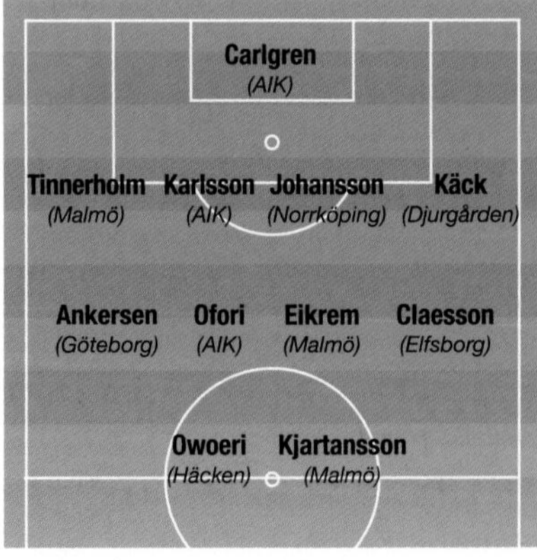

NATIONAL TEAM

International tournament appearances

FIFA World Cup (11) 1934 (2nd round), 1938 (4th), 1950 (3rd), 1958 (runners-up), 1970, 1974 (2nd phase), 1978, 1990, 1994 (3rd), 2002 (2nd round), 2006 (2nd round)
UEFA European Championship (6) 1992 (semi-finals), 2000, 2004 (qtr-finals), 2008, 2012, 2016

Top five all-time caps

Anders Svensson (148); Thomas Ravelli (143); Andreas Isaksson (133); Kim Källström (131); Olof Mellberg (117)

Top five all-time goals

Zlatan Ibrahimović (62); Sven Rydell (49); Gunnar Nordahl (43); Henrik Larsson (37); Gunnar Gren (32)

Results 2016/17

06/09/16	Netherlands (WCQ)	H	Solna	D	1-1	*Berg (42)*
07/10/16	Luxembourg (WCQ)	A	Luxembourg	W	1-0	*Lustig (58)*
10/10/16	Bulgaria (WCQ)	H	Solna	W	3-0	*Toivonen (39), Hiljemark (45), Lindelöf (58)*
11/11/16	France (WCQ)	A	Saint-Denis	L	1-2	*Forsberg (55)*
15/11/16	Hungary	A	Budapest	W	2-0	*Sam Larsson (30), Kiese Thelin (67)*
08/01/17	Ivory Coast	N	Abu Dhabi (UAE)	L	1-2	*Kanon (39og)*
12/01/17	Slovakia B	N	Abu Dhabi (UAE)	W	6-0	*Isak (19), Moberg Karlsson (51), Andersson (59, 79), Frick (89), Ghoddos (90+2)*
25/03/17	Belarus (WCQ)	H	Solna	W	4-0	*Forsberg (19p, 49), Berg (57), Kiese Thelin (78)*
28/03/17	Portugal	A	Funchal	W	3-2	*Claesson (57, 76), João Cancelo (90+3og)*
09/06/17	France (WCQ)	H	Solna	W	2-1	*Durmaz (43), Toivonen (90+3)*
13/06/17	Norway	A	Oslo	D	1-1	*Armenteros (81)*

Appearances 2016/17

Coach: Jan Andersson	29/09/62		NED	LUX	BUL	FRA	Hun	Civ	Svk	BLR	Por	FRA	Nor	Caps	Goals
Robin Olsen	08/01/90	København (DEN)	G	G	G	G				G		G		10	-
Mikael Lustig	13/12/86	Celtic (SCO)	D	D						D	s70	D		58	4
Victor Lindelöf	17/07/94	Benfica (POR)	D	D	D	D	s46					D		12	1
Andreas Granqvist	16/04/85	Krasnodar (RUS)	D	D	D	D	D46			D	D46	D		63	3
Oscar Wendt	24/10/85	Mönchengladbach (GER)	D		s74		D							28	-
Markus Rohdén	11/05/91	Crotone (ITA)	M76				M						s68	9	1
Alexander Fransson	02/04/94	Basel (SUI)	M	s79			s81							5	-
Oscar Hiljemark	28/06/92	Palermo (ITA) /Genoa (ITA)	M	M	M	s66	M			M	s89		M68	18	2
Emil Forsberg	23/10/91	RB Leipzig (GER)	M	M	M74	M				M		M	s69	27	5
John Guidetti	15/04/92	Celta (ESP)	A64	A70	s85	A73	s74					s88	A68	19	1
Marcus Berg	17/08/86	Panathinaikos (GRE)	A87	A	A85					A	s87	A88		47	12
Christoffer Nyman	05/10/92	Braunschweig (GER)	s64	s88			A				A87		A	9	-
Emir Kujovic	22/06/88	Gent (BEL)	s76											5	1
Jimmy Durmaz	22/03/89	Toulouse (FRA)	s87	M88	M	M87				M85	s67	M76		41	3
Martin Olsson	17/05/88	Norwich (ENG)		D	D63									40	5
Albin Ekdal	28/07/89	Hamburg (GER)		M79	M	M66				M69		M77		30	-
Ola Toivonen	03/07/86	Toulouse (FRA)		s70	A	A				A74		A		50	11
Emil Krafth	02/08/94	Bologna (ITA)			D	D	D73				D70		D	9	-
Ludwig Augustinsson	21/04/94	København (DEN)			s63	D				D		D		8	-
Jakob Johansson	21/06/90	AEK Athens (GRE)				M	M81			s69	M	M	s70	9	-
Isaac Kiese Thelin	24/06/92	Bordeaux (FRA) /Anderlecht (BEL)				s73	A74			s74	A			12	2
Pontus Jansson	13/02/91	Leeds (ENG)				s87	D			D	s46		D70	13	-
Kristoffer Nordfeldt	23/06/89	Swansea (ENG)					G						G	7	-
Sam Larsson	10/04/93	Heerenveen (NED)					M65				M67		M69	3	1
Viktor Claesson	02/01/92	Elfsborg /Krasnodar (RUS)					s65	M	M	s85	M	s76	M	13	3
Linus Wahlqvist	11/11/96	Norrköping					s73	D	D					5	-
Peter Abrahamsson	18/07/88	Häcken						G						1	-
Emil Salomonsson	28/04/89	Göteborg						D	s76					8	1
Pa Konate	25/04/94	Malmö						D46						3	-
Franz Brorsson	30/01/96	Malmö						D						1	-
Oscar Lewicki	14/07/92	Malmö						M74	M60					14	-
Kristoffer Olsson	30/06/95	Midtjylland (DEN)						M74						1	-
Nicklas Bärkroth	19/01/92	Norrköping						M62	s85					6	-
Sebastian Andersson	15/07/91	Norrköping						A	A85					2	2
Per Frick	14/04/92	Elfsborg						A62	s71					2	1
Joakim Nilsson	06/02/94	Elfsborg						s46	D60					3	-
Alexander Isak	21/09/99	AIK						s62	A71					2	1
David Moberg Karlsson	20/03/94	Norrköping						s62	M60					2	1
Joel Allansson	03/11/92	Randers (DEN)						s74	M					2	-
Saman Ghoddos	06/09/93	Östersund						s74	s60					2	1
Andreas Linde	24/07/93	Molde (NOR)							G					1	-
Anton Tinnerholm	26/02/91	Malmö							D76					7	-
Jacob Une Larsson	08/04/94	Djurgården							D					1	-
Filip Dagerstål	01/02/97	Norrköping							s60					1	-
Ken Sema	30/09/93	Östersund							s60					1	-
Karl-Johan Johnsson	28/01/90	Guingamp (FRA)									G			4	-
Filip Helander	22/04/93	Bologna (ITA)									D89		D	2	-
Niklas Hult	13/02/90	Panathinaikos (GRE)									D		D	6	-
Sebastian Larsson	06/06/85	Sunderland (ENG)									M	s77	M	90	6
Samuel Armenteros	27/05/90	Heracles (NED)											s68	1	1

EUROPE

IFK Norrköping

CHAMPIONS LEAGUE

Second qualifying round - Rosenborg BK (NOR)
A 1-3 *Andersson (70)*
Vaikla, Fjóluson, Johansson, Nyman, Wahlqvist, Blomqvist (Citaku 90+1), Bärkroth (Hadenius 67), Telo, Andersson, Sjölund, Tekie (Smith 67). Coach: Jens Gustafsson (SWE)
H 3-2 *Andersson (57, 77), Nyman (59)*
Vaikla, Fjóluson (Dagerstål 90+1), Johansson, Nyman, Wahlqvist, Blomqvist (Hadenius 74), Bärkroth, Telo, Smith (Tekie 59), Andersson, Sjölund. Coach: Jens Gustafsson (SWE)

BK Häcken

EUROPA LEAGUE

Second qualifying round - Cork City FC (IRL)
H 1-1 *Owoeri (83)*
Abrahamsson, Sudic, Wahlström, Schüller, Paulinho, Mensah, Ericsson (Savage 57), Arkivuo (Binaku 78), Owoeri, Mohammed (J Andersson 66), Gustafsson. Coach: Peter Gerhardsson (SWE)
Red card: Mensah 63
A 0-1
Abrahamsson, Sudic, Wahlström, Schüller (Ericsson 64), Paulinho, Abubakari, Arkivuo, Owoeri (Jeremejeff 74), Mohammed (Savage 45+1), Gustafsson, J Andersson. Coach: Peter Gerhardsson (SWE)

IFK Göteborg

EUROPA LEAGUE

First qualifying round - Llandudno FC (WAL)
H 5-0 *Engvall (11), Rieks (12), Salomonsson (36), Hysén (79, 81)*
Alvbåge, Salomonsson, Aleesami, Eriksson (Pettersson 76), Albæk, Rieks, Smedberg-Dalence (Karlsson Lagemyr 53), Boman (Hysén 65), Engvall, Rogne, Bjärsmyr. Coach: Jörgen Lennartsson (SWE)
A 2-1 *Smedberg-Dalence (36), Sköld (54)*
Dahlberg, Albæk (Eriksson 63), Hysén (Boman 80), Smedberg-Dalence, Jónsson, Sköld, Pettersson, Karlsson Lagemyr (Rieks 80), Nordström, Bjärsmyr, Leksell. Coach: Jörgen Lennartsson (SWE)

Second qualifying round - GKS Piast Gliwice (POL)
A 3-0 *Rogne (2), Hysén (35), Engvall (86)*
Alvbåge, Salomonsson, Aleesami, Eriksson, Albæk, Rieks, Ankersen (Smedberg-Dalence 82), Hysén (Engvall 80), Boman (Pettersson 87), Rogne, Bjärsmyr. Coach: Jörgen Lennartsson (SWE)
H 0-0
Alvbåge, Salomonsson, Aleesami, Albæk (Eriksson 69), Rieks (Ankersen 63), Hysén (Sköld 78), Smedberg-Dalence, Engvall, Pettersson, Rogne, Bjärsmyr. Coach: Jörgen Lennartsson (SWE)

Third qualifying round - HJK Helsinki (FIN)
H 1-2 *Salomonsson (73)*
Alvbåge, Salomonsson, Aleesami, Eriksson, Albæk, Rieks, Ankersen, Hysén (Engvall 79), Smedberg-Dalence (Karlsson Lagemyr 65), Rogne, Bjärsmyr (Jónsson 46). Coach: Jörgen Lennartsson (SWE)
A 2-0 *Boman (35), Ankersen (82)*
Alvbåge, Salomonsson, Aleesami, Eriksson, Albæk, Rieks, Ankersen, Smedberg-Dalence (Pettersson 86), Boman, Rogne, Bjärsmyr. Coach: Jörgen Lennartsson (SWE)

Play-offs - Qarabağ FK (AZE)
H 1-0 *Albæk (56)*
Alvbåge, Salomonsson, Jamieson, Albæk, Rieks (Nordström 88), Ankersen, Hysén (Smedberg-Dalence 83), Boman, Pettersson, Rogne, Bjärsmyr. Coach: Jörgen Lennartsson (SWE)
A 0-3
Alvbåge, Salomonsson, Jamieson, Eriksson (Smedberg-Dalence 83), Albæk, Rieks, Ankersen, Hysén (Ómarsson 72), Boman (Pettersson 72), Rogne, Bjärsmyr. Coach: Jörgen Lennartsson (SWE)

AIK

EUROPA LEAGUE

First qualifying round - Bala Town FC (WAL)
H 2-0 *Affane (27), Johansson (52)*
Carlgren, Karlsson, Johansson, Ofori, Sundgren, Strandberg, Ishizaki, Gravius (Jönsson Salétros 74), Kpozo, Isak (Avdic 83), Affane (Blomberg 68). Coach: Rikard Norling (SWE)
A 2-0 *Avdic (8), Strandberg (24)*
Carlgren, Johansson, Blomberg, Avdic, Väisänen, Ofori (Affane 72), Sundgren, Strandberg (Isak 63), Ishizaki (Yasin 46), Jönsson Salétros, Kpozo. Coach: Rikard Norling (SWE)

Second qualifying round - Europa FC (GIB)
H 1-0 *Strandberg (89)*
Carlgren, Hauksson (Sundgren 78), Karlsson, Avdic, Ofori, Ishizaki, Hooiveld, Gravius (Strandberg 46), Kpozo, Isak, Affane (Blomberg 68). Coach: Rikard Norling (SWE)
A 1-0 *Markkanen (55)*
Carlgren, Hauksson, Johansson, Blomberg, Markkanen (Yasin 78), Väisänen (Kpozo 88), Ofori, Sundgren, Hooiveld, Jönsson Salétros, Affane (Ishizaki 46). Coach: Rikard Norling (SWE)

Third qualifying round - Panathinaikos FC (GRE)
A 0-1
Carlgren, Hauksson, Karlsson, Johansson, Blomberg, Avdic (Jönsson Salétros 87), Markkanen, Ofori, Sundgren, Ishizaki (Yasin 65), Kpozo. Coach: Rikard Norling (SWE)
H 0-2
Carlgren, Hauksson, Karlsson, Johansson, Blomberg (Yasin 61), Markkanen, Ofori, Sundgren, Ishizaki (Jönsson Salétros 78), Hooiveld, Affane (Avdic 62). Coach: Rikard Norling (SWE)

DOMESTIC LEAGUE CLUB-BY-CLUB

AIK

1891 • Friends Arena (54,329) • aikfotboll.se

Major honours
Swedish League (11) 1900, 1901, 1911, 1914, 1916, 1923, 1932, 1937, 1992, 1998, 2009; Swedish Cup (8) 1949, 1950, 1976, 1985, 1996, 1997, 1999, 2009

Coach: Andreas Alm;
(13/05/16) Rikard Norling

2016					
03/04	h	Sundsvall	D	1-1	*Brustad*
07/04	a	Östersund	W	2-0	*Strandberg, Isak*
11/04	h	Göteborg	D	3-3	*Hauksson, Ishizaki, Brustad*
17/04	a	Norrköping	L	1-4	*Strandberg*
25/04	h	Elfsborg	W	2-1	*Isak, Jönsson Salétros*
28/04	a	Helsingborg	L	1-2	*Strandberg*
02/05	h	Jönköping	D	0-0	
08/05	h	Häcken	W	3-2	*Strandberg 2, Yasin*
16/05	h	Djurgården	W	2-0	*Ishizaki, Hauksson*
20/05	a	Falkenberg	W	3-2	*Strandberg 2, Hauksson*
23/05	a	Gefle	W	1-0	*Isak*
28/05	h	Örebro	D	0-0	
10/07	a	Kalmar	D	1-1	*Ishizaki*
17/07	h	Malmö	D	1-1	*Avdic*
24/07	a	Hammarby	W	3-0	*Hauksson, Markkanen, Ofori*
31/07	h	Falkenberg	W	2-0	*Markkanen 2*
07/08	a	Malmö	L	0-2	
13/08	h	Helsingborg	W	2-1	*Markkanen, Sundgren (p)*
21/08	a	Örebro	W	2-0	*Obasi, Isak*
28/08	h	Hammarby	D	0-0	
11/09	a	Sundsvall	W	3-1	*Avdic, og (Tranberg), Markkanen*
18/09	h	Gefle	W	1-0	*Markkanen*
21/09	a	Djurgården	W	3-0	*Isak 2, Obasi*
25/09	a	Elfsborg	D	2-2	*Obasi 2*
02/10	h	Norrköping	W	6-0	*Ishizaki, Isak 2, Ofori, Obasi, Markkanen*
16/10	h	Östersund	W	2-0	*Isak, Obasi*
24/10	a	Göteborg	L	0-1	
27/10	h	Häcken	W	2-1	*Väisänen, Markkanen*
31/10	a	Jönköping	D	0-0	
06/11	h	Kalmar	W	3-1	*Isak, Sundgren (p), Ofori*

No	Name	Nat	DoB	Pos	Aps	(s)	Gls
39	Amin Affane		21/01/94	M	7	(12)	
10	Denni Avdic		05/09/88	A	8	(7)	2
8	Johan Blomberg		14/06/87	M	16	(5)	
7	Fredrik Brustad	NOR	22/06/89	A	4	(7)	2
35	Patrik Carlgren		08/01/92	G	28		
14	John Chibuike	NGA	10/10/88	M		(7)	
28	Niclas Eliasson		07/12/95	M	3	(2)	
20	Dickson Etuhu	NGA	08/06/82	M	1	(1)	
31	Christos Gravius		14/10/97	A	3	(6)	
2	Haukur Hauksson	ISL	01/09/91	D	15	(3)	4
26	Jos Hooiveld	NED	22/04/83	D	11		
36	Alexander Isak		21/09/99	A	19	(5)	10
24	Stefan Ishizaki		15/05/82	M	26	(1)	4
4	Nils-Eric Johansson		13/01/80	D	28		
29	Anton Jönsson Salétros		12/04/96	M	15	(4)	1
3	Per Karlsson		02/01/86	D	26		
32	Patrick Kpozo	GHA	15/07/97	D	11		
34	Oscar Linnér		23/02/97	G	2		
11	Eero Markkanen	FIN	03/07/91	A	9	(13)	8
7	Chinedu Obasi	NGA	01/06/86	M	9	(1)	6
17	Ebenezer Ofori	GHA	01/07/95	M	24	(3)	3
22	Carlos Strandberg		14/04/96	A	11	(1)	7
21	Daniel Sundgren		22/11/90	D	24		2
15	Sauli Väisänen	FIN	05/06/94	D	18	(4)	1
19	Ahmed Yasin	IRQ	21/04/91	M	12	(6)	1

Djurgårdens IF

1891 • Tele2Arena (33,000) • dif.se

Major honours
Swedish League (11) 1912, 1915, 1917, 1920, 1955, 1959, 1964, 1966, 2002, 2003, 2005; Swedish Cup (4) 1990, 2002, 2004, 2005

Coach: Per Olsson;
(03/08/16) Mark Dempsey (ENG)

2016					
03/04	a	Örebro	W	2-0	*Johnson, Colley*
07/04	h	Falkenberg	W	5-0	*Johnson 2, Ranégie (p), Walker, Colley*
10/04	a	Gefle	W	2-1	*Johnson, Walker*
19/04	h	Hammarby	L	1-3	*Johnson*
24/04	a	Malmö	L	0-1	
28/04	a	Elfsborg	L	0-3	
02/05	h	Östersund	W	3-0	*Moon, Johnson, Ranégie*
09/05	a	Göteborg	L	1-2	*Sabovic*
16/05	a	AIK	L	0-2	
19/05	h	Kalmar	L	0-3	
22/05	h	Helsingborg	W	3-0	*Johnson, Berntsen, Karlström*
29/05	a	Häcken	L	1-3	*Ranégie*
09/07	h	Norrköping	L	0-1	
18/07	a	Jönköping	L	0-1	
25/07	h	Sundsvall	L	1-3	*Kadewere*
01/08	a	Kalmar	L	1-2	*Walker*
08/08	h	Göteborg	W	3-1	*Olunga 2, Ranégie*
14/08	h	Elfsborg	D	2-2	*Olunga, Eriksson*
20/08	a	Östersund	L	0-1	
27/08	h	Gefle	W	2-1	*Gunnarsson, Olunga*
11/09	a	Falkenberg	W	2-1	*Ranégie, Olunga*
18/09	h	Malmö	W	3-1	*Eriksson, Olunga 2*
21/09	h	AIK	L	0-3	
26/09	a	Norrköping	W	3-1	*Gunnarsson, Olunga, Berntsen*
02/10	h	Örebro	W	3-2	*Une Larsson, Faltsetas, Käck*
17/10	a	Hammarby	L	2-4	*Walker, Ranégie*
24/10	h	Jönköping	L	0-2	
27/10	a	Helsingborg	W	2-1	*Olunga 2*
31/10	h	Häcken	W	1-0	*Kadewere*
06/11	a	Sundsvall	W	5-2	*Olunga 2, El Kabir, Kadewere, Eriksson*

No	Name	Nat	DoB	Pos	Aps	(s)	Gls
10	Daniel Berntsen	NOR	04/04/93	M	14	(11)	2
2	Tim Björkström		08/01/91	D	22		
27	Kebba Ceesay	GAM	14/11/87	D	14		
15	Omar Colley	GAM	24/10/92	D	16	(1)	2
58	Othman El Kabir	NED	17/07/91	M	12	(1)	1
77	Magnus Eriksson		08/04/90	A	17		3
6	Alexander Faltsetas		04/07/87	M	25	(1)	1
28	Niklas Gunnarsson	NOR	27/04/91	D	13		2
19	Marcus Hansson		12/02/90	M	18	(1)	
12	Kenneth Høie	NOR	11/09/79	G	15		
1	Andreas Isaksson		03/10/81	G	8		
11	Amadou Jawo		26/09/84	A	3	(12)	
20	Sam Johnson	LBR	06/05/93	A	12		7
25	Oskar Jonsson		24/01/97	G	1		
24	Tino Kadewere	ZIM	05/01/96	A	8	(13)	3
5	Stefan Karlsson		15/12/88	D	3	(2)	
22	Jesper Karlström		21/06/95	M	10	(5)	1
3	Elliot Käck		18/09/89	D	30		1
21	Mihlali Mayambela	RSA	25/08/96	M	1	(7)	
7	Moon Seon-Min	KOR	09/06/92	M	6	(4)	1
23	Hampus Nilsson		17/07/90	G	6		
17	Michael Olunga	KEN	26/03/94	A	18	(9)	12
9	Haris Radetinac	SRB	28/10/85	M	1	(1)	
13	Mathias Ranégie		14/06/84	A	20	(5)	6
14	Besard Sabovic		05/01/98	M	3	(4)	1
31	Filip Tasic		12/11/98	M		(1)	
4	Jacob Une Larsson		08/04/94	D	10	(3)	1
8	Kevin Walker		03/08/89	M	24	(1)	4

IF Elfsborg

1904 • Borås Arena (16,284) • elfsborg.se

Major honours
Swedish League (6) 1936, 1939, 1940, 1961, 2006, 2012; Swedish Cup (3) 2001, 2003, 2014

Coach: Magnus Haglund

2016					
03/04	a	Häcken	L	1-2	*Lundqvist*
07/04	h	Hammarby	W	4-1	*Prodell, Claesson, og (Magyar), Rohdén (p)*
10/04	a	Kalmar	L	2-3	*Hedlund, Prodell*
18/04	h	Malmö	L	0-1	
25/04	a	AIK	L	1-2	*Prodell*
28/04	h	Djurgården	W	3-0	*L Nilsson, Claesson, Prodell*
01/05	a	Falkenberg	W	2-1	*Hedlund, Bajrami*
07/05	h	Gefle	W	2-0	*L Nilsson, Hedlund*
15/05	a	Örebro	L	0-1	
18/05	a	Sundsvall	W	3-1	*Prodell 2, Rohdén (p)*
22/05	h	Jönköping	D	3-3	*Rohdén, Frick, Prodell*
29/05	a	Norrköping	D	0-0	
10/07	a	Helsingborg	W	4-2	*L Nilsson, Rohdén, Randrup, Lundevall*
17/07	h	Göteborg	D	1-1	*Hedlund*
25/07	h	Östersund	W	3-1	*Prodell, Claesson 2*
30/07	a	Östersund	D	0-0	
07/08	h	Häcken	L	2-4	*Hedlund, Prodell*
14/08	a	Djurgården	D	2-2	*Frick, Prodell*
22/08	h	Sundsvall	W	4-0	*Jönsson, Jebali 3*
28/08	a	Jönköping	L	0-1	
10/09	h	Kalmar	D	1-1	*Claesson*
18/09	h	Falkenberg	W	5-0	*Claesson (p), Gustavsson, Prodell, Jebali, Lundevall*
22/09	a	Malmö	L	0-1	
25/09	h	AIK	D	2-2	*Prodell, Frick*
02/10	a	Gefle	D	2-2	*Frick, Jebali*
16/10	h	Helsingborg	W	1-0	*Claesson*
23/10	a	Hammarby	W	4-2	*Claesson, Frick, Lundevall, Jebali*
26/10	h	Norrköping	W	2-1	*Prodell, Manns*
31/10	a	Göteborg	D	2-2	*Frick 2*
06/11	h	Örebro	W	2-1	*Lundevall, Jebali*

No	Name	Nat	DoB	Pos	Aps	(s)	Gls
20	Emir Bajrami		07/03/88	M	9	(8)	1
27	Thomas Kind Bendiksen	NOR	08/08/89	M		(9)	
16	Viktor Claesson		02/01/92	M	29		8
29	Ibrahim Dresevic		24/01/97	D	1	(1)	
17	Per Frick		14/04/92	A	7	(17)	7
7	Daniel Gustavsson		29/08/90	M	10		1
24	Viktor Götesson		14/07/95	A		(3)	
21	Henning Hauger	NOR	17/07/85	M	16	(5)	
19	Simon Hedlund		11/03/93	M	17		5
5	Jørgen Horn	NOR	07/06/87	D	20		
11	Issam Jebali	TUN	25/12/91	A	14	(1)	7
6	Jon Jönsson		08/07/83	D	19	(2)	1
28	Rami Kaib		08/05/97	D	3	(2)	
10	Simon Lundevall		23/09/88	M	22	(7)	4
3	Adam Lundqvist		20/03/94	D	25		1
2	Jesper Manns		05/08/95	D	24	(4)	1
12	Joakim Nilsson		06/02/94	D	16	(4)	
9	Lasse Nilsson		03/01/82	A	8	(4)	3
31	Simon Olsson		14/09/97	M	4		
22	Viktor Prodell		29/02/88	A	27	(3)	13
4	Anders Randrup	DEN	16/07/88	D	13	(3)	1
7	Marcus Rohdén		11/05/91	M	15		4
15	Rasmus Rosenqvist		17/07/96	M	1	(1)	
1	Kevin Stuhr Ellegaard	DEN	23/05/86	G	30		

SWEDEN

Falkenbergs FF

1928 • Falkenbergs IP (6,000) • falkenbergsff.se

Coach: Hans Eklund

2016					
03/04	h	Göteborg	L	0-2	
07/04	a	Djurgården	L	0-5	
10/04	h	Östersund	L	1-2	*Jakobsen*
16/04	a	Helsingborg	L	1-3	*Svensson*
22/04	h	Norrköping	W	2-1	*Nilsson, Juel-Nielsen*
27/04	a	Jönköping	D	1-1	*Krizanovic*
01/05	h	Elfsborg	L	1-2	*Nazari (p)*
09/05	a	Sundsvall	L	1-2	*Juel-Nielsen*
15/05	h	Häcken	L	1-4	*Kwakwa*
20/05	h	AIK	L	2-3	*Juel-Nielsen 2*
23/05	a	Malmö	L	0-2	
29/05	h	Kalmar	L	1-2	*Svensson*
09/07	a	Gefle	W	2-1	*Nazari, Araba*
17/07	a	Hammarby	D	3-3	*J Karlsson 2, Sjöstedt*
23/07	h	Örebro	L	1-3	*Krizanovic*
31/07	a	AIK	L	0-2	
06/08	h	Jönköping	L	0-5	
12/08	a	Göteborg	L	0-2	
21/08	h	Gefle	D	1-1	*J Karlsson*
28/08	a	Örebro	L	2-3	*J Karlsson, Rodevåg*
11/09	h	Djurgården	L	1-2	*Rodevåg*
18/09	a	Elfsborg	L	0-5	
21/09	a	Kalmar	L	0-3	
26/09	h	Hammarby	L	0-2	
01/10	a	Östersund	L	1-6	*J Karlsson*
15/10	h	Sundsvall	D	1-1	*J Karlsson*
23/10	a	Norrköping	L	1-2	*J Karlsson*
26/10	h	Malmö	L	0-3	
30/10	h	Helsingborg	L	1-4	*Rodevåg*
06/11	a	Häcken	L	0-7	

No	Name	Nat	DoB	Pos	Aps	(s)	Gls
18	Hakeem Araba	ENG	12/02/91	A	11	(13)	1
12	Christoffer Carlsson		15/01/89	M	21	(1)	
25	Felipe Carvalho	URU	18/09/93	D	14		
30	Thomas Drage	NOR	20/02/92	M	11	(1)	
10	Alexander Jakobsen	DEN	18/03/94	A	10	(1)	1
4	Daniel Johansson		28/07/87	D	3	(1)	
33	Tibor Joza		10/08/86	D	15	(2)	
21	Thomas Juel-Nielsen	DEN	18/06/90	D	28		4
17	Jesper Karlsson		25/07/98	A	20	(6)	7
14	Per Karlsson		20/04/89	D	15	(1)	
8	Tobias Karlsson		25/02/75	D	3	(2)	
42	Zlatan Krizanovic		17/05/91	A	11	(8)	2
23	Enock Kwakwa	GHA	02/07/94	M	16	(2)	1
16	Alexander Lundin		25/10/92	G	12		
1	Otto Martler		14/04/87	G	18		
77	Kamal Mustafa		22/07/91	M	3	(17)	
19	Amin Nazari		26/04/93	M	20	(3)	2
9	Gustaf Nilsson		23/05/97	A	5		1
70	Lord Ofosuhene	GHA	30/03/94	A	3		
20	Akseli Pelvas	FIN	08/02/89	A	6	(8)	
15	Stefan Rodevåg		11/06/80	A	14	(8)	3
2	Rasmus Sjöstedt		28/02/92	D	23	(2)	1
7	David Svensson		09/04/84	M	25		2
3	Edi Sylisufaj		08/05/99	M		(3)	
11	Johannes Vall		19/10/92	D	23	(2)	
6	Erik Zetterberg		16/02/97	M		(2)	

Gefle IF

1882 • Gavlevallen (6,500) • gefleiffotboll.se

Coach: Roger Sandberg; (02/05/16) Thomas Andersson

2016					
03/04	h	Helsingborg	D	1-1	*Skrabb*
07/04	a	Sundsvall	W	2-1	*Bååth, Williams*
10/04	h	Djurgården	L	1-2	*Skrabb*
17/04	a	Jönköping	L	0-1	
23/04	h	Östersund	D	0-0	
28/04	a	Häcken	L	1-6	*Bertilsson*
02/05	h	Göteborg	L	2-6	*Williams 2*
07/05	a	Elfsborg	L	0-2	
14/05	a	Malmö	L	0-3	
19/05	h	Örebro	L	0-4	
23/05	h	AIK	L	0-1	
29/05	a	Hammarby	L	1-2	*Bertilsson*
09/07	h	Falkenberg	L	1-2	*Skrabb*
18/07	h	Kalmar	W	4-2	*Oremo, Bertilsson, Hjelte, Skrabb*
23/07	a	Norrköping	L	0-2	
30/07	h	Hammarby	L	0-2	
05/08	a	Helsingborg	W	3-2	*Bertilsson, Oremo, Lantto*
13/08	h	Norrköping	D	0-0	
21/08	a	Falkenberg	D	1-1	*Skrabb*
27/08	a	Djurgården	L	1-2	*Bertilsson*
12/09	h	Häcken	D	2-2	*og (Wahlström), Rauschenberg*
18/09	a	AIK	L	0-1	
21/09	h	Jönköping	L	0-1	
26/09	a	Örebro	D	2-2	*Bertilsson, Skrabb*
02/10	h	Elfsborg	D	2-2	*Williams, Oremo*
17/10	a	Göteborg	D	3-3	*Skrabb, Rauschenberg (p), Nadeau*
21/10	h	Sundsvall	D	1-1	*Bertilsson*
26/10	a	Kalmar	W	1-0	*Bellander*
30/10	h	Malmö	W	1-0	*Williams*
06/11	a	Östersund	W	4-2	*Lantto, Oremo 2, Bertilsson*

No	Name	Nat	DoB	Pos	Aps	(s)	Gls
19	Abdul-Basit Adam	GHA	13/02/95	A		(5)	
25	Andreas Andersson		27/02/91	G	22		
20	Emil Bellander		05/01/94	A		(6)	1
13	Johan Bertilsson		15/02/88	M	30		8
21	Kwame Bonsu	GHA	25/09/94	M	13	(10)	
12	Anders Bååth		13/04/91	M	17	(5)	1
5	Jacob Ericsson		17/09/93	D	12	(7)	
6	Jesper Florén		11/09/90	D	28		
1	Emil Hedvall		09/06/83	G	8		
15	Jacob Hjelte		11/08/96	A	1	(14)	1
4	Anton Lans		17/04/91	D	12	(2)	
17	Jonas Lantto		22/05/87	M	27	(2)	2
26	Albin Lohikangas		20/08/98	D		(2)	
2	Joshua Nadeau	FRA	12/09/94	D	21		1
7	Robin Nilsson		15/09/88	M	29		
9	Johan Oremo		24/10/86	A	19	(8)	5
14	Jens Portin	FIN	13/12/84	D	18	(1)	
11	York Rafael		17/03/99	A		(1)	
29	Martin Rauschenberg	DEN	15/01/92	D	29		2
8	Simon Skrabb	FIN	19/01/95	A	28		7
18	Tshutshu Tshakasua		15/05/97	M		(3)	
10	Dioh Williams	LBR	08/01/84	A	16	(6)	5

IFK Göteborg

1904 • Nya Gamla Ullevi (19,000) • ifkgoteborg.se

Major honours
UEFA Cup (2) 1982, 1987; Swedish League (18) 1908, 1910, 1918, 1935, 1942, 1958, 1969, 1982, 1983, 1984, 1987, 1990, 1991, 1993, 1994, 1995, 1996, 2007; Swedish Cup (7) 1979, 1982, 1983, 1991 (autumn), 2008, 2013, 2015

Coach: Jörgen Lennartsson

2016					
03/04	a	Falkenberg	W	2-0	*Albæk (p), Hysén*
06/04	h	Häcken	W	1-0	*Rieks*
11/04	a	AIK	D	3-3	*Hysén 2, Jónsson*
17/04	h	Kalmar	D	1-1	*Salomonsson*
24/04	a	Örebro	L	2-3	*Boman, Rieks*
27/04	h	Malmö	L	0-3	*(w/o; match abandoned after 77 mins at 0-0)*
02/05	a	Gefle	W	6-2	*og (Bertilsson), Smedberg-Dalence, Ankersen 2, Hysén, Karlsson Lagemyr*
09/05	h	Djurgården	W	2-1	*Engvall, Hysén*
15/05	a	Östersund	L	0-2	
19/05	h	Norrköping	D	1-1	*Salomonsson*
23/05	h	Hammarby	W	2-1	*Smedberg-Dalence, Boman*
29/05	a	Helsingborg	W	3-1	*Ankersen, Engvall, Karlsson Lagemyr*
10/07	h	Sundsvall	W	4-1	*Engvall, Salomonsson, Boman, Pettersson*
17/07	a	Elfsborg	D	1-1	*Boman*
24/07	h	Jönköping	W	2-1	*Albæk 2*
31/07	a	Jönköping	D	1-1	*Hysén*
08/08	a	Djurgården	L	1-3	*Pettersson*
12/08	h	Falkenberg	W	2-0	*Smedberg-Dalence, Salomonsson (p)*
21/08	a	Hammarby	L	0-2	
28/08	h	Helsingborg	W	2-0	*Ómarsson, Ankersen*
12/09	a	Malmö	L	1-3	*og (Jeremejeff)*
19/09	a	Häcken	D	2-2	*Salomonsson (p), Ómarsson*
22/09	h	Örebro	W	3-2	*Hysén 2, Ómarsson*
26/09	h	Östersund	W	2-0	*Rieks, Ómarsson*
02/10	a	Kalmar	L	2-4	*Hysén 2*
17/10	h	Gefle	D	3-3	*Salomonsson, Rieks, Ankersen*
24/10	h	AIK	W	1-0	*Ómarsson*
27/10	a	Sundsvall	W	3-1	*Ankersen 2, Ómarsson*
31/10	h	Elfsborg	D	2-2	*Salomonsson (p), Albæk*
06/11	a	Norrköping	L	1-3	*Sabah*

No	Name	Nat	DoB	Pos	Aps	(s)	Gls
7	Mads Albæk	DEN	14/01/90	M	26		4
13	Mauricio Albornoz		10/03/88	D	4	(3)	
4	Haitam Aleesami	NOR	31/07/91	D	15		
1	John Alvbåge		10/08/82	G	29		
9	Jakob Ankersen	DEN	22/11/90	M	29		7
30	Mattias Bjärsmyr		03/01/86	D	23		
16	Mikael Boman		14/07/88	A	10	(5)	4
25	Erik Dahlin		28/04/89	G	1		
19	Gustav Engvall		29/04/96	A	12	(4)	3
6	Sebastian Eriksson		31/01/89	M	26	(2)	
3	Hjörtur Hermannsson	ISL	08/02/95	D	6	(1)	
10	Tobias Hysén		09/03/82	A	15	(13)	10
3	Scott Jamieson	AUS	13/10/88	D	10	(1)	
22	Adam Johansson		21/02/83	D		(1)	
14	Hjálmar Jónsson	ISL	29/07/80	D	6	(1)	1
26	Patrik Karlsson Lagemyr		18/12/96	A	2	(9)	2
17	Prosper Kasim	GHA	15/12/96	A		(1)	
20	Alexander Leksell		14/02/97	D		(1)	
27	Billy Nordström		18/09/95	D	5	(3)	
13	Elías Már Ómarsson	ISL	18/01/95	A	12	(1)	6
24	Tom Pettersson		25/05/90	M	7	(12)	2
8	Søren Rieks	DEN	07/04/87	M	20	(2)	4
28	Thomas Rogne	NOR	29/06/90	D	22	(1)	
18	Lawson Sabah	GHA	02/04/97	M	3	(8)	1
2	Emil Salomonsson		28/04/89	D	29		7
20	Victor Sköld		31/07/89	A		(2)	
11	Martin Smedberg-Dalence	BOL	10/05/84	M	18	(9)	3

Hammarby Fotboll

1915 • Tele2Arena (33,000) • hammarbyfotboll.se

Major honours
Swedish League (1) 2001

Coach: Nanne Bergstrand

2016

Date		Opponent		Score	Scorers
04/04	h	Östersund	D	1-1	*Sætra*
07/04	a	Elfsborg	L	1-4	*Smárason*
10/04	h	Helsingborg	W	5-1	*Israelsson 3, Alex, Söderqvist*
19/04	a	Djurgården	W	3-1	*Alex 2, Israelsson*
23/04	h	Jönköping	D	1-1	*og (Calisir)*
26/04	a	Norrköping	L	1-3	*Israelsson*
01/05	h	Sundsvall	D	1-1	*Haglund*
09/05	a	Örebro	L	2-3	*Alex, og (Almebäck)*
14/05	a	Kalmar	D	1-1	*Israelsson*
18/05	h	Malmö	L	2-3	*Rômulo, Israelsson*
23/05	a	Göteborg	L	1-2	*Sævarsson*
29/05	h	Gefle	W	2-1	*Israelsson, Alex*
09/07	a	Häcken	L	2-4	*Smárason (p), Bakircioglü (p)*
17/07	h	Falkenberg	D	3-3	*Bakircioglü, Khalili, Magyar*
24/07	h	AIK	L	0-3	
30/07	a	Gefle	W	2-0	*Haglund, Bakircioglü (p)*
07/08	h	Kalmar	W	2-1	*Bakircioglü (p), Persson*
15/08	a	Sundsvall	D	0-0	
21/08	h	Göteborg	W	2-0	*Haglund, Bakircioglü*
28/08	a	AIK	D	0-0	
12/09	h	Örebro	D	1-1	*Aidoo*
16/09	a	Jönköping	W	1-0	*Bakircioglü*
22/09	h	Häcken	L	2-3	*Israelsson, Solheim*
26/09	a	Falkenberg	W	2-0	*Israelsson, Dibba*
30/09	a	Helsingborg	W	1-0	*Rômulo*
17/10	h	Djurgården	W	4-2	*Rômulo 3, Smárason*
23/10	h	Elfsborg	L	2-4	*Dibba, Solheim*
26/10	a	Östersund	L	0-2	
30/10	h	Norrköping	D	1-1	*Smárason*
06/11	a	Malmö	L	0-3	

No	Name	Nat	DoB	Pos	Aps	(s)	Gls
6	Joseph Aidoo	GHA	29/09/95	D	14		1
7	Alex	BRA	21/08/90	A	20	(8)	5
10	Kennedy Bakircioglü		02/11/80	M	21	(6)	6
9	Stefan Batan		20/03/85	D	7	(2)	
17	Pa Dibba		15/10/87	A	7	(3)	2
5	Philip Haglund		22/03/87	M	22	(1)	3
21	Melker Hallberg		20/10/95	M	12		
4	Erik Israelsson		25/02/89	M	27	(2)	10
26	Dusan Jajic		04/07/98	M	1	(2)	
55	Imad Khalili	PLE	03/04/87	A	3	(14)	1
1	Ögmundur Kristinsson	ISL	19/06/89	G	30		
27	Isac Lidberg		08/09/98	A	1	(4)	
3	Richard Magyar		03/05/91	D	18	(2)	1
8	Johan Persson		20/06/84	M	22		1
20	Amadaiya Rennie	LBR	17/03/90	M		(2)	
16	Rômulo	BRA	02/11/91	A	10	(16)	5
18	Oliver Silverholt		22/06/94	D	1		
11	Arnór Smárason	ISL	07/09/88	M	26	(1)	4
77	Mats Solheim	NOR	03/12/87	D	16		2
23	Lars Sætra	NOR	24/07/91	D	18	(1)	1
2	Birkir Már Sævarsson	ISL	11/11/84	D	27		1
34	Måns Söderqvist		08/02/93	A	2	(5)	1
14	Fredrik Torsteinbø	NOR	13/03/91	M	14	(8)	
66	David Boo Wiklander		03/10/84	D	11	(2)	

Helsingborgs IF

1907 • Olympia (17,200) • hif.se

Major honours
Swedish League (5) 1933, 1934, 1941, 1999, 2011; Swedish Cup (5) 1941, 1998, 2006, 2010, 2011

Coach: Henrik Larsson

2016

Date		Opponent		Score	Scorers
03/04	a	Gefle	D	1-1	*J Larsson*
07/04	h	Örebro	L	1-3	*Bojanic*
10/04	a	Hammarby	L	1-5	*Johansson*
16/04	h	Falkenberg	W	3-1	*Hallenius, Eriksson, Bojanic*
25/04	a	Kalmar	W	3-2	*Bojanic, Johansson, Hallenius*
28/04	h	AIK	W	2-1	*J Larsson 2*
02/05	a	Norrköping	L	0-3	
08/05	h	Malmö	W	2-1	*J Larsson, Rusike*
13/05	a	Jönköping	D	1-1	*Helstrup*
18/05	h	Östersund	D	1-1	*A Wede*
22/05	a	Djurgården	L	0-3	
29/05	h	Göteborg	L	1-3	*Dahlberg*
10/07	h	Elfsborg	L	2-4	*Dahlberg, J Larsson*
16/07	a	Sundsvall	W	2-0	*Rusike, Dahlberg*
24/07	h	Häcken	L	0-2	
31/07	a	Häcken	D	1-1	*A Wede*
05/08	h	Gefle	L	2-3	*Atakora, Ralani*
13/08	a	AIK	L	1-2	*og (Väisänen)*
20/08	h	Kalmar	L	0-1	
28/08	a	Göteborg	L	0-2	
11/09	a	Östersund	L	0-2	
18/09	h	Norrköping	L	1-2	*A Wede (p)*
21/09	h	Sundsvall	W	2-1	*Samuel, A Wede*
25/09	a	Malmö	L	0-2	
30/09	h	Hammarby	L	0-1	
16/10	a	Elfsborg	L	0-1	
23/10	a	Örebro	D	0-0	
27/10	h	Djurgården	L	1-2	*P Larsson*
30/10	a	Falkenberg	W	4-1	*J Larsson 2, Ralani, Rusike (p)*
06/11	h	Jönköping	W	2-0	*Helstrup, Dahlberg*

No	Name	Nat	DoB	Pos	Aps	(s)	Gls
13	Alexander Achinioti-Jönsson		17/04/96	M	5	(9)	
4	Christoffer Andersson		22/10/78	D	5	(2)	
27	Lalawélé Atakora	TOG	09/11/90	M	19	(4)	1
25	Felix Bindelöv		23/02/97	D	10	(1)	
29	Jesper Björkman		29/04/93	D	1	(2)	
19	Darijan Bojanic		28/12/94	M	12	(5)	3
41	Tomer Chencinski	CAN	01/12/84	G	19		
8	Martin Christensen	DEN	23/12/87	M	15	(7)	
16	Mikael Dahlberg		16/03/85	A	8	(4)	4
11	Adam Eriksson		13/07/90	D	30		1
15	Linus Hallenius		01/04/89	A	11	(7)	2
3	Frederik Helstrup	DEN	16/03/93	D	26		2
2	Carl Johansson		23/05/94	D	5	(1)	2
6	Andreas Landgren		17/03/89	D	16	(1)	
22	Jesper Lange	DEN	11/01/86	A	6	(3)	
18	Jordan Larsson		27/06/97	A	24	(3)	7
26	Peter Larsson		30/04/84	D	24		1
7	Viktor Ljung		19/04/91	D	1		
5	Johan Mårtensson		16/02/89	M	20	(1)	
35	Jonatan Olsson		09/02/93	D	2	(1)	
1	Matt Pyzdrowski	USA	17/08/86	G	11		
14	Bradley Ralani	RSA	04/10/87	M	12	(2)	2
9	Matthew Rusike	ZIM	28/06/90	A	10	(15)	3
21	Monday Samuel	NGA	12/11/93	M	11	(2)	1
37	Max Svensson		19/06/98	A		(2)	
10	Anton Wede		20/04/90	M	23	(4)	4
20	Carl Wede		20/04/90	M	4	(3)	
55	Moustafa Zeidan		07/06/98	A		(2)	

BK Häcken

1940 • Bravida Arena (6,500) • bkhacken.se

Major honours
Swedish Cup (1) 2016

Coach: Peter Gerhardsson

2016

Date		Opponent		Score	Scorers
03/04	h	Elfsborg	W	2-1	*Paulinho, Mohammed*
06/04	a	Göteborg	L	0-1	
09/04	h	Norrköping	L	1-2	*A Andersson*
15/04	a	Östersund	L	1-2	*Sandberg*
24/04	h	Sundsvall	L	0-1	
28/04	h	Gefle	W	6-1	*Savage 2, Makondele 2, Owoeri, Arkivuo*
01/05	a	Malmö	L	0-3	
08/05	h	AIK	L	2-3	*Paulinho 2*
15/05	a	Falkenberg	W	4-1	*Jeremejeff, Gustafsson, Paulinho 2*
18/05	h	Jönköping	W	3-1	*Arkivuo, Gustafsson, Jeremejeff*
22/05	a	Kalmar	D	1-1	*Paulinho*
29/05	h	Djurgården	W	3-1	*Paulinho 2, Owoeri*
09/07	h	Hammarby	W	4-2	*Ericsson, Owoeri 2, Savage*
17/07	a	Örebro	D	0-0	
24/07	a	Helsingborg	W	2-0	*Owoeri, Mashamaite*
31/07	h	Helsingborg	D	1-1	*Owoeri*
07/08	a	Elfsborg	W	4-2	*Owoeri 2, Gustafsson, Kamara*
10/08	a	Norrköping	L	1-3	*og (Sjölund)*
14/08	h	Örebro	L	0-1	
28/08	h	Östersund	W	3-1	*Mohammed, Owoeri, Mashamaite*
12/09	a	Gefle	D	2-2	*Kamara 2*
19/09	h	Göteborg	D	2-2	*Owoeri, Kamara*
22/09	a	Hammarby	W	3-2	*Kamara, Abubakari, Farnerud*
26/09	a	Sundsvall	D	0-0	
01/10	h	Malmö	L	2-4	*Owoeri, Farnerud*
16/10	a	Jönköping	D	1-1	*Paulinho*
23/10	h	Kalmar	L	2-3	*Owoeri (p), Wahlström*
27/10	a	AIK	L	1-2	*Owoeri*
31/10	a	Djurgården	L	0-1	
06/11	h	Falkenberg	W	7-0	*Farnerud, Schüller, Mohammed, Owoeri 4*

No	Name	Nat	DoB	Pos	Aps	(s)	Gls
26	Peter Abrahamsson		18/07/88	G	29		
12	Mohammed Abubakari	GHA	15/02/86	M	27		1
20	Niclas Andersén		05/08/92	D		(1)	
28	Adam Andersson		11/11/96	M	6	(9)	1
27	Joel Andersson		11/11/96	D	25	(2)	
15	Kari Arkivuo	FIN	23/06/83	D	22	(2)	2
17	Gustav Berggren		07/09/97	M	2	(6)	
25	Egzon Binaku		27/08/95	D	4	(6)	
14	Martin Ericsson		04/09/80	M	12	(5)	1
9	Alexander Farnerud		01/05/84	M	10	(1)	3
22	Samuel Gustafsson		11/01/95	M	18		3
18	Alexander Jeremejeff		12/10/93	A	7	(2)	2
93	Alhassan Kamara	SLE	13/01/93	A	7	(7)	5
1	Christoffer Källqvist		26/08/83	G	1		
7	Rasmus Lindgren		29/11/84	M	14		
24	René Makondele	COD	20/04/82	M	4	(9)	2
4	Tefu Mashamaite	RSA	27/09/84	D	4		2
13	Baba Mensah	GHA	20/08/94	D	2	(5)	
21	Nasiru Mohammed	GHA	06/06/94	M	21	(5)	3
19	John Owoeri	NGA	13/01/87	A	19	(7)	17
10	Paulinho	BRA	09/03/86	A	8	(3)	9
9	Dardan Rexhepi		16/02/92	A		(1)	
23	Simon Sandberg		25/03/94	D	11	(1)	1
8	Demba Savage	GAM	17/06/88	A	12	(7)	3
6	Rasmus Schüller	FIN	18/06/91	M	17	(1)	1
3	Jasmin Sudic		24/11/90	D	18	(3)	
7	Niels Vorthoren	NED	21/02/88	M	3		
5	Emil Wahlström		02/03/87	D	27		1

Jönköpings Södra IF

1922 • Stadsparksvallen (6,321) • jonkopingssodra.se

Coach: Jimmy Thelin

2016

Date		Opponent	Res	Score	Scorers
02/04	a	Kalmar	W	1-0	*Cibicki*
06/04	h	Malmö	W	3-2	*Cibicki 2, Smylie*
11/04	a	Örebro	L	1-2	*Thelin*
17/04	h	Gefle	W	1-0	*Smylie*
23/04	a	Hammarby	D	1-1	*Thelin*
27/04	h	Falkenberg	D	1-1	*Smylie*
02/05	a	AIK	D	0-0	
08/05	h	Norrköping	L	0-2	
13/05	h	Helsingborg	D	1-1	*Cibicki*
18/05	a	Häcken	L	1-3	*Cibicki*
22/05	a	Elfsborg	D	3-3	*Svensson, Silka, Cibicki*
28/05	h	Sundsvall	D	1-1	*Cibicki*
10/07	a	Östersund	L	0-1	
18/07	h	Djurgården	W	1-0	*Thelin*
24/07	a	Göteborg	L	1-2	*Cibicki*
31/07	h	Göteborg	D	1-1	*Fendrich*
06/08	a	Falkenberg	W	5-0	*Smylie, Thelin 2 (1p), Gojani, Kozica*
15/08	h	Östersund	D	1-1	*Thelin*
22/08	a	Malmö	L	1-4	*Cala*
28/08	h	Elfsborg	W	1-0	*Cibicki*
11/09	a	Norrköping	L	1-5	*Smylie*
16/09	h	Hammarby	L	0-1	
21/09	a	Gefle	W	1-0	*Eriksson*
24/09	h	Kalmar	L	0-1	
01/10	a	Sundsvall	L	1-3	*Thelin*
16/10	h	Häcken	D	1-1	*Smylie*
24/10	a	Djurgården	W	2-0	*Smylie, Kozica*
27/10	h	Örebro	D	1-1	*Aasmundsen*
31/10	h	AIK	D	0-0	
06/11	a	Helsingborg	L	0-2	

No	Name	Nat	DoB	Pos	Aps	(s)	Gls
15	Stian Aasmundsen	NOR	02/11/89	M	7	(8)	1
28	Álex Portillo	ESP	06/11/92	D	12		
23	Anton Cajtoft		13/02/94	G	3		
30	Cala	ESP	02/03/90	M	3	(3)	1
26	André Calisir		13/06/90	D	28		
22	Pawel Cibicki		09/01/94	A	24	(2)	9
31	Pär Eriksson		21/07/88	M	1	(10)	1
5	Fredric Fendrich		27/01/88	M	26	(2)	1
1	Fran Marmolejo	ESP	19/01/88	G	1		
24	Robert Gojani		19/10/92	M	25	(1)	1
8	Joakim Karlsson		04/02/89	D	26		
7	Dzenis Kozica		28/04/93	M	25	(5)	2
25	Damir Mehic		18/04/87	G	26	(1)	
14	Tobias Nilsson		20/02/86	D	1	(7)	
10	Moses Ogbu	NGA	07/02/91	A	3	(9)	
16	Viktor Rönneklev		16/08/82	D	21	(1)	
18	Liridon Silka	KOS	17/07/90	M	1	(10)	1
3	Tom Siwe		02/03/87	D	27	(1)	
17	Daryl Smylie	NIR	10/09/85	M	25	(1)	7
12	Jesper Svensson		06/03/90	M	9	(16)	1
2	Jonathan Tamimi Syberg		10/12/94	D	6	(4)	
9	Tommy Thelin		22/09/83	A	30		7

Kalmar FF

1910 • Guldfågeln Arena (12,105) • kalmarff.se

Major honours
Swedish League (1) 2008; Swedish Cup (3) 1981, 1987, 2007

Coach: Peter Swärdh

2016

Date		Opponent	Res	Score	Scorers
02/04	h	Jönköping	L	0-1	
06/04	a	Norrköping	L	1-4	*Antonsson*
10/04	h	Elfsborg	W	3-2	*Diouf 2, Johansson*
17/04	a	Göteborg	D	1-1	*Eriksson*
25/04	h	Helsingborg	L	2-3	*Antonsson, Eriksson*
28/04	a	Sundsvall	D	1-1	*Antonsson*
02/05	h	Örebro	W	3-2	*Antonsson 2, Diouf*
07/05	a	Östersund	L	0-1	
14/05	h	Hammarby	D	1-1	*Antonsson*
19/05	a	Djurgården	W	3-0	*Antonsson 2, Ring*
22/05	h	Häcken	D	1-1	*Antonsson (p)*
29/05	a	Falkenberg	W	2-1	*Eriksson, Antonsson*
10/07	h	AIK	D	1-1	*R Elm*
18/07	a	Gefle	L	2-4	*Romarinho, Ismael*
23/07	a	Malmö	D	1-1	*V Elm*
01/08	h	Djurgården	W	2-1	*og (Colley), Romarinho*
07/08	a	Hammarby	L	1-2	*Romarinho*
14/08	h	Malmö	D	1-1	*Ring*
20/08	a	Helsingborg	W	1-0	*Eid*
27/08	h	Norrköping	L	0-1	
10/09	a	Elfsborg	D	1-1	*Eriksson*
17/09	h	Östersund	W	2-0	*Anier, Ismael*
21/09	h	Falkenberg	W	3-0	*Ring 2, Hallberg*
24/09	a	Jönköping	W	1-0	*Thorbjörnsson*
02/10	h	Göteborg	W	4-2	*Romarinho 2, Ring, Eid*
16/10	a	Örebro	L	1-2	*Eriksson*
23/10	a	Häcken	W	3-2	*Romarinho, Eriksson, Söderqvist*
26/10	h	Gefle	L	0-1	
30/10	h	Sundsvall	W	2-0	*Söderqvist, Eriksson*
06/11	a	AIK	L	1-3	*Romarinho*

No	Name	Nat	DoB	Pos	Aps	(s)	Gls
12	Lumala Abdu	UGA	21/07/97	A	1	(9)	
5	Viktor Agardius		23/10/89	D	11	(1)	
19	Henri Anier	EST	17/12/90	A	7	(2)	1
9	Marcus Antonsson		08/05/91	A	12		10
4	Marko Biskupovic	CHI	30/07/89	D	28		
27	Pape Alioune Diouf	SEN	22/06/89	A	6	(1)	3
18	Mahmoud Eid	PLE	26/06/93	A	3	(7)	2
16	David Elm		10/01/83	A	6	(8)	
6	Rasmus Elm		17/03/88	M	15	(3)	1
23	Viktor Elm		13/11/85	M	21	(1)	1
18	Pär Ericsson		21/07/88	A		(1)	
10	Tobias Eriksson		19/03/85	M	24		7
34	Herman Hallberg		22/05/97	M	8	(7)	1
32	Lucas Hägg-Johansson		11/07/94	G	1		
22	Svante Ingelsson		04/06/98	M	2	(9)	
7	Ismael	BRA	01/12/94	M	29		2
20	Carl Johansson		07/06/96	M	5	(7)	1
14	Stefan Larsson		21/01/83	D	16	(1)	
21	Anton Maikkula		03/02/97	D	2		
13	Emin Nouri	AZE	22/07/85	D	27		
11	Jonathan Ring		05/12/91	M	23	(5)	5
29	Romarinho	BRA	10/08/85	M	28	(1)	7
24	Filip Sachpekidis		03/07/97	M	3	(10)	
3	Sebastian Starke Hedlund		05/04/95	D	9	(2)	
1	Ole Söderberg		20/07/90	G	29		
9	Måns Söderqvist		08/02/93	M	8	(5)	2
2	Markus Thorbjörnsson		01/10/87	D	6	(3)	1

Malmö FF

1910 • Swedbank Stadion (24,000) • mff.se

Major honours
Swedish League (19) 1944, 1949, 1950, 1951, 1953, 1965, 1967, 1970, 1971, 1974, 1975, 1977, 1986, 1988, 2004, 2010, 2013, 2014, 2016; Swedish Cup (14) 1944, 1946, 1947, 1951, 1953, 1967, 1973, 1974, 1975, 1978, 1980, 1984, 1986, 1989

Coach: Allan Kuhn (DEN)

2016

Date		Opponent	Res	Score	Scorers
02/04	h	Norrköping	W	3-1	*Christiansen, Berget (p), Rakip*
06/04	a	Jönköping	L	2-3	*Bengtsson, Berget*
11/04	h	Sundsvall	L	1-2	*Molins*
18/04	a	Elfsborg	W	1-0	*Rosenberg*
24/04	h	Djurgården	W	1-0	*Carvalho*
27/04	a	Göteborg	W	3-0	*(w/o; match abandoned after 77 mins at 0-0)*
01/05	h	Häcken	W	3-0	*Kjartansson 3*
08/05	a	Helsingborg	L	1-2	*Eikrem*
14/05	h	Gefle	W	3-0	*Molins 2, Rodić*
18/05	a	Hammarby	W	3-2	*Kjartansson, Christiansen, Eikrem*
23/05	h	Falkenberg	W	2-0	*Rosenberg, Kjartansson*
28/05	a	Östersund	W	4-1	*Rosenberg, Kjartansson 3*
11/07	h	Örebro	W	1-0	*Berget*
17/07	a	AIK	D	1-1	*Kjartansson*
23/07	h	Kalmar	D	1-1	*Kjartansson*
01/08	a	Örebro	W	3-0	*Kjartansson 2, Rosenberg (p)*
07/08	h	AIK	W	2-0	*Eikrem, Christiansen*
14/08	a	Kalmar	D	1-1	*Christiansen*
22/08	h	Jönköping	W	4-1	*Bengtsson, Kjartansson, Christiansen, Jeremejeff*
28/08	a	Sundsvall	W	1-0	*Kjartansson*
12/09	h	Göteborg	W	3-1	*Rosenberg 2, Jeremejeff*
18/09	a	Djurgården	L	1-3	*Eikrem*
22/09	h	Elfsborg	W	1-0	*Rakip*
25/09	h	Helsingborg	W	2-0	*Christiansen, Svanberg*
01/10	a	Häcken	W	4-2	*Adu, Berget, Jeremejeff, Sana*
16/10	a	Norrköping	W	2-1	*Árnason, Jeremejeff*
22/10	h	Östersund	L	0-3	
26/10	a	Falkenberg	W	3-0	*Berget, Svanberg, Jeremejeff*
30/10	a	Gefle	L	0-1	
06/11	h	Hammarby	W	3-0	*Berget, Rosenberg 2*

No	Name	Nat	DoB	Pos	Aps	(s)	Gls
8	Enoch Kofi Adu	GHA	14/09/90	M	17	(1)	1
29	Fredrik Andersson		25/10/88	G	2	(1)	
21	Kári Árnason	ISL	13/10/82	D	24		1
17	Rasmus Bengtsson		26/06/86	D	18		2
23	Jo Inge Berget	NOR	11/09/90	A	25		6
33	Teddy Bergqvist		16/03/99	A		(1)	
31	Franz Brorsson		30/01/96	D	16	(2)	
25	Felipe Carvalho	URU	18/09/93	D	1	(1)	1
7	Anders Christiansen	DEN	08/06/90	M	21	(1)	6
19	Magnus Wolff Eikrem	NOR	08/08/90	M	19	(4)	4
37	Dennis Hadzikadunic		09/07/98	D		(1)	
11	Alexander Jeremejeff		12/10/93	A	10	(5)	5
18	Piotr Johansson		28/02/95	M		(3)	
24	Vidar Örn Kjartansson	ISL	11/03/90	A	18	(2)	14
2	Pa Konate		25/04/94	D	15	(7)	
6	Oscar Lewicki		14/07/92	M	19	(5)	
10	Guillermo Molins		26/09/88	M	3	(4)	3
5	Erdal Rakip		13/02/96	M	12	(15)	2
20	Vladimir Rodić	MNE	07/09/93	M	3	(5)	1
9	Markus Rosenberg		27/09/82	A	19	(3)	8
4	Behrang Safari		09/02/85	D	11		
22	Tobias Sana		11/07/89	M	4	(7)	1
32	Mattias Svanberg		05/01/99	M	2	(4)	2
3	Anton Tinnerholm		26/02/91	D	29		
26	Andreas Vindheim	NOR	14/08/95	D	2	(4)	
1	Johan Wiland		24/01/81	G	28		
13	Yoshimar Yotún	PER	07/04/90	D	12	(7)	

IFK Norrköping

1897 • Östgötaporten (17,234) • ifknorrkoping.se

Major honours
Swedish League (13) 1943, 1945, 1946, 1947, 1948, 1952, 1956, 1957, 1960, 1962, 1963, 1989, 2015; Swedish Cup (6) 1943, 1945, 1969, 1988, 1991 (spring), 1994

Coach: Jan Andersson; (01/06/16) Jens Gustafsson

2016

Date		Opponent		Score	Scorers
02/04	a	Malmö	L	1-3	*Nyman*
06/04	h	Kalmar	W	4-1	*Tkalčić, Fjóluson, Kujovic, Telo*
09/04	a	Häcken	W	2-1	*Nyman, Andersson*
17/04	h	AIK	W	4-1	*Nyman, og (Karlsson), Andersson, Tkalčić*
22/04	a	Falkenberg	L	1-2	*Hadenius*
26/04	h	Hammarby	W	3-1	*Wahlqvist, Blomqvist, Traustason (p)*
02/05	h	Helsingborg	W	3-0	*Nyman, Kujovic 2 (1p)*
08/05	a	Jönköping	W	2-0	*Nyman, Kujovic*
15/05	h	Sundsvall	W	3-1	*Kujovic (p), Andersson, Tkalčić*
19/05	a	Göteborg	D	1-1	*Traustason*
22/05	a	Örebro	D	2-2	*Kujovic 2*
29/05	h	Elfsborg	D	0-0	
09/07	a	Djurgården	W	1-0	*Andersson*
16/07	h	Östersund	D	3-3	*Bärkroth, Nyman, Andersson*
23/07	h	Gefle	W	2-0	*Sjölund, Blomqvist*
30/07	a	Sundsvall	W	2-1	*Nyman 2*
07/08	h	Örebro	W	3-1	*Blomqvist, Johansson, Sjölund*
10/08	h	Häcken	W	3-1	*Nyman (p), Andersson, Moberg Karlsson*
13/08	a	Gefle	D	0-0	
27/08	a	Kalmar	W	1-0	*og (Biskupovic)*
11/09	h	Jönköping	W	5-1	*Moberg Karlsson, Andersson 2, Holmberg 2*
18/09	a	Helsingborg	W	2-1	*Andersson, Eliasson*
21/09	a	Östersund	W	2-0	*Andersson 2*
26/09	h	Djurgården	L	1-3	*Holmberg*
02/10	a	AIK	L	0-6	
16/10	h	Malmö	L	1-2	*Bärkroth*
23/10	h	Falkenberg	W	2-1	*Wahlqvist, Andersson*
26/10	a	Elfsborg	L	1-2	*Bärkroth (p)*
30/10	a	Hammarby	D	1-1	*Holmberg*
06/11	h	Göteborg	W	3-1	*Andersson 2, Bärkroth*

No	Name	Nat	DoB	Pos	Aps	(s)	Gls
19	Sebastian Andersson		15/07/91	A	22	(8)	14
8	Nicklas Bärkroth		19/01/92	M	17	(5)	4
7	Andreas Blomqvist		05/05/92	M	15	(3)	3
26	Adin Budkva		11/01/98	M		(3)	
2	Henrik Castegren		28/03/96	D		(4)	
24	Gentrit Citaku		25/02/96	M		(1)	
25	Filip Dagerstål		01/02/97	M	15	(1)	
22	Niclas Eliasson		07/12/95	M	8	(5)	1
16	Joel Enarsson		27/06/93	A		(2)	
15	Marcus Falk-Olander		21/05/87	D	9	(2)	
3	Jón Gudni Fjóluson	ISL	10/04/89	D	15	(1)	1
21	Andreas Hadenius		18/03/91	D	3	(17)	1
17	Karl Holmberg		03/03/93	A	7	(5)	4
4	Andreas Johansson		10/03/82	D	30		1
10	Emir Kujovic		22/06/88	A	9		7
31	Michael Langer	AUT	06/01/85	G	13		
91	David Mitov Nilsson	MKD	12/01/91	G	5		
9	David Moberg Karlsson		20/03/94	M	10	(6)	2
5	Christoffer Nyman		05/10/92	A	20		9
20	Daniel Sjölund	FIN	22/04/83	M	27		2
14	Eric Smith		08/01/97	M	2	(8)	
27	Tesfaldet Tekie		04/06/97	M	20	(6)	
11	Christopher Telo		04/11/89	D	24	(3)	1
30	Nikola Tkalčić	CRO	03/12/89	D	10		3
9	Arnór Ingvi Traustason	ISL	30/04/93	M	9		2
1	Andreas Vaikla	EST	19/02/97	G	12	(1)	
6	Linus Wahlqvist		11/11/96	D	28		2

GIF Sundsvall

1903 • Norrporten Arena (8,500) • gifsundsvall.se

Coach: Joel Cedergren & Roger Franzén; (17/09/16) Joel Cedergren

2016

Date		Opponent		Score	Scorers
03/04	a	AIK	D	1-1	*Sigurjónsson*
07/04	h	Gefle	L	1-2	*Silva*
11/04	a	Malmö	W	2-1	*Sonko Sundberg, Hasani*
18/04	h	Örebro	W	3-1	*Dibba 2, Sigurjónsson*
24/04	h	Häcken	W	1-0	*Gerson (p)*
28/04	h	Kalmar	D	1-1	*Gerson (p)*
01/05	a	Hammarby	D	1-1	*Sigurjónsson*
09/05	h	Falkenberg	W	2-1	*Sigurjónsson, Silva*
15/05	a	Norrköping	L	1-3	*Eklund*
18/05	h	Elfsborg	L	1-3	*Dibba*
21/05	h	Östersund	W	5-0	*Dibba, Sigurjónsson 2, Sonko Sundberg, Silva*
28/05	a	Jönköping	D	1-1	*Silva*
10/07	a	Göteborg	L	1-4	*Dibba*
16/07	h	Helsingborg	L	0-2	
25/07	a	Djurgården	W	3-1	*Silva 2, Granat*
30/07	h	Norrköping	L	1-2	*Silva*
06/08	a	Östersund	L	0-4	
15/08	h	Hammarby	D	0-0	
22/08	a	Elfsborg	L	0-4	
28/08	h	Malmö	L	0-1	
11/09	h	AIK	L	1-3	*Albornoz*
16/09	a	Örebro	D	3-3	*Wilson, Eklund, Gerson (p)*
21/09	a	Helsingborg	L	1-2	*Gerson*
26/09	h	Häcken	D	0-0	
01/10	h	Jönköping	W	3-1	*Wilson 3*
15/10	a	Falkenberg	D	1-1	*Wilson*
21/10	a	Gefle	D	1-1	*Larsson*
27/10	h	Göteborg	L	1-3	*Eklund*
30/10	a	Kalmar	L	0-2	
06/11	h	Djurgården	L	2-5	*Sonko Sundberg, Wilson*

No	Name	Nat	DoB	Pos	Aps	(s)	Gls
27	Mauricio Albornoz		10/03/88	M	4	(8)	1
5	Erik Björkander		11/06/96	D	4		
15	Marcus Danielsson		08/04/89	D	30		
14	Pa Dibba	GAM	15/10/87	A	17		5
9	Johan Eklund		30/05/84	A	9	(13)	3
14	Joel Enarsson		27/06/93	A	1	(4)	
8	Lars Gerson	LUX	05/02/90	M	24		4
26	Erik Granat		09/08/95	M	15	(8)	1
12	Shpëtim Hasani	KOS	10/08/82	M		(14)	1
21	Eric Larsson		15/07/91	D	29		1
32	Jonathan Morsay		15/10/97	M	4	(1)	
17	Tommy Naurin		17/05/84	G	30		
3	Dennis Olsson		03/10/94	D	22		
11	Sebastian Rajalakso		23/09/88	M	8	(14)	
18	Robbin Sellin		12/04/90	M	15	(7)	
6	Rúnar Már Sigurjónsson	ISL	18/06/90	M	12		6
22	Stefan Silva		11/03/90	A	30		7
19	Noah Sonko Sundberg		06/06/96	D	22	(1)	3
7	Kristinn Steindórsson	ISL	29/04/90	M	14	(2)	
20	Smajl Suljevic		15/07/94	M	13	(7)	
16	Robin Tranberg		12/04/90	M	16	(2)	
30	Peter Wilson		09/10/96	M	10	(2)	6
4	Stefan Ålander		25/04/83	D	1	(1)	

Örebro SK

1908 • Behrn Arena (12,674) • oskfotboll.se

Coach: Alexander Axén

2016

Date		Opponent		Score	Scorers
03/04	h	Djurgården	L	0-2	
07/04	a	Helsingborg	W	3-1	*Almebäck, Gerzic, Kamara*
11/04	h	Jönköping	W	2-1	*Astrit Ajdarevic, Gustavsson*
18/04	a	Sundsvall	L	1-3	*Åhman Persson*
24/04	h	Göteborg	W	3-2	*Åhman Persson, Sema 2*
27/04	a	Östersund	W	4-2	*Holmberg 2, Gustavsson 2*
02/05	a	Kalmar	L	2-3	*Gustavsson, Sema*
09/05	h	Hammarby	W	3-2	*Nordmark, Astrit Ajdarevic, Hines-Ike*
15/05	h	Elfsborg	W	1-0	*Moberg*
19/05	a	Gefle	W	4-0	*Holmberg, Valgardsson, Astrit Ajdarevic, Sema*
22/05	h	Norrköping	D	2-2	*Sema, Gustavsson*
28/05	a	AIK	D	0-0	
11/07	a	Malmö	L	0-1	
17/07	h	Häcken	D	0-0	
23/07	a	Falkenberg	W	3-1	*Ring, Sema, Gustavsson*
01/08	h	Malmö	L	0-3	
07/08	a	Norrköping	L	1-3	*Nordmark*
14/08	a	Häcken	W	1-0	*Broberg*
21/08	h	AIK	L	0-2	
28/08	h	Falkenberg	W	3-2	*Gerzic, Besara, Sema*
12/09	a	Hammarby	D	1-1	*Besara*
16/09	h	Sundsvall	D	3-3	*Omoh, Besara, Broberg (p)*
22/09	a	Göteborg	L	2-3	*Besara, Astrit Ajdarevic*
26/09	h	Gefle	D	2-2	*Björnqvist, Sköld (p)*
02/10	a	Djurgården	L	2-3	*Sema, Ayaz*
16/10	h	Kalmar	W	2-1	*Gerzic, Sköld*
23/10	h	Helsingborg	D	0-0	
27/10	a	Jönköping	D	1-1	*Sköld*
31/10	h	Östersund	L	1-5	*Åhman Persson*
06/11	a	Elfsborg	L	1-2	*Gerzic*

No	Name	Nat	DoB	Pos	Aps	(s)	Gls
11	Alfred Ajdarevic		20/06/98	M		(1)	
8	Astrit Ajdarevic		17/04/90	M	24	(1)	4
14	Michael Almebäck		04/04/88	D	29		1
7	Ferhad Ayaz		10/10/94	M	2	(8)	1
17	Nahir Besara		25/02/91	M	11	(2)	4
12	Daniel Björnqvist		08/01/89	D	26		1
9	Martin Broberg		24/09/90	M	15	(6)	2
45	Carl Ekstrand Hamrén		17/06/96	D	1		
25	Nordin Gerzic		09/11/83	M	27		4
90	Daniel Gustavsson		29/08/90	M	17		6
2	Patrik Haginge		02/04/85	D		(3)	
3	Brendan Hines-Ike	USA	30/11/94	D	5	(12)	1
17	Karl Holmberg		03/03/93	A	11	(3)	3
1	Oscar Jansson		23/12/90	G	18		
10	Alhassan Kamara	SLE	16/03/93	A	5	(5)	1
15	Martin Lorentzson		21/07/84	D	7	(1)	
13	Jonathan Lundberg		27/10/97	A		(6)	
5	Erik Moberg		05/07/86	D	25		1
16	Daniel Nordmark		04/01/88	M	7	(13)	2
29	Michael Omoh	NGA	29/08/91	A	4	(11)	1
19	Sebastian Ring		18/04/95	D	18	(3)	1
30	Jakob Rinne		20/06/93	G	12		
23	Maic Sema		02/12/88	M	20	(9)	8
10	Victor Sköld		31/07/89	A	13	(1)	3
4	Hjörtur Logi Valgardsson	ISL	27/09/88	D	6	(1)	1
6	Robert Åhman Persson		26/03/87	M	27		3

SWEDEN

Östersunds FK

1996 • Jämtkraft Arena (6,200) • ostersundsfotbollsklubb.se

Major honours
Swedish Cup (1) 2017

Coach: Graham Potter (ENG)

2016

Date		Opponent		Score	Scorers
04/04	a	Hammarby	D	1-1	*Ghoddos*
07/04	h	AIK	L	0-2	
10/04	a	Falkenberg	W	2-1	*Smajic, Stadler*
15/04	h	Häcken	W	2-1	*Mukiibi, Nouri*
23/04	a	Gefle	D	0-0	
27/04	h	Örebro	L	2-4	*Atta 2*
02/05	a	Djurgården	L	0-3	
07/05	h	Kalmar	W	1-0	*Mukiibi*
15/05	h	Göteborg	W	2-0	*Mukiibi, Ghoddos*
18/05	a	Helsingborg	D	1-1	*Stadler*
21/05	a	Sundsvall	L	0-5	
28/05	h	Malmö	L	1-4	*Dyer*
10/07	h	Jönköping	W	1-0	*Dyer*
16/07	a	Norrköping	D	3-3	*Nouri (p), Ghoddos 2*
25/07	a	Elfsborg	L	1-3	*Dyer*
30/07	h	Elfsborg	D	0-0	
06/08	h	Sundsvall	W	4-0	*Stadler, Ghoddos, Nouri (p), Aiesh*
15/08	a	Jönköping	D	1-1	*Dyer*
20/08	h	Djurgården	W	1-0	*Sema*
28/08	a	Häcken	L	1-3	*Edwards*
11/09	h	Helsingborg	W	2-0	*Edwards, Dyer*
17/09	a	Kalmar	L	0-2	
21/09	h	Norrköping	L	0-2	
26/09	a	Göteborg	L	0-2	
01/10	h	Falkenberg	W	6-1	*Dyer 2, Gero 2, Nouri (p), Sema*
16/10	a	AIK	L	0-2	
22/10	a	Malmö	W	3-0	*Ghoddos 2, Bachirou*
26/10	h	Hammarby	W	2-0	*Gero, Edwards*
31/10	a	Örebro	W	5-1	*Dyer, Sema 2, Ghoddos 2 (1p)*
06/11	h	Gefle	L	2-4	*Dyer, Ghoddos*

No	Name	Nat	DoB	Pos	Aps	(s)	Gls
10	Hosem Aiesh		14/04/95	M	5	(10)	1
5	Walid Atta	ETI	28/08/86	D	16	(4)	2
21	Fouad Bachirou	COM	15/04/90	M	18	(4)	1
6	Douglas Bergqvist		29/03/93	D	20	(3)	
27	Jamal Blackman	ENG	27/10/93	G	12		
23	Alex Dyer	MSR	11/06/90	M	25	(1)	9
17	Curtis Edwards	ENG	12/01/94	M	10	(2)	3
18	Alhaji Gero	NGA	10/10/93	A	12	(10)	3
93	Saman Ghoddos		06/09/93	M	25	(2)	10
8	Jamie Hopcutt	ENG	15/11/92	M		(1)	
27	Piotr Johansson		28/02/95	M	3	(4)	
39	Stefan Karlsson		15/12/88	D	13	(2)	
1	Aly Keita		08/12/86	G	12		
25	Samuel Mensah	GHA	19/05/89	D	7	(5)	
24	Ronald Mukiibi		16/09/91	D	20	(1)	3
16	Hampus Nilsson		17/07/90	G	6		
22	Brwa Nouri	IRQ	23/01/87	M	27		4
29	Michael Omoh	NGA	29/08/91	A	4	(3)	
31	Sotirios Papagiannopoulos	GRE	05/09/90	D	22		
7	Monday Samuel	NGA	12/11/93	M	2	(3)	
12	Ken Sema		30/09/93	M	16	(7)	4
9	Emir Smajic		03/02/89	A	4	(5)	1
14	Bobo Sollander Jansson		26/06/85	D	2	(3)	
20	Gabriel Somi		24/08/91	D	12	(3)	
11	Andrew Stadler	USA	01/05/88	A	10	(11)	3
19	Dennis Widgren		28/03/94	D	27	(3)	

Top goalscorers

17 John Owoeri (Häcken)

14 Vidar Örn Kjartansson (Malmö)
Sebastian Andersson (Norrköping)

13 Viktor Prodell (Elfsborg)

12 Michael Olunga (Djurgården)

10 Alexander Isak (AIK)
Tobias Hysén (Göteborg)
Erik Israelsson (Hammarby)
Marcus Antonsson (Kalmar)
Saman Ghoddos (Östersund)

Promoted clubs

IK Sirius FK

1907 • Studenternas IP (8,000) • siriusfotboll.se

Coach: Kim Bergstrand

AFC United

2007 • Skytteholms IP (3,500) • afc-eskilstuna.se

Coach: Özcan Melkemichel

Halmstads BK

1914 • Örjans Vall (15,500) • hbk.se

Major honours
Swedish League (4) 1976, 1979, 1997, 2000;
Swedish Cup (1) 1995

Coach: Jan Jönsson

Second level final table 2016

		Pld	W	D	L	F	A	Pts
1	IK Sirius FK	30	18	7	5	54	23	61
2	AFC United	30	18	7	5	50	20	61
3	Halmstads BK	30	16	6	8	43	28	54
4	Dalkurd FF	30	14	11	5	41	24	53
5	Varbergs BoIS FC	30	14	6	10	33	37	48
6	Åtvidabergs FF	30	13	5	12	53	53	44
7	Trelleborgs FF	30	10	10	10	39	35	40
8	GAIS Göteborg	30	9	12	9	45	36	39
9	Örgryte IS	30	11	6	13	42	44	39
10	IK Frej Täby	30	9	11	10	38	42	38
11	IFK Värnamo	30	8	11	11	35	40	35
12	Degerfors IF	30	8	9	13	34	54	33
13	Syrianska FC	30	7	11	12	26	37	32
14	Assyriska FF	30	6	10	14	36	47	28
15	Ljungskile SK	30	6	8	16	34	48	26
16	Ängelholms FF	30	4	8	18	22	57	20

Promotion/Relegation play-offs

(17/11/16 & 20/11/16)
Halmstad 1-1 Helsingborg
Helsingborg 1-2 Halmstad
(Halmstad 3-2)

DOMESTIC CUP

Svenska Cupen 2016/17

SECOND ROUND

(24/08/16)
Arameisk-Syrianska 3-0 Assyriska
Brommapojkarna 4-2 Frej Täby
Enskede 0-3 Sirius
Gamla Upsala 1-2 Hammarby
Gnosjö 0-4 Helsingborg
Grebbestad 0-3 Kalmar
Karlstad 0-4 Örebro
Lidköping 0-2 Trelleborg
IFK Luleå 0-2 AIK
Nyköping 2-1 AFC United
Onsala 0-6 Ängelholm
Sandviken 1-2 Åtvidaberg
Smedby 1-5 Djurgården
Söderhamn 0-1 Gefle
Torslanda 0-2 Värnamo
Täby 0-2 Dalkurd
Utsikten 0-4 Falkenberg
Viken 0-9 Degerfors
Vänersborg 2-0 Jönköping
Västerås 0-4 Norrköping
Växjö 1-11 Häcken
Ytterhogdal 2-2 Syrianska *(aet; 4-2 on pens)*
Öster 0-3 GAIS

(25/08/16)
Gauthiod 0-7 Elfsborg
Hässleholm 0-4 Halmstad
Höllviken 1-2 Örgryte *(aet)*
Kristianstad 3-3 Ljungskile *(aet; 3-2 on pens)*
Landskrona 3-1 Malmö
Norrtälje 1-0 Sundsvall
Torn 1-3 Varberg
(06/09/16)
Sollentuna 0-2 Östersund
(13/10/16)
Oskarshamn 0-6 Göteborg

NB: Ängelholm withdrew before group stage; Ljungskile took their place.

THIRD ROUND

Group 1

(18/02/17)
Kristianstad 1-3 Dalkurd

(19/02/17)
AIK 1-0 GAIS

(25/02/17)
Dalkurd 2-2 GAIS
Kristianstad 0-3 AIK

(05/03/17)
AIK 0-0 Dalkurd
GAIS 1-2 Kristianstad

Final standings
1 AIK 7 pts *(qualified)*
2 Dalkurd 5 pts; 3 Kristianstad 3 pts;
4 GAIS 1 pt *(eliminated)*

Group 2

(18/02/17)
Vänersborg 2-2 Halmstad

(19/02/17)
Norrköping 1-1 Örgryte

(25/02/17)
Halmstad 4-0 Örgryte
Vänersborg 2-2 Norrköping

(04/03/17)
Norrköping 7-0 Halmstad
Örgryte 1-3 Vänersborg

Final standings
1 Norrköping 5 pts *(qualified)*
2 Vänersborg 5 pts; 3 Halmstad 4 pts;
4 Örgryte 1 pt *(eliminated)*

Group 3

(18/02/17)
Göteborg 3-2 Ljungskile

(19/02/17)
Arameisk-Syrianska 0-5 Sirius

(25/02/17)
Sirius 2-0 Ljungskile

(26/02/17)
Göteborg 6-0 Arameisk-Syrianska

(04/03/17)
Göteborg 2-2 Sirius
Ljungskile 2-0 Arameisk-Syrianska

Final standings
1 Göteborg 7 pts *(qualified)*
2 Sirius 7 pts; 3 Ljungskile 3 pts;
4 Arameisk-Syrianska 0 pts *(eliminated)*

Group 4

(18/02/17)
Ytterhogdal 0-3 Falkenberg

(19/02/17)
Elfsborg 2-2 Värnamo

(25/02/17)
Falkenberg 1-1 Värnamo

(26/02/17)
Ytterhogdal 0-3 Elfsborg

(05/03/17)
Elfsborg 6-1 Falkenberg
Värnamo 1-0 Ytterhogdal

Final standings
1 Elfsborg 7 pts *(qualified)*
2 Värnamo 5 pts; 3 Falkenberg 4 pts;
4 Ytterhogdal 0 pts *(eliminated)*

Group 5

(19/02/17)
Kalmar 1-1 Trelleborg
Landskrona 2-1 Gefle

(26/02/17)
Gefle 1-2 Trelleborg
Landskrona 2-2 Kalmar

(04/03/17)
Kalmar 3-0 Gefle
Trelleborg 2-1 Landskrona

Final standings
1 Trelleborg 7 pts *(qualified)*
2 Kalmar 5 pts; 3 Landskrona 4 pts;
4 Gefle 0 pts *(eliminated)*

Group 6

(18/02/17)
Brommapojkarna 3-0 Helsingborg

(20/02/17)
Djurgården 1-2 Degerfors

(26/02/17)
Helsingborg 2-3 Degerfors

(27/02/17)
Brommapojkarna 1-1 Djurgården

(04/03/17)
Degerfors 1-4 Brommapojkarna
Djurgården 1-0 Helsingborg

Final standings
1 Brommapojkarna 7 pts *(qualified)*
2 Degerfors 6 pts; 3 Djurgården 4 pts;
4 Helsingborg 0 pts *(eliminated)*

Group 7

(18/02/17)
Nyköping 2-3 Hammarby
Östersund 2-1 Varberg

(25/02/17)
Nyköping 1-5 Östersund

(26/02/17)
Hammarby 3-3 Varberg

(05/03/17)
Varberg 1-1 Nyköping
Östersund 1-0 Hammarby

Final standings
1 Östersund 9 pts *(qualified)*
2 Hammarby 4 pts; 3 Varberg 2 pts;
4 Nyköping 1 pt *(eliminated)*

Group 8

(18/02/17)
Norrtälje 0-4 Häcken
Örebro 1-1 Åtvidaberg

(25/02/17)
Häcken 3-1Åtvidaberg
Norrtälje 0-5 Örebro

(05/03/17)
Örebro 1-1 Häcken
Åtvidaberg 6-0 Norrtälje

Final standings
1 Häcken 7 pts *(qualified)*
2 Örebro 5 pts; 3 Åtvidaberg 4 pts;
4 Norrtälje 0 pt *(eliminated)*

QUARTER-FINALS

(11/03/17)
Göteborg 1-2 Norrköping *(Boman 80; Holmberg 56, 68)*

Östersund 4-1 Trelleborg *(Bertilsson 7, Nouri 27p, Ghoddos 48, Bojanic 90+2; Islamovic 87)*

(12/03/17)
Elfsborg 1-2 Brommapojkarna *(Jebali 10; Kabran 2, Gyökeres 83)*

Häcken 3-0 AIK *(Lindgren 70, Kamara 89, Paulinho 90+4p)*

SEMI-FINALS

(18/03/17)
Häcken 1-3 Östersund *(Kamara 32; Pettersson 6, Ghoddos 30, 87)*

(19/03/17)
Norrköping 4-0 Brommapojkarna *(Fjóluson 20, Holmberg 29, 66, Eliasson 64)*

FINAL

(13/04/17)
Jämtkraft Arena, Ostersund
ÖSTERSUNDS FK 4 *(Mensah 8, Aiesh 18, Gero 83, Ghoddos 86)*
IFK NORRKÖPING 1 *(Wahlqvist 54)*
Referee: *Al Hakim*
ÖSTERSUND: *Keita, Mensah, Bergqvist, Pettersson, Widgren, Aiesh (Papagiannapoulos 66), Nouri, Edwards, Sema, Gero (Hopcutt 90+2), Ghoddos (Björkström 90)*
NORRKÖPING: *Langer, Wahlqvist, Smith, Johansson, Telo, Bärkroth, Dagerstål (Hadenius 79), Sjölund, Eliasson (Thórarinsson 75), Holmberg, Andersson*

Free-scoring Östersund won seven games out of seven en route to a first Swedish Cup triumph

SWITZERLAND

Schweizerischer Fussballverband/Association Suisse de Football (SFV/ASF)

Address	Worbstrasse 48, Postfach CH-3000 Bern 15	**President**	Peter Gilliéron
Tel	+41 31 950 8111	**General secretary**	Alex Miescher
Fax	+41 31 950 8181	**Media officer**	Marco von Ah
E-mail	sfv.asf@football.ch	**Year of formation**	1895
Website	football.ch		

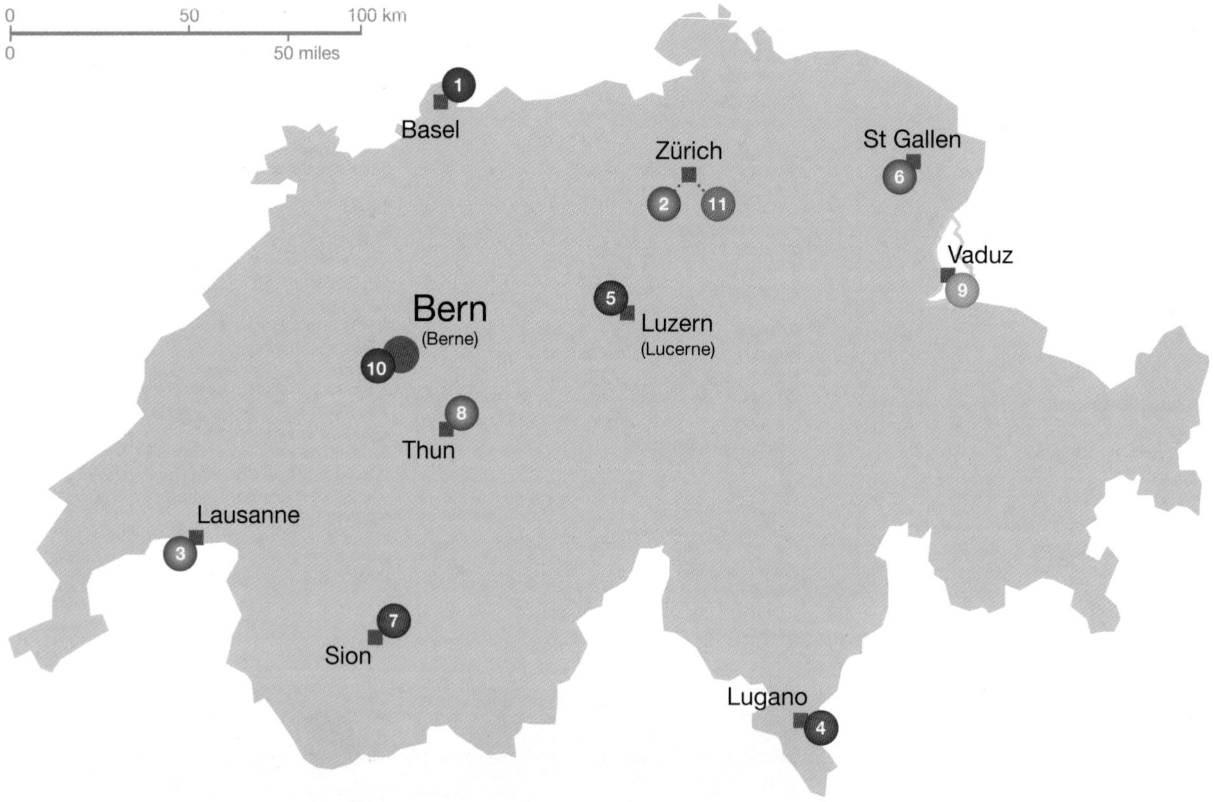

0 50 100 km
0 50 miles

Basel 1
Zürich 2 11
St Gallen 6
Vaduz 9
Bern (Berne) 10
Luzern (Lucerne) 5
Thun 8
Lausanne 3
Sion 7
Lugano 4

SUPER LEAGUE CLUBS

  1 **FC Basel 1893**

 2 **Grasshopper Club Zürich**

 3 **FC Lausanne-Sport**

 4 **FC Lugano**

 5 **FC Luzern**

 6 **FC St Gallen**

 7 **FC Sion**

 8 **FC Thun**

 9 **FC Vaduz**

 10 **BSC Young Boys**

PROMOTED CLUB

  11 **FC Zürich**

KEY

- UEFA Champions League
- UEFA Europa League
- Promoted
- Relegated

Unchallenged Basel in league of their own

The song remained the same in Switzerland's Super League as FC Basel won the title for a record-extending eighth season in a row. Coach Urs Fischer's second campaign in charge was practically a repeat of his first as the Red-and-Blues ran away from the pack early on and were never remotely in danger of being caught.

There was also a Swiss Cup triumph to savour for Fischer's team, three second-half goals in the Geneva final ending the remarkable record of opponents FC Sion, who had been victorious on all 13 of their previous appearances in the fixture.

Domestic double joy for serial champions

Sion finally defeated in Swiss Cup final

Perfect season for Petković's national team

Domestic league

Basel's 20th league title was never in doubt once they began the campaign by beating all of their Super League opponents one after the other, those nine successive wins enabling the defending champions to open up a huge lead with only a quarter of the season elapsed. FC Thun finally halted that victory surge on 1 October, but it was not until the onset of winter that Basel were finally beaten, 3-1 by second-placed Young Boys in Berne. However, even that setback could not prevent Fischer's men from entering the mid-season break 12 points clear of their closest pursuers from the capital.

There was no let-up in the spring. Victories remained a matter of routine, and on 28 April, with an unprecedented six fixtures still outstanding, Basel's eighth successive Super League triumph was complete as their 30th game of the season produced their 24th win, 2-1 away to FC Luzern. There would be an understandable easing-off in the closing weeks, including a second defeat, again by Young Boys at the Stade de Suisse, but Basel still managed to improve on virtually all of their vital statistics from the previous, equally dominant, campaign, amassing more points, scoring more goals and finding the net at least once in every game. Their margin of victory was also bigger, 17 points separating them from second-placed Young Boys, who finished with the same number of points (69) as they had registered in 2015/16.

Key to the champions' continued success were dependable stalwarts such as goalkeeper Tomáš Vaclík, defenders Michael Lang and Marek Suchý and midfielders Matías Delgado and Luca Zuffi, while there were excellent first-time contributions from on-loan Ivory Coast striker Seydou Doumbia, who scored a golden boot-winning tally of 20 goals, and Norwegian international Mohamed Elyounoussi.

Powered by the 18 goals of Guillaume Hoarau, Young Boys took the runners-up spot – and the second UEFA Champions League place – for the third year running. Once again they did so with room to spare ahead of third place, which this time was filled, thanks to a storming late run under Italian coach Paolo Tramezzani, by surprise package FC Lugano. The other UEFA Europa League places were seized by Sion and Luzern, while Liechtenstein's FC Vaduz went down, to be replaced, as expected, by Challenge League champions FC Zürich.

Domestic cup

One of European football's more remarkable sequences of success finally ended on 25 May 2017 when Sion lost a Swiss Cup final. It was 14th time unlucky for them as second-period strikes from Delgado, Adama Traoré and Lang gave Basel a 3-0 win that brought the club a 12th victory in the competition and a sixth league and cup double.

Europe

Basel's domestic dominance was not felt in Europe, where Fischer's team finished bottom of their UEFA Champions League group with just two points. There would be no post-Christmas Swiss presence on the continental stage for the first time in seven years as both Young Boys and FC Zürich failed to progress from their UEFA Europa League group, the Berne club having earlier received a pasting from Borussia Mönchengladbach in their UEFA Champions League play-off.

National team

Switzerland won all of their opening six 2018 FIFA World Cup qualifiers, plus a friendly against Belarus, to make 2016/17 a season of perfection for Vladimir Petković's side. With a trip to Portugal still to come, first place in Group B was far from assured, but having defeated the European champions – albeit without the injured Cristiano Ronaldo – 2-0 in Basel on matchday one and then claimed maximum points against the other teams in the section, a play-off berth was all but guaranteed for a country seeking to participate in a fourth successive World Cup.

DOMESTIC SEASON AT A GLANCE

Super League 2016/17 final table

			Home					Away					Total					
		Pld	W	D	L	F	A	W	D	L	F	A	W	D	L	F	A	Pts
1	**FC Basel 1893**	**36**	**13**	**5**	**0**	**50**	**17**	**13**	**3**	**2**	**42**	**18**	**26**	**8**	**2**	**92**	**35**	**86**
2	BSC Young Boys	36	13	2	3	52	24	7	7	4	20	20	20	9	7	72	44	69
3	FC Lugano	36	8	5	5	30	24	7	3	8	22	37	15	8	13	52	61	53
4	FC Sion	36	9	2	7	32	23	6	4	8	28	32	15	6	15	60	55	51
5	FC Luzern	36	7	6	5	33	26	7	2	9	29	40	14	8	14	62	66	50
6	FC Thun	36	7	4	7	33	33	4	8	6	25	30	11	12	13	58	63	45
7	FC St Gallen	36	7	3	8	21	23	4	5	9	22	34	11	8	17	43	57	41
8	Grasshopper Club Zürich	36	7	4	7	28	24	3	4	11	19	37	10	8	18	47	61	38
9	FC Lausanne-Sport	36	3	5	10	25	31	6	3	9	26	31	9	8	19	51	62	35
10	FC Vaduz	36	3	6	9	21	32	4	3	11	24	46	7	9	20	45	78	30

European qualification 2017/18

Champion/Cup winner: FC Basel 1893 (group stage)

BSC Young Boys (third qualifying round)

FC Lugano (group stage)
FC Sion (third qualifying round)
FC Luzern (second qualifying round)

Top scorer	Seydou Doumbia (Basel), 20 goals
Relegated club	FC Vaduz
Promoted club	FC Zürich
Cup final	FC Basel 1893 3-0 FC Sion

Player of the season

Guillaume Hoarau
(BSC Young Boys)

The former Paris Saint-Germain and France striker maintained his excellent productivity in the Swiss Super League, following up his 17 goals in 2014/15 and 18 in 2015/16 with another 18-goal haul in 2016/17 to help Young Boys to a third successive runners-up spot. Hoarau struck twice in a 3-1 home win over Basel – the champions' first defeat – and was an ever-present danger with his aerial power, physical presence and clinical finishing. The lanky 33-year-old also scored five of Young Boys' seven goals in the UEFA Europa League group stage.

Newcomer of the season

Mohamed Elyounoussi
(FC Basel 1893)

A replacement at Basel for Schalke-bound Breel Embolo, Elyounoussi arrived from Norwegian club Molde on a four-year contract and enjoyed an outstanding debut season in the Swiss Super League. The Morocco-born 22-year-old – cousin of fellow Norwegian international Tarik Elyounoussi – became a fundamental figure in Urs Fischer's side and scored ten league goals, including a 36-minute hat-trick in a 4-0 win over Lugano in the first game after the winter break. He also registered his first goal for Norway in a June friendly against Sweden.

Team of the season

(4-4-2)

Coach: Fischer *(Basel)*

NATIONAL TEAM

International tournament appearances

FIFA World Cup (10) 1934, 1938 (qtr-finals), 1950, 1954 (qtr-finals), 1962, 1966, 1994 (2nd round), 2006 (2nd round), 2010, 2014 (2nd round)
UEFA European Championship (4) 1996, 2004, 2008, 2016 (round of 16)

Top five all-time caps

Heinz Hermann (118); Alain Geiger (112); Stéphane Chapuisat (103); Johann Vogel (94); **Stephan Lichtsteiner** (90)

Top five all-time goals

Alexander Frei (42); Xam Abegglen & Kubilay Türkyilmaz (34); André Abegglen & Jacky Fatton (29)

Results 2016/17

06/09/16	Portugal (WCQ)	H	Basel	W	2-0	*Embolo (24), Mehmedi (30)*
07/10/16	Hungary (WCQ)	A	Budapest	W	3-2	*Seferovic (51), Rodriguez (67), Stocker (89)*
10/10/16	Andorra (WCQ)	A	Andorra la Vella	W	2-1	*Schär (19p), Mehmedi (77)*
13/11/16	Faroe Islands (WCQ)	H	Lucerne	W	2-0	*Derdiyok (27), Lichtsteiner (83)*
25/03/17	Latvia (WCQ)	H	Geneva	W	1-0	*Drmic (66)*
01/06/17	Belarus	H	Neuchatel	W	1-0	*Shaqiri (9)*
09/06/17	Faroe Islands (WCQ)	A	Torshavn	W	2-0	*Xhaka (36), Shaqiri (59)*

Appearances 2016/17

Coach: Vladimir Petković	15/08/63		POR	HUN	AND	FRO	LVA	Blr	FRO	Caps	Goals
Yann Sommer	17/12/88	Mönchengladbach (GER)	G	G		G	G		G	27	-
Stephan Lichtsteiner	16/01/84	Juventus (ITA)	D70	D		D	D		D	90	6
Fabian Schär	20/12/91	Hoffenheim (GER)	D	D	D	D	D			29	7
Johan Djourou	18/01/87	Hamburg (GER)	D			D	D	D65	D	69	2
Ricardo Rodriguez	25/08/92	Wolfsburg (GER)	D	D	D	D				45	1
Valon Behrami	19/04/85	Watford (ENG)	M	M		M		M	M	75	2
Granit Xhaka	27/09/92	Arsenal (ENG)	M 93*		M	M	M	s65	M	53	7
Breel Embolo	14/02/97	Schalke (GER)	M	M	M					17	2
Blerim Dzemaili	12/04/86	Bologna (ITA) /Montreal Impact (USA)	M89	M		M80	M		M86	57	7
Admir Mehmedi	16/03/91	Leverkusen (GER)	M	M88	M	M	M	A	M62	53	7
Haris Seferovic	22/02/92	Eintracht Frankfurt (GER)	A78	A72	A	s87	A83	s65	A78	41	8
Silvan Widmer	05/03/93	Udinese (ITA)	s70					D46		9	-
Eren Derdiyok	12/06/88	Galatasaray (TUR)	s78	s72		A87			s78	57	11
Gelson Fernandes	02/09/86	Rennes (FRA)	s89	s81	M66		M64	s65		64	2
Nico Elvedi	30/09/96	Mönchengladbach (GER)		D	s46			D46		4	-
Xherdan Shaqiri	10/10/91	Stoke (ENG)		M81	M80		M77	M	M	62	20
Valentin Stocker	12/04/89	Hertha (GER)		s88	s80	M69				36	6
Roman Bürki	14/11/90	Dortmund (GER)			G			G		7	-
Timm Klose	09/05/88	Norwich (ENG)			D46			s46		16	-
Michael Lang	08/02/91	Basel			D					20	2
Denis Zakaria	20/11/96	Young Boys			s66					3	-
Edimilson Fernandes	15/04/96	West Ham (ENG)				s69		M65		2	-
Renato Steffen	03/11/91	Basel				s80				5	-
François Moubandje	21/06/90	Toulouse (FRA)					D	D	D	14	-
Josip Drmic	08/08/92	Mönchengladbach (GER)					s64			26	9
Steven Zuber	17/08/91	Hoffenheim (GER)					s77	M65	s62	3	-
Remo Freuler	15/04/92	Atalanta (ITA)					s83	M46	s86	3	-
Fabian Frei	08/01/89	Mainz (GER)						s46		10	1
Florent Hadergjonaj	31/07/94	Ingolstadt (GER)						s46		1	-
Manuel Akanji	19/07/95	Basel							D	1	-

EUROPE

FC Basel 1893

Group A

Match 1 - PFC Ludogorets Razgrad (BUL)

H 1-1 *Steffen (79)*

Vaclík, Traoré, Lang, Zuffi (Fransson 70), Bjarnason, Delgado (Callà 82), Steffen, Suchý, Janko (Doumbia 40), Balanta, Xhaka. Coach: Urs Fischer (SUI)

Match 2 - Arsenal FC (ENG)

A 0-2

Vaclík, Traoré, Lang, Zuffi (Elyounoussi 71), Bjarnason (Delgado 79), Steffen, Fransson, Suchý, Balanta, Xhaka, Doumbia (Šporar 57). Coach: Urs Fischer (SUI)

Match 3 - Paris Saint-Germain (FRA)

A 0-3

Vaclík, Traoré, Lang, Serey Dié (Janko 78), Bjarnason, Delgado (Zuffi 70), Steffen, Suchý, Balanta, Xhaka, Doumbia (Šporar 61). Coach: Urs Fischer (SUI)

Match 4 - Paris Saint-Germain (FRA)

H 1-2 *Zuffi (76)*

Vaclík, Traoré, Gaber (Šporar 69), Serey Dié, Bjarnason, Delgado (Zuffi 59), Steffen, Suchý, Balanta, Xhaka, Doumbia (Janko 59). Coach: Urs Fischer (SUI)

Red card: Serey Dié 84

Match 5 - PFC Ludogorets Razgrad (BUL)

A 0-0

Vaclík, Traoré, Lang, Zuffi, Bjarnason (Callà 85), Delgado (Šporar 80), Suchý, Balanta, Elyounoussi, Xhaka, Doumbia (Janko 79). Coach: Urs Fischer (SUI)

Match 6 - Arsenal FC (ENG)

H 1-4 *Doumbia (78)*

Vaclík, Traoré, Lang, Serey Dié (Zuffi 74), Delgado (Doumbia 54), Steffen, Suchý, Janko, Balanta, Elyounoussi (Callà 60), Xhaka. Coach: Urs Fischer (SUI)

BSC Young Boys

Third qualifying round - FC Shakhtar Donetsk (UKR)

A 0-2

Mvogo, Vilotić, Bertone, Sulejmani (Wüthrich 58), Lecjaks, Gerndt (Kubo 48), Ravet, Rochat, Sutter (Hadergjonaj 80), Sanogo, Hoarau. Coach: Adi Hütter (AUT)

Red card: Vilotić 55

H 2-0 (aet; 4-2 on pens) *Kubo (54, 60)*

Mvogo, Von Bergen, Bertone (Gajić 111), Sulejmani, Lecjaks, Ravet (Hadergjonaj 88), Rochat, Sutter (Obexer 116), Kubo, Sanogo, Hoarau. Coach: Adi Hütter (AUT)

Play-offs - VfL Borussia Mönchengladbach (GER)

H 1-3 *Sulejmani (56)*

Mvogo, Vilotić, Bertone, Sulejmani (Schick 86), Lecjaks, Ravet, Gajić (Zakaria 73), Rochat, Sutter, Kubo (Frey 73), Hoarau. Coach: Adi Hütter (AUT)

A 1-6 *Ravet (79)*

Mvogo, Von Bergen (Kubo 46), Bertone, Sulejmani (Schick 46), Lecjaks, Ravet, Frey (Duah 69), Rochat, Wüthrich, Sutter, Zakaria. Coach: Adi Hütter (AUT)

Group B

Match 1 - Olympiacos FC (GRE)

H 0-1

Mvogo, Von Bergen, Bertone, Sulejmani, Lecjaks, Ravet (Duah 86), Frey (Schick 78), Rochat, Sutter, Zakaria, Kubo. Coach: Adi Hütter (AUT)

Match 2 - FC Astana (KAZ)

A 0-0

Mvogo, Von Bergen, Bertone, Sulejmani (Schick 81), Lecjaks, Ravet, Frey (Duah 81), Sutter, Nuhu, Zakaria, Kubo (Aebischer 90+1). Coach: Adi Hütter (AUT)

Match 3 - APOEL FC (CYP)

H 3-1 *Hoarau (18, 52, 82p)*

Mvogo, Von Bergen, Lecjaks, Ravet (Duah 88), Schick (Bertone 80), Sutter, Nuhu, Zakaria, Kubo, Sanogo, Hoarau (Frey 84). Coach: Adi Hütter (AUT)

Match 4 - APOEL FC (CYP)

A 0-1

Mvogo, Von Bergen, Lecjaks, Ravet (Mbabu 65), Schick, Sutter, Nuhu, Zakaria (Bertone 80), Kubo (Frey 80), Sanogo, Hoarau. Coach: Adi Hütter (AUT)

Red card: Mbabu 67

Match 5 - Olympiacos FC (GRE)

A 1-1 *Hoarau (58)*

Mvogo, Von Bergen, Bertone, Sulejmani (Gerndt 58), Lecjaks, Schick (Frey 88), Sutter, Zakaria, Sanogo (Duah 77), Benito, Hoarau. Coach: Adi Hütter (AUT)

Match 6 - FC Astana (KAZ)

H 3-0 *Frey (63), Hoarau (66), Schick (71)*

Mvogo, Von Bergen, Bertone, Gerndt, Schick, Sutter, Nuhu, Obexer (Benito 67), Sanogo, Aebischer (Frey 61), Hoarau (Duah 78). Coach: Adi Hütter (AUT)

FC Zürich

Group L

Match 1 - Villarreal CF (ESP)

A 1-2 *Sadiku (2)*

Vaņins, Winter (Schönbächler 65), Sadiku, Nef, Kukeli, Bangura, Kecojević, Brunner, Sarr (Yapi Yapo 57), Rodriguez (Čavuševič 84), Voser. Coach: Uli Forte (SUI)

Match 2 - Osmanlıspor (TUR)

H 2-1 *Schönbächler (45+1), Čavuševič (79)*

Vaņins, Koné (Rodriguez 55), Nef, Buff (Yapi Yapo 88), Kukeli, Čavuševič, Kecojević, Brunner, Schönbächler (Winter 70), Sarr, Voser. Coach: Uli Forte (SUI)

Match 3 - FC Steaua Bucureşti (ROU)

A 1-1 *Koné (86)*

Vaņins, Koné, Winter (Schönbächler 73), Nef, Buff, Kecojević, Brunner (Marchesano 84), Sarr (Čavuševič 78), Rodriguez, Yapi Yapo, Voser. Coach: Uli Forte (SUI)

Match 4 - FC Steaua Bucureşti (ROU)

H 0-0

Vaņins, Winter (Koné 65), Nef, Buff (Schönbächler 75), Kukeli, Čavuševič, Kecojević, Brunner, Sarr, Rodriguez, Voser (Stettler 29). Coach: Uli Forte (SUI)

Match 5 - Villarreal CF (ESP)

H 1-1 *Rodriguez (87p)*

Vaņins, Koné, Marchesano, Nef, Kukeli (Sadiku 79), Bangura, Kecojević, Brunner (Rodriguez 69), Schönbächler, Sarr, Voser (Winter 69). Coach: Uli Forte (SUI)

Match 6 - Osmanlıspor (TUR)

A 0-2

Vaņins, Winter, Nef, Kukeli, Čavuševič (Schönbächler 67), Bangura, Kecojević, Brunner (Sadiku 60), Sarr, Rodriguez, Voser (Koné 77). Coach: Uli Forte (SUI)

FC Luzern

Third qualifying round - US Sassuolo Calcio (ITA)

H 1-1 *M Schneuwly (8)*

Zibung, Lustenberger, Hyka (Grether 54), Jantscher, Puljić, M Schneuwly, C Schneuwly, Ricardo Costa, Itten (Juric 63), Haas, Neumayr. Coach: Markus Babbel (GER)

A 0-3

Zibung, Lustenberger, Hyka (Oliveira 72), Jantscher, Puljić (Sarr 11), M Schneuwly, C Schneuwly, Ricardo Costa, Kryeziu, Haas, Neumayr (Arnold 72). Coach: Markus Babbel (GER)

Red card: Ricardo Costa 38

DOMESTIC LEAGUE CLUB-BY-CLUB

Grasshopper Club Zürich

EUROPA LEAGUE

Second qualifying round - KR Reykjavík (ISL)

A 3-3 *Munsy (18), Gjorgjev (36), Caio (59)*

Mall, Pnishi, Sigurjónsson, Bašić, Brahimi (Kamberi 68), Lavanchy, Munsy (Tabakovic 78), Caio, Bamert, Lüthi, Gjorgjev (Andersen 62). Coach: Pierluigi Tami (SUI)

H 2-1 *Sigurjónsson (45, 68)*

Mall, Pnishi (Källström 63), Sigurjónsson, Bašić, Andersen (Kamberi 73), Brahimi, Lavanchy, Munsy, Caio (Gjorgjev 66), Bamert, Lüthi. Coach: Pierluigi Tami (SUI)

W

Third qualifying round - Apollon Limassol FC (CYP)

H 2-1 *Tabakovic (11), Lavanchy (90+3)*

Mall, Antonov, Källström, Pnishi, Sigurjónsson, Bašić, Andersen (Brahimi 77), Tabakovic (Munsy 46), Bamert, Kamberi (Lavanchy 71), Lüthi. Coach: Pierluigi Tami (SUI)

A 3-3 (aet) *Andersen (77), Caio (103), Gjorgjev (120+1)*

Mall, Källström (Gjorgjev 91), Pnishi, Sigurjónsson (Brahimi 90+3), Bašić, Andersen, Lavanchy, Munsy (Tabakovic 86), Caio, Bamert, Lüthi. Coach: Pierluigi Tami (SUI)

Play-offs - Fenerbahçe SK (TUR)

A 0-3

Vasić, Källström, Pnishi, Sigurjónsson (Brahimi 84), Bašić, Lavanchy, Munsy, Caio (Kamberi 74), Bamert, Lüthi, Gjorgjev (Andersen 64). Coach: Pierluigi Tami (SUI)

H 0-2

Mall, Antonov, Pnishi, Sigurjónsson, Andersen (Alpsoy 81), Brahimi, Tabakovic, Rhyner, Kareem (Kamberi 68), Lüthi, Gjorgjev. Coach: Pierluigi Tami (SUI)

FC Basel 1893

1893 • St Jakob-Park (37,994) • fcb.ch

Major honours

Swiss League (20) 1953, 1967, 1969, 1970, 1972, 1973, 1977, 1980, 2002, 2004, 2005, 2008, 2010, 2011, 2012, 2013, 2014, 2015, 2016, 2017;
Swiss Cup (12) 1933, 1947, 1963, 1967, 1975, 2002, 2003, 2007, 2008, 2010, 2012, 2017

Coach: Urs Fischer

Date		Opponent		Score	Scorers
2016					
24/07	h	Sion	W	3-0	*Delgado 2 (1p), Doumbia*
31/07	a	Vaduz	W	5-1	*Janko, Delgado (p), Elyounoussi, Steffen, Doumbia*
07/08	a	Luzern	W	3-2	*Suchý, Janko 2*
10/08	h	Young Boys	W	3-0	*Zuffi, Bjarnason, og (Vilotić)*
20/08	h	Lugano	W	4-1	*Suchý, Steffen, Doumbia, Lang*
28/08	a	Thun	W	3-0	*Lang, Janko, Zuffi*
10/09	h	Grasshoppers	W	3-1	*Bjarnason, Doumbia 2*
21/09	a	Lausanne	W	2-1	*Bjarnason, Balanta*
24/09	a	St Gallen	W	3-1	*Delgado, og (Gelmi), Doumbia (p)*
01/10	h	Thun	D	1-1	*Callà*
15/10	h	Luzern	W	3-0	*Doumbia, Lang, Elyounoussi*
22/10	a	Lugano	D	2-2	*Delgado, Callà (p)*
29/10	a	Grasshoppers	W	2-0	*Delgado 2 (1p)*
05/11	h	Lausanne	W	2-1	*Suchý, Janko*
19/11	h	Vaduz	W	6-0	*Doumbia 2, Elyounoussi, Lang, Bjarnason, Callà*
27/11	a	Sion	W	2-1	*Delgado, Janko*
03/12	a	Young Boys	L	1-3	*Delgado (p)*
10/12	h	St Gallen	W	1-0	*Janko*
2017					
04/02	h	Lugano	W	4-0	*Elyounoussi 3, Janko*
11/02	a	Thun	W	2-0	*og (Schindelholz), Doumbia*
19/02	h	Lausanne	W	4-3	*Doumbia 2, Akanji, Janko*
26/02	h	Luzern	W	3-1	*Suchý, og (Lucas), Janko*
05/03	a	Vaduz	D	1-1	*Zuffi*
12/03	a	Sion	W	1-0	*Lang*
18/03	h	Grasshoppers	W	1-0	*Zuffi*
01/04	a	St Gallen	W	3-0	*Akanji 2, Janko*
09/04	h	Young Boys	D	1-1	*Elyounoussi*
15/04	a	Lausanne	W	4-0	*Lang, Elyounoussi 2, Šporar*
22/04	h	Vaduz	D	2-2	*Delgado, Doumbia*
28/04	a	Luzern	W	2-1	*Doumbia, Steffen*
07/05	a	Lugano	D	2-2	*Fransson, Zuffi*
14/05	h	Thun	D	3-3	*Steffen, Elyounoussi, Serey Dié*
18/05	h	Sion	D	2-2	*Janko, Doumbia*
21/05	a	Young Boys	L	1-2	*Doumbia*
28/05	a	Grasshoppers	W	3-1	*Akanji, Doumbia 2*
02/06	h	St Gallen	W	4-1	*Doumbia 2, Steffen, Janko*

No	Name	Nat	DoB	Pos	Aps	(s)	Gls
36	Manuel Akanji		19/07/95	D	14	(1)	4
23	Éder Balanta	COL	28/02/93	D	18	(1)	1
8	Birkir Bjarnason	ISL	27/05/88	M	9	(4)	4
77	Jean-Paul Boëtius	NED	22/03/94	M	1	(1)	
33	Kevin Bua		11/08/93	M	1	(2)	
39	Davide Callà		06/10/84	M	11	(16)	3
10	Matías Delgado	ARG	15/12/82	M	28	(1)	10
88	Seydou Doumbia	CIV	31/12/87	A	15	(10)	20
24	Mohamed Elyounoussi	NOR	04/08/94	M	24	(8)	10
15	Alexander Fransson	SWE	02/04/94	M	12	(13)	1
4	Omar Gaber	EGY	30/01/92	D	9	(3)	
26	Daniel Høegh	DEN	06/01/91	D	7	(3)	
21	Marc Janko	AUT	25/06/83	A	13	(11)	13
20	Dereck Kutesa		06/12/97	M	1	(2)	
5	Michael Lang		08/02/91	D	31		6
27	Neftali Manzambi		23/04/97	A		(2)	
13	Djordje Nikolić	SRB	13/04/97	G	1		
28	Raoul Petretta		24/03/97	D	5		
42	Charles Pickel		15/05/97	M		(1)	
25	Blas Riveros	PAR	03/02/98	D	7	(1)	
31	Dominik Schmid		10/03/98	M	1		
6	Serey Dié	CIV	07/11/84	M	10	(6)	1
9	Andraž Šporar	SVN	27/02/94	A	9	(9)	1
11	Renato Steffen		03/11/91	M	26	(4)	5
17	Marek Suchý	CZE	29/03/88	D	33		4
3	Adama Traoré	CIV	03/02/90	D	20	(3)	
1	Tomáš Vaclík	CZE	29/03/89	G	34		
18	Germano Vailati		30/08/80	G	1		
34	Taulant Xhaka	ALB	28/03/91	M	29	(1)	
7	Luca Zuffi		27/03/90	M	26	(5)	5

SWITZERLAND

Grasshopper Club Zürich

1886 • Letzigrund (26,104) • gcz.ch

Major honours

Swiss League (27) 1898, 1900, 1901, 1905, 1921, 1927, 1928, 1931, 1937, 1939, 1942, 1943, 1945, 1952, 1956, 1971, 1978, 1982, 1983, 1984, 1990, 1991, 1995, 1996, 1998, 2001, 2003; Swiss Cup (19) 1926, 1927, 1932, 1934, 1937, 1938, 1940, 1941, 1942, 1943, 1946, 1952, 1956, 1983, 1988, 1989, 1990, 1994, 2013

Coach: Pierluigi Tami; (12/03/17) Carlos Bernegger (ARG)

Date		Opponent		Score	Scorers
2016					
24/07	h	Lausanne	W	2-0	*Caio 2*
31/07	a	Luzern	L	3-4	*Andersen, Caio 2*
07/08	a	St Gallen	L	1-2	*Caio*
11/08	a	Thun	L	1-2	*Munsy*
21/08	h	Sion	W	2-1	*Tabakovic, Caio*
28/08	h	Young Boys	W	4-1	*Munsy, Lavanchy, Sigurjónsson, Caio (p)*
10/09	a	Basel	L	1-3	*Sigurjónsson*
22/09	a	Lugano	L	0-2	
25/09	h	Vaduz	W	2-1	*Sigurjónsson 2*
02/10	h	Luzern	W	3-2	*Munsy, Sigurjónsson, Hunziker*
16/10	a	Sion	L	2-4	*Bašić, Munsy*
23/10	a	Young Boys	L	0-4	
29/10	h	Basel	L	0-2	
06/11	a	Vaduz	D	0-0	
19/11	h	Thun	D	1-1	*Caio*
26/11	h	St Gallen	D	2-2	*Andersen, Caio*
04/12	a	Lausanne	W	2-1	*Sigurjónsson, Lavanchy*
11/12	h	Lugano	D	0-0	
2017					
04/02	h	Thun	L	0-1	
11/02	a	Lugano	L	0-3	
19/02	h	Sion	L	0-1	
25/02	h	Young Boys	L	2-3	*Dabbur, og (Mvogo)*
05/03	a	Luzern	D	1-1	*Sigurjónsson*
11/03	h	Vaduz	L	1-2	*Bergström*
18/03	a	Basel	L	0-1	
02/04	a	Lausanne	D	0-0	
08/04	h	St Gallen	W	3-1	*Dabbur 2, Caio*
17/04	a	Young Boys	W	1-0	*Dabbur*
22/04	h	Luzern	W	4-1	*Caio 2, Bamert, Dabbur*
30/04	h	Lugano	L	0-1	
06/05	a	Vaduz	W	4-2	*Caio, Andersen 2, Vilotić*
14/05	h	Lausanne	D	1-1	*Dabbur*
17/05	a	Thun	L	1-3	*Andersen*
21/05	a	St Gallen	L	1-4	*Dabbur*
28/05	h	Basel	L	1-3	*Caio*
02/06	a	Sion	D	1-1	*Andersen*

No	Name	Nat	DoB	Pos	Aps	(s)	Gls
31	Harun Alpsoy		03/03/97	M	1	(1)	
10	Lucas Andersen	DEN	13/09/94	M	28	(5)	6
3	Nemanja Antonov	SRB	06/05/95	D	26	(2)	
30	Nedim Bajrami		28/02/99	M	2	(5)	
24	Jan Bamert		09/03/98	D	25	(2)	1
8	Marko Bašić	CRO	25/05/88	M	15	(1)	1
13	Emil Bergström	SWE	19/05/93	D	18		1
11	Mërgim Brahimi	KOS	08/08/92	M	21	(8)	
21	Caio	BRA	29/05/86	M	33	(1)	14
9	Munas Dabbur	ISR	14/05/92	A	12	(1)	7
32	Valon Fazliu	KOS	02/02/96	M	2	(2)	
35	Nikola Gjorgjev	MKD	22/08/97	M	4	(14)	
29	Levent Gülen		24/02/94	D		(1)	
17	Nicolas Hunziker		23/02/96	A	6	(8)	1
4	Kim Källström	SWE	24/08/82	M	16		
26	Florian Kamberi		08/03/95	A	1	(3)	
25	Sherko Kareem	IRN	25/05/96	A	1	(2)	
14	Numa Lavanchy		25/08/93	D	35		2
22	Benjamin Lüthi		30/11/88	D	5	(2)	
18	Joël Mall		05/04/91	G	16		
20	Ridge Munsy	COD	09/07/89	A	17	(15)	4
26	Patrick Olsen	DEN	23/04/94	M	2	(4)	
23	Charles Pickel		15/05/97	M	12		
6	Alban Pnishi	KOS	20/10/90	D	20	(4)	
28	Petar Pusic		25/01/99	M		(1)	
29	Arijan Qollaku	ALB	04/02/97	D	1		
23	Jean-Pierre Rhyner		16/03/96	D	1		
7	Rúnar Már Sigurjónsson	ISL	18/06/90	M	29	(2)	7
19	Haris Tabakovic		20/06/94	A	7	(12)	1
1	Vaso Vasić	SRB	26/04/90	G	20		
4	Milan Vilotić	SRB	21/10/86	D	13		1
22	Cédric Zesiger		24/06/98	D	7		

FC Lausanne-Sport

1896 • Olympique de la Pontaise (8,500) • lausanne-sport.ch

Major honours

Swiss League (7) 1913, 1932, 1935, 1936, 1944, 1951, 1965; Swiss Cup (9) 1935, 1939, 1944, 1950, 1962, 1964, 1981, 1998, 1999

Coach: Fabio Celestini

Date		Opponent		Score	Scorers
2016					
24/07	a	Grasshoppers	L	0-2	
31/07	h	Thun	D	4-4	*Margiotta, Pak, Torres, Marcus Diniz*
06/08	a	Sion	W	3-1	*Margiotta, Torres (p), Margairaz*
11/08	h	St Gallen	W	1-0	*Margairaz*
20/08	a	Young Boys	L	2-7	*Campo, Pak*
27/08	a	Lugano	D	1-1	*Campo*
11/09	h	Vaduz	W	5-0	*Kololli 2, Custodio, Campo, Pak*
21/09	h	Basel	L	1-2	*Margiotta*
24/09	a	Luzern	W	3-1	*Margiotta 2, Torres*
02/10	h	Lugano	W	4-1	*Marcus Diniz, Araz, Custodio (p), Margiotta*
15/10	a	Thun	L	0-1	
23/10	h	Sion	L	0-2	
30/10	h	Luzern	L	2-3	*Lotomba, Pak*
05/11	a	Basel	L	1-2	*Margiotta*
20/11	a	St Gallen	L	0-2	
27/11	h	Young Boys	L	1-2	*Ben Khalifa*
04/12	h	Grasshoppers	L	1-2	*Margiotta*
10/12	a	Vaduz	D	1-1	*Ben Khalifa*
2017					
05/02	h	Luzern	D	4-4	*Ben Khalifa 3, Kololli (p)*
12/02	a	St Gallen	L	1-2	*Kololli*
19/02	a	Basel	L	3-4	*Kololli 2 (1p), Campo*
26/02	h	Sion	L	0-1	
04/03	a	Lugano	L	1-2	*Campo*
12/03	h	Young Boys	D	0-0	
19/03	a	Vaduz	W	1-0	*Torres*
02/04	h	Grasshoppers	D	0-0	
08/04	a	Thun	W	4-2	*Ben Khalifa 3, Kololli*
15/04	h	Basel	L	0-4	
23/04	a	Sion	W	1-0	*Torres*
29/04	h	Vaduz	L	1-3	*Torres*
07/05	h	St Gallen	L	0-1	
14/05	a	Grasshoppers	D	1-1	*Torres*
17/05	a	Luzern	W	3-0	*Torres, Campo, Kololli (p)*
20/05	h	Thun	D	0-0	
28/05	h	Lugano	L	1-2	*Ben Khalifa*
02/06	a	Young Boys	L	0-2	

No	Name	Nat	DoB	Pos	Aps	(s)	Gls
8	Musa Araz		17/01/94	M	20	(3)	1
25	Nassim Ben Khalifa		13/01/92	A	16	(7)	9
11	Samuele Campo		06/07/95	M	29	(5)	6
1	Thomas Castella		30/06/93	G	25	(1)	
17	Olivier Custodio		10/02/95	M	24	(4)	2
35	Danny Da Silva		03/03/93	G	3		
20	Maxime Dominguez		01/02/96	M	3	(1)	
6	Elton Monteiro	POR	22/02/94	D	30		
15	Juan Esnáider	ESP	31/01/92	A		(1)	
13	Paolo Frascatore	ITA	04/01/92	D	1		
16	Nicolas Gétaz		11/06/91	D	26	(3)	
7	Benjamin Kololli	KOS	15/05/92	D	24	(2)	8
23	Jordan Lotomba		29/09/98	M	20	(5)	1
18	Andrea Maccoppi	ITA	22/01/87	M	17		
4	Jérémy Manière		26/07/91	D	28	(1)	
12	Marcus Diniz	BRA	01/08/87	D	29	(1)	2
5	Xavier Margairaz		07/01/84	M	3	(20)	2
19	Francesco Margiotta	ITA	15/07/93	A	18		8
22	Kevin Martin		13/06/95	G	8	(1)	
10	Kevin Méndez	URU	10/01/96	M		(6)	
9	Pak Kwang-ryong	PRK	27/09/92	A	22	(8)	4
14	Alexandre Pasche		31/05/91	M	16	(11)	
33	Taye Taiwo	NGA	16/04/85	D	11	(2)	
28	Yeltsin Tejeda	CRC	17/03/92	M	5	(6)	
24	Xavier Tomas	FRA	04/01/86	D	2	(1)	
37	Gabriel Torres	PAN	31/10/88	A	16	(14)	8
21	Ming-Yang Yang		11/07/95	M		(4)	

FC Lugano

1908 • Cornaredo (6,390) • fclugano.com

Major honours

Swiss League (3) 1938, 1941, 1949; Swiss Cup (3) 1931, 1968, 1993

Coach: Andrea Manzo (ITA); (20/12/16) Paolo Tramezzani (ITA)

Date		Opponent		Score	Scorers
2016					
23/07	h	Luzern	L	1-2	*Ceesay*
30/07	a	Young Boys	W	2-1	*Alioski, og (Von Bergen)*
07/08	h	Vaduz	L	0-2	
10/08	h	Sion	W	3-1	*Alioski 2 (1p), Sabbatini*
20/08	a	Basel	L	1-4	*Rosseti*
27/08	h	Lausanne	D	1-1	*Alioski*
11/09	a	St Gallen	W	2-0	*Alioski, Aguirre*
22/09	h	Grasshoppers	W	2-0	*Rosseti, Alioski*
25/09	a	Thun	D	2-2	*Sabbatini, Alioski*
02/10	a	Lausanne	L	1-4	*Piccinocchi*
16/10	h	Young Boys	D	0-0	
22/10	h	Basel	D	2-2	*Mariani, Alioski (p)*
29/10	a	Sion	L	1-5	*Rosseti*
06/11	h	St Gallen	L	2-3	*Alioski, Mariani*
20/11	a	Luzern	L	1-2	*Rosseti*
27/11	a	Vaduz	L	1-5	*Mariani*
04/12	h	Thun	D	1-1	*Mariani*
11/12	a	Grasshoppers	D	0-0	
2017					
04/02	a	Basel	L	0-4	
11/02	h	Grasshoppers	W	3-0	*Sabbatini, Carlinhos Júnior, Sadiku*
19/02	a	Vaduz	D	1-1	*Sadiku*
26/02	a	St Gallen	W	1-0	*Sadiku*
04/03	h	Lausanne	W	2-1	*Sadiku, Alioski*
12/03	a	Thun	L	2-5	*Carlinhos Júnior, Sadiku*
19/03	h	Young Boys	L	0-2	
02/04	a	Luzern	W	2-0	*Mizrahi, Carlinhos Júnior*
09/04	h	Sion	W	4-2	*Alioski 3 (2p), Sadiku*
17/04	h	Thun	W	2-1	*og (Facchinetti), Alioski*
23/04	a	Young Boys	W	2-1	*Alioski, Sadiku*
30/04	a	Grasshoppers	W	1-0	*Mariani*
07/05	h	Basel	D	2-2	*Alioski (p), Sadiku*
13/05	a	Sion	L	0-2	
16/05	h	St Gallen	W	3-2	*Mariani 2, Črnigoj*
20/05	h	Vaduz	W	2-1	*Sadiku, Mariani*
28/05	a	Lausanne	W	2-1	*og (Lotomba), Carlinhos Júnior*
02/06	h	Luzern	L	0-1	

No	Name	Nat	DoB	Pos	Aps	(s)	Gls
21	Rodrigo Aguirre	ARG	01/10/94	A	9		1
7	Ezgjan Alioski	MKD	12/02/92	M	34		16
10	Mattia Bottani		24/05/91	M	1		
11	Carlinhos Júnior	BRA	08/08/94	M	7	(9)	4
29	Assan Ceesay	GAM	17/03/94	A	3	(9)	1
33	Domen Črnigoj	SVN	18/11/95	M	24	(6)	1
41	Eray Cümart		04/02/98	D	12		
5	Vladimir Golemić	SRB	28/06/91	D	33		
3	Goran Jozinović	CRO	27/08/90	D	18		
20	Davide Mariani		19/05/91	M	34		8
92	Bruno Martignoni		13/12/92	D	2	(2)	
91	Dragan Mihajlovic		22/08/91	D	30	(3)	
8	Ofir Mizrahi	ISR	04/12/93	A	10	(12)	1
4	Marco Padalino		08/12/83	D	10	(4)	
15	Pepín	EQG	14/08/96	M		(5)	
18	Mario Piccinocchi	ITA	21/02/95	M	21	(1)	1
99	Andrés Ponce	VEN	11/11/96	A	2	(6)	
19	Antoine Rey		25/08/86	M	2	(18)	
27	Lorenzo Rosseti	ITA	05/08/94	A	9	(2)	4
11	Karim Rossi		01/05/94	A		(2)	
22	Steve Rouiller		09/06/84	D	10	(4)	
30	Francesco Russo	ITA	23/12/81	G	4		
14	Jonathan Sabbatini	URU	31/03/88	M	28	(1)	3
10	Armando Sadiku	ALB	27/05/91	A	16		9
23	Mirko Salvi		14/02/94	G	32	(1)	
28	Fulvio Sulmoni		04/01/86	D	31		
6	Orlando Urbano	ITA	09/06/84	D	1	(3)	
17	Bálint Vécsei	HUN	13/07/93	M	13	(6)	

FC Luzern

1901 • swissporarena (16,490) • fcl.ch

Major honours

Swiss League (1) 1989; Swiss Cup (2) 1960, 1992

Coach: Markus Babbel (GER)

2016

23/07 a Lugano W 2-1 *Neumayr, M Schneuwly (p)*
31/07 h Grasshoppers W 4-3 *Juric 2 (1p), Hyka, Puljić*
07/08 h Basel L 2-3 *Hyka 2*
10/08 a Vaduz W 3-1 *M Schneuwly 2, Itten*
21/08 h Thun W 3-0 *Neumayr, M Schneuwly, Oliveira*
28/08 a St Gallen L 0-3
10/09 a Young Boys L 1-2 *M Schneuwly*
21/09 h Sion D 2-2 *M Schneuwly, og (Lüchinger)*
24/09 h Lausanne L 1-3 *M Schneuwly*
02/10 a Grasshoppers L 2-3 *Rodriguez, Neumayr (p)*
15/10 a Basel L 0-3
23/10 h St Gallen W 3-0 *Juric, Puljić, C Schneuwly*
30/10 a Lausanne W 3-2 *M Schneuwly 2, Neumayr (p)*
06/11 h Young Boys D 2-2 *Haas, M Schneuwly*
20/11 h Lugano W 2-1 *Ricardo Costa, Puljić*
26/11 a Thun W 2-1 *Puljić, Rodriguez*
03/12 h Vaduz W 3-0 *Neumayr, Hyka 2*
11/12 a Sion L 1-3 *Hyka*

2017

05/02 a Lausanne D 4-4 *Affolter, M Schneuwly, Neumayr, Itten*
12/02 h Young Boys W 4-1 *Oliveira, Kryeziu, Rodriguez, Neumayr (p)*
18/02 h Thun D 1-1 *Rodriguez*
26/02 a Basel L 1-3 *Affolter*
05/03 h Grasshoppers D 1-1 *Schürpf*
11/03 a St Gallen D 1-1 *Juric*
18/03 h Sion D 0-0
02/04 h Lugano L 0-2
09/04 a Vaduz W 2-0 *Schürpf, M Schneuwly*
17/04 h St Gallen W 2-0 *Kryeziu, Itten*
22/04 a Grasshoppers L 1-4 *Knezevic*
28/04 h Basel L 1-2 *M Schneuwly*
06/05 a Thun L 1-3 *M Schneuwly*
14/05 a Young Boys L 1-4 *Juric*
17/05 h Lausanne L 0-3
21/05 a Sion W 3-2 *Juric, Rodriguez 2*
28/05 h Vaduz D 2-2 *Juric, Schürpf*
02/06 a Lugano W 1-0 *Juric*

No	Name	Nat	DoB	Pos	Aps	(s)	Gls
16	François Affolter		13/03/91	D	24	(4)	2
6	Remo Arnold		17/01/97	M	2	(3)	
17	Simon Grether		20/05/92	D	18	(3)	
32	Nicolas Haas		23/01/96	M	17	(6)	1
8	Jahmir Hyka	ALB	08/03/88	M	12	(3)	6
30	Cédric Itten		27/12/96	A	15	(13)	3
10	Jakob Jantscher	AUT	08/01/89	M	1	(3)	
9	Tomi Juric	AUS	22/07/91	A	22	(8)	8
33	Stefan Knezevic		30/10/96	D	8		1
31	Hekuran Kryeziu	KOS	12/02/93	M	28	(4)	2
5	Lucas	BRA	22/07/92	D	7		
7	Claudio Lustenberger		06/01/87	D	32		
77	Markus Neumayr	GER	26/03/86	M	27	(4)	7
37	João Oliveira		06/01/96	M	5	(10)	2
21	Jonas Omlin		10/01/94	G	14		
13	Tomislav Puljić	CRO	21/03/83	D	11	(1)	4
20	Ricardo Costa	POR	16/05/81	D	33		1
68	Francisco Rodriguez		14/09/95	M	17	(8)	6
23	Sally Sarr	MTN	06/05/86	D		(4)	
19	Christian Schneuwly		07/02/88	M	32		1
15	Marco Schneuwly		27/03/85	A	27	(6)	14
11	Pascal Schürpf		15/07/89	M	5	(5)	3
14	Jérôme Thiesson		06/08/87	D	9	(1)	
35	Filip Ugrinic		05/01/99	M	6	(15)	
42	Idriz Voca		15/05/97	D	2	(1)	
1	David Zibung		10/01/84	G	22		

FC St Gallen

1879 • kybunpark (19,456) • fcsg.ch

Major honours

Swiss League (2) 1904, 2000; Swiss Cup (1) 1969

Coach: Joe Zinnbauer (GER); (04/05/17) Giorgio Contini (SUI)

2016

23/07 h Young Boys L 0-2
30/07 a Sion L 1-2 *Aleksić*
07/08 h Grasshoppers W 2-1 *Buess, Tafer*
11/08 a Lausanne L 0-1
21/08 a Vaduz L 0-2
28/08 h Luzern W 3-0 *Buess, Aratore, Chabbi*
11/09 h Lugano L 0-2
20/09 a Thun W 2-1 *Bunjaku, Ajeti*
24/09 h Basel L 1-3 *Aratore*
02/10 a Young Boys D 2-2 *Buess, Bunjaku*
16/10 h Vaduz L 0-2
23/10 a Luzern L 0-3
30/10 h Thun D 0-0
06/11 a Lugano W 3-2 *Ajeti, Bunjaku, Aratore (p)*
20/11 h Lausanne W 2-0 *Buess, Tafer*
26/11 a Grasshoppers D 2-2 *Ajeti, Wittwer*
04/12 h Sion W 2-1 *Ajeti 2*
10/12 a Basel L 0-1

2017

05/02 a Vaduz D 1-1 *Ajeti*
12/02 h Lausanne W 2-1 *Haggui, Ajeti*
18/02 a Young Boys D 2-2 *Ajeti, Buess*
26/02 h Lugano L 0-1
05/03 a Sion W 2-1 *Tafer 2*
11/03 h Luzern D 1-1 *Tafer*
19/03 a Thun D 2-2 *Ajeti, Aratore*
01/04 h Basel L 0-3
08/04 a Grasshoppers L 1-3 *Wittwer*
17/04 a Luzern L 0-2
23/04 h Thun L 1-2 *Tafer*
30/04 h Young Boys L 0-2
07/05 a Lausanne W 1-0 *Ajeti*
13/05 h Vaduz W 2-0 *Haggui, Barnetta (p)*
16/05 a Lugano L 2-3 *og (Mihajlovic), Toko*
21/05 h Grasshoppers W 4-1 *Aleksić, Tafer 2, Wiss*
28/05 h Sion D 1-1 *Gelmi*
02/06 a Basel L 1-4 *Aleksić*

No	Name	Nat	DoB	Pos	Aps	(s)	Gls
27	Albian Ajeti		26/02/97	A	22	(7)	10
23	Danijel Aleksić	SRB	30/04/91	A	14	(10)	3
4	Martin Angha		22/01/94	D	14	(1)	
22	Marco Aratore		04/06/91	M	32	(4)	4
51	Boris Babic		10/11/97	A	1	(4)	
85	Tranquillo Barnetta		22/05/85	M	15	(1)	1
11	Roman Buess		21/09/92	A	25	(4)	5
10	Albert Bunjaku	KOS	29/11/83	A	8	(4)	3
7	Seifedin Chabbi	AUT	04/07/93	A	2	(4)	1
13	Lucas Cueto	GER	24/03/96	M		(13)	
80	Gianluca Gaudino	GER	11/11/96	M	12	(6)	
14	Roy Gelmi		01/03/95	D	24	(3)	1
15	Mohamed Gouaida	TUN	15/05/93	M	5	(8)	
21	Karim Haggui	TUN	20/01/84	D	27	(1)	2
36	Silvan Hefti		25/10/97	D	33		
8	Steven Lang		03/09/87	M		(1)	
1	Daniel Lopar		19/04/85	G	32		
19	Mario Mutsch	LUX	03/09/84	D	11	(5)	
10	Sejad Salihović	BIH	08/10/84	M	6	(7)	
3	Kofi Schulz	GER	21/07/89	D	15	(5)	
25	Dejan Stojanovic	AUT	19/07/93	G	4		
9	Yannis Tafer	FRA	11/02/91	M	20	(15)	8
28	Nzuzi Toko	COD	20/11/90	M	29		1
6	Alain Wiss		21/08/90	D	16	(4)	1
16	Andreas Wittwer		05/10/90	M	29	(1)	2

FC Sion

1909 • Tourbillon (14,283) • fc-sion.ch

Major honours

Swiss League (2) 1992, 1997; Swiss Cup (13) 1965, 1974, 1980, 1982, 1986, 1991, 1995, 1996, 1997, 2006, 2009, 2011, 2015

Coach: Didier Tholot (FRA); (22/08/16) Peter Zeidler (GER); (25/04/17) Sébastien Fournier

2016

24/07 a Basel L 0-3
30/07 h St Gallen W 2-1 *Mujangi Bia, Sierro*
06/08 h Lausanne L 1-3 *Ziegler*
10/08 a Lugano L 1-3 *Ziegler*
21/08 a Grasshoppers L 1-2 *Mujangi Bia*
27/08 h Vaduz W 3-1 *Gekas, Carlitos, Léo Itaperuna*
11/09 h Thun W 1-0 *Ziegler (p)*
21/09 a Luzern D 2-2 *Ziegler, Akolo*
25/09 h Young Boys D 0-0
01/10 a Vaduz W 5-2 *Konaté, Akolo, Mveng, Assifuah 2*
16/10 h Grasshoppers W 4-2 *Akolo 2, Ziegler 2 (2p)*
23/10 a Lausanne W 2-0 *Ziegler 2 (1p)*
29/10 h Lugano W 5-1 *Gekas 2, Akolo, Karlen, Salatic*
05/11 a Thun W 3-2 *Konaté 2, Sierro*
20/11 a Young Boys L 3-4 *Konaté 2, Akolo*
27/11 h Basel L 1-2 *Karlen*
04/12 a St Gallen L 1-2 *Zverotić*
11/12 h Luzern W 3-1 *Akolo 2, Carlitos*

2017

05/02 a Young Boys L 1-3 *Akolo*
12/02 h Vaduz W 4-2 *Akolo 2, Mujangi Bia 2*
19/02 a Grasshoppers W 1-0 *Mujangi Bia*
26/02 a Lausanne W 1-0 *Akolo*
05/03 h St Gallen L 1-2 *Paulo Ricardo*
12/03 h Basel L 0-1
18/03 a Luzern D 0-0
01/04 h Thun W 2-1 *Carlitos, Akolo*
09/04 a Lugano L 2-4 *Konaté, Constant*
15/04 a Vaduz W 1-0 *N'Doye*
23/04 h Lausanne L 0-1
30/04 a Thun L 1-2 *Akolo*
07/05 h Young Boys L 0-1
13/05 h Lugano W 2-0 *og (Sulmoni), Konaté (p)*
18/05 a Basel D 2-2 *Akolo, Constant*
21/05 h Luzern L 2-3 *Mujangi Bia, Konaté*
28/05 a St Gallen D 1-1 *Paulo Ricardo*
02/06 h Grasshoppers D 1-1 *Maceiras*

No	Name	Nat	DoB	Pos	Aps	(s)	Gls
13	Chadrac Akolo	COD	01/04/95	M	29	(5)	15
21	Ebenezer Assifuah	GHA	03/07/93	A	3	(11)	2
15	Arthur Boka	CIV	02/04/83	D	3		
10	Carlitos	POR	06/09/82	M	26	(2)	3
11	Kévin Constant	GUI	10/05/87	M	10	(1)	2
21	Frederico Da Costa		17/05/99	A	1	(6)	
7	Edimilson Fernandes		15/04/96	M	4	(1)	
18	Kevin Fickentscher		06/07/88	G	1		
22	Daniel Follonier		18/01/94	M	1	(10)	
33	Theofanis Gekas	GRE	23/05/80	A	6	(6)	3
66	Joaquim Adão	ANG	14/07/92	M	20	(9)	
12	Grégory Karlen		30/01/95	M	22	(6)	2
14	Moussa Konaté	SEN	03/04/93	A	28	(5)	8
4	Léo Lacroix		27/02/92	D	5		
89	Léo Itaperuna	BRA	12/04/89	A	3	(16)	1
50	Nicolas Lüchinger		16/10/94	D	30		
62	Quentin Maceiras		10/10/95	D	2		1
1	Anton Mitryushkin	RUS	08/02/96	G	35		
17	Pa Modou	GAM	26/12/89	D	24		
27	Bruno Morgado		16/12/97	D	4	(4)	
63	Geoffrey Mujangi Bia	BEL	12/08/89	M	9	(7)	6
8	Freddy Mveng	CMR	29/05/92	M	6	(2)	1
34	Birama N'Doye	SEN	27/03/94	M	11	(1)	1
6	Paulo Ricardo	BRA	13/07/94	D	10	(5)	2
45	Aimery Pinga		06/01/98	A		(1)	
5	Veroljub Salatic		14/11/85	M	28	(1)	1
19	Vincent Sierro		08/10/95	M	12	(5)	2
87	Jérémy Taravel	FRA	17/04/87	D	3	(2)	
11	Martin Zeman	CZE	28/03/89	M	2	(1)	
3	Reto Ziegler		16/01/86	D	25		8
31	Elsad Zverotić	MNE	31/10/86	D	33		1

SWITZERLAND

FC Thun

1898 • Stockhorn Arena (10,014) • fcthun.ch

Coach: Jeff Saibene (LUX); (19/03/17) (Mauro Lustrinelli)

2016

24/07	h	Vaduz	D	1-1	*Rapp*
31/07	a	Lausanne	D	4-4	*Rapp (p), Geissmann, Schirinzi, Peyretti*
06/08	a	Young Boys	L	1-4	*Fassnacht*
11/08	h	Grasshoppers	W	2-1	*Schindelholz, Fassnacht*
21/08	a	Luzern	L	0-3	
28/08	h	Basel	L	0-3	
11/09	a	Sion	L	0-1	
20/09	h	St Gallen	L	1-2	*Geissmann*
25/09	h	Lugano	D	2-2	*Hediger, Fassnacht*
01/10	a	Basel	D	1-1	*Tosetti*
15/10	h	Lausanne	W	1-0	*Fassnacht*
22/10	a	Vaduz	W	3-2	*Sorgić 2, Geissmann*
30/10	a	St Gallen	D	0-0	
05/11	h	Sion	L	2-3	*Bürki, Sorgić*
19/11	a	Grasshoppers	D	1-1	*Fassnacht*
26/11	h	Luzern	L	1-2	*Schindelholz*
04/12	a	Lugano	D	1-1	*Peyretti*
11/12	h	Young Boys	L	2-3	*Tosetti, Sorgić*

2017

04/02	a	Grasshoppers	W	1-0	*Sorgić*
11/02	h	Basel	L	0-2	
18/02	a	Luzern	D	1-1	*Sorgić*
25/02	h	Vaduz	W	4-3	*Fassnacht, Sorgić, Nélson Ferreira, Lauper*
04/03	a	Young Boys	L	2-3	*Fassnacht, Sorgić*
12/03	h	Lugano	W	5-2	*Fassnacht 2, Rapp 2 (2p), Sorgić*
19/03	h	St Gallen	D	2-2	*Schirinzi, Hediger*
01/04	a	Sion	L	1-2	*Rapp*
08/04	h	Lausanne	L	2-4	*Sorgić, Schirinzi*
17/04	a	Lugano	L	1-2	*Sorgić*
23/04	a	St Gallen	W	2-1	*Bürgy (p), Sorgić*
30/04	h	Sion	W	2-1	*og (Lüchinger), Rapp*
06/05	h	Luzern	W	3-1	*Facchinetti, Rapp, Fassnacht*
14/05	a	Basel	D	3-3	*Sorgić 3*
17/05	h	Grasshoppers	W	3-1	*Rapp, Geissmann, Reinmann*
20/05	a	Lausanne	D	0-0	
28/05	h	Young Boys	D	0-0	
02/06	a	Vaduz	W	3-1	*Rapp, Tosetti, Geissmann*

No	Name	Nat	DoB	Pos	Aps	(s)	Gls
2	Ayrton Ribeiro	POR	09/09/97	D		(1)	
25	Kevin Bigler		05/10/92	M	12	(2)	
32	Nicolas Bürgy		07/08/95	D	12		1
4	Marco Bürki		10/07/93	D	25		1
10	Carlinhos	BRA	22/06/94	M	6	(1)	
19	Omer Dzonlagic		25/05/95	M		(5)	
7	Mickaël Facchinetti		15/02/91	D	31		1
1	Guillaume Faivre		20/02/87	G	29		
16	Christian Fassnacht		11/11/93	M	34	(1)	10
6	Joël Geissmann		03/03/93	M	21	(6)	5
31	Stefan Glarner		21/11/87	D	34		
28	Mike Hauswirth		15/11/97	D		(1)	
17	Dennis Hediger		22/09/86	M	34		2
39	Sven Joss		18/07/94	D	3	()	
30	Sandro Lauper		25/10/96	M	24	(2)	1
42	Ivan Markovic		15/06/97	A		(2)	
21	Nélson Ferreira	POR	26/05/82	M	2	(12)	1
23	Norman Peyretti	FRA	06/02/94	M	11	(18)	2
13	Simone Rapp		01/10/92	A	23	(10)	9
26	Thomas Reinmann		09/04/83	D	18	(1)	1
18	Francesco Ruberto		19/03/93	G	7		
14	Nicolas Schindelholz		12/02/88	D	9	(1)	2
27	Enrico Schirinzi	ITA	14/11/84	D	4	(12)	3
9	Dejan Sorgić	SRB	15/09/89	A	24	(8)	15
33	Marvin Spielmann		23/02/96	M	2	(9)	
11	Matteo Tosetti		15/02/92	M	30	(5)	3
3	Colin Trachsel		28/09/97	D	1	(1)	

FC Vaduz

1932 • Rheinpark (6,127) • fcvaduz.li

Major honours
Liechtenstein Cup (45) 1949, 1952, 1953, 1954, 1956, 1957, 1958, 1959, 1960, 1961, 1962, 1966, 1967, 1968, 1969, 1970, 1971, 1974, 1980, 1985, 1986, 1988, 1990, 1992, 1995, 1996, 1998, 1999, 2000, 2001, 2002, 2003, 2004, 2005, 2006, 2007, 2008, 2009, 2010, 2011, 2013, 2014, 2015, 2016, 2017

Coach: Giorgio Contini; (07/03/17) (Daniel Hasler (LIE)); (22/03/17) Roland Vrabec (GER)

2016

24/07	a	Thun	D	1-1	*Messaoud*
31/07	h	Basel	L	1-5	*Grippo*
07/08	a	Lugano	W	2-0	*og (Sulmoni), Muntwiler*
10/08	h	Luzern	L	1-3	*Kukuruzović*
21/08	h	St Gallen	W	2-0	*Costanzo (p), Muntwiler*
27/08	a	Sion	L	1-3	*Brunner*
11/09	a	Lausanne	L	0-5	
21/09	h	Young Boys	D	0-0	
25/09	a	Grasshoppers	L	1-2	*Kukuruzović*
01/10	h	Sion	L	2-5	*Burgmeier, Costanzo*
16/10	a	St Gallen	W	2-0	*Costanzo (p), Burgmeier*
22/10	h	Thun	L	2-3	*Burgmeier, Brunner*
30/10	a	Young Boys	L	0-5	
06/11	h	Grasshoppers	D	0-0	
19/11	a	Basel	L	0-6	
27/11	h	Lugano	W	5-1	*Kukuruzović, Mathys 3, Hasler*
03/12	a	Luzern	L	0-3	
10/12	h	Lausanne	D	1-1	*Costanzo (p)*

2017

05/02	h	St Gallen	D	1-1	*Costanzo*
12/02	a	Sion	L	2-4	*Costanzo, Avdijaj*
19/02	h	Lugano	D	1-1	*Grippo*
25/02	a	Thun	L	3-4	*Brunner, Janjatovic 2 (1p)*
05/03	h	Basel	D	1-1	*Avdijaj*
11/03	a	Grasshoppers	W	2-1	*Grippo, Zárate*
19/03	h	Lausanne	L	0-1	
02/04	a	Young Boys	L	2-3	*Zárate, Muntwiler*
09/04	h	Luzern	L	0-2	
15/04	h	Sion	L	0-1	
22/04	a	Basel	D	2-2	*Brunner, Kukuruzović*
29/04	a	Lausanne	W	3-1	*Kukuruzović, og (Castella), og (Méndez)*
06/05	h	Grasshoppers	L	2-4	*Zárate, Avdijaj*
13/05	a	St Gallen	L	0-2	
17/05	h	Young Boys	W	1-0	*Bühler*
20/05	a	Lugano	L	1-2	*Borgmann*
28/05	a	Luzern	D	2-2	*Turkes, Mathys*
02/06	h	Thun	L	1-3	*Zárate*

No	Name	Nat	DoB	Pos	Aps	(s)	Gls
7	Albion Avdijaj	ALB	12/01/94	A	16	(7)	3
21	Axel Borgmann	GER	08/07/94	D	29	(1)	1
24	Maurice Brunner		29/01/91	D	15	(10)	4
11	Franz Burgmeier	LIE	07/04/82	M	8	(6)	3
29	Mario Bühler		05/01/92	D	21	(2)	1
12	Ramon Cecchini		30/08/90	M		(2)	
8	Diego Ciccone		21/07/87	M	20	(4)	
16	Moreno Costanzo		20/02/88	M	24		6
30	Yones Felfel	DEN	24/11/95	A	1		
33	Maximilian Göppel	LIE	31/08/97	D	14	(2)	
3	Simone Grippo		12/12/88	D	28		3
20	Nicolas Hasler	LIE	04/05/91	M	27	(4)	1
31	Dejan Janjatovic	GER	25/02/92	M	3	(5)	2
1	Peter Jehle	LIE	22/01/82	G	9		
4	Thomas Konrad	GER	05/11/89	D	18	(3)	
25	Stjepan Kukuruzović	CRO	07/06/89	M	31	(4)	5
17	Marco Mathys		05/07/87	M	14	(11)	4
10	Ali Messaoud	FRA	13/04/91	M	1	(3)	1
27	Philipp Muntwiler		25/02/87	M	32		3
2	Marvin Pfründer		28/01/94	D	4		
13	Pascal Schürpf		15/07/89	M	6	(9)	
22	Benjamin Siegrist		31/01/92	G	27		
23	Caleb Stanko	USA	26/07/93	M	20	(6)	
5	Matthias Strohmaier	GER	11/03/94	D	1		
9	Aldin Turkes		22/04/96	A	9	(15)	1
10	Gonzalo Zárate	ARG	06/08/84	A	18	(13)	4

BSC Young Boys

1898 • Stade de Suisse (31,789) • bscyb.ch

Major honours
Swiss League (11) 1903, 1909, 1910, 1911, 1920, 1929, 1957, 1958, 1959, 1960, 1986; Swiss Cup (6) 1930, 1945, 1953, 1958, 1977, 1987

Coach: Adi Hütter (AUT)

2016

23/07	a	St Gallen	W	2-0	*Bertone, Kubo*
30/07	h	Lugano	L	1-2	*Hoarau (p)*
06/08	h	Thun	W	4-1	*Frey, og (Lauper), Hoarau 2 (1p)*
10/08	a	Basel	L	0-3	
20/08	h	Lausanne	W	7-2	*Hoarau, Ravet, Schick, Sutter, Lecjaks, Kubo, Frey*
28/08	a	Grasshoppers	L	1-4	*Frey*
10/09	h	Luzern	W	2-1	*Sulejmani 2*
21/09	a	Vaduz	D	0-0	
25/09	a	Sion	D	0-0	
02/10	h	St Gallen	D	2-2	*Bertone, Duah*
16/10	a	Lugano	D	0-0	
23/10	h	Grasshoppers	W	4-0	*Ravet (p), Kubo, Zakaria, Frey*
30/10	h	Vaduz	W	5-0	*Hoarau 2, Kubo, Bertone, Frey*
06/11	a	Luzern	D	2-2	*og (Haas), Kubo*
20/11	h	Sion	W	4-3	*Sulejmani, Hoarau 2 (1p), Schick*
27/11	a	Lausanne	W	2-1	*Hoarau 2*
03/12	h	Basel	W	3-1	*Hoarau 2, Mbabu*
11/12	a	Thun	W	3-2	*Hoarau, Sanogo, Frey*

2017

05/02	h	Sion	W	3-1	*Rochat, Hoarau, Schick*
12/02	a	Luzern	L	1-4	*Ravet*
18/02	h	St Gallen	D	2-2	*Hoarau (p), Assalé*
25/02	a	Grasshoppers	W	3-2	*Assalé 2, Hoarau (p)*
04/03	h	Thun	W	3-2	*Sulejmani, og (Bürki), Sanogo*
12/03	a	Lausanne	D	0-0	
19/03	a	Lugano	W	2-0	*Sulejmani, Hoarau*
02/04	h	Vaduz	W	3-2	*Hoarau (p), Frey, Assalé*
09/04	a	Basel	D	1-1	*Ravet*
17/04	h	Grasshoppers	L	0-1	
23/04	h	Lugano	L	1-2	*Aebischer*
30/04	a	St Gallen	W	2-0	*Gerndt 2*
07/05	a	Sion	W	1-0	*Sulejmani*
14/05	h	Luzern	W	4-1	*Sulejmani 2, Assalé, Frey*
17/05	a	Vaduz	L	0-1	
21/05	h	Basel	W	2-1	*Assalé, Schick*
28/05	a	Thun	D	0-0	
02/06	h	Lausanne	W	2-0	*Ravet 2*

No	Name	Nat	DoB	Pos	Aps	(s)	Gls
51	Michel Aebischer		06/01/97	M	8	(6)	1
17	Roger Assalé	CIV	13/11/93	A	10	(3)	6
80	Loris Benito		07/01/92	D	6	(1)	
6	Leonardo Bertone		14/03/94	M	23	(7)	3
26	Nicolas Bürgy		07/08/95	D		(2)	
18	Kwadwo Duah		24/02/97	M	1	(5)	1
11	Michael Frey		19/07/94	A	19	(10)	8
14	Milan Gajić	SRB	17/11/86	M	3	(3)	
9	Alexander Gerndt	SWE	14/07/86	A	7	(9)	2
3	Florent Hadergjonaj		31/07/94	D	2		
99	Guillaume Hoarau	FRA	05/03/84	A	19	(2)	18
39	Sven Joss		18/07/94	D	8	(2)	
31	Yuya Kubo	JPN	24/12/93	A	10	(4)	5
8	Jan Lecjaks	CZE	09/08/90	D	25	(6)	1
43	Kevin Mbabu		19/04/95	D	17	(4)	1
18	Yvon Mvogo		06/06/94	G	35		
24	Kasim Nuhu	GHA	22/06/95	D	18		
32	Linus Obexer		05/06/97	D	2	(3)	
10	Yoric Ravet	FRA	12/09/89	M	28	(4)	6
21	Alain Rochat		01/02/83	D	24		1
35	Sékou Sanogo	CIV	05/05/89	M	18	(3)	2
19	Thorsten Schick	AUT	19/05/90	M	19	(11)	4
7	Miralem Sulejmani	SRB	05/12/88	M	22	(5)	8
16	Tauljant Sulejmanov	MKD	15/11/96	M		(7)	
23	Scott Sutter		13/05/86	D	15	(4)	1
4	Milan Vilotić	SRB	21/10/86	D	2	(1)	
5	Steve von Bergen		10/06/83	D	28		
1	Marco Wölfli		22/08/82	G	1		
22	Gregory Wüthrich		04/12/94	D	3		
28	Denis Zakaria		20/11/96	M	23		1

Top goalscorers

20 Seydou Doumbia (Basel)

18 Guillaume Hoarau (Young Boys)

16 Ezgjan Alioski (Lugano)

15 Chadrac Akolo (Sion)
Dejan Sorgić (Thun)

14 Caio (Grasshoppers)
Marc Schneuwly (Luzern)

13 Marc Janko (Basel)

10 Matías Delgado (Basel)
Mohamed Elyounoussi (Basel)
Albian Ajeti (St Gallen)
Christian Fassnacht (Thun)

Promoted club

FC Zürich

1896 • Letzigrund (26,104) • fcz.ch

Major honours
Swiss League: (12) 1902, 1924, 1963, 1966, 1968, 1974, 1975, 1976, 1981, 2006, 2007, 2009; Swiss Cup: (9) 1966, 1970, 1972, 1973, 1976, 2000, 2005, 2014, 2016

Coach: Uli Forte

Second level final table 2016/17

		Pld	W	D	L	F	A	Pts
1	FC Zürich	36	26	7	3	91	30	85
2	Neuchâtel Xamax FCS	36	22	7	7	66	36	73
3	Servette FC	36	18	8	10	55	43	62
4	FC Schaffhausen	36	16	3	17	64	59	51
5	FC Aarau	36	13	6	17	57	64	45
6	FC Winterthur	36	11	8	17	45	62	41
7	FC Wohlen	36	12	3	21	42	60	39
8	FC Chiasso	36	9	10	17	43	63	37
9	FC Le Mont	36	8	11	17	31	54	35
10	FC Wil 1900	36	10	7	19	35	58	34

NB FC Le Mont did not receive licence for 2017/18 season, enabling FC Wil 1900 to avoid relegation; FC Wil 1900 – 3 pts deducted.

DOMESTIC CUP

Schweizer Cup/Coupe de Suisse 2016/17

FIRST ROUND

(10/08/16)
Bubendorf 1-2 Zug

(13/08/16)
Arbedo 0-5 Neuchâtel Xamax
Binningen 2-1 Münsingen
Conthey 1-4 Bellinzona
Grenchen 0-2 Iliria
Gunzwil 2-0 Vernier
Klingnau 0-6 Tuggen
La Chaux-de-Fonds 0-2 Zürich
Meyrin 1-3 Wohlen
Moutier 0-3 Lugano
Oberwallis Naters 1-4 Luzern
Romontois 1-6 Sion
Rümlang 2-5 Seuzach
Seefeld Zürich 1-2 Köniz
Ticino 4-0 Uzwil
Veltheim 0-6 Young Boys
Wabern 0-5 Brühl St Gallen
Yverdon Sport 1-4 Winterthur

(14/08/16)
Bazenheid 2-1 Red Star Zürich
Breitenrain 3-1 Servette
Calcio Kreuzlingen 1-0 Cham
Donneloye 0-14 Le Mont
Dulliken 0-3 Chiasso
Genolier-Begnins 1-3 Azzurri 90
Kriens 2-1 Thun
La Sarraz-Eclépens 0-3 Schaffhausen
Lancy 1-2 Lausanne-Sport
Old Boys 0-2 Grasshoppers *(aet)*
Rapperswil-Jona 0-1 Basel
Stade-Lausanne-Ouchy 4-2 Wil
Zollbrück 0-5 Aarau

(15/08/16)
Black Stars 2-3 St Gallen

SECOND ROUND

(16/09/16)
Breitenrain 0-1 Aarau
Köniz 3-1 Lausanne-Sport

(17/09/16)
Azzurri 90 2-3 Kriens
Binningen 1-2 Brühl St Gallen
Calcio Kreuzlingen 1-1 Tuggen *(aet; 5-6 on pens)*
Chiasso 1-0 Wohlen
Gunzwil 1-4 Lugano
Le Mont 0-1 St Gallen
Seuzach 1-4 Grasshoppers
Stade-Lausanne-Ouchy 0-3 Winterthur
Ticino 0-3 Luzern

(18/09/16)
Bazenheid 1-7 Young Boys
Bellinzona 0-2 Zürich
Iliria 1-4 Schaffhausen
Neuchâtel Xamax 3-4 Sion
Zug 0-1 Basel

THIRD ROUND

(26/10/16)
Aarau 2-0 Lugano
Kriens 5-3 Brühl St Gallen *(aet)*
Tuggen 1-4 Basel
Winterthur 2-1 Chiasso
Young Boys 5-0 Grasshoppers

(27/10/16)
Köniz 1-1 Luzern *(aet; 4-5 on pens)*
Zürich 2-1 St Gallen

(02/11/16)
Schaffhausen 2-5 Sion *(aet)*

QUARTER-FINALS

(01/03/17)
Aarau 3-5 Luzern *(Josipovic 28, Ciarrocchi 41, Tréand 51; Juric 2, 54, Neumayr 3, C Schneuwly 36, M Schneuwly 76)*

Young Boys 2-2 Winterthur *(Hoarau 8, Bertone 39; Silvio 61, Sutter 66) (aet; 3-5 on pens)*

(02/03/17)
Basel 3-1 Zürich *(Janko 21, Lang 42, Steffen 75; Buff 3)*

Sion 5-1 Kriens *(Mujangi Bia 45, 78, Konaté 65, 67, 83; Thali 32)*

SEMI-FINALS

(05/04/17)
Sion 0-0 Luzern *(aet; 6-5 on pens)*

Winterthur 1-3 Basel *(Cani 88; Delgado 54p, Akanji 85, Fransson 90+4p)*

FINAL

(25/05/17)
Stade de Genève, Geneva
FC BASEL 1893 3 *(Delgado 47, Traoré 62, Lang 89)*
FC SION 0
Referee: *Klossner*
BASEL: *Vaclík, Lang, Suchý, Akanji, Traoré, Xhaka, Zuffi (Fransson 90+3), Elyounoussi, Delgado (Serey Dié 81), Steffen, Doumbia (Janko 88)*
SION: *Mitryushkin, Lüchinger, Zverotić, Ziegler, Modou (Carlitos 63), Constant, Salatic, Karlen (Mujangi Bia 70), Akolo (Léo Itaperuna 79), Joaquim Adão, Konaté*

Basel ended Sion's perfect record in the Swiss Cup final with a comprehensive 3-0 victory in Geneva to complete the domestic double

TURKEY

Türkiye Futbol Federasyonu (TFF)

Address	Hasan Doğan Milli Takımlar Kamp ve Eğitim Tesisleri Riva, Beykoz TR-İstanbul
Tel	+90 216 554 5100
Fax	+90 216 319 1945
E-mail	intdept@tff.org
Website	tff.org

President	Yıldırım Demirören
General secretary	Kadir Kardaş
Media officer	Bahri Çiftçi
Year of formation	1923

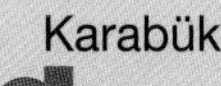

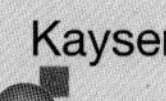

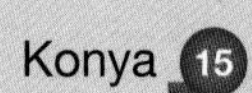

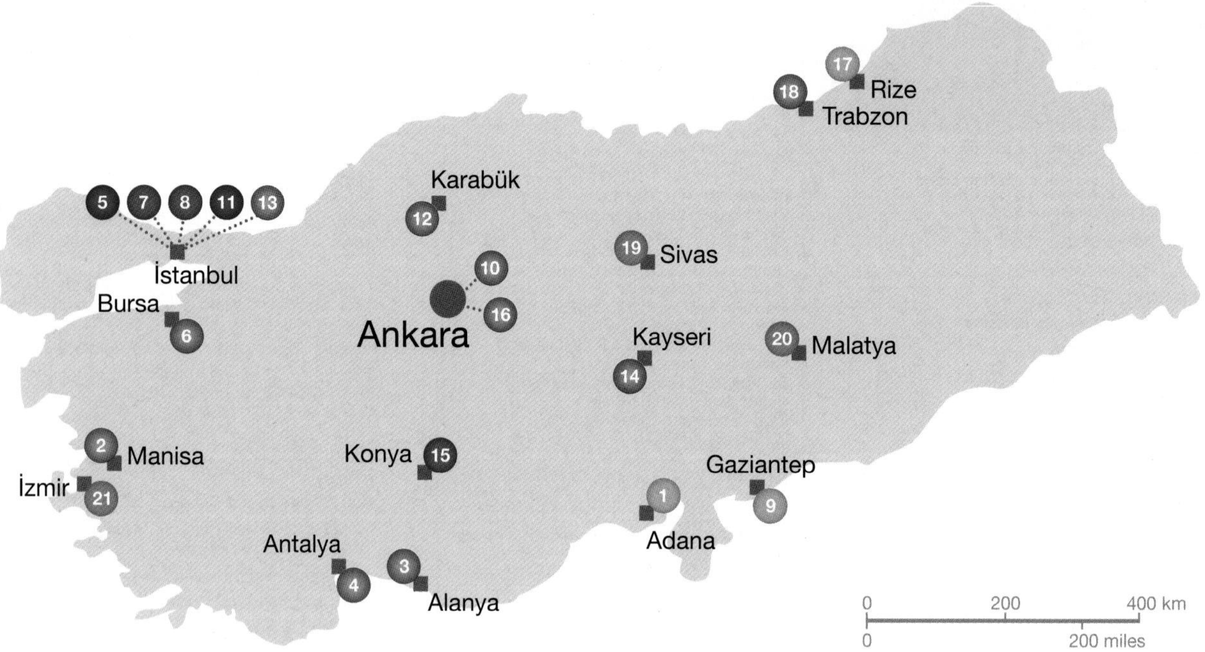

SÜPER LİG CLUBS

 1 **Adanaspor AŞ**

 2 **Akhisar Belediyespor**

 3 **Alanyaspor**

 4 **Antalyaspor**

 5 **Beşiktaş JK**

 6 **Bursaspor**

 7 **Fenerbahçe SK**

 8 **Galatasaray AŞ**

 9 **Gaziantepspor**

 10 **Gençlerbirliği SK**

 11 **İstanbul Başakşehir**

 12 **Kardemir Karabükspor**

 13 **Kasımpaşa SK**

 14 **Kayserispor**

 15 **Konyaspor**

 16 **Osmanlıspor**

 17 **Rizespor**

 18 **Trabzonspor AŞ**

PROMOTED CLUBS

  19 **Sivasspor**

 20 **Yeni Malatyaspor**

 21 **Göztepe SK**

KEY

- UEFA Champions League
- UEFA Europa League
- Promoted
- Relegated

More Süper Lig glory for Beşiktaş

Beşiktaş's 15th Turkish title arrived just 12 months after their 14th as experienced former Turkey coach Şenol Güneş led the Istanbul club down the path to Süper Lig success for the second season in a row.

There was a concerted challenge to their crown from city rivals, but not from traditional powerhouses Fenerbahçe and Galatasaray, who both had a season to forget. Instead it was İstanbul Başakşehir, led by another ex-Turkey boss in Abdullah Avcı, who pushed Beşiktaş all the way. They also reached the final of the cup, only to be defeated on penalties by first-time winners Konyaspor.

Black Eagles successfully defend league title

İstanbul Başakşehir battle bravely to the end

Cup win gives Konyaspor a first major trophy

Domestic league

Beşiktaş had not made a successful defence of the Turkish title for a quarter of a century, and their chances of doing so in 2016/17 appeared to lessen when two key players, Mario Gomez and José Sosa, both left in pre-season. However, the club had a long-standing reputation for its resistance to adversity, and they started the new campaign with a flourish, winning nine of their first 15 games and drawing the others.

Such form would normally have secured a place at the Süper Lig summit, but Beşiktaş were not alone in getting off to a storming start. Indeed, when the league closed down for its short winter break, İstanbul Başakşehir were the only team without a defeat to their name, Beşiktaş's unbeaten run having hit the buffers a week earlier with a 2-1 loss at Kasımpaşa.

One point in arrears at Christmas, Beşiktaş finally claimed top spot in late January when they won 4-1 at Alanyaspor a day after İstanbul Başakşehir were finally beaten, 1-0 at Fenerbahçe. As in 2015/16, the Super Eagles proved resilient front-runners. İstanbul Başakşehir pursued them with purpose, their challenge sustained by the mid-season arrival of Emmanuel Adebayor, who scored a hat-trick in a 4-0 win against a faltering Galatasaray and another goal – to add to a double from teenage wonderkid Cengiz Ünder – as his team defeated Beşiktaş 3-1 at home in the all-important head-to-head. But, that defeat apart, the champions were too consistent, and they wrapped up the title with a 4-0 win at Gaziantepspor on the penultimate weekend.

Brazilian playmaker Talisca, on loan from Benfica, scored twice in that game and was the outstanding newcomer to a side in which several of the previous season's champions, such as centre-back Marcelo, midfield duo Atiba Hutchinson and Oğuzhan Özyakup, winger Ricardo Quaresma and 20-goal striker Cenk Tosun, again made invaluable contributions. Having never won his country's national title prior to 2015/16, Şenol Güneş now became the first Turkish coach to do so back to back.

İstanbul Başakşehir's valiant effort earned them second place and a crack at the UEFA Champions League, but there were only UEFA Europa League qualifying spots for Fenerbahçe and Galatasaray, who both finished 13 points adrift of Beşiktaş. Both teams lacked a prolific marksman, although a couple of golden oldies did shine elsewhere, 33-year-old Brazilian Vágner Love topping the scorers' charts with 23 goals for Alanyaspor while 36-year-old Samuel Eto'o struck 18 times for fifth-placed Antalyaspor.

Domestic cup

Four days after conceding defeat in the Süper Lig, İstanbul Başakşehir suffered further frustration when they lost the Turkish Cup final on penalties to Konyaspor following a goalless draw in Eskisehir. Konyaspor's victory not only earned them a first major trophy but also put them in the group stage of the UEFA Europa League for the second season running.

Europe

It was a busy European season for Turkish clubs, with Beşiktaş leading the way. They spurned a good opportunity to reach the UEFA Champions League knockout phase for the first time but did make it to the UEFA Europa League quarter-finals, where only a penalty shoot-out defeat by Lyon prevented further progress. Osmanlıspor were surprise group winners in the same competition, while Fenerbahçe, under new coach Dick Advocaat, also advanced to the round of 32 before coming a cropper against FC Krasnodar.

National team

A slow start had endangered Turkey's UEFA EURO 2016 qualifying campaign, and there were more early agonies for Fatih Terim's team as they drew at home to Ukraine and lost – again – in Iceland. Nine points from their next three games, against Kosovo (twice) and Finland, were essential, and they duly got them, thereby re-emerging as bona fide contenders in a tightly-contested Group I headed by Croatia.

DOMESTIC SEASON AT A GLANCE

Süper Lig 2016/17 final table

			Home					Away					Total					
		Pld	W	D	L	F	A	W	D	L	F	A	W	D	L	F	A	Pts
1	**Beşiktaş JK**	**34**	**13**	**4**	**0**	**44**	**15**	**10**	**4**	**3**	**29**	**15**	**23**	**8**	**3**	**73**	**30**	**77**
2	İstanbul Başakşehir	34	12	5	0	39	15	9	5	3	24	13	21	10	3	63	28	73
3	Fenerbahçe SK	34	8	6	3	28	15	10	4	3	32	17	18	10	6	60	32	64
4	Galatasaray AŞ	34	11	0	6	37	17	9	4	4	28	23	20	4	10	65	40	64
5	Antalyaspor	34	9	4	4	20	16	8	3	6	27	24	17	7	10	47	40	58
6	Trabzonspor AŞ	34	6	5	6	22	18	8	4	5	17	16	14	9	11	39	34	51
7	Akhisar Belediyespor	34	9	2	6	29	18	5	4	8	17	24	14	6	14	46	42	48
8	Gençlerbirliği SK	34	8	6	3	19	9	4	4	9	14	25	12	10	12	33	34	46
9	Konyaspor	34	6	5	6	20	21	5	5	7	20	24	11	10	13	40	45	43
10	Kasımpaşa SK	34	8	4	5	31	24	4	3	10	15	26	12	7	15	46	50	43
11	Kardemir Karabükspor	34	10	4	3	24	12	2	3	12	14	36	12	7	15	38	48	43
12	Alanyaspor	34	8	1	8	35	32	4	3	10	19	33	12	4	18	54	65	40
13	Osmanlıspor	34	3	6	8	15	24	6	5	6	22	21	9	11	14	37	45	38
14	Bursaspor	34	7	3	7	19	22	4	2	11	15	36	11	5	18	34	58	38
15	Kayserispor	34	6	3	8	23	23	4	5	8	24	35	10	8	16	47	58	38
16	Rizespor	34	6	4	7	24	23	4	2	11	20	30	10	6	18	44	53	36
17	Gaziantepspor	34	4	2	11	15	29	3	3	11	15	36	7	5	22	30	65	26
18	Adanaspor AŞ	34	4	3	10	20	32	2	4	11	13	30	6	7	21	33	62	25

European qualification 2017/18

Champion: Beşiktaş JK (group stage)
İstanbul Başakşehir (third qualifying round)

Cup winner: Konyaspor (group stage)
Fenerbahçe SK (third qualifying round)
Galatasaray AŞ (second qualifying round)

Top scorer Vágner Love (Alanyaspor), 23 goals
Relegated clubs Adanaspor AŞ, Gaziantepspor, Rizespor
Promoted clubs Sivasspor, Yeni Malatyaspor, Göztepe SK
Cup final Konyaspor 0-0 İstanbul Başakşehir *(aet; 4-1 on pens)*

Player of the season

Talisca
(Beşiktaş JK)

Beşiktaş are generally renowned for their discipline, efficiency and hard work. However, their 2016/17 title win was as much down to craft as graft, and a plentiful supply of the former was supplied by Talisca, a tall, left-footed Brazilian with a special talent for accurate set-pieces and spectacular goals. The only disappointment for Beşiktaş fans was that he was only on loan to the club from Benfica – against whom, with delicious irony, he scored a brilliant late equaliser on his return to Lisbon in the UEFA Champions League.

Newcomer of the season

Cengiz Ünder
(İstanbul Başakşehir)

After a couple of seasons in the shadows at second-tier Altınordu, Cengiz found himself under the Süper Lig spotlight in 2016/17, and it was a stage on which he established himself as one of Turkey's finest young prospects. İstanbul Başakşehir were the happy beneficiaries of the 19-year-old's exceptional talent, which was supplemented by a willingness and ability to rise to the big occasion – as he did in the two big games against Beşiktaş, which provided three of his seven goals. Alert to his potential, Roma paid €13m to lure him to Italy in July.

Team of the season

(4-2-3-1)

Coach: Şenol Güneş *(Beşiktaş)*

NATIONAL TEAM

International tournament appearances

FIFA World Cup (2) 1954, 2002 (3rd)
UEFA European Championship (4) 1996, 2000 (qtr-finals), 2008 (semi-finals), 2016

Top five all-time caps

Rüştü Reçber (120); Hakan Şükür (112); Bülent Korkmaz (102); **Arda Turan** (97); Tugay Kerimoğlu (94)

Top five all-time goals

Hakan Şükür (51); **Burak Yılmaz** (23); Tuncay Şanlı (22); Lefter Küçükandonyadis (21); Cemil Turan, Metin Oktay & Nihat Kahveci (19)

Results 2016/17

31/08/16	Russia	H	Antalya	D	0-0	
05/09/16	Croatia (WCQ)	A	Zagreb	D	1-1	*Hakan Çalhanoğlu (45+2)*
06/10/16	Ukraine (WCQ)	H	Konya	D	2-2	*Ozan Tufan (45+1), Hakan Çalhanoğlu (81p)*
09/10/16	Iceland (WCQ)	A	Reykjavik	L	0-2	
12/11/16	Kosovo (WCQ)	H	Antalya	W	2-0	*Burak Yılmaz (51), Volkan Şen (55)*
24/03/17	Finland (WCQ)	H	Antalya	W	2-0	*Cenk Tosun (9, 13)*
27/03/17	Moldova	H	Eskisehir	W	3-1	*Emre Mor (14), Ahmet Çalık (24), Cengiz Ünder (51)*
05/06/17	FYR Macedonia	A	Skopje	D	0-0	
11/06/17	Kosovo (WCQ)	A	Shkoder (ALB)	W	4-1	*Volkan Şen (6), Cengiz Ünder (31), Burak Yılmaz (61), Ozan Tufan (82)*

Appearances 2016/17

Coach: Fatih Terim	04/09/53		Rus	CRO	UKR	ISL	KOS	FIN	Mda	Mkd	KOS	Caps	Goals
Volkan Babacan	11/08/88	İstanbul Başakşehir	G	G	G	G	G	G		G	G	28	-
Şener Özbayraklı	23/01/90	Fenerbahçe	D	D	D	D			D			13	-
Serdar Aziz	23/10/90	Galatasaray	D67	D								11	1
Çağlar Söyüncü	23/05/96	Freiburg (GER)	D						D	D	D	5	-
İsmail Köybaşı	10/07/89	Fenerbahçe	D46	D				D		D46	s85	25	-
Ozan Tufan	23/03/95	Fenerbahçe	M	M	M77	M43				M	M	33	4
Mehmet Topal	03/03/86	Fenerbahçe	M	D	M	D	D	D			D	69	1
Hakan Çalhanoğlu	08/02/94	Leverkusen (GER)	M62	M	M	M	M					26	8
Emre Mor	24/07/97	Dortmund (GER)	M85	M85	M	A		s72	M83	s61	s80	12	1
Volkan Şen	07/07/87	Fenerbahçe	M46	s85	s77	M66	M76	M			M80	26	2
Cenk Tosun	07/06/91	Beşiktaş	A62	A71	A	s59	s87	A84	s83	s61		19	5
Hasan Ali Kaldırım	09/12/89	Fenerbahçe	s46				D			s46	D85	20	-
Kaan Ayhan	10/11/94	Düsseldorf (GER)	s46	M53	s46	M			s69	D		6	-
Enes Ünal	10/05/97	Twente (NED)	s62		A46			s84	A76	A46		6	-
Yunus Mallı	24/02/92	Mainz (GER) /Wolfsburg (GER)	s62				s46	M63	s83	M61		12	-
Ahmet Çalık	26/02/94	Gençlerbirliği /Galatasaray	s67	s53			D		D			8	1
Okay Yokuşlu	09/03/94	Trabzonspor	s85	M				s63	M			5	-
Olcay Şahan	26/05/87	Beşiktaş /Trabzonspor		s71				M72		M46		29	2
Ömer Toprak	21/07/89	Leverkusen (GER)			D	D		D				26	2
Hakan Balta	23/03/83	Galatasaray			D46							50	2
Caner Erkin	04/10/88	Beşiktaş			D	D						51	2
Tolga Ciğerci	23/03/92	Galatasaray			s46	s43						2	-
Yasin Öztekin	19/03/87	Galatasaray				M59						6	-
Mevlüt Erdinç	25/02/87	Metz (FRA)				s66						35	8
Gökhan Gönül	04/01/85	Beşiktaş					D	D		D	D	64	1
Selçuk İnan	10/02/85	Galatasaray					M	M		s46	M	59	8
Oğuzhan Özyakup	23/09/92	Beşiktaş					M46		M64		M73	26	1
Arda Turan	30/01/87	Barcelona (ESP)					M	M		M61		97	17
Burak Yılmaz	15/07/85	Beijing Guoan (CHN)					A87			s79	A	50	23
Cengiz Ünder	14/07/97	İstanbul Başakşehir					s76		M83	s46	M	4	2
Onur Kıvrak	01/01/88	Trabzonspor							G46			13	-
Güray Vural	11/06/88	Kayserispor							D			1	-
Emre Çolak	20/05/91	Deportivo (ESP)							M69	M79		4	-
Harun Tekin	17/06/89	Bursaspor							s46			1	-
Deniz Türüç	29/01/93	Kayserispor							s64			1	-
Serdar Gürler	14/09/91	Gençlerbirliği							s76			1	-
Yusuf Yazıcı	29/01/97	Trabzonspor									s73	1	-

EUROPE

Beşiktaş JK

CHAMPIONS LEAGUE

Group B
Match 1 - SL Benfica (POR)
A 1-1 *Talisca (90+3)*
Tolga Zengin, Adriano (Cenk Tosun 63), Tošić, Ricardo Quaresma, Aboubakar (Olcay Şahan 81), Hutchinson, Oğuzhan Özyakup (Talisca 46), Marcelo, Beck, Inler, Caner Erkin. Coach: Şenol Güneş (TUR)
Match 2 - FC Dynamo Kyiv (UKR)
H 1-1 *Ricardo Quaresma (29)*
Fabricio, Adriano (Cenk Tosun 68), Tošić, Ricardo Quaresma, Aboubakar (Kerim Koyunlu 85), Hutchinson, Arslan (Inler 77), Marcelo, Beck, Caner Erkin, Talisca. Coach: Şenol Güneş (TUR)
Match 3 - SSC Napoli (ITA)
A 3-2 *Adriano (12), Aboubakar (38, 86)*
Fabricio, Adriano (Inler 70), Tošić, Ricardo Quaresma, Aboubakar, Hutchinson, Arslan (Cenk Tosun 75), Necip Uysal (Talisca 90), Marcelo, Beck, Caner Erkin. Coach: Şenol Güneş (TUR)
Match 4 - SSC Napoli (ITA)
H 1-1 *Ricardo Quaresma (79p)*
Fabricio, Adriano, Tošić (Cenk Tosun 24), Ricardo Quaresma, Aboubakar, Hutchinson, Arslan, Marcelo, Beck, Rhodolfo, Inler (Oğuzhan Özyakup 66). Coach: Şenol Güneş (TUR)
Match 5 - SL Benfica (POR)
H 3-3 *Cenk Tosun (58), Ricardo Quaresma (83p), Aboubakar (89)*
Fabricio, Adriano, Tošić (Atınç Nukan 60), Ricardo Quaresma, Aboubakar, Hutchinson, Oğuzhan Özyakup, Arslan (Inler 46), Marcelo, Beck, Gökhan Gönül (Cenk Tosun 46). Coach: Şenol Güneş (TUR)
Match 6 - FC Dynamo Kyiv (UKR)
A 0-6
Fabricio, Adriano, Tošić, Ricardo Quaresma (Kerim Koyunlu 70), Aboubakar, Olcay Şahan (Gökhan Gönül 46), Hutchinson, Oğuzhan Özyakup, Arslan (Cenk Tosun 46), Marcelo, Beck. Coach: Şenol Güneş (TUR)
Red cards: Beck 29, Aboubakar 56

EUROPA LEAGUE

Round of 32 - Hapoel Beer-Sheva FC (ISR)
A 3-1 *William (42og), Cenk Tosun (60), Hutchinson (90+3)*
Fabricio, Mitrović, Tošić, Ricardo Quaresma (Inler 90), Hutchinson, Arslan (Talisca 74), Necip Uysal, Cenk Tosun (Ömer Şişmanoğlu 90+2), Marcelo, Babel, Gökhan Gönül. Coach: Şenol Güneş (TUR)
H 2-1 *Aboubakar (17), Cenk Tosun (87)*
Fabricio, Tošić, Ricardo Quaresma (Arslan 61), Aboubakar (Cenk Tosun 79), Necip Uysal (Oğuzhan Özyakup 72), Marcelo, Beck, Atınç Nukan, Babel, Inler, Talisca. Coach: Şenol Güneş (TUR)

Round of 16 - Olympiacos FC (GRE)
A 1-1 *Aboubakar (53)*
Fabricio, Adriano, Tošić, Ricardo Quaresma, Aboubakar (Cenk Tosun 82), Hutchinson, Arslan (Oğuzhan Özyakup 46), Marcelo, Babel, Gökhan Gönül, Talisca (Inler 90+2). Coach: Şenol Güneş (TUR)
H 4-1 *Aboubakar (10), Babel (22, 75), Cenk Tosun (84)*
Fabricio, Mitrović, Adriano, Tošić, Ricardo Quaresma (Cenk Tosun 83), Aboubakar, Hutchinson, Oğuzhan Özyakup (Necip Uysal 60), Babel, Gökhan Gönül, Talisca (Inler 90+1). Coach: Şenol Güneş (TUR)
Red card: Aboubakar 39

Quarter-finals - Olympique Lyonnais (FRA)
A 1-2 *Babel (15)*
Fabricio, Mitrović (Necip Uysal 64), Adriano, Tošić, Hutchinson, Oğuzhan Özyakup (Arslan 74), Cenk Tosun (Inler 86), Marcelo, Babel, Gökhan Gönül, Talisca. Coach: Şenol Güneş (TUR)
H 2-1 (aet; 6-7 on pens) *Talisca (27, 58)*
Fabricio, Mitrović, Adriano (Beck 77), Tošić, Ricardo Quaresma (Arslan 117), Hutchinson, Oğuzhan Özyakup (Necip Uysal 94), Cenk Tosun, Babel, Gökhan Gönül, Talisca. Coach: Şenol Güneş (TUR)

Fenerbahçe SK

CHAMPIONS LEAGUE

Third qualifying round - AS Monaco FC (FRA)
H 2-1 *Emenike (39, 61)*
Ertuğrul Taşkıran, Hasan Ali Kaldırım, Kjær, Souza, Ozan Tufan, Fernandão, Van der Wiel (Stoch 90+2), Emenike (Chahechouhe 71), Neustädter, Škrtel, Salih Uçan (Şener Özbayraklı 82). Coach: Filipe Almeida (POR)
A 1-3 *Emenike (53)*
Ertuğrul Taşkıran, Hasan Ali Kaldırım (Stoch 78), Kjær (Mehmet Topal 36), Souza (Chahechouhe 69), Ozan Tufan, Fernandão, Van der Wiel, Emenike, Neustädter, Škrtel, Salih Uçan. Coach: Vítor Pereira (POR)

EUROPA LEAGUE

Play-offs - Grasshopper Club Zürich (SUI)
H 3-0 *Chahechouhe (4), Stoch (72, 90+1)*
Volkan Demirel, Hasan Ali Kaldırım, Mehmet Topal, Ozan Tufan, Fernandão (Van Persie 68), Van der Wiel, Emenike, Neustädter, Škrtel, Salih Uçan, Chahechouhe (Stoch 68). Coach: Dick Advocaat (NED)
A 2-0 *Fernandão (77), Stoch (84)*
Volkan Demirel, Hasan Ali Kaldırım (İsmail Köybaşı 73), Kjær, Mehmet Topal, Alper Potuk, Ozan Tufan, Van Persie (Fernandão 68), Van der Wiel, Škrtel, Salih Uçan (Chahechouhe 53), Stoch. Coach: Dick Advocaat (NED)

Group A
Match 1 - FC Zorya Luhansk (UKR)
A 1-1 *Kjær (90+5)*
Volkan Demirel, Hasan Ali Kaldırım, Kjær, Mehmet Topal, Souza, Alper Potuk (Emenike 73), Sow, Şener Özbayraklı, Škrtel, Salih Uçan (Ozan Tufan 46), Stoch (Van Persie 58). Coach: Dick Advocaat (NED)
Match 2 - Feyenoord (NED)
H 1-0 *Emenike (18)*
Volkan Demirel, Hasan Ali Kaldırım (İsmail Köybaşı 77), Kjær, Mehmet Topal, Souza, Ozan Tufan, Sow, Van der Wiel, Emenike (Van Persie 77), Škrtel, Lens (Alper Potuk 86). Coach: Dick Advocaat (NED)
Match 3 - Manchester United FC (ENG)
A 1-4 *Van Persie (83)*
Volkan Demirel, Hasan Ali Kaldırım, Kjær (Emenike 46), Mehmet Topal, Souza, Alper Potuk, Van Persie, Şener Özbayraklı, Volkan Şen (İsmail Köybaşı 69), Neustädter, Škrtel. Coach: Dick Advocaat (NED)
Match 4 - Manchester United FC (ENG)
H 2-1 *Sow (2), Lens (59)*
Volkan Demirel, Hasan Ali Kaldırım, Kjær, Mehmet Topal, Souza, Alper Potuk (Neustädter 82), Sow (İsmail Köybaşı 86), Şener Özbayraklı, Volkan Şen (Emenike 68), Škrtel, Lens. Coach: Dick Advocaat (NED)
Match 5 - FC Zorya Luhansk (UKR)
H 2-0 *Stoch (59), Kjær (67)*
Volkan Demirel, Hasan Ali Kaldırım, Kjær, Mehmet Topal, Souza, Alper Potuk, Sow (Salih Uçan 86), Şener Özbayraklı, Volkan Şen (Neustädter 73), Emenike (Stoch 46), Škrtel. Coach: Dick Advocaat (NED)
Match 6 - Feyenoord (NED)
A 1-0 *Sow (22)*
Volkan Demirel, Hasan Ali Kaldırım, Kjær, Mehmet Topal (Neustädter 86), Souza, Alper Potuk, Van Persie (Emenike 75), Sow, Şener Özbayraklı, Škrtel, Lens (Volkan Şen 70). Coach: Dick Advocaat (NED)

Round of 32 - FC Krasnodar (RUS)
A 0-1
Volkan Demirel, Hasan Ali Kaldırım, Kjær, Mehmet Topal, Souza, Alper Potuk, Sow (Ozan Tufan 72), Şener Özbayraklı, Emenike (Fernandão 72), Neustädter, Lens. Coach: Dick Advocaat (NED)
H 1-1 *Souza (41)*
Volkan Demirel (Fabiano 71), Kjær, Mehmet Topal, Souza, Alper Potuk, Van Persie, Sow (Fernandão 71), Şener Özbayraklı (Volkan Şen 71), İsmail Köybaşı, Škrtel, Lens. Coach: Dick Advocaat (NED)

Konyaspor

EUROPA LEAGUE

Group H
Match 1 - FC Shakhtar Donetsk (UKR)
H 0-1
Serkan Kırıntılı, Douglas, Ali Turan, Jønsson (Halil İbrahim Sönmez 85), Ömer Ali Şahiner, Ali Çamdalı, Bajić (Hora 70), Milošević (Meha 76), Hadžiahmetović, Vuković, Skubic. Coach: Aykut Kocaman (TUR)
Match 2 - KAA Gent (BEL)
A 0-2
Serkan Kırıntılı, Douglas, Ali Turan, Jønsson (Volkan Fındıklı 40), Ömer Ali Şahiner, Ali Çamdalı, Bajić, Milošević (Halil İbrahim Sönmez 81), Hadžiahmetović (Meha 65), Vuković, Skubic. Coach: Aykut Kocaman (TUR)
Match 3 - SC Braga (POR)
H 1-1 *Milošević (9)*
Serkan Kırıntılı, Volkan Fındıklı, Douglas, Ali Turan, Ömer Ali Şahiner (Meha 46), Ali Çamdalı, Bajić, Milošević, Hadžiahmetović (Halil İbrahim Sönmez 82), Vuković, Skubic. Coach: Aykut Kocaman (TUR)
Match 4 - SC Braga (POR)
A 1-3 *Rangelov (30)*
Serkan Kırıntılı, Volkan Fındıklı, Ali Turan (Ali Çamdalı 46), Jønsson, Rangelov (Bajić 76), Milošević, Hadžiahmetović (Ömer Ali Şahiner 46), Meha, Abdülkerim Bardakcı, Mehmet Uslu, Skubic. Coach: Aykut Kocaman (TUR)
Red card: Skubic 54
Match 5 - FC Shakhtar Donetsk (UKR)
A 0-4
Serkan Kırıntılı, Volkan Fındıklı, Selim Ay, Ömer Ali Şahiner, Ali Çamdalı (Meha 16), Milošević (Halil İbrahim Sönmez 63), Mbamba, Hadžiahmetović, Abdülkerim Bardakcı, Mehmet Uslu, Hora (Bajić 83). Coach: Aykut Kocaman (TUR)
Match 6 - KAA Gent (BEL)
H 0-1
Serkan Kırıntılı, Volkan Fındıklı, Douglas, Selim Ay, Jønsson, Ömer Ali Şahiner (Milošević 73), Mbamba, Vuković, Meha (Hadžiahmetović 87), Hora (Bajić 66), Skubic. Coach: Aykut Kocaman (TUR)

İstanbul Başakşehir

Third qualifying round - HNK Rijeka (CRO)
H 0-0
Volkan Babacan, Yalçın Ayhan, Emre Belözoğlu, Epureanu, Višća, Mehmet Batdal (Çikalleshi 85), Doka Madureira (Cengiz Ünder 76), Eren Albayrak, Mahmut Tekdemir, Holmén (Mossoró 59), Uğur Uçar. Coach: Abdullah Avcı (TUR)
A 2-2 *Višća (42, 74)*
Volkan Babacan, Yalçın Ayhan, Emre Belözoğlu, Epureanu, Višća, Mossoró (Holmén 84), Mehmet Batdal, Doka Madureira (Cengiz Ünder 64), Eren Albayrak, Mahmut Tekdemir, Uğur Uçar (Cenk Ahmet Alkılıç 64). Coach: Abdullah Avcı (TUR)

Play-offs - FC Shakhtar Donetsk (UKR)
H 1-2 *Emre Belözoğlu (56p)*
Volkan Babacan, Yalçın Ayhan, Ferhat Öztorun, Emre Belözoğlu (Holmén 75), Epureanu, Višća, Mossoró, Doka Madureira (Cengiz Ünder 46), Mahmut Tekdemir, Cenk Ahmet Alkılıç (Dieng 72), Çikalleshi. Coach: Abdullah Avcı (TUR)
A 0-2
Volkan Babacan, Ferhat Öztorun, Rotman, Emre Belözoğlu (Holmén 28), Epureanu, Eren Albayrak, Attamah, Cengiz Ünder, Hakan Özmert (Mossoró 78), Cenk Ahmet Alkılıç (Uğur Uçar 46), Çikalleshi. Coach: Abdullah Avcı (TUR)

Osmanlıspor

Second qualifying round - FC Zimbru Chisinau (MDA)
A 2-2 *Numan Çürüksu (12), Engin Bekdemir (77)*
Karčemarskas, Vršajević, Mehmet Güven, Lawal (Rusescu 64), Webó (Engin Bekdemir 76), Ndiaye, Procházka, Umar, Delarge (Erdal Kılıçaslan 87), Muhammed Bayır, Numan Çürüksu. Coach: Mustafa Akçay (TUR)
H 5-0 *Umar (16p, 26, 50), Erdal Kılıçaslan (74), Rusescu (83)*
Karčemarskas, Vršajević, Mehmet Güven, Webó (Rusescu 75), Ndiaye, Tiago Pinto, Procházka, Umar, Delarge, Musa Çağıran (Engin Bekdemir 14; Erdal Kılıçaslan 38), Numan Çürüksu. Coach: Mustafa Akçay (TUR)

Third qualifying round - Nõmme Kalju FC (EST)
H 1-0 *Tiago Pinto (74)*
Karčemarskas, Vršajević, Mehmet Güven, Webó (Diabaté 81), Ndiaye, Erdal Kılıçaslan (Rusescu 71), Tiago Pinto, Procházka, Umar, Delarge (Lawal 89), Numan Çürüksu. Coach: Mustafa Akçay (TUR)
A 2-0 *Numan Çürüksu (4), Delarge (29)*
Karčemarskas, Vršajević, Mehmet Güven, Ndiaye (Lawal 54), Erdal Kılıçaslan, Tiago Pinto, Procházka, Rusescu (Tugay Kaçar 79), Umar (Diabaté 70), Delarge, Numan Çürüksu. Coach: Mustafa Akçay (TUR)

Play-offs - FC Midtjylland (DEN)
A 1-0 *Banggaard (20og)*
Karčemarskas, Vršajević, Mehmet Güven, Lawal (Musa Çağıran 61), Webó (Rusescu 77), Ndiaye, Erdal Kılıçaslan (Muhammed Bayır 77), Tiago Pinto, Procházka, Delarge, Numan Çürüksu. Coach: Mustafa Akçay (TUR)
H 2-0 *Tiago Pinto (20, 50)*
Karčemarskas, Koray Altınay (Muhammed Bayır 82), Lawal, Webó (Diabaté 66), Ndiaye, Tiago Pinto, Procházka, Umar, Delarge (Erdal Kılıçaslan 74), Musa Çağıran, Numan Çürüksu. Coach: Mustafa Akçay (TUR)

Group L
Match 1 - FC Steaua Bucureşti (ROU)
H 2-0 *Diabaté (64p), Umar (74)*
Karčemarskas, Koray Altınay, Aykut Demir, Lawal, Ndiaye, Diabaté (Rusescu 78), Tiago Pinto, Regattin, Umar (Delarge 75), Musa Çağıran (Maher 84), Numan Çürüksu. Coach: Mustafa Akçay (TUR)
Match 2 - FC Zürich (SUI)
A 1-2 *Maher (73)*
Karčemarskas, Vršajević, Aykut Demir, Lawal, Ndiaye, Tiago Pinto, Regattin, Rusescu (Diabaté 72), Delarge (Umar 67), Musa Çağıran (Maher 61), Numan Çürüksu. Coach: Mustafa Akçay (TUR)
Match 3 - Villarreal CF (ESP)
H 2-2 *Rusescu (23, 24)*
Hakan Arıkan, Vršajević, Aykut Demir, Lawal (Mehmet Güven 39), Ndiaye, Tiago Pinto, Rusescu (Regattin 80), Umar, Delarge, Numan Çürüksu, Maher (Procházka 57). Coach: Mustafa Akçay (TUR)
Red card: Mehmet Güven 53
Match 4 - Villarreal CF (ESP)
A 2-1 *Webó (8), Rusescu (75)*
Hakan Arıkan, Webó (Rusescu 73), Ndiaye, Tiago Pinto, Procházka, Umar, Delarge (Regattin 67), Muhammed Bayır, Musa Çağıran (Aykut Demir 86), Numan Çürüksu, Maher. Coach: Mustafa Akçay (TUR)
Match 5 - FC Steaua Bucureşti (ROU)
A 1-2 *Ndiaye (30)*
Karčemarskas, Vršajević (Muhammed Bayır 75), Ndiaye, Tiago Pinto, Regattin, Procházka, Rusescu, Delarge (Erdal Kılıçaslan 69), Musa Çağıran, Numan Çürüksu, Maher (Lawal 61). Coach: Mustafa Akçay (TUR)
Match 6 - FC Zürich (SUI)
H 2-0 *Delarge (73), Erdal Kılıçaslan (89)*
Karčemarskas, Vršajević, Mehmet Güven, Webó (Rusescu 78), Ndiaye, Tiago Pinto, Regattin (Erdal Kılıçaslan 87), Procházka, Delarge (Umar 74), Numan Çürüksu, Maher. Coach: Mustafa Akçay (TUR)

Round of 32 - Olympiacos FC (GRE)
A 0-0
Karčemarskas, Vršajević, Ndiaye, Tiago Pinto, Regattin, Luíz Carlos (Maher 87), Procházka, Delarge (Rusescu 81), Musa Çağıran, Bifouma (Mehmet Güven 90+4), Numan Çürüksu. Coach: Mustafa Akçay (TUR)
H 0-3
Karčemarskas, Vršajević, Webó, Ndiaye, Tiago Pinto (Muhammed Bayır 66), Regattin (Delarge 75), Procházka, Musa Çağıran (Mehmet Güven 74), Bifouma, Numan Çürüksu, Maher. Coach: Mustafa Akçay (TUR)

DOMESTIC LEAGUE CLUB-BY-CLUB

Adanaspor AŞ

1954 • 5 Ocak Fatih Terim (16,095) • adanaspor.com.tr

Coach; (Eyüp Arın); (01/09/16) Krunoslav Jurčić (CRO); (06/12/16) (Eyüp Arın); (23/12/16) Levent Şahin; (10/04/17) (Eyüp Arın)

2016					
19/08	h	Bursaspor	L	1-2	*Renan Diniz*
27/08	a	Kasımpaşa	D	1-1	*Renan Diniz*
10/09	h	Gaziantepspor	D	0-0	
18/09	a	Osmanlıspor	L	0-1	
26/09	h	Alanyaspor	W	3-2	*Tevfik, Gueye, Cem*
02/10	a	Konyaspor	L	0-1	
15/10	h	Karabükspor	L	1-2	*Gueye (p)*
22/10	a	Akhisar	L	0-1	
29/10	h	Galatasaray	L	0-1	
06/11	a	Rizespor	D	2-2	*Roni 2*
19/11	h	Beşiktaş	L	1-2	*Gueye (p)*
26/11	a	Antalyaspor	L	0-1	
04/12	h	Gençlerbirliği	L	0-2	
09/12	a	Trabzonspor	L	1-4	*Renan Foguinho*
18/12	h	Kayserispor	W	2-1	*Ahmet Dereli, Cem*
24/12	h	İstanbul Başakşehir	D	1-1	*Gueye*
2017					
15/01	a	Fenerbahçe	D	2-2	*Gueye, Roni*
21/01	a	Bursaspor	W	1-0	*Gueye*
30/01	h	Kasımpaşa	W	3-0	*(w/o; original result 2-0 Roni, Digão)*
13/02	a	Gaziantepspor	L	0-1	
19/02	h	Osmanlıspor	L	1-5	*Roni*
25/02	a	Alanyaspor	L	1-4	*Gueye (p)*
05/03	h	Konyaspor	L	0-1	
11/03	a	Karabükspor	L	0-2	
18/03	h	Akhisar	W	2-1	*Gueye, Ahmet Dereli*
03/04	a	Galatasaray	L	0-4	
09/04	h	Rizespor	L	1-3	*Gueye*
24/04	a	Beşiktaş	L	2-3	*Roni, Gueye*
30/04	h	Antalyaspor	L	2-5	*Roni, Ahmet Dereli*
06/05	a	Gençlerbirliği	W	1-0	*Maurício Ramos*
13/05	h	Trabzonspor	D	1-1	*Renan Foguinho*
20/05	a	Kayserispor	D	1-1	*Renan Foguinho*
27/05	a	İstanbul Başakşehir	L	1-2	*Cem*
03/06	h	Fenerbahçe	L	1-3	*Koman*

No	Name	Nat	DoB	Pos	Aps	(s)	Gls
8	Ahmet Bahçıvan		27/02/96	M	1	(11)	
7	Ahmet Dereli		22/09/92	A	6	(16)	3
17	Barış Memiş		05/01/90	M		(1)	
88	Bekir Yılmaz		06/03/88	M	18	(3)	
11	Canberk Dilaver		01/06/83	D	2	(2)	
27	Cem Özdemir		27/07/92	M	15	(11)	3
53	Didi	BRA	25/05/91	D	23		
22	Digão	BRA	12/03/93	D	30		1
29	Edgar	BRA	03/01/87	A	6	(7)	
21	Emre Uruç		10/04/94	D	5	(8)	
90	Fırat Kaplan		16/07/98	M		(3)	
9	Magaye Gueye	SEN	06/07/90	A	29	(3)	10
66	Halil İbrahim Pehlivan		21/08/83	D	4		
26	Charles Itandje	CMR	02/11/82	G	12		
46	İrfan Can Eğribayat		30/06/98	G	2		
18	Goran Karačić	BIH	18/08/96	G	12		
77	Vladimir Koman	HUN	16/03/89	M	30	(1)	1
5	Maurício Ramos	BRA	10/04/85	D	29		1
1	Mert Akyüz		02/10/93	G	8		
33	Renan Diniz	BRA	27/02/93	D	19		2
32	Renan Foguinho	BRA	09/09/89	M	25	(2)	3
99	Reynaldo	BRA	24/08/89	A	2	(7)	
80	Roni	BRA	26/01/91	M	28	(1)	7
6	Sami Can Keskin		14/08/93	M	14	(9)	
97	Serbay Can		10/06/97	D		(1)	
20	Tevfik Altındağ		26/10/88	M	26	(4)	1
3	Ousmane Viera	CIV	21/12/86	D	13	(2)	
10	Vinícius	BRA	03/08/93	A	15	(1)	

TURKEY

Akhisar Belediyespor

1970 • 19 Mayıs, Manisa (16,597) • akhisarspor.com

Coach: Cihat Arslan; (04/09/16) Tolunay Kafkas; (23/03/17) Okan Buruk

2016					
21/08	a	Kayserispor	W	2-0	*Rodallega, Miguel Lopes*
27/08	h	Galatasaray	L	1-3	*Vaz Té*
11/09	a	Rizespor	L	0-1	
18/09	h	Beşiktaş	L	0-2	
23/09	a	Antalyaspor	D	0-0	
30/09	h	Gençlerbirliği	D	0-0	
16/10	a	Trabzonspor	D	0-0	
22/10	h	Adanaspor	W	1-0	*Rodallega*
30/10	a	İstanbul Başakşehir	L	1-5	*Rodallega*
06/11	h	Fenerbahçe	L	1-3	*Rodallega*
19/11	a	Bursaspor	D	0-0	
26/11	h	Kasımpaşa	W	1-0	*Sissoko*
04/12	a	Gaziantepspor	W	2-1	*Özer, Muğdat*
11/12	h	Osmanlıspor	L	1-2	*Vaz Té*
18/12	a	Alanyaspor	D	0-0	
25/12	h	Konyaspor	W	1-0	*Vaz Té*
2017					
14/01	a	Karabükspor	L	0-1	
21/01	h	Kayserispor	D	0-0	
28/01	a	Galatasaray	L	0-6	
12/02	h	Rizespor	W	1-0	*Mustafa*
19/02	a	Beşiktaş	L	1-3	*Olcan*
25/02	h	Antalyaspor	W	3-0	*Özer 2, Aykut*
06/03	a	Gençlerbirliği	L	0-2	
13/03	h	Trabzonspor	L	1-3	*Çikalleshi*
18/03	a	Adanaspor	L	1-2	*Mustafa*
01/04	h	İstanbul Başakşehir	W	2-1	*Vaz Té, Çikalleshi*
09/04	a	Fenerbahçe	L	1-3	*Vaz Té (p)*
23/04	h	Bursaspor	W	5-1	*Olcan 2, Mustafa, Çikalleshi, Vaz Té*
30/04	a	Kasımpaşa	W	2-0	*Vaz Té, Olcan*
08/05	h	Gaziantepspor	W	6-0	*og (Wallace), Çikalleshi 2, Vaz Té 2 (1p), Larsson*
14/05	a	Osmanlıspor	W	4-0	*Custódio, Özer, Olcan, og (Procházka)*
22/05	h	Alanyaspor	W	3-0	*Miguel Lopes, Çikalleshi, Özer*
27/05	a	Konyaspor	W	3-0	*og (Skubic), Miguel Lopes, Vaz Té*
02/06	h	Karabükspor	L	2-3	*Çikalleshi, Vaz Té (p)*

No	Name	Nat	DoB	Pos	Aps	(s)	Gls
18	Enoch Kofi Adu	GHA	14/09/90	M	1	(2)	
25	Alper Uludağ		11/12/90	D	1		
6	Aykut Çeviker		03/01/90	M	10	(8)	1
30	Jeremy Bokila	COD	14/11/88	A		(4)	
35	Bora Körk		09/06/80	G	11		
88	Caner Osmanpaşa		15/01/88	D	33		
90	Mervan Celik	SWE	28/05/90	M	5	(2)	
27	Custódio	POR	24/05/83	M	28		1
37	Sokol Çikalleshi	ALB	27/07/90	A	11	(3)	7
2	Douglão	BRA	15/08/86	D	6		
26	Fatih Öztürk		22/12/86	G	11		
16	Hasan Ali Adıgüzel		03/04/00	M	1	(3)	
89	Kadir Keleş		01/01/88	D	12	(1)	
12	Daniel Larsson	SWE	15/01/87	M	1	(8)	1
1	Milan Lukač	SRB	04/10/85	G	12		
13	Miguel Lopes	POR	19/12/86	D	31		3
7	Muğdat Çelik		03/01/90	A	3	(18)	1
22	Mustafa Yumlu		25/09/87	D	12		3
21	Landry N'Guémo	CMR	28/11/85	M	11		
29	Olcan Adın		30/09/85	M	14	(2)	5
11	Onur Ayık		28/01/90	M	10	(15)	
15	Orhan Taşdelen		06/02/87	D	6	(3)	
19	Ömer Bayram		27/07/91	D	28	(1)	
5	Özer Hurmacı		20/11/86	M	27	(2)	5
23	Hugo Rodallega	COL	25/07/85	A	17		4
28	Miral Samardžič	SVN	17/02/87	D	3		
17	Sami	GNB	18/12/88	A	3	(2)	
53	Serdar Kesimal		24/01/89	D	8		
20	Abdoul Sissoko	MLI	20/03/90	M	15	(5)	1
10	Soner Aydoğdu		05/01/91	M	21	(6)	
14	Tolga Ünlü		10/09/89	D	3	(1)	
9	Ricardo Vaz Té	POR	01/10/86	A	19	(12)	11

Alanyaspor

1948 • Bahçesehir Okulları Stadyumu (10,842) • alanyaspor.org.tr

Coach: Hüseyin Kalpar; (16/01/17) (Mustafa Camunak); (27/01/17) Safet Sušić (BIH)

2016					
20/08	a	Beşiktaş	L	1-4	*Emre Akbaba (p)*
26/08	h	Antalyaspor	W	2-1	*Guerrier, Ayité*
10/09	a	Gençlerbirliği	D	0-0	
17/09	h	Trabzonspor	W	3-0	*Emre Akbaba, Guerrier, Sefa*
26/09	a	Adanaspor	L	2-3	*Ba, Guerrier*
02/10	h	İstanbul Başakşehir	L	0-5	
16/10	a	Fenerbahçe	D	1-1	*Daniel Candeias*
22/10	h	Bursaspor	L	0-2	
31/10	a	Kasımpaşa	L	1-2	*Sackey*
05/11	h	Gaziantepspor	W	4-3	*Emre Akbaba, Daniel Candeias, Guerrier, Vágner Love*
19/11	a	Osmanlıspor	L	0-2	
25/11	h	Kayserispor	W	3-0	*Sackey, Vágner Love (p), Emre Akbaba (p)*
04/12	h	Konyaspor	L	2-3	*Taha, Vágner Love*
11/12	a	Karabükspor	W	2-0	*Vágner Love 2 (1p)*
18/12	h	Akhisar	D	0-0	
25/12	a	Galatasaray	L	1-5	*Shahbazzadeh*
2017					
14/01	h	Rizespor	L	2-3	*Vágner Love, Plet*
23/01	h	Beşiktaş	L	1-4	*Vágner Love (p)*
28/01	a	Antalyaspor	L	1-2	*Vágner Love*
11/02	h	Gençlerbirliği	W	3-0	*Fernandes, Vágner Love, Emre Akbaba*
20/02	a	Trabzonspor	D	0-0	
25/02	h	Adanaspor	W	4-1	*Vágner Love (p), Omeruo, Fernandes, Emre Akbaba*
05/03	a	İstanbul Başakşehir	L	1-2	*Fernandes*
10/03	h	Fenerbahçe	L	2-3	*Fernandes, Vágner Love*
19/03	a	Bursaspor	W	3-1	*Efecan, Vágner Love 2 (1p)*
01/04	h	Kasımpaşa	W	3-1	*Vágner Love 2, Tzavellas*
08/04	a	Gaziantepspor	W	3-2	*Vágner Love, Fernandes, Daniel Candeias*
22/04	h	Osmanlıspor	L	0-1	
29/04	a	Kayserispor	L	0-3	
06/05	a	Konyaspor	W	3-2	*Vágner Love 2 (1p), Fernandes*
14/05	h	Karabükspor	W	4-2	*Vágner Love 3, Daniel Candeias*
22/05	a	Akhisar	L	0-3	
29/05	h	Galatasaray	L	2-3	*Vágner Love 2 (1p)*
03/06	a	Rizespor	L	0-1	

No	Name	Nat	DoB	Pos	Aps	(s)	Gls
6	Ismail Aissati	MAR	16/08/88	M	9	(3)	
9	Jonathan Ayité	TOG	21/07/85	A	2	(9)	1
33	Abdoulaye Ba	SEN	01/01/91	D	10		1
3	Berkan Emir		08/02/88	D	13	(10)	
4	Birol Parlak		01/03/90	D	3	(2)	
13	Carlos García	ESP	29/04/84	D	8	(1)	
91	Cenk Ahmet Alkılıç		09/12/87	D	2	(4)	
23	Daniel Candeias	POR	23/02/88	M	29		4
5	Deniz Vural		11/07/88	M	7	(2)	
7	Efecan Karaca		16/11/89	M	20	(4)	1
10	Emre Akbaba		04/10/92	M	33	(1)	6
24	Emre Nefiz		24/11/94	M	3	(8)	
20	Erhan Kartal		01/03/93	D	2	(2)	
78	Júnior Fernandes	CHI	10/04/88	A	14		6
38	Mamadou Fofana	MLI	21/01/98	D	1		
89	Lamine Gassama	SEN	20/10/89	D	29		
14	Gökay İravul		17/10/92	M		(2)	
77	Wilde-Donald Guerrier	HAI	31/03/89	M	12	(12)	4
1	Haydar Yılmaz		19/01/84	G	25		
16	Guy-Michel Landel	GUI	07/07/90	M	4	(1)	
94	Darko Lazić	SRB	19/07/94	D	3	(1)	
21	Fabrice N'Sakala	COD	21/07/90	D	26	(1)	
44	Kenneth Omeruo	NGA	17/10/93	D	26		1
29	Glynor Plet	NED	20/01/87	A	1	(9)	1
2	Isaac Sackey	GHA	04/04/94	M	22	(1)	2
32	Sefa Yılmaz		14/02/90	M	2	(7)	1
8	Sajjad Shahbazzadeh	IRN	23/01/90	A	2	(2)	1
15	Nuru Suley	GHA	11/06/92	D	7		
88	Taha Yalçıner		12/01/87	M	8	(10)	1
31	Georgios Tzavellas	GRE	26/11/87	D	15		1
99	Vágner Love	BRA	11/06/84	A	27	(1)	23
37	Zdeněk Zlámal	CZE	05/11/85	G	9		

Antalyaspor

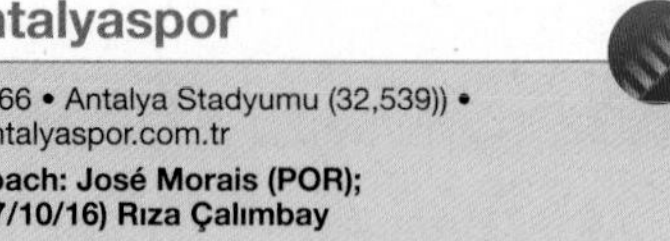

1966 • Antalya Stadyumu (32,539)) • antalyaspor.com.tr

Coach: José Morais (POR); (07/10/16) Rıza Çalımbay

2016					
21/08	h	Osmanlıspor	D	0-0	
26/08	a	Alanyaspor	L	1-2	*Zeki*
11/09	h	Konyaspor	L	1-3	*Eto'o*
16/09	a	Karabükspor	L	2-3	*Diego Ângelo, Deniz*
23/09	h	Akhisar	D	0-0	
02/10	a	Galatasaray	L	1-3	*Deniz*
17/10	h	Rizespor	D	1-1	*Deniz*
23/10	a	Beşiktaş	L	0-3	
31/10	a	Kayserispor	W	1-0	*Eto'o (p)*
05/11	h	Gençlerbirliği	W	1-0	*Eto'o (p)*
21/11	a	Trabzonspor	W	1-0	*Chico*
26/11	h	Adanaspor	W	1-0	*Ramon*
03/12	a	İstanbul Başakşehir	D	2-2	*Eto'o 2 (1p)*
12/12	h	Fenerbahçe	W	1-0	*Yekta*
19/12	a	Bursaspor	L	1-2	*Deniz*
25/12	h	Kasımpaşa	W	2-1	*Makoun, Ramon*
2017					
15/01	a	Gaziantepspor	W	3-0	*Etame, Chico, Deniz*
22/01	a	Osmanlıspor	W	2-1	*Etame, Eto'o*
28/01	h	Alanyaspor	W	2-1	*Eto'o 2*
12/02	a	Konyaspor	D	1-1	*El Kabir*
18/02	h	Karabükspor	W	1-0	*Eto'o*
25/02	a	Akhisar	L	0-3	
06/03	h	Galatasaray	L	2-3	*Etame, Deniz*
12/03	a	Rizespor	W	2-1	*Deniz, Etame*
19/03	h	Beşiktaş	D	0-0	
01/04	h	Kayserispor	W	2-1	*Eto'o, El Kabir*
08/04	a	Gençlerbirliği	D	1-1	*Eto'o*
22/04	h	Trabzonspor	L	0-3	
30/04	a	Adanaspor	W	5-2	*Deniz, Eto'o 3, El-Kabir*
05/05	h	İstanbul Başakşehir	L	0-1	
13/05	a	Fenerbahçe	W	1-0	*Deniz*
20/05	h	Bursaspor	W	2-1	*Eto'o 2*
27/05	a	Kasımpaşa	W	3-0	*Eto'o, Ramon, Deniz*
02/06	h	Gaziantepspor	W	4-1	*Drole 2, Zeki, Eto'o*

No	Name	Nat	DoB	Pos	Aps	(s)	Gls
92	Atakan Cangöz		30/03/92	M		(1)	
8	Charles	BRA	14/02/85	M	28	(1)	
20	Chico	BRA	02/02/87	D	19	(4)	2
28	Ondřej Čelůstka	CZE	18/06/89	D	34		
90	Danilo	BRA	15/01/90	M	25	(3)	
63	Deniz Kadah		02/03/86	A	27	(2)	10
3	Diego Ângelo	BRA	17/02/86	D	29	(1)	1
66	Doğukan Sinik		21/01/99	M		(1)	
55	Jean Armel Drole	CIV	18/06/97	A	1	(1)	2
14	Moestafa El Kabir	MAR	05/10/88	A	8	(3)	3
77	Emre Güral		05/04/89	A	1	(8)	
99	Mbilla Etame	CMR	22/06/88	M	23	(5)	4
9	Samuel Eto'o	CMR	10/03/81	A	28	(2)	18
35	Ferhat Kaplan		07/01/89	G	18		
32	Sašo Fornezzi	SVN	11/12/82	G	15		
22	Harun Alpsoy		03/03/97	M	1	(1)	
6	Kenan Horić	BIH	13/09/90	M	1	(8)	
22	Samuel Inkoom	GHA	01/06/89	D	1		
11	Milan Jevtović	SRB	13/06/93	A		(7)	
17	Jean II Makoun	CMR	29/05/83	M	5	(3)	1
1	Ozan Özenç		07/01/93	G	1	(1)	
31	Ramon	BRA	06/05/88	D	17	(4)	3
30	Amadaiya Rennie	LBR	17/03/90	A	1	(1)	
25	Rıdvan Şimşek		17/01/91	D	4	(1)	
23	Sakıb Aytaç		24/11/91	D	24	(3)	
24	Salih Dursun		12/07/91	D	14	(2)	
33	Sandro	BRA	15/03/89	M	6	(6)	
10	Serdar Özkan		01/01/87	M	6	(13)	
18	Yekta Kurtuluş		11/12/85	M	10	(15)	1
97	Yusuf Çelik		27/06/96	D	2		
7	Zeki Yıldırım		15/01/91	M	25	(4)	2

Beşiktaş JK

1903 • Vodafone Park (41,903) • bjk.com.tr

Major honours
Turkish League (15) 1957, 1958, 1960, 1966, 1967, 1982, 1986, 1990, 1991, 1992, 1995, 2003, 2009, 2016, 2017; Turkish Cup (9) 1975, 1989, 1990, 1994, 1998, 2006, 2007, 2009, 2011

Coach: Şenol Güneş

Date		Opponent			Scorers
2016					
20/08	h	Alanyaspor	W	4-1	*Oğuzhan, Olcay, Cenk 2 (1p)*
26/08	a	Konyaspor	D	2-2	*Olcay, Cenk*
10/09	h	Karabükspor	W	3-1	*Cenk, Ömer, Oğuzhan (p)*
18/09	a	Akhisar	W	2-0	*Talisca, og (Rodallega)*
24/09	h	Galatasaray	D	2-2	*Marcelo, Cenk*
01/10	a	Rizespor	W	1-0	*Adriano*
15/10	a	Kayserispor	W	1-0	*Ömer*
23/10	h	Antalyaspor	W	3-0	*Aboubakar, Talisca 2*
28/10	a	Gençlerbirliği	D	1-1	*Talisca*
05/11	h	Trabzonspor	W	2-1	*Rhodolfo, Cenk (p)*
19/11	a	Adanaspor	W	2-1	*Aboubakar, Cenk (p)*
26/11	h	İstanbul Başakşehir	D	1-1	*Marcelo*
03/12	a	Fenerbahçe	D	0-0	
10/12	h	Bursaspor	W	2-1	*Cenk 2 (2p)*
17/12	a	Kasımpaşa	L	1-2	*Cenk*
24/12	h	Gaziantepspor	W	1-0	*Aboubakar*
2017					
16/01	a	Osmanlıspor	W	2-0	*Talisca, Cenk*
23/01	a	Alanyaspor	W	4-1	*Cenk, Babel, Ricardo Quaresma (p), Marcelo*
30/01	h	Konyaspor	W	5-1	*Babel, Oğuzhan, Cenk 3 (1p)*
10/02	a	Karabükspor	L	1-2	*Aboubakar*
19/02	h	Akhisar	W	3-1	*Cenk, Talisca, Atınç*
27/02	a	Galatasaray	W	1-0	*Talisca*
04/03	h	Rizespor	W	1-0	*Gökhan*
12/03	h	Kayserispor	D	2-2	*Aboubakar 2*
19/03	a	Antalyaspor	D	0-0	
02/04	h	Gençlerbirliği	W	3-0	*Oğuzhan, Talisca, Babel*
08/04	a	Trabzonspor	W	4-3	*Cenk, Aboubakar, Talisca, Hutchinson*
24/04	h	Adanaspor	W	3-2	*Aboubakar, Talisca, Tošić*
30/04	a	İstanbul Başakşehir	L	1-3	*Ba*
07/05	h	Fenerbahçe	D	1-1	*Aboubakar*
15/05	a	Bursaspor	W	2-0	*Cenk, Aboubakar*
20/05	h	Kasımpaşa	W	4-1	*Aboubakar, Ricardo Quaresma (p), Talisca, Babel*
28/05	a	Gaziantepspor	W	4-0	*Babel, Oğuzhan, Talisca 2*
03/06	h	Osmanlıspor	W	4-0	*Cenk 2, Tošić, Aboubakar*

No	Name	Nat	DoB	Pos	Aps	(s)	Gls
9	Vincent Aboubakar	CMR	22/01/92	A	16	(11)	12
3	Adriano	BRA	26/10/84	D	24	(7)	1
18	Tolgay Arslan	GER	16/08/90	M	18	(12)	
33	Atınç Nukan		20/07/93	D	7	(1)	1
99	Demba Ba	SEN	25/05/85	A		(2)	1
49	Ryan Babel	NED	19/12/86	M	18		5
32	Andreas Beck	GER	13/03/87	D	8	(9)	
88	Caner Erkin		04/10/88	D	6	(2)	
23	Cenk Tosun		07/06/91	A	29	(4)	20
1	Fabricio	ESP	31/12/87	G	32		
77	Gökhan Gönül		04/01/85	D	27	(2)	1
13	Atiba Hutchinson	CAN	08/02/83	M	28		1
80	Gökhan Inler	SUI	27/06/84	M	5	(9)	
21	Kerim Koyunlu		19/11/93	M	1	(6)	
30	Marcelo	BRA	20/05/87	D	32		3
2	Matej Mitrović	CRO	10/11/93	D	2	(5)	
20	Necip Uysal		24/01/91	M	5	(12)	
15	Oğuzhan Özyakup		23/09/92	M	28	(1)	5
10	Olcay Şahan		26/05/87	M	8	(3)	2
17	Ömer Şişmanoğlu		01/08/89	A	2	(6)	2
22	Aras Özbiliz	ARM	09/03/90	M		(1)	
44	Rhodolfo	BRA	11/08/86	D	3	(2)	1
7	Ricardo Quaresma	POR	26/09/83	M	26	(3)	2
94	Talisca	BRA	01/02/94	M	21	(1)	13
29	Tolga Zengin		10/10/83	G	2	(1)	
6	Duško Tošić	SRB	19/01/85	D	26		2

Bursaspor

1963 • Büyükşehir Belediye Stadyumu (43,331) • bursaspor.org.tr

Major honours
Turkish League (1) 2010; Turkish Cup (1) 1986

Coach: Hamza Hamzaoğlu; (21/01/17) (Tunahan Akdoğan); (30/01/17) Mutlu Topçu

Date		Opponent			Scorers
2016					
19/08	a	Adanaspor	W	2-1	*Ertuğrul, Batalla*
28/08	h	İstanbul Başakşehir	L	0-2	
11/09	a	Fenerbahçe	W	1-0	*Batalla*
16/09	h	Kayserispor	W	3-1	*Batalla, Jorquera, Sercan*
25/09	h	Kasımpaşa	W	1-0	*Jorquera*
01/10	a	Gaziantepspor	L	2-3	*Batalla, Del Valle*
16/10	h	Osmanlıspor	D	0-0	
22/10	a	Alanyaspor	W	2-0	*Jorquera 2*
29/10	h	Konyaspor	W	2-0	*Kubilay, Batalla*
05/11	a	Karabükspor	D	0-0	
19/11	h	Akhisar	D	0-0	
25/11	a	Galatasaray	L	1-3	*Kubilay*
05/12	h	Rizespor	W	2-1	*Yılmaz 2*
10/12	a	Beşiktaş	L	1-2	*Emre*
19/12	h	Antalyaspor	W	2-1	*Kubilay, Batalla*
26/12	a	Gençlerbirliği	L	1-3	*Kubilay*
2017					
13/01	h	Trabzonspor	L	1-2	*Kubilay*
21/01	h	Adanaspor	L	0-1	
29/01	a	İstanbul Başakşehir	L	0-1	
11/02	h	Fenerbahçe	D	1-1	*Batalla (p)*
17/02	a	Kayserispor	L	0-2	
24/02	a	Kasımpaşa	L	0-4	
04/03	h	Gaziantepspor	W	2-1	*İsmail, John*
11/03	a	Osmanlıspor	D	1-1	*Yılmaz (p)*
19/03	h	Alanyaspor	L	1-3	*Yılmaz (p)*
02/04	a	Konyaspor	L	0-2	
07/04	h	Karabükspor	W	3-0	*Kubilay, Sercan, Erdem (p)*
23/04	a	Akhisar	L	1-5	*Batalla*
01/05	h	Galatasaray	L	0-5	
07/05	a	Rizespor	L	0-6	
15/05	h	Beşiktaş	L	0-2	
20/05	a	Antalyaspor	L	1-2	*Sinan*
28/05	h	Gençlerbirliği	L	1-2	*Jorquera*
03/06	a	Trabzonspor	W	2-1	*Jorquera, Batalla*

No	Name	Nat	DoB	Pos	Aps	(s)	Gls
10	Pablo Batalla	ARG	16/01/84	M	31		9
23	Aziz Behich	AUS	16/12/90	D	32		
5	Bilal Kısa		22/06/83	M	5	(8)	
28	Yonathan Del Valle	VEN	28/05/90	M	18	(3)	1
3	Emre Taşdemir		08/08/95	D	2	(4)	1
22	Erdem Özgenç		22/08/84	D	13	(4)	1
24	Ertuğrul Ersoy		13/02/97	D	20		1
14	Ricardo Faty	SEN	04/08/86	M	19	(5)	
17	Furkan Soyalp		12/06/95	M		(1)	
1	Harun Tekin		17/06/89	G	34		
4	İsmail Konuk		16/01/88	D	23		1
11	Joshua John	NED	01/10/88	M	16	(6)	1
8	Cristóbal Jorquera	CHI	04/08/88	M	19	(11)	6
25	Boban Jovič	SVN	25/06/91	D	5	(1)	
18	Kubilay Kanatsızkuş		28/03/97	A	20	(9)	6
70	Mert Örnek		12/02/97	M	2	(4)	
7	Merter Yüce		18/02/85	M	22	(4)	
15	Tomáš Necid	CZE	13/08/89	A	2	(4)	
33	Onur Atasayar		01/01/95	D	9	(2)	
9	Sercan Yıldırım		05/04/90	A	4	(19)	2
2	Serdar Kurtuluş		23/07/87	D	6		
12	Sinan Bakış		22/04/94	A	5	(7)	1
66	Tomáš Sivok	CZE	15/09/83	D	21		
30	Bogdan Stancu	ROU	28/06/87	A	8	(4)	
6	Şamil Çinaz		08/03/86	M	20	(3)	
88	Deniz Yılmaz	AZE	26/02/88	A	18	(1)	4

Fenerbahçe SK

1907 • Şükrü Saraçoğlu (50,509) • fenerbahce.org

Major honours
Turkish League (19) 1959, 1961, 1964, 1965, 1968, 1970, 1974, 1975, 1978, 1983, 1985, 1989, 1996, 2001, 2004, 2005, 2007, 2011, 2014; Turkish Cup (6) 1968, 1974, 1979, 1983, 2012, 2013

Coach: Vítor Pereira (POR); (17/08/16) Dick Advocaat (NED)

Date		Opponent			Scorers
2016					
21/08	a	İstanbul Başakşehir	L	0-1	
28/08	h	Kayserispor	D	3-3	*Kjær, Ozan, Alper*
11/09	h	Bursaspor	L	0-1	
19/09	a	Kasımpaşa	W	5-1	*Souza, Ozan, Emenike, Sow, İsmail*
25/09	h	Gaziantepspor	W	2-1	*Emenike, Souza*
02/10	a	Osmanlıspor	D	1-1	*Van Persie*
16/10	h	Alanyaspor	D	1-1	*Mehmet*
24/10	a	Konyaspor	W	1-0	*Emenike (p)*
30/10	h	Karabükspor	W	5-0	*Van Persie 2 (1p), Škrtel, Chahechouhe, Lens*
06/11	a	Akhisar	W	3-1	*Van Persie, Chahechouhe, og (Fatih)*
20/11	h	Galatasaray	W	2-0	*Van Persie 2 (1p)*
27/11	a	Rizespor	W	5-1	*Sow 3, Chahechouhe, İsmail*
03/12	h	Beşiktaş	D	0-0	
12/12	a	Antalyaspor	L	0-1	
19/12	h	Gençlerbirliği	W	3-0	*Sow 2, Fernandão*
26/12	a	Trabzonspor	W	3-0	*Fernandão (p), Sow, Lens*
2017					
15/01	h	Adanaspor	D	2-2	*Mehmet, Fernandão (p)*
22/01	h	İstanbul Başakşehir	W	1-0	*Ozan*
29/01	a	Kayserispor	L	1-4	*Mehmet*
11/02	a	Bursaspor	D	1-1	*Sow (p)*
19/02	h	Kasımpaşa	D	0-0	
26/02	a	Gaziantepspor	D	1-1	*Lens*
05/03	h	Osmanlıspor	W	1-0	*Mehmet*
10/03	a	Alanyaspor	W	3-2	*og (Omeruo), Fernandão, Chahechouhe*
17/03	h	Konyaspor	L	2-3	*Škrtel, Sow*
01/04	a	Karabükspor	W	1-0	*Van Persie*
09/04	h	Akhisar	W	3-1	*og (Miguel Lopes), Souza, Lens*
23/04	a	Galatasaray	W	1-0	*Souza*
30/04	h	Rizespor	W	2-1	*Sow 2*
07/05	a	Beşiktaş	D	1-1	*og (Marcelo)*
13/05	h	Antalyaspor	L	0-1	
22/05	a	Gençlerbirliği	W	2-1	*Van Persie 2 (1p)*
27/05	h	Trabzonspor	D	1-1	*Sow*
03/06	a	Adanaspor	W	3-1	*Souza, Chahechouhe, Emenike*

No	Name	Nat	DoB	Pos	Aps	(s)	Gls
7	Alper Potuk		08/04/91	M	25	(4)	1
92	Aatif Chahechouhe	MAR	02/07/86	M	13	(5)	5
29	Emmanuel Emenike	NGA	10/05/87	A	9	(7)	4
13	Ertuğrul Taşkıran		05/11/89	G		(1)	
40	Fabiano	BRA	29/02/88	G	6		
9	Fernandão	BRA	27/03/87	A	7	(6)	4
3	Hasan Ali Kaldırım		09/12/89	D	28	(1)	
22	İsmail Köybaşı		10/07/89	D	11	(3)	2
11	Olexandr Karavayev	UKR	02/06/92	M		(3)	
4	Simon Kjær	DEN	26/03/89	D	27		1
77	Jeremain Lens	NED	24/11/87	M	25	(1)	4
5	Mehmet Topal		03/03/86	M	29		4
33	Roman Neustädter	RUS	18/02/88	M	12	(6)	
8	Ozan Tufan		23/03/95	M	14	(8)	3
48	Salih Uçan		06/01/94	M	4	(7)	
6	Souza	BRA	11/02/89	M	29	(1)	5
17	Moussa Sow	SEN	19/01/86	A	16	(9)	12
99	Miroslav Stoch	SVK	19/10/89	M	2	(7)	
19	Şener Özbayraklı		23/01/90	D	18	(1)	
37	Martin Škrtel	SVK	15/12/84	D	31		2
23	Gregory van der Wiel	NED	03/02/88	D	11		
10	Robin van Persie	NED	06/08/83	A	14	(10)	9
1	Volkan Demirel		27/10/81	G	28		
20	Volkan Şen		07/07/87	M	14	(12)	
53	Yiğithan Güveli		16/05/98	D	1		

TURKEY

Galatasaray AŞ

1905 • Türk Telekom Stadyumu (52,600) • galatasaray.org

Major honours
UEFA Cup (1) 2000; UEFA Super Cup (1) 2000; Turkish League (20) 1962, 1963, 1969, 1971, 1972, 1973, 1987, 1988, 1993, 1994, 1997, 1998, 1999, 2000, 2002, 2006, 2008, 2012, 2013, 2015; Turkish Cup (17) 1963, 1964, 1965, 1966, 1973, 1976, 1982, 1985, 1991, 1993, 1996, 1999, 2000, 2005, 2014, 2015, 2016

Coach: Jan Olde Riekerink (NED); (15/02/17) Igor Tudor (CRO)

Date		Opponent		Score	Scorers
2016					
22/08	h	Karabükspor	W	1-0	*Derdiyok*
27/08	a	Akhisar	W	3-1	*Derdiyok, Yasin, Bruma*
10/09	a	Kayserispor	D	1-1	*Yasin*
17/09	h	Rizespor	W	2-0	*Derdiyok 2*
24/09	a	Beşiktaş	D	2-2	*Derdiyok, Bruma*
02/10	h	Antalyaspor	W	3-1	*Selçuk, Podolski 2*
15/10	a	Gençlerbirliği	W	1-0	*Bruma*
22/10	h	Trabzonspor	L	0-1	
29/10	a	Adanaspor	W	1-0	*Bruma*
04/11	h	İstanbul Başakşehir	L	1-2	*Sinan*
20/11	a	Fenerbahçe	L	0-2	
25/11	h	Bursaspor	W	3-1	*Yasin, Sneijder, Derdiyok*
04/12	a	Kasımpaşa	W	2-1	*Podolski, Bruma*
11/12	h	Gaziantepspor	W	3-1	*Yasin 3*
18/12	a	Osmanlıspor	D	2-2	*Yasin, Semih*
25/12	h	Alanyaspor	W	5-1	*De Jong, og (Gassama), Sneijder, Derdiyok, Josué*
2017					
14/01	a	Konyaspor	W	1-0	*Sabri*
21/01	a	Karabükspor	L	1-2	*Yasin*
28/01	h	Akhisar	W	6-0	*Semih, Bruma 2, Yasin, Selçuk (p), Sinan*
12/02	h	Kayserispor	L	1-2	*Derdiyok*
18/02	a	Rizespor	D	1-1	*Podolski*
27/02	h	Beşiktaş	L	0-1	
06/03	a	Antalyaspor	W	3-2	*Bruma, Derdiyok 2*
11/03	h	Gençlerbirliği	W	3-2	*Selçuk 2 (1p), Podolski*
18/03	a	Trabzonspor	L	0-2	
03/04	h	Adanaspor	W	4-0	*Podolski, Mendes Rodrigues, Selçuk 2 (2p)*
10/04	a	İstanbul Başakşehir	L	0-4	
23/04	h	Fenerbahçe	L	0-1	
01/05	a	Bursaspor	W	5-0	*Bruma 2, Ahmet, Podolski, Yasin*
06/05	h	Kasımpaşa	L	1-3	*Sneijder*
14/05	a	Gaziantepspor	W	2-1	*Josué, Sneijder*
19/05	h	Osmanlıspor	W	2-0	*Sneijder, Sinan*
29/05	a	Alanyaspor	W	3-2	*Bruma, Sinan 2*
03/06	h	Konyaspor	W	2-1	*Sinan 2*

No	Name	Nat	DoB	Pos	Aps	(s)	Gls
3	Ahmet Çalık		26/02/94	D	12	(2)	1
20	Bruma	POR	24/10/94	M	30		11
23	Lionel Carole	FRA	12/04/91	D	26		
39	Luis Cavanda	BEL	02/01/91	D	3	(4)	
21	Aurélien Chedjou	CMR	20/06/85	D	14	(1)	
34	Nigel de Jong	NED	30/11/84	M	12	(6)	1
9	Eren Derdiyok	SUI	12/06/88	A	18	(13)	10
22	Hakan Balta		23/03/83	D	22		
5	Hamit Altıntop		08/12/82	M		(4)	
30	Josué	POR	17/09/90	M	9	(15)	2
14	Martin Linnes	NOR	20/09/91	D	13	(5)	
16	Garry Mendes Rodrigues	CPV	27/11/90	M	5	(11)	1
1	Fernando Muslera	URU	16/06/86	G	34		
11	Lukas Podolski	GER	04/06/85	A	19	(7)	7
55	Sabri Sarıoğlu		26/07/84	D	25	(3)	1
8	Selçuk İnan		10/02/85	M	32		6
26	Semih Kaya		24/02/91	D	18	(2)	2
4	Serdar Aziz		23/10/90	D	5		
18	Sinan Gümüş		15/01/94	M	7	(11)	7
10	Wesley Sneijder	NED	09/06/84	M	25	(3)	5
27	Tolga Ciğerci		23/03/92	M	20	(4)	
7	Yasin Öztekin		19/03/87	M	25	(3)	10

Gaziantepspor

1969 • Kamil Ocak (16,981); Gaziantep Stadyumu (35,502) • gaziantepspor.org.tr

Coach: İsmail Kartal; (07/12/16) (Tahsin Tan); (12/12/16) İbrahim Üzülmez; (24/01/17) Bülent Uygum

Date		Opponent		Score	Scorers
2016					
21/08	a	Gençlerbirliği	L	0-2	
27/08	h	Trabzonspor	W	1-0	*Orkan*
10/09	a	Adanaspor	D	0-0	
18/09	h	İstanbul Başakşehir	L	0-1	
25/09	a	Fenerbahçe	L	1-2	*Ghilas*
01/10	h	Bursaspor	W	3-2	*Ghilas, Kangwa 2*
15/10	a	Kasımpaşa	D	0-0	
21/10	h	Kayserispor	L	1-2	*Ghilas (p)*
29/10	h	Osmanlıspor	W	3-1	*İlhan, Angan, og (Vršajević)*
05/11	a	Alanyaspor	L	3-4	*og (Omeruo), Kangwa, İlhan (p)*
19/11	h	Konyaspor	L	0-3	
26/11	a	Karabükspor	L	0-2	
04/12	h	Akhisar	L	1-2	*Musa*
11/12	a	Galatasaray	L	1-3	*Elyasa*
18/12	h	Rizespor	L	1-2	*Van Hintum*
24/12	a	Beşiktaş	L	0-1	
2017					
15/01	h	Antalyaspor	L	0-3	
29/01	a	Trabzonspor	L	0-4	
13/02	h	Adanaspor	W	1-0	*Ben-Hatira*
18/02	a	İstanbul Başakşehir	D	0-0	
26/02	h	Fenerbahçe	D	1-1	*Sefa*
04/03	a	Bursaspor	L	1-2	*Marcinho*
11/03	h	Kasımpaşa	L	0-2	
18/03	a	Kayserispor	W	4-3	*Ghilas 3, İlhan*
02/04	a	Osmanlıspor	W	2-0	*Ghilas, Ben-Hatira*
08/04	h	Alanyaspor	L	2-3	*Marquinhos Pedroso, Ghilas (p)*
12/04	h	Gençlerbirliği	L	0-1	
21/04	a	Konyaspor	W	2-1	*Kangwa, Muhammet*
28/04	h	Karabükspor	D	0-0	
08/05	a	Akhisar	L	0-6	
14/05	h	Galatasaray	L	1-2	*Thiam*
20/05	a	Rizespor	L	0-2	
28/05	h	Beşiktaş	L	0-4	
02/06	a	Antalyaspor	L	1-4	*Serkan*

No	Name	Nat	DoB	Pos	Aps	(s)	Gls
5	Abdülkadir Kayalı		30/01/91	M	19	(5)	
17	Alpay Koçaklı		19/09/98	D	2	(5)	
19	Davy Claude Angan	CIV	20/09/87	M	8	(10)	1
26	Barış Yardımcı		16/08/92	D	28		
32	Änis Ben-Hatira	TUN	18/07/88	M	12	(2)	2
22	Bruno Mota	BRA	22/05/95	M	2	(2)	
8	Doğanay Kılıç		08/06/96	M	5	(2)	
3	Elyasa Süme		13/08/83	D	25	(3)	1
7	Emre Nefiz		24/11/94	M	3	(2)	
34	Eren Ersu		21/04/94	G	2		
66	Mohammed Fatau	GHA	24/12/92	M	17	(4)	
99	Nabil Ghilas	ALG	20/04/90	A	28	(1)	8
83	Gökhan Değirmenci		21/03/89	G	13		
20	Muhammet Ildiz	AUT	14/05/91	M	17	(2)	
1	Charles Itandje	CMR	02/11/82	G	5		
23	İlhan Parlak		18/01/87	A	16	(8)	3
11	Evans Kangwa	ZAM	21/06/94	M	14	(10)	4
15	Sergei Kislyak	BLR	06/08/87	M	10	(2)	
85	Daniel Kolář	CZE	27/10/85	M	8	(3)	
9	Daniel Larsson	SWE	15/01/87	M	9	(3)	
70	Marcinho	BRA	14/05/86	M	12	(1)	1
2	Marquinhos Pedroso	BRA	04/10/93	D	14		1
18	Muhammet Demir		10/01/92	A	2	(5)	1
77	Musa Nizam		08/09/90	D	15	(2)	1
10	Orkan Çınar		29/01/96	M	5	(10)	1
48	Paulo Victor	BRA	12/01/87	G	14		
14	Anton Putilo	BLR	10/06/87	M	5	(8)	
27	František Rajtoral	CZE	12/03/86	D	11	(1)	
61	Sefa Yılmaz		14/02/90	M	9	(4)	1
97	Serkan Bakan		01/01/01	M	1	(1)	1
6	Şenol Can		03/04/83	D	3	(1)	
55	Khaly Thiam	SEN	07/01/94	M	11		1
4	Bart van Hintum	NED	16/01/87	D	15		1
25	Wallace	BRA	26/12/87	D	14		
93	Yunus Şencay		04/02/97	M		(1)	

Gençlerbirliği SK

1923 • 19 Mayıs (19,209) • genclerbirligi.org.tr

Major honours
Turkish Cup (2) 1987, 2001

Coach: İbrahim Üzülmez; (08/11/16) Ümit Özat

Date		Opponent		Score	Scorers
2016					
21/08	h	Gaziantepspor	W	2-0	*Stancu, Muriqi*
28/08	a	Osmanlıspor	D	2-2	*Serdar, Stancu (p)*
10/09	h	Alanyaspor	D	0-0	
18/09	a	Konyaspor	D	1-1	*Serdar*
25/09	h	Karabükspor	W	2-0	*Landel, İrfan Can*
30/09	a	Akhisar	D	0-0	
15/10	h	Galatasaray	L	0-1	
21/10	a	Rizespor	L	1-2	*Muriqi*
28/10	h	Beşiktaş	D	1-1	*Serdar*
05/11	a	Antalyaspor	L	0-1	
20/11	a	Kayserispor	W	2-0	*Matei, Serdar*
27/11	h	Trabzonspor	D	0-0	
04/12	a	Adanaspor	W	2-0	*Serdar (p), Rantie*
10/12	h	İstanbul Başakşehir	D	0-0	
19/12	a	Fenerbahçe	L	0-3	
26/12	h	Bursaspor	W	3-1	*Serdar 2, Uğur*
2017					
15/01	a	Kasımpaşa	L	0-3	
29/01	h	Osmanlıspor	D	1-1	*Serdar (p)*
11/02	a	Alanyaspor	L	0-3	
19/02	h	Konyaspor	W	2-0	*Serdar 2*
26/02	a	Karabükspor	L	0-1	
05/03	h	Akhisar	W	2-0	*Luccas Claro, Aydın*
11/03	a	Galatasaray	L	2-3	*Khalili, Selçuk (p)*
19/03	h	Rizespor	W	1-0	*Aydın*
02/04	a	Beşiktaş	L	0-3	
08/04	h	Antalyaspor	D	1-1	*Aydın*
12/04	a	Gaziantepspor	W	1-0	*Serdar*
22/04	h	Kayserispor	W	2-1	*Serdar 2*
29/04	a	Trabzonspor	D	0-0	
06/05	h	Adanaspor	L	0-1	
13/05	a	İstanbul Başakşehir	L	1-2	*Rantie*
22/05	h	Fenerbahçe	L	1-2	*Selçuk*
28/05	a	Bursaspor	W	2-1	*Rantie, Issah*
02/06	h	Kasımpaşa	W	1-0	*Muriqi*

No	Name	Nat	DoB	Pos	Aps	(s)	Gls
5	Ahmet Çalık		26/02/94	D	16		
2	Ahmet Oğuz		16/01/93	D	31		
79	Anıl Karaer		04/07/88	D	13		
20	Aydın Karabulut		25/01/88	M	25	(6)	3
22	Bady	BRA	27/04/89	M	2	(5)	
4	Fernat Görgülü		28/10/91	D		(1)	
33	Halil İbrahim Pehlivan		21/08/93	D	1	(1)	
1	Johannes Hopf	SWE	16/06/87	G	32		
23	Kamal Issah	GHA	30/08/92	M	14	(7)	1
17	İrfan Can Kahveci		15/07/95	M	12	(3)	1
55	Abdul Khalili	SWE	07/06/92	M	26	(3)	1
66	Ante Kulušić	CRO	06/06/86	D	5	(1)	
16	Guy-Michel Landel	GUI	07/07/90	M	9	(3)	1
12	Luccas Claro	BRA	02/10/91	D	17		1
30	Cosmin Matei	ROU	30/09/91	M	2	(10)	1
18	Agon Mehmeti	ALB	20/11/89	A		(1)	
11	Marko Milinković	SRB	16/04/88	M	3	(8)	
77	Murat Duruer		15/01/88	M	3	(6)	
12	Nihat Şahin		15/09/89	G	2		
9	Vedat Muriqi	KOS	24/04/94	A	15	(18)	3
67	Orhan Şam		01/06/86	D	3		
15	Sergei Politevich	BLR	09/04/90	D	28		
31	Tokelo Rantie	RSA	08/09/90	A	10	(10)	3
14	Jonathan Ring	SWE	05/12/91	M	2	(4)	
21	Selçuk Şahin		31/01/81	M	28		2
7	Serdar Gürler		14/09/91	M	31		13
10	Bogdan Stancu	ROU	28/06/87	A	9	(1)	2
8	Aleksandar Šćekić	MNE	12/12/91	M	3	(8)	
3	Uğur Çiftçi		04/05/92	D	28	(2)	1
93	Umut Sözen		27/01/90	M	1	(1)	
88	Etien Velikonja	SVN	26/12/88	A	3	(3)	

İstanbul Başakşehir

2014 • Başakşehir Fatih Terim (17,300) • ibfk.com.tr

Coach: Abdullah Avcı

2016

21/08	h	Fenerbahçe	W	1-0	*Mossoró*
28/08	a	Bursaspor	W	2-0	*Mossoró, Mustafa*
10/09	h	Kasımpaşa	W	3-1	*Višća, Mossoró, Hakan*
18/09	a	Gaziantepspor	W	1-0	*og (Van Hintum)*
24/09	h	Osmanlıspor	D	2-2	*Napoleoni 2*
02/10	a	Alanyaspor	W	5-0	*Višća, Mehmet, Epureanu, Cengiz, Mustafa*
16/10	h	Konyaspor	D	1-1	*Mehmet*
23/10	a	Karabükspor	W	2-0	*Emre (p), Mehmet*
30/10	h	Akhisar	W	5-1	*Cengiz, Višća 2, Mahmut, Mossoró*
04/11	a	Galatasaray	W	2-1	*Mehmet, Yalçın*
21/11	h	Rizespor	W	2-1	*Emre, Epureanu*
26/11	a	Beşiktaş	D	1-1	*Cengiz*
03/12	h	Antalyaspor	D	2-2	*Mahmut, Mossoró*
10/12	a	Gençlerbirliği	D	0-0	
17/12	h	Trabzonspor	W	1-0	*Višća*
24/12	a	Adanaspor	D	1-1	*Attamah*

2017

14/01	h	Kayserispor	W	5-0	*Mehmet, Emre (p), Višća, og (Stevanović), Cengiz*
22/01	a	Fenerbahçe	L	0-1	
29/01	h	Bursaspor	W	1-0	*İrfan Can*
12/02	a	Kasımpaşa	L	0-4	
18/02	h	Gaziantepspor	D	0-0	
26/02	a	Osmanlıspor	W	1-0	*Mustafa*
05/03	h	Alanyaspor	W	2-1	*Višća, Mustafa*
12/03	a	Konyaspor	W	3-0	*Yalçın, Adebayor, Cengiz*
19/03	h	Karabükspor	D	3-3	*Doka Madureira, Višća, Adebayor*
01/04	a	Akhisar	L	1-2	*Yalçın*
10/04	h	Galatasaray	W	4-0	*Adebayor 3, Mustafa*
22/04	a	Rizespor	D	3-3	*Alparslan, Mustafa, Emre (p)*
30/04	h	Beşiktaş	W	3-1	*Cengiz 2, Adebayor*
05/05	a	Antalyaspor	W	1-0	*Napoleoni*
13/05	h	Gençlerbirliği	W	2-1	*Mossoró, Mustafa*
21/05	a	Trabzonspor	D	0-0	
27/05	h	Adanaspor	W	2-1	*Doka Madureira, Napoleoni*
03/06	a	Kayserispor	W	1-0	*Bekir*

No	Name	Nat	DoB	Pos	Aps	(s)	Gls
26	Emmanuel Adebayor	TOG	26/02/84	A	10	(1)	6
39	Alparslan Erdem		11/12/88	D	9	(1)	1
15	Joseph Attamah	GHA	22/05/94	M	11	(4)	1
14	Bekir Irtegün		20/04/84	D	10	(1)	1
17	Cengiz Ünder		14/07/97	M	31	(1)	7
34	Cenk Ahmet Alkılıç		09/12/87	M	2	(1)	
99	Sokol Çikalleshi	ALB	27/07/90	A	1	(1)	
29	Cheikhou Dieng	SEN	23/11/93	M		(1)	
10	Doka Madureira	BRA	11/02/84	M	2	(9)	2
25	Emre Belözoğlu		07/09/80	M	26	(1)	4
6	Alexandru Epureanu	MDA	27/09/86	D	30		2
11	Eren Albayrak		23/04/91	D	18	(6)	
3	Ferhat Öztorun		08/05/87	D	7	(1)	
20	Hakan Özmert		03/06/85	M	2	(7)	1
23	Samuel Holmén	SWE	28/06/84	M	7	(10)	
77	İrfan Can Kahveci		15/07/95	M	5	(7)	1
80	Júnior Caiçara	BRA	27/04/89	D	13	(1)	
21	Mahmut Tekdemir		20/01/88	M	24	(2)	2
9	Mehmet Batdal		24/02/86	A	18	(3)	5
8	Mossoró	BRA	04/07/83	M	31	(1)	6
19	Mustafa Pektemek		11/08/88	A	4	(27)	7
18	Stefano Napoleoni	ITA	26/06/86	A	3	(13)	4
86	Ufuk Ceylan		23/06/86	G	1		
33	Uğur Uçar		05/04/87	D	17	(1)	
7	Edin Višća	BIH	17/02/90	M	32	(2)	8
1	Volkan Babacan		11/08/88	G	33		
2	Yalçın Ayhan		01/05/82	D	27		3

Kardemir Karabükspor

1969 • Dr Necmettin Şeyhoğlu (12,400) • kardemirkarabukspor.org.tr

Coach: Igor Tudor (CRO); (15/02/17) (Levent Açıkgöz); (21/02/17) Zoran Barisic (AUT)

2016

22/08	a	Galatasaray	L	0-1	
28/08	h	Rizespor	W	3-0	*Yatabaré, Traoré, Skúlason*
10/09	a	Beşiktaş	L	1-3	*Traoré*
16/09	h	Antalyaspor	W	3-2	*Tănase, Traoré 2*
25/09	a	Gençlerbirliği	L	0-2	
01/10	h	Trabzonspor	W	4-0	*Yatabaré, Latovlevici, Traoré, og (Zeki)*
15/10	a	Adanaspor	W	2-1	*Traoré, Zec*
23/10	h	İstanbul Başakşehir	L	0-2	
30/10	a	Fenerbahçe	L	0-5	
05/11	h	Bursaspor	D	0-0	
20/11	a	Kasımpaşa	D	2-2	*Skúlason, Barış*
26/11	h	Gaziantepspor	W	2-0	*Yatabaré, Traoré (p)*
04/12	a	Osmanlıspor	L	1-2	*Latovlevici*
11/12	h	Alanyaspor	L	0-2	
18/12	h	Konyaspor	D	1-1	*Yatabaré*
25/12	a	Kayserispor	L	0-2	

2017

14/01	h	Akhisar	W	1-0	*Latovlevici*
21/01	h	Galatasaray	W	2-1	*Seleznyov (p), Serdar*
28/01	a	Rizespor	L	0-1	
10/02	h	Beşiktaş	W	2-1	*Zec, Seleznyov*
18/02	a	Antalyaspor	L	0-1	
26/02	h	Gençlerbirliği	W	1-0	*Seleznyov (p)*
03/03	a	Trabzonspor	L	0-1	
11/03	h	Adanaspor	W	2-0	*Tănase 2*
19/03	a	İstanbul Başakşehir	D	3-3	*Seleznyov, Bliyznychenko, Papp*
01/04	h	Fenerbahçe	L	0-1	
07/04	a	Bursaspor	L	0-3	
21/04	h	Kasımpaşa	D	0-0	
28/03	a	Gaziantepspor	D	0-0	
08/05	h	Osmanlıspor	W	1-0	*Seleznyov (p)*
14/05	a	Alanyaspor	L	2-4	*Seleznyov (p), Yatabaré*
21/05	a	Konyaspor	L	0-3	
28/05	h	Kayserispor	D	2-2	*Serdar, Yatabaré*
02/06	a	Akhisar	W	3-2	*Zec 3 (1p)*

No	Name	Nat	DoB	Pos	Aps	(s)	Gls
1	Adriano	BRA	12/03/83	G	5	(1)	
78	Ahmet Şahin		22/03/78	G	26		
90	Marius Alexe	ROU	22/02/90	A		(1)	
22	Barış Başdaş		17/01/90	D	28	(1)	1
17	André Biyogo Poko	GAB	07/03/93	M	26	(2)	
97	Andriy Bliyznychenko	UKR	24/07/94	M	10	(2)	1
6	Ceyhun Gülselam		25/12/87	M	30		
34	Çınar Tarhan		20/05/97	M		(1)	
5	Valerică Găman	ROU	25/02/89	D	14	(3)	
99	Fatih Atik		25/06/84	M	1		
42	Hakan Aslantaş		26/08/85	D	5	(4)	
7	İlhan Depe		10/09/92	M	7	(17)	
68	İshak Doğan		08/08/90	D	1	(1)	
11	Kerim Zengin		13/04/85	D	15	(2)	
44	Elvis Kokalović	CRO	17/07/88	D	6	(2)	
14	Iasmin Latovlevici	ROU	11/05/86	D	30		3
21	Dejan Lazarevič	SVN	15/02/90	M	11	(9)	
24	Nahmut Akan		14/07/94	M		(1)	
13	Dany Nounkeu	CMR	11/04/86	D	31		
8	Osman Çelik		27/11/91	M	1	(3)	
4	Paul Papp	ROU	11/11/89	D	10	(2)	1
10	Isaac Promise	NGA	02/12/87	A		(3)	
20	Vladimir Rodić	MNE	07/09/93	M	1	(5)	
87	Olexandr Rybka	UKR	10/04/87	G	3		
29	Yevhen Seleznyov	UKR	20/07/85	A	15	(1)	6
23	Serdar Deliktaş		04/08/86	A	5	(11)	2
16	Ólafur Ingi Skúlason	ISL	01/04/83	M	18	(7)	2
25	Talha Sanuç		17/12/99	D		(1)	
30	Cristian Tănase	ROU	18/02/87	M	26	(3)	3
12	Abdou Traoré	BFA	28/12/88	A	16	(1)	7
9	Mustapha Yatabaré	MLI	26/01/86	A	19	(7)	6
28	Ermin Zec	BIH	18/02/88	M	14	(6)	5

Kasımpaşa SK

1921 • Recep Tayyip Erdoğan (14,234) • kasimpasaspor.org.tr

Coach: Rıza Çalımbay; (16/09/16) Kemal Özdeş

2016

20/08	a	Trabzonspor	L	0-2	
27/08	h	Adanaspor	D	1-1	*Shala*
10/09	a	İstanbul Başakşehir	L	1-3	*Otigba*
19/09	h	Fenerbahçe	L	1-5	*Tunay (p)*
25/09	a	Bursaspor	L	0-1	
01/10	h	Kayserispor	W	3-1	*Adem, Veysel, Batuhan*
15/10	h	Gaziantepspor	D	0-0	
23/10	a	Osmanlıspor	W	2-1	*Pavelka, Adem (p)*
31/10	h	Alanyaspor	W	2-1	*Adem, Turgut Doğan*
06/11	a	Konyaspor	L	1-2	*Adem*
20/11	h	Karabükspor	D	2-2	*André Castro, Titi*
26/11	a	Akhisar	L	0-1	
04/12	h	Galatasaray	L	1-2	*Eduok*
10/12	a	Rizespor	W	1-0	*Eduok*
17/12	h	Beşiktaş	W	2-1	*Tunay, og (Gökhan)*
25/12	a	Antalyaspor	L	1-2	*Koita*

2017

15/01	h	Gençlerbirliği	W	3-0	*Titi (p), Adem, Pavelka*
22/01	h	Trabzonspor	L	0-1	
30/01	a	Adanaspor	L	0-3	*(w/o; original result 0-2)*
12/02	h	İstanbul Başakşehir	W	4-0	*Titi, Adem, Eduok, André Castro*
19/02	a	Fenerbahçe	D	0-0	
24/02	h	Bursaspor	W	4-0	*Titi (p), Koita 2, Tunay*
05/03	a	Kayserispor	D	2-2	*Titi (p), André Castro*
11/03	a	Gaziantepspor	W	2-0	*André Castro, Guanca*
18/03	h	Osmanlıspor	W	3-2	*Adem 3*
01/04	a	Alanyaspor	L	1-3	*Koita*
10/04	h	Konyaspor	D	1-1	*Veysel*
21/04	a	Karabükspor	D	0-0	
30/04	h	Akhisar	L	0-2	
06/05	a	Galatasaray	W	3-1	*André Castro 2, Turgut Doğan*
12/05	h	Rizespor	W	4-2	*Guanca (p), Turgut Doğan, Titi, Batuhan*
20/05	a	Beşiktaş	L	1-4	*Eduok*
27/05	h	Antalyaspor	L	0-3	
02/06	a	Gençlerbirliği	L	0-1	

No	Name	Nat	DoB	Pos	Aps	(s)	Gls
5	Abdullah Durak		01/04/87	M	25	(3)	
10	Adem Büyük		30/08/87	M	24		9
66	Ahmed Ildız		29/11/96	M		(8)	
8	André Castro	POR	02/04/88	M	32	(1)	6
33	Batuhan Altıntaş		14/03/96	A	5	(9)	2
3	Vasil Bozhikov	BUL	02/06/88	D	4	(5)	
13	Samuel Eduok	NGA	31/01/94	M	20	(9)	4
34	Eray Birniçan		20/07/88	G	3		
14	Franck Etoundi	CMR	30/08/90	A	3	(1)	
20	Cristian Guanca	ARG	26/03/93	M	2	(10)	2
18	Hasan Bilal		12/08/98	M	2	(2)	
9	Bengali-Fodé Koita	FRA	21/10/90	A	16	(4)	4
10	Mert Ilıman		02/01/89	A		(5)	
2	Kenny Otigba	HUN	29/08/92	D	14	(1)	1
12	David Pavelka	CZE	18/05/91	M	21	(4)	2
90	Strahil Popov	BUL	31/08/90	D	32	(1)	
1	Ramazan Köse		12/05/88	G	31		
6	Loret Sadiku	KOS	28/07/91	M	22	(3)	
7	Herolind Shala	KOS	01/02/92	M	1	(9)	1
4	Titi	BRA	12/03/88	D	33		6
11	Tunay Torun		21/04/90	M	21	(4)	3
17	Turgut Doğan Şahin		02/02/88	M	8	(17)	3
31	Olivier Veigneau	FRA	16/07/85	D	30	(1)	
88	Veysel Sarı		25/07/88	D	25	(3)	2

TURKEY

Kayserispor

1966 • Kadir Has (32,864) • kayserispor.org.tr

Major honours
Turkish Cup (1) 2008

Coach: Hakan Kutlu; (06/12/16) (Ertuğrul Seçme); (11/01/17) Sergen Yalçın; (24/04/17) Mesut Bakkal

Date		Opponent		Score	Scorers
2016					
21/08	h	Akhisar	L	0-2	
28/08	a	Fenerbahçe	D	3-3	*Welliton 2, Budak*
10/09	h	Galatasaray	D	1-1	*Welliton*
16/09	a	Bursaspor	L	1-3	*Nakoulma*
25/09	h	Rizespor	W	2-1	*Sow, Welliton*
01/10	a	Kasımpaşa	L	1-3	*Welliton*
15/10	h	Beşiktaş	L	0-1	
21/10	a	Gaziantepspor	W	2-1	*Deniz 2 (1p)*
31/10	h	Antalyaspor	L	0-1	
06/11	a	Osmanlıspor	D	1-1	*Nakoulma*
20/11	h	Gençlerbirliği	L	0-2	
25/11	a	Alanyaspor	L	0-3	
05/12	h	Trabzonspor	L	0-1	
11/12	a	Konyaspor	L	0-1	
18/12	a	Adanaspor	L	1-2	*Deniz*
25/12	h	Karabükspor	W	2-0	*Deniz (p), Welliton*
2017					
14/01	a	İstanbul Başakşehir	L	0-5	
21/01	a	Akhisar	D	0-0	
29/01	h	Fenerbahçe	W	4-1	*Umut Bulut, Güray 2, Welliton*
12/02	a	Galatasaray	W	2-1	*Mabiala, Levent*
17/02	h	Bursaspor	W	2-0	*Welliton, Rotman*
24/02	a	Rizespor	W	4-2	*Lawal, Güray, Welliton 2*
05/03	h	Kasımpaşa	D	2-2	*Deniz, Lawal*
12/03	a	Beşiktaş	D	2-2	*Umut Bulut, og (Beck)*
18/03	h	Gaziantepspor	L	3-4	*Umut Bulut, Deniz 2 (1p)*
01/04	a	Antalyaspor	L	1-2	*Ryan Mendes*
09/04	h	Osmanlıspor	L	1-4	*Deniz (p)*
22/04	a	Gençlerbirliği	L	1-2	*Deniz (p)*
29/04	h	Alanyaspor	W	3-0	*Mabiala, Welliton 2*
06/05	a	Trabzonspor	W	3-2	*Deniz, Lawal 2*
12/05	h	Konyaspor	W	2-1	*Mabiala, Lawal*
20/05	h	Adanaspor	D	1-1	*Sow*
28/05	a	Karabükspor	D	2-2	*Umut Bulut, Deniz*
03/06	h	İstanbul Başakşehir	L	0-1	

No	Name	Nat	DoB	Pos	Aps	(s)	Gls
16	Ali Ahamada	FRA	19/08/91	G	17	(1)	
3	Anıl Karaer		04/07/88	D	12	(2)	
27	Ufuk Budak	AZE	26/05/90	D	9	(3)	1
10	Deniz Türüç		29/01/93	M	32		11
2	Douglão	BRA	15/08/86	D	2	(3)	
38	Efe Halil Özarslan		29/03/90	D	1		
26	Erdem Beytaş		30/04/98	M		(2)	
89	Erkam Reşmen		29/11/89	D	3	(1)	
23	Erkan Kaş		10/09/91	D	12	(1)	
14	Furkan Yaman		08/01/96	A	1	(1)	
77	Güray Vural		11/06/88	M	12	(1)	3
42	Hakan Aslantaş		26/08/85	D	13	(3)	
76	Jean-Armel Kana-Biyik	CMR	03/07/89	D	25	(2)	
8	Kubilay Sönmez		17/06/94	M	11	(7)	
12	Raheem Lawal	NGA	04/05/90	M	16		5
4	Levent Gülen		24/02/94	D	28	(2)	1
6	Larrys Mabiala	COD	08/10/87	D	28		3
19	Mert Ilıman		08/10/95	M	1	(1)	
30	Mert Özyıldırım		28/02/95	D		(3)	
35	Srdjan Mijailović	SRB	10/11/93	M	13	(2)	
1	Muammer Yıldırım		14/09/90	G	17	(1)	
17	Murat Duruer		15/01/88	M	3	(4)	
22	Prejuce Nakoulma	BFA	21/04/87	M	13		2
24	Landry N'Guémo	CMR	28/11/85	M		(9)	
5	Rajko Rotman	SVN	19/03/89	M	16		1
34	Ryan Mendes	CPV	08/01/90	A	1	(5)	1
7	Samba Sow	MLI	29/04/89	M	18	(7)	2
15	Miladin Stevanović	SRB	11/02/96	D	1	(1)	
20	Alain Traoré	BFA	31/12/88	M	3	(9)	
9	Umut Bulut		15/03/83	A	26	(4)	4
13	Umut Sönmez		20/06/93	M	6	(8)	
18	Silvestre Varela	POR	02/02/85	A	11	(4)	
11	Welliton	BRA	22/10/86	A	23	(5)	12

Konyaspor

1922 • Konya Büyükşehir (41,981) • konyaspor.org.tr

Major honours
Turkish Cup (1) 2017

Coach: Aykut Kocaman

Date		Opponent		Score	Scorers
2016					
20/08	a	Rizespor	D	1-1	*Vuković*
26/08	h	Beşiktaş	D	2-2	*Bajić 2*
11/09	a	Antalyaspor	W	3-1	*Ömer Ali 2, Rangelov*
18/09	h	Gençlerbirliği	D	1-1	*og (Uğur)*
24/09	a	Trabzonspor	L	0-1	
02/10	h	Adanaspor	W	1-0	*Vuković*
16/10	a	İstanbul Başakşehir	D	1-1	*Bajić*
24/10	h	Fenerbahçe	L	0-1	
29/10	a	Bursaspor	L	0-2	
06/11	h	Kasımpaşa	W	2-1	*Ömer Ali, Bajić*
19/11	a	Gaziantepspor	W	3-0	*Bajić 2, Hadžiahmetović*
28/11	h	Osmanlıspor	D	1-1	*Bajić*
04/12	a	Alanyaspor	W	3-2	*og (Berkan), Bajić, Vuković (p)*
11/12	h	Kayserispor	W	1-0	*Ali Çamdalı*
18/12	a	Karabükspor	D	1-1	*Rangelov*
25/12	a	Akhisar	L	0-1	
2017					
14/01	h	Galatasaray	L	0-1	
21/01	h	Rizespor	W	2-1	*Milošević, Bajić*
30/01	a	Beşiktaş	L	1-5	*og (Tošić)*
12/02	h	Antalyaspor	D	1-1	*Bajić*
19/02	a	Gençlerbirliği	L	0-2	
25/02	h	Trabzonspor	D	1-1	*Rangelov*
05/03	a	Adanaspor	W	1-0	*Jønsson*
12/03	h	İstanbul Başakşehir	L	0-3	
17/03	a	Fenerbahçe	W	3-2	*Bajić 2, Ömer Ali*
02/04	h	Bursaspor	W	2-0	*Skubic, Milošević*
10/04	a	Kasımpaşa	D	1-1	*Bajić*
21/04	h	Gaziantepspor	L	1-2	*Vuković (p)*
01/05	a	Osmanlıspor	D	0-0	
06/05	h	Alanyaspor	L	2-3	*Bajić 2*
12/05	a	Kayserispor	L	1-2	*Bajić*
21/05	h	Karabükspor	W	3-0	*Bajic, Ömer Ali, Hora*
27/05	h	Akhisar	L	0-3	
03/06	a	Galatasaray	L	1-2	*Selim*

No	Name	Nat	DoB	Pos	Aps	(s)	Gls
25	Abdülaziz Demircan		05/02/91	G	1		
42	Abdülkerim Bardakçı		07/09/94	D	4	(2)	
8	Ali Çamdalı		22/02/84	M	25	(5)	1
17	Ali Dere		29/09/92	M	1	(1)	
4	Ali Turan		06/09/83	D	23	(2)	
10	Riad Bajić	BIH	06/05/94	A	25	(7)	17
19	Can Demir Aktav		31/08/94	D		(1)	
3	Barry Douglas	SCO	04/09/89	D	20	(2)	
15	Emre Can Atila		02/09/96	M		(1)	
21	Moryké Fofana	CIV	23/11/91	M	7	(6)	
18	Amir Hadžiahmetović	BIH	08/03/97	M	25	(5)	1
61	Halil İbrahim Sönmez		01/10/90	A	7	(13)	
88	Ioan Hora	ROU	21/08/88	A	3	(11)	1
6	Jens Jønsson	DEN	10/01/93	M	21	(3)	1
1	Kaya Tarakçı		23/04/81	G	3		
14	Marc Mbamba	CMR	15/10/88	M	4	(3)	
27	Alban Meha	KOS	26/04/86	M	6	(9)	
54	Mehmet Uslu		25/02/88	D	14		
11	Deni Milošević	BIH	09/03/95	M	20	(11)	2
7	Ömer Ali Şahiner		02/01/92	M	26	(5)	5
9	Dimitar Rangelov	BUL	09/02/83	A	19	(7)	3
5	Selim Ay		31/07/91	D	6	(2)	1
30	Serkan Kırıntılı		15/02/85	G	30		
89	Nejc Skubic	SVN	13/06/89	D	31		1
2	Volkan Fındıklı		13/10/90	M	26	(5)	
26	Jagoš Vuković	SRB	10/06/88	D	27		4

Osmanlıspor

1978 • Osmanlı (19,626) • osmanlispor.com.tr

Coach: Mustafa Akçay; (22/03/17) Hamza Hamzaoğlu

Date		Opponent		Score	Scorers
2016					
21/08	a	Antalyaspor	D	0-0	
28/08	h	Gençlerbirliği	D	2-2	*Delarge, Mehmet*
11/09	a	Trabzonspor	W	2-0	*Ndiaye, Rusescu*
18/09	h	Adanaspor	W	1-0	*Ndiaye*
24/09	a	İstanbul Başakşehir	D	2-2	*Musa, Ndiaye (p)*
02/10	h	Fenerbahçe	D	1-1	*Ndiaye (p)*
16/10	a	Bursaspor	D	0-0	
23/10	h	Kasımpaşa	L	1-2	*Ndiaye*
29/10	a	Gaziantepspor	L	1-3	*Umar*
06/11	h	Kayserispor	D	1-1	*Mehmet*
19/11	h	Alanyaspor	W	2-0	*Webó, Musa*
28/11	a	Konyaspor	D	1-1	*og (Vuković)*
04/12	h	Karabükspor	W	2-1	*Musa, Numan*
11/12	a	Akhisar	W	2-1	*og (Serdar), Umar*
18/12	h	Galatasaray	D	2-2	*Webó 2*
25/12	a	Rizespor	W	1-0	*Musa (p)*
2017					
16/01	h	Beşiktaş	L	0-2	
22/01	h	Antalyaspor	L	1-2	*Webó*
29/01	a	Gençlerbirliği	D	1-1	*Musa*
11/02	h	Trabzonspor	L	0-1	
19/02	a	Adanaspor	W	5-1	*Ndiaye, Webó, Maher, Bifouma, Musa*
26/02	h	İstanbul Başakşehir	L	0-1	
05/03	a	Fenerbahçe	L	0-1	
11/03	h	Bursaspor	D	1-1	*Umar*
18/03	a	Kasımpaşa	L	2-3	*Webó 2*
02/04	h	Gaziantepspor	L	0-2	
09/04	a	Kayserispor	W	4-1	*Umar 2 (1p), Mehmet, Webó (p)*
22/04	a	Alanyaspor	W	1-0	*Webó*
01/05	h	Konyaspor	D	0-0	
08/05	a	Karabükspor	L	0-1	
14/05	h	Akhisar	L	0-4	
19/05	a	Galatasaray	L	0-2	
28/05	h	Rizespor	L	1-2	*Maher*
03/06	a	Beşiktaş	L	0-4	

No	Name	Nat	DoB	Pos	Aps	(s)	Gls
13	Ahmet Eyüp Türkaslan		11/09/94	G	1		
5	Aykut Demir		22/10/88	D	6	(3)	
39	Thievy Bifouma	CGO	13/05/92	A	11	(5)	1
54	Burak Ağaoğlu		23/03/99	A		(1)	
28	Dzon Delarge	CGO	24/06/90	M	11	(10)	1
14	Cheick Diabaté	MLI	25/04/88	A	3	(5)	
7	Engin Bekdemir		07/02/92	M	1	(2)	
11	Erdal Kılıçaslan		23/08/84	M	1	(14)	
1	Hakan Arıkan		17/08/82	G	6		
99	Žydrūnas Karčemarskas	LTU	24/05/83	G	27		
4	Koray Altınay		11/10/91	D	6	(4)	
8	Raheem Lawal	NGA	04/05/90	M		(3)	
20	Luíz Carlos	BRA	05/07/85	M	8	(3)	
93	Adam Maher	NED	20/07/93	M	15	(9)	2
6	Mehmet Güven		30/07/87	M	26	(1)	3
33	Muhammed Bayır		05/02/89	D	14	(4)	
35	Musa Çağıran		17/11/92	M	23	(3)	6
10	Pape Alioune Ndiaye	SEN	27/10/90	M	26		6
61	Numan Çürüksu		02/12/84	D	32		1
21	Václav Procházka	CZE	08/05/84	D	29		
17	Adrien Regattin	MAR	22/08/91	M	23	(5)	
24	Raul Rusescu	ROU	09/07/88	A	6	(16)	1
22	Sinan Kurt		02/03/95	M		(1)	
3	Łukasz Szukała	POL	26/05/84	D	1	(1)	
15	Tiago Pinto	POR	01/02/88	D	25		
40	Tugay Kaçar		01/01/94	M		(1)	
27	Aminu Umar	NGA	06/03/95	M	22	(3)	5
2	Avdija Vršajević	BIH	06/03/86	D	25	(1)	
9	Pierre Webó	CMR	20/01/82	A	26	(3)	9

Rizespor

1953 • Yeni Rize Şehir (15,485) •
caykurrizespor.org.tr

Coach: Hikmet Karaman

Date		Opponent		Score	Scorers
2016					
20/08	h	Konyaspor	D	1-1	*Emrah*
28/08	a	Karabükspor	L	0-3	
11/09	h	Akhisar	W	1-0	*Atiemwen*
17/09	a	Galatasaray	L	0-2	
25/09	a	Kayserispor	L	1-2	*Jantscher (p)*
01/10	h	Beşiktaş	L	0-1	
17/10	a	Antalyaspor	D	1-1	*Ahmet İlhan*
21/10	h	Gençlerbirliği	W	2-1	*Jantscher, Kweuke (p)*
30/10	a	Trabzonspor	D	2-2	*Kweuke 2*
06/11	h	Adanaspor	D	2-2	*Jantscher, Robin*
21/11	a	İstanbul Başakşehir	L	1-2	*Jantscher*
27/11	h	Fenerbahçe	L	1-5	*Yacoubi*
05/12	a	Bursaspor	L	1-2	*Recep*
10/12	h	Kasımpaşa	L	0-1	
18/12	a	Gaziantepspor	W	2-1	*Kweuke, Saâdane*
25/12	h	Osmanlıspor	L	0-1	
2017					
14/01	a	Alanyaspor	W	3-2	*Kweuke 2, Ismail*
21/01	a	Konyaspor	L	1-2	*Recep*
28/01	h	Karabükspor	W	1-0	*Kweuke*
12/02	a	Akhisar	L	0-1	
18/02	h	Galatasaray	D	1-1	*Özgür*
24/02	h	Kayserispor	L	2-4	*Kweuke 2 (1p)*
04/03	a	Beşiktaş	L	0-1	
12/03	h	Antalyaspor	L	1-2	*Özgür*
19/03	a	Gençlerbirliği	L	0-1	
02/04	h	Trabzonspor	L	0-1	
09/04	a	Adanaspor	W	3-1	*Kweuke (p), Saâdane, Petrucci*
22/04	h	İstanbul Başakşehir	D	3-3	*Süleyman, og (Júnior Caiçara), Özgür (p)*
30/04	a	Fenerbahçe	L	1-2	*Aynaoğlu*
07/05	h	Bursaspor	W	6-0	*Kweuke 2, Oğulcan, Recep, Edomwonyi, Igiebor*
12/05	a	Kasımpaşa	L	2-4	*Jantscher, Recep*
20/05	h	Gaziantepspor	W	2-0	*Edomwonyi, Kweuke*
28/05	a	Osmanlıspor	W	2-1	*Petrucci, Kweuke*
03/06	h	Alanyaspor	W	1-0	*Süleyman (p)*

No	Name	Nat	DoB	Pos	Aps	(s)	Gls
78	Ahmet İlhan Özek		01/01/88	M	14	(4)	1
24	Iyayi Atiemwen	NGA	24/01/96	A	3	(1)	1
20	Oğuz Han Aynaoğlu	DEN	22/03/92	M	5	(6)	1
1	Abdoulaye Diallo	SEN	30/03/92	G	19		
34	Bright Edomwonyi	NGA	24/07/94	A	13	(3)	2
10	Emrah Başsan		17/04/92	M	7	(5)	1
5	Ali Faez	IRQ	09/09/94	D	12	(2)	
27	Matic Fink	SVN	27/02/90	D	7		
23	Gökhan Akkan		01/05/95	G	15		
40	Emmanuel Nosa Igiebor	NGA	09/11/90	M	6	(7)	1
53	Dhurgham Ismail	IRQ	23/05/94	D	29	(3)	1
7	Jakob Jantscher	AUT	08/01/89	M	21	(7)	5
9	Leonard Kweuke	CMR	12/07/87	A	25	(3)	14
17	Mehmet Akyüz		02/01/86	M	5	(10)	
2	Godfrey Oboabona	NGA	16/08/90	D	26		
19	Oğulcan Çağlayan		22/03/96	A	14	(11)	1
77	Orhan Ovacıklı		23/11/88	D	21	(2)	
60	Özgür Çek		03/01/91	D	9	(10)	3
4	Davide Petrucci	ITA	05/10/91	M	27	(3)	2
21	Recep Niyaz		01/01/95	M	13	(8)	4
6	Robin Yalçın		25/01/94	M	23	(3)	1
16	Marwane Saâdane	MAR	17/01/92	M	25	(2)	2
18	Süleyman Koç		09/06/89	D	8	(2)	2
8	Patryk Tuszyński	POL	13/12/89	A	7	(8)	
80	Ümit Kurt		02/05/91	D	17		
30	Mohamed Ali Yacoubi	TUN	05/10/90	D	3	(2)	1

Trabzonspor AŞ

1967 • Hüseyin Avni Aker (24,169);
Şenol Güneş Spor Kompleksi (41,513) •
trabzonspor.org.tr

Major honours
Turkish League (6) 1976, 1977, 1979, 1980, 1981, 1984; Turkish Cup (8) 1977, 1978, 1984, 1992, 1995, 2003, 2004, 2010

Coach: Ersun Yanal

Date		Opponent		Score	Scorers
2016					
20/08	h	Kasımpaşa	W	2-0	*Onazi 2*
27/08	a	Gaziantepspor	L	0-1	
11/09	h	Osmanlıspor	L	0-2	
17/09	a	Alanyaspor	L	0-3	
24/09	h	Konyaspor	W	1-0	*Yusuf Erdoğan*
01/10	a	Karabükspor	L	0-4	
16/10	h	Akhisar	D	0-0	
22/10	a	Galatasaray	W	1-0	*N'Doye*
30/10	h	Rizespor	D	2-2	*Mehmet, Uğur (p)*
05/11	a	Beşiktaş	L	1-2	*Yusuf Erdoğan*
21/11	h	Antalyaspor	L	0-1	
27/11	a	Gençlerbirliği	D	0-0	
05/12	a	Kayserispor	W	1-0	*Bero*
09/12	h	Adanaspor	W	4-1	*Yusuf Erdoğan 2, Mehmet 2 (1p)*
17/12	a	İstanbul Başakşehir	L	0-1	
26/12	h	Fenerbahçe	L	0-3	
2017					
13/01	a	Bursaspor	W	2-1	*Yusuf Yazıcı, Uğur*
22/01	a	Kasımpaşa	W	1-0	*Más*
29/01	h	Gaziantepspor	W	4-0	*Castillo 2, Yusuf Yazıcı, Uğur (p)*
11/02	a	Osmanlıspor	W	1-0	*Olcay*
20/02	h	Alanyaspor	D	0-0	
25/02	a	Konyaspor	D	1-1	*Rodallega*
03/03	h	Karabükspor	W	1-0	*Okay*
13/03	a	Akhisar	W	3-1	*N'Doye 2, Uğur (p)*
18/03	h	Galatasaray	W	2-0	*N'Doye, Yusuf Yazıcı*
02/04	a	Rizespor	W	1-0	*N'Doye*
08/04	h	Beşiktaş	L	3-4	*Okay, Castillo, Rodallega*
22/04	a	Antalyaspor	W	3-0	*Rodallega 2, Uğur*
29/04	h	Gençlerbirliği	D	0-0	
06/05	h	Kayserispor	L	2-3	*Rodallega, Uğur (p)*
13/05	a	Adanaspor	D	1-1	*Yusuf Yazıcı*
21/05	h	İstanbul Başakşehir	D	0-0	
27/05	a	Fenerbahçe	D	1-1	*Bero*
03/06	h	Bursaspor	L	1-2	*Rodallega*

No	Name	Nat	DoB	Pos	Aps	(s)	Gls
19	Abdülkadir Ömür		25/06/99	M		(2)	
33	Serge Akakpo	TOG	15/10/87	D	1	(3)	
23	Esteban Alvarado	CRC	28/04/89	G	2	(1)	
35	Aytaç Kara		28/03/93	M	8	(9)	
21	Matúš Bero	SVK	06/09/95	M	14	(9)	2
11	Fabián Castillo	COL	17/06/92	M	21	(7)	3
4	Ján Ďurica	SVK	10/12/81	D	27	(1)	
7	Güray Vural		11/06/88	M	6	(2)	
88	Luis Ibáñez	ARG	15/07/88	D	2	(3)	
47	João Pereira	POR	25/02/94	D	17		
3	Emmanuel Más	ARG	15/01/89	D	18		1
6	Carl Medjani	ALG	15/05/85	M	9	(4)	
8	Mehmet Ekici		25/03/90	M	15		3
10	Muhammet Demir		10/01/92	A	4	(5)	
25	Mustafa Akbaş		30/05/90	D	11	(4)	
22	Mustafa Yumlu		25/09/87	D	6	(2)	
14	Dame N'Doye	SEN	21/02/85	A	22	(5)	5
5	Okay Yokuşlu		09/03/94	M	27	(2)	2
20	Olcay Şahan		26/05/87	M	17		1
17	Ogenyi Onazi	NGA	25/12/92	M	30	(2)	2
1	Onur Kıvrak		01/01/88	G	32		
28	Hugo Rodallega	COL	25/07/85	A	10	(5)	6
90	Ramil Şeydayev	AZE	15/03/96	A		(1)	
9	Suk Hyun-jun	KOR	29/06/91	A	5	(5)	
15	Uğur Demirok		08/07/88	D	28		6
32	Yusuf Erdoğan		07/08/92	M	11	(13)	4
97	Yusuf Yazıcı		29/01/97	M	17	(1)	4
2	Zeki Yavru		05/09/91	D	14	(3)	

Top goalscorers

23	Vágner Love (Alanyaspor)
20	Cenk Tosun (Beşiktaş)
18	Samuel Eto'o (Antalyaspor)
17	Riad Bajić (Konyaspor)
14	Leonard Kweuke (Rizespor)
13	Talisca (Beşiktaş) Serdar Gürler (Gençlerbirliği)
12	Vincent Aboubakar (Beşiktaş) Moussa Sow (Fenerbahçe) Welliton (Kayserispor)

Promoted clubs

Sivasspor

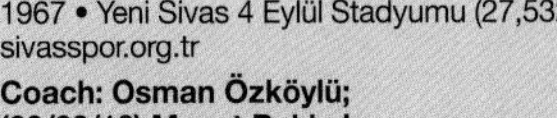

1967 • Yeni Sivas 4 Eylül Stadyumu (27,532) •
sivasspor.org.tr

Coach: Osman Özköylü;
(30/09/16) Mesut Bakkal;
(24/03/17) Samet Aybaba

Yeni Malatyaspor

1986 • Malatya İnönü (10,411) •
yenimalatyaspor.org.tr

Coach: İrfan Buz

Göztepe SK

1925 • İzmir Atatürk Stadyumu (51,295);
Bornova Stadyumu (6,041) • goztepe.org.tr

Major honours
Turkish Cup (2) 1969, 1970

Coach: Okan Buruk;
(22/03/17) Yılmaz Vural

Second level final table 2016/17

		Pld	W	D	L	F	A	Pts
1	Sivasspor	34	17	11	6	51	27	62
2	Yeni Malatyaspor	34	18	7	9	47	40	61
3	Eskişehirspor	34	16	11	7	62	44	56
4	Boluspor	33	16	6	12	56	53	54
5	Göztepe SK	34	15	8	11	55	51	53
6	Giresunspor	34	15	8	11	40	34	53
7	Altınordu	34	14	11	9	45	37	53
8	Ümraniyespor	34	12	12	10	42	38	48
9	Balıkesirspor	34	10	12	12	56	48	42
10	Elazığspor	34	12	11	11	43	35	41
11	Denizlispor	34	11	10	13	46	45	40
12	Manisaspor	34	11	9	14	47	53	39
13	Gaziantep BB	34	9	10	15	37	46	37
14	Adana Demirspor	34	8	15	11	47	51	36
15	Samsunspor	34	9	9	16	27	46	36
16	Şanlıurfaspor	34	9	9	16	38	46	36
17	Bandırmaspor	34	9	8	17	43	52	35
18	Mersin İdman Yurdu	34	6	11	17	35	71	26

NB Elazığspor – 6 pts deducted; Adana Demirspor, Denizlispor, Eskişehirspor, Manisaspor & Mersin İdman Yurdu– 3pts deducted.

Promotion play-offs

(25/05/17 & 29/05/17)
Giresunspor 3-3 Eskişehirspor
Eskişehirspor 1-0 Giresunspor
(Eskişehirspor 4-3)

Göztepe 2-0 Boluspor
Boluspor 0-2 Göztepe
(Göztepe 4-0)

(04/06/17)
Göztepe 1-1 Eskişehirspor *(aet; 3-2 on pens)*

DOMESTIC CUP

Türkiye Kupası 2016/17

SECOND ROUND

(20/09/16)
Afyonspor 2-1 Karşıyaka
Alanyaspor 0-1 Sancaktepe Belediye Spor
Elazığspor 6-4 Sarayönü Belediyespor
Ofspor 5-3 Karabükspor
Orhangazispor 2-3 Kayserispor *(aet)*

(21/09/16)
24 Erzincanspor 3-2 Adanaspor
Adana Demirspor 1-3 BB Erzurumspor
Amed Sportif Faaliyetler 2-0 Niğde Belediyespor
Ankara Adliye Spor 0-3 Menemen Belediye Spor
Bandırmaspor 3-1 Yeşil Bursa
Boluspor 4-0 Nevşehir Spor Gençlik
Büyükçekmece Tepecik Spor 2-2 Manavgatspor *(aet; 6-5 on pens)*
Cizre Spor 0-2 Aydınspor 1968
Darıca Gençlerbirliği 2-0 Ankaragücü
Dersim Spor 1-0 Eskişehirspor
Düzyurtspor 2-0 1461 Trabzon
Elaziz Belediyespor 4-2 Tokatspor
Hatayspor 0-1 Balıkesirspor
İnegölspor 3-0 Halide Edip Adıvarspor
Kahramanmaraşspor 2-1 Hacettepe Spor
Karagümrük 1-0 Giresunspor
Karaman Belediyespor 2-3 Gümüşhanespor
Kastamonuspor 1966 1-2 Tuzlaspor
Kayseri Erciyesspor 0-1 Yeni Amasya Spor
Keçiörengücü 2-0 Anadolu Üsküdar 1908 Spor
Kırıkhanspor 1-3 Fethiyespor *(aet)*
Kırklarelispor 2-1 Etimesgut Belediye Spor
Kocaeli Birlik Spor 2-0 Sakaryaspor
Konya Anadolu Selçukspor 1-0 Altınordu
Manisa BB Spor 2-4 Rizespor
Manisaspor 1-3 Çorum Belediyespor *(aet)*
Nazilli Belediyespor 3-0 Kartalspor
Pendikspor 3-2 Türk Metal Kırıkkale Spor
Samsunspor 1-1 Diyarbekir Spor *(aet; 5-4 on pens)*
Sarıyer 1-0 Bodrum Belediyesi Bodrumspor
Silivrispor 1-1 Ümraniyespor *(aet; 2-4 on pens)*
Sivas Belediye Spor 1-2 Bucaspor *(aet)*
Trabzonspor 6-0 Serhat Ardahan Spor
Yeni Malatyaspor 4-0 Kurtalan Spor
Yomraspor 0-0 İstanbulspor *(aet; 4-1 on pens)*
Zonguldak Kömürspor 1-2 Şanlıurfaspor

(22/09/16)
Bayrampaşa 0-1 Bursaspor
BUGSAŞ Spor 2-0 Sultanbeyli Belediyespor
Denizlispor 2-1 Kemerspor 2003
Eyüpspor 0-2 Gaziantepspor
Gaziantep BB Spor 0-0 Düzcespor *(aet; 3-2 on pens)*
Göztepe 5-0 Kütahyaspor
Kızılcabölükspor 5-1 Mersin İdman Yurdu
Sivasspor 3-1 Tire 1922 Spor

THIRD ROUND

(25/10/16)
24 Erzincanspor 2-1 Yeni Malatyaspor
Amed Sportif Faaliyetler 2-1 Keçiörengücü
Bandırmaspor 2-2 Sancaktepe Belediye Spor *(aet; 3-4 on pens)*
Elazığspor 1-1 Ofspor *(aet; 4-1 on pens)*
Galatasaray 5-1 Dersim Spor
Gaziantepspor 1-0 Düzyurtspor
Kızılcabölükspor 2-1 Kocaeli Birlik Spor *(aet)*
Pendikspor 0-1 Gençlerbirliği
Rizespor 3-0 Fethiyespor

(26/10/16)
Afyonspor 1-1 Ümraniyespor *(aet; 4-5 on pens)*
Akhisar Belediye 5-2 Nazilli Belediyespor
Balıkesirspor 0-0 Darıca Gençlerbirliği *(aet; 1-4 on pens)*
BB Erzurumspor 1-4 Tuzlaspor
Boluspor 1-0 Elaziz Belediyespor *(aet)*
Bursaspor 3-0 Yomraspor
Büyükçekmece Tepecik Spor 0-2 Şanlıurfaspor
Çorum Belediyespor 1-2 Trabzonspor *(aet)*
Gümüşhanespor 2-1 Konya Anadolu Selçukspor
İnegölspor 3-2 Sarıyer
Kırklarelispor 2-1 Gaziantep BB Spor
Samsunspor 1-4 Menemen Belediye Spor
Sivasspor 3-2 BUGSAŞ Spor

(27/10/16)
Aydınspor 1968 1-0 Antalyaspor
Karagümrük 0-3 Göztepe
Kasımpaşa 2-0 Kahramanmaraşspor
Kayserispor 1-0 Bucaspor
Yeni Amasya 1-0 Denizlispor

GROUP STAGE

Group A

(30/11/16)
Şanlıurfaspor 4-1 Kırklarelispor
(01/12/16)
Osmanlıspor 2-1 Gaziantepspor
(14/12/16)
Gaziantepspor 0-3 Şanlıurfaspor
Kırklarelispor 1-3 Osmanlıspor
(21/12/16)
Gaziantepspor 2-0 Kırklarelispor
Osmanlıspor 1-2 Şanlıurfaspor
(27/12/16)
Kırklarelispor 0-4 Gaziantepspor
(29/12/16)
Şanlıurfaspor 0-3 Osmanlıspor
(19/01/17)
Gaziantepspor 2-0 Osmanlıspor
Kırklarelispor 0-2 Şanlıurfaspor
(25/01/17)
Osmanlıspor 3-0 Kırklarelispor
(26/01/17)
Şanlıurfaspor 1-0 Gaziantepspor

Final standings
1 Şanlıurfaspor 15 pts; 2 Osmanlıspor 12 pts *(qualified)*
3 Gaziantepspor 9 pts; 4 Kırklarelispor 0 pts *(eliminated)*

Group B

(01/12/16)
Rizespor 5-0 İnegölspor
Sancaktepe Belediye Spor 1-2 Kasımpaşa
(13/12/16)
Kasımpaşa 1-6 Rizespor
(14/12/16)
İnegölspor 1-2 Sancaktepe Belediye Spor
(20/12/16)
Kasımpaşa 3-2 İnegölspor
(21/12/16)
Sancaktepe Belediye Spor 0-1 Rizespor
(27/12/16)
Rizespor 4-1 Sancaktepe Belediye Spor
(28/12/16)
İnegölspor 1-3 Kasımpaşa
(17/01/17)
İnegölspor 0-0 Rizespor
(18/01/17)
Kasımpaşa 6-1 Sancaktepe Belediye Spor
(24/01/17)
Sancaktepe Belediye Spor 0-0 İnegölspor
(25/01/17)
Rizespor 2-3 Kasımpaşa

Final standings
1 Kasımpaşa 15 pts; 2 Rizespor 13 pts *(qualified)*
3 Sancaktepe Belediye Spor 4 pts;
4 İnegölspor 2 pts *(eliminated)*

Group C

(30/11/16)
Fenerbahçe 1-2 Gençlerbirliği
Menemen Belediye Spor 2-1 Amed Sportif Faaliyetler
(15/12/16)
Amed Sportif Faaliyetler 1-1 Fenerbahçe
Gençlerbirliği 3-0 Menemen Belediye Spor
(22/12/16)
Menemen Belediye Spor 0-1 Fenerbahçe
(29/12/16)
Fenerbahçe 6-0 Menemen Belediye Spor
Gençlerbirliği 6-0 Amed Sportif Faaliyetler
(08/01/17)
Amed Sportif Faaliyetler 0-5 Gençlerbirliği
(18/01/17)
Amed Sportif Faaliyetler 2-2 Menemen Belediye Spor
Gençlerbirliği 2-2 Fenerbahçe
(25/01/17)
Fenerbahçe 3-0 Amed Sportif Faaliyetler
Menemen Belediye Spor 3-2 Gençlerbirliği

Final standings
1 Gençlerbirliği 13 pts; 2 Fenerbahçe 11 pts *(qualified)*
3 Menemen Belediye Spor 7 pts: 4 Amed Sportif Faaliyetler 2 pts *(eliminated)*

Group D

(29/11/16)
Darıca Gençlerbirliği 1-2 Beşiktaş
Kayserispor 3-0 Boluspor
(13/12/16)
Boluspor 3-1 Darıca Gençlerbirliği
(14/12/16)
Beşiktaş 2-1 Kayserispor
(20/12/16)
Boluspor 1-1 Beşiktaş
(22/12/16)
Kayserispor 3-1 Darıca Gençlerbirliği
(27/12/16)
Beşiktaş 2-0 Boluspor
(28/12/16)
Darıca Gençlerbirliği 2-1 Kayserispor
(17/01/17)
Boluspor 0-0 Kayserispor
(19/01/17)
Beşiktaş 3-0 Darıca Gençlerbirliği
(26/01/17)
Darıca Gençlerbirliği 1-1 Boluspor
Kayserispor 1-1 Beşiktaş

Final standings
1 Beşiktaş 14 pts; 2 Kayserispor 8 pts *(qualified)*
3 Boluspor 6 pts; 4 Darıca Gençlerbirliği 4 pts *(eliminated)*

Group E

(30/11/16)
Galatasaray 1-1 Elazığspor
Tuzlaspor 4-0 24 Erzincanspor
(13/12/16)
Elazığspor 0-1 Tuzlaspor
(14/12/16)
24 Erzincanspor 1-1 Galatasaray
(20/12/16)
Elazığspor 0-4 24 Erzincanspor
(21/12/16)
Galatasaray 2-1 Tuzlaspor
(27/12/16)
24 Erzincanspor 3-2 Elazığspor
(28/12/16)
Tuzlaspor 3-2 Galatasaray
(17/01/17)
24 Erzincanspor 0-1 Tuzlaspor
Elazığspor 1-4 Galatasaray
(24/01/17)
Galatasaray 6-2 24 Erzincanspor
Tuzlaspor 1-1 Elazığspor

Final standings
1 Tuzlaspor 13 pts; 2 Galatasaray 11 pts *(qualified)*
3 24 Erzincanspor 7 pts; 4 Elazığspor 2 pts *(eliminated)*

Group F

(29/11/16)
Sivasspor 0-1 Göztepe
Yeni Amasya Spor 0-1 İstanbul Başakşehir
(13/12/16)
Göztepe 2-0 Yeni Amasya Spor
İstanbul Başakşehir 2-0 Sivasspor
(20/12/16)
İstanbul Başakşehir 6-2 Göztepe
Yeni Amasya Spor 2-3 Sivasspor
(27/12/16)
Sivasspor 3-1 Yeni Amasya Spor
(28/12/16)
Göztepe 0-2 İstanbul Başakşehir
(18/01/17)
Göztepe 0-2 Sivasspor
(19/01/17)
İstanbul Başakşehir 0-0 Yeni Amasya Spor
(25/01/17)
Sivasspor 0-0 İstanbul Başakşehir
(26/01/17)
Yeni Amasya Spor 3-2 Göztepe

Final standings
1 İstanbul Başakşehir 14 pts; 2 Sivasspor 10 pts *(qualified)*
3 Göztepe 6 pts; 4 Yeni Amasya Spor 4 pts *(eliminated)*

Group G

(29/11/16)
Ümraniyespor 3-1 Aydınspor 1968
(30/11/16)
Akhisar 3-3 Bursaspor
(14/12/16)
Aydınspor 1968 2-2 Akhisar
(15/12/16)
Bursaspor 3-0 Ümraniyespor
(21/12/16)
Ümraniyespor 1-2 Akhisar
(22/12/16)
Aydınspor 1968 1-0 Bursaspor
(28/12/16)
Akhisar 0-1 Ümraniyespor
(29/12/16)
Bursaspor 1-1 Aydınspor 1968
(17/01/17)
Bursaspor 1-4 Akhisar
(18/01/17)
Aydınspor 1968 0-1 Ümraniyespor
(24/01/17)
Akhisar 1-0 Aydınspor 1968
(25/01/17)
Ümraniyespor 0-1 Bursaspor

Final standings
1 Akhisar 11 pts; 2 Ümraniyespor 9 pts *(qualified)*
3 Bursaspor 8 pts; 4 Aydınspor 1968 5 pts *(eliminated)*

Group H

(01/12/16)
Kızılcabölükspor 0-4 Konyaspor
Trabzonspor 1-2 Gümüşhanespor
(14/12/16)
Konyaspor 0-0 Trabzonspor
(15/12/16)
Gümüşhanespor 1-0 Kızılcabölükspor
(21/12/16)
Gümüşhanespor 1-1 Konyaspor
(22/12/16)
Trabzonspor 5-0 Kızılcabölükspor
(28/12/16)
Konyaspor 3-0 Gümüşhanespor
(29/12/16)
Kızılcabölükspor 1-1 Trabzonspor
(17/01/17)
Konyaspor 1-0 Kızılcabölükspor
(18/01/17)
Gümüşhanespor 0-0 Trabzonspor
(24/01/17)
Kızılcabölükspor 1-1 Gümüşhanespor
(26/01/17)
Trabzonspor 1-0 Konyaspor

Final standings
1 Konyaspor 11 pts; 2 Gümüşhanespor 9 pts *(qualified)*
3 Trabzonspor 9 pts; 4 Kızılcabölükspor 2 pts *(eliminated)*

ROUND OF 16

(04/02/17)
Gençlerbirliği 2-3 Kayserispor
İstanbul Başakşehir 2-1 Galatasaray
Şanlıurfaspor 1-2 Rizespor *(aet)*
Tuzlaspor 1-4 Sivasspor

(05/02/17)
Akhisar 3-1 Gümüşhanespor
Beşiktaş 0-1 Fenerbahçe
Kasımpaşa 1-0 Osmanlıspor *(aet)*
Konyaspor 2-1 Ümraniyespor *(aet)*

QUARTER FINALS

(28/02/17 & 05/04/17)
Kasımpaşa 2-0 Rizespor *(Popov 63, Koita 90)*
Rizespor 2-2 Kasımpaşa *(Yacoubi 9, Kweuke; Adem 38, 90+3)*
(Kasımpaşa 4-2)

(01/03/17 & 04/04/17)
İstanbul Başakşehir 1-1 Akhisar *(Napoleoni 25; Vaz Té)*
Akhisar 0-2 İstanbul Başakşehir *(Adebayor 24, Mehmet 90+4)*
(İstanbul Başakşehir 3-1)

(01/03/17 & 06/04/17)
Sivasspor 0-0 Konyaspor
Konyaspor 3-2 Sivasspor *(Rangelov 34p, Fofana 43, 78; Ergin 37, Emre 58)*
(Konyaspor 3-2)

(02/03/17 & 05/04/17)
Kayserispor 0-3 Fenerbahçe *(Fernandão 45, 71, Erkan 76og)*
Fenerbahçe 3-0 Kayserispor *(Chahechouhe 31, Souza 35, Volkan Şen 83)*
(Fenerbahçe 6-0)

SEMI FINALS

(26/04/17 & 17/05/17)
İstanbul Başakşehir 2-2 Fenerbahçe *(Cengiz 7, 11; Ozan 12, Van Persie 61)*
Fenerbahçe 2-2 İstanbul Başakşehir *(Sow 71, Ozan 88; Emre 41, Holmén 86) (aet)*
(4-4; İstanbul Başakşehir 10-9 on pens)

(27/04/17 & 16/05/17)
Kasımpaşa 3-2 Konyaspor *(Pavelka 82, Adem 85, Eduok 86; Hadžiahmetović 17, Bajić 44)*
Konyaspor 2-0 Kasımpaşa *(Bajić 17p, 57)*
(Konyaspor 4-3)

FINAL

(31/05/17)
Yeni Stadyum, Eskisehir
KONYASPOR 0
İSTANBUL BAŞAKŞEHİR 0
(aet; 4-1 on pens)
Referee: *Aydınus*
KONYASPOR: *Serkan, Skubic, Ali Turan (Hora 118), Vuković, Douglas, Ali Çamdalı, Jønsson (Volkan 77), Ömer Ali, Milošević (Fofana 106), Hadžiahmetović, Bajić*
İSTANBUL BAŞAKŞEHİR: *Volkan, Uğur, Bekir, Epureanu, Eren (Alparslan 73), Emre, Mahmut, Višća, Mossoró, Cengiz, Adebayor (Mustafa 80; Napoleoni 106)*

Konyaspor are Turkish Cup winners for the first time

UKRAINE

Federatsiya Futbola Ukrainy (FFU)

Address	Provulok Laboratorniy 7-A PO Box 55 UA-01133 Kyiv	**President**	Andriy Pavelko
		General secretary	Yuriy Zapisotskiy
		Media officer	Olexandr Hlyvynskiy
Tel	+380 44 521 0535	**Year of formation**	1991
Fax	+380 44 522 8513	**National stadium**	NSC Olimpiyskiy, Kyiv (70,050)
E-mail	info@ffu.org.ua		
Website	ffu.org.ua		

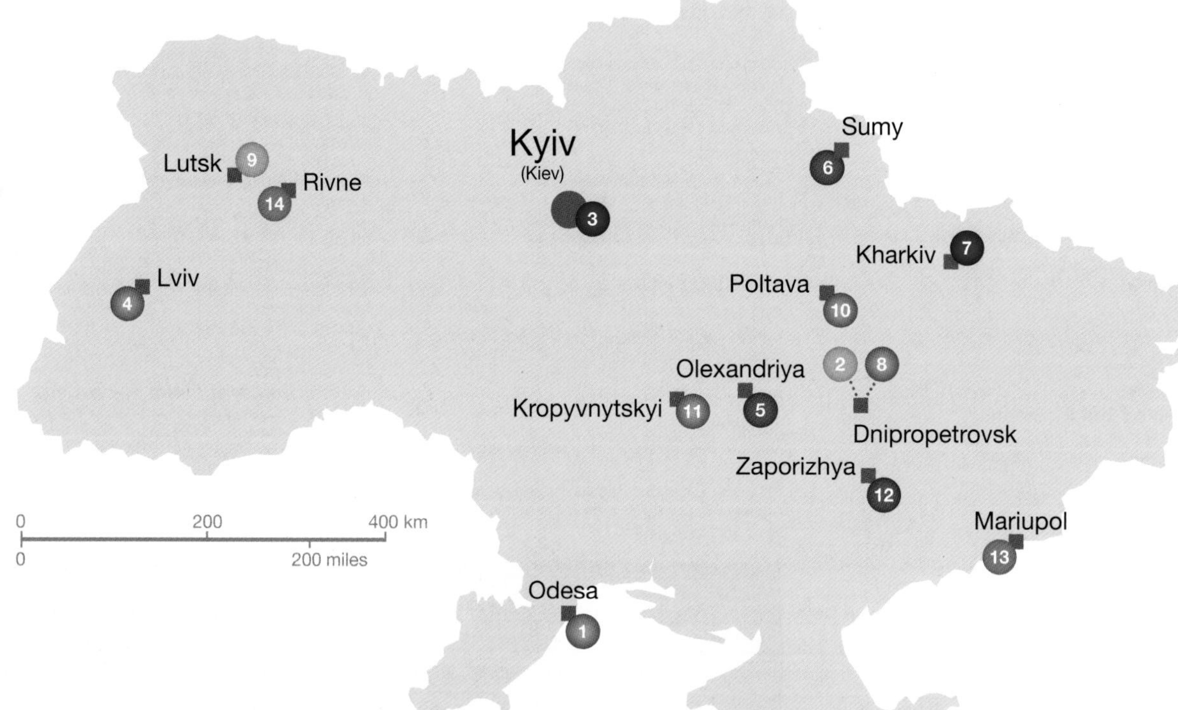

PREMIER LEAGUE CLUBS

1 **FC Chornomorets Odesa**

2 **FC Dnipro Dnipropetrovsk**

3 **FC Dynamo Kyiv**

4 **FC Karpaty Lviv**

5 **FC Olexandriya**

6 **FC Olimpik Donetsk**

7 **FC Shakhtar Donetsk**

8 **FC Stal Kamianske**

9 **FC Volyn Lutsk**

10 **FC Vorskla Poltava**

11 **FC Zirka Kropyvnytskyi**

12 **FC Zorya Luhansk**

PROMOTED CLUBS

13 **FC Illychivets Mariupol**
NB Renamed FC Mariupol for 2016/17 season

14 **NK Veres Rivne**

KEY

- UEFA Champions League
- UEFA Europa League
- Promoted
- Relegated

Show of strength from Shakhtar

Still displaced from their home town and their splendid Donbass Arena, Shakhtar Donetsk spent half a season based in Lviv and the other in Kharkiv, but despite the disruption they dominated the new-look Premier League from start to its protracted finish to displace arch-rivals Dynamo Kyiv as Ukrainian champions.

There was a domestic cup win to celebrate, too, for Shakhtar's new coach Paulo Fonseca as he led the team to a 1-0 victory over Dynamo in the final, but Europe turned out to be a bittersweet experience for the man brought in to replace long-serving Mircea Lucescu.

New coach Paulo Fonseca leads Pitmen to double

Dynamo Kyiv finish runners-up in league and cup

Record-equalling 11th cup win for Orange-and-Blacks

Domestic league

Shakhtar's new Portuguese coach, plucked from Braga, had the benefit of sharing the native tongue of the club's large Brazilian contingent, and harmony appeared to be coursing through the team as they began the post-Lucescu era – all 12 years of it – with a string of victories that was only interrupted by a 1-1 draw at home to the defending champions. Seeking a hat-trick of league titles for the first time since their nine-titles-in-a-row sequence ended in 2001, Dynamo also started well, but shock home defeats by Vorskla Poltava and Zorya sandwiched the draw against Shakhtar, and from that moment on they were always in trouble.

Shakhtar's efficiency was ruthless. By the time they drew breath in mid-December, after an exhausting autumn schedule, they had won 16 of their 18 matches and drawn the other two. A thrilling 4-3 away win over Dynamo in the last round before the winter break increased their lead at the top to 13 points, and it was up to 14 when the Premier League was cut in half in late March.

The second phase of the new two-tiered format provided Shakhtar with two further matches against Dynamo, but victory in the first of those, 1-0 in Kyiv, effectively ended the title race, with the Orange-and-Blacks' landmark tenth title being officially confirmed a fortnight later when they beat third-placed Zorya Luhansk 3-2 in Kharkiv.

Shakhtar closed the season with a 1-1 draw at Olexandriya, which meant they scored in all 32 matches. The goals were spread around the team, with only Argentinian striker Facundo Ferreyra reaching double figures. Seven Brazilians got on the scoresheet and there was even a goal for evergreen skipper Darijo Srna, who thus maintained his record of scoring in each of his 14 seasons at the club. The golden boot went to Srna's counterpart at Dynamo Kyiv, Andriy Yarmolenko, and the runners-up even outscored the champions, although Shakhtar had the better defence, in which seasoned Ukrainian internationals Andriy Pyatov, Yaroslav Rakitskiy and Olexandr Kucher continued to provide a secure and reliable service.

Domestic cup

The Shakhtar defence kept arguably its most important clean sheet of the season in the Ukrainian Cup final. Staged in their temporary Kharkiv home, the match was heading for extra time when Marlos, Shakhtar's Brazilian playmaker, scored a fantastic solo goal to win the game 1-0 and keep the trophy in his club's possession. The victory was Shakhtar's 11th in the competition, equalling their defeated opponents' all-time record.

Europe

For the first time in seven seasons Shakhtar were not involved in the UEFA Champions League group stage, a penalty shoot-out defeat to Swiss side Young Boys transferring them to the UEFA Europa League, where they bossed their group, winning all six matches, before snatching defeat from the jaws of victory against Celta Vigo in the round of 32. Dynamo had a rough ride in the UEFA Champions League, failing to win a group game until, already eliminated, they signed out by thrashing Beşiktaş 6-0.

National team

Legendary striker Andriy Shevchenko took over the Ukrainian national team reins after the shambles of UEFA EURO 2016, and with six of the team's ten 2018 FIFA World Cup group fixtures played, there was a reasonable chance that he might lead his country across the border to the finals of a competition he graced as a player in 2006. Yarmolenko and Artem Kravets both scored in three successive qualifiers as the team made an unbeaten start, but a 1-0 defeat by Croatia in Zagreb provided a first setback before a 2-1 win in Finland steered Shevchenko's men back on course for a top-two final placing in a highly competitive Group I.

DOMESTIC SEASON AT A GLANCE

Premier League 2016/17 final table

			Home					Away					Total					
		Pld	W	D	L	F	A	W	D	L	F	A	W	D	L	F	A	Pts
1	**FC Shakhtar Donetsk**	**32**	**11**	**3**	**2**	**31**	**13**	**14**	**2**	**0**	**35**	**11**	**25**	**5**	**2**	**66**	**24**	**80**
2	FC Dynamo Kyiv	32	11	0	5	35	16	10	4	2	34	17	21	4	7	69	33	67
3	FC Zorya Luhansk	32	8	1	7	27	19	8	5	3	18	12	16	6	10	45	31	54
4	FC Olimpik Donetsk	32	7	5	4	18	20	4	6	6	15	24	11	11	10	33	44	44
5	FC Olexandriya	32	7	6	3	27	16	3	4	9	14	27	10	10	12	41	43	40
6	FC Chornomorets Odesa	32	5	5	6	12	17	5	3	8	13	20	10	8	14	25	37	38
7	FC Vorskla Poltava	32	5	7	4	17	14	6	2	8	15	18	11	9	12	32	32	42
8	FC Stal Kamianske	32	6	2	8	18	18	5	6	5	9	13	11	8	13	27	31	41
9	FC Zirka Kropyvnytskyi	32	7	5	4	18	13	2	2	12	11	30	9	7	16	29	43	34
10	FC Karpaty Lviv	32	6	4	6	18	19	3	5	8	17	22	9	9	14	35	41	30
11	FC Dnipro Dnipropetrovsk	32	4	6	6	18	19	4	7	5	13	21	8	13	11	31	40	13
12	FC Volyn Lutsk	32	3	3	10	10	17	1	1	14	7	34	4	4	24	17	51	10

NB League splits into top and bottom halves after 22 games, after which the clubs play exclusively against teams in their group.
FC Dnipro Dnipropetrovsk – 24 pts deducted; FC Karpaty Lviv & FC Volyn Lutsk – 6 pts deducted.

European qualification 2017/18

Champion/Cup winner: FC Shakhtar Donetsk (group stage)

FC Dynamo Kyiv (third qualifying round)

FC Zorya Luhansk (group stage)
FC Olimpik Donetsk (third qualifying round)
FC Olexandriya (third qualifying round)

Top scorer	Andriy Yarmolenko (Dynamo Kyiv), 15 goals
Relegated clubs	FC Volyn Lutsk, FC Dnipro Dnipropetrovsk
Promoted clubs	FC Illychivets Mariupol, NK Veres Rivne
Cup final	FC Shakhtar Donetsk 1-0 FC Dynamo Kyiv

Player of the season

Marlos
(FC Shakhtar Donetsk)

As ever, there was a sizeable Brazilian contribution towards Shakhtar's achievements in 2016/17. Nine players from South America's largest country donned the club's orange-and-black shirts during coach Paulo Fonseca's debut season at the club, and while Bernard, Dentinho, Fred, Ismaily and Taison all had their moments, it was Marlos, in his third season, who outshone his compatriots. A creative midfielder happy to operate out wide or through the centre, he saved his best until last with a wonderful late goal to beat Dynamo Kyiv in the Ukrainian Cup final.

Newcomer of the season

Artem Besedin
(FC Dynamo Kyiv)

After a lean loan spell at hometown club Metalist Kharkiv in 2015/16, Besedin returned to Dynamo eager to make his mark in the Premier League. At first he was used by coach Serhiy Rebrov only as a deputy to Júnior Moraes, but when the free-scoring Brazilian was despatched on loan to Chinese club Tianjin Quanjian, the 21-year-old Ukrainian youth international seized his chance, leading the Dynamo attack in style and ending the season with nine league goals, plus his first senior caps for Ukraine and a crucial World Cup qualifying goal against Finland.

Team of the season
(4-4-1-1)

Coach: Paulo Fonseca *(Shakhtar)*

NATIONAL TEAM

International tournament appearances

FIFA World Cup (1) 2006 (qtr-finals)
UEFA European Championship (2) 2012, 2016

Top five all-time caps

Anatoliy Tymoshchuk (144); Andriy Shevchenko (111); Oleh Gusev (98); **Ruslan Rotan** (93); Olexandr Shovkovskiy (92)

Top five all-time goals

Andriy Shevchenko (48); **Andriy Yarmolenko** (29); Serhiy Rebrov (15); **Yevhen Konoplyanka** (14); Oleh Gusev (13)

Results 2016/17

05/09/16	Iceland (WCQ)	H	Kyiv	D	1-1	*Yarmolenko (41)*
06/10/16	Turkey (WCQ)	A	Konya	D	2-2	*Yarmolenko (24p), Kravets (27)*
09/10/16	Kosovo (WCQ)	H	Krakow (POL)	W	3-0	*Kravets (31), Yarmolenko (81), Rotan (87)*
12/11/16	Finland (WCQ)	H	Odessa	W	1-0	*Kravets (25)*
15/11/16	Serbia	H	Kharkiv	W	2-0	*Shakhov (38), Yarmolenko (87p)*
24/03/17	Croatia (WCQ)	A	Zagreb	L	0-1	
06/06/17	Malta	N	Graz (AUT)	L	0-1	
11/06/17	Finland (WCQ)	A	Tampere	W	2-1	*Konoplyanka (51), Besedin (75)*

Appearances 2016/17

Coach: Andriy Shevchenko	**29/09/76**		**ISL**	**TUR**	**KOS**	**FIN**	**Srb**	**CRO**	**Mal**	**FIN**	**Caps**	**Goals**
Andriy Pyatov	28/06/84	Shakhtar Donetsk	G	G	G	G		G	G	G	74	-
Bohdan Butko	13/01/91	Shakhtar Donetsk	D	D	D	D	D	D	s46	D	26	-
Olexandr Kucher	22/10/82	Shakhtar Donetsk	D	D	D	D		D	D46		57	2
Yaroslav Rakitskiy	03/08/89	Shakhtar Donetsk	D			D			D46	D	46	4
Eduard Sobol	20/04/95	Zorya	D	D	D	D			s46	s87	6	-
Taras Stepanenko	08/08/89	Shakhtar Donetsk	M	M	M	M		M	M46	M	39	3
Andriy Yarmolenko	23/10/89	Dynamo Kyiv	M	M	M	M	s65	M	M46	M	70	29
Yevhen Konoplyanka	29/09/89	Schalke (GER)	M	M81	M79	M83		M	s46	M87	63	14
Serhiy Sydorchuk	02/05/91	Dynamo Kyiv	M63	s46			M46	s77	M46		19	2
Olexandr Zinchenko	15/12/96	PSV (NED)	A90	M46	M63	M67	s76				11	1
Viktor Kovalenko	14/02/96	Shakhtar Donetsk	A	M	M	M89		M85	M46	M76	13	-
Roman Zozulya	17/11/89	Betis (ESP)	s63	s73	s84		A62				33	4
Yevhen Shakhov	30/11/90	PAOK (GRE)	s90			s89	M76		s46		4	1
Ivan Ordets	08/07/92	Shakhtar Donetsk		D	D		D	D	s46	D	8	1
Artem Kravets	03/06/89	Granada (ESP)		A73	A84	A		A59			17	7
Ivan Petryak	13/03/94	Zorya		s81			s46				3	-
Ruslan Rotan	29/10/81	Dnipro			s63	s67	s46	M77			93	8
Olexandr Karavayev	02/06/92	Zorya			s79		M46				5	-
Viktor Tsygankov	15/11/97	Dynamo Kyiv				s83	M65		s46		3	-
Denys Boyko	29/01/88	Málaga (ESP)					G				5	-
Serhiy Krivtsov	15/03/91	Shakhtar Donetsk					D		s46		3	-
Artem Fedetskiy	26/04/85	Darmstadt (GER)					D				53	2
Maxym Malyshev	24/12/92	Shakhtar Donetsk					M		s46		3	-
Artem Besedin	31/03/96	Dynamo Kyiv					s62	s85	s46	s65	4	1
Mykola Matviyenko	02/05/96	Karpaty						D	D46	D	3	-
Yevhen Seleznyov	20/07/85	Karabükspor (TUR)						s59	A46	A65	55	11
Mykola Morozyuk	17/01/88	Dynamo Kyiv							D46		14	1
Ruslan Malinovskiy	04/05/93	Genk (BEL)							M46	M	5	-
Volodymyr Shepelev	01/06/97	Dynamo Kyiv							s46	s76	2	-

EUROPE

FC Dynamo Kyiv

Group B
Match 1 - SSC Napoli (ITA)
H 1-2 *Garmash (26)*
Shovkovskiy, Antunes, Yarmolenko, Júnior Moraes (Gladkiy 87), Tsygankov (Gusev 73), Sydorchuk, Rybalka (Korzun 82), Garmash, Vida, Makarenko, Khacheridi. Coach: Serhiy Rebrov (UKR)
Red card: Sydorchuk 68
Match 2 - Beşiktaş JK (TUR)
A 1-1 *Tsygankov (65)*
Rudko, Antunes, Morozyuk, Yarmolenko, Júnior Moraes (Gladkiy 78), Rybalka, Garmash, Vida, González (Tsygankov 62), Buyalskiy (Korzun 22), Khacheridi. Coach: Serhiy Rebrov (UKR)
Match 3 - SL Benfica (POR)
H 0-2
Rudko, Danilo Silva, Antunes, Yarmolenko, Júnior Moraes, Sydorchuk (Gladkiy 80), Korzun, Vida, González (Tsygankov 71), Fedorchuk (Buyalskiy 56), Khacheridi. Coach: Serhiy Rebrov (UKR)
Match 4 - SL Benfica (POR)
A 0-1
Rudko, Morozyuk, Júnior Moraes, Tsygankov (Besedin 61), Sydorchuk (Orikhovskiy 76), Rybalka, Vida, González, Makarenko, Buyalskiy (Gromov 87), Khacheridi. Coach: Serhiy Rebrov (UKR)
Match 5 - SSC Napoli (ITA)
A 0-0
Rudko, Morozyuk, Yarmolenko, Tsygankov (González 60), Sydorchuk (Orikhovskiy 67), Rybalka, Garmash, Vida, Makarenko, Khacheridi, Besedin (Júnior Moraes 81). Coach: Serhiy Rebrov (UKR)
Match 6 - Beşiktaş JK (TUR)
H 6-0 *Besedin (9), Yarmolenko (30p), Buyalskiy (32), González (45+3), Sydorchuk (60), Júnior Moraes (77)*
Rudko, Antunes, Yarmolenko, Sydorchuk (Korzun 66), Rybalka, Vida, González (Tsygankov 69), Burda, Buyalskiy , Khacheridi, Besedin (Júnior Moraes 76). Coach: Serhiy Rebrov (UKR)

FC Shakhtar Donetsk

Third qualifying round - BSC Young Boys (SUI)
H 2-0 *Bernard (27), Seleznyov (75)*
Pyatov, Stepanenko, Fred, Bernard, Marlos, Ordets, Eduardo (Seleznyov 71), Taison (Dentinho 77), Ismaily, Srna, Krivtsov. Coach: Paulo Fonseca (POR)
A 0-2 (aet; 2-4 on pens)
Pyatov, Stepanenko, Fred, Dentinho (Wellington Nem 75), Marlos, Ordets, Eduardo (Seleznyov 62), Taison, Ismaily, Srna, Krivtsov (Rakitskiy 120). Coach: Paulo Fonseca (POR)

Play-offs - İstanbul Başakşehir (TUR)
A 2-1 *Çikalleshi (24og), Kovalenko (41)*
Pyatov, Kucher, Stepanenko, Fred, Marlos, Ferreyra (Eduardo 70), Taison (Wellington Nem 80), Ismaily, Srna, Rakitskiy, Kovalenko (Malyshev 87). Coach: Paulo Fonseca (POR)
H 2-0 *Attamah (22og), Marlos (71p)*
Pyatov, Kucher, Stepanenko, Fred (Malyshev 72), Marlos, Ferreyra (Eduardo 77), Taison, Ismaily, Srna, Rakitskiy, Kovalenko (Wellington Nem 83). Coach: Paulo Fonseca (POR)

Group H
Match 1 - Konyaspor (TUR)
A 1-0 *Ferreyra (75)*
Pyatov, Butko, Kucher, Stepanenko, Fred, Bernard (Taison 67), Marlos, Ferreyra (Eduardo 90), Ismaily, Rakitskiy, Kovalenko (Malyshev 90+3). Coach: Paulo Fonseca (POR)
Match 2 - SC Braga (POR)
H 2-0 *Stepanenko (5), Kovalenko (56)*
Pyatov, Butko, Kucher, Stepanenko, Fred, Bernard, Marlos (Taison 74), Ordets, Ferreyra (Dentinho 85), Ismaily, Kovalenko (Malyshev 90+1). Coach: Paulo Fonseca (POR)
Red card: Fred 47
Match 3 - KAA Gent (BEL)
H 5-0 *Kovalenko (12), Ferreyra (30), Bernard (46), Taison (75), Malyshev (85)*
Pyatov, Kucher, Stepanenko, Bernard (Taison 74), Marlos, Malyshev, Ferreyra (Eduardo 81), Ismaily, Srna, Rakitskiy, Kovalenko (Dentinho 37). Coach: Paulo Fonseca (POR)
Match 4 - KAA Gent (BEL)
A 5-3 *Marlos (36p), Taison (41), Stepanenko (45+3), Fred (68), Ferreyra (87)*
Pyatov, Kucher, Stepanenko (Malyshev 72), Fred, Bernard, Marlos, Ferreyra, Taison (Dentinho 71), Ismaily, Srna, Rakitskiy (Ordets 78). Coach: Paulo Fonseca (POR)
Match 5 - Konyaspor (TUR)
H 4-0 *Abdülkerim Bardakcı (11og), Dentinho (36), Eduardo (66), Bernard (74)*
Shevchenko, Dentinho, Bernard, Malyshev, Ordets, Matviyenko, Taison (Eduardo 64), Srna, Krivtsov, Boryachuk (Stepanenko 79), Kovalenko (Tankovskiy 46). Coach: Paulo Fonseca (POR)
Match 6 - SC Braga (POR)
A 4-2 *Krivtsov (22, 62), Taison (39, 66)*
Shevchenko, Butko, Dentinho, Marlos (Bernard 58), Malyshev, Ordets, Tankovskiy (Fred 61), Matviyenko, Taison, Krivtsov, Boryachuk (Ferreyra 66). Coach: Paulo Fonseca (POR)

Round of 32 - RC Celta de Vigo (ESP)
A 1-0 *Blanco (27)*
Pyatov, Fred, Dentinho (Kovalenko 46), Marlos (Márcio Azevedo 90+3), Malyshev, Ordets, Taison (Bernard 84), Ismaily, Srna, Rakitskiy, Blanco. Coach: Paulo Fonseca (POR)
H 0-2 (aet)
Pyatov, Fred, Marlos, Malyshev (Boryachuk 112), Ordets, Taison (Bernard 83), Ismaily, Srna, Rakitskiy, Kovalenko (Stepanenko 73), Blanco. Coach: Paulo Fonseca (POR)

FC Zorya Luhansk

Group A
Match 1 - Fenerbahçe SK (TUR)
H 1-1 *Grechishkin (52)*
Shevchenko, Sivakov, Chaikovskiy, Kamenyuka, Petryak (Paulinho 73), Kulach (Hordiyenko 87), Rafael Forster, Karavayev, Ljubenović (Opanasenko 83), Grechishkin, Sobol. Coach: Yuriy Vernydub (UKR)
Match 2 - Manchester United FC (ENG)
A 0-1
Shevchenko, Sivakov, Chaikovskiy (Hordiyenko 80), Kamenyuka, Petryak, Kulach (Paulinho 60), Rafael Forster, Karavayev, Ljubenović (Lipartia 76), Grechishkin, Sobol. Coach: Yuriy Vernydub (UKR)
Match 3 - Feyenoord (NED)
A 0-1
Shevchenko, Sivakov, Hordiyenko (Kharatin 65), Kamenyuka, Petryak (Paulinho 58), Kulach (Ljubenović 46), Lipartia, Rafael Forster, Karavayev, Grechishkin, Sobol. Coach: Yuriy Vernydub (UKR)
Match 4 - Feyenoord (NED)
H 1-1 *Rafael Forster (44)*
Shevchenko, Chaikovskiy, Petryak, Kharatin, Rafael Forster, Karavayev, Ljubenović (Paulinho 62), Grechishkin, Opanasenko (Kamenyuka 30), Bonaventure (Kulach 55), Sobol. Coach: Yuriy Vernydub (UKR)

Match 5 - Fenerbahçe SK (TUR)
A 0-2
Shevchenko, Sivakov, Chaikovskiy, Kamenyuka (Opanasenko 35), Petryak (Bonaventure 57), Kharatin, Kulach (Paulinho 69), Rafael Forster, Karavayev, Grechishkin, Sobol. Coach: Yuriy Vernydub (UKR)
Red card: Sobol 90+2
Match 6 - Manchester United FC (ENG)
H 0-2
Levchenko, Sukhovskiy, Sivakov, Chaikovskiy, Petryak, Kharatin (Grechishkin 57), Rafael Forster, Karavayev, Bezborodko (Bonaventure 54), Ljubenović (Lipartia 72), Opanasenko. Coach: Yuriy Vernydub (UKR)

FC Vorskla Poltava

EUROPA LEAGUE

Third qualifying round - NK Lokomotiva Zagreb (CRO)
A 0-0
Shust, Siminin (Sapai 72), Perduta, Sklyar, Kobakhidze, Tkachuk, Khlebas, Chesnakov, Dityatyev, Rebenok (Bartulović 66), Zarichnyuk (Kolomoyets 56). Coach: Vasyl Sachko (UKR)
H 2-3 *Perić (49og), Chesnakov (74)*
Shust, Perduta, Sklyar (Holodyuk 70), Kobakhidze, Tkachuk, Bartulović, Khlebas (Zarichnyuk 74), Chesnakov, Sapai (Rebenok 60), Kolomoyets, Dityatyev. Coach: Vasyl Sachko (UKR)

FC Olexandriya

EUROPA LEAGUE

Third qualifying round - HNK Hajduk Split (CRO)
H 0-3
Levanidov, Mykytsei, Kulish (Yaremchuk 62), Ponomar, Zhichikov (Leonov 77), Zaporozhan, Hitchenko, Shendryk, Banada, Kozak (Hrytsuk 73), Basov. Coach: Volodymyr Sharan (UKR)
A 1-3 *Starenkiy (13)*
Novak, Mykytsei, Myagkov, Ponomar (Hrytsuk 46), Yaremchuk (Kulish 73), Tsurikov, Hitchenko, Shendryk, Starenkiy (Putrash 57), Banada, Kozak. Coach: Volodymyr Sharan (UKR)

DOMESTIC LEAGUE CLUB-BY-CLUB

FC Chornomorets Odesa

1936 • Chornomorets (34,164) • chernomorets.odessa.ua
Major honours
Ukrainian Cup (2) 1992, 1994
Coach: Olexandr Babych

Date		Opponent		Score	Scorers
2016					
23/07	a	Vorskla	L	0-1	
30/07	h	Shakhtar	L	1-4	*Filimonov*
07/08	a	Zorya	L	0-4	
14/08	h	Olimpik	W	3-0	*Martynenko 2, Barylko*
21/08	a	Zirka	W	1-0	*Khocholava*
27/08	a	Volyn	W	1-0	*Kabayev*
11/09	h	Olexandriya	W	1-0	*og (Hitchenko)*
17/09	a	Karpaty	D	0-0	
25/09	h	Dnipro	D	0-0	
01/10	a	Stal	W	2-1	*Korkishko, Khoblenko*
15/10	h	Dynamo	D	1-1	*og (Khacheridi)*
23/10	h	Vorskla	L	1-2	*Korkishko*
29/10	a	Shakhtar	L	0-2	
06/11	h	Zorya	D	0-0	
19/11	a	Olimpik	L	0-1	
26/11	h	Zirka	W	2-1	*Korkishko, Andriyevskiy*
03/12	h	Volyn	D	0-0	
11/12	a	Olexandriya	L	1-2	*Kovalets*
2017					
26/02	h	Karpaty	W	1-0	*Smirnov*
04/03	a	Dnipro	D	1-1	*Khoblenko*
11/03	h	Stal	L	0-1	
17/03	a	Dynamo	L	1-2	*Khocholava*
01/04	h	Olimpik	D	0-0	
09/04	a	Shakhtar	W	2-1	*Andriyevskiy, Jorge Elias*
16/04	h	Olexandriya	W	1-0	*Korkishko*
23/04	a	Zorya	W	2-1	*Korkishko 2 (1p)*
30/04	h	Dynamo	L	1-4	*Tatarkov*
06/05	a	Olimpik	L	0-1	
13/05	h	Shakhtar	L	0-3	
21/05	a	Olexandriya	D	1-1	*Korkishko*
26/05	h	Zorya	L	0-1	
31/05	a	Dynamo	L	1-2	*Andriyevskiy (p)*

No	Name	Nat	DoB	Pos	Aps	(s)	Gls
3	Rizvan Ablitarov		18/04/89	D	12		
8	Olexandr Andriyevskiy		25/06/94	M	19	(5)	3
2	Olexandr Azatskiy		13/01/94	D	21	(2)	
33	Volodymyr Barylko		29/01/94	A	8	(9)	1
71	Dmytro Bezruk		30/03/96	G	7		
12	Yevhen Borovyk		02/03/85	G	17		
94	Oleh Danchenko		01/08/94	D	22	(2)	
16	Artem Filimonov		21/02/94	M	16		1
23	Sheriff Isa	NGA	10/11/90	M		(1)	
26	Jorge Elias	BRA	05/06/91	A	3	(5)	1
22	Vladyslav Kabayev		01/09/95	M	16	(9)	1
10	Vladyslav Kalitvintsev		04/01/93	M	9	(3)	
1	Danylo Kanevtsev		26/07/96	G	8		
96	Olexandr Kapliyenko		07/03/96	D	8	(1)	
10	Artur Karnoza		02/08/90	M		(4)	
9	Olexiy Khoblenko		04/04/94	A	22	(5)	2
5	David Khocholava	GEO	08/02/93	D	24		2
7	Dmytro Korkishko		04/05/90	M	24	(3)	7
6	Kyrylo Kovalets		02/07/93	M	16	(11)	1
20	Valeriy Kutsenko		02/11/86	M	2	(1)	
27	Serhiy Lyulka		22/02/90	D	25		
25	Yevheniy Martynenko		25/06/93	D	16		2
20	Olexandr Mashnin		20/03/90	M		(6)	
14	Yevhen Murashov		09/05/95	A		(1)	
99	Mykola Musolitin		21/01/99	M	3	(9)	
32	Serhiy Petko		23/01/94	D	4		
18	Sílvio	BRA	04/05/94	A	2	(5)	
11	Yevhen Smirnov		16/04/93	M	20		1
17	Mykyta Tatarkov		04/01/95	M	17	(4)	1
75	Maxym Tretyakov		06/03/96	M	11	(9)	

FC Dnipro Dnipropetrovsk

1918 • Dnipro-Arena (31,003) • fcdnipro.ua
Major honours
USSR League (2) 1983, 1988; USSR Cup (1) 1989
Coach: Dmytro Mykhaylenko

Date		Opponent		Score	Scorers
2016					
24/07	h	Volyn	W	5-0	*Balanyuk 2, Kohut, Vakulko, Kochergin*
31/07	h	Stal	D	1-1	*Blyznychenko (p)*
06/08	a	Dynamo	L	0-1	
13/08	h	Vorskla	D	1-1	*Blyznychenko (p)*
21/08	a	Shakhtar	L	0-4	
26/08	h	Zorya	W	2-0	*Rotan, Balanyuk*
11/09	a	Olimpik	L	0-3	
17/09	h	Zirka	L	0-1	
25/09	a	Chornomorets	D	0-0	
01/10	h	Olexandriya	L	1-4	*Kochergin*
16/10	a	Karpaty	D	1-1	*Kohut*
22/10	a	Volyn	L	0-3	
30/10	a	Stal	D	1-1	*Vakulko*
06/11	h	Dynamo	L	1-2	*Rotan*
20/11	a	Vorskla	W	2-1	*Rotan, Luchkevych*
27/11	h	Shakhtar	L	0-2	
03/12	a	Zorya	W	3-2	*Kochergin 2, Luchkevych*
09/12	h	Olimpik	D	1-1	*Rotan*
2017					
26/02	a	Zirka	D	1-1	*Rotan*
04/03	h	Chornomorets	D	1-1	*Dovbyk*
11/03	a	Olexandriya	D	0-0	
17/03	h	Karpaty	D	0-0	
01/04	h	Zirka	W	1-0	*Nağıyev*
09/04	a	Karpaty	D	2-2	*Dovbyk 2*
15/04	h	Stal	D	0-0	
22/04	h	Vorskla	W	2-0	*Kochergin, Dovbyk*
30/04	a	Volyn	W	1-0	*Cheberko (p)*
07/05	a	Zirka	D	1-1	*Cheberko*
14/05	h	Karpaty	L	2-3	*Kochergin, Dovbyk*
20/05	a	Stal	W	1-0	*Balanyuk*
27/05	a	Vorskla	L	0-1	
31/05	h	Volyn	L	0-3	*(w/o; match abandoned after 47 mins at 1-0 Dovbyk)*

No	Name	Nat	DoB	Pos	Aps	(s)	Gls
3	Volodymyr Adamyuk		17/07/91	D	27	(1)	
36	Anderson Pico	BRA	04/11/88	D	3	(3)	
17	Denys Balanyuk		16/01/97	A	15	(10)	4
1	Olexiy Bashtanenko		16/03/94	G	3		
7	Andriy Blyznychenko		24/07/94	M	10	(5)	2
11	Yevheniy Bokhashvili		05/01/93	A	2	(1)	
14	Yevhen Cheberko		23/01/98	M	7	(7)	2
14	Yevhen Cheberyachko		19/06/83	D	14		
15	Artem Dovbyk		21/06/97	A	17	(4)	6
10	Vladyslav Kochergin		30/04/96	M	16	(9)	6
25	Ihor Kohut		07/03/96	M	12	(10)	2
18	Denys Kostyshyn		31/08/97	A		(1)	
87	Oleh Kozhushko		17/02/98	M	2	(11)	
4	Serhiy Kravchenko		24/04/83	M	15		
7	Maxym Lopyrionok		13/04/95	D	20		
24	Valeriy Luchkevych		11/01/96	M	10		2
12	Andriy Lunin		11/02/99	G	22		
99	Maxym Lunyov		22/05/98	A	15	(6)	
33	Dmitri Nağıyev	AZE	27/11/95	M	11	(2)	1
28	Serhiy Nazarenko		16/02/80	M	1	(3)	
7	Yehor Nazaryna		10/07/97	M		(1)	
89	Serhiy Politylo		09/01/89	M	13	(1)	
8	Volodymyr Polyoviy		28/07/85	D	18	(1)	
29	Ruslan Rotan		29/10/81	M	17	(2)	5
77	Denys Shelikhov		23/06/89	G	7		
39	Olexandr Svatok		27/09/94	D	31		
9	Yuriy Vakulko		10/11/97	M	22	(4)	2
2	Alexandru Vlad	ROU	06/12/89	D	22		

UKRAINE

FC Dynamo Kyiv

1927 • NSC Olimpiyskiy (70,050); Chornomorets, Odesa (34,164) • fcdynamo.kiev.ua

Major honours
UEFA Cup Winners' Cup (2) 1975, 1986;
UEFA Super Cup (1) 1975;
USSR League (13) 1961, 1966, 1967, 1968, 1971, 1974, 1975, 1977, 1980, 1981, 1985, 1986, 1990;
Ukrainian League (15) 1993, 1994, 1995, 1996, 1997, 1998, 1999, 2000, 2001, 2003, 2004, 2007, 2009, 2015, 2016;
USSR Cup (9) 1954, 1964, 1966, 1974, 1978, 1982, 1985, 1987, 1990;
Ukrainian Cup (11) 1993, 1996, 1998, 1999, 2000, 2003, 2005, 2006, 2007, 2014, 2015

Coach: Serhiy Rebrov

2016

Date		Opponent		Score	Scorers
23/07	h	Olexandriya	W	5-1	*Júnior Moraes 3 (1p), Buyalskiy, Vida*
31/07	a	Karpaty	W	2-0	*Yarmolenko 2*
06/08	h	Dnipro	W	1-0	*Júnior Moraes*
14/08	a	Stal	W	2-1	*Garmash, Antunes*
20/08	h	Volyn	W	2-1	*Morozyuk, Garmash*
27/08	h	Vorskla	L	0-2	
09/09	a	Shakhtar	D	1-1	*Gusev (p)*
18/09	h	Zorya	L	0-1	
24/09	a	Olimpik	W	4-0	*Tsygankov, Júnior Moraes (p), González, Fedorchuk*
02/10	h	Zirka	W	2-0	*Sydorchuk, Tsygankov*
15/10	a	Chornomorets	D	1-1	*Júnior Moraes*
23/10	a	Olexandriya	D	1-1	*González*
29/10	h	Karpaty	W	4-1	*Besedin, Vida, Morozyuk, Orikhovskiy*
06/11	a	Dnipro	W	2-1	*Besedin, Sydorchuk*
19/11	h	Stal	W	2-1	*Khacheridi, Makarenko*
26/11	a	Volyn	W	4-1	*Júnior Moraes 3, Yarmolenko*
03/12	a	Vorskla	D	2-2	*Sydorchuk, Yarmolenko (p)*
12/12	h	Shakhtar	L	3-4	*Júnior Moraes, Rybalka, Besedin*

2017

Date		Opponent		Score	Scorers
25/02	a	Zorya	W	2-1	*Garmash, Besedin*
04/03	h	Olimpik	W	1-0	*Besedin*
12/03	a	Zirka	L	0-2	
17/03	h	Chornomorets	W	2-1	*Yarmolenko, Sydorchuk*
02/04	a	Olexandriya	W	4-1	*Besedin, Garmash, Yarmolenko 2 (1p)*
09/04	h	Olimpik	W	4-0	*Besedin, Yarmolenko 2, Garmash*
14/04	a	Zorya	W	1-0	*Garmash*
21/04	h	Shakhtar	L	0-1	
30/04	a	Chornomorets	W	4-1	*Yarmolenko 2 (1p), Besedin, Vida*
07/05	h	Olexandriya	W	6-0	*Yarmolenko (p), Besedin, Garmash 2, Morozyuk, Tsygankov*
13/05	a	Olimpik	L	1-2	*Burda*
21/05	h	Zorya	L	1-2	*Morozyuk*
26/05	a	Shakhtar	W	3-2	*Garmash, Yarmolenko 2 (1p)*
31/05	h	Chornomorets	W	2-1	*González, Yarmolenko*

No	Name	Nat	DoB	Pos	Aps	(s)	Gls
5	Antunes	POR	01/04/87	D	19		1
41	Artem Besedin		31/03/96	A	12	(10)	9
26	Mykyta Burda		24/03/95	D	5		1
29	Vitaliy Buyalskiy		06/01/93	M	17	(4)	1
2	Danilo Silva	BRA	24/11/86	D	5		
6	Aleksandar Dragovic	AUT	06/03/91	D	4		
32	Valeriy Fedorchuk		05/10/88	M	2	(6)	1
19	Denys Garmash		19/04/90	M	17	(8)	9
7	Olexandr Gladkiy		24/08/87	A	4	(4)	
25	Derlis González	PAR	20/03/94	M	15	(3)	3
77	Artem Gromov		14/01/90	M	5	(4)	
20	Oleh Gusev		25/04/83	M	2	(4)	1
11	Júnior Moraes	BRA	04/04/87	A	11	(5)	10
44	Tamás Kádár	HUN	14/03/90	D	10		
34	Yevhen Khacheridi		28/07/87	D	12		1
18	Nikita Korzun	BLR	06/03/95	M	5	(6)	
35	Maxym Koval		09/12/92	G	7		
21	Mykyta Kravchenko		14/06/97	M	1		
27	Yevhen Makarenko		21/05/91	D	10		1
9	Mykola Morozyuk		17/01/88	D	25	(3)	4
14	Zurab Ochigava		18/05/95	D	4	(4)	
48	Pavlo Orikhovskiy		13/05/96	M	2	(1)	1
4	Aleksandar Pantić	SRB	11/04/92	D	13		
72	Artur Rudko		07/05/92	G	17		
17	Serhiy Rybalka		01/04/90	M	17	(9)	1
8	Volodymyr Shepelev		01/06/97	M	10	(2)	
1	Olexandr Shovkovskiy		02/01/75	G	8		
16	Serhiy Sydorchuk		02/05/91	M	24	(3)	4
15	Viktor Tsygankov		15/11/97	M	11	(9)	3
40	Olexandr Tymchyk		20/01/97	D	2		
24	Domagoj Vida	CRO	29/04/89	D	28		3
20	Roman Yaremchuk		27/11/95	A	5	(4)	
10	Andriy Yarmolenko		23/10/89	M	23	(5)	15

FC Karpaty Lviv

1963 • Arena Lviv (34,915) • fckarpaty.lviv.ua

Major honours
USSR Cup (1) 1969

Coach: (Serhiy Zaytsev); (07/10/16) Oleg Dulub (BLR)

2016

Date		Opponent		Score	Scorers
23/07	a	Stal	W	3-0	*Chachua, Blanco 2*
31/07	h	Dynamo	L	0-2	
07/08	a	Vorskla	D	1-1	*Hrysio*
12/08	h	Shakhtar	L	2-3	*Blanco, Chachua*
21/08	a	Zorya	L	1-2	*Lobai*
28/08	h	Olimpik	L	0-2	
11/09	a	Zirka	L	0-1	
17/09	h	Chornomorets	D	0-0	
25/09	a	Olexandriya	L	2-3	*Ksionz, Chachua*
02/10	a	Volyn	D	1-1	*Khudobyak*
16/10	h	Dnipro	D	1-1	*Blanco*
22/10	h	Stal	L	0-1	
29/10	a	Dynamo	L	1-4	*Zaviyskiy*
05/11	h	Vorskla	W	1-0	*Blanco*
19/11	a	Shakhtar	L	1-2	*Ksionz (p)*
27/11	h	Zorya	D	2-2	*Khudobyak, Blanco*
11/12	h	Zirka	L	2-3	*Blanco, Chachua*

2017

Date		Opponent		Score	Scorers
26/02	a	Chornomorets	L	0-1	
05/03	h	Olexandriya	W	1-0	*Khudobyak*
11/03	h	Volyn	W	2-1	*Gladkiy, Khudobyak*
17/03	a	Dnipro	D	0-0	
26/03	a	Olimpik	D	0-0	
02/04	h	Stal	W	2-0	*Gladkiy 2 (1p)*
09/04	h	Dnipro	D	2-2	*og (Svatok), Khudobyak*
15/04	a	Vorskla	D	0-0	
23/04	h	Volyn	W	1-0	*Hutsulyak*
29/04	a	Zirka	L	2-3	*Gladkiy, Hutsulyak*
07/05	a	Stal	L	1-2	*Nesterov*
14/05	a	Dnipro	W	3-2	*Ksionz, Nesterov, Hrysio*
21/05	h	Vorskla	L	0-1	
27/05	a	Volyn	W	1-0	*Hutsulyak*
31/05	h	Zirka	W	2-1	*Nesterov, Matviyenko*

No	Name	Nat	DoB	Pos	Aps	(s)	Gls
9	Gustavo Blanco	ARG	05/11/91	A	17		7
40	Ihor Bohach		03/05/96	M		(3)	
66	Yevhen Borovyk		02/03/85	G	14		
11	Ambrosiy Chachua		02/04/94	M	16	(14)	4
28	Yevhen Chumak		25/08/95	M	1	(2)	
34	Olexiy Dityatyev		07/11/88	D	13		
8	Artem Filimonov		21/02/94	M	7	(1)	
21	Olexandr Gladkiy		24/08/84	A	13		4
27	Oleh Holodyuk		02/01/88	M	6		
47	Maxym Hrysio		14/05/96	M	10	(16)	2
9	Olexiy Hutsulyak		25/12/97	A	7	(6)	3
77	Gegam Kadimyan	ARM	19/10/92	M	3	(4)	
77	Viktor Khomchenko		11/11/94	M		(3)	
16	Ihor Khudobyak		20/02/85	M	29		5
48	Dmytro Klyots		15/04/96	M	15	(2)	
8	Volodymyr Kostevych		23/10/92	M	16		
3	Vasyl Kravets		20/08/97	D	12	(3)	
7	Pavlo Ksionz		02/01/87	M	19	(3)	3
70	Ivan Lobai		21/05/96	D	28	(1)	1
79	Andriy Markovych		25/06/95	D		(4)	
22	Mykola Matviyenko		02/05/96	D	14		1
94	Denys Miroshnychenko		11/10/94	D	17	(9)	
23	Roman Mysak		09/09/91	G	4		
5	Andriy Nesterov		02/07/90	D	30		3
26	Artur Novotryasov		19/07/92	M	8		
98	Gabriel Okechukwu	NGA	26/08/95	A		(2)	
1	Roman Pidkivka		09/05/95	G	14		
19	Serhiy Rudyka		14/06/88	M	1	(4)	
17	Maxym Salamakha		17/07/96	A		(2)	
10	Shina	BRA	02/08/96	A		(2)	
27	Vadym Strashkevych		21/04/94	A		(1)	
88	Nazar Verbniy		26/07/97	M	15	(4)	
74	Nazar Vyzdryk		27/04/96	D		(1)	
21	Kostyantyn Yaroshenko		12/09/86	M	4	(1)	
73	Taras Zaviyskiy		12/04/95	M	4	(3)	1
20	Dmytro Zayikin		06/04/97	A		(1)	
42	Yevhen Zubeyko		30/09/89	D	15	(1)	

FC Olexandriya

1948 • CSC Nika (7,000) • fco.com.ua

Coach: Volodymyr Sharan

2016

23/07 a Dynamo L 1-5 *Banada*
31/07 h Vorskla W 3-2 *Starenkiy, Zaporozhan, Hrytsuk*
07/08 a Shakhtar L 0-1
13/08 h Zorya L 0-1
20/08 a Olimpik W 2-0 *Chorniy, Zaporozhan (p)*
28/08 h Zirka W 4-0 *Chorniy, Hitchenko, Hrytsuk, Ponomar*
11/09 a Chornomorets L 0-1
18/09 a Volyn D 1-1 *Polyarus*
25/09 h Karpaty W 3-2 *Zaporozhan (p), Ponomar, og (Lobai)*
01/10 a Dnipro W 4-1 *Ponomar, Yaremchuk 2, Mykytsei*
16/10 h Stal W 2-0 *Starenkiy, Kulish*
23/10 h Dynamo D 1-1 *Ponomar*
30/10 a Vorskla D 2-2 *Yaremchuk 2*
06/11 h Shakhtar L 1-2 *Yaremchuk*
19/11 a Zorya W 2-1 *Mykytsei, Kulish*
27/11 h Olimpik D 1-1 *Ponomar*
04/12 a Zirka D 1-1 *Shendryk*
11/12 h Chornomorets W 2-1 *Mykytsei, Hrytsuk*

2017

25/02 h Volyn W 6-0 *Hrytsuk (p), Kulish 4, og (Zaderetskiy)*
05/03 a Karpaty L 0-1
11/03 h Dnipro D 0-0
18/03 a Stal L 1-4 *Starenkiy*
02/04 h Dynamo L 1-4 *Ohyrya*
09/04 h Zorya D 0-0
16/04 a Chornomorets L 0-1
22/04 h Olimpik W 1-0 *Polyarus*
30/04 a Shakhtar L 0-1
07/05 a Dynamo L 0-6
13/05 a Zorya L 0-1
21/05 h Chornomorets D 1-1 *Hrytsuk (p)*
26/05 a Olimpik D 0-0
31/05 h Shakhtar D 1-1 *Starenkiy*

No	Name	Nat	DoB	Pos	Aps	(s)	Gls
44	Yevhen Banada		29/02/92	M	23		1
87	Serhiy Basov		19/01/87	D	22	(1)	
5	Valeriy Bondarenko		03/02/94	D	4	(3)	
77	Vakhtang Chanturishvili	GEO	05/08/93	M		(4)	
25	Serhiy Chebotayev		07/03/88	D	19		
13	Artem Chorniy		23/10/89	M	8	(7)	2
17	Andriy Hitchenko		02/10/84	D	17	(1)	1
22	Vasyl Hrytsuk		21/11/87	M	21	(4)	5
72	Mykhailo Kozak		20/01/91	M	8	(5)	
7	Stanislav Kulish		08/02/89	A	8	(12)	6
6	Dmytro Leonov		06/11/88	M	5	(13)	
24	Vladyslav Levanidov		23/02/93	G	15	(1)	
8	Pavlo Myagkov		30/12/92	M	3	(6)	
3	Stanislav Mykytsei		07/09/89	D	12		3
54	Andriy Novak		06/12/88	G	17		
4	Vladyslav Ohyrya		03/04/90	M	18	(3)	1
14	Artem Polyarus		05/07/92	M	15	(5)	2
9	Vitaliy Ponomar		31/05/90	A	26	(5)	5
10	Volodymyr Priyomov		02/10/86	A	1	(6)	
40	Yuriy Putrash		29/01/90	D	4	(2)	
26	Anton Shendryk		26/05/86	D	23		1
3	Serhiy Siminin		09/10/87	D	9		
27	Serhiy Starenkiy		20/09/84	M	16	(7)	4
11	Andriy Tsurikov		05/10/92	D	23		
10	Roman Yaremchuk		27/11/95	A	11	(3)	5
15	Andriy Zaporozhan		21/03/83	M	23	(1)	3
12	Maxym Zhichikov		07/11/92	M	1	(2)	

FC Olimpik Donetsk

2001 • Yuvileiniy, Sumy (25,830); Arena Lviv, Lviv (34,915); Tsentralniy, Cherkasy (10,321); Dynamo im. Valeriy Lobanovskiy, Kyiv (16,873); Vorskla im. Olexiy Butovskiy, Poltava (24,795); Zirka, Kropyvnytskyi (14,628) • olimpik.com.ua

Coach: Roman Sanzhar

2016

24/07 a Zorya L 0-3
30/07 a Volyn D 2-2 *Postupalenko, Petrov*
07/08 h Zirka W 4-2 *Matyazh, Shestakov, Postupalenko, Kornev*
14/08 a Chornomorets L 0-3
20/08 h Olexandriya L 0-2
28/08 a Karpaty W 2-0 *Lysenko 2*
11/09 h Dnipro W 3-0 *Bogdanov 3*
17/09 a Stal W 3-2 *Postupalenko, Bogdanov, Hryn*
24/09 h Dynamo L 0-4
01/10 a Vorskla W 2-1 *Hryn, Shestakov*
15/10 h Shakhtar D 1-1 *Matyazh*
23/10 h Zorya L 0-2
29/10 h Volyn W 2-1 *Postupalenko, Hryshko*
05/11 a Zirka W 2-1 *Petrov, Postupalenko*
19/11 h Chornomorets W 1-0 *Matyazh*
27/11 a Olexandriya D 1-1 *Matyazh (p)*
09/12 a Dnipro D 1-1 *Tanchyk*

2017

25/02 h Stal D 0-0
04/03 a Dynamo L 0-1
11/03 h Vorskla W 3-2 *Rhasalla, Hryshko, Matyazh*
17/03 a Shakhtar D 1-1 *Postupalenko*
26/03 h Karpaty D 0-0
01/04 a Chornomorets D 0-0
09/04 a Dynamo L 0-4
15/04 h Shakhtar L 0-4
22/04 a Olexandriya L 0-1
30/04 h Zorya D 1-1 *Nemchaninov*
06/05 h Chornomorets W 1-0 *Brikner*
13/05 h Dynamo W 2-1 *Serhiychuk, Postupalenko*
21/05 a Shakhtar D 1-1 *Serhiychuk*
26/05 h Olexandriya D 0-0
31/05 a Zorya L 0-2

No	Name	Nat	DoB	Pos	Aps	(s)	Gls
5	Artem Baranovskiy		17/03/90	D	9	(1)	
22	Stanislav Bilenkiy		02/08/98	A		(1)	
90	Andriy Bogdanov		21/01/90	M	22	(1)	4
27	Ivan Brikner		30/06/93	D	6	(7)	1
8	Volodymyr Doronin		15/01/93	M	14	(1)	
7	Maxym Drachenko		28/01/90	M	3	(3)	
24	Vitaliy Fedoriv		21/10/87	D	7	(10)	
15	Vitaliy Hemeha		10/01/94	M	3	(1)	
9	Vitaliy Hoshkoderya		08/01/88	M	21	(6)	
94	Serhiy Hryn		06/06/94	M	13	(7)	2
4	Dmytro Hryshko		02/12/85	D	23		2
32	Vladis-Emmerson Illoy-Ayyet		07/10/95	D	18	(3)	
45	Vladyslav Khomutov		04/06/98	M	3	(14)	
19	Illya Kornev		01/11/96	A	1	(4)	1
31	Yaroslav Kotlyarov		19/11/97	G	1	(2)	
21	Volodymyr Lysenko		20/04/88	A	7	(4)	2
1	Zauri Makharadze		24/03/93	G	31		
20	Ivan Matyazh		15/02/88	A	17	(7)	5
23	Dmytro Nemchaninov		27/01/90	D	26	(3)	1
33	Yaroslav Oliynyk		14/03/91	D	15	(5)	
3	Temur Partsveniya		06/07/91	D	11	(2)	
26	Kyrylo Petrov		22/06/90	D	15		2
14	Anton Postupalenko		28/08/88	M	19	(3)	7
11	Mohammed Rhasalla	MAR	15/09/93	A	13		1
7	Mykhailo Serhiychuk		29/07/91	A	6	(3)	2
17	Serhiy Shestakov		12/04/90	M	27	(1)	2
34	Volodymyr Tanchyk		17/10/91	M	10	(4)	1
44	Yevheniy Tsymbalyuk		19/06/96	M	10	(2)	
25	Ihor Zhurakhovskiy		19/09/94	M	1		

FC Shakhtar Donetsk

1936 • Arena Lviv, Lviv (34,915); Metalist, Kharkiv (38,633); Dynamo im. Valeriy Lobanovskiy, Kyiv (16,873) • shakhtar.com

Major honours

UEFA Cup (1) 2009; Ukrainian League (10) 2002, 2005, 2006, 2008, 2010, 2011, 2012, 2013, 2014, 2017; USSR Cup (4) 1961, 1962, 1980, 1983; Ukrainian Cup (11) 1995, 1997, 2001, 2002, 2004, 2008, 2011, 2012, 2013, 2016, 2017

Coach: Paulo Fonseca (POR)

2016

22/07 h Zirka W 4-1 *Bernard, Taison, Eduardo, og (Kovaliov)*
30/07 a Chornomorets W 4-1 *Seleznyov, Fred, Eduardo, Kovalenko*
07/08 h Olexandriya W 1-0 *Ismaily*
12/08 a Karpaty W 3-2 *Stepanenko, Kovalenko, Marlos*
21/08 h Dnipro W 4-0 *Ordets, Dentinho, Marlos, Ferreyra*
28/08 a Stal W 1-0 *Ferreyra*
09/09 h Dynamo D 1-1 *Dentinho*
18/09 a Vorskla W 1-0 *Taison*
24/09 h Volyn W 3-0 *og (Kychak), Ordets, Boryachuk*
02/10 h Zorya W 1-0 *Ferreyra*
15/10 a Olimpik D 1-1 *Ordets*
23/10 a Zirka W 3-0 *og (Pereyra), Boryachuk, Ferreyra*
29/10 h Chornomorets W 2-0 *Ferreyra, Dentinho*
06/11 a Olexandriya W 2-1 *Dentinho, Ferreyra*
19/11 h Karpaty W 2-1 *Srna, Ferreyra*
27/11 a Dnipro W 2-0 *Kovalenko 2*
04/12 h Stal W 2-0 *Marlos (p), Taison*
12/12 a Dynamo W 4-3 *og (Khacheridi) 2, Fred, Ferreyra*

2017

26/02 h Vorskla W 2-1 *Kovalenko, Ferreyra*
05/03 a Volyn W 1-0 *Kovalenko*
12/03 a Zorya W 2-1 *Bernard, Malyshev*
17/03 h Olimpik D 1-1 *Blanco*
02/04 a Zorya W 2-1 *Blanco, Taison*
09/04 h Chornomorets L 1-2 *Bernard*
15/04 a Olimpik W 4-0 *Taison, Bernard, Kovalenko, Ferreyra (p)*
21/04 a Dynamo W 1-0 *Ferreyra*
30/04 h Olexandriya W 1-0 *Ferreyra*
06/05 h Zorya W 3-2 *Ferreyra, Ismaily, Ordets*
13/05 a Chornomorets W 3-0 *og (Ablitarov), Blanco 2*
21/05 h Olimpik D 1-1 *Butko*
26/05 h Dynamo L 2-3 *Alan Patrick, Dentinho*
31/05 a Olexandriya D 1-1 *Boryachuk*

No	Name	Nat	DoB	Pos	Aps	(s)	Gls
29	Alan Patrick	BRA	13/05/91	M	3	(6)	1
20	Giorgi Arabidze	GEO	04/03/97	A	1		
10	Bernard	BRA	08/09/92	M	20	(4)	4
99	Gustavo Blanco	ARG	05/11/91	A	9	(2)	4
41	Andriy Boryachuk		23/04/96	A	2	(5)	3
2	Bohdan Butko		13/01/91	D	10	(1)	1
9	Dentinho	BRA	19/01/89	M	11	(12)	5
22	Eduardo	CRO	25/02/83	A	7	(3)	2
19	Facundo Ferreyra	ARG	14/03/91	A	13	(7)	13
8	Fred	BRA	05/03/93	M	18		2
31	Ismaily	BRA	11/01/90	D	27	(1)	2
32	Anton Kanibolotskiy		16/05/88	G	1		
52	Ihor Kiryukhantsev		21/01/96	D		(1)	
14	Vasyl Kobin		24/05/85	D	1	(1)	
74	Viktor Kovalenko		14/02/96	M	21	(7)	7
38	Serhiy Krivtsov		15/03/91	D	5	(1)	
5	Olexandr Kucher		22/10/82	D	20	(2)	
55	Oleh Kudryk		17/10/96	G	1		
17	Maxym Malyshev		24/12/92	M	14	(10)	1
66	Márcio Azevedo	BRA	05/02/86	D	3		
11	Marlos	BRA	07/06/88	M	25	(5)	3
18	Ivan Ordets		08/07/92	D	18	(2)	4
49	Olexandr Pikhalionok		07/05/97	M		(1)	
30	Andriy Pyatov		28/06/84	G	28		
44	Yaroslav Rakitskiy		03/08/89	D	21		
7	Yevhen Seleznyov		20/07/85	A	2	(1)	1
26	Mykyta Shevchenko		26/01/93	G	2		
33	Darijo Srna	CRO	01/05/82	D	23		1
6	Taras Stepanenko		08/08/89	M	20	(7)	1
28	Taison	BRA	13/01/88	M	17	(7)	5
24	Vyacheslav Tankovskiy		16/08/95	M	4		
29	Andriy Totovytskiy		20/01/93	M		(1)	
12	Wellington Nem	BRA	06/02/92	M	2	(5)	
59	Olexandr Zubkov		03/08/96	M	3	(5)	

UKRAINE

FC Stal Kamianske

1926 • Meteor, Dnipropetrovsk (24,381) • fcstal.com

Coach: Eric van der Meer (NED); (10/08/16) Joop Gall (NED); (15/01/17) Leonid Kuchuk (BLR)

Date		Opponent		Score	Scorers
2016					
23/07	h	Karpaty	L	0-3	
31/07	a	Dnipro	D	1-1	*Comvalius*
06/08	h	Volyn	W	1-0	*Deul*
14/08	h	Dynamo	L	1-2	*Ishchenko*
21/08	a	Vorskla	D	0-0	
28/08	h	Shakhtar	L	0-1	
10/09	a	Zorya	D	2-2	*Karikari, Vasin*
17/09	h	Olimpik	L	2-3	*Karasyuk, Comvalius (p)*
25/09	a	Zirka	D	0-0	
01/10	h	Chornomorets	L	1-2	*Karikari*
16/10	a	Olexandriya	L	0-2	
22/10	a	Karpaty	W	1-0	*Kalenchuk*
30/10	h	Dnipro	D	1-1	*Comvalius*
04/11	a	Volyn	W	1-0	*Comvalius (p)*
19/11	a	Dynamo	L	1-2	*Comvalius*
26/11	h	Vorskla	L	0-1	
04/12	a	Shakhtar	L	0-2	
11/12	h	Zorya	L	0-2	
2017					
25/02	a	Olimpik	D	0-0	
05/03	h	Zirka	W	3-0	*Karasyuk, Vasin (p), Debelko*
11/03	a	Chornomorets	W	1-0	*Vasin*
18/03	h	Olexandriya	W	4-1	*Karikari 3 (1p), Deul (p)*
02/04	a	Karpaty	L	0-2	
08/04	h	Volyn	W	2-0	*Karikari 2*
15/04	a	Dnipro	D	0-0	
23/04	h	Zirka	W	1-0	*Leandro*
29/04	a	Vorskla	L	0-2	
07/05	h	Karpaty	W	2-1	*Debelko, Karasyuk*
12/05	a	Volyn	W	1-0	*Debelko*
20/05	h	Dnipro	L	0-1	
27/05	a	Zirka	W	1-0	*Vasin*
31/05	h	Vorskla	D	0-0	

No	Name	Nat	DoB	Pos	Aps	(s)	Gls
12	Olexandr Bandura		30/05/86	G	4		
99	Sylvano Comvalius	NED	10/08/87	A	12	(5)	5
14	Erixon Danso	ARU	22/07/89	M	3	(5)	
93	Roman Debelko		08/08/93	A	8	(12)	3
10	Boy Deul	NED	30/08/87	M	10	(8)	2
3	Olexiy Dovhiy		02/11/89	M	4	(2)	
32	Mykola Ishchenko		09/03/83	D	24	(2)	1
6	Maxym Kalenchuk		05/12/89	M	29	(1)	1
91	Roman Karasyuk		27/03/91	M	26	(4)	3
16	Kwame Karikari	GHA	21/01/92	A	17	(9)	7
21	Yuriy Klymchuk		05/05/97	M	2	(3)	
4	Anton Kravchenko		23/03/91	D	8	(5)	
17	Orest Kuzyk		17/05/95	M	2	(3)	
2	Leandro	BRA	26/06/85	D	14		1
18	Edgar Malakyan	ARM	22/09/90	M	21	(5)	
8	Gor Malakyan	ARM	12/06/94	M	13	(6)	
25	Mykhailo Meskhi		26/02/97	M		(1)	
88	Maryan Mysyk		02/10/96	M	11	(5)	
79	Yuriy Pankiv		03/11/84	G	28		
20	Pavlo Paşayev	AZE	04/01/88	D	28	(1)	
15	Artem Shabanov		07/03/92	D	13		
13	Miloš Stamenković	SRB	01/06/90	D	27	(4)	
39	Denys Vasin		04/03/89	M	18	(7)	4
7	Serhiy Voronin		24/03/87	D	14		
94	Maxym Zaderaka		07/09/94	M	16	(6)	

FC Volyn Lutsk

1960 • Avanhard (10,792); Ukraina, Lviv (27,925) • fcvolyn.net

Coach: Vitaliy Kvartsyaniy

Date		Opponent		Score	Scorers
2016					
24/07	a	Dnipro	L	0-5	
30/07	h	Olimpik	D	2-2	*Khomchenko, Herasymyuk*
06/08	a	Stal	L	0-1	
13/08	h	Zirka	W	1-0	*og (Bayenko)*
20/08	a	Dynamo	L	1-2	*Petrov*
27/08	h	Chornomorets	L	0-1	
11/09	a	Vorskla	L	1-2	*Didenko (p)*
18/09	h	Olexandriya	D	1-1	*Petrov*
24/09	a	Shakhtar	L	0-3	
02/10	h	Karpaty	D	1-1	*Petrov*
15/10	a	Zorya	L	0-2	
22/10	h	Dnipro	W	3-0	*Memeshev, Dudyk, Shapoval*
29/10	a	Olimpik	L	1-2	*Dudyk*
04/11	h	Stal	L	0-1	
20/11	a	Zirka	L	0-2	
26/11	h	Dynamo	L	1-4	*Didenko*
03/12	a	Chornomorets	D	0-0	
10/12	h	Vorskla	L	0-1	
2017					
25/02	a	Olexandriya	L	0-6	
05/03	h	Shakhtar	L	0-1	
11/03	a	Karpaty	L	1-2	*Dudyk*
19/03	h	Zorya	L	0-1	
01/04	a	Vorskla	L	0-2	
08/04	a	Stal	L	0-2	
14/04	h	Zirka	W	1-0	*Petrov*
23/04	a	Karpaty	L	0-1	
30/04	h	Dnipro	L	0-1	
05/05	h	Vorskla	L	0-1	
12/05	h	Stal	L	0-1	
20/05	a	Zirka	L	0-2	
27/05	h	Karpaty	L	0-1	
31/05	a	Dnipro	W	3-0	*(w/o; match abandoned after 47 mins at 0-1)*

No	Name	Nat	DoB	Pos	Aps	(s)	Gls
61	Roman Babyak		28/02/98	D	1	(1)	
17	Andriy Bogdanov		21/01/90	M	1		
48	Olexandr Chepelyuk		05/09/97	M	14	(10)	
59	Yaroslav Deda		28/05/99	A	7	(4)	
99	Anatoliy Didenko		09/06/82	A	16	(1)	2
78	Vladyslav Dmytrenko		24/05/00	A	2	(3)	
97	Artem Dudyk		02/01/97	M	16	(8)	3
24	Miha Goropevšek	SVN	12/03/91	D	18	(4)	
7	Oleh Herasymyuk		25/09/86	M	21		1
79	Bohdan Hladun		10/06/99	A		(1)	
30	Oleh Humenyuk		03/05/83	D	1		
60	Roman Ilnytskiy		30/01/98	M	1	(3)	
94	Viktor Khomchenko		11/11/94	M	9		1
86	Yevhen Kotyun		31/07/96	M	2	(1)	
89	Dmytro Kozban		27/04/89	A	2		
1	Artem Kychak		16/05/89	G	17		
18	Serhiy Loginov		24/08/90	D	22		
76	Andriy Lyashenko		11/06/98	M	5	(11)	
73	Andriy Marchuk		25/06/97	G	7		
80	Ruslan Marushka		23/08/98	D	4	(2)	
67	Serhiy Melynyshyn		26/05/97	D	7	(3)	
9	Redvan Memeshev		15/08/93	M	26		1
42	Vitaliy Nedilko		21/08/82	G	7		
25	Andriy Nykytyuk		16/08/94	M	1	(10)	
26	Roman Nykytyuk		09/09/93	D	21	(1)	
38	Serhiy Petrov		21/05/97	A	27	(2)	4
47	Yuriy Romanyuk		06/05/97	D	26	(2)	
13	Artem Shabanov		07/03/92	D	14		
50	Roman Shandruk		29/05/98	M	1	(1)	
22	Vladyslav Shapoval		08/09/95	D	23	(2)	1
65	Yuriy Teterenko		22/01/97	M	14	(6)	
58	Oleh Trakalo		14/02/98	D	1	(1)	
54	Serhiy Trykosh		12/10/98	M	1	(1)	
20	Dmytro Zaderetskiy		03/08/94	M	16	(10)	
84	Roman Zhmurko		27/07/97	G	1		

FC Vorskla Poltava

1955 • Vorskla im. Olexiy Butovskiy (24,795) • vorskla.com.ua

Major honours
Ukrainian Cup (1) 2009

Coach: Vasyl Sachko

Date		Opponent		Score	Scorers
2016					
23/07	h	Chornomorets	W	1-0	*Khlebas*
31/07	a	Olexandriya	L	2-3	*Kolomoyets, Khlebas*
07/08	h	Karpaty	D	1-1	*Kolomoyets*
13/08	a	Dnipro	D	1-1	*Khlebas*
21/08	h	Stal	D	0-0	
27/08	a	Dynamo	W	2-0	*Kolomoyets 2*
11/09	h	Volyn	W	2-1	*Khlebas, Tursunov*
18/09	h	Shakhtar	L	0-1	
24/09	a	Zorya	L	1-2	*Dityatyev*
01/10	h	Olimpik	L	1-2	*Chesnakov*
16/10	a	Zirka	L	0-2	
23/10	a	Chornomorets	W	2-1	*Kolomoyets 2*
30/10	h	Olexandriya	D	2-2	*Kobakhidze, Odaryuk*
05/11	a	Karpaty	L	0-1	
20/11	h	Dnipro	L	1-2	*Tursunov*
26/11	a	Stal	W	1-0	*Rebenok*
03/12	h	Dynamo	D	2-2	*Tursunov, Rebenok*
10/12	a	Volyn	W	1-0	*Odaryuk*
2017					
26/02	a	Shakhtar	L	1-2	*Khlebas*
05/03	h	Zorya	L	1-2	*Sharpar (p)*
11/03	a	Olimpik	L	2-3	*Khlebas, Zahorulko*
18/03	h	Zirka	D	0-0	
01/04	h	Volyn	W	2-0	*Sharpar, Khlebas*
08/04	a	Zirka	L	0-1	
15/04	h	Karpaty	D	0-0	
22/04	a	Dnipro	L	0-2	
29/04	h	Stal	W	2-0	*Sharpar (p), Rebenok*
05/05	a	Volyn	W	1-0	*Myakushko*
14/05	h	Zirka	D	1-1	*Khlebas*
21/05	a	Karpaty	W	1-0	*Sharpar*
27/05	h	Dnipro	W	1-0	*Sharpar*
31/05	a	Stal	D	0-0	

No	Name	Nat	DoB	Pos	Aps	(s)	Gls
24	Oleh Barannyk		20/03/92	A		(1)	
11	Mladen Bartulović	CRO	05/10/86	M	8	(8)	
17	Volodymyr Chesnakov		12/02/88	D	28		1
33	Olexandr Chizhov		10/08/86	D	12		
44	Ardin Dallku	ALB	01/11/94	D	10	(1)	
54	Olexiy Dityatyev		07/11/88	D	16		1
27	Oleh Holodyuk		02/01/88	M	7		
16	Serhiy Ichanskiy		01/09/95	M		(1)	
13	Dmytro Khlebas		09/05/94	A	23	(6)	8
7	Aleksandre Kobakhidze	GEO	11/02/87	M	16	(1)	1
26	Yuriy Kolomoyets		22/03/90	A	11	(2)	6
38	Serhiy Kosovskiy		19/05/98	M		(1)	
29	Dmytro Kravchenko		25/02/95	M	21	(2)	
3	Roman Kunev		20/09/90	D		(5)	
10	Serhiy Myakushko		15/04/93	M	10	(4)	1
12	Dmytro Nepogodov		17/02/88	G	13		
19	Volodymyr Odaryuk		13/02/94	A	15	(3)	2
5	Oleh Ostapenko		11/06/97	D		(1)	
4	Ihor Perduta		15/11/90	D	27	(1)	
79	Andriy Pylyavskiy		04/12/88	D	7	(1)	
82	Pavlo Rebenok		23/07/85	M	24	(5)	3
40	Taras Sakhiv		19/11/97	D	2	(5)	
23	Vadym Sapai		07/02/86	D	11	(1)	
12	Bohdan Sarnavskiy		29/01/95	G	3		
25	Dmytro Shapoval		17/06/96	A		(1)	
11	Vyacheslav Sharpar		02/06/87	M	13		5
1	Bohdan Shust		04/03/86	G	16		
3	Serhiy Siminin		09/10/87	D	12		
6	Olexandr Sklyar		26/02/91	M	8	(7)	
8	Andriy Tkachuk		18/11/87	M	21	(2)	
10	Sanzhar Tursunov	UZB	29/12/86	M	9	(3)	3
9	Artur Zahorulko		13/02/93	A	6	(18)	1
99	Yevhen Zarichnyuk		03/02/89	M	3	(6)	

FC Zirka Kropyvnytskyi

1911 • Zirka (14,628); Slavutych Arena, Zaporizhya (11,756) • fczirka.com.ua

Coach: Serhiy Lavrynenko; (18/08/16) (Dario Drudi (ARG); (15/11/16) Roman Monarev

2016					
22/07	a	Shakhtar	L	1-4	*Sitalo*
30/07	h	Zorya	D	1-1	*Cucerenco (p)*
07/08	a	Olimpik	L	2-4	*Lupashko, Zahalskiy*
13/08	a	Volyn	L	0-1	
21/08	h	Chornomorets	L	0-1	
28/08	a	Olexandriya	L	0-4	
11/09	h	Karpaty	W	1-0	*Favorov (p)*
17/09	a	Dnipro	W	1-0	*Moya*
25/09	h	Stal	D	0-0	
02/10	a	Dynamo	L	0-2	
16/10	h	Vorskla	W	2-0	*Moya, Popov*
23/10	h	Shakhtar	L	0-3	
30/10	a	Zorya	L	1-2	*Zahalskiy (p)*
05/11	h	Olimpik	L	1-2	*Favorov*
20/11	h	Volyn	W	2-0	*Favorov, Bilonoh*
26/11	a	Chornomorets	L	1-2	*Bilonoh*
04/12	h	Olexandriya	D	1-1	*Batsula*
11/12	a	Karpaty	W	3-2	*Batsula, Pereyra, Cucerenco*
2017					
26/02	h	Dnipro	D	1-1	*Sitalo*
05/03	a	Stal	L	0-3	
12/03	h	Dynamo	W	2-0	*Batsula, Polehenko*
18/03	a	Vorskla	D	0-0	
01/04	a	Dnipro	L	0-1	
08/04	h	Vorskla	W	1-0	*Ekiza*
16/04	a	Volyn	L	0-1	
23/04	a	Stal	L	0-1	
29/04	h	Karpaty	W	3-2	*Bilonoh, Zahalskiy (p), Drachenko*
07/05	h	Dnipro	D	1-1	*Pereyra*
14/05	a	Vorskla	D	1-1	*Zahalskiy*
20/05	h	Volyn	W	2-0	*Eseola, Sitalo*
27/05	h	Stal	L	0-1	
31/05	a	Karpaty	L	1-2	*Pryadun*

No	Name	Nat	DoB	Pos	Aps	(s)	Gls
50	Olexandr Akymenko		05/09/85	A	1	(8)	
11	Andriy Batsula		06/02/92	D	26		3
29	Volodymyr Bayenko		09/02/90	D	14		
26	Dmytro Bilonoh		26/05/95	M	8	(8)	3
77	Olexiy Chichikov		30/09/87	M	12	(4)	
28	Yevhen Chumak		25/08/95	M	2	(3)	
18	Alexandr Cucerenco	MDA	01/10/91	D	20	(1)	2
10	Oleh Dopilka		12/03/86	D	2		
7	Maxym Drachenko		28/01/90	M	11		1
27	Kyrylo Dryshlyuk		16/09/99	M	5	(2)	
32	Borja Ekiza	ESP	06/03/88	M	10		1
10	Aderinsona Eseola		28/06/91	A	7	(3)	1
20	Dmytro Fateyev		21/06/94	D	14		
10	Artem Favorov		19/03/94	A	5	(6)	3
17	Aitor Fernández	ESP	23/08/86	M	7	(1)	
30	Hennadiy Ganev		15/05/90	G	1		
7	Vitaliy Gavrysh		18/03/86	M	6		
7	Ihor Kalinin		11/11/95	D	2	(3)	
27	Olexandr Kochura		07/03/86	M		(2)	
55	Maxym Kovaliov		20/03/89	D	13		
99	Roman Loktionov		18/10/86	A	1	(5)	
8	Vladyslav Lupashko		04/12/86	M	15	(2)	1
41	Roman Lyopka		26/01/97	G	3		
23	Olexandr Matkobozhyk		03/01/98	D	2	(1)	
16	Jonathan Moya	CRC	06/01/92	A	6	(5)	2
5	Nailson	BRA	24/02/94	D	3		
44	Yevhen Past		16/03/88	G	28		
4	Federico Pereyra	ARG	04/01/89	D	22		2
28	Pavlo Polehenko		06/01/95	M	15	(4)	1
95	Roman Popov		29/06/95	M	5	(8)	1
29	Maxym Pryadun		17/02/97	M	2	(1)	1
9	Artem Shchedriy		09/11/92	M	17	(10)	
14	Artem Sitalo		01/08/89	A	29	(1)	3
21	Ihor Zahalskiy		19/05/91	M	23	(5)	4
15	Olexiy Zbun		09/06/97	M	6	(2)	
99	Mykyta Zhukov		19/03/95	M	4	(5)	
13	Olexandr Zozulya		11/04/96	D		(1)	
24	Ruslan Zubkov		24/11/91	M	5	(4)	

FC Zorya Luhansk

1923 • Slavutych Arena, Zaporizhya (11,756) • zarya-lugansk.com

Major honours
USSR League (1) 1972

Coach: Yuriy Vernydub

2016					
24/07	h	Olimpik	W	3-0	*Bonaventure, Ljubenović, Tkachuk*
30/07	a	Zirka	D	1-1	*Hordiyenko*
07/08	h	Chornomorets	W	4-0	*Karavayev 2, Petryak, Chaikovskiy*
13/08	a	Olexandriya	W	1-0	*Petryak*
21/08	h	Karpaty	W	2-1	*Hordiyenko, Karavayev*
26/08	a	Dnipro	L	0-2	
10/09	h	Stal	D	2-2	*Ljubenović, Karavayev*
18/09	a	Dynamo	W	1-0	*Opanasenko*
24/09	h	Vorskla	W	2-1	*Ljubenović, Paulinho*
02/10	a	Shakhtar	L	0-1	
15/10	h	Volyn	W	2-0	*Kulach, Rafael Forster (p)*
23/10	a	Olimpik	W	2-0	*Rafael Forster 2 (2p)*
30/10	h	Zirka	W	2-1	*Petryak, Kulach*
06/11	a	Chornomorets	D	0-0	
19/11	h	Olexandriya	L	1-2	*Petryak*
27/11	a	Karpaty	D	2-2	*Sukhovskiy, Ljubenović*
03/12	h	Dnipro	L	2-3	*Bezborodko, Karavayev*
11/12	a	Stal	W	2-0	*Karavayev, Bonaventure*
2017					
25/02	h	Dynamo	L	1-2	*Bonaventure*
05/03	a	Vorskla	W	2-1	*Grechishkin, Kalitvintsev (p)*
12/03	h	Shakhtar	L	1-2	*Kharatin*
19/03	a	Volyn	W	1-0	*Rafael Forster (p)*
01/04	h	Shakhtar	L	1-2	*Bonaventure*
09/04	a	Olexandriya	D	0-0	
14/04	h	Dynamo	L	0-1	
23/04	h	Chornomorets	L	1-2	*Rafael Forster*
30/04	a	Olimpik	D	1-1	*Paulinho*
06/05	a	Shakhtar	L	2-3	*Kharatin, Bonaventure*
13/05	h	Olexandriya	W	1-0	*Rafael Forster (p)*
21/05	a	Dynamo	W	2-1	*Checher, Bonaventure*
26/05	a	Chornomorets	W	1-0	*Paulinho*
31/05	h	Olimpik	W	2-0	*Sobol, Petryak*

No	Name	Nat	DoB	Pos	Aps	(s)	Gls
36	Ruslan Babenko		08/07/92	M	2	(3)	
21	Denys Bezborodko		31/05/94	A	3	(2)	1
42	Emmanuel Bonaventure	NGA	15/11/97	A	19	(3)	6
4	Ihor Chaikovskiy		07/10/91	M	17		1
44	Vyacheslav Checher		15/12/80	D	15		1
77	Oleh Chuvayev		25/10/89	G	1		
24	Dmytro Grechishkin		22/09/91	M	21	(3)	1
5	Artem Hordiyenko		04/03/91	M	18	(2)	2
17	Gegam Kadimyan	ARM	19/10/92	M		(4)	
15	Vladyslav Kalitvintsev		04/01/93	M	7	(2)	1
6	Mykyta Kamenyuka		03/06/85	D	14	(1)	
20	Olexandr Karavayev		02/06/92	M	16	(1)	6
8	Ihor Kharatin		02/02/95	M	15	(4)	2
9	Vladyslav Kulach		07/05/93	A	6	(8)	2
17	Yaroslav Kvasov		05/03/92	A		(2)	
91	Ihor Levchenko		23/02/91	G	6		
10	Jaba Lipartia	GEO	16/11/87	M	17	(10)	
22	Željko Ljubenović	SRB	09/07/81	M	13	(13)	4
39	Yevhen Opanasenko		25/08/90	D	18	(3)	1
11	Paulinho	BRA	29/05/93	A	19	(12)	3
34	Ivan Petryak		13/03/94	M	24	(4)	5
99	Andriy Pylyavskiy		04/12/88	D	6	(1)	
12	Rafael Forster	BRA	23/07/90	D	25		6
23	Mykhailo Shershen		27/04/95	D	1		
1	Olexiy Shevchenko		24/02/92	G	25		
3	Mikhail Sivakov	BLR	16/01/88	D	13	(1)	
95	Eduard Sobol		20/04/95	D	14	(7)	1
2	Artem Sukhovskiy		06/12/92	D	15	(2)	1
27	Yevheniy Tkachuk		27/06/91	D	1	(1)	1
16	Hryhoriy Yarmash		04/01/85	D	1	(1)	

Top goalscorers

15	Andriy Yarmolenko (Dynamo)
13	Facundo Ferreyra (Shakhtar)
11	Gustavo Blanco (Karpaty/Shakhtar)
10	Júnior Moraes (Dynamo)
9	Artem Besedin (Dynamo)
	Denys Garmash (Dynamo)
8	Dmytro Khlebas (Vorskla)
7	Dmytro Korkishko (Chornomorets)
	Anton Postupalenko (Olimpik)
	Viktor Kovalenko (Shakhtar)
	Kwame Karikari (Stal)

UKRAINE

Promoted clubs

FC Illychivets Mariupol

1960 • Illychivets (12,680) • fcilich.com
Coach: Olexandr Sevidov

NK Veres Rivne

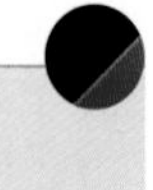

1957 • Avanhard (3,300); Izotop, Varash (3,000) • veres.club
Coach: Volodymyr Mazyar; (25/04/17) (Yuriy Virt)

Second level final table 2016/17

		Pld	W	D	L	F	A	Pts
1	FC Illychivets Mariupol	34	25	6	3	61	21	81
2	FC Desna Chernihiv	34	22	8	4	55	23	74
3	NK Veres Rivne	34	20	7	7	62	32	67
4	FC Helios Kharkiv	34	16	10	8	31	22	58
5	FC Kolos Kovalivka	34	16	9	9	52	38	57
6	FC Naftovyk-Ukrnafta Okhtyrka	34	15	9	10	47	29	54
7	FC Avanhard Kramatorsk	34	14	10	10	32	28	52
8	FC Cherkaskiy Dnipro Cherkasy	34	12	12	10	30	29	48
9	FC Obolon-Brovar Kyiv	34	12	9	13	37	37	45
10	FC Arsenal Kyiv	34	12	9	13	38	39	45
11	FC Hirnyk-Sport Horishni Plavni	34	12	7	15	47	54	43
12	FC Poltava	34	13	4	17	33	43	40
13	FC Inhulets Petrove	34	10	8	16	33	45	38
14	MFC Mykolaiv	34	11	4	19	35	44	37
15	FC Sumy	34	8	12	14	34	44	36
16	FSC Bukovyna Chernivtsi	34	8	9	17	27	40	33
17	FC Skala Stryi	34	5	5	24	25	58	20
18	FC Ternopil	34	3	6	25	17	70	15

NB FC Poltava – 3 pts deducted;
FC Desna Chernihiv did not obtain licence for Premier League; NK Veres Rivne promoted instead.

DOMESTIC CUP

Kubok Ukraïny 2016/17

SECOND ROUND

(21/09/16)
Cherkaskiy Dnipro Cherkasy 1-3 Stal Kamianske
Desna Chernihiv 1-0 Arsenal Kyiv
Illychivets Mariupol 2-0 Ternopil
Myr Hornostaivka 1-2 Veres Rivne
Naftovyk-Ukrnafta Okhtyrka 2-0 Chornomorets Odesa
Nyva Vinnytsya 0-2 Mykolaiv
Perlyna Odesa 0-0 Karpaty Lviv *(aet; 4-5 on pens)*
Poltava 1-0 Zirka Kropyvnytskyi
Volyn Lutsk 2-1 Olimpik Donetsk

(22/09/16)
Real Farma Odesa 0-2 Obolon-Brovar Kyiv

Byes – Dnipro, Dynamo Kyiv, Olexandriya, Shakhtar Donetsk, Vorskla Poltava, Zorya Luhansk

THIRD ROUND

(26/10/16)
Desna Chernihiv 0-0 Dnipro *(aet; 6-7 on pens)*
Dynamo Kyiv 5-2 Zorya Luhansk *(aet)*
Illychivets Mariupol 1-1 Stal Kamianske *(aet; 4-2 on pens)*
Mykolaiv 0-0 Obolon-Brovar Kyiv *(aet; 5-4 on pens)*
Naftovyk-Ukrnafta Okhtyrka 2-1 Volyn Lutsk
Poltava 2-1 Karpaty Lviv
Shakhtar Donetsk 2-1 Olexandriya
Veres Rivne 0-1 Vorskla Poltava

QUARTER-FINALS

(26/11/16)
Mykolaiv 0-0 Illychivets Mariupol *(aet; 4-2 on pens)*

(30/11/16)
Dnipro 1-0 Vorskla Poltava *(Balanyuk 73)*

(05/04/17)
Naftovyk-Ukrnafta Okhtyrka 0-1 Dynamo Kyiv *(Garmash 44)*

Poltava 0-3 Shakhtar Donetsk *(w/o)*

SEMI-FINALS

(26/04/17)
Mykolaiv 0-4 Dynamo Kyiv *(Yarmolenko (45+1, 81p, 90+1, Kádár 44)*

Shakhtar Donetsk 1-0 Dnipro *(Taison 68)*

FINAL

(17/05/17)
Metalist, Kharkiv
FC SHAKHTAR DONETSK 1 *(Marlos 80)*
FC DYNAMO KYIV 0
Referee: *Trukhanov*
SHAKHTAR: *Pyatov, Srna, Kucher, Rakitskiy, Ismaily, Stepanenko, Kovalenko (Malyshev 84), Marlos, Taison, Bernard (Zubkov 90+1), Ferreyra (Ordets 90+2)*
DYNAMO: *Koval, Pantić, Vida, Kádár (Tsygankov 84), Morozyuk, Shepelev, Sydorchuk (Rybalka 67), Antunes, Yarmolenko, Garmash, Besedin*

The Brazilian flag is to the fore as Shakhtar celebrate their 1-0 victory against Dynamo Kyiv in the Ukrainian Cup final

WALES

Cymdeithas Bêl-droed Cymru / Football Association of Wales (FAW)

Address	11/12 Neptune Court, Vanguard Way GB-Cardiff CF24 5PJ
Tel	+44 29 2043 5830
Fax	+44 29 2049 6953
E-mail	info@faw.co.uk
Website	faw.org.uk

President	David Griffiths
General secretary	Jonathan Ford
Media officer	Ian Gwyn Hughes
Year of formation	1876
National stadium	Cardiff City Stadium, Cardiff (33,280)

PREMIER LEAGUE CLUBS

 1 **Aberystwyth Town FC**

 2 **AUK Broughton FC**

 3 **Bala Town FC**

 4 **Bangor City FC**

 5 **Cardiff Metropolitan University FC**

 6 **Carmarthen Town AFC**

 7 **Cefn Druids AFC**

 8 **Connah's Quay FC**

 9 **Llandudno FC**

 10 **Newtown AFC**

 11 **Rhyl FC**

 12 **The New Saints FC**

PROMOTED CLUBS

 13 **Prestatyn Town FC**

 14 **Barry Town United FC**

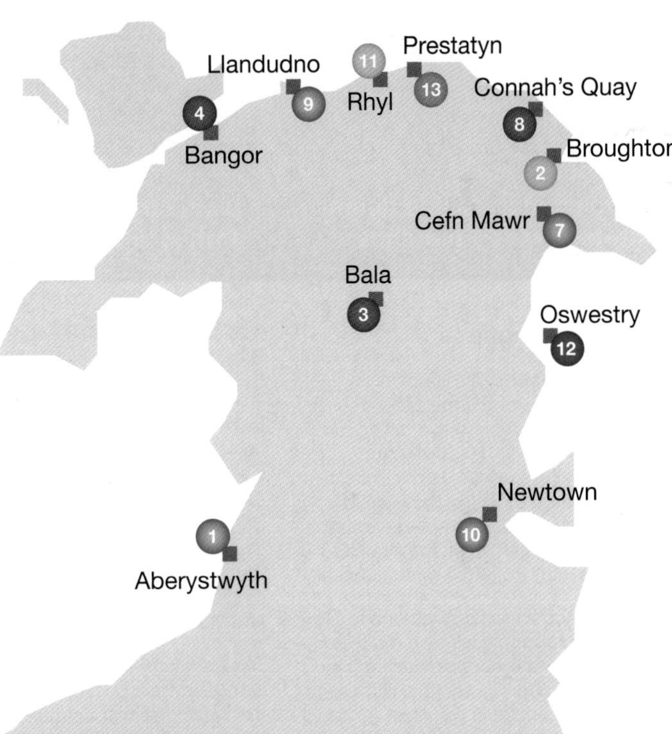

KEY

- UEFA Champions League
- UEFA Europa League
- Promoted
- Relegated

0 100 200 km
0 100 miles

No let-up from The New Saints

The New Saints' sixth Welsh Premier League title in a row was achieved in record-breaking fashion as Craig Harrison's team won every one of their 21 matches before the turn of the year. There were still seven fixtures outstanding when they wrapped up proceedings in early March.

A fourth successive domestic double was denied the perennial champions, however, when Bala Town, third in the league below runners-up Connah's Quay, came from behind to defeat them 2-1 in the final of the Welsh Cup.

Winning start to title defence stretches to 21 matches

Sixth straight league title and 11th in all

Bala Town upset champions in cup final

Domestic league

Arguably the hottest pre-season favourites in any of Europe's top divisions, TNS's superiority was so marked that but for a 94th-minute equaliser by Newtown's Jamie Price in their 22nd league fixture, they would have done the double over every other team in the division when the Premier League split in two at the end of January.

From mid-August to late December, TNS were an unstoppable winning machine. No other side took six points from their opening two fixtures, whereas Harrison's side were victorious in their first 21. Most of those wins were one-sided, and in one of them TNS actually reached double figures, routing Rhyl 10-0. By New Year's Eve the defending champions had not just amassed a maximum 63 points but breached their opponents' defences no fewer than 74 times.

It was a disappointment, of course, to TNS and their fans that the winning run eventually ended – although not before word spread around the principality of a world record having been set – but even though the team eventually lost three times, they still ended up with an impressive collection of statistics, notably a 100% success rate at home, 101 goals and a 27-point gap between themselves and Connah's Quay, whose last-day 0-0 draw at Cardiff Metropolitan University was sufficient to take second place as Bala, runners-up in each of the previous two campaigns, were beaten 6-4 by TNS.

Evidently a class apart from the competition, TNS possessed most of the league's standout individuals, among them Alex Darlington and New Zealander Greg Draper, the club's joint-top scorers with 15 goals apiece, defenders Simon Spender, Steve Saunders and Chris Marriott and midfield trio Jon Routledge, Ryan Brobbel and Polish playmaker Adrian Cieślewicz.

The Oswestry-based club's 11th title extended their own competition record in the Welsh Premier League's landmark 25th year. The next best-placed club, seven-time winners Barry Town, had gone into administration and been relegated from the top flight in 2004, but they finally made it back, under the new name of Barry Town United, in tandem with runaway northern feeder league champions Prestatyn.

Domestic cup

TNS won a third successive Welsh League Cup in January when a 12-minute hat-trick from Craig Seargeant helped them to a 4-0 victory against Barry, but there would be no treble hat-trick as Bala, who had lost all four league games to TNS, staged a stunning late fightback to beat the champions 2-1 with late goals from Jordan Evans and Kieran Smith. Victory brought Bala their first major trophy as TNS for once ended up on the losing side in what would be manager Harrison's final game in charge, the six-time title-winner departing for Hartlepool United.

Europe

TNS won a European tie for the fourth time, defeating Tre Penne of San Marino, but the bigger headlines were made by Connah's Quay, who, on their European debut, sensationally knocked out Norwegian side Stabæk, a 1-0 away win following a goalless draw in north Wales.

National team

The euphoria of UEFA EURO 2016 carried Chris Coleman's Wales side into the 2018 FIFA World Cup qualifying campaign high on confidence, and optimism remained rife after an opening Gareth Bale-inspired 4-0 home win against Moldova was followed by a 2-2 draw in Austria. However, two home draws against Georgia and Serbia – in which, as in Vienna, Wales surrendered leads – stopped the team in their tracks, and although further one-pointers in Dublin and Belgrade kept up the team's unbeaten run, it was victories not draws that Coleman's charges required in their final four fixtures to keep alive the country's hopes of participating at a World Cup for the first time in 60 years.

DOMESTIC SEASON AT A GLANCE

Premier League 2016/17 final table

			Home					Away					Total					
		Pld	W	D	L	F	A	W	D	L	F	A	W	D	L	F	A	Pts
1	**The New Saints FC**	**32**	**16**	**0**	**0**	**55**	**6**	**12**	**1**	**3**	**46**	**20**	**28**	**1**	**3**	**101**	**26**	**85**
2	Connah's Quay FC	32	9	5	2	25	11	7	5	4	20	13	16	10	6	45	24	58
3	Bala Town FC	32	8	6	2	33	18	8	3	5	28	28	16	9	7	61	46	57
4	Bangor City FC	32	11	0	5	30	20	5	4	7	23	33	16	4	12	53	53	52
5	Carmarthen Town AFC	32	4	4	8	21	29	6	5	5	19	17	10	9	13	40	46	39
6	Cardiff Metropolitan University FC	32	6	3	7	28	23	4	3	9	13	18	10	6	16	41	41	36
7	Newtown AFC	32	5	8	3	34	26	7	1	8	25	15	12	9	11	59	41	45
8	Cefn Druids AFC	32	6	5	5	27	27	3	7	6	13	21	9	12	11	40	48	39
9	Llandudno FC	32	3	6	7	12	21	4	8	4	19	24	7	14	11	31	45	35
10	Aberystwyth Town FC	32	5	2	9	19	29	5	2	9	22	34	10	4	18	41	63	34
11	Rhyl FC	32	6	3	7	18	21	2	3	11	20	55	8	6	18	38	76	30
12	AUK Broughton FC	32	4	3	9	18	36	1	3	12	19	42	5	6	21	37	78	21

NB League splits into top and bottom halves after First Phase of 22 games, with each team playing a further ten matches (home and away) exclusively against clubs from its half of the table.

European qualification 2017/18

Champion: The New Saints FC (first qualifying round)

Cup Winner: Bala Town FC (first qualifying round)

Connah's Quay FC (first qualifying round)
Bangor City FC (first qualifying round)

Top scorer	Jason Oswell (Newtown) 22 goals
Relegated clubs	AUK Broughton FC, Rhyl FC
Promoted clubs	Prestatyn Town FC, Barry Town United FC
Cup final	Bala Town FC 2-1 The New Saints FC

Player of the season

Jason Oswell
(Newtown AFC)

A third season at Newtown ended well for Oswell as the 24-year-old collected the Welsh Premier League top scorer prize, thus ending the three-year reign of Chris Venables. Most of the striker's goals came after the league split, which, with Newtown in the relegation group, somewhat devalued the prize, but his final tally of 22 was nevertheless seven more than anyone else managed and it also included three hat-tricks. There would be no chance of the Englishman defending his golden boot in 2017/18, however, as he opted to further his career at Stockport County.

Newcomer of the season

Henry Jones
(Bangor City FC)

An all-action midfielder who once captained the Wales Under-21 side, Jones joined Bangor from English Premier League club Swansea City in the summer of 2016 and proved himself to be a huge asset for the north Wales club, starting 27 league games and scoring ten goals, his tally rising to double figures with the opener in a 3-0 home win over champions TNS. The 23-year-old was voted young player of the season after helping Bangor win the UEFA Europa League qualifying play-offs, but he left for English non-league outfit Fylde in the summer.

Team of the season

(4-3-1-2)

Coach: Coach: Harrison *(TNS)*

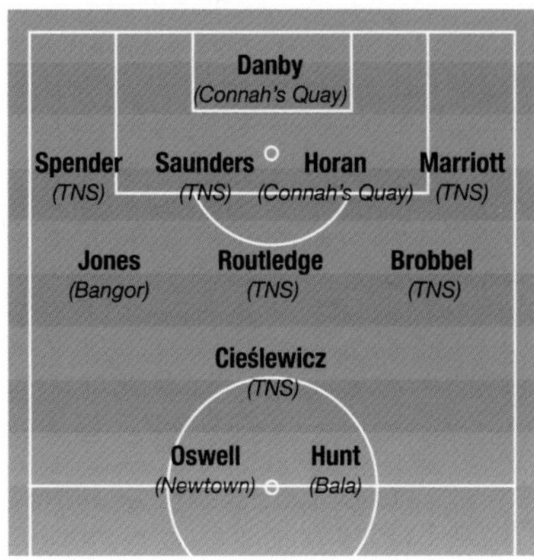

WALES

NATIONAL TEAM

International tournament appearances
FIFA World Cup (1) 1958 (qtr-finals)
UEFA European Championship (1) 2016 (semi-finals)

Top five all-time caps
Neville Southall (92); Gary Speed (85); **Chris Gunter** (79); Craig Bellamy (78); Dean Saunders (75)

Top five all-time goals
Ian Rush (28); **Gareth Bale** (26); Ivor Allchurch & Trevor Ford (23); Dean Saunders (22)

Results 2016/17

05/09/16	Moldova (WCQ)	H	Cardiff	W	4-0	*Vokes (38), Allen (44), Bale (51, 90+5p)*
06/10/16	Austria (WCQ)	A	Vienna	D	2-2	*Allen (22), Wimmer (45+1og)*
09/10/16	Georgia (WCQ)	H	Cardiff	D	1-1	*Bale (10)*
12/11/16	Serbia (WCQ)	H	Cardiff	D	1-1	*Bale (30)*
24/03/17	Republic of Ireland (WCQ)	A	Dublin	D	0-0	
11/06/17	Serbia (WCQ)	A	Belgrade	D	1-1	*Ramsey (35p)*

Appearances 2016/17

Coach: Chris Coleman	**10/06/70**		**MDA**	**AUT**	**GEO**	**SRB**	**IRL**	**SRB**	**Caps**	**Goals**
Wayne Hennessey	24/01/87	Crystal Palace (ENG)	G	G	G	G	G	G	68	-
Chris Gunter	21/07/89	Reading (ENG)	D	D	D	D	D	D	79	-
James Chester	23/01/89	Aston Villa (ENG)	D	D	D	D	D	D	23	-
Ashley Williams	23/08/84	Everton (ENG)	D82	D	D	D	D	D	71	2
Ben Davies	24/04/93	Tottenham (ENG)	D	D	D		D	D	30	-
Neil Taylor	07/02/89	Swansea (ENG) /Aston Villa (ENG)	D	D91	D70	D	D 69*		39	1
Joe Ledley	23/01/87	Crystal Palace (ENG)	M67	M	M73	M84	M72	M	73	4
Joe Allen	14/03/90	Stoke (ENG)	M	M56		M	M	M	36	2
Andy King	29/10/88	Leicester (ENG)	M	M	M61				39	2
Sam Vokes	21/10/89	Burnley (ENG)	A75	A77	A	A	s46	A86	50	8
Gareth Bale	16/07/89	Real Madrid (ESP)	A	A	A	M	A		66	26
Emyr Huws	30/09/93	Cardiff (ENG)	s67	s91	s73			s73	11	1
Hal Robson-Kanu	21/05/89	West Brom (ENG)	s75	s77	s61	A68	A46		40	4
James Collins	23/08/83	West Ham (ENG)	s82						50	3
David Edwards	03/02/86	Wolves (ENG)		s56	M	s84		M73	39	3
David Cotterill	04/12/87	Birminghan (ENG)			s70				24	2
Aaron Ramsey	26/12/90	Arsenal (ENG)				M	M	M	47	12
Tom Lawrence	13/01/94	Ipswich (ENG)				s68		s86	6	-
Ashley Richards	12/04/91	Cardiff (ENG)					s72	D	12	-

EUROPE

The New Saints FC

First qualifying round - SP Tre Penne (SMR)

H 2-1 *Quigley (13), Mullan (40)*

Harrison, Spender, Marriott, Baker, Routledge, Brobbel, Mullan, Rawlinson, Cieślewicz (Parry 71), Quigley (Draper 85), Edwards. Coach: Craig Harrison (ENG)

A 3-0 *Quigley (45), Edwards (47), Draper (90)*

Harrison, Spender (Pryce 76), Marriott, Baker, Routledge, Brobbel (Seargeant 88), Mullan, Rawlinson, Cieślewicz, Quigley (Draper 82), Edwards. Coach: Craig Harrison (ENG)

Second qualifying round - APOEL FC (CYP)

H 0-0

Harrison, Marriott, Baker, Routledge, Brobbel (Williams 72), Mullan, Rawlinson, Cieślewicz (Parry 89), Quigley, Edwards (Seargeant 36), Pryce. Coach: Craig Harrison (ENG)

A 0-3

Harrison, Spender, Marriott, Baker, Routledge, Seargeant, Brobbel (Parry 90), Mullan (Draper 86), Rawlinson, Cieślewicz (Saunders 80), Quigley. Coach: Craig Harrison (ENG)

Bala Town FC

First qualifying round - AIK (SWE)

A 0-2

Morris, Valentine, Stephens, Stuart Jones, Stuart J Jones, Connolly (M Jones 69), Sheridan, Smith, Davies, Thompson (Hayes 56), Burke (Crowther 83). Coach: Colin Caton (WAL)

H 0-2

Morris, Valentine, Stephens, Stuart Jones, Stuart J Jones, Connolly, M Jones (Thompson 65), Sheridan, Smith (Hayes 74), DavieStuart (Crowther 65), Burke. Coach: Colin Caton (WAL)

Llandudno FC

First qualifying round - IFK Göteborg (SWE)

A 0-5

Roberts, Taylor, Joyce (Tierney 77), Shaw, Hughes, Thomas (Dawson 57), Marc Williams, Reed, Mike Williams, Dix, Buckley (Owen 70). Coach: Alan Morgan (WAL)

H 1-2 *Hughes (72)*

Roberts, Taylor, Joyce, Shaw (Peate 58), Evans (Dawson 70), Hughes, Marc Williams, Owen (Riley 65), Mike Williams, Dix, Buckley. Coach: Alan Morgan (WAL)

Connah's Quay FC

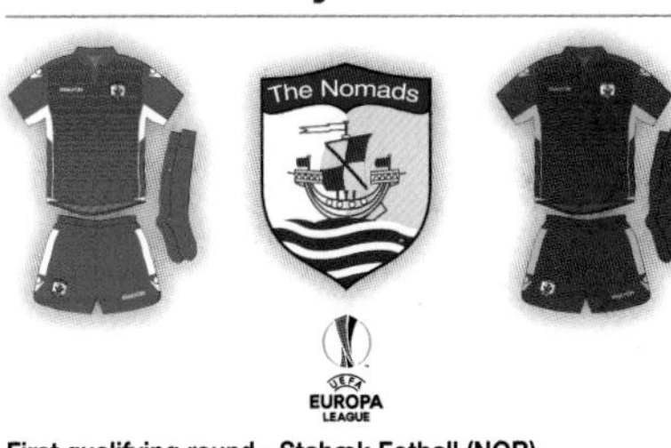

First qualifying round - Stabæk Fotball (NOR)

H 0-0

Danby, Disney, Kearney, Horan, Harrison, Morris, Woolfe, J Owen, Baynes, Short, Wilde (Davies 89). Coach: Andy Morrison (SCO)

A 1-0 *Morris (15)*

Danby, Disney (M Owen 68), Kearney, Horan, Harrison, Morris, Woolfe (Smith 80), J Owen, Baynes, Short, Wilde (Davies 84). Coach: Andy Morrison (SCO)

Red card: Disney 78

Second qualifying round - FK Vojvodina (SRB)

A 0-1

Danby, Kearney, Horan, Harrison, Morris, Smith, Woolfe, J Owen (M Owen 89), Baynes, Short, Wilde (Davies 81). Coach: Andy Morrison (SCO)

H 1-2 *Wilde (65)*

Danby, Disney (Davies 55), Kearney, Horan, Morris, Smith, Woolfe, J Owen (M Owen 70), Baynes, Short, Wilde (Ruane 84). Coach: Andy Morrison (SCO)

DOMESTIC LEAGUE CLUB-BY-CLUB

Aberystwyth Town FC

1884 • Park Avenue (2,502) • atfc.org.uk

Major honours
Welsh Cup (1) 1900

Manager: Matthew Bishop (ENG); (22/03/17) Wayne Jones

Date		Opponent		Score	Scorers
2016					
14/08	a	TNS	L	1-2	*C Jones*
21/08	a	Broughton	W	1-0	*Kellaway*
28/08	a	Llandudno	W	1-0	*Evans*
31/08	a	Rhyl	L	1-3	*B Davies*
03/09	a	Bangor	L	0-4	
10/09	h	Carmarthen	L	0-3	
18/09	a	Connah's Quay	L	0-4	
20/09	a	Carmarthen	W	5-0	*Borrelli, Kellaway 3, March*
24/09	a	Cardiff MU	L	0-1	
01/10	h	TNS	L	1-5	*C Jones (p)*
14/10	h	Rhyl	W	4-0	*Mullock, Kellaway, Borrelli 2*
23/10	h	Llandudno	D	0-0	
29/10	h	Broughton	W	3-1	*Borrelli 2, C Jones (p)*
05/11	h	Connah's Quay	L	1-3	*C Jones*
11/11	a	Bala	L	0-4	
25/11	h	Bala	L	1-3	*March*
16/12	a	Cefn Druids	W	3-0	*Kellaway, Borrelli, Georgievsky*
20/12	h	Bangor	L	0-3	
26/12	h	Newtown	W	1-0	*March*
31/12	a	Newtown	D	2-2	*Clarke 2*
2017					
07/01	h	Cefn Druids	L	0-1	
14/01	h	Cardiff MU	L	0-2	
04/02	h	Broughton	W	1-0	*Sherbon*
11/02	a	Cefn Druids	L	1-2	*Owen*
18/02	h	Llandudno	L	3-4	*Sherbon, Borrelli, C Jones (p)*
03/03	a	Rhyl	D	2-2	*M Jones (p), Kellaway*
10/03	h	Newtown	L	0-4	
18/03	a	Broughton	L	2-4	*Kellaway, M Jones*
25/03	h	Cefn Druids	D	0-0	
09/04	a	Llandudno	W	2-0	*M Jones, Melvin*
14/04	h	Rhyl	W	4-0	*Borrelli 2, Owen 2*
22/04	a	Newtown	L	1-6	*Ewart*

No	Name	Nat	DoB	Pos	Aps	(s)	Gls
19	Daniel Alfei		23/02/92	D	18		
5	Phil Baker	ENG	04/11/82	D	5		
5	Will Bell	ENG	29/09/94	D	14	(5)	
11	Luke Borrelli		28/03/91	A	31		9
6	Joe Clarke		13/09/91	M	19		2
18	Lewis Coyle	ENG	07/07/88	A	1	(6)	
22	Josh Crowl		21/11/99	A		(1)	
6	Jamie Crowther		10/02/92	M	8	(3)	
9	Blake Davies		24/03/98	A	5	(10)	1
3	Cledan Davies		10/03/90	D	14	(5)	
15	Jonathan Evans		10/03/93	A	3	(5)	1
25	Sion Ewart		22/12/98	D		(3)	1
16	Kostya Georgievsky	NIR	28/06/96	M	5	(10)	1
9	Lee Healey	ENG	13/11/86	A		(3)	
21	Chris Jones		12/09/89	M	20	(3)	5
20	Dafydd Jones		05/06/98	M	2	(3)	
23	Mark Jones		01/05/89	A	7	(1)	3
7	Geoff Kellaway	ENG	07/04/86	M	22	(5)	8
17	Kurtis March		30/04/93	D	18	(7)	3
15	Malcolm Melvin	ENG	08/05/95	A	10		1
26	Chris Mullock		16/09/88	G	24		1
10	John Owen		18/08/82	A	6	(4)	3
2	Dylan Rees		17/09/96	D	6	(1)	
1	Dominic Richards	ENG	26/01/95	G	8		
14	Jack Rimmer		29/03/99	D	4	(6)	
4	Sam Rodon		27/05/93	D	27	(1)	
18	Elliot Scotcher		30/03/94	D	2		
8	Luke Sherbon	ENG	06/06/86	M	22	(1)	2
12	Greg Walters		10/01/95	M	5	(2)	
2	Ricky Watts		07/11/91	D	16	(1)	
13	Ryan Wollacott	ENG	01/12/94	D	30		

WALES

AUK Broughton FC

1946 • The Airfield (1,500) • airbusfc.com
Manager: Andy Thomas

Date		Opponent	Result		Scorers
2016					
14/08	h	Cardiff MU	W	1-0	*Gray*
21/08	h	Aberystwyth	L	0-1	
27/08	a	Carmarthen	L	1-2	*Gray*
30/08	a	Llandudno	L	0-2	
04/09	h	TNS	L	1-4	*Gray*
10/09	a	Rhyl	L	1-3	*Gray*
18/09	h	Cefn Druids	W	3-2	*Menagh, Fraughan, Gray*
20/09	a	Cefn Druids	D	2-2	*Fraughan, Gray*
24/09	a	Newtown	W	4-2	*Ryan Edwards 2, Gray, Menagh*
01/10	h	Llandudno	L	2-3	*Ryan Edwards, McGinn*
16/10	a	Bala	D	3-3	*Monteiro 2, McGinn (p)*
22/10	h	Carmarthen	D	1-1	*Menagh*
29/10	a	Aberystwyth	L	1-3	*Spittle*
05/11	h	Newtown	L	0-2	
13/11	a	Cardiff MU	L	0-2	
19/11	h	Rhyl	L	0-3	
25/11	a	TNS	L	0-4	
17/12	a	Bangor	L	1-2	*Hulley*
20/12	h	Bala	L	2-4	*Murphy, Gray*
26/12	h	Connah's Quay	L	0-3	
30/12	a	Connah's Quay	L	1-5	*Ryan Edwards*
2017					
14/01	h	Bangor	W	4-2	*og (Hart), Jackson, O'Neill 2*
04/02	a	Aberystwyth	L	0-1	
10/02	h	Llandudno	D	0-0	
18/02	h	Rhyl	L	0-2	
04/03	a	Newtown	L	1-4	*Gray*
10/03	h	Cefn Druids	D	0-0	
18/03	h	Aberystwyth	W	4-2	*Ryan J Edwards 2, Tomassen, Spittle*
25/03	a	Llandudno	D	2-2	*Deakin, Gray*
08/04	a	Rhyl	L	1-2	*Tomassen*
14/04	h	Newtown	L	0-7	
22/04	a	Cefn Druids	L	1-3	*Anoruo*

No	Name	Nat	DoB	Pos	Aps	(s)	Gls
28	Obi Anoruo	NGA	28/08/91	A	5	(1)	1
16	Leon Clowes	ENG	27/02/92	M	4		
4	Paul Connolly	ENG	29/09/83	D	12		
6	Jake Cook	ENG	10/06/95	M	2		
11	Reece Deakin	ENG	12/12/96	A	6	(2)	1
20	Dominic Doherty	ENG	15/12/97	M		(5)	
7	Ryan Edwards		22/06/88	D	29	(2)	4
6	Ryan Joseph Edwards		25/05/94	M	16	(2)	2
32	Zebb Edwards		08/05/99	M	4	(5)	
33	Ryan Fraughan	ENG	06/04/84	A	17	(5)	2
9	Tony Gray	ENG	06/12/84	A	30		10
26	Rhys Hewitt		12/01/98	D	1		
14	Jake Hulley	ENG	08/09/93	D	17	(3)	1
3	Bailey Jackson	ENG	22/02/97	D	16	(5)	1
15	Rhys Jones		25/11/97	M		(4)	
6	Josh Malden	ENG	28/11/96	M		(2)	
2	Tom Matthews	ENG	12/12/97	D	17		
22	Matty McGinn	ENG	27/06/83	D	19	(1)	2
24	Jamie Menagh	ENG	14/09/93	M	18	(1)	3
34	Kevin Monteiro	FRA	21/03/94	D	7	(6)	2
31	James Murphy	ENG	31/01/97	M	18	(11)	1
21	Ryan Neild	ENG	26/09/95	G	25	(1)	
17	Liam O'Neill	ENG	12/06/97	M	4	(9)	2
36	Lee Owens	ENG	29/06/86	D	8	(1)	
1	Shaun Pearson		16/08/90	G	7		
2	Connor Roberts-Nurse	ENG	08/09/93	D	2	(1)	
24	Blake Robinson	ENG	26/04/99	M		(1)	
4	Glenn Rule	ENG	30/11/89	M	10	(1)	
5	Jonny Spittle	ENG	13/08/94	D	22	(1)	2
25	Steve Tomassen	ENG	03/10/93	M	9		2
11	Ryan Wignall	ENG	28/03/89	M	6	(3)	
8	Ashley Williams	ENG	08/10/87	M	21	(2)	

Bala Town FC

1880 • Maes Tegid (1,200) • balatownfc.co.uk
Major Honours
Welsh Cup (1) 2017
Manager: Colin Caton

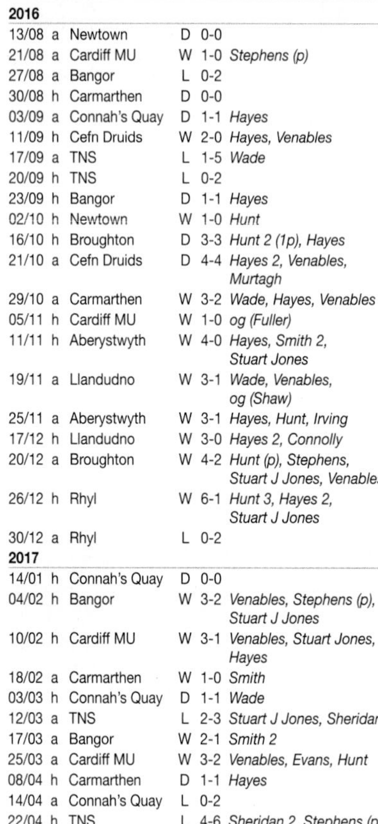

Date		Opponent	Result		Scorers
2016					
13/08	a	Newtown	D	0-0	
21/08	a	Cardiff MU	W	1-0	*Stephens (p)*
27/08	a	Bangor	L	0-2	
30/08	h	Carmarthen	D	0-0	
03/09	a	Connah's Quay	D	1-1	*Hayes*
11/09	h	Cefn Druids	W	2-0	*Hayes, Venables*
17/09	a	TNS	L	1-5	*Wade*
20/09	h	TNS	L	0-2	
23/09	h	Bangor	D	1-1	*Hayes*
02/10	h	Newtown	W	1-0	*Hunt*
16/10	h	Broughton	D	3-3	*Hunt 2 (1p), Hayes*
21/10	a	Cefn Druids	D	4-4	*Hayes 2, Venables, Murtagh*
29/10	a	Carmarthen	W	3-2	*Wade, Hayes, Venables*
05/11	h	Cardiff MU	W	1-0	*og (Fuller)*
11/11	h	Aberystwyth	W	4-0	*Hayes, Smith 2, Stuart Jones*
19/11	a	Llandudno	W	3-1	*Wade, Venables, og (Shaw)*
25/11	a	Aberystwyth	W	3-1	*Hayes, Hunt, Irving*
17/12	h	Llandudno	W	3-0	*Hayes 2, Connolly*
20/12	a	Broughton	W	4-2	*Hunt (p), Stephens, Stuart J Jones, Venables*
26/12	h	Rhyl	W	6-1	*Hunt 3, Hayes 2, Stuart J Jones*
30/12	a	Rhyl	L	0-2	
2017					
14/01	h	Connah's Quay	D	0-0	
04/02	h	Bangor	W	3-2	*Venables, Stephens (p), Stuart J Jones*
10/02	h	Cardiff MU	W	3-1	*Venables, Stuart Jones, Hayes*
18/02	a	Carmarthen	W	1-0	*Smith*
03/03	h	Connah's Quay	D	1-1	*Wade*
12/03	a	TNS	L	2-3	*Stuart J Jones, Sheridan*
17/03	a	Bangor	W	2-1	*Smith 2*
25/03	a	Cardiff MU	W	3-2	*Venables, Evans, Hunt*
08/04	h	Carmarthen	D	1-1	*Hayes*
14/04	a	Connah's Quay	L	0-2	
22/04	h	TNS	L	4-6	*Sheridan 2, Stephens (p), Thompson*

No	Name	Nat	DoB	Pos	Aps	(s)	Gls
15	Will Bell	ENG	29/09/94	D		(2)	
88	Nathan Burke	ENG	15/09/95	M	20	(1)	
7	Mark Connolly	ENG	02/07/84	M	13	(6)	1
15	Jamie Crowther		10/02/92	M		(1)	
50	Joel Darlington		24/11/98	A		(1)	
16	Tony Davies	ENG	05/07/84	D	2		
22	Ryan Edwards		25/05/94	M	7	(5)	
50	Jordan Evans		23/09/95	D	7	(1)	1
12	Ryan Goldston		28/10/98	G	1		
9	Mike Hayes	ENG	21/11/87	A	20	(10)	15
18	Lee Hunt	ENG	05/06/82	A	12	(3)	9
26	John Irving	ENG	17/09/88	D	14	(1)	1
8	Mark Jones		15/08/84	M	5	(10)	
4	Stuart Jones	ENG	28/08/86	D	30		2
5	Stuart J Jones		14/03/84	D	25		4
23	Alex Lynch		04/04/95	G	7		
1	Ashley Morris		31/03/84	G	24		
6	Conall Murtagh	NIR	29/06/85	M	18	(4)	1
29	Lee Owens	ENG	29/06/86	D	6	(1)	
10	Ian Sheridan	ENG	12/03/89	A	9	(9)	3
11	Kieran Smith	ENG	06/03/92	A	19	(1)	5
3	Anthony Stephens	ENG	21/01/94	M	29		4
27	Dave Thompson	ENG	27/02/91	D	24	(2)	1
2	Ryan Valentine		19/08/82	D	10	(5)	
25	Chris Venables		23/07/85	M	30		8
14	Ryan Wade	ENG	22/01/88	M	20	(5)	4

Bangor City FC

1876 • Nantporth (3,000) • bangorcityfc.co.uk
Major honours
Welsh League (3) 1994, 1995, 2011; Welsh Cup (8) 1889, 1896, 1962, 1998, 2000, 2008, 2009, 2010
Manager: Andy Legg;
(23/11/16) Ian Dawes (ENG);
(29/03/17) Gary Taylor-Fletcher (ENG)

Date		Opponent	Result		Scorers
2016					
12/08	h	Cefn Druids	W	2-1	*Nardiello, Jones*
21/08	h	Connah's Quay	L	0-2	
27/08	h	Bala	W	2-0	*Allen, Nardiello*
31/08	h	Newtown	W	2-1	*Reed, G Roberts (p)*
03/09	h	Aberystwyth	W	4-0	*G Roberts 2 (1p), Reed, Edwards*
11/09	a	TNS	L	0-4	
17/09	a	Carmarthen	D	1-1	*G Roberts (p)*
20/09	a	Rhyl	L	0-1	
23/09	a	Bala	D	1-1	*Nardiello*
02/10	h	Cardiff MU	W	2-1	*Nardiello 2*
16/10	a	Connah's Quay	D	2-2	*Branco, Shaw*
22/10	h	Rhyl	W	3-2	*Branco, Nardiello, Jones*
28/10	a	Cefn Druids	W	3-2	*Davies, G Roberts, Miley*
05/11	h	TNS	L	1-2	*G Roberts (p)*
13/11	a	Newtown	W	2-1	*Jones, Shaw*
19/11	a	Cardiff MU	L	0-4	
26/11	h	Carmarthen	L	1-2	*Shaw*
17/12	h	Broughton	W	2-1	*Nardiello, Miley*
20/12	a	Aberystwyth	W	3-0	*Allen 2, Branco*
26/12	h	Llandudno	W	2-1	*Jones, Cavanagh*
2017					
01/01	a	Llandudno	L	0-1	
14/01	a	Broughton	L	2-4	*Connolly, Nardiello*
04/02	a	Bala	L	2-3	*Nardiello, Branco*
10/02	h	Connah's Quay	W	2-1	*Jones 2*
18/02	h	Cardiff MU	W	3-2	*Jones 2, Rittenberg*
04/03	a	TNS	L	0-4	
11/03	a	Carmarthen	W	3-2	*Nardiello 3 (1p)*
17/03	h	Bala	L	1-2	*Miley*
25/03	a	Connah's Quay	D	1-1	*Branco*
09/04	a	Cardiff MU	W	3-2	*Rittenberg, Wilson, Jones*
14/04	h	TNS	W	3-0	*Jones, Nardiello, Taylor-Fletcher*
22/04	h	Carmarthen	L	0-2	

No	Name	Nat	DoB	Pos	Aps	(s)	Gls
8	Damien Allen	ENG	01/08/86	M	22	(2)	3
22	Christoph Aziamale	GER	18/12/97	A		(3)	
20	Alex Boss		09/10/98	A	1	(2)	
19	Sion Bradley		20/02/98	M		(2)	
91	Branco	BRA	14/07/91	A	10	(12)	5
17	Shaun Cavanagh		18/12/97	A		(7)	1
4	Leon Clowes	ENG	27/02/92	D	14		
30	Paul Connolly	ENG	29/09/83	D	14		1
21	Jordan Davies		18/08/98	D	14		1
14	Oscar Durnin	ENG	12/04/95	M		(3)	
11	Sion Edwards		01/08/87	M	7	(8)	1
16	Danny Gosset		30/09/94	M	26	(2)	
23	Matthew Hall	ENG	17/10/97	G	1		
3	Sam Hart	ENG	29/11/91	D	10	(4)	
31	Michael Higdon	ENG	02/09/83	A	3		
15	River Humphreys	ENG	12/09/90	M	4		
7	Bradley Jackson	ENG	20/10/96	M	9	(1)	
27	Henry Jones		18/09/93	M	27		10
15	Jaques Kpohomouh		12/03/97	M	2		
10	Christian Langos	CGO	09/09/94	A	2	(7)	
29	Jack Metcalfe	ENG	25/12/91	M	1	(2)	
5	Anthony Miley	ENG	30/08/92	D	22	(2)	3
9	Daniel Nardiello		22/10/82	A	26	(3)	13
24	Cai Owen		12/07/98	D		(1)	
30	Pavel Vieira	GNB	15/02/92	M	1	(1)	
28	Adam Pritchard		12/10/97	D		(1)	
7	Jamie Reed		13/08/87	A	11	(9)	2
10	Dean Rittenberg	ENG	13/05/96	A	10		2
1	Connor Roberts		08/12/92	G	31		
6	Gary Roberts	ENG	04/02/87	M	24		6
25	Brayden Shaw	ENG	25/02/97	M	18		3
25	Gary Taylor-Fletcher	ENG	04/06/81	A	10		1
31	Sergio Uyi	NGA	22/06/93	D	5	(1)	
2	Laurence Wilson	ENG	10/10/86	D	14	(1)	1
14	Yalania Baio	POR	10/10/94	M	6	(1)	
23	Ashley Young	ENG	14/07/90	M	7	(3)	

Cardiff Metropolitan University FC

2000 • Cyncoed Campus (1,875) • cardiffmetsu.co.uk/mens-football

Manager: Christian Edwards; (04/02/17) Wayne Allison (ENG)

Date		Opponent		Score	Scorers
2016					
14/08	a	Broughton	L	0-1	
21/08	h	Bala	L	0-1	
27/08	a	Cefn Druids	D	0-0	
31/08	h	TNS	L	1-2	*Philpott*
04/09	a	Rhyl	L	0-1	
11/09	h	Connah's Quay	L	1-2	*Roscrow*
18/09	a	Llandudno	W	1-0	*McCarthy (p)*
20/09	h	Newtown	W	2-1	*og (Sutton), W Evans*
24/09	h	Aberystwyth	W	1-0	*Baker*
02/10	a	Bangor	L	1-2	*Lewis*
16/10	h	Cefn Druids	W	5-0	*Corsby 2, Lam 2, Baker*
23/10	a	Connah's Quay	D	0-0	
30/10	h	Rhyl	W	4-0	*E Evans, W Evans, McCarthy (p), Lam*
05/11	a	Bala	L	0-1	
13/11	h	Broughton	W	2-0	*Roscrow, Corsby*
19/11	h	Bangor	W	4-0	*E Evans 3, Littlemore*
27/11	h	Llandudno	D	1-1	*Roscrow*
10/12	a	TNS	L	1-3	*W Evans*
17/12	a	Newtown	W	1-0	*W Evans*
26/12	a	Carmarthen	D	0-0	
31/12	h	Carmarthen	L	1-3	*Roscrow*
2017					
14/01	a	Aberystwyth	W	2-0	*Roscrow, McCarthy (p)*
04/02	a	TNS	L	0-2	
10/02	a	Bala	L	1-3	*McCarthy (p)*
18/02	a	Bangor	L	2-3	*E Evans, Spencer*
04/03	h	Carmarthen	D	2-2	*Baker, Lewis*
11/03	a	Connah's Quay	L	0-2	
18/03	h	TNS	L	0-5	
25/03	h	Bala	L	2-3	*Baker, Roscrow*
09/04	h	Bangor	L	2-3	*McCarthy, Thomas*
14/04	a	Carmarthen	W	4-0	*McCarthy (p), W Evans, Thomas, E Evans*
22/04	h	Connah's Quay	D	0-0	

No	Name	Nat	DoB	Pos	Aps	(s)	Gls
8	Chris Baker		29/11/93	M	15	(14)	4
20	Josh Barnett	ENG	30/10/92	M	7	(2)	
22	Liam Black		02/07/94	D	10	(2)	
6	Ben Bowler	ENG	12/03/95	M	24	(2)	
10	Charlie Corsby	ENG	14/10/91	M	32		3
7	Eliot Evans	ENG	26/11/91	M	28	(2)	6
15	Will Evans		01/07/97	M	19	(6)	5
1	Will Fuller	ENG	07/07/93	G	32		
17	Gwion Howell		12/02/97	A		(2)	
11	Jordan Lam	ENG	16/08/94	M	27	(5)	3
18	Joel Letori	ENG	10/01/94	D	17	(1)	
5	Emlyn Lewis		14/06/96	D	29		2
14	Jon Littlemore		10/12/94	A	3	(16)	1
3	Kyle McCarthy	ENG	12/04/93	D	28		6
33	Thomas Moseley	ENG	13/05/96	M		(1)	
21	Harry Owen	ENG	15/02/96	A	1	(3)	
2	Isaac Philpott	ENG	31/05/95	D	8		1
9	Adam Roscrow		17/02/95	A	26	(4)	6
12	Dan Spencer	ENG	19/05/93	A	8	(17)	1
40	Mart Swindlehurst	ENG	21/03/96	D	4		
27	Matt Taylor		01/02/97	D	4	(1)	
39	Rhys Thomas		20/12/97	A	2	(2)	2
4	Bradley Woolridge	ENG	16/12/92	D	28		

Carmarthen Town AFC

1948 • Richmond Park (3,000) • carmarthentownafc.co.uk

Major honours
Welsh Cup (1) 2007

Manager: Mark Aizlewood

Date		Opponent		Score	Scorers
2016					
13/08	h	Connah's Quay	D	0-0	
20/08	a	Newtown	L	2-4	*Bailey, Jones*
27/08	h	Broughton	W	2-1	*Jones (p), Bassett*
30/08	a	Bala	D	0-0	
03/09	h	Llandudno	L	0-1	
10/09	a	Aberystwyth	W	3-0	*og (Bell), Lewis, L Thomas*
17/09	h	Bangor	D	1-1	*Vincent*
20/09	h	Aberystwyth	L	0-5	
25/09	a	TNS	L	1-2	*Morgan*
02/10	a	Connah's Quay	L	0-1	
15/10	h	Newtown	W	3-1	*L Thomas 2, Vincent*
22/10	a	Broughton	D	1-1	*Carroll*
29/10	h	Bala	L	2-3	*og (Connolly), Vincent*
05/11	a	Rhyl	W	1-0	*Harling*
13/11	h	Cefn Druids	D	2-2	*Jones 2*
18/11	h	TNS	L	2-4	*Vincent, Carroll*
26/11	a	Bangor	W	2-1	*L Thomas, Surman*
10/12	a	Llandudno	L	0-2	
17/12	h	Rhyl	W	5-0	*Bassett, Jones, L Thomas 2, Carroll*
26/12	h	Cardiff MU	D	0-0	
31/12	a	Cardiff MU	W	3-1	*Jones 2 (1p), L Thomas*
2017					
14/01	a	Cefn Druids	D	0-0	
04/02	a	Connah's Quay	W	1-0	*Morgan*
11/02	h	TNS	W	1-0	*L Thomas*
18/02	h	Bala	L	0-1	
04/03	a	Cardiff MU	D	2-2	*Surman, L Thomas*
11/03	h	Bangor	L	2-3	*M Thomas, L Thomas*
18/03	h	Connah's Quay	L	1-3	*Cummings*
25/03	a	TNS	L	0-2	
08/04	a	Bala	D	1-1	*L Thomas (p)*
14/04	h	Cardiff MU	L	0-4	
22/04	a	Bangor	W	2-0	*L Thomas 2*

No	Name	Nat	DoB	Pos	Aps	(s)	Gls
19	Dwaine Bailey		24/04/92	M	20	(4)	1
11	Kyle Bassett		10/09/88	A	16	(5)	2
7	Declan Carroll		04/07/93	D	23	(3)	3
31	Rhodri Cole		21/07/99	M		(3)	
2	Luke Cummings		25/10/91	D	7	(2)	1
16	Jordan Ellis		01/07/94	M		(3)	
15	Liam Griffiths		17/09/93	A	6	(4)	
3	Craig Hanford		08/07/84	D	19	(7)	
10	Lewis Harling		11/06/92	M	14	(4)	1
1	Lee Idzi		08/02/88	G	32		
28	Luke James-Raymond		18/11/97	M		(1)	
9	Mark Jones		01/05/89	A	20	(3)	7
4	Jordan Knott		13/09/93	D	14	(1)	
25	Kieran Lewis		26/06/93	M	29	(1)	1
14	Ceri Morgan		22/01/91	M	29	(1)	2
12	Dan Sheehan		22/12/90	D	23	(2)	
21	Neil Smothers		08/12/77	M		(1)	
6	Lee Surman		03/04/86	D	27		2
20	Danny Thomas		13/05/85	M	1	(9)	
18	Liam Thomas		06/11/91	M	31		13
8	Matthew Thomas		18/07/92	A	13	(11)	1
5	Dave Vincent		17/06/90	D	28	(2)	4

Cefn Druids AFC

1872 • The Rock (2,500) • cefndruidsafc.co.uk

Major Honours
Welsh Cup (8) 1880, 1881, 1882, 1885, 1886, 1898, 1899, 1904

Manager: Huw Griffiths

Date		Opponent		Score	Scorers
2016					
12/08	a	Bangor	L	1-2	*S Cook*
20/08	a	Rhyl	W	3-0	*Bowen, Barrow, Eden*
27/08	h	Cardiff MU	D	0-0	
31/08	h	Connah's Quay	D	0-0	
04/09	a	Newtown	D	1-1	*Bowen*
11/09	a	Bala	L	0-2	
18/09	a	Broughton	L	2-3	*og (Hulley), Ruane*
20/09	h	Broughton	D	2-2	*Blenkinsop, Bowen*
25/09	a	Llandudno	D	0-0	
30/09	h	Rhyl	W	4-3	*Bowen, Ruane 2 (1p), Pritchard*
16/10	a	Cardiff MU	L	0-5	
21/10	h	Bala	D	4-4	*Pritchard 2, Ruane, Hesp*
28/10	h	Bangor	L	2-3	*Eckersley, Ruane*
04/11	h	Llandudno	L	1-3	*Pritchard*
13/11	a	Carmarthen	D	2-2	*Pritchard (p), M Cook*
25/11	h	Newtown	W	1-0	*Hesp*
13/12	a	Connah's Quay	L	0-1	
16/12	h	Aberystwyth	L	0-3	
26/12	a	TNS	L	0-4	
30/12	h	TNS	L	0-2	
2017					
07/01	a	Aberystwyth	W	1-0	*Eden*
14/01	h	Carmarthen	D	0-0	
04/02	a	Rhyl	W	2-0	*Hesp, Ruane*
11/02	h	Aberystwyth	W	2-1	*Peate, Ruane*
17/02	h	Newtown	L	1-2	*Roper*
03/03	a	Llandudno	D	0-0	
10/03	a	Broughton	D	0-0	
17/03	h	Rhyl	W	4-1	*Ruane 2, Pritchard, Healing*
25/03	a	Aberystwyth	D	0-0	
08/04	a	Newtown	D	1-1	*Ruane*
14/04	h	Llandudno	W	3-2	*Pritchard 2, Ruane*
22/04	h	Broughton	W	3-1	*Peate, Blenkinsop, Hesp*

No	Name	Nat	DoB	Pos	Aps	(s)	Gls
16	Naim Arsan		14/12/93	M	28	(2)	
6	Jordan Barrow	ENG	18/10/93	M	27	(3)	1
9	Steve Blenkinsop	ENG	03/02/89	A	11	(12)	2
11	Aaron Bowen	ENG	30/03/91	A	12	(2)	4
90	Filippo Casaretto	ITA	23/11/90	G	1		
12	Theodorakis Chrisokhou	ENG	09/05/97	D		(1)	
8	Matty Cook	ENG	07/09/85	M	9	(4)	1
7	Stuart Cook	ENG	29/03/86	G	1		
7	Stuart Cook	ENG	29/03/86	M	26	(1)	1
25	Tommy Cooney	IRL	05/09/95	M		(3)	
5	Matthew Eckersley	ENG	17/01/89	D	30		1
17	Adam Eden		20/05/92	A	3	(12)	2
19	Fisnik Hajdari	ENG	16/03/97	M	14	(4)	
23	Jordan Harper	ENG	07/09/96	A	1	(9)	
14	Ellis Healing	ENG	11/05/96	M	4	(4)	1
4	Adam Hesp		30/08/91	D	27	(3)	4
25	River Humphreys	ENG	12/09/90	D	1		
17	Joshua Jones		05/05/98	A		(4)	
1	Michael Jones	ENG	03/12/87	G	26		
13	Daniel Lloyd	ENG	17/09/89	G	4		
2	Kyle Parle	ENG	24/02/95	D	26	(2)	
20	Gareth Partridge		26/09/91	M	5	(4)	
15	Nathan Peate	ENG	19/01/88	M	12		2
3	Max Penk	ENG	17/02/93	D	1		
24	Jake Phillips		31/01/97	D	6	(1)	
10	Michael Pritchard		10/12/91	A	31		8
21	Corey Roper		13/09/95	M	26	(1)	1
26	Ashley Ruane	ENG	26/06/85	M	20	(1)	11
20	Jonathon Taylor		12/05/89	A		(4)	
18	Joe Williams		22/12/96	A		(3)	

WALES

Connah's Quay FC

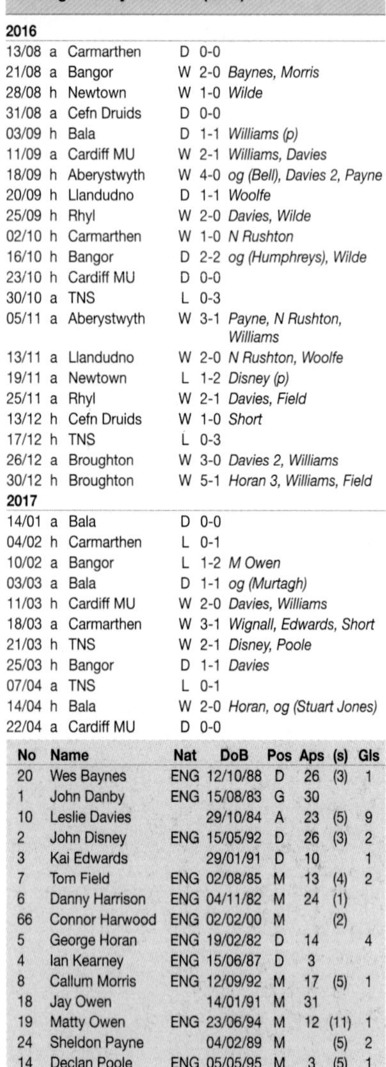

1946 • Deeside Stadium (4,000) • the-nomads.co.uk

Manager: Andy Morrison (SCO)

Date		Opponent		Score	Scorers
2016					
13/08	a	Carmarthen	D	0-0	
21/08	a	Bangor	W	2-0	*Baynes, Morris*
28/08	h	Newtown	W	1-0	*Wilde*
31/08	a	Cefn Druids	D	0-0	
03/09	h	Bala	D	1-1	*Williams (p)*
11/09	a	Cardiff MU	W	2-1	*Williams, Davies*
18/09	h	Aberystwyth	W	4-0	*og (Bell), Davies 2, Payne*
20/09	h	Llandudno	D	1-1	*Woolfe*
25/09	h	Rhyl	W	2-0	*Davies, Wilde*
02/10	h	Carmarthen	W	1-0	*N Rushton*
16/10	h	Bangor	D	2-2	*og (Humphreys), Wilde*
23/10	h	Cardiff MU	D	0-0	
30/10	a	TNS	L	0-3	
05/11	a	Aberystwyth	W	3-1	*Payne, N Rushton, Williams*
13/11	a	Llandudno	W	2-0	*N Rushton, Woolfe*
19/11	a	Newtown	L	1-2	*Disney (p)*
25/11	a	Rhyl	W	2-1	*Davies, Field*
13/12	h	Cefn Druids	W	1-0	*Short*
17/12	h	TNS	L	0-3	
26/12	a	Broughton	W	3-0	*Davies 2, Williams*
30/12	h	Broughton	W	5-1	*Horan 3, Williams, Field*
2017					
14/01	a	Bala	D	0-0	
04/02	h	Carmarthen	L	0-1	
10/02	a	Bangor	L	1-2	*M Owen*
03/03	a	Bala	D	1-1	*og (Murtagh)*
11/03	h	Cardiff MU	W	2-0	*Davies, Williams*
18/03	a	Carmarthen	W	3-1	*Wignall, Edwards, Short*
21/03	h	TNS	W	2-1	*Disney, Poole*
25/03	h	Bangor	D	1-1	*Davies*
07/04	a	TNS	L	0-1	
14/04	h	Bala	W	2-0	*Horan, og (Stuart Jones)*
22/04	a	Cardiff MU	D	0-0	

No	Name	Nat	DoB	Pos	Aps	(s)	Gls
20	Wes Baynes	ENG	12/10/88	D	26	(3)	1
1	John Danby	ENG	15/08/83	G	30		
10	Leslie Davies		29/10/84	A	23	(5)	9
2	John Disney	ENG	15/05/92	D	26	(3)	2
3	Kai Edwards		29/01/91	D	10		1
7	Tom Field	ENG	02/08/85	M	13	(4)	2
6	Danny Harrison	ENG	04/11/82	M	24	(1)	
66	Connor Harwood	ENG	02/02/00	M		(2)	
5	George Horan	ENG	19/02/82	D	14		4
4	Ian Kearney	ENG	15/06/87	D	3		
8	Callum Morris	ENG	12/09/92	M	17	(5)	1
18	Jay Owen		14/01/91	M	31		
19	Matty Owen	ENG	23/06/94	M	12	(11)	1
24	Sheldon Payne		04/02/89	M		(5)	2
14	Declan Poole	ENG	05/05/95	M	3	(5)	1
17	Chris Rimmer	ENG	02/07/92	D	1	(3)	
9	Ashley Ruane	ENG	26/06/85	A	1	(3)	
28	Jon Rushton		17/05/90	G	2		
11	Nick Rushton		03/02/92	A	10	(3)	3
21	Lewis Short	ENG	11/06/90	M	19	(8)	2
15	Sean Smith	ENG	12/12/94	D	19	(5)	
17	Ryan Wignall	ENG	28/03/89	M	7	(2)	1
22	Mike Wilde	ENG	27/08/83	A	11	(9)	3
12	Matty Williams		05/11/82	A	24	(2)	6
16	Nathan Woolfe	ENG	06/10/88	M	26	(2)	2

Llandudno FC

1988 • Parc Maesdu (1,503) • llandudnotownfc.co.uk

Manager: Alan Morgan

Date		Opponent		Score	Scorers
2016					
14/08	a	Rhyl	D	0-0	
20/08	h	TNS	L	0-5	
28/08	h	Aberystwyth	L	0-1	
30/08	h	Broughton	W	2-0	*Owen, Buckley*
03/09	a	Carmarthen	W	1-0	*Joyce*
10/09	h	Newtown	D	0-0	
18/09	h	Cardiff MU	L	0-1	
20/09	a	Connah's Quay	D	1-1	*Marc Williams*
25/09	h	Cefn Druids	D	0-0	
01/10	a	Broughton	W	3-2	*Mike Williams, Riley, Buckley*
15/10	a	TNS	L	0-5	
23/10	a	Aberystwyth	D	0-0	
29/10	a	Newtown	D	0-0	
04/11	a	Cefn Druids	W	3-1	*Owen, Mike Williams, Riley*
13/11	h	Connah's Quay	L	0-2	
19/11	h	Bala	L	1-3	*Mike Williams*
27/11	a	Cardiff MU	D	1-1	*Owen*
10/12	h	Carmarthen	W	2-0	*Thomas (p), Hughes*
17/12	a	Bala	L	0-3	
26/12	a	Bangor	L	1-2	*Thomas (p)*
2017					
01/01	h	Bangor	W	1-0	*Marc Williams*
14/01	h	Rhyl	D	2-2	*Reed, Joyce*
04/02	h	Newtown	L	1-2	*Hart (p)*
10/02	a	Broughton	D	0-0	
18/02	a	Aberystwyth	W	4-3	*Hart (p), Mike Williams, Hughes, Marc Williams*
03/03	h	Cefn Druids	D	0-0	
10/03	h	Rhyl	D	1-1	*Marc Williams*
19/03	a	Newtown	D	2-2	*Hughes, Shaw*
25/03	h	Broughton	D	2-2	*Shaw, Marc Williams*
09/04	h	Aberystwyth	L	0-2	
14/04	a	Cefn Druids	L	2-3	*Thomas, Marc Williams*
22/04	a	Rhyl	D	1-1	*Reed*

No	Name	Nat	DoB	Pos	Aps	(s)	Gls
23	Lewis Buckley		10/12/91	M	23	(3)	2
11	Joe Chaplin		11/10/92	A		(2)	
17	Jamal Crawford	ENG	26/11/97	M	5	(3)	
19	Liam Dawson	ENG	12/01/91	A	5	(10)	
20	Thomas Dix	ENG	13/10/91	M	29		
7	Gareth Evans		29/04/87	M	11	(6)	
16	Sam Hart	ENG	29/11/91	D	10		2
8	Danny Hughes		28/05/88	M	30		3
21	Ben Jago	ENG	04/09/96	M	6	(3)	
24	Owain Jones		11/01/99	A		(3)	
3	James Joyce		03/11/94	D	26		2
22	Sean McCaffery		19/06/98	M	1	(8)	
11	John Owen		18/08/92	A	19	(2)	3
39	Robbie Parry		18/10/94	M	3		
5	Nathan Peate	ENG	25/09/91	D	3	(5)	
15	Jamie Reed		13/08/87	A	9	(1)	2
14	Leo Riley	ENG	09/01/96	M	8	(13)	2
1	David Roberts	ENG	10/12/88	G	32		
15	Dean Seager		19/09/94	A		(1)	
4	Daniel Shaw	ENG	19/04/96	M	28	(2)	2
2	Danny Taylor	ENG	01/09/91	D	32		
9	Lee Thomas		14/06/84	A	12	(14)	3
10	Marc Williams		27/07/88	M	26		6
18	Mike Williams		27/10/86	D	30		4
6	Tom Williams		15/11/97	M	4	(2)	

Newtown AFC

1875 • Latham Park (6,000) • newtownafc.co.uk

Major honours
Welsh Cup (2) 1879, 1895

Manager: Chris Hughes

Date		Opponent		Score	Scorers
2016					
13/08	h	Bala	D	0-0	
20/08	h	Carmarthen	W	4-2	*Oswell 2, Mitchell, Kershaw*
28/08	a	Connah's Quay	L	0-1	
31/08	a	Bangor	L	1-2	*Oswell*
04/09	h	Cefn Druids	D	1-1	*C Williams (I) (p)*
10/09	a	Llandudno	D	0-0	
17/09	h	Rhyl	D	3-3	*Oswell 3*
20/09	a	Cardiff MU	L	1-2	*Oswell*
24/09	h	Broughton	L	2-4	*Fletcher, Oswell*
02/10	a	Bala	L	0-1	
15/10	a	Carmarthen	L	1-3	*Boundford*
23/10	a	TNS	L	0-1	
29/10	h	Llandudno	D	0-0	
05/11	a	Broughton	W	2-0	*Mitchell, Stephens (p)*
13/11	h	Bangor	L	1-2	*Sutton*
19/11	h	Connah's Quay	W	2-1	*C Williams (II), Mitchell*
25/11	a	Cefn Druids	L	0-1	
10/12	a	Rhyl	W	3-1	*Oswell, Kershaw, A Jones*
17/12	h	Cardiff MU	L	0-1	
26/12	a	Aberystwyth	L	0-1	
31/12	h	Aberystwyth	D	2-2	*Mitchell, Boundford*
2017					
14/01	h	TNS	D	3-3	*Mitchell, Rushton, Price*
04/02	a	Llandudno	W	2-1	*Oswell, Rushton*
11/02	h	Rhyl	W	3-2	*Oswell 2, Rushton*
17/02	a	Cefn Druids	W	2-1	*Kershaw, Rushton*
04/03	h	Broughton	W	4-1	*Oswell, Fletcher 2, Mills-Evans*
10/03	a	Aberystwyth	W	4-0	*Oswell 3, Rushton*
19/03	h	Llandudno	D	2-2	*Boundford, Oswell*
26/03	a	Rhyl	W	2-0	*Kenton, Oswell*
08/04	h	Cefn Druids	D	1-1	*Oswell*
14/04	h	Broughton	W	7-0	*Fletcher, Mills-Evans, Oswell 3, Sutton, Stephens*
22/04	h	Aberystwyth	W	6-1	*Rushton 3, Edwards, Kershaw, Boundford*

No	Name	Nat	DoB	Pos	Aps	(s)	Gls
9	Luke Boundford		30/01/88	D	23	(4)	4
16	Gavin Cadwallader	ENG	18/04/86	D	1	(3)	
3	Stefan Edwards		10/10/89	D	14	(5)	1
25	Will Evans	ENG	11/08/00	M		(1)	
23	Alex Fletcher	ENG	17/11/96	M	24	(6)	4
20	Tom Goodwin		12/01/90	M	27		
22	Jack Steven Hughes		12/02/90	D	4		
12	Andy Jones	ENG	23/03/85	D	12	(3)	1
1	David Jones		03/02/90	G	25		
2	Joe Kenton	ENG	19/05/98	M		(7)	1
18	Ryan Kershaw		21/09/95	M	16	(13)	4
5	Kieran Mills-Evans	ENG	11/10/92	D	23	(2)	2
7	Neil Mitchell	ENG	01/04/88	A	29	(3)	5
17	Joe Newton	ENG	17/09/95	M	6	(6)	
10	Jason Oswell	ENG	07/10/92	A	30	(1)	22
13	Jack Perry	ENG	31/10/97	G	7		
15	Jamie Price	ENG	22/07/88	M	20	(2)	1
8	Nick Rushton		03/02/92	A	11		8
4	Ross Stephens		28/05/85	M	11	(7)	2
6	Shane Sutton		31/01/89	D	30		2
14	Jordan Wells	ENG	18/10/96	D	3	(6)	
11	Craig Williams (I)		28/01/83	A	8	(1)	1
19	Craig Williams (II)		21/12/87	M	28		1

Rhyl FC

1879 • Belle Vue (3,000) • rhylfc.co.uk

Major honours
Welsh League (2) 2004, 2009; Welsh Cup (4) 1952, 1953, 2004, 2006

Manager: Niall McGuinness

2016					
14/08	h	Llandudno	D	0-0	
20/08	h	Cefn Druids	L	0-3	
28/08	a	TNS	L	0-10	
31/08	h	Aberystwyth	W	3-1	*Buckley, Lamb 2*
04/09	h	Cardiff MU	W	1-0	*Hughes*
10/09	h	Broughton	W	3-1	*T Jones, A Jones 2*
17/09	a	Newtown	D	3-3	*og (Sutton), Ahmadi, Hughes*
20/09	h	Bangor	W	1-0	*T Jones*
25/09	a	Connah's Quay	L	0-2	
30/09	a	Cefn Druids	L	3-4	*A Jones, Simpson, Lamb*
14/10	a	Aberystwyth	L	0-4	
22/10	a	Bangor	L	2-3	*Pierce, Ahmadi*
30/10	a	Cardiff MU	L	0-4	
05/11	h	Carmarthen	L	0-1	
19/11	a	Broughton	W	3-0	*Lamb 2, Hughes*
25/11	h	Connah's Quay	L	1-2	*Z Edwards*
10/12	h	Newtown	L	1-3	*Ahmadi*
14/12	h	TNS	L	1-2	*Lamb*
17/12	a	Carmarthen	L	0-5	
26/12	a	Bala	L	1-6	*Lamb*
30/12	h	Bala	W	2-0	*T Jones, A Jones*
2017					
14/01	a	Llandudno	D	2-2	*A Jones 2*
04/02	h	Cefn Druids	L	0-2	
11/02	a	Newtown	L	2-3	*Halewood, Pierce (p)*
18/02	a	Broughton	W	2-0	*Lewis, T Jones*
03/03	h	Aberystwyth	D	2-2	*Davies, T Jones*
10/03	a	Llandudno	D	1-1	*Halewood*
17/03	a	Cefn Druids	L	1-4	*Lewis*
26/03	h	Newtown	L	0-2	
08/04	h	Broughton	W	2-1	*Rimmer, Lewis*
14/04	a	Aberystwyth	L	0-4	
22/04	h	Llandudno	D	1-1	*A Jones*

No	Name	Nat	DoB	Pos	Aps	(s)	Gls
10	Jack Abraham	ENG	02/10/90	M	5		
19	Porya Ahmadi	IRN	18/11/93	A	9	(5)	3
17	Andreas Alvarado		17/10/90	A		(1)	
15	Christoph Aziamale	GER	18/12/97	A		(1)	
8	James Bell		11/04/96	M	21		
22	James Brewerton		17/11/79	D	8	(2)	
21	Oliver Buckley		06/06/95	A	9	(11)	1
24	Dan Collins	AUS	15/06/96	D	12		
19	Lewis Coyle	ENG	07/07/88	A	6	(1)	
13	Rory Crowther	ENG	29/12/96	G	2	(1)	
25	Josh Davies		02/04/94	A	6	(2)	1
29	Oliver Durkin	ENG	28/08/98	M		(2)	
11	Sion Edwards		01/08/87	M	1	(1)	
14	Zyaac Edwards		30/05/97	M	13	(7)	1
1	Owen Evans		29/11/96	G	20		
26	Luke Fitzpatrick		13/11/98	D		(1)	
5	Stefan Halewood		19/05/88	D	18	(2)	2
3	Tom Hartley	ENG	21/11/91	D	28	(1)	
25	Kieran Hilditch		31/05/92	D	1		
11	Robert Hughes		22/04/92	M	14	(3)	3
6	Alex Jones		04/08/94	A	22	(1)	7
24	James Jones		04/08/84	D	4		
23	Ryan Jones		07/01/96	M		(4)	
9	Toby Jones		25/08/92	A	29	(1)	5
27	Carl Lamb	ENG	10/11/84	A	12	(5)	7
12	Christian Langos	CGO	09/09/94	A	1	(9)	
1	Dan Lavercombe	ENG	16/09/96	G	10		
20	Steve Lewis	ENG	10/11/87	A	5	(3)	3
15	Levi Mackin	ENG	04/04/86	A		(1)	
12	Jordan Miller		29/02/92	M	10	(4)	
28	Iwan Murray		08/08/00	M		(1)	
20	Rakim Newton		02/12/97	M	7	(2)	
7	Kristian Pierce		11/11/93	A	20	(5)	2
15	Chris Rimmer	ENG	02/07/92	D	9	(1)	1
4	Michael Sharples		23/05/99	D	20		
2	Aaron Simpson		19/10/95	D	18	(2)	1
16	Michael Walsh	ENG	30/05/86	M	4	(4)	
12	Alun Webb		28/12/93	A	1		
18	Jamie Whitehouse		04/03/96	D		(1)	
23	Ashley Young	ENG	14/07/90	M	7	(3)	

The New Saints FC

1959 • Park Hall (3,000) • tnsfc.co.uk

Major honours
Welsh League (11) 2000, 2005, 2006, 2007, 2010, 2012, 2013, 2014, 2015, 2016, 2017; Welsh Cup (6) 1996, 2005, 2012, 2014, 2015, 2016

Manager: Craig Harrison (ENG)

2016					
14/08	h	Aberystwyth	W	2-1	*Brobbel, Cieślewicz*
20/08	a	Llandudno	W	5-0	*Cieślewicz, Quigley, Seargeant 2 (1p), Brobbel*
28/08	h	Rhyl	W	10-0	*Edwards, Quigley 2, Spender, Marriott, Brobbel, Draper 3, Farleigh*
31/08	a	Cardiff MU	W	2-1	*Seargeant 2 (1p)*
04/09	a	Broughton	W	4-1	*Rawlinson, Darlington 2, Seargeant*
11/09	h	Bangor	W	4-0	*Darlington 2, Saunders, Mullan*
17/09	h	Bala	W	5-1	*Saunders, Draper, Seargeant 2 (2p), Parry*
20/09	a	Bala	W	2-0	*Parry, Darlington*
25/09	h	Carmarthen	W	2-1	*Draper 2*
01/10	a	Aberystwyth	W	5-1	*Draper 2, Edwards, Saunders, og (Bell)*
15/10	h	Llandudno	W	5-0	*Darlington 2, Parry, Brobbel 2*
23/10	h	Newtown	W	1-0	*Parry*
30/10	h	Connah's Quay	W	3-0	*Fletcher, Seargeant, Routledge*
05/11	a	Bangor	W	2-1	*Draper, Darlington*
18/11	a	Carmarthen	W	4-2	*og (Surman), Seargeant (p), Parry, Draper*
25/11	h	Broughton	W	4-0	*Routledge 2, Edwards, Quigley*
10/12	h	Cardiff MU	W	3-1	*Edwards, og (Lewis), Cieślewicz*
14/12	a	Rhyl	W	2-1	*Darlington 2 (1p)*
17/12	a	Connah's Quay	W	3-0	*Quigley, Draper, Rawlinson*
26/12	h	Cefn Druids	W	4-0	*Darlington, Cieślewicz 2, Draper*
30/12	a	Cefn Druids	W	2-0	*Edwards, Routledge*
2017					
14/01	a	Newtown	D	3-3	*Edwards, Draper, Cieślewicz*
04/02	h	Cardiff MU	W	2-0	*Cieślewicz, Darlington (p)*
11/02	a	Carmarthen	L	0-1	
04/03	h	Bangor	W	4-0	*Cieślewicz, Mullan 2, Saunders*
12/03	h	Bala	W	3-2	*Cieślewicz, Darlington (p), Mullan*
18/03	a	Cardiff MU	W	5-0	*Darlington 2, og (Barnett), Draper, Cieślewicz*
21/03	a	Connah's Quay	L	1-2	*Jones*
25/03	h	Carmarthen	W	2-0	*Brobbel, Cieślewicz*
07/04	h	Connah's Quay	W	1-0	*Draper*
14/04	a	Bangor	L	0-3	
22/04	a	Bala	W	6-4	*Cieślewicz, Brobbel, Quigley 3, Parry*

No	Name	Nat	DoB	Pos	Aps	(s)	Gls
25	Sam Ashworth		27/01/00	M		(1)	
4	Phil Baker	ENG	04/11/82	D	6	(6)	
8	Ryan Brobbel	ENG	05/03/93	M	31		7
21	Adrian Cieślewicz	POL	16/11/90	M	12	(5)	12
20	Alex Darlington		26/12/88	A	22	(8)	15
9	Greg Draper	NZL	13/08/89	A	22	(9)	15
23	Aeron Edwards		16/02/88	M	26	(1)	6
24	Jacob Farleigh	ENG	16/11/98	M		(4)	1
10	Wes Fletcher	ENG	28/02/91	A	4	(12)	1
1	Paul Harrison	ENG	18/12/84	G	30		
31	Aron Hughes Jones		31/07/99	M		(1)	
27	James Jones		13/03/87	D	4	(3)	1
18	Mihai Leca	ROU	14/04/92	D	2	(2)	
3	Chris Marriott	ENG	24/09/89	D	25	(1)	1
12	Tom Matthews	ENG	12/12/97	D		(1)	
14	Jamie Mullan	ENG	10/02/88	M	7	(11)	4
11	Robbie Parry		18/10/94	M	13	(3)	6
26	Ryan Pryce	ENG	30/06/97	D	10	(7)	
22	Scott Quigley	ENG	02/09/92	A	11	(7)	8
16	Connell Rawlinson		22/09/91	D	28		2
6	Jon Routledge	ENG	23/11/89	M	29		4
15	Steve Saunders	SCO	30/03/91	D	28	(1)	4
7	Christian Seargeant	ENG	13/09/86	M	11	(5)	9
2	Simon Spender		15/11/85	D	29		1
30	Andrew Wycherley		28/05/98	G	2		

Top goalscorers

22	Jason Oswell (Newtown)
15	Mike Hayes (Bala)
	Alex Darlington (TNS)
	Greg Draper (TNS)
13	Daniel Nardiello (Bangor)
	Liam Thomas (Carmarthen)
12	Adrian Cieślewicz (TNS)
11	Ashley Ruane (Cefn Druids)
	Nick Rushton (Connah's Quay/Newtown)
10	Tony Gray (Broughton)
	Henry Jones (Bangor)

UEFA Europa League qualification play-offs

SEMI-FINALS

(06/05/17)
Bangor 3-2 Newtown *(Taylor-Fletcher 5, Nardiello 12, G Roberts 75; Boundford 19, Mitchell 26)*

(07/05/17)
Carmarthen 1-2 Cardiff MU *(Griffiths 48; Roscrow 60, Corsby 90)*

FINAL

(13/05/17)
Bangor 1-0 Cardiff MU *(Rittenberg 31)*

Promoted clubs

Prestatyn Town FC

1910 • Bastion Road (2,300) • ptfconline.co.uk

Major honours
Welsh Cup (1) 2013

Manager: Neil Gibson

Barry Town United FC

1912 • Jenner Park (2,000) • no website

Major honours
Welsh League (7) 1996, 1997, 1998, 1999, 2001, 2002, 2003; Welsh Cup (6) 1955, 1994, 1997, 2001, 2002, 2003

Manager: Gavin Chesterfield

Second level final tables 2016/17

North		Pld	W	D	L	F	A	Pts
1	Prestatyn Town FC	30	26	2	2	114	35	80
2	Caernarfon Town FC	30	19	7	4	83	45	64
3	Gresford Athletic FC	30	18	2	10	67	47	56
4	CPD Porthmadog FC	30	16	2	12	64	48	50
5	Flint Town United FC	30	14	6	10	62	47	48
6	Caersws FC	30	15	3	12	61	59	48
7	Holywell Town FC	30	14	8	8	52	45	50
8	Holyhead Hotspur FC	30	12	6	12	57	52	42
9	Guilsfield FC	30	12	7	11	53	45	43
10	Denbigh Town FC	30	10	8	12	57	62	38
11	Ruthin Town FC	30	10	3	17	49	72	33
12	CPD Penrhyncoch FC	30	9	7	14	39	48	31
13	Llanfair United FC	30	7	4	19	36	69	25
14	Mold Alexandria FC	30	7	4	19	44	91	25
15	Conwy Borough FC	30	7	3	20	53	83	24
16	Buckley Town FC	30	6	4	20	38	81	22

NB CPD Penrhyncoch FC - 3pts deducted.

South		Pld	W	D	L	F	A	Pts
1	Barry Town United FC	30	20	6	4	69	18	66
2	Penybont FC	30	19	4	7	73	41	61
3	Goytre AFC	30	18	4	8	80	49	58
4	Haverfordwest County FC	30	16	6	8	55	47	54
5	Caerau (Ely) FC	30	13	9	8	57	50	48
6	Cwmbran Celtic FC	30	14	3	13	60	50	45
7	Undy AFC	30	13	2	15	53	53	41
8	Afan Lido FC	30	13	5	12	46	49	41
9	Taffs Well AFC	30	12	4	14	40	48	40
10	Goytre United FC	30	10	9	11	44	37	39
11	Cambrian & Clydach Vale BGC	30	10	7	13	41	49	37
12	Ton Pentre AFC	30	10	6	14	51	61	36
13	Port Talbot Town FC	30	10	5	15	41	57	35
14	Monmouth Town FC	30	9	6	15	49	74	33
15	Caldicot Town FC	30	7	2	21	36	65	23
16	Risca United FC	30	6	2	22	38	85	20

NB Afan Lido FC - 3pts deducted.

DOMESTIC CUP

Welsh Cup 2016/17

THIRD ROUND

(02/12/16)
Llanelli 5-1 Ynysgerwn

(03/12/16)
Aberystwyth 2-0 Holywell
Bala 6-1 Caldicot
Caernarfon 3-1 Carmarthen
Cardiff MU 4-0 Porthmadog
Connah's Quay 3-2 Goytre United
Greenfield 0-3 Guilsfield
Haverfordwest 1-0 Afan Lido
Llandudno 0-2 Goytre FC *(Goytre subsequently expelled; Llandudno reinstated)*
Llanfair 1-0 Corwen
Newtown 0-3 TNS
Penybont 4-1 Broughton
Prestatyn 2-1 Holyhead *(aet)*
Rhyl 6-0 Penrhyncoch

(10/12/16)
Cefn Druids 2-0 Llantwit Major
Ton Pentre 0-2 Bangor

FOURTH ROUND

(28/01/17)
Aberystwyth 1-5 Prestatyn
Bala 4-1 Penybont *(aet)*
Bangor 4-0 Llandudno
Caernarfon 3-2 Rhyl *(aet)*
Guilsfield 4-2 Cardiff MU
Haverfordwest 1-5 Connah's Quay
Llanfair 4-1 Cefn Druids
TNS 7-0 Llanelli

QUARTER-FINALS

(25/02/17)
Guilsfield 0-3 Bala *(Wade 41, Venables 70, Irving 86)*

Llanfair 0-7 Caernarfon *(Edwards 5, 24, Lloyd 12, Breese 48, 63, Thomas 76, Clive Williams 81)*

Prestatyn 2-2 Connah's Quay *(Williams 6, Maher 42; Edwards 46 Baynes 82)*
(aet; 3-4 on pens)

TNS 2-1 Bangor *(Draper 105, Cieślewicz 116; Jones 94) (aet)*

SEMI-FINALS

(01/04/17)
Caernarfon 1-3 Bala *(Stuart J Jones 28og; Hunt 77, 90, Smith 89)*

Connah's Quay 0-3 TNS *(Cieślewicz 71, Edwards 74, Mullan 81)*

FINAL

(30/04/17)
Nantporth, Bangor
BALA TOWN FC 2 *(Evans 77, Smith 85)*
THE NEW SAINTS FC 1 *(Draper 55)*
Referee: *Jones*
BALA: *Morris, Irving, Stuart J Jones, Stuart Jones, Thompson, Burke, Stephens, Smith, Venables, Sheridan (Wade 71), Hunt (Evans 65)*
TNS: *Harrison, Spender, Rawlinson, Saunders, Marriott, Edwards, Routledge, Cieślewicz, Brobbel (Darlington 87), Mullan (Seargeant 87), Draper (Quigley 74)*

Bala Town upset the odds as they came from behind to defeat champions TNS 2-1 in the Welsh Cup final

UEFA Events Calendar 2017/18

National team

2018 FIFA World Cup European Qualifiers

31/08-05/09/2017	Qualifying round matches
05-10/10/2017	Qualifying round matches
13/10/2017	Play-off draw (Zurich, Switzerland)
09-11/11/2017	Play-off matches, first leg
12-14/11/2017	Play-off matches, second leg

2018 FIFA World Cup Final tournament

01/12/2017	Final tournament draw (Moscow, Russia)
14/06-15/07/2018	Final tournament (Russia)

2019 UEFA European Under-21 Championship

01-05/09/2017	Qualifying round matches
02-10/10/2017	Qualifying round matches
06-14/11/2017	Qualifying round matches
19-27/03/2018	Qualifying round matches
07-08/06/2018	Qualifying round matches

Club

2017/18 UEFA Champions League

24/08/2017	Group stage draw (Monaco)
12-13/09/2017	Group stage, Matchday 1
26-27/09/2017	Group stage, Matchday 2
17-18/10/2017	Group stage, Matchday 3
31/10-01/11/2017	Group stage, Matchday 4
21-22/11/2017	Group stage, Matchday 5
05-06/12/2017	Group stage, Matchday 6
11/12/2017	Round of 16 draw (Nyon, Switzerland)
13-14/02/2018	Round of 16, first leg
20-21/02/2018	Round of 16, first leg
06-07/03/2018	Round of 16, second leg
13-14/03/2018	Round of 16, second leg
16/03/2018	Quarter-final draw (Nyon, Switzerland)
03-04/04/2018	Quarter-finals, first leg
10-11/04/2018	Quarter-finals, second leg
13/04/2018	Semi-final draw (Nyon, Switzerland)
24-25/04/2018	Semi-final, first leg
01-02/05/2018	Semi-final, second leg
26/05/2018	Final (Kyiv, Ukraine)

2017/18 UEFA Europa League

25/08/2017	Group stage draw (Monaco)
14/09/2017	Group stage, Matchday 1
28/09/2017	Group stage, Matchday 2
19/10/2017	Group stage, Matchday 3
02/11/2017	Group stage, Matchday 4
23/11/2017	Group stage, Matchday 5
07/12/2017	Group stage, Matchday 6
11/12/2017	Round of 32 draw (Nyon, Switzerland)
15/02/2018	Round of 32, first leg
22/02/2018	Round of 32, second leg
23/02/2018	Round of 16 draw (Nyon, Switzerland)
08/03/2018	Round of 16, first leg
15/03/2018	Round of 16, second leg
16/03/2018	Quarter-final draw (Nyon, Switzerland)
05/04/2018	Quarter-finals, first leg
12/04/2018	Quarter-finals, second leg
13/04/2018	Semi-final draw (Nyon, Switzerland)
26/04/2018	Semi-final, first leg
03/05/2018	Semi-final, second leg
16/05/2018	Final (Lyon, France)

2017/18 UEFA Youth League

24/08/2017	Group stage draw (Monaco)
29/08/2017	First and second round draw (Nyon, Switzerland)
12-13/09/2017	Group stage, Matchday 1
26-27/09/2017	Group stage, Matchday 2
27/09/2017	First round, first leg matches
17-18/10/2017	Group stage, Matchday 3
18/10/2017	First round, second leg matches
31/10-01/11/2017	Group stage, Matchday 4
01/11/2017	Second round, first leg matches
21-22/11/2017	Group stage, Matchday 5
22/11/2017	Second round, second leg matches
05-06/12/2017	Group stage, Matchday 6
11/12/2017	Play-off draw (Nyon, Switzerland)
06-07/02/2018	Play-off matches
09/02/18	Knockout round draw (Nyon, Switzerland)
20-21/02/2018	Round of 16 matches
13-14/03/2018	Quarter-final matches
20-23/04/2018	Final Four (Nyon, Switzerland)

2017 FIFA Club World Cup

06-16/12/2017	Final tournament (UAE)

Youth & Amateur

2017/18 UEFA European Under-19 Championship

03/10-14/11/2017	Qualifying round matches
06/12/2017	Elite round draw (Nyon, Switzerland)
19-27/03/2018	Elite round matches
21/06/2018	Final tournament draw (tbd, Finland)
16-29/07/2018	Final tournament (Finland)

2018/19 UEFA European Under-19 Championship

06/12/2017	Qualifying round draw (Nyon, Switzerland)

2017/18 UEFA European Under-17 Championship

27/09-01/11/2017	Qualifying round matches
06/12/2017	Elite round draw (Nyon, Switzerland)
01-31/03/2018	Elite round matches
05/04/2018	Final tournament draw (tbd, England)
04-20/05/2018	Final tournament (England)

2018/19 UEFA European Under-17 Championship

06/12/2017	Qualifying round draw (Nyon, Switzerland)

2018/19 Regions' Cup

06/12/2017	Preliminary and intermediate round draw (Nyon, Switzerland)
03-10/03/2018	Preliminary round matches

Women's

2017/18 UEFA Women's Champions League

01/09/2017	Round of 32 draw (Nyon, Switzerland)
04-05/10/2017	Round of 32, first leg
11-12/10/2017	Round of 32, second leg
16/10/2017	Round of 16 draw (Nyon, Switzerland)
08-09/11/2017	Round of 16, first leg
15-16/11/2017	Round of 16, second leg
24/11/2017	Quarter-final and Semi-final draw (Nyon, Switzerland)
21-22/03/2018	Quarter-finals, first leg
28-29/03/2018	Quarter-finals, second leg
21-22/04/2018	Semi-finals, first leg
28-29/04/2018	Semi-finals, second leg
24/05/2018	Final (Kyiv, Ukraine)

2017/18 UEFA European Women's Under-19 Championship

08/09-31/10/2017	Qualifying round matches
24/11/2017	Elite round draw (Nyon, Switzerland)
02-10/04/2018	Elite round matches
22/05/2018	Final tournament draw (tbd, Switzerland)
18-30/07/2018	Final tournament (Switzerland)

2018/19 UEFA European Women's Under-19 Championship

24/11/2017	Qualifying round draw (Nyon, Switzerland)

2017/18 UEFA European Women's Under-17 Championship

22/09-29/10/2017	Qualifying round matches
24/11/2017	Elite round draw (Nyon, Switzerland)
01/02-16/04/2018	Elite round matches
17/04/2018	Final tournament draw (tbd, Lithuania)
09-21/05/2018	Final tournament (Lithuania)

2018/19 UEFA European Women's Under-17 Championship

24/11/2017	Qualifying round draw (Nyon, Switzerland)

Futsal

UEFA Futsal EURO 2018

10-13/09/2017	Play-off matches, first leg
24-27/09/2017	Play-off matches, second leg
tbd	Final tournament draw (Ljubljana, Slovenia)
30/01-10/02/2018	Final tournament (Slovenia)

2017/18 UEFA Futsal Cup

22-27/08/2017	Preliminary round matches
10-15/10/2017	Main round matches
19/10/2017	Elite round draw
21-26/11/2017	Elite round matches
19/03/2018	Final tournament draw (tbd)
19-22/04/2018	Final tournament (tbd)

tbd = to be decided